THE CHIEF ELIZABETHAN DRAMATISTS

THE ELIZABETHAN DRAMATISTS

THE CHIEF ELIZABETHAN DRAMATISTS

EXCLUDING SHAKESPEARE

Selected Plays

BY

LYLY, PEELE, GREENE, MARLOWE, KYD, CHAPMAN, JONSON
DEKKER, MARSTON, HEYWOOD, BEAUMONT, FLETCHER
WEBSTER, MIDDLETON, MASSINGER, FORD, SHIRLEY

EDITED FROM THE ORIGINAL QUARTOS AND FOLIOS
WITH NOTES, BIOGRAPHIES, AND BIBLIOGRAPHIES

BY

WILLIAM ALLAN NEILSON, Ph. D.
PROFESSOR OF ENGLISH, HARVARD UNIVERSITY

HOUGHTON MIFFLIN COMPANY

The Riverside Press Cambridge

COPYRIGHT, 1939, BY WILLIAM ALLAN NEILSON

COPYRIGHT, 1911, BY WILLIAM ALLAN NEILSON

PR
1263
.N35

The Riverside Press

CAMBRIDGE · MASSACHUSETTS

PRINTED IN THE U.S.A.

PREFACE

THE aim in the selection of the plays in this volume has been twofold : first, to present typical examples of the work of the most important of Shakespeare's contemporaries, so that, read with Shakespeare's own writings, they might afford a view of the development of the English drama through its most brilliant period ; secondly, to present, as far as it was possible in one volume, the most distinguished plays of that period, regarded merely from the point of view of their intrinsic value. It is clear that these two purposes could not always be perfectly combined ; but it is hoped that each has been in good measure achieved without undue sacrifice of the other, and that the interests of the academic student and the general reader have been fairly harmonized.

In the treatment of the text, the same principles have been followed as in the editor's edition of Shakespeare's works in the Cambridge Poets Series. Each play has been printed from the most authentic text accessible, and emendations have been adopted sparingly. Modern stage directions, and divisions into scenes and acts which do not appear in the original editions, have been distinguished by square brackets ; modern notes of place at the beginning of scenes have been relegated to the footnotes ; and indications given by the early copies of the authors' intentions with regard to the reading of the metre have been carefully preserved, especially in the matter of elided vowels. It is probable that, in the case of most of the present plays, the final *-ed* of verbs was intended to be pronounced as a separate syllable whenever it is spelled in full. The spelling and punctuation have been modernized throughout, except when the older spelling implied a different pronunciation.

The footnotes give the most important variant readings, and explanations of obsolete expressions ; and the Additional Notes at the end of the volume supply information with regard to the circumstances of publication, date, and sources of each play. In accordance with the plan of the Chief Poets Series, to which the volume belongs, there have been added concise biographical sketches and a selected bibliography of the dramatic work of each author. In view of the full bibliographies printed recently in Professor Schelling's *Elizabethan Drama* and in *The Cambridge History of English Literature*, vols. v and vi, it has not seemed advisable to attempt to give exhaustive bibliographies at the expense of reducing the number of dramas. All collected editions of the dramatists concerned are, however, mentioned ; all separate editions of the plays here printed ; a complete list of each author's dramas, with the dates of the original editions ; and a selection of the more important critical and biographical articles and books. Attention may also be called to the complete index of all the *dramatis personae* who have speaking parts, and to the index of songs.

In the selection of the thirty plays to be included I have received valuable advice from many friends and colleagues on the faculties of many colleges and universities ; so many that a complete acknowledgment would be impracticable, a partial one invidious. For all such help I am deeply grateful. I have also received courtesies from the authorities of the Boston Public Library, the Boston Athenaeum, and the Harvard College Library, which have enabled me to add to the authority of my texts by a first-hand collation of a number of the original quartos.

Printing from so great a variety of sources and from so many different authors, I have found it difficult to preserve perfect uniformity of treatment, and have doubtless at times failed of accuracy. Any corrections which may occur to students of the Elizabethan drama who use the volume will be warmly welcomed.

W. A. N.

CAMBRIDGE, MASSACHUSETTS, January, 1911.

CONTENTS

ENDYMION

THE MAN IN THE MOON

BY

JOHN LYLY

[DRAMATIS PERSONAE

ENDYMION, in love with Cynthia.
EUMENIDES, his friend, in love with Semele.
CORSITES, a Captain, in love with Tellus.
PANELION, } Lords of Cynthia's Court.
ZONTES, }
PYTHAGORAS, the Greek Philosopher.
GYPTES, an Egyptian Soothsayer.
GERON, an old man, husband to Dipsas.
SIR TOPHAS, a Braggart.
DARES, Page to Eumenides.
SAMIAS, Page to Endymion.
EPITON, Page to Sir Tophas.

Master Constable.
First Watchman.
Second Watchman.

CYNTHIA, the Queen.
TELLUS, in love with Endymion.
FLOSCULA, her friend.
SEMELE, loved by Eumenides.
SCINTILLA, } Waiting-maids.
FAVILLA, }
DIPSAS, an old Enchantress.
BAGOA, her servant.

Watchmen; Fairies; Three Ladies and an Old Man in the Dumb Show.]

THE PROLOGUE

MOST high and happy Princess, we must tell you a tale of the Man in the Moon, which, if it seem ridiculous for the method, or superfluous for the matter, or for the means incredible, for three faults we can make but one excuse: it is a tale of the Man in the Moon.

It was forbidden in old time to dispute of Chimæra because it was a fiction: we hope in our times none will apply pastimes,[1] because they are fancies; for there liveth none under the sun that knows what to make of the Man in the Moon. We present neither comedy, nor tragedy, nor story, nor anything but that whosoever heareth may say this: Why, here is a tale of the Man in the Moon.

ACT I

SCENE I.[2]

[*Enter*] ENDYMION *and* EUMENIDES.

Endymion. I find, Eumenides, in all things both variety to content, and satiety to glut, saving only in my affections, which are so staid, and withal so stately, that I can neither satisfy my heart with love, nor mine eyes with wonder. [5 My thoughts, Eumenides, are stitched to the stars, which being as high as I can see, thou mayest imagine how much higher they are than I can reach.

Eum. If you be enamoured of anything [10 above the moon, your thoughts are ridiculous, for that things immortal are not subject to affections; if allured or enchanted with these transitory things under the moon, you show yourself senseless to attribute such lofty [15 titles to such [low][3] trifles.

End. My love is placed neither under the moon nor above.

¹ Interpret the play as referring to political or other events.
² In the Gardens of Cynthia's Palace.
³ So Bond. Old edd. *love.*

Eum. I hope you be not sotted[4] upon the Man in the Moon.   20

End. No; but settled either to die or possess the moon herself.

Eum. Is Endymion mad, or do I mistake? Do you love the moon, Endymion?

End. Eumenides, the moon.   25

Eum. There was never any so peevish[5] to imagine the moon either capable of affection or shape of a mistress; for as impossible it is to make love fit to her humour, which no man knoweth, as a coat to her form, which con- [30 tinueth not in one bigness whilst she is measuring. Cease off, Endymion, to feed so much upon fancies. That melancholy blood must be purged which draweth you to a dotage no less miserable than monstrous.   35

End. My thoughts have no veins, and yet un-less they be let blood, I shall perish.

Eum. But they have vanities, which being re-formed, you may be restored.

End. O, fair Cynthia, why do others term [40 thee unconstant whom I have ever found un-movable? Injurious time, corrupt manners, unkind men, who, finding a constancy not to be matched in my sweet mistress, have christened

⁴ Infatuated with.   ⁵ Foolish.

her with the name of wavering, waxing, and [45 waning! Is she inconstant that keepeth a settled course; which, since her first creation, altereth not one minute in her moving? There is nothing thought more admirable or commendable in the sea than the ebbing and flowing; [50 and shall the moon, from whom the sea taketh this virtue, be accounted fickle for increasing and decreasing? Flowers in their buds are nothing worth till they be blown, nor are blossoms accounted till they be ripe fruit; and shall [55 we then say they be changeable for that they grow from seeds to leaves, from leaves to buds, from buds to their perfection? Then, why be not twigs that become trees, children that become men, and mornings that grow to even- [60 ings, termed wavering, for that they continue not at one stay? Ay, but Cynthia, being in her fulness, decayeth, as not delighting in her greatest beauty, or withering when she should be most honoured. When malice cannot object [65 anything, folly will, making that a vice which is the greatest virtue. What thing (my mistress excepted), being in the pride of her beauty and latter minute of her age, that waxeth young again? Tell me, Eumenides, what is he that [70 having a mistress of ripe years and infinite virtues, great honours and unspeakable beauty, but would wish that she might grow tender again, getting youth by years, and never-decaying beauty by time; whose fair face neither the [75 summer's blaze can scorch, nor winter's blast chap, nor the numbering of years breed altering of colours? Such is my sweet Cynthia, whom time cannot touch because she is divine, nor will offend because she is delicate. O Cyn- [80 thia, if thou shouldst always continue at thy fulness, both gods and men would conspire to ravish thee. But thou, to abate the pride of our affections, dost detract from thy perfections, thinking it sufficient if once in a month [85 we enjoy a glimpse of thy majesty; and then, to increase our griefs, thou dost decrease thy gleams, coming out of thy royal robes, wherewith thou dazzlest our eyes, down into thy swathe clouts,[1] beguiling our eyes; and then —   90

Eum. Stay there, Endymion; thou that committest idolatry, wilt straight blaspheme, if thou be suffered. Sleep would do thee more good than speech: the moon heareth thee not, or if she do, regardeth thee not.   95

End. Vain Eumenides, whose thoughts never grow higher than the crown of thy head! Why troublest thou me, having neither head to conceive the cause of my love or a heart to receive the impressions? Follow thou thine own for- [100 tunes, which creep on the earth, and suffer me to fly to mine, whose fall, though it be desperate, yet shall it come by daring. Farewell. *[Exit*

Eum. Without doubt Endymion is bewitched; otherwise in a man of such rare virtues there [105 could not harbour a mind of such extreme madness. I will follow him, lest in this fancy of the moon he deprive himself of the sight of the sun.

                   Exit.

SCENE II.[2]

[Enter] TELLUS and FLOSCULA.

Tellus. Treacherous and most perjured Endymion, is Cynthia the sweetness of thy life and the bitterness of my death? What revenge may be devised so full of shame as my thoughts are replenished with malice? Tell me, Floscula, [5 if falseness in love can possibly be punished with extremity of hate? As long as sword, fire, or poison may be hired, no traitor to my love shall live unrevenged. Were thy oaths without number, thy kisses without measure, thy sighs [10 without end, forged to deceive a poor credulous virgin, whose simplicity had been worth thy favour and better fortune? If the gods sit unequal beholders of injuries, or laughers at lovers' deceits, then let mischief be as well for- [15 given in women as perjury winked at in men.

Flosc. Madam, if you would compare the state of Cynthia with your own, and the height of Endymion his thoughts with the meanness of your fortune, you would rather yield than [20 contend, being between you and her no comparison; and rather wonder than rage at the greatness of his mind, being affected with a thing more than mortal.

Tellus. No comparison, Floscula? And [25 why so? Is not my beauty divine, whose body is decked with fair flowers, and veins are vines, yielding sweet liquor to the dullest spirits; whose ears are corn, to bring strength; and whose hairs are grass, to bring abundance? [30 Doth not frankincense and myrrh breathe out of my nostrils, and all the sacrifice of the gods breed in my bowels? Infinite are my creatures, without which neither thou, nor Endymion, nor any, could love or live.   35

Flosc. But know you not, fair lady, that Cynthia governeth all things? Your grapes would be but dry husks, your corn but chaff, and all your virtues vain, were it not Cynthia that preserveth the one in the bud and nourisheth the [40 other in the blade, and by her influence both comforteth all things, and by her authority commandeth all creatures. Suffer, then, Endymion to follow his affections, though to obtain her be impossible, and let him flatter himself in his [45 own imaginations, because they are immortal.

Tellus. Loath I am, Endymion, thou shouldest die, because I love thee well; and that thou shouldest live, it grieveth me, because thou lovest Cynthia too well. In these extremities, [50 what shall I do? Floscula, no more words; I am resolved. He shall neither live nor die.

Flosc. A strange practice,[3] if it be possible.

Tellus. Yes, I will entangle him in such a sweet net that he shall neither find the means [55 to come out, nor desire it. All allurements of pleasure will I cast before his eyes, insomuch that he shall slake that love which he now voweth to Cynthia, and burn in mine, of which he seemeth careless. In this languishing, be- [60 tween my amorous devices and his own loose desires, there shall such dissolute thoughts take

---

root in his head, and over his heart grow so thick a skin, that neither hope of preferment, nor fear of punishment, nor counsel of the wisest, nor [65 company of the worthiest, shall alter his humour, nor make him once to think of his honour.

Flosc. A revenge incredible, and, if it may be, unnatural.

Tellus. He shall know the malice of a wo- [70 man to have neither mean nor end; and of a woman deluded in love to have neither rule nor reason. I can do it; I must; I will! All his virtues will I shadow with vices; his person (ah, sweet person!) shall he deck with such rich [75 robes as he shall forget it is his own person; his sharp wit (ah, wit too sharp that hath cut off all my joys!) shall he use in flattering of my face and devising sonnets in my favour. The prime of his youth and pride of his time shall be spent [80 in melancholy passions, careless behaviour, untamed thoughts, and unbridled affections.

Flosc. When this is done, what then? Shall it continue till his death, or shall he dote forever in this delight? 85

Tellus. Ah, Floscula, thou rendest my heart in sunder in putting me in remembrance of the end.

Flosc. Why, if this be not the end, all the rest is to no end. 90

Tellus. Yet suffer me to imitate Juno, who would turn Jupiter's lovers to beasts on the earth, though she knew afterwards they should be stars in heaven.

Flosc. Affection that is bred by enchant- [95 ment is like a flower that is wrought in silk, — in colour and form most like, but nothing at all in substance or savour.

Tellus. It shall suffice me if the world talk that I am favoured of Endymion. 100

Flosc. Well, use your own will; but you shall find that love gotten with witchcraft is as unpleasant as fish taken with medicines [1] unwholesome.

Tellus. Floscula, they that be so poor that [105 they have neither net nor hook will rather poison dough than pine with hunger; and she that is so oppress'd with love that she is neither able with beauty nor wit to obtain her friend, will rather use unlawful means than try in- [110 tolerable pains. I will do it. *Exit.*

Flosc. Then about it. Poor Endymion, what traps are laid for thee because thou honourest one that all the world wondereth at! And what plots are cast to make thee unfortunate that [115 studiest of all men to be the faithfulest! *Exit.*

SCENE III.[2]

[Enter] DARES and SAMIAS.

Dares. Now our masters are in love up to the ears, what have we to do but to be in knavery up to the crowns?

Samias. Oh, that we had Sir Tophas, that brave squire, in the midst of our mirth, — *et* [5 *ecce autem,* " Will you see the Devil ",—

[1] Caught with poisoned dough-balls.
[2] The same.

Enter SIR TOPHAS [and EPITON].

Top. Epi!

Epi. Here, sir.

Top. I brook not this idle humour of love; it tickleth not my liver, from whence the love- [10 mongers in former ages seemed to infer they should proceed.

Epi. Love, sir, may lie in your lungs, — and, I think it doth, and that is the cause you blow and are so pursy. 11

Top. Tush, boy, I think it but some device of the poet to get money.

Epi. A poet? What's that?

Top. Dost thou not know what a poet is?

Epi. No. 20

Top. Why, fool, a poet is as much as one should say — a poet. [*Noticing* DARES *and* SAMIAS.] But soft, yonder be two wrens; shall I shoot at them?

Epi. They are two lads. 25

Top. Larks or wrens, I will kill them.

Epi. Larks! Are you blind? They are two little boys.

Top. Birds or boys, they are both but a pittance for my breakfast; therefore have at [30 them, for their brains must as it were embroider my bolts.[3]

Sam. Stay your courage, valiant knight, for your wisdom is so weary that it stayeth itself.

Dar. Why, Sir Tophas, have you for- [35 gotten your old friends?

Top. Friends? *Nego argumentum.*

Sam. And why not friends?

Top. Because *amicitia* (as in old annals we find) is *inter pares.* Now, my pretty com- [40 panions, you shall see how unequal you be to me; but I will not cut you quite off, you shall be my half-friends for reaching to my middle; so far as from the ground to the waist I will be your friend. 45

Dar. Learnedly. But what shall become of the rest of your body, from the waist to the crown?

Top. My children, *quod supra vos nihil ad vos;* you must think the rest immortal, be- [50 cause you cannot reach it.

Epi. Nay, I tell ye my master is more than a man.

Dar. And thou less than a mouse.

Top. But what be you two? 55

Sam. I am Samias, page to [Eumenides].

Dar. And I Dares, page to [Endymion].

Top. Of what occupation are your masters?

Dar. Occupation, you clown! Why, they are honourable and warriors. 60

Top. Then are they my prentices.

Dar. Thine! And why so?

Top. I was the first that ever devised war, and therefore by Mars himself given me for my arms a whole armory; and thus I go, as you [65 see, clothed with artillery. It is not silks, milksops, nor tissues, nor the fine wool of Seres,[4]

[3] Blunt arrows.
[4] Wool of Seres, Chinese silk. Old edd. read *Ceres.* Bond *Seres.*

but iron, steel, swords, flame, shot, terror, clamour, blood, and ruin, that rocks asleep my thoughts, which never had any other cradle [70 but cruelty. Let me see, do you not bleed?

Dar. Why so?

Top. Commonly my words wound.

Sam. What then do your blows?

Top. Not only [wound],[1] but also confound. 75

Sam. How darest thou come so near thy master, Epi? Sir Tophas, spare us.

Top. You shall live: — you, Samias, because you are little; you, Dares, because you are no bigger; and both of you, because you are but [80 two; for commonly I kill by the dozen, and have for every particular adversary a peculiar weapon.

Sam. May we know the use, for our better skill in war?

Top. You shall. Here is a bird-bolt for the [85 ugly beast the blackbird.

Dar. A cruel sight.

Top. Here is the musket for the untamed or, as the vulgar sort term it, the wild mallard.[2]

Sam. O desperate attempt! 90

Edi. Nay, my master will match them.

Dar. Ay, if he catch them.

Top. Here is a spear and shield, and both necessary, the one to conquer, the other to subdue or overcome the terrible trout, which al- [95 though he be under the water, yet tying a string to the top of my spear and an engine of iron to the end of my line, I overthrow him, and then herein I put him.

Sam. O wonderful war! [*Aside.*] Dares, [100 didst thou ever hear such a dolt?

Dar. [*Aside.*] All the better; we shall have good sport hereafter, if we can get leisure.

Sam. [*Aside.*] Leisure! I will rather lose my master's service than his company! Look [105 how he struts. [*To* Sir Tophas.] But what is this? Call you it your sword?

Top. No, it is my simitar; which I, by construction often studying to be compendious, call my smiter. [110

Dar. What, are you also learned, sir?

Top. Learned? I am all Mars and Ars.

Sam. Nay, you are all mass and ass.

Top. Mock you me? You shall both suffer, yet with such weapons as you shall make choice [115 of the weapon wherewith you shall perish. Am I all a mass or lump; is there no proportion in me? Am I all ass; is there no wit in me? Epi, prepare them to the slaughter.

Sam. I pray, sir, hear us speak! We call [120 you mass, which your learning doth well understand is all man, for *mas, maris* is a man. Then *as* (as you know) is a weight, and we for your virtues account you a weight.

Top. The Latin hath saved your lives, the [125 which a world of silver could not have ransom'd. I understand you, and pardon you.

Dar. Well, Sir Tophas, we bid you farewell, and at our next meeting we will be ready to do you service. 130

Top. Samias, I thank you: Dares, I thank you: but especially I thank you both.

1 Old edd. *confound.*　　2 Drake.

Sam. [*Aside.*] Wisely. Come, next time we'll have some pretty gentlewomen with us to walk, for without doubt with them he will [135 be very dainty.

Dar. Come, let us see what our masters do; it is high time. *Exeunt* [Samias *and* Dares.]

Top. Now will I march into the field, where, if I cannot encounter with my foul [140 enemies, I will withdraw myself to the river, and there fortify for fish, for there resteth no minute free from fight.

　　　　Exeunt [Sir Tophas *and* Epiton.] 145

Scene IV.[3]

[*Enter at one side*] Floscula *and* Tellus, [*at the other*] Dipsas.

Tellus. Behold, Floscula, we have met with the woman by chance that we sought for by travel. I will break my mind to her without ceremony or circumstance, lest we lose that time in advice that should be spent in execu- [5 tion.

Flosc. Use your discretion; I will in this case neither give counsel nor consent, for there cannot be a thing more monstrous than to force affection by sorcery, neither do I imagine [10 anything more impossible.

Tellus. Tush, Floscula, in obtaining of love, what impossibilities will I not try? And for the winning of Endymion, what impieties will I not practise? Dipsas, whom as many honour for [15 age as wonder at for cunning, listen in few words to my tale, and answer in one word to the purpose, for that neither my burning desire can afford long speech, nor the short time I have to stay many delays. Is it possible by herbs, [20 stones, spells, incantation, enchantment, exorcisms, fire, metals, planets, or any practice,[4] to plant affection where it is not, and to supplant it where it is?

Dipsas. Fair lady, you may imagine that [25 these hoary hairs are not void of experience, nor the great name that goeth of my cunning to be without cause. I can darken the sun by my skill and remove the moon out of her course; I can restore youth to the aged and make [30 hills without bottoms; there is nothing that I cannot do but that only which you would have me do: and therein I differ from the gods, that I am not able to rule hearts; for were it in my power to place affection by appointment, I [35 would make such evil appetites, such inordinate lusts, such cursed desires, as all the world should be filled both with superstitious heats and extreme love.

Tellus. Unhappy Tellus, whose desires are [40 so desperate that they are neither to be conceived of any creature, nor to be cured by any art!

Dipsas. This I can: breed slackness in love, though never root it out. What is he whom [45 you love, and what she that he honoureth?

Tellus. Endymion, sweet Endymion is he that hath my heart; and Cynthia, too, too fair

3 The same.　　　4 Plot.

comparison, for other captains kill and beat, and there is nothing you kill, but you also eat.

Top. I will draw out their guts out of their bellies, and tear the flesh with my teeth, so mortal is my hate, and so eager my un- 90 staunched stomach.

Epi. [*Aside.*] My master thinks himself the valiantest man in the world if he kill a wren ; so warlike a thing he accounteth to take away life, though it be from a lark.   95

Top. Epi, I find my thoughts to swell and my spirit to take wings, insomuch that I cannot continue within the compass of so slender combats.

Favil. This passeth !   ⎫   100
Scint. Why, is he not mad ?   ⎬ [*Aside.*]
Sam. No, but a little vainglorious. ⎭

Top. Epi !
Epi. Sir.
Top. I will encounter that black and cruel 105 enemy that beareth rough and untewed[1] locks upon his body, whose sire throweth down the strongest walls, whose legs are as many as both ours, on whose head are placed most horrible horns by nature as a defence from all harms. 110

Epi. What mean you, master, to be so desperate ?

Top. Honour inciteth me, and very hunger compelleth me.

Epi. What is that monster ?   115
Top. The monster *Ovis.* I have said, — let thy wits work.

Epi. I cannot imagine it. Yet let me see, — a " black enemy " with " rough locks." It may be a sheep, and *Ovis* is a sheep. His sire so [120 strong : a ram is a sheep's sire, that being also an engine of war. Horns he hath, and four legs, — so hath a sheep. Without doubt, this monster is a black sheep. Is it not a sheep that you mean ?   125

Top. Thou hast hit it: that monster will I kill and sup with.

Sam. [*Aside.*] Come let us take him off.

[SAMIAS, DARES, FAVILLA, *and* SCINTILLA *come forward.*] Sir Tophas, all hail !   130

Top. Welcome, children ; I seldom cast mine eyes so low as to the crowns of your heads, and therefore pardon me that I spake not all this while.

Dar. No harm done. Here be fair ladies [135 come to wonder at your person, your valour, your wit, the report whereof hath made them careless of their own honours, to glut their eyes and hearts upon yours.

Top. Report cannot but injure me, for that [140 not knowing fully what I am, I fear she hath been a niggard in her praises.

Scint. No, gentle knight, report hath been prodigal, for she hath left you no equal, nor herself credit, so much hath she told, yet no [145 more than we now see.

Dar. A good wench.

Favil. If there remain as much pity toward women as there is in you courage against your enemies, then shall we be happy, who, hear- [150

ing of your person, came to see it, and seeing it are now in love with it.

Top. Love me, ladies ? I easily believe it, but my tough heart receiveth no impression with sweet words. Mars may pierce it, [155 Venus shall not paint on it.

Favil. A cruel saying.

Sam. [*Aside.*] There 's a girl.

Dar. Will you cast these ladies away, and all for a little love ? Do but speak kindly.   160

Top. There cometh no soft syllable within my lips ; custom hath made my words bloody and my heart barbarous. That pelting[2] word love, how waterish it is in my mouth ; it carrieth no sound. Hate, horror, death, are [165 speeches that nourish my spirits. I like honey, but I care not for the bees ; I delight in music, but I love not to play on the bagpipes ; I can vouchsafe to hear the voice of women, but to touch their bodies, I disdain it as a [170 thing childish and fit for such men as can digest nothing but milk.

Scint. A hard heart ! Shall we die for your love and find no remedy ?

Top. I have already taken a surfeit.   175

Epi. Good master, pity them.

Top. Pity them, Epi ? No, I do not think that this breast shall be pest'red with such a foolish passion. What is that the gentlewoman carrieth in a chain ?   180

Epi. Why, it is a squirrel.

Top. A squirrel ? O gods, what things are made for money !

Dar. Is not this gentleman over-wise ?

Favil. I could stay all day with him, if [185 I feared not to be shent.[3]

Scint. Is it not possible to meet again ?

Dar. Yes, at any time.

Favil. Then let us hasten home.

Scint. Sir Tophas, the god of war deal [190 better with you than you do with the god of love.

Favil. Our love we may dissemble, digest we cannot ; but I doubt not but time will hamper you and help us.   195

Top. I defy time, who hath no interest in my heart. Come, Epi, let me to the battle with that hideous beast. Love is as pap, and hath no relish in my taste because it is not terrible.

[*Exeunt* Sir TOPHAS *and* EPITON.]

Dar. Indeed a black sheep is a perilous [20c beast ; but let us in till another time.

Favil. I shall long for that time.   *Exeunt.*

SCENE III.[4]

[*Enter*] ENDYMION.

End. No rest, Endymion ! Still uncertain how to settle thy steps by day or thy thoughts by night ! Thy truth is measured by thy fortune, and thou art judged unfaithful because thou art unhappy. I will see if I can beguile [5 myself with sleep, and if no slumber will take hold in my eyes, yet will I embrace the golden thoughts in my head, and wish to melt by mus-

---

ing ; that as ebony, which no fire can scorch, is yet consumed with sweet savours, so my heart, [10 which cannot be bent by the hardness of fortune, may be bruised by amorous desires. On yonder bank never grew anything but lunary,[1] and hereafter I will never have any bed but that bank. O Endymion, Tellus was fair. But [15 what availeth beauty without wisdom ? Nay, Endymion, she was wise. But what availeth wisdom without honour ? She was honourable, Endymion ; belie her not. Ay, but how obscure is honour without fortune. Was she not for- [20 tunate whom so many followed ? Yes, yes, but base is fortune without majesty : thy majesty, Cynthia, all the world knoweth and wondereth at, but not one in the world that can imitate it or comprehend it. No more, Endymion. Sleep [25 or die. Nay, die, for to sleep, it is impossible ; — and yet I know not how it cometh to pass, I feel such a heaviness both in mine eyes and heart that I am suddenly benumbed, yea, in every joint. It may be weariness, for when [30 did I rest ? It may be deep melancholy, for when did I not sigh ? Cynthia ! Ay, so ; — I say, Cynthia !   *He falls asleep.*

[*Enter* DIPSAS *and* BAGOA.]

Dipsas. Little dost thou know, Endymion, when thou shalt wake, for hadst thou placed [35 thy heart as low in love as thy head lieth now in sleep, thou mightest have commanded Tellus, whom now, instead of a mistress, thou shalt find a tomb. These eyes must I seal up by art, not nature, which are to be opened neither by [40 art nor nature. Thou that layest down with golden locks shalt not awake until they be turned to silver hairs ; and that chin on which scarcely appeareth soft down shall be filled with bristles as hard as broom. Thou shalt sleep [45 out thy youth and flowering time, and become dry hay before thou knewest thyself green grass ; and ready by age to step into the grave when thou wakest, that was youthful in the court when thou laidest thee down to sleep. [50 The malice of Tellus hath brought this to pass, which if she could not have intreated of me by fair means, she would have commanded by menacing, for from her gather we all our simples to maintain our sorceries. [*To* BAGOA.] 55 Fan with this hemlock over his face, and sing the enchantment for sleep, whilst I go in and finish those ceremonies that are required in our art. Take heed ye touch not his face, for the fan is so seasoned that whoso it toucheth with [60 a leaf shall presently die, and over whom the wind of it breatheth, he shall sleep forever.

Bagoa. Let me alone ; I will be careful. [*Exit* DIPSAS.] What hap hadst thou, Endymion, to come under the hands of Dipsas ? O fair En- [65 dymion, how it grieveth me that that fair face must be turned to a withered skin and taste the pains of death before it feel the reward of love !

[1] Moonwort. " I have heard of an herb called Lunary that being bound to the pulses of the sick cause nothing but dreams of weddings and dances." Act III, Sc. 3, *Sapho and Phao.* (Baker.)

I fear Tellus will repent that which the heavens themselves seemed to rue. But I hear Dipsas [70 coming ! I dare not repine, lest she make me pine, and rock me into such a deep sleep that I shall not awake to my marriage.

Re-enter DIPSAS.

Dipsas. How now, have you finished ?
Bagoa. Yea.   [75
Dipsas. Well then, let us in ; and see that you do not so much as whisper that I did this, for if you do, I will turn thy hairs to adders and all thy teeth in thy head to tongues. Come away, come away.   *Exeunt* [DIPSAS *and* BAGOA]. [80

A DUMB SHOW[2] [*representing the dream of Endymion*].

Music sounds. Three ladies enter: one with a knife and a looking-glass, who, by the procurement of one of the other two, offers to stab Endymion as he sleeps ; but the third wrings her hands, lamenteth, offering still to prevent it, but dares [85 not. At last, the first lady looking in the glass, casts down the knife.   *Exeunt.*

Enter an ancient man with books with three leaves ; offers the same twice. Endymion refuseth. He rendeth[3] two, and offers the third, [90 where he stands awhile ; and then Endymion offers to take it.   *Exit* [*the Old Man*].

ACT III

SCENE I.[4]

[*Enter*] CYNTHIA, TELLUS, [SEMELE, EUMENIDES, CORSITES, PANELION, *and* ZONTES.]

Cynthia. Is the report true, that Endymion is stricken into such a dead sleep that nothing can either wake him or move him ?
Eum. Too true, madam, and as much to be pitied as wondered at.   *5
Tellus. As good sleep and do no harm as wake and do no good.
Cynth. What maketh you, Tellus, to be so short ? The time was Endymion only was.
Eum. It is an old saying, madam, that a [10 waking dog doth afar off bark at a sleeping lion.
Sem. It were good, Eumenides, that you took a nap with your friend, for your speech beginneth to be heavy.   [15
Eum. Contrary to your nature, Semele, which hath been always accounted light.
Cynth. What, have we here before my face these unseemly and malapert overthwarts![5] I will tame your tongues and your thoughts, [20 and make your speeches answerable to your duties, and your conceits fit for my dignity, else will I banish you both my person and the world.
Eum. Pardon, I humbly ask ; but such is my unspotted faith to Endymion that whatsoever [25

[2] *Dumb show.* Omitted in first edition. Given by Blount in 1632.   [3] Blount reads *readeth.*
[4] In the Gardens of the Palace.   [5] Wranglings.

seemeth a needle to prick his finger is a dagger
to wound my heart.

Cynth. If you be so dear to him, how hap-
peneth it you neither go to see him, nor search
for remedy for him?   [30

Eum. I have seen him to my grief, and sought
recure with despair, for that I cannot imagine
who should restore him that is the wonder to
all men. Your Highness, on whose hands the
compass of the earth is at command, though [35
not in possession, may show yourself both
worthy your sex, your nature, and your favour,
if you redeem that honourable Endymion,
whose ripe years foretell rare virtues, and whose
unmellowed conceits promise ripe counsel.   [40

Cynth. I have had trial of Endymion, and
conceive greater assurance of his age than I
could hope of his youth.

Tellus. But timely, madam, crooks that tree
that will be a cammock,[1] and young it pricks [45
that will be a thorn; and therefore he that
began without care to settle his life, it is a sign
without amendment he will end it.

Cynth. Presumptuous girl, I will make thy
tongue an example of unrecoverable dis-   [50
pleasure. Corsites, carry her to the castle in the
desert, there to remain and weave.

Cors. Shall she work stories or poetries?

Cynth. It skilleth[2] not which. Go to, in both;
for she shall find examples infinite in either [55
what punishment long tongues have. Eumenides, if either the soothsayers in Egypt, or the
enchanters in Thessaly, or the philosophers in
Greece, or all the sages of the world can find
remedy, I will procure it; therefore, dispatch [60
with all speed: you, Eumenides, into Thessaly; you, Zontes, into Greece, because you are
acquainted in Athens; you, Panelion, to Egypt;
saying that Cynthia sendeth, and if you will,
commandeth.   [65

Eum. On bowed knee I give thanks, and with
wings on my legs, I fly for remedy.

Zon. We are ready at your highness' command, and hope to return to your full content.

Cynth. It shall never be said that Cynthia, [70
whose mercy and goodness filleth the heavens
with joys and the world with marvels, will
suffer either Endymion or any to perish, if he
may be protected.

Eum. Your Majesty's words have been al- [75
ways deeds, and your deeds virtues.   *Exeunt.*

Scene II.[3]

[*Enter*] Corsites *and* Tellus.

Cors. Here is the castle, fair Tellus, in which
you must weave, till either time end your days,
or Cynthia her displeasure. I am sorry so fair a
face should be subject to so hard a fortune, and
that the flower of beauty, which is honoured [5
in courts, should here wither in prison.

Tellus. Corsites, Cynthia may restrain the
liberty of my body, of my thoughts she cannot;
and therefore do I esteem myself most free,
though I am in greatest bondage.   10

Cors. Can you then feed on fancy, and subdue the malice of envy by the sweetness of
imagination?

Tellus. Corsites, there is no sweeter music to
the miserable than despair; and therefore [15
the more bitterness I feel, the more sweetness
I find; for so vain were liberty, and so unwelcome the following of higher fortune, that I
choose rather to pine in this castle than to be a
prince in any other court.   20

Cors. A humour contrary to your years and
nothing agreeable to your sex; the one commonly allured with delights, the other always
with sovereignty.

Tellus. I marvel, Corsites, that you being [25
a captain, who should sound nothing but terror
and suck nothing but blood, can find in your
heart to talk such smooth words, for that it
agreeth not with your calling to use words so
soft as that of love.   30

Cors. Lady, it were unfit of wars to discourse
with women, into whose minds nothing can sink
but smoothness; besides, you must not think
that soldiers be so rough-hewn, or of such
knotty mettle, that beauty cannot allure, [35
and you, being beyond perfection, enchant.

Tellus. Good Corsites, talk not of love, but
let me to my labour. The little beauty I have
shall be bestowed on my loom, which I now
mean to make my lover.   40

Cors. Let us in, and what favor Corsites can
show, Tellus shall command.

Tellus. The only favour I desire is now and
then to walk.   *Exeunt.*

Scene III.[4]

[*Enter*] Sir Tophas *and* Epiton.

Tophas. Epi!

Epi. Here, sir.

Tophas. Unrig me. Heigho!

Epi. What's that?

Tophas. An interjection, whereof some are [5
of mourning: as *eho, vah.*[5]

Epi. I understand you not.

Tophas. Thou seest me.

Epi. Ay.

Tophas. Thou hearest me.   10

Epi. Ay.

Tophas. Thou feelest me.

Epi. Ay.

Tophas. And not understand'st me?

Epi. No.   15

Tophas. Then am I but three-quarters of a
noun substantive. But alas, Epi, to tell thee
the troth, I am a noun adjective.

Epi. Why?

Tophas. Because I cannot stand without [20
another.

Epi. Who is that?

Tophas. Dipsas.

Epi. Are you in love?

Tophas. No; but love hath, as it were, [25

---

[1] A crooked tree.   [2] Matters.   [3] Before a castle.

[4] In the Gardens of the Palace.
[5] Here, and below, the allusions are to W. Lilly's Latin
Grammar.

milk'd my thoughts and drained from my heart
the very substance of my accustomed courage;
it worketh in my head like new wine, so as I
must hoop my sconce with iron, lest my head
break, and so I bewray [1] my brains. But, I [30
pray thee, first discover me in all parts, that I
may be like a lover, and then will I sigh and
die. Take my gun and give me a gown : *Cedant
arma togæ.*[2]

Epi. Here.　　　　　　　　　　　　　35

Tophas. Take my sword and shield and give
me beard-brush and scissors : *Bella gerant alii,
tu Pari semper ama.*[3]

Epi. Will you be trimm'd, sir ?

Tophas. Not yet; for I feel a contention [40
within me whether I shall frame the bodkin
beard or the bush. But take my pike and give
me pen : *Dicere quæ puduit, scribere jussit amor.*[4]

Epi. I will furnish you, sir.

Tophas. Now, for my bow and bolts give [45
me ink and paper, for my smiter a pen-knife ;
for

　　*Scalpellum, calami, atramentum, charta, libelli,
　　Sint semper studiis arma parata meis.*[5]

Epi. Sir, will you give over wars and play [50
with that bauble called love ?

Tophas. Give over wars ? No, Epi, *Militat
omnis amans, et habet sua castra Cupido.*[6]

Epi. Love hate made you very eloquent, but
your face is nothing fair.　　　　　　　55

Tophas. *Non formosus erat, sed erat facundus
Ulysses.*[7]

Epi. Nay, I must seek a new master if you
can speak nothing but verses.

Tophas. *Quicquid conabar dicere, versus* [60
erat.[8] Epi, I feel all Ovid *De Arte Amandi* lie
as heavy at my heart as a load of logs. Oh,
what a fine, thin hair hath Dipsas! What a
pretty low forehead! What a tall and stately
nose! What little hollow eyes! What great [65
and goodly lips! How harmless she is, being
toothless, — her fingers fat and short, adorned
with long nails like a bittern! In how sweet a
proportion her cheeks hang down to her breasts
like dugs and her paps to her waist like bags! [70
What a low stature she is, and yet what a great
foot she carrieth! How thrifty must she be in
whom there is no waist! How virtuous is she
like to be, over whom no man can be jealous!

Epi. Stay, master, you forget yourself.　　75

Tophas. O Epi, even as a dish melteth by the
fire, so doth my wit increase by love.

Epi. Pithily, and to the purpose! But what,
begin you to nod ?

Tophas. Good Epi, let me take a nap; for [80
as some man may better steal a horse than another look over the hedge, so divers shall be
sleepy when they would fainest take rest.
　　　　　　　　　　　　　　He sleeps.

---

[1] Disclose.
[2] Cicero, *De Officiis,* i. 22, 76.
[3] Adapted from Ovid, *Heroides,* xvii. 254.
[4] Ovid, *Her.* iv. 10.
[5] These lines seem to be Lyly's own.
[6] Ovid, *Amores,* i. 9. 1.
[7] Ovid, *Ars Amatoria,* ii. 123.
[8] Ovid, *Tristia,* iv. 10. 26.

Epi. Who ever saw such a woodcock![9] Love
Dipsas! Without doubt all the world will [85
now account him valiant, that ventureth on her
whom none durst undertake. But here cometh
two wags.

Enter DARES and SAMIAS.

Sam. Thy master hath slept his share.

Dar. I think he doth it because he would [90
not pay me my board-wages.

Sam. It is a thing most strange : and I think
mine will never return, so that we must both
seek new masters, for we shall never live by
our manners.　　　　　　　　　　95

Epi. If you want masters, join with me and
serve Sir Tophas, who must needs keep more
men, because he is toward marriage.

Sam. What, Epi, where's thy master ?

Epi. Yonder, sleeping in love.　　　　100

Dar. Is it possible ?

Epi. He hath taken his thoughts a hole lower,
and saith, seeing it is the fashion of the world,
he will vail[10] bonnet to beauty.

Sam. How is he attired ?　　　　　　105

Epi. Lovely.

Dar. Whom loveth this amorous knight ?

Epi. Dipsas.

Sam. That ugly creature ? Why, she is a
fool, a scold, fat, without fashion, and quite [110
without favour.

Epi. Tush, you be simple ; my master hath
a good marriage.

Dar. Good! As how ?

Epi. Why, in marrying Dipsas he shall [115
have every day twelve dishes of meat to his
dinner, though there be none but Dipsas with
him : four of flesh, four of fish, four of fruit.

Sam. As how, Epi ?

Epi. For flesh these : woodcock, goose, [120
bittern, and rail.

Dar. Indeed, he shall not miss, if Dipsas be
there.

Epi. For fish these : crab, carp, lump, and
pouting.　　　　　　　　　　　　125

Sam. Excellent, for of my word she is both
crabbish, lumpish, and carping.

Epi. For fruit these : fritters, medlars, har-
tichokes, and lady-longings. Thus you see he
shall fare like a king, though he be but a [130
beggar.

Dar. Well, Epi, dine thou with him, for I
had rather fast than see her face. But see, thy
master is asleep; let us have a song to wake
this amorous knight.　　　　　　　　135

Epi. Agreed.

Sam. Content.

THE FIRST SONG.[11]

　　Epi. Here snores Tophas,
　　　That amorous ass,
　　Who loves Dipsas,　　　　　　　140
　　With face so sweet,
　　Nose and chin meet.

All three. { At sight of her each Fury skips
　　　　　　{ And flings into her lap their whips.

---

[9] Simpleton.　　　　　[10] Take off.
[11] The Song appears first in Blount's edition.

Dar. Holla, holla in his ear.   145
Sam. The witch, sure, thrust her fingers there.
Epi. Cramp him, or wring the fool by th' nose ;
Dar. Or clap some burning flax to his toes.
Sam. What music 's best to wake him ?
Epi. Bow-wow, let bandogs shake him !   150
Dar. Let adders hiss in 's ear ;
Sam. Else earwigs wriggle there.
Epi. No, let him batten [1] ; when his tongue
Once goes, a cat is not worse strung.
All three. { But if he ope nor mouth nor eyes, [155
         { He may in time sleep himself wise.

Top. Sleep is a binding of the senses, love a
loosing.
Epi. [*Aside.*] Let us hear him awhile.
Top. There appeared in my sleep a goodly [160
owl, who, sitting upon my shoulder, cried
"Twit, twit"; and before mine eyes presented
herself the express image of Dipsas. I mar-
velled what the owl said, till at the last I perceived "Twit, twit," "To it, to it," only [165
by contraction admonished by this vision to
make account of my sweet Venus.
Sam. Sir Tophas, you have overslept yourself.
Top. No, youth, I have but slept over [170
my love.
Dar. Love? Why, it is impossible that into
so noble and unconquered a courage love
should creep, having first a head as hard to
pierce as steel, then to pass to a heart [175
arm'd with a shirt of mail.
Epi. Ay, but my master yawning one day in
the sun, Love crept into his mouth before he
could close it, and there kept such a tumbling
in his body that he was glad to untruss [2] [180
the points of his heart and entertain Love as a
stranger.
Top. If there remain any pity in you, plead
for me to Dipsas.
Dar. Plead ! Nay, we will press her to it. [185
[*Aside to* SAMIAS.] Let us go with him to Dipsas, and there shall we have good sport. — But,
Sir Tophas, when shall we go? For I find my
tongue voluble, and my heart venturous, and
all myself like myself.   190
Sam. [*Aside to* DARES.] Come, Dares, let us
not lose him until we find our masters, for as
long as he liveth, we shall lack neither mirth
nor meat.
Epi. We will traverse.[3] Will you go, sir ? 195
Top. I *prœ, sequar.*[4]   *Exeunt.*

SCENE IV.[5]

[*Enter*] EUMENIDES *and* GERON.

Eum. Father, your sad music being tuned on
the same key that my hard fortune is, hath so
melted my mind that I wish to hang at your
mouth's end till my life end.
Ger. These tunes, gentleman, have I been [5
accustomed with these fifty winters, having no
other house to shroud myself but the broad
heavens; and so familiar with me hath use
made misery that I esteem sorrow my chiefest

[1] Grow fat.   [3] So Baker. Old edd. *Travice.*
[2] To untie the laces.   [4] Terence, *Andria*, I. i. 144.
[5] A desert place, with a fountain.

solace, and welcomest is that guest to me [10
that can rehearse the saddest tale or the blood-
iest tragedy.
Eum. A strange humour. Might I inquire the
cause ?
Ger. You must pardon me if I deny to tell [15
it, for knowing that the revealing of griefs is,
as it were, a renewing of sorrow, I have vowed
therefore to conceal them, that I might not only
feel the depth of everlasting discontentment,
but despair of remedy. But whence are you ? [20
What fortune hath thrust you to this distress ?
Eum. I am going to Thessaly, to seek remedy
for Endymion, my dearest friend, who hath
been cast into a dead sleep almost these twenty
years, waxing old and ready for the grave, [25
being almost but newly come forth of the cradle.
Ger. You need not for recure travel far, for
whoso can clearly see the bottom of this fountain shall have remedy for anything.
Eum. That methinketh is impossible. Why, [30
what virtue can there be in water ?
Ger. Yes, whosoever can shed the tears of a
faithful lover shall obtain anything he would.
Read these words engraven about the brim.
Eum. Have you known this by experience, [35
or is it placed here of purpose to delude men ?
Ger. I only would have experience of it, and
then should there be an end of my misery ; and
then would I tell the strangest discourse that
ever yet was heard.   40
Eum. Ah, Eumenides !
Ger. What lack you, gentleman ; are you not
well ?
Eum. Yes, father, but a qualm that often
cometh over my heart doth now take hold of [45
me. But did never any lovers come hither ?
Ger. Lusters, but not lovers ; for often have
I seen them weep, but never could I hear they
saw the bottom.
Eum. Came there women also ?   50
Ger. Some.
Eum. What did they see ?
Ger. They all wept, that the fountain over-
flowed with tears, but so thick became the
water with their tears that I could scarce [55
discern the brim, much less behold the bottom.
Eum. Be faithful lovers so scant ?
Ger. It seemeth so, for yet heard I never of
any.
Eum. Ah, Eumenides, how art thou per- [60
plexed ! Call to mind the beauty of thy sweet
mistress and the depth of thy never-dying affections. How oft hast thou honoured her, not only
without spot, but suspicion of falsehood ! And
how hardly hath she rewarded thee without [65
cause or colour of despite. How secret hast
thou been these seven years, that hast not, nor
once darest not to name her, for discontenting
her. How faithful, that hast offered to die for
her, to please her ! Unhappy Eumenides ! [70
Ger. Why, gentleman, did you once love ?
Eum. Once? Ay, father, and ever shall.
Ger. Was she unkind and you faithful ?
Eum. She of all women the most froward,
and I of all creatures the most fond.   [75
Ger. You doted then, not loved, for affection

is grounded on virtue, and virtue is never peevish ; or on beauty, and beauty loveth to be
praised.

Eum. Ay, but if all virtuous ladies should [80
yield to all that be loving, or all amiable gentlewomen entertain all that be amorous, their
virtues would be accounted vices, and their
beauties deformities ; for that love can be but
between two, and that not proceeding of him [85
that is most faithful but most fortunate.

Ger. I would you were so faithful that your
tears might make you fortunate.

Eum. Yea, father, if that my tears clear not
this fountain, then may you swear it is but a [90
mere mockery.

Ger. So saith every one yet that wept.

Eum. Ah, I faint, I die ! Ah, sweet Semele,
let me alone, and dissolve, by weeping, into
water.   [*He gazes into the fountain.*] [95

Ger. This affection seemeth strange : if he
see nothing, without doubt this dissembling
passeth, for nothing shall draw me from the
belief.

Eum. Father, I plainly see the bottom, [100
and there in white marble engraven these
words : *Ask one for all, and but one thing at all.*

Ger. O fortunate Eumenides, (for so have I
heard thee call thyself,) let me see. I cannot discern any such thing. I think thou dreamest. [105

Eum. Ah, father, thou art not a faithful
lover, and therefore canst not behold it.

Ger. Then ask, that I may be satisfied by
the event, and thyself blessed.

Eum. Ask ? So I will. And what shall I [110
do but ask, and whom should I ask but Semele,
the possessing of whose person is a pleasure that
cannot come within the compass of comparison ;
whose golden locks seem most curious when
they seem most careless ; whose sweet looks [115
seem most alluring when they are most chaste ;
and whose words the more virtuous they are,
the more amorous they be accounted ? I pray
thee, Fortune, when I shall first meet with fair
Semele, dash my delight with some light dis- [120
grace, lest embracing sweetness beyond measure, I take a surfeit without recure. Let her
practise her accustomed coyness that I may diet
myself upon my desires ; otherwise the fulness
of my joys will diminish the sweetness, and [125
I shall perish by them before I possess them.

Why do I trifle the time in words ? The least
minute being spent in the getting of Semele is
more worth than the whole world ; therefore
let me ask. What now, Eumenides ! Whither [130
art thou drawn? Hast thou forgotten both
friendship and duty, care of Endymion, and the
commandment of Cynthia? Shall he die in a
leaden sleep because thou sleepest in a golden
dream ? Ay, let him sleep ever, so I slumber [135
but one minute with Semele. Love knoweth
neither friendship nor kindred. Shall I not
hazard the loss of a friend for the obtaining of
her for whom I would often lose myself ? Fond [1]
Eumenides, shall the enticing beauty of a [140
most disdainful lady be of more force than the

         [1] **Foolish.**

rare fidelity of a tried friend ? The love of men
to women is a thing common and of course ; the
friendship of man to man infinite and immortal.
Tush ! Semele doth possess my love. Ay, [145
but Endymion hath deserved it. I will help
Endymion. I found Endymion unspotted in his
truth. Ay, but I shall find Semele constant in
her love. I will have Semele. What shall I do ?
Father, thy gray hairs are embassadors of [150
experience. Which shall I ask ?

Ger. Eumenides, release Endymion, for all
things, friendship excepted, are subject to fortune : love is but an eye-worm, which only
tickleth the head with hopes and wishes ; [155
friendship the image of eternity, in which there
is nothing movable, nothing mischievous. As
much difference as there is between beauty and
virtue, bodies and shadows, colours and life, so
great odds is there between love and friend- [160
ship.

Love is a chameleon, which draweth nothing
into the mouth but air, and nourisheth nothing
in the body but lungs. Believe me, Eumenides,
desire dies in the same moment that beauty [165
sickens, and beauty fadeth in the same instant
that it flourisheth. When adversities flow, then
love ebbs ; but friendship standeth stiffly in
storms. Time draweth wrinkles in a fair face,
but addeth fresh colours to a fast friend, [170
which neither heat, nor cold, nor misery, nor
place, nor destiny, can alter or diminish. O
friendship, of all things the most rare, and
therefore most rare because most excellent,
whose comforts in misery is always sweet, [175
and whose counsels in prosperity are ever fortunate ! Vain love, that, only coming near to
friendship in name, would seem to be the same
or better in nature !

Eum. Father, I allow your reasons, and [180
will therefore conquer mine own. Virtue shall
subdue affections, wisdom lust, friendship
beauty. Mistresses are in every place, and as
common as hares on Athos, bees in Hybla,
fowls in the air ; but friends to be found [185
are like the phœnix in Arabia, but one ; or the
philadelphi in Arays, never above two. I will
have Endymion. Sacred fountain, in whose
bowels are hidden divine secrets, I have in-
creased your waters with the tears of un- [190
spotted thoughts, and therefore let me receive
the reward you promise. Endymion, the truest
friend to me, and faithfulest lover to Cynthia,
is in such a dead sleep that nothing can wake or
move him.   [195

Ger. Dost thou see anything ?

Eum. I see in the same pillar these words :
*When she whose figure of all is the perfectest,
and never to be measured ; always one, yet never
the same ; still inconstant, yet never wavering ;* [200
*shall come and kiss Endymion in his sleep, he
shall then rise, else never.* This is strange.

Ger. What see you else ?

Eum. There cometh over mine eyes either
a dark mist, or upon the fountain a deep [205
thickness, for I can perceive nothing. But how
am I deluded, or what difficult, nay impossible,
thing is this ?

Ger. Methinketh it easy.
Eum. Good father, and how? 210
Ger. Is not a circle of all figures the perfectest?
Eum. Yes.
Ger. And is not Cynthia of all circles the most absolute? 215
Eum. Yes.
Ger. Is it not impossible to measure her, who still worketh by her influence, never standing at one stay?
Eum. Yes. 220
Ger. Is she not always Cynthia, yet seldom in the same bigness; always wavering in her waxing or waning, that our bodies might the better be governed, our seasons the dailier give their increase; yet never to be removed from her [225 course, as long as the heavens continue theirs?
Eum. Yes.
Ger. Then who can it be but Cynthia, whose virtues being all divine must needs bring things to pass that be miraculous? Go, humble thy- [230 self to Cynthia; tell her the success, of which myself shall be a witness. And this assure thyself, that she that sent to find means for his safety will now work her cunning.
Eum. How fortunate am I, if Cynthia be [235 she that may do it!
Ger. How fond[1] art thou, if thou do not believe it!
Eum. I will hasten thither that I may entreat on my knees for succour, and embrace in [240 mine arms my friend.
Ger. I will go with thee, for unto Cynthia must I discover all my sorrows, who also must work in me a contentment.
Eum. May I now know the cause? 245
Ger. That shall be as we walk, and I doubt not but the strangeness of my tale will take away the tediousness of our journey.
Eum. Let us go.
Ger. I follow. *Exeunt.* [250

ACT IV

SCENE I.[2]

[Enter] TELLUS.

Tellus. I marvel Corsites giveth me so much liberty, — all the world knowing his charge to be so high and his nature to be most strange, — who hath so ill entreated ladies of great honour that he hath not suffered them to look out [5 of windows, much less to walk abroad. It may be he is in love with me, for (Endymion, hardhearted Endymion, excepted) what is he that is not enamour'd of my beauty? But what respectest thou the love of all the world? En- [10 dymion hates me. Alas, poor Endymion, my malice hath exceeded my love, and thy faith to Cynthia quenched my affections. Quenched, Tellus? Nay, kindled them afresh; insomuch that I find scorching flames for dead embers, [15 and cruel encounters of war in my thoughts instead of sweet parleys. Ah, that I might once

[1] Foolish.   [2] Before Corsites' Castle.

again see Endymion! Accursed girl, what hope hast thou to see Endymion, on whose head already are grown gray hairs, and whose life [20 must yield to nature, before Cynthia end her displeasure. Wicked Dipsas, and most devilish Tellus, the one for cunning too exquisite, the other for hate too intolerable! Thou wast commanded to weave the stories and poetries [25 wherein were showed both examples and punishments of tattling tongues, and thou hast only embroidered the sweet face of Endymion, devices of love, melancholy imaginations, and what not, out of thy work, that thou shouldst [30 study to pick out of thy mind. But here cometh Corsites. I must seem yielding and stout; full of mildness, yet tempered with a majesty; for if I be too flexible, I shall give him more hope than I mean; if too froward, enjoy less liberty [35 than I would. Love him I cannot, and therefore will practise that which is most contrary[3] to our sex, to dissemble.

Enter CORSITES.

Cor. Fair Tellus, I perceive you rise with the lark, and to yourself sing with the nightin- 40 gale.
Tellus. My lord, I have no playfellow but fancy; being barred of all company, I must question with myself, and make my thoughts my friends. [45
Cor. I would you would account my thoughts also your friends, for they be such as are only busied in wondering at your beauty and wisdom; and some such as have esteemed your fortune too hard; and divers of that kind [50 that offer to set you free, if you will set them free.
Tellus. There are no colours so contrary as white and black, nor elements so disagreeing as fire and water, nor anything so opposite as [55 men's thoughts and their words.
Cor. He that gave Cassandra the gift of prophesying, with the curse that, spake she never so true, she should never be believed, hath I think poisoned the fortune of men, [60 that uttering the extremities of their inward passions are always suspected of outward perjuries.
Tellus. Well, Corsites, I will flatter myself and believe you. What would you do to en- [65 joy my love?
Cor. Set all the ladies of the castle free, and make you the pleasure of my life: more I cannot do, less I will not.
Tellus. These be great words, and fit your [70 calling; for captains must promise things impossible. But will you do one thing for all?
Cor. Anything, sweet Tellus, that am ready for all.
Tellus. You know that on the lunary bank [75 sleepeth Endymion.
Cor. I know it.
Tellus. If you will remove him from that place by force, and convey him into some obscure cave by policy, I give you here the [80

[3] Bond emends to *customary.*

faith of an unspotted virgin that you only shall
possess me as a lover, and in spite of malice
have me for a wife.

Cor. Remove him, Tellus! Yes, Tellus, he
shall be removed, and that so soon as [1] thou [85]
shalt as much commend my diligence as my
force. I go.

Tellus. Stay, will yourself attempt it?

Cor. Ay, Tellus; as I would have none partaker of my sweet love, so shall none be [90]
partners of my labors. But I pray thee go at
your best leisure, for Cynthia beginneth to rise,
and if she discover our love, we both perish, for
nothing pleaseth her but the fairness of virginity. All things must be not only without [95]
lust but without suspicion of lightness.

Tellus. I will depart, and go you to Endymion.

Cor. I fly, Tellus, being of all men the most
fortunate. *Exit.* [100]

Tellus. Simple Corsites, I have set thee about
a task, being but a man, that the gods themselves cannot perform, for little dost thou know
how heavy his head lies, how hard his fortune;
but such shifts must women have to deceive [105]
men, and under colour of things easy, entreat
that which is impossible; otherwise we should
be cumb'red with importunities, oaths, sighs,
letters, and all implements of love, which to
one resolved to the contrary are most loath- [110]
some. I will in, and laugh with the other ladies
at Corsites' sweating. *Exit.*

SCENE II.[2]

[Enter] SAMIAS and DARES.

Sam. Will thy master never awake?

Dar. No; I think he sleeps for a wager. But
how shall we spend the time? Sir Tophas is so
far in love that he pineth in his bed and cometh
not abroad. 5

Sam. But here cometh Epi in a pelting chafe.[3]

[Enter EPITON.]

Epi. A pox of all false proverbs, and were a
proverb a page, I would have him by the ears!

Sam. Why art thou angry?

Epi. Why? You know it is said, "The [10]
tide tarrieth no man."

Sam. True.

Epi. A monstrous lie; for I was tied two
hours, and tarried for one to unloose me.

Dar. Alas, poor Epi! 15

Epi. Poor! No, no, you base-conceited
slaves, I am a most complete gentleman, although I be in disgrace with Sir Tophas.

Dar. Art thou out with him?

Epi. Ay, because I cannot get him a lodg- [20]
ing with Endymion. He would fain take a nap
for forty or fifty years.

Dar. A short sleep, considering our long life.

Sam. Is he still in love?

Epi. In love? Why he doth nothing but [25]
make sonnets.

Sam. Canst thou remember any one of his
poems?

Epi. Ay, this is one: —

The beggar, Love, that knows not where to lodge, [30]
  At last within my heart, when I slept,
          He crept,
  I wak'd, and so my fancies began to fodge.[4]

Sam. That's a very long verse.

Epi. Why, the other was short. The first [35]
is called from the thumb to the little finger;
the second from the little finger to the elbow;
and some he hath made to reach to the crown
of his head, and down again to the sole of his
foot. It is set to the tune of the black [40]
Saunce[5]; *ratio est*, because Dipsas is a black
saint.

Dar. Very wisely. But pray thee, Epi, how
art thou complete; and being from thy master,
what occupation wilt thou take? 45

Epi. Know,[6] my hearts, I am an absolute
Microcosmus, a petty world of myself: my
library is my head, for I have no other books
but my brains; my wardrobe on my back, for
I have no more apparel than is on my body; [50]
my armory at my fingers' ends, for I use no
other artillery than my nails; my treasure in
my purse. *Sic omnia mea mecum porto.*[7]

Dar. Good!

Epi. Know,[8] sirs, my palace is pav'd with [55]
grass, and tiled with stars, for *Cælo tegitur qui
non habet urnam,*[9] — he that hath no house must
lie in the yard.

Sam. A brave resolution! But how wilt thou
spend thy time? 60

Epi. Not in any melancholy sort; for mine
exercise I will walk horses.

Dar. Too bad!

Epi. Why, is it not said, "It is good walking when one hath his horse in his hand"? [65]

Sam. Worse and worse! But how wilt thou
live?

Epi. By angling. Oh, 'tis a stately occupation
to stand four hours in a cold morning, and to
have his nose bitten with frost before his [70]
bait be mumbled with a fish.

Dar. A rare attempt! But wilt thou never
travel?

Epi. Yes, in a western barge, when with a
good wind and lusty pugs,[10] one may go ten [75]
miles in two days.

Sam. Thou art excellent at thy choice. But
what pastime wilt thou use? None?

Epi. Yes, the quickest of all.

Sam. What, dice? [80]

Epi. No, when I am in haste, one-and-twenty
games at chess, to pass a few minutes.

Dar. A life for a little lord, and full of
quickness.

---

[1] That.
[2] In the Gardens of the Palace.
[3] Irritable humour.
[4] Move.
[5] Black Sanctus, a hymn to Saint Satan.
[6] So Baker. Old edd. read *No*.
[7] Quoted by Cicero in *Paradoxa Stoicorum*, i. 1, as
from Bias (Baker).
[8] So Baker. Old edd. read *Now*.
[9] Lucan, vii. 819.
[10] Fellows.

Epi. Tush, let me alone! But I must [85
needs see if I can find where Endymion lieth,
and then go to a certain fountain hard by,
where they say faithful lovers shall have all
things they will ask. If I can find out any of
these, *Ego et magister meus erimus in tuto,* I [90
and my master shall be friends. He is resolved
to weep some three or four pailfuls to avoid the
rheum of love that wambleth [1] in his stomach.

Enter [Master Constable *and* Two] Watch-
[men].

Sam. Shall we never see thy master, Dares?
Dar. Yes; let us go now, for to-morrow [95
Cynthia will be there.
Epi. I will go with you; — but how shall we
see for the Watch?
Sam. Tush, let me alone! I 'll begin to them.
Masters, God speed you.　　　　　　　　[100
1 *Watch.* Sir boy, we are all sped already.
Epi. [*Aside.*] So methinks, for they smell all
of drink, like a beggar's beard.
Dar. But I pray, sirs, may we see Endymion?　　　　　　　　　　　　　　　105
2 *Watch.* No, we are commanded in Cynthia's name, that no man shall see him.
Sam. No man! Why, we are but boys.
1 *Watch.* Mass, neighbours, he says true, for
if I swear I will never drink my liquor by [110
the quart, and yet call for two pints, I think
with a safe conscience I may carouse both.
Dar. Pithily, and to the purpose.
2 *Watch.* Tush, tush, neighbours, take me
with you.[2]　　　　　　　　　　　115
Sam. [*Aside.*] This will grow hot.
Dar. [*Aside.*] Let them alone.
2 *Watch.* If I say to my wife, "Wife, I
will have no raisins in my pudding," she puts in
currants; small raisins are raisins, and boys [120
are men: even as my wife should have put no
raisins in my pudding, so shall there no boys
see Endymion.
Dar. Learnedly.
Epi. Let Master Constable speak; I think [125
he is the wisest among you.
Master Constable. You know, neighbours, 't is
an old said saw, "Children and fools speak
true."
All. True.　　　　　　　　　　　130
Mast. Const. Well, there you see the men be
the fools, because it is provided from the children.
Dar. Good.
Mast. Const. Then, say I, neighbours, that [135
children must not see Endymion, because children and fools speak true.
Epi. O wicked application!
Sam. Scurvily brought about!
1 *Watch.* Nay, he says true, and therefore [140
till Cynthia have been here, he shall not be un-
covered. Therefore, away!
Dar. [*Aside to Sam. and Epi.*] A watch, quoth
you! A man may watch seven years for a
wise word, and yet go without it. Their wits [145
are all as rusty as their bills. — But come on,

Master Constable, shall we have a song before
we go?
Mast. Const. With all my heart.

THE SECOND SONG.[3]

Watch. Stand! Who goes there?　　　　150
We charge you appear
'Fore our constable here,
In the name of the Man in the Moon.
To us billmen relate
Why you stagger so late,　　　　　　155
And how you come drunk so soon.
Pages. What are ye, scabs?
Watch.　　　　　　　　The Watch;
This the Constable.
Pages.　　　　　A patch.[4]
Const. Knock 'em down unless they all stand:
If any run away,　　　　　　　　160
'T is the old watchman's play,
To reach him a bill of his hand.
Pages. O gentlemen, hold,
Your gowns freeze with cold,
And your rotten teeth dance in your head;　165
Epi. Wine, nothing shall cost ye;
Sam. Nor huge fires to roast ye;
Dares. Then soberly let us be led.
Const. Come, my brown bills, we 'll roar,[5]
Bounce loud at tavern door,　　　　　170
Omnes. And i' th' morning steal all to bed.
　　　　　　　　　　　　　Exeunt.

SCENE III.[6]

CORSITES *solus.* [ENDYMION *lies asleep on the
lunary bank.*]

Corsites. I am come in sight of the lunary
bank. Without doubt Tellus doteth upon me,
and cunningly, that I might not perceive her
love, she hath set me to a task that is done before it is begun. Endymion, you must change [5
your pillow, and if you be not weary of sleep, I
will carry you where at ease you shall sleep your
fill. It were good that without more ceremonies
I took him, lest being espied, I be entrapt, and
so incur the displeasure of Cynthia, who [10
commonly setteth watch that Endymion have
no wrong. [*He tries to lift Endymion.*] What
now, is your mastership so heavy, or are you
nail'd to the ground? Not stir one whit! Then
use all thy force, though he feel it and wake. [15
What, stone-still? Turn'd, I think, to earth
with lying so long on the earth. Didst not thou,
Corsites, before Cynthia, pull up a tree that
forty years was fast'ned with roots and
wreathed in knots to the ground? Didst not [20
thou, with main force, pull open the iron gates
which no ram or engine could move? Have my
weak thoughts made brawn-fallen my strong
arms, or is it the nature of love, or the quintessence of the mind, to breed numbness or [25
litherness,[7] or I know not what languishing
in my joints and sinews, being but the base
strings of my body? Or doth the remembrance
of Tellus so refine my spirits into a matter so
subtle and divine that the other fleshy parts [30
cannot work whilst they muse? Rest thyself,
rest thyself; nay, rend thyself in pieces, Cor-

---

[1] Rumbles.　　　　　　　[2] Let me understand
[3] This song appears first in Blount's edition.
[4] Fool.　　　　　　　[6] In the Grove. till v. 54.
[5] Swagger.　　　　　　[7] Languor

sites, and strive, in spite of love, fortune, and nature, to lift up this dulled body, heavier than dead and more senseless than death.   35

Enter Fairies.

But what are these so fair fiends that cause my hairs to stand upright and spirits to fall down? Hags,— out alas, nymphs, I crave pardon. Ay me, out! what do I hear!

[*The Fairies dance, and with a song pinch him, and he falleth asleep. They kiss Endymion and depart.*

THE THIRD SONG [1] BY FAIRIES

Omnes. Pinch him, pinch him, black and blue,   40
Saucy mortals must not view
What the Queen of Stars is doing,
Nor pry into our fairy wooing.
1 *Fairy.* Pinch him blue,
2 *Fairy.* And pinch him black;   45
3 *Fairy.* Let him not lack
Sharp nails to pinch him blue and red,
Till sleep has rock'd his addle head.
4 *Fairy.* For the trespass he hath done,
Spots o'er all his flesh shall run.   50
Kiss Endymion, kiss his eyes,
Then to our midnight heidegyes. [2] *Exeunt* [Fairies].

[*Enter, at the side of the stage*[3] *opposite* CORSITES,]
CYNTHIA, FLOSCULA, SEMELE, PANELION,
ZONTES, PYTHAGORAS, *and* GYPTES. [COR-
SITES *sleeps still.*]

Cynth. You see, Pythagoras, what ridiculous opinions you hold, and I doubt not but you are now of another mind.   55
Pythag. Madam, I plainly perceive that the perfection of your brightness hath pierced through the thickness that covered my mind; insomuch that I am no less glad to be reformed than ashamed to remember my [60 grossness.
Gyptes. They are thrice fortunate that live in your palace where truth is not in colours but life, virtues not in imagination but execution.
Cynth. I have always studied to have rather [65 living virtues than painted gods, the body of truth than the tomb. But let us walk to Endymion; it may be it lieth in your arts to deliver him; as for Eumenides, I fear he is dead.   [70
Pythag. I have alleged all the natural reasons I can for such a long sleep.
Gyptes. I can do nothing till I see him.
Cynth. Come, Floscula; I am sure you are glad that you shall behold Endymion.   [75
Flosc. I were blessed, if I might have him recovered.
Cynth. Are you in love with his person?
Flosc. No, but with his virtue.
Cynth. What say you, Semele?   80
Sem. Madam, I dare say nothing for fear I offend.
Cynth. Belike you cannot speak except you be spiteful; but as good be silent as saucy. Panelion, what punishment were fit for [85

1 Appears first in Blount's edition.
2 A country dance.   3 Now the Gardens.

Semele, in whose speech and thoughts is only contempt and sourness?
Panel. I love not, madam, to give any judgment; yet, sith Your Highness commandeth, I think to commit her tongue close prisoner [90 to her mouth.
Cynth. Agreed. Semele, if thou speak this twelvemonth, thou shalt forfeit thy tongue. Behold Endymion! [4] Alas, poor gentleman, hast thou spent thy youth in sleep, that once [95 vowed all to my service! Hollow eyes, gray hairs, wrinkled cheeks, and decayed limbs! Is it destiny or deceit that hath brought this to pass? If the first, who could prevent thy wretched stars? If the latter, I would I [100 might know thy cruel enemy. I favoured thee, Endymion, for thy honour, thy virtues, thy affections; but to bring thy thoughts within the compass of thy fortunes, I have seemed strange, that I might have thee staid; and [105 now are thy days ended before my favour begin. But whom have we here? Is it not Corsites?
Zon. It is, but more like a leopard than a man.
Cynth. Awake him. [*Zontes wakens Corsites.*] How now, Corsites, what make you here? [110 How came you deformed? Look on thy hands, and then seest thou the picture of thy face.
Cors. Miserable wretch, and accursed! How am I deluded! Madam, I ask pardon for my offence, and you see my fortune deserveth pity. [115
Cynth. Speak on; thy offence cannot deserve greater punishment: but see thou rehearse the truth, else shalt thou not find me as thou wishest me.
Cors. Madam, as it is no offence to be in [120 love, being a man mortal, so I hope can it be no shame to tell with whom, my lady being heavenly. Your Majesty committed to my charge fair Tellus, whose beauty in the same moment took my heart captive that I undertook to carry [125 her body prisoner. Since that time have I found such combats in my thoughts between love and duty, reverence and affection, that I could neither endure the conflict, nor hope for the conquest.   130
Cynth. In love? A thing far unfitting the name of a captain, and (as I thought) the tough and unsmoothed nature of Corsites. But forth!
Cors. Feeling this continual war, I thought [135 rather by parley to yield than by certain danger to perish. I unfolded to Tellus the depth of my affections, and framed my tongue to utter a sweet tale of love, that was wont to sound nothing but threats of war. She, too fair to be [140 true and too false for one so fair, after a nice denial, practised a notable deceit, commanding me to remove Endymion from this cabin, and carry him to some dark cave; which I, seeking to accomplish, found impossible; and so by [145 fairies or fiends have been thus handled.
Cynth. How say you, my lords, is not Tellus always practising of some deceits? In sooth, Corsites, thy face is now too foul for a lover, and thine heart too fond for a soldier. You [150

4 Again in the Grove.

see when warriors become wantons how their manners alter with their faces. Is it not a shame, Corsites, that having lived so long in Mars his camp, thou shouldst now be rocked in Venus's cradle? Dost thou wear Cupid's [155 quiver at thy girdle and make lances of looks? Well, Corsites, rouse thyself and be as thou hast been; and let Tellus, who is made all of love, melt herself in her own looseness.

Cors. Madam, I doubt not but to recover [160 my former state, for Tellus's beauty never wrought such love in my mind as now her deceit hath despite; and yet to be revenged of a woman were a thing than love itself more womanish.

Gyptes. These spots, gentleman, are to be [165 worn out, if you rub them over with this lunary; so that in place where you received this maim you shall find a medicine.

Cors. I thank you for that. The gods bless me from love and these pretty ladies that [170 haunt this green.

Flosc. Corsites, I would Tellus saw your amiable face. [SEMELE *laughs.*]

Zont. How spitefully Semele laugheth, that dare not speak. 175

Cynth. Could you not stir Endymion with chat doubled strength of yours?

Cors. Not so much as his finger with all my force.

Cynth. Pythagoras and Gyptes, what [180 think you of Endymion? What reason is to be given, what remedy?

Pyth. Madam, it is impossible to yield reason for things that happen not in compass of nature. It is most certain that some strange en- [185 chantment hath bound all his senses.

Cynth. What say you, Gyptes?

Gyptes. With Pythagoras, that it is enchantment, and that so strange that no art can undo it, for that heaviness argueth a malice unre- [190 movable in the enchantress, and that no power can end it, till she die that did it, or the heavens show some means more than miraculous.

Flosc. O Endymion, could spite itself devise a mischief so monstrous as to make thee dead [195 with life, and living, being altogether dead? Where others number their years, their hours, their minutes, and step to age by stairs, thou only hast thy years and times in a cluster, being old before thou rememb'rest thou wast young. [200

Cynth. No more, Floscula; pity doth him no good: I would anything else might; and I vow by the unspotted honour of a lady he should not miss it. But is this all, Gyptes, that is to be done? 205

Gyptes. All as yet. It may be that either the enchantress shall die or else be discovered; if either happen, I will then practise the utmost of my art. In the mean season, about this grove would I have a watch, and the first living [210 thing that toucheth Endymion to be taken.

Cynth. Corsites, what say you, will you undertake this?

Cors. Good madam, pardon me! I was overtaken[1] too late. I should rather break into [215

the midst of a main battle than again fall into the hands of those fair babies.

Cynth. Well, I will provide others. Pythagoras and Gyptes, you shall yet remain in my court, till I hear what may be done in this [220 matter.

Pyth. We attend.

Cynth. Let us go in.   *Exeunt.*

ACT V

SCENE I.[2]

[*Enter*] SAMIAS *and* DARES.

Samias. Eumenides hath told such strange tales as I may well wonder at them, but never believe them.

Dar. The other old man, what a sad speech used he, that caused us almost all to weep. [5 Cynthia is so desirous to know the experiment of her own virtue, and so willing to ease Endymion's hard fortune, that she no sooner heard the discourse but she made herself in a readiness to try the event. 10

Sam. We will also see the event. But whilst here cometh Cynthia with all her train. Let us sneak in amongst them.

Enter CYNTHIA, FLOSCULA, SEMELE, [EUMENIDES,] PANELION, *etc.*

Cynth. Eumenides, it cannot sink into my head that I should be signified by that sa- [15 cred fountain, for many things are there in the world to which those words may be applied.

Eum. Good madam, vouchsafe but to try; else shall I think myself most unhappy that I asked not my sweet mistress. 20

Cynth. Will you not yet tell me her name?

Eum. Pardon me, good madam, for if Endymion awake, he shall; myself have sworn never to reveal it.

Cynth. Well, let us to Endymion. I will [25 not be so stately, good Endymion, not to stoop to do thee good; and if thy liberty consist in a kiss from me, thou shalt have it; and although my mouth hath been heretofore as untouched as my thoughts, yet now to recover thy life, [30 though to restore thy youth it be impossible, I will do that to Endymion which yet never mortal man could boast of heretofore, nor shall ever hope for hereafter.   *She kisseth him.*

Eum. Madam, he beginneth to stir. 35

Cynth. Soft, Eumenides; stand still.

Eum. Ah, I see his eyes almost open.

Cynth. I command thee once again, stir not. I will stand behind him.

Pan. What do I see? Endymion almost [40 awake?

Eum. Endymion, Endymion, art thou deaf or dumb, or hath this long sleep taken away thy memory? Ah, my sweet Endymion, seest thou not Eumenides, thy faithful friend, thy faith- [45 ful Eumenides, who for thy safety hath been

---

[1] Overcome.   [2] In the Grove.

careless of his own content ? Speak, Endymion !
Endymion ! Endymion !
End. Endymion ? I call to mind such a
name.   50
Eum. Hast thou forgotten thyself, Endy-
mion ? Then do I not marvel thou rememb'rest
not thy friend. I tell thee thou art Endymion,
and I Eumenides. Behold also Cynthia, by
whose favour thou art awaked, and by whose [55
virtue thou shalt continue thy natural course.
Cynth. Endymion, speak, sweet Endymion !
Knowest thou not Cynthia ?
End. O heavens, whom do I behold ? Fair
Cynthia, divine Cynthia ?   60
Cynth. I am Cynthia, and thou Endymion.
End. "Endymion"! What do I hear[1]? What,
a gray beard, hollow eyes, withered body, decayed limbs, — and all in one night ?
Eum. One night ! Thou hast here slept [65
forty years, — by what enchantress as yet it is
not known, — and behold, the twig to which
thou laid'st thy head is now become a tree.
Callest thou not Eumenides to remembrance ?
End. Thy name I do remember by the [70
sound, but thy favour[2] I do not yet call to mind ;
only divine Cynthia, to whom time, fortune,
destiny, and death are subject, I see and remember, and in all humility I regard and reverence.   75
Cynth. You have good cause to remember
Eumenides, who hath for thy safety forsaken
his own solace.
End. Am I that Endymion who was wont in
court to lead my life, and in justs, tourneys, [80
and arms, to exercise my youth ? Am I that
Endymion ?
Eum. Thou art that Endymion, and I Eumenides : wilt thou not yet call me to remembrance ?   85
End. Ah, sweet Eumenides, I now perceive
thou art he, and that myself have the name of
Endymion ; but that this should be my body I
doubt, for how could my curled locks be turned
to gray hairs and my strong body to a dying [90
weakness, having waxed old, and not knowing
it.
Cynth. Well, Endymion, arise. [*Endymion,
trying to rise, sinks back.*] A while sit down, for
that thy limbs are stiff and not able to stay [95
thee, and tell what hast thou seen in thy sleep
all this while, — what dreams, visions, thoughts,
and fortunes ; for it is impossible but in so long
time thou shouldst see things strange.
End. Fair Cynthia, I will rehearse what [100
I have seen, humbly desiring that when I exceed in length, you give me warning, that I
may end ; for to utter all I have to speak would
be troublesome, although haply the strangeness
may somewhat abate the tediousness.   105
Cynth. Well, Endymion, begin.
End. Methought I saw a lady passing fair,
but very mischievous, who in the one hand carried a knife with which she offered to cut my
throat, and in the other a looking-glass, [110
wherein seeing how ill anger became ladies, she

refrained from intended violence. She was accompanied with other damsels, one of which,
with a stern countenance, and as it were with
a settled malice engraven in her eyes, [115
provoked her to execute mischief ; another,
with visage sad, and constant only in sorrow,
with her arms crossed, and watery eyes, seemed
to lament my fortune, but durst not offer to
prevent the force. I started in my sleep, [120
feeling my very veins to swell and my sinews
to stretch with fear, and such a cold sweat be-
dewed all my body that death itself could not
be so terrible as the vision.
Cynth. A strange sight ! Gyptes, at our [125
better leisure, shall expound it.
End. After long debating with herself, mercy
overcame anger, and there appeared in her
heavenly face such a divine majesty mingled
with a sweet mildness that I was ravished [130
with the sight above measure, and wished that I
might have enjoyed the sight without end : and
so she departed with the other ladies, of which
the one retained still an unmovable cruelty,
the other a constant pity.   135
Cynth. Poor Endymion, how wast thou affrighted ! What else ?
End. After her, immediately appeared an
aged man with a beard as white as snow, carrying in his hand a book with three leaves, [140
and speaking, as I remember, these words :
"Endymion, receive this book with three
leaves, in which are contained counsels, policies, and pictures," and with that he offered me
the book, which I rejected ; wherewith, [145
moved with a disdainful pity, he rent the first
leaf in a thousand shivers. The second time he
offered it, which I refused also ; at which,
bending his brows, and pitching his eyes fast
to the ground, as though they were fixed [150
to the earth and not again to be removed, then
suddenly casting them up to the heavens, he
tore in a rage the second leaf, and offered the
book only with one leaf. I know not whether
fear to offend or desire to know some [155
strange thing moved me : I took the book, and
so the old man vanished.
Cynth. What didst thou imagine was in the
last leaf ?
End. There portray'd to life, with a cold [160
quaking in every joint, I beheld many wolves
barking at thee, Cynthia, who having ground
their teeth to bite, did with striving bleed
themselves to death. There might I see Ingratitude with an hundred eyes gazing for bene- [165
fits, and with a thousand teeth gnawing on the
bowels wherein she was bred ; Treachery stood
all clothed in white, with a smiling countenance, but both her hands bathed in blood ; Envy
with a pale and meagre face (whose body [170
was so lean that one might tell all her bones,
and whose garment was so tatter'd that it was
easy to number every thread) stood shooting at
stars, whose darts fell down again on her
own face. There might I behold drones or [175
beetles — I know not how to term them —
creeping under the wings of a princely eagle,
who, being carried into her nest, sought there

---

¹ Or *here*. Old edd. read *heere*.   ² *Appearance*.

to suck that vein that would have killed the eagle. I mused that things so base should [180 attempt a fact so barbarous, or durst imagine a thing so bloody. And many other things, madam, the repetition whereof may at your better leisure seem more pleasing, for bees surfeit sometimes with honey, and the gods are [185 glutted with harmony, and your highness may be dulled with delight.

Cynth. I am content to be dieted ; therefore, let us in. Eumenides, see that Endymion be well tended, lest either eating immoderately or [190 sleeping again too long, he fall into a deadly surfeit or into his former sleep. See this also be proclaimed : that whosoever will discover this practice shall have of Cynthia infinite thanks and no small rewards.   195

      Exeunt [all except ENDYMION, EUMENIDES, FLOSCULA *and* SEMELE.]

Flosc. Ah, Endymion, none so joyful as Floscula of thy restoring.

Eum. Yes, Floscula, let Eumenides be somewhat gladder, and do not that wrong to the settled friendship of a man as to compare it [200 with the light affection of a woman. Ah, my dear friend Endymion, suffer me to die with gazing at thee.

End. Eumenides, thy friendship is immortal and not to be conceived ; and thy good [205 will, Floscula, better than I have deserved ; but let us all wait on Cynthia. I marvel Semele speaketh not a word.

Eum. Because if she do, she loseth her tongue.   210

End. But how prospereth your love ?

Eum. I never yet spake word since your sleep.

End. I doubt not but your affection is old and your appetite cold.   215

Eum. No, Endymion, thine hath made it stronger, and now are my sparks grown to flames and my fancies almost to frenzies : but let us follow, and within we will debate all this matter at large.   *Exeunt.* [220

SCENE II.[1]

[Enter] Sir TOPHAS *and* EPITON.

Top. Epi, Love hath justled my liberty from the wall, and taken the upper hand of my reason.

Epi. Let me then trip up the heels of your affection and thrust your good will into the [5 gutter.

Top. No, Epi, Love is a lord of misrule and keepeth Christmas in my corps.

Epi. No doubt there is good cheer : what dishes of delight doth his lordship feast you [10 withal?

Top. First, with a great platter of plum porridge of pleasure, wherein is stewed the mutton of distrust.

Epi. Excellent love-pap.[2]   [15

Top. Then cometh a pie of patience, a hen

---

of honey, a goose of gall, a capon of care, and many other viands, some sweet and some sour, which proveth love to be, as it was said of in old years, *Dulce venenum.*   20

Epi. A brave banquet !

Top. But, Epi, I pray thee feel on my chin ; something pricketh me. What dost thou feel or see?

Epi. There are three or four little hairs.   25

Top. I pray thee call it my beard. How shall I be troubled when this young spring[3] shall grow to a great wood !

Epi. Oh, sir, your chin is but a quiller[4] yet ; you will be most majestical when it is full- [30 fledged. But I marvel that you love Dipsas, that old crone.

Top. Agnosco veteris vestigia flammæ[5]*;* I love the smoke of an old fire.

Epi. Why she is so cold that no fire can [35 thaw her thoughts.

Top. It is an old goose, Epi, that will eat no oats ; old kine will kick, old rats gnaw cheese, and old sacks will have much patching. I prefer an old coney before a rabbit-sucker,[6] [40 and an ancient hen before a young chicken-peeper.

Epi. [*Aside.*] *Argumentum ab antiquitate ;* my master loveth antique work.

Top. Give me a pippin that is withered [45 like an old wife !

Epi. Good, sir.

Top. Then, — *a contrario sequitur argumentum,* — give me a wife that looks like an old pippin.   50

Epi. [*Aside.*] Nothing hath made my master a fool but flat scholarship.

Top. Knowest thou not that old wine is best ?

Epi. Yes.

Top. And thou knowest that like will to[7] [55 like ?

Epi. Ay.

Top. And thou knowest that Venus loved the best wine ?

Epi. So.   60

Top. Then I conclude that Venus was an old woman in an old cup of wine, for *est Venus in vinis, ignis in igne fuit.*[8]

Epi. O *lepidum caput,*[9] O madcap master ! You were worthy to win Dipsas, were she as [65 old again, for in your love you have worn the nap of your wit quite off and made it threadbare. But soft, who comes here ?

[Enter SAMIAS *and* DARES.]

Top. My solicitors.

Sam. All hail, Sir Tophas ; how feel you [70 yourself ?

Top. Stately in every joint, which the common people term stiffness. Doth Dipsas stoop ? Will she yield ? Will she bend ?

Dar. Oh, sir, as much as you would wish, [75 for her chin almost toucheth her knees.

Epi. Master, she is bent, I warrant you.

---

[3] Grove.
[4] An unfledged bird.
[5] Virgil, *Æneid,* iv. 23.
[6] A sucking rabbit.
[7] Old edd. *be.*
[8] Adapted from Ovid, *Ars Amat.* i. 244.
[9] Terence, *Adelphi,* v. 9. 9.

Top. What conditions doth she ask ?
Sam. She hath vowed she will never love any that hath not a tooth in his head less than [80 she.
Top. How many hath she ?
Dar. One.
Epi. That goeth hard, master, for then you must have none.   85
Top. A small request, and agreeable to the gravity of her years. What should a wise man do with his mouth full of bones like a charnel-house ? The turtle true hath ne'er a tooth.
Sam. [*Aside.*] Thy master is in a notable [90 vein, that will lose his teeth to be like a turtle.
Epi. [*Aside.*] Let him lose his tongue, too; I care not.
Dar. Nay, you must also have no nails, for she long since hath cast hers.   95
Top. That I yield to. What a quiet life shall Dipsas and I lead when we can neither bite nor scratch ! You may see, youths, how age provides for peace.
Sam. [*Aside.*] How shall we do to make [100 him leave his love, for we never spake to her ?
Dar. [*Aside.*] Let me alone. [*To* Sir Tophas.] She is a notable witch, and hath turned her maid Bagoa to an aspen tree, for bewraying her secrets.   105
Top. I honour her for her cunning, for now when I am weary of walking on two legs, what a pleasure may she do me to turn me to some goodly ass, and help me to four.
Dar. Nay, then I must tell you the [110 truth. Her husband, Geron, is come home, who this fifty years hath had her to wife.
Top. What do I hear ? Hath she an husband ? Go to the sexton and tell him Desire is dead, and will him to dig his grave. O [115 heavens, an husband ! What death is agreeable to my fortune ?
Sam. Be not desperate, and we will help you to find a young lady.
Top. I love no grissels[1]; they are so brit- [120 tle they will crack like glass, or so dainty that if they be touched they are straight of the fashion of wax ; *animus majoribus instat*,[2] I desire old matrons. What a sight would it be to embrace one whose hair were as orient as [125 the pearl, whose teeth shall be so pure a watchet[3] that they shall stain the truest turquoise, whose nose shall throw more beams from it than the fiery carbuncle, whose eyes shall be environ'd about with redness ex- [130 ceeding the deepest coral, and whose lips might compare with silver for the paleness ! Such a one if you can help me to, I will by piecemeal curtail my affections towards Dipsas, and walk my swelling thoughts till they be cold.   135
Epi. Wisely provided. How say you, my friends, will you angle for my master's cause ?
Sam. Most willingly.
Dar. If we speed him not shortly, I will burn my cap. We will serve him of the spades, [140 and dig an old wife out of the grave that shall be answerable to his gravity.

Top. Youths, adieu ; he that bringeth me first news, shall possess mine inheritance.
                                    [*Exit* Sir Tophas.]
Dar. What, is thy master landed ?   145
Epi. Know you not that my master is *liber tenens* ?
Sam. What 's that ?
Epi. A freeholder. But I will after him.
Sam. And we to hear what news of En- [150 dymion for the conclusion.   *Exeunt.*

[*Enter*] Panelion *and* Zontes.

Pan. Who would have thought that Tellus, being so fair by nature, so honourable by birth, so wise by education, would have entered into a mischief to the gods so odious, to men so detestable, and to her friend so malicious.   5
Zon. If Bagoa had not bewrayed it, how then should it have come to light ? But we see that gold and fair words are of force to corrupt the strongest men, and therefore able to work silly women like wax.   10
Pan. I marvel what Cynthia will determine in this cause.
Zon. I fear, as in all causes : — hear of it in justice, and then judge of it in mercy ; for how can it be that she that is unwilling to punish [15 her deadliest foes with disgrace, will revenge injuries of her train with death.
Pan. That old witch, Dipsas, in a rage, having understood her practice to be discovered, turned poor Bagoa to an aspen tree. But let [20 us make haste and bring Tellus before Cynthia, for she was coming out after us.
Zon. Let us go.   *Exeunt.*

[*Enter*,] Cynthia, Semele, Floscula, Dipsas, Endymion, Eumenides, [Geron, Pythagoras, Gyptes, *and* Sir Tophas].

Cynth. Dipsas, thy years are not so many as thy vices, yet more in number than commonly [25 nature doth afford or justice should permit. Hast thou almost these fifty years practised that detested wickedness of witchcraft ? Wast thou, so simple as for to know the nature of simples, of all creatures to be most sinful ? Thou hast [30 threat'ned to turn my course awry and alter by thy damnable art the government that I now possess by the eternal gods ; but know thou, Dipsas, and let all the enchanters know, that Cynthia, being placed for light on earth, is also [35 protected by the powers of heaven. Breathe out thou mayest words ; gather thou mayest herbs ; find out thou mayest stones agreeable to thine art ; yet of no force to appal my heart, in which courage is so rooted, and constant [40 persuasion of the mercy of the gods so grounded, that all thy witchcraft I esteem as weak as the world doth thy case wretched. This noble gentleman, Geron, once thy husband but now thy mortal hate, didst thou procure to live in [45 a desert, almost desperate ; Endymion, the flower of my court and the hope of succeeding

---

[1] Girls.   [2] Ovid, *Ars Amat.*, ii. 535.   [3] Pale blue.

[4] The same.

time, hast thou bewitched by art, before thou wouldst suffer him to flourish by nature.

Dipsas. Madam, things past may be re- [50 pented, not recalled : there is nothing so wicked that I have not done, nor anything so wished for as death ; yet among all the things that I committed, there is nothing so much tormenteth my rented and ransack'd thoughts as that in [55 the prime of my husband's youth I divorced him by my devilish art ; for which if to die might be amends, I would not live till to-morrow ; if to live and still be more miserable would better content him, I would wish of all creatures to [60 be oldest and ugliest.

Geron. Dipsas, thou hast made this difference between me and Endymion, that being both young, thou hast caused me to wake in melancholy, losing the joys of my youth, and him [65 to sleep, not rememb'ring youth.

Cynth. Stay, here cometh Tellus ; we shall now know all.

[*Re-enter* PANELION *and* ZONTES, *with* CORSITES *and* TELLUS.]

Cors. I would to Cynthia thou couldst make as good an excuse in truth as to me thou hast [70 done by wit.

Tellus. Truth shall be mine answer, and therefore I will not study for an excuse.

Cynth. Is it possible, Tellus, that so few years should harbour so many mischiefs ? Thy [75 swelling pride have I borne, because it is a thing that beauty maketh blameless, which the more it exceedeth fairness in measure, the more it stretcheth itself in disdain. Thy devices against Corsites I smile at, for that wits, the sharper [80 they are, the shrewder [1] they are ; but this unacquainted [2] and most unnatural practice with a vile enchantress against so noble a gentleman as Endymion I abhor as a thing most malicious, and will revenge as a deed most monstrous. [85 And as for you, Dipsas, I will send you into the desert amongst wild beasts, and try whether you can cast lions, tigers, boars, and bears into as dead a sleep as you did Endymion, or turn them to trees, as you have done Bagoa. But tell me, [90 Tellus, what was the cause of this cruel part, far unfitting thy sex, in which nothing should be but simpleness, and much disagreeing from thy face, in which nothing seemed to be but softness. 95

Tellus. Divine Cynthia, by whom I receive my life and am content to end it, I can neither excuse my fault without lying, nor confess it without shame ; yet were it possible that in so heavenly thoughts as yours there could fall [100 such earthly motions as mine, I would then hope, if not to be pardoned without extreme punishment, yet to be heard without great marvel.

Cynth. Say on, Tellus ; I cannot imagine any thing that can colour such a cruelty. 105

Tellus. Endymion, that Endymion, in the prime of his youth, so ravish'd my heart with love, that to obtain my desires I could not find means, nor to resist them reason. What was

she that favoured not Endymion, being [110 young, wise, honourable, and virtuous ; besides, what metal was she made of (be she mortal) that is not affected with the spice, nay, infected with the poison of that not-to-be-expressed yet always-to-be-felt love, which breaketh the [115 brains and never bruiseth the brow, consumeth the heart and never toucheth the skin, and maketh a deep scar to be seen before any wound at all be felt.[3] My heart, too tender to withstand such a divine fury, yielded to [120 love. Madam, I, not without blushing, confess [I] yielded to love.

Cynth. A strange effect of love, to work such an extreme hate. How say you, Endymion ? All this was for love ? 125

End. I say, madam, then the gods send me a woman's hate.

Cynth. That were as bad, for then by contrary you should never sleep. But on, Tellus ; let us hear the end. 130

Tellus. Feeling a continual burning in all my bowels, and a bursting almost in every vein, I could not smother the inward fire, but it must needs be perceived by the outward smoke ; and by the flying abroad of divers sparks, [135 divers judged of my scalding flames. Endymion, as full of art as wit, marking mine eyes, (in which he might see almost his own,) my sighs, (by which he might ever hear his name sounded,) aimed at my heart, in which he [140 was assured his person was imprinted, and by questions wrung out that which was ready to burst out. When he saw the depth of my affections, he swore that mine in respect of his were as fumes to Ætna, valleys to Alps, ants [145 to eagles, and nothing could be compared to my beauty but his love and eternity. Thus drawing a smooth shoe upon a crooked foot, he made me believe that (which all of our sex willingly acknowledge) I was beautiful, and [150 to wonder (which indeed is a thing miraculous) that any of his sex should be faithful.

Cynth. Endymion, how will you clear yourself ?

End. Madam, by mine own accuser. 155

Cynth. Well, Tellus, proceed ; but briefly, lest taking delight in uttering thy love, thou offend us with the length of it.

Tellus. I will, madam, quickly make an end of my love and my tale. Finding continual [160 increase of my tormenting thoughts, and that the enjoying of my love made deeper wounds than the entering into it, I could find no means to ease my grief but to follow Endymion, and continually to have him in the object of [165 mine eyes who had me slave and subject to his love. But in the moment that I feared his falsehood and tried myself most in mine affections, I found — ah, grief, even then I lost myself ! — I found him in most melancholy and desperate [170 terms cursing his stars, his state, the earth, the heavens, the world, and all for the love of —

Cynth. Of whom ? Tellus, speak boldly.

---

[1] Wickeder.   [2] Unheard of.

[3] Bond transposes *scar* and *wound ;* and *seen* and *felt.*

Tellus. Madam, I dare not utter, for fear to offend.   175

Cynth. Speak, I say ; who dare take offence, if thou be commanded by Cynthia ?

Tellus. For the love of Cynthia.

Cynth. For my love, Tellus ? That were strange. Endymion, is it true ?   180

End. In all things, madam, Tellus doth not speak false.

Cynth. What will this breed to in the end ? Well, Endymion, we shall hear all.

Tellus. I, seeing my hopes turned to mis- [185 haps, and a settled dissembling towards me, and an immovable desire to Cynthia, forgetting both myself and my sex, fell into this unnatural hate ; for knowing your virtues, Cynthia, to be immortal, I could not have an imagination to with- [190 draw him ; and finding mine own affections unquenchable, I could not carry the mind that any else should possess what I had pursued. For though in majesty, beauty, virtue, and dignity, I always humbled and yielded myself [195 to Cynthia, yet in affections I esteemed myself equal with the goddesses, and all other creatures, according to their states, with myself ; for stars to their bigness have their lights, and the sun hath no more, and little pitchers, when [200 they can hold no more, are as full as great vessels that run over. Thus, madam, in all truth have I uttered the unhappiness of my love and the cause of my hate, yielding wholly to that divine judgment which never erred for want of [205 wisdom or envied for too much partiality.

Cynth. How say you, my lords, to this matter ? But what say you, Endymion ; hath Tellus told truth ?

End. Madam, in all things but in that [210 she said I loved her and swore to honour her.

Cynth. Was there such a time whenas for my love thou didst vow thyself to death, and in respect of it loathed thy life ? Speak, Endymion ; I will not revenge it with hate.   215

End. The time was, madam, and is, and ever shall be, that I honoured your highness above all the world, but to stretch it so far as to call it love I never durst. There hath none pleased mine eye but Cynthia, none delighted [220 mine ears but Cynthia, none possessed my heart but Cynthia. I have forsaken all other fortunes to follow Cynthia, and here I stand ready to die, if it please Cynthia. Such a difference hath the gods set between our states that all must be [225 duty, loyalty, and reverence ; nothing (without it vouchsafe your highness) be termed love. My unspotted thoughts, my languishing body, my discontented life, let them obtain by princely favour that which to challenge they [230 must not presume, only wishing of impossibilities ; with imagination of which I will spend my spirits, and to myself, that no creature may hear, softly call it love ; and if any urge to utter what I whisper, then will I name it honour. [235 From this sweet contemplation if I be not driven, I shall live of all men the most content, taking more pleasure in mine aged thoughts than ever I did in my youthful actions.

Cynth. Endymion, this honourable respect [240

of thine shall be christened love in thee, and my reward for it, favour. Persevere, Endymion, in loving me, and I account more strength in a true heart than in a walled city. I have laboured to win all, and study to keep such as I [245 have won ; but those that neither my favour can move to continue constant, nor my offered benefits get to be faithful, the gods shall either reduce to truth, or revenge their treacheries with justice. Endymion, continue as thou hast [250 begun, and thou shalt find that Cynthia shineth not on thee in vain.

End. Your Highness hath blessed me, and your words have again restored my youth ; methinks I feel my joints strong and these [255 mouldy hairs to moult, and all by your virtue, Cynthia, into whose hands the balance that weigheth time and fortune are committed.

Cynth. What, young again ! Then it is pity to punish Tellus.   260

Tellus. Ah, Endymion, now I know thee and ask pardon of thee ; suffer me still to wish thee well.

End. Tellus, Cynthia must command what she will.   265

Flosc. Endymion, I rejoice to see thee in thy former estate.

End. Good Floscula, to thee also am I in my former affections.

Eum. Endymion, the comfort of my life, [270 how am I ravished with a joy matchless, saving only the enjoying of my mistress.

Cynth. Endymion, you must now tell who Eumenides shrineth for his saint.

End. Semele, madam.   275

Cynth. Semele, Eumenides ? Is it Semele, the very wasp of all women, whose tongue stingeth as much as an adder's tooth ?

Eum. It is Semele, Cynthia, the possessing of whose love must only prolong my life.   280

Cynth. Nay, sith Endymion is restored, we will have all parties pleased. Semele, are you content after so long trial of his faith, such rare secrecy, such unspotted love, to take Eumenides ? Why speak you not ? Not a word ? [285

End. Silence, madam, consents ; that is most true.

Cynth. It is true, Endymion. Eumenides, take Semele ; take her, I say.

Eum. Humble thanks, madam ; now only [290 do I begin to live.

Sem. A hard choice, madam, either to be married if I say nothing, or to lose my tongue if I speak a word. Yet do I rather choose to have my tongue cut out than my heart distem- [295 pered : I will not have him.

Cynth. Speaks the parrot ! She shall nod hereafter with signs. Cut off her tongue, nay her head, that having a servant of honourable birth, honest manners, and true love, will not be [300 persuaded.

Sem. He is no faithful lover, madam, for then would he have asked his mistress.

Ger. Had he not been faithful, he had never seen into the fountain, and so lost his friend [305 and mistress.

Eum. Thine own thoughts, sweet Semele,

witness against thy words, for what hast thou found in my life but love? And as yet what have I found in my love but bitterness? [310 Madam, pardon Semele, and let my tongue ransom hers.

Cynth. Thy tongue, Eumenides! What, shouldst thou live wanting a tongue to blaze the beauty of Semele! Well, Semele, I will [315 not command love, for it cannot be enforced; let me entreat it.

Sem. I am content your highness shall command, for now only do I think Eumenides faithful, that is willing to lose his tongue for my [320 sake; yet loath, because it should do me better service. Madam, I accept of Eumenides.

Cynth. I thank you, Semele.

Eum. Ah, happy Eumenides, that hast a friend so faithful and a mistress so fair! [325 With what sudden mischief will the gods daunt this excess of joy? Sweet Semele, I live or die as thou wilt.

Cynth. What shall become of Tellus? Tellus, you know Endymion is vowed to a service [330 from which death cannot remove him. Corsites casteth still a lovely look towards you. How say you, will you have your Corsites, and so receive pardon for all that is past?

Tellus. Madam, most willingly.   335

Cynth. But I cannot tell whether Corsites be agreed.

Cors. Ay, madam, more happy to enjoy Tellus than the monarchy of the world.

Eum. Why, she caused you to be pinch'd [340 with fairies.

Cors. Ay, but her fairness hath pinched my heart more deeply.

Cynth. Well, enjoy thy love. But what have you wrought in the castle, Tellus?   345

Tellus. Only the picture of Endymion.

Cynth. Then so much of Endymion as his picture cometh to, possess and play withal.

Cors. Ah, my sweet Tellus, my love shall be as thy beauty is, matchless.   350

Cynth. Now it resteth, Dipsas, that if thou wilt forswear that vile art of enchanting, Geron hath promised again to receive thee; otherwise, if thou be wedded to that wickedness, I must and will see it punished to the uttermost.   355

Dipsas. Madam, I renounce both substance and shadow of that most horrible and hateful trade, vowing to the gods continual penance, and to your highness obedience.

Cynth. How say you, Geron; will you ad- [360 mit her to your wife?

Ger. Ay, with more joy than I did the first day, for nothing could happen to make me happy but only her forsaking that lewd[1] and detestable course. Dipsas, I embrace thee.   3v.

Dipsas. And I thee, Geron, to whom I will hereafter recite the cause of these my first follies.

Cynth. Well, Endymion, nothing resteth now but that we depart. Thou hast my favour; [370 Tellus her friend; Eumenides in Paradise with his Semele; Geron content with Dipsas.

Sir Top. Nay, soft; I cannot handsomely go to bed without Bagoa.

Cynth. Well, Sir Tophas, it may be there [375 are more virtues in me than myself knoweth of, for Endymion I awaked, and at my words he waxed young. I will try whether I can turn this tree again to thy true love.

Top. Turn her to a true love or false, so [380 she be a wench I care not.

Cynth. Bagoa, Cynthia putteth an end to thy hard fortunes; for, being turn'd to a tree for revealing a truth, I will recover thee again, if in my power be the effect of truth.   385

[BAGOA *recovers human shape.*]

Top. Bagoa, a bots[2] upon thee!

Cynth. Come, my lords, let us in. You, Gyptes and Pythagoras, if you can content yourselves in our court, to fall from vain follies of philosophers to such virtues as are here practised, [390 you shall be entertained according to your deserts, for Cynthia is no stepmother to strangers.

Pythag. I had rather in Cynthia's court spend ten years than in Greece one hour.

Gyptes. And I choose rather to live by [395 the sight of Cynthia than by the possessing of all Egypt.

Cynth. Then follow.

Eum. We all attend.   *Exeunt.*

---

[1] Mean, base.
[2] Worms. A comic execration.

THE EPILOGUE

A MAN walking abroad, the Wind and Sun strove for sovereignty, the one with his blast, the other with his beams. The Wind blew hard; the man wrapped his garment about him harder: it blust'red more strongly; he then girt it fast to him. "I cannot prevail," said the Wind. The Sun, casting her crystal beams, began to warm the man; he unloosed his gown: yet it shined brighter; he then put it off. "I yield," said the Wind, "for if thou continue shining, he will also put off [5 his coat."

Dread Sovereign, the malicious that seek to overthrow us with threats, do but stiffen our thoughts, and make them sturdier in storms; but if your highness vouchsafe with your favourable beams to glance upon us, we shall not only stoop, but with all humility lay both our hands and hearts at your majesty's feet.   1C

THE OLD WIVES TALE

BY

GEORGE PEELE

[DRAMATIS PERSONAE

SACRAPANT.
First Brother, named CALYPHA.
Second Brother, named THELEA.
EUMENIDES.
ERESTUS.
LAMPRISCUS.
HUANEBANGO.
COREBUS.
WIGGEN.
Churchwarden.
Sexton.
Ghost of JACK.

Friar, Harvest-men, Furies, Fiddlers, &c.

DELIA, sister to CALYPHA and THELEA.
VENELIA, betrothed to ERESTUS.
ZANTIPPA, } daughters to LAMPRISCUS.
CELANTA,   }
Hostess.

ANTIC.
FROLIC.
FANTASTIC.
CLUNCH, a smith.
MADGE, his wife.]

Enter ANTIC, FROLIC, *and* FANTASTIC.

Ant. How now, fellow Frolic![1] What, all amort?[2] Doth this sadness become thy madness? What though we have lost our way in the woods, yet never hang the head as though thou hadst no hope to live till to-morrow; for [5 Fantastic and I will warrant thy life to-night for twenty in the hundred.

Fro. Antic and Fantastic, as I am frolic franion,[3] never in all my life was I so dead slain. What, to lose our way in the wood, [10 without either fire or candle, so uncomfortable! *O cælum! O terra! O Maria!* O Neptune!

Fan. Why makes thou it so strange, seeing Cupid hath led our young master to the fair lady, and she is the only saint that he hath [15 sworn to serve?

Fro. What resteth, then, but we commit him to his wench, and each of us take his stand up in a tree, and sing out our ill fortune to the tune of "*O man in desperation*"? 20

Ant. Desperately spoken, fellow Frolic, in the dark; but seeing it falls out thus, let us rehearse the old proverb:

> "Three merry men, and three merry men,
> And three merry men be we;   25
> I in the wood, and thou on the ground,
> And Jack sleeps in the tree."

Fan. Hush! a dog in the wood, or a wooden[4] dog! O comfortable hearing! I had even as lief the chamberlain of the White Horse had [30 called me up to bed.

Fro. Either hath this trotting cur gone out of his circuit, or else are we near some village, which should not be far off, for I perceive the

Enter [CLUNCH] *a smith, with a lantern and candle.*

glimmering of a glow-worm, a candle, or a [35 cat's eye, my life for a halfpenny! In the name of my own father, be thou ox or ass that appearest, tell us what thou art.

Smith. What am I? Why, I am Clunch the smith. What are you? What make you in [40 my territories at this time of the night?

Ant. What do we make, dost thou ask? Why, we make faces for fear; such as if thy mortal eyes could behold, would make thee water th' long seams of thy side slops,[5] [45 smith.

Fro. And, in faith, sir, unless your hospitality do relieve us, we are like to wander, with a sorrowful heigh-ho, among the owlets and hob-goblins of the forest. Good Vulcan, for [50 Cupid's sake that hath cozened us all, befriend us as thou mayst; and command us howsoever, whereso r, whensoever, in whatsoever, for ever and r.

Smith. l, masters, it seems to me you [55 have lost your way in the wood; in considera-tion whereof, if you will go with Clunch to his cottage, you shall have house-room and a good fire to sit by, although we have no bedding to put you in.   60

All. O blessed smith, O bountiful Clunch!

Smith. For your further entertainment, it shall be as it may be, so and so.

A dog barks [*within*].

Hark![6] this is Ball my dog, that bids you all welcome in his own language. Come, take [65 heed for stumbling on the threshold. — Open door, Madge; take in guests.

---

[1] Q *Franticke.*   [3] A gay fellow.
[2] Dejected.   [4] With a pun on *wood*, mad.

[5] Long wide trousers.
[6] The scene is now at the cottage.

Enter [MADGE, *an*] *old woman.*

Madge.[1] Welcome, Clunch, and good fellows all, that come with my good-man. For my good-man's sake, come on, sit down ; here is [70 a piece of cheese, and a pudding of my own making.

Ant. Thanks, gammer ; a good example for the wives of our town.

Fro. Gammer, thou and thy good-man sit [75 lovingly together ; we come to chat, and not to eat.

Smith. Well, masters, if you will eat nothing, take away. Come, what do we to pass away the time ? Lay a crab in the fire to roast for [80 lamb's-wool.[2] What, shall we have a game at trump[3] or ruff[3] to drive away the time ? How say you ?

Fan. This smith leads a life as merry as a king with Madge his wife. Sirrah Frolic, I [85 am sure thou art not without some round or other ; no doubt but Clunch can bear his part.

Fro. Else think you me ill brought up ; so set to it when you will.   *They sing.*

SONG.

Whenas the rye reach to the chin,   90
And chopcherry, chopcherry ripe within,
Strawberries swimming in the cream,
And school-boys playing in the stream ;
Then, O, then, O, then, O, my true-love said,
Till that time come again   95
She could not live a maid.

Ant. This sport does well ; but methinks, gammer, a merry winter's tale would drive away the time trimly. Come, I am sure you are not without a score.   100

Fan. I'faith, gammer, a tale of an hour long were as good as an hour's sleep.

Fro. Look you, gammer, of the giant and the king's daughter, and I know not what. I have seen the day, when I was a little one, [105 you might have drawn me a mile after you with such a discourse.

Madge. Well, since you be so importunate, my good-man shall fill the pot and get him to bed ; they that ply their work must keep [110 good hours. One of you go lie with him ; he is a clean-skinned man I tell you, without either spavin or wind-gall : so I am content to drive away the time with an old wives' winter's tale.

Fan. No better hay in Devonshire ; o' my [115 word, gammer, I'll be one of your audience.

Fro. And I another, that's flat.

Ant. Then must I to bed with the good-man. — *Bona nox*, gammer. — Good night, Frolic.

Smith. Come on, my lad, thou shalt take [120 thy unnatural rest with me.

Exit ANTIC *and the smith.*

Fro. Yet this vantage shall we have of them in the morning, to be ready at the sight thereof extempore.

[1] Madge is called *old woman* in the speech-tags throughout in Q.
[2] A drink made of ale and the pulp of roasted crab-apples.
[3] A common card game.

Madge. Now this bargain, my masters, [125 must I make with you, that you will say hum and ha to my tale, so shall I know you are awake.

Both. Content, gammer, that will we do.

Madge. Once upon a time, there was a [130 king, or a lord, or a duke, that had a fair daughter, the fairest that ever was, as white as snow and as red as blood ; and once upon a time his daughter was stolen away ; and he sent all his men to seek out his daughter ; and he [135 sent so long, that he sent all his men out of his land.

Fro. Who drest his dinner, then ?

Madge. Nay, either hear my tale, or kiss my tail.   [140

Fan. Well said ! On with your tale, gammer.

Madge. O Lord, I quite forgot ! There was a conjurer, and this conjurer could do any thing, and he turned himself into a great dragon, and carried the king's daughter away in his [145 mouth to a castle that he made of stone ; and there he kept her I know not how long, till at last all the king's men went out so long that her two brothers went to seek her. O, I forget ! she (he, I would say,) turned a proper[4] [150 young man to a bear in the night, and a man in the day, and keeps[5] by a cross that parts three several ways ; and he made his lady run mad — Gods me bones, who comes here ?

Enter the Two Brothers.

Fro. Soft, gammer, here some come to [155 tell your tale for you.

Fan. Let them alone ; let us hear what they will say.

1 Bro. Upon these chalky cliffs of Albion We are arrived now with tedious toil ;   160 And compassing the wide world round about, To seek our sister, to seek fair Delia forth, Yet cannot we so much as hear of her.

2 Bro. O fortune cruel, cruel and unkind ! Unkind in that we cannot find our sister,   165 Our sister, hapless in her cruel chance ! Soft ! who have we here ?

Enter Senex [ERESTUS] *at the cross, stooping to gather.*

1 Bro. Now, father, God be your speed ! What do you gather there ?

Erest.[6] Hips and haws, and sticks and [170 straws, and things that I gather on the ground, my son.

1 Bro. Hips and haws, and sticks and straws ! Why, is that all your food, father ?

Erest. Yea, son.   175

2 Bro. Father, here is an alms-penny for me ; and if I speed in that I go for, I will give thee as good a gown of grey as ever thou didst wear.

1 Bro. And, father, here is another alms- [180 penny for me ; and if I speed in my journey. I

[4] Handsome.
[5] [The young man] lives.
[6] Erestus is called *old man* in the speech-tags throughout in Q.

will give thee a palmer's staff of ivory, and a
scallop-shell of beaten gold.
Erest. Was she fair?
2 *Bro.* Ay, the fairest for white, and the [185
purest for red, as the blood of the deer, or the
driven snow.
Erest. Then hark well, and mark well, my
old spell:
Be not afraid of every stranger;
Start not aside at every danger;   190
Things that seem are not the same;
Blow a blast at every flame;
For when one flame of fire goes out,
Then comes your wishes well about:
If any ask who told you this good,   195
Say, the white bear of England's wood.
1 *Bro.* Brother, heard you not what the old
man said?
" Be not afraid of every stranger;
Start not aside for every danger;
Things that seem are not the same;   200
Blow a blast at every flame;
[For when one flame of fire goes out,
Then comes your wishes well about:]
If any ask who told you this good,
Say, the white bear of England's wood."   205
2 *Bro.* Well, if this do us any good.
Well fare the white bear of England's
wood!
                Exeunt [*the* Two Brothers].
Erest. Now sit thee here, and tell a heavy
tale,
Sad in thy mood, and sober in thy cheer;
Here sit thee now, and to thyself relate   210
The hard mishap of thy most wretched state.
In Thessaly I liv'd in sweet content,
Until that fortune wrought my overthrow;
For there I wedded was unto a dame,
That liv'd in honour, virtue, love, and fame. 215
But Sacrapant, that cursed sorcerer,
Being besotted with my beauteous love,
My dearest love, my true betrothed wife,
Did seek the means to rid me of my life.
But worse than this, he with his chanting
spells   220
Did turn me straight unto an ugly bear;
And when the sun doth settle in the west,
Then I begin to don my ugly hide.
And all the day I sit, as now you see,
And speak in riddles, all inspir'd with rage, [225
Seeming an old and miserable man,
And yet I am in April of my age.

Enter VENELIA *his lady, mad; and goes in again.*

See where Venelia, my betrothed love,
Runs madding, all enrag'd, about the woods,
All by his cursed and enchanting spells. —   [230

Enter LAMPRISCUS *with a pot of honey.*

But here comes Lampriscus, my discontented
neighbour. How now, neighbour! You look toward the ground as well as I; you muse on
something.
Lamp. Neighbour, on nothing but on the [235
matter I so often moved to you. If you do anything for charity, help me: if for neighbour-

hood or brotherhood, help me: never was one
so cumbered as is poor Lampriscus; and to begin, I pray receive this pot of honey, to [240
mend your fare.
Erest. Thanks, neighbour, set it down;
honey is always welcome to the bear. And now,
neighbour, let me hear the cause of your
coming.   245
Lamp. I am, as you know, neighbour, a man
unmarried; and lived so unquietly with my two
wives, that I keep every year holy the day
wherein I buried them both: the first was on
Saint Andrew's day, the other on Saint [250
Luke's.
Erest. And now, neighbour, you of this
country say, your custom is out. But on with
your tale, neighbour.
Lamp. By my first wife, whose tongue [555
wearied me alive, and sounded in my ears like
the clapper of a great bell, whose talk was a
continual torment to all that dwelt by her or
lived nigh her, you have heard me say I had a
handsome daughter.   260
Erest. True, neighbour.
Lamp. She it is that afflicts me with her continual clamours, and hangs on me like a bur.
Poor she is, and proud she is; as poor as a
sheep new-shorn, and as proud of her hopes [265
as a peacock of her tail well-grown.
Erest. Well said, Lampriscus! You speak it
like an Englishman.
Lamp. As curst as a wasp, and as froward as
a child new-taken from the mother's teat; [270
she is to my age as smoke to the eyes or as
vinegar to the teeth.
Erest. Holily praised, neighbour. As much
for the next.
Lamp. By my other wife I had a daughter [275
so hard-favoured, so foul and ill-faced, that I
think a grove full of golden trees, and the
leaves of rubies and diamonds, would not be a
dowry answerable to her deformity.
Erest. Well, neighbour, now you have [280
spoke, hear me speak. Send them to the well
for the water of life; there shall they find
their fortunes unlooked for. Neighbour, farewell.   *Exit.*
Lamp. Farewell, and a thousand! And [285
now goeth poor Lampriscus to put in execution
this excellent counsel.   *Exit.*
Fro. Why, this goes round without a fiddling-
stick: but, do you hear, gammer, was this the
man that was a bear in the night and a man [290
in the day?
Madge. Ay, this is he; and this man that
came to him was a beggar, and dwelt upon a
green. But soft! who comes here? O, these
are the harvest-men; ten to one they sing a [295
song of mowing.

Enter the Harvest-men *a-singing, with this song*
double repeated.

All ye that lovely lovers be,
Pray you for me.
Lo, here we come a-sowing, a-sowing,
And sow sweet fruits of love;   306
In your sweet hearts well may it prove!
                                        Exeunt.

Enter HUANEBANGO *with his two-hand sword,*
and BOOBY,[1] *the clown.*

Fan. Gammer, what is he?

Madge. O, this is one that is going to the conjurer. Let him alone; hear what he says.

Huan. Now, by Mars and Mercury, [305 Jupiter and Janus, Sol and Saturnus, Venus and Vesta, Pallas and Proserpina, and by the honour of my house, Polimackeroeplacidus, it is a wonder to see what this love will make silly fellows adventure, even in the wane of their [310 wits and infancy of their discretion. Alas, my friend! what fortune calls thee forth to seek thy fortune among brazen gates, enchanted towers, fire and brimstone, thunder and lightning? Beauty, I tell thee, is peerless, and [315 she precious whom thou affectest. Do off these desires, good countryman; good friend, run away from thyself; and, so soon as thou canst, forget her, whom none must inherit but he that can monsters tame, labours achieve, riddles [320 absolve, loose enchantments, murder magic, and kill conjuring, — and that is the great and mighty Huanebango.

Booby. Hark you, sir, hark you. First know I have here the flirting feather, and have [325 given the parish the start for the long stock : [2] now, sir, if it be no more but running through a little lightning and thunder, and "riddle me, riddle me what's this?" I'll have the wench from the conjurer, if he were ten conjurers. [330

Huan. I have abandoned the court and honourable company, to do my devoir against this sore sorcerer and mighty magician: if this lady be so fair as she is said to be, she is mine, she is mine; *meus, mea, meum, in contemptum* [335 *omnium grammaticorum.*

Booby. O *falsum Latinum!*
The fair maid is *minum,*
Cum apurtinantibus gibletis and all.

Huan. If she be mine, as I assure myself [340 the heavens will do somewhat to reward my worthiness, she shall be allied to none of the meanest gods, but be invested in the most famous stock of Huanebango, — Polimackeroeplacidus my grandfather, my father Per- [345 gopolineo, my mother Dionora de Sardinia, famously descended.

Booby. Do you hear, sir? Had not you a cousin that was called Gusteceridis?

Huan. Indeed, I had a cousin that some- [350 time followed the court unfortunately, and his name Bustegusteceridis.

Cor. O Lord, I know him well! He is the knight of the neat's-feet.

Huan. O, he loved no capon better! He [355 hath oftentimes deceived his boy of his dinner ; that was his fault, good Bustegusteceridis.

Booby. Come, shall we go along?

[*Enter* ERESTUS *at the cross.*]

Soft! here is an old man at the cross; let us ask him the way thither. — Ho, you gaffer! [360

---

[1] Later, *Corebus.*
[2] The clown appears to be priding himself on his finery — his plume and long stockings.

I pray you tell where the wise man the conjurer dwells.

Huan. Where that earthly goddess keepeth her abode, the commander of my thoughts, and fair mistress of my heart. 365

Erest. Fair enough, and far enough from thy fingering, son.

Huan. I will follow my fortune after mine own fancy, and do according to mine own discretion. 370

Erest. Yet give something to an old man before you go.

Huan. Father, methinks a piece of this cake might serve your turn.

Erest. Yea, son. 375

Huan. Huanebango giveth no cakes for alms ; ask of them that give gifts for poor beggars. — Fair lady, if thou wert once shrined in this bosom, I would buckler thee haratantara.
Exit.

Booby. Father, do you see this man? You [380 little think he'll run a mile or two for such a cake, or pass [3] for a pudding. I tell you, father, he has kept such a begging of me for a piece of this cake! Whoo! he comes upon me with "a superfantial substance, and the foison [4] of [385 the earth," that I know not what he means. If he came to me thus, and said, "My friend Booby," or so, why, I could spare him a piece with all my heart; but when he tells me how God hath enriched me above other fellows [390 with a cake, why, he makes me blind and deaf at once. Yet, father, here is a piece of cake for you, as hard as the world goes.[5] [*Gives cake.*]

Erest. Thanks, son, but list to me ; He shall be deaf when thou shalt not see. 395 Farewell, my son : things may so hit, Thou mayst have wealth to mend thy wit.

Cor. Farewell, father, farewell; for I must make haste after my two-hand sword that is gone before. *Exeunt omnes.* [400

Enter SACRAPANT *in his study.*

Sac. The day is clear, the welkin bright and grey,
The lark is merry and records [6] her notes ;
Each thing rejoiceth underneath the sky,
But only I, whom heaven hath in hate,
Wretched and miserable Sacrapant. 405
In Thessaly was I born and brought up ;
My mother Meroe hight,[7] a famous witch,
And by her cunning I of her did learn
To change and alter shapes of mortal men.
There did I turn myself into a dragon, 410
And stole away the daughter to the king,
Fair Delia, the mistress of my heart ;
And brought her hither to revive the man
That seemeth young and pleasant to behold,
And yet is aged, crooked, weak, and numb. [415
Thus by enchanting spells I do deceive
Those that behold and look upon my face ;
But well may I bid youthful years adieu.

---

[3] Care.
[4] Abundance.
[5] However hard the times may be.
[6] Sings.
[7] Called.

Enter DELIA *with a pot in her hand.*

See where she comes from whence my sorrows
    grow!
How now, fair Delia! where have you been? [420
Del. At the foot of the rock for running
water, and gathering roots for your dinner, sir.
Sac. Ah, Delia, fairer art thou than the
running water, yet harder far than steel or
adamant!   425
Del. Will it please you to sit down, sir?
Sac. Ay, Delia, sit and ask me what thou
wilt,
Thou shalt have it brought into thy lap.
Del. Then, I pray you, sir, let me have the
best meat from the King of England's table, [430
and the best wine in all France, brought in by
the veriest knave in all Spain.
Sac. Delia, I am glad to see you so pleasant.
Well, sit thee down. —
Spread, table, spread,   435
Meat, drink, and bread,
Ever may I have
What I ever crave,
When I am spread,
For meat for my black cock,   440
And meat for my red.

Enter a Friar *with a chine of beef and a pot of
wine.*

Here, Delia, will ye fall to?
Del. Is this the best meat in England?
Sac. Yea.
Del. What is it?   445
Sac. A chine of English beef, meat for a
king and a king's followers.
Del. Is this the best wine in France?
Sac. Yea.
Del. What wine is it?   450
Sac. A cup of neat wine of Orleans, that never
came near the brewers in England.
Del. Is this the veriest knave in all Spain?
Sac. Yea.
Del. What, is he a friar?   455
Sac. Yea, a friar indefinite, and a knave in-
finite.
Del. Then, I pray ye, Sir Friar, tell me before
you go, which is the most greediest English-
man?   460
Fri. The miserable and most covetous usurer.
Sac. Hold thee there, friar. (*Exit* Friar.)
But, soft!
Who have we here? Delia, away, be gone!

Enter the Two Brothers.

Delia, away! for beset are we. —
But heaven or hell shall rescue her for me. [465
    [*Exeunt* DELIA *and* SACRAPANT.]
1 *Bro.* Brother, was not that Delia did
    appear,
Or was it but her shadow that was here?
2 *Bro.* Sister, where art thou? Delia, come
    again!
He calls, that of thy absence doth complain. —
Call out, Calypha, that she may hear,   470
And cry aloud, for Delia is near.
Echo. Near.

1 *Bro.* Near! O, where? Hast thou any
    tidings?
Echo. Tidings.
2 *Bro.* Which way is Delia, then; or that,
    or this?   475
Echo. This.
1 *Bro.* And may we safely come where
    Delia is?
Echo. Yes.
2 *Bro.* Brother, remember you the white
bear of England's wood?   x
"Start not aside for every danger,
Be not afeard of every stranger;
Things that seem are not the same."
1 *Bro.*
Why do we not, then, courageously enter? [485
2 *Bro.* Then, brother, draw thy sword and
follow me.

Re-enter [SACRAPANT] *the Conjurer: it lightens
and thunders; the* Second Brother *falls down.*

1 *Bro.* What, brother, dost thou fall?
Sac. Ay, and thou too, Calypha.

The First Brother *falls down. Enter* Two Furies.

Adeste, dæmones! Away with them:
Go carry them straight to Sacrapanto's cell, [490
There in despair and torture for to dwell.
    [*Exeunt* Furies *with the* Two Brothers.]
These are Thenores' sons of Thessaly,
That come to seek Delia their sister forth;
But, with a potion I to her have given,
My arts have made her to forget herself.   495
    Removes a turf, and shows a light in a glass.
See here the thing which doth prolong my life,
With this enchantment I do any thing;
And till this fade, my skill shall still endure,
And never none shall break this little glass,
But she that's neither wife, widow, nor
maid.   500
Then cheer thyself; this is thy destiny,
Never to die but by a dead man's hand. *Exit.*

Enter EUMENIDES, *the wandering knight, and*
[ERESTUS] *the old man at the cross.*

Eum. Tell me, Time,
Tell me, just Time, when shall I Delia see?
When shall I see the loadstar of my life?   505
When shall my wand'ring course end with her
    sight,
Or I but view my hope, my heart's delight?
    [*Seeing* Erestus.]
Father, God speed! If you tell fortunes, I pray,
good father, tell me mine.
Erest. Son, I do see in thy face   510
Thy blessed fortune work apace.
I do perceive that thou hast wit;
Beg of thy fate to govern it,
For wisdom govern'd by advice,
Makes many fortunate and wise.   515
Bestow thy alms, give more than all,
Till dead men's bones come at thy call.
Farewell, my son! Dream of no rest,
Till thou repent that thou didst best. *Exit.*
Eum. This man hath left me in a laby-
rinth: 520
He biddeth me give more than all,
Till dead men's bones come at my call·

He biddeth me dream of no rest,
Till I repent that I do best.

[*Lies down and sleeps.*]

Enter WIGGEN, COREBUS,[1] Churchwarden, *and*
Sexton.

Wig. You may be ashamed, you whoreson [525
scald Sexton and Churchwarden, if you had
any shame in those shameless faces of yours, to
let a poor man lie so long above ground unburied. A rot on you all, that have no more
compassion of a good fellow when he is gone ! [530

Church.[2] What, would you have us to bury
him, and to answer it ourselves to the parish ?

Sex. Parish me no parishes ; pay me my fees,
and let the rest run on in the quarter's accounts, and put it down for one of your good [535
deeds, o' God's name ! for I am not one that
curiously stands upon merits.

Cor. You whoreson, sodden-headed sheep's-
face, shall a good fellow do less service and
more honesty to the parish, and will you not, [540
when he is dead, let him have Christmas burial ?

Wig. Peace, Corebus ! As sure as Jack is
Jack, the frolic'st franion amongst you, and I,
Wiggen, his sweet sworn brother, Jack shall
have his funerals, or some of them shall lie [545
on God's dear earth for it, that 's once.[3]

Church. Wiggen, I hope thou wilt do no more
than thou dar'st answer.

Wig. Sir, sir, dare or dare not, more or less,
answer or not answer, do this, or have this. [550

Sex. Help, help, help !

WIGGEN *sets upon the parish with a pike-staff* :[4]

EUMENIDES *awakes and comes to them.*

Eum. Hold thy hands, good fellow.

Cor. Can you blame him, sir, if he take
Jack's part against this shake-rotten parish
that will not bury Jack ?   555

Eum. Why, what was that Jack ?

Cor. Who, Jack, sir ? Who, our Jack, sir ?
As good a fellow as ever trod upon neat's-
leather.

Wig. Look you, sir ; he gave fourscore [560
and nineteen mourning gowns to the parish
when he died, and because he would not make
them up a full hundred, they would not bury
him : was not this good dealing ?

Church. O Lord, sir, how he lies ! He was [565
not worth a halfpenny, and drunk out every
penny ; and now his fellows, his drunken companions would have us to bury him at the
charge of the parish. An we make many such
matches, we may pull down the steeple, sell [570
the bells, and thatch the chancel. He shall lie
above ground till he dance a galliard about the
church-yard, for Steven Loach.

Wig. Sic argumentaris, Domine Loach ; —
" an we make many such matches, we may [575
pull down the steeple, sell the bells, and thatch
the chancel ! " — in good time, sir, and hang
yourselves in the bell-ropes, when you have

<hr>

[1] Previously, *Booby, the clown.*   [2] Q. *Simon.*
[3] That 's flat.
[4] In Q. *Wiggen . . . pike-staff* appears as part of
Sexton's speech.

done. *Domine, opponens præpono tibi hanc
quæstionem,* whether will you have the [580
ground broken or your pates broken first ? For
one of them shall be done presently, and to
begin mine,[5] I 'll seal it upon your coxcomb.

Eum. Hold thy hands, I pray thee, good
fellow ; be not too hasty.   585

Cor. You capon's face, we shall have you
turned out of the parish one of these days, with
never a tatter to your arse ; then you are in
worse taking than Jack.

Eum. Faith, and he is bad enough. This [590
fellow does but the part of a friend, to seek to
bury his friend. How much will bury him ?

Wig. Faith, about some fifteen or sixteen
shillings will bestow him honestly.

Sex. Ay, even thereabouts, sir.   59?

Eum. Here, hold it, then : —[*aside.*] and
I have left me but one poor three half-pence.
Now do I remember the words the old man
spake at the cross, " Bestow all thou hast,"
and this is all, " till dead men's bones come [600
at thy call." — Here, hold it [*gives money*] ; and
so farewell.

Wig. God, and all good, be with you, sir !
[*Exit* EUMENIDES.] Nay, you cormorants, I 'll
bestow one peal of[6] Jack at mine own [605
proper costs and charges.

Cor. You may thank God the long staff and
the bilbo-blade crossed not your coxcomb. —
Well, we 'll to the church-stile[7] and have a pot,
and so trill-lill.   [*Exit with* WIGGEN.] [610

Church. }
Sex.   } Come, let 's go.   *Exeunt.*

Fan. But, hark you, gammer, methinks this
Jack bore a great sway in the parish.

Madge. O, this Jack was a marvellous [615
fellow ! he was but a poor man, but very well
beloved. You shall see anon what this Jack will
come to.

Enter the Harvest-men *singing, with women in
their hands.*

Fro. Soft ! who have we here ? Our amorous
harvesters.   620

Fan. Ay, ay, let us sit still, and let them
alone.

Here they begin to sing, the song doubled.

Lo, here we come a-reaping, a-reaping,
To reap our harvest-fruit !
And thus we pass the year so long,   625
And never be we mute.

Exeunt the Harvest-men.

Enter HUANEBANGO *and* COREBUS, *the clown.*

Fro. Soft ! who have we here ?

Madge. O, this is a choleric gentleman ! All
you that love your lives, keep out of the smell
of his two-hand sword. Now goes he to the [630
conjurer.

Fan. Methinks the conjurer should put the
fool into a juggling-box.

Huan. Fee, fa, fum,
Here is the Englishman, —   635

<hr>

[5] Open the argument from my side. (Bullen).   [6] On-
[7] Where the ale-house often stood.

Conquer him that can, —
Come for his lady bright,
To prove himself a knight,
And win her love in fight.
Cor. Who-haw, Master Bango, are you [640
here? Hear you, you had best sit down here,
and beg an alms with me.
Huan. Hence, base cullion! Here is he that
commandeth ingress and egress with his
weapon, and will enter at his voluntary, [645
whosoever saith no.

A voice and flame of fire; HUANEBANGO
falleth down.

Voice. No.
Madge. So with that they kissed, and spoiled
the edge of as good a two-hand sword as ever
God put life in. Now goes Corebus in, spite [650
of the conjurer.

Enter [SACRAPANT] *the Conjurer and* [Two
Furies].

Sac. Away with him into the open fields,
To be a ravening prey to crows and kites:
[HUAN. *is carried out by the* Two Furies.]
And for this villain, let him wander up and
down,
In naught but darkness and eternal night. [655
        Strikes COREBUS *blind.*
Cor. Here hast thou slain Huan, a slashing
knight,
And robbed poor Corebus of his sight.   *Exit.*
Sac. Hence, villain, hence! — Now I have
unto Delia
Given a potion of forgetfulness,
That, when she comes, she shall not know her
brothers.   660
Lo, where they labour, like to country-slaves,
With spade and mattock, on this enchanted
ground!
Now will I call her by another name;
For never shall she know herself again,
Until that Sacrapant hath breath'd his last. [665
See where she comes.

Enter DELIA.

Come hither, Delia, take this goad; here hard
At hand two slaves do work and dig for gold:
Gore them with this, and thou shalt have
enough.   *Gives her a goad.*
Del. Good sir, I know not what you mean. [670
Sac. [*aside.*] She hath forgotten to be Delia,
But not forgot the same she should forget;
But I will change her name. —
Fair Berecynthia, so this country calls you,
Go ply these strangers, wench; they dig for
gold.   *Exit.* [675
Del. O heavens, how
Am I beholding to this fair young man!
But I must ply these strangers to their work:
See where they come.

Enter the Two Brothers *in their shirts, with
spades, digging.*

1 *Bro.* O brother, see where Delia is!   680
2 *Bro.* O Delia,
Happy are we to see thee here!

Del. What tell you me of Delia, prating
swains?
I know no Delia, nor know I what you mean.
Ply you your work, or else you 're like to
smart.   685
1 *Bro.* Why, Delia, know'st thou not thy
brothers here?
We come from Thessaly to seek thee forth;
And thou deceiv'st thyself, for thou art Delia.
Del. Yet more of Delia? Then take this,
and smart.   [*Pricks them with the goad.*]
What, feign you shifts for to defer your
labour?   690
Work, villains, work; it is for gold you dig.
2 *Bro.* Peace, brother, peace: this vild[1]
enchanter
Hath ravisht Delia of her senses clean,
And she forgets that she is Delia.
1 *Bro.* Leave, cruel thou, to hurt the
miserable. —   695
Dig, brother, dig, for she is hard as steel.

Here they dig, and descry a light [*in a glass*]
under a little hill.

2 *Bro.* Stay, brother; what hast thou
descried?
Del. Away, and touch it not; 't is something
that
My lord hath hidden there.
                    Covers the light again.

Re-enter SACRAPANT.

Sac. Well said![2] thou plyest these pioners[3]
well. —   700
Go get you in, you labouring slaves.
                    [*Exeunt the* Two Brothers.]
Come, Berecynthia, let us in likewise,
And hear the nightingale record her notes.
                                          Exeunt.

Enter ZANTIPPA, *the curst daughter, to the Well*
[*of Life*], *with a pot in her hand.*

Zan. Now for a husband, house, and home:
God send a good one or none, I pray God! [705
My father hath sent me to the well for the
water of life, and tells me, if I give fair words,
I shall have a husband. But here comes

Enter [CELANTA], *the foul wench, to the Well for
water with a pot in her hand.*

Celanta, my sweet sister. I 'll stand by and hear
what she says.   710
Cel. My father hath sent me to the well for
water, and he tells me, if I speak fair, I shall
have a husband, and none of the worst. Well,
though I am black,[4] I am sure all the world
will not forsake me; and, as the old proverb [715
is, though I am black, I am not the devil.
Zan. Marry-gup with a murrain,[5] I know
wherefore thou speak'st that: but go thy ways
home as wise as thou camest, or I 'll set thee
home with a wanion.[6]   720
    *Here she strikes her pitcher against her
sister's, and breaks them both, and then exit.*

---

[1] Vile.   [2] Well done.   [3] Diggers.   [4] Ugly.
[5] Plague take you!   [6] With a vengeance. The origin of the phrase is uncertain.

Cel. I think this be the curstest quean in the world. You see what she is, a little fair, but as proud as the devil, and the veriest vixen that lives upon God's earth. Well, I 'll let her alone, and go home and get another pitcher, and, [725 for all this, get me to the well for water. *Exit.*

Enter two Furies out of the Conjurer's cell and lay HUANEBANGO *by the Well of Life [and then exeunt.] Re-enter* ZANTIPPA *with a pitcher to the well.*

Zan. Once again for a husband ; and, in faith, Celanta, I have got the start of you ; belike husbands grow by the well-side. Now my father says I must rule my tongue. Why, alas, [730 what am I, then? A woman without a tongue is as a soldier without his weapon. But I 'll have my water, and be gone.

Here she offers to dip her pitcher in, and a Head *speaks in the well.*

Head. Gently dip, but not too deep,
For fear you make the golden beard to weep. 735
Fair maiden, white and red,
Stroke me smooth, and comb my head,
And thou shalt have some cockell-bread.[1]
Zan. What is this?
"Fair maiden, white and red, 740
Comb me smooth, and stroke m, nead,
And thou shalt have some cockell-bread"?
"Cockell" callest thou it, boy? Faith, I 'll give you cockell-bread.

She breaks her pitcher upon the Head: *then it thunders and lightens ; and* HUANEBANGO, *who is deaf and cannot hear, rises up.*

Huan. Philida, phileridos, pamphilida, florida, flortos : 745
Dub dub-a-dub, bounce, quoth the guns, with a sulphurous huff-snuff : [2]
Wakt with a wench, pretty peat, pretty love, and my sweet pretty pigsnie,[3]
Just by thy side shall sit surnamed great Huanebango:
Safe in my arms will I keep thee, threat Mars or thunder Olympus.
Zan. [*aside.*] Foh, what greasy groom [750 have we here ? He looks as though he crept out of the backside of the well, and speaks like a drum perisht at the west end.
Huan. O, that I might, — but I may not, woe to my destiny therefore ! — [4]
Kiss that I clasp ! but I cannot. Tell me, my destiny, wherefore ? 755
Zan. [*aside.*] Whoop! now I have my dream. Did you never hear so great a wonder as this? Three blue beans in a blue bladder, rattle, bladder, rattle.
Huan. [*aside.*] I 'll now set my counte- [760 nance, and to her in prose, it may be, this rim-ram-ruff [5] is too rude an encounter. — Let me, fair lady, if you be at leisure, revel with your

[1] Used as a love charm.
[2] Apparently a parody of Stanyhurst's hexameters.
[3] Pig's eye, darling.
[4] A quotation from Harvey's *Encomium Lauri.*
[5] Chaucer's phrase for alliteration.

sweetness, and rail upon that cowardly conjurer, that hath cast me, or congealed me [765 rather, into an unkind sleep, and polluted my carcass.
Zan. [*aside.*] Laugh, laugh, Zantippa ; thou hast thy fortune, a fool and a husband under one.
Huan. Truly, sweet-heart, as I seem, [770 about some twenty years, the very April of mine age.
Zan. [*aside.*] Why, what a prating ass is this!
Huan. Her coral lips, her crimson chin,
Her silver teeth so white within, 775
Her golden locks, her rolling eye,
Her pretty parts, let them go by,
Heigh-ho, hath wounded me,
That I must die this day to see !
Zan. By Gogs-bones, thou art a flouting [780 knave. "Her coral lips, her crimson chin"! ka,[6] wilshaw !
Huan. Her, my own, and my own because mine, and mine because mine, ha, ha ! Above a thousand pounds in possibility, and things [785 fitting thy desire in possession.
Zan. [*aside.*] The sot thinks I ask of his lands. Lob [7] be your comfort, and cuckold be your destiny ! — Hear you, sir ; an if you will have us, you had best say so betime. 790
Huan. True, sweet-heart, and will royalize thy progeny with my pedigree. *Exeunt.*

Enter EUMENIDES, *the wandering knight.*

Eum. Wretched Eumenides, still unfortunate,
Envied by fortune and forlorn by fate,
Here pine and die, wretched Eumenides, 795
Die in the spring, the April of my age !
Here sit thee down, repent what thou hast done ?
I would to God that it were ne'er begun !

Enter [the GHOST OF] JACK.

[*G. of*] *Jack.* You are well overtaken, sir.
Eum. Who 's that ? 800
[*G. of*] *Jack.* You are heartily well met, sir.
Eum. Forbear, I say ; who is that which pincheth me ?
[*G. of*] *Jack.* Trusting in God, good Master Eumenides, that you are in so good health as [805 all your friends were at the making hereof, God give you good morrow, sir ! Lack you not a neat, handsome, and cleanly young lad, about the age of fifteen or sixteen years, that can run by your horse, and, for a need, make [810 your mastership's shoes as black as ink ? How say you, sir ?
Eum. Alas, pretty lad, I know not how to keep myself, and much less a servant, my pretty boy ; my state is so bad. 815
[*G. of*] *Jack.* Content yourself, you shall not be so ill a master but I 'll be as bad a servant. Tut, sir, I know you, though you know not me. Are not you the man, sir, deny it if you can, sir, that came from a strange place [820 in the land of Catita, where Jack-an-apes flies with his tail in his mouth, to seek out a lady

[6] Quoth he.
[7] "Lob's pound" meant "the thralldom of a hen pecked married man." (Bullen.)

as white as snow and as red as blood? Ha, ha!
nave I touched you now?

Eum. [*aside.*] I think this boy be a spirit. [825
— How knowest thou all this?

[*G. of*] *Jack.* Tut, are not you the man,
sir, deny it if you can, sir, that gave all the
money you had to the burying of a poor man,
and but one three half-pence left in your [830
purse? Content you, sir, I 'll serve you, that is
flat.

Eum. Well, my lad, since thou art so im-
por[tu]nate, I am content to entertain thee, not
as a servant, but a copartner in my journey. [835
But whither shall we go? for I have not any
money more than one bare three half-pence.

G. [*of*] *Jack.* Well, master, content yourself,
for if my divination be not out, that shall be
spent at the next inn or alehouse we come [840
to : for, master, I know you are passing hungry;
therefore I 'll go before and provide dinner until
that you come ; no doubt but you 'll come fair
and softly after.

Eum. Ay, go before ; I 'll follow thee.   845

[*G. of*] *Jack.* But do you hear, master? Do
you know my name?

Eum. No, I promise thee, not yet.

[*G. of*] *Jack.* Why, I am Jack.   *Exit.*

Eum. Jack ! Why, be it so, then.   850

Enter the Hostess *and* Jack, *setting meat on the
table ; and Fiddlers come to play.* Eumenides
walketh up and down, and will eat no meat.

Host. How say you, sir? Do you please to sit
down ?

Eum. Hostess, I thank you, I have no great
stomach.

Host. Pray, sir, what is the reason your [855
master is so strange ? Doth not this meat please
him ?

[*G. of*] *Jack.* Yes, hostess, but it is my master's fashion to pay before he eats ; therefore,
a reckoning, good hostess.   860

Host. Marry, shall you, sir, presently. *Exit.*

Eum. Why, Jack, what dost thou mean?
Thou knowest I have not any money ; therefore,
sweet Jack, tell me what shall I do ?

[*G. of*] *Jack.* Well, master, look in your [865
purse.

Eum. Why, faith, it is a folly, for I have no
money.

[*G. of*] *Jack.* Why, look you, master ; do so
much for me.   870

Eum. [*looking into his purse.*] Alas, Jack, my
purse is full of money !

[*G. of*] *Jack.* " Alas," master ! does that word
belong to this accident? Why, methinks I
should have seen you cast away your cloak, [875
and in a bravado dance a galliard round about
the chamber. Why, master, your man can
teach you more wit than this.

[*Re-enter* Hostess.]

Come, hostess, cheer up my master.

Host. You are heartily welcome ; and if it [880
please you to eat of a fat capon, a fairer bird, a
finer bird, a sweeter bird, a crisper bird, a
neater bird, your worship never eat of.

Eum. Thanks, my fine, eloquent hostess.

[*G. of*] *Jack.* But hear you, master, one [685
word by the way. Are you content I shall be
halves in all you get in your journey ?

Eum. I am, Jack, here is my hand.

[*G. of*] *Jack.* Enough, master, I ask no more.

Eum. Come, hostess, receive your money ; [890
and I thank you for my good entertainment.
     [*Gives money.*]

Host. You are heartily welcome, sir.

Eum. Come, Jack, whither go we now?

[*G. of*] *Jack.* Marry, master, to the conjurer's presently.   895

Eum. Content, Jack.— Hostess, farewell.
     Exeunt.

Enter Corebus [*blind*]*, and* Celanta, *the foul
wench, to the Well for water.*

Cor. Come, my duck, come : I have now got
a wife. Thou art fair, art thou not ?

Cel. My Corebus, the fairest alive ; make no
doubt of that.   900

Cor. Come, wench, are we almost at the well ?

Cel. Ay, Corebus, we are almost at the well
now. I 'll go fetch some water ; sit down while
I dip my pitcher in.

Voice. Gently dip, but not too deep,   905
For fear you make the golden beard to weep.

A Head *comes up with ears of corn, and she
combs them into her lap.*

Fair maiden, white and red,
Comb me smooth, and stroke my head,
And thou shalt have some cockell-bread.

A [Second] Head *comes up full of gold ; she
combs it into her lap.*[1]

[*Sec. Head.*] Gently dip, but not too deep, [910
For fear thou make the golden beard to weep.
Fair maid, white and red,
Comb me smooth, and stroke my head,
And every hair a sheaf shall be,
And every sheaf a golden tree.   915

Cel. O, see, Corebus, I have comb'd a great
deal of gold into my lap, and a great deal of
corn !

Cor. Well said,[2] wench ! now we shall have
just enough. God send us coiners to coin our [92c
gold. But come, shall we go home, sweet-heart ?

Cel. Nay, come, Corebus, I will lead you.

Cor. So, Corebus, things have well hit ;
Thou hast gotten wealth to mend thy wit.
     Exeunt.

Enter [*the* Ghost of] Jack *and* [Eumenides]
the wandering knight.

[*G. of*] *Jack.* Come away, master, come.   925

Eum. Go along, Jack, I 'll follow thee. Jack,
they say it is good to go cross-legged, and say
his prayers backward ; how sayest thou ?

[*G. of*] *Jack.* Tut, never fear, master ; let me
alone. Here sit you still ; speak not a word ; [930
and because you shall not be enticed with his
enchanting speeches, with this same wool I 'll

---

[1] This stage direction occurs in Q after *tree.*
[2] Well done !

stop your ears: and so, master, sit still, for I
must to the conjurer. *Exit.*

Enter [SACRAPANT] *the Conjurer to the wandering knight.*

Sac. How now! What man art thou that sits
so sad? 935
Why dost thou gaze upon these stately trees
Without the leave and will of Sacrapant?
What, not a word but mum? Then, Sacrapant,
Thou art betray'd.

Re-enter [*the* GHOST OF] JACK *invisible, and
takes off* SACRAPANT'S *wreath from his head,
and his sword out of his hand.*

What hand invades the head of Sacrapant? [940
What hateful Fury doth envy my happy state?
Then, Sacrapant, these are thy latest days.
Alas, my veins are numb'd, my sinews
shrink,
My blood is pierc'd, my breath fleeting away,
And now my timeless date is come to end! [945
He in whose life his actions hath[1] been so foul,
Now in his death to hell descends his soul.
He dieth.

[*G. of*] *Jack.* O, sir, are you gone? Now I hope
we shall have some other coil. — Now, master,
how like you this? The conjurer he is [950
dead, and vows never to trouble us more. Now
get you to your fair lady, and see what you can
do with her. — Alas, he heareth me not all this
while; but I will help that.
Pulls the wool out of the ears of EUMENIDES.

Eum. How now, Jack! What news? 955

[*G. of*] *Jack.* Here, master, take this sword,
and dig with it at the foot of this hill.

EUMENIDES *digs, and spies a light* [*in a glass*].

Eum. How now, Jack! What is this?

[*G. of*] *Jack.* Master, without this the conjurer could do nothing; and so long as this [960
light lasts, so long doth his art endure, and this
being out, then doth his art decay.

Eum. Why, then, Jack, I will soon put out
this light.

[*G. of*] *Jack.* Ay, master, how? 965

Eum. Why, with a stone I'll break the glass,
and then blow it out.

[*G. of*] *Jack.* No, master, you may as soon
break the smith's anvil as this little vial; nor the
biggest blast that ever Boreas blew cannot [970
blow out this little light; but she that is neither
maid, wife, nor widow. Master, wind this horn,
and see what will happen.

EUMENIDES *winds the horn. Here enters* VENELIA, *and breaks the glass, and blows out the
light, and goeth in again.*

So, master, how like you this? This is she that
ran madding in the woods, his betrothed love [975
that keeps the cross; and now, this light being
out, all are restored to their former liberty.
And now, master, to the lady that you have so
long looked for.

[1] Qy. Read *life's* for *life his?*

The GHOST OF JACK *draweth a curtain, and
there* DELIA *sitteth asleep.*

Eum. God speed, fair maid, sitting alone, [980
— there is once; God speed, fair maid, — there
is twice; God speed, fair maid, — that is
thrice.

Del. Not so, good sir, for you are by.

[*G. of*] *Jack.* Enough, master, she hath [985
spoke; now I will leave her with you. [*Exit.*]

Eum. Thou fairest flower of these western
parts,
Whose beauty so reflecteth in my sight
As doth a crystal mirror in the sun;
For thy sweet sake I have crost the frozen
Rhine;[2] 990
Leaving fair Po, I sail'd up Danuby
As far as Saba, whose enhancing streams
Cut twixt the Tartars and the Russians;
These have I crost for thee, fair Delia:
Then grant me that which I have su'd for
long. 995

Del. Thou gentle knight, whose fortune is so
good
To find me out and set my brothers free,
My faith, my heart, my hand I give to thee.

Eum. Thanks, gentle madam; but here
comes Jack; thank him, for he is the [1000
best friend that we have.

Re-enter [*the* GHOST OF] JACK, *with a head in
his hand.*

How now, Jack! What hast thou there?

[*G. of*] *Jack.* Marry, master, the head of the
conjurer.

Eum. Why, Jack, that is impossible; he [1005
was a young man.

[*G. of*] *Jack.* Ah, master, so he deceived
them that beheld him! But he was a miserable, old, and crooked man, though to each
man's eye he seemed young and fresh; for, [1010
master, this conjurer took the shape of the old
man that kept the cross, and that old man was
in the likeness of the conjurer. But now, master,
wind your horn.

EUMENIDES *winds his horn. Enter* VENELIA,
the Two Brothers, *and* [ERESTUS] *he that was
at the cross.*

Eum. Welcome, Erestus! welcome, fair
Venelia! 1014
Welcome, Thelea and Calypha both!
Now have I her that I so long have sought;
So saith fair Delia, if we have your consent.

1 Bro. Valiant Eumenides, thou well deservest
To have our favours; so let us rejoice 1020
That by thy means we are at liberty.
Here may we joy each in other's sight,
And this fair lady have her wandering knight.

[*G. of*] *Jack.* So, master, now ye think you
have done; but I must have a saying to [1025
you. You know you and I were partners, I to
have half in all you got.

[2] This and the next three lines are found, with slight
variations, in Greene's *Orlando Furioso.* (Dyce.)

Eum. Why, so thou shalt, Jack.

[*G. of*] *Jack.* Why, then, master, draw your sword, part your lady, let me have half of [1030 her presently.

Eum. Why, I hope, Jack, thou dost but jest. I promised thee half I got, but not half my lady.

[*G. of*] *Jack.* But what else, master? [1035 Have you not gotten her? Therefore divide her straight, for I will have half; there is no remedy.

Eum. Well, ere I will falsify my word unto my friend, take her all. Here, Jack, I 'll [1040 give her thee.

[*G. of*] *Jack.* Nay, neither more nor less, master, but even just half.

Eum. Before I will falsify my faith unto my friend, I will divide her. Jack, thou shalt [1045 have half.

1 Bro. Be not so cruel unto our sister, gentle knight.

2 Bro. O, spare fair Delia! She deserves no death.   1050

Eum. Content yourselves; my word is passed to him. -- Therefore prepare thyself, Delia, for thou must die.

Del. Then farewell, world! Adieu, Eumenides!

EUMENIDES *offers to strike, and* [*the* GHOST OF] JACK *stays him.*

[*G. of*] *Jack.* Stay, master; it is suffi- [1055 cient I have tried your constancy. Do you now remember since you paid for the burying of a poor fellow?

Eum. Ay, very well, Jack.

[*G. of*] *Jack.* Then, master, thank that [1060 good deed for this good turn; and so God be witn you all!   *Leaps down in the ground.*

Eum. Jack, what, art thou gone? Then farewell, Jack! --

Come, brothers, and my beauteous Delia,
Erestus, and thy dear Venelia,   1065
We will to Thessaly with joyful hearts.

All. Agreed: we follow thee and Delia.

Exeunt all [*except* FROLIC, FANTASTIC, *and* MADGE].

Fan. What, gammer, asleep?

Madge. By the mass, son, 't is almost day; and my windows shut at the cock's-crow.   1070

Fro. Do you hear, gammer? Methinks this Jack bore a great sway amongst them.

Madge. O, man, this was the ghost of the poor man that they kept such a coil to bury; and that makes him to help the wander- [1075 ing knight so much. But come, let us in: we will have a cup of ale and a toast this morning, and so depart.[1]

Fan. Then you have made an end of your tale, gammer?   1080

Madge. Yes, faith: when this was done, I took a piece of bread and cheese, and came my way; and so shall you have, too, before you go, to your breakfast.   [*Exeunt.*]

---

[1] Separate.

THE HONOURABLE HISTORY OF FRIAR BACON AND FRIAR BUNGAY

BY

ROBERT GREENE

[DRAMATIS PERSONAE

KING HENRY THE THIRD.
EDWARD, Prince of Wales, his son.
EMPEROR OF GERMANY.
KING OF CASTILE.
LACY, Earl of Lincoln.
WARREN, Earl of Sussex.
ERMSBY, a gentleman.
RALPH SIMNELL, the King's Fool.
FRIAR BACON.
MILES, Friar Bacon's poor scholar.
FRIAR BUNGAY.
JAQUES VANDERMAST, a German.
BURDEN, }
MASON, } Doctors of Oxford.
CLEMENT, }
LAMBERT, } gentlemen.
SERLSBY, }

Two Scholars, their sons.
The Keeper of Fressingfield.
THOMAS, } farmers' sons.
RICHARD, }
Constable.
A Post.
Lords, Country Clowns, &c.

ELINOR, daughter to the King of Castile.
MARGARET, the Keeper's daughter of Fressingfield.
JOAN, a country wench.
Hostess of the Bell at Henley.

A DEVIL.
Spirit in the shape of HERCULES.
A dragon shooting fire.]

[SCENE I.] [1]

Enter PRINCE EDWARD *malcontented, with*
LACY, WARREN, ERMSBY, *and* RALPH
SIMNELL.

Lacy. Why looks my lord like to a troubled
sky
When heaven's bright shine is shadow'd with a
fog?
Alate [2] we ran the deer, and through the lawns
Stripp'd [3] with our nags the lofty frolic bucks
That scudded 'fore the teasers [4] like the wind.
Ne'er was the deer of merry Fressingfield   6
So lustily pull'd down by jolly mates,
Nor shar'd the farmers such fat venison,
So frankly dealt, this hundred years before;
Nor have I seen my lord more frolic in the
chase,   10
And now — chang'd to a melancholy dump.
War. After the prince got to the Keeper's
lodge,
And had been jocund in the house awhile,
Tossing off ale and milk in country cans,
Whether it was the country's sweet content,   15
Or else the bonny damsel fill'd us drink,
That seem'd so stately in her stammel [5] red,
Or that a qualm did cross his stomach then, —
But straight he fell into his passions.
Erms. Sirrah Ralph, what say you to your
master?   20
Shall he thus all amort [6] live malcontent?

1 Framlingham.   2 Of late.
3 Outstripped.   4 Dogs that roused the game.
5 A woollen cloth.   6 Dejected.

Ralph. Hearest thou, Ned? — Nay, look if
he will speak to me!
P. Edw. What say'st thou to me, fool?
Ralph. I prithee, tell me, Ned, art thou in [25
love with the Keeper's daughter?
P. Edw. How if I be, what then?
Ralph. Why, then, sirrah, I'll teach thee
how to deceive Love.
P. Edw. How, Ralph?   30
Ralph. Marry, Sirrah Ned, thou shalt put on
my cap and my coat and my dagger, and I will
put on thy clothes and thy sword; and so thou
shalt be my fool.
P. Edw. And what of this?   35
Ralph. Why, so thou shalt beguile Love; for
Love is such a proud scab, that he will never
meddle with fools nor children. Is not Ralph's
counsel good, Ned?
P. Edw. Tell me, Ned Lacy, didst thou mark
the maid,   40
How lively in her country-weeds she look'd?
A bonnier wench all Suffolk cannot yield: —
All Suffolk! nay, all England holds none such.
Ralph. Sirrah Will Ermsby, Ned is deceived.
Erms. Why, Ralph?   45
Ralph. He says all England hath no such,
and I say, and I'll stand to it, there is one better
in Warwickshire.
War. How provest thou that, Ralph?
Ralph. Why, is not the abbot a learned man, [50
and hath read many books, and thinkest thou
he hath not more learning than thou to choose
a bonny wench? Yes, I warrant thee, by his
whole grammar.

Erms. A good reason, Ralph.   55
P. Edw. I tell thee, Lacy, that her sparkling
eyes
Do lighten forth sweet love's alluring fire ;
And in her tresses she doth fold the looks
Of such as gaze upon her golden hair ;   59
Her bashful white, mix'd with the morning's red,
Luna doth boast upon her lovely cheeks ;
Her front is beauty's table, where she paints
The glories of her gorgeous excellence ;
Her teeth are shelves of precious marguerites,[1]
Richly enclos'd with ruddy coral cliffs.   65
Tush, Lacy, she is Beauty's over-match,
If thou survey'st her curious imagery.[2]
Lacy. I grant, my lord, the damsel is as fair
As simple Suffolk's homely towns can yield ;
But in the court be quainter dames than she,   70
Whose faces are enrich'd with honour's taint,[3]
Whose beauties stand upon the stage of Fame,
And vaunt their trophies in the Courts of Love.
P. Edw. Ah, Ned, but hadst thou watch'd
her as myself,
And seen the secret beauties of the maid,   75
Their courtly coyness were but foolery.
Erms. Why, how watch'd you her, my lord ?
P. Edw. Whenas she swept like Venus
through the house,
And in her shape fast folded up my thoughts,
Into the milk-house went I with the maid,   80
And there amongst the cream-bowls she did
shine
As Pallas 'mongst her princely huswifery.
She turn'd her smock over her lily arms,
And div'd them into milk to run her cheese ;
But, whiter than the milk, her crystal skin,   85
Checked with lines of azure, made her blush[4]
That art or nature durst bring for compare.
Ermsby, if thou hadst seen, as I did note it
well,
How Beauty play'd the huswife, how this girl,
Like Lucrece, laid her fingers to the work,   90
Thou wouldst, with Tarquin, hazard Rome
and all
To win the lovely maid of Fressingfield.
Ralph. Sirrah Ned, wouldst fain have her ?
P. Edw. Ay, Ralph.
Ralph. Why, Ned, I have laid the plot in [95
my head ; thou shalt have her already.
P. Edw. I 'll give thee a new coat, an learn
me that.
Ralph. Why, Sirrah Ned, we 'll ride to Oxford to Friar Bacon. O, he is a brave scholar, [100
sirrah ; they say he is a brave necromancer, that
he can make women of devils, and he can juggle
cats into costermongers.
P. Edw. And how then, Ralph ?
Ralph. Marry, sirrah, thou shalt go to [105
him : and because thy father Harry shall not miss
thee, he shall turn me into thee ; and I 'll to the
court, and I 'll prince it out ; and he shall make
thee either a silken purse full of gold, or else
a fine wrought smock.   110
P. Edw. But how shall I have the maid ?
Ralph. Marry, sirrah, if thou be'st a silken

purse full of gold, then on Sundays she 'll hang
thee by her side, and you must not say a word.
Now, sir, when she comes into a great [115
press of people, for fear of the cutpurse, on a
sudden she 'll swap thee into her plackerd ; [5]
then, sirrah, being there, you may plead for
yourself.
Erms. Excellent policy !   120
P. Edw. But how if I be a wrought smock ?
Ralph. Then she 'll put thee into her chest
and lay thee into lavender, and upon some good
day she 'll put thee on ; and at night when you
go to bed, then being turned from a smock [125
to a man, you may make up the match.
Lacy. Wonderfully wisely counselled, Ralph.
P. Edw. Ralph shall have a new coat.
Ralph. God thank you when I have it on my
back, Ned.   130
P. Edw. Lacy, the fool hath laid a perfect
plot ;
For-why[6] our country Margaret is so coy,
And stands so much upon her honest points,
That marriage or no market with the maid.
Ermsby, it must be necromantic spells   135
And charms of art that must enchain her love,
Or else shall Edward never win the girl.
Therefore, my wags, we 'll horse us in the
morn,
And post to Oxford to this jolly friar :   139
Bacon shall by his magic do this deed.   [way
War. Content, my lord ; and that 's a speedy
To wean these headstrong puppies from the
teat.
P. Edw. I am unknown, not taken for the
prince ;
They only deem us frolic courtiers,
That revel thus among our liege's game ;   145
Therefore I have devis'd a policy.
Lacy, thou know'st next Friday is Saint
James',[7]
And then the country flocks to Harleston fair ;
Then will the Keeper's daughter frolic there,
And over-shine the troop of all the maids   150
That come to see and to be seen that day.
Haunt thee disguis'd among the country-swains,
Feign thou 'rt a farmer's son, not far from
thence,
Espy her loves, and who she liketh best ;
Cote[8] him, and court her, to control[9] the
clown ;   155
Say that the courtier tired all in green,
That help'd her handsomely to run her cheese,
And fill'd her father's lodge with venison,
Commends him, and sends fairings to herself.
Buy something worthy of her parentage,   160
Not worth her beauty ; for, Lacy, then the
fair
Affords no jewel fitting for the maid.
And when thou talk'st of me, note if she
blush ;
O, then she loves : but if her cheeks wax pale,
Disdain it is. Lacy, send how she fares,   165
And spare no time nor cost to win her loves.

[1] Pearls.   [2] Rare appearance.   [3] Tint.
[4] Would have made that woman blush whom art, etc.

[5] Placket, slit in a woman's skirt.
[6] Because.
[7] July 25.
[8] Outstrip.
[9] Overmaster.

Lacy. I will, my lord, so execute this charge
As if that Lacy were in love with her.
    P. Edw. Send letters speedily to Oxford of
      the news.
    Ralph. And, Sirrah Lacy, buy me a thou- [170
sand thousand million of fine bells.
    Lacy. What wilt thou do with them, Ralph?
    Ralph. Marry, every time that Ned sighs for
the Keeper's daughter, I 'll tie a bell about him ;
and so within three or four days I will send [175
word to his father Harry that his son and my
master Ned is become Love's morris-dance.
    P. Edw. Well, Lacy, look with care unto
      thy charge,
And I will haste to Oxford to the friar,
That he by art and thou by secret gifts   180
Mayst make me lord of merry Fressingfield.
    Lacy. God send your honour your heart's
      desire.
                        Exeunt.

[SCENE II.][1]

Enter FRIAR BACON, *with* MILES *his poor
Scholar, with books under his arm; with them*
BURDEN, MASON, *and* CLEMENT, *three Doctors.*

    Bacon. Miles, where are you?
    Miles. Hic sum, docíssime et reverendíssime
doctor.
    Bacon. Attulisti nos libros meos de necroman-
tia ?   5
    Miles. Ecce quam bonum et quam jucundum
habitare libros in unum !
    Bacon. Now, masters of our academic state,
That rule in Oxford, viceroys in your place,
Whose heads contain maps of the liberal arts,   10
Spending your time in depth of learned skill,
Why flock you thus to Bacon's secret cell,
A friar newly stall'd in Brazen-nose?
Say what 's your mind, that I may make reply.
    Burd. Bacon, we hear that long we have
      suspect,   15
That thou art read in magic's mystery ;
In pyromancy, to divine by flames ;
To tell, by hydromatic, ebbs and tides ;
By aeromancy to discover doubts,
To plain out questions, as Apollo did.   20
    Bacon. Well, Master Burden, what of all this ?
    Miles. Marry, sir, he doth but fulfil, by re-
hearsing of these names, the fable of the Fox
and the Grapes ; that which is above us pertains
nothing to us.   25
    Burd. I tell thee, Bacon, Oxford makes re-
      port,
Nay, England, and the court of Henry says,
Thou 'rt making of a brazen head by art,
Which shall unfold strange doubts and apho-
      risms,
And read a lecture in philosophy ;   30
And, by the help of devils and ghastly fiends,
Thou mean'st, ere many years or days be past,
To compass England with a wall of brass.
    Bacon. And what of this ?
    Miles. What of this, master ! Why, he doth [35

---

[1] Friar Bacon's cell at Brazenose.

speak mystically; for he knows, if your skill
fail to make a brazen head, yet Mother Waters'
strong ale will fit his turn to make him have a
copper nose.
    Clem. Bacon, we come not grieving at thy
      skill,   40
But joying that our académy yields
A man suppos'd the wonder of the world ;
For if thy cunning work these miracles,
England and Europe shall admire thy fame,
And Oxford shall in characters of brass,   45
And statues, such as were built up in Rome,
Etérnize Friar Bacon for his art.
    Mason. Then, gentle friar, tell us thy intent.
    Bacon. Seeing you come as friends unto the
      friar,
Resolve you,[2] doctors, Bacon can by books   50
Make storming Boreas thunder from his cave,
And dim fair Luna to a dark eclipse.
The great arch-ruler, potentate of hell,
Trembles when Bacon bids him or his fiends
Bow to the force of his pentagonon.[3]   55
What art can work, the frolic friar knows;
And therefore will I turn my magic books,
And strain out necromancy to the deep.
I have contriv'd and fram'd a head of brass
(I made Belcephon hammer out the stuff),   60
And that by art shall read philosophy ;
And I will strengthen England by my skill,
That if ten Cæsars liv'd and reign'd in Rome,
With all the legions Europe doth contain,
They should not touch a grass of English
      ground.   65
The work that Ninus rear'd at Babylon,
The brazen walls fram'd by Semiramis,
Carv'd out like to the portal of the sun,
Shall not be such as rings the English strand
From Dover to the market-place of Rye.   70
    Burd. Is this possible ?
    Miles. I'll bring ye two or three witnesses.
    Burd. What be those ?
    Miles. Marry, sir, three or four as honest
devils and good companions as any be in hell. [75
    Mason. No doubt but magic may do much in
this ;
For he that reads but mathematic rules
Shall find conclusions that avail to work
Wonders that pass the common sense of men.
    Burd. But Bacon roves[4] a bow beyond his
      reach,   80
And tells of more than magic can perform,
Thinking to get a fame by fooleries.
Have I not pass'd as far in state of schools,
And read of many secrets ? Yet to think
That heads of brass can utter any voice,   85
Or more, to tell of deep philosophy, —
This is a fable Æsop had forgot.
    Bacon. Burden, thou wrong'st me in detract-
ing thus ;
Bacon loves not to stuff himself with lies.
But tell me 'fore these doctors, if thou dare, 90
Of certain questions I shall move to thee.
    Burd. I will: ask what thou can.

---

[2] Be assured.
[3] Pentagram, the five-rayed star supposed to have
magical properties.
[4] Aims, tries to shoot with.

Miles. Marry, sir, he'll straight be on your pick-pack,[1] to know whether the feminine or the masculine gender be most worthy.   95

Bacon. Were you not yesterday, Master Burden, at Henley upon the Thames?

Burd. I was; what then?

Bacon. What book studied you thereon all night?   100

Burd. I! none at all; I read not there a line.

Bacon. Then, doctors, Friar Bacon's art knows naught.

Clem. What say you to this, Master Burden? Doth he not touch you?

Burd. I pass not of [2] his frivolous speeches.   105

Miles. Nay, Master Burden, my master, ere he hath done with you, will turn you from a doctor to a dunce, and shake you so small, that he will leave no more learning in you than is in Balaam's ass.   110

Bacon. Masters, for that learned Burden's skill is deep,
And sore he doubts of Bacon's cabalism,
I'll show you why he haunts to Henley oft:
Not, doctors, for to taste the fragrant air,
But there to spend the night in alchemy,   115
To multiply with secret spells of art;
Thus private steals he learning from us all.
To prove my sayings true, I'll show you straight
The book he keeps at Henley for himself.

Miles. Nay, now my master goes to conjuration, take heed.   120

Bacon. Masters, stand still, fear not, I'll show you but his book.   *Here he conjures.*
Per omnes deos infernales, Belcephon!

Enter a Woman with a shoulder of mutton on a spit, and a Devil.

Miles. O master, cease your conjuration, or you spoil all; for here's a she-devil come [125 with a shoulder of mutton on a spit. You have marr'd the devil's supper; but no doubt he thinks our college fare is slender, and so hath sent you his cook with a shoulder of mutton, to make it exceed.   130

Hostess. O, where am I, or what's become of me?

Bacon. What art thou?

Hostess. Hostess at Henley, mistress of the Bell.

Bacon. How camest thou here?

Hostess. As I was in the kitchen 'mongst the maids,   135
Spitting the meat 'gainst supper for my guests,
A motion [3] mov'd me to look forth of door:
No sooner had I pried into the yard,
But straight a whirlwind hoisted me from thence,
And mounted me aloft unto the clouds.   140
As in a trance, I thought nor feared naught,
Nor know I where or whither I was ta'en,
Nor where I am nor what these persons be.

Bacon. No? Know you not Master Burden?

Hostess. O, yes, good sir, he is my daily guest. —   145

What, Master Burden! 't was but yesternight
That you and I at Henley play'd at cards.

Burd. I know not what we did. — A pox of all conjuring friars!

Clem. Now, jolly friar, tell us, is this the book   150
That Burden is so careful to look on?

Bacon. It is. — But, Burden, tell me now,
Think'st thou that Bacon's necromantic skill
Cannot perform his head and wall of brass,
When he can fetch thine hostess in such post?   155

Miles. I'll warrant you, master, if Master Burden could conjure as well as you, he would have his book every night from Henley to study on at Oxford.

Mason. Burden,   160
What, are you mated [4] by this frolic friar? —
Look how he droops; his guilty conscience
Drives him to bash,[5] and makes his hostess blush.

Bacon. Well, mistress, for I will not have you miss'd,
You shall to Henley to cheer up your guests   165
'Fore supper gin. — Burden, bid her adieu;
Say farewell to your hostess 'fore she goes. —
Sirrah, away, and set her safe at home.

Hostess. Master Burden, when shall we see you at Henley?   170
              Exeunt Hostess *and* Devil.

Burd. The devil take thee and Henley too.

Miles. Master, shall I make a good motion?

Bacon. What's that?

Miles. Marry, sir, now that my hostess is gone to provide supper. conjure up another [175 spirit, and send Doctor Burden flying after.

Bacon. Thus, rulers of our academic state,
You have seen the friar frame his art by proof;
And as the college called Brazen-nose
Is under him, and he the master there,   180
So surely shall this head of brass be fram'd,
And yield forth strange and uncouth aphorisms,
And hell and Hecate shall fail the friar,
But I will circle England round with brass.

Miles. So be it *et nunc et semper, amen.*   185
                     Exeunt.

[SCENE III.] [6]

Enter MARGARET, *the fair maid of Fressingfield, and* JOAN; THOMAS, [RICHARD,] *and other* Clowns; *and* LACY *disguised in country apparel.*

Thom. By my troth, Margaret, here's a weather is able to make a man call his father " whoreson": if this weather hold, we shall have hay good cheap, and butter and cheese at Harleston will bear no price.   5

Mar. Thomas, maids when they come to see the fair
Count not to make a cope [7] for dearth of hay;
When we have turn'd our butter to the salt,
And set our cheese safely upon the racks,

Then let our fathers price it as they please. 10
We country sluts of merry Fressingfield
Come to buy needless naughts to make us fine,
And look that young men should be frank this
　day,
And court us with such fairings as they can.
Phœbus is blithe, and frolic looks from heaven,
As when he courted lovely Semele, 16
Swearing the pedlars shall have empty packs,
If that fair weather may make chapmen buy.
　Lacy. But, lovely Peggy, Semele is dead,
And therefore Phœbus from his palace pries, 20
And, seeing such a sweet and seemly saint,
Shows all his glories for to court yourself.
　Mar. This is a fairing, gentle sir, indeed,
To soothe me up with such smooth flattery;
But learn of me, your scoff's too broad be-
　fore. — [1] 25
Well, Joan, our beauties must abide their jests;
We serve the turn in jolly Fressingfield.
　Joan. Margaret, a farmer's daughter for a
　farmer's son:
I warrant you, the meanest of us both
Shall have a mate to lead us from the church.
But, Thomas, what's the news? What, in a
　dump? 31
Give me your hand, we are near a pedlar's
　shop;
Out with your purse, we must have fairings
　now.
　Thom. Faith, Joan, and shall. I'll bestow a
fairing on you, and then we will to the tavern, [35
and snap off a pint of wine or two.
　　All this while LACY *whispers*
　　　MARGARET *in the ear.*
　Mar. Whence are you, sir? Of Suffolk? For
　your terms
Are finer than the common sort of men.
　Lacy. Faith, lovely girl, I am of Beccles by,
Your neighbour, not above six miles from
　hence, 40
A farmer's son, that never was so quaint [2]
But that he could do courtesy to such dames.
But trust me, Margaret, I am sent in charge
From him that revell'd in your father's house,
And fill'd his lodge with cheer and venison, 45
Tired in green. He sent you this rich purse,
His token that he help'd you run your cheese,
And in the milkhouse chatted with yourself.
　Mar. To me?
　Lacy. You forget yourself; [3] 50
Women are often weak in memory.
　Mar. O, pardon, sir, I call to mind the man.
'Twere little manners to refuse his gift,
And yet I hope he sends it not for love;
For we have little leisure to debate of that. 55
　Joan. What, Margaret! blush not; maids
must have their loves.
　Thom. Nay, by the mass, she looks pale as
if she were angry.
　Rich. Sirrah, are you of Beccles? I pray,
how doth Goodman Cob? My father bought a [60
horse of him.— I'll tell you, Margaret, 'a were
good to be a gentleman's jade, for of all things

---

[1] In the face of it. [3] Qq. give these words to Mar.
[2] Fastidious.

the foul hilding [4] could not abide a doong-
cart.
　Mar. [*aside.*] How different is this farmer
　from the rest 65
That erst as yet have pleas'd my wand'ring
　sight!
His words are witty, quickened with a smile,
His courtesy gentle, smelling of the court;
Facile and debonair in all his deeds,
Proportion'd as was Paris, when, in grey, [5] 70
He courted Œnon in the vale by Troy.
Great lords have come and pleaded for my love:
Who but the Keeper's lass of Fressingfield?
And yet methinks this farmer's jolly son
Passeth the proudest that hath pleas'd mine
　eye. 76
But, Peg, disclose not that thou art in love,
And show as yet no sign of love to him,
Although thou well wouldst wish him for thy
　love;
Keep that to thee till time doth serve thy turn.
To show the grief wherein thy heart doth
　burn. — 80
Come, Joan and Thomas, shall we to the
　fair?
You, Beccles man, will not forsake us now?
　Lacy. Not whilst I may have such quaint
girls as you.
　Mar. Well, if you chance to come by Fres-
singfield,
Make but a step into the Keeper's lodge, 85
And such poor fare as woodmen can afford,
Butter and cheese, cream and fat venison,
You shall have store, and welcome therewithal.
　Lacy. Gramercies, Peggy; look for me ere
　long. *Exeunt.*

[SCENE IV.] [6]

Enter [KING] HENRY THE THIRD, *the* EMPEROR,
　the KING OF CASTILE, ELINOR, *his daughter,*
　and VANDERMAST, *a German.*

　K. Hen. Great men of Europe, monarchs of
　the west,
Ring'd with the walls of old Oceanus,
Whose lofty surge is like the battlements
That compass'd high-built Babel in with
　towers,
Welcome, my lords, welcome, brave western
　kings, 5
To England's shore, whose promontory cliffs
Show Albion is another little world;
Welcome says English Henry to you all;
Chiefly unto the lovely Elinor,
Who dar'd for Edward's sake cut through the
　seas, 10
And venture as Agenor's damsel through the
　deep,
To get the love of Henry's wanton son.
　K. of Cast. England's rich monarch, brave
　Plantagenet,
The Pyren Mounts swelling above the clouds,
That ward the wealthy Castile in with walls, 15
Could not detain the beauteous Elinor;

---

[4] A term of contempt. [6] Hampton Court.
[5] *I. e.* shepherd's garb.

But, hearing of the fame of Edward's youth,
She dar'd to brook Neptunus' haughty pride,
And bide the brunt of froward Æolus.   19
Then may fair England welcome her the more.

Elin. After that English Henry by his lords
Had sent Prince Edward's lovely counterfeit,
A present to the Castile Elinor,
The comely portrait of so brave a man,
The virtuous fame discoursed of his deeds,   25
Edward's courageous resolution,
Done at the Holy Land 'fore Damas' walls,
Led both mine eye and thoughts in equal links
To like so of the English monarch's son,
That I attempted perils for his sake.   30

Emp. Where is the prince, my lord?
K. Hen. He posted down, not long since,
     from the court,
To Suffolk side, to merry Framlingham,
To sport himself amongst my fallow deer;
From thence, by packets sent to Hampton-
     house,   35
We hear the prince is ridden with his lords
To Oxford, in the académy there
To hear dispute amongst the learned men.
But we will send forth letters for my son,
To will him come from Oxford to the court.   40

Emp. Nay, rather, Henry, let us, as we be,
Ride for to visit Oxford with our train.
Fain would I see your universities,
And what learn'd men your académy yields.
From Hapsburg have I brought a learned clerk
To hold dispute with English orators.   45
This doctor, surnam'd Jaques Vandermast,
A German born, pass'd into Padua,
To Florence and to fair Bologna,
To Paris, Rheims, and stately Orleans,   50
And, talking there with men of art, put down
The chiefest of them all in aphorisms,[1]
In magic, and the mathematic rules:
Now let us, Henry, try him in your schools.

K. Hen. He shall, my lord; this motion likes
me well.   55
We'll progress straight to Oxford with our
     trains,
And see what men our académy brings. —
And, wonder Vandermast, welcome to me.
In Oxford shalt thou find a jolly friar
Call'd Friar Bacon, England's only flower: 60
Set him but nonplus in his magic spells,
And make him yield in mathematic rules,
And for thy glory I will bind thy brows,
Not with a poet's garland made of bays,
But with a coronet of choicest gold.   65
Whilst,[2] then, we set[3] to Oxford with our
     troops,
Let's in and banquet in our English court.
             Exeunt.

[SCENE V.][4]

Enter RALPH SIMNELL *in* [PRINCE] EDWARD'S
apparel; and [PRINCE] EDWARD, WARREN,
and ERMSBY, *disguised.*

Ralph. Where be these vagabond knaves,
that they attend no better on their master?

P. Edw. If it please your honour, we are all
ready at an inch.[5]

Ralph. Sirrah Ned, I'll have no more post- [1
horse to ride on: I'll have another fetch.[6]

Erms. I pray you, how is that, my lord?

Ralph. Marry, sir, I'll send to the Isle of Ely
for four or five dozen of geese, and I'll have them
tied six and six together with whip-cord. [10
Now upon their backs will I have a fair field-
bed with a canopy; and so, when it is my pleasure, I'll flee into what place I please. This will
be easy.

War. Your honour hath said well; but [15
shall we to Brazen-nose College before we pull
off our boots?

Erms. Warren, well motion'd; we will to the
     friar
Before we revel it within the town. —
Ralph, see you keep your countenance like a
     prince.   20

Ralph. Wherefore have I such a company of
cutting[7] knaves to wait upon me, but to keep
and defend my countenance against all mine
enemies? Have you not good swords and bucklers?   25

Enter [FRIAR] BACON *and* MILES.

Erms. Stay, who comes here?

War. Some scholar; and we'll ask him where
Friar Bacon is.

Bacon. Why, thou arrant dunce, shall I never
make thee good scholar? Doth not all the [30
town cry out and say, Friar Bacon's subsizer[8] is
the greatest blockhead in all Oxford? Why,
thou canst not speak one word of true Latin.

Miles. No, sir? yes. What is this else? *Ego
sum tuus homo,* " I am your man": I warrant [35
you, sir, as good Tully's phrase as any is in Oxford.

Bacon. Come on, sirrah; what part of speech
is *Ego?*

Miles. Ego, that is " I "; marry, *nomen* [40
substantivo.

Bacon. How prove you that?

Miles. Why, sir, let him prove himself an 'a
will; I can be heard, felt, and understood.

Bacon. O gross dunce!   *Beats him.* [45

P. Edw. Come, let us break off this dispute
between these two. — Sirrah, where is Brazen-
nose College?

Miles. Not far from Coppersmith's Hall.

P. Edw. What, dost thou mock me?   50

Miles. Not I, sir: but what would you at
Brazen-nose?

Erms. Marry, we would speak with Friar
Bacon.

Miles. Whose men be you?   55

Erms. Marry, scholar, here's our master.

Ralph. Sirrah, I am the master of these good
fellows; mayst thou not know me to be a lord
by my reparrel?   59

Miles. Then here's good game for the hawk;
for here's the master-fool and a covey of cox-

---

[1] Definitions, statements of scientific principles.
[2] Till.   [3] Q$_1$ *fit;* Q$_2$ *sit.* Qy. *flit?*   [4] Oxford: a street.

[5] At hand, at any instant.   [6] Trick.   [7] Swaggering.
[8] A student who received free board and tuition, and,
formerly, performed menial services.

combs. One wise man, I think, would spring you all.

P. Edw. Gog's wounds! Warren, kill him.

War. Why, Ned, I think the devil be in [65 my sheath; I cannot get out my dagger.

Erms. Nor I mine. 'Swounds, Ned, I think I am bewitcht.

Miles. A company of scabs! The proudest of you all draw your weapon, if he can. —   70
[*Aside.*]
See how boldly I speak, now my master is by.

P. Edw. I strive in vain; but if my sword be shut
And conjur'd fast by magic in my sheath,
Villain, here is my fist.
          Strikes MILES *a box on the ear.*

Miles. O, I beseech you conjure his hands [75 too, that he may not lift his arms to his head, for he is light-fingered!

Ralph. Ned, strike him; I 'll warrant thee by mine honour.

Bacon. What means the English prince to wrong my man?   80

P. Edw. To whom speak'st thou?

Bacon. To thee.

P. Edw. Who art thou.

Bacon. Could you not judge when all your swords grew fast,
That Friar Bacon was not far from hence?   85
Edward, King Henry's son and Prince of Wales,
Thy fool disguis'd cannot conceal thyself.
I know both Ermsby and the Sussex Earl,
Else Friar Bacon had but little skill.
Thou com'st in post from merry Fressing-field,   90
Fast-fancied [1] to the Keeper's bonny lass,
To crave some succour of the jolly friar;
And Lacy, Earl of Lincoln, hast thou left
To treat [2] fair Margaret to allow thy loves;   94
But friends are men, and love can baffle lords;
The earl both woos and courts her for himself.

War. Ned, this is strange; the friar knoweth all.

Erms. Apollo could not utter more than this.

P. Edw. I stand amaz'd to hear this jolly friar
Tell even the very secrets of my thoughts. —
But, learned Bacon, since thou know'st the cause   101
Why I did post so fast from Fressingfield,
Help, friar, at a pinch, that I may have
The love of lovely Margaret to myself,   104
And, as I am true Prince of Wales, I 'll give
Living and lands to strength thy college state.

War. Good friar, help the prince in this.

Ralph. Why, servant Ned, will not the friar do it? Were not my sword glued to my scab-bard by conjuration, I would cut off his [110 head, and make him do it by force.

Miles. In faith, my lord, your manhood and your sword is all alike; they are so fast conjured that we shall never see them.

Erms. What, doctor, in a dump? Tush, help the prince,   115
And thou shalt see how liberal he will prove.

[1] Tied by love.   [2] Entreat.

Bacon. Crave not such actions greater dumps than these?
I will, my lord, strain out my magic spells;
For this day comes the earl to Fressingfield,   119
And 'fore that night shuts in the day with dark,
They 'll be betrothed each to other fast.
But come with me; we 'll to my study straight,
And in a glass prospective I will show
What 's done this day in merry Fressingfield.

P. Edw. Gramercies, Bacon; I will quite thy pain.   125

Bacon. But send your train, my lord, into the town;
My scholar shall go bring them to their inn.
Meanwhile we 'll see the knavery of the earl.

P. Edw. Warren, leave me: — and, Ermsby, take the fool;
Let him be master, and go revel it,   130
Till I and Friar Bacon talk awhile.

War. My lord.

Ralph. Faith, Ned, and I 'll lord it out till thou comest. I 'll be Prince of Wales over all the black-pots [3] in Oxford.   *Exeunt.* [135

[SCENE VI.] [4]

FRIAR BACON *and* [PRINCE] EDWARD *go into the study.* [5]

Bacon. Now, frolic Edward, welcome to my cell;
Here tempers Friar Bacon many toys,
And holds this place his consistory-court,
Wherein the devils plead homage to his words,
Within this glass prospective thou shalt see
This day what 's done in merry Fressingfield
'Twixt lovely Peggy and the Lincoln Earl.

P. Edw. Friar, thou glad 'st me. Now shall Edward try
How Lacy meaneth to his sovereign lord.

Bacon. Stand there and look directly in the glass.   10

Enter MARGARET *and* FRIAR BUNGAY.

What sees my lord?

P. Edw. I see the Keeper's lovely lass appear,
As brightsome [6] as the paramour of Mars,
Only attended by a jolly friar.

Bacon. Sit still, and keep the crystal in your eye.   15

Mar. But tell me, Friar Bungay, is it true [7]
That this fair courteous country swain,
Who says his father is a farmer nigh,
Can be Lord Lacy, Earl of Lincolnshire?

Bun. Peggy, 't is true, 't is Lacy for my life,   20
Or else mine art and cunning both doth fail,
Left by Prince Edward to procure his loves;
For he in green, that help you run your cheese,
Is son to Henry and the Prince of Wales.

Mar. Be what he will, his lure is but for lust.   25

[3] Leathern wine jugs.
[4] Friar Bacon's Cell.
[5] This stage-direction shows that the change of scene took place only in the minds of the audience.
[6] Qq. *bright-sunne.* Gayley suggests *sunne-bright.*
[7] The Prince does not hear the following dialogue.

But did Lord Lacy like poor Margaret,
Or would he deign to wed a country lass,
Friar, I would his humble handmaid be,
And for great wealth quite him with cour-
   tesy.   29
Bun. Why, Margaret, dost thou love him ?
Mar. His personage, like the pride of vaunt-
   ing Troy,
Might well avouch to shadow [1] Helen's scape : [2]
His wit is quick and ready in conceit,
As Greece afforded in her chiefest prime :
Courteous, ah friar, full of pleasing smiles !   35
Trust me, I love too much to tell thee more ;
Suffice to me he 's England's paramour.
Bun. Hath not each eye that view'd thy
   pleasing face
Surnamed thee Fair Maid of Fressingfield ?
Mar. Yes, Bungay ; and would God the
   lovely earl   40
Had that in *esse* that so many sought.
Bun. Fear not, the friar will not be behind
To show his cunning to entangle love.
P. Edw. I think the friar courts the bonny
   wench;
Bacon, methinks he is a lusty churl.   45
Bacon. Now look, my lord.

   Enter LACY [*disguised as before*].

P. Edw. Gog's wounds, Bacon, here comes
Lacy !
Bacon. Sit still, my lord, and mark the
   comedy.
Bun. Here 's Lacy, Margaret ; step aside
   awhile.   *They withdraw.*
Lacy. Daphne, the damsel that caught
   Phœbus fast,   51
And lock'd him in the brightness of her looks,
Was not so beauteous in Apollo's eyes
As is fair Margaret to the Lincoln Earl.
Recant thee, Lacy, thou art put in trust :   55
Edward, thy sovereign's son, hath chosen thee,
A secret friend, to court her for himself,
And dar'st thou wrong thy prince with treach-
   ery ?
Lacy, love makes no exception of a friend,
Nor deems it of a prince but as a man.   60
Honour bids thee control [3] him in his lust ;
His wooing is not for to wed the girl,
But to entrap her and beguile the lass.
Lacy, thou lov'st, then brook not such abuse,
But wed her, and abide thy prince's frown ;   65
For better die than see her live disgrac'd.
Mar. Come, friar, I will shake him from his
   dumps. —   [*Comes forward.*]
How cheer you, sir ? A penny for your thought !
You 're early up, pray God it be the near. [4]
What, come from Beccles in a morn so soon? 70
Lacy. Thus watchful are such men as live in
   love,
Whose eyes brook broken slumbers for their
   sleep.
I tell thee, Peggy, since last Harleston fair
My mind hath felt a heap of passions.

   1 Excuse.
   2 So Gayley. Qq. *cape*. Other edd. *rape*.
   3 Check, overmaster.
   4 Nearer (to your purpose).

Mar. A trusty man, that court it for your
   friend.   75
Woo you still for the courtier all in green ?
I marvel that he sues not for himself.
Lacy. Peggy,
I pleaded first to get your grace for him ;
But when mine eyes survey'd your beauteous
   looks,   80
Love, like a wag, straight div'd into my heart,
And there did shrine the idea of yourself.
Pity me, though I be a farmer's son,
And measure not my riches, but my love.   84
Mar. You are very hasty ; for to garden well,
Seeds must have time to sprout before they
   spring :
Love ought to creep as doth the dial's shade,
For timely [5] ripe is rotten too-too soon.
Bun. [*coming forward.*] *Deus hic* ; room for a
   merry friar !
What, youth of Beccles, with the Keeper's
   lass ?   90
'T is well ; but tell me, hear you any news ?
Mar. No, friar. What news ?
Bun. Hear you not how the pursuivants do
   post
With proclamations through each country-
   town ?   94
Lacy. For what, gentle friar ? Tell the news.
Bun. Dwell'st thou in Beccles, and hear'st
   not of these news ?
Lacy, the Earl of Lincoln, is late fled
From Windsor court, disguised like a swain,
And lurks about the country here unknown.
Henry suspects him of some treachery,   100
And therefore doth proclaim in every way,
That who can take the Lincoln Earl shall have,
Paid in the Exchequer, twenty thousand crowns.
Lacy. The Earl of Lincoln ! Friar, thou art
   mad.
It was some other ; thou mistak'st the man.   105
The Earl of Lincoln ! Why, it cannot be.
Mar. Yes, very well, my lord, for you are he :
The Keeper's daughter took you prisoner.
Lord Lacy, yield, I 'll be your gaoler once.
P. Edw. How familiar they be, Bacon !   110
Bacon. Sit still, and mark the sequel of their
   loves.
Lacy. Then am I double prisoner to thyself.
Peggy, I yield. But are these news in jest ?
Mar. In jest with you, but earnest unto me ;
For-why [6] these wrongs do wring me at the
   heart.   115
Ah, how these earls and noblemen of birth
Flatter and feign to forge poor women's ill !
Lacy. Believe me, lass, I am the Lincoln
   Earl ;
I not deny but, tired thus in rags,
I liv'd disguis'd to win fair Peggy's love.   120
Mar. What love is there where wedding ends
   not love ?
Lacy. I meant, fair girl, to make thee Lacy's
   wife.
Mar. I little think that earls will stoop so low.
Lacy. Say, shall I make thee countess ere I
   sleep ?

   5 Prematurely.   6 Because.

Mar. Handmaid unto the earl, so please himself ;   125
A wife in name, but servant in obedience.
Lacy. The Lincoln Countess, for it shall be so :
I 'll plight the bands, and seal it with a kiss.
P. Edw. Gog's wounds, Bacon, they kiss ! I 'll
stab them.   130
    Bacon. O, hold your hands, my lord, it is the
glass !
    P. Edw. Choler to see the traitors gree so
well
Made me think the shadows substances.
    Bacon. 'T were a long poniard, my lord, to
reach between
Oxford and Fressingfield ; but sit still and see
more.   135
    Bun. Well, Lord of Lincoln, if your loves be
knit,
And that your tongues and thoughts do both
agree,
To avoid ensuing jars, I 'll hamper up the
match.
I 'll take my portace[1] forth and wed you
here :
Then go to bed and seal[2] up your desires.   140
    Lacy. Friar, content. — Peggy, how like you
this ?
    Mar. What likes my lord is pleasing unto me.
    Bun. Then hand-fast hand, and I will to my
book.
    Bacon. What sees my lord now ?
    P. Edw. Bacon, I see the lovers hand in
hand,   145
The friar ready with his portace there
To wed them both : then am I quite undone.
Bacon, help now, if e'er thy magic serv'd ;
Help, Bacon ! Stop the marriage now,
If devils or necromancy may suffice,   150
And I will give thee forty thousand crowns.
    Bacon. Fear not, my lord, I 'll stop the jolly
friar
For[3] mumbling up his orisons this day.
    Lacy. Why speak'st not, Bungay ? Friar, to
thy book.
    Bungay is mute, crying, " Hud, hud.''
    Mar. How look'st thou, friar, as a man dis-
traught ?   155
Reft of thy senses, Bungay ? Show by signs,
If thou be dumb, what passions holdeth thee.
    Lacy. He 's dumb indeed. Bacon hath with
his devils
Enchanted him, or else some strange disease
Or apoplexy hath possess'd his lungs.   160
But, Peggy, what he cannot with his book,
We 'll 'twixt us both unite it up in heart.
    Mar. Else let me die, my lord, a miscreant.
    P. Edw. Why stands Friar Bungay so
amaz'd ?
    Bacon. I have struck him dumb, my lord ;
and, if your honour please,   165
I 'll fetch this Bungay straightway from Fres-
singfield
And he shall dine with us in Oxford here.
    P. Edw. Bacon, do that, and thou contentest
me.

Lacy. Of courtesy, Margaret, let us lead the
friar
Unto thy father's lodge, to comfort him   170
With broths, to bring him from this hapless
trance.
    Mar. Or else, my lord, we were passing un-
kind
To leave the friar so in his distress.

Enter a Devil, who carries off BUNGAY *on his
back.*

O, help, my lord ! a devil, a devil, my lord !
Look how he carries Bungay on his back !   175
Let 's hence, for Bacon's spirits be abroad.
                            Exit [*with* LACY].
    P. Edw. Bacon, I laugh to see the jolly friar
Mounted upon the devil, and how the earl
Flees with his bonny lass for fear.
As soon as Bungay is at Brazen-nose,   180
And I have chatted with the merry friar,
I will in post hie me to Fressingfield,
And quite these wrongs on Lacy ere 't be long.
    Bacon. So be it, my lord ; but let us to our
dinner ;
For ere we have taken our repast awhile,   185
We shall have Bungay brought to Brazen-nose.
                              Exeunt.

[SCENE VII.][4]

Enter three doctors, BURDEN, MASON, *and*
CLEMENT.

    Mason. Now that we are gathered in the
Regent-house,
It fits us talk about the king's repair,[5]
For he, trooped with all the western kings,
That lie alongst the Dantzic seas by east,
North by the clime of frosty Germany,   5
The Almain monarch, and the Saxon duke,
Castile and lovely Elinor with him,
Have in their jests resolv'd for Oxford town.
    Burd. We must lay plots of stately tragedies.
Strange comic shows, such as proud Roscius   10
Vaunted before the Roman emperors,
To welcome all the western potentates.
    Clem. But more ; the king by letters hath
foretold
That Frederick, the Almain emperor,
Hath brought with him a German of esteem,   15
Whose surname is Don Jaques Vandermast,
Skilful in magic and those secret arts.
    Mason. Then must we all make suit unto the
friar,
To Friar Bacon, that he vouch this task,
And undertake to countervail in skill   20
The German ; else there 's none in Oxford can
Match and dispute with learned Vandermast.
    Burd. Bacon, if he will hold the German
play,
Will teach him what an English friar can do.
The devil, I think, dare not dispute with him.   25
    Clem. Indeed, Mas doctor, he [dis]pleasur'd
you,
In that he brought your hostess with her spit
From Henley, posting unto Brazen-nose.

---

[1] Portable breviary.   [2] Gayley *scale,* as Q.   [3] From.   [4] The Regent-house at Oxford.   [5] Visit.

Burd. A vengeance on the friar for his pains!
But leaving that, let 's hie to Bacon straight,　30
To see if he will take this task in hand.
Clem. Stay, what rumour is this? The town
is up in a mutiny. What hurly-burly is this?

Enter a Constable, *with* RALPH SIMNELL, WAR-
REN, ERMSBY, [*all three disguised as before*],
and MILES.

Cons. Nay, masters, if you were ne'er so
good, you shall before the doctors to answer [35
your misdemeanour.
Burd. What 's the matter, fellow?
Cons. Marry, sir, here 's a company of rufflers,
that, drinking in the tavern, have made a great
brawl, and almost killed the vintner.　40
Miles. Salve, Doctor Burden!
This lubberly lurden,[1]
Ill-shap'd and ill-faced,
Disdain'd and disgraced,
What he tells unto *vobis*　45
Mentitur de nobis.
Burd. Who is the master and chief of this
crew?
*Miles. Ecce asinum mundi
Fugura rotundi,*　50
Neat, sheat,[2] and fine,
As brisk as a cup of wine.
Burd. What are you?
Ralph. I am, father doctor, as a man would
say, the bell-wether of this company; these [55
are my lords, and I the Prince of Wales.
Clem. Are you Edward, the king's son?
Ralph. Sirrah Miles, bring hither the tapster
that drew the wine, and, I warrant, when they
see how soundly I have broke his head, [60
they 'll say 't was done by no less man than a
prince.
Mason. I cannot believe that this is the Prince
of Wales.
War. And why so, sir?　65
Mason. For they say the prince is a brave
and a wise gentleman.
War. Why, and think'st thou, doctor, that
he is not so?
Dar'st thou detract and derogate from him,
Being so lovely and so brave a youth?　70
Erms. Whose face, shining with many a
sug'red smile,
Bewrays that he is bred of princely race.
Miles. And yet, master doctor,
To speak like a proctor,
And tell unto you　75
What is veriment and true;
To cease of this quarrel,
Look but on his apparel;
Then mark but my talis,
He is great Prince of Walis,　80
The chief of our *gregis,*
And *filius regis:*
Then 'ware what is done,
For he is Henry's white[3] son.
Ralph. Doctors, whose doting night-caps are [85
not capable of my ingenious dignity, know that
I am Edward Plantagenet, whom if you dis-

¹ Worthless fellow.　² Trim (?) (Cent. Dict.)　³ Darling.

please will make a ship that shall hold all your
colleges, and so carry away the niniversity with
a fair wind to the Bankside in Southwark. [90
—How sayest thou, Ned Warren, shall I not
do it?
War. Yes, my good lord; and, if it please
your lordship, I will gather up all your old
pantofles, and with the cork[4] make you a [95
pinnace of five-hundred ton, that shall serve
the turn marvellous well, my lord.
Erms. And I, my lord, will have pioners to
undermine the town, that the very gardens and
orchards be carried away for your summer- [100
walks.
Miles. And I, with *scientia*
And great *diligentia,*
Will conjure and charm,
To keep you from harm;　105
That *utrum horum mavis,*
Your very great *navis,*
Like Barclay's[5] ship,
From Oxford do skip
With colleges and schools,　110
Full-loaden with fools.
Quid dicis ad hoc,
Worshipful *Domine* Dawcock?
Clem. Why, hare-brain'd courtiers, are you
drunk or mad,
To taunt us up with such scurrility?　115
Deem you us men of base and light esteem,
To bring us such a fop for Henry's son? —
Call out the beadles and convey them hence
Straight to Bocardo:[6] let the roisters lie
Close clapt in bolts, until their wits be tame.　120
Erms. Why, shall we to prison, my lord?
Ralph. What sayest, Miles, shall I honour
the prison with my presence?
Miles. No, no: out with your blades,
And hamper these jades;　125
Have a flurt and a crash,
Now play revel-dash,
And teach these sacerdos
That the Bocardos,
Like peasants and elves,　130
Are meet for themselves.
Mason. To the prison with them, constable.
War. Well, doctors, seeing I have sported
me
With laughing at these mad and merry wags,
Know that Prince Edward is at Brazen-nose, 135
And this, attired like the Prince of Wales,
Is Ralph, King Henry's only loved fool;
I, Earl of Sussex, and this Ermsby,
One of the privy-chamber to the king;
Who, while the prince with Friar Bacon stays,
Have revell'd it in Oxford as you see.　141
Mason. My lord, pardon us, we knew not
what you were:
But courtiers may make greater scapes than
these.
Wilt please your honour dine with me to-day?
War. I will, Master doctor, and satisfy [145

⁴ From the soles of the slippers.
⁵ Qq. *Bartlets,* perhaps rightly, as Greene may have
intended Miles to corrupt the name of the author of
The Ship of Fooles.
⁶ The old north gate of Oxford, used as a prison.

the vintner for his hurt; only I must desire you
to imagine him all this forenoon the Prince of
Wales.
Mason. I will, sir.
Ralph. And upon that I will lead the way; [¹⁵⁰
only I will have Miles go before me, because I
have heard Henry say that wisdom must go before majesty.   *Exeunt.*

[SCENE VIII.]¹

Enter PRINCE EDWARD *with his poniard in his
hand,* LACY, *and* MARGARET.

P. Edw. Lacy, thou canst not shroud thy
    traitorous thoughts,
Nor cover, as did Cassius, all his wiles;
For Edward hath an eye that looks as far
As Lynceus from the shores of Græcia.
Did not I sit in Oxford by the friar,   5
And see thee court the maid of Fressingfield,
Sealing thy flattering fancies with a kiss?
Did not proud Bungay draw his portace forth,
And, joining hand in hand, had married you,
If Friar Bacon had not struck him dumb,   10
And mounted him upon a spirit's back,
That we might chat at Oxford with the friar?
Traitor, what answer'st? Is not all this true?
Lacy. Truth all, my lord; and thus I make
    reply:
At Harleston fair, there courting for your grace,
Whenas mine eye survey'd her curious shape,   15
And drew the beauteous glory of her looks
To dive into the centre of my heart,
Love taught me that your honour did but jest,
That princes were in fancy² but as men;   20
How that the lovely maid of Fressingfield
Was fitter to be Lacy's wedded wife
Than concubine unto the Prince of Wales.
P. Edw. Injurious Lacy, did I love thee
    more
Than Alexander his Hephæstion?   25
Did I unfold the passions of my love,
And lock them in the closet of thy thoughts?
Wert thou to Edward second to himself,
Sole friend, and partner of his secret loves?
And could a glance of fading beauty break   30
Th' enchained fetters of such private friends?
Base coward, false, and too effeminate
To be corrival³ with a prince in thoughts!
From Oxford have I posted since I din'd,
To quite a traitor 'fore that Edward sleep.   35
Mar. 'T was I, my lord, not Lacy stept awry:
For oft he su'd and courted for yourself,
And still woo'd for the courtier all in green;
But I, whom fancy made but over-fond,
Pleaded myself with looks as if I lov'd;   40
I fed mine eye with gazing on his face,
And still bewitch'd lov'd Lacy with my looks;
My heart with sighs, mine eyes pleaded with
    tears,
My face held pity and content at once,
And more I could not cipher-out by signs,   45
But that I lov'd Lord Lacy with my heart.
Then, worthy Edward, measure with thy mind
If women's favours will not force men fall,

If beauty, and if darts of piercing love,
Are not of force to bury thoughts of friends. 50
P. Edw. I tell thee, Peggy, I will have thy
    loves;
Edward or none shall conquer Margaret
In frigates bottom'd with rich Sethin⁴ planks,
Topt with the lofty firs of Lebanon,
Stemm'd and incas'd with burnish'd ivory,   55
And over-laid with plates of Persian wealth,
Like Thetis shalt thou wanton on the waves,
And draw the dolphins to thy lovely eyes,
To dance lavoltas in the purple streams:
Sirens, with harps and silver psalteries,   60
Shall wait with music at thy frigate's stem,
And entertain fair Margaret with their lays.
England and England's wealth shall wait on
    thee;
Britain shall bend unto her prince's love,
And do due homage to thine excellence,   65
If thou wilt be but Edward's Margaret.
Mar. Pardon, my lord: if Jove's great royalty
Sent me such presents as to Danaë;
If Phœbus, tired in Latona's webs,
Come courting from the beauty of his lodge;   70
The dulcet tunes of frolic Mercury, —
Nor all the wealth heaven's treasury affords
Should make me leave Lord Lacy or his love.
P. Edw. I have learn'd at Oxford, then, this
    point of schools, ——
Ablata causa, tollitur effectus: 75
Lacy, the cause that Margaret cannot love
Nor fix her liking on the English prince,
Take him away, and then th' effects will fail.
Villain, prepare thyself; for I will bathe
My poniard in the bosom of an earl.   80
Lacy. Rather than live, and miss fair Mar-
    garet's love,
Prince Edward, stop not at the fatal doom,
But stab it home: end both my loves and life.
Mar. Brave Prince of Wales, honoured for
    royal deeds,
'T were sin to stain fair Venus' courts with
    blood;   85
Love's conquest ends, my lord, in courtesy.
Spare Lacy, gentle Edward; let me die,
For so both you and he do cease your loves.
P. Edw. Lacy shall die as traitor to his lord.
Lacy. I have deserv'd it, Edward; act it
    well.   90
Mar. What hopes the prince to gain by Lacy's
    death?
P. Edw. To end the loves 'twixt him and
    Margaret.
Mar. Why, thinks King Henry's son that
    Margaret's love
Hangs in th' uncertain balance of proud time?
That death shall make a discord of our
    thoughts?   95
No, stab the earl, and, 'fore the morning sun
Shall vaunt him thrice over the lofty east,
Margaret will meet her Lacy in the heavens.
Lacy. If aught betides to lovely Margaret
That wrongs or wrings her honour from con-
    tent,   100
Europe's rich wealth nor England's monarchy

---

¹ Fressingfield.   ² Love.   ³ Sharer.   ⁴ Shittim.

Should not allure Lacy to over-live.
Then, Edward, short my life, and end her loves.
   Mar. Rid[1] me, and keep a friend worth
    many loves.
   Lacy. Nay, Edward, keep a love worth many
    friends.   105
   Mar. An if thy mind be such as fame hath
    blaz'd,
Then, princely Edward, let us both abide
The fatal resolution of thy rage.
Banish thou fancy and embrace revenge,
And in one tomb knit both our carcases,   110
Whose hearts were linked in one perfect love.
   P. Edw. [*aside.*] Edward, art thou that fa-
    mous Prince of Wales,
Who at Damasco beat the Saracens,
And brought'st home triumph on thy lance's
    point?
And shall thy plumes be pull'd by Venus
    down?   115
Is't princely to dissever lovers' leagues,
To part such friends as glory in their loves?
Leave, Ned, and make a virtue of this fault,
And further Peg and Lacy in their loves:
So in subduing fancy's passion,   120
Conquering thyself, thou gett'st the richest
    spoil. ——
Lacy, rise up. Fair Peggy, here's my hand.
The Prince of Wales hath conquered all his
    thoughts,
And all his loves he yields unto the earl.
Lacy, enjoy the maid of Fressingfield;   125
Make her thy Lincoln Countess at the church,
And Ned, as he is true Plantagenet,
Will give her to thee frankly for thy wife.
   Lacy. Humbly I take her of my sovereign,
As if that Edward gave me England's right, 130
And rich'd me with the Albion diadem.
   Mar. And doth the English prince mean true?
Will he vouchsafe to cease his former loves,
And yield the title of a country maid
Unto Lord Lacy?   135
   P. Edw. I will, fair Peggy, as I am true lord.
   Mar. Then, lordly sir, whose conquest is as
    great,
In conquering love, as Cæsar's victories,
Margaret, as mild and humble in her thoughts
As was Aspasia unto Cyrus' self,   140
Yields thanks, and, next Lord Lacy, doth en-
    shrine
Edward the second secret in her heart.
   P. Edw. Gramercy, Peggy. Now that vows
    are past,
And that your loves are not to be revolt,[2]
Once, Lacy, friends again. Come, we will post
To Oxford; for this day the king is there,   146
And brings for Edward Castile Elinor.
Peggy, I must go see and view my wife:
I pray God I like her as I loved thee.
Beside, Lord Lincoln, we shall hear dispute 150
'Twixt Friar Bacon and learned Vandermast.
Peggy, we'll leave you for a week or two.
   Mar. As it please Lord Lacy; but love's fool-
    ish looks
Think footsteps miles and minutes to be hours.

   Lacy. I'll hasten, Peggy, to make short re-
    turn. ——   155
But please your honour go unto the lodge,
We shall have butter, cheese, and venison;
And yesterday I brought for Margaret
A lusty bottle of neat claret-wine:
Thus can we feast and entertain your grace. 160
   P. Edw. 'T is cheer, Lord Lacy, for an em-
    peror,
If he respect the person and the place.
Come, let us in; for I will all this night
Ride post until I come to Bacon's cell.
                    Exeunt.

[SCENE IX.][3]

Enter KING HENRY, *the* EMPEROR, *the* KING
   OF CASTILE, ELINOR, VANDERMAST, *and*
   BUNGAY.

   Emp. Trust me, Plantagenet, these Oxford
    schools
Are richly seated near the river-side:
The mountains full of fat and fallow deer,
The battling[4] pastures lade with kine and
    flocks,
The town gorgeous with high-built colleges,   5
And scholars seemly in their grave attire,
Learned in searching principles of art.——
What is thy judgment, Jaques Vandermast?
   Van. That lordly are the buildings of the
    town,   9
Spacious the rooms, and full of pleasant walks;
But for the doctors, how that they be learned,
It may be meanly, for aught I can hear.
   Bun. I tell thee, German, Hapsburg holds
    none such,
None read so deep as Oxenford contains.
There are within our academic state   15
Men that may lecture in Germany
To all the doctors of your Belgic schools.
   K. Hen. Stand to him, Bungay, charm this
    Vandermast,
And I will use thee as a royal king.
   Van. Wherein darest thou dispute with
    me?   20
   Bun. In what a doctor and a friar can.
   Van. Before rich Europe's worthies put thou
    forth
The doubtful question unto Vandermast.
   Bun. Let it be this, — Whether the spirits of
pyromancy or geomancy be most predomi- [25
nant in magic?
   Van. I say, of pyromancy.
   Bun. And I, of geomancy.
   Van. The cabalists that write of magic
    spells,
As Hermes, Melchie, and Pythagoras,   30
Affirm that, 'mongst the quadruplicity
Of elemental essence, *terra* is but thought
To be a *punctum* squared[5] to the rest;
And that the compass of ascending elements
Exceed in bigness as they do in height;   35
Judging the concave circle of the sun
To hold the rest in his circumference.
If, then, as Hermes says, the fire be great'st,

---

    [1] Get rid of.   [2] Overturned.   [3] Oxford.   [4] Fattening.   [5] Compared.

Purest, and only giveth shape to spirits,
Then must these dæmones that haunt that place
Be every way superior to the rest. 41
  Bun. I reason not of elemental shapes,
Nor tell I of the concave latitudes,
Noting their essence nor their quality,
But of the spirits that pyromancy calls, 45
And of the vigour of the geomantic fiends.
I tell thee, German, magic haunts the ground,
And those strange necromantic spells,
That work such shows and wondering in the
    world,
Are acted by those geomantic spirits 50
That Hermes calleth *terræ filii.*
The fiery spirits are but transparent shades,
That lightly pass as heralds to bear news ;
But earthly fiends, clos'd in the lowest deep,
Dissever mountains, if they be but charg'd, 55
Being more gross and massy in their power.
  Van. Rather these earthly geomantic spirits
Are dull and like the place where they remain ;
For when proud Lucifer fell from the heavens,
The spirits and angels that did sin with him, 60
Retain'd their local essence as their faults,
All subject under Luna's continent.
They which offended less hang in the fire,
And second faults did rest within the air ;
But Lucifer and his proud-hearted fiends 65
Were thrown into the centre of the earth,
Having less understanding than the rest,
As having greater sin and lesser grace.
Therefore such gross and earthly spirits do serve
For jugglers, witches, and vile sorcerers ; 70
Whereas the pyromantic genii
Are mighty, swift, and of far-reaching power.
But grant that geomancy hath most force ;
Bungay, to please these mighty potentates,
Prove by some instance what thy art can do. 75
  Bun. I will.
  Emp. Now, English Harry, here begins the
    game ;
We shall see sport between these learned men.
  Van. What wilt thou do ?
  Bun. Show thee the tree, leav'd with refined
    gold, 80
Whereon the fearful dragon held his seat,
That watch'd the garden call'd Hesperides,
Subdu'd and won by conquering Hercules.
  Van. Well done !

Here BUNGAY *conjures, and the tree appears
with the dragon shooting fire.*

  K. Hen. What say you, royal lordings, to my
    friar ? 85
Hath he not done a point of cunning skill ?
  Van. Each scholar in the necromantic spells
Can do as much as Bungay hath perform'd.
But as Alcmena's bastard raz'd this tree,
So will I raise him up as when he liv'd, 90
And cause him pull the dragon from his seat,
And tear the branches piecemeal from the root.—
Hercules ! *Prodi, prodi,* Hercules !

  HERCULES *appears in his lion's skin.*

  Her. Quis me vult ?
  Van. Jove's bastard son, thou Libyan Her-
    cules, 95

Pull off the sprigs from off the Hesperian tree,
As once thou didst to win the golden fruit.
  Her. Fiat.   *Begins to break the branches.*
  Van. Now, Bungay, if thou canst by magic
    charm
The fiend, appearing like great Hercules, 100
From pulling down the branches of the tree,
Then art thou worthy to be counted learned.
  Bun. I cannot.
  Van. Cease, Hercules, until I give thee
    charge.—
Mighty commander of this English isle, 105
Henry, come from the stout Plantagenets,
Bungay is learn'd enough to be a friar ;
But to compare with Jaques Vandermast,
Oxford and Cambridge must go seek their cells
To find a man to match him in his art. 110
I have given non-plus to the Paduans,
To them of Sien, Florence, and Bologna,
Rheims, Louvain, and fair Rotterdam,
Frankfort, Lutetia,[1] and Orleans :
And now must Henry, if he do me right, 115
Crown me with laurel, as they all have done.

Enter BACON.

  Bacon. All hail to this royal company,
That sit to hear and see this strange dispute ! —
Bungay, how stand'st thou as a man amaz'd ?
What, hath the German acted more than
    thou ? 120
  Van. What art thou that questions thus ?
  Bacon. Men call me Bacon.
  Van. Lordly thou look'st, as if that thou wert
    learn'd ;
Thy countenance as if science held her seat
Between the circled archers of thy brows. 125
  K. Hen. Now, monarchs, hath the German
    found his match.
  Emp. Bestir thee, Jaques, take not now the
    foil,
Lest thou dost lose what foretime thou didst
    gain.
  Van. Bacon, wilt thou dispute ?
  Bacon. No, 130
Unless he were more learn'd than Vandermast :
For yet, tell me, what hast thou done ?
  Van. Rais'd Hercules to ruinate that tree
That Bungay mounted by his magic spells.
  Bacon. Set Hercules to work. 135
  Van. Now, Hercules, I charge thee to thy
    task ;
Pull off the golden branches from the root.
  Her. I dare not. See'st thou not great Bacon
    here,
Whose frown doth act more than thy magic
    can ?
  Van. By all the thrones, and dominations, 140
Virtues, powers, and mighty hierarchies,
I charge thee to obey to Vandermast.
  Her. Bacon, that bridles headstrong Bel-
    cephon,
And rules Asmenoth, guider of the north,
Binds me from yielding unto Vandermast. 145
  K. Hen. How now, Vandermast ! Have you
met with your match ?

---

[1] *I. e.* Paris. Qq. *Lutrecia.*

Van. Never before was 't known to Vander-
    mast
That men held devils in such obedient awe.
Bacon doth more than art, or else I fail.   150
   Emp. Why, Vandermast, art then over-
    come ? —
Bacon, dispute with him, and try his skill.
   Bacon. I come not, monarchs, for to hold dis-
    pute
With such a novice as is Vandermast ;
I came to have your royalties to dine   155
With Friar Bacon here in Brazen-nose ;
And, for this German troubles but the place,
And holds this audience with a long suspence,
I 'll send him to his académy hence.——   159
Thou Hercules, whom Vandermast did raise,
Transport the German unto Hapsburg straight,
That he may learn by travail, 'gainst the spring,
More secret dooms and aphorisms of art.
Vanish the tree, and thou away with him !

Exit the spirit [of HERCULES] *with* VANDER-
   MAST *and the tree.*

   Emp. Why, Bacon, whither dost thou send
    him ?   165
   Bacon. To Hapsburg ; there your highness at
    return
Shall find the German in his study safe.
   K. Hen. Bacon, thou hast honour'd England
    with thy skill,
And made fair Oxford famous by thine art ;
I will be English Henry to thyself.   170
But tell me, shall we dine with thee to-day ?
   Bacon. With me, my lord ; and while I fit
    my cheer,
See where Prince Edward comes to welcome
    you,
Gracious as the morning-star of heaven.
                        Exit.

*Enter [*PRINCE] EDWARD, LACY, WARREN,
   ERMSBY.

   Emp. Is this Prince Edward, Henry's royal
    son ?   175
How martial is the figure of his face !
Yet lovely and beset with amorets.[1]
   K. Hen. Ned, where hast thou been ?
   P. Edw. At Framlingham, my lord, to try
    your bucks
If they could scape the teasers [2] or the toil.   180
But hearing of these lordly potentates
Landed, and progress'd up to Oxford town,
I posted to give entertain to them :
Chief, to the Almain monarch ; next to him,
And joint with him, Castile and Saxony   185
Are welcome as they may be to the English court.
Thus for the men : but see, Venus appears,
Or one that overmatcheth Venus in her shape !
Sweet Elinor, beauty's high-swelling pride,
Rich nature's glory and her wealth at once,   190
Fair of all fairs, welcome to Albion ;
Welcome to me, and welcome to thine own,
If that thou deign'st the welcome from myself.
   Elin. Martial Plantagenet, Henry's high-
    minded son,

The mark that Elinor did count her aim,   195
I lik'd 'fore I saw thee : now I love,
And so as in so short a time I may ;
Yet so as time shall never break that so,
And therefore so accept of Elinor.
   K. of Cast. Fear not, my lord, this couple
    will agree,   200
If love may creep into their wanton eyes : ——
And therefore, Edward, I accept thee here,
Without suspence, as my adopted son.
   K. Hen. Let me that joy in these consorting
    greets,
And glory in these honours done to Ned,   205
Yield thanks for all these favours to my son,
And rest a true Plantagenet to all.

Enter MILES *with a cloth and trenchers and
   salt.*

   Miles. Salvete, omnes reges,
That govern your *greges*
In Saxony and Spain,   210
In England and in Almain !
For all this frolic rabble
Must I cover the table
With trenchers, salt, and cloth ;
And then look for your broth.   215
   Emp. What pleasant fellow is this ?
   K. Hen. 'Tis, my lord, Doctor Bacon's poor
    scholar.
   Miles [aside.] My master hath made me
sewer [3] of these great lords ; and, God knows, [220
I am as serviceable at a table as a sow is under
an apple-tree. 'T is no matter ; their cheer shall
not be great, and therefore what skills where the
salt stand, before or behind ?   [*Exit.*]
   K. of Cast. These scholars know more skill in
    axioms,   225
How to use quips and sleights of sophistry,
Than for to cover courtly for a king.

Re-enter MILES *with a mess of pottage and broth ;
   and, after him,* BACON.

   Miles. Spill, sir ? why, do you think I never
carried twopenny chop [4] before in my life ? ——
By your leave, *nobile decus,*   230
For here comes Doctor Bacon's *pecus,*
Being in his full age
To carry a mess of pottage.
   Bacon. Lordings, admire [5] not if your cheer
be this,
For we must keep our academic fare ;   235
No riot where philosophy doth reign :
And therefore, Henry, place these potentates,
And bid them fall unto their frugal cates.
   Emp. Presumptuous friar ! What, scoff'st
thou at a king ?
What, dost thou taunt us with thy peasants'
    fare,   240
And give us cates fit for country swains ?——
Henry, proceeds this jest of thy consent,
To twit us with [6] a pittance of such price ?
Tell me, and Frederick will not grieve thee long.
   K. Hen. By Henry's honour, and the royal
    faith   245

---

[1] Love-kindling looks.   [2] See note on I. 5.

[3] A servant who sets the table.
[4] Chopped meat in broth (?) (N. E. D.)
[5] Wonder.   [6] Qq. *with such.*

The English monarch beareth to his friend,
I knew not of the friar's feeble fare,
Nor am I pleas'd he entertains you thus.
  Bacon. Content thee, Frederick, for I show'd
    the cates,
To let thee see how scholars use to feed;   250
How little meat refines our English wits.——
Miles, take away, and let it be thy dinner.
  Miles. Marry, sir, I will.
This day shall be a festival-day with me;
For I shall exceed in the highest degree. [*Exit.*]
  Bacon. I tell thee, monarch, all the German
    peers   255
Could not afford thy entertainment such,
So royal and so full of majesty,
As Bacon will present to Frederick.
The basest waiter that attends thy cups   260
Shall be in honours greater than thyself;
And for thy cates, rich Alexandria drugs,[1]
Fetch'd by carvels from Egypt's richest straits,
Found in the wealthy strand of Africa,
Shall royalize the table of my king;   265
Wines richer than th' Egyptian courtesan
Quaff'd to Augustus' kingly countermatch,
Shall be carous'd in English Henry's feast;
Candy shall yield the richest of her canes;
Persia, down her Volga by canoes,   270
Send down the secrets of her spicery;
The Afric dates, myrobalans[2] of Spain,
Conserves and suckets[3] from Tiberias,
Cates from Judæa, choicer than the lamp[4]
That fired Rome with sparks of gluttony,   275
Shall beautify the board for Frederick:
And therefore grudge not at a friar's feast.
                 [*Exeunt.*]

[SCENE X.][5]

Enter two gentlemen, LAMBERT *and* SERLSBY,
with the Keeper.

  Lam. Come, frolic Keeper of our liege's game,
Whose table spread hath ever venison
And jacks[6] of wine to welcome passengers,
Know I 'm in love with jolly Margaret,
That overshines our damsels as the moon   5
Dark'neth the brightest sparkles of the night.
In Laxfield here my land and living lies:
I 'll make thy daughter jointer[7] of it all,
So thou consent to give her to my wife;
And I can spend five hundred marks a-year.   10
  Ser. I am the lands-lord, Keeper, of thy holds,
By copy all thy living lies in me;
Laxfield did never see me raise my due:
I will enfeoff fair Margaret in all,
So she will take her to a lusty squire.   15
  Keep. Now, courteous gentles, if the Keep-
    er's girl
Hath pleas'd the liking fancy of you both,
And with her beauty hath subdu'd your
    thoughts,
'T is doubtful to decide the question.
It joys me that such men of great esteem   20
Should lay their liking on this base estate,

And that her state should grow so fortunate
To be a wife to meaner men than you.
But sith such squires will stoop to keeper's fee,[8]
I will, to avoid displeasure of you both,   25
Call Margaret forth, and she shall make her
    choice.   *Exit.*
  Lam. Content, Keeper; send her unto us.
Why, Serlsby, is thy wife so lately dead,
Are all thy loves so lightly passed over,
As thou canst wed before the year be out?   30
  Ser. I live not, Lambert, to content the dead,
Nor was I wedded but for life to her:
The grave ends and begins a married state.

Enter MARGARET.

  Lam. Peggy, the lovely flower of all towns,
Suffolk's fair Helen, and rich England's star,   35
Whose beauty, tempered with her huswifery,
Makes England talk of merry Fressingfield!
  Ser. I cannot trick it up with poesies,
Nor paint my passions with comparisons,
Nor tell a tale of Phœbus and his loves: 40
But this believe me,—Laxfield here is mine,
Of ancient rent seven hundred pounds a-year,
And if thou canst but love a country squire,
I will enfeoff thee, Margaret, in all.
I cannot flatter; try me, if thou please.   45
  Mar. Brave neighbouring squires, the stay
    of Suffolk's clime,
A keeper's daughter is too base in gree[9]
To match with men accounted of such worth:
But might I not displease, I would reply.
  Lam. Say, Peggy; naught shall make us dis-
    content.   50
  Mar. Then, gentles, note that love hath little
    stay,
Nor can the flames that Venus sets on fire
Be kindled but by fancy's motion:
Then pardon, gentles, if a maid's reply.
Be doubtful, while[10] I have debated with my-
    self,   55
Who, or of whom, love shall constrain me like.
  Ser. Let it be me; and trust me, Margaret,
The meads environed with the silver streams,
Whose battling pastures fatt'neth all my flocks,
Yielding forth fleeces stapled with such wool |60
As Leominster[11] cannot yield more finer stuff,
And forty kine with fair and burnish'd heads,
With strouting[12] dugs that paggle[13] to the ground,
Shall serve thy dairy, if thou wed with me.
  Lam. Let pass the country wealth, as flocks
    and kine,   65
And lands that wave with Ceres' golden
    sheaves,
Filling my barns with plenty of the fields;
But, Peggy, if thou wed thyself to me,
Thou shalt have garments of embroid'red silk,
Lawns, and rich net-works for thy head-at-
    tire: 70
Costly shall be thy fair habiliments,
If thou wilt be but Lambert's loving wife.
  Mar. Content you, gentles, you have proffer'd
    fair,
And more than fits a country maid's degree;

---

[1] Spices	[5] Fressingfield.
[2] A variety of plums.	[6] Pitchers.
[3] Confectionery.	[7] Jointure, or jointress.
[4] Lamprey (?) (Ward).	

[8] Estate (Gayley).	[11] Qq. *Lempster* (phonetic).
[9] Degree.	[12] Strutting, swelling.
[10] Till.	[13] Hang loosely (N. E. D.).

But give me leave to counsel me a time,   75
For fancy blooms not at the first assault ;
Give me but ten days' respite, and I will
  reply,
Which or to whom myself affectionates.
   Ser. Lambert, I tell thee, thou'rt importunate;
Such beauty fits not such a base esquire :   80
It is for Serlsby to have Margaret.
   Lam. Think'st thou with wealth to overreach
  me ?
Serlsby, I scorn to brook thy country braves.
I dare thee, coward, to maintain this wrong,
At dint of rapier, single in the field.   85
   Ser. I 'll answer, Lambert, what I have
avouch'd. ——
Margaret, farewell ; another time shall serve.
                        Exit.
   Lam. I 'll follow. — Peggy, farewell to thy-
  self ;
Listen how well I 'll answer for thy love. *Exit.*
   Mar. How Fortune tempers lucky haps with
  frowns,   90
And wrongs me with the sweets of my delight !
Love is my bliss, and love is now my bale.
Shall I be Helen in my froward [1] fates,
As I am Helen in my matchless hue,
And set rich Suffolk with my face afire ?   95
If lovely Lacy were but with his Peggy,
The cloudy darkness of his bitter frown
Would check the pride of these aspiring squires.
Before the term of ten days be expired,
Whenas they look for answer of their loves,   100
My lord will come to merry Fressingfield,
And end their fancies and their follies both :
Till when, Peggy, be blithe and of good cheer.

Enter a Post *with a letter and a bag of gold.*

   Post. Fair lovely damsel, which way leads
this path ?
How might I post me unto Fressingfield ?   105
Which footpath leadeth to the Keeper's lodge ?
   Mar. Your way is ready, and this path is right;
Myself do dwell hereby in Fressingfield,
And if the Keeper be the man you seek,
I am his daughter : may I know the cause ?   110
   Post. Lovely, and once beloved of my lord,—
No marvel if his eye was lodg'd so low,
When brighter beauty is not in the heavens, —
The Lincoln Earl hath sent you letters here,
And, with them, just an hundred pounds in
  gold.   115
Sweet, bonny wench, read them, and make
  reply.
   Mar. The scrolls that Jove sent Danaë,
Wrapt in rich closures of fine burnish'd gold,
Were not more welcome than these lines to me.
Tell me, whilst that I do unrip the seals,   120
Lives Lacy well ? How fares my lovely lord ?
   Post. Well, if that wealth may make men to
live well.
   Mar. (*reads*) *The blooms of the almond-tree
grow in a night, and vanish in a morn ; the flies
hæmeræ,[2] fai; Peggy, take life with the sun,* [125
*and die with the dew ; fancy that slippeth in with
a gaze, goeth out with a wink ; and too timely* [3]

   [1] Qq. *forward.*   [2] Ephemeræ.   [3] Premature.

*loves have ever the shortest length. I write this as
thy grief, and my folly, who at Fressingfield loved
that which time hath taught me to be but mean* [130
*dainties. Eyes are dissemblers, and fancy is but
queasy ; therefore know, Margaret, I have chosen
a Spanish lady to be my wife, chief waiting-woman
to the Princess Elinor ; a lady fair, and no less
fair than thyself, honourable and wealthy. In* [135
*that I forsake thee, I leave thee to thine own lik-
ing ; and for thy dowry I have sent thee an hundred pounds ; and ever assure thee of my favour,
which shall avail thee and thine much.*
     Farewell.   *Not thine, nor his own,* [140
                          EDWARD LACY.
Fond Ate, doomer of bad-boding fates,
That wraps proud Fortune in thy snaky locks,
Didst thou enchant my birth-day with such stars
As light'ned mischief from their infancy ?   145
If heavens had vow'd, if stars had made decree,
To show on me their froward influence,
If Lacy had but lov'd, heavens, hell, and all
Could not have wrong'd the patience of my mind.
   Post. It grieves me, damsel ; but the earl is
forc'd   150
To love the lady by the king's command.
   Mar. The wealth combin'd within the English
shelves,
Europe's commander, nor the English king,
Should not have mov'd the love of Peggy from
her lord.
   Post. What answer shall I return to my
lord ?   155
   Mar. First, for thou cam'st from Lacy whom
I lov'd, —
Ah, give me leave to sigh at every thought ! —
Take thou, my friend, the hundred pound he
sent,
For Margaret's resolution craves no dower.
The world shall be to her as vanity ;   160
Wealth, trash ; love, hate ; pleasure, despair :
For I will straight to stately Framlingham,
And in the abbey there be shorn a nun,
And yield my loves and liberty to God.
   Fellow, I give thee this, not for the news,   165
For those be hateful unto Margaret,
But for thou 'rt Lacy's man, once Margaret's
love.
   Post. What I have heard, what passions I
have seen,
I 'll make report of them unto the earl.
   Mar. Say that she joys his fancies be at
rest,   170
And prays that his misfortune may be hers.
                            Exeunt.

              [SCENE XI.] [4]

Enter FRIAR BACON *drawing the curtains with a
white stick, a book in his hand, and a lamp
lighted by him ; and the* Brazen Head, *and*
MILES *with weapons by him.*

   Bacon. Miles, where are you ?
   Miles. Here, sir.
   Bacon. How chance you tarry so long ?

   [4] Friar Bacon's cell.

Miles. Think you that the watching of the Brazen Head craves no furniture? I warrant [5 you, sir, I have so armed myself that if all your devils come, I will not fear them an inch.

Bacon. Miles,
Thou know'st that I have dived into hell,
And sought the darkest palaces of fiends; 10
That with my magic spells great Belcephon
Hath left his lodge and kneeled at my cell;
The rafters of the earth rent from the poles,
And three-form'd Luna hid her silver looks,
Trembling upon her concave continent, 15
When Bacon read upon his magic book.
With seven years' tossing necromantic charms,
Poring upon dark Hecat's principles,
I have fram'd out a monstrous head of brass,
That, by the enchanting forces of the devil, 20
Shall tell out strange and uncouth aphorisms,
And girt fair England with a wall of brass.
Bungay and I have watch'd these threescore days,
And now our vital spirits crave some rest.
If Argus liv'd, and had his hundred eyes, 25
They could not over-watch Phobetor's night.
Now, Miles, in thee rests Friar Bacon's weal:
The honour and renown of all his life
Hangs in the watching of this Brazen Head;
Therefore I charge thee by the immortal God, 30
That holds the souls of men within his fist,
This night thou watch; for ere the morning-star
Sends out his glorious glister on the north,
The head will speak: then, Miles, upon thy life,
Wake me; for then by magic art I 'll work 35
To end my seven years' task with excellence.
If that a wink but shut thy watchful eye,
Then farewell Bacon's glory and his fame!
Draw close the curtains, Miles: now, for thy life,
Be watchful, and — *Here he falleth asleep.* [40

Miles. So; I thought you would talk yourself asleep anon; and 't is no marvel, for Bungay on the days, and he on the nights, have watched just these ten and fifty days: now this is the night, and 'tis my task, and no more. Now, [45 Jesus bless me, what a goodly head it is! and a nose! you talk of *nos autem glorificare;* but here 's a nose that I warrant may be called *nos autem populare* for the people of the parish. Well, I am furnished with weapons: now, [50 sir, I will set me down by a post, and make it as good as a watchman to wake me, if I chance to slumber. I thought, Goodman Head, I would call you out of your *memento.* . . . Passion o' God, I have almost broke my pate! Up, Miles, to [55 your task; take your brown-bill [1] in your hand; here 's some of your master's hobgoblins abroad.
With this a great noise. The Head *speaks.*
The Brazen Head. Time is!

Miles. Time is! Why, Master Brazen-head, have you such a capital nose, and answer [60 you with syllables, "Time is"? Is this all my master's cunning, to spend seven years' study about "Time is"? Well, sir, it may be we shall have some better orations of it anon. Well, I 'll watch you as narrowly as ever you were [65 watched, and I 'll play with you as the night-

ingale with the slow-worm; I 'll set a prick against my breast. Now rest there, Miles. Lord have mercy upon me, I have almost killed myself! [*A great noise.*] Up, Miles; list how [70 they rumble.
The Brazen Head. Time was!

Miles. Well, Friar Bacon, you spent your seven-years' study well, that can make your head speak but two words at once, "Time [75 was." Yea, marry, time was when my master was a wise man, but that was before he began to make the Brazen Head. You shall lie while [2] your arse ache, an your head speak no better. Well, I will watch, and walk up and down, [80 and be a peripatetian and a philosopher of Aristotle's stamp. [*A great noise.*] What, a fresh noise? Take thy pistols in hand, Miles.

Here the Head *speaks, and a lightning flashes forth, and a hand appears that breaks down the* Head *with a hammer.*

The Brazen Head. Time is past!

Miles. Master, master, up! Hell 's broken [85 loose! Your head speaks; and there 's such a thunder and lightning, that I warrant all Oxford is up in arms. Out of your bed, and take a brown-bill in your hand; the latter day is come. 90
Bacon. Miles, I come. O, passing warily watch'd!
Bacon will make thee next himself in love.
When spake the head?

Miles. When spake the head! Did not you say that he should tell strange principles of [95 philosophy? Why, sir, it speaks but two words at a time.
Bacon. Why, villain, hath it spoken oft?
Miles. Oft! ay, marry, hath it, thrice; but in all those three times it hath uttered but [100 seven words.
Bacon. As how?
Miles. Marry, sir, the first time he said "Time is," as if Fabius Cumentator should have pronounced a sentence; [the second [105 time] he said, "Time was"; and the third time, with thunder and lightning, as in great choler, he said, "Time is past."
Bacon. 'T is past indeed. Ah, villain! time is past:
My fame, my glory, all are past. — [110
Bacon, the turrets of thy hope are ruin'd down,
Thy seven years' study lieth in the dust:
Thy Brazen Head lies broken through a slave
That watch'd, and would not when the head did will. —
What said the head first? 115
Miles. Even, sir, "Time is."
Bacon. Villain, if thou hadst call'd to Bacon then,
If thou hadst watch'd, and wak'd the sleepy friar,
The Brazen Head had uttered aphorisms,
And England had been circled round with brass: 12[0]
But proud Asmenoth, ruler of the north,

---

[1] Halbert.   [2] Till.

And Demogorgon, master of the fates,
Grudge that a mortal man should work so much.
Hell trembled at my deep-commanding spells,
Fiends frown'd to see a man their over-
    match;   125
Bacon might boast more than a man might
    boast.
But now the braves of Bacon hath an end,
Europe's conceit of Bacon hath an end,
His seven years' practice sorteth to ill end:
And, villain, sith my glory hath an end,   130
I will appoint thee to some fatal end.
Villain, avoid! get thee from Bacon's sight!
Vagrant, go roam and range about the world,
And perish as a vagabond on earth!
  Miles. Why, then, sir, you forbid me your
    service?   135
  Bacon. My service, villain! with a fatal curse,
That direful plagues and mischief fall on thee.
  Miles. 'T is no matter, I am against you with
the old proverb, — The more the fox is cursed,[1]
the better he fares. God be with you, [140
sir. I 'll take but a book in my hand, a wide-
sleeved gown on my back, and a crowned cap
on my head, and see if I can want promotion.
  Bacon. Some fiend or ghost haunt on thy
    weary steps,
Until they do transport thee quick to hell; 145
For Bacon shall have never merry day,
To lose the fame and honour of his head.
                        Exeunt.

[SCENE XII.][2]

Enter the EMPEROR, *the* KING OF CASTILE,
  KING HENRY, ELINOR, PRINCE EDWARD,
  LACY, *and* RALPH [SIMNELL].

  Emp. Now, lovely prince, the prime of Al-
    bion's wealth,
How fare the Lady Elinor and you?
What, have you courted and found Castile fit
To answer England in equivalence?   4
Will 't be a match 'twixt bonny Nell and thee?
  P. Edw. Should Paris enter in the courts of
    Greece,
And not lie fettered in fair Helen's looks?
Or Phœbus scape those piercing amorets
That Daphne glanced at his deity?
Can Edward, then, sit by a flame and freeze, 10
Whose heat puts Helen and fair Daphne down?
Now, monarchs, ask the lady : we gree.
  K. Hen. What, madam, hath my son found
    grace or no?
  Elin. Seeing, my lord, his lovely counterfeit,
And hearing how his mind and shape agreed, 15
I come not, troop'd with all this warlike train,
Doubting of love, but so affectionate
As Edward hath in England what he won in
  Spain.
  K. of Cast. A match, my lord; these wantons
    needs must love:
Men must have wives, and women will be
    wed.   20
Let 's haste the day to honour up the rites.
  Ralph. Sirrah Harry, shall Ned marry Nell?

  K. Hen. Ay, Ralph: how then?
  Ralph. Marry, Harry, follow my counsel:
send for Friar Bacon to marry them, for he 'll [25
so conjure him and her with his necromancy,
that they shall love together like pig and lamb
whilst they live.
  K. of Cast. But hearest thou, Ralph, art thou
content to have Elinor to thy lady?   30
  Ralph. Ay, so she will promise me two things.
  K. of Cast. What 's that, Ralph?
  Ralph. That she will never scold with Ned,
nor fight with me. — Sirrah Harry, I have put
her down with a thing unpossible.   35
  K. Hen. What 's that, Ralph?
  Ralph. Why, Harry, didst thou ever see that
a woman could both hold her tongue and her
hands? No: but when egg-pies grows on apple-
trees, then will thy grey mare prove a bag- [40
piper.
  Emp. What say the Lord of Castile and the
Earl of Lincoln, that they are in such earnest
and secret talk?
  K. of Cast. I stand, my lord, amazed at his
    talk,   45
How he discourseth of the constancy
Of one surnam'd, for beauty's excellence,
The Fair Maid of merry Fressingfield.
  K. Hen. 'T is true, my lord, 't is wondrous
    for to hear;
Her beauty passing Mars's paramour,   50
Her virgin's right as rich as Vesta's was.
Lacy and Ned hath told me miracles.
  K. of Cast. What says Lord Lacy? Shall she
be his wife?
  Lacy. Or else Lord Lacy is unfit to live. —
May it please your highness give me leave to
  post   55
To Fressingfield, I 'll fetch the bonny girl,
And prove, in true appearance at the court,
What I have vouched often with my tongue.
  K. Hen. Lacy, go to the 'querry of my stable,
And take such coursers as shall fit thy turn; 60
Hie thee to Fressingfield, and bring home the
  lass;
And, for her fame flies through the English
  coast,
If it may please the Lady Elinor,
One day shall match your excellence and her.
  Elin. We Castile ladies are not very coy; 65
Your highness may command a greater boon:
And glad were I to grace the Lincoln Earl
With being partner of his marriage-day.
  P. Edw. Gramercy, Nell, for I do love the
  lord,
As he that 's second to myself in love.   70
  Ralph. You love her? — Madam Nell, never
believe him you, though he swears he loves you.
  Elin. Why, Ralph?
  Ralph. Why, his love is like unto a tapster's
glass that is broken with every touch; for [75
he loved the fair maid of Fressingfield once out
of all ho.[3] — Nay, Ned, never wink upon me; I
care not, I.
  K. Hen. Ralph tells all; you shall have a
good secretary of him. —   80

---

[1] With a pun on *coursed* and *fares*, goes. [2] At Court.

                                  [3] Excessively.

But, Lacy, haste thee post to Fressingfield ;
For ere thou hast fitted all things for her
　　state,
The solemn marriage-day will be at hand.
　　Lacy. I go, my lord.　　　　　　*Exit.*
　　Emp. How shall we pass this day, my lord ?　85
　　K. Hen. To horse, my lord ; the day is passing
　　fair,
We 'll fly the partridge, or go rouse the deer.
Follow, my lords ; you shall not want for sport.
　　　　　　　　　　　　　　　　Exeunt.

[SCENE XIII.] [1]

Enter FRIAR BACON *with* FRIAR BUNGAY *to his
cell.*

　Bun. What means the friar that frolick'd it
　　of late,
To sit as melancholy in his cell
As if he had neither lost nor won to-day ?
　Bacon. Ah, Bungay, my Brazen Head is
　　spoil'd,
My glory gone, my seven years' study lost !　　5
The fame of Bacon, bruited through the world,
Shall end and perish with this deep disgrace.
　Bun. Bacon hath built foundation of his fame
So surely on the wings of true report,
With acting strange and uncouth miracles,　　10
As this cannot infringe what he deserves.
　Bacon. Bungay, sit down, for by prospective
　　skill
I find this day shall fall out ominous ;
Some deadly act shall 'tide me ere I sleep ;
But what and wherein little can I guess.　　15
My mind is heavy, whatsoe'er shall hap.

*Enter two Scholars, sons to Lambert and Serlsby.
Knock.*

　Bacon. Who 's that knocks ?
　Bun. Two scholars that desire to speak with
　　you.
　Bacon. Bid them come in. —
Now, my youths, what would you have ?　　20
　First Schol. Sir, we are Suffolk-men and neigh-
　　bouring friends ;
Our fathers in their countries lusty squires ;
Their lands adjoin : in Cratfield mine doth dwell,
And his in Laxfield. We are college-mates,
Sworn brothers, as our fathers live as friends.　25
　Bacon. To what end is all this ?
　Second Schol. Hearing your worship kept
　　within your cell
A glass prospective, wherein men might see
Whatso their thoughts or hearts' desire could
　　wish,
We come to know how that our fathers fare.　30
　Bacon. My glass is free for every honest
　　man.
Sit down, and you shall see ere long, how
Or in what state your friendly fathers live.
Meanwhile, tell me your names.
　First Schol. Mine Lambert.　　　　　35
　Second Schol. And mine Serlsby.
　Bacon. Bungay, I smell there will be a tra-
　　gedy.

　　　　　　　1 Friar Bacon's cell.

Enter LAMBERT *and* SERLSBY *with rapiers and
daggers.*

　Lam. Serlsby, thou hast kept thine hour like
　　a man :
Thou 'rt worthy of the title of a squire,
That durst, for proof of thy affection　　　40
And for thy mistress' favour, prize [2] thy blood.
Thou know 'st what words did pass at Fressing-
　　field,
Such shameless braves as manhood cannot brook:
Ay, for I scorn to bear such piercing taunts,
Prepare thee, Serlsby ; one of us will die.　45
　Ser. Thou see'st I single [meet] thee [in] the
　　field,
And what I spake, I 'll maintain with my sword.
Stand on thy guard, I cannot scold it out.
An if thou kill me, think I have a son,
That lives in Oxford in the Broadgates-hall,　50
Who will revenge his father's blood with blood.
　Lam. And, Serlsby, I have there a lusty
　　boy,
That dares at weapon buckle with thy son,
And lives in Broadgates too, as well as thine.
But draw thy rapier, for we'll have a bout.　55
　Bacon. Now, lusty younkers, look within the
　　glass,
And tell me if you can decern your sires.
　First Schol. Serlsby, 't is hard ; thy father
　　offers wrong,
To combat with my father in the field.
　Second Schol. Lambert, thou liest, my father's
　　is th' abuse,　　　　　　　　　　　60
And thou shalt find it, if my father harm.
　Bun. How goes it, sirs ?
　First Schol. Our fathers are in combat hard
　　by Fressingfield.
　Bacon. Sit still, my friends, and see the event.
　Lam. Why stand'st thou, Serlsby ? Doubt'st
　　thou of thy life ?　　　　　　　65
A veney,[3] man ! fair Margaret craves so much.
　Ser. Then this for her.
　First Schol. Ah. well thrust !
　Second Schol. But mark the ward.

[LAMBERT *and* SERLSBY] *fight and kill each
other.*

　Lam. O, I am slain !　　　　　　　70
　Ser. And I, — Lord have mercy on me !
　First Schol. My father slain ! — Serlsby, ward
　　that.
　Second Schol. And so is mine ! — Lambert,
　　I 'll quite thee well.
　　The two Scholars *stab each other [and die].*
　Bun. O strange stratagem !
　Bacon. See, friar, where the fathers both lie
　　dead !　　　　　　　　　　　75
Bacon, thy magic doth effect this massacre ;
This glass prospective worketh many woes ;
And therefore seeing these brave lusty Brutes,[4]
These friendly youths, did perish by thine
　　art,
End all thy magic and thine art at once.　　80
The poniard that did end the fatal [5] lives,
Shall break the cause efficient of their woes.

　2 Venture.　　　　　3 Bout.
　4 Britons (?) bloods (?)　　5 Doomed.

So fade the glass, and end with it the shows
That necromancy did infuse the crystal with.
                              Breaks the glass.
Bun. What means learn'd Bacon thus to
   break his glass?   85
Bacon. I tell thee, Bungay, it repents me sore
That ever Bacon meddled in this art.
The hours I have spent in pyromantic spells,
The fearful tossing in the latest night
Of papers full of necromantic charms,   90
Conjuring and adjuring devils and fiends,
With stole and alb and strange pentagonon ;
The wresting of the holy name of God,
As Soter, Eloim, and Adonai,
Alpha, Manoth, and Tetragrammaton,   95
With praying to the five-fold powers of heaven,
Are instances that Bacon must be damn'd
For using devils to countervail his God. —
Yet, Bacon, cheer thee, drown not in despair :
Sins have their salves, repentance can do
   much :   100
Think Mercy sits where Justice holds her seat,
And from those wounds those bloody Jews did
   pierce,
Which by thy magic oft did bleed afresh,
From thence for thee the dew of mercy drops,
To wash the wrath of high Jehovah's ire,   105
And make thee as a new-born babe from sin. —
Bungay, I'll spend the remnant of my life
In pure devotion, praying to my God
That he would save what Bacon vainly lost.
                              Exeunt.

[SCENE XIV.] [1]

Enter MARGARET *in nun's apparel, the* Keeper,
   her father, and their Friend.

Keeper. Margaret, be not so headstrong in
   these vows :
O, bury not such beauty in a cell,
That England hath held famous for the hue !
Thy father's hair, like to the silver blooms
That beautify the shrubs of Africa,   5
Shall fall before the dated time of death,
Thus to forgo his lovely Margaret.
Mar. Ah, father, when the harmony of
   heaven
Soundeth the measures of a lively faith,
The vain illusions of this flattering world   10
Seem odious to the thoughts of Margaret.
I loved once, — Lord Lacy was my love ;
And now I hate myself for that I lov'd,
And doted more on him than on my God ;
For this I scourge myself with sharp repents.   15
But now the touch of such aspiring sins
Tells me all love is lust but love of heavens ;
That beauty us'd for love is vanity :
The world contains naught but alluring baits,
Pride, flattery, and inconstant thoughts.   20
To shun the pricks of death, I leave the world,
And vow to meditate on heavenly bliss,
To live in Framlingham a holy nun,
Holy and pure in conscience and in deed ;
And for to wish all maids to learn of me   25
To seek heaven's joy before earth's vanity.

Friend. And will you, then, Margaret, be
shorn a nun, and so leave us all ?
Mar. Now farewell world, the engine of all
   woe !
Farewell to friends and father ! Welcome
   Christ !   30
Adieu to dainty robes ! This base attire
Better befits an humble mind to God
Than all the show of rich habiliments.
Love — O love ! and, with fond love, farewell
Sweet Lacy, whom I loved once so dear !   35
Ever be well, but never in my thoughts,
Lest I offend to think on Lacy's love :
But even to that, as to the rest, farewell !

Enter LACY, WARREN, *and* ERMSBY, *booted
   and spurred.*

Lacy. Come on, my wags, we're near the
   Keeper's lodge.
Here have I oft walk'd in the watery meads,   40
And chatted with my lovely Margaret.
War. Sirrah Ned, is not this the Keeper ?
Lacy. 'T is the same.
Erm. The old lecher hath gotten holy mut-
ton [2] to him : a nun, my lord.   45
Lacy. Keeper, how far'st thou ? Holla, man,
   what cheer ?
How doth Peggy, thy daughter and my love ?
Keeper. Ah, good my lord ! O, woe is me
   for Peggy !
See where she stands clad in her nun's attire,
Ready for to be shorn in Framlingham ;   50
She leaves the world because she left your love.
O, good my lord, persuade her if you can !
Lacy. Why, how now, Margaret ! What, a
   malcontent ?
A nun ? What holy father taught you this,
To task yourself to such a tedious life   55
As die a maid ? 'T were injury to me,
To smother up such beauty in a cell.
Mar. Lord Lacy, thinking of thy former miss,
How fond [3] the prime of wanton years were
   spent
In love (O, fie upon that fond conceit,   60
Whose hap and essence hangeth in the eye !),
I leave both love and love's content at once,
Betaking me to Him that is true love,
And leaving all the world for love of Him.
Lacy. Whence, Peggy, comes this metamor-
   phosis ?   65
What, shorn a nun, and I have from the court
Posted with coursers to convey thee hence
To Windsor, where our marriage shall be kept ?
Thy wedding-robes are in the tailor's hands.
Come, Peggy, leave these peremptory vows.   70
Mar. Did not my lord resign his interest,
And make divorce 'twixt Margaret and him ?
Lacy. 'T was but to try sweet Peggy's con-
   stancy.
But will fair Margaret leave her love and lord ?
Mar. Is not heaven's joy before earth's fading
   bliss,   75
And life above sweeter than life in love ?
Lacy. Why, then, Margaret will be shorn a
   nun ?

: Fraesingfield.

[2] A lewd woman.   [3] Foolishly.

Mar. Margaret hath made a vow which may
     not be revok'd.
War. We cannot stay, my lord ; an if she be
     so strict,
Our leisure grants us not to woo afresh.   80
Erms. Choose you, fair damsel, yet the choice
     is yours, —
Either a solemn nunnery or the court,
God or Lord Lacy. Which contents you best,
To be a nun or else Lord Lacy's wife ?
Lacy. A good motion. — Peggy, your answer
must be short.   85
Mar. The flesh is frail : my lord doth know it
     well,
That when he comes with his enchanting face,
Whatso'er betide, I cannot say him nay.
Off goes the habit of a maiden's heart,
And. seeing fortune will, fair Framlingham,   90
And all the show of holy nuns, farewell !
Lacy for me, if he will be my lord.
Lacy. Peggy, thy lord, thy love, thy husband.
Trust me, by truth of knighthood, that the king
Stays for to marry matchless Elinor,   95
Until I bring thee richly to the court,
That one day may both marry her and thee. —
How say'st thou, Keeper ? Art thou glad of this?
Keep. As if the English king had given
The park and deer of Fressingfield to me.   100
Erm. I pray thee, my Lord of Sussex, why
art thou in a brown study ?
War. To see the nature of women ; that
be they never so near God, yet they love to die
in a man's arms.   105
Lacy. What have you fit for breakfast ? We
have hied
And posted all this night to Fressingfield.
Mar. Butter and cheese, and umbles of a deer,
Such as poor keepers have within their lodge.
Lacy. And not a bottle of wine ?   110
Mar. We'll find one for my lord.
Lacy. Come, Sussex, let us in: we shall have
more,
For she speaks least, to hold her promise sure.
                          Exeunt.

[SCENE XV.] [1]

Enter a Devil *to seek* MILES.

Dev. How restless are the ghosts of hellish
     spirits,
When every charmer with his magic spells
Calls us from nine-fold-trenched Phlegethon,
To scud and over-scour the earth in post
Upon the speedy wings of swiftest winds !   5
Now Bacon hath rais'd me from the darkest
     deep,
To search about the world for Miles his man,
For Miles, and to torment his lazy bones
For careless watching of his Brazen Head.
See where he comes. O, he is mine !   10

Enter MILES *with a gown and a corner-cap.*

Miles. A scholar, quoth you ! marry, sir, I
would I had been made a bottle-maker when I
was made a scholar ; for I can get neither to

be a deacon, reader, nor schoolmaster, no, not
the clerk of a parish. Some call me dunce ; [15
another saith, my head is as full of Latin as an
egg's full of oatmeal. Thus I am tormented,
that the devil and Friar Bacon haunts me.
— Good Lord, here's one of my master's devils !
I'll go speak to him. — What, Master Plu- [20
tus, how cheer you ?
Dev. Dost thou know me ?
Miles. Know you, sir ! Why, are not you
one of my master's devils, that were wont to
come to my master, Doctor Bacon, at Bra- [25
zen-nose ?
Dev. Yes, marry, am I.
Miles. Good Lord, Master Plutus, I have
seen you a thousand times at my master's, and
yet I had never the manners to make you [30
drink. But, sir, I am glad to see how conform-
able you are to the statute. — I warrant you,
he's as yeomanly a man as you shall see:
mark you, masters, here's a plain honest man,
without welt or guard.[2] But I pray you, sir, [35
do you come lately from hell ?
Dev. Ay, marry : how then ?
Miles. Faith, 't is a place I have desired long
to see. Have you not good tippling-houses there ?
May not a man have a lusty fire there, a [40
pot of good ale, a pair [3] of cards, a swinging
piece of chalk, and a brown toast that will clap
a white waistcoat [4] on a cup of good drink ?
Dev. All this you may have there.
Miles. You are for me, friend, and I am for [45
you. But I pray you, may I not have an office
there ?
Dev. Yes, a thousand. What wouldst thou be ?
Miles. By my troth, sir, in a place where I
may profit myself. I know hell is a hot place, [50
and men are marvellous dry, and much drink
is spent there ; I would be a tapster.
Dev. Thou shalt.
Miles. There's nothing lets me from going
with you, but that 't is a long journey, and [55
I have never a horse.
Dev. Thou shalt ride on my back.
Miles. Now surely here's a courteous devil
that, for to pleasure his friend, will not stick
to make a jade of himself. — But I pray [60
you, goodman friend, let me move a question
to you.
Dev. What's that ?
Miles. I pray you, whether is your pace a trot
or an amble ?   65
Dev. An amble.
Miles. 'T is well ; but take heed it be not a
trot : but 't is no matter, I'll prevent it.
Dev. What dost ?
Miles. Marry, friend, I put on my spurs ; [70
for if I find your pace either a trot or else uneasy, I'll put you to a false gallop ; I'll make
you feel the benefit of my spurs.
Dev. Get up upon my back.
         [MILES *mounts on the* Devil's *back.*]
Miles. O Lord, here's even a goodly mar- [75
vel, when a man rides to hell on the devil's back!
                       Exeunt, roaring.

---

[1] Friar Bacon's cell.

[2] Trimmings or facings.   [3] Pack.   [4] Of froth.

[SCENE XVI.][1]

Enter the EMPEROR *with a pointless sword ; next
the* KING OF CASTILE *carrying a sword with
a point;* LACY *carrying the globe;* PRINCE
EDWARD ;* WARREN *carrying a rod of gold
with a dove on it :* ERMSBY *with a crown and
sceptre; the* QUEEN ; [PRINCESS ELINOR] *with
the Fair Maid of Fressingfield on her left
hand;* KING HENRY; BACON; *with other Lords
attending.*

P. Edw. Great potentates, earth's miracles
    for state,
Think that Prince Edward humbles at your
    feet,
And, for these favours, on his martial sword
He vows perpetual homage to yourselves,
Yielding these honours unto Elinor.   5
K. Hen. Gramercies, lordings ; old Planta-
    genet,
That rules and sways the Albion diadem,
With tears discovers these conceived joys,
And vows requital, if his men-at-arms,
The wealth of England, or due honours done 10
To Elinor, may quite his favourites.
But all this while what say you to the dames
That shine like to the crystal lamps of heaven ?
Emp. If but a third were added to these two,
They did surpass those gorgeous images   15
That gloried Ida with rich beauty's wealth.
Mar. 'Tis I, my lords, who humbly on my knee
Must yield her orisons to mighty Jove
For lifting up his handmaid to this state,
Brought from her homely cottage to the court, 20
And grac'd with kings, princes, and emperors ;
To whom (next to the noble Lincoln Earl)
I vow obedience, and such humble love
As may a handmaid to such mighty men.
P. Elin. Thou martial man that wears the
    Almain crown,   25
And you the western potentates of might,
The Albion princess, English Edward's wife,
Proud that the lovely star of Fressingfield,
Fair Margaret, Countess to the Lincoln Earl, 29
Attends on Elinor, — gramercies, lord, for her,—
'T is I give thanks for Margaret to you all,
And rest for her due bounden to yourselves.
K. Hen. Seeing the marriage is solémnized,
Let 's march in triumph to the royal feast. —
But why stands Friar Bacon here so mute ?   35

[1] The Court

Bacon. Repentant for the follies of my youth,
That magic's secret mysteries misled,
And joyful that this royal marriage
Portends such bliss unto this matchless realm.
K. Hen. Why, Bacon,   40
What strange event shall happen to this land ?
Or what shall grow from Edward and his
    queen ?
Bacon. I find by deep prescience of mine art,
Which once I temp'red in my secret cell,
That here where Brute did build his Troyno-
    vant,   45
From forth the royal garden of a king
Shall flourish out so rich and fair a bud [2]
Whose brightness shall deface proud Phœbus'
    flower,
And over-shadow Albion with her leaves.
Till then Mars shall be master of the field,   50
But then the stormy threats of wars shall cease :
The horse shall stamp as careless of the pike,
Drums shall be turn'd to timbrels of delight ;
With wealthy favours plenty shall enrich
The strand that gladded wand'ring Brute to
    see,   55
And peace from heaven shall harbour in these
    leaves
That gorgeous beautifies this matchless flower:
Apollo's heliotropion then shall stoop,
And Venus' hyacinth shall vail [3] her top ;
Juno shall shut her gilliflowers up,   60
And Pallas' bay shall 'bash her brightest green ;
Ceres' carnation, in consórt with those,
Shall stoop and wonder at Diana's rose.
K. Hen. This prophecy is mystical. ——
But, glorious commanders of Europa's love,   65
That make fair England like that wealthy isle
Circled with Gihon and [swift] [4] Euphrates,
In royalizing Henry's Albion
With presence of your princely mightiness, —
Let 's march : the tables all are spread,   70
And viands, such as England's wealth affords,
Are ready set to furnish out the boards.
You shall have welcome, mighty potentates :
It rests to furnish up this royal feast,
Only your hearts be frolic ; for the time   75
Craves that we taste of naught but jouissance.
Thus glories England over all the west.
                        Exeunt omnes
Omne tulit punctum qui miscuit utile dulci.

[2] This prophecy refers, as usual, to Elizabeth.
[3] Lower.   [4] So Dyce. Qq. *first.*

TAMBURLAINE THE GREAT

BY

CHRISTOPHER MARLOWE

PART THE FIRST

[DRAMATIS PERSONAE

MYCETES, King of Persia.
COSROE, his Brother.
ORTYGIUS,
CENEUS,
MEANDER, } Persian Lords and Captains.
MENAPHON,
THERIDAMAS,
TAMBURLAINE, a Scythian Shepherd.
TECHELLES, } his Followers.
USUMCASANE, }
BAJAZETH, Emperor of the Turks.
KING OF ARABIA.
KING of FEZ
KING of MOROCCO.

KING of ARGIER (Algiers).
SOLDAN of EGYPT.
GOVERNOR of DAMASCUS.
AGYDAS, } Median Lords.
MAGNETES, }
CAPOLIN, an Egyptian Captain.
PHILEMUS, a Messenger.
Bassoes, Lords, Citizens, Moors, Soldiers, and Attendants.
ZENOCRATE, Daughter of the Soldan of Egypt.
ANIPPE, her Maid.
ZABINA, Wife of Bajazeth.
EBEA, her Maid.
Virgins of Damascus.]

THE PROLOGUE

FROM jigging veins of rhyming mother wits,
And such conceits as clownage keeps in pay,
We'll lead you to the stately tent of war,
Where you shall hear the Scythian Tamburlaine
Threat'ning the world with high astounding terms,
And scourging kingdoms with his conquering sword.
View but his picture in this tragic glass,
And then applaud his fortunes as you please.

ACT I

SCENE I.

*Enter] MYCETES, COSROE, MEANDER, THERI-
DAMAS, ORTYGIUS, CENEUS, [MENAPHON,]
with others.*

Myc. Brother Cosroe, I find myself aggriev'd,
Yet insufficient to express the same,
For it requires a great and thund'ring speech:
Good brother, tell the cause unto my lords;
I know you have a better wit than I.   5
Cos. Unhappy Persia, that in former age
Hast been the seat of mighty conquerors,
That, in their prowess and their policies,
Have triumph'd over Afric and the bounds
Of Europe, where the sun dares scarce appear   10
For freezing meteors and congealed cold,
Now to be rul'd and governed by a man
At whose birthday Cynthia with Saturn join'd,
And Jove, the Sun, and Mercury denied
To shed [their] influence in his fickle brain !   15
Now Turks and Tartars shake their swords at thee,
Meaning to mangle all thy provinces.
Myc. Brother, I see your meaning well enough,

And through your planets I perceive you think
I am not wise enough to be a king;   20
But I refer me to my noblemen
That know my wit, and can be witnesses.
I might command you to be slain for this:
Meander, might I not?
Meand. Not for so small a fault, my sovereign
lord.   25
Myc. I mean it not, but yet I know I might;
Yet live; yea, live, Mycetes wills it so.
Meander, thou, my faithful counsellor,
Declare the cause of my conceived grief,
Which is, God knows, about that Tamburlaine,
That, like a fox in midst of harvest time,   31
Doth prey upon my flocks of passengers;
And, as I hear, doth mean to pull my plumes:
Therefore 't is good and meet for to be wise.
Meand. Oft have I heard your majesty com-
plain   35
Of Tamburlaine, that sturdy Scythian thief,
That robs your merchants of Persepolis
Trading by land unto the Western Isles,
And in your confines with his lawless train
Daily commits incivil [1] outrages,   40
Hoping (misled by dreaming prophecies)
To reign in Asia, and with barbarous arms

1 Uncivilized.

To make himself the monarch of the East;
But ere he march in Asia, or display
His vagrant ensign in the Persian fields,   45
Your grace hath taken order by Theridamas,
Charg'd with a thousand horse, to apprehend
And bring him captive to your highness' throne.
    Myc. Full true thou speak'st, and like thyself,
     my lord,
Whom I may term a Damon for thy love: 50
Therefore 'tis best, if so it like you all,
To send my thousand horse incontinent [1]
To apprehend that paltry Scythian.
How like you this, my honourable lords?
Is it not a kingly resolution?   55
    Cos. It cannot choose, because it comes from
     you.
    Myc. Then hear thy charge, valiant Theri-
     damas,
The chiefest captain of Mycetes' host,
The hope of Persia, and the very legs
Whereon our State doth lean as on a staff,   60
That holds us up, and foils our neighbour foes.
Thou shalt be leader of this thousand horse,
Whose foaming gall with rage and high disdain
Have sworn the death of wicked Tamburlaine.
Go frowning forth; but come thou smiling
     home,   65
As did Sir Paris with the Grecian dame;
Return with speed — time passeth swift away;
Our life is frail, and we may die to-day.
    Ther. Before the moon renew her borrowed
     light,
Doubt not, my lord and gracious sovereign,   70
But Tamburlaine and that Tartarian rout,
Shall either perish by our warlike hands,
Or plead for mercy at your highness' feet.
    Myc. Go, stout Theridamas, thy words are
     swords,   74
And with thy looks thou conquerest all thy foes;
I long to see thee back return from thence,
That I may view these milk-white steeds of mine
All loaden with the heads of killed men,
And from their knees e'en to their hoofs below
Besmear'd with blood that makes a dainty
     show.   80
    Ther. Then now, my lord, I humbly take my
     leave.
    Myc. Theridamas, farewell! ten thousand
     times.   *Exit* THERIDAMAS.
Ah, Menaphon, why stay'st thou thus behind,
When other men press forward for renown?
Go, Menaphon, go into Scythia;   85
And foot by foot follow Theridamas.
    Cos. Nay, pray you let him stay; a greater
     [task]
Fits Menaphon than warring with a thief.
Create him Prorex [2] of all Africa,
That he may win the Babylonians' hearts   90
Which will revolt from Persian government,
Unless they have a wiser king than you.
    Myc. " Unless they have a wiser king than
     you!"
These are his words; Meander, set them down.
    Cos. And add this to them — that all Asia   95
Laments to see the folly of their king.

    Myc. Well, here I swear by this my royal
     seat, —
    Cos. You may do well to kiss it then.
    Myc. Emboss'd with silk as best beseems
     my state,
To be reveng'd for these contemptuous words.
Oh, where is duty and allegiance now?   101
Fled to the Caspian or the Ocean main?
What shall I call thee? Brother? — No, a foe;
Monster of nature! Shame unto thy stock
That dar'st presume thy sovereign for to mock!
Meander, come: I am abus'd, Meander.   106
     Exeunt all but COSROE *and* MENAPHON.
    Men. How now, my lord? What, mated [3] and
     amaz'd
To hear the king thus threaten like himself!
    Cos. Ah, Menaphon, I pass [4] not for his
     threats;
The plot is laid by Persian noblemen   110
And captains of the Median garrisons
To crown me Emperor of Asia;
But this it is that doth excruciate
The very substance of my vexed soul —   114
To see our neighbours that were wont to quake
And tremble at the Persian monarch's name,
Now sit and laugh our regiment [5] to scorn;
And that which might resolve [6] me into tears,
Men from the farthest equinoctial line   119
Have swarm'd in troops into the Eastern India,
Lading their ships with gold and precious stones,
And made their spoils from all our provinces.
    Men. This should entreat your highness to
     rejoice,
Since Fortune gives you opportunity
To gain the title of a conqueror   125
By curing of this maimed empery.
Afric and Europe bordering on your land,
And continent to your dominions,
How easily may you, with a mighty host,
Pass into Græcia, as did Cyrus once,   130
And cause them to withdraw their forces home,
Lest you subdue the pride of Christendom.
           [*Trumpet within.*]
    Cos. But, Menaphon, what means this
     trumpet's sound?
    Men. Behold, my lord, Ortygius and the rest
Bringing the crown to make you Emperor!   135

Enter ORTYGIUS *and* CENEUS *bearing a crown
         with others.*

    Orty. Magnificent and mighty Prince Cosroe,
We, in the name of other Persian states [7]
And commons of this mighty monarchy,
Present thee with th' imperial diadem.
    Cen. The warlike soldiers and the gentlemen,
That heretofore have fill'd Persepolis   141
With Afric captains taken in the field,
Whose ransom made them march in coats of
     gold,
With costly jewels hanging at their ears,
And shining stones upon their lofty crests,   145
Now living idle in the walled towns,
Wanting both pay and martial discipline,
Begin in troops to threaten civil war,

---

[1] Forthwith.   [2] Viceroy.

[3] Confounded.   [5] Rule.   [7] Persons of state.
[4] Care.   [6] Dissolve.

And openly exclaim against the king:
Therefore, to stay all sudden mutinies,   150
We will invest your highness Emperor,
Whereat the soldiers will conceive more joy
Than did the Macedonians at the spoil
Of great Darius and his wealthy host.
  Cos. Well, since I see the state of Persia
        droop   155
And languish in my brother's government,
I willingly receive th' imperial crown,
And vow to wear it for my country's good,
In spite of them shall malice my estate.
  Orty. And in assurance of desir'd success, 160
We here do crown thee monarch of the East,
Emperor of Asia and Persia;
Great Lord of Media and Armenia;
Duke of Africa and Albania,
Mesopotamia and of Parthia,   165
East India and the late-discovered isles ;
Chief Lord of all the wide, vast Euxine sea,
And of the ever-raging Caspian lake.
Long live Cosroe, mighty Emperor !
  Cos. And Jove may [1] never let me longer live
Than I may seek to gratify your love,   171
And cause the soldiers that thus honour me
To triumph over many provinces !
By whose desires of discipline in arms
I doubt not shortly but to reign sole king, 175
And with the army of Theridamas,
(Whither we presently will fly, my lords)
To rest secure against my brother's force.
  Orty. We knew, my lord, before we brought
        the crown,
Intending your investion [2] so near   180
The residence of your despised brother,
The lords would not be too exasperate
To injure or suppress your worthy title ;
Or, if they would, there are in readiness
Ten thousand horse to carry you from hence,
In spite of all suspected enemies.   186
  Cos. I know it well, my lord, and thank you all.
  Orty. Sound up the trumpets then. God save
        the King !   [*Trumpets sound.*] *Exeunt.*

SCENE II.

[*Enter*] TAMBURLAINE *leading* ZENOCRATE,
TECHELLES, USUMCASANE, [AGYDAS, MAG-
NETES] *and other* Lords, *and* Soldiers, *loaden
with treasure.*

  Tamb. Come, lady, let not this appal your
        thoughts ;
The jewels and the treasure we have ta'en
Shall be reserv'd, and you in better state,
Than if you were arriv'd in Syria,
Even in the circle of your father's arms,   5
The mighty Soldan of Egyptia.
  Zeno. Ah, shepherd ! pity my distressed
        plight,
(If, as thou seemst, thou art so mean a man,)
And seek not to enrich thy followers
By lawless rapine from a silly maid,   10
Who travelling with these Median lords
To Memphis, from my uncle's country, Media,[3]

Where all my youth I have been governed,
Have pass'd the army of the mighty Turk,
Bearing his privy signet and his hand   15
To safe conduct us thorough Africa.
  Mag. And since we have arriv'd in Scythia,
Besides rich presents from the puissant Cham,
We have his highness' letters to command
Aid and assistance, if we stand in need.   20
  Tamb. But now you see these letters and
        commands
Are countermanded by a greater man ;
And through my provinces you must expect
Letters of conduct from my mightiness,
If you intend to keep your treasure safe.   25
But, since I love to live at liberty,
As easily may you get the Soldan's crown
As any prizes out of my precinct ;
For they are friends that help to wean my state
Till men and kingdoms help to strengthen it, 30
And must maintain my life exempt from servi-
        tude.—
But, tell me, madam, is your grace betroth'd ?
  Zeno. I am — my lord — for so you do im-
        port.
  Tamb. I am a lord, for so my deeds shall
        prove :
And yet a shepherd by my parentage.   35
But, lady, this fair face and heavenly hue
Must grace his bed that conquers Asia,
And means to be a terror to the world,
Measuring the limits of his empery
By east and west, as Phœbus doth his course. 40
Lie here ye weeds that I disdain to wear !
This complete armour and this curtle-axe [4]
Are adjuncts more beseeming Tamburlaine.
And, madam, whatsoever you esteem
Of this success and loss unvalued,[5]   45
Both may invest you Empress of the East ;
And these that seem but silly country swains
May have the leading of so great an host,
As with their weight shall make the mountains
        quake,
Even as when windy exhalations   50
Fighting for passage, tilt within the earth.
  Tech. As princely lions, when they rouse
        themselves,
Stretching their paws, and threat'ning herds of
        beasts,
So in his armour looketh Tamburlaine.
Methinks I see kings kneeling at his feet,   55
And he with frowning brows and fiery looks,
Spurning their crowns from off their captive
        heads.
  Usum. And making thee and me, Techelles,
        kings,
That even to death will follow Tamburlaine.
  Tamb. Nobly resolv'd, sweet friends and fol-
        lowers !   60
These lords, perhaps, do scorn our estimates,
And think we prattle with distempered spirits ;
But since they measure out deserts so mean,
That in conceit bear empires on our spears,
Affecting thoughts coequal with the clouds.   65

---

[4] The curtle-axe (Fr. *coutelasse*) was not an axe, but
a short curved sword, the modern cutlass.
[5] Invaluable.

[1] May Jove.   [2] Investiture.
[3] Early edd. read *of Medea.*

They shall be kept our forced followers,
Till with their eyes they view us emperors.
Zeno. The gods, defenders of the innocent,
Will never prosper your intended drifts,
That thus oppress poor friendless passengers. 70
Therefore at least admit us liberty,
Even as thou hop'st to be eternised,
By living Asia's mighty Emperor.
Agyd. I hope our lady's treasure and our own
May serve for ransom to our liberties.   75
Return our mules and empty camels back,
That we may travel into Syria,
Where her betrothed lord Alcidamas,
Expects th' arrival of her highness' person.
Mag. And wheresoever we repose ourselves, 80
We will report but well of Tamburlaine.
Tamb. Disdains Zenocrate to live with me?
Or you, my lords, to be my followers?
Think you I weigh this treasure more than you?
Not all the gold in India's wealthy arms   85
Shall buy the meanest soldier in my train.
Zenocrate, lovelier than the love of Jove,
Brighter than is the silver Rhodope,
Fairer than whitest snow on Scythian hills, —
Thy person is more worth to Tamburlaine,   90
Than the possession of the Persian crown,
Which gracious stars have promis'd at my birth.
A hundred Tartars shall attend on thee,
Mounted on steeds swifter than Pegasus;
Thy garments shall be made of Median silk,   95
Enchas'd with precious jewels of mine own,
More rich and valurous[1] than Zenocrate's.
With milk-white harts upon an ivory sled,
Thou shalt be drawn amidst the frozen pools,
And scale the icy mountains' lofty tops,   100
Which with thy beauty will be soon resolv'd.
My martial prizes with five hundred men,
Won on the fifty-headed Volga's waves,
Shall we all offer to Zenocrate, —
And then myself to fair Zenocrate.   105
Tech. What now! — in love?
Tamb. Techelles, women must be flattered:
But this is she with whom I am in love.

Enter a Soldier.

Sold. News! news!
Tamb. How now, what's the matter?   110
Sold. A thousand Persian horsemen are at
hand,
Sent from the king to overcome us all.
Tamb. How now, my lords of Egypt, and
Zenocrate!
How! — must your jewels be restor'd again,
And I that triumph'd so be overcome?   115
How say you, lordings, — is not this your hope?
Agyd. We hope yourself will willingly restore
them.
Tamb. Such hope, such fortune, have the
thousand horse.
Soft ye, my lords, and sweet Zenocrate!
You must be forced from me ere you go.   120
A thousand horsemen! — We five hundred
foot! —
An odds too great for us to stand against.
But are they rich? And is their armour good?

Sold. Their plumed helms are wrought with
beaten gold,   124
Their swords enamell'd, and about their necks
Hangs massy chains of gold, down to the waist.
In every part exceeding brave[2] and rich.
Tamb. Then shall we fight courageously with
them?
Or look you I should play the orator?
Tech. No; cowards and faint-hearted runa-
ways   130
Look for orations when the foe is near.
Our swords shall play the orator for us.
Usum. Come! let us meet them at the moun-
tain foot,
And with a sudden and an hot alarum,
Drive all their horses headlong down the hill. 135
Tech. Come, let us march!
Tamb. Stay, Techelles! ask a parley first.

The Soldiers *enter.*

Open the mails,[3] yet guard the treasure sure;
Lay out our golden wedges to the view,   139
That their reflections may amaze the Persians;
And look we friendly on them when they come,
But if they offer word or violence,
We'll fight five hundred men-at-arms to one,
Before we part with our possession.   144
And 'gainst the general we will lift our swords,
And either lance his greedy thirsting throat,
Or take him prisoner, and his chain shall serve
For manacles, till he be ransom'd home.
Tech. I hear them come; shall we encounter
them?
Tamb. Keep all your standings and not stir a
foot,   150
Myself will bide the danger of the brunt.

Enter THERIDAMAS *with others.*

Ther. Where is this Scythian Tamburlaine?
Tamb. Whom seek'st thou, Persian? — I am
Tamburlaine.
Ther. Tamburlaine! —
A Scythian shepherd so embellished   155
With nature's pride and richest furniture!
His looks do menace Heaven and dare the gods:
His fiery eyes are fix'd upon the earth,
As if he now devis'd some stratagem,   159
Or meant to pierce Avernus' darksome vaults
To pull the triple-headed dog from hell.
Tamb. Noble and mild this Persian seems to
be,
If outward habit judge the inward man.
Tech. His deep affections make him passion-
ate.
Tamb. With what a majesty he rears his
looks!   165
In thee, thou valiant man of Persia,
I see the folly of thy emperor.
Art thou but captain of a thousand horse,
That by characters graven in thy brows,
And by thy martial face and stout aspéct,   170
Deserv'st to have the leading of an host!
Forsake thy king, and do but join with me,
And we will triumph over all the world.
I hold the Fates bound fast in iron chains,

---

[1] Valuable.   [2] Fine.   [3] Trunks.

And with my hand turn Fortune's wheel about:
And sooner shall the sun fall from his sphere 175
Than Tamburlaine be slain or overcome.
Draw forth thy sword, thou mighty man-at-
arms,
Intending but to raze my charmed skin,
And Jove himself will stretch his hand from
Heaven 180
To ward the blow and shield me safe from harm.
See how he rains down heaps of gold in showers,
As if he meant to give my soldiers pay !
And as a sure and grounded argument,
That I shall be the monarch of the East, 185
He sends this Soldan's daughter rich and brave,
To be my Queen and portly Emperess.
If thou wilt stay with me, renowned man,
And lead thy thousand horse with my condúct,
Besides thy share of this Egyptian prize, 190
Those thousand horse shall sweat with martial
spoil
Of conquered kingdoms and of cities sack'd.
Both we will walk upon the lofty clifts,
And Christian merchants [1] that with Russian
stems
Plough up huge furrows in the Caspian sea, 195
Shall vail [2] to us, as lords of all the lake.
Both we will reign as consuls of the earth,
And mighty kings shall be our senators.
Jove sometimes masked in a shepherd's weed,
And by those steps that he hath scal'd the Heav-
ens 200
May we become immortal like the gods.
Join with me now in this my mean estate,
(I call it mean because, being yet obscure,
The nations far remov'd admire me not,) 204
And when my name and honour shall be spread
As far as Boreas claps his brazen wings,
Or fair Boötes sends his cheerful light,
Then shalt thou be competitor [3] with me,
And sit with Tamburlaine in all his majesty.
    Ther. Not Hermes, prolocutor to the gods, 210
Could use persuasions more pathetical.
    Tamb. Nor are Apollo's oracles more true,
Than thou shalt find my vaunts substantial.
    Tech. We are his friends, and if the Persian
king
Should offer present dukedoms to our state, 215
We think it loss to make exchange for that
We are assur'd of by our friend's success.
    Usum. And kingdoms at the least we all
expect,
Besides the honour in assured conquests,
Where kings shall crouch unto our conquering
swords, 220
And hosts of soldiers stand amaz'd at us ;
When with their fearful tongues they shall con-
fess
These are the men that all the world admires.
    Ther. What strong enchantments 'tice my
yielding soul !
Are these resolved nobles [4] Scythians ? 225
But shall I prove a traitor to my king ?
    Tamb. No, but the trusty friend of Tambur-
laine.

    Ther. Won with thy words, and conquered
with thy looks,
I yield myself, my men, and horse to thee,
To be partaker of thy good or ill, 230
As long as life maintains Theridamas.
    Tamb. Theridamas, my friend, take here my
hand,
Which is as much as if I swore by Heaven
And call'd the gods to witness of my vow.
Thus shall my heart be still combin'd with thine
Until our bodies turn to elements, 236
And both our souls aspire celestial thrones.
Techelles and Casane, welcome him !
    Tech. Welcome, renowned Persian, to us all !
    Usum. Long may Theridamas remain with
us ! 240
    Tamb. These are my friends, in whom I more
rejoice
Than doth the King of Persia in his crown,
And by the love of Pylades and Orestes,
Whose statues we adore in Scythia,
Thyself and them shall never part from me 245
Before I crown you kings in Asia.
Make much of them, gentle Theridamas,
And they will never leave thee till the death.
    Ther. Nor thee nor them, thrice noble Tam-
burlaine,
Shall want my heart to be with gladness pierc'd
To do you honour and security. 251
    Tamb. A thousand thanks, worthy Therida-
mas.
And now fair madam, and my noble lords,
If you will willingly remain with me
You shall have honours as your merits be ; 255
Or else you shall be forc'd with slavery.
    Agyd. We yield unto thee, happy Tambur-
laine.
    Tamb. For you then, madam, I am out of
doubt.
    Zeno. I must be pleas'd perforce. Wretched
Zenocrate !   *Exeunt.* 260

ACT II

SCENE I.

[*Enter*] COSROE, MENAPHON, ORTYGIUS, CEN-
EUS, *with other* Soldiers.

    Cos. Thus far are we towards Theridamas,
And valiant Tamburlaine, the man of fame,
The man that in the forehead of his fortune
Bears figures of renown and miracle.
But tell me, that hast seen him, Menaphon, 5
What stature wields he, and what person-
age ?
    Men. Of stature tall, and straightly fashioned,
Like his desire, lift upwards and divine ;
So large of limbs, his joints so strongly knit,
Such breadth of shoulders as might mainly bear
Old Atlas' burden ; 'twixt his manly pitch, [5] 11
A pearl, more worth than all the world, is
plac'd,

---

[1] Merchantmen.
[2] Lower their flags.
[3] Partner.
[4] Early edd. *noble.*

[5] Originally the height to which a falcon soared,
hence for height in general. Here it means the shoulders.

Wherein by curious sovereignty of art
Are fix'd his piercing instruments of sight,
Whose fiery circles bear encompassed   15
A heaven of heavenly bodies in their spheres,
That guides his steps and actions to the throne,
Where honour sits invested royally:
Pale of complexion, wrought in him with passion,
Thirsting with sovereignty and love of arms; 20
His lofty brows in folds do figure death,
And in their smoothness amity and life;
About them hangs a knot of amber hair,
Wrapped in curls, as fierce Achilles' was,
On which the breath of Heaven delights to
play,   25
Making it dance with wanton majesty. —
His arms and fingers, long, and sinewy,[1]
Betokening valour and excess of strength —
In every part proportioned like the man
Should make the world subdu'd to Tambur-
laine.   30
  Cos. Well hast thou pourtray'd in thy terms
of life
The face and personage of a wondrous man;
Nature doth strive with Fortune and his stars
To make him famous in accomplish'd worth;
And well his merits show him to be made   35
His fortune's master and the king of men,
That could persuade at such a sudden pinch,
With reasons of his valour and his life,
A thousand sworn and overmatching foes.
Then, when our powers in points of swords are
join'd   40
And clos'd in compass of the killing bullet,
Though strait the passage and the port[2] be made
That leads to palace of my brother's life,
Proud is his fortune if we pierce it not.
And when the princely Persian diadem   45
Shall overweigh his weary witless head,
And fall like mellowed fruit with shakes of
death,
In fair Persia, noble Tamburlaine
Shall be my regent and remain as king.
  Orty. In happy hour we have set the crown 50
Upon your kingly head, that seeks our honour
In joining with the man ordain'd by Heaven,
To further every action to the best.
  Cen. He that with shepherds and a little spoil
Durst, in disdain of wrong and tyranny,   55
Defend his freedom 'gainst a monarchy,
What will he do supported by a king,
Leading a troop of gentlemen and lords,
And stuff'd with treasure for his highest
thoughts!
  Cos. And such shall wait on worthy Tambur-
laine.   60
Our army will be forty thousand strong,
When Tamburlaine and brave Theridamas
Have met us by the river Araris;
And all conjoin'd to meet the witless king,
That now is marching near to Parthia,   65
And with unwilling soldiers faintly arm'd,
To seek revenge on me and Tamburlaine,
To whom, sweet Menaphon, direct me straight.
  Men. I will, my lord.

                               Exeunt.

¹ So Dyce. Early edd read *snowy.*   ² Gate.

Scene II.

[*Enter*] Mycetes, Meander, *with other* Lords
and Soldiers.

  Myc. Come, my Meander, let us to this gear.
I tell you true, my heart is swoln with wrath
On this same thievish villain, Tamburlaine,
And on that false Cosroe, my traitorous brother.
Would it not grieve a king to be so abus'd   5
And have a thousand horsemen ta'en away?
And, which is worst, to have his diadem
Sought for by such scald[3] knaves as love him
not?
I think it would; well then, by Heavens I
swear,
Aurora shall not peep out of her doors,   10
But I will have Cosroe by the head,
And kill proud Tamburlaine with point of
sword.
Tell you the rest, Meander; I have said.
  Meand. Then having past Armenian deserts
now,   14
And pitch'd our tents under the Georgian hills,
Whose tops are covered with Tartarian thieves,
That lie in ambush, waiting for a prey,
What should we do but bid them battle
straight,
And rid the world of those detested troops?
Lest, if we let them linger here awhile,   20
They gather strength by power of fresh sup-
plies.
This country swarms with vile outrageous men
That live by rapine and by lawless spoil,
Fit soldiers for the wicked Tamburlaine;
And he that could with gifts and promises   25
Inveigle him that led a thousand horse,
And make him false his faith unto his king,
Will quickly win such as are like himself.
Therefore cheer up your minds; prepare to
fight:
He that can take or slaughter Tamburlaine   30
Shall rule the province of Albania:
Who brings that traitor's head, Theridamas,
Shall have a government in Media,
Beside the spoil of him and all his train:
But if Cosroe, (as our spials[4] say,   35
And as we know) remains with Tamburlaine,
His highness' pleasure is that he should live,
And be reclaim'd with princely lenity.

                      [*Enter* a Spy.]

  A Spy. A hundred horsemen of my com-
pany
Scouting abroad upon these champaign plains 40
Have view'd the army of the Scythians,
Which make reports it far exceeds the king's.
  Meand. Suppose they be in number infinite,
Yet being void of martial discipline
All running headlong after greedy spoils,   45
And more regarding gain than victory,
Like to the cruel brothers of the earth,
Sprung of the teeth of dragons venomous,
Their careless swords shall lance their fellows'
throats,
And make us triumph in their overthrow   50

³ Scurvy.   ⁴ Spies.

Myc. Was there such brethren, sweet Mean-
   der, say,
That sprung of teeth of dragons venomous?
   Meand. So poets say, my lord.
   Myc. And 't is a pretty toy to be a poet.
Well, well, Meander, thou art deeply read,   55
And having thee, I have a jewel sure.
Go on, my lord, and give your charge, I say;
Thy wit will make us conquerors to-day.
   Meand. Then, noble soldiers, to entrap these
   thieves,
That live confounded in disordered troops,   60
If wealth or riches may prevail with them,
We have our camels laden all with gold,
Which you that be but common soldiers
Shall fling in every corner of the field;
And while the base-born Tartars take it up,   65
You, fighting more for honour than for gold,
Shall massacre those greedy-minded slaves;
And when their scattered army is subdu'd,
And you march on their slaughtered carcases,
Share equally the gold that bought their lives, 70
And live like gentlemen in Persia.
Strike up the drum and march courageously!
Fortune herself doth sit upon our crests.
   Myc. He tells you true, my masters: so he
does.
Drums, why sound ye not, when Meander
   speaks?   75
                        Exeunt [drums sounding].

SCENE III.

[Enter] COSROE, TAMBURLAINE, THERIDAMAS,
TECHELLES, USUMCASANE, *and* ORTYGIUS,
with others.

   Cos. Now, worthy Tamburlaine, have I re-
   pos'd
In thy approved fortunes all my hope.
What think'st thou, man, shall come of our at-
   tempts?
For even as from assured oracle,
I take thy doom for satisfaction.   5
   Tamb. And so mistake you not a whit, my
   lord;
For fates and oracles [of] Heaven have sworn
To royalise the deeds of Tamburlaine,
And make them blest that share in his at-
   tempts.
And doubt you not but, if you favour me,   10
And let my fortunes and my valour sway
To some direction in your martial deeds,
The world will strive with hosts of men-at-arms,
To swarm unto the ensign I support:
The host of Xerxes, which by fame is said   15
To drink the mighty Parthian Araris,
Was but a handful to that we will have.
Our quivering lances, shaking in the air,
And bullets, like Jove's dreadful thunderbolts,
Enroll'd in flames and fiery smouldering mists, 20
Shall threat the gods more than Cyclopian wars:
And with our sun-bright armour as we march,
We'll chase the stars from Heaven and dim
   their eyes
That stand and muse at our admired arms.
   Ther. You see, my lord. what working words
   he hath: 25

But when you see his actions [top][1] his speech,
Your speech will stay or so extol his worth
As I shall be commended and excus'd
For turning my poor charge to his direction.
And these his two renowmed friends, my lord,   30
Would make one thirst and strive to be retain'd
In such a great degree of amity.
   Tech. With duty and with amity we yield
Our utmost service to the fair Cosroe.
   Cos. Which I esteem as portion of my crown,
Usumcasane and Techelles both,   36
When she[2] that rules in Rhamnus' golden
   gates,
And makes a passage for all prosperous arms,
Shall make me solely Emperor of Asia,
Then shall your meeds and valours be advanc'd
To rooms of honour and nobility.   41
   Tamb. Then haste, Cosroe, to be king alone,
That I with these, my friends, and all my men
May triumph in our long-expected fate.
The king, your brother, is now hard at hand;   45
Meet with the fool, and rid your royal shoul-
   ders
Of such a burden as outweighs the sands
And all the craggy rocks of Caspia.

   [Enter a Messenger.]

   Mes. My lord, we have discovered the enemy
Ready to charge you with a mighty army.   50
   Cos. Come, Tamburlaine! now whet thy
   winged sword,
And lift thy lofty arm into the clouds,
That it may reach the King of Persia's crown,
And set it safe on my victorious head.   54
   Tamb. See where it is, the keenest curtle-axe
That e'er made passage thorough Persian arms,
These are the wings shall make it fly as swift
As doth the lightning or the breath of Heaven,
And kill as sure as it swiftly flies.   59
   Cos. Thy words assure me of kind success;
Go valiant soldier, go before and charge
The fainting army of that foolish king.
   Tamb. Usumcasane and Techelles, come!
We are enow to scare the enemy,
And more than needs to make an emperor.   64
                       [Exeunt] to the battle.

[SCENE IV.]

MYCETES *comes out alone with his crown in his
hand, offering to hide it.*

   Myc. Accurs'd be he that first invented war!
They knew not, ah, they knew not, simple men,
How those were hit by pelting cannon shot,
Stand staggering like a quivering aspen leaf
Fearing the force of Boreas' boisterous blasts. 5
In what a lamentable case were I
If Nature had not given me wisdom's lore!
For kings are clouts[3] that every man shoots at,
Our crown the pin[4] that thousands seek to
   cleave;

---

[1] Surpass. Early edd. read *stop.*

[2] Nemesis, who had a temple at Rhamnus in Attica.
(Bullen.)

[3] The white mark in the target at which the archers
aimed.

[4] The peg in the centre which fastened the clout.

Therefore in policy I think it good 10
To hide it close; a goodly stratagem,
And far from any man that is a fool:
So shall I not be known; or if I be,
They cannot take away my crown from me.
Here will I hide it in this simple hole. 15

Enter TAMBURLAINE.

Tamb. What, fearful coward, straggling from
the camp,
When kings themselves are present in the field?
Myc. Thou liest.
Tamb. Base villain! darest thou give the lie?
Myc. Away; I am the king; go; touch me
not. 20
Thou break'st the law of arms, unless thou
kneel
And cry me "mercy, noble king."
Tamb. Are you the witty King of Persia?
Myc. Ay, marry am I: have you any suit to
me?
Tamb. I would entreat you speak but three
wise words. 25
Myc. So I can when I see my time.
Tamb. Is this your crown?
Myc. Ay, didst thou ever see a fairer?
Tamb. You will not sell it, will you?
Myc. Such another word and I will have 30
thee executed. Come, give it me!
Tamb. No; I took it prisoner.
Myc. You lie; I gave it you.
Tamb. Then 't is mine.
Myc. No; I mean I let you keep it. 35
Tamb. Well; I mean you shall have it again.
Here; take it for a while: I lend it thee,
'Till I may see thee hemm'd with armed men;
Then shalt thou see me pull it from thy head:
Thou art no match for mighty Tamburlaine. 40
[*Exit.*]
Myc. O gods! Is this Tamburlaine the thief?
I marvel much he stole it not away.
Trumpets sound to the battle, and he runs in.

[SCENE V.]

[*Enter*] COSROE, TAMBURLAINE, THERIDAMAS,
MENAPHON, MEANDER, ORTYGIUS, TECHEL-
LES, USUMCASANE, *with others*

Tamb. Hold thee, Cosroe! wear two imperial
crowns;
Think thee invested now as royally,
Even by the mighty hand of Tamburlaine,
As if as many kings as could encompass thee 4
With greatest pomp, had crown'd thee emperor.
Cos. So do I, thrice renowned man-at-arms,
And none shall keep the crown but Tambur-
laine.
Thee do I make my regent of Persia,
And general lieutenant of my armies.
Meander, you, that were our brother's guide, 10
And chiefest counsellor in all his acts,
Since he is yielded to the stroke of war,
On your submission we with thanks excuse,
And give you equal place in our affairs.
Meand. Most happy Emperor, in humblest
terms 15

I vow my service to your majesty,
With utmost virtue of my faith and duty.
Cos. Thanks, good Meander: then, Cosroe
reign,
And govern Persia in her former pomp!
Now send embassage to thy neighbour kings, 20
And let them know the Persian king is
chang'd,
From one that knew not what a king should do,
To one that can command what 'longs thereto.
And now we will to fair Persepolis,
With twenty thousand expert soldiers. 25
The lords and captains of my brother's camp
With little slaughter take Meander's course,
And gladly yield them to my gracious rule.
Ortygius and Menaphon, my trusty friends,
Now will I gratify your former good, 30
And grace your calling with a greater sway.
Orty. And as we ever aim'd at your behoof,
And sought your state all honour it deserv'd,
So will we with our powers and our lives
Endeavour to preserve and prosper it. 35
Cos. I will not thank thee, sweet Ortygius;
Better replies shall prove my purposes.
And now, Lord Tamburlaine, my brother's
camp
I leave to thee and to Theridamas,
To follow me to fair Persepolis. 40
Then will we march to all those Indian mines,
My witless brother to the Christians lost,
And ransom them with fame and usury.
And till thou overtake me, Tamburlaine,
(Staying to order all the scattered troops,) 45
Farewell, lord regent and his happy friends!
I long to sit upon my brother's throne.
Meand. Your majesty shall shortly have your
wish,
And ride in triumph through Persepolis.
Exeunt all but TAMBURLAINE, TECHELLES,
THERIDAMAS, *and* USUMCASANE.
Tamb. "And ride in triumph through Perse-
polis!" 50
Is it not brave to be a king, Techelles?
Usumcasane and Theridamas,
Is it not passing brave to be a king,
"And ride in triumph through Persepolis"?
Tech. O, my lord, 't is sweet and full of pomp.
Usum. To be a king is half to be a god. 56
Ther. A god is not so glorious as a king
I think the pleasure they enjoy in Heaven,
Cannot compare with kingly joys in earth.
To wear a crown enchas'd with pearl and gold,
Whose virtues carry with it life and death; 61
To ask and have, command and be obeyed;
When looks breed love, with looks to gain the
prize, —
Such power attractive shines in princes' eyes!
Tamb. Why say, Theridamas, wilt thou be a
king? 66
Ther. Nay, though I praise it, I can live with-
out it.
Tamb. What says my other friends? Will
you be kings?
Tech. I, if I could, with all my heart, my lord.
Tamb. Why, that 's well said, Techelles; so
would I,
And so would you, my masters, would you not?

Usum. What then, my lord ? 71
Tamb. Why then, Casane, shall we wish for aught
The world affords in greatest novelty,
And rest attemptless, faint, and destitute ?
Methinks we should not: I am strongly mov'd,
That if I should desire the Persian crown, 76
I could attain it with a wondrous ease.
And would not all our soldiers soon consent,
If we should aim at such a dignity ?
Ther. I know they would with our persua-
sions. 80
Tamb. Why then, Theridamas, I 'll first assay
To get the Persian kingdom to myself ;
Then thou for Parthia ; they for Scythia and Media ;
And, if I prosper, all shall be as sure
As if the Turk, the pope, Afric, and Greece, 85
Came creeping to us with their crowns apace.[1]
Tech. Then shall we send to this triumphing king,
And bid him battle for his novel crown ?
Usum. Nay, quickly then, before his room be hot.
Tamb. 'T will prove a pretty jest, in faith, my friends. 90
Ther. A jest to charge on twenty thousand men !
I judge the purchase[2] more important far.
Tamb. Judge by thyself, Theridamas, not me ;
For presently Techelles here shall haste
To bid him battle ere he pass too far, 95
And lose more labour than the game will quite.[3]
Then shalt thou see this Scythian Tamburlaine
Make but a jest to win the Persian crown.
Techelles, take a thousand horse with thee,
And bid him turn him back to war with us, 100
That only made him king to make us sport.
We will not steal upon him cowardly,
But give him warning and more warriors.
Haste thee, Techelles ; we will follow thee.
[*Exit* TECHELLES.]
What saith Theridamas ? 105
Ther.   Go on for me. *Exeunt.*

SCENE VI.

[*Enter*] COSROE, MEANDER, ORTYGIUS, MENA-
PHON, *with other* Soldiers.

Cos. What means this devilish shepherd to aspire
With such a giantly presumption
To cast up hills against the face of Heaven,
And dare the force of angry Jupiter ?
But as he thrust them underneath the hills, 5
And press'd out fire from their burning jaws,
So will I send this monstrous slave to hell,
Where flames shall ever feed upon his soul.
Meand. Some powers divine, or else infernal, mix'd
Their angry seeds at his conception ; 10
For he was never sprung of human race,
Since with the spirit of his fearful pride

He dare so doubtlessly resolve of rule,
And by profession be ambitious.
Orty. What god, or fiend, or spirit of the earth, 15
Or monster turned to a manly shape,
Or of what mould or mettle he be made,
What star or state[4] soever govern him,
Let us put on our meet encount'ring minds
And in detesting such a devilish thief, 20
In love of honour and defence of right,
Be arm'd against the hate of such a foe,
Whether from earth, or hell, or Heaven, he grow.
Cos. Nobly resolv'd, my good Ortygius ;
And since we all have suck'd one wholesome air, 26
And with the same proportion of elements
Resolve, I hope we are resembled,
Vowing our loves to equal death and life.
Let 's cheer our soldiers to encounter him,
That grievous image of ingratitude, 30
That fiery thirster after sovereignty,
And burn him in the fury of that flame,
That none can quench but blood and empery.
Resolve, my lords and loving soldiers, now
To save your king and country from decay. 35
Then strike up, drum ; and all the stars that make
The loathsome circle of my dated life,
Direct my weapon to his barbarous heart,
That thus opposeth him against the gods,
And scorns the powers that govern Persia ! 40
[*Exeunt.*]

[SCENE VII.]

Enter to the battle, and after the battle enter Cos-
ROE, *wounded*, TAMBURLAINE, THERIDAMAS,
TECHELLES, USUMCASANE, *with others.*

Cos. Barbarous and bloody Tamburlaine,
Thus to deprive me of my crown and life !
Treacherous and false Theridamas,
Even at the morning of my happy state,
Scarce being seated in my royal throne, 5
To work my downfall and untimely end !
An uncouth pain torments my grieved soul,
And death arrests the organ of my voice,
Who, ent'ring at the breach thy sword hath made,
Sacks every vein and artier[5] of my heart. — 10
Bloody and insatiate Tamburlaine !
Tamb. The thirst of reign and sweetness of a crown
That caus'd the eldest son of heavenly Ops,
To thrust his doting father from his chair,
And place himself in the empyreal Heaven, 15
Mov'd me to manage arms against thy state.
What better precedent than mighty Jove ?
Nature that fram'd us of four elements,
Warring within our breasts for regiment,[6]
Doth teach us all to have aspiring minds : 20
Our souls, whose faculties can comprehend
The wondrous architecture of the world,
And measure every wand'ring planet's course,
Still climbing after knowledge infinite,
And always moving as the restless spheres, 25

---

[1] Ed. of 1605, *apeece.*   [2] Booty.   [3] Requite.   [4] Dyce emends to *fate.*   [5] Artery.   [6] Rule.

Wills us to wear ourselves, and never rest,
Until we reach the ripest fruit of all,
That perfect bliss and sole felicity,
The sweet fruition of an earthly crown.
 Ther. And that made me to join with Tam-
  burlaine :   30
For he is gross and like the massy earth,
That moves not upwards, nor by princely deeds
Doth mean to soar above the highest sort.
 Tech. And that made us the friends of Tam-
  burlaine,
To lift our swords against the Persian king. 35
 Usum. For as, when Jove did thrust old Sat-
  urn down,
Neptune and Dis gain'd each of them a crown,
So do we hope to reign in Asia,
If Tamburlaine be plac'd in Persia.
 Cos. The strangest men that ever nature
  made !   40
I know not how to take their tyrannies.
My bloodless body waxeth chill and cold,
And with my blood my life slides through my
  wound;
My soul begins to take her flight to hell,
And summons all my senses to depart. — 45
The heat and moisture, which did feed each
  other,
For want of nourishment to feed them both,
Is dry and cold ; and now doth ghastly death,
With greedy talons gripe my bleeding heart,
And like a harpy tires [1] on my life. 50
Theridamas and Tamburlaine, I die :
And fearful vengeance light upon you both !
     [Cosroe *dies.* Tamburlaine] *takes*
      the crown and puts it on.
 Tamb. Not all the curses which the Furies
  breathe,
Shall make me leave so rich a prize as this.
Theridamas, Techelles, and the rest, 55
Who think you now is King of Persia ?
 All. Tamburlaine ! Tamburlaine !
 Tamb. Though Mars himself, the angry god
  of arms,
And all the earthly potentates conspire
To dispossess me of this diadem, 60
Yet will I wear it in despite of them,
As great commander of this eastern world,
If you but say that Tamburlaine shall reign.
 All. Long live Tamburlaine and reign in
  Asia !
 Tamb. So now it is more surer on my head, 65
Than if the gods had held a parliament,
And all pronounc'd me King of Persia.
         [*Exeunt.*]

ACT III

Scene I.

[*Enter*] Bajazeth, *the* Kings *of* Fez, Morocco, *and* Argier,[2] *with others in great pomp.*

 Baj. Great Kings of Barbary and my portly
  bassoes,[3]
We hear the Tartars and the eastern thieves,

Under the conduct of one Tamburlaine,
Presume a bickering with your emperor, 4
And thinks to rouse us from our dreadful siege
Of the famous Grecian Constantinople.
You know our army is invincible ;
As many circumcised Turks we have,
And warlike bands of Christians renied,[4]
As hath the ocean or the Terrene sea [5] 10
Small drops of water when the moon begins
To join in one her semicircled horns.
Yet would we not be brav'd with foreign power,
Nor raise our siege before the Grecians yield,
Or breathless lie before the city walls. 15
 K. of Fez. Renowmed Emperor, and mighty
  general,
What, if you sent the bassoes of your guard
To charge him to remain in Asia,
Or else to threaten death and deadly arms
As from the mouth of mighty Bajazeth. 20
 Baj. Hie thee, my basso, fast to Persia,
Tell him thy lord, the Turkish Emperor,
Dread Lord of Afric, Europe, and Asia,
Great King and conqueror of Græcia,
The ocean, Terrene, and the Coal-black sea,[6] 25
The high and highest monarch of the world,
Wills and commands (for say not I entreat),
Not once to set his foot on Africa,
Or spread his colours [forth] in Græcia,
Lest he incur the fury of my wrath. 30
Tell him I am content to take a truce,
Because I hear he bears a valiant mind :
But if, presuming on his silly power,
He be so mad to manage arms with me,
Then stay thou with him ; say, I bid thee so : 35
And if, before the sun have measured Heaven
With triple circuit, thou regreet us not,
We mean to take his morning's next arise
For messenger he will not be reclaim'd,
And mean to fetch thee in despite of him. 40
 Bas. Most great and puissant monarch of the
  earth,
Your basso will accomplish your behest,
And show your pleasure to the Persian,
As fits the legate of the stately Turk. *Exit.*
 K. of Arg. They say he is the King of Persia ;
But, if he dare attempt to stir your siege, 45
'T were requisite he should be ten times more,
For all flesh quakes at your magnificence.
 Baj. True, Argier ; and tremble at my looks.
 K. of Mor. The spring is hind'red by your
  smothering host, 50
For neither rain can fall upon the earth,
Nor sun reflex his virtuous beams thereon,
The ground is mantled with such multitudes.
 Baj. All this is true as holy Mahomet ;
And all the trees are blasted with our breaths.
 K. of Fez. What thinks your greatness best
  to be achiev'd 55
In pursuit of the city's overthrow ?
 Baj. I will the captive pioners of Argier
Cut off the water that by leaden pipes
Runs to the city from the mountain Carnon. 60
Two thousand horse shall forage up and down,
That no relief or succour come by land :

---

 [1] Preys. [2] Algiers. [3] Pashas.

 [4] Christians who have abjured their faith
 [5] The Mediterranean. [6] The Black Sea.

And all the sea my galleys countermand.
Then shall our footmen lie within the trench,
And with their cannons mouth'd like Orcus'
gulf,   65
Batter the walls, and we will enter in;
And thus the Grecians shall be conquered.
                Exeunt.

            SCENE II.

[*Enter*] ZENOCRATE, AGYDAS, ANIPPE, *with
              others.*

[*Agyd.*] Madam Zenocrate, may I presume
To know the cause of these unquiet fits,
That work such trouble to your wonted rest ?
'T is more than pity such a heavenly face
Should by heart's sorrow wax so wan and pale,   5
When your offensive rape by Tamburlaine,
(Which of your whole displeasures should be
    most,)
Hath seem'd to be digested long ago.
    Zeno. Although it be digested long ago,
As his exceeding favours have deserv'd,   10
And might content the Queen of Heaven, as well
As it hath chang'd my first conceiv'd disdain,
Yet since a farther passion feeds my thoughts
With ceaseless and disconsolate conceits,
Which dyes my looks so lifeless as they are,   15
And might, if my extremes had full events,
Make me the ghastly counterfeit of death.
    Agyd. Eternal heaven sooner be dissolv'd,
And all that pierceth Phœbus' silver eye,
Before such hap fall to Zenocrate !   20
    Zeno. Ah, life and soul, still hover in his
       breast
And leave my body senseless as the earth.
Or else unite you to his life and soul,
That I may live and die with Tamburlaine !

Enter [*behind*] TAMBURLAINE, TECHELLES, *and
             others.*

    Agyd. With Tamburlaine ! Ah, fair Zeno-
       crate,   25
Let not a man so vile and barbarous,
That holds you from your father in despite,
And keeps you from the honours of a queen,
(Being suppos'd his worthless concubine,)
Be honoured with your love but for necessity. 30
So, now the mighty Soldan hears of you,
Your highness needs not doubt but in short time
He will with Tamburlaine's destruction
Redeem you from this deadly servitude.
    Zeno. [Agydas,] leave to wound me with these
       words,   35
And speak of Tamburlaine as he deserves.
The entertainment we have had of him
Is far from villany [1] or servitude,
And might in noble minds be counted princely.
    Agyd. How can you fancy one that looks so
       fierce,   40
Only dispos'd to martial stratagems ?
Who, when he shall embrace you in his arms,
Will tell how many thousand men he slew ;
And when you look for amorous discourse,
Will rattle forth his facts [2] of war and blood, 45
Too harsh a subject for your dainty ears.

    Zeno. As looks the Sun through Nilus' flow-
       ing stream,
Or when the Morning holds him in her arms,
So looks my lordly love, fair Tamburlaine ;
His talk much sweeter than the Muses' song 50
They sung for honour 'gainst Pierides ;
Or when Minerva did with Neptune strive:
And higher would I rear my estimate
Than Juno, sister to the highest god,
If I were match'd with mighty Tamburlaine. 55
    Agyd. Yet be not so inconstant in your love;
But let the young Arabian live in hope
After your rescue to enjoy his choice.
You see though first the King of Persia,
Being a shepherd, seem'd to love you much, 60
Now in his majesty he leaves those looks,
Those words of favour, and those comfortings,
And gives no more than common courtesies.
    Zeno. Thence rise the tears that so distain my
       cheeks,
Fearing his love through my unworthiness. — 65
       TAMBURLAINE *goes to her and takes
          her away lovingly by the hand,
          looking wrathfully on* AGYDAS,
          and says nothing. [*Exeunt all but
          AGYDAS.]
    Agyd. Betray'd by fortune and suspicious
       love,
Threat'ned with frowning wrath and jealousy,
Surpris'd with fear of hideous revenge,
I stand aghast ; but most astoniéd [1]
To see his choler shut in secret thoughts,   70
And wrapt in silence of his angry soul.
Upon his brows was portray'd ugly death ;
And in his eyes the furies of his heart
That shone as comets, menacing revenge,
And casts a pale complexion on his cheeks.   75
As when the seaman sees the Hyades
Gather an army of Cimmerian clouds,
(Auster and Aquilon with winged steeds,
All sweating, tilt about the watery Heavens,
With shivering spears enforcing thunder claps, 80
And from their shields strike flames of light-
    ning,)
All fearful folds his sails and sounds the main,
Lifting his prayers to the Heavens for aid
Against the terror of the winds and waves,
So fares Agydas for the late-felt frowns,   85
That sent a tempest to my daunted thoughts,
And makes my soul divine her overthrow.

Re-enter TECHELLES *with a naked dagger.*

    Tech. See you, Agydas, how the king salutes
       you ?
He bids you prophesy what it imports.   *Exit.*
    Agyd. I prophesied before, and now I prove 90
The killing frowns of jealousy and love.
He needed not with words confirm my fear,
For words are vain where working tools pre-
    sent
The naked action of my threat'ned end :
It says, Agydas, thou shalt surely die,   95
And of extremities elect the least ;
More honour and less pain it may procure
To die by this resolved hand of thine,

       [1] Subjection.   [2] Deeds.   [1] Astonished.

Than stay the torments he and Heaven have
   sworn. 99
Then haste, Agydas, and prevent the plagues
Which thy prolonged fates may draw on thee.
Go, wander, free from fear of tyrant's rage,
Removed from the torments and the hell
Wherewith he may excruciate thy soul,
And let Agydas by Agydas die, 105
And with this stab slumber eternally.
           Stabs himself.

[*Re-enter* TECHELLES *with* USUMCASANE.]

Tech. Usumcasane, see, how right the man
Hath hit the meaning of my lord, the king.
Usum. Faith, and Techelles, it was manly
   done;
And since he was so wise and honourable, 110
Let us afford him now the bearing hence,
And crave his triple-worthy burial.
Tech. Agreed, Casane; we will honour him.
        [*Exeunt bearing out the body.*]

SCENE III.

[*Enter*] TAMBURLAINE, TECHELLES, USUMCA-
SANE, THERIDAMAS, *a* BASSO, ZENOCRATE,
[ANIPPE,] *with others.*

Tamb. Basso, by this thy lord and master
   knows
I mean to meet him in Bithynia:
See how he comes! Tush, Turks are full of
   brags,
And menace more than they can well perform.
He meet me in the field, and fetch thee hence!
Alas! poor Turk! his fortune is too weak 6
To encounter with the strength of Tamburlaine.
View well my camp, and speak indifferently;
Do not my captains and my soldiers look
As if they meant to conquer Africa? 10
Bas. Your men are valiant, but their num-
   ber few,
And cannot terrify his mighty host.
My lord, the great commander of the world,
Besides fifteen contributory kings,
Hath now in arms ten thousand Janissaries, 15
Mounted on lusty Mauritanian steeds,
Brought to the war by men of Tripoli;
Two hundred thousand footmen that have serv'd
In two set battles fought in Græcia:
And for the expedition of this war, 20
If he think good, can from his garrisons
Withdraw as many more to follow him.
Tech. The more he brings the greater is the
   spoil,
For when they perish by our warlike hands,
We mean to seat our footmen on their steeds, 25
And rifle all those stately Janisars.
Tamb. But will those kings accompany your
   lord?
Bas. Such as his highness please; but some
   must stay
To rule the provinces he late subdu'd.
Tamb. [*To his* Officers.] Then fight coura-
   geously: their crowns are yours; 30
This hand shall set them on your conquering
   heads,
That made me Emperor of Asia.

Usum. Let him bring millions infinite of men,
Unpeopling Western Africa and Greece,
Yet we assure us of the victory. 35
Ther. Even he that in a trice vanquish'd two
   kings,
More mighty than the Turkish emperor,
Shall rouse him out of Europe, and pursue
His scattered army till they yield or die.
Tamb. Well said, Theridamas; speak in that
   mood; 40
For *will* and *shall* best fitteth Tamburlaine,
Whose smiling stars give him assured hope
Of martial triumph ere he meet his foes.
I that am term'd the scourge and wrath of God,
The only fear and terror of the world, 45
Will first subdue the Turk, and then enlarge
Those Christian captives, which you keep as
   slaves,
Burdening their bodies with your heavy chains,
And feeding them with thin and slender fare;
That naked row about the Terrene sea, 50
And when they chance to breathe and rest a space,
Are punish'd with bastones [1] so grievously,
That they lie panting on the galley's side,
And strive for life at every stroke they give.
These are the cruel pirates of Argier, 55
That damned train, the scum of Africa,
Inhabited with straggling runagates,
That make quick havoc of the Christian blood;
But, as I live, that town shall curse the time
That Tamburlaine set foot in Africa. 60

Enter BAJAZETH *with his* Bassoes, *and contribu-*
tory KINGS [*of* FEZ, MOROCCO, *and* ARGIER;
ZABINA *and* EBEA].

Baj. Bassoes and Janissaries of my guard,
Attend upon the person of your lord,
The greatest potentate of Africa.
Tamb. Techelles and the rest, prepare your
   swords;
I mean to encounter with that Bajazeth. 65
Baj. Kings of Fez, Moroccus, and Argier,
He calls me Bajazeth, whom you call Lord!
Note the presumption of this Scythian slave!
I tell thee, villain, those that lead my horse
Have to their names titles of dignity, 70
And dar'st thou bluntly call me Bajazeth?
Tamb. And know, thou Turk, that those
   which lead my horse,
Shall lead thee captive thorough Africa;
And dar'st thou bluntly call me Tamburlaine?
Baj. By Mahomet my kinsman's sepulchre,
And by the holy Alcoran I swear, 76
He shall be made a chaste and lustless eunuch,
And in my sarell [2] tend my concubines;
And all his captains that thus stoutly stand,
Shall draw the chariot of my emperess, 80
Whom I have brought to see their overthrow.
Tamb. By this my sword, that conquer'd
   Persia,
Thy fall shall make me famous through the
   world.
I will not tell thee how I'll handle thee,
But every common soldier of my camp 85
Shall smile to see thy miserable state.

[1] Sticks. Ital. *bastone.*   [2] Seraglio.

K. of Fez. What means the mighty Turkish
    emperor,
To talk with one so base as Tamburlaine?
K. of Mor. Ye Moors and valiant men of Bar-
    bary,
How can ye suffer these indignities?   90
K. of Arg. Leave words, and let them feel
    your lances' points
Which glided through the bowels of the Greeks.
Baj. Well said, my stout contributory kings:
Your threefold army and my hugy[1] host
Shall swallow up these base-born Persians.   95
Tech. Puissant, renowmed, and mighty Tam-
    burlaine,
Why stay we thus prolonging all their lives?
Ther. I long to see those crowns won by our
    swords,
That we may reign as kings of Africa.
Usum. What coward would not fight for such
    a prize?   100
Tamb. Fight all courageously, and be you
    kings;
I speak it, and my words are oracles.
Baj. Zabina, mother of three braver boys
Than Hercules, that in his infancy
Did pash[2] the jaws of serpents venomous;   105
Whose hands are made to gripe a warlike lance,
Their shoulders broad for complete armour fit,
Their limbs more large, and of a bigger size,
Than all the brats ysprung from Typhon's loins;
Who, when they come unto their father's age,
Will batter turrets with their manly fists; — 111
Sit here upon this royal chair of state,
And on thy head wear my imperial crown,
Until I bring this sturdy Tamburlaine,
And all his captains bound in captive chains. 115
Zab. Such good success happen to Bajazeth!
Tamb. Zenocrate, the loveliest maid alive,
Fairer than rocks of pearl and precious stone,
The only paragon of Tamburlaine,
Whose eyes are brighter than the lamps of
    Heaven   120
And speech more pleasant than sweet harmony!
That with thy looks canst clear the darkened sky,
And calm the rage of thund'ring Jupiter,
Sit down by her, adorned with my crown,
As if thou wert the Empress of the world.   125
Stir not, Zenocrate, until thou see
Me march victoriously with all my men,
Triumphing over him and these his kings,
Which I will bring as vassals to thy feet;
Till then take thou my crown, vaunt of my
    worth,   130
And manage words with her, as we will arms.
Zeno. And may my love, the King of Persia,
Return with victory and free from wound!
Baj. Now shalt thou feel the force of Turkish
    arms,
Which lately made all Europe quake for fear.   135
I have of Turks, Arabians, Moors, and Jews,
Enough to cover all Bithynia.
Let thousands die; their slaughtered carcasses
Shall serve for walls and bulwarks to the rest
And as the heads of Hydra, so my power,   140
Subdued, shall stand as mighty as before.

If they should yield their necks unto the sword,
Thy soldiers' arms could not endure to strike
So many blows as I have heads for thee.
Thou know'st not, foolish, hardy Tamburlaine,
What 't is to meet me in the open field,   145
That leave no ground for thee to march upon.
    Tamb. Our conquering swords shall marshal
        us the way
We use to march upon the slaughtered foe,   149
Trampling their bowels with our horses' hoofs;
Brave horses bred on the white Tartarian hills;
My camp is like to Julius Cæsar's host,
That never fought but had the victory;
Nor in Pharsalia was there such hot war
As these, my followers, willingly would have. 155
Legions of spirits fleeting[3] in the air
Direct our bullets and our weapons' points,
And make your[4] strokes to wound the senseless
    lure,[5]
And when she sees our bloody colours spread,
Then Victory begins to take her flight,   160
Resting herself upon my milk-white tent.—
But come, my lords, to weapons let us fall;
The field is ours, the Turk, his wife, and all.
                        Exit with his followers.
Baj. Come, kings and bassoes, let us glut our
    swords,   164
That thirst to drink the feeble Persians' blood.
                        Exit with his followers.
Zab. Base concubine, must thou be plac'd by
    me,
That am the empress of the mighty Turk?
Zeno. Disdainful Turkess and unreverend
    boss![6]
Call'st thou me concubine, that am betroth'd
Unto the great and mighty Tamburlaine?   170
Zab. To Tamburlaine, the great Tartarian
    thief!
Zeno. Thou wilt repent these lavish words of
    thine,
When thy great basso-master and thyself
Must plead for mercy at his kingly feet,
And sue to me to be your advocate.   175
Zab. And sue to thee! I tell thee, shameless
    girl,
Thou shalt be laundress to my waiting maid! —
How lik'st thou her, Ebea? Will she serve?
Ebea. Madam, she thinks, perhaps, she is too
    fine,
But I shall turn her into other weeds,   180
And make her dainty fingers fall to work.
Zeno. Hear'st thou, Anippe, how thy drudge
    doth talk?
And how my slave, her mistress, menaceth?
Both for their sauciness shall be employed   184
To dress the common soldiers' meat and drink,
For we will scorn they should come near our-
    selves.
Anip. Yet sometimes let your highness send
    for them
To do the work my chambermaid disdains.
                        They sound the battle within.[7]

2 Floating.   4 Qq. *our.*
5 Perhaps in the sense of "decoy." Ellis suggests
"light" from Fr. *lueur.* Dyce conj. *air.*
6 Contemptuously used of a woman.
7 Early edd. add *and stay.*

1 Huge.   2 Dash to pieces.

Zeno. Ye gods and powers that govern Persia,
And made my lordly love her worthy king,   190
Now strengthen him against the Turkish Baj-
   azeth,
And let his foes, like flocks of fearful roes
Pursu'd by hunters, fly his angry looks,
That I may see him issue conqueror!
Zab. Now, Mahomet, solicit God himself,   195
And make him rain down murdering shot from
   Heaven
To dash the Scythians' brains, and strike them
   dead,
That dare to manage arms with him
That offered jewels to thy sacred shrine,
When first he warr'd against the Christians!   200
     [They sound] to the battle again.
Zeno. By this the Turks lie welt'ring in
   their blood,
And Tamburlaine is Lord of Africa.
Zab. Thou art deceiv'd. — I heard the trump-
   ets sound
As when my emperor overthrew the Greeks,
And led them captive into Africa.   205
Straight will I use thee as thy pride deserves:
Prepare thyself to live and die my slave.
Zeno. If Mahomet should come from Heaven
   and swear
My royal lord is slain or conquered,
Yet should he not persuade me otherwise   210
But that he lives and will be conqueror.

BAJAZETH *flies and* [TAMBURLAINE] *pursues
him. The battle short, and they enter.* BAJAZETH
is overcome.

   Tamb. Now, king of bassoes, who is conqueror?
Baj. Thou, by the fortune of this damned
   [foil].[1]
Tamb. Where are your stout contributory
   kings?

Re-enter TECHELLES, THERIDAMAS, *and* USUM-
   CASANE.

   Tech. We have their crowns, their bodies
   strow the field.   215
Tamb. Each man a crown! Why, kingly
fought, i' faith.
Deliver them into my treasury.
Zeno. Now let me offer to my gracious lord
His royal crown again so highly won.
Tamb. Nay, take the Turkish crown from her,
   Zenocrate,   220
And crown me Emperor of Africa.
Zab. No, Tamburlaine: though now thou gat
   the best,
Thou shalt not yet be lord of Africa.
Ther. Give her the crown, Turkess: you were
best.
     He takes it from her, and gives it to
     ZENOCRATE.
Zab. Injurious villains! thieves! runagates!
How dare you thus abuse my majesty?   226
Ther. Here, madam, you are Empress; she is
none.
Tamb. Not now, Theridamas; her time is
past.

   [1] Defeat. Early edd. read *soile.*

The pillars that have bolstered up those terms,
Are fallen in clusters at my conquering feet.   230
   Zab. Though he be prisoner, he may be ran-
   somed.
Tamb. Not all the world shall ransom Bajazeth.
Baj. Ah, fair Zabina! we have lost the field;
And never had the Turkish emperor
So great a foil by any foreign foe.   235
Now will the Christian miscreants be glad,
Ringing with joy their superstitious bells,
And making bonfires for my overthrow.
But, ere I die, those foul idolaters
Shall make me bonfires with their filthy bones.
For though the glory of this day be lost,   241
Afric and Greece have garrisons enough
To make me sovereign of the earth again.
Tamb. Those walled garrisons will I subdue,
And write myself great lord of Africa.   245
So from the East unto the furthest West
Shall Tamburlaine extend his puissant arm.
The galleys and those pilling[2] brigandines,
That yearly sail to the Venetian gulf,
And hover in the Straits for Christians' wrack,
Shall lie at anchor in the isle Asant,[3]   251
Until the Persian fleet and men of war,
Sailing along the oriental sea,
Have fetch'd about the Indian continent,
Even from Persepolis to Mexico,   255
And thence unto the straits of Jubalter;[4]
Where they shall meet and join their force in one
Keeping in awe the bay of Portingale,[5]
And all the ocean by the British shore;
And by this means I'll win the world at last.   260
Baj. Yet set a ransom on me, Tamburlaine.
Tamb. What, think'st thou Tamburlaine es-
   teems thy gold?
I'll make the kings of India, ere I die,
Offer their mines to sue for peace to me,
And dig for treasure to appease my wrath.   265
Come, bind them both, and one lead in the
   Turk;
The Turkess let my love's maid lead away.
             Thy bind them.
Baj. Ah, villains! — dare you touch my
   sacred arms?
O Mahomet! — O sleepy Mahomet!
Zab. O cursed Mahomet, that makes us thus
The slaves to Scythians rude and barbarous!   271
   Tamb. Come, bring them in; and for this
   happy conquest,
Triumph and solemnise a martial feast. *Exeunt.*

ACT IV

SCENE I.

[*Enter the*] SOLDAN *of* EGYPT, *with three or four*
   Lords, CAPOLIN, [*and a* Messenger].

   Sold. Awake, ye men of Memphis! Hear the
   clang
Of Scythian trumpets! Hear the basilisks[6]

   [2] Plundering.
   [3] Zante. (Bullen.)
   [4] Gibraltar.
   [5] Biscay.
   [6] Pieces of ordnance, so called from their fancied
resemblance to the fabulous serpent of that name.
(Cunningham.)

That, roaring, shake Damascus' turrets down!
The rogue of Volga holds Zenocrate,
The Soldan's daughter, for his concubine,   5
And with a troop of thieves and vagabonds,
Hath spread his colours to our high disgrace,
While you, faint-hearted, base Egyptians,
Lie slumbering on the flowery banks of Nile,
As crocodiles that unaffrighted rest,   10
While thund'ring cannons rattle on their skins.
    Mess. Nay, mighty Soldan, did your greatness
        see
The frowning looks of fiery Tamburlaine,
That with his terror and imperious eyes
Commands the hearts of his associates,   15
It might amaze your royal majesty.
    Sold. Villain, I tell thee, were that Tambur-
        laine
As monstrous[1] as Gorgon,[2] prince of hell,
The Soldan would not start a foot from him.
But speak, what power hath he?
    Mess.   Mighty lord,   20
Three hundred thousand men in armour clad,
Upon their prancing steeds disdainfully
With wanton paces trampling on the ground:
Five hundred thousand footmen threat'ning
        shot,
Shaking their swords, their spears, and iron bills,
Environing their standard round, that stood   26
As bristle-pointed as a thorny wood:
Their warlike engines and munition
Exceed the forces of their martial men.
    Sold. Nay, could their numbers countervail
        the stars,   30
Or ever-drizzling drops of April showers,
Or withered leaves that Autumn shaketh down
Yet would the Soldan by his conquering power,
So scatter and consume them in his rage,
That not a man should live to rue their fall.   35
    Capo. So might your highness, had you time
        to sort
Your fighting men, and raise your royal host;
But Tamburlaine, by expedition,
Advantage takes of your unreadiness.   39
    Sold. Let him take all th' advantages he can.
Were all the world conspir'd to fight for him,
Nay, were he devil, as he is no man,
Yet in revenge of fair Zenocrate,
Whom he detaineth in despite of us,
This arm should send him down to Erebus,   45
To shroud his shame in darkness of the night.
    Mess. Pleaseth your mightiness to under-
        stand,
His resolution far exceedeth all.
The first day when he pitcheth down his tents,
White is their hue, and on his silver crest,   50
A snowy feather spangled white he bears,
To signify the mildness of his mind,
That, satiate with spoil, refuseth blood.
But when Aurora mounts the second time
As red as scarlet is his furniture;   55
Then must his kindled wrath be quench'd with
        blood,
Not sparing any that can manage arms;
But if these threats move not submission,
Black are his colours, black pavilion;

His spear, his shield, his horse, his armour,
        plumes,   60
And jetty feathers menace death and hell!
Without respect of sex, degree, or age,
He razeth all his foes with fire and sword.
    Sold. Merciless villain! Peasant, ignorant
Of lawful arms or martial discipline!   65
Pillage and murder are his usual trades;
The slave usurps the glorious name of war.
See, Capolin, the fair Arabian king,
That hath been disappointed by this slave
Of my fair daughter and his princely love,   70
May have fresh warning to go war with us,
And be reveng'd for her disparagement.
                                            [Exeunt.]

                    SCENE II.

[Enter] TAMBURLAINE, TECHELLES, THERIDA
    MAS, USUMCASANE, ZENOCRATE, ANIPPE,
    two Moors *drawing* BAJAZETH *in his cage,
    and his wife* [ZABINA] *following him.*

    Tamb. Bring out my footstool.
                            They take him out of the cage.
    Baj. Ye holy priests of heavenly Mahomet,
That, sacrificing, slice and cut your flesh,
Staining his altars with your purple blood;
Make Heaven to frown and every fixed star   5
To suck up poison from the moorish fens,
And pour it in this glorious[3] tyrant's throat!
    Tamb. The chiefest God, first mover of that
        sphere,
Enchas'd with thousands ever-shining lamps,
Will sooner burn the glorious frame of Hea-
        ven,   10
Than it should so conspire my otherthrow.
But, villain! thou that wishest this to me,
Fall prostrate on the low disdainful earth,
And be the footstool of great Tamburlaine,
That I may rise into my royal throne.   15
    Baj. First shalt thou rip my bowels with thy
        sword,
And sacrifice my heart to death and hell,
Before I yield to such a slavery.
    Tamb. Base villain, vassal, slave to Tambur-
        laine!
Unworthy to embrace or touch the ground,   1
That bears the honour of my royal weight;
Stoop, villain, stoop!—Stoop! for so he bids
That may command thee piecemeal to be torn,
Or scattered like the lofty cedar trees
Struck with the voice of thund'ring Jupiter.   21
    Baj. Then, as I look down to the damned
        fiends,
Fiends look on me! and thou, dread god of hell
With ebon sceptre strike this hateful earth,
And make it swallow both of us at once!
    [TAMBURLAINE] *gets up upon him to his chair*
    Tamb. Now clear the triple region of the
        air,   3
And let the majesty of Heaven behold
Their scourge and terror tread on emperors.
Smile stars, that reign'd at my nativity,
And dim the brightness of their neighbour
        lamps!

---

[1] Trisyllabic here.   [2] Demogorgon.   [3] Vain-glorious, boastful.

Disdain to borrow light of Cynthia ! 35
For I, the chiefest lamp of all the earth,
First rising in the East with mild aspect,
But fixœd now in the meridian line,
Will send up fire to your turning spheres,
And cause the sun to borrow light of you. 40
My sword struck fire from his coat of steel,
Even in Bithynia, when I took this Turk ;
As when a fiery exhalation,
Wrapt in the bowels of a freezing cloud
Fighting for passage, make[s] the welkin crack,
And casts a flash of lightning to the earth : 46
But ere I march to wealthy Persia,
Or leave Damascus and th' Egyptian fields,
As was the fame of Clymene's brain-sick son,
That almost brent the axle-tree of Heaven, 50
So shall our swords, our lances, and our shot
Fill all the air with fiery meteors :
Then, when the sky shall wax as red as blood,
It shall be said I made it red myself,
To make me think of nought but blood and war. 55
 Zab. Unworthy king, that by thy cruelty
Unlawfully unsurp'st the Persian seat,
Dar'st thou, that never saw an emperor
Before thou met my husband in the field,
Being his captive, thus abuse his state, 60
Keeping his kingly body in a cage,
That roofs of gold and sun-bright palaces
Should have prepar'd to entertain his grace ?
And treading him beneath thy loathsome feet,
Whose feet the kings of Africa have kiss'd. 65
 Tech. You must devise some torment worse,
  my lord,
To make these captives rein their lavish
  tongues.
 Tamb. Zenocrate, look better to your slave.
 Zeno. She is my handmaid's slave, and she
  shall look
That these abuses flow not from her tongue : 70
Chide her, Anippe.
 Anip. Let these be warnings for you then,
  my slave,
How you abuse the person of the king ;
Or else I swear to have you whipt, stark-nak'd.
 Baj. Great Tamburlaine, great in my over-
  throw, 75
Ambitious pride shall make thee fall as low,
For treading on the back of Bajazeth,
That should be horsed on four mighty kings.
 Tamb. Thy names and titles and thy dignities
Are fled from Bajazeth and remain with me, 80
That will maintain 't against a world of kings.
Put him in again.
   [*They put him back into the cage.*]
 Baj. Is this a place for mighty Bajazeth ?
Confusion light on him that helps thee thus !
 Tamb. There, whiles he lives, shall Bajazeth
  be kept ; 85
And, where I go, be thus in triumph drawn ;
And thou, his wife, shalt feed him with the
  scraps
My servitors shall bring thee from my board ;
For he that gives him other food than this
Shall sit by him and starve to death himself ; 90
This is my mind and I will have it so.
Not all the kings and emperors of the earth,

If they would lay their crowns before my feet,
Shall ransom him or take him from his cage.
The ages that shall talk of Tamburlaine, 95
Even from this day to Plato's wondrous year,
Shall talk how I have handled Bajazeth ;
These Moors, that drew him from Bithynia
To fair Damascus, where we now remain,
Shall lead him with us wheresoe'er we go. 100
Techelles, and loving followers,
Now may we see Damascus' lofty towers,
Like to the shadows of Pyramides,
That with their beauties grac'd the Memphian
  fields.
The golden statue[1] of their feathered bird 105
That spreads her wings upon the city walls
Shall not defend it from our battering shot.
The townsmen mask in silk and cloth of gold,
And every house is as a treasury :
The men, the treasure, and the town is ours.
 Ther. Your tents of white now pitch'd before
  the gates, 111
And gentle flags of amity display'd,
I doubt not but the governor will yield,
Offering Damascus to your majesty.
 Tamb. So shall he have his life and all the
  rest. 115
But if he stay until the bloody flag
Be once advanc'd on my vermilion tent,
He dies, and those that kept us out so long.
And when they see me march in black array,
With mournful streamers hanging down their
  heads, 120
Were in that city all the world contain'd,
Not one should scape, but perish by our swords.
 Zeno. Yet would you have some pity for my
  sake,
Because it is my country's, and my father's.
 Tamb. Not for the world, Zenocrate, if I've
  sworn. 125
Come ; bring in the Turk.   *Exeunt.*

SCENE III.

[*Enter the*] SOLDAN, [*the* KING *of*] ARABIA, CA-
POLIN, *with streaming colours and* Soldiers.

 Sold. Methinks we march as Meleager did,
Environ'd with brave Argolian knights,
To chase the savage Calydonian boar,
Or Cephalus with lusty Theban youths
Against the wolf that angry Themis sent 5
To waste and spoil the sweet Aonian fields,
A monster of five hundred thousand heads,
Compact of rapine, piracy, and spoil.
The scum of men, the hate and scourge of God,
Raves in Egyptia and annoyeth us. 10
My lord, it is the bloody Tamburlaine,
A sturdy felon and a base-bred thief,
By murder raised to the Persian crown,
That dares control us in our territories.
To tame the pride of this presumptuous beast, 15
Join your Arabians with the Soldan's power,
Let us unite our royal bands in one,
And hasten to remove Damascus' siege.
It is a blemish to the majesty
And high estate of mighty emperors, 20

---

[1] Early edd. read *stature.*

That such a base usurping vagabond
Should brave a king, or wear a princely crown.
  K. of Arab. Renowmed Soldan, have you
lately heard
The overthrow of mighty Bajazeth
About the confines of Bithynia ?   25
The slavery wherewith he persecutes
The noble Turk and his great emperess ?
  Sold. I have, and sorrow for his bad success ;
But, noble lord of great Arabia,
Be so persuaded that the Soldan is   30
No more dismay'd with tidings of his fall
Than in the haven when the pilot stands
And views a stranger's ship rent in the winds,
And shivered against a craggy rock ;
Yet in compassion of his wretched state,   35
A sacred vow to Heaven and him I make,
Confirming it with Ibis' holy name,
That Tamburlaine shall rue the day, the hour,
Wherein he wrought such ignominious wrong
Unto the hallowed person of a prince,   40
Or kept the fair Zenocrate so long
As concubine, I fear, to feed his lust.
  K. of Arab. Let grief and fury hasten on re-
venge ;
Let Tamburlaine for his offences feel
Such plagues as Heaven and we can pour on
him.   45
I long to break my spear upon his crest,
And prove the weight of his victorious arm ;
For Fame, I fear, hath been too prodigal
In sounding through the world his partial praise,
  Sold. Capolin, hast thou survey'd our
powers ?   50
  Capol. Great Emperors of Egypt and Arabia,
The number of your hosts united is
A hundred and fifty thousand horse ;
Two hundred thousand foot, brave men-at-
arms,
Courageous, and full of hardiness,   55
As frolic as the hunters in the chase
Of savage beasts amid the desert woods.
  K. of Arab. My mind presageth fortunate
success ;
And, Tamburlaine, my spirit doth foresee
The utter ruin of thy men and thee.   60
  Sold. Then rear your standards ; let your
sounding drums
Direct our soldiers to Damascus' walls.
Now, Tamburlaine, the mighty Soldan comes,
And leads with him the great Arabian king,
To dim thy baseness and obscurity,   65
Famous for nothing but for theft and spoil ;
To raze and scatter thy inglorious crew
Of Scythians and slavish Persians.   *Exeunt.*

SCENE IV.

The Banquet ; and to it cometh TAMBURLAINE,
all in scarlet, [ZENOCRATE,] THERIDAMAS,
TECHELLES, USUMCASANE, *the Turk* [BAJA-
ZETH *in his cage,* ZABINA,] *with others.*

  Tamb. Now hang our bloody colours by Da-
mascus,
Reflexing hues of blood upon their heads,
While they walk quivering on their city walls,
Half dead for fear before they feel my wrath :

Then let us freely banquet and carouse   5
Full bowls of wine unto the god of war
That means to fill your helmets full of gold,
And make Damascus spoils as rich to you,
As was to Jason Colchos' golden fleece. —
And now, Bajazeth, hast thou any stomach ?   10
  Baj. Ay, such a stomach, cruel Tamburlaine,
as I could willingly feed upon thy blood-raw
heart.
  Tamb. Nay thine own is easier to come by ;
pluck out that, and 't will serve thee and thy [15
wife. Well, Zenocrate, Techelles, and the rest,
fall to your victuals.
  Baj. Fall to, and never may your meat digest !
Ye Furies, that can mask invisible,
Dive to the bottom of Avernus' pool,   20
And in your hands bring hellish poison up
And squeeze it in the cup of Tamburlaine !
Or, winged snakes of Lerna, cast your stings,
And leave your venoms in this tyrant's dish !
  Zab. And may this banquet prove as ominous
As Progne's to th' adulterous Thracian king,   26
That fed upon the substance of his child.
  Zeno. My lord, how can you [tamely][1] suffer
these
Outrageous curses by these slaves of yours ?
  Tamb. To let them see, divine Zenocrate,   30
I glory in the curses of my foes,
Having the power from the imperial Heaven
To turn them all upon their proper heads.
  Tech. I pray you give them leave, madam ;
this speech is a goodly refreshing to them.   35
  Ther. But if his highness would let them be
fed, it would do them more good.
  Tamb. Sirrah, why fall you not to ? Are you
so daintily brought up, you cannot eat your own
flesh ?   40
  Baj. First, legions of devils shall tear thee in
pieces.
  Usum. Villain, know'st thou to whom thou
speakest ?
  Tamb. O, let him alone. Here ; eat, sir ; [45
take it from my sword's point, or I'll thrust it to
thy heart. *Bajazeth takes it and stamps upon it.*
  Ther. He stamps it under his feet, my lord.
  Tamb. Take it up, villain, and eat it ; or I
will make thee slice the brawns of thy arms [50
into carbonadoes[2] and eat them.
  Usum. Nay, 't were better he kill'd his
wife, and then she shall be sure not to be
starv'd, and he be provided for a month's victual
beforehand.   55
  Tamb. Here is my dagger : despatch her while
she is fat ; for if she live but a while longer,
she will fall into a consumption with fretting,
and then she will not be worth the eating.
  Ther. Dost thou think that Mahomet will [60
suffer this ?
  Tech. 'Tis like he will when he cannot let[3]
it.
  Tamb. Go to ; fall to your meat. — What, not
a bit ! Belike he hath not been watered to- [65
day ; give him some drink.
*They give Bajazeth water to drink,
and he flings it on the ground.*

---

[1] Dyce conj.   [2] Slices for broiling.   [3] Hinder.

Tamb. Fast, and welcome, sir, while[1] hunger make you eat. How now, Zenocrate, doth not the Turk and his wife make a goodly show at a banquet ?   70

Zeno. Yes, my lord.

Ther. Methinks, 't is a great deal better than a consort[2] of music.

Tamb. Yet music would do well to cheer up Zenocrate. Pray thee tell why thou art so [75 sad ? If thou wilt have a song, the Turk shall strain his voice. But why is it ?

Zeno. My lord, to see my father's town besieg'd,
The country wasted where myself was born,
How can it but afflict my very soul ?   80
If any love remain in you, my lord,
Or if my love unto your majesty
May merit favour at your highness' hands,
Then raise your siege from fair Damascus' walls,
And with my father take a friendly truce.   85

Tamb. Zenocrate, were Egypt Jove's own land,
Yet would I with my sword make Jove to stoop.
I will confute those blind geographers
That make a triple region in the world,
Excluding regions which I mean to trace,   90
And with this pen[3] reduce them to a map,
Calling the provinces, cities, and towns,
After my name and thine, Zenocrate.
Here at Damascus will I make the point
That shall begin the perpendicular ;   95
And would'st thou have me buy thy father's love
With such a loss ? — Tell me, Zenocrate.

Zeno. Honour still wait on happy Tamburlaine !
Yet give me leave to plead for him, my lord.

Tamb. Content thyself : his person shall be safe   100
And all the friends of fair Zenocrate,
If with their lives they will be pleas'd to yield,
Or may be forc'd to make me Emperor ;
For Egypt and Arabia must be mine. —
Feed, you slave ! Thou may'st think thy- [105
self happy to be fed from my trencher.

Baj. My empty stomach, full of idle heat,
Draws bloody humours from my feeble parts,
Preserving life by hasting cruel death.
My veins are pale, my sinews hard and dry, 110
My joints benumb'd : unless I eat, I die.

Zab. Eat, Bajazeth. Let us live in spite of them, looking[4] some happy power will pity and enlarge[5] us.

Tamb. Here, Turk ; wilt thou have a clean [115
trencher ?

Baj. Ay, tyrant, and more meat.

Tamb. Soft, sir ; you must be dieted ; too much eating will make you surfeit.

Ther. So it would, my lord, specially hav- [120
ing so small a walk and so little exercise.

Enter a second course of crowns.

Tamb. Theridamas, Techelles, and Casane, here are the cates you desire to finger, are they not ?

---

[1] Until.   [3] Holding out his sword.   [5] Free.
[2] Band.   [4] Expecting.

Ther. Ay, my lord ; but none save kings must feed with these.   124

Tech. 'T is enough for us to see them, and for Tamburlaine only to enjoy them.

Tamb. Well ; here is now to the Soldan of Egypt, the King of Arabia, and the Governor [130
of Damascus. Now take these three crowns, and pledge me, my contributory kings. I crown you here, Theridamas, King of Argier ; Techelles, King of Fez ; and Usumcasane, King of Moroccus. How say you to this, Turk ? These are [135
not your contributory kings.

Baj. Nor shall they long be thine, I warrant them.

Tamb. Kings of Argier, Moroccus, and of Fez,
You that have march'd with happy Tamburlaine 140
As far as from the frozen [plage[6]] of Heaven
Unto the watery morning's ruddy bower,[7]
And thence by land unto the torrid zone,
Deserve these titles I endow you with
By [valour[8]] and by magnanimity.   145
Your births shall be no blemish to your fame,
For virtue is the fount whence honour springs
And they are worthy she investeth kings.

Ther. And since your highness hath so well vouchsaf'd,
If we deserve them not with higher meeds
Than erst our states and actions have retain'd 150
Take them away again and make us slaves.

Tamb. Well said, Theridamas ; when holy fates
Shall 'stablish me in strong Egyptia,
We mean to travel to th' antartic pole,
Conquering the people underneath our feet, 155
And be renowm'd as never emperors were.
Zenocrate, I will not crown thee yet,
Until with greater honours I be grac'd.

                       [*Exeunt.*]

ACT V

SCENE I.

[*Enter*] *the* GOVERNOR *of* DAMASCUS, *with three or four* Citizens, *and four* Virgins, *with branches of laurel in their hands.*

Gov. Still doth this man, or rather god of war,
Batter our walls and beat our turrets down ;
And to resist with longer stubbornness
Or hope of rescue from the Soldan's power,
Were but to bring our wilful overthrow,   5
And make us desperate of our threat'ned lives.
We see his tents have now been altered
With terrors to the last and cruellest hue.
His coal-black colours everywhere advanc'd
Threaten our city with a general spoil ;   10
And if we should with common rites of arms
Offer our safeties to his clemency,
I fear the custom, proper to his sword,
Which he observes as parcel of his fame,
Intending so to terrify the world,   15

---

[6] Shore : Fr. *plage.* Early edd. read *place.*
[7] First two edd. read *hower*.
[8] Early edd. *value.*

By any innovation or remorse
Will never be dispens'd with till our deaths.
Therefore, for these our harmless virgins' sakes,
Whose honours and whose lives rely on him,
Let us have hope that their unspotted prayers, 20
Their blubbered cheeks, and hearty, humble
   moans,
Will melt his fury into some remorse,[1]
And use us like a loving conqueror.
  1 Virg. If humble suits or imprecations,[2]
(Uttered with tears of wretchedness and blood 25
Shed from the heads and hearts of all our sex,
Some made your wives and some your children)
Might have entreated your obdurate breasts
To entertain some care of our securities
Whiles only danger beat upon our walls,   30
These more than dangerous warrants of our
   death
Had never been erected as they be,
Nor you depend on such weak helps as we.
  Gov. Well, lovely virgins, think our country's
   care,
Our love of honour, loath to be inthrall'd   35
To foreign powers and rough imperious yokes,
Would not with too much cowardice or fear,
(Before all hope of rescue were denied)
Submit yourselves and us to servitude.
Therefore in that your safeties and our own, 40
Your honours, liberties, and lives were weigh'd
In equal care and balance with our own,
Endure as we the malice of our stars,
The wrath of Tamburlaine, and power of wars;
Or be the means the overweighing heavens   45
Have kept to qualify[3] these hot extremes,
And bring us pardon in your cheerful looks.
  2 Virg. Then here before the majesty of
   Heaven
And holy patrons of Egyptia,
With knees and hearts submissive we entreat 50
Grace to our words and pity to our looks
That this device may prove propitious,
And through the eyes and ears of Tamburlaine
Convey events of mercy to his heart;
Grant that these signs of victory we yield   55
May bind the temples of his conquering head,
To hide the folded furrows of his brows,
And shadow his displeased countenance
With happy looks of ruth and lenity.
Leave us, my lord, and loving countrymen;   60
What simple virgins may persuade, we will.
  Gov. Farewell, sweet virgins, on whose safe
   return
Depends our city, liberty, and lives.   *Exeunt.*

SCENE II.

[Enter] TAMBURLAINE, *all in black and very melancholy,* TECHELLES, THERIDAMAS, USUMCASANE, *with others.*

  Tamb. What, are the turtles fray'd[4] out of
   their nests?
Alas, poor fools! must you be first shall feel
The sworn destruction of Damascus?
They knew my custom; could they not as well
Have sent ye out when first my milk-white flags, 5

Through which sweet Mercy threw her gentle
   beams,
Reflexing[5] them on your disdainful eyes,
As now, when fury and incensed hate
Flings slaughtering terror from my coal-black
   tents,
And tells for truth submission[6] comes too late?
  1 Virg. Most happy King and Emperor of the
   earth,
Image of honour and nobility,
For whom the powers divine have made the
   world,
And on whose throne the holy Graces sit;
In whose sweet person is compris'd the sum 15
Of Nature's skill and heavenly majesty;
Pity our plights! O pity poor Damascus!
Pity old age, within whose silver hairs
Honour and reverence evermore have reign'd!
Pity the marriage bed, where many a lord,   20
In prime and glory of his loving joy,
Embraceth now with tears of ruth and blood
The jealous body of his fearful wife,
Whose cheeks and hearts, so punish'd with conceit
To think thy puissant, never-stayed arm   25
Will part their bodies, and prevent their souls
From heavens of comfort yet their age might
   bear,
Now wax all pale and withered to the death,
As well for grief our ruthless governor
Hath thus refus'd the mercy of thy hand,   30
(Whose sceptre angels kiss and furies dread,)
As for their liberties, their loves, or lives!
O then for these, and such as we ourselves,
For us, our infants, and for all our bloods,
That never nourish'd thought against thy rule, 35
Pity, O pity, sacred Emperor,
The prostrate service of this wretched town,
And take in sign thereof this gilded wreath;
Whereto each man of rule hath given his hand,
And wish'd, as worthy subjects, happy means 40
To be investers of thy royal brows
Even with the true Egyptian diadem!
  Tamb. Virgins, in vain ye labour to prevent
That which mine honour swears shall be performed.
Behold my sword! what see you at the point?
  1 Virg. Nothing but fear and fatal steel,
   my lord.   45
  Tamb. Your fearful minds are thick and
   misty then;
For there sits Death, there sits imperious Death
Keeping his circuit[7] by the slicing edge.
But I am pleas'd you shall not see him there;
He now is seated on my horsemen's spears,   50
And on their points his fleshless body feeds.
Techelles, straight go charge a few of them
To charge these dames, and show my servant,
   Death,
Sitting in scarlet on their armed spears.   55
  Virgins. O pity us!
  Tamb. Away with them, I say, and show them
   Death.   *They take them away.*
I will not spare these proud Egyptians,

---

[1] Pity.   [2] Prayers.   [3] Moderate.   [4] Frightened.

[5] Later edd. emend to *Reflexed . . . their.*
[6] Early edd. read *submissions.*   [7] Court.

Nor change my martial observations
For all the wealth of Gihon's golden waves,   60
Or for the love of Venus, would she leave
The angry god of arms and lie with me.
They have refus'd the offer of their lives,
And know my customs are as peremptory
As wrathful planets, death, or destiny.   65

Re-enter TECHELLES.

What, have your horsemen shown the virgins
   Death?
Tech. They have, my lord, and on Damascus'
   walls
Have hoisted up their slaughtered carcases.
Tamb. A sight as baneful to their souls, I
   think,
As are Thessalian drugs or mithridate:[1]   70
But go, my lords, put the rest to the sword.
       Exeunt [all except TAMBURLAINE].
Ah, fair Zenocrate! divine Zenocrate!
Fair is too foul an epithet for thee,
That in thy passion[2] for thy country's love,
And fear to see thy kingly father's harm,   75
With hair dishevell'd wip'st thy watery cheeks;
And, like to Flora in her morning's pride
Shaking her silver tresses in the air,
Rain'st on the earth resolved[3] pearl in showers,
And sprinklest sapphires on thy shining face,   80
Where Beauty, mother to the Muses, sits
And comments volumes with her ivory pen,
Taking instructions from thy flowing eyes;
Eyes when that Ebena steps to Heaven,
In silence of thy solemn evening's walk,   85
Making the mantle of the richest night,
The moon, the planets, and the meteors, light;
There angels in their crystal armours fight
A doubtful battle with my tempted thoughts
For Egypt's freedom, and the Soldan's life;   90
His life that so consumes Zenocrate,
Whose sorrows lay more siege unto my soul,
Than all my army to Damascus' walls:
And neither Persia's sovereign, nor the Turk
Troubled my senses with conceit of foil[4]   95
So much by much as doth Zenocrate.
What is beauty, saith my sufferings, then?
If all the pens that ever poets held
Had fed the feeling of their masters' thoughts,
And every sweetness that inspir'd their hearts, 101
Their minds, and muses on admired themes;
If all the heavenly quintessence they still[5]
From their immortal flowers of poesy,
Wherein, as in a mirror, we perceive
The highest reaches of a human wit;   105
If these had made one poem's period,
And all combin'd in beauty's worthiness,
Yet should there hover in their restless heads
One thought, one grace, one wonder, at the least,
Which into words no virtue can digest.   110
But how unseemly is it for my sex,
My discipline of arms and chivalry,
My nature, and the terror of my name,
To harbour thoughts effeminate and faint!
Save only that in beauty's just applause,   115

With whose instinct the soul of man is
   touch'd; —
And every warrior that is rapt with love
Of fame, of valour, and of victory,
Must needs have beauty beat on his conceits:
I thus conceiving and subduing both   120
That which hath stoop'd the [chiefest][6] of the
   gods,
Even from the fiery-spangled veil of Heaven,
To feel the lowly[7] warmth of shepherds' flames,
And mask[8] in cottages of strowed reeds,[9]
Shall give the world to note, for all my birth, 125
That virtue solely is the sum of glory,
And fashions men with true nobility. —
Who's within there?

      Enter two or three [Attendants].

Hath Bajazeth been fed to-day?
Atten. Ay, my lord.   130
Tamb. Bring him forth; and let us know if
the town be ransack'd.   [*Exeunt* Attendants.]

Enter TECHELLES, THERIDAMAS, USUMCA-
      SANE, *and others.*

Tech. The town is ours, my lord, and fresh
   supply
Of conquest and of spoil is offered us.
Tamb. That's well, Techelles; what's the
   news?   135
Tech. The Soldan and the Arabian king to-
   gether,
March on us with such eager violence,
As if there were no way but one with us.
Tamb. No more there is not, I warrant thee,
   Techelles.
      They bring in the Turk [and ZABINA].
Ther. We know the victory is ours, my lord;
But let us save the reverend Soldan's life,   141
For fair Zenocrate that so laments his state.
Tamb. That will we chiefly see unto, Theri-
   damas,
For sweet Zenocrate, whose worthiness
Deserves a conquest over every heart.   145
And now, my footstool, if I lose the field,
You hope of liberty and restitution?
Here let him stay, my masters, from the tents,
Till we have made us ready for the field.
Pray for us, Bajazeth; we are going.   150
    Exeunt [all except BAJAZETH *and* ZABINA].
Baj. Go, never to return with victory!
Millions of men encompass thee about,
And gore thy body with as many wounds!
Sharp, forked arrows light upon thy horse!
Furies from the black Cocytus lake   155
Break up the earth, and with their firebrands
Enforce thee run upon the baneful pikes!
Volleys of shot pierce through thy charmed
   skin,
And every bullet dipt in poisoned drugs!
Or roaring cannons sever all thy joints,   160
Making thee mount as high as eagles soar!
Zab. Let all the swords and lances in the
   field

---

[1] An antidote distilled from poisons. (Bullen.)
[2] Sorrow.   [4] Idea of defeat.
[3] Dissolved.   [5] Distil.

[6] Emend. Dyce. Early edd. read *stopt the tempest.*
[7] Conj. Collier. Early edd. read *lonely.*
[8] Early edd. *martch.*
[9] Emend. Dyce. Early edd. read *weeds.*

Stick in his breast as in their proper rooms!
At every pore let blood come dropping forth,
That ling'ring pains may massacre his heart, 165
And madness send his damned soul to hell!
  Baj. Ah, fair Zabina! we may curse his
      power,
The heavens may frown, the earth for anger
      quake,
But such a star hath influence in his sword, 169
As rules the skies and countermands the gods
More than Cimmerian Styx or Destiny ;
And then shall we in this detested guise,
With shame, with hunger, and with horror
      [stay,][1]
Griping our bowels with retorqued[2] thoughts,
And have no hope to end our ecstasies. 175
  Zab. Then is there left no Mahomet, no God,
No Fiend, no Fortune, nor no hope of end
To our infamous, monstrous slaveries.
Gape, earth, and let the fiends infernal view
A hell as hopeless and as full of fear 180
As are the blasted banks of Erebus,
Where shaking ghosts with ever-howling
      groans
Hover about the ugly ferryman,
To get a passage to Elysium ?
Why should we live ? O, wretches, beggars,
      slaves! 185
Why live we, Bajazeth, and build up nests
So high within the region of the air
By living long in this oppression,
That all the world will see and laugh to scorn
The former triumphs of our mightiness 190
In this obscure infernal servitude ?
  Baj. O life, more loathsome to my vexed
      thoughts
Than noisome parbreak[3] of the Stygian
      snakes,
Which fills the nooks of hell with standing air,
Infecting all the ghosts with cureless griefs! 195
O dreary engines[4] of my loathed sight,
That sees my crown, my honour, and my name
Thrust under yoke and thraldom of a thief,
Why feed ye still on day's accursed beams
And sink not quite into my tortur'd soul? 200
You see my wife, my queen, and emperess,
Brought up and propped by the hand of fame,
Queen of fifteen contributory queens,
Now thrown to rooms of black abjection,
Smeared with blots of basest drudgery, 205
And villainess[5] to shame, disdain, and misery.
Accursed Bajazeth, whose words of ruth,
(That would with pity cheer Zabina's heart,
And make our souls resolve[6] in ceaseless tears;)
Sharp hunger bites upon, and gripes the root [210
From whence the issues of my thoughts do
      break ;
O poor Zabina ! O my queen ! my queen !
Fetch me some water for my burning breast,
To cool and comfort me with longer date,
That in the short'ned sequel of my life 215
I may pour forth my soul into thine arms
With words of love, whose moaning intercourse

---

[1] Emend. Dyce. Early edd. *aie.* Qy. *die?*
[2] Bent back.   [4] *I. e.* eyes.   [6] Dissolve.
[3] Vomit.   [5] Slave.

Hath hitherto been stay'd with wrath and hate
Of our expressless bann'd inflictions.
  Zab. Sweet Bajazeth, I will prolong thy life,
As long as any blood or spark of breath 221
Can quench or cool the torments of my grief.
                              She goes out.
  Baj. Now, Bajazeth, abridge thy baneful
      days,
And beat thy brains out of thy conquer'd head,
Since other means are all forbidden me 225
That may be ministers of my decay.
O, highest lamp of ever-living Jove,
Accursed day ! infected with my griefs,
Hide now thy stained face in endless night,
And shut the windows of the lightsome
      heavens ! 230
Let ugly Darkness with her rusty coach,
Engirt with tempests, wrapt in pitchy clouds,
Smother the earth with never-fading mists,
And let her horses from their nostrils breathe
Rebellious winds and dreadful thunder-claps, 235
That in this terror Tamburlaine may live,
And my pin'd soul, resolv'd in liquid air,
May still excruciate his tormented thoughts !
Then let the stony dart of senseless cold
Pierce through the centre of my withered heart,
And make a passage for my loathed life ! 241
      He brains himself against the cage.

Re-enter ZABINA.

  Zab. What do mine eyes behold ? My hus-
      band dead !
His skull all riven in twain ! His brains dash'd
      out,
The brains of Bajazeth, my lord and sovereign !
O Bajazeth, my husband and my lord ! 245
O Bajazeth ! O Turk ! O Emperor !
Give him his liquor ? Not I. Bring milk and
fire, and my blood I bring him again. — Tear me
in pieces ! Give me the sword with a ball of wild-
fire upon it. — Down with him ! Down with [250
him ! — Go to my child ! Away ! Away ! Away !
Ah, save that infant ! save him, save him ! —
I, even I, speak to her. — The sun was down ;
streamers white, red, black, here, here, here !
— Fling the meat in his face — Tamburlaine,
Tamburlaine ! — Let the soldiers be buried. [256
— Hell ! Death ! Tamburlaine ! Hell ! — Make
ready my coach, my chair, my jewels. I come !
I come ! I come !
      She runs against the cage and brains herself.

[Enter] ZENOCRATE *with* ANIPPE.

  Zeno. Wretched Zenocrate ! that liv'st to see
Damascus' walls dy'd with Egyptians' blood, 261
Thy father's subjects and thy countrymen ;
Thy streets strow'd with dissevered joints of
      men
And wounded bodies gasping yet for life:
But most accurst, to see the sun-bright troop 265
Of heavenly virgins and unspotted maids,
(Whose looks might make the angry god of
      arms
To break his sword and mildly treat of love)
On horsemen's lances to be hoisted up
And guiltlessly endure a cruel death: 270
For every fell and stout Tartarian steed,

That stampt on others with their thund'ring
  hoofs,
When all their riders charg'd their quivering
  spears,
Began to check the ground and rein themselves,
Gazing upon the beauty of their looks.   275
Ah Tamburlaine! wert thou the cause of this
That term'st Zenocrate thy dearest love?
Whose lives were dearer to Zenocrate
Than her own life, or aught save thine own love.
But see another bloody spectacle!   280
Ah, wretched eyes, the enemies of my heart,
How are ye glutted with these grievous objects,
And tell my soul more tales of bleeding ruth!
See, see, Anippe, if they breathe or no.
  Anippe. No breath, nor sense, nor motion in
    them both;   285
Ah, madam! this their slavery hath enforc'd,
And ruthless cruelty of Tamburlaine.
  Zeno. Earth, cast up fountains from thy en-
    trails,
And wet thy cheeks for their untimely deaths!
Shake with their weight in sign of fear and
  grief!   290
Blush, Heaven, that gave them honour at their
  birth
And let them die a death so barbarous!
Those that are proud of fickle empery
And place their chiefest good in earthly pomp,
Behold the Turk and his great Emperess!   295
Ah, Tamburlaine! my love! sweet Tambur-
  laine!
That fight'st for sceptres and for slippery
  crowns,
Behold the Turk and his great Emperess!
Thou, that in conduct of thy happy stars
Sleep'st every night with conquests on thy
  brows,   300
And yet would'st shun the wavering turns of
  war,
In fear and feeling of the like distress
Behold the Turk and his great Emperess!
Ah, mighty Jove and holy Mahomet,
Pardon my love!—O, pardon his contempt   305
Of earthly fortune and respect of pity,
And let not conquest, ruthlessly pursu'd,
Be equally against his life incens'd
In this great Turk and hapless Emperess!
And pardon me that was not mov'd with ruth
To see them live so long in misery!   311
Ah, what may chance to thee, Zenocrate?
  Anippe. Madam, content yourself, and be re-
    solv'd
Your love hath Fortune so at his command,
That she shall stay and turn her wheel no more,
As long as life maintains his mighty arm   316
That fights for honour to adorn your head.

  Enter [PHILEMUS,] *a* Messenger.

  Zeno. What other heavy news now brings
Philemus?
  Phil. Madam, your father, and the Arabian
king,
The first affecter of your excellence,   320
Comes now, as Turnus 'gainst Æneas did,
Armed with lance into the Egyptian fields,
Ready for battle 'gainst my lord, the king.

  Zeno. Now shame and duty, love and fear
presents
A thousand sorrows to my martyred soul.   325
Whom should I wish the fatal victory
When my poor pleasures are divided thus
And rack'd by duty from my cursed heart?
My father and my first-betrothed love
Must fight against my life and present love; 330
Wherein the change I use condemns my faith,
And makes my deeds infamous through the
  world:
But as the gods, to end the Troyans' toil,
Prevented Turnus of Lavinia
And fatally enrich'd Æneas' love,   335
So, for a final issue to my griefs,
To pacify my country and my love
Must Tamburlaine by their resistless powers
With virtue of a gentle victory
Conclude a league of honour to my hope;   340
Then, as the Powers divine have pre-ordain'd,
With happy safety of my father's life
Send like defence of fair Arabia.
      They sound to the battle [*within*]: *and*
        TAMBURLAINE *enjoys the victory. After,*
        [*the* KING *of*] ARABIA *enters wounded.*
  K. of Arab. What cursed power guides the
murdering hands
Of this infamous tyrant's soldiers   345
That no escape may save their enemies,
Nor fortune keep themselves from victory?
Lie down, Arabia, wounded to the death,
And let Zenocrate's fair eyes behold
That, as for her thou bear'st these wretched
  arms,   350
Even so for her thou diest in these arms,
Leaving thy blood for witness of thy love.
  Zeno. Too dear a witness for such love, my
lord,
Behold Zenocrate! the cursed object,
Whose fortunes never mastered her griefs; 355
Behold her wounded, in conceit, for thee,
As much as thy fair body is for me.
  K. of Arab. Then shall I die with full, con-
tented heart,
Having beheld divine Zenocrate,
Whose sight with joy would take away my life
As now it bringeth sweetness to my wound, 361
If I had not been wounded as I am.
Ah! that the deadly pangs I suffer now,
Would lend an hour's licence to my tongue,
To make discourse of some sweet accidents 365
Have chanc'd thy merits in this worthless bond-
  age;
And that I might be privy to the state
Of thy deserv'd contentment, and thy love;
But, making now a virtue of thy sight
To drive all sorrow from my fainting soul, 370
Since death denies me farther cause of joy,
Depriv'd of care, my heart with comfort dies,
Since thy desired hand shall close mine eyes.
                                        [*He dies.*]

Re-enter TAMBURLAINE, *leading the* SOLDAN,
  TECHELLES, THERIDAMAS, USUMCASANE,
  with others.

  Tamb. Come, happy father of Zenocrate,
A title higher than thy Soldan's name: 375

Though my right hand have thus enthralled
    thee,
Thy princely daughter here shall set thee free ;
She that hath calm'd the fury of my sword,
Which had ere this been bath'd in streams of
    blood
As vast and deep as Euphrates or Nile.   380
  Zeno. O sight thrice welcome to my joyful
    soul,
To see the king, my father, issue safe
From dangerous battle of my conquering love !
  Sold. Well met, my only dear Zenocrate,   384
Though with the loss of Egypt and my crown.
  Tamb. 'T was I, my lord, that got the victory,
And therefore grieve not at your overthrow,
Since I shall render all into your hands,
And add more strength to your dominions
Than ever yet confirm'd th' Egyptian crown.
The god of war resigns his room to me,   391
Meaning to make me general of the world.
Jove, viewing me in arms, looks pale and wan,
Fearing my power should pull him from his
    throne.
Where'er I come the Fatal Sisters sweat,   395
And grisly Death, by running to and fro,
To do their ceaseless homage to my sword ;
And here in Afric, where it seldom rains,
Since I arriv'd with my triumphant host,
Have swelling clouds, drawn from wide-gasp-
    ing wounds,   400
Been oft resolv'd in bloody purple showers,
A meteor that might terrify the earth,
And make it quake at every drop it drinks.
Millions of souls sit on the banks of Styx,
Waiting the back return of Charon's boat ;   405
Hell and Elysium swarm with ghosts of men,
That I have sent from sundry foughten fields,
To spread my fame through hell and up to
    Heaven.
And see, my lord, a sight of strange import,   409
Emperors and kings lie breathless at my feet.
The Turk and his great Empress, as it seems,
Left to themselves while we were at the fight,
Have desperately despatch'd their slavish lives ;
With them Arabia, too, hath left his life ;
All sights of power to grace my victory :   415
And such are objects fit for Tamburlaine ;
Wherein, as in a mirror, may be seen
His honour, that consists in shedding blood,
When men presume to manage arms with him.
  Sold. Mighty hath God and Mahomet made
    thy hand,   420
Renowned Tamburlaine ! to whom all kings
Of force must yield their crowns and emperies ;
And I am pleas'd with this my overthrow,
If, as beseems a person of thy state,
Thou hast with honour us'd Zenocrate.   425

  Tamb. Her state and person wants no pomp,
    you see ;
And for all blot of foul inchastity
I record Heaven her heavenly self is clear.
Then let me find no further time to grace   429
Her princely temples with the Persian crown.
But here these kings that on my fortunes wait,
And have been crown'd for proved worthiness,
Even by this hand that shall establish them,
Shall now, adjoining all their hands with mine,
Invest her here my Queen of Persia.   435
What saith the noble Soldan and Zenocrate !
  Sold. I yield with thanks and protestations
Of endless honour to thee for her love.
  Tamb. Then doubt I not but fair Zenocrate
Will soon consent to satisfy us both.   440
  Zeno. Else should I much forget myself, my
    lord.
  Ther. Then let us set the crown upon her
    head,
That long hath ling'red for so high a seat.
  Tech. My hand is ready to perform the deed ;
For now her marriage-time shall work us rest.
  Usum. And here 's the crown, my lord ; help
    set it on.   446
  Tamb. Then sit thou down, divine Zenocrate ;
And here we crown thee Queen of Persia,
And all the kingdoms and dominions
That late the power of Tamburlaine subdu'd.
As Juno, when the giants were suppress'd,   451
That darted mountains at her brother Jove,
So looks my love, shadowing in her brows
Triumphs and trophies for my victories ;
Or as Latona's daughters, bent to arms,   455
Adding more courage to my conquering mind.
To gratify the sweet Zenocrate,
Egyptians, Moors, and men of Asia,
From Barbary unto the western India,
Shall pay a yearly tribute to thy sire ;   460
And from the bounds of Afric to the banks
Of Ganges shall his mighty arm extend.
And now, my lords and loving followers,
That purchas'd kingdoms by your martial
    deeds,
Cast off your armour, put on scarlet robes,   465
Mount up your royal places of estate,
Environed with troops of noblemen,
And there make laws to rule your provinces.
Hang up your weapons on Alcides' post,
For Tamburlaine takes truce with all the world.
Thy first-betrothed love, Arabia,   471
Shall we with honour, as beseems, entomb,
With this great Turk and his fair Emperess.
Then, after all these solemn exequies,
We will our [1] rites of marriage solemnise.   475
                     [*Exeunt.*]

   [1] Early edd. read *our celebrated.*

THE TRAGICAL HISTORY OF DR. FAUSTUS

BY

CHRISTOPHER MARLOWE

[DRAMATIS PERSONAE

THE POPE.
CARDINAL OF LORRAIN.
EMPEROR OF GERMANY.
DUKE OF VANHOLT.
FAUSTUS.
VALDES and CORNELIUS, Friends to FAUSTUS.
WAGNER, Servant to FAUSTUS.
Clown.
ROBIN.
RALPH.
Vintner.
Horse-Courser.
Knight.

Old Man.
Scholars, Friars, and **Attendants.**
DUCHESS OF VANHOLT.
LUCIFER.
BELZEBUB.
MEPHISTOPHILIS.
Good Angel.
Evil Angel.
The Seven Deadly Sins.
Devils.
Spirits in the shape of ALEXANDER THE GREAT, of his
Paramour, and of HELEN of TROY.
CHORUS.]

Enter CHORUS

Chorus. Not marching now in fields of Thrasi-
mene,
Where Mars did mate[1] the Carthaginians;
Nor sporting in the dalliance of love,
In courts of kings where state is overturn'd;
Nor in the pomp of proud audacious deeds, 5
Intends our Muse to vaunt his heavenly verse:
Only this, gentlemen, — we must perform
The form of Faustus' fortunes, good or bad.
To patient judgments we appeal our plaud,[2]
And speak for Faustus in his infancy. 10
Now is he born, his parents base of stock,
In Germany, within a town call'd Rhodes;[3]
Of riper years to Wittenberg he went,
Whereas his kinsmen chiefly brought him up.
So soon he profits in divinity, 15
The fruitful plot of scholarism grac'd,[4]
That shortly he was grac'd with doctor's name,
Excelling all whose sweet delight disputes
In heavenly matters of theology;
Till swollen with cunning,[5] of a self-conceit, 20
His waxen wings[6] did mount above his reach,
And, melting, Heavens conspir'd his overthrow;
For, falling to a devilish exercise,
And glutted [now] with learning's golden gifts,
He surfeits upon cursed necromancy. 25
Nothing so sweet as magic is to him,
Which he prefers before his chiefest bliss.
And this the man that in his study sits! *Exit.*

[SCENE I.]

Enter FAUSTUS *in his Study*

Faust. Settle my studies, Faustus, and begin
To sound the depth of that thou wilt profess[7];
Having commence'd, be a divine in show.
Yet level[8] and at the end of every art,
And live and die in Aristotle's works. 5
Sweet Analytics,[9] 't is thou hast ravish'd me,
Bene disserere est finis logices.
Is to dispute well logic's chiefest end?
Affords this art no greater miracle?
Then read no more, thou hast attain'd the end;
A greater subject fitteth Faustus' wit. 11
Bid ὂν καὶ μὴ ὂν[10] farewell; Galen come,
Seeing *Ubi desinit Philosophus, ibi incipit Medi-
cus;*[11]
Be a physician, Faustus, heap up gold,
And be eternis'd for some wondrous cure. 15
Summum bonum medicinæ sanitas,[12]
" The end of physic is our body's health."
Why, Faustus, hast thou not attain'd that end?
Is not thy common talk sound Aphorisms?[13]
Are not thy bills[14] hung up as monuments, 20
Whereby whole cities have escap'd the plague,
And thousand desperate maladies been eas'd?
Yet art thou still but Faustus and a man.
Wouldst thou make men to live eternally,

---

[1] Confound. But Hannibal was victorious at Lake
Trasumennus, B. c. 217.
[2] For applause.
[3] Roda, in the Duchy of Saxe-Altenburg, near Jena.
[4] The garden of scholarship being adorned by him.
[5] Knowledge.
[6] An allusion to the myth of Icarus, who flew too near
the sun.

[7] Teach publicly.
[8] Aim.
[9] Logic.
[10] This is Mr. Bullen's emendation of Q₁, *Oncay-
maeon,* a corruption of the Aristotelian phrase for " being and not being."
[11] " Where the philosopher leaves off, there the physician begins."
[12] This and the previous quotation are from Aristotle.
[13] Medical maxims.
[14] Announcements.

Or, being dead, raise them to life again?   25
Then this profession were to be esteem'd.
Physic, farewell. — Where is Justinian?
                                    [Reads.]
Si una eademque res legatur duobus, alter rem,
    alter valorem rei, &c. [1]
A pretty case of paltry legacies!   [Reads.]
Exhæreditare filium non potest pater nisi,
    &c. [2]   30
Such is the subject of the Institute [3]
And universal Body of the Law. [4]
His [5] study fits a mercenary drudge,
Who aims at nothing but external trash;
Too servile and illiberal for me.   35
When all is done, divinity is best;
Jerome's Bible, [6] Faustus, view it well.
                                    [Reads.]
Stipendium peccati mors est. Ha! *Stipendium,*
    &c.
" *The reward of sin is death.*" That's hard.
                                    [Reads.]
Si peccasse negamus, fallimur, et nulla est in nobis
    veritas.
"If we say that we have no sin we deceive our-
selves, and there's no truth in us." Why then,
belike we must sin and so consequently die.
Ay, we must die an everlasting death.
What doctrine call you this, *Che sera sera,*   45
"What will be shall be?" Divinity, adieu!
These metaphysics of magicians
And necromantic books are heavenly;
Lines, circles, scenes, letters, and characters, 49
Ay, these are those that Faustus most desires.
O what a world of profit and delight,
Of power, of honour, of omnipotence
Is promis'd to the studious artisan!
All things that move between the quiet poles
Shall be at my command. Emperors and kings
Are but obeyed in their several provinces,   56
Nor can they raise the wind or rend the clouds;
But his dominion that exceeds [7] in this
Stretcheth as far as doth the mind of man.
A sound magician is a mighty god: 60
Here, Faustus, try thy [8] brains to gain a deity.
Wagner!

                Enter WAGNER.

Commend me to my dearest friends,
The German Valdes and Cornelius;
Request them earnestly to visit me.
Wag. I will, sir.   *Exit.* 65
Faust. Their conference will be a greater
    help to me
Than all my labours, plod I ne'er so fast.

            Enter GOOD ANGEL *and* EVIL ANGEL.

G. Ang. O Faustus! lay that damned book
    aside,

1 "If one and the same thing is bequeathed to two
persons, one gets the thing and the other the value of
the thing."
2 "A father cannot disinherit the son except," etc.
3 Of Justinian, under whom the Roman law was
codified.
4 Q1, *Church.*   7 Excels.
5 Its.   8 Q3, *tire my.*
* The Vulgate.

And gaze not upon it lest it tempt thy soul,
And heap God's heavy wrath upon thy head. 70
Read, read the Scriptures: that is blasphemy.
E. Ang. Go forward, Faustus, in that famous
    art,
Wherein all Nature's treasure is contain'd:
Be thou on earth as Jove is in the sky,
Lord and commander of these elements.   74
                        Exeunt [Angels.]
Faust. How am I glutted with conceit [9] of this!
Shall I make spirits fetch me what I please,
Resolve me of all ambiguities,
Perform what desperate enterprise I will?
I'll have them fly to India for gold,   80
Ransack the ocean for orient pearl,
And search all corners of the new-found wo:ld
For pleasant fruits and princely delicates;
I'll have them read me strange philosophy
And tell the secrets of all foreign kings;   85
I'll have them wall all Germany with brass,
And make swift Rhine circle fair Wittenberg;
I'll have them fill the public schools with [silk]. [10]
Wherewith the students shall be bravely clad;
I'll levy soldiers with the coin they bring,   90
And chase the Prince of Parma from our land, [11]
And reign sole king of all the provinces;
Yea, stranger engines for the brunt of war
Than was the fiery keel [12] at Antwerp's bridge,
I'll make my servile spirits to invent.   95
Come, German Valdes and Cornelius,
And make me blest with your sage conference.

        Enter VALDES *and* CORNELIUS. [13]

Valdes, sweet Valdes, and Cornelius,
Know that your words have won me at the last
To practise magic and concealed arts: 100
Yet not your words only, but mine own fantasy,
That will receive no object, for my head
But ruminates on necromantic skill.
Philosophy is odious and obscure,
Both law and physic are for petty wits;   105
Divinity is basest of the three,
Unpleasant, harsh, contemptible, and vile:
'T is magic, magic, that hath ravish'd me.
Then, gentle friends, aid me in this attempt;
And I that have with concise syllogisms   110
Gravell'd the pastors of the German church,
And made the flow'ring pride of Wittenberg
Swarm to my problems, as the infernal spirits
On sweet Musæus, [14] when he came to hell,
Will be as cunning as Agrippa was,   115
Whose shadows made all Europe honour him.
Vald. Faustus, these books, thy wit, and our
    experience
Shall make all nations to canónise us.
As Indian Moors [15] obey their Spanish lords,
So shall the subjects [16] of every element   120

9 Idea.
10 Emend. Dyce. Qq. *skill.*
11 The Netherlands, over which Parma re-established
the Spanish dominion.
12 A ship filled with explosives used to blow up a
bridge built by Parma in 1585 at the siege of Antwerp.
13 The famous Cornelius Agrippa. German Valdes is
not known.
14 Cf. Virgil, *Aeneid,* vi. 667.   16 Q4, *spirits.*
15 American Indians.

Be always serviceable to us three ;
Like lions shall they guard us when we please ;
Like Almain rutters[1] with their horsemen's
   staves,
Or Lapland giants, trotting by our sides ;
Sometimes like women or unwedded maids, 125
Shadowing more beauty in their airy brows
Than have the white breasts of the queen of love :
From Venice shall they drag huge argosies,
And from America the golden fleece
That yearly stuffs old Philip's treasury ;   130
If learned Faustus will be resolute.

Faust. Valdes, as resolute am I in this
As thou to live ; therefore object it not.

Corn. The miracles that magic will perform
Will make thee vow to study nothing else.   135
He that is grounded in astrology,
Enrich'd with tongues, well seen[2] in minerals,
Hath all the principles magic doth require.
Then doubt not, Faustus, but to be renowm'd,
And more frequented for this mystery   140
Than heretofore the Delphian Oracle.
The spirits tell me they can dry the sea,
And fetch the treasure of all foreign wracks,
Ay, all the wealth that our forefathers hid
Within the massy entrails of the earth ;   145
Then tell me, Faustus, what shall we three
  want ?

Faust. Nothing, Cornelius ! O this cheers my
  soul !
Come show me some demonstrations magical,
That I may conjure in some lusty grove,
And leave these joys in full possession.   150

Vald. Then haste thee to some solitary grove,
And bear wise Bacon's[3] and Albanus's[4]
  works,
The Hebrew Psalter and New Testament;
And whatsoever else is requisite   154
We will inform thee ere our conference cease.

Corn. Valdes, first let him know the words of
  art ;
And then, all other ceremonies learn'd,
Faustus may try his cunning by himself.

Vald. First I 'll instruct thee in the rudiments,
And then wilt thou be perfecter than I.   160

Faust. Then come and dine with me, and
  after meat,
We 'll canvass every quiddity[5] thereof ;
For ere I sleep I 'll try what I can do :
This night I 'll conjure though I die therefore.
                Exeunt.

[SCENE II.][6]

Enter two SCHOLARS.

1 *Schol.* I wonder what 's become of Faustus that was wont to make our schools ring
with *sic probo* ?[7]

---

[1] Troopers. Germ. *Reiters.*   [3] Roger Bacon.
[2] Versed.
[4] Perhaps Pietro d'Abano, a medieval alchemist;
perhaps a misprint for Albertus (Magnus), the great
schoolman.
[5] Fine point.
[6] Before Faustus's House.
[7] " Thus I prove " — a common formula in scholastic
discussions.

---

2 *Schol.* That shall we know, for see here
comes his boy.   5

Enter WAGNER.

1 *Schol.* How now, sirrah ! Where 's thy
master ?

Wag. God in heaven knows !

2 *Schol.* Why, dost not thou know ?

Wag. Yes, I know. But that follows not.   10

1 *Schol.* Go to, sirrah ! Leave your jesting,
and tell us where he is.

Wag. That follows not necessary by force of
argument, that you, being licentiate, should
stand upon 't : therefore, acknowledge your [15
error and be attentive.

2 *Schol.* Why, didst thou not say thou
knew'st ?

Wag. Have you any witness on 't ?

1 *Schol.* Yes, sirrah, I heard you.   20

Wag. Ask my fellow if I be a thief.

2 *Schol.* Well, you will not tell us ?

Wag. Yes, sir, I will tell you ; yet if you
were not dunces, you would never ask me such
a question ; for is not he *corpus naturale* ?[8] and
is not that *mobile* ? Then wherefore should [26
you ask me such a question ? But that I am by
nature phlegmatic, slow to wrath, and prone to
lechery (to love, I would say), it were not for
you to come within forty foot of the place [30
of execution, although I do not doubt to see
you both hang'd the next sessions. Thus having
triumph'd over you, I will set my countenance
like a precisian,[9] and begin to speak thus : —
Truly, my dear brethren, my master is within
at dinner, with Valdes and Cornelius, as this [36
wine, if it could speak, would inform your worships ; and so the Lord bless you, preserve you,
and keep you, my dear brethren, my dear brethren.   *Exit.* 40

1 *Schol.* Nay, then, I fear he has fallen into
that damned Art, for which they two are infamous through the world.

2 *Schol.* Were he a stranger, and not allied
to me, yet should I grieve for him. But come,
let us go and inform the Rector, and see if he [46
by his grave counsel can reclaim him.

1 *Schol.* O, I fear me nothing can reclaim
him.

2 *Schol.* Yet let us try what we can do.   50
                  Exeunt.

[SCENE III.][10]

Enter FAUSTUS *to conjure.*

Faust. Now that the gloomy shadow of the
  earth
Longing to view Orion's drizzling look,
Leaps from th' antarctic world unto the sky,
And dims the welkin with her pitchy breath,
Faustus, begin thine incantations,   5
And try if devils will obey thy hest,
Seeing thou hast pray'd and sacrific'd to them.
Within this circle is Jehovah's name,

---

[8] " ' *Corpus naturale seu mobile* ' is the current
scholastic expression for the subject-matter of Physics."
(Ward.)
[9] Puritan.   [10] A Grove.

Forward and backward anagrammatis'd,
The breviated names of holy saints,   10
Figures of every adjunct[1] to the Heavens,
And characters of signs and erring stars,[2]
By which the spirits are enforc'd to rise:
Then fear not, Faustus, but be resolute,
And try the uttermost magic can perform.   15
   Sint mihi Dei Acherontis propitii! Valeat nu-
men triplex Jehovae! Ignei, aerii, aquatani
spiritus, salvete! Orientis princeps Belzebub,
inferni ardentis monarcha, et Demogorgon, pro-
pitiamus vos, ut appareat et surgat Mephisto- [20
philis. Quid tu moraris? Per Jehovam, Gehen-
nam, et consecratum aquam quam nunc spargo,
signumque crucis quod nunc facio, et per vota
nostra, ipse nunc surgat nobis dicatus Mephisto-
philis![3]   25

     Enter [MEPHISTOPHILIS] *a Devil.*

I charge thee to return and change thy shape;
Thou art too ugly to attend on me.
Go, and return an old Franciscan friar;
That holy shape becomes a devil best.
                 Exit Devil.
I see there's virtue in my heavenly words;   30
Who would not be proficient in this art?
How pliant is this Mephistophilis,
Full of obedience and humility!
Such is the force of magic and my spells.
[Now,] Faustus, thou art conjuror laureate,   35
Thou canst command great Mephistophilis:
Quin regis Mephistophilis fratris imagine.[4]

Re-enter MEPHISTOPHILIS [*like a Franciscan*
Friar].

   Meph. Now, Faustus, what would'st thou
     have me do?
   Faust. I charge thee wait upon me whilst I
     live,
To do whatever Faustus shall command,   40
Be it to make the moon drop from her sphere,
Or the ocean to overwhelm the world.
   Meph. I am a servant to great Lucifer,
And may not follow thee without his leave;
No more than he commands must we perform.   45
   Faust. Did he not charge thee to appear to
     me?
   Meph. No, I came hither of mine own accord.
   Faust. Did not my conjuring speeches raise
     thee? Speak:
   Meph. That was the cause, but yet *per acci-*
     dens;
For when we hear one rack[5] the name of God,
Abjure the Scriptures and his Saviour Christ,   51

[1] Every star belonging to.
[2] Planets.
[3] "Be propitious to me, gods of Acheron! May the triple deity of Jehovah prevail! Spirits of fire, air, water, hail! Belzebub, Prince of the East, monarch of burning hell, and Demogorgon, we propitiate ye, that Mephistophilis may appear and rise. Why dost thou delay? By Jehovah, Gehenna, and the holy water which now I sprinkle, and the sign of the cross which now I make, and by our prayer, may Mephistophilis now summoned by us arise!'"
[4] "For indeed thou hast power in the image of thy brother Mephistophilis."
[5] Twist in anagrams.

We fly in hope to get his glorious soul;
Nor will we come, unless he use such means
Whereby he is in danger to be damn'd:
Therefore the shortest cut for conjuring   55
Is stoutly to abjure the Trinity,
And pray devoutly to the Prince of Hell.
   Faust. So Faustus hath
Already done; and holds this principle,
There is no chief but only Belzebub,   60
To whom Faustus doth dedicate himself.
This word "damnation" terrifies not him,
For he confounds hell in Elysium; [6]
His ghost be with the old philosophers!
But, leaving these vain trifles of men's souls,   65
Tell me what is that Lucifer thy lord?
   Meph. Arch-regent and commander of all
     spirits.
   Faust. Was not that Lucifer an angel once?
   Meph. Yes, Faustus, and most dearly lov'd
     of God.
   Faust. How comes it then that he is Prince
     of devils?   70
   Meph. O, by aspiring pride and insolence;
For which God threw him from the face of
     Heaven.
   Faust. And what are you that you live with
     Lucifer?
   Meph. Unhappy spirits that fell with Lucifer,
Conspir'd against our God with Lucifer,   75
And are for ever damn'd with Lucifer.
   Faust. Where are you damn'd?
   Meph. In hell.
   Faust. How comes it then that thou art out
     of hell?
   Meph. Why this is hell, nor am I out of it.   80
Think'st thou that I who saw the face of God,
And tasted the eternal joys of Heaven,
Am not tormented with ten thousand hells,
In being depriv'd of everlasting bliss?
O Faustus! leave these frivolous demands,   85
Which strike a terror to my fainting soul.
   Faust. What, is great Mephistophilis so pas-
     sionate[7]
For being depriv'd of the joys of Heaven?
Learn thou of Faustus manly fortitude,
And scorn those joys thou never shalt possess.
Go bear these tidings to great Lucifer: 90
Seeing Faustus hath incurr'd eternal death
By desperate thoughts against Jove's deity,
Say he surrenders up to him his soul,
So he will spare him four and twenty years,   95
Letting him live in all voluptuousness;
Having thee ever to attend on me;
To give me whatsoever I shall ask,
To tell me whatsoever I demand,
To slay mine enemies, and aid my friends,   100
And always be obedient to my will.
Go and return to mighty Lucifer,
And meet me in my study at midnight,
And then resolve[8] me of thy master's mind.
   Meph. I will, Faustus.   *Exit.* 105
   Faust. Had I as many souls as there be stars,
I'd give them all for Mephistophilis.
By him I'll be great Emperor of the world.

[6] Heaven and hell are indifferent to him.
[7] Sorrowful.   [8] Inform.

And make a bridge through the moving air,
To pass the ocean with a band of men ;   110
I 'll join the hills that bind the Afric shore,
And make that [country] continent to Spain,
And both contributory to my crown.
The Emperor shall not live but by my leave,
Nor any potentate of Germany.   115
Now that I have obtain'd what I desire,
I 'll live in speculation[1] of this art
Till Mephistophilis return again.   *Exit.*

[SCENE IV.][2]

Enter WAGNER *and the* CLOWN.

Wag. Sirrah, boy, come hither.
Clown. How, boy ! Swowns, boy ! I hope you
have seen many boys with such pickadevaunts[3]
as I have. Boy, quotha !
Wag. Tell me, sirrah, hast thou any comings
in ?   6
Clown. Ay, and goings out too. You may see
else.
Wag. Alas, poor slave ! See how poverty jest-
eth in his nakedness ! The villain is bare and [10
out of service, and so hungry that I know he
would give his soul to the devil for a shoulder
of mutton, though it were blood-raw.
Clown. How ? My soul to the Devil for a
shoulder of mutton, though 't were blood-raw ! [15
Not so, good friend. By 'r Lady, I had need
have it well roasted and good sauce to it, if I
pay so dear.
Wag. Well, wilt thou serve me, and I 'll
make thee go like *Qui mihi discipulus?*[4]   20
Clown. How, in verse ?
Wag. No, sirrah ; in beaten silk and stavesacre.[5]
Clown. How, how, Knave's acre ![6] Ay, I
thought that was all the land his father left [25
him. Do you hear ? I would be sorry to rob you
of your living.
Wag. Sirrah, I say in stavesacre.
Clown. Oho ! Oho ! Stavesacre ! Why, then,
belike if I were your man I should be full of
vermin.   31
Wag. So thou shalt, whether thou beest with
me or no. But, sirrah, leave your jesting,
and bind yourself presently unto me for seven
years, or I 'll turn all the lice about thee into
familiars, and they shall tear thee in pieces.   36
Clown. Do you hear, sir ? You may save that
labour ; they are too familiar with me already. Swowns ! they are as bold with my
flesh as if they had paid for [their] meat and [40
drink.
Wag. Well, do you hear, sirrah ? Hold, take
these guilders.   [*Gives money.*]
Clown. Gridirons ! what be they ?
Wag. Why, French crowns.   45
Clown. Mass, but for the name of French
crowns, a man were as good have as many Eng-

1 Study.   2 A street.
3 Beards cut to a sharp point (Fr. *pic-à-devant*).
4 Dyce points out that these are the first words of
W. Lily's " *Ad discipulos carmen de moribus.*"
5 A kind of larkspur, used for destroying lice.
6 A mean street in London.

lish counters. And what should I do with
these?
Wag. Why, now, sirrah, thou art at an [50
hour's warning, whensoever and wheresoever
the Devil shall fetch thee.
Clown. No, no. Here, take your gridirons
again.
Wag. Truly I 'll none of them.   55
Clown. Truly but you shall.
Wag. Bear witness I gave them him.
Clown. Bear witness I give them you again.
Wag. Well, I will cause two devils presently
to fetch thee away — Baliol and Belcher.   60
Clown. Let your Baliol and your Belcher
come here, and I 'll knock them, they were
never so knockt since they were devils. Say I
should kill one of them, what would folks say ?
" Do you see yonder tall fellow in the round [65
slop ?[7] — he has kill'd the devil." So I should
be call'd Kill-devil all the parish over.

Enter two DEVILS : *the* Clown *runs up and down
crying.*

Wag. Baliol and Belcher ! Spirits, away !
      Exeunt Devils.
Clown. What, are they gone ? A vengeance
on them, they have vile long nails ! There [70
was a he-devil, and a she-devil ! I 'll tell you how
you shall know them : all he-devils has horns,
and all she-devils has clifts and cloven feet.
Wag. Well, sirrah, follow me.
Clown. But, do you hear — if I should serve
you, would you teach me to raise up Banios [76
and Belcheos ?
Wag. I will teach thee to turn thyself to anything ; to a dog, or a cat, or a mouse, or a rat,
or anything.   80
Clown. How ! a Christian fellow to a dog or
a cat, a mouse or a rat ! No, no, sir. If you
turn me into anything, let it be in the likeness
of a little pretty frisky flea, that I may be here
and there and everywhere. Oh, I 'll tickle [85
the pretty wenches' plackets ; I 'll be amongst
them, i' faith.
Wag. Well, sirrah, come.
Clown. But, do you hear, Wagner ?
Wag. How ! — Baliol and Belcher !   90
Clown. O Lord ! I pray, sir, let Banio and
Belcher go sleep.
Wag. Villain — call me Master Wagner, and
let thy left eye be diametarily[8] fixt upon my
right heel, with *quasi vestigias nostras insistere.*[9]
      Exit.
Clown. God forgive me, he speaks Dutch [96
fustian. Well, I 'll follow him, I 'll serve him
that 's flat.   *Exit.*

[SCENE V.]

Enter FAUSTUS *in his study.*

Faust. Now, Faustus, must
Thou needs be damn'd, and canst thou not be
sav'd :
What boots it then to think of God or Heaven ?
Away with such vain fancies, and despair :

7 Short wide breeches.   8 For *diametrically.*
9 " As if to tread in my tracks."

Despair in God, and trust in Belzebub.   5
Now go not backward : no, Faustus, be resolute.
Why waverest thou ? O, something soundeth
    in mine ears
" Abjure this magic, turn to God again ! "
Ay, and Faustus will turn to God again.
To God ? — He loves thee not —   10
The God thou serv'st is thine own appetite,
Wherein is fix'd the love of Belzebub ;
To him I 'll build an altar and a church,
And offer lukewarm blood of new-born babes.

Enter GOOD ANGEL *and* EVIL [ANGEL]

G. Ang. Sweet Faustus, leave that execrable
    art.   15
Faust. Contrition, prayer, repentance ! What
    of them ?
G. Ang. O, they are means to bring thee unto
    Heaven.
E. Ang. Rather illusions, fruits of lunacy,
That makes men foolish that do trust them
    most.
G. Ang. Sweet Faustus, think of Heaven, and
    heavenly things.   20
E. Ang. No, Faustus, think of honour and
    of wealth.   *Exeunt* [ANGELS.]
Faust. Of wealth !
Why, the signiory of Emden [1] shall be mine.
When Mephistophilis shall stand by me,
What God can hurt thee, Faustus ? Thou art
    safe ;   25
Cast no more doubts. Come, Mephistophilis,
And bring glad tidings from great Lucifer ; —
Is 't not midnight ? Come, Mephistophilis ;
Veni, veni, Mephistophile !

Enter MEPHISTOPHILIS.

Now tell me, what says Lucifer thy lord ?   30
Meph. That I shall wait on Faustus whilst
    he lives,
So he will buy my service with his soul.
Faust. Already Faustus hath hazarded that
    for thee.
Meph. But, Faustus, thou must bequeath it
    solemnly,
And write a deed of gift with thine own blood,
For that security craves great Lucifer.   36
If thou deny it, I will back to hell.
Faust. Stay, Mephistophilis ! and tell me what
    good
Will my soul do thy lord.
Meph.   Enlarge his kingdom.
Faust. Is that the reason why he tempts us
    thus ?   40
*Meph. Solamen miseris socios habuisse dolo-
ris.* [2]
Faust. Why, have you any pain that torture
    others ?
Meph. As great as have the human souls of
    men.
But tell me, Faustus, shall I have thy soul ?
And I will be thy slave, and wait on thee,   45
And give thee more than thou hast wit to ask.

---

[1] Emden, near the mouth of the river Ems, was an
important commercial town in Elizabethan times.
[2] "Misery loves company."

Faust. Ay, Mephistophilis, I give it thee.
Meph. Then Faustus, stab thine arm cour-
    ageously.
And bind thy soul that at some certain day
Great Lucifer may claim it as his own ;   50
And then be thou as great as Lucifer.
Faust. [*stabbing his arm.*] Lo, Mephistophilis,
    for love of thee,
I cut mine arm, and with my proper blood
Assure my soul to be great Lucifer's,
Chief lord and regent of perpetual night !   55
View here the blood that trickles from mine
    arm.
And let it be propitious for my wish.
Meph. But, Faustus, thou must
Write it in manner of a deed of gift.
Faust. Ay, so I will. [*Writes.*] But, Mephis-
    tophilis,   60
My blood congeals, and I can write no more.
Meph. I 'll fetch thee fire to dissolve it
    straight.   *Exit.*
Faust. What might the staying of my blood
    portend ?
Is it unwilling I should write this bill ?
Why streams it not that I may write afresh ?   65
Faustus gives to thee his soul. Ah, there it stay'd.
Why should'st thou not ? Is not thy soul thine
    own ?
Then write again, *Faustus gives to thee his soul.*

Re-enter MEPHISTOPHILIS *with a chafer of coals.*

Meph. Here 's fire. Come, Faustus, set it on.
Faust. So now the blood begins to clear
    again ;   70
Now will I make an end immediately. [*Writes.*]
Meph. O what will not I do to obtain his
    soul.   [*Aside.*]
Faust. Consummatum est : [3] this bill is ended,
And Faustus hath bequeath'd his soul to Luci-
    fer —
But what is this inscription on mine arm ?   75
Homo, fuge ! [4] Whither should I fly ?
If unto God, he 'll throw me down to hell.
My senses are deceiv'd ; here 's nothing writ : —
I see it plain ; here in this place is writ
Homo, fuge ! Yet shall not Faustus fly.   80
Meph. I 'll fetch him somewhat to delight his
    mind.   *Exit.*

Re-enter [MEPHISTOPHILIS] *with Devils, giving
crowns and rich apparel to* FAUSTUS, *and
dance, and then depart.*

Faust. Speak, Mephistophilis, what means
    this show ?
Meph. Nothing, Faustus, but to delight thy
    mind withal,
And to show thee what magic can perform.
Faust. But may I raise up spirits when I
    please ?   85
Meph. Ay, Faustus, and do greater things
    than these.
Faust. Then there 's enough for a thousand
    souls.
Here, Mephistophilis, receive this scroll,
A deed of gift of body and of soul :

---

[3] " It is finished."   [4] " Man, fly ! "

But yet conditionally that thou perform 90
All articles prescrib'd between us both.
Meph. Faustus, I swear by hell and Lucifer
To effect all promises between us made.
Faust. Then hear me read them : *On these*
conditions following. First, that Faustus may [95
be a spirit in form and substance. Secondly, that
Mephistophilis shall be his servant, and at his
command. Thirdly, that Mephistophilis shall do
for him and bring him whatsoever [*he desires*].
Fourthly, that he shall be in his chamber or [100
house invisible. Lastly, that he shall appear to the
said John Faustus, at all times, in what form
or shape soever he pleases. I, John Faustus, of
Wittenberg, Doctor, by these presents do give both
body and soul to Lucifer, Prince of the East, [105
and his minister, Mephistophilis ; and furthermore
grant unto them, that twenty-four years being ex-
pired, the articles above written inviolate, full
power to fetch or carry the said John Faustus,
body and soul, flesh, blood, or goods, into their [110
habitation wheresoever. By me, John Faustus.
Meph. Speak, Faustus, do you deliver this as
your deed ?
Faust. Ay, take it, and the Devil give thee
good on 't.
Meph. Now, Faustus, ask what thou wilt. 114
Faust. First will I question with thee about hell.
Tell me where is the place that men call hell ?
Meph. Under the heavens.
Faust. Ay, but whereabout ?
Meph. Within the bowels of these elements,
Where we are tortur'd and remain for ever ; 120
Hell hath no limits, nor is circumscrib'd
In one self place ; for where we are is hell,
And where hell is there must we ever be :
And, to conclude, when all the world dissolves,
And every creature shall be purified, 125
All places shall be hell that is not Heaven.
Faust. Come, I think hell 's a fable.
Meph. Ay, think so still, till experience
change thy mind.
Faust. Why, think'st thou then that Faustus
shall be damn'd ? 129
Meph. Ay, of necessity, for here 's the scroll
Wherein thou hast given thy soul to Lucifer.
Faust. Ay, and body too ; but what of that ?
Think'st thou that Faustus is so fond[1] to ima-
gine
That, after this life, there is any pain ?
Tush ; these are trifles, and mere old wives'
tales. 135
Meph. But, Faustus, I am an instance to
prove the contrary,
For I am damned, and am now in hell.
Faust. How ! now in hell !
Nay, an this be hell, I 'll willingly be damn'd
here ;
What ? walking, disputing, &c. ? 140
But, leaving off this, let me have a wife,
The fairest maid in Germany ;
For I am wanton and lascivious,
And cannot live without a wife.
Meph. How — a wife ? 145
I prithee, Faustus, talk not of a wife.

[1] Foolish.

Faust. Nay, sweet Mephistophilis, fetch me
one, for I will have one.
Meph. Well — thou wilt have one. Sit there
till I come :
I 'll fetch thee a wife in the Devil's name.
[*Exit.*]

Re-enter MEPHISTOPHILIS *with a* Devil *dressed*
like a woman, with fireworks.

Meph. Tell [me,] Faustus, how dost thou like
thy wife ? 150
Faust. A plague on her for a hot whore !
Meph. Tut, Faustus,
Marriage is but a ceremonial toy ;
And if thou lovest me, think no more of it.
I 'll cull thee out the fairest courtesans, 155
And bring them every morning to thy bed ;
She whom thine eye shall like, thy heart shall
have,
Be she as chaste as was Penelope,
As wise as Saba,[2] or as beautiful
As was bright Lucifer before his fall. 160
Here, take this book, peruse it thoroughly :
[*Gives a book.*]
The iterating[3] of these lines brings gold ;
The framing of this circle on the ground
Brings whirlwinds, tempests, thunder and
lightning ;
Pronounce this thrice devoutly to thyself, 165
And men in armour shall appear to thee,
Ready to execute what thou desir'st.
Faust. Thanks, Mephistophilis ; yet fain
would I have a book wherein I might behold
all spells and incantations, that I might raise [170
up spirits when I please.
Meph. Here they are, in this book.
Turns to them.
Faust. Now would I have a book where I
might see all characters and planets of the
heavens, that I might know their motions and [175
dispositions.
Meph. Here they are too. *Turns to them.*
Faust. Nay, let me have one book more, —
and then I have done, — wherein I might see
all plants, herbs, and trees that grow upon [180
the earth.
Meph. Here they be.
Faust. O, thou art deceived.
Meph. Tut, I warrant thee. *Turns to them.*
[*Exeunt.*

[SCENE VI.[4]

Enter FAUSTUS *and* MEPHISTOPHILIS.]

Faust. When I behold the heavens, then I
repent,
And curse thee, wicked Mephistophilis,
Because thou hast depriv'd me of those joys.
Meph. Why, Faustus,
Thinkest thou Heaven is such a glorious thing ? 5
I tell thee 't is not half so fair as thou,
Or any man that breathes on earth.
Faust. How provest thou that ?
Meph. 'T was made for man, therefore is man
more excellent.

[2] The Queen of Sheba.   [3] Repeating.
[4] The same.

Faust. If it were made for man, 't was made
    for me ;   10
I will renounce this magic and repent.

Enter GOOD ANGEL *and* EVIL ANGEL.

G. Ang. Faustus, repent ; yet God will pity
    thee.
E. Ang. Thou art a spirit ; God cannot pity
    thee.
Faust. Who buzzeth in mine ears I am a
    spirit ?
Be I a devil, yet God may pity me ;   15
Ay, God will pity me if I repent.
E. Ang. Ay, but Faustus never shall repent.
                  Exeunt [ANGELS.]
Faust. My heart 's so hard'ned I cannot re-
    pent.
Scarce can I name salvation, faith, or heaven,
But fearful echoes thunder in mine ears   20
" Faustus, thou art damn'd ! " Then swords
    and knives,
Poison, gun, halters, and envenom'd steel
Are laid before me to despatch myself,
And long ere this I should have slain myself,
Had not sweet pleasure conquer'd deep despair.
Have I not made blind Homer sing to me   26
Of Alexander's love and Œnon's death ?
And hath not he that built the walls of Thebes
With ravishing sound of his melodious harp,
Made music with my Mephistophilis ?   30
Why should I die then, or basely despair ?
I am resolv'd : Faustus shall ne'er repent.
Come, Mephistophilis, let us dispute again,
And argue of divine astrology.
Tell me, are there many heavens above the
    moon ?   35
Are all celestial bodies but one globe,
As is the substance of this centric earth ?
Meph. As are the elements, such are the
    spheres
Mutually folded in each other's orb,
And, Faustus,   40
All jointly move upon one axletree
Whose terminine is term'd the world's wide pole;
Nor are the names of Saturn, Mars, or Jupiter
Feign'd, but are erring stars.
Faust. But tell me, have they all one motion,
both *situ et tempore ?* [1]   46
Meph. All jointly move from east to west in
twenty-four hours upon the poles of the world ;
but differ in their motion upon the poles of the
zodiac.   50
Faust. Tush !
These slender trifles Wagner can decide ;
Hath Mephistophilis no greater skill ?
Who knows not the double motion of the
    planets ?
The first is finish'd in a natural day ;   55
The second thus : as Saturn in thirty years ;
Jupiter in twelve ; Mars in four ; the Sun, Venus,
and Mercury in a year ; the moon in twenty-
eight days. Tush, these are freshmen's supposi-
tions. But tell me, hath every sphere a domin-
ion or *intelligentia ?*   61
Meph. Ay.

      [1] " In direction and in time ? "

Faust. How many heavens, or spheres, are
there ?
Meph. Nine : the seven planets, the firma-
ment, and the empyreal heaven.   66
Faust. Well, resolve me in this question :
Why have we not conjunctions, oppositions,
aspects, eclipses, all at one time, but in some
years we have more, in some less ?   70
Meph. Per inæqualem motum respecta totius. [2]
Faust. Well, I am answered. Tell me who
    made the world.
Meph. I will not.
Faust. Sweet Mephistophilis, tell me.
Meph. Move me not, for I will not tell thee.
Faust. Villain, have I not bound thee to tell
    me anything ?   76
Meph. Ay, that is not against our kingdom ;
    but this is.
Think thou on hell, Faustus, for thou art
    damn'd.
Faust. Think, Faustus, upon God that made
    the world.
Meph. Remember this.   80
Faust. Ay, go, accursed spirit, to ugly hell.
'T is thou hast damn'd distressed Faustus' soul.
Is 't not too late ?

Re-enter GOOD ANGEL *and* EVIL ANGEL.

E. Ang. Too late.
G. Ang. Never too late, if Faustus can repent.
E. Ang. If thou repent, devils shall tear thee
    in pieces.   86
G. Ang. Repent, and they shall never raze
    thy skin.
                  Exeunt [ANGELS.]
Faust. Ah, Christ, my Saviour,
Seek to save distressed Faustus' soul.

Enter LUCIFER, BELZEBUB, *and* MEPHISTO-
PHILIS.

Luc. Christ cannot save thy soul, for he is
    just ;   90
There 's none but I have interest in the same.
Faust. O, who art thou that look'st so terrible ?
Luc. I am Lucifer,
And this is my companion-prince in hell.
Faust. O Faustus ! they are come to fetch
    away thy soul !   95
Luc. We come to tell thee thou dost injure us ;
Thou talk'st of Christ contrary to thy promise ;
Thou should'st not think of God : think of the
    Devil,
And of his dam, too.
Faust. Nor will I henceforth : pardon me in
    this,   100
And Faustus vows never to look to Heaven,
Never to name God, or to pray to him,
To burn his Scriptures, slay his ministers,
And make my spirits pull his churches down.
Luc. Do so, and we will highly gratify thee.
Faustus, we are come from hell to show thee [105
some pastime. Sit down, and thou shalt see all
the Seven Deadly Sins appear in their proper
shapes.

    [2] " On account of their unequal motion in relation to
the whole."

Faust. That sight will be pleasing unto me,
As Paradise was to Adam the first day   111
Of his creation.

Luc. Talk not of Paradise nor creation, but
mark this show: talk of the Devil, and nothing
else. — Come away!   115

Enter the SEVEN DEADLY SINS.

Now, Faustus, examine them of their several
names and dispositions.

Faust. What art thou — the first?

Pride. I am Pride. I disdain to have any
parents. I am like to Ovid's flea: I can [120
creep into every corner of a wench; sometimes,
like a periwig, I sit upon her brow; or like a
fan of feathers, I kiss her lips; indeed I do —
what do I not? But, fie, what a scent is here!
I'll not speak another word, except the [125
ground were perfum'd, and covered with cloth
of arras.

Faust. What art thou — the second?

Covet. I am Covetousness, begotten of an old
churl in an old leathern bag; and might I [130
have my wish I would desire that this house and
all the people in it were turn'd to gold, that I
might lock you up in my good chest. O, my
sweet gold!

Faust. What art thou — the third?   135

Wrath. I am Wrath. I had neither father
nor mother: I leapt out of a lion's mouth when
I was scarce half an hour old; and ever since
I have run up and down the world with this
ease[1] of rapiers wounding myself when I [140
had nobody to fight withal. I was born in hell;
and look to it, for some of you shall be my
father.

Faust. What art thou — the fourth?

Envy. I am Envy, begotten of a chim- [145
ney sweeper and an oyster-wife. I cannot read,
and therefore wish all books were burnt. I am
lean with seeing others eat. O that there would
come a famine through all the world, that
all might die, and I live alone! then thou [150
should'st see how fat I would be. But must thou
sit and I stand! Come down with a vengeance!

Faust. Away, envious rascal! What art thou
-- the fifth?

Glut. Who, I, sir? I am Gluttony. My [155
parents are all dead, and the devil a penny they
have left me, but a bare pension, and that is
thirty meals a day and ten bevers[2] — a small
trifle to suffice nature. O, I come of a royal parentage! My grandfather was a Gammon [160
of Bacon, my grandmother a Hogshead of
Claret-wine; my godfathers were these, Peter
Pickleherring, and Martin Martlemas-beef.[3] O,
but my godmother, she was a jolly gentlewoman,
and well beloved in every good town and [165
city; her name was Mistress Margery March-
beer. Now, Faustus, thou hast heard all my
progeny, wilt thou bid me to supper?

Faust. No, I'll see thee hanged: thou wilt eat
up all my victuals.   170

[1] Pair.   [2] Refreshments between meals.
[3] Martlemas or Martinmas was "the customary time
for hanging up provisions to dry which had been salted
for the winter." (Nares.)

Glut. Then the Devil choke thee!

Faust. Choke thyself, glutton! Who art thou
— the sixth?

Sloth. I am Sloth. I was begotten on a sunny
bank, where I have lain ever since; and [175
you have done me great injury to bring me from
thence: let me be carried thither again by
Gluttony and Lechery. I'll not speak another
word for a king's ransom.

Faust. What are you, Mistress Minx, the
seventh and last?   180

Lech. Who, I, sir? I am one that loves an
inch of raw mutton better than an ell of fried
stockfish; and the first letter of my name begins
with Lechery.

Luc. Away to hell, to hell! (*Exeunt the* SINS.)
— Now, Faustus, how dost thou like this?   185

Faust. O, this feeds my soul!

Luc. Tut, Faustus, in hell is all manner of
delight.

Faust. O might I see hell, and return again.
How happy were I then!   190

Luc. Thou shalt; I will send for thee at midnight.
In meantime take this book; peruse it throughly,
And thou shalt turn thyself into what shape
thou wilt.

Faust. Great thanks, mighty Lucifer!
This will I keep as chary as my life.   195

Luc. Farewell, Faustus, and think on the
Devil.

Faust. Farewell, great Lucifer! Come, Mephistophilis.

Exeunt omnes.

Enter WAGNER.[4]

Wagner. Learned Faustus,
To know the secrets of astronomy,
Graven in the book of Jove's high firmament,
Did mount himself to scale Olympus' top,   200
Being seated in a chariot burning bright,
Drawn by the strength of yoky dragons' necks,
He now is gone to prove cosmography,
And, as I guess, will first arrive at Rome,   205
To see the Pope and manner of his court,
And take some part of holy Peter's feast,
That to this day is highly solemnis'd.   *Exit.*

[SCENE VII.][5]

Enter FAUSTUS *and* MEPHISTOPHILIS.

Faust. Having now, my good Mephistophilis,
Past with delight the stately town of Trier,[6]
Environ'd round with airy mountain-tops,
With walls of flint, and deep entrenched lakes,
Not to be won by any conquering prince;   5
From Paris next, coasting the realm of France,
We saw the river Maine fall into Rhine,
Whose banks are set with groves of fruitful vines;
Then up to Naples, rich Campania,
Whose buildings fair and gorgeous to the eye, 10
The streets straight forth, and pav'd with
finest brick,
Quarter the town in four equivalents.

[4] Later edd. give this speech to Chorus.
[5] The Pope's Privy-chamber.   [6] Treves.

There saw we learned Maro's[1] golden tomb,
The way he cut, an English mile in length,
Thorough a rock of stone in one night's space ; [15]
From thence to Venice, Padua, and the rest,
In one of which a sumptuous temple stands,
That threats the stars with her aspiring top,
Thus hitherto has Faustus spent his time :
But tell me, now, what resting-place is this ? [20]
Hast thou, as erst I did command,
Conducted me within the walls of Rome ?

Meph. Faustus, I have ; and because we
will not be unprovided, I have taken up[2] his
Holiness' privy-chamber for our use. [25]

Faust. I hope his Holiness will bid us welcome.

Meph. Tut, 'tis no matter, man, we'll be
bold with his good cheer.
And now, my Faustus, that thou may'st per-
ceive
What Rome containeth to delight thee with, [30]
Know that this city stands upon seven hills
That underprop the groundwork of the same.
[Just through the midst runs flowing Tiber's
stream,
With winding banks that cut it in two parts :]
Over the which four stately bridges lean, [35]
That make safe passage to each part of Rome :
Upon the bridge call'd Ponto Angelo
Erected is a castle passing strong,
Within whose walls such store of ordnance are,
And double cannons, fram'd of carved brass, [40]
As match the days within one complete year ;
Besides the gates and high pyramides,
Which Julius Cæsar brought from Africa.

Faust. Now by the kingdoms of infernal rule,
Of Styx, of Acheron, and the fiery lake [45]
Of ever-burning Phlegethon, I swear
That I do long to see the monuments
And situation of bright-splendent Rome :
Come therefore, let 's away.

Meph. Nay, Faustus, stay ; I know you 'd fain
see the Pope, [50]
And take some part of holy Peter's feast,
Where thou shalt see a troop of bald-pate friars,
Whose *summum bonum* is in belly-cheer.

Faust. Well, I 'm content to compass then
some sport,
And by their folly make us merriment. [55]
Then charm me, [Mephistophilis,] that I
May be invisible, to do what I please
Unseen of any whilst I stay in Rome.
[MEPHISTOPHILIS *charms him.*]

Meph. So, Faustus, now [59]
Do what thou wilt, thou shalt not be discern'd.

Sound a sennet.[3] *Enter the* POPE *and the* CAR-
DINAL *of* LORRAIN *to the banquet, with* FRIARS
attending.

Pope. My Lord of Lorrain, wilt please you
draw near ?

Faust. Fall to, and the devil choke you an[4]
you spare !

[1] Virgil, who was reputed a magician in the Middle
Ages, was buried at Naples.
[2] Engaged.
[3] " A particular set of notes on the trumpet or cornet,
different from a flourish." (Nares.)   [4] If.

Pope. How now ! Who 's that which spake ?
— Friars, look about.

1 *Friar.* Here 's nobody, if it like your Holiness. [64]

Pope. My lord, here is a dainty dish was sent
me from the Bishop of Milan.

Faust. I thank you, sir.   *Snatches it.*

Pope. How now ! Who 's that which snatch'd
the meat from me ? Will no man look ? My [69]
Lord, this dish was sent me from the Cardinal
of Florence.

Faust. You say true ; I 'll ha 't. [*Snatches it.*]

Pope. What, again ! My lord, I 'll drink to
your Grace.

Faust. I 'll pledge your Grace. [75]
[*Snatches the cup.*]

C. of Lor. My lord, it may be some ghost
newly crept out of purgatory, come to beg a
pardon of your Holiness.

Pope. It may be so. Friars, prepare a dirge
to lay the fury of this ghost. Once again, my [80]
lord, fall to.   *The* POPE *crosseth himself.*

Faust. What, are you crossing of yourself ?
Well, use that trick no more I would advise you.
[*The* POPE] *crosses* [*himself*] *again.*
Well, there 's the second time. Aware the third,
I give you fair warning. [85]
[*The* POPE] *crosses* [*himself*] *again,*
and FAUSTUS *hits him a box of the*
ear ; and they all run away.
Come on, Mephistophilis, what shall we do ?

Meph. Nay, I know not. We shall be curs'd
with bell, book, and candle.

Faust. How ! bell, book, and candle,— candle,
book, and bell,
Forward and backward to curse Faustus to hell !
Anon you shall hear a hog grunt, a calf bleat,
and an ass bray, [90]
Because it is Saint Peter's holiday.

Re-enter all the FRIARS *to sing the Dirge.*

1 *Friar.* Come, brethren, let 's about our
business with good devotion.

They sing :

Cursed be he that stole away his Holiness' meat
from the table ! *Maledicat Dominus !*[5]
Cursed be he that struck his Holiness a blow
on the face ! *Maledicat Dominus !* [95]
Cursed be he that took Friar Sandelo a blow on
the pate ! *Maledicat Dominus !*
Cursed be he that disturbeth our holy dirge !
Maledicat Dominus !
Cursed be he that took away his Holiness' wine !
Maledicat Dominus ! Et omnes sancti !
Amen !
[MEPHISTOPHILIS *and* FAUSTUS]
beat the FRIARS, *and fling fire-*
works among them : and so exeunt.

Enter CHORUS.

Chorus. When Faustus had with pleasure
ta'en the view
Of rarest things, and royal courts of kings, [100]

[5] " May the Lord curse him."
[6] " And all the saints."

He stay'd his course, and so returned home;
Where such as bear his absence but with grief,
I mean his friends, and near'st companions,
Did gratulate his safety with kind words,
And in their conference of what befell,   105
Touching his journey through the world and air,
They put forth questions of Astrology,
Which Faustus answer'd with such learned skill,
As they admir'd and wond'red at his wit.
Now is his fame spread forth in every land;   110
Amongst the rest the Emperor is one,
Carolus the Fifth, at whose palace now
Faustus is feasted 'mongst his noblemen.
What there he did in trial of his art,   114
I leave untold — your eyes shall see perform'd.
                                        Exit.

[Scene VIII.] [1]

Enter Robin *the Ostler with a book in his hand.*

Robin. O, this is admirable! here I ha' stolen
one of Dr. Faustus, conjuring books, and i'
faith I mean to search some circles for my
own use. Now will I make all the maidens in
our parish dance at my pleasure, stark naked [5
before me; and so by that means I shall see
more than e'er I felt or saw yet.

Enter Ralph *calling* Robin.

Ralph. Robin, prithee come away; there's a
gentleman tarries to have his horse, and he
would have his things rubb'd and made clean. [10
He keeps such a chafing with my mistress about
it; and she has sent me to look thee out. Prithee
come away.

Robin. Keep out, keep out, or else you are
blown up; you are dismemb'red, Ralph: keep [15
out, for I am about a roaring piece of work.

Ralph. Come, what dost thou with that same
book? Thou canst not read.

Robin. Yes, my master and mistress shall
find that I can read, he for his forehead, she [20
for her private study; she's born to bear with
me, or else my art fails.

Ralph. Why, Robin, what book is that?

Robin. What book! Why, the most intolerable book for conjuring that e'er was invented
by any brimstone devil.   26

Ralph. Canst thou conjure with it?

Robin. I can do all these things easily with it:
first, I can make thee drunk with ippocras [2] at
any tabern in Europe for nothing; that's one
of my conjuring works.   31

Ralph. Our Master Parson says that's nothing.

Robin. True, Ralph; and more, Ralph, if thou
hast any mind to Nan Spit, our kitchenmaid,
then turn her and wind her to thy own use [35
as often as thou wilt, and at midnight.

Ralph. O brave Robin, shall I have Nan
Spit, and to mine own use? On that condition
I'll feed thy devil with horsebread as long as
he lives, of free cost.   40

Robin. No more, sweet Ralph: let's go and
make clean our boots, which lie foul upon our
hands, and then to our conjuring in the Devil's
name.   *Exeunt.*

An Inn-yard.
Wine mixed with sugar and spices.

[Scene IX.] [3]

Enter Robin *and* Ralph *with a silver goblet.*

Robin. Come, Ralph, did not I tell thee we
were for ever made by this Doctor Faustus'
book? *Ecce signum,* here's a simple purchase [4]
for horsekeepers; our horses shall eat no hay
as long as this lasts.   *

Enter the Vintner.

Ralph. But, Robin, here comes the vintner.

Robin. Hush! I'll gull him supernaturally.
Drawer, I hope all is paid: God be with you.
Come, Ralph.

Vint. Soft, sir; a word with you. I must [10
yet have a goblet paid from you, ere you go.

Robin. I, a goblet, Ralph; I, a goblet! I
scorn you, and you are but a [5] &c. I, a goblet!
search me.

Vint. I mean so, sir, with your favour.   15
                              [*Searches him.*]

Robin. How say you now?

Vint. I must say somewhat to your fellow.
You, sir!

Ralph. Me, sir! me, sir! search your fill.
[Vintner *searches him.*] Now, sir, you may be
ashamed to burden honest men with a matter [21
of truth.

Vint. Well, t' one of you hath this goblet
about you.

Robin. [*Aside.*] You lie, drawer, 'tis afore [25
me. — Sirrah you, I'll teach ye to impeach
honest men; stand by; — I'll scour you for a
goblet! — stand aside you had best, I charge
you in the name of Belzebub. Look to the
goblet, Ralph.   [*Aside to* Ralph.] 30

Vint. What mean you, sirrah?

Robin. I'll tell you what I mean. *Reads
[from a book.] Sanctobulorum, Periphrasticon*
— Nay, I'll tickle you, vintner. Look to the
goblet, Ralph.   [*Aside to* Ralph.] 35
*Polypragmos Belseborams framanto pacostiphos
tostu, Mephistophilis, &c.*   [*Reads.*]

Enter Mephistophilis, *sets squibs at their backs,
[and then exit]. They run about.*

Vint. O *nomine Domini!* [6] what meanest thou,
Robin? Thou hast no goblet.

Ralph. Peccatum peccatorum! [7] Here's [40
thy goblet, good vintner.
          [*Gives the goblet to* Vintner, *who exit.*]

Robin. Misericordia pro nobis! [8] What shall
I do? Good Devil, forgive me now, and I'll
never rob thy library more.

Re-enter to them Mephistophilis.

Meph. Monarch of hell, under whose black
          survey   45
Great potentates do kneel with awful fear,
Upon whose altars thousand souls do lie,
How am I vexed with these villains' charms?
From Constantinople am I hither come
Only for pleasure of these damned slaves.   50

3 An Inn.   4 Gain.
5 The abuse was left to the actor's inventiveness.
6 "In the name of the Lord."
7 "Sin of sins."   8 "Mercy on us."

Robin. How from Constantinople? You have had a great journey. Will you take sixpence in your purse to pay for your supper, and be-gone?

Meph. Well, villains, for your presumption, [55 I transform thee into an ape, and thee into a dog; and so begone.   *Exit.*

Robin. How, into an ape? That's brave! I'll have fine sport with the boys. I'll get nuts and apples enow.   60

Ralph. And I must be a dog.

Robin. I' faith thy head will never be out of **the** pottage pot.   *Exeunt.*

[SCENE X.][1]

Enter EMPEROR, FAUSTUS, *and a* KNIGHT *with attendants.*

Emp. Master Doctor Faustus, I have heard strange report of thy knowledge in the black art, how that none in my empire nor in the whole world can compare with thee for the rare effects of magic; they say thou hast a familiar [5 spirit, by whom thou canst accomplish what thou list. This, therefore, is my request, that thou let me see some proof of thy skill, that mine eyes may be witnesses to confirm what mine ears have heard reported; and here I [10 swear to thee by the honour of mine imperial crown, that, whatever thou doest, thou shalt be no ways prejudiced or endamaged.

Knight. I' faith he looks much like a con-juror.   *Aside.* 15

Faust. My gracious sovereign, though I must confess myself far inferior to the report men have published, and nothing answerable [2] to the honour of your imperial majesty, yet for that love and duty binds me thereunto, I am con- [20 tent to do whatsoever your majesty shall com-mand me.

Emp. Then, Doctor Faustus, mark what I shall say.

As I was sometime solitary set
Within my closet, sundry thoughts arose   25
About the honour of mine ancestors,
How they had won by prowess such exploits,
Got such riches, subdued so many kingdoms,
As we that do succeed, or they that shall
Hereafter possess our throne, shall   30
(I fear me) ne'er attain to that degree
Of high renown and great authority;
Amongst which kings is Alexander the Great,
Chief spectacle of the world's pre-eminence,
The bright shining of whose glorious acts   35
Lightens the world with his [3] reflecting beams,
As, when I heard but motion [4] made of him,
It grieves my soul I never saw the man.
If, therefore, thou by cunning of thine art 39
Canst raise this man from hollow vaults below,
Where lies entomb'd this famous conqueror,
And bring with him his beauteous paramour,
Both in their right shapes, gesture, and attire
They us'd to wear during their time of life,
Thou shalt both satisfy my just desire,   45
And give me cause to praise thee whilst I live.

[1] The Court of the Emperor.   [2] Proportionate.
[3] I+.   [4] Mention.

Faust. My gracious lord, I am ready to ac-complish your request so far forth as by art, and power of my Spirit, I am able to per-form.   50

Knight. I' faith that's just nothing at all.
                                       Aside.

Faust. But, if it like your Grace, it is not in my ability to present before your eyes the true substantial bodies of those two deceased prin-ces, which long since are consumed to dust. 55

Knight. Ay, marry, Master Doctor, now there's a sign of grace in you, when you wil confess the truth.   *Aside.*

Faust. But such spirits as can lively resemble Alexander and his paramour shall appear before your Grace in that manner that they best [60 liv'd in, in their most flourishing estate; which I doubt not shall sufficiently content your im-perial majesty.

Emp. Go to, Master Doctor, let me see them presently.   66

Knight. Do you hear, Master Doctor? You bring Alexander and his paramour before the Emperor!

Faust. How then, sir?   70

Knight. I' faith that's as true as Diana turn'd me to a stag!

Faust. No, sir, but when Actæon died, he left the horns for you. Mephistophilis, be-gone.   *Exit* MEPHISTOPHILIS. [75

Knight. Nay, an you go to conjuring, I'll be-gone.   *Exit.*

Faust. I'll meet with you anon for inter-rupting me so. Here they are, my gracious lord.   80

Re-enter MEPHISTOPHILIS *with* [SPIRITS *in the shape of*] ALEXANDER *and his* PARAMOUR.

Emp. Master Doctor, I heard this lady while she liv'd had a wart or mole in her neck: how shall I know whether it be so or no?

Faust. Your Highness may boldly go and see.
                                       Exeunt [Spirits.]

Emp. Sure these are no spirits, but the [85 true substantial bodies of those two deceased princes.

Faust. Will t please your Highness now to send for the knight that was so pleasant with me here of late?   90

Emp. One of you call him forth.
                                       [*Exit* Attendant.]

Re-enter the KNIGHT *with a pair of horns on his head.*

How now, sir knight! why I had thought thou had'st been a bachelor, but now I see thou hast a wife, that not only gives thee horns, but makes thee wear them. Feel on thy head.   95

Knight. Thou damned wretch and execrable dog,
Bred in the concave of some monstrous rock,
How darest thou thus abuse a gentleman?
Villain, I say, undo what thou hast done!

Faust. O, not so fast, sir; there's no haste; [100 but, good, are you remember'd how you crossed me in my conference with the Emperor? think I have met with you for it.

Emp. Good Master Doctor, at my entreaty release him; he hath done penance sufficient. [105

Faust. My gracious lord, not so much for the injury he off'red me here in your presence, as to delight you with some mirth, hath Faustus worthily requited this injurious knight; [109 which, being all I desire, I am content to release him of his horns: and, sir knight, hereafter speak well of scholars. Mephistophilis, transform him straight. [MEPHISTOPHILIS *removes the horns.*] Now, my good lord, having done my duty I humbly take my leave. 115

Emp. Farewell, Master Doctor; yet, ere you go, Expect from me a bounteous reward. *Exeunt.*

[SCENE XI.]¹

[*Enter* FAUSTUS *and* MEPHISTOPHILIS.]

Faust. Now, Mephistophilis, the restless course
That Time doth run with calm and silent foot,
Short'ning my days and thread of vital life,
Calls for the payment of my latest years;
Therefore, sweet Mephistophilis, let us   5
Make haste to Wittenberg.

Meph. What, will you go on horseback or on foot?

Faust. Nay, till I'm past this fair and pleasant green,
I'll walk on foot.

Enter a HORSE-COURSER.

Horse-C. I have been all this day seeking [10 one Master Fustian: mass, see where he is! God save you, Master Doctor!

Faust. What, horse-courser! You are well met.

Horse-C. Do you hear, sir? I have brought [15 you forty dollars for your horse.

Faust. I cannot sell him so: if thou likest him for fifty, take him.

Horse-C. Alas, sir, I have no more. — I pray you speak for me. 20

Meph. I pray you let him have him: he is an honest fellow, and he has a great charge, neither wife nor child.

Faust. Well, come, give me your money. [HORSE-COURSER *gives* FAUSTUS *the money.*] 25 My boy will deliver him to you. But I must tell you one thing before you have him; ride him not into the water at any hand.

Horse-C. Why, sir, will he not drink of all waters? 30

Faust. O yes, he will drink of all waters, but ride him not into the water: ride him over hedge or ditch, or where thou wilt, but not into the water.

Horse-C. Well, sir. — Now I am made man [35 for ever. I'll not leave my horse for forty. If he had but the quality of hey-ding-ding, hey-ding-ding, I'd make a brave living on him: he has a buttock as slick as an eel. [*Aside.*] Well, God b' wi' ye, sir, your boy will deliver him me: but [40 hark ye, sir; if my horse be sick or ill at ease, if I bring his water to you, you'll tell me what it is?

Exit HORSE-COURSER.

¹ A Green · afterwards. the house of Faustus.

Faust. Away, you villain; what, dost think I am a horse-doctor?
What art thou, Faustus, but a man condemn'd to die?   45
Thy fatal time doth draw to final end;
Despair doth drive distrust unto my thoughts:
Confound these passions with a quiet sleep:
Tush, Christ did call the thief upon the cross;
Then rest thee, Faustus, quiet in conceit.   50

Sleeps in his chair.

Re-enter HORSE-COURSER, *all wet, crying.*

Horse-C. Alas, alas! Doctor Fustian, quotha? Mass, Doctor Lopus² was never such a doctor. Has given me a purgation has purg'd me of forty dollars; I shall never see them more. But yet, like an ass as I was, I would not be ruled [55 by him, for he bade me I should ride him into no water. Now I, thinking my horse had had some rare quality that he would not have had me known of, I, like a venturous youth, rid him into the deep pond at the town's end. I was [60 no sooner in the middle of the pond, but my horse vanish'd away, and I sat upon a bottle of hay, never so near drowning in my life. But I'll seek out my Doctor, and have my forty dollars again, or I'll make it the dearest horse! — [65 O, yonder is his snipper-snapper. — Do you hear? You hey-pass,³ where's your master?

Meph. Why, sir, what would you? You cannot speak with him.

Horse-C. But I will speak with him. 70

Meph. Why, he's fast asleep. Come some other time.

Horse-C. I'll speak with him now, or I'll break his glass windows about his ears.

Meph. I tell thee he has not slept this [75 eight nights.

Horse-C. An he have not slept this eight weeks, I'll speak with him.

Meph. See where he is, fast asleep. 79

Horse-C. Ay, this is he. God save you, Master Doctor! Master Doctor, Master Doctor Fustian! — Forty dollars, forty dollars for a bottle of hay!

Meph. Why, thou seest he hears thee not.

Horse-C. So ho, ho! — so ho, ho! (*Hollas in* [85 *his ear.*) No, will you not wake? I'll make you wake ere I go. (*Pulls* FAUSTUS *by the leg, and pulls it away.*) Alas, I am undone! What shall I do?

Faust. O my leg, my leg! Help, Mephisto- [90 philis! call the officers. My leg, my leg!

Meph. Come, villain, to the constable.

Horse-C. O lord, sir, let me go, and I'll give you forty dollars more.

Meph. Where be they? 95

Horse-C. I have none about me. Come to my ostry⁴ and I'll give them you.

Meph. Begone quickly.

HORSE-COURSER *runs away.*

Faust. What, is he gone? Farewell he! [99 Faustus has his leg again, and the horse-courser,

² Dr. Lopez, physician to Queen Elizabeth, hanged in 1594 on the charge of conspiring to poison the Queen.
³ A juggler's term, like "presto, fly!" Hence applied to the juggler himself. (Bullen.)   ⁴ Inn.

I take it, a bottle of hay for his labour. Well, this trick shall cost him forty dollars more.

Enter WAGNER.

How now, Wagner, what's the news with thee?

Wag. Sir, the Duke of Vanholt doth ear- [105 nestly entreat your company.

Faust. The Duke of Vanholt! an honourable gentleman, to whom I must be no niggard of my cunning. Come, Mephistophilis, let's away to him.   *Exeunt.* [110

[SCENE XII.] 1

Enter the DUKE [*of* VANHOLT], *the* DUCHESS, [FAUSTUS, *and* MEPHISTOPHILIS.]

Duke. Believe me, Master Doctor, this merriment hath much pleased me.

Faust. My gracious lord, I am glad it contents you so well. — But it may be, madam, you take no delight in this. I have heard that great- [5 bellied women do long for some dainties or other. What is it, madam? Tell me, and you shall have it.

Duchess. Thanks, good Master Doctor; and for I see your courteous intent to pleasure [10 me, I will not hide from you the thing my heart desires; and were it now summer, as it is January and the dead time of the winter, I would desire no better meat than a dish of ripe grapes.

Faust. Alas, madam, that's nothing! [15 Mephistophilis, begone. (*Exit* MEPHISTOPHILIS.) Were it a greater thing than this, so it would content you, you should have it.

Re-enter MEPHISTOPHILIS *with the grapes.*

Here they be, madam; wilt please you taste on them?   20

Duke. Believe me, Master Doctor, this makes me wonder above the rest, that being in the dead time of winter, and in the month of January, how you should come by these grapes.

Faust. If it like your Grace, the year is [25 divided into two circles over the whole world, that, when it is here winter with us, in the contrary circle it is summer with them, as in India, Saba, and farther countries in the East; and by means of a swift spirit that I have, [30 I had them brought hither, as ye see. — How do you like them, madam; be they good?

Duchess. Believe me, Master Doctor, they be the best grapes that I e'er tasted in my life before.   35

Faust. I am glad they content you so, madam.

Duke. Come, madam, let us in, where you must well reward this learned man for the great kindness he hath show'd to you.

Duchess. And so I will, my lord; and [40 whilst I live, rest beholding for this courtesy.

Faust. I humbly thank your Grace.

Duke. Come, Master Doctor, follow us and receive your reward.   *Exeunt.*

1 The Court of the Duke of Vanholt.

[SCENE XIII.] 2

Enter WAGNER, *solus.*

Wag. I think my master means to die shortly,
For he hath given to me all his goods;
And yet, methinks, if that death were near,
He would not banquet and carouse and swill
Amongst the students, as even now he doth,   5
Who are at supper with such belly-cheer
As Wagner ne'er beheld in all his life.
See where they come! Belike the feast is ended.

Enter FAUSTUS, *with two or three* SCHOLARS [*and* MEPHISTOPHILIS.]

1 *Schol.* Master Doctor Faustus, since our conference about fair ladies, which was the [10 beautifullest in all the world, we have determined with ourselves that Helen of Greece was the admirablest lady that ever lived: therefore, Master Doctor, if you will do us that favour, as to let us see that peerless dame of Greece, [15 whom all the world admires for majesty, we should think ourselves much beholding unto you.

Faust. Gentlemen,
For that I know your friendship is unfeigned,
And Faustus' custom is not to deny   20
The just requests of those that wish him well,
You shall behold that peerless dame of Greece,
No otherways for pomp and majesty
Than when Sir Paris cross'd the seas with her,
And brought the spoils to rich Dardania.   25
Be silent, then, for danger is in words.

            Music sounds, and HELEN *passeth over the stage.*

2 *Schol.* Too simple is my wit to tell her praise,
Whom all the world admires for majesty.

3 *Schol.* No marvel though the angry Greeks pursu'd
With ten years' war the rape of such a queen, 30
Whose heavenly beauty passeth all compare.

1 *Schol.* Since we have seen the pride of Nature's works,
And only paragon of excellence,

            Enter an OLD MAN.

Let us depart; and for this glorious deed
Happy and blest be Faustus evermore.   35

Faustus. Gentlemen, farewell — the same I wish to you.

            Exeunt SCHOLARS [*and* WAGNER].

Old Man. Ah, Doctor Faustus, that I might prevail
To guide thy steps unto the way of life,
By which sweet path thou may'st attain the goal
That shall conduct thee to celestial rest!   40
Break heart, drop blood, and mingle it with tears,
Tears falling from repentant heaviness
Of thy most vile and loathsome filthiness,
The stench whereof corrupts the inward soul
With such flagitious crimes of heinous sins   45
As no commiseration may expel,
But mercy, Faustus, of thy Saviour sweet,
Whose blood alone must wash away thy guilt.

Faust. Where art thou, Faustus? Wretch, what hast thou done?
Damn'd art thou, Faustus, damn'd; despair and die!   50

2 A room in the house of Faustus.

Hell calls for right, and with a roaring voice
Says " Faustus ! come ! thine hour is [almost]
    come ! "
And Faustus [now] will come to do thee right.
        MEPHISTOPHILIS *gives him a dagger.*
Old Man. Ah stay, good Faustus, stay thy
    desperate steps !
I see an angel hovers o'er thy head,   55
And, with a vial full of precious grace,
Offers to pour the same into thy soul :
Then call for mercy, and avoid despair.
Faust. Ah, my sweet friend, I feel
Thy words do comfort my distressed soul.   60
Leave me a while to ponder on my sins.
Old Man. I go, sweet Faustus, but with heavy
    cheer,
Fearing the ruin of thy hopeless soul.   [*Exit.*]
Faust. Accursed Faustus, where is mercy now?
I do repent ; and yet I do despair ;   65
Hell strives with grace for conquest in my
    breast :
What shall I do to shun the snares of death ?
Meph. Thou traitor, Faustus, I arrest thy soul
For disobedience to my sovereign lord ;
Revolt, or I 'll in piecemeal tear thy flesh.   70
Faust. Sweet Mephistophilis, entreat thy lord
To pardon my unjust presumption,
And with my blood again I will confirm
My former vow I made to Lucifer.
Meph. Do it now then quickly, with unfeigned
    heart,   75
Lest danger do attend thy drift.
        [FAUSTUS *stabs his arm and writes
        on a paper with his blood.*]
Faust. Torment, sweet friend, that base and
    crooked age,[1]
That durst dissuade me from my Lucifer,
With greatest torments that our hell affords.
Meph. His faith is great, I cannot touch his
    soul ;   80
But what I may afflict his body with
I will attempt, which is but little worth.
Faust. One thing, good servant, let me crave
    of thee,
To glut the longing of my heart's desire, —
That I might have unto my paramour   85
That heavenly Helen, which I saw of late,
Whose sweet embracings may extinguish clean
These thoughts that do dissuade me from my
    vow,
And keep mine oath I made to Lucifer.
Meph. Faustus, this or what else thou shalt
    desire   90
Shall be perform'd in twinkling of an eye.
        Re-enter HELEN.
Faust. Was this the face that launch'd a
    thousand ships,
And burnt the topless [2] towers of Ilium ?
Sweet Helen, make me immortal with a kiss.
                                    [*Kisses her.*]
Her lips suck [3] forth my soul ; see where it
    flies ! —   95
Come, Helen, come, give me my soul again.

    [1] Old Man.
    [2] Unsurpassed in height.
    [3] Qq1-3 read *sucke*.

Here will I dwell, for Heaven be in these lips,
And all is dross that is not Helena.
        Enter OLD MAN.
I will be Paris, and for love of thee,
Instead of Troy, shall Wittenberg be sack'd; 100
And I will combat with weak Menelaus,
And wear thy colours on my plumed crest ;
Yea, I will wound Achilles in the heel,
And then return to Helen for a kiss.
Oh, thou art fairer than the evening air   105
Clad in the beauty of a thousand stars ;
Brighter art thou than flaming Jupiter
When he appear'd to hapless Semele :
More lovely than the monarch of the sky
In wanton Arethusa's azur'd arms :   110
And none but thou shalt be my paramour.
                                    Exeunt.
Old Man. Accursed Faustus, miserable man,
That from thy soul exclud'st the grace of
    Heaven,
And fly'st the throne of his tribunal seat !
        Enter DEVILS.
Satan begins to sift me with his pride :   115
As in this furnace God shall try my faith,
My faith, vile hell, shall triumph over thee.
Ambitious fiends ! see how the heavens smiles
At your repulse, and laughs your state to scorn !
Hence, hell ! for hence I fly unto my God. 120
                                    Exeunt.

                [SCENE XIV.][4]
        Enter FAUSTUS *with the* SCHOLARS.
Faust. Ah, gentlemen !
1 Schol. What ails Faustus ?
Faust. Ah, my sweet chamber-fellow, had I
lived with thee, then had I lived still ! but now
I die eternally. Look, comes he not, comes he [5
not ?
2 Schol. What means Faustus ?
3 Schol. Belike he is grown into some sickness
by being over solitary.
1 Schol. If it be so, we 'll have physicians to [10
cure him. 'T is but a surfeit. Never fear, man.
Faust. A surfeit of deadly sin that hath
damn'd both body and soul.
2 Schol. Yet, Faustus, look up to Heaven ; remember God's mercies are infinite.   15
Faust. But Faustus' offences can never be
pardoned : the serpent that tempted Eve may
be sav'd, but not Faustus. Ah, gentlemen, hear
me with patience, and tremble not at my
speeches ! Though my heart pants and quiv- [20
ers to remember that I have been a student here
these thirty years, oh, would I had never seen
Wittenberg, never read book ! And what wonders I have done, all Germany can witness, yea,
the world ; for which Faustus hath lost both [25
Germany and the world, yea Heaven itself, Heaven, the seat of God, the throne of the blessed,
the kingdom of joy ; and must remain in hell
for ever, hell, ah, hell, for ever ! Sweet friends !
what shall become of Faustus being in hell for
ever ?   37

    [4] The same.

3 Schol. Yet, Faustus, call on God.

Faust. On God, whom Faustus hath abjur'd!
on God, whom Faustus hath blasphemed! Ah,
my God, I would weep, but the Devil draws [35
in my tears. Gush forth blood instead of tears!
Yea, life and soul! Oh, he stays my tongue!
I would lift up my hands, but see, they hold
them, they hold them!

All. Who, Faustus?   40

Faust. Lucifer and Mephistophilis. Ah,
gentlemen, I gave them my soul for my cunning!

All. God forbid!

Faust. God forbade it indeed; but Faustus [45
hath done it. For vain pleasure of twenty-four
years hath Faustus lost eternal joy and felicity.
I writ them a bill with mine own blood: the
date is expired; the time will come, and he will
fetch me.   50

1 Schol. Why did not Faustus tell us of this before, that divines might have prayed for thee?

Faust. Oft have I thought to have done so;
but the Devil threat'ned to tear me in pieces if
I nam'd God; to fetch both body and soul if I [55
once gave ear to divinity: and now 't is too late.
Gentlemen, away! lest you perish with me.

2 Schol. Oh, what shall we do to save Faustus?

Faust. Talk not of me, but save yourselves,
and depart.   60

3 Schol. God will strengthen me. I will stay
with Faustus.

1 Schol. Tempt not God, sweet friend; but let
us into the next room, and there pray for him.

Faust. Ay, pray for me, pray for me! and [65
what noise soever ye hear, come not unto me,
for nothing can rescue me.

2 Schol. Pray thou, and we will pray that God
may have mercy upon thee.

Faust. Gentlemen, farewell! If I live till [70
morning I 'll visit you: if not — Faustus is gone
to hell.

All. Faustus, farewell!

Exeunt SCHOLARS. *The clock strikes eleven.*

Faust. Ah, Faustus,
Now hast thou but one bare hour to live,   75
And then thou must be damn'd perpetually!
Stand still, you ever-moving spheres of Heaven,
That time may cease, and midnight never
    come;
Fair Nature's eye, rise, rise again and make
Perpetual day; or let this hour be but   80
A year, a month, a week, a natural day,
That Faustus may repent and save his soul!
O lente, lente, currite noctis equi! [1]
The stars move still, [2] time runs, the clock will
    strike,
The Devil will come, and Faustus must be
    damn'd.   85
O, I 'll leap up to my God! Who pulls me down?
See, see where Christ's blood streams in the fir-
    mament!
One drop would save my soul — half a drop: ah,
    my Christ!

---

[1] "Run softly, softly, horses of the night." — Ovid's
Amores, i. 13.

[2] Without ceasing.

Ah, rend not my heart for naming of my
    Christ!   89
Yet will I call on him: O spare me, Lucifer! —
Where is it now? 'T is gone; and see where God
Stretcheth out his arm, and bends his ireful
    brows!
Mountain and hills come, come and fall on me,
And hide me from the heavy wrath of God!
No! no!   95
Then will I headlong run into the earth;
Earth gape! O no, it will not harbour me!
You stars that reign'd at my nativity,
Whose influence hath allotted death and hell,
Now draw up Faustus like a foggy mist   100
Into the entrails of yon labouring clouds,
That when they vomit forth into the air,
My limbs may issue from their smoky mouths,
So that my soul may but ascend to Heaven.
    The watch strikes [the half hour].
Ah, half the hour is past! 'T will all be past
    anon!   105
O God!
If thou wilt not have mercy on my soul,
Yet for Christ's sake whose blood hath ransom'd
    me,
Impose some end to my incessant pain;
Let Faustus live in hell a thousand years —   110
A hundred thousand, and at last be sav'd!
O, no end is limited to damned souls!
Why wert thou not a creature wanting soul?
Or why is this immortal that thou hast?
Ah, Pythagoras' metempsychosis! were that
    true,   115
This soul should fly from me. and I be chang'd
Unto some brutish beast! All beasts are happy,
For, when they die,
Their souls are soon dissolv'd in elements;   119
But mine must live, still to be plagu'd in hell.
Curst be the parents that engend'red me!
No, Faustus: curse thyself: curse Lucifer
That hath depriv'd thee of the joys of Heaven.
    The clock striketh twelve.
O, it strikes, it strikes! Now, body, turn to air,
Or Lucifer will bear thee quick to hell.   125
    Thunder and lightning.
O soul, be chang'd into little water-drops,
And fall into the ocean — ne'er be found.
My God! my God! look not so fierce on me!

Enter DEVILS.

Adders and serpents, let me breathe awhile!
Ugly hell, gape not! come not, Lucifer!   130
I 'll burn my books! — Ah Mephistophilis!
    Exeunt [DEVILS *with* FAUSTUS.]

Enter CHORUS.

[*Cho.*] Cut is the branch that might have
    grown full straight,
And burned is Apollo's laurel bough,
That sometimes grew within this learned man.
Faustus is gone; regard his hellish fall,   135
Whose hapless fortune may exhort the wise
Only to wonder at unlawful things,
Whose deepness doth entice such forward wits
To practise more than heavenly power permits.
    [*Exit.*]
Terminat hora diem, terminat author opus.   140

THE JEW OF MALTA

BY

CHRISTOPHER MARLOWE

[DRAMATIS PERSONAE.

BARABAS, a wealthy Jew.
FERNEZE, Governor of Malta.
DON LODOWICK, his Son.
SELIM CALYMATH, Son of the Grand Seignior.
MARTIN DEL Bosco, Vice-Admiral of Spain.
DON MATHIAS, a Gentleman.
ITHAMORE, slave of Barabas.
JACOMO, ⎱ Friars.
BARNARDINE. ⎰
PILIA-BORSA, a Bully.
Two Merchants.

Three Jews.
Knights, Bassoes, Officers, Reader, Guard,
    Messengers, Slaves, and Carpenters.

KATHERINE, mother of MATHIAS.
ABIGAIL, Daughter of BARABAS.
BELLAMIRA, a Courtesan.
Abbess.
Two Nuns.

MACHIAVEL, Speaker of the Prologue.

SCENE. — Malta.]

[THE PROLOGUE.]

MACHIAVEL.

ALBEIT the world think Machiavel is dead,
Yet was his soul but flown beyond the Alps,
And, now the Guise [1] is dead, is come from France
To view this land and frolic with his friends.
To some perhaps my name is odious,   5
But such as love me guard me from their tongues;
And let them know that I am Machiavel,
And weigh not men, and therefore not men's words.
Admir'd I am of those that hate me most.
Though some speak openly against my books,   10
Yet will they read me, and thereby attain
To Peter's chair; and when they cast me off,
Are poison'd by my climbing followers.
I count religion but a childish toy,
And hold there is no sin but ignorance.   15
"Birds of the air will tell of murders past!"
I am asham'd to hear such fooleries.
Many will talk of title to a crown:
What right had Cæsar to the empery? [2]
Might first made kings, and laws were then most sure   20
When, like the Draco's, they were writ in blood.
Hence comes it that a strong-built citadel
Commands much more than letters can import;
Which maxim had [but] Phalaris observ'd,
He had never bellowed, in a brazen bull,   25
Of great ones' envy. O' the poor petty wights
Let me be envi'd and not pitied!
But whither am I bound? I come not, I,
To read a lecture here in Britain,
But to present the tragedy of a Jew,   30
Who smiles to see how full his bags are cramm'd,
Which money was not got without my means.
I crave but this — grace him as he deserves,
And let him not be entertain'd the worse
Because he favours me.   [Exit.]   35

---

1. The Duc de Guise, who had organised the Massacre of St. Bartholomew in 1572, was assassinated in 1588.
2. Q. Empire.

[ACT I

SCENE I.]

Enter BARABAS *in his counting-house, with heaps of gold before him.*

Bar. So that of thus much that return was made :
And of the third part of the Persian ships,
There was the venture summ'd and satisfied.
As for those Samnites, [1] and the men of Uz,
That bought my Spanish oils and wines of Greece,   5
Here have I purs'd their paltry silverlings.
Fie, what a trouble 't is to count this trash !
Well fare the Arabians, who so richly pay
The things they traffic for with wedge of gold,
Whereof a man may easily in a day   10
Tell [2] that which may maintain him all his life.
The needy groom that never fing'red groat,
Would make a miracle of thus much coin ;
But he whose steel-barr'd coffers are cramm'd full,
And all his lifetime hath been tired,   15
Wearying his fingers' ends with telling it,
Would in his age be loth to labour so,
And for a pound to sweat himself to death.
Give me the merchants of the Indian mines,
That trade in metal of the purest mould ;   20
The wealthy Moor, that in the eastern rocks
Without control can pick his riches up,
And in his house heap pearl like pebble-stones,
Receive them free, and sell them by the weight ;
Bags of fiery opals, sapphires, amethysts,   25
Jacinths, hard topaz, grass-green emeralds,
Beauteous rubies, sparkling diamonds,
And seld-seen [3] costly stones of so great price
As one of them indifferently rated,
And of a carat of this quantity,   30
May serve in peril of calamity
To ransom great kings from captivity.
This is the ware wherein consists my wealth ;
And thus methinks should men of judgment frame
Their means of traffic from the vulgar trade,   35
And as their wealth increaseth, so inclose
Infinite riches in a little room.
But now how stands the wind ?
Into what corner peers my halcyon's bill ? [4]
Ha ! to the east ? Yes. See, how stands the vanes ?   40
East and by south : why, then, I hope my ships
I sent for Egypt and the bordering isles
Are gotten up by Nilus' winding banks ;
Mine argosy from Alexandria,
Loaden with spice and silks, now under sail,   45
Are smoothly gliding down by Candy shore
To Malta, through our Mediterranean sea.
But who comes here ? How now ?

Enter a Merchant.

Merch. Barabas, thy ships are safe,
Riding in Malta-road : and all the merchants   50

[1] Q. *Samintes.* Recent edd. *Sabans.*
[2] Count.   [3] Seldom seen.
[4] A stuffed halcyon, or kingfisher, was used as a
  eather vane.

With other merchandise are safe arriv'd,
And have sent me to know whether yourself
Will come and custom [5] them.
Bar. The ships are safe thou say'st, and richly fraught ?
Merch. They are.
Bar. Why then go bid them come ashore,
And bring with them their bills of entry.   56
I hope our credit in the custom-house
Will serve as well as I were present there.
Go send 'em threescore camels, thirty mules,
And twenty waggons to bring up the ware.   60
But art thou master in a ship of mine,
And is thy credit not enough for that ?
Merch. The very custom barely comes to more
Than many merchants of the town are worth,
And therefore far exceeds my credit, sir.   65
Bar. Go tell 'em the Jew of Malta sent thee, man :
Tush ! who amongst 'em knows not Barabas ?
Merch. I go.
Bar. So then, there 's somewhat come.
Sirrah, which of my ships art thou master of ?
Merch. Of the *Speranza*, sir.
Bar. And saw'st thou not
Mine argosy at Alexandria ?   71
Thou could'st not come from Egypt, or by Caire,
But at the entry there into the sea,
Where Nilus pays his tribute to the main,
Thou needs must sail by Alexandria.   75
Merch. I neither saw them, nor inquir'd of them :
But this we heard some of our seamen say,
They wond'red how you durst with so much wealth
Trust such a crazed vessel, and so far.
Bar. Tush, they are wise ! I know her and her strength.   80
[But] go, go thou thy ways, discharge thy ship,
And bid my factor bring his loading in.
                                   [*Exit* Merch.]
And yet I wonder at this argosy.

Enter a second Merchant.

2 Merch. Thine argosy from Alexandria,
Know, Barabas, doth ride in Malta-road,   81
Laden with riches, and exceeding store
Of Persian silks, of gold, and orient pearl.
Bar. How chance you came not with those other ships
That sail'd by Egypt ?
2 Merch. Sir, we saw 'em not.
Bar. Belike they coasted round by Candy shore   90
About their oils, or other businesses.
But 't was ill done of you to come so far
Without the aid or conduct of their ships.
2 Merch. Sir, we were wafted by a Spanish fleet,
That never left us till within a league,   95
That had the galleys of the Turk in chase.
Bar. O ! they were going up to Sicily. —
Well, go,
And bid the merchants and my men despatch
And come ashore, and see the fraught discharg'd.   100

[5] Enter them at the custom-house.

2 *Merch.* I go.   *Exit.*
Bar. Thus trowls our fortune in by land and
    sea,
And thus are we on every side enrich'd.
These are blessings promis'd to the Jews,
And herein was old Abram's happiness.   105
What more may Heaven do for earthly man
Than thus to pour out plenty in their laps,
Ripping the bowels of the earth for them,
Making the sea their servant,[1] and the winds
To drive their substance with successful blasts?
Who hateth me but for my happiness?   111
Or who is honour'd now but for his wealth?
Rather had I, a Jew, be hated thus,
Than pitied in a Christian poverty;
For I can see no fruits in all their faith, 115
But malice, falsehood, and excessive pride,
Which methinks fits not their profession.
Haply some hapless man hath conscience,
And for his conscience lives in beggary.
They say we are a scatter'd nation: 120
I cannot tell, but we have scambled[2] up
More wealth by far than those that brag of
    faith.
There 's Kirriah Jairim, the great Jew of Greece,
Obed in Bairseth, Nones in Portugal,
Myself in Malta, some in Italy,   125
Many in France, and wealthy every one;
Ay, wealthier far than any Christian.
I must confess we come not to be kings;
That 's not our fault: alas, our number 's few,
And crowns come either by succession,   130
Or urg'd by force; and nothing violent
Oft have I heard tell, can be permanent.
Give us a peaceful rule, make Christians kings,
That thirst so much for principality.
I have no charge,[3] nor many children,   135
But one sole daughter, whom I hold as dear
As Agamemnon did his Iphigen;
And all I have is hers. But who comes here?

    Enter three Jews.[4]

1 *Jew.* Tush, tell not me; 't was done of
    policy.
2 *Jew.* Come, therefore, let us go to Bara-
    bas,   140
For he can counsel best in these affairs;
And here he comes.
Bar.   Why, how now, countrymen!
Why flock you thus to me in multitudes?
What accident 's betided to the Jews?
1 *Jew.* A fleet of warlike galleys, Barabas, 145
Are come from Turkey, and lie in our road;
And they this day sit in the council-house
To entertain them and their embassy.
Bar. Why, let 'em come, so they come not to
    war;
Or let 'em war, so we be conquerors:—   150
Nay, let 'em combat, conquer, and kill all!
So they spare me, my daughter, and my wealth.
                     Aside.
1 *Jew.* Were it for confirmation of a league,
They would not come in warlike manner thus.

2 *Jew.* I fear their coming will afflict us all.
Bar. Fond[5] men! what dream you of their
    multitudes?   156
What need they treat of peace that are in
    league?
The Turks and those of Malta are in league.
Tut, tut, there is some other matter in 't.
1 *Jew.* Why, Barabas, they come for peace or
    war.   160
Bar. Haply for neither, but to pass along
Towards Venice by the Adriatic Sea;
With[6] whom they have attempted many times,
But never could effect their stratagem.
3 *Jew.* And very wisely said. It may be so.
2 *Jew.* But there 's a meeting in the senate-
    house,   166
And all the Jews in Malta must be there.
Bar. Hum; all the Jews in Malta must be
    there?
Ay, like enough. Why, then, let every man
Provide him, and be there for fashion-sake. 170
If anything shall there concern our state,
Assure yourselves I 'll look — unto myself.
                     Aside.
1 *Jew.* I know you will. Well, brethren, let
    us go.
2 *Jew.* Let 's take our leaves. Farewell, good
    Barabas.
Bar. Do so. Farewell, Zaareth; farewell,
    Temainte.   [*Exeunt* Jews.] 175
And, Barabas, now search this secret out;
Summon thy senses, call thy wits together:
These silly men mistake the matter clean.
Long to the Turk did Malta contribute;
Which tribute, all in policy, I fear,   18
The Turks have let increase to such a sum
As all the wealth of Malta cannot pay;
And now by that advantage thinks, belike,
To seize upon the town: ay, that he seeks.
Howe'er the world go, I 'll make sure for one,
And seek in time to intercept the worst,   18
Warily guarding that which I ha' got.
Ego mihimet sum semper proximus.[7]
Why, let 'em enter, let 'em take the town.
                     [*Exit.*]

    [SCENE II.][8]

Enter [FERNEZE,] *Governor of Malta,* Knights,
    [*and* Officers;] *met by* Bassoes *of the Turk;*
    CALYMATH.

Fern. Now, Bassoes,[9] what demand you at
    our hands?
1 *Bas.* Know, Knights of Malta, that we
    came from Rhodes,
From Cyprus, Candy, and those other Isles
That lie betwixt the Mediterranean seas.
Fern. What 's Cyprus, Candy, and those
    other Isles   5
To us or Malta? What at our hands demand ye?
Cal. The ten years' tribute that remains
    unpaid.
Fern. Alas! my lord, the sum is over-great,
I hope your highness will consider us.

---

[1] Q *servants*   [3] Expenses.
[2] Scrambled.
[4] Some edd. suppose the scene to be shifted here to a
street.

[5] Foolish   [6] Against.
[7] Misquoted from Terence's *Andria,* iv. 1, 12. The
words should be " Proximus sum egomet mihi." (Ellis.)
[8] Inside the council-house.   [9] Bashaws or Pashas

Cal. I wish, grave governor, 't were in my
     power   10
To favour you, but 't is my father's cause,
Wherein I may not, nay, I dare not dally.
    Fern. Then give us leave, great Selim Caly-
     math. [*Consults apart with the* Knights.]
    Cal. Stand all aside, and let the knights
     determine,
And send to keep our galleys under sail,   15
For happily [1] we shall not tarry here. —
Now, governor, how are you resolv'd ?
    Fern. Thus: since your hard conditions are
     such
That you will needs have ten years' tribute past,
We may have time to make collection   20
Amongst the inhabitants of Malta for 't.
    1 *Bas.* That 's more than is in our com-
     mission.
    Cal. What, Callipine ! a little courtesy.
Let 's know their time, perhaps it is not long ;
And 't is more kingly to obtain by peace   25
Than to enforce conditions by constraint.
What respite ask you, governors ?
    Fern.   But a month.
    Cal. We grant a month, but see you keep
     your promise.
Now launch our galleys back again to sea,
Where we 'll attend [2] the respite you have ta'en,
And for the money send our messenger.   31
Farewell, great governor and brave Knights of
     Malta.
    Fern. And all good fortune wait on Caly-
     math! *Exeunt* [CALYMATH *and* Bassoes.]
Go one and call those Jews of Malta hither:
Were they not summon'd to appear to-day ?   35
    Off. They were, my lord, and here they come.

       Enter BARABAS *and three* Jews.

    1 *Knight.* Have you determined what to say
     to them ?
    Fern. Yes, give me leave: — and, Hebrews,
     now come near.
From the Emperor of Turkey is arriv'd
Great Selim Calymath, his highness' son,   40
To levy of us ten years' tribute past,
Now then, here know that it concerneth us —
    Bar. Then, good my lord, to keep your quiet
     still,
Your lordship shall do well to let them have it.
    Fern. Soft, Barabas, there 's more longs to 't
     than so.   45
To what this ten years' tribute will amount,
That we have cast,[3] but cannot compass it
By reason of the wars that robb'd our store ;
And therefore are we to request your aid.
    Bar. Alas, my lord, we are no soldiers ;   50
And what 's our aid against so great a prince ?
    1 *Knight.* Tut, Jew, we know thou art no
     soldier ;
Thou art a merchant and a monied man,
And 't is thy money, Barabas, we seek.   54
    Bar. How, my lord ! my money ?
    Fern.   Thine and the rest.
For, to be short, amongst you 't must be had.
    1 *Jew.* Alas, my lord, the most of us are poor.

    Fern. Then let the rich increase your por-
     tions.
    Bar. Are strangers with your tribute to be
     tax'd ?
    2 *Knight.* Have strangers leave with us to
     get their wealth ?   60
Then let them with us contribute.
    Bar. How ! Equally ?
    Fern.   No, Jew, like infidels.
For through our sufferance of your hateful lives,
Who stand accursed in the sight of Heaven,
These taxes and afflictions are befall'n,   65
And therefore thus we are determined.
Read there the articles of our decrees.
    Reader. "First, the tribute-money of the
Turks shall all be levied amongst the Jews, and
each of them to pay one half of his estate."   70
    Bar. How, half his estate ? I hope you mean
     not mine.   [*Aside.*]
    Fern. Read on.
    Reader. "Secondly, he that denies [4] to pay
shall straight become a Christian."
    Bar. How, a Christian ? Hum, what 's here
     to do ?   [*Aside.*] 75
    Reader. "Lastly, he that denies this shall
absolutely lose all he has."
    All three Jews. O my lord, we will give half.
    Bar. O earth-mettl'd villains, and no
     Hebrews born !
And will you basely thus submit yourselves   80
To leave your goods to their arbitrament ?
    Fern. Why, Barabas, wilt thou be christened ?
    Bar. No, governor, I will be no convertite.[5]
    Fern. Then pay thy half.
    Bar. Why, know you what you did by this
     device ?   85
Half of my substance is a city's wealth.
Governor, it was not got so easily ;
Nor will I part so slightly therewithal.
    Fern. Sir, half is the penalty of our decree,
Either pay that, or we will seize on all.   90
    Bar. Corpo di Dio ! stay ! you shall have half ;
Let me be us'd but as my brethren are.
    Fern. No, Jew, thou hast denied the articles,
And now it cannot be recall'd.
             [*Exeunt* Officers, *on a sign from*
             FERNEZE.]
    Bar. Will you then steal my goods ?   95
Is theft the ground of your religion ?
    Fern. No, Jew, we take particularly thine
To save the ruin of a multitude ;
And better one want for the common good
Than many perish for a private man.   100
Yet, Barabas, we will not banish thee,
But here in Malta, where thou gott'st thy
     wealth,
Live still ; and, if thou canst, get more.
    Bar. Christians, what or how can I multiply ?
Of naught is nothing made.   105
    1 *Knight.* From naught at first thou cam'st
     to little wealth,
From little unto more, from more to most.
If your first curse fall heavy on thy head,
And make thee poor and scorn'd of all the world,
'T is not our fault, but thy inherent sin.   110

Bar. What, bring you Scripture to confirm
    your wrongs?
Preach me not out of my possessions.
Some Jews are wicked, as all Christians are;
But say the tribe that I descended of
Were all in general cast away for sin,   115
Shall I be tried by their transgression?
The man that dealeth righteously shall live;
And which of you can charge me otherwise?
  Fern. Out, wretched Barabas!
Sham'st thou not thus to justify thyself,   120
As if we knew not thy profession?
If thou rely upon thy righteousness,
Be patient and thy riches will increase.
Excess of wealth is cause of covetousness:
And covetousness, O, 't is a monstrous sin.   125
  Bar. Ay, but theft is worse. Tush! take not
    from me then,
For that is theft; and if you rob me thus,
I must be forc'd to steal and compass more.
  1 *Knight.* Grave governor, list not to his ex-
    claims.
Convert his mansion to a nunnery;   130

         Re-enter Officers.

His house will harbour many holy nuns.
  Fern. It shall be so. Now, officers, have you
    done?
  Off. Ay, my lord, we have seiz'd upon the
    goods
And wares of Barabas, which being valued,
Amount to more than all the wealth in Malta. 135
And of the other we have seized half.
  [*Fern.*] Then we 'll take order for the residue.
  Bar. Well then, my lord, say, are you satis-
    fied?
You have my goods, my money, and my wealth,
My ships, my store, and all that I enjoy'd;   140
And, having all, you can request no more;
Unless your unrelenting flinty hearts
Suppress all pity in your stony breasts,
And now shall move you to bereave my life.
  Fern. No, Barabas, to stain our hands with
    blood   145
Is far from us and our profession.
  Bar. Why, I esteem the injury far less
To take the lives of miserable men
Than be the causers of their misery.
You have my wealth, the labour of my life, 150
The comfort of mine age, my children's hope,
And therefore ne'er distinguish of the wrong.
  Fern. Content thee, Barabas, thou hast
    naught but right.
  Bar. Your extreme right does me exceeding
    wrong:
But take it to you, i' the devil's name.   155
  Fern. Come, let us in, and gather of these
    goods
The money for this tribute of the Turk.
  1 *Knight.* 'T is necessary that be look'd
    unto;
For if we break our day, we break the league,
And that will prove but simple [1] policy.   160
      Exeunt [*all except* BARABAS *and*
      the Jews.]
  Bar. Ay, policy! that's their profession,
        [1] Foolish.

And not simplicity, as they suggest.
The plagues of Egypt, and the curse of Heaven,
Earth's barrenness, and all men's hatred
Inflict upon them, thou great *Primus Motor!* 165
And here upon my knees, striking the earth,
I ban their souls to everlasting pains
And extreme tortures of the fiery deep,
That thus have dealt with me in my distress.
  1 *Jew.* O yet be patient, gentle Barabas. 170
  Bar. O silly brethren, born to see this day,
Why stand you thus unmov'd with my laments?
Why weep you not to think upon my wrongs?
Why pine not I, and die in this distress?
  1 *Jew.* Why, Barabas, as hardly can we
    brook   175
The cruel handling of ourselves in this;
Thou seest they have taken half our goods.
  Bar. Why did you yield to their extortion?
You were a multitude, and I but one;
And of me only have they taken all.   180
  1 *Jew.* Yet, Brother Barabas, remember
    Job.
  Bar. What tell you me of Job? I wot his
    wealth
Was written thus: he had seven thousand
    sheep,
Three thousand camels, and two hundred yoke
Of labouring oxen, and five hundred   185
She-asses: but for every one of those,
Had they been valued at indifferent rate,
I had at home, and in mine argosy,
And other ships that came from Egypt last,
As much as would have bought his beasts and
    him,   190
And yet have kept enough to live upon:
So that not he, but I may curse the day,
Thy fatal birth-day, forlorn Barabas;
And henceforth wish for an eternal night, 194
That clouds of darkness may inclose my flesh,
And hide these extreme sorrows from mine
    eyes:
For only I have toil'd to inherit here
The months of vanity and loss of time,
And painful nights, have been appointed me. [1]
  2 *Jew.* Good Barabas, be patient.   200
  Bar. Ay;
Pray, leave me in my patience. You that
Were ne'er possess'd of wealth, are pleas'd
    with want;
But give him liberty at least to mourn,
That in a field amidst his enemies   205
Doth see his soldiers slain, himself disarm'd,
And knows no means of his recovery.
Ay, let me sorrow for this sudden chance;
'T is in the trouble of my spirit I speak;
Great injuries are not so soon forgot.   210
  1 *Jew.* Come, let us leave him; in his ireful
    mood
Our words will but increase his ecstasy. [2]
  2 *Jew.* On, then; but trust me 't is a
    misery
To see a man in such affliction.—
Farewell, Barabas!   *Exeunt* [*the three* Jews.]
  Bar.   Ay, fare you well. 215

[1] For I have toiled only to inherit the months, etc.,
  which have been, etc.
[2] Violent emotion.

See the simplicity of these base slaves,
Who, for the villains have no wit themselves,
Think me to be a senseless lump of clay
That will with every water wash to dirt.
No, Barabas is born to better chance,   220
And fram'd of finer mould than common men,
That measure naught but by the present time.
A reaching thought will search his deepest wits,
And cast [1] with cunning for the time to come:
For evils are apt to happen every day. —   225

Enter ABIGAIL. [2]

But wither wends my beauteous Abigail?
O! what has made my lovely daughter sad?
What, woman! moan not for a little loss:
Thy father has enough in store for thee.
  Abig. Not for myself, but aged Barabas;   230
Father, for thee lamenteth Abigail.
But I will learn to leave these fruitless tears,
And, urg'd thereto with my afflictions,
With fierce exclaims run to the senate-house,
And in the senate reprehend them all,   235
And rend their hearts with tearing of my hair,
Till they reduce [3] the wrongs done to my father.
  Bar. No, Abigail, things past recovery
Are hardly cur'd with exclamations.
Be silent, daughter, sufferance breeds ease, 240
And time may yield us an occasion
Which on the sudden cannot serve the turn.
Besides, my girl, think me not all so fond [4]
As negligently to forego so much
Without provision for thyself and me: 245
Ten thousand portagues,[5] besides great pearls,
Rich costly jewels, and stones infinite,
Fearing the worst of this before it fell,
I closely hid.
  Abig.   Where, father?
  Bar.   In my house, my girl.
  Abig. Then shall they ne'er be seen of Bara-
    bas: 250
For they have seiz'd upon thy house and wares.
  Bar. But they will give me leave once more,
    I trow,
To go into my house.
  Abig.   That may they not:
For there I left the governor placing nuns,
Displacing me; and of thy house they mean 255
To make a nunnery, where none but their own
    sect [6]
Must enter in; men generally barr'd.
  Bar. My gold! my gold! and all my wealth
    is gone!
You partial heavens, have I deserv'd this
    plague?
What, will you thus oppose me, luckless stars, 260
To make me desperate in my poverty?
And knowing me impatient in distress,
Think me so mad as I will hang myself,
That I may vanish o'er the earth in air,
And leave no memory that e'er I was?   265
No, I will live; nor loathe I this my life:
And, since you leave me in the ocean thus

To sink or swim, and put me to my shifts,
I 'll rouse my senses and awake myself.   269
Daughter, I have it! Thou perceiv'st the plight
Wherein these Christians have oppressed me.
Be rul'd by me, for in extremity
We ought to make bar of no policy.
  Abig. Father, whate'er it be to injure them
That have so manifestly wronged us,   275
What will not Abigail attempt?
  Bar.   Why, so;
Then thus, thou told'st me they have turn'd
    my house
Into a nunnery, and some nuns are there?
  Abig. I did.
  Bar.   Then, Abigail, there must my girl
Entreat the abbess to be entertain'd.   280
  Abig. How, as a nun?
  Bar.   Ay, daughter, for religion
Hides many mischiefs from suspicion.
  Abig. Ay, but, father, they will suspect me
    there.
  Bar. Let 'em suspect; but be thou so precise
As they may think it done of holiness.   285
Entreat 'em fair, and give them friendly
    speech,
And seem to them as if thy sins were great,
Till thou has gotten to be entertain'd.
  Abig. Thus, father, shall I much dissemble.
  Bar.   Tush!
As good dissemble that thou never mean'st, 290
As first mean truth and then dissemble it.
A counterfeit profession is better
Than unseen hypocrisy.
  Abig. Well, father, say [that] I be entertain'd,
What then shall follow?
  Bar.   This shall follow then:
There have I hid, close underneath the plank 296
That runs along the upper-chamber floor,
The gold and jewels which I kept for thee.
But here they come; be cunning, Abigail.
  Abig. Then, father, go with me.
  Bar.   No, Abigail, in this
It is not necessary I be seen;   301
For I will seem offended with thee for 't.
Be close,[7] my girl, for this must fetch my gold.
                [They retire.]

Enter Friars [JACOMO *and* BARNARDINE, *Ab-*
  bess,] *and a* Nun.

  F. Jac. Sisters,   304
We now are almost at the new-made nunnery.
  Abb. The better; for we love not to be seen.
'T is thirty winters long since some of us
Did stray so far amongst the multitude.
  F. Jac. But, madam, this house
And waters [8] of this new-made nunnery   310
Will much delight you.
  Abb. It may be so; but who comes here?
          *[*ABIGAIL *comes forward.]*
  Abig. Grave abbess, and you, happy virgins'
    guide,
Pity the state of a distressed maid.
  Abb. What art thou, daughter?   315
  Abig. The hopeless daughter of a hapless Jew,

---

[1] Plan.
[2] The scene seems to change here from the Council-
house to the neighbourhood of Scene I.
[3] Redress.   [5] Portuguese gold coins.
[4] Foolish.   [6] Sex.
[7] Secretive.
[8] So Q. "cloisters," "gardens," and "quarters,"
have been conjectured as emendations.

The Jew of Malta, wretched Barabas;
Sometimes the owner of a goodly house,
Which they have now turn'd to a nunnery.
  Abb. Well, daughter, say, what is thy suit
with us?   320
  Abig. Fearing the afflictions which my father
feels
Proceed from sin, or want of faith in us,
I'd pass away my life in penitence,
And be a novice in your nunnery,
To make atonement for my labouring soul.   325
  F. Jac. No doubt, brother, but this pro-
ceedeth of the spirit.
  F. Barn. Ay, and a moving spirit too,
brother; but come,
Let us entreat she may be entertain'd.
  Abb. Well, daughter, we admit you for a
nun.   329
  Abig. First let me as a novice learn to frame
My solitary life to your strait laws,
And let me lodge where I was wont to lie.
I do not doubt, by your divine precepts
And mine own industry, but to profit much.
  Bar. As much, I hope, as all I hid is worth.
                        Aside.
  Abb. Come, daughter, follow us.   336
  Bar. [*coming forward.*] Why, how now, Abi-
gail, what makest thou
Amongst these hateful Christians?
  F. Jac. Hinder her not, thou man of little
faith,   339
For she has mortified herself.
  Bar.   How! mortified?
  F. Jac. And is admitted to the sisterhood.
  Bar. Child of perdition, and thy father's
shame!
What wilt thou do among these hateful fiends?
I charge thee on my blessing that thou leave
These devils, and their damned heresy.   345
  Abig. Father, give me—   [*She goes to him.*]
  Bar. (*Whispers to her.*) Nay, back, Abi-
gail, —
And think upon the jewels and the gold;
The board is marked thus that covers it. —
Away, accursed, from thy father's sight.
  F. Jac. Barabas, although thou art in mis-
belief,   350
And wilt not see thine own afflictions,
Yet let thy daughter be no longer blind.
  Bar. Blind friar, I reck not thy persua-
sions,—
(The board is marked thus + that covers it.)
        [*Aside to* Abigail *in a whisper.*]
For I had rather die than see her thus.   355
Wilt thou forsake me too in my distress,
Seduced daughter? (Go, forget not!)   *Aside.*
Becomes it Jews to be so credulous?—
(To-morrow early I'll be at the door.)   *Aside.*
No, come not at me; if thou wilt be damn'd,
Forget me, see me not, and so be gone.—   361
(Farewell, remember to-morrow morning.)—
                        Aside.
Out, out, thou wretch!
    [*Exeunt, on one side* Barabas, *on
the other side* Friars, Abbess,
Nun, *and* Abigail; *as they are
going out,*]

Enter Mathias.

  Math. Who's this? Fair Abigail, the rich
Jew's daughter,
Become a nun! Her father's sudden fall   365
Has humbled her and brought her down to
this.
Tut, she were fitter for a tale of love,
Than to be tired out with orisons;
And better would she far become a bed,
Embraced in a friendly lover's arms,   370
Than rise at midnight to a solemn mass.

Enter Lodowick.

  Lod. Why, how now, Don Mathias! in a
dump?
  Math. Believe me, noble Lodowick, I have
seen
The strangest sight, in my opinion,
That ever I beheld.
  Lod.   What was't I prithee? 375
  Math. A fair young maid, scarce fourteen
years of age,
The sweetest flower in Cytherea's field,
Cropt from the pleasures of the fruitful earth,
And strangely metamorphos'd [to a] nun.
  Lod. But say, what was she?
  Math.   Why, the rich Jew's daughter.
  Lod. What, Barabas, whose goods were
lately seiz'd?   381
Is she so fair?
  Math.   And matchless beautiful,
As, had you seen her, 'would have mov'd your
heart,
Though countermin'd with walls of brass, to
love,
Or at the least to pity.   385
  Lod. And if she be so fair as you report,
'T were time well spent to go and visit her.
How say you, shall we?
  Math. I must and will, sir; there's no remedy.
  Lod. And so will I too, or it shall go hard.
Farewell, Mathias.
  Math.   Farewell, Lodowick.   391
                       Exeunt [*severally.*]

ACT II

[Scene I.][1]

Enter Barabas *with a light.*

  Bar. Thus, like the sad presaging raven,
that tolls
The sick man's passport in her hollow beak,
And in the shadow of the silent night
Doth shake contagion from her sable wings,
Vex'd and tormented runs poor Barabas   5
With fatal curses towards these Christians.
The incertain pleasures of swift-footed Time
Have ta'en their flight, and left me in despair;
And of my former riches rests no more
But bare remembrance, like a soldier's scar,   10
That has no further comfort for his maim.

[1] The scene is before Barabas's house, now a nunnery.

O thou, that with a fiery pillar led'st
The sons of Israel through the dismal shades,
Light Abraham's offspring, and direct the
hand
Of Abigail this night; or let the day   15
Turn to eternal darkness after this!
No sleep can fasten on my watchful eyes,
Nor quiet enter my distemper'd thoughts,
Till I have answer of my Abigail.

Enter ABIGAIL *above.*

Abig. Now have I happily espi'd a time   20
To search the plank my father did appoint;
And here behold, unseen, where I have found
The gold, the pearls, and jewels, which he hid.
  Bar. Now I remember those old women's
words,   24
Who in my wealth[1] would tell me winter's tales,
And speak of spirits and ghosts that glide by
night
About the place where treasure hath been hid:
And now methinks that I am one of those;
For whilst I live, here lives my soul's sole hope,
And, when I die, here shall my spirit walk.   30
  Abig. Now that my father's fortune were so
good
As but to be about this happy place!
'T is not so happy: yet when we parted last,
He said he would attend me in the morn.
Then, gentle sleep, where'er his body rests, 35
Give charge to Morpheus that he may dream
A golden dream, and of the sudden walk,[2]
Come and receive the treasure I have found.
  Bar. Bueno para todos mi ganado no era.[3]
As good go on as sit so sadly thus.   40
But stay, what star shines yonder in the east?
The loadstar of my life, if Abigail.
Who's there?
  Abig.   Who's that?
  Bar.   Peace, Abigail, 't is I.
  Abig. Then, father, here receive thy happiness.
  Bar. Hast thou 't?   *She throws down bags.*
  Abig. Here, hast thou 't? There's more, and
more, and more.   46
  Bar. O my girl,
My gold, my fortune, my felicity!
Strength to my soul, death to mine enemy!
Welcome the first beginner of my bliss!   50
O Abigail, Abigail, that I had thee here too!
Then my desires were fully satisfied:
But I will practise thy enlargement thence.
O girl! O gold! O beauty! O my bliss!
                          Hugs his bags.
  Abig. Father, it draweth towards midnight
now,   55
And 'bout this time the nuns begin to wake;
To shun suspicion, therefore, let us part.
  Bar. Farewell, my joy, and by my fingers
take
A kiss from him that sends it from his soul.
                      [*Exit* ABIGAIL *above.*]
Now Phœbus ope the eyelids of the day,   60

And for the raven wake the morning lark,
That I may hover with her in the air;
Singing o'er these, as she does o'er her young,
Hermoso placer de los dineros.[4]   *Exit.*

[SCENE II.][5]

Enter Governor [FERNEZE], DEL BOSCO, *and*
Knights.

Fern. Now, captain, tell us whither thou art
bound?
Whence is thy ship that anchors in our road?
And why thou cam'st ashore without our
leave?
  Bosc. Governor of Malta, hither am I bound;
My Ship, *The Flying Dragon*, is of Spain,   5
And so am I: del Bosco is my name;
Vice-admiral unto the Catholic King.
  1 *Knight.* 'T is true, my lord, therefore entreat him well.
  Bosc. Our fraught[6] is Grecians, Turks, and
Afric Moors.
For late upon the coast of Corsica,   10
Because we vail'd[7] not to the [Turkish][8] fleet,
Their creeping galleys had us in the chase:
But suddenly the wind began to rise,
And then we luff'd and tack'd[9] and fought at
ease:
Some have we fir'd, and many have we sunk;   15
But one amongst the rest became our prize.
The captain's slain, the rest remain our slaves,
Of whom we would make sale in Malta here.
  Fern. Martin del Bosco, I have heard of thee:
Welcome to Malta, and to all of us;   20
But to admit a sale of these thy Turks
We may not, nay, we dare not give consent
By reason of a tributary league.
  1 *Knight.* Del Bosco, as thou lov'st and
honour'st us,
Persuade our governor against the Turk;   25
This truce we have is but in hope of gold,
And with that sum he craves might we wage war.
  Bosc. Will Knights of Malta be in league
with Turks,
And buy it basely too for sums of gold?
My lord, remember that, to Europe's shame,   30
The Christian Isle of Rhodes, from whence you
came,
Was lately lost, and you were stated[10] here
To be at deadly enmity with Turks.
  Fern. Captain, we know it, but our force is
small.
  Bosc. What is the sum that Calymath requires?   35
  Fern. A hundred thousand crowns.
  Bosc. My lord and king hath title to this isle,
And he means quickly to expel you hence;
Therefore be rul'd by me, and keep the gold.
I 'll write unto his majesty for aid,   40
And not depart until I see you free.
  Fern. On this condition shall thy Turks be
sold.

---

[1] Bullen emends to *youth.*   [2] Dyce emends to *wake.*
[3] Span. "My herd was not good for all"; *i. e.,* different people judged me differently.

[4] Span. "Beautiful pleasure of money."
[5] The Council-house.   [8] Q. Spanish.
[6] Freight.   [9] So Dyce. Q. *left and tooke.*
[7] Lowered our flags.   [10] Established.

Go, officers, and set them straight in show.
              [*Exeunt* Officers.]
Bosco, thou shalt be Malta's general;
We and our warlike Knights will follow thee 45
Against these barbarous misbelieving Turks.
  Bosc. So shall you imitate those you succeed:
For when their hideous force environ'd Rhodes,
Small though the number was that kept the
     town,
They fought it out, and not a man surviv'd 50
To bring the hapless news to Christendom.
  Fern. So will we fight it out. Come, let's
     away!
Proud daring Calymath, instead of gold,
We'll send thee bullets wrapt in smoke and
     fire.
Claim tribute where thou wilt, we are resolv'd,
Honour is bought with blood and not with
     gold.   *Exeunt.* 55
         [SCENE III.][1]

Enter Officers *with* [ITHAMORE *and other*] Slaves.

  1 *Off.* This is the market-place, here let 'em
     stand:
Fear not their sale, for they'll be quickly
     bought.
  2 *Off.* Every one's price is written on his
     back,
And so much must they yield or not be sold.
  1 *Off.* Here comes the Jew; had not his
     goods been seiz'd, 5
He'd give us present money for them all.

          Enter BARABAS.

  Bar. In spite of these swine-eating Chris-
     tians, —
Unchosen nation, never circumcis'd,
Such as (poor villains!) were ne'er thought
     upon.
Till Titus and Vespasian conquer'd us, — 10
Am I become as wealthy as I was.
They hop'd my daughter would ha' been a nun;
But she's at home, and I have bought a house
As great and fair as is the governor's;
And there in spite of Malta will I dwell, 15
Having Ferneze's hand, whose heart I'll have;
Ay, and his son's too, or it shall go hard.
I am not of the tribe of Levi, I,
That can so soon forget an injury. 19
We Jews can fawn like spaniels when we please;
And when we grin we bite, yet are our looks
As innocent and harmless as a lamb's.
I learn'd in Florence how to kiss my hand,
Heave up my shoulders when they call me
     dog,
And duck as low as any barefoot friar; 25
Hoping to see them starve upon a stall,
Or else be gather'd for in our synagogue,
That, when the offering-basin comes to me,
Even for charity I may spit into 't.
Here comes Don Lodowick, the governor's son,
One that I love for his good father's sake. 31

         Enter LODOWICK.

  Lod. I hear the wealthy Jew walked this
     way.
        [1] The market-place.

I'll seek him out, and so insinuate,
That I may have a sight of Abigail;
For Don Mathias tells me she is fair. 35
  Bar. [*Aside.*] Now will I show myself
To have more of the serpent than the dove;
This is — more knave than fool.
  Lod. Yond' walks the Jew; now for fair
     Abigail.
  Bar. [*Aside.*] Ay, ay, no doubt but she's at
     your command. 40
  Lod. Barabas, thou know'st I am the gover-
     nor's son.
  Bar. I would you were his father, too, sir;
That's all the harm I wish you. [*Aside.*] The
     slave looks
Like a hog's-cheek new singed.
  Lod. Whither walk'st thou, Barabas? 45
  Bar. No further: 't is a custom held with us,
That when we speak with Gentiles like to
     you,
We turn into the air to purge ourselves:
For unto us the promise doth belong.
  Lod. Well, Barabas, canst help me to a dia-
     mond? 50
  Bar. O, sir, your father had my diamonds.
Yet I have one left that will serve your
     turn: —
I mean my daughter: but ere he shall have her
I'll sacrifice her on a pile of wood.
I ha' the poison of the city for him, 55
And the white leprosy.   *Aside.*
  Lod. What sparkle does it give without a
     foil?[2]
  Bar. The diamond that I talk of ne'er was
     foil'd: —[3]
  [*Aside.*] But when he touches it, it will be
     foil'd: —
Lord Lodowick, it sparkles bright and fair. 60
  Lod. Is it square or pointed, pray let me
     know.
  Bar. Pointed it is, good sir — but not for
     you.   *Aside.*
  Lod. I like it much the better.
  Bar.   So do I too.
  Lod. How shows it by night?
  Bar.   Outshines Cynthia's rays:
— You'll like it better far o' nights than days.
                       Aside. 65
  Lod. And what's the price?
  Bar. [*Aside.*] Your life an if you have it. —
O my lord,
We will not jar about the price; come to my
     house
And I will give 't your honour — with a ven-
     geance.   *Aside.*
  Lod. No, Barabas, I will deserve it first. 70
  Bar. Good sir,
Your father has deserv'd it at my hands,
Who, of mere charity and Christian ruth,
To bring me to religious purity,
And as it were in catechising sort, 75
To make me mindful of my mortal sins,
Against my will, and whether I would or no,
Seiz'd all I had, and thrust me out o' doors,

   [2] Gold or silver leaf placed under a gem to increase its
brilliance.
   [3] Defiled, punning on *foil.*

And made my house a place for nuns most
    chaste.
Lod. No doubt your soul shall reap the fruit
    of it.   80
Bar. Ay, but, my lord, the harvest is far off.
And yet I know the prayers of those nuns
And holy friars, having money for their pains,
Are wondrous ; — and indeed do no man good —
                    Aside.
And seeing they are not idle, but still doing, 85
'T is likely in time may reap some fruit,
I mean in fulness of perfection.
   Lod. Good Barabas, glance [1] not at our holy
    nuns.
   Bar. No, but I do it through a burning
    zeal, —
Hoping ere long to set the house afire ;   90
For though they do a while increase and
    multiply
I 'll have a saying to that nunnery. —   *Aside.*
As for the diamond, sir, I told you of,
Come home and there 's no price shall make
    us part,
Even for your honourable father's sake. — 95
It shall go hard but I will see your death. —
                    Aside.
But now I must be gone to by a slave.
   Lod. And, Barabas, I 'll bear thee company.
   Bar. Come then — here 's the market-place.
What 's the price of this slave? Two hundred
    crowns!   100
Do the Turks weigh so much ?
   1 *Off.*   Sir, that 's his price.
   Bar. What, can he steal that you demand
    so much?
Belike he has some new trick for a purse ;
And if he has, he is worth three hundred
    plates,[2]
So that, being bought, the town-seal might be
    got   105
To keep him for his lifetime from the gallows.
The sessions day is critical to thieves,
And few or none 'scape but by being purg'd.
   Lod. Rat'st thou this Moor but at two hun-
    dred plates?
   1 *Off.* No more, my lord.   110
   Bar. Why should this Turk be dearer than
    that Moor ?
   1 *Off.* Because he is young and has more
    qualities.
   Bar. What, hast thou the philosopher's stone?
An thou hast, break my head with it, I 'll for-
    give thee.   115
   Slave. No, sir ; I can cut and shave.
   Bar. Let me see, sirrah, are you not an old
    shaver ?
   Slave. Alas, sir ! I am a very youth.
   Bar. A youth? I 'll buy you, and marry [120
you to Lady Vanity, if you do well.
   Slave. I will serve you, sir.
   Bar. Some wicked trick or other. It may be,
under colour of shaving, thou 'lt cut my throat
for my goods. Tell me, hast thou thy health
well ?   126
   Slave. Ay, passing well.

   Bar. So much the worse ; I must have one
that 's sickly, an 't be but for sparing victuals :
't is not a stone of beef a day will maintain [130
you in these chops ; let me see one that 's some-
what leaner.
   1 *Off.* Here 's a leaner, how like you him?
   Bar. Where wast thou born ?
   Itha. In Thrace ; brought up in Arabia. 135
   Bar. So much the better, thou art for my
    turn.
An hundred crowns ? I 'll have him ; there 's
    the coin.   [*Gives money.*]
   1 *Off.* Then mark him, sir, and take him
    hence.
   Bar. Ay, mark him, you were best, for this
    is he
That by my help shall do much villainy.   140
                  [*Aside.*]
My lord, farewell. Come, sirrah, you are mine.
As for the diamond, it shall be yours ;
I pray, sir, be no stranger at my house,
All that I have shall be at your command.

Enter MATHIAS *and his* Mother [KATHERINE]

   Math. What makes the Jew and Lodowick
    so private ?   145
I fear me 't is about fair Abigail.   [*Aside.*]
   Bar. Yonder comes Don Mathias, let us
    stay ;[3]   [*Exit* LODOWICK.]
He loves my daughter, and she holds him dear :
But I have sworn to frustrate both their hopes,
And be reveng'd upon the governor.   150
   Kath. This Moor is comeliest, is he not ?
    Speak, son.
   Math. No, this is the better, mother ; view
    this well.
   Bar. Seem not to know me here before your
    mother,
Lest she mistrust the match that is in hand.
When you have brought her home, come to my
    house ;   155
Think of me as thy father ; son, farewell.
   Math. But wherefore talk'd Don Lodowick
    with you ?
   Bar. Tush ! man, we talk'd of diamonds, not
    of Abigail.
   Kath. Tell me, Mathias, is not that the
    Jew ?
   Bar. As for the comment on the Maccabees,
I have it, sir, and 't is at your command.   161
   Math. Yes, madam, and my talk with him was
About the borrowing of a book or two.
   Kath. Converse not with him, he 's cast off
    from heaven.
Thou hast thy crowns, fellow ; come, let 's
    away.   165
   Math. Sirrah, Jew, remember the book.
   Bar. Marry will I, sir.
          Exeunt [MATHIAS *and his* Mother].
   Off.   Come, I have made
A reasonable market ; let 's away.
        [*Exeunt* Officers *with* Slaves.]
   Bar. Now let me know thy name, and there-
    withal
Thy birth, condition, and profession.   170

---

[1] Make insinuations.   [2] Pieces of silver coin.   [3] Break off our conversation.

Itha. Faith, sir, my birth is but mean; my
    name's
Ithamore; my profession what you please.
  Bar. Hast thou no trade? Then listen to my
    words,
And I will teach [thee] that shall stick by thee:
First be thou void of these affections,   175
Compassion, love, vain hope, and heartless fear;
Be mov'd at nothing, see thou pity none,
But to thyself smile when the Christians
    moan.
  Itha. O brave! Master, I worship your nose [1]
    for this.
  Bar. As for myself, I walk abroad o' nights
And kill sick people groaning under walls: 181
Sometimes I go about and poison wells;
And now and then, to cherish Christian thieves,
I am content to lose some of my crowns,
That I may, walking in my gallery,   185
See 'em go pinion'd along by my door.
Being young, I studied physic, and began
To practise first upon the Italian;
There I enrich'd the priests with burials,
And always kept the sextons' arms in ure [2]   190
With digging graves and ringing dead men's
    knells:
And after that was I an engineer,
And in the wars 'twixt France and Germany,
Under pretence of helping Charles the Fifth,
Slew friend and enemy with my stratagems.   195
Then after that was I an usurer,
And with extorting, cozening, forfeiting,
And tricks belonging unto brokery,
I fill'd the jails with bankrupts in a year,
And with young orphans planted hospitals,   200
And every moon made some or other mad,
And now and then one hang himself for grief,
Pinning upon his breast a long great scroll
How I with interest tormented him.
But mark how I am blest for plaguing them;   205
I have as much coin as will buy the town.
But tell me now, how hast thou spent thy
    time?
  Itha. 'Faith, master,
In setting Christian villages on fire,
Chaining of eunuchs, binding galley-slaves.   210
One time I was an ostler in an inn,
And in the night-time secretly would I steal
To travellers' chambers, and there cut their
    throats.
Once at Jerusalem, where the pilgrims kneel'd,
I strowed powder on the marble stones,   215
And therewithal their knees would rankle so,
That I have laugh'd a-good [3] to see the crip-
    ples
Go limping home to Christendom on stilts.
  Bar. Why this is something. Make account
    of me
As of thy fellow, we are villains both;   220
Both circumcised, we hate Christians both.
Be true and secret, thou shalt want no gold.
But stand aside, here comes Don Lodowick.

[1] Barabas was represented on the stage with a large
false nose. In Rowley's *Search for Money* (1609) allusion is made to the "artificiall Jewe of Maltaes nose."
(Ellis.)
  [2] Practice.   [3] In good earnest.

Enter LODOWICK.

  Lod. O Barabas, well met;
Where is the diamond you told me of?   225
  Bar. I have it for you, sir; please you walk
    in with me.
What ho, Abigail! open the door, I say.

Enter ABIGAIL [*with letters*].

  Abig. In good time, father; here are letters
    come
From Ormus, and the post stays here within.
  Bar. Give me the letters. — Daughter, do   230
    you hear,
Entertain Lodowick the governor's son
With all the courtesy you can afford;
Provided that you keep your maidenhead.
Use him as if he were a Philistine,
Dissemble, swear, protest, vow love to him,   235
He is not of the seed of Abraham. —   *Aside.*
I am a little busy, sir, pray pardon me.
Abigail, bid him welcome for my sake.
  Abig. For your sake and his own he's welcome
    hither.
  Bar. Daughter, a word more; kiss him; speak
    him fair,   240
And like a cunning Jew so cast about,
That ye be both made sure [4] ere you come nigh.
                           [*Aside.*]
  Abig. O father! Don Mathias is my love.
  Bar. I know it: yet I say, make love to him;
Do, it is requisite it should be so —   [*Aside.*]
Nay, on my life, it is my factor's hand —   246
But go you in, I'll think upon the account.

[*Exeunt* ABIGAIL *and* LODOWICK *into the house.*]

The account is made, for Lodowick — dies.
My factor sends me word a merchant's fled
That owes me for a hundred tun of wine.   250
I weigh it thus much [*snapping his fingers*]; I
    have wealth enough.
For now by this has he kiss'd Abigail;
And she vows love to him, and he to her.
As sure as Heaven rain'd manna for the Jews,
So sure shall he and Don Mathias die: 255
His father was my chiefest enemy.

Enter MATHIAS.

Whither goes Don Mathias? Stay awhile.
  Math. Whither, but to my fair love Abigail?
  Bar. Thou know'st, and Heaven can witness
    it is true,
That I intend my daughter shall be thine.   260
  Math. Ay, Barabas, or else thou wrong'st
    me much.
  Bar. O, Heaven forbid I should have such a
    thought.
Pardon me though I weep: the governor's son
Will, whether I will or no, have Abigail:
He sends her letters, bracelets, jewels, rings.
  Math. Does she receive them?   266
  Bar. She? No, Mathias, no, but sends them
    back,
And when he comes, she locks herself up fast;
Yet through the keyhole will he talk to her,
While she runs to the window looking out,   270

[4] Affianced.

When you should come and hale him from the door.

Math. O treacherous Lodowick!

Bar. Even now as I came home, he slipt me in,
And I am sure he is with Abigail.

Math. I 'll rouse him thence.   175

Bar. Not for all Malta, therefore sheathe your sword.
If you love me, no quarrels in my house;
But steal you in, and seem to see him not;
I 'll give him such a warning ere he goes
As he shall have small hopes of Abigail.   280
Away, for here they come.

Re-enter LODOWICK *and* ABIGAIL.

Math. What, hand in hand! I cannot suffer this.

Bar. Mathias, as thou lov'st me, not a word.

Math. Well, let it pass, another time shall serve.   *Exit [into the house.]*

Lod. Barabas, is not that the widow's son?

Bar. Ay, and take heed, for he hath sworn your death.   286

Lod. My death? What, is the base-born peasant mad?

Bar. No, no, but happily he stands in fear
Of that which you, I think, ne'er dream upon,
My daughter here, a paltry silly girl.   290

Lod. Why, loves she Don Mathias?

Bar. Doth she not with her smiling answer you?

Abig. [*Aside.*] He has my heart; I smile against my will.

Lod. Barabas, thou know'st I 've lov'd thy daughter long.

Bar. And so has she done you, even from a child.   295

Lod. And now I can no longer hold my mind.

Bar. Nor I the affection that I bear to you.

Lod. This is thy diamond, tell me shall I have it?

Bar. Win it, and wear it, it is yet unfoil'd.[1]
O! but I know your lordship would disdain   300
To marry with the daughter of a Jew;
And yet I 'll give her many a golden cross [2]
With Christian posies round about the ring.

Lod. 'T is not thy wealth, but her that I esteem,
Yet crave I thy consent.   305

Bar. And mine you have, yet let me talk to her. —
This offspring of Cain, this Jebusite,
That never tasted of the Passover,
Nor e'er shall see the land of Canaan,
Nor our Messias that is yet to come;   310
This gentle maggot, Lodowick, I mean,
Must be deluded. Let him have thy hand,
But keep thy heart till Don Mathias comes.
          Aside.

Abig. What, shall I be betroth'd to Lodowick?

Bar. It 's no sin to deceive a Christian;   315
For they themselves hold it a principle,

Faith is not to be held with heretics;
But all are heretics that are not Jews;
This follows well, and therefore, daughter, fear not. —   [*Aside.*]
I have entreated her, and she will grant.   320

Lod. Then, gentle Abigail, plight thy faith to me.

Abig. I cannot choose, seeing my father bids,
Nothing but death shall part my love and me.

Lod. Now have I that for which my soul hath long'd.   324

Bar. So have not I, but yet I hope I shall.
          Aside.

Abig. [*Aside.*] O wretched Abigail, what hast thou done?

Lod. Why on the sudden is your colour chang'd?

Abig. I know not, but farewell, I must be gone.

Bar. Stay her, but let her not speak one word more.

Lod. Mute o' the sudden! Here 's a sudden change.   330

Bar. O, muse not at it, 't is the Hebrews' guise,
That maidens new betroth'd should weep awhile.
Trouble her not; sweet Lodowick, depart:
She is thy wife, and thou shalt be mine heir.

Lod. O, is 't the custom? Then I am resolv'd:[3]   335
But rather let the brightsome heavens be dim,
And nature's beauty choke with stifling clouds,
Than my fair Abigail should frown on me. —
There comes the villain, now I 'll be reveng'd.

Re-enter MATHIAS.

Bar. Be quiet, Lodowick, it is enough   340
That I have made thee sure [4] to Abigail.

Lod. Well, let him go.   *Exit.*

Bar. Well, but for me, as you went in at doors
You had been stabb'd, but not a word on 't now;
Here must no speeches pass, nor swords be drawn.   345

Math. Suffer me, Barabas, but to follow him.

Bar. No; so shall I, if any hurt be done,
Be made an accessory of your deeds.
Revenge it on him when you meet him next.

Math. For this I 'll have his heart.   350

Bar. Do so; lo, here I give thee Abigail.

Math. What greater gift can poor Mathias have?
Shall Lodowick rob me of so fair a love?
My life is not so dear as Abigail.

Bar. My heart misgives me, that, to cross your love,   355
He 's with your mother; therefore after him.

Math. What, is he gone unto my mother?

Bar. Nay, if you will, stay till she comes herself.

Math. I cannot stay; for if my mother come,
She 'll die with grief.   360
          Exit

---

[1] Q. *unsoyl'd.* But cf. II. iii. 58.

[2] A piece of money with a cross marked on it.

[3] Satisfied.

[4] Betrothed thee.

Abig. I cannot take my leave of him for tears.

Father, why have you thus incens'd them both?

Bar. What's that to thee?

Abig. I'll make 'em friends again.

Bar. You'll make 'em friends! Are there not Jews enow 364
In Malta, but thou must dote upon a Christian?

Abig. I will have Don Mathias; he is my love.

Bar. Yes, you shall have him.—Go, put her in.

Itha. Ay, I'll put her in. [*Puts* ABIGAIL *in.*]

Bar. Now tell me, Ithamore, how lik'st thou this?

Itha. Faith, master, I think by this 370
You purchase both their lives; is it not so?

Bar. True; and it shall be cunningly performd.

Itha. O master, that I might have a hand in this.

Bar. Ay, so thou shalt, 't is thou must do the deed.

Take this, and bear it to Mathias straight, 375
[*Gives a letter.*]
And tell him that it comes from Lodowick.

Itha. 'T is poison'd, is it not?

Bar. No, no, and yet it might be done that way.

It is a challenge feign'd from Lodowick. 379

Itha. Fear not; I will so set his heart afire,
That he shall verily think it comes from him.

Bar. I cannot choose but like thy readiness:
Yet be not rash, but do it cunningly.

Itha. As I behave myself in this, employ me hereafter.

Bar. Away then. *Exit* ITHAMORE.

So, now will I go in to Lodowick, 386
And, like a cunning spirit, feign some lie,
Till I have set 'em both at enmity. *Exit.*

ACT III

[SCENE I.][1]

Enter [BELLAMIRA,] *a Courtesan.*

Bell. Since this town was besieg'd, my gain grows cold.

The time has been that, but for one bare night,
A hundred ducats have been freely given:
But now against my will I must be chaste;
And yet I know my beauty doth not fail. 5
From Venice merchants, and from Padua
Were wont to come rare-witted gentlemen,
Scholars I mean, learned and liberal;
And now, save Pilia-Borsa, comes there none,
And he is very seldom from my house; 10
And here he comes.

Enter PILIA-BORSA.

Pilia. Hold thee, wench, there's something for thee to spend. [*Shews a bag of silver.*]

Bell. 'T is silver. I disdain it.

Pilia. Ay, but the Jew has gold, 15
And I will have it, or it shall go hard.

Court. Tell me, how cam'st thou by this?

Pilia. Faith, walking the back-lanes, through the gardens, I chanc'd to cast mine eye up to the Jew's counting-house, where I saw some [20 bags of money, and in the night I clamber'd up with my hooks, and, as I was taking my choice, I heard a rumbling in the house; so I took only this, and run my way. But here's the Jew's man. 25

Enter ITHAMORE.

Bell. Hide the bag.

Pilia. Look not towards him, let's away. Zoons, what a looking thou keep'st; thou'lt betray's anon.
[*Exeunt* BELLAMIRA *and* PILIA-BORSA.]

Itha. O the sweetest face that ever I beheld! I know she is a courtesan by her attire. Now [30 would I give a hundred of the Jew's crowns that I had such a concubine.

Well, I have deliver'd the challenge in such sort, As meet they will, and fighting die; brave sport! *Exit.*

[SCENE II.][2]

Enter MATHIAS.

Math. This is the place; now Abigail shall see
Whether Mathias holds her dear or no.

Enter LODOWICK.

Math. [*reading*].[3] What, dares the villain write in such base terms?

Lod. I did it; and revenge it if thou dar'st. *They fight.*

Enter BARABAS, *above* [*on a balcony*].

Bar. O! bravely fought; and yet they thrust not home. 5
Now, Lodovico! now, Mathias! So ——
[*Both fall.*]
So now they have show'd themselves to be tall[4] fellows.

[*Cries within.* Part 'em, part 'em.

Bar. Ay, part 'em now they are dead. Farewell, farewell. *Exit.*

Enter FERNEZE, KATHERINE [*and* Attendants].

Fern. What sight is this!—my Lodowick slain! 10
These arms of mine shall be thy sepulchre.

Kath. Who is this? My son Mathias slain!

Fern. O Lodowick! had'st thou perish'd by the Turk,
Wretched Ferneze might have veng'd thy death.

Kath. Thy son slew mine, and I'll revenge his death. 15

Fern. Look, Katherine, look!—thy son gave mine these wounds.

[1] Outside of Bellamira's house.
[2] A street.
[3] Q. places *reading* after *Enter Lodowick*
[4] Brave.

Kath. O leave to grieve me, I am griev'd
    enough.
Fern. O ! that my sighs could turn to lively
    breath ;
And these my tears to blood, that he might live.
Kath. Who made them enemies ?   20
Fern. I know not, and that grieves me most
    of all.
Kath. My son lov'd thine.
Fern.   And so did Lodowick him.
Kath. Lend me that weapon that did kill my
    son,
And it shall murder me.
Fern. Nay, madam, stay ; that weapon was
    my son's,   25
And on that rather should Ferneze die.
Kath. Hold, let 's inquire the causers of their
    deaths,
That we may venge their blood upon their
    heads.
Fern. Then take them up, and let them be
    interr'd
Within one sacred monument of stone ;   30
Upon which altar I will offer up
My daily sacrifice of sighs and tears,
And with my prayers pierce impartial heavens,
Till they [reveal] the causers of our smarts,
Which forc'd their hands divide united hearts.
Come, Katherina, our losses equal are ;   36
Then of true grief let us take equal share.
                    Exeunt [with the bodies].

[SCENE III.][1]

Enter ITHAMORE.

Itha. Why, was there ever seen such villany,
So neatly plotted, and so well perform'd ?
Both held in hand, and flatly both beguil'd ?

Enter ABIGAIL.

Abig. Why, how now, Ithamore, why
    laugh'st thou so ?
Itha. O mistress, ha ! ha ! ha !   5
Abig. Why, what ail'st thou ?
Itha. O my master !
Abig. Ha !
Itha. O mistress ! I have the bravest, gravest,
secret, subtle, bottle-nos'd knave to my master,
that ever gentleman had.   11
Abig. Say, knave, why rail'st upon my father
thus ?
Itha. O, my master has the bravest policy.
Abig. Wherein ?
Itha. Why, know you not ?
Abig. Why, no.   16
Itha. Know you not of Mathias' and Don
Lodowick's disaster ?
Abig. No, what was it ?
Itha. Why, the devil invented a challenge, [20
my master writ it, and I carried it, first to
Lodowick, and *imprimis* to Mathias.
And then they met, [and,] as the story says,
In doleful wise they ended both their days.
Abig. And was my father furtherer of their
deaths ?   25

[1] A room in Barabas's house.

Itha. Am I Ithamore ?
Abig. Yes.
Itha. So sure did your father write, and I
carry the challenge.
Abig. Well, Ithamore, let me request thee
this :   30
Go to the new-made nunnery, and inquire
For any of the friars of Saint Jacques,
And say, I pray them come and speak with me.
Itha. I pray, mistress, will you answer me
but one question ?   35
Abig. Well, sirrah, what is 't ?
Itha. A very feeling one : have not the nuns
fine sport with the friars now and then ?
Abig. Go to, sirrah sauce, is this your ques-
tion ? Get ye gone.   40
Itha. I will, forsooth, mistress.   *Exit.*
Abig. Hard-hearted father, unkind Barabas !
Was this the pursuit [2] of thy policy !
To make me show them favour severally,   44
That by my favour they should both be
    slain ?
Admit thou lov'dst not Lodowick for his sire, [3]
Yet Don Mathias ne'er offended thee :
But thou wert set upon extreme revenge,
Because the [sire] [4] dispossess'd thee once,
And could'st not venge it, but upon his son,   50
Nor on his son, but by Mathias' means ;
Nor on Mathias, but by murdering me.
But I perceive there is no love on earth,
Pity in Jews, nor piety in Turks.   54
But here comes cursed Ithamore, with the friar.

Enter ITHAMORE *and* Friar [JACOMO].

F. Jac. Virgo, salve.
Itha. When ! duck you !
Abig. Welcome, grave friar ; Ithamore, be-
    gone.   *Exit* [ITHAMORE].
Know, holy sir, I am bold to solicit thee.
F. Jac. Wherein ?   60
Abig. To get me be admitted for a nun.
F. Jac. Why, Abigail, it is not yet long since
That I did labour thy admission,
And then thou did'st not like that holy life.
Abig. Then were my thoughts so frail and
    unconfirm'd,   65
And I was chain'd to follies of the world :
But now experience, purchased with grief,
Has made me see the difference of things.
My sinful soul, alas, hath pac'd too long
The fatal labyrinth of misbelief,   70
Far from the Sun [5] that gives eternal life.
F. Jac. Who taught thee this ?
Abig.   The abbess of the house,
Whose zealous admonition I embrace :
O, therefore, Jacomo, let me be one,
Although unworthy, of that sisterhood.   75
F. Jac. Abigail, I will, but see thou change
no more,
For that will be most heavy to thy soul.
Abig. That was my father's fault.
F. Jac.   Thy father's ! how ?
Abig. Nay, you shall pardon me. [*Aside.*] O
    Barabas,

---

[2] Object.   [4] Q. *Pryor. Sire,* Tucker Brooke
[3] Q. *sinne.*   [5] Q. *Sonne.*

Though thou deservest hardly at my hands,   80
Yet never shall these lips bewray[1] thy life.
  F. Jac. Come, shall we go?
  Abig.   My duty waits on you.
                                  Exeunt.

[SCENE IV.][2]

Enter BARABAS, *reading a letter.*

  Bar. What, Abigail become a nun again!
False and unkind[3]; what, hast thou lost thy
    father?
And all unknown, and unconstrain'd of me,
Art thou again got to the nunnery?
Now here she writes, and wills me to repent.   5
Repentance! *Spurca!* what pretendeth[4] this?
I fear she knows — 'tis so — of my device
In Don Mathias' and Lodovico's deaths.
If so, 't is time that it be seen into;
For she that varies from me in belief   10
Gives great presumption that she loves me not;
Or loving, doth dislike of something done.
But who comes here?

[*Enter* ITHAMORE.]

              O Ithamore, come near;
Come near, my love; come near, thy master's
    life.
My trusty servant, nay, my second [self]:[5]   15
For I have now no hope but even in thee,
And on that hope my happiness is built.
When saw'st thou Abigail?
  Itha.   To-day.
  Bar.   With whom?
  Itha. A friar.
  Bar. A friar! false villain, he hath done the
    deed.   20
  Itha. How, sir?
  Bar. Why, made mine Abigail a nun.
  Itha. That's no lie, for she sent me for him.
  Bar. O unhappy day!
False, credulous, inconstant Abigail!
But let 'em go: and, Ithamore, from hence   25
Ne'er shall she grieve me more with her dis-
    grace;
Ne'er shall she live to inherit aught of mine,
Be blest of me, nor come within my gates,
But perish underneath my bitter curse,
Like Cain by Adam for his brother's death.   30
  Itha. O master!
  Bar. Ithamore, entreat not for her, I am
    mov'd,
And she is hateful to my soul and me:
And 'less[6] I yield to this that I entreat,
I cannot think but that thou hat'st my life.   35
  Itha. Who, I, master? Why, I'll run to some
    rock,
And throw myself headlong into the sea;
Why, I'll do anything for your sweet sake.
  Bar. O trusty Ithamore, no servant, but my
    friend,
I here adopt thee for mine only heir,   40
All that I have is thine when I am dead,
And whilst I live use half; spend as myself.
Here take my keys, — I'll give 'em thee anon.

Go buy thee garments; but thou shalt not
  want:
Only know this, that thus thou art to do: 45
But first go fetch me in the pot of rice
That for our supper stands upon the fire.
  Itha. [*Aside.*] I hold my head my master's
    hungry.— I go, sir.   *Exit.*
  Bar. Thus every villain ambles after wealth,
Although he ne'er be richer than in hope.   50
But, hush't!

        Re-enter ITHAMORE *with the pot.*

  Itha. Here 't is, master.
  Bar.   Well said, Ithamore.
What, hast thou brought the ladle with thee too?
  Itha. Yes, sir, the proverb says he that eats
with the devil had need of a long spoon. I have
brought you a ladle.   55
  Bar. Very well, Ithamore, then now be se-
    cret;
And for thy sake, whom I so dearly love,
Now shalt thou see the death of Abigail,
That thou may'st freely live to be my heir.
  Itha. Why, master, will you poison her [60
with a mess of rice porridge? That will preserve
life, make her round and plump, and batten[7]
more than you are aware.
  Bar. Ay, but, Ithamore, seest thou this?
It is a precious powder that I bought   65
Of an Italian in Ancona once,
Whose operation is to bind, infect,
And poison deeply, yet not appear
In forty hours after it is ta'en.
  Itha. How, master?   70
  Bar. Thus, Ithamore.
This even they use in Malta here, — 't is called
Saint Jacques' Even,— and then I say they use
To send their alms unto the nunneries.
Among the rest bear this, and set it there;   75
There's a dark entry where they take it in,
Where they must neither see the messenger,
Nor make inquiry who hath sent it them.
  Itha. How so?
  Bar. Belike there is some ceremony in't.   80
There, Ithamore, must thou go place this pot!
Stay, let me spice it first.
  Itha. Pray do, and let me help you, master.
Pray let me taste first.
  Bar. Prythee do [ITHAMORE *tastes*]. What
say'st thou now?   85
  Itha. Troth, master, I'm loth such a pot of
pottage should be spoil'd.
  Bar. Peace, Ithamore, 't is better so than
spar'd.
Assure thyself thou shalt have broth by the eye,[8]
My purse, my coffer, and myself is thine.   90
  Itha. Well, master, I go.
  Bar. Stay, first let me stir it, Ithamore.
As fatal be it to her as the draught
Of which great Alexander drunk and died:
And with her let it work like Borgia's wine,   95
Whereof his sire, the Pope, was poisoned.
In few,[9] the blood of Hydra, Lerna's bane,
The juice of hebon,[10] and Cocytus' breath,

---

[1] Reveal.   [3] Unnatural.   [5] Q. *life.*
[2] The same.   [4] Meaneth.   [6] Q. *least.*

[7] Feed.   [8] In abundance.   [9] In short
[10] A poison not certainly identified.

And all the poisons of the Stygian pool
Break from the fiery kingdom ; and in this   100
Vomit your venom and invenom her
That like a fiend hath left her father thus.
  Itha. [*Aside.*] What a blessing has he given 't !
Was ever pot of rice porridge so sauc'd ! — What
shall I do with it ?   105
  Bar. O, my sweet Ithamore, go set it down,
And come again so soon as thou hast done,
For I have other business for thee.
  Itha. Here 's a drench to poison a whole stable
of Flanders mares. I 'll carry 't to the nuns [110
with a powder.
  Bar. And the horse pestilence to boot ; away !
  Itha. I am gone.
Pay me my wages, for my work is done. *Exit.*
  Bar. I 'll pay thee with a vengeance, Itha-
more.   *Exit.* 115

[SCENE V.]¹

Enter FERNEZE, DEL BOSCO, Knights, *and*
Basso.

  Fern. Welcome, great basso ; how fares Caly-
math ?
What wind drives you thus into Malta-road ?
  Bas. The wind that bloweth all the world
besides, —
Desire of gold.
  Fern.   Desire of gold, great sir ?
That 's to be gotten in the Western Ind :   5
In Malta are no golden minerals.
  Bas. To you of Malta thus saith Calymath :
The time you took for respite is at hand,
For the performance of your promise pass'd,
And for the tribute-money I am sent.   10
  Fern. Basso, in brief, shalt have no tribute
here,
Nor shall the heathens live upon our spoil.
First will we raze the city walls ourselves,
Lay waste the island, hew the temples down,
And, shipping off our goods to Sicily,   15
Open an entrance for the wasteful sea,
Whose billows beating the resistless banks,
Shall overflow it with their refluence.
  Bas. Well, Governor, since thou hast broke
the league
By flat denial of the promis'd tribute,   20
Talk not of razing down your city walls.
You shall not need trouble yourselves so far,
For Selim Calymath shall come himself,
And with brass bullets batter down your towers,
And turn proud Malta to a wilderness   25
For these intolerable wrongs of yours ;
And so farewell.
  Fern. Farewell.   [*Exit* Basso.]
And now, you men of Malta, look about,
And let 's provide to welcome Calymath.   30
Close your portcullis, charge your basilisks,²
And as you profitably take up arms,
So now courageously encounter them ;
For by this answer, broken is the league,
And naught is to be look'd for now but wars, 35
And naught to us more welcome is than wars.
                                       Exeunt.

¹ The council-house.   ² Cannon.

[SCENE VI.]³

Enter Friar [JACOMO] *and* Friar [BARNARDINE].

  F. [*Jac.*] O, brother, brother, all the nuns are
sick,
And physic will not help them ; they must die
  F. [*Barn.*] The abbess sent for me to be con
fess'd :
O, what a sad confession will there be !
  F. Jac. And so did fair Maria send for me. 1
I 'll to her lodging ; hereabouts she lies. *Exit.*

Enter ABIGAIL.

  F. Barn. What, all dead, save only Abigail ?
  Abig. And I shall die too, for I feel death
coming.
Where is the friar that convers'd with me ?   9
  F. Barn. O, he is gone to see the other nuns.
  Abig. I sent for him, but seeing you are come,
Be you my ghostly father : and first know,
That in this house I liv'd religiously,
Chaste, and devout, much sorrowing for my sins ;
But ere I came ——   15
  F. Barn. What then ?
  Abig. I did offend high Heaven so grievously,
As I am almost desperate for my sins ;
And one offence torments me more than all.
You knew Mathias and Don Lodowick ?   20
  F. Barn. Yes, what of them ?
  Abig. My father did contract me to 'em both :
First to Don Lodowick ; him I never lov'd ;
Mathias was the man that I held dear,
And for his sake did I become a nun.   25
  F. Barn. So, say how was their end ?
  Abig. Both jealous of my love, envied⁴ each
other,
And by my father's practice,⁵ which is there
Set down at large, the gallants were both slain.
                          [*Gives a written paper.*]
  F. Barn. O monstrous villainy !   30
  Abig. To work my peace, this I confess to
thee ;
Reveal it not, for then my father dies.
  F. Barn. Know that confession must not be
reveal'd,
The canon law forbids it, and the priest
That makes it known, being degraded first,   35
Shall be condemn'd, and then sent to the fire.
  Abig. So I have heard ; pray, therefore keep
it close.⁶
Death seizeth on my heart : ah, gentle friar,
Convert my father that he may be sav'd,
And witness that I die a Christian. [*Dies.*] 40
  F. Barn. Ay, and a virgin too ; that grieves
me most.
But I must to the Jew and exclaim on him,
And make him stand in fear of me.

Re-enter Friar [JACOMO].

  F. Jac. O brother, all the nuns are dead, let 's
bury them.
  F. Barn. First help to bury this, then go with
me   45
And help me to exclaim against the Jew.

³ The interior of a convent.   ⁵ Plot.
⁴ Hated.   ⁶ Secret.

F. Jac. Why, what has he done?
F. Barn. A thing that makes me tremble to
unfold.
F. Jac. What, has he crucified a child?
F. Barn. No, but a worse thing: 't was told
me in shrift,   50
Thou know'st 't is death an if it be reveal'd.
Come, let 's away.   *Exeunt.*

ACT IV

[SCENE I.]¹

Enter BARABAS *and* ITHAMORE. *Bells within.*

Bar. There is no music to² a Christian's
knell:
How sweet the bells ring now the nuns are dead,
That sound at other times like tinker's pans!
I was afraid the poison had not wrought;
Or, though it wrought, it would have done no
good,   5
For every year they swell, and yet they live;
Now all are dead, not one remains alive.
Itha. That 's brave, master, but think you it
will not be known?
Bar. How can it, if we two be secret?   10
Itha. For my part fear you not.
Bar. I 'd cut thy throat if I did.
Itha. And reason too.
But here 's a royal monastery hard by;
Good master, let me poison all the monks.   15
Bar. Thou shalt not need, for now the nuns
are dead
They 'll die with grief.
Itha. Do you not sorrow for your daughter's
death?
Bar. No, but I grieve because she liv'd so
long.
An Hebrew born, and would become a Chris-
tian!   20
*Cazzo,*³ *diabolo.*

Enter Friar JACOMO *and* Friar BARNARDINE.

Itha. Look, look, master, here come two re-
ligious caterpillars.
Bar. I smelt 'em ere they came.   24
Itha. God-a-mercy, nose! Come, let 's begone.
F. Barn. Stay, wicked Jew, repent, I say,
and stay.
F. Jac. Thou hast offended, therefore must
be damn'd.
Bar. I fear they know we sent the poison'd
broth.
Itha. And so do I, master; therefore speak
'em fair.
F. Barn. Barabas, thou hast ——   30
F. Jac. Ay, that thou hast ——
Bar. True, I have money, what though I
have?
F. Barn. Thou art a ——
F. Jac. Ay, that thou art, a ——
Bar. What needs all this? I know I am a Jew.
F. Barn. Thy daughter ——   36

F. Jac. Ay, thy daughter ——
Bar. O speak not of her! then I die with
grief.
F. Barn. Remember that ——
F. Jac. Ay, remember that ——   40
Bar. I must needs say that I have been a
great usurer.
F. Barn. Thou hast committed ——
Bar. Fornication — but that was in another
country; and besides, the wench is dead.
F. Barn. Ay, but, Barabas,   45
Remember Mathias and Don Lodowick.
Bar. Why, what of them?
F. Barn. I will not say that by a forg'd chal-
lenge they met.
Bar. [*Aside.*] She has confest, and we are
both undone, —
My bosom inmates! —— but I must dis-
semble. —   *Aside.*
O holy friars, the burden of my sins   51
Lie heavy on my soul; then pray you tell me,
Is 't not too late now to turn Christian?
I have been zealous in the Jewish faith,
Hard-hearted to the poor, a covetous wretch, 55
That would for lucre's sake have sold my soul.
A hundred for a hundred I have ta'en;
And now for store of wealth may I compare
With all the Jews of Malta; but what is
wealth?
I am a Jew, and therefore am I lost.   60
Would penance serve [to atone]⁴ for this my
sin,
I could afford to whip myself to death ——
Itha. And so could I; but penance will not
serve.
Bar. To fast, to pray, and wear a shirt of
hair,
And on my knees creep to Jerusalem.   65
Cellars of wine, and sollars⁵ full of wheat,
Warehouses stuff'd with spices and with drugs,
Whole chests of gold, in bullion, and in coin,
Besides I know not how much weight in pearl,
Orient and round, have I within my house; 70
At Alexandria, merchandise unsold:
But yesterday two ships went from this town,
Their voyage will be worth ten thousand crowns.
In Florence, Venice, Antwerp, London, Seville,
Frankfort, Lubeck, Moscow, and where not, 75
Have I debts owing; and in most of these,
Great sums of money lying in the banco;
All this I 'll give to some religious house
So I may be baptiz'd, and live therein.
F. Jac. O good Barabas, come to our house.
F. Barn. O no, good Barabas, come to our
house;   81
And, Barabas, you know ——
Bar. I know that I have highly sinn'd.
You shall convert me, you shall have all my
wealth.
F. Jac. O Barabas, their laws are strict. 85
Bar. I know they are, and I will be with you.
F. Barn. They wear no shirts, and they go
barefoot too.
Bar. Then 't is not for me; and I am resolv'd
You shall confess me, and have all my goods.

---

¹ A street.   ² Equal to.   ³ A petty oath. (Italian).

⁴ Dyce emend. Q. omits.   ⁵ Lofts.

F. Jac. Good Barabas, come to me.   90
Bar. You see I answer him, and yet he stays ;
Rid him away, and go you home with me.
F. Jac. I 'll be with you to-night.
Bar. Come to my house at one o'clock this
    night.
F. Jac. You hear your answer, and you may
    be gone.   95
F. Barn. Why, go, get you away.
F. Jac. I will not go for thee.
F. Barn. Not ! then I 'll make thee, [rogue].[1]
F. Jac. How, dost call me rogue ? *They fight.*
Itha. Part 'em, master, part 'em.   100
[*Bar.*] This is mere frailty, brethren ; be con-
    tent.
Friar Barnardine, go you with Ithamore :
You know my mind, let me alone with him.
                    [*Aside to* F. BARNARDINE.]
F. Jac. Why does he go to thy house ? Let
    him be gone.
Bar. I 'll give him something and so stop his
    mouth.   105

Exit [ITHAMORE *with* Friar BARNARDINE]

I never heard of any man but he
Malign'd the order of the Jacobins :
But do you think that I believe his words ?
Why, brother, you converted Abigail ;
And I am bound in charity to requite it,   110
And so I will. O Jacomo, fail not, but come.
    F. Jac. But, Barabas, who shall be your god-
    fathers ?
For presently you shall be shriv'd.
    Bar. Marry, the Turk[2] shall be one of my
    godfathers,
But not a word to any of your covent.[3]   115
    F. Jac. I warrant thee, Barabas.   *Exit.*
    Bar. So, now the fear is past, and I am safe,
For he that shriv'd her is within my house ;
What if I murder'd him ere Jacomo comes ?
Now I have such a plot for both their lives   120
As never Jew nor Christian knew the like :
One turn'd my daughter, therefore he shall die ;
The other knows enough to have my life,
Therefore 't is not requisite he should live.
But are not both these wise men to suppose   125
That I will leave my house, my goods, and all,
To fast and be well whipt ? I 'll none of that.
Now, I 'll feast you, lodge you, give you fair words,
And after that, I and my trusty Turk —   130
No more, but so : it must and shall be done.
                    [*Exit.*]

[SCENE II.][4]

Enter [BARABAS *and*] ITHAMORE.

Bar. Ithamore, tell me, is the friar asleep ?
Itha. Yes ; and I know not what the reason is,
Do what I can he will not strip himself,
Nor go to bed, but sleeps in his own clothes.
I fear me he mistrusts what we intend.   5
Bar. No, 't is an order which the friars use.
Yet, if he knew our meanings, could he scape ?

Itha. No, none can hear him, cry he ne'er so
    loud.
Bar. Why, true, therefore did I place him
    there.
The other chambers open towards the street.   10
Itha. You loiter, master ; wherefore stay we
    thus ?
O how I long to see him shake his heels.
Bar. Come on, sirrah.
Off with your girdle, make a handsome noose.
        [ITHAMORE *takes off his girdle and
        ties a noose in it.*]
Friar, awake !   15
        [*They put the noose round the* Friar's
        neck.]
F. Barn. What, do you mean to strangle me ?
Itha. Yes, 'cause you use to confess.
Bar. Blame not us but the proverb, " Con-
fess and be hanged." Pull hard !
F. Barn. What, will you [have][5] my life ?   20
Bar. Pull hard, I say. — You would have had
    my goods.
Itha. Ay, and our lives too, therefore pull
    amain.   [*They strangle him.*]
'T is neatly done, sir, here 's no print at all.
Bar. Then is it as it should be ; take him up.
Itha. Nay, master, be rul'd by me a little.   25
[*Stands the body upright against the wall and puts
a staff in its hand.*] So, let him lean upon his
staff. Excellent ! he stands as if he were beg-
ging of bacon.[6]
Bar. Who would not think but that this friar
    liv'd ?   30
What time o' night is 't now, sweet Ithamore ?
Itha. Towards one.
Bar. Then will not Jacomo be long from
    hence.   [*Exeunt.*]

[SCENE III.][7]

Enter Friar JACOMO.

F. Jac. This is the hour wherein I shall pro-
    ceed ;[8]
O happy hour wherein I shall convert
An infidel, and bring his gold into
Our treasury !
But soft, is not this Barnardine ? It is ;   5
And, understanding I should come this way,
Stands here a purpose, meaning me some wrong,
And intercept my going to the Jew. —
Barnardine !
Wilt thou not speak ? Thou think'st I see thee
    not ;   10
Away, I 'd wish thee, and let me go by.
No, wilt thou not ? Nay, then, I 'll force my way :
And see, a staff stands ready for the purpose :
As thou lik'st that, stop me another time.
        [*Takes the staff and] strikes the
        body, which falls down.*]

Enter BARABAS [*and* ITHAMORE].

Bar. Why, how now, Jacomo, what hast thou
    done ?   15

1 So Tucker Brooke. Q. *goe.*
2 Ithamore.   3 Convent.
4 A room in the house of Barabas.
5 Q. *save.*
6 It would appear from the following scene that the
body was stood up outside of the house.
7 Outside Barabas's house.   8 Succeed.

F. Jac. Why, stricken him that would have struck at me.

Bar. Who is it? Barnardine! Now out, alas, he's slain!

Itha. Ay, master, he's slain; look how his brains drop out on's nose. 19

F. Jac. Good sirs, I have done't, but nobody knows it but you two; I may escape.

Bar. So might my man and I hang with you for company.

Itha. No, let us bear him to the magistrates.

F. Jac. Good Barabas, let me go. 25

Bar. No, pardon me; the law must have its course.
I must be forc'd to give in evidence,
That being importun'd by this Barnardine
To be a Christian, I shut him out,
And there he sat. Now I, to keep my word, 30
And give my goods and substance to your house,
Was up thus early; with intent to go
Unto your friary, because you stay'd.[1]

Itha. Fie upon 'em, master; will you turn Christian when holy friars turn devils and [35 murder one another?

Bar. No, for this example I'll remain a Jew:
Heaven bless me! What, a friar a murderer?
When shall you see a Jew commit the like?

Itha. Why, a Turk could ha' done no more. 40

Bar. To-morrow is the sessions; you shall to it.
Come, Ithamore, let's help to take him hence.

F. Jac. Villains, I am a sacred person; touch me not.

Bar. The law shall touch you, we'll but lead you, we.
'Las, I could weep at your calamity! 45
Take in the staff too, for that must be shown:
Law wills that each particular be known.

Exeunt.

[SCENE IV.][2]

Enter Courtesan [BELLAMIRA] *and* PILIA-BORSA.

Bell. Pilia-Borsa, did'st thou meet with Ithamore?

Pilia. I did.

Bell. And did'st thou deliver my letter?

Pilia. I did.

Bell. And what think'st thou? Will he come? 5

Pilia. I think so, and yet I cannot tell; for at the reading of the letter he look'd like a man of another world.

Bell. Why so?

Pilia. That such a base slave as he should [10 be saluted by such a tall[3] man as I am, from such a beautiful dame as you.

Bell. And what said he?

Pilia. Not a wise word, only gave me a nod, as who should say, "Is it even so?" and so I [15 left him, being driven to a non-plus at the critical aspect of my terrible countenance.

Bell. And where didst meet him?

Pilia. Upon mine own freehold, within forty feet of the gallows, conning his neck-verse, [20 I take it, looking of[4] a friar's execution, whom I saluted with an old hempen proverb, *Hodie tibi, cras mihi,* and so I left him to the mercy of the hangman: but the exercise[5] being done, see where he comes. 25

Enter ITHAMORE.

Itha. I never knew a man take his death so patiently as this friar. He was ready to leap off ere the halter was about his neck; and when the hangman had put on his hempen tippet, he made such haste to his prayers, as if he had [30 had another cure to serve. Well, go whither he will, I'll be none of his followers in haste: and, now I think on't, going to the execution, a fellow met with me with a muschatoes[6] like a raven's wing, and a dagger with a hilt like a warm- [35 ing-pan, and he gave me a letter from one Madam Bellamira, saluting me in such sort as if he had meant to make clean my boots with his lips; the effect was, that I should come to her house. I wonder what the reason is; it [40 may be she sees more in me than I can find in myself: for she writes further, that she loves me ever since she saw me, and who would not requite such love? Here's her house, and here she comes, and now would I were gone; I am [45 not worthy to look upon her.

Pilia. This is the gentleman you writ to.

Itha. [*Aside.*] Gentleman! he flouts me; what gentry can be in a poor Turk of tenpence? I'll be gone. 50

Bell. Is't not a sweet-fac'd youth, Pilia?

Itha. [*Aside.*] Again, "sweet youth!" — Did not you, sir, bring the sweet youth a letter?

Pilia. I did, sir, and from this gentlewoman, who, as myself, and the rest of the family, [55 stand or fall at your service.

Bell. Though woman's modesty should hale me back,
I can withhold no longer; welcome, sweet love.

Itha. [*Aside.*] Now am I clean, or rather foully, out of the way. 60

Bell. Whither so soon?

Itha. [*Aside.*] I'll go steal some money from my master to make me handsome.—Pray pardon me, I must go and see a ship discharg'd.

Bell. Canst thou be so unkind to leave me thus? 65

Pilia. An ye did but know how she loves you, sir.

Itha. Nay, I care not how much she loves me—Sweet Bellamira, would I had my master's wealth for thy sake!

Pilia. And you can have it, sir, an if you please. 70

Itha. If 'twere above ground, I could and would have it; but he hides and buries it up, as partridges do their eggs, under the earth.

Pilia. And is't not possible to find it out?

Itha. By no means possible. 75

Bell. [*Aside to* PILIA-BORSA.] What shall we do with this base villain then?

---

[1] Delayed.

[2] A verandah of Bellamira's house. [3] Brave.

[4] At. [5] Service. [6] Mustachios

Pilia. [*Aside to her.*] Let me alone; do but
you speak him fair.
But, [sir.] you know some secrets of the Jew,
Which, if they were reveal'd, would do him
harm.   79
Itha. Ay, and such as — Go to, no more! I 'll
make him send me half he has, and glad he
scapes so too. Pen and ink! I 'll write unto
him; we 'll have money straight.
Pilia. Send for a hundred crowns at least.
[ITHAMORE] *writes.*
Itha. Ten hundred thousand crowns. "Master
Barabas."   85
Pilia. Write not so submissively, but threat-
'ning him.
Itha. [*writing.*] "Sirrah, Barabas, send me a
hundred crowns."
Pilia. Put in two hundred at least.
Itha. [*writing.*] "I charge thee send me three
hundred by this bearer, and this shall be [90
your warrant: if you do not — no more, but so."
Pilia. Tell him you will confess.
Itha. [*writing.*] "Otherwise I 'll confess all."
— Vanish, and return in a twinkle.
Pilia. Let me alone; I 'll use him in his
kind.   95
[*Exit* PILIA-BORSA *with the letter.*]
Itha. Hang him, Jew!
Bell. Now, gentle Ithamore, lie in my lap.—
Where are my maids? Provide a running[1] ban-
quet;
Send to the merchant, bid him bring me silks,
Shall Ithamore, my love, go in such rags? 100
Itha. And bid the jeweller come hither too.
Bell. I have no husband, sweet; I 'll marry
thee.
Itha. Content: but we will leave this paltry
land,
And sail from hence to Greece, to lovely Greece.
I 'll be thy Jason, thou my golden fleece; 105
Where painted carpets o'er the meads are
hurl'd,
And Bacchus' vineyards overspread the world;
Where woods and forests go in goodly green,
I 'll be Adonis, thou shalt be Love's Queen.
The meads, the orchards, and the primrose-
lanes,   110
Instead of sedge and reed, bear sugar-canes;
Thou in those groves, by Dis above,
Shalt live with me and be my love.
Bell. Whither will I not go with gentle Itha-
more?

Re-enter PILIA-BORSA.

Itha. How now! hast thou the gold?   115
Pilia. Yes.
Itha. But came it freely? Did the cow give
down her milk freely?
Pilia. At reading of the letter, he star'd and
stamp'd and turn'd aside. I took him by [120
the beard, and look'd upon him thus; told him
he were best to send it; then he hugg'd and
embrac'd me.
Itha. Rather for fear than love.
Pilia. Then, like a Jew, he laugh'd and [125

jeer'd, and told me he iov'd me for your sake,
and said what a faithful servant you had been.
Itha. The more villain he to keep me thus.
Here 's goodly 'parel, is there not?   129
Pilia. To conclude. he gave me ten crowns.
[*Gives the money to* ITHAMORE.]
Itha. But ten? I 'll not leave him worth a
grey groat. Give me a ream[2] of paper; we 'll
have a kingdom of gold for 't.
Pilia. Write for five hundred crowns.   134
Itha. [*writing.*] "Sirrah, Jew, as you love your
life send me five hundred crowns, and give the
bearer one hundred." Tell him I must have 't.
Pilia. I warrant your worship shall have 't.
Itha. And if he ask why I demand so much.
tell him I scorn to write a line under a hundred
crowns.   141
Pilia. You 'd make a rich poet, sir. I am
gone.   *Exit.*
Itha. Take thou the money: spend it for my
sake.
Bell. 'T is not thy money, but thyself I
weigh;
Thus Bellamira esteems of gold.   145
[*Throws it aside.*]
But thus of thee.   *Kisses him.*
Itha. That kiss again! she runs division[3] of
my lips.
What an eye she casts on me! It twinkles like
a star.
Bell. Come, my dear love, let 's in and sleep
together.   149
Itha. O, that ten thousand nights were put
in one, that we might sleep seven years together
afore we wake!
Bell. Come, amorous wag, first banquet, and
then sleep.   *Exeunt.*

[SCENE V.][4]

Enter BARABAS, *reading a letter.*

Bar. "Barabas, send me three hundred
crowns. —"
Plain Barabas! O, that wicked courtesan!
He was not wont to call me Barabas.
"Or else I will confess:" ay, there it goes:
But, if I get him, *coupe de gorge* for that.   6
He sent a shaggy totter'd[5] staring slave,
That when he speaks draws out his grisly
beard,
And winds it twice or thrice about his ear:
Whose face has been a grindstone for men's
swords;
His hands are hack'd, some fingers cut quite
off;   10
Who, when he speaks, grunts like a hog, and
looks
Like one that is employ'd in catzerie[6]
And crossbiting,[7] — such a rogue
As is the husband to a hundred whores:
And I by him must send three hundred crowns!
Well, my hope is, he will not stay there still: 16
And when he comes, — O, that he were but here!

2 The early form of *realm* had no "l."
3 A musical term.
4 The street.
5 Tattered.
6 Knavery.
7 Playing sham husband to a courtesan.

1 Hasty.

Enter PILIA-BORSA.

Pilia. Jew, I must ha' more gold.
Bar. Why, want'st thou any of thy tale ? [1]
Pilia. No; but three hundred will not serve
his turn.   21
Bar. Not serve his turn, sir ?
Pilia. No, sir; and, therefore, I must have
five hundred more.
Bar. I 'll rather ——   25
Pilia. O good words, sir, and send it you
were best ! See, there 's his letter. [*Gives letter.*]
Bar. Might he not as well come as send ?
Pray bid him come and fetch it; what he writes
for you, ye shall have straight.   30
Pilia. Ay, and the rest too, or else ——
Bar. [*Aside.*] I must make this villain
away.— Please you dine with me, sir ; — and
you shall be most heartily poison'd.

                         Aside.
Pilia. No, God-a-mercy. Shall I have these
crowns ?   35
Bar. I cannot do it, I have lost my keys.
Pilia. O, if that be all, I can pick ope your locks.
Bar. Or climb up to my counting-house win-
dow : you know my meaning.
Pilia. I know enough, and therefore talk not
to me of your counting-house. The gold ! or [41
know, Jew, it is in my power to hang thee.
Bar. [*Aside.*] I am betray'd. —
'T is not five hundred crowns that I esteem,
I am not mov'd at that : this angers me,   45
That he, who knows I love him as myself,
Should write in this imperious vein. Why, sir,
You know I have no child, and unto whom
Should I leave all but unto Ithamore ?
Pilia. Here 's many words, but no crowns.
The crowns !   50
Bar. Commend me to him, sir, most humbly,
And unto your good mistress, as unknown.
Pilia. Speak, shall I have 'em, sir ?
Bar.   Sir, here they are. —
                     [*Gives money.*]
O, that I should part with so much gold! —
Here, take 'em, fellow, with as good a will——
[*Aside*] ; As I would see thee hang'd.—O, love
stops my breath :   56
Never lov'd man servant as I do Ithamore !
Pilia. I know it, sir.
Bar. Pray, when, sir, shall I see you at my
house ?
Pilia. Soon enough, to your cost, sir. Fare
you well.   *Exit.*   60
Bar. Nay, to thine own cost, villain, if thou
com'st !
Was ever Jew tormented as I am ?
To have a shag-rag knave to come, —
Three hundred crowns, — and then five hundred
crowns !
Well, I must seek a means to rid 'em all,   65
And presently ; for in his villany
He will tell all he knows, and I shall die for 't.
I have it :
I will in some disguise go see the slave,   69
And how the villain revels with my gold. *Exit.*

     [1] Sum, number.

[SCENE VI.] [2]

Enter Courtezan [BELLAMIRA,] ITHAMORE, *and*
PILIA-BORSA.

Bell. I 'll pledge thee, love, and therefore
drink it off.
Itha. Say'st thou me so ? Have at it ; and, do
you hear ?   [*Whispers.*]
Bell. Go to, it shall be so.
Itha. Of that condition I will drink it up.
Here 's to thee !
Bell.   Nay, I 'll have all or none.   5
Itha. There, if thou lov'st me, do not leave a
drop.
Bell. Love thee ! fill me three glasses.
Itha. Three and fifty dozen, I 'll pledge thee.
Pilia. Knavely spoke, and like a knight-at-
arms.
Itha. Hey, *Rivo Castiliano !* [3] a man 's a man !
Bell. Now to the Jew.   11
Itha. Ha ! to the Jew, and send me money he
were best.
Pilia. What would 'st thou do if he should
send thee none ?
Itha. Do nothing ; but I know what I know ;
he 's a murderer.
Bell. I had not thought he had been so brave
a man.   15
Itha. You knew Mathias and the governor's
son ; he and I killed 'em both, and yet never
touch'd 'em.
Pilia. O, bravely done.   20
Itha. I carried the broth that poison'd the
nuns ; and he and I, snickle hand too fast, [4]
strangled a friar.
Bell. You two alone ?
Itha. We two ; and 't was never known, nor
never shall be for me.   26
Pilia. [*Aside to* BELLAMIRA.] This shall with
me unto the governor.
Bell. [*Aside to* PILIA-BORSA.] And fit it
should : but first let 's ha' more gold, —
Come, gentle Ithamore, lie in my lap.
Itha. Love me little, love me long. Let music
rumble   30
Whilst I in thy incony [5] lap do tumble.

Enter BARABAS, *with a lute, disguis'd.*

Bell. A French musician ! Come, let 's hear
your skill.
Bar. Must tuna my lute for sound, twang,
twang, first.
Itha. Wilt drink, Frenchman ? Here 's to [35
thee with a —— Pox on this drunken hiccup !
Bar. Gramercy, monsieur.
Bell. Prythee, Pilia-Borsa, bid the fiddler
give me the posy in his hat there.
Pilia. Sirrah, you must give my mistress
your posy.   41
Bar. À votre commandement, madame.
Bell. How sweet, my Ithamore, the flowers
smell !

     [2] A verandah of Bellamira's house.
     [3] A familar Bacchanalian exclamation
     [4] Probably corrupt. " Snickle " is a noose.
     [5] Dainty, sweet.

Itha. Like thy breath, sweetheart ; no violet
like 'em.   45
Pilia. Foh ! methinks they stink like a holly-
hock.
Bar. [*Aside.*] So, now I am reveng'd upon
'em all.
The scent thereof was death ; I poison'd it.
Itha. Play, fiddler, or I 'll cut your cat's guts
into chitterlings.   51
Bar. Pardonnez moi, be no in tune yet ; so
now, now all be in.
Itha. Give him a crown, and fill me out more
wine.
Pilia. There 's two crowns for thee ; play.   55
Bar. (*Aside.*) How liberally the villain gives
me mine own gold !   [*Plays.*]
Pilia. Methinks he fingers very well.
Bar. (*Aside.*) So did you when you stole my
gold.   60
Pilia. How swift he runs !
Bar. (*Aside.*) You run swifter when you
threw my gold out of my window.
Bell. Musician, hast been in Malta long ?
Bar. Two, three, four month, madame.   65
Itha. Dost not know a Jew, one Barabas ?
Bar. Very mush ; monsieur, you no be his
man ?
Pilia. His man ?
Itha. I scorn the peasant ; tell him so.   70
Bar. [*Aside.*] He knows it already.
Itha. 'T is a strange thing of that Jew, he
lives upon pickled grasshoppers and sauc'd
mushrooms.
Bar. (*Aside.*) What a slave 's this ? The gov-
ernor feeds not as I do.   76
Itha. He never put on clean shirt since he was
circumcis'd.
Bar. (*Aside.*) O rascal ! I change myself twice
a day.   80
Itha. The hat he wears, Judas left under the
elder when he hang'd himself. [1]
Bar. (*Aside.*) 'T was sent me for a present
from the great Cham.
Pilia. A musty [2] slave he is ; — Whither now,
fiddler ?   86
Bar. Pardonnez moi, monsieur, me be no well.
                                                       Exit.
Pilia. Farewell, fiddler ! One letter more to
the Jew.
Bell. Prythee, sweet love, one more, and
write it sharp.   90
Itha. No, I 'll send by word of mouth now.
— Bid him deliver thee a thousand crowns, by
the same token, that the nuns lov'd rice,
that Friar Barnardine slept in his own clothes ;
any of 'em will do it.   95
Pilia. Let me alone to urge it, now I know
the meaning.
Itha. The meaning has a meaning. Come
let 's in.
To undo a Jew is charity, and not sin. *Exeunt.*

---

[1] Referring to the tradition that Judas Iscariot
hanged himself on an elder-tree.
[2] Q. masty.

ACT V

[SCENE I.] [2]

Enter FERNEZE, Knights, DEL BOSCO, [*and*
Officers].

Fern. Now, gentlemen, betake you to your
arms,
And see that Malta be well fortifi'd ;
And it behoves you to be resolute ;
For Calymath, having hover'd here so long,
Will win the town, or die before the walls.   5
1 *Knight.* And die he shall, for we will never
yield.

Enter COURTESAN [BELLAMIRA] *and* PILIA-
BORSA.

Bell. O, bring us to the governor.
Fern. Away with her ! she is a courtesan.
Bell. Whate'er I am, yet, governor, hear me
speak ;   9
I bring thee news by whom thy son was slain :
Mathias did it not ; it was the Jew.
Pilia. Who, besides the slaughter of these
gentlemen,
Poison'd his own daughter and the nuns,
Strangled a friar and I know not what   14
Mischief beside.
Fern.   Had we but proof of this ——
Bell. Strong proof, my lord ; his man 's now
at my lodging,
That was his agent ; he 'll confess it all.
Fern. Go fetch him straight [*Exeunt* Officers].
I always fear'd that Jew.

Enter [Officers *with*] BARABAS *and* ITHAMORE.

Bar. I 'll go alone ; dogs ! do not hale me
thus.
Itha. Nor me neither, I cannot outrun you,
constable : — O my belly !   21
Bar. [*Aside.*] One dram of powder more had
made all sure.
What a damn'd slave was I !
Fern. Make fires, heat irons, let the rack be
fetch'd.
1 *Knight.* Nay, stay, my lord ; 't may be he
will confess.   25
Bar. Confess ! what mean you, lords ? Who
should confess ?
Fern. Thou and thy Turk ; 't was you that
slew my son.
Itha. Guilty, my lord, I confess. Your son
and Mathias were both contracted unto Abi-
gail ; he forg'd a counterfeit challenge.   30
Bar. Who carried that challenge ?
Itha. I carried it, I confess ; but who writ it ?
Marry, even he that strangled Barnardine,
poison'd the nuns and his own daughter.
Fern. Away with him ! his sight is death to
me.   35
Bar. For what, you men of Malta ? Hear me
speak :
She is a courtesan, and he a thief,

---

[2] The council-house.

And he my bondman. Let me have law,
For none of this can prejudice my life.
  Fern. Once more, away with him; you shall
    have law.   40
  Bar. [*Aside.*] Devils, do your worst! I'll
live in spite of you. —
As these have spoke, so be it to their souls! —
[*Aside.*] I hope the poison'd flowers will work
anon.
        Exeunt [Officers *with* BARABAS
        and ITHAMORE, BELLAMIRA *and*
        PILIA-BORSA].

     Enter [KATHERINE.][1]

  Kath. Was my Mathias murder'd by the Jew?
Ferneze, 't was thy son that murder'd him.   45
  Fern. Be patient, gentle madam, it was he;
He forg'd the daring challenge made them fight.
  Kath. Where is the Jew? Where is that
murderer?
  Fern. In prison till the law has pass'd on him.

    Re-enter [First] Officer.

1 *Off.* My lord, the courtesan and her man
  are dead: 50
So is the Turk and Barabas the Jew.
  Fern. Dead!
1 *Off.* Dead, my lord, and here they bring
his body.
  Bosco. This sudden death of his is very
strange.
  Fern. Wonder not at it, sir, the Heavens are
just;   55
Their deaths were like their lives, then think
not of 'em.
Since they are dead, let them be buried;
For the Jew's body, throw that o'er the walls,
To be a prey for vultures and wild beasts. —
So now away, and fortify the town.   *Exeunt.*   60

       [SCENE II.]

  [BARABAS *discovered rising.*][2]

  Bar. What, all alone? Well fare, sleepy
drink.
I'll be reveng'd on this accursed town:
For by my means Calymath shall enter in.
I'll help to slay their children and their wives,
To fire the churches, pull their houses down,   5
Take my goods too, and seize upon my lands.
I hope to see the governor a slave,
And, rowing in a galley, whipt to death.

   Enter CALYMATH, Bassoes, *and* Turks.

  Caly. Whom have we there, a spy?
  Bar. Yes, my good lord, one that can spy a
place   10
Where you may enter, and surprise the town:
My name is Barabas: I am a Jew.
  Caly. Art thou that Jew whose goods we
heard were sold
For tribute-money?
  Bar.   The very same, my lord:
And since that time they have hir'd a slave, my
man,   15

To accuse me of a thousand villanies:
I was imprison'd, but escap'd their hands.
  Caly. Did'st break prison?
  Bar. No, no;
I drank of poppy and cold mandrake juice;   20
And being asleep, belike they thought me dead,
And threw me o'er the walls: so, or how else,
The Jew is here, and rests at your command.
  Caly. 'T was bravely done: but tell me,
Barabas,   24
Canst thou, as thou report'st, make Malta ours?
  Bar. Fear not, my lord, for here against the
sluice[3]
The rock is hollow, and of purpose digg'd
To make a passage for the running streams
And common channels of the city.
Now, whilst you give assault unto the walls,   30
I'll lead five hundred soldiers through the vault,
And rise with them i' th' middle of the town,
Open the gates for you to enter in;
And by this means the city is your own.   34
  Caly. If this be true, I'll make thee governor.
  Bar. And if it be not true, then let me die.
  Caly. Thou'st doom'd thyself. Assault it
presently.[4]   *Exeunt.*

      [SCENE III.][5]

Alarums. Enter [CALYMATH, Bassoes,] Turks,
  and BARABAS, *with* FERNEZE *and* Knights
  prisoners.

  Caly. Now vail[6] your pride, you captive
Christians,
And kneel for mercy to your conquering foe.
Now where's the hope you had of haughty
Spain?
Ferneze, speak, had it not been much better   4
To keep[7] thy promise than be thus surpris'd?
  Fern. What should I say? We are captives
and must yield.
  Caly. Ay, villains, you must yield, and under
Turkish yokes
Shall groaning bear the burden of our ire;
And, Barabas, as erst we promis'd thee,
For thy desert we make thee governor;   10
Use them at thy discretion.
  Bar.   Thanks, my lord.
  Fern. O fatal day, to fall into the hands
Of such a traitor and unhallowed Jew!
What greater misery could Heaven inflict?
  Caly. 'T is our command: and, Barabas, we
give   15
To guard thy person these our Janizaries:
Entreat them well, as we have used thee.
And now, brave bassoes, come, we'll walk
about
The ruin'd town, and see the wrack we
made: —   19
Farewell, brave Jew; farewell, great Barabas!
     Exeunt [CALYMATH *and* Bassoes].
  Bar. May all good fortune follow Calymath!
And now, as entrance to our safety,
To prison with the governor and these
Captains, his consorts and confederates.

3 Conj. Collier. Q. *truce.*   6 Lower.
4 At once.   7 Q. *kept.*
5 An open place in the city.

Fern. O villain ! Heaven will be reveng'd on
thee.   25
    Exeunt [Turks, *with* FERNEZE *and*
    Knights.]
Bar. Away ! no more ; let him not trouble me.[1]
Thus hast thou gotten, by thy policy,
No simple place, no small authority.
I now am governor of Malta ; true, —
But Malta hates me, and, in hating me,   30
My life 's in danger, and what boots it thee,
Poor Barabas, to be the governor,
Whenas thy life shall be at their command ?
No, Barabas. this must be look'd into ;
And since by wrong thou got'st authority,   35
Maintain it bravely by firm policy,
At least unprofitably lose it not :
For he that liveth in authority,
And neither gets him friends, nor fills his bags,
Lives like the ass, that Aesop speaketh of,   40
That labours with a load of bread and wine,
And leaves it off to snap on thistle-tops :
But Barabas will be more circumspect.
Begin betimes ; occasion's bald behind ;
Slip not thine opportunity, for fear too late   45
Thou seek'st for much, but canst not compass
it. —
Within here !

   Enter FERNEZE, *with a* Guard.

Fern. My lord ?
Bar. Ay, "lord ; " thus slaves will learn.
Now, governor ; — stand by there, wait within.
        [*Exeunt* Guard.]
This is the reason that I sent for thee :
Thou seest thy life and Malta's happiness   50
Are at my arbitrement ; and Barabas
At his discretion may dispose of both ;
Now tell me, governor, and plainly too,
What think'st thou shall become of it and thee ?
Fern. This, Barabas ; since things are in thy
power,   55
I see no reason but of Malta's wrack,
Nor hope of thee but extreme cruelty ;
Nor fear I death, nor will I flatter thee.
Bar. Governor, good words ; be not so furious.
'T is not thy life which can avail me aught ;   60
Yet you do live, and live for me you shall :
And, as for Malta's ruin, think you not
'T were slender policy for Barabas
To dispossess himself of such a place ?
For sith, as once you said, 't is in[2] this isle,   65
In Malta here, that I have got my goods,
And in this city still have had success,
And now at length am grown your governor,
Yourselves shall see it shall not be forgot :
For, as a friend not known but in distress,   70
I 'll rear up Malta, now remediless.
Fern. Will Barabas recover Malta's loss ?
Will Barabas be good to Christians ?
Bar. What wilt thou give me, governor, to
procure
A dissolution of the slavish bands   75
Wherein the Turk hath yok'd your land and you ?
What will you give me if I render you

[1] The scene is here supposed to shift to the governor's
residence inside the citadel.
[2] *'T is in,* Cunningham emend. Q. *within.*

The life of Calymath, surprise his men,
And in an outhouse of the city shut
His soldiers, till I have consum'd 'em all with
fire ?   80
What will you give him that procureth this ?
Fern. Do but bring this to pass which thou
pretendest,
Deal truly with us as thou intimatest,
And I will send amongst the citizens,
And by my letters privately procure   85
Great sums of money for thy recompense
Nay more, do this, and live thou governor still.
Bar. Nay, do thou this, Ferneze, and be free ;
Governor, I enlarge thee ; live with me,
Go walk about the city, see thy friends :   90
Tush, send not letters to 'em, go thyself,
And let me see what money thou canst make.
Here is my hand that I 'll set Malta free :
And thus we cast it : to a solemn feast
I will invite young Selim Calymath,   95
Where be thou present only to perform
One stratagem that I 'll impart to thee,
Wherein no danger shall betide thy life,
And I will warrant Malta free for ever.   99
Fern. Here is my hand ; believe me, Barabas,
I will be there, and do as thou desirest.
When is the time ?
Bar. Governor, presently :
For Calymath, when he hath view'd the town,
Will take his leave and sail toward Ottoman.
Fern. Then will I, Barabas, about his coin, 100
And bring it with me to thee in the evening.
Bar. Do so, but fail not ; now farewell, Fern-
eze ! —   [*Exit* FERNEZE.]
And thus far roundly goes the business :
Thus loving neither, will I live with both,
Making a profit of my policy ;   110
And he from whom my most advantage comes
Shall be my friend.
This is the life we Jews are us'd to lead ;
And reason too, for Christians do the like.
Well, now about effecting this device ;   115
First to surprise great Selim's soldiers,
And then to make provision for the feast,
That at one instant all things may be done.
My policy detests prevention :
To what event my secret purpose drives,   120
I know ; and they shall witness with their lives.
          Exit.

     [SCENE IV.][3]

   Enter CALYMATH *and* Bassoes.

Caly. Thus have we view'd the city, seen the
sack
And caus'd the ruins to be new-repair'd,
Which with our bombards'[4] shot and basilisk
We rent in sunder at our entry :
And now I see the situation,
And how secure this conquer'd island stands
Environ'd with the Mediterranean Sea,
Strong-countermin'd with other petty isles ;
And, toward Calabria, back'd by Sicily,
Where Syracusian Dionysius reign'd,   10
Two lofty turrets that command the town.
I wonder how it could be conquer'd thus.

[3] Outside the city walls   [4] Cannons'.

Enter a Messenger.

Mess. From Barabas, Malta's governor, I bring
A message unto mighty Calymath ;
Hearing his sovereign was bound for sea,   15
To sail to Turkey, to great Ottoman,
He humbly would entreat your majesty
To come and see his homely citadel,
And banquet with him ere thou leav'st the isle.
Caly. To banquet with him in his citadel ?   20
I fear me, messenger, to feast my train
Within a town of war so lately pillag'd
Will be too costly and too troublesome :
Yet would I gladly visit Barabas,
For well has Barabas deserv'd of us.   25
Mess. Selim, for that, thus saith the governor,
That he hath in his store a pearl so big,
So precious, and withal so orient,
As, be it valued but indifferently,
The price thereof will serve to entertain   30
Selim and all his soldiers for a month ;
Therefore he humbly would entreat your
highness
Not to depart till he has feasted you.
Caly. I cannot feast my men in Malta-walls,
Except he place his tables in the streets.   35
Mess. Know, Selim, that there is a monastery
Which standeth as an outhouse to the town :
There will he banquet them ; but thee at home,
With all thy bassoes and brave followers.
Caly. Well, tell the governor we grant his
suit,   40
We 'll in this summer evening feast with him.
Mess. I shall, my lord.   *Exit.*
Caly. And now, bold bassoes, let us to our
tents,
And meditate how we may grace us best
To solemnize our governor's great feast.   45
Exeunt.

[SCENE V.] [1]

Enter FERNEZE, Knights, *and* DEL BOSCO.

Fern. In this, my countrymen, be rul'd by me,
Have special care that no man sally forth
Till you shall hear a culverin discharg'd
By him that bears the linstock, kindled thus ;
Then issue out and come to rescue me,   5
For happily I shall be in distress,
Or you released of this servitude.
1 Knight. Rather than thus to live as Turk-
ish thralls,
What will we not adventure ?
Fern. On then, begone.
Knights.   Farewell, grave governor !   10
[*Exeunt on one side* Knights *and* DEL
BOSCO ; *on the other* FERNEZE.]

[SCENE VI.] [2]

Enter, above, [BARABAS,] *with a hammer, very
busy ; [and* Carpenters].

Bar. How stands the cords ? How hang these
hinges ? Fast ?
Are all the cranes and pulleys sure ?

[1] A street in Malta.
[2] A hall in the citadel, with a gallery at the end.

1 Carp.   All fast.
Bar. Leave nothing loose, all levell'd to my
mind.
Why now I see that you have art indeed.
There, carpenters, divide that gold amongst
you :   [*Gives money.*] 5
Go swill in bowls of sack and muscadine !
Down to the cellar, taste of all my wines.
1 Carp. We shall, my lord, and thank you.
Exeunt [Carpenters].
Bar. And, if you like them, drink your fill
and die :
For so I live, perish may all the world !   10
Now, Selim Calymath, return me word
That thou wilt come, and I am satisfied.

Enter Messenger.

Now, sirrah, what, will he come ?
Mess. He will ; and has commanded all his
men
To come ashore, and march through Malta
streets,   15
That thou may'st feast them in thy citadel.
Bar. Then now are all things as my wish
would have 'em,
There wanteth nothing but the governor's pelf,
And see, he brings it.

Enter FERNEZE.

Now, governor, the sum.
Fern. With free consent, a hundred thousand
pounds.
Bar. Pounds, say'st thou, governor ? Well,
since it is no more,
I 'll satisfy myself with that ; nay, keep it still,
For if I keep not promise, trust not me.
And, governor, now partake my policy :
First, for his army ; they are sent before,   25
Enter'd the monastery, and underneath
In several places are field-pieces pitch'd,
Bombards, whole barrels full of gunpowder
That on the sudden shall dissever it,
And batter all the stones about their ears,   30
Whence none can possibly escape alive.
Now as for Calymath and his consorts
Here have I made a dainty gallery,
The floor whereof, this cable being cut,
Doth fall asunder ; so that it doth sink   35
Into a deep pit past recovery.
Here, hold that knife [*throws down a knife*], and
when thou seest he comes,
And with his bassoes shall be blithely set,
A warning-piece shall be shot off from the tower,
To give thee knowledge when to cut the cord [40
And fire the house ; say, will not this be brave ?
Fern. O excellent ! here, hold thee, Barabas,
I trust thy word, take what I promis'd thee.
Bar. No, governor, I 'll satisfy thee first,
Thou shalt not live in doubt of anything.   45
Stand close,[3] for here they come [FERNEZE *re-
tires*]. Why, is not this
A kingly kind of trade to purchase towns
By treachery and sell 'em by deceit ?
Now tell me, worldlings, underneath the sun
If greater falsehood ever has been done ?   50

[3] Concealed.

Enter CALYMATH *and* Bassoes.

Caly. Come, my companion bassoes; see, I pray,
How busy Barabas is there above
To entertain us in his gallery;
Let us salute him. Save thee, Barabas!
　Bar. Welcome, great Calymath!　　　　55
　Fern. [*Aside.*] How the slave jeers at him.
　Bar. Will 't please thee, mighty Selim Calymath,
To ascend our homely stairs?
　Caly.　　　　　　　Ay, Barabas; —
Come bassoes, attend.[1]
　Fern. [*coming forward.*] Stay, Calymath!　60
For I will show thee greater courtesy
Than Barabas would have afforded thee.
　Knight [*within.*] Sound a charge there!
　　　A charge [*sounded within.* FERN-
　　　EZE] *cuts the cord :* [*the floor of the
　　　gallery gives way, and* BARABAS
　　　falls into] *a caldron.*

[*Enter* DEL BOSCO *and* Knights.]

Caly. How now! what means this?
Bar. Help, help me! Christians, help!　65
Fern. See, Calymath, this was devis'd for thee!
Caly. Treason! treason! bassoes, fly!
Fern. No, Selim, do not fly;
See his end first, and fly then if thou canst.　69
Bar. O help me, Selim! help me, Christians!
Governor, why stand you all so pitiless?
Fern. Should I in pity of thy plaints or thee,
Accursed Barabas, base Jew, relent?
No, thus I 'll see thy treachery repaid,
But wish thou hadst behav'd thee otherwise.　75
Bar. You will not help me, then?
Fern.　　　　　　No, villain, no.
Bar. And, villains, know you cannot help me now. —
Then, Barabas, breathe forth thy latest [hate,][2]
And in the fury of thy torments strive
To end thy life with resolution.　　　　80
Know, governor, 't was I that slew thy son;
I fram'd the challenge that did make them meet.
Know, Calymath, I aim'd thy overthrow,
And had I but escap'd this stratagem,
I would have brought confusion on you all,　85
Damn'd Christians, dogs, and Turkish infidels!
But now begins the extremity of heat
To pinch me with intolerable pangs.

Die, life! fly, soul! tongue, curse thy fill, and die!　　　　　　　　　　　　[*Dies.*]
Caly. Tell me, you Christians, what doth this portend?　　　　　　　　　　90
Fern. This train he laid to have entrapp'd thy life.
Now, Selim, note the unhallowed deeds of Jews:
Thus he determin'd to have handled thee,
But I have rather chose to save thy life.
Caly. Was this the banquet he prepar'd for us?　　　　　　　　　　　　98
Let 's hence, lest further mischief be pretended.[3]
Fern. Nay, Selim, stay; for since we have thee here,
We will not let thee part so suddenly:
Besides, if we should let thee go, all 's one,
For with thy galleys could'st thou not get hence,　　　　　　　　　　　100
Without fresh men to rig and furnish them.
Caly. Tush, governor, take thou no care for that,
My men are all aboard,
And do attend my coming there by this.
Fern. Why heard'st thou not the trumpet sound a charge?　　　　　　　105
Caly. Yes, what of that?
Fern.　　　Why then the house was fir'd,
Blown up, and all thy soldiers massacred.
Caly. O monstrous treason!
Fern.　　　　　　A Jew's courtesy:
For he that did by treason work our fall,
By treason hath delivered thee to us.　110
Know, therefore, till thy father hath made good
The ruins done to Malta and to us,
Thou canst not part; for Malta shall be freed,
Or Selim ne'er return to Ottoman.
Caly. Nay, rather, Christians, let me go to Turkey,　　　　　　　　　114
In person there to mediate[4] your peace;
To keep me here will naught advantage you.
Fern. Content thee, Calymath, here thou must stay,
And live in Malta prisoner; for come all the world
To rescue thee, so will we guard us now,　120
As sooner shall they drink the ocean dry
Than conquer Malta, or endanger us.
So march away, and let due praise be given
Neither to Fate nor Fortune, but to Heaven.
　　　　　　　　　　　　　[*Exeunt.*

---

[1] Dyce, *ascend.*　　[2] Cunningham emend. Q. *fate.*

[3] Intended.　　[4] Q *meditate.*

THE TROUBLESOME REIGN AND LAMENTABLE DEATH OF EDWARD THE SECOND

BY

CHRISTOPHER MARLOWE.

[ACT I]

[SCENE I.] [1]

Enter GAVESTON, *reading on a letter that was
brought him from the King.*

  Gaveston. " My father is deceas'd ! Come,
    Gaveston,
And share the kingdom with thy dearest
    friend."
Ah ! words that make me surfeit with delight !
What greater bliss can hap to Gaveston
Than live and be the favourite of a king !   5
Sweet prince, I come ; these, these thy amorous
    lines
Might have enforc'd me to have swum from
    France,
And, like Leander, gasp'd upon the sand,
So thou would'st smile, and take me in thine
    arms.
The sight of London to my exil'd eyes   10
Is as Elysium to a new-come soul ;
Not that I love the city, or the men,
But that it harbours him I hold so dear —
The king, upon whose bosom let me die,[2]
And with the world be still at enmity.   15
What need the arctic people love starlight,
To whom the sun shines both by day and
    night ?

Farewell base stooping to the lordly peers !
My knee shall bow to none but to the king.
As for the multitude, that are but sparks   20
Rak'd up in embers of their poverty ; —
Tanti.[3] I 'll fawn first on the wind
That glanceth at my lips, and flyeth away.

Enter three Poor Men.

But how now, what are these ?
  Poor Men. Such as desire your worship 's
    service.   25
  Gav. What canst thou do ?
  1 *P. Man.* I can ride.
  Gav. But I have no horses. — What art
    thou ?
  2 *P. Man.* A traveller.
  Gav. Let me see : thou would'st do well   30
To wait at my trencher and tell me lies at
    dinner time ;
And as I like your discoursing, I 'll have
    you. —
And what art thou ?
  3 *P. Man.* A soldier that hath serv'd
    against the Scot.
  Gav. Why, there are hospitals for such as   35
I have no war, and therefore, sir, begone.
  3 *P. Man.* Farewell, and perish by a sol-
    dier's hand,
That would'st reward them with an hospital.

---

[1] A street in London.
[2] Dyce emends to *lie.* *Die* may be used in the sense
of " swoon."

[3] " So much for them."

Gav. Ay, ay, these words of his move me as much
As if a goose should play the porpentine,   40
And dart her plumes, thinking to pierce my breast.
But yet it is no pain to speak men fair ;
I 'll flatter these, and make them live in hope. —   [*Aside.*]
You know that I came lately out of France,
And yet I have not view'd my lord the king ;   45
If I speed well, I 'll entertain you all.
All. We thank your worship.
Gav. I have some business : leave me to myself.
All. We will wait here about the court.
                Exeunt.
Gav. Do. — These are not men for me :   50
I must have wanton poets, pleasant wits,
Musicians, that with touching of a string
May draw the pliant king which way I please.
Music and poetry is his delight ;
Therefore I 'll have Italian masks by night,   55
Sweet speeches, comedies, and pleasing shows ;
And in the day, when he shall walk abroad,
Like sylvan nymphs my pages shall be clad ;
My men, like satyrs grazing on the lawns,
Shall with their goat-feet dance an antic hay.[1]
Sometime a lovely boy in Dian's shape,   61
With hair that gilds the water as it glides,
Crownets of pearl about his naked arms,
And in his sportful hands an olive tree,
To hide those parts which men delight to see,   65
Shall bathe him in a spring ; and there hard by,
One like Actaeon peeping through the grove
Shall by the angry goddess be transform'd,
And running in the likeness of an hart
By yelping hounds pull'd down, and seem to die ; —   70
Such things as these best please his majesty,
My lord. — Here comes the king, and the nobles
From the parliament. I 'll stand aside.
                [*Retires.*]

Enter KING [EDWARD], LANCASTER, *the* Elder
MORTIMER, Young MORTIMER ; EDMUND,
EARL *of* KENT ; GUY, EARL *of* WARWICK,
and [Attendants].

K. Edw. Lancaster !
Lan. My lord.   75
Gav. That Earl of Lancaster do I abhor.
                [*Aside.*]
K. Edw. Will you not grant me this ? — In spite of them
I 'll have my will ; and these two Mortimers,
That cross me thus, shall know I am displeas'd.
                [*Aside.*]
E. Mor. If you love us, my lord, hate Gaveston.   80
Gav. That villain Mortimer ! I 'll be his death.   [*Aside.*]
Y. Mor. Mine uncle here, this earl, and I myself
Were sworn to your father at his death,
That he should ne'er return into the realm ;

     [1] A rural dance.

And know, my lord, ere I will break my oath,
This sword of mine, that should offend your foes,   86
Shall sleep within the scabbard at thy need,
And underneath thy banners march who will,
For Mortimer will hang his armour up.
   Gav. Mort Dieu !   [*Aside.*]
   K. Edw. Well, Mortimer, I 'll make thee rue these words.   91
Beseems it thee to contradict thy king ?
Frown'st thou thereat, aspiring Lancaster ?
The sword shall plane the furrows of thy brows,
And hew these knees that now are grown so stiff.   95
I will have Gaveston ; and you shall know
What danger 't is to stand against your king.
   Gav. Well done, Ned !   [*Aside.*]
   Lan. My lord, why do you thus incense your peers,
That naturally would love and honour you   100
But for that base and obscure Gaveston ?
Four earldoms have I, besides Lancaster —
Derby, Salisbury, Lincoln, Leicester, —
These will I sell, to give my soldiers pay,
Ere Gaveston shall stay within the realm ;   105
Therefore, if he be come, expel him straight.
   Kent. Barons and earls, your pride hath made me mute ;
But now I 'll speak, and to the proof, I hope.
I do remember, in my father's days,
Lord Percy of the north, being highly mov'd,
Braved Moubery[2] in presence of the king ;   111
For which, had not his highness lov'd him well,
He should have lost his head ; but with his look
The undaunted spirit of Percy was appeas'd,
And Moubery and he were reconcil'd :   115
Yet dare you brave the king unto his face ? —
Brother, revenge it, and let these their heads
Preach upon poles, for trespass of their tongues.
   War. O, our heads !
   K. Edw. Ay, yours ; and therefore I would wish you grant —   120
   War. Bridle thy anger, gentle Mortimer.
   Y. Mor. I cannot, nor I will not ; I must speak. —
Cousin, our hands I hope shall fence our heads,
And strike off his that makes you threaten us.   124
Come, uncle, let us leave the brain-sick king,
And henceforth parle with our naked swords.
   E. Mor. Wiltshire hath men enough to save our heads.
   War. All Warwickshire will love him for my sake.[3]
   Lan. And northward Gaveston hath many friends. —
Adieu, my lord ; and either change your mind,   130
Or look to see the throne, where you should sit,
To float in blood ; and at thy wanton head,
The glozing[4] head of thy base minion thrown.
       Exeunt [*all except* KING EDWARD,
       KENT, GAVESTON, *and* Attendants].

     [2] Mowbray, but the Q. spelling indicates the pronunciation.
     [3] This line and the next are ironical.   [4] Flattering.

K. Edw. I cannot brook these haughty men-
　　aces.
Am I a king, and must be overrul'd? —   135
Brother, display my ensigns in the field ;
I 'll bandy [1] with the barons and the earls,
And either die or live with Gaveston.
　　Gav. I can no longer keep me from my
　　　　lord.   [*Comes forward.*]
　　K. Edw. What, Gaveston ! welcome ! — Kiss
　　not my hand —   140
Embrace me, Gaveston, as I do thee.
Why should'st thou kneel? Know'st thou not
who I am ?
Thy friend, thyself, another Gaveston !
Not Hylas was more mourn'd of Hercules,
Than thou hast been of me since thy exile.   145
　　Gav. And since I went from hence, no soul
　　　　in hell
Hath felt more torment than poor Gaveston.
　　K. Edw. I know it. — Brother, welcome
　　home my friend.
Now let the treacherous Mortimers conspire,
And that high-minded Earl of Lancaster :   150
I have my wish, in that I joy thy sight ;
And sooner shall the sea o'erwhelm my land,
Than bear the ship that shall transport thee
hence.
I here create thee Lord High Chamberlain,
Chief Secretary to the state and me,   155
Earl of Cornwall, King and Lord of Man.
　　Gav. My lord, these titles far exceed my
　　　　worth.
　　Kent. Brother, the least of these may well
　　suffice
For one of greater birth than Gaveston.
　　K. Edw. Cease, brother, for I cannot brook
　　these words.   160
Thy worth, sweet friend, is far above my gifts.
Therefore, to equal it, receive my heart.
If for these dignities thou be envíed,
I 'll give thee more ; for, but to honour thee,
Is Edward pleas'd with kingly regiment? [2]   165
Fear'st [3] thou thy person? Thou shalt have a
guard.
Wantest thou gold? Go to my treasury.
Wouldst thou be lov'd and fear'd? Receive my
seal ;
Save or condemn, and in our name command
Whatso thy mind effects, or fancy likes,   170
　　Gav. It shall suffice me to enjoy your love,
Which whiles I have, I think myself as great
As Caesar riding in the Roman street,
With captive kings at his triumphant car.

Enter the BISHOP *of* COVENTRY.

　　K. Edw. Whither goes my lord of Coventry
　　so fast?   175
　　B. of Cov. To celebrate your father's exe-
　　quies.
But is that wicked Gaveston return'd ?
　　K. Edw. Ay, priest, and lives to be reveng'd
　　on thee,
That wert the only cause of his exile.
　　Gav. 'T is true; and but for reverence of
　　these robes,   180

Thou should'st not plod one foot beyond this
　　place.
　　B. of Cov. I did no more than I was bound
　　to do;
And, Gaveston, unless thou be reclaim'd,
As then I did incense the parliament,
So will I now, and thou shalt back to France.
　　Gav. Saving your reverence, you must pardon
　　me.   186
　　K. Edw. Throw off his golden mitre, rend
　　his stole,
And in the channel [4] christen him anew.
　　Kent. Ah, brother, lay not violent hands on
　　him !
For he 'll complain unto the see of Rome.   190
　　Gav. Let him complain unto the see of hell ;
I 'll be reveng'd on him for my exile.
　　K. Edw. No, spare his life, but seize upon
　　his goods.
Be thou lord bishop and receive his rents,
And make him serve thee as thy chaplain.   195
I give him thee — here, use him as thou wilt.
　　Gav. He shall to prison, and there die in bolts.
　　K. Edw. Ay, to the Tower, the Fleet, or
　　where thou wilt.
　　B. of Cov. For this offence, be thou accurst
　　of God !
　　K. Edw. Who 's there? Convey this priest
　　to the Tower.   200
　　B. of Cov. True, true.[5]
　　K. Edw. But in the meantime, Gaveston,
　　away,
And take possession of his house and goods.
Come, follow me, and thou shalt have my guard
To see it done, and bring thee safe again.   205
　　Gav. What should a priest do with so fair a
　　house ?
A prison may best beseem his holiness.
　　　　　　　　　　　　　　　　　　[*Exeunt.*]

[SCENE II.] [6]

Enter [*on one side*] *both the* MORTIMERS ; [*on the
other,*] WARWICK *and* LANCASTER.

　　War. 'T is true, the bishop is in the Tower.
And goods and body given to Gaveston.
　　Lan. What ! will they tyrannise upon the
　　church ?
Ah, wicked king ! accursed Gaveston !
This ground, which is corrupted with their
steps,   5
Shall be their timeless [7] sepulchre or mine.
　　Y. Mor. Well, let that peevish Frenchman
　　guard him sure ;
Unless his breast be sword-proof he shall die.
　　E. Mor. How now ! why droops the Earl of
　　Lancaster ?
　　Y. Mor. Wherefore is Guy of Warwick dis-
　　content ?   10
　　Lan. That villain Gaveston is made an earl.
　　E. Mor. An earl !
　　War. Ay, and besides Lord Chamberlain of
　　the realm,
And Secretary too, and Lord of Man.

---

[1] Contend.　　　[2] Rule.　　　[3] Fear'st for.

[4] Gutter.
[5] *I. e.,* You have used the true word " Convey " (=
steal).
[6] Westminster.　　　[7] Untimely.

E. Mor. We may not, nor we will not suffer
   this.   15
Y. Mor. Why post we not from hence to levy
   men ?
Lan. "My Lord of Cornwall" now at every
   word !
And happy is the man whom he vouchsafes,
For vailing of his bonnet,[1] one good look.
Thus, arm in arm, the king and he doth march :
Nay more, the guard upon his lordship waits ; 21
And all the court begins to flatter him.
War. Thus leaning on the shoulder of the
   king,
He nods and scorns and smiles at those that
   pass.
E. Mor. Doth no man take exceptions at
   the slave ?   25
Lan. All stomach[2] him, but none dare speak
   a word.
Y. Mor. Ah, that bewrays[3] their baseness,
   Lancaster !
Were all the earls and barons of my mind,
We 'll hale him from the bosom of the king,
And at the court-gate hang the peasant up,   30
Who, swoln with venom of ambitious pride,
Will be the ruin of the realm and us.

Enter the [ARCH]BISHOP *of* CANTERBURY [*and
   an* Attendant.]

War. Here comes my lord of Canterbury's
   grace.
Lan. His countenance bewrays he is dis-
   pleas'd.
A. of Cant. First were his sacred garments
   rent and torn,   35
Then laid they violent hands upon him ; next
Himself imprisoned, and his goods asseiz'd :
This certify the Pope ; — away, take horse,
                                     [*Exit Attend.*]
Lan. My lord, will you take arms against the
   king ?
A. of Cant. What need I ? God himself is up
   in arms,   40
When violence is offered to the church.
Y. Mor. Then will you join with us, that be
   his peers,
To banish or behead that Gaveston ?
A. of Cant. What else, my lords ? for it con-
   cerns me near ;
The bishopric of Coventry is his.   45

Enter QUEEN [ISABELLA].

Y. Mor. Madam, whither walks your majesty
   so fast ?
Q. Isab. Unto the forest, gentle Mortimer,
To live in grief and baleful discontent ;
For now my lord the king regards me not,
But dotes upon the love of Gaveston.   50
He claps his cheeks, and hangs about his neck,
Smiles in his face, and whispers in his ears ;
And when I come he frowns, as who should say,
"Go whither thou wilt, seeing I have Gaveston."
E. Mor. Is it not strange that he is thus
   bewitch'd ?   55

Y. Mor. Madam, return unto the court again.
That sly inveigling Frenchman we 'll exile,
Or lose our lives ; and yet, ere that day come,
The king shall lose his crown ; for we have
   power,
And courage too, to be reveng'd at full.   60
Q. Isab. But yet lift not your swords against
   the king.
Lan. No ; but we will lift Gaveston from
   hence.
War. And war must be the means, or he 'll
   stay still.
Q. Isab. Then let him stay ; for rather than
   my lord
Shall be oppress'd by civil mutinies,   65
I will endure a melancholy life,
And let him frolic with his minion.
A. of Cant. My lords, to ease all this, but
   hear me speak : —
We and the rest, that are his counsellors,
Will meet, and with a general consent   70
Confirm him banishment with our hands and
   seals.
Lan. What we confirm the king will frustrate.
Y. Mor. Then may we lawfully revolt from
   him.
War. But say, my lord, where shall this
   meeting be ?
A. of Cant. At the New Temple.   75
Y. Mor. Content.
A. of Cant. And, in the meantime, I 'll en-
   treat you all
To cross to Lambeth, and there stay with
   me.
Lan. Come then, let 's away.
Y. Mor. Madam, farewell !   80
Q. Isab. Farewell, sweet Mortimer, and, for
   my sake,
Forbear to levy arms against the king.
Y. Mor. Ay, if words will serve ; if not, I
   must.   [*Exeunt.*]

[SCENE III.][4]

Enter GAVESTON *and* KENT.

Gav. Edmund, the mighty Prince of Lancas-
   ter,
That hath more earldoms than an ass can bear,
And both the Mortimers, two goodly men,
With Guy of Warwick, that redoubted knight,
Are gone toward Lambeth — there let them
   remain !   [*Exeunt.*] 5

[SCENE IV.][5]

Enter Nobles [LANCASTER, WARWICK, PEM-
BROKE, *the* Elder MORTIMER, Young MORTI-
MER, *the* ARCHBISHOP *of* CANTERBURY *and*
Attendants].

Lan. Here is the form of Gaveston's exile :
May it please your lordship to subscribe your
   name.
A. of Cant. Give me the paper.
          [*He subscribes, as do the others after him.*]

---

[1] Removing it as a mark of respect.
[2] Feel resentment at.   [3] Shows.
[4] A street in London.   [5] The New Temple.

Lan. Quick, quick, my lord ; I long to write
  my name.
War. But I long more to see him banish'd
  hence.   5
Y. Mor. The name of Mortimer shall fright
  the king,
Unless he be declin'd from that base peasant.

Enter KING [EDWARD,] GAVESTON, [*and* KENT].

K. Edw. What, are you mov'd that Gaveston
  sits here ?
It is our pleasure ; we will have it so.
Lan. Your grace doth well to place him by
  your side,   10
For nowhere else the new earl is so safe.
E. Mor. What man of noble birth can brook
  this sight ?
Quam male conveniunt ! [1]
See what a scornful look the peasant casts !
Pem. Can kingly lions fawn on creeping
  ants ?   15
War. Ignoble vassal, that like Phaeton
Aspir'st unto the guidance of the sun !
Y. Mor. Their downfall is at hand, their
  forces down ;
We will not thus be fac'd and over-peer'd.
K. Edw. Lay hands on that traitor Mortimer !
E. Mor. Lay hands on that traitor Gaves-
  ton !   21
Kent. Is this the duty that you owe your
  king ?
War. We know our duties — let him know
  his peers.
K. Edw. Whither will you bear him ? Stay,
  or ye shall die.
E. Mor. We are no traitors; therefore threaten
  not.   25
Gav. No, threaten not, my lord, but pay
  them home !
Were I a king ——
Y. Mor. Thou villain, wherefore talk'st thou
  of a king,
That hardly art a gentleman by birth ?
K. Edw. Were he a peasant, being my
  minion,   30
I'll make the proudest of you stoop to him.
Lan. My lord, you may not thus disparage
  us. —
Away, I say, with hateful Gaveston !
E. Mor. And with the Earl of Kent that
  favours him.
    [*Attendants remove* KENT *and* GAVESTON.]
K. Edw. Nay, then, lay violent hands upon
  your king.   35
Here, Mortimer, sit thou in Edward's throne ;
Warwick and Lancaster, wear you my crown.
Was ever king thus over-rul'd as I ?
Lan. Learn then to rule us better, and the
  realm.
Y. Mor. What we have done, our heart-blood
  shall maintain.   40
War. Think you that we can brook this up-
  start pride ?
K. Edw. Anger and wrathful fury stops my
  speech.

A. of Cant. Why are you mov'd ? Be patient,
  my lord,
And see what we your counsellors have done.
Y. Mor. My lords, now let us all be resolute, 45
And either have our wills, or lose our lives.
K. Edw. Meet you for this, proud overdaring
  peers ?
Ere my sweet Gaveston shall part from me,
This isle shall fleet [2] upon the ocean,
And wander to the unfrequented Inde.   50
A. of Cant. You know that I am legate to
  the Pope.
On your allegiance to the see of Rome,
Subscribe, as we have done, to his exile.
Y. Mor. Curse him, if he refuse ; and then
  may we
Depose him and elect another king.   55
K. Edw. Ay, there it goes ! but yet I will
  not yield.
Curse me, depose me, do the worst you can.
Lan. Then linger not, my lord, but do it
  straight.
A. of Cant. Remember how the bishop was
  abus'd !   59
Either banish him that was the cause thereof,
Or I will presently discharge these lords
Of duty and allegiance due to thee.
K. Edw. [*Aside.*] It boots me not to threat ; I
  must speak fair. —
The legate of the Pope will be obey'd.
My lord, you shall be Chancellor of the realm ;
Thou, Lancaster, High Admiral of our fleet ; 66
Young Mortimer and his uncle shall be earls ;
And you, Lord Warwick, President of the
  North ;
And thou, of Wales. If this content you not,
Make several kingdoms of this monarchy,   70
And share it equally amongst you all,
So I may have some nook or corner left,
To frolic with my dearest Gaveston.
A. of Cant. Nothing shall alter us, we are
  resolv'd.
Lan. Come, come, subscribe.   75
Y. Mor. Why should you love him whom the
  world hates so ?
K. Edw. Because he loves me more than all
  the world.
Ah, none but rude and savage-minded men
Would seek the ruin of my Gaveston ;
You that be noble-born should pity him.   80
War. You that are princely-born should
  shake him off.
For shame subscribe, and let the lown [3] depart.
E. Mor. Urge him, my lord.
A. of Cant. Are you content to banish him
  the realm ?
K. Edw. I see I must, and therefore am
  content.   85
Instead of ink, I'll write it with my tears.
                      [*Subscribes.*]
Y. Mor. The king is love-sick for his minion.
K. Edw. 'T is done ; and now, accursed hand,
  fall off !
Lan. Give it me ; I'll have it publish'd in
  the streets.

---

[1] "How ill they agree ! "   [2] Float.   [3] Fellow.

Y. Mor. I 'll see him presently despatch'd
    away.   90
A. of Cant. Now is my heart at ease.
War.   And so is mine.
Pem. This will be good news to the common
    sort.
E. Mor. Be it or no, he shall not linger here.
        Exeunt all except KING EDWARD.
K. Edw. How fast they run to banish him I
    love!
They would not stir, were it to do me good.   95
Why should a king be subject to a priest?
Proud Rome! that hatchest such imperial
    grooms,
For these thy superstitious taper-lights,
Wherewith thy antichristian churches blaze,
I 'll fire thy crazed buildings, and enforce   100
The papal towers to kiss the lowly ground!
With slaughtered priests make Tiber's channel
    swell,
And banks rais'd higher with their sepulchres!
As for the peers, that back the clergy thus,
If I be king, not one of them shall live.   105

        Re-enter GAVESTON.

Gav. My lord, I hear it whispered everywhere,
That I am banish'd, and must fly the land.
K. Edw. 'T is true, sweet Gaveston — O! were
    it false!
The legate of the Pope will have it so,
And thou must hence, or I shall be depos'd.   110
But I will reign to be reveng'd of them;
And therefore, sweet friend, take it patiently.
Live where thou wilt, I 'll send thee gold
    enough;
And long thou shalt not stay, or if thou dost,   114
I 'll come to thee; my love shall ne'er decline.
Gav. Is all my hope turn'd to this hell of
    grief?
K. Edw. Rend not my heart with thy too
    piercing words:
Thou from this land, I from myself am ban-
    ish'd.
Gav. To go from hence grieves not poor
    Gaveston;
But to forsake you, in whose gracious looks   120
The blessedness of Gaveston remains,
For nowhere else seeks he felicity.
K. Edw. And only this torments my wretched
    soul
That, whether I will or no, thou must depart.
Be governor of Ireland in my stead,   125
And there abide till fortune call thee home.
Here take my picture, and let me wear thine;
        [They exchange pictures.]
O, might I keep thee here as I do this,
Happy were I! but now most miserable!   129
Gav. 'T is something to be pitied of a king.
K. Edw. Thou shalt not hence — I 'll hide
    thee, Gaveston.
Gav. I shall be found, and then 't will grieve
    me more.
K. Edw. Kind words and mutual talk makes
    our grief greater;
Therefore, with dumb embracement, let us
    part. —
Stay, Gaveston, I cannot leave thee thus.   135

Gav. For every look, my lord [1] drops down a
    tear.
Seeing I must go, do not renew my sorrow.
K. Edw. The time is little that thou hast to
    stay,
And, therefore, give me leave to look my fill.
But come, sweet friend, I 'll bear thee on thy
    way.   140
Gav. The peers will frown.
K. Edw. I pass [2] not for their anger. — Come
    let 's go;
O that we might as well return as go.

    Enter EDMUND *and* QUEEN ISABELLA.

Q. Isab. Whither goes my lord?
K. Edw. Fawn not on me, French strumpet!
    Get thee gone!   145
Q. Isab. On whom but on my husband should
    I fawn?
Gav. On Mortimer! with whom, ungentle
    queen —
I say no more. Judge you the rest, my lord.
Q. Isab. In saying this, thou wrong'st me,
    Gaveston.   149
Is 't not enough that thou corrupt'st my lord,
And art a bawd to his affections,
But thou must call mine honour thus in ques-
    tion?
Gav. I mean not so; your grace must pardon
    me.
K. Edw. Thou art too familiar with that
    Mortimer,
And by thy means is Gaveston exil'd;   155
But I would wish thee reconcile the lords,
Or thou shalt ne'er be reconcil'd to me.
Q. Isab. Your highness knows it lies not in
    my power.
K. Edw. Away then! touch me not. — Come,
    Gaveston.
Q. Isab. Villain! 't is thou that robb'st me
    of my lord.   160
Gav. Madam, 't is you that rob me of my
    lord.
K. Edw. Speak not unto her; let her droop
    and pine.
Q. Isab. Wherein, my lord, have I deserv'd
    these words?
Witness the tears that Isabella sheds,
Witness this heart, that, sighing for thee,
    breaks,   165
How dear my lord is to poor Isabel.
K. Edw. And witness Heaven how dear thou
    art to me!
There weep; for till my Gaveston be repeal'd,
Assure thyself thou com'st not in my sight.
        Exeunt EDWARD *and* GAVESTON.
Q. Isab. O miserable and distressed queen!
Would, when I left sweet France and was em-
    bark'd,   171
That charming Circes, walking on the waves,
Had chang'd my shape, or at the marriage-day
The cup of Hymen had been full of poison,
Or with those arms that twin'd about my neck
I had been stifled, and not liv'd to see   175
The king my lord thus to abandon me!

                      ———
[1] Altered to *love* in Dodsley. &c.   [2] Care.

Like frantic Juno will I fill the earth
With ghastly murmur of my sighs and cries ;
For never doted Jove on Ganymede   180
So much as he on cursed Gaveston.
But that will more exasperate his wrath ;
I must entreat him, I must speak him fair,
And be a means to call home Gaveston.
And yet he'll ever dote on Gaveston ;   185
And so am I for ever miserable.

Re-enter Nobles [LANCASTER, WARWICK, PEM-
   BROKE, *the* Elder MORTIMER, *and* Young
   MORTIMER] *to the* Queen.

Lan. Look where the sister of the King of
   France
Sits wringing of her hands, and beats her
   breast !
War. The king, I fear, hath ill-entreated
   her.
Pem. Hard is the heart that injures such a
   saint.   190
Y. Mor. I know 't is 'long of Gaveston she
   weeps.
E. Mor. Why ? He is gone.
Y. Mor.   Madam, how fares your grace ?
Q. Isab. Ah, Mortimer ! now breaks the
   king's hate forth,
And he confesseth that he loves me not.
Y. Mor. Cry quittance, madam, then ; and
   love not him.   195
Q. Isab. No, rather will I die a thousand
   deaths !
And yet I love in vain ; — he 'll ne'er love me.
La . Fear ye not, madam ; now his minion 's
   gone,
His wanton humour will be quickly left.   199
Q. Isab. O never, Lancaster ! I am enjoin'd
To sue upon you all for his repeal ;
This wills my lord, and this must I perform,
Or else be banish'd from his highness' presence.
Lan. For his repeal ? Madam, he comes not
   back,
Unless the sea cast up his shipwrack'd body.   205
War. And to behold so sweet a sight as that,
There 's none here but would run his horse to
   death.
Y. Mor. But, madam, would you have us
   call him home ?
Q. Isab. Ay, Mortimer, for till he be restor'd,
The angry king hath banish'd me the court ;   210
And, therefore, as thou lov'st and tend'rest me,
Be thou my advocate unto these peers.
Y. Mor. What ! would you have me plead for
   Gaveston ?
E. Mor. Plead for him he that will, I am
   resolv'd
Lan. And so am I, my lord. Dissuade the
   queen.   215
Q. Isab. O Lancaster ! let him dissuade the
   king,
For 't is against my will he should return.
War. Then speak not for him, let the peas-
   ant go.
Q. Isab. 'T is for myself I speak, and not for
   him.
Pem. No speaking will prevail, and therefore
   cease.   220

Y. Mor. Fair queen, forbear to angle for the
   fish
Which, being caught, strikes him that takes it
   dead ;
I mean that vile torpedo, Gaveston,
That now, I hope, floats on the Irish seas.
Q. Isab. Sweet Mortimer, sit down by me
   awhile,   225
And I will tell thee reasons of such weight
As thou wilt soon subscribe to his repeal.
Y. Mor. It is impossible ; but speak your
   mind.
Q. Isab. Then thus, — but none shall hear it
   but ourselves.
            [*Talks to* Young MORTIMER *apart.*]
Lan. My lords, albeit the queen win Morti-
   mer,   230
Will you be resolute, and hold with me ?
E. Mor. Not I, against my nephew.
Pem. Fear not, the queen's words cannot
   alter him.
War. No ? Do but mark how earnestly she
   pleads !
Lan. And see how coldly his looks make
   denial !   235
War. She smiles ; now for my life his mind
   is chang'd !
Lan. I 'll rather lose his friendship, I, than
   grant.
Y. Mor. Well, of necessity it must be so.
My lords, that I abhor base Gaveston,
I hope your honours make no question,   240
And therefore, though I plead for his repeal,
'T is not for his sake, but for our avail ;
Nay for the realm's behoof, and for the
   king's.
Lan. Fie, Mortimer, dishonour not thyself !
Can this be true, 't was good to banish him ?   245
And is this true,[1] to call him home again ?
Such reasons make white black, and dark night
   day.
Y. Mor. My lord of Lancaster, mark the re-
   spect.[2]
Lan. In no respect can contraries be true.
Q. Isab. Yet, good my lord, hear what he
   can allege.   250
War. All that he speaks is nothing ; we are
   resolv'd.
Y. Mor. Do you not wish that Gaveston were
   dead ?
Pem. I would he were !
Y. Mor. Why, then, my lord, give me but
   leave to speak.
E. Mor. But, nephew, do not play the so-
   phister.   255
Y. Mor. This which I urge is of a burning zeal
To mend the king, and do our country good.
Know you not Gaveston hath store of gold,
Which may in Ireland purchase him such
   friends
As he will front the mightiest of us all ?   260
And whereas he shall live and be belov'd,
'T is hard for us to work his overthrow.
War. Mark you but that, my lord of Lan-
   caster.

---

[1] Qy. for *true* read *good* (?)   [2] Consideration

Y. Mor. But were he here, detested as he is,
How easily might some base slave be suborn'd
To greet his lordship with a poniard,   266
And none so much as blame the murderer,
But rather praise him for that brave attempt,
And in the chronicle enrol his name
For purging of the realm of such a plague!   270
Pem. He saith true.
   Lan. Ay, but how chance this was not done
      before?
   Y. Mor. Because, my lords, it was not
      thought upon.
Nay, more, when he shall know it lies in us
To banish him, and then to call him home,   275
'T will make him vail [1] the top-flag of his pride,
And fear to offend the meanest nobleman.
   E. Mor. But how if he do not, nephew?
   Y. Mor. Then may we with some colour [2] rise
      in arms;
For howsoever we have borne it out,   280
'T is treason to be up against the king.
So we shall have the people of our side,
Which for his father's sake lean to the king,
But cannot brook a night-grown mushroom,
Such a one as my lord of Cornwall is,   285
Should bear us down of the nobility.
And when the commons and the nobles join,
'T is not the king can buckler Gaveston;
We 'll pull him from the strongest hold he hath.
My lords, if to perform this I be slack,   290
Think me as base a groom as Gaveston.
   Lan. On that condition, Lancaster will grant.
   War. And so will Pembroke and I.
   E. Mor. And I.   294
   Y. Mor. In this I count me highly gratified,
And Mortimer will rest at your command.
   Q. Isab. And when this favour Isabel for-
      gets,
Then let her live abandon'd and forlorn.—
But see, in happy time, my lord the king,
Having brought the Earl of Cornwall on his
      way,   300
Is new return'd. This news will glad him much,
Yet not so much as me. I love him more
Than he can Gaveston; would he lov'd me
But half so much, then were I treble-blest.

   Re-enter KING EDWARD, *mourning.*

   K. Edw. He 's gone, and for his absence thus
      I mourn.   305
Did never sorrow go so near my heart
As doth the want of my sweet Gaveston;
And could my crown's revenue bring him back,
I would freely give it to his enemies,
And think I gain'd, having bought so dear a
      friend.   310
   Q. Isab. Hark! how he harps upon his minion.
   K. Edw. My heart is as an anvil unto sorrow,
Which beats upon it like the Cyclops' hammers,
And with the noise turns up my giddy brain,
And makes me frantic for my Gaveston;   315
Ah! had some bloodless Fury rose from hell,
And with my kingly sceptre struck me dead,
When I was forc'd to leave my Gaveston!
   Lan. Diablo! What passions call you these?

<hr>

[1] Lower.   [2] Pretext.

Q. Isab. My gracious lord, I come to bring
   you news.   320
K. Edw. That you have parley'd with your
   Mortimer!
Q. Isab. That Gaveston, my lord, shall be
   repeal'd.
K. Edw. Repeal'd! The news is too sweet to
   be true?
Q. Isab. But will you love me, if you find it so?
K. Edw. If it be so, what will not Edward
   do?   325
Q. Isab. For Gaveston, but not for Isabel.
K. Edw. For thee, fair queen, if thou lov'st
   Gaveston.
I 'll hang a golden tongue about thy neck,
Seeing thou hast pleaded with so good success. 330
Q. Isab. No other jewels hang about my neck
Than these, my lord; nor let me have more
      wealth
Than I may fetch from this rich treasury.
O how a kiss revives poor Isabel!
K. Edw. Once more receive my hand; and
   let this be
A second marriage 'twixt thyself and me.   335
Q. Isab. And may it prove more happy than
   the first!
My gentle lord, bespeak these nobles fair,
That wait attendance for a gracious look,
And on their knees salute your majesty.
K. Edw. Courageous Lancaster, embrace thy
   king!   340
And, as gross vapours perish by the sun,
Even so let hatred with thy sovereign's smile.
Live thou with me as my companion.
Lan. This salutation overjoys my heart.
K. Edw. Warwick shall be my chiefest
   counsellor: 345
These silver hairs will more adorn my court
Than gaudy silks, or rich embroidery.
Chide me, sweet Warwick, if I go astray.
War. Slay me, my lord, when I offend your
   grace.
K. Edw. In solemn triumphs, and in public
   shows,   350
Pembroke shall bear the sword before the king.
Pem. And with this sword Pembroke will
   fight for you.
K. Edw. But wherefore walks young Morti-
   mer aside?
Be thou commander of our royal fleet;
Or, if that lofty office like thee not,   355
I make thee here Lord Marshal of the realm.
Y. Mor. My lord, I 'll marshal so your ene-
   mies,
As England shall be quiet, and you safe.
K. Edw. And as for you, Lord Mortimer of
   Chirke,   359
Whose great achievements in our foreign war
Deserves no common place nor mean reward,
Be you the general of the levied troops,
That now are ready to assail the Scots.
E. Mor. In this your grace hath highly
   honoured me,
For with my nature war doth best agree.   365
Q. Isab. Now is the King of England rich
   and strong,
Having the love of his renowned peers,

K. Edw. Ay, Isabel, ne'er was my heart so
light.
Clerk of the crown, direct our warrant forth
For Gaveston to Ireland:

[*Enter* BEAUMONT *with warrant.*]

Beaumont, fly   370
As fast as Iris or Jove's Mercury.
Beau. It shall be done, my gracious lord.
[*Exit.*]
K. Edw. Lord Mortimer, we leave you to
your charge.
Now let us in, and feast it royally.   374
Against our friend the Earl of Cornwall comes,
We'll have a general tilt and tournament;
And then his marriage shall be solemnis'd.
For wot you not that I have made him sure [1]
Unto our cousin, the Earl of Gloucester's heir?
Lan. Such news we hear, my lord.   380
K. Edw. That day, if not for him, yet for my
sake,
Who in the triumph will be challenger,
Spare for no cost; we will requit your love.
War. In this, or aught, your highness shall
command us.
K. Edw. Thanks, gentle Warwick: come,
let's in and revel.   385
Exeunt all except the MORTIMERS.
E. Mor. Nephew, I must to Scotland; thou
stayest here.
Leave now t' oppose thyself against the king.
Thou seest by nature he is mild and calm,
And seeing his mind so dotes on Gaveston,
Let him without controlment have his will.   390
The mightiest kings have had their minions:
Great Alexander loved Hephestion;
The conquering Hercules [2] for Hylas wept;
And for Patroclus stern Achilles droopt:
And not kings only, but the wisest men: 395
The Roman Tully lov'd Octavius;
Grave Socrates, wild Alcibiades.
Then let his grace, whose youth is flexible,
And promiseth as much as we can wish,
Freely enjoy that vain, light-headed earl;   400
For riper years will wean him from such toys.
Y. Mor. Uncle, his wanton humour grieves
not me;
But this I scorn, that one so basely born
Should by his sovereign's favour grow so pert,
And riot it with the treasure of the realm.   405
While soldiers mutiny for want of pay,
He wears a lord's revenue on his back,
And Midas-like, he jets [3] it in the court,
With base outlandish cullions [4] at his heels,   409
Whose proud fantastic liveries make such show
As if that Proteus, god of shapes, appear'd.
I have not seen a dapper Jack so brisk;
He wears a short Italian hooded cloak
Larded with pearl, and, in his Tuscan cap,
A jewel of more value than the crown.   415
While others walk below, the king and he
From out a window laugh at such as we,
And flout our train, and jest at our attire.
Uncle, 'tis this that makes me impatient.

E. Mor. But, nephew, now you see the king
is chang'd.   420
Y. Mor. Then so am I, and live to do him
service:
But whiles I have a sword, a hand, a heart,
I will not yield to any such upstart.
You know my mind; come, uncle, let's away.
Exeunt

[ACT II]

[SCENE I.] [5]

Enter [Young] SPENCER *and* BALDOCK.

Bald. Spencer, seeing that our lord th' Earl
of Gloucester's dead,
Which of the nobles dost thou mean to serve?
Y. Spen. Not Mortimer, nor any of his side,
Because the king and he are enemies.
Baldock, learn this of me, a factious lord   5
Shall hardly do himself good, much less us;
But he that hath the favour of a king,
May with one word advance us while we live.
The liberal Earl of Cornwall is the man   9
On whose good fortune Spencer's hope depends.
Bald. What, mean you then to be his fol-
lower?
Y. Spen. No, his companion; for he loves me
well,
And would have once preferr'd me to the king. [6]
Bald. But he is banish'd; there's small hope
of him.
Y. Spen. Ay, for a while; but, Baldock,
mark the end.   15
A friend of mine told me in secrecy
That he's repeal'd, and sent for back again;
And even now a post came from the court
With letters to our lady from the king;
And as she read she smil'd, which makes me
think   20
It is about her lover Gaveston.
Bald. 'Tis like enough; for since he was
exil'd
She neither walks abroad, nor comes in sight.
But I had thought the match had been broke off, 24
And that his banishment had chang'd her mind.
Y. Spen. Our lady's first love is not wavering;
My life for thine, she will have Gaveston.
Bald. Then hope I by her means to be pre-
ferr'd,
Having read unto her since she was a child.
Y. Spen. Then, Baldock, you must cast the
scholar off,   30
And learn to court it like a gentleman.
'Tis not a black coat and a little band,
A velvet-cap'd coat, fac'd before with serge,
And smelling to a nosegay all the day,
Or holding of a napkin in your hand,   35
Or saying a long grace at a table's end,
Or making low legs [7] to a nobleman,
Or looking downward with your eyelids close,
And saying, "Truly, an't may please your
honour,"
Can get you any favour with great men;   40

---

[1] Affianced him.
[2] Qq. *Hector*.
[3] Struts.
[4] Scoundrels.

[5] Gloucester's house.
[6] Advanced me to the king's service.
[7] Bows.

You must be proud, bold, pleasant, resolute,
And now and then stab, as occasion serves.
   Bald. Spencer, thou know'st I hate such for-
mal toys,
And use them but of mere hypocrisy.
Mine old lord whiles he liv'd was so precise,   45
That he would take exceptions at my buttons,
And being like pin's heads, blame me for the
bigness;
Which made me curate-like in mine attire,
Though inwardly licentious enough
And apt for any kind of villainy.   50
I am none of these common pedants, I,
That cannot speak without *propterea quod*.[1]
   Y. Spen. But one of those that saith *quando-
quidem*,[2]
And hath a special gift to form a verb.
   Bald. Leave off this jesting, here my lady
comes.   55

   Enter the Lady [KING EDWARD'S Niece.]

   Niece. The grief for his exile was not so much
As is the joy of his returning home.
This letter came from my sweet Gaveston: —
What need'st thou, love, thus to excuse thyself?
I know thou couldst not come and visit me.   60
[*Reads.*] " I will not long be from thee, though
I die."
This argues the entire love of my lord;
[*Reads.*] " When I forsake thee, death seize on
my heart: "
But stay thee here where Gaveston shall sleep.
        [*Puts the letter into her bosom.*]
Now to the letter of my lord the king.—   65
He wills me to repair unto the court,
And meet my Gaveston. Why do I stay,
Seeing that he talks thus of my marriage-day?
Who 's there? Baldock!
See that my coach be ready, I must hence.   70
   Bald. It shall be done, madam.
   Niece. And meet me at the park-pale pre-
sently.   *Exit* BALDOCK.
Spencer, stay you and bear me company,
For I have joyful news to tell thee of.
My lord of Cornwall is a-coming over,   75
And will be at the court as soon as we.
   Y. Spen. I knew the king would have him
home again.
   Niece. If all things sort [3] out as I hope they will,
Thy service, Spencer, shall be thought upon.
   Y. Spen. I humbly thank your ladyship.   80
   Niece. Come, lead the way; I long till I am
there.   [*Exeunt.*]

       [SCENE II.][4]

Enter KING EDWARD, QUEEN ISABELLA, KENT,
LANCASTER, Young MORTIMER, WARWICK,
PEMBROKE, *and* Attendants.

   K. Edw. The wind is good, I wonder why he
stays;
I fear me he is wrack'd upon the sea.
   Q. Isab. Look, Lancaster, how passionate [5]
he is,
And still his mind runs on his minion!

   Lan. My lord,—   5
   K. Edw. How now! what news? Is Gaveston
arriv'd?
   Y. Mor. Nothing but Gaveston! — What
means your grace?
You have matters of more weight to think upon;
The King of France sets foot in Normandy.
   K. Edw. A trifle! we 'll expel him when we
please.   10
But tell me, Mortimer, what 's thy device
Against the stately triumph we decreed?
   Y. Mor. A homely one, my lord, not worth
the telling.
   K. Edw. Pray thee let me know it.
   Y. Mor. But, seeing you are so desirous, thus
it is: 15
A lofty cedar-tree, fair flourishing,
On whose top-branches kingly eagles perch,
And by the bark a canker [6] creeps me up,
And gets into the highest bough of all:
The motto, *Aeque tandem*.[7]   20
   K. Edw. And what is yours, my lord of Lan-
caster?
   Lan. My lord, mine 's more obscure than
Mortimer's.
Pliny reports there is a flying fish
Which all the other fishes deadly hate,
And therefore, being pursued, it takes the air:
No sooner is it up, but there 's a fowl   25
That seizeth it; this fish, my lord, I bear:
The motto this: *Undique mors est*.[8]
   K. Edw. Proud Mortimer! ungentle Lancas-
ter!
Is this the love you bear your sovereign?   30
Is this the fruit your reconcilement bears?
Can you in words make show of amity,
And in your shields display your rancorous
minds?
What call you this but private libelling
Against the Earl of Cornwall and my brother?
   Q. Isab. Sweet husband, be content, they all
love you.   35
   K. Edw. They love me not that hate my
Gaveston.
I am that cedar, shake me not too much;
And you the eagles; soar ye ne'er so high,
I have the jesses [9] that will pull you down;   40
And *Aeque tandem* shall that canker cry
Unto the proudest peer of Britainy.
Though thou compar'st him to a flying fish,
And threatenest death whether he rise or fall,
'Tis not the hugest monster of the sea,   45
Nor foulest harpy that shall swallow him.
   Y. Mor. If in his absence thus he favours
him,
What will he do whenas he shall be present?
   Lan. That shall we see; look where his lord-
ship comes.

       Enter GAVESTON.

   K. Edw. My Gaveston!   50
Welcome to Tynemouth! Welcome to thy
friend!

---

[1] Lat. "because."   [3] Turn.   [5] Sorrowful.
[2] Lat. "since."   [4] Before Tynemouth Castle.

[6] Canker-worm.   [8] Lat. "On all sides is death."
[7] Lat. "Justly at length."
[9] The straps round a hawk's legs, to which the falconer's leash was fastened.

Thy absence made me droop and pine away;
For, as the lovers of fair Danae,
When she was lock'd up in a brazen tower,
Desir'd her more, and wax'd outrageous,   55
So did it fare [1] with me; and now thy sight
Is sweeter far than was thy parting hence
Bitter and irksome to my sobbing heart.

Gav. Sweet lord and king, your speech pre-
venteth [2] mine,
Yet have I words left to express my joy: 60
The shepherd nipt with biting winter's rage
Frolics not more to see the painted spring,
Than I do to behold your majesty.

K. Edw. Will none of you salute my Gaveston?

Lan. Salute him? yes. Welcome, Lord Chamberlain!   65

Y. Mor. Welcome is the good Earl of Cornwall!

War. Welcome, Lord Governor of the Isle
of Man!

Pem. Welcome, Master Secretary!

Kent. Brother, do you hear them?

K. Edw. Still will these earls and barons use
me thus.   70

Gav. My lord, I cannot brook these injuries.

Q. Isab. [*Aside.*] Aye me, poor soul, when
these begin to jar.

K. Edw. Return it to their throats, I'll be
thy warrant.

Gav. Base, leaden earls, that glory in your
birth,
Go sit at home and eat your tenants' beef;   75
And come not here to scoff at Gaveston,
Whose mounting thoughts did never creep so
low
As to bestow a look on such as you.

Lan. Yet I disdain not to do this for you.
[*Draws his sword and offers to stab*
GAVESTON.]

K. Edw. Treason! treason! where's the
traitor?   80

Pem. Here! here!

K. Edw. Convey hence Gaveston; they'll
murder him.

Gav. The life of thee shall salve this foul
disgrace.

Y. Mor. Villain! thy life, unless I miss mine
aim.   [*Wounds* GAVESTON.]

Q. Isab. Ah! furious Mortimer, what hast
thou done?   85

Y. Mor. No more than I would answer, were
he slain.
[*Exit* GAVESTON *with* Attendants.]

K. Edw. Yes, more than thou canst answer,
though he live.
Dear shall you both abye [3] this riotous deed.
Out of my presence! Come not near the court.

Y. Mor. I'll not be barr'd the court for
Gaveston.   90

Lan. We'll hale him by the ears unto the
block.

K. Edw. Look to your own heads; his is
sure enough.

[1] Qq. 1594–1612, *sure.*   [2] Anticipateth.
[3] Pay for.

War. Look to your own crown, if you back
him thus.

Kent. Warwick, these words do ill beseem
thy years.

K. Edw. Nay, all of them conspire to cross
me thus;   95
But if I live, I'll tread upon their heads
That think with high looks thus to tread me
down.
Come, Edmund, let's away and levy men,
'T is war that must abate these barons' pride.
Exeunt KING [EDWARD, QUEEN
ISABELLA *and* KENT].

War. Let's to our castles, for the king is
mov'd.   100

Y. Mor. Mov'd may he be, and perish in his
wrath!

Lan. Cousin, it is no dealing with him now,
He means to make us stoop by force of arms;
And therefore let us jointly here protest,
To persecute that Gaveston to the death.   105

Y. Mor. By heaven, the abject villain shall
not live!

War. I'll have his blood, or die in seeking it.

Pem. The like oath Pembroke takes.

Lan. And so doth Lancaster.
Now send our heralds to defy the king;   110
And make the people swear to put him down.

Enter a Messenger. [4]

Y. Mor. Letters! From whence?

Mess. From Scotland, my lord.
[*Giving letters to* MORTIMER.]

Lan. Why, how now, cousin, how fares all
our friends?

Y. Mor. My uncle's taken prisoner by the
Scots.   115

Lan. We'll have him ransom'd, man; be of
good cheer.

Y. Mor. They rate his ransom at five thou-
sand pound.
Who should defray the money but the king,
Seeing he is taken prisoner in his wars?
I'll to the king.   120

Lan. Do, cousin, and I'll bear thee company.

War. Meantime, my lord of Pembroke and
myself
Will to Newcastle here, and gather head. [5]

Y. Mor. About it then, and we will follow
you.

Lan. Be resolute and full of secrecy.   125

War. I warrant you. [*Exit with* PEMBROKE.]

Y. Mor. Cousin, and if he will not ransom
him,
I'll thunder such a peal into his ears,
As never subject did unto his king.

Lan. Content, I'll bear my part — Holla!
who's there?   130

[*Enter* Guard.]

Y. Mor. Ay, marry, such a guard as this
doth well.

Lan. Lead on the way.

Guard. Whither will your lordships?

Y. Mor. Whither else but to the king.   134

[4] Qq. *Poast.*   [5] An army.

Guard. His highness is dispos'd to be alone.
Lan. Why, so he may, but we will speak to
　him.
Guard. You may not in, my lord.
Y. Mor. May we not?

[*Enter* KING EDWARD *and* KENT.]

K. Edw. How now!
What noise is this? Who have we there?
Is 't you?　　　　　　　　　[*Going.*] 140
Y. Mor. Nay, stay, my lord, I come to bring
　you news;
Mine uncle 's taken prisoner by the Scots.
K. Edw. Then ransom him.
Lan. 'T was in your wars; you should ransom
　him.
Y. Mor. And you shall ransom him, or
　else ——　　　　　　　　　　　145
Kent. What! Mortimer, you will not threaten
　him?
K. Edw. Quiet yourself, you shall have the
　broad seal,
To gather for him thoroughout the realm.
Lan. Your minion Gaveston hath taught you
　this.
Y. Mor. My lord, the family of the Morti-
　mers　　　　　　　　　　　　150
Are not so poor, but, would they sell their land,
'T would levy men enough to anger you.
We never beg, but use such prayers as these.
K. Edw. Shall I still be haunted thus?
Y. Mor. Nay, now you 're here alone, I 'll
　speak my mind.　　　　　　　155
Lan. And so will I, and then, my lord, fare-
　well.
Y. Mor. The idle triumphs, masques, lasciv-
　ious shows,
And prodigal gifts bestow'd on Gaveston,
Have drawn thy treasury dry, and made thee
　weak;
The murmuring commons, overstretched,
　[break].[1]　　　　　　　　　　160
Lan. Look for rebellion, look to be depos'd.
Thy garrisons are beaten out of France,
And, lame and poor, lie groaning at the gates.
The wild O' Neill, with swarms of Irish kerns,[2]
Lives uncontroll'd within the English pale.　165
Unto the walls of York the Scots made road,
And unresisted drave away rich spoils.
Y. Mor. The haughty Dane commands the
　narrow seas,
While in the harbour ride thy ships unrigg'd.
Lan. What foreign prince sends thee ambas-
　sadors?　　　　　　　　　　　170
Y. Mor. Who loves thee, but a sort[3] of flat-
　terers?
Lan. Thy gentle queen, sole sister to Valois,
Complains that thou hast left her all forlorn.
Y. Mor. Thy court is naked, being bereft of
　those　　　　　　　　　　　　174
That make a king seem glorious to the world;
I mean the peers, whom thou should'st dearly
　love.
Libels are cast again thee in the street;
Ballads and rhymes made of thy overthrow.

Lan. The Northern borderers seeing their
　houses burnt,
Their wives and children slain, run up and
　down,　　　　　　　　　　　180
Cursing the name of thee and Gaveston.
Y. Mor. When wert thou in the field with
　banner spread,
But once? and then thy soldiers marcht like
　players,
With garish robes, not armour; and thyself,
Bedaub'd with gold, rode laughing at the rest,
Nodding and shaking of thy spangled crest, 186
Where women's favours hung like labels down.
Lan. And therefore came it, that the fleer-
　ing[4] Scots,
To England's high disgrace, have made this jig:
"Maids of England, sore may you mourn,— 190
　For your lemans[5] you have lost at Bannocks-
　　bourn,—[6]
　With a heave and a ho!
What weeneth the King of England,
So soon to have won Scotland?—
　With a rombelow!"　　　　　　195
Y. Mor. Wigmore[7] shall fly, to set my uncle
　free.
Lan. And when 't is gone, our swords shall
　purchase more.
If ye be mov'd, revenge it as you can;
Look next to see us with our ensigns spread.

　　　　　　　Exit [*with* Young MORTIMER].

K. Edw. My swelling heart for very anger
　breaks!　　　　　　　　　　　200
How oft have I been baited by these peers,
And dare not be reveng'd, for their power is
　great!
Yet, shall the crowing of these cockerels
Affright a lion? Edward, unfold thy paws,
And let their lives' blood slake thy fury's hun-
　ger.　　　　　　　　　　　　205
If I be cruel and grow tyrannous,
Now let them thank themselves, and rue too
　late.
Kent. My lord, I see your love to Gaveston
Will be the ruin of the realm and you,
For now the wrathful nobles threaten wars, 210
And therefore, brother, banish him for ever.
K. Edw. Art thou an enemy to my Gaveston?
Kent. Ay, and it grieves me that I favoured
　him.
K. Edw. Traitor, begone! whine thou with
　Mortimer.　　　　　　　　　214
Kent. So will I, rather than with Gaveston.
K. Edw. Out of my sight, and trouble me no
　more!
Kent. No marvel though thou scorn thy noble
　peers,
When I thy brother am rejected thus.
K. Edw. Away!　　　　　　*Exit* KENT.
Poor Gaveston, that has no friend but me, 220
Do what they can, we 'll live in Tynemouth here,
And, so I walk with him about the walls,
What care I though the earls begirt us round?—
Here comes she that is cause of all these jars.

---

[4] Jeering.　　　　　　　　[5] Lovers.
[6] Bannockburn was not yet fought. The rhyme is
taken from the Chronicles.
[7] Young Mortimer's estate.

[1] So Dodsley. Qq. *hath.*　　[2] Foot soldiers.　　[3] Band.

Enter QUEEN ISABELLA *with* [KING EDWARD'S
Niece, *two*] Ladies, [GAVESTON,] BALDOCK
and Young SPENCER.

Q. Isab. My lord, 'tis thought the earls are
up in arms.   225
K. Edw. Ay, and 'tis likewise thought you
favour 'em.
Q. Isab. Thus do you still suspect me with-
out cause?
Niece. Sweet uncle! speak more kindly to
the queen.
Gav. My lord, dissemble with her, speak her
fair.
K. Edw. Pardon me, sweet, I forgot my-
self.   230
Q. Isab. Your pardon is quickly got of Isabel.
K. Edw. The younger Mortimer is grown so
brave,
That to my face he threatens civil wars.
Gav. Why do you not commit him to the
Tower?
K. Edw. I dare not, for the people love him
well.   235
Gav. Why, then we'll have him privily made
away.
K. Edw. Would Lancaster and he had both
carous'd
A bowl of poison to each other's health!
But let them go, and tell me what are these?
Niece. Two of my father's servants whilst he
liv'd,—   240
Mayst please your grace to entertain them
now.
K. Edw. Tell me, where wast thou born?
What is thine arms?
Bald. My name is Baldock, and my gentry
I fetcht from Oxford, not from heraldry.
K. Edw. The fitter art thou, Baldock, for my
turn.   245
Wait on me, and I'll see thou shalt not want.
Bald. I humbly thank your majesty.
K. Edw. Knowest thou him, Gaveston?
Gav.   Ay, my lord;
His name is Spencer, he is well allied;
For my sake, let him wait upon your grace;   250
Scarce shall you find a man of more desert.
K. Edw. Then, Spencer, wait upon me; for
his sake
I'll grace thee with a higher style ere long.
Y. Spen. No greater titles happen unto me,
Than to be favoured of your majesty!   255
K. Edw. Cousin, this day shall be your mar-
riage-feast.
And, Gaveston, think that I love thee well
To wed thee to our niece, the only heir
Unto the Earl of Gloucester late deceas'd.
Gav. I know, my lord, many will stomach [1]
me,   260
But I respect neither their love nor hate.
K. Edw. The headstrong barons shall not
limit me:
He that I list to favour shall be great.
Come, let's away; and when the marriage ends,
Have at the rebels, and their 'complices!   265
                                   Exeunt.

[1] Feel resentment at.

Enter KENT, LANCASTER, Young MORTIMER,
WARWICK, PEMBROKE, [*and others*].

Kent. My lords, of love to this our native land
I come to join with you and leave the king;
And in your quarrel and the realm's behoof
Will be the first that shall adventure life.
Lan. I fear me, you are sent of policy,   5
To undermine us with a show of love.
War. He is your brother, therefore have we
cause
To cast [3] the worst, and doubt of your revolt.
Kent. Mine honour shall be hostage of my
truth;
If that will not suffice, farewell, my lords.   10
Y. Mor. Stay, Edmund; never was Planta-
genet
False to his word, and therefore trust we thee.
Pem. But what's the reason you should leave
him now?
Kent. I have inform'd the Earl of Lancaster.
Lan. And it sufficeth. Now, my lords, know
this,   15
That Gaveston is secretly arriv'd,
And here in Tynemouth frolics with the king.
Let us with these our followers scale the walls,
And suddenly surprise them unawares.   19
Y. Mor. I'll give the onset.
War.   And I'll follow thee.
Y. Mor. This tottered[4] ensign of my ancestors,
Which swept the desert shore of that dead sea
Whereof we got the name of Mortimer,
Will I advance upon these castle-walls.
Drums, strike alarum, raise them from their
sport,   25
And ring aloud the knell of Gaveston!
Lan. None be so hardy as to touch the king;
But neither spare you Gaveston nor his friends.
                                   Exeunt.

Enter KING EDWARD *and* Young SPENCER.

K. Edw. O tell me, Spencer, where is Gaveston?
Spen. I fear he is slain, my gracious lord.
K. Edw. No, here he comes; now let them
spoil and kill.

[*Enter* QUEEN ISABELLA, KING EDWARD'S
Niece, GAVESTON, *and* Nobles.]

Fly, fly, my lords, the earls have got the hold;
Take shipping and away to Scarborough;   5
Spencer and I will post away by land.
Gav. O stay, my lord, they will not injure
you.
K. Edw. I will not trust them; Gaveston,
away!
Gav. Farewell, my lord.
K. Edw. Lady, farewell.   10
Niece. Farewell, sweet uncle, till we meet
again.

[2] Near Tynemouth Castle.   [3] Suspect.
[4] Tattered.   [5] Near Tynemouth Castle.

K. Edw. Farewell, sweet Gaveston; and farewell, niece.

Q. Isab. No farewell to poor Isabel thy queen?

K. Edw. Yes, yes, for Mortimer, your lover's sake. *Exeunt all but* QUEEN ISABELLA.

Q. Isab. Heavens can witness I love none but you!   15
From my embracements thus he breaks away.
O that mine arms could close this isle about,
That I might pull him to me where I would!
Or that these tears that drizzle from mine eyes
Had power to mollify his stony heart,   20
That when I had him we might never part.

Enter the Barons, [LANCASTER, WARWICK, Young MORTIMER, *and others*]. *Alarums.*

Lan. I wonder how he scap'd!
Y. Mor.   Who's this? The queen!
Q. Isab. Ay, Mortimer, the miserable queen,
Whose pining heart her inward sighs have blasted,
And body with continual mourning wasted.   25
These hands are tir'd with haling of my lord
From Gaveston, from wicked Gaveston,
And all in vain; for, when I speak him fair,
He turns away, and smiles upon his minion.
Y. Mor. Cease to lament, and tell us where's the king?   30
Q. Isab. What would you with the king?
Is't him you seek?
Lan. No, madam, but that cursed Gaveston.
Far be it from the thought of Lancaster
To offer violence to his sovereign.
We would but rid the realm of Gaveston: 35
Tell us where he remains, and he shall die.
Q. Isab. He's gone by water unto Scarborough;
Pursue him quickly, and he cannot scape;
The king hath left him, and his train is small.
War. Foreslow [1] no time, sweet Lancaster;
let's march.   40
Y. Mor. How comes it that the king and he is parted?
Q. Isab. That thus your army, going several ways,
Might be of lesser force; and with the power
That he intendeth presently to raise,
Be easily suppress'd; therefore be gone.   45
Y. Mor. Here in the river rides a Flemish hoy; [2]
Let's all aboard, and follow him amain.
Lan. The wind that bears him hence will fill our sails.
Come, come aboard, 't is but an hour's sailing.
Y. Mor. Madam, stay you within this castle here.   50
Q. Isab. No, Mortimer, I'll to my lord the king.
Y. Mor. Nay, rather sail with us to Scarborough.
Q. Isab. You know the king is so suspicious,
As if he hear I have but talk'd with you,
Mine honour will be call'd in question;   55
And therefore, gentle Mortimer, be gone.

[1] Delay.   [2] A small vessel.

Y. Mor. Madam, I cannot stay to answer you,
But think of Mortimer as he deserves.
     [*Exeunt all except* QUEEN ISABELLA.]
Q. Isab. So well hast thou deserv'd sweet Mortimer,
As Isabel could live with thee for ever!   60
In vain I look for love at Edward's hand,
Whose eyes are fix'd on none but Gaveston;
Yet once more I'll importune him with prayers.
If he be strange and not regard my words,
My son and I will over into France,   65
And to the king my brother there complain,
How Gaveston hath robb'd me of his love:
But yet I hope my sorrows will have end,
And Gaveston this blessed day be slain.   *Exit.*

[SCENE V.] [3]

Enter GAVESTON, *pursued.*

Gav. Yet, lusty lords, I have escap'd your hands,
Your threats, your 'larums, and your hot pursuits;
And though divorced from King Edward's eyes,
Yet liveth Pierce of Gaveston unsurpris'd, [4]
Breathing, in hope (*malgrado* [5] all your beards,   5
That muster rebels thus against your king),
To see his royal sovereign once again.

Enter the Nobles, [WARWICK, LANCASTER, PEMBROKE, Young MORTIMER, Soldiers, JAMES, *and other* Attendants of PEMBROKE].

War. Upon him, soldiers, take away his weapons.
Y. Mor. Thou proud disturber of thy country's peace,
Corrupter of thy king, cause of these broils,   10
Base flatterer, yield! and were it not for shame,
Shame and dishonour to a soldier's name,
Upon my weapon's point here shouldst thou fall,
And welter in thy gore.
Lan.   Monster of men!
That, like the Greekish strumpet, [6] train'd [7] to arms   15
And bloody wars so many valiant knights;
Look for no other fortune, wretch, than death!
King Edward is not here to buckler thee.
War. Lancaster, why talk'st thou to the slave?   19
Go, soldiers, take him hence, for, by my sword,
His head shall off. Gaveston, short warning
Shall serve thy turn; it is our country's cause
That here severely we will execute
Upon thy person. Hang him at a bough.   24
Gav. My lord! —
War.   Soldiers, have him away; —
But for thou wert the favourite of a king,
Thou shalt have so much honour at our hands —
Gav. I thank you all, my lords: then I perceive,
That heading is one, and hanging is the other,
And death is all.   30

[3] The open country.   [6] Helen of Troy.
[4] Uncaptured.   [7] Drew.
[5] Ital. "in spite of."

Enter Earl of ARUNDEL.

Lan. How now, my lord of Arundel?
Arun. My lords, King Edward greets you all
    by me.
War. Arundel, say your message.
Arun.   His majesty,
Hearing that you had taken Gaveston,
Entreateth you by me, yet but he may   35
See him before he dies; for why, he says,
And sends you word, he knows that die he shall ;
And if you gratify his grace so far,
He will be mindful of the courtesy.   39
War. How now?
Gav.   Renowned Edward, how thy name
Revives poor Gaveston !
War.   No, it needeth not ;
Arundel, we will gratify the king
In other matters ; he must pardon us in this.
Soldiers, away with him !
Gav.   Why, my lord of Warwick,
Will not these delays beget my hopes ?   45
I know it, lords, it is this life you aim at,
Yet grant King Edward this.
Y. Mor.   Shalt thou appoint
What we shall grant? Soldiers, away with him !
Thus will we gratify the king :
We 'll send his head by thee ; let him bestow 50
His tears on that, for that is all he gets
Of Gaveston, or else his senseless trunk.
Lan. Not so, my lords, lest he bestow more
    cost
In burying him than he hath ever earn'd.
Arun. My lords, it is his majesty's request, 55
And in the honour of a king he swears,
He will but talk with him, and send him back.
War. When? can you tell ? Arundel, no ; we
    wot
He that the care of his realm remits,
And drives his nobles to these exigents [1]   60
For Gaveston, will, if he sees [2] him once,
Violate any promises to possess him.
Arun. Then if you will not trust his grace in
    keep,
My lords, I will be pledge for his return.   64
Y. Mor. 'T is honourable in thee to offer this ;
But for we know thou art a noble gentleman,
We will not wrong thee so, to make away
A true man for a thief.
Gav. How mean'st thou, Mortimer? That is
    over-base.
Y. Mor. Away, base groom, robber of king's
    renown !   70
Question with thy companions and thy mates.
Pem. My Lord Mortimer, and you, my lords,
    each one,
To gratify the king's request therein,
Touching the sending of this Gaveston,
Because his majesty so earnestly   75
Desires to see the man before his death,
I will upon mine honour undertake
To carry him, and bring him back again ;
Provided this, that you my lord of Arundel 79
Will join with me.

    [1] Extremities.
    [2] Cunningham's emendation for Q. *zease*.

War.   Pembroke, what wilt thou do ?
Cause yet more bloodshed ? Is it not enough
That we have taken him, but must we now
Leave him on " had I wist," [3] and let him go ?
Pem. My lords, I will not over-woo your
    honours,
But if you dare trust Pembroke with the pris-
    oner,   85
Upon mine oath, I will return him back.
Arun. My lord of Lancaster, what say you in
    this ?
Lan. Why, I say, let him go on Pembroke's
    word.
Pem. And you, Lord Mortimer ?   89
Y. Mor. How say you, my lord of Warwick ?
War. Nay, do your pleasures, I know how
    't will prove.
Pem. Then give him me.
Gav.   Sweet sovereign, yet I come
To see thee ere I die.
War.   Yet not perhaps,
If Warwick's wit and policy prevail. [*Aside.*]
Y. Mor. My lord of Pembroke, we deliver
    him you ;   95
Return him on your honour. Sound, away !
        Exeunt all except PEMBROKE, AR-
        UNDEL, GAVESTON, [JAMES, *and
        other*] Attendants *of* PEMBROKE.
Pem. My lord [Arundel,] you shall go with
    me.
My house is not far hence ; out of the way
A little, but our men shall go along.
We that have pretty wenches to our wives, 100
Sir, must not come so near and baulk their lips.
Arun. 'T is very kindly spoke, my lord of
    Pembroke ;
Your honour hath an adamant of power
To draw a prince.
Pem.   So, my lord. Come hither, James :
I do commit this Gaveston to thee,   105
Be thou this night his keeper ; in the morning
We will discharge thee of thy charge. Be gone.
Gav. Unhappy Gaveston, whither goest thou
    now ?
        Exit with [JAMES *and the other*] At-
        tendants.
Horse-boy. My lord, we 'll quickly be at Cob-
    ham.   *Exeunt.*

[ACT III]

[SCENE I.] [4]

Enter GAVESTON *mourning,* [JAMES *and other*]
    Attendants *of* PEMBROKE.

    Gav. O treacherous Warwick ! thus to wrong
        thy friend.
    James. I see it is your life these arms pursue.
    Gav. Weaponless must I fall, and die in
        bands ?
    O ! must this day be period of my life ?
    Centre of all my bliss ! An ye be men,   5
    Speed to the king.

    [3] " Had I known — the exclamation of those who
    repent of what they have rashly done." (Dyce.)
    [4] The open country.

Enter WARWICK *and his company.*

War.　　　My lord of Pembroke's men,
Strive you no longer — I will have that Gaveston.
James. Your lordship does dishonour to yourself,
And wrong our lord, your honourable friend.
War. No, James, it is my country's cause I
follow.　　　　　　　　　　　10
Go, take the villain ; soldiers, come away.
We 'll make quick work. Commend me to your
master,
My friend, and tell him that I watch'd it well.
Come, let thy shadow[1] parley with King Edward.
Gav. Treacherous earl, shall I not see the
king ?　　　　　　　　　　15
War. The king of Heaven, perhaps ; no other
king.
Away !　　*Exeunt* WARWICK *and his men with*
GAVESTON.

James. Come, fellows, it booted not for us to
strive,
We will in haste go certify our lord.　*Exeunt.*

[SCENE II.][2]

Enter KING EDWARD *and* [Young] SPENCER,
[BALDOCK, *and* Nobles *of the* KING'S *side, and*
Soldiers] *with drums and fifes.*

K. Edw. I long to hear an answer from the
barons
Touching my friend, my dearest Gaveston.
Ah ! Spencer, not the riches of my realm
Can ransom him ! Ah, he is mark'd to die !
I know the malice of the younger Mortimer,　5
Warwick I know is rough, and Lancaster
Inexorable, and I shall never see
My lovely Pierce, my Gaveston again !
The barons overbear me with their pride.
Y. Spen. Were I King Edward, England's
sovereign,　　　　　　　　10
Son to the lovely Eleanor of Spain,
Great Edward Longshanks' issue, would I bear
These braves, this rage, and suffer uncontroll'd
These barons thus to beard me in my land,
In mine own realm ? My lord, pardon my
speech :　　　　　　　　　15
Did you retain your father's magnanimity,
Did you regard the honour of your name,
You would not suffer thus your majesty
Be counterbuff'd of [3] your nobility.
Strike off their heads, and let them preach on
poles !　　　　　　　　　20
No doubt, such lessons they will teach the rest,
As by their preachments they will profit much,
And learn obedience to their lawful king.
K. Edw. Yea, gentle Spencer, we have been
too mild,
Too kind to them ; but now have drawn our
sword,　　　　　　　　　25
And if they send me not my Gaveston,
We 'll steel it[4] on their crest, and poll their
tops.

[1] Ghost.
[2] Near Boroughbridge, in Yorkshire.
[3] Checked by.　　　[4] Use our steel.

Bald. This haught[5] resolve becomes your
majesty,
Not to be tied to their affection,
As though your highness were a schoolboy still,
And must be aw'd and govern'd like a child.　31

Enter the Elder SPENCER, *with his truncheon and*
Soldiers.

E. Spen. Long live my sovereign, the noble
Edward,
In peace triumphant, fortunate in wars !
K. Edw. Welcome, old man, com'st thou in
Edward's aid ?
Then tell thy prince of whence, and what thou
art.　　　　　　　　　35
E. Spen. Lo, with a band of bowmen and of
pikes,
Brown bills and targeteers, four hundred
strong,
Sworn to defend King Edward's royal right,
I come in person to your majesty,
Spencer, the father of Hugh Spencer there,　40
Bound to your highness everlastingly,
For favour done, in him, unto us all.
K. Edw. Thy father, Spencer ?
Y. Spen.　　　True, an it like your grace,
That pours, in lieu of all your goodness shown,
His life, my lord, before your princely feet.　45
K. Edw. Welcome ten thousand times, old
man, again.
Spencer, this love, this kindness to thy king,
Argues thy noble mind and disposition.
Spencer, I here create thee Earl of Wiltshire,
And daily will enrich thee with our favour,　50
That, as the sunshine, shall reflect o'er thee.
Beside, the more to manifest our love,
Because we hear Lord Bruce doth sell his land,
And that the Mortimers are in hand[6] withal,
Thou shalt have crowns of us t' outbid the
barons :　　　　　　　　　55
And, Spencer, spare them not, but lay it on.
Soldiers, a largess, and thrice welcome all !
Y. Spen. My lord, here comes the queen.

Enter QUEEN [ISABELLA,] *and her son* [PRINCE
EDWARD,] *and* LEVUNE, a Frenchman.

K. Edw. Madam, what news ?
Q. Isab. News of dishonour, lord, and discontent.　　　　　　　　　60
Our friend Levune, faithful and full of trust,
Informeth us, by letters and by words,
That Lord Valois our brother, King of France,
Because your highness hath been slack in homage,
Hath seized Normandy into his hands.　65
These be the letters, this the messenger.
K. Edw. Welcome, Levune. Tush, Sib, if
this be all
Valois and I will soon be friends again. —
But to my Gaveston ; shall I never see,
Never behold thee now ? — Madam in this matter,　　　　　　　　　70
We will employ you and your little son ;
You shall go parley with the king of France. —
Boy, see you bear you bravely to the king,
And do your message with a majesty.

[5] High-spirited.　　[6] Negotiating.

P. Edw. Commit not to my youth things of
more weight   75
Than fits a prince so young as I to bear,
And fear not, lord and father, Heaven's great
beams
On Atlas' shoulder shall not lie more safe,
Than shall your charge committed to my trust.

Q. Isab. Ah, boy ! this towardness makes thy
mother fear   80
Thou art not mark'd to many days on earth.

K. Edw. Madam, we will that you with speed
be shipp'd,
And this our son ; Levune shall follow you
With all the haste we can despatch him hence.
Choose of our lords to bear you company,   85
And go in peace ; leave us in wars at home.

Q. Isab. Unnatural wars, where subjects
brave their king ;
God end them once ! My lords, I take my leave,
To make my preparation for France.

    [*Exit with* PRINCE EDWARD.]

Enter [ARUNDEL].[1]

K. Edw. What, Lord [Arundel,] dost thou
come alone ?   90

Arun. Yea, my good lord, for Gaveston is
dead.

K. Edw. Ah, traitors ! have they put my
friend to death ?
Tell me, Arundel, died he ere thou cam'st,
Or didst thou see my friend to take his death ?

Arun. Neither, my lord ; for as he was sur-
pris'd,   95
Begirt with weapons and with enemies round,
I did your highness' message to them all ;
Demanding him of them, entreating rather,
And said, upon the honour of my name,
That I would undertake to carry him   100
Unto your highness, and to bring him back.

K. Edw. And tell me, would the rebels deny
me that ?

Y. Spen. Proud recreants !

K. Edw.   Yea, Spencer, traitors all.

Arun. I found them at the first inexorable ;
The Earl of Warwick would not bide the hear-
ing,   105
Mortimer hardly ; Pembroke and Lancaster
Spake least : and when they flatly had denied,
Refusing to receive me pledge for him,
The Earl of Pembroke mildly thus bespake ;
" My lords, because our sovereign sends for
him,   110
And promiseth he shall be safe return'd,
I will this undertake, to have him hence,
And see him re-delivered to your hands."

K. Edw. Well, and how fortunes [it] that he
came not ?

Y. Spen. Some treason, or some villainy, was
cause.   115

Arun. The Earl of Warwick seiz'd him on his
way ;
For being delivered unto Pembroke's men,
Their lord rode home thinking his prisoner safe ;
But ere he came, Warwick in ambush lay,

And bare him to his death ; and in a trench   120
Strake off his head, and march'd unto the camp.

Y. Spen. A bloody part, flatly 'gainst law of
arms !

K. Edw. O shall I speak, or shall I sigh and
die !

Y. Spen. My lord, refer your vengeance to the
sword
Upon these barons ; hearten up your men ;   125
Let them not unreveng'd murder your friends !
Advance your standard, Edward, in the field,
And march to fire them from their starting holes.

K. Edw. (*kneeling.*) By earth, the common
mother of us all,
By Heaven, and all the moving orbs thereof,   130
By this right hand, and by my father's sword,
And all the honours 'longing to my crown,
I will have heads and lives for him, as many
As I have manors, castles, towns, and towers ! —
    [*Rises.*]
Treacherous Warwick ! traitorous Mortimer !   135
If I be England's king, in lakes of gore
Your headless trunks, your bodies will I trail,
That you may drink your fill, and quaff in blood,
And stain my royal standard with the same,
That so my bloody colours may suggest   140
Remembrance of revenge immortally
On your accursed traitorous progeny,
You villains, that have slain my Gaveston !
And in this place of honour and of trust,
Spencer, sweet Spencer, I adopt thee here :   145
And merely of our love we do create thee
Earl of Gloucester, and Lord Chamberlain.
Despite of times, despite of enemies.

Y. Spen. My lord, here 's a messenger from
the barons.
Desires access unto your majesty.   150

K. Edw. Admit him near.

Enter the Herald *from the Barons with his coat
of arms.*

Her. Long live King Edward, England's lawful lord !

K. Edw. So wish not they, I wis, that sent
thee hither.
Thou com'st from Mortimer and his 'complices,
A ranker rout of rebels never was.   155
Well, say thy message.

Her. The barons up in arms, by me salute
Your highness with long life and happiness ;
And bid me say, as plainer to your grace,
That if without effusion of blood   160
You will this grief have ease and remedy,
That from your princely person you remove
This Spencer, as a putrifying branch,
That deads the royal vine, whose golden leaves
Empale your princely head, your diadem,   165
Whose brightness such pernicious upstarts dim,
Say they ; and lovingly advise your grace,
To cherish virtue and nobility,
And have old servitors in high esteem,
And shake off smooth dissembling flatterers.   170
This granted, they, their honours, and their
lives,
Are to your highness vow'd and consecrate.

Y. Spen. Ah, traitors ! will they still display
their pride ?

K. Edw. Away, tarry no answer, but be
gone!
Rebels, will they appoint their sovereign   175
His sports, his pleasures, and his company?
Yet, ere thou go, see how I do divorce
                    Embraces SPENCER.
Spencer from me. — Now get thee to thy
lords,
And tell them I will come to chastise them
For murdering Gaveston; hie thee, get thee
gone!   180
Edward with fire and sword follows at thy heels.
                    [*Exit* Herald.]
My lords, perceive you how these rebels swell?
Soldiers, good hearts, defend your sovereign's
right,
For now, even now, we march to make them
stoop.   184
Away!   *Exeunt. Alarums, excursions, a great
fight, and a retreat [sounded, within].*

[SCENE III.][1]

Re-enter KING EDWARD, *the* Elder SPENCER,
Young SPENCER, *and* Noblemen *of the*
KING'S *side.*

K. Edw. Why do we sound retreat? Upon
them, lords!
This day I shall pour vengeance with my sword
On those proud rebels that are up in arms
And do confront and countermand their king.
    Y. Spen. I doubt it not, my lord, right will
prevail.   5
    E. Spen. 'T is not amiss, my liege, for either
part
To breathe awhile; our men, with sweat and
dust
All chokt well near, begin to faint for heat;
And this retire refresheth horse and man.
    Y. Spen. Here come the rebels.   10

Enter the Barons, Young MORTIMER, LANCAS-
TER, WARWICK, PEMBROKE, *and others.*

Y. Mor. Look, Lancaster, yonder is Edward
Among his flatterers.
    Lan.   And there let him be
Till he pay dearly for their company.
    War. And shall, or Warwick's sword shall
smite in vain.
    K. Edw. What, rebels, do you shrink and
sound retreat?   15
    Y. Mor. No, Edward, no; thy flatterers faint
and fly.
    Lan. Thou 'd best betimes forsake them, and
their trains,[2]
For they 'll betray thee, traitors as they are.
    Y. Spen. Traitor on thy face, rebellious Lan-
caster!
    Pem. Away, base upstart, brav'st thou
nobles thus?   20
    E. Spen. A noble attempt and honourable
deed,
Is it not, trow ye, to assemble aid,
And levy arms against your lawful king!

---

[1] Battle-field at Boroughbridge in Yorkshire.
[2] Plots. T. Brooke emend. Qq. *Th'ad . . . thee.*

K. Edw. For which ere long their heads shall
satisfy,
T' appease the wrath of their offended king.   25
    Y. Mor. Then, Edward, thou wilt fight it to
the last,
And rather bathe thy sword in subjects' blood,
Than banish that pernicious company?
    K. Edw. Ay, traitors all, rather than thus be
brav'd,
Make England's civil towns huge heaps of
stones,   30
And ploughs to go about our palace-gates.
    War. A desperate and unnatural resolution!
Alarum! to the fight!
St. George for England, and the barons' right!
    K. Edw. Saint George for England, and King
Edward's right!   35
[*Alarums. Exeunt the two parties severally.*]

[SCENE IV.][3]

Enter KING EDWARD [*and his followers,*] *with
the* Barons [*and* KENT], *captives.*

K. Edw. Now, lusty lords, now, not by chance
of war,
But justice of the quarrel and the cause,
Vail'd[4] is your pride; methinks you hang the
heads,
But we 'll advance[5] them, traitors. Now 't is time
To be aveng'd on you for all your braves,   5
And for the murder of my dearest friend,
To whom right well you knew our soul was
knit,
Good Pierce of Gaveston, my sweet favourite.
Ah, rebels! recreants! you made him away.
    Kent. Brother, in regard of thee, and of thy
land,   10
Did they remove that flatterer from thy throne.
    K. Edw. So, sir, you have spoke; away,
avoid our presence!   [*Exit* KENT.]
Accursed wretches, was 't in regard of us,
When we had sent our messenger to request
He might be spar'd to come to speak with us,
And Pembroke undertook for his return,   16
That thou, proud Warwick, watch'd the pris-
oner,
Poor Pierce, and headed him 'gainst law of
arms?
For which thy head shall overlook the rest,
As much as thou in rage outwent'st the rest.   20
    War. Tyrant, I scorn thy threats and men-
aces;
It is but temporal that thou canst inflict.
    Lan. The worst is death, and better die to
live
Than live in infamy under such a king.
    K. Edw. Away with them, my lord of Win-
chester!   25
These lusty leaders, Warwick and Lancaster,
I charge you roundly — off with both their
heads!
Away!
    War. Farewell, vain world!
    Lan.   Sweet Mortimer, farewell.
    Y. Mor. England, unkind to thy nobility,   30

---

[3] The same.   [4] Lowered.   [5] Raise.

Groan for this grief, behold how thou art
    maim'd !
K. Edw. Go take that haughty Mortimer to
    the Tower,
There see him safe bestow'd ; and for the rest,
Do speedy execution on them all.
Begone !
    Y. Mor.   What, Mortimer ! can ragged stony   35
        walls
Immure thy virtue that aspires to Heaven ?
No, Edward, England's scourge, it may not be ;
Mortimer's hope surmounts his fortune far.
    [The captive Barons are led off.]
K. Edw. Sound drums and trumpets ! March
    with me, my friends,   40
Edward this day hath crown'd him king anew.
        Exeunt all except Young SPENCER,
            LEVUNE, and BALDOCK.
Y. Spen. Levune, the trust that we repose in
    thee,
Begets the quiet of King Edward's land.
Therefore begone in haste, and with advice
Bestow that treasure on the lords of France,   45
That, therewith all enchanted, like the guard
That suffered Jove to pass in showers of gold
To Danaë, all aid may be denied
To Isabel, the queen, that now in France
Makes friends, to cross the seas with her young
    son,   50
And step into his father's regiment.[1]
Levune. That's it these barons and the subtle
    queen
Long levell'd at.
Bal.   Yea, but, Levune, thou seest
These barons lay their heads on blocks to-
    gether ;
What they intend, the hangman frustrates
    clean.   55
Levune. Have you no doubt, my lords, I'll
    clap so close
Among the lords of France with England's gold,
That Isabel shall make her plaints in vain,
And France shall be obdurate with her tears.
Y. Spen. Then make for France amain ;
    Levune, away !   60
Proclaim King Edward's wars and victories.
                                        Exeunt.

[ACT IV]

[SCENE I.][2]

Enter KENT.

Kent. Fair blows the wind for France ; blow
    gentle gale,
Till Edmund be arriv'd for England's good !
Nature, yield to my country's cause in this.
A brother ? No, a butcher of thy friends !
Proud Edward, dost thou banish me thy pres-
    ence ?   5
But I'll to France, and cheer the wronged
    queen,
And certify what Edward's looseness is.
Unnatural king ! to slaughter noblemen

And cherish flatterers ! Mortimer, I stay   9
Thy sweet escape : stand gracious, gloomy night,
To his device.

        Enter Young MORTIMER, disguised.

Y. Mor.   Holla ! who walketh there ?
Is 't you, my lord ?
Kent.   Mortimer, 'tis I ;
But hath thy potion wrought so happily ?
Y. Mor. It hath, my Lord ; the warders all
    asleep,
I thank them, gave me leave to pass in peace.   15
But hath your grace got shipping unto France ?
Kent. Fear it not.   Exeunt.

[SCENE II.][3]

Enter QUEEN [ISABELLA] and her son [PRINCE EDWARD].

Q. Isab. Ah, boy ! our friends do fail us all
    in France.
The lords are cruel, and the king unkind ;
What shall we do ?
P. Edw.   Madam, return to England,
And please my father well, and then a fig
For all my uncle's friendship here in France.   5
I warrant you, I'll win his highness quickly ;
'A loves me better than a thousand Spencers.
Q. Isab. Ah, boy, thou art deceiv'd, at least
    in this,
To think that we can yet be tun'd together ;
No, no, we jar too far. Unkind Valois !   10
Unhappy Isabel ! when France rejects,
Whither, oh ! whither dost thou bend thy
    steps ?

        Enter SIR JOHN of HAINAULT.

Sir J. Madam, what cheer ?
Q. Isab.   Ah ! good Sir John of Hainault,
Never so cheerless, nor so far distrest.
Sir J. I hear, sweet lady, of the king's un-
    kindness ;   15
But droop not, madam ; noble minds contemn
Despair. Will your grace with me to Hainault,
And there stay time's advantage with your
    son ?
How say you, my lord, will you go with your
    friends,
And share of[4] all our fortunes equally ?   20
P. Edw. So pleaseth the queen, my mother,
    me it likes.
The King of England, nor the court of France,
Shall have me from my gracious mother's side,
Till I be strong enough to break a staff ;   24
And then have at the proudest Spencer's head.
Sir J. Well said, my lord.
Q. Isab. O, my sweet heart, how do I moan
    thy wrongs,
Yet triumph in the hope of thee, my joy !
Ah, sweet Sir John ! even to the utmost verge
Of Europe, or the shore of Tanais,   30
Will we with thee to Hainault — so we will : —
The marquis is a noble gentleman ;
His grace, I dare presume, will welcome me.
But who are these ?

----

[1] Rule.   [2] Near the Tower of London.

[3] Paris.   [4] T. Brooke emend. Qq. shake off.

Enter KENT *and* Young MORTIMER.

Kent.   Madam, long may you live,
Much happier than your friends in England do !
Q. Isab. Lord Edmund and Lord Mortimer
alive !   36
Welcome to France ! The news was here, my
lord,
That you were dead, or very near your death.
Y. Mor. Lady, the last was truest of the
twain ;
But Mortimer, reserv'd for better hap,   40
Hath shaken off the thraldom of the Tower,
And lives t' advance your standard, good my
lord.
P. Edw. How mean you ? An[1] the king, my
father, lives ?
No, my Lord Mortimer, not I, I trow.
Q. Isab. Not, son ! why not ? I would it were
no worse.   45
But, gentle lords, friendless we are in France.
Y. Mor. Monsieur le Grand, a noble friend of
yours,
Told us, at our arrival, all the news :
How hard the nobles, how unkind the king
Hath show'd himself ; but, madam, right makes
room   50
Where weapons want ; and, though a many
friends
Are made away, away, as Warwick, Lancaster,
And others of our party and faction ;
Yet have we friends, assure your grace, in Eng-
land
Would cast up caps, and clap their hands for
joy,   55
To see us there, appointed[2] for our foes.
Kent. Would all were well, and Edward well
reclaim'd,
For England's honour, peace, and quietness.
Y. Mor. But by the sword, my lord, 't must
be deserv'd ;[3]
The king will ne'er forsake his flatterers.   60
Sir J. My lord of England, sith th' ungentle
king
Of France refuseth to give aid of arms
To this distressed queen his sister here,
Go you with her to Hainault. Doubt ye not,   64
We will find comfort, money, men, and friends
Ere long, to bid the English king a base.[4]
How say, young prince ? What think you of
the match ?
P. Edw. I think King Edward will outrun
us all.
Q. Isab. Nay, son, not so ; and you must not
discourage
Your friends, that are so forward in your aid. 70
Kent. Sir John of Hainault, pardon us, I pray ;
These comforts that you give our woful queen
Bind us in kindness all at your command.
Q. Isab. Yea, gentle brother ; and the God of
heaven
Prosper your happy motion, good Sir John.   75
Y. Mor. This noble gentleman, forward in
arms,

1 If.   2 Equipped.   3 Earned.
4 Challenge. A reference to the game of prisoner's
base.

Was born, I see, to be our anchor-hold.
Sir John of Hainault, be it thy renown,
That England's queen and nobles in distress,
Have been by thee restor'd and comforted.   80
Sir J. Madam, along, and you my lords, with
me,
That England's peers may Hainault's welcome
see.   [*Exeunt.*]
                    [SCENE III.][5]

Enter KING [EDWARD,] ARUNDEL, *the* Elder
and Younger SPENCER, *with others.*

K. Edw. Thus after many threats of wrath-
ful war,
Triumpheth England's Edward with his friends;
And triumph, Edward, with his friends uncon-
troll'd !
My lord of Gloucester, do you hear the news ?
Y. Spen. What news, my lord ?   5
K. Edw. Why, man, they say there is great
execution
Done through the realm ; my lord of Arundel,
You have the note, have you not ?
Arun. From the Lieutenant of the Tower,
my lord.
K. Edw. I pray let us see it. [*Takes the note.*]
What have we there ?   10
Read it, Spencer.
          [*Hands the note to*] Young SPEN-
                CER [*who*] *reads the names.*
Why, so ; they bark'd apace a month ago :
Now, on my life, they 'll neither bark nor bite.
Now, sirs, the news from France ? Gloucester,
I trow
The lords of France love England's gold so well
As Isabella gets no aid from thence.   16
What now remains ? Have you proclaim'd,
my lord,
Reward for them can bring in Mortimer ?
Y. Spen. My lord, we have ; and if he be in
England,
'A will be had ere long, I doubt it not.   20
K. Edw. If, dost thou say ? Spencer, as true
as death,
He is in England's ground ; our portmasters
Are not so careless of their king's command.

                    Enter a Post.

How now, what news with thee ? From whence
come these ?
Post. Letters, my lord, and tidings forth of
France ; —   25
To you, my lord of Gloucester, from Levune.
          [*Gives letters to* Young SPENCER.]
K. Edw. Read.
Y. Spen. (*reads*).
" My duty to your honour premised, &c., I
have, according to instructions in that behalf,
dealt with the King of France his lords, and [30
effected that the queen, all discontented and
discomforted, is gone : whither, if you ask, with
Sir John of Hainault, brother to the marquis,
into Flanders. With them are gone Lord Edmund, and the Lord Mortimer, having in their [35
company divers of your nation, and others ; and,

5 The Royal Palace, London.

as constant report goeth, they intend to give
King Edward battle in England, sooner than
he can look for them. This is all the news of
import.   40
     Your honour's in all service, LEVUNE."
  K. Edw. Ah, villains! hath that Mortimer
     escap'd?
With him is Edmund gone associate?
And will Sir John of Hainault lead the round?
Welcome, a' God's name, madam, and your son;
England shall welcome you and all your rout. 46
Gallop apace, bright Phoebus, through the sky,
And dusky night, in rusty iron car,
Between you both shorten the time, I pray,
That I may see that most desired day   50
When we may meet these traitors in the field.
Ah, nothing grieves me but my little boy
Is thus misled to countenance their ills.
Come, friends, to Bristow,[1] there to make us
     strong;
And, winds, as equal be to bring them in,   55
As you injurious were to bear them forth!
                                      [*Exeunt.*]

[SCENE IV.][2]

Enter QUEEN [ISABELLA], *her son,* [PRINCE
EDWARD,] KENT, Young MORTIMER, *and* SIR
JOHN [*of* HAINAULT].

  Q. Isab. Now, lords, our loving friends and
     countrymen,
Welcome to England all, with prosperous
     winds!
Our kindest friends in Belgia have we left,
To cope with friends at home; a heavy case
When force to force is knit, and sword and
     glaive   5
In civil broils make kin and countrymen
Slaughter themselves in others, and their sides
With their own weapons gor'd! But what's the
     help?
Misgoverned kings are cause of all this wrack;
And, Edward, thou art one among them all,   10
Whose looseness hath betray'd thy land to spoil,
Who made the channels overflow with blood.
Of thine own people patron shouldst thou be,
But thou——   14
  Y. Mor. Nay, madam, if you be a warrior,
You must not grow so passionate in speeches.
Lords,
Sith that we are by sufferance of Heaven
Arriv'd and armed in this prince's right,
Here for our country's cause swear we to him 20
All homage, fealty, and forwardness;
And for the open wrongs and injuries
Edward hath done to us, his queen and land,
We come in arms to wreak it with the sword;
That England's queen in peace may repossess
Her dignities and honours; and withal   26
We may remove these flatterers from the king,
That havocs England's wealth and treasury.
  Sir J. Sound trumpets, my lord, and forward
     let us march.
Edward will think we come to flatter him.   30
  Kent. I would he never had been flattered
     more.   [*Exeunt.*]

----
[1] Bristol.   [2] Near Harwich.

[SCENE V.][3]

Enter KING EDWARD, BALDOCK, *and* Young
SPENCER, *flying about the stage.*

  Y. Spen. Fly, fly, my lord! the queen is
     over-strong;
Her friends do multiply, and yours do fail.
Shape we our course to Ireland, there to
     breathe.
  K. Edw. What! was I born to fly and run
     away,
And leave the Mortimers conquerors behind? 5
Give me my horse, and let's reinforce our
     troops:
And in this bed of honour die with fame.
  Bald. O no, my lord, this princely resolution
Fits not the time; away! we are pursu'd.
                                      [*Exeunt.*]

Enter KENT, *with sword and target.*

  Kent. This way he fled, but I am come too
     late.   10
Edward, alas! my heart relents for thee.
Proud traitor, Mortimer, why dost thou chase
Thy lawful king, thy sovereign, with thy sword?
Vile wretch! and why hast thou, of all unkind,
Borne arms against thy brother and thy king?
Rain showers of vengeance on my cursed head,
Thou God, to whom in justice it belongs   17
To punish this unnatural revolt!
Edward, this Mortimer aims at thy life!
O fly him, then! But, Edmund, calm this rage,
Dissemble, or thou diest; for Mortimer   21
And Isabel do kiss, while they conspire;
And yet she bears a face of love forsooth.
Fie on that love that hatcheth death and hate!
Edmund, away! Bristow to Longshanks' blood
Is false. Be not found single for suspect:[4] 26
Proud Mortimer pries near unto thy walks.

Enter QUEEN [ISABELLA,] PRINCE [EDWARD,]
Young MORTIMER, *and* SIR JOHN *of* HAI-
NAULT.

  Q. Isab. Successful battle gives the God of
     kings
To them that fight in right and fear his wrath.
Since then successfully we have prevailed,   30
Thanked be Heaven's great architect, and you.
Ere farther we proceed, my noble lords,
We here create our well-beloved son,
Of love and care unto his royal person,
Lord Warden of the realm, and sith the fates 35
Have made his father so unfortunate,
Deal you, my lords, in this, my loving lords,
As to your wisdoms fittest seems in all.
  Kent. Madam, without offence, if I may ask,
How will you deal with Edward in his fall? 40
  P. Edw. Tell me, good uncle, what Edward
     do you mean?
  Kent. Nephew, your father; I dare not call
     him king.
  Y. Mor. My lord of Kent, what needs these
     questions?
'T is not in her controlment, nor in ours,
But as the realm and parliament shall please, 45

----
[3] Near Bristol.   [4] Lest you are suspected.

So shall your brother be disposed of. —
I like not this relenting mood in Edmund.
Madam, 't is good to look to him betimes.
                    [*Aside to the* QUEEN.]
  Q. Isab. My lord, the Mayor of Bristow
    knows our mind.
  Y. Mor. Yea, madam, and they scape not
    easily   50
That fled the field.
  Q. Isab.   Baldock is with the king,
A goodly chancellor, is he not, my lord ?
  Sir J. So are the Spencers, the father and
    the son.
  Kent. This Edward is the ruin of the realm.

Enter RICE AP HOWELL *and the* Mayor of Bristol, *with the* Elder SPENCER [*prisoner, and*
  Attendants].

  Rice. God save Queen Isabel, and her princely
    son !   55
Madam, the mayor and citizens of Bristow,
In sign of love and duty to this presence,
Present by me this traitor to the state,
Spencer, the father to that wanton Spencer,
That, like the lawless Catiline of Rome,   60
Revelled in England's wealth and treasury.
  Q. Isab. We thank you all.
  Y. Mor.   Your loving care in this
Deserveth princely favours and rewards.
But where 's the king and the other Spencer fled?
  Rice. Spencer the son, created Earl of Glou-
    cester,   65
Is with that smooth-tongu'd scholar Baldock
    gone
And shipt but late for Ireland with the king.
  Y. Mor. [*Aside.*] Some whirlwind fetch them
    back or sink them all ! —
They shall be started thence, I doubt it not.
  P. Edw. Shall I not see the king my father
    yet ?   70
  Kent. [*Aside.*] Unhappy 's Edward, chas'd
    from England's bounds.
  Sir J. Madam, what resteth, why stand you
    in a muse ?
  Q. Isab. I rue my lord's ill-fortune ; but alas !
Care of my country call'd me to this war.
  Y. Mor. Madam, have done with care and
    sad complaint ;   75
Your king hath wrong'd your country and him-
    self,
And we must seek to right it as we may.
Meanwhile, have hence this rebel to the block.
Your lordship cannot privilege your head.
  E. Spen. Rebel is he that fights against his
    prince ;   80
So fought not they that fought in Edward's right.
  Y. Mor. Take him away, he prates.
         [*Exeunt* Attendants *with the* Elder
        SPENCER.]
              You, Rice ap Howell,
Shall do good service to her majesty,
Being of countenance in your country here,
To follow these rebellious runagates.   85
We in meanwhile, madam, must take advice
How Baldock, Spencer, and their complices
May in their fall be followed to their end.
                            Exeunt.

[SCENE VI.] [1]

Enter the Abbot, Monks, [KING] EDWARD,
  Young SPENCER, *and* BALDOCK [*the three latter disguised*].

  Abbot. Have you no doubt, my lord ; have
    you no fear ;
As silent and as careful we will be,
To keep your royal person safe with us,
Free from suspect and fell invasion
Of such as have your majesty in chase,   5
Yourself, and those your chosen company,
As danger of this stormy time requires.
  K. Edw. Father, thy face should harbour no
    deceit.
O ! hadst thou ever been a king, thy heart,
Pierced deeply with sense of my distress,   10
Could not but take compassion of my state.
Stately and proud, in riches and in train,
Whilom I was, powerful, and full of pomp :
But what is he whom rule and empery
Have not in life or death made miserable ?   15
Come, Spencer ; come, Baldock, come, sit down
    by me ;
Make trial now of that philosophy,
That in our famous nurseries of arts
Thou suck'dst from Plato and from Aristotle.
Father, this life contemplative is Heaven.   20
O that I might this life in quiet lead !
But we, alas ! are chas'd ; and you, my friends,
Your lives and my dishonour they pursue.
Yet, gentle monks, for treasure, gold, nor fee,
Do you betray us and our company.   25
  Monks. Your grace may sit secure, if none but
    we
Do wot of your abode.
  Y. Spen. Not one alive ; but shrewdly I sus-
    pect
A gloomy fellow in a mead below.
'A gave a long look after us, my lord ;   30
And all the land I know is up in arms,
Arms that pursue our lives with deadly hate.
  Bald. We were embark'd for Ireland,
    wretched we !
With awkward winds and [with] sore tempests
    driven
To fall on shore, and here to pine in fear   35
Of Mortimer and his confederates.
  K. Edw. Mortimer ! who talks of Mortimer ?
Who wounds me with the name of Mortimer,
That bloody man ?   Good father, on thy lap
Lay I this head, laden with mickle care.   40
O might I never open these eyes again !
Never again lift up this drooping head !
O never more lift up this dying heart !
  Y. Spen. Look up, my lord. — Baldock, this
    drowsiness
Betides no good ; here even we are betray'd.   45

Enter, with Welsh hooks, RICE AP HOWELL, *a*
  Mower, *and* LEICESTER.

  Mow. Upon my life, these be the men ye seek.
  Rice. Fellow, enough. — My lord, I pray be
    short,
A fair commission warrants what we do.

            [1] The abbey of Neath.

Leices. The queen's commission, urged by
Mortimer ;
What cannot gallant Mortimer with the queen ?
Alas ! see where he sits, and hopes unseen   51
T' escape their hands that seek to reave his life.
Too true it is, *Quem dies vidit veniens superbum,*
Hunc dies vidit fugiens jacentem.[1]
But, Leicester, leave to grow so passionate.   55
Spencer and Baldock, by no other names,
I do arrest you of high treason here.
Stand not on titles, but obey th' arrest ;
'T is in the name of Isabel the queen.
My lord, why droop you thus ?   60
   K. Edw. O day, the last of all my bliss on
earth !
Centre of all misfortune ! O my stars,
Why do you lour unkindly on a king ?
Comes Leicester, then, in Isabella's name
To take my life, my company from me ?   65
Here, man, rip up this panting breast of mine,
And take my heart in rescue of my friends !
   Rice. Away with them !
   Y. Spen.   It may become thee yet
To let us take our farewell of his grace.
   Abbot. My heart with pity earns [2] to see this
sight, —   70
[*Aside.*] A king to bear these words and proud
commands.
   K. Edw. Spencer, ah, sweet Spencer, thus
then must we part ?
   Y. Spen. We must, my lord, so will the an-
gry Heavens.
   K. Edw. Nay, so will hell and cruel Morti-
mer ;
The gentle Heavens have not to do in this.   75
   Bald. My lord, it is in vain to grieve or storm.
Here humbly of your grace we take our leaves ;
Our lots are cast ; I fear me, so is thine.
   K. Edw. In Heaven we may, in earth ne'er
shall we meet :   79
And, Leicester, say, what shall become of us ?
   Leices. Your majesty must go to Killing-
worth.[3]
   K. Edw. Must ! it is somewhat hard, when
kings *must* go.
   Leices. Here is a litter ready for your grace,
That waits your pleasure, and the day grows old.
   Rice. As good be gone, as stay and be be-
nighted.   85
   K. Edw. A litter hast thou ? Lay me in a
hearse,
And to the gates of hell convey me hence ;
Let Pluto's bells ring out my fatal knell,
And hags howl for my death at Charon's shore,
For friends hath Edward none but these and
these,   90
And these must die under a tyrant's sword.
   Rice. My lord, be going ; care not for these,
For we shall see them shorter by the heads.
   K. Edw. Well, that shall be, shall be : part
we must !   94
Sweet Spencer, gentle Baldock, part we must !
Hence feigned weeds ! unfeigned are my woes ;
[*Throws off his disguise.*]

[1] " Whom the dawn sees proud, evening sees prostrate." Seneca, *Thyestes*, 613.
[2] Yearns, grieves.   [3] Kenilworth.

Father, farewell ! Leicester, thou stay'st for
me,
And go I must. Life, farewell, with my friends.
           Exeunt EDWARD *and* LEICESTER.
   Y. Spen. O ! is he gone ? Is noble Edward
gone ?
Parted from hence, never to see us more ?   100
Rent, sphere of Heaven ! and, fire, forsake thy
orb !
Earth, melt to air ! gone is my sovereign,
Gone, gone, alas ! never to make return.
   Bald. Spencer, I see our souls are fleeted
hence ;
We are depriv'd the sunshine of our life :   105
Make for a new life, man ; throw up thy eyes,
And heart, and hand to Heaven's immortal
throne ;
Pay nature's debt with cheerful countenance ;
Reduce we all our lessons unto this :   109
To die, sweet Spencer, therefore live we all ;
Spencer, all live to die, and rise to fall.
   Rice. Come, come, keep these preachments
till you come to the place appointed. You,
and such as you are, have made wise work in
England. Will your lordships away ?   115
   Mow. Your lordship, I trust, will remember
me ?
   Rice. Remember thee, fellow ! what else ?
Follow me to the town.   [*Exeunt.*]

[ACT V]

[SCENE I.][4]

Enter KING [EDWARD,] LEICESTER, *the* BISHOP
[*of* WINCHESTER] *for the crown* [*and* TRUSSEL].

   Leices. Be patient, good my lord, cease to
lament,
Imagine Killingworth Castle were your court,
And that you lay for pleasure here a space,
Not of compulsion or necessity.
   K. Edw. Leicester, if gentle words might
comfort me,   5
Thy speeches long ago had eas'd my sorrows ;
For kind and loving hast thou always been.
The griefs of private men are soon allay'd,
But not of kings. The forest deer, being struck,
Runs to an herb that closeth up the wounds ;   10
But, when the imperial lion's flesh is gor'd,
He rends and tears it with his wrathful paw,
[And] highly scorning that the lowly earth
Should drink his blood, mounts up into the air.
And so it fares with me, whose dauntless mind
The ambitious Mortimer would seek to curb,   16
And that unnatural queen, false Isabel,
That thus hath pent and mew'd me in a prison ;
For such outrageous passions cloy my soul,
As with the wings of rancour and disdain   20
Full often am I soaring up to Heaven,
To plain me to the gods against them both.
But when I call to mind I am a king,
Methinks I should revenge me of my wrongs,
That Mortimer and Isabel have done.   25
But what are kings, when regiment [5] is gone,

[4] A room in Kenilworth Castle.   [5] Rule

But perfect shadows in a sunshine day?
My nobles rule, I bear the name of king;
I wear the crown, but am controll'd by them,
By Mortimer, and my unconstant queen, 30
Who spots my nuptial bed with infamy;
Whilst I am lodg'd within this cave of care,
Where sorrow at my elbow still attends,
To company my heart with sad laments,
That bleeds within me for this strange ex-
change. 35
But tell me, must I now resign my crown,
To make usurping Mortimer a king?
B. of Win. Your grace mistakes; it is for
England's good,
And princely Edward's right we crave the
crown.
K. Edw. No, 't is for Mortimer, not Edward's
head; 40
For he 's a lamb, encompassed by wolves,
Which in a moment will abridge his life.
But if proud Mortimer do wear this crown,
Heavens turn it to a blaze of quenchless fire!
Or like the snaky wreath of Tisiphon, 45
Engirt the temples of his hateful head;
So shall not England's vine be perished,
But Edward's name survives, though Edward
dies.
Leices. My lord, why waste you thus the time
away?
They stay your answer; will you yield your
crown? 50
K. Edw. Ah, Leicester, weigh how hardly I
can brook
To lose my crown and kingdom without cause;
To give ambitious Mortimer my right,
That like a mountain overwhelms my bliss, 54
In which extreme my mind here murdered is.
But what the heavens appoint, I must obey!
Here, take my crown; the life of Edward too;
[*Taking off the crown.*]
Two kings in England cannot reign at once.
But stay awhile, let me be king till night,
That I may gaze upon this glittering crown; 60
So shall my eyes receive their last content,
My head, the latest honour due to it,
And jointly both yield up their wished right.
Continue ever thou celestial sun;
Let never silent night possess this clime: 65
Stand still you watches of the element;
All times and seasons, rest you at a stay,
That Edward may be still fair England's
king!
But day's bright beam doth vanish fast away,
And needs I must resign my wished crown. 70
Inhuman creatures! nurs'd with tiger's milk!
Why gape you for your sovereign's overthrow!
My diadem I mean, and guiltless life.
See, monsters, see, I 'll wear my crown again!
[*He puts on the crown.*]
What, fear you not the fury of your king? 75
But, hapless Edward, thou art fondly [1] led;
They pass [2] not for thy frowns as late they did,
But seek to make a new-elected king;
Which fills my mind with strange despairing
thoughts,

Which thoughts are martyred with endless
torments, 80
And in this torment comfort find I none,
But that I feel the crown upon my head;
And therefore let me wear it yet awhile.
Trus. My lord, the parliament must have
present news,
And therefore say, will you resign or no? 85
The KING *rageth.*
K. Edw. I 'll not resign, but whilst I live [be
king.] [3]
Traitors, be gone and join with Mortimer!
Elect, conspire, install, do what you will: —
Their blood and yours shall seal these treach-
eries!
B. of Win. This answer we 'll return, and so
farewell. [*Going with* TRUSSEL.] 90
Leices. Call them again, my lord, and speak
them fair;
For if they go, the prince shall lose his right.
K. Edw. Call thou them back, I have no
power to speak.
Leices. My lord, the king is willing to resign.
B. of Win. If he be not, let him choose. 95
K. Edw. O would I might, but heavens and
earth conspire
To make me miserable! Here receive my
crown;
Receive it? No, these innocent hands of mine
Shall not be guilty of so foul a crime.
He of you all that most desires my blood, 100
And will be call'd the murderer of a king,
Take it. What, are you mov'd? Pity you me?
Then send for unrelenting Mortimer,
And Isabel, whose eyes, being turn'd to steel,
Will sooner sparkle fire than shed a tear. 105
Yet stay, for rather than I 'll look on them,
Here, here! [*Gives the crown.*]
Now, sweet God of Heaven,
Make me despise this transitory pomp,
And sit for aye enthronized in Heaven!
Come, death, and with thy fingers close my
eyes, 110
Or if I live, let me forget myself.
B. of Win. My lord —
K. Edw. Call me not lord; away — out of my
sight!
Ah, pardon me: grief makes me lunatic!
Let not that Mortimer protect my son; 115
More safety is there in a tiger's jaws,
Than his embracements. Bear this to the queen,
Wet with my tears, and dried again with sighs;
[*Gives a handkerchief.*]
If with the sight thereof she be not mov'd,
Return it back and dip it in my blood. 120
Commend me to my son, and bid him rule
Better than I. Yet how have I transgress'd,
Unless it be with too much clemency?
Trus. And thus most humbly do we take our
leave. 124
K. Edw. Farewell; [*Exeunt the* BISHOP
of WINCHESTER *and* TRUSSEL.]
I know the next news that they bring
Will be my death; and welcome shall it be;
To wretched men, death is felicity.

---

[1] Foolishly.   [2] Care.

[3] Qq. omit. Added by Dodsley.

Enter BERKELEY,[1] [*who gives a paper to* LEICESTER].

Leices. Another post! what news brings he?
K. Edw. Such news as I expect — come, Berkeley, come,
And tell thy message to my naked breast.   130
  Berk. My lord, think not a thought so villainous
Can harbour in a man of noble birth.
To do your highness service and devoir,
And save you from your foes, Berkeley would die.
  Leices. My lord, the council of the queen commands   135
That I resign my charge.
  K. Edw. And who must keep me now? Must you, my lord?
  Berk. Ay, my most gracious lord; so 't is decreed.
  K. Edw. [*taking the paper.*] By Mortimer, whose name is written here!   139
Well may I rend his name that rends my heart!
                    [*Tears it.*]
This poor revenge has something eas'd my mind.
So may his limbs be torn, as is this paper!
Hear me, immortal Jove, and grant it too!
  Berk. Your grace must hence with me to Berkeley straight.
  K. Edw. Whither you will; all places are alike,   145
And every earth is fit for burial.
  Leices. Favour him, my lord, as much as lieth in you.
  Berk. Even so betide my soul as I use him.
  K. Edw. Mine enemy hath pitied my estate,
And that 's the cause that I am now remov'd.
  Berk. And thinks your grace that Berkeley will be cruel?   151
  K. Edw. I know not; but of this am I assured,
That death ends all, and I can die but once.
Leicester, farewell!
  Leices. Not yet, my lord; I 'll bear you on your way.   *Exeunt.*   155

[SCENE II.] [2]

Enter QUEEN ISABELLA *and* Young MORTIMER.

Y. Mor. Fair Isabel, now have we our desire;
The proud corrupters of the light-brain'd king
Have done their homage to the lofty gallows,
And he himself lies in captivity.
Be rul'd by me, and we will rule the realm.   5
In any case take heed of childish fear,
For now we hold an old wolf by the ears,
That, if he slip, will seize upon us both,
And gripe the sorer, being gript himself.
Think therefore, madam, that imports us much
To erect[3] your son with all the speed we may,   11
And that I be protector over him;
For our behoof will bear the greater sway
Whenas a king's name shall be under writ.

[1] Old edd. *Bartley*, showing pronunciation.
[2] The Royal Palace, London.   [3] Crown.

Q. Isab. Sweet Mortimer, the life of Isabel,
Be thou persuaded that I love thee well,   15
And therefore, so the prince my son be safe,
Whom I esteem as dear as these mine eyes,
Conclude against his father what thou wilt,
And I myself will willingly subscribe.   20
  Y. Mor. First would I hear news that he were depos'd,
And then let me alone to handle him.

Enter Messenger.

Letters! from whence?
  Mess.   From Killingworth, my lord.
  Q. Isab. How fares my lord the king?
  Mess. In health, madam, but full of pensiveness.   25
  Q. Isab. Alas, poor soul, would I could ease his grief!

[*Enter the* BISHOP *of* WINCHESTER *with the crown.*]

Thanks, gentle Winchester. [*To the* Messenger.]
  Sirrah, be gone.   [*Exit* Messenger.]
  B. of Win. The king hath willingly resign'd his crown.
  Q. Isab. O happy news! send for the prince, my son.
  B. of Win. Further, or this letter was seal'd, Lord Berkeley came,   30
So that he now is gone from Killingworth;
And we have heard that Edmund laid a plot
To set his brother free; no more but so.
The lord of Berkeley is so pitiful
As Leicester that had charge of him before.   35
  Q. Isab. Then let some other be his guardian.
  Y. Mor. Let me alone, here is the privy seal.
                    [*Exit the* BISHOP *of* WINCHESTER.]
Who 's there? — Call hither Gurney and Matrevis.   [*To* Attendants *within.*]
To dash the heavy-headed Edmund's drift,   39
Berkeley shall be discharg'd, the king remov'd,
And none but we shall know where he lieth.
  Q. Isab. But, Mortimer, as long as he survives,
What safety rests for us, or for my son?
  Y. Mor. Speak, shall he presently be despatch'd and die?
  Q. Isab. I would he were, so 't were not by my means.   45

Enter MATREVIS *and* GURNEY.

Y. Mor. Enough. —
Matrevis, write a letter presently
Unto the lord of Berkeley from ourself
That he resign the king to thee and Gurney;   49
And when 't is done, we will subscribe our name.
  Mat. It shall be done, my lord.
  Y. Mor.   Gurney.
  Gur.   My lord.
  Y. Mor. As thou intend'st to rise by Mortimer,
Who now makes Fortune's wheel turn as he please,
Seek all the means thou canst to make him droop,   54
And neither give him kind word nor good look.
  Gur. I warrant you, my lord.

Y. Mor. And this above the rest: because we hear
That Edmund casts[1] to work his liberty,
Remove him still from place to place by night,
Till at the last he come to Killingworth, 　60
And then from thence to Berkeley back again;
And by the way, to make him fret the more,
Speak curstly to him, and in any case
Let no man comfort him; if he chance to weep,
But amplify his grief with bitter words. 　65
　　Mat. Fear not, my lord, we'll do as you command.
　　Y. Mor. So now away; post thitherwards amain.
　　Q. Isab. Whither goes this letter? To my lord the king?
Commend me humbly to his majesty,
And tell him that I labour all in vain 　70
To ease his grief, and work his liberty;
And bear him this as witness of my love.
　　　　　　　　　　　　[Gives a ring.]
　　Mat. I will, madam.　　*Exit with* GURNEY.

Enter PRINCE [EDWARD,] *and* KENT *talking with him.*

　　Y. Mor. Finely dissembled. Do so still, sweet queen.
Here comes the young prince with the Earl of Kent. 　75
　　Q. Isab. Something he whispers in his childish ears.
　　Y. Mor. If he have such access unto the prince,
Our plots and stratagems will soon be dash'd.
　　Q. Isab. Use Edmund friendly, as if all were well.
　　Y. Mor. How fares my honourable lord of Kent? 　80
　　Kent. In health, sweet Mortimer. How fares your grace?
　　Q. Isab. Well, if my lord your brother were enlarg'd.
　　Kent. I hear of late he hath depos'd himself.
　　Q. Isab. The more my grief.
　　Y. Mor.　　　　　　And mine.
　　Kent. [*Aside.*]　　Ah, they do dissemble!
　　Q. Isab. Sweet son, come hither, I must talk with thee. 　85
　　Y. Mor. You being his uncle, and the next of blood,
Do look to be protector o'er the prince.
　　Kent. Not I, my lord; who should protect the son,
But she that gave him life? I mean the queen.
　　P. Edw. Mother, persuade me not to wear the crown: 　90
Let him be king—I am too young to reign.
　　Q. Isab. But be content, seeing 't is his highness' pleasure.
　　P. Edw. Let me but see him first, and then I will.
　　Kent. Ay, do, sweet nephew.
　　Q. Isab. Brother, you know it is impossible.
　　P. Edw. Why, is he dead? 　96
　　Q. Isab. No, God forbid!

　　Kent. I would those words proceeded from your heart.
　　Y. Mor. Inconstant Edmund, dost thou favour him,
That wast the cause of his imprisonment? 　100
　　Kent. The more cause have I now to make amends.
　　Y. Mor. [*Aside to Q. Isab.*] I tell thee, 't is not meet that one so false
Should come about the person of a prince. —
My lord, he hath betray'd the king his brother,
And therefore trust him not. 　105
　　P. Edw. But he repents, and sorrows for it now.
　　Q. Isab. Come, son, and go with this gentle lord and me.
　　P. Edw. With you I will, but not with Mortimer.
　　Y. Mor. Why, youngling, 'sdain'st thou so of Mortimer?
Then I will carry thee by force away. 　110
　　P. Edw. Help, uncle Kent! Mortimer will wrong me.
　　Q. Isab. Brother Edmund, strive not; we are his friends;
Isabel is nearer than the Earl of Kent.
　　Kent. Sister, Edward is my charge, redeem him.
　　Q. Isab. Edward is my son, and I will keep him. 　115
　　Kent. Mortimer shall know that he hath wrong'd me! —
[*Aside.*] Hence will I haste to Killingworth Castle,
And rescue aged Edward from his foes.
To be reveng'd on Mortimer and thee.
　　　　　　Exeunt [on one side QUEEN ISA-
　　　　　　BELLA, PRINCE EDWARD, *and*
　　　　　　Young MORTIMER; *on the other*
　　　　　　KENT.]

[SCENE III.][2]

Enter MATREVIS *and* GURNEY [*and* Soldiers,] *with* KING [EDWARD].

　　Mat. My lord, be not pensive, we are your friends;
Men are ordain'd to live in misery,
Therefore come, — dalliance dangereth our lives.
　　K. Edw. Friends, whither must unhappy Edward go? 　5
Will hateful Mortimer appoint no rest?
Must I be vexed like the nightly bird,
Whose sight is loathsome to all winged fowls?
When will the fury of his mind assuage?
When will his heart be satisfied with blood?
If mine will serve, unbowel straight this breast,
And give my heart to Isabel and him; 　11
It is the chiefest mark they level[3] at.
　　Gur. Not so my liege, the queen hath given this charge
To keep your grace in safety;
Your passions make your dolours to increase.
　　K. Edw. This usage makes my misery to increase. 　16

But can my air of life continue long
When all my senses are annoy'd with stench?
Within a dungeon England's king is kept,
Where I am starv'd for want of sustenance.　20
My daily diet is heart-breaking sobs,
That almost rents the closet of my heart.
Thus lives old Edward not reliev'd by any,
And so must die, though pitied by many.
O, water, gentle friends, to cool my thirst,　25
And clear my body from foul excrements!
　　Mat. Here's channel [1] water, as our charge is
　　given.
Sit down, for we'll be barbers to your grace.
　　K. Edw. Traitors, away! What, will you
　　murder me,
Or choke your sovereign with puddle water?　30
　　Gur. No; but wash your face, and shave
　　away your beard,
Lest you be known and so be rescued.
　　Mat. Why strive you thus? Your labour is in
　　vain!
　　K. Edw. The wren may strive against the
　　lion's strength,
But all in vain: so vainly do I strive　35
To seek for mercy at a tyrant's hand.
　　They wash him with puddle water,
　　and shave his beard away.
Immortal powers! that knows the painful cares
That wait upon my poor distressed soul,
O level all your looks upon these daring men,
That wrongs their liege and sovereign, Eng-
　　land's king!　40
O Gaveston, 'tis for thee I am wrong'd,
For me, both thou and both the Spencers died!
And for your sakes a thousand wrongs I'll take.
The Spencers' ghosts, wherever they remain,　44
Wish well to mine; then tush, for them I'll die.
　　Mat. 'Twixt theirs and yours shall be no en-
　　mity.
Come, come away; now put the torches out,
We'll enter in by darkness to Killingworth.

Enter KENT.

　　Gur. How now, who comes there?
　　Mat. Guard the king sure: it is the Earl of
　　Kent.　50
　　K. Edw. O gentle brother, help to rescue me!
　　Mat. Keep them asunder; thrust in the king.
　　Kent. Soldiers, let me but talk to him one word.
　　Gur. Lay hands upon the earl for this assault.
　　Kent. Lay down your weapons, traitors! Yield
　　the king!　55
　　Mat. Edmund, yield thou thyself, or thou
　　shalt die.
　　Kent. Base villains, wherefore do you gripe
　　me thus?
　　Gur. Bind him and so convey him to the court.
　　Kent. Where is the court but here? Here is
　　the king;
And I will visit him; why stay you me?　60
　　Mat. The court is where Lord Mortimer re-
　　mains;
Thither shall your honour go; and so farewell.
　　Exeunt MATREVIS *and* GURNEY,
　　with KING EDWARD.

　　Kent. O miserable is that commonweal,
Where lords keep courts, and kings are lockt
　　in prison!
　　Sol. Wherefore stay we? On, sirs, to the
　　court!　65
　　Kent. Ay, lead me whither you will, even to
　　my death,
Seeing that my brother cannot be releas'd.
　　　　　　　　　　　　　　　　　Exeunt.

　　　　　　　[SCENE IV.] [2]

Enter YOUNG MORTIMER, *alone.*

　　Y. Mor. The king must die, or Mortimer
　　goes down;
The commons now begin to pity him.
Yet he that is the cause of Edward's death,
Is sure to pay for it when his son's of age;
And therefore will I do it cunningly.　5
This letter, written by a friend of ours,
Contains his death, yet bids them save his life.
　　　　　　　　　　　　　　　　　[*Reads.*]
" *Edwardum occidere nolite timere, bonum est:*
Fear not to kill the king, 'tis good he die."
But read it thus, and that's another sense:　10
"*Edwardum occidere nolite, timere bonum est:*
Kill not the king, 'tis good to fear the worst."
Unpointed as it is, thus shall it go,
That, being dead, if it chance to be found,
Matrevis and the rest may bear the blame,　15
And we be quit that caus'd it to be done.
Within this room is lock'd the messenger
That shall convey it, and perform the rest;
And by a secret token that he bears,
Shall he be murdered when the deed is done. —
Lightborn, come forth!　21

[*Enter* LIGHTBORN.]

Art thou as resolute as thou wast?
　　Light. What else, my lord? And far more
　　resolute.
　　Y. Mor. And hast thou cast [3] how to ac-
　　complish it?
　　Light. Ay, ay, and none shall know which way
　　he died.　25
　　Y. Mor. But at his looks, Lightborn, thou
　　wilt relent.
　　Light. Relent! ha, ha! I use much to relent.
　　Y. Mor. Well, do it bravely, and be secret.
　　Light. You shall not need to give instructions;
'Tis not the first time I have kill'd a man.　30
I learn'd in Naples how to poison flowers;
To strangle with a lawn [4] thrust through the
　　throat;
To pierce the windpipe with a needle's point;
Or whilst one is asleep, to take a quill
And blow a little powder in his ears;　35
Or open his mouth and pour quicksilver down.
And yet I have a braver way than these.
　　Y. Mor. What's that?
　　Light. Nay, you shall pardon me; none shall
　　know my tricks.
　　Y. Mor. I care not how it is, so it be not
　　spied.　40
Deliver this to Gurney and Matrevis.
　　　　　　　　　　　　　　　[*Gives letter.*]

At every ten mile end thou hast a horse.
Take this ; [*Gives money*] away ! and never see
   me more.
  Light. No ?
  Y. Mor. No ;   45
Unless thou bring me news of Edward's death.
  Light. That will I quickly do. Farewell, my
   lord.   [*Exit.*]
  Y. Mor. The prince I rule, the queen do I
   command,
And with a lowly congé to the ground,
The proudest lords salute me as I pass ;   50
I seal, I cancel, I do what I will.
Fear'd am I more than lov'd ; — let me be fear'd,
And when I frown, make all the court look
   pale.
I view the prince with Aristarchus' eyes,
Whose looks were as a breeching to a boy.   55
They thrust upon me the protectorship,
And sue to me for that that I desire.
While at the council-table, grave enough,
And not unlike a bashful puritan,
First I complain of imbecility,   60
Saying it is *onus quam gravissimum*,[1]
Till being interrupted by my friends,
Suscepi that *provinciam*[2] as they term it ;
And to conclude, I am Protector now.
Now is all sure : the queen and Mortimer   65
Shall rule the realm, the king ; and none rule us.
Mine enemies will I plague, my friends advance ;
And what I list command who dare control ?
Major sum quam cui possit fortuna nocere.[3]
And that this be the coronation-day,   70
It pleaseth me, and Isabel the queen.
               [*Trumpets within.*]
The trumpets sound, I must go take my place.

Enter the young KING, QUEEN [ISABELLA,] *the*
  ARCHBISHOP [*of* CANTERBURY,] *Champion*
  and Nobles.

  A. of Cant. Long live King Edward, by the
   grace of God
King of England and Lord of Ireland !
  Cham. If any Christian, Heathen, Turk, or
   Jew,   75
Dares but affirm that Edward's not true king,
And will avouch his saying with the sword,
I am the champion that will combat him.
  Y. Mor. None comes, sound trumpets.
              [*Trumpets sound.*]
  K. Edw. Third. Champion, here's to thee.
              [*Gives a purse.*]
  Q. Isab. Lord Mortimer, now take him to
   your charge.   80

  Enter Soldiers, *with* KENT *prisoner.*

  Y. Mor. What traitor have we there with
   blades and bills ?
  Sol. Edmund, the Earl of Kent.
  K. Edw. Third.   What hath he done ?
  Sol. 'A would have taken the king away per-
   force,
As we were bringing him to Killingworth.

---

[1] Lat. "a very heavy burden."
[2] Lat. "I have undertaken that office."
[3] Lat. "I am too great for fortune to injure." Ovid,
Metamorphoses, vi. 195.

  Y. Mor. Did you attempt this rescue, Ed-
   mund ? Speak.   85
  Kent. Mortimer, I did ; he is our king,
And thou compell'st this prince to wear the
   crown.
  Y. Mor. Strike off his head ! he shall have
   martial law.
  Kent. Strike off my head ! Base traitor, I defy
   thee !
  K. Edw. Third. My lord, he is my uncle, and
   shall live.   90
  Y. Mor. My lord, he is your enemy, and shall
   die.
  Kent. Stay, villains !
  K. Edw. Third. Sweet mother, if I cannot
   pardon him,
Entreat my Lord Protector for his life.
  Q. Isab. Son, be content ; I dare not speak a
   word.   95
  K. Edw. Third. Nor I, and yet methinks I
   should command ;
But, seeing I cannot, I 'll entreat for him —
My lord, if you will let my uncle live,
I will requite it when I come to age.
  Y. Mor. 'T is for your highness' good, and
   for the realm's. —   100
How often shall I bid you bear him hence ?
  Kent. Art thou king ? Must I die at thy com-
   mand ?
  Y. Mor. At our command — Once more away
   with him.
  Kent. Let me but stay and speak ; I will not go.
Either my brother or his son is king,   105
And none of both them thirst for Edmund's
   blood :
And therefore, soldiers, whither will you hale
   me ?
      Soldiers *hale* KENT *away, and carry*
        him to be beheaded.
  K. Edw. Third. What safety may I look for
   at his hands,
If that my uncle shall be murdered thus ?
  Q. Isab. Fear not, sweet boy, I 'll guard thee
   from thy foes ;   110
Had Edmund liv'd, he would have sought thy
   death.
Come, son, we 'll ride a-hunting in the park.
  K. Edw. Third. And shall my uncle Edmund
   ride with us ?
  Q. Isab. He is a traitor ; think not on him ;
   come.   *Exeunt.*

           [SCENE V.][4]

    Enter MATREVIS *and* GURNEY.

  Mat. Gurney, I wonder the king dies not,
Being in a vault up to the knees in water,
To which the channels of the castle run,
From whence a damp continually ariseth,
That were enough to poison any man,   5
Much more a king brought up so tenderly.
  Gur. And so do I, Matrevis : yesternight
I opened but the door to throw him meat,
And I was almost stifled with the savour.
  Mat. He hath a body able to endure   10

---

[4] Berkeley Castle.

More than we can inflict: and therefore now
Let us assail his mind another while.

Gur. Send for him out thence, and I will anger him.

Mat. But stay, who's this?

Enter LIGHTBORN.

Light.　　　　My Lord Protector greets you.
　　　　　　　　　　　　　　　　[*Gives letter.*]

Gur. What's here? I know not how to construe it.　　　　　　　　　　　　　　15

Mat. Gurney, it was left unpointed for the nonce;[1]

"*Edwardum occidere nolite timere,*"
That's his meaning.

Light. Know ye this token? I must have the king.　　　　　　　　　　[*Gives token.*]

Mat. Ay, stay awhile, thou shalt have answer straight. —　　　　　　　　20

[*Aside.*] This villain's sent to make away the king.

Gur. [*Aside.*] I thought as much.

Mat. [*Aside.*] And when the murder's done,
See how he must be handled for his labour.

Pereat iste![2] Let him have the king. —　　24
What else? Here is the keys, this is the lake,[3]
Do as you are commanded by my lord.

Light. I know what I must do. Get you away.
Yet be not far off, I shall need your help;
See that in the next room I have a fire,
And get me a spit, and let it be red-hot.　　30

Mat. Very well.

Gur.　　　　　Need you anything besides?

Light. What else? A table and a feather-bed.

Gur. That's all?

Light. Ay, ay; so, when I call you, bring it in.

Mat. Fear not thou that.　　　　　　35

Gur. Here's a light, to go into the dungeon.
　　　[*Gives a light, and then exit with
　　　　　　　　　　　　MATREVIS.*]

Light. So now
Must I about this gear;[4] ne'er was there any
So finely handled as this king shall be.　　39
For, here's a place indeed, with all my heart!

K. Edw. Who's there? What light is that?
　　Wherefore com'st thou?

Light. To comfort you, and bring you joyful
　　news.

K. Edw. Small comfort finds poor Edward in
　　thy looks.
Villain, I know thou com'st to murder me.　44

Light. To murder you, my most gracious lord!
Far is it from my heart to do you harm.
The queen sent me to see how you were used,
For she relents at this your misery:
And what eyes can refrain from shedding tears,
To see a king in this most piteous state?　　50

K. Edw. Weep'st thou already? List awhile
　　to me
And then thy heart, were it as Gurney's is,
Or as Matrevis', hewn from the Caucasus,
Yet will it melt, ere I have done my tale.　54
This dungeon where they keep me is the sink
Wherein the filth of all the castle falls.

Light. O villains!

K. Edw. And there in mire and puddle have
　　I stood
This ten days' space; and, lest that I should
　　sleep,
One plays continually upon a drum.　　60
They give me bread and water, being a king;
So that, for want of sleep and sustenance,
My mind's distempered, and my body's numb'd,
And whether I have limbs or no I know not.　64
O, would my blood dropp'd out from every vein,
As doth this water from my tattered robes.
Tell Isabel, the queen, I look'd not thus,
When for her sake I ran at tilt in France,
And there unhors'd the Duke of Cleremont.

Light. O speak no more, my lord! this breaks
　　my heart.　　　　　　　　70
Lie on this bed, and rest yourself awhile.

K. Edw. These looks of thine can harbour
　　nought but death:
I see my tragedy written in thy brows.
Yet stay awhile; forbear thy bloody hand,
And let me see the stroke before it comes,　75
That even then when I shall lose my life,
My mind may be more steadfast on my God.

Light. What means your highness to mistrust
　　me thus?

K. Edw. What mean'st thou to dissemble
　　with me thus?

Light. These hands were never stain'd with
　　innocent blood,　　　　　　80
Nor shall they now be tainted with a king's.

K. Edw. Forgive my thought for having such
　　a thought.
One jewel have I left; receive thou this.
　　　　　　　　　　　　[*Giving jewel.*]
Still fear I, and I know not what's the cause,
But every joint shakes as I give it thee.　　85
O, if thou harbour'st murder in thy heart,
Let this gift change thy mind, and save thy
　　soul!
Know that I am a king: O, at that name
I feel a hell of grief! Where is my crown?
Gone, gone! and do I remain alive?　　90

Light. You're overwatch'd,[5] my lord; lie down
　　and rest.

K. Edw. But that grief keeps me waking, I
　　should sleep;
For not these ten days have these eye-lids clos'd.
Now as I speak they fall, and yet with fear
Open again. O wherefore sitt'st thou here?　95

Light. If you mistrust me, I'll begone, my
　　lord.

K. Edw. No, no, for if thou mean'st to murder me,
Thou wilt return again, and therefore stay.

Light. He sleeps.

K. Edw. [*waking.*] O let me not die yet!
　　Stay, O stay awhile!　　　　　100

Light. How now, my lord?

K. Edw. Something still buzzeth in mine
　　ears,
And tells me if I sleep I never wake;
This fear is that which makes me tremble thus.
And therefore tell me, wherefore art thou come?

---

[1] Purposely
[2] Lat. "Let this man die."
[3] Perhaps for "lock."
[4] Business.
[5] Worn out with waking.

Light. To rid thee of thy life. — Matrevis, come! 106

[*Enter* MATREVIS *and* GURNEY.]

K. Edw. I am too weak and feeble to re-
sist : —
Assist me, sweet God, and receive my soul !
Light. Run for the table.
K. Edw. O spare me, or despatch me in a
   trice.   [MATREVIS *brings in a table.*] 110
Light. So, lay the table down, and stamp on it,
But not too hard, lest that you bruise his body.
          [KING EDWARD *is murdered.*]
Mat. I fear me that this cry will raise the
   town,
And therefore, let us take horse and away. 114
Light. Tell me, sirs, was it not bravely done ?
Gur. Excellent well : take this for thy reward.
   GURNEY *stabs* LIGHTBORN [*who dies*].
Come, let us cast the body in the moat,
And bear the king's to Mortimer our lord :
Away !   *Exeunt* [*with the bodies*].

[SCENE VI.][1]

Enter Young MORTIMER *and* MATREVIS.

Y. Mor. Is 't done, Matrevis, and the mur-
   derer dead ?
Mat. Ay, my good lord ; I would it were un-
   done !
Y. Mor. Matrevis, if thou now growest peni-
   tent
I 'll be thy ghostly father ; therefore choose,
Whether thou wilt be secret in this,   5
Or else die by the hand of Mortimer.
Mat. Gurney, my lord, is fled, and will, I fear,
Betray us both, therefore let me fly.
Y. Mor. Fly to the savages !
Mat. I humbly thank your honour. [*Exit.*] 10
Y. Mor. As for myself, I stand as Jove's huge
   tree,
And others are but shrubs compar'd to me.
All tremble at my name, and I fear none ;
Let 's see who dare impeach me for his death !

Enter QUEEN ISABELLA.

Q. Isab. Ah, Mortimer, the king my son hath
   news   15
His father's dead, and we have murdered
   him !
Y. Mor. What if he have ? The king is yet a
   child.
Q. Isab. Ay, but he tears his hair, and wrings
   his hands,
And vows to be reveng'd upon us both.
Into the council-chamber he is gone,   20
To crave the aid and succour of his peers.
Ay me ! see here he comes, and they with him.
Now, Mortimer, begins our tragedy.

Enter KING [EDWARD THE THIRD], LORDS
[*and* Attendants].

1 Lord. Fear not, my lord, know that you are
   a king.
K. Edw. Third. Villain ! —   25

[1] The Royal Palace, London.

Y. Mor. How now, my lord !
K. Edw. Third. Think not that I am frighted
   with thy words !
My father 's murdered through thy treachery ;
And thou shalt die, and on his mournful hearse
Thy hateful and accursed head shall lie,   30
To witness to the world, that by thy means
His kingly body was too soon interr'd.
Q. Isab. Weep not, sweet son !
K. Edw. Third. Forbid me not to weep, he
   was my father ;
And, had you lov'd him half so well as I,   35
You could not bear his death thus patiently.
But you, I fear, conspir'd with Mortimer.
1 Lord. Why speak you not unto my lord the
   king ?
Y. Mor. Because I think scorn to be accus'd.
Who is the man dares say I murdered him ?   40
K. Edw. Third. Traitor ! in me my loving
   father speaks,
And plainly saith, 't was thou that murd'redst
   him.
Y. Mor. But has your grace no other proof
   than this ?
K. Edw. Thrd. Yes, if this be the hand of
   Mortimer.   [*Shewing letter.*]
Y. Mor. [*Aside.*] False Gurney hath betray'd
   me and himself.   45
Q. Isab. [*Aside.*] I fear'd as much ; murder
   cannot be hid.
Y. Mor. It is my hand ; what gather you by
   this ?
K. Edw. Third. That thither thou didst send
   a murderer.
Y. Mor. What murderer ? Bring forth the
   man I sent.
K. Edw. Third. Ah, Mortimer, thou knowest
   that he is slain ;   50
And so shalt thou be too. — Why stays he here ?
Bring him unto a hurdle, drag him forth ;
Hang him, I say, and set his quarters up ;
But bring his head back presently to me.
Q. Isab. For my sake, sweet son, pity Morti-
   mer !   55
Y. Mor. Madam, entreat not, I will rather
   die,
Than sue for life unto a paltry boy.
K. Edw. Third. Hence with the traitor ! with
   the murderer !
Y. Mor. Base Fortune, now I see, that in thy
   wheel
There is a point, to which when men aspire,   60
They tumble headlong down: that point I
   touch'd,
And, seeing there was no place to mount up
   higher,
Why should I grieve at my declining fall ? —
Farewell, fair queen ; weep not for Mortimer,
That scorns the world, and, as a traveller,   65
Goes to discover countries yet unknown.
K. Edw. Third. What ! suffer you the traitor
   to delay ?
          [Young MORTIMER *is taken away
          by* 1 Lord *and* Attendants.]
Q. Isab. As thou receivedst thy life from
   me,
Spill not the blood of gentle Mortimer !

K. Edw. Third. This argues that you spilt
    my father's blood,   70
Else would you not entreat for Mortimer.
  Q. Isab. I spill his blood? No!
  K. Edw. Third. Ay, madam, you; for so the
    rumour runs.
  Q. Isab. That rumour is untrue; for loving
    thee,
Is this report rais'd on poor Isabel.   75
  K. Edw. Third. I do not think her so unnat-
    ural.
  2 Lord. My lord, I fear me it will prove too
    true.
  K. Edw. Third. Mother, you are suspected
    for his death,
And therefore we commit you to the Tower
Till farther trial may be made thereof;   80
If you be guilty, though I be your son,
Think not to find me slack or pitiful.
  Q. Isab. Nay, to my death, for too long have
    I liv'd
Whenas my son thinks to abridge my days.
  K. Edw. Third. Away with her, her words
    enforce these tears,   85
And I shall pity her if she speak again.
  Q. Isab. Shall I not mourn for my beloved
    lord,
And with the rest accompany him to his grave?
  2 Lord. Thus, madam, 't is the king's will
    you shall hence.

  Q. Isab. He hath forgotten me; stay, I am his
    mother.   90
  2 Lord. That boots not; therefore, gentle
    madam, go.
  Q. Isab. Then come, sweet death, and rid me
    of this grief.   [*Exit.*]

[*Re-enter* 1 Lord, *with the head of* Young Mor-
    timer.]

  1 Lord. My lord, here is the head of Morti-
    mer.
  K. Edw. Third. Go fetch my father's hearse,
    where it shall lie;
And bring my funeral robes.
           [*Exeunt* Attendants.]
            Accursed head,   95
Could I have rul'd thee then, as I do now,
Thou had'st not hatch'd this monstrous treach-
    ery! —
Here comes the hearse; help me to mourn, my
    lords.

[*Re-enter* Attendants *with the hearse and funeral
    robes.*]

Sweet father, here unto thy murdered ghost
I offer up this wicked traitor's head;   1.
And let these tears, distilling from mine eyes,
Be witness of my grief and innocency.
              [*Exeunt*.

THE SPANISH TRAGEDY

OR

HIERONIMO IS MAD AGAIN

BY

THOMAS KYD

[DRAMATIS PERSONAE

Ghost of Andrea, a Spanish nobleman, } Chorus.
Revenge,
KING OF SPAIN.
DON CYPRIAN, DUKE OF CASTILE, his brother.
LORENZO, the Duke's son.
BEL-IMPERIA, Lorenzo's sister.
VICEROY OF PORTUGAL.
BALTHAZAR, his son.
DON PEDRO, the Viceroy's brother.
HIERONIMO, Marshal of Spain.
ISABELLA, his wife.
HORATIO, their son.
Spanish General.
Deputy.
DON BAZULTO, an old man.
Three Citizens.
Portuguese Ambassador.
ALEXANDRO, } Portuguese Noblemen.
VILLUPPO,

Two Portuguese.
PEDRINGANO, Bel-imperia's servant.
CHRISTOPHIL, Bel-imperia's custodian.
Lorenzo's Page.
SERBERINE, Balthazar's servant.
Isabella's Maid.
Messenger.
Hangman.
SOLIMAN, Sultan of Turkey (Balthazar), } In
ERASTUS, Knight of Rhodes (Lorenzo), } Hieronimo's
THE BASHAW (Hieronimo), } Play.
PERSEDA (Bel-imperia),
Three Kings and three Knights in the first Dumb-show.
Hymen and two torch-bearers in the second.
BAZARDO, a Painter, } In the additions to
PEDRO and JAQUES, Hieronimo's } the play.
servants,
Army, Royal Suites, Noblemen, Halberdiers, Officers,
Three Watchmen, Servants, etc.]

ACT I

[SCENE I: INDUCTION.]

Enter the GHOST OF ANDREA, *and with him*
REVENGE.

  Ghost. When this eternal substance of my
    soul
Did live imprison'd in my wanton flesh,
Each in their function serving other's need,
I was a courtier in the Spanish court.
My name was Don Andrea; my descent,   5
Though not ignoble, yet inferior far
To gracious fortunes of my tender youth:
For there in prime and pride of all my years,
By duteous service and deserving love,
In secret I possess'd a worthy dame,   10
Which hight sweet Bel-imperia by name.
But in the harvest of my summer joys
Death's winter nipp'd the blossoms of my bliss,
Forcing divorce betwixt my love and me.
For in the late conflict with Portingale   15
My valour drew me into danger's mouth
Till life to death made passage through my
    wounds.
When I was slain, my soul descended straight
To pass the flowing stream of Acheron;
But churlish Charon, only boatman there,   20
Said that, my rites of burial not perform'd,
I might not sit amongst his passengers.
Ere Sol had slept three nights in Thetis' lap,
And slak'd his smoking chariot in her flood,
By Don Horatio, our knight marshal's son,   25

My funerals and obsequies were done.
Then was the ferryman of hell content
To pass me over to the slimy strand,
That leads to fell Avernus' ugly waves.
There, pleasing Cerberus with honey'd speech, 30
I pass'd the perils of the foremost porch.
Not far from hence, amidst ten thousand
    souls,
Sat Minos, Aeacus, and Rhadamanth;
To whom no sooner 'gan I make approach,
To crave a passport for my wand'ring ghost, 35
But Minos, in graven leaves of lottery,
Drew forth the manner of my life and death.
"This knight," quoth he, "both liv'd and died
    in love;
And for his love tried fortune of the wars;
And by war's fortune lost both love and life." 40
"Why then," said Aeacus, "convey him hence,
To walk with lovers in our fields of love,
And spend the course of everlasting time
Under green myrtle-trees and cypress shades."
"No, no," said Rhadamanth, "it were not
    well,   45
With loving souls to place a martialist.
He died in war, and must to martial fields,
Where wounded Hector lives in lasting pain,
And Achilles' Myrmidons do scour the plain."
Then Minos, mildest censor of the three, 50
Made this device to end the difference:
"Send him," quoth he, "to our infernal king,
To doom him as best seems his majesty."
To this effect my passport straight was drawn.
In keeping on my way to Pluto's court, 55

Through dreadful shades of ever-glooming
　　night,
I saw more sights than thousand tongues can
　　tell,
Or pens can write, or mortal hearts can think.
Three ways there were: that on the right-hand
　　side
Was ready way unto the 'foresaid fields,　　60
Where lovers live and bloody martialists ;
But either sort contain'd within his bounds.
The left-hand path, declining fearfully,
Was ready downfall to the deepest hell,
Where bloody Furies shakes their whips of
　　steel,　　65
And poor Ixion turns an endless wheel ;
Where usurers are chok'd with melting gold,
And wantons are embrac'd with ugly snakes,
And murderers groan with never-killing
　　wounds,
And perjur'd wights scalded in boiling lead,　70
And all foul sins with torments overwhelm'd.
'Twixt these two ways I trod the middle path,
Which brought me to the fair Elysian green,
In midst whereof there stands a stately tower,
The walls of brass, the gates of adamant.　75
Here finding Pluto with his Proserpine,
I show'd my passport, humbled on my knee ;
Whereat fair Proserpine began to smile,
And begg'd that only she might give my doom.
Pluto was pleas'd, and seal'd it with a kiss.　80
Forthwith, Revenge, she rounded [1] thee in th'
　　ear,
And bade thee lead me through the gates of
　　horn, [2]
Where dreams have passage in the silent night.
No sooner had she spoke, but we were here —
I wot not how — in twinkling of an eye.　85
　　Revenge. Then know, Andrea, that thou art
　　arriv'd
Where thou shalt see the author of thy death,
Don Balthazar, the prince of Portingale,
Depriv'd of life by Bel-imperia.
Here sit we down to see the mystery,　90
And serve for Chorus in this tragedy.

[Scene II.] [3]

Enter Spanish King, General, Castile,
　　and Hieronimo.

　　King. Now say, lord General, how fares our
　　camp ?
　　Gen. All well, my sovereign liege, except
　　some few
That are deceas'd by fortune of the war.
　　King. But what portends thy cheerful
　　countenance,
And posting to our presence thus in haste ?　5
Speak, man, hath fortune given us victory ?
　　Gen. Victory, my liege, and that with little
　　loss.
　　King. Our Portingals will pay us tribute
　　then ?
　　Gen. Tribute and wonted homage there-
　　withal.

[3] Whispered.　　　　[2] See *Aeneid,* vi. 893.
[1] The Court of Spain.

　　King. Then bless'd be heaven and guider of
　　the heavens,　10
From whose fair influence such justice flows.
　　Cast. O *multum dilecte Deo, tibi militat
　　aether,*
Et conjuratae curt ato poplite gentes
Succumbunt : recti soror est victoria juris. [4]
　　King. Thanks to my loving brother of
　　Castile.　15
But, General, unfold in brief discourse
Your form of battle and your war's success,
That, adding all the pleasure of thy news
Unto the height of former happiness,
With deeper wage and greater dignity　20
We may reward thy blissful chivalry.
　　Gen. Where Spain and Portingale do jointly
　　knit
Their frontiers, leaning on each other's bound,
There met our armies in their proud array ;
Both furnish'd well, both full of hope and
　　fear,　25
Both menacing alike with daring shows,
Both vaunting sundry colours of device,
Both cheerly sounding trumpets, drums, and
　　fifes,
Both raising dreadful clamours to the sky,
That valleys, hills, and rivers made rebound,　30
And heav'n itself was frighted with the sound.
Our battles both were pitch'd in squadron form,
Each corner strongly fenc'd with wings of shot ;
But ere we join'd and came to push of pike,
I brought a squadron of our readiest shot　35
From out our rearward to begin the fight :
They brought another wing t' encounter us.
Meanwhile, our ordnance play'd on either side,
And captains strove to have their valours
　　tried.
Don Pedro, their chief horsemen's colonel,　40
Did with his cornet [5] bravely make attempt
To break the order of our battle ranks :
But Don Rogero, worthy man of war,
March'd forth against him with our musketeers,
And stopp'd the malice of his fell approach.　45
While they maintain hot skirmish to and fro,
Both battles join, and fall to handy-blows,
Their violent shot resembling th' ocean's rage,
When, roaring loud, and with a swelling tide,
It beats upon the rampiers of huge rocks,　50
And gapes to swallow neighbour-bounding
　　lands.
Now, while Bellona rageth here and there,
Thick storms of bullets ran like winter's hail,
And shivered lances dark the troubled air.
　　　　Pede pes et cuspide cuspis ; 55
Arma sonant armis, vir petiturque viro. [6]
On every side drop captains to the ground,
And soldiers, some ill-maim'd, some slain out-
　　right :
Here falls a body sund'red from his head,
There legs and arms lie bleeding on the
　　grass,　60
Mingled with weapons and unbowell'd steeds,

[4] Adapted from Claudian's *De Tertio Consulatu
Honorii,* 96-98.
[5] Troop of cavalry.
[6] A combination of phrases from Statius, Virgil, and
Curtius.

That scattering overspread the purple plain.
In all this turmoil, three long hours and more,
The victory to neither part inclin'd ;
Till Don Andrea, with his brave lanciers,　　65
In their main battle made so great a breach,
That, half dismay'd, the multitude retir'd :
But Balthazar, the Portingals' young prince,
Brought rescue, and encourag'd them to stay.
Here-hence the fight was eagerly renew'd,　　70
And in that conflict was Andrea slain :
Brave man at arms, but weak to Balthazar.
Yet while the prince, insulting over him,
Breath'd out proud vaunts, sounding to our reproach,
Friendship and hardy valour join'd in one　　75
Prick'd forth Horatio, our knight marshal's son,
To challenge forth that prince in single fight.
Not long between these twain the fight endur'd,
But straight the prince was beaten from his horse,
And forc'd to yield him prisoner to his foe.　　80
When he was taken, all the rest they fled,
And our carbines pursu'd them to the death,
Till, Phoebus waving [1] to the western deep,
Our trumpeters were charg'd to sound retreat.
　　King. Thanks, good lord General, for these good news ;　　85
And for some argument of more to come,
Take this and wear it for thy sovereign's sake.
　　　　　　　　　　　Gives him his chain.
But tell me now, hast thou confirm'd a peace?
　　Gen. No peace, my liege, but peace conditional,
That if with homage tribute be well paid,　　90
The fury of your forces will be stay'd :
And to this peace their viceroy hath subscrib'd,
　　　　　　　　　　　Gives the King a paper.
And made a solemn vow that, during life,
His tribute shall be truly paid to Spain.
　　King. These words, these deeds, become thy person well.　　95
But now, knight marshal, frolic with thy king,
For 't is thy son that wins this battle's prize.
　　Hier. Long may he live to serve my sovereign liege,
And soon decay, unless he serve my liege.
　　King. Nor thou, nor he, shall die without reward.　　*A tucket* [2] *afar off.*　　100
What means this warning of this trumpet's sound?
　　Gen. This tells me that your grace's men of war,
Such as war's fortune hath reserv'd from death,
Come marching on towards your royal seat,
To show themselves before your majesty ;　　105
For so I gave in charge at my depart.
Whereby by demonstration shall appear
That all, except three hundred or few more,
Are safe return'd, and by their foes enrich'd.

The Army *enters;* BALTHAZAR, *between* LO-
RENZO *and* HORATIO, *captive.*

　　King. A gladsome sight ! I long to see them here.　　*They enter and pass by.*　　110

Was that the warlike prince of Portingale,
That by our nephew was in triumph led ?
　　Gen. It was, my liege, the prince of Portingale.
　　King. But what was he that on the other side
Held him by th' arm, as partner of the prize ?　　115
　　Hier. That was my son, my gracious sovereign ;
Of whom though from his tender infancy
My loving thoughts did never hope but well,
He never pleas'd his father's eyes till now,
Nor fill'd my heart with over-cloying joys.　　120
　　King. Go, let them march once more about these walls,
That, staying them, we may confer and talk
With our brave prisoner and his double guard.
　　　　　　　　　　　[*Exit a messenger.*]
Hieronimo, it greatly pleaseth us
That in our victory thou have a share,　　125
By virtue of thy worthy son's exploit.

Enter again.

Bring hither the young prince of Portingale :
The rest march on ; but, ere they be dismiss'd,
We will bestow on every soldier
Two ducats and on every leader ten,　　130
That they may know our largess welcomes them.
　　　　　Exeunt all but [*the* KING], BALTHA-
　　　　　ZAR, LORENZO *and* HORATIO.
Welcome, Don Balthazar ! welcome, nephew !
And thou, Horatio, thou art welcome too.
Young prince, although thy father's hard misdeeds,
In keeping back the tribute that he owes,　　135
Deserve but evil measure at our hands,
Yet shalt thou know that Spain is honourable.
　　Bal. The trespass that my father made in peace
Is now controll'd [3] by fortune of the wars ;
And cards once dealt, it boots not ask why so.　　140
His men are slain, a weakening to his realm ;
His colours seiz'd, a blot unto his name ;
His son distress'd, a cor'sive [4] to his heart :
These punishments may clear his late offence.
　　King. Ay, Balthazar, if he observe this truce,　　145
Our peace will grow the stronger for these wars.
Meanwhile live thou, though not in liberty,
Yet free from bearing any servile yoke ;
For in our hearing thy deserts were great,
And in our sight thyself art gracious.　　150
　　Bal. And I shall study to deserve this grace.
　　King. But tell me — for their holding makes me doubt —
To which of these twain art thou prisoner ?
　　Lor. To me, my liege.
　　Hor.　　　　　　　　To me, my sovereign.
　　Lor. This hand first took his courser by the reins.　　155
　　Hor. But first my lance did put him from his horse.

---

[1] Moving.　　　　[2] Flourish of trumpets.　　　　[3] Curbed.　　　　[4] Corrosive.

Lor. I seiz'd his weapon, and enjoy'd it first.
Hor. But first I forc'd him lay his weapons
down.
King. Let go his arm, upon our privilege.
                        They let him go.
Say, worthy prince, to whether did'st thou
yield?   160
Bal. To him in courtesy, to this perforce.
He spake me fair, this other gave me strokes;
He promis'd life, this other threat'ned death;
He won my love, this other conquer'd me,
And, truth to say, I yield myself to both.   165
    Hier. But that I know your grace for just
                        and wise,
And might seem partial in this difference,
Enforc'd by nature and by law of arms
My tongue should plead for young Horatio's
right.
He hunted well that was a lion's death,   170
Not he that in a garment wore his skin;
So hares may pull dead lions by the beard.
King. Content thee, marshal, thou shalt have
                        no wrong;
And, for thy sake, thy son shall want no right.
Will both abide the censure of my doom?   175
    Lor. I crave no better than your grace
awards.
Hor. Nor I, although I sit beside my right.
King. Then by my judgment, thus your strife
shall end:
You both deserve, and both shall have reward.
Nephew, thou took'st his weapon and his
horse: 180
His weapons and his horse are thy reward.
Horatio, thou didst force him first to yield:
His ransom therefore is thy valour's fee;
Appoint the sum, as you shall both agree.
But, nephew, thou shalt have the prince in
guard,   185
For thine estate best fitteth such a guest:
Horatio's house were small for all his train.
Yet, in regard thy substance passeth his,
And that just guerdon may befall desert,
To him we yield the armour of the prince.   190
How likes Don Balthazar of this device?
Bal. Right well, my liege, if this proviso were,
That Don Horatio bear us company,
Whom I admire and love for chivalry.
King. Horatio, leave him not that loves thee
so. —   195
Now let us hence to see our soldiers paid,
And feast our prisoner as our friendly guest.
                        Exeunt.

[SCENE III.]¹

Enter VICEROY, ALEXANDRO, VILLUPPO.

Vic. Is our ambassador despatch'd for Spain?
Alex. Two days, my liege, are past since his
depart.
Vic. And tribute-payment gone along with
him?
Alex. Ay, my good lord.   4
Vic. Then rest we here awhile in our unrest,
And feed our sorrows with some inward sighs,
For deepest cares break never into tears.

¹ The Court of Portugal.

But wherefore sit I in a regal throne?
This better fits a wretch's endless moan.
                        Falls to the ground.
Yet this is higher than my fortunes reach,   10
And therefore better than my state deserves.
Ay, ay, this earth, image of melancholy,
Seeks him whom fates adjudge to misery.
Here let me lie; now am I at the lowest.
    Qui jacet in terra, non habet unde cadat. 15
    In me consumpsit vires fortuna nocendo;
    *Nil superest ut jam possit obesse magis.*²
Yes, Fortune may bereave me of my crown:
Here, take it now; — let Fortune do her worst,
She will not rob me of this sable weed.   20
O no, she envies none but pleasant things.
Such is the folly of despiteful chance!
Fortune is blind, and sees not my deserts;
So is she deaf, and hears not my laments;
And could she hear, yet is she wilful-mad,   25
And therefore will not pity my distress.
Suppose that she could pity me, what then?
What help can be expected at her hands
Whose foot [is] standing on a rolling stone,
And mind more mutable than fickle winds?   30
Why wail I, then, where's hope of no redress?
O yes, complaining makes my grief seem less.
My late ambition hath distain'd my faith;
My breach of faith occasion'd bloody wars;
Those bloody wars have spent my treasury;³   35
And with my treasury³ my people's blood;
And with their blood, my joy and best belov'd,
My best belov'd, my sweet and only son.
O, wherefore went I not to war myself?
The cause was mine; I might have died for
both.   40
My years were mellow, his but young and green,
My death were natural, but his was forc'd.
    Alex. No doubt, my liege, but still the prince
survives.
Vic. Survives! Ay, where?
Alex. In Spain, a prisoner by mischance of
war.   45
Vic. Then they have slain him for his father's
fault.
Alex. That were a breach to common law of
arms.
Vic. They reck no laws that meditate re-
venge.
Alex. His ransom's worth will stay from foul
revenge.
Vic. No; if he liv'd, the news would soon be
here.   50
Alex. Nay, evil news fly faster still than
good.
Vic. Tell me no more of news, for he is
dead.
Vil. My sovereign, pardon the author of ill
news,
And I'll bewray⁴ the fortune of thy son.
Vic. Speak on, I'll guerdon thee, whate'er it
be.   55
Mine ear is ready to receive ill news;
My heart grown hard 'gainst mischief's battery.
Stand up, I say, and tell thy tale at large.

² The source of this passage has not been found.
³ So Manly. Qq. *treasure.*   ⁴ Reveal.

Vil. Then hear that truth which these mine
　　eyes have seen.
When both the armies were in battle join'd,　60
Don Balthazar, amidst the thickest troops,
To win renown did wondrous feats of arms.
Amongst the rest, I saw him, hand to hand,
In single fight with their lord-general;
Till Alexandro, that here counterfeits　　65
Under the colour of a duteous friend,
Discharg'd his pistol at the prince's back
As though he would have slain their general:
But therewithal Don Balthazar fell down;
And when he fell, then we began to fly:　70
But, had he liv'd, the day had sure been ours.
　　Alex. O wicked forgery! O traitorous mis-
　　creant!
　　Vic. Hold thou thy peace! But now, Vil-
　　luppo, say,
Where then became [1] the carcase of my son?
　　Vil. I saw them drag it to the Spanish tents.
　　Vic. Ay, ay, my nightly dreams have told me
　　this. —　　　　　　　　　　　　　　　76
Thou false, unkind, unthankful, traitorous
　　beast,
Wherein had Balthazar offended thee,
That thou shouldst thus betray him to our foes?
Was 't Spanish gold that bleared so thine eyes　80
That thou couldst see no part of our deserts?
Perchance, because thou art Terceira's [2] lord,
Thou hadst some hope to wear this diadem,
If first my son and then myself were slain;
But thy ambitious thought shall break thy
　　neck.　　　　　　　　　　　　　　85
Ay, this was it that made thee spill his blood;
　　Takes the crown and puts it on again.
But I 'll now wear it till thy blood be spilt.
　　Alex. Vouchsafe, dread sovereign, to hear
　　me speak.
　　Vic. Away with him! His sight is second
　　hell.
Keep him till we determine of his death:　　90
　　　　　　　　　　[They take him out.] [3]
If Balthazar be dead, he shall not live.
Villuppo, follow us for thy reward.
　　　　　　　　　　　　Exit Viceroy.
　　Vil. Thus have I with an envious, forged
　　tale
Deceiv'd the king, betray'd mine enemy,
And hope for guerdon of my villany.　*Exit.*　95

[SCENE IV.] [4]

Enter HORATIO *and* BEL-IMPERIA.

　　Bel. Signior Horatio, this is the place and
　　hour,
Wherein I must entreat thee to relate
The circumstance of Don Andrea's death,
Who, living, was my garland's sweetest flower,
And in his death hath buried my delights.　5
　　Hor. For love of him and service to yourself,
I nill [5] refuse this heavy doleful charge;
Yet tears and sighs, I fear, will hinder me.
When both our armies were enjoin'd in fight,
Your worthy chevalier amidst the thick'st,　10

For glorious cause still aiming at the fairest,
Was at the last by young Don Balthazar
Encount'red hand to hand. Their fight was
　　long,
Their hearts were great, their clamours mena-
　　cing,
Their strength alike, their strokes both dan-
　　gerous.　　　　　　　　　　　　15
But wrathful Nemesis, that wicked power,
Envying at Andrea's praise and worth,
Cut short his life, to end his praise and worth.
She, she herself, disguis'd in armour's mask —
As Pallas was before proud Pergamus —　20
Brought in a fresh supply of halberdiers,
Which paunch'd [6] his horse, and ding'd [7] him to
　　the ground.
Then young Don Balthazar with ruthless rage,
Taking advantage of his foe's distress,
Did finish what his halberdiers begun,　　25
And left not, till Andrea's life was done.
Then, though too late, incens'd with just re-
　　morse, [8]
I with my band set forth against the prince,
And brought him prisoner from his halberdiers.
　　Bel. Would thou hadst slain him that so slew
　　my love!　　　　　　　　　　　　30
But then was Don Andrea's carcase lost?
　　Hor. No, that was it for which I chiefly
　　strove,
Nor stepp'd I back till I recover'd him.
I took him up, and wound him in mine arms;
And wielding [9] him unto my private tent,　35
There laid him down, and dew'd him with my
　　tears,
And sigh'd and sorrowed as became a friend.
But neither friendly sorrow, sighs, nor tears
Could win pale Death from his usurped right.
Yet this I did, and less I could not do:　　40
I saw him honoured with due funeral.
This scarf I pluck'd from off his lifeless arm,
And wear it in remembrance of my friend.
　　Bel. I know the scarf: would he had kept it
　　still!
For had he liv'd, he would have kept it still, 45
And worn it for his Bel-imperia's sake;
For 't was my favour at his last depart.
But now wear thou it both for him and me;
For after him thou hast deserv'd it best.
But for thy kindness in his life and death,　50
Be sure, while Bel-imperia's life endures,
She will be Don Horatio's thankful friend.
　　Hor. And, madam, Don Horatio will not
　　slack
Humbly to serve fair Bel-imperia.
But now, if your good liking stand thereto,　55
I 'll crave your pardon to go seek the prince;
For so the duke, your father, gave me charge.
　　Bel. Ay, go, Horatio, leave me here alone;
For solitude best fits my cheerless mood.
　　　　　　　　　　　　Exit HORATIO.
Yet what avails to wail Andrea's death,　　60
From whence Horatio proves my second love?
Had he not lov'd Andrea as he did,
He could not sit in Bel-imperia's thoughts.

---

[1] What became of.　　　[4] The Court of Spain.
[2] An island in the Azores.　[5] Ne will, will not.
[3] Add. Manly.

[6] Stab in the belly, disembowel.　[8] Vexation.
[7] Knocked.　　　　　　　　　[9] Carrying

But how can love find harbour in my breast
Till I revenge the death of my belov'd ?   65
Yes, second love shall further my revenge !
I 'll love Horatio, my Andrea's friend,
The more to spite the prince that wrought his
    end ;
And where Don Balthazar, that slew my love,
Himself now pleads for favour at my hands,   70
He shall, in rigour of my just disdain,
Reap long repentance for his murderous deed.
For what was 't else but murderous cowardice,
So many to oppress one valiant knight,
Without respect of honour in the fight ?   75
And here he comes that murd'red my delight.

Enter LORENZO *and* BALTHAZAR.

Lor. Sister, what means this melancholy
    walk ?
Bel. That for a while I wish no company.
Lor. But here the prince is come to visit you.
Bel. That argues that he lives in liberty.   80
Bal. No, madam, but in pleasing servitude.
Bel. Your prison then, belike, is your conceit.
Bal. Ay, by conceit my freedom is enthrall'd.
Bel. Then with conceit enlarge yourself
    again.
Bal. What, if conceit have laid my heart to
    gage ?   85
Bel. Pay that you borrowed, and recover it.
Bal. I die, if it return from whence it lies.
Bel. A heartless man, and live ? A miracle !
Bal. Ay, lady, love can work such miracles.
Lor. Tush, tush, my lord ! let go these am-
    bages,[1]   90
And in plain terms acquaint her with your love.
Bel. What boots complaint, when there 's no
    remedy ?
Bal. Yes, to your gracious self must I com-
    plain,
In whose fair answer lies my remedy,
On whose perfection all my thoughts attend, 95
On whose aspect mine eyes find beauty's bower,
In whose translucent breast my heart is lodg'd.
Bel. Alas, my lord, these are but words of
    course,[2]
And but devis'd[3] to drive me from this place.
    She, in going in, lets fall her glove,
    which HORATIO, *coming out, takes*
    up.
Hor. Madam, your glove.   100
Bel. Thanks, good Horatio ; take it for thy
    pains.
Bal. Signior Horatio stoop'd in happy time !
Hor. I reap'd more grace than I deserv'd or
    hop'd.
Lor. My lord, be not dismay'd for what is
    past :
You know that women oft are humorous.[4] 105
These clouds will overblow with little wind ;
Let me alone, I 'll scatter them myself.
Meanwhile, let us devise to spend the time
In some delightful sports and revelling.
Hor. The king, my lords, is coming hither
    straight,   110

---

[1] Circumlocutions. [3] So 1599. Allde, 1594, *devise.*
[2] Formal phrases. [4] Capricious, whimsical.

To feast the Portingal ambassador ;
Things were in readiness before I came.
Bal. Then here it fits us to attend the king,
To welcome hither our ambassador,   114
And learn my father and my country's health.

[SCENE V.][5]

Enter the Banquet, Trumpets, the KING, *and*
Ambassador.

King. See, lord Ambassador, how Spain en-
    treats
Their prisoner Balthazar, thy viceroy's son.
We pleasure more in kindness than in wars.
Amb. Sad is our king, and Portingale la-
    ments,
Supposing that Don Balthazar is slain.   5
Bal. So am I ! — slain by beauty's tyranny.
You see, my lord, how Balthazar is slain :
I frolic with the Duke of Castile's son,
Wrapp'd every hour in pleasures of the court,
And grac'd with favours of his majesty.   10
King. Put off your greetings, till our feast be
    done ;
Now come and sit with us, and taste our cheer.
                    Sit to the banquet.
Sit down, young prince, you are our second
    guest ;
Brother, sit down ; and, nephew, take your
    place.
Signior Horatio, wait thou upon our cup ;   15
For well thou hast deserved to be honoured.
Now, lordings, fall to ; Spain is Portugal,
And Portugal is Spain : we both are friends ;
Tribute is paid, and we enjoy our right.
But where is old Hieronimo, our marshal ?   20
He promis'd us, in honour of our guest,
To grace our banquet with some pompous[6] jest.

Enter HIERONIMO, *with a drum, three knights,*
each his scutcheon ; then he fetches three kings ;
they take their crowns and them captive.

Hieronimo, this masque contents mine eye,
Although I sound not well the mystery.
Hier. The first arm'd knight, that hung his
    scutcheon up,   25
        He takes the scutcheon and gives it
        to the KING.
Was English Robert, Earl of Gloucester,
Who, when King Stephen bore sway in Albion,
Arriv'd with five and twenty thousand men
In Portingale, and by success of war
Enforc'd the king, then but a Saracen,   30
To bear the yoke of the English monarchy.
King. My lord of Portingale, by this you see
That which may comfort both your king and
    you,
And make your late discomfort seem the less.
But say, Hieronimo, what was the next ?   35
Hier. The second knight, that hung his
    scutcheon up,   *He doth as he did before.*
Was Edmund, Earl of Kent in Albion,
When English Richard wore the diadem.
He came likewise, and razed Lisbon walls,
And took the King of Portingale in fight ;   40

---

[5] The same.   [6] Stately.

For which and other such-like service done
He after was created Duke of York.
King. This is another special argument,
That Portingale may deign to bear our yoke,
When it by little England hath been yok'd.   45
But now, Hieronimo, what were the last?
Hier. The third and last, not least, in our
        account,   *Doing as before.*
Was, as the rest, a valiant Englishman,
Brave John of Gaunt, the Duke of Lancaster,
As by his scutcheon plainly may appear.   50
He with a puissant army came to Spain,
And took our King of Castile prisoner.
Amb. This is an argument for our viceroy
That Spain may not insult for her success,
Since English warriors likewise conquered
        Spain,   55
And made them bow their knees to Albion.
King. Hieronimo, I drink to thee for this de-
        vice,
Which hath pleas'd both the ambassador and
        me:
Pledge me, Hieronimo, if thou love the king.
        Takes the cup of Horatio.
My lord, I fear we sit but over-long,   60
Unless our dainties were more delicate;
But welcome are you to the best we have.
Now let us in, that you may be despatch'd:
I think our council is already set.
        Exeunt omnes.

[CHORUS.]

Andrea. Come we for this from depth of un-
        derground,   65
To see him feast that gave me my death's
        wound?
These pleasant sights are sorrow to my soul:
Nothing but league, and love, and banqueting?
Revenge. Be still, Andrea; ere we go from
        hence,
I'll turn their friendship into fell despite,   70
Their love to mortal hate, their day to night,
Their hope into despair, their peace to war,
Their joys to pain, their bliss to misery.

ACT II

[SCENE I.] [1]

Enter LORENZO *and* BALTHAZAR.

Lor. My lord, though Bel-imperia seem thus
        coy,
Let reason hold you in your wonted joy.
In time the savage bull sustains the yoke, [2]
In time all haggard [3] hawks will stoop to lure,
In time small wedges cleave the hardest oak, 5
In time the flint is pierc'd with softest shower,
And she in time will fall from her disdain,
And rue the sufferance of your friendly pain.
Bal. No, she is wilder, and more hard withal,

[1] Palace of Don Cyprian.
[2] Lines 3-6, 9-10 are taken almost literally from Watson's *Hecatompathia*, *Sonnet* 47. Watson copied Se-
rafino.
[3] Wayward.

Than beast, or bird, or tree, or stony wall.   10
But wherefore blot I Bel-imperia's name?
It is my fault, not she, that merits blame.
My feature is not to content her sight,
My words are rude and work her no delight.
The lines I send her are but harsh and ill,   15
Such as do drop from Pan and Marsyas' quill.
My presents are not of sufficient cost,
And being worthless, all my labour's lost.
Yet might she love me for my valiancy:
Ay, but that's sland'red by captivity.   20
Yet might she love me to content her sire:
Ay, but her reason masters his desire.
Yet might she love me as her brother's friend:
Ay, but her hopes aim at some other end.
Yet might she love me to uprear her state: 25
Ay, but perhaps she hopes some nobler mate.
Yet might she love me as her beauty's thrall:
Ay, but I fear she cannot love at all.
Lor. My lord, for my sake leave this ecstasy,
And doubt not but we'll find some remedy.   30
Some cause there is that lets you not be lov'd;
First that must needs be known, and then re-
        mov'd.
What, if my sister love some other knight?
Bal. My summer's day will turn to winter's
        night.
Lor. I have already found a stratagem   35
To sound the bottom of this doubtful theme.
My lord, for once you shall be rul'd by me;
Hinder me not, whate'er you hear or see.
By force or fair means will I cast about
To find the truth of all this question out.   40
Ho, Pedringano!
Ped.   *Signior!*
Lor.   *Vien qui presto.*

Enter PEDRINGANO.

Ped. Hath your lordship any service to com-
        mand me?
Lor. Ay, Pedringano, service of import;
And — not to spend the time in trifling words —
Thus stands the case: it is not long, thou
        know'st,   45
Since I did shield thee from my father's wrath,
For thy conveyance [4] in Andrea's love,
For which thou wert adjudg'd to punishment.
I stood betwixt thee and thy punishment,
And since, thou knowest how I have favoured
        thee.   50
Now to these favours will I add reward,
Not with fair words, but store of golden coin,
And lands and living join'd with dignities,
If thou but satisfy my just demand.   54
Tell truth, and have me for thy lasting friend.
Ped. Whate'er it be your lordship shall de-
        mand,
My bounden duty bids me tell the truth,
If case [5] it lie in me to tell the truth.
Lor. Then, Pedringano, this is my demand:
Whom loves my sister Bel-imperia?   60
For she reposeth all her trust in thee.
Speak, man, and gain both friendship and re-
        ward:
I mean, whom loves she in Andrea's place?

[4] Secret behavior.   [5] In case.

Ped. Alas, my lord, since Don Andrea's death
I have no credit with her as before,   65
And therefore know not, if she love or no.
  Lor. Nay, if thou dally, then I am thy foe,
                              Draws his sword.
And fear shall force what friendship cannot win.
Thy death shall bury what thy life conceals ;
Thou diest for more esteeming her than me.   70
  Ped. O, stay, my lord !
  Lor. Yet speak the truth, and I will guerdon
                              thee,
And shield thee from whatever can ensue,
And will conceal whate'er proceeds from thee.
But if thou dally once again, thou diest.   75
  Ped. If madam Bel-imperia be in love ——
  Lor. What, villain ! Ifs and ands ?
                              Offers to kill him.
  Ped. O, stay, my lord ! She loves Horatio.
                      BALTHAZAR *starts back.*
  Lor. What, Don Horatio, our knight mar-
                              shal's son ?
  Ped. Even him, my lord.   80
  Lor. Now say but how know'st thou he is her
                              love,
And thou shalt find me kind and liberal.
Stand up, I say, and fearless tell the truth.
  Ped. She sent him letters, which myself
                              perus'd,
Full-fraught with lines and arguments of love,
Preferring him before Prince Balthazar.   86
  Lor. Swear on this cross[1] that what thou
                              say's[t] is true,
And that thou wilt conceal what thou hast told.
  Ped. I swear to both, by him that made us all.
  Lor. In hope thine oath is true, here's thy
                              reward ;   90
But if I prove thee perjur'd and unjust,
This very sword whereon thou took'st thine
                              oath
Shall be the worker of thy tragedy.
  Ped. What I have said is true, and shall —
                              for me —
Be still conceal'd from Bel-imperia.   95
Besides, your honour's liberality
Deserves my duteous service, even till death.
  Lor. Let this be all that thou shalt do for me :
Be watchful when and where these lovers meet,
And give me notice in some secret sort.   100
  Ped. I will, my lord.
  Lor. Then shalt thou find that I am liberal.
Thou know'st that I can more advance thy state
Than she ; be therefore wise, and fail me not.
Go and attend her, as thy custom is,   105
Lest absence make her think thou dost amiss.
                              Exit PEDRINGANO.
Why so : *tam armis quam ingenio :*
Where words prevail not, violence prevails ;
But gold doth more than either of them both.
How likes Prince Balthazar this stratagem ? 110
  Bal. Both well and ill ; it makes me glad and
                              sad :
Glad, that I know the hinderer of my love ;
Sad, that I fear she hates me whom I love :
Glad, that I know on whom to be reveng'd ;
Sad, that she 'll fly me, if I take revenge.   115

Yet must I take revenge, or die myself,
For love resisted grows impatient.
I think Horatio be my destin'd plague :
First, in his hand he brandished a sword,
And with that sword he fiercely waged war, 120
And in that war he gave me dangerous wounds,
And by those wounds he forced me to yield,
And by my yielding I became his slave.
Now in his mouth he carries pleasing words,
Which pleasing words do harbour sweet con-
                              ceits,   125
Which sweet conceits are lim'd with sly deceits,
Which sly deceits smooth Bel-imperia's ears,
And through her ears dive down into her heart,
And in her heart set him, where I should stand.
Thus hath he ta'en my body by his force,   130
And now by sleight would captivate my soul ;
But in his fall I 'll tempt the destinies,
And either lose my life, or win my love.
  Lor. Let 's go, my lord ; your staying stays
                              revenge.
Do you but follow me, and gain your love :   135
Her favour must be won by his remove. *Exeunt.*

[SCENE II.][2]

Enter HORATIO *and* BEL-IMPERIA.

  Hor. Now, madam, since by favour of your
                              love
Our hidden smoke is turn'd to open flame,
And that with looks and words we feed our
                              thought
(Two chief contents, where more cannot be had) ;
Thus, in the midst of love's fair blandishments,
Why show you sign of inward languishments,   6
              PEDRINGANO *showeth all to the*
              PRINCE *and* LORENZO, *placing*
              them in secret.
  Bel. My heart, sweet friend, is like a ship at
                              sea :
She wisheth port, where, riding all at ease,
She may repair what stormy times have worn,
And leaning on the shore, may sing with joy   10
That pleasure follows pain, and bliss annoy.
Possession of thy love is th' only port,
Wherein my heart, with fears and hopes long
                              toss'd,
Each hour doth wish and long to make resort,
There to repair the joys that it hath lost,   15
And, sitting safe, to sing in Cupid's choir
That sweetest bliss is crown of love's desire.
              BALTHAZAR *and* LORENZO *above.*
  Bal. O sleep, mine eyes, see not my love pro-
                              fan'd ;
Be deaf, my ears, hear not my discontent ;
Die, heart ; another joys what thou deserv'st. 20
  Lor. Watch still, mine eyes, to see this love
                              disjoin'd ;
Hear still, mine ears, to hear them both lament ;
Live, heart, to joy at fond Horatio's fall.
  Bel. Why stands Horatio speechless all this
                              while ?   24
  Hor. The less I speak, the more I meditate.
  Bel. But whereon dost thou chiefly meditate?
  Hor. On dangers past, and pleasures to ensue.

---

[1] Sword-hilt.

[2] The same.

Bal. On pleasures past, and dangers to ensue.
Bel. What dangers and what pleasures dost
     thou mean ?
Hor. Dangers of war, and pleasures of our
     love.   30
Lor. Dangers of death, but pleasures none at
     all.
Bel. Let dangers go, thy war shall be with
     me :
But such a war as breaks no bond of peace.
Speak thou fair words, I 'll cross them with fair
     words ;
Send thou sweet looks, I 'll meet them with
     sweet looks ;   35
Write loving lines, I 'll answer loving lines ;
Give me a kiss, I 'll countercheck thy kiss :
Be this our warring peace, or peaceful war.
Hor. But, gracious madam, then appoint the
     field,
Where trial of this war shall first be made.   40
Bal. Ambitious villain, how his boldness
     grows !
Bel. Then be thy father's pleasant bower the
     field,
Where first we vow'd a mutual amity :
The court were dangerous, that place is safe.
Our hour shall be, when Vesper 'gins to rise,   45
That summons home distressful travellers.[1]
There none shall hear us but the harmless birds;
Haply the gentle nightingale
Shall carol us asleep, ere we be ware,
And, singing with the prickle at her breast,   50
Tell our delight and mirthful dalliance.
Till then each hour will seem a year and more.
Hor. But, honey-sweet and honourable love,
Return we now into your father's sight ;
Dangerous suspicion waits on our delight.   55
Lor. Ay, danger mixed with jealous[2] despite
Shall send thy soul into eternal night.   *Exeunt.*

[SCENE III.][3]

Enter KING OF SPAIN, PORTINGALE AMBAS-
     SADOR, DON CYPRIAN, *etc.*

King. Brother of Castile, to the prince's love
What says your daughter Bel-imperia ?
Cyp. Although she coy it,[4] as becomes her
     kind,
And yet dissemble that she loves the prince,
I doubt it, but she will stoop in time.   5
And were she froward, which she will not be,
Yet herein shall she follow my advice,
Which is to love him, or forgo my love.
King. Then, lord Ambassador of Portingale,
Advise thy king to make this marriage up,   10
For strengthening of our late-confirmed league ;
I know no better means to make us friends.
Her dowry shall be large and liberal :
Besides that she is daughter and half-heir
Unto our brother here, Don Cyprian,   15
And shall enjoy the moiety of his land,
I 'll grace her marriage with an uncle's gift,
And this it is, in case the match go forward :

The tribute which you pay, shall be releas'd ;
And if by Balthazar she have a son,   20
He shall enjoy the kingdom after us.
Amb. I 'll make the motion to my sovereign
     liege,
And work it, if my counsel may prevail.
King. Do so, my lord, and if he give consent,
I hope his presence here will honour us,   25
In celebration of the nuptial day ;
And let himself determine of the time.
Amb. Will 't please your grace command me
     aught beside ?
King. Commend me to the king, and so fare-
     well.
But where 's Prince Balthazar to take his leave ?
Amb. That is perform'd already, my good
     lord.   31
King. Amongst the rest of what you have in
     charge,
The prince's ransom must not be forgot :
That 's none of mine, but his that took him
     prisoner ;
And well his forwardness deserves reward.   35
It was Horatio, our knight marshal's son.
Amb. Between us there 's a price already
     pitch'd,
And shall be sent with all convenient speed.
King. Then once again farewell, my lord.
Amb. Farewell, my lord of Castile, and the
     rest.   *Exit.* [40
King. Now, brother, you must take some
     little pains
To win fair Bel-imperia from her will.
Young virgins must be ruled by their friends.
The prince is amiable, and loves her well ;
If she neglect him and forgo his love,   45
She both will wrong her own estate and ours.
Therefore, whiles I do entertain the prince
With greatest pleasure that our court affords,
Endeavour you to win your daughter's thought :
If she give back,[5] all this will come to naught. 50
                                        Exeunt.

[SCENE IV.][6]

Enter HORATIO, BEL-IMPERIA, *and* PEDRIN-
     GANO.

Hor. Now that the night begins with sable
     wings
To overcloud the brightness of the sun,
And that in darkness pleasures may be done :
Come, Bel-imperia, let us to the bower,
And there in safety pass a pleasant hour.   5
Bel. I follow thee, my love, and will not back,
Although my fainting heart controls [7] my
     soul.
Hor. Why, make you doubt of Pedringano's
     faith ?
Bel. No, he is as trusty as my second self. —
Go, Pedringano, watch without the gate,   10
And let us know if any make approach.
Ped. [*Aside.*] Instead of watching, I 'll de-
     serve more gold
By fetching Don Lorenzo to this match.
                             Exit PEDRINGANO.
Hor. What means thy love ?

---

[1] *Travailers* and *travellers* were not distinguished in
Elizabethan spelling.
[2] Kittredge suggests *mix'd with jealous.* (Manly.)
[3] The Court of Spain.   [4] Pretend to be shy.
[5] Refuse.   [6] Hieronimo's garden.   [7] Checks.

Bel.   I know not what myself;
And yet my heart foretells me some mischance.
Hor. Sweet, say not so; fair fortune is our
friend,   16
And heavens have shut up day to pleasure us.
The stars, thou see'st, hold back their twink-
ling shine,
And Luna hides herself to pleasure us.
Bel. Thou hast prevail'd; I 'll conquer my
misdoubt,   20
And in thy love and counsel drown my fear.
I fear no more; love now is all my thoughts.
Why sit we not? for pleasure asketh ease.
Hor. The more thou sitt'st within these leafy
bowers,
The more will Flora deck it with her flowers. 25
Bel. Ay, but if Flora spy Horatio here,
Her jealous eye will think I sit too near.
Hor. Hark, madam, how the birds record [1] by
night,
For joy that Bel-imperia sits in sight.
Bel. No, Cupid counterfeits the nightin-
gale,   30
To frame sweet music to Horatio's tale.
Hor. If Cupid sing, then Venus is not far:
Ay, thou art Venus, or some fairer star.
Bel. If I be Venus, thou must needs be Mars;
And where Mars reigneth, there must needs be
wars.   35
Hor. Then thus begin our wars: put forth
thy hand,
That it may combat with my ruder hand.
Bel. Set forth thy foot to try the push of
mine.
Hor. But first my looks shall combat against
thine.
Bel. Then ward thyself: I dart this kiss at
thee.   40
Hor. Thus I retort the dart thou threw'st at
me.
Bel. Nay, then to gain the glory of the field,
My twining arms shall yoke and make thee
yield.
Hor. Nay, then my arms are large and strong
withal:
Thus elms by vines are compass'd, till they
fall.   45
Bel. O, let me go; for in my troubled eyes
Now may'st thou read that life in passion dies.
Hor. O, stay a while, and I will die with
thee;
So shalt thou yield, and yet have conquer'd
me.
Bel. Who 's there? Pedringano? We are be-
tray'd!   50

Enter LORENZO, BALTHAZAR, SERBERINE,
PEDRINGANO, *disguised.*

Lor. My lord, away with her, take her
aside. —
O, sir, forbear: your valour is already tried.
Quickly despatch, my masters.
                    They hang him in the arbour.
Hor.   What, will you murder me?
Lor. Ay, thus, and thus: these are the fruits
of love.   *They stab him.*
                    [1] Sing.

Bel. O, save his life, and let me die for him!
O, save him, brother; save him, Balthazar: 56
I lov'd Horatio; but he lov'd not me.
Bal. But Balthazar loves Bel-imperia.
Lor. Although his life were still ambitious,
proud,
Yet is he at the highest now he is dead.   60
Bel. Murder! murder! Help, Hieronimo,
help!
Lor. Come, stop her mouth; away with her.
                                      Exeunt.

Enter HIERONIMO *in his shirt, etc.*

Hier. What outcries pluck me from my naked
bed,
And chill my throbbing heart with trembling
fear,
Which never danger yet could daunt before?
Who calls Hieronimo? Speak, here I am.   6[?]
I did not slumber; therefore 't was no dream.
No, no, it was some woman cried for help,
And here within this garden did she cry,
And in this garden must I rescue her. —   70
But stay, what murd'rous spectacle is this?
A man hang'd up and all the murderers gone!
And in my bower, to lay the guilt on me!
This place was made for pleasure, not for death.
                          He cuts him down.
Those garments that he wears I oft have
seen —   75
Alas, it is Horatio, my sweet son!
O no, but he that whilom was my son!
O, was it thou that call'dst me from my bed?
O speak, if any spark of life remain:
I am thy father; who hath slain my son?   8[?]
What savage monster, not of human kind,
Hath here been glutted with thy harmless blood,
And left thy bloody corpse dishonoured here,
For me, amidst these dark and deathful shades,
To drown thee with an ocean of my tears?   8[?]
O heavens, why made you night to cover sin?
By day this deed of darkness had not been.
O earth, why didst thou not in time devour
The vild [2] profaner of this sacred bower?
O poor Horatio, what hadst thou misdone,   90
To leese [3] thy life, ere life was new begun?
O wicked butcher, whatsoe'er thou wert,
How could thou strangle virtue and desert?
Ay me most wretched, that have lost my joy,
In leesing my Horatio, my sweet boy!   95

Enter ISABELLA.

Isab. My husband's absence makes my heart
to throb: —
Hieronimo!
Hier. Here, Isabella, help me to lament;
For sighs are stopp'd, and all my tears are spent.
Isab. What world of grief! my son Horatio!
O, where 's the author of this endless woe? 101
Hier. To know the author were some ease of
grief,
For in revenge my heart would find relief.
Isab. Then is he gone? and is my son gone
too?
O, gush out, tears, fountains and floods of tears; 105

[2] Vile.   [3] Lose.

Blow, sighs, and raise an everlasting storm ;
For outrage fits our cursed wretchedness.
¹ [*Ay me, Hieronimo, sweet husband, speak !*
Hier. He supp'd with us to-night, frolic and
   merry,
And said he would go visit Balthazar   110
At the duke's palace; there the prince doth lodge.
He had no custom to stay out so late :
He may be in his chamber; some go see.
Roderigo, ho!

    Enter PEDRO *and* JAQUES.

Isab. Ay me, he raves! — Sweet Hieronimo! 115
Hier. True, all Spain takes note of it.
Besides, he is so generally belov'd ;
His majesty the other day did grace him
With waiting on his cup : these be favours,
Which do assure me he cannot be short-liv'd.   120
Isab. Sweet Hieronimo!
Hier. I wonder how this fellow got his clothes! —
Sirrah, sirrah, I'll know the truth of all.
Jaques, run to the Duke of Castile's presently,
And bid my son Horatio to come home :   125
I and his mother have had strange dreams to-night.
Do ye hear me, sir ?
Jaques.   *Ay, sir.*
Hier.   *Well, sir, be gone.*
Pedro, come hither; know'st thou who this is?
Ped. Too well, sir.
Hier. Too well! Who, who is it? Peace, Isabella!
Nay, blush not, man.
         It is my lord Horatio. 131
Hier. Ha, ha, St. James! but this doth make me
   laugh,
That there are more deluded than myself.
Ped. Deluded?
Hier.   *Ay:*
I would have sworn myself, within this hour,   135
That this had been my son Horatio :
His garments are so like.
Ha! are they not great persuasions?
Isab. O, would to God it were not so!
Hier. Were not, Isabella? Dost thou dream it is?
Can thy soft bosom entertain a thought 141
That such a black deed of mischief should be done
On one so pure and spotless as our son ?
Away, I am ashamed.
Isab.   *Dear Hieronimo,*
Cast a more serious eye upon thy grief;   145
Weak apprehension gives but weak belief.
Hier. It was a man, sure, that was hang'd up
   here ;
A youth, as I remember : I cut him down.
If it should prove my son now after all —
Say you ? say you? — Light! lend me a taper;
Let me look again. — O God!   151
Confusion, mischief, torment, death and hell,
Drop all your stings at once in my cold bosom,
That now is stiff with horror : kill me quickly !
Be gracious to me, thou infective ² *night,* 155
And drop this deed of murder down on me ;
Gird in my waste of grief with thy large darkness,
And let me not survive to see the light

May put me in the mind I had a son.
Isab. O sweet Horatio! O my dearest son! 160
Hier. How strangely had I lost my way to grief!]
Sweet, lovely rose, ill-pluckt before thy
   time,
Fair, worthy son, not conquer'd, but betray'd,
I'll kiss thee now, for words with tears are
   stay'd.
Isab. And I'll close up the glasses of his sight,
For once these eyes were only my delight. 166
Hier. See'st thou this handkercher besmear'd
   with blood ?
It shall not from me, till I take revenge.
See'st thou those wounds that yet are bleeding
   fresh ?
I'll not entomb them, till I have reveng'd.   170
Then will I joy amidst my discontent ;
Till then my sorrow never shall be spent
Isab. The heavens are just ; murder cannot
   be hid :
Time is the author both of truth and right,
And time will bring this treachery to light. 175
Hier. Meanwhile, good Isabella, cease thy
   plaints,
Or, at the least, dissemble them awhile :
So shall we sooner find the practice out,
And learn by whom all this was brought about.
Come, Isabel, now let us take him up,   180
          They take him up.
And bear him in from out this cursed place.
I'll say his dirge ; singing fits not this case.

O aliquis mihi quas pulchrum ver educat herbas,
   Hieronimo sets his breast unto his sword.
Misceat, et nostro detur medicina dolori ;
Aut, si qui faciunt annorum oblivia, succos   185
Praebeat: ipse metam magnum quaecunque per
   orbem
Gramina Sol pulchras effert in luminis oras ;
Ipse bibam quicquid meditatur saga veneni,
Quicquid et herbarum vi caeca nenia nectit :
Omnia perpetiar, lethum quoque, dum semel omnis
Noster in extincto moriatur pectore sensus. — 291
Ergo tuos oculos nunquam, mea vita, videbo,
Et tua perpetuus sepelivit lumina somnus?
Emoriar tecum : sic, juvat ire sub umbras. —
At tamen absistam properato cedere letho, 195
*Ne mortem vindicta tuam tam nulla sequatur.*³
   Here he throws it from him and
      bears the body away.

      [CHORUS.]

Andrea. Brought'st thou me hither to in-
   crease my pain ?
I look'd that Balthazar should have been slain ;
But 't is my friend Horatio that is slain,
And they abuse fair Bel-imperia,   200
On whom I doted more than all the world,
Because she lov'd me more than all the world.
Revenge. Thou talk'st of harvest, when the
   corn is green :
The end is crown of every work well done ;
The sickle comes not, till the corn be ripe.   205
Be still ; and ere I lead thee from this place,
I'll show thee Balthazar in heavy case.

---

¹ First passage of additions begins here.
² Infectious.

³ A cento of passages from Virgil, Tibullus, and others.

ACT III

[SCENE I.] [1]

Enter VICEROY OF PORTINGALE, Nobles, ALEXANDRO, VILLUPPO.

Vic. Infortunate condition of kings,
Seated amidst so many helpless doubts !
First we are plac'd upon extremest height,
And oft supplanted with exceeding hate,
But ever subject to the wheel of chance ;   5
And at our highest never joy we so
As we both doubt and dread our overthrow.
So striveth not the waves with sundry winds
As Fortune toileth in the affairs of kings,
That would be fear'd, yet fear to be belov'd,   10
Sith fear or love to kings is flattery.
For instance, lordings, look upon your king,
By hate deprived of his dearest son,
The only hope of our successive line.
Nob. I had not thought that Alexandro's
    heart   15
Had been envenom'd with such extreme hate ;
But now I see that words have several works,
And there's no credit in the countenance.
Vil. No ; for, my lord, had you beheld the
    train [2]
That feigned love had colour'd in his looks,   20
When he in camp consorted [3] Balthazar,
Far more inconstant had you thought the sun,
That hourly coasts [4] the centre of the earth,
Than Alexandro's purpose to the prince.
Vic. No more, Villuppo, thou hast said
    enough,   25
And with thy words thou slay'st our wounded
    thoughts.
Nor shall I longer dally with the world,
Procrastinating Alexandro's death.
Go some of you, and fetch the traitor forth,
That, as he is condemned, he may die.   30

Enter ALEXANDRO *with a* Nobleman *and halberts.*

Nob. In such extremes will nought but patience serve.
Alex. But in extremes what patience shall I
    use ?
Nor discontents it me to leave the world,
With whom there nothing can prevail but wrong.
Nob. Yet hope the best.
Alex.   'T is heaven is my hope.   35
As for the earth, it is too much infect
To yield me hope of any of her mould.
Vic. Why linger ye ? Bring forth that daring
    fiend,
And let him die for his accursed deed.
Alex. Not that I fear the extremity of death
(For nobles cannot stoop to servile fear)   41
Do I, O king, thus discontented live.
But this, O this, torments my labouring soul,
That thus I die suspected of a sin
Whereof, as heav'ns have known my secret
    thoughts,   45
So am I free from this suggestion.

Vic. No more, I say ! to the tortures !
    When ? [5]
Bind him, and burn his body in those flames,
            They bind him to a stake.
That shall prefigure those unquenched fires
Of Phlegethon, prepared for his soul.   50
Alex. My guiltless death will be aveng'd on
    thee,
On thee, Villuppo, that hath malic'd [6] thus,
Or for thy meed hast falsely me accus'd.
Vil. Nay, Alexandro, if thou menace me,
I 'll lend a hand to send thee to the lake   55
Where those thy words shall perish with thy
    works,
Injurious traitor ! monstrous homicide !

Enter AMBASSADOR.

Amb. Stay, hold a while ;
And here — with pardon of his majesty —
Lay hands upon Villuppo.
Vic.   Ambassador,   60
What news hath urg'd this sudden entrance ?
Amb. Know, sovereign lord, that Balthazar
    doth live.
Vic. What say'st thou ? Liveth Balthazar
    our son ?
Amb. Your highness' son, Lord Balthazar,
    doth live ;
And, well entreated in the court of Spain,   65
Humbly commends him to your majesty.
These eyes beheld ; and these my followers,
With these, the letters of the king's commends,
            Gives him letters.
Are happy witnesses of his highness' health.
    *The King looks on the letters, and
        proceeds.*
Vic. "Thy son doth live, your tribute is re-
    ceiv'd ;   70
Thy peace is made, and we are satisfied.
The rest resolve upon as things propos'd
For both our honours and thy benefit."
Amb. These are his highness' farther articles.
            He gives him more letters.
Vic. Accursed wretch, to intimate these ills 75
Against the life and reputation
Of noble Alexandro ! Come, my lord, unbind
    him. —
Let him unbind thee, that is bound to death,
To make a quital [7] for thy discontent.
            They unbind him.
Alex. Dread lord, in kindness [8] you could do
    no less   80
Upon report of such a damned fact ;
But thus we see our innocence hath sav'd
The hopeless life which thou, Villuppo, sought
By thy suggestions to have massacred.
Vic. Say, false Villuppo, wherefore didst thou
    thus   85
Falsely betray Lord Alexandro's life ?
Him whom thou know'st that no unkindness else
But even the slaughter of our dearest son
Could once have mov'd us to have misconceiv'd.
Alex. Say, treacherous Villuppo, tell the
    king :   90

---

[1] The Court of Portugal.
[2] Guile.
[3] Accompanied.
[4] Moves round.
[5] An exclamation of impatience.
[6] Slandered.
[7] Requital.
[8] Nature.

Wherein[1] hath Alexandro us'd thee ill?
   Vil. Rent with remembrance of so foul a
      deed,
My guilty soul submits me to thy doom ;
For not for Alexandro's injuries,
But for reward and hope to be preferr'd,   95
Thus have I shamelessly hazarded his life.
   Vic. Which, villain, shall be ransom'd with
      thy death ;
And not so mean[2] a torment as we here
Devis'd for him who, thou said'st, slew our son,
But with the bitt'rest torments and extremes 100
That may be yet invented for thine end.
          ALEXANDRO *seems to entreat.*
Entreat me not ; go, take the traitor hence :
                    Exit VILLUPPO.
And, Alexandro, let us honour thee
With public notice of thy loyalty. —
To end those things articulated here   105
By our great lord, the mighty King of Spain,
We with our council will deliberate.
Come, Alexandro, keep us company·   *Exeunt.*

[SCENE II.][3]

Enter HIERONIMO.

   Hier. O eyes ! no eyes, but fountains fraught
      with tears ;
O life ! no life, but lively form of death ;
O world ! no world, but mass of public wrongs,
Confus'd and fill'd with murder and misdeeds !
O sacred heav'ns ! if this unhallowed deed,   5
If this inhuman and barbarous attempt,
If this incomparable murder thus
Of mine, but now no more my son,
Shall unreveal'd and unrevenged pass,
How should we term your dealings to be just, 10
If you unjustly deal with those that in your
      justice trust ?
The night, sad secretary to my moans,
With direful visions wake my vexed soul,
And with the wounds of my distressful son
Solicit me for notice of his death.   15
The ugly fiends do sally forth of hell,
And frame my steps to unfrequented paths,
And fear my heart with fierce inflamed thoughts.
The cloudy day my discontents records,
Early begins to register my dreams,   20
And drive me forth to seek the murderer.
Eyes, life, world, heav'ns, hell, night, and day,
See, search, shew, send some man, some mean,
    that may —   *A letter falleth.*
What 's here ? a letter ? Tush ! it is not so !—
A letter written to Hieronimo !   *Red ink.* 25
" For want of ink, receive this bloody writ.
Me hath my hapless brother hid from thee ;
Revenge thyself on Balthazar and him :
For these were they that murdered thy son.
Hieronimo, revenge Horatio's death,   30
And better fare than Bel-imperia doth."
What means this unexpected miracle ?
My son slain by Lorenzo and the prince !
What cause had they Horatio to malign ?
Or what might move thee, Bel-imperia,   35

To accuse thy brother, had he been the mean ?
Hieronimo, beware ! — thou art betray'd,
And to entrap thy life this train is laid.
Advise thee therefore, be not credulous :
This is devised to endanger thee,   40
That thou, by this, Lorenzo shouldst accuse ;
And he, for thy dishonour done, should draw
Thy life in question and thy name in hate.
Dear was the life of my beloved son,
And of his death behoves me be reveng'd ; 45
Then hazard not thine own, Hieronimo,
But live t' effect thy resolution.
I therefore will by circumstances[4] try,
What I can gather to confirm this writ ;
And, heark'ning near the Duke of Castile's
    house,   50
Close, if I can, with Bel-imperia,
To listen more, but nothing to bewray.

Enter PEDRINGANO.

Now, Pedringano !
   Ped.   Now, Hieronimo !
   Hier. Where 's thy lady ?
   Ped.   I know not ; here 's my lord.

Enter LORENZO.

   Lor. How now, who 's this ? Hieronimo ?
   Hier.   My lord.
   Ped. He asketh for my lady Bel-imperia. 55
   Lor. What to do, Hieronimo ? The duke,
      my father, hath
Upon some disgrace awhile remov'd her hence ;
But, if it be ought I may inform her of,
Tell me, Hieronimo, and I 'll let her know it. 60
   Hier. Nay, nay, my lord, I thank you ; it
      shall not need.
I had a suit unto her, but too late,
And her disgrace makes me unfortunate.
   Lor. Why so, Hieronimo ? Use me.
   Hier. O no, lord, I dare not ; it must not be. 65
I humbly thank your lordship.
   [5] [*Hier.*   *Who ? You, my lord ?*
I reserve your favour for a greater honour ;
This is a very toy, my lord, a toy.
   Lor. All 's one, Hieronimo, acquaint me with it.
   Hier. I' faith, my lord, it is an idle thing ; 70
I must confess I ha' been too slack, too tardy,
Too remiss unto your honour.
   Lor.   *How now, Hieronimo ?*
   Hier. In troth, my lord, it is a thing of nothing :
The murder of a son, or so ——
A thing of nothing, my lord !]
   Lor.   Why then, farewell. 75
   Hier. My grief no heart, my thoughts no
      tongue can tell.   *Exit.*
   Lor. Come hither, Pedringano, see'st thou
      this ?
   Ped. My lord, I see it, and suspect it too.
   Lor. This is that damned villain Serberine
That hath, I fear, reveal'd Horatio's death. 80
   Ped. My lord, he could not, 't was so lately
      done ;
And since he hath not left my company.

---

[1] So Hazlitt. Qq. *Or wherein.*
[2] Moderate.   [3] The Court of Spain.
[4] Indirect means.
[5] Second passage of additions begins here, replacing
Hieronimo's speech in ll. 65-66.

Lor. Admit he have not, his condition's such,
As fear or flattering words may make him false.
I know his humour, and therewith repent   85
That e'er I us'd him in this enterprise.
But, Pedringano, to prevent the worst,
And 'cause I know thee secret as my soul,
Here, for thy further satisfaction, take thou this,   *Gives him more gold.*
And hearken to me — thus it is devis'd :   90
This night thou must (and, prithee, so resolve),
Meet Serberine at Saint Luigi's Park —
Thou know'st 't is here hard by behind the house ;
There take thy stand, and see thou strike him sure,
For die he must, if we do mean to live.   95
Ped. But how shall Serberine be there, my lord ?
Lor. Let me alone ; I 'll send to him to meet
The prince and me, where thou must do this deed.
Ped. It shall be done, my lord, it shall be done ;
And I 'll go arm myself to meet him there.   100
Lor. When things shall alter, as I hope they will,
Then shalt thou mount for this ; thou know'st my mind.   *Exit* PEDRINGANO.
Che le Ieron ! [1]

Enter PAGE.

Page.   My lord ?
Lor.   Go, sirrah,
To Serberine, and bid him forthwith meet
The prince and me at Saint Luigi's Park,   105
Behind the house ; this evening, boy !
Page.   I go, my lord.
Lor. But, sirrah, let the hour be eight o'clock :
Bid him not fail.
Page.   I fly, my lord.   *Exit.*
Lor. Now to confirm the complot thou hast cast
Of all these practices, I 'll spread the watch,   110
Upon precise commandment from the king,
Strongly to guard the place where Pedringano
This night shall murder hapless Serberine.
Thus must we work that will avoid distrust ;
Thus must we practise to prevent mishap,   115
And thus one ill another must expulse.
This sly enquiry of Hieronimo
For Bel-imperia breeds suspicion,
And this suspicion bodes a further ill.
As for myself, I know my secret fault,   120
And so do they ; but I have dealt for them :
They that for coin their souls endangered,
To save my life, for coin shall venture theirs ;
And better it 's that base companions [2] die
Than by their life to hazard our good haps.   125
Nor shall they live, for me to fear their faith :
I 'll trust myself, myself shall be my friend ;
For die they shall, —
Slaves are ordained to no other end.   *Exit.*

[1] Unintelligible. Probably a corruption of a call to the **Page.**   [2] Fellows.

Enter PEDRINGANO, *with a pistol.*

Ped. Now, Pedringano, bid thy pistol hold,
And hold on, Fortune ! once more favour me ;
Give but success to mine attempting spirit,
And let me shift for taking of mine aim.
Here is the gold : this is the gold propos'd ;   5
It is no dream that I adventure for,
But Pedringano is possess'd thereof.
And he that would not strain his conscience
For him that thus his liberal purse hath stretch'd,
Unworthy such a favour, may he fail,   10
And, wishing, want when such as I prevail.
As for the fear of apprehension,
I know, if need should be, my noble lord
Will stand between me and ensuing harms ;
Besides, this place is free from all suspect :   15
Here therefore will I stay and take my stand.

Enter the Watch.

1 *Watch.* I wonder much to what intent it is
That we are thus expressly charg'd to watch.
2 *Watch.* 'T is by commandment in the king's own name.
3 *Watch.* But we were never wont to watch and ward   20
So near the duke his brother's house before.
2 *Watch.* Content yourself, stand close, there 's somewhat in 't.

Enter SERBERINE.

Ser. Here, Serberine, attend and stay thy pace ;
For here did Don Lorenzo's page appoint
That thou by his command shouldst meet with him.   25
How fit a place — if one were so dispos'd —
Methinks this corner is to close with one.
Ped. Here comes the bird that I must seize upon.
Now, Pedringano, or never, play the man !
Ser. I wonder that his lordship stays so long,   30
Or wherefore should he send for me so late ?
Ped. For this, Serberine ! — and thou shalt ha 't.   *Shoots the dag.* [4]
So, there he lies ; my promise is perform'd.

The Watch.

1 *Watch.* Hark, gentlemen, this is a pistol shot.
2 *Watch.* And here 's one slain ; — stay the murderer.   35
Ped. Now by the sorrows of the souls in hell,   *He strives with the* Watch. [5]
Who first lays hand on me, I 'll be his priest.
3 *Watch.* Sirrah, confess, and therein play the priest,
Why hast thou thus unkindly kill'd the man ?
Ped. Why ? Because he walk'd abroad so late.   40

[3] Saint Luigi's Park.   [4] Pistol.
[5] Murder him (be present at his death).

3 *Watch.* Come, sir, you had been better
          kept your bed,
Than have committed this misdeed so late.
2 *Watch.* Come, to the marshal's with the
          murderer!
1 *Watch.* On to Hieronimo's! help me here
To bring the murd'red body with us too.   45
    Ped. Hieronimo? Carry me before whom you
          will.
Whate'er he be, I 'll answer him and you;
And do your worst, for I defy you all. *Exeunt.*

[SCENE IV.]¹

Enter LORENZO *and* BALTHAZAR.

    Bal. How now, my lord, what makes you
          rise so soon?
    Lor. Fear of preventing our mishaps too
          late.
    Bal. What mischief is it that we not mis-
          trust?
    Lor. Our greatest ills we least mistrust, my
          lord,
And inexpected harms do hurt us most.   5
    Bal. Why, tell me, Don Lorenzo, tell me,
          man,
If ought concerns our honour and your own.
    Lor. Nor you, nor me, my lord, but both in
          one;
For I suspect — and the presumption 's great —
That by those base confederates in our fault   10
Touching the death of Don Horatio,
We are betray'd to old Hieronimo.
    Bal. Betray'd, Lorenzo? Tush! it cannot be.
    Lor. A guilty conscience, urged with the
          thought
Of former evils, easily cannot err.   15
I am persuaded — and dissuade me not —
That all 's revealed to Hieronimo.
And therefore know that I have cast it thus:—

Enter Page.

But here 's the page. How now? what news
          with thee?
    Page. My lord, Serberine is slain.
    Bal.   Who? Serberine, my man?   20
    Page. Your highness' man, my lord.
    Lor.   Speak, page, who murdered him?
    Page. He that is apprehended for the fact.²
    Lor. Who?
    Page.   Pedringano.
    Bal. Is Serberine slain, that lov'd his lord so
          well?
Injurious villain, murderer of his friend!   25
    Lor. Hath Pedringano murdered Serberine?
My lord, let me entreat you to take the pains
To exasperate and hasten his revenge
With your complaints unto my lord the king.
This their dissension breed a greater doubt.   30
    Bal. Assure thee, Don Lorenzo, he shall die,
Or else his highness hardly shall deny.³
Meanwhile I 'll haste the marshal-sessions,
For die he shall for this his damned deed.
          Exit BALTHAZAR.

    Lor. Why so, this fits our former policy,   35
And thus experience bids the wise to deal.
I lay the plot; he prosecutes the point:
I set the trap; he breaks the worthless twigs,
And sees not that wherewith the bird was
          lim'd.⁴
Thus hopeful men, that mean to hold their
          own,   40
Must look like fowlers to their dearest friends.
He runs to kill whom I have holp⁵ to catch,
And no man knows it was my reaching fetch.⁶
'T is hard to trust unto a multitude,
Or any one, in mine opinion,   45
When men themselves their secrets will reveal.

Enter a Messenger *with a letter.*

Boy!
    Page. My lord.
    Lor. What 's he?
    Mes.   I have a letter to your lordship.
    Lor. From whence?
    Mes.   From Pedringano that 's imprison'd.
    Lor. So he is in prison then?
    Mes.   Ay, my good lord.   50
    Lor. What would he with us? — He writes
          us here,
To stand good lord, and help him in distress. —
Tell him I have his letters, know his mind;
And what we may, let him assure him of.
Fellow, begone; my boy shall follow thee.   55
          Exit Messenger.
This works like wax; yet once more try thy
          wits.
Boy, go, convey this purse to Pedringano;
Thou know'st the prison, closely⁷ give it him,
And be advis'd that none be there about.
Bid him be merry still, but secret;   60
And though the marshal-sessions be to-day,
Bid him not doubt of his delivery.
Tell him his pardon is already sign'd,
And thereon bid him boldly be resolv'd:
For, were he ready to be turned off —⁸   65
As 't is my will the uttermost be tried —
Thou with his pardon shalt attend him still.
Show him this box, tell him his pardon 's in 't;
But open 't not, an if thou lov'st thy life,
But let him wisely keep his hopes unknown.   70
He shall not want while Don Lorenzo lives.
Away!
    Page. I go, my lord, I run.
    Lor. But, sirrah, see that this be cleanly⁹
          done.   *Exit* Page.
Now stands our fortune on a tickle point,
And now or never ends Lorenzo's doubts.   75
One only thing is uneffected yet,
And that 's to see the executioner.
But to what end? I list not trust the air
With utterance of our pretence¹⁰ therein,
For fear the privy whisp'ring of the wind   80
Convey our words amongst unfriendly ears,
That lie too open to advantages.
E' quel che voglio io, nessun lo sa;
Intendo io: quel mi basterà.   *Exit.*

---

⁴ Snared.   ⁵ Helped.
⁶ Deep-reaching device. Qq. have dialect form *fatch.*
⁷ Secretly.   ⁹ Cleverly.
⁸ Hanged.   ¹⁰ Intention.

¹ Palace of Don Cyprian.   ³ Resist with difficulty.
² Deed.

[SCENE V.]¹

Enter Boy with the box.

Boy. My master hath forbidden me to look
in this box ; and, by my troth, 't is likely, if he
had not warned me, I should not have had so
much idle time ; for we men's-kind in our mi-
nority are like women in their uncertainty : [5
that they are most forbidden, they will soonest
attempt : so I now.——By my bare honesty,
here 's nothing but the bare empty box ! Were it
not sin against secrecy, I would say it were a
piece of gentlemanlike knavery. I must go [10
to Pedringano, and tell him his pardon is in
this box ; nay, I would have sworn it, had I not
seen the contrary. I cannot choose but smile
to think how the villain will flout the gallows,
scorn the audience, and descant on the [15
hangman, and all presuming of his pardon from
hence. Will 't not be an odd jest for me to stand
and grace every jest he makes, pointing my
finger at this box, as who would say, " Mock on,
here 's thy warrant." Is 't not a scurvy jest [20
that a man should jest himself to death ? Alas !
poor Pedringano, I am in a sort sorry for thee ;
but if I should be hanged with thee, I cannot
weep. *Exit.*

[SCENE VI.]²

Enter HIERONIMO *and the* Deputy.

Hier. Thus must we toil in other men's ex-
tremes,
That know not how to remedy our own ;
And do them justice, when unjustly we,
For all our wrongs, can compass no redress.
But shall I never live to see the day,   5
That I may come, by justice of the heavens,
To know the cause that may my cares allay ?
This toils my body, this consumeth age,
That only I to all men just must be,
And neither gods nor men be just to me.   10
Dep. Worthy Hieronimo, your office asks
A care to punish such as do transgress.
Hier. So is 't my duty to regard his death
Who, when he liv'd, deserv'd my dearest blood.
But come, for that we came for : let 's begin,   15
For here lies that which bids me to be gone.

Enter Officers, Boy, *and* PEDRINGANO, *with a
letter in his hand, bound.*

Dep. Bring forth the prisoner, for the court
is set.
Ped. Gramercy, boy, but it was time to come ;
For I had written to my lord anew
A nearer matter that concerneth him,   20
For fear his lordship had forgotten me.
But sith he hath remember'd me so well —
Come, come, come on, when shall we to this
gear ?³
Hier. Stand forth, thou monster, murderer
of men,
And here, for satisfaction of the world,   25
Confess thy folly, and repent thy fault :
For there 's thy place of execution.

¹ A street.   ² A Court of Justice.   ³ Business.

Ped. This is short work. Well, to your
marshalship
First I confess — nor fear I death therefore —
I am the man, 't was I slew Serberine.   30
But, sir, then you think this shall be the place,
Where we shall satisfy you for this gear ?
Dep. Ay, Pedringano.
Ped.   Now I think not so.
Hier. Peace, impudent ; for thou shalt find
it so ;   34
For blood with blood shall, while I sit as judge,
Be satisfied, and the law discharg'd.
And though myself cannot receive the like,
Yet will I see that others have their right.
Despatch : the fault 's approved⁴ and confess'd,
And by our law he is condemn'd to die.   40
Hangm. Come on, sir, are you ready ?
Ped. To do what, my fine, officious knave ?
Hangm. To go to this gear.
Ped. O sir, you are too forward : thou
wouldst fain furnish me with a halter, to [45
disfurnish me of my habit.⁵ So I should go out
of this gear, my raiment, into that gear, the
rope. But, hangman, now I spy your knavery,
I 'll not change without boot,⁶ that 's flat.
Hangm. Come, sir.
Ped. So, then, I must up ?   50
Hangm. No remedy.
Ped. Yes, but there shall be for my coming
down.
Hangm. Indeed, here 's a remedy for that.   55
Ped. How ? Be turn'd off ?
Hangm. Ay, truly. Come, are you ready ? I
pray, sir, despatch ; the day goes away.
Ped. What, do you hang by the hour ? If
you do, I may chance to break your old
custom.   61
Hangm. Faith, you have reason ; for I am
like to break your young neck.
Ped. Dost thou mock me, hangman ? Pray
God, I be not preserved to break your knave's
pate for this.   66
Hangm. Alas, sir ! you are a foot too low to
reach it, and I hope you will never grow so high
while I am in the office.
Ped. Sirrah, dost see yonder boy with [70
the box in his hand ?
Hangm. What, he that points to it with his
finger ?
Ped. Ay, that companion.
Hangm. I know him not ; but what of [75
him ?
Ped. Dost thou think to live till his old
doublet will make thee a new truss ?
Hangm. Ay, and many a fair year after, to
truss up many an honester man than either
thou or he.   81
Ped. What hath he in his box, as thou
think'st ?
Hangm. Faith, I cannot tell, nor I care not
greatly ; methinks you should rather hearken
to your soul's health.   86
Ped. Why, sirrah, hangman, I take it that
that is good for the body is likewise good for

⁴ Proved.
⁵ The hangman got the clothes of the criminals he
executed.   ⁶ Advantage.

the soul: and it may be, in that box is balm for
both.   90
Hangm. Well, thou art even the merriest
piece of man's flesh that e'er groan'd at my
office door!
Ped. Is your roguery become an office with
a knave's name?   95
Hangm. Ay, and that shall all they witness
that see you seal it with a thief's name.
Ped. I prithee, request this good company to
pray with me.
Hangm. Ay, marry, sir, this is a good motion.
My masters, you see here's a good fellow.   101
Ped. Nay, nay, now I remember me, let them
alone till some other time; for now I have no
great need.
Hier. I have not seen a wretch so impudent.
O monstrous times, where murder's set so
light,   106
And where the soul, that should be shrin'd in
heaven,
Solely delights in interdicted things,
Still wand'ring in the thorny passages,
That intercepts itself of [1] happiness.   110
Murder! O bloody monster! God forbid   —
A fault so foul should 'scape unpunished.
Despatch, and see this execution done! —
This makes me to remember thee, my son.
                              Exit HIERONIMO.
Ped. Nay, soft, no haste.   115
Dep. Why, wherefore stay you? Have you
hope of life?
Ped. Why, ay!
Hangm.   As how?
Ped. Why, rascal, by my pardon from the
king.
Hangm. Stand you on that? Then you shall
off with this.   *He turns him off.*
Dep. So, executioner; — convey him hence;
But let his body be unburied: 121
Let not the earth be choked or infect
With that which heav'n contemns, and men
neglect.   *Exeunt.*

[SCENE VII.] [2]

Enter HIERONIMO.

Hier. Where shall I run to breathe abroad
my woes,
My woes, whose weight hath wearied the earth?
Or mine exclaims, that have surcharg'd the air
With ceaseless plaints for my deceased son?
The blust'ring winds, conspiring with my
words,   5
At my lament have mov'd the leafless trees,
Disrob'd the meadows of their flow'red green,
Made mountains marsh with spring-tides of my
tears,
And broken through the brazen gates of hell.
Yet still tormented is my tortured soul   10
With broken sighs and restless passions,
That, winged, mount; and, hovering in the air,
Beat at the windows of the brightest heavens,
Soliciting for justice and revenge:
But they are plac'd in those empyreal [3] heights,15

Where, countermur'd [4] with walls of diamond,
I find the place impregnable; and they
Resist my woes, and give my words no way.

Enter Hangman *with a letter.*

Hangm. O lord, sir! God bless you, sir! the
man, sir, Petergade, sir, he that was so full [20
of merry conceits ——
Hier. Well, what of him?
Hangm. O lord, sir, he went the wrong way;
the fellow had a fair commission to the contrary.
Sir, here is his passport; I pray you, sir, we [25
have done him wrong.
Hier. I warrant thee, give it me.
Hangm. You will stand between the gallows
and me?
Hier. Ay, ay.
Hangm. I thank your lord worship.   30
                              Exit Hangman.
Hier. And yet, though somewhat nearer me
concerns,
I will, to ease the grief that I sustain,
Take truce with sorrow while I read on this.
" My lord, I write,[5] as mine extremes requir'd,
That you would labour my delivery: 35
If you neglect, my life is desperate,
And in my death I shall reveal the troth.
You know, my lord, I slew him for your sake,
And was confed'rate with the prince and you;
Won by rewards and hopeful promises,   40
I holp to murder Don Horatio too." —
Holp he to murder mine Horatio?
And actors in th' accursed tragedy
Wast thou, Lorenzo, Balthazar and thou,
Of whom my son, my son deserv'd so well?   45
What have I heard, what have mine eyes be-
held?
O sacred heavens, may it come to pass
That such a monstrous and detested deed,
So closely smother'd, and so long conceal'd,
Shall thus by this be venged or reveal'd?   50
Now see I what I durst not then suspect,
That Bel-imperia's letter was not feign'd.
Nor feigned she, though falsely they have
wrong'd
Both her, myself, Horatio, and themselves.
Now may I make compare 'twixt hers and this,
Of every accident I ne'er could find   55
Till now, and now I feelingly perceive
They did what heav'n unpunish'd would not
leave.
O false Lorenzo! are these thy flattering looks?
Is this the honour that thou didst my son?   60
And Balthazar — bane to thy soul and me! —
Was this the ransom he reserv'd thee for?
Woe to the cause of these constrained wars!
Woe to thy baseness and captivity,
Woe to thy birth, thy body, and thy soul,   65
Thy cursed father, and thy conquer'd self!
And bann'd with bitter execrations be
The day and place where he did pity thee!
But wherefore waste I mine unfruitful words,
When nought but blood will satisfy my woes? 70
I will go plain me to my lord the king,
And cry aloud for justice through the court,

---

[1] Hinder it from.   [2] Hieronimo's house.
          [3] So Schick. Qq. *imperial.*

[4] Doubly fenced·   [5] Manly emends to *writ.*

Wearing the flints with these my withered feet;
And either purchase justice by entreats,
Or tire them all with my revenging threats.   75
                                    Exit.

[SCENE VIII.] [1]

Enter ISABELLA *and her* Maid.

Isab. So that you say this herb will purge
      the eye,
And this, the head? —
Ah! — but none of them will purge the heart!
No, there's no medicine left for my disease,
Nor any physic to recure the dead.   5
                              She runs lunatic.
Horatio! O, where's Horatio?
  Maid. Good madam, affright not thus your-
      self
With outrage [2] for your son Horatio:
He sleeps in quiet in the Elysian fields.
  Isab. Why, did I not give you gowns and
      goodly things,   10
Bought you a whistle and a whipstalk too,
To be revenged on their villanies?
  Maid. Madam, these humours do torment my
      soul.
  Isab. My soul — poor soul, thou talk'st [3] of
      things
Thou know'st not what — my soul hath silver
      wings,   15
That mounts me up unto the highest heavens;
To heaven? Ay, there sits my Horatio,
Back'd with a troop of fiery Cherubins,
Dancing about his newly healed wounds,   19
Singing sweet hymns and chanting heav'nly notes,
Rare harmony to greet his innocence,
That died, ay died, a mirror in our days.
But say, where shall I find the men, the mur-
      derers,
That slew Horatio? Whither shall I run
To find them out that murdered my son?   25
                                    Exeunt.

[SCENE IX.] [4]

BEL-IMPERIA *at a window.*

Bel. What means this outrage that is off'red
      me?
Why am I thus sequest'red from the court?
No notice! Shall I not know the cause
Of these my secret and suspicious ills?
Accursed brother, unkind murderer,   5
Why bend'st [5] thou thus thy mind to martyr me?
Hieronimo, why writ I of thy wrongs,
Or why art thou so slack in thy revenge?
Andrea, O Andrea! that thou saw'st
Me for thy friend Horatio handled thus,   10
And him for me thus causeless murdered! —
Well, force perforce, I must constrain myself
To patience, and apply me [6] to the time,
Till heaven, as I have hop'd, shall set me free.

Enter CHRISTOPHIL.

Chris. Come, madam Bel-imperia, this may
      not be.   *Exeunt.* 15

¹ The same.   ³ 1623. Earlier edd. *talkes.*
² Outcry.   ⁴ Palace of Don Cyprian.
⁵ 1623. Earlier edd. *bends.*   ⁶ Adapt myself.

[SCENE X.] [7]

Enter LORENZO, BALTHAZAR, *and the* Page.

Lor. Boy, talk no further; thus far things go
      well.
Thou art assur'd that thou sawest him dead?
  Page. Or else, my lord, I live not.
  Lor.   That's enough.
As for his resolution in his end,
Leave that to him with whom he sojourns now. 5
Here, take my ring and give it Christophil,
And bid him let my sister be enlarg'd,
And bring her hither straight. —   *Exit* Page.
This that I did was for a policy,
To smooth and keep the murder secret,   10
Which, as a nine-days' wonder, being o'erblown,
My gentle sister will I now enlarge.
  Bal. And time, Lorenzo: for my lord the
      duke,
You heard, enquired for her yester-night.
  Lor. Why, and my lord, I hope you heard me
      say   15
Sufficient reason why she kept away;
But that's all one. My lord, you love her?
  Bal.   Ay.
  Lor. Then in your love beware; deal cun-
      ningly:
Salve all suspicions, only soothe [8] me up;
And if she hap to stand on terms [9] with us — 20
As for her sweetheart and concealment so —
Jest with her gently: under feigned jest
Are things conceal'd that else would breed un-
      rest.
But here she comes.

Enter BEL-IMPERIA.

                    Now, sister, —
  Bel.   Sister? No!
Thou art no brother, but an enemy;   25
Else wouldst thou not have us'd thy sister so:
First, to affright me with thy weapons drawn,
And with extremes abuse my company; [10]
And then to hurry me, like whirlwind's rage,
Amidst a crew of thy confederates,   30
And clap me up where none might come at me,
Nor I at any to reveal my wrongs.
What madding fury did possess thy wits?
Or wherein is't that I offended thee?
  Lor. Advise you better, Bel-imperia,   35
For I have done you no disparagement;
Unless, by more discretion than deserv'd,
I sought to save your honour and mine own.
  Bel. Mine honour? Why, Lorenzo, wherein
      is't
That I neglect my reputation so,   40
As you, or any, need to rescue it?
  Lor. His highness and my father were resolv'd
To come confer with old Hieronimo
Concerning certain matters of estate
That by the viceroy was determined.   45
  Bel. And wherein was mine honour touch'd
      in that?
  Bal. Have patience, Bel-imperia; hear the
      rest.

⁷ The same.   ⁹ Haggle, hold out.
⁸ Back.   ¹⁰ Companion.

Lor. Me, next in sight, as messenger they sent
To give him notice that they were so nigh :
Now when I came, consorted with the prince, 50
And unexpected in an arbour there
Found Bel-imperia with Horatio —
Bel. How then ?
Lor. Why, then, remembering that old dis-
grace,
Which you for Don Andrea had endur'd, 55
And now were likely longer to sustain,
By being found so meanly accompanied,
Thought rather — for I knew no readier mean —
To thrust Horatio forth my father's way.
Bal. And carry you obscurely somewhere
else, 60
Lest that his highness should have found you
there.
Bel. Ev'n so, my lord ? And you are witness
That this is true which he entreateth of ?
You, gentle brother, forg'd this for my sake,
And you, my lord, were made his instrument ?
A work of worth, worthy the noting too ! 66
But what's the cause that you conceal'd me
since ?
Lor. Your melancholy, sister, since the news
Of your first favourite Don Andrea's death,
My father's old wrath hath exasperate. 70
Bal. And better was 't for you, being in dis-
grace,
To absent yourself, and give his fury place.
Bel. But why had I no notice of his ire ?
Lor. That were to add more fuel to your fire,
Who burnt like Aetna for Andrea's loss. 75
Bel. Hath not my father then enquir'd for me?
Lor. Sister, he hath, and this, excus'd I thee.
He whispereth in her ear.
But Bel-imperia, see the gentle prince ;
Look on thy love, behold young Balthazar,
Whose passions by thy presence are increas'd; 80
And in whose melancholy thou may'st see
Thy hate, his love ; thy flight, his following thee.
Bel. Brother, you are become an orator —
I know not, I, by what experience —
Too politic for me, past all compare, 85
Since last I saw you ; but content yourself :
The prince is meditating higher things.
Bal. 'T is of thy beauty, then, that conquers
kings ;
Of those thy tresses, Ariadne's twines,
Wherewith my liberty thou hast surpris'd ; 90
Of that thine ivory front, my sorrow's map,
Wherein I see no haven to rest my hope.
Bel. To love and fear, and both at once, my
lord,
In my conceit, are things of more import
Than women's wits are to be busied with. 95
Bal. 'T is I that love.
Bel.　　　　　　　Whom ?
Bal.　　　　　　　　　　　Bel-imperia.
Bel. But I that fear.
Bal.　　　　　　Whom ?
Bel.　　　　　　　　　　Bel-imperia.
Lor. Fear yourself ?
Bel.　　　　　Ay, brother.
Lor.　　　　　　　　　　How ?
Bel.　　　　　　　　　　　　　As those
That what they love are loth and fear to lose.

Bal. Then, fair, let Balthazar your keeper
be. 100
Bel. No, Balthazar doth fear as well as we :
Et [1] *tremulo metui pavidum junxere timorem* —
Est [2] *vanum stolidae proditionis opus.*
Lor. Nay, and you argue things so cunningly,
We 'll go continue this discourse at court. 105
Bal. Led by the loadstar of her heavenly
looks,
Wends poor oppressed Balthazar,
As o'er the mountains walks the wanderer,
Incertain to effect his pilgrimage.　　*Exeunt.*

[SCENE XI.] [3]

Enter two PORTINGALES, *and* HIERONIMO *meets
them.*

1 *Port.* By your leave, sir.
Hier. [4] ['*T is neither as you think, nor as you
think,*
Nor as you think ; you're wide all.
*These slippers are not mine, they were my son Ho-
ratio's.*
My son ? and what's a son ? A thing begot 5
Within a pair of minutes — thereabout ;
A lump bred up in darkness, and doth serve
To ballace [5] *these light creatures we call women ;*
And, at nine months' end, creeps forth to light.
What is there yet in a son, 10
To make a father dote, rave, or run mad ?
Being born, it pouts, cries, and breeds teeth.
What is there yet in a son ? He must be fed,
Be taught to go, and speak. Ay, or yet
Why might not a man love a calf as well ? 15
Or melt in passion o'er a frisking kid,
As for a son ? Methinks, a young bacon,
Or a fine little smooth horse colt,
Should move a man as much as doth a son :
For one of these, in very little time, 20
Will grow to some good use; whereas a son,
The more he grows in stature and in years,
The more unsquar'd, unbevell'd, [6] *he appears,*
Reckons his parents among the rank of fools,
Strikes care upon their heads with his mad riots, 25
Makes them look old before they meet with age.
This is a son ! — And what a loss were this,
Consider'd truly ? —— O, but my Horatio
Grew out of reach of these insatiate humours :
He lov'd his loving parents ; 30
He was my comfort, and his mother's joy,
The very arm that did hold up our house :
Our hopes were stored up in him,
None but a damned murderer could hate him.
He had not seen the back of nineteen year, 35
When his strong arm unhors'd
The proud Prince Balthazar, and his great mind,
Too full of honour, took him unto [7] *mercy,*
That valiant, but ignoble Portingale !
Well, heaven is heaven still ! 40
And there is Nemesis, and Furies,
And things call'd whips,
And they sometimes do meet with murderers :

---

[1] So Hazlitt. Qq. *Est.*　　　　　[3] A street.
[2] So Schick. Qq. *Et.*
[4] Third passage of additions begins here.
[5] Ballast.　　[6] Unpolished.　　[7] Qq. *us to*

They do not always scape, that is some comfort.
Ay, ay, ay ; and then time steals on,   45
And steals, and steals, till violence leaps forth
Like thunder wrapt in a ball of fire,
And so doth bring confusion to them all.]
Good leave have you : nay, I pray you go,
For I 'll leave you, if you can leave me so.   50
2 *Port.* Pray you, which is the next way to
my lord the duke's ?
Hier. The next way from me.
1 *Port.*   To his house, we mean.
Hier. O, hard by : 't is yon house that you
see.
2 *Port.* You could not tell us if his son were
there ?
Hier. Who, my Lord Lorenzo ?
1 *Port.*   Ay, sir.
*He goeth in at one door and comes
out at another.*
Hier.   O, forbear !
For other talk for us far fitter were.   55
But if you be importunate to know
The way to him, and where to find him out,
Then list to me, and I 'll resolve your doubt.
There is a path upon your left-hand side   60
That leadeth from a guilty conscience
Unto a forest of distrust and fear —
A darksome place, and dangerous to pass :
There shall you meet with melancholy thoughts,
Whose baleful humours if you but uphold,   65
It will conduct you to despair and death —
Whose rocky cliffs when you have once beheld,
Within a hugy dale of lasting night,
That, kindled with the world's iniquities,
Doth cast up filthy and detested fumes : —   70
Not far from thence, where murderers have built
A habitation for their cursed souls,
There, in a brazen cauldron, fix'd by Jove,
In his fell wrath, upon a sulphur flame,
Yourselves shall find Lorenzo bathing him   75
In boiling lead and blood of innocents.
1 *Port.* Ha, ha, ha !
Hier. Ha, ha, ha ! Why, ha, ha, ha ! Fare-
well, good ha, ha, ha !   *Exit.*
2 *Port.* Doubtless this man is passing lunatic,
Or imperfection of his age doth make him dote.
Come, let 's away to seek my lord the duke.   81
Exeunt.

[SCENE XII.][1]

Enter HIERONIMO, *with a poniard in one hand
and a rope in the other.*

Hier. Now, sir, perhaps I come and see the
king ;
The king sees me, and fain would hear my suit :
Why, is not this a strange and seld-seen[2] thing,
That standers-by with toys should strike me
mute ?
Go to, I see their shifts, and say no more.   5
Hieronimo, 't is time for thee to trudge.
Down by the dale that flows with purple gore
Standeth a fiery tower ; there sits a judge
Upon a seat of steel and molten brass,
And 'twixt his teeth he holds a fire-brand,   10
That leads unto the lake where hell doth stand.

[1] The Court of Spain.   [2] Seldom seen.

Away, Hieronimo ! to him be gone ;
He 'll do thee justice for Horatio's death.
Turn down this path : thou shalt be with him
straight ;
Or this, and then thou need'st not take thy
breath :   15
This way or that way ? —— Soft and fair, not
so :
For if I hang or kill myself, let 's know
Who will revenge Horatio's murder then ?
No, no ! fie, no ! pardon me, I 'll none of that.
He flings away the dagger and halter.
This way I 'll take, and this way comes the
king :   20
And here I 'll have a fling at him, that 's flat ;
And, Balthazar, I 'll be with thee to bring,[3]
And thee, Lorenzo ! Here 's the king — nay, stay ;
And here, ay here — there goes the hare away.[4]

Enter KING, AMBASSADOR, CASTILE, *and* LO-
RENZO.

King. Now show, ambassador, what our vice-
roy saith :   25
Hath he receiv'd the articles we sent ?
Hier. Justice, O justice to Hieronimo.
Lor. Back ! see'st thou not the king is busy ?
Hier.   O, is he so ?
King. Who is he that interrupts our business ?
Hier. Not I. [*Aside.*] Hieronimo, beware ! go
by, go by !   30
Amb. Renowned King, he hath receiv'd and
read
Thy kingly proffers, and thy promis'd league ;
And, as a man extremely over-joy'd
To hear his son so princely entertain'd,
Whose death he had so solemnly bewail'd,   35
This for thy further satisfaction
And kingly love he kindly lets thee know :
First, for the marriage of his princely son
With Bel-imperia, thy beloved niece,
The news are more delightful to his soul,   40
Than myrrh or incense to the offended heavens.
In person, therefore, will he come himself,
To see the marriage rites solemnized,
And, in the presence of the court of Spain,
To knit a sure inexplicable[5] band   45
Of kingly love and everlasting league
Betwixt the crowns of Spain and Portingal.
There will he give his crown to Balthazar,
And make a queen of Bel-imperia.
King. Brother, how like you this our vice-
roy's love ?   50
Cast. No doubt, my lord, it is an argument
Of honourable care to keep his friend,
And wondrous zeal to Balthazar his son ;
Nor am I least indebted to his grace,
That bends his liking to my daughter thus.   55
Amb. Now last, dread lord, here hath his
highness sent
(Although he send not that his son return)
His ransom due to Don Horatio.

[3] Give thee a lesson.
[4] This phrase usually means, "There the matter
ends." Perhaps here it might mean, "There begins the
chase."
[5] *I. e.* inextricable, which some modern edd. read.
Allde, *inexecrable.*

Hier. Horatio! who calls Horatio?
King. And well rememb'red: thank his majesty.   60
Here, see it given to Horatio.
Hier. Justice, O, justice, justice, gentle king!
King. Who is that? Hieronimo?
Hier. Justice, O, justice! O my son, my son!
My son, whom naught can ransom or redeem!
Lor. Hieronimo, you are not well-advis'd.   66
Hier. Away, Lorenzo, hinder me no more;
For thou hast made me bankrupt of my bliss.
Give me my son! you shall not ransom him!
Away! I 'll rip the bowels of the earth,   70
He diggeth with his dagger.
And ferry over to th' Elysian plains,
And bring my son to show his deadly wounds.
Stand from about me!
I 'll make a pickaxe of my poniard,
And here surrender up my marshalship;   75
For I 'll go marshal up the fiends in hell,
To be avenged on you all for this.
King. What means this outrage?
Will none of you restrain his fury?
Hier. Nay, soft and fair! you shall not need
to strive.   80
Needs must he go that the devils drive.   *Exit.*
King. What accident hath happ'd Hieronimo?
I have not seen him to demean him so.
Lor. My gracious lord, he is with extreme
pride,
Conceiv'd of young Horatio his son   85
And covetous of having to himself
The ransom of the young prince Balthazar,
Distract, and in a manner lunatic.
King. Believe me, nephew, we are sorry for 't:
This is the love that fathers bear their sons.   90
But, gentle brother, go give to him this gold,
The prince's ransom; let him have his due.
For what he hath, Horatio shall not want;
Haply Hieronimo hath need thereof.
Lor. But if he be thus helplessly distract,   95
'T is requisite his office be resign'd,
And giv'n to one of more discretion.
King. We shall increase his melancholy so.
'T is best that we see further in it first,
Till when, ourself will execute[1] the place.   100
And, brother, now being in the ambassador,
That he may be a witness of the match
'Twixt Balthazar and Bel-imperia,
And that we may prefix a certain time,
Wherein the marriage shall be solemniz'd,   105
That we may have thy lord, the viceroy, here.
Amb. Therein your highness highly shall content
His majesty, that longs to hear from hence.
King. On, then, and hear you, lord ambassador ——   *Exeunt.*

[SCENE XIIA.][2]

[3][Enter JAQUES and PEDRO.

Jaq. I wonder, Pedro, why our master thus
At midnight sends us with our torches light,
When man, and bird, and beast, are all at rest,
Save those that watch for rape and bloody murder.

[1] So Collier. Qq. *exempt.*
[2] Hieronimo's garden.
[3] Fourth passage of additions.

Ped. O Jaques, know thou that our master's
mind   5
Is much distraught, since his Horatio died,
And — now his aged years should sleep in rest,
His heart in quiet — like a desperate man,
Grows lunatic and childish for his son.
Sometimes, as he doth at his table sit,   10
He speaks as if Horatio stood by him;
Then starting in a rage, falls on the earth,
Cries out, "Horatio, where is my Horatio?"
So that with extreme grief and cutting sorrow
There is not left in him one inch of man: 14
See, where he comes.

Enter HIERONIMO.

Hier. I pry through every crevice of each wall,
Look on each tree, and search through every brake,
Beat at the bushes, stamp our grandam earth,
Dive in the water, and stare up to heaven,   20
Yet cannot I behold my son Horatio. —
How now, who's there? Spirits, spirits?
Ped. We are your servants that attend you, sir.
Hier. What make you with your torches in the
dark?
Ped. You bid us light them, and attend you here.
Hier. No, no, you are deceiv'd! not I; — you are
deceiv'd!   26
Was I so mad to bid you light your torches now?
Light me your torches at the mid of noon,
When-as the sun-god rides in all his glory;
Light me your torches then.
Ped.   *Then we burn*[4] *daylight.*
Hier. Let it be burnt; Night is a murderous
slut,   31
That would not have her treasons to be seen;
And yonder pale-fac'd Hecate there, the moon,
Doth give consent to that is done in darkness;
And all those stars that gaze upon her face,   35
Are aglets[5] *on her sleeve, pins on her train;*
And those that should be powerful and divine,
Do sleep in darkness when they most should shine.
Ped. Provoke them not, fair sir, with tempting
words:
The heav'ns are gracious, and your miseries   40
And sorrow makes you speak you know not what.
Hier. Villain, thou liest! and thou dost nought
But tell me I am mad. Thou liest, I am not mad!
I know thee to be Pedro, and he Jaques.   44
I 'll prove it to thee; and were I mad, how could I?
Where was she that same night when my Horatio
*Was murd'red? She should have shone: search thou
the book.*
*Had the moon shone, in my boy's face there was a
kind of grace,*
*That I know — nay, I do know — had the murderer
seen him,*   49
His weapon would have fall'n and cut the earth,
Had he been fram'd of naught but blood and death.
Alack! when mischief doth it knows not what,
What shall we say to mischief?

Enter ISABELLA.

Isab. Dear Hieronimo, come in a-doors;
O, seek not means so to increase thy sorrow.   55

[4] Waste.   [5] Metal ornaments, orig. points of laces.

Hier. Indeed, Isabella, we do nothing here ;
I do not cry : ask Pedro, and ask Jaques ;
Not I indeed ; we are very merry, very merry.
Isab. *How ? be merry here, be merry here ?*
Is not this the place, and this the very tree,   60
Where my Horatio died, where he was murdered ?
Hier. *Was — do not say what : let her weep it out.*
This was the tree ; I set it of a kernel :
And when our hot Spain could not let it grow,
But that the infant and the human sap   65
Began to wither, duly twice a morning
Would I be sprinkling it with fountain-water.
At last it grew and grew, and bore and bore,
Till at the length
It grew a gallows, and did bear our son ;   70
It bore thy fruit and mine — O wicked, wicked
    plant !
        One knocks within at the door.
See, who knocks there.
        Ped.   *It is a painter, sir.*
Hier. *Bid him come in, and paint some comfort,*
For surely there's none lives but painted comfort.
Let him come in ! — One knows not what may   75
    chance :
God's will that I should set this tree ! — but even so
Masters ungrateful servants rear from nought,
And then they hate them that did bring them up.

        Enter the Painter.

Paint. *God bless you, sir.*   79
Hier. *Wherefore ? Why, thou scornful villain ?*
How, where, or by what means should I be bless'd ?
Isab. *What wouldst thou have, good fellow ?*
Paint.   *Justice, madam.*
Hier. *O ambitious beggar !*
Wouldst thou have that that lives not in the world ?
Why, all the undelved mines cannot buy   85
An ounce of justice !
'T is a jewel so inestimable. I tell thee,
God hath engross'd all justice in his hands,
And there is none but what comes from him.
Paint.   *O, then I see*
That God must right me for my murd'red son.   90
Hier. *How, was thy son murdered ?*
Paint. *Ay, sir ; no man did hold a son so dear.*
Hier. *What, not as thine ? That's a lie,*
As massy as the earth. I had a son
Whose least unvalued hair did weigh   95
A thousand of thy sons : and he was murdered.
Paint. *Alas, sir, I had no more but he.*
Hier. *Nor I, nor I : but this same one of mine*
Was worth a legion. But all is one.
Pedro, Jaques, go in a-doors ; Isabella, go,   100
And this good fellow here and I
Will range this hideous orchard up and down,
Like to two lions reaved of their young.
Go in a-doors, I say.
        [Exeunt. The painter and he sits down.
            Come, let's talk wisely now.
Was thy son murdered ?
Paint.   *Ay, sir.*
Hier.   *So was mine.*   105
How dost take it ? Art thou not sometimes mad ?
Is there no tricks[1] that comes before thine eyes ?

        [1] Illusions.

Paint. *O Lord, yes, sir.*
Hier. *Art a painter ? Canst paint me a tear, or a*
wound, a groan, or a sigh ? Canst paint me such [110
a tree[2] as this ?
Paint. *Sir, I am sure you have heard of my*
painting : my name's Bazardo.
Hier. *Bazardo! Afore God, an excellent fellow.*
Look you, sir, do you see ? I'd have you paint me [115
[for] my gallery, in your oil-colours matted,[3] and
draw me five years younger than I am — do ye
see, sir, let five years go ; let them go like the marshal
of Spain — my wife Isabella standing by me, with
a speaking look to my son Horatio, which should [120
intend to this or some such-like purpose : "God bless
thee, my sweet son," and my hand leaning upon his
head, thus, sir ; do you see ? May it be done ?
Paint. *Very well, sir.*
Hier. *Nay, I pray, mark me, sir. Then, sir,* [125
would I have you paint me this tree, this very tree.
Canst paint a doleful cry ?
Paint. *Seemingly, sir.*
Hier. *Nay, it should cry ; but all is one. Well,*
sir, paint me a youth run through and through [130
with villains' swords, hanging upon this tree. Canst
thou draw a murderer ?
Paint. *I'll warrant you, sir ; I have the pattern*
of the most notorious villains that ever lived in all
Spain.   135
Hier. *O, let them be worse, worse : stretch thine*
art, and let their beards be of Judas his own colour ;
and let their eye-brows jutty over : in any case ob-
serve that. Then, sir, after some violent noise,
bring me forth in my shirt, and my gown under [140
mine arm, with my torch in my hand, and my
sword reared up, thus : — and with these words :
"What noise is this ? Who calls Hieronimo ?"
May it be done ?
Paint. *Yea, sir.*   145
Hier. *Well, sir; then bring me forth, bring me*
through alley and alley, still with a distracted coun-
tenance going along, and let my hair heave up my
night-cap. Let the clouds scowl, make the moon
dark, the stars extinct, the winds blowing, the bells [150
tolling, the owls shrieking, the toads croaking, the
minutes jarring,[4] and the clock striking twelve. And
then at last, sir, starting, behold a man hanging,
and tottering and tottering, as you know the wind
will wave a man, and I with a trice to cut him [155
down. And looking upon him by the advantage of
my torch, find it to be my son Horatio. There you
may [show] a passion, there you may show a pas-
sion ! Draw me like old Priam of Troy, crying,
"The house is a-fire, the house is a-fire, as [160
the torch over my[5] head !" Make me curse, make
me rave, make me cry, make me mad, make me well
again, make me curse hell, invocate heaven, and in
the end leave me in a trance — and so forth.
Paint. *And is this the end ?*   165
Hier. *O no, there is no end ; the end is death and*
madness ! As I am never better than when I am
mad ; then methinks I am a brave fellow, then I do
wonders ; but reason abuseth me, and there's the tor-
ment, there's the hell. At the last, sir, bring me to [170

2 Q. 1602, *A teare.*   4 Ticking.
3 Dulled, unburnished.   5 So 1602.   Later Qq. *thy.*

one of the murderers: were he as strong as Hector,
thus would I tear and drag him up and down.

He beats the painter in, then comes
out again, with a book in his
hand.]

[SCENE XIII.]¹

Enter HIERONIMO, *with a book in his hand.*

[*Hier.*] *Vindicta mihi!*
Ay, heaven will be reveng'd of every ill;
Nor will they suffer murder unrepaid.
Then stay, Hieronimo, attend their will:
For mortal men may not appoint their time!   5
" *Per scelus semper tutum est sceleribus iter.*"
Strike, and strike home, where wrong is off'red
    thee;
For evils unto ills conductors be,
And death's the worst of resolution.
For he that thinks with patience to contend   10
To quiet life, his life shall easily end. —
" *Fata si miseros juvant, habes salutem;*
Fata si vitam negant, habes sepulchrum" :
If destiny thy miseries do ease,
Then hast thou health, and happy shalt thou be ;
If destiny deny thee life, Hieronimo,   16
Yet shalt thou be assured of a tomb ;
If neither, yet let this thy comfort be :
Heaven covereth him that hath no burial.
And to conclude, I will revenge his death !   20
But how ? Not as the vulgar wits of men,
With open, but inevitable ills,²
As by a secret, yet a certain mean,
Which under kindship³ will be cloaked best.
Wise men will take their opportunity,   25
Closely and safely fitting things to time.
But in extremes advantage hath no time ;
And therefore all times fit not for revenge.
Thus therefore will I rest me in unrest,
Dissembling quiet in unquietness,   30
Not seeming that I know their villanies,
That my simplicity may make them think
That ignorantly I will let all slip ;
For ignorance, I wot, and well they know,
*Remedium malorum iners est.*⁴   35
Nor ought avails it me to menace them,
Who, as a wintry storm upon a plain,
Will bear me down with their nobility.
No, no, Hieronimo, thou must enjoin
Thine eyes to observation, and thy tongue   40
To milder speeches than thy spirit affords,
Thy heart to patience, and thy hands to rest,
Thy cap to courtesy, and thy knee to bow,
Till to revenge thou know when, where, and
    how.   *A noise within.*
How now, what noise ? What coil⁵ is that you
    keep ?   45

[*Enter a* Servant.]

Serv. Here are a sort⁶ of poor petitioners
That are importunate, and it shall please you,
    sir,
That you should plead their cases to the king.

¹ Hieronimo's house.
² Not with open but with inevitable injuries.
³ Kindness.   ⁵ Turmoil.
⁴ From Seneca's *Oedipus*, 515.   ⁶ Group, band.

Hier. That I should plead their several ac-
    tions ?
Why, let them enter, and let me see them.   50

Enter three Citizens *and an* Old Man.

1 *Cit.* So, I tell you this : for learning and
    for law,
There is not any advocate in Spain
That can prevail, or will take half the pain
That he will, in pursuit of equity.
Hier. Come near, you men, that thus impor-
    tune me. —   55
[*Aside.*]   Now must I bear a face of gravity ;
For thus I us'd, before my marshalship,
To plead in causes as corregidor.⁷ —
Come on, sirs, what's the matter ?
2 *Cit.*   Sir, an action.
Hier. Of battery ?
1 *Cit.*   Mine of debt.
Hier.   Give place.
2 *Cit.* No, sir, mine is an action of the case.⁸
3 *Cit.* Mine an *ejectione firmae*⁹ by a lease.   62
Hier. Content you, sirs ; are you determined
That I should plead your several actions ?
1 *Cit.* Ay, sir, and here's my declaration.   65
2 *Cit.* And here's my band.
3 *Cit.*   And here's my lease.
                They give him papers.
Hier. But wherefore stands yon silly man so
    mute,
With mournful eyes and hands to heaven up-
    rear'd ?
Come hither, father, let me know thy cause.
Senex. O worthy sir, my cause, but slightly
    known,   70
May move the hearts of warlike Myrmidons,
And melt the Corsic rocks with ruthful tears.
Hier. Say, father, tell me, what's thy suit ?
Senex.   No, sir, could my woes
Give way unto my most distressful words,
Then should I not in paper, as you see,   75
With ink bewray what blood began in me.
Hier. What's here ? " The humble supplica·
    tion
Of Don Bazulto for his murd'red son."
Senex. Ay, sir.
Hier.   No, sir, it was my murd'red son :
O my son, my son, O my son Horatio !   80
But mine, or thine, Bazulto, be content.
Here, take my handkercher and wipe thine eyes,
Whiles wretched I in thy mishaps may see
The lively portrait of my dying self.
                He draweth out a bloody napkin.
O no, not this ; Horatio, this was thine ;   85
And when I dy'd it in thy dearest blood,
This was a token 'twixt thy soul and me,
That of thy death revenged I should be.
But here, take this, and this — what, my
    purse ? —
Ay, this, and that, and all of them are thine ;
For all as one are our extremities.   91
1 *Cit.* O, see the kindness of Hieronimo !

⁷ Advocate. Properly, magistrate.
⁸ " A universal remedy given for all personal wrongs
. . . so called because the plaintiff's whole case . . . is
set forth at length in the original writ." (Blackstone.)
⁹ A writ to eject a tenant.

2 Cit. This gentleness shows him a gentle-
man.
Hier. See, see, O see thy shame, Hieronimo!
See here a loving father to his son!   95
Behold the sorrows and the sad laments,
That he delivereth for his son's decease!
If love's effects so strive[1] in lesser things,
If love enforce such moods in meaner wits,
If love express such power in poor estates,   100
Hieronimo, as when[2] a raging sea,
Toss'd with the wind and tide, o'erturneth[3] then
The upper billows, course of waves to keep,
Whilst lesser waters labour in the deep,
Then sham'st thou not, Hieronimo, to neglect
The sweet revenge of thy Horatio?   106
Though on this earth justice will not be found,
I'll down to hell, and in this passion
Knock at the dismal gates of Pluto's court,
Getting by force, as once Alcides did,   110
A troop of Furies and tormenting hags
To torture Don Lorenzo and the rest.
Yet lest the triple-headed porter should
Deny my passage to the slimy strand,
The Thracian poet thou shalt counterfeit.   115
Come on, old father, be my Orpheus,
And if thou canst[4] no notes upon the harp,
Then sound the burden of thy sore heart's grief,
Till we do gain that Proserpine may grant
Revenge on them that murdered my son.   120
Then will I rent and tear them, thus and thus,
Shivering their limbs in pieces with my teeth.
                           Tears the papers.
1 Cit. O sir, my declaration!
             Exit Hieronimo, and they after.
2 Cit.   Save my bond!

        Enter HIERONIMO.

2 Cit. Save my bond!
3 Cit. Alas, my lease! it cost me ten pound,
And you, my lord, have torn the same.   126
Hier. That cannot be, I gave it never a
   wound.
Show me one drop of blood fall from the same!
How is it possible I should slay it then?
Tush, no; run after, catch me if you can.   130
        Exeunt all but the Old Man. BA-
        ZULTO *remains till* HIERONIMO
        *enters again, who, staring him in
        the face, speaks.*
Hier. And art thou come, Horatio, from the
   depth,
To ask for justice in this upper earth,
To tell thy father thou art unreveng'd,
To wring more tears from Isabella's eyes,
Whose lights are dimm'd with over-long la-
   ments?   135
Go back, my son, complain to Aeacus,
For here's no justice; gentle boy, begone,
For justice is exiled from the earth:
Hieronimo will bear thee company.
Thy mother cries on righteous Rhadamanth   140
For just revenge against the murderers.

[1] Qq. *strives.*
[2] So Kittredge in Manly. Qq. *when as.*
[3] So Hawkins. Early Qq. *ore turnest.* Later Qq. *ore-
turned.*
[4] Hast skill in.

Senex. Alas, my lord, whence springs this
   troubled speech?
Hier. But let me look on my Horatio.
Sweet boy, how art thou chang'd in death's
   black shade!
Had Proserpine no pity on thy youth,   145
But suffered thy fair crimson-colour'd spring
With withered winter to be blasted thus?
Horatio, thou art older than thy father.
Ah, ruthless fate,[5] that favour thus transforms!
Baz. Ah, my good lord, I am not your young
   son.   150
Hier. What, not my son? Thou then a Fury
   art,
Sent from the empty kingdom of black night
To summon me to make appearance
Before grim Minos and just Rhadamanth,
To plague Hieronimo that is remiss,   155
And seeks not vengeance for Horatio's death.
Baz. I am a grieved man, and not a ghost,
That came for justice for my murdered son.
Hier. Ay, now I know thee, now thou nam'st
   thy son.
Thou art the lively image of my grief;   160
Within thy face my sorrows I may see.
Thy eyes are gumm'd with tears, thy cheeks
   are wan,
Thy forehead troubled, and thy mutt'ring lips
Murmur sad words abruptly broken off
By force of windy sighs thy spirit breathes;   165
And all this sorrow riseth for thy son:
And selfsame sorrow feel I for my son.
Come in, old man, thou shalt to Isabel.
Lean on my arm: I thee, thou me, shalt stay,
And thou, and I, and she will sing a song,   170
Three parts in one, but all of discords fram'd—:
Talk not of chords, but let us now be gone,
For with a cord Horatio was slain.   *Exeunt.*

        [SCENE XIV.][6]

Enter KING OF SPAIN, *the* DUKE, VICEROY, *and*
   LORENZO, BALTHAZAR, DON PEDRO, *and*
   BEL-IMPERIA.

King. Go, brother, it is the Duke of Castile's
   cause;
Salute the Viceroy in our name.
Cast.   I go.
Vic. Go forth, Don Pedro, for thy nephew's
   sake,
And greet the Duke of Castile.
Ped.   It shall be so.
King. And now to meet these Portuguese: 5
For as we now are, so sometimes were these,
Kings and commanders of the western Indies.
Welcome, brave Viceroy, to the court of Spain,
And welcome all his honourable train!
'T is not unknown to us for why you come,   10
Or have so kingly cross'd the seas:
Sufficeth it, in this we note the troth
And more than common love you lend to us.
So is it that mine honourable niece
(For it beseems us now that it be known)   15
Already is betroth'd to Balthazar:

[5] So Dodsley. Qq. *Father.*
[6] The Court of Spain.

And by appointment and our condescent [1]
To-morrow are they to be married.
To this intent we entertain thyself,
Thy followers, their pleasure, and our peace. 20
Speak, men of Portingal, shall it be so?
If ay, say so; if not, say flatly no.
  Vic. Renowmed King, I come not, as thou
      think'st,
With doubtful followers, unresolved men,
But such as have upon thine articles   25
Confirm'd thy motion, and contented me.
Know, sovereign, I come to solemnize
The marriage of thy beloved niece,
Fair Bel-imperia, with my Balthazar, —
With thee, my son; whom sith I live to see, 30
Here take my crown, I give it her and thee;
And let me live a solitary life,
In ceaseless prayers,
To think how strangely heaven hath thee pre-
      serv'd.
  King. See, brother, see, how nature strives
      in him!   35
Come, worthy Viceroy, and accompany
Thy friend with thine extremities; [2]
A place more private fits this princely mood.
  Vic. Or here, or where your highness thinks
      it good.
            Exeunt all but CASTILE *and* LORENZO.
  Cast. Nay, stay, Lorenzo, let me talk with
      you.   40
See'st thou this entertainment of these kings?
  Lor. I do, my lord, and joy to see the same.
  Cast. And know'st thou why this meeting is?
  Lor. For her, my lord, whom Balthazar doth
      love,
And to confirm their promised marriage.   45
  Cast. She is thy sister?
  Lor.   Who, Bel-imperia? Ay,
My gracious lord, and this is the day,
That I have long'd so happily to see.
  Cast. Thou wouldst be loth that any fault of
      thine
Should intercept her in her happiness?   50
  Lor. Heavens will not let Lorenzo err so
      much.
  Cast. Why then, Lorenzo, listen to my words:
It is suspected, and reported too,
That thou, Lorenzo, wrong'st Hieronimo,
And in his suits towards his majesty   55
Still keep'st him back, and seek'st to cross his
      suit.
  Lor. That I, my lord ——?
  Cast. I tell thee, son, myself have heard it
      said,
When (to my sorrow) I have been ashamed
To answer for thee, though thou art my son. 60
Lorenzo, know'st thou not the common love
And kindness that Hieronimo hath won
By his deserts within the court of Spain?
Or see'st thou not the king my brother's care
In his behalf, and to procure his health?   65
Lorenzo, shouldst thou thwart his passions,
And he exclaim against thee to the king,
What honour were 't in this assembly,
Or what a scandal were 't among the kings

To hear Hieronimo exclaim on thee?   70
Tell me — and look thou tell me truly too —
Whence grows the ground of this report in
      court?
  Lor. My lord, it lies not in Lorenzo's power
To stop the vulgar, liberal of their tongues.
A small advantage makes a water-breach,   75
And no man lives that long contenteth all.
  Cast. Myself have seen thee busy to keep
      back
Him and his supplications from the king.
  Lor. Yourself, my lord, hath seen his passions,
That ill beseem'd the presence of a king: 80
And, for I pitied him in his distress,
I held him thence with kind and courteous
      words
As free from malice to Hieronimo
As to my soul, my lord.
  Cast. Hieronimo, my son, mistakes thee then.
  Lor. My gracious father, believe me, so he
      doth.   85
But what's a silly man, distract in mind
To think upon the murder of his son?
Alas! how easy is it for him to err!
But for his satisfaction and the world's,   90
'T were good, my lord, that Hieronimo and I
Were reconcil'd, if he misconster me.
  Cast. Lorenzo, thou hast said; it shall be so.
Go one of you, and call Hieronimo.

        Enter BALTHAZAR *and* BEL-IMPERIA.

  Bal. Come, Bel-imperia, Balthazar's content,
My sorrow's ease and sovereign of my bliss, 95
Sith heaven hath ordain'd thee to be mine:
Disperse those clouds and melancholy looks,
And clear them up with those thy sun-bright
      eyes,
Wherein my hope and heaven's fair beauty lies.
  Bel. My looks, my lord, are fitting for my
      love,   101
Which, new-begun, can show no brighter yet.
  Bal. New-kindled flames should burn as
      morning sun.
  Bel. But not too fast, lest heat and all be
      done.
I see my lord my father.
  Bal.   Truce, my love;   105
I will go salute him.
  Cast.   Welcome, Balthazar,
Welcome, brave prince, the pledge of Castile's
      peace!
And welcome, Bel-imperia! — How now, girl?
Why com'st thou sadly to salute us thus?
Content thyself, for I am satisfied: 110
It is not now as when Andrea liv'd;
We have forgotten and forgiven that,
And thou art graced with a happier love. —
But, Balthazar, here comes Hieronimo;
I 'll have a word with him.   115

        Enter HIERONIMO *and a* Servant.

  Hier. And where's the duke?
  Serv.   Yonder.
  Hier.   Even so. —
What new device have they devised, trow? [3]

---

[1] Consent.   [2] Extreme show of feeling.

[3] Think you.

Pocas palabras ! [1] mild as the lamb !
Is 't I will be reveng'd ? No, I am not the man.
Cast. Welcome, Hieronimo. 120
Lor. Welcome, Hieronimo.
Bal. Welcome, Hieronimo.
Hier. My lords, I thank you for Horatio.
Cast. Hieronimo, the reason that I sent
To speak with you, is this.
Hier.   What, so short ? 125
Then I 'll be gone, I thank you for 't.
Cast. Nay, stay, Hieronimo ! — go call him,
son.
Lor. Hieronimo, my father craves a word
with you.
Hier. With me, sir ? Why, my lord, I thought
you had done.
Lor. No ; [*Aside*] would he had !
Cast.   Hieronimo, I hear
You find yourself aggrieved at my son, 131
Because you have not access unto the king ;
And say 't is he that intercepts your suits.
Hier. Why, is not this a miserable thing, my
lord ?
Cast. Hieronimo, I hope you have no cause,
And would be loth that one of your deserts 136
Should once have reason to suspect my son,
Considering how J think of you myself.
Hier. Your son Lorenzo ! Whom, my noble
lord ?
The hope of Spain, mine honourable friend ? 140
Grant me the combat of them, if they dare :
    Draws out his sword.
I 'll meet him face to face, to tell me so !
These be the scandalous reports of such
As love not me, and hate my lord too much.
Should I suspect Lorenzo would prevent 145
Or cross my suit, that lov'd my son so well ?
My lord, I am asham'd it should be said.
Lor. Hieronimo, I never gave you cause.
Hier. My good lord, I know you did not.
Cast.   There then pause ;
And for the satisfaction of the world, 150
Hieronimo, frequent my homely house,
The Duke of Castile, Cyprian's ancient seat ;
And when thou wilt, use me, my son, and it :
But here, before Prince Balthazar and me,
Embrace each other, and be perfect friends. 155
Hier. Ay, marry, my lord, and shall.
Friends, quoth he ? See, I 'll be friends with
you all :
Especially with you, my lovely lord ;
For divers causes it is fit for us
That we be friends : the world 's suspicious, 160
And men may think what we imagine not.
Bal. Why, this is friendly done, Hieronimo.
Lor. And that I hope old grudges are for-
got.
Hier. What else ? It were a shame it should
not be so.
Cast. Come on, Hieronimo, at my request ; 165
Let us entreat your company to-day. *Exeunt.*
Hier. Your lordship's to command. — Pah !
keep your way :
Chi mi fa più carezze che non suole,
Tradito mi ha, o tradir mi vuole.   [*Exit.*

1 Span. " few words."

[CHORUS.]

Enter GHOST *and* REVENGE.

Ghost. Awake, Erichtho ! Cerberus, awake !
Solicit Pluto, gentle Proserpine ! 171
To combat, Acheron and Erebus !
For ne'er, by Styx and Phlegethon in hell,[2]
Nor ferried Charon to the fiery lakes
Such fearful sights, as poor Andrea sees.[3] 175
Revenge, awake !
Revenge.   Awake ? For why ?
Ghost. Awake, Revenge ; for thou art ill-ad-
vis'd
To sleep away what thou art warn'd to watch !
Revenge. Content thyself, and do not trouble
me.
Ghost. Awake, Revenge, if love — as love
hath had — 180
Have yet the power or prevalence in hell !
Hieronimo with Lorenzo is join'd in league,
And intercepts our passage to revenge.
Awake, Revenge, or we are woe-begone !
Revenge. Thus worldlings ground what they
have dream'd upon.[4] 185
Content thyself, Andrea : though I sleep,
Yet is my mood soliciting their souls.
Sufficeth thee that poor Hieronimo
Cannot forget his son Horatio.
Nor dies Revenge, although he sleep awhile ;
For in unquiet, quietness is feign'd, 191
And slumb'ring is a common worldly wile.
Behold, Andrea, for an instance, how
Revenge hath slept, and then imagine thou,
What 't is to be subject to destiny. 195

Enter a Dumb-Show.

Ghost. Awake, Revenge ; reveal this mystery.
Revenge. Lo ! the two first the nuptial torches
bore
As brightly burning as the mid-day's sun ;
But after them doth Hymen hie as fast,
Clothed in sable and a saffron robe, 200
And blows them out, and quencheth them with
blood,
As discontent that things continue so.
Ghost. Sufficeth me ; thy meaning 's under-
stood,
And thanks to thee and those infernal powers
That will not tolerate a lover's woe. 205
Rest thee, for I will sit to see the rest.
Revenge. Then argue not, for thou hast thy
request.   *Exeunt.*

ACT IV

[SCENE I.] [5]

Enter BEL-IMPERIA *and* HIERONIMO.

Bel. Is this the love thou bear'st Horatio ?
Is this the kindness that thou counterfeits ?
Are these the fruits of thine incessant tears ?

2 Qq. read *in hell* at end of l. 3. The passage is clearly
corrupt.
3 Early Qq. read *see.*
4 Rely upon what they have dreamed.
5 Palace of Don Cyprian.

Hieronimo, are these thy passions,
Thy protestations and thy deep laments,   5
That thou wert wont to weary men withal?
O unkind father! O deceitful world!
With what excuses canst thou show thyself [1]
From this dishonour and the hate of men,
Thus to neglect the loss and life of him   10
Whom both my letters and thine own belief
Assures thee to be causeless slaughtered?
Hieronimo, for shame, Hieronimo,
Be not a history to after-times
Of such ingratitude unto thy son.   15
Unhappy mothers of such children then!
But monstrous fathers to forget so soon
The death of those whom they with care and
    cost
Have tend'red so, thus careless should be lost.
Myself, a stranger in respect of thee,   20
So lov'd his life, as still I wish their deaths.
Nor shall his death be unreveng'd by me,
Although I bear it out for fashion's sake;
For here I swear, in sight of heaven and earth,
Shouldst thou neglect the love thou shouldst
    retain,   25
And give it over and devise no more,
Myself should send their hateful souls to hell
That wrought his downfall with extremest
    death.
    Hier. But may it be that Bel-imperia
Vows such revenge as she hath deign'd to say?   30
Why, then I see that heaven applies our drift,[2]
And all the saints do sit soliciting
For vengeance on those cursed murderers.
Madam, 't is true, and now I find it so,
I found a letter, written in your name,   35
And in that letter, how Horatio died.
Pardon, O pardon, Bel-imperia,
My fear and care in not believing it;
Nor think I thoughtless think upon a mean
To let his death be unreveng'd at full.   40
And here I vow — so you but give consent,
And will conceal my resolution —
I will ere long determine of their deaths
That causeless thus have murdered my son.
    Bel. Hieronimo, I will consent, conceal,   45
And ought that may effect for thine avail,
Join with thee to revenge Horatio's death.
    Hier. On, then; [and] whatsoever I devise,
Let me entreat you, grace my practices,
For-why[3] the plot 's already in mine head.   50
Here they are.

    Enter BALTHAZAR *and* LORENZO.

    Bal.   How now, Hieronimo?
What, courting Bel-imperia?
    Hier.   Ay, my lord;
Such courting as, I promise you,
She hath my heart, but you, my lord, have hers.
    Lor. But now, Hieronimo, or never,   55
We are to entreat your help.
    Hier.   My help?
Why, my good lords, assure yourselves of me;
For you have giv'n me cause, — ay, by my faith
    have you!

[1] Qq. insert after l. 8, *With what dishonour and the
hate of men.*
[2] Supports our intention.   [3] Because.

    Bal. It pleas'd you, at the entertainment of
    the ambassador,
To grace the king so much as with a show.   60
Now, were your study so well furnished,
As, for the passing of the first night's sport,
To entertain my father with the like,
Or any such-like pleasing motion,
Assure yourself, it would content them well.   65
    Hier. Is this all?
    Bal.   Ay, this is all.
    Hier. Why then, I 'll fit you; say no more.
When I was young, I gave my mind
And plied myself to fruitless poetry;
Which though it profit the professor naught,   70
Yet is it passing pleasing to the world.
    Lor. And how for that?
    Hier.   Marry, my good lord, thus: —
And yet methinks, you are too quick with us —
When in Toledo there I studied,
It was my chance to write a tragedy,   75
See here, my lords —   *He shows them a book.*
Which, long forgot, I found this other day.
Now would your lordships favour me so much
As but to grace me with your acting it —
I mean each one of you to play a part —   80
Assure you it will prove most passing strange,
And wondrous plausible[4] to that assembly.
    Bal. What, would you have us play a trag-
    edy?
    Hier. Why, Nero thought it no disparage-
    ment,
And kings and emperors have ta'en delight   85
To make experience of their wits in plays.
    Lor. Nay, be not angry, good Hieronimo;
The prince but ask'd a question.
    Bal. In faith, Hieronimo, an you be in earnest,
I 'll make one.
    Lor.   And I another.   90
    Hier. Now, my good lord, could you entreat
Your sister Bel-imperia to make one?
For what 's a play without a woman in it?
    Bel. Little entreaty shall serve me, Hieron-
    imo;
For I must needs be employed in your play.   95
    Hier. Why, this is well. I tell you, lordings,
It was determined to have been acted
By gentlemen and scholars too,
Such as could tell what to speak.
    Bal.   And now
It shall be play'd by princes and courtiers,   100
Such as can tell how to speak:
If, as it is our country manner,
You will but let us know the argument.
    Hier. That shall I roundly. The chronicles
    of Spain
Record this written of a knight of Rhodes: 105
He was betroth'd, and wedded at the length,
To one Perseda, an Italian dame,
Whose beauty ravish'd all that her beheld,
Especially the soul of Soliman,
Who at the marriage was the chiefest guest.   110
By sundry means sought Soliman to win
Perseda's love, and could not gain the same.
Then 'gan he break his passions to a friend,
One of his bashaws,[5] whom he held full dear.

[4] Pleasing.   [5] Usual Elizabethan form of *pacha.*

Her had this bashaw long solicited,   115
And saw she was not otherwise to be won,
But by her husband's death, this knight of
    Rhodes,
Whom presently by treachery he slew.
She, stirr'd with an exceeding hate therefore,
As cause of this slew Soliman,   120
And, to escape the bashaw's tyranny,
Did stab herself: and this the tragedy.
    Lor. O excellent!
    Bel.   But say, Hieronimo,
What then became of him that was the bashaw?
    Hier. Marry, thus: mov'd with remorse of
        his misdeeds,   125
Ran to a mountain-top, and hung himself.
    Bal. But which of us is to perform that part?
    Hier. O, that will I, my lords; make no doubt
        of it.
I 'll play the murderer, I warrant you;
For I already have conceited that.   130
    Bal. And what shall I?
    Hier. Great Soliman, the Turkish emperor.
    Lor. And I?
    Hier.   Erastus, the knight of Rhodes.
    Bel. And I?
    Hier.   Perseda, chaste and resolute.
And here, my lords, are several abstracts
    drawn,   135
For each of you to note your parts,
And act it, as occasion 's off'red you.
You must provide a Turkish cap,
A black mustachio and a falchion;
            Gives a paper to BALTHAZAR.
You with a cross, like to a knight of Rhodes; 140
            Gives another to LORENZO.
And, madam, you must attire yourself
            He giveth BEL-IMPERIA *another.*
Like Phoebe, Flora, or the huntress [Dian],[1]
Which to your discretion shall seem best.
And as for me, my lords, I 'll look to one,
And, with the ransom that the viceroy sent, 145
So furnish and perform this tragedy,
As all the world shall say, Hieronimo
Was liberal in gracing of it so.
    Bal. Hieronimo, methinks a comedy were
        better.
    Hier. A comedy?   150
Fie! comedies are fit for common wits;
But to present a kingly troop withal,
Give me a stately-written tragedy;
Tragoedia cothurnata, fitting kings,
Containing matter, and not common things. 155
My lords, all this must be performed,
As fitting for the first night's revelling.
The Italian tragedians were so sharp of wit,
That in one hour's meditation
They would perform anything in action.   160
    Lor. And well it may; for I have seen the
        like
In Paris 'mongst the French tragedians.
    Hier. In Paris? mass! and well remembered!
There 's one thing more that rests for us to do.
    Bal. What is that, Hieronimo? Forget not
        anything.   165
    Hier. Each one of us

[1] Supplied by Kittredge (Manly).

Must act his part in unknown languages,
That it may breed the more variety:
As you, my lord, in Latin, I in Greek,
You in Italian; and for because I know   170
That Bel-imperia hath practised the French,
In courtly French shall all her phrases be.
    Bel. You mean to try my cunning then, Hier-
        onimo?
    Bal. But this will be a mere confusion
And hardly shall we all be understood.   175
    Hier. It must be so; for the conclusion
Shall prove the invention[2] and all was good:
And I myself in an oration,
And with a strange and wondrous show besides,
That I will have there behind a curtain,   180
Assure yourself, shall make the matter known;
And all shall be concluded in one scene,
For there 's no pleasure ta'en in tediousness.
    Bal. How like you this?
    Lor.   Why, thus my lord:
We must resolve to soothe his humours up. 185
    Bal. On then, Hieronimo; farewell till soon.
    Hier. You 'll ply this gear?
    Lor.   I warrant you.
            Exeunt all but HIERONIMO.
    Hier.   Why so:
Now shall I see the fall of Babylon.
Wrought by the heavens in this confusion.
And if the world like not this tragedy,   190
Hard is the hap of old Hieronimo.   *Exit.*

[SCENE II.][3]

Enter ISABELLA *with a weapon.*

    Isab. Tell me no more! — O monstrous homi-
        cides!
Since neither piety or pity moves
The king to justice or compassion,
I will revenge myself upon this place,
Where thus they murdered my beloved son.   5
            She cuts down the arbour.
Down with these branches and these loathsome
    boughs
Of this unfortunate and fatal pine!
Down with them, Isabella; rent them up,
And burn the roots from whence the rest is
    sprung!
I will not leave a root, a stalk, a tree,   10
A bough, a branch, a blossom, nor a leaf,
No, not an herb within this garden-plot, —
Accursed complot[4] of my misery!
Fruitless for ever may this garden be,
Barren the earth, and blissless whosoever 15
Imagines not to keep it unmanur'd![5]
An eastern wind, commix'd with noisome airs,
Shall blast the plants and the young saplings;
The earth with serpents shall be pestered,
And passengers, for fear to be infect,   20
Shall stand aloof, and, looking at it, tell:
"There, murd'red, died the son of Isabel."
Ay, here he died, and here I him embrace:

[2] Boas gives *intention* as Qq. reading.
[3] Hieronimo's garden.
[4] Usually conspiracy; here, accomplice (to accommo-
    date the pun).
[5] Untilled.

See, where his ghost solicits with his wounds
Revenge on her that should revenge his death. 25
Hieronimo, make haste to see thy son ;
For sorrow and despair hath cited me
To hear Horatio plead with Rhadamanth.
Make haste, Hieronimo, to hold excus'd [1]
Thy negligence in pursuit of their deaths   30
Whose hateful wrath bereav'd him of his breath.
Ah, nay, thou dost delay their deaths,
Forgives the murderers of thy noble son,
And none but I bestir me — to no end !
And as I curse this tree from further fruit,   35
So shall my womb be cursed for his sake ;
And with this weapon will I wound the breast,
The hapless breast, that gave Horatio suck.
                              She stabs herself.

[SCENE III.] [2]

Enter HIERONIMO ; he knocks up the curtain.
Enter the DUKE of CASTILE.

Cast. How now, Hieronimo, where 's your
         fellows,
That you take all this pain ?
Hier. O sir, it is for the author's credit,
To look that all things may go well.
But, good my lord, let me entreat your grace, 5
To give the king the copy of the play :
This is the argument of what we show.
Cast. I will, Hieronimo.
Hier. One thing more, my good lord.
Cast. What 's that ?
Hier.   Let me entreat your grace 10
That, when the train are pass'd into the gallery,
You would vouchsafe to throw me down the
         key.
Cast. I will, Hieronimo.   *Exit* CASTILE.
Hier. What, are you ready, Balthazar ?
Bring a chair and a cushion for the king.   15

Enter BALTHAZAR, *with a chair.*

Well done, Balthazar ! hang up the title :
Our scene is Rhodes. What, is your beard on ?
Bal. Half on ; the other is in my hand.
Hier. Despatch for shame ; are you so long ?
                              Exit BALTHAZAR.
Bethink thyself, Hieronimo,   20
Recall thy wits, recount thy former wrongs
Thou hast receiv'd by murder of thy son,
And lastly, not least ! how Isabel,
Once his mother and thy dearest wife,
All woe-begone for him, hath slain herself.   25
Behoves thee then, Hieronimo, to be reveng'd !
The plot is laid of dire revenge :
On, then, Hieronimo, pursue revenge ;
For nothing wants but acting of revenge !
                              Exit Hieronimo.

[SCENE IV.] [3]

Enter Spanish KING, VICEROY, *the* DUKE OF
CASTILE, *and their train [to the gallery].* [4]

King. Now, Viceroy, shall we see the tragedy
Of Soliman, the Turkish emperor,

Perform'd of pleasure by your son the prince,
My nephew Don Lorenzo, and my niece.   4
Vic. Who ? Bel-imperia ?
King.   Ay, and Hieronimo, our marshal,
At whose request they deign to do 't themselves.
These be our pastimes in the court of Spain.
Here, brother, you shall be the bookkeeper :
This is the argument of that they show.
                      He giveth him a book.
Gentlemen, this play of Hieronimo, in sundry [10
languages, was thought good to be set down in Eng-
lish, more largely, for the easier understanding to
every public reader.

Enter BALTHAZAR, BEL-IMPERIA, *and* HIERO-
NIMO.

Bal. Bashaw, that Rhodes is ours, yield heavens
         the honour,
And holy Mahomet, our sacred prophet !   15
And be thou grac'd with every excellence
That Soliman can give, or thou desire.
But thy desert in conquering Rhodes is less
Than in reserving this fair Christian nymph,
Perseda, blissful lamp of excellence,   20
Whose eyes compel, like powerful adamant,
The warlike heart of Soliman to wait.
King. See, Viceroy, that is Balthazar, your
         son,
That represents the emperor Soliman :
How well he acts his amorous passion !   25
Vic. Ay, Bel-imperia hath taught him that.
Cast. That 's because his mind runs all on
         Bel-imperia.
Hier. Whatever joy earth yields, betide your
         majesty.
Bal. Earth yields no joy without Perseda's love.
Hier. Let then Perseda on your grace attend. 30
Bal. She shall not wait on me, but I on her :
Drawn by the influence of her lights, I yield.
But let my friend, the Rhodian knight, come forth,
Erasto, dearer than my life to me,
That he may see Perseda, my belov'd.   35

Enter ERASTO.

King. Here comes Lorenzo : look upon the
         plot,
And tell me, brother, what part plays he ?
Bel. Ah, my Erasto, welcome to Perseda.
Lor. Thrice happy is Erasto that thou liv'st ;
Rhodes' loss is nothing to Erasto's joy ;   60
Sith his Perseda lives, his life survives.
Bal. Ah, bashaw, here is love between Erasto
And fair Perseda, sovereign of my soul.
Hier. Remove Erasto, mighty Soliman,
And then Perseda will be quickly won.   45
Bal. Erasto is my friend ; and while he lives,
Perseda never will remove her love.
Hier. Let not Erasto live to grieve great Soliman.
Bal. Dear is Erasto in our princely eye.
Hier. But if he be your rival, let him die.   50
Bal. Why, let him die ! — so love commandeth me.
Yet grieve I that Erasto should so die.
Hier. Erasto, Soliman saluteth thee,
And lets thee wit by me his highness' will,
Which is, thou shouldst be thus employ'd.
                              Stabs him.

---

[1] Make excuses for.   [3] The same.
[2] Palace of Don Cyprian.   [4] Added by Manly.

Bel.   *Ay me !*
Erasto ! See, Soliman, Erasto 's slain !   56
     Bal. Yet liveth Soliman to comfort thee.
Fair queen of beauty, let not favour die,
But with a gracious eye behold his grief
That with Perseda's beauty is increas'd,   60
If by Perseda his grief be not releas'd.
     Bel. Tyrant, desist soliciting vain suits ;
Relentless are mine ears to thy laments,
As thy butcher is pitiless and base,
Which seiz'd on my Erasto, harmless knight.   65
Yet by thy power thou thinkest to command,
And to thy power Perseda doth obey ;
But, were she able, thus she would revenge
Thy treacheries on thee, ignoble prince :
                                        Stabs him.
And on herself she would be thus reveng'd.   70
                                        Stabs herself.
King. Well said ! — Old marshal, this was
     bravely done !
Hier. But Bel-imperia plays Perseda well !
Vic. Were this in earnest, Bel-imperia,
You would be better to my son than so.   74
King. But now what follows for Hieronimo ?
Hier. Marry, this follows for Hieronimo :
Here break we off our sundry languages,
And thus conclude I in our vulgar tongue.
Haply you think — but bootless are your
     thoughts —
That this is fabulously counterfeit,   80
And that we do as all tragedians do, —
To die to-day, for fashioning our scene,
The death of Ajax or some Roman peer,
And in a minute starting up again,
Revive to please to-morrow's audience.   85
No, princes ; know I am Hieronimo,
The hopeless father of a hapless son,
Whose tongue is tun'd to tell his latest tale,
Not to excuse gross errors in the play.   89
I see, your looks urge instance of these words ;
Behold the reason urging me to this !
                                    Shows his dead son.
See here my show, look on this spectacle !
Here lay my hope, and here my hope hath end ;
Here lay my heart, and here my heart was slain ;
Here lay my treasure, here my treasure lost ; 95
Here lay my bliss, and here my bliss bereft :
But hope, heart, treasure, joy, and bliss,
All fled, fail'd, died, yea, all decay'd with this.
From forth these wounds came breath that gave
     me life ;
They murd'red me that made these fatal
     marks.   100
The cause was love, whence grew this mortal
     hate ;
The hate, Lorenzo and young Balthazar ;
The love, my son to Bel-imperia.
But night, the coverer of accursed crimes,
With pitchy silence hush'd these traitors'
     harms,   105
And lent them leave, for they had sorted [1] lei-
     sure
To take advantage in my garden-plot
Upon my son, my dear Horatio.
There merciless they butcher'd up my boy,   109

In black, dark night, to pale, dim, cruel death,
He shrieks : I heard — and yet, methinks, I
     hear —
His dismal outcry echo in the air.
With soonest speed I hasted to the noise,
Where hanging on a tree I found my son,
Through-girt [2] with wounds, and slaught'red as
     you see.   115
And griev'd I, think you, at this spectacle ?
Speak, Portuguese, whose loss resembles mine :
If thou canst weep upon thy Balthazar,
'T is like I wail'd for my Horatio.
And you, my lord, whose reconciled son   120
March'd in a net, and thought himself unseen,
And rated me for brainsick lunacy,
With "God amend that mad Hieronimo !" —
How can you brook our play's catastrophe ?
And here behold this bloody handkercher,   125
Which at Horatio's death I weeping dipp'd
Within the river of his bleeding wounds :
It as propitious, see, I have reserved,
And never hath it left my bloody heart,
Soliciting remembrance of my vow   130
With these, O, these accursed murderers :
Which now perform'd, my heart is satisfied.
And to this end the bashaw I became
That might revenge me on Lorenzo's life,
Who therefore was appointed to the part,   135
And was to represent the knight of Rhodes,
That I might kill him more conveniently.
So, Viceroy, was this Balthazar, thy son,
That Soliman which Bel-imperia,
In person of Perseda, murdered ;   140
Solely appointed to that tragic part
That she might slay him that offended her.
Poor Bel-imperia miss'd her part in this :
For though the story saith she should have
     died,
Yet I of kindness, and of care to her,   145
Did otherwise determine of her end ;
But love of him whom they did hate too much
Did urge her resolution to be such.
And, princes, now behold Hieronimo,
Author and actor in this tragedy,   150
Bearing his latest fortune in his fist ;
And will as resolute conclude his part,
As any of the actors gone before.
And, gentles, thus I end my play ;
Urge no more words : I have no more to say.   155
                        He runs to hang himself.
     King. O hearken, Viceroy ! Hold, Hiero-
     nimo !
Brother, my nephew and thy son are slain !
     Vic. We are betray'd ; my Balthazar is
     slain !
Break ope the doors ; run, save Hieronimo.
                        They break in and hold Hieronimo.
Hieronimo, do but inform the king of these
     events :   160
Upon mine honour, thou shalt have no harm.
     Hier. Viceroy, I will not trust thee with my
     life,
Which I this day have offered to my son.
Accursed wretch !   164
Why stay'st thou him that was resolv'd to die ?

---

[1] Chosen.

[2] Pierced, from *gird*, to smite.

King. Speak, traitor! damned, bloody mur-
    derer, speak!
For now I have thee, I will make thee speak.
Why hast thou done this undeserving deed?
    Vic. Why hast thou murdered my Baltha-
    zar?
    Cast. Why hast thou butchered both my
    children thus?   170
    Hier. O, good words!
As dear to me was my Horatio
As yours, or yours, or yours, my lord, to you.
My guiltless son was by Lorenzo slain,
And by Lorenzo and that Balthazar   175
Am I at last revenged thoroughly,
Upon whose souls may heavens be yet aveng'd
With greater far than these afflictions.
    Cast. But who were thy confederates in this?
    Vic. That was thy daughter Bel-imperia; 180
For by her hand my Balthazar was slain:
I saw her stab him.
    King.   Why speak'st thou not?
    Hier. What lesser liberty can kings afford
Than harmless silence?   Then afford it me.
Sufficeth, I may not, nor I will not tell thee. 185
    King. Fetch forth the tortures: traitor as
    thou art,
I 'll make thee tell.
    Hier.   Indeed,
Thou may'st torment me as his wretched son
Hath done in murd'ring my Horatio;
But never shalt thou force me to reveal   190
The thing which I have vow'd inviolate.
And therefore, in despite of all thy threats,
Pleas'd with their deaths, and eas'd with their
    revenge,
First take my tongue, and afterwards my heart.
                He bites out his tongue.
[1 *Hier. But are you sure they are dead?*
  Cast.   *Ay, slave,*[2] *too sure.*
  Hier. What, and yours too?   196
  Vic. Ay, all are dead; not one of them survive.
  Hier. Nay, then I care not; come, and we shall
    be friends;
Let us lay our heads together:
See, here's a goodly noose will hold them all. 200
  Vic. O damned devil, how secure[3] *he is!*
  Hier. Secure? Why, dost thou wonder at it?
I tell thee, Viceroy, this day I have seen revenge,
And in that sight am grown a prouder monarch,
Than ever sat under the crown of Spain. 205
Had I as many lives as there be stars,
As many heavens to go to, as those lives,
I'd give them all, ay, and my soul to boot,
But I would see thee ride in this red pool.
  Cast. But who were thy confederates in this? 210
  Vic. That was thy daughter Bel-imperia;
For by her hand my Balthazar was slain:
I saw her stab him.
  Hier. O, good words!
As dear to me was my Horatio, 215
As yours, or yours, or yours, my lord, to you.
My guiltless son was by Lorenzo slain,
And by Lorenzo and that Balthazar
Am I at last revenged thoroughly,

Upon whose souls may heavens be yet avenged 220
With greater far than these afflictions.
Methinks, since I grew inward with revenge,
I cannot look with scorn enough on death.
  King. What, dost thou mock us, slave? — Bring
  tortures forth. 224
  Hier. Do, do, do: and meantime I'll torture you.
You had a son, as I take it; and your son
Should ha' been married to your daughter:
Ha, was it not so? — You had a son too,
He was my liege's nephew; he was proud
And politic; had he liv'd, he might ha' come 230
To wear the crown of Spain, I think 't was so: —
'T was I that kill'd him; look you, this same hand,
'T was it that stabb'd his heart — do ye see? this
  hand —
For one Horatio, if you ever knew him: a youth,
One that they hang'd up in his father's garden; 235
One that did force your valiant son to yield,
While your more valiant son did take him prisoner.
  Vic. *Be deaf, my senses; I can hear no more.*
  King. *Fall, heaven, and cover us with thy sad*
  ruins. 239
  Cast. *Roll all the world within thy pitchy cloud.*
  Hier. *Now do I applaud what I have acted.*
Nunc iners cadat [4] manus!
Now to express the rupture of my part, —
First take my tongue, ana afterward my heart.]
    King. O monstrous resolution of a wretch! 245
See, Viceroy, he hath bitten forth his tongue,
Rather than to reveal what we requir'd.
    Cast. Yet can he write.
    King. And if in this he satisfy us not,
We will devise th' extremest kind of death 250
That ever was invented for a wretch.
          Then he makes signs for a knife to
          mend his pen.
    Cast. O, he would have a knife to mend his
    pen.
    Vic. Here, and advise thee that thou write
    the troth. —
Look to my brother! save Hieronimo!
          He with a knife stabs the DUKE *and*
          himself.
    King. What age hath ever heard such mon-
    strous deeds? 255
My brother, and the whole succeeding hope
That Spain expected after my decease!
Go, bear his body hence, that we may mourn
The loss of our beloved brother's death,
That he may be entomb'd whate'er befall. 260
I am the next, the nearest, last of all.
    Vic. And thou, Don Pedro, do the like for us:
Take up our hapless son, untimely slain;
Set me with him, and he with woeful me,
Upon the main-mast of a ship unmann'd, 265
And let the wind and tide haul me along
To Scylla's barking and untamed gulf,
Or to the loathsome pool of Acheron,
To weep our want for my sweet Balthazar:
Spain hath no refuge for a Portingale. 270
      The trumpets sound a dead march; the
      KING OF SPAIN *mourning after his*
      brother's body, and the KING OF POR-
      TINGAL *bearing the body of his son.*

---

1 Fifth passage of additions, replacing ll. 171-194.
2 Some Qq. read *slaine*.   3 Assured.
4 Schick emend. Early Qq. *mors caede* or *mers cadae*.

[CHORUS.]

Enter GHOST *and* REVENGE.

Ghost. Ay, now my hopes have end in their
    effects,
When blood and sorrow finish my desires :
Horatio murdered in his father's bower ;
Vild Serberine by Pedringano slain ;
False Pedringano hang'd by quaint device ; 5
Fair Isabella by herself misdone ;
Prince Balthazar by Bel-imperia stabb'd ;
The Duke of Castile and his wicked son
Both done to death by old Hieronimo ;
My Bel-imperia fall'n as Dido fell, 10
And good Hieronimo slain by himself :
Ay, these were spectacles to please my soul !
Now will I beg at lovely Proserpine
That, by the virtue of her princely doom,
I may consort [1] my friends in pleasing sort, 15
And on my foes work just and sharp revenge.
I 'll lead my friend Horatio through those fields,
Where never-dying wars are still inur'd ; [2]
I 'll lead fair Isabella to that train,
Where pity weeps, but never feeleth pain ; 20
I 'll lead my Bel-imperia to those joys,
That vestal virgins and fair queens possess ;
I 'll lead Hieronimo where Orpheus plays,
Adding sweet pleasure to eternal days. 24

[1] Select, group.   [2] Carried on.

But say, Revenge, for thou must help, or none,
Against the rest how shall my hate be shown ?
  Rev. This hand shall hale them down to
    deepest hell,
Where none but Furies, bugs, [3] and tortures
    dwell.
  Ghost. Then, sweet Revenge, do this at my
    request :
Let me be judge, and doom them to unrest. 30
Let loose poor Tityus from the vulture's gripe,
And let Don Cyprian supply his room ;
Place Don Lorenzo on Ixion's wheel,
And let the lover's endless pains surcease 34
(Juno forgets old wrath, and grants him ease) :
Hang Balthazar about Chimaera's neck,
And let him there bewail his bloody love,
Repining at our joys that are above ;
Let Serberine go roll the fatal stone,
And take from Sisyphus his endless moan ; 40
False Pedringano, for his treachery,
Let him be dragg'd through boiling Acheron,
And there live, dying still in endless flames,
Blaspheming gods and all their holy names.
  Rev. Then haste we down to meet thy friends
    and foes : 45
To place thy friends in ease, the rest in woes ;
For here though death hath end their misery,
I 'll there begin their endless tragedy. *Exeunt.*

[3] Terrors, bugbears.

BUSSY D'AMBOIS

BY

GEORGE CHAPMAN

[DRAMATIS PERSONAE

HENRY III., King of France.
Monsieur, his brother.
THE DUKE OF GUISE.
MONTSURRY, a Count.
BUSSY D'AMBOIS.
BARRISOR, ⎫
L'ANOU, ⎬ Courtiers; enemies of D'Ambois.
PYRRHOT, ⎭
BRISAC, ⎫ Courtiers; friends of D'Ambois.
MELYNELL, ⎭
FRIAR COMOLET.
MAFFE, steward to Monsieur.
NUNTIUS.

Murderers.
BEHEMOTH, ⎫
CARTOPHYLAX, ⎬ Spirits.
UMBRA of FRIAR.

ELENOR, Duchess of Guise.
TAMYRA, Countess of Montsurry.
BEAUPRE, niece to Elenor.
PERO, maid to Tamyra.
CHARLOTTE, maid to Beaupre.
PYRA, a court lady.
ANNAPELLE, maid to Elenor.
Lords, Ladies, Pages, &c.

SCENE. — *Paris.*]

PROLOGUE

NOT out of confidence that none but we [1]
Are able to present this tragedy,
Not out of envy at the grace of late
It did receive, nor yet to derogate
From their deserts who [2] give out boldly that 5
They move with equal feet on the same flat;
Neither for all nor any of such ends
We offer it, gracious and noble friends,
To your review; we, far from emulation
And (charitably judge) from imitation, 10
With this work entertain you, a piece known
And still believ'd in Court to be our own.
To quit our claim, doubting our right or merit,
Would argue in us poverty of spirit
Which we must not subscribe to. Field [3] is
gone, 15
Whose action first did give it name, and one [4]
Who came the nearest to him, is denied
By his gray beard to show the height and
pride
Of D'Ambois' youth and bravery; yet to hold
Our title still a-foot, and not grow cold 20
By giving it o'er, a third man [5] with his best
Of care and pains defends our interest;
As Richard [6] he was lik'd, nor do we fear
In personating D'Ambois he'll appear
To faint, or go less, so [7] your free consent, 25
As heretofore, give him encouragement.

---

[1] The company of actors — the "King's men."
[2] A rival company which had given the play.
[3] Nathaniel Field, b. 1587; one of the "King's men."
[4] Not identified.
[5] Supposed to be Ilyard Swanston.
[6] Perhaps Ricardo, in Massinger's *Picture.* (Phelps).
[7] If.

ACT I

SCENE I. [8]

Enter BUSSY D'AMBOIS, *poor.*

Bu. Fortune, not Reason, rules the state of
things,
Reward goes backwards, Honour on his head;
Who is not poor, is monstrous; only need
Gives form and worth to every human seed.
As cedars beaten with continual storms, 5
So great men flourish; and do imitate
Unskilful statuaries, who suppose,
In forming a Colossus, if they make him
Straddle enough, strut, and look big, and gape,
Their work is goodly: so men merely great 10
In their affected gravity of voice,
Sourness of countenance, manners' cruelty,
Authority, wealth, and all the spawn of fortune,
Think they bear all the kingdom's worth before
them;
Yet differ not from those colossic statues, 15
Which, with heroic forms without o'erspread,
Within are nought but mortar, flint, and lead.
Man is a torch borne in the wind; a dream
But of a shadow, summ'd with all his substance;
And as great seamen, using all their wealth 20
And skills in Neptune's deep invisible paths,
In tall ships richly built and ribb'd with brass,
To put a girdle round about the world,
When they have done it (coming near their
haven)
Are glad to give a warning-piece, [9] and call 25
A poor, staid fisherman, that never past

---

[8] A glade, near the Court.
[9] Discharge a signal shot.

His country's sight, to waft and guide them in :
So when we wander furthest through the waves
Of glassy Glory, and the gulfs of State,   29
Topt with all titles, spreading all our reaches,
As if each private arm would sphere the earth,
We must to Virtue for her guide resort,
Or we shall shipwrack in our safest port.
                              Procumbit.

[*Enter*] Monsieur, *with two* Pages.

[*Mo.*] There is no second place in numerous
          state [1]
That holds more than a cipher ; in a king   35
All places are contain'd. His word and looks
Are like the flashes and the bolts of Jove ;
His deeds inimitable, like the sea   38
That shuts still as it opes, and leaves no tracts
Nor prints of precedent for mean men's facts : [2]
There 's but a thread betwixt me and a crown :
I would not wish it cut, unless by nature ;
Yet to prepare me for that possible fortune,
'T is good to get resolved spirits about me.
I follow'd D'Ambois to this green retreat ;   45
A man of spirit beyond the reach of fear,
Who (discontent with his neglected worth)
Neglects the light, and loves obscure abodes ;
But he is young and haughty, apt to take
Fire at advancement, to bear state and flour-
          ish ;   50
In his rise therefore shall my bounties shine.
None loathes the world so much, nor loves to
          scoff it,
But gold and grace will make him surfeit of it.
What, D'Ambois ?
     Bu.   He, sir.
     Mo.   Turn'd to earth, alive ?
Up, man ; the sun shines on thee.
     Bu.   Let it shine :
I am no mote to play in 't, as great men are.   55
     Mo. Call'st thou men great in state, motes
          in the sun ?
They say so that would have thee freeze in
          shades,
They (like the gross Sicilian gourmandist)
Empty their noses in the cates [3] they love,   60
That none may eat but they. Do thou but bring
Light to the banquet Fortune sets before thee,
And thou wilt loathe lean darkness like thy
          death.
Who would believe thy mettle could let sloth
Rust and consume it ? If Themistocles   65
Had liv'd obscur'd thus in th'Athenian State,
Xerxes had made both him and it his slaves.
If brave Camillus had lurkt so in Rome,
He had not five times been Dictator there,
Nor four times triumpht. If Epaminondas   70
(Who liv'd twice twenty years obscur'd in
          Thebes)
Had liv'd so still, he had been still unnam'd,
And paid his country nor himself their right ;
But putting forth his strength, he rescu'd both
From imminent ruin ; and, like burnisht steel,   75
After long use he shin'd ; for as the light
Not only serves to show, but render us

----

1 Punning on (1) the series of numbers ; (2) a populous
kingdom. (Boas.)
2 Deeds.   3 Delicacies.

Mutually profitable ; so our lives
In acts exemplary, not only win
Ourselves good names, but do to others give   80
Matter for virtuous deeds, by which we live.
     Bu. What would you wish me ?
     Mo.   Leave the troubled streams,
And live, as thrivers do, at the well-head.
     Bu. At the well-head ? Alas, what should I
          do
With that enchanted glass ? See devils there ?
Or, like a strumpet, learn to set my looks   86
In an eternal brake,[4] or practise juggling,
To keep my face still fast, my heart still loose ;
Or bear (like dame's schoolmistresses their rid-
          dles)
Two tongues, and be good only for a shift ; [5]   90
Flatter great lords, to put them still in mind
Why they were made lords ; or please humor-
          ous [6] ladies
With a good carriage, tell them idle tales
To make their physic work ; spend a man's life
In sights and visitations, that will make   95
His eyes as hollow as his mistress' heart :
To do none good, but those that have no need ;
To gain being forward, though you break for
          haste
All the commandments ere you break your fast ;
But believe backwards, make your period   100
And creed's last article, " I believe in God " ;
And (hearing villanies preacht) t'unfold their
          art.
Learn to commit them : 't is a great man's part.
Shall I learn this there ?
     Mo.   No, thou need'st not learn,
Thou hast the theory ; now go there and prac-
          tise.   105
     Bu. Ay, in a threadbare suit ; when men
          come there,
They must have high naps, [7] and go from thence
          bare :
A man may drown the parts [8] of ten rich men
In one poor suit ; brave barks [9] and outward
          gloss
Attract Court loves, be in parts ne'er so gross.
     Mo. Thou shalt have gloss enough, and all
          things fit   111
T'enchase in all show thy long-smothered spirit :
Be rul'd by me then. The old Scythians
Painted blind Fortune's powerful hands with
          wings,
To show her gifts come swift and suddenly,   115
Which, if her favourite be not swift to take,
He loses them for ever. Then be wise :
Stay but awhile here, and I 'll send to thee.
                    Exit Monsieur *with* Pages.
     Bu. What will he send ? Some crowns ? It is
          to sow them   119
Upon my spirit, and make them spring a crown
Worth millions of the seed-crowns he will send.
Like to disparking [10] noble husbandmen,
He 'll put his plow into me, plow me up.
But his unsweating thrift is policy,

----

4 A frame for holding an object fixed.
5 Equivocation, trickery.   8 Abilities.
6 Whimsical.   9 Fine coverings.
7 Clothes with rich surface.
10 Changing parks into plow-land.

And learning-hating policy is ignorant   125
To fit his seed-land soil; a smooth plain ground
Will never nourish any politic seed.
I am for honest actions, not for great:
If I may bring up a new fashion,
And rise in Court for virtue, speed his plow! 130
The King hath known me long as well as he,
Yet could my fortune never fit the length
Of both their understandings till this hour.
There is a deep nick in Time's restless wheel
For each man's good, when which nick comes,
    it strikes;   135
As rhetoric yet works not persuasion,
But only is a mean to make it work,
So no man riseth by his real merit,
But when it cries "clink" in his raiser's spirit.
Many will say, that cannot rise at all,   140
Man's first hour's rise is first step to his fall.
I'll venture that; men that fall low must die,
As well as men cast headlong from the sky.

Enter MAFFE.

Ma. Humour of princes! Is this wretch
    endu'd
With any merit worth a thousand crowns?   145
Will my lord have me be so ill a steward
Of his revenue, to dispose a sum
So great with so small cause as shows in him?
I must examine this. Is your name D'Ambois?
Bu.   Sir?
Ma.   Is your name D'Ambois?
Bu.   Who have we here? 150
Serve you the Monsieur?
Ma.   How?
Bu.   Serve you the Monsieur?
Ma. Sir, y'are very hot. I do serve the Mon-
    sieur;
But in such place as gives me the command
Of all his other servants. And because
His grace's pleasure is to give your good   155
His pass[1] through my command, methinks you
    might
Use me with more respect.
Bu.   Cry you mercy![2]
Now you have opened my dull eyes, I see you,
And would be glad to see the good you speak
    of.
What might I call your name?
Ma.   Monsieur Maffe.
Bu. Monsieur Maffe? Then, good Monsieur
    Maffe,   161
Pray let me know you better.
Ma.   Pray do so,
That you may use me better. For yourself,
By your no better outside, I would judge you
To be some poet; have you given my lord   165
Some pamphlet?
Bu.   Pamphlet?
Ma.   Pamphlet, sir, I say.
Bu. Did your great master's goodness leave
    the good
That is to pass your charge to my poor use,
To your discretion?
Ma.   Though he did not, sir,
I hope 'tis no rude office to ask reason   170

[1] Its passage.   [2] Beg pardon!

How that his grace gives me in charge, goes
    from me?
Bu. That's very perfect, sir.
Ma.   Why, very good, sir;
I pray then give me leave; if for no pamphlet,
May I not know what other merit in you,   174
Makes his compunction willing to relieve you?
Bu. No merit in the world, sir.
Ma.   That is strange.
Y'are a poor soldier, are you?
Bu.   That I am, sir.
Ma. And have commanded?
Bu.   Ay, and gone without, sir.
Ma. [*Aside.*] I see the man; a hundred
    crowns will make him   179
Swagger and drink healths to his grace's bounty,
And swear he could not be more bountiful;
So there's nine hundred crowns sav'd.—Here,
    tall soldier,
His grace hath sent you a whole hundred crowns.
Bu. A hundred, sir? Nay, do his highness
    right;
I know his hand is larger, and perhaps   185
I may deserve more than my outside shows.
I am a scholar, as I am a soldier,
And I can poetise; and (being well encourag'd)
May sing his fame for giving; yours for deliver-
    ing   189
(Like a most faithful steward) what he gives.
Ma. What shall your subject be?
Bu.   I care not much
If to his bounteous grace I sing the praise
Of fair great noses, and to you of long ones.
What qualities have you, sir, beside your chain[3]
And velvet jacket?[3] Can your worship dance?
Ma. A pleasant fellow, faith; it seems my
    lord   196
Will have him for his jester; and by'r lady,
Such men are now no fools; 'tis a knight's place.
If I (to save his grace some crowns) should urge
    him
T'abate his bounty, I should not be heard;   200
I would to heaven I were an errant ass,
For then I should be sure to have the ears
Of these great men, where now their jesters
    have them.
'Tis good to please him, yet I'll take no notice
Of his preferment, but in policy   205
Will still be grave and serious, lest he think
I fear his wooden dagger.[4] Here, sir Ambo!
Bu. How, Ambo, sir?
Ma.   Ay, is not your name Ambo?
Bu. You call'd me lately D'Ambois; has
    your worship
So short a head?
Ma.   I cry thee mercy, D'Ambois.
A thousand crowns I bring you from my lord.
If you be thrifty, and play the good husband,
    you may make   212
This a good standing living: 'tis a bounty
His highness might perhaps have bestow'd bet-
    ter.
Bu. Go, y'are a rascal; hence, away, you
    rogue!   215

[3] Badges of a steward's office.
[4] The weapon of the Fool, as of the Vice in The Mor-
alities.

Ma. What mean you, sir?
Bu.   Hence! prate no more!
Or, by thy villain's blood, thou prat'st thy last!
A barbarous groom grudge at his master's
  bounty!
But since I know he would as much abhor   219
His hind should argue what he gives his friend,
Take that, sir, for your aptness to dispute.
                    [*Strikes him.*] *Exit.*
Ma. These crowns are set in blood; blood be
  their fruit.   *Exit.*

[SCENE II.]¹

[*Enter*] HENRY, GUISE, MONTSURRY, ELENOR,
  TAMYRA, BEAUPRE, PERO, CHARLOTTE,
  PYRA, ANNABELLE.

He. Duchess of Guise, your grace is much en-
  richt
In the attendance of that English virgin,
That will initiate her prime of youth
(Dispos'd to Court conditions) under the hand
Of your preferr'd instructions and command,   5
Rather than any in the English Court,
Whose ladies are not matcht in Christendom
For graceful and confirm'd behaviours;
More than the Court, where they are bred, is
  equall'd.
Gu. I like not their Court fashion; it is too
  crestfall'n   10
In all observance, making demigods
Of their great nobles; and of their old queen,
An ever-young and most immortal goddess.
Mo. No question she's the rarest queen in
  Europe.
Gu. But what's that to her immortality?   15
He. Assure you, cousin Guise, so great a cour-
  tier,
So full of majesty and royal parts,
No queen in Christendom may vaunt herself.
Her Court approves it, that's a Court indeed,
Not mixt with clowneries us'd in common
  houses,   20
But, as Courts should be, th' abstracts of their
  kingdoms,
In all the beauty, state, and worth they hold;
So is hers, amply, and by her inform'd.
The world is not contracted in a man
With more proportion and expression,   25
Than in her Court, her kingdom. Our French
  Court
Is a mere mirror of confusion to it:
The king and subject, lord and every slave,
Dance a continual hay;² our rooms of state
Kept like our stables; no place more observ'd
Than a rude market-place: and though our
  custom   31
Keep this assur'd confusion from our eyes,
'Tis ne'er the less essentially unsightly,
Which they would soon see, would they change
  their form   34
To this of ours, and then compare them both;
Which we must not affect,³ because in kingdoms

Where the king's change doth breed the sub-
  ject's terror,
Pure innovation is more gross than error.
Mo. No question we shall see them imitate
(Though afar off) the fashions of our Courts,   40
As they have ever ap'd us in attire.
Never were men so weary of their skins,
And apt to leap out of themselves as they;
Who, when they travel⁴ to bring forth rare men,
Come home, delivered of a fine French suit.   45
Their brains lie with their tailors, and get babies
For their most complete issue; he's sole heir
To all the moral virtues that first greets
The light with a new fashion, which becomes
  them
Like apes, disfigur'd with the attires of men.   50
He. No question they much wrong their real
  worth
In affectation of outlandish scum;
But they have faults, and we more; they fool-
  ish-proud
To jet⁵ in others' plumes so haughtily;
We proud, that they are proud of foolery,   55
Holding our worths more complete for their
  vaunts.

Enter Monsieur, D'AMBOIS.

Mo. Come, mine own sweetheart, I will enter
  thee.
Sir, I have brought a gentleman to Court,
And pray you would vouchsafe to do him grace.
He. D'Ambois, I think?
Bu.   That's still my name, my lord,   60
Though I be something altered in attire.
He. We like your alteration, and must tell you
We have expected th' offer of your service;
For we (in fear to make mild virtue proud)
Use not to seek her out in any man.
Bu. Nor doth she use to seek out any man:
He that will win must woo her; [she's not
  shameless.]⁶
Mo. I urg'd her modesty in him, my lord,
And gave her those rites that he says she
  merits.
He. If you have woo'd and won, then, brother,
  wear him.   70
Mo. Th' art mine, sweetheart. See, here's the
  Guise's Duchess,
The Countess of Montsurreau, Beaupre.
Come, I'll enseam⁷ thee. Ladies, y'are too many
To be in council; I have here a friend
That I would gladly enter in your graces.   75
Bu. Save you, ladies.
Du. If you enter him in our graces, my lord,
methinks by his blunt behaviour he should come
out of himself.
Ta. Has he never been courtier, my lord?   80
Mo. Never, my lady.
Be. And why did the toy take him in th' head
now?
Bu. 'Tis leap-year, lady, and therefore very
good to enter a courtier.   85
He. Mark, Duchess of Guise, there is one is
  not bashful.

---

¹ A room in the Court. From a misplaced stage-direction in Sc. I (Q. 1641), it appears that Henry and
Guise are playing chess here.
² A boisterous country dance.   ³ Desire.
⁴ "Travel" and "travail" were not distinguished in
Elizabethan spelling.
⁵ Strut.   ⁶ From Qq. of 1607, 8.   ⁷ Introduce.

Du. No, my lord, he is much guilty of the bold extremity.

Ta. The man's a courtier at first sight.

Bu. I can sing pricksong,[1] lady, at first sight; and why not be a courtier as suddenly? 90

Be. Here's a courtier rotten before he be ripe.

Bu. Think me not impudent, lady ; I am yet no courtier ; I desire to be one, and would gladly take entrance, madam, under your princely colours. 95

Enter BARRISOR, L'ANOU, PYRRHOT.

Du. Soft, sir, you must rise by degrees, first being the servant[2] of some common lady, or knight's wife ; then a little higher to a lord's wife ; next a little higher to a countess ; yet a little higher to a duchess, and then turn the ladder. 101

Bu. Do you allow a man, then, four mistresses when the greatest mistress is allowed but three servants ?

Du. Where find you that statute, sir ? 105

Bu. Why, be judged by the groom-porters.[3]

Du. The groom-porters ?

Bu. Ay, madam ; must not they judge of all gamings i' th' Court ?

Du. You talk like a gamester. 110

Gu. Sir, know you me ?

Bu. My lord ?

Gu. I know not you. Whom do you serve ?

Bu. Serve, my lord ?

Gu. Go to, companion,[4] your courtship's too saucy. 116

Bu. [*Aside.*] Saucy ! Companion ! 'T is the Guise, but yet those terms might have been spared of the guiserd.[5] Companion ! He's jealous, by this light. Are you blind of that side, duke ? I'll to her again for that. — Forth, [121 princely mistress, for the honour of courtship. Another riddle !

Gu. Cease your courtship, or by heaven I'll cut your throat. 125

Bu. Cut my throat ? Cut a whetstone, young Accius Naevius,[6] Do as much with your tongue, as he did with a razor. Cut my throat !

Ba. What new-come gallant have we here, that dares mate[7] the Guise thus ? 130

L'A. 'Sfoot, 't is D'Ambois. The duke mistakes him, on my life, for some knight of the new edition.[8]

Bu. Cut my throat ! I would the king fear'd thy cutting of his throat no more than I fear thy cutting of mine. 136

Gu. I'll do 't, by this hand.

Bu. That hand dares not do 't. Y'ave cut too many throats already, Guise ; and robb'd the realm of many thousand souls, more precious than thine own. — Come madam, talk on. [141

---

[1] Music written with points.   [2] Lover.

[3] Officials of the English court who furnished cards, dice, etc. and decided gaming disputes.

[4] Fellow.

[5] The point is obscure. Perhaps, gizzard = throat.

[6] A Roman augur who cut a whetstone before Tarquin.

[7] Checkmate, overcome.

[8] Recent creation. An allusion to the lavish practice of James I.

'Sfoot, can you not talk? Talk on, I say; another riddle?

Py. Here's some strange distemper.

Ba. Here's a sudden transmigration with D'Ambois, — out of the knight's ward[9] into the duchess' bed.

L'A. See what a metamorphosis a brave suit can work. 149

Py. 'Slight, step to the Guise and discover him.

Ba. By no means ; let the new suit work, we'll see the issue.

Gu. Leave your courting. 154

Bu. I will not. — I say, mistress, and I will stand unto it, that if a woman may have three servants, a man may have three-score mistresses.

Gu. Sirrah, I'll have you whipt out of the Court for this insolence. 160

Bu. Whipt ? Such another syllable out a th' presence, if thou dar'st, for thy dukedom.

Gu. Remember, poltroon.

Mo. Pray thee, forbear. 164

Bu. Passion of death ! Were not the king here, he should strow the chamber like a rush.

Mo. But leave courting his wife, then.

Bu. I will not. I'll court her in despite of him. Not court her ! Come, madam, talk on, fear me nothing. [*To Guise.*] Well may'st thou drive thy master from the Court, but never [171 D'Ambois.

Mo. His great heart will not down; 't is like the sea,

That partly by his own internal heat,
Partly the stars' daily and nightly motion, 175
Their heat and light, and partly of the place,
The divers frames, but chiefly by the moon,
Bristled with surges, never will be won
(No, not when th' hearts of all those powers are burst)
To make retreat into his settled home, 180
Till he be crown'd with his own quiet foam.

He. You have the mate.[10] Another ?

Gu. No more.   *Flourish short.*
            Exit GUISE, *after him the* King,
                Monsieur *whispering.*

Ba. Why, here's the lion, scar'd with the throat of a dunghill cock, a fellow that has [185 newly shak'd off his shackles; now does he crow for that victory.

L'A. 'T is one of the best jigs that ever was acted. 189

Py. Whom does the Guise suppose him to be, trow ?

L'A. Out of doubt, some new denizen'd lord, and thinks that suit newly drawn out a' th' mercer's books. 194

Ba. I have heard of a fellow, that by a fixt imagination looking upon a bull-baiting, had a visible pair of horns grew out of his forehead; and I believe this gallant, overjoyed with the conceit of Monsieur's cast[11] suit, imagines himself to be the Monsieur. 200

L'A. And why not ; as well as the ass, stalk-

---

[9] A part of the " Counter " prison.

[10] Checkmate.   [11] Cast off.

ing in the lion's case,[1] bare himself like a lion,
braying all the huger beasts out of the forest ?
Py. Peace, he looks this way.   204
Ba. Marry, let him look, sir. What will you
say now if the Guise be gone to fetch a blanket[2]
for him ?
L'A. Faith, I believe it for his honour sake.
Py. But, if D'Ambois carry it clean ?[3]
                              Exeunt Ladies.
Ba. True, when he curvets in the blanket.
Py. Ay, marry, sir.   211
L'A. 'Sfoot, see how he stares on 's.
Ba. Lord bless us, let 's away.
Bu. Now, sir, take your full view ; how does
the object please ye ?   215
Ba. If you ask my opinion, sir, I think your
suit sits as well as if 't had been made for you.
Bu. So, sir, and was that the subject of your
ridiculous jollity ?
L'A. What 's that to you, sir ?   220
Bu. Sir, I have observ'd all your fleerings ;[4]
and resolve yourselves ye shall give a strict ac-
count for 't.

Enter BRISAC, MELYNELL.

Ba. Oh, miraculous jealousy ![5] Do you think
yourself such a singular subject for laughter [225
that none can fall into the matter of our merriment but you ?
L'A. This jealousy of yours, sir, confesses
some close defect in yourself, that we never
dream'd of.   230
Py. We held discourse of a perfum'd ass, that
being disguis'd in a lion's case, imagin'd himself a lion. I hope that toucht not you.
Bu. So, sir ; your descants[6] do marvellous
well fit this ground. We shall meet where [235
your buffoonly laughters will cost ye the best
blood in your bodies.
Ba. For life's sake let 's be gone; he 'll kill 's
outright else.
Bu. Go, at your pleasures, I 'll be your ghost
to haunt you ; an ye sleep an 't, hang me.   241
L'A. Go, go, sir ; court your mistress.
Py. And be advis'd ; we shall have odds
against you.
Bu. Tush ! valour stands not in number ; I 'll
maintain it, that one man may beat three [246
boys.
Br. Nay, you shall have no odds of him in
number, sir ; he 's a gentleman as good as the
proudest of you, and ye shall not wrong him.
Ba. Not, sir ?   251
Me. Not, sir : though he be not so rich, he 's
a better man than the best of you ; and I will
not endure it.
L'A. Not you, sir ?   255
Br. No, sir, not I.
Bu. I should thank you for this kindness, if
I thought these perfum'd musk-cats (being out
of this privilege) durst but once mew at us.

---

[1] Skin.   [4] Sneers.
[2] To toss him.   [5] Suspicion.
[3] Come off superior.
[6] *Descant* and *ground* are used with a play on the ordinary meanings and the musical ones of accompani-
ment, variation.

Ba. Does your confident spirit doubt that,
sir ? Follow us and try.   261
L'A. Come, sir, we 'll lead you a dance.
                              Exeunt.

ACT II

SCENE I.[7]

[*Enter*] HENRY, GUISE, MONTSURRY, *and* Attendants.

He. This desperate quarrel sprung out of
    their envies
To D'Ambois' sudden bravery,[8] and great
    spirit.
Gu. Neither is worth their envy.
He.   Less than either
Will make the gall of envy overflow.
She feeds on outcast entrails like a kite ;   5
In which foul heap, if any ill lies hid,
She sticks her beak into it, shakes it up,
And hurls it all abroad, that all may view it.
Corruption is her nutriment ; but touch her
With any precious ointment, and you kill her.
Where she finds any filth in men, she feasts, 11
And with her black throat bruits it through
    the world
(Being sound and healthful). But if she but
    taste
The slenderest pittance of commended virtue,
She surfeits on it, and is like a fly   15
That passes all the body's soundest parts,
And dwells upon the sores ; or if her squint eye
Have power to find none there, she forges some.
She makes that crooked ever which is straight ;
Calls valour giddiness, justice tyranny ;   20
A wise man may shun her, she not herself ;
Whithersoever she flies from her harms,
She bears her foes still claspt in her own arms :
And therefore, Cousin Guise, let us avoid her.

Enter Nuntius.

Nu. What Atlas or Olympus lifts his head   25
So far past covert, that with air enough
My words may be inform'd, and from their
    height
I may be seen, and heard through all the world ?
A tale so worthy, and so fraught with wonder
Sticks in my jaws, and labours with event.   30
He. Comest thou from D'Ambois ?
Nu.   From him, and the rest,
His friends and enemies ; whose stern fight I
    saw,
And heard their words before and in the fray.
He. Relate at large what thou hast seen and
    heard.
Nu. I saw fierce D'Ambois and his two brave
    friends   35
Enter the field, and at their heels their foes ;
Which were the famous soldiers, Barrisor,
L'Anou, and Pyrrhot, great in deeds of arms :
All which arriv'd at the evenest piece of earth
The field afforded, the three challengers   40
Turn'd head, drew all their rapiers, and stood
    rankt :

---

[7] A room in the Court.   [8] Finery.

When face to face the three defendants met
  them,
Alike prepar'd, and resolute alike.
Like bonfires of contributory wood
Every man's look show'd, fed with either's
  spirit;   45
As one had been a mirror to another,
Like forms of life and death, each took from
  other;
And so were life and death mixt at their
  heights,
That you could see no fear of death, for life,
Nor love of life, for death; but in their brows 50
Pyrrho's opinion in great letters shone:
That life and death in all respects are one.
  He. Past there no sort of words at their en-
  counter?
  Nu. As Hector, 'twixt the hosts of Greece
  and Troy,   54
(When Paris and the Spartan king should end
The nine years' war) held up his brazen lance
For signal that both hosts should cease from
  arms,
And hear him speak: so Barrisor advis'd,[1]
Advanc'd his naked rapier 'twixt both sides,
Ript[2] up the quarrel, and compar'd six lives 60
Then laid in balance with six idle words;
Offer'd remission and contrition too;
Or else that he and D'Ambois might conclude
The others' dangers. D'Ambois lik'd the last;
But Barrisor's friends (being equally engag'd 65
In the main quarrel) never would expose
His life alone to that they all deserv'd.
And, for the other offer of remission,
D'Ambois (that like a laurel put in fire
Spark'd and spit) did much more than scorn 70
That his wrong should incense him so like chaff
To go so soon out; and like lighted paper
Approve his spirit at once both fire and ashes.
So drew they lots and in them fates appointed
That Barrisor should fight with fiery D'Am-
  bois;   75
Pyrrhot with Melynell; with Brisac L'Anou:
And then like flame and powder they commixt,
So spritely, that I wisht they had been spirits,
That the ne'er-shutting wounds, they needs
  must open,
Might as they open'd shut, and never kill. 80
But D'Ambois' sword (that light'ned as it flew)
Shot like a pointed comet at the face
Of manly Barrisor; and there it stuck.
Thrice pluckt he[3] at it, and thrice drew on
  thrusts,
From him[4] that of himself was free as fire; 85
Who[4] thrust still as he[3] pluckt, yet (past belief)
He[3] with his subtle eye, hand, body, scapt.
At last, the deadly bitten point tugg'd off,
On fell his yet undaunted foe so fiercely
That (only made more horrid with his wound) 90
Great D'Ambois shrunk, and gave a little
  ground;
But soon return'd, redoubled[5] in his danger,
And at the heart of Barrisor seal'd his anger.
Then, as in Arden I have seen an oak

---

[1] Cautious.   [3] D'Ambois.
[2] Explained the source.   [4] Barrisor.
[6] Risking himself a second time.

Long shook with tempests, and his lofty top 95
Bent to his root, which being at length made
  loose
Even groaning with his weight) he 'gan to nod
This way and that, as loth his curled brows
(Which he had oft wrapt in the sky with
  storms)   99
Should stoop: and yet, his radical fibres burst,
Storm-like he fell, and hid the fear-cold earth;
So fell stout Barrisor, that had stood the shocks
Of ten set battles in your highness' war,
'Gainst the sole soldier of the world, Navarre.
  Gu. Oh, piteous and horrid murder!
  [*Mont.*]   Such a life
Methinks had metal in it to survive   106
An age of men.
  He.   Such often soonest end.
Thy felt report calls on, we long to know
On what events the other have arriv'd.
  Nu. Sorrow and fury, like two opposite fumes
Met in the upper region of a cloud,   111
At the report made by this worthy's fall,
Brake from the earth, and with them rose Re-
  venge,
Ent'ring with fresh powers his two noble
  friends;
And under that odds fell surcharg'd[6] Brisac, 115
The friend of D'Ambois, before fierce L'Anou;
Which D'Ambois seeing, as I once did see,
In my young travels through Armenia,
An angry unicorn in his full career
Charge with too swift a foot a jeweller   120
That watcht him for the treasure of his brow,[7]
And, ere he could get shelter of a tree,
Nail him with his rich antler to the earth;
So D'Ambois ran upon reveng'd L'Anou,
Who eying th' eager point borne in his face, 125
And giving back, fell back, and in his fall
His foe's uncurbed sword stopt in his heart;
By which time all the life-strings of the
  tw' other
Were cut, and both fell as their spirits flew
Upwards; and still hunt honour at the view: 130
And now, of all the six, sole D'Ambois stood
Untoucht, save only with the others' blood.
  He. All slain outright?
  Nu.   All slain outright but he,
Who kneeling in the warm life of his friends,
(All freckled with the blood his rapier rain'd) 135
He kist their pale cheeks, and bade both fare-
  well;
And see the bravest man the French earth
  bears!   [*Exit* Nuntius.]

  Enter Monsieur D'Ambois *bare.*[8]

  Bu. Now is the time; y' are princely vow'd
  my friend;
Perform it princely, and obtain my pardon.
  Mo. Else heaven forgive not me! Come on,
  brave friend! —   140
If ever nature held herself her own,
When the great trial of a king and subject
Met in one blood, both from one belly springing;
Now prove her virtue and her greatness one,
Or make the t' one the greater with t' other, 145

---

[6] Overwhelmed.   [7] The horn.   [8] Bare-headed.

(As true kings should) and for your brother's
love,
(Which is a special species of true virtue)
Do that you could not do, not being a king.
   He. Brother, I know your suit; these wilful
     murders
Are ever past our pardon.
   Mo.   Manly slaughter 150
Should never bear th' account of wilful murder;
It being a spice [1] of justice, where with life
Offending past law,[2] equal life is laid
In equal balance, to scourge that offence
By law of reputation, which to men   155
Exceeds all positive law, and what that [3] leaves
To true men's valours (not prefixing rights
Of satisfaction, suited to their wrongs)
A free man's eminence may supply and take.
   He. This would make every man that thinks
     him wrong'd   160
Or is offended, or in wrong or right,
Lay on this violence, and all vaunt themselves
Law-menders and suppliers,[4] though mere
     butchers;
Should this fact [5] (though of justice [6]) be for-
     given?
   Mo. Oh, no, my lord; it would make cowards
     fear   165
To touch the reputations of true men
When only they are left to imp [7] the law.
Justice will soon distinguish murderous minds
From just revengers. Had my friend been slain,
(His enemy surviving) he should die,   170
Since he had added to a murder'd fame
(Which was in his intent) a murdered man,
And this had worthily been wilful murder:
But my friend only sav'd his fame's dear life,
Which is above life, taking th' under value, 175
Which in the wrong it did, was forfeit to him;
And in this fact only preserves a man
In his uprightness; worthy to survive
Millions of such as murder men alive.
   He. Well, brother, rise, and raise your friend
     withal   180
From death to life; and D'Ambois, let your life
(Refin'd, by passing through this merited death)
Be purg'd from more such foul pollution;
Nor on your scape nor valour more presuming
To be again so daring.
   Bu.   My lord,   185
I loathe as much a deed of unjust death
As law itself doth; and to tyrannize,
Because I have a little spirit to dare
And power to do, as to be tyranniz'd.
This is a grace that (on my knees redoubled [8]),
I crave to double this, my short life's gift; 191
And shall your royal bounty centuple,
That I may so make good what Law and nature
Have given me for my good; since I am free,
(Offending no just law), let no law make 195
By any wrong it does, my life her slave:
When I am wrong'd, and that law fails to right
     me,

Let me be king myself (as man was made),
And do a justice that exceeds the law;
If my wrong pass the power of single valour 200
To right and expiate, then be you my king,
And do a right, exceeding law and nature,
Who to himself is law, no law doth need,
Offends no law, and is a king indeed.
   He. Enjoy what thou entreat'st; we give but
     ours.   205
   Bu. What you have given, my lord, is ever
     yours.   *Exit* Rex *cum* [MONTSURRY]
   Gu. Mort dieu! who would have pardon'd
     such a murder?   *Exit.*
   Mo. Now vanish horrors into Court attrac-
     tions,
For which let this balm make thee fresh and
     fair.
And now forth with thy service to the
     duchess,   210
As my long love will to Montsurry's countess.
                             Exit.
   Bu. To whom my love hath long been vow'd
     in heart,
Although in hand for show I held the duchess.
And now through blood and vengeance, deeds
     of height
And hard to be achiev'd, 't is fit I make   215
Attempt of her perfection. I need fear
No check in his rivality,[9] since her virtues
Are so renown'd, and he of all dames hated.
                             Exit.

[SCENE II.] [10]

MONTSURRY, TAMYRA, BEAUPRE, PERO,
     CHARLOTTE, PYRA.

   Mont. He will have pardon, sure.
   Ta.   'T were pity, else:
For though his great spirit something over-
     flow,
All faults are still borne that from greatness
     grow;
But such a sudden courtier saw I never.
   Be. He was too sudden, which indeed was
     rudeness.   5
   Ta. True, for it argued his no due conceit [11]
Both of the place and greatness of the persons,
Nor of our sex: all which (we all being
     strangers
To his encounter) should have made more
     manners   9
Deserve more welcome.
   Mont.   All this fault is found
Because he lov'd the duchess and left you.
   Ta. Alas, love give her joy; I am so far
From envy of her honour, that I swear,
Had he encounter'd me with such proud slight.
I would have put that project [12] face of his 15
To a more test than did her duchesship.
   Be. Why (by your leave, my lord) I 'll speak
     it here,
Although she be my aunt, she scarce was
     modest,
When she perceiv'd the duke her husband
     take

---

[1] Species, kind.
[2] In a way not recog-
nized by law.
[3] *I. e.* positive law.
[4] Substitutes.

[5] Deed.
[6] Done in the name of justice.
[7] Piece out.
[8] A second time kneeling.

[9] Rivalry.
[10] A room in Montsurry's house.
[11] Conception.
[12] Forward.

Those late exceptions to her servant's court-
        ship,   20
To entertain him.
    Ta.   Ay, and stand him still,
Letting her husband give her servant place.
Though he did manly, she should be a woman.

            Enter GUISE.

[*Gu.*] D'Ambois is pardon'd! Where 's a
        king? Where law?
See how it runs, much like a turbulent sea,   25
Here high and glorious as it did contend
To wash the heavens and make the stars more
        pure,
And here so low, it leaves the mud of hell
To every common view; come, Count Mont-
        surry,   29
We must consult of this.
    Ta.   Stay not, sweet lord.
    Mont. Be pleas'd, I 'll straight return.
                        Exit cum GUISE.
    Ta.   Would that would please me!
    Be. I 'll leave you, madam, to your passions;
I see there 's change of weather in your looks.
                        Exit cum suis.
    Ta. I cannot cloak it; but, as when a fume,
Hot, dry, and gross, within the womb of earth
Or in her superficies begot,   36
When extreme cold hath struck it to her
        heart,
The more it is comprest, the more it rageth;
Exceeds his prison's strength that should con-
        tain it,
And then it tosseth temples in the air,   40
All bars made engines to his insolent fury;
So, of a sudden, my licentious fancy
Riots within me: not my name and house
Nor my religion, to this hour observ'd,
Can stand above it. I must utter that   45
That will in parting break more strings in me
Than death when life parts; and that holy man
That, from my cradle, counsell'd for my soul,
I now must make an agent for my blood.[1]   49

            Enter Monsieur.

    Mo. Yet, is my mistress gracious?
    Ta.   Yet unanswered?
    Mo. Pray thee regard thine own good, if not
        mine,
And cheer my love for that; you do not know
What you may be by me, nor what without
        me;
I may have power t' advance and pull down
        any.
    Ta. That 's not my study. One way I am
        sure   55
You shall not pull down me; my husband's
        height
Is crown to all my hopes; and his retiring
To any mean state, shall be my aspiring;
My honour 's in mine own hands, spite of kings.
    Mo. Honour, what 's that? Your second
        maidenhead: 60
And what is that? A word. The word is gone,
The thing remains: the rose is pluckt, the
        stalk

Abides; an easy loss where no lack 's found.
Believe it, there 's as small lack in the loss
As there is pain i' th' losing; archers ever   65
Have two strings to a bow; and shall great
        Cupid
(Archer of archers both in men and women,)
Be worse provided than a common archer?
A husband and a friend all wise wives have.
    Ta. Wise wives they are that on such strings
        depend,   70
With a firm husband joining a loose friend!
    Mo. Still you stand on your husband, so do
        all
The common sex of you, when y' are encounter'd
With one ye cannot fancy. All men know   74
You live in Court, here, by your own election,
Frequenting all our common sports and tri-
        umphs,
All the most youthful company of men:
And wherefore do you this? To please your
        husband?
'T is gross and fulsome: if your husband's
        pleasure
Be all your object, and you aim at honour   80
In living close to him, get you from Court;
You may have him at home; these common
        put-offs
For common women serve: "My honour!
        Husband!"
Dames maritorious[2] ne'er were meritorious.
Speak plain, and say, "I do not like you, sir, 85
Y' are an ill-favour'd fellow in my eye;"
And I am answer'd.
    Ta.   Then, I pray, be answer'd:
For in good faith, my lord, I do not like you
In that sort[3] you like,
    Mo.   Then have at you, here!
Take (with a politic hand) this rope of pearl,   90
And though you be not amorous, yet be wise:
Take me for wisdom; he that you can love
Is ne'er the further from you.
    Ta.   Now it comes
So ill prepar'd, that I may take a poison,
Under a medicine as good cheap as it;   95
I will not have it were it worth the world.
    Mo. Horror of death; could I but please your
        eye,
You would give me the like, ere you would lose
        me.
"Honour and husband!"
    Ta.   By this light, my lord,
Y' are a vile fellow, and I 'll tell the king   100
Your occupation of dishonouring ladies
And of his Court. A lady cannot live
As she was born, and with that sort of
        pleasure
That fits her state, but she must be defam'd
With an infamous lord's detraction.   105
Who would endure the Court if these attempts
Of open and profest lust must be borne?
Who 's there? Come on, dame; you are at your
        book
When men are at your mistress; have I taught
        you
Any such waiting-woman's quality?   110

---

[1] Satisfying my passion.   [2] Excessively fond of their husbands.   [3] Way.

Mo. Farewell, good " husband."
　　　　　　　　　　　　Exit Monsieur.
Mont. 　　　　　　　　Farewell, wicked lord.

　　　　　Enter MONTSURRY.

Mont. Was not the Monsieur here ?
Ta. 　　　　　　Yes, to good purpose ;
And your cause is as good to seek him too,
And haunt his company.
Mont. 　　　　　Why, what 's the matter ?
Ta. Matter of death, were I some husbands'
　　wife. 　　　　　　　　　　　　　　115
I cannot live at quiet in my chamber,
For opportunities [1] almost to rapes
Offer'd me by him.
Mont. 　　　　Pray thee bear with him.
Thou know'st he is a bachelor and a courtier,
Ay, and a prince ; and their prerogatives 　120
Are to their laws, as to their pardons are
Their reservations, after Parliaments —
One quits another ; form gives all their essence.
That prince doth high in virtue's reckoning
　stand
That will entreat a vice, and not command. 　125
So far bear with him ; should another man
Trust to his privilege, he should trust to death.
Take comfort, then, my comfort, nay, triumph
And crown thyself, thou part'st with victory ; [2]
My presence is so only dear to thee 　　　　130
That other men's appear worse than they be.
For this night yet, bear with my forced
　absence ;
Thou know'st my business ; and with how
　much weight.
My vow hath charg'd it.
Ta. 　　　　True, my lord, and never
My fruitless love shall let [3] your serious honour ;
Yet, sweet lord, do not stay ; you know my
　soul 　　　　　　　　　　　　　　135
Is so long time without me, and I dead,
As you are absent.
Mont. 　　　　By this kiss, receive
My soul for hostage, till I see my love.
Ta. The morn shall let me see you.
Mont. 　　　　　　　　With the sun
I 'll visit thy more comfortable [4] beauties. 　141
Ta. This is my comfort, that the sun hath
　left
The whole world's beauty ere my sun leaves me.
Mont. 'T is late night now indeed ; farewell,
　my light. 　　　　　　　　　　*Exit.*
Ta. Farewell, my light and life ; — but not
　in him, 　　　　　　　　　　　　145
In mine own dark love and light bent to
　another.
Alas that in the wane [5] of our affections
We should supply it with a full dissembling,
In which each youngest maid is grown a
　mother ;
Frailty is fruitful, one sin gets another. 　　150
Our loves like sparkles are that brightest shine
When they go out, most vice shows most
　divine. —
Go, maid, to bed ; lend me your book, I pray ;

[1] Importunities.
[2] That thou comest
off victorious.
[3] Hinder.
[4] Comforting.
[5] Emend. Dilke. Qq. *wave.*

Not like yourself for form ; I 'll this night
　trouble
None of your services. Make sure the doors, 155
And call your other fellows to their rest.
Pe. I will, — [*Aside.*] yet I will watch to know
　why you watch. 　　　　　　　*Exit.*
Ta. Now all ye peaceful regents of the
　night,
Silently-gliding exhalations,
Languishing winds, and murmuring falls of
　waters, 　　　　　　　　　　　　160
Sadness of heart and ominous secureness,
Enchantments, dead sleeps, all the friends of
　rest,
That ever wrought upon the life of man,
Extend your utmost strengths ; and this
　charm'd hour 　　　　　　　　　165
Fix like the centre ; [6] make the violent wheels
Of Time and Fortune stand ; and great Ex-
　istence
(The Maker's treasury) now not seem to be,
To all but my approaching friends and me.
They come, alas, they come ! Fear, fear and
　hope
Of one thing, at one instant fight in me ; 　170
I love what most I loathe, and cannot live
Unless I compass that which holds my death ;
For life 's mere death, loving one that loathes me,
And he I love will loathe me, when he sees
I fly my sex, my virtue, my renown, 　　　175
To run so madly on a man unknown.
　　　　　　　　　　　The vault opens.
See, see, a vault is opening that was never
Known to my lord and husband, nor to any
But him that brings the man I love, and me.
How shall I look on him ? How shall I live,
And not consume in blushes ? I will in, 　181
And cast myself off,[7] as I ne'er had been.[8] *Exit.*

　　Ascendit Friar *and* D'AMBOIS.

Fr. Come, worthiest son, I am past measure
　glad,
That you (whose worth I have approv'd so
　long)
Should be the object of her fearful love ; 　185
Since both your wit and spirit can adapt
Their full force to supply her utmost weakness.
You know her worths and virtues, for report
Of all that know is to a man a knowledge : 　189
You know besides, that our affections' storm,
Rais'd in our blood, no reason can reform.
Though she seek them their satisfaction
(Which she must needs, or rest unsatisfied)
Your judgment will esteem her peace thus
　wrought, 　　　　　　　　　　　194
Nothing less dear than if yourself had sought ;
And (with another colour, which my art
Shall teach you to lay on) yourself must seem
The only agent, and the first orb move [9]
In this our set and cunning world of love.
Bu. Give me the colour, my most honour'd
　father, 　　　　　　　　　　　200
And trust my cunning then to lay it on.

[6] Centre of the earth.
[7] Undress.
[8] Supply *watching here.*
[9] *Primum mobile*, the prime moving sphere of the
Ptolemaic system.

Fr. 'T is this, good son ; Lord Barrisor (whom
　　you slew)
Did love her dearly, and with all fit means
Hath urg'd his acceptation, of all which
She keeps one letter written in his blood.　205
You must say thus, then, that you heard from
　　me
How much herself was toucht in conscience
With a report (which is in truth dispers't)
That your main quarrel grew about her love,
Lord Barrisor imagining your courtship　210
Of the great Guise's Duchess in the presence,
Was by you made to his elected mistress ;
And so made me your mean now to resolve her,
Choosing (by my direction) this night's depth
For the more clear avoiding of all note　215
Of your presumed presence : and with this
(To clear her hands of such a lover's blood)
She will so kindly thank and entertain you,
Methinks I see how), ay, and ten to one,
Show you the confirmation in his blood,　220
Lest you should think report and she did feign,
That you shall so have circumstantial means
To come to the direct, which must be used :
For the direct is crooked ; love comes flying ;
The height of love is still won with denying.　225
　Bu. Thanks, honour'd father.
　Fr.　　　　　　She must never know
That you know anything of any love
Sustain'd on her part : for, learn this of me,
In anything a woman does alone,
If she dissemble, she thinks 't is not done ;　230
If not dissemble, [1] nor a little chide,
Give her her wish, she is not satisfi'd ;
To have a man think that she never seeks,
Does her more good than to have all she likes :
This frailty sticks in them beyond their sex,
Which to reform, reason is too perplex :　236
Urge reason to them, it will do no good ;
Humour (that is the chariot of our food
In everybody) must in them be fed,
To carry their affections by it bred.　240
Stand close.

Enter TAMYRA *with a book.*

　Ta. Alas, I fear my strangeness will retire
　　him.
If he go back, I die ; I must prevent it,
And cheer his onset with my sight at least,
And that 's the most ; though every step he
　　takes　245
Goes to my heart. I 'll rather die than seem
Not to be strange to that I most esteem.
　Fr. Madam.
　Ta.　　　　Ah !
　Fr.　　　　　　You will pardon me, I hope,
That so beyond your expectation,
And at a time for visitants so unfit,　250
I (with my noble friend here) visit you.
You know that my access at any time
Hath ever been admitted ; and that friend
That my care will presume to bring with me
Shall have all circumstance of worth in him　255
To merit as free welcome as myself.
　Ta. Oh, father ! but at this suspicious hour

[1] If she has no chance to dissemble.

You know how apt best men are to suspect us,
In any cause that makes suspicious shadow
No greater than the shadow of a hair :　260
And y' are to blame. What though my lord and
　　husband
Lie forth to-night, and, since I cannot sleep
When he is absent, I sit up to-night ;
Though all the doors are sure, and all our
　　servants
As sure bound with their sleeps ; yet there is
　　One　265
That wakes above, whose eye no sleep can
　　bind.
He sees through doors, and darkness, and our
　　thoughts ;
And therefore as we should avoid with fear
To think amiss ourselves before his search,
So should we be as curious to shun　270
All cause that other think not ill of us.
　Bu. Madam, 't is far from that ; I only
　　heard
By this my honour'd father, that your con-
　　science
Made some deep scruple with a false report
That Barrisor's blood should something touch
　　your honour,　275
Since he imagin'd I was courting you,
When I was bold to change words with the
　　duchess,
And therefore made his quarrel ; his long love
And service, as I hear, being deeply vowed　279
To your perfections, which my ready presence,
Presum'd on with my father at this season
For the more care of your so curious [2] honour,
Can well resolve [3] your conscience, is most
　　false.
　Ta. And is it therefore that you come, good
　　sir ?　284
Then crave I now your pardon and my father's,
And swear your presence does me so much
　　good,
That all I have it binds to your requital.
Indeed, sir, 't is most true that a report
Is spread, alleging that his love to me
Was reason of your quarrel, and because　2k
You shall not think I feign it for my glory
That he importun'd me for his court service, [4]
I 'll show you his own hand, set down in blood
To that vain purpose. Good sir, then come in.
Father, I thank you now a thousand-fold.　29.
　　　　　　　Exit TAMYRA *and* D'AMBOIS.
　Fr. May it be worth it to you, honour'd
　　daughter.　　　　　　　*Descendit* Friar.

ACT III

SCENE I. [5]

Enter D'AMBOIS, TAMYRA, *with a chain of
pearl.*

　Bu. Sweet mistress, cease ! Your conscience
　　is too nice, [6]
And bites too hotly of the Puritan spice.

[2] Fastidiously guarded.　　　　[3] Assure.
[4] *Service* was the conventional term for courtly love.
[5] A room in Montsurry's house.　　[6] Scrupulous.

Ta. Oh, my dear servant,[1] in thy close em-
  braces,
I have set open all the doors of danger
To my encompast honour, and my life.   5
Before I was secure against death and hell,
But now am subject to the heartless fear
Of every shadow and of every breath,
And would change firmness with an aspen leaf ;
So confident a spotless conscience is,   10
So weak a guilty. Oh, the dangerous siege
Sin lays about us, and the tyranny
He exercises when he hath expugn'd ! [2]
Like to the horror of a winter's thunder,
Mixt with a gushing storm, that suffer nothing
To stir abroad on earth but their own rages, 16
Is sin, when it hath gathered head above us :
No roof, no shelter can secure us so,
But he will drown our cheeks in fear or woe.
  Bu. Sin is a coward, madam, and insults   20
But on our weakness, in his truest valour ; [3]
And so our ignorance tames us, that we let
His shadows fright us : and like empty clouds,
In which our faulty apprehensions forge
The forms of dragons, lions, elephants,   25
When they hold no proportion, the sly charms
Of the witch, Policy, makes him like a monster
Kept only to show men for servile money.
That false hag often paints him in her cloth
Ten times more monstrous than he is in troth. 30
In three of us, the secret of our meeting
Is only guarded, and three friends as one
Have ever been esteem'd : as our three powers
That in our one soul are as one united :
Why should we fear then ? For myself I swear 35
Sooner shall torture be the sire to pleasure,
And health be grievous to one long time sick,
Than the dear jewel of your fame in me
Be made an outcast to your infamy ;
Nor shall my value (sacred to your virtues)   40
Only give free course to it, from myself :
But make it fly out of the mouths of kings
In golden vapours and with awful wings.
  Ta. It rests [4] as all kings' seals were set in
thee.
Now let us call my father, whom I swear   45
I could extremely chide, but that I fear
To make him so suspicious of my love
Of which, sweet servant, do not let him know
For all the world.
  Bu.   Alas ! he will not think it. 49
  Ta. Come, then — ho ! Father, ope, and take
your friend.   *Ascendit* Friar.
  Fr. Now, honour'd daughter, is your doubt
resolv'd ?
  Ta. Ay, father, but you went away too soon.
  Fr. Too soon ?
  Ta. Indeed you did, you should have stayed ;
Had not your worthy friend been of your bring-
ing,
And that contains all laws to temper me,   55
Not all the fearful danger that besieged us,
Had aw'd my throat from exclamation.
  Fr. I know your serious disposition well.
Come, son, the morn comes on.

  [1] Lover.   [2] Taken by storm.
  [3] If his valor be truly estimated.
  [4] Remains inviolable.

Bu.   Now, honour'd mistress,
Till farther service call, all bliss supply you. 60
  Ta. And you this chain of pearl, and my
love only.
                Descendit Friar *and* D'AMBOIS.
It is not I, but urgent destiny,
That (as great statesmen for their general end
In politic justice, make poor men offend)
Enforceth my offence to make it just.   65
What shall weak dames do, when th' whol
  work of nature
Hath a strong finger in each one of us ?
Needs must that sweep away the silly cobweb
Of our still-undone labours ; that lays still
Our powers to it : as to the line, the stone, 70
Not to the stone, the line should be oppos'd ; [5]
We cannot keep our constant course in virtue :
What is alike at all parts ? Every day
Differs from other : every hour and minute,
Ay, every thought in our false clock of life   75
Ofttimes inverts the whole circumference :
We must be sometimes one, sometimes another.
Our bodies are but thick clouds to our souls,
Through which they cannot shine when they
  desire :
When all the stars, and even the sun himself, 80
Must stay the vapours' times that he exhales
Before he can make good his beams to us ;
Oh, how can we, that are but motes to him,
Wand'ring at random in his ordered rays,
Disperse our passions' fumes, with our weak
  labours,   85
That are more thick and black than all earth's
  vapours ?

                Enter MONTSURRY.

  Mont. Good day, my love ; what, up and
ready [6] too !
  Ta. Both, my dear lord ; not all this night
made I
Myself unready, or could sleep a wink.
  Mont. Alas ! what troubled my true love, my
peace,   90
From being at peace within her better self ?
Or how could sleep forbear to seize thine eyes
When he might challenge them as his just
  prize ?
  Ta. I am in no power earthly, but in yours ;
To what end should I go to bed, my lord,   95
That wholly mist the comfort of my bed ?
Or how should sleep possess my faculties,
Wanting the proper closer of mine eyes ?
  Mont. Then will I never more sleep nigh
from thee.
All mine own business, all the king's affairs, 100
Shall take the day to serve them ; every night
I 'll ever dedicate to thy delight.
  Ta. Nay, good my lord, esteem not my de-
  sires
Such doters on their humours that my judgment
Cannot subdue them to your worthier pleasure ;
A wife's pleas'd husband must her object be   106
In all her acts, not her sooth'd fantasy.

  [5] As the stone is made to accord with the line, and
not vice versa, so nature brings our powers into accord
with her will.
  [6] Dressed.

Mont. Then come, my love, now pay those
    rites to sleep
Thy fair eyes owe him ; shall we now to bed ?
   Ta. Oh, no, my lord ; your holy friar says 110
All couplings in the day that touch the bed
Adulterous are, even in the married ;
Whose grave and worthy doctrine, well I know,
Your faith in him will liberally allow.[1]   114
   Mont. He 's a most learned and religious man ;
Come to the presence then, and see great
    D'Ambois
(Fortune's proud mushroom shot up in a night)
Stand like an Atlas under our King's arm ;
Which greatness[2] with him Monsieur now en-
    vies
As bitterly and deadly as the Guise.   120
   Ta. What, he that was but yesterday his
    maker,
His raiser and preserver ?
   Mont.   Even the same.
Each natural agent works but to this end,
To render that it works on like itself ;
Which since the Monsieur in his act on D'Am-
    bois   125
Cannot to his ambitious end effect,
But that, quite opposite, the King hath power
In his love borne to D'Ambois, to convert
The point of Monsieur's aim on his own breast,
He turns his outward love to inward hate. 130
A prince's love is like the lightning's fume,
Which no man can embrace, but must con-
    sume.   *Exeunt.*

[SCENE II.][3]

Enter HENRY, D'AMBOIS, Monsieur, GUISE,
Duchess, ANNABELLE, CHARLOTTE, Attendants.

   He. Speak home, my Bussy ; thy impartial
    words
Are like brave falcons that dare truss[4] a fowl
Much greater than themselves ; flatterers are
    kites
That check at[5] sparrows ; thou shalt be my
    eagle,
And bear my thunder underneath thy wings ;
Truth's words like jewels hang in th' ears of
    kings.   6
   Bu. Would I might live to see no Jews hang
    there
Instead of jewels ; sycophants, I mean,
Who use truth like the devil, his true foe,
Cast by the angel to the pit of fears,   10
And bound in chains ; truth seldom decks kings'
    ears.
Slave Flattery (like a rippier's[6] legs roll'd up
In boots of hay ropes) with kings' soothed guts
Swaddl'd and strappl'd,[7] now lives only free.
Oh, 't is a subtle knave ; how like the plague 15
Unfelt he strikes into the brain of man.
And rageth in his entrails, when he can,
Worse than the poison of a red-hair'd man ![8]

<hr>

[1] Approve.
[2] High favor.
[3] A room in the Court.
[4] Seize.
[5] Pursue.
[6] Fisherman.
[7] Bound.
[8] A traitor : Judas's hair was represented as red in
old paintings, tapestries, etc.

He. Fly at him and his brood ; I cast thee off,
And once more give thee surname of mine
    eagle.   20
   Bu. I 'll make you sport enough, then ; let
    me have
My lucerns[9] too, or dogs inur'd to hunt
Beasts of most rapine, but to put them up,[10]
And if I truss not, let me not be trusted.
Show me a great man (by the people's voice, 25
Which is the voice of God) that by his great-
    ness
Bombasts[11] his private roofs with public riches ;
That affects royalty, rising from a clapdish ; [12]
That rules so much more by[13] his suffering king,
That he makes kings of his subordinate
    slaves :   30
Himself and them graduate like woodmongers,
Piling a stack of billets from the earth,
Raising each other into steeples' heights ;
Let him convey this on the turning props
Of Protean law, and, his own counsel keeping,
Keep all upright ; let me but hawk at him, 36
I 'll play the vulture, and so thump his liver,
That, like a huge unlading Argosy,
He shall confess all, and you then may hang
    him.
Show me a clergyman, that is in voice   40
A lark of heaven, in heart a mole of earth ;
That hath good living, and a wicked life ;
A temperate look, and a luxurious gut ;
Turning the rents of his superfluous cures
Into your pheasants and your partridges ; 45
Venting their quintessence as men read He-
    brew ; [14]
Let me but hawk at him, and, like the other,
He shall confess all, and you then may hang him.
Show me a lawyer that turns sacred law
(The equal rend'rer of each man his own, 50
The scourge of rapine and extortion,
The sanctuary and impregnable defence
Of retir'd learning and besieged virtue)
Into a harpy, that eats all but 's own,
Into the damned sins it punisheth ; 55
Into the synagogue of thieves and atheists,
Blood into gold, and justice into lust ;
Let me but hawk at him, as at the rest,
He shall confess all, and you then may hang him.

Enter MONTSURRY, TAMYRA, *and* PERO.

   Gu. Where will you find such game as you
    would hawk at ?   60
   Bu. I 'll hawk about your house for one of
    them.
   Gu. Come, y' are a glorious[15] ruffian, and run
    proud
Of the King's headlong graces. Hold your
    breath,
Or, by that poison'd vapour, not the King
Shall back your murderous valour against me.

<hr>

[9] Hunting dogs.   [10] Start them.   [11] Stuffs out.
[12] Dish carried by beggars, who clapped the lid to attract notice.
[13] *I. e.* by the sufferance or indulgence of his king.
Qq. 1607, 8 read *than.*
[14] *I. e.* backwards. Reversing the proper use of his
income.
[15] Boastful.

Bu. I would the King would make his pres-
ence free   66
But for one bout betwixt us : by the reverence
Due to the sacred space 'twixt kings and sub-
jects,
Here would I make thee cast that popular
purple,
In which thy proud soul sits and braves thy
sovereign.   70
Mo. Peace, peace, I pray thee peace.
Bu.   Let him peace first
That made the first war.
Mo.   He 's the better man.
Bu. And therefore may do worst ?
Mo.   He has more titles.
Bu. So Hydra had more heads.
Mo.   He 's greater known.
Bu. His greatness is the people's ; mine's
mine own.   75
Mo. He 's nobler[1] born.
Bu.   He is not, I am noble;
And noblesse in his blood hath no gradation,
But in his merit.
Gu.   Th' art not nobly born,
But bastard to the Cardinal of Ambois.
Bu. Thou liest, proud Guiserd. Let me fly,
my lord.   80
He. Not in my face, my eagle ; violence flies
The sanctuaries of a prince's eyes.
Bu. Still shall we chide and foam upon this
bit ?
Is the Guise only great in faction ?
Stands he not by himself ? Proves he th' opin-
ion   85
That men's souls are without them ? Be a duke,
And lead me to the field.
Gu.   Come, follow me.
He. Stay them ! Stay, D' Ambois. Cousin
Guise, I wonder
Your honour'd disposition brooks so ill
A man so good, that only would uphold   90
Man in his native noblesse, from whose fall
All our dimensions rise ; that in himself
(Without the outward patches of our frailty,
Riches and honour) knows he comprehends
Worth with the greatest. Kings had never
borne   95
Such boundless empire over other men,
Had all maintain'd the spirit and state of
D' Ambois ;
Nor had the full impartial hand of nature
That all things gave in her original[2]   99
Without these definite terms of mine and thine,
Been turn'd unjustly to the hand of Fortune,
Had all preserv'd her in her prime, like D' Am-
bois.
No envy, no disjunction had dissolv'd,
Or pluck'd one stick out of the golden faggot
In which the world of Saturn[3] bound our lives,
Had all been held together with the nerves, 105
The genius, and th' ingenious[4] soul of D' Am-
bois.
Let my hand therefore be the Hermean rod[5]

[1] Qq. *noble.*   [3] The fabled Golden Age.
[2] In the beginning.   [4] Qq. 1607, 8 read *ingenuous.*
[5] The caduceus which was wreathed with two serpents that clung to it when separated by Hermes.

To part and reconcile, and so conserve you,
As my combin'd embracers and supporters. 110
Bu. 'T is our king's motion, and we shall not
seem
To worst eyes womanish, though we change
thus soon
Never so great grudge for his greater pleas-
ure.
Gu. I seal to that ; and, so the manly freedom
That you so much profess, hereafter prove
not   115
A bold and glorious license to deprave,[6]
To me his hand shall hold the Hermean virtue
His grace affects, in which submissive sign
On this his sacred right hand I lay mine.
Bu. 'T is well, my lord, and so your worthy
greatness   120
Decline not to the greater insolence,
Nor make you think it a prerogative
To rack men's freedoms with the ruder wrongs ;
My hand (stuck full of laurel, in true sign
'T is wholly dedicate to righteous peace)   125
In all submission kisseth th' other side.
He. Thanks to ye both ; and kindly I invite
ye
Both to a banquet, where we 'll sacrifice
Full cups to confirmation of your loves ;   129
At which, fair ladies, I entreat your presence ;
And hope you, madam, will take one carouse
For reconcilement of your lord and servant.
Du. If I should fail, my lord, some other
lady
Would be found there to do that for my servant.
Mo. Any of these here ?
Du.   Nay, I know not that.
Bu. Think your thoughts like my mistress ',
honour'd lady ?   136
Ta. I think not on you, sir ; y' are one I
know not.
Bu. Cry you mercy, madam.
Mont.   Oh, sir, has she met you ?
Exeunt HENRY, D'AMBOIS, Ladies.
Mo. What had my bounty drunk when it
rais'd him ?
Gu. Y' ave stuck us up a very worthy flag, 140
That takes more wind than we with all our
sails.
Mo. Oh, so he spreads and flourishes.
Gu.   He must down ;
Upstarts should never perch too near a crown.
Mo. 'T is true, my lord ; and as this doting
hand,   144
Even out of earth, like Juno, struck this giant,
So Jove's great ordinance shall be here impli'd
To strike him under th' Etna of his pride ;
To which work lend your hands, and let us
cast[7]
Where we may set snares for his ranging great-
ness.   149
I think it best, amongst our greatest women ;
For there is no such trap to catch an upstart
As a loose downfall ; for you know their falls
Are th' ends of all men's rising. If great men
And wise make scapes[8] to please advantage[9]

[6] Slander.   [7] Plan.   [8] Escapades.
[9] To give advantage to their enemies.

'T is with a woman : women that worst may   155
Still hold men's candles ;[1] they direct and
    know
All things amiss in all men ; and their women [2]
All things amiss in them ; through whose
    charm'd mouths,
We may see all the close scapes[3] of the Court.
When the most royal beast of chase, the hart,
(Being old and cunning in his lairs and haunts)
Can never be discovered to the bow,   162
The piece,[4] or hound ; yet where, behind some
    quitch,[5]
He breaks his gall, and rutteth with his hind,
The place is markt, and by his venery   165
He still is taken. Shall we then attempt
The chiefest mean to that discovery here,
And court our greatest ladies' chiefest women
With shows of love and liberal promises ?   169
'T is but our breath. If something given in hand
Sharpens their hopes of more, 't will be well
    ventur'd.
  Gu. No doubt of that ; and 't is the cun-
    ning'st point
Of your devis'd investigation.
  Mo.   I have broken
The ice to it already with the woman
Of your chaste lady, and conceive good hope   175
I shall wade thorough to some wished shore
At our next meeting.
  Mont.   Nay, there 's small hope there.
  Gu. Take say[6] of her, my lord, she comes
    most fitly.
  Mo. Starting back ?

Enter CHARLOTTE, ANNABELLE, PERO.

  Gu. Y' are engag'd, indeed.   180
  An. Nay, pray, my lord, forbear.
  Mont. What, skittish, servant ?
  An. No, my lord, I am not so fit for your service.
  Ch. Pray pardon me now, my lord ; my lady
excepts me.   186
  Gu. I 'll satisfy her expectation, as far as an
uncle may.
  Mo. Well said ; a spirit of courtship of all
hands. Now mine own Pero, hast thou re-   190
memb'red me for the discovery I entreated thee
make of thy mistress? Speak boldly, and be
sure of all things I have sworn to thee.
  Pe. Building on that assurance, my lord, I
may break ; and much the rather, because [195
my lady hath not trusted me with that I can
tell you ; for now I cannot be said to betray her.
  Mo. That 's all one, so we reach our objects.
Forth, I beseech thee.
  Pe. To tell you truth, my lord, I have made
a strange discovery.   201
  Mo. Excellent, Pero, thou reviv'st me. May
I sink quick to perdition if my tongue discover[7] it.
  Pe. 'T is thus, then : this last night, my lord
lay forth, and I watching my lady's sitting [206
up, stole up at midnight from my pallet ; and
(having before made a hole both through the

---

wall and arras to her inmost chamber) I saw
D'Ambois and herself reading a letter.   216
  Mo. D'Ambois ?
  Pe. Even he, my lord.
  Mo. Dost thou not dream, wench ?
  Pe. I swear he is the man.
  Mo. The devil he is, and thy lady his [21F
dam ! Why, this was the happiest shot that ever
flew ! The just plague of hypocrisy levell'd it.
Oh, the infinite regions betwixt a woman's
tongue and her heart ! Is this our goddess of [219
chastity ? I thought I could not be so slighted
if she had not her fraught besides, and therefore plotted this with her woman, never dreaming of D'Ambois. Dear Pero, I will advance
thee for ever ; but tell me now, — God's precious, it transforms me with admiration[8] — [225
sweet Pero, whom should she trust with this
conveyance ? Or, all the doors being made sure,
how should his conveyance be made ?
  Pe. Nay, my lord, that amazes[9] me ; I cannot
by any study so much as guess at it.   230
  Mo. Well, let 's favour our apprehensions with
forbearing that a little ; for if my heart
were not hoopt with adamant, the conceit[10] of
this would have burst it. But hark thee.
                                        Whispers.
  [*Ch.* I swear to you grace, all that I can [235
conjecture touching my lady your niece, is a
strong affection she bears to the English Mylor.
  Gu. All, quod you ? 'T is enough, I assure
you, but tell me.][11]
  Mont. I pray thee, resolve me : the duke [240
will never imagine that I am busy about 's
wife : hath D'Ambois any privy access to her ?
  An. No, my lord ; D'Ambois neglects her, as
she takes it, and is therefore suspicious that
either your lady, or the Lady Beaupre [245
hath closely[12] entertain'd him.
  Mont. By 'r lady, a likely suspicion, and
very near the life, [if she marks it,][13] especially
of my wife.
  Mo. Come, we'll disguise all with seeming [250
only to have courted.— Away, dry palm ! sh'as
a liver as dry as a biscuit ; a man may go a
whole voyage with her, and get nothing but
tempests from her windpipe.
  Gu. Here 's one, I think, has swallowed a [255
porcupine, she casts pricks from her tongue so.
  Mont. And here 's a peacock seems to have
devour'd one of the Alps, she has so swelling a
spirit, and is so cold of her kindness.   259
  Ch. We are no windfalls, my lord ; ye must
gather us with the ladder of matrimony, or
we 'll hang till we be rotten.
  Mo. Indeed, that 's the way to make ye right
openarses.[15] But, alas ! ye have no portions fit
for such husbands as we wish you.   265
  Pe. Portions, my lord ? Yes, and such portions as your principality cannot purchase.
  Mo. What, woman ? what are those portions ?
  Pe. Riddle my riddle, my lord.
  Mo. Ay, marry, wench, I think thy portion [270

---

[8] Wonder.   [9] Bewilders.   [10] Thought.
[11] These two speeches are omitted in Q 1641.
[12] Secretly.   [14] A sign of chastity.
[13] Q. 1641 omits.   [15] Medlars.

---

[1] Be accomplices,   [4] Gun.   [6] Make trial.
[2] Waiting-women.   [5] Grass.   [7] Reveal.
[3] Escapades.

is a right riddle, a man shall never find it out
But let 's hear it.
Pe. You shall, my lord.
What 's that, that being most rare 's most cheap ?
That when you sow, you never reap ?   275
That when it grows most, most you thin 1 *it ?*
And still you lose it when you win it ;
That when 't is commonest, 't is dearest,
And when 't is farthest off, 't is nearest ?

Mo. Is this your great portion ?   280
Pe. Even this, my lord.
Mo. Believe me, I cannot riddle it.
Pe. No, my lord : 't is my chastity, which you
shall neither riddle nor fiddle.
Mo. Your chastity ? Let me begin with the [285
end of it ; how is a woman's chastity nearest
a man when 't is furthest off ?
Pe. Why, my lord, when you cannot get it,
it goes to th' heart on you : and that, I think,
comes most near you : and I am sure it [290
shall be far enough off. And so we leave you to
our mercies.   *Exeunt* Women.
Mo. Farewell, riddle.
Gu. Farewell, medlar.
Mont. Farewell, winter plum.   295
Mo. Now, my lords, what fruit of our inquisition ? Feel you nothing budding yet ? Speak,
good my Lord Montsurry.
Mont. Nothing but this : D'Ambois is thought
negligent in observing the duchess, and [300
therefore she is suspicious that your niece or my
wife closely entertains him.
Mo. Your wife, my lord ? Think you that
possible ?
Mont. Alas, I know she flies him like her last
hour.   306
Mo. Her last hour ? Why, that comes upon
her the more she flies it. Does D'Ambois so,
think you ?
Mont. That 's not worth the answering. 'T is
miraculous to think with what monsters [311
women's imaginations engross them when they
are once enamour'd, and what wonders they
will work for their satisfaction. They will make
sheep valiant, a lion fearful.   315
Mo. [*Aside.*] And an ass confident. — Well,
my lord, more will come forth shortly ; get you
to the banquet.
Gu. Come, my lord ; I have the blind side of
one of them.   *Exit* GUISE *cum* MONTSURRY. 320
Mo. Oh, the unsounded sea of women's bloods,
That when 't is calmest, is most dangerous ;
Not any wrinkle creaming in their faces
When in their hearts are Scylla and Charybdis,
Which still are hid in dark and standing fogs, 325
Where never day shines, nothing never grows
But weeds and poisons, that no statesman knows,
Nor Cerberus ever saw the damned nooks
Hid with the veils of women's virtuous looks.
²But what a cloud of sulphur have I drawn 330

---

1 Boas emend. Qq. *in.*
2 In place of the following fifteen lines, Qq. 1607, 8
read,

I will conceal all yet, and give more time
To D'Ambois' trial, now upon my hook.

Up to my bosom in this dangerous secret !
Which if my haste with any spark should light,
Ere D'Ambois were engag'd in some sure plot,
I were blown up ; he would be sure my death.
Would I had never known it, for before 335
I shall persuade th' importance to Montsurry,
And make him with some studied stratagem
Train D'Ambois to his wreak, his maid may
tell it,
Or I (out of my fiery thirst to play
With the fell tiger, up in darkness tied, 340
And give it some light) make it quite break
loose.
I fear it, afore heaven, and will not see
D'Ambois again, till I have told Montsurry
And set a snare with him to free my fears :
Who 's there ?

Enter MAFFE.

Ma.   My lord ?
Mo.   Go call the Count Montsurry,
And make the doors fast ; I will speak with
none   345
Till he come to me.
Ma.   Well, my lord. *Exiturus.*
Mo.   Or else
Send you some other, and see all the doors
Made safe yourself, I pray ; haste, fly about it.
Ma. You 'll speak with none but with the
Count Montsurry ?   350
Mo. With none but he, except it be the Guise.
Ma. See even by this, there 's one exception
more !
Your grace must be more firm in the command,
Or else shall I as weakly execute.   355
The Guise shall speak with you ?
Mo.   He shall, I say.
Ma. And Count Montsurry ?
Mo.   Ay, and Count Montsurry.
Ma. Your grace must pardon me, that I am
bold
To urge the clear and full sense of your pleasure ;
Which whensoever I have known, I hope 360
Your grace will say, I hit it to a hair.
Mo. You have.
Ma.   I hope so, or I would be glad —
Mo. I pray thee get thee gone, thou art so
tedious
In the strict form of all thy services
That I had better have one negligent. 365
You hit my pleasure well, when D'Ambois hit
you ;
Did you not, think you ?
Ma.   D'Ambois ? Why, my lord —
Mo. I pray thee talk no more, but shut the
doors :
Do what I charge thee.
Ma.   I will, my lord, and yet
I would be glad the wrong I had of D'Ambois —
Mo. Precious ! then it is a fate that plagues
me   371

He awes my throat, else, like Sybilla's care,
It should breathe oracles. I fear him strangely,
And may resemble his advanced valour
Unto a spirit rais'd without a circle,
Endangering him that ignorantly rais'd him,
And for whose fury he hath learn'd no limit.

In this man's foolery ; I may be murdered
While he stands on protection of his folly.
Avaunt about thy charge.
Ma.   I go, my lord. —
I had my head broke in his faithful service ; 375
I had no suit the more, nor any thanks,
And yet my teeth must still be hit with D'Am-
    bois :
D'Ambois, my lord, shall know —
Mo.   The devil and D'Ambois !
                      Exit MAFFE.
How am I tortur'd with this trusty fool !
Never was any curious in his place   380
To do things justly, but he was an ass ;
We cannot find one trusty that is witty,[1]
And therefore bear their disproportion.
Grant thou, great star and angel of my life,
A sure lease of it but for some few days,   385
That I may clear my bosom of the snake
I cherish there, and I will then defy
All check to it but Nature's, and her altars
Shall crack with vessels crown'd with every
    liquor
Drawn from her highest and most bloody hu-
    mours.   390
I fear him strangely, his advanced valour
Is like a spirit rais'd without a circle,
Endangering him that ignorantly rais'd him,
And for whose fury he hath learnt no limit.

        Enter MAFFE *hastily.*

Ma. I cannot help it: what should I do
    more ?   395
As I was gathering a fit guard to make
My passage to the doors, and the doors sure,
The man of blood is enter'd.
Mo.   Rage of death !
If I had told the secret, and he knew it,
Thus had I been endanger'd.

        Enter D'AMBOIS.

                    My sweet heart !
How now, what leap'st thou at ?
Bu.   O royal object !
Mo. Thou dream'st, awake ; object in th'
    empty air ?   402
Bu. Worthy the brows of Titan, worth his
    chair.
Mo. Pray thee, what mean'st thou ?
Bu.   See you not a crown
Impale the forehead of the great King Mon-
    sieur ?   405
Mo. Oh, fie upon thee !
Bu.   Prince, that is the subject
Of all these your retir'd and sole discourses.
Mo. Wilt thou not leave that wrongful sup-
    position ?
Bu. Why wrongful, to suppose the doubtless
    right
To the succession worth the thinking on ? 410
Mo. Well, leave these jests. How I am over-
    joyed
With thy wish'd presence, and how fit thou
    com'st,
For of mine honour I was sending for thee.

              [1] Clever, sensible.

Bu. To what end ?
Mo.   Only for thy company,
Which I have still in thought ; but that 's no
    payment   415
On thy part made with personal appearance.
Thy absence so long suffered, oftentimes
Put me in some little doubt thou dost not love
    me.
Wilt thou do one thing therefore now sincerely ?
Bu. Ay, anything, but killing of the King.
Mo. Still in that discord, and ill-taken note ?
How most unseasonable thou play'st the
    cuckoo,   422
In this thy fall of friendship !
Bu.   Then do not doubt,
That there is any act within my nerves
But killing of the King, that is not yours. 425
Mo. I will not, then ; to prove which by my
    love
Shown to thy virtues, and by all fruits else
Already sprung from that still-flourishing tree,
With whatsoever may hereafter spring,
I charge thee utter (even with all the freedom
Both of thy noble nature and thy friendship) 431
The full and plain state of me in thy thoughts.
Bu. What, utter plainly what I think of
    you ?
Mo. Plain as truth.
Bu. Why, this swims quite against the stream
    of greatness ;   435
Great men would rather hear their flatteries,
And if they be not made fools, are not wise.
Mo. I am no such great fool, and therefore
    charge thee
Even from the root of thy free heart, display
    me.
Bu. Since you affect [2] it in such serious terms,
If yourself first will tell me what you think 441
As freely and as heartily of me,
I 'll be as open in my thoughts of you.
Mo. A bargain, of mine honour ; and make
    this,
That prove we in our full dissection   445
Never so foul, live still the sounder friends.
Bu. What else, sir ? Come, pay me home ;
    I 'll bide it bravely.
Mo. I will swear. I think thee then a man
That dares as much as a wild horse or tiger ;
As headstrong and as bloody ; and to feed 450
The ravenous wolf of thy most cannibal valour,
(Rather than not employ it) thou wouldst turn
Hackster [3] to any whore, slave to a Jew
Or English usurer, to force possessions
(And cut men's throats) of mortgaged estates ;
Or thou wouldst 'tire thee like a tinker's
    strumpet,   456
And murder market-folks, quarrel with sheep,
And run as mad as Ajax ; serve a butcher,
Do anything but killing of the King :
That in thy valour th' art like other naturals [4]
That have strange gifts in nature, but no soul 461
Diffus'd quite through, to make them of a piece,
But stop at humours that are more absurd,
Childish and villanous than that hackster,
    whore,

    [2] Desire.   [3] Professional gallant.   [4] Idiots.

Slave, cut-throat, tinker's bitch, compar'd
　　before;　　　　　　　　　　　　　　　465
And in those humours wouldst envy, betray,
Slander, blaspheme, change each hour a reli-
　　gion;
Do anything but killing of the King:
That in thy valour (which is still the dung-hill,
To which hath reference all filth in thy house)
Th' art more ridiculous and vain-glorious　471
Than any mountebank, and impudent
Than any painted bawd; which, not to soothe
And glorify thee like a Jupiter Hammon,
Thou eat'st thy heart in vinegar; and thy gall
Turns all thy blood to poison, which is cause　476
Of that toad-pool that stands in thy complexion,
And makes thee with a cold and earthy moisture,
(Which is the dam of putrefaction)
As plague to thy damn'd pride, rot as thou
　　liv'st;　　　　　　　　　　　　　　　480
To study calumnies and treacheries;
To thy friends' slaughters like a screech-owl
　　sing,
And do all mischiefs — but to kill the King.
　　Bu. So! have you said?
　　Mo.　　　　How think'st thou? Do I flatter?
Speak I not like a trusty friend to thee?　485
　　Bu. That ever any man was blest withal.
So here's for me. I think you are (at worst)
No devil, since y' are like to be no king;
Of which, with any friend of yours, I 'll lay
This poor stillado [1] here, 'gainst all the stars,
Ay, and 'gainst all your treacheries, which are
　　more;　　　　　　　　　　　　　　　491
That you did never good, but to do ill;
But ill of all sorts, free and for itself:
That (like a murdering piece, making lanes in
　　armies,
The first man of a rank, the whole rank falling)
If you have wrong'd one man, you are so far　496
From making him amends that all his race,
Friends, and associates, fall into your chase:
That y' are for perjuries the very prince
Of all intelligencers; [2] and your voice　500
Is like an eastern wind, that where it flies
Knits nets of caterpillars, with which you catch
The prime of all the fruits the kingdom yields.
That your political head is the curst fount
Of all the violence, rapine, cruelty,　505
Tyranny, and atheism flowing through the
　　realm.
That y 'ave a tongue so scandalous, 't will cut
The purest crystal; and a breath that will
Kill to [3] that wall a spider. You will jest
With God, and your soul to the devil tender　510
For lust; kiss horror, and with death engender.
That your foul body is a Lernean fen
Of all the maladies breeding in all men;
That you are utterly without a soul;　514
And, for your life, the thread of that was spun
When Clotho slept, and let her breathing rock [4]
Fall in the dirt; and Lachesis still draws it,
Dipping her twisting fingers in a bowl
Defil'd, and crown'd with virtue's forced soul.
And lastly (which I must for gratitude　520

---

[1] Stiletto　　[2] Spies.　　[3] At the distance of.
[4] " The distaff from whence she draws the breath of
life." (Dilke.)

Ever remember) that of all my height
And dearest life, you are the only spring,
Only in royal hope to kill the king.
　　Mo. Why, now I see thou lov'st me. Come
to the banquet.　　　　　　　　　*Exeunt.*

ACT IV

SCENE I.[5]

[*Enter*] HENRY, Monsieur, *with a letter;* GUISE,
MONTSURRY, BUSSY, ELENOR, TAMYRA,
BEAUPRE, PERO, CHARLOTTE, ANNABELLE,
PYRA, *with four* Pages.

　　He. Ladies, ye have not done our banquet
　　right,
Nor lookt upon it with those cheerful rays
That lately turn'd your breaths to floods of
　　gold;
Your looks, methinks, are not drawn out with
　　thoughts
So clear and free as heretofore, but foul,　5
As if the thick complexions of men
Govern'd within them.
　　Bu.　　　　'T is not like, my lord,
That men in women rule, but contrary;
For as the moon (of all things God created)
Not only is the most appropriate image　10
Or glass to show them how they wax and wane,
But in her height and motion likewise bears
Imperial influences that command
In all their powers, and make them wax and
　　wane;　　　　　　　　　　　　　　14
So women, that (of all things made of nothing)
Are the most perfect idols of the moon,
Or still-unwean'd sweet moon-calves with white
　　faces,
Not only are patterns of change to men,
But as the tender moonshine of their beauties
Clears or is cloudy, make men glad or sad;　20
So then they rule in men, not men in them.
　　Mo. But here the moons are chang'd, (as the
　　King notes)
And either men rule in them, or some power
Beyond their voluntary faculty,
For nothing can recover their lost faces.　25
　　Mont. None can be always one: our griefs and
　　joys
Hold several sceptres in us, and have times
For their divided empires: which grief now, in
　　them
Doth prove as proper to his diadem.
　　Bu. And grief 's a natural sickness of the
　　blood,　　　　　　　　　　　　　30
That time to part asks, as his coming had;
Only slight fools griev'd suddenly are glad.
A man may say t' a dead man, " Be reviv'd,"
As well as to one sorrowful, " Be not griev'd,"
And therefore, princely mistress,[6] in all wars　35
Against these base foes that insult on weakness,
And still fight hous'd behind the shield of Na-
　　ture,
Of privilege, law, treachery, or beastly need,

---

[5] The Banqueting Hall in the Court.
[6] Duchess of Guise.

Your servant [1] cannot help ; authority here
Goes with corruption: something like some
   states, 40
That back worst men : valour to them must creep
That, to themselves left, would fear him asleep.
Du. Ye all take that for granted that doth
   rest
Yet to be prov'd ; we all are as we were,
As merry and as free in thought as ever. 45
Gu. And why then can ye not disclose your
   thoughts ?
Ta. Methinks the man hath answer'd for us
   well.
Mo. The man ? Why, madam, d' ye not know
   his name ?
Ta. Man is a name of honour for a king : 49
Additions [2] take away from each chief thing:
The school of modesty not to learn learns dames:
They sit in high forms [3] there, that know men's
   names.
Mo. [*to* BUSSY.] Hark ! sweetheart, here's a
   bar set to your valour ;
It cannot enter here ; no, not to notice 54
Of what your name is. Your great eagle's beak
(Should you fly at her) had as good encounter
An Albion cliff, as her more craggy liver. [4]
Bu. I 'll not attempt her, sir ; her sight and
   name
(By which I only know her) doth deter me. 59
He. So do they all men else.
Mo.   You would say so
If you knew all.
Ta.   Knew all, my lord ? What mean you ?
Mo. All that I know, madam.
Ta.   That you know ? Speak it.
Mo. No, 't is enough. I feel it.
He.   But, methinks
Her courtship is more pure than heretofore ; 64
True courtiers should be modest, but not nice ; [5]
Bold, but not impudent ; pleasure love, not vice.
Mo. Sweetheart ! come hither, what if one
   should make
Horns at Montsurry ? Would it not strike him
   jealous
Through all the proofs of his chaste lady's vir-
   tues ?
Bu. If he be wise, not. 70
Mo. What ? Not if I should name the gard-
   ener
That I would have him think hath grafted him ?
Bu. So the large licence that your greatness
   uses
To jest at all men may be taught indeed
To make a difference of the grounds you play
   on, 75
Both in the men you scandal, and the matter.
Mo. As how ? as how ?
Bu.   Perhaps led with a train,
Where you may have your nose made less and
   slit,
Your eyes thrust out.
Mo.   Peace, peace, I pray thee peace. 79
Who dares do that ? The brother of his king ?

[1] D'Ambois, who still keeps up the pretence of being
the Duchess's courtly lover.
[2] Titles.   [4] Supposed seat of passion.
[3] *I. e.* in disgrace.   [5] Over-fastidious.

Bu. Were your king brother in you ; all your
   powers
(Stretcht in the arms of great men and their
   bawds),
Set close down by you ; all your stormy laws
Spouted with lawyers' mouths, and gushing
   blood
Like to so many torrents; all your glories 85
Making you terrible, like enchanted flames
Fed with bare cockscombs [6] and with crooked
   hams ; [6]
All your prerogatives, your shames, and tor-
   tures ;
All daring heaven, and opening hell about
   you ; — 89
Were I the man ye wrong'd so and provok'd,
Though ne'er so much beneath you, like a box-
   tree
I would out of the roughness of my root
Ram hardness, in my lowness, and like death
Mounted on earthquakes, I would trot through
   all
Honours and horrors, thorough foul and fair, 95
And from your whole strength toss you into the
   air.
Mo. Go, th' art a devil ; such another spirit
Could not be 'still'd from all th' Armenian dra-
   gons.
O my love's glory ! Heir to all I have,
(That 's all I can say, and that all I swear) 100
If thou outlive me, as I know thou must,
Or else hath nature no proportion'd end
To her great labours ; she hath breath'd a mind
Into thy entrails, of desert to swell
Into another great Augustus Cæsar ; 105
Organs and faculties fitted to her greatness ;
And should that perish like a common spirit,
Nature 's a courtier and regards no merit.
He. Here 's nought but whispering with us ;
   like a calm
Before a tempest, when the silent air 110
Lays her soft ear close to the earth to hearken
For that she fears steals on to ravish her ;
Some fate doth join our ears to hear it coming.
Come, my brave eagle, let 's to covert fly ;
I see almighty Aether in the smoke 115
Of all his clouds descending ; and the sky
Hid in the dim ostents [7] of tragedy.
   Exit HENRY *with* D'AMBOIS *and* Ladies.
Gu. Now stir the humour, and begin the
   brawl.
Mont. The King and D'Ambois now are
   grown all one. 119
Mo. Nay, they are two, [8] my lord.
Mont.   How 's that ?
Mo.   No more.
Mont. I must have more, my lord.
Mo.   What, more than two ?
Mont. How monstrous is this !
Mo.   Why ?
Mont.   You make me horns.
Mo. Not I ; it is a work without my power,
Married men's ensigns are not made with fin-
   gers.

[6] Signs of the sycophant.
[7] Manifestations.
[8] Monsieur here makes the gesture of the cuckold.

Of divine fabric they are, not men's hands. 125
Your wife, you know, is a mere [1] Cynthia,
And she must fashion horns out of her nature.
  Mont. But doth she — dare you charge her?
Speak, false prince.
  Mo. I must not speak, my lord; but if you 'll
use
The learning of a nobleman, and read, 130
Here 's something to those points; soft, you
must pawn [2]
Your honour having read it to return it.
  Mont. Not I. I pawn my honour for a pa-
per!
  Mo. You must not buy it under.
          Exeunt GUISE *and* Monsieur.
  Mont.　　　　　　　　Keep it then,
And keep fire in your bosom.
  Ta.　　　　　　　　What says he?
  Mont. You must make good the rest.
  Ta.　　　　　　　How fares my lord?
Takes my love anything to heart he says? 137
  Mont. Come y' are a ——
  Ta.　　　　　　What, my lord?
  Mont.　　　　　　The plague of Herod
Feast in his rotten entrails.
  Ta.　　　　　　Will you wreak
Your anger's just cause given by him, on me?
  Mont. By him?
  Ta.　　　By him, my lord. I have admir'd [3]
You could all this time be at concord with him,
That still hath play'd such discords on your hon-
our. 143
  Mont. Perhaps 't is with some proud string of
my wife's.
  Ta. How 's that, my lord?
  Mont.　　Your tongue will still admire, 145
Till my head be the miracle of the world.
  Ta. Oh, woe is me!　　*She seems to swound.*
  Pe.　　What does your lordship mean?
Madam, be comforted; my lord but tries you.
Madam! Help, good my lord, are you not
mov'd?
Do your set looks print in your words your
thoughts? 150
Sweet lord, clear up those eyes,
Unbend that masking forehead; whence is it
You rush upon her with these Irish wars,
More full of sound than hurt? But it is enough;
You have shot home, your words are in her
heart; 155
She has not liv'd to bear a trial now.
  Mont. Look up, my love. and by this kiss re-
ceive
My soul amongst the spirits for supply
To thine, chas'd with my fury.
  Ta.　　　　　　Oh, my lord,
I have too long liv'd to hear this from you. 160
  Mont. 'T was from my troubled blood, and
not from me.
I know not how I fare; a sudden night
Flows through my entrails, and a headlong
chaos
Murmurs within me, which I must digest,
And not drown her in my confusions, 165
That was my life's joy, being best inform'd.

     Absolute.　　**2 Pledge.**　　**3 Wondered.**

Sweet, you must needs forgive me, that my love
(Like to a fire disdaining his suppression)
Rag'd being discourag'd; my whole heart is
wounded 169
When any least thought in you is but toucht,
And shall be till I know your former merits;
Your name and memory altogether crave
In just oblivion their eternal grave;
And then you must hear from me, there's no
mean
In any passion I shall feel for you. 175
Love is a razor, cleansing being well us'd,
But fetcheth blood still being the least abus'd.
To tell you briefly all: the man that left me
When you appear'd, did turn me worse than
woman,
And stabb'd me to the heart thus, with his fin-
gers.[4] 180
  Ta. Oh, happy woman! Comes my stain from
him,
It is my beauty, and that innocence proves
That slew Chimaera, rescued Peleus
From all the savage beasts in Pelion;
And rais'd the chaste Athenian prince [5] from
hell; 185
All suffering with me, they for women's lusts,
I for a man's, that the Augean stable
Of his foul sin would empty in my lap.
How his guilt shunn'd me, sacred innocence
That where thou fear'st, art dreadful! [6] and his
face 190
Turn'd in flight from thee, that had thee in
chase!
Come, bring me to him; I will tell the serpent
Even to his venom'd teeth (from whose curst
seed
A pitcht field starts up 'twixt my lord and me)
That his throat lies, and he shall curse his fin-
gers, 195
For being so govern'd by his filthy soul.
  Mont. I know not if himself will vaunt t' have
been
The princely author of the slavish sin,
Or any other; he would have resolv'd [7] me
Had you not come; not by his word, but writing,
Would I have sworn to give it him again, 201
And pawn'd mine honour to him for a paper.
  Ta. See how he flies me still; 't is a foul heart
That fears his own hand. Good my lord, make
haste
To see the dangerous paper; papers hold
Oft-times the forms and copies of our souls, 206
And, though the world despise them, are the
prizes
Of all our honours; make your honour then
A hostage for it, and with it confer
My nearest woman here, in all she knows; 210
Who (if the sun or Cerberus could have seen
Any stain in me) might as well as they;
And, Pero, here I charge thee by my love,
And all proofs of it (which I might call bounties),
By all that thou hast seen seem good in me, 215
And all the ill which thou shouldst spit from
thee,

    4 Making horns.　　　　**5** Hippolytus.
    6 Art feared even by those thou fearest.
    7 Informed.

By pity of the wound this touch hath given me,
Not as thy mistress now, but a poor woman,
To death given over, rid me of my pains,   219
Pour on thy powder ; clear thy breast of me ;
My lord is only here ; here speak thy worst,
Thy best will do me mischief. If thou spar'st me,
Never shine good thought on thy memory !
Resolve, my lord, and leave me desperate.

  Pe. My lord ! My lord hath play'd a prodi-
    gal's part,   225
To break his stock for nothing ; and an insolent,
To cut a gordian when he could not loose it.
What violence is this, to put true fire
To a false train ? to blow up long-crown'd peace
With sudden outrage, and believe a man   230
Sworn to the shame of women, 'gainst a woman,
Born to their honours ? But I will to him.

  Ta. No, I will write (for I shall never more
Meet with the fugitive) where I will defy him,
Were he ten times the brother of my king.   235
To him, my lord, and I 'll to cursing him.
                      Exeunt.

          [SCENE II.]¹

    Enter D'AMBOIS *and* Friar.

  Bu. I am suspicious, my most honour'd
    father,
By some of Monsieur's cunning passages,
That his still ranging and contentious nostrils,
To scent the haunts of mischief have so us'd
The vicious virtue of his busy sense,   5
That he trails hotly of him, and will rouse him,
Driving him all enrag'd and foaming, on us ;
And therefore have entreated your deep skill
In the command of good aërial spirits,
To assume these magic rites, and call up one   10
To know if any have reveal'd unto him
Anything touching my dear love and me.

  Fr. Good son, you have amaz'd me but to make
The least doubt of it, it concerns so nearly
The faith and reverence of my name and order.
Yet will I justify, upon my soul,   16
All I have done.
If any spirit i' the earth or air
Can give you the resolve,² do not despair.

Music. TAMYRA *enters with* PERO, *her maid,*
        bearing a letter.

  Ta. Away, deliver it :   *Exit* PERO.
                O may thy lines
Fill'd with the poison of a woman's hate   21
When he shall open them, shrink up his curst
    eyes
With torturous darkness, such as stands in hell,
Stuck full of inward horrors, never lighted ;
With which are all things to be fear'd, af-
    frighted ;   25
[Father !

    Ascendit BUSSY *with* Friar.]³

  Bu.   How is it with my honour'd mistress ?
  Ta. O servant, help, and save me from the
    gripes

  ¹ A room in Montsurry's house.
  ² Certainty.
  ³ Q. 1641 omits. But we must suppose that D'Ambois
and the Friar have withdrawn during Pero's presence.

Of shame and infamy. Our love is known :
Your Monsieur hath a paper where is writ
Some secret tokens that decipher it.   30

  Bu. What cold dull northern brain, what fool
    but he
Durst take into his Epimethean breast
A box of such plagues as the danger yields
Incurr'd in this discovery ? He had better
Ventur'd his breast in the consuming reach   35
Of the hot surfeits cast out of the clouds,
Or stood the bullets that (to wreak the sky)
The Cyclops ram in Jove's artillery.

  Fr. We soon will take the darkness from his
    face
That did that deed of darkness ; we will know   40
What now the Monsieur and your husband do ;
What is contain'd within the secret paper
Offer'd by Monsieur, and your love's events :
To which ends, honour'd daughter, at your mo-
    tion,
I have put on these exorcising rites,   45
And, by my power of learned holiness
Vouchsaft me from above, I will command
Our resolution⁴ of a raised spirit.

  Ta. Good father, raise him in some beauteous
    form
That with least terror I may brook his sight.   50

  Fr. Stand sure together, then, whate'er ye
    see,
And stir not, as ye tender all our lives.
           He puts on his robes.
*Occidentalium legionum spiritualium imperator
(magnus ille Behemoth) veni, veni, comitatus cum
Asaroth locotenente invicto. Adjuro te per Stygis* [55
*inscrutabilia arcana, per ipsos irremeabiles anfrac-
tus Averni : adesto o Behemoth, tu cui pervia sunt
Magnatum scrinia ; veni, per Noctis & tenebrarum
abdita profundissima ; per labentia sidera ; per ipsos
motus horarum furtivos, Hecatesque altum silen-* [60
*tium. Appare in forma spiritali, lucente, splendida
& amabili.*

    [*Thunder. Ascendit* Behemoth *with*
        Cartophylax *and other spirits.*]

  Beh. What would the holy Friar ?
  Fr.   I would see
What now the Monsieur and Montsurry do ;
And see the secret paper that the Monsieur   65
Offer'd to Count Montsurry, longing much
To know on what events the secret loves
Of these two honour'd persons shall arrive.

  Beh. Why call'dst thou me to this accursed
    light
To these light purposes ? I am emperor   70
Of that inscrutable darkness where are hid
All deepest truths, and secrets never seen,
All which I know ; and command legions
Of knowing spirits that can do more than
    these.
Any of this my guard that circle me   75
In these blue fires, and out of whose dim fumes
Vast murmurs use to break, and from their
    sounds
Articulate voices, can do ten parts more
Than open such slight truths as you require.

  Fr. From the last night's black depth I call'd
    up one   80

  ⁴ Information.

Of the inferior ablest ministers,
And he could not resolve me. Send one then
Out of thine own command, to fetch the paper
That Monsieur hath to show to Count Montsurry.
Beh. I will. Cartophylax, thou that properly
Hast in thy power all papers so inscrib'd,   86
Glide through all bars to it and fetch that paper.
Cartoph. I will.   *A torch removes.*
Fr. Till he returns, great prince of darkness,
Tell me if Monsieur and the Count Montsurry
Are yet encounter'd ?
Beh.   Both them and the Guise
Are now together.
Fr.   Show us all their persons,   91
And represent the place, with all their actions.
Beh. The spirit will straight return ; and then
I 'll show thee.
See, he is come ; why brought'st thou not the paper ?
Cartoph. He hath prevented me, and got a spirit
Rais'd by another, great in our command,   96
To take the guard of it before I came.
Beh. This is your slackness, not t' invoke our powers
When first your acts set forth to their effects ;
Yet shall you see it and themselves. Behold
They come here, and the Earl now holds the paper.   101

Enter Monsieur, Guise, Montsurry, *with a paper.*

Bu. May we not hear them ?
Fr.   No, be still and see.
Bu. I will go fetch the paper.
Fr.   Do not stir ;
There's too much distance and too many locks
'Twixt you and them, how near soe'er they seem,
For any man to interrupt their secrets.   106
Ta. O honour'd spirit, fly into the fancy
Of my offended lord, and do not let him
Believe what there the wicked man hath written.
Beh. Persuasion hath already enter'd him   110
Beyond reflection ; peace till their departure !

Mo.[1] There is a glass of ink[2] where you may see
How to make ready black-fac'd tragedy.
You now discern, I hope, through all her paintings,
Her gasping wrinkles, and fame's sepulchres.   115
Gu. Think you he feigns, my lord ? What hold you now ?
Do we malign your wife, or honour you ?
Mo. What, stricken dumb ! Nay fie, lord, be not daunted ;
Your case is common ; were it ne'er so rare,
Bear it as rarely. Now to laugh were manly.   120
A worthy man should imitate the weather
That sings in tempests, and being clear is silent.
Gu. Go home, my lord, and force your wife to write
Such loving lines to D'Ambois as she us'd.
When she desir'd his presence,
Mo.   Do, my lord,   125

[1] Monsieur, Guise, and Montsurry presumably appear at the back of the stage.
[2] *I. e.* a written document.

And make her name her conceal'd messenger,
That close and most inennerable[3] pander,
That passeth all our studies to exquire ;[4]
By whom convey the letter to her love :
And so you shall be sure to have him come   130
Within the thirsty reach of your revenge ;
Before which, lodge an ambush in her chamber
Behind the arras, of your stoutest men
All close[5] and soundly arm'd ; and let them share
A spirit amongst them that would serve a thousand.   135

Enter Pero *with a letter.*

Gu. Yet stay a little ; see, she sends for you.
Mo. Poor, loving lady ; she 'll make all good yet,
Think you not so, my lord ?
    Montsurry *stabs* Pero *and exit.*
Gu.   Alas, poor soul !
Mo. That was cruelly done, i' faith.
Pe.   'T was nobly done.
And I forgive his lordship from my soul.   140
Mo. Then much good do 't thee, Pero ! Hast a letter ?
Pe. I hope it rather be a bitter volume
Of worthy curses for your perjury.
Gu. To you, my lord.
Mo.   To me ? Now, out upon her.
Gu. Let me see, my lord.   145
Mo. You shall presently. How fares my Pero ?

Enter Servant.

Who 's there ? Take in this maid, sh'as caught a clap,
And fetch my surgeon to her. Come, my lord,
We 'll now peruse our letter.
    Exeunt Monsieur, Guise. *Lead her out.*
Pe.   Furies rise
Out of the black lines, and torment his soul.   150

Ta. Hath my lord slain my woman ?
Beh.   No, she lives.
Fr. What shall become of us ?
Beh.   All I can say,
Being call'd thus late, is brief, and darkly this :
If D'Ambois' mistress dye not her[6] white hand
In her forc'd blood, he shall remain untoucht :
So, father, shall yourself, but by yourself.   156
To make this augury plainer : when the voice
Of D'Ambois shall invoke me, I will rise,
Shining in greater light : and show him all
That will betide ye all. Meantime be wise,
And curb his valour with your policies.   161
    Descendit cum suis.
Bu. Will he appear to me when I invoke him ?
Fr. He will, be sure.
Bu.   It must be shortly then :
For his dark words have tied my thoughts on knots,
Till he dissolve, and free them.
Ta.   In meantime,   165
Dear servant, till your powerful voice revoke[7] him,

[3] Indescribable.   [5] Hidden.   [7] Call back.
[4] Find out.   [6] Qq. *his.*

Be sure to use the policy he advis'd ;
Lest fury in your too quick knowledge taken
Of our abuse, and your defence of me,
Accuse me more than any enemy ;   170
And, father, you must on my lord impose
Your holiest charges, and the Church's power
To temper his hot spirit and disperse
The cruelty and the blood I know his hand
Will shower upon our heads, if you put not   175
Your finger to the storm, and hold it up,
As my dear servant here must do with Monsieur.
   Bu. I 'll soothe his plots, and strow my hate
     with smiles,
Till all at once the close mines of my heart
Rise at full date, and rush into his blood.   180
I 'll bind his arm in silk, and rub his flesh,
To make the vein swell, that his soul may gush
Into some kennel, where it longs to lie,
And policy shall be flankt [1] with policy.
Yet shall the feeling centre where we meet   185
Groan with the weight of my approaching feet ;
I 'll make th' inspired thresholds of his court
Sweat with the weather of my horrid steps,
Before I enter ; yet will I appear
Like calm security before a ruin.   190
A politician must, like lightning, melt
The very marrow, and not taint the skin :
His ways must not be seen ; the superficies
Of the green centre [2] must not taste his feet,
When hell is plow'd up with his wounding
    tracts ;
And all his harvest reapt by hellish facts.   196
                    Exeunt.

ACT V

Scene I. [3]

Montsurry *bare, unbraced, pulling* Tamyra *in by the hair ;* Friar. *One bearing light, a standish* [4] *and paper, which sets a table.*

   Ta. Oh, help me, father.
   Fr.   Impious earl, forbear.
Take violent hand from her, or by mine order
The King shall force thee.
   Mont.   'T is not violent ;
Come you not willingly ?
   Ta.   Yes, good my lord.
   Fr. My lord, remember that your soul must
     seek   5
Her peace, as well as your revengeful blood.
You ever to this hour have prov'd yourself
A noble, zealous, and obedient son,
T' our holy mother ; be not an apostate.
Your wife's offence serves not, were it the
    worst   10
You can imagine, without greater proofs,
To sever your eternal bonds and hearts ;
Much less to touch her with a bloody hand ;
Nor is it manly, much less husbandly,
To expiate any frailty in your wife   15
With churlish strokes or beastly odds of
    strength.
The stony birth of clouds [5] will touch no laurel,

Nor any sleeper ; your wife is your laurel,
And sweetest sleeper ; do not touch her then ;
Be not more rude than the wild seed of vapour,[24]
To her that is more gentle than that rude ;
In whom kind nature suffer'd one offence
But to set off her other excellence.
   Mont. Good father, leave us ; interrupt no
    more
The course I must run for mine honour sake. 25
Rely on my love to her, which her fault
Cannot extinguish. Will she but disclose
Who was the secret minister of her love,
And through what maze he serv'd it, we are
    friends.
   Fr. It is a damn'd work to pursue those
    secrets   30
That would ope more sin, and prove springs of
    slaughter ;
Nor is 't a path for Christian feet to tread,
But out of all way to the health of souls,
A sin impossible to be forgiven ;
Which he that dares commit——   35
   Mont. Good father, cease your terrors ;
Tempt not a man distracted ; I am apt
To outrages that I shall ever rue ;
I will not pass the verge that bounds a Christian,
Nor break the limits of a man nor husband.   40
   Fr. Then Heaven inspire you both with
    thoughts and deeds
Worthy his high respect, and your own souls.
   Ta. Father !
   Fr.   I warrant thee, my dearest daughter,
He will not touch thee ; think'st thou him a
    pagan ?
His honour and his soul lies for thy safety.   45
                    Exit.
   Mont. Who shall remove the mountain from
    my breast ?
Stand [in] [6] the opening furnace of my thoughts,
And set fit outcries for a soul in hell ?
             Montsurry *turns a key.*
For now it nothing fits my woes to speak
But thunder, or to take into my throat   50
The trump of heaven, with whose determinate [7]
    blast
The winds shall burst, and the devouring seas
Be drunk up in his sounds ; that my hot woes
(Vented enough) I might convert to vapour,
Ascending from my infamy unseen ;   55
Shorten the world, preventing [8] the last breath
That kills the living and regenerates death.[9]
   Ta. My lord, my fault (as you may censure [10]
    it
With too strong arguments) is past your pardon :
But how the circumstances may excuse me   60
Heaven knows, and your more temperate mind
    hereafter
May let my penitent miseries make you know.
   Mont. Hereafter ? 'T is a suppos'd infinite,
That from this point will rise eternally.
Fame grows in going ; in the scapes [11] of virtue 65
Excuses damn her : they be fires in cities
Enrag'd with those winds that less lights ex-
    tinguish.

---

  [1] Outflanked.   [4] Case for pen and ink.
  [2] Earth.   [5] Thunderbolt.
  [3] A room in Montsurry's house.

  [6] Qq. omit. Boas emend.   [9] The dead.
  [7] Final. (Boas.)   [10] Judge.
  [8] Anticipating.   [11] Escapades.

Come, syren, sing, and dash against my rocks
Thy ruffian galley, rigg'd with quench for lust ;
Sing, and put all the nets into thy voice   70
With which thou drew'st into thy strumpet's lap
The spawn of Venus ; and in which ye danc'd ;
That, in thy lap's stead, I may dig his tomb,
And quit his manhood with a woman's sleight,
Who never is deceiv'd in her deceit.   75
Sing (that is, write), and then take from mine
    eyes
The mists that hide the most inscrutable pander
That ever lapt up[1] an adulterous vomit,
That I may see the devil, and survive
To be a devil, and then learn to wive ;   80
That I may hang him, and then cut him down,
Then cut him up, and with my soul's beams
    search
The cranks and caverns of his brain, and study
The errant wilderness of a woman's face ;
Where men cannot get out, for[2] all the comets   85
That have been lighted at it ; though they know
That adders lie a-sunning in their smiles,
That basilisks drink their poison from their eyes,
And no way there to coast out to their hearts ;
Yet still they wander there, and are not stay'd   90
Till they be fetter'd, nor secure before
All cares devour them ; nor in human consort
Till they embrace within their wife's two
    breasts
All Pelion and Cythaeron with their beasts.   94
Why write you not ?
    Ta.   O good my lord, forbear
In wreak[3] of great faults, to engender greater,
And make my love's corruption generate
    murder.
    Mont. It follows needfully as child and
    parent ;
The chain-shot of thy lust is yet aloft,
And it must murder ; 'tis thine own dear
    twin :   100
No man can add height to a woman's sin.
Vice never doth her just hate so provoke,
As when she rageth under virtue's cloak.
Write ! for it must be — by this ruthless steel,
By this impartial torture, and the death   105
Thy tyrannies have invented in my entrails,
To quicken life in dying, and hold up
The spirits in fainting, teaching to preserve,
Torments in ashes, that will ever last.   109
Speak ! Will you write ?
    Ta.   Sweet lord, enjoin my sin
Some other penance than what makes it
    worse ;
Hide in some gloomy dungeon my loath'd face,
And let condemned murderers let me down
(Stopping their noses) my abhorred food :
Hang me in chains, and let me eat these arms
That have offended ; bind my face to face   116
To some dead woman, taken from the cart
Of execution, till death and time
In grains of dust dissolve me ; I'll endure ;
Or any torture that your wrath's invention   120
Can fright all pity from the world withal ;
But to betray a friend with show of friendship,
That is too common for the rare revenge

Your rage affecteth. Here then are my breasts,
Last night your pillows ; here my wretched
    arms,   125
As late the wished confines of your life ;
Now break them as you please, and all the
    bounds
Of manhood, noblesse, and religion.
    Mont. Where all these have been broken,
    they are kept,
In doing their justice there with any show   130
Of the like cruel cruelty ; thine arms have lost
Their privilege in lust, and in their torture
Thus they must pay it.   Stabs her.
    Ta.   O Lord !
    Mont.   Till thou writest,
I'll write in wounds (my wrong's fit characters)
Thy right of sufferance. Write.
    Ta.   Oh, kill me, kill me ; 135
Dear husband, be not crueller than death.
You have beheld some Gorgon ; feel, oh, feel
How you are turn'd to stone. With my heart-
    blood
Dissolve yourself again, or you will grow
Into the image of all tyranny.   140
    Mont. As thou art of adultery ; I will ever
Prove thee my parallel, being most a monster ;
Thus I express thee yet.   Stabs her again.
    Ta.   And yet I live.
    Mont. Ay, for thy monstrous idol is not done
    yet ;
This tool hath wrought enough ; now, torture,
    use   145

            Enter Servants.

This other engine[4] on th' habituate powers
Of her thrice-damn'd and whorish fortitude.
Use the most madding pains in her that ever
Thy venoms soak'd through, making most of
    death ;
That she may weigh her wrongs with them,
    and then   150
Stand vengeance on thy steepest rock, a victor.
    Ta. Oh, who is turn'd into my lord and hus-
    band ?
Husband ! My lord ! None but my lord and
    husband !
Heaven, I ask thee remission of my sins,
Not of my pains ; husband, oh, help me, hus-
    band !   155

            Ascendit Friar *with a sword drawn.*

    Fr. What rape of honour and religion —
Oh, wrack of nature !   *Falls and dies.*
    Ta.   Poor man ; oh, my father.
Father, look up ; oh, let me down, my lord,
And I will write.
    Mont.   Author of prodigies !
What new flame breaks out of the firmament, 160
That turns up counsels never known before ?
Now is it true, earth moves, and heaven stands
    still ;
Even heaven itself must see and suffer ill.
The too huge bias of the world hath sway'd
Her back part upwards, and with that she
    braves   165

---

[1] Hid.   [2] In spite of.   [3] Revenge.

[4] Tamyra is now put on the rack.

This hemisphere, that long her mouth hath
mockt;
The gravity of her religious face,
(Now grown too weighty with her sacrilege,
And here discern'd sophisticate enough)
Turns to th' antipodes; and all the forms   170
That her illusions have imprest in her,
Have eaten through her back; and now all see,
How she is riveted with hypocrisy.
Was this the way? Was he the mean betwixt
you?
Ta. He was, he was, kind worthy man, he
was.   175
Mont. Write, write a word or two.
Ta.   I will, I will.
I 'll write, but with my blood, that he may see
These lines come from my wounds, and not
from me.   *Writes.*
Mont. Well might he die for thought; me-
thinks the frame
And shaken joints of the whole world should
crack   180
To see her parts so disproportionate;
And that his[1] general beauty cannot stand
Without these stains in the particular man.
Why wander I so far? Here, here was she
That was a whole world without spot to me,
Though now a world of spots. Oh, what a
lightning   186
Is man's delight in women! What a bubble
He builds his state, fame, life on, when he
marries!
Since all earth's pleasures are so short and small,
The way t' enjoy it, is t' abjure it all.   190
Enough! I must be messenger myself,
Disguis'd like this strange creature. In, I 'll
after,
To see what guilty light gives this cave eyes,
And to the world sing new impieties.

      He puts the Friar *in the vault and
      follows. She wraps herself in the
      arras. Exeunt* [*servants*].

[SCENE II.][2]

Enter Monsieur *and* GUISE.

Mo. Now shall we see that Nature hath no
end
In her great works responsive to their worths,
That she, that makes so many eyes and souls
To see and foresee, is stark blind herself;
And as illiterate men say Latin prayers   5
By rote of heart and daily iteration,
Not knowing what they say,[3] so Nature lays
A deal of stuff together, and by use,
Or by the mere necessity of matter,
Ends such a work, fills it, or leaves it empty   10

---

[1] *Her,* referring to world, would be expected. *His*
seems to refer to *man,* in next line.
[2] A room in Montsurry's house.
[3] In place of *Not . . . say,* Qq. 1607, 8 read,
*In whose hot zeal a man would think they knew
What they ran so away with, and were sure
To have rewards proportion'd to their labours;
Yet may implore their own confusions
For anything they know, which often times
It falls out they incur.*

Of strength or virtue, error or clear truth,
Not knowing what she does; but usually
Gives that which she calls merit to a man,
And belief must arrive[4] him on huge riches,
Honour, and happiness, that effects his ruin;   15
Even as in ships of war, whose lasts[5] of powder
Are laid, men think,[6] to make them last, and
guard them,
When a disorder'd spark, that powder taking,
Blows up with sudden violence and horror
Ships that kept empty, had sail'd long, with
terror.[7]   20
Gu. He that observes, but like a worldly man,
That which doth oft succeed, and by th' events
Values the worth of things, will think it true
That Nature works at random, just with you;
But with as much proportion she may make   25
A thing that from the feet up to the throat
Hath all the wondrous fabric man should have,
And leave it headless, for a perfect man,
As give a full man valour, virtue, learning,
Without an end more excellent than those,   30
On whom she no such worthy part bestows.
Mo. Yet shall you see it here; here will be
one
Young, learned, valiant, virtuous, and full
mann'd;
One on whom Nature spent so rich a hand
That with an ominous eye she wept to see   35
So much consum'd her virtuous treasury.[8]
Yet, as the winds sing through a hollow tree,
And (since it lets them pass through) lets it
stand;
But a tree solid (since it gives no way
To their wild rage) they rend up by the root;   40
So this whole man,
(That will not wind with every crooked way,
Trod by the servile world) shall reel and fall
Before the frantic puffs of blind-born chance,
That pipes through empty men, and makes them
dance.   45
Not so the sea raves on the Lybian sands,
Tumbling her billows in each other's neck;
Not so the surges of the Euxine sea
(Near to the frosty pole, where free Boötes
From those dark deep waves turns his radiant
team)   50
Swell, being enrag'd even from their inmost
drop,
As Fortune swings about the restless state
Of virtue, now thrown into all men's hate.

Enter MONTSURRY *disguis'd with the* Murderers.

Away, my lord, you are perfectly disguis'd,   54
Leave us to lodge your ambush.
Mont.   Speed me, vengeance. *Exit.*
Mo. Resolve, my masters, you shall meet with
one
Will try what proofs your privy coats[9] are made
on;
When he is ent'red, and you hear us stamp,
Approach, and make all sure.
Murd.   We will, my lord. *Exeunt.*

---

[4] Bring.
[5] Loads.
[6] Boas amends to *methinks.*
[7] To their enemies. (Boas.)
[8] Store of virtues.
[9] Coats of mail.

[SCENE III.] [1]

D'AMBOIS *with two* Pages *with tapers.*

Bu. Sit up to-night, and watch; I'll speak
　　with none
But the old Friar, who bring to me.
Pa.　　　　　　　We will, sir. *Exeunt.*
Bu. What violent heat is this? Methinks the
　　fire
Of twenty lives doth on a sudden flash
Through all my faculties; the air goes high　5
In this close chamber, and the frighted earth
　　　　　　　　　　　　　　　Thunder.
Trembles, and shrinks beneath me; the whole
　　house
Nods with his shaken burthen.

Enter Umbra Friar.

　　　　　　　　Bless me, heaven!
Um. Note what I want, dear son, and be fore-
　　warn'd;
O there are bloody deeds past and to come.　10
I cannot stay; a fate doth ravish me;
I'll meet thee in the chamber of thy love. *Exit.*
Bu. What dismal change is here; the good
　　old Friar
Is murder'd; being made known to serve my
　　love;　　　　　　　　　　　　　　　14
And now his restless spirit would forewarn me
Of some plot dangerous and imminent.
Note what he wants? He wants his upper weed,
He wants his life and body; which of these
Should be the want he means, and may supply
　　me　　　　　　　　　　　　　　　19
With any fit forewarning? This strange vision
(Together with the dark prediction
Us'd by the Prince of Darkness that was rais'd
By this embodied shadow) stir my thoughts
With reminiscion [2] of the spirit's promise,
Who told me that by any invocation　　25
I should have power to raise him, though it
　　wanted
The powerful words and decent rights of art.
Never had my set brain such need of spirit
T' instruct and cheer it; now, then, I will claim
Performance of his free and gentle vow　30
T' appear in greater light, and make more plain
His rugged oracle. I long to know
How my dear mistress fares, and be inform'd
What hand she now holds on the troubled blood
Of her incensed lord. Methought the spirit　35
(When he had utter'd his perplext presage)
Threw his chang'd countenance headlong into
　　clouds,
His forehead bent, as it would hide his face,
He knockt his chin against his dark'ned breast,
And struck a churlish silence through his
　　powers.　　　　　　　　　　　　　40
Terror of darkness! O, thou king of flames!
That with thy music-footed horse dost strike
The clear light out of crystal on dark earth,
And hurl'st instructive fire about the world,　44
Wake, wake the drowsy and enchanted night,
That sleeps with dead eyes in this heavy riddle!
Or thou great prince of shades, where never sun

Sticks his **far-darted** beams, whose eyes are
　　made
To shine in darkness, and see ever best
Where men are blindest, open now the heart　50
Of thy abashed oracle, that, for fear
Of some ill it includes, would fain lie hid,
And rise thou with it in thy greater light.
　　　　　Thunders. Surgit Spiritus cum suis.
Beh. Thus to observe my vow of apparition
In greater light, and explicate thy fate,　55
I come; and tell thee that if thou obey
The summons that thy mistress next will send
　　thee,
Her hand shall be thy death.
Bu.　　　　　　When will she send?
Beh. Soon as I set again, where late I rose.59
Bu. Is the old Friar slain?
Beh.　　　　　　No, and yet lives not.
Bu. Died he a natural death?
Beh.　　　　　　He did.
Bu.　　　　　　　　　Who then
Will my dear mistress send?
Beh.　　　　　　I must not tell thee.
Bu. Who lets [3] thee?
Beh.　　　Fate.
Bu.　　　　　　Who are fate's ministers?
Beh. The Guise and Monsieur.
Bu.　　　　　　A fit pair of shears
To cut the threads of kings and kingly spirits,
And consorts fit to sound forth harmony,　60
Set to the falls of kingdoms: shall the hand
Of my kind mistress kill me?
Beh.　　　　　If thou yield
To her next summons, y 'are fair-warn'd: fare-
　　well!　　　　　　　*Thunders. Exit.*
Bu. I must fare well, however, though I die,
My death consenting [4] with his augury.　71
Should not my powers obey when she commands,
My motion must be rebel to my will,
My will to life: if, when I have obey'd,
Her hand should so reward me, they must arm
　　it,　　　　　　　　　　　　　75
Bind me or force it: or, I lay my life,
She rather would convert it many times
On her own bosom, even to many deaths;
But were there danger of such violence,
I know 't is far from her intent to send;　80
And who she should send is as far from thought,
Since he is dead, whose only mean she us'd.
　　　　　　　　　　　　　　Knocks.
Who 's there! Look to the door, and let him in,
Though politic Monsieur or the violent Guise.

Enter MONTSURRY, *like the* Friar, *with a letter
written in blood.*

Mont. Hail to my worthy son.
Bu.　　　　　Oh, lying spirit! [5]
To say the Friar was dead; I 'll now believe　86

Nothing of all his forg'd predictions.
My kind and honour'd father, well reviv'd,
I have been frighted with your death and mine,
And told my mistress' hand should be my death
If I obey'd this summons.
 Mont.   I believ'd 91
Your love had been much clearer than to give
Any such doubt a thought, for she is clear,
And having freed her husband's jealousy
(Of which her much abus'd hand here is witness)
She prays, for urgent cause, your instant pres-
 ence. 96
 Bu. Why, then your prince of spirits may be
  call'd
The prince of liars.
 Mont.   Holy Writ so calls him.
 Bu. What, writ in blood?
 Mont.   Ay, 't is the ink of lovers.
 Bu. O, 't is a sacred witness of her love. 100
So much elixir of her blood as this
Dropt in the lightest dame, would make her firm
As heat to fire; and, like to all the signs,[1]
Commands the life confin'd in all my veins.
O, how it multiplies my blood with spirit, 105
And makes me apt t' encounter death and hell.
But come, kind father, you fetch me to heaven,
And to that end your holy weed was given.
        Exeunt.

[SCENE IV.] [2]

Thunder. Intrat Umbra Friar, *and discovers*
TAMYRA.

 Um. Up with these stupid thoughts, still
  loved daughter,
And strike away this heartless trance of an-
 guish.
Be like the sun, and labour in eclipses;
Look to the end of woes: oh, can you sit
Mustering the horrors of your servant's slaugh-
 ter 5
Before your contemplation, and not study [3]
How to prevent it? Watch when he shall rise,
And with a sudden outcry of his murder,
Blow [4] his retreat before he be revenged.
 Ta. O father, have my dumb woes wak'd
  your death? 10
When will our human griefs be at their height?
Man is a tree that hath no top in cares,
No root in comforts; all his power to live
Is given to no end, but t' have power to grieve.
 Um. It is the misery of our creation. 15
Your true friend,
Led by your husband, shadowed in my weed,
Now enters the dark vault.
 Ta.   But, my dearest father,
Why will not you appear to him yourself,
And see that none of these deceits annoy him?
 Um. My power is limited; alas! I cannot. 21
All that I can do — See, the cave opens.
    Exit. D'AMBOIS *at the gulf.*

---

[1] Of the zodiac. [2] A room in Montsurry's house.
[3] In place of the first six lines, Qq. 1607, 8 **read**;
Revive those stupid thoughts, and sit not thus
Gathering the horrors of your servant's slaughter
(So urg'd by your hand, and so imminent)
Into an idle fancy; but devise
[4] Give the signal for.

 Ta. Away, my love, away; thou wilt be
  murder'd!

 Enter Monsieur *and* GUISE *above.*

 Bu. Murder'd; I know not what that He-
  brew means:
That word had ne'er been nam'd had all been
 D'Ambois. 25
Murder'd? By heaven he is my murderer
That shows me not a murderer; what such bug [5]
Abhorreth not the very sleep of D'Ambois?
Murder'd? Who dares give all the room I see
To D'Ambois' reach? or look with any odds [3]
His fight i' th' face, upon whose hand sits
 death;
Whose sword hath wings, and every feather
 pierceth?
If I scape Monsieur's 'pothecary shops,
Foutre [6] for Guise's shambles! 'T was ill
 plotted;
They should have maul'd me here, 35
When I was rising. I am up and ready.
Let in my politic visitants, let them in,
Though ent'ring like so many moving armours,
Fate is more strong than arms and sly than
 treason,
And I at all parts buckl'd in my fate. 40
 Mo. }
 Gu. } Why enter not the coward villains?
 Bu. Dare they not come?

 Enter Murderers *with* Friar *at the other door.*

 Ta.   They come.
 1 Mur.   Come all at once.
 Um. Back, coward murderers, back.
 Omn.   Defend us, heaven.
     Exeunt all but the first.
 1 Mur. Come ye not on?
 Bu.   No, slave, nor goest thou off.
     [*Strikes at him.*]
Stand you so firm? Will it not enter here? 45
You have a face yet; so in thy life's flame
I burn the first rites to my mistress' fame.
 Um. Breathe thee, brave son, against the
  other charge.
 Bu. Oh, is it true then that my sense first told
  me?
Is my kind father dead?
 Ta.   He is, my love. 50
'T was the Earl, my husband, in his weed that
 brought thee.
 Bu. That was a speeding sleight,[7] and well
 resembled.
Where is that angry Earl? My lord, come
 forth
And show your own face in your own affair;
Take not into your noble veins the blood 55
Of these base villains, nor the light reports
Of blister'd tongues for clear and weighty
 truth:
But me against the world, in pure defence
Of your rare lady, to whose spotless name
I stand here as a bulwark, and project 60
A life to her renown, that ever yet

---

[5] Terrifying thing. [6] An expression of contempt.
[7] Successful trick.

Hath been untainted, even in envy's eye,
And where it would protect a sanctuary.
Brave Earl, come forth, and keep your scandal
in ;
'T is not our fault if you enforce the spot   65
Nor the wreak [1] yours if you perform it not.

Enter MONTSURRY, *with all the* Murderers.

Mont. Cowards, a fiend or spirit beat ye off !
They are your own faint spirits that have forg'd
The fearful shadows that your eyes deluded.   69
The fiend was in you ; cast him out then, thus.
          D'AMBOIS *hath* MONT. *down.*
Ta. Favour my lord, my love, O, favour him !
Bu. I will not touch him : take your life, my
          lord,
And be appeas'd.   *Pistols shot within.*
          O, then the coward Fates
Have maim'd themselves, and ever lost their
          honour.
Um. What have ye done, slaves ? Irreligious
          lord !   75
Bu. Forbear them, father ; 't is enough for
          me
That Guise and Monsieur, death and destiny,
Come behind D'Ambois. Is my body, then,
But penetrable flesh ? And must my mind
Follow my blood ? Can my divine part add
No aid to th' earthly in extremity ?   81
Then these divines are but for form, not fact.[2]
Man is of two sweet courtly friends compact,
A mistress and a servant ; let my death
Define life nothing but a courtier's breath.   85
Nothing is made of nought, of all things made,
Their abstract being a dream but of a shade.
I 'll not complain to earth yet, but to heaven,
And, like a man, look upwards even in death.
And if Vespasian thought in majesty   90
An emperor might die standing, why not I ?
          She offers to help him.
Nay, without help, in which I will exceed him ;
For he died splinted with his chamber grooms.
Prop me, true sword, as thou hast ever done :
The equal thought I bear of life and death   95
Shall make me faint on no side ; I am up.
Here like a Roman statue I will stand
Till death hath made me marble. Oh, my fame,
Live in despite of murder ; take thy wings
And haste thee where the grey-ey'd morn per-
          fumes   100
Her rosy chariot with Sabaean spices ;
Fly, where the evening from th' Iberian vales,
Takes on her swarthy shoulders Hecate,
Crown'd with a grove of oaks ; fly where men
          feel
The burning axletree ; and those that suffer   105
Beneath the chariot of the snowy Bear ;
And tell them all that D'Ambois now is hast-
          ing
To the eternal dwellers ; that a thunder
Of all their sighs together (for their frailties
Beheld in me) may quit my worthless fall   110
With a fit volley for my funeral.

---

[1] Vengeance.
[2] Then these teachers of divinity deal with figments,
not realities. (Boas.)

Um. Forgive thy murderers.
Bu.   I forgive them all ;
And you, my lord, their fautor ;[3] for true sign
Of which unfeign'd remission, take my sword ;
Take it, and only give it motion,   115
And it shall find the way to victory
By his own brightness, and th' inherent valour
My fight hath 'still'd into 't, with charms of
          spirit.
Now let me pray you that my weighty blood
Laid in one scale of your impartial spleen,   120
May sway the forfeit of my worthy love
Weigh'd in the other ; and be reconcil'd
With all forgiveness to your matchless wife.
Ta. Forgive thou me, dear servant, and this
          hand
That led thy life to this unworthy end ;   125
Forgive it, for the blood with which 't is stain'd,
In which I writ the summons of thy death ;
The forced summons, by this bleeding wound,
By this here in my bosom ; and by this
That makes me hold up both my hands im-
          bru'd   130
For thy dear pardon.
Bu.   O, my heart is broken.
Fate, nor these murderers, Monsieur, nor the
          Guise,
Have any glory in my death, but this,
This killing spectacle, this prodigy.
My sun is turn'd to blood, in whose red beams
Pindus and Ossa, hid in drifts of snow   135
Laid on my heart and liver, from their veins
Melt like two hungry torrents, eating rocks
Into the ocean of all human life,
And make it bitter, only with my blood.   140
O frail condition of strength, valour, virtue,
In me (like warning fire upon the top
Of some steep beacon on a steeper hill)
Made to express it : like a falling star
Silently glanc'd, that like a thunderbolt   145
Lookt to have struck [4] and shook the firmament.
          Moritur.
Um. [My terrors are struck inward, and no
          more
My penance will allow they shall enforce
Earthly afflictions but upon myself.][5]
Farewell, brave relics of a complete man !   150
Look up and see thy spirit made a star,
Join flames with Hercules, and when thou
          sett'st
Thy radiant forehead in the firmament,
Make the vast crystal crack with thy receipt ;
Spread to a world of fire ; and th' aged sky   155
Cheer with new sparks of old humanity.
          [*To* MONT.] Son of the earth, whom my un-
          rested soul,
Rues t' have begotten in the faith of heaven ;
[Since thy revengeful spirit hath rejected
The charity it commands, and the remission   160
To serve and worship the blind rage of blood ;][5]
Assay to gratulate [6] and pacify
The soul fled from this worthy by performing
The Christian reconcilement he besought   164

---

[3] Patron.   [4] Boas emend. Qq. *stuck.*
[5] Q. 1641 omits these lines.
[6] Gratify.

Betwixt thee and thy lady. Let her wounds
Manlessly [1] digg'd in her, be eas'd and cur'd
With balm of thine own tears ; or be assur'd
Never to rest free from my haunt and horror.
   Mont. See how she merits this, still kneeling
    by,   169
And mourning his fall more than her own fault.
   Um. Remove, dear daughter, and content
    thy husband ;
So piety wills thee, and thy servant's peace.
   Ta. O wretched piety, that art so distract
In thine own constancy, and in thy right
Must be unrighteous. If I right my friend, 175
I wrong my husband ; if his wrong I shun,
The duty of my friend I leave undone.
Ill plays on both sides ; here and there it riseth ;
No place, no good, so good but ill compriseth.
[My soul more scruple breeds, than my blood,
    sin.   180
Virtue imposeth more than any stepdame ;] [2]
O had I never married but for form,
Never vow'd faith but purpos'd to deceive,
Never made conscience of any sin,
But cloak'd it privately and made it common ;
Nor never honour'd been in blood or mind, 186
Happy had I been then, as others are
Of the like licence ; I had then been honour'd ;
Liv'd without envy ; custom had benumb'd
All sense of scruple, and all note of frailty ; 190
My fame had been untouch'd, my heart un-
    broken :
But (shunning all) I strike on all offence,
O husband ! Dear friend ! O my conscience !
   Mo. Come, let 's away ; my senses are not
    proof   194
Against those plaints.
             Exeunt GUISE, Monsieur: D'AM-
             BOIS *is borne off.*
   Mont. I must not yield to pity, nor to love
So servile and so traitorous. Cease, my blood,
To wrastle with my honour, fame, and judg-
    ment. —
Away ! Forsake my house ; forbear complaints
Where thou hast bred them : here all things
    [are] full   200
Of their own shame and sorrow; leave my
    house.

---

     [1] Inhumanly.   [2] Omitted in Q 1641.

   Ta. Sweet lord, forgive me, and I will be
    gone,
And till these wounds, that never balm shall close
Till death hath enter'd at them, so I love them,
Being opened by your hands, by death be cur'd,
I never more will grieve you with my sight, 206
Never endure that any roof shall part
Mine eyes and heaven; but to the open deserts
(Like to a hunted tigress) I will fly,
Eating my heart, shunning the steps of men,
And look on no side till I be arriv'd.   211
   Mont. I do forgive thee, and upon my knees,
With hands held up to heaven, wish that mine
    honour
Would suffer reconcilement to my love ;
But since it will not, honour never serve
My love with flourishing object till it sterve : [3]
And as this taper, though it upwards look, 217
Downwards must needs consume, so let our love ;
As having lost his honey, the sweet taste
Runs into savour, and will needs retain   220
A spice of his first parents, till, like life,
It sees and dies ; so let our love ; and lastly,
As when the flame is suffer'd to look up,
It keeps his lustre, but, being thus turn'd
    down,
(His natural course of useful light inverted), 225
His own stuff puts it out ; so let our love.
Now turn from me, as here I turn from thee,
And may both points of heaven's straight axle-
    tree
Conjoin in one, before thyself and me.
                     Exeunt severally.

EPILOGUE

WITH many hands you have seen D'Ambois
    slain,
Yet by your grace he may revive again,
And every day grow stronger in his skill
To please, as we presume he is in will.
The best deserving actors of the time   [4]
Had their ascents, and by degrees did climb
To their full height, a place to study due.
To make him tread in their path lies in you ·
He 'll not forget his makers, but still prove
His thankfulness as you increase your love   [10]

---

     [3] Perish.

EVERY MAN IN HIS HUMOUR

BY

BEN JONSON

THE PERSONS OF THE PLAY

KNOWELL, an old Gentleman.
EDWARD KNOWELL, his Son.
BRAINWORM, the Father's Man.
[GEORGE] DOWNRIGHT, a plain Squire.
WELLBRED, his Half-Brother.
KITELY, a Merchant.
CAPTAIN BOBADILL, a Paul's Man.[1]
MASTER STEPHEN, a Country Gull.
MASTER MATHEW, the Town Gull.
[THOMAS] CASH, Kitely's Man.

[OLIVER] COB, a Water-bearer.
JUSTICE CLEMENT, an old merry Magistrate.
ROGER FORMAL, his Clerk.
[Wellbred's Servant.]

DAME KITELY, Kitely's Wife.
MISTRESS BRIDGET, his Sister.
TIB, Cob's Wife.

[Servants, etc.]

SCENE. — *London.*

PROLOGUE

THOUGH need make many poets, and some such
As art and nature have not better'd much;
Yet ours for want hath not so lov'd the stage,
As he dare serve th' ill customs of the age,
Or purchase your delight at such a rate,   5
As, for it, he himself must justly hate:
To make a child now swaddled, to proceed
Man, and then shoot up, in one beard and weed,
Past threescore years; or, with three rusty swords,
And help of some few foot-and-half-foot words,   10
Fight over York and Lancaster's long jars,
And in the tyring-house[2] bring wounds to scars.
He rather prays you will be pleas'd to see
One such to-day, as other plays should be;
Where neither chorus wafts you o'er the seas,   15
Nor creaking throne comes down the boys to please;
Nor nimble squib is seen to make afeard
The gentlewomen; nor roll'd bullet heard
To say, it thunders; nor tempestuous drum
Rumbles, to tell you when the storm doth come;   20
But deeds, and language, such as men do use,
And persons, such as comedy would choose,
When she would shew an image of the times,
And sport with human follies, not with crimes;
Except we make 'em such, by loving still   25
Our popular errors, when we know they're ill.
I mean such errors as you 'll all confess,
By laughing at them, they deserve no less:
Which when you heartily do, there 's hope left then,
You, that have so grac'd monsters, may like men.   30

ACT I

SCENE I. [3]

[*Enter*] KNOWELL, [*at the door of his house.*]

Know. A goodly day toward, and a fresh
    morning.—
Brainworm!

---

[1] A frequenter of the aisle of St. Paul's Cathedral.
[2] Dressing-room.   [3] A street in London.

[*Enter* BRAINWORM.]

Call up your young master: bid him rise, sir.
Tell him, I have some business to employ him.
    Brai. I will, sir, presently.
    Know.   But hear you, sirrah,
If he be at his book, disturb him not.
    Brai. Well, sir.   [*Exit.*]
    Know. How happy yet should I esteem my-
    self,
Could I, by any practice, wean the boy

From one vain course of study he affects.　10
He is a scholar, if a man may trust
The liberal voice of fame in her report,
Of good account in both our Universities,
Either of which hath favour'd him with graces:
But their indulgence must not spring in me　15
A fond [1] opinion that he cannot err.
Myself was once a student, and, indeed,
Fed with the self-same humour he is now,
Dreaming on nought but idle poetry,
That fruitless and unprofitable art,　20
Good unto none, but least to the professors;
Which then I thought the mistress of all knowledge;
But since, time and the truth have wak'd my judgment,
And reason taught me better to distinguish
The vain from th' useful learnings.

[*Enter* MASTER STEPHEN.]

Cousin Stephen,　25
What news with you, that you are here so early?
Step. Nothing, but e'en come to see how you do, uncle.
Know. That's kindly done; you are welcome, coz.　30
Step. Ay, I know that, sir; I would not ha' come else. How does my cousin Edward, uncle?
Know. O, well, coz; go in and see; I doubt he be scarce stirring yet.　34
Step. Uncle, afore I go in, can you tell me, an he have e'er a book of the sciences of hawking and hunting; I would fain borrow it.
Know. Why, I hope you will not a hawking now, will you?　39
Step. No, wusse; [2] but I'll practise against next year, uncle. I have bought me a hawk, and a hood, and bells, and all; I lack nothing but a book to keep it by.
Know. Oh, most ridiculous!
Step. Nay, look you now, you are angry, [45 uncle. — Why, you know an a man have not skill in the hawking and hunting languages now-a-days, I'll not give a rush for him: they are more studied than the Greek, or the Latin. [49 He is for no gallant's company without 'em; and by gadslid [3] I scorn it, I, so I do, to be a consort for every humdrum: hang 'em, scroyles! [4] there's nothing in 'em i' the world. What do you talk on it? Because I dwell at Hogsden, [5] [54 I shall keep company with none but the archers of Finsbury, or the citizens that come a ducking to Islington ponds! A fine jest, i' faith! 'Slid, [3] a gentleman mun [6] show himself like a gentleman. Uncle, I pray you be not angry; I know what I have to do, I trow, I am no [60 novice.
Know. You are a prodigal, absurd coxcomb, go to!
Nay, never look at me, 't is I that speak;
Take 't as you will, sir, I'll not flatter you.
Ha' you not yet found means enow to waste　65

[1] Foolish.　　　　[2] I-wis, certainly.
[3] By God's eyelid — one of the frequent oaths by parts of Christ's body.
[4] Scabs, scurvy fellows.　　[5] Hoxton.　　[6] Must.

That which your friends have left you, but you must
Go cast away your money on a kite,
And know not how to keep it, when you ha' done?
O, it's comely! This will make you a gentleman!　60
Well, cousin, well, I see you are e'en past hope
Of all reclaim. — Ay, so, now you are told on 't,
You look another way. —
Step. 　　　　What would you ha' me do?
Know. What would I have you do? I'll tell you, kinsman;
Learn to be wise, and practise how to thrive;
That would I have you do: and not to spend　75
Your coin on every bauble that you fancy,
Or every foolish brain that humours you.
I would not have you to invade each place,
Nor thrust yourself on all societies,
Till men's affections, or your own desert,　80
Should worthily invite you to your rank.
He that is so respectless in his courses,
Oft sells his reputation at cheap market.
Nor would I you should melt away yourself
In flashing bravery, [7] lest, while you affect [8]　85
To make a blaze of gentry to the world,
A little puff of scorn extinguish it;
And you be left like an unsavoury snuff,
Whose property is only to offend.
I'd ha' you sober, and contain yourself,　90
Not that your sail be bigger than your boat;
But moderate your expenses now, at first,
As you may keep the same proportion still:
Nor stand so much on your gentility,
Which is an airy and mere borrow'd thing,　95
From dead men's dust and bones; and none of
yours,
Except you make, or hold it. Who comes here?

SCENE II.[9]

KNOWELL, STEPHEN. [*Enter a*] Servant.

Serv. Save you, gentlemen!
Step. Nay, we do not stand much on our gentility, friend; yet you are welcome: and I assure you mine uncle here is a man of a thousand a year, Middlesex land. He has but one son in [5 all the world, I am his next heir, at the common law, master Stephen, as simple as I stand here, if my cousin die, as there's hope he will. I have a pretty living o' mine own too, beside, hard by here.　10
Serv. In good time, sir.
Step. In good time, sir! Why, and in very good time, sir! You do not flout, friend, do you?
Serv. Not I, sir.
Step. Not you, sir! you were not best, sir; [15 an you should, here be them can perceive it, and that quickly too; go to: and they can give it again soundly too, an need be.
Serv. Why, sir, let this satisfy you; good faith, I had no such intent.　20
Step. Sir, an I thought you had, I would talk with you, and that presently.[10]

[7] Waste your means on showy clothes.　　[8] Desire
[9] The same. The scene-divisions are Jonson's.
[10] At once.

Serv. Good master Stephen, so you may, sir,
at your pleasure.

Step. And so I would, sir, good my saucy [25
companion! An you were out o' mine uncle's
ground, I can tell you; though I do not stand
upon my gentility neither, in 't.

Know. Cousin, cousin, will this ne'er be left?

Step. Whoreson, base fellow! a mechanical [30
serving-man! By this cudgel, an 't were not for
shame, I would ——

Know. What would you do, you peremptory
gull? [1]
If you cannot be quiet, get you hence.
You see the honest man demeans himself   35
Modestly tow'rds you, giving no reply
To your unseason'd, quarrelling, rude fashion;
And still you huff [2] it, with a kind of carriage
As void of wit, as of humanity.
Go, get you in; 'fore heaven, I am asham'd   40
Thou hast a kinsman's interest in me.
                    [*Exit* MASTER STEPHEN.]

Serv. I pray, sir, is this master Knowell's
house?

Know. Yes, marry is it, sir.   44

Serv. I should inquire for a gentleman here,
one master Edward Knowell; do you know any
such, sir, I pray you?

Know. I should forget myself else, sir.

Serv. Are you the gentleman? Cry you mercy, sir: I was requir'd by a gentleman i' the [50
city, as I rode out at this end o' the town, to deliver you this letter, sir.

Know. To me, sir! What do you mean? pray
you remember your court'sy. [3] [*Reads.*] *To his
most selected friend, master Edward Knowell.* [55
What might the gentleman's name be, sir, that
sent it? Nay, pray you be cover'd.

Serv. One master Wellbred, sir.

Know. Master Wellbred! a young gentleman,
is he not?   60

Serv. The same, sir; master Kitely married
his sister; the rich merchant i' the Old Jewry.

Know. You say very true. — Brainworm!

[*Enter* BRAINWORM.]

Brai. Sir.   64

Know. Make this honest friend drink here:
pray you, go in.

                    [*Exeunt* BRAINWORM *and* Servant.]
This letter is directed to my son;
Yet I am Edward Knowell too, and may,
With the safe conscience of good manners, use
The fellow's error to my satisfaction.   70
Well, I will break it ope (old men are curi-
ous),
Be it but for the style's sake and the phrase,
To see if both do answer my son's praises,
Who is almost grown the idolater
Of this young Wellbred. What have we here?   75
What 's this?
[*Reads.*] Why, Ned, I beseech thee, hast thou
forsworn all thy friends i' the Old Jewry? or
dost thou think us all Jews that inhabit there?
Yet, if thou dost, come over, and but see our [79

---

frippery; [4] change an old shirt for a whole smock
with us: do not conceive that antipathy between
us and Hogsden, as was between Jews and hogs-
flesh. Leave thy vigilant father alone, to
number over his green apricots, evening and [84
morning, o' the north-west wall. An I had been
his son, I had sav'd him the labour long since,
if taking in all the young wenches that pass by
at the back-door, and coddling [5] every kernel
of the fruit for 'em, would ha' serv'd. But [89
prithee, come over to me quickly this morning;
I have such a present for thee! — our Turkey
company never sent the like to the Grand Signior. One is a rhymer, sir, o' your own batch,
your own leaven; but doth think himself poet-
major o' the town, willing to be shown, and [95
worthy to be seen. The other — I will not venture his description with you, till you come, because I would ha' you make hither with an
appetite. If the worst of 'em be not worth your
journey, draw your bill of charges, as un- [100
conscionable as any Guildhall verdict will give it
you, and you shall be allow'd your viaticum. [6]
                    From the Windmill. [7]
From the Bordello it might come as well,
The Spittle, or Piet-hatch. [8] Is this the man
My son hath sung so, for the happiest wit,   105
The choicest brain, the times have sent us
forth!
I know not what he may be in the arts,
Nor what in schools; but, surely, for his man-
ners,
I judge him a profane and dissolute wretch;
Worse by possession of such great good gifts,110
Being the master of so loose a spirit.
Why, what unhallow'd ruffian would have
writ
In such a scurrilous manner to a friend!
Why should he think I tell [9] my apricots,
Or play the Hesperian dragon with my fruit, 115
To watch it? Well, my son, I 'd thought
You'd had more judgment t' have made elec-
tion
Of your companions, than t' have ta'en on
trust
Such petulant, jeering gamesters, that can spare
No argument or subject from their jest.   120
But I perceive affection makes a fool
Of any man too much the father. — Brainworm!

[*Enter* BRAINWORM.]

Brai. Sir.

Know. Is the fellow gone that brought this
letter?

Brai. Yes, sir, a pretty while since.

Know. And where 's your young master?   125

Brai. In his chamber, sir.

Know. He spake not with the fellow, did he?

Brai. No, sir, he saw him not.

Know. Take you this letter, and deliver it my
son; but with no notice that I have open'd it, on
your life.   131

Brai. O Lord, sir! that were a jest indeed.
                    [*Exit.*]

---

[1] Fool.   [2] Swagger.
[3] Put on your hat. Cf. *Love's Labour 's Lost*, V. i. 103.

[4] Old clothes shop.   [7] A tavern.
[5] Stewing.   [8] Places of ill-fame.
[6] Travelling expenses.   [9] Count.

Know. I am resolv'd I will not stop his jour-
   ney,
Nor practise any violent means to stay
The unbridled course of youth in him; for
   that   135
Restrain'd grows more impatient; and in kind
Like to the eager, but the generous[1] greyhound,
Who ne'er so little from his game withheld,
Turns head, and leaps up at his holder's throat.
There is a way of winning more by love   140
And urging of the modesty, than fear:
Force works on servile natures, not the free.
He that's compell'd to goodness, may be good,
But 't is but for that fit; where others, drawn
By softness and example, get a habit.   145
Then, if they stray, but warn 'em, and the same
They should for virtue 've done, they 'll do for
   shame.   [*Exit.*]

SCENE III.[2]

[*Enter*] E. KNOWELL, [*with a letter in his hand,
   followed by*] BRAINWORM.

E. Know. Did he open it, say'st thou?
Brai. Yes, o' my word, sir, and read the contents.
E. Know. That scarce contents me. What
countenance, prithee, made he i' the reading of
it? Was he angry or pleas'd?   6
Brai. Nay, sir, I saw him not read it, nor open
it, I assure your worship.
E. Know. No! How know'st thou then that
he did either?   10
Brai. Marry, sir, because he charg'd me, on
my life, to tell nobody that he open'd it;
which, unless he had done, he would never fear
to have it reveal'd.
E. Know. That's true: well, I thank thee,
Brainworm.   16

[*Enter* STEPHEN.]

Step. O, Brainworm, didst thou not see a fel-
low here in what-sha'-call-him doublet? He
brought mine uncle a letter e'en now.
Brai. Yes, master Stephen; what of him? 20
Step. O, I ha' such a mind to beat him ——
where is he, canst thou tell?
Brai. Faith, he is not of that mind: he is gone,
master Stephen.
Step. Gone! which way? When went he?
How long since?   26
Brai. He is rid hence; he took horse at the
street-door.
Step. And I staid i' the fields! Whoreson
Scanderbag[3] rogue! O that I had but a horse
to fetch him back again!   31
Brai. Why, you may ha' my master's gelding,
to save your longing, sir.
Step. But I ha' no boots, that's the spite on't.
Brai. Why, a fine wisp of hay, roll'd hard,
master Stephen.   36

---

[1] Well-bred.
[2] A room in Knowell's house.
[3] The Albanian patriot, Castriot, whose life was translated from the French in 1596; known also as Iskander
(Alexander) Bey, whence *Scanderbeg* or *Scanderbag*.

Step. No, faith, it's no boot to follow him
now: let him e'en go and hang. Prithee, help
to truss[4] me a little: he does so vex me ——
Brai. You'll be worst vex'd when you are [40
truss'd, master Stephen. Best keep unbrac'd,
and walk yourself till you be cold; your choler
may founder you else.
Step. By my faith, and so I will, now thou
tell'st me on't. How dost thou like my leg,
Brainworm?   46
Brai. A very good leg, master Stephen; but
the woollen stocking does not commend it so
well.   49
Step. Foh! the stockings be good enough,
now summer is coming on, for the dust: I 'll
have a pair of silk again'[5] winter, that I go to
dwell in the town. I think my leg would shew
in a silk hose ——   54
Brai. Believe me, master Stephen, rarely well.
Step. In sadness,[6] I think it would; I have a
reasonable good leg.
Brai. You have an excellent good leg, master
Stephen; but I cannot stay to praise it longer
now, and I am very sorry for it.   [*Exit.*] 60
Step. Another time will serve, Brainworm,
Gramercy for this.
E. Know. Ha, ha, ha! (*Laughs, having read
the letter.*)
Step. 'Slid, I hope he laughs not at me; an he
do ——   65
E. Know. Here was a letter indeed, to be intercepted by a man's father, and do him good
with him! He cannot but think most virtuously,
both of me, and the sender, sure, that make the
careful costermonger of him in our familiar [70
epistles. Well, if he read this with patience I'll
be gelt, and troll ballads for Master John
Trundle[7] yonder, the rest of my mortality. It
is true, and likely, my father may have as much
patience as another man, for he takes much [75
physic; and oft taking physic makes a man
very patient. But would your packet, Master
Wellbred, had arriv'd at him in such a minute of his patience! then we had known the end
of it, which now is doubtful, and threatens ——
[*sees* MASTER STEPHEN.] What, my wise [81
cousin! Nay, then I 'll furnish our feast with one
gull more toward the mess. He writes to me of
a brace, and here's one, that's three: oh, for a
fourth! Fortune, if ever thou 'lt use thine eyes,
I entreat thee ——   86
Step. Oh, now I see who he laughed at: he
laughed at somebody in that letter. By this
good light, an he had laughed at me ——   89
E. Know. How now, cousin Stephen, melancholy?
Step. Yes, a little: I thought you had laughed
at me, cousin.
E. Know. Why, what an I had, coz? What
would you ha' done?   95
Step. By this light, I would ha' told mine
uncle.

---

[4] Tie the laces which took the place of buttons. It
was also slang for beat.
[5] Against, in preparation for.
[6] Seriously.   [7] A printer.

E. Know. Nay, if you would ha' told your
uncle, I did laugh at you, coz.

Step. Did you, indeed?   100

E. Know. Yes, indeed.

Step. Why then ——

E. Know. What then?

Step. I am satisfied ; it is sufficient.   104

E. Know. Why, be so, gentle coz: and, I
pray you, let me entreat a courtesy of you. I
am sent for this morning by a friend i' the
Old Jewry, to come to him ; it is but crossing
over the fields to Moorgate. Will you bear me
company? I protest it is not to draw you into
bond or any plot against the state, coz.   111

Step. Sir, that's all one an 't were ; you
shall command me twice so far as Moorgate, to
do you good in such a matter. Do you think I
would leave you? I protest ——   115

E. Know. No, no, you shall not protest, coz.

Step. By my fackings,[1] but I will, by your
leave : — I 'll protest more to my friend, than
I 'll speak of at this time.

E. Know. You speak very well, coz.   120

Step. Nay, not so neither, you shall pardon
me : but I speak to serve my turn.

E. Know. Your turn, coz! Do you know what
you say? A gentleman of your sort,[2] parts, [124
carriage, and estimation, to talk o' your turn [3
i' this company, and to me alone, like a tankard-
bearer at a conduit! fie! A wight that,
hitherto, his every step hath left the stamp of
a great foot behind him, as every word the [129
savour of a strong spirit, and he! this man! so
grac'd, gilded, or, to use a more fit metaphor,
so tin-foil'd by nature, as not ten housewives'
pewter again' a good time,[4] shows more bright
to the world than he! and he! (as I said last,
so I say again, and still shall say it) this [135
man! to conceal such real ornaments as these,
and shadow their glory, as a milliner's wife does
her wrought stomacher, with a smoky lawn, or a
black cyprus![5] O, coz! it cannot be answer'd; [139
go not about it. Drake's old ship[6] at Deptford
may sooner circle the world again. Come, wrong
not the quality of your desert, with looking
downward, coz ; but hold up your head, so : and
let the idea of what you are be portrayed i' your
face, that men may read i' your physnomy, *Here
within this place is to be seen the true, rare,* [146
and accomplish'd monster, or miracle of nature,
which is all one. What think you of this, coz?

Step. Why, I do think of it : and I will be
more proud, and melancholy, and gentleman-
like, than I have been, I 'll insure you.   151

E. Know. Why, that's resolute, master
Stephen! — [*Aside.*] Now, if I can but hold him
up to his height, as it is happily begun, it will
do well for a suburb humour : we may hap have
a match with the city, and play him for forty [156
pound. — Come, coz.

Step. I 'll follow you.

E. Know. Follow me! You must go before.

---

[1] Faith, a minced oath.   [2] Rank.

[3] Water-carriers (tankard-bearers) were paid at so
much a " turn " or journey from the conduit.

[4] In preparation for a festivity.

[5] Crape.   [6] *The Golden Hind.*

Step. Nay, an I must, I will. Pray you shew
me, good cousin.   [*Exeunt.*]   161

SCENE IV.[7]

[*Enter*] MASTER MATHEW.

Mat. I think this be the house. What, ho!

[*Enter* COB.]

Cob. Who's there? O, master Mathew! gi'
your worship good morrow.

Mat. What, Cob! how dost thou, good Cob?
Dost thou inhabit here, Cob?   5

Cob. Ay, sir, I and my lineage ha' kept a
poor house here, in our days.

Mat. Thy lineage, monsieur Cobb! What lineage, what lineage?

Cob. Why, sir, an ancient lineage, and a [10
princely. Mine ance'try came from a king's belly
no worse man ; and yet no man either, by your
worship's leave, I did lie in that, but herring,
the king of fish (from his belly I proceed), one
o' the monarchs o' the world, I assure you. [15
The first red herring that was broil'd in Adam
and Eve's kitchen, do I fetch my pedigree from,
by the harrot's[8] book. His cob[9] was my great,
great, mighty-great grandfather.

Mat. Why mighty, why mighty, I pray
thee?   21

Cob. O, it was a mighty while ago, sir, and a
mighty great cob.

Mat. How know'st thou that?

Cob. How know I! why, I smell his ghost
ever and anon.   26

Mat. Smell a ghost! O unsavoury jest! and
the ghost of a herring cob?

Cob. Ay, sir. With favour of your worship's
nose, master Mathew, why not the ghost of [30
a herring cob, as well as the ghost of Rasher
Bacon?

Mat. Roger Bacon, thou would'st say.

Cob. I say Rasher Bacon. They were both
broil'd o' the coals ; and a man may smell broil'd
meat, I hope! You are a scholar ; upsolve [36
me that now.

Mat. O raw ignorance! — Cob, canst thou
shew me of a gentleman, one captain Bobadill,
where his lodging is?   40

Cob. O, my guest, sir, you mean.

Mat. Thy guest! alas, ha, ha!

Cob. Why do you laugh, sir? Do you not
mean captain Bobadill?

Mat. Cob, pray thee advise thyself well ; do [45
not wrong the gentleman, and thyself too. I
dare be sworn, he scorns thy house ; he! he lodge
in such a base obscure place as thy house! Tut,
I know his disposition so well, he would not lie
in thy bed if thou 'dst gi' it him.   50

Cob. I will not give it him though, sir. Mass,
I thought somewhat was in 't, we could not
get him to bed all night. Well, sir, though he
lie not o' my bed, he lies o' my bench ; an 't
please you to go up, sir, you shall find him with
two cushions under his head, and his cloak [56
wrapt about him, as though he had neither won

---

[7] Lane before Cob's house.   [8] Herald's.

[9] Usually, the head of a herring ; in this play, a herring.

nor lost, and yet, I warrant, he ne'er cast [1] better in his life, than he has done to-night.

Mat. Why, was he drunk? 60

Cob. Drunk, sir! you hear not me say so. Perhaps he swallow'd a tavern-token, [2] or some such device, sir; I have nothing to do withal. I deal with water and not with wine. — Gi' me my tankard there, ho! — God b' wi' you, sir. It's six o'clock: I should ha' carried two [66 turns by this. What ho! my stopple! [3] come.

[*Enter* TIB *with a water-tankard.*]

Mat. Lie in a water-bearer's house! a gentleman of his havings! Well, I'll tell him my mind. 70

Cob, What, Tib; shew this gentleman up to the captain. [*Exit* TIB *with* MASTER MATHEW.] Oh, an my house were the Brazen-head [4] now! faith it would e'en speak *Moe* [5] fools yet. You should have some now would take this Mas- [75 ter Mathew to be a gentleman, at the least. His father's an honest man, a worshipful fishmonger, and so forth; and now does he creep and wriggle into acquaintance with all the brave gallants about the town, such as my guest is (O, [81 my guest is a fine man!), and they flout him (is invincibly. He useth every day to a merchant's house where I serve water, one master Kitely's, i' the Old Jewry; and here's the jest, he is in love with my master's sister, Mrs. Bridget, and calls her "Mistress"; and there he will sit [86 you a whole afternoon sometimes, reading o' these same abominable, vile (a pox on 'em! I cannot abide them), rascally verses, poyetry, poyetry, and speaking of interludes; 't will [90 make a man burst to hear him. And the wenches, they do so jeer, and ti-he at him. — Well, should they do so much to me, I'd forswear them all, by the foot of Pharaoh! There's an oath! How many water-bearers shall you [95 hear swear such an oath? O, I have a guest — he teaches me — he does swear the legiblest of any man christ'ned: *By St. George! The foot of Pharaoh! The body of me! As I am a gentleman and a soldier!* such dainty oaths! and withal [100 he does take this same filthy roguish tobacco, the finest and cleanliest! It would do a man good to see the fumes come forth at 's tonnels. [6] — Well, he owes me forty shillings, my wife lent him out of her purse, by sixpence a time, besides his lodging: I would I had it! I shall ha' it, he says, the next action. Helter skelter, hang [107 sorrow, care 'll kill a cat, up-tails all, and a louse for the hangman! [*Exit.*]

SCENE V.[7]

BOBADILL *is discovered lying on his bench.*

Bob. Hostess, hostess!

[*Enter* TIB.]

Tib. What say you, sir?

Bob. A cup o' thy small beer, sweet hostess.

Tib. Sir, there's a gentleman below would speak with you.

Bob. A gentleman! 'odso, I am not within.

Tib. My husband told me you were, sir.

Bob. What a plague — what meant he?

Mat. (*below.*) Captain Bobadill!

Bob. Who's there! — Take away the bason, good hostess; — Come up, sir. 11

Tib. He would desire you to come up, sir. You come into a cleanly house, here!

[*Enter* MATHEW.]

Mat. Save you, sir; save you, captain!

Bob. Gentle master Mathew! Is it you, sir? Please you sit down. 16

Mat. Thank you, good captain; you may see I am somewhat audacious.

Bob. Not so, sir. I was requested to supper last night by a sort [8] of gallants, where you [20 were wish'd for, and drunk to, I assure you.

Mat. Vouchsafe me, by whom, good captain?

Bob. Marry, by young Wellbred, and others. — Why, hostess, a stool here for this gentleman.

Mat. No haste, sir, 't is very well. 25

Bob. Body o' me! it was so late ere we parted last night, I can scarce open my eyes yet; I was but new risen, as you came. How passes the day abroad, sir? you can tell.

Mat. Faith, some half hour to seven. Now, [30 trust me, you have an exceeding fine lodging here, very neat, and private.

Bob. Ay, sir: sit down, I pray you. Master Mathew, in any case possess no gentlemen of our acquaintance with notice of my lodging. 35

Mat. Who? I, sir? No.

Bob. Not that I need to care who know it, for the cabin is convenient; but in regard I would not be too popular, and generally visited, as some are. 40

Mat. True, captain, I conceive you.

Bob. For, do you see, sir, by the heart of valour in me, except it be to some peculiar and choice spirits, to whom I am extraordinarily engag'd, as yourself, or so, I could not extend [45 thus far.

Mat. O Lord, sir! I resolve [9] so.

Bob. I confess I love a cleanly and quiet privacy, above all the tumult and roar of fortune. What new book ha' you there? What! "Go [50 by, Hieronymo?" [10]

Mat. Ay: did you ever see it acted? Is 't not well penn'd?

Bob. Well penn'd! I would fain see all the poets of these times pen such another play [55 as that was: they'll prate and swagger, and keep a stir of art and devices, when, as I am a gentleman, read 'em, they are the most shallow, pitiful, barren fellows that live upon the face of the earth again. 60

Mat. Indeed here are a number of fine speeches in this book. *O eyes, no eyes, but fountains fraught with tears!* There's a conceit! *Fountains fraught with tears! O life, no life, but lively form of death!* — another. *O world, no* [65

---

[1] Pun on *cast*, to throw dice, and to vomit.
[2] A cant term for getting drunk. (Reed.)　[3] Stopper.
[4] See Greene's *Friar Bacon and Friar Bungay*.
[5] More.　[6] Nostrils.　[7] Room in Cob's house.

[8] Company.　　　[9] I am sure of it.
[10] See *The Spanish Tragedy*, from Act. III of which Mathew reads the lines below.

world, but mass of public wrongs! — a third. *Con-*
fus'd and fill'd with murder and misdeeds! —
a fourth. O, the muses! Is 't not excellent?
Is 't not simply the best that ever you heard,
captain? Ha! how do you like it?   70

Bob. 'T is good.

Mat. To thee, the purest object to my sense,
The most refined essence heaven covers,
Send I these lines, wherein I do commence
The happy state of turtle-billing lovers.   75
If they prove rough, unpolish'd, harsh, and rude,
Haste made the waste : thus mildly I conclude.

Bob. Nay, proceed, proceed. Where 's this?
BOBADILL *is making himself ready*
all this while.

Mat. This, sir! a toy o' mine own, in my
nonage; the infancy of my muses. But [80
when will you come and see my study? Good
faith, I can shew you some very good things I
have done of late. — That boot becomes your
leg passing well, captain, methinks.

Bob. So, so; it 's the fashion gentlemen [85
now use.

Mat. Troth, captain, and now you speak o'
the fashion, master Wellbred's elder brother
and I are fall'n out exceedingly. This other
day, I happ'ned to enter into some discourse [90
of a hanger, [1] which, I assure you, both for
fashion and workmanship, was most peremptory [2] beautiful and gentlemanlike : yet he condemn'd, and cri'd it down for the most pied [3]
and ridiculous that he ever saw.   95

Bob. Squire Downright, the half-brother,
was 't not?

Mat. Ay, sir, he.

Bob. Hang him, rook! [4] he! why he has no
more judgment than a malt-horse. By St. [100
George, I wonder you 'ld lose a thought upon
such an animal; the most peremptory [2] absurd
clown of Christendom, this day, he is holden. I
protest to you, as I am a gentleman and a soldier, I ne'er chang'd words with his like. [105
By his discourse, he should eat nothing but hay ;
he was born for the manger, pannier, or pack-
saddle. He has not so much as a good phrase in
his belly, but all old iron and rusty proverbs : a
good commodity for some smith to make [110
hob-nails of.

Mat. Ay, and he thinks to carry it away [5]
with his manhood still, where he comes : he
brags he will gi' me the bastinado, as I hear.

Bob. How! he the bastinado! How came [115
he by that word, trow?

Mat. Nay, indeed, he said cudgel me; I
term'd it so, for my more grace.

Bob. That may be ; for I was sure it was none
of his word : but when, when said he so?   120

Mat. Faith, yesterday, they say ; a young
gallant, a friend of mine, told me so.

Bob. By the foot of Pharaoh, an 't were my
case now, I should send him a chartel [6] presently.
The bastinado! a most proper and sufficient [125

dependence,[7] warranted by the great Caranza.[8]
Come hither, you shall chartel him ; I 'll show
you a trick or two you shall kill him with at
pleasure ; the first stoccata,[9] if you will, by this
air.   130

Mat. Indeed, you have absolute knowledge i'
the mystery, I have heard, sir.

Bob. Of whom, of whom, ha' you heard it,
I beseech you ?

Mat. Troth, I have heard it spoken of di- [135
vers, that you have very rare, and un-in-one-
breath-utterable skill, sir.

Bob. By heaven, no, not I ; no skill i' the
earth ; some small rudiments i' the science, as to
know my time, distance, or so. I have pro- [140
fest it more for noblemen and gentlemen's use,
than mine own practice, I assure you. — Hostess, accommodate us with another bed-staff here
quickly. [*Enter* TIB.] Lend us another bed-staff
— the woman does not understand the words [145
of action. — Look you, sir : exalt not your point
above this state, at any hand, and let your poniard maintain your defence, thus : — give it the
gentleman, and leave us. [*Exit* TIB.] So, sir.
Come on : O, twine your body more about, [150
that you may fall to a more sweet, comely,
gentleman-like guard ; so! indifferent : hollow
your body more, sir, thus : now, stand fast o'
your left leg, note your distance, keep your due
proportion of time. — Oh, you disorder your [155
point most irregularly !

Mat. How is the bearing of it now, sir ?

Bob. O, out of measure ill. A well experi-
enc'd hand would pass upon you at pleasure.

Mat. How mean you, sir, pass upon me ?   160

Bob. Why, thus, sir, — make a thrust at me
— [MASTER MATHEW *pushes at* BOBADILL]
come in upon the answer, control your point,
and make a full career at the body. The best-
practis'd gallants of the time name it the pas-
sado ; a most desperate thrust, believe it.   [166

Mat. Well, come, sir.

Bob. Why, you do not manage your weapon
with any facility or grace to invite me. I have
no spirit to play with you ; your dearth of [170
judgment renders you tedious.

Mat. But one venue,[10] sir.

Bob. "Venue!" fie ; the most gross denomi-
nation as ever I heard. O, the "stoccata,"
while you live, sir ; note that. — Come put [175
on your cloak, and we 'll go to some private
place where you are acquainted ; some tavern,
or so — and have a bit. I 'll send for one of
these fencers, and he shall breathe [11] you, by my
direction ; and then I will teach you your [180
trick : you shall kill him with it at the first, if
you please. Why, I will learn you, by the true
judgment of the eye, hand, and foot, to control
any enemy's point i' the world. Should your
adversary confront you with a pistol, 't were [185
nothing, by this hand! You should, by the
same rule, control his bullet, in a line, except it
were hail shot, and spread. What money have
you about you, master Mathew ?

---

[1] A strap by which a weapon was hung from the
girdle.
[2] A mere intensive, common in Elizabethan fashionable slang.   [3] Variegated.
[4] Fool, humbug.   [5] Domineer.   [6] Challenge.

[7] Ground for a duel.
[8] Author of the *Philosophy of Arms*, 1569.
[9] Thrust.   [10] Bout.   [11] Exercise.

Mat. Faith, I ha' not past a two shillings [190
or so.

Bob. 'T is somewhat with the least; but
come; we will have a bunch of radish and salt
to taste our wine, and a pipe of tobacco to close
the orifice of the stomach: and then we 'll [195
call upon young Wellbred. Perhaps we shall
meet the Corydon [1] his brother there, and put
him to the question.   [*Exeunt.*]

ACT II

Scene I.[2]

[*Enter*] Kitely, Cash, Downright.

Kit. Thomas, come hither.
There lies a note within upon my desk;
Here take my key: it is no matter neither. —
Where is the boy?
Cash.   Within, sir, i' the warehouse.
Kit. Let him tell over straight that Spanish
gold,   5
And weigh it, with th' pieces of eight.[3] Do you
See the delivery of those silver stuffs
To Master Lucar: tell him, if he will,
He shall ha' the grograns [4] at the rate I told him,
And I will meet him on the Exchange anon.   10
Cash. Good, sir.   [*Exit.*]
Kit. Do you see that fellow, brother Down-
right?
Dow. Ay, what of him?
Kit.   He is a jewel, brother.
I took him of a child up at my door,
And christ'ned him, gave him mine own name,
Thomas: 15
Since bred him at the Hospital; [5] where proving
A toward imp, I call'd him home, and taught
him
So much, as I have made him my cashier,
And giv'n him, who had none, a surname, Cash:
And find him in his place so full of faith,   20
That I durst trust my life into his hands.
Dow. So would not I in any bastard's, brother,
As it is like he is, although I knew
Myself his father. But you said you 'd somewhat
To tell me, gentle brother: what is 't, what is 't?
Kit. Faith, I am very loath to utter it,   26
As fearing it may hurt your patience;
But that I know your judgment is of strength,
Against the nearness of affection ——
Dow. What need this circumstance? [6] Pray
you, be direct.   30
Kit. I will not say how much I do ascribe
Unto your friendship, nor in what regard
I hold your love; but let my past behaviour,
And usage of your sister, [both] [7] confirm
How well I 've been affected to your ——   35
Dow. You are too tedious; come to the mat-
ter, the matter.

---

[1] Rustic.
[2] The Old Jewry. A hall in Kitely's house.
[3] Coins worth eight reals, or a little more than two
dollars.
[4] Cloth partly made of silk.
[5] Christ's Hospital, then a school for foundlings.
[6] Indirect approach to the matter.   [7] Fol. *but.*

Kit. Then, without further ceremony, thus.
My brother Wellbred, sir, I know not how,
Of late is much declin'd in what he was,
And greatly alter'd in his disposition.   40
When he came first to lodge here in my house,
Ne'er trust me if I were not proud of him:
Methought he bare himself in such a fashion,
So full of man, and sweetness in his carriage,
And what was chief, it show'd not borrowed in
him,   45
But all he did became him as his own,
And seem'd as perfect, proper, and possest,
As breath with life, or colour with the blood.
But now, his course is so irregular,
So loose, affected, and depriv'd of grace,   50
And he himself withal so far fall'n off
From that first place, as scarce no note remains,
To tell men's judgments where he lately stood.
He 's grown a stranger to all due respect,
Forgetful of his friends; and, not content   55
To stale [8] himself in all societies,
He makes my house here common as a mart,
A theatre, a public receptacle
For giddy humour, and diseased riot;
And here, as in a tavern, or a stews,   60
He and his wild associates spend their hours,
In repetition of lascivious jests,
Swear, leap, drink, dance, and revel night by
night,
Control my servants; and, indeed, what not?
Dow. 'Sdeins, [9] I know not what I should [65
say to him, i' the whole world! He values me
at a crack'd three-farthings, for aught I see. It
will never out o' the flesh that 's bred i' the bone.
I have told him enough, one would think, if that
would serve; but counsel to him is as good [70
as a shoulder of mutton to a sick horse. Well!
he knows what to trust to, for [10] George: let him
spend, and spend, and domineer, till his heart
ache; an he think to be reliev'd by me, when
he is got into one o' your city pounds, the [75
counters, he has the wrong sow by the ear, i'
faith; and claps his dish [11] at the wrong man's
door. I 'll lay my hand o' my halfpenny, ere I
part with 't to fetch him out, I 'll assure him.
Kit. Nay, good brother, let it not trouble you
thus.   80
Dow. 'Sdeath! he mads me; I could eat my
very spur-leathers for anger! But, why are you
so tame? Why do you not speak to him, and
tell him how he disquiets your house?
Kit. O, there are divers reasons to dissuade,
brother.   85
But, would yourself vouchsafe to travail in it
(Though but with plain and easy circumstance),
It would both come much better to his sense,
And savour less of stomach,[12] or of passion.
You are his elder brother, and that title   90
Both gives and warrants you authority,
Which, by your presence seconded, must breed
A kind of duty in him, and regard;
Whereas, if I should intimate the least,

---

[8] Make cheap.
[9] An oath of obscure meaning, sometimes explained
as *Disdain.* Query, *God's veins?*
[10] 'Fore.   [11] Like a beggar with dish and clapper.
[12] Resentment.

It would but add contempt to his neglect, 95
Heap worse on ill, make up a pile of hatred,
That in the rearing would come tott'ring down,
And in the ruin bury all our love.
Nay, more than this, brother ; if I should speak,
He would be ready, from his heat of humour, [1]
And overflowing of the vapour in him, 101
To blow the ears of his familiars
With the false breath of telling what disgraces
And low disparagements I had put upon him :
Whilst they, sir, to relieve him in the fable, [2] 105
Make their loose comments upon every word,
Gesture, or look, I use ; mock me all over,
From my flat cap [3] unto my shining shoes ; [3]
And, out of their impetuous rioting phant'sies,
Beget some slander that shall dwell with me. 110
And what would that be, think you ? Marry, this :
They would give out, because my wife is fair,
Myself but lately married, and my sister
Here sojourning a virgin in my house,
That I were jealous ! — nay, as sure as death, 115
That they would say ; and, how that I had
　quarrell'd
My brother purposely, thereby to find
An apt pretext to banish them my house.
　Dow. Mass, perhaps so ; they 're like enough
　to do it.
　Kit. Brother, they would, believe it ; so
　should I, 120
Like one of these penurious quack-salvers,
But set the bills up [4] to mine own disgrace,
And try experiments upon myself ;
Lend scorn and envy opportunity
To stab my reputation and good name —— 125

SCENE II.[5]

KITELY, DOWNRIGHT. [*Enter*] MATHEW [*struggling with*] BOBADILL.

　Mat. I will speak to him.
　Bob. Speak to him ! away ! By the foot of
Pharaoh, you shall not ! you shall not do him
that grace. — The time of day to you, gentleman o' the house. Is master Wellbred stirring ?
　Dow. How then ? What should he do ? 6
　Bob. Gentleman of the house, it is to you. Is
he within, sir ?
　Kit. He came not to his lodging to-night, sir,
I assure you. 10
　Dow. Why, do you hear ? You !
　Bob. The gentleman citizen hath satisfied
me ;
I 'll talk to no scavenger. [*Exeunt* BOB. *and*
MAT.]
　Dow. How ! scavenger ! Stay, sir, stay !
　Kit. Nay, brother Downright. 15
　Dow. 'Heart ! stand you away, an you love me.
　Kit. You shall not follow him now, I pray
you, brother, good faith you shall not ; I will
overrule you.
　Dow. Ha ! scavenger ! Well, go to, I say [20
little ; but, by this good day (God forgive me I
should swear), if I put it up [6] so, say I am the
rankest cow that ever pist. 'Sdeins, an I swallow

this, I 'll ne'er draw my sword in the sight of
Fleet-street again while I live ; I 'll sit in a [25
barn with madge-howlet, and catch mice first.
Scavenger ! heart ! — and I 'll go near to fill that
huge tumbrel-slop [7] of yours with somewhat, an
I have good luck : your Garagantua breech cannot carry it away so. 30
　Kit. Oh, do not fret yourself thus ; never
think on 't.
　Dow. These are my brother's consorts, these !
These are his cam'rades, his walking mates !
He 's a gallant, a cavaliero too, right hangman
cut ! Let me not live, an I could not find in [35
my heart to swinge the whole ging [8] of 'em, one
after another, and begin with him first. I am
griev'd it should be said he is my brother, and
take these courses. Well, as he brews, so shall
he drink, for George, again. Yet he shall [40
hear on 't, and that tightly too, an I live, i' faith.
　Kit. But, brother, let your reprehension, then,
Run in an easy current, not o'er high
Carried with rashness, or devouring choler ;
But rather use the soft persuading way, 45
Whose powers will work more gently, and compose
Th' imperfect thoughts you labour to reclaim ;
More winning than enforcing the consent.
　Dow. Ay, ay, let me alone for that, I warrant
you. 49
　Kit. How now ! (*Bell rings.*) Oh, the bell rings
to breakfast. Brother, I pray you go in, and
bear my wife company till I come ; I 'll but give
order for some despatch of business to my servants. [*Exit* DOWNRIGHT.]

SCENE III. [9]

KITELY, [*Enter*] COB.

　Kit. What, Cob ! our maids will have you by
the back, i' faith, for coming so late this morning.
　Cob. Perhaps so, sir ; take heed somebody
have not them by the belly, for walking so late
in the evening. 6
　　　　　He passes by with his tankard.
　Kit. Well ; yet my troubled spirit 's somewhat eas'd,
Though not repos'd in that security
As I could wish : but I must be content,
Howe'er I set a face on 't to the world. 10
Would I had lost this finger at a venture,
So Wellbred had ne'er lodged within my house.
Why 't cannot be, where there is such resort
Of wanton gallants and young revellers,
That any woman should be honest long. 15
Is 't like that factious beauty will preserve
The public weal of chastity unshaken,
When such strong motives muster and make
　head [10]
Against her single peace ? No, no : beware.
When mutual appetite doth meet to treat, 20
And spirits of one kind and quality
Come once to parley in the pride of blood,

---
[1] Temper.　　[3] Marks of the citizen.　　[5] The same.
[2] Narrative.　　[4] Advertise.　　[6] Endure it.

[7] Large puffed breeches.
[8] Gang.　　　　[9] The same.
[10] Gather their forces : a military phrase.

It is no slow conspiracy that follows.
Well, to be plain, if I but thought the time
Had answer'd their affections,[1] all the world 25
Should not persuade me but I were a cuckold.
Marry, I hope they ha' not got that start;
For opportunity hath balk'd 'em yet,
And shall do still, while I have eyes and ears
To attend the impositions of my heart. 30
My presence shall be as an iron bar
'Twixt the conspiring motions of desire:
Yea, every look or glance mine eye ejects
Shall check occasion, as one doth his slave,
When he forgets the limits of prescription. 35

[*Enter* DAME KITELY.]

Dame K. Sister Bridget, pray you fetch down
the rose-water, above in the closet. — Sweetheart, will you come in to breakfast?
Kit. An she have overheard me now!——
Dame Kit. I pray thee, good muss,[2] we stay
for you. 41
Kit. By heaven, I would not for a thousand
angels.[3]
Dame K. What ail you, sweet-heart? are you
not well? Speak, good muss. 45
Kit. Troth my head aches extremely on a
sudden.
Dame K. [*putting her hand to his forehead.*] O,
the Lord!
Kit. How now! What? 50
Dame K. Alas, how it burns! Muss, keep
you warm; good truth it is this new disease,[4]
there 's a number are troubled withal. For love's
sake, sweet-heart, come in out of the air.
Kit. How simple, and how subtle are her an-
swers! 55
A new disease, and many troubled with it?
Why true; she heard me, all the world to
nothing.
Dame K. I pray thee, good sweet-heart, come
in; the air will do you harm, in troth.
Kit. The air! she has me i' the wind.[5] — [60
Sweet-heart, I 'll come to you presently, 't will
away, I hope.
Dame K. Pray Heaven it do. [*Exit.*]
Kit. A new disease! I know not, new or old,
But it may well be call'd poor mortals' plague;[65]
For, like a pestilence, it doth infect
The houses of the brain. First it begins
Solely to work upon the phantasy,
Filling her seat with such pestiferous air
As soon corrupts the judgment; and from
thence 70
Sends like contagion to the memory:
Still each to other giving the infection,
Which as a subtle vapour spreads itself
Confusedly through every sensive part,
Till not a thought or motion in the mind 75
Be free from the black poison of suspect.[6]
Ah! but what misery is it to know this?

Or, knowing it, to want the mind's erection
In such extremes? Well, I will once more strive,
In spite of this black cloud, myself to be, 80
And shake the fever off that thus shakes me.
[*Exit.*]

[*Enter*] BRAINWORM [*disguised like a maimed
Soldier.*]

Brai. 'Slid, I cannot choose but laugh to see
myself translated thus, from a poor creature to
a creator; for now must I create an intolerable
sort[8] of lies, or my present profession loses the
grace: and yet the lie, to a man of my coat, is [5
as ominous a fruit as the fico.[9] O, sir, it holds
for good polity ever, to have that outwardly in
vilest estimation, that inwardly is most dear to
us: so much for my borrowed shape. Well, the
troth is, my old master intends to follow my [10
young master, dry-foot,[10] over Moorfields to
London, this morning; now, I knowing of this
hunting-match, or rather conspiracy, and to insinuate with my young master (for so must we
that are blue waiters,[11] and men of hope and [15
service do, or perhaps we may wear motley at
the year's end, and who wears motley,[12] — you
know), have got me afore in this disguise, de-
termining here to lie in ambuscado, and intercept him in the mid-way. If I can but get his [20
cloak, his purse, and his hat, nay, any thing to
cut him off, that is, to stay his journey, *Veni,
vidi, vici,* I may say with Captain Caesar, I am
made for ever, i' faith. Well, now I must practise to get the true garb of one of these lance- [25
knights, my arm here, and my —— [Odso! my]
young master, and his cousin, master Stephen,
as I am true counterfeit man of war, and no
soldier! [*Exit.*]

[*Enter* E. KNOWELL *and* STEPHEN.]

E. Know. So, sir! and how then, coz? 30
Step. 'Sfoot! I have lost my purse, I think.
E. Know. How! lost your purse? Where?
When had you it?
Step. I cannot tell; stay.
Brai. 'Slid, I am afraid they will know me:
would I could get by them! 36
E. Know. What, ha' you it?
Step. No; I think I was bewitcht, I ——
[*Cries.*]
E. Know. Nay, do not weep the loss: hang
it, let it go. 40
Step. Oh, it 's here. No, an it had been lost,
I had not car'd, but for a jet ring mistress Mary
sent me.
E. Know. A jet ring! O the posy, the posy?
Step. Fine, i' faith. — 45
　　　Though Fancy sleep,
　　　My love is deep.

[1] The opportunity had suited their desires.
[2] Mouse.
[3] Coins worth about $2.50.
[4] The fever of which Prince Henry died.
[5] Has got the scent of my suspicions.
[6] Suspicion.
[7] Moorfields.　　　　　　[8] Lot.
[9] To give the lie to a soldier is as fatal a thing as to
make the gesture of insult called the fig (thrusting out
the thumb between two fingers).
[10] Explained both as meaning to track by scent of the
foot, and by foot-marks without scent.
[11] Servants, who then wore blue livery.
[12] The fool.

Meaning, that though I did not fancy her, yet she loved me dearly.

E. Know. Most excellent! 50

Step. And then I sent her another, and my poesie was,

> The deeper the sweeter,
> I'll be judg'd by St. Peter.

E. Know. How, by St. Peter? I do not [55 conceive that.

Step. Marry, St. Peter, to make up the metre.

E. Know. Well, there the saint was your good patron, he help'd you at your need; thank him, thank him. 60

Re-enter BRAINWORM.

Brai. I cannot take leave on 'em so; 1 will venture, come what will. — Gentlemen, please you change a few crowns for a very excellent good blade here? I am a poor gentleman, a soldier, one that, in the better state of my for- [65 tunes, scorn'd so mean a refuge; but now it is the humour of necessity to have it so. You seem to be gentlemen well affected to martial men, else I should rather die with silence, than live with shame: however, vouchsafe to remem- [70 ber it is my want speaks, not myself; this condition agrees not with my spirit.

E. Know. Where hast thou serv'd?

Brai. May it please you, sir, in all the late wars of Bohemia, Hungary, Dalmatia, Po- [75 land, — where not, sir? I have been a poor servitor by sea and land any time this fourteen years, and follow'd the fortunes of the best commanders in Christendom. I was twice shot at the taking of Aleppo, once at the relief [80 of Vienna; I have been at Marseilles, Naples, and the Adriatic gulf, a gentleman-slave in the galleys, thrice; where I was most dangerously shot in the head, through both the thighs; and yet, being thus maim'd, I am void of main- [85 tenance, nothing left me but my scars, the noted marks of my resolution.

Step. How will you sell this rapier, friend?

Brai. Generous sir, I refer it to your own judgment; you are a gentleman, give me [90 what you please.

Step. True, I am a gentleman, I know that, friend; but what though? I pray you say, what would you ask?

Brai. I assure you, the blade may become [95 the side or thigh of the best prince in Europe.

E. Know. Ay, with a velvet scabbard, I think.

Step. Nay, an 't be mine, it shall have a velvet scabbard, coz, that 's flat; I 'd not wear it, as it is, an you would give me an angel. 100

Brai. At your worship's pleasure, sir; [STEPHEN *examines the blade*] nay, 't is a most pure Toledo.

Step. I had rather it were a Spaniard. But tell me, what shall I give you for it? An it had a silver hilt —— 106

E. Know. Come, come, you shall not buy it. Hold, there 's a shilling, fellow; take thy rapier.

Step. Why, but I will buy it now, because you say so; and there 's another shilling, fellow; 1 scorn to be out-bidden. What, shall I walk [111 with a cudgel, like Higginbottom, and may have a rapier for money!

E. Know. You may buy one in the city.

Step. Tut! I 'll buy this i' the field, so I will: I have a mind to 't, because 't is a field [116 rapier. Tell me your lowest price.

E. Know. You shall not buy it, I say.

Step. By this money, but I will, though I give more than 't is worth. 120

E. Know. Come away, you are a fool.

Step. Friend, I am a fool, that 's granted; but I 'll have it, for that word's sake. Follow me for your money.

Brai. At your service, sir. [*Exeunt.*] 125

SCENE V.[1]

[*Enter*] KNOWELL.

Know. I cannot lose the thought yet of this letter
Sent to my son; nor leave t' admire[2] the change
Of manners, and the breeding of our youth
Within the kingdom, since myself was one. —
When I was young, he liv'd not in the stews 5
Durst have conceiv'd a scorn, and utter'd it,
On a gray head; age was authority
Against a buffoon, and a man had then
A certain reverence paid unto his years,
That had none due unto his life: so much 10
The sanctity of some prevail'd for others.
But now we all are fall'n; youth, from their fear,
And age, from that which bred it, good example.
Nay, would ourselves were not the first, e'en parents, 14
That did destroy the hopes in our own children;
Or they not learn'd our vices in their cradles,
And suck'd in our ill customs with their milk!
Ere all their teeth be born, or they can speak,
We make their palates cunning; the first words
We form their tongues with, are licentious jests:
Can it call "whore"? cry "bastard"? O, then, kiss it! 21
A witty child! Can 't swear? The father's darling!
Give it two plums. Nay, rather than 't shall learn
No bawdy song, the mother herself will teach it!
But this is in the infancy, the days 25
Of the long coat; when it puts on the breeches,
It will put off all this. Ay, it is like,
When it is gone into the bone already!
No, no; this dye goes deeper than the coat,
Or shirt, or skin; it stains into the liver 30
And heart, in some: and, rather than it should not,
Note what we fathers do! Look how we live!
What mistresses we keep! at what expense!
In our sons' eyes, where they may handle our gifts,
Hear our lascivious courtships, see our dalliance,
Taste of the same provoking meats with us, 36
To ruin of our states! Nay, when our own
Portion is fled, to prey on the remainder,
We call them into fellowship of vice;
Bait 'em with the young chamber-maid, to seal,[3]

---

[1] Another part of Moorfields. [2] Wonder at

[3] Probably, to agree to the sale of family estates.

And teach 'em all bad ways to buy affliction. 41
This is one path ; but there are millions more,
In which we spoil our own, with leading them.
Well, I thank heaven, I never yet was he
That travell'd with my son, before sixteen,   45
To shew him the Venetian courtesans ;
Nor read the grammar of cheating I had made,
To my sharp boy, at twelve ; repeating still
The rule, *Get money ; still, get money, boy ;*
No matter by what means ; money will do   50
More, boy, than my lord's letter. Neither have I
Drest snails or mushrooms curiously before him,
Perfum'd my sauces, and taught him how to
    make 'em ;
Preceding still, with my gray gluttony,
At all the ord'naries, and only fear'd   55
His palates should degenerate, not his manners.
These are the trade of fathers now ; however,
My son, I hope, hath met within my threshold
None of these household precedents, which are
    strong
And swift to rape youth to their precipice.   60
But let the house at home be ne'er so clean
Swept, or kept sweet from filth, nay dust and
    cobwebs,
If he will live abroad with his companions,
In dung and leystals,[1] it is worth a fear ;
Nor is the danger of conversing less   65
Than all that I have mention'd of example.

[*Enter* Brainworm, *disguised as before.*]

Brai. [*Aside.*] My master ! nay, faith, have
at you ; I am flesht now, I have sped so well. —
Worshipful sir, I beseech you, respect the estate
of a poor soldier ; I am asham'd of this base [70
course of life, — God 's my comfort — but extremity provokes me to 't : what remedy ?
Know. I have not for you, now.
Brai. By the faith I bear unto truth, gentleman, it is no ordinary custom in me, but [75
only to preserve manhood. I protest to you, a
man I have been : a man I may be, by your
sweet bounty.
Know. Pray thee, good friend, be satisfied.
Brai. Good sir, by that hand, you may do [80
the part of a kind gentleman, in lending a poor
soldier the price of two cans of beer, a matter
of small value : the king of heaven shall pay you,
and I shall rest thankful. Sweet worship —— 85
Know. Nay, an you be so importunate ——
Brai. Oh, tender sir ! need will have its
course ; I was not made to this vile use. Well,
the edge of the enemy could not have abated
me so much : it 's hard when a man hath serv'd
in his prince's cause, and be thus (*Weeps*). [90
Honourable worship, let me derive a small piece
of silver from you, it shall not be given in the
course of time.[2] By this good ground, I was fain
to pawn my rapier last night for a poor supper ;
I had suck'd the hilts long before, I am a [95
pagan else. Sweet honour ——
Know. Believe me, I am taken with some
    wonder,
To think a fellow of thy outward presence,

---

[1] Dirt-heaps.
[2] Probably this means that ultimately it will turn out
to have been a loan.

Should, in the frame and fashion of his mind,
Be so degenerate, and sordid-base.   100
Art thou a man, and sham'st thou not to beg ?
To practise such a servile kind of life ?
Why, were thy education ne'er so mean,
Having thy limbs, a thousand fairer courses
Offer themselves to thy election.   105
Either the wars might still supply thy wants,
Or service of some virtuous gentleman,
Or honest labour ; nay, what can I name,
But would become thee better than to beg :
But men of thy condition feed on sloth,   110
As doth the beetle on the dung she breeds in ;
Nor caring how the metal of your minds
Is eaten with the rust of idleness.
Now, afore me, whate'er he be, that should
Relieve a person of thy quality,   115
While thou insist'st in this loose desperate
    course,
I would esteem the sin not thine, but his.
    Brai. Faith, sir, I would gladly find some
other course, if so ——
    Know. Ay, you 'd gladly find it, but you will
not seek it.   121
    Brai. Alas, sir, where should a man seek ?
In the wars, there 's no ascent by desert in these
days ; but —— and for service, would it were as
soon purchas'd,[3] as wisht for ! The air 's my [125
comfort. — |*Sighs*] — I know what I would say.
    Know. What 's thy name ?
    Brai. Please you, Fitz-Sword, sir.
    Know. Fitz-Sword !
Say that a man should entertain thee now,   130
Wouldst thou be honest, humble, just, and true?
    Brai. Sir, by the place and honour of a sol-
    dier ——
    Know. Nay, nay, I like not these affected
oaths. Speak plainly, man, what think'st thou
of my words ?   135
    Brai. Nothing, sir, but wish my fortunes were
as happy as my service should be honest.
    Know. Well, follow me, I 'll prove thee, if
    thy deeds
Will carry a proportion to thy words.   [*Exit.*]
    Brai. Yes, sir, straight ; I 'll but garter [140
my hose. Oh that my belly were hoopt now,
for I am ready to burst with laughing ! never
was bottle or bagpipe fuller. ' Slid, was there
ever seen a fox in years to betray himself thus !
Now shall I be possest of all his counsels ; [145
and, by that conduit, my young master. Well,
he is resolv'd to prove[4] my honesty ; faith, and
I 'm resolv'd to prove his patience : oh, I shall
abuse[5] him intolerably. This small piece of service will bring him clean out of love with [150
the soldier for ever. He will never come within
the sign of it, the sight of a cassock,[6] or a mus-
ket-rest again. He will hate the musters at
Mile-end for it, to his dying day. It 's no matter,
let the world think me a bad counterfeit, if [155
I cannot give him the slip[7] at an instant. Why,
this is better than to have staid his journey.
Well, I 'll follow him. Oh, how I long to be
employed !   [*Exit.*]

---

[3] Gained.   [4] Test.   [5] Deceive.
[6] A soldier's loose overcoat.
[7] A pun. *Slip* also meant counterfeit money.

ACT III

Scene I.[1]

[*Enter*] Master Mathew, Wellbred, *and* Bobadill.

Mat. Yes, faith, sir, we were at your lodging to seek you too.

Wel. Oh, I came not there to-night.

Bob. Your brother delivered us as much.

Wel. Who, my brother Downright?   5

Bob. He. Mr. Wellbred, I know not in what kind you hold me; but let me say to you this: as sure as honour, I esteem it so much out of the sunshine of reputation, to throw the least beam of regard upon such a ——   10

Wel. Sir, I must hear no ill words of my brother.

Bob. I protest to you, as I have a thing to be sav'd about me, I never saw any gentleman-like part ——   15

Wel. Good captain, faces about[2] to some other discourse.

Bob. With your leave, sir, an there were no more men living upon the face of the earth, I should not fancy him, by St. George!   20

Mat. Troth, nor I; he is of a rustical cut, I know not how: he doth not carry himself like a gentleman of fashion.

Wel. Oh, master Mathew, that's a grace peculiar but to a few, *quos aequus amavit Jupiter*.   25

Mat. I understand you, sir.

Wel. No question, you do, — [*Aside.*] or do you not, sir.

Enter E. Knowell [*and* Stephen].

Ned Knowell! by my soul, welcome: how dost thou, sweet spirit, my genius? 'Slid, I shall love Apollo and the mad Thespian girls[3] the better, [31 while I live, for this, my dear Fury; now I see there's some love in thee. Sirrah, these be the two I writ to thee of: nay, what a drowsy humour is this now! Why dost thou not speak?   35

E. Know. Oh, you are a fine gallant; you sent me a rare letter.

Wel. Why, was't not rare?

E. Know. Yes, I'll be sworn, I was ne'er guilty of reading the like; match it in all [40 Pliny, or Symmachus's epistles, and I'll have my judgment burn'd in the ear for a rogue: make much of thy vein, for it is inimitable. But I marle[4] what camel it was, that had the carriage of it; for, doubtless, he was no ordinary beast that brought it.   46

Wel. Why?

E. Know. "Why?" say'st thou! Why, dost thou think that any reasonable creature, especially in the morning, the sober time of the day too, could have mista'en my father for me?   51

Wel. 'Slid, you jest, I hope.

E. Know. Indeed, the best use we can turn it to, is to make a jest on't, now: but I'll assure you, my father had the full view of your [55 flourishing style some hour before I saw it.

---

[1] The Old Jewry. A room in the Windmill Tavern.
[2] A military term: face the opposite direction.
[3] The Muses.   [4] Marvel.

Wel. What a dull slave was this! But, sirrah, what said he to it, i' faith?

E. Know. Nay, I know not what he said; but I have a shrewd guess what he thought.   60

Wel. What, what?

E. Know. Marry, that thou art some strange, dissolute young fellow, and I — a grain or two better, for keeping thee company.

Wel. Tut! that thought is like the moon in [65 her last quarter, 't will change shortly. But, sirrah, I pray thee be acquainted with my two hang-by's here; thou wilt take exceeding pleasure in 'em if thou hear'st 'em once go; my [69 wind-instruments; I'll wind 'em up —— But what strange piece of silence is this? The sign of the Dumb Man?

E. Know. Oh, sir, a kinsman of mine, one that may make your music the fuller, an he please; he has his humour, sir.   75

Wel. Oh, what is't, what is't?

E. Know. Nay, I'll neither do your judgment nor his folly that wrong, as to prepare your apprehension; I'll leave him to the mercy o' your search; if you can take him, so!   80

Wel. Well, captain Bobadill, master Mathew, pray you know this gentleman here; he is a friend of mine, and one that will deserve your affection. — I know not your name, sir (*to* [84 Stephen), but I shall be glad of any occasion to render me more familiar to you.

Step. My name is master Stephen, sir; I am this gentleman's own cousin, sir; his father is mine uncle, sir. I am somewhat melancholy, [89 but you shall command me, sir, in whatsoever is incident to a gentleman.

Bob. (*to* E. Knowell.) Sir, I must tell you this, I am no general[5] man; but for master Wellbred's sake (you may embrace it at what height of favour you please), I do communi- [95 cate with you, and conceive you to be a gentleman of some parts; I love few words.

E. Know. And I fewer, sir; I have scarce enough to thank you.   99

Mat. But are you, indeed, sir, so given to it?

Step. Ay, truly, sir, I am mightily given to melancholy.

Mat. Oh, it's your only fine humour, sir: your true melancholy breeds your perfect fine wit, sir. I am melancholy myself, diver times, sir, and then do I no more but take pen and [106 paper presently, and overflow you half a score, or a dozen of sonnets at a sitting.

E. Know. (*Aside.*) Sure he utters them then by the gross.   110

Step. Truly, sir, and I love such things out of measure.

E. Know. I' faith, better than in measure, I'll undertake.

Mat. Why, I pray you, sir, make use of my study; it's at your service.   116

Step. I thank you, sir, I shall be bold I warrant you; have you a stool there to be melancholy upon?

Mat. That I have, sir, and some papers [120 there of mine own doing, at idle hours, that

---

[5] Open to general acquaintance.

you'll say there's some sparks of wit in 'em,
when you see them.

Wel. [*Aside.*] Would the sparks would kindle once, and become a fire amongst 'em! I [125
might see self-love burnt for her heresy.

Step. Cousin, is it well? Am I melancholy
enough?

E. Know. Oh ay, excellent.

Wel. Captain Bobadill, why muse you so? [130

E. Know. He is melancholy too.

Bob. Faith, sir, I was thinking of a most honourable piece of service, was perform'd to-
morrow, being St. Mark's day, shall be some
ten years now.　　　　　　　　　　135

E. Know. In what place, captain?

Bob. Why, at the beleag'ring of Strigonium,[1]
where, in less than two hours, seven hundred
resolute gentlemen, as any were in Europe, lost
their lives upon the breach. I'll tell you, gen- [140
tlemen, it was the first, but the best leaguer that
ever I beheld with these eyes, except the taking
in [2] of — what do you call it? [3] last year, by the
Genoways; [4] but that, of all other, was the most
fatal and dangerous exploit that ever I was [145
rang'd in, since I first bore arms before the face
of the enemy, as I am a gentleman and a soldier!

Step. So! I had as lief as an angel I could
swear as well as that gentleman.　　　　150

E. Know. Then, you were a servitor at both,
it seems; at Strigonium, and what do you call 't?

Bob. O lord, sir! By St. George, I was the
first man that ent'red the breach; and had
I not effected it with resolution, I had been
slain if I had had a million of lives.　　　156

E. Know. 'T was pity you had not ten; a cat's
and your own, i' faith. But, was it possible?

Mat. Pray you mark this discourse, sir.

Step. So I do.　　　　　　　　　　160

Bob. I assure you, upon my reputation, 't is
true, and yourself shall confess.

E. Know. [*Aside.*] You must bring me to the
rack, first.　　　　　　　　　　　164

Bob. Observe me judicially, sweet sir: they
had planted me three demi-culverins [5] just in
the mouth of the breach; now, sir, as we were
to give on,[6] their master-gunner (a man of no
mean skill and mark, you must think), con- [169
fronts me with his linstock,[7] ready to give fire;
I, spying his intendment, discharg'd my petro-
nel [8] in his bosom, and with these single arms,
my poor rapier, ran violently upon the Moors
that guarded the ordnance, and put 'em pell-
mell to the sword.　　　　　　　　175

Wel. To the sword! To the rapier, captain.

E. Know. Oh, it was a good figure observ'd,
sir. But did you all this, captain, without hurt-
ing your blade?

Bob. Without any impeach o' the earth: [180
you shall perceive, sir. [*Shews his rapier.*] It is
the most fortunate weapon that ever rid on poor

gentleman's thigh. Shall I tell you, sir? You
talk of Morglay, Excalibur, Durindana,[9] or so;
tut! I lend no credit to that is fabled of 'em. [185
I know the virtue of mine own, and therefore
I dare the boldlier maintain it.

Step. I marle whether it be a Toledo or no.

Bob. A most perfect Toledo, I assure you,
sir.　　　　　　　　　　　　　190

Step. I have a countryman of his here.

Mat. Pray you, let's see, sir; yes, faith, it is.

Bob. This a Toledo? Pish!

Step. Why do you pish, captain?　　　194

Bob. A Fleming, by heaven! I'll buy them
for a guilder a-piece, an I would have a thousand
of them.

E. Know. How say you, cousin? I told you
thus much.　　　　　　　　　　　199

Wel. Where bought you it, master Stephen?

Step. Of a scurvy rogue soldier: a hundred
of lice go with him! He swore it was a Toledo.

Bob. A poor provant [10] rapier, no better.

Mat. Mass, I think it be indeed, now I look
on 't better.　　　　　　　　　　205

E. Know. Nay, the longer you look on 't, the
worse. Put it up, put it up.

Step. Well, I will put it up; but by — I have
forgot the captain's oath, I thought to ha'
sworn by it — an e'er I meet him ——　　210

Wel. O, it is past help now, sir; you must
have patience.

Step. Whoreson, coney-catching [11] rascal! I
could eat the very hilts for anger.　　　214

E. Know. A sign of good digestion; you have
an ostrich stomach, cousin.

Step. A stomach! Would I had him here,
you should see an I had a stomach.[12]

Wel. It's better as 't is. — Come, gentlemen,
shall we go?　　　　　　　　　　220

SCENE II.[13]

E. KNOWELL, MASTER STEPHEN, WELLBRED,
BOBADILL, MASTER MATHEW.

[*Enter*] BRAINWORM, [*disguised as before.*]

E. Know. A miracle, cousin; look here, look
here!

Step. Oh — God's lid. By your leave, do you
know me, sir?

Brai. Ay, sir, I know you by sight.　　　5

Step. You sold me a rapier, did you not?

Brai. Yes, marry, did I, sir.

Step. You said it was a Toledo, ha?

Brai. True, I did so.

Step. But it is none.　　　　　　　10

Brai. No, sir, I confess it; it is none.

Step. Do you confess it? Gentlemen, bear
witness, he has confest it: — By God's will, an
you had not confest it ——

E. Know. Oh, cousin, forbear, forbear!　15

Step. Nay, I have done, cousin.

---

[1] Gran, in Hungary, retaken from the Turks in 1597.
[2] Capture.
[3] He called it *Tortosa* in the Quarto.
[4] Genoese.　　　[5] A kind of cannon.　　[6] Charge.
[7] Stick to hold the lint for firing a cannon.
[8] Carbine.
[9] The swords of Bevis, Arthur, and Orlando, in the romances.
[10] Such as was regularly supplied to the common sol-dier.
[11] Swindling.
[12] Punning on *stomach* in the sense of courage.
[13] The same

Wel. Why, you have done like a gentleman ; he has confest it, what would you more ?

Step. Yet, by his leave, he is a rascal, under his favour, do you see.   20

E. Know. Ay, by his leave, he is, and under favour : a pretty piece of civility ! Sirrah, how dost thou like him ?

Wel. Oh, it 's a most precious fool, make much on him. I can compare him to nothing [25 more happily than a drum ; for every one may play upon him.

E. Know No, no, a child's whistle were far the fitter.

Brai. Shall I entreat a word with you ?   30

E. Know. With me, sir ? You have not another Toledo to sell, ha' you ?

Brai. You are conceited,[1] sir. Your name is Master Knowell, as I take it ?

E. Know. You are i' the right; you mean [35 not to proceed in the catechism, do you ?

Brai. No, sir ; I am none of that coat.

E. Know. Of as bare a coat, though. Well, say, sir.   39

Brai. [*taking* E. KNOW. *aside.*] Faith, sir, I am but servant to the drum [2] extraordinary, and indeed, this smoky varnish being washt off, and three or four patches remov'd, I appear your worship's in reversion, after the decease of your good father, — Brainworm.   45

E. Know. Brainworm ! 'Slight, what breath of a conjurer hath blown thee hither in this shape ?

Brai. The breath o' your letter, sir, this morning ; the same that blew you to the Windmill, and your father after you.   51

E. Know. My father !

Brai. Nay, never start, 't is true ; he has follow'd you over the fields by the foot, as you would do a hare i' the snow.   55

E. Know. Sirrah Wellbred, what shall we do, sirrah ? My father is come over after me.

Wel. Thy father ! Where is he ?

Brai. At justice Clement's house, in Coleman-street, where he but stays my return ; and then ——   61

Wel. Who 's this ? Brainworm !

Brai. The same, sir.

Wel. Why how, in the name of wit, com'st thou transmuted thus ?   65

Brai. Faith, a device, a device ; nay, for the love of reason, gentlemen, and avoiding the danger, stand not here ; withdraw, and I 'll tell you all.   69

Wel. But art thou sure he will stay thy return ?

Brai. Do I live, sir ? What a question is that !

Wel. We 'll prorogue his expectation, then, a little : Brainworm, thou shalt go with us. — Come on, gentlemen. — Nay, I pray thee, [75 sweet Ned, droop not ; 'heart, an our wits be so wretchedly dull, that one old plodding brain can outstrip us all, would we were e'en prest [3] to make porters of, and serve out the remnant

---

[1] Witty.
[2] An allusion to the tricky servant in *Jack Drum's Entertainment.*
[3] Impressed.

of our days in Thames-street, or at Custom- [80 house quay, in a civil war against the carmen !

Brai. Amen, amen, amen, say I.   [*Exeunt.*]

Scene III.[4]

[*Enter*] KITELY and CASH.

Kit. What says he, Thomas ? Did you speak with him ?

Cash. He will expect you, sir, within this half hour.

Kit. Has he the money ready, can you tell ?

Cash. Yes, sir, the money was brought in last night.

Kit. O, that is well ; fetch me my cloak, my cloak ! —   [*Exit* CASH.]   5
Stay, let me see, an hour to go and come ;
Ay, that will be the least ; and then 't will be
An hour before I can dispatch with him,
Or very near ; well, I will say two hours.
Two hours ! ha ! things never dreamt of yet,   10
May be contriv'd, ay, and effected too,
In two hours' absence ; well, I will not go.
Two hours ! No, fleering Opportunity,
I will not give your subtilty that scope.
Who will not judge him worthy to be robb'd,   15
That sets his doors wide open to a thief,
And shews the felon where his treasure lies ?
Again, what earthy spirit but will attempt
To taste the fruit of beauty's golden tree,
When leaden sleep seals up the dragon's eyes ?
I will not go. Business, go by for once.   21
No, beauty, no ; you are of too good caract [5]
To be left so, without a guard, or open.
Your lustre, too, 'll inflame at any distance,
Draw courtship to you, as a jet doth straws ;   25
Put motion in a stone, strike fire from ice,
Nay, make a porter leap you with his burden.
You must be then kept up, close, and well watch'd,
For, give you opportunity, no quick-sand
Devours or swallows swifter ! He that lends   30
His wife, if she be fair, or time or place,
Compels her to be false. I will not go !
The dangers are too many : — and then the dressing
Is a most main attractive ! Our great heads
Within this city never were in safety   35
Since our wives wore these little caps. I 'll change 'em ;
I 'll change 'em straight in mine : mine shall no more
Wear three-piled [6] acorns, to make my horns ache,[7]
Nor will I go ; I am resolv'd for that.

[*Re-enter* CASH *with a cloak.*]

Carry in my cloak again. Yet stay. Yet do, too :
I will defer going, on all occasions.   41

Cash. Sir, Snare, your scrivener, will be there with th' bonds.

Kit. That 's true : fool on me ! I had clean forgot it ;
I must go. What 's a clock ?

---

[4] Kitely's warehouse.   [5] Carat, value, quality.
[6] Velvet of the best quality.
[7] Note the execrable pun on *acorns* and *horns ache.*

Cash.   Exchange-time,[1] sir.
Kit. 'Heart, then will Wellbred presently be
          here too,   45
With one or other of his loose consorts.
I am a knave if I know what to say,
What course to take, or which way to resolve.
My brain, methinks, is like an hour-glass,
Wherein my imaginations run like sands,   50
Filling up time; but then are turn'd and turn'd:
So that I know not what to stay upon,
And less, to put in act. — It shall be so.
Nay, I dare build upon his secrecy,
He knows not to deceive me. — Thomas!
Cash.   Sir.   55
Kit. Yet now I have bethought me, too, I will
          not. —
Thomas, is Cob within?
Cash.   I think he be, sir.
Kit. But he 'll prate too, there is no speech
          of him.
No, there were no man o' the earth to[2] Thomas,
If I durst trust him; there is all the doubt.   60
But should he have a chink in him, I were gone.
Lost i' my fame for ever, talk for th' Ex-
          change!
The manner he hath stood with, till this present,
Doth promise no such change: what should I
          fear then?
Well, come what will, I 'll tempt my fortune
          once.   65
Thomas — you may deceive me, but, I hope —
Your love to me is more—
Cash.   Sir, if a servant's
Duty, with faith, may be call'd love, you are
More than in hope, you are possess'd of it.
Kit. I thank you heartily, Thomas: give me
          your hand: 70
With all my heart, good Thomas. I have,
          Thomas,
A secret to impart unto you — but,
When once you have it, I must seal your lips
          up;
So far I tell you, Thomas.
Cash.   Sir, for that ——
Kit. Nay, hear me out. Think I esteem you,
          Thomas,   75
When I will let you in thus to my private.
It is a thing sits nearer to my crest,
Than thou art 'ware of, Thomas; if thou
          should'st
Reveal it, but ——
Cash.   How, I reveal it?
Kit.   Nay,
I do not think thou would'st; but if thou
          should'st,   80
'T were a great weakness.
Cash.   A great treachery:
Give it no other name.
Kit.   Thou wilt not do 't, then?
Cash. Sir, if I do, mankind disclaim me ever!
Kit. He will not swear, he has some reserva-
          tion,
Some conceal'd purpose, and close[3] meaning
          sure;   85

Else, being urg'd so much, how should he choose
But lend an oath to all this protestation?
He 's no precisian,[4] that I 'm certain of,
Nor rigid Roman Catholic: he 'll play
At fayles,[5] and tick-tack;[5] I have heard him
          swear.   90
What should I think of it? Urge him again,
And by some other way? I will do so.
Well, Thomas, thou hast sworn not to dis-
          close: —
Yes, you did swear?
Cash.   Not yet, sir, but I will,
Please you ——
Kit.   No, Thomas, I dare take thy word,
But, if thou wilt swear, do as thou think'st
          good;   95
I am resolv'd[6] without it; at thy pleasure.
Cash. By my soul's safety then, sir, I protest,
My tongue shall ne'er take knowledge of a word
Deliver'd me in nature of your trust.
Kit. It is too much; these ceremonies need   100
          not;
I know thy faith to be as firm as rock.
Thomas, come hither, near; we cannot be
Too private in this business. So it is, —
[*Aside.*] Now he has sworn, I dare the safelier
          venture.   105
I have of late, by divers observations ——
[*Aside.*] But whether his oath can bind him,
          yea, or no,
Being not taken lawfully?[7] Ha! say you?
I will ask council ere I do not proceed : —
Thomas, it will be now too long to stay,   110
I 'll spy some fitter time soon, or to-morrow.
Cash. Sir, at your pleasure.
Kit.   I will think: — and, Thomas,
I pray you search the books 'gainst my return,
For the receipts 'twixt me and Traps.
Cash.   I will, sir.
Kit. And hear you, if your mistress' brother,
          Wellbred,   115
Chance to bring hither any gentlemen
Ere I come back, let one straight bring me word.
Cash. Very well, sir.
Kit.   To the Exchange, do you hear?
Or here in Coleman-street, to justice Clement's.
Forget it not, nor be not out of the way.   120
Cash. I will not, sir.
Kit.   I pray you have a care on 't.
Or, whether he come or no, if any other,
Stranger, or else; fail not to send me word.
Cash. I shall not, sir.
Kit.   Be 't your special business
Now to remember it.
Cash.   Sir, I warrant you.   125
Kit. But, Thomas, this is not the secret,
          Thomas,
I told you of.
Cash.   No, sir; I do suppose it.
Kit. Believe me, it is not.
Cash.   Sir, I do believe you.
Kit. By heaven it is not, that 's enough. But,
          Thomas,
I would not you should utter it, do you see, 130

---

1 Ten o'clock, according to the Q.
2 Compared to.   3 Secret.

4 Puritan.
5 Games of chance, somewhat like back-gammon.
6 Convinced.   7 Before a magistrate.

To any creature living; yet I care not.
Well, I must hence. Thomas, conceive thus
much;
It was a trial of you, when I meant
So deep a secret to you; I mean not this, 134
But that I have to tell you; this is nothing, this.
But, Thomas, keep this from my wife, I charge
you,
Lock'd up in silence, midnight, buried here.—
No greater hell than to be slave to fear. [*Exit.*]
*Cash. Lock'd up in silence, midnight, buried
here!*
Whence should this flood of passion, trow, take
head? ha! 140
Best dream no longer of this running humour,
For fear I sink; the violence of the stream
Already hath transported me so far,
That I can feel no ground at all. But soft—
Oh, 't is our water-bearer: somewhat has crost
him now. 145

Scene IV.[1]

Cash. [*Enter*] Cob, [*hastily*].

Cob. Fasting-days! what tell you me of fasting-days? 'Slid, would they were all on a light
fire for me! They say the whole world shall be
consum'd with fire one day, but would I had
these Ember-weeks and villanous Fridays [5
burnt in the mean time, and then —
Cash. Why, how now, Cob? What moves
thee to this choler, ha?
Cob. Collar, master Thomas! I scorn your
collar, I, sir; I am none o' your cart-horse, [10
though I carry and draw water. An you offer to
ride me with your collar or halter either, I may
hap shew you a jade's trick, sir.
Cash. O, you 'll slip your head out of the
collar? Why, goodman Cob, you mistake me. 15
Cob. Nay, I have my rheum, and I can be
angry as well as another, sir.
Cash. Thy rheum, Cob! Thy humour, thy
humour — thou mistak'st.[2]
Cob. Humour! mack,[3] I think it be so in- [20
deed. What is that humour? Some rare thing,
I warrant.
Cash. Marry I 'll tell thee, Cob: it is a gentleman-like monster, bred in the special gallantry
of our time, by affectation, and fed by folly. 25
Cob. How! must it be fed?
Cash. Oh ay, humour is nothing if it be not
fed; didst thou never hear that? It 's a common
phrase, *Feed my humour.*
Cob. I 'll none on it: humour, avaunt! I know
you not, be gone! Let who will make hun- [31
gry meals for your monstership, it shall not be
I. Feed you, quoth he! 'Slid, I ha' much ado
to feed myself; especially on these lean rascally
days too; an 't had been any other day but a [35
fasting-day — a plague on them all for me! By
this light, one might have done the commonwealth good service, and have drown'd them all
i' the flood, two or three hundred thousand
years ago. O, I do stomach[4] them hugely. I [40

---
[1] The same.
[2] *Humour* had displaced *rheum* as the fashionable
word for whim, mood.
[3] Mass.
[4] Resent.

have a maw[5] now, and 't were for sir Bevis his
horse, against 'em.
Cash. I pray thee, good Cob, what makes thee
so out of love with fasting days?
Cob. Marry, that which will make any man [45
out of love with 'em, I think; their bad conditions, an you will needs know. First, they are of
a Flemish breed, I am sure on 't, for they raven
up more butter than all the days of the week
beside; next, they stink of fish and leek-porridge
miserably; thirdly, they 'll keep a man de- [51
voutly hungry all day, and at night send him
supperless to bed.
Cash. Indeed, these are faults, Cob. 54
Cob. Nay, an this were all, 't were something;
but they are the only known enemies to my
generation. A fasting-day no sooner comes, but
my lineage goes to wrack; poor cobs! they
smoke for it, they are made martyrs o' the grid-
iron, they melt in passion: and your maids [60
too know this, and yet would have me turn Hannibal,[6] and eat my own flesh and blood. My
princely coz (*Pulls out a red herring*), fear nothing; I have not the heart to devour you, an I
might be made as rich as king Cophetua. O that
I had room for my tears, I could weep salt- [66
water enough now to preserve the lives of ten
thousand of my kin! But I may curse none but
these filthy almanacs; for an 't were not for
them, these days of persecution would never [70
be known. I 'll be hang'd an some fishmonger's
son do not make of 'em, and puts in more fasting-days than he should do, because he would
utter[7] his father's dried stock-fish and stinking
conger. 75
Cash. 'Slight, peace! Thou 'lt be beaten like
a stock-fish else. Here is master Mathew. Now
must I look out for a messenger to my master.
[*Exeunt.*]

Scene V.[8]

[*Enter*] Wellbred, E. Knowell, Brainworm, Mathew, Bobadill, *and* Stephen.

Wel. Beshrew me, but it was an absolute
good jest, and exceedingly well carried!
E. Know. Ay, and our ignorance maintain'd
it as well, did it not?
Wel. Yes, faith; but was it possible thou [5
shouldst not know him? I forgive master
Stephen, for he is stupidity itself.
E. Know. 'Fore God, not I, an I might have
been join'd patten[9] with one of the seven wise
masters for knowing him. He had so written [10
himself into the habit of one of your poor [11
infantry, your decay'd, ruinous, worm-eaten
gentlemen of the round;[11] such as have vowed
to sit on the skirts of the city, let your provost
and his half-dozen of halberdiers do what [15
they can; and have translated begging out of
the old hackney-pace to a fine easy amble, and
made it run as smooth off the tongue as a shove-
groat shilling.[12] Into the likeness of one of these

---
[5] Stomach, appetite.
[6] Cannibal.
[7] Sell.
[8] The same.
[9] By a patent.
[10] Twisted.
[11] Under-officers who went the rounds, inspecting
sentries, etc.
[12] A smooth shilling used for playing shovel-board.

reformados [1] had he moulded himself so per- [20
fectly, observing every trick of their action, as,
varying the accent, swearing with an emphasis,
indeed, all with so special and exquisite a grace,
that, hadst thou seen him, thou wouldst have
sworn he might have been sergeant-major, [2] if
not lieutenant-colonel to the regiment.　　　26

Wel. Why, Brainworm, who would have
thought thou hadst been such an artificer ?

E. Know. An artificer ! an architect. Except
a man had studied begging all his life time, [30
and been a weaver of language from his infancy
for the clothing of it, I never saw his rival.

Wel. Where got'st thou this coat, I marle ? [3]

Brai. Of a Houndsditch man, sir, one of the
devil's near kinsmen, a broker.　　　35

Wel. That cannot be, if the proverb hold ;
for *A crafty knave needs no broker.*

Brai. True, sir ; but I did *need a broker,
ergo* ——

Wel. Well put off : — *no crafty knave,* you 'll
say.　　　41

E. Know. Tut, he has more of these shifts.

Brai. And yet, where I have one the broker
has ten, [4] sir.

[*Re-enter* CASH.]

Cash. Francis ! Martin ! Ne'er a one to be
found now ? What a spite 's this !　　　46

Wel. How now, Thomas ? Is my brother
Kitely within ?

Cash. No, sir, my master went forth e'en
now ; but master Downright is within. — Cob !
what, Cob ! Is he gone too ?　　　51

Wel. Whither went your master, Thomas,
canst thou tell ?

Cash. I know not : to justice Clement's, I
think, sir. — Cob !

E. Know. Justice Clement ! what 's he ?　　　56

Wel. Why, dost thou not know him ? He is
a city-magistrate, a justice here, an excellent
good lawyer, and a great scholar ; but the only
mad, merry old fellow in Europe. I show'd
him you the other day.　　　61

E. Know. Oh, is that he ? I remember him
now. Good faith, and he is a very strange presence methinks ; it shows as if he stood out of the
rank from other men : I have heard many [65
of his jests i' the University. They say he will
commit a man for taking the wall of his horse.

Wel. Ay, or wearing his cloak on one shoulder, or serving of God ; any thing indeed, if it
come in the way of his humour.　　　70

CASH *goes in and out calling.*

Cash. Gasper ! Martin ! Cob ! 'Heart, where
should they be, trow ?

Bob. Master Kitely's man, pray thee vouchsafe us the lighting of this match.　　　74

Cash. Fire on your match ! No time but now
to *vouchsafe ?* — Francis ! Cob !　　　[*Exit.*]

Bob. Body o' me ! here 's the remainder of
seven pound since yesterday was seven-night.

'T is your right Trinidado : [5] did you never take
any, master Stephen ?　　　80

Step. No, truly, sir ; but I 'll learn to take it
now, since you commend it so.

Bob. Sir, believe me upon my relation, for
what I tell you, the world shall not reprove. I
have been in the Indies, where this herb grows,
where neither myself, nor a dozen gentlemen [85
more of my knowledge, have received the taste
of any other nutriment in the world, for the
space of one-and-twenty weeks, but the fume
of this simple [6] only ; therefore it cannot be but
't is most divine. Further, take it in the na- [91
ture, in the true kind ; so, it makes an antidote,
that, had you taken the most deadly poisonous
plant in all Italy, it should expel it, and clarify
you, with as much ease as I speak. And for [95
your green wound, — your Balsamum and your
St. John's wort, are all mere gulleries and trash
to it, especially your Trinidado : your Nicotian [7]
is good too. I could say what I know of the
virtue of it, for the expulsion of rheums, [100
raw humours, crudities, obstructions, with a
thousand of this kind ; but I profess myself no
quacksalver. Only thus much ; by Hercules, I
do hold it, and will affirm it before any prince
in Europe, to be the most sovereign and pre- [105
cious weed that ever the earth tend'red to the
use of man.

E. Know. This speech would ha' done de-
cently in a tobacco-trader's mouth.

[*Re-enter* CASH *with* COB.]

Cash. At justice Clement's he is, in the [110
middle of Coleman-street.

Cob. Oh, oh !

Bob. Where 's the match I gave thee, master
Kitely's man ?　　　114

Cash. Would his match and he, and pipe and all,
were at Sancto Domingo ! I had forgot it. [*Exit.*]

Cob. By God's me, I marle what pleasure or
felicity they have in taking this roguish tobacco. It 's good for nothing but to choke a
man, and fill him full of smoke and embers. [120
There were four died out of one house last
week with taking of it, and two more the
bell went for yesternight ; one of them, they
say, will ne'er scape it ; he voided a bushel of
soot yesterday, upward and downward. By [125
the stocks, an there were no wiser men than I,
I 'd have it present whipping, man or woman,
that should but deal with a tobacco pipe. Why,
it will stifle them all in the end, as many as use
it ; it 's little better than ratsbane or rosaker. [8] 130

BOBADILL *beats him with a cudgel.*

All. Oh, good captain, hold, hold !

Bob. You base cullion, you !

Re-enter CASH.

Cash. Sir, here 's your match. — Come, thou
must needs be talking too, thou 'rt well enough
serv'd.　　　135

---

[1] Disbanded soldiers.　　　[2] Major, at that time.
[3] Marvel.
[4] Punning on the meanings of *shifts : devices,* and
changes of clothes.

[5] Tobacco from Trinidad was much prized.　　　[6] Herb.
[7] Tobacco named from M. Nicot, French ambassador
to Portugal in 1559. It is usually a generic name, and
the specific use here may be an intentional mistake.
[8] Common poisons.

Cob. Nay, he will not meddle with his match,
I warrant you. Well, it shall be a dear beating,
an I live.

Bob. Do you prate, do you murmur ?   139

E. Know. Nay, good captain, will you regard
the humour of a fool ? Away, knave.

Wel. Thomas, get him away.
                              [*Exit* CASH *with* COB.]

Bob. A whoreson filthy slave, a dung-worm,
an excrement ! Body o' Caesar, but that I scorn
to let forth so mean a spirit, I 'd have stabb'd
him to the earth.   146

Wel. Marry, the law forbid, sir !

Bob. By Pharaoh's foot, I would have done it.

Step. Oh, he swears most admirably ! By
Pharaoh's foot ! Body o' Caesar ! — I shall [150
never do it, sure. Upon mine honour, and by St.
George ! — No, I have not the right grace.

Mat. Master Stephen, will you any ? By this air,
the most divine tobacco that ever I drunk.[1] 154

Step. None, I thank you, sir. O, this gentleman does it rarely too : but nothing like the
other. By this air ! As I am a gentleman !
By ——   [*Exeunt* BOB. *and* MAT.]

Brai. Master, glance, glance ! master Wellbred !   STEPHEN *is practising to the post.* 160

Step. As I have somewhat to be saved, I protest ——

Wel. You are a fool ; it needs no affidavit.

E. Know. Cousin, will you any tobacco ?

Step. I, sir ! Upon my reputation ——

E. Know. How now, cousin !   165

Step. I protest, as I am a gentleman, but no
soldier, indeed ——

Wel. No, master Stephen ! As I remember,
your name is ent'red in the artillery-garden. 169

Step. Ay, sir, that 's true. Cousin, may I
swear " as I am a soldier " by that ?

E. Know. O yes, that you may ; it is all you
have for your money.

Step. Then, as I am a gentleman and a sol-
dier, it is " divine tobacco ! "   175

Wel. But soft, where 's master Mathew ? Gone ?

Brai. No, sir ; they went in here.

Wel. O let 's follow them. Master Mathew is
gone to salute his mistress in verse ; we shall
ha' the happiness to hear some of his poetry [180
now ; he never comes unfurnish'd. — Brainworm !

Step. Brainworm ! Where ? Is this Brainworm ?

E. Know. Ay, cousin ; no words of it, upon
your gentility.   185

Step. Not I, body o' me ! By this air ! St.
George ! and the foot of Pharaoh !

Wel. Rare ! Your cousin's discourse is simply
drawn out with oaths.   189

E. Know. 'T is larded with 'em ; a kind of
French dressing, if you love it.   [*Exeunt.*]

SCENE VI.[2]

[Enter] KITELY, COB.

Kit. Ha ! how many are there, sayest thou ?

Cob. Marry, sir, your brother, master Wellbred ——

Kit. Tut, beside him : what strangers are
there, man ?

Cob. Strangers ? let me see, one, two ; mass,
I know not well, there are so many.   5

Kit. How ! so many ?

Cob. Ay, there 's some five or six of them at
the most.

Kit. [*Aside.*] A swarm, a swarm !
Spite of the devil, how they sting my head
With forked stings, thus wide and large ! — But,
    Cob,   10
How long hast thou been coming hither, Cob ?

Cob. A little while, sir.

Kit. Didst thou come running ?

Cob. No, sir.

Kit. [*Aside.*] Nay, then I am familiar with
thy haste.   15
Bane to my fortunes ! what meant I to marry ?
I, that before was rankt in such content,
My mind at rest too, in so soft a peace,
Being free master of mine own free thoughts, 19
And now become a slave ? What ! never sigh,
Be of good cheer, man ; for thou art a cuckold :
'T is done, 't is done ! Nay, when such flowing-
    store,
Plenty itself, falls in[to] my wife's lap,
The cornucopiae will be mine, I know. —
But, Cob,   25
What entertainment had they ? I am sure
My sister and my wife would bid them wel-
    come : ha ?

Cob. Like enough, sir ; yet I heard not a word
of it.

Kit. No ; —
[*Aside.*] Their lips were seal'd with kisses, and
    the voice,   30
Drown'd in a flood of joy at their arrival,
Had lost her motion, state, and faculty. —
Cob, which of them was 't that first kist my wife,
My sister, I should say ? My wife, alas !
I fear not her ; ha ! who was it say'st thou ?   35

Cob. By my troth, sir, will you have the
truth of it ?

Kit. Oh, ay, good Cob, I pray thee heartily.

Cob. Then I am a vagabond, and fitter for
Bridewell than your worship's company, if I
saw any body to be kist, unless they would [40
have kist the post [3] in the middle of the warehouse ; for there I left them all at their tobacco,
with a pox !

Kit. How ! were they not gone in then ere
thou cam'st !

Cob. O no, sir.   45

Kit. Spite of the devil ! what do I stay here then ?
Cob, follow me.   [*Exit.*]

Cob. Nay, soft and fair ; I have eggs on the
spit ; [4] I cannot go yet, sir. Now am I, for some
five and fifty reasons, hammering, hammer- [50
ing revenge : oh for three or four gallons of
vinegar, to sharpen my wits ! Revenge, vinegar
revenge, vinegar and mustard revenge ! Nay,
an he had not lien in my house, 't would never
have griev'd me ; but being my guest, one that, [55
I 'll be sworn, my wife has lent him her smock

---

[1] Smoked.

[2] A room in Justice Clement's house in Coleman St.

[3] *To kiss the post* was a phrase meaning to be shut
out.

[4] Business to attend to.

off her back, while his own shirt has been at washing; pawn'd her neckerchers for clean bands for him; sold almost all my platters, to buy him tobacco; and he to turn monster of [60] ingratitude, and strike his lawful host! Well, I hope to raise up an host of fury for't: here comes justice Clement.

SCENE VII.[1]

COB. [Enter] JUSTICE CLEMENT, KNOWELL, FORMAL.

Clem. What's master Kitely gone, Roger?

Form. Ay, sir.

Clem. 'Heart o' me! what made him leave us so abruptly? — How now, sirrah! what make you here? What would you have, ha?   5

Cob. An't please your worship, I am a poor neighbour of your worship's ——

Clem. A poor neighbour of mine! Why, speak, poor neighbour.

Cob. I dwell, sir, at the sign of the Water- [10] tankard, hard by the Green Lattice:[2] I have paid scot and lot[3] there any time this eighteen years.

Clem. To the Green Lattice?

Cob. No, sir, to the parish. Marry, I have [15] seldom scapt scot-free at the Lattice.

Clem. O, well; what business has my poor neighbour with me?

Cob. An't like your worship, I am come to crave the peace of your worship.   20

Clem. Of me, knave! Peace of me, knave! Did I ever hurt thee, or threaten thee, or wrong thee, ha?

Cob. No, sir; but your worship's warrant for one that has wrong'd me, sir. His arms are at [25] too much liberty, I would fain have them bound to a treaty of peace, an my credit could compass it with your worship.

Clem. Thou goest far enough about for't, I am sure.   30

Know. Why, dost thou go in danger of thy life for him, friend?

Cob. No, sir; but I go in danger of my death every hour, by his means; an I die within a twelve-month and a day,[4] I may swear by the law of the land that he kill'd me.   36

Clem. How, how, knave, swear he kill'd thee, and by the law? What pretence, what colour, hast thou for that?

Cob. Marry, an't please your worship, both black and blue; colour enough, I warrant you. [41] I have it here to shew your worship.

[*Shows his bruises.*]

Clem. What is he that gave you this, sirrah?

Cob. A gentleman and a soldier, he says he is, of the city here.   45

Clem. A soldier o' the city! What call you him?

Cob. Captain Bobadill.

Clem. Bobadill! and why did he bob[5] and beat you, sirrah? How began the quarrel betwixt you, ha? Speak truly, knave, I advise you.   50

Cob. Marry, indeed, an't please your worship,

only because I spake against their vagrant tobacco, as I came by 'em when they were taking on't; for nothing else.

Clem. Ha! you speak against tobacco? For- [55] mal, his name.

Form. What's your name, sirrah?

Cob. Oliver, sir, Oliver Cob, sir.

Clem. Tell Oliver Cob he shall go to the jail, Formal.   60

Form. Oliver Cob, my master, justice Clement, says you shall go to the jail.

Cob. O, I beseech your worship, for God's sake, dear master justice!   64

Clem. God's precious! an such drunkards and tankards as you are, come to dispute of tobacco once, I have done. Away with him!

Cob. O, good master justice! — Sweet old gentleman!   [*To* KNOWELL.]

Know. "Sweet Oliver," would I could do [70] thee any good! — Justice Clement, let me intreat you, sir.

Clem. What! a thread-bare rascal, a beggar, a slave that never drunk out of better than piss-pot metal[6] in his life! and he to deprave and [75] abuse the virtue of an herb so generally receiv'd in the courts of princes, the chambers of nobles, the bowers of sweet ladies, the cabins of soldiers! — Roger, away with him? By God's precious —— I say, go to.   80

Cob. Dear master justice, let me be beaten again, I have deserv'd it: but not the prison, I beseech you.

Know. Alas, poor Oliver!

Clem. Roger, make him a warrant: — he shall not go, I but fear[7] the knave.   86

Form. Do not stink, sweet Oliver, you shall not go; my master will give you a warrant.

Cob. O, the Lord maintain his worship, his worthy worship!   90

Clem. Away, dispatch him.

[*Exeunt* FORMAL *and* COB.]

— How now, master Knowell, in dumps, in dumps! Come, this becomes not.

Know. Sir, would I could not feel my cares.

Clem. Your cares are nothing: they are [95] like my cap, soon put on, and as soon put off. What! your son is old enough to govern himself; let him run his course, it's the only way to make him a staid man. If he were an unthrift, a ruffian, a drunkard, or a licentious liver, [100] then you had reason; you had reason to take care: but, being none of these, mirth's my witness, an I had twice so many cares as you have, I'd drown them all in a cup of sack. Come, come, let's try it: I muse[8] your parcel of a [105] soldier returns not all this while.   *Exeunt.*

ACT IV

SCENE I.[9]

[*Enter*] DOWNRIGHT *and* DAME KITELY.

Dow. Well, sister, I tell you true; and you'll find it so in the end.

<hr>

[1] The same.   [2] A tavern.   [3] Rates and taxes.
[4] The legal limit of time in defining murder.
[5] Strike.

[6] Pewter.   [7] Frighten.   [8] Wonder.
[9] A room in Kitely's house.

Dame K. Alas, brother, what would you have me to do? I cannot help it; you see my brother brings 'em in here; they are his friends. 5

Dow. His friends! his fiends. 'Slud! they do nothing but haunt him up and down like a sort of unlucky spirits, and tempt him to all manner of villainy that can be thought of. Well, by this light, a little thing would make me play [10 the devil with some of 'em : an 't were not more for your husband's sake than anything else, I 'd make the house too hot for the best on 'em; they should say, and swear, hell were broken loose, ere they went hence. But, by God's will, 't is nobody's fault but yours; for an you had [16 done as you might have done, they should have been parboil'd, and bak'd too, every mother's son, ere they should ha' come in, e'er a one of 'em. 20

Dame K. God's my life! did you ever hear the like? What a strange man is this! Could I keep out all them, think you? I should put myself against half a dozen men, should I? Good faith, you'd mad the patient'st body in the [25 world, to hear you talk so, without any sense or reason.

SCENE II.[1]

DOWNRIGHT, DAME KITELY. [*Enter*] MISTRESS BRIDGET, MASTER MATHEW, *and* BOBADILL; [*followed, at a distance, by*] WELLBRED, E. KNOWELL, STEPHEN, *and* BRAINWORM.

Brid. Servant,[2] in troth you are too prodigal Of your wit's treasure, thus to pour it forth Upon so mean a subject as my worth.

Mat. You say well, mistress, and I mean as well.

Dow. Hoy-day, here is stuff! 5

Wel. O, now stand close;[3] pray Heaven, she can get him to read! He should do it of his own natural impudency.

Brid. Servant, what is this same, I pray you?

Mat. Marry, an elegy, an elegy, an odd toy ——

Dow. To mock an ape withal![4] O, I could [11 sew up his mouth, now.

Dame K. Sister, I pray you let 's hear it.

Dow. Are you rhyme-given too?

Mat. Mistress, I 'll read it, if you please. 15

Brid. Pray you do, servant.

Dow. O, here 's no foppery! Death! I can endure the stocks better. [*Exit.*]

E. Know. What ails thy brother? Can he not hold his water at reading of a ballad? 20

Wel. O, no; a rhyme to him is worse than cheese, or a bag-pipe; but mark; you lose the protestation.

Mat. Faith, I did it in a humour; I know not how it is; but please you come near, sir. This [25 gentleman has judgment, he knows how to censure of a —— pray you, sir, you can judge?

Step. Not I, sir; upon my reputation, and by the foot of Pharaoh!

Wel. O, chide your cousin for swearing. 30

E. Know. Not I, so long as he does not forswear himself.

---

[1] The same. [2] Lover. [3] Aside.
[4] To gull a fool with. Proverbial.

Bob. Master Mathew, you abuse the expectation of your dear mistress, and her fair sister. Fie! while you live, avoid this prolixity. 35

Mat. I shall, sir, well; *incipere dulce.*[5]

E. Know. How, *insipere dulce!* "a sweet thing to be a fool," indeed!

Wel. What, do you take *incipere* in that sense? 40

E. Know. You do not, you! This was your villainy, to gull him with a mot.

Wel. O, the benchers'[6] phrase : *pauca verba, pauca verba!*

Mat. [*Reads.*] *Rare creature, let me speak without offence,* 45
Would God my rude words had the influence
To rule thy thoughts, as thy fair looks do mine,
Then shouldst thou be his prisoner, who is thine.

E. Know. This is "Hero and Leander." 49

Wel. O, ay : peace, we shall have more of this.

Mat. *Be not unkind and fair : misshapen stuff*
Is of behaviour boisterous and rough.

Wel. How like you that, sir?

MASTER STEPHEN *answers with shaking his head.*

E. Know. 'Slight, he shakes his head like a bottle, to feel an there be any brain in it. 55

Mat. But observe the catastrophe, now :
And I in duty will exceed all other,
As you in beauty do excel Love's mother.

E. Know. Well, I 'll have him free of the wit-brokers, for he utters nothing but stol'n remnants. 61

Wel. O, forgive it him.

E. Know. A filching[7] rogue, hang him! — and from the dead! It 's worse than sacrilege. [64

[WELLBRED, E. KNOWELL, *and* MASTER STEPHEN *come forward.*]

Wel. Sister, what ha' you here? Verses? Pray you, let 's see. Who made these verses? They are excellent good.

Mat. O, Master Wellbred, 't is your disposition to say so, sir. They were good i ' the morning : I made them *ex tempore* this morning.

Wel. How! *ex tempore?* 71

Mat. Ay, would I might be hang'd else; ask Captain Bobadill; he saw me write them, at the —— pox on it! — the Star, yonder.

Brai. Can he find in his heart to curse the stars so? 76

E. Know. Faith, his are even with him; they ha' curst him enough already.

Step. Cousin, how do you like this gentleman's verses? 80

E. Know. O, admirable! the best that ever I heard, coz.

Step. Body o' Caesar, they are admirable! the best that I ever heard, as I am a soldier! 84

[*Re-enter* DOWNRIGHT.]

Dow. I am vext, I can hold ne'er a bone of me still. 'Heart, I think they mean to build and breed here.

Wel. Sister, you have a simple servant here,

---

[5] It is sweet to begin.
[6] Variously explained as ale-house loafers, and justices.
[7] Thieving.

that crowns your beauty with such encomi- [89 ums and devices; you may see what it is to be the mistress of a wit that can make your perfections so transparent, that every blear eye may look through them, and see him drown'd over head and ears in the deep well of desire. Sister Kitely, I marvel you get you not a servant that can rhyme, and do tricks too. 96

Dow. O monster! impudence itself! tricks!

Dame K. Tricks, brother! what tricks?

Brid. Nay, speak, I pray you, what tricks?

Dame K. Ay, never spare any body here; [100 but say, what tricks?

Brid. Passion of my heart, do tricks!

Wel. 'Slight, here's a trick vied and revied![1] Why, you monkeys, you, what a cater-wauling do you keep! Has he not given you rhymes and verses and tricks? 106

Dow. O, the fiend!

Wel. Nay, you lamp of virginity, that take it in snuff[2] so, come, and cherish this tame poetical fury in your servant; you'll be begg'd [110 else shortly for a concealment:[3] go to, reward his muse. You cannot give him less than a shilling in conscience, for the book he had it out of cost him a teston[4] at least. How now, gallants! [114 Master Mathew! Captain! what, all sons of silence? No spirit?

Dow. Come, you might practise your ruffian tricks somewhere else, and not here, I wuss;[5] this is no tavern nor drinking-school, to vent your exploits in. 120

Wel. How now; whose cow has calv'd?

Dow. Marry, that has mine, sir. Nay, boy, never look askance at me for the matter; I'll tell you of it, I, sir; you and your companions mend yourselves when I ha' done. 125

Wel. My companions!

Dow. Yes, sir, your companions, so I say; I am not afraid of you, nor them neither; your hangbyes here. You must have your poets and your potlings,[6] your soldados and foolados to [130 follow you up and down the city; and here they must come to domineer and swagger. — Sirrah, you ballad-singer, and Slops[7] your fellow there, get you out, get you home; or by this steel, I'll cut off your ears, and that presently. 135

Wel. 'Slight, stay, let's see what he dare do; cut off his ears! cut a whetstone. You are an ass, do you see? Touch any man here, and by this hand I'll run my rapier to the hilts in you. 140

Dow. Yea, that would I fain see, boy.

They all draw, and they of the house make out to part them.

Dame K. O Jesu! murder! Thomas! Gasper!

Brid. Help, help! Thomas!

---

[1] *To vie* and *revie* meant to stake a sum and cover it with a higher.
[2] Are offended.
[3] This is a reference to the unauthorized holding of sequestered lands, such as those which had belonged to the monasteries. Elizabeth had appointed commissions to search such holdings or "concealments," which her courtiers often "begged."
[4] Sixpence.
[5] I-wis, assuredly.
[6] Topers.
[7] Loose breeches: Bobadill.

E. Know. Gentlemen, forbear, I pray you. 144

Bob. Well, sirrah, you Holofernes; by my hand, I will pink your flesh full of holes with my rapier for this; I will, by this good heaven! Nay, let him come, let him come, gentlemen; by the body of St. George, I'll not kill him.

Offer to fight again, and are parted.

Cash. Hold, hold, good gentlemen. 150

Dow. You whoreson, bragging coystril![8]

SCENE III.[9]

To them [enter] KITELY.

Kit. Why, how now! what's the matter, what's the stir here?

Whence springs the quarrel? Thomas! where is he?

Put up your weapons, and put off this rage.

My wife and sister, they are the cause of this.

What, Thomas! where is the knave? 5

Cash. Here, sir.

Wel. Come, let's go; this is one of my brother's ancient humours, this.

Step. I am glad nobody was hurt by his ancient humour. 10

[Exeunt WELLBRED, STEPHEN, E. KNOWELL, BOBADILL, and BRAINWORM.]

Kit. Why, how now, brother, who enforc'd this brawl?

Dow. A sort[10] of lewd rake-hells, that care neither for God nor the devil. And they must come here to read ballads, and roguery, and [14 trash! I'll mar the knot of 'em ere I sleep, perhaps; especially Bob there, he that's all manner of shapes: and Songs and Sonnets, his fellow.

Brid. Brother, indeed you are too violent, Too sudden in your humour: and you know 20 My brother Wellbred's temper will not bear Any reproof, chiefly in such a presence, Where every slight disgrace he should receive Might wound him in opinion and respect. 24

Dow. Respect! what talk you of respect among such as ha' nor spark of manhood nor good manners? 'Sdeins, I am asham'd to hear you! respect! *[Exit.]*

Brid. Yes, there was one a civil gentleman, And very worthily demean'd himself. 30

Kit. O, that was some love of yours, sister.

Brid. A love of mine! I would it were no worse, brother;

You'd pay my portion sooner than you think for.

Dame K. Indeed he seem'd to be a gentle- [34 man of a very exceeding fair disposition, and of excellent good parts.

[Exeunt DAME KITELY and BRIDGET.]

Kit. Her love, by heaven! my wife's minion. *Fair disposition! excellent good parts!* Death! these phrases are intolerable. Good parts! how should she know his parts? 40 His parts! Well, well, well, well, well, well; It is too plain, too clear: Thomas, come hither. What, are they gone?

---

[8] Lackey. [9] The same. [10] Band.

Cash.   Ay, sir, they went in.
My mistress and your sister ——

Kit. Are any of the gallants within?   45
Cash. No, sir, they are all gone.
Kit.   Art thou sure of it?
Cash. I can assure you, sir.
Kit. What gentleman was that they prais'd
so, Thomas?
Cash. One, they call him Master Knowell, [50
a handsome young gentleman, sir.
Kit. Ay, I thought so; my mind gave me as
            much.
I 'll die, but they have hid him i' the house
Somewhere; I 'll go and search; go with me,
Thomas: 54
Be true to me, and thou shalt find me a master.
                            [*Exeunt.*]

Scene IV.[1]

[*Enter*] Cob.

Cob. [*knocks at the door.*] What, Tib! Tib, I
say!
Tib. [*within.*] How now, what cuckold is that
knocks so hard?

Enter Tib.

O, husband! is it you? What 's the news?   5
Cob. Nay, you have stunn'd me, i' faith; you
ha' giv'n me a knock o' the forehead will stick
by me. Cuckold! 'Slid, cuckold!
Tib. Away, you fool! did I know it was you
that knockt? Come, come, you may call me
as bad when you list.   11
Cob. May I? Tib, you are a whore.
Tib. You lie in your throat, husband.
Cob. How, the lie! and in my throat too! do
you long to be stabb'd, ha?   15
Tib. Why, you are no soldier, I hope.
Cob. O, must you be stabb'd by a soldier?
Mass, that 's true! When was Bobadill here,
your captain? that rogue, that foist,[2] that
fencing Burgullion?[3] I 'll tickle him, i' faith.
Tib. Why, what 's the matter, trow?   21
Cob. O, he has basted me rarely, sumptuously!
but I have it here in black and white [*Pulls out
the warrant*], for his black and blue shall pay
him. O, the justice, the honestest old brave [25
Trojan in London; I do honour the very flea
of his dog. A plague on him, though, he put me
once in a villanous filthy fear; marry, it
vanished away like the smoke of tobacco; but I
was smokt[4] soundly first. I thank the devil, [30
and his good angel, my guest. Well, wife, or
Tib, which you will, get you in, and lock the
door; I charge you let nobody in to you, wife;
nobody in to you; those are my words: not
Captain Bob himself, nor the fiend in his [35
likeness. You are a woman, you have flesh and
blood enough in you to be tempted; therefore
keep the door shut upon all comers.
Tib. I warrant you, there shall nobody enter
here without my consent.   40

---

[1] The lane before Cob's house.
[2] Cheat.   [3] Bully.
[4] Usually, found out; but here, apparently, frightened.

Cob. Nor with your consent, sweet Tib; and
so I leave you.
Tib. It 's more than you know, whether you
leave me so.
Cob. How?   45
Tib. Why, *sweet.*
Cob. Tut, sweet or sour, thou art a flower.
Keep close thy door, I ask no more. [*Exeunt.*]

Scene V.[5]

[*Enter*] E. Knowell, Wellbred, Stephen,
and Brainworm, [*disguised as before.*]

E. Know. Well, and Brainworm, perform this
business happily, and thou makest a purchase
of my love for ever.
Wel. I' faith, now let thy spirits use their
best faculties: but, at any hand, remember [5
the message to my brother; for there 's no
other means to start him.
Brai. I warrant you, sir; fear nothing; I have
a nimble soul has wakt all forces of my
phant'sie by this time, and put 'em in true [10
motion. What you have possest[6] me withal,
I 'll discharge it amply, sir; make it no question.   [*Exit.*]
Wel. Forth, and prosper, Brainworm. Faith,
Ned, how dost thou approve of my abilities in
this device?   16
E. Know. Troth, well, howsoever; but it will
come excellent if it take.
Wel. Take, man! why it cannot choose but
take, if the circumstances miscarry not: [20
but, tell me ingenuously, dost thou affect my
sister Bridget as thou pretend'st?
E. Know. Friend, am I worth belief?
Wel. Come, do not protest. In faith, she is
a maid of good ornament, and much mod- [25
esty; and, except I conceiv'd very worthily of
her, thou should'st not have her.
E. Know. Nay, that, I am afraid, will be a
question yet, whether I shall have her, or no.
Wel. 'Slid, thou shalt have her; by this light
thou shalt.   31
E. Know. Nay, do not swear.
Wel. By this hand thou shalt have her; I 'll
go fetch her presently. 'Point but where to
meet, and as I am an honest man I 'll bring her.
E. Know. Hold, hold, be temperate.   36
Wel. Why, by —— what shall I swear by?
Thou shalt have her, as I am ——
E. Know. Pray thee, be at peace, I am
satisfied; and do believe thou wilt omit no [40
offered occasion to make my desires complete.
Wel. Thou shalt see, and know, I will not.
                            [*Exeunt.*]

Scene VI.[7]

[*Enter*] Formal and Knowell.

Form. Was your man a soldier, sir?
Know.   Ay, a knave;
I took him begging o' the way, this morning,
As I came over Moorfields.

---

[5] A room in the Windmill Tavern.
[6] Informed.   [7] The Old Jewry.

[*Enter* BRAINWORM, *disguised as before.*]

O, here he is ! — you 've made fair speed, believe
me,
Where, i' the name of sloth, could you be
thus ?   5
Brai. Marry, peace be my comfort, where I
thought I should have had little comfort of
your worship's service.
Know. How so ?   9
Brai. O, sir, your coming to the city, your
entertainment of me, and your sending me to
watch——indeed all the circumstances either of
your charge, or my employment, are as open to
your son, as to yourself.
Know. How should that be, unless that
villain, Brainworm,   15
Have told him of the letter, and discover'd
All that I strictly charg'd him to conceal ?
'T is so.
Brai. I am partly o' the faith, 't is so,
indeed.
Know. But, how should he know thee to be
my man ?   20
Brai. Nay, sir, I cannot tell ; unless it be by
the black art. Is not your son a scholar, sir ?
Know. Yes, but I hope his soul is not allied
Unto such hellish practice : if it were,
I had just cause to weep my part in him,   25
And curse the time of his creation.
But, where didst thou find them, Fitz-Sword ?
Brai. You should rather ask where they
found me, sir ; for I 'll be sworn, I was going
along in the street, thinking nothing, when, [30
of a sudden, a voice calls, " Mr. Knowell's
man ! " another cries, " Soldier ! " and thus
half a dozen of 'em, till they had call'd me
within a house, where I no sooner came, but
they seem'd men, and out flew all their [35
rapiers at my bosom, with some three or four
score oaths to accompany them ; and all to tell
me, I was but a dead man, if I did not confess
where you were, and how I was employed, and
about what ; which when they could not get [40
out of me (as, I protest, they must ha' dissected,
and made an anatomy [1] o' me first, and so I
told 'em), they lock'd me up into a room i' the
top of a high house, whence by great miracle
(having a light heart) I slid down by a [45
bottom [2] of packthread into the street, and so
scapt. But, sir, thus much I can assure you,
for I heard it while I was lockt up, there were
a great many rich merchants and brave citizens'
wives with 'em at a feast ; and your son, [50
master Edward, withdrew with one of 'em, and
has 'pointed to meet her anon at one Cob's
house, a water-bearer that dwells by the Wall.
Now, there your worship shall be sure to take
him, for there he preys, and fail he will
not.   56
Know. Nor will I fail to break his match, I
doubt not.
Go thou along with justice Clement's man,
And stay there for me. At one Cob's house,
say'st thou ?   59

¹ Skeleton.   ² Ball.

Brai. Ay, sir, there you shall have him.
[*Exit* KNOWELL.] Yes — invisible ! Much wench,
or much son ! 'Slight, when he has staid there
three or four hours, travailing with the expectation of wonders, and at length be deliver'd of air ! O the sport that I should then [65
take to look on him, if I durst ! But now, I
mean to appear no more afore him in this
shape : I have another trick to act yet. O
that I were so happy as to light on a nupson [3]
now of this justice's novice ! — Sir, I make you
stay somewhat long.   71
Form. Not a whit, sir. Pray you what do you
mean, sir ?
Bra. I was putting up some papers.
Form. You ha' been lately in the wars, sir,
it seems.   76
Brai. Marry have I, sir, to my loss, and expense of all, almost.
Form. Troth, sir, I would be glad to bestow a bottle of wine o' you, if it please you to
accept it——   81
Brai. O, sir——
Form. But to hear the manner of your
services, and your devices in the wars. They
say they be very strange, and not like those [85
a man reads in the Roman histories, or sees at
Mile-end.[4]
Brai. No, I assure you, sir ; why at any time
when it please you, I shall be ready to discourse to you all I know ; [*Aside.*] — and more
too somewhat.   91
Form. No better time than now, sir ; we 'll go
to the Windmill ; there we shall have a cup of
neat grist,[5] we call it. I pray you, sir, let me
request you to the Windmill.   95
Brai. I 'll follow you, sir ; [*Aside.*] — and
make grist o' you, if I have good luck.
                                        [*Exeunt.*]

SCENE VII.[6]

[*Enter*] MATHEW, E. KNOWELL, BOBADILL,
STEPHEN.

Mat. Sir, did your eyes ever taste the like
clown of him where we were to-day, Mr. Wellbred's half-brother ? I think the whole earth
cannot shew his parallel, by this daylight.
E. Know. We were now speaking of him : [5
captain Bobadill tells me he is fall'n foul o' you
too.
Mat. O, ay, sir, he threat'ned me with the
bastinado.
Bob. Ay, but I think, I taught you pre- [10
vention this morning, for that. You shall kill
him beyond question, if you be so generously
minded.
Mat. Indeed, it is a most excellent trick.
                                        [*Fences.*]
Bob. O, you do not give spirit enough to [15
your motion ; you are too tardy, too heavy !
O, it must be done like lightning, hay !
                                Practises at a post.
Mat. Rare, captain !

³ Simpleton.
⁴ Where the city bands trained.
⁵ Slang for liquor : the product of the Windmill.
⁶ Moorfields.

Bob. Tut! 'tis nothing, an't be not done in a ── *punto.*[1]   20

E. Know. Captain, did you ever prove yourself upon any of our masters of defence here?

Mat. O good sir! yes, I hope he has.

Bob. I will tell you, sir. Upon my first coming to the city, after my long travel for know- [25 ledge in that mystery only, there came three or four of 'em to me, at a gentleman's house, where it was my chance to be resident at that time, to intreat my presence at their schools: and withal so much importun'd me that, [30 I protest to you as I am a gentleman, I was asham'd of their rude demeanour out of all measure. Well, I told 'em that to come to a public school, they should pardon me, it was opposite, in diameter, to my humour; but if [35 so be they would give their attendance at my lodging, I protested to do them what right or favour I could, as I was a gentleman, and so forth.

E. Know. So, sir! then you tried their skill?

Bob. Alas, soon tried: you shall hear, sir. [41 Within two or three days after, they came; and, by honesty, fair sir, believe me, I grac'd them exceedingly, shew'd them some two or three tricks of prevention have purchas'd [45 'em since a credit to admiration. They cannot deny this; and yet now they hate me; and why? Because I am excellent; and for no other vile reason on the earth.

E. Know. This is strange and barbarous, [50 as ever I heard.

Bob. Nay, for a more instance of their preposterous natures, but note, sir. They have assaulted me some three, four, five, six of them together, as I have walkt alone in divers skirts i' the town, as Turnbull, Whitechapel, [56 Shoreditch,[2] which were then my quarters; and since, upon the Exchange, at my lodging, and at my ordinary: where I have driven them afore me the whole length of a street, in the [60 open view of all our gallants, pitying to hurt them, believe me. Yet all this lenity will not o'ercome their spleen; they will be doing with the pismire,[3] raising a hill a man may spurn abroad with his foot at pleasure. By myself, [65 I could have slain them all, but I delight not in murder. I am loth to bear any other than this bastinado for 'em: yet I hold it good polity not to go disarm'd, for though I be skilful, I may be oppress'd with multitudes.   70

E. Know. Ay, believe me, may you, sir: and in my conceit, our whole nation should sustain the loss by it, if it were so.

Bob. Alas, no? what's a peculiar[4] man to a nation? Not seen.   75

E. Know. O, but your skill, sir.

Bob. Indeed, that might be some loss; but who respects it? I will tell you, sir, by the way of private, and under seal; I am a gentleman, and live here obscure, and to myself; but [80 were I known to her majesty and the lords, ── observe me, ── I would undertake, upon this poor head and life, for the public benefit of the state, not only to spare the entire lives of her subjects in general; but to save the one half, [85 nay, three parts of her yearly charge in holding war, and against what enemy soever. And how would I do it, think you?

E. Know. Nay, I know not, nor can I conceive.   90

Bob. Why thus, sir. I would select nineteen more, to myself, throughout the land; gentlemen they should be of good spirit, strong and able constitution; I would choose them by an instinct, a character that I have: and I would teach these nineteen the special rules, as your [96 *punto*, your *reverso*, your *stoccata*, your *imbroccato*, your *passada*, your *montanto*;[5] till they could all play very near, or altogether, as well as myself. This done, say the enemy were forty thousand strong, we twenty would come into the [101 field the tenth of March, or thereabouts; and we would challenge twenty of the enemy; they could not in their honour refuse us: well, we would kill them; challenge twenty more, kill [105 them; twenty more, kill them; twenty more, kill them too; and thus would we kill every man his twenty a day, that's twenty score; twenty score, that's two hundred;[6] two hundred a day, five days a thousand: forty thousand; forty times five, five times forty, two hundred [111 days kills them all up by computation. And this will I venture my poor gentleman-like carcase to perform, provided there be no treason practis'd upon us, by fair and discreet manhood; [115 that is, civilly by the sword.

E. Know. Why, are you so sure of your hand, captain, at all times?

Bob. Tut! never miss thrust, upon my reputation with you.   120

E. Know. I would not stand in Downright's state then, an you meet him, for the wealth of any one street in London.

Bob. Why, sir, you mistake me: if he were here now, by this welkin, I would not draw my weapon on him. Let this gentleman do his [126 mind; but I will bastinado him, by the bright sun, wherever I meet him.

Mat. Faith, and I'll have a fling at him, at my distance.   130

E. Know. 'God's so, look where he is! yonder he goes.

            DOWNRIGHT *walks over the stage.*

Dow. What peevish luck have I, I cannot meet with these bragging rascals?

Bob. It is not he, is it?   135

E. Know. Yes, faith, it is he.

Mat. I'll be hang'd, then, if that were he.

E. Know. Sir, keep your hanging good for some greater matter, for I assure you that was he.   140

Step. Upon my reputation, it was he.

Bob. Had I thought it had been he, he must not have gone so: but I can hardly be induc'd to believe it was he yet.

E. Know. That I think, sir.   145

---

[1] Moment.
[2] All low districts.
[3] Ant.
[4] Individual.
[5] Italian terms of fencing.
[6] "Bobadill is too much of a borrower to be an accurate reckoner." (Gifford.)

[*Re-enter* DOWNRIGHT.]

But see, he is come again.

Dow. O, Pharaoh's foot, have I found you?
Come, draw, to your tools ; draw, gipsy, or I 'll
thrash you.

Bob. Gentleman of valour, I do believe in
thee ; hear me ——   151

Dow. Draw your weapon then.

Bob. Tall[1] man, I never thought on it till
now —— body of me, I had a warrant of the
peace served on me, even now as I came along,
by a water-bearer; this gentleman saw it, [156
Master Mathew.

Dow. 'S death ! you will not draw then?

Beats and disarms him. MATHEW *runs away.*

Bob. Hold, hold ! under thy favour forbear !

Dow. Prate again, as you like this, you [160
whoreson foist[2] you ! You 'll "control[3] the
point," you ! Your consort is gone ; had he staid
he had shar'd with you, sir.   [*Exit.*]

Bob. Well, gentlemen, bear witness, I was
bound to the peace, by this good day.   165

E. Know. No, faith, it 's an ill day, captain,
never reckon it other: but, say you were bound
to the peace, the law allows you to defend yourself : that 'll prove but a poor excuse.

Bob. I cannot tell, sir ; I desire good con- [170
struction in fair sort. I never sustain'd the
like disgrace, by heaven ! Sure I was struck
with a planet thence, for I had no power to
touch my weapon.

E. Know. Ay, like enough ; I have heard of
many that have been beaten under a planet : [176
go, get you to a surgeon. 'Slid ! an these be
your tricks, your *passadas,* and your *montan-
tos,* I 'll none of them. [*Exit* BOBADILL.] O, manners ! that this age should bring forth such [180
creatures ! that nature should be at leisure to
make them ! Come, coz.

Step. Mass, I 'll ha' this cloak.

E. Know. 'Od's will, 't is Downright's.

Step. Nay, it 's mine now, another might have
ta'en up as well as I : I 'll wear it, so I will. 186

E. Know. How an he see it? He 'll challenge it, assure yourself.

Step. Ay, but he shall not ha' it ; I 'll say I
bought it.   190

E. Know. Take heed you buy it not too dear,
coz.   [*Exeunt.*]

SCENE VIII.[4]

[*Enter*] KITELY, WELLBRED, DAME KITELY,
and BRIDGET.

Kit. Now, trust me, brother, you were much
to blame,
T' incense his anger, and disturb the peace
Of my poor house, where there are sentinels
That every minute watch to give alarms
Of civil war, without adjection[5]   5
Of your assistance or occasion.

Wel. No harm done, brother, I warrant you.
Since there is no harm done, anger costs a man
nothing ; and a tall man is never his own man
till he be angry. To keep his valour in ob- [10

scurity, is to keep himself as it were in a cloak-
bag. What's a musician, unless he play? What's
a tall man unless he fight ? For, indeed, all this
my wise brother stands upon absolutely ; and
that made me fall in with him so resolutely. 15

Dame K. Ay, but what harm might have
come of it, brother !

Wel. Might, sister ? So might the good warm
clothes your husband wears be poison'd, for any
thing he knows : or the wholesome wine he [20
drank, even now at the table.

Kit. [*Aside.*] Now, God forbid ! O me ! now
I remember
My wife drank to me last, and chang'd the cup,
And bade me wear this cursed suit to-day.
See, if Heaven suffer murder undiscover'd ! — 25
I feel me ill ; give me some mithridate,[6]
Some mithridate and oil, good sister, fetch me;
O, I am sick at heart, I burn, I burn.
If you will save my life, go fetch it me.

Wel. O strange humour ! my very breath [30
has poison'd him.

Brid. Good brother, be content, what do you
mean?
The strength of these extreme conceits[7] will kill
you.

Dame K. Beshrew your heart-blood, brother
Wellbred, now,
For putting such a toy into his head !   35

Wel. Is a fit simile a toy ? Will he be poison'd
with a simile ? Brother Kitely, what a strange
and idle imagination is this ! For shame, be
wiser. O' my soul, there 's no such matter. 38

Kit. Am I not sick ? How am I then not poison'd ?
Am I not poison'd ? How am I then so sick ?

Dame K. If you be sick, your own thoughts
make you sick.

Wel. His jealousy is the poison he has taken.

Enter BRAINWORM, *disguised like justice Clement's man.*

Brai. Master Kitely, my master, justice [44
Clement, salutes you ; and desires to speak with
you with all possible speed.

Kit. No time but now, when I think I am sick,
very sick ! Well, I will wait upon his worship.
Thomas ! Cob ! I must seek them out, and set
'em sentinels till I return. Thomas ! Cob ! [50
Thomas !   [*Exit.*]

Wel. This is perfectly rare, Brainworm ;
[*Takes him aside.*] but how got'st thou this apparel of the justice's man ?   54

Brai. Marry, sir, my proper fine pen-man
would needs bestow the grist o' me, at the
Windmill, to hear some martial discourse;
where I so marshall'd him, that I made him
drunk with admiration : and, because too much
heat was the cause of his distemper, I stript [60
him stark naked as he lay along asleep, and
borrowed his suit to deliver this counterfeit
message in, leaving a rusty armour, and an old
brown bill to watch him till my return ; which
shall be, when I ha' pawn'd his apparel, and [65
spent the better part o' the money, perhaps.

Wel. Well, thou art a successful merry knave.

---

[1] Bold.   [2] Cheat.   [3] Beat down.
[4] A room in Kitely's house.   [5] Addition.
[6] Used as a general antidote.   [7] Fancies.

Brainworm: his absence will be a good subject for more mirth. I pray thee return to thy young master, and will him to meet me and my [70 sister Bridget at the Tower[1] instantly; for here, tell him, the house is so stor'd with jealousy, there is no room for love to stand upright in. We must get our fortunes committed to some larger prison, say; and than the Tower, I [75 know no better air, nor where the liberty of the house may do us more present service. Away!
[*Exit* BRAINWORM.]

[*Re-enter* KITELY, *talking aside to* CASH.]

Kit. Come hither, Thomas. Now my secret's ripe,
And thou shalt have it: lay to both thine ears.
Hark what I say to thee. I must go forth, Thomas;   80
Be careful of thy promise, keep good watch,
Note every gallant, and observe him well,
That enters in my absence to thy mistress:
If she would shew him rooms, the jest is stale,
Follow 'em, Thomas, or else hang on him,   85
And let him not go after; mark their looks;
Note if she offer but to see his band,
Or any other amorous toy about him;
But praise his leg, or foot: or if she say
The day is hot, and bid him feel her hand,   90
How hot it is; O, that's a monstrous thing!
Note me all this, good Thomas, mark their sighs,
And if they do but whisper, break 'em off:
I'll bear thee out in it. Wilt thou do this?
Wilt thou be true, my Thomas?
Cash.   As truth's self, sir. 95
Kit. Why, I believe thee. Where is Cob, now? Cob!   [*Exit.*]
Dame K. He's ever calling for Cob: I wonder how he employs Cob so.
Wel. Indeed, sister, to ask how he employs Cob, is a necessary question for you that are [100 his wife, and a thing not very easy for you to be satisfied in; but this I'll assure you, Cob's wife is an excellent bawd, sister, and oftentimes your husband haunts her house; marry, to what end? I cannot altogether accuse him; imagine [105 you what you think convenient: but I have known fair hides have foul hearts ere now, sister.
Dame K. Never said you truer than that, brother, so much I can tell you for your learning. Thomas, fetch your cloak and go with me. [110
[*Exit* CASH.]
I'll after him presently: I would to fortune I could take him there, i' faith. I'd return him his own, I warrant him!   [*Exit.*]
Wel. So, let 'em go; this may make sport anon. Now, my fair sister-in-law, that you knew but [115 how happy a thing it were to be fair and beautiful.
Brid. That touches not me, brother.
Wel. That's true; that's even the fault of it; for indeed, beauty stands a woman in no [120 stead, unless it procure her touching. — But, sister, whether it touch you or no, it touches your beauties; and I am sure they will abide the touch; an they do not, a plague of all cer-

use,[2] say I! and it touches me too in part, [125 though not in the —— Well, there's a dear and respected friend of mine, sister, stands very strongly and worthily affected toward you, and hath vow'd to inflame whole bonfires of zeal at his heart, in honour of your perfections. I [130 have already engag'd my promise to bring you where you shall hear him confirm much more. Ned Knowell is the man, sister: there's no exception against the party. You are ripe for a husband; and a minute's loss to such an [135 occasion is a great trespass in a wise beauty. What say you, sister? On my soul he loves you; will you give him the meeting?
Brid. Faith, I had very little confidence in mine own constancy, brother, if I durst not [140 meet a man: but this motion of yours savours of an old knight adventurer's servant a little too much, methinks.
Wel. What's that, sister?
Brid. Marry, of the squire.[3]   145
Wel. No matter if it did, I would be such an one for my friend. But see, who is return'd to hinder us!

[*Re-enter* KITELY.]

Kit. What villany is this? Call'd out on a false message!
This was some plot; I was not sent for. —Bridget,   150
Where is your sister?
Brid.   I think she be gone forth, sir.
Kit. How! is my wife gone forth? Whither, for God's sake?
Brid. She's gone abroad with Thomas.
Kit. Abroad with Thomas! oh, that villain dors[4] me:
He hath discover'd all unto my wife.   155
Beast that I was, to trust him! Whither, I pray you
Went she?
Brid.   I know not, sir.
Wel.   I'll tell you, brother,
Whither I suspect she's gone.
Kit.   Whither, good brother?
Wel. To Cob's house, I believe: but, keep my counsel.
Kit. I will, I will: to Cob's house! Doth she haunt Cob's?   160
She's gone a' purpose now to cuckold me
With that lewd rascal, who, to win her favour,
Hath told her all.   [*Exit.*]
Wel.   Come, he is once more gone,
Sister, let's lose no time; th' affair is worth it.
[*Exeunt.*]

SCENE IX.[5]

[*Enter*] MATHEW *and* BOBADILL.

Mat. I wonder, captain, what they will say of my going away, ha?
Bob. Why, what should they say, but as of a discreet gentleman; quick, wary, respectful of nature's fair lineaments? and that's all.   5
Mat. Why so! but what can they say of your beating?

---

[1] "As the Tower was extra-parochial, it probably afforded some facility to private marriages." (Gifford.)

[2] White lead, used as a cosmetic.
[3] Used in the sense of pander.

[4] Fools.
[5] A street

Bob. A rude part, a touch with soft wood, a kind of gross battery us'd, laid on strongly, borne most patiently; and that 's all.   10
Mat. Ay, but would any man have offered it in Venice, as you say?
Bob. Tut! I assure you, no: you shall have there your *nobilis*, your *gentilezza*, come in bravely upon your reverse, stand you close, [15 stand you firm, stand you fair, save your *retricato* with his left leg, come to the *assalto* with the right, thrust with brave steel, defy your base wood! But wherefore do I awake this remembrance? I was fascinated, by Jupiter; fascinated, but I will be unwitch'd and reveng'd by law.   21
Mat. Do you hear? Is it not best to get a warrant, and have him arrested and brought before justice Clement?
Bob. It were not amiss? Would we had it!   25

[Enter BRAINWORM *disguised as* FORMAL.]

Mat. Why, here comes his man; let 's speak to him.
Bob. Agreed, do you speak.
Mat. Save you, sir.
Brai. With all my heart, sir.   30
Mat. Sir, there is one Downright hath abus'd this gentleman and myself, and we determine to make our amends by law. Now, if you would do us the favour to procure a warrant to [34 bring him afore your master, you shall be well considered, I assure you, sir.
Brai. Sir, you know my service is my living; such favours as these gotten of my master is his only preferment,[1] and therefore you must [39 consider me as I may make benefit of my place.
Mat. How is that, sir?
Brai. Faith, sir, the thing is extraordinary, and the gentleman may be of great account; yet, be he what he will, if you will lay me down a brace of angels in my hand you shall [45 have it, otherwise not.
Mat. How shall we do, captain? He asks a brace of angels; you have no money?
Bob. Not a cross,[2] by fortune.
Mat. Nor I, as I am a gentleman, but two- [50 pence left of my two shillings in the morning for wine and radish: let 's find him some pawn.
Bob. Pawn! we have none to the value of his demand.
Mat. O, yes; I 'll pawn this jewel in my [55 ear, and you may pawn your silk stockings, and pull up your boots, they will ne'er be mist: it must be done now.
Bob. Well, an there be no remedy, I 'll step aside and pull 'em off.   *[Withdraws.]*   60
Mat. Do you hear, sir? We have no store of money at this time, but you shall have good pawns; look you, sir, this jewel, and that gentleman's silk stockings; because we would have it dispatch'd ere we went to our chambers.   65
Brai. I am content, sir; I will get you the warrant presently.[3] What 's his name, say you? Downright?
Mat. Ay, ay, George Downright.

---

[1] The only preferment he gives me.   [2] Penny.
[3] Forthwith.

Brai. What manner of man is he?   70
Mat. A tall big man, sir; he goes in a cloak most commonly of silk-russet, laid about with russet lace.
Brai. 'T is very good, sir.
Mat. Here, sir, here 's my jewel.   75
Bob. [*returning.*] And here are stockings.
Brai. Well, gentlemen, I 'll procure you this warrant presently; but who will you have to serve it?
Mat. That 's true, captain: that must be [80 consider'd.
Bob. Body o' me I know not; 't is service of danger.
Brai. Why, you were best get one o' the varlets o' the city,[4] a serjeant: I 'll appoint you one, if you please.   86
Mat. Will you, sir? Why, we can wish no better.
Bob. We 'll leave it to you, sir.
                    [Exeunt BOB. *and* MAT.]
Brai. This is rare! Now will I go and pawn this cloak of the justice's man's at the brok- [90 er's for a varlet's suit, and be the varlet myself; and get either more pawns, or more money of Downright, for the arrest.   *[Exit.]*

SCENE X.[5]

[Enter] KNOWELL.

Know. Oh, here it is; I am glad I have found it now;
Ho! who is within here?
Tib. [*within.*] I am within, sir? What 's your pleasure?
Know. To know who is within besides yourself.
Tib. Why, sir, you are no constable, I hope?
Know. O, fear you the constable? Then I doubt not   6
You have some guests within deserve that fear.
I 'll fetch him straight.

[Enter TIB.]

                    O' God's name, sir!
Know. Go to; come tell me, is not young Knowell here?
Tib. Young Knowell! I know none such, sir, o' mine honesty.   10
Know. Your honesty, dame! It flies too lightly from you.
There is no way but fetch the constable.
Tib. The constable! the man is mad, I think.
                    [Exit, and claps to the door.]

[Enter DAME KITELY *and* CASH.]

Cash. Ho! who keeps house here?
Know. O, this is the female copesmate[6] of my son: 15
Now shall I meet him straight.
Dame K.   Knock, Thomas, hard.
Cash. Ho, goodwife!

[Re-enter TIB.]

Tib. Why, what 's the matter with you?
Dame K. Why, woman, grieves it you to ope your door?

---

[4] Bailiff.   [5] The lane before Cob's house.
[6] Companion.

Belike you get something to keep it shut.
Tib. What mean these questions, pray ye? 20
Dame K. So strange you make it! Is not my
husband here?
Know. Her husband!
Dame K. My tried husband, master Kitely?
Tib. I hope he needs not to be tried here.
Dame K. No, dame, he does it not for need,
but pleasure. 24
Tib. Neither for need nor pleasure is he here.
Know. This is but a device to balk me withal:

[*Enter* KITELY, *muffled in his cloak.*]

Soft, who is this? 'T is not my son disguis'd?
Dame K. (*spies her husband come, and runs to
him.*) O, sir, have I forestall'd your honest
market?
Found your close[1] walks? You stand amaz'd
now, do you? 29
I' faith, I am glad I have smokt[2] you yet at last.
What is your jewel, trow? In, come, let 's see her;
Fetch forth your huswife, dame; if she be
fairer,
In any honest judgment, than myself,
I 'll be content with it: but she is change, 35
She feeds you fat, she soothes your appetite,
And you are well! Your wife, an honest woman,
Is meat twice sod[3] to you, sir! O, you treach-
our![4]
Know. She cannot counterfeit thus palpably.
Kit. Out on thy more than strumpet's impu-
dence!
Steal'st thou thus to thy haunts? and have I
taken 40
Thy bawd and thee, and thy companion,
                        (*pointing to old* KNOWELL)
This hoary-headed letcher, this old goat,
Close at your villainy, and would'st thou 'scuse it
With thy stale harlot's jest, accusing me?
O, old incontinent (*to* KNOWELL), dost thou not
shame, 45
When all thy powers in chastity is spent,
To have a mind so hot, and to entice,
And feed th' enticements of a lustful woman?
Dame K. Out, I defy thee, I, dissembling
wretch!
Kit. Defy me, strumpet! Ask thy pander[5]
here, 50
Can he deny it; or that wicked elder?
Know. Why, hear you, sir.
Kit.   Tut, tut, tut; never speak:
Thy guilty conscience will discover thee.
Know. What lunacy is this, that haunts this
man?
Kit. Well, good wife BA'D,[6] Cob's wife, and
you,
That make your husband such a hoddy-doddy;[7]
And you, young apple-squire, and old cuckold-
maker;
I 'll ha' you every one before a justice:
Nay, you shall answer it, I charge you go.
Know. Marry, with all my heart, sir, I go
willingly; 60
Though I do taste this as a trick put on me,

[1] Secret.   [2] Found.   [3] Boiled.   [4] Traitor.
[6] F, has in margin *By Thomas, i. e.* referring to Cash.
[5] Apparently a poor pun on *bad* and *bawd.*   [7] Dupe.

To punish my impertinent search, and justly,
And half forgive my son for the device.
Kit. Come, will you go?
Dame K.   Go! to thy shame believe it.

[*Enter* COB.]

Cob. Why, what 's the matter here, what 's
here to do? 65
Kit. O, Cob, art thou come? I have been
abus'd,
And i' thy house; was never man so wrong'd!
Cob. 'Slid, in my house, my master Kitely!
Who wrongs you in my house?
Kit. Marry, young lust in old, and old in
young here: 70
Thy wife 's their bawd, here have I taken 'em.
Cob. How, bawd! is my house come to that?
Am I preferr'd thither? Did I not charge you
to keep your doors shut, Isbel? and do you let
'em lie open for all comers? 75
          He falls upon his wife and beats her.
Know. Friend, know some cause, before thou
beat'st thy wife.
This 's madness in thee.
Cob.   Why, is there no cause?
Kit. Yes, I 'll shew cause before the justice,
Cob:
Come, let her go with me.
Cob.   Nay, she shall go.
Tib. Nay, I will go. I 'll see an you may [80
be allow'd to make a bundle o' hemp[8] o' your
right and lawful wife thus, at every cuckoldy
knave's pleasure. Why do you not go?
Kit. A bitter quean! Come, we will ha' you
tam'd.   [*Exeunt.*]

SCENE XI.[9]

[*Enter*] BRAINWORM, [*disguised as a City Serjeant.*]

Brai. Well, of all my disguises yet, now am
I most like myself, being in this serjeant's gown.
A man of my present profession never counterfeits, till he lays hold upon a debtor and says
he 'rests him; for then he brings him to all [5
manner of unrest. A kind of little kings we
are, bearing the diminutive of a mace, made
like a young artichoke, that always carries
pepper and salt in itself. Well, I know not what
danger I undergo by this exploit; pray Hea- [10
ven I come well off!

[*Enter* MATHEW *and* BOBADILL.]

Mat. See, I think, yonder is the varlet, by his
gown.
Bob. Let 's go in quest of him.
Mat. 'Save you, friend! Are not you here by
appointment of justice Clement's man? 15
Brai. Yes, an't please you, sir; he told me
two gentlemen had will'd him to procure a
warrant from his master, which I have about
me, to be serv'd on one Downright.
Mat. It is honestly done of you both; and [20
see where the party comes you must arrest;
serve it upon him quickly, afore he be aware.
Bob. Bear back, master Mathew.

[8] Hemp is prepared by beating.   [9] A street.

[*Enter* STEPHEN *in* DOWNRIGHT'S *cloak.*]

Brai. Master Downright, I arrest you i' the queen's name, and must carry you afore a [25 justice by virtue of this warrant.

Step. Me, friend! I am no Downright, I; I am master Stephen. You do not well to arrest me, I tell you, truly; I am in nobody's bonds nor books, I would you should know it. A plague [30 on you heartily, for making me thus afraid afore my time!

Brai. Why, now are you deceived, gentlemen?

Bob. He wears such a cloak, and that deceived us: but see, here 'a comes indeed; this [35 is he, officer.

[*Enter* DOWNRIGHT.]

Dow. Why how now, signior gull! Are you turn'd filcher of late! Come, deliver my cloak.

Step. Your cloak, sir! I bought it even now, in open market. 40

Brai. Master Downright, I have a warrant I must serve upon you, procur'd by these two gentlemen.

Dow. These gentlemen! These rascals!
[*Offers to beat them.*]

Brai. Keep the peace, I charge you in her majesty's name. 46

Dow. I obey thee. What must I do, officer?

Brai. Go before master justice Clement, to answer what they can object against you, sir. I will use you kindly, sir.

Mat. Come, let 's before, and make[1] the justice, captain. 50

Bob. The varlet 's a tall man, afore heaven!
[*Exeunt* BOB. *and* MAT.]

Dow. Gull, you 'll gi' me my cloak.

Step. Sir, I bought it, and I 'll keep it. 53

Dow. You will?

Step. Ay, that I will.

Dow. Officer, there 's thy fee, arrest him.

Brai. Master Stephen, I must arrest you.

Step. Arrest me! I scorn it. There, take your cloak, I 'll none on 't. 61

Dow. Nay, that shall not serve your turn now, sir. Officer, I 'll go with thee to the justice's; bring him along.

Step. Why, is not here your cloak? What would you have? 66

Dow. I 'll ha' you answer it, sir.

Brai. Sir, I 'll take your word, and this gentleman's too, for his appearance.

Dow. I 'll ha' no words taken: bring him along.

Brai. Sir, I may choose to do that, I may [71 take bail.

Dow. 'T is true, you may take bail, and choose at another time; but you shall not now, varlet. Bring him along, or I 'll swinge you. 75

Brai. Sir, I pity the gentleman's case; here 's your money again.

Dow. 'Sdeins, tell not me of my money; bring him away, I say.

Brai. I warrant you he will go with you of himself, sir. 81

Dow. Yet more ado?

[1] Prepare.

Brai. [*Aside.*] I have made a fair mash on 't.

Step. Must I go?

Brai. I know no remedy, master Stephen. 85

Dow. Come along afore me here; I do not love your hanging look behind.

Step. Why, sir, I hope you cannot hang me for it: can he, fellow?

Brai. I think not, sir; it is but a whipping matter, sure. 91

Step. Why then let him do his worst, I am resolute. [*Exeunt.*]

ACT V

SCENE I.[2]

[*Enter*] CLEMENT, KNOWELL, KITELY, DAME KITELY, TIB, CASH, COB, Servants.

Clem. Nay, but stay, stay, give me leave: my chair, sirrah. — You, master Knowell, say you went thither to meet your son?

Know. Ay, sir.

Clem. But who directed you thither? 5

Know. That did mine own man, sir.

Clem. Where is he?

Know. Nay, I know not now; I left him with your clerk, and appointed him to stay here for me. 10

Clem. My clerk! about what time was this?

Know. Marry, between one and two, as I take it.

Clem. And what time came my man with the false message to you, master Kitely? 15

Kit. After two, sir.

Clem. Very good: but, mistress Kitely, how chance that you were at Cob's, ha?

Dame K. An't please you, sir, I 'll tell you: my brother Wellbred told me that Cob's house was a suspected place —— 21

Clem. So it appears, methinks: but on.

Dame K. And that my husband us'd thither daily.

Clem. No matter, so he us'd himself well, mistress. 26

Dame K. True, sir: but you know what grows by such haunts oftentimes.

Clem. I see rank fruits of a jealous brain, mistress Kitely: but did you find your hus- [30 band there, in that case as you suspected?

Kit. I found her there, sir.

Clem. Did you so? That alters the case. Who gave you knowledge of your wife's being there?

Kit. Marry, that did my brother Wellbred. 35

Clem. How, Wellbred first tell her; then tell you after! Where is Wellbred?

Kit. Gone with my sister, sir, I know not whither. 39

Clem. Why this is a mere trick, a device; you are gull'd in this most grossly all. Alas, poor wench! wert thou beaten for this?

Tib. Yes, most pitifully, an 't please you.

Cob. And worthily, I hope, if it shall prove so. 45

Clem. Ay, that 's like, and a piece of a sentence. ——

[2] Coleman St. A hall in Justice Clement's house.

[*Enter a* Servant.]

How now, sir! what's the matter?
Serv. Sir, there's a gentleman i' the court
without, desires to speak with your worship. 50
Clem. A gentleman! what is he?
Serv. A soldier, sir, he says.
Clem. A soldier! Take down my armour, my
sword quickly. A soldier speak with me! Why,
when, knaves! Come on, come on. (*Arms him-* [55
self); hold my cap there, so; give me my gorget,[1]
my sword: stand by, I will end your matters
anon.——Let the soldier enter. [*Exit Servant.*]

SCENE II. [2]

[CLEMENT, KNOWELL, *etc. Enter*] BOBADILL,
[followed by] MATHEW.

Now, sir, what ha' you to say to me? [3]
Bob. By your worship's favour——
Clem. Nay, keep out, sir; I know not your
pretence. — You send me word, sir, you are a
soldier; why, sir, you shall be answer'd here: [5
here be them have been amongst soldiers. Sir,
your pleasure.
Bob. Faith, sir, so it is, this gentleman and
myself have been most uncivilly wrong'd and
beaten by one Downright, a coarse fellow [10
about the town here; and for mine own part, I
protest, being a man in no sort given to this
filthy humour of quarrelling, he hath assaulted
me in the way of my peace, despoil'd me of
mine honour, disarm'd me of my weapons, [15
and rudely laid me along in the open streets,
when I not so much as once offer'd to resist him.
Clem. O, God's precious! is this the soldier?
Here, take my armour off quickly, 't will make
him swoon, I fear; he is not fit to look on 't, [20
that will put up a blow.
Mat. An't please your worship, he was bound
to the peace.
Clem. Why, an he were, sir, his hands were
not bound, were they? 25

[*Re-enter* Servant.]

Serv. There's one of the varlets of the city,
sir, has brought two gentlemen here; one, upon
your worship's warrant.
Clem. My warrant?
Serv. Yes, sir; the officer says, procur'd by
these two.
Clem. Bid him come in. [*Exit* Servant.] Set 31
by this picture.[4]

SCENE III.[5]

[CLEMENT, BOBADILL, *etc. Enter*] DOWNRIGHT,
STEPHEN, *and* BRAINWORM [*disguised as
before*].

What, Master Downright! Are you brought in at
Mr. Freshwater's[6] suit here? [7]
Dow. I' faith, sir, and here's another brought
at my suit.

---
[1] Armor for the throat.   [2] The same.
[3] In F, at end of Sc. I.   [4] Mere picture of a soldier.
[5] The same.
[6] A freshwater soldier was one who had never crossed
the sea, *i. e.* had seen no service.
[7] In F, at end of Sc. 2.

Clem. What are you, sir? 5
Step. A gentleman, sir. O, uncle!
Clem. Uncle! Who? Master Knowell?
Know. Ay, sir; this is a wise kinsman of
mine. 9
Step. God's my witness, uncle, I am wrong'd
here monstrously; he charges me with stealing
of his cloak, and would I might never stir, if I
did not find it in the street by chance.
Dow. O, did you find it now? You said you
bought it ere-while. 15
Step. And you said, I stole it. Nay, now my
uncle is here, I'll do well enough with you.
Clem. Well, let this breathe awhile. You that
have cause to complain there, stand forth. Had
you my warrant for this gentleman's appre- [20
hension?
Bob. Ay, an't please your worship.
Clem. Nay, do not speak in passion[8] so.
Where had you it?
Bob. Of your clerk, sir. 25
Clem. That's well! an my clerk can make
warrants, and my hand not at 'em! Where is
the warrant — officer, have you it?
Brai. No, sir. Your worship's man, Master
Formal, bid me do it for these gentlemen, [30
and he would be my discharge.
Clem. Why, Master Downright, are you such
a novice, to be serv'd and never see the warrant?
Dow. Sir, he did not serve it on me. 35
Clem. No! how then?
Dow. Marry, sir, he came to me, and said he
must serve it, and he would use me kindly,
and so —— 39
Clem. O, God's pity, was it so, sir? *He must
serve it!* Give me my long sword there, and
help me off. So, come on, sir varlet, *I must* cut
off your legs, sirrah [BRAINWORM *kneels*]; nay,
stand up, *I'll use you kindly;* I *must* cut off
your legs, I say. 45
       Flourishes over him with his long sword.
Brai. O, good sir, I beseech you; nay, good
master justice!
Clem. I *must* do it, there is no remedy; I
must cut off your legs, sirrah, I *must* cut off
your ears, you rascal, I *must* do it: I *must* [50
cut off your nose, I *must* cut off your head.
Brai. O, good your worship!
Clem. Well, rise; how dost thou do now?
Dost thou feel thyself well? Hast thou no
harm? 55
Brai. No, I thank your good worship, sir.
Clem. Why so! I said I must cut off thy
legs, and I must cut off thy arms, and I must
cut off thy head; but I did not do it: so you
said you must serve this gentleman with my [60
warrant, but you did not serve him. You knave,
you slave, you rogue, do you say you *must*,
sirrah! Away with him to the jail; I'll teach
you a trick for your *must*, sir.
Brai. Good sir, I beseech you, be good to [65
me.
Clem. Tell him he shall to the jail; away with
him, I say.
Brai. Nay, sir, if you will commit me, it

---
[8] Melancholy emotion.

shall be for committing more than this: I will [70
not lose by my travail any grain of my fame,
certain.   [*Throws off his serjeant's gown.*]
  Clem. How is this?
  Know. My man Brainworm!
  Step. O, yes, uncle; Brainworm has been
with my cousin Edward and I all this day.   76
  Clem. I told you all there was some device.
  Brai. Nay, excellent justice, since I have laid
myself thus open to you, now stand strong for
me; both with your sword and your balance.   80
  Clem. Body o' me, a merry knave! give me
a bowl of sack. If he belong to you, Master
Knowell, I bespeak your patience.
  Brai. That is it I have most need of. Sir, if
you'll pardon me only, I'll glory in all the [85
rest of my exploits.
  Know. Sir, you know I love not to have my
favours come hard from me. You have your
pardon, though I suspect you shrewdly for being of counsel with my son against me.   90
  Brai. Yes, faith, I have, sir, though you retain'd me doubly this morning for yourself:
first, as Brainworm; after, as Fitz-Sword. I was
your reform'd soldier, sir. 'Twas I sent you to
Cob's upon the errand without end.   95
  Know. Is it possible? or that thou should'st
disguise thy language so as I should not know
thee?
  Brai. O, sir, this has been the day of my
metamorphosis. It is not that shape alone [100
that I have run through to-day. I brought this
gentleman, master Kitely, a message too, in
the form of master Justice's man here, to draw
him out o' the way, as well as your worship,
while master Wellbred might make a convey- [105
ance of mistress Bridget to my young master.
  Kit. How! my sister stol'n away?
  Know. My son is not married, I hope.
  Brai. Faith, sir, they are both as sure as love,
a priest, and three thousand pound, which [110
is her portion, can make 'em; and by this time
are ready to bespeak their wedding-supper at
the Windmill, except some friend here prevent
'em, and invite 'em home.
  Clem. Marry, that will I; I thank thee for [115
putting me in mind on't. Sirrah, go you and
fetch them hither upon my warrant. [*Exit* Servant.] Neither's friends have cause to be sorry,
if I know the young couple aright. Here, I
drink to thee for thy good news. But I pray [120
thee, what hast thou done with my man, Formal?
  Brai. Faith, sir, after some ceremony past,
as making him drunk, first with story, and then
with wine, (but all in kindness,) and strip- [125
ping him to his shirt, I left him in that cool
vein; departed, sold your worship's warrant to
these two, pawn'd his livery for that varlet's
gown, to serve it in; and thus have brought
myself by my activity to your worship's consideration.   131
  Clem. And I will consider thee in another
cup of sack. Here's to thee, which having
drunk off this my sentence: Pledge me. Thou
hast done, or assisted to nothing, in my [135
judgment, but deserves to be pardon'd for the

wit of the offence. If thy master, or any man
here, be angry with thee, I shall suspect his
ingine,[1] while I know him, for't. How now,
what noise is that?   146

  [*Enter* Servant.]

  Serv. Sir, it is Roger is come home.
  Clem. Bring him in, bring him in.

SCENE IV.[2]

To them [*enter*] FORMAL [*in a suit of armour.*]

What! drunk? In arms against me? Your
reason, your reason for this?[3]
  Form. I beseech your worship to pardon me;
I happen'd into ill company by chance, that
cast me into a sleep, and stript me of all my [5
clothes.
  Clem. Well, tell him I am Justice Clement,
and do pardon him: but what is this to your
armour? What may that signify?
  Form. An't please you, sir, it hung up i' [10
the room where I was stript; and I borrow'd it
of one of the drawers[4] to come home in, because
I was loth to do penance through the street i'
my shirt.
  Clem. Well, stand by a while.   15

SCENE V.[2]

To them [*enter*] E. KNOWELL, WELLBRED, *and*
BRIDGET.

Who be these? O, the young company; welcome, welcome! Gi' you joy. Nay, mistress
Bridget, blush not; you are not so fresh a bride,
but the news of it is come hither afore you.
Master bridegroom, I ha' made your peace, [5
give me your hand: so will I for all the rest ere
you forsake my roof.[5]
  E. Know. We are the more bound to your humanity, sir.
  Clem. Only these two have so little of man in
'em, they are no part of my care.   11
  Wel. Yes, sir, let me pray you for this gentleman, he belongs to my sister the bride.
  Clem. In what place, sir?
  Wel. Of her delight, sir, below the stairs, [15
and in public: her poet, sir.
  Clem. A poet! I will challenge him myself
presently at extempore,
    Mount up thy Phlegon,[6] *Muse, and testify*
      How Saturn, sitting in an ebon cloud,   20
    Disrobed his podex, white as ivory,
      And through the welkin thund'red all aloud.
  Wel. He is not for extempore, sir: he is all for
the pocket muse; please you command a sight
of it.   25
  Clem. Yes, yes, search him for a taste of his
vein.   [*They search* MATHEW's *pockets.*]
  Wel. You must not deny the queen's justice,
sir, under a writ o' rebellion.   28
  Clem. What! all this verse? Body o' me, he

---

1 Wit.
2 The same.
3 In F, at end of Sc. 3.
4 Waiters.
5 In F, at end of Sc. 4.
6 One of the horses of the Sun's chariot.

carries a whole realm,[1] a commonwealth of paper in his hose. Let us see some of his subjects. [*Reads.*]

Unto the boundless ocean of thy face,
Runs this poor river, charg'd with streams of eyes.[2]
How! this is stol'n. 35

E. Know. A parody! a parody! with a kind of miraculous gift, to make it absurder than it was.

Clem. Is all the rest of this batch? Bring me a torch; lay it together, and give fire. [40 Cleanse the air. [*Sets the papers on fire.*] Here was enough to have infected the whole city, if it had not been taken in time. See, see, how our poet's glory shines! brighter and brighter! still it increases! O, now it 's at the highest; [45 and now it declines as fast. You may see, *sic transit gloria mundi!*

Know. There's an emblem for you, son, and your studies. 49

Clem. Nay, no speech or act of mine be drawn against such as profess it worthily. They are not born every year, as an alderman. There goes more to the making of a good poet, than a sheriff. Master Kitely, you look upon me! — though I live i' the city here, amongst you, I [55 will do more reverence to him, when I meet him, than I will to the mayor out of his year. But these paper-pedlars! these ink-dabblers! they cannot expect reprehension or reproach; they have it with the fact. 60

E. Know. Sir, you have sav'd me the labour of a defence.[3]

---

[1] Punning on *ream.*
[2] Parodied from Daniel, *Sonnet to Delia.*
[3] The following passage occurs in Q₁ at this point:

Giu. Call you this poetry?
Lo. ju. Poetry! Nay, then call blasphemy religion,
Call devils angels, and sin piety;
Let all things be preposterously transchanged.
Lo. se. Why, how now, son? What, are you startled
now?
Hath the brize* prickt you, ha? Go to! You see
How abjectly your poetry is rankt
In general opinion.
Lo. ju. Opinion! O God, let gross opinion
Sink and be damn'd as deep as Barathrum!
If it may stand with your most wisht content,
I can refell† opinion and approve
The state of poesy, such as it is,
Blessed, eternal, and most true divine.
Indeed, if you will look on poesy
As she appears in many, poor and lame,
Patch'd up in remnants and old worn-out rags,
Half starv'd for want of her peculiar food,
Sacred invention,— then I must confirm
Both your conceit and censure of her merit:
But view her in her glorious ornaments,
Attired in the majesty of art,
Set high in spirit with the precious taste
Of sweet philosophy, and, which is most,
Crown'd with the rich traditions of a soul
That hates to have her dignity profan'd
With any relish of an earthly thought,
Oh, then how proud a presence doth she bear!
Then is she like herself, fit to be seen
Of none but grave and consecrated eyes.
Nor is it any blemish to her fame
That such keen, ignorant, and blasted wits,

*Gad-fly.   †Refute.

Clem. It shall be discourse for supper between your father and me, if he dare under- [64 take me. But to dispatch away these: you sign o' the soldier, and picture o' the poet, (but both so false, I will not ha' you hang'd out at my door till midnight,) while we are at supper, you two shall penitently fast it out in my court without; and, if you will, you may pray there [70 that we may be so merry within as to forgive or forget you when we come out. Here 's a third, because we tender your safety, shall watch you, he is provided for the purpose.[4] — Look to your charge, sir. 75

Step. And what shall I do?

Clem. O! I had lost a sheep an he had not bleated: why, sir, you shall give master Downright his cloak; and I will intreat him to take it. A trencher and a napkin you shall [80 have i' the buttery, and keep Cob and his wife company here; whom I will intreat first to be reconcil'd; and you to endeavour with your wit to keep 'em so.

Step. I 'll do my best. 85

Cob. Why, now I see thou art honest, Tib, I receive thee as my dear and mortal wife again.

Tib. And I you, as my loving and obedient husband. 90

Clem. Good compliment! It will be their bridal night too. They are married anew. Come, I conjure the rest to put off all discontent. You, master Downright, your anger; you, master Knowell, your cares; Master Kitely and his wife, their jealousy. 96

For, I must tell you both, while that is fed,
Horns i' the mind are worse than o' the head.

Kit. Sir, thus they go from me; kiss me, sweetheart. 100

See what a drove of horns fly in the air,
Wing'd with my cleansed and my credulous
breath!
Watch 'em, suspicious eyes, watch where they fall.
See, see! on heads that think they 've none at
all!
O, what a plenteous world of this will come! 105
When air rains horns, all may be sure of some.[5]
I ha' learn'd so much verse out of a jealous man's part in a play.

Clem. 'T is well, 't is well! This night we 'll dedicate to friendship, love, and laughter. 110 Master bridegroom, take your bride and lead; every one, a fellow. Here is my mistress, Brainworm! to whom all my addresses of courtship shall have their reference: whose adventures this day, when our grandchildren shall [115 hear to be made a fable, I doubt not but it shall find both spectators and applause. [*Exeunt.*]

---

[4] Formal, in his armor.   [5] F, *fame.*

Such brainless gulls, should utter their stolen wares
With such applauses in our vulgar ears;
Or that their slubber'd lines have current pass
From the fat judgments of the multitude;
But that this barren and infected age
Should set no difference 'twixt these empty spirits
And a true poet; than which reverend names
Nothing can more adorn humanity.

SEJANUS, HIS FALL

BY

BEN JONSON

Non hic Centauros, non Gorgonas, Harpyiasque Invenies : Hominem pagina nostra sapit.

PERSONS OF THE PLAY

TIBERIUS, [Emperor].
DRUSUS SENIOR, [Nephew of Tiberius].
NERO, ⎫ [Sons
DRUSUS JUNIOR, ⎬ of
CALIGULA, ⎭ Germanicus].
[LUCIUS] ARRUNTIUS, ⎫
[CAIUS] SILIUS, ⎪ [Gentlemen
[TITIUS] SABINUS, ⎬ opposed
[MARCUS] LEPIDUS, ⎪ to
[CREMUTIUS] CORDUS, ⎪ Sejanus].
[ASINIUS] GALLUS, ⎭
REGULUS, [Consul].
TERENTIUS,
[GRACINUS] LACO.
EUDEMUS, [a Physician].
RUFUS.
SEJANUS.
LATIARIS.
VARRO, [Consul].
[SERTORIUS] MACRO.
COTTA.
[DOMITIUS] AFER.

HATERIUS.
SANQUINIUS.
POMPONIUS.
[JULIUS] POSTHUMUS.
[FULCINUS] TRIO, Consul.
MINUTIUS.
SATRIUS [SECUNDUS].
[PINNARIUS] NATTA.
OPSIUS.

AGRIPPINA, [Widow of Germanicus].
LIVIA, [Wife of Drusus senior].
SOSIA, [Wife of C. Silius].
Tribuni.
Praecones.
Flamen.
Tubicines.
Nuntius.
Lictores.
Ministri.
Tibicines.
Servus, [etc.].

SCENE. — *Rome.*

TO THE

NO LESS NOBLE BY VIRTUE THAN BLOOD,

ESME, LORD AUBIGNY

MY LORD, — If ever any ruin were so great as to survive, I think this be one I send you, The Fall of Sejanus. It is a poem, that, if I well remember, in your lordship's sight, suffer'd no less violence from our people here, than the subject of it did from the rage of the people of Rome; but with a different fate, as, I hope, merit; [1] for this hath outliv'd their malice, and begot itself a greater favour than he lost, the love of good men. Amongst whom, if I make your lordship the first it thanks, it is not without a just confession of the bond your benefits have, and ever shall hold upon me,

Your Lordship's most faithful honourer,
BEN. JONSON.

TO THE READERS [2]

THE following and voluntary labours [3] of my friends, prefixed to my book, have relieved me in much whereat, without them, I should necessarily have touched. Now I will only use three or four short and needful notes, and so rest.

First, if it be objected, that what I publish is no true poem, in the strict laws of time, I confess it : as also in the want of a proper chorus ; whose habit and moods are such and so difficult, as not any, whom I have seen, since the ancients, no, not they who have most presently affected laws, have yet come in the way of. Nor is it needful, or almost possible in these our times, and to such auditors as commonly things are presented, to observe the old state and splendour of dramatic poems, with preservation of any popular delight. But of this I shall take more seasonable cause to speak, in my observations upon Horace his Art of Poetry, which, with the text translated, I

[1] *I. e.* with a different merit.   [2] Only in Q.   [3] Commendatory verses.

intend shortly to publish.[1] In the meantime, if in truth of argument, dignity of persons, gravity and height of elocution, fulness and frequency of sentence, I have discharged the other offices of a tragic writer, let not the absence of these forms be imputed to me, wherein I shall give you occasion hereafter, and without my boast, to think I could better prescribe, than omit the due use for want of a convenient knowledge.

The next is, lest in some nice nostril the quotations might savour affected, I do let you know, that I abhor nothing more ; and I have only done it to show my integrity in the story, and save myself in those common torturers that bring all wit to the rack ; whose noses are ever like swine spoiling and rooting up the Muses' gardens ; and their whole bodies like moles, as blindly working under earth, to cast any, the least, hills upon virtue.

Whereas they are in Latin, and the work in English, it was presupposed none but the learned would take the pains to confer them ; the authors themselves being all in the learned tongues, save one,[2] with whose English side I have had little to do. To which it may be required, since I have quoted the page, to name what editions I followed : *Tacit. Lips. in quarto, Antwerp, edit,* 1600. *Dio. folio, Hen. Steph.* 1592. For the rest, as *Sueton. Seneca,* &c., the chapter doth sufficiently direct, or the edition is not varied.

Lastly, I would inform you, that this book, in all numbers, is not the same with that which was acted on the public stage ; wherein a second pen[3] had good share : in place of which, I have rather chosen to put weaker, and, no doubt, less pleasing, of mine own, than to defraud so happy a genius of his right by my loathed usurpation.

Fare you well, and if you read farther of me, and like, I shall not be afraid of it, though you praise me out.

Neque enim mihi cornea fibra est.

But that I should plant my felicity in your general saying, *good*, or *well*, &c., were a weakness which tne better sort of you might worthily contemn, if not absolutely hate me for.

BEN. JONSON ;
and no such,

Quem
Palma negata macrum, donata reducit opimum.

THE ARGUMENT

AELIUS SEJANUS, son to Seius Strabo, a gentleman of Rome, and born at Vulsinium ; after his long service in court, first under Augustus ; afterward, Tiberius ; grew into that favour with the latter, and won him by those arts, as there wanted nothing but the name to make him a co-partner of the Empire. Which greatness of his, Drusus, the Emperor's son, not brooking ; after many smother'd dislikes, it one day breaking out, the prince struck him publicly on the face. To revenge which disgrace, Livia, the wife of Drusus (being before corrupted by him to her dishonour, and the discovery of her husband's counsels) Sejanus practiseth with, together with her physician, called Eudemus, and one Lygdus, an eunuch, to poison Drusus. This their inhuman act having successful and unsuspected passage, it emboldeneth Sejanus to farther and more insolent projects, even the ambition of the Empire ; where finding the lets[4] he must encounter to be many and hard, in respect of the issue of Germanicus, who were next in hope for the succession, he deviseth to make Tiberius' self his means ; and instils into his ears many doubts and suspicions, both against the princes, and their mother Agrippina ; which Caesar jealously heark'ning to, as covetously consenteth to their ruin, and their friends'. In this time, the better to mature and strengthen his design, Sejanus labours to marry Livia, and worketh with all his ingine,[5] to remove Tiberius from the knowledge of public business, with allurements of a quiet and retired life ; the latter of which, Tiberius, out of a proneness to lust, and a desire to hide those unnatural pleasures which he could not so publicly practise, embraceth : the former enkindleth his fears, and there gives him first cause of doubt or suspect towards Sejanus : against whom he raiseth in private a new instrument, one Sertorius Macro, and by him underworketh, discovers the other's counsels, his means, his ends, sounds the affections of the senators, divides, distracts them : at last, when Sejanus least looketh, and is most secure ; with pretext of doing him an unwonted honour in the senate, he trains[6] him from his guards, and with a long doubtful letter, in one day hath him suspected, accused, condemned, and torn in pieces by the rage of the people. [This do we advance, as a mark of terror to all traitors, and treasons ; to show how just the heavens are, in pouring and thundering down a weighty vengeance on their unnatural intents, even to the worst princes ; much more to those, for guard of whose piety and virtue the angels are in continual watch, and God himself miraculously working.][7]

---

[1] Lost in the burning of his study.   [2] Tacitus, translated by Grenaway.
[3] Not identified. Shakespeare and Fletcher have been suggested.
[4] Hindrances.   [5] Ingenuity.   [6] Beguiles.
[7] Only in Q, in apparent allusion to King James and the Gunpowder Plot.

ACT I

[SCENE I.][1]

[*Enter*] SABINUS *and* SILIUS, [*followed by*] LA-
TIARIS.

Sab. Hail, Caius Silius![2]
Sil.   Titius Sabinus,[3] hail!
You're rarely met in court,
Sab.   Therefore, well met.
Sil. 'T is true: indeed, this place is not our
   sphere.
Sab. No, Silius, we are no good inginers.[4]
We want the fine arts, and their thriving use 5
Should make us grac'd, or favour'd of the
   times:
We have no shift of faces, no cleft tongues,
No soft and glutinous bodies, that can stick,
Like snails, on painted walls; or, on our breasts,
Creep up, to fall from that proud height, to
   which   ¬
We did by slavery,[5] not by service climb.
We are no guilty men, and then no great;
We have nor place in court, office in state,
That we can say,[6] we owe unto our crimes:
We burn with no black secrets,[7] which can
   make   15
Us dear to the pale authors; or live fear'd
Of their still waking jealousies, to raise
Ourselves a fortune, by subverting theirs.
We stand not in the lines, that do advance
To that so courted point.

[*Enter* SATRIUS *and* NATTA *at a distance.*]
Sil.   But yonder lean 20
A pair that do.
Sab. [*salutes* LATIARIS.] Good cousin Latiaris.[8]
Sil. Satrius Secundus,[9] and Pinnarius Natta,[10]
The great Sejanus' clients: there be two,
Know more than honest counsels; whose close[11]
   breasts,   24
Were they ripp'd up to light, it would be found
A poor and idle [12] sin to which their trunks
Had not been made fit organs. These can lie,
Flatter, and swear, forswear,[13] deprave, inform,
Smile, and betray; make guilty men; then beg
The forfeit lives, to get their livings; cut 30
Men's throats with whisp'rings; sell to gaping
   suitors
The empty smoke that flies about the palace;
Laugh when their patron laughs; sweat when
   he sweats;
Be hot and cold with him; change every mood,

Habit, and garb, as often as he varies; 35
Observe him, as his watch observes his clock;[14]
And, true as turquoise in the dear lord's ring,[15]
Look well or ill with him:[16] ready to praise
His lordship, if he spit, or but piss fair, 39
Have an indifferent stool, or break wind well;
Nothing can scape their catch.
Sab.   Alas! these things
Deserve no note, conferr'd[17] with other vile
And filthier flatteries,[18] that corrupt the times,
When, not alone our gentries chief are fain
To make their safety from such sordid acts, 45
But all our consuls,[19] and no little part
Of such as have been praetors, yea, the most
Of senators,[20] that else not use their voices,
Start up in public senate, and there strive
Who shall propound most abject things, and
   base;   50
So much, as oft Tiberius hath been heard,
Leaving the court, to cry,[21] O race of men,
Prepar'd for servitude! — which show'd that he
Who least the public liberty could like,
As loathly brook'd their flat servility.
Sil. Well, all is worthy of us, were it more,
Who with our riots, pride, and civil hate,
Have so provok'd the justice of the gods:
We, that, within these fourscore years, were
   born
Free, equal lords of the triumphed world, 60
And knew no masters but affections;
To which betraying first our liberties,
We since became the slaves to one man's lusts;
And now to many:[22] every minist'ring spy
That will accuse and swear, is lord of you, 65
Of me, of all, our fortunes and our lives.
Our looks are call'd to question,[23] and our
   words,
How innocent soever, are made crimes;
We shall not shortly dare to tell our dreams,
Or think, but 't will be treason.
Sab.   Tyrants' arts 70
Are to give flatterers grace; accusers, power;
That those may seem to kill whom they devour.

[*Enter* CORDUS *and* ARRUNTIUS.]
Now, good Cremutius Cordus.[24]
Cor. [*salutes* SABINUS.] Hail to your lordship!
Nat. Who's that salutes your cousin?
Lat.   'T is one Cordus,   *They whisper.*
A gentleman of Rome: one that has writ 75

---

[1] A state room in the Palace.
[2] *De Caio Silio, vid. Tacit.* Lips. edit. quarto. *Ann.*
Lib. i pag. ii. Lib. II. p. 28 *et* 33. All such notes giving
authorities are Jonson's own, and are retained through
one scene for their characteristic value.
[3] *De Titio Sabino, vid. Tacit.* Lib. iv. p. 79.
[4] Intriguers.   [6] *Juv. Sat.* I. v. 75.
[5] *Tac. Ann.* I. 2.   [7] *Ibid.* III. v. 49, *etc.*
[8] *De Latiari, cons. Tacit. Ann.* iv. 94, *et Dion,* Step.
edit. fol. lviii. 711.
[9] *De Satrio Secundo et*
[10] *Pinnario Natta, leg. Tacit. Ann.* iv. 83. *Et de
Satrio cons. Senec. Consol. ad Marciam.*
[11] Secret.   [12] Empty, useless.
[13] *Vid. Sen. de Benef.* iii. 26.

[14] The pocket-watch, in Jonson's days, was constantly
regulated by the motion of the clock, at that time the
more accurate machine of the two. (Gifford.)
[15] This belief in the sympathetic nature of the turquoise is often alluded to.
[16] *Juv. Sat.* iii. 105, *etc.*   [18] *Vid. Tacit. Ann.* i. 3
[17] Compared.   [19] *Ibid.* iii. 69.
[20] *Pedarii.* (Senators not yet on the censor's roll,
who had no vote of their own, but could merely assent
to that of another.)
[21] *Tacit. Ann.* iii. 69.
[22] *Legs Tacit. Ann.* i. 24, *de Romano, Hispano, etc.*
ibid. et iii. 61, 62. *Juv. Sat.* X. v. 87. *Suet. Tib.* cap. 61.
[23] *Vid. Tacit. Ann.* i. 4. *et* iii. 62. *Suet. Tib.* cap. 61.
Senec. de Benef. iii. 26.
[24] *De Crem. Cordo. vid. Tacit. Ann.* iv. 83, 84. *Senec.
Cons. ad Marciam. Dio.* lvii. 710. *Suet. Aug.* c. 35.
Tib. c. 61. *Cal.* c. 16.

Annals of late, they say, and very well.
  Nat. Annals? Of what times?
  Lat.   I think of Pompey's,[1]
And Caius Caesar's; and so down to these.
  Nat. How stands he affected to the present
       state?
Is he or Drusian,[2] or Germanican,   80
Or ours, or neutral?
  Lat.   I know him not so far.
  Nat. Those times are somewhat queasy[3] to
       be toucht.
Have you or seen or heard part of his work?
  Lat. Not I; he means they shall be public
       shortly.
  Nat. O, Cordus do you call him?
  Lat.   Ay. [*Exeunt* NATTA *and* SATRIUS.]
  Sab.   But these our times   85
Are not the same, Arruntius.[4]
  Arr.   Times! The men,
The men are not the same! 'T is we are base,
Poor, and degenerate from th' exalted strain
Of our great fathers. Where is now the soul
Of god-like Cato? he, that durst be good,   90
When Caesar durst be evil; and had power,
As not to live his slave, to die his master?
Or where's the constant Brutus, that being
    proof
Against all charm of benefits, did strike
So brave a blow into the monster's heart   95
That sought unkindly[5] to captive his country?
O, they are fled the light! Those mighty spirits
Lie rak'd up with their ashes in their urns,
And not a spark of their eternal fire
Glows in a present bosom. All's but blaze,   100
Flashes, and smoke, wherewith we labour so;
There's nothing Roman in us; nothing good,
Gallant, or great. 'T is true that Cordus says,
" Brave Cassius was the last of all that race."

DRUSUS *passes by* [*attended by* HATERIUS, *etc.*]

  Sab. Stand by! Lord Drusus.[6]
  Hat.   Th' emp'ror's son! Give place. 105
  Sil. I like the prince well.
  Arr.   A riotous youth,[7]
There's little hope of him.
  Sab.   That fault his age
Will, as it grows, correct. Methinks he bears
Himself each day more nobly than other;
And wins no less on men's affections,   110
Than doth his father lose. Believe me, I love
    him;
And chiefly for opposing to Sejanus.[8]
  Sil. And I, for gracing his young kinsmen
    so,[9]
The sons[10] of prince Germanicus:[11] it shows

[1] *Suet. Aug. c.* 35.
[2] *Vid. de faction. Tacit. Ann.* ii. 39 *et* iv. 79.
[3] Ticklish.
[4] *De Lu. Arrun. isto vid. Tacit. Ann.* i. 6 *et* iii. 60, *et Dion. Rom. Hist.* Lib. 58.
[5] Unnaturally.
[6] *Lege de Druso Tacit. Ann.* i. 9. *Suet. Tib. c.* 52. *Dio. Rom. Hist.* lvii. 699.   [8] *Vid. Tacit. Ann.* iv. 74.
[7] *Tacit. Ann.* iii. 62.   [9] *Ibid.* iv. 75, 76.
[10] *Nero, Drusus, Caius qui in castris genitus, et Caligula nominatus. Ibid.* i.
[11] *De Germanico cons. ibid.* i. 14, *et Dion. Rom. Hist.* lvii. 694.

A gallant clearness in him, a straight mind, 115
That envies not, in them, their father's name.
  Arr. His name was, while he liv'd, above all
    envy ;
And, being dead, without it. O, that man!
If there were seeds of the old virtue left,   119
They liv'd in him.
  Sil.   He had the fruits, Arruntius,
More than the seeds :[12] Sabinus and myself
Had means to know him within; and can report him.
We were his followers, he would call us friends ;
He was a man most like to virtue; in all,
And every action, nearer to the gods   125
Than men, in nature ; of a body as fair
As was his mind ; and no less reverend
In face than fame :[13] he could so use his state,
Temp'ring his greatness with his gravity,
As it avoided all self-love in him,   130
And spite in others. What his funerals lack'd
In images and pomp, they had suppli'd
With honourable sorrow, soldiers' sadness,
A kind of silent mourning, such as men,
Who know no tears but from their captives,
    use   135
To show in so great losses.
  Cor.   I thought once,
Considering their forms, age, manner of deaths,
The nearness of the places where they fell,
T' have parallel'd him with great Alexander :
For both were of best feature, of high race, 140
Year'd but to thirty, and, in foreign lands,
By their own people alike made away.
  Sab. I know not, for his death, how you
    might wrest it :
But, for his life, it did as much disdain
Comparison with that voluptuous, rash,   145
Giddy, and drunken Macedon's, as mine
Doth with my bondman's. All the good in him,
His valour, and his fortune, he made his ;
But he had other touches of late Romans,   149
That more did speak him :[14] Pompey's dignity,
The innocence of Cato, Caesar's spirit,
Wise Brutus' temp'rance : and every virtue,
Which, parted unto others, gave them name,
Flow'd mixt in him. He was the soul of good-
    ness ;
And all our praises of him are like streams 155
Drawn from a spring, that still rise full, and
    leave
The part remaining greatest.
  Arr.   I am sure
He was too great for us,[15] and that they knew
Who did remove him hence.
  Sab.   When men grow fast
Honour'd and lov'd, there is a trick in state, 160
(Which jealous princes never fail to use)
How to decline that growth, with fair pretext,
And honourable colours of employment,
Either by embassy, the war, or such,
To shift them forth into another air,   165

[12] *Tacit. Ann.* iv. 79.
[13] *Ibid.* ii. 47, *et Dion. Rom. Hist.* lvii. 705.
[14] *Vid. apud Vell. Paterc.* Lips. 4 to. pp. 35–47, *istorum hominum characteres.*
[15] *Vid. Tacit. Ann.* ii. 28, 34. *Dio. Rom. Hist.* lvii. 705.

Where they may purge, and lessen ; so was he : [1]
And had his seconds there, sent by Tiberius
And his more subtile dam, to discontent him ;
To breed and cherish mutinies ; detract
His greatest actions ; give audacious check   170
To his commands ; and work to put him out
In open act of treason. All which snares
When his wise cares prevented,[2] a fine poison
Was thought on, to mature their practices.
   Cor. Here comes Sejanus.[3]
   Sil.   Now observe the stoops,   175
The bendings, and the falls.
   Arr.   Most creeping base !

[*Enter*] Sejanus, Terentius, Satrius,
          [Natta,] etc.

                    They pass over the stage.
   Sej. I note 'em well : no more. Say you ?
   Sat.   My lord,
There is a gentleman of Rome would buy ——
   Sej. How call you him you talk'd with ?
   Sat.   Please your worship,
It is Eudemus,[4] the physician   180
To Livia, Drusus' wife.
   Sej.   On with your suit.
Would buy, you said ——
   Sat.   A tribune's place, my lord.
   Sej. What will he give ?
   Sat.   Fifty sestertia.[5]
   Sej. Livia's physician, say you, is that fellow ?
   Sat. It is, my lord. Your lordship's answer ?
   Sej.   To what ?   185
   Sat. The place, my lord. 'T is for a gentle-
man
Your lordship will well like of, when you see
him,
And one that you may make yours, by the
grant.
   Sej. Well, let him bring his money, and his
name.
   Sat. Thank your lordship. He shall, my
lord.
   Sej. Come hither.   190
Know you this same Eudemus ? Is he learn'd ?
   Sat. Reputed so, my lord, and of deep prac-
tice.
   Sej. Bring him in to me, in the gallery ;
And take you cause to leave us there together :
I would confer with him, about a grief. — On !
          [*Exeunt* Sejanus, Satrius, Ter-
          entius, *etc.*]
   Arr. So ! yet another ? yet ? O desperate
state   196
Of grov'ling honour ! Seest thou this, O sun,
And do we see thee after ? Methinks, day
Should lose his light, when men do lose their
shames,

[1] Con *Tacit. Ann.* ii. 39, *de occultis mandatis Pisoni,
et postea,* pp. 42, 43, 48. *Orat. D. Celeris. Est Tibi Au-
gustae conscientia est Caesaris favor, sed in occulto,
etc. Leg. Suet. Tib.* c. 52. *Dio.* p. 706.
[2] *Vid. Tacit. Ann.* ii. 46, 47. *Lib.* iii. 54, *et Suet. Cal.*
c. 1 *et* 2.
[3] *De Sejano vid. Tacit. Ann.* i. 9. *Lib.* iv. *princip.
et per tot. Suet. Tib. Dio.* lvii. lviii. *et Plin. et Senec.*
[4] *De Eudemo isto vid. Tacit. Ann.* iv. 74.
[5] *Monetae nostrae* 375 *lib. vid. Budaeum de asse,* ii.

And for the empty circumstance of life,   200
Betray their cause of living.
   Sil.   Nothing so.[6]
Sejanus can repair, if Jove should ruin.
He is the now court-god ; and well applied
With sacrifice of knees, of crooks, and cringe,
He will do more than all the house of heav'n   205
Can for a thousand hecatombs. 'T is he
Makes us our day, or night ; hell and elysium
Are in his look. We talk of Rhadamanth,
Furies, and firebrands ; but 't is his frown   209
That is all these ; where, on the adverse part,
His smile is more than e'er yet poets feign'd
Of bliss, and shades, nectar ——
   Arr.   A serving boy !
I knew him, at Caius' [7] trencher, when for hire
He prostituted his abused body
To that great gourmand, fat Apicius :   215
And was the noted pathic [8] of the time.
   Sab. And, now,[9] the second face of the whole
world !
The partner of the empire, hath his image
Rear'd equal with Tiberius, borne in ensigns ;
Commands, disposes every dignity.   220
Centurions, tribunes, heads of provinces,
Praetors, and consuls ; all that heretofore
Rome's general suffrage gave, is now his sale,
The gain, or rather spoil of all the earth,
One, and his house, receives.
   Sil.   He hath of late   225
Made him a strength too, strangely, by reduc-
ing
All the praetorian bands into one camp,
Which he commands : pretending that the sol-
dier,
By living loose and scatter'd, fell to riot ;
And that if any sudden enterprise   230
Should be attempted, their united strength
Would be far more than sever'd ; and their life
More strict, if from the city more remov'd.
   Sab. Where now he builds what kind of forts
he please,
Is heard to court the soldier by his name,   235
Woos, feasts the chiefest men of action,
Whose wants, nor loves, compel them to be his.
And though he ne'er were liberal by kind,[10]
Yet to his own dark ends, he' s most profuse,
Lavish, and letting fly he cares not what   240
To his ambition.
   Arr.   Yet hath he ambition ?
Is there that step in state can make him higher,
Or more, or anything he is, but less ?
   Sil. Nothing but emp'ror.
   Arr.   The name Tiberius,
I hope, will keep, howe'er he hath foregone   245
The dignity and power.
   Sil.   Sure, while he lives.
   Arr. And dead, it comes to Drusus. Should
he fail,

[6] *De ingenio, moribus, et potentia Sejani, leg. Tacit.
Ann.* iv. 74. *Dio. Rom. Hist.* lvii. 708.
[7] *Caius divi Augusti nepos. Cons. Tacit. Ann.* iv. 74
et Dio. lvii. 706.
[8] A male prostitute.
[9] *Juv. Sat.* X. v. 63, *etc. Tacit. Ibid. Dion. ibid. et
sic passim.*
[10] Nature.

To the brave issue of Germanicus ;
And they are three : [1] too many — ha ? for him
To have a plot upon ?
  Sil.   I do not know   250
The heart of his designs ; but sure their face
Looks farther than the present.
  Arr.   By the gods,
If I could guess he had but such a thought,
My sword should cleave him down from head
    to heart,
But I would find it out ; and with my hand 255
I 'd hurl his panting brain about the air
In mites as small as atomi t' undo
The knotted bed ——
  Sab.   You are observ'd, Arruntius.
  Arr. (*Turns to* SEJANUS' *clients.*) Death ! I
    dare tell him so ; and all his spies.
You, sir, I would, do you look ? and you.
  Sab.   Forbear. 260
           [SCENE II.] [2]

      [*Enter*] SATRIUS, EUDEMUS.

  Sat. Here he will instant be ; let 's walk a
    turn ;
You 're in a muse, Eudemus ?
  Eud.   Not I, sir.
[*Aside.*] I wonder he should mark me out so.
    Well,
Jove and Apollo form it for the best !
  Sat. Your fortune 's made unto you now,
    Eudemus,   5
If you can but lay hold upon the means ;
Do but observe his humour, and — believe
    it —
He is the noblest Roman, where he takes —

        [*Enter* SEJANUS.]

Here comes his lordship.
  Sej.   Now, good Satrius.
  Sat. This is the gentleman, my lord.
  Sej.   Is this ? 10
Give me your hand, we must be more ac-
    quainted.
Report, sir, hath spoke out your art and learn-
    ing :
And I am glad I have so needful cause,
However in itself painful and hard,
To make me known to so great virtue —
    Look,   15
Who 's that, Satrius ? [*Exit* SAT.] I have a
    grief, sir,
That will desire your help. Your name 's Eude-
    mus ?
  Eud. Yes.
  Sej.   Sir ?
  Eud.   It is, my lord.
  Sej.   I hear you are
Physician to Livia, the princess.
  Eud. I minister unto her, my good lord. 20
  Sej. You minister to a royal lady, then.
  Eud. She is, my lord, and fair.
  Sej.   That 's understood
Of all their sex, who are or would be so ;

  [1] *Nero, Drusus, et Caligula. — Tacit. ibid.*
  [2] The same. The scene divisions are Gifford's. Jonson
did not sub-divide the Acts in this play.

And those that would be, physic soon can make
    'em :
For those that are, their beauties fear no col-
    ours.[3]   25
  Eud. Your lordship is conceited. [4]
  Sej.   Sir, you know it,
And can, if need be, read a learned lecture
On this, and other secrets. 'Pray you, tell me,
What more of ladies, besides Livia,
Have you your patients ?
  Eud.   Many, my good lord. 30
The great Augusta, Urgulania,
Mutilia Prisca, and Plancina ; divers —
  Sej. And all these tell you the particulars
Of every several grief ? how first it grew,
And then increas'd ; what action caused that ;
What passion that ; and answer to each point 35
That you will put 'em ?
  Eud.   Else, my lord, we know not
How to prescribe the remedies.
  Sej.   Go to,
You are a subtile nation, you physicians !
And grown the only cabinets in court   40
To ladies' privacies. Faith, which of these
Is the most pleasant lady in her physic ?
Come, you are modest [5] now.
  Eud.   'T is fit, my lord.
  Sej. Why, sir, I do not ask you of their
    urines,
Whose smell 's most violet, or whose siege is
    best,   45
Or who makes hardest faces on her stool,
Which lady sleeps with her own face a nights,
Which puts her teeth off, with her clothes, in
    court,
Or, which her hair, which her complexion,
And, in which box she puts it. These were
    questions   50
That might, perhaps, have put your gravity
To some defence of blush. But, I inquir'd,
Which was the wittiest, merriest, wantonest ?
Harmless interrogatories, but conceits. ——
Methinks Augusta should be most perverse, 55
And froward in her fit.
  Eud.   She 's so, my lord.
  Sej. I knew it : and Mutilia the most jocund.
  Eud. 'T is very true, my lord.
  Sej.   And why would you
Conceal this from me, now ? Come, what is
    Livia ?
I know she 's quick and quaintly spirited, 60
And will have strange thoughts, when she is at
    leisure :
She tells 'em all to you ?
  Eud.   My noblest lord,
He breathes not in the Empire, or on earth,
Whom I would be ambitious to serve
(In any act that may preserve mine honour) 65
Before your lordship.
  Sej.   Sir, you can lose no honour,
By trusting aught to me. The coarsest act
Done to my service, I can so requite
As all the world shall style it honourable :
Your idle, virtuous definitions, 70
Keep honour poor, and are as scorn'd as vain :

  [3] Need fear nothing.   [4] Jocular.   [5] Reserved.

Those deeds breathe honour that do suck in
    gain.
  Eud. But, good my lord, if I should thus
    betray
The counsels of my patient, and a lady's
Of her high place and worth, what might your
    lordship,   75
(Who presently are to trust me with your own)
Judge of my faith?
  Sej.   Only the best, I swear.
Say now that I should utter you my grief,
And with it the true cause; that it were love,
And love to Livia: you should tell her this: 80
Should she suspect your faith? I would you
    could
Tell me as much from her; see if my brain
Could be turn'd jealous.[1]
  Eud.   Happily,[2] my lord,
I could in time tell you as much and more;
So I might safely promise but the first   85
To her from you.
  Sej.   As safely, my Eudemus,
I now dare call thee so, as I have put
The secret into thee.
  Eud.   My lord ——
  Sej.   Protest not,
Thy looks are vows to me; use only speed,
And but affect her with Sejanus' love,   90
Thou art a man made to make consuls. Go.
  Eud. My lord, I'll promise you a private
    meeting.
This day together.
  Sej.   Canst thou?
  Eud.   Yes.
  Sej.   The place?
  Eud. My gardens, whither I shall fetch your
    lordship.
  Sej. Let me adore my Aesculapius.   95
Why, this indeed is physic! and outspeaks
The knowledge of cheap drugs, or any use
Can be made out of it! more comforting
Than all your opiates, juleps, apozems,[3]
Magistral[4] syrups, or ——Begone, my friend,
Not barely styled, but created so;   101
Expect things greater than thy largest hopes,
To overtake thee. Fortune shall be taught
To know how ill she hath deserv'd thus long,
To come behind thy wishes. Go, and speed ——
                      [*Exit* Eudemus.]
Ambition makes more trusty slaves than need.
These fellows, by the favour of their art,   107
Have still the means to tempt; oft-times the
    power.
If Livia will be now corrupted, then
Thou hast the way, Sejanus, to work out   110
His secrets, who, thou know'st, endures thee not,
Her husband, Drusus: and to work against
    them.
Prosper it, Pallas, thou that better'st wit;
For Venus hath the smallest share in it.

[*Enter*] Tiberius, Drusus, [*attended.*] *One*
    kneels to Tiberius.

  Tib. We not endure these flatteries; let him
    stand;   115

Our empire, ensigns, axes, rods, and state
Take not away our human nature from us:
Look up on us, and fall before the gods.
  Sej. How like a god speaks Cæsar!
  Arr. [*Aside to* Cordus.]   There, observe!
He can endure that second, that's no flattery.
O, what is it proud slime will not believe,   121
Of his own worth, to hear it equal prais'd
Thus with the gods!
  Cor.   He did not hear it, sir.
  Arr. He did not? Tut, he must not, we think
    meanly.
'T is your most courtly known confederacy,   125
To have your private parasite redeem
What he, in public subtilety, will lose
To making him a name.
  Hat.   Right mighty lord ——
                    [*Gives him letters.*]
  Tib. We must make up our ears' 'gainst these
    assaults
Of charming tongues; we pray you use no
    more
These contumelies to us; style not us   131
Or lord, or mighty, who profess ourself
The servant of the senate, and are proud
T' enjoy them our good, just, and favouring
    lords.
  Cor. Rarely dissembled!
  Arr.   Prince-like to the life.   135
  Sab. When power that may command, so
    much descends,
Their bondage, whom it stoops to, it intends.
  Tib. Whence are these letters?
  Hat.   From the senate.
  Tib.   So.
Whence these?   [Lat. *gives him letters.*]
  Lat.   From thence too.
  Tib.   Are they sitting now?
  Lat. They stay thy answer, Caesar.
  Sil.   If this man   140
Hath but a mind allied unto his words,
How blest a fate were it to us, and Rome!
We could not think[5] that state for which to
    change,
Although the aim were our old liberty:
The ghosts of those that fell for that, would
    grieve   145
Their bodies liv'd not, now, again to serve.
Men are deceiv'd, to think there can be thrall
Beneath a virtuous prince. Wish'd liberty
Ne'er lovelier looks, than under such a crown.
But, when his grace is merely but lip-good,   150
And that no longer than he airs himself
Abroad in public, there, to seem to shun
The strokes and stripes of flatterers, which
    within
Are lechery unto him, and so feed
His brutish sense with their afflicting sound,   155
As, dead to virtue, he permits himself
Be carried like a pitcher by the ears,
To every act of vice: this is a case
Deserves our fear, and doth presage the nigh
And close approach of blood and tyranny.   160
Flattery is midwife unto prince's rage:
And nothing sooner doth help forth a tyrant,

---

[1] Suspicious.   [2] Perhaps.   [3] Decoctions.   [4] Sovereign.   [5] Think of.

Than that and whisperers' grace, who have the
  time,
The place, the power, to make all men offenders.
  Arr. He should be told this ; and be bid dis-
    semble   165
With fools and blind men : we that know the
  evil,
Should hunt the palace-rats, or give them
  bane.[1]
Fright hence these worse than ravens, that
  devour
The quick, where they but prey upon the dead :
He shall be told it.
  Sab.   Stay, Arruntius,   170
We must abide our opportunity,
And practise what is fit, as what is needful.
It is not safe t' enforce a sovereign's ear :
Princes hear well, if they at all will hear.
  Arr. Ha, say you so? well ! In the mean
    time, Jove,   175
(Say not but I do call upon thee now,)
Of all wild beasts preserve me from a tyrant ;
And of all tame. a flatterer.
  Sil.   'T is well pray'd.
  Tib. [*having read the letters.*] Return the lords
    this voice : We are their creature,
And it is fit a good and honest prince,   180
Whom they, out of their bounty, have in-
  structed
With so dilate[2] and absolute a power,
Should owe the office of it to their service,
And good of all and every citizen.
Nor shall it e'er repent us to have wish'd   185
The senate just and fav'ring lords unto us,
Since their free loves do yield no less defence
T' a prince's state, than his own innocence.
Say then, there can be nothing in their thought
Shall want to please us, that hath pleased them ;
Our suffrage rather shall prevent[3] than stay 191
Behind their wills : 't is empire to obey,
Where such, so great, so good determine.
Yet, for the suit of Spain t' erect a temple
In honour of our mother and our self,   195
We must, with pardon of the senate, not
Assent thereto. Their lordships may object
Our not denying the same late request
Unto the Asian cities : we desire
That our defence for suffering that be known 200
In these brief reasons, with our after purpose.
Since deified Augustus hind'red not
A temple to be built at Pergamum,
In honour of himself and sacred Rome
We, that have all his deeds and words observ'd
Ever, in place of laws, the rather follow'd   206
That pleasing precedent, because with ours,
The senate's reverence, also, there was join'd.
But as, t' have once receiv'd it, may deserve
The gain of pardon ; so, to be ador'd   210
With the continu'd style and note[4] of gods,
Through all the provinces, were wild ambition,
And no less pride : yea, ev'n Augustus' name
Would early vanish, should it be profan'd   214
With such promiscuous flatteries. For our part,
We here protest it, and are covetous

Posterity should know it, we are mortal ;
And can but deeds of men : 't were glory
  enough,
Could we be truly a prince. And they shall add
Abounding grace unto our memory,   220
That shall report us worthy our forefathers,
Careful of your affairs, constant in dangers,
And not afraid of any private frown
For public good. These things shall be to us
Temples and statues, reared in your minds,   225
The fairest, and most during imag'ry :
For those of stone or brass, if they become
Odious in judgment of posterity,
Are more contemn'd as dying sepulchres,
Than ta'en for living monuments. We then 230
Make here our suit, alike to gods and men ;
The one, until the period of our race,
T' inspire us with a free and quiet mind,
Discerning both divine and human laws ;
The other, to vouchsafe us after death,   235
An honourable mention, and fair praise,
T' accompany our actions and our name :
The rest of greatness princes may command,
And, therefore, may neglect ; only, a long,
A lasting, high, and happy memory   240
They should, without being satisfied, pursue :
Contempt of fame begets contempt of virtue.
  Nat. Rare !
  Sat.   Most divine !
  Sej.   The oracles are ceas'd,
That only Caesar, with their tongue, might
  speak.
  Arr. Let me be gone : most felt and open
    this !   245
  Cor. Stay.
  Arr.   What ! to hear more cunning and fine
    words,
With their sound flatter'd ere their sense be
  meant?
  Tib. Their choice of Antium, there to place
    the gift,
Vow'd to the goddess[5] for our mother's health,
We will the senate know, we fairly like ;   250
As also of their grant to Lepidus,
For his repairing the Aemilian place,
And restoration of those monuments :
Their grace, too, in confining of Silanus
To th' other isle Cithera, at the suit   255
Of his religious sister, much commends
Their policy, so temp'red with their mercy.
But for the honours which they have decreed
To our Sejanus, to advance[6] his statue
In Pompey's theatre, (whose ruining fire   260
His vigilance and labour kept restrain'd
In that one loss,) they have therein outgone
Their own great wisdoms, by their skilful choice
And placing of their bounties on a man
Whose merit more adorns the dignity   265
Than that can him ; and gives a benefit,
In taking, greater than it can receive.
Blush not, Sejanus, thou great aid of Rome,
Associate of our labours, our chief helper ;
Let us not force thy simple modesty   270
With off'ring at[7] thy praise, for more we cannot,

Since there 's no voice can take [1] it. No man here
Receive our speeches as hyperboles :
For we are far from flattering our friend,
Let envy know, as from the need to flatter.   275
Nor let them ask the causes of our praise :
Princes have still their grounds rear'd with themselves,
Above the poor low flats of common men ;
And who will search the reasons of their acts,
Must stand on equal bases. Lead, away :   280
Our loves unto the senate.

      [*Exeunt* TIB., SEJAN., NATTA., HAT.,
         SAT., Officers, *etc.*]

Arr.   Caesar !
Sab.   Peace.
Cor. Great Pompey's theatre was never ruin'd
Till now, that proud Sejanus hath a statue
Rear'd on his ashes.
Arr.   Place the shame of soldiers   284
Above the best of generals ? Crack the world,
And bruise the name of Romans into dust,
Ere we behold it !
Sil.   Check your passion ;
Lord Drusus tarries.
Dru.   Is my father mad,
Weary of life and rule, lords, thus to heave   289
An idol up with praise ? Make him his mate,
His rival in the empire ?
Arr.   O, good prince !
Dru. Allow him statues, titles, honours, such
As he himself refuseth ?
Arr.   Brave, brave Drusus !
Dru. The first ascents to sovereignty are hard ;
But ent'red once, there never wants or means,
Or ministers, to help th' aspirer on.   296
Arr. True, gallant Drusus.
Dru.   We must shortly pray
To Modesty, that he will rest contented —
Arr. Ay, where he is, and not write emp'ror.

Re-enter SEJANUS, [SATRIUS, LATIARIS,]
       Clients, *etc.*

Sej. There is your bill, and yours ; bring you
your man.   [*To* SATRIUS.]   300
I have mov'd for you, too, Latiaris.
Dru.   What !
Is your vast greatness grown so blindly bold,
That you will over us ?
Sej.   Why then give way.
Dru. Give way, Colossus ! Do you lift ? Advance you ?
Take that !   *Strikes him.*
Arr. Good ! brave ! excellent, brave prince !   305
Dru. Nay, come, approach. [*Draws his sword.*]
What, stand you off ? at gaze ?
It looks too full of death for thy cold spirits.
Avoid mine eye, dull camel, or my sword
Shall make thy brav'ry fitter for a grave,
Than for a triumph. I'll advance [2] a statue   310
O' your own bulk ; but 't shall be on the cross,

Where I will nail your pride at breadth and length,
And crack those sinews, which are yet but stretch'd
With your swoln fortune's rage.
Arr.   A noble prince !
All. A Castor, a Castor, a Castor, a Castor.
           [*Exeunt all but* SEJANUS.]
Sej. He that, with such wrong mov'd, can
bear it through   316
With patience, and an even mind, knows how
To turn it back. Wrath cover'd carries fate :
Revenge is lost, if I profess my hate.
What was my practice [3] late, I 'll now pursue,
As my fell justice : this hath styl'd it new.   321
                   [*Exit.*]

     CHORUS — of musicians.

ACT II

[SCENE I.] [4]

[*Enter*] SEJANUS, LIVIA, EUDEMUS.

Sej. Physician, thou art worthy of a province,
For the great favours done unto our loves ;
And, but that greatest Livia bears a part
In the requital of thy services,
I should alone despair of aught like means   5
To give them worthy satisfaction.
Liv. Eudemus, I will see it, shall receive
A fit and full reward for his large merit. —
But for this potion we intend to Drusus,
(No more our husband, now) whom shall we
choose   10
As the most apt and abled instrument,
To minister it to him ?
Eud.   I say, Lygdus.
Sej. Lygdus ? What 's he ?
Liv.   An eunuch Drusus loves.
Eud. Ay, and his cup-bearer.
Sej.   Name not a second.
If Drusus love him, and he have that place,   15
We cannot think a fitter.
Eud.   True, my lord ;
For free access and trust are two main aids.
Sej. Skilful physician !
Liv.   But he must be wrought
To th' undertaking, with some labour'd art.
Sej. Is he ambitious ?
Liv.   No.
Sej.   Or covetous ?   20
Liv. Neither.
Eud.   Yet, gold is a good general charm.
Sej. What is he, then ?
Liv.   Faith, only wanton, light.
Sej. How ! is he young ? and fair ?
Eud.   A delicate youth.
Sej. Send him to me, I 'll work him. — Royal
lady,
Though I have lov'd you long, and with that
height   25
Of zeal and duty, like the fire, which more
It mounts it trembles, thinking nought could
add

---

     [1] Achieve.   [2] Raise.   [3] Treasonous plot.   [4] The garden of Eudemus.

Unto the fervour which your eye had kindled;
Yet, now I see your wisdom, judgment, strength,
Quickness, and will, to apprehend the means 30
To your own good and greatness, I protest
Myself through rarified, and turn'd all flame
In your affection. Such a spirit as yours,
Was not created for the idle second
To a poor flash, as Drusus; but to shine 35
Bright as the moon among the lesser lights,
And share the sov'reignty of all the world.
Then Livia triumphs in her proper sphere,
When she and her Sejanus shall divide
The name of Caesar, and Augusta's star 40
Be dimm'd with glory of a brighter beam:
When Agrippina's fires are quite extinct,
And the scarce-seen Tiberius borrows all
As little light from us, whose folded arms
Shall make one perfect orb! [*Knocking within.*]
    Who's that? Eudemus, 45
Look. [*Exit* EUDEMUS.] 'T is not Drusus, lady,
do not fear.
   Liv. Not I, my lord: my fear and love of him
Left me at once.
   Sej.   Illustrious lady, stay ——
   Eud. [*within.*] I 'll tell his lordship.

        [*Re-enter* EUDEMUS.]

   Sej.   Who is it, Eudemus?
   Eud. One of your lordship's servants brings
you word 50
The emp'ror hath sent for you.
   Sej.   O! where is he?—
With your fair leave, dear princess, I 'll but ask
A question, and return.   *He goes out.*
   Eud.   Fortunate princess!
How are you blest in the fruition
Of this unequall'd man, the soul of Rome, 55
The Empire's life, and voice of Caesar's world!
   Liv. So blessed, my Eudemus, as to know
The bliss I have, with what I ought to owe
The means that wrought it. How do I look to-
day?
   Eud. Excellent clear, believe it. This same
fucus[1] 60
Was well laid on.
   Liv.   Methinks 't is here not white.
   Eud. Lend me your scarlet, lady. 'T is the sun,
Hath giv'n some little taint unto the ceruse;[2]
You should have us'd of the white oil I gave
you.
Sejanus for your love! his very name 65
Commandeth above Cupid or his shafts ——
        [*Paints her cheek.*]
   Liv. Nay, now you 've made it worse.
   Eud.   I 'll help it straight ——
And but pronounc'd, is a sufficient charm
Against all rumour; and of absolute power
To satisfy for any lady's honour. —— 70
   Liv. What do you now, Eudemus?
   Eud.   Make a light fucus,
To touch you o'er withal. — Honour'd Sejanus!
What act, though ne'er so strange and insolent,
But that addition will at least bear out,
If 't do not expiate?

   Liv.   Here, good physician. 75
   Eud. I like this study to preserve the love
Of such a man, that comes not every hour
To greet the world. — 'T is now well, lady; you
should
Use of the dentifrice I prescrib'd you too, 79
To clear your teeth, and the prepar'd pomatum,
To smooth the skin. — A lady cannot be
Too curious of her form, that still would hold
The heart of such a person, made her captive,
As you have his; who, to endear him more
In your clear eye, hath put away his wife, 85
The trouble of his bed and your delights,
Fair Apicata, and made spacious room
To your new pleasures.
   Liv.   Have not we return'd
That with our hate to Drusus, and discovery
Of all his counsels?
   Eud.   Yes, and wisely, lady. 90
The ages that succeed, and stand far off
To gaze at your high prudence, shall admire,
And reckon it an act without[4] your sex:
It hath that rare appearance. Some will think
Your fortune could not yield a deeper sound, 95
Than mixt with Drusus; but, when they shall
hear
That and the thunder of Sejanus meet,
Sejanus, whose high name doth strike the stars,
And rings about the concave; great Sejanus,
Whose glories, style, and titles are himself, 100
The often iterating of Sejanus;
They then will lose their thoughts, and be
asham'd
To take acquaintance of them.

        [*Re-enter* SEJANUS.]
   Sej.   I must make
A rude departure, lady; Caesar sends 104
With all his haste both of command and prayer.
Be resolute in our plot; you have my soul,
As certain yours as it is my body's.
And, wise physician, so prepare the poison,
As you may lay the subtile operation
Upon some natural disease of his: 110
Your eunuch send to me. I kiss your hands,
Glory of ladies, and commend my love
To your best faith and memory.
   Liv.   My lord,
I shall but change[5] your words. Farewell. Yet,
this
Remember for your heed, he loves you not; 115
You know what I have told you; his designs
Are full of grudge and danger; we must use
More than a common speed.
   Sej.   Excellent lady,
How you do fire my blood!
   Liv.   Well, you must go?
The thoughts be best, are least set forth to
show.   [*Exit* SEJANUS.]
   Eud. When will you take some physic, lady?
   Liv.   When 121
I shall, Eudemus: but let Drusus' drug
Be first prepar'd.
   Eud. Were Lygdus made,[6] that 's done;

---

[1] Cosmetic.   [2] White lead, used as a cosmetic.

[3] Counterbalanced.   [4] Beyond the powers of.
[5] Reciprocate.   [6] Prepared for our purposes.

I have it ready. And, to-morrow morning
I 'll send you a perfume, first to resolve   125
And procure sweat, and then prepare a bath
To cleanse and clear the cutis ;[1] against when
I 'll have an excellent new fucus made,
Resistive 'gainst the sun, the rain, or wind,
Which you shall lay on with a breath, or oil,   130
As you best like, and last some fourteen hours.
This change came timely, lady, for your health,
And the restoring your complexion,
Which Drusus' choler had almost burnt up ;
Wherein your fortune hath prescrib'd you bet-
ter   135
Than art could do.

Liv.   Thanks, good physician,
I 'll use my fortune, you shall see, with rever-
ence.
Is my coach ready ?

Eud.   It attends your highness.
                                  [Exeunt.]

[SCENE II.][2]

[Enter] SEJANUS.

Sej. If this be not revenge, when I have done
And made it perfect, let Egyptian slaves,
Parthians, and barefoot Hebrews brand my face,
And print my body full of injuries.
Thou lost thyself, child Drusus, when thou
    thought'st   5
Thou couldst outskip my vengeance, or outstand
The power I had to crush thee into air.
Thy follies now shall taste what kind of man
They have provok'd, and this thy father's house
Crack in the flame of my incensed rage,   10
Whose fury shall admit no shame or mean. —
Adultery ! it is the lightest ill
I will commit. A race of wicked acts
Shall flow out of my anger, and o'erspread
The world's wide face, which no posterity   15
Shall e'er approve, nor yet keep silent : things,
That for their cunning, close,[3] and cruel mark
Thy father would wish his, and shall, perhaps,
Carry the empty name, but we the prize.
On, then, my soul, and start not in thy course ;
Though heav'n drop sulphur, and hell belch out
    fire,   21
Laugh at the idle terrors : tell proud Jove,
Between his power and thine there is no odds :
'T was only fear first in the world made gods.

[Enter] TIBERIUS *[attended.]*

Tib. Is yet Sejanus come ?

Sej.   He 's here, dread Caesar.

Tib. Let all depart that chamber, and the
    next.   26
                [Exeunt Attendants.]
Sit down, my comfort. When the master prince
Of all the world, Sejanus, saith he fears,
Is it not fatal ?

Sej.   Yes, to those are fear'd.

Tib. And not to him ?

Sej.   Not if he wisely turn   30
That part of fate he holdeth, first on them.

Tib. That nature, blood, and laws of kind
    forbid.

Sej. Do policy and state forbid it ?

Tib.   No.

Sej. The rest of poor respects, then let go by;
State[4] is enough to make th' act just, them
    guilty.   35

Tib. Long hate pursues such acts.

Sej.   Whom hatred frights,
Let him not dream of sov'reignty.

Tib.   Are rites
Of faith, love, piety, to be trod down,
Forgotten, and made vain ?

Sej.   All for a crown.
The prince who shames a tyrant's name to bear,
Shall never dare do anything but fear ;   41
All the command of sceptres quite doth perish,
If it begin religious thoughts to cherish :
Whole empires fall, sway'd by those nice[5] re-
    spects ;
It is the licence of dark deeds protects   45
Ev'n states most hated, when no laws resist
The sword, but that it acteth what it list.

Tib. Yet so, we may do all things cruelly,
Not safely.

Sej.   Yes, and do them thoroughly.

Tib. Knows yet Sejanus whom we point at ?

Sej.   Ay,   50
Or else my thought, my sense, or both do err :
'T is Agrippina.

Tib.   She, and her proud race.

Sej. Proud ! dangerous, Caesar : for in them
    apace
The father's spirit shoots up. Germanicus
Lives in their looks, their gait, their form, t'
    upbraid us   55
With his close death, if not revenge the same.

Tib. The act 's not known.

Sej.   Not prov'd ; but whisp'ring Fame
Knowledge and proof doth to the jealous[6] give,
Who, than to fail,[7] would their own thought be-
    lieve.
It is not safe the children draw long breath,   60
That are provoked by a parent's death.

Tib. It is as dangerous to make them hence,
If nothing but their birth be their offence.

Sej. Stay, till they strike at Caesar ; then
    their crime
Will be enough ; but late and out of time   65
For him to punish.

Tib.   Do they purpose it ?

Sej. You know, sir, thunder speaks not till
    it hit.
Be not secure ;[8] none swiftlier are opprest
Than they whom confidence betrays to rest.
Let not your daring make your danger such :   70
All power 's to be fear'd, where 't is too much.
The youths are of themselves hot, violent,
Full of great thought ; and that male-spirited
    dame,
Their mother, slacks no means to put them on,
By large allowance, popular presentings,   75
Increase of train and state, suing for titles ;
Hath them commended with like prayers, like
    vows,

---

[1] Skin.   [2] An apartment in the Palace.   [3] Secret.
[4] Reasons of state.   [5] Foolishly fastidious.
[6] Suspicious.
[7] Rather than fail of proof would accept their own
thought as such.   [8] Over-confident.

To the same gods, with Caesar : days and nights
She spends in banquets and ambitious feasts
For the nobility ; where Caius Silius,   80
Titius Sabinus, old Arruntius,
Asinius Gallus, Furnius, Regulus,
And others of that discontented list,
Are the prime guests. There, and to these, she tells
Whose niece she was, whose daughter, and
      whose wife.   85
And then must they compare her with Augusta,
Ay, and prefer her too ; commend her form,
Extol her fruitfulness, at which a shower
Falls for the memory of Germanicus.
Which they blow over straight with windy
      praise   90
And puffing hopes of her aspiring sons ;
Who, with these hourly ticklings, grow so
      pleas'd,
And wantonly conceited of themselves,
As now they stick not to believe they 're such
As these do give them out ; and would be
      thought   95
More than competitors,[1] immediate heirs.
Whilst to their thirst of rule, they win the rout
(That 's still the friend of novelty) with hope
Of future freedom, which on every change
That greedily, though emptily expects.   100
Caesar, 't is age in all things breeds neglects,
And princes that will keep old dignity
Must not admit too youthful heirs stand by ;
Not their own issue ; but so darkly set
As shadows are in picture, to give height   105
And lustre to themselves.
Tib.   We will command
Their rank thoughts down, and with a stricter
      hand
Than we have yet put forth ; their trains must
      bate,[2]
Their titles, feasts, and factions.
Sej.   Or your state.
But how, sir, will you work ?
Tib.   Confine 'em.
Sej.   No.   110
They are too great, and that too faint a blow
To give them now ; it would have serv'd at first,
When with the weakest touch their knot had
      burst.
But now, your care must be, not to detect
The smallest cord, or line of your suspect ;   115
For such, who know the weight of princes' fear,
Will, when they find themselves discover'd,
      rear
Their forces, like seen snakes, that else would
      lie
Roll'd in their circles, close. Nought is more
      high,
Daring, or desperate, than offenders found ;   120
Where guilt is, rage and courage doth abound.
The course must be, to let 'em still swell up,
Riot, and surfeit on blind Fortune's cup ;
Give 'em more place, more dignities, more style,
Call 'em to court, to senate ; in the while,   125
Take from their strength some one or twain or
      more,

Of the main fautors[3] (it will fright thy store),
And, by some by-occasion. Thus, with sleight
You shall disarm first ; and they, in night
Of their ambition,[4] not perceive the train,   130
Till in the engine[5] they are caught and slain.
Tib. We would not kill, if we knew how to
      save ;
Yet, than a throne, 't is cheaper give a grave.
Is there no way to bind them by deserts ?
Sej. Sir, wolves do change their hair, but not
      their hearts.   135
While thus your thought unto a mean[6] is tied,
You neither dare enough, nor do provide.
All modesty is fond,[7] and chiefly where
The subject is no less compell'd to bear,
Than praise his sov'reign's acts.
Tib.   We can no longer   140
Keep on our mask to thee, our dear Sejanus ;
Thy thoughts are ours, in all, and we but prov'd
Their voice, in our designs, which by assenting
Hath more confirm'd us, then if heart'ning Jove
Had, from his hundred statues, bid us strike,   145
And at the stroke clickt all his marble thumbs.
But who shall first be struck ?
Sej.   First, Caius Silius ;
He is the most of mark, and most of danger :
In power and reputation equal strong,
Having commanded an imperial army   150
Seven years together, vanquish'd Sacrovir
In Germany, and thence obtain'd to wear
The ornaments triumphal. His steep fall,
By how much it doth give the weightier crack,
Will send more wounding terror to the rest,   155
Command them stand aloof, and give more way
To our surprising of the principal.
Tib. But what, Sabinus ?
Sej.   Let him grow awhile,
His fate is not yet ripe : we must not pluck
At all together, lest we catch ourselves.   160
And there 's Arruntius too, he only talks.
But Sosia, Silius' wife, would be wound in
Now, for she hath a fury in her breast,
More than hell ever knew ; and would be sent
Thither in time. Then is there one Cremutius
Cordus, a writing fellow, they have got   165
To gather notes of the precedent times,
And make them into Annals ; a most tart
And bitter spirit, I hear : who, under colour   169
Of praising those, doth tax[8] the present state,
Censures[9] the men, the actions, leaves no trick,
No practice unexamin'd, parallels
The times, the governments ; a profest champion
For the old liberty ——
Tib.   A perishing wretch !
As if there were that chaos bred in things,   175
That laws and liberty would not rather choose
To be quite broken, and ta'en hence by us,
Than have the stain to be preserv'd by such.
Have we the means to make these guilty first ?
Sej. Trust that to me : let Caesar, by his
      power,   180
But cause a formal meeting of the senate,
I will have matter and accusers ready.

[1] Partners.   [2] Lesson.

[3] Supporters.   [7] Moderate measures
[4] Blinded by ambition.   are foolish.
[5] Contrivance.   [8] Accuse.
[6] Middle course.   [9] Passes judgment on.

Tib. But how ? Let us consult.
Sej.   We shall misspend
The time of action. Counsels are unfit
In business where all rest is more pernicious 185
Than rashness can be. Acts of this close kind
Thrive more by execution than advice.
There is no ling'ring in that work begun,
Which cannot praised be, until through done.
Tib. Our edict shall forthwith command a
     court.   190
While I can live, I will prevent earth's fury :
Ἐμοῦ θανόντος γαῖα μιχθήτω πυρί.[1]
                                    [*Exit.*]

[*Enter* JULIUS] POSTHUMUS.

Pos. My lord Sejanus ——
Sej.   Julius Posthumus !
Come with my wish ! What news from Agrip-
     pina's ?
Pos. Faith, none. They all lock up them-
     selves a' late,   195
Or talk in character ; I have not seen
A company so chang'd. Except they had
Intelligence by augury of our practice —
Sej. When were you there ?
Pos.   Last night.
Sej.   And what guests found you ?
Pos. Sabinus, Silius, (the old list,) Arruntius,
Furnius, and Gallus.
Sej.   Would not these talk ?
Pos.   Little. 201
And yet we offered choice of argument.[2]
Satrius was with me.
Sej.   Well : 't is guilt enough
Their often meeting. You forgot t' extol
The hospitable lady ?
Pos.   No ; that trick   205
Was well put home, and had succeeded too,
But that Sabinus cough'd a caution out ;
For she began to swell.
Sej.   And may she burst !
Julius, I would have you go instantly
Unto the palace of the great Augusta,   210
And, by your kindest friend, get swift access ;
Acquaint her with these meetings : tell the
     words
You brought me th' other day, of Silius,
Add somewhat to 'em. Make her understand
The danger of Sabinus, and the times,   215
Out of his closeness. Give Arruntius' words
Of malice against Caesar ; so, to Gallus :
But, above all, to Agrippina. Say,
As you may truly, that her infinite pride,
Propt with the hopes of her too fruitful womb,
With popular studies gapes for sovereignty,   221
And threatens Caesar. Pray Augusta then,
That for her own, great Caesar's, and the pub-
Lic safety, she be pleas'd to urge these dangers.
Caesar is too secure,[3] he must be told,   225
And best he 'll take it from a mother's tongue.
Alas ! what is 't for us to sound, t' explore,
To watch, oppose, plot, practise, or prevent,
If he, for whom it is so strongly labour'd,
Shall, out of greatness and free spirit, be   230

[1] " When I am dead, let the earth be mingled with
fire."
[2] Subject.   [3] Confident, unsuspicious.

Supinely negligent ? Our city 's now
Divided as in time o' th' civil war,
And men forbear not to declare themselves
Of Agrippina's party. Every day
The faction multiplies ; and will do more,   235
If not resisted : you can best enlarge it,
As you find audience. Noble Posthumus,
Commend me to your Prisca : and pray her,
She will solicit this great business
To earnest and most present execution,   240
With all her utmost credit with Augusta,
Pos. I shall not fail in my instructions. [*Exit.*]
Sej. This second, from his mother, will well
     urge
Our late design, and spur on Caesar's rage ;
Which else might grow remiss. The way to put
A prince in blood, is to present the shapes   246
Of dangers greater than they are, like late
Or early shadows : and, sometimes, to feign
Where there are none, only to make him fear.
His fear will make him cruel : and once ent'red
He doth not easily learn to stop, or spare   251
Where he may doubt. This have I made my
     rule
To thrust Tiberius into tyranny,
And make him toil to turn aside those blocks,
Which I alone could not remove with safety. 255
Drusus once gone, Germanicus' three sons
Would clog my way ; whose guards have too
     much faith
To be corrupted : and their mother known
Of too unreprov'd[4] a chastity
To be attempted, as light Livia was.   260
Work then, my art, on Caesar's fears, as they
On those they fear, till all my lets[5] be clear'd,
And he in ruins of his house, and hate
Of all his subjects, bury his own state ;
When with my peace, and safety, I will rise,   265
By making him the public sacrifice.   [*Exit.*]

[SCENE III.][6]

[*Enter*] SATRIUS, NATTA.

Sat. They 're grown exceeding circumspect,
     and wary.
Nat. They have us in the wind : and yet Ar-
     runtius
Cannot contain himself.
Sat.   Tut, he 's not yet
Look'd after ; there are others more desir'd,
That are more silent.
Nat.   Here he comes. Away ! [*Exeunt.*]

[*Enter*] SABINUS, ARRUNTIUS, CORDUS.

Sab. How is it, that these beagles haunt the
     house   6
Of Agrippina ?
Arr.   O, they hunt, they hunt !
There is some game here lodg'd, which they
     must rouse,
To make the great ones sport.
Cor.   Did you observe
How they inveigh'd 'gainst Caesar ?
Arr.   Ay, baits, baits

[4] Blameless.
[5] Obstacles. F_1 betts.
[6] A room in Agrippina's house.

For us to bite at : would I have my flesh   11
Torn by the public hook, these qualified hang-
    men
Should be my company.
Cor.   Here comes another.
       [DOM. AFER *passes over the stage.*]
   Arr. Ay, there 's a man, Afer the orator !   14
One that hath phrases, figures, and fine flowers,
To strew his rhetoric with, and doth make
    haste,
To get him note or name by any offer
Where blood or gain be objects ; steeps his
    words,
When he would kill, in artificial tears :
The crocodile of Tiber ! him I love,   20
That man is mine ; he hath my heart and voice
When I would curse ! he, he.
   Sab.   Contemn the slaves,
Their present lives will be their future graves.
                       [*Exeunt.*]

          [SCENE IV.] [1]

[*Enter*] SILIUS, AGRIPPINA, NERO, SOSIA.

   Sil. May 't please your highness not forget
    yourself ;
I dare not, with my manners, to attempt
Your trouble farther.
   Agr.   Farewell, noble Silius !
   Sil. Most royal princess.
   Agr.   Sosia stays with us ?
   Sil. She is your servant, and doth owe your
    grace   5
An honest, but unprofitable love.
   Agr. How can that be, when there 's no gain
    but virtue's ?
   Sil. You take the moral, not the politic
    sense.
I meant, as she is bold, and free of speech,
Earnest to utter what her zealous thought   10
Travails withal, in honour of your house ;
Which act, as it is simply borne in her,
Partakes of love and honesty ; but may,
By th' over-often, and unseason'd use,
Turn to your loss and danger : for your state   15
Is waited on by envies, as by eyes ;
And every second guest your tables take
Is a fee'd spy, to observe who goes, who comes ;
What conference you have, with whom, where,
    when,
What the discourse is, what the looks, the
    thoughts   20
Of ev'ry person there, they do extract,
And make into a substance.
   Agr.   Hear me, Silius.
Were all Tiberius' body stuck with eyes,
And ev'ry wall and hanging in my house
Transparent, as this lawn I wear, or air ;   25
Yea, had Sejanus both his ears as long
As to my inmost closet, I would hate
To whisper any thought, or change an act,
To be made Juno's rival. Virtue's forces
Show ever noblest in conspicuous courses.   30
   Sil. 'T is great, and bravely spoken, like the
    spirit
Of Agrippina : yet, your highness knows,

     [1] Another apartment in the same.

There is nor loss nor shame in providence ; [2]
Few can, what all should do, beware enough.
You may perceive with what officious face,   35
Satrius, and Natta, Afer, and the rest
Visit your house of late, t' inquire the secrets ;
And with what bold and privileg'd art, they
    rail
Against Augusta, yea, and at Tiberius ;
Tell tricks of Livia, and Sejanus : all   40
T' excite, and call your indignation on,
That they might hear it at more liberty.
   Agr. You 're too suspicious, Silius.
   Sil.   Pray the gods,
I be so, Agrippina ; but I fear   44
Some subtile practice. They that durst to strike
At so exampless, and unblam'd a life,
As that of the renown'd Germanicus,
Will not sit down with that exploit alone :
He threatens many that hath injur'd one.
   Nero. 'T were best rip forth their tongues,
    sear out their eyes,   50
When next they come.
   Sos.   A fit reward for spies.

          [*Enter*] DRUSUS JUN.

   Dru. jun. Hear you the rumour ?
   Agr.   What ?
   Dru. jun.   Drusus is dying.
   Agr. Dying !
   Nero.   That 's strange !
   Agr.   You were with him yesternight.
   Dru. jun. One met Eudemus the physician,
Sent for, but now ; who thinks he cannot live.   55
   Sil. Thinks ! If it be arriv'd at that, he
    knows,
Or none.
   Agr. 'T is quick ! What should be his disease ?
   Sil. Poison, poison——
   Agr.   How, Silius !
   Nero.   What 's that ?
   Sil. Nay, nothing. There was late a certain
    blow
Giv'n o' the face.
   Nero.   Ay, to Sejanus.
   Sil.   True.   60
   Dru. jun. And what of that ?
   Sil.   I 'm glad I gave it not.
   Nero. But there is somewhat else ?
   Sil.   Yes, private meetings,
With a great lady at a physician's,
And a wife turn'd away—
   Nero.   Ha !
   Sil.   Toys, mere toys :
What wisdom's now i' th' streets, i' th' common
    mouth ?   65
   Dru. jun. Fears, whisp'rings, tumults, noise,
    I know not what :
They say the Senate sit.
   Sil.   I 'll thither straight ;
And see what 's in the forge.
   Agr.   Good Silius, do ;
Sosia and I will in.
   Sil.   Haste you, my lords,
To visit the sick prince ; tender your loves,   70
And sorrows to the people. This Sejanus,

           [2] Caution.

Trust my divining soul, hath plots on all :
No tree, that stops his prospect, but must fall.
                                            [*Exeunt.*]
        CHORUS — of Musicians.

ACT III

[SCENE I.]

The Senate.

[*Enter*] Praecones, Lictores, SEJANUS, VARRO,
        LATIARIS, COTTA, *and* AFER.

   Sej. 'T is only you must urge against him,
        Varro ;
Nor I, nor Caesar may appear therein,
Except in your defence, who are the consul ;
And, under colour of late enmity   4
Between your father and his, may better do it,
As free from all suspicion of a practice. [1]
Here be your notes, what points to touch at ;
        read :
Be cunning in them. Afer has them too.
   Var. But is he summon'd ?
   Sej.   No. It was debated
By Caesar, and concluded as most fit   10
To take him unprepar'd.
   Afer.   And prosecute
All under name of treason.
   Var.   I conceive.

[*Enter* SABINUS, GALLUS, LEPIDUS, *and* AR-
        RUNTIUS.]

   Sab. Drusus being dead, Caesar will not be
        here.
   Gal. What should the business of this senate
        be ?
   Arr. That can my subtle whisperers tell you :
        we   15
That are the good-dull-noble lookers-on.
Are only call'd to keep the marble warm.
What should we do with those deep mysteries,
Proper to these fine heads ? Let them alone. 19
Our ignorance may, perchance, help us be sav'd
From whips and furies.
   Gal.   See, see, see their action !
   Arr. Ay, now their heads do travail, now
        they work ;
Their faces run like shittles ; they are weaving
Some curious cobweb to catch flies.
   Sab.   Observe,
They take their places.
   Arr.   What, so low !
   Gal.   O yes, 25
They must be seen to flatter Caesar's grief,
Though but in sitting.
   Var.   Bid us silence.
   Prae.   Silence.
   Var. " Fathers conscript, may this our pre-
        sent meeting
Turn fair and fortunate to the commonwealth ! "

   [*Enter* SILIUS [*and other* Senators.]

   Sej. See, Silius enters.
   Sil.   Hail, grave fathers !

   Lic.   Stand. 30
Silius, forbear thy place.
   Sen.   How !
   Prae.   Silius, stand forth,
The consul hath to charge thee.
   Lic.   Room for Caesar
   Arr. Is he come too ! Nay then expect a
        trick.
   Sab. Silius accus'd ! Sure he will answer
        nobly.

        [*Enter*] TIBERIUS [*attended.*]

   Tib. We stand amazed, fathers, to behold 35
This general dejection. Wherefore sit
Rome's consuls thus dissolv'd, as they had lost
All the remembrance both of style and place ?
It not becomes. No woes are of fit weight
To make the honour of the Empire stoop :   40
Though I, in my peculiar self may meet
Just reprehension, that so suddenly,
And in so fresh a grief, would greet the senate,
When private tongues, of kinsmen and allies,
Inspir'd with comforts, lothly are endur'd,   45
The face of men not seen, and scarce the day,
To thousands that communicate [2] our loss.
Nor can I argue these of weakness, since
They take but natural ways ; yet I must seek 49
For stronger aids, and those fair helps draw out
From warm embraces of the commonwealth.
Our mother, great Augusta, 's struck with
        time,
Our self imprest with aged characters,
Drusus is gone, his children young and babes ;
Our aims must now reflect on those that may
Give timely succour to these present ills,   55
And are our only glad-surviving hopes,
The noble issue of Germanicus,
Nero and Drusus : might it please the consul
Honour them in, they both attend without.   60
I would present them to the senate's care,
And raise those suns of joy that should drink
        up
These floods of sorrow in your drowned eyes.
   Arr. By Jove, I am not Oedipus enough
To understand this Sphinx.
   Sab.   The princes come. 65

        [*Enter*] NERO, DRUSUS JUNIOR.

   Tib. Approach you, noble Nero, noble Dru-
        sus.
These princes, fathers, when their parent died,
I gave unto their uncle, with this prayer,
That though he 'd proper issue of his own,
He would no less bring up, and foster these,   70
Than that self-b'ood ; and by that act confirm
Their worths to him, and to posterity.
Drusus ta'en hence, I turn my prayers to you,
And 'fore our country and our gods, beseech
You take, and rule Augustus' nephew's sons,   75
Sprung of the noblest ancestors ; and so
Accomplish both my duty, and your own.
Nero, and Drusus, these shall be to you
In place of parents, these your fathers, these ;
And not unfitly : for you are so born,   80
As all your good or ill 's the commonwealth's.

───────
[1] Plot.

[2] Share.

Receive them, you strong guardians ; and blest
　　gods,
Make all their actions answer to their bloods :
Let their great titles find increase by them,
Not they by titles. Set them, as in place,　　85
So in example, above all the Romans :
And may they know no rivals but themselves.
Let Fortune give them nothing, but attend
Upon their virtue : and that still come forth　89
Greater than hope, and better than their fame.
Relieve me, fathers, with your general voice.
　　Senators. " May all the gods consent to Cae-
　　　　sar's wish,
And add to any honours that may crown
The hopeful issue of Germanicus ! "
　　Tib. We thank you, reverend fathers, in
　　　　their right.　　　　　　　　　　　　95
　　Arr. [*Aside.*] If this were true, now ! but the
　　　　space, the space
Between the breast and lips ! Tiberius' heart
Lies a thought farther than another man's.
　　Tib. My comforts are so flowing in my joys,
As, in them, all my streams of grief are lost, 100
No less than are land-waters in the sea,
Or showers in rivers ; though their cause was
　　such,
As might have sprinkled ev'n the gods with
　　tears :
Yet, since the greater doth embrace the less,
We covetously obey.
　　Arr. (Aside.)[1]　　Well acted, Caesar.　 105
　　Tib. And now I am the happy witness made
Of your so much desir'd affections
To this great issue, I could wish the Fates
Would here set peaceful period to my days ;
However, to my labours I entreat　　　　　110
And beg it of this senate, some fit ease.
　　Arr. (Aside.)[1] Laugh, fathers, laugh : ha '
　　　　you no spleens[2] about you ?
　　Tib. The burden is too heavy I sustain
On my unwilling shoulders ; and I pray
It may be taken off, and reconferr'd　　　115
Upon the consuls, or some other Roman,
More able, and more worthy.
　　Arr. (Aside.)[1]　　　　Laugh on still.
　　Sab. Why, this doth render all the rest sus-
　　　　pected !
　　Gal. It poisons all.
　　Arr.　　　　　　O, do you taste it then ?
　　Sab. It takes away my faith to anything　120
He shall hereafter speak.
　　Arr.　　　　　　Ay, to pray that,
Which would be to his head as hot as thunder,
' Gainst which he wears that charm,[3] should
　　but the court
Receive him at his word.
　　Gal.　　　　　Hear !
　　Tib.　　　　　　　　For myself
I know my weakness, and so little covet,　 125
Like some gone past, the weight that will op-
　　press me,
As my ambition is the counter-point.
　　Arr. (Aside.)[1] Finely maintain'd ; good still !

[1] These speeches marked (*Aside*) are placed in pa-
rentheses in the Folio.
[2] The supposed seat of mirth and other emotions.
[3] A wreath of laurel. (Jonson.)

　　Sej.　　　　　But Rome, whose blood,
Whose nerves, whose life, whose very frame
　　relies
On Caesar's strength, no less than heaven on
　　Atlas,　　　　　　　　　　　　　　130
Cannot admit it but with general ruin.
　　Arr. (Aside.) Ah ! are you there to bring him
　　　　off ?
　　Sej.　　　　Let Caesar
No more then urge a point so contrary
To Caesar's greatness, the griev'd senate's vows,
Or Rome's necessity.
　　Gal. (Aside.)　　He comes about ——　 135
　　Arr. (Aside.) More nimbly than Vertumnus.
　　Tib.　　　　　　　For the public,
I may be drawn to show I can neglect
All private aims, though I affect my rest ;
But if the senate still command me serve,
I must be glad to practise my obedience.　 140
　　Arr. (Aside.) You must and will, sir. We do
　　　　know it.
　　Senators.　　" Caesar,
Live long and happy, great and royal Caesar ;
The gods preserve thee and thy modesty,
Thy wisdom and thy innocence ! "
　　Arr. (Aside.)　　　　　Where is 't ?
The prayer is made before the subject.
　　Senators.　　　　　　" Guard 145
His meekness, Jove, his piety, his care,
His bounty —— "
　　Arr. [*Aside.*]　And his subtilty, I 'll put in :
Yet he 'll keep that himself, without the gods.
All prayers are vain for him.
　　Tib.　　　　　We will not hold
Your patience, fathers, with long answer ; but
Shall still contend to be what you desire,　 151
And work to satisfy so great a hope.
Proceed to your affairs.
　　Arr. [*Aside.*]　　Now, Silius, guard thee ;
The curtain 's drawing. Afer advanceth.
　　Prae.　　　　　　　　Silence !
　　Afer. Cite Caius Silius.
　　Prae.　　　　　　　Caius Silius !
　　Sil.　　　　　　　　　　Here. 155
　　Afer. The triumph that thou hadst in Ger-
　　　　many
For thy late victory on Sacrovir,
Thou hast enjoy'd so freely, Caius Silius,
As no man it envi'd thee ; nor would Caesar 159
Or Rome admit, that thou wert then defrauded
Of any honours thy deserts could claim
In the fair service of the commonwealth ;
But now, if after all their loves and graces,
(Thy actions, and their courses being discover'd)
It shall appear to Caesar and this senate,　 165
Thou hast defil'd those glories with thy
　　crimes ——
　　Sil. Crimes !
　　Afer.　　　Patience, Silius.
　　Sil.　　　　　　Tell thy mule of patience ;
I am a Roman. What are my crimes ? Proclaim
　　them.
Am I too rich, too honest for the times ?
Have I or treasure, jewels, land, or houses 170
That some informer gapes for ? Is my strength
Too much to be admitted, or my knowledge ?
These now are crimes.

Afer.   Nay, Silius, if the name
Of crime so touch thee, with what impotence
Wilt thou endure the matter to be search'd? 175
  Sil. I tell thee, Afer, with more scorn than
      fear:
Employ your mercenary tongue and art.
Where 's my accuser?
  Var.   Here.
  Arr.   Varro, the consul!
Is he thrust in?
  Var.   'T is I accuse thee, Silius.
Against the majesty of Rome and Caesar,   180
I do pronounce thee here a guilty cause,
First of beginning and occasioning,
Next, drawing out the war in Gallia,
For which thou late triumph'st; dissembling
      long
That Sacrovir to be an enemy,   185
Only to make thy entertainment more:
Whilst thou, and thy wife Sosia, poll'd[1] the
      province;
Wherein, with sordid-base desire of gain,
Thou hast discredited thy actions' worth,
And been a traitor to the state.
  Sil.   Thou liest.   190
  Arr. I thank thee, Silius; speak so still and
      often.
  Var. If I not prove it, Caesar, but unjustly
Have call'd him into trial, here I bind
Myself to suffer what I claim 'gainst him;   194
And yield to have what I have spoke, confirm'd
By judgment of the court, and all good men.
  Sil. Caesar, I crave to have my cause deferr'd,
Till this man's consulship be out.
  Tib.   We cannot,
Nor may we grant it.
  Sil.   Why? Shall he design[2]
My day of trial? Is he my accuser,   200
And must he be my judge?
  Tib.   It hath been usual,
And is a right that custom hath allow'd
The magistrate, to call forth private men
And to appoint their day: which privilege
We may not in the consul see infring'd,   205
By whose deep watches and industrious care
It is so labour'd, as the commonwealth
Receive no loss, by any oblique course.
  Sil. Caesar, thy fraud is worse than violence.
  Tib. Silius, mistake us not, we dare not use
The credit of the consul to thy wrong;   211
But only do preserve his place and power,
So far as it concerns the dignity
And honour of the state.
  Arr.   Believe him, Silius.
  Cot. Why, so he may, Arruntius.
  Arr.   I say so; 215
And he may choose too.
  Tib.   By the Capitol,
And all our gods, but that the dear republic,
Our sacred laws, and just authority
Are interess'd therein, I should be silent. 219
  Afer. Please Caesar to give way unto his trial,
He shall have justice.
  Sil.   Nay, I shall have law;
Shall I not, Afer? Speak.

---

[1] Plundered by extortion.   [2] Name.

Afer.   Would you have moe?
  Sil. No, my well-spoken man, I would no
      more;
Nor less: might I enjoy it natural,
Not taught to speak unto your present ends, 225
Free from thine, his, and all your unkind hand-
      ling,
Furious enforcing, most unjust presuming,
Malicious, and manifold applying,
Foul wresting, and impossible construction.
  Afer. He raves, he raves.
  Sil.   Thou durst not tell me so, 230
Hadst thou not Caesar's warrant. I can see
Whose power condemns me.
  Var.   This betrays his spirit:
This doth enough declare him what he is.
  Sil. What am I? speak.
  Var.   An enemy to the state.
  Sil. Because I am an enemy to thee,   235
And such corrupted ministers o' the state,
That here art made a present instrument
To gratify it with thine own disgrace.
  Sej. This, to the consul, is most insolent,
And impious!
  Sil.   Ay, take part. Reveal yourselves. 240
Alas! I scent not your confed'racies,
Your plots, and combinations! I not know
Minion Sejanus hates me; and that all
This boast of law, and law, is but a form,
A net of Vulcan's filing, a mere ingine,   245
To take that life by a pretext of justice,
Which you pursue in malice! I want brain
Or nostril to persuade me, that your ends
And purposes are made to what they are,
Before my answer! O, you equal gods,   250
Whose justice not a world of wolf-turn'd men
Shall make me to accuse (howe'er provoke),
Have I for this so oft engag'd myself?
Stood in the heat and fervour of a fight,
When Phoebus sooner hath forsook the day   255
Than I the field, against the blue-ey'd Gauls,
And crisped Germans? when our Roman eagles
Have fann'd the fire with their labouring wings,
And no blow dealt, that left not death behind
      it?
When I have charg'd, alone, into the troops 260
Of curl'd Sicambrians, routed them, and came
Not off with backward ensigns of a slave,
But forward marks, wounds on my breast and
      face,
Were meant to thee, O Caesar, and thy Rome?
And have I this return! Did I, for this,   265
Perform so noble, and so brave defeat,
On Sacrovir! O Jove, let it become me
To boast my deeds, when he, whom they con-
      cern,
Shall thus forget them.
  Afer.   Silius, Silius,   269
These are the common customs of thy blood,
When it is high with wine, as now with rage.
This well agrees with that intemperate vaunt,
Thou lately mad'st at Agrippina's table,
That, when all other of the troops were prone
To fall into rebellion, only yours   275
Remain'd in their obedience. You were he
That sav'd the Empire, which had then been
      lost

Had but your legions there rebell'd, or mutin'd;
Your virtue met, and fronted every peril. 279
You gav'st to Caesar and to Rome their surety.
Their name, their strength, their spirit, and
    their state,
Their being was a donative from you.
Arr. Well worded, and most like an orator.
Tib. Is this true, Silius?
Sil.   Save thy question, Caesar,
Thy spy of famous credit hath affirm'd it. 285
Arr. Excellent Roman!
Sab.   He doth answer stoutly.
Sej. If this be so, there needs no farther cause
Of crime against him.
Var.   What can more impeach
The royal dignity and state of Caesar,
Than to be urged with a benefit 290
He cannot pay.
Cot.   In this, all Caesar's fortune
Is made unequal to the courtesy.
Lat. His means are clean destroy'd that
    should requite.
Gal. Nothing is great enough for Silius' merit.
Arr. Gallus on that side too?
Sil.   Come, do not hunt,
And labour so about for circumstance, 296
To make him guilty, whom you have fore-
    doom'd:
Take shorter ways, I'll meet your purposes.
The words were mine, and more I now will say:
Since I have done thee that great service,
    Caesar, 300
Thou still hast fear'd me; and, in place of grace,
Return'd me hatred: so soon all best turns,
With doubtful princes, turn deep injuries
In estimation, when they greater rise
Than can be answer'd. Benefits, with you, 305
Are of no longer pleasure, than you can
With ease restore them; that transcended once,
Your studies are not how to thank, but kill.
It is your nature, to have all men slaves
To you, but you acknowledging to none. 310
The means that makes your greatness, must not
    come
In mention of it; if it do, it takes
So much away, you think: and that which
    help'd
Shall soonest perish, if it stand in eye, 314
Where it may front, or but upbraid the high.
Cot. Suffer him speak no more.
Var.   Note but his spirit.
Afer. This shows him in the rest.
Lat.   Let him be censur'd. [1]
Sej. He hath spoke enough to prove him
    Caesar's foe.
Cot. His thoughts look through his words.
Sej.   A censure.
Sil.   Stay,
Stay, most officious senate, I shall straight 320
Delude thy fury. Silius hath not plac'd
His guards within him, against fortune's spite,
So weakly but he can escape your gripe
That are but hands of fortune: she herself, 324
When virtue doth oppose, must lose her threats.
All that can happen in humanity,

      [1] Judged.

The frown of Caesar, proud Sejanus' hatred,
Base Varro's spleen, and Afer's bloodying
    tongue,
The senate's servile flattery, and these
Must'red to kill, I'm fortified against, 330
And can look down upon: they are beneath me.
It is not life whereof I stand enamour'd
Nor shall my end make me accuse my fate.
The coward and the valiant man must fall, 334
Only the cause, and manner how, discerns them:
Which then are gladdest, when they cost us
    dearest.
Romans, if any here be in this senate,
Would know to mock Tiberius' tyranny,
Look upon Silius, and so learn to die.
        [*Stabs himself.*]
Var. O desperate act!
Arr.   An honourable hand! 340
Tib. Look, is he dead?
Sab.   'T was nobly struck, and home.
Arr. My thought did prompt him to it. Fare-
    well, Silius.
Be famous ever for thy great example.
Tib. We are not pleas'd in this sad accident,
That thus hath stalled, [2] and abus'd our mercy,
Intended to preserve thee, noble Roman, 346
And to prevent thy hopes.
Arr.   Excellent wolf!
Now he is full he howls.
Sej.   Caesar doth wrong
His dignity and safety thus to mourn
The deserv'd end of so profest a traitor; 350
And doth, by this his lenity, instruct
Others as factious to the like offence.
Tib. The confiscation merely of his state
Had been enough.
Arr.   O, that was gap'd for then?
Var. Remove the body.
Sej.   Let citation 355
Go out for Sosia.
Gal.   Let her be proscrib'd:
And for the goods, I think it fit that half
Go to the treasure, half unto the children.
Lep. With leave of Caesar, I would think
    that fourth 359
Part, which the law doth cast on the informers,
Should be enough; the rest go to the children:
Wherein the prince shall show humanity,
And bounty; not to force them by their want,
Which in their parent's trespass they deserv'd,
To take ill courses.
Tib.   It shall please us.
Arr.   Ay, 365
Out of necessity. This Lepidus
Is grave and honest, and I have observ'd
A moderation still in all his censures,[3]
Sab. And bending to the better —— Stay,
    who's this?
Cremutius Cordus! What! is he brought in?
Arr. More blood unto the banquet! Noble
    Cordus, 371
I wish thee good; be as thy writings, free
And honest.
Tib.   What is he?
Sej.   For th' *Annals*, Caesar.

      [2] Forestalled.   [3] Judgments.

[*Enter*] Praeco. SATRIUS *and* NATTA, [*with*]
　　CREMUTIUS CORDUS, [*guarded.*]

Prae. Cremutius Cordus!
Cor.　　　　　　　　　　Here.
Prae.　　　　　　　　　Satrius Secundus,
Pinnarius Natta, you are his accusers.　375
　Arr. Two of Sejanus' blood-hounds, whom he
　　breeds
With human flesh, to bay at citizens.
　Afer. Stand forth before the Senate, and con-
　front him.
　Sat. I do accuse thee here, Cremutius Cordus,
To be a man factious and dangerous,　380
A sower of sedition in the state,
A turbulent and discontented spirit,
Which I will prove from thine own writings,
　here,
The *Annals* thou hast publish'd ; where thou
　bit'st
The present age, and with a viper's tooth,　385
Being a member of it, dar'st that ill
Which never yet degenerous bastard did
Upon his parent.
　Nat.　　　　　To this I subscribe ;
And, forth[1] a world of more particulars,
Instance in only one : comparing men　390
And times, thou praisest Brutus, and affirm'st
That Cassius was the last of all the Romans.
　Cot. How ! what are we then ?
　Var.　　　　　　What is Caesar ! Nothing ?
　Afer. My lords, this strikes at every Roman's
　private,
In whom reigns gentry and estate of spirit,　395
To have a Brutus brought in parallel,
A parricide, an enemy of his country,
Rank'd, and preferr'd to any real worth
That Rome now holds. This is most strangely
　invective,
Most full of spite, and insolent upbraiding,　400
Nor is 't the time alone is here dispriz'd,
But the whole man of time, yea, Caesar's self
Brought in disvalue ; and he aim'd at most,
By oblique glance of his licentious pen.
Caesar, if Cassius were the last of Romans,　405
Thou hast no name.
　Tib.　　　Let 's hear him answer. Silence !
　Cor. So innocent I am of fact, my lords,
As but my words are argu'd : yet those words
Not reaching either prince or prince's parent ;
The which your law of treason comprehends.
Brutus and Cassius I am charg'd t' have
　prais'd ;　411
Whose deeds, when many more, besides myself,
Have writ, not one hath mention'd without
　honour.
Great Titus Livius, great for eloquence
And faith amongst us, in his History　415
With so great praises Pompey did extol,
As oft Augustus call'd him a Pompeian :
Yet this not hurt their friendship. In his book
He often names Scipio, Afranius,
Yea, the same Cassius, and this Brutus too,　420
As worthiest men ; not thieves and parricides,
Which notes upon their fames are now impos'd.

Asinius Pollio's writings quite throughout
Give them a noble memory ; so Messala　424
Renown'd his general, Cassius : yet both these
Liv'd with Augustus, full of wealth and hon-
　ours.
To Cicero's book, where Cato was heav'd up
Equal with heaven, what else did Caesar answer,
Being then dictator, but with a penn'd oration,
As if before the judges? Do but see　430
Antonius' letters ; read but Brutus' pleadings :
What vile reproach they hold against Augustus,
False, I confess, but with much bitterness.
The epigrams of Bibaculus and Catullus
Are read, full stuft with spite of both the Cae-
　sars ;　435
Yet deified Julius, and no less Augustus,
Both bore them, and contemn'd them : I not
　know,
Promptly to speak it, whether done with more
Temper, or wisdom ; for such obloquies
If they despised be, they die suppprest ;　440
But if with rage acknowledg'd, they are confest.
The Greeks I slip, whose licence not alone,
But also lust did scape unpunished :
Or where some one, by chance, exception took,
He words with words reveng'd. But, in my
　work,　445
What could be aim'd more free,[2] or farther off
From the time's scandal, than to write of those
Whom death from grace or hatred had ex-
　empted ?
Did I, with Brutus and with Cassius,
Arm'd and possess'd of the Philippi fields,　450
Incense the people in the civil cause,
With dangerous speeches? Or do they, being
　slain
Seventy years since, as by their images,
Which not the conqueror hath defac'd, appears,
Retain that guilty memory with writers ?　455
Posterity pays every man his honour ;
Nor shall there want, though I condemned am,
That will not only Cassius well approve,
And of great Brutus' honour mindful be,
But that will also mention make of me.　460
　Arr. Freely and nobly spoken !
　Sab.　　　　　　With good temper ;
I like him, that he is not mov'd with passion.
　Arr. He puts 'em to their whisper.
　Tib.　　　　　　Take him hence ;
We shall determine of him at next sitting.
　　　　　[*Exeunt* Officers *with* CORDUS.]
　Cot. Mean time, give order, that his books be
　　burnt,　465
To the aediles.
　Sej.　　　You have well advis'd.
　Afer. It fits not such licentious things should
　live
T' upbraid the age.
　Arr.　　　If th' age were good, they might.
　Lat. Let 'em be burnt.
　Gal.　　　All sought, and burnt to-day.
　Prae. The court is up ; lictors, resume the
　　fasces.　470
　　　　[*Exeunt all but*] ARRUNTIUS, SAB-
　　　　INUS, *and* LEPIDUS.

---

[1] Out of.　　　　　　　　　[2] Innocent.

Arr. Let them be burnt ! O, how ridiculous
Appear the senate's brainless diligence,
Who think they can, with present power, ex-
    tinguish
The memory of all succeeding times !
Sab. 'T is true ; when, contrary, the punish-
    ment   475
Of wit doth make th' authority increase.
Nor do they aught, that use this cruelty
Of interdiction, and this rage of burning,
But purchase to themselves rebuke and shame,
And to the writers an eternal name.   480
Lep. It is an argument the times are sore,
When virtue cannot safely be advanc'd,
Nor vice reprov'd.
Arr.   Ay, noble Lepidus ;
Augustus well foresaw what we should suffer
Under Tiberius, when he did pronounce   485
The Roman race most wretched, that should
    live
Between so slow jaws, and so long a bruising.
                                              [*Exeunt.*]

[SCENE II.]¹

[*Enter*] TIBERIUS *and* SEJANUS.

Tib. This business hath succeeded well, Se-
    janus ;
And quite remov'd all jealousy of practice²
'Gainst Agrippina, and our nephews. Now,
We must bethink us how to plant our ingines
For th' other pair, Sabinus and Arruntius,   5
And Gallus too ; howe'er he flatter us,
His heart we know.
Sej.   Give it some respite, Caesar.
Time shall mature, and bring to perfect crown,
What we, with so good vultures, have begun :
Sabinus shall be next.
Tib.   Rather Arruntius.   10
Sej. By any means, preserve him. His frank
    tongue
Being lent the reins, would take away all
    thought
Of malice, in your course against the rest :
We must keep him to stalk with.
Tib.   Dearest head,
To thy most fortunate design I yield it.   15
Sej. Sir, I have been so long train'd up in
    grace,
First with your father, great Augustus ; since,
With your most happy bounties so familiar ;
As I not sooner would commit my hopes
Or wishes to the gods, than to your ears.   20
Nor have I ever yet been covetous
Of over-bright and dazzling honours ; rather
To watch and travail in great Caesar's safety,
With the most common soldier.
Tib.   'T is confest.
Sej. The only gain, and which I count most
    fair   25
Of all my fortunes, is, that mighty Caesar
Has thought me worthy his alliance. Hence
Begin my hopes.
Tib.   Umph !
Sej.   I have heard, Augustus,
In the bestowing of his daughter, thought

But even of gentlemen of Rome : if so —   30
I know not how to hope so great a favour —
But if a husband should be sought for Livia,
And I be had in mind, as Caesar's friend,
I would but use the glory of the kindred.   34
It should not make me slothful, or less caring
For Caesar's state ; it were enough to me
It did confirm, and strengthen my weak house,
Against the now-unequal opposition
Of Agrippina ; and for dear regard
Unto my children, this I wish : myself   40
Have no ambition farther than to end
My days in service of so dear a master.
Tib. We cannot but commend thy piety,
Most lov'd Sejanus, in acknowledging
Those bounties ; which we, faintly, such re-
    member. —   45
But to thy suit. The rest of mortal men,
In all their drifts and counsels, pursue profit ;
Princes alone are of a different sort,
Directing their main actions still to fame :   49
We therefore will take time to think and answer.
For Livia she can best, herself, resolve
If she will marry, after Drusus, or
Continue in the family ; besides,
She hath a mother, and a grandam yet,   54
Whose nearer counsels she may guide her by :
But I will simply deal. That enmity
Thou fear'st in Agrippina, would burn more,
If Livia's marriage should, as 't were in parts,
Divide th' imperial house ; an emulation
Between the women might break forth ; and
    discord   60
Ruin the sons and nephews on both hands.
What if it cause some present difference ?
Thou art not safe, Sejanus, if thou prove³ it.
Canst thou believe, that Livia, first the wife
To Caius Caesar, then to Drusus, now   65
Will be contented to grow old with thee,
Born but a private gentleman of Rome,
And raise thee with her loss, if not her shame ?
Or say that I should wish it, canst thou think
The senate, or the people (who have seen   70
Her brother, father, and our ancestors,
In highest place of empire) will endure it ?
The state thou hold'st already, is in talk ;
Men murmur at thy greatness ; and the nobles
Stick not, in public, to upbraid thy climbing   75
Above our father's favours, or thy scale :
And dare accuse me, from their hate to thee.
Be wise, dear friend. We would not hide these
    things,
For friendship's dear respect : nor will we stand
Adverse to thine, or Livia's designments.   80
What we have purpos'd to thee, in our thought,
And with what near degrees of love to bind
    thee,
And make thee equal to us, for the present
We will forbear to speak. Only, thus much
Believe, our lov'd Sejanus, we not know   85
That height in blood or honour, which thy
    virtue
And mind to us, may not aspire with merit.
And this we 'll publish on all watch'd occasion
The senate or the people shall present.

<hr>

¹ A room in the Palace.   ² Suspicion of conspiracy.   ³ Test, attempt.

Sej. I am restor'd, and to my sense again,   90
Which I had lost in this so blinding suit.
Caesar hath taught me better to refuse,
Than I knew how to ask. How pleaseth Caesar
T' embrace my late advice for leaving Rome ?
Tib. We are resolv'd.
Sej.   Here are some motives more,   95
                    [*Gives him a paper.*]
Which I have thought on since, may more con-
    firm.
Tib. Careful Sejanus ! we will straight peruse
    them :
Go forward in our main design, and prosper.
                                    [*Exit.*]
Sej. If those but take, I shall. Dull, heavy
    Caesar !
Wouldst thou tell me, thy favours were made
    crimes,   100
And that my fortunes were esteem'd thy faults,
That thou for me wert hated, and not think
I would with winged haste prevent that change,
When thou might'st win all to thyself again,
By forfeiture of me ? Did those fond words   105
Fly swifter from thy lips than this my brain,
This sparkling forge, created me an armour
T' encounter chance and thee ? Well, read my
    charms,
And may they lay that hold upon thy senses,   109
As thou hadst snuft up hemlock, or ta'en down
The juice of poppy and mandrakes. Sleep,
Voluptuous Caesar, and security
Seize on thy stupid powers, and leave them dead
To public cares ; awake but to thy lusts,
The strength of which makes thy libidinous
    soul   115
Itch to leave Rome ! and I have thrust it on ;
With blaming of the city business,
The multitude of suits, the confluence
Of suitors : then their importunacies,
The manifold distractions he must suffer,   120
Besides ill-rumours, envies, and reproaches,
All which a quiet and retired life,
Larded with ease and pleasure, did avoid :
And yet for any weighty and great affair,   124
The fittest place to give the soundest counsels.
By this I shall remove him both from thought
And knowledge of his own most dear affairs ;
Draw all dispatches through my private hands ;
Know his designments, and pursue mine own ;
Make mine own strengths by giving suits and
    places,   130
Conferring dignities and offices ;
And these that hate me now, wanting access
To him, will make their envy none, or less :
For when they see me arbiter of all,
They must observe ; or else with Caesar fall. 135
                                    [*Exit.*]

[Scene III.]¹

[*Enter*] Tiberius.

Tib. To marry Livia ! will no less, Sejanus,
Content thy aims ? No lower object ? Well !
Thou know'st how thou art wrought into our
    trust ;
Woven in our design ; and think'st we must

¹ Another room in the same.

Now use thee, whatso'er thy projects are :   5
'T is true. But yet with caution and fit care ;
And, now we better think — Who 's there with-
    in ?

[*Enter an* Officer.]

Off. Caesar !
Tib. [*Aside.*] To leave our journey off, were sin
'Gainst our decreed delights ; and would appear
Doubt ; or, what less becomes a prince, low
    fear.   10
Yet doubt hath law, and fears have their ex-
    cuse,
Where princes' states plead necessary use ;
As ours doth now : more in Sejanus' pride,
Than all fell Agrippina's hates beside.
Those are the dreadful enemies, we raise   15
With favours, and make dangerous with praise ;
The injur'd by us may have will alike,
But 't is the favourite hath the power to strike ;
And fury ever boils more high and strong,
Heat² with ambition, than revenge of wrong. 20
'T is then a part of supreme skill, to grace
No man too much ; but hold a certain space
Between th' ascender's rise and thine own flat,³
Lest, when all rounds be reach'd, his aim be
    that.
'T is thought. — Is Macro in the palace ? see : 25
If not, go seek him, to come to us. [*Exit* Officer.]
He
Must be the organ we must work by now ;
Though none less apt for trust : need doth al-
    low
What choice would not. I have heard that
    aconite,
Being timely taken, hath a healing might   30
Against the scorpion's stroke ; the proof we 'll
    give :
That, while two poisons wrastle, we may live.
He hath a spirit too working to be us'd
But to th' encounter of his like ; excus'd
Are wiser sov'reigns then, that raise one ill   35
Against another, and both safely kill :
The prince that feeds great natures, they will
    sway him ;
Who nourisheth a lion, must obey him. —

[*Re-enter* Officer *with*] Macro.

Macro, we sent for you.
Mac.   I heard so, Caesar.
Tib. Leave us a while.   [*Exit* Officer.]
            When you shall know, good Macro,
The causes of our sending, and the ends,   41
You will then hearken nearer ; and be pleas'd
You stand so high both in our choice and
    trust.
Mac. The humblest place in Caesar's choice
    or trust,
May make glad Macro proud ; without ambi-
    tion,   45
Save to do Caesar service.
Tib.   Leave your courtings.
We are in purpose, Macro, to depart
The city for a time, and see Campania ;
Not for our pleasures, but to dedicate

² Heated.   ³ Level.

A pair of temples, one to Jupiter　　　50
At Capua; th' other at Nola, to Augustus:
In which great work, perhaps our stay will be
Beyond our will produc'd. Now, since we are
Not ignorant what danger may be born
Out of our shortest absence, in a state　　55
So subject unto envy, and embroil'd
With hate and faction; we have thought on thee,
Amongst a field of Romans, worthiest Macro,
To be our eye and ear: to keep strict watch
On Agrippina, Nero, Drusus; ay,　　60
And on Sejanus: not that we distrust
His loyalty, or do repent one grace,
Of all that heap we have conferr'd on him;
For that were to disparage our election,
And call that judgment now in doubt, which then　　65
Seem'd as unquestion'd as an oracle—
But greatness hath his cankers. Worms and moths
Breed out of too fit matter, in the things
Which after they consume, transferring quite
The substance of their makers int' themselves.
Macro is sharp, and apprehends: besides,　　71
I know him subtile, close, wise, and well read
In man, and his large nature; he hath studied
Affections, passions, knows their springs, their ends,
Which way, and whether they will work: 't is proof　　75
Enough of his great merit that we trust him.
Then to a point (because our conference
Cannot be long without suspicion):
Here, Macro, we assign thee both to spy,
Inform, and chastise; think, and use thy means,
Thy ministers, what, where, on whom thou wilt;　　81
Explore, plot, practise: all thou dost in this
Shall be, as if the senate or the laws
Had giv'n it privilege, and thou thence styl'd
The saviour both of Caesar and of Rome.　　85
We will not take thy answer but in act:
Whereto, as thou proceed'st, we hope to hear
By trusted messengers. If 't be inquir'd
Wherefore we call'd you, say you have in charge
To see our chariots ready, and our horse.　　90
Be still our lov'd and, shortly, honour'd Macro.
　　　　　　　　　　　　　[Exit.]

Mac. I will not ask why Caesar bids do this;
But joy, that he bids me. It is the bliss
Of courts to be employ'd, no matter how;
A prince's power makes all his actions virtue.　95
We, whom he works by, are dumb instruments,
To do, but not inquire: his great intents
Are to be serv'd, not search'd. Yet, as that bow
Is most in hand whose owner best doth know　99
T' affect[1] his aims; so let that statesman hope
Most use, most price, can hit his prince's scope.[2]
Nor must he look at what or whom to strike,
But loose[3] at all; each mark must be alike.
Were it to plot against the fame, the life

Of one with whom I twinn'd; remove a wife 105
From my warm side, as lov'd as is the air;
Practise away each parent; draw mine heir
In compass,[4] though but one; work all my kin
To swift perdition; leave no untrain'd engine
For friendship, or for innocence; nay, make 110
The gods all guilty; I would undertake
This, being impos'd me, both with gain and ease:
The way to rise is to obey and please.
He that will thrive in state, he must neglect 114
The trodden paths that truth and right respect;
And prove new, wilder ways: for virtue there
Is not that narrow thing she is elsewhere.
Men's fortune there is virtue; reason their will;
Their licence, law; and their observance, skill.
Occasion is their foil; conscience, their stain; 170
Profit their lustre; and what else is, vain.
If then it be the lust of Caesar's power
T' have rais'd Sejanus up, and in an hour
O'erturn him, tumbling, down from height of all;
We are his ready engine: and his fall 125
May be our rise. It is no uncouth[5] thing
To see fresh buildings from old ruins spring.
　　　　　　　　　　　　　[Exit.]

　　CHORUS — of Musicians.

ACT IV

[SCENE I.][6]

[Enter] GALLUS, AGRIPPINA.

Gal. You must have patience, royal Agrippina.
Agr. I must have vengeance first; and that were nectar
Unto my famish'd spirits. O, my fortune,
Let it be sudden thou prepar'st against me;
Strike all my powers of understanding blind,　5
And ignorant of destiny to come!
Let me not fear, that cannot hope.
Gal.　　　　　　　　　Dear princess.
These tyrannies on yourself are worse than Caesar's.
Agr. Is this the happiness of being born great?
Still to be aim'd at? still to be suspected? 1/
To live the subject of all jealousies?
At least the colour[7] made, if not the ground
To every painted danger? Who would not
Choose once to fall, than thus to hang for ever?
Gal. You might be safe if you would —
Agr.　　　　　　What, my Gallus! 15
Be lewd Sejanus' strumpet? Or the bawd
To Caesar's lusts, he now is gone to practise?
Not these are safe, where nothing is. Yourself,
While thus you stand but by me, are not safe.
Was Silius safe? Or the good Sosia safe? 20
Or was my niece, dear Claudia Pulchra, safe,
Or innocent Furnius? they that latest have
(By being made guilty) added reputation

---

[1] Effect.　　　[2] Aim.　　　[3] Shoot.

[4] Entrap mine heir.
[5] Unknown.
[6] An apartment in Agrippina's house.
[7] Pretext, with a pun.

To Afer's eloquence? O, foolish friends,
Could not so fresh example warn your loves,   25
But you must buy my favours with that loss
Unto yourselves ; and when you might perceive
That Caesar's cause of raging must forsake
    him,
Before his will! Away, good Gallus, leave me.
Here to be seen, is danger ; to speak, treason : 30
To do me least observance, is call'd faction.
You are unhappy in me, and I in all.
Where are my sons Nero and Drusus? We
Are they be shot at ; let us fall apart ;
Not in our ruins sepulchre our friends.   35
Or shall we do some action like offence,[1]
To mock their studies that would make us
    faulty,
And frustrate practice by preventing[2] it ?
The danger's like : for what they can contrive,
They will make good. No innocence is safe   40
When power contests : nor can they trespass
    more,
Whose only being[3] was all crime before.

[*Enter* NERO, DRUSUS, *and* CALIGULA.]

Ner. You hear Sejanus is come back from
    Caesar ?
Gal. No. How? disgrac'd ?
Dru.   More graced now than ever.
Gal. By what mischance ?
Cal.   A fortune like enough
Once to be bad.
Dru.   But turn'd too good to both. 46
Gal. What was 't ?
Ner.   Tiberius sitting at his meat,
In a farm-house they call Spelunca, sited
By the sea-side, among the Fundane hills,
Within a natural cave ; part of the grot,   50
About the entry, fell, and overwhelm'd
Some of the waiters ; others ran away :
Only Sejanus with his knees, hands, face,
O'erhanging Caesar, did oppose himself
To the remaining ruins, and was found   55
In that so labouring posture by the soldiers
That came to succour him. With which adven-
    ture,
He hath so fixt himself in Caesar's trust,
As thunder cannot move him, and is come
With all the height of Caesar's praise to Rome.
Agr. And power to turn those ruins all on
    us,   61
And bury whole posterities beneath them.
Nero, and Drusus, and Caligula,
Your places are the next, and therefore most
In their offence. Think on your birth and
    blood,   65
Awake your spirits, meet their violence ;
'T is princely when a tyrant doth oppose,
And is a fortune sent to exercise
Your virtue, as the wind doth try strong trees,
Who by vexation[4] grow more sound and firm.
After your father's fall, and uncle's fate, 71
What can you hope, but all the change of stroke
That force or sleight can give? Then stand
    upright ;

And though you do not act, yet suffer nobly : 74
Be worthy of my womb, and take strong cheer;
What we do know will come, we should not
    fear.   [*Exeunt.*]

[SCENE II.][5]

[*Enter*] MACRO.

Mac. Return'd so soon ! Renew'd in trust
    and grace !
Is Caesar then so weak, or hath the place
But wrought this alteration with the air ;
And he, on next remove, will all repair ?
Marco, thou art engag'd : and what before   5
Was public, now must be thy private more.
The weal of Caesar, fitness did imply ;
But thine own fate confers necessity
On thy employment ; and the thoughts borne
    nearest   9
Unto ourselves, move swiftest still, and dearest.
If he recover, thou art lost ; yea, all
The weight of preparation to his fall
Will turn on thee, and crush thee : therefore
    strike
Before he settle, to prevent the like
Upon thyself. He doth his vantage know,   15
That makes it home,[6] and gives the foremost
    blow.   [*Exit.*]

[SCENE III.][7]

[*Enter*] LATIARIS, RUFUS, *and* OPSIUS.

Lat. It is a service great Sejanus will
See well requited, and accept of nobly.
Here place yourselves between the roof and
    ceiling ;
And when I bring him to his words of danger,
Reveal yourselves, and take him.
Ruf.   Is he come ? 5
Lat. I 'll now go fetch him.   [*Exit.*]
Ops.   With good speed. — I long
To merit from the state in such an action.
Ruf. I hope it will obtain the consulship
For one of us.
Ops.   We cannot think of less,
To bring in one so dangerous as Sabinus.   10
Ruf. He was a follower of Germanicus,
And still is an observer[8] of his wife
And children, though they be declin'd in grace ;
A daily visitant, keeps them company
In private and in public, and is noted   15
To be the only client of the house :
Pray Jove, he will be free to Latiaris.
Ops. He 's alli'd to him, and doth trust him
    well.
Ruf. And he 'll requite his trust !
Ops.   To do an office
So grateful to the state, I know no man   20
But would strain nearer bands than kin-
    dred —
Ruf.   List !
I hear them come.
Ops.   Shift to our holes with silence.
                            [*They retire.*]

---

[1] Like the offences we are charged with.
[2] Anticipating.   [3] Mere existence.   [4] Tossing.
[3] The street.
[6] Follows it up to the utmost.
[7] An upper room of Agrippina's house.
[8] One who pays respectful attentions.

[Re-enter] LATIARIS, SABINUS.

Lat. It is a noble constancy you show
To this afflicted house; that not like others,
The friends of season, you do follow fortune, 25
And, in the winter of their fate, forsake
The place whose glories warm'd you. You are
　　just,
And worthy such a princely patron's love,
As was the world's-renown'd Germanicus,
Whose ample merit when I call to thought, 30
And see his wife and issue objects made
To so much envy, jealousy, and hate;
It makes me ready to accuse the gods
Of negligence, as men of tyranny.
Sab. They must be patient, so must we.
Lat.　　　　　　　　　　O Jove,
What will become of us or of the times, 36
When, to be high or noble, are made crimes,
When land and treasure are most dangerous
　　faults?
Sab. Nay, when our table, yea our bed, as-
　　saults
Our peace and safety? When our writings are
By any envious instruments, that dare 41
Apply them to the guilty, made to speak
What they will have to fit their tyrannous
　　wreak?
When ignorance is scarcely innocence;
And knowledge made a capital offence? 45
When not so much, but the bare empty shade
Of liberty, is reft[1] us; and we made
The prey to greedy vultures and vile spies,
That first transfix us with their murdering
　　eyes? 49
Lat. Methinks the genius of the Roman race
Should not be so extinct, but that bright flame
Of liberty might be reviv'd again,
(Which no good man but with his life should
　　lose)
And we not sit like spent and patient fools,
Still puffing in the dark at one poor coal, 55
Held on by hope, till the last spark is out.
The cause is public, and the honour, name,
The immortality of every soul,
That is not bastard or a slave in Rome,
Therein concern'd: whereto, if men would
　　change 60
The weari'd arm, and for the weighty shield
So long sustain'd, employ the facile sword,
We might have soon assurance of our vows.
This ass's fortitude doth tire us all:
It must be active valour must redeem 65
Our loss, or none. The rock and our hard steel
Should meet t' enforce those glorious fires
　　again,
Whose splendour cheer'd the world, and heat
　　gave life
No less than doth the sun's.
Sab.　　　　　　　　'T were better stay
In lasting darkness, and despair of day, 70
No ill should force the subject undertake
Against the sovereign, more than hell should
　　make
The gods do wrong. A good man should and
　　must

　　　　　　　¹ *reft,* F₁. Qy. *left?*

Sit rather down with loss than rise unjust;
Though, when the Romans first did yield them-
　　selves 75
To one man's power, they did not mean their
　　lives,
Their fortunes, and their liberties should be
His absolute spoil, as purchas'd by the sword.
Lat. Why, we are worse, if to be slaves, and
　　bond 79
To Caesar's slave, be such, the proud Sejanus!
He that is all, does all, gives Caesar leave
To hide his ulcerous and anointed face,
With his bald crown at Rhodes, while he here
　　stalks
Upon the heads of Romans and their princes,
Familiarly to empire.
Sab.　　　　　　　Now you touch 85
A point indeed, wherein he shows his art,
As well as power.
Lat.　　　　　　And villany in both.
Do you observe where Livia lodges? How
Drusus came dead? What men have been cut off?
Sab. Yes, those are things remov'd. I nearer
　　lookt 90
Into his later practice, where he stands
Declar'd a master in his mystery.
First, ere Tiberius went, he wrought his fear
To think that Agrippina sought his death.
Then put those doubts in her; sent her oft
　　word, 95
Under the show of friendship, to beware
Of Caesar, for he laid to poison her:
Drave them to frowns, to mutual jealousies,
Which, now, in visible hatred are burst out.
Since, he hath had his hired instruments 100
To work on Nero, and to heave him up;
To tell him Caesar's old, that all the people,
Yea, all the army have their eyes on him;
That both do long to have him undertake 104
Something of worth, to give the world a hope;
Bids him to court their grace: the easy youth
Perhaps gives ear, which straight he writes to
　　Caesar;
And with this comment: "See yon dangerous
　　boy;
Note but the practice of the mother, there;
She's tying him for purposes at hand, 110
With men of sword." Here's Caesar put in
　　fright
'Gainst son and mother. Yet he leaves not thus,
The second brother, Drusus, a fierce nature,
And fitter for his snares, because ambitious
And full of envy, him he clasps and hugs, 115
Poisons with praise, tells him what hearts he
　　wears,
How bright he stands in popular expectance;
That Rome doth suffer with him in the wrong
His mother does him, by preferring Nero: 119
Thus sets he them asunder, each 'gainst other,
Projects the course that serves him to condemn,
Keeps in opinion of a friend to all,
And all drives on to ruin.
Lat.　　　　　　　Caesar sleeps,
And nods at this.
Sab.　　　　　　Would he might ever sleep,
Bogg'd in his filthy lusts!
　　　　　　　　　　*[*OPSIUS *and* RUFUS *rush in.]*

Ops.　　　　　　　Treason to Caesar ! 125
Ruf. Lay hands upon the traitor, Latiaris,
Or take the name thyself.
Lat.　　　　　　　I am for Caesar.
Sab. Am I then catch'd ?
Ruf.　　　　How think you, sir ? You are.
Sab. Spies of this head, so white, so full of
　　　years !
Well, my most reverend monsters, you may live
To see yourself thus snar'd.
Ops.　　　　　　　Away with him ! 131
Lat. Hale him away.
Ruf.　　　　　To be a spy for traitors,
Is honourable vigilance.
Sab.　　　　　You do well,
My most officious instruments of state,
Men of all uses. Drag me hence, away.　　135
The year is well begun, and I fall fit
To be an off'ring to Sejanus. Go !
Ops. Cover him with his garments, hide his
　　　face.
Sab. It shall not need. Forbear your rude as-
　　　sault.
The fault 's not shameful, villany makes a
　　　fault.　　　　　　[*Exeunt.*] 140

[SCENE IV.][1]

[*Enter*] MACRO, CALIGULA.

Mac. Sir, but observe how thick your dan-
　　　gers meet
In his clear drifts![2] Your mother and your
　　　brothers,
Now cited to the senate ; their friend Gallus,
Feasted to-day by Caesar, since committed !
Sabinus here we met, hurried to fetters :　　5
The senators all struck with fear and silence,
Save those whose hopes depend not on good
　　　means,
But force their private prey from public spoil.
And you must know, if here you stay, your state
Is sure to be the subject of his hate,　　10
As now the object.
Cal.　　　What would you advise me ?
Mac. To go for Capreae presently ; and there
Give up yourself entirely to your uncle.
Tell Caesar (since your mother is accus'd
To fly for succours to Augustus' statue,　　15
And to the army, with your brethren) you
Have rather chose to place your aids in him
Than live suspected ; or in hourly fear
To be thrust out, by bold Sejanus' plots :
Which you shall confidently urge to be　　20
Most full of peril to the state, and Caesar,
As being laid to his peculiar ends,
And not to be let run with common safety.
All which, upon the second, I 'll make plain,
So both shall love and trust with Caesar gain.
Cal. Away then, let 's prepare us for our
　　　journey.　　　　　　[*Exeunt.*] 26

[SCENE V.][3]

[*Enter*] ARRUNTIUS.

Arr. Still dost thou suffer, heaven ! Will no
　　　flame,

---

　　　1 The street before Agrippina's house.
　　　2 Plans, purposes.
　　　3 Another part of the street.

No heat of sin, make thy just wrath to boil
In thy distemp'red bosom, and o'erflow
The pitchy blazes of impiety,
Kindled beneath thy throne ! Still canst thou
　　　sleep,　　　　　　　　　5
Patient, while vice doth make an antic face
At thy dread power, and blow dust and smoke
Into thy nostrils ! Jove, will nothing wake thee?
Must vile Sejanus pull thee by the beard,
Ere thou wilt open thy black-lidded eye,　　10
And look him dead ? Well ! snore on, dreaming
　　　gods ;
And let this last of that proud giant-race
Heave mountain upon mountain 'gainst your
　　　state. —
Be good unto me, Fortune and you powers,
Whom I, expostulating, have profan'd ;　　15
I see (what 's equal with a prodigy)
A great, a noble Roman, and an honest,
Live an old man ! —

[*Enter* LEPIDUS.][4]

　　　　　　O Marcus Lepidus,
When is our turn to bleed ? Thyself and I,
Without our boast, are a'most all the few　　20
Left to be honest in these impious times.
Lep. What we are left to be, we will be, Lu-
　　　cius ;
Though tyranny did stare as wide as death,
To fright us from it.
Arr.　　　　'T hath so on Sabinus.
Lep. I saw him now drawn from the Gemo-
　　　nies,[5]　　　　　　　　　25
And what increas'd the direness of the fact,
His faithful dog, upbraiding all us Romans,
Never forsook the corpse, but, seeing it thrown
Into the stream, leap'd in, and drown'd with it.
Arr. O act, to be envi'd him of us men !　　30
We are the next the hook lays hold on, Marcus :
What are thy arts, good patriot, teach them me,
That have preser'r'd thy hairs to this white
　　　dye,
And kept so reverend and so dear a head
Safe on his comely shoulders ?
Lep.　　　　　　Arts, Arruntius ! 35
None, but the plain and passive fortitude,
To suffer and be silent ; never stretch
These arms against the torrent ; live at home,
With my own thoughts and innocence about me,
Not tempting the wolves' jaws : these are my
　　　arts.　　　　　　　　　40
Arr. I would begin to study 'em, if I thought
They would secure me. May I pray to Jove
In secret and be safe ? ay, or aloud,
With open wishes, so I do not mention
Tiberius or Sejanus ? Yes, I must,　　45
If I speak out. 'T is hard, that. May I think,
And not be rackt ? What danger is 't to dream,
Talk in one's sleep, or cough ? Who knows the
　　　law ?
May I shake my head without a comment ? say
It rains, or it holds up, and not be thrown　　50
Upon the Gemonies ? These now are things,
Whereon men's fortune, yea, their fate depends.

---

　　　4 After *impious times* in F.
　　　5 Steps on the Aventine Hill, down which the bodies
　　　of executed criminals were thrown into the Tiber.

Nothing hath privilege 'gainst the violent ear.
No place, no day, no hour, we see, is free,
(Not our religious and most sacred times)   55
From some one kind of cruelty: all matter,
Nay, all occasion pleaseth. Madmen's rage,
The idleness of drunkards, women's nothing,
Jester's simplicity, all, all is good
That can be catcht at. Nor is now th' event   60
Of any person, or for any crime,
To be expected ;[1] for 't is always one :
Death, with some little difference of place,
Or time —— What 's this ?   Prince Nero,
    guarded !

[Enter] LACO *and* NERO *[with* GUARDS.]

Lac. On, lictors, keep your way.   My lords,
    forbear.   65
On pain of Caesar's wrath, no man attempt
Speech with the prisoner.
Ner.   Noble friends, be safe ;
To lose yourselves for words, were as vain
    hazard,
As unto me small comfort. Fare you well.
Would all Rome's suff'rings in my fate did
    dwell !   70
Lac. Lictors, away.
Lep.   Where goes he, Laco ?
Lac.   Sir,
He 's banished into Pontia by the senate.
Arr. Do I see, and hear, and feel ? May I
    trust sense,
Or doth my phant'sie form it ?
Lep.   Where 's his brother ?
Lac. Drusus is prisoner in the palace.
Arr.   Ha !   75
I smell it now : 't is rank. Where's Agrippina ?
Lac. The princess is confin'd to Pandataria.
Arr. Bolts, Vulcan ; bolts for Jove ! Phoebus,
    thy bow ;
Stern Mars, thy sword ; and, blue-ey'd Maid,
    thy spear ;
Thy club, Alcides : all the armoury   80
Of heaven is too little ! — Ha ! to guard
The gods, I meant. Fine, rare dispatch ! This
    same
Was swiftly borne ! Confin'd, imprison'd, ban-
    ish'd ?
Most tripartite ! The cause, sir ?
Lac.   Treason.
Arr.   O !
The complement of all accusings ! That   85
Will hit, when all else fails.
Lep.   This turn is strange !
But yesterday the people would not hear,
Far less objected, but cri'd Caesar's letters
Were false and forg'd ; that all these plots were
    malice ;
And that the ruin of the prince's house   90
Was practis'd 'gainst his knowledge. Where are
    now
Their voices, now that they behold his heirs
Lock'd up, disgrac'd, led into exile ?
Arr.   Hush'd,
Drown'd in their bellies. Wild Sejanus' breath
Hath, like a whirlwind, scatter'd that poor
    dust,   95

---

1 Awaited with uncertainty.

With his rude blast. — We 'll talk no treason,
    sir,   *Turns to* LACO, *and the rest.*
If that be it you stand for. Fare you well.
We have no need of horse-leeches. Good spy,
Now you are spi'd, be gone.
    [Exeunt LACO, NERO, *and* Guards.]
Lep.   I fear you wrong him :
He hath the voice to be an honest Roman.   100
Arr. And trusted to this office ! Lepidus,
I 'd sooner trust Greek Sinon than a man
Our state employs. He 's gone : and being gone,
I dare tell you, whom I dare better trust,
That our night-ey'd Tiberius doth not see   105
His minion's drifts ; or, if he do, he 's not
So arrant subtile, as we fools do take him ;
To breed a mongrel up, in his own house,
With his own blood, and, if the good gods
    please,
At his own throat flesh him to take a leap.   110
I do not beg it, heav'n ; but if the fates
Grant it these eyes, they must not wink.
Lep.   They must
Not see it, Lucius.
Arr.   Who should let[2] 'em ?
Lep.   Zeal,
And duty ; with the thought he is our prince.
Arr. He is our monster : forfeited to vice   115
So far, as no rack'd virtue can redeem him.
His loathed person fouler than all crimes :
An emp'ror only in his lusts. Retir'd,
From all regard of his own fame, or Rome's,
Into an obscure island, where he lives   120
Acting his tragedies with a comic face,
Amidst his rout of Chaldees : spending hours,
Days, weeks, and months, in the unkind[3] abuse
Of grave astrology, to the bane of men,
Casting the scope of men's nativities,   125
And having found aught worthy in their for-
    tune,
Kill, or precipitate them in the sea,
And boast he can mock fate. Nay, muse not :
    these
Are far from ends of evil, scarce degrees.
He hath his slaughter-house at Capreae ;   130
Where he doth study murder as an art ;
And they are dearest in his grace that can
Devise the deepest tortures. Thither, too,
He hath his boys, and beauteous girls ta'en up
Out of our noblest houses, the best form'd,   135
Best nurtur'd, and most modest ; what 's their
    good,
Serves to provoke his bad. Some are allur'd,
Some threat'ned ; others, by their friends de-
    tain'd,
Are ravish'd hence, like captives, and, in sight
Of their most grieved parents, dealt away   1)
Unto his spintries,[4] sellaries,[5] and slaves
Masters of strange and new commented lusts,
For which wise nature hath left not a name.
To this (what most strikes us, and bleeding
    Rome)
He is, with all his craft, become the ward   145
To his own vassal, a stale catamite.[4]
Whom he, upon our low and suffering necks,

---

2 Hinder.   4 Male prostitutes.
3 Unnatural.   5 Lewd persons.

Hath raised from excrement to side the gods,
And have his proper sacrifice in Rome :
Which Jove beholds, and yet will sooner rive 150
A senseless oak with thunder than his trunk !

[*Re-enter*] LACO, POMPONIUS, MINUTIUS.

Lac. These letters make men doubtful what
t' expect.
Whether his coming, or his death.
Pom. Troth, both :
And which comes soonest, thank the gods for.
Arr. (*Aside.*) List !
Their talk is Caesar ; I would hear all voices. 155
    [ARRUNT. *and* LEPIDUS *stand aside.*]
Min. One day, he 's well ; and will return to
Rome ;
The next day, sick ; and knows not when to
hope it.
Lac. True; and to-day, one of Sejanus' friends
Honour'd by special writ ; and on the morrow
Another punish'd ——
Pom. By more special writ. 160
Min. This man receives his praises of Seja-
nus,
A second but slight mention, a third none,
A fourth rebukes : and thus he leaves the senate
Divided and suspended, all uncertain.
Lac. These forked tricks, I understand 'em
not : 165
Would he would tell us whom he loves or hates,
That we might follow, without fear or doubt.
Arr. (*Aside.*) Good Heliotrope ! Is this your
honest man ?
Let him be yours so still ; he is my knave.
Pom. I cannot tell, Sejanus still goes on, 170
And mounts, we see ; new statues are advanc'd,[1]
Fresh leaves of titles, large inscriptions read,
His fortune sworn by, himself new gone out
Caesar's colleague in the fifth consulship ;
More altars smoke to him than all the gods : 175
What would be more ? [choke him,
Arr. (*Aside.*) That the dear smoke would
[That would I more.
Lep. Peace, good Arruntius.][2]
Lat. But there are letters come, they say,
ev'n now,
Which do forbid that last.
Min. Do you hear so ?
Lac. Yes.
Pom. By Castor that 's the worst.
Arr. (*Aside.*) By Pollux, best.
Min. I did not like the sign, when Regulus, 182
Whom all we know no friend unto Sejanus,
Did, by Tiberius' so precise command,
Succeed a fellow in the consulship :
It boded somewhat.
Pom. Not a mote. His partner,
Fulcinius Trio, is his own, and sure. — 186
Here comes Terentius.

[*Enter* TERENTIUS]

He can give us more.
[*They whisper with* TERENTIUS.]
Lep. I 'll ne'er believe but Caesar hath some
scent

1 Raised.   2 F₁ omits.

Of bold Sejanus' footing. These cross points
Of varying letters, and opposing consuls, 190
Mingling his honours and his punishments,
Feigning now ill, now well, raising Sejanus,
And then depressing him, as now of late
In all reports we have it, cannot be
Empty of practice : 't is Tiberius' art, 195
For, having found his favourite grown too great,
And with his greatness strong ; that all the sol-
diers
Are, with their leaders, made at his devotion ;
That almost all the senate are his creatures,
Or hold on him their main dependencies, 200
Either for benefit, or hope, or fear ;
And that himself hath lost much of his own,
By parting unto him ; and, by th' increase
Of his rank lusts and rages, quite disarm'd
Himself of love, or other public means 205
To dare an open contestation ;
His subtilty hath chose this doubling line,
To hold him even in : not so to fear him,
As wholly put him out, and yet give check
Unto his farther boldness. In mean time, 210
By his employments, makes him odious
Unto the staggering rout, whose aid, in fine,
He hopes to use, as sure, who, when they sway,
Bear down, o'erturn all objects in their way. 214
Arr. You may be a Lynceus, Lepidus : yet I
See no such cause, but that a political tyrant,
Who can so well disguise it, should have ta'en
A nearer way : feign'd honest, and come home
To cut his throat, by law.
Lep. Ay, but his fear
Would ne'er be mask'd, allbe his vices were.
Pom. His lordship then is still in grace ?
Ter. Assure you,
Never in more, either of grace or power. 222
Pom. The gods are wise and just.
Arr. (*Aside.*) The fiends they are,
To suffer thee belie 'em.
Ter. I have here
His last and present letters, where he writes
him, 225
"The partner of his cares," and "his Seja-
nus." —
Lac. But is that true, if 't is prohibited
To sacrifice unto him ?
Ter. Some such thing
Caesar makes scruple of, but forbids it not ;
No more than to himself : says he could wish
It were forborne to all.
Lac. Is it no other ? 231
Ter. No other, on my trust. For your more
surety,
Here is that letter too.
Arr. (*Aside.*) How easily
Do wretched men believe what they would
have ! 234
Looks this like plot ?
Lep. (*Aside.*) Noble Arruntius, stay.
Lac. He names him here without his titles.
Lep. (*Aside.*) Note !
Arr. (*Aside.*) Yes, and come off your notable
fool. I will.
Lac. No other than Sejanus.
Pom. That 's but haste
In him that writes : here he gives large amends

Mar. And with his own hand written?
Pom.   Yes.
Lac.   Indeed?
Ter. Believe it, gentlemen, Sejanus' breast
Never receiv'd more full contentments in,   242
Than at this present.
Pom.   Takes he well th' escape
Of young Caligula, with Macro?
Ter.   Faith,
At the first air it somewhat troubled him.   245
Lep. (*Aside.*) Observe you?
Arr. (*Aside.*)   Nothing; riddles. Till ⊥ see
Sejanus struck, no sound thereof strikes me.
            [*Exeunt* ARRUNTIUS *and* LEPIDUS.]
Pom. I like it not. I muse he'd not attempt
Somewhat against him in the consulship,
Seeing the people 'gin to favour him.   250
Ter. He doth repent it now; but he's em-
      ploy'd
Pagonianus after him: and he holds
That correspondence there, with all that are
Near about Caesar, as no thought can pass
Without his knowledge, thence, in act to front
      him.   255
Pom. I gratulate the news.
Lac.   But how comes Macro
So in trust and favour with Caligula?
Pom. O, sir, he has a wife; and the young
      prince
An appetite: he can look up and spy
Flies in the roof, when there are fleas i' bed; 260
And hath a learned nose t' assure his sleeps.
Who to be favour'd of the rising sun,
Would not lend little of his waning moon?
It is the saf'st ambition. Noble Terentius!
Ter. The night grows fast upon us. At your
      service.   265
                                        [*Exeunt.*]

CHORUS — of Musicians.

ACT V

[SCENE I.]¹

[*Enter*] SEJANUS.

Sej. Swell, swell, my joys; and faint not to
      declare
Yourselves as ample as your causes are.
I did not live till now: this my first hour,
Wherein I see my thoughts reach'd by my
      power.
But this, and gripe my wishes. Great and high,
The world knows only two, that's Rome and I. 6
My roof receives me not; 'tis air I tread;
And, at each step, I feel my advanced head
Knock out a star in heaven! Rear'd to this
      height,
All my desires seem modest, poor, and slight,
That did before sound impudent; 'tis place, 11
Not blood, discerns the noble and the base.
Is there not something more than to be Caesar?
Must we rest there? It irks t' have come so far,
To be so near a stay. Caligula,   15
Would thou stood'st stiff, and many in our way!

¹ An apartment in Sejanus's house.

Winds lose their strength, when they do empty
      fly,
Unmet of woods or buildings; great fires die,
That want their matter to withstand them: so,
It is our grief, and will be our loss, to know 20
Our power shall want opposites; unless
The gods, by mixing in the cause, would bless
Our fortune with their conquest. That were
      worth
Sejanus' strife, durst fates but bring it forth.

[*Enter*] TERENTIUS.

Ter. Safety to great Sejanus!
Sej.   Now, Terentius? 25
Ter. Hears not my lord the wonder?
Sej.   Speak it; no.
Ter. I meet it violent in the people's mouths,
Who run in routs to Pompey's theatre,
To view your statue; which, they say, sends
      forth
A smoke, as from a furnace, black and dread-
      ful.   30
Sej. Some traitor hath put fire in: you, go
      see,
And let the head be taken off, to look
What 't is. [*Exit* TERENTIUS.] Some slave hath
      practis'd an imposture
To stir the people. — How now! Why return
      you?

[*Re-enter* TERENTIUS, *with*] SATRIUS *and*
                  NATTA.

Sat. The head, my lord, already is ta'en
      off,   35
I saw it; and, at opening, there leapt out
A great and monstrous serpent.
Sej.   Monstrous! Why?
Had it a beard, and horns? no heart? a
      tongue
Forked as flattery? Look'd it of the hue
To such as live in great men's bosoms? Was 40
The spirit of it Macro's?
Nat.   May it please
The most divine Sejanus, in my days,
(And by his sacred fortune, I affirm it,)
I have not seen a more extended, grown,
Foul, spotted, venomous, ugly—
Sej.   O, the fates! 45
What a wild muster's here of attributes,
T' express a worm, a snake!
Ter.   But how that should
Come there, my lord?
Sej.   What, and you too, Terentius!
I think you mean to make 't a prodigy
In your reporting.
Ter.   Can the wise Sejanus 50
Think heav'n hath meant it less?
Sej.   O, superstition!
Why, then the falling of our bed, that brake
This morning, burd'ned with the populous
      weight
Of our expecting clients, to salute us;
Or running of the cat betwixt our legs,   55
As we set forth unto the Capitol,
Were prodigies.
Ter.   I think them ominous:
And would they had not happ'ned! As, to-day,

The fate of some your servants: who declining[1]
Their way, not able, for the throng, to follow,
Slipt down the Gemonies, and brake their
necks! 61
Besides, in taking your last augury,
No prosperous bird appear'd; but croaking
ravens
Flagg'd up and down, and from the sacrifice
Flew to the prison, where they sat all night, 65
Beating the air with their obstreperous beaks!
I dare not counsel, but I could entreat,
That great Sejanus would attempt the gods
Once more with sacrifice.
Sej. What excellent fools
Religion makes of men! Believes Terentius, 70
If these were dangers, as I shame to think
them,
The gods could change the certain course of fate?
Or, if they could they would, now in a moment,
For a beeve's fat, or less, be brib'd t' invert
Those long decrees? Then think the gods, like
flies, 75
Are to be taken with the steam of flesh,
Or blood, diffus'd about their altars: think
Their power as cheap as I esteem it small.
Of all the throng that fill th' Olympian hall,
And, without pity, lade poor Atlas' back, 80
I know not that one deity, but Fortune,
To whom I would throw up, in begging smoke,
One grain of incense; or whose ear I'd buy
With thus much oil. Her I indeed adore;
And keep her grateful image in my house, 85
Sometimes belonging to a Roman king,
But now call'd mine, as by the better style:
To her I care not, if, for satisfying
Your scrupulous phant'sies, I go offer. Bid
Our priest prepare us honey, milk, and poppy, 90
His masculine odours, and night-vestments: say
Our rites are instant; which perform'd, you'll
see
How vain, and worthy laughter, your fears be.
[*Exeunt.*]

[SCENE II.][2]

[*Enter*] COTTA *and* POMPONIUS.

Cot. Pomponius, whither in such speed?
Pom. I go.
To give my lord Sejanus notice ——
Cot. What?
Pom. Of Macro.
Cot. Is he come?
Pom. Ent'red but now
The house of Regulus.
Cot. The opposite consul!
Pom. Some half hour since.
Cot. And by night too! Stay, sir; 5
I'll bear you company.
Pom. Along then. [*Exeunt.*]

[SCENE III.][3]

[*Enter*] MACRO, REGULUS, [*and* Attendant.]

Mac. 'T is Caesar's will to have a frequent
senate;

[1] Turning out of the way.
[2] A street.
[3] A room in Regulus's house.

And therefore must your edict lay deep mulct
On such as shall be absent.
Reg. So it doth.
Bear it my fellow consul to adscribe.[4]
Mac. And tell him it must early be pro-
claim'd: 5
The place Apollo's temple. [*Exit* Attendant.]
Reg. That's rememb'red.
Mac. And at what hour?
Reg. Yes.
Mac. You do forget
To send one for the provost of the watch.
Reg. I have not: here he comes.

[*Enter*] LACO.

Mac. Gracinus Laco,
You are a friend most welcome: by and by, 10
I'll speak with you. — You must procure this list
Of the praetorian cohorts, with the names
Of the centurions, and their tribunes.
Reg. Ay.
Mac. I bring you letters, and a health from
Caesar.
Lac. Sir, both come well.
Mac. And, hear you? with your note, 15
Which are the eminent men, and most of
action.
Reg. That shall be done you too. *Goes out.*
Mac. Most worthy Laco, —
Caesar salutes you. — Consul! death and furies!
Gone now! — The argument will please you,
sir. —
Ho! Regulus! The anger of the gods 20
Follow your diligent legs, and overtake 'em,
In likeness of the gout!

Re-enter REGULUS.

O, my good lord,
We lackt you present; I would pray you send
Another to Fulcinius Trio, straight,
To tell him you will come and speak with
him: 25
The matter we'll devise, to stay him there,
While I with Laco do survey the watch.
REGULUS goes out again.
What are your strengths, Gracinus?
Lac. Seven cohorts.
Mac. You see what Caesar writes; and — Gone
again!
H' as sure a vein of mercury in his feet. —— 30
Know you what store of the praetorian soldiers
Sejanus holds about him, for his guard?
Lac. I cannot the just[5] number; but I think
Three centuries.
Mac. Three! good.
Lac. At most not four.
Mac. And who be those centurions?
Lac. That the consul 35
Can best deliver you.
Mac. When he's away!
Spite on his nimble industry! — Gracinus,
You find what place you hold, there, in the
trust
Of royal Caesar?
Lac. Ay, and I am ——

[4] Sign. [5] Precise.

Mac.   Sir,   39
The honours there propos'd are but beginnings
Of his great favours.
Lac.   They are more ——
Mac.   I heard him
When he did study what to add.
Lac.   My life,
And all I hold ——
Mac.   You were his own first choice!
Which doth confirm as much as you can speak;
And will, if we succeed, make more —— Your
    guards   45
Are seven cohorts, you say?
Lac.   Yes.
Mac.   Those we must
Hold still in readiness and undischarg'd.
Lac. I understand so much. But how it
    can ——
Mac. Be done without suspicion, you'll
    object?

Re-enter REGULUS.

Reg. What's that.
Lac.   The keeping of the watch in arms, 50
When morning comes.
Mac.   The senate shall be met, and set
So early in the temple, as all mark
Of that shall be avoided.
Reg.   If we need,
We have commission to possess the palace, 54
Enlarge Prince Drusus, and make him our chief.
Mac. (Aside.) That secret would have burnt
    his reverend mouth,
Had he not spit it out now. —— By the gods,
You carry things too —— Let me borrow a man
Or two, to bear these —— That of freeing
    Drusus,
Caesar projected as the last and utmost;   60
Not else to be rememb'red.

[*Enter Servants.*]

Reg.   Here are servants.
Mac. These to Arruntius, these to Lepidus.
This bear to Cotta, this to Latiaris.
If they demand you of me, say I have ta'en
Fresh horse and am departed. [*Exeunt Ser-*
    vants.] You, my lord,   65
To your colleague, and be you sure to hold him
With long narration of the new fresh favours,
Meant to Sejanus, his great patron; I,
With trusted Laco, here, are for the guards:
Then, to divide. For night hath many eyes, 70
Whereof, though most do sleep, yet some are
    spies.   [*Exeunt.*]

[SCENE IV.]¹

[*Enter*] Praecones, Flamen, [Tubicines, Tibicines,] Ministri, SEJANUS, TERENTIUS, SATRI-
US, [NATTA,] *etc.*

Prae. Be all profane far hence; fly, fly far off:
Be absent far; far hence be all profane!
    Tubicines² *and* Tibicines³ *sound*
        while the Flamen *washeth.*
Fla. We have been faulty, but repent us now.

¹ A chapel in Sejanus's house.
² Trumpeters.   ³ Flute-players.

And bring pure hands, pure vestments, and pure
    minds.   4
1 Min. Pure vessels.
2 Min.   And pure offerings.
3 Min.   Garlands pure.
Fla. Bestow your garlands: and, with rever-
    ence place
The vervain⁴ on the altar.
Prae.   Favour your tongues.
    While they sound again, the Flamen
    takes of the honey with his finger,
    and tastes, then ministers to all the
    rest: so of the milk in an earthen
    vessel, he deals about; which done,
    he sprinkleth upon the altar, milk;
    then imposeth the honey, and kin-
    dleth his gums, and after censing
    about the altar, placeth his censer
    thereon, into which they put sev-
    eral branches of poppy, and the
    music ceasing, proceed.
Fla. Great mother Fortune, queen of human
    state,
Rectress of action, arbitress of fate,
To whom all sway, all power, all empire bows,
Be present, and propitious to our vows!   11
Prae. Favour it with your tongues.
Min. Be present, and propitious to our vows!
Accept our off'ring, and be pleas'd, great god-
    dess.   14
Ter. See, see, the image stirs!
Sat.   And turns away!
Nat. Fortune averts her face!
Fla.   Avert, you gods,
The prodigy. Still! still! some pious rite
We have neglected. Yet, heav'n be appeas'd,
And be all tokens false or void, that speak   19
Thy present wrath!
Sej.   Be thou dumb, scrupulous priest:
And gather up thyself, with these thy wares,
Which I, in spite of thy blind mistress, or
Thy juggling mystery, religion, throw
Thus scorned on the earth.
        [*Overturns the statue and the altar.*]
                    Nay, hold thy look
Averted till I woo thee turn again;   25
And thou shalt stand, to all posterity,
Th' eternal game and laughter, with thy neck
Writh'd to thy tail, like a ridiculous cat.
Avoid⁵ these fumes, these superstitious lights,
And all these cos'ning⁶ ceremonies; you,   30
Your pure and spiced⁷ conscience!
        [*Exeunt all but* SEJANUS, TEREN-
        TIUS, SATRIUS, *and* NATTA.]
                    I, the slave
And mock of fools, (scorn on my worthy head!)
That have been titled and ador'd a god,
Yea sacrific'd unto, myself, in Rome,
No less than Jove: and I be brought to do   35
A peevish giglot⁸ rites! Perhaps the thought
And shame of that made Fortune turn her face,
Knowing herself the lesser deity,
And but my servant. — Bashful queen, if so,
Sejanus thanks thy modesty. — Who's that? 40

⁴ Verbena, "herb of grace."
⁵ Remove.   ⁶ Cheating.
⁷ Absurdly scrupulous.   ⁸ Wench.

[*Enter*] Pomponius *and* Minutius.

Pom. His fortune suffers, till he hears my
    news:
I have waited here too long. Macro, my lord——
Sej. Speak lower and withdraw.
                   [*Takes him aside.*]
Ter.   Are these things true ?
Min. Thousands are gazing at it in the streets.
Sej. What 's that ?
Ter.   Minutius tells us here, my lord, 45
That a new head being set upon your statue,
A rope is since found wreath'd about it ! and,
But now, a fiery meteor in the form
Of a great ball was seen to roll along   49
The troubled air, where yet it hangs unperfect,
The amazing wonder of the multitude !
Sej. No more. That Macro 's come, is more
    than all !
Ter. Is Macro come ?
Pom.   I saw him.
Ter.   Where ? with whom ?
Pom. With Regulus.
Sej.   Terentius !
Ter.   My lord.
Sej. Send for the tribunes, we will straight
    have up   55
More of the soldiers for our guard. [*Exit* Ter.]
    Minutius,
We pray you go for Cotta, Latiaris,
Trio the consul, or what senators
You know are sure, and ours. [*Exit* Min.] You,
    my good Natta.
For Laco, provost of the watch. [*Exit* Nat.]
Now, Satrius,   60
The time of proof comes on ; arm all our ser-
    vants,
And without tumult. [*Exit* Sat.] You, Pom-
    ponius,
Hold some good correspondence with the consul :
Attempt him, noble friend. [*Exit* Pomp.] These
    things begin
To look like dangers, now, worthy my fates. 65
Fortune, I see thy worst : let doubtful states,
And things uncertain hang upon thy will ;
Me surest death shall render certain still.
Yet, why is now my thought turn'd toward
    death,
Whom fates have let go on so far in breath, 70
Uncheck'd or unreprov'd ? I, that did help
To fell the lofty cedar of the world
Germanicus ; that at one stroke cut down
Drusus, that upright elm ; wither'd his vine ;
Laid Silius and Sabinus, two strong oaks,   75
Flat on the earth ; besides those other shrubs,
Cordus and Sosia, Claudia Pulchra,
Furnius and Gallus, which I have grubb'd up ;
And since, have set my axe so strong and deep
Into the root of spreading Agrippine ;   80
Lopt off and scatter'd her proud branches,
    Nero,
Drusus ; and Caius too, although replanted.
If you will, Destinies, that after all,
I faint now ere I touch my period,
You are but cruel ; and I already have done 85
Things great enough. All Rome hath been my
    slave :

The senate sate an idle looker-on,
And witness of my power ; when I have blush'd
More to command than it to suffer : [1] all
The fathers have sat ready and prepar'd   90
To give me empire, temples, or their throats,
When I would ask 'em ; and, what crowns the
    top,
Rome, senate, people, all the world have seen
Jove but my equal ; Caesar but my second.
'T is then your malice, Fates, who, but your
    own,   95
Envy and fear t' have any power long known.
                                  [*Exit.*]

[SCENE V.] [2]

[*Enter*] Terentius *and* Tribunes.

Ter. Stay here : I 'll give [3] his lordship you
    are come.

[*Enter*] Minutius, Cotta, Latiaris.

Min. Marcus Terentius, pray you tell my lord
Here 's Cotta, and Latiaris.
Ter.   Sir, I shall. [*Exit.*]
Cot. My letter is the very same with yours ;
Only requires me to be present there,   5
And give my voice to strengthen his design.
Lat. Names he not what it is ?
Cot.   No, nor to you.
Lat. 'T is strange and singular doubtful !
Cot.   So it is.
It may be all is left to lord Sejanus.

[*Enter*] Natta *and* Gracinus Laco.

Nat. Gentlemen, where 's my lord ?
Tri.   We wait him here. 10
Cot. The provost Laco ! What 's the news ?
Lat.   My lord ——

[*Enter*] Sejanus.

Sej. Now, my right dear, noble, and trusted
    friends,
How much I am a captive to your kindness !
Most worthy Cotta, Latiaris, Laco,
Your valiant hand ; and, gentlemen, your loves.
I wish I could divide myself unto you ;   15
Or that it lay within our narrow powers,
To satisfy for so enlarged bounty.
Gracinus, we must pray you, hold your guards
Unquit when morning comes. Saw you the con-
    sul ?   20
Min. Trio will presently be here, my lord.
Cot. They are but giving order for the edict,
To warn the senate ?
Sej.   How ! the senate ?
Lac.   Yes.
This morning in Apollo's temple ——
Cot.   We
Are charg'd by letter to be there, my lord. 25
Sej. By letter ! Pray you let 's see.
Lat.   Knows not his lordship ?
Cot. It seems so !
Sej. A senate warn'd ! without my know-
    ledge !
And on this sudden ! Senators by letters
Required to be there ! Who brought these ?

     ¹ Permit.   **² A room in the same.**   **³ Tell**

Cot. Macro. 30
Sej. Mine enemy! And when?
Cot. This midnight.
Sej. Time,
With ev'ry other circumstance, doth give
It hath some strain of engine[1] in 't! — How
  now?

[*Enter*] SATRIUS.

Sat. My lord, Sertorius Macro is without,
Alone, and prays t' have private conference 35
In business of high nature with your lordship,
He says to me, and which regards you much.
Sej. Let him come here.
Sat. Better, my lord, withdraw:
You will betray what store and strength of
  friends
Are now about you; which he comes to spy. 40
Sej. Is he not arm'd?
Sat. We'll search him.
Sej. No; but take,
And lead him to some room, where you con-
  ceal'd
May keep a guard upon us. [*Exit* SAT.] Noble
  Laco,
You are our trust; and till our own cohorts
Can be brought up, your strengths must be our
  guard. 45
Now, good Minutius, honour'd Latiaris,
             He salutes them humbly.
Most worthy and my most unwearied friends;
I return instantly.   [*Exit.*]
Lat.   Most worthy lord!
Cot. His lordship is turn'd instant kind, me-
  thinks;
I have not observ'd it in him heretofore. 50
1 *Tri.* 'T is true, and it becomes him nobly.
Min.   I
Am rapt withal.
2 *Tri.*   By Mars, he has my lives,
Were they a million, for this only grace.
Lac. Ay, and to name a man!
Lat.   As he did me!
Min. And me!   [and fortunes
Lat. Who would not spend his life
To purchase but the look of such a lord? 56
Lac. [*Aside.*] He that would nor be lord's
  fool, nor the world's.   [*Exeunt.*]

[SCENE VI.][2]

Enter SEJANUS, MACRO, *and* SATRIUS.

Sej. Macro! most welcome, as most coveted
  friend!
Let me enjoy my longings. When arriv'd you?
Mac. About the noon of night.
Sej. Satrius, give leave. [*Exit* SATRIUS.]
Mac. I have been, since I came, with both
  the consuls,
On a particular design from Caesar. 5
Sej. How fares it with our great and royal
  master?
Mac. Right plentifully well; as with a prince

[1] Element of trickery.
[2] Another room in the same.

That still holds out the great proportion
Of his large favours, where his judgment hath
Made once divine election: like the god 10
That wants not, nor is wearied to bestow
Where merit meets his bounty, as it doth
In you, already the most happy, and, ere
The sun shall climb the south, most high Sej-
  anus.
Let not my lord be amus'd.[3] For to this end 15
Was I by Caesar sent for to the isle,
With special caution to conceal my journey;
And thence had my despatch as privately
Again to Rome; charg'd to come here by night;
And only to the consuls make narration 20
Of his great purpose: that the benefit
Might come more full, and striking, by how
  much
It was less look'd for, or aspir'd by you,
Or least informed to the common thought.
Sej. What may this be? Part of myself,
  dear Macro, 25
If good, speak out; and share with your Sejanus.
Mac. If bad, I should for ever loathe myself
To be the messenger to so good a lord.
I do exceed my instructions to acquaint
Your lordship with thus much; but 't is my
  venture 30
On your retentive wisdom: and because
I would no jealous scruple should molest
Or rack your peace of thought. For I assure
My noble lord, no senator yet knows
The business meant: though all by several let-
  ters 35
Are warned to be there, and give their voices,
Only to add unto the state and grace
Of what is purpos'd.
Sej.   You take pleasure, Macro,
Like a coy wench, in torturing your lover. 39
What can be worth this suffering?
Mac.   That which follows,
The tribunitial dignity and power:
Both which Sejanus is to have this day
Conferr'd upon him, and by public senate.
Sej. Fortune be mine again! [*Aside.*] Thou
  hast satisfied
For thy suspected loyalty.
Mac.   My lord, 45
I have no longer time, the day approacheth,
And I must back to Caesar.
Sej.   Where's Caligula?
Mac. That I forgot to tell your lordship.
  Why,
He lingers yonder about Capreae,
Disgrac'd; Tiberius hath not seen him yet. 50
He needs would thrust himself to go with me,
Against my wish or will; but I have quitted
His forward trouble,[4] with as tardy note
As my neglect or silence could afford him. 54
Your lordship cannot now command me aught,
Because I take no knowledge that I saw you;
But I shall boast to live to serve your lordship;
And so take leave.
Sej.   Honest and worthy Macro;
Your love and friendship. [*Exit* MACRO.]
  Who's there? Satrius,

[3] Amazed.   [4] His troublesome forwardness.

Attend my honourable friend forth. — O! 60
How vain and vile a passion is this fear,
What base uncomely things it makes men do!
Suspect their noblest friends, as I did this,
Flatter poor enemies, entreat their servants,
Stoop, court, and catch at the benevolence 65
Of creatures unto whom, within this hour,
I would not have vouchsaf'd a quarter-look,
Or piece of face! By you that fools call gods,
Hang all the sky with your prodigious signs,
Fill earth with monsters, drop the scorpion
            down 70
Out of the zodiac, or the fiercer lion,
Shake off the loos'ned globe from her long hinge,
Roll all the world in darkness, and let loose
Th' enraged winds to turn up groves and towns!
When I do fear again, let me be struck 75
With forked fire, and unpitied die;
Who fears, is worthy of calamity.   [Exit.]

[SCENE VII.]¹

[Enter TERENTIUS, MINUTIUS, LACO, COTTA,
LATIARIS, and] POMPONIUS; REGULUS, TRIO,
[and others, on different sides.]

Pom. Is not my lord here?
Ter.   Sir, he will be straight.
Cot. What news, Fulcinius Trio?
Tri.   Good, good tidings;
But keep it to yourself. My lord Sejanus
Is to receive this day in open senate
The tribunitial dignity.
Cot.   Is 't true?   5
Tri. No words, not to your thought: but, sir,
        believe it.
Lat. What says the consul?
Cot.   Speak it not again:
He tells me that to-day my lord Sejanus——
Tri. I must entreat you, Cotta, on your honour
Not to reveal it.
Cot.   On my life, sir.
Lat.   Say.   10
Cot. Is to receive the tribunitial power,
But, as you are an honourable man,
Let me conjure you not to utter it;
For it is trusted to me with that bond.
Lat. I am Harpocrates.
Ter.   Can you assure it? 15
Pom. The consul told it me; but keep it close.
Min. Lord Latiaris, what 's the news?
Lat.   I 'll tell you;
But you must swear to keep it secret.

[Enter] SEJANUS.

Sej. I knew the Fates had on their distaff left
More of our thread, than so.
Reg.   Hail, great Sejanus! 20
Tri. Hail, the most honour'd!
Cot.   Happy!
Lat.   High Sejanus!
Sej. Do you bring prodigies too?
Tri.   May all presage
Turn to those fair effects, whereof we bring
Your lordship news.
Reg.   May 't please my lord withdraw.

¹ Another room in the same.

Sej. Yes: — I will speak with you anon.
                To some that stand by.
Ter.   My lord, 25
What is your pleasure for the tribunes?
Sej.   Why,
Let 'em be thankt and sent away.
Min.   My lord——
Lac. Will 't please your lordship to command
        me——
Sej.   No:
You are troublesome.
Min.   The mood is chang'd.
Tri.   Not speak,
Nor look!
Lac.   Ay, he is wise, will make him friends
Of such who never love but for their ends. 31
                [Exeunt.]

[SCENE VIII.]²

[Enter] ARRUNTIUS and LEPIDUS, divers other
        Senators passing by them.

Arr. Ay, go, make haste; take heed you be
        not last
To tender your "All Hail" in the wide hall
Of huge Sejanus: run a lictor's pace:
Stay not to put your robes on; but away
With the pale troubled ensigns of great friend-
        ship 5
Stampt i' your face! Now, Marcus Lepidus,
You still believe your former augury?
Sejanus must go downward! You perceive
His wane approaching fast!
Lep.   Believe me, Lucius,
I wonder at this rising.
Arr.   Ay, and that we 10
Must give our suffrage to it. You will say,
It is to make his fall more steep and grievous:
It may be so. But think it, they that can
With idle wishes 'say³ to bring back time:
In cases desperate, all hope is crime. 15
See, see! what troops of his officious friends
Flock to salute my lord, and start before
My great proud lord! to get a lord-like nod!
Attend my lord unto the senate-house! 19
Bring back my lord! like servile ushers, make
Way for my lord! proclaim his idol lordship,
More than ten criers, or six noise of trumpets!⁴
Make legs, kiss hands, and take a scatter'd hair
From my lord's eminent shoulder! See, San-
        guinius,
With his slow belly, and his dropsy! Look, 25
What toiling haste he makes! Yet here 's
        another
Retarded with the gout, will be afore him.
Get thee Liburnian porters, thou gross fool,
To bear thy obsequious fatness, like thy peers.
They met! The gout returns, and his great
        carriage. 30

Lictors, Consuls, [REGULUS and TRIO] SEJA-
NUS, [SATRIUS, SANGUINIUS, HATERIUS, and
many other Senators] pass over the stage.

Lict. Give way, make place, room for the
        consul!

² A space before the Temple of Apollo.   ³ Essay, try.
⁴ Bands of trumpeters.

San.   Hail,
Hail, great Sejanus!
   Hat.   Hail, my honour'd lord!
   Arr. We shall be markt anon, for our not
Hail.
   Lep. That is already done.
   Arr.   It is a note.
Of upstart greatness, to observe and watch   35
For these poor trifles, which the noble mind
Neglects and scorns.
   Lep.   Ay, and they think themselves
Deeply dishonour'd where they are omitted,
As if they were necessities that helpt
To the perfection of their dignities;   40
And hate the men that but refrain 'em.
   Arr.   O!
There is a farther cause of hate. Their breasts
Are guilty that we know their obscure springs
And base beginnings; thence the anger grows.
On. Follow.   [*Exeunt.*]   45

[SCENE IX.]¹

[Enter] MACRO *and* LACO.

   Mac. When all are ent'red, shut the temple
doors;
And bring your guards up to the gate.
   Lac.   I will.
   Mac. If you shall hear commotion in the sen-
ate,
Present yourself: and charge on any man   4
Shall offer to come forth.
   Loc.   I am instructed. [*Exeunt.*]

[SCENE X.]²

The Senate.

HATERIUS, TRIO, SANGUINIUS, COTTA, REGU-
LUS, SEJANUS, POMPONIUS, LATIARIS, LEPI-
DUS, ARRUNTIUS; Praecones, Lictores.

   Hat. How well his lordship looks to-day!
   Tri.   As if
He had been born, or made for this hour's
state.
   Cot. Your fellow consul's come about, me-
thinks?
   Tri. Ay, he is wise,
   San.   Sejanus trusts him well.
   Tri. Sejanus is a noble, bounteous lord.   5
   Hat. He is so, and most valiant.
   Lat.   And most wise.
   [1] *Sen.* He's everything.
   Lat.   Worthy of all, and more
Than bounty can bestow.
   Tri.   This dignity
Will make him worthy.
   Pom.   Above Caesar.
   San.   Tut,
Caesar is but the rector of an isle,   10
He of the Empire.
   Tri.   Now he will have power
More to reward than ever.
   Cot.   Let us look
We be not slack in giving him our voices.
   Lat. Not I.

¹ Another part of the same.
² The Temple of Apollo.

San.   Nor I.
   Cot.   The readier we seem
To propagate his honours, will more bind   15
His thoughts to ours.
   Hat.   I think right with your lordship;
It is the way to have us hold our places.
   San. Ay, and get more.
   Lat.   More office and more titles.
   Pom. I will not lose the part I hope to share
In these his fortunes, for my patrimony.   20
   Lat. See how Arruntius sits, and Lepidus!
   Tri. Let 'em alone, they will be markt anon.
   1 *Sen.* I'll do with others.
   2 *Sen.*   So will I.
   3 *Sen.*   And I.
Men grow not in the state but as they are planted
Warm in his favours.
   Cot.   Noble Sejanus!   25
   Hat. Honour'd Sejanus!
   Lat.   Worthy and great Sejanus!
   Arr. Gods! how the sponges open and take
in
And shut again! Look, look! is not he blest
That gets a seat in eye-reach of him! more
That comes in ear, or tongue-reach? O but
most   30
Can claw his subtile elbow, or with a buz
Fly-bow his ears?
   Praet.   Proclaim the senate's peace,
And give last summons by the edict.
   Prae.   Silence!
In the name of Caesar, and the senate, silence!
   "Memmius Regulus, and Fulcinius Trio, [35
consuls, these present kalends of June, with the
first light, shall hold a senate in the temple of
Apollo Palatine: all that are fathers, and are
regist'red fathers, that have right of ent'ring
the senate, we warn or command you be fre- [40
quently present, take knowledge the business
is the commonwealth's: whosoever is absent,
his fine or mulct will be taken, his excuse will
not be taken."
   Tri. Note who are absent, and record their
names.   45
   Reg. Fathers conscript, may what I am to
utter
Turn good and happy for the commonwealth!
And thou, Apollo, in whose holy house
We here are met, inspire us all with truth,
And liberty of censure to our thought!   50
The majesty of great Tiberius Caesar
Propounds to this grave senate, the bestowing
Upon the man he loves, honour'd Sejanus,
The tribunitial dignity and power:
Here are his letters, signed with his signet.   55
What pleaseth now the fathers to be done?
   Sen. Read, read 'em, open, publicly read
'em.
   Cot. Caesar hath honour'd his own greatness
much
In thinking of this act.
   Tri.   It was a thought
Happy, and worthy Caesar.
   Lat.   And the lord   60
As worthy it, on whom it is directed!
   Hat. Most worthy!
   San.   Rome did never boast the virtue

That could give envy bounds, but his: Sejanus ——
[1] *Sen.* Honour'd and noble!
[2] *Sen.*   Good and great Sejanus!   64
Arr. O, most tame slavery, and fierce flattery!
Prae.   Silence!   (*Reads.*)
"Tiberius Caesar to the Senate greeting.
If you, conscript fathers, with your children,
be in health, it is abundantly well : we with our
friends here are so. The care of the commonwealth, howsoever we are remov'd in person, [70
cannot be absent to our thought : although, oftentimes, even to princes most present, the
truth of their own affairs is hid ; than which
nothing falls out more miserable to a state, or
makes the art of governing more difficult. [75
But since it hath been our easeful happiness to
enjoy both the aids and industry of so vigilant
a senate, we profess to have been the more indulgent to our pleasures, not as being careless
of our office, but rather secure of the necessity.
Neither do these common rumours of many, [81
and infamous libels published against our retirement, at all afflict us ; being born more out
of men's ignorance than their malice : and will,
neglected, find their own grave quickly ; [85
whereas, too sensibly acknowledg'd, it would
make their obloquy ours. Nor do we desire their
authors, though found, be censur'd, since in a
free state, as ours, all men ought to enjoy both
their minds and tongues free."   90
Arr. (*Aside.*) The lapwing, the lapwing!
"Yet in things which shall worthily and more
near concern the majesty of a prince, we hold
fear to be so unnaturally cruel to our own fame,
as to neglect them. True it is, conscript fathers,
that we have raised Sejanus from obscure, [96
and almost unknown gentry,"
Sen. (*Aside.*) How, how!
"to the highest and most conspicuous point of
greatness, and, we hope, deservingly ; yet [100
not without danger : it being a most bold hazard
in that sov'reign who, by his particular love to
one, dares adventure the hatred of all his other
subjects."
Arr. (*Aside.*) This touches ; the blood turns.
"But we affy[1] in your loves and under- [106
standings, and do no way suspect the merit of
our Sejanus, to make our favours offensive to
any."
Sen. (*Aside.*) O! good, good.   110
"Though we could have wished his zeal had
run a calmer course against Agrippina and our
nephews, howsoever the openness of their actions declared them delinquents ; and that he
would have rememb'red no innocence is so [115
safe, but it rejoiceth to stand in the sight of
mercy : the use of which in us he hath so quite
taken away toward them, by his loyal fury, as
now our clemency would be thought but wearied cruelty, if we should offer to exercise it."
Arr. (*Aside.*) I thank him ; there I look'd
for 't. A good fox!   121
"Some there be that would interpret this his

public severity to be particular ambition ; and
that, under a pretext of service to us, he
doth but remove his own lets :[2] alleging the [125
strengths he hath made to himself, by the praetorian soldiers, by his faction in court and senate, by the offices he holds himself, and confers
on others, his popularity and dependents, his
urging and almost driving us to this our un- [130
willing retirement, and, lastly, his aspiring to
be our son-in-law."
Sen. (*Aside.*) This is strange!
Arr. (*Aside.*) I shall anon believe your vultures.[3] Marcus.
"Your wisdoms, conscript fathers, are able [135
to examine, and censure[4] these suggestions. But
were they left to our absolving voice, we durst
pronounce them, as we think them, most malicious."
Sen. (*Aside.*) O, he has restor'd all ; list!   140
"Yet are they offer'd to be averr'd, and on the
lives of the informers. What we should say, or
rather what we should not say, lords of the senate, if this be true, our gods and goddesses confound us if we know! Only we must think, [145
we have plac'd our benefits ill ; and conclude,
that in our choice, either we were wanting to
the gods, or the gods to us."
         The Senators *shift their places.*
Arr. (*Aside.*) The place grows hot ; they shift.
"We have not been covetous, honourable [150
fathers, to change ; neither is it now any new
lust that alters our affection, or old loathing :
but those needful jealousies of state, that warn
wiser princes hourly to provide their safety ;
and do teach them how learned a thing it is [155
to beware of the humblest enemy ; much more
of those great ones, whom their own employ'd
favours have made fit for their fears."
[1] *Sen.* (*Aside.*) Away.
[2] *Sen.* (*Aside.*)   Sit farther.
Cot. (*Aside.*)   Let's remove ——
Arr. (*Aside.*) Gods! how the leaves drop off,
this little wind!   162
"We therefore desire, that the offices he
holds be first seized by the senate ; and him-
self suspended from all exercise of place or
power —— "
Sen. (*Aside.*) How!   165
San. [*Thrusting by.*] By your leave.   [rius?
Arr. Come, porpoise. (*Aside.*) Where's Hate-
His gout keeps him most miserably constant! —
Your dancing shows a tempest.
Sej.   Read no more.
Reg. Lords of the senate, hold your seats:
read on.
Sej. These letters, they are forg'd.
Reg.   A guard! sit still.   170

       Enter Laco, *with the* Guards.

Arr. There's change!
Reg.   Bid silence, and read forward.
Prae. Silence! —"and himself suspended from
all exercise of place or power, but till due and
mature trial be made of his innocency, which
yet we can faintly apprehend the necessity to [175

---

[1] Trust.   [2] Obstacles.   [3] Referring to augury.   [4] Judge.

doubt. If, conscript fathers, to your more searching wisdoms, there shall appear farther cause
— or of farther proceeding, either to seizure of
lands, goods, or more — it is not our power that
shall limit your authority, or our favour [180
that must corrupt your justice : either were dishonourable in you, and both uncharitable to
ourself. We would willingly be present with
your counsels in this business ; but the danger
of so potent a faction, if it should prove [185
so, forbids our attempting it : except one of the
consuls would be entreated for our safety, to
undertake the guard of us home ; then we
should most readily adventure. In the meantime, it shall not be fit for us to impor- [190
tune so judicious a senate, who know how much
they hurt the innocent that spare the guilty ;
and how grateful a sacrifice to the gods is the
life of an ingrateful person. We reflect not in
this on Sejanus, (notwithstanding, if you [195
keep an eye upon him — and there is Latiaris,
a senator, and Pinnarius Natta, two of his most
trusted ministers ; and so profest, whom we desire not to have apprehended,) but as the necessity of the cause exacts it."   200
Reg. A guard on Latiaris !
Arr.   O, the spy,
The reverend spy is caught ! Who pities him ?
Reward, sir, for your service : now, you ha'
    done
Your property,[1] you see what use is made !
    [*Exeunt* LATIARIS *and* NATTA *guarded.*]
Hang up the instrument.
Sej.   Give leave.
Lac.   Stand, stand ! 205
He comes upon his death, that doth advance
An inch toward my point.
Sej.   Have we no friends here ?
Arr. Husht ! Where now are all the hails and
    acclamations ?

            [*Enter*] MACRO.

Mac. Hail to the consuls, and this noble
    senate !
Sej. [*Aside.*] Is Macro here ? O, thou art
    lost, Sejanus !   210
Mac. Sit still, and unaffrighted, reverend
    fathers ;
Macro, by Caesar's grace the new-made pro-
    vost,
And now possest of the praetorian bands,
An honour late belong'd to that proud man,
Bids you be safe : and to your constant doom [2] 215
Of his deservings, offers you the surety
Of all the soldiers, tribunes, and centurions,
Receiv'd in our command.
Reg.   Sejanus, Sejanus,
Stand forth, Sejanus !
Sej.   Am I call'd !
Mac.   Ay, thou,
Thou insolent monster, art bid stand.
Sej.   Why, Macro, 220
It hath been otherwise between you and I ;
This court, that knows us both, hath seen a
    difference,

---

[1] Performed your office.   [2] Firm judgment.

And can, if it be pleas'd to speak, confirm
Whose insolence is most.
Mac.   Come down, Typhoeus.
If mine be most, lo ! thus I make it more ;   225
Kick up thy heels in air, tear off thy robe,
Play with thy beard and nostrils. Thus 't is fit
(And no man take compassion of thy state)
To use th' ingrateful viper, tread his brains
Into the earth.
Reg.   Forbear.
Mac.   If I could lose   230
All my humanity now, 't were well to torture
So meriting a traitor. — Wherefore, fathers,
Sit you amaz'd and silent ; and not censure
This wretch, who, in the hour he first rebell'd
'Gainst Caesar's bounty, did condemn himself ?
Phlegra, the field where all the sons of earth
Muster'd against the gods, did ne'er acknow-
    ledge   237
So proud and huge a monster.
Reg.   Take him hence ;
And all the gods guard Caesar !
Tri.   Take him hence.
Hat. Hence.
Cot.   To the dungeon with him.
San.   He deserves it. 240
Sen. Crown all our doors with bays.
San.   And let an ox,
With gilded horns and garlands, straight be led
Unto the Capitol.
Hat.   And sacrific'd
To Jove, for Caesar's safety.
Tri.   All our gods
Be present still to Caesar !
Cot.   Phoebus.
San.   Mars. 245
Hat. Diana.
San.   Pallas.
Sen.   Juno, Mercury,
All guard him !
Mac.   Forth thou prodigy of men.
                        [*Exit* SEJANUS, *guarded.*]
Cot. Let all the traitor's titles be defac'd.
Tri. His images and statues be pull'd down.
Hat. His chariot-wheels be broken.
Arr.   And the legs
Of the poor horses, that deserved nought,   251
Let them be broken too !
Lep.   O violent change,
And whirl of men's affections !
Arr.   Like, as both
Their bulks and souls were bound on Fortune's
    wheel,
And must act only with her motion.   255
    [*Exeunt all but*] LEPIDUS *and* ARRUN-
                            TIUS.
Lep. Who would depend upon the popular
    air,
Or voice of men, that have to-day beheld
That which, if all the gods had fore-declar'd,
Would not have been believ'd Sejanus' fall ?
He that this morn rose proudly as the sun,   260
And, breaking through a mist of clients'
    breath,
Came on as gaz'd at and admir'd as he,
When superstitious Moors salute his light !
That had our servile nobles waiting him

As common grooms ; and hanging on his look
No less than human life on destiny !   266
That had men's knees as frequent as the gods ;
And sacrifices more than Rome had altars :
And this man fall ! fall ? ay, without a look
That durst appear his friend, or lend so much
Of vain relief, to his chang'd state, as pity ! 271
    Arr. They that before, like gnats, play'd in
        his beams,
And throng'd to circumscribe him, now not
        seen,
Nor deign to hold a common seat with him !
Others, that waited him unto the senate,   275
Now inhumanely ravish him to prison,
Whom but this morn they follow'd as their
        lord !
Guard through the streets, bound like a fugi-
        tive,
Instead of wreaths give fetters, strokes for
        stoops :
Blind shame for honours, and black taunts for
        titles !   280
Who would trust slippery Chance ?
    Lep.   They that would make
Themselves her spoil ; and foolishly forget,
When she doth flatter, that she comes to prey.
Fortune, thou hadst no deity, if men
Had wisdom : we have placed thee so high,   285
By fond belief in thy felicity.
(*Shout within.*) The gods guard Caesar ! All the
        gods guard Caesar !

[*Re-enter* MACRO,] REGULUS, [*and divers*],
        Senators.

    Mac. Now, great Sejanus, you that aw'd the
        state,
And sought to bring the nobles to your whip ;
That would be Caesar's tutor, and dispose   290
Of dignities and offices ! that had
The public head still bare to your designs,
And made the general voice to echo yours !
That look'd for salutations twelve score off,
And would have pyramids, yea, temples, rear'd
To your huge greatness ; now you lie as flat 296
As was your pride advanc'd !¹
    Reg.   Thanks to the gods !
    Sen. And praise to Macro, that hath saved
        Rome !
Liberty, liberty, liberty ! Lead on,
And praise to Macro, that hath saved Rome ! 300
        [*Exeunt all but*] ARRUNTIUS *and* LEPI-
            DUS.
    Arr. I prophesy, out of the senate's flattery,
That this new fellow, Macro, will become
A greater prodigy in Rome than he
That now is fall'n.

        [*Enter* TERENTIUS.]

    Ter.   O you, whose minds are good,
And have not forc'd all mankind from your
        breasts ;   305
That yet have so much stock of virtue left
To pity guilty states, when they are wretched :
Lend your soft ears to hear, and eyes to weep
Deeds done by men, beyond the acts of furies.

        ¹ Raised.

The eager multitude (who never yet   310
Knew why to love or hate, but only pleas'd
T' express their rage of power) no sooner heard
The murmur of Sejanus in decline,
But with that speed and heat of appetite,
With which they greedily devour the way   315
To some great sports, or a new theatre,
They fill'd the Capitol, and Pompey's Cirque
Where, like so many mastiffs biting stones,
As if his statues now were sensitive   319
Of their wild fury ; first, they tear them down ;
Then fast'ning ropes, drag them along the
        streets,
Crying in scorn, " This, this was that rich head
Was crown'd with garlands, and with odours,
        this
That was in Rome so reverenced ! Now
The furnace and the bellows shall to work, 325
The great Sejanus crack, and piece by piece
Drop in the founder's pit."
    Lep.   O popular rage !
    Ter. The whilst the senate at the temple of
        Concord
Make haste to meet again, and thronging cry,
" Let us condemn him, tread him down in water,
While he doth lie upon the bank ; away ! " 331
While some, more tardy, cry unto their bearers,
" He will be censur'd ere we come ; run, knaves,"
And use that furious diligence, for fear
Their bondmen should inform against their
        slackness,   335
And bring their quaking flesh unto the hook.
The rout, they follow with confused voice,
Crying they 're glad, say they could ne'er abide
        him ;
Inquire what man he was, what kind of face,
What beard he had, what nose, what lips ?
        protest   340
They ever did presage he 'd come to this ;
They never thought him wise, nor valiant ; ask
After his garments, when he dies, what death ;
And not a beast of all the herd demands
What was his crime, or who were his accusers,
Under what proof or testimony he fell.   346
There came, says one, a huge long-worded
        letter
From Capreae against him. Did there so ?
O, they are satisfied ; no more.
    Lep.   Alas !
They follow Fortune, and hate men condemn'd,
Guilty or not.
    Arr.   But had Sejanus thriv'd   351
In his design, and prosperously opprest
The old Tiberius ; then, in that same minute,
These very rascals, that now rage like furies,
Would have proclaim'd Sejanus emperor.   356
    Lep. But what hath follow'd ?
    Ter.   Sentence by the senate,
To lose his head ; which was no sooner off,
But that and th' unfortunate trunk were seiz'd
By the rude multitude ; who not content
With what the forward justice of the state 360
Officiously had done, with violent rage
Have rent it limb from limb. A thousand heads,
A thousand hands, ten thousand tongues and
        voices,
Employ'd at once in several acts of malice !

Old men not staid with age, virgins with shame,
Late wives with loss of husbands, mothers of
   children,   366
Losing all grief in joy of his sad fall,
Run quite transported with their cruelty !
These mounting at his head, these at his face,
These digging out his eyes, those with his brain
Sprinkling themselves, their houses and their
   friends ;   371
Others are met, have ravish'd thence an arm,
And deal small pieces of the flesh for favours ;
These with a thigh, this hath cut off his hands,
And this his feet; these fingers, and these
   toes ;   375
That hath his liver, he his heart: there wants
Nothing but room for wrath, and place for
   hatred !
What cannot oft be done, is now o'erdone.
The whole, and all of what was great Sejanus,
And, next to Caesar, did possess the world,   380
Now torn and scatter'd, as he needs no grave
Each little dust covers a little part :
So lies he nowhere, and yet often buried !

[Enter] NUNTIUS.

Arr. More of Sejanus ?
Nun.   Yes.
Lep.   What can be added ?
We know him dead.
Nun.   Then there begin your pity.   385
There is enough behind to melt ev'n Rome,
And Caesar into tears ; since never slave
Could yet so highly offend, but tyranny,
In tormenting him, would make him worth la-
   menting.
A son and daughter to the dead Sejanus,   390
(Of whom there is not now so much remaining
As would give fast'ning to the hangman's
   hook,)
Have they drawn forth for farther sacrifice ;
Whose tenderness of knowledge, unripe years,
And childish silly innocence was such,   395
As scarce would lend them feeling of their
   danger :
The girl so simple, as she often askt
Where they would lead her ? for what cause
   they dragg'd her ?
Cried, she would do no more : that she could
   take
Warning with beating. And because our
   laws   400
Admit no virgin immature to die,
The wittily and strangely cruel Macro
Deliver'd her to be deflower'd and spoil'd
By the rude lust of the licentious hangman,   404
Then to be strangled with her harmless brother.
Lep. O, act most worthy hell, and lasting
   night,
To hide it from the world !
Nun.   Their bodies thrown
Into the Gemonies, (I know not how,

Or by what accident return'd,) the mother,
Th' expulsed [1] Apicata, finds them there ;   410
Whom when she saw lie spread on the degrees, [2]
After a world of fury on herself,
Tearing her hair, defacing of her face,
Beating her breasts and womb, kneeling amaz'd,
Crying to heaven, then to them ; at last,   415
Her drowned voice gat up above her woes,
And with such black and bitter execrations
As might affright the gods, and force the sun
Run backward to the east ; nay, make the old
Deformed chaos rise again, t' o'erwhelm   420
Them, us, and all the world, she fills the air,
Upbraids the heavens with their partial dooms,
Defies their tyrannous powers, and demands,
What she, and those poor innocents have trans-
   gress'd,
That they must suffer such a share in ven-
   geance,   425
Whilst Livia, Lygdus, and Eudemus live,
Who, as she says, and firmly vows to prove it
To Caesar and the senate, poison'd Drusus ?
Lep. Confederates with her husband !
Nun.   Ay.
Lep.   Strange act !
Arr. And strangely open'd. What says now
   my monster,   430
The multitude ? They reel now, do they not ?
Nun. Their gall is gone, and now they 'gin
   to weep
The mischief they have done.
Arr.   I thank 'em, rogues.
Nun. Part are so stupid, or so flexible,
As they believe him innocent ; all grieve :   435
And some, whose hands yet reek with his warm
   blood,
And grip the part which they did tear of him,
Wish him collected and created new.
Lep. How Fortune plies her sports, when she
   begins
To practise 'em ! pursues, continues, adds,   440
Confounds with varying her impassion'd moods !
Arr. Dost thou hope, Fortune, to redeem thy
   crimes,
To make amend for thy ill placed favours,
With these strange punishments ! Forbear,
   you things
That stand upon the pinnacles of state,   445
To boast your slippery height ; when you do
   fall,
You pash [3] yourselves in pieces, ne'er to rise ;
And he that lends you pity, is not wise.
Ter. Let this example move the insolent man
Not to grow proud and careless of the gods.   450
It is an odious wisdom to blaspheme,
Much more to slighten, or deny their powers :
For whom the morning saw so great and high,
Thus low and little, 'fore the even doth lie.

[Exeunt.]

---

[1] Divorced.   [2] Steps.   [3] Dash, bruise.

VOLPONE; OR, THE FOX

BY

BEN JONSON

THE PERSONS OF THE PLAY

VOLPONE, a Magnifico.
MOSCA, his Parasite.
VOLTORE, an Advocate.
CORBACCIO, an old Gentleman.
CORVINO, a Merchant.
BONARIO, a young Gentleman, [son to Corbaccio.]
[SIR] POLITIC WOULD-BE, a Knight.
PEREGRINE, a Gentleman Traveller.
NANO, a Dwarf.
CASTRONE, an Eunuch.
ANDROGYNO, an Hermaphrodite.

Grege [or Mob].
Commandadori, Officers [of Justice.]
Mercatori, three Merchants.
Avocatori, four Magistrates.
Notario, the Register.

Fine Madame WOULD-BE, the Knight's Wife.
CELIA, [Corvino] the Merchant's Wife.

Servitore, a Servant, [two Waiting-] women, &c.

SCENE. — *Venice.*

THE ARGUMENT

V OLPONE, childless, rich, feigns sick, despairs,
O ffers his state to hopes of several heirs,
L ies languishing : his parasite receives
P resents of all, assures, deludes ; then weaves
O ther cross plots, which ope themselves, are told.   5
N ew tricks for safety are sought ; they thrive : when, bold,
E ach tempts th' other again, and all are sold.

PROLOGUE

Now, luck yet send us, and a little wit
   Will serve to make our play hit ;
According to the palates of the season,
   Here is rhyme, not empty of reason.
This we were bid to credit from our poet,   5
   Whose true scope, if you would know it,
In all his poems still hath been this measure,
   To mix profit with your pleasure ;
And not as some, whose throats their envy failing,
   Cry hoarsely, " All he writes is railing : "   10
And when his plays come forth, think they can flout them,
   With saying, he was a year about them.
To this there needs no lie, but this his creature,
   Which was two months since no feature :
And though he dares give them five lives to mend it,   15
   'T is known, five weeks fully penn'd it,
From his own hand, without a coadjutor,
   Novice, journeyman, or tutor.
Yet thus much I can give you as a token
   Of his play's worth, no eggs are broken,   20
Nor quaking custards with fierce teeth affrighted,
   Wherewith your rout are so delighted ;
Nor hales he in a gull, old ends reciting,
   To stop gaps in his loose writing ;
With such a deal of monstrous and forc'd action,   25
   As might make Bethlem [1] a faction :

---

[1] Bedlam ; the madhouse.

Nor made he his play for jests stol'n from each table,
  But makes jests to fit his fable;
And so presents quick comedy refin'd,
  As best critics have design'd;   30
The laws of time, place, persons he observeth,
  From no needful rule he swerveth,
All gall and copperas [1] from his ink he draineth,
  Only a little salt remaineth,
Wherewith he'll rub your cheeks, till, red with laughter,   35
  They shall look fresh a week after.

ACT I

SCENE I. [2]

[Enter] VOLPONE, MOSCA.

Volp. Good morning to the day; and next,
    my gold!
Open the shrine, that I may see my saint.
    [MOSCA *withdraws the curtain, and*
    discovers piles of gold, plate
    jewels, etc.]
Hail the world's soul, and mine! More glad
    than is
The teeming earth to see the long'd-for sun
Peep through the horns of the celestial Ram,   5
Am I, to view thy splendour dark'ning his;
That lying here, amongst my other hoards,
Show'st like a flame by night, or like the day
Struck out of chaos, when all darkness fled
Unto the centre.[3] O thou son of Sol,   10
But brighter than thy father, let me kiss,
With adoration, thee, and every relic
Of sacred treasure in this blessed room.
Well did wise poets, by thy glorious name,
Title that age which they would have the best;
Thou being the best of things, and far tran-
    scending   16
All style of joy, in children, parents, friends,
Or any other waking dream on earth:
Thy looks when they to Venus did ascribe,
They should have given her twenty thousand
    Cupids;   20
Such are thy beauties and our loves! Dear
    saint,
Riches, the dumb god, that giv'st all men
    tongues,
That canst do nought, and yet mak'st men do
    all things;
The price of souls; even hell, with thee to
    boot,   24
Is made worth heaven. Thou art virtue, fame,
Honour, and all things else. Who can get thee,
He shall be noble, valiant, honest, wise —— [4]
    Mos. And what he will, sir. Riches are in
    fortune
A greater good than wisdom is in nature.
    Volp. True, my beloved Mosca. Yet I glory
More in the cunning purchase of my wealth,   31
Than in the glad possession, since I gain

[1] Green vitriol, used in making ink.
[2] A room in Volpone's house.
[3] Centre of the earth.
[4] Gifford and others have noted that in this splendid
speech Jonson is indebted to Pindar, Euripides, and
Horace.

No common way; I use no trade, no venture;
I wound no earth with ploughshares, I fat no
    beasts
To feed the shambles; have no mills for iron,   35
Oil, corn, or men, to grind them into powder;
I blow no subtle glass, expose no ships
To threat'nings of the furrow-faced sea;
I turn no monies in the public bank,
No usure private.
    Mos.   No, sir, nor devour   40
Soft prodigals. You shall ha' some will swal-
    low
A melting heir as glibly as your Dutch
Will pills of butter, and ne'er purge for it;
Tear forth the fathers of poor families
Out of their beds, and coffin them alive   45
In some kind clasping prison, where their bones
May be forthcoming, when the flesh is rotten:
But your sweet nature doth abhor these
    courses;
You loathe the widow's or the orphan's tears
Should wash your pavements, or their piteous
    cries   50
Ring in your roofs, and beat the air for ven-
    geance.
    Volp. Right, Mosca; I do loathe it.
    Mos.   And, besides, sir,
You are not like the thresher that doth stand
With a huge flail, watching a heap of corn,   54
And, hungry, dares not taste the smallest grain,
But feeds on mallows, and such bitter herbs;
Nor like the merchant, who hath fill'd his
    vaults
With Romagnia, rich and Candian wines,
Yet drinks the lees of Lombard's vinegar:
You will not lie in straw, whilst moths and
    worms   60
Feed on your sumptuous hangings and soft
    beds;
You know the use of riches, and dare give now
From that bright heap, to me, your poor ob-
    server,
Or to your dwarf, or your hermaphrodite,
Your eunuch, or what other household trifle   65
Your pleasure allows maintenance —
    Vol.   Hold thee, Mosca,
Take of my hand; thou strik'st on truth in all,
And they are envious term thee parasite.
Call forth my dwarf, my eunuch, and my fool,
And let 'em make me sport.   [*Exit* Mos.]
                    What should I do,   70
But cocker up my genius, and live free
To all delights my fortune calls me to?
I have no wife, no parent, child, ally,
To give my substance to; but whom I make

Must be my heir; and this makes men observe [1]
  me: 75
This draws new clients daily to my house,
Women and men of every sex and age,
That bring me presents, send me plate, coin,
  jewels,
With hope that when I die (which they expect
Each greedy minute) it shall then return 80
Tenfold upon them; whilst some, covetous
Above the rest, seek to engross me whole,
And counter-work the one unto the other,
Contend in gifts, as they would seem in love:
All which I suffer, playing with their hopes, 85
And am content to coin 'em into profit,
And look upon their kindness, and take more,
And look on that; still bearing them in hand,[2]
Letting the cherry knock against their lips,
And draw it by their mouths, and back again.—
How now! 91

SCENE II.[3]

[*To him re-enter*] MOSCA, [*with*] NANO, AN-
DROGYNO, *and* CASTRONE.

Nan. "Now, room for fresh gamesters, who
  do will you to know,
They do bring you neither play nor university
  show;
And therefore do intreat you that whatsoever
  they rehearse,
May not fare a whit the worse, for the false
  pace of the verse.
If you wonder at this, you will wonder more ere
  we pass, 5
For know, here [4] is inclos'd the soul of Pytha-
  goras,
That juggler divine, as hereafter shall follow;
Which soul, fast and loose, sir, came first from
  Apollo,
And was breath'd into Aethalides, Mercurius
  his son,
Where it had the gift to remember all that ever
  was done. 10
From thence it fled forth, and made quick
  transmigration
To goldy-lock'd Euphorbus, who was kill'd in
  good fashion,
At the siege of old Troy, by the cuckold of
  Sparta.
Hermotimus was next (I find it in my charta).
To whom it did pass, where no sooner it was
  missing, 15
But with one Pyrrhus of Delos it learn'd to go
  a-fishing;
And thence did it enter the sophist of Greece.
From Pythagore, she went into a beautiful
  piece,
Hight Aspasia, the meretrix; and the next toss
  of her
Was again of a whore, she became a philosopher,
Crates the cynick, as itself doth relate it: 21
Since kings, knights, and beggars, knaves, lords,
  and fools gat it,

Besides ox and ass, camel, mule, goat, and
  brock,[5]
In all which it hath spoke, as in the cobbler's
  cock.[6] 24
But I come not here to discourse of that matter,
Or his one, two, or three, or his great oath,
  BY QUATER! [7]
His musics, his trigon,[8] his golden thigh,
Or his telling how elements shift; but I
Would ask, how of late thou hast suffer'd
  translation,
And shifted thy coat in these days of reforma-
  tion. 30
And. Like one of the reform'd, a fool, as you
  see,
Counting all old doctrine heresy.
Nan. But not on thine own forbid meats
  hast thou ventur'd?
And. On fish, when first a Carthusian I en-
  ter'd.
Nan. Why, then thy dogmatical silence hath
  left thee? 35
And. Of that an obstreperous lawyer bereft me.
Nan. O wonderful change, when sir lawyer
  forsook thee!
For Pythagore's sake, what body then took thee?
And. A good dull mule.
Nan.   And how! by that means
Thou wert brought to allow of the eating of
  beans? 40
And. Yes.   [thou pass?
Nan.   But from the mule into whom didst
And. Into a very strange beast, by some
  writers call'd an ass;
By others a precise,[9] pure, illuminate brother
Of those devour flesh, and sometimes one
  another;
And will drop you forth a libel, or a sanctifi'd lie,
Betwixt every spoonful of a nativity-pie.[10] 46
Nan. Now quit thee, for heaven, of that
  profane vision.
And gently report thy next transmigration.
And. To the same that I am.
Nan.   A creature of delight,
And, what is more than a fool, an hermaphro-
  dite! 50
Now, prithee, sweet soul, in all thy variation,
Which body wouldst thou choose to keep up
  thy station?
And. Troth, this I am in: even here would
  I tarry.
Nan. 'Cause here the delight of each sex
  thou canst vary?
And. Alas, those pleasures be stale and for-
  saken; 55
No, 'tis your fool wherewith I am so taken,
The only one creature that I can call blessed;
For all other forms I have prov'd most dis-
  tressed.
Nan. Spoke true, as thou wert in Pythagoras
  still.
This learned opinion we celebrate will, 60

[1] Pay obsequious attention to.
[2] Deceiving by false hopes.
[3] The same. The scene divisions are Jonson's.
[4] In Androgyno.

[5] Badger.
[6] This interlude is based on Lucian's dialogue between
a cobbler and a cock.
[7] Quatre, the four in dice.   [9] Puritanical.
[8] A triangular lyre.   [10] Christmas-pie.

Fellow eunuch, as behoves us, with all our wit
        and art,
To dignify that whereof ourselves are so great
        and special a part."
  Volp. Now, very, very pretty! Mosca, this
Was thy invention?
  Mos.   If it please my patron,
Not else.
  Volp. It doth, good Mosca.
  Mos.   Then it was, sir. 65

[NANO and CASTRONE *sing.*]

SONG.

"Fools, they are the only nation
  Worth men's envy or admiration;
  Free from care or sorrow-taking,
  Selves and others merry making:
  All they speak or do is sterling.   70
  Your fool he is your great man's darling,
  And your ladies' sport and pleasure;
  Tongue and bauble are his treasure.
  E'en his face begetteth laughter,
  And he speaks truth free from slaughter;[1] 75
  He 's the grace of every feast,
  And sometimes the chiefest guest;
  Hath his trencher and his stool,
  When wit waits upon the fool.
  O, who would not be   80
  He, he, he?"

                          One knocks without.

  Volp. Who's that? Away! Look, Mosca.
        Fool, begone!
          [*Exeunt* NANO, CAST. *and* ANDRO.]
  Mos. 'Tis Signior Voltore, the advocate;
I know him by his knock.
  Volp.   Fetch me my gown,
My furs, and night-caps; say my couch is
        changing   85
And let him entertain himself awhile
Without i' th' gallery. [*Exit* MOSCA.] Now,
        now my clients
Begin their visitation! Vulture, kite,
Raven, and gorcrow,[2] all my birds of prey, 89
That think me turning carcase, now they come:
I am not for 'em yet.

[*Re-enter* MOSCA, *with the gown, etc.*]

                          How now! the news?
  Mos. A piece of plate, sir.
  Volp.   Of what bigness?
  Mos.   Huge,
Massy, and antique, with your name inscrib'd,
And arms engraven.
  Volp.   Good! and not a fox 94
Stretcht on the earth, with fine delusive sleights,
Mocking a gaping crow? ha, Mosca!
  Mos.   Sharp, sir.
  Volp. Give me my furs.
                          [*Puts on his sick dress.*]
        Why dost thou laugh so, man?
  Mos. I cannot choose, sir, when I apprehend
What thoughts he has without now, as he
        walks: 99
That this might be the last gift he should give,
That this would fetch you; if you died to-day,

And gave him all, what he should be to-morrow;
What large return would come of all his ven-
        tures;   103
How he should worshipp'd be, and reverenc'd;
Ride with his furs, and foot cloths; waited on
By herds of fools and clients; have clear way
Made for his mule, as letter'd as himself;
Be call'd the great and learned advocate: 108
And then concludes, there 's nought impossible.
  Volp. Yes, to be learned, Mosca.
  Mos.   O, no: rich
Implies it. Hood an ass with reverend purple,
So you can hide his two ambitious[3] ears,
And he shall pass for a cathedral doctor.
  Volp. My caps, my caps, good Mosca. Fetch
        him in.   114
  Mos. Stay, sir; your ointment for your eyes.
  Volp.   That's true;
Dispatch, dispatch: I long to have possession
Of my new present.
  Mos.   That, and thousands more,
I hope to see you lord of.
  Volp.   Thanks, kind Mosca.
  Mos. And that, when I am lost in blended
        dust,
And hundreds such as I am, in succession — 120
  Volp. Nay, that were too much, Mosca.
  Mos.   You shall live
Still to delude these harpies.
  Volp.   Loving Mosca!
'T is well: my pillow now, and let him enter.
                              [*Exit* MOSCA.]
Now, my feign'd cough, my phthisic, and my
        gout,
My apoplexy, palsy, and catarrhs,   125
Help, with your forced functions, this my pos-
        ture,
Wherein, this three year, I have milk'd their
        hopes.
He comes; I hear him — Uh! [*coughing*] uh!
        uh! uh! O ——

SCENE III[4]

VOLPONE; [*re-enter* MOSCA, [*introducing*] VOL-
TORE [*with a piece of plate.*]

  Mos. You still are what you were, sir. Only
        you,
Of all the rest, are he commands his love,
And you do wisely to preserve it thus,
With early visitation, and kind notes
Of your good meaning to him, which, I know,   5
Cannot but come most grateful. Patron! sir!
Here 's Signior Voltore is come ——
  Volp. [*Faintly.*]   What say you?
  Mos. Sir, Signior Voltore is come this morn-
        ing
To visit you.
  Volp. I thank him.
  Mos.   And hath brought
A piece of antique plate, bought of St. Mark,[5]
With which he here presents you.

---

[1] With impunity.   [2] Carrion crow.

[3] With a reference to the etymological sense of
"moving round."

[4] The same.

[5] At one of the goldsmith's shops beside St. Mark's.

Volp.   He is welcome. 11
Pray him to come more often.
Mos.   Yes.
Volt.   What says he?
Mos. He thanks you, and desires you see him
often.
Volp. Mosca.
Mos.   My patron!
Volp. Bring him near, where is he?
I long to feel his hand.
Mos.   The plate is here, sir. 15
Volt. How fare you, sir?
Volp.   I thank you, Signior Voltore;
Where is the plate? mine eyes are bad.
Volt. [*putting it into his hands.*]   I 'm sorry
To see you still thus weak.
Mos. [*Aside.*]   That he 's not weaker.
Volp. You are too munificent.
Volt.   No, sir; would to heaven
I could as well give health to you, as that
plate!   20
Volp. You give, sir, what you can; I thank
you. Your love
Hath taste in this, and shall not be unanswer'd:
I pray you see me often.
Volt.   Yes, I shall, sir.
Volp. Be not far from me.
Mos.   Do you observe that, sir?
Volp. Hearken unto me still; it will concern
you.   25
Mos. You are a happy man, sir; know your
good.
Volp. I cannot now last long ——
Mos. (*Aside.*)   You are his heir, sir.
Volt. (*Aside.*) Am I?
Volp.   I feel me going: Uh! uh! uh! uh!
I 'm sailing to my port. Uh! uh! uh! uh!
And I am glad I am so near my haven.   30
Mos. Alas, kind gentleman! Well, we must
all go ——
Volt. But, Mosca ——
Mos.   Age will conquer.
Volt.   Prithee, hear me;
Am I inscrib'd his heir for certain?
Mos.   Are you!
I do beseech you, sir, you will vouchsafe
To write me i' your family. All my hopes   35
Depend upon your worship: I am lost
Except the rising sun do shine on me.
Volt. It shall both shine, and warm thee,
Mosca.
Mos.   Sir,
I am a man that hath not done your love
All the worst offices: here I wear your keys,   40
See all your coffers and your caskets lock'd,
Keep the poor inventory of your jewels,
Your plate, and monies; am your steward, sir,
Husband your goods here.
Volt.   But am I sole heir?
Mos. Without a partner, sir: confirm'd this
morning: 45
The wax is warm yet, and the ink scarce dry
Upon the parchment.
Volt.   Happy, happy me!
By what good chance, sweet Mosca?
Mos.   Your desert, sir;
I know no second cause.

Volt.   Thy modesty
Is loth to know it; well, we shall requite it.   50
Mos. He ever lik'd your course, sir; that
first took him.
I oft have heard him say how he admir'd
Men of your large profession, that could speak
To every cause, and things mere contraries,
Till they were hoarse again, yet all be law;   55
That, with most quick agility, could turn,
And return; [1] make knots, and undo them;
Give forked counsel; take provoking gold
On either hand, and put it up; these men,
He knew, would thrive with their humility.   60
And, for his part, he thought he should be blest
To have his heir of such a suff'ring spirit,
So wise, so grave, of so perplex'd a tongue,
And loud withal, that would not wag, nor
scarce
Lie still, without a fee; when every word   65
Your worship but lets fall, is a chequin! —
                              Another knocks.
Who 's that? one knocks; I would not have
you seen, sir.
And yet — pretend you came and went in haste;
I 'll fashion an excuse — and, gentle sir,
When you do come to swim in golden lard,   70
Up to the arms in honey, that your chin
Is borne up stiff with fatness of the flood,
Think on your vassal; but remember me:
I ha' not been your worst of clients.
Volt.   Mosca! ——
Mos. When will you have your inventory
brought, sir?   75
Or see a copy of the will? — Anon!
I 'll bring them to you, sir. Away, begone,
Put business i' your face.   [*Exit* VOLTORE.]
Volp. [*Springing up.*] Excellent Mosca!
Come hither, let me kiss thee.
Mos.   Keep you still, sir.
Here is Corbaccio.
Volp.   Set the plate away: 80
The vulture 's gone, and the old raven 's come.

SCENE IV. [2]

MOSCA, VOLPONE.

Mos. Betake you to your silence, and your
sleep.
Stand there and multiply. [*Putting the plate to
the rest.*] Now we shall see
A wretch who is indeed more impotent
Than this can feign to be; yet hopes to hop
Over his grave.

                      [*Enter* CORBACCIO.]

                Signior Corbaccio!   5
You 're very welcome, sir.
Corb.   How does your patron?
Mos. Troth, as he did, sir; no amends.
Corb.   What! mends he?
Mos. No, sir: he 's rather worse.
Corb.   That 's well. Where is he?
Mos. Upon his couch, sir, newly fall'n asleep.
Corb. Does he sleep well?

---

[1] Gifford emends to *re-turn; could.*
[2] The same.

Mos.　　　　No wink, sir, all this night, 10
Nor yesterday; but slumbers.
Corb.　　　　Good! he should take
Some counsel of physicians: I have brought
　　him
An opiate here, from mine own doctor.
Mos. He will not hear of drugs.
Corb.　　　　Why? I myself
Stood by while 't was made, saw all th' ingre-
　　dients; 15
And know it cannot but most gently work:
My life for his, 't is but to make him sleep.
Volp. [*Aside.*] Ay, his last sleep, if he would
　　take it.
Mos.　　　Sir,
He has no faith in physic.
Corb.　　　　Say you, say you?
Mos. He has no faith in physic: he does
　　think 20
Most of your doctors are the greater danger,
And worse disease, t' escape. I often have
Heard him protest that your physician
Should never be his heir.
Corb.　　　　Not I his heir?
Mos. Not your physician, sir.
Corb.　　　　O, no, no, no, 25
I do not mean it.
Mos.　　　No, sir, nor their fees
He cannot brook: he says they flay a man
Before they kill him.
Corb.　　　　Right, I do conceive you.
Mos. And then they do it by experiment;
For which the law not only doth absolve 'em,
But gives them great reward: and he is loth 31
To hire his death so.
Corb.　　　　It is true, they kill
With as much licence as a judge.
Mos.　　　　Nay, more;
For he but kills, sir, where the law condemns,
And these can kill him too.
Corb.　　　　Ay, or me; 35
Or any man. How does his apoplex?
Is that strong on him still?
Mos.　　　　Most violent.
His speech is broken, and his eyes are set,
His face drawn longer than 't was wont ——
Corb.　　　　How! how!
Stronger than he was wont?
Mos.　　　No, sir; his face 40
Drawn longer than 't was wont.
Corb.　　　O, good!
Mos.　　　His mouth
Is ever gaping, and his eyelids hang.
Corb.　　　　Good.
Mos. A freezing numbness stiffens all his
　　joints,
And makes the colour of his flesh like lead.
Corb.　　　　'T is good.
Mos. His pulse beats slow, and dull.
Corb.　　　　Good symptoms still. 45
Mos. And from his brain ——
Corb.　　　Ha? How? Not from his brain?
Mos. Yes, sir, and from his brain —
Corb.　　　I conceive you; good.
Mos. Flows a cold sweat, with a continual
　　rheum,
Forth the resolved corners of his eyes.

Corb. Is 't possible? Yet I am better, ha! 50
How does he with the swimming of his head?
Mos. O, sir, 't is past the scotomy;[1] he now
Hath lost his feeling, and hath left to snort:
You hardly can perceive him, that he breathes.
Corb. Excellent, excellent! sure I shall out-
　　last him: 55
This makes me young again, a score of years.
Mos. I was a-coming for you, sir.
Corb.　　　Has he made his will?
What has he giv'n me?
Mos.　　　No, sir.
Corb.　　　Nothing! ha?
Mos. He has not made his will, sir.
Corb.　　　Oh, oh, oh!
What then did Voltore, the lawyer, here? 60
Mos. He smelt a carcase, sir, when he but
　　heard
My master was about his testament;
As I did urge him to it for your good ——
Corb. He came unto him, did he? I thought
　　so.
Mos. Yes, and presented him this piece of
　　plate. 65
Corb. To be his heir?
Mos.　　　I do not know, sir.
Corb.　　　True:
I know it too.
Mos. [*Aside.*] By your own scale, sir.
Corb.　　　Well,
I shall prevent him yet. See, Mosca, look,
Here I have brought a bag of bright chequins,[2]
Will quite lay down his plate.
Mos. [*taking the bag.*]　　Yea, marry, sir. 70
This is true physic, this your sacred medicine;
No talk of opiates to this great elixir!
Corb. 'T is *aurum palpabile*, if not *potabile*.
Mos. It shall be minister'd to him in his bowl.
Corb. Ay, do, do, do.
Mos.　　　Most blessed cordial! 75
This will recover him.
Corb.　　　Yes, do, do, do.
Mos. I think it were not best, sir.
Corb.　　　What?
Mos.　　　To recover him.
Corb. O, no, no, no; by no means.
Mos.　　　Why, sir, this
Will work some strange effect, if he but feel it.
Corb. 'T is true, therefore forbear; I'll take
　　my venture: 80
Give me 't again.
Mos.　　　At no hand: pardon me:
You shall not do yourself that wrong, sir. I
Will so advise you, you shall have it all.
Corb. How?　　　　　　[no man
Mos.　　All, sir; 't is your right, your own;
Can claim a part: 't is yours without a rival, 85
Decreed by destiny.
Corb.　　　How, how, good Mosca?
Mos. I'll tell you, sir. This fit he shall re-
　　cover, —
Corb. I do conceive you.
Mos.　　　And on first advantage
Of his gain'd sense, will I re-importune him

[1] Imperfect sight, with giddiness.
[2] Ital. *zecchino*, a sequin; a coin worth about two dollars.

Unto the making of his testament :   90
And show him this.   [*Pointing to the money.*]
   Corb.   Good, good.
   Mos.   'T is better yet,
If you will hear, sir.
   Corb.   Yes, with all my heart.
   Mos. Now would I counsel you, make home
    with speed ;
There, frame a will ; whereto you shall inscribe
My master your sole heir.
   Corb.   And disinherit 95
My son ?
   Mos. O, sir, the better : for that colour[1]
Shall make it much more taking.
   Corb.   O, but colour ?
   Mos. This will, sir, you shall send it unto me.
Now, when I come to inforce, as I will do,
Your cares, your watchings, and your many
    prayers, 100
Your more than many gifts, your this day's
    present,
And last, produce your will ; where, without
    thought,
Or least regard, unto your proper issue,
A son so brave, and highly meriting,
The stream of your diverted love hath thrown
    you 105
Upon my master, and made him your heir ;
He cannot be so stupid, or stone-dead,
But out of conscience and mere gratitude ——
   Corb. He must pronounce me his ?
   Mos.   'T is true.
   Corb.   This plot
Did I think on before.
   Mos.   I do believe it. 110
   Corb. Do you not believe it ?
   Mos.   Yes, sir,
   Corb.   Mine own project.
   Mos. Which, when he hath done, sir ——
   Corb.   Publish'd me his heir ?
   Mos. And you so certain to survive him ——
   Corb.   Ay.
   Mos. Being so lusty a man ——
   Corb.   'T is true.
   Mos.   Yes, sir ——
   Corb. I thought on that too. See, how he
    should be 115
The very organ to express my thoughts !
   Mos. You have not only done yourself a
    good ——
   Corb. But multipli'd it on my son.
   Mos.   'T is right, sir.
   Corb. Still, my invention.
   Mos.   'Las, sir ! heaven knows,
It hath been all my study, all my care, 120
(I e'en grow gray withal,) how to work
    things ——
   Corb. I do conceive, sweet Mosca.
   Mos.   You are he
For whom I labour here.
   Corb.   Ay, do, do, do :
I 'll straight about it.   [*Going.*]
   Mos. [*Aside.*]   Rook go with you,[2] raven !
   Corb. I know thee honest.
   Mos.   You do lie, sir !

   Corb.   And —— 125
   Mos. Your knowledge is no better than your
    ears, sir.
   Corb. I do not doubt to be a father to thee.
   Mos. Nor I to gull my brother of his blessing.
   Corb. I may ha' my youth restor'd to me,
    why not ?
   Mos. Your worship is a precious ass !
   Corb.   What sayst thou ?
   Mos. I do desire your worship to make haste,
    sir. 131
   Corb. 'T is done, 't is done ; I go.   [*Exit.*]
   Volp. [*leaping from his couch.*] O, I shall
    burst !
Let out my sides, let out my sides ——
   Mos.   Contain
Your flux of laughter, sir : you know this hope
Is such a bait, it covers any hook. 135
   Volp. O, but thy working, and thy placing it !
I cannot hold ; good rascal, let me kiss thee :
I never knew thee in so rare a humour.
   Mos. Alas, sir, I but do as I am taught ;
Follow your grave instructions ; give 'em
    words ; 140
Pour oil into their ears, and send them hence.
   Volp. 'T is true, 't is true. What a rare pun-
    ishment
Is avarice to itself !
   Mos.   Ay, with our help, sir.
   Volp. So many cares, so many maladies,
So many fears attending on old age. 145
Yea, so often call'd on, as no wish
Can be more frequent with 'em, their limbs
    faint,
Their senses dull, their seeing, hearing, going,
All dead before them ; yea, their very teeth,
Their instruments of eating, failing them : 150
Yet this is reckon'd life ! Nay, here was one,
Is now gone home, that wishes to live longer !
Feels not his gout, nor palsy ; feigns himself
Younger by scores of years, flatters his age
With confident belying it, hopes he may 155
With charms like Aeson, have his youth re-
    stor'd ;
And with these thoughts so battens, as if fate
Would be as easily cheated on as he,
And all turns air ! Who 's that there, now ? a
    third !   *Another knocks.*
   Mos. Close, to your couch again ; I hear his
    voice. 160
It is Corvino, our spruce merchant.
   Volp.   [*Lies down as before.*] Dead.
   Mos. Another bout, sir, with your eyes
    [*Anointing them*]. Who 's there ?

SCENE V.[3]

MOSCA, VOLPONE. [*Enter*] CORVINO.

Signior Corvino ! come most wish'd for ! O,
How happy were you, if you knew it, now !
   Corv. Why ? what ? wherein ?
   Mos.   The tardy hour is come, sir.
   Corv. He is not dead ?
   Mos.   Not dead, sir, but as good ;
He knows no man.

     Pretence.   [2] May you be rooked, or cheated.

      [3] The same.

Corv.   How shall I do then?
Mos.   Why, sir? 5
Corv. I have brought him here a pearl.
Mos.   Perhaps he has
So much remembrance left as to know you,
    sir :
He still calls on you ; nothing but your name
Is in his mouth. Is your pearl orient,[1] sir ?
Corv. Venice was never owner of the like. 10
Volp. [*faintly.*] Signior Corvino !
Mos.   Hark !
Volp.   Signior Corvino.
Mos. He calls you ; step and give it him. —
    He 's here, sir.
And he has brought you a rich pearl.
Corv.   How do you, sir ?
Tell him it doubles the twelve carat.
Mos.   Sir,
He cannot understand, his hearing 's gone ; 15
And yet it comforts him to see you ——
Corv.   Say
I have a diamond for him, too.
Mos.   Best show 't, sir ;
Put it into his hand : 't is only there
He apprehends : he has his feeling yet.
See how he grasps it !
Corv.   'Las, good gentleman ! 20
How pitiful the sight is !
Mos.   Tut, forget, sir.
The weeping of an heir should still be laughter
Under a visor.
Corv.   Why, am I his heir ?
Mos. Sir, I am sworn, I may not show the
    will
Till he be dead ; but here has been Corbaccio,
Here has been Voltore, here were others too, 26
I cannot number 'em, they were so many ;
All gaping here for legacies : but I,
Taking the vantage of his naming you,
Signior Corvino, Signior Corvino, took 30
Paper, and pen, and ink, and there I ask'd
    him
Whom he would have his heir ! *Corvino*. Who
Should be executor ? *Corvino*. And
To any question he was silent to,
I still interpreted the nods he made, 35
Through weakness, for consent : and sent home
Nothing bequeath'd them, but to cry and curse.
Corv. O, my dear Mosca. (*They embrace.*)
    Does he not perceive us ?
Mos. No more than a blind harper. He knows
    no man,
No face of friend, nor name of any servant, 40
Who 't was that fed him last, or gave him
    drink :
Not those he hath begotten, or brought up,
Can he remember.
Corv.   Has he children ?
Mos.   Bastards,
Some dozen, or more, that he begot on beggars,
Gypsies, and Jews, and black-moors, when he
    was drunk. 45
Knew you not that, sir ? 't is the common
    fable,

The dwarf, the fool, the eunuch, are all his ;
He 's the true father of his family,
In all save me : — but he has giv'n 'em nothing.
Corv. That 's well, that 's well ! Art sure he
    does not hear us ? 50
Mos. Sure, sir ! why, look you, credit your
    own sense.   [*Shouts in* VOL.'*s ear.*]
The pox approach, and add to your diseases,
If it would send you hence the sooner, sir,
For your incontinence, it hath deserv'd it
Throughly and throughly, and the plague to
    boot ! — 55
You may come near, sir. — Would you would
    once close
Those filthy eyes of yours, that flow with slime
Like two frog-pits ; and those same hanging
    cheeks,
Cover'd with hide instead of skin — Nay, help,
    sir [2] ——
That look like frozen dish-clouts set on end ! 60
Corv. Or like an old smok'd wall, on which
    the rain
Ran down in streaks !
Mos.   Excellent, sir ! speak out :
You may be louder yet ; a culverin
Discharged in his ear would hardly bore it.
Corv. His nose is like a common sewer, still
    running. 65
Mos. 'T is good ! And what his mouth ?
Corv.   A very draught.
Mos. O, stop it up ——
Corv.   By no means.
Mos.   Pray you, let me :
Faith I could stifle him rarely with a pillow
As well as any woman that should keep him.
Corv. Do as you will ; but I 'll begone.
Mos.   Be so ; 70
It is your presence makes him last so long.
Corv. I pray you use no violence.
Mos.   No, sir ! why ?
Why should you be thus scrupulous, pray you,
    sir ?
Corv. Nay, at your discretion.
Mos.   Well, good sir, be gone.
Corv. I will not trouble him now to take [3] my
    pearl. 75
Mos. Puh ! nor your diamond. What a need-
    less care
Is this afflicts you ? Is not all here yours ?
Am not I here, whom you have made your
    creature ?
That owe my being to you ?
Corv.   Grateful Mosca ! 79
Thou art my friend, my fellow, my compan-
    ion,
My partner, and shalt share in all my fortunes.
Mos. Excepting one.
Corv.   What 's that ?
Mos.   Your gallant wife, sir. [*Exit* CORV.]
Now is he gone : we had no other means
To shoot him hence but this.
Volp.   My divine Mosca ! 84
Thou hast to-day outgone thyself. Who 's there ?
                Another knocks.

---

[1] Used for " brilliant " as well as " oriental."

[2] To Corvino, to join in the abuse.

[3] Take from Volpone's hand, which had closed on it.

I will be troubled with no more. Prepare
Me music, dances, banquets, all delights;
The Turk is not more sensual in his pleasures
Than will Volpone. [*Exit* Mos.] Let me see; a pearl!
A diamond! plate! chequins! Good morning's purchase.[1]   90
Why, this is better than rob churches, yet;
Or fat, by eating, once a month, a man ——

[*Re-enter* Mosca.]

Who is 't?
   Mos.   The beauteous Lady Would-be, sir,
Wife to the English knight, Sir Politic Would-be,
(This is the style, sir, is directed me,)   95
Hath sent to know how you have slept to-night,
And if you would be visited?
   Volp.   Not now:
Some three hours hence.
   Mos.   I told the squire[2] so much.
   Volp. When I am high with mirth and wine;
then then: 99
'Fore heaven, I wonder at the desperate valour
Of the bold English, that they dare let loose
Their wives to all encounters!
   Mos.   Sir, this knight
Had not his name for nothing, he is *politic*,
And knows, howe'er his wife affect strange airs,
She hath not yet the face to be dishonest: 105
But had she Signior Corvino's wife's face ——
   Volp. Hath she so rare a face?
   Mos.   O, sir, the wonder,
The blazing star of Italy! a beauty ripe as harvest!
Whose skin is whiter than a swan all over,   110
Than silver, snow, or lilies; a soft lip,
Would tempt you to eternity of kissing!
And flesh that melteth in the touch to blood!
Bright as your gold, and lovely as your gold!
   Volp. Why had not I known this before?
   Mos.   Alas, sir,   115
Myself but yesterday discover'd it.
   Volp. How might I see her?
   Mos.   O, not possible;
She 's kept as warily as is your gold;
Never does come abroad, never takes air
But at a windore. All her looks are sweet,   120
As the first grapes or cherries, and are watch'd
As near as they are.
   Volp.   I must see her.
   Mos.   Sir,
There is a guard of ten spies thick upon her,
All his whole household; each of which is set
Upon his fellow, and have all their charge,   125
When he goes out, when he comes in, examin'd.
   Volp. I will go see her, though but at her windore.
   Mos. In some disguise then.
   Volp.   That is true; I must
Maintain mine own shape still the same: we 'll think.   [*Exeunt.*]

[1] Booty.   [2] Messenger, go-between.

ACT II

Scene I.[3]

[*Enter*] Sir Politic Would-be, *and* Peregrine.

   Sir P. Sir, to a wise man, all the world 's his soil:
It is not Italy, nor France, nor Europe,
That must bound me, if my fates call me forth.
Yet I protest, it is no salt desire
Of seeing countries, shifting a religion,   5
Nor any disaffection to the state
Where I was bred, and unto which I owe
My dearest plots, hath brought me out, much less
That idle, antique, stale, grey-headed project
Of knowing men's minds and manners, with Ulysses!   10
But a peculiar humour of my wife's
Laid for this height of Venice, to observe,
To quote,[4] to learn the language, and so forth ——
I hope you travel, sir, with licence?
   Per.   Yes.
   Sir P. I dare the safelier converse —— How long, sir,   15
Since you left England?
   Per.   Seven weeks.
   Sir P.   So lately!
You have not been with my lord ambassador?
   Per. Not yet, sir.   [climate?
   Sir P. Pray you, what news, sir, vents our
I heard last night a most strange thing reported
By some of my lord's followers, and I long   20
To hear how 't will be seconded.
   Per.   What was 't, sir?
   Sir P. Marry, sir, of a raven that should build
In a ship royal of the king 's.
   Per. [*Aside.*]   This fellow,
Does he gull me, trow? or is gull'd? Your name, sir?
   Sir P. My name is Politic Would-be.
   Per. [*Aside.*]   O, that speaks him.   25
A knight, sir?
   Sir P.   A poor knight, sir.
   Per.   Your lady
Lies[5] here in Venice, for intelligence
Of tires and fashions, and behaviour,
Among the courtesans? The fine Lady Would-be?
   Sir P. Yes, sir; the spider and the bee oft-times   30
Suck from one flower.
   Per.   Good Sir Politic,
I cry you mercy; I have heard much of you:
'T is true, sir, of your raven.
   Sir P.   On your knowledge?
   Per. Yes, and your lion's whelping in the Tower.
   Sir P. Another whelp![6]
   Per.   Another, sir.

[3] St. Mark's Place; a retired corner before Corvino's house.
[4] To make note of.   [5] Stays.
[6] A lion is recorded by Stow to have been born in the Tower of London, Aug. 5, 1604, the first born in captivity in England.

Sir P.　　　　　　　　　Now heaven ! 35
What prodigies be these ? The fires at Berwick!
And the new star ! These things concurring,
　　strange,
And full of omen ! Saw you those meteors ?
Per. I did, sir.
Sir P.　Fearful ! Pray you, sir, confirm me,
Were there three porpoises seen above the
　　bridge,　　　　　　　　　　　40
As they give out ?
Per.　　　　　Six, and a sturgeon, sir.
Sir P. I am astonish'd.
Per.　　　　Nay, sir, be not so ;
I 'll tell you a greater prodigy than these.
Sir P.　What should these things portend ?
Per.　　　　　　　The very day
(Let me be sure) that I put forth from London,
There was a whale discover'd in the river,　46
As high as Woolwich, that had waited there,
Few know how many months, for the subver-
　　sion
Of the Stode fleet.
Sir P.　　Is 't possible ? Believe it,
'T was either sent from Spain, or the arch-
　　duke's :　　　　　　　　　　50
Spinola's whale, upon my life, my credit !
Will they not leave these projects ? Worthy sir,
Some other news.
Per.　　Faith, Stone the fool is dead,
And they do lack a tavern fool extremely.
Sir P. Is Mass Stone dead ?
Per.　　　　He 's dead, sir ; why, I hope 55
You thought him not immortal ? — [*Aside.*] O,
　　this knight,
Were he well known, would be a precious thing
To fit our English stage : he that should write
But such a fellow, should be thought to feign
Extremely, if not maliciously.
Sir P.　　　　　Stone dead ! 60
Per. Dead. — Lord ! how deeply, sir, you ap-
　　prehend it !
He was no kinsman to you ?
Sir P.　　　　That I know of.
Well ! that same fellow was an unknown fool.
Per. And yet you knew him, it seems ?
Sir P.　　　　　I did so. Sir,
I knew him one of the most dangerous heads 65
Living within the state, and so I held him.
Per. Indeed, sir ?
Sir P.　　While he liv'd, in action,
He has receiv'd weekly intelligence,
Upon my knowledge, out of the Low Countries,
For all parts of the world, in cabbages ;　70
And those dispens'd again to ambassadors,
In oranges, musk-melons, apricots,
Lemons, pome-citrons, and such-like ; some-
　　times
In Colchester oysters, and your Selsey cockles.
Per. You make me wonder.
Sir P.　　Sir, upon my knowledge. 75
Nay, I 've observ'd him, at your public ordinary,
Take his advertisement [1] from a traveller,
A conceal'd statesman, in a trencher of meat ;
And instantly, before the meal was done,
Convey an answer in a tooth-pick.

[1] Information.

Per.　　　　　　　Strange ! 80
How could this be, sir ?
Sir P.　　Why, the meat was cut
So like his character, and so laid as he
Must easily read the cipher.
Per.　　　　I have heard,
He could not read, sir.
Sir P.　　So 't was given out,
In policy, by those that did employ him :　85
But he could read, and had your languages,
And to 't, as sound a noddle ——
Per.　　　　I have heard, sir,
That your baboons were spies, and that they
　　were
A kind of subtle nation near to China.
Sir P. Ay, ay, your Mamaluchi. Faith, they
　　had　　　　　　　　　　90
Their hand in a French plot or two ; but they
Were so extremely giv'n to women, as
They made discovery of all : yet I
Had my advices here, on Wednesday last,
From one of their own coat, they were return'd,
Made their relations, as the fashion is,　96
And now stand fair for fresh employment.
Per. [*Aside.*]　　　　　Heart !
This Sir Pol will be ignorant of nothing. ——
It seems, sir, you know all.
Sir P.　　Not all, sir ; but
I have some general notions. I do love　100
To note and to observe : though I live out,
Free from the active torrent, yet I 'd mark
The currents and the passages of things
For mine own private use ; and know the ebbs
And flows of state.
Per.　　Believe it, sir, I hold　105
Myself in no small tie [2] unto my fortunes,
For casting me thus luckily upon you,
Whose knowledge, if your bounty equal it,
May do me great assistance, in instruction
For my behaviour, and my bearing, which　110
Is yet so rude and raw.
Sir P.　　Why ? came you forth
Empty of rules for travel ?
Per.　　Faith, I had
Some common ones, from out that vulgar
　　grammar,
Which he that cri'd Italian to me, taught me.
Sir P. Why, this it is that spoils all our
　　brave bloods,　　　　　　　115
Trusting our hopeful gentry unto pedants,
Fellows of outside, and mere bark. You seem
To be a gentleman of ingenuous race : ——
I not profess it, but my fate hath been
To be, where I have been consulted with,　120
In this high kind, touching some great men's
　　sons,
Persons of blood and honour. ——
Per.　　Who be these, sir ?

SCENE II.

[*To them enter*] MOSCA *and* NANO [*disguised,
followed by persons with materials for erecting
a stage.*]

Mos. Under that window, there 't must be.
The same.

[2] Obligation.

Sir P. Fellows, to mount a bank. Did your instructor
In the dear tongues, never discourse to you
Of the Italian mountebanks?
Per.   Yes, sir.
Sir P.   Why,
Here shall you see one.
Per.   They are quacksalvers,
Fellows that live by venting oils and drugs.   6
Sir P. Was that the character he gave you of them?
Per. As I remember.
Sir P.   Pity his ignorance.
They are the only knowing men of Europe!
Great general scholars, excellent physicians,   10
Most admir'd statesmen, profest favourites
And cabinet counsellors to the greatest princes;
The only languag'd men of all the world!
Per. And, I have heard, they are most lewd [1]
impostors;
Made all of terms and shreds; no less beliers   15
Of great men's favours, than their own vile medicines;
Which they will utter upon monstrous oaths;
Selling that drug for twopence, ere they part,
Which they have valu'd at twelve crowns before.
Sir P. Sir, calumnies are answer'd best with silence.   20
Yourself shall judge. — Who is it mounts, my friends?
Mos. Scoto of Mantua,[2] sir.
Sir P.   Is 't he? Nay, then
I 'll proudly promise, sir, you shall behold
Another man than has been phant'sied [3] to you.
I wonder yet, that he should mount his bank,   25
Here in this nook, that has been wont t' appear
In face of the Piazza! — Here he comes.

[*Enter* VOLPONE, *disguised as a mountebank Doctor, and followed by a crowd of people.*]

Volp. Mount, zany. [*To* NANO.]
Mob. Follow, follow, follow, follow!
Sir P. See how the people follow him! he 's a man   30
May write ten thousand crowns in bank here. Note,

[VOLPONE *mounts the stage.*]

Mark but his gesture: — I do use to observe
The state he keeps in getting up.
Per.   'T is worth it, sir.
Volp. "Most noble gentlemen, and my [34
worthy patrons! It may seem strange that I,
your Scoto Mantuano, who was ever wont to fix
my bank in the face of the public Piazza, near
the shelter of the Portico to the Procuratia,
should now, after eight months' absence from
this illustrious city of Venice, humbly retire [40
myself into an obscure nook of the Piazza."
Sir P. Did not I now object the same?
Per.   Peace, sir.
Volp. "Let me tell you: I am not, as your
Lombard proverb saith, cold on my feet; or

[1] Ignorant.
[2] The name of an Italian juggler who was in England about this time. (Gifford.)
[3] Misrepresented.

content to part with my commodities at a [45
cheaper rate than I am accustom'd: look not
for it. Nor that the calumnious reports of that
impudent detractor, and shame to our profession (Alessandro Buttone, I mean), who gave
out, in public, I was condemn'd *a' sforzato* [4] [50
to the galleys, for poisoning the Cardinal Bem-
bo's — cook, hath at all attach'd, much less dejected me. No, no, worthy gentlemen; to tell
you true, I cannot endure to see the rabble of
these ground *ciarlitani*,[5] that spread their [55
cloaks on the pavement, as if they meant to do
feats of activity, and then come in lamely, with
their mouldy tales out of Boccacio, like stale
Tabarin,[6] the fabulist: some of them discoursing their travels, and of their tedious cap- [60
tivity in the Turk's galleys, when, indeed, were
the truth known, they were the Christian's galleys, where very temperately they eat bread,
and drunk water, as a wholesome penance, enjoin'd them by their confessors, for base pil- [65
feries."
Sir P. Note but his bearing, and contempt of these.
Volp. "These turdy-facy-nasty-paty-lousy-
fartical rogues, with one poor groat's-worth of [69
unprepar'd antimony, finely wrapt up in several
scartoccios,[7] are able, very well, to kill their
twenty a week, and play; yet these meagre,
starv'd spirits, who have half stopt the organs of their minds with earthy oppilations,[8] [74
want not their favourers among your shrivell'd
salad-eating artisans, who are overjoy'd that
they may have their half-pe'rth of physic;
though it purge 'em into another world, 't
makes no matter."
Sir P. Excellent! ha' you heard better language, sir?   80
Volp. "Well, let 'em go. And, gentlemen,
honourable gentlemen, know, that for this time,
our bank, being thus removed from the
clamours of the *canaglia* [9] shall be the scene of
pleasure and delight; for I have nothing [85
to sell, little or nothing to sell."
Sir P. I told you, sir, his end.
Per.   You did so, sir.
Volp. "I protest, I, and my six servants, are
not able to make of this precious liquor so fast
as it is fetch'd away from my lodging by [90
gentlemen of your city; strangers of the Terra
firma;[10] worshipful merchants; ay, and senators
too: who, ever since my arrival, have detain'd
me to their uses, by their splendidous liberali-
ties. And worthily; for, what avails your [95
rich man to have his magazines stuft with *mos*
cadelli, or of the purest grape, when his physicians prescribe him, on pain of death, to drink
nothing but water cocted [11] with aniseeds? O [99

[4] Ital. "With hard labor."
[5] Petty charlatans, impostors.
[6] A French charlatan of the early seventeenth century, whose jests were published.
[7] Folds of paper.
[8] Obstructions.
[9] Rabble.
[10] Continental possessions of Venice. (Gifford.)
[11] Boiled.

health ! health ! the blessing of the rich ! the
riches of the poor ! who can buy thee at too dear
a rate, since there is no enjoying this world without thee ? Be not then so sparing of your
purses, honourable gentlemen, as to abridge the
natural course of life —— "   105
Per. You see his end.
Sir P.   Ay, is 't not good ?
Volp. "For when a humid flux, or catarrh,
by the mutability of air, falls from your head
into an arm or shoulder, or any other part; take
you a ducket, or your chequin of gold, and [110
apply to the place affected : see what good
effect it can work. No, no, 't is this blessed
unguento,[1] this rare extraction, that hath only
power to disperse all malignant humours, that
proceed either of hot, cold, moist, or windy
causes —— "   116
Per. I would he had put in dry too.
Sir P.   Pray you observe.
Volp. "To fortify the most indigest and crude
stomach, ay, were it of one that, through extreme weakness, vomited blood, applying only [120
a warm napkin to the place, after the unction
and fricace ;[2] — for the *vertigine*[3] in the head,
putting but a drop into your nostrils, likewise
behind the ears ; a most sovereign and ap- [124
prov'd remedy ; the *mal caduco*,[4] cramps, con-
vulsions, paralyses, epilepsies, *tremorcordia*, retir'd nerves, ill vapours of the spleen, stoppings
of the liver, the stone, the strangury, *hernia
ventosa*, *iliaca passio* ;[5] stops a *dysenteria* immediately ; easeth the torsion [6] of the small [130
guts ; and cures *melancholia hypocondriaca*, being taken and appli'd, according to my printed
receipt. (*Pointing to his bill and his glass*.) For
this is the physician, this the medicine ; this
counsels, this cures ; this gives the direction, [135
this works the effect ; and, in sum, both together may be term'd an abstract of the theoric
and practic in the Aesculapian art. 'T will cost
you eight crowns. And, — Zan Fritada, prithee
sing a verse extempore in honour of it."   140
Sir P. How do you like him, sir ?
Per.   Most strangely, I !
Sir P. Is not his language rare ?
Per.   But alchemy,
I never heard the like ; or Broughton's [7] books.

[NANO *sings.*]

Had old Hippocrates, or Galen,
That to their books put med'cines all in,   145
But they had known this secret, they had never
(Of which they will be guilty ever)
Been murderers of so much paper,
Or wasted many a hurtless taper ;
No Indian drug had e'er been fam'd,   150
Tobacco, sassafras not nam'd ;
Ne yet of guacum one small stick, sir,
Nor Raymund Lully's [8] great elixir.

---

1 Ointment.   4 Epilepsy.
2 An oil to be rubbed in.   5 Colic.
3 Giddiness.   6 Gripes.
7 An eccentric theologian of the time. See *The Alchemist.*
8 The well-known alchemist of the fourteenth century.

Ne had been known the Danish Gonswart,[9]
Or Paracelsus, with his long sword.[10]   155

Per. All this, yet, will not do ; eight crowns
is high.
Volp. "No more. — Gentlemen, if I had but
time to discourse to you the miraculous effects
of this my oil, surnam'd Oglio del Scoto ; with
the countless catalogue of those I have [160
cur'd of th' aforesaid, and many more diseases;
the patents and privileges of all the princes and
commonwealths of Christendom ; or but the
depositions of those that appear'd on my part,
before the signiory of the Sanita and most [165
learned College of Physicians ; where I was
authoris'd, upon notice taken of the admirable
virtues of my medicaments, and mine own excellency in matter of rare and unknown secrets,
not only to disperse them publicly in this [170
famous city, but in all the territories, that happily joy under the government of the most pious
and magnificent states of Italy. But may
some other gallant fellow say, 'O, there be
divers that make profession to have as good, [175
and as experimented receipts as yours:' indeed,
very many have assay'd, like apes, in imitation
of that, which is really and essentially in me,
to make of this oil ; bestow'd great cost in [179
furnaces, stills, alembics, continual fires, and
preparation of the ingredients (as indeed there
goes to it six hundred several simples, besides
some quantity of human fat, for the conglutina-
tion, which we buy of the anatomists), but when
these practitioners come to the last decoc- [185
tion, blow, blow, puff, puff, and all flies in
fumo :[11] ha, ha, ha ! Poor wretches ! I rather
pity their folly and indiscretion, than their
loss of time and money ; for those may be recover'd by industry : but to be a fool born, is a
disease incurable.   191
"For myself, I always from my youth have
endeavour'd to get the rarest secrets, and book
them, either in exchange, or for money ; I
spar'd nor cost nor labour, where anything [195
was worthy to be learned. And, gentlemen,
honourable gentlemen, I will undertake, by
virtue of chymical art, out of the honourable
hat that covers your head, to extract the four
elements ; that is to say, the fire, air, water, [200
and earth, and return you your felt without burn
or stain. For, whilst others have been at the
ballo,[12] I have been at my book ; and am now
past the craggy paths of study, and come to
the flowery plains of honour and reputation." 205
Sir P. I do assure you, sir, that is his aim.
Volp. "But to our price — "
Per.   And that withal, Sir Pol.
Volp. "You all know, honourable gentlemen,
I never valu'd this *ampulla*, or vial, at less than
eight crowns ; but for this time, I am con- [210
tent to be depriv'd of it for six ; six crowns is
the price, and less in courtesy I know you cannot offer me ; take it or leave it, howsoever.

---

9 Unknown.
10 In the hilt of which he carried his familiar.
11 In smoke.
12 Ball; dancing.

ooth it and I am at your service. I ask you not as
the value of the thing, for then I should de- [215
mand of you a thousand crowns, so the Cardinals Montalto, Fernese, the great Duke of Tus-
cany, my gossip,[1] with divers other princes,
have given me; but I despise money. Only to
show my affection to you, honourable gentle- [220
men, and your illustrious State here, I have
neglected the messages of these princes, mine
own offices, fram'd my journey hither, only to
present you with the fruits of my travels. —[224
Tune your voices once more to the touch of your
instruments, and give the honourable assembly
some delightful recreation."

Per. What monstrous and most painful circumstance
Is here, to get some three or four gazettes,[2]
Some threepence i' the whole! for that 't will
come to.   230

[NANO *sings*.]

You that would last long, list to my song,
Make no more coil, but buy of this oil.
Would you be ever fair and young?
Stout of teeth, and strong of tongue?
Tart of palate? quick of ear?   235
Sharp of sight? of nostril clear?
Moist of hand? and light of foot?
Or, I will come nearer to 't,
Would you live free from all diseases?
Do the act your mistress pleases,   240
Yet fright all aches[3] from your bones?
Here 's a med'cine for the nones.[4]

Volp. "Well, I am in a humour at this time
to make a present of the small quantity my
coffer contains; to the rich in courtesy, and [245
to the poor for God's sake. Wherefore now
mark: I ask'd you six crowns; and six crowns,
at other times, you have paid me; you shall not
give me six crowns, nor five, nor four, nor three,
nor two, nor one; nor half a ducat; no, nor a [250
moccinigo.[5] Sixpence it will cost you, or six hundred pound — expect no lower price, for, by the
banner of my front, I will not bate a bagatine,[6]
— that I will have, only, a pledge of your loves,
to carry something from amongst you, to [255
show I am not contemn'd by you. Therefore,
now, toss your handkerchiefs, cheerfully, cheerfully; and be advertis'd, that the first heroic
spirit that deigns to grace me with a handkerchief, I will give it a little remembrance of [260
something beside, shall please it better than if
I had presented it with a double pistolet."[7]

Per. Will you be that heroic spark, Sir Pol?
CELIA, *at the window, throws down
her handkerchief.*

O, see! the windore has prevented[8] you.

[1] Lit. god-parent; usually, familiar friend.
[2] A small Venetian coin, worth about three farthings.
The name was transferred to the news-sheets bought
for it.
[3] Pron. *aitches*.
[4] For the purpose.
[5] A coin used in Venice, worth about ninepence.
[6] An Italian coin worth about one third of a farthing.
[7] A Spanish coin.
[8] Anticipated.

Volp. "Lady, I kiss your bounty; and for [265
this timely grace you have done your poor Scoto of Mantua, I will return you, over and above
my oil, a secret of that high and inestimable nature, shall make you for ever enamour'd on that
minute, wherein your eye first descended [270
on so mean, yet not altogether to be despis'd,
an object. Here is a powder conceal'd in this
paper, of which, if I should speak to the
worth, nine thousand volumes were but as one
page, that page as a line, that line as a word; [275
so short is this pilgrimage of man (which some
call life) to the expressing of it. Would I reflect
on the price? Why, the whole world is but as
an empire, that empire as a province, that province as a bank, that bank as a private purse [280
to the purchase of it. I will only tell you; it is
the powder that made Venus a goddess (given
her by Apollo), that kept her perpetually young,
clear'd her wrinkles, firm'd her gums, fill'd
her skin, colour'd her hair; from her de- [285
riv'd to Helen, and at the sack of Troy unfortunately lost: till now, in this our age, it was
as happily recover'd, by a studious antiquary,
out of some ruins of Asia, who sent a moiety
of it to the court of France (but much [290
sophisticated), wherewith the ladies there now
colour their hair. The rest, at this present, remains with me; extracted to a quintessence: so
that, wherever it but touches, in youth it perpetually preserves, in age restores the com- [295
plexion; seats your teeth, did they dance like
virginal jacks,[9] firm as a wall: makes them
white as ivory, that were black as ——"

SCENE III.[10]

[*To them enter*] CORVINO.

Cor. Spite o' the devil, and my shame! come
down here;
Come down! — No house but mine to make
your scene?
Signior Flaminio, will you down, sir? down?
What, is my wife your Franciscina, sir?
No windows on the whole Piazza, here,   5
To make your properties, but mine? but mine?

Beats away [VOLPONE, NANO, *etc.*]
Heart! ere to-morrow I shall be new christen'd,
And called the Pantalone di Besogniosi,[11]
About the town.
Per.   What should this mean, Sir Pol?
Sir P. Some trick of state, believe it; I will
home.   10
Per. It may be some design on you.
Sir P.   I know not.
I 'll stand upon my guard.
Per.   It is your best, sir.
Sir P. This three weeks, all my advices, all
my letters,
They have been intercepted.
Per.   Indeed, sir!
Best have a care.
Sir P.   Nay, so I will.

[9] Small pieces of wood to which were attached the
quills which struck the strings of the virginal.
[10] The same.   [11] Ital. "Fool of the Beggars."

Per.   This knight, 15
I may not lose him, for my mirth, till night.
                                              [*Exeunt.*]

Scene IV.[1]

[*Enter*] VOLPONE, MOSCA.

Volp. O, I am wounded !
Mos.   Where, sir ?
Volp.   Not without ;
Those blows were nothing : I could bear them
        ever.
But angry Cupid, bolting from her eyes,
Hath shot himself into me like a flame ;
Where now he flings about his burning heat, 5
As in a furnace an ambitious fire
Whose vent is stopt. The fight is all within
        me.
I cannot live, except thou help me, Mosca ;
My liver melts, and I, without the hope
Of some soft air from her refreshing breath, 10
Am but a heap of cinders.
Mos.   'Las, good sir,
Would you had never seen her !
Volp.   Nay, would thou
Hadst never told me of her !
Mos.   Sir, 't is true ;
I do confess I was unfortunate,
And you unhappy ; but I 'm bound in con-
        science,   15
No less than duty, to effect my best
To your release of torment, and I will, sir.
Volp. Dear Mosca, shall I hope ?
Mos.   Sir, more than dear,
I will not bid you to despair of aught
Within a human compass.
Volp.   O, there spoke 20
My better angel. Mosca, take my keys,
Gold, plate, and jewels, all 's at thy devotion ;
Employ them how thou wilt : nay, coin me
        too :
So thou in this but crown my longings, Mosca.
Mos. Use but your patience.
Volp.   So I have.
Mos.   I doubt not. 25
To bring success to your desires.
Volp.   Nay, then,
I not repent me of my late disguise.
Mos. If you can horn him, sir, you need not.
Volp.   True :
Besides, I never meant him for my heir.
Is not the colour o' my beard and eyebrows 30
To make me known ?
Mos.   No jot.
Volp.   I did it well.
Mos. So well, would I could follow you in
        mine,
With half the happiness ! and yet I would
Escape your epilogue.[2]
Volp.   But were they gull'd
With a belief that I was Scoto ?
Mos.   Sir, 35
Scoto himself could hardly have distinguish'd !
I have not time to flatter you now ; we 'll part :
And as I prosper, so applaud my art. [*Exeunt.*]

----

    [1] A room in Volpone's house.
    [2] *I. e.* the beating from Corvino.

Scene V.[3]

[*Enter*] CORVINO, [*with his sword in his hand,
        dragging in*] CELIA.

Corv. Death of mine honour, with the city's
        fool !
A juggling, tooth-drawing, prating mounte-
        bank !
And at a public windore ! where, whilst he,
With his strain'd action, and his dole of faces,[4]
To his drug-lecture draws your itching ears, 5
A crew of old, unmarri'd, noted lechers,
Stood leering up like satyrs : and you smile
Most graciously, and fan your favours forth,
To give your hot spectators satisfaction !
What, was your mountbank their call ? their
        whistle ?   10
Or were you enamour'd on his copper rings,
His saffron jewel, with the toad-stone in 't,
Or his embroid'red suit, with the cope-stitch,
Made of a hearse cloth ? or his old tilt-feather ?
Or his starch'd beard ! Well, you shall have
        him, yes !   15
He shall come home, and minister unto you
The fricace for the mother.[5] Or, let me see,
I think you 'd rather mount ; would you not
        mount ?
Why, if you 'll mount, you may ; yes, truly,
        you may !
And so you may be seen, down to the foot. 20
Get you a cittern, Lady Vanity,
And be a dealer with the virtuous man ;
Make one. I 'll but protest myself a cuckold,
And save your dowry. I 'm a Dutchman, I !
For if you thought me an Italian,   25
You would be damn'd ere you did this, you
        whore !
Thou 'dst tremble to imagine that the murder
Of father, mother, brother, all thy race,
Should follow, as the subject of my justice.
Cel. Good sir, have patience.
Corv.   What couldst thou propose [6] 30
Less to thyself, than in this heat of wrath,
And stung with my dishonour, I should strike
This steel into thee, with as many stabs
As thou wert gaz'd upon with goatish eyes ?
Cel. Alas, sir, be appeas'd ! I could not think
My being at the windore should more now 36
Move your impatience than at other times.
Corv. No ! not to seek and entertain a parley
With a known knave, before a multitude !
You were an actor with your handkerchief, 40
Which he most sweetly kist in the receipt,
And might, no doubt, return it with a letter,
And point the place where you might meet ;
        your sister's,
Your mother's, or your aunt's might serve the
        turn.
Cel. Why, dear sir, when do I make these
        excuses,   45
Or ever stir abroad, but to the church ?
And that so seldom ——
Corv.   Well, it shall be less ;
And thy restraint before was liberty,

----

    [3] A room in Corvino's house.   [5] Hysteria.
    [4] Grimaces.   [6] Expect.

To what I now decree: and therefore mark
　me.
First, I will have this bawdy light damm'd
　up; 　　　　　　　　　　　　　　50
And till 't be done, some two or three yards
　off,
I 'll chalk a line; o'er which if thou but chance
To set thy desp'rate foot, more hell, more
　horror,
More wild remorseless rage shall seize on thee,
Than on a conjuror that had heedless left 　55
His circle's safety ere his devil was laid.
Then here 's a lock which I will hang upon
　thee,
And, now I think on 't, I will keep thee back-
　wards;
Thy lodging shall be backwards: thy walks
　backwards;
Thy prospect, all be backwards; and no plea-
　sure, 　　　　　　　　　　　　　　60
That thou shalt know but backwards: nay,
　since you force
My honest nature, know, it is your own,
Being too open, makes me use you thus:
Since you will not contain your subtle nostrils
In a sweet room, but they must snuff the air 　65
Of rank and sweaty passengers. (Knock within.)
　One knocks.
Away, and be not seen, pain of thy life;
Nor look toward the windore; if thou dost ——
Nay, stay, hear this —— let me not prosper,
　whore,
But I will make thee an anatomy, 　　70
Dissect thee mine own self, and read a lecture
Upon thee to the city, and in public.
Away! —　　　　　　　　　[Exit CELIA.]

　　　　　[Enter SERVANT.]

　　　Who 's there?
Ser.　　　　　'T is Signior Mosca, sir.

　　　SCENE VI.[1]

　　CORVINO. Enter MOSCA.

Corv. Let him come in. His master 's dead;
　there 's yet
Some good to help the bad. —— My Mosca, wel-
　come!
I guess your news.
　Mos.　　　　I fear you cannot, sir.
　Corv. Is 't not his death?
　Mos.　　　　Rather the contrary.
　Corv. Not his recovery?
　Mos.　　　　Yes, sir.
　Corv.　　　　I am curs'd, 　5
I am bewitch'd, my crosses meet to vex me.
How? how? how? how?
　Mos.　　　　Why, sir, with Scoto's oil;
Corbaccio and Voltore brought of it,
Whilst I was busy in an inner room ——
　Corv. Death! that damn'd mountebank! but
　for the law 　　　　　　　　　　10
Now, I could kill the rascal: it cannot be
His oil should have that virtue. Ha' not I
Known him a common rogue, come fiddling
　in

　　　　　1 The same.

To the osteria,[2] with a tumbling whore,
And, when he has done all his forc'd tricks,
　been glad 　　　　　　　　　　　15
Of a poor spoonful of dead wine, with flies
　in 't?
It cannot be. All his ingredients
Are a sheep's gall, a roasted bitch's marrow,
Some few sod [3] earwigs, pounded caterpillars,
A little capon's grease, and fasting spittle: 　20
I know them to a dram.
　Mos.　　　　I know not, sir;
But some on 't, there, they pour'd into his ears,
Some in his nostrils, and recover'd him;
Applying but the fricace.
　Corv.　　　　Pox o' that fricace!
　Mos. And since, to seem the more officious 　25
And flatt'ring of his health, there, they have had,
At extreme fees, the college of physicians
Consulting on him, how they might restore
　him;
Where one would have a cataplasm [4] of spices,
Another a flay'd ape clapp'd to his breast, 　30
A third would have it a dog, a fourth an oil,
With wild cats' skins: at last, they all resolv'd
That to preserve him, was no other means
But some young woman must be straight sought
　out,
Lusty, and full of juice, to sleep by him; 　35
And to this service most unhappily,
And most unwillingly, am I now employ'd,
Which here I thought to pre-acquaint you with,
For your advice, since it concerns you most;
Because I would not do that thing might cross
Your ends, on whom I have my whole depend-
　ence, sir; 　　　　　　　　　　41
Yet, if I do it not they may delate [5]
My slackness to my patron, work me out
Of his opinion; and there all your hopes,
Ventures, or whatsoever, are all frustrate! 　45
I do but tell you, sir. Besides, they are all
Now striving who shall first present him; there-
　fore ——
I could entreat you, briefly conclude somewhat;
Prevent 'em if you can.
　Corv.　　　　Death to my hopes,
This is my villanous fortune! Best to hire 　50
Some common courtesan.
　Mos.　　　　Ay, I thought on that, sir;
But they are all so subtle, full of art —
And age again doting and flexible,
So as — I cannot tell — we may, perchance,
Light on a quean may cheat us all.
　Corv.　　　　'T is true. 　55
　Mos. No, no: it must be one that has no
　tricks, sir,
Some simple thing, a creature made [6] unto it;
Some wench you may command. Ha' you no
　kinswoman?
Gods so — Think, think, think, think, think,
　think, think, sir.
One o' the doctors offer'd there his daughter.
　Corv. How?
　Mos.　　　　Yes, Signior Lupo, the physician. 　61
　Corv. His daughter!

　　2 The inn.　　　4 Poultice.　　　6 Prepared.
　　3 Boiled.　　　5 Accuse.

Mos.   And a virgin, sir. Why, alas,
He knows the state of 's body, what it is :
That nought can warm his blood, sir, but a fe-
    ver ;
Nor any incantation raise his spirit :   65
A long forgetfulness hath seiz'd that part.
Besides, sir, who shall know it ? Some one or
    two —
    Corv. I pray thee give me leave. [*Walks
        aside.*] If any man
But I had had this luck — The thing in 't self,
I know, is nothing. — Wherefore should not
    I   70
As well command my blood and my affections
As this dull doctor ? In the point of honour,
The cases are all one of wife and daughter.
    Mos. [*Aside.*] I hear him coming.[1]
    Corv.   She shall do 't : 't is done.
Slight ! if this doctor, who is not engag'd,   75
Unless 't be for his counsel, which is nothing,
Offer his daughter, what should I, that am
So deeply in ? I will prevent him : Wretch !
Covetous wretch ! — Mosca, I have determin'd.
    Mos. How, sir ?   [wot of 80
    Corv.   We 'll make all sure. The party you
Shall be mine own wife, Mosca.
    Mos.   Sir, the thing,
But that I would not seem to counsel you,
I should have motion'd [2] to you, at the first :
And make your count,[3] you have cut all their
    throats.[4]
Why, 't is directly taking a possession !   85
And in his next fit, we may let him go.
'T is but to pull the pillow from his head,
And he is throttled : it had been done before
But for your scrupulous doubts.
    Corv.   Ay, a plague on 't,
My conscience fools my wit ! Well, I 'll be
    brief,   90
And so be thou, lest they should be before us.
Go home, prepare him, tell him with what
    zeal
And willingness I do it : swear it was
On the first hearing, as thou mayst do, truly,
Mine own free motion.
    Mos.   Sir, I warrant you, 95
I 'll so possess him with it, that the rest
Of his starv'd clients shall be banish'd all ;
And only you receiv'd. But come not, sir,
Until I send, for I have something else
To ripen for your good, you must not know 't.
    Corv. But do not you forget to send now.
    Mos.   Fear not. [*Exit.*]   101

[Scene VII.] [5]

Corvino.

    Corv. Where are you, wife ? My Celia !
        wife !

[*Enter* Celia.]

                    — What, blubb'ring ?
Come, dry those tears. I think thou thought'st
    me in earnest ;

---

1 Coming into my trap.   2 Proposed.
3 Reckon on it.   4 Outdone them all.   5 The same.

Ha ! by this light I talk'd so but to try thee :
Methinks, the lightness of the occasion
Should have confirm'd thee. Come, I am not
    jealous.   5
    Cel. No ?
    Corv.   Faith I am not, I, nor never was ;
It is a poor unprofitable humour.
Do not I know, if women have a will,
They 'll do 'gainst all the watches o' the
    world,
And that the fiercest spies are tam'd with gold ?
Tut, I am confident in thee, thou shalt see 't ; 11
And see I 'll give thee cause too, to believe it.
Come kiss me. Go, and make thee ready
    straight,
In all thy best attire, thy choicest jewels,
Put 'em all on, and, with 'em, thy best
    looks :   15
We are invited to a solemn feast,
At old Volpone's, where it shall appear
How far I am free from jealousy or fear.
                              [*Exeunt.*]

ACT III

Scene I.[6]

[*Enter*] Mosca.

    Mos. I fear I shall begin to grow in love
With my dear self, and my most prosp'rous
    parts,
They do so spring and burgeon ; I can feel
A whimsy i' my blood : I know not how,
Success hath made me wanton. I could skip   5
Out of my skin now, like a subtle snake,
I am so limber. O ! your parasite
Is a most precious thing, dropt from above,
Not bred 'mongst clods and clodpoles, here on
    earth.
I muse, the mystery [7] was not made a science, 10
It is so liberally profest ! Almost
All the wise world is little else, in nature,
But parasites or sub-parasites. And yet
I mean not those that have your bare town-art,
To know who 's fit to feed them ; have no
    house,   15
No family, no care, and therefore mould
Tales for men's ears, to bait that sense ; or get
Kitchen-invention, and some stale receipts
To please the belly, and the groin ; nor those,
With their court dog-tricks, that can fawn and
    fleer,   20
Make their revenue out of legs [8] and faces,
Echo my lord, and lick away a moth :
But your fine elegant rascal, that can rise
And stoop, almost together, like an arrow ;
Shoot through the air as nimbly as a star ;   25
Turn short as doth a swallow ; and be here,
And there, and here, and yonder, all at once ;
Present to any humour, all occasion ;
And change a visor swifter than a thought ! 29
This is the creature had the art born with him ;
Toils not to learn it, but doth practise it
Out of most excellent nature : and such sparks
Are the true parasites, others but their zanies.

---

6 A street.   7 Profession.   8 Bows.

SCENE II.[1]

MOSCA. [*Enter*] BONARIO.

Who 's this? Bonario, old Corbaccio's son?
The person I was bound to seek. Fair sir,
You are happ'ly met.
    Bon.   That cannot be by thee.
    Mos. Why, sir?   [leave me:
    Bon.   Nay, pray thee know thy way, and
I would be loth to interchange discourse   5
With such a mate[2] as thou art.
    Mos.   Courteous sir,
Scorn not my poverty.
    Bon.   Not I, by heaven;
But thou shalt give me leave to hate thy baseness.
    Mos. Baseness!
    Bon.   Ay; answer me, is not thy sloth
Sufficient argument? thy flattery?   10
Thy means of feeding?
    Mos.   Heaven be good to me!
These imputations are too common, sir,
And easily stuck on virtue when she 's poor.
You are unequal[3] to me, and however
Your sentence may be righteous, yet you are not,   15
That, ere you know me, thus proceed in censure:
St. Mark bear witness 'gainst you, 't is inhuman.
               [*Weeps.*]
    Bon. [*Aside.*] What! does he weep? the sign
is soft and good:
I do repent me that I was so harsh.
    Mos. 'T is true, that, sway'd by strong necessity,   20
I am enforc'd to eat my careful bread
With too much obsequy; 't is true, beside,
That I am fain to spin mine own poor raiment
Out of my mere observance, being not born
To a free fortune: but that I have done   25
Base offices, in rending friends asunder,
Dividing families, betraying counsels,
Whisp'ring false lies, or mining men with praises,
Train'd their credulity with perjuries,
Corrupted chastity, or am in love   30
With mine own tender ease, but would not rather
Prove the most rugged and laborious course,
That might redeem my present estimation,
Let me here perish, in all hope of goodness.
    Bon. [*Aside.*] This cannot be a personated
passion. —   35
I was to blame, so to mistake thy nature;
Prithee forgive me: and speak out thy business.
    Mos. Sir, it concerns you; and though I may seem
At first to make a main offence in manners,
And in my gratitude unto my master,   40
Yet for the pure love which I bear all right,
And hatred of the wrong, I must reveal it.
This very hour your father is in purpose
To disinherit you ——
    Bon.   How!
    Mos.   And thrust you forth,

As a mere stranger to his blood: 't is true, sir.
The work no way engageth me, but as   45
I claim an interest in the general state
Of goodness and true virtue, which I hear
T' abound in you; and for which mere respect,
Without a second aim, sir, I have done it.   50
    Bon. This tale hath lost thee much of the
late trust
Thou hadst with me; it is impossible.
I know not how to lend it any thought,
My father should be so unnatural.
    Mos. It is a confidence that well becomes   55
Your piety; and form'd, no doubt, it is
From your own simple innocence: which makes
Your wrong more monstrous and abhorr'd. But,
sir,
I now will tell you more. This very minute,
It is, or will be doing; and if you   60
Shall be but pleas'd to go with me, I 'll bring
you,
I dare not say where you shall see, but where
Your ear shall be a witness of the deed;
Hear yourself written bastard, and profest
The common issue of the earth.
    Bon.   I 'm maz'd!   65
    Mos. Sir, if I do it not, draw your just sword,
And score your vengeance on my front and
face;
Mark me your villain: you have too much
wrong,
And I do suffer for you, sir. My heart   69
Weeps blood in anguish ——
    Bon.   Lead; I follow thee. [*Exeunt.*]

SCENE III.[4]

[*Enter*] VOLPONE, NANO, ANDROGYNO, CASTRONE.

    Volp. Mosca stays long, methinks. — Bring
forth your sports,
And help to make the wretched time more
sweet.
    Nan. "Dwarf, fool, and eunuch, well met
here we be.
A question it were now, whether of us three,
Being all the known delicates of a rich man,   5
In pleasing him, claim the precedency can?"
    Cas. "I claim for myself."
    And.   "And so doth the fool."
    Nan. "'T is foolish indeed: let me set you
both to school.
First for your dwarf, he 's little and witty,
And everything, as it is little, is pretty;   10
Else why do men say to a creature of my shape,
So soon as they see him, 'It 's a pretty little
ape'?
And why a pretty ape, but for pleasing imitation
Of greater men's actions, in a ridiculous fashion?   14
Beside, this feat[5] body of mine doth not crave
Half the meat, drink, and cloth, one of your
bulks will have.
Admit your fool's face be the mother of laughter,

Yet, for his brain, it must always come after:
And though that do feed him, it's a pitiful case,
His body is beholding to such a bad face."   20
                                   One knocks.
Volp. Who's there? My couch; away! look!
      Nano, see: [*Exeunt* AND. *and* CAS.]
Give me my caps first — go, inquire. [*Exit*
      NANO.] Now, Cupid
Send it be Mosca, and with fair return!
      Nan. [*within.*] It is the beauteous madam —
Volp.   Would-be — is it?
Nan. The same.
Volp. Now torment on me! Squire her in; 25
For she will enter, or dwell here for ever:
Nay, quickly. [*Retires to his couch.*] That my fit
      were past! I fear
A second hell too, that my loathing this
Will quite expel my appetite to the other:
Would she were taking now her tedious leave.
Lord, how it threats me what I am to suffer! 31

SCENE IV.[1]

[*To him enter*] NANO, LADY POLITIC WOULD-BE.

Lady P. I thank you, good sir. Pray you
      signify
Unto your patron I am here. — This band
Shows not my neck enough. — I trouble you, sir;
Let me request you bid one of my women
Come hither to me. In good faith, I am drest 5
Most favourably to-day! It is no matter:
'T is well enough.

            [*Enter* 1 Waiting-woman.]

            Look, see these petulant things,
How they have done this!
Volp.   [*Aside.*] I do feel the fever
Ent'ring in at mine ears; O, for a charm,
To fright it hence!
Lady P.   Come nearer: is this curl 10
In his right place, or this? Why is this higher
Than all the rest? You ha' not wash'd your
      eyes yet!
Or do they not stand even i' your head?
Where is your fellow? call her. [*Exit* 1 Woman.]
Nan.   Now, St. Mark
Deliver us! anon she'll beat her women,   15
Because her nose is red.

            [*Re-enter* 1 *with* 2 Woman.]

Lady P.   I pray you view
This tire,[2] forsooth: are all things apt, or no?
1 *Wom.* One hair a little here sticks out, for-
      sooth.
Lady P. Does 't so, forsooth! and where was
      your dear sight,
When it did so, forsooth! What now! bird-
      ey'd?[3]   20
And you, too? Pray you, both approach and
      mend it.
Now, by that light I muse you 're not asham'd!
I, that have preach'd these things so oft unto
      you,
Read you the principles, argu'd all the grounds,
Disputed every fitness, every grace,   25

Call'd you to counsel of so frequent dressings —
Nan. (*Aside.*) More carefully than of your
      fame or honour.
Lady P. Made you acquainted what an ample
      dowry
The knowledge of these things would be unto
      you,
Able alone to get you noble husbands   30
At your return: and you thus to neglect it!
Besides, you seeing what a curious nation
Th' Italians are, what will they say of me?
"The English lady cannot dress herself."
Here's a fine imputation to our country!   35
Well, go your ways, and stay i' the next room.
This fucus[4] was too coarse too; it's no matter.—
Good sir, you 'll give 'em entertainment?
            [*Exeunt* NANO *and* Waiting-women.]
Volp. The storm comes toward me.   [*pone*?
Lady P. [*Goes to the couch.*] How does my Vol-
Volp. Troubl'd with noise, I cannot sleep; I
      dreamt   40
That a strange fury ent'red now my house,
And, with the dreadful tempest of her breath,
Did cleave my roof asunder.
Lady P.   Believe me, and I
Had the most fearful dream, could I remem-
      ber 't —
Volp. [*Aside.*] Out on my fate! I have given
      her the occasion   45
How to torment me: she will tell me hers.
Lady P. Methought the golden mediocrity,
Polite, and delicate ——
Volp.   O, if you do love me,
No more: I sweat, and suffer, at the mention
Of any dream; feel how I tremble yet.   50
Lady P. Alas, good soul! the passion of the
      heart.
Seed-pearl were good now, boil'd with syrup of
      apples,
Tincture of gold, and coral, citron-pills,
Your elecampane[5] root, myrobalanes[6] ——
Volp. Ay me, I have ta'en a grasshopper by
      the wing!7   55
Lady P. Burnt silk and amber. You have
      muscadel
Good i' the house ——
Volp.   You will not drink, and part?
Lady P. No, fear not that. I doubt we shall
      not get
Some English saffron, half a dram would
      serve;   59
Your sixteen cloves, a little musk, dried mints;
Bugloss, and barley-meal ——
Volp.   [*Aside.*] She's in again!
Before I feign'd diseases, now I have one.
Lady P. And these appli'd with a right
      scarlet cloth.
Volp. [*Aside.*] Another flood of words! a
      very torrent!
Lady P. Shall I, sir, make you a poultice?
Volp.   No, no, no.   65
I'm very well, you need prescribe no more.

---

1 The same.   2 Head-dress.   3 Short-sighted(?)

4 Paint for the face.
5 Horse-heal, a medicinal herb.
6 An astringent kind of plum.
7 "The faster you hold them by the wings, the louder
they scream."

Lady P. I have a little studied physic; but now
I 'm all for music, save, i' the forenoons,
An hour or two for painting. I would have
A lady, indeed, to have all letters and arts,   70
Be able to discourse, to write, to paint,
But principal, as Plato holds, your music,
And so does wise Pythagoras, I take it,
Is your true rapture: when there is concent 1
In face, in voice, and clothes: and is, indeed, 75
Our sex's chiefest ornament.
    Volp.   The poet
As old in time as Plato, and as knowing,
Says that your highest female grace is silence.
    Lady P. Which of your poets? Petrarch, or
        Tasso, or Dante?
Guarini? Ariosto? Aretine?   80
Cieco di Hadria? I have read them all.
    Volp. [*Aside.*] Is everything a cause to my
        destruction?
    Lady P. I think I have two or three of 'em
        about me.
    Volp. [*Aside.*] The sun, the sea, will sooner
        both stand still   84
Than her eternal tongue! nothing can scape it.
    Lady P. Here 's Pastor Fido ——
    Volp.   [*Aside.*] Profess obstinate silence;
That 's now my safest.
    Lady P.   All our English writers,
I mean such as are happy in th' Italian,
Will deign to steal out of this author, mainly;
Almost as much as from Montagnié: 90
He has so modern and facile a vein,
Fitting the time, and catching the court-ear!
Your Petrarch is more passionate, yet he,
In days of sonnetting, trusted 'em with much:
Dante is hard, and few can understand him. 95
But for a desperate wit, there 's Aretine;
Only his pictures are a little obscene ——
You mark me not.
    Volp.   Alas, my mind 's perturb'd.
    Lady P. Why, in such cases, we must cure
        ourselves,
Make use of our philosophy ——
    Volp.   Oh me!   100
    Lady P. And as we find our passions do
        rebel,
Encounter them with reason, or divert 'em,
By giving scope unto some other humour
Of lesser danger: as, in politic bodies,
There 's nothing more doth overwhelm the
        judgment,   105
And cloud the understanding, than too much
Settling and fixing, and, as 't were, subsiding
Upon one object. For the incorporating
Of these same outward things, into that part
Which we call mental, leaves some certain
        faeces   110
That stop the organs, and, as Plato says,
Assassinate our knowledge.
    Volp.   [*Aside.*] Now, the spirit
Of patience help me!
    Lady P.   Come, in faith, I must
Visit you more a days; and make you well:
Laugh and be lusty.

        1 Harmony.

    Volp. [*Aside.*] My good angel save me! 115
    Lady P. There was but one sole man in all
        the world
With whom I e'er could sympathise; and he
Would lie you, often, three, four hours together
To hear me speak; and be sometime so rapt,
As he would answer me quite from the pur-
        pose,   120
Like you, and you are like him, just. I 'll dis-
        course,
An 't be but only, sir, to bring you asleep,
How we did spend our time and loves together,
For some six years.
    Volp.   Oh, oh, oh, oh, oh, oh!
    Lady P. For we were coaetanei,2 and brought
        up ——   125
    Volp. Some power, some fate, some fortune
        rescue me!

SCENE V.3

[*To them enter*] MOSCA.

    Mos. God save you, madam!
    Lady P.   Good sir.
    Volp.   Mosca! welcome,
Welcome to my redemption.
    Mos.   Why, sir?
    Volp.   Oh,
Rid me of this my torture, quickly, there;
My madam with the everlasting voice:
The bells, in time of pestilence, ne'er made   5
Like noise, or were in that perpetual motion!
The Cock-pit comes not near it. All my house,
But now, steam'd like a bath with her thick
        breath,
A lawyer could not have been heard; nor scarce
Another woman, such a hail of words   10
She has let fall. For hell's sake, rid her hence.
    Mos. Has she presented?
    Volp.   Oh, I do not care;
I 'll take her absence upon any price,
With any loss.
    Mos.   Madam ——
    Lady P.   I ha' brought your patron
A toy, a cap here, of mine own work.
    Mos.   'T is well. 15
I had forgot to tell you I saw your knight
Where you would little think it.——
    Lady P.   Where?
    Mos.   Marry,
Where yet, if you make haste, you may appre-
        hend him,
Rowing upon the water in a gondole,
With the most cunning courtesan of Venice.   20
    Lady P. Is 't true?
    Mos.   Pursue 'em, and believe your eyes:
Leave me to make your gift.
              [*Exit* LADY P. *hastily.*]
              I knew 't would take:
For, lightly, they that use themselves most
        licence,
Are still most jealous.
    Volp.   Mosca, hearty thanks
For thy quick fiction, and delivery of me.   25
Now to my hopes, what sayst thou?

        2 Of the same age.   3 The same.

[*Re-enter* LADY P. WOULD-BE.]

Lady P. But do you hear, sir? ——
Volp. Again! I fear a paroxysm.
Lady P. Which way
Row'd they together?
Mos. Toward the Rialto.
Lady P. I pray you lend me your dwarf.   29
Mos. I pray you take him. [*Exit* LADY P.]
Your hopes, sir, are like happy blossoms, fair,
And promise timely fruit, if you will stay
But the maturing; keep you at your couch,
Corbaccio will arrive straight, with the will;
When he is gone, I 'll tell you more. [*Exit.*]
Volp. My blood,   35
My spirits are return'd; I am alive:
And, like your wanton gamester at primero,
Whose thought had whisper'd to him, not go [1]
    less,
Methinks I lie, and draw [2] —— for an encounter.[2]

SCENE VI. [3]

[*Enter*] MOSCA, BONARIO.

Mos. Sir, here conceal'd [*Opening a door*] you
    may hear all. But, pray you,
Have patience, sir; [*One knocks.*] the same's
    your father knocks:
I am compell'd to leave you. [*Exit.*]
Bon. Do so. — Yet
Cannot my thought imagine this a truth.
    [*Goes in.*]

SCENE VII.[4]

[*Enter*] MOSCA, CORVINO, CELIA. —

Mos. Death on me! you are come too soon,
    what meant you?
Did not I say I would send?
Corv. Yes, but I fear'd
You might forget it, and then they prevent us.
Mos. Prevent! [*Aside.*] Did e'er man haste
    so for his horns?
A courtier would not ply it so for a place.   5
— Well, now there is no helping it, stay here;
I 'll presently return. [*Exit.*]
Corv. Where are you, Celia?
You know not wherefore I have brought you
    hither?
Cel. Not well, except you told me.
Corv. Now I will:
Hark hither. [*They retire to one side.*]

[*Re-enter* MOSCA.]
    [word,
Mos. (*to* BONARIO) Sir, your father hath sent
It will be half an hour ere he come;   11
And therefore, if you please to walk the while
Into that gallery — at the upper end,
There are some books to entertain the time:
And I 'll take care no man shall come unto you,
    sir.   15
Bon. Yes, I will stay there. — [*Aside.*] I do
    doubt this fellow. [*Exit.*]

――――――
[1] Hazard.
[2] Terms in primero. Volpone is lying in the alcove at
the back of the stage, and at the end of the scene the
curtains close on him.
[3] The same.   [4] The same.

Mos. [*Looking after him.*] There; he is far
    enough; he can hear nothing:
And for his father, I can keep him off.[5]
Corv. Nay, now, there is no starting back,
    and therefore,
Resolve upon it: I have so decreed.   20
It must be done. Nor would I move 't afore,
Because I would avoid all shifts and tricks,
That might deny me.
Cel. Sir, let me beseech you,
Affect not these strange trials; if you doubt
My chastity, why, lock me up for ever;   25
Make me the heir of darkness. Let me live
Where I may please your fears, if not your trust.
Corv. Believe it, I have no such humour, I.
All that I speak I mean; yet I 'm not mad;   29
Not horn-mad, you see? Go to, show yourself
Obedient, and a wife.
Cel. O heaven!
Corv. I say it,
Do so.
Cel. Was this the train?
Corv. I 've told you reasons;
What the physicians have set down; how much
It may concern me; what my engagements are;
My means, and the necessity of those means   35
For my recovery: wherefore, if you be
Loyal and mine, be won, respect my venture.
Cel. Before your honour?
Corv. Honour! tut, a breath:
There 's no such thing in nature; a mere term
Invented to awe fools. What is my gold   40
The worse for touching, clothes for being look'd
    on?
Why, this 's no more. An old decrepit wretch,
That has no sense, no sinew; takes his meat
With others' fingers: only knows to gape
When you do scald his gums; a voice, a shadow;
And what can this man hurt you?
Cel. [*Aside.*] Lord! what spirit   46
Is this hath ent'red him?
Corv. And for your fame,
That 's such a jig; as if I would go tell it,
Cry it on the Piazza! Who shall know it
But he that cannot speak it, and this fellow,   50
Whose lips are i' my pocket? Save yourself,
(If you'll proclaim 't, you may,) I know no other
Should come to know it.
Cel. Are heaven and saints then nothing?
Will they be blind or stupid?
Corv. How!
Cel. Good sir,
Be jealous still, emulate them; and think   55
What hate they burn with toward every sin.
Corv. I grant you: if I thought it were a sin
I would not urge you. Should I offer this
To some young Frenchman, or hot Tuscan blood
That had read Aretine, conn'd all his prints,   60
Knew every quirk within lust's labyrinth,
And were profest critic in lechery;
And I would look upon him, and applaud him,
This were a sin: but here, 't is contrary,
A pious work, mere charity for physic,   65
And honest polity, to assure mine own.

――――――
[5] At this point, Mosca goes back and opens the curtains, discovering Volpone on his couch.

Cel. O heaven! canst thou suffer such a change?

Volp. Thou art mine honour, Mosca, and my pride,

My joy, my tickling, my delight! Go bring 'em.

Mos. [*Advancing.*] Please you draw near, sir.

Corv.   Come on, what ——

You will not be rebellious? By that light —— 71

Mos. Sir, Signior Corvino, here, is come to see you.

Volp. Oh!

Mos. And hearing of the consultation had,

So lately, for your health, is come to offer,

Or rather, sir, to prostitute ——

Corv.   Thanks, sweet Mosca. 75

Mos. Freely, unask'd, or unintreated ——

Corv.   Well.

Mos. As the true fervent instance of his love,

His own most fair and proper wife; the beauty

Only of price in Venice ——

Corv.   'T is well urg'd.

Mos. To be your comfortress, and to preserve you. 80

Volp. Alas, I am past, already! Pray you, thank him

For his good care and promptness; but for that,

'T is a vain labour e'en to fight 'gainst heaven;

Applying fire to stone — uh, uh, uh, uh!
[*Coughing.*]

Making a dead leaf grow again. I take 85

His wishes gently, though; and you may tell him

What I have done for him: marry, my state is hopeless.

Will him to pray for me; and to use his fortune

With reverence when he comes to 't.

Mos.   Do you hear, sir?

Go to him with your wife.

Corv.   Heart of my father! 90

Wilt thou persist thus? Come, I pray thee, come.

Thou seest 't is nothing, Celia. By this hand

I shall grow violent. Come, do 't, I say.

Cel. Sir, kill me, rather: I will take down poison,

Eat burning coals, do anything ——

Corv.   Be damn'd! 95

Heart, I will drag thee hence home by the hair;

Cry thee a strumpet through the streets; rip up

Thy mouth unto thine ears; and slit thy nose,

Like a raw rochet![1] — Do not tempt me; come,

Yield, I am loth — Death! I will buy some slave 100

Whom I will kill, and bind thee to him alive;

And at my windore hang you forth, devising

Some monstrous crime, which I, in capital letters,

Will eat into thy flesh with aquafortis, 104

And burning cor'sives,[2] on this stubborn breast.

Now, by the blood thou hast incens'd, I 'll do it!

Cel. Sir, what you please, you may; I am your martyr.

1 "A *rochet* or *rouget*, so named from its *red colour*, is a fish of the gurnet kind, but not so large." (Whalley.)

2 Corrosives.

Corv. Be not thus obstinate, I ha' not deserv'd it:

Think who it is intreats you. Prithee, sweet; —

Good faith, thou shalt have jewels, gowns, attires, 110

What thou wilt think, and ask. Do but go kiss him.

Or touch him but. For my sake. At my suit —

This once. No! not! I shall remember this.

Will you disgrace me thus? Do you thirst my undoing?

Mos. Nay, gentle lady, be advis'd.

Corv.   No, no. 115

She has watch'd her time. God's precious, this is scurvy,

'T is very scurvy; and you are ——

Mos.   Nay, good sir.

Corv. An arrant locust — by heaven, a locust! —

Whore, crocodile, that hast thy tears prepar'd,

Expecting how thou 'lt bid 'em flow ——

Mos.   Nay, pray you, sir! 120

She will consider.

Cel.   Would my life would serve

To satisfy ——   [him,

Corv. 'Sdeath! if she would but speak to him,

And save my reputation, 't were somewhat;

But spitefully to affect my utter ruin!

Mos. Ay, now you have put your fortune in her hands. 125

Why i' faith, it is her modesty, I must quit her.

If you were absent, she would be more coming;

I know it: and dare undertake for her.

What woman can before her husband? Pray you,

Let us depart and leave her here.

Corv.   Sweet Celia, 130

Thou mayest redeem all yet; I 'll say no more:

If not, esteem yourself as lost. Nay, stay there.
[*Exit with* MOSCA.]

Cel. O God, and his good angels! whither, whither,

Is shame fled human breasts? that with such ease, 134

Men dare put off your honours, and their own?

Is that, which ever was a cause of life,

Now plac'd beneath the basest circumstance,

And modesty an exile made, for money?

Volp. Ay, in Corvino, and such earth-fed minds,   *He leaps from his couch.*

That never tasted the true heaven of love. 140

Assure thee, Celia, he that would sell thee,

Only for hope of gain, and that uncertain,

He would have sold his part of Paradise

For ready money, had he met a cope-man,[3]

Why art thou maz'd to see me thus reviv'd?

Rather applaud thy beauty's miracle; 146

'T is thy great work, that hath, not now alone,

But sundry times rais'd me, in several shapes,

And, but this morning, like a mountebank,

To see thee at thy windore: ay, before 150

I would have left my practice, for thy love,

In varying figures, I would have contended

With the blue Proteus, or the horned flood.[4]

Now art thou welcome.

3 Chapman, merchant.

4 "Acheloüs, of whose 'contention' there is a pretty story in Ovid." (Gifford.)

Cel.   Sir !
Volp.   Nay, fly me not,
Nor let thy false imagination   155
That I was bed-rid, make thee think I am so :
Thou shalt not find it. I am now as fresh,
As hot, as high, and in as jovial plight
As, when, in that so celebrated scene,
At recitation of our comedy,   160
For entertainment of the great Valois,
I acted young Antinous ; and attracted
The eyes and ears of all the ladies present,
To admire each graceful gesture, note, and
    footing.   [*Sings.*]

SONG[1]

Come, my Celia, let us prove   165
    While we can, the sports of love,
    Time will not be ours for ever,
    He, at length, our good will sever ;
    Spend not then his gifts in vain :
    Suns that set may rise again ;   170
    But if once we lose this light,
    'T is with us perpetual night.
    Why should we defer our joys ?
    Fame and rumour are but toys.
    Cannot we delude the eyes   175
    Of a few poor household spies ?
    Or his easier ears beguile,
    Thus removed by our wile ?
    'T is no sin love's fruits to steal ;
    But the sweet thefts to reveal :   180
    To be taken, to be seen,
    These have crimes accounted been.

Cel. Some serene[2] blast me, or dire lightning
    strike
'I is my offending face !
Volp.   Why droops my Celia ?
Thou hast, in place of a base husband found   185
A worthy lover : use thy fortune well,
With secrecy and pleasure. See, behold,
What thou art queen of ; not in expectation,
As I feed others : but possess'd and crown'd.
See, here, a rope of pearl ; and each more orient[3]
Then the brave Aegyptian queen carous'd :   191
Dissolve and drink 'em. See, a carbuncle,
May put out both the eyes of our St. Mark ;
A diamond would have bought Lollia Paulina,
When she came in like star-light, hid with
    jewels   195
That were the spoils of provinces ; take these
And wear, and lose 'em ; yet remains an ear-
    ring
To purchase them again, and this whole state.
A gem but worth a private patrimony
Is nothing ; we will eat such at a meal.   200
The heads of parrots, tongues of nightingales,
The brains of peacocks, and of estriches,
Shall be our food, and, could we get the phoe-
    nix,
Though nature lost her kind, she were our dish.
Cel. Good sir, these things might move a
    mind affected   205
With such delights ; but I, whose innocence
Is all I can think wealthy, or worth th' enjoy-
    ing,

---

[1] Imitated, in part, from Catullus.
[2] Mildew.   [3] Brilliant.

And which, once lost, I have nought to lose be-
    yond it,
Cannot be taken with these sensual baits :
If you have conscience ——
Volp.   'T is the beggar's virtue ;
If thou hast wisdom, hear me, Celia.   211
Thy baths shall be the juice of July-flowers,
Spirit of roses, and of violets,
The milk of unicorns, and panthers' breath   214
Gather'd in bags, and mix'd with Cretan wines.
Our drink shall be prepared gold and amber ;
Which we will take until my roof whirl round
With the vertigo : and my dwarf shall dance,
My eunuch sing, my fool make up the antic,   219
Whilst we, in changed shapes, act Ovid's tales,
Thou, like Europa now, and I like Jove,
Then I like Mars, and thou like Erycine :
So of the rest, till we have quite run through,
And wearied all the fables of the gods.   224
Then will I have thee in more modern forms,
Attired like some sprightly dame of France,
Brave Tuscan lady, or proud Spanish beauty ;
Sometimes unto the Persian sophy's wife ;
Or the grand signior's mistress ; and for change,
To one of our most artful courtesans,   230
Or some quick Negro, or cold Russian ;
And I will meet thee in as many shapes :
Where we may so transfuse our wand'ring souls
Out at our lips, and score up sums of pleasures,
    [*Sings.*]

    That the curious shall not know   235
    How to tell them as they flow ;
    And the envious, when they find
    What their number is, be pin'd.

Cel. If you have ears that will be pierc'd —
    or eyes
That can be open'd — a heart that may be
    touch'd —   240
Or any part that yet sounds man about you —
If you have touch of holy saints — or heaven —
Do me the grace to let me scape : — if not,
Be bountiful and kill me. You do know,
I am a creature, hither ill betray'd,   245
By one whose shame I would forget it were :
If you will deign me neither of these graces,
Yet feed your wrath, sir, rather than your lust,
(It is a vice comes nearer manliness,)
And punish that unhappy crime of nature,   250
Which you miscall my beauty : flay my face,
Or poison it with ointments for seducing
Your blood to this rebellion. Rub these hands
With what may cause an eating leprosy,
E'en to my bones and marrow : anything   255
That may disfavour me, save in my honour —
And I will kneel to you, pray for you, pay down
A thousand hourly vows, sir, for your health ;
Report, and think you virtuous ——
Volp.   Think me cold,
Frozen, and impotent, and so report me ?   260
That I had Nestor's hernia, thou wouldst think.
I do degenerate, and abuse my nation,
To play with opportunity thus long ;
I should have done the act, and then have par-
    ley'd.
Yield, or I 'll force thee.   [*Seizes her.*]
Cel.   O ! just God !

Volp.   In vain —— 265
Bon. (*leaps out from where* MOSCA *had placed
   him.*) Forbear, foul ravisher! libidinous
   swine!
Free the forc'd lady, or thou diest, impostor.
But that I'm loth to snatch thy punishment
Out of the hand of justice, thou shouldst yet
Be made the timely sacrifice of vengeance, 270
Before this altar and this dross, thy idol. ——
Lady, let's quit the place, it is the den
Of villany; fear nought, you have a guard:
And he ere long shall meet his just reward. 274
                 [*Exeunt* BON. *and* CEL.]
Volp. Fall on me, roof, and bury me in ruin!
Become my grave, that wert my shelter! O!
I am unmask'd, unspirited, undone,
Betray'd to beggary, to infamy ——

[SCENE VIII.]¹

VOLPONE. [*Enter*] MOSCA, [*wounded and bleeding.*]

Mos. Where shall I run, most wretched shame
   of men,
To beat out my unlucky brains?
Volp.   Here, here.
What! dost thou bleed?
Mos.   O, that his well-driv'n sword
Had been so courteous to have cleft me down
Unto the navel, ere I liv'd to see   5
My life, my hopes, my spirits, my patron, all
Thus desperately engaged by my error!
Volp. Woe on thy fortune!
Mos.   And my follies, sir.
Volp. Thou hast made me miserable.
Mos.   And myself, sir.
Who would have thought he would have hear-
   k'ned so?   10
Volp. What shall we do?
Mos.   I know not; if my heart
Could expiate the mischance, I'd pluck it out.
Will you be pleas'd to hang me, or cut my
   throat?
And I'll requite you, sir. Let's die like
   Romans,²
Since we have liv'd like Grecians.
              They knock without.
Volp.   Hark! who's there? 15
I hear some footing; officers, the saffi,³
Come to apprehend us! I do feel the brand
Hissing already at my forehead; now
Mine ears are boring.
Mos.   To your couch, sir, you,
Make that place good, however. [VOLPONE *lies
   down as before.*] Guilty men   20
Suspect what they deserve still. Signior Cor-
   baccio!

[SCENE IX.]⁴

[*To them enter*] CORBACCIO.

Corb. Why, how now, Mosca?
Mos.   O, undone, amaz'd, sir.
Your son, I know not by what accident,

Acquainted with your purpose to my patron,
Touching your will, and making him your heir,
Ent'red our house with violence, his sword
   drawn,   5
Sought for you, called you wretch, unnatural,
Vow'd he would kill you.
Corb.   Me!
Mos.   Yes, and my patron.
Corb. This act shall disinherit him indeed:
Here is the will.
Mos.   'Tis well, sir.
Corb.   Right and well:
Be you as careful now for me.

     [*Enter* VOLTORE *behind.*]

Mos.   My life, sir,   10
Is not more tender'd; I am only yours.
Corb. How does he? Will he die shortly,
   think'st thou?
Mos.   I fear
He'll outlast May.
Corb.   To-day?
Mos.   No, last out May, sir.
Corb. Couldst thou not gi' him a dram?
Mos.   O, by no means, sir.
Corb. Nay, I'll not bid you.
Volt. [*coming forward.*] This is a knave, I
   see.   15
Mos. [*Aside, seeing* VOLT.] How! Signior Vol-
   tore! did he hear me?
Volt.   Parasite!
Mos. Who's that?—O, sir, most timely wel-
   come—
Volt.   Scarce,
To the discovery of your tricks, I fear.
You are his, *only*? And mine also, are you not?
Mos. Who? I, sir!
Volt.   You, sir. What device is this 20
About a will?
Mos.   A plot for you, sir.
Volt.   Come,
Put not your foists⁵ upon me; I shall scent 'em.
Mos. Did you not hear it?
Volt.   Yes, I hear Corbaccio
Hath made your patron there his heir.
Mos.   'Tis true,
By my device, drawn to it by my plot,   25
With hope ——
Volt.   Your patron should reciprocate?
And you have promis'd?
Mos.   For your good I did, sir.
Nay, more, I told his son, brought, hid him
   here,
Where he might hear his father pass the deed;
Being persuaded to it by this thought, sir,   30
That the unnaturalness, first, of the act,
And then his father's oft disclaiming in him,
(Which I did mean t' help on), would sure en-
   rage him
To do some violence upon his parent,   34
On which the law should take sufficient hold,
And you be stated in a double hope.
Truth be my comfort, and my conscience,
My only aim was to dig you a fortune
Out of these two rotten sepulchres ——

---

¹ The same.   ³ Bailiff's attendants.
² *I. e.* by suicide.   ⁴ The same.

                    ⁵ Deceits.

Volt. I cry thee mercy, Mosca.
Mos.   — Worth your patience, 40
And your great merit, sir. And see the change!
Volt. Why, what success?
Mos.   Most hapless! you must help, sir.
Whilst we expected th' old raven, in comes
Corvino's wife, sent hither by her husband ——
Volt. What, with a present?
Mos.   No, sir, on visitation; 45
(I 'll tell you how anon;) and staying long,
The youth he grows impatient, rushes forth,
Seizeth the lady, wounds me, makes her swear
(Or he would murder her, that was his vow)
T' affirm my patron to have done her rape: 50
Which how unlike it is, you see! and hence,
With that pretext he 's gone, t' accuse his
    father,
Defame my patron, defeat you ——
Volt.   Where 's her husband?
Let him be sent for straight.
Mos.   Sir, I 'll go fetch him.
Volt. Bring him to the Scrutineo.[1]
Mos.   Sir, I will. 55
Volt. This must be stopt.
Mos.   O you do nobly, sir.
Alas, 't was labour'd all, sir, for your good;
Nor was there want of counsel in the plot:
But Fortune can, at any time, o'erthrow
The projects of a hundred learned clerks, sir. 60
Corb. [*listening.*] What 's that?
Volt.   Wilt please you, sir, to go along?
    [*Exit* CORBACCIO, *followed by* VOL-
       TORE.]
Mos. Patron, go in, and pray for our success.
Volp. [*rising from his couch.*] Need makes
    devotion: heaven your labour bless!
                                   [*Exeunt.*]

ACT IV

SCENE I.[2]

[*Enter*] SIR POLITIC WOULD-BE, PEREGRINE.

Sir P. I told you, sir, it was a plot; you see
What observation is! You mention'd me
For some instructions: I will tell you, sir,
(Since we are met here in this height of Venice,)
Some few particulars I have set down, 5
Only for this meridian, fit to be known
Of your crude traveller; and these are these.
I will not touch, sir, at your phrase, or clothes,
For they are old.
Per.   Sir, I have better.
Sir P.   Pardon,
I meant, as they are themes.
Per.   O, sir, proceed: 10
I 'll slander you no more of wit, good sir.
Sir P. First, for your garb, it must be grave
    and serious,
Very reserv'd and lockt; not tell a secret
On any terms, not to your father; scarce
A fable, but with caution: make sure choice 15
Both of your company and discourse; beware
You never speak a truth ——
Per.   How!

1 Senate House.   2 A street.

Sir P.   Not to strangers,
For those be they you must converse with
    most;
Others I would not know, sir, but at distance
So as I still might be a saver in them: 20
You shall have tricks else past upon you hourly.
And then, for your religion, profess none,
But wonder at the diversity of all;
And, for your part, protest, were there no other
But simply the laws o' th' land, you could con-
    tent you. 25
Nic. Machiavel and Monsieur Bodin,[3] both
Were of this mind. Then must you learn the
    use
And handling of your silver fork at meals,
The metal of your glass; (these are main mat-
    ters
With your Italian;) and to know the hour 30
When you must eat your melons and your figs.
Per. Is that a point of state too?
Sir P.   Here it is:
For your Venetian, if he see a man
Preposterous in the least, he has him straight;
He has; he strips him. I 'll acquaint you, sir, 35
I now have liv'd here 't is some fourteen months:
Within the first week of my landing here,
All took me for a citizen of Venice,
I knew the forms so well ——
Per. [*Aside.*]   And nothing else.
Sir P. I had read Contarene,[4] took me a
    house, 40
Dealt with my Jews to furnish it with mov-
    ables —
Well, if I could but find one man, one man
To mine own heart, whom I durst trust, I
    would ——
Per. What, what, sir?
Sir P. Make him rich; make him a fortune:
He should not think again. I would command
    it. 45
Per. As how?
Sir P.   With certain projects that I have;
Which I may not discover.
Per. [*Aside.*]   If I had
But one to wager with, I would lay odds now,
He tells me instantly.
Sir P.   One is, and that
I care not greatly who knows, to serve the state
Of Venice with red herrings for three years, 51
And at a certain rate, from Rotterdam,
Where I have correspondence. There 's a letter,
Sent me from one o' th' states, and to that pur-
    pose:
He cannot write his name, but that 's his
    mark. 55
Per. He is a chandler?
Sir P.   No, a cheesemonger.
There are some others too with whom I treat
About the same negotiation;
And I will undertake it: for 't is thus.
I 'll do 't with ease, I have cast[5] it all. Your
    hoy[6] 60
Carries but three men in her, and a boy;
And she shall make me three returns a year:

3 A famous French lawyer.
4 Gasp. Contarini, author of a work on Venice.
5 Reckoned.   6 A small passenger sloop.

So if there come but one of three, I save ;
If two, I can defalk : [1] — but this is now,
If my main project fail.
　Per.　　　　　Then you have others ? 65
　Sir P. I should be loth to draw the subtle
air
Of such a place, without my thousand aims.
I 'll not dissemble, sir : where'er I come,
I love to be considerative ; and 't is true,
I have at my free hours thought upon 70
Some certain goods unto the state of Venice,
Which I do call my Cautions ; and, sir, which
I mean, in hope of pension, to propound
To the Great Council, then unto the Forty, 74
So to the Ten. My means are made already —
　Per. By whom ?　　　　　[be obscure,
　Sir P.　　　Sir, one that though his place
Yet he can sway, and they will hear him. He 's
A *commandadore.*
　Per.　　　　What ! a common serjeant ?
　Sir P. Sir, such as they are, put it in their
mouths,
What they should say, sometimes ; as well as
greater :　　　　　　　　　　　　　80
I think I have my notes to show you —
　　　　　　　　[*Searching his pockets.*]
　Per.　　　　　　　Good sir.
　Sir P. But you shall swear unto me, on your
gentry,
Not to anticipate —
　Per.　　　　I, sir !
　Sir P.　　　　　Nor reveal
A circumstance —— My paper is not with me.
　Per. O, but you can remember, sir.
　Sir P.　　　　　My first is 85
Concerning tinder-boxes. You must know,
No family is here without its box.
Now, sir, it being so portable a thing,
Put case, that you or I were ill affected
Unto the state, sir ; with it in our pockets, 90
Might not I go into the Arsenal,
Or you come out again, and none the wiser ?
　Per. Except yourself, sir.
　Sir P.　　　　Go to, then. I therefore
Advertise to the state, how fit it were
That none but such as were known patriots, 95
Sound lovers of their country, should be suf-
fer'd
T' enjoy them in their houses ; and even those
Seal'd at some office, and at such a bigness
As might not lurk in pockets.
　Per.　　　　　Admirable !
　Sir P. My next is, how t' inquire, and be re-
solv'd 100
By present demonstration, whether a ship,
Newly arriv'd from Soria,[2] or from
Any suspected part of all the Levant,
Be guilty of the plague : and where they use
To lie out forty, fifty days, sometimes, 105
About the Lazaretto, for their trial ;
I 'll save that charge and loss unto the merchant,
And in an hour clear the doubt.
　Per.　　　　　Indeed, sir !
　Sir P. Or —— I will lose my labour.
　Per.　　　　My faith, that 's much.

Sir. P. Nay, sir, conceive me. It will cost me
in onions,　　　　　　　　　　　　110
Some thirty livres ——
　Per.　　　Which is one pound sterling.
　Sir P. Beside my waterworks : for this I do,
sir.
First, I bring in your ship 'twixt two brick
walls ;
But those the state shall venture. On the one
I strain me a fair tarpauling, and in that 115
I stick my onions, cut in halves ; the other
Is full of loopholes, out of which I thrust
The noses of my bellows ; and those bellows
I keep, with waterworks, in perpetual motion,
Which is the easiest matter of a hundred. 120
Now, sir, your onion, which doth naturally
Attract th' infection, and your bellows blow-
ing
The air upon him, will show instantly,
By his chang'd colour, if there be contagion ;
Or else remain as fair as at the first. 125
Now it is known, 't is nothing.
　Per.　　　　　You are right, sir.
　Sir P. I would I had my note.
　Per.　　　　Faith, so would I :
But you ha' done well for once, sir.
　Sir P.　　　　Were I false,
Or would be made so, I could show you reasons
How I could sell this state now to the Turk, 130
Spite of their galleys, or their ——
　　　　　　[*Examining his papers.*]
　Per.　　　　Pray you, Sir Pol.
　Sir P. I have 'em not about me.
　Per.　　　　That I fear'd.
They are there, sir ?
　Sir P.　　　No, this is my diary,
Wherein I note my actions of the day. 134
　Per. Pray you let 's see, sir. What is here ?
Notandum,　　　　　　[*Reads.*]
" A rat had gnawn my spur-leathers ; notwith-
standing,
I put on new, and did go forth ; but first
I threw three beans over the threshold. Item,
I went and bought two toothpicks, whereof
one 140
I burst immediately, in a discourse
With a Dutch merchant, 'bout *ragion' del stato.*[3]
From him I went and paid a *moccinigo* [4]
For piecing my silk stockings ; by the way
I cheapen'd [5] sprats ; and at St. Mark's I
urin'd."
'Faith these are politic notes !
　Sir P.　　　　Sir, I do slip 145
No action of my life, but thus I quote [6] it.
　Per. Believe me, it is wise !
　Sir P.　　　　Nay, sir, read forth.

SCENE II.[7]

[*Enter, at a distance,*] LADY POLITIC WOULD-
BE, NANO, [*and two* Waiting]-women.

　Lady P. Where should this loose knight be,
trow ? Sure he 's hous'd.
　Nan. Why, then he 's fast.

---

[1] Cut off. reduce.　　　　[2] Syria.
[3] Politics.　　　　[4] About ninepence.
[5] Bargained for.　　[6] Note.　[7] The same.

Lady P.   Ay, he plays both [1] with me.
I pray you stay. This heat will do more harm
To my complexion than his heart is worth.
(I do not care to hinder, but to take him.)   5
How it comes off!   [*Rubbing her cheeks.*]
1 *Wom.*   My master's yonder.
Lady P.   Where?
2 *Wom.* With a young gentleman.
Lady P.   That same's the party:
In man's apparel! Pray you, sir, jog my
    knight:
I will be tender to his reputation,
However he demerit.
Sir P. [*seeing her*] My lady!
Per.   Where?   10
Sir P. 'T is she indeed, sir; you shall know
    her. She is,
Were she not mine, a lady of that merit,
For fashion and behaviour; and for beauty
I durst compare ——
Per.   It seems you are not jealous,
That dare commend her.
Sir P.   Nay, and for discourse —— 15
Per. Being your wife, she cannot miss that.
Sir. P. [*introducing* PER.]   Madam,
Here is a gentleman, pray you, use him fairly;
He seems a youth, but he is ——
Lady P.   None.
Sir P.   Yes one
Has put his face as soon into the world ——
Lady P. You mean, as early? But to-day?
Sir P.   How's this? 20
Lady P. Why, in this habit, sir; you appre-
    hend me.
Well, Master Would-be, this doth not become
    you;
I had thought the odour, sir, of your good name
Had been more precious to you; that you would
    not
Have done this dire massacre on your honour;
One of your gravity, and rank besides!   26
But knights, I see, care little for the oath
They make to ladies; chiefly their own ladies.
Sir P. Now, by my spurs, the symbol of my
    knighthood ——
Per. [*Aside.*] Lord, how his brain is humbl'd
    for an oath!   30
Sir P. I reach [2] you not.
Lady P.   Right, sir, your polity
May bear it through thus. Sir, a word with you.
                                        [*To* PER.]
I would be loth to contest publicly
With any gentlewoman, or to seem
Froward, or violent, as the courtier says;   35
It comes too near rusticity in a lady,
Which I would shun by all means: and how-
    ever
I may deserve from Master Would-be, yet
T' have one fair gentlewoman thus be made
The unkind instrument to wrong another,   40
And one she knows not, ay, and to perséver;
In my poor judgment, is not warranted
From being a solecism in our sex,
If not in manners.

---

[1] Both "fast and loose," the name of a game.
[2] Understand.

Per.   How is this!
Sir P.   Sweet madam,
Come nearer to your aim.
Lady P.   Marry, and will, sir. 45
Since you provoke me with your impudence,
And laughter of your light land-syren here,
Your Sporus, your hermaphrodite ——
Per.   What's here?
Poetic fury and historic storms!   49
Sir P. The gentleman, believe it, is of worth
And of our nation.
Lady P.   Ay, your Whitefriars nation.[3]
Come, I blush for you, Master Would-be, I;
And am asham'd you should ha' no more fore-
    head
Than thus to be the patron, or St. George,
To a lewd harlot, a base fricatrice,[4]   55
A female devil, in a male outside.
Sir P.   Nay,
An you be such a one, I must bid adieu
To your delights. The case appears too liquid.
                                        [*Exit.*]
Lady P. Ay, you may carry 't clear, with
    you state-face!
But for your carnival concupiscence,   60
Who here is fled for liberty of conscience,
From furious persecution of the marshal,
Her will I disc'ple.[5]
Per.   This is fine, i' faith!
And do you use this often? Is this part
Of your wit's exercise, 'gainst you have occa-
    sion?   65
Madam ——
Lady P. Go to, sir.
Per.   Do you hear me, lady?
Why, if your knight have set you to beg shirts,
Or to invite me home, you might have done it
A nearer way by far.
Lady P.   This cannot work you
Out of my snare.
Per.   Why, am I in it, then? 70
Indeed your husband told me you were fair,
And so you are; only your nose inclines,
That side that's next the sun, to the queen-
    apple.[6]
Lady P. This cannot be endur'd by any pa-
    tience.

SCENE III.[7]

[*To them enter*] MOSCA.

Mos. What is the matter, madam?
Lady P.   If the senate
Right not my quest in this, I will protest 'em
To all the world no aristocracy.
Mos. What is the injury, lady?
Lady P.   Why, the callet[4]
You told me of, here I have ta'en disguis'd.   5
Mos. Who? this! what means your lady-
    ship? The creature
I mention'd to you is apprehended now,
Before the senate; you shall see her ——
Lady P.   Where?

---

[3] Whitefriars was at this time a privileged spot, in which fraudulent debtors, gamblers, prostitutes, and other outcasts of society usually resided. (Gifford.)
[4] Prostitute.   [5] Disciple, discipline.
[6] The queen-apple is red within.   [7] The same.

Mos. I 'll bring you to her. This young gen-
    tleman,
I saw him land this morning at the port.   10
  Lady P. Is 't possible ! how has my judg-
    ment wander'd ?
Sir, I must, blushing, say to you, I have err'd ;
And plead your pardon.
    Per.   What, more changes yet !
  Lady P. I hope you ha' not the malice to
    remember
A gentlewoman 's passion. If you stay   15
In Venice here, please you to use me, sir ——
  Mos. Will you go, madam ?
  Lady P.   Pray you, sir, use me ; in faith,
The more you see me the more I shall conceive
You have forgot our quarrel.
[*Exeunt* Lady Would-be, Mosca, Nano, *and*
          Waiting-women.]
  Per.   This is rare !
Sir Politic Would-be ? No, Sir Politic Bawd,   20
To bring me thus acquainted with his wife !
Well, wise Sir Pol, since you have practis'd
    thus
Upon my freshman-ship, I 'll try your salt-head,
What proof it is against a counter-plot.
                         [*Exit.*]

Scene IV.[1]

[*Enter*] Voltore, Corbaccio, Corvino,
      Mosca.

  Volt. Well, now you know the carriage of the
    business,
Your constancy is all that is requir'd
Unto the safety of it.
  Mos.   Is the lie
Safely convey'd[2] amongst us ? Is that sure ?
Knows every man his burden ?
  Corv.   Yes.
  Mos.   Then shrink not. 5
  Corv. But knows the advocate the truth ?
  Mos.   O, sir,
By no means ; I devis'd a formal tale,
That salv'd your reputation. But be valiant,
    sir.
  Corv. I fear no one but him that this his
    pleading
Should make him stand for a co-heir ——
  Mos.   Co-halter !   10
Hang him ; we will but use his tongue, his noise,
As we do croaker's[3] here.
  Corv.   Ay, what shall he do ?
  Mos. When we ha' done, you mean ?
  Corv.   Yes.
  Mos.   Why, we 'll think ;
Sell him for mummia :[4] he 's half dust al-
    ready. ——
Do you not smile, (*to* Voltore) to see this
    buffalo,[5]
How he doth sport it with his head ? [*Aside.*]
    I should,
If all were well and past. — Sir, (*to* Corbaccio)
    only you

1 The Scrutineo, or Senate House.
2 Arranged.   3 Corbaccio's.
4 A medicine, supposed to be made of the oozing from
mummies.
5 Horned animal — the usual joke on cuckolds.

Are he that shall enjoy the crop of all,
And these not know for whom they toil.
  Corb.   Ay, peace.
  Mos. (*turning to* Corvino.) But you shall eat
    it. [*Aside.*] Much ! — Worshipful sir, (*to*
    Voltore)   20
Mercury sit upon your thund'ring tongue,
Or the French Hercules, and make your lan-
    guage
As conquering as his club, to beat along,
As with a tempest, flat, our adversaries ;
But much more yours, sir.
  Volt.   Here they come, ha' done. 25
  Mos. I have another witness, if you need, sir,
I can produce.
  Volt.   Who is it ?
  Mos.   Sir, I have her.

Scene V.[6]

[*Enter*] 4 Avocatori, [*and take their seats,*] Bo-
    nario, Celia, Notario, Commandadori, Saffi,
    and other Officers of Justice.]

  1 Avoc. The like of this the senate never
    heard of.
  2 Avoc. 'T will come most strange to them
    when we report it.
  4 Avoc. The gentlewoman has been ever
    held
Of unreproved name.
  3 Avoc.   So has the youth.
  4 Avoc. The more unnatural part that of his
    father.   5
  2 Avoc. More of the husband.
  1 Avoc.   I not know to give
His act a name, it is so monstrous !
  4 Avoc. But the impostor, he 's a thing
    created.
T' exceed example !
  1 Avoc.   And all after-times !
  2 Avoc. I never heard a true voluptuary   10
Describ'd but him.
  3 Avoc.   Appear yet those were cited ?
  Not. All but the old magnifico, Volpone.
  1 Avoc. Why is not he here ?
  Mos.   Please your fatherhoods,
Here is his advocate : himself 's so weak,
So feeble ——
  4 Avoc. Who are you ?
  Bon.   His parasite,   15
His knave, his pander. I beseech the court
He may be forc'd to come, that your grave eyes
May bear strong witness of his strange impost-
    ures.
  Volt. Upon my faith and credit with your
    virtues.
He is not able to endure the air.   20
  2 Avoc. Bring him.
  3 Avoc.   We will see him.
  4 Avoc.   Fetch him.
  Volt. Your fatherhoods' fit pleasures be
    obey'd ;   [*Exeunt* Officers.]
But sure, the sight will rather move your pities
Than indignation. May it please the court,
In the mean time, he may be heard in me.   25

6 The same.

I know this place most void of prejudice,
And therefore crave it, since we have no reason
To fear our truth should hurt our cause.
3 *Avoc.* Speak free.
Volt. Then know, most honour'd fathers, I
must now
Discover to your strangely abus'd ears,   30
The most prodigious and most frontless piece
Of solid impudence, and treachery,
That ever vicious nature yet brought forth
To shame the state of Venice. This lewd
woman,
That wants no artificial looks or tears   35
To help the vizor she has now put on,
Hath long been known a close adulteress
To that lascivious youth there ; not suspected,
I say, but known, and taken in the act   39
With him ; and by this man, the easy husband,
Pardon'd ; whose timeless bounty makes him
now
Stand here, the most unhappy, innocent person,
That ever man's own goodness made accus'd.
For these not knowing how to owe a gift
Of that dear grace, but with their shame ; be-
ing plac'd   45
So began all powers of their gratitude,
Began to hate the benefit ; and in place
Of thanks, devise t' extirp the memory
Of such an act: wherein I pray your father-
hoods
To observe the malice, yea, the rage of crea-
tures   50
Discover'd in their evils : and what heart
Such take, ev'n from their crimes : — but that
anon
Will more appear. — This gentleman, the
father,
Hearing of this foul fact, with many others,
Which daily struck at his too tender ears,   55
And griev'd in nothing more than that he could
not
Preserve himself a parent (his son's ills
Growing to that strange flood), at last decreed
To disinherit him.
1 *Avoc.* These be strange turns !
2 *Avoc.* The young man's fame was ever
fair and honest.   60
Volt. So much more full of danger is his vice,
That can beguile so, under shade of virtue.
But, as I said, my honour'd sires, his father
Having this settled purpose, by what means
To him betray'd, we know not, and this day   65
Appointed for the deed ; that parricide,
I cannot style him better, by confederacy
Preparing this his paramour to be there,
Ent'red Volpone's house (who was the man,
Your fatherhoods must understand, design'd   70
For the inheritance), there sought his father : —
But with what purpose sought he him, my
lords ?
I tremble to pronounce it, that a son
Unto a father, and to such a father,
Should have so foul, felonious intent !   75
It was to murder him : when being prevented
By his more happy absence, what then did he ?
Not check his wicked thoughts ; no, now new
deeds ;

(Mischief doth never end where it begins)
An act of horror, fathers ! He dragg'd forth   80
The aged gentleman that had there lain bed-
rid
Three years and more, out of his innocent couch,
Naked upon the floor ; there left him ; wounded
His servant in the face ; and with this strumpet,
The stale [1] to his forg'd practice, who was glad
To be so active, — (I shall here desire   85
Your fatherhoods to note but my collections,
As most remarkable, —) thought at once to
stop
His father's ends, discredit his free choice
In the old gentleman, redeem themselves,   90
By laying infamy upon this man,
To whom, with blushing, they should owe
their lives.
1 *Avoc.* What proofs have you of this ?
Bon. Most honour'd fathers,
I humbly crave there be no credit given
To this man's mercenary tongue.
2 *Avoc.* Forbear.   95
Bon. His soul moves in his fee.
3 *Avoc.* O, sir.
Bon. This fellow,
For six sols [2] more would plead against his
Maker.
1 *Avoc.* You do forget yourself.
Volt. Nay, nay, grave fathers,
Let him have scope: can any man imagine   99
That he will spare his accuser, that would not
Have spar'd his parent ?
1 *Avoc.* Well, produce your proofs.
Cel. I would I could forget I were a creature.
Volt. Signior Corbaccio !
[CORBACCIO *comes forward.*]
4 *Avoc.* What is he ?
Volt. The father.
2 *Avoc.* Has he had an oath ?
Not. Yes.
Corb. What must I do now ?   104
Not. Your testimony 's crav'd.
Corb. Speak to the knave ?
I 'll ha' my mouth first stopt with earth ; my
heart
Abhors his knowledge : I disclaim in [3] him.
1 *Avoc.* But for what cause ?
Corb. The mere portent of nature !
He is an utter stranger to my loins.   109
Bon. Have they made you to [4] this ?
Corb. I will not hear thee,
Monster of men, swine, goat, wolf, parricide !
Speak not, thou viper.
Bon. Sir, I will sit down,
And rather wish my innocence should suffer
Than I resist the authority of a father.   114
Volt. Signior Corvino !
[CORVINO *comes forward.*]
2 *Avoc.* This is strange.
1 *Avoc.* Who 's this ?
Not. The husband.
4 *Avoc.* Is he sworn ?
Not. He is.
3 *Avoc.* Speak then.

---

[1] Stalking horse, mask to his false plot.
[2] A *sol* = about a franc.   [3] Disown.
[4] Prepared you to do.

Corv. This woman, please your fatherhoods,
is a whore,
Of most hot exercise, more than a partridge,
Upon record ——
1 *Avoc.*   No more.
Corv.   Neighs like a jennet. 119
Not. Preserve the honour of the court.
Corv.   I shall,
And modesty of your most reverend ears.
And yet I hope that I may say, these eyes
Have seen her glu'd unto that piece of cedar,
That fine well timber'd gallant : and that here
The letters may be read, thorough the horn,[1] 125
That make the story perfect.
Mos.   Excellent ! sir.
Corv. [*Aside to* MOSCA.] There is no shame in
this now, is there ?
Mos.   None.
Corv. Or if I said, I hop'd that she were on-
ward
To her damnation, if there be a hell
Greater than whore and woman, a good Catho-
lic   130
May make the doubt.
3 *Avoc.*   His grief hath made him frantic.
1 *Avoc.* Remove him hence.
2 *Avoc.*   Look to the woman.
                                CELIA *swoons.*
Corv.   Rare !
Prettily feign'd again !
4 *Avoc.*   Stand from about her.
1 *Avoc.* Give her the air.
3 *Avoc.* What can you say ? [*To* MOSCA.]
Mos.   My wound,
May it please your wisdoms, speaks for me, receiv'd   135
In aid of my good patron, when he mist
His sought-for father, when that well-taught
dame
Had her cue giv'n her to cry out, "A rape ! "
Bon. O most laid [2] impudence ! Fathers —
3 *Avoc.*   Sir, be silent ; 139
You had your hearing free, so must they theirs.
2 *Avoc.* I do begin to doubt th' imposture
here.
4 *Avoc.* This woman has too many moods.
Volt.   Grave fathers,
She is a creature of a most profest
And prostituted lewdness.
Corv.   Most impetuous, 144
Unsatisfi'd, grave fathers !
Volt.   May her feignings
Not take your wisdoms : but this day she baited
A stranger, a grave knight, with her loose eyes,
And more lascivious kisses. This man saw 'em
Together on the water, in a gondola.
Mos. Here is the lady herself, that saw them
too,   150
Without ; who then had in the open streets
Pursu'd them, but for saving her knight's hon-
our.
1 *Avoc.* Produce that lady.
2 *Avoc.*   Let her come. [*Exit* MOSCA.]

[1] Playing upon the *horns* of the cuckold and the
horn-book.
[2] Well-contriv'd.

4 *Avoc.*   These things,
They strike with wonder.
3 *Avoc.*   I am turn'd a stone.

SCENE VI.[3]

[*To them re-enter*] MOSCA [*with*] LADY
                WOULD-BE.

Mos. Be resolute, madam.
Lady P.   Ay, this same is she.
                        [*Pointing to* CELIA.]
Out, thou chameleon harlot ! now thine eyes
Vie tears with the hyena. Dar'st thou look
Upon my wronged face ? I cry your pardons,
I fear I have forgettingly transgrest   5
Against the dignity of the court ——
2 *Avoc.*   No, madam.
Lady P. And been exorbitant ——
2 *Avoc.*   You have not, lady.
4 *Avoc.* These proofs are strong.
Lady P.   Surely, I had no purpose
To scandalize your honours, or my sex's.
3 *Avoc.* We do believe it.
Lady P.   Surely you may believe it. 10
2 *Avoc.* Madam, we do.
Lady P.   Indeed you may ; my breeding
Is not so coarse ——
4 *Avoc.*   We know it.
Lady P.   To offend
With pertinacy ——
3 *Avoc.*   Lady ——
Lady P.   Such a presence !
No surely.
1 *Avoc.* We will think it.
Lady P.   You may think it.
1 *Avoc.* Let her o'ercome. What witnesses
have you,   15
To make good your report ?
Bon.   Our consciences.
Cel. And heaven, that never fails the inno-
cent.
1 *Avoc.* These are no testimonies.
Bon.   Not in your courts,
Where multitude and clamour overcomes.
1 *Avoc.* Nay, then you do wax insolent.

VOLPONE *is brought in, as impotent.*

Volt.   Here, here, 20
The testimony comes that will convince,
And put to utter dumbness their bold tongues !
See here, grave fathers, here 's the ravisher,
The rider on men's wives, the great impostor,
The grand voluptuary ! Do you not think   25
These limbs should affect venery ? or these
eyes
Covet a concubine ? Pray you mark these
hands ;
Are they not fit to stroke a lady's breasts ?
Perhaps he doth dissemble !
Bon.   So he does.
Volt. Would you ha' him tortur'd ?
Bon.   I would have him prov'd. 30
Volt. Best try him then with goads, or burn-
ing irons ;
Put him to the strappado : I have heard

[3] The same.

The rack hath cur'd the gout; faith, give it
    him,
And help him of a malady; be courteous.   34
I 'll undertake, before these honour'd fathers,
He shall have yet as many left diseases,
As she has known adulterers, or thou strumpets.
O, my most equal hearers, if these deeds,
Acts of this bold and most exorbitant strain,
May pass with suff'rance, what one citizen   40
But owes the forfeit of his life, yea, fame,
To him that dares traduce him? Which of you
Are safe, my honour'd fathers? I would ask,
With leave of your grave fatherhoods, if their
    plot
Have any face or colour like to truth?   45
Or if, unto the dullest nostril here,
It smell not rank, and most abhorred slander?
I crave your care of this good gentleman,
Whose life is much endanger'd by their fable;
And as for them, I will conclude with this,   50
That vicious persons, when they 're hot, and
    flesh'd
In impious acts, their constancy [1] abounds:
Damn'd deeds are done with greatest confi-
    dence.
  1 *Avoc.* Take 'em to custody, and sever
    them.
  2 *Avoc.* 'T is pity two such prodigies should
    live.   55
  1 *Avoc.* Let the old gentleman be return'd
    with care.
          [*Exeunt* Officers *with* VOLPONE.]
I 'm sorry our credulity wrong'd him.
  4 *Avoc.* These are two creatures!
  3 *Avoc.*   I 've an earthquake in me.
  2 *Avoc.* Their shame, ev'n in their cradles,
    fled their faces.
  4 *Avoc.* You have done a worthy service to
    the state, sir,   60
In their discovery.   [*To* VOLT.]
  1 *Avoc.*   You shall hear, ere night,
What punishment the court decrees upon 'em.
      [*Exeunt* Avocat., Not., *and* Officers
           with BONARIO *and* CELIA.]
  Volt. We thank your fatherhoods. How like
    you it?
  Mos.   Rare.
I d ha' your tongue, sir, tipt with gold for
    this;
I 'd ha' you be the heir to the whole city;   65
The earth I 'd have want men ere you want
    living:
They 're bound to erect your statue in St.
    Mark's.
Signior Corvino, I would have you go
And show yourself that you have conquer'd.
  Corv.   Yes.
  Mos. It was much better that you should pro-
    fess   70
Yourself a cuckold thus, than that the other
Should have been prov'd.
  Corv.   Nay, I consider'd that:
Now it is her fault.
  Mos.   Then it had been yours.
  Corv. True; I do doubt this advocate still.

  Mos.   I' faith.
You need not, I dare ease you of that care.   75
  Corv. I trust thee, Mosca.   [*Exit.*]
  Mos.   As your own soul, sir.
  Corb.   Mosca!
  Mos. Now for your business, sir.
  Corb.   How! ha' you business?
  Mos. Yes, yours, sir,
  Corb.   O, none else?
  Mos.   None else, not I.
  Corb. Be careful then.
  Mos.   Rest you with both your eyes, sir.
  Corb. Dispatch it.
  Mos.   Instantly.
  Corb.   And look that all,   80
Whatever, be put in, jewels, plate, moneys,
Household stuff, bedding, curtains.
  Mos.   Curtain-rings, sir:
Only the advocate's fee must be deducted.
  Corb. I 'll pay him now; you 'll be too prod-
    igal.
  Mos. Sir, I must tender it.
  Corb.   Two chequins is well.   85
  Mos. No, six, sir.
  Corb.   'T is too much.
  Mos.   He talk'd a great while;
You must consider that, sir.
  Corb.   Well, there 's three——
  Mos. I 'll give it him.
  Corb.   Do so, and there 's for thee. [*Exit.*]
  Mos. [*Aside.*] Bountiful bones! What horrid
    strange offence
Did he commit 'gainst nature, in his youth,   90
Worthy this age? — You see, sir, [*to* VOLT.] how
    I work
Unto your ends; take you no notice.
  Volt.   No,
I 'll leave you.
  Mos.   All is yours, the devil and all,
Good advocate!— Madam, I 'll bring you
    home.
  Lady P. No, I 'll go see your patron.
  Mos.   That you shall not: 95
I 'll tell you why. My purpose is to urge
My patron to reform his will, and for
The zeal you 've shown to-day, whereas before
You were but third or fourth, you shall be
    now   99
Put in the first; which would appear as begg'd
If you were present. Therefore——
  Lady P.   You shall sway me. [*Exeunt.*]

ACT V

SCENE I.[2]

[*Enter*] VOLPONE.

  Volp. Well, I am here, and all this brunt is
    past.
I ne'er was in dislike with my disguise
Till this fled moment: here 't was good, in pri-
    vate;
But in your public, —*cave* whilst I breathe.   4
'Fore God, my left leg 'gan to have the cramp,

---

[1] boldness.

[2] A room in Volpone's house.

And I apprehended straight some power had
    struck me
With a dead palsy. Well! I must be merry,
And shake it off. A many of these fears
Would put me into some villanous disease,
Should they come thick upon me: I 'll prevent
    'em.   10
Give me a bowl of lusty wine, to fright
This humour from my heart. (*Drinks.*) Hum,
    hum, hum!
'T is almost gone already; I shall conquer.
Any device now of rare ingenious knavery,   14
That would possess me with a violent laughter,
Would make me up again. (*Drinks again.*) So,
    so, so, so!
This heat is life; 't is blood by this time: —
    Mosca!

SCENE II.[1]

VOLPONE. [*Enter*] MOSCA.

Mos. How now, sir? Does the day look clear
    again?
Are we recover'd, and wrought out of error,
Into our way, to see our path before us?
Is our trade free once more?
    Volp.   Exquisite Mosca!
Mos. Was it not carri'd learnedly?
    Volp.   And stoutly: 5
Good wits are greatest in extremities.
    Mos. It were folly beyond thought to trust
Any grand act unto a cowardly spirit.
You are not taken with it enough, methinks.
    Volp. O, more than if I had enjoy'd the
        wench: 10
The pleasure of all woman-kind 's not like it.
    Mos. Why, now you speak, sir. We must
        here be fix'd;
Here we must rest; this is our masterpiece;
We cannot think to go beyond this.
    Volp.   True,
Thou hast play'd thy prize, my precious Mosca.
    Mos.   Nay, sir, 15
To gull the court —
    Volp.   And quite divert the torrent
Upon the innocent.
    Mos.   Yes, and to make
So rare a music out of discords —
    Volp.   Right.
That yet to me 's the strangest, how thou 'st
    borne it!
That these, being so divided 'mongst them-
    selves,   20
Should not scent somewhat, or in me or thee,
Or doubt their own side.
    Mos.   True, they will not see 't.
Too much light blinds 'em, I think. Each of
    'em
Is so possest and stuft with his own hopes
That anything unto the contrary,   25
Never so true, or never so apparent,
Never so palpable, they will resist it —
    Volp. Like a temptation of the devil.
    Mos.   Right, sir.
Merchants may talk of trade, and your great
    signiors

Of land that yields well; but if Italy   30
Have any glebe more fruitful than these fellows,
I am deceiv'd. Did not your advocate rare?
    Volp. O — "My most honour'd fathers, my
        grave fathers,
Under correction of your fatherhoods,
What face of truth is here? If these strange
    deeds   35
May pass, most honour'd fathers " — I had
    much ado
To forbear laughing.
    Mos.   It seem'd to me, you sweat, sir.
    Volp. In troth, I did a little.
    Mos.   But confess, sir,
Were you not daunted?
    Volp.   In good faith, I was
A little in a mist, but not dejected;   40
Never but still myself.
    Mos.   I think it, sir.
Now, so truth help me, I must needs say this,
    sir,
And out of conscience for your advocate,
He has taken pains, in faith, sir, and deserv'd,
In my poor judgment, I speak it under favour, 45
Not to contrary you, sir, very richly —
Well — to be cozen'd.
    Volp.   Troth, and I think so too,
By that I heard him in the latter end.
    Mos. O, but before, sir: had you heard him
    first
Draw it to certain heads, then aggravate,   50
Then use his vehement figures — I look'd still
When he would shift a shirt; and doing this
Out of pure love, no hope of gain —
    Volp.   'T is right.
I cannot answer him, Mosca, as I would,
Not yet; but for thy sake, at thy entreaty,   55
I will begin, even now — to vex 'em all,
This very instant.
    Mos.   Good sir.
    Volp.   Call the dwarf
And eunuch forth.
    Mos.   Castrone, Nano!

[*Enter* CASTRONE *and* NANO.]

Nano.   Here.
Volp. Shall we have a jig now?
    Mos.   What you please, sir.
Volp.   Go,
Straight give out about the streets, you two, 60
That I am dead; do it with constancy,
Sadly,[2] do you hear? Impute it to the grief
Of this late slander.
            [*Exeunt* CAST. *and* NANO.]
    Mos.   What do you mean, sir?
    Volp.   O,
I shall have instantly my Vulture, Crow,
Raven, come flying hither, on the news,   65
To peck for carrion, my she-wolf, and all,
Greedy, and full of expectation —
    Mos. And then to have it ravish'd from their
        mouths!
    Volp. 'T is true. I will ha' thee put on a
        gown,   69
And take upon thee, as thou wert mine heir;

---
[1] The same.   [2] Seriously.

Show 'em a will. Open that chest, and reach
Forth one of those that has the blanks; I 'll
    straight
Put in thy name.
 Mos.   It will be rare, sir.
      [Gives him a paper.]
 Volp.   Ay,
When they e'en gape, and find themselves de-
    luded ——   74
 Mos. Yes.   [patch,
 Volp. And thou use them scurvily! Dis-
Get on thy gown.
 Mos. [putting on a gown.] But what, sir, if
    they ask
After the body?
 Volp. Say, it was corrupted.
 Mos. I 'll say it stunk, sir; and was fain to
    have it
Coffin'd up instantly, and sent away.
 Volp. Anything; what thou wilt. Hold,
    here 's my will.   80
Get thee a cap, a count-book, pen and ink,
Papers afore thee; sit as thou wert taking
An inventory of parcels. I 'll get up
Behind the curtain, on a stool, and hearken:
Sometime peep over. see how they do look,   85
With what degrees their blood doth leave their
    faces.
O, 't will afford me a rare meal of laughter!
 *Mos. [putting on a cap, and setting out the
    table, &c.]* Your advocate will turn stark
    dull upon it.
 Volp. It will take off his oratory's edge.   89
 Mos. But your clarissimo, old roundback, he
Will crump you like a hog-louse, with the touch.
 Volp. And what Corvino?
 Mos.   O, sir, look for him,
To-morrow morning, with a rope and dagger,
To visit all the streets; he must run mad,
My lady too, that came into the court,   95
To bear false witness for your worship ——
 Volp.   Yes,
And kiss'd me 'fore the fathers, when my face
Flow'd all with oils ——
 Mos.   And sweat, sir. Why, your gold
Is such another med'cine, it dries up
All those offensive savours: it transforms   100
The most deformed, and restores them lovely,
As 't were the strange poetical girdle.[1] Jove
Could not invent t' himself a shroud more subtle
To pass Acrisius'[2] guards. It is the thing
Makes all the world her grace, her youth, her
    beauty.   105
 Volp. I think she loves me.
 Mos.   Who? The lady, sir?
She 's jealous of you.
 Volp.   Dost thou say so?
       [Knocking within.]
 Mos.   Hark.
There 's some already.
 Volp. Look.
 Mos.   It is the Vulture;
He has the quickest scent.
 Volp.   I 'll to my place,
Thou to thy posture. *[Goes behind the curtain.]*

----

[1] Cestus. (Jonson.)   [2] The father of Danaë.

 Mos.   I am set.
 Volp.   But, Mosca, 110
Play the artificer now, torture 'em rarely.

Scene III.[3]

Mosca. [Enter] Voltore.

 Volt. How now, my Mosca?
 Mos. [writing]. "Turkey carpets, nine —— "
 Volt. Taking an inventory! that is well.
 Mos. "Two suits of bedding, tissue —— "
 Volt.   Where 's the will?
Let me read that the while.

  [Enter Servants with Corbaccio *in a chair.]*

 Corb.   So, set me down,
And get you home. *[Exeunt Servants.[*5
 Volt.   Is he come now, to trouble us?
 Mos. "Of cloth of gold, two more —— "
 Corb.   Is it done, Mosca?
 Mos. "Of several velvets, eight —— "
 Volt.   I like his care.
 Corb. Dost thou not hear?

    [Enter Corvino.]

 Corv.   Ha! is the hour come, Mosca?
 Volp. Ay, now they muster.
    Peeps from behind a traverse.
 Corv. What does the advocate here, 10
Or this Corbaccio?
 Corb.   What do these here?

  [Enter Lady Pol. Would-be.]

 Lady P.   Mosca!
Is his thread spun?
 Mos.   "Eight chests of linen —— "
 Volp.   O,
My fine Dame Would-be, too!
 Corv.   Mosca, the will,
That I may show it these, and rid 'em
hence.
 Mos. "Six chests of diaper, four of dam-
ask." — There.   15
  *[Gives them the will carelessly, over
   his shoulder.]*
 Corb. Is that the will?
 Mos. "Down-beds, and bolsters —— "
 Volp.   Rare!
Be busy still. Now they begin to flutter:
They never think of me. Look, see, see, see!
How their swift eyes run over the long deed,
Unto the name, and to the legacies,   20
What is bequeath'd them there ——
 Mos. "Ten suits of hangings —— "
 Volp. Ay, in their garters, Mosca. Now their
hopes
Are at the gasp.
 Volt. Mosca the heir.
 Corb.   What 's that?
 Volp. My advocate is dumb; look to my
 merchant,
He 's heard of some strange storm, a ship is
lost,   25
He faints; my lady will swoon. Old glazen-eyes,
He hath not reach'd his despair yet.

----

[3] The same.

Corb.   All these
Are out of hope; I am, sure, the man.
                       [*Takes the will.*]
Corv.   But, Mosca ——
Mos. "Two cabinets ——"
Corv.   Is this in earnest?
Mos.   "One
Of ebony ——"
Corv.   Or do you but delude me?   30
Mos. "The other, mother of pearl." — I'm
very busy,
Good faith, it is a fortune thrown upon me —
"Item, one salt of agate " — not my seeking.
Lady P. Do you hear, sir?   [bear,
Mos.   "A perfum'd box " — Pray you for-
You see I'm troubl'd — "made of an onyx——"
Lady P.   How!   35
Mos. To-morrow or next day, I shall be at
leisure
To talk with you all.
Corv.   Is this my large hope's issue?
Lady P. Sir, I must have a fairer answer.
Mos.   Madam!
Marry, and shall: pray you, fairly quit my
house.
Nay, raise no tempest with your looks; but
hark you,   40
Remember what your ladyship off'red me
To put you in an heir; go to, think on it:
And what you said e'en your best madams
did
For maintenance; and why not you? Enough.
Go home, and use the poor Sir Pol, your knight,
well,   45
For fear I tell some riddles; go, be melancholic.
                       [*Exit* LADY WOULD-BE.]
Volp. O, my fine devil!
Corv.   Mosca, pray you a word.
Mos. Lord! will not you take your dispatch
hence yet?
Methinks, of all, you should have been th' ex-
ample.
Why should you stay here? With what thought,
what promise?   50
Hear you; do you not know, I know you an
ass,
And that you would most fain have been a wit-
tol
If fortune would have let you? that you are
A declar'd cuckold, on good terms? This
pearl,
You'll say, was yours? right: this diamond?   55
I'll not deny't, but thank you. Much here
else?
It may be so. Why, think that these good works
May help to hide your bad. I'll not betray
you;
Although you be but extraordinary,
And have it only in title, it sufficeth: 60
Go home, be melancholy too, or mad.
                       [*Exit* CORVINO.]
Volp. Rare Mosca! how his villany becomes
him!
Volt. Certain he doth delude all these for
me.
Corb. Mosca the heir!
Volp.   O, his four eyes have found it.

Corb. I am cozen'd, cheated, **by a parasite**.
slave;   65
Harlot,[1] th' hast gull'd me.
Mos.   Yes, sir. Stop your mouth,
Or I shall draw the only tooth is left.
Are not you he, that filthy covetous wretch,
With the three legs, that here, in hope of prey,
Have, any time this three years, snuff'd about,
With your most grov'ling nose, and would
have hir'd   71
Me to the pois'ning of my patron, sir?
Are not you he that have to-day in court
Profess'd the disinheriting of your son?
Perjur'd yourself? Go home, and die, and
stink?   75
If you but croak a syllable, all comes out:
Away, and call your porters! [*Exit* CORBACCIO.]
Go, go, stink.
Volp. Excellent varlet!
Volt.   Now, my faithful Mosca,
I find thy constancy ——
Mos.   Sir!
Volt.   Sincere.
Mos. [*writing.*]   "A table
Of porphyry " — I marle[2] you'll be thus
troublesome.   80
Volt. Nay, leave off now, they are gone.
Mos.   Why, who are you?
What! who did send for you? O, cry you mercy,
Reverend sir! Good faith, I am griev'd for
you,
That any chance of mine should thus defeat
Your (I must needs say) most deserving trav-
ails: 85
But I protest, sir, it was cast upon me,
And I could almost wish to be without it,
But that the will o' the dead must be observ'd.
Marry, my joy is that you need it not;
You have a gift, sir (thank your education),   90
Will never let you want, while there are men,
And malice, to breed causes.[3] Would I had
But half the like, for all my fortune, sir!
If I have any suits, as I do hope,
Things being so easy and direct, I shall not,   95
I will make bold with your obstreperous aid,
Conceive me — for your fee, sir. In mean time,
You that have so much law, I know ha' the
conscience
Not to be covetous of what is mine.
Good sir, I thank you for my plate; 't will
help   100
To set up a young man. Good faith, you look
As you were costive; best go home and purge,
sir.   [*Exit* VOLTORE.]
Volp. [*comes from behind the curtain.*] Bid him
eat lettuce[4] well. My witty mischief,
Let me embrace thee. O that I could now
Transform thee to a Venus! — Mosca, go,   105
Straight take my habit of clarissimo,
And walk the streets; be seen, torment 'em
more:
We must pursue, as well as plot. Who would
Have lost this feast?
Mos.   I doubt it will lose them.

[1] Fellow: formerly used of both sexes.
[2] Marvel.
[3] Law-suits.   [4] To make him sleep.

Volp. O, my recovery shall recover all.   110
That I could now but think on some disguise
To meet 'em in, and ask 'em questions :
How I would vex 'em still at every turn !
Mos. Sir, I can fit you.
Volp.   Canst thou ?
Mos.   Yes, I know
One o' the commandadori, sir, so like you ;   115
Him will I straight make drunk, and bring
    you his habit.
Volp. A rare disguise, and answering thy brain!
O, I will be a sharp disease unto 'em.
Mos. Sir, you must look for curses ——
Volp.   Till they burst ;
The Fox fares ever best when he is curst.   120
                                    [*Exeunt.*]

SCENE IV.[1]

[*Enter*] PEREGRINE [*disguised and*] *three* Mer-
    catori.

Per. Am I enough disguis'd ?
1 Mer.   I warrant you.
Per. All my ambition is to fright him only.
2 Mer. If you could ship him away, 't were
    excellent.
3 Mer. To Zant, or to Aleppo ?
Per.   Yes, and ha' his
Adventures put i' th' Book of Voyages,   5
And his gull'd story regist'red for truth.
Well, gentlemen, when I am in a while,
And that you think us warm in our discourse,
Know your approaches.
1 Mer.   Trust it to our care.   9
                          [*Exeunt* Merchants.]

[*Enter* Waiting-woman.]

Per. Save you, fair lady! Is Sir Pol within?
Wom. I do not know, sir.
Per.   Pray you say unto him
Here is a merchant, upon earnest business,
Desires to speak with him.
Wom.   I will see, sir. [*Exit.*]
Per.   Pray you.
I see the family is all female here.

[*Re-enter* Waiting-woman.]

Wom. He says, sir, he has weighty affairs of
    state,   15
That now require him whole ; some other time
You may possess him.
Per.   Pray you say again,
If those require him whole, these will exact him,
Whereof I bring him tidings. [*Exit* Woman.]
                    What might be
His grave affair of state now ! How to make   20
Bolognian sausages here in Venice, sparing
One o' th' ingredients ?

[*Re-enter* Waiting-woman.]

Wom.   Sir, he says, he knows
By your word " tidings," that you are no
    statesman,
And therefore wills you stay.
Per.   Sweet, pray you return him ;
I have not read so many proclamations,   25

    [1] A hall in Sir Politic's house.

And studied them for words, as he has done ——
But — here he deigns to come. [*Exit* Woman.]

[*Enter* SIR POLITIC.]

Sir P.   Sir, I must crave
Your courteous pardon. There hath chanc'd to-
    day
Unkind disaster 'twixt my lady and me ;
And I was penning my apology,   30
To give her satisfaction, as you came now.
Per. Sir, I am griev'd I bring you worse dis-
    aster :
The gentleman you met at th' port to-day,
That told you he was newly arriv'd ——
Sir P.   Ay, was
A fugitive punk ?
Per.   No, sir, a spy set on you :   35
And he has made relation to the senate,
That you profest to him to have a plot
To sell the State of Venice to the Turk.
Sir P. O me !   [time,
Per. For which warrants are sign'd by this
To apprehend you, and to search your study   40
For papers ——
Sir P.   Alas, sir, I have none, but notes
Drawn out of play-books ——
Per.   All the better, sir.
Sir P. And some essays. What shall I do ?
Per.   Sir, best
Convey yourself into a sugar-chest ;
Or, if you could lie round, a frail[2] were rare ;   45
And I could send you aboard.
Sir P.   Sir, I but talk'd so,
For discourse sake merely. [*They knock without.*]
Per.   Hark ! they are there.
Sir P. I am a wretch, a wretch !
Per.   What will you do, sir ?
Have you ne'er a currant-butt to leap into ?
They 'll put you to the rack ; you must be
    sudden.   50
Sir P. Sir, I have an engine[3] ——
3 Mer. [*within.*]   Sir Politic Would-be !
2 Mer. [*within.*] Where is he ?
Sir P. That I 've thought upon before time.
Per. What is it ?
Sir P.   I shall ne'er endure the torture.
Marry, it is, sir, of a tortoise-shell,
Fitted for these extremities : pray you, sir, help
    me.   55
Here I 've a place, sir, to put back my legs,
Please you to lay it on, sir, [*Lies down while*
    PER. *places the shell upon him.*] — with
    this cap,
And my black gloves. I 'll lie, sir, like a
    tortoise,
Till they are gone.
Per.   And call you this an engine ?
Sir P. Mine own device. —— Good sir, bid my
    wife's women   60
To burn my papers.   [*Exit* PER.]

The three Merchants *rush in.*

1 Mer.   Where is he hid ?
3 Mer.   We must,
And will sure find him.
2 Mer.   Which is his study ?

    [2] Rush-basket.   [3] Contrivance

[*Re-enter* PEREGRINE.]

1 *Mer.*   What
Are you, sir?
   Per.   I 'm a merchant, that came here
To look upon this tortoise?
3 *Mer.*   How!
1 *Mer.*   St. Mark!
What beast is this?
   Per.   It is a fish.
2 *Mer.*   Come out here! 65
   Per. Nay, you may strike him, sir, and tread
     upon him;
He 'll bear a cart.
1 *Mer.*   What, to run over him?
   Per.   Yes, sir.
3 *Mer.* Let 's jump upon him.
2 *Mer.*   Can he not go?
   Per.   He creeps, sir.
1 *Mer.* Let 's see him creep.
   Per.   No, good sir, you will hurt him. 69
2 *Mer.* Heart, I will see him creep, or prick
     his guts.
3 *Mer.* Come out here!
   Per.   Pray you, sir, creep a little.
1 *Mer.*   Forth.
2 *Mer.* Yet further.
   Per.   Good sir! — Creep.
2 *Mer.*   We 'll see his legs.
      They pull off the shell and discover
       him.
3 *Mer.* Gods so, he has garters!
1 *Mer.*   Ay, and gloves!
2 *Mer.*   Is this
Your fearful tortoise?
   Per. [*discovering himself.*] Now, Sir Pol,
     we 're even;
For your next project I shall be prepar'd: 75
I am sorry for the funeral of your notes, sir.
1 *Mer.* 'T were a rare motion[1] to be seen in
     Fleet-street.
2 *Mer.* Ay, in the Term.
1 *Mer.*   Or Smithfield, in the fair.
3 *Mer.* Methinks 't is but a melancholic
     sight.
   Per. Farewell, most politic tortoise!
         [*Exeunt* PER. *and Merchants.*]

[*Re-enter* Waiting-woman.]

Sir P.   Where 's my lady? 80
Knows she of this?
   Wom.   I know not, sir.
   Sir P.   Enquire. —
O, I shall be the fable of all feasts,
The freight of the gazetti, [1] ship-boys' tale;
And, which is worst, even talk for ordinaries.
   Wom. My lady 's come most melancholic
     home,   85
And says, sir, she will straight to sea, for
     physic.
   Sir P. And I, to shun this place and clime
     for ever,
Creeping with house on back, and think it well
To shrink my poor head in my politic shell.
                 [*Exeunt.*]

   [1] Show.   [2] The theme of the newspapers.

SCENE V.[3]

[*Enter*] MOSCA *in the habit of a clarissimo, and*
   VOLPONE *in that of a commandadore.*

Volp. Am I then like him?
   Mos.   O, sir, you are he;
No man can sever you.
   Volp.   Good.
   Mos.   But what am I?
   Volp. 'Fore heaven, a brave clarissimo; thou
     becom'st it!
Pity thou wert not born one.
   Mos. [*Aside.*]   If I hold
My made one, 't will be well.
   Volp.   I 'll go and see 5
What news first at the court.   [*Exit.*]
   Mos.   Do so. My Fox
Is out of his hole, and ere he shall re-enter,
I 'll make him languish in his borrow'd case,[4]
Except he come to composition with me. —
Androgyno, Castrone, Nano!

[*Enter* ANDROGYNO, CASTRONE, *and* NANO.]

All.   Here. 10
   Mos. Go, recreate yourselves abroad; go,
     sport. —   [*Exeunt.*]
So, now I have the keys, and am possest.
Since he will needs be dead afore his time,
I 'll bury him, or gain by 'm: I 'm his heir,
And so will keep me, till he share at least. 15
To cozen him of all, were but a cheat
Well plac'd; no man would construe it a sin:
Let his sport pay for 't. This is call'd the Fox-
     trap.   [*Exit.*]

SCENE VI.[5]

[*Enter*] CORBACCIO, CORVINO.

Corb. They say the court is set.
   Corv.   We must maintain
Our first tale good, for both our reputations.
   Corb. Why, mine 's no tale: my son would
     there have kill'd me.
   Corv. That 's true, I had forgot: — mine is,
     I 'm sure.
But for your will, sir.
   Corb.   Ay, I 'll come upon him 5
For that hereafter, now his patron 's dead.

[*Enter* VOLPONE.]

Volp. Signior Corvino! and Corbaccio! sir,
Much joy unto you.
   Corv.   Of what?
   Volp.   The sudden good
Dropt down upon you ——
   Corb.   Where?
   Volp.   And none knows how,
From old Volpone, sir.
   Corb.   Out, arrant knave! 10
   Volp. Let not your too much wealth, sir,
     make you furious.
   Corb. Away, thou varlet.
   Volp.   Why, sir?
   Corb.   Dost thou mock me?

   [3] A room in Volpone's house.
   [4] Disguise.   [5] A street.

Volp. You mock the world, sir ; did you not change wills ?

Corb. Out, harlot !

Volp.   O ! belike you are the man,
Signior Corvino ? Faith, you carry it well ;   15
You grow not mad withal ; I love your spirit :
You are not over-leaven'd with your fortune.
You should ha' some would swell now, like a
     wine-fat,
With such an autumn. — Did he gi' you all,
     sir ?

Corb. Avoid, you rascal !

Volp.   Troth, your wife has shown   20
Herself a very woman ; but you are well,
You need not care, you have a good estate,
To bear it out, sir, better by this chance :
Except Corbaccio have a share.

Corb.   Hence, varlet.

Volp. You will not be acknown, sir ; why,
     'tis wise.   25
Thus do all gamesters, at all games, dissemble :
No man will seem to win. [*Exeunt* CORVINO *and*
     CORBACCIO.] Here comes my vulture,
Heaving his beak up i' the air, and snuffing.

SCENE VII.[1]

VOLPONE. [*Enter*] VOLTORE.

Volt. Outstript thus, by a parasite ! a slave,
Would run on errands, and make legs for
     crumbs !
Well, what I 'll do ——

Volp.   The court stays for your worship.
I e'en rejoice, sir, at your worship's happiness,
And that it fell into so learned hands,   5
That understand the fing'ring ——

Volt.   What do you mean ?

Volp. I mean to be a suitor to your worship,
For the small tenement, out of reparations,[2]
That, at the end of your long row of houses,
By the Piscaria : it was, in Volpone's time,   10
Your predecessor, ere he grew diseas'd,
A handsome, pretty, custom'd[3] bawdy-house
As any was in Venice, none disprais'd ;
But fell with him : his body and that house
Decay'd together.

Volt.   Come, sir, leave your prating. 15

Volp. Why, if your worship give me but your
     hand
That I may ha' the refusal, I have done.
'T is a mere toy to you, sir ; candle-rents ;
As your learn'd worship knows——

Volt.   What do I know ?

Volp. Marry, no end of your wealth, sir ; God
     decrease it !   20

Volt. Mistaking knave ! what, mock'st thou
     my misfortune ?   [*Exit.*]

Volt. His blessing on your heart, sir ; would
     't were more ! ——
Now to my first again, at the next corner.
                        [*Exit.*]

---

[1] The same.   [3] Well-frequented.
[2] Out of repair.

SCENE VIII.[4]

[*Enter*] CORBACCIO *and* CORVINO ; — (MOSCA *passant.*)

Corb. See, in our habit ![5] see the impudent
     varlet !

Corv. That I could shoot mine eyes at him,
     like gun-stones !

[*Enter* VOLPONE.]

Volp. But is this true, sir, of the parasite ?

Corb. Again, t' afflict us ! monster !

Volp.   In good faith, sir,
I 'm heartily griev'd, a beard of your grave
     length   5
Should be so over-reach'd. I never brook'd
That parasite's hair ; methought his nose should
     cozen :[6]
There still was somewhat in his look, did promise
The bane of a clarissimo.

Corb.   Knave——

Volp.   Methinks
Yet you, that are so traded i' the world,   10
A witty merchant, the fine bird, Corvino,
That have such moral emblems on your name,
Should not have sung your shame, and dropt
     your cheese,
To let the Fox laugh at your emptiness.

Corv. Sirrah, you think the privilege of the
     place,   15
And your red saucy cap, that seems to me
Nail'd to your jolt-head with those two chequins,
Can warrant your abuses ; come you hither :
You shall perceive, sir, I dare beat you ; approach.

Volp. No haste, sir, I do know your valour
     well,   20
Since you durst publish what you are, sir.

Corv.   Tarry,
I 'd speak with you.

Volp.   Sir, sir, another time——

Corv. Nay, now.

Volp.   O lord, sir ! I were a wise man,
Would stand the fury of a distracted cuckold.
                 MOSCA *walks by them.*

Corb. What, come again !

Volp.   Upon 'em, Mosca ; save me. 25

Corb. The air 's infected where he breathes.

Corv.   Let 's fly him.
           [*Exeunt* CORV. *and* CORB.]

Volp. Excellent basilisk ! turn upon the vulture.

SCENE IX.[7]

MOSCA, VOLPONE. [*Enter*] VOLTORE.

Volt. Well, flesh-fly, it is summer with you
     now ;
Your winter will come on.

Mos.   Good advocate,
Prithee not rail, nor threaten out of place thus ;
Thou 'lt make a solecism, as madam says.

---

[4] The Scrutineo, or Senate House.
[5] Dressed like a clarissimo, or gentleman.
[6] Swindle.   [7] The same.

Get you a biggin[1] more; your brain breaks
   loose.   [*Exit.*] 5
Volt. Well sir.   [slave,
  Volp. Would you ha' me beat the insolent
Throw dirt upon his first good clothes?
Volt.   This same
Is doubtless some familiar.
  Volp.   Sir, the court,
In troth, stays for you. I am mad, a mule
That never read Justinian, should get up, 10
And ride an advocate. Had you no quirk
To avoid gullage, sir, by such a creature?
I hope you do but jest; he has not done 't:
This 's but confederacy to blind the rest.
You are the heir?
  Volt.   A strange, officious, 15
Troublesome knave! thou dost torment me.
  Volp.   I know ——
It cannot be, sir, that you should be cozen'd;
'T is not within the wit of man to do it;
You are so wise, so prudent; and 't is fit 19
That wealth and wisdom still should go to-
   gether.   [*Exeunt.*]

Scene X.[2]

[*Enter*] 4 Avocatori, Notario, BONARIO, CELIA,
  CORBACCIO, CORVINO, Commandadori, [Saffi,
  etc.]

1 Avoc. Are all the parties here?
Not.   All but th' advocate.
2 Avoc. And here he comes.

[*Enter* VOLTORE *and* VOLPONE.]

1 Avoc. Then bring them forth to sentence.
Volt. O, my most honour'd fathers, let your
  mercy
Once win upon your justice, to forgive —
I am distracted ——
  Volp.   (*Aside.*) What will he do now?
  Volt.   O, 5
I know not which t' address myself to first;
Whether your fatherhoods, or these innocents —
  Corv. (*Aside.*) Will he betray himself?
  Volt.   Whom equally
I have abus'd, out of most covetous ends ——
  Corv. The man is mad!
  Corb.   What 's that?
  Corv.   He is possest. 10
  Volt. For which, now struck in conscience,
  here I prostrate
Myself at your offended feet, for pardon.
  1, 2 Avoc. Arise.
  Cel.   O heaven, how just thou art!
  Volp.   I 'm caught
I' mine own noose ——
  Corv. [*to* CORBACCIO.] Be constant, sir;
  nought now   14
Can help but impudence.
  1 Avoc.   Speak forward.
  Com.   Silence!
  Volt. It is not passion in me, reverend
  fathers,
But only conscience, conscience, my good sires,

That makes me now tell truth. That parasite,
That knave, hath been the instrument of all. 18
  1 Avoc. Where is that knave? Fetch him.
  Volp.   I go.   [*Exit.*]
  Corv.   Grave fathers,
This man 's distracted; he confest it now:
For, hoping to be old Volpone's heir,
Who now is dead ——
  3 Avoc.   How!
  2 Avoc.   Is Volpone dead?
  Corv. Dead since, grave fathers.
  Bon.   O sure vengeance!
  1 Avoc.   Stay,
Then he was no deceiver?
  Volt.   O no, none: 25
This parasite, grave fathers.
  Corv.   He does speak
Out of mere envy, 'cause the servant 's made
The thing he gap'd for. Please your father-
  hoods,
This is the truth, though I 'll not justify
The other, but he may be some-deal faulty. 30
  Volt. Ay, to your hopes, as well as mine, Cor-
  vino:
But I 'll use modesty.[3] Pleaseth your wisdoms,
To view these certain notes, and but confer[4]
  them;
And as I hope favour, they shall speak clear
  truth.   35
  Corv. The devil has ent'red him!
  Bon.   Or bides in you.
  4 Avoc. We have done ill, by a public officer
To send for him, if he be heir.
  2 Avoc.   For whom?
  4 Avoc. Him that they call the parasite.
  3 Avoc.   'T is true,
He is a man of great estate, now left.
  4 Avoc. Go you, and learn his name, and say
  the court   40
Entreats his presence here, to the clearing
Of some few doubts.   [*Exit* Notary.]
  2 Avoc.   This same 's a labyrinth!
  1 Avoc. Stand you unto your first report?
  Corv.   My state,
My life, my fame ——
  Bon.   Where is 't?
  Corv.   Are at the stake.
  1 Avoc. Is yours so too?
  Corb.   The advocate 's a knave, 45
And has a forked tongue ——
  2 Avoc.   Speak to the point.
  Corb. So is the parasite too.
  1 Avoc.   This is confusion.
  Volt. I do beseech your fatherhoods, read but
  those —   [*Giving them papers.*]
  Corv. And credit nothing the false spirit hath
  writ:
It cannot be but he 's possest, grave fathers. 50
               [*The scene closes.*]

Scene XI.[5]

[*Enter*] VOLPONE.

Volp. To make a snare for mine own neck!
  and run

---

[1] Barrister's cap.
[2] The same.
[3] Moderation.   [4] Compare.   [5] A street.

My head into it, wilfully! with laughter!
When I had newly scap'd, was free and clear,
Out of mere wantonness! O, the dull devil
Was in this brain of mine when I devis'd it,   5
And Mosca gave it second; he must now
Help to sear up this vein, or we bleed dead.

[*Enter* NANO, ANDROGYNO, *and* CASTRONE.]

How now! Who let you loose? Whither go
          you now?
What, to buy gingerbread, or to drown kit-
          lings?
Nan. Sir, Master Mosca call'd us out of doors,
And bid us all go play, and took the keys.   11
And. Yes.   [*Why*, so!
Volp.   Did Master Mosca take the keys?
I'm farther in. These are my fine conceits!
I must be merry, with a mischief to me!   14
What a vile wretch was I, that could not bear
My fortune soberly? I must ha' my crochets,
And my conundrums! Well, go you, and seek
          him:
His meaning may be truer than my fear.
Bid him, he straight come to me to the court;
Thither will I, and, if 't be possible,   20
Unscrew my advocate, upon new hopes:
When I provok'd him, then I lost myself.
                                        [*Exeunt.*]

SCENE XII.[1]

Avocatori, [BONARIO, CELIA, CORBACCIO, COR-
VINO, Commandadori, Saffi,] *etc.*, [*as before.*]

1 *Avoc.* These things can ne'er be reconcil'd.
He here   [*showing the papers*]
Professeth that the gentleman was wrong'd,
And that the gentlewoman was brought thither,
Forc'd by her husband, and there left.
Volt.   Most true.
Cel. How ready is heaven to those that
          pray!
1 *Avoc.*   But that   5
Volpone would have ravish'd her, he holds
Utterly false, knowing his impotence.
Corv. Grave fathers, he's possest; again, I
          say,
Possest: nay, if there be possession, and
Obsession, he has both.
3 *Avoc.*   Here comes our officer.   10

[*Enter* VOLPONE.]

Volp. The parasite will straight be here,
          grave fathers.
2 *Avoc.* You might invent some other name,
          sir varlet.
3 *Avoc.* Did not the notary meet him?
Volp.   Not that I know.
4 *Avoc.* His coming will clear all.
2 *Avoc.*   Yet it is misty.
Volt. May 't please your fatherhoods ——
Volp. (*whispers* VOLT.)   Sir, the parasite   15
Will'd me to tell you that his master lives;
That you are still the man; your hopes the
          same;
And this was only a jest ——
Volt.   How?

Volp.   Sir, to try
If you were firm, and how you stood affected.
Volt. Art sure he lives?
Volp.   Do I live, sir?
Volt.   O me!
I was too violent.
Volp.   Sir, you may redeem it.   21
They said you were possest; fall down, and
          seem so:
I'll help to make it good. (VOLTORE *falls.*)
          God bless the man! ——
Stop your wind hard, and swell — See, see, see,
          see!
He vomits crooked pins! His eyes are set,   24
Like a dead hare's hung in a poulter's shop!
His mouth 's running away! Do you see, signior?
Now it is in his belly.
Corv.   Ay, the devil!
Volp. Now in his throat.
Corv.   Ay, I perceive it plain.
Volp. 'T will out, 't will out! stand clear.
See where it flies,   30
In shape of a blue toad, with a bat's wings!
Do you not see it, sir?
Corb.   What? I think I do.
Corv. 'T is too manifest.
Volp.   Look! he comes t' himself!
Volt. Where am I?
Volp.   Take good heart, the worst is past, sir.
You're dispossest.
1 *Avoc.*   What accident is this!   35
2 *Avoc.* Sudden and full of wonder!
3 *Avoc.*   If he were
Possest, as it appears, all this is nothing.
Corv. He has been often subject to these fits.
1 *Avoc.* Show him that writing: — do you
          know it, sir?
Volp. (*whispers* VOLT.) Deny it, sir, forswear
          it; know it not.   40
Volt. Yes, I do know it well, it is my hand;
But all that it contains is false.
Bon.   O practice![2]
2 *Avoc.* What maze is this!
1 *Avoc.*   Is he not guilty then,
Whom you there name the parsite?
Volt.   Grave fathers,
No more than his good patron, old Volpone.   45
4 *Avoc.* Why, he is dead.
Volt.   O no, my honour'd fathers,
He lives ——
1 *Avoc.*   How! lives?
Volt.   Lives.
2 *Avoc.*   This is subtler yet!
3 *Avoc.* You said he was dead.
Volt.   Never.
3 *Avoc.*   You said so.
Corv.   I heard so.
4 *Avoc.* Here comes the gentleman; make
          him way.

[*Enter* MOSCA.]

3 *Avoc.*   A stool,
4 *Avoc.* [*Aside.*] A proper man; and were
          Volpone dead,   50
A fit match for my daughter.

3 Avoc.   Give him way.
Volp. [*Aside to* Mos.] Mosca, I was a'most
lost ; the advocate
Had betray'd all ; but now it is recover'd ;
All 's on the hinge again —— Say I am living.
Mos. What busy knave is this ! — Most rev-
erend fathers,   55
I sooner had attended your grave pleasures,
But that my order for the funeral
Of my dear patron did require me ——
Volp. [*Aside.*]   Mosca !
Mos. Whom I intend to bury like a gentle-
man.
Volp. [*Aside.*] Ay, quick, and cozen me of all.
2 Avoc.   Still stranger !   60
More intricate !
1 Avoc.   And come about again !
4 Avoc. [*Aside.*] It is a match, my daughter
is bestow'd.
Mos. [*Aside to* Volp.] Will you gi' me half ?
Volp.   First I 'll be hang'd.
Mos.   I know
Your voice is good, cry not so loud.
1 Avoc.   Demand
The advocate. — Sir, did you not affirm   65
Volpone was alive ?
Volp.   Yes, and he is ;
This gent'man told me so. — [*Aside to* Mos.]
Thou shalt have half.
Mos. Whose drunkard is this same ? Speak,
some that know him :
I never saw his face. — [*Aside to* Volp.] I can-
not now
Afford it you so cheap.
Volp.   No !
1 Avoc.   What say you ? 70
Volt. The officer told me.
Volp.   I did, grave fathers,
And will maintain he lives, with mine own life,
And that this creature [*points to* Mos.] told
me. [*Aside.*] — I was born
With all good stars my enemies.
Mos.   Most grave fathers,
If such an insolence as this must pass   75
Upon me, I am silent : 't was not this
For which you sent, I hope.
2 Avoc.   Take him away.
Volp. Mosca !
3 Avoc.   Let him be whipt.
Volp.   Wilt thou betray me ?
Cozen me ?
3 Avoc. And taught to bear himself
Toward a person of his rank.
4 Avoc.   Away.   80
     [*The* Officers *seize* Volpone.]
Mos. I humbly thank your fatherhoods.
Volp.   Soft, soft : [*Aside.*] Whipt !
And lose all that I have ! If I confess,
It cannot be much more.
4 Avoc.   Sir, are you married ?
Volp. They 'll be alli'd anon ; I must be re-
solute ;   84
The Fox shall here uncase.
     Puts off his disguise.
Mos.   Patron !
Volp.   Nay, now
My ruin shall not come alone ; your match

I 'll hinder sure : my substance shall not glue
you,
Nor screw you into a family.
Mos.   Why, patron !
Volp. I am Volpone, and this is my knave ;
     [*Pointing to* Mosca.]
This [*to* Volt.], his own knave; this [*to* Corb.],
avarice's fool ;   90
This [*to* Corv.], a chimera of wittol, fool, and
knave :
And, reverend fathers, since we all can hope
Nought but a sentence, let 's not now despair it.
You hear me brief.
Corv.   May it please your fatherhoods ——
Com.   Silence. 94
1 Avoc. The knot is now undone by miracle.
2 Avoc. Nothing can be more clear.
3 Avoc.   Or can more prove
These innocent.
1 Avoc.   Give 'em their liberty.
Bon. Heaven could not long let such gross
crimes be hid.
2 Avoc. If this be held the highway to get
riches,   99
May I be poor !
3 Avoc. This 's not the gain, but torment.
1 Avoc. These possess wealth, as sick men
possess fevers,
Which trulier may be said to possess them.
2 Avoc. Disrobe that parasite.
Corv. Mos.   Most honour'd fathers ——
1 Avoc. Can you plead aught to stay the
course of justice ?   104
If you can, speak.
Corv. Volt.   We beg favour.
Cel.   And mercy.
1 Avoc. You hurt your innocence, suing for
the guilty.
Stand forth ; and first the parasite. You appear
T' have been the chiefest minister, if not plot-
ter,
In all these lewd impostures, and now, lastly,
Have with your impudence abus'd [1] the court,
And habit of a gentleman of Venice,   111
Being a fellow of no birth or blood :
For which our sentence is, first, thou be whipt ;
Then live perpetual prisoner in our galleys.   114
Volp. I thank you for him.
Mos.   Bane to thy wolfish nature !
1 Avoc. Deliver him to the saffi.[2] [Mosca *is
carried out.*] Thou, Volpone,
By blood and rank a gentleman, canst not fall
Under like censure ; but our judgment on thee
Is, that thy substance all be straight confiscate
To the hospital of the Incurabili :   120
And since the most was gotten by imposture,
By feigning lame, gout, palsy, and such dis-
eases,
Thou art to lie in prison, cramp'd with irons,
Till thou be'st sick and lame indeed. Remove
him.   [*He is taken from the Bar.*]
Volp. This is called mortifying of a Fox.   125
1 Avoc. Thou, Voltore, to take away the
scandal
Thou hast giv'n all worthy men of thy profes-
sion,

---

[1] Deceived.   [2] Under-bailiff.

Art banish'd from their fellowship, and our state.
Corbaccio! — bring him near. We here possess
Thy son of all thy state, and confine thee   130
To the monastery of San Spirito;
Where, since thou knew'st not how to live well here.
Thou shalt be learn'd to die well.
 Corb   Ha! what said he?
 Com. You shall know anon, sir.
 1 *Avoc.*   Thou, Corvino, shalt
Be straight embark'd from thine own house,
Round about Venice, through the Grand Canal,
Wearing a cap, with fair long ass's ears,   135
Instead of horns! and so to mount, a paper
Pinn'd on thy breast, to the Berlina.[1]
 Corv.   Yes, 139
And have mine eyes beat out with stinking fish,
Bruis'd fruit, and rotten eggs — 't is well. I 'm glad
I shall not see my shame yet.
 1 *Avoc.*   And to expiate
Thy wrongs done to thy wife, thou art to send her

[1] Pillory.

Home to her father, with her dowry trebled:
And these are all your judgments.
 All.   Honour'd fathers —— 145
 1 *Avoc.* Which may not be revok'd. Now you begin,
When crimes are done and past, and to be punish'd,
To think what your crimes are. Away with them!
Let all that see these vices thus rewarded,
Take heart, and love to study 'em. Mischiefs feed   150
Like beasts, till they be fat, and then they bleed. [*Exeunt.*]

VOLPONE [*comes forward*].

" The seasoning of a play is the applause.
Now, though the Fox be punish'd by the laws,
He yet doth hope, there is no suff'ring due,   154
For any fact [2] which he hath done 'gainst you;
If there be, censure him; here he doubtful stands:
If not, fare jovially, and clap your hands."
        [*Exit.*]

[2] Deed.

THE ALCHEMIST

BY

BEN JONSON

THE PERSONS OF THE PLAY

SUBTLE, the ALCHEMIST.
FACE, the House-keeper.
DOL COMMON, their colleague.
DAPPER, a [Lawyer's] clerk.
DRUGGER, a Tobacco-man.
LOVEWIT, Master of the House.
[Sir] EPICURE MAMMON, a Knight.

[PERTINAX] SURLY, a Gamester.
TRIBULATION [WHOLESOME], a Pastor of Amsterdam.
ANANIAS, a Deacon there.
KASTRIL, the angry boy.
DAME PLIANT, his sister, a Widow.
Neighbours.
Officers, Mutes.

SCENE. — *London.*

[TO THE READER [1]

IF thou beest more, thou art an understander, and then I trust thee. If thou art one that tak'st up, and but a pretender, beware at what hands thou receiv'st thy commodity; for thou wert never more fair in the way to be coz'ned than in this age in poetry, especially in plays: wherein now the concupiscence of jigs and dances [2] so reigneth, as to run away from nature and be afraid of her is the only point of art that tickles the spectators. But how out of purpose and place do I name art, when the professors are grown so obstinate contemners of it, and presumers on their own naturals, [3] as they are deriders of all diligence that way, and, by simple mocking at the terms when they understand not the things, think to get off wittily with their ignorance! Nay, they are esteem'd the more learned and sufficient for this by the multitude, [4] through their excellent vice [5] of judgment. For they commend writers as they do fencers or wrastlers; who, if they come in robustiously and put for it with a great deal of violence, are receiv'd for the braver fellows; when many times their own rudeness is the cause of their disgrace, and a little touch of their adversary gives all that boisterous force the foil. [6] I deny not but that these men who always seek to do more than enough may some time happen on some thing that is good and great; but very seldom: and when it comes, it doth not recompence the rest of their ill. It sticks out, perhaps, and is more eminent, because all is sordid and vile about it; as lights are more discern'd in a thick darkness than a faint shadow. I speak not this out of a hope to do good on any man against his will; for I know, if it were put to the question of theirs and mine, the worse would find more suffrages, because the most favour common errors. But I give thee this warning, that there is a great difference between those that (to gain the opinion of copie [7]) utter [8] all they can, however unfitly, and those that use election and a mean. For it is only the disease of the unskillful to think rude things greater than polish'd, or scatter'd more numerous than compos'd.]

ARGUMENT

T HE sickness hot, [9] a master quit, for fear,
H is house in town, and left one servant there.
E ase him corrupted, and gave means to know
A Cheater and his punk; [10] who now brought low,
L eaving their narrow practice, were become
C oz'ners [11] at large; and only wanting some
H ouse to set up, and with him they here contract,
E ach for a share, and all begin to act.
M uch company they draw, and much abuse, [12]
I n casting figures, [13] telling fortunes, news,
S elling of flies, [14] flat bawdry, with the stone, [15]
T ill it, and they, and all in fume [16] are gone.

1 Printed in Q. only.
2 Hoe's copy of the Q. reads *Daunces, and Antikes* for *jigs and dances.*
3 Natural gifts.
4 Hoe's Q. *Many.*
5 Surpassing defect.
6 Defeat.
7 *Copia,* copiousness.
8 Publish.
9 The plague raging.
10 Mistress.
11 Swindlers.
12 Deceive.
13 Calculating the future.
14 Familiar spirits.
15 Philosophers' stone.
16 Smoke.

PROLOGUE

FORTUNE, that favours fools, these two short hours
  We wish away, both for your sakes and ours,
Judging spectators; and desire in place,
  To th' author justice, to ourselves but grace.
Our scene is London, 'cause we would make known,   5
  No country's mirth is better than our own.
No clime breeds better matter for your whore,
  Bawd, squire, impostor, many persons more,
Whose manners, now call'd humours, feed the stage;
  And which have still been subject for the rage   10
Or spleen of comic writers. Though this pen
  Did never aim to grieve, but better men;
Howe'er the age he lives in doth endure
  The vices that she breeds, above their cure.
But when the wholesome remedies are sweet,   15
  And, in their working gain and profit meet,
He hopes to find no spirit so much diseas'd,
  But will with such fair correctives be pleas'd.
For here he doth not fear who can apply.
  If there be any that will sit so nigh   20
Unto the stream, to look what it doth run,
  They shall find things, they'd think, or wish, were done;
They are so natural follies, but so shown,
  As even the doers may see, and yet not own.

ACT I

SCENE I.[1]

[*Enter*] FACE, [*in a captain's uniform, with his sword drawn, and*] SUBTLE [*with a vial, quarrelling, and followed by*] DOL COMMON.

Face. Believe 't, I will.
Sub.   Thy worst. I fart at thee.
Dol. Ha' you your wits? Why, gentlemen! for love——
Face. Sirrah, I'll strip you——
Sub.   What to do? Lick figs[2]
Out at my——   [sleights.[3]
Face.   Rogue, rogue!—out of all your
Dol. Nay, look ye, sovereign, general, are you madmen?   5
Sub. O, let the wild sheep loose. I'll gum your silks
With good strong water, an you come.
Dol.   Will you have
The neighbours hear you? Will you betray all?
Hark! I hear somebody.
Face.   Sirrah——
Sub.   I shall mar
All that the tailor has made, if you approach. 10
Face. You most notorious whelp, you insolent slave,
Dare you do this?
Sub.   Yes, faith; yes, faith.
Face.   Why, who
Am I, my mongrel, who am I?
Sub.   I'll tell you,
Since you know not yourself.
Face.   Speak lower, rogue.

   [1] A room in Lovewit's house.
   [2] Rabelais, Bk. IV. ch. 45.
      Drop your tricks.

Sub. Yes. You were once (time's not long past) the good,   15
Honest, plain, livery-three-pound-thrum,[4] that kept
Your master's worship's house here in the Friars,[5]
For the vacations——
Face.   Will you be so loud?
Sub. Since, by my means, translated suburb-captain.
Face. By your means, doctor dog!
Sub.   Within man's memory,   20
All this I speak of.
Face.   Why, I pray you, have I
Been countenanc'd by you, or you by me?
Do but collect, sir, where I met you first.
Sub. I do not hear well.
Face.   Not of this, I think it.
But I shall put you in mind, sir;—at Pie-corner,   25
Taking your meal of steam in, from cooks' stalls,
Where, like the father of hunger, you did walk
Piteously costive, with your pinch'd-horn-nose,
And your complexion of the Roman wash,[6]
Stuck full of black and melancholic worms,   30
Like powder-corns[7] shot at the artillery-yard.
Sub. I wish you could advance your voice a little.
Face. When you went pinn'd up in the several rags
You had rak'd and pick'd from dunghills, before day;
Your feet in mouldy slippers, for your kibes;[8]
A felt of rug,[9] and a thin threaden cloak,   34
That scarce would cover your no-buttocks——

   [4] Poorly paid servant.
   [5] The precinct of Blackfriars.
   [6] *I. e.* sallow.   [8] Chilblains.
   [7] Grains of powder.   [9] A hat of coarse material.

Sub. So, sir!
Face. When all your alchemy, and your alge-
bra,
Your minerals, vegetals, and animals,
Your conjuring, coz'ning;[1] and your dozen of
trades, 40
Could not relieve your corpse with so much
linen
Would make you tinder, but to see a fire;
I ga' you count'nance, credit for your coals,
Your stills, your glasses, your materials;
Built you a furnace, drew you customers, 45
Advanc'd all your black arts; lent you, beside,
A house to practise in ——
Sub. Your master's house!
Face. Where you have studied the more
thriving skill
Of bawdry, since.
Sub. Yes, in your master's house.
You and the rats here kept possession. 50
Make it not strange.[2] I know you were one
could keep
The buttery-hatch still lock'd, and save the
chippings,
Sell the dole beer to aqua-vitae men,[3]
The which, together with your Christmas vails[4]
At post-and-pair,[5] your letting out of coun-
ters,[6] 55
Made you a pretty stock, some twenty marks,
And gave you credit to converse with cobwebs,
Here, since your mistress' death hath broke up
house.
Face. You might talk softlier, rascal.
Sub. No, you scarab,
I'll thunder you in pieces. I will teach you 60
How to beware to tempt a Fury again
That carries tempest in his hand and voice.
Face. The place has made you valiant.
Sub. No, your clothes.
Thou vermin, have I ta'en thee out of dung,
So poor, so wretched, when no living thing 65
Would keep thee company, but a spider or
worse?
Rais'd thee from brooms, and dust, and wat'r-
ing-pots,
Sublim'd thee, and exalted thee, and fix'd thee
In the third region,[7] call'd our state of grace?
Wrought thee to spirit, to quintessence, with
pains 70
Would twice have won me the philosopher's
work?
Put thee in words and fashion? made thee fit
For more than ordinary fellowships?
Giv'n thee thy oaths, thy quarrelling dimen-
sions?
Thy rules to cheat at horse-race, cock-pit, cards,
Dice, or whatever gallant tincture[8] else? 76
Made thee a second in mine own great art?
And have I this for thanks! Do you rebel?
Do you fly out i' the projection?[9]
Would you be gone now?

Dol. Gentlemen, what mean you? 80
Will you mar all?
Sub. Slave, thou hadst had no name ——
Dol. Will you undo yourselves with civil
war?
Sub. Never been known, past *equi clibanum,*
The heat of horse-dung, under ground, in cel-
lars,
Or an ale-house darker than deaf John's; been
lost 85
To all mankind, but laundresses and tapsters,
Had not I been.
Dol. Do you know who hears you, sovereign?
Face. Sirrah —— [were civil.
Dol. Nay, general, I thought you
Face. I shall turn desperate, if you grow thus
loud,
Sub. And hang thyself, I care not.
Face. Hang thee, collier,
And all thy pots and pans, in picture I will, 91
Since thou hast mov'd me ——
Dol. [*Aside*] O, this'll o'erthrow all.
Face. Write thee up bawd in Paul's; have
all thy tricks
Of coz'ning with a hollow coal, dust, scrapings.
Searching for things lost, with a sieve and
shears, 95
Erecting figures in your rows of houses,[10]
And taking in of shadows with a glass,
Told in red letters; and a face cut for thee,
Worse than Gamaliel Ratsey's.[11]
Dol. Are you sound?
Ha' you your senses, masters?
Face. I will have 100
A book, but rarely reckoning thy impostures,
Shall prove a true philosopher's stone to
printers.
Sub. Away, you trencher-rascal!
Face. Out, you dog-leech!
The vomit of all prisons ——
Dol. Will you be
Your own destructions, gentlemen?
Face. Still spew'd out 105
For lying too heavy o' the basket.[12]
Sub. Cheater!
Face. Bawd!
Sub. Cow-herd!
Face. Conjurer!
Sub. Cutpurse!
Face. Witch!
Dol. O me!
We are ruin'd, lost! Ha' you no more regard
To your reputations? Where's your judgment?
'Slight, 109
Have yet some care of me, o' your republic——
Face. Away, this brach![13] I'll bring thee,
rogue, within
The statute of sorcery, tricesimo tertio
Of Harry the Eighth:[14] ay, and perhaps thy neck
Within a noose, for laund'ring gold and barbing
it.[15]

---

[1] Swindling.   [2] Don't pretend to forget.
[3] Sell the beer intended for the poor to liquor-dealers.
[4] Tips.   [5] A game of cards.
[6] *I. e.,* to the card-players.
[7] Technical jargon of alchemy.   [8] Accomplishment.
[9] At the moment when success is near.

[10] Astrological tricks.   [11] A notorious highwayman.
[12] Eating more than his share of rations.
[13] Bitch.
[14] 33 Henry VIII, the first act against witchcraft in England.
[15] "Sweating" and clipping the coinage.

Dol. You 'll bring your head within a cocks-
    comb, will you ?[1]   115
        She catcheth out FACE *his sword, and*
        breaks SUBTLE'S *glass.*
And you, sir, with your menstrue ![2] — Gather
    it up.
'Sdeath, you abominable pair of stinkards,
Leave off your barking, and grow one again,
Or, by the light that shines, I 'll cut your throats.
I 'll not be made a prey unto the marshal   120
For ne'er a snarling dog-bolt[3] o' you both.
Ha' you together cozen'd all this while,
And all the world, and shall it now be said,
You 've made most courteous shift to cozen
    yourselves ?
[*To* FACE.] You will accuse him ! You will
    " bring him in
Within the statute ! " Who shall take your
    word ?   126
A whoreson, upstart, apocryphal captain,
Whom not a Puritan in Blackfriars will trust
So much as for a feather : and you, too,
                        [*to* SUBTLE]
Will give the cause, forsooth ! You will insult,
And claim a primacy in the divisions !   131
You must be chief ! As if you, only, had
The powder to project[4] with, and the work
Were not begun out of equality !   134
The venture tripartite ! All things in common !
Without priority ! 'Sdeath ! you perpetual curs,
Fall to your couples again, and cozen kindly,
And heartily, and lovingly, as you should,
And lose not the beginning of a term,
Or, by this hand, I shall grow factious too,   140
And take my part, and quit you.
Face.   'T is his fault ;
He ever murmurs, and objects his pains,
And says, the weight of all lies upon him.
Sub. Why, so it does.
Dol.   How does it ? Do not we
Sustain our parts ?
Sub.   Yes, but they are not equal. 145
Dol. Why, if your part exceed to-day, I hope
Ours may to-morrow match it.
Sub.   Ay, they *may.*
Dol. May, murmuring mastiff ! Ay, and do.
    Death on me !
Help me to throttle him.
            [*Seizes* SUB. *by the throat.*]
Sub.   Dorothy ! Mistress Dorothy !
'Ods precious, I 'll do anything. What do you
    mean ?   150
Dol. Because o' your fermentation and ciba-
    tion ?[5]
Sub. Not I, by heaven ——
Dol.   Your Sol and Luna —— help me.
                        [*To* FACE.]
Sub. Would I were hang'd then ! I 'll conform
    myself.
Dol. Will you, sir ? Do so then, and quickly:
    swear.
Sub. What should I swear ?
Dol.   To leave your faction,[6] sir,
And labour kindly in the common work.   155

Sub. Let me not breathe if I meant aught be-
    side.
I only us'd those speeches as a spur
To him.
Dol. I hope we need no spurs, sir. Do we ?
Face. 'Slid, prove to-day who shall shark
    best.
Sub. Agreed.   160
Dol. Yes, and work close and friendly.
Sub.   'Slight, the knot
Shall grow the stronger for this breach, with
    me.   [*They shake hands.*]
Dol. Why, so, my good baboons ! Shall we go
    make
A sort[7] of sober, scurvy, precise neighbours,
That scarce have smil'd twice sin' the king came
    in,[8]   165
A feast of laughter at our follies ? Rascals,
Would run themselves from breath, to see me
    ride,
Or you t' have but a hole to thrust your heads in,[9]
For which you should pay ear-rent ?[10] No, agree.
And may Don Provost ride a feasting long,   170
In his old velvet jerkin and stain'd scarfs,
My noble sovereign, and worthy general,
Ere we contribute a new crewel[11] garter
To his most worsted worship.
Sub.   Royal Dol !
Spoken like Claridiana,[12] and thyself.   175
Face. For which at supper, thou shalt sit in
    triumph,
And not be styl'd Dol Common, but Dol Pro-
    per,
Dol Singular: the longest cut at night,
Shall draw thee for his Dol Particular.
              [*Bell rings without.*]
Sub. Who 's that ? One rings. To the window.
Dol : [*Exit* DOL.] — Pray heav'n,   180
The master do not trouble us this quarter.
Face. O, fear not him. While there dies one
    a week
O' the plague, he 's safe from thinking toward
    London.
Beside, he 's busy at his hop-yards now ;
I had a letter from him. If he do,   185
He 'll send such word, for airing o' the house,
As you shall have sufficient time to quit it :
Though we break up a fortnight, 't is no mat-
    ter.

              Re-enter DOL.

Sub. Who is it, Dol ?
Dol.   A fine young quodling.[13]
Face.   O,
My lawyer 's clerk, I lighted on last night,   190
In Holborn, at the Dagger. He would have
(I told you of him) a familiar,
To rifle with at horses, and win cups.
Dol. O, let him in.
Sub.   Stay. Who shall do 't ?
Face.   Get you   194
Your robes on ; I will meet him, as going out.

---

[1] Halter.   [2] A liquid which dissolves solids.
[3] A contemptible fellow.   [4] Transmute metals.
[5] Alchemical terms.   Quarreling.

[7] Group.   [8] Seven years before.
[9] In the pillory.   [10] Have your ears cut off.
[11] Familiar puns.
[12] The heroine of the " Mirror of Knighthood."
[13] Green apple, a youth.

Dol. And what shall I do?
Face.   Not be seen; away! [*Exit* Dol.]
Seem you very reserv'd.
  Sub.   Enough.   [*Exit.*]
  Face. [*aloud and retiring.*] God be wi' you,
    sir,
I pray you let him know that I was here:
His name is Dapper. I would gladly have staid,
    but ——

Scene II. [1]

FACE.

Dap. [*within.*] Captain, I am here. [doctor.
Face. Who 's that? — He 's come, I think,

[*Enter* DAPPER.]

Good faith, sir, I was going away.
  Dap.   In truth,
I am very sorry, captain.
  Face.   But I thought
Sure I should meet you.
  Dap.   Ay, I am very glad.
I had a scurvy writ or two to make,   5
And I had lent my watch last night to one
That dines to-day at the sheriff's, and so was
    robb'd
Of my pass-time.[2]

[*Re-enter* SUBTLE *in his velvet cap and gown.*]
                  Is this the cunning-man?
  Face. This is his worship.
  Dap.   Is he a doctor?
  Face.   Yes.
  Dap. And ha' you broke[3] with him, captain?
  Face.   Ay.
  Dap.   And how? 10
  Face. Faith, he does make the matter, sir, so
    dainty,[4]
I know not what to say.
  Dap.   Not so, good captain.
  Face. Would I were fairly rid on 't, believe
    me.
  Dap. Nay, now you grieve me, sir. Why
    should you wish so?
I dare assure you, I 'll not be ungrateful. 15
  Face. I cannot think you will, sir. But the
    law
Is such a thing —— and then he says, Read's[5]
    matter
Falling so lately ——
  Dap.   Read! he was an ass,
And dealt, sir, with a fool.
  Face.   It was a clerk, sir. 19
  Dap. A clerk!
  Face. Nay, hear me, sir. You know the law
Better, I think ——
  Dap.   I should, sir, and the danger:
You know, I show'd the statute to you.
  Face.   You did so.
  Dap. And will I tell then! By this hand of
    flesh,
Would it might never write good courthand
    more,

1 The same. The scene-divisions are Jonson's.
2 Watch.   3 Opened the matter.
4 Has such scruples.
5 A magician recently convicted.

If I discover.[6] What do you think of me, 27
That I am a chiaus?[7]
  Face.   What 's that?
  Dap.   The Turk was here.
As one would say, do you think I am a Turk?
  Face. I 'll tell the doctor so.
  Dap.   Do, good sweet captain.
  Face. Come, noble doctor, pray thee let 's
    prevail;
This is the gentleman, and he is no chiaus. 30
  Sub. Captain, I have return'd you all my an-
    swer.
I would do much, sir, for your love —— But
    this
I neither may, nor can.
  Face.   Tut, do not say so.
You deal now with a noble fellow, doctor,
One that will thank you richly; and he 's no
    chiaus: 35
Let that, sir, move you.
  Sub.   Pray you, forbear ——
  Face.   He has
Four angels here.
  Sub.   You do me wrong, good sir.
  Face. Doctor, wherein? To tempt you with
    these spirits?
  Sub. To tempt my art and love, sir, to my
    peril.
'Fore heav'n, I scarce can think you are my
    friend,   40
That so would draw me to apparent danger.
  Face. I draw you! A horse draw you, and a
    halter,
You, and your flies[8] together ——
  Dap.   Nay, good captain.
  Face. That know no difference of men.
  Sub.   Good words, sir.
  Face. Good deeds, sir, doctor dogs'-meat.
    'Slight, I bring you   45
No cheating Clim o' the Cloughs[9] or Claribels,[10]
That look as big as five-and-fifty, and flush;[11]
And spit out secrets like hot custard ——
  Dap.   Captain!
  Face. Nor any melancholic underscribe,
Shall tell the vicar; but a special gentle, 50
That is the heir to forty marks a year,
Consorts with the small poets of the time,
Is the sole hope of his old grandmother;
That knows the law, and writes you six fair
    hands,
Is a fine clerk, and has his ciph'ring perfect. 55
Will take his oath o' the Greek Xenophon,[12]
If need be, in his pocket; and can court
His mistress out of Ovid.
  Dap.   Nay, dear captain ——
  Face. Did you not tell me so?
  Dap.   Yes; but I'd ha' you
Use master doctor with some more respect. 60

6 Reveal.
7 A Turkish interpreter, like the one who had recently cheated some merchants.
8 Familiar spirits.   9 An outlaw hero.
10 Probably a hero of romance. The name occurs in
Spenser.
11 Five-and-fifty was the highest number to stand on
at the old game of Primero. If a flush accompanied this,
the hand swept the table. (Gifford.)
12 The Q. reads *Testament.*

Face. Hang him, proud stag, with his broad
    velvet head ! —
But for your sake, I 'd choke ere I would change
An article of breath with such a puck-fist ! [1]
Come, let 's be gone.   [*Going.*]
Sub.   Pray you le' me speak with you.
Dap. His worship calls you, captain.
Face.   I am sorry
I e'er embark'd myself in such a business.   65
Dap. Nay, good sir ; he did call you.
Face.   Will he take then ?
Sub. First, hear me ——
Face.   Not a syllable, 'less you take.
Sub. Pray ye, sir ——
Face.   Upon no terms but an *assumpsit.*[2]
Sub. Your humour must be law.
             He takes the money.
Face.   Why now, sir, talk.   70
Now I dare hear you with mine honour. Speak.
So may this gentleman too.
Sub.   Why, sir ——
       [*Offering to whisper* FACE.]
Face.   No whisp'ring.
Sub. 'Fore heav'n, you do not apprehend the
    loss
You do yourself in this.
Face.   Wherein ? for what ?
Sub. Marry, to be so importunate for one   75
That, when he has it, will undo you all :
He 'll win up all the money i' the town.
Face. How ?   [gamester,
Sub.   Yes, and blow up gamester after
As they do crackers in a puppet-play.
If I do give him a familiar,   80
Give you him all you play for ; never set [3] him :
For he will have it.
Face.   You 're mistaken, doctor.
Why, he does ask one but for cups and horses,
A rifling [4] fly ; none o' your great familiars.
Dap. Yes, captain, I would have it for all
    games.   85
Sub. I told you so.
Face. [*taking* DAP. *aside.*] 'Slight, that is a
    new business !
I understood you, a tame bird, to fly
Twice in a term, or so, on Friday nights,
When you had left the office ; for a nag
Of forty or fifty shillings.
Dap.   Ay, 't is true, sir ;   90
But I do think, now, I shall leave the law,
And therefore ——
Face.   Why, this changes quite the case.
Do you think that I dare move him ?
Dap.   If you please, sir ;
All 's one to him, I see.
Face.   What ! for that money ?   94
I cannot with my conscience ; nor should you
Make the request, methinks.
Dap.   No, sir, I mean
To add consideration.
Face.   Why, then, sir,
I 'll try. [*Goes to* SUBTLE.] Say that it were for
    all games, doctor ?
Sub. I say then, not a mouth shall eat for him

1 Niggard.
2 That he has undertaken the affair.
    Stake against.   4 To be used in raffles.

At any ordinary,[5] but o' the score,[6]   100
That is a gaming mouth, conceive me.
Face.   Indeed !
Sub. He 'll draw you all the treasure of the
    realm,
If it be set him.
Face.   Speak you this from art ?
Sub. Ay, sir, and reason too, the ground of
    art.
He is o' the only best complexion,   105
The queen of Fairy loves.
Face.   What ! Is he ?
Sub.   Peace.
He 'll overhear you. Sir, should she but see
    him ——
Face. What ?
Sub.   Do not you tell him.
Face.   Will he win at cards too ?
Sub. The spirits of dead Holland, living
    Isaac,[7]   110
You 'd swear, were in him ; such a vigorous luck
As cannot be resisted. 'Slight, he 'll put
Six o' your gallants to a cloak,[8] indeed.
Face. A strange success, that some man shall
    be born to !
Sub. He hears you, man ——
Dap.   Sir, I 'll not be ingrateful.
Face. Faith, I have a confidence in his good
    nature :   115
You hear, he says he will not be ingrateful.
Sub. Why, as you please ; my venture follows
    yours.
Face. Troth, do it, doctor ; think him trusty,
    and make him.
He may make us both happy in an hour ;
Win some five thousand pound, and send us
    two on 't.   120
Dap. Believe it, and I will, sir.
Face.   And you shall, sir.
You have heard all ?   FACE *takes him aside.*
Dap.   No, what was 't ? Nothing, I, sir.
Face. Nothing ?
Dap.   A little, sir.
Face.   Well, a rare star
Reign'd at your birth.
Dap.   At mine, sir ! No.
Face.   The doctor
Swears that you are ——
Sub.   Nay, captain, you 'll tell all now. 125
Face. Allied to the queen of Fairy.
Dap.   Who ! That I am ?
Believe it, no such matter ——
Face.   Yes, and that
You were born with a caul o' your head.
Dap.   Who says so ?
Face.   Come
You know it well enough, though you dissemble
    it.   129
Dap. I' fac,[9] I do not ; you are mistaken.
Face.   How !

5 Table d'hôte restaurant.
6 The gamblers (who frequented ordinaries) will be
so impoverished through his winnings that they will
have to eat on credit.
7 Supposed to refer to two alchemists, but the dates
do not agree.
   8 Strip to the cloak.   9 Faith.

Swear by your fac, and in a thing so known
Unto the doctor? How shall we, sir, trust you
I' the other matter? Can we ever think,
When you have won five or six thousand pound,
You'll send us shares in 't, by this rate?
Dap.   By Jove, sir, 135
I'll win ten thousand pound, and send you half.
I' fac 's no oath.
Sub.   No, no, he did but jest.
Face. Go to. Go thank the doctor. He's your
    friend,
To take it so.
Dap.   I thank his worship.
Face.   So!
Another angel.
Dap.   Must I?
Face.   Must you! 'Slight, 140
What else is thanks? Will you be trivial? —
    Doctor,   [DAPPER *gives him the money.*]
When must he come for his familiar?
Dap. Shall I not ha' it with me?
Sub.   O, good sir!
There must a world of ceremonies pass;
You must be bath'd and fumigated first: 145
Besides, the queen of Fairy does not rise
Till it be noon.
Face.   Not if she danc'd to-night.
Sub. And she must bless it.
Face.   Did you never see
Her royal grace yet?
Dap.   Whom?
Face.   Your aunt of Fairy?
Sub. Not since she kist him in the cradle,
    captain;   150
I can resolve you that.
Face.   Well, see her grace,
Whate'er it cost you, for a thing that I know.
It will be somewhat hard to compass; but
However, see her. You are made, believe it, 154
If you can see her. Her grace is a lone woman,
And very rich; and if she take a fancy,
She will do strange things. See her, at any hand.
'Slid, she may hap to leave you all she has!
It is the doctor's fear.
Dap.   How will't be done, then?
Face. Let me alone, take you no thought. Do
    you   160
But say to me, "Captain, I'll see her grace."
Dap. "Captain, I'll see her grace."
Face.   Enough.   *One knocks without.*
Sub.   Who's there?
Anon. — [*Aside to* FACE.] Conduct him forth
by the back way.
Sir, against one o'clock prepare yourself;
Till when you must be fasting; only take 165
Three drops of vinegar in at your nose,
Two at your mouth, and one at either ear;
Then bathe your fingers' ends and wash your
    eyes,
To sharpen your five senses, and cry *hum* 169
Thrice, and then *buz* as often; and then come.
                   [*Exit.*]
Face. Can you remember this?
Dap.   I warrant you.
Face. Well then, away. It is but your bestow-
    ing
Some twenty nobles 'mong her grace's servants.

And put on a clean shirt. You do not know 174
What grace her grace may do you in clean linen.
           [*Exeunt* FACE *and* DAPPER.]

SCENE III.[1]

Sub. [*within.*] Come in! Good wives, I pray
    you forbear me now;
Troth, I can do you no good till afternoon. —
      [*Enter* SUBTLE, *followed by* DRUGGER.]
Sub. What is your name, say you? **Abel**
    Drugger?
Drug.   Yes, sir.
Sub. A seller of tobacco?
Drug.   Yes, sir.
Sub.   Umph!
Free of the grocers?[2]
Drug.   Ay, an't please you.
Sub.   Well —— 5
Your business, Abel?
Drug.   This, an't please your worship;
I am a young beginner, and am building
Of a new shop, an 't like your worship, just
At corner of a street: — Here is the plot[3]
on 't ——   9
And I would know by art, sir, of your worship,
Which way I should make my door, by necro-
    mancy,
And where my shelves; and which should be
    for boxes,
And which for pots. I would be glad to thrive,
    sir:
And I was wish'd[4] to your worship by a gentle-
    man,
One Captain Face, that says you know men's
    planets,   15
And their good angels, and their bad.
Sub.   I do,
If I do see 'em ——
           [*Enter* FACE.]
Face.   What! my honest Abel?
Thou art well met here.
Drug.   Troth, sir, I was speaking,
Just as your worship came here, of your worship.
I pray you speak for me to master doctor. 20
Face. He shall do anything. Doctor, do you
    hear?
This is my friend, Abel, an honest fellow;
He lets me have good tobacco, and he does not
Sophisticate it with sack-lees or oil,
Nor washes it in muscadel and grains, 25
Nor buries it in gravel, under ground,
Wrapp'd up in greasy leather, or piss'd clouts:
But keeps it in fine lily pots, that, open'd,
Smell like conserve of roses, or French beans.
He has his maple block,[5] his silver tongs, 30
Winchester pipes, and fire of juniper:[6]
A neat, spruce, honest fellow, and no gold-
    smith.[7]

    [1] The same.
    [2] *I. e.* a member of the Grocers' Company.
    [3] Plan.   [4] Recommended.
    [5] On which tobacco was shredded.
    [6] The coals of which were used to light pipes.
    [7] Usurer.

Sub. He's a fortunate fellow, that I am sure on.

Face. Already, sir, ha' you found it? Lo thee, Abel!

Sub. And in right way toward riches ——

Face.   Sir!

Sub.   This summer. 35
He will be of the clothing of his company,[1]
And next spring call'd to the scarlet ;[2] spend
what he can.

Face. What, and so little beard?

Sub.   Sir, you must think,
He may have a receipt to make hair come:
But he 'll be wise, preserve his youth, and fine
for 't ;   40
His fortune looks for him another way.

Face. 'Slid, doctor, how canst thou know this
so soon?
I am amus'd[3] at that.

Sub.   By a rule, captain,
In metoposcopy,[4] which I do work by ;   44
A certain star i' the forehead, which you see
not.
Your chestnut or your olive-colour'd face
Does never fail : and your long ear doth promise.
I knew 't, by certain spots, too, in his teeth,
And on the nail of his mercurial finger.

Face. Which finger's that?

Sub.   His little finger. Look. 50
You were born upon a Wednesday?

Drug.   Yes, indeed, sir.

Sub. The thumb, in chiromancy, we give
Venus ;
The forefinger to Jove ; the midst to Saturn ;
The ring to Sol ; the least to Mercury,   55
Who was the lord, sir, of his horoscope,
His house of life being Libra ; which forshow'd
He should be a merchant, and should trade with
balance.

Face. Why, this is strange! Is it not, honest
Nab?

Sub. There is a ship now coming from Ormus,
That shall yield him such a commodity   60
Of drugs —— This is the west, and this the
south? [*Pointing to the plan.*]

Drug. Yes, sir.

Sub.   And those are your two sides?

Drug.   Ay, sir.

Sub. Make me your door then, south ; your
broad side, west :
And on the east side of your shop, aloft,
Write Mathlai, Tarmiel, and Baraborat ;   65
Upon the north part, Rael, Velel, Thiel.
They are the names of those Mercurial spirits
That do fright flies from boxes.

Drug.   Yes, sir.

Sub.   And
Beneath your threshold, bury me a loadstone 69
To draw in gallants that wear spurs : the rest,
They 'll seem[5] to follow.

Face.   That 's a secret, Nab!

Sub. And, on your stall, a puppet, with a
vice

And a court-fucus,[6] to call city-dames:
You shall deal much with minerals.

Drug.   Sir, I have.
At home, already ——

Sub.   Ay, I know, you 've arsenic, 75
Vitriol, sal-tartar, argaile,[7] alkali,
Cinoper :[8] I know all. — This fellow, captain,
Will come, in time, to be a great distiller,
And give a say[9] — I will not say directly,
But very fair — at the philosopher's stone.   80

Face. Why, how now, Abel! is this true?

Drug. [*Aside to* FACE.]   Good captain,
What must I give?

Face.   Nay, I 'll not counsel thee.
Thou hear'st what wealth (he says, spend what
thou canst),
Thou 'rt like to come to.

Drug.   I would gi' him a crown.

Face. A crown! and toward such a fortune?
Heart,   85
Thou shalt rather gi' him thy shop. No gold
about thee?

Drug. Yes, I have a portague,[10] I ha' kept
this half-year.

Face. Out on thee, Nab! 'Slight, there was
such an offer—
Shalt keep 't no longer, I 'll gi' it him for thee.
Doctor,
Nab prays your worship to drink this, and
swears   90
He will appear more grateful, as your skill
Does raise him in the world.

Drug.   I would entreat
Another favour of his worship.

Face.   What is 't, Nab?

Drug. But to look over, sir, my almanac,
And cross out my ill-days,[11] that I may neither
Bargain, nor trust upon them.

Face.   That he shall, Nab : 96
Leave it, it shall be done, 'gainst afternoon.

Sub. And a direction for his shelves.

Face.   Now, Nab,
Art thou well pleas'd, Nab?

Drug. 'Thank, sir, both your worships. 99

Face. Away. [*Exit* DRUGGER.]
Why, now, you smoky persecutor of nature!
Now do you see, that something 's to be done,
Beside your beech-coal, and your cor'sive[12]
waters,
Your crosslets,[13] crucibles, and cucurbites ?[14]
You must have stuff brought home to you, to
work on :   105
And yet you think, I am at no expense
In searching out these veins, then following
'em,
Then trying 'em out. 'Fore God, my intelligence
Costs me more money than my share oft comes
to,
In these rare works.

Sub.   You 're pleasant, sir. — How now! 110

---

[1] Wear the livery.   [4] A branch of physiognomy.
[2] Be sheriff.   [5] Be seen.
[3] Amazed.
[6] Paint for the face.   [7] Tartar deposited by wine.
[8] Cinnabar, mercuric sulphid.
[9] Assay.
[10] A gold coin worth about three pounds, twelve shillings.
[11] Unlucky days.   [12] Corrosive.   [13] Crucible.
[14] Glass retort, shaped like a gourd.

Scene IV.[1]

Face, Subtle. [*Enter*] Dol.

Sub. What says my dainty Dolkin?
Dol.   Yonder fish-wife
Will not away. And there 's your giantess,
The bawd of Lambeth.
 Sub.   Heart, I cannot speak with 'em.
Dol. Not afore night, I have told 'em in a voice,
Thorough the trunk, like one of your familiars.
But I have spied Sir Epicure Mammon ——
 Sub.   Where? 6
Dol. Coming along, at far end of the lane,
Slow of his feet, but earnest of his tongue
To one that 's with him.
 Sub.   Face, go you and shift.
Dol, you must presently make ready too. 10
       [*Exit* Face.]
 Dol. Why, what 's the matter?
 Sub.   O, I did look for him
With the sun's rising: marvel he could sleep!
This is the day I am to perfect for him
The magisterium, our great work, the stone;
And yield it, made, into his hands; of which 15
He has, this month, talk'd as he were possess'd.
And now he 's dealing pieces on 't away.
Methinks I see him ent'ring ordinaries,
Dispensing for the pox, and plaguy houses,
Reaching his dose, walking Moorfields for lepers, 20
And off'ring citizens' wives pomander[2]-bracelets,
As his preservative, made of the elixir;
Searching the 'spital, to make old bawds young;
And the highways, for beggars to make rich.
I see no end of his labours. He will make 25
Nature asham'd of her long sleep; when art,
Who 's but a step-dame, shall do more than she,
In her best love to mankind, ever could.
If his dream last, he 'll turn the age to gold.
       [*Exeunt.*]

ACT II

Scene I.[3]

[*Enter*] Sir Epicure Mammon *and* Surly.

Mam. Come on, sir. Now you set your foot on shore
In *Novo Orbe*;[4] here 's the rich Peru:
And there within, sir, are the golden mines,
Great Solomon's Ophir! He was sailing to 't
Three years, but we have reach'd it in ten months. 5
This is the day wherein, to all my friends,
I will pronounce the happy word, Be rich;
This day you shall be spectatissimi.[5]
You shall no more deal with the hollow die, 9
Or the frail card; no more be at charge of keeping
The livery-punk[6] for the young heir, that must

[1] The same.
[2] A ball of perfume carried against infection.
[3] An outer room in Lovewit's house.
[4] The New World. [5] Most gazed at.
[6] Female accomplice in swindling heirs out of property.

Seal, at all hours, in his shirt: no more,
If he deny, ha' him beaten to 't, as he is
That brings him the commodity; no more
Shall thirst of satin, or the covetous hunger 15
Of velvet entrails[7] for a rude-spun cloak,
To be display'd at Madam Augusta's, make
The sons of Sword and Hazard fall before
The golden calf, and on their knees, whole nights,
Commit idolatry with wine and trumpets: 20
Or go a feasting after drum and ensign.
No more of this. You shall start up young viceroys,
And have your punks and punkettees, my Surly.
And unto thee I speak it first, Be rich.
Where is my Subtle there? Within, ho!
 [Face. *within.*]   Sir, 25
He 'll come to you by and by.
 Mam.   That is his fire-drake,[8]
His Lungs, his Zephyrus, he that puffs his coals,
Till he firk[9] nature up, in her own centre.
You are not faithful,[10] sir. This night I 'll change
All that is metal in my house to gold: 30
And, early in the morning, will I send
To all the plumbers and the pewterers,
And buy their tin and lead up; and to Lothbury
For all the copper.
 Sur. What, and turn that, too?
Mam. Yes, and I 'll purchase Devonshire and Cornwall, 35
And make them perfect Indies! You admire now?
 Sur. No, faith.
 Mam. But when you see th' effects of the Great Med'cine,
Of which one part projected on a hundred
Of Mercury, or Venus, or the Moon, 40
Shall turn it to as many of the Sun;[11]
Nay, to a thousand, so *ad infinitum:*
You will believe me.
 Sur. Yes, when I see 't, I will.
But if my eyes do cozen me so, and I
Giving 'em no occasion, sure I 'll have 45
A whore, shall piss 'em out next day.
 Mam.   Ha! why?
Do you think I fable with you? I assure you,
He that has once the flower of the sun,
The perfect ruby, which we call elixir,
Not only can do that, but by its virtue, 50
Can confer honour, love, respect, long life;
Give safety, valour, yea, and victory,
To whom he will. In eight and twenty days,
I 'll make an old man of fourscore, a child.
 Sur. No doubt; he 's that already.
 Mam. Nay, I mean, 55
Restore his years, renew him, like an eagle,
To the fifth age; make him get sons and daughters,
Young giants; as our philosophers have done,
The ancient patriarchs, afore the flood,
But taking, once a week, on a knife's point, 60
The quantity of a grain of mustard of it;
Become stout Marses, and beget young Cupids.

[7] Lining.   [9] Stir, rouse.
[8] Dragon.   [10] Believing.
[11] Turn mercury, copper, or silver into gold.

Sur. The decay'd vestals of Pickt-hatch [1]
would thank you,
That keep the fire alive there.
Mam. 'T is the secret
Of nature naturiz'd 'gainst all infections,   65
Cures all diseases coming of all causes ;
A month's grief in a day, a year's in twelve ;
And, of what age soever, in a month.
Past all the doses of your drugging doctors.
I 'll undertake, withal, to fright the plague   70
Out o' the kingdom in three months.
Sur.   And I 'll
Be bound, the players shall sing your praises
then,
Without their poets.[2]
Mam.   Sir, I 'll do 't. Meantime,
I 'll give away so much unto my man,
Shall serve th' whole city with preservative   75
Weekly ; each house his dose, and at the
rate ——
Sur. As he that built the Water-work does
with water ?
Mam. You are incredulous.
Sur.   Faith, I have a humour,
I would not willingly be gull'd.[3] Your stone
Cannot transmute me.
Mam.   Pertinax Surly,   80
Will you believe antiquity ? Records ?
I 'll show you a book where Moses, and his
sister,
And Solomon have written of the art ;
Ay, and a treatise penn'd by Adam ——
Sur.   How !
Mam. Of the philosopher's stone, and in High
Dutch.   85
Sur. Did Adam write, sir, in High Dutch ?
Mam.   He did ;
Which proves it was the primitive tongue.
Sur.   What paper ?
Mam. On cedar board.
Sur.   O that, indeed, they say,
Will last 'gainst worms.
Mam.   'T is like your Irish wood
'Gainst cobwebs. I have a piece of Jason's
fleece too,   90
Which was no other than a book of alchemy,
Writ in large sheepskin, a good fat ram-vellum.
Such was Pythagoras' thigh, Pandora's tub,
And all that fable of Medea's charms,   94
The manner of our work ; the bulls, our furnace,
Still breathing fire ; our argent-vive,[4] the
dragon :
The dragon's teeth, mercury sublimate,
That keeps the whiteness, hardness, and the
biting ;
And they are gather'd into Jason's helm,   99
Th' alembic, and then sow'd in Mars his field,
And thence sublim'd so often, till they 're fix'd.
Both this, th' Hesperian garden, Cadmus' story,
Jove's shower, the boon of Midas, Argus' eyes,
Boccace his Demogorgon,[5] thousands more,   104
All abstract riddles of our stone. — How now !

[1] A disreputable locality.
[2] The theatres were closed when the plague was prevalent.
[3] Fooled.   [4] Quicksilver.
[5] According to Boccaccio, the ancestor of all the gods.

SCENE II.[6]

MAMMON, SURLY. [*Enter*] FACE, [*as a Servant.*]

Mam. Do we succeed ? Is our day come ?
And holds it ?
Face. The evening will set red upon you, sir ;
You have colour for it, crimson : the red fer-
ment
Has done his office ; three hours hence prepare
you
To see projection.
Mam.   Pertinax, my Surly,   5
Again I say to thee, aloud, BE RICH.
This day thou shalt have ingots ; and to-morrow
Give lords th' affront. — Is it, my Zephyrus,
right ?
Blushes the bolt's-head ?[7]
Face.   Like a wench with child, sir,
That were but now discover'd to her master. 10
Mam. Excellent witty Lungs ! — My only care
is
Where to get stuff enough now, to project on ;[8]
This town will not half serve me.
Face.   No, sir ? Buy
The covering off o' churches.
Mam.   That 's true.
Face.   Yes.
Let 'em stand bare, as do their auditory ;[9] 15
Or cap 'em new with shingles.
Mam.   No, good thatch :
Thatch will lie light upo' the rafters, Lungs.
Lungs, I will manumit thee from the furnace ;
I will restore thee thy complexion, Puff,
Lost in the embers ; and repair this brain,   20
Hurt wi' the fume o' the metals.
Face.   I have blown, sir,
Hard, for your worship ; thrown by many a
coal,
When 't was not beech ; weigh'd those I put in,
just
To keep your heat still even. These blear'd
eyes
Have wak'd to read your several colours, sir, 25
Of the pale citron, the green lion, the crow,
The peacock's tail, the plumed swan.
Mam.   And lastly,
Thou hast descried the flower, the *sanguis agni* ?
Face. Yes, sir.
Mam.   Where 's master ?
Face.   At 's prayers, sir, he ;
Good man, he 's doing his devotions   30
For the success.
Mam.   Lungs, I will set a period
To all thy labours ; thou shalt be the master
Of my seraglio.
Face.   Good, sir.
Mam.   But do you hear ?
I 'll geld you, Lungs.
Face.   Yes, sir.
Mam.   For I do mean
To have a list of wives and concubines   35
Equal with Solomon, who had the stone
Alike with me ; and I will make me a back
With the elixir, that shall be as tough

[6] The same.   [8] Transmute.
[7] A kind of flask.   [9] Congregation.

As Hercules, to encounter fifty a night.—
Thou 'rt sure thou saw 'st it blood ?
  Face.   Both blood and spirit, sir.   40
  Mam. I will have all my beds blown up, not
    stuft ;
Down is too hard : and then, mine oval room
Fill' d with such pictures as Tiberius took
From Elephantis, and dull Aretine
But coldly imitated. Then, my glasses   45
Cut in more subtle angles, to disperse
And multiply the figures, as I walk
Naked between my succubae.[1] My mists
I 'll have of perfume, vapour'd 'bout the room,
To lose our selves in ; and my baths, like pits   50
To fall into ; from whence we will come forth,
And roll us dry in gossamer and roses.—
Is it arrived at ruby ? —— Where I spy
A wealthy citizen, or [a] rich lawyer,
Have a sublim'd pure wife, unto that fellow   55
I 'll send a thousand pound to be my cuckold.
  Face. And I shall carry it ?
  Mam.   No. I 'll ha' no bawds
But fathers and mothers : they will do it best,
Best of all others. And my flatterers
Shall be the pure and gravest of divines,   60
That I can get for money. My mere fools,
Eloquent burgesses, and then my poets
The same that writ so subtly of the fart,
Whom I will entertain still for that subject.
The few that would give out themselves to be   65
Court and town-stallions, and, each-where, bely
Ladies who are known most innocent, for
    them,—
Those will I beg, to make me eunuchs of :
And they shall fan me with ten estrich tails
A-piece, made in a plume to gather wind.   70
We will be brave, Puff, now we ha' the med'-
    cine.
My meat shall all come in, in Indian shells,
Dishes of agate set in gold, and studded
With emeralds, sapphires, hyacinths, and ru-
    bies.
The tongues of carps, dormice, and camels'
    heels,   75
Boil'd i' the spirit of sol, and dissolv'd pearl
(Apicius' diet, 'gainst the epilepsy) :
And I will eat these broths with spoons of am-
    ber,
Headed with diamond and carbuncle.
My foot-boy shall eat pheasants, calver'd sal-
    mons,[2]   80
Knots,[3] godwits, lampreys : I myself will have
The beards of barbel[4] serv'd, instead of salads ;
Oil'd mushrooms ; and the swelling unctuous
    paps
Of a fat pregnant sow, newly cut off,
Drest with an exquisite and poignant sauce ;   85
For which, I 'll say unto my cook, *There 's gold ;
Go forth, and be a knight.*
  Face.   Sir, I 'll go look
A little, how it heightens.   [*Exit.*]
  Mam.   Do.— My shirts
I 'll have of taffeta-sarsnet,[5] soft and light
As cobwebs ; and for all my other raiment,   90

¹ Mistresses.   ⁴ A fish.
² Salmon elaborately prepared.   ⁵ Soft silk.
³ Robin-snipes.

It shall be such as might provoke the Persian,
Were he to teach the world riot anew.
My gloves of fishes and birds' skins, perfum'd
With gums of paradise, and Eastern air ——
  Sur. And do you think to have the stone with
    this ?   95
  Mam. No, I do think t' have all this with
    the stone.
  Sur. Why, I have heard he must be *homo
    frugi,*[6]
A pious, holy, and religious man,
One free from mortal sin, a very virgin.
  Man. That makes it, sir ; he is so. But I buy
    it ;   100
My venture brings it me. He, honest wretch,
A notable, superstitious, good soul,
Has worn his knees bare, and his slippers bald,
With prayer and fasting for it : and, sir, let him
Do it alone, for me, still. Here he comes.   105
Not a profane word afore him ; 't is poison.—

SCENE III.[7]

MAMMON, SURLY. [*Enter*] SUBTLE.

  Mam. Good morrow, father.
  Sub.   Gentle son, good morrow,
And to your friend there. What is he is with
    you ?
  Mam. An heretic, that I did bring along,
In hope, sir, to convert him.
  Sub.   Son, I doubt
You 're covetous, that thus you meet your time
I' the just[8] point, prevent[9] your day at morn-
    ing.   6
This argues something worthy of a fear
Of importune and carnal appetite.
Take heed you do not cause the blessing leave
    you,
With your ungovern'd haste. I should be sorry
To see my labours, now e'en at perfection,   11
Got by long watching and large patience,
Not prosper where my love and zeal hath plac'd
    'em.
Which (heaven I call to witness, with your self,
To whom I have pour'd my thoughts) in all my
    ends,   15
Have look'd no way, but unto public good,
To pious uses, and dear charity,
Now grown a prodigy with men. Wherein
If you, my son, should now prevaricate,
And to your own particular lusts employ   20
So great and catholic a bliss, be sure
A curse will follow, yea, and overtake
Your subtle and most secret ways.
  Mam.   I know, sir ;
You shall not need to fear me ; I but come
To ha' you confute this gentleman.
  Sur.   Who is,   25
Indeed, sir, somewhat costive of belief
Toward your stone ; would not be gull'd.
  Sub.   Well, son,
All that I can convince him in, is this,
The work is done, bright Sol is in his robe.
We have a med'cine of the triple soul,   30

⁶ A virtuous man.   ⁸ Exact.
⁷ The same.   ⁹ Anticipate.

The glorified spirit. Thanks be to heaven,
And make us worthy of it ! — Ulen Spiegel! [1]
  Face. [*within.*] Anon, sir.
  Sub.   Look well to the register.
And let your heat still lessen by degrees,
To the aludels.[2]   35
  Face. [*within.*] Yes, sir.
  Sub.   Did you look
O' the bolt's head yet ?
  Face. [*within.*] Which? On D, sir ?
  Sub.   Ay;
What 's the complexion ?
  Face. [*within.*] Whitish.
  Sub.   Infuse vinegar, 40
To draw his volatile substance and his tincture :
And let the water in glass E be filt'red,
And put into the gripe's egg.[3] Lute [4] him well ;
And leave him clos'd *in balneo.*[5]
  Face. [*within.*]   I will, sir.
  Sur. What a brave language here is ! next to
    canting.[6]   45
  Sub. I have another work you never saw,
    son,
That three days since past the philosopher's
    wheel,
In the lent heat of Athanor ; [7] and 's become
Sulphur o' Nature.
  Mam.   But 't is for me ?
  Sub.   What need you ?
You have enough, in that is, perfect.
  Mam.   O, but —— 50
  Sub. Why, this is covetise !
  Mam.   No, I assure you,
I shall employ it all in pious uses,
Founding of colleges and grammar schools,
Marrying young virgins, building hospitals,
And, now and then, a church.

            [*Re-enter* FACE]

  Sub.   How now !
  Face.   Sir, please you, 55
Shall I not change the filter ?
  Sub.   Marry, yes ;
And bring me the complexion of glass B.
                    [*Exit* FACE.]
  Mam. Ha' you another ?
  Sub.   Yes, son ; were I assur'd
Your piety were firm, we would not want
The means to glorify it : but I hope the best. 60
I mean to tinct C in sand-heat to-morrow,
And give him imbibition.[8]
  Mam.   Of white oil ?
  Sub. No, sir, of red. F is come over the helm
    too,
I thank my maker, in S. Mary's bath.
And shows *lac virginis.* Blessed be heaven ! 65
I sent you of his faeces there calcin'd :
Out of that calx, I ha' won the salt of mercury.
  Mam. By pouring on your rectified water ?
  Sub. Yes, and reverberating in Athanor.

---

1 The hero of a well-known German jest-book.
2 A pear-shaped vessel, open at both ends.
3 An egg-shaped vessel. *Gripe* is griffin.
4 Seal with clay.
5 A dish of warm water.   7 An alchemical furnace.
6 Rogues' slang.   8 Absorption.

            [*Re-enter* FACE.]

How now ! what colour says it ?
  Face.   The ground black, **sir.** 70
  Mam. That 's your crow's head ?
  Sur.   Your cock's comb's, is it not ?
  Sub. No, 't is not perfect. Would it were the
    crow !
That work wants something.
  Sur. [*Aside.*]   O, I look'd for this,
The hay 's [9] a pitching.
  Sub.   Are you sure you loos'd 'em
In their own menstrue ? [10]
  Face.   Yes, sir, and then married 'em, 75
And put 'em in a bolt's-head nipp'd to digestion,
According as you bade me, when I set
The liquor of Mars to circulation
In the same heat.
  Sub.   The process then was right. 79
  Face. Yes, by the token, sir, the retort brake,
And what was sav'd was put into the pellican,
And sign'd with Hermes' seal.
  Sub.   I think 't was so.
We should have a new amalgama.
  Sur. [*Aside.*]   O, this ferret
Is rank as any polecat.
  Sub.   But I care not ;
Let him e'en die ; we have enough beside, 85
In embrion. H has his white shirt on ?
  Face.   Yes, sir,
He 's ripe for inceration, he stands warm,
In his ash-fire. I would not you should let
Any die now, if I might counsel, sir,
For luck's sake to the rest : it is not good. 90
  Mam. He says right.
  Sur. (*Aside.*)   Ay, are you bolted ?
  Face.   Nay, I know 't, sir,
I 've seen th' ill fortune. What is some three
    ounces
Of fresh materials ?
  Mam.   Is 't no more ?
  Face.   No more, sir,
Of gold, t' amalgam with some six of mercury.
  Mam. Away, here 's money. What will serve ?
  Face.   Ask him, sir. 95
  Mam. How much ?
  Sub.   Give him nine pound : you may gi' him
  Sur. Yes, twenty, and be cozen'd, do.
  Mam.   There 't is. [*Gives* FACE *the money.*]
  Sub. This needs not ; but that you will have
    it so,
To see conclusions of all : for two
Of our inferior works are at fixation, 100
A third is in ascension. Go your ways.
Ha' you set the oil of Luna in kemia ?
  Face. Yes, sir.
  Sub.   And the philosopher's vinegar ?
  Face.   Ay. [*Exit.*]
  Sur. We shall have a salad !
  Mam.   When do you make projection ?
  Sub. Son, be not hasty, I exalt our med'cine,
By hanging him *in balneo vaporoso,* 105
And giving him solution ; then congeal him ;
And then dissolve him ; then again congeal him ;

---

9 A net for catching rabbits.
10 Dissolving fluids.

For look, how oft I iterate the work,
So many times I add unto his virtue.   110
As, if at first one ounce convert a hundred,
After his second loose, he 'll turn a thousand ;
His third solution, ten ; his fourth, a hundred ;
After his fifth, a thousand thousand ounces
Of any imperfect metal, into pure   115
Silver or gold, in all examinations,
As good as any of the natural mine.
Get you your stuff here against afternoon,
Your brass, your pewter, and your andirons.
    Mam. Not those of iron ?
    Sub.   Yes, you may bring them too ;   120
We 'll change all metals.
    Sur.   I believe you in that.
    Mam. Then I may send my spits ?
    Sub.   Yes, and your racks.
    Sur. And dripping-pans, and pot-hangers,
       and hooks ?
Shall he not ?
    Sub.   If he please.
    Sur.   — To be an ass.   124
    Sub. How, sir !
    Mam. This gent'man you must bear withal.
I told you he had no faith.
    Sur.   And little hope, sir ;
But much less charity, should I gull myself.
    Sub. Why, what have you observ'd, sir, in
       our art,
Seems so impossible ?
    Sur.   But your whole work, no more.
That you should hatch gold in a furnace, sir,
As they do eggs in Egypt !
    Sub.   Sir, do you   131
Believe that eggs are hatch'd so ?
    Sur.   If I should ?
    Sub. Why, I think that the greater miracle.
No egg but differs from a chicken more
Than metals in themselves.
    Sur.   That cannot be.   135
The egg 's ordain'd by nature to that end,
And is a chicken *in potentia.*
    Sub. The same we say of lead and other
      metals,
Which would be gold if they had time.
    Mam.   And that
Our art doth further.
    Sub.   Ay, for 't were absurd   140
To think that nature in the earth bred gold
Perfect i' the instant : something went before.
There must be remote matter.
    Sur.   Ay, what is that ?
    Sub. Marry, we say ——
    Mam.   Ay, now it heats : stand, father,
Pound him to dust.
    Sub.   It is, of the one part,   145
A humid exhalation, which we call
Materia liquida, or the unctuous water ;
On th' other part, a certain crass and viscous
Portion of earth ; both which, concorporate,
Do make the elementary matter of gold ;   150
Which is not yet *propria materia,*
But common to all metals and all stones ;
For, where it is forsaken of that moisture,
And hath more dryness, it becomes a stone :
Where it retains more of the humid fatness,   155
It turns to sulphur, or to quicksilver.

Who are the parents of all other metals.
Nor can this remote matter suddenly
Progress so from extreme unto extreme,   159
As to grow gold, and leap o'er all the means.
Nature doth first beget th' imperfect, then
Proceeds she to the perfect. Of that airy
And oily water, mercury is engend'red ;
Sulphur o' the fat and earthy part ; the one,   164
Which is the last, supplying the place of male,
The other of the female, in all metals.
Some do believe hermaphrodeity,
That both do act and suffer. But these two
Make the rest ductile, malleable, extensive.
And even in gold they are ; for we do find   170
Seeds of them by our fire, and gold in them ;
And can produce the species of each metal
More perfect thence, than nature doth in earth.
Beside, who doth not see in daily practice
Art can beget bees, hornets, beetles, wasps,   175
Out of the carcases and dung of creatures ;
Yea, scorpions of an herb, being rightly plac'd ?
And these are living creatures, far more perfect
And excellent than metals.
    Mam.   Well said, father !
Nay, if he take you in hand, sir, with an argu-
      ment,   180
He 'll bray you in a mortar.
    Sur.   Pray you, sir, stay.
Rather than I 'll be bray'd, sir, I 'll believe
That Alchemy is a pretty kind of game,
Somewhat like tricks o' the cards, to cheat a
     man
With charming.
    Sub.   Sir ?
    Sur.   What else are all your terms,   185
Whereon no one o' your writers 'grees with
      other ?
Of your elixir, your *lac virginis,*
Your stone, your med'cine, and your chryso-
      sperm,
Your sal, your sulphur, and your mercury,   189
Your oil of height, your tree of life, your blood,
Your marchesite, your tutie, your magnesia,
Your toad, your crow, your dragon, and your
      panther ;
Your sun, your moon, your firmament, your
      adrop,
Your lato, azoch, zernich, chibrit, heautarit,   194
And then your red man, and your white woman,
With all your broths, your menstrues, and ma-
      terials
Of piss and egg-shells, women's terms, man's
      blood,
Hair o' the head, burnt clouts, chalk, merds,
      and clay,
Powder of bones, scalings of iron, glass,
And worlds of other strange ingredients,   200
Would burst a man to name ?
    Sub.   And all these, nam'd,
Intending but one thing ; which art our writers
Us'd to obscure their art.
    Mam.   Sir, so I told him —
Because [1] the simple idiot should not learn it,
And make it vulgar.
    Sub.   Was not all the knowledge   205

    [1] In order that.

Of the Aegyptians writ in mystic symbols?
Speak not the scriptures oft in parables?
Are not the choicest fables of the poets,
That were the fountains and first springs of
    wisdom,
Wrapt in perplexed allegories?
    Mam.   I urg'd that, 210
And clear'd to him, that Sisyphus was damn'd
To roll the ceaseless stone, only because
He would have made ours common. (DOL *is
    seen*) [*at the door.*] — Who is this?
    Sub. God's precious! — What do you mean?
Go in, good lady,
Let me entreat you. [DOL *retires.*] — Where's
    this varlet?

[*Re-enter* FACE.]

Face.   Sir.   215
Sub. You very knave! do you use me thus?
Face.   Wherein, sir?
Sub. Go in and see, you traitor. Go!
                            [*Exit* FACE.]
Mam.   Who is it, sir?
Sub. Nothing, sir; nothing.
Mam.   What's the matter, good sir?
I have not seen you thus distemp'red: who is 't?
Sub. All arts have still had, sir, their adver-
    saries;   220
But ours the most ignorant. —

FACE *returns.*

                            What now?
Face. 'T was not my fault, sir; she would
    speak with you.
Sub. Would she, sir! Follow me. [*Exit.*]
Mam. [*stopping him.*] Stay, Lungs.
Face.   I dare not, sir.
Mam. How! pray thee, stay.
Face. She's mad, sir, and sent hither — 225
Mam. Stay, man; what is she?
Face.   A lord's sister, sir.
He'll be mad too. —
Mam. I warrant thee. — Why sent hither?
Face. Sir, to be cur'd.
Sub. [*within.*] Why, rascal!
Face.   Lo you! — Here, sir! *Exit.*
Mam. 'Fore God, a Bradamante, a brave
    piece.
Sur. Heart, this is a bawdy-house! I'll be
    burnt else.   230
Mam. O, by this light, no: do not wrong him.
    He's
Too scrupulous that way: it is his vice.
No, he's a rare physician, do him right,
An excellent Paracelsian, and has done
Strange cures with mineral physic. He deals all
With spirits, he; he will not hear a word   236
Of Galen; or his tedious recipes. —

FACE *again.*

                            How now, Lungs!
Face. Softly, sir; speak softly. I meant
To ha' told your worship all. This must not
    hear.
Mam. No, he will not be gull'd; let him alone.
Face. You're very right, sir; she is a most
    rare scholar.   241

And is gone mad with studying Broughton's[1]
    works.
If you but name a word touching the Hebrew,
She falls into her fit, and will discourse
So learnedly of genealogies,   245
As you would run mad too, to hear her, sir.
Mam. How might one do t' have conference
    with her, Lungs?
Face. O, divers have run mad upon the con-
    ference.
I do not know, sir: I am sent in haste
To fetch a vial.
Sur.   Be not gull'd, Sir Mammon. 250
Mam. Wherein? Pray ye, be patient.
Sur.   Yes, as you are,
And trust confederate knaves and bawds and
    whores.
Mam. You are too foul, believe it. — Come
    here, Ulen,
One word.
Face.   I dare not, in good faith. [*Going.*]
Mam.   Stay, knave.
Face. He's extreme angry that you saw her,
    sir.   255
Mam. Drink that. [*Gives him money.*] What
    is she when she's out of her fit?
Face. O, the most affablest creature, sir! so
    merry!
So pleasant! She'll mount you up, like quick-
    silver,
Over the helm; and circulate like oil,
A very vegetal: discourse of state,   260
Of mathematics, bawdry, anything ——
Mam. Is she no way accessible? no means,
No trick to give a man a taste of her —— wit ——
Or so?
[*Sub. within.*] Ulen!
Face.   I'll come to you again, sir. [*Exit.*]
Mam. Surly, I did not think one o' your
    breeding   266
Would traduce personages of worth.
Sur.   Sir Epicure,
Your friend to use; yet still loth to be gull'd:
I do not like your philosophical bawds.
Their stone is lechery enough to pay for, 270
Without this bait.
Mam.   Heart, you abuse yourself.
I know the lady, and her friends, and means,
The original of this disaster. Her brother
Has told me all.
Sur.   And yet you ne'er saw her
Till now!   275
Mam. O yes, but I forgot. I have, believe
    it,
One o' the treacherous'st memories, I do think,
Of all mankind.
Sur.   What call you her brother?
Mam.   My lord ——
He wi' not have his name known, now I think
    on 't.
Sur. A very treacherous memory!
Mam.   O' my faith —— 280
Sur. Tut, if you ha' it not about you, pass it
Till we meet next.
Mam.   Nay, by this hand, 't is true.

---

[1] A learned eccentric of the time.

He 's one I honour, and my noble friend ;
And I respect his house.
Sur.　　　　　　　　　　Heart ! can it be
That a grave sir, a rich, that has no need,　285
A wise sir, too, at other times, should thus,
With his own oaths, and arguments, make hard
　means
To gull himself ? An this be your elixir,
Your *lapis mineralis,* and your lunary,
Give me your honest trick yet at primero,　290
Or gleek, [1] and take your *lutum sapientis,*
Your *menstruum simplex !* I 'll have gold before
　you,
And with less danger of the quicksilver,
Or the hot sulphur.

[*Re-enter* FACE.]

Face. Here 's one from Captain Face, sir.　295
　　　　　　　　　　　　　(*To* SURLY.)
Desires you meet him i' the Temple-church,
Some half-hour hence, and upon earnest busi-
　ness.
Sir, (*whispers* MAMMON) if you please to quit us
　now, and come
Again within two hours, you shall have
My master busy examining o' the works ;　300
And I will steal you in unto the party,
That you may see her converse. — Sir, shall I
　say
You 'll meet the captain's worship?
Sur.　　　　　Sir, I will. — [*Walks aside.*]
But, by attorney, and to a second purpose.
Now, I am sure it is a bawdy-house ;　305
I 'll swear it, were the marshal here to thank
　me :
The naming this commander doth confirm it.
Don Face ! why, he 's the most authentic dealer
I' these commodities, the superintendent
To all the quainter traffickers in town !　310
He is the visitor, and does appoint
Who lies with whom, and at what hour ; what
　price ;
Which gown, and in what smock ; what fall ; [2]
　what tire.[3]
Him will I prove, by a third person, to find
The subtleties of this dark labyrinth :　315
Which if I do discover, dear Sir Mammon,
You 'll give your poor friend leave, though no
　philosopher,
To laugh ; for you that are, 't is thought, shall
　weep.
Face. Sir, he does pray you 'll not forget.
Sur.　　　　　　　　　I will not, sir.
Sir Epicure, I shall leave you.　　　[*Exit.*]
Mam.　　　　　I follow you straight.　320
Face. But do so, good sir, to avoid suspicion.
This gent'man has a parlous head.
Mam.　　　　　　But wilt thou, Ulen,
Be constant to thy promise ?
Face.　　　　　　　As my life, sir.
Mam. And wilt thou insinuate what I am,
　and praise me,
And say I am a noble fellow ?
Face.　　　　　O, what else, sir ?　325

And that you 'll make her royal with the stone,
An empress ; and yourself King of Bantam.
Mam. Wilt thou do this ?
Face.　　　　　　Will I, sir !
Mam.　　　　　　Lungs, my Lungs !
I love thee.
Face. Send your stuff, sir, that my master
May busy himself about projection.　　330
Mam. Thou 'st witch'd me, rogue : take, go.
　　　　　　　　　[*Gives him money.*]
Face.　　　　　Your jack, and all, sir.
Mam. Thou art a villain — I will send my
　jack,
And the weights too. Slave, I could bite thine
　ear.
Away, thou dost not care for me.
Face.　　　　　　　Not I, sir !
Mam. Come, I was born to make thee, my
　good weasel,　　335
Set thee on a bench, and ha' thee twirl a chain
With the best lord's vermin of 'em all.
Face.　　　　　　　　Away, sir.
Mam. A count, nay, a count palatine ——
Face.　　　　　　　Good sir, go.
Mam. Shall not advance thee better : no, nor
　faster.　　　　　　[*Exit.*]

SCENE IV.[4]

FACE. [*Re-enter*] SUBTLE *and* DOL.

Sub. Has he bit ? has he bit ?
Face.　　　　　And swallow'd, too, my
　Subtle.
I ha' given him line, and now he plays, i' faith.
Sub. And shall we twitch him ?
Face.　　　　　Thorough both the gills.
A wench is a rare bait, with which a man
No sooner 's taken, but he straight firks mad.[5] 5
Sub. Dol, my Lord What's-hum's sister, you
　must now
Bear yourself *statelich.*
Dol.　　　　　O, let me alone,
I 'll not forget my race, I warrant you.
I 'll keep my distance, laugh and talk aloud ;
Have all the tricks of a proud scurvy lady,　10
And be as rude 's her woman.
Face.　　　　Well said, sanguine ![6]
Sub. But will he send his andirons ?
Face.　　　　　　　His jack too,
And 's iron shoeing-horn ; I ha' spoke to him.
　Well,
I must not lose my wary gamester yonder.
Sub. O, Monsieur Caution, that will not be
　gull'd ?　　　　　　　15
Face. Ay,
If I can strike a fine hook into him, now ! —
The Temple-church, there I have cast mine an-
　gle.
Well, pray for me. I 'll about it.
　　　　　　　　　(*One knocks.*)
Sub. What, more gudgeons ![7]　　20
Dol, scout, scout ! [DOL *goes to the window.*)
Stay, Face, you must go to the door ;
'Pray God it be my anabaptist — Who is 't, Dol ?

---

1 Games at cards.　　　3 A head-dress.
2 A collar, or a veil.

4 The same.　　　6 Red cheeks.
5 Runs mad.　　　7 Easy dupes.

Dol. I know him not: he looks like a gold-
end-man.[1]

Sub. Gods so! 't is he, he said he would send
— what call you him?
The sanctified elder, that should deal　25
For Mammon's jack and andirons. Let him in.
Stay, help me off, first, with my gown. [*Exit*
FACE *with the gown.*] Away,
Madam, to your withdrawing chamber. Now,
　　　　　　　　　　　　　　[*Exit* DOL.]
In a new tune, new gesture, but old language.—
This fellow is sent from one negotiates with me
About the stone too, for the holy brethren　31
Of Amsterdam, the exil'd saints, that hope
To raise their discipline[2] by it. I must use him
In some strange fashion now, to make him ad-
mire me.

SCENE V.[3]

SUBTLE. [*Enter*] ANANIAS.

Where is my drudge?　　　　　　　[*Aloud.*]

[*Enter*] FACE.

Face. 　　　　　　　　　　Sir!
Sub. 　　　　　Take away the recipient,
And rectify your menstrue from the phlegma.
Then pour it on the Sol, in the cucurbite,
And let 'em macerate together.
Face. 　　　　　　　　　　Yes, sir.
And save the ground?
Sub. 　　　　　　　No: *terra damnata*　5
Must not have entrance in the work. — Who
are you?
Ana. A faithful brother,[4] if it please you.
Sub. 　　　　　　　　What 's that?
A Lullianist? a Ripley?[5] *Filius artis?*
Can you sublime and dulcify? Calcine?
Know you the sapor pontic? Sapor stiptic?　10
Or what is homogene, or heterogene?
Ana. I understand no heathen language,
truly.
Sub. Heathen! You Knipperdoling?[6] Is Ars
sacra,
Or chrysopoeia, or spagyrica,
Or the pamphysic, or panarchic knowledge,　15
A heathen language?
Ana. 　　　　　Heathen Greek, I take it.
Sub. How! Heathen Greek?
Ana. 　　　　　All 's heathen but the Hebrew.
Sub. Sirrah my varlet, stand you forth and
speak to him
Like a philosopher: answer i' the language.
Name the vexations, and the martyrizations　20
Of metals in the work.
Face. 　　　　　Sir, putrefaction,
Solution, ablution, sublimation,
Cohobation, calcination, ceration, and
Fixation.
Sub. This is heathen Greek, to you, now! —
And when comes vivification?

---

[1] A man who buys broken remnants of gold.
[2] Puritan form of church government.
[3] The same.
[4] A Puritan. Subtle wilfully misunderstands.
[5] A follower of Raymond Lully (1235-1315) or George
Ripley (d. *cir.* 1490), well-known alchemical writers.
[6] An Anabaptist leader.

Face. 　　　　　　After mortification.　25
Sub. What 's cohobation?
Face. 　　　　　'T is the pouring on
Your *aqua regis*, and then drawing him off,
To the trine circle of the seven spheres.
Sub. What 's the proper passion of metals?
Face. 　　　　　　　　　Malleation.
Sub. What 's your *ultimum supplicium auri?*
Face. 　　　　　　　Antimonium.　30
Sub. This 's heathen Greek to you! — And
what 's your mercury?
Face. A very fugitive, he will be gone, sir.
Sub. How know you him?
Face. 　　　　　By his viscosity,
His oleosity, and his suscitability.
Sub. How do you sublime him?
Face. 　　　　　With the calce of egg-shells,　35
White marble, talc.
Sub. 　　　　Your magisterium now,
What 's that?
Face. 　　Shifting, sir, your elements,
Dry into cold, cold into moist, moist into hot,
Hot into dry.
Sub. 　　This is heathen Greek to you still!
Your *lapis philosophicus?*
Face. 　　　　　'T is a stone,　40
And not a stone; a spirit, a soul, and a body:
Which if you do dissolve, it is dissolv'd;
If you coagulate, it is coagulated;
If you make it to fly, it flieth.
Sub. 　　　　Enough. [*Exit* FACE.]
This 's heathen Greek to you! What are you,
sir?　45
Ana. Please you, a servant of the exil'd
brethren,
That deal with widows' and with orphans'
goods,
And make a just account unto the saints:
A deacon.
Sub. O, you are sent from Master Wholesome,
Your teacher?
Ana. 　　　From Tribulation Wholesome,　51
Our very zealous pastor.
Sub. 　　　Good! I have
Some orphans' goods to come here.
Ana. 　　　　Of what kind, sir?
Sub. Pewter and brass, andirons and kitchen-
ware,
Metals, that we must use our med'cine on:　55
Wherein the brethren may have a penn'orth
For ready money.
Ana. 　　　Were the orphans' parents
Sincere professors?
Sub. 　　　Why do you ask?
Ana. 　　　　　　Because
We then are to deal justly, and give, in truth,
Their utmost value.
Sub. 　　　'Slid, you 'd cozen else,　60
An if their parents were not of the faithful! —
I will not trust you, now I think on it,
Till I ha' talk'd with your pastor. Ha' you
brought money
To buy more coals?
Ana. 　　　No, surely.
Sub. 　　　　　No? How so?
Ana. The brethren bid me say unto you,
sir,

Surely, they will not venture any more   65
Till they may see projection.
Sub.   How !
Ana.   You 've had
For the instruments, as bricks, and lome, and
    glasses,
Already thirty pound ; and for materials,
They say, some ninety more: and they have
    heard since,
That one, at Heidelberg, made it of an egg,   70
And a small paper of pin-dust.
Sub.   What 's your name ?
Ana. My name is Ananias.
Sub   Out, the varlet
That cozen'd the apostles ! Hence, away !
Flee, mischief ! had your holy consistory   75
No name to send me, of another sound
Than wicked Ananias ? Send your elders
Hither, to make atonement for you, quickly,
And gi' me satisfaction ; or out goes
The fire ; and down th' alembics, and the fur-
    nace,   80
Piger Henricus, or what not. Thou wretch !
Both *sericon* and *bufo* shall be lost,
Tell 'em. All hope of rooting out the bishops,
Or th' anti-Christian hierarchy shall perish,
If they stay threescore minutes : the aqueity,
Terreity, and sulphureity   85
Shall run together again, and all be annull'd,
Thou wicked Ananias ! [*Exit* ANANIAS.] This
    will fetch 'em,
And make 'em haste towards their gulling
    more.
A man must deal like a rough nurse, and fright
Those that are froward, to an appetite.   91

SCENE VI.[1]

SUBTLE. [*Enter*] FACE [*in his uniform, followed
by*] DRUGGER.

Face. He 's busy with his spirits, but we 'll
    upon him.
Sub. How now ! What mates, what Bayards[2]
    ha' we here ?
Face. I told you he would be furious. — Sir,
    here 's Nab
Has brought you another piece of gold to look
    on ;
— We must appease him. Give it me, — and
    prays you,   5
You would devise — what is it, Nab ?
Drug.   A sign, sir.
Face. Ay, a good lucky one, a thriving sign,
    doctor.
Sub. I was devising now.
Face. [*Aside to* SUBTLE.] 'Slight, do not say
    so,
He will repent he ga' you any more. —
What say you to his constellation, doctor,   10
The Balance ?
Sub.   No, that way is stale and common.
A townsman born in Taurus, gives the bull,
Or the bull's head : in Aries, the ram, —
A poor-device ! No, I will have his name   14
Form'd in some mystic character; whose *radii,*

Striking the senses of the passers-by,
Shall, by a virtual [3] influence, breed affections,
That may result upon the party owns it :
As thus ——   19
Face. Nab !
Sub.   He first shall have *a bell,* that 's *Abel;*
And by it standing one whose name is *Dee,*[4]
In a *rug*[5] gown, there 's *D,* and *Rug,* that 's
    drug
And right anenst him a dog snarling *er ;*
There 's Drugger, Abel Drugger. That 's his
    sign.
And here 's now mystery and hieroglyphic !   25
Face. Abel, thou art made.
Drug.   Sir, I do thank his worship.
Face. Six o' thy legs[6] more will not do it,
    Nab.
He has brought you a pipe of tobacco, doctor.
Drug.   Yes, sir ;
I have another thing I would impart ——   29
Face. Out with it, Nab.
Drug.   Sir, there is lodg'd, hard by me,
A rich young widow ——
Face.   Good ! a bona roba ?[7]
Drug. But nineteen at the most.
Face.   Very good, Abel.
Drug. Marry, she 's not in fashion yet ; she
    wears
A hood, but 't stands a cop.[8]
Face.   No matter, Abel.
Drug. And I do now and then give her a fu-
    cus[9] ——   35
Face. What ! dost thou deal, Nab ?
Sub.   I did tell you, captain.
Drug. And physic too, sometime, sir ; for
    which she trusts me
With all her mind. She 's come up here of pur-
    pose
To learn the fashion.
Face.   Good (his match too !) — On, Nab.
Drug. And she does strangely long to know
    her fortune.   40
Face. God's lid, Nab, send her to the doctor,
    hither.
Drug. Yes, I have spoke to her of his worship
    already ;
But she 's afraid it will be blown abroad,
And hurt her a marriage.
Face.   Hurt it ! 't is the way
To heal it, if 't were hurt ; to make it more   45
Follow'd and sought. Nab, thou shalt tell her
    this.
She 'll be more known, more talk'd of ; and your
    widows
Are ne'er of any price till they be famous ;
Their honour is their multitude of suitors.   50
Send her, it may be thy good fortune. What !
Thou dost not know ?
Drug.   No, sir, she 'll never marry
Under a knight : her brother has made a vow.

---

[3] Due to the virtue or power of the device.
[4] A reference to Dr. Dee, the famous magician and
astrologer, who died in 1608.
[5] Of coarse frieze.   [6] Bows.   [7] Handsome wench.
[8] Peaked (?) or straight on the top of her head, instead of tilted (?).
[9] Paint for her face.

---

[1] The same.   [2] Blind horses.

Face. What! and dost thou despair, my little
Nab,
Knowing what the doctor has set down for thee,
And seeing so many o' the city dubb'd?   55
One glass o' thy water, with a madam I know,
Will have it done, Nab. What's her brother? a
knight?
Drug. No, sir, a gentleman newly warm in 's
land, sir,
Scarce cold in his one and twenty, that does
govern
His sister here; and is a man himself   60
Of some three thousand a year, and is come up
To learn to quarrel, and to live by his wits,
And will go down again, and die i' the country.
Face. How! to quarrel?
Drug.   Yes, sir, to carry quarrels,
As gallants do; to manage 'em by line.   65
Face. 'Slid, Nab, the doctor is the only
man
In Christendom for him. He has made a table,
With mathematical demonstrations,
Touching the art of quarrels: he will give him
An instrument to quarrel by. Go, bring 'em
both,   70
Him and his sister. And, for thee, with her
The doctor happ'ly may persuade. Go to:
'Shalt give his worship a new damask suit
Upon the premises.
Sub.   O, good captain!
Face.   He shall;
He is the honestest fellow, doctor. Stay not,   75
No offers; bring the damask, and the parties.
Drug. I'll try my power, sir.
Face.   And thy will too, Nab.
Sub. 'T is good tobacco, this! What is 't an
ounce?
Face. He'll send you a pound, doctor.
Sub.   O no.
Face.   He will do 't.
It is the goodest soul!—Abel, about it.   80
Thou shalt know more anon. Away, be gone.
                    [*Exit* Abel.]
A miserable rogue, and lives with cheese,
And has the worms. That was the cause, in-
deed,
Why he came now: he dealth with me in pri-
vate,   84
To get a med'cine for 'em.
Sub.   And shall, sir. This works.
Face. A wife, a wife for one on 's, my dear
Subtle!
We'll e'en draw lots, and he that fails, shall
have
The more in goods, the other has in tail.
Sub. Rather the less; for she may be so light   90
She may want grains.
Face.   Ay; or be such a burden,
A man would scarce endure her for the whole.
Sub. Faith, best let 's see her first, and then
determine.
Face. Content: but Dol must ha' no breath
on 't.
Sub.   Mum.
Away you, to your Surly yonder, catch him.
Face. Pray God I ha' not staid too long.   95
Sub.   I fear it. [*Exeunt.*]

ACT III

Scene I.[1]

[*Enter*] Tribulation [Wholesome] *and* Ananias.

Tri. These chastisements are common to the
saints,
And such rebukes we of the separation
Must bear with willing shoulders, as the trials
Sent forth to tempt our frailties.
Ana.   In pure zeal,   5
I do not like the man; he is a heathen,
And speaks the language of Canaan, truly.
Tri. I think him a profane person indeed.
Ana.   He bears
The visible mark of the beast in his forehead.
And for his stone, it is a work of darkness,
And with philosophy blinds the eyes of man.   10
Tri. Good brother, we must bend unto all
means
That may give furtherance to the holy cause.
Ana. Which his cannot: the sanctified cause
Should have a sanctified course.
Tri.   Not always necessary:
The children of perdition are oft times   15
Made instruments even of the greatest works.
Beside, we should give somewhat to man's
nature,
The place he lives in, still about the fire,
And fume of metals, that intoxicate
The brain of man, and make him prone to
passion.   20
Where have you greater atheists than your
cooks?
Or more profane, or choleric, than your glass-
men?
More anti-Christian than your bell-founders?
What makes the devil so devilish, I would ask
you,
Sathan, our common enemy, but his being   25
Perpetually about the fire, and boiling
Brimstone and arsenic? We must give, I say,
Unto the motives, and the stirrers up
Of humours in the blood. It may be so,
When as the work is done, the stone is made,   30
This heat of his may turn into a zeal,
And stand up for the beauteous discipline
Against the menstruous cloth and rag of Rome.
We must await his calling, and the coming
Of the good spirit. You did fault, t' upbraid
him   35
With the brethren's blessing of Heidelberg,
weighing
What need we have to hasten on the work,
For the restoring of the silenc'd saints, [2]
Which ne'er will be but by the philosopher's
stone.
And so a learned elder, one of Scotland,   40
Assur'd me; *aurum potabile* being
The only med'cine for the civil magistrate,
T' incline him to a feeling of the cause;
And must be daily us'd in the disease.
Ana. I have not edified more, truly, by man;

---

[1] The lane before Lovewit's house.
[2] Non-conformist ministers not allowed to preach.

Not since the beautiful light first shone on
    me :   46
And I am sad my zeal hath so offended.
    Tri. Let us call on him then.
    Ana.   The motion 's good,
And of the spirit ; I will knock first. [*Knocks.*]
        Peace be within ! [*The door is opened,
        and they enter.*]

SCENE II.[1]

[*Enter*] SUBTLE, [*followed by*] TRIBULATION
    and ANANIAS.

    Sub. O, are you come? 'T was time. Your
        threescore minutes
Were at last thread, you see ; and down had
        gone
Furnus acediae, turris circulatorius :
Limbec, bolt's-head, retort, and pelican
Had all been cinders. Wicked Ananias !   5
Art thou return'd ? Nay, then it goes down
        yet.
    Tri. Sir, be appeased ; he is come to humble
Himself in spirit, and to ask your patience,
If too much zeal hath carried him aside
From the due path.
    Sub.   Why, this doth qualify !   10
    Tri. The brethren had no purpose, verily,
To give you the least grievance ; but are ready
To lend their willing hands to any project
The spirit and you direct.
    Sub.   This qualifies more !
    Tri. And for the orphans' goods, let them be
        valu'd,   15
Or what is needful else to the holy work,
It shall be numb'red ; here, by me, the saints
Throw down their purse before you.
    Sub.   This qualifies most !
Why, thus it should be, now you understand.
Have I discours'd so unto you of our stone,   20
And of the good that it shall bring your cause ?
Show'd you (beside the main of hiring forces
Abroad, drawing the Hollanders, your friends,
From th' Indies, to serve you, with all their fleet)
That even the med'cinal use shall make you a
        faction   25
And party in the realm ? As, put the case,
That some great man in state, he have the
        gout,
Why, you but send three drops of your elixir,
You help him straight : there you have made a
        friend.
Another has the palsy or the dropsy,   30
He takes of your incombustible stuff,
He 's young again : there you have made a
        friend.
A lady that is past the feat of body,
Though not of mind, and hath her face decay'd
Beyond all cure of paintings, you restore   35
With the oil of talc : there you have made a
        friend ;
And all her friends. A lord that is a leper,
A knight that has the bone-ache, or a squire
That hath both these, you make 'em smooth
        and sound

With a bare fricace[2] of your med'cine ; still   40
You increase your friends.
    Tri.   Ay, 't is very pregnant.
    Sub. And then the turning of this lawyer's
        pewter
To plate at Christmas——
    Ana.   Christ-tide, I pray you.
    Sub. Yet, Ananias !
    Ana.   I have done.
    Sub.   Or changing
His parcel[3] gilt to massy gold. You cannot   45
But raise you friends. Withal, to be of power
To pay an army in the field, to buy
The King of France out of his realms, or Spain
Out of his Indies. What can you not do
Against lords spiritual or temporal,   50
That shall oppone[4] you ?
    Tri.   Verily, 't is true.
We may be temporal lords ourselves, I take it.
    Sub. You may be anything, and leave off to
        make
Long-winded exercises ; or suck up
Your *ha !* and *hum !* in a tune. I not deny, 55
But such as are not graced in a state,
May, for their ends, be adverse in religion,
And get a tune to call the flock together :
For, to say sooth, a tune does much with women
And other phlegmatic people ; it is your bell. 60
    Ana. Bells are profane ; a tune may be re-
        ligious.
    Sub. No warning with you? Then farewell
        my patience.
Slight, it shall down ; I will not be thus tortur'd.
    Tri. I pray you, sir.
    Sub.   All shall perish. I have spoke it.
    Tri. Let me find grace, sir, in your eyes ; the
        man,   65
He stands corrected : neither did his zeal,
But as your self, allow a tune somewhere,
Which now, being tow'rd[5] the stone, we shall
        not need.
    Sub. No, nor your holy vizard,[6] to win widows
To give you legacies ; or make zealous wives   70
To rob their husbands for the common cause :
Nor take the start of bonds broke but one day,
And say they were forfeited by providence.
Nor shall you need o'er night to eat huge meals,
To celebrate your next day's fast the better ; 75
The whilst the brethren and the sisters hum-
        bled,
Abate the stiffness of the flesh. Nor cast
Before your hungry hearers scrupulous bones ;[7]
As whether a Christian may hawk or hunt,
Or whether matrons of the holy assembly   80
May lay their hair out, or wear doublets,
Or have that idol, starch, about their linen.
    Ana. It is indeed an idol.
    Tri.   Mind him not, sir.
I do command thee, spirit (of zeal, but trouble),
To peace within him ! Pray you, sir, go on.   85
    Sub. Nor shall you need to libel 'gainst the
        prelates,
And shorten so your ears[8] against the hearing

---

    1 A room in Lovewit's house.

    2 Rubbing.   3 Partly.   4 Oppose.
    5 Near possession of.   6 Set expression of face.
    7 The dry bones of discussion on such scruples.
    8 Have your ears cut off in the pillory.

Of the next wire-drawn grace. Nor of necessity
Rail against plays, to please the alderman
Whose daily custard you devour; nor lie   90
With zealous rage till you are hoarse. Not one
Of these so singular arts. Nor call yourselves
By names of Tribulation, Persecution,
Restraint, Long-patience, and such like,
  affected
By the whole family or wood [1] of you,   95
Only for glory, and to catch the ear
Of the disciple.
  Tri.   Truly, sir, they are
Ways that the godly brethren have invented,
For propagation of the glorious cause,
As very notable means, and whereby also   100
Themselves grow soon, and profitably, famous.
  Sub. O, but the stone, all 's idle to 't! No-
    thing!
The art of angels, nature's miracle,
The divine secret that doth fly in clouds
From east to west: and whose tradition   105
Is not from men, but spirits.
  Ana.   I hate traditions;
I do not trust them——
  Tri.   Peace!
  Ana.   They are popish all.
I will not peace: I will not——
  Tri.   Ananias!
  Ana. Please the profane, to grieve the godly;
    I may not.
  Sub. Well, Ananias, thou shalt overcome.   110
  Tri. It is an ignorant zeal that haunts him, sir:
But truly else a very faithful brother,
A botcher, [2] and a man by revelation
That hath a competent knowledge of the truth.
  Sub. Has he a competent sum there i' the
    bag   115
To buy the goods within? I am made guardian,
And must, for charity and conscience' sake,
Now see the most be made for my poor orphan;
Though I desire the brethren, too, good gainers:
There they are within. When you have view'd
    and bought 'em,   120
And ta'en the inventory of what they are,
They are ready for projection; there 's no more
To do: cast on the med'cine, so much silver
As there is tin there, so much gold as brass,
I 'll gi' it you in by weight.
  Tri.   But how long time,   125
Sir, must the saints expect yet?
  Sub.   Let me see,
How 's the moon now? Eight, nine, ten days
    hence,
He will be silver potate; then three days
Before he citronise.[3] Some fifteen days,
The magisterium [4] will be perfected.   130
  Ana. About the second day of the third week,
In the ninth month?
  Sub.   Yes, my good Ananias.
  Tri. What will the orphans' goods arise to,
    think you?

Sub. Some hundred marks, as much as fill'd
    three cars,
Unladed now: you 'll make six millions of
    'em——   135
But I must ha' more coals laid in.
  Tri.   How?
  Sub.   Another load,
And then we ha' finish'd. We must now in-
    crease
Our fire to *ignis ardens;* [5] we are past
Fimus equinus, balnei, cineris,[6]
And all those lenter [7] heats. If the holy purse
Should with this draught fall low, and that the
    saints   141
Do need a present sum, I have a trick
To melt the pewter, you shall buy now in-
    stantly,
And with a tincture make you as good Dutch
    dollars
As any are in Holland.
  Tri.   Can you so?   145
  Sub. Ay, and shall bide the third examination.
  Ana. It will be joyful tidings to the brethren.
  Sub. But you must carry it secret.
  Tri.   Ay; but stay,
This act of coining, is it lawful?
  Ana.   Lawful!
We know no magistrate: or, if we did,   150
This 's foreign coin.
  Sub.   It is no coining, sir.
It is but casting.
  Tri.   Ha! you distinguish well:
Casting of money may be lawful.
  Ana.   'T is, sir.
  Tri. Truly, I take it so.
  Sub.   There is no scruple,
Sir, to be made of it; believe Ananias;   155
This case of conscience he is studied in.
  Tri. I 'll make a question of it to the bre-
    thren.
  Ana. The brethren shall approve it lawful,
    doubt not.
Where shall 't be done?
  Sub. For that we 'll talk anon. *Knock without.*
There 's some to speak with me. Go in, I pray
    you,   160
And view the parcels. That 's the inventory.
I 'll come to you straight. [*Exeunt* TRIB. *and*
    ANA.] Who is it?—Face! appear.

Scene III.[8]

SUBTLE. [*Enter*] FACE [*in his uniform*].

  Sub. How now! good prize?
  Face.   Good pox! Yond' costive cheater
Never came on.
  Sub.   How then?
  Face.   I ha' walk'd the round
Till now, and no such thing.
  Sub.   And ha' you quit him?
  Face. Quit him! An hell would quit him too,
    he were happy.
'Slight! would you have me stalk like a mill-
    jade,   5

---

[1] Assembly.
[2] Tailor. But the term was used generally of Puritans.
[3] Become the color of citron—a stage in the process of producing the stone.
[4] Full accomplishment

[5] Fiery heat.
[6] Heat from horse-dung, warm bath, ashes.
[7] Milder.   [8] The same.

All day, for one that will not yield us grains?
I know him of old.
 Sub.   O, but to ha' gull'd him,
Had been a mastery.
 Face.   Let him go, black boy!
And turn thee, that some fresh news may pos-
  sess thee.
A noble count, a don of Spain (my dear 10
Delicious compeer, and my party[1]-bawd),
Who is come hither private for his conscience
And brought munition with him, six great
 slops,[2]
Bigger than three Dutch hoys,[3] beside round
 trunks,[4]   14
Furnish'd with pistolets,[5] and pieces of eight,[6]
Will straight be here, my rogue, to have thy
 bath,
(That is the colour,[7]) and to make his batt'ry
Upon our Dol, our castle, our cinqueport,
Our Dover pier, our what thou wilt. Where is
 she?
She must prepare perfumes, delicate linen, 20
The bath in chief, a banquet, and her wit,
Where is the doxy?
 Sub.   I'll send her to thee:
And but despatch my brace of little John Ley-
 dens[8]
And come again myself.
 Face.   Are they within then?
Sub. Numb'ring the sum.
 Face. How much?
 Sub.   A hundred marks, boy. [*Exit.*]
Face. Why, this is a lucky day. Ten pounds
 of Mammon!   26
Three o' my clerk! A portague o' my grocer!
This o' the brethren! Beside reversions
And states to come, i' the widow, and my count!
My share to-day will not be bought for forty ——

[Enter DOL.*]*

Dol.   What? 30
Face. Pounds, dainty Dorothy! Art thou so
 near?
Dol. Yes; say, lord general, how fares our
 camp?
Face. As with the few that had entrench'd
 themselves
Safe, by their discipline, against a world, Dol,
And laugh'd within those trenches, and grew
 fat   35
With thinking on the booties, Dol, brought in
Daily by their small parties. This dear hour,
A doughty don is taken with my Dol;
And thou mayst make his ransom what thou
 wilt,
My Dousabel;[9] he shall be brought here, fet-
 ter'd   40
With thy fair looks, before he sees thee; and
 thrown
In a down-bed, as dark as any dungeon;

Where thou shalt keep him waking with thy
 drum;
Thy drum, my Dol, thy drum; till he be tame
As the poor blackbirds were i' the great frost,
Or bees are with a bason; and so hive him 46
I' the swan-skin coverlid and cambric sheets,
Till he work honey and wax, my little God's-
 gift.[10]
 Dol. What is he, general?
 Face.   An adalantado,[11] 49
A grandee, girl. Was not my Dapper here yet?
Dol. No.
Face. Nor my Drugger?
 Dol.   Neither.
 Face.   A pox on 'em,
They are so long a furnishing! such stinkards
Would not be seen upon these festival days. —

[Re-enter SUBTLE.*]*

How now! ha' you done?
 Sub.   Done. They are gone: the sum
Is here in bank, my Face. I would we knew 55
Another chapman who would buy 'em outright.
Face. 'Slid, Nab shall do't against he ha' the
 widow,
To furnish household.
 Sub. Excellent, well thought on:
Pray God he come.
 Face.   I pray he keep away
Till our new business be o'erpast.
 Sub.   But, Face, 60
How camst thou by this secret don?
 Face.   A spirit
Brought me th' intelligence in a paper here,
As I was conjuring yonder in my circle
For Surly; I ha' my flies[12] abroad. Your bath
Is famous, Subtle, by my means. Sweet Dol, 65
You must go tune your virginal, no losing
O' the least time. And — do you hear? — good
 action!
Firk like a flounder; kiss like a scallop, close;
And tickle him with thy mother-tongue. His
 great
Verdugoship[13] has not a jot of language; 70
So much the easier to be cozen'd, my Dolly.
He will come here in a hir'd coach, obscure,
And our own coachman, whom I have sent as
 guide,
No creature else. (*One knocks.*) Who's that?
            [Exit DOL.*]*
 Sub.   It is not he?
Face. O no, not yet this hour.

[Re-enter DOL.*]*

 Sub.   Who is't?
 Dol.   Dapper, 75
Your clerk.
 Face. God's will then, Queen of Fairy,
On with your tire; [*Exit* DOL.*] and, doctor, with
 your robes.
Let's despatch him for God's sake.
 Sub.   'Twill be long.

---

[1] Partner.   [3] Passenger sloops.
[2] Large breeches.   [4] Trunk hose.
[5] A Spanish gold coin worth about 16s. 8d.
[6] A coin worth about 4s. 6d.
[7] Pretext.
[8] Puritans, from the name of the Anabaptist leader.
[9] *I. e. douce et belle;* sweetheart

[10] Referring to the literal meaning of *Dorothea.*
[11] A Spanish governor. [12] Familiars.
[13] Verdugo is a Spanish name, but the precise allusion
is uncertain.

Face. I warrant you, take but the cues I give
  you,
It shall be brief enough. [*Goes to the window.*]
'Slight, here are more !   80
Abel, and I think the angry boy, the heir,
That fain would quarrel.
  Sub.   And the widow ?
  Face.   No,
Not that I see. Away !   [*Exit* SUB.]

SCENE IV.[1]

FACE. [*Enter*] DAPPER.

Face.   O, sir, you are welcome.
The doctor is within a moving for you ;
I have had the most ado to win him to it ! —
He swears you 'll be the darling o' the dice :
He never heard her highness dote till now.[2]   5
Your aunt has giv'n you the most gracious
  words
That can be thought on.
  Dap.   Shall I see her grace ?
Face. See her, and kiss her too. —

[*Enter* ABEL, *followed by* KASTRIL.]

                          What, honest Nab !
Hast brought the damask ?
  Nab.   No, sir ; here 's tobacco.
Face. 'T is well done, Nab ; thou 'lt bring
  the damask too ?   10
Drug. Yes. Here 's the gentleman, captain,
  Master Kastril,
I have brought to see the doctor.
  Face.   Where 's the widow ?
Drug. Sir, as he likes, his sister, he says,
  shall come.
Face. O, is it so ? Good time. Is your name
Kastril, sir ?
  Kas. Ay, and the best o' the Kastrils, I 'd
  be sorry else,   15
By fifteen hundred a year.[3] Where is this
  doctor ?
My mad tobacco-boy here tells me of one
That can do things. Has he any skill ?
  Face.   Wherein, sir ?
Kas. To carry a business, manage a quarrel
  fairly,
Upon fit terms.
  Face.   It seems, sir, you 're but young 20
About the town, that can make that a question.
Kas. Sir, not so young but I have heard
  some speech
Of the angry boys,[4] and seen 'em take tobacco ;
And in his shop ; and I can take it too.
And I would fain be one of 'em, and go down
And practise i' the country.
  Face.   Sir, for the duello, 26
The doctor, I assure you, shall inform you,
To the least shadow of a hair ; and show you
An instrument he has of his own making,
Wherewith, no sooner shall you make report 30
Of any quarrel, but he will take the height on 't
Most instantly, and tell in what degree

---

[1] The same.   [2] Folio adds (*he says*).
[3] *I. e.* he is £1500 a year richer than any other of
the Kastrils.
[4] Roysterers, young bloods.

Of safety it lies in, or mortality.
And how it may be borne, whether in a right
  line,
Or a half circle ; or may else be cast   35
Into an angle blunt, if not acute :
And this he will demonstrate. And then, rules
To give and take the lie by.
  Kas.   How ! to take it ?
Face. Yes, in oblique he 'll show you, or in
  circle ;[5]
But ne'er in diameter.[6] The whole town   40
Study his theorems, and dispute them ordinarily
At the eating academies.
  Kas.   But does he teach
Living by the wits too ?
  Face.   Anything whatever.
You cannot think that subtlety but he reads it.
He made me a captain. I was a stark pimp,   45
Just o' your standing, 'fore I met with him ;
It 's not two months since. I 'll tell you his
  method :
First, he will enter you at some ordinary.
Kas. No, I 'll not come there : you shall par-
  don me.
  Face.   For why, sir ?
Kas. There 's gaming there, and tricks.
  Face.   Why, would you be   50
A gallant, and not game ?
  Kas. Ay, 't will spend a man.
Face. Spend you ! It will repair you when
  you are spent.
How do they live by their wits there, that have
  vented
Six times your fortunes ?
  Kas. What, three thousand a year !
Face. Ay, forty thousand.
  Kas.   Are there such ?
  Face.   Ay, sir,   55
And gallants yet. Here 's a young gentleman
Is born to nothing,— [*Points to* DAPPER.] forty
  marks a year
Which I count nothing : — he 's to be initiated,
And have a fly o' the doctor. He will win you
By unresistible luck, within this fortnight,   60
Enough to buy a barony. They will set him
Upmost, at the groom porter's,[7] all the Christ-
  mas :
And for the whole year through at every place
Where there is play, present him with the
  chair,   64
The best attendance, the best drink, sometimes
Two glasses of Canary, and pay nothing ;
The purest linen and the sharpest knife,
The partridge next his trencher : and somewhere
The dainty bed, in private, with the dainty.
You shall ha' your ordinaries bid for him,   70
As playhouses for a poet ; and the master
Pray him aloud to name what dish he affects,
Which must be butter'd shrimps : and those
  that drink
To no mouth else, will drink to his, as being
The goodly president mouth of all the board. 75
  Kas. Do you not gull one ?

---

[5] The lie circumstantial.   [6] The lie direct.
[7] An officer of the royal household, having charge o
the cards, dice, etc. He had the privilege of keepin
open table at Christmas.

Face.   'Ods my life ! Do you think it ?
You shall have a cast commander, (can but get
In credit with a glover, or a spurrier,
For some two pair of either's ware aforehand,)
Will, by most swift posts, dealing [but] with
    him,   80
Arrive at competent means to keep himself,
His punk, and naked boy, in excellent fashion,
And be admir'd for 't.
Kas.   Will the doctor teach this ?
Face. He will do more, sir : when your land
    is gone,
(As men of spirit hate to keep earth long),   85
In a vacation,[1] when small money is stirring,
And ordinaries suspended till the term,
He 'll show a perspective,[2] where on one side
You shall behold the faces and the persons
Of all sufficient young heirs in town,   90
Whose bonds are current for commodity ;[3]
On th' other side, the merchants' forms, and
    others,
That without help of any second broker,
Who would expect a share, will trust such par-
    cels :
In the third square, the very street and sign   95
Where the commodity dwells, and does but
    wait
To be deliver'd, be it pepper, soap,
Hops, or tobacco, oatmeal, woad,[4] or cheeses.
All which you may so handle, to enjoy
To your own use, and never stand oblig'd.   100
Kas. I' faith ! is he such a fellow ?
Face.   Why, Nab here knows him.
And then for making matches for rich widows,
Young gentlewomen, heirs, the fortunat'st
    man !
He 's sent to, far and near, all over England,   104
To have his counsel, and to know their fortunes.
Kas. God 's will, my suster shall see him.
Face.   I 'll tell you, sir,
What he did tell me of Nab. It 's a strange
    thing —
(By the way, you must eat no cheese, Nab, it
    breeds melancholy,
And that same melancholy breeds worms) but
    pass it : —   109
He told me, honest Nab here was ne'er at tavern
But once in 's life.
Drug.   Truth, and no more I was not.
Face. And then he was so sick ——
Drug.   Could he tell you that too ?
Face. How should I know it ?
Drug.   In troth, we had been a shooting,
And had a piece of fat ram-mutton to supper,
That lay so heavy o' my stomach ——
Face.   And he has no head   115
To bear any wine ; for what with the noise o'
    the fiddlers,
And care of his shop, for he dares keep no ser-
    vants ——
Drug. My head did so ache ——

Face.   As he was fain to be brought home.
The doctor told me : and then a good old
    woman ——
Drug. Yes, faith, she dwells in Seacoal-lane,
    — did cure me,   120
With sodden ale, and pellitory[5] o' the wall ;
Cost me but twopence. I had another sickness
Was worse than that.
Face.   Ay, that was with the grief
Thou took'st for being cess'd[6] at eighteen-
    pence,
For the waterwork.
Drug.   In truth, and it was like   125
T' have cost me almost my life.
Face.   Thy hair went off ?
Drug. Yes, sir ; 't was done for spite.
Face.   Nay, so says the doctor.
Kas. Pray thee, tobacco-boy, go fetch my
    suster ;
I 'll see this learned boy before I go ;
And so shall she.
Face.   Sir, he is busy now :   130
But if you have a sister to fetch hither,
Perhaps your own pains may command her
    sooner ;
And he by that time will be free.
Kas.   I go. [*Exit.*]
Face. Drugger, she 's thine : the damask ! —
    [*Exit* ABEL.] Subtle and I
Must wrastle for her. [*Aside.*] Come on, Master
    Dapper,   135
You see how I turn clients here away,
To give your cause dispatch ; ha' you perform'd
The ceremonies were enjoin'd you ?
Dap.   Yes, o' the vinegar,
And the clean shirt.
Face.   'T is well : that shirt may do you
More worship than you think. Your aunt 's a-
    fire,   140
But that she will not show it, t' have a sight of
    you.
Ha' you provided for her grace's servants ?
Dap. Yes, here are six score Edward shil-
    lings.
Face.   Good !
Dap. And an old Harry's sovereign.
Face.   Very good !
Dap. And three James shillings, and an
    Elizabeth groat,   145
Just twenty nobles.[7]
Face.   O, you are too just.
I would you had had the other noble in Maries.
Dap. I have some Philip and Maries.
Face.   Ay, those same
Are best of all : where are they ? Hark, the
    doctor.

SCENE V.[8]

FACE, DAPPER. [*Enter*] SUBTLE, *disguised
like a priest of Fairy [with a strip of cloth].*

Sub. [*in a feigned voice.*] Is yet her grace's
    cousin come ?
Face.   He is come.
Sub. And is he fasting ?

---

[1] Of the law-courts.   [2] A magic glass.
[3] The reference is to the "commodity" fraud, in
which a borrower was obliged to take part of a loan in
merchandise, which the lender frequently bought back
by agents for much less than it represented in the loan.
[4] A plant used for a dye.

[5] A herb.   [7] A noble was worth 6s. 8d.
[6] Assessed, taxed.   [8] The same.

Face.   Yes.
Sub.   And hath cried "hum"?
Face. Thrice, you must answer.
Dap.   Thrice.
Sub.   And as oft "buz"?
Face. If you have, say.
Dap.   I have.
Sub.   Then, to her cuz,
Hoping that he hath vinegar'd his senses,   5
As he was bid, the Fairy queen dispenses,
By me, this robe, the petticoat of Fortune;
Which that he straight put on, she doth impor-
tune.
And though to Fortune near be her petticoat,   9
Yet nearer is her smock, the queen doth note:
And therefore, even of that a piece she hath
sent,
Which, being a child, to wrap him in was rent;
And prays him for a scarf he now will wear it,
With as much love as then her grace did tear it,
About his eyes, (*They blind him with the rag.*) to
show he is fortunate.   15
And, trusting unto her to make his state,
He 'll throw away all worldly pelf about him;
Which that he will perform, she doth not doubt
him.
Face. She need not doubt him, sir. Alas, he
has nothing
But what he will part withal as willingly,   20
Upon his grace's word — throw away your
purse —
As she would ask it: — handkerchiefs and all —
She cannot bid that thing but he 'll obey. —
If you have a ring about you, cast it off,
Or a silver seal at your wrist; her grace will
send (*He throws away, as they bid him.*)   25
Her fairies here to search you, therefore deal
Directly [1] with her highness: if they find
That you conceal a mite, you are undone.
Dap. Truly, there 's all.
Face.   All what?
Dap.   My money; truly.
Face. Keep nothing that is transitory about
you.   30
[*Aside to* SUBTLE.] Bid Dol play music. — Look,
the elves are come

                    DOL. *enters with a cittern.*

To pinch you, if you tell not the truth. Advise
you.   *They pinch him.*
Dap. O! I have a paper with a spur-ryal [2]
in 't.
Face.   Ti, ti.
They knew 't, they say.
Sub.   Ti, ti, ti, ti. He has more yet.
Face. Ti, ti-ti-ti. I' the other pocket?
Sub.   Titi, titi, titi, titi, titi.   35
They must pinch him or he will never confess,
they say.   [*They pinch him again.*]
Dap. O, O!
Face. Nay, pray you, hold: he is her grace's
nephew
Ti, ti, ti? What care you? Good faith, you
shall care. —   39
Deal plainly, sir, and shame the fairies. Show
You are innocent.

---

[1] Uprightly.   [2] A gold coin worth 15s.

Dap.   By this good light, I ha' nothing.
Sub. Ti, ti, ti, ti, to, ta. He does equivocate
she says:
Ti, ti do ti, ti ti do, ti da; and swears by the
light when he is blinded.
Dap. By this good dark, I ha' nothing but a
half-crown   44
Of gold about my wrist, that my love gave me;
And a leaden heart I wore sin' she forsook
me.
Face. I thought 't was something. And would
Your aunt's displeasure for these trifles? Come,
I had rather you had thrown away twenty half-
crowns.   [*Takes it off.*]
You may wear your leaden heart still. — How
now!   50
Sub. What news, Dol?
Dol. Yonder 's your knight, Sir Mammon.
Face. God's lid, we never thought of him till
now!
Where is he?
Dol.   Here hard by. He 's at the door.
Sub. And you are not ready now! Dol, get
his suit.   [*Exit* DOL.]
He must not be sent back.
Face.   O, by no means.   55
What shall we do with this same puffin [3] here,
Now he 's o' the spit?
Sub.   Why, lay him back awhile,
With some device.

          [*Re-enter* DOL *with* FACE'S *clothes.*]

                    — Ti, ti, ti, ti, ti, ti. Would her grace
speak with me?
I come. — Help, Dol!   *Knocking without.*
                    there? Sir Epicure,
Face. (*speaks through the keyhole.*) — Who 's
My master 's i' the way. Please you to walk   60
Three or four turns, but till his back be turn'd,
And I am for you. — Quickly, Dol!
Sub.   Her grace
Commends her kindly to you, Master Dapper.
Dap. I long to see her grace.
Sub.   She now is set
At dinner in her bed, and she has sent you   65
From her own private trencher, a dead mouse,
And a piece of gingerbread, to be merry withal,
And stay your stomach, lest you faint with
fasting:
Yet if you could hold out till she saw you, she
says,
It would be better for you.
Face.   Sir, he shall   70
Hold out, an 't were this two hours, for her
highness;
I can assure you that. We will not lose
All we ha' done. ——
Sub.   He must not see, nor speak
To anybody, till then.
Face.   For that we 'll put, sir,
A stay in 's mouth.
Sub.   Of what?
Face.   Of gingerbread.   75
Make you it fit. He that hath pleas'd her grace

---

[3] A sort of sea-bird; used contemptuously of a puffed-
up person.

Thus far, shall not now crinkle [1] for a little. ——
Gape, sir, and let him fit you.

> [*They thrust a gag of gingerbread
> into his mouth.*]

Sub.   —— Where shall we now
Bestow him ?
Dol.   I' the privy. ——
Sub.   Come along, sir,   80
I must now show you Fortune's privy lodgings.
Face. Are they perfum'd, and his bath ready?
Sub.   All:
Only the fumigation 's somewhat strong.
Face. [*speaking through the keyhole.*] Sir Epi-
cure, I am yours, sir, by and by.

> [*Exeunt with* DAPPER.]

ACT IV

Scene I.[2]

[*Enter*] FACE *and* MAMMON.

Face. O, sir, you 're come i' the only finest
time. ——
Mam. Where 's master ?
Face.   Now preparing for projection, sir.
Your stuff will be all chang'd shortly.
Mam.   Into gold ?
Face. To gold and silver, sir.
Mam.   Silver I care not for.
Face. Yes, sir, a little to give beggars.
Mam.   Where 's the lady ?   5
Face. At hand here. I ha' told her such brave
things o' you,
Touching your bounty and your noble spirit ——
Mam.   Hast thou ?
Face. As she is almost in her fit to see you.
But, good sir, no divinity i' your conference,
For fear of putting her in rage. ——
Mam.   I warrant thee.   10
Face. Six men [sir] will not hold her down.
And then,
If the old man should hear or see you ——
Mam.   Fear not.
Face. The very house, sir, would run mad.
You know it,
How scrupulous he is, and violent,
'Gainst the least act of sin. Physic or mathema-
tics,   15
Poetry, state,[3] or bawdry, as I told you,
She will endure, and never startle ; but
No word of controversy.
Mam.   I am school'd, good Ulen.
Face. And you must praise her house, remem-
ber that,
And her nobility.
Mam.   Let me alone :   20
No herald, no, nor antiquary, Lungs,
Shall do it better. Go.
Face. [*Aside.*]   Why, this is yet
A kind of modern happiness,[4] to have
Dol Common for a great lady.   [*Exit.*]
Mam.   Now, Epicure,
Heighten thyself, talk to her all in gold ;   25

---

[1] Turn aside from his purpose.
[2] A room in Lovewit's house.
[3] Politics.
[4] Up-to-date appropriateness.

Rain her as many showers as Jove did drops
Unto his Danaë ; show the god a miser,
Compar'd with Mammon. What ! the stone will
do 't.
She shall feel gold, taste gold, hear gold, sleep
gold ;
Nay, we will *concumbere* gold : I will be puissant,
And mighty in my talk to her. —

> [*Re-enter* FACE *with* DOL *richly dressed.*]

Here she comes.   31
Face. To him, Dol, suckle him. This is the
noble knight
I told your ladyship ——
Mam.   Madam, with your pardon,
I kiss your vesture.
Dol.   Sir, I were uncivil
If I would suffer that ; my lip to you, sir.   35
Mam. I hope my lord your brother be in
health, lady.
Dol. My lord my brother is, though I no lady,
sir.
Face. [*Aside.*] Well said, my Guinea bird.
Mam.   Right noble madam ——
Face. [*Aside.*] O, we shall have most fierce
idolatry.
Mam. 'T is your prerogative.
Dol.   Rather your courtesy.   40
Mam. Were there nought else t' enlarge your
virtues to me,
These answers speak your breeding and your
blood.
Dol. Blood we boast none, sir ; a poor baron's
daughter.
Mam. Poor ! and gat you ? Profane not. Had
your father
Slept all the happy remnant of his life   45
After that act, lien but there still, and panted,
He 'd done enough to make himself, his issue,
And his posterity noble.
Dol.   Sir, although
We may be said to want the gilt and trappings,
The dress of honour, yet we strive to keep   50
The seeds and the materials.
Mam.   I do see
The old ingredient, virtue, was not lost,
Nor the drug money us'd to make your com-
pound.
There is a strange nobility i' your eye,
This lip, that chin ! Methinks you do resemble
One o' the Austriac princes.
Face. [*Aside.*]   Very like !   55
Her father was an Irish costermonger.
Mam. The house of Valois just had such a
nose,
And such a forehead yet the Medici
Of Florence boast.
Dol.   Troth, and I have been lik'ned   60
To all these princes.
Face. [*Aside.*] I 'll be sworn, I heard it.
Mam. I know not how ! it is not any one,
But e'en the very choice of all their features.
Face. [*Aside.*] I 'll in, and laugh.   [*Exit.*]
Mam.   A certain touch, or air,
That sparkles a divinity beyond   65
An earthly beauty !
Dol.   O, you play the courtier.

Mam. Good lady, gi' me leave ——
Dol.   In faith, I may not,
To mock me, sir.
Mam.   To burn i' this sweet flame ;
The phoenix never knew a nobler death.
Dol. Nay, now you court the courtier, and
destroy   70
What you would build. This art, sir, i' your
words,
Calls your whole faith in question.
Mam.   By my soul ——
Dol. Nay, oaths are made o' the same air, sir.
Mam.   Nature
Never bestow'd upon mortality
A more unblam'd, a more harmonious feature ;
She play'd the step-dame in all faces else :   75
Sweet madam, le' me be particular ——
Dol. Particular, sir ! I pray you, know your
distance.
Mam. In no ill sense, sweet lady : but to ask
How your fair graces pass the hours ? I see   80
You're lodg'd here, i' the house of a rare man,
An excellent artist : but what 's that to you ?
Dol. Yes, sir ; I study here the mathematics,
And distillation.
Mam.   O, I cry your pardon.
He 's a divine instructor ! can extract   85
The souls of all things by his art ; call all
The virtues, and the miracles of the sun,
Into a temperate furnace ; teach dull nature
What her own forces are. A man, the emp'ror
Has courted above Kelly ; [1] sent his medals   90
And chains, t' invite him.
Dol.   Ay, and for his physic, sir ——
Mam. Above the art of Aesculapius,
That drew the envy of the thunderer !
I know all this, and more.
Dol.   Troth, I am taken, sir,
Whole with these studies that contemplate na-
ture.   95
Mam. It is a noble humour ; but this form
Was not intended to so dark a use.
Had you been crooked, foul, of some coarse
mould,
A cloister had done well ; but such a feature,
That might stand up the glory of a kingdom,
To live recluse is a mere solecism,   101
Though in a nunnery. It must not be.
I muse, my lord your brother will permit it :
You should spend half my land first, were I he.
Does not this diamond better on my finger   105
Than i' the quarry ?
Dol.   Yes.
Mam.   Why, you are like it.
You were created, lady, for the light.
Here, you shall wear it ; take it, the first pledge
Of what I speak, to bind you to believe me.
Dol. In chains of adamant ?
Mam.   Yes, the strongest bands.   110
And take a secret too. — Here, by your side,
Doth stand this hour the happiest man in Europe.
Dol. You are contented, sir ?
Mam.   Nay, in true being,
The envy of princes and the fear of states.

----

[1] The partner of Dee, the astrologer. He and Dee
visited the emperor, Rodolph II, at Prague in 1584.

Dol. Say you so, Sir Epicure ?
Mam.   Yes, and thou shalt prove it,   115
Daughter of honour. I have cast mine eye
Upon thy form, and I will rear this beauty
Above all styles.
Dol.   You mean no treason, sir ?
Mam. No, I will take away that jealousy.
I am the lord of the philosopher's stone,   120
And thou the lady.
Dol.   How, sir ! ha' you that ?
Mam. I am the master of the mastery.[2]
This day the good old wretch here o' the house
Has made it for us : now he 's at projection.
Think therefore thy first wish now, let me hear
it ;   125
And it shall rain into thy lap, no shower,
But floods of gold, whole cataracts, a deluge,
To get a nation on thee.
Dol.   You are pleas'd, sir,
To work on the ambition of our sex.
Mam. I am pleas'd the glory of her sex should
know,   130
This nook here of the Friars is no climate
For her to live obscurely in, to learn
Physic and surgery, for the constable's wife
Of some odd hundred in Essex ; but come forth,
And taste the air of palaces ; eat, drink   135
The toils of empirics, and their boasted prac-
tice ;
Tincture of pearl, and coral, gold, and amber ;
Be seen at feasts and triumphs ; have it ask'd,
What miracle she is ; set all the eyes
Of court a-fire, like a burning glass,   140
And work 'em into cinders, when the jewels
Of twenty states adorn thee, and the light
Strikes out the stars that, when thy name is
mention'd,
Queens may look pale ; and, we but showing our
love,
Nero's Poppaea may be lost in story !   145
Thus will we have it.
Dol.   I could well consent, sir.
But in a monarchy, how will this be ?
The prince will soon take notice, and both seize
You and your stone, it being a wealth unfit
For any private subject.
Mam.   If he knew it.   150
Dol. Yourself do boast it, sir.
Mam.   To thee, my life.
Dol. O, but beware, sir ! You may come to
end
The remnant of your days in a loath'd prison,
By speaking of it.
Mam.   'T is no idle fear.   154
We 'll therefore go with all, my girl, and live
In a free state, where we will eat our mullets,
Sous'd in high-country wines, sup pheasants'
eggs,
And have our cockles boil'd in silver shells ;
Our shrimps to swim again, as when they liv'd,
In a rare butter made of dolphins' milk,   160
Whose cream does look like opals ; and with
these
Delicate meats set ourselves high for pleasure,
And take us down again, and then renew

----

[2] The art of transmutation.

Our youth and strength with drinking the
   elixir,
And so enjoy a perpetuity   165
Of life and lust! And thou shalt ha' thy ward-
   robe
Richer than Nature's, still to change thyself,
And vary oft'ner, for thy pride, than she,
Or Art, her wise and almost-equal servant.

              [*Re-enter* FACE.]

  Face. Sir, you are too loud. I hear you every
   word   170
Into the laboratory. Some fitter place;
The garden, or great chamber above. How like
   you her?
  Mam. Excellent! Lungs. There's for thee.
              [*Gives him money.*]
  Face.   But do you hear?
Good sir, beware, no mention of the rabbins.
  Mam. We think not on 'em.
            [*Exeunt* MAM. *and* DOL.]
  Face.   O, it is well, sir. — Subtle!   175

SCENE II.[1]

FACE. [*Enter*] SUBTLE.

Dost thou not laugh?
  Sub.   Yes; are they gone?
  Face.   All's clear.
  Sub. The widow is come.
  Face.   And your quarreling disciple?
  Sub. Ay.
  Face. I must to my captainship again then.
  Sub. Stay, bring 'em in first.
  Face.   So I meant. What is she?
A bonnibel?
  Sub. I know not.
  Face.   We'll draw lots: 5
You'll stand to that?
  Sub.   What else?
  Face.   O, for a suit,
To fall now like a curtain, flap!
  Sub.   To th' door, man.
  Face. You'll ha' the first kiss, 'cause I am
   not ready.   [*Exit.*]
  Sub. Yes, and perhaps hit you through both
   the nostrils.[2]   9
  Face. [*within.*] Who would you speak with?
  Kas. [*within.*]   Where's the captain?
  Face. [*within.*]   Gone, sir,
About some business.
  Kas. [*within.*] Gone!
  Face. [*within.*]   He'll return straight.
But, master doctor, his lieutenant, is here.

     [*Enter* KASTRIL, *followed by* Dame PLIANT.]

  Sub. Come near, my worshipful boy, *my
   terrae fili,*
That is, my boy of land; make thy approaches:
Welcome; I know thy lusts and thy desires,   15
And I will serve and satisfy 'em. Begin,
Charge me from thence, or thence, or in this
   line;
Here is my centre: ground thy quarrel.
  Kas.   You lie.

  Sub. How, child of wrath and anger! the
   loud lie?
For what, my sudden boy?
  Kas.   Nay, that look you to,   20
I am aforehand.
  Sub.   O, this is no true grammar,
And as ill logic! You must render causes,
   child,
Your first and second intentions, know your
   canons
And your divisions, moods, degrees, and differ-
   ences,
Your predicaments, substance, and accident,   25
Series extern and intern, with their causes,
Efficient, material, formal, final,
And ha' your elements perfect?
  Kas.   What is this?
The angry[3] tongue he talks in?
  Sub.   That false precept,
Of being aforehand, has deceiv'd a number,   30
And made 'em enter quarrels oftentimes
Before they were aware; and afterward,
Against their wills.
  Kas.   How must I do then, sir?
  Sub. I cry this lady mercy; she should first
Have been saluted. (*Kisses her.*) I do call you
   lady,   35
Because you are to be one ere 't be long,
My soft and buxom widow.
  Kas.   Is she, i' faith?
  Sub. Yes, or my art is an egregious liar.
  Kas. How know you?
  Sub.   By inspection on her forehead,   39
And subtlety of her lip, which must be tasted
Often to make a judgment. (*Kisses her again.*)
'Slight, she melts
Like a myrobolane.[4] Here is yet a line,
In *rivo frontis,*[5] tells me he is no knight.
  Dame P. What is he then, sir?
  Sub.   Let me see your hand.
O, your *linea fortunae* makes it plain;   45
And *stella* here in *monte Veneris.*
But, most of all, *junctura annularis.*[6]
He is a soldier, or a man of art, lady,
But shall have some great honour shortly.
  Dame P.   Brother,
He's a rare man, believe me!

      [*Re-enter* FACE, *in his uniform.*]

  Kas.   Hold your peace.   50
Here comes t' other rare man. — 'Save you,
   captain.
  Face. Good Master Kastril! Is this your
   sister?
  Kas. Ay, sir.
Please you to kuss her, and be proud to know
   her.
  Face. I shall be proud to know you, lady.
              [*Kisses her.*]
  Dame P.   Brother,
He calls me lady, too.
  Kas.   Ay, peace: I heard it.   55
            [*Takes her aside.*]

---

[1] The same.   [2] "Put your nose out of joint."
[3] Swaggering.
[4] A kind of dried plum, esteemed as a sweetmeat.
[5] Frontal vein.
[6] These are the cant phrases of palmistry.

Face. The count is come.
Sub.   Where is he ?
Face.   At the door.
Sub. Why, you must entertain him.
Face.   What will you do
With these the while ?
Sub.   Why, have 'em up, and show 'em
Some fustian book, or the dark glass.
Face.   'Fore God,
She is a delicate dabchick ! I must have her.
                         [*Exit.*]
Sub. [*Aside.*] Must you ! Ay, if your fortune
will, you must. —   61
Come, sir, the captain will come to us presently :
I 'll ha' you to my chamber of demonstrations,
Where I 'll show you both the grammar and
    logic,
And rhetoric of quarreling ; my whole method
Drawn out in tables ; and my instrument,   66
That hath the several scales upon 't shall make
    you
Able to quarrel at a straw's-breadth by moon-
    light.
And, lady, I 'll have you look in a glass,   69
Some half an hour, but to clear your eyesight,
Against you see [1] your fortune ; which is greater
Than I may judge upon the sudden, trust me.
                         [*Exeunt.*]

SCENE III.[2]

[*Enter*] FACE.

Face. Where are you, doctor ?
Sub. [*within.*]   I 'll come to you presently.
Face. I will ha' this same widow, now I ha'
    seen her,
On any composition.

[*Enter* SUBTLE]

Sub.   What do you say ?
Face. Ha' you dispos'd of them ?
Sub.   I ha' sent 'em up.
Face. Subtle, in troth, I needs must have this
    widow.   5
Sub. Is that the matter ?
Face.   Nay, but hear me.
Sub.   Go to.
If you rebel once, Dol shall know it all :
Therefore be quiet, and obey your chance.
Face. Nay, thou art so violent now. Do but
    conceive,
Thou art old, and canst not serve ——
Sub.   Who cannot ? I ?   10
'Slight, I will serve her with thee, for a ——
Face.   Nay,
But understand : I 'll gi' you composition.[3]
Sub. I will not treat with thee. What ! sell
    my fortune ?
'T is better than my birthright. Do not mur-
    mur :
Win her, and carry her. If you grumble, Dol   15
Knows it directly.
Face.   Well, sir, I am silent.
Will you go help to fetch in Don in state ?
                         [*Exit.*]

---

[1] In preparation for seeing.
[2] The same.   [3] Recompense.

Sub. I follow you, sir. We must keep **Face**
    in awe,
Or he will overlook us like a tyrant.

[*Re-enter* FACE, *introducing*] SURLY *like a Span-
          iard.*

Brain of a tailor ! who comes here ? Don John !
*Sur. Senores, beso las manos a vuestras merce-
    des.*[4]   21
Sub. Would you had stoop'd a little, and
    kist our *anos.*
Face. Peace, Subtle !
Sub.   Stab me ; I shall never hold, man.
He looks in that deep ruff like a head in a plat-
    ter,
Serv'd in by a short cloak upon two trestles.   25
Face. Or what do you say to a collar of
    brawn,[5] cut down
Beneath the souse,[6] and wriggled with a knife ?
Sub. 'Slud, he does look too fat to be a Span-
    iard.
Face. Perhaps some Fleming or some Hol-
    lander got him
In d'Alva's time ; Count Egmont's bastard.
Sub.   Don,   30
Your scurvy, yellow, Madrid face is welcome.
Sur. Gratia.
Sub.   He speaks out of a fortification.
Pray God he ha' no squibs in those deep sets.[7]
Sur. Por dios, senores,[8] *muy linda casa !*
Sub. What says he ?
Face.   Praises the house, I think ;   35
I know no more but 's action.
Sub.   Yes, the *casa,*
My precious Diego, will prove fair enough
To cozen you in. Do you mark ? You shall
Be cozened, Diego.[9]
Face.   Cozened, do you see,
My worthy Donzel,[10] cozened.
Sur.   *Entiendo.*[11]   40
Sub. Do you intend it ? So do we, dear Don.
Have you brought pistolets [12] or portagues,
My solemn Don ? [*To* FACE.] Dost thou feel any?
Face. (*Feels his pockets.*)   Full.
Sub. You shall be emptied, Don, pumped and
    drawn
Dry, as they say.
Face.   Milked, in troth, sweet Don.   45
Sub. See all the monsters ; the great lion of
    all, Don.
*Sur. Con licencia, se puede ver a esta se-
    nora ?*[13]
Sub. What talks he now ?
Face.   Of the senora.
Sub.   O, Don,
This is the lioness, which you shall see
Also, my Don.

---

[4] Spanish. " Gentlemen, I kiss your hands."
[5] Neck of a boar, or boar's flesh rolled.
[6] Ear.
[7] The deep plaits of his *ruff.*
[8] " Gad, sirs, a very pretty house."
[9] Spaniard. Strictly, Spanish for *James.*
[10] Diminutive of *Don.*
[11] " I understand."
[12] Spanish gold coin, worth about 16s. 8d.
[13] " If you please, may I see the lady ? "

Face. 'Slid, Subtle, how shall we do? 50
Sub. For what?
Face. Why, Dol's employ'd, you know.
Sub. That's true.
'Fore heav'n I know not: he must stay, that's all.
Face. Stay! that he must not by no means.
Sub. No! why?
Face. Unless you'll mar all. 'Slight, he'll suspect it;
And then he will not pay, not half so well. 55
This is a travell'd punk-master, and does know
All the delays; a notable hot rascal,
And looks already rampant.
Sub. 'Sdeath, and Mammon
Must not be troubled.
Face. Mammon! in no case.
Sub. What shall we do then?
Face. Think: you must be sudden.[1] 60
*Sur. Entiendo que la senora es tan hermosa,
que codicio tan a verla como la bien aventuranza
de mi vida.*[2]
Face. Mi vida! 'Slid, Subtle, he puts me in mind o' the widow.
What dost thou say to draw her to 't, ha! 65
And tell her 't is her fortune? All our venture
Now lies upon 't. It is but one man more,
Which on 's chance to have her: and beside,
There is no maidenhead to be fear'd or lost.
What dost thou think on 't, Subtle?
Sub. Who, I? why —— 70
Face. The credit of our house too is engag'd.[3]
Sub. You made me an offer for my share erewhile.
What wilt thou gi' me, i' faith?
Face. O, by that light
I'll not buy now. You know your doom[4] to me.
E'en take your lot, obey your chance, sir; win her, 75
And wear her — out for me.
Sub. 'Slight, I'll not work her then.
Face. It is the common cause; therefore bethink you.
Dol else must know it, as you said.
Sub. I care not.
Sur. Senores, porque se tarda tanto?[5]
Sub. Faith, I am not fit, I am old.
Face. That's now no reason, sir.
Sur. Puede ser de hazer burla de mi amor?[6] 81
Face. You hear the Don too? By this air I call,
And loose the hinges. Dol!
Sub. A plague of hell ——
Face. Will you then do?
Sub. You're a terrible rogue!
I'll think of this. Will you, sir, call the widow?
Face. Yes, and I'll take her too with all her faults, 86
Now I do think on 't better.
Sub. With all my heart, sir;
Am I discharg'd o' the lot?

Face. As you please.
Sub. Hands. [*They shake hands.*]
Face. Remember now, that upon any change
You never claim her.
Sub. Much good joy and health to you, sir, 90
Marry a whore! Fate, let me wed a witch first.
Sur. Por estas honradas barbas [7] ——
Sub. He swears by his beard.
Dispatch, and call the brother too. [*Exit* FACE.]
*Sur. Tengo duda, senores, que no me hagan
alguna traycion.*[8] 95
Sub. How, issue on? Yes, *praesto, senor.*
Please you
Enthratha the chambratha, worthy don:
Where if you please the fates, in your *bathada,*
You shall be soak'd, and strok'd, and tubb'd, and rubb'd,
And scrubb'd, and fubb'd,[9] dear don, before you go. 100
You shall in faith, my scurvy baboon don,
Be curried, claw'd, and flaw'd,[10] and taw'd,[11] indeed.
I will the heartlier go about it now,
And make the widow a punk so much the sooner,
To be reveng'd on this impetuous Face: 105
The quickly doing of it is the grace.
[*Exeunt* SUB. *and* SURLY.]

SCENE IV.[12]

[*Enter*] FACE, KASTRIL, *and* Dame PLIANT.

[*Face.*] Come, lady: I knew the doctor would not leave
Till he had found the very nick of her fortune.
Kas. To be a countess, say you?
[*Face.*][13] A Spanish countess, sir.
Dame P. Why, is that better than an English countess?
Face. Better! 'Slight, make you that a question, lady? 5
Kas. Nay, she is a fool, captain, you must pardon her.
Face. Ask from your courtier to your innsof-court-man,
To your mere milliner; they will tell you all,
Your Spanish jennet is the best horse; your Spanish
Stoop is the best garb;[14] your Spanish beard 10
Is the best cut; your Spanish ruffs are the best
Wear; your Spanish pavin the best dance;
Your Spanish titillation in a glove
The best perfume: and for your Spanish pike,
And Spanish blade, let your poor captain speak. —
Here comes the doctor.

[*Enter* SUBTLE *with a paper.*]

Sub. My most honour'd lady,
For so I am now to style you, having found

---

[1] Quick about it.
[2] "I understand that the lady is so handsome that I am as eager to see her as the good fortune of my life."
[3] Involved.   [4] Agreement.
[5] "Sirs, why so long delay?"
[6] "Can it be to make sport of my love?"
[7] "By this honored beard ——"
[8] "I fear, sirs, that you are playing me some trick."
[9] Cheated.   [10] Cracked.
[11] Soaked, like a hide being tanned.
[12] Another room in the same.
[13] Folio gives this line also to KASTRIL.
[14] Bodily carriage.

By this my scheme,[1] you are to undergo
An honourable fortune very shortly, 19
What will you say now, if some ——
Face. I ha' told her all, sir,
And her right worshipful brother here, that she
    shall be
A countess ; do not delay 'em, sir ; a Spanish
    countess.
Sub. Still, my scarce-worshipful captain, you
    can keep
No secret ! Well, since he has told you, madam,
Do you forgive him, and I do.
Kas. She shall do that, sir ; 25
I 'll look to it ; 't is my charge.
Sub. Well then : nought rests
But that she fit her love now to her fortune.
Dame P. Truly I shall never brook a Span-
    iard.
Sub. No ?
Dame P. Never sin' eighty-eight[2] could I
    abide 'em,
And that was some three years afore I was born,
    in truth. 30
Sub. Come, you must love him, or be miser-
    able ;
Choose which you will.
Face. By this good rush, persuade her,
She will cry[3] strawberries else within this
    twelve month.
Sub. Nay, shads and mackerel, which is
    worse.
Face. Indeed, sir !
Kas. God's lid, you shall love him, or I 'll kick
    you.
Dame P. Why, 35
I 'll do as you will ha' me, brother.
Kas. Do,
Or by this hand I 'll maul you.
Face. Nay, good sir,
Be not so fierce.
Sub. No, my enraged child ;
She will be rul'd. What, when she comes to
    taste
The pleasures of a countess ! to be courted —— 40
Face. And kiss'd and ruffled !
Sub. Ay, behind the hangings.
Face. And then come forth in pomp !
Sub. And know her state !
Face. Of keeping all th' idolators o' the
    chamber
Barer to her, than at their prayers !
Sub. Is serv'd
Upon the knee !
Face. And has her pages, ushers, 45
Footmen, and coaches——
Sub. Her six mares ——
Face. Nay, eight !
Sub. To hurry her through London, to th' Ex-
    change,[4]
Bet'lem,[5] the China-houses[6] ——
Face. Yes, and have

1 Horoscope.
2 *I.e.*, since 1588, the year of the "Invincible Armada."
3 Sell on the street.
4 There were shops in the Royal Exchange.
5 The madhouse was often visited for entertainment.
6 Shops with merchandise from China.

The citizens gape at her, and praise her tires,[7]
And my lord's goose-turd bands,[8] that rides
    with her ! 50
Kas. Most brave ! By this hand, you are not
    my suster
If you refuse.
Dame P. I will not refuse, brother.

[*Enter* SURLY.]

*Sur. Que es esto, senores, que non se venga ?
Esta tardanza me mata !* [9]
Face. It is the count come :
The doctor knew he would be here, by his art.
*Sub. En gallanta, madama, Don ! gallantis-
    sima !* 56
*Sur. Por todos los dioses, la mas acabada
Hermosura, que he visto en ma vida !* [10]
Face. Is 't not a gallant language that they
    speak ?
Kas. An admirable language ! Is 't not
    French ? 60
Face. No, Spanish, sir.
Kas. It goes like law French,
And that, they say, is the court-liest language.
Face. List, sir.
*Sur. El sol ha perdido su lumbre, con el
Resplandor que trae esta dana ! Valga me dios !* [11]
Face. H' admires your sister.
Kas. Must not she make curt'sy. 65
Sub. 'Ods will, she must go to him, man, and
    kiss him !
It is the Spanish fashion, for the women
To make first court.
Face. 'T is true he tells you, sir :
His art knows all.
Sur. Porque no se acude ? [12]
Kas. He speaks to her, I think.
Face. That he does, sir. 70
*Sur. Por el amor de dios, que es esto que se
    tarda ?* [13]
Kas. Nay, see : she will not understand him !
    Gull, Noddy.
Dame P. What say you, brother ?
Kas. Ass, my suster,
Go kuss him, as the cunning man would ha' you ;
I 'll thrust a pin i' your buttocks else.
Face. O no, sir. 75
*Sur. Senora mia, mi persona muy indigna esta
Allegar a tanta hermosura.* [14]
Face. Does he not use her bravely ?
Kas. Bravely, i' faith !
Face. Nay, he will use her better.
Kas. Do you think so ?
Sur. Senora, si sera servida, entremos. [15] 80

[*Exit with* Dame PLIANT.]

7 Head-dresses.
8 In greenish-yellow liveries.
9 "Why does n't she come, sirs ? This delay is killing
me."
10 "By all the gods, the most perfect beauty I have
seen in my life."
11 "The sun has lost his light with the splendor this
lady brings, so help me God."
12 "Why don't you draw near ? "
13 "For the love of God, why this delay ? "
14 "Madam, my person is unworthy to approach
such beauty."
15 "Madam, at your service, let us go in."

Kas. Where does he carry her?
Face.   Into the garden, sir;
Take you no thought: I must interpret for
        her.
Sub. Give Dol the word.
        [*Aside to* FACE, *who goes out.*]
        — Come, my fierce child, advance,
We'll to our quarreling lesson again.
Kas.   Agreed.
I love a Spanish boy with all my heart.   85
Sub. Nay, and by this means, sir, you shall be
        brother
To a great count.
Kas.   Ay, I knew that at first.
This match will advance the house of the Kas-
        trils.
Sub. 'Pray God your sister prove but pliant!
Kas.   Why,
Her name is so, by her other husband.
Sub.   How!   90
Kas. The Widow Pliant. Knew you not that?
Sub.   No, faith, sir;
Yet, by the erection of her figure,[1] I guess'd
        it.
Come, let's go practise.
Kas.   Yes, but do you think, doctor,
I e'er shall quarrel well?
Sub.   I warrant you. [*Exeunt.*]

SCENE V.[2]

[*Enter*] DOL [*followed by*] MAMMON.

DOL (*in her fit of talking*). *For after Alex-
        ander's death* —— [3]
Mam.   Good lady ——
*Dol. That Perdiccas and Antigonus were slain,
The two that stood, Seleuc' and Ptolomy* ——
Mam.   Madam —
*Dol. Make up the two legs, and the fourth beast,
That was Gog-north and Egypt-south: which
        after   5
Was called Gog-iron-leg and South-iron-leg* ——
Mam.   Lady ——
*Dol. And then Gog-horned. So was Egypt,
        too:
Then Egypt-clay-leg, and Gog-clay-leg* ——
Mam.   Sweet madam ——
*Dol. And last Gog-dust, and Egypt-dust, which
        fall
In the last link of the fourth chain. And these* 10
Be stars in story, which none see, or look at ——
Mam. What shall I do?
Dol.   *For, as he says, except
We call the rabbins, and the heathen Greeks* ——
Mam. Dear lady ——
Dol.   *To come from Salem, and from Athens,
And teach the people of Great Britain* ——

[*Enter* FACE *hastily, in his servant's dress.*]

Face.   What's the matter, sir?   15
*Dol. To speak the tongue of Eber and Ja-
        van* ——

[1] By her horoscope, with a pun on her bearing.
[2] Another room in the same.
[3] Doll's ravings are taken almost at random from
the headings of columns, preface, etc., of the *Concent
of Scripture*, by Hugh Broughton.

Mam.   O,
She's in her fit.
Dol.   *We shall know nothing* ——
Face.   Death, sir,
We are undone!
Dol.   *Where then a learned linguist
Shall see the ancient us'd communion
Of vowels and consonants* ——
Face.   My master will hear!   20
*Dol. A wisdom, which Pythagoras held most
        high* ——
Mam. Sweet honourable lady!
Dol.   *To comprise
All sounds of voices, in few marks of letters.*
Face. Nay, you must never hope to lay her
        now.   (*They all speak together.*)
Dol. And so we may arrive by Talmud skill,[4]   25
*And profane Greek, to raise the building up
Of Helen's house against the Ismaelite,
King of Thogarma, and his habergions
Brimstony, blue, and fiery; and the force
Of king Abaddon, and the beast of Cittim:*   30
*Which rabbi David Kimchi, Onkelos,
And Aben Ezra do interpret Rome.*
Face. How did you put her into't?
Mam.   Alas, I talkt
Of a fifth monarchy I would erect   34
With the philosopher's stone, by chance, and she
Falls on the other four straight.
Face.   Out of Broughton!
I told you so. 'Slid, stop her mouth.
Mam.   Is't best?
Face. She'll never leave else. If the old man
        hear her,
We are but faeces, ashes.
Sub. [*within.*] What's to do there?
Face. O, we are lost! Now she hears him,
        she is quiet.   40

[*Enter* SUBTLE;] *upon* SUBTLE's *entry they
        disperse.*

Mam. Where shall I hide me!
Sub.   How! What sight is here?
Close[5] deeds of darkness, and that shun the
        light!
Bring him again. Who is he? What, my son!
O, I have liv'd too long.
Mam.   Nay, good, dear father,
There was no unchaste purpose.
Sub.   Not? and flee me   45
When I come in?
Mam.   That was my error.
Sub.   Error?
Guilt, guilt, my son; give it the right name.
        No marvel
If I found check in our great work within,
When such affairs as these were managing!   49
Mam. Why, have you so?
Sub.   It has stood still this half hour:
And all the rest of our less works gone back.
Where is the instrument of wickedness,
My lewd false drudge?

[4] In the early editions this speech is printed in parallel columns with the dialogue immediately following,
to indicate simultaneous utterance.
[5] Secret.

Mam.   Nay, good sir, blame not him ;
Believe me, 't was against his will or know-
    ledge :   54
I saw her by chance.
Sub.   Will you commit more sin,
T' excuse a varlet ?
Mam.   By my hope, 't is true, sir.
Sub. Nay, then I wonder less, if you, for
    whom
The blessing was prepar'd, would so tempt
    heaven,
And lose your fortunes.
Mam.   Why, sir ?
Sub.   This will retard
The work a month at least.
Mam.   Why, if it do,   60
What remedy ? But think it not, good father :
Our purposes were honest.[1]
Sub.   As they were,
So the reward will prove. (*A great crack and
    noise within.*) — How now ! ay me !
God and all saints be good to us. ——

[*Re-enter* FACE.]

                         What 's that ?   64
Face. O, sir, we are defeated ! All the works
Are flown *in fumo*,[2] every glass is burst ;
Furnace and all rent down, as if a bolt
Of thunder had been driven through the house.
Retorts, receivers, pelicans,[3] bolt heads,[4]   69
All struck in shivers !
    (SUBTLE *falls down as in a swoon.*)
                         Help, good sir ! alas,
Coldness and death invades him. Nay, Sir
    Mammon,
Do the fair offices of a man ! You stand,
As you were readier to depart than he.
                         (*One knocks.*)
Who 's there ? My lord her brother is come.
Mam.   Ha, Lungs !
Face. His coach is at the door. Avoid his
    sight,   75
For he 's as furious as his sister 's mad.
Mam. Alas !
Face.   My brain is quite undone with
    the fume, sir,
I ne'er must hope to be mine own man again.
Mam. Is all lost, Lungs ? Will nothing be
    preserv'd
Of all our cost ?
Face.   Faith, very little, sir ;   80
A peck of coals or so, which is cold comfort,
    sir.
Mam. O, my voluptuous mind ! I am justly
    punish'd.
Face. And so am I, sir.
Mam.   Cast from all my hopes ——
Face. Nay, certainties, sir.
Mam.   By mine own base affections.
Sub. (*seeming to come to himself.*) O, the curst
    fruits of vice and lust !
Mam.   Good father,   85
It was my sin. Forgive it.
Sub.   Hangs my roof

¹ Chaste.   ² Into smoke.
³ An alembic of a particular shape.
⁴ A globular flask.

Over us still, and will not fall, O justice,
Upon us, for this wicked man !
Face.   Nay, look, sir,
You grieve him now with staying in his sight.
Good sir, the nobleman will come too, and take
    you,   90
And that may breed a tragedy.
Mam.   I 'll go.
Face. Ay, and repent at home, sir. It may be,
For some good penance you may ha' it yet ;
A hundred pound to the box at Bet'lem [5] ——
Mam.   Yes.
Face. For the restoring such as — ha' their
    wits.
Mam. I 'll do 't.   95
Face. I 'll send one to you to receive it.
Mam.   Do.
Is no projection left ?
Face.   All flown, or stinks, sir.
Mam. Will nought be sav'd that 's good for
    med'cine, think'st thou ?
Face. I cannot tell, sir. There will be per-
    haps
Something about the scraping of the shards, 100
Will cure the itch, — though not your itch of
    mind, sir. [*Aside.*]
It shall be sav'd for you, and sent home. Good
    sir,
This way, for fear the lord shall meet you.
                         [*Exit* MAMMON.]
Sub. [*raising his head.*]   Face !
Face. Ay.
Sub.   Is he gone ?
Face.   Yes, and as heavily
As all the gold he hop'd for were in 's blood. 105
Let us be light though.
Sub. [*leaping up.*]   Ay, as balls, and bound
And hit our heads against the roof for joy :
There 's so much of our care now cast away.
Face. Now to our don.
Sub.   Yes, your young widow by this time
Is made a countess, Face ; she 's been in tra-
    vail   110
Of a young heir for you.
Face.   Good, sir.
Sub.   Off with your case,[6]
And greet her kindly, as a bridegroom should,
After these common hazards.
Face.   Very well, sir.
Will you go fetch Don Diego off the while ?
Sub. And fetch him over too, if you 'll be
    pleas'd, sir.   115
Would Dol were in her place, to pick his pock-
    ets now !
Face. Why, you can do 't as well, if you
    would set to 't.
I pray you prove your virtue.[7]
Sub.   For your sake, sir. [*Exeunt.*]

SCENE VI.[8]

[*Enter*] SURLY *and* Dame PLIANT.

Sur. Lady, you see into what hands you are
    fall'n ;

⁵ The lunatic asylum.   ⁶ His costume as Lungs.
⁷ Capacity.   ⁸ Another room in the same.

'Mongst what a nest of villains ! and how near
Your honour was t' have catch'd a certain clap,
Through your credulity, had I but been
So punctually forward, as place, time,　　5
And other circumstance would ha' made a man ;
For you 're a handsome woman : would you were
　　wise too !
I am a gentleman come here disguis'd,
Only to find the knaveries of this citadel ;
And where I might have wrong'd your honour,
　　and have not,　　10
I claim some interest in your love. You are,
They say, a widow, rich ; and I 'm a bachelor,
Worth nought : your fortunes may make me a
　　man,
As mine ha' preserv'd you a woman. Think
　　upon it,
And whether I have deserv'd you or no.
　　Dame P.　　　　　　　　I will, sir.　15
　　Sur. And for these household-rogues, let me
　　alone
To treat with them.

　　　　　　[*Enter* SUBTLE.]

　　Sub.　　　　　How doth my noble Diego,
And my dear madam countess ? Hath the count
Been courteous, lady ? liberal and open ?
Donzel,[1] methinks you look melancholic,　20
I do not like the dulness of your eye ;
It hath a heavy cast, 't is upsee Dutch,[2]
And says you are a lumpish whore-master.
Be lighter, I will make your pockets so.
　　　　　　　(*He falls to picking of them.*)
　　Sur. [*throws open his cloak.*] Will you, don
　　bawd and pick-purse ? [*Strikes him down.*]
　　How now ! Reel you ?　　25
Stand up, sir, you shall find, since I am so heavy,
I 'll gi' you equal weight.
　　Sub.　　　　　　　Help ! murder !
　　Sur.　　　　　　　　No, sir,
There 's no such thing intended. A good cart[3]
And a clean whip shall ease you of that fear.
I am the Spanish don that should be cozened,　30
Do you see ? Cozened ? Where 's your Captain
　　Face,
That parcel[4]-broker, and whole-bawd, all ras-
　　cal ?

　　　　　[*Enter* FACE *in his uniform.*]

　　Face. How, Surly !
　　Sur.　　O, make your approach, good captain.
I 've found from whence your copper rings and
　　spoons
Come now, wherewith you cheat abroad in tav-
　　erns.　　35
'T was here you learn'd t' anoint your boot with
　　brimstone,
Then rub men's gold on 't for a kind of touch,
And say, 't was naught, when you had chang'd
　　the colour,
That you might ha't for nothing. And this doc-
　　tor,
Your sooty, smoky-bearded compeer, he　40

　　[1] Diminutive of Don.
　　[2] As if you had been drinking heavy Dutch beer.
　　[3] Referring to the punishment inflicted on bawds.
　　[4] Part.

Will close you so much gold, in a bolt's-head,
And, on a turn, convey i' the stead another
With sublim'd mercury, that shall burst i' the
　　heat,
And fly out all *in fumo !* Then weeps Mammon ;
Then swoons his worship. Or, [FACE *slips out.*]
　　he is the Faustus,　　45
That casteth figures[5] and can conjure, cures
Plagues, piles, and pox, by the ephemerides.[6]
And holds intelligence with all the bawds
And midwives of three shires : while you send
　　in —
Captain ! — what ! is he gone ? — damsels with
　　child,　　50
Wives that are barren, or the waiting-maid
With the green sickness. [*Seizes* SUBTLE *as he
　　is retiring.*] — Nay, sir, you must tarry,
Though he be scap'd ; and answer by the ears,
　　sir.

　　　　　　　　SCENE VII.[7]

[*Re-enter*] FACE [*with*] KASTRIL [*to*] SURLY [*and*]
　　　　　　　　　SUBTLE.

　　Face. Why, now 's the time, if ever you will
　　quarrel
Well, as they say, and be a true-born child :
The doctor and your sister both are abus'd.[8]
　　Kas. Where is he ? Which is he ? He is a
　　slave.
Whate'er he is, and the son of a whore. — Are
　　you　　5
The man, sir, I would know ?
　　Sur.　　　　　　I should be loth, sir,
To confess so much.
　　Kan.　　　　Then you lie i' your throat.
　　Sur.　　　　　　　　　How !
　　Face. [*To* KASTRIL.] A very arrant rogue, sir,
　　and a cheater,
Employ'd here by another conjurer
That does not love the doctor, and would cross
　　him　　10
If he knew how.
　　Sur.　　　Sir, you are abus'd.
　　Kas.　　　　　　　　　You lie :
And 't is no matter.
　　Face.　　　　Well said, sir ! He is
The impudent'st rascal ——
　　Sur. You are indeed. Will you hear me, sir ?
　　Face. By no means : bid him be gone.
　　Kas.　　　　　　　Begone, sir, quickly.
　　Sur. This is strange ! — Lady, do you inform
　　your brother.　　15
　　Face. There is not such a foist[9] in all the
　　town.
The doctor had him presently ; and finds yet
The Spanish count will come here. — Bear up,
　　Subtle.　　　　　　　　[*Aside.*]
　　Sub. Yes, sir, he must appear within this
　　hour.
　　Face. And yet this rogue would come in a
　　disguise,　　20
By the temptation of another spirit,
To trouble our art, though he could not hurt it !
　　Kas.　　　　　　　　　　　　Ay,

　　[5] Horoscopes.
　　[6] Astrological almanacs.
　　[7] The same.
　　[8] Cheated.
　　[9] Rascal.

I know — Away, [*To his sister.*] you talk like a
    foolish mauther.[1]
Sur. Sir, all is truth she says.
Face.   Do not believe him, sir. **14**
He is the lying'st swabber! Come your ways, sir.
Sur. You are valiant out of company!
Kas.   Yes, how then, sir?

[*Enter* DRUGGER *with a piece of damask.*]

Face. Nay, here's an honest fellow too that
    knows him,
And all his tricks. (Make good what I say,
    Abel.)
This cheater would ha' cozen'd thee o' the
    widow. —   [*Aside to* DRUG.]
He owes this honest Drugger here seven pound,
He has had on him in twopenny'orths of to-
    bacco.   **31**
Drug. Yes, sir. And he has damn'd himself
    three terms to pay me.
Face. And what does he owe for lotium?[2]
Drug.   Thirty shillings, sir;
And for six syringes.
Sur.   Hydra of villainy!
Face. Nay, sir, you must quarrel him out o'
    the house.
Kas.   I will: **35**
— Sir, if you get not out o' doors, you lie;
And you are a pimp.
Sur.   Why, this is madness, sir,
Not valour in you; I must laugh at this.
Kas. It is my humour; you are a pimp and a
    trig.[3]
And an Amadis de Gaul, or a Don Quixote.   **40**
Drug. Or a knight o' the curious coxcomb,
    do you see?

[*Enter* ANANIAS.]

Ana. Peace to the household!
Kas.   I'll keep peace for no man.
Ana. Casting of dollars is concluded lawful.
Kas. Is he the constable?
Sub.   Peace, Ananias.
Face.   No, sir.
Kas. Then you are an otter, and a shad, a
    whit,   **45**
A very tim.[4]
Sur. You'll hear me, sir?
Kas.   I will not.
Ana. What is the motive?
Sub.   Zeal in the young gentleman,
Against his Spanish slops.
Ana.   They are profane,
Lewd, superstitious, and idolatrous breeches.
Sur. New rascals!
Kas.   Will you be gone, sir?
Ana.   Avoid, Sathan!   **50**
Thou art not of the light! That ruff of pride
About thy neck, betrays thee; and is the same
With that which the unclean birds, in seventy-
    seven,[5]
Were seen to prank it with on divers coasts:
Thou look'st like antichrist, in that lewd hat.   **55**

1 Girl.   2 A lotion.   3 Dandy.
4 Kastril's terms of abuse are not meant to be appropriate.
5 The allusion here has not been explained.

Sur. I must give way.
Kas.   Be gone, sir.
Sur.   But I'll take
A course with you. ——
Ana.   Depart, proud Spanish fiend!
Sur. Captain and doctor.
Ana.   Child of perdition!
Kas.   Hence, sir! — [*Exit* SURLY.]
Did I not quarrel bravely?
Face.   Yes, indeed, sir.
Kas. Nay, an I give my mind to't, I shall
    do't.   **60**
Face. O, you must follow, sir, and threaten
    him tame:
He'll turn again else.
Kas.   I'll re-turn him then. [*Exit.*]
Face. Drugger, this rogue prevented us, for
    thee:
We had determin'd that thou should'st ha'
    come
In a Spanish suit, and ha' carried her so; and
    he,   **65**
A brokerly slave, goes, puts it on himself.
Hast brought the damask?
Drug.   Yes, sir.
Face.   Thou must borrow
A Spanish suit. Hast thou no credit with the
    players?
Drug. Yes, sir; did you never see me play
    the Fool?
Face. I know not, Nab; — thou shalt, if I
    can help it. —   [*Aside.*]   **70**
Hieronimo's[6] old cloak, ruff, and hat will serve;
I'll tell thee more when thou bring'st 'em.
                [*Exit* DRUGGER.] SUBTLE *hath
                whisper'd with* ANAN. *this while.*
Ana.   Sir, I know.
The Spaniard hates the brethren, and hath
    spies
Upon their actions: and that this was one
I make no scruple. — But the holy synod   **75**
Have been in prayer and meditation for it;
And 'tis reveal'd no less to them than me,
That casting of money is most lawful.
Sub.   True.
But here I cannot do it: if the house
Should chance to be suspected, all would out, **80**
And we be lock'd up in the Tower for ever,
To make gold there for th' state, never come
    out;
And then are you defeated.
Ana.   I will tell
This to the elders and the weaker brethren,
That the whole company of the separation   **85**
May join in humble prayer again.
Sub.   And fasting.
Ana. Yea, for some fitter place. The peace
    of mind
Rest with these walls!   [*Exit.*]
Sub.   Thanks, courteous Ananias.
Face. What did he come for?
Sub.   About casting dollars,
Presently out of hand. And so I told him,   **90**
A Spanish minister came here to spy,
Against the faithful ——

6 In Kyd's *Spanish Tragedy.*

Face.   I conceive. Come, Subtle,
Thou art so down upon the least disaster!
How wouldst thou ha' done, if I had not helpt
thee out?
    Sub. I thank thee, Face, for the angry boy,
i' faith.   95
    Face. Who would ha' lookt[1] it should ha'
been that rascal
$urly? He had dy'd his beard and all. Well,
sir.
Here's damask come to make you a suit.
    Sub.   Where's Drugger?
    Face. He is gone to borrow me a Spanish
habit;   99
I'll be the count now.
    Sub.   But where's the widow?
    Face. Within, with my lord's sister; Madam
Dol
Is entertaining her.
    Sub.   By your favour, Face,
Now she is honest, I will stand again.
    Face. You will not offer it?
    Sub.   Why?
    Face.   Stand to your word,
Or — here comes Dol. She knows ——
    Sub.   You 're tyrannous still. 105

    [*Enter* DOL *hastily.*]

Face. — Strict for my right. — How now, Dol!
Hast told her,
The Spanish count will come?
    Dol.   Yes; but another is come,
You little lookt for!
    Face.   Who's that?
    Dol.   Your master;
The master of the house.
    Sub.   How, Dol!
    Face.   She lies,
This is some trick. Come, leave your quiblins,[2]
Dorothy.   110
    Dol. Look out and see.
           [FACE *goes to the window.*]
    Sub.   Art thou in earnest?
    Dol.   'Slight,
Forty o' the neighbours are about him, talking.
    Face. 'T is he, by this good day.
    Dol.   'T will prove ill day
For some on us.
    Face.   We are undone, and taken.
    Dol. Lost, I'm afraid.
    Sub.   You said he would not come, 115
While there died one a week within the liber-
ties.[3]
    Face. No: 't was within the walls.
    Sub.   Was 't so? Cry you mercy.
I thought the liberties. What shall we do now,
Face?
    Face. Be silent: not a word, if he call or
knock.   119
I 'll into mine old shape again and meet him,
Of Jeremy, the butler. I' the meantime,
Do you two pack up all the goods and pur-
chase[4]

---

[1] Expected.   [2] Quibbles.
[3] The district outside the walls subject to the city
authorities.
[4] Stolen goods, booty.

That we can carry i' the two trunks. I 'll keep
him
Off for to-day, if I cannot longer: and then   124
At night, I 'll ship you both away to Ratcliff,
Where we will meet to-morrow, and there we 'll
share.
Let Mammon's brass and pewter keep the cel-
lar;
We 'll have another time for that. But, Dol,
Prithee go heat a little water quickly;   129
Subtle must shave me. All my captain's beard
Must off, to make me appear smooth Jeremy.
You 'll do it?
    Sub.   Yes, I 'll shave you as well as I can.
    Face. And not cut my throat, but trim me?
    Sub.   You shall see, sir. [*Exeunt.*]

ACT V

SCENE I.[5]

[*Enter*] LOVEWIT, [*with several of the*] Neighbours.

    Love. Has there been such resort, say you?
    1 *Nei.*   Daily, Sir.
    2 *Nei.* And nightly, too.
    3 *Nei.*   Ay, some as brave as lords.
    4 *Nei.* Ladies and gentlewomen.
    5 *Nei.*   Citizens' wives.
    1 *Nei.* And knights.
    6 *Nei.*   In coaches.
    2 *Nei.*   Yes, and oyster-women.
    1 *Nei.* Beside other gallants.
    3 *Nei.*   Sailors' wives.
    4 *Nei.*   Tobacco men.   5
    5 *Nei.* Another Pimlico.[6]
    Love.   What should my knave advance,
To draw this company? He hung out no ban-
ners
Of a strange calf with five legs to be seen,
Or a huge lobster with six claws?
    6 *Nei.*   No, sir.
    3 *Nei.* We had gone in then, sir.
    Love.   He has no gift 10
Of teaching i' the nose[7] that e'er I knew of.
You saw no bills set up that promis'd cure
Of agues or the tooth-ache?
    2 *Nei.*   No such thing, sir!
    Love. Nor heard a drum struck for baboons
or puppets?
    5 *Nei.* Neither, sir.
    Love.   What device should he bring forth
now?   15
I love a teeming wit as I love my nourishment:
'Pray God he ha' not kept such open house,
That he hath sold my hangings, and my bed-
ding!
I left him nothing else. If he have eat 'em,   20
A plague o' the moth, say I! Sure he has got
Some bawdy pictures to call all this ging;[8]

---

[5] Before Lovewit's door.
[6] A summer resort, where the citizens had cakes and
ale.
[7] Like a Puritan preacher.
[8] Gang.

The Friar and the Nun ; or the new motion [1]
Of the knight's courser covering the parson's
   mare ;
The boy of six year old, with the great thing : 24
Or 't may be, he has the fleas that run at tilt
Upon a table, or some dog to dance.
When saw you him ?
   1 *Nei.*   Who, sir, Jeremy ?
   2 *Nei.*   Jeremy butler ?
We saw him not this month.
   Love.   How !
   4 *Nei.*   Not these five weeks, sir.
   [6] *Nei.* These six weeks, at the least.
   Love.   You amaze me, neighbours !
   5 *Nei.* Sure, if your worship know not where
   he is,   30
He 's slipt away.
   6 *Nei.*   Pray God he be not made away.
                          He knocks.
   Love. Ha ! it 's no time to question, then.
   6 *Nei.*   About
Some three weeks since I heard a doleful cry,
As I sat up a-mending my wife's stockings.
   Love. This 's strange that none will answer !
   Did'st thou hear   35
A cry, sayst thou ?
   6 *Nei.*   Yes, sir, like unto a man
That had been strangled an hour, and could not
   speak.
   2 *Nei.* I heard it, too, just this day three
   weeks, at two o'clock
Next morning.
   Love. These be miracles, or you make 'em so !
A man an hour strangled, and could not speak,
And both you heard him cry ?
   3 *Nei.*   Yes, downward, sir. 41
   Love. Thou art a wise fellow. Give me thy
   hand, I pray thee.
What trade art thou on ?
   3 *Nei.*   A smith, an 't please your worship.
   Love. A smith ! Then lend me thy help to
   get this door open.
   3 *Nei.* That I will presently, sir, but fetch
   my tools —   [*Exit.*] 45
   1 *Nei.* Sir, best to knock again afore you
   break it.

Scene II.[2]

Lovewit, Neighbours.

[**Love.** *Knocks again.*] I will.

   [*Enter* Face *in his butler's livery.*]

   Face.   What mean you, sir ?
   1, 2, 4 *Nei.*   O, here 's Jeremy !
   Face. Good sir, come from the door.
   Love.   Why, what 's the matter ?
   Face. Yet farther, you are too near yet.
   Love.   I ' the name of wonder,
What means the fellow ?
   Face.   The house, sir, has been visited.
   Love. What, with the plague ? Stand thou
   then farther.
   Face.   No, sir,
I had it not.

     [1] Puppet show.   [2] The same.

   Love.   Who had it then ? I left
None else but thee 'i the house.
   Face.   Yes, sir, my fellow,
The cat that kept the buttery, had it on her
A week before I spied it ; but I got her
Convey'd away i' the night : and so I shut 10
The house for a month ——
   Love.   How !
   Face.   Purposing then, sir,
To have burnt rose-vinegar, treacle, and tar,
And ha' made it sweet, that you should ne'er
Because I knew the news would but afflict you,
   sir.
   Love. Breathe less, and farther off ! Why this
   is stranger :   15
The neighbours tell me all here that the doors
Have still been open ——
   Face.   How, sir !
   Love.   Gallants, men and women,
And of all sorts, tag-rag, been seen to flock here
In threaves, [3] these ten weeks, as to a second
   Hogsden,
In days of Pimlico and Eye-bright.[4]
   Face.   Sir, 20
Their wisdoms will not say so.
   Love.   To-day they speak
Of coaches and gallants ; one in a French hood
Went in, they tell me ; and another was seen
In a velvet gown at the window : divers more
Pass in and out.   [then,
   Face.   They did pass through the doors
Or walls, I assure their eye-sights, and their
   spectacles ;   24
For here, sir, are the keys, and here have been,
In this my pocket, now above twenty days !
And for before, I kept the fort alone there.
But that 't is yet not deep i' the afternoon, 30
I should believe my neighbours had seen double
Through the black pot, [5] and made these ap-
   paritions !
For, on my faith to your worship, for these
   three weeks
And upwards, the door has not been open'd.
   Love.   Strange !
   1 *Nei.* Good faith, I think I saw a coach.
   2 *Nei.*   And I too, 35
I 'd ha' been sworn.
   Love.   Do you but think it now ?
And but one coach ?
   4 *Nei.*   We cannot tell, sir : Jeremy
Is a very honest fellow.
   Face.   Did you see me at all ?
   1 *Nei.* No ; that we are sure on.
   2 *Nei.*   I 'll be sworn o' that.
   Love. Fine rogues to have your testimonies
   built on !   40

   [*Re-enter third* Neighbour, *with his tools.*]

   3 *Nei.* Is Jeremy come !
   1 *Nei.* O yes ; you may leave your tools ;
We were deceiv'd, he says.
   2 *Nei.*   He 's had the keys ;
And the door has been shut these three weeks.

   [3] Lit., two dozen sheaves ; droves.
   [4] A suburban tavern, eclipsed as a resort by Pimlico.
   [5] With drinking.

3 *Nei.*　　　　　　　　　　Like enough.
Love. Peace, and get hence, you changelings.

[*Enter* SURLY *and* MAMMON.]

Face. [*Aside.*]　　　　　　　Surly come.
And Mammon made acquainted! They'll tell
all.　　　　　　　　　　　　　　　45
How shall I beat them off? What shall I do?
Nothing's more wretched than a guilty con-
　science.

SCENE III.[1]

SURLY, MAMMON, LOVEWIT, FACE, Neigh-
　　　bours.

Sur. No, sir, he was a great physician. This,
It was no bawdy-house, but a mere chancel!
You knew the lord and his sister.
Mam.　　　　　　Nay, good Surly. ——
Sur. The happy word, BE RICH ——
Mam.　　　　　　Play not the tyrant. —
Sur. Should be to-day pronounc'd to all your
　friends,　　　　　　　　　　　　5
And where be your andirons now? And your
　brass pots,
That should ha' been golden flagons, and great
　wedges?
Mam. Let me but breathe. What, they ha'
　shut their doors,
Methinks!　　　　　*He and* SURLY *knock.*
Sur. Ay, now 'tis holiday with them.
Mam.　　　　　　　　　　Rogues,
Cozeners, impostors, bawds!
Face.　　　　　What mean you, sir? 10
Mam. To enter if we can.
Face.　　　　　Another man's house!
Here is the owner, sir; turn you to him,
And speak your business.
Mam.　　　　　Are you, sir, the owner?
Love. Yes, sir.　　　　　　　[cheaters!
Mam.　　　And are those knaves within, your
Love. What knaves, what cheaters?
Mam.　　　　　　Subtle and his Lungs. 15
Face. The gentleman is distracted, sir! No
　lungs
Nor lights ha' been seen here these three weeks,
　sir,
Within these doors upon my word.
Sur.　　　　　　　　Your word,
Groom arrogant!
Face.　　　　Yes, sir, I am the housekeeper,
And know the keys ha' not been out o' my
　hands.　　　　　　　　　　　20
Sur. This 's a new Face.
Face.　　　　You do mistake the house, sir:
What sign was 't at?
Sur.　　　　You rascal! This is one
Of the confedcracy. Come, let's get officers,
And force the door.
Love.　　　　Pray you stay, gentlemen.
Sur. No, sir, we'll come with warrant.
Mam.　　　　　Ay, and then 25
We shall ha' your doors open.
　　　　　　　[*Exeunt* MAM. *and* SUR.]
Love.　　　　　　What means this?

Face. I cannot tell, sir.
1 *Nei.*　　　These are two o' the gallants
That we do think we saw.
Face.　　　　Two o' the fools!
You talk as idly as they. Good faith, sir,
I think the moon has craz'd 'em all. — [*Aside.*]
　O me,　　　　　　　　　　　30

[*Enter* KASTRIL.]

The angry boy come too! He'll make a noise,
And ne'er away till he have betray'd us all.
Kas. (*knocking.*) What, rogues, bawds, slaves,
　you'll open the door anon!
Punk, cockatrice, my suster! By this light 34
I'll fetch the marshal to you. You are a whore
To keep your castle ——
Face.　　　Who would you speak with, sir?
Kas. The bawdy doctor, and the cozening
　captain,
And puss my suster.
Love.　　　　This is something, sure.
Face. Upon my trust, the doors were never
　open, sir.
Kas. I have heard all their tricks told me
　twice over,　　　　　　　　　　40
By the fat knight and the lean gentleman.
Love. Here comes another.

[*Enter* ANANIAS *and* TRIBULATION.]

Face.　　　　　　　Ananias too!
And his pastor!
Tri.　　　The doors are shut against us.
　　　　　　They beat too, at the door.
Ana. Come forth, you seed of sulphur, sons
　of fire!
Your stench it is broke forth; abomination 45
Is in the house.
Kas.　　　Ay, my suster's there.
Ana.　　　　　　　The place,
It is become a cage of unclean birds.
Kas. Yes, I will fetch the scavenger, and the
　constable.
Tri. You shall do well.
Ana.　　　We'll join to weed them out.
Kas. You will not come then, punk devise,[2]
　my suster!　　　　　　　　　　50
Ana. Call her not sister; she's a harlot verily.
Kas. I'll raise the street.
Love.　　　Good gentleman, a word.
Ana. Satan avoid, and hinder not our zeal!
　　　　　[*Exeunt* ANA., TRIB., *and* KAST.]
Love. The world's turn'd Bet'lem.
Face.　　　These are all broke loose,
Out of St. Katherine's, where they use to keep
The better sort of mad-folks.
1 *Nei.*　　　　　All these persons 55
We saw go in and out here.
2 *Nei.*　　　　　Yes, indeed, sir.
3 *Nei.* These were the parties.
Face.　　　Peace, you drunkards! Sir,
I wonder at it. Please you to give me leave
To touch the door; I'll try an the lock be
　chang'd.　　　　　　　　　　60
Love. It mazes me!
Face. [*goes to the door.*]　　Good faith, sir, I
　believe

---

1 The same.　　　　　　2 Perfect harlot.

There 's no such thing : 't is all *deceptio visus*.[1] —
[*Aside.*] Would I could get him away.
  Dap. [*within.*] Master captain ! Master doc-
    tor !
  Love. Who 's that ?
  Face. [*Aside.*] Our clerk within, that I for-
    got ! — I know not, sir.   65
  Dap. [*within.*] For God's sake, when will her
    grace be at leisure ?
  Face.   Ha !
Illusions, some spirit o' the air ! — [*Aside.*] His
    gag is melted,
And now he sets out the throat.
  Dap. [*within.*]   I am almost stifled ——
  Face. [*Aside.*] Would you were together.
  Love.   'T is i' the house.
Ha ! list.
  Face. Believe it, sir, i' the air.
  Love.   Peace, you. 70
  Dap. [*within.*] Mine aunt's grace does not use
    me well.
  Sub. [*within.*] You fool,
Peace, you 'll mar all.
  Face. [*speaks through the keyhole, while* LOVE-
    WIT *advances to the door unobserved.*] Or
    you will else, you rogue.
  Love. O, is it so ? Then you converse with
    spirits ! —
Come, sir. No more o' your tricks, good Jeremy.
The truth, the shortest way.
  Face.   Dismiss this rabble, sir. — 75
[*Aside.*] What shall I do ? I am catch'd.
  Love.   Good neighbours,
I thank you all. You may depart. [*Exeunt*
    Neighbours.*] — Come, sir,
You know that I am an indulgent master ;
And therefore conceal nothing. What 's your
    medicine,
To draw so many several sorts of wild fowl ? 80
  Face. Sir, you were wont to affect mirth
    and wit —
But here 's no place to talk on 't i' the street.
Give me but leave to make the best of my for-
    tune,
And only pardon me th' abuse of your house :
It 's all I beg. I 'll help you to a widow, 85
In recompense, that you shall gi' me thanks for,
Will make you seven years younger, and a rich
    one.
'T is but your putting on a Spanish cloak :
I have her within. You need not fear the house ;
It was not visited.
  Love.   But by me, who came 90
Sooner than you expected.
  Face.   It is true, sir.
'Pray you forgive me.
  Love. Well : let's see your widow. [*Exeunt.*]

SCENE IV.[2]

[*Enter*] SUBTLE [*leading in*] DAPPER, [*with his
    eyes bound as before*].

  Sub. How ! ha' you eaten your gag ?
  Dap.   Yes, faith, it crumbled
Away i' my mouth.

  Sub.   You ha' spoil'd all then.
  Dap.   No !
I hope my aunt of Fairy will forgive me.
  Sub. Your aunt's a gracious lady ; but in
    troth
You were to blame.
  Dap.   The fume did overcome me, 5
And I did do 't to stay my stomach. 'Pray you
So satisfy her grace.

[*Enter* FACE *in his uniform.*]

           Here comes the captain.
  Face. How now ! Is his mouth down ?
  Sub.   Ay, he has spoken !
  Face. A pox, I heard him, and you too. He 's
    undone then. —
[*Aside to* SUBTLE.] I have been fain to say, the
    house is haunted 10
With spirits, to keep churl back.
  Sub.   And hast thou done it ?
  Face. Sure, for this night.
  Sub.   Why, then triumph and sing
Of Face so famous, the precious king
Of present wits.
  Face.   Did you not hear the coil 15
About the door ?
  Sub.   Yes, and I dwindled [3] with it.
  Face. Show him his aunt, and let him be dis-
    patch'd :
I 'll send her to you.   [*Exit* FACE.]
  Sub.   Well, sir, your aunt her grace
Will give you audience presently, on my suit,
And the captain's word that you did not eat
    your gag
In any contempt of her highness.
              [*Unbinds his eyes.*]
  Dap.   Not I, in troth, sir. 20

[*Enter*] DOL *like the Queen of Fairy.*

  Sub. Here she is come. Down o' your knees
    and wriggle :
She has a stately presence. [DAPPER *kneels and
    shuffles towards her.*] Good ! Yet nearer,
And bid, God save you !
  Dap.   Madam !
  Sub.   And your aunt.
  Dap. And my most gracious aunt, God save
    your grace.
  Dol. Nephew, we thought to have been angry
    with you ; 25
But that sweet face of yours hath turn'd the
    tide,
And made it flow with joy, that ebb'd of love.
Arise, and touch our velvet gown.
  Sub.   The skirts,
And kiss 'em. So !
  Dol.   Let me now stroke that head.
*Much, nephew, shalt thou win, much shalt thou
    spend ;* 30
Much shalt thou give away, much shalt thou lend.
  Sub. [*Aside.*] Ay, much ! indeed. — Why do
    you not thank her grace ?
  Dap. I cannot speak for joy.
  Sub.   See, the kind wretch !
Your grace's kinsman right.

---

[1] Optical illusion.   [2] A room in the same.

[3] Shrank with fear.

Dol.   Give me the bird. ——
Here is your fly in a purse, about your neck,
cousin ;   35
Wear it, and feed it about this day sev'n-night,
On your right wrist ——
Sub.   Open a vein with a pin
And let it suck but once a week ; till then,
You must not look on 't.
Dol.   No : and, kinsman,
Bear yourself worthy of the blood you came on.
Sub. Her grace would ha' you eat no more
    Woolsack [1] pies,   41
Nor Dagger [1] frumety.[2]
Dol.   Nor break his fast
In Heaven [1] and Hell.[1]
Sub.   She 's with you everywhere !
Nor play with costermongers, at mumchance,[3]
    traytrip,[3]
God-make-you-rich [3] (when as your aunt has
    done it) ; but keep   45
The gallant'st company, and the best
    games ——
Dap.   Yes, sir.
Sub. Gleek [3] and primero ; [3] and what you
get, be true to us.
Dap. By this hand, I will.
Sub.   You may bring 's a thousand pound
Before to-morrow night, if but three thousand
Be stirring, an you will.
Dap.   I swear I will then. 50
Sub. Your fly will learn you all games.
Face. [*within.*]   Ha' you done there ?
Sub. Your grace will command him no more
    duties ?
Dol.   No :
But come and see me often. I may chance
To leave him three or four hundred chests of
    treasure,   54
And some twelve thousand acres of fairy land,
If he game well and comely with good game-
    sters.
Sub. There 's a kind aunt : kiss her departing
    part. —
But you must sell your forty mark a year
    now.
Dap. Ay, sir, I mean.
Sub.   Or, give 't away ; pox on 't !
Dap. I 'll gi' 't mine aunt. I 'll go and fetch
    the writings.   [*Exit.*] 60
Sub. 'T is well ; away.

[*Re-enter* FACE.]

Face.   Where 's Subtle ?
Sub.   Here : what news ?
Face. Drugger is at the door ; go take his
    suit,
And bid him fetch a parson presently.
Say he shall marry the widow. Thou shalt
    spend   64
A hundred pound by the service !
                                    [*Exit* SUBTLE.]
                        Now, Queen Dol,
Have you pack'd up all ?
Dol.   Yes.

Face.   And how do you like
The Lady Pliant ?
Dol.   A good dull innocent.

[*Re-enter* SUBTLE.]

Sub. Here 's your Hieronimo's cloak and hat.
Face.   Give me 'em.
Sub. And the ruff too ?
Face.   Yes ; I 'll come to you presently.
                                              [*Exit.*]
Sub. Now he is gone about his project, Dol, 70
I told you of, for the widow.
Dol.   'T is direct
Against our articles.
Sub.   Well, we will fit him, wench.
Hast thou gull'd her of her jewels or her brace-
    lets ?
Dol. No ; but I will do 't.
Sub.   Soon at night, my Dolly,
When we are shipt, and all our goods aboard, 75
Eastward for Ratcliff, we will turn our course
To Brainford, westward, if thou sayst the
    word,
And take our leaves of this o'erweening rascal.
This peremptory Face.
Dol.   Content ; I 'm weary of him.
Sub. Thou 'st cause, when the slave will run
    at wiving, Dol,   80
Against the instrument that was drawn be-
    tween us.
Dol. I 'll pluck his bird as bare as I can.
Sub.   Yes, tell her
She must by any means address some present
To th' cunning man, make him amends for
    wronging
His art with her suspicion ; send a ring,   85
Or chain of pearl ; she will be tortur'd else
Extremely in her sleep, say, and ha' strange
    things
Come to her. Wilt thou ?
Dol.   Yes.
Sub.   My fine flitter-mouse,[4]
My bird o' the night ! We 'll tickle it at the
    Pigeons,[5]   89
When we have all, and may unlock the trunks,
And say, this 's mine, and thine ; and thine,
    and mine.   *They kiss.*

Re-enter FACE.

Face. What now ! a billing ?
Sub.   Yes, a little exalted
In the good passage of our stock-affairs.
Face. Drugger has brought his parson ; take
    him in, Subtle,
And send Nab back again to wash his face.   95
Sub. I will : and shave himself ?   [*Exit.*]
Face.   If you can get him.
Dol. You are hot upon it, Face, whate'er it
    is !
Face. A trick that Dol shall spend ten pound
    a month by.

[*Re-enter* SUBTLE.]

Is he gone ?
Sub.   The chaplain waits you i' the hall, sir.

---

[1] Names of taverns.   [2] Wheat boiled in milk.
        [3] Games of chance.

[4] Bat.   [5] An inn at Brentford.

Face. I 'll go bestow him. [*Exit.*]
Dol. He 'll now marry her instantly.
Sub. He cannot yet, he is not ready. Dear Dol, 101
Cozen her of all thou canst. To deceive him
Is no deceit, but justice, that would break
Such an inextricable tie as ours was.
Dol. Let me alone to fit him.

[*Re-enter* FACE.]

Face. Come, my venturers,
You ha' pack'd up all? Where be the trunks?
Bring forth. 106
Sub. Here.
Face. Let us see 'em. Where 's the money?
Sub. Here,
In this.
Face. Mammon's ten pound; eight score before:
The brethren's money this. Drugger's and Dapper's.
What paper 's that?
Dol. The jewel of the waiting maid's, 110
That stole it from her lady, to know certain —
Face. If she should have precedence of her mistress?
Dol. Yes.
Face. What box is that?
Sub. The fish-wives' rings, I think,
And th' ale-wives' single money.[1] Is 't not, Dol?
Dol. Yes; and the whistle that the sailor's wife 115
Brought you to know an her husband were with Ward.[2]
Face. We 'll wet it to-morrow; and our silver beakers
And tavern cups. Where be the French petticoats
And girdles and hangers?
Sub. Here, i' the trunk,
And the bolts of lawn.
Face. Is Drugger's damask there,
And the tobacco?
Sub. Yes.
Face. Give me the keys. 121
Dol. Why you the keys?
Sub. No matter, Dol; because
We shall not open 'em before he comes.
Face. 'Tis true, you shall not open them, indeed;
Nor have 'em forth, do you see? Not forth, Dol.
Dol. No! 125
Face. No, my smock-rampant. The right is, my master
Knows all, has pardon'd me, and he will keep 'em.
Doctor, 't is true — you look — for all your figures:
I sent for him, indeed. Wherefore, good partners,
Both he and she, be satisfied: for here 130
Determines[3] the indenture tripartite
'Twixt Subtle, Dol, and Face. All I can do

Is to help you over the wall, o' the back-side,
Or lend you a sheet to save your velvet gown, Dol.
Here will be officers presently, bethink you 135
Of some course suddenly to scape the dock;
For thither you 'll come else. (*Some knock.*)
Hark you, thunder.
Sub. You are a precious fiend!
Offi. [*without.*] Open the door.
Face. Dol, I am sorry for thee i' faith; but hear'st thou?
It shall go hard but I will place thee somewhere: 140
Thou shalt ha' my letter to Mistress Amo —
Dol. Hang you.
Face. Or Madam Caesarean.
Dol. Pox upon you, rogue,
Would I had but time to beat thee!
Face. Subtle,
Let 's know where you 'll set up next; I will send you 144
A customer now and then, for old acquaintance.
What new course have you?
Sub. Rogue, I 'll hang myself;
That I may walk a greater devil than thou,
And haunt thee i' the flock-bed and the buttery. [*Exeunt.*]

SCENE V.[4]

[*Enter*] LOVEWIT [*in the Spanish dress, with the* Parson. *Loud knocking at the door.*]

Love. What do you mean, my masters?
Mam. [*without.*] Open your door,
Cheaters, bawds, conjurers.
Offi. [*without.*] Or we 'll break it open.
Love. What warrant have you?
Offi. [*without.*] Warrant enough, sir, doubt not,
If you 'll not open it.
Love. Is there an officer there?
Offi. [*without.*] Yes, two or three for failing.[5]
Love. Have but patience, 5
And I will open it straight.

[*Enter* FACE, *as butler.*]

Face. Sir, ha' you done?
Is it a marriage? Perfect?
Love. Yes, my brain.
Face. Off with your ruff and cloak then; be yourself, sir.
Sur. [*without.*] Down with the door.
Kas. [*without.*] 'Slight, ding[6] it open.
Love. [*opening the door.*] Hold,
Hold, gentlemen, what means this violence? 10

[MAMMON, SURLY, KASTRIL, ANANIAS, TRIBULATION *and* Officers *rush in.*]

Mam. Where is this collier?
Sur. And my Captain Face?
Mam. These day-owls.
Sur. That are birding[7] in men's purses.
Mam. Madam Suppository.
Kas. Doxy, my suster.

---

[1] Small change.   [2] A famous pirate.   [3] Ends.
[4] An outer room in the same.   [6] Break.
[5] For fear of failing.   [7] Stealing.

Ana.   Locusts.
Of the foul pit.
Tri.   Profane as Bel and the Dragon.
Ana. Worse than the grasshoppers, or the lice
    of Egypt.   15
Love. Good gentlemen, hear me. Are you
    officers,
And cannot stay this violence ?
1 *Offi.*   Keep the peace.
Love. Gentlemen, what is the matter? Whom
    do you seek ?
Mam. The chemical cozener.
Sur.   And the captain pander.
Kas. The nun my suster.
Mam.   Madam Rabbi.
Ana.   Scorpions,   20
And caterpillars.
Love.   Fewer at once, I pray you.
1 *Offi.* One after another, gentlemen, I
    charge you,
By virtue of my staff.
Ana.   They are the vessels
Of pride, lust, and the cart.
Love.   Good zeal, lie still
A little while.
Tri.   Peace, Deacon Ananias.   25
Love. The house is mine here, and the doors
    are open ;
If there be any such persons as you seek for,
Use your authority, search on o' God's name,
I am but newly come to town, and finding
This tumult 'bout my door, to tell you true,   30
It somewhat maz'd me ; till my man here, fear-
    ing
My more displeasure, told me he had done
Somewhat an insolent part, let out my house
(Belike presuming on my known aversion
From any air o' the town while there was sick-
    ness),   35
To a doctor and a captain: who, what they are
Or where they be, he knows not.
Mam.   Are they gone ?
Love. You may go in and search, sir. (MAM-
    MON, ANA., *and* TRIB. *go in.*) Here, I find
The empty walls worse than I left 'em, smok'd,
A few crack'd pots, and glasses, and a furnace ;
The ceiling fill'd with poesies of the candle,   41
And " Madam with a dildo "[1] writ o' the walls.
Only one gentlewoman I met here
That is within, that said she was a widow ——
Kas. Ay, that 's my suster ; I 'll go thump
    her. Where is she ?   [*Goes in.*]   45
Love. And should ha' married a Spanish count,
    but he,
When he came to 't, neglected her so grossly,
That I, a widower, am gone through with her.
Sur. How ! have I lost her then ?
Love.   Were you the don, sir ?
Good faith, now she does blame you extremely,
    and says   50
You swore, and told her you had ta'en the pains
To dye your beard, and umber o'er your face,
Borrowed a suit, and ruff, all for her love :
And then did nothing. What an oversight
And want of putting forward, sir, was this !   55

Well fare an old harquebusier[2] yet,
Could prime his powder, and give fire, and hit,
All in a twinkling !   MAMMON *comes forth.*
Mam.   The whole nest are fled !
Love. What sort of birds were they ?
Mam.   A kind of choughs,[3]
Or thievish daws, sir, that have pickt my
    purse,   60
Of eight score and ten pounds within these five
    weeks,
Beside my first materials ; and my goods,
That lie i' the cellar, which I am glad they ha'
    left,
I may have home yet.
Love.   Think you so, sir ?
Mam.   Ay.
Love. By order of law, sir, but not otherwise.
Mam. Not mine own stuff !
Love.   Sir, I can take no knowledge   65
That they are yours, but by public means.
If you can bring certificate that you were gull'd
    of 'em,
Or any formal writ out of a court,
That you did cozen yourself, I will not hold
    them.   70
Mam. I 'll rather lose 'em.
Love.   That you shall not, sir,
By me, in troth ; upon these terms, they 're
    yours.
What, should they ha' been, sir, turn'd into
    gold, all ?
Mam.   No.
I cannot tell. — It may be they should. — What
    then ?
Love. What a great loss in hope have you
    sustain'd !   75
Mam. Not I ; the commonwealth has.
Face.   Ay, he would ha' built
The city new ; and made a ditch about it
Of silver, should have run with cream from
    Hogsden ;
That every Sunday in Moorsfields the younk-
    ers,
And tits[4] and tom-boys should have fed on,
    gratis.   80
Mam. I will go mount a turnip-cart, and
    preach
The end o' the world within these two months.
    Surly,
What ! in a dream ?
Sur.   Must I needs cheat myself
With that same foolish vice of honesty !
Come, let us go and hearken out the rogues :   85
That Face I 'll mark for mine, if e'er I meet him.
Face. If I can hear of him, sir, I 'll bring you
    word
Unto your lodging ; for in troth, they were
    strangers
To me ; I thought 'em honest as myself, sir.
                          They come forth.

[*Re-enter* ANANIAS *and* TRIBULATION.]

Tri. 'T is well, the saints shall not lose all
    yet. Go   90
And get some carts ——

---

[1] Probably a fragment of a song.

[2] Musketeer.   [3] Crow.   [4] Wenches.

Love. For what, my zealous friends?
Ana. To bear away the portion of the right-
eous
Out of this den of thieves.
Love. What is that portion?
Ana. The goods sometimes the orphans', that
the brethren
Bought with their silver pence.
Love. What, those i' the cellar, 95
The knight Sir Mammon claims?
Ana. I do defy
The wicked Mammon, so do all the brethren,
Thou profane man! I ask thee with what con-
science
Thou canst advance that idol against us,
That have the seal?[1] Were not the shillings
numb'red 100
That made the pounds; were not the pounds
told out
Upon the second day of the fourth week,
In the eighth month, upon the table dormant,
The year of the last patience of the saints,
Six hundred and ten?
Love. Mine earnest vehement botcher, 105
And deacon also, I cannot dispute with you:
But if you get you not away the sooner,
I shall confute you with a cudgel.
Ana. Sir!
Tri. Be patient, Ananias.
Ana. I am strong,
And will stand up, well girt, against an host 110
That threaten Gad in exile.
Love. I shall send you
To Amsterdam, to your cellar.
Ana. I will pray there,
Against thy house. May dogs defile thy walls,
And wasps and hornets breed beneath thy roof,
This seat of falsehood, and this cave of coz'-
nage! [*Exeunt* ANA. *and* TRIB.]

Enter DRUGGER.

Love. Another too?
Drug. Not I, sir, I am no brother. 116
Love. (*beats him.*) Away, you Harry Nicho-
las![2] do you talk? [*Exit* DRUG.]
Face. No, this was Abel Drugger. Good sir,
go, (*To the* Parson.)
And satisfy him; tell him all is done:
He staid too long a washing of his face. 120
The doctor, he shall hear of him at Westches-
ter;
And of the captain, tell him, at Yarmouth, or
Some good port-town else, lying for a wind.
[*Exit* Parson.]
If you can get off the angry child now, sir ——

[*Enter* KASTRIL, *dragging in* his sister.]

Kas. Come on, you ewe, you have match'd
most sweetly, ha' you not? 125
Did not I say, I would never ha' you tupt
But by a dubb'd boy,[3] to make you a lady-
tom?

[1] That are sealed as God's people.
[2] The founder of the fanatical sect called "The
Family of Love."
[3] Knight.

'Slight, you are a mammet![4] O, I could touse
you now.
Death, mun[5] you marry with a pox!
Love. You lie, boy;
As sound as you; and I 'm aforehand with you.
Kas. Anon! 130
Love. Come, will you quarrel? I will feize[6]
you, sirrah;
Why do you not buckle to your tools?
Kas. God's light,
This is a fine old boy as e'er I saw!
Love. What, do you change your copy now?
Proceed;
Here stands my dove: stoop[7] at her if you
dare. 135
Kas. 'Slight, I must love him! I cannot
choose, i' faith,
An I should be hang'd for 't! Suster, I protest,
I honour thee for this match.
Love. O, do you so, sir?
Kas. Yes, an thou canst take tobacco and
drink, old boy,
I 'll give her five hundred pound more to her
marriage, 140
Than her own state.
Love. Fill a pipe full, Jeremy.
Face. Yes; but go in and take it, sir.
Love. We will.
I will be rul'd by thee in anything, Jeremy.
Kas. 'Slight, thou art not hide-bound, thou
art a jovy[8] boy! 144
Come, let us in, I pray thee, and take our whiffs.
Love. Whiff in with your sister, brother boy.
[*Exeunt* KAS. *and* Dame P.]
That master
That had receiv'd such happiness by a ser-
vant,
In such a widow, and with so much wealth,
Were very ungrateful, if he would not be
A little indulgent to that servant's wit, 150
And help his fortune, though were some small
strain
Of his own candour.[9] [*Advancing.*] Therefore,
gentlemen,
And kind spectators, if I have outstript
An old man's gravity, or strict canon, think 154
What a young wife and a good brain may do;
Stretch age's truth sometimes, and crack it
too.
Speak for thyself, knave.
Face. So I will, sir. [*Advancing to the front of
the stage.*] Gentlemen,
My part a little fell in this last scene,
Yet 't was decorum.[10] And though I am clean
Got off from Subtle, Surly, Mammon, Dol, 160
Hot Ananias, Dapper, Drugger, all
With whom I traded; yet I put myself
On you, that are my country:[11] and this pelf
Which I have got, if you do quit me, rests,
To feast you often, and invite new guests. 165
[*Exeunt.*]

[4] Puppet.   [5] Must.   [6] Beat.
[7] A term of falconry: used in punning allusion to the
name of Kastril, which means hawk.
[8] Jovial.   [10] Dramatic propriety.
[9] Fair reputation.   [11] Jury.

THE SHOEMAKERS' HOLIDAY

BY

THOMAS DEKKER

[DRAMATIS PERSONAE

THE KING.	ROGER, commonly called HODGE, } EYRE's Journeymen.
THE EARL OF CORNWALL.	FIRK,
SIR HUGH LACY, Earl of Lincoln.	RALPH,
ROWLAND LACY, otherwise HANS, } His Nephews.	LOVELL, a Courtier.
ASKEW	DODGER, a Servant to the EARL OF LINCOLN.
SIR ROGER OATELY, Lord Mayor of London.	A Dutch Skipper.
Master HAMMON,	A Boy.
Master WARNER, } Citizens of London.	ROSE, Daughter of SIR ROGER.
Master SCOTT,	SYBIL, her Maid.
SIMON EYRE, the Shoemaker.	MARGERY, Wife of SIMON EYRE.
	JANE, Wife of RALPH.

Courtiers, Attendants, Officers, Soldiers, Hunters, Shoemakers, Apprentices, Servants.

SCENE. — *London* and *Old Ford*.]

THE PROLOGUE

As it was pronounced before the Queen's Majesty

As wretches in a storm, expecting day,
With trembling hands and eyes cast up to heaven,
Make prayers the anchor of their conquer'd hopes,
So we, dear goddess, wonder of all eyes,
Your meanest vassals, through mistrust and fear   5
To sink into the bottom of disgrace
By our imperfect pastimes, prostrate thus
On bended knees, our sails of hope do strike,
Dreading the bitter storms of your dislike.
Since then, unhappy men, our hap is such   10
That to ourselves ourselves no help can bring,
But needs must perish, if your saint-like ears,
Locking the temple where all mercy sits,
Refuse the tribute of all begging tongues ;
Oh, grant, bright mirror of true chastity,   15
From those life-breathing stars, your sun-like eyes,
One gracious smile ; for your celestial breath
Must send us life, or sentence us to death.

ACT I

SCENE I.[1]

Enter the LORD MAYOR *and the* EARL OF LINCOLN.

Linc. My lord mayor, you have sundry times
Feasted myself and many courtiers more ;
Seldom or never can we be so kind
To make requital of your courtesy.
But leaving this, I hear my cousin Lacy   5
Is much affected to[2] your daughter Rose.

[1] A street in London.   [2] In love with.

L. Mayor. True, my good lord, and she loves
him so well
That I mislike her boldness in the chase.
Linc. Why, my lord mayor, think you it then
a shame,
To join a Lacy with an Oateley's name ?   10
L. Mayor. Too mean is my poor girl for his
high birth ;
Poor citizens must not with courtiers wed,
Who will in silks and gay apparel spend
More in one year than I am worth, by far :
Therefore your honour need not doubt[3] my
girl.   15

[3] Fear.

Linc. Take heed, my lord, advise you what
    you do !
A verier unthrift lives not in the world,
Than is my cousin ; for I 'll tell you what :
'T is now almost a year since he requested
To travel countries for experience.   20
I furnish him with coin, bills of exchange,
Letters of credit, men to wait on him,
Solicited my friends in Italy
Well to respect him. But, to see the end,
Scant had he journey'd through half Germany,
But all his coin was spent, his men cast off,   26
His bills embezzl'd,[1] and my jolly coz,[2]
Asham'd to show his bankrupt presence here,
Became a shoemaker in Wittenberg,
A goodly science for a gentleman   30
Of such descent ! Now judge the rest by this :
Suppose your daughter have a thousand pound,
He did consume me more in one half year :
And make him heir to all the wealth you have
One twelvemonth's rioting will waste it all.   35
Then seek, my lord, some honest citizen
To wed your daughter to.
L. Mayor.   I thank your lordship.
[*Aside.*] Well, fox, I understand your subtil-
    ty. —
As for your nephew, let your lordship's eye
But watch his actions, and you need not fear,
For I have seen my daughter far enough.   41
And yet your cousin Rowland might do well,
Now he hath learn'd an occupation :
And yet I scorn to call him son-in-law.
Linc. Ay, but I have a better trade for him.
I thank his grace, he hath appointed him   46
Chief colonel of all those companies
Must'red in London and the shires about,
To serve his highness in those wars of France.
See where he comes ! —

Enter LOVELL, LACY, *and* ASKEW.

                Lovell, what news with you ?
Lovell. My Lord of Lincoln, 't is his highness'
    will,   51
That presently[3] your cousin ship for France
With all his powers ; he would not for a mil-
    lion,
But they should land at Dieppe within four
    days.
Linc. Go certify his grace, it shall be done.
                            Exit LOVELL.
Now, cousin Lacy, in what forwardness   56
Are all your companies ?
Lacy.   All well prepar'd.
The men of Hertfordshire lie at Mile-end,
Suffolk and Essex train in Tothill-fields,
The Londoners and those of Middlesex,   60
All gallantly prepar'd in Finsbury,
With frolic spirits long for their parting hour.
L. Mayor. They have their imprest,[4] coats,
    and furniture ;[5]
And, if it please your cousin Lacy come
To the Guildhall, he shall receive his pay ;   65
And twenty pounds besides my brethren

[1] Wasted.
[2] Cousin ; used of any relative not of one's immediate family.
[3] At once.   [4] Advance-pay.   [5] Equipment.

Will freely give him, to approve our loves
We bear unto my lord, your uncle here.
Lacy. I thank your honour.
Linc.   Thanks, my good lord mayor.   69
L. Mayor. At the Guildhall we will expect
    your coming.   *Exit.*
Linc. To approve your loves to me ? No sub-
    tilty
Nephew, that twenty pound he doth bestow
For joy to rid you from his daughter Rose.
But, cousins both, now here are none but
    friends,
I would not have you cast an amorous eye   75
Upon so mean a project as the love
Of a gay, wanton, painted citizen.
I know, this churl even in the height of scorn
Doth hate the mixture of his blood with thine.
I pray thee, do thou so ! Remember, coz,   80
What honourable fortunes wait on thee.
Increase the king's love, which so brightly
    shines,
And gilds thy hopes. I have no heir but thee, —
And yet not thee, if with a wayward spirit
Thou start from the true bias[6] of my love.   85
Lacy. My lord, I will for honour, not desire
Of land or livings, or to be your heir,
So guide my actions in pursuit of France,
As shall add glory to the Lacies' name.
Linc. Coz, for those words here 's thirty Por-
    tuguese,[7]   90
And, nephew Askew, there 's a few for you.
Fair Honour, in her loftiest eminence,
Stays in France for you, till you fetch her
    thence.
Then, nephews, clap swift wings on your de-
    signs.   94
Begone, begone, make haste to the Guildhall ;
There presently I 'll meet you. Do not stay :
Where honour [beckons][8] shame attends delay.
                                Exit.
Askew. How gladly would your uncle have
    you gone !
Lacy. True, coz, but I 'll o'erreach his policies.
I have some serious business for three days,   100
Which nothing but my presence can dispatch.
You, therefore, cousin, with the companies,
Shall haste to Dover ; there I 'll meet with
    you :
Or, if I stay past my prefixed time,   104
Away for France ; we 'll meet in Normandy.
The twenty pounds my lord mayor gives to me
You shall receive, and these ten Portuguese,
Part of mine uncle's thirty. Gentle coz,
Have care to our great charge ; I know, your
    wisdom
Hath tried itself in higher consequence.   110
Askew. Coz, all myself am yours : yet have
    this care,
To lodge in London with all secrecy ;
Our uncle Lincoln hath, besides his own,
Many a jealous eye, that in your face
Stares only to watch means for your disgrace.
Lacy. Stay, cousin, who be these ?   116

[6] Inclination.
[7] A gold coin, worth about three pounds twelve
shillings.
[8] Qq. *become.* Malone emend.

Enter SIMON EYRE, [MARGERY] *his wife,*
HODGE, FIRK, JANE, *and* RALPH *with a
piece.*[1]

Eyre. Leave whining, leave whining! Away
with this whimp'ring, this puling, these blub-
b'ring tears, and these wet eyes! I'll get thy
husband discharg'd, I warrant thee, sweet
Jane; go to!   121
Hodge. Master, here be the captains.
Eyre. Peace, Hodge; husht, ye knave, husht!
Firk. Here be the cavaliers and the colonels,
master.   125
Eyre. Peace, Firk; peace, my fine Firk!
Stand by with your pishery-pashery,[2] away!
I am a man of the best presence; I'll speak to
them, an[3] they were Popes. — Gentlemen, captains, colonels, commanders! Brave men, [130]
brave leaders, may it please you to give me audience. I am Simon Eyre, the mad shoemaker of
Tower Street; this wench with the mealy mouth
that will never tire, is my wife, I can tell you;
here's Hodge, my man and my foreman; [135]
here's Firk, my fine firking[4] journeyman, and
this is blubbered Jane. All we come to be suitors
for this honest Ralph. Keep him at home, and as
I am a true shoemaker and a gentleman of the
gentle craft, buy spurs yourself, and I'll [140]
find ye boots these seven years.
Marg. Seven years, husband?
Eyre. Peace, midriff,[5] peace! I know what
I do. Peace!   144
Firk. Truly, master cormorant,[6] you shall
do God good service to let Ralph and his wife
stay together. She's a young new-married woman; if you take her husband away from her
a-night, you undo her; she may beg in the day-
time; for he's as good a workman at a prick
and an awl as any is in our trade.   151
Jane. O let him stay, else I shall be undone.
Firk. Ay, truly, she shall be laid at one side
like a pair of old shoes else, and be occupied
for no use.   155
Lacy. Truly, my friends it lies not in my
power:
The Londoners are press'd,[7] paid, and set
forth
By the lord mayor; I cannot change a man.
Hodge. Why, then you were as good be a corporal as a colonel, if you cannot discharge [160]
one good fellow; and I tell you true, I think
you do more than you can answer, to press a
man within a year and a day of his marriage.
Eyre. Well said, melancholy Hodge; gramercy, my fine foreman.   165
Marg. Truly, gentlemen, it were ill done for
such as you, to stand so stiffly against a poor
young wife, considering her case, she is new-
married; but let that pass. I pray, deal not
roughly with her; her husband is a young man,
and but newly ent'red; but let that pass.   171
Eyre. Away with your pishery-pashery, your
pols and your edipols![8] Peace, midriff; si-

lence, Cicely Bumtrinket! Let your head
speak.   145
Firk. Yea, and the horns too, master.
Eyre. Too soon, my fine Firk, too soon!
Peace, scoundrels! See you this man? Captains, you will not release him? Well, let him
go; he's a proper shot; let him vanish! [180]
Peace, Jane, dry up thy tears, they'll make his
powder dankish.[9] Take him, brave men, [130]
tor of Troy was an hackney to him, Hercules
and Termagant[10] scoundrels, Prince Arthur's
Round-table — by the Lord of Ludgate — [185]
ne'er fed such a tall,[11] such a dapper swordman;
by the life of Pharaoh, a brave resolute sword-
man! Peace, Jane! I say no more, mad knaves.
Firk. See, see, Hodge, how my master raves
in commendation of Ralph!   190
Hodge. Ralph, th' art a gull,[12] by this hand,
an thou goest not.
Askew. I am glad, good Master Eyre, it is my
hap
To meet so resolute a soldier.
Trust me, for your report and love to him, 195
A common slight regard shall not respect him.
Lacy. Is thy name Ralph?
Ralph.   Yes, sir.
Lacy.   Give me thine hand;
Thou shalt not want, as I am a gentleman.
Woman, be patient; God, no doubt, will send
Thy husband safe again; but he must go,   200
His country's quarrel says it shall be so.
Hodge. Th' art a gull, by my stirrup, if thou
dost not go. I will not have thee strike thy
gimlet into these weak vessels; prick thine
enemies, Ralph.   205

Enter DODGER.

Dodger. My lord, your uncle on the Tower-
hill
Stays with the lord-mayor and the aldermen,
And doth request you, with all speed you may,
To hasten thither.
Askew.   Cousin, let's go.
Lacy. Dodger, run you before, tell them we
come,   214
This Dodger is mine uncle's parasite,
Exit DODGER.
The arrant'st varlet that e'er breath'd on earth;
He sets more discord in a noble house
By one day's broaching of his pickthank tales,[13]
Than can be salv'd[14] again in twenty years, 215
And he, I fear, shall go with us to France,
To pry into our actions.
Askew.   Therefore, coz,
It shall behove you to be circumspect.
Lacy. Fear not, good cousin. — Ralph, hie to
your colours. [*Exit* LACY *and* ASKEW.]
Ralph. I must, because there's no remedy;
But, gentle master and my loving dame,   221
As you have always been a friend to me,
So in mine absence think upon my wife.
Jane. Alas, my Ralph.
Marg.   She cannot speak for weeping. 224

---

[1] Piece of leather.   [5] Used as a term of contempt.
[2] Twiddle-twaddle.   [6] Quibbling on *colonel*.
[3] If.   [7] Impressed into service.
[4] Frisky, tricky.   [8] Solemn declarations.

[9] Damp.   [11] Brave.
[10] An imaginary Saracen god. [12] Fool.
[13] Tales told to curry favor.
[14] Healed.

Eyre. Peace, you crack'd groats,[1] you mustard tokens,[2] disquiet not the brave soldier. Go thy ways, Ralph!

Jane. Ay, ay, you bid him go; what shall I do
When he is gone?

Firk. Why, be doing with me or my fellow Hodge; be not idle.   231

Eyre. Let me see thy hand, Jane. This fine hand, this white hand, these pretty fingers must spin, must card, must work; work, you bombast cotton-candle-quean; work for your living, [235 with a pox to you. — Hold thee, Ralph, here's five sixpences for thee; fight for the honour of the gentle craft, for the gentlemen shoemakers. the courageous cordwainers, the flower of St. Martin's, the mad knaves of Bedlam, Fleet [240 Street, Tower Street and Whitechapel; crack me the crowns of the French knaves; a pox on them, crack them; fight, by the Lord of Ludgate; fight, my fine boy!

Firk. Here, Ralph, here's three two- [245 pences; two carry into France, the third shall wash our souls at parting, for sorrow is dry. For my sake, firk the *Basa mon cues.*

Hodge. Ralph, I am heavy at parting; but here's a shilling for thee. God send[3] thee to [250 cram thy slops[4] with French crowns, and thy enemies' bellies with bullets.

Ralph. I thank you, master, and I thank you all.
Now, gentle wife, my loving lovely Jane,
Rich men, at parting, give their wives rich gifts,   255
Jewels and rings, to grace their lily hands.
Thou know'st our trade makes rings for women's heels:
Here take this pair of shoes, cut out by Hodge,
Stitch'd by my fellow Firk, seam'd by myself,
Made up and pink'd[5] with letters for thy name.   260
Wear them, my dear Jane, for thy husband's sake,
And every morning when thou pull'st them on,
Remember me, and pray for my return.
Make much of them; for I have made them so
That I can know them from a thousand mo.   265

Drum sounds. Enter the LORD MAYOR, *the* EARL OF LINCOLN, LACY, ASKEW, DODGER, *and* Soldiers. *They pass over the stage;* RALPH *falls in amongst them;* FIRK *and the rest cry* "Farewell," *etc., and so exeunt.*

ACT II

SCENE I.[6]

Enter ROSE, *alone, making a garland.*

Rose. Here sit thou down upon this flow'ry bank

[1] Four-penny piece.
[2] Yellow spots on the body denoting the infection of the plague.
[3] Grant.
[4] Breeches (-pockets).
[5] Perforated.
[6] A garden at Old Ford.

And make a garland for thy Lacy's head.
These pinks, these roses, and these violets,
These blushing gilliflowers, these marigolds,
The fair embroidery of his coronet,   5
Carry not half such beauty in their cheeks,
As the sweet count'nance of my Lacy doth.
O my most unkind father! O my stars,
Why lower'd you so at my nativity,
To make me love, yet live robb'd of my love?
Here as a thief am I imprisoned   11
For my dear Lacy's sake within those walls,
Which by my father's cost were builded up
For better purposes. Here must I languish
For him that doth as much lament, I know,   15
Mine absence, as for him I pine in woe.

Enter SYBIL.

Sybil. Good morrow, young mistress. I am sure you make that garland for me, against[7] I shall be Lady of the Harvest.

Rose. Sybil, what news at London?   20

Sybil. None but good; my lord mayor, your father, and master Philpot, your uncle, and Master Scot, your cousin, and Mistress Frigbottom by Doctors' Commons, do all, by my troth, send you most hearty commendations. [25

Rose. Did Lacy send kind greetings to his love?

Sybil. O yes, out of cry, by my troth. I scant knew him; here 'a wore a scarf; and here a scarf, here a bunch of feathers, and here precious stones and jewels, and a pair [30 of garters, — O, monstrous! like one of our yellow silk curtains at home here in Old Ford House here, in Master Belly-mount's chamber. I stood at our door in Cornhill, look'd at him, he at me indeed, spake to him, but he not [35 to me, not a word; marry go-up, thought I, with a wanion! [8] He pass'd by me as proud —Marry foh! are you grown humorous,[9] thought I; and so shut the door, and in I came.

Rose. O Sybil, how dost thou my Lacy wrong!   40
My Rowland is as gentle as a lamb,
No dove was ever half so mild as he.

Sybil. Mild? yea, as a bushel of stamp crabs.[10] He lookt upon me as sour as verjuice.[11] Go thy ways, thought I, thou may'st be much [45 in my gaskins,[12] but nothing in my netherstocks.[13] This is your fault, mistress, to love him that loves not you; he thinks scorn to do as he's done to; but if I were as you, I'd cry, "Go by, Jeronimo, go by!" [14]   50

I'd set mine old debts against my new driblets,
And the hare's foot against the goose giblets,
For if ever I sigh, when sleep I should take,
Pray God I may lose my maidenhead when I wake.

Rose. Will my love leave me then, and go to France?   55

Sybil. I know not that, but I am sure I see

[7] In preparation.
[8] With a vengeance.
[9] Capricious.
[10] Crushed crab-apples.
[11] Juice of green fruits.
[12] Wide trousers.
[13] Stockings. The meaning seems to be that though we may be acquainted, we are not intimate friends.
[14] A phrase from Kyd's *Spanish Tragedy.*

him stalk before the soldiers. By my troth,
he is a proper[1] man ; but he is proper that
proper doth. Let him go snick-up,[2] young
mistress.   60
  Rose. Get thee to London, and learn per-
    fectly
Whether my Lacy go to France, or no.
Do this, and I will give thee for thy pains
My cambric apron and my Romish gloves,
My purple stockings and a stomacher.   65
Say, wilt thou do this, Sybil, for my sake ?
  Sybil. Will I, quoth 'a ? At whose suit ? By
my troth, yes, I 'll go. A cambric apron, gloves,
a pair of purple stockings, and a stomacher !
I 'll sweat in purple, mistress, for you ;   [70
I 'll take anything that comes a' God's name.
O rich ! a cambric apron ! Faith, then have at
'up tails all.' I 'll go jiggy-joggy to London,
and be here in a trice, young mistress.   *Exit.*
  Rose. Do so, good Sybil. Meantime wretched I
Will sit and sigh for his lost company. *Exit.* [76

Scene II.[3]

Enter LACY, *like a Dutch Shoemaker.*

  Lacy. How many shapes have gods and kings
    devis'd,
Thereby to compass their desired loves !
It is no shame for Rowland Lacy, then,
To clothe his cunning with the gentle craft,
That, thus disguis'd, I may unknown possess 5
The only happy presence of my Rose.
For her have I forsook my charge in France,
Incurr'd the king's displeasure, and stirr'd up
Rough hatred in mine uncle Lincoln's breast.
O love, how powerful art thou, that canst change
High birth to baseness, and a noble mind   11
To the mean semblance of a shoemaker !
But thus it must be ; for her cruel father,
Hating the single union of our souls,   14
Has secretly convey'd my Rose from London,
To bar me of her presence ; but I trust,
Fortune and this disguise will further me
Once more to view her beauty, gain her sight.
Here in Tower Street with Eyre the shoemaker
Mean I a while to work ; I know the trade, 20
I learnt it when I was in Wittenberg.
Then cheer thy hoping spirits, be not dismay'd,
Thou canst not want : do Fortune what she can,
The gentle craft is living for a man.   *Exit.*

Scene III.[4]

Enter EYRE, *making himself ready.*[5]

  Eyre. Where be these boys, these girls, these
drabs, these scoundrels ? They wallow in the fat
brewiss[6] of my bounty, and lick up the crumbs
of my table, yet will not rise to see my walks
cleansed. Come out, you powder-beef[7] queans !
What, Nan ! what, Madge Mumble-crust. [6
Come out, you fat midriff-swag-belly-whores,
and sweep me these kennels[8] that the noisome
stench offend not the noses of my neighbours.

What, Firk, I say ; what, Hodge ! Open my [10
shop windows ! What, Firk, I say !

Enter FIRK.

  Firk. O master, is 't you that speak bandog[9]
and Bedlam[10] this morning ? I was in a dream,
and mused what madman was got into the street
so early. Have you drunk this morning that [15
your throat is so clear ?
  Eyre. Ah, well said, Firk ; well said, Firk. To
work, my fine knave, to work ! Wash thy face,
and thou 't be more blest.
  Firk. Let them wash my face that will eat [20
it. Good master, send for a souse-wife,[11] if you'll
have my face cleaner.

Enter HODGE.

  Eyre. Away, sloven ! avaunt, scoundrel ! —
Good-morrow, Hodge ; good-morrow, my fine
foreman.   25
  Hodge. O master, good-morrow ; y' are an
early stirrer. Here 's a fair morning. — Good-
morrow, Firk, I could have slept this hour.
Here 's a brave day towards.[12]
  Eyre. Oh, haste to work, my fine foreman, [30
haste to work.
  Firk. Master, I am dry as dust to hear my
fellow Roger talk of fair weather ; let us pray
for good leather, and let clowns and plough-
boys and those that work in the fields pray [35
for brave days. We work in a dry shop ; what
care I if it rain ?

Enter EYRE's *wife* [MARGERY].

  Eyre. How now, Dame Margery, can you see
to rise ? Trip and go, call up the drabs, your
maids.   40
  Marg. See to rise ? I hope 't is time enough,
't is early enough for any woman to be seen
abroad. I marvel how many wives in Tower
Street are up so soon. Gods me, 't is not noon,
— here 's a yawling !![13]   45
  Eyre. Peace, Margery, peace ! Where 's Cicely
Bumtrinket, your maid ? She has a privy fault,
she farts in her sleep. Call the quean up ; if my
men want shoe-thread, I 'll swinge her in a stirrup.   50
  Firk. Yet, that 's but a dry beating ; here 's
still a sign of drought.

Enter LACY [*disguised*], *singing.*

  Lacy. Der was een bore van Gelderland
          Frolick sie byen ;
      He was als dronck he cold nyet stand,
          Upsolce sie byen.   56
      Tap eens de canneken,
      Drincke, schone mannekin.[14]

---

[9] Watch dog.   [10] Madman.
[11] A woman who washed and pickled pigs' faces.
[12] Coming.   [13] Bawling.
[14] The language is, of course, meant for Dutch.

  There was a boor from Gelderland,
          Jolly they be ;
      He was so drunk he could not stand,
          Drunken (?) they be :
      Clink then the cannikin,
      Drink, pretty mannikin !

---

[1] Handsome.   [5] Dressing himself.
[2] Go and be hanged ! [6] Beef broth.
[3] A street in London. [7] Salted beef.
[4] Before Eyre's house. [8] Gutters.

Firk. Master, for my life, yonder 's a bro- [59 ther of the gentle craft ; if he bear not Saint Hugh's bones,[1] I 'll forfeit my bones ; he 's some uplandish workman : hire him, good master, that I may learn some gibble-gabble ; 't will make us work the faster. 64

Eyre. Peace, Firk ! A hard world ! Let him pass, let him vanish ; we have journeymen enow. Peace, my fine Firk !

Marg. Nay, nay, y' are best follow your man's counsel ; you shall see what will come on 't. We have not men enow, but we must entertain [70 every butter-box ;[2] but let that pass.

Hodge. Dame, 'fore God, if my master follow your counsel, he 'll consume little beef. He shall be glad of men an he can catch them.

Firk. Ay, that he shall. 75

Hodge. 'Fore God, a proper man, and I warrant, a fine workman. Master, farewell ; dame, adieu ; if such a man as he cannot find work, Hodge is not for you. *Offers to go.*

Eyre. Stay, my fine Hodge. 80

Firk. Faith, an your foreman go, dame, you must take a journey to seek a new journeyman ; if Roger remove, Firk follows. If Saint Hugh's bones shall not be set a-work, I may prick mine all in the walls, and go play. Fare ye well, master ; good-bye, dame. 86

Eyre. Tarry, my fine Hodge, my brisk foreman ! Stay, Firk ! Peace, pudding-broth ! By the Lord of Ludgate, I love my men as my life. Peace, you gallimaufry ![3] Hodge, if he [90 want work, I 'll hire him. One of you to him ; stay, — he comes to us.

Lacy. Goeden dach, meester, ende u vro oak.[4]

Firk. Nails,[5] if I should speak after him without drinking, I should choke. And you, [95 friend Oake, are you of the gentle craft ?

Lacy. Yaw, yaw, ik bin den skomawker.[6]

Firk. Den skomaker, quoth 'a ! And hark you, skomaker, have you all your tools, a good rubbing-pin, a good stopper, a good dresser, your [100 four sorts of awls, and your two balls of wax, your paring knife, your hand-and-thumb-leathers, and good St. Hugh's bones to smooth up your work ? 104

Lacy. Yaw, yaw ; be niet vorveard. Ik hab al de dingen voour mack skoees groot and cleane.[7]

Firk. Ha, ha ! Good master, hire him ; he 'll make me laugh so that I shall work more in mirth than I can in earnest.

Eyre. Hear ye, friend, have ye any skill in [110 the mystery[8] of cordwainers ?

Lacy. Ik weet niet wat yow seg ; ich verstaw you niet.[9]

Firk. Why, thus, man : [*Imitating by ges-* [114 *ture a shoemaker at work.*] Ich verste u niet, quoth 'a.

Lacy. Yaw, yaw, yaw ; ick can dat wel doen.[10]

Firk. Yaw, yaw ! He speaks yawing like a jackdaw that gapes to be fed with cheese-curds. Oh, he 'll give a villanous pull at a [120 can of double-beer ; but Hodge and I have the vantage, we must drink first, because we are the eldest journeymen.

Eyre. What is thy name ?

Lacy. Hans — Hans Meulter. 125

Eyre. Give me thy hand ; th' art welcome. — Hodge, entertain him ; Firk, bid him welcome ; come, Hans. Run, wife, bid your maids, your trullibubs,[11] make ready my fine men's breakfasts. To him, Hodge ! 130

Hodge. Hans, th' art welcome ; use thyself friendly, for we are good fellows ; if not, thou shalt be fought with, wert thou bigger than a giant.

Firk. Yea, and drunk with, wert thou Gar- [135 gantua. My master keeps no cowards, I tell thee. — Ho, boy, bring him an heel-block, here 's a new journeyman.

[*Enter Boy.*]

Lacy. O, ich wersto you ; ich moet een halve dossen cans betaelen ; here, boy, nempt dis skill-ing, tap eens freelicke.[12] [*Exit Boy.*] 141

Eyre. Quick, snipper-snapper, away ! Firk, scour thy throat ; thou shalt wash it with Castilian liquor.

[*Enter Boy.*]

Come, my last of the fives, give me a can. Have to thee, Hans ; here, Hodge ; here, Firk ; [146 drink, you mad Greeks, and work like true Trojans, and pray for Simon Eyre, the shoemaker. — Here, Hans, and th' art welcome.

Firk. Lo, dame, you would have lost a good fellow that will teach us to laugh. This [151 beer came hopping in well.

Marg. Simon, it is almost seven.

Eyre. Is 't so, Dame Clapper-dudgeon ?[13] Is 't seven a clock, and my men's breakfast not ready ? Trip and go, you sous'd conger,[14] [156 away ! Come, you mad hyperboreans ; follow me, Hodge ; follow me, Hans ; come after, my fine Firk ; to work, to work a while, and then to breakfast. *Exit.*

Firk. Soft ! Yaw, yaw, good Hans, though [161 my master have no more wit but to call you afore me, I am not so foolish to go behind you, I being the elder journeyman. *Exeunt.*

SCENE IV.[15]

[*Halloaing within.*] *Enter* WARNER *and* HAM-MON, *like Hunters.*

Ham. Cousin, beat every brake, the game 's not far,

---

[1] The bones of St. Hugh were supposed to have been made into shoemaker's tools.
[2] Dutchman.
[3] A dish of different hashed meats. The word is sometimes used contemptuously of a versatile person, but is applied to Margery without much appropriateness.
[4] *Good-day, master, and your wife too.*
[5] An oath.
[6] *Yes, yes, I am a shoemaker.*
[7] *Yes, yes ; be not afraid. I have everything to make boots big and little.*
[8] Trade.
[9] *I don't know what you say ; I don't understand you.*
[10] *Yes, yes ; I can do that well.* [11] Slatterns.
[12] *O, I understand you ; I must pay for half-a-dozen cans ; here, boy, take this shilling, tap once freely.*
[13] Slang for beggar.
[14] Conger-eel. [15] A field near Old Ford.

This way with winged feet he fled from death,
Whilst the pursuing hounds, scenting his steps,
Find out his highway to destruction.
Besides, the miller's boy told me even now, 5
He saw him take soil,[1] and he halloaed him,
Affirming him to have been so embost [2]
That long he could not hold.
Warn. If it be so,
'T is best we trace these meadows by Old Ford.

[*A noise of* Hunters *within. Enter a Boy.*]

Ham. How now, boy? Where 's the deer?
speak, saw'st thou him? 11
Boy. O yea; I saw him leap through a hedge,
and then over a ditch, then at my lord mayor's
pale, over he skipt me, and in he went me, and
" holla " the hunters cried, and " there, [15
boy; there, boy! " But there he is, a' mine
honesty.
Ham. Boy, Godamercy. Cousin, let 's away;
I hope we shall find better sport to-day. 18
Exeunt.

SCENE V.[3]

[*Hunting within.*] *Enter* ROSE *and* SYBIL.

Rose. Why, Sybil, wilt thou prove a forester?
Sybil. Upon some, no. Forester? Go by; no,
faith, mistress. The deer came running into
the barn through the orchard and over the
pale; I wot well, I lookt as pale as a new cheese
to see him. But whip, says Goodman Pin- [6
close, up with his flail, and our Nick with a
prong, and down he fell, and they upon him,
and I upon them. By my troth, we had such
sport; and in the end we ended him; his throat
we cut, flay'd him, unhorn'd him, and my [11
lord mayor shall eat of him anon, when he
comes. *Horns sound within.*
Rose. Hark, hark, the hunters come; y' are
best take heed,
They 'll have a saying to you for this deed. 15

Enter HAMMON, WARNER, Huntsmen, *and*
Boy.

Ham. God save you, fair ladies.
Sybil. Ladies! O gross! [4]
Warn. Came not a buck this way?
Rose. No, but two does.
Ham. And which way went they? Faith,
we 'll hunt at those.
Sybil. At those? Upon some, no. When, can
you tell?
Warn. Upon some, ay.
Sybil. Good Lord!
Warn. Wounds! [5] Then farewell! 20
Ham. Boy, which way went he?
Boy. This way, sir, he ran.
Ham. This way he ran indeed, fair Mistress
Rose;
Our game was lately in your orchard seen.
Warn. Can you advise, which way he took
his flight?
Sybil. Follow your nose; his horns will guide
you right. 25

[1] Cover.
[2] Exhausted.
[3] The garden at Old Ford.
[4] Stupid.
[5] An oath.

Warn. Th' art a mad wench.
Sybil. O, rich!
Rose. Trust me, not I.
It is not like that the wild forest-deer
Would come so near to places of resort;
You are deceiv'd, he fled some other way.
Warn. Which way, my sugar-candy, can
you shew? 30
Sybil. Come up, good honeysops, upon some,
no.
Rose. Why do you stay, and not pursue your
game?
Sybil. I 'll hold my life, their hunting-nags
be lame.
Ham. A deer more dear is found within this
place.
Rose. But not the deer, sir, which you had
in chase. 35
Ham. I chas'd the deer, but this dear chaseth
me.
Rose. The strangest hunting that ever I see.
But where 's your park? *She offers to go away.*
Ham. 'T is here: O stay!
Rose. Impale me, and then I will not stray.
Warn. They wrangle, wench; we are more
kind than they. 40
Sybil. What kind of hart is that dear heart
you seek?
Warn. A hart, dear heart.
Sybil. Who ever saw the like?
Rose. To lose your heart, is 't possible you
can?
Ham. My heart is lost.
Rose. Alack, good gentleman!
Ham. This poor lost heart would I wish you
might find. 45
Rose. You, by such luck, might prove your
hart a hind.
Ham. Why Luck had horns, so have I heard
some say.
Rose. Now, God, an 't be his will, send Luck
into your way.

Enter the LORD MAYOR *and* Servants.

L. Mayor. What, Master Hammon? Welcome
to Old Ford!
Sybil. Gods pittikins,[6] hands off, sir! Here 's
my lord. 50
L. Mayor. I hear you had ill luck, and lost
your game.
Ham. 'T is true, my lord.
L. Mayor. I am sorry for the same.
What gentleman is this?
Ham. My brother-in-law.
L. Mayor. Y' are welcome both; sith For-
tune offers you
Into my hands, you shall not part from hence,
Until you have refresht your wearied limbs. 56
Go, Sybil, cover the board! You shall be guest
To no good cheer, but even a hunter's feast.
Ham. I thank your lordship. —Cousin, on
my life,
For our lost venison I shall find a wife. 60
Exeunt [all but MAYOR].
L. Mayor. In, gentlemen; I 'll not be absent
long. —

[6] By God's pity.

This Hammon is a proper gentleman,
A citizen by birth, fairly allied ;
How fit an husband were he for my girl !
Well, I will in, and do the best I can,　　65
To match my daughter to this gentleman.
　　　　　　　　　　　　　　　　　　Exit.

ACT III

Scene I.[1]

Enter Lacy [*as* Hans], Skipper, Hodge, *and*
　　　　　　　　Firk.

Skip. *Ick sal yow wat seggen, Hans ; dis skip
dat comen from Candy, is all vol, by Got's sacrament, van sugar, civet, almonds, cambrick, end
alle dingen, towsand towsand ding. Nempt it,
Hans, nempt it vor v meester. Daer be de bils* [5
*van laden. Your meester Simon Eyre sal hae good
copen. Wat seggen yow, Hans ?*[2]
Firk. *Wat seggen de reggen de copen, slopen*
—laugh, Hodge, laugh !　　9
Hans. *Mine liever broder Firk, bringt Meester
Eyre tot det signe vn Swannekin ; daer sal yow
finde dis skipper end me. Wat seggen yow, broder
Firk ? Doot it, Hodge.*[3] Come, skipper.
　　　　　　　　　　　　　　　　　　Exeunt.
Firk. Bring him, quoth you ? Here 's no [14
knavery, to bring my master to buy a ship
worth the lading of two or three hundred
thousand pounds. Alas, that 's nothing ; a trifle,
a bauble, Hodge.
Hodge. The truth is, Firk, that the merchant
owner of the ship dares not shew his head, [20
and therefore this skipper that deals for him,
for the love he bears to Hans, offers my master
Eyre a bargain in the commodities. He shall
have a reasonable day of payment ; he may sell [24
the wares by that time, and be an huge gainer
himself.
Firk. Yea, but can my fellow Hans lend my
master twenty porpentines as an earnest penny ?
Hodge. Portuguese, thou wouldst say ; here [29
they be, Firk ; hark, they jingle in my pocket
like St. Mary Overy's bells.

Enter Eyre *and his* Wife [Margery].

Firk. Mum, here comes my dame and my
master. She 'll scold, on my life, for loitering
this Monday ; but all 's one, let them all say
what they can, Monday 's our holiday.　　35

Marg. You sing, Sir Sauce, but I beshrew your heart.
　I fear, for this your singing we shall smart.

Firk. Smart for me, dame ; why, dame, why ?
Hodge. Master, I hope you 'll not suffer my
dame to take down your journeymen.　　40

---

[1] A room in Eyre's house.
[2] I'll tell you what, Hans ; this ship that is come from
Candia, is quite full, by God's sacrament, of sugar, civet,
almonds, cambric, and all things ; a thousand, thousand
things. Take it, Hans, take it for your master. There
are the bills of lading. Your master, Simon Eyre, shall
have a good bargain. What say you, Hans ?
[3] My dear brother Firk, bring Master Eyre to the sign
of the Swan ; there shall you find the skipper and me.
What say you, brother Firk. Do it, Hodge.

Firk. If she take me down, I 'll take her up ?
yea, and take her down too, a button-hole lower.
Eyre. Peace, Firk ; not I, Hodge ; by the
life of Pharaoh, by the Lord of Ludgate, by
this beard, every hair whereof I value at a [45
king's ransom, she shall not meddle with you. —
Peace, you bombast-cotton-candle-quean ; away,
queen of clubs ; quarrel not with me and my
men, with me and my fine Firk ; I 'll firk you,
if you do.　　50
Marg. Yea, yea, man, you may use me as
you please ; but let that pass.
Eyre. Let it pass, let it vanish away ; peace !
Am I not Simon Eyre ? Are not these my [54
brave men, brave shoemakers, all gentlemen of
the gentle craft ? Prince am I none, yet am I
nobly born, as being the sole son of a shoemaker. Away, rubbish ! vanish, melt ; melt ;
like kitchen-stuff.　　59
Marg. Yea, yea, 't is well ; I must be call'd
rubbish, kitchen-stuff, for a sort[4] of knaves.
Firk. Nay, dame, you shall not weep and
wail in woe for me. Master, I 'll stay no
longer ; here 's an inventory of my shop-tools.
Adieu, master ; Hodge, farewell.　　65
Hodge. Nay, stay, Firk ; thou shalt not go
alone.
Marg. I pray, let them go ; there be moe
maids than Mawkin, more men than Hodge,
and more fools than Firk.　　70
Firk. Fools ? Nails ! if I tarry now, I would
my guts might be turn'd to shoe-thread.
Hodge. And if I stay, I pray God I may be
turn'd to a Turk, and set in Finsbury[5] for boys
to shoot at. — Come, Firk.　　75
Eyre. Stay, my fine knaves, you arms of my
trade, you pillars of my profession. What,
shall a tittle-tattle's words make you forsake
Simon Eyre ? — Avaunt, kitchen-stuff ! Rip,
you brown-bread Tannikin ; out of my sight !
Move me not ! Have not I ta'en you from sell- [81
ing tripes in Eastcheap, and set you in my shop,
and made you hail-fellow with Simon Eyre,
the shoemaker ? And now do you deal thus [84
with my journeymen ? Look, you powder-beef-
quean, on the face of Hodge, here 's a face
for a lord.
Firk. And here 's a face for any lady in
Christendom.　　89
Eyre. Rip, you chitterling, avaunt ! Boy, bid
the tapster of the Boar's Head fill me a dozen
cans of beer for my journeymen.
Firk. A dozen cans ? O, brave ! Hodge, now
I 'll stay.
Eyre. [*in a low voice to the Boy.*] An the [95
knave fills any more than two, he pays for
them. [*Exit Boy. Aloud.*] — A dozen cans of
beer for my journeymen. [*Re-enter Boy.*] Here,
you mad Mesopotamians, wash your livers [99
with this liquor. Where be the odd ten ? — No
more, Madge, no more. — Well said.[6] Drink
and to work ! — What work dost thou, Hodge ?
What work ?

---

[4] Set.
[5] Finsbury was a famous practising ground for arch
ery.
　　　　　　　　　　[6] Well done.

Hodge. I am a making a pair of shoes for my lord mayor's daughter, Mistress Rose.   105
Firk. And I a pair of shoes for Sybil, my lord's maid. I deal with her.
Eyre. Sybil? Fie, defile not thy fine workmanly fingers with the feet of kitchenstuff [109 and basting-ladles. Ladies of the court, fine ladies, my lads, commit their feet to our apparelling; put gross work to Hans. Yark[1] and seam, yark and seam!
Firk. For yarking and seaming let me alone, an I come to 't.   115
Hodge. Well, master, all this is from the bias.[2] Do you remember the ship my fellow Hans told you of? The skipper and he are both drinking at the Swan. Here be the Portu-[119 guese to give earnest. If you go through with it, you cannot choose but be a lord at least.
Firk. Nay, dame, if my master prove not a lord, and you a lady, hang me.
Marg. Yea, like enough, if you may loiter and tipple thus.   125
Firk. Tipple, dame? No, we have been bargaining with Skellum Skanderbag:[3] can you Dutch spreaken for a ship of silk Cyprus, laden with sugar-candy.   129

Enter Boy *with a velvet coat and an Alderman's gown.* EYRE *puts them on.*

Eyre. Peace, Firk; silence, Tittle-tattle! Hodge, I 'll go through with it. Here 's a sealring, and I have sent for a guarded gown[4] and a damask cassock. See where it comes; look here, Maggy; help me, Firk; apparel me, Hodge; silk and satin, you mad Philistines, [135 silk and satin.
Firk. Ha, ha, my master will be as proud as a dog in a doublet, all in beaten[5] damask and velvet.   139
Eyre. Softly, Firk, for rearing[6] of the nap, and wearing threadbare my garments. How dost thou like me, Firk? How do I look, my fine Hodge?
Hodge. Why, now you look like yourself, master. I warrant you, there 's few in the [145 city but will give you the wall,[7] and come upon you with[8] the right worshipful.
Firk. Nails, my master looks like a threadbare cloak new turn'd and drest. Lord, Lord, [149 to see what good raiment doth! Dame, dame, are you not enamoured?
Eyre. How say'st thou, Maggy, am I not brisk? Am I not fine?
Marg. Fine? By my troth, sweetheart, very fine! By my troth, I never likt thee so well [155 in my life, sweetheart; but let that pass. I warrant, there be many women in the city have not such handsome husbands, but only for their apparel; but let that pass too.   159

1 Prepare.   2 Beside the point.
3 German: Schelm, a scoundrel. Skanderbag, or Scander Beg (*i. e.* Lord Alexander), a Turkish name for John Kastriota, the Albanian hero, who freed his country from the yoke of the Turks (1443–1467). (Warnke and Proescholdt.)
4 A robe ornamented with guards or facings.
5 Stamped.   7 Yield precedence.
6 Ruffling.   8 Address you as.

Re-enter HANS *and* SKIPPER.

Hans. Godden day, mester. Dis be de skipper dat heb de skip van marchandice; de commodity ben good; nempt it, master, nempt it.[9]
Eyre. Godamercy, Hans; welcome, skipper. Where lies this ship of merchandise?   164
Skip. De skip ben in revere; dor be van sugar, civet, almonds, cambrick, and a towsand, towsand tings, gotz sacrament; nempt it, mester: ye sal heb good copen.[10]
Firk. To him, master! O sweet master! [169 O sweet wares! Prunes, almonds, sugar-candy, carrot-roots, turnips, O brave fatting meat! Let not a man buy a nutmeg but yourself.
Eyre. Peace, Firk! Come, skipper, I 'll go aboard with you. — Hans, have you made him drink?   175
Skip. Yaw, yaw, ic heb veale gedrunck.[11]
Eyre. Come, Hans, follow me. Skipper, thou shalt have my countenance in the city.
                                        Exeunt.
Firk. Yaw heb veale gedrunck, quoth 'a. They may well be called butter-boxes, when [180 they drink fat veal and thick beer too. But come, dame, I hope you 'll chide us no more.
Marg. No, faith, Firk; no, perdy,[12] Hodge. I do feel honour creep upon me, and which is more, a certain rising in my flesh; but let that pass.   186
Firk. Rising in your flesh do you feel, say you? Ay, you may be with child, but why should not my master feel a rising in his flesh, having a gown and a gold ring on? But you are such a shrew, you 'll soon pull him down. 191
Marg. Ha, ha! prithee, peace! Thou mak'st my worship laugh; but let that pass. Come, I 'll go in; Hodge, prithee, go before me; Firk, follow me.   195
Firk. Firk doth follow: Hodge, pass out in state.   *Exeunt.*

SCENE II.[13]

Enter the EARL OF LINCOLN *and* DODGER.

Linc. How now, good Dodger, what 's the news in France?
Dodger. My lord, upon the eighteenth day of May
The French and English were prepar'd to fight;
Each side with eager fury gave the sign
Of a most hot encounter. Five long hours   5
Both armies fought together; at the length
The lot of victory fell on our side.
Twelve thousand of the Frenchmen that day died,
Four thousand English, and no man of name
But Captain Hyam and young Ardington,   10
Two gallant gentlemen, I knew them well.

9 Good day, master. This is the skipper that has the ship of merchandise; the commodity is good; take it, master, take it.
10 The ship lies in the river; there are sugar, civet, almonds, cambric, and a thousand thousand things. By God's sacrament, take it, master; you shall have a good bargain.
11 Yes, yes, I have drunk well.
12 Fr. Par Dieu.
13 London: a room in Lincoln's house.

Linc. But Dodger, prithee, tell me, in this
    fight
How did my cousin Lacy bear himself?
Dodger. My lord, your cousin Lacy was not
    there.
Linc. Not there?
Dodger.   No, my good lord.
Linc.   Sure, thou mistakest. 15
I saw him shipp'd, and a thousand eyes beside
Were witnesses of the farewells which he gave,
When I, with weeping eyes, bid him adieu.
Dodger, take heed.
Dodger.   My lord, I am advis'd [1]
That what I spake is true: to prove it so,   20
His cousin Askew, that suppli'd his place,
Sent me for him from France, that secretly
He might convey himself thither.
Linc.   Is 't even so?
Dares he so carelessly venture his life
Upon the indignation of a king?   25
Has he despis'd my love, and spurn'd those
    favours
Which I with prodigal hand pour'd on his head?
He shall repent his rashness with his soul;
Since of my love he makes no estimate,
I'll make him wish he had not known my
    hate.   30
Thou hast no other news?
Dodger.   None else, my lord.
Linc. None worse I know thou hast. — Pro-
    cure the king
To crown his giddy brows with ample honours,
Send him chief colonel, and all my hope   34
Thus to be dash'd! But 't is in vain to grieve,
One evil cannot a worse relieve.
Upon my life, I have found out his plot;
That old dog, Love, that fawn'd upon him so,
Love to that puling girl, his fair-cheek'd Rose,
The lord mayor's daughter, hath distracted
    him,   40
And in the fire of that love's lunacy
Hath he burnt up himself, consum'd his credit,
Lost the king's love, yea, and I fear, his life,
Only to get a wanton to his wife,
Dodger, it is so.
Dodger.   I fear so, my good lord.   45
Linc. It is so — nay, sure it cannot be!
I am at my wits' end, Dodger!
Dodger.   Yea, my lord.
Linc. Thou art acquainted with my neph-
    ew's haunts,
Spend this gold for thy pains; go seek him out.
Watch at my lord mayor's — there if he live, 50
Dodger, thou shalt be sure to meet with him.
Prithee, be diligent.— Lacy, thy name
Liv'd once in honour, now 't is dead in shame.—
Be circumspect.   *Exit.*
Dodger. I warrant you, my lord.   *Exit.*

Scene III.[2]

Enter the L. Mayor *and* Master Scott.

L. Mayor. Good Master Scott, I have been
    bold with you,

[2] Certainly informed.
[3] London: a room in the Lord Mayor's house.

To be a witness to a wedding-knot
Betwixt young Master Hammon and my daugh-
    ter.
O, stand aside; see where the lovers come.

Enter Master Hammon *and* Rose.

Rose. Can it be possible you love me so?   5
No, no, within those eyeballs I espy
Apparent likelihoods of flattery.
Pray now, let go my hand.
Ham.   Sweet Mistress Rose,
Misconstrue not my words, nor misconceive
Of my affection, whose devoted soul   10
Swears that I love thee dearer than my heart.
Rose. As dear as your own heart? I judge it
    right,
Men love their hearts best when th' are out of
    sight.
Ham. I love you, by this hand.
Rose.   Yet hands off now!
If flesh be frail, how weak and frail 's your vow!
Ham. Then by my life I swear.
Rose.   Then do not brawl; 16
One quarrel loseth wife and life and all.
Is not your meaning thus?
Ham.   In faith, you jest.
Rose. Love loves to sport; therefore leave
    love, y' are best.
L. Mayor. What? square[3] they, Master
    Scott?
Scott. Sir, never doubt,   20
Lovers are quickly in, and quickly out.
Ham. Sweet Rose, be not so strange in fancy-
    ing me.
Nay, never turn aside, shun not my sight:
I am not grown so fond, to fond[4] my love
On any that shall quit it with disdain;   25
If you will love me, so; — if not, farewell.
L. Mayor. Why, how now, lovers, are you
    both agreed?
Ham. Yes, faith, my lord.
L. Mayor. 'T is well, give me your hand,
Give me yours, daughter. — How now, both pull
    back!
What means this, girl?
Rose.   I mean to live a maid. 30
Ham. (*Aside.*) But not to die one; pause, ere
    that be said.
L. Mayor. Will you still cross me, still be
    obstinate?
Ham. Nay, chide her not, my lord, for doing
    well;
If she can live an happy virgin's life,
'T is far more blessed than to be a wife.   35
Rose. Say, sir, I cannot: I have made a vow,
Whoever be my husband, 't is not you.
L. Mayor. Your tongue is quick; but Master
    Hammon, know,
I bade you welcome to another end.
Ham. What, would you have me pule and
    pine and pray,   40
With "lovely lady," "mistress of my heart,"
"Pardon your servant," and the rhymer play,
Railing on Cupid and his tyrant's-dart;
Or shall I undertake some martial spoil,

[3] Quarrel.   [4] Found, set; a pun upon fond.

Wearing your glove at tourney and at tilt,   45
And tell how many gallants I unhors'd —
Sweet, will this pleasure you?
Rose.   Yea, when wilt begin?
What, love rhymes, man? Fie on that deadly
    sin!
  L. Mayor. If you will have her, I 'll make
    her agree.
  Ham. Enforced love is worse than hate to me.
[*Aside.*] There is a wench keeps shop in the   51
To her will I — it is not wealth I seek.   *Old Change,*
I have enough — and will prefer her love
Before the world. — [*Aloud.*] My good lord
    mayor, adieu,
Old love for me, I have no luck with new.
                                    Exit.
  L. Mayor. Now, mammet,[1] you have well
    behav'd yourself,   56
But you shall curse your coyness if I live. —
Who 's within there? See you convey your mis-
    tress
Straight to th' Old Ford! I 'll keep you
    straight enough,
Fore God, I would have sworn the puling girl
Would willingly accepted Hammon's love;   61
But banish him, my thoughts! — Go, minion,
    in!   *Exit* ROSE.
Now tell me, Master Scott, would you have
    thought
That Master Simon Eyre, the shoemaker,
Had been of wealth to buy such merchandise?
  Scott. 'T was well, my lord, your honour and
    myself   66
Grew partners with him; for your bills of lading
Shew that Eyre's gains in one commodity
Rise at the least to full three thousand pound
Besides like gain in other merchandise.   70
  L. Mayor. Well, he shall spend some of his
    thousands now,
For I have sent for him to the Guildhall.

Enter EYRE.

See, where he comes. — Good morrow, Master
    Eyre.
  Eyre. Poor Simon Eyre, my lord, your shoe-
    maker.
  L. Mayor. Well, well, it likes[2] yourself to
    term you so.   75

Enter DODGER.

Now Master Dodger, what 's the news with
    you?
  Dodger. I 'd gladly speak in private to your
    honour.
  L. Mayor. You shall, you shall. — Master
    Eyre and Master Scott,
I have some business with this gentleman;
I pray, let me entreat you to walk before   80
To the Guildhall; I 'll follow presently.
Master Eyre, I hope ere noon to call you sheriff.
  Eyre. I would not care, my lord, if you might
    call me
King of Spain. — Come, Master Scott.
                        [*Exeunt* EYRE *and* SCOTT.]

  L. Mayor. Now, Master Dodger, what 's the
    news you bring?   85
  Dodger. The Earl of Lincoln by me greets
    your lordship,
And earnestly requests you, if you can,
Inform him where his nephew Lacy keeps.
  L. Mayor. Is not his nephew Lacy now in
    France?
  Dodger. No, I assure your Lordship, but dis-
    guis'd   90
Lurks here in London.
  L. Mayor.   London? Is 't even so?
It may be; but upon my faith and soul,
I know not where he lives, or whether he lives:
So tell my Lord of Lincoln. — Lurk in London?
Well, Master Dodger, you perhaps may start
    him;   95
Be but the means to rid him into France,
I 'll give you a dozen angels[3] for your pains:
So much I love his honour, hate his nephew.
And, prithee, so inform thy lord from me.
  Dodger. I take my leave.   *Exit* DODGER.
  L. Mayor. Farewell, good Master Dodger.
Lacy in London? I dare pawn my life,   101
My daughter knows thereof, and for that cause
Deni'd young Master Hammon in his love.
Well, I am glad I sent her to Old Ford.
Gods Lord, 't is late! to Guildhall I must hie;
I know my brethren stay[4] my company. *Exit.* 106

SCENE IV.[5]

Enter FIRK, *Eyre's wife* [MARGERY, LACY *as*]
    HANS, *and* ROGER.

  Marg. Thou goest too fast for me, Roger. O,
    Firk.
  Firk. Ay, forsooth.
  Marg. I pray thee, run — do you hear? — run
to Guildhall, and learn if my husband, Mas- [5
ter Eyre, will take that worshipful vocation of
Master Sheriff upon him. Hie thee, good Firk.
  Firk. Take it? Well, I go; an he should not
take it, Firk swears to forswear him. Yes, forsooth, I go to Guildhall.   10
  Marg. Nay, when? Thou art too compendious and tedious.
  Firk. O rare, your excellence is full of eloquence; how like a new cart-wheel my dame
speaks, and she looks like an old musty ale- [15
bottle[6] going to scalding.
  Marg. Nay, when? Thou wilt make me melancholy.
  Firk. God forbid your worship should fall
into that humour; — I run.   *Exit.* [20
  Marg. Let me see now, Roger and Hans.
  Hodge. Ay, forsooth, dame — mistress, I
should say, but the old term so sticks to the
roof of my mouth, I can hardly lick it off.
  Marg. Even what thou wilt, good Roger; [25
dame is a fair name for any honest Christian;
but let that pass. How dost thou, Hans?
  Hans. Mee tanck you, vro.[7]
  Marg. Well, Hans and Roger, you see, God
hath blest your master, and, perdy, if ever [30

----

1 *Puppet, doll.*   2 *Pleases.*

3 Coins worth about 10s. each.   4 Wait for.
5 London: a room in Eyre's house.
6 Ale-kegs made of wood.   7 *I thank you, mistress!*

he comes to be Master Sheriff of London
— as we are all mortal — you shall see, I will
have some odd thing or other in a corner for
your: I will not be your back-friend ;[1] but let
that pass. Hans, pray thee, tie my shoe.   35
Hans. *Yaw, ic sal, vro.*[2]
Marg. Roger, thou know'st the length of my
foot; as it is none of the biggest, so I thank
God, it is handsome enough; prithee, let me
have a pair of shoes made, cork, good Roger, [40
wooden heel too.
Hodge. You shall.
Marg. Art thou acquainted with never a
farthingale-maker, nor a French hood-maker ?
I must enlarge my bum, ha, ha ! How shall [45
I look in a hood, I wonder ! Perdy, oddly I
think.
Hodge. [*Aside.*] As a cat out of a pillory. —
Very well, I warrant you, mistress.
Marg. Indeed, all flesh is grass ; and, [50
Roger, canst thou tell where I may buy a good
hair ?
Hodge. Yes, forsooth, at the poulterer's in
Gracious Street.
Marg. Thou art an ungracious wag : perdy, [55
I mean a false hair for my periwig.
Hodge. Why, mistress, the next time I cut
my beard, you shall have the shavings of it ;
but they are all true hairs.
Marg. It is very hot, I must get me a fan [60
or else a mask.
Hodge. [*Aside.*] So you had need, to hide
your wicked face.
Marg. Fie, upon it, how costly this world's
calling is ; perdy, but that it is one of the won- [65
derful works of God, I would not deal with it.
— Is not Firk come yet ? Hans, be not so sad,
let it pass and vanish, as my husband's worship
says.
Hans. *Ick bin vrolicke, lot see yow soo.*[3]   70
Hodge. Mistress, will you drink[4] a pipe of
tobacco ?
Marg. Oh, fie upon it, Roger, perdy ! These
filthy tobacco-pipes are the most idle slavering
baubles that ever I felt. Out upon it ! God [75
bless us, men look not like men that use them.

Enter RALPH, *being lame.*

Hodge. What, fellow Ralph ? Mistress, look
here, Jane's husband ! Why, how now, lame ?
Hans, make much of him, he 's a brother of our
trade, a good workman, and a tall[5] soldier. [80
Hans. You be welcome, broder.
Marg. Perdy, I knew him not. How dost
thou, good Ralph ? I am glad to see thee well.
Ralph. I would to God you saw me, dame, as
well
As when I went from London into France.   85
Marg. Trust me, I am sorry, Ralph, to see
thee impotent. Lord, how the wars have made
him sunburnt ! The left leg is not well ; 't was
a fair gift of God the infirmity took not hold a
little higher, considering thou camest from [90
France ; but let that pass.

[1] Faithless friend.
[2] *Yes, I shall, mistress !*
[3] *I am merry ; let 's see you so !*
[4] Smoke.
[5] Brave.

Ralph. I am glad to see you well, and I rejoice
To hear that God hath blest my master so
Since my departure.
Marg. Yea, truly, Ralph, I thank my [95
Maker ; but let that pass.
Hodge. And, sirrah Ralph, what news, what
news in France ?
Ralph. Tell me, good Roger, first, what news
in England ?
How does my Jane ? When didst thou see my
wife ?   100
Where lives my poor heart ? She 'll be poor in-
deed,
Now I want limbs to get whereon to feed.
Hodge. Limbs ? Hast thou not hands, man ?
Thou shalt never see a shoemaker want bread,
though he have but three fingers on a hand. 105
Ralph. Yet all this while I hear not of my
Jane.
Marg. O Ralph, your wife, — perdy, we know
not what 's become of her. She was here a
while, and because she was married, grew more
stately than became her ; I checkt her, and [110
so forth ; away she flung, never returned, nor
said bye nor bah ; and, Ralph, you know, " ka
me, ka thee."[6] And, so as I tell ye —— Roger,
is not Firk come yet ?
Hodge. No, forsooth.   115
Marg. And so, indeed, we heard not of her,
but I hear she lives in London ; but let that
pass. If she had wanted, she might have opened
her case to me or my husband, or to any of my
men ; I am sure, there 's not any of them, [120
perdy, but would have done her good to his
power. Hans, look if Firk be come.
Hans. *Yaw, ik sal, vro.*[7]   *Exit* HANS.
Marg. And so, as I said — but, Ralph, why
dost thou weep ? Thou knowest that naked [125
we came out of our mother's womb, and naked
we must return ; and, therefore, thank God for
all things.
Hodge. No, faith, Jane is a stranger here ; but,
Ralph, pull up a good heart, I know thou [130
hast one. Thy wife, man, is in London ; one told
me, he saw her a while ago very brave[8] and
neat ; we 'll ferret her out, an London hold
her.
Marg. Alas, poor soul, he 's overcome [135
with sorrow ; he does but as I do, weep for the
loss of any good thing. But, Ralph, get thee
in, call for some meat and drink, thou shalt
find me worshipful towards thee.
Ralph. I thank you, dame ; since I want
limbs and lands,   140
I 'll trust to God, my good friends, and my
hands.   *Exit.*

Enter HANS *and* FIRK *running.*

Firk. Run, good Hans ! O Hodge, O mistress !
Hodge, heave up thine ears ; mistress, smug up[9]
your looks ; on with your best apparel ; my
master is chosen, my master is called, nay, [145
condemn'd by the cry of the country to be
sheriff of the city for this famous year now to

[6] Scratch me, and I 'll scratch thee.
[7] *Yes, I shall, dame.*
[8] Fine.
[9] Brighten up.

come. And, time now being, a great many men
in black gowns were askt for their voices and
their hands, and my master had all their [150
fists about his ears presently, and they cried
'Ay, ay, ay, ay,'—and so I came away —
    Wherefore without all other grieve
I do salute you, Mistress Shrieve.[1]

Hans. Yaw, my mester is de groot man, de [155
shrieve.

Hodge. Did not I tell you, mistress? Now I
may boldly say: Good-morrow to your worship.

Marg. Good-morrow, good Roger. I thank [160
you, my good people all. — Firk, hold up thy
hand : here 's a three-penny piece for thy tidings.

Firk. 'T is but three-half-pence, I think.
Yes, 't is three-pence, I smell the rose.[2]   165

Hodge. But, mistress, be rul'd by me, and
do not speak so pulingly.

Firk. 'T is her worship speaks so, and not
she. No, faith, mistress, speak me in the old
key: " To it, Firk ; " " there, good Firk ; " [170
" ply your business, Hodge ; " " Hodge, with a
full mouth ; " " I 'll fill your bellies with good
cheer, till they cry twang."

Enter EYRE *wearing a gold chain.*

Hans. See, myn liever broder, heer compt my
meester.[3]   175

Marg. Welcome home, Master Shrieve ; I
pray God continue you in health and wealth.

Eyre. See here, my Maggy, a chain, a gold
chain for Simon Eyre. I shall make thee a
lady ; here 's a French hood for thee ; on with [180
it, on with it ! dress thy brows with this flap of
a shoulder of mutton,[4] to make thee look
lovely. Where be my fine men? Roger, I 'll
make over my shop and tools to thee; Firk, thou
shalt be the foreman ; Hans, thou shalt have [185
an hundred for twenty.[5] Be as mad knaves as
your master Sim Eyre hath been, and you shall
live to be sheriffs of London. — How dost thou
like me, Margery? Prince am I none, yet [189
am I princely born. Firk, Hodge, and Hans !

All Three. Ay, forsooth, what says your worship, Master Sheriff ?

Eyre. Worship and honour, you Babylonian
knaves, for the gentle craft. But I forgot myself, I am bidden by my lord mayor to din- [195
ner to Old Ford ; he 's gone before, I must after.
Come, Madge, on with your trinkets ! Now, my
true Trojans, my fine Firk, my dapper Hodge,
my honest Hans, some device, some odd crat-
chets, some morris, or such like, for the [200
honour of the gentlemen shoemakers. Meet me
at Old Ford, you know my mind. Come,
Madge, away. Shut up the shop, knaves, and
make holiday.   *Exeunt.*

---

[1] Sheriff.

[2] " The three-farthing silver pieces of Queen Elizabeth had the profile of the sovereign with a rose at the
back of her head." (Dyce.)

[3] See, my dear brothers, here comes my master.

[4] The flap of a hood trimmed with fur or sheep's
wool. (Rhys.)

[5] I. e. for the twenty Portuguese previously lent.

Firk. O rare! O brave ! Come, Hodge; follow me, Hans ;   [206
We 'll be with them for a morris-dance.
                             Exeunt.

SCENE V.[6]

Enter the LORD MAYOR, [ROSE,] EYRE, *his*
wife [MARGERY] *in a French hood*, SYBIL, *and*
other Servants.

L. Mayor. Trust me, you are as welcome to
    Old Ford
As I myself.

Marg.   Truly, I thank your lordship.

L. Mayor. Would our bad cheer were worth
    the thanks you give.

Eyre. Good cheer, my lord mayor, fine cheer !
A fine house, fine walls, all fine and neat.   5

L. Mayor. Now, by my troth, I 'll tell thee,
    Master Eyre,
It does me good, and all my brethren,
That such a madcap fellow as thyself
Is ent'red into our society.

Marg. Ay, but, my lord, he must learn now to
    put on gravity.   10

Eyre. Peace, Maggy, a fig for gravity ! When
I go to Guildhall in my scarlet gown, I 'll look
as demurely as a saint, and speak as gravely as
a justice of peace ; but now I am here at Old
Ford, at my good lord mayor's house, let it [15
go by, vanish, Maggy, I 'll be merry ; away with
flip-flap, these fooleries, these gulleries. What,
honey? Prince am I none, yet am I princely
born. What says my lord mayor ?

L. Mayor. Ha, ha, ha! I had rather than [20
a thousand pound, I had an heart but half so
light as yours.

Eyre. Why, what should I do, my lord ? A
pound of care pays not a dram of debt. Hum,
let 's be merry, whiles we are young ; old age, [25
sack and sugar will steal upon us, ere we be
aware.

THE FIRST THREE MEN'S SONG[7]

O the month of May, the merry month of May,
  So frolick, so gay, and so green, so green, so green !
O, and then did I unto my true love say :   30
  " Sweet Peg, thou shalt be my summer's queen !

" Now the nightingale, the pretty nightingale,
  The sweetest singer in all the forest's choir,
Entreats thee, sweet Peggy, to hear thy true love's tale ;
  Lo, yonder she sitteth, her breast against a brier.   35

" But O, I spy the cuckoo, the cuckoo, the cuckoo ;
  See where she sitteth : come away, my joy ;
Come away, I prithee : I do not like the cuckoo
  Should sing where my Peggy and I kiss and toy."

O the month of May, the merry month of May,   40
  So frolick, so gay, and so green, so green, so green !
And then did I unto my true love say :
  " Sweet Peg, thou shalt be my summer's queen ! "

L. Mayor. It 's well done. Mistress Eyre, pray,
    give good counsel
To my daughter.   45

---

[6] A room at Old Ford.

[7] A catch for three voices. It is by no means certain
at what point in the play the songs were introduced.

Marg. I hope, Mistress Rose will have the
grace to take nothing that's bad.
L. Mayor. Pray God she do; for i' faith,
Mistress Eyre,
I would bestow upon that peevish girl
A thousand marks more than I mean to give her
Upon condition she'd be rul'd by me.   51
The ape still crosseth me. There came of late
A proper gentleman of fair revenues,
Whom gladly I would call son-in-law:
But my fine cockney would have none of him.
You'll prove a coxcomb for it, ere you die: 56
A courtier, or no man, must please your eye.
Eyre. Be rul'd, sweet Rose: th'art ripe
for a man. Marry not with a boy that has no
more hair on his face than thou hast on thy [60
cheeks. A courtier, wash, go by, stand not upon
pishery-pashery: those silken fellows are but
painted images, outsides, outsides, Rose; their
inner linings are torn. No, my fine mouse, marry
me with a gentleman grocer like my lord [65
mayor, your father; a grocer is a sweet trade:
plums, plums. Had I a son or daughter should
marry out of the generation and blood of the
shoemakers, he should pack. What, the gentle
trade is a living for a man through Europe,
through the world.   71
            A noise within of a tabor and a pipe.
L. Mayor. What noise is this?
Eyre. O my lord mayor, a crew of good fellows that for love to your honour are come
hither with a morris-dance. Come in, my Mesopotamians, cheerily.   76

Enter HODGE, HANS, RALPH, FIRK, *and other*
Shoemakers, *in a morris; after a little dancing, the* LORD MAYOR *speaks.*

L. Mayor. Master Eyre, are all these shoe-
makers?
Eyre. All cordwainers, my good lord mayor.
Rose. [*Aside.*] How like my Lacy looks yond
shoemaker!
Hans. [*Aside.*] O that I durst but speak unto
my love!   80
L. Mayor. Sybil, go fetch some wine to make
these drink. You are all welcome.
All. We thank your lordship.
            ROSE *takes a cup of wine and goes*
                                    to HANS.
Rose. For his sake whose fair shape thou re-
present'st,
Good friend I drink to thee.   85
Hans. *Ic bedancke, good frister.*[1]
Marg. I see, Mistress Rose, you do not
want judgment; you have drunk to the proper-
est man I keep.
Firk. Here be some have done their parts to
be as proper as he.   91
L. Mayor. Well, urgent business calls me
back to London.
Good fellows, first go in and taste our cheer;
And to make merry as you homeward go,
Spend these two angels in beer at Stratford-
    Bow.   95
Eyre. To these two, my mad lads, Sim Eyre

            [1] *I thank you, good maid!*

adds another; then cheerily, Firk; tickle
it, Hans, and all for the honour of shoemakers.
                        All go dancing out.
L. Mayor. Come, Master Eyre, let's have
your company.   *Exeunt.*
Rose. Sybil, what shall I do?   100
Sybil. Why, what's the matter?
Rose. That Hans the shoemaker is my love
Lacy,
Disguis'd in that attire to find me out.
How should I find the means to speak with
him?   104
Sybil. What, mistress, never fear; I dare
venture my maidenhead to nothing, and that's
great odds, that Hans the Dutchman, when
we come to London, shall not only see and speak
with you, but in spite of all your father's poli-
cies steal you away and marry you. Will not
this please you?   111
Rose. Do this, and ever be assured of my love.
Sybil. Away, then, and follow your father to
London, lest your absence cause him to suspect
something: 115
To-morrow, if my counsel be obey'd,
I'll bind you prentice to the gentle trade.
                            [*Exeunt.*]

ACT IV

SCENE I.[2]

JANE *in a Seamster's shop, working; enter* Mas-
    ter HAMMON, *muffled: he stands aloof.*

Ham. Yonder's the shop, and there my fair
love sits.
She's fair and lovely, but she is not mine.
O, would she were! Thrice have I courted her,
Thrice hath my hand been moist'ned with her
hand,
Whilst my poor famisht eyes do feed on that 5
Which made them famish. I am unfortunate:
I still love one, yet nobody loves me.
I muse in other men what women see
That I so want! Fine Mistress Rose was coy,
And this too curious![3] Oh, no, she is chaste, 10
And for she thinks me wanton, she denies
To cheer my cold heart with her sunny eyes.
How prettily she works! Oh pretty hand!
Oh happy work! It doth me good to stand
Unseen to see her. Thus I oft have stood   15
In frosty evenings, a light burning by her,
Enduring biting cold, only to eye her.
One only look hath seem'd as rich to me
As a king's crown; such is love's lunacy.
Muffled I'll pass along, and by that try   20
Whether she know me.
Jane.   Sir, what is't you buy?
What is't you lack, sir, calico, or lawn,
Fine cambric shirts, or bands, what will you
buy?
Ham. [*Aside.*] That which thou wilt not sell.
    Faith, yet I'll try: —
How do you sell this handkerchief?
Jane.   Good cheap. 25

            [2] A street in London.   [3] Fastidious.

Ham. And how these ruffs ?
Jane.   Cheap too.
Ham.   And how this band ?
Jane. Cheap too.   [hand ?
Ham.   All cheap; how sell you then this
Jane. My hands are not to be sold.
Ham.   To be given then !
Nay, faith, I come to buy.
Jane.   But none knows when.
Ham. Good sweet, leave work a little while ;
    let 's play.   30
Jane. I cannot live by keeping holiday.
Ham. I 'll pay you for the time which shall
    be lost.
Jane. With me you shall not be at so much
    cost.
Ham. Look, how you wound this cloth, so you
    wound me.
Jane. It may be so.
Ham.   'T is so.
Jane.   What remedy ?   35
Ham. Nay, faith, you are too coy.
Jane.   Let go my hand.
Ham. I will do any task at your command,
I would let go this beauty, were I not
In mind to disobey you by a power
That controls kings : I love you !
Jane.   So, now part.   40
Ham. With hands I may, but never with my
    heart.
In faith, I love you.
Jane.   I believe you do.
Ham. Shall a true love in me breed hate in
    you ?
Jane. I hate you not.
Ham.   Then you must love ?
Jane.   I do.
What are you better now ? I love not you.
Ham. All this, I hope, is but a woman's fray,   45
That means, " Come to me," when she cries,
    " Away ! "
In earnest, mistress, I do not jest,
A true chaste love hath ent'red in my breast.
I love you dearly, as I love my life,   50
I love you as a husband loves a wife ;
That, and no other love, my love requires.
Thy wealth, I know, is little ; my desires
Thirst not for gold. Sweet, beauteous Jane,
    what 's mine   54
Shall, if thou make myself thine, all be thine.
Say, judge, what is thy sentence, life or death ?
Mercy or cruelty lies in thy breath.
Jane. Good sir, I do believe you love me
    well ;
For 't is a silly conquest, silly pride
For one like you — I mean a gentleman —   60
To boast that by his love-tricks he hath brought
Such and such women to his amorous lure ;
I think you do not so, yet many do,
And make it even a very trade to woo.
I could be coy, as many women be,   65
Feed you with sunshine smiles and wanton
    looks,
But I detest witchcraft ; say that I
Do constantly believe, you constant have ——
Ham. Why dost thou not believe me ?
Jane.   I believe you ;   69

But yet, good sir, because I will not grieve you
With hopes to taste fruit which will never fall,
In simple truth this is the sum of all :
My husband lives, at least, I hope he lives.
Prest was he to these bitter wars in France ;
Bitter they are to me by wanting him.   75
I have but one heart, and that heart 's his due.
How can I then bestow the same on you ?
Whilst he lives, his I live, be it ne'er so poor,
And rather be his wife than a king's whore.
Ham. Chaste and dear woman, I will not
    abuse thee,   80
Although it cost my life, if thou refuse me.
Thy husband, prest for France, what was his
    name ?
Jane. Ralph Damport.
Ham.   Damport ? — Here 's a letter sent
From France to me, from a dear friend of
    mine,
A gentleman of place ; here he doth write   85
Their names that have been slain in every
    fight.
Jane. I hope death's scroll contains not my
    love's name.
Ham. Cannot you read ?
Jane.   I can.
Ham.   Peruse the same.
To my remembrance such a name I read
Amongst the rest. See here.
Jane.   Ay me, he 's dead !   90
He 's dead ! If this be true, my dear heart 's
    slain !
Ham. Have patience, dear love.
Jane.   Hence, hence !
Ham.   Nay, sweet Jane,
Make not poor sorrow proud with these rich
    tears.
I mourn thy husband's death, because thou
    mourn'st.
Jane. That bill is forg'd ; 't is sign'd by for-
    gery.   95
Ham. I 'll bring thee letters sent besides to
    many,
Carrying the like report : Jane, 't is too true.
Come, weep not : mourning, though it rise from
    love,
Helps not the mourned, yet hurts them that
    mourn.
Jane. For God's sake, leave me.
Ham.   Whither dost thou turn ?   100
Forget the dead, love them that are alive ;
His love is faded, try how mine will thrive.
Jane. 'T is now no time for me to think on
    love.
Ham. 'T is now best time for you to think on
    love,
Because your love lives not.
Jane.   Though he be dead,   105
My love to him shall not be buried ;
For God's sake, leave me to myself alone.
Ham. 'T would kill my soul, to leave thee
    drown'd in moan.
Answer me to my suit, and I am gone ;
Say to me yea or no.
Jane.   No.
Ham.   Then farewell !   110
One farewell will not serve, I come again :

Come, dry these wet cheeks; tell me, faith,
    sweet Jane,
Yea or no, once more.
  Jane.   Once more I say no ;
Once more be gone, I pray ; else will I go.
  Ham. Nay, then I will grow rude, by this
    white hand,   115
Until you change that cold " no " ; here I 'll
    stand
Till by your hard heart ——
  Jane.   Nay, for God's love, peace !
My sorrows by your presence more increase.
Not that you thus are present, but all grief
Desires to be alone ; therefore in brief   120
Thus much I say, and saying bid adieu :
If ever I wed man, it shall be you.
  Ham. O blessed voice ! Dear Jane, I 'll urge
    no more,
Thy breath hath made me rich.
  Jane.   Death makes me poor.
                         Exeunt.

SCENE II.[1]

HODGE, *at his shop-board,* RALPH, FIRK, HANS,
    and a Boy *at work.*

  All. Hey, down a down, down derry.
  Hodge. Well said, my hearts ; ply your work
to-day, we loit'red yesterday ; to it pell-mell,
that we may live to be lord mayors, or aldermen
at least.   5
  Firk. Hey, down a down, derry.
  Hodge. Well said, i' faith ! How say'st thou,
Hans, doth not Firk tickle it ?
  Hans. *Yaw, mester.*
  Firk. Not so neither, my organ-pipe [10
squeaks this morning for want of liquoring.
Hey, down a down, derry !
  Hans. *Forward, Firk, tow best un jolly young-*
ster. Hort, I, mester, ic bid yo, cut me un pair
vampres vor Mester Jeffre's boots.[2]   15
  Hodge. Thou shalt, Hans.
  Firk. Master !
  Hodge. How now, boy ?
  Firk. Pray, now you are in the cutting vein,
cut me out a pair of counterfeits,[3] or else [20
my work will not pass current ; hey, down a
down !
  Hodge. Tell me, sirs, are my cousin Mrs.
Priscilla's shoes done ?   24
  Firk. Your cousin ? No, master ; one of your
aunts, hang her ; let them alone.
  Ralph. I am in hand with them ; she gave
charge that none but I should do them for her.
  Firk. Thou do for her ? Then 't will be a [29
lame doing, and that she loves not. Ralph, thou
might'st have sent her to me, in faith, I would
have yarked and firked your Priscilla. Hey,
down a down, derry. This gear will not hold.
  Hodge. How say'st thou, Firk, were we not
merry at Old Ford ?   35
  Firk. How, merry ! Why, our buttocks went

jiggy-joggy like a quagmire. Well, Sir Roger
Oatmeal, if I thought all meal of that nature,
I would eat nothing but bagpuddings.   39
  Ralph. Of all good fortunes my fellow Hans
had the best.
  Firk. 'T is true, because Mistress Rose drank
to him.
  Hodge. Well, well, work apace. They say,
seven of the aldermen be dead, or very sick.
  Firk. I care not, I 'll be none.   45
  Ralph. No, nor I ; but then my Master Eyre
will come quickly to be lord mayor.

Enter SYBIL.

  Firk. Whoop, yonder comes Sybil.
  Hodge. Sybil, welcome, i' faith ; and how
dost thou, mad wench ?   50
  Firk. Sib-whore, welcome to London.
  Sybil. Godamercy, sweet Firk ; good lord,
Hodge, what a delicious shop you have got !
You tickle it, i' faith.   54
  Ralph. Godamercy, Sybil, for our good cheer
at Old Ford.
  Sybil. That you shall have, Ralph.
  Firk. Nay, by the mass, we had tickling
cheer, Sybil ; and how the plague dost thou [59
and Mistress Rose and my lord mayor ? I put
the women in first.
  Sybil. Well, Godamercy ; but God's me, I for-
get myself, where 's Hans the Fleming ?
  Firk. Hark, butter-box, now you must [6.
yelp out some *spreken.*
  Hans. *Wat begaie you ? Vat vod you, Frister ?*[4]
  Sybil. Marry, you must come to my young
mistress, to pull on her shoes you made last.
  Hans. *Vare ben your egle fro, vare ben your*
mistris ?[5]   70
  Sybil. Marry, here at our London house in
Cornhill.
  Firk. Will nobody serve her turn but Hans ?
  Sybil. No, sir. Come, Hans, I stand upon
needles.   75
  Hodge. Why then, Sybil, take heed of prick-
ing.
  Sybil. For that let me alone. I have a trick in
my budget. Come, Hans.
  Hans. *Yaw, yaw, iz sall meete yo gane.*[6]   80
                   Exit HANS *and* SYBIL.
  Hodge. Go, Hans, make haste again. Come,
who lacks work ?
  Firk. I, master, for I lack my breakfast ; 't is
munching-time, and past.   84
  Hodge. Is 't so ? Why, then leave work,
Ralph. To breakfast ! Boy, look to the tools.
Come, Ralph ; come, Firk.   *Exeunt.*

SCENE III.[7]

Enter a Serving-man.

  Serv. Let me see now, the sign of the Last in
Tower Street. Mass, yonder 's the house. What,
haw ! Who 's within ?

---

[1] London : a street before Hodge's shop.
[2] *Forward, Firk, thou art a jolly youngster. Hark,*
ay, master, I pray you cut me a pair of vamps for Mas-
ter Jeffrey's boots. Vamps are the upper leathers of a
shoe.
[3] *Counterfeits* sometimes means vamps.

[4] *What do you want, what would you, girl ?*
[5] *Where is your noble lady, where is your mistress ?*
[6] *Yes, yes, I shall go with you.*
[7] The same.

Enter RALPH.

Ralph. Who calls there? What want you, sir?

Serv. Marry, I would have a pair of shoes made for a gentlewoman against to-morrow morning. What, can you do them?

Ralph. Yes, sir, you shall have them. But what length's her foot? 10

Serv. Why you must make them in all parts like this shoe; but, at any hand, fail not to do them, for the gentlewoman is to be married very early in the morning.

Ralph. How? by this shoe must it be made? By this? Are you sure, sir, by this? 16

Serv. How, by this? Am I sure, by this? Art thou in thy wits? I tell thee, I must have a pair of shoes dost thou mark me? A pair of shoes, two shoes, made by this very shoe, this same [20 shoe, against to-morrow morning by four a clock. Dost understand me? Canst thou do't?

Ralph. Yes, sir, yes — I — I — I can do't. By this shoe, you say? I should know this shoe. Yes, sir, yes, by this shoe, I can do't. Four [25 a clock, well. Whither shall I bring them?

Serv. To the sign of the Golden Ball in Watling Street; enquire for one Master Hammon, a gentleman, my master.

Ralph. Yea, sir; by this shoe, you say? 30

Serv. I say, Master Hammon at the Golden Ball; he's the bridegroom, and these shoes are for his bride.

Ralph. They shall be done by this shoe. Well, well, Master Hammon at the Golden Shoe — I would say, the Golden Ball; very well, very [36 well. But I pray you, sir, where must Master Hammon be married?

Serv. At Saint Faith's Church, under Paul's. But what's that to thee? Prithee, dispatch those shoes, and so farewell. *Exit.* 41

Ralph. By this shoe, said he. How am I amaz'd
At this strange accident! Upon my life,
This was the very shoe I gave my wife,
When I was prest for France; since when, alas!
I never could hear of her. It is the same, 46
And Hammon's bride no other but my Jane.

Enter FIRK.

Firk. 'Snails,[1] Ralph, thou hast lost thy part of three pots, a countryman of mine gave me to breakfast. 50

Ralph. I care not; I have found a better thing.

Firk. A thing? Away! Is it a man's thing, or a woman's thing?

Ralph. Firk, dost thou know this shoe?

Firk. No, by my troth; neither doth that [56 know me! I have no acquaintance with it, 'tis a mere stranger to me.

Ralph. Why, then I do; this shoe, I durst be sworn,
Once covered the instep of my Jane. 60
This is her size, her breadth, thus trod my love;

---
[1] A corruption of "God's nails."

These true-love knots I prickt. I hold my life,
By this old shoe I shall find out my wife.

Firk. Ha, ha! Old shoe, that wert new! How a murrain came this ague-fit of foolishness [65 upon thee?

Ralph. Thus, Firk: even now here came a serving-man;
By this shoe would he have a new pair made
Against to-morrow morning for his mistress,
That's to be married to a gentleman. 70
And why may not this be my sweet Jane?

Firk. And why may'st not thou be my sweet ass?
Ha, ha!

Ralph. Well, laugh and spare not! But the truth is this:
Against to-morrow morning I'll provide 75
A lusty crew of honest shoemakers,
To watch the going of the bride to church.
If she prove Jane, I'll take her in despite
From Hammon and the devil, were he by.
If it be not my Jane, what remedy? 80
Hereof I am sure, I shall live till I die,
Although I never with a woman lie. *Exit.*

Firk. Thou lie with a woman to build nothing but Cripplegates! Well, God sends fools fortune, and it may be, he may light upon [85 his matrimony by such a device; for wedding and hanging goes by destiny. *Exit.*

SCENE IV.[2]

Enter [LACY *as*] HANS *and* ROSE, *arm in arm.*

Hans. How happy am I by embracing thee!
Oh, I did fear such cross mishaps did reign
That I should never see my Rose again.

Rose. Sweet Lacy, since fair opportunity
Offers herself to further our escape, 5
Let not too over-fond esteem of me
Hinder that happy hour. Invent the means,
And Rose will follow thee through all the world.

Hans. Oh, how I surfeit with excess of joy,
Made happy by thy rich perfection! 10
But since thou pay'st sweet interest to my hopes,
Redoubling love on love, let me once more
Like to a bold-fac'd debtor crave of thee
This night to steal abroad, and at Eyre's house,
Who now by death of certain aldermen 15
Is mayor of London, and my master once,
Meet thou thy Lacy, where in spite of change,
Your father's anger, and mine uncle's hate,
Our happy nuptials will we consummate.

Enter SYBIL.

Sybil. Oh God, what will you do, mistress? [20
Shift for yourself, your father is at hand! He's coming, he's coming! Master Lacy, hide yourself in my mistress! For God's sake, shift for yourselves!

Hans. Your father come! Sweet Rose, what shall I do? 25
Where shall I hide me? How shall I escape?

Rose. A man, and want wit in extremity?

---
[2] London: a room in the Lord Mayor's house.

Come, come, be Hans still, play the shoemaker,
Pull on my shoe.

Enter the LORD MAYOR.

Hans. Mass, and that 's well rememb'red.
Sybil. Here comes your father.   30
*Hans. Forware, metresse, 't is un good skow, it
ral vel dute, or ye sal neit betallen.*[1]
Rose. Oh God, it pincheth me; what will you
do?
Hans. [*Aside.*] Your father's presence pincheth, not the shoe.   34
Lord Mayor. Well done; fit my daughter
well, and she shall please thee well.
*Hans. Yaw, yaw, ick weit dat well; forware,
't is un good skoo, 't is gimait van neitz leither:
se euer, mine here.*[2]

Enter a Prentice.

L. Mayor. I do believe it. — What 's the news
with you?   40
Prentice. Please you, the Earl of Lincoln at
the gate
Is newly lighted, and would speak with you.
L. Mayor. The Earl of Lincoln come to speak
with me?
Well, well, I know his errand. Daughter Rose,
Send hence your shoemaker, dispatch, have
done!   45
Syb, make things handsome! Sir boy, follow
me.   *Exit.*
Hans. Mine uncle come! Oh, what may this
portend?
Sweet Rose, this of our love threatens an end.
Rose. Be not dismay'd at this; whate'er be-
fall,
Rose is thine own. To witness I speak truth, 50
Where thou appoint'st the place, I 'll meet
with thee.
I will not fix a day to follow thee,
But presently[3] steal hence. Do not reply:
Love which gave strength to bear my father's
hate,
Shall now add wings to further our escape.   55
          Exeunt.

SCENE V.[4]

Enter the LORD MAYOR *and the* EARL OF LIN-
COLN.

L. Mayor. Believe me, on my credit, I speak
truth:
Since first your nephew Lacy went to France.
I have not seen him. It seem'd strange to me,
When Dodger told me that he stay'd behind,
Neglecting the high charge the king imposed. 5
Lincoln. Trust me, Sir Roger Oateley, I did
think
Your counsel had given head to this attempt,
Drawn to it by the love he bears your child.
Here I did hope to find him in your house;
But now I see mine error, and confess,   10
My judgment wrong'd you by conceiving so.

[1] *Indeed, mistress, 't is a good shoe, it shall fit well, or
you shall not pay.*
[2] *Yes, yes, I know that well; indeed, 't is a good shoe,
't is made of neat's leather; see here, good sir!*
[3] *At once.*   [4] *Another room in the same house.*

L. Mayor. Lodge in my house, say you?
Trust me, my lord,
I love your nephew Lacy too too dearly,
So much to wrong his honour; and he hath
done so,   14
That first gave him advice to stay from France.
To witness I speak truth, I let you know
How careful I have been to keep my daughter
Free from all conference or speech of him;
Not that I scorn your nephew, but in love
I bear your honour, lest your noble blood   20
Should by my mean worth be dishonoured.
Lincoln. [*Aside.*] How far the churl's tongue
wanders from his heart! —
Well, well, Sir Roger Oateley, I believe you,
With more than many thanks for the kind love
So much you seem to bear me. But, my lord, 25
Let me request your help to seek my nephew,
Whom if I find, I 'll straight embark for France.
So shall your Rose be free, my thoughts at rest,
And much care die which now lies in my breast.

Enter SYBIL.

Sybil. Oh Lord! Help, for God's sake! [30
My mistress; oh, my young mistress!
L. Mayor. Where is thy mistress? What 's
become of her?
Sybil. She 's gone, she 's fled!
L. Mayor. Gone! Whither is she fled?   35
Sybil. I know not, forsooth; she 's fled out of
doors with Hans the shoemaker; I saw them
scud, scud, scud, apace, apace!
L. Mayor. Which way? What, John! Where
be my men? Which way?   40
Sybil. I know not, an it please your worship.
L. Mayor. Fled with a shoemaker? Can this
be true?
Sybil. Oh Lord, sir, as true as God 's in
Heaven.
Lincoln. Her love turn'd shoemaker? I am
glad of this.
L. Mayor. A Fleming butter-box, a shoe-
maker!   45
Will she forget her birth, requite my care
With such ingratitude? Scorn'd she young
Hammon
To love a honniken,[5] a needy knave?
Well, let her fly, I 'll not fly after her,   49
Let her starve, if she will: she 's none of mine.
Lincoln. Be not so cruel, sir.

Enter FIRK *with shoes.*

Sybil.   I am glad, she 's scapt.
L. Mayor. I 'll not account of her as of my
child.
Was there no better object for her eyes,
But a foul drunken lubber, swill-belly,
A shoemaker? That 's brave!   55
Firk. Yea, forsooth; 't is a very brave shoe,
and as fit as a pudding.
L. Mayor. How now, what knave is this?
From whence comest thou?
Firk. No knave, sir. I am Firk the shoe- [60
maker, lusty Roger's chief lusty journeyman,
and I have come hither to take up the pretty

[5] Simpleton (?).

leg of sweet Mistress Rose, and thus hoping
your worship is in as good health, as I was at
the making hereof, I bid you farewell, yours, [65
Firk.

L. Mayor. Stay, stay, Sir Knave!

Lincoln. Come hither, shoemaker!

Firk. 'T is happy the knave is put before the
shoemaker, or else I would not have vouch- [70
safed to come back to you. I am moved, for I
stir.

L. Mayor. My lord, this villain calls us
knaves by craft.

Firk. Then 't is by the gentle craft, and [75
to call one knave gently, is no harm. Sit your
worship merry! Syb, your young mistress —
I 'll so bob[1] them, now my Master Eyre is lord
mayor of London.

L. Mayor. Tell me, sirrah, whose man are [80
you?

Firk. I am glad to see your worship so merry.
I have no maw to this gear, no stomach as yet
to a red petticoat.   *Pointing to* SYBIL.

Lincoln. He means not, sir, to woo you to his
maid,   85
But only doth demand whose man you are.

Firk. I sing now to the tune of Rogero.
Roger, my fellow, is now my master.

Lincoln. Sirrah, know'st thou one Hans, a
shoemaker?   90

Firk. Hans, shoemaker? Oh yes, stay, yes,
I have him. I tell you what, I speak it in secret:
Mistress Rose and he are by this time — no, not
so, but shortly are to come over one another
with "Can you dance the shaking of the [95
sheets?" It is that Hans — [*Aside.*] I 'll so
gull[1] these diggers![2]

L. Mayor. Know'st thou, then, where he is?

Firk. Yes, forsooth; yea, marry!

Lincoln. Canst thou, in sadness[3] ——   100

Firk. No, forsooth, no, marry!

L. Mayor. Tell me, good honest fellow, where
he is,
And thou shalt see what I 'll bestow on thee.

Firk. Honest fellow? No, sir; not so, sir;
my profession is the gentle craft; I care not [105
for seeing, I love feeling; let me feel it here;
aurium tenus, ten pieces of gold; *genuum tenus,*
ten pieces of silver; and then Firk is your man
— [*Aside.*] in a new pair of stretchers.[4]

L. Mayor. Here is an angel, part of thy re-
ward,   110
Which I will give thee; tell me where he is.

Firk. No point. Shall I betray my brother?
No! Shall I prove Judas to Hans? No! Shall
I cry treason to my corporation? No, I shall
be firkt and yerkt then. But give me your [115
angel; your angel shall tell you.

Lincoln. Do so, good fellow; 't is no hurt to
thee.

Firk. Send simpering Syb away.

L. Mayor. Huswife, get you in.   119
                                                Exit SYBIL.

Firk. Pitchers have ears, and maids have
wide mouths; but for Hans Prauns, upon my

word, to-morrow morning he and young Mistress Rose go to this gear, they shall be married
together, by this rush, or else turn Firk to a
firkin of butter, to tan leather withal.   125

L. Mayor. But art thou sure of this?

Firk. Am I sure that Paul's steeple is a
handful higher than London Stone,[5] or that
the Pissing-Conduit[6] leaks nothing but pure [129
Mother Bunch?[7] Am I sure I am lusty Firk?
God's nails, do you think I am so base to gull
you?

Lincoln. Where are they married? Dost thou
know the church?   134

Firk. I never go to church, but I know the
name of it; it is a swearing church — stay a
while, 't is — ay, by the mass, no, no, — 't is —
ay, by my troth, no, nor that; 't is — ay, by my
faith, that, that, 't is, ay, by my Faith's
Church under Paul's Cross. There they shall [140
be knit like a pair of stockings in matrimony;
there they 'll be inconie.[8]

Lincoln. Upon my life, my nephew Lacy
walks
In the disguise of this Dutch shoemaker.

Firk. Yes, forsooth.   145

Lincoln. Doth he not, honest fellow?

Firk. No, forsooth; I think Hans is nobody
but Hans, no spirit.

L. Mayor. My mind misgives me now, 't is
so, indeed.

Lincoln. My cousin speaks the language,
knows the trade.   150

L. Mayor. Let me request your company,
my lord;
Your honourable presence may, no doubt,
Refrain their headstrong rashness, when myself
Going alone perchance may be o'erborne.
Shall I request this favour?

Lincoln.   This, or what else. 155

Firk. Then you must rise betimes, for they
mean to fall to their hey-pass and repass,[9]
pindy-pandy, which hand will you have, very
early.

L. Mayor. My care shall every way equal
their haste.   160
This night accept your lodging in my house,
The earlier shall we stir, and at Saint Faith's
Prevent this giddy hare-brain'd nuptial.
This traffic of hot love shall yield cold gains:
They ban[10] our loves, and we 'll forbid their
banns.   *Exit.* 165

Lincoln. At Saint Faith's Church thou say'st?

Firk. Yes, by their troth.

Lincoln. Be secret, on thy life.   *Exit.*

Firk. Yes, when I kiss your wife! Ha, ha,
here 's no craft in the gentle craft. I came [170
hither of purpose with shoes to Sir Roger's
worship, whilst Rose, his daughter, is be cony-
catcht by Hans. Soft now; these two gulls
will be at Saint Faith's Church to-morrow [174
morning, to take Master Bridegroom and Mis-

---

[1] Fool.   [2] *I. e.* diggers for information.
[3] Seriously.   [4] Stretchers of the truth, lies.

[5] A stone which marked the centre from which the
old Roman roads radiated.
[6] A small conduit near the Royal Exchange.
[7] Mother Bunch was a well-known ale-wife.
[8] A pretty sight.   [10] Curse
[9] Conjuring terms.

tress Bride napping, and they, in the mean time, shall chop up the matter at the Savoy. But the best sport is, Sir Roger Oateley will find my fellow lame Ralph's wife going to [179 marry a gentleman, and then he 'll stop her instead of his daughter. Oh brave ! there will be fine tickling sport. Soft now, what have I to do ? Oh, I know ; now a mess of shoemakers meet at the Woolsack in Ivy Lane, to cozen [1] my gentleman of lame Ralph's wife, that 's [185 true.

Alack, alack !
Girls, hold out tack !
For now smocks for this jumbling
Shall go to wrack. 190
Exit.

ACT V

Scene I.[2]

Enter Eyre, *his wife* [Margery], Hans, *and* Rose.

Eyre. This is the morning, then; stay, my bully, my honest Hans, is it not ?

Hans. This is the morning that must make us two happy or miserable ; therefore, if you —— 5

Eyre. Away with these ifs and ans, Hans, and these et caeteras ! By mine honour, Rowland Lacy, none but the king shall wrong thee. Come, fear nothing, am not I Sim Eyre ? Is not Sim Eyre lord mayor of London ? Fear no- [10 thing, Rose : let them all say what they can ; dainty, come thou to me — laughest thou ?

Marg. Good my lord, stand her friend in what thing you may.

Eyre. Why, my sweet Lady Madgy, think [15 you Simon Eyre can forget his fine Dutch journeyman ? No, vah ! Fie, I scorn it, it shall never be cast in my teeth, that I was unthankful. Lady Madgy, thou had'st never cover'd thy Saracen's head with this French flap, nor [20 loaden thy bum with this farthingale, ('t is trash, trumpery, vanity) ; Simon Eyre had never walk'd in a red petticoat, nor wore a chain of gold, but for my fine journeyman's Portuguese. — And shall I leave him ? No ! Prince am I [25 none, yet bear a princely mind.

Hans. My lord, 't is time for us to part from hence.

Eyre. Lady Madgy, Lady Madgy, take two or three of my pie-crust-eaters, my buff-jerkin varlets, that do walk in black gowns at [30 Simon Eyre's heels ; take them, good Lady Madgy ; trip and go, my brown queen of periwigs, with my delicate Rose and my jolly Rowland to the Savoy ; see them linkt, countenance the marriage ; and when it is done, cling, [35 cling together, you Hamborow turtle-doves. I 'll bear you out, come to Simon Eyre ; come, dwell with me, Hans, thou shalt eat mine'd-pies and marchpane.[3] Rose, away, cricket ; trip and go, my Lady Madgy, to the Savoy ; Hans, wed, and to bed ; kiss, and away ! Go, vanish !

---
[1] Cheat.   [2] A room in Eyre's house.
[3] A sweetmeat made of sugar and almonds.

Marg. Farewell, my lord. 42
Rose. Make haste, sweet love.
Marg. She 'd fain the deed were done.
Hans. Come, my sweet Rose ; faster than deer we 'll run. 45
Exeunt Hans, Rose, *and* Margery.
Eyre. Go, vanish, vanish ! Avaunt, I say ! By the Lord of Ludgate, it 's a mad life to be a lord mayor ; it 's a stirring life, a fine life, a velvet life, a careful life. Well, Simon Eyre, yet set a good face on it, in the honour of Saint [50 Hugh. Soft, the king this day comes to dine with me, to see my new buildings ; his majesty is welcome, he shall have good cheer, delicate cheer, princely cheer. This day, my fellow prentices of London come to dine with me too, [55 they shall have fine cheer, gentlemanlike cheer. I promised the mad Cappadocians, when we all served at the Conduit together, that if ever I came to be mayor of London, I would feast them all, and I 'll do 't, I 'll do 't, by the life [60 of Pharaoh ; by this beard, Sim Eyre will be no flincher. Besides, I have procur'd that upon every Shrove-Tuesday, at the sound of the pancake bell, my fine dapper Assyrian lads shall clap up their shop windows, and away. [65 This is the day, and this day they shall do 't, they shall do 't.

Boys, that day are you free, let masters care,
And prentices shall pray for Simon Eyre.
Exit.

Scene II.[4]

Enter Hodge, Firk, Ralph, *and five or six* Shoemakers, *all with cudgels or such weapons.*

Hodge. Come, Ralph ; stand to it, Firk. My masters, as we are the brave bloods of the shoemakers, heirs apparent to Saint Hugh, and perpetual benefactors to all good fellows, thou shalt have no wrong : were Hammon a king [5 of spades, he should not delve in thy close without thy sufferance. But tell me, Ralph, art thou sure 't is thy wife ?

Ralph. Am I sure this is Firk ? This morning, when I strokt on her shoes,[5] I lookt upon [10 her, and she upon me, and sighed, askt me if ever I knew one Ralph. Yes, said I. For his sake, said she — tears standing in her eyes — and for thou art somewhat like him, spend this piece of gold. I took it ; my lame leg and [15 my travel beyond sea made me unknown. All is one for that : I know she 's mine.

Firk. Did she give thee this gold ? O glorious glittering gold ! She 's thine own, 't is thy wife, and she loves thee ; for I 'll stand to 't, [20 there 's no woman will give gold to any man, but she thinks better of him than she thinks of them she gives silver to. And for Hammon, neither Hammon nor hangman shall wrong thee in London ! Is not our old master Eyre, [25 lord mayor ? Speak, my hearts.

All. Yes, and Hammon shall know it to his cost.

---
[4] A street near St. Faith's Church.
[5] Fitted.

Enter HAMMON, *his man*, JANE, *and* Others.

Hodge. Peace, my bullies; yonder they come.   29
Ralph. Stand to 't, my hearts. Firk, let me speak first.
Hodge. No, Ralph, let me. — Hammon, whither away so early?
Ham. Unmannerly, rude slave, what 's that to thee?   34
Firk. To him, sir? Yes, sir, and to me, and others. Good-morrow, Jane, how dost thou? Good Lord, how the world is changed with you! God be thanked!
Ham. Villains, hands off! How dare you touch my love?   39
All. Villains? Down with them! Cry clubs for prentices![1]
Hodge. Hold, my hearts! Touch her, Hammon? Yea, and more than that: we 'll carry her away with us. My masters and gentlemen, never draw your bird-spits; shoemakers are steel to the back, men every inch of them, [46 all spirit.
All of Hammon's side. Well, and what of all this?
Hodge. I 'll show you. — Jane, dost thou [50 know this man? 'Tis Ralph, I can tell thee; nay, 't is he in faith, though he be lam'd by the wars. Yet look not strange, but run to him, fold him about the neck and kiss him.
Jane. Lives then my husband? Oh God, let me go,   55
Let me embrace my Ralph.
Ham.   What means my Jane?
Jane. Nay, what meant you, to tell me, he was slain?
Ham. Pardon me, dear love, for being misled.
[*To* RALPH.] 'T was rumour'd here in London, thou wert dead.
Firk. Thou seest he lives. Lass, go, pack home with him.   60
Now, Master Hammon, where 's your mistress, your wife?
Serv. 'Swounds, master, fight for her! Will you thus lose her?
All. Down with that creature! Clubs! Down with him!   65
Hodge. Hold, hold!
Ham. Hold, fool! Sirs, he shall do no wrong. Will my Jane leave me thus, and break her faith?
Firk. Yea, sir! She must, sir! She shall, sir! What then? Mend it!   70
Hodge. Hark, fellow Ralph, follow my counsel: set the wench in the midst, and let her choose her man, and let her be his woman.
Jane. Whom shall I choose? Whom should my thoughts affect
But him whom Heaven hath made to be my love?   75
Thou art my husband, and these humble weeds Make thee more beautiful than all his wealth. Therefore, I will but put off his attire,

Returning it into the owner's hand,
And after ever be thy constant wife.   80
Ham. Not a rag, Jane! The law 's on our side: he that sows in another man's ground, forfeits his harvest. Get thee home, Ralph; follow him, Jane; he shall not have so much as a busk-point[2] from thee.   85
Firk. Stand to that, Ralph; the appurtenances are thine own. Hammon, look not at her!
Serv. O, swounds, no!   89
Firk. Blue coat, be quiet, we 'll give you a new livery else; we 'll make Shrove Tuesday Saint George's Day for you. Look not, Hammon, leer not! I 'll firk you! For thy head now, one glance, one sheep's eye, anything, at her! Touch not a rag, lest I and my brethren beat you to clouts.   96
Serv. Come, Master Hammon, there 's no striving here.
Ham. Good fellows, hear me speak; and, honest Ralph,
Whom I have injured most by loving Jane,
Mark what I offer thee: here in fair gold   100
Is twenty pound, I 'll give it for thy Jane;
If this content thee not, thou shalt have more.
Hodge. Sell not thy wife, Ralph; make her not a whore.
Ham. Say, wilt thou freely cease thy claim in her,
And let her be my wife?
All.   No, do not, Ralph.   105
Ralph. Sirrah Hammon, Hammon, dost thou think a shoemaker is so base to be a bawd to his own wife for commodity? Take thy gold, choke with it! Were I not lame, I would make thee eat thy words.   110
Firk. A shoemaker sell his flesh and blood? Oh indignity!
Hodge. Sirrah, take up your pelf, and be packing.
Ham. I will not touch one penny, but in lieu Of that great wrong I offered thy Jane,   116
To Jane and thee I give that twenty pound. Since I have fail'd of her, during my life, I vow, no woman else shall be my wife. Farewell, good fellows of the gentle trade: 120 Your morning mirth my mourning day hath made.   *Exit.*
Firk. [*to the* Serving-man.] Touch the gold creature, if you dare! Y' are best be trudging. Here, Jane, take thou it. Now let 's home, my hearts.   125
Hodge. Stay! Who comes here? Jane, on again with thy mask!

Enter the EARL OF LINCOLN, *the* LORD MAYOR, *and* Servants.

Lincoln. Yonder 's the lying varlet mockt us so.
L. Mayor. Come hither, sirrah!
Firk. I, sir? I am sirrah? You mean me, do you not?   130
Lincoln. Where is my nephew married?

---

[1] " Clubs " was the rallying cry of the London apprentices.

[2] A lace with a tag, which fastened the busk, or piece of wood or whalebone used to keep the stays in position.

Firk. Is he married ? God give him joy, I am glad of it. They have a fair day, and the sign is in a good planet, Mars in Venus.

L. Mayor. Villain, thou toldst me that my daughter Rose 135 This morning should be married at Saint Faith's ; We have watch'd there these three hours at the least, Yet see we no such thing.

Firk. Truly, I am sorry for 't ; a bride's a pretty thing. 140

Hodge. Come to the purpose. Yonder 's the bride and bridegroom you look for, I hope. Though you be lords, you are not to bar by your authority men from women, are you ?

L. Mayor. See, see, my daughter 's maskt.

Lincoln. True, and my nephew, 145 To hide his guilt, counterfeits him lame.

Firk. Yea, truly ; God help the poor couple, they are lame and blind.

L. Mayor. I 'll ease her blindness.

Lincoln. I 'll his lameness cure. 149

Firk. Lie down, sirs, and laugh ! My fellow Ralph is taken for Rowland Lacy, and Jane for Mistress Damask Rose. This is all my knavery.

L. Mayor. What, have I found you, minion ?

Lincoln. O base wretch ! Nay, hide thy face, the horror of thy guilt Can hardly be washt off. Where are thy powers ? 155 What battles have you made ? O yes, I see, Thou fought'st with Shame, and Shame hath conquer'd thee. This lameness will not serve.

L. Mayor. Unmask yourself.

Lincoln. Lead home your daughter.

L. Mayor. Take your nephew hence. 159

Ralph. Hence ! Swounds, what mean you ? Are you mad ? I hope you cannot enforce my wife from me. Where 's Hammon ?

L. Mayor. Your wife ?

Lincoln. What, Hammon ? 164

Ralph. Yea, my wife ; and, therefore, the proudest of you that lay hands on her first, I 'll lay my crutch 'cross his pate.

Firk. To him, lame Ralph ! Here 's brave sport ! 169

Ralph. Rose call you her ? Why, her name is Jane. Look here else ; do you know her now ? [*Unmasking* JANE.]

Lincoln. Is this your daughter ?

L. Mayor. No, nor this your nephew. My Lord of Lincoln, we are both abus'd By this base, crafty varlet. 174

Firk. Yea, forsooth, no varlet ; forsooth, no base ; forsooth, I am but mean ; no crafty neither, but of the gentle craft.

L. Mayor. Where is my daughter Rose ? Where is my child ?

Lincoln. Where is my nephew Lacy married ?

Firk. Why, here is good lac'd mutton,[1] as I promist you. 181

Lincoln. Villain, I 'll have thee punisht for this wrong.

[1] A slang term for a woman.

Firk. Punish the journeyman villain, but not the journeyman shoemaker.

Enter DODGER.

Dodger. My lord, I come to bring unwelcome news. 185 Your nephew Lacy and your daughter Rose Early this morning wedded at the Savoy, None being present but the lady mayoress. Besides, I learnt among the officers, 189 The lord mayor vows to stand in their defence 'Gainst any that shall seek to cross the match.

Lincoln. Dares Eyre the shoemaker uphold the deed ?

Firk. Yes, sir, shoemakers dare stand in a woman's quarrel, I warrant you, as deep as another, and deeper too. 195

Dodger. Besides, his grace to-day dines with the mayor ; Who on his knees humbly intends to fall And beg a pardon for your nephew's fault.

Lincoln. But I 'll prevent him ! Come, Sir Roger Oateley ; The king will do us justice in this cause. 200 Howe'er their hands have made them man and wife, I will disjoin the match, or lose my life. *Exeunt.*

Firk. Adieu. Monsieur Dodger ! Farewell, fools ! Ha, ha ! Oh, if they had stay'd, I [204 would have so lamb'd[2] them with flouts ! O heart, my codpiece-point is ready to fly in pieces every time I think upon Mistress Rose. But let that pass, as my lady mayoress says.

Hodge. This matter is answer'd. Come, Ralph ; home with thy wife. Come, my fine [210 shoemakers, let 's to our master's the new lord mayor, and there swagger this Shrove Tuesday. I 'll promise you wine enough, for Madge keeps the cellar.

All. O rare ! Madge is a good wench. 215

Firk. And I 'll promise you meat enough, for simp'ring Susan keeps the larder. I 'll lead you to victuals, my brave soldiers ; follow your captain. O brave ! Hark, hark ! *Bell rings.* [219

All. The pancake-bell[3] rings, the pancake-bell ! Trilill, my hearts !

Firk. Oh brave ! Oh sweet bell ! O delicate pancakes ! Open the doors, my hearts, and shut up the windows ! keep in the house, let out [224 the pancakes ! Oh rare, my hearts ! Let 's march together for the honour of Saint Hugh to the great new hall[4] in Gracious Street corner, which our master, the new lord mayor, hath built.

Ralph. O the crew of good fellows that will dine at my lord mayor's cost to-day ! 230

Hodge. By the Lord, my lord mayor is a most brave man. How shall prentices be bound to pray for him and the honour of the gentlemen shoemakers ! Let 's feed and be fat with my lord's bounty. 235

Firk. O musical bell, still ! O Hodge, O my brethren ! There 's cheer for the heavens : venison-pasties walk up and down piping hot, like

[2] Whipped.
[3] A bell rung on the morning of Shrove Tuesday.
[4] Leadenhall.

sergeants; beef and brewess [1] comes march- [239]
ing in dry-vats,[2] fritters and pancakes comes
trowling in in wheel-barrows; hens and oranges
hopping in porters'-basket, collops and eggs in
scuttles,[3] and tarts and custards comes quaver-
ing in in malt-shovels.

Enter more Prentices.

All. Whoop, look here, look here! 245
Hodge. How now, mad lads, whither away so
fast?
1 Prentice. Whither? Why, to the great
new hall, know you not why? The lord [249]
mayor hath bidden all the prentices in London
to breakfast this morning.
All. Oh brave shoemakers, oh brave lord of
incomprehensible good-fellowship! Whoo!
Hark you! The pancake-bell rings. 254
                    Cast up caps.
Firk. Nay, more, my hearts! Every Shrove-
Tuesday is our year of jubilee; and when the
pancake-bell rings, we are as free as my lord
mayor; we may shut up our shops, and make
holiday; I'll have it call'd Saint Hugh's Holi-
day. 260
All. Agreed, agreed! Saint Hugh's Holiday.
Hodge. And this shall continue for ever.
All. Oh brave! Come, come, my hearts!
Away, away!
Firk. O eternal credit to us of the gentle
craft! March fair, my hearts! Oh rare! 265
                    Exeunt.

SCENE III.[4]

Enter the KING *and his* Train *over the stage.*

King. Is our lord mayor of London such a
gallant?
Nobleman. One of the merriest madcaps in
your land.
Your grace will think, when you behold the man,
He's rather a wild ruffian than a mayor.
Yet thus much I'll ensure your majesty, 5
In all his actions that concern his state
He is as serious, provident, and wise,
As full of gravity amongst the grave,
As any mayor hath been these many years.
King. I am with child [5] till I behold this huff-
cap.[6] 10
But all my doubt is, when we come in presence,
His madness will be dasht clean out of counte-
nance.
Nobleman. It may be so, my liege.
King.   Which to prevent,
Let some one give him notice, 't is our pleasure
That he put on his wonted merriment. 15
Set forward!
All. On afore! *Exeunt.*

SCENE IV.[7]

Enter EYRE, HODGE, FIRK, RALPH, *and other*
Shoemakers, *all with napkins on their shoulders.*

Eyre. Come, my fine Hodge, my jolly gentlemen shoemakers; soft, where be these canni-

[1] Beef broth. [3] Hods. [6] Swaggerer.
[2] Barrels. [4] A street in London. [7] A great hall.
        [5] In suspense.

bals, these varlets, my officers? Let them all
walk and wait upon my brethren; for my meaning is, that none but shoemakers, none but the [5]
livery of my company shall in their satin hoods
wait upon the trencher of my sovereign.
Firk. O my lord, it will be rare!
Eyre. No more, Firk; come, lively! Let your
fellow-prentices want no cheer; let wine be [10]
plentiful as beer, and beer as water. Hang these
penny-pinching fathers, that cram wealth in innocent lamb-skins. Rip, knaves, avaunt! Look
to my guests!
Hodge. My lord, we are at our wits' end [15]
for room; those hundred tables will not feast
the fourth part of them.
Eyre. Then cover me those hundred tables
again, and again, till all my jolly prentices be
feasted. Avoid, Hodge! Run, Ralph! Frisk [20]
about, my nimble Firk! Carouse me fathom-
healths to the honour of the shoemakers. Do
they drink lively, Hodge? Do they tickle it,
Firk?
Firk. Tickle it? Some of them have taken [25]
their liquor standing so long that they can stand
no longer; but for meat, they would eat it an
they had it.
Eyre. Want they meat? Where's this swag-
belly, this greasy kitchen stuff cook? Call [30]
the varlet to me! Want meat? Firk, Hodge,
lame Ralph, run, my tall men, beleaguer the
shambles, beggar all Eastcheap, serve me whole
oxen in chargers, and let sheep whine upon the
tables like pigs for want of good fellows to [35]
eat them. Want meat? Vanish, Firk! Avaunt,
Hodge!
Hodge. Your lordship mistakes my man Firk;
he means, their bellies want meat, not the
boards; for they have drunk so much, they [40]
can eat nothing.

THE SECOND THREE MEN'S SONG

Cold 's the wind, and wet 's the rain,
  Saint Hugh be our good speed:
Ill is the weather that bringeth no gain,
  Nor helps good hearts in need. 45

Trowl [8] the bowl, the jolly nut-brown bowl,
  And here, kind mate, to thee:
Let 's sing a dirge for Saint Hugh's soul,
  And down it merrily.

Down a down heydown a down, 50
  (*Close with the tenor boy*)
Hey derry derry, down a down!
Ho, well done; to me let come!
Ring, compass, gentle joy.

Trowl the bowl, the nut-brown bowl,
  And here, kind mate, to thee: etc. 55
  *Repeat as often as there be men to drink;
  and at last when all have drunk, this verse:*
Cold 's the wind, and wet 's the rain,
  Saint Hugh be our good speed:
Ill is the weather that bringeth no gain,
  Nor helps good hearts in need.

Enter HANS, ROSE, *and* Wife [MARGERY].

Marg. Where is my lord? 62
Eyre. How now, Lady Madgy?

        [8] Pass.

Marg. The king's most excellent majesty is new come; he sends me for thy honour; one of his most worshipful peers bade me tell thou must be merry, and so forth; but let that pass. 65

Eyre. Is my sovereign come? Vanish, my tall shoemakers, my nimble brethren; look to my guests, the prentices. Yet stay a little! How now, Hans? How looks my little Rose? 69

Hans. Let me request you to remember me. I know, your honour easily may obtain
Free pardon of the king for me and Rose,
And reconcile me to my uncle's grace.

Eyre. Have done, my good Hans, my honest journeyman; look cheerily! I'll fall upon [75 both my knees, till they be as hard as horn, but I'll get thy pardon.

Marg. Good my lord, have a care what you speak to his grace. 79

Eyre. Away, you Islington whitepot![1] hence, you hopper-arse! hence, you barley-pudding, full of maggots! you broiled carbonado![2] avaunt, avaunt, avoid, Mephistophiles! Shall Sim Eyre learn to speak of you, Lady Madgy? Vanish, Mother Miniver-cap; vanish, go, trip and go; [85 meddle with your partlets[3] and your pishery-pashery, your flewes[4] and your whirligigs; go, rub,[5] out of mine alley! Sim Eyre knows how to speak to a Pope, to Sultan Soliman, to Tamburlaine, an he were here, and shall I melt, [90 shall I droop before my sovereign? No, come, my Lady Madgy! Follow me, Hans! About your business, my frolic free-booters! Firk, frisk about, and about, and about, for the honour of mad Simon Eyre, lord mayor of London. 95

Firk. Hey, for the honour of the shoemakers!
Exeunt.

SCENE V.[6]

{ *long flourish, or two. Enter the* KING, *Nobles,* EYRE, *his Wife* [MARGERY], LACY, ROSE. LACY *and* ROSE *kneel.*

King. Well, Lacy, though the fact was very foul
Of your revolting from our kingly love
And your own duty, yet we pardon you.
Rise both, and, Mistress Lacy, thank my lord mayor
For your young bridegroom here. 5

Eyre. So, my dear liege, Sim Eyre and my brethren, the gentlemen shoemakers, shall set your sweet majesty's image cheek by jowl by Saint Hugh for this honour you have done poor Simon Eyre. I beseech your grace, pardon [10 my rude behaviour; I am a handicraftsman, yet my heart is without craft; I would be sorry at my soul, that my boldness should offend my king.

King. Nay, I pray thee, good lord mayor, be even as merry 15
As if thou wert among thy shoemakers;
It does me good to see thee in this humour.

---

[1] "A dish, made of milk, eggs, and sugar, baked in a pot." (Webster.)
[2] A steak cut crossways.   [3] Ruffs for the neck.
[4] Flaps; as resembling the hanging chaps of a hound.
[5] Obstruction, a term in bowling.
[6] An open yard before the hall.

Eyre. Say'st thou me so, my sweet Diocle-sian? Then, hump! Prince am I none, yet am I princely born. By the Lord of Ludgate, my liege, I'll be as merry as a pie.[7] 21

King. Tell me, in faith, mad Eyre, how old thou art.

Eyre. My liege, a very boy, a stripling, a younker; you see not a white hair on my head, not a gray in this beard. Every hair, I as- [25 sure thy majesty, that sticks in this beard, Sim Eyre values at the King of Babylon's ransom, Tamar Cham's beard was a rubbing brush to't: yet I'll shave it off, and stuff tennis-balls with it, to please my bully king. 30

King. But all this while I do not know your age.

Eyre. My liege, I am six and fifty year old, yet I can cry hump! with a sound heart for the honour of Saint Hugh. Mark this old wench, my king: I danc'd the shaking of the sheets [35 with her six and thirty years ago, and yet I hope to get two or three young lord mayors, ere I die. I am lusty still, Sim Eyre still. Care and cold lodging brings white hairs. My sweet Majesty, let care vanish, cast it upon thy nobles, [40 it will make thee look always young like Apollo, and cry hump! Prince am I none, yet am I princely born.

King. Ha, ha!
Say, Cornwall, didst thou ever see his like? 45
Nobleman. Not I, my lord.

Enter the EARL OF LINCOLN *and the* LORD MAYOR.

King.   Lincoln, what news with you?
Lincoln. My gracious lord, have care unto yourself,
For there are traitors here.
All.   Traitors? Where? Who?
Eyre. Traitors in my house? God forbid! [49 Where be my officers? I'll spend my soul, ere my king feel harm.
King. Where is the traitor, Lincoln?
Lincoln.   Here he stands.
King. Cornwall, lay hold on Lacy! — Lincoln, speak,
What canst thou lay unto thy nephew's charge?
Lincoln. This, my dear liege: your Grace, to do me honour, 55
Heapt on the head of this degenerate boy
Desertless favours; you made choice of him
To be commander over powers in France.
But he——
King. Good Lincoln, prithee, pause a while!
Even in thine eyes I read what thou wouldst speak. 60
I know how Lacy did neglect our love,
Ran himself deeply, in the highest degree,
Into vile treason——
Lincoln.   Is he not a traitor?
King. Lincoln, he was; now have we pard-'ned him.
'Twas not a base want of true valour's fire, 63
That held him out of France, but love's desire.
Lincoln. I will not bear his shame upon my back.

---

[7] Magpie.

King. Nor shalt thou, Lincoln; I forgive you
  both.
Lincoln. Then, good my liege, forbid the boy
  to wed
One whose mean birth will much disgrace his
  bed.   70
King. Are they not married?
Lincoln.   No, my liege.
Both.   We are.
King. Shall I divorce them then? O be it far
That any hand on earth should dare untie
The sacred knot, knit by God's majesty;   74
I would not for my crown disjoin their hands
That are conjoin'd in holy nuptial bands.
How say'st thou, Lacy, wouldst thou lose thy
  Rose?
Lacy. Not for all India's wealth, my sover-
  eign.
King. But Rose, I am sure, her Lacy would
  forego?
Rose. If Rose were askt that question, she'd
  say no.   80
King. You hear them, Lincoln?
Lincoln.   Yea, my liege, I do.
King. Yet canst thou find i' th' heart to part
  these two?
Who seeks, besides you, to divorce these lovers?
L. Mayor. I do, my gracious lord, I am her
  father.
King. Sir Roger Oateley, our last mayor, I
  think?   85
Nobleman. The same, my liege.
King.   Would you offend Love's laws?
Well, you shall have your wills, you sue to me,
To prohibit the match. Soft, let me see —
You both are married, Lacy, art thou not?
Lacy. I am, dread sovereign.
King.   Then, upon thy life,   90
I charge thee, not to call this woman wife.
L. Mayor. I thank your grace.
Rose.   O my most gracious lord!
                                          Kneels.
King. Nay, Rose, never woo me; I tell you
  true,
Although as yet I am a bachelor,
Yet I believe I shall not marry you.   95
Rose. Can you divide the body from the soul,
Yet make the body live?
King.   Yea, so profound?
I cannot, Rose, but you I must divide.
This fair maid, bridegroom, cannot be your
  bride.
Are you pleas'd, Lincoln? Oateley, are you
  pleas'd?   100
Both. Yes, my lord.
King.   Then must my heart be eas'd;
For, credit me, my conscience lives in pain,
Till these whom I divorc'd, be join'd again.
Lacy, give me thy hand; Rose, lend me thine!
Be what you would be! Kiss now! So, that's
  fine.   105
At night, lovers, to bed! — Now, let me see,
Which of you all mislikes this harmony.
L. Mayor. Will you then take from me my
  child perforce?
King. Why tell me, Oateley: shines not Lacy's
  name   109

As bright in the world's eye as the gay beams
Of any citizen?
Lincoln.   Yea, but, my gracious lord,
I do mislike the match far more than he;
Her blood is too too base.
King.   Lincoln, no more.
Dost thou not know that love respects no blood,
Cares not for difference of birth or state?   115
The maid is young, well born, fair, virtuous,
A worthy bride for any gentleman.
Besides, your nephew for her sake did stoop
To bear necessity, and, as I hear,
Forgetting honours and all courtly pleasures, 120
To gain her love, became a shoemaker.
As for the honour which he lost in France,
Thus I redeem it: Lacy, kneel thee down! —
Arise, Sir Rowland Lacy! Tell me now,   124
Tell me in earnest, Oateley, canst thou chide,
Seeing thy Rose a lady and a bride?
L. Mayor. I am content with what your grace
  hath done.
Lincoln. And I, my liege, since there's no
  remedy.
King. Come on, then, all shake hands: I'll
  have you friends;
Where there is much love, all discord ends.   130
What says my mad lord mayor to all this love?
Eyre. O my liege, this honour you have done
to my fine journeyman here, Rowland Lacy, and
all these favours which you have shown to [134
me this day in my poor house, will make Simon
Eyre live longer by one dozen of warm summers
more than he should.
King. Nay, my mad lord mayor, that shall
  be thy name;
If any grace of mine can length thy life,
One honour more I'll do thee: that new build-
  ing,[1]   140
Which at thy cost in Cornhill is erected,
Shall take a name from us; we'll have it call'd
The Leadenhall, because in digging it
You found the lead that covereth the same.   144
Eyre. I thank your majesty.
Marg.   God bless your grace!
King. Lincoln, a word with you!

Enter HODGE, FIRK, RALPH, *and more* Shoemakers.

Eyre. How now, my mad knaves? Peace,
speak softly, yonder is the king.
King. With the old troop which there we
  keep in pay,
We will incorporate a new supply.   150
Before one summer more pass o'er my head,
France shall repent, England was injured.
What are all those?
Lacy.   All shoemakers, my liege,
Sometime my fellows; in their companies
I liv'd as merry as an emperor.   155
King. My mad lord mayor, are all these shoe-
  makers?

---

1 "A. D. 1419. This year Sir Symon Eyre built Leadenhall, at his proper expense, as it now appears, and
gave the same to the City to be employed as a public
granary for laying up corn against a time of scarcity."
—Maitland's *History and Survey of London*, II. 187.
According to Stow, Eyre was a draper, became Mayor
in 1445, and died in 1459.

Eyre. All shoemakers, my liege ; all gentlemen of the gentle craft, true Trojans, courageous cordwainers ; they all kneel to the shrine of
holy Saint Hugh.   160
All the Shoemakers. God save your majesty !
King. Mad Simon, would they anything with
us ?
Eyre. Mum, mad knaves ! Not a word ! I 'll
do 't ; I warrant you. They are all beggars, my
liege ; all for themselves, and I for them [165
all on both my knees do entreat, that for the
honour of poor Simon Eyre and the good of his
brethren, these mad knaves, your grace would
vouchsafe some privilege to my new Leadenhall,
that it may be lawful for us to buy and sell
leather there two days a week.   171
King. Mad Sim, I grant your suit, you shall
have patent
To hold two market-days in Leadenhall,
Mondays and Fridays, those shall be the times.
Will this content you ?
All.   Jesus bless your grace ! 175
Eyre. In the name of these my poor brethren
shoemakers, I most humbly thank your grace.
But before I rise, seeing you are in the giving
vein and we in the begging, grant Sim Eyre one
boon more.   180
King. What is it, my lord mayor ?
Eyre. Vouchsafe to taste of a poor banquet
that stands sweetly waiting for your sweet pre-
sence.   184

King. I shall undo thee, Eyre, only with feasts ;
Already have I been too troublesome ;
Say, have I not ?
Eyre. O my dear king, Sim Eyre was taken
unawares upon a day of shroving,[1] which I [189
promist long ago to the prentices of London.
For, an 't please your highness, in time past,
I bare the water-tankard,[2] and my coat
Sits not a whit the worse upon my back ;
And then, upon a morning, some mad boys,
It was Shrove Tuesday, even as 't is now,   195
gave me my breakfast, and I swore then by the
stopple of my tankard, if ever I came to be
lord mayor of London, I would feast all the
prentices. This day, my liege, I did it, and the
slaves had an hundred tables five times covered ;
they are gone home and vanisht,   201
Yet add more honour to the gentle trade,
Taste of Eyre's banquet, Simon 's happy
made.
King. Eyre, I will taste of thy banquet, and
will say,
I have not met more pleasure on a day.   205
Friends of the gentle craft, thanks to you all,
Thanks, my kind lady mayoress, for our
cheer. —
Come, lords, a while let 's revel it at home !
When all our sports and banquetings are done,
Wars must right wrongs which Frenchmen
have begun.   *Exeunt.* 210

---

[1] Merry-making.   [2] As an apprentice.

THE HONEST [1] WHORE

PART I

BY

THOMAS DEKKER

[DRAMATIS PERSONAE

GASPARO TREBAZZI, Duke of Milan.
HIPPOLITO, a Count.
CASTRUCHIO.
SINEZI.
PIORATTO.
FLUELLO.
MATHEO.
BENEDICT, a Doctor.
ANSELMO, a Friar.
FUSTIGO, Brother of Viola.
CANDIDO, a Linen-draper.
GEORGE, his Servant.
First Prentice.

Second Prentice.
CRAMBO,
POLI.
ROGER, Servant of Bellafront.
Porter,
Sweeper.
Madmen, Servants, etc.

INFELICE, Daughter of the Duke.
BELLAFRONT, a Harlot.
VIOLA, Wife of Candido.
Mistress FINGERLOCK, a Bawd.

SCENE. — *Milan and the Neighbourhood.*]

ACT I.

SCENE I. [2]

Enter at one door a Funeral (a coronet lying on the hearse, scutcheons and garlands hanging on the sides), attended by GASPARO TREBAZZI, Duke of Milan, CASTRUCHIO, SINEZI, PIORATTO, FLUELLO, *and others. At another door enter* HIPPOLITO, *in discontented appearance; and* MATHEO, *a Gentleman, his friend, labouring to hold him back.*

Duke. Behold, yon comet shows his head again !
Twice hath he thus at cross-turns thrown on us
Prodigious [3] looks ; twice hath he troubled
The waters of our eyes. See, he 's turn'd wild : —
Go on, in God's name.
Cas., Sin.   On afore there, ho ! 5
Duke. Kinsmen and friends, take from your manly sides
Your weapons to keep back the desperate boy
From doing violence to the innocent dead.
Hip. I prithee, dear Matheo ——
Mat.   Come, you 're mad !
Hip. I do arrest thee, murderer ! Set down,
Villains, set down that sorrow, 't is all mine. 11
Duke. I do beseech you all, for my blood's sake
Send hence your milder spirits, and let wrath
Join in confederacy with your weapons' points ;

[1] Chaste.   [2] A street in Milan.   [3] Portentous.

If he proceed to vex us, let your swords 15
Seek out his bowels : funeral grief loathes words.
All. Set on.
Hip.   Set down the body !
Mat.   O my lord !
You 're wrong ! I 'th' open street ? You see she 's dead.
Hip. I know she is not dead.
Duke.   Frantic young man,
Wilt thou believe these gentlemen ? — Pray speak. — 20
Thou dost abuse my child, and mock'st the tears
That here are shed for her. If to behold
Those roses withered, that set out her cheeks ;
That pair of stars that gave her body light,
Dark'ned and dim for ever ; all those rivers 25
That fed her veins with warm and crimson streams
Frozen and dried up : if these be signs of death,
Then is she dead. Thou unreligious youth,
Art not asham'd to empty all these eyes
Of funeral tears, a debt due to the dead, 30
As mirth is to the living ? Sham'st thou not
To have them stare on thee ? Hark, thou art curst
Even to thy face, by those that scarce can speak.
Hip. My lord ——   [dead ?
Duke. What would'st thou have ? Is she not
Hip. Oh, you ha' kill'd her by your cruelty !
Duke. Admit I had, thou kill'st her now again ;
And art more savage than a barbarous Moor. 37
Hip. Let me but kiss her pale and bloodless lip.
Duke. O fie, fie, fie.

Hip. Or if not touch her, let me look on her.
Mat. As you regard your honour ——
Hip.   Honour? Smoke! 41
Mat. Or if you lov'd her living, spare her now.
Duke. Ay, well done, sir, you play the gentleman. ——
Steal hence ; — 't is nobly done ; — away ; — I 'll join
My force to yours, to stop this violent torment [1] —   45
Pass on.
                    Exeunt with funeral, [all except the
                    DUKE, HIPPOLITO *and* MATHEO].
Hip. Matheo, thou dost wound me more.
Mat. I give you physic, noble friend, not wounds.
Duke. O, well said, well done, a true gentleman!
Alack, I know the sea of lovers' rage
Comes rushing with so strong a tide, it beats 50
And bears down all respects of life, of honour,
Of friends, of foes! Forget her, gallant youth.
Hip. Forget her?
Duke.   Nay, nay, be but patient ;
For-why [2] death's hand hath su'd a strict divorce
'Twixt her and thee. What 's beauty but a corse ?   55
What but fair sand-dust are earth's purest forms ?
Queen's bodies are but trunks to put in worms.
Mat. Speak no more sentences, my good lord, but slip hence ; you see they are but fits ; I 'll rule him, I warrant ye. Ay, so, tread gingerly ; your grace is here somewhat too long already. [*Exit* DUKE.] 'Sblood, the jest were now, if, [62 having ta'en some knocks o' th' pate already, he should get loose again, and like a mad ox, toss my new black cloaks into the kennel.[3] I must humour his lordship. — My Lord Hip- [66 polito, is it in your stomach to go to dinner ?
Hip. Where is the body ?
Mat. The body, as the duke spake very wisely, is gone to be worm'd.   70
Hip. I cannot rest ; I 'll meet it at next turn : I 'll see how my love looks.
                    MATHEO *holds him in 's arms.*
Mat. How your love looks ? Worse than a scare-crow. Wrestle not with me : the great fellow gives the fall for a ducat.   75
Hip. I shall forget myself.
Mat. Pray, do so, leave yourself behind yourself, and go whither you will. 'Sfoot, do you long to have base rogues that maintain a Saint Anthony's fire in their noses by nothing but [80 twopenny ale, make ballads of you ? If the duke had but so much mettle in him, as is in a cobbler's awl, he would ha' been a vext thing : he and his train had blown you up, but that their powder has taken the wet of cowards. You 'll bleed three pottles of Alicant,[4] by [86 this light, if you follow 'em, and then we shall have a hole made in a wrong place, to have surgeons roll thee up like a baby in swaddling clouts.   90

---

[1] Dyce conj. *torrent.*   [2] Because.   [3] Gutter.
[4] A red Spanish wine made at Alicant.

Hip. What day is to-day, Matheo ?
Mat. Yea marry, this is an easy question : why to-day is — let me see — Thursday.
Hip. Oh! Thursday.   94
Mat. Here 's a coil [5] for a dead commodity. 'Sfoot, women when they are alive are but dead commodities, for you shall have one woman lie upon many men's hands.
Hip. She died on Monday then.   99
Mat. And that 's the most villanous day of all the week to die in : and she was well, and eat a mess of water-gruel on Monday morning.
Hip. Ay ? It cannot be
Such a bright taper should burn out so soon.
Mat. O yes, my lord. So soon ? Why, I ha' known them that at dinner have been as [106 well, and had so much health, that they were glad to pledge it, yet before three a'clock have been found dead — drunk.
Hip. On Thursday buried! and on Monday died!   110
Quick haste, by'rlady.[6] Sure her winding sheet Was laid out 'fore [7] her body ; and the worms That now must feast with her, were even bespoke,
And solemnly invited like strange guests.   114
Mat. Strange feeders they are indeed, my lord, and, like your jester, or young courtier, will enter upon any man's trencher without bidding.
Hip. Curst be that day for ever that robb'd her
Of breath, and me of bliss ! Henceforth let it stand
Within the wizard's book (the calendar)   120
Markt with a marginal finger, to be chosen
By thieves, by villains, and black murderers,
As the best day for them to labour in.
If henceforth this adulterous bawdy world
Be got with child with treason, sacrilege,   125
Atheism, rapes, treacherous friendship, perjury,
Slander (the beggar's sin), lies (sin of fools),
Or any other damn'd impieties,
On Monday let 'em be delivered.
I swear to thee, Matheo, by my soul,   130
Hereafter weekly on that day I 'll glue
Mine eye-lids down, because they shall not gaze
On any female cheek. And being lockt up
In my close [8] chamber, there I 'll meditate
On nothing but my Infelice's end,   135
Or on a dead man's skull draw out mine own.
Mat. You 'll do all these good works now every Monday, because it is so bad ; but I hope upon Tuesday morning I shall take you with a wench.   140
Hip. If ever, whilst frail blood through my veins run,
On woman's beams I throw affection,
Save her that 's dead ; or that I loosely fly
To th' shore of any other wafting eye,
Let me not prosper, Heaven ! I will be true,
Even to her dust and ashes : could her tomb 146
Stand whilst I liv'd, so long that it might rot,
That should fall down, but she be ne'er forgot.
Mat. If you have this strange monster, hon-

---

[5] Turmoil.   [6] By our lady.   [7] Q. *for.*   [8] Private.

esty,[1] in your belly, why so jig-makers[2] and chroniclers shall pick something out of you; [151 but an I smell not you and a bawdy house out within these ten days, let my nose be as big as an English bag-pudding. I'll follow your lordship, though it be to the place aforenamed. *Exeunt.*

[SCENE II.][3]

Enter FUSTIGO *in some fantastic Sea-suit at one door, a* Porter *meets him at another.*

Fus. How now, porter, will she come?

Por. If I may trust a woman, sir, she will come.

Fus. There's for thy pains [*gives money*]. God-amercy, if I ever stand in need of a wench that will come with a wet finger,[4] porter, thou [5 shalt earn my money before any clarissimo[5] in Milan; yet, so God sa'[6] me, she's mine own sister, body and soul, as I am a Christian gentle-man. Farewell; I'll ponder till she come. Thou hast been no bawd in fetching this woman, I [10 assure thee.

Por. No matter if I had, sir; better men than porters are bawds.

Fus. O God, sir, many that have borne offi-ces. But, porter, art sure thou went'st into [15 a true[7] house?

Por. I think so, for I met with no thieves.

Fus. Nay, but art sure it was my sister Viola?

Por. I am sure, by all superscriptions, it was the party you ciphered.   20

Fus. Not very tall?

Por. Nor very low; a middling woman.

Fus. 'T was she, 'faith 't was she. A pretty plump cheek, like mine?   24

Por. At a blush,[8] a little very much like you.

Fus. Godso, I would not for a ducat she had kickt up her heels, for I ha' spent an abomina-tion this voyage; marry, I did it amongst sail-ors and gentlemen. There's a little modicum more, porter, for making thee stay [*gives* [30 *money*]; farewell, honest porter.

Por. I am in your debt, sir; God preserve you.   *Exit.*

Enter VIOLA.

Fus. Not so, neither, good porter. God's lid, yonder she comes. Sister Viola, I am glad to [35 see you stirring: it's news to have me here, is 't not, sister?

Vio. Yes, trust me. I wond'red who should be so bold to send for me. You're welcome to Milan, brother.

Fus. Troth, sister, I heard you were mar- [41 ried to a very rich chuff,[9] and I was very sorry for it, that I had no better clothes, and that made me send; for you know we Milaners love to strut upon Spanish leather. And how do all our friends?   46

Vio. Very well. You ha' travelled enough now, I trow, to sow your wild oats.

Fus. A pox on 'em! wild oats? I ha' not an oat to throw at a horse. Troth, sister, I ha'

sowed my oats, and reapt two hundred ducats [50 if I had 'em here. Marry, I must entreat you to lend me some thirty or forty till the ship come. By this hand, I'll discharge at my day, by this hand.   55

Vio. These are your old oaths.

Fus. Why, sister, do you think I'll forswear my hand?

Vio. Well, well, you shall have them. Put yourself into better fashion, because I must em-ploy you in a serious matter.   61

Fus. I'll sweat like a horse if I like the mat-ter.

Vio. You ha' cast off all your old swaggering humours?

Fus. I had not sail'd a league in that great [66 fishpond, the sea, but I cast up my very gall.

Vio. I am the more sorry, for I must employ a true swaggerer.

Fus. Nay by this iron, sister, they shall find I am powder and touch-box, if they put fire [71 once into me.

Vio. Then lend me your ears.

Fus. Mine ears are yours, dear sister.

Vio. I am married to a man that has wealth enough, and wit enough.   76

Fus. A linen-draper, I was told, sister.

Vio. Very true, a grave citizen; I want noth-ing that a wife can wish from a husband: but here's the spite, he has not all things belong-ing to a man.   81

Fus. God's my life, he's a very mandrake,[10] or else (God bless us) one a' these whiblins,[11] and that's worse, and then all the children that he gets lawfully of your body, sister, are bastards by a statute.   86

Vio. O, you run over me too fast, brother; I have heard it often said, that he who cannot be angry is no man. I am sure my husband is a man in print,[12] for all things else save only in this, no tempest can move him.   91

Fus. 'Slid, would he had been at sea with us! he should ha' been mov'd, and mov'd again, for I'll be sworn, la, our drunken ship reel'd like a Dutchman.

Vio. No loss of goods can increase in him [96 a wrinkle, no crabbed language make his coun-tenance sour, the stubbornness of no servant shake him; he has no more gall in him than a dove, no more sting than an ant; musician [100 will he never be, yet I find much music in him, but he loves no frets,[13] and is so free from anger, that many times I am ready to bite off my tongue, because it wants that virtue which all women's tongues have, to anger their husbands. Brother, mine can by no thunder turn him [106 into a sharpness.

Fus. Belike his blood, sister, is well brew'd then.   109

Vio. I protest to thee, Fustigo, I love him most affectionately; but I know not—I ha'

---

[10] The allusion is to the fancied resemblance of the roots of the mandrake to the human figure.

[11] "Query Whimlings — idiots." (Rhys.)

[12] A perfect man.

[13] A common pun on *fret*, the ridge on which the strings of a musical instrument are stopped.

[1] Chastity.   [4] Readily.   [7] Honest.
[2] Song-makers.   [5] Grandee.   [8] Glance.
[3] Another street.   [6] Save.   [9] Churl.

such a tickling within me — such a strange longing ; nay verily I do long.

Fus. Then you 're with child, sister, by all
signs and tokens ; nay, I am partly a physician,
and partly something else. I ha' read Al- [116
bertus Magnus, and Aristotle's Emblems.

Vio. You 're wide a' th' bow hand [1] still, brother: my longings are not wanton, but wayward.
I long to have my patient husband eat up a
whole porcupine, to the intent, the bristling [121
quills may stick about his lips like a Flemish
mustachio, and be shot at me. I shall be leaner
than the new moon, unless I can make him
horn-mad.[2]   125

Fus. 'Sfoot, half a quarter of an hour does
that ; make him a cuckold.

Vio. Pooh, he would count such a cut no unkindness.   129

Fus. The honester citizen he ; then make him
drunk and cut off his beard.

Vio. Fie, fie, idle, idle ! He 's no Frenchman,
to fret at the loss of a little scald [3] hair. No,
brother, thus it shall be — you must be secret.

Fus. As your mid-wife, I protest, sister, or
a barber-surgeon.   136

Vio. Repair to the Tortoise here in St. Christopher's Street ; I will send you money ; turn
yourself into a brave [4] man : instead of the arms
of your mistress, let your sword and your [140
military scarf hang about your neck.

Fus. I must have a great horseman's French
feather too, sister.

Vio. O, by any means, to show your light
head, else your hat will sit like a coxcomb. [145
To be brief, you must be in all points a most
terribly wide-mouth'd swaggerer.

Fus. Nay, for swaggering points let me alone.

Vio. Resort then to our shop, and, in my
husband's presence, kiss me, snatch rings, [150
jewels, or any thing, so you give it back again,
brother, in secret.

Fus. By this hand, sister.

Vio. Swear as if you came but new from
knighting.   155

Fus. Nay, I 'll swear after four hundred a
year.

Vio. Swagger worse than a lieutenant among
freshwater soldiers,[5] call me your love, your
ingle,[6] your cousin, or so ; but sister at no [160
hand.

Fus. No, no, it shall be cousin, or rather coz ;
that 's the gulling word between the citizens'
wives and their mad-caps that man [7] 'em to the
garden ; to call you one a' mine aunts,[8] sis- [165
ter, were as good as call you arrant whore ; no,
no, let me alone to cousin you rarely.

Vio. H 'as heard I have a brother, but never
saw him, therefore put on a good face.

Fus. The best in Milan, I warrant.   170

Vio. Take up wares, but pay nothing, rifle
my bosom, my pocket, my purse, the boxes for

money to dice withal ; but, brother, you must
give all back again in secret.   174

Fus. By this welkin that here roars I will, or
else let me never know what a secret is : why,
sister, do you think I 'll cony-catch [9] you, when
you are my cousin ? God 's my life, then I were
a stark ass. If I fret not his guts, beg me for a
fool.[10]   180

Vio. Be circumspect, and do so then. Farewell.

Fus. The Tortoise, sister ! I 'll stay there ;
forty ducats.   *Exit.*

Vio. Thither I 'll send. — This law can none
deny,   184
Women must have their longings, or they die.
                                           Exit.

[SCENE III.] [11]

[*Enter*] GASPARO *the* Duke, Doctor BENEDICT,
       and two Servants.

Duke. Give charge that none do enter ; lock
       the doors —   [*Speaking as he enters.*]
And fellows, what your eyes and ears receive,
Upon your lives trust not the gadding air
To carry the least part of it. The glass, the
       hour-glass !

Doct. Here, my lord.

Duke.   Ah, 't is near [12] spent ! 5
But, Doctor Benedict, does your art speak
       truth ?
Art sure the soporiferous stream will ebb,
And leave the crystal banks of her white body
Pure as they were at first, just at the hour ?

Doct. Just at the hour, my lord.

Duke.   Uncertain her : 10
       [*A curtain is drawn back and* INFE-
       LICE *discovered lying on a couch.*]
Softly ! — See,[13] doctor, what a coldish heat
Spreads over all her body !

Doct.   Now it works.
The vital spirits that by a sleepy charm
Were bound up fast, and threw an icy rust [14]
On her exterior parts, now 'gin to break ; 15
Trouble her not, my lord.

Duke.   Some stools ! You call'd
For music, did you not ? Oh ho, it speaks,
                                         [*Music.*]
It speaks ! Watch, sirs, her waking, note those
       sands.
Doctor, sit down. A dukedom that should
       weigh
Mine own down twice, being put into one scale,
And that fond [15] desperate boy, Hippolito, 21
Making the weight up, should not at my hands
Buy her i' th' other, were her state more light
Than hers, who makes a dowry up with alms.
Doctor, I 'll starve her on the Apennine 25
Ere he shall marry her. I must confess
Hippolito is nobly born ; a man —
Did not mine enemies' blood boil in his veins —
Whom I would court to be my son-in-law ;

But princes, whose high spleens for empery
swell,　　　　　　　　　　　　　　　　30
Are not with easy art made parallel.
　Servants. She wakes, my lord.
　Duke.　　　　　　Look, Doctor Benedict —
I charge you on your lives, maintain for truth
What e'er the doctor or myself aver,
For you shall bear her hence to Bergamo.　　35
　Inf. O God, what fearful dreams !
　　　　　　　　　　　　　　[*Wakening.*]
　Doct.　　　　　　　　Lady.
　Inf.　　　　　　　　　　　　Ha !
　Duke.　　　　　　　　　　　　　Girl.
Why, Infelice, how is 't now, ha ? Speak.
　Inf. I 'm well — what makes this doctor here ?
　— I 'm well.
　Duke. Thou wert not so even now, sickness'
　　　　　pale hand
Laid hold on thee even in the midst[1] of feast-
　　ing ;　　　　　　　　　　　　　40
And when a cup crown'd with thy lover's
　　health
Had touch'd thy lips, a sensible cold dew
Stood on thy cheeks, as if that death had wept
To see such beauty alter.
　Inf.　　　　　　　　I remember
I sate at banquet, but felt no such change.　45
　Duke. Thou hast forgot, then, how a mes-
　　　　　senger
Came wildly in, with this unsavoury news,
That he was dead ?
　Inf.　　　What messenger ? Who 's dead ?
　Duke. Hippolito. Alack ! wring not thy
　　　　　hands.　　　　　　　　　49
　Inf. I saw no messenger, heard no such news.
　Doct. Trust me you did, sweet lady.
　Duke.　　　　　　　La, you now !
　1 Ser. Yes, indeed, madam.
　Duke.　　　La, you now. — 'T is well, good
　　　　　knaves ![2]
　Inf. You ha' slain him, and now you 'll mur-
　　　　　der me.
　Duke. Good Infelice, vex not thus thyself.
Of this the bad report before did strike　　55
So coldly to thy heart, that the swift currents
Of life were all frozen up ——
　Inf.　　　　　　　　It is untrue,
'T is most untrue, O most unnatural father !
　Duke. And we had much to do by art's best
　　　　　cunning,
To fetch life back again.
　Doct.　　　　　Most certain, lady.　60
　Duke. Why, la, you now, you'll not believe
　　　　　me. Friends,
Sweat we not all ? Had we not much to do ?
　Servants. Yes, indeed, my lord, much.
　Duke. Death drew such fearful pictures in
　　　　　thy face,
That were Hippolito alive again,　　　　65
I 'd kneel and woo the noble gentleman
To be thy husband : now I sore repent
My sharpness to him, and his family.
Nay, do not weep for him ; we all must die. —
Doctor, this place where she so oft hath seen　70
His lively presence, hurts[3] her, does it not ?

　Doct. Doubtless, my lord, it does.
　Duke.　　　　　　It does, it does :
Therefore, sweet girl, thou shalt to Bergamo.
　Inf. Even where you will ; in any place there 's
　　　　　woe.
　Duke. A coach is ready ; Bergamo doth
　　　　　stand　　　　　　　　　　　75
In a most wholesome air, sweet walks ; there 's
　　deer,
Ay, thou shalt hunt and send us venison,
Which like some goddess in the Cyprian groves,
Thine own fair hand shall strike. — Sirs, you
　　shall teach her
To stand, and how to shoot ; ay, she shall hunt :
Cast off this sorrow. In, girl, and prepare　81
This night to ride away to Bergamo.
　Inf. O most unhappy maid !　　　*Exit.*
　Duke.　　　　　　Follow her close.
No words that she was buried, on your lives !
Or that her ghost walks now after she 's dead ;
I 'll hang you if you name a funeral.　　86
　1 Ser. I 'll speak Greek, my lord, ere I speak
　　that deadly word.
　2 Ser. And I 'll speak Welsh, which is harder
　　than Greek.　　　　*Exeunt* [*Servants*].　90
　Duke. Away, look to her. — Doctor Benedict,
Did you observe how her complexion altered
Upon his name and death? Oh, would 'twere true.
　Doct. It may, my lord.
　Duke.　　　May ! How ? I wish his death.
　Doct. And you may have your wish ; say but
　　the word,　　　　　　　　　　95
And 't is a strong spell to rip up his grave.
I have good knowledge with Hippolito ;
He calls me friend, I 'll creep into his bosom,
And sting him there to death ; poison can do 't.
　Duke. Perform it ; I 'll create thee half mine
　　heir.　　　　　　　　　　　　100
　Doct. It shall be done, although the fact[4] be
　　foul.
　Duke. Greatness hides sin, the guilt upon my
　　soul !　　　　　　　　　　　*Exeunt.*

[SCENE IV.][5]

Enter CASTRUCHIO, PIORATTO, *and* FLUELLO.

　Cas. Signor Pioratto, Signor Fluello, shall 's
be merry ? Shall 's play the wags now ?
　Flu. Ay, any thing that may beget the child
of laughter.
　Cas. Truth, I have a pretty sportive conceit
new crept into my brain, will move excellent [5
mirth.
　Pio. Let 's ha 't, let 's ha 't ; and where shall
the scene of mirth lie ?
　Cas. At Signor Candido's house, the patient
man, nay, the monstrous patient man. They [10
say his blood is immoveable, that he has taken
all patience from a man, and all constancy from
a woman.
　Flu. That makes so many whores now-a-days.
　Cas. Ay, and so many knaves too.　　15
　Pio. Well, sir.
　Cas. To conclude, the report goes, he 's so
mild, so affable, so suffering, that nothing indeed can move him : now do but think what

---

[1] Q2 *deadst.*　　[2] Q2 *God knows.*　　[3] Q2 *haunts.*

[4] Deed.　　[5] A street.

sport it will be to make this fellow, the mir- [20
ror of patience, as angry, as vext, and as mad
as an English cuckold.

Flu. O, 't were admirable mirth, that; but
how will 't be done, signor?

Cas. Let me alone, I have a trick, a con- [25
ceit, a thing, a device will sting him, i' faith, if
he have but a thimbleful of blood in 's belly, or
a spleen not so big as a tavern token.[1]

Pio. Thou stir him? Thou move him? Thou
anger him? Alas, I know his approved tem- [30
per. Thou vex him? Why he has a patience
above man's injuries: thou may'st sooner raise
a spleen in an angel, than rough humour in him.
Why, I 'll give you instance for it. This wonderfully temper'd Signor Candido upon a time [35
invited home to his house certain Neapolitan
lords, of curious taste, and no mean palates,
conjuring his wife, of all loves,[2] to prepare cheer
fitting for such honourable trencher-men. She
— just of a woman's nature, covetous to try [40
the uttermost of vexation, and thinking at last
to get the start of his humour — willingly neglected the preparation, and became unfurnish,
not only of dainty, but of ordinary dishes. He,
according to the mildness of his breast, en- [45
tertained the lords, and with courtly discourse
beguiled the time, as much as a citizen might
do. To conclude, they were hungry lords, for
there came no meat in; their stomachs were
plainly gull'd,[3] and their teeth deluded, and, [50
if anger could have seiz'd a man, there was
matter enough i' faith to vex any citizen in the
world, if he were not too much made a fool by
his wife.

Flu. Ay, I 'll swear for 't. 'Sfoot, had it [55
been my case, I should ha' play'd mad tricks
with my wife and family. First, I would ha'
spitted the men, stew'd the maids, and bak'd
the mistress, and so served them in.

Pio. Why 't would ha' tempted any blood but
his,   60
And thou to vex him? thou to anger him
With some poor shallow jest?

Cas. 'Sblood, Signor Pioratto, you that disparage my conceit, I 'll wage a hundred ducats
upon the head on 't, that it moves him, frets [65
him, and galls him.

Pio. Done, 't is a lay,[4] join golls[5] on 't: witness Signor Fluello.

Cas. Witness: 't is done.
Come, follow me: the house is not far off,   70
I 'll thrust him from his humour, vex his breast,
And win a hundred ducats by one jest. *Exeunt.*

[SCENE V.][6]

Enter [VIOLA] CANDIDO's *wife*, GEORGE, *two*
Prentices *in the shop.*

Vio. Come, you put up your wares in good
order here, do you not, think you? One piece
cast this way, another that way! You had need
have a patient master indeed.   4

---

[1] A piece of brass or copper money, coined by tavern-
keepers and other tradesmen for small change.
[2] For love's sake.   [4] Bet.
[1] Cheated.   [5] Hands.   [6] Candido's shop.

Geo. [*Aside.*] Ay, I 'll be sworn, for we have
a curst mistress.

Vio. You mumble, do you? mumble? I
would your master or I could be a note more
angry, for two patient folks in a house spoil all
the servants that ever shall come under them. 10

1 *Pren.* [*Aside.*] You patient! Ay, so is the
devil when he is horn-mad.

Enter CASTRUCHIO, FLUELLO, *and* PIORATTO.

Geo.[7] Gentlemen, what do you lack?[8]
1 *Pren.*[7] What is 't you buy?
2 *Pren.*[7] See fine hollands, fine cambrics,
fine lawns.   16
Geo. What is 't you lack?
2 *Pren.* What is 't you buy?
Cas. Where 's Signor Candido, thy master?
Geo. Faith, signor, he 's a little negotiated,[9]
he 'll appear presently.   21
Cas. Fellow, let 's see a lawn, a choice one,
sirrah.
Geo. The best in all Milan, gentlemen, and
this is the piece. I can fit you gentlemen [25
with fine calicoes too for doublets, the only
sweet fashion now, most delicate and courtly, a
meek gentle calico, cut upon two double affable
taffetas, — ah, most neat, feat, and unmatch-
able!   30
Flu. A notable voluble-tongu'd villain.
Pio. I warrant this fellow was never begot
without much prating.
Cas. What, and is this she, sayest thou?
Geo. Ay, and the purest she that ever you [35
finger'd since you were a gentleman. Look how
even she is, look how clean she is, ha! as even
as the brow of Cynthia, and as clean as your
sons and heirs when they ha' spent all.
Cas. Pooh, thou talk'st — pox on 't, 't is [40
rough.
Geo. How? Is she rough? But if you bid[10]
pox on 't, sir, 't will take away the roughness
presently.
Flu. Ha, signor; has he fitted your French [45
curse?
Geo. Look you, gentlemen, here 's another.
Compare them I pray, *compara Virgilium cum
Homero*, compare virgins with harlots.
Cas. Pooh, I ha' seen better, and as you [50
term them, evener and cleaner.
Geo. You may see further for your mind, but
trust me, you shall not find better for your
body.

Enter CANDIDO.

Cas. O here he comes, let 's make as though
we pass,   55
Come, come, we 'll try in some other shop.
Cand. How now? What 's the matter?
Geo. The gentlemen find fault with this
lawn, fall out with it, and without a cause too.
Cand. Without a cause?   60
And that makes you to let 'em pass away.
Ah, may I crave a word with you, gentlemen?
Flu. He calls us.

---

[7] Qq. give first three speeches to *All Three.*
[8] The shopkeeper's common cry at this period.
[9] Engaged.   [10] Pray, invoke.

Cas.   Makes the better for the jest.
Cand. I pray come near, you 're very wel-
come, gallants.   64
Pray pardon my man's rudeness, for I fear me
H 'as talkt above a prentice with you. Lawns!
                              [*Showing lawns.*]
Look you, kind gentlemen, this — no — ay —
this:
Take this upon my honest-dealing faith,
To be a true weave, not too hard nor slack,
But e'en as far from falsehood as from black. 70
Cas. Well, how do you rate it?
Cand. Very consciouably, eighteen shillings
a yard.
Cas. That 's too dear: how many yards does
the whole piece contain, think you?   75
Cand. Why, some seventeen yards, I think,
or thereabouts.
How much would serve your turn, I pray?
Cas. Why, let me see — would it were better
too!
Cand. Truth 't is the best in Milan, at few
words.
Cas. Well, let me have then — a whole penny-
worth.   80
Cand. Ha, ha! you 're a merry gentleman.
Cas. A penn'orth I say.
Cand. Of lawn!
Cas. Of lawn? Ay, of lawn, a penn'orth.
'Sblood, dost not hear? A whole penn'orth,
are you deaf?   86
Cand. Deaf? no, sir; but I must tell you,
Our wares do seldom meet such customers.
Cas. Nay, an you and your lawns be so
squeamish, fare you well.   90
Cand. Pray stay; a word, pray, signor: for
what purpose is it, I beseech you?
Cas. 'Sblood, what 's that to you: I 'll have
a penny-worth.   94
Cand. A penny-worth! Why you shall. I 'll
serve you presently.[1]
2 *Pren.* 'Sfoot, a penny-worth, mistress!
Vio. A penny-worth! Call you these gentle-
men?
Cas. No, no: not there.   100
Cand. What then, kind gentlemen, what, at
this corner here?
Cas. No, nor there neither;
I 'll have it just in the middle, or else not.   104
Cand. Just in the middle — ha — you shall
too: what, —
Have you a single penny?
Cas. Yes, here 's one.
Cand. Lend it me, I pray.
Flu. An excellent followed jest!
Vio. What, will he spoil the lawn now?   110
Cand. Patience, good wife.
Vio. Ay, that patience makes a fool of you.
— Gentlemen, you might ha' found some other
citizen to have made a kind gull[2] on, besides
my husband.   115
Cand. Pray, gentlemen, take her to be a
woman;
Do not regard her language. — O kind soul,
Such words will drive away my customers.

Vio. Customers with a murrain![3] Call you
these customers?   120
Cand. Patience, good wife.
Vio. Pox a' your patience.
Geo. 'Sfoot, mistress, I warrant these are
some cheating companions.[4]   124
Cand. Look you, gentlemen, there 's your
ware; I thank you, I have your money here;
pray know my shop, pray let me have your
custom.
Vio. Custom, quoth 'a!
Cand. Let me take more of your money.   130
Vio. You had need so.
Pio. Hark in thine ear, thou 'st lost an hun-
dred ducats.
Cas. Well, well, I know 't: is 't possible that
homo   134
Should be nor man, nor woman: not once mov'd;
No not at such an injury, not at all!
Sure he 's a pigeon, for he has no gall.
Flu. Come, come, you 're angry though you
smother it:
You 're vext i' faith; confess.
Cand.   Why, gentlemen,
Should you conceit me to be vext or mov'd? 140
He has my ware, I have his money for 't,
And that 's no argument I 'm angry: no:
The best logician cannot prove me so.
Flu. Oh, but the hateful name of a penn'orth
of lawn,
And then cut i' th' middle of the piece.   145
Pah, I guess it by myself, 't would move a lamb
Were he a linen-draper, 't would, i' faith.
Cand. Well, give me leave to answer you for
that:
We are set here to please all customers,   149
Their humours and their fancies; — offend none,
We get by many, if we leese[5] by one.
May be his mind stood to no more than that,
A penn'orth serves him, and 'mongst trades
't is found,
Deny a penn'orth, it may cross a pound.   154
Oh, that that means to thrive, with patient eye
Must please the devil if he come to buy!
Flu. O wondrous man, patient 'bove wrong
or woe,
How blest were men, if women could be so!
Cand. And to express how well my breast is
pleas'd,
And satisfied in all: — George fill a beaker. 160
                                   Exit GEORGE.
I 'll drink unto that gentleman, who lately
Bestow'd his money with me.
Vio.   God 's my life,
We shall have all our gains drunk out in beak-
ers,
To make amends for pennyworths of lawn!   164

[*Re*]-enter GEORGE [*with beaker*].

Cand. Here wife, begin you to the gentleman.
Vio. I begin to him!   [*Spills the wine.*]
Cand.   George, fill 't up again:
'T was my fault, my hand shook. *Exit* GEORGE.
Pio.   How strangely this doth show!
A patient man linkt with a waspish shrew.

---

[1] At once.   [2] Dupe.   [3] Plague.   [4] Fellows.   [5] Lose.

Flu. [*Aside.*] A silver and gilt beaker : I 've
  a trick   169
To work upon that beaker, sure 't will fret him ;
It cannot choose but vex him. — Signor Castru-
  chio,
In pity to thee I have a conceit,
Will save thy hundred ducats yet ; 't will do 't,
And work him to impatience.
Cas.   Sweet Fluello,
I should be bountiful to that conceit.   175
Flu. Well, 't is enough.

    [*Re*]-*enter* GEORGE [*with beaker.*]

Cand.   Here, gentlemen, to you,
I wish your custom, you 're exceeding welcome.
                [*Drinks.*]
Cas. I pledge you, Signor Candido —
                [*Drinks.*]
Here you that must receive a hundred ducats.
Pio. I 'll pledge them deep, i' faith, Castru-
  chio. —   180
Signor Fluello.   [*Drinks.*]
Flu.   Come : play 't off to me ;
I am your last man.
Cand.   George, supply the cup.
    [*Exit* GEORGE *who returns with
      beaker filled.*]
Flu. So, so, good honest George, —
Here Signor Candido, all this to you.   184
Cand. O, you must pardon me, I use it not.[1]
Flu. Will you not pledge me then ?
Cand.   Yes, but not that :
Great love is shown in little.
Flu.   Blurt[2] on your sentences !
'Sfoot, you shall pledge me all.
Cand.   Indeed I shall not.
Flu. Not pledge me ? 'Sblood, I 'll carry
  away the beaker then.
Cand. The beaker ? Oh ! that at your pleas-
  sure, sir.   190
Flu. Now by this drink I will.   [*Drinks.*]
Cas.   Pledge him, he 'll do 't else.
Flu. So : I ha' done you right on my thumb-
  nail,[3]
What, will you pledge me now ?
Cand.   You know me, sir,
I am not of that sin.
Flu.   Why, then, farewell :
I 'll bear away the beaker by this light.   195
Cand. That 's as you please ; 't is very good.
Flu. Nay, it doth please me, and as you say,
'T is a very good one. Farewell, Signor Candido.
Pio. Farewell, Candido.
Cand. You 're welcome, gentlemen.
Cas.   Art not mov'd yet ?   200
I think his patience is above our wit.
       Exeunt [CASTRUCHIO, FLUELLO,
      carrying off the beaker, and PIO-
      RATTO.]
Geo. I told you before, mistress, they were
all cheaters.   203
Vio. Why fool ! why husband ! why madman !

---

[1] I am not accustomed to drink whole beakers full.
[2] An exclamation of contempt, equivalent to "a fig
for." (Dyce.)
[3] Emptied the cup so completely that the remaining
  drop will stand on the thumb-nail.

I hope you will not let 'em sneak away so with
a silver and gilt beaker, the best in the house
too. — Go, fellows, make hue and cry after
them.
Cand. Pray let your tongue lie still, all will
  be well. —
Come hither, George, hie to the constable,   210
And in calm order wish him to attach them.
Make no great stir, because they 're gentlemen,
And a thing partly done in merriment.
'T is but a size above a jest thou know'st,
Therefore pursue it mildly. Go, begone,   215
The constable 's hard by, bring him along, —
Make haste again.   *Exit* GEORGE.
Vio. O you 're a goodly patient woodcock,[4]
are you not now ? See what your patience comes
to : every one saddles you, and rides you ; [220
you 'll be shortly the common stone-horse[5] of
Milan : a woman 's well holpt up with such a
meacock.[6] I had rather have a husband that
would swaddle[7] me thrice a day, than such a
one, that will be gull'd twice in half-an-hour. [225
Oh, I could burn all the wares in my shop for
anger.
Cand. Pray wear a peaceful temper ; be my
  wife,
That is, be patient ; for a wife and husband
Share but one soul between them : this being
  known,   230
Why should not one soul then agree in one ?
                Exit.
Vio. Hang your agreements ! but if my
beaker be gone. —

Re-enter CASTRUCHIO, FLUELLO, PIORATTO,
    and GECRGE.

Cand. Oh, here they come.   234
Geo. The constable, sir, let 'em come along
with me, because[8] there should be no wond'-
ring : he stays at door.
Cas. Constable, Goodman Abram.[9]
Flu. Now Signor Candido, 'sblood, why do
you attach us ?   240
Cas. 'Sheart ! attach us !
Cand.   Nay swear not, gallants,
Your oaths may move your souls, but not move
  me ;
You have a silver beaker of my wife's.
Flu. You say not true : 't is gilt.
Cand.   Then you say true ;
And being gilt, the guilt lies more on you.   245
Cas. I hope y' are not angry, sir.
Cand. Then you hope right ; for I 'm not angry.
Flu. No, but a little mov'd.
Cand. I mov'd ! 'T was you were mov'd, you
  were brought hither.
Cas. But you, out of your anger and impa
  tience,   25
Caus'd us to be attacht.
Cand.   Nay, you misplace it
Out of my quiet sufferance I did that,
And not of any wrath. Had I shown anger,
I should have then pursu'd you with the law,

---

[4] Simpleton.   [6] Milksop.
[5] Stallion.   [7] Beat.   [8] In order that
[9] A beggar who pretended madness was called an
Abraham man.

And hunted you to shame, as many worldlings
Do build their anger upon feebler grounds ;   256
The more 's the pity ; many lose their lives
For scarce so much coin as will hide their palm :
Which is most cruel ; those have vexed spirits
That pursue lives. In this opinion rest,   260
The loss of millions could not move my breast.

Flu. Thou art a blest man, and with peace
dost deal ;
Such a meek spirit can bless a commonweal.

Cand. Gentlemen, now 't is upon eating-time,
Pray part not hence, but dine with me to-day.

Cas. I never heard a carter yet say nay   266
To such a motion. I 'll not be the first.

Pio. Nor I.

Flu. Nor I.   269

Cand. The constable shall bear you company.
George, call him in : let the world say what it
can,
Nothing can drive me from a patient man.
Exeunt.

[ACT II]

[SCENE I.]¹

Enter ROGER *with a stool, cushion, looking-glass
and chafing-dish ; those being set down, he pulls
out of his pocket a phial with white colour in it,
and two boxes, one with white another red
painting ; he places all things in order, and a
candle by them, singing with the ends of old
ballads as he does it. At last* BELLAFRONT, *as
he rubs his cheek with the colours, whistles
within.*

Rog. Anon, forsooth.

Bell. [*within.*] What are you playing the
rogue about ?

Rog. About you, forsooth ; I 'm drawing up
a hole in your white silk stocking.   5

Bell. Is my glass there ? and my boxes of
complexion ?

Rog. Yes, forsooth : your boxes of complexion
are here, I think : yes, 't is here. Here 's your
two complexions, — [*Aside.*] and if I had all [10
the four complexions, I should ne'er set a good
face upon 't. Some men I see, are born under hard-favoured planets as well as women.
Zounds, I look worse now than I did before !
and it makes her face glister most damna- [15
bly. There 's knavery in daubing, I hold my
life ; or else this is only female pomatum.

Enter BELLAFRONT *not full ready,² without a
gown ; she sits down ; with her bodkin³ curls
her hair ; and colours her lips.*

Bell. Where 's my ruff and poker,⁴ you blockhead ?

Rog. Your ruff, your poker, are engend'ring
together upon the cupboard of the court, or [21
the court cupboard.⁵

Bell. Fetch 'em. Is the pox in your hams,
you can go no faster ?   [*Strikes him.*]

¹ A room in Bellafront's house.
² Dressed.   ⁴ A stick used for plaiting ruffs.
³ Frizzling iron.   ⁵ Sideboard.

Rog. Would the pox were in your fingers, [25
unless you could leave flinging ! Catch. *Exit.*

Bell. I 'll catch you, you dog, by and by : do
you grumble ?   *She sings.*

Cupid is a God, as naked as my nail,
I 'll whip him with a rod, if he my true love fail.

[*Re-enter* ROGER *with ruff and poker.*]

Rog. There 's your ruff, shall I poke it ?   31

Bell. Yes, honest Roger — no, stay ; prithee,
good boy, hold here.

[*Sings.* ROGER *holds the glass and candle.*]

Down, down, down, down, I fall down and arise, —
down —
I never shall arise.   35

Rog. Troth, mistress, then leave the trade if
you shall never rise.

Bell. What trade, Goodman Abram ?

Rog. Why that of down and arise, or the
falling trade.   40

Bell. I 'll fall with you by and by.

Rog. If you do I know who shall smart for 't.
Troth, mistress, what do I look like now ?

Bell. Like as you are ; a panderly sixpenny
rascal.   45

Rog. I may thank you for that : in faith, I
look like an old proverb, "Hold the candle before the devil."

Bell. Ud's life, I 'll stick my knife in your guts
an you prate to me so ! — What ?   *She sings.*

Well met, pug, the pearl of beauty : umh, umh.   51
How now, Sir Knave ? you forget your duty, umh, umh,
Marry muff⁶ sir, are you grown so dainty ; fa, la, la, etc.
Is it you, sir ? the worst of twenty, fa, la, la, leera, la.

Pox on you, how dost thou hold my glass ?   55

Rog. Why, as I hold your door : with my
fingers.

Bell. Nay, pray thee, sweet honey Roger,
hold up handsomely.   [*Sings.*]

Sing pretty wantons warble, etc.   60

We shall ha' guests to-day, I lay my little
maidenhead ; my nose itches so.

Rog. I said so too last night, when our fleas
twinged me.   64

Bell. So, poke my ruff now ; my gown, my
gown ! Have I my fall ?⁷ Where 's my fall,
Roger ?

Rog. Your fall, forsooth, is behind.
One knocks.

Bell. God 's my pittikins !⁸ some fool or other
knocks.   70

Rog. Shall I open to the fool, mistress ?

Bell. And all these baubles lying thus ?
Away with it quickly. — Ay, ay, knock, and
be damn'd, whosoever you be ! — So : give the
fresh salmon line now : let him come ashore. [75
[*Exit* ROGER.] He shall serve for my breakfast,
though he go against my stomach.

ROGER *fetch in* FLUELLO, CASTRUCHIO, *and*
PIORATTO.

Flu. Morrow, coz.

Cas. How does my sweet acquaintance ?

⁶ An expression of contempt.
⁷ A kind of collar, falling flat round the neck.
⁸ A corruption of "God 's my pity."

Pio. Save thee, little marmoset : how dost thou, good, pretty rogue ? 81

Bell. Well, God-a-mercy, good, pretty rascal.

Flu. Roger, some light, I prithee.

Rog. You shall, signor, for we that live here in this vale of misery are as dark as hell. 85

Exit for a candle.

Cas. Good tobacco, Fluello ?

Flu. Smell.

Pio. It may be tickling gear : for it plays with my nose already.

Re-enter ROGER [*with candle*].

Rog. Here 's another light angel,[1] signor. 90

Bell. What, you pied curtal,[2] what 's that you are neighing ?

Rog. I say God send us the light of Heaven, or some more angels.

Bell. Go fetch some wine, and drink half of it.

Rog. I must fetch some wine, gentlemen, and drink half of it. 95

Flu. Here Roger.

Cas. No, let me send, prithee.

Flu. Hold, you cankerworm.

Rog. You shall send both, if you please, signors. 100

Pio. Stay, what 's best to drink a' mornings ?

Rog. Hippocras,[3] sir, for my mistress, if I fetch it, is most dear to her.

Flu. Hippocras ? There then, here 's a teston[4] for you, you snake. 105

Rog. Right sir, here 's three shillings and six-pence for a pottle[5] and a manchet.[6] *Exit.*

Cas. Here 's most Herculanean[7] tobacco ; ha' some, acquaintance ? 109

Bell. Faugh, not I, makes your breath stink like the piss of a fox. Acquaintance, where supt you last night ?

Cas. At a place, sweet acquaintance, where your health danc'd the canaries,[8] i' faith : you should ha' been there. 115

Bell. I there among your punks ![9] Marry, faugh, hang' em ; I scorn 't. Will you never leave sucking of eggs in other folk's hens' nests ? 119

Cas. Why, in good troth, if you 'll trust me, acquaintance, there was not one hen at the board ; ask Fluello.

Flu. No, faith, coz, none but cocks. Signor Malavella drunk to thee. 124

Bell. O, a pure beagle ; that horse-leech there ?

Flu. And the knight, Sir Oliver Lollio, swore he would bestow a taffeta petticoat on thee, but to break his fast with thee. 129

Bell. With me ? I 'll choke him then, hang him, molecatcher ! It 's the dreaming'st snotty-nose.

Pio. Well, many took that Lollio for a fool, but he 's a subtle fool. 134

Bell. Ay, and he has fellows : of all filthy,

dry-fisted knights, I cannot abide that he should touch me.

Cas. Why, wench ? Is he scabbed ?

Bell. Hang him, he 'll not live to be so honest, nor to the credit to have scabs about him ; [140 his betters have 'em : but I hate to wear out any of his coarse knight-hood, because he 's made like an alderman's night-gown, fac'd all with cony[10] before, and within nothing but fox. This sweet Oliver will eat mutton[11] till he [145 be ready to burst, but the lean-jaw'd slave will not pay for the scraping of his trencher.

Pio. Plague him ; set him beneath the salt, and let him not touch a bit, till every one has had his full cut. 150

Flu. Lord Ello, the gentleman-usher, came in to us too ; marry 't was in our cheese, for he had been to borrow money for his lord, of a citizen. 154

Cas. What an ass is that lord, to borrow money of a citizen !

Bell. Nay, God 's my pity, what an ass is that citizen to lend money to a lord !

Enter MATHEO *and* HIPPOLITO ; HIPPOLITO *saluting the company, as a stranger, walks off.*[12] ROGER *comes in sadly behind them, with a pottle pot, and stands aloof off.*

Mat. Save you, gallants. Signor Fluello, exceedingly well met, as I may say. 160

Flu. Signor Matheo, exceedingly well met too, as I may say.

Mat. And how fares my little pretty mistress ? 164

Bell. Ee'n as my little pretty servant ; sees three court dishes before her, and not one good bit in them : — How now ? Why the devil stand'st thou so ? Art in a trance ?

Rog. Yes, forsooth. 169

Bell. Why dost not fill out their wine ?

Rog. Forsooth, 't is fill'd out already : all the wine that the signors have bestow'd upon you is cast away ; a porter ran a little[13] at me, and so fac'd me down that I had not a drop. 174

Bell. I 'm accurst to let such a withered arti-choke-faced rascal grow under my nose. Now you look like an old he-cat, going to the gal-lows. I 'll be hang'd if he ha' not put up the money to cony-catch[14] us all. 179

Rog. No, truly, forsooth, 't is not put up yet.

Bell. How many gentlemen hast thou served thus ?

Rog. None but five hundred, besides prenti-ces and serving-men. 184

Bell. Dost think I 'll pocket it up at thy hands ?

Rog. Yes, forsooth, I fear you will pocket it up.

Bell. Fie, fie, cut my lace, good servant ; I shall ha' the mother[15] presently, I 'm so vext at this horse-plum.[16] 191

Flu. Plague, not for a scald[17] pottle of wine !

---

[1] A gold coin worth about ten shillings.
[2] A docked horse.
[3] Spiced and sweetened wine.
[4] Sixpence.
[5] Half a gallon.
[6] A roll of fine bread.
[7] Q₂ *Herculian.*
[8] A sprightly dance.
[9] Prostitutes.
[10] Rabbit-skin.
[11] " Mutton " was slang for a light woman.
[12] Retires to the background.
[13] Dyce suggests *tilt.*
[14] Cheat.
[15] Hysterics.
[16] A small red plum.
[17] Paltry.

Mat. Nay, sweet Bellafront, for a little pig's wash!

Cas. Here Roger, fetch more. [*Gives money.*] A mischance, i' faith, acquaintance. 196

Bell. Out of my sight, thou ungodly puritanical creature.

Rog. For the t' other pottle? Yes, forsooth.

Bell. Spill that too. [*Exit* ROGER.] What gentleman is that, servant? Your friend? 201

Mat. Gods so; a stool, a stool! If you love me mistress, entertain this gentleman respectively,[1] and bid him welcome.

Bell. He 's very welcome, — pray, sir, sit. 205

Hip. Thanks, lady.

Flu. Count Hippolito, is 't not? Cry you mercy, signor; you walk here all this while, and we not heard you! Let me bestow a stool upon you, beseech you; you are a stranger here, we know the fashions a' th' house. 211

Cas. Please you be here, my lord?
[*Offers*] tobacco.

Hip. No, good Castruchio.

Flu. You have abandoned the Court, I see, my lord, since the death of your mistress. Well, [215 she was a delicate piece. — Beseech you, sweet, come let us serve under the colours of your acquaintance still for all that. — Please you to meet here at [the] lodging of my coz, I shall bestow a banquet upon you. 220

Hip. I never can deserve this kindness, sir. What may this lady be, whom you call coz?

Flu. Faith, sir, a poor gentlewoman, of passing good carriage; one that has some suits in law, and lies here in an attorney's house. 225

Hip. Is she married?

Flu. Ha, as all your punks are, a captain's wife, or so. Never saw her before, my lord?

Hip. Never, trust me : a goodly creature! 229

Flu. By gad, when you know her as we do, you 'll swear she is the prettiest, kindest, sweetest, most bewitching honest ape under the pole. A skin, your satin is not more soft, nor lawn whiter. 234

Hip. Belike, then, she 's some sale [2] courtesan.

Flu. Troth, as all your best faces are, a good wench.

Hip. Great pity that she 's a good wench. 239

Mat. Thou shalt ha', i' faith, mistress. — How now, signors? What, whispering? Did not I lay a wager I should take you, within seven days, in a house of vanity?

Hip. You did; and, I beshrew your heart, you 've won. 245

Mat. How do you like my mistress?

Hip. Well, for such a mistress; better, if your mistress be not your master. — I must break manners, gentlemen; fare you well.

Mat. 'Sfoot, you shall not leave us. 250

Bell. The gentleman likes not the taste of our company,

All. Beseech you stay.

Hip. Trust me, my affairs beckon for me; pardon me, 255

Mat. Will you call for me half an hour hence here?

[1] Respectfully.   [2] For sale.

Hip. Perhaps I shall.

Mat. Perhaps? faugh! I know you can swear to me you will. 260

Hip. Since you will press me, on my word, I will.   *Exit.*

Bell. What sullen picture is this, servant?

Mat. It 's Count Hippolito, the brave count.

Pio. As gallant a spirit as any in Milan, [265 you sweet Jew.

Flu. Oh! he 's a most essential gentleman, coz.

Cas. Did you never hear of Count Hippolito, acquaintance? 270

Bell. Marry, muff a' your counts, an be no more life in 'em.

Mat. He 's so malcontent! Sirrah [3] Bellafront, and you be honest gallants, let 's sup together, and have the count with us : — thou shalt [275 sit at the upper end, punk.[4]

Bell. Punk, you sous'd [5] gurnet?

Mat. King's truce! Come, I 'll bestow the supper to have him but laugh.

Cas. He betrays his youth too grossly to [280 that tyrant melancholy.

Mat. All this is for a woman.

Bell. A woman? Some whore! What sweet jewel is 't?

Pio. Would she heard you! 285

Flu. Troth, so would I.

Cas. And I, by Heaven.

Bell. Nay, good servant, what woman?

Mat. Pah!

Bell. Prithee, tell me; a buss,[6] and tell [290 me. I warrant he 's an honest fellow, if he take on thus for a wench. Good rogue, who?

Mat. By th' Lord I will not, must not, faith, mistress. Is 't a match, sirs? this night, at th' Antelope : ay, for there 's best wine, and good boys. 296

All. It 's done; at th' Antelope.

Bell. I cannot be there to-night.

Mat. Cannot? By th' Lord you shall.

Bell. By the Lady I will not. Shall! 300

Flu. Why, then, put it off till Friday; wu't come then, coz?

Bell. Well.

Re-enter ROGER.

Mat. You 're the waspishest ape. Roger, put your mistress in mind to sup with us on [305 Friday next. You 're best come like a madwoman, without a band, in your waistcoat,[7] and the linings of your kirtle outward, like every common hackney [8] that steals out at the back gate of her sweet knight's lodging. 310

Bell. Go, go, hang yourself!

Cas. It 's dinner-time, Matheo; shall 's hence?

All. Yes, yes. — Farewell, wench.   *Exeunt.*

Bell. Farewell, boys. — Roger, what wine sent they for? 314

Rog. Bastard wine,[9] for if it had been truly begotten, it would not ha' been asham'd to

[3] The term sirrah was applied often to women as well as to men.

[4] Prostitute.   [5] Pickled.   [6] Kiss.

[7] *I. e.* without your upper dress.

[8] Harlot.   [9] A sweet Spanish wine.

come in. Here 's six shillings to pay for nursing
the bastard.

Bell. A company of rooks![1] O good sweet
Roger, run to the poulter's, and buy me some
fine larks !   321

Rog. No woodcocks ? [1]

Bell. Yes, faith, a couple, if they be not dear.

Rog. I 'll buy but one, there 's one already
here.   *Exit.*

Enter HIPPOLITO.

Hip. Is the gentleman, my friend, departed.
mistress ?   326

Bell. His back is but new turn'd, sir.

Hip.   Fare you well.

Bell. I can direct you to him.

Hip.   Can you, pray?

Bell. If you please, stay, he 'll not be absent
long.

Hip. I care not much.

Bell.   Pray sit, forsooth.

Hip.   I 'm hot.   330
If I may use your room, I 'll rather walk.

Bell. At your best pleasure. — Whew ! some
rubbers [2] there !

Hip. Indeed, I 'll none : — indeed I will not:
thanks.

Pretty fine lodging. I perceive my friend
Is old in your acquaintance.

Bell.   Troth, sir, he comes 335
As other gentlemen, to spend spare hours.
If yourself like our roof, such as it is,
Your own acquaintance may be as old as his.

Hip. Say I did like ; what welcome should I
find ?

Bell. Such as my present fortunes can afford.

Hip. But would you let me play Matheo's
part ?   341

Bell. What part ?   [you, kiss.

Hip.   Why, embrace you: dally with
Faith, tell me, will you leave him and love me ?

Bell. I am in bonds to no man, sir.

Hip.   Why then,
You 're free for any man ; if any, me.   345
But I must tell you, lady, were you mine,
You should be all mine ; I could brook no
sharers,
I should be covetous, and sweep up all.
I should be pleasure's usurer ; faith, I should.

Bell. O fate !

Hip.   Why sigh you, lady? May I know ?

Bell. 'T has never been my fortune yet to
single   351
Out that one man, whose love could fellow
mine,
As I have ever wisht it. O my stars !
Had I but met with one kind gentleman,
That would have purchas'd sin alone to him-
self,   355
For his own private use, although scarce pro-
per,[3]
Indifferent handsome ; meetly legg'd and
thigh'd ;
And my allowance reasonable, i' faith,
According to my body, by my troth,

I would have been as true unto his pleasures,
Yea, and as royal to his afternoons,   361
As ever a poor gentlewoman could be.

Hip. This were well now to one but newly
fledg'd,
And scarce a day old in this subtle world ;
'T were pretty art, good bird-lime, cunning
net ;   365
But come, come, faith, confess: how many
men
Have drunk this self-same protestation,
From that red 'ticing lip ?

Bell.   Indeed, not any.

Hip. "Indeed," and blush not !

Bell.   No, in truth, not any.

Hip. "Indeed ! " "In truth ! " — how warily
you swear !   370
'T is well, if ill it be not ; yet had I
The ruffian in me, and were drawn before you
But in light colours, I do know indeed,
You could not swear *indeed*, but thunder oaths
That should shake Heaven, drown the harmo-
nious spheres,   375
And pierce a soul that lov'd her maker's hon-
our
With horror and amazement.

Bell.   Shall I swear ? —
Will you believe me then ?

Hip.   Worst then of all ;
Our sins by custom, seem at last but small.
Were I but o'er your threshold, a next man, 380
And after him a next, and then a fourth,
Should have this golden hook, and lascivious
bait,
Thrown out to the full length. Why let me tell
you :
I ha' seen letters sent from that white hand,
Tuning such music to Matheo's ear.   385

Bell. Matheo ! that 's true, but believe it, I
No sooner had laid hold upon your presence,
But straight mine eye convey'd you to my
heart.

Hip. Oh, you cannot feign with me ! Why, I
know, lady,
This is the common passion of you all,   390
To hook in a kind gentleman, and then
Abuse his coin, conveying it to your lover,
And in the end you show him a French trick,
And so you leave him, that a coach may run
Between his legs for breath.

Bell.   Oh, by my soul,   395
Not I ! therein I 'll prove an honest whore,
In being true to one, and to no more.

Hip. If any be dispos'd to trust your oath,
Let him : I 'll not be he. I know you feign
All that you speak ; ay, for a mingled harlot 400
Is true in nothing but in being false.
What ! shall I teach you how to loath yourself ?
And mildly too, not without sense or reason.

Bell. I am content ; I would feign loath myself
If you not love me.

Hip.   Then if your gracious blood 405
Be not all wasted, I shall assay to do 't.
Lend me your silence, and attention.
You have no soul, that makes you weigh so
light ;

---

[1] Simpletons.   [2] Towels.   [3] Fine-looking.

Heaven's treasure bought it :   409
And half-a-crown hath sold it : — for your body
Is like the common-shore, that still receives
All the town's filth. The sin of many men
Is within you ; and thus much I suppose,
That if all your committers stood in rank,
They'd make a lane, in which your shame
     might dwell,   415
And with their spaces reach from hence to hell.
Nay, shall I urge it more ? there has been
     known
As many by one harlot, maim'd and dismem-
     b'red,
As would ha' stuft an hospital : this I might
Apply to you, and perhaps do you right.   420
O you're as base as any beast that bears, —
Your body is e'en hir'd, and so are theirs.
For gold and sparkling jewels, if he can,
You'll let a Jew get you with Christian :
Be he a Moor, a Tartar, though his face   425
Look uglier than a dead man's skull.
Could the devil put on a human shape,
If his purse shake out crowns, up then he
     gets ;
Whores will be rid to hell with golden bits.
So that you're crueller than Turks, for they   430
Sell Christians only, you sell yourselves away.
Why, those that love you, hate you : and will
     term you
Liquorish [1] damnation ; with themselves half-
     sunk
After the sin is laid out, and e'en curse
Their fruitless riot ; for what one begets   435
Another poisons ; lust and murder hit :
A tree being often shook, what fruit can knit ?
     Bell. O me unhappy !
     Hip.   I can vex you more :
A harlot is like Dunkirk, true to none,
Swallows both English, Spanish, fulsome
     Dutch,   440
Back-door'd Italian, last of all, the French,
And he sticks to you, faith, gives you your
     diet,
Brings you acquainted, first with Monsieur
     Doctor,
And then you know what follows.
     Bell.   Misery.
Rank, stinking, and most loathsome misery. 445
     Hip. Methinks a toad is happier than a
     whore ;
That with one poison swells, with thousands
     more
The other stocks her veins. Harlot ? fie, fie !
You are the miserablest creatures breathing,
The very slaves of nature ; mark me else :   450
You put on rich attires, others' eyes wear them,
You eat, but to supply your blood with sin :
And this strange curse e'en haunts you to your
     graves.
From fools you get, and spend it upon slaves.
Like bears and apes, you're baited and show
     tricks   455
For money ; but your bawd the sweetness licks.
Indeed, you are their journey-women, and do
All base and damn'd works they list set you
     to ;

So that you ne'er are rich ; for do but show me,
In present memory, or in ages past,   460
The fairest and most famous courtesan,
Whose flesh was dear'st ; that rais'd the price
     of sin,
And held it up ; to whose intemperate bosom,
Princes, earls, lords, the worst has been a
     knight,
The mean'st a gentleman, have off'red up   465
Whole hecatombs of sighs, and rain'd in
     showers
Handfuls of gold ; yet, for all this, at last
Diseases suckt her marrow, then grew so poor,
That she has begg'd e'en at a beggar's door.
And (wherein Heav'n has a finger) when this
     idol,   470
From coast to coast, has leapt on foreign
     shores,
And had more worship than th' outlandish
     whores ;
When several nations have gone over her,
When for each several city she has seen,
Her maidenhead has been new, and been sold
     dear ;   475
Did live well there, and might have died un-
     known,
And undefam'd ; back comes she to her own,
And there both miserably lives and dies,
Scorn'd even of those that once ador'd her
     eyes,
As if her fatal circled life thus ran,   480
Her pride should end there where it first be-
     gan.
What [2] do you weep to hear your story read ?
Nay, if you spoil your cheeks, I'll read no
     more.
     Bell. O yes, I pray, proceed :
Indeed, 't will do me good to weep, indeed.   485
     Hip. To give those tears a relish, this I add,
You're like the Jews, scatter'd, in no place
     certain ;
Your days are tedious, your hours burden-
     some :
And were 't not for full suppers, midnight re-
     vels,
Dancing, wine, riotous meetings, which do
     drown   490
And bury quite in you all virtuous thoughts,
And on your eyelids hang so heavily,
They have no power to look so high as Hea-
     ven, —
You'd sit and muse on nothing but despair,
Curse that devil Lust, that so burns up your
     blood,   495
And in ten thousand shivers break your glass
For his temptation. Say you taste delight,
To have a golden gull from rise to set,
To mete [3] you in his hot luxurious arms,   499
Yet your nights pay for all. I know you dream
Of warrants, whips, and beadles, and then
     start
At a door's windy creak : think every weasel
To be a constable, and every rat
A long-tail'd officer. Are you now not slaves ?
Oh, you've damnation without pleasure for it !

---

[1] Luscivious.   [2] Why.   [3] Measure.

Such is the state of harlots. To conclude: 506
When you are old and can well paint no more,
You turn bawd, and are then worse than before :
Make use of this : farewell.
   Bell.   Oh, I pray, stay.
   Hip. I see Matheo comes not : time hath
barr'd me ;   510
Would all the harlots in the town had heard
me.   *Exit.*
   Bell. Stay yet a little longer ! No ? quite
gone !
Curst be that minute — for it was no more,
So soon a maid is chang'd into a whore —
Wherein I first fell ! Be it for ever black !   515
Yet why should sweet Hippolito shun mine eyes,
For whose true love I would become pure-hon-
est,
Hate the world's mixtures, and the smiles of
gold ?
Am I not fair ? Why should he fly me then ?   519
Fair creatures are desir'd, not scorn'd of men.
How many gallants have drunk healths to me,
Out of their dagger'd arms, and thought them
blest,
Enjoying but mine eyes at prodigal feasts !
And does Hippolito detest my love ?   524
Oh, sure their heedless lusts but flatt'red me,
I am not pleasing, beautiful, nor young.
Hippolito hath spied some ugly blemish,
Eclipsing all my beauties : I am foul.
Harlot ! Ay, that's the spot that taints my
soul.   529
What ! has he left his weapon here behind him
And gone forgetful ? O fit instrument
To let forth all the poison of my flesh !
Thy master hates me, 'cause my blood hath
rang'd :
But when 't is forth, then he 'll believe I 'm
chang'd.

[As she is about to stab herself] re-enter HIPPO-
LITO.

   Hip. Mad woman, what art doing ?
   Bell.   Either love me,   535
Or split my heart upon thy rapier's point :
Yet do not neither ; for thou then destroy'st
That which I love thee for — thy virtues.
Here, here ;
            [Gives sword to HIPPOLITO.]
Th' art crueller, and kill'st me with disdain :   539
To die so, sheds no blood, yet 't is worse pain.
            Exit HIPPOLITO.
Not speak to me ! Not bid farewell ? A scorn ?
Hated ! this must not be ; some means I 'll
try.
Would all whores were as honest now as I !
            Exit.

[ACT III]

SCENE [I.]

Enter CANDIDO, *his wife* [VIOLA], GEORGE, *and
two Prentices in the shop :* FUSTIGO *enters,
walking by.*

   Geo. See, gentlemen, what you lack ; a fine
holland, a fine cambric : see what you buy.

   1 Pren. Holland for shirts, cambric for bands;
what is 't you lack ?
   Fus. [*Aside.*] 'Sfoot, I lack 'em all ; nay, [5
more, I lack money to buy 'em. Let me see,
let me look again : mass, this is the shop. —
What coz ! sweet coz ! how dost, i' faith, since
last night after candlelight ? We had good sport,
i' faith, had we not ? And when shall 's laugh [10
again ?
   Vio. When you will, cousin.
   Fus. Spoke like a kind Lacedemonian. I see
yonder 's thy husband.
   Vio. Ay, there 's the sweet youth, God bless
him !   16
   Fus. And how is 't, cousin ? and how, how
is 't, thou squall ? [1]
   Vio. Well, cousin, how fare you ?
   Fus. How fare I ? For sixpence a-meal, [20
wench, as well as heart can wish, with calves'
chaldrons,[2] and chitterlings ; [3] besides, I have
a punk after supper, as good as a roasted apple.
   Cand. Are you my wife's cousin ?
   Fus. I am, sir ; what hast thou to do with
that ?   25
   Cand. O, nothing, but y' are welcome.
   Fus. The devil's dung in thy teeth ! I 'll be
welcome whether thou wilt or no, I. — What
ring 's this, coz ? Very pretty and fantastical,
i' faith ! let 's see it.   30
   Vio. Pooh ! nay, you wrench my finger.
   Fus. I ha' sworn I 'll ha 't, and I hope you
will not let my oaths be crackt in [4] the ring, will
you ? [*Seizes the ring.*] I hope, sir, you are not
malicholly [5] at this, for all your great looks. [35
Are you angry ?
   Cand. Angry ? Not I, sir, nay if she can part
So easily with her ring, 't is with my heart.
   Geo. Suffer this, sir, and suffer all. A whore-
son gull, to —   40
   Cand. Peace, George, when she has reapt
what I have sown,
She 'll say, one grain tastes better of her own,
Than whole sheaves gather'd from another's
land.
Wit 's never good, till bought at a dear hand.
   Geo. But in the mean-time she makes an ass
of some body.   46
   2 Pren. See, see, see, sir, as you turn your
back they do nothing but kiss.
   Cand. No matter, let 'em ; when I touch her
lip,
I shall not feel his kisses, no, nor miss   50
Any of her lip : no harm in kissing is.
Look to your business, pray, make up your
wares.
   Fus. Troth, coz, and well rememb'red. I
would thou wouldst give me five yards of lawn,
to make my punk some falling bands [6] a' [55
the fashion ; three falling one upon another, for
that 's the new edition now. She 's out of linen
horribly, too ; troth, sh'as never a good smock
to her back neither, but one that has a great
many patches in 't, and that I 'm fain to [60

   [1] Wench.   [2] Calves' fry.   [3] Tripe.
   [4] *I. e.* false, like an uncurrent coin.
   [5] A corruption of the word " melancholy."
   [6] Collars lying flat on the neck.

wear myself for want of shift, too. Prithee, put
me into wholesome napery, and bestow some
clean commodities upon us.

Vio. Reach me those cambrics, and the lawns
hither.

Cand. What to do, wife? To lavish out my
goods upon a fool?

Fus. Fool? Snails, eat[1] the fool, or I'll so
batter your crown, that it shall scarce go for
five shillings. 70

2 Pren. Do you hear, sir? You're best be
quiet, and say a fool tells you so.

Fus. Nails, I think so, for thou tell'st me.

Cand. Are you angry, sir, because I nam'd
thee fool?

Trust me, you are not wise in my own house 75
And to my face to play the antic thus.
If you'll needs play the madman, choose a stage
Of lesser compass, where few eyes may note
Your action's error: but if still you miss,
As here you do, for one clap, ten will hiss. 80

Fus. Zounds, cousin, he talks to me, as if I
were a scurvy tragedian.

2 Pren. Sirrah George, I ha' thought upon a
device, how to break his pate, beat him soundly,
and ship him away. 85

Geo. Do 't.

2 Pren. I'll go in, pass through the house,
give some of our fellow-prentices the watch-
word when they shall enter; then come and
fetch my master in by a wile, and place one [90
in the hall to hold him in conference, whilst we
cudgel the gull out of his coxcomb.

　　　　　　　　　[Exit 2 Prentice.]

Geo. Do 't; away, do 't.

Vio. Must I call twice for these cambrics and
lawns? 95

Cand. Nay see, you anger her, George;
prithee despatch.

1 Pren. Two of the choicest pieces are in the
warehouse, sir.

Cand. Go fetch them presently. 100
　　　　　　　　　Exit 1 Prentice.

Fus. Ay, do, make haste, sirrah.

Cand. Why were you such a stranger all this
while, being my wife's cousin?

Fus. Stranger? No sir, I'm a natural Milaner
born. 105

Cand. I perceive still it is your natural guise
to mistake[2] me, but you are welcome, sir; I
much wish your acquaintance.

Fus. My acquaintance? I scorn that, i' faith;
I hope my acquaintance goes in chains of [110
gold three and fifty times double: — you know
who I mean, coz; the posts of his gate are a-
painting too.[3]

Re-enter the 2 *Prentice.*

2 Pren. Signor Pandulfo the merchant desires conference with you. 115

Cand. Signor Pandulfo? I'll be with him
straight,
Attend your mistress and the gentleman. *Exit.*

<hr>

[1] Retract.　　　　　　[2] Misunderstand.

[3] In allusion to the painting of a citizen's gateposts
on his promotion to be sheriff, so as to display official
notices the better. (Rhys.)

<hr>

Vio. When do you show those pieces?

Fus. Ay, when do you show those pieces?

Prentices. [*within.*] Presently, sir, presently:
we are but charging them. 121

Fus. Come, sirrah: you flat-cap,[4] where be
these whites?

[Re-enter 1 *Prentice with pieces.]*

Geo. Flat-cap? Hark in your ear, sir, you're
a flat fool, an ass, a gull, and I'll thrum[5] you.
— Do you see this cambric, sir? 125

Fus. 'Sfoot coz, a good jest, did you hear
him? He told me in my ears, I was a " flat
fool, an ass, a gull, and I'll thrum you: — do
you see this cambric, sir?"

Vio. What, not my men, I hope? 130

Fus. No, not your men, but one of your men,
i' faith.

1 Pren. I pray, sir, come hither, what say you
to this? Here's an excellent good one. 134

Fus. Ay, marry, this likes[6] me well; cut me
off some half-score yards.

2 Pren. Let your whores cut; you're an impudent coxcomb; you get none, and yet I'll
thrum you. — A very good cambric, sir. 139

Fus. Again, again, as God judge me! 'Sfoot,
coz, they stand thrumming here with me all
day, and yet I get nothing.

1 Pren. A word, I pray, sir, you must not be
angry. Prentices have hot bloods, young fellows.
— What say you to this piece? Look you, [145
't is so delicate, so soft, so even, so fine a thread,
that a lady may wear it.

Fus. 'Sfoot, I think so; if a knight marry
my punk, a lady shall wear it. Cut me off
twenty yards; thou 'rt an honest lad. 150

1 Pren. Not without money, gull, and I'll
thrum you too.

All. Gull, we'll thrum you.

Fus. O Lord, sister, did you not hear something cry thrum? Zounds, your men here make
a plain ass of me. 156

Vio. What, to my face so impudent?

Geo. Ay, in a cause so honest, we'll not suffer
Our master's goods to vanish moneyless.

Vio. You will not suffer them?

2 Pren. 　　　　No, and you may blush, 160
In going about to vex so mild a breast,
As is our master's.

Vio. 　　　　Take away those pieces,
Cousin, I give them freely.

Fus. Mass, and I'll take 'em as freely.

All. We'll make you lay 'em down again
more freely. 165
　　　　　[They all attack FUSTIGO *with their
　　　　　　clubs.]*

Vio. Help, help! my brother will be murdered.

Re-enter CANDIDO.

Cand. How now, what coil[7] is here? Forbear
I say.
　　　　　[Exeunt all the Prentices *except the
　　　　　　1 and* 2.]

Geo. He calls us flat-caps, and abuses us.

<hr>

[4] Citizen.　　[5] Beat.　　[6] Pleases.　　[7] Turmoil

Cand. Why, sirs, do such examples flow from me?

Vio. They're of your keeping, sir. Alas, poor brother. 170

Fus. I 'faith they ha' pepper'd me, sister ; look, dost not spin? Call you these prentices? I 'll ne'er play at cards more when clubs is trump. I have a goodly coxcomb, sister, have I not? 175

Cand. Sister and brother? Brother to my wife?

Fus. If you have any skill in heraldry, you may soon know that ; break but her pate, and you shall see her blood and mine is all one.

Cand. A surgeon ! run, a surgeon ! [*Exit* 1 Prentice.] Why then wore you that forged name of cousin? 182

Fus. Because it 's a common thing to call coz and ningle [1] now-a-days all the world over.

Cand. Cousin ! A name of much deceit, folly, and sin, 185
For under that common abused word,
Many an honest-temp'red citizen
Is made a monster, and his wife train'd out
To foul adulterous action, full of fraud.
I may well call that word, a city's bawd. 190

Fus. Troth, brother, my sister would needs ha' me take upon me to gull your patience a little : but it has made double gules [2] on my coxcomb.

Vio. What, playing the woman? Blabbing now, you fool? 195

Cand. Oh, my wife did but exercise a jest upon your wit.

Fus. 'Sfoot, my wit bleeds for 't, methinks.

Cand. Then let this warning more of sense afford ;
The name of cousin is a bloody word. 200

Fus. I 'll ne'er call coz again whilst I live, to have such a coil about it. This should be a coronation day ; for my head runs claret lustily.
Exit.

Enter an Officer.

Cand. Go, wish [3] the surgeon to have great respect — *Exit* 2 Prentice. 204
How now, my friend ? What, do they sit to-day?

Offi. Yes, sir, they expect you at the senate-house.

Cand. I thank your pains ; I 'll not be last man there. — *Exit* Officer.
My gown, George, go, my gown. [*Exit* GEORGE.]
A happy land,
Where grave men meet each cause to under-stand ;
Whose consciences are not cut out in bribes 210
To gull the poor man's right ; but in even scales,
Peize [4] rich and poor, without corruption's vails. [5]

Re-enter GEORGE.

Come, where 's the gown?

Geo.   I cannot find the key, sir.

Cand. Request it of your mistress.

Vio. Come not to me for any key ;   215

[1] Mine ingle, *i. e.* my intimate.
[2] The heraldic term for red.
[3] Desire.   [4] Weigh.   [5] Perquisites.

I 'll not be troubled to deliver it.

Cand. Good wife, kind wife, it is a needful trouble, but for my gown !

Vio. Moths swallow down your gown !
You set my teeth on edge with talking on 't. 220

Cand. Nay, prithee, sweet, — I cannot meet without it,
I should have a great fine set on my head.

Vio. Set on your coxcomb ; tush, fine me no fines.

Cand. Believe me, sweet, none greets the senate-house,
Without his robe of reverence, — that's his gown. 225

Vio. Well, then, you 're like to cross that custom once ;
You get nor key, nor gown ; and so depart. —
[*Aside.*] This trick will vex him sure, and fret his heart.   *Exit.*

Cand. Stay, let me see, I must have some device, — 229
My cloak 's too short : fie, fie, no cloak will do 't ;
It must be something fashioned like a gown,
With my arms out. Oh George, come hither, George ;
I prithee, lend me thine advice.

Geo. Troth, sir, were 't any but you, they would break open chest. 235

Cand. O no! break open chest ! that 's a thief's office.
Therein you counsel me against my blood ;
'Twould show impatience that : any meek means
I would be glad to embrace. Mass, I have got it.
Go, step up, fetch me down one of the carpets, [6]
The saddest[7]-colour'd carpet, honest George, 241
Cut thou a hole i' th' middle for my neck,
Two for mine arms. Nay, prithee, look not strange.

Geo. I hope you do not think, sir, as you mean.

Cand. Prithee, about it quickly, the hour chides me ; 245
Warily, George, softly, take heed of eyes.
Exit GEORGE.
Out of two evils he 's accounted wise,
That can pick out the least ; the fine impos'd
For an un-gowned senator, is about
Forty crusadoes, [8] the carpet not 'bove four. 250
Thus have I chosen the lesser evil yet,
Preserv'd my patience, foil'd her desperate wit.

Re-enter GEORGE [*with carpet*].

Geo. Here, sir, here 's the carpet.

Cand. O well done, George, we 'll cut it just i' th' midst. [*They cut the carpet.*]
'T is very well ; I thank thee : help it on. 255

Geo. It must come over your head, sir, like a wench's petticoat.

Cand. Thou 'rt in the right, good George ; it must indeed.
Fetch me a night-cap ; for I 'll gird it close,

[6] Table covers.   [7] Quietest.
[8] Portuguese coins, worth about 2s. 10d. each, but varying in value.

As if my health were queasy : 't will show well
For a rude, careless night-gown, will 't not,
think'st ?   260
Geo. Indifferent well, sir, for a night-gown,
being girt and pleated.
Cand. Ay, and a night-cap on my head.
Geo. That 's true sir, I 'll run and fetch one,
and a staff.   Exit.
Cand. For thus they cannot choose but con-
ster[1] it,   265
One that is out of health, takes no delight,
Wears his apparel without appetite,
And puts on heedless raiment without form. —

Re-enter GEORGE [*with night-cap and staff*].

So, so, kind George, [*puts on night-cap*] — be
secret now ; and, prithee, do not laugh at me
till I 'm out of sight.   271
Geo. I laugh ? Not I, sir.
Cand.   Now to the senate-house.
Methinks, I 'd rather wear, without a frown,
A patient carpet, than an angry gown.   Exit.
Geo. Now, looks my master just like one [275
of our carpet knights, only he 's somewhat the
honester of the two.

Re-enter VIOLA.

Vio. What, is your master gone ?
Geo. Yes, forsooth, his back is but new
turn'd.
Vio. And in his cloak ? Did he not vex and
swear ?   280
Geo. [*Aside.*] No, but he'll make you swear
anon. —
No indeed, he went away like a lamb.
Vio. Key, sink to hell ! Still patient, patient
still ?
I am with child[2] to vex him. Prithee, George,
If e'er thou look'st for favour at my hands,   285
Uphold one jest for me.
Geo.   Against my master ?
Vio. 'T is a mere jest, in faith. Say, wilt
thou do 't ?
Geo. Well, what is 't ?
Vio. Here, take this key ; thou know'st
where all things lie.
Put on thy master's best apparel, gown,   290
Chain, cap, ruff, every thing, be like himself ;
And 'gainst his coming home, walk in the shop ;
Feign the same carriage, and his patient look,
'T will breed but a jest, thou know'st ; speak,
wilt thou ?
Geo. 'T will wrong my master's patience.
Vio.   Prithee, George.   295
Geo. Well, if you 'll save me harmless, and
put me under covert barn,[3] I am content to
please you, provided it may breed no wrong
against him.
Vio. No wrong at all. Here take the key, be
gone.   300
If any vex him, this ; if not this, none. *Exeunt.*

[1] Construe.
[2] *I. e.* I long.
[3] When he may rob under protection. *Barn* is a corruption of *baron*, and in law a wife is said to be under
covert baron, being sheltered by marriage under her
husband. (Dyce.)

SCENE [II].[4]

Enter a Bawd [Mistress FINGERLOCK] *and*
ROGER.

Miss F. O Roger, Roger, where 's your mistress, where 's your mistress ? There 's the
finest, neatest gentleman at my house, but
newly come over. Oh, where is she, where is
she, where is she ?   5
Rog. My mistress is abroad, but not amongst
'em. My mistress is not the whore now that
you take her for.
Mis. F. How ? Is she not a whore ? Do you
go about to take away her good name, [10
Roger ? You are a fine pander indeed.
Rog. I tell you, Madonna Fingerlock, I am
not sad for nothing ; I ha' not eaten one good
meal this three and thirty days. I had wont
to get sixteen pence by fetching a pottle [15
of hippocras ; but now those days are past.
We had as good things, Madonna Fingerlock,
she within doors, and I without, as any poor
young couple in Milan.
Mis. F. God 's my life, and is she chang'd [20
now ?
Rog. I ha' lost by her squeamishness more
than would have builded twelve bawdy-houses.
Mis. F. And had she no time to turn honest
but now ? What a vile woman is this ! [25
Twenty pound a night, I 'll be sworn, Roger, in
good gold and no silver. Why here was a time !
If she should ha' pickt out a time, it could not
be better : gold enough stirring ; choice of men,
choice of hair, choice of beards, choice of [30
legs, and choice of every, every, everything. It
cannot sink into my head, that she should be
such an ass, Roger, I never believe it.
Rog. Here she comes now.

Enter BELLAFRONT.

Mis. F. O sweet madonna, on with your [35
loose gown, your felt[5] and your feather ; there 's
the sweetest, prop'rest,[6] gallantest gentleman
at my house ; he smells all of musk and ambergris, his pocket full of crowns, flame-coloured
doublet, red satin hose, carnation silk stock- [40
ings, and a leg, and a body, — oh !
Bell. Hence thou, our sex's monster, poison-
ous bawd,
Lust's factor, and damnation's orator !
Gossip of hell ! were all the harlots' sins
Which the whole world contains, numb'red to-
gether,   45
Thine far exceeds them all : of all the creatures
That ever were created, thou art basest.
What serpent would beguile thee of thy office ?
It is detestable : for thou livest
Upon the dregs of harlots, guard'st the door,   50
Whilst couples are dancing. O coarse devil !
Thou art the bastard's curse, thou brand'st his
birth ;
The lecher's French disease, for thou dry-
suck'st him ;
The harlot's poison, and thine own confusion.

[4] An outer apartment in Bellafront's house.
[5] Hat.   [6] Handsomest.

Mis. F. Marry come up, with a pox! Have [55
you nobody to rail against but your bawd now?
Bell. And you, knave pander, kinsman to a
bawd.
Rog. You and I, madonna, are cousins.
Bell. Of the same blood and making, near al-
lied;
Thou, that slave to sixpence, base metall'd
villain!   60
Rog. Sixpence? Nay, that's not so: I never
took under two shillings four-pence; I hope I
know my vocation.
Bell. I know not against which most to in-
veigh;
For both of you are damn'd so equally.   65
Thou never spar'st for oaths, swear'st any thing,
As if thy soul were made of shoe-leather:
"God damn me, gentlemen, if she be within!"
When in the next room she's found dallying.
Rog. If it be my vocation to swear, every [70
man in his vocation. I hope my betters swear
and damn themselves, and why should not I?
Bell. Roger, you cheat kind gentlemen.
Rog. The more gulls they.
Bell. Slave, I cashier thee.   75
Mis. F. An you do cashier him, he shall be
entertain'd.
Rog. Shall I? Then blurt a' your service.
Bell. As hell would have it, entertain'd by you!
I dare the devil himself to match those two. 80
                                                     Exit.
Mis. F. Marry gup,[1] are you grown so holy,
so pure, so honest with a pox?
Rog. Scurvy honest punk! But stay, ma-
donna, how must our agreement be now? for,
you know, I am to have all the comings-in at
the hall-door, and you at the chamber-door. 86
Mis F. True, Roger, except my vails.[2]
Rog. Vails? What vails?
Mis. F. Why as thus: if a couple come in a
coach, and light to lie down a little, then, [90
Roger, that's my fee, and you may walk
abroad; for the coachman himself is their pander.
Rog. Is 'a so? In truth I have almost forgot,
for want of exercise. But how if I fetch this [95
citizen's wife unto that gull, and that madonna
to that gallant, how then?
Mis. F. Why then, Roger, you are to have
sixpence a lane;[3] so many lanes, so many sixpences.   100
Rog. Is't so? Then I see we two shall agree,
and live together.
Mis. F. Ay, Roger, so long as there be any
taverns and bawdy-houses in Milan.   *Exeunt.*

SCENE [III].[4]

Enter BELLAFRONT *with lute, pen, ink, and
paper being placed before her.*

SONG.

[*Bell.*]
    The courtier's flattering jewels,
    Temptation's only fuels;

---

1 Go up, get out.   2 Perquisites.
3 Assignation (?) Customer (?) Pair (?)
4 A chamber in Bellafront's house.

    The lawyer's ill-got moneys,
    That suck up poor bees' honeys;
    The citizen's son's riot,   5
    The gallant's costly diet:
    Silks and velvets, pearls and ambers,
    Shall not draw me to their chambers.
        Silks and velvets, &c.

                                              She writes.

Oh, 't is in vain to write! it will not please; 10
Ink on this paper would ha' but presented
The foul black spots that stick upon my soul,
And rather made me loathsomer, than wrought
My love's impression in Hippolito's thought. 14
No, I must turn the chaste leaves of my breast,
And pick out some sweet means to breed my
    rest.
Hippolito, believe me, I will be
As true unto thy heart, as thy heart to thee,
And hate all men, their gifts and company! 19

Enter MATHEO, CASTRUCHIO, FLUELLO, *and*
PIORATTO.

Mat. You, goody punk, *subaudi*[5] cockatrice,
oh y'are a sweet whore of your promise, are
you not, think you? How well you came to
supper to us last night! Mew, a whore, and
break her word! Nay, you may blush, and hold
down your head at it well enough. 'Sfoot, [25
ask these gallants if we stay'd not till we were
as hungry as sergeants.
Flu. Ay, and their yeomen too.
Cas. Nay, faith, acquaintance, let me tell
you, you forgat yourself too much. We had [30
excellent cheer, rare vintage, and were drunk
after supper.
Pio. And when we were in, our woodcocks,[6]
sweet rogue, a brace of gulls, dwelling here in
the city, came in, and paid all the shot.   35
Mat. Pox on her! let her alone.
Bell. Oh, I pray do, if you be gentlemen;
I pray, depart the house. Beshrew the door
For being so easily entreated! Faith,
I lent but little ear unto your talk;   40
My mind was busied otherwise, in troth,
And so your words did unregarded pass.
Let this suffice, — I am not as I was.
Flu. I am not what I was? No, I'll be sworn
thou art not; for thou wert honest at five, [45
and now th' art a punk at fifteen. Thou wert
yesterday a simple whore, and now th' art a
cunning, cony-catching[7] baggage to-day.
Bell. I'll say I'm worse; I pray, forsake me
then:
I do desire you leave me, gentlemen,   50
And leave yourselves. O be not what you are,
Spendthrifts of soul and body!
Let me persuade you to forsake all harlots,
Worse than the deadliest poisons, they are
    worse:
For o'er their souls hangs an eternal curse.   55
In being slaves to slaves, their labours perish;
They're seldom blest with fruit; for ere it
    blossoms,
Many a worm confounds it.
They have no issue but foul ugly ones,   59
That run along with them, e'en to their graves;

---

5 Understand.   6 Simpletons.   7 Cheating.

For, 'stead of children, they breed rank diseases,
And all you gallants can bestow on them
Is that French infant, which ne'er acts, but
   speaks.
What shallow son and heir, then, foolish gal-
   lants,
Would waste all his inheritance, to purchase 65
A filthy, loath'd disease? and pawn his body
To a dry evil: that usury's worst of all,
When th' interest will eat out the principal.
   Mat. [*Aside.*] 'Sfoot, she gulls 'em the best!
This is always her fashion, when she would be [70
rid of any company that she cares not for, to
enjoy mine alone.
   Flu. What's here? Instructions, admoni-
tions, and caveats? Come out, you scabbard
of vengeance. 75
   Mat. Fluello, spurn your hounds when they
foist,[1] you shall not spurn my punk, I can tell
you: my blood is vext.
   Flu. Pox a' your blood! make it a quarrel. 79
   Mat. You're a slave! Will that serve turn?
   All. 'Sblood, hold, hold!
   Cas. Matheo, Fluello, for shame, put up!
   Bell. O how many thus
Mov'd with a little folly, have let out
Their souls in brothel houses! fell down and
   died 85
Just at their harlot's foot, as 't were in pride.
   Flu. Matheo, we shall meet.
   Mat. Ay, ay; any where, saving at church;
Pray take heed we meet not there.
   Flu. Adieu, damnation!
   Cas.   Cockatrice, farewell! 90
   Pio. There's more deceit in women, than in
hell.
               Exeunt [CASTRUCHIO, FLUELLO,
                  and PIORATTO].
   Mat. Ha, ha, thou dost gull 'em so rarely, so
naturally! If I did not think thou hadst been
in earnest!
Thou art a sweet rogue for 't i' faith. 95
   Bell. Why are not you gone too, Signor
Matheo?
I pray depart my house: you may believe me,
In troth, I have no part of harlot in me.
   Mat. How's this?
   Bell. Indeed, I love you not: but hate you
   worse 100
Than any man, because you were the first
Gave money for my soul: you brake the ice,
Which after turn'd a puddle; I was led
By your temptation to be miserable.
I pray, seek out some other that will fall, 105
Or rather, I pray seek out none at all.
   Mat. Is 't possible to be impossible! An hon-
est whore! I have heard many honest wenches
turn strumpets with a wet finger,[2] but for a har-
lot to turn honest is one of Hercules' labours. [110
It was more easy for him in one night to make
fifty queans, than to make one of them honest
again in fifty years. Come, I hope thou dost
but jest.
   Bell. 'T is time to leave off jesting; I had almost 115

        [1] Stink.   [2] Readily.

Jested away salvation. I shall love you,
If you will soon forsake me.
   Mat.   God be with thee!
   Bell. O tempt no more women! Shun their
   weighty curse!
Women, at best, are bad, make them not worse.
You gladly seek our sex's overthrow; 120
But not to raise our states. For all your wrongs,
Will you vouchsafe me but due recompense,
To marry with me?
   Mat. How! marry with a punk, a cockatrice,
a harlot? Marry, faugh, I'll be burnt through
the nose first. 126
   Bell. Why, la, these are your oaths! you love
   to undo us,
To put Heaven from us, whilst our best hours
   waste;
You love to make us lewd, but never chaste.
   Mat. I'll hear no more of this, this ground
   upon; 130
Thou 'rt damn'd for alt'ring thy religion. *Exit.*
   Bell. Thy lust and sin speak so much. Go
   thou, my ruin,
The first fall my soul took! By my example
I hope few maidens now will put their heads
Under men's girdles; who least trusts is most
   wise: 135
Men's oaths do cast a mist before our eyes.
My best of wit, be ready! Now I go,
By some device to greet Hippolito.

[ACT IV]

SCENE [I].[3]

Enter a Servant, *setting out a table, on which he
places a skull, a picture* [*of* INFELICE], *a book,
and a taper.*

   Ser. So, this is Monday morning, and now
must I to my huswifery. Would I had been
created a shoemaker, for all the gentle craft
are gentlemen every Monday by their copy,[4]
and scorn then to work one true stitch. My [5
master means sure to turn me into a student,
for here's my book, here my desk, here my
light, this my close chamber, and here my punk:
so that this dull drowsy first day of the week
makes me half a priest, half a chandler, half [10
a painter, half a sexton, ay, and half a bawd;
for all this day my office is to do nothing but
keep the door. To prove it, look you, this good
face and yonder gentleman, so soon as ever my
back is turn'd, will be naught together. 15

Enter HIPPOLITO.

   Hip. Are all the windows shut?
   Ser. Close, sir, as the fist of a courtier that
hath stood in three reigns.
   Hip. Thou art a faithful servant, and ob-
   serv'st
The calendar both of my solemn vows, 20
And ceremonious sorrow. Get thee gone;

        [3] A chamber in Hippolito's house.
        [4] Certificate of membership in the craft.

I charge thee on thy life, let not the sound
Of any woman's voice pierce through that door.
  Ser. If they do, my lord, I'll pierce some of
    them;
What will your lordship have to breakfast? 25
  Hip. Sighs.
  Ser. What to dinner?
  Hip. Tears.
  Ser. The one of them, my lord, will fill you
too full of wind, the other wet you too much. [30
What to supper?
  Hip. That which now thou canst not get me,
the constancy of a woman.
  Ser. Indeed that's harder to come by than
ever was Ostend.[1] 35
  Hip. Prithee, away.
  Ser. I'll make away myself presently, which
few servants will do for their lords; but rather
help to make them away. Now to my door-
keeping; I hope to pick something out of it. 40
                  Exit.
  Hip. [*taking up* INFELICE'S *picture.*] My In-
    felice's face, her brow, her eye,
The dimple on her cheek! and such sweet skill,
Hath from the cunning workman's pencil flown,
These lips look fresh and lively as her own, 44
Seeming to move and speak. 'Las! now I see,
The reason why fond[2] women love to buy
Adulterate complexion! Here, 't is read:
False colours last after the true be dead.
Of all the roses grafted on her cheeks,
Of all the graces dancing in her eyes, 50
Of all the music set upon her tongue,
Of all that was past woman's excellence,
In her white bosom, — look! a painted board
Circumscribes all. Earth can no bliss afford,
Nothing of her but this. This cannot speak, 55
It has no lap for me to rest upon,
No lip worth tasting; here the worms will feed,
As in her coffin. Hence, then, idle art!
True love's best pictur'd in a true-love's heart.
Here art thou drawn, sweet maid, till this be
    dead; 60
So that thou liv'st twice, twice art buried.
Thou figure of my friend, lie there. What's
  here?   [*Takes up the skull.*]
Perhaps this shrewd pate was mine enemy's:
'Las! say it were; I need not fear him now!
For all his braves, his contumelions breath, 65
His frowns, though dagger-pointed, all his plot,
Though ne'er so mischievous, his Italian pills,
His quarrels, and that common fence, his law,
See, see, they're all eaten out! Here's not left
  one:
How clean they're pickt away to the bare
  bone! 70
How mad are mortals, then, to rear great
  names
On tops of swelling houses! or to wear out
Their fingers' ends in dirt, to scrape up gold!
Not caring, so that sumpter-horse, the back,
Be hung with gaudy trappings, with what
  coarse— 75

Yea, rags most beggarly, they clothe the soul:
Yet, after all, their gayness looks thus foul.
What fools are men to build a garish tomb,
Only to save the carcase whilst it rots,
To maintain 't long in stinking, make good car-
  rion, 80
But leave no good deeds to preserve them
  sound!
For good deeds keep men sweet, long above
  ground.
And must all come to this? fools, wise, all
  hither?
Must all heads thus at last be laid[3] together?
Draw me my picture then, thou grave neat
  workman, 85
After this fashion, not like this; these colours
In time, kissing but air, will be kist off:
But here's a fellow; that which he lays on
Till doomsday alters not complexion.
Death's the best painter then: they that draw
  shapes, 90
And live by wicked faces, are but God's apes.
They come but near the life, and there they
  stay;
This fellow draws life too: his art is fuller,
The pictures which he makes are without
  colour. 94

          Re-enter Servant.

  Ser. Here's a person would speak with you,
sir.
  Hip. Hah!
  Ser. A parson, sir, would speak with you.
  Hip. Vicar? 99
  Ser. Vicar! No, sir; has too good a face to
be a vicar yet; a youth, a very youth.
  Hip. What youth? Of man or woman?
    Lock the doors.
  Ser. If it be a woman, marrow-bones[4] and
potato pies[4] keep me from meddling with her,
for the thing has got the breeches! 'T is a [105
male-varlet sure, my lord, for a woman's tailor
ne'er measur'd him.
  Hip. Let him give thee his message and be
gone.
  Ser. He says he's Signor Matheo's man, but
I know he lies. 110
  Hip. How dost thou know it?
  Ser. 'Cause he has ne'er a beard. 'T is his
boy, I think, sir, whosoe'er paid for his nursing.
  Hip. Send him and keep the door.
                [*Exit* Servant.]
  (*Reads.*) " *Fata si liceat mihi,* 115
Fingere arbitrio meo,
Temperem zephyro levi
Vela."[5]
I'd sail were I to choose, not in the ocean;
Cedars are shaken, when shrubs do feel no
  bruise. 120

Enter BELLAFRONT, *like a* Page, [*with a letter*].

How? from Matheo?
  Bell.   Yes, my lord.
  Hip.   Art sick?

---

[1] Ostend held out for three years and ten weeks, and
was eventually captured by the Marquis of Spinola on
Sept. 8, 1604.
[2] Foolish.

[3] Q 1635, *brought.*
[4] Used as provocatives.   [5] Seneca, *Oedipus,* 882.

Bell. Not all in health, my lord.
Hip.   Keep off.
Bell.   I do.—
[*Aside.*] Hard fate when women are compell'd
      to woo.
Hip. This paper does speak nothing.
Bell.   Yes, my lord,
Matter of life, it speaks, and therefore writ 125
In hidden character: to me instruction
My master gives, and, 'less you please to stay
Till you both meet, I can the text display.
Hip. Do so ; read out.
Bell.   I am already out.[1] 129
Look on my face, and read the strangest story !
Hip. What, villain, ho ?——

Re-enter Servant.

Ser. Call you, my lord ?
Hip. Thou slave, thou hast let in the devil !
Ser. Lord bless us, where ? He 's not cloven,
my lord, that I can see: besides the devil goes [135
more like a gentleman than a page. Good my
lord, *Buon coraggio.*[2]
Hip. Thou hast let in a woman in man's shape.
And thou art damn'd for 't.   139
Ser. Not damn'd I hope for putting in a
woman to a lord,
Hip. Fetch me my rapier,— do not ; I shall
kill thee.
Purge this infected chamber of that plague,
That runs upon me thus. Slave, thrust her
hence.   144
Ser. Alas, my lord, I shall never be able to
thrust her hence without help ! Come, mer-
maid, you must to sea again.
Bell. Hear me but speak, my words shall be
all music ;
Hear me but speak.   [*Knocking within.*
Hip.   Another beats the door,
T 'other she-devil ! look.
Ser. Why, then, hell 's broke loose. 150
Hip. Hence ; guard the chamber: let no
      more come on,   *Exit* [Servant].
One woman serves for man's damnation —
Beshrew thee, thou dost make me violate
The chastest and most sanctimonious vow,
That e'er was ent'red in the court of Heaven !
I was, on meditation's spotless wings,   156
Upon my journey thither ; like a storm
Thou beat'st my ripened cogitations,
Flat to the ground ; and like a thief dost stand,
To steal devotion from the holy land.   160
Bell. If woman were thy mother — if thy
      heart,
Be not all marble, or if 't marble be,
Let my tears soften it, to pity me —
I do beseech thee, do not thus with scorn
Destroy a woman !
Hip.   Woman, I beseech thee, 165
Get thee some other suit, this fits thee not ;
I would not grant it to a kneeling queen,
I cannot love thee, nor I must not: see
                    [*Points to* INFELICE'S *picture.*]
The copy of that obligation,
Where my soul 's bound in heavy penalties. 170

Bell. She 's dead, you told me ; she 'll let fall
      her suit.
Hip. My vows to her fled after her to
      Heaven.
Were thine eyes clear as mine, thou might'st
      behold her,
Watching upon yon battlements of stars,—
How I observe them ! Should I break my bond,
This board would rive in twain, these wooden
      lips   176
Call me most perjur'd villain. Let it suffice,
I ha' set thee in the path ; is 't not a sign
I love thee, when with one so most most dear,
I 'll have thee fellows ? All are fellows there. 180
Bell. Be greater than a king ; save not a body,
But from eternal shipwrack keep a soul.
If not, and that again sin's path I tread,
The grief be mine, the guilt fall on thy head !
Hip. Stay, and take physic for it ; read this
      book,   185
Ask counsel of this head, what 's to be done :
He 'll strike it dead, that 't is damnation
If you turn Turk again. Oh, do it not !
Though Heaven cannot allure you to do well,
From doing ill let hell fright you ; and learn
      this,   190
The soul whose bosom lust did never touch,
Is God's fair bride, and maidens' souls are
      such :
The soul that leaving chastity's white shore,
Swims in hot sensual streams, is the devil's
      whore.—

Re-enter Servant [*with letter*].

How now, who comes ?   195
Ser. No more knaves, my lord, that wear
smocks : here 's a letter from Doctor Benedict.
I would not enter his man, though he had hairs
at his mouth, for fear he should be a woman,
for some women have beards ; marry, they [200
are half-witches. 'Slid ! you are a sweet youth
to wear a cod-piece, and have no pins to stick
upon 't.
Hip. I 'll meet the doctor, tell him ; yet to-
night
I cannot : but at morrow rising sun   205
I will not fail.— Go, woman ; fare thee well.
            Exeunt [HIPPOLITO *and* Servant].
Bell. The lowest fall can be but into hell ;
It does not move him : I must therefore fly
From this undoing city, and with tears
Wash off all anger from my father's brow : 210
He cannot sure but joy, seeing me new born.
A woman honest first, and then turn whore,
Is, as with me, common to thousands more ; 213
But from a strumpet to turn chaste, that sound
Has oft been heard, that woman hardly found.
                                        Exit.

SCENE [II].[3]

Enter FUSTIGO, CRAMBO, *and* POLI.

Fus. Hold up your hands, gentlemen, here 's
one, two, three [*giving money*] — nay, I warrant
they are sound pistoles, and without flaws ; I
had them of my sister and I know she uses to

---

[1] Have nothing to say.   [2] Ital. *Good courage.*

[3] A street.

put [up] nothing that's crackt — four, five, [5
six, seven, eight, and nine; by this hand bring
me but a piece of his blood, and you shall have
nine more. I'll lurk in a tavern not far off, and
provide supper to close up the end of the tragedy. The linen-draper's, remember. Stand [10
to't, I beseech you, and play your parts perfectly.

Cram. Look you, signor, 't is not your gold
that we weigh —

Fus. Nay, nay, weigh it and spare not; if [15
it lack one grain of corn, I'll give you a bushel
of wheat to make it up.

Cram. But by your favour, signor, which of
the servants is it? because we'll punish justly.

Fus. Marry, 't is the head man; you shall [20
taste him by his tongue; a pretty, tall, prating
fellow, with a Tuscalonian beard.

Poli. Tuscalonian? Very good.

Fus. God's life, I was ne'er so thrummed
since I was a gentleman. My coxcomb was [25
dry beaten, as if my hair had been hemp.

Cram. We'll dry-beat some of them.

Fus. Nay, it grew so high, that my sister
cried out murder, very manfully. I have her
consent, in a manner, to have him pepper'd; [30
else I'll not do't, to win more than ten cheaters
do at a rifling.[1] Break but his pate, or so, only
his mazer,[2] because I'll have his head in a
cloth as well as mine; he's a linen-draper, and
may take enough. I could enter mine action [35
of battery against him, but we may perhaps be
both dead and rotten before the lawyers would
end it.

Cram. No more to do, but ensconce yourself
i' th' tavern; provide no great cheer, a [40
couple of capons, some pheasants, plovers, an
orangeado[3]-pie, or so: but how bloody howso-
e'er the day be, sally you not forth.

Fus. No, no; nay, if I stir, somebody shall
stink. I'll not budge; I'll lie like a dog in [45
a manger.

Cram. Well, well, to the tavern, let not our
supper be raw, for you shall have blood enough,
your bellyful.

Fus. That's all, so God sa' me, I thirst [50
after; blood for blood, bump for bump, nose for
nose, head for head, plaster for plaster; and so
farewell. What shall I call your names? because I'll leave word, if any such come to the
bar. 55

Cram. My name is Corporal Crambo.

Poli. And mine, Lieutenant Poli. *Exit.*

Cram. Poli is as tall a man as ever opened
oyster; I would not be the devil to meet Poli.
Farewell. 60

Fus. Nor I, by this light, if Poli be such a
Poli. *Exeunt.*

[SCENE III.]

Enter Candido's wife [VIOLA] *in her shop, and
the two Prentices.*

Vio. What's a'clock now?

2 Pren. 'T is almost twelve.

---

[3] A game with dice. [2] Mazzard, the head.
[5] Candied orange-peel.

Vio. That's well,
The Senate will leave wording presently:
But is George ready?

2 Pren. Yes, forsooth, he's furbisht.

Vio. Now, as you ever hope to win my favour,
Throw both your duties and respects on him 5
With the like awe as if he were your master;
Let not your looks betray it with a smile
Or jeering glance to any customer;
Keep a true settled countenance, and beware
You laugh not, whatsoe'er you hear or see. 10

2 Pren. I warrant you, mistress, let us alone
for keeping our countenance: for, if I list,
there's ne'er a fool in all Milan shall make me
laugh, let him play the fool never so like an ass,
whether it be the fat court-fool, or the lean [15
city-fool.

Vio. Enough then, call down George.

2 Pren. I hear him coming.

Enter GEORGE [*in* CANDIDO'S *apparel*].

Vio. Be ready with your legs[4] then; let me
see
How courtesy would become him. — Gallantly!
Beshrew my blood, a proper seemly man. 20
Of a choice carriage, walks with a good port!

Geo. I thank you, mistress, my back's broad
enough, now my master's gown's on.

Vio. Sure, I should think it were the least of
sin,
To mistake the master, and to let him in. 25

Geo. 'T were a good Comedy of Errors that,
i' faith.

2 Pren. Whist, whist! my master.

Enter CANDIDO, [*dressed as before in the carpet
he stares at* GEORGE,] *and exit presently.*

Vio. You all know your tasks. George's my life,
what's that he has got on's back? Who can tell?

Geo. [*Aside.*] That can I, but I will not. 30

Vio. Girt about him like a madman! What,
has he lost his cloak too? This is the maddest
fashion that e'er I saw. What said he, George,
when he passed by thee? 34

Geo. Troth, mistress, nothing: not so much
as a bee, he did not hum; not so much as a
bawd, he did not hem; not so much as a cuckold, he did not ha; neither hum, hem, nor ha;
only stared me in the face, passed along, and
made haste in, as if my looks had worked [40
with him, to give him a stool.

Vio. Sure he's vext now, this trick has mov'd
his spleen,
He's anger'd now, because he utt'red nothing;
And wordless wrath breaks out more violent.
May be he'll strive for place, when he comes
down, 45
But if thou lov'st me, George, afford him none.

Geo. Nay, let me alone to play my master's
prize,[5] as long as my mistress warrants me. I'm
sure I have his best clothes on, and I scorn to
give place to any that is inferior in apparel [50
to me; that's an axiom, a principle, and is ob-

---

[4] Bows.
[5] A quibble. There were three degrees in fencing, the
master's, the provost's, and the scholar's, for each of
which a "prize was played."

serv'd as much as the fashion. Let that persuade you then, that I'll shoulder with him for the upper hand in the shop, as long as this chain will maintain it.   55
Vio. Spoke with the spirit of a master, though with the tongue of a prentice.

Re-enter CANDIDO *like a* Prentice.

Why how now, madman? What in your tricksy-coats?
Cand. O peace, good mistress.

Enter CRAMBO *and* POLI.

See, what you lack? What is't you buy? [60
Pure calicoes, fine hollands, choice cambrics, neat lawns? See, what you buy? Pray come near, my master will use you well, he can afford you a penny-worth.
Vio. Ay, that he can, out of a whole piece of lawn, i' faith.   66
Cand. Pray see your choice here, gentlemen.
Vio. O fine fool! what, a madman! a patient madman! Who ever heard of the like? Well, sir, I'll fit you and your humour presently. [70
What, cross-points? I'll untie 'em all in a trice:
I'll vex you i' faith: boy take your cloak, quick, come.   *Exit* [*with* 1 Prentice].
Cand. Be covered, George, this chain and welted[1] gown
Bare to this coat? Then the world's upside down.   75
Geo. Umh, umh, hum.
Cram. That's the shop, and there's the fellow.
Poli. Ay, but the master is walking in there.
Cram. No matter, we'll in.
Poli. 'Sblood, dost long to lie in limbo?
Cram. An limbo be in hell, I care not.   80
Cand. Look you, gentlemen, your choice: cambrics?
Cram. No, sir, some shirting.
Cand. You shall.
Cram. Have you none of this strip'd canvas for doublets?   85
Cand. None strip'd, sir, but plain.
2 *Pren.* I think there be one piece strip'd within.
Geo. Step, sirrah, and fetch it, hum, hum, hum.

[*Exit* 2 Pren., *and returns with the piece.*]

Cand. Look you, gentleman, I'll make but one spreading, here's a piece of cloth, fine, [90
yet shall wear like iron. 'T is without fault; take this upon my word, 't is without fault.
Cram. Then 't is better than you, sirrah.
Cand. Ay, and a number more. Oh, that each soul
Were but as spotless as this innocent white,   95
And had as few breaks in it!
Cram.   'T would have some then:
There was a fray here last day in this shop.
Cand. There was, indeed, a little flea-biting.

Poli. A gentleman had his pate broke; call you that but a flea-biting?   100
Cand. He had so.
Cram. Zounds, do you stand to it?
                          He strikes him.
Geo. 'Sfoot, clubs, clubs! Prentices, down with 'em!

[*Enter several* Prentices *with clubs, who disarm* CRAMBO *and* POLI.]

Ah, you rogues, strike a citizen in's shop?
Cand. None of you stir, I pray; forbear, good George.   105
Cram. I beseech you, sir, we mistook our marks; deliver us our weapons.
Geo. Your head bleeds, sir; cry clubs!
Cand. I say you shall not; pray be patient,
Give them their weapons. Sirs, y' are best be gone;   110
I tell you here are boys more tough than bears.
Hence, lest more fists do walk about your ears.
Cram., Poli. We thank you, sir.   *Exeunt.*
Cand.   You shall not follow them;
Let them alone, pray; this did me no harm.
Troth, I was cold, and the blow made me warm,
I thank 'em for 't: besides, I had decreed[2]   116
To have a vein prickt, I did mean to bleed:
So that there's money sav'd. They're honest men,
Pray use 'em well when they appear again.   119
Geo. Yes, sir, we'll use 'em like honest men.
Cand. Ay, well said, George, like honest men, though they be arrant knaves, for that's the phrase of the city. Help to lay up these wares.

Re-enter his Wife *with* Officers.

Vio. Yonder he stands.
1 *Off.*   What in a prentice-coat?
Vio. Ay, ay; mad, mad; pray take heed.   125
Cand. How now! what news with them?
What make they with my wife?
Officers. is she attach'd? — Look to your wares.
Vio. He talks to himself: oh, he's much gone indeed.
1 *Off.* Pray, pluck up a good heart, be not so fearful: 130
Sirs, hark, we'll gather to him by degrees.
Vio. Ay, ay, by degrees I pray. Oh me!
What makes he with the lawn in his hand?
He'll tear all the ware in my shop.   134
1 *Off.* Fear not, we'll catch him on a sudden.
Vio. Oh! you had need do so; pray take heed of your warrant.
1 *Off.* I warrant, mistress. Now, Signor Candido.
Cand. Now, sir, what news with you, sir?
Vio. What news with you? he says: oh, he's far gone!   140
1 *Off.* I pray, fear nothing; let's alone with him.
Signor, you look not like yourself, methinks, —
Steal you a' t' other side; — you're chang'd, you're alt'red.
Cand. Chang'd sir, why true, sir. Is change strange? 'T is not

---

1 With ornamental border.   2 Decided.

The fashion unless it alter! Monarchs turn 145
To beggars, beggars creep into the nests
Of princes, masters serve their prentices,
Ladies their serving-men, men turn to women.
1 Off. And women turn to men.
Cand. Ay, and women turn to men, you say
true. Ha, ha, a mad world, a mad world. 151
　　　　　[Officers *seize* CANDIDO.]
1 Off. Have we caught you, sir?
Cand. Caught me? Well, well, you have
　　caught me.
Vio. He laughs in your faces.
Geo. A rescue, prentices! my master's catch-
poll'd. 155
1 Off. I charge you, keep the peace, or have
　　your legs
Gartered with irons! We have from the duke
A warrant strong enough for what we do.
Cand. I pray, rest quiet, I desire no rescue.
Vio. La, he desires no rescue, 'las poor
heart, 160
He talks against himself.
Cand. 　　　　　Well, what's the matter?
1 Off. Look to that arm. Pray, make sure
work, double the cord. [Officers *bind* CANDIDO.]
Cand. Why, why?
Vio. Look how his head goes. Should he get
but loose, 165
Oh 't were as much as all our lives were worth!
1 Off. Fear not, we 'll make all sure for our
　　own safety.
Cand. Are you at leisure now? Well, what's
　　the matter?
Why do I enter into bonds thus, ha?
1 Off. Because y'are mad, put fear upon your
wife. 170
Vio. Oh ay, I went in danger of my life every
minute.
Cand. What, am I mad, say you, and I not
　　know it?
1 Off. That proves you mad, because you
　　know it not.
Vio. Pray talk to him as little as you can, 175
You see he's too far spent.
Cand. 　　　　Bound, with strong cord!
A sister's thread, i' faith, had been enough,
To lead me anywhere. — Wife, do you long?
You are mad too, or else you do me wrong.
Geo. But are you mad indeed, master?
Cand. 　　　　My wife says so, 180
And what she says, George, is all truth, you
　　know. —
And whither now, to Bethlem Monastery?
Ha! whither?
1 Off. 　　Faith, e'en to the madmen's pound.
Cand. A' God's name! still I feel my patience
　　sound. *Exeunt* [Officers *with* CANDIDO].
Geo. Come, we 'll see whither he goes. If [185
the master be mad, we are his servants, and must
follow his steps; we 'll be mad-caps too. Fare-
well, mistress, you shall have us all in Bedlam.
　　　　　Exeunt [GEORGE *and* Prentices].
Vio. I think I ha' fitted you too, you and
　　your clothes.
If this move not his patience, nothing can; 190
I 'll swear then I 've a saint, and not a man.
　　　　　　　　　　　　　　[*Exit.*]

SCENE [IV].[1]

Enter DUKE, Doctor [BENEDICT], FLUELLO,
　　CASTRUCHIO, *and* PIORATTO.

Duke. Give us a little leave.
　　　　[*Exeunt* FLUELLO, CASTRUCHIO,
　　　　　and PIORATTO.]
　　　　　　　Doctor, your news.
Doct. I sent for him, my lord; at last he
　　came,
And did receive all speech that went from me,
As gilded pills made to prolong his health. 4
My credit with him wrought it; for some men
Swallow even empty hooks, like fools that fear
No drowning where 't is deepest, 'cause 't is clear.
In th' end we sat and eat: a health I drank
To Infelice's sweet departed soul.
This train [2] I knew would take.
Duke. 　　　　　'T was excellent. 10
Doct. He fell with such devotion on his knees,
To pledge the same —
Duke. 　　　　Fond, superstitious fool!
Doct. That had he been inflam'd with zeal of
　　prayer,
He could not pour 't out with more reverence.
About my neck he hung, wept on my cheek. 15
Kist it, and swore he would adore my lips,
Because they brought forth Infelice's name.
Duke. Ha, ha! alack, alack.
Doct. The cup he lifts up high, and thus he
　　said;
"Here, noble maid!" — drinks, and was poi-
　　soned. 20
Duke. And died?
Doct. 　　　　And died, my lord.
Duke. 　　　　　Thou in that word
Hast piec'd mine aged hours out with more years
Than thou hast taken from Hippolito.
A noble youth he was, but lesser branches 24
Hind'ring the greater's growth, must be lopt off,
And feed the fire. Doctor, we 're now all thine,
And use us so: be bold.
Doct. 　　　　Thanks, gracious lord —
My honoured lord: —
Duke. 　　Hum.
Doct. I do beseech your grace to bury deep,
This bloody act of mine.
Duke. 　　　　Nay, nay, for that, 30
Doctor, look you to 't, me it shall not move;
They 're curst that ill do, not that ill do love.
Doct. You throw an angry forehead on my
　　face:
But be you pleas'd backward thus far to look,
That for your good, this evil I undertook — 35
Duke. Ay, ay, we conster [3] so.
Doct. And only for your love.
Duke. 　　　　Confest: ' tis true.
Doct. Nor let it stand against me as a bar
To thrust me from your presence; nor believe
As princes have quick thoughts, that now my
　　finger 40
Being dipt in blood, I will not spare the hand,
But that for gold,— as what can gold not do?—
I may be hir'd to work the like on you.

----

[1] Grounds near the Duke's Palace.
[2] Device.　　　　[3] Construe.

Duke. Which to prevent —
Doct.   'T is from my heart as far.
Duke. No matter, doctor ; 'cause I 'll fearless
sleep,   45
And that you shall stand clear of that suspicion,
I banish thee for ever from my court.
This principle is old, but true as fate,
Kings may love treason, but the traitor hate.
        Exit.
Doct. Is 't so ? Nay then, duke, your stale
principle,   50
With one as stale, the doctor thus shall quit.
He falls himself that digs another's pit.

Enter the Doctor's Man.

How now ! where is he ? will he not meet me ?
Man. Meet you, sir ? He might have met with
three fencers in this time, and have received [55
less hurt than by meeting one doctor of physic.
Why, sir, he has walkt under the old abbey-
wall yonder this hour, till he 's more cold than a
citizen's country house in Janivere. You may
smell him behind, sir : la, you, yonder he comes.

Enter HIPPOLITO.

Doct. Leave me.   61
Man. I 'th' lurch, if you will.   *Exit.*
Doct. O my most noble friend !
Hip.   Few but yourself,
Could have entic'd me thus, to trust the air
With my close sighs. You sent for me ; what
news ?   65
Doct. Come, you must doff this black, dye that
pale cheek
Into his own colour, go, attire yourself
Fresh as a bridegroom when he meets his bride.
The duke has done much treason to thy love ;
'T is now reveal'd, 't is now to be reveng'd.   70
Be merry, honour'd friend, thy lady lives.
Hip. What lady ?
Doct.   Infelice, she 's reviv'd.
Reviv'd ? Alack ! death never had the heart,
To take breath from her.
Hip.   Umh : I thank you, sir,
Physic prolongs life, when it cannot save ;   75
This helps not my hopes, mine are in their
grave,
You do some wrong to mock me.
Doct.   By that love
Which I have ever borne you, what I speak
Is truth : the maiden lives ; that funeral,   79
Duke's tears, the mourning, was all counterfeit.
A sleepy draught coz'ned the world and you :
I was his minister, and then chamb'red up,
To stop discovery.
Hip.   O treacherous duke !
Doct. He cannot hope so certainly for bliss,
As he believes that I have poison'd you.   85
He woo'd me to 't ; I yielded, and confirm'd
him
In his most bloody thoughts.
Hip.   A very devil !
Doct. Her did he closely coach to Bergamo,
And thither —
Hip.   Will I ride. Stood Bergamo   89
In the low countries of black hell, I 'll to her.
Doct. You shall to her, but not to Bergamo.

How passion makes you fly beyond yourself !
Much of that weary journey I ha' cut off ;
For she by letters hath intelligence
Of your supposed death, her own interment,   95
And all those plots which that false duke, her
father,
Has wrought against you ; and she 'll meet
you —
Hip. Oh, when ?
Doct. Nay, see ; how covetous are your desires.
Early to-morrow morn.
Hip.   Oh where, good father ?   100
Doct. At Bethlem Monastery : are you pleas'd
now ?
Hip. At Bethlem Monastery ! The place well
fits ;
It is the school where those that lose their wits
Practise again to get them. I am sick
Of that disease ; all love is lunatic.   105
Doct. We 'll steal away this night in some
disguise.
Father Anselmo, a most reverend friar,
Expects our coming ; before whom we 'll lay
Reasons so strong, that he shall yield in bands
Of holy wedlock to tie both your hands.   110
Hip. This is such happiness.
That to believe it, 't is impossible.
Doct. Let all your joys then die in misbelief ;
I will reveal no more.
Hip.   O yes, good father,
I am so well acquainted with despair,   115
I know not how to hope : I believe all.
Doct. We 'll hence this night. Much must be
done, much said ;
But if the doctor fail not in his charms,
Your lady shall ere morning fill these arms.
Hip. Heavenly physician ! for thy fame shall
spread,   120
That mak'st two lovers speak when they be
dead.   *Exeunt.*

[ACT V]

[SCENE I.]¹

Enter Candido's *wife* [VIOLA *with a petition*]
and GEORGE. PIORATTO *meets them.*

Vio. Oh watch, good George, watch which
way the duke comes.
Geo. Here comes one of the butterflies ; ask him.
Vio. Pray, sir, comes the duke this way ?
Pio. He 's upon coming, mistress.   5
Vio. I thank you, sir. [*Exit* PIORATTO.]
George, are there many mad folks where thy
master lies ?
Geo. Oh yes, of all countries some ; but especially mad Greeks, they swarm. Troth, [10
mistress, the world is altered with you ; you
had not wont to stand thus with a paper humbly complaining : but you 're well enough serv'd ;
provender prickt ² you, as it does many of our
city wives besides.   15
Vio. Dost think, George, we shall get him
forth ?

Geo. Truly, mistress, I cannot tell ; I think
you 'll hardly get him forth. Why, 't is strange!
'Sfoot, I have known many women that [20
have had mad rascals to their husbands, whom
they would belabour by all means possible to
keep 'em in their right wits ; but of a woman to
long to turn a tame man into a madman, why the
devil himself was never us 'd so by his dam. 25

Vio. How does he talk, George ? Ha ! good
George, tell me.

Geo. Why, you 're best go see.

Vio. Alas, I am afraid!

Geo. Afraid ! you had more need be [30
asham'd. He may rather be afraid of you.

Vio. But, George, he 's not stark mad, is he ?
He does not rave, he is not horn-mad, George,
is he ?

Geo. Nay I know not that, but he talks [35
like a justice of peace, of a thousand matters,
and to no purpose.

Vio. I 'll to the monastery. I shall be mad till
I enjoy him, I shall be sick until I see him; yet
when I do see him I shall weep out mine eyes. 40

Geo. I 'd fain see a woman weep out her eyes !
That 's as true as to say, a man's cloak burns,
when it hangs in the water. I know you 'll weep,
mistress, but what says the painted cloth ? [1]

> Trust not a woman when she cries,   45
> For she 'll pump water from her eyes
> With a wet finger,[2] and in faster showers
> Than April when he rains down flowers.

Vio. Ay, but George, that painted cloth is
worthy to be hanged up for lying. All women [50
have not tears at will, unless they have good
cause.

Geo. Ay, but mistress, how easily will they
find a cause, and as one of our cheese-trenchers[3]
says very learnedly,   55

> As out of wormwood bees suck honey,
> As from poor clients lawyers firk money,
> As parsley from a roasted cony :
> So, though the day be ne'er so funny,
> If wives will have it rain, down then it drives,   60
> The calmest husbands make the stormiest wives.

Vio. Tame, George. But I ha' done storming now.

Geo. Why that 's well done. Good mistress,
throw aside this fashion of your humour, be [65
not so fantastical in wearing it ; storm no more,
long no more. This longing has made you come
short of many a good thing that you might have
had from my master. Here comes the duke.

Enter DUKE, FLUELLO, PIORATTO, *and* SINEZI.

Vio. O, I beseech you, pardon my offence, 70
In that I durst abuse your grace's warrant ;
Deliver forth my husband, good my lord.

Duke. Who is her husband ?

Flu.   Candido, my lord.

Duke. Where is he ?

Vio.   He 's among the lunatics ;

---

[1] A cheap substitute for tapestry, frequently adorned
with mottoes and verses.

[2] Readily.

[3] Cheese-trenchers used to be inscribed with proverbial phrases.

He was a man made up without a gall ;   75
Nothing could move him, nothing could convert
His meek blood into fury ; yet like a monster,
I often beat at the most constant rock
Of his unshaken patience, and did long
To vex him.

Duke. Did you so ?

Vio.   And for that purpose 80
Had warrant from your grace, to carry him
To Bethlem Monastery, whence they will not
free him
Without your grace's hand that sent him in.

Duke. You have long'd fair ; 't is you are mad,
I fear ;
It 's fit to fetch him thence, and keep you
there.   85
If he be mad, why would you have him forth ?

Geo. An please your grace, he 's not stark
mad, but only talks like a young gentleman,
somewhat fantastically, that 's all. There 's a
thousand about your court, city, and coun- [90
try madder than he.

Duke. Provide a warrant, you shall have our
hand.

Geo. Here 's a warrant ready drawn, my lord.

Duke. Get pen and ink, get pen and ink.
                                [*Exit* GEORGE.]

Enter CASTRUCHIO.

Cas. Where is my lord the duke ?

Duke.   How now ! more madmen ? 95

Cas. I have strange news, my lord.

Duke.   Of what ? Of whom ?

Cas. Of Infelice, and a marriage.

Duke. Ha ! where ? with whom ?

Cas.   Hippolito.

Re-enter GEORGE, *with pen and ink.*

Geo. Here, my lord.

Duke. Hence, with that woman ! Void the
room !   100

Flu. Away ! the duke 's vext.

Geo. Whoop, come, mistress, the duke 's mad
too.

                Exeunt [VIOLA *and* GEORGE].

Duke. Who told me that Hippolito was dead ?

Cas. He that can make any man dead, the doctor : but, my lord, he 's as full of life as wild- [105
fire, and as quick. Hippolito, the doctor, and
one more rid hence this evening ; the inn at
which they light is Bethlem Monastery ; Infelice comes from Bergamo and meets them there.
Hippolito is mad, for he means this day to [110
be married ; the afternoon is the hour, and Friar
Anselmo is the knitter.

Duke. From Bergamo ? Is 't possible ? it cannot be.
It cannot be.

Cas.   I will not swear, my lord ;
But this intelligence I took from one   115
Whose brains work in the plot.

Duke.   What 's he ?

Cas.   Matheo.

Flu. Matheo knows all.

Pior.   He 's Hippolito's bosom.

Duke. How far stands Bethlem hence ?

All.   Six or seven miles.

Duke. Is 't so ? Not married till the afternoon :
Stay, stay, let 's work out some prevention.
    How !   120
This is most strange ; can none but mad men
    serve
To dress their wedding dinner ? All of you
Get presently to horse, disguise yourselves
Like country-gentlemen,
Or riding citizens, or so : and take   125
Each man a several path, but let us meet
At Bethlem Monastery ; some space of time
Being spent between the arrival each of other,
As if we came to see the lunatics.
To horse, away ! Be secret on your lives.   130
Love must be punisht that unjustly thrives.
            Exeunt [all but Fluello].
Flu. Be secret on your lives ! Castruchio,
You 're but a scurvy spaniel. Honest lord,
Good lady ! Zounds, their love is just, 't is
    good,   134
And I 'll prevent you, though I swim in blood.
                                            Exit.

[Scene II.]¹

Enter Friar Anselmo, Hippolito, Matheo,
    and Infelice.

Hip. Nay, nay, resolve,² good father, or
    deny.
Ans. You press me to an act both full of
    danger
And full of happiness ; for I behold
Your father's frowns, his threats, nay, perhaps
    death
To him that dare do this : yet, noble lord,   5
Such comfortable beams break through these
    clouds
By this blest marriage, that your honour'd word
Being pawn'd in my defence, I will tie fast
The holy wedding-knot.
Hip.   Tush, fear not the duke.
Ans. O son ! wisely to fear, is to be free from
    fear.   10
Hip. You have our words, and you shall have
    our lives,
To guard you safe from all ensuing danger.
Mat. Ay, ay, chop 'em up, and away.
Ans. Stay, when is 't fit for me, and safest for
    you,
To entertain this business ?
Hip.   Not till the evening.   15
Ans. Be 't so, there is a chapel stands hard
    by,
Upon the west end of the abbey wall ;
Thither convey yourselves, and when the sun
Hath turn'd his back upon this upper world,
I 'll marry you ; that done, no thund'ring voice
Can break the sacred bond : yet, lady, here   21
You are most safe.
Inf.   Father, your love 's most dear.
Mat. Ay, well said ; lock us into some little
room by ourselves, that we may be mad for an
hour or two.   25
Hip. O, good Matheo, no, let 's make no
    noise.

---

¹ An apartment in Bethlem Monastery.
² Consent.

Mat. How ! no noise ! Do you know where
you are ? 'Sfoot, amongst all the madcaps
in Milan ; so that to throw the house out at
window will be the better, and no man will [³⁰
suspect that we lurk here to steal mutton.³ The
more sober we are, the more scurvy ⁴ 't is. And
though the friar tell us that here we are safest,
I am not of his mind ; for if those lay here that
had lost their money, none would ever look [³⁵
after them ; but here are none but those that
have lost their wits, so that if hue and cry be
made, hither they 'll come ; and my reason is,
because none goes to be married till he be stark
mad.   40
Hip. Muffle yourselves, yonder 's Fluello.

Enter Fluello.

Mat.   Zounds !
Flu. O my lord, these cloaks are not for this
rain ! The tempest is too great. I come sweat-
ing to tell you of it, that you may get out of it.
Mat. Why, what 's the matter ?   44
Flu. What 's the matter ? You have matter'd
it fair ; the duke 's at hand.
All. The duke ?
Flu.   The very duke.
Hip.   Then all our plots
Are turn'd upon our heads   and we 're blown up
With our own underminings. 'Sfoot, how comes
    he ?   50
What villain durst betray our being here ?
Flu. Castruchio told the duke, and Matheo
here told Castruchio.
Hip. Would you betray me to Castruchio ?
Mat. 'Sfoot, he damn'd himself to the pit [⁵⁵
of hell, if he spake on 't again.
Hip. So did you swear to me : so were you
damn'd.
Mat. Pox on 'em, and there be no faith in
men, if a man shall not believe oaths. He took
bread and salt, by this light, that he would [⁶⁰
never open his lips.
Hip. O God, O God !
Ans.   Son, be not desperate,
Have patience, you shall trip your enemy
Down by his own slights.⁵ How far is the duke
    hence ?
Flu. He 's but new set out ; Castruchio, [⁶⁵
Pioratto, and Sinezi come along with him. You
have time enough yet to prevent ⁶ them, if you
have but courage.
Ans. Ye shall steal secretly into the chapel,
And presently be married. If the duke   70
Abide here still, spite of ten thousand eyes,
You shall scape hence like friars.
Hip. O blest disguise ! O happy man !
Ans. Talk not of Happiness till your clos'd
    hand
Have her by th' forehead, like the lock of
    Time.   75
Be nor too slow, nor hasty, now you climb
Up to the tower of bliss ; only be wary
And patient, that 's all. If you like my plot,
Build and despatch ; if not, farewell, then not.

---

³ *I. e.* to steal a wench.   ⁵ Artifices.
⁴ Suspicious.   ⁶ Anticipate.

Hip. O yes, we do applaud it! we'll dispute   80
No longer, but will hence and execute.
Fluello, you'll stay here: let us be gone.
The ground that frighted lovers tread upon
Is stuck with thorns.
Ans.   Come, then, away, 'tis meet,
To escape those thorns, to put on winged feet. [85
    Exeunt [ANSELMO, HIPPOLITO, *and*
    INFELICE].

Mat. No words, I pray, Fluello, for 't stands
us upon.
Flu. Oh, sir, let that be your lesson!
    [*Exit* MATHEO.]
Alas, poor lovers! On what hopes and fears
Men toss themselves for women! When she's
    got,   90
The best has in her that which pleaseth not.

Enter to FLUELLO *the* DUKE, CASTRUCHIO, PIO-
RATTO, *and* SINEZI *from several doors, muffled.*

Duke. Who's there?
Cas.   My lord.
Duke.   Peace; send that "lord" away.
A lordship will spoil all; let's be all fellows.
What's he?
Cas. Fluello, or else, Sinezi, by his little [95
legs.
All. All friends, all friends.
Duke. What? Met upon the very point of
    time?
Is this the place?
Pio.   This is the place, my lord.
Duke. Dream you on lordships? Come no
more "lords," I pray: 100
You have not seen these lovers yet?
All.   Not yet.
Duke. Castruchio, art thou sure this wedding
    feat
Is not till afternoon?
Cas.   So 't is given out, my lord.
Duke. Nay, nay, 'tis like; thieves must ob-
    serve their hours;
Lovers watch minutes like astronomers;   105
How shall the interim hours by us be spent?
Flu. Let's all go to see the madmen.
All. Mass, content.

Enter a Sweeper.[1]

Duke. Oh, here comes one; question him,
question him.   110
Flu. Now, honest fellow? dost thou belong
to the house?
Sweep. Yes, forsooth, I am one of the implements; I sweep the madmen's rooms, and fetch
straw for 'em, and buy chains to tie 'em, [115
and rods to whip 'em. I was a mad wag myself
here, once, but I thank Father Anselmo, he
lasht me into my right mind again.
Duke. Anselmo is the friar must marry them;
Question him where he is.   120
Cas. And where is Father Anselmo now?
Sweep. Marry, he's gone but e'en now.
Duke. Ah, well done. — Tell me, whither is
he gone?

Sweep. Why to God a'mighty.
Flu. Ha, ha! this fellow's a fool, talks [124
idly.
Pio. Sirrah, are all the mad folks in Milan
brought hither?
Sweep. How, all? There's a question indeed! Why if all the mad folks in Milan [130
should come hither, there would not be left ten
men in the city.
Duke. Few gentlemen or courtiers here, ha?
Sweep. O yes, abundance, abundance!
Lands no sooner fall into their hands, [135
but straight they run out a' their wits. Citizens' sons and heirs are free of the house by
their fathers' copy.[2] Farmers' sons come hither
like geese, in flocks, and when they ha' sold all
their cornfields, here they sit and pick the [140
straws.
Sin. Methinks you should have women here
as well as men.
Sweep. Oh, ay, a plague on 'em, there's no
ho![3] with 'em; they're madder than March [145
hares.
Flu. Are there no lawyers amongst you?
Sweep. Oh no, not one; never any lawyer.
We dare not let a lawyer come in, for he'll
make 'em mad faster than we can recover [150
'em.
Duke. And how long is 't ere you recover any
of these?
Sweep. Why, according to the quantity of the
moon that's got into 'em. An alderman's [155
son will be mad a great while, a very great
while, especially if his friends left him well. A
whore will hardly come to her wits again. A
puritan, there's no hope of him, unless he may
pull down the steeple, and hang himself i' [160
th' bell-ropes.
Flu. I perceive all sorts of fish come to your
net.
Sweep. Yes, in truth, we have blocks[4] for all
heads; we have good store of wild-oats [165
here; for the courtier is mad at the citizen, the
citizen is mad at the countryman; the shoemaker is mad at the cobbler, the cobbler at the
carman; the punk is mad that the merchant's
wife is no whore, the merchant's wife is mad [170
that the punk is so common a whore. Gods so,
here's Father Anselmo; pray say nothing that
I tell tales out of the school.   *Exit.*

Re-enter ANSELMO [*and* Servants].

All. God bless you, father.
Ans.   I thank you, gentlemen.
Cas. Pray, may we see some of those wretched
souls,   175
That here are in your keeping?
Ans.   Yes, you shall;
But, gentlemen, I must disarm you then.
There are of mad men, as there are of tame,
All humour'd not alike: we have here some,
So apish and fantastic, play with a feather,   180
And, though 't would grieve a soul to see God's
image
So blemisht and defac'd, yet do they act

---

[1] Qq. *Enter Towne like a Sweeper.*

[2] Citizenship.   [3] Check.   [4] Moulds for hats, or hats.

Such antic and such pretty lunacies,
That spite of sorrow they will make you smile.
Others again we have like hungry lions,　185
Fierce as wild-bulls, untameable as flies,
And these have oftentimes from strangers'
　　　sides
Snatcht rapiers suddenly, and done much harm,
Whom if you 'll see, you must be weaponless.

All. With all our hearts.
　　　　　　[*Giving their weapons to* Anselmo.]
Ans.　　　Here, take these weapons in.— 190
　　　　　　[*Exit* Servant *with weapons.*]
Stand off a little, pray ; so, so, 't is well.
I 'll show you here a man that was sometimes
A very grave and wealthy citizen ;
Has serv'd a prenticeship to this misfortune,
Been here seven years, and dwelt in Ber-
　　gamo.　　195
Duke. How fell he from his wits ?
Ans.　　　By loss at sea ;
I 'll stand aside, question him you alone,
For if he spy me, he 'll not speak a word,
Unless he 's th'roughly vext.
　　　Discovers an old man, *wrapt in a net.*
Flu.　　　Alas, poor soul !
Cas. A very old man.　200
Duke. God speed, father !
1 Mad. God speed the plough, thou shalt not
speed me.
Pio. We see you, old man, for all you dance
in a net.　205
1 Mad. True, but thou wilt dance in a halter,
and I shall not see thee.
Ans. Oh do not vex him, pray.
Cas. Are you a fisherman, father ?
1 Mad. No, I am neither fish nor flesh.　210
Flu. What do you with that net then ?
1 Mad. Dost not see, fool ? There 's a fresh
salmon in 't ; if you step one foot further, you 'll
be over shoes, for you see I 'm over head and
ears in the salt-water : and if you fall into [215
this whirl-pool where I am, y' are drown'd :
y 'are a drown'd rat. I am fishing here for five
ships, but I cannot have a good draught, for my
net breaks still, and breaks ; but I 'll break some
of your necks an I catch you in my clutches. [220
Stay, stay, stay, stay, stay, where 's the wind ?
where 's the wind ? where 's the wind ? where 's
the wind ? Out, you gulls, you goose-caps,[1] you
gudgeon-eaters ![2] Do you look for the wind in
the heavens ? Ha, ha, ha, ha ! no, no ! Look [225
there, look there, look there ! the wind is always
at that door : hark how it blows, puff, puff,
puff !
All. Ha, ha, ha !
1 Mad. Do you laugh at God's creatures ? [230
Do you mock old age, you rogues ? Is this gray
beard and head counterfeit that you cry, ha, ha,
ha ? Sirrah, art not thou my eldest son ?
Pio. Yes, indeed, father.
1 Mad. Then th' art a fool, for my eldest [235
son had a polt-foot,[3] crooked legs, a verjuice[4]
face, and a pear-colour'd beard. I made him a
scholar, and he made himself a fool. — Sirrah,
thou there : hold out thy hand.

Duke. My hand ? Well, here 't is.　240
1 Mad. Look, look, look, look ! Has he not
long nails, and short hair ?
Flu. Yes, monstrous short hair, and abominable long nails.
1 Mad. Ten-penny nails, are they not ?　245
Flu. Yes, ten-penny nails.
1 Mad. Such nails had my second boy. Kneel
down, thou varlet, and ask thy father's blessing. Such nails had my middlemost son, and I
made him a promoter :[5] and he scrapt, and [250
scrapt, and scrapt, till he got the devil and all :
but he scrapt thus, and thus, and thus, and it
went under his legs, till at length a company
of kites, taking him for carrion, swept up all,
all, all, all, all, all, all. If you love your [255
lives, look to yourselves : see, see, see, see, the
Turks' galleys are fighting with my ships !
Bounce goes the guns ! Oooh ! cry the men !
Rumble, rumble, go the waters ! Alas, there ;
't is sunk, 't is sunk : I am undone, I am un- [260
done ! You are the damn'd pirates have undone
me : you are, by the Lord, you are, you are ! —
Stop 'em — you are !
Ans. Why, how now sirrah ! Must I fall to
tame you ?　265
1 Mad. Tame me ! No, I 'll be madder than
a roasted cat. See, see, I am burnt with gun-
powder, — these are our close fights !
Ans. I 'll whip you, if you grow unruly thus.
1 Mad. Whip me ? Out you toad ! Whip [270
me ? What justice is this, to whip me because
I am a beggar ? Alas ! I am a poor man : a very
poor man ! I am starv'd, and have had no meat
by this light, ever since the great flood ; I am
a poor man.　275
Ans. Well, well, be quiet, and you shall have
meat.
1 Mad. Ay, ay, pray do ; for, look you, here
be my guts : these are my ribs — you may look
through my ribs — see how my guts come out ! [280
These are my red guts, my very guts, oh, oh !
Ans. Take him in there.
　　　　　　[*Servants remove* 1 Madman.]
All. A very piteous sight.
Cas. Father, I see you have a busy charge.
Ans. They must be us'd like children, pleas'd
with toys.　285
And anon whipt for their unruliness.
I 'll show you now a pair quite different
From him that 's gone. He was all words ; and
　　these
Unless you urge 'em, seldom spend their speech,
But save their tongues.
　　[*Opens another door, from which enter*
　　　2 *and* 3 *Madmen.*]
　　　　　　La, you ; this hithermost
Fell from the happy quietness of mind　291
About a maiden that he lov'd, and died.
He followed her to church, being full of
　　tears,
And as her body went into the ground,
He fell stark mad. This is a married man,　295
Was jealous of a fair, but, as some say,
A very virtuous wife ; and that spoil'd him.

---

[1] Simpletons.　[2] Dupes.　[3] Club foot.　[4] Sour, crabbed.

[5] Informer.

3 Mad.[1] All these are whoremongers, and lay with my wife: whore, whore, whore, whore, whore!

Flu. Observe him.   300

3 Mad. Gaffer shoemaker, you pull'd on my wife's pumps, and then crept into her pantofles:[2] lie there, lie there!—This was her tailor. [*304* You cut out her loose-bodied gown, and put in a yard more than I allowed her; lie there by the shoemaker. O master doctor! are you here? You gave me a purgation, and then crept into my wife's chamber to feel her pulses, and [*309* you said, and she said, and her maid said, that they went pit-a-pat, pit-a-pat, pit-a-pat. Doctor, I'll put you anon into my wife's urinal. Heigh, come aloft, Jack! This was her school-master, and taught her to play upon the virginals, [*314* and still his jacks[3] leapt up, up. You prickt[4] her out nothing but bawdy lessons, but I'll prick you all, fiddler—doctor—tailor—shoe-maker—shoemaker—fiddler—doctor—tailor! So! lie with my wife again, now.   319

Cas. See how he notes the other, now he feeds.

3 Mad. Give me some porridge.
2 Mad. I'll give thee none.
3 Mad. Give me some porridge.
2 Mad. I'll not give thee a bit.   325
3 Mad. Give me that flap-dragon.[5]
2 Mad. I'll not give thee a spoonful. Thou liest, it's no dragon, 't is a parrot that I bought for my sweetheart, and I'll keep it.
3 Mad. Here's an almond for parrot.[6]   330
2 Mad. Hang thyself!
3 Mad. Here's a rope for parrot.[6]
2 Mad. Eat it, for I'll eat this.
3 Mad. I'll shoot at thee, an thou 't give me none.   335
2 Mad. Wu't thou?
3 Mad. I'll run a tilt at thee, an thou 't give me none.
2 Mad. Wu't thou? Do an thou dar'st.
3 Mad. Bounce!   [*Strikes him.*] 340
2 Mad. O—oh! I am slain! Murder, murder, murder! I am slain; my brains are beaten out.
Ans. How now, you villains! Bring me whips: I'll whip you.   345
2 Mad. I am dead! I am slain! ring out the bell, for I am dead.
Duke. How will you do now, sirrah? You ha' kill'd him.   349
3 Mad. I'll answer 't at sessions: he was eat-ing of almond-butter, and I long'd for 't. The child had never been delivered out of my belly, if I had not kill'd him. I'll answer 't at sessions, so my wife may be burnt i' th' hand, too. [*354*
Ans. Take 'em in both: bury him, for he's dead.

---

[1] The Qq. read 2 *Mad.* for 3 *Mad.* and 3 *Mad.* for 2 *Mad.*
[2] Slippers.
[3] Pieces of wood fixed to the key-levers of virginals, spinets, and harpsichords, which rose when the keys were pressed down.
[4] Wrote in musical notes.
[5] A raisin floating on burning brandy.
[6] A proverbial phrase.

2 Mad. Indeed, I am dead; put me, I pray, into a good pit-hole.
3 Mad. I'll answer 't at sessions.   352
[*Servants remove 2 and 3 Madmen.*]

Enter BELLAFRONT *mad.*

Ans. How now, huswife, whither gad you?
Bell. A-nutting forsooth. How do you, gaffer? How do you, gaffer? There's a French curtsey for you, too.
Flu. 'T is Bellafront!
Pio. 'T is the punk, by th' Lord!   365
Duke. Father, what's she, I pray?
Ans.   As yet I know not,
She came in but this day; talks little idly,
And therefore has the freedom of the house.
Bell. Do not you know me?—nor you?—nor you?—nor you?   370
All. No, indeed.
Bell. Then you are an ass,—and you an ass,—and you are an ass,—for I know you.
Ans. Why, what are they? Come, tell me, what are they?   375
Bell. They're fish-wives, will you buy any gudgeons?
God's santy![7] yonder come friars, I know them too.—

Enter HIPPOLITO, MATHEO, *and* INFELICE *disguised in the habits of* Friars.

How do you, friar?
Ans. Nay, nay, away, you must not trouble friars.—   379
[*Aside to* HIPPOLITO, *etc.*] The duke is here, speak nothing.
Bell. Nay, indeed, you shall not go: we'll run at barley-break first, and you shall be in hell.[8]   384
Mat. My punk turn'd mad whore, as all her fellows are!
Hip. Say nothing; but steal hence, when you spy time.
Ans. I'll lock you up, if you're unruly: fie!
Bell. Fie! Marry, so, they shall not go in-deed, till I ha' told 'em their fortunes. 390
Duke. Good father, give her leave.
Bell. Ay, pray, good father, and I'll give you my blessing.
Ans. Well then, be brief, but if you're thus unruly,
I'll have you lockt up fast.   395
Pio. Come, to their fortunes.
Bell. Let me see, one, two, three, and four. I'll begin with the little friar[9] first. Here's a fine hand, indeed! I never saw friar have such a dainty hand: here's a hand for a lady! [*400* Here's your fortune:—
You love a friar better than a nun;
Yet long you'll love no friar, nor no friar's son.
Bow a little, the line of life is out, yet I'm afraid,

---

[7] A corruption of God's sanctity or God's saints. (Steevens.)
[8] In the game of barley-break the ground was divided into three compartments, the middle one of which was called "hell."
[9] *I. e.* Infelice.

For all you 're holy, you 'll not die a maid. 405
God give you joy !
Now to you, Friar Tuck.
  Mat. God send me good luck !
  Bell. You love one, and one loves you :
You 're a false knave, and she 's a Jew, 410
Here is a dial that false ever goes —
  Mat. O your wit drops !
  Bell.   Troth, so does your nose —
Nay let 's shake hands with you too ; pray open,
here 's a fine hand !
Ho friar, ho ! God be here ! 415
So he had need. You 'll keep good cheer,
Here 's a free table,[1] but a frozen breast,
For you 'll starve those that love you best ;
Yet you have good fortune, for if I 'm no liar,
Then you are no friar, nor you, nor you no friar,
Haha, haha !   *Discovers them.* 421
  Duke. Are holy habits cloaks for villany ?
Draw all your weapons !
  Hip. Do ; draw all your weapons.
  Duke. Where are your weapons ? Draw ! 425
  All. The friar has gull'd us of 'em.
  Mat.   O rare trick !
You ha' learnt one mad point of arithmetic.
  Hip. Why swells your spleen so high ?
Against what bosom
Would you your weapons draw ? Her's ? 'T is
your daughter's : 429
Mine ? 'T is your son's.
  Duke.   Son ?
  Mat.   Son, by yonder sun.
  Hip. You cannot shed blood here but 't is
your own ;
To spill your own blood were damnation.
Lay smooth that wrinkled brow, and I will
throw
Myself beneath your feet:
Let it be rugged still and flinted ore, 435
What can come forth but sparkles, that will
burn
Yourself and us ? She 's mine ; my claim 's most
good ;
She 's mine by marriage, though she 's yours by
blood.
  [*Ans. kneeling.*] I have a hand, dear lord,
deep in this act,
For I foresaw this storm, yet willingly 440
Put forth to meet it. Oft have I seen a father
Washing the wounds of his dear son in tears,
A son to curse the sword that struck his father,
Both slain i' th' quarrel of your families. 444
Those scars are now ta'en off ; and I beseech you
To seal our pardon ! All was to this end,
To turn the ancient hates of your two houses
To fresh green friendship, that your loves might
look
Like the spring's forehead, comfortably sweet ;
And your vext souls in peaceful union meet. 450
Their blood will now be yours, yours will be
theirs,
And happiness shall crown your silver hairs.
  Flu. You see, my lord, there 's now no rem-
edy.

[1] A quibble. "Table" also meant the palm of the
hand. (Dyce.)

  All. Beseech your lordship !
  Duke. You beseech fair, you have me in place
fit 455
To bridle me. — Rise friar, you may be glad
You can make madmen tame, and tame men mad.
Since Fate hath conquer'd, I must rest content;
To strive now, would but add new punishment.
I yield unto your happiness ; be blest, 460
Our families shall henceforth breathe in rest.
  All. Oh, happy change !
  Duke.   Your's now is my content,
I throw upon your joys my full consent.
  Bell. Am not I a good girl, for finding [46?
"the friar in the well ? "[2] Gods so, you are a
brave man ! Will not you buy me some sugar-
plums, because I am so good a fortune-teller ?
  Duke. Would thou hadst wit, thou pretty
soul, to ask,
As I have will to give. 469
  Bell. Pretty soul ? A pretty soul is better
than a pretty body. Do not you know my pretty
soul ? I know you. Is not your name Matheo ?
  Mat. Yes, lamb.
  Bell. Baa lamb ! there you lie, for I am mutton.[3] — Look, fine man ! he was mad for me [475
once, and I was mad for him once, and he was
mad for her once, and were you never mad ?
Yes, I warrant ; I had a fine jewel once, a very
fine jewel, and that naughty man stole it away
from me, — a very fine and a rich jewel. 480
  Duke. What jewel, pretty maid ?
  Bell. Maid ? Nay, that 's a lie. O, 't was a very
rich jewel, called a maidenhead, and had not
you it, leerer ?
  Mat. Out, you mad ass ! away. 485
  Duke. Had he thy maidenhead ?
He shall make thee amends, and marry thee.
  Bell. Shall he ? O brave Arthur of Bradley[4]
then !
  Duke. And if he bear the mind of a gentleman,
I know he will. 491
  Mat. I think I rifled her of some such paltry
jewel.
  Duke. Did you ? Then marry her ; you see
the wrong
Has led her spirits into a lunacy. 495
  Mat. How ? Marry her, my lord ? 'Sfoot,
marry a madwoman ? Let a man get the tam-
est wife he can come by, she 'll be mad enough
afterward, do what he can.
  Duke. Nay then, Father Anselmo here shall
do his best, 500
To bring her to her wits ; and will you then ?
  Mat. I cannot tell, I may choose.
  Duke. Nay, then, law shall compel. I tell you,
sir,
So much her hard fate moves me, you should
not breathe
Under this air, unless you married her. 505
  Mat. Well, then, when her wits stand in their
right place,
I 'll marry her.
  Bell. I thank your grace. — Matheo, thou art
mine.

[2] The name of a well-known tale.
[3] A prostitute.
[4] An allusion to a ballad of that name.

I am not mad, but put on this disguise,
Only for you, my lord ; for you can tell   510
Much wonder of me ; but you are gone : farewell.
Matheo, thou didst first turn my soul black,
Now make it white again. I do protest,
I 'm pure as fire now, chaste as Cynthia's breast.
Hip. I durst be sworn, Matheo, she 's indeed.
Mat. Cony-catch, gull'd ! Must I sail in your
      fly-boat,   516
Because I helpt to rear your main-mast first ?
Plague 'found [1] you for 't, 't is well.
The cuckold's stamp goes current in all nations,
Some men ha' horns giv'n them at their crea-
      tions ;   520
If I be one of those, why so : 't is better
To take a common wench, and make her good,
Than one that simpers, and at first will scarce
Be tempted forth over the threshold door,
Yet in one se'nnight, zounds, turns arrant
      whore !   525
Come wench, thou shalt be mine, give me thy
      golls,[2]
We 'll talk of legs hereafter.— See, my lord,
God give us joy !
All. God give you joy !   529

Enter Candido's wife [VIOLA] and GEORGE.

Geo. Come mistress, we are in Bedlam now ;
mass and see, we come in pudding-time, for
here 's the duke.
Vio. My husband, good my lord !
Duke. Have I thy husband ?   534
Cast. It 's Candido, my lord, he 's here among
the lunatics. Father Anselmo, pray fetch him
forth. [*Exit* ANSELMO.] This mad woman is his
wife, and though she were not with child, yet
did she long most spitefully to have her [539
husband mad ; and because she would be sure
he should turn Jew, she placed him here in
Bethlem. Yonder he comes.

Enter CANDIDO with ANSELMO.

Duke. Come hither, signor ; are you mad ?
Cand. You are not mad.
Duke. Why, I know that.   545
Cand. Then may you know I am not mad,
      that know
You are not mad, and that you are the duke.
None is mad here but one. — How do you, wife ?
What do you long for now ? — Pardon, my
      lord :   549
She had lost her child's nose else. I did cut out
Pennyworths of lawn, the lawn was yet mine
      own :
A carpet was my gown, yet 't was mine own :
I wore my man's coat, yet the cloth mine own :

Had a crackt crown, the crown was yet mine
      own.   554
She says for this I 'm mad : were her words true,
I should be mad indeed. O foolish skill ![3]
Is patience madness ? I 'll be a madman still.
Vio. Forgive me, and I 'll vex your spirit no
      more.   [*Kneels.*]
Duke. Come, come, we 'll have you friends ;
join hearts, join hands.   560
Cand. See, my lord, we are even, —
Nay, rise, for ill deeds kneel unto none but
      Heaven.
Duke. Signor, methinks patience has laid on
      you
Such heavy weight, that you should loathe it——
Cand.   Loathe it !
Duke. For he whose breast is tender, blood
      so cool,   565
That no wrongs heat it, is a patient fool.
What comfort do you find in being so calm ?
Cand. That which green wounds receive from
      sovereign balm.   568
Patience, my lord ! why, 't is the soul of peace ;
Of all the virtues, 't is nearest kin to Heaven ;
It makes men look like gods. The best of men
That e'er wore earth about him, was a sufferer,
A soft, meek, patient, humble, tranquil spirit,
The first true gentleman that ever breath'd.
The stock of patience, then, cannot be poor ; 575
All it desires, it has ; what monarch more ?
It is the greatest enemy to law
That can be ; for it doth embrace all wrongs,
And so chains up lawyers' and women's tongues.
' T is the perpetual prisoner's liberty,   580
His walks and orchards : 't is the bond slave's
      freedom,
And makes him seem proud of each iron chain,
As though he wore it more for state than pain :
It is the beggars' music, and thus sings,   584
Although their bodies beg, their souls are kings.
O my dread liege ! It is the sap of bliss
Rears us aloft, makes men and angels kiss.
And last of all, to end a household strife,
It is the honey 'gainst a waspish wife.
Duke. Thou giv'st it lively colours : who dare
      say   590
He 's mad, whose words march in so good array ?
'T were sin all women should such husbands
      have,
For every man must then be his wife's slave.
Come, therefore, you shall teach our court to
      shine,
So calm a spirit is worth a golden mine.   595
Wives with meek husbands that to vex them
      long,
In Bedlam must they dwell, else dwell they
      wrong.   *Exeunt.*

---

[1] Confound.   [2] Hands.   [3] Reason.

THE HONEST WHORE

PART II

BY

THOMAS DEKKER

ACT I

SCENE I.[1]

Enter at one door BERALDO, CAROLO, FONTI-
NELL, *and* ASTOLFO, *with* Serving-men, *or*
Pages, *attending on them; at another door enter*
LODOVICO, *meeting them.*

Lod. Good day, gallants.
All. Good morrow, sweet Lodovico.
Lod. How dost thou, Carolo?
Car. Faith, as the physicians do in a plague,
see the world sick, and am well myself.   5
Fon. Here's a sweet morning, gentlemen.
Lod. Oh, a morning to tempt Jove from his
ningle,[2] Ganymede; which is but to give dairy-
wenches green gowns as they are going a-milk-
ing. What, is thy lord stirring yet?   10
Ast. Yes, he will not be horst this hour, sure.
Ber. My lady swears he shall, for she longs
to be at court.
Car. Oh, we shall ride switch and spur;
would we were there once.   15

Enter BRYAN, *the* Footman.

Lod. How now, is thy lord ready?
Bry. No, so crees sa'[3] me; my lady will have
some little ting in her pelly first.
Car. Oh, then they 'll to breakfast.
Lod. Footman, does my lord ride i 'th' coach
with my lady, or on horseback?   21
Bry. No, foot, la; my lady will have me lord
sheet wid her, my lord will sheet in de one side,
and my lady sheet in de toder side.   *Exit.*

---

[1] A hall in Hippolito's house.
[2] Darling.   [3] Christ save.

Lod. My lady sheet in de toder side! Did [25
you ever hear a rascal talk so like a pagan?
Is 't not strange that a fellow of his star, should
be seen here so long in Italy, yet speak so from[4]
a Christian?

Enter ANTONIO GEORGIO, *a poor scholar* [*with
a book*].

Ast. An Irishman in Italy! that so strange!
Why, the nation have running heads.   31
                    Exchange walk.[5]
Lod. Nay, Carolo, this is more strange, I ha'
been in France, there's few of them. Marry,
England they count a warm chimney corner,
and there they swarm like crickets to the crevice of a brew-house; but sir, in England I [36
have noted one thing.
All. What's that, what's that of England?
Lod. Marry this, sir,— What 's he yonder? 39
Ber. A poor fellow would speak with my lord.
Lod. In England, sir,— troth, I ever laugh
when I think on 't: to see a whole nation
be markt i 'th' forehead, as a man may say,
with one iron: why, sir, there all costermongers
are Irishmen.   45
Car. Oh, that 's to show their antiquity, as
coming from Eve, who was an apple-wife, and
they take after the mother.
All. Good, good! ha, ha!
Lod. Why, then, should all your chimney- [50
sweepers likewise be Irishmen? Answer that
now; come, your wit.
Car. Faith, that 's soon answered; for St.
Patrick, you know, keeps purgatory; he makes

---

[4] Unlike.
[5] Promenade, as on the Exchange.

the fire, and his countrymen could do nothing, [55
if they cannot sweep the chimneys.
All. Good again.
Lod. Then, sir, have you many of them, like
this fellow, especially those of his hair, footmen
to noblemen and others, and the knaves are [60
very faithful where they love. By my faith,
very proper men, many of them, and as active
as the clouds,— whirr, hah !
All. Are they so ?
Lod. And stout ! exceeding stout; why, I [65
warrant, this precious wild villain, if he were
put to 't, would fight more desperately than
sixteen Dunkirks.[1]
Ast. The women, they say, are very fair.
Lod. No, no, our country *bona-robas*,[2] [70
oh ! are the sugarest, delicious rogues !
Ast. Oh, look, he has a feeling of them !
Lod. Not I, I protest. There 's a saying
when they commend nations. It goes, the Irishman for his hand, the Welshmen for a leg, [75
the Englishman for a face, the Dutchman for a
beard.
Fon. I' faith, they may make swabbers[3] of
them.
Lod. The Spaniard, — let me see, — for a
little foot, I take it ; the Frenchman,— what [81
a pox hath he ? And so of the rest. Are they
at breakfast yet ? Come walk.
Ast. This Lodovico is a notable tongued fellow.
Fon. Discourses well.   85
Ber. And a very honest gentleman.
Ast. Oh ! he 's well valued by my lord.

Enter BELLAFRONT, *with a petition.*

Fon. How now, how now, what 's she ?
Ber. Let 's make towards her.
Bell. Will it be long, sir, ere my lord come [90
forth ?
Ast. Would you speak with my lord ?
Lod. How now, what 's this, a nurse's bill ?
Hath any here got thee with child and now will
not keep it ?   95
Bell. No, sir, my business is unto my lord.
Lod. He 's about his own wife's now, he 'll
hardly dispatch two causes in a morning.
Ast. No matter what he says, fair lady ; he 's
a knight, there 's no hold to be taken at his
words.   101
Fon. My lord will pass this way presently.
Ber. A pretty, plump rogue.
Ast. A good lusty, bouncing baggage.
Ber. Do you know her ?   105
Lod. A pox on her, I was sure her name was
'n my table-book once. I know not of what cut
her die is now, but she has been more common
than tobacco; this is she that had the name of
the Honest Whore.   110
All. Is this she ?
Lod. This is the blackamoor that by washing
was turned white ; this is the birding-piece new
scoured ; this is she that, if any of her religion
can be saved, was saved by my lord Hippolito.
Ast. She has been a goodly creature.   116

Lod. She has been ! that 's the epitaph of all
whores. I 'm well acquainted with the poor
gentleman her husband. Lord ! what fortunes
that man has overreached ! She knows not [120
me, yet I have been in her company ; I scarce
know her, for the beauty of her cheek hath,
like the moon, suff'red strange eclipses since I
beheld it : but women are like medlars, — no
sooner ripe but rotten :   125
A woman last was made, but is spent first,
Yet man is oft proved in performance worst.
All. My lord is come.

Enter HIPPOLITO, INFELICE, *and two* Waiting-
women.

Hip. We ha' wasted half this morning. Mor-
row, Lodovico.   130
Lod. Morrow, madam.
Hip. Let 's away to horse.
All. Ay, ay, to horse, to horse.
Bell. I do beseech your lordship, let your
eye read o'er this wretched paper.   135
Hip. I 'm in haste ; pray thee, good woman,
take some apter time.
Inf. Good woman, do.
Bell. Oh, 'las ! it does concern a poor man's
life.   140
Hip. Life ! — Sweetheart, seat yourself, I 'll
but read this and come.
Lod. What stockings have you put on this
morning, madam ? If they be not yellow,[4]
change them ; that paper is a letter from some
wench to your husband.   146
Inf. Oh sir, that cannot make me jealous.
Exeunt [*all except* HIPPOLITO, BEL-
LAFRONT, *and* ANTONIO].
Hip. Your business, sir ? To me ?
Ant. Yes, my good lord.   148
Hip. Presently, sir.— Are you Matheo's wife ?
Bell. That most unfortunate woman.
Hip. I 'm sorry these storms are fallen on
him ; I love Matheo,
And any good shall do him ; he and I
Have seal'd two bonds of friendship, which
are strong
In me, however fortune does him wrong.   155
He speaks here he 's condemned. Is 't so ?
Bell. Too true.
Hip. What was he whom he killed ? Oh, his
name 's here ;
Old Giacomo, son to the Florentine ;
Giacomo, a dog, that, to meet profit,   160
Would to the very eyelids wade in blood
Of his own children. Tell Matheo,
The duke, my father, hardly shall deny
His signed pardon. 'Twas fair fight, yes,
If rumour's tongue go true ; so writes he
here.—   165
To-morrow morning I return from court,
Pray be you here then. — I 'll have done, sir,
straight : —   [*To* ANTONIO.]
But in troth say, are you Matheo's wife ?
You have forgot me.
Bell.   No, my lord.
Hip.   Your turner,

---

[1] Dunkirk pirates.   [2] Courtesans.
[3] Mop for cleaning decks, etc.

[4] Yellow was typical of jealousy.

That made you smooth to run an even bias,   170
You know I lov'd you when your very soul
Was full of discord : art not a good wench still ?
   Bell. Umph, when I had lost my way to
    Heaven, you show'd it:
I was new born that day.

            Re-enter LODOVICO.

   Lod. 'Sfoot, my lord, your lady asks if [175
you have not left your wench yet ? When you
get in once, you never have done. Come, come,
come, pay your old score, and send her packing ;
come.
   Hip. Ride softly on before, I 'll o'ertake
you.   181
   Lod. Your lady swears she 'll have no riding
on before, without ye.
   Hip. Prithee, good Lodovico.
   Lod. My lord, pray hasten.   185
   Hip. I come.   [*Exit* LODOVICO.]
To-morrow let me see you, fare you well ;
Commend me to Matheo. Pray one word more :
Does not your father live about the court ?
   Bell. I think he does, but such rude spots of
    shame   190
Stick on my cheek, that he scarce knows my
    name.
   Hip. Orlando Friscobaldo, is 't not ?
   Bell. Yes, my lord.
   Hip. What does he for you ?
   Bell.   All he should : when children
From duty start, parents from love may swerve.
He nothing does ; for nothing I deserve.   196
   Hip. Shall I join him unto you, and restore
you to wonted grace ?
   Bell. It is impossible.   [*Exit* BELLAFRONT.]
   Hip. It shall be put to trial : fare you well.
The face I would not look on ! Sure then 't was
    rare,   201
When, in despite of grief, 't is still thus fair.
Now, sir, your business with me.
   Ant.   I am bold
T' express my love and duty to your lordship
In these few leaves,
   Hip.   A book !
   Ant.   Yes, my good lord. 205
   Hip. Are you a scholar ?
   Ant.   Yes, my lord, a poor one.
   Hip. Sir, you honour me.
Kings may be scholars' patrons, but, faith, tell
    me,
To how many hands besides hath this bird
    flown,
How many partners share with me ?
   Ant.   Not one, 210
In troth, not one : your name I held more dear.
I 'm not, my lord, of that low character.
   Hip. Your name I pray ?
   Ant.   Antonio Georgio.
   Hip. Of Milan ?
   Ant.   Yes, my lord,
   Hip.   I 'll borrow leave
To read you o'er, and then we 'll talk : till then
Drink up this gold ; good wits should love good
    wine ;   216
This of your loves, the earnest that of mine. —
                    [*Gives money.*]

            Re-enter BRYAN.

How now, sir, where 's your lady? Not gone yet ?
   Bry. I fart di lady is run away from dee, a
mighty deal of ground ; she sent me back [220
for dine own sweet face. I pray dee come, my
lord, away, wu't tow go now ?
   Hip. Is the coach gone ? Saddle my horse,
the sorrel.   224
   Bry. A pox a' de horse's nose, he is a lousy
rascally fellow. When I came to gird his belly,
his scurvy guts rumbled ; di horse farted in my
face, and dow knowest, an Irishman cannot
abide a fart. But I have saddled de hobby-horse,
di fine hobby is ready. I pray dee, my good [230
sweet lord, wi't tow go now, and I will run to
de devil before dee ?
   Hip. Well, sir. — I pray let 's see you, master
scholar.   234
   Bry. Come, I pray dee, wu't come, sweet
face ? Go.   *Exeunt.*

             SCENE II.[1]

Enter LODOVICO, CAROLO, ASTOLFO, *and* BER-
    ALDO.

   Lod. Godso, gentlemen, what do we forget ?
   All. What ?
   Lod. Are not we all enjoined as this day, —
Thursday is 't not ? Ay, as that day to be at the
linen-draper's house at dinner ?   5
   Car. Signor Candido, the patient man.
   Ast. Afore Jove, true, upon this day he 's
married.
   Ber. I wonder, that being so stung with a
wasp before, he dares venture again to [10
come about the eaves amongst bees.
   Lod. Oh 't is rare sucking a sweet honey comb !
Pray Heaven his old wife be buried deep enough,
that she rise not up to call for her dance ! The
poor fiddlers' instruments would crack for [15
it ; she 'd tickle them. At any hand let 's try
what mettle is in his new bride ; if there be
none, we 'll put in some. Troth, it 's a very noble citizen, I pity he should marry again ; I 'll
walk along, for it is a good old fellow.   20
   Car. I warrant the wives of Milan would give
any fellow twenty thousand ducats, that could
but have the face to beg of the duke, that all
the citizens in Milan might be bound to the
peace of patience, as the linen-draper is.   25
   Lod. Oh, fie upon 't ! 't would undo all us that
are courtiers ; we should have no whoo with the
wenches then.

            Enter HIPPOLITO.

   All. My lord 's come.
   Hip. How now, what news ?   30
   All. None.
   Lod. Your lady is with the duke, her father.
   Hip. And we 'll to them both presently —

     Enter ORLANDO FRISCOBALDO.

Who 's that !
   All. Signor Friscobaldo.   33

      ¹ An apartment in the Duke's Palace.

Hip. Friscobaldo, oh! pray call him, and
leave me; we two have business.
Car. Ho Signor! Signor Friscobaldo! The
Lord Hippolito.
        Exeunt [*all but* HIPPOLITO *and*
            FRISCOBALDO].
Orl. My noble lord: my Lord Hippolito! [40
the duke's son! his brave daughter's brave husband! how does your honour'd lordship! Does
your nobility remember so poor a gentleman as
Signor Orlando Friscobaldo! old mad Orlando!
Hip. Oh, sir, our friends! they ought to be [45
unto us as our jewels, as dearly valued, being
locked up, and unseen, as when we wear them
in our hands. I see, Friscobaldo, age hath not
command of your blood; for all Time's sickle
has gone over you, you are Orlando still.   50
Orl. Why, my lord, are not the fields mown
and cut down, and stript bare, and yet wear
they not pied coats again? Though my head be
like a leek, white, may not my heart be like the
blade, green?   55
Hip. Scarce can I read the stories on your
brow,
Which age hath writ there; you look youthful
still.
Orl. I eat snakes,[1] my lord, I eat snakes. My
heart shall never have a wrinkle in it, so long
as I can cry "Hem," with a clear voice.   60
Hip. You are the happier man, sir.
Orl. Happy man? I'll give you, my lord, the
true picture of a happy man. I was turning
leaves over this morning, and found it; an ex-
cellent Italian painter drew it; if I have it in [65
the right colours, I'll bestow it on your lord-
ship.
Hip. I stay for it.
Orl. He that makes gold his wife, but not
his whore,
He that at noon-day walks by a prison door, 70
He that i' th' sun is neither beam nor mote,
He that's not mad after a petticoat,
He for whom poor men's curses dig no grave,
He that is neither lord's nor lawyer's slave,
He that makes this his sea, and that his
shore,   75
He that in 's coffin is richer than before,
He that counts youth his sword, and age his
staff,
He whose right hand carves his own epitaph,
He that upon his deathbed is a swan,
And dead, no crow — he is a happy man.   80
Hip. It's very well; I thank you for this pic-
ture.
Orl. After this picture, my lord, do I strive
to have my face drawn: for I am not covetous,
am not in debt; sit neither at the duke's [85
side, nor lie at his feet. Wenching and I have
done; no man I wrong, no man I fear, no man
I fee; I take heed how far I walk, because I
know corner's my home; I would not die like
a rich man, to carry nothing away save a [90
winding sheet; but like a good man, to leave
Orlando behind me. I sowed leaves in my
youth, and I reap now books in my age. I fill

this hand, and empty this; and when the bell
shall toll for me, if I prove a swan, and go [95
singing to my nest, why so! If a crow! throw
me out like a carrion, and pick out mine eyes.
May not old Friscobaldo, my lord, be merry
now! ha?
Hip. You may; would I were partner in [100
your mirth.
Orl. I have a little, have all things. I have
nothing; I have no wife, I have no child, have
no chick; and why should not I be in my jo-
cundare?[2]   105
Hip. Is your wife then departed?
Orl. She's an old dweller in those high countries, yet not from me. Here, she's here: but,
before me, when a knave and a quean are married, they commonly walk like serjeants [110
together: but a good couple are seldom parted.
Hip. You had a daughter too, sir, had you not?
Orl. O my lord! this old tree had one branch,
and but one branch growing out of it. It was
young, it was fair, it was straight; I prun'd [115
it daily, drest it carefully, kept it from the
wind, help 'd it to the sun, yet for all my skill
in planting, it grew crooked, it bore crabs. I
hewed it down; what's become of it, I neither
know, nor care.   120
Hip. Then I can tell you what's become of it;
That branch is wither'd.
Orl.   So 't was long ago.
Hip. Her name I think was Bellafront; she's
dead.
Orl. Ha? dead?
Hip. Yes; what of her was left, not worth
the keeping,   125
Even in my sight was thrown into a grave.
Orl. Dead! my last and best peace go with
her! I see Death's a good trencherman;
he can eat coarse homely meat, as well as the
daintiest.   130
Hip. Why, Friscobaldo, was she homely?
Orl. O my lord! a strumpet is one of the
devil's vines; all the sins, like so many poles,
are stuck upright out of hell, to be her props,
that she may spread upon them. And when [135
she's ripe, every slave has a pull at her, then
must she be prest. The young beautiful grape
sets the teeth of lust on edge, yet to taste
that lickerish [3] wine, is to drink a man's own
damnation. Is she dead?   140
Hip. She's turned to earth.
Orl. Would she were turn'd to Heaven!
Umph, is she dead? I am glad the world has
lost one of his idols; no whoremonger will at
midnight beat at the doors. In her grave [145
sleep all my shame, and her own; and all my
sorrows, and all her sins!
Hip. I'm glad you 're wax, not marble;
you are made
Of man's best temper; there are now good
hopes
That all these heaps of ice about your heart, 150
By which a father's love was frozen up,
Are thaw'd in these sweet showers, fetcht from
your eyes;

---

[1] A supposed recipe for restoring youth. (Dyce.)

[2] Merriment.   [3] Tempting.

We are ne'er like angels till our passion dies.
She is not dead, but lives under worse fate ; 154
I think she 's poor ; and, more to clip her wings,
Her husband at this hour lies in the jail,
For killing of a man. To save his blood,
Join all your force with mine : mine shall be
shown :
The getting of his life preserves your own.   159
Orl. In my daughter, you will say ! Does she
live then ? I am sorry I wasted tears upon a
harlot ; but the best is I have a handkercher to
drink them up ; soap can wash them all out
again. Is she poor ?
Hip. Trust me, I think she is.   165
Orl. Then she 's a right strumpet ; I ne'er
knew any of their trade rich two years together.
Sieves can hold no water, nor harlots hoard
up money ; they have many vents, too many
sluices to let it out ; taverns, tailors, bawds, [170
panders, fiddlers, swaggerers, fools, and knaves
do all wait upon a common harlot's trencher.
She is the gallipot to which these drones fly,
not for love to the pot, but for the sweet sucket [1]
within it, her money, her money.   175
Hip. I almost dare pawn my word, her bosom
Gives warmth to no such snakes. When did
you see her ?
Orl. Not seventeen summers.
Hip. Is your hate so old ?   179
Orl. Older ; it has a white head, and shall
never die till she be buried : her wrongs shall be
my bedfellow.
Hip. Work yet his life, since in it lives her
fame.
Orl. No let him hang, and half her infamy de-
parts out of the world. I hate him for her ; [185
he taught her first to taste poison ; I hate her
for herself, because she refused my physic.
Hip. Nay, but Friscobaldo ! —
Orl. I detest her, I defy [2] both ; she 's not
mine, she 's —   190
Hip. Hear her but speak.
Orl. I love no mermaids, I 'll not be caught
with a quail-pipe. [3]
Hip. You 're now beyond all reason.   194
Orl. I am then a beast. Sir, I had rather be
a beast, and not dishonour my creation, than be
a doting father, and like Time, be the destruc-
tion of mine own brood.
Hip. 'T is 't dotage to relieve your child, being
poor ?   199
Orl. Is 't fit for an old man to keep a whore ?
Hip. 'T is charity, too.
Orl. 'T is foolery ; relieve her !
Were her cold limbs stretcht out upon a bier,
I would not sell this dirt under my nails
To buy her an hour's breath, nor give this hair,
Unless it were to choke her.   206
Hip. Fare you well, for I 'll trouble you no
more.   *Exit.*
Orl. And fare you well, sir. Go thy ways ;
we have few lords of thy making, that love
wenches for their honesty. 'Las my girl ! [210
art thou poor ? Poverty dwells next door to

despair, there 's but a wall between them. Despair is one of hell's catch-poles ; and lest that
devil arrest her, I 'll to her. Yet she shall not
know me ; she shall drink of my wealth, [215
as beggars do of running water, freely, yet
never know from what fountain's head it flows.
Shall a silly bird pick her own breast to nourish
her young ones, and can a father see his child
starve ? That were hard ; the pelican does [220
it, and shall not I ? Yes, I will victual the
camp for her, but it shall be by some stratagem.
That knave there, her husband, will be hanged,
I fear ; I 'll keep his neck out of the noose if I
can, he shall not know how.   225

Enter two Serving-men.

How now, knaves ? Whither wander you ?
1 *Ser.* To seek your worship.
Orl. Stay, which of you has my purse ? What
money have you about you ?   229
2 *Ser.* Some fifteen or sixteen pounds, sir.
Orl. Give it me. [*Takes purse.*] — I think
I have some gold about me ; yes, it 's well. Leave
my lodging at court, and get you home. Come,
sir, though I never turned any man out of
doors, yet I 'll be so bold as to pull your coat
over your ears.   236
[ORLANDO *puts on the coat of* 1
Serving-man, *and gives him in
exchange his cloak.*]
1 *Ser.* What do you mean to do, sir ?
Orl. Hold thy tongue, knave ; take thou my
cloak. I hope I play not the paltry merchant
in this bart'ring ; bid the steward of my [240
house sleep with open eyes in my absence, and to
look to all things. Whatsoever I command by
letters to be done by you, see it done. So, does
it sit well ?   244
2 *Ser.* As if it were made for your worship.
Orl. You proud varlets, you need not be
ashamed to wear blue, [4] when your master is
one of your fellows. Away, do not see me.
Both. This is excellent.   *Exeunt.* 249
Orl. I should put on a worse suit, too ; perhaps I will. My vizard is on ; now to this
masque. Say I should shave off this honour of
an old man, or tie it up shorter. Well, I will
spoil a good face for once.
My beard being off, how should I look ? Even
like   255
A winter cuckoo, or unfeather'd owl ;
Yet better lose this hair, than lose her soul.
Exit.

[SCENE III.] [5]

Enter CANDIDO, LODOVICO, CAROLO, [ASTOL-
FO], *other guests, and* Bride *with* Prentices.

Cand. O gentlemen, so late ! Y' are very
welcome, pray sit down.
Lod. Carolo, did'st e'er see such a nest of
caps ? [6]
Ast. Methinks it 's a most civil and most
comely sight.
Lod. What does he i' th' middle look like ? [5]

---

[1] Confection.   [2] Renounce.
[3] Used by fowlers to allure quails.

[4] The color of servants' livery.
[5] A room in Candido's house.   [6] Citizens.

Ast. Troth, like a spire steeple in a country
village overpeering so many thatcht houses.

Lod. It 's rather a long pike-staff against so
many bucklers without pikes ;[1] they sit for all
the world like a pair of organs,[2] and he 's the
tall great roaring pipe i' th' midst.   11

Ast. Ha, ha, ha, ha !

Cand. What 's that you laugh at, signors ?

Lod. Troth, shall I tell you, and aloud I 'll
   tell it ;
We laugh to see, yet laugh we not in scorn,   15
Amongst so many caps that long hat worn.

[1 *Guest.*] Mine is as tall a felt as any is this
day in Milan, and therefore I love it, for the
block[3] was cleft out for my head, and fits me
to a hair.   20

Cand. Indeed you 're good observers ; it
shows strange :
But gentlemen, I pray neither contemn,
Nor yet deride a civil ornament ;
I could build so much in the round cap's praise,
That 'bove this high roof, I this flat would
raise.

Lod. Prithee, sweet bridegroom, do 't.   26

Cand. So all these guests will pardon me, I 'll
   do 't.

All. With all our hearts.

Cand. Thus, then, in the cap's honour :
To every sex, and state, both nature, time,   30
The country's laws, yea, and the very clime
Do allot distinct habits ; the spruce courtier
Jets[4] up and down in silk ; the warrior
Marches in buff ; the clown plods on in gray :
But for these upper garments thus I say,   35
The seaman has his cap, par'd without brim ;
The gallant's head is feather'd, that fits him ;
The soldier has his morion,[5] women ha' tires ;[6]
Beasts have their head-pieces, and men ha'
theirs.

Lod. Proceed.   40

Cand. Each degree has his fashion, it 's fit
then,
One should be laid by for the citizen,
And that 's the cap which you see swells not
high,
For caps are emblems of humility.
It is a citizen's badge, and first was worn   45
By th' Romans ; for when any bondman's turn
Came to be made a freeman, thus 't was said,
He to the cap was call'd, that is, was made
Of Rome a freeman ; but was first close shorn :
And so a citizen's hair is still short worn.   50

Lod. That close shaving made barbers a
company,
And now every citizen uses it.

Cand. Of geometric figures the most rare,
And perfect'st, are the circle and the square ;
The city and the school much build upon   55
These figures, for both love proportion.
The city-cap is round, the scholar's square,
To show that government and learning are
The perfect'st limbs i' th' body of a state ;
For without them, all 's disproportionate.   60
If the cap had no honour, this might rear it,

The reverend fathers of the law do wear it.
It 's light for summer, and in cold it sits
Close to the skull, a warm house for the wits ;
It shows the whole face boldly, 't is not made
As if a man to look on 't were afraid,   66
Nor like a draper's shop with broad dark shed,
For he 's no citizen that hides his head.
Flat caps as proper are to city gowns,
As to armours helmets, or to kings their crowns.
Let then the city-cap by none be scorn'd,   71
Since with it princes' heads have been adorn'd.
If more the round cap's honour you would know,
How would this long gown with this steeple[7]
show ?

All. Ha, ha, ha ! most vile, most ugly.   75

Cand. Pray, signor, pardon me, 't was done
   in jest.

Bride. A cup of claret wine there.

1 Pren. Wine ? yes, forsooth, wine for the
   bride.

Car. You ha' well set out the cap, sir.

Lod. Nay, that 's flat.   80

Cand. A health !

Lod. Since his cap 's round, that shall go
round. Be bare,
For in the cap's praise all of you have share.
    [*They bare their heads and drink.*
    As 1 Prentice *offers the wine to the*
    Bride,] *she hits him on the lips,*
    [*breaking the glass*].
The bride 's at cuffs.

Cand. Oh, peace, I pray thee ; thus far off I
   stand,   85
I spied the error of my servants ;
She call'd for claret, and you fill'd out sack.
That cup give me, 't is for an old man's back,
And not for hers. Indeed, 't was but mistaken ;
Ask all these else.

Guests.   No faith, 't was but mistaken.

1 Pren. Nay, she took it right enough.   91

Cand. Good Luke, reach her that glass of
   claret.
Here mistress bride, pledge me there.

Bride.   Now I 'll none. *Exit.*

Cand. How now ?

Lod.   Look what your mistress ails.

1 Pren. Nothing, sir, but about filling a
wrong glass, — a scurvy trick.   96

Cand. I pray you, hold your tongue. — My
servant there tells me she is not well.

Guests. Step to her, step to her.

Lod. A word with you : do ye hear ? This
wench, your new wife, will take you down in [101
your wedding shoes, unless you hang her up in
her wedding garters ?

Cand. How, hang her in her garters ?   104

Lod. Will you be a tame pigeon still ? Shall
your back be like a tortoise shell, to let carts
go over it, yet not to break ? This she-cat will
have more lives than your last puss had, and
will scratch worse, and mouse you worse : look
to 't.   110

Cand. What would you have me do, sir ?

Lod. What would I have you do ? Swear,
swagger, brawl, fling ! for fighting it 's no mat-

---

[1] Spikes in the centre of bucklers.
[2] A pipe organ.
[3] The model for the hat.
[4] Struts.
[5] Head-piece.
[6] Head-dresses.

[7] The steeple-like hat worn by 1 Guest.

ter, we ha' had knocking pusses enow already;
you know, that a woman was made of the rib
of a man, and that rib was crooked. The [116
moral of which is, that a man must from his
beginning be crooked to his wife. Be you like
an orange to her; let her cut you never so fair,
be you sour as vinegar. Will you be ruled by me?

Cand. In any thing that's civil, honest, and
just.   122

Lod. Have you ever a prentice's suit will fit
me?

Cand. I have the very same which myself
wore.   126

Lod. I'll send my man for't within this half
hour, and within this two hours I'll be your
prentice. The hen shall not overcrow the cock;
I'll sharpen your spurs.   130

Cand. It will be but some jest, sir?

Lod. Only a jest: farewell, come, Carolo.
           Exeunt [LODOVICO, CAROLO, *and*
                  ASTOLFO].

All. We'll take our leaves, sir, too.

Cand.   Pray conceit not ill
Of my wife's sudden rising. This young knight,
Sir Lodovico, is deep seen in physic,   135
And he tells me, the disease, called the mother,[1]
Hangs on my wife, it is a vehement heaving
And beating of the stomach, and that swelling
Did with the pain thereof cramp up her arm,
That hit his lips, and brake the glass, — no
  harm,   140
It was no harm!

Guests.   No, signor, none at all.

Cand. The straightest arrow may fly wide by
  chance.
But come, we'll close this brawl up in some
       dance.   *Exeunt.*

[ACT II]

[SCENE I.][2]

Enter BELLAFRONT *and* MATHEO.

Bell. O my sweet husband! wert thou in thy
grave and art alive again? Oh welcome, welcome!

Mat. Dost know me? My cloak, prithee, lay't
up. Yes, faith, my winding-sheet was taken [5
out of lavender, to be stuck with rosemary:[3] I
lackt but the knot here, or here; yet if I had had
it, I should ha' made a wry mouth at the world
like a plaice: but, sweetest villain, I am here
now and I will talk with thee soon.   10

Bell. And glad am I th' art here.

Mat. Did these heels caper in shackles? Ah!
my little plump rogue, I'll bear up for all this,
and fly high. *Catso catso.*[4]

Bell. Matheo?   15

Mat. What sayest, what sayest? O brave
fresh air! a pox on these grates and gingling
of keys, and rattling of iron. I'll bear up, I'll
fly high, wench, hang toff.[5]

---

[1] Hysteria.   [2] A room in Matheo's house.
[3] Rosemary was an emblem of remembrance.
[4] Ital. A term of abuse or contempt.
[5] A vague exclamation. Hang it all! (?)

Bell. Matheo, prithee, make thy prison thy
  glass,   20
And in it view the wrinkles and the scars
By which thou wert disfigur'd: viewing them,
  mend them.

Mat. I'll go visit all the mad rogues now,
and the good roaring boys.[6]

Bell. Thou dost not hear me?   25

Mat. Yes, faith, do I.

Bell. Thou has been in the hands of misery,
and ta'en strong physic; prithee now be sound.

Mat. Yes 'Sfoot, I wonder how the inside
of a tavern looks now. Oh, when shall I [30
bizzle, bizzle.[7]

Bell. Nay, see, thou'rt thirsty still for poi·
  son! Come,
I will not have thee swagger.

Mat.   Honest ape's face!

Bell. 'T is that sharp'ned an axe to cut thy
  throat.
Good love, I would not have thee sell thy sub-
  stance   35
And time, worth all, in those damn'd shops of
  hell;
Those dicing houses, that stand never well
But when they stand most ill; that four-squar'd
  sin[8]
Has almost lodg'd us in the beggar's inn.
Besides, to speak which even my soul does
  grieve,   40
A sort[9] of ravens have hung upon thy sleeve,
And fed upon thee: good Mat, if you please,
Scorn to spread wing amongst so base as
  these;
By them thy fame is speckled, yet it shows
Clear amongst them; so crows are fair with
  crows.   45
Custom in sin, gives sin a lovely dye;
Blackness in Moors is no deformity.

Mat. Bellafront, Bellafront, I protest to
thee, I swear, as I hope for my soul, I will
turn over a new leaf. The prison I confess [50
has bit me; the best man that sails in such a
ship, may be lousy.   [*Knocking within.*]

Bell. One knocks at door.

Mat. I'll be the porter. They shall see a jail
cannot hold a brave spirit, I'll fly high.   55
                                                Exit.

Bell. How wild is his behaviour! Oh, I fear
He's spoil'd by prison, he's half damn'd comes
  there.
But I must sit all storms: when a full sail
His fortunes spread, he lov'd me; being now
  poor,
I'll beg for him, and no wife can do more.   60

Re-enter MATHEO, *with* ORLANDO *like a* Serv-
                  ing-man.

Mat. Come in, pray! would you speak with
me, sir?

Orl. Is your name Signor Matheo?

Mat. My name is Signor Matheo.

Orl. Is this gentlewoman your wife, sir? 65

Mat. This gentlewoman is my wife, sir.

---

[6] Roystering gallants.   [8] Dicing.
[7] Drink deep.   [9] Band.

Orl. The Destinies spin a strong and even thread of both your loves! — [*Aside.*] The mother's own face, I ha' not forgot that. — I 'm an old man, sir, and am troubled with a [70 whoreson salt rheum, that I cannot hold my water. — Gentlewoman, the last man I served was your father.

Bell. My father? Any tongue that sounds his name,

Speaks music to me; welcome, good old man! How does my father? Lives he? Has he health?   76

How does my father? — [*Aside.*] I so much do shame him,

So much do wound him, that I scarce dare name him.

Orl. I can speak no more.

Mat. How, old lad, what, dost cry?   80

Orl. The rheum still, sir, nothing else; I should be well season'd, for mine eyes lie in brine. Look you, sir, I have a suit to you.

Mat. What is 't, my little white-pate?

Orl. Troth, sir, I have a mind to serve your worship.   86

Mat. To serve me? Troth, my friend, my fortunes are, as a man may say —

Orl. Nay, look you, sir, I know, when all sins are old in us, and go upon crutches, that cov- [90 etousness does but then lie in her cradle; 't is not so with me. Lechery loves to dwell in the fairest lodging, and covetousness in the oldest buildings, that are ready to fall : but my white head, sir, is no inn for such a gossip. If a [95 serving-man at my years be not stored with biscuit enough, that has sailed about the world, to serve him the voyage out of his life, and to bring him East home, ill pity but all his days should be fasting days. I care not so much [100 for wages, for I have scraped a handful of gold together. I have a little money, sir, which I would put into your worship's hands, not so much to make it more —   104

Mat. No, no, you say well, thou sayest well; but I must tell you, — How much is the money, sayest thou?

Orl. About twenty pound, sir.

Mat. Twenty pound? Let me see : that shall bring thee in, after ten *per centum per annum*, —   111

Orl. No, no, no, sir, no : I cannot abide to have money engender : fie upon this silver lechery, fie! If I may have meat to my mouth, and rags to my back, and a flock-bed to [115 snort upon when I die, the longer liver take all.

Mat. A good old boy, i' faith! If thou servest me, thou shalt eat as *I* eat, drink as *I* drink, lie as *I* lie, and ride as *I* ride.

Orl. [*Aside.*] That 's if you have money [120 to hire horses.

Mat. Front, what dost thou think on 't? This good old lad here shall serve me.

Bell. Alas, Matheo, wilt thou load a back That is already broke?   125

Mat. Peace, pox on you, peace. There 's a trick in 't, I fly high; it shall be so, Front, as I tell you. Give me thy hand, thou shalt serve me i 'faith : welcome. As for your money —

Orl. Nay, look you, sir, I have it here.   130

Mat. Pish, keep it thyself, man, and then thou 'rt sure 't is safe.

Orl. Safe ! an 't were ten thousand ducats, your worship should be my cash-keeper. I have heard what your worship is, an excellent [135 dunghill cock, to scatter all abroad ; but I 'll venture twenty pounds on 's head.

[*Gives money to* MATHEO.]

Mat. And didst thou serve my worshipful father-in-law, Signor Orlando Friscobaldo, that madman, once?   140

Orl. I served him so long, till he turned me out of doors.

Mat. It 's a notable chuff ;[1] I ha' not seen him many a day.

Orl. No matter an you ne'er see him ; [145 it 's an arrant grandee, a churl, and as damn'd a cut-throat.

Bell. Thou villain, curb thy tongue! Thou art a Judas,

To sell thy master's name to slander thus.

Mat. Away, ass! He speaks but truth, thy father is a —   151

Bell. Gentleman.

Mat. And an old knave. There 's more deceit in him than in sixteen 'pothecaries: it 's a devil ; thou may'st beg, starve, hang, damn ! does he send thee so much as a cheese ?   156

Orl. Or so much as a gammon of bacon ; he 'll give it his dogs first.

Mat. A jail, a jail.

Orl. A Jew, a Jew, sir.   160

Mat. A dog !

Orl. An English mastiff, sir.

Mat. Pox rot out his old stinking garbage !

Bell. Art not asham'd to strike an absent man thus ?

Art not asham'd to let this vild [2] dog bark, 165 And bite my father thus ? I 'll not endure it. Out of my doors, base slave !

Mat. Your doors ? a vengeance ! I shall live to cut that old rogue's throat, for all you take his part thus.   170

Orl. [*Aside.*] He shall live to see thee hang'd first.

Enter HIPPOLITO.

Mat. Gods so, my lord, your lordship is most welcome.

I 'm proud of this, my lord.

Hip.   Was bold to see you. Is that your wife ?

Mat.   Yes, sir.

Hip.   I 'll borrow her lip. 175

[*Kisses* BELLAFRONT.]

Mat. With all my heart, my lord.

Orl.   Who 's this, I pray, sir.

Mat. My Lord Hippolito : what 's thy name ?

Orl.   Pacheco.

Mat. Pacheco, fine name : thou seest, Pacheco, I keep company with no scoundrels, nor base fellows.   180

Hip. Came not my footman to you?

Bell.   Yes, my lord.

---

[1] Notorious churl.   [2] Vile.

Hip. I sent by him a diamond and a letter,
Did you receive them?
Bell.　　　　　　　Yes, my lord, I did.
Hip. Read you the letter?
Bell.　　　　　　O'er and o'er 't is read.
Hip. And, faith, your answer?
Bell.　　　　　Now the time 's not fit, 185
You see, my husband 's here.
Hip.　　　　　I 'll now then leave you,
And choose mine hour; but ere I part away,
Hark you, remember I must have no nay. —
Matheo, I will leave you.
Mat.　　　　　A glass of wine.
Hip. Not now, I 'll visit you at other times.
You 're come off well, then? 191
Mat. Excellent well, I thank your lordship. I
owe you my life, my lord; and will pay my
best blood in any service of yours.
Hip. I 'll take no such dear payment. [195
Hark you, Matheo, I know the prison is a gulf.
If money run low with you, my purse is yours:
call for it.
Mat. Faith, my lord, I thank my stars, they
send me down some; I cannot sink, so long as
these bladders hold. 201
Hip. I will not see your fortunes ebb; pray, try.
To starve in full barns were fond [1] modesty.
Mat. Open the door, sirrah.
Hip. Drink this, and anon, I pray thee, [205
give thy mistress this.
　　　[*Gives to* FRISCOBALDO, *who opens
　　　　the door, first money, then a purse,
　　　　and] exit.*
Orl. O noble spirit, if no worse guests here
　　　dwell,
My blue coat sits on my old shoulders well.
Mat. The only royal fellow, he 's bounteous
as the Indies. What 's that he said to thee, [210
Bellafront?
Bell. Nothing.
Mat. I prithee, good girl.
Bell. Why, I tell you, nothing.
Mat. Nothing? It 's well. Tricks! that I [215
must be beholden to a scald hot-liver'd goatish
gallant, to stand with my cap in my hand, and
vail [2] bonnet, when I ha' spread as lofty sails
as himself. Would I had been hanged. No-
thing? Pacheco, brush my cloak. 220
Orl. Where is 't, sir?
Mat. Come, we 'll fly high.
Nothing? There 's a whore still in thy eye.
　　　　　　　　　　　　　　Exit.
Orl. [*Aside.*] My twenty pounds fly high. O
　　　wretched woman! 224
This varlet 's able to make Lucrece common. —
How now, mistress?
Has my master dy'd you into this sad colour?
Bell. Fellow, begone I pray thee; if thy
　　　tongue
Itch after talk so much, seek out thy master.
Thou 'rt a fit instrument for him. 230
Orl. Zounds, I hope he will not play upon me!
Bell. Play on thee? No, you two will fly to-
　　　gether,
Because you 're roving arrows of one feather.

Would thou wouldst leave my house; thou ne'er
　　　shalt please me!
Weave thy nets ne'er so high, 235
Thou shalt be but a spider in mine eye.
Thou 'rt rank with poison: poison temper'd
　　　well
Is food for health; but thy black tongue doth
　　　swell
With venom, to hurt him that gave thee bread.
To wrong men absent, is to spurn the dead; 240
And so did'st thou thy master, and my father.
Orl. You have small reason to take his part;
for I have heard him say five hundred times,
you were as arrant a whore as ever stiff'ned
tiffany neckcloths in water-starch upon a [245
Saturday i' th' afternoon.
Bell. Let him say worse. When for the
　　　earth's offence
Hot vengeance through the marble clouds is
　　　driven,
Is 't fit earth shoot again those darts at heaven?
Orl. And so if your father call you whore [250
you 'll not call him old knave. — [*Aside.*] Friscobaldo, she carries thy mind up and down;
she 's thine own flesh, blood, and bone. — Troth,
mistress, to tell you true, the fireworks that
ran from me upon lines against my good [255
old master, your father, were but to try how
my young master, your husband, loved such
squibs: but it 's well known, I love your father as myself; I 'll ride for him at midnight,
run for you by owl-light; I 'll die for him, [260
drudge for you; I 'll fly low, and I 'll fly high,
as my master says, to do you good, if you 'll forgive me.
Bell. I am not made of marble; I forgive
　　　thee. 264
Orl. Nay, if you were made of marble, a good
stone-cutter might cut you. I hope the twenty
pound I delivered to my master is in a sure
hand.
Bell. In a sure hand, I warrant thee, for
　　　spending.
Orl. I see my young master is a mad-cap, [270
and a *bonus socius.*[3] I love him well, mistress:
yet as well as I love him, I 'll not play the knave
with you. Look you, I could cheat you of this
purse full of money; but I am an old lad, and
I scorn to cony-catch:[4] yet I ha' been dog [275
at a cony in my time. [*Gives purse.*]
Bell. A purse? Where hadst it?
Orl. The gentleman that went away whisper'd in mine ear, and charged me to give it
you. 280
Bell. The Lord Hippolito?
Orl. Yes, if he be a lord, he gave it me.
Bell. 'T is all gold.
Orl. 'T is like so. It may be, he thinks you
want money, and therefore bestows his alms [285
bravely, like a lord.
Bell. He thinks a silver net can catch the
　　　poor;
Here 's bait to choke a nun, and turn her
　　　whore.
Wilt thou be honest to me? 28[?]

---

[1] Foolish.　　　　　[2] Lower, take off.　　　　　[3] Boon companion.　　　　　[4] Cheat.

Orl. As your nails to your fingers, which I think never deceived you.

Bell. Thou to this lord shalt go, commend me to him,
And tell him this, the town has held out long,
Because within 't was rather true than strong ;
To sell it now were base. Say 't is no hold 295
Built of weak stuff, to be blown up with gold.
He shall believe thee by this token, or this ;
If not, by this. [*Giving purse, ring, and letters.*
Orl. Is this all ?
Bell. This is all.
Orl. [*Aside.*] Mine own girl still !
Bell. A star may shoot, not fall. *Exit.*
Orl. A star ? nay, thou art more than the [300
moon, for thou hast neither changing quarters,
nor a man standing in thy circle with a bush
of thorns. Is 't possible the Lord Hippolito,
whose face is as civil as the outside of a dedi-
catory book, should be a muttonmonger ?[1] A [305
poor man has but one ewe, and this grandee
sheep-biter leaves whole flocks of fat wethers,
whom he may knock down, to devour this.
I 'll trust neither lord nor butcher with quick
flesh for this trick ; the cuckoo, I see now, [310
sings all the year, though every man cannot
hear him ; but I 'll spoil his notes. Can neither
love-letters, nor the devil's common pick-locks,
gold, nor precious stones make my girl draw up
her percullis ?[2] Hold out still, wench. 315
All are not bawds, I see now, that keep doors,
Nor all good wenches that are markt for
whores. [*Exit.*

[SCENE II.][3]

Enter CANDIDO, *and* LODOVICO *like a* Prentice.

Lod. Come, come, come, what do ye lack,
sir ? What do ye lack, sir ? What is 't ye lack,
sir ? Is not my worship well suited ? Did you
ever see a gentleman better disguised ?
Cand. Never, believe me, signor. 5
Lod. Yes, but when he has been drunk.
There be prentices would make mad gallants,
for they would spend all, and drink, and whore,
and so forth ; and I see we gallants could make
mad prentices. How does thy wife like me ? [10
Nay, I must not be so saucy, then I spoil all.
Pray you how does my mistress like me ?
Cand. Well ; for she takes you for a very
simple fellow.
Lod. And they that are taken for such are [15
commonly the arrantest knaves : but to our
comedy, come.
Cand. I shall not act it ; chide, you say, and
fret,
And grow impatient : I shall never do 't.
Lod. 'Sblood, cannot you do as all the [20
world does, counterfeit ?
Cand. Were I a painter, that should live by
drawing
Nothing but pictures of an angry man,
I should not earn my colours ; I cannot do 't.
Lod. Remember you're a linen-draper, and [25
that if you give your wife a yard, she 'll take

an ell : give her not therefore a quarter of your
yard, not a nail.
Cand. Say I should turn to ice, and nip her
love
Now 't is but in the bud.
Lod. Well, say she 's nipt. 30
Cand. It will so overcharge her heart with
grief,
That like a cannon, when her sighs go off,
She in her duty either will recoil,
Or break in pieces and so die : her death,
By my unkindness might be counted murder. 35
Lod. Die ? never, never. I do not bid you
beat her, nor give her black eyes, nor pinch
her sides ; but cross her humours. Are not
baker's arms the scales of justice ? Yet is not
their bread light ? And may not you, I pray, [40
bridle her with a sharp bit, yet ride her gently?
Cand. Well, I will try your pills.
Do you your faithful service, and be ready
Still at a pinch to help me in this part,
Or else I shall be out clean. 45
Lod. Come, come, I 'll prompt you.
Cand. I 'll call her forth now, shall I ?
Lod. Do, do, bravely.
Cand. Luke, I pray, bid your mistress to
come hither.
Lod. Luke, I pray, bid your mistress to come
hither. 50
Cand. Sirrah, bid my wife come to me : why,
when ?[4]
1 Pren. (*within.*) Presently, sir, she comes.
Lod. La, you, there 's the echo ! She comes.

Enter BRIDE.

Bride. What is your pleasure with me ?
Cand. Marry, wife,
I have intent ; and you see this stripling here, 55
He bears good will and liking to my trade,
And means to deal in linen.
Lod. Yes, indeed, sir, I would deal in linen,
if my mistress like me so well as I like her.
Cand. I hope to find him honest, pray ; good
wife, 60
Look that his bed and chamber be made
ready.
Bride. You 're best to let him hire me for his
maid.
I look to his bed ? Look to 't yourself.
Cand. Even so ?
I swear to you a great oath —
Lod. [*Aside.*] Swear, cry "Zounds ! " — 64
Cand. I will not — go to, wife — I will not —
Lod. [*Aside.*] That your great oath ?
Cand. Swallow these gudgeons ![5]
Lod. [*Aside.*] Well said !
Bride. Then fast, then you may choose.
Cand. You know at table
What tricks you play'd, swagger'd, broke
glasses, fie ! 70
Fie, fie, fie ! and now before my prentice here,
You make an ass of me, thou — what shall I
call thee ?
Bride. Even what you will.

---

[1] Whoremonger. [2] Portcullis.
[3] Before Candido's shop.

[4] An expression of impatience.
[5] Be so imposed upon.

Lod. [*Aside.*]   Call her arrant whore.
Cand. [*Aside.*] Oh fie, by no means! then
          she'll call me cuckold. —
Sirrah, go look to th' shop.— How does this
          show ?   75
Lod. [*Aside.*] Excellent well — I'll go look to
          the shop, sir.
Fine cambrics, lawns ; what do you lack ?
                              Exit [*into the shop*].
Cand. A curst cow's milk I ha' drunk once
          before,
And 't was so rank in taste, I 'll drink no more.
Wife, I 'll tame you.
Bride.   You may, sir, if you can, 80
But at a wrestling I have seen a fellow
Limb'd like an ox, thrown by a little man.
Cand. And so you 'll throw me ? — Reach
          me, knaves, a yard !
Lod. A yard for my master.
          [LODOVICO *returns from the shop*
          with a yard-wand and followed by
          Prentices.]
1 *Pren.* My master is grown valiant.   85
Cand. I 'll teach you fencing tricks.
Prentices. Rare, rare ! a prize ![1]
Lod. What will you do, sir ?
Cand. Marry, my good prentice, nothing but
          breathe my wife.   90
Bride. Breathe me with your yard ?
Lod. No, he 'll but measure you out, forsooth.
Bride. Since you 'll needs fence, handle your
          weapon well,
For if you take a yard, I 'll take an ell.
Reach me an ell !
Lod.   An ell for my mistress.   95
          [*Brings an ell-wand from the shop.*]
Keep the laws of the noble science, sir, and
measure weapons with her ; your yard is a
plain heathenish weapon. 'T is too short, she
may give you a handful, and yet you 'll not
reach her.   100
Cand. Yet I ha' the longer arm. — Come fall
          to 't roundly,
And spare not me, wife, for I 'll lay 't on
          soundly :
If o'er husbands their wives will needs be mas-
          ters,
We men will have a law to win 't at wasters.[2]
Lod. 'T is for the breeches, is 't not ?
Cand.   For the breeches !   105
Bride. Husband, I 'm for you, I 'll not strike
          in jest.
Cand. Nor I.
Bride.   But will you sign to one request ?
Cand. What 's that ?
Bride. Let me give the first blow.
Cand. The first blow, wife ? [*Aside to* LOD.]
          Shall I ? Prompt ?
Lod.   Let her ha 't :   109
If she strike hard, in to her, and break her pate.
Cand. A bargain : strike !
Bride.   Then guard you from this blow,
For I play all at legs, but 't is thus low.
                              She kneels.
Behold, I 'm such a cunning fencer grown,

I keep my ground, yet down I will be thrown
With the least blow you give me ; I disdain   115
The wife that is her husband's sovereign.
She that upon your pillow first did rest,
They say, the breeches wore, which I detest :
The tax which she impos'd on you, I abate you;
If me you make your master, I shall hate you. 120
The world shall judge who offers fairest play ;
You win the breeches, but I win the day.
Cand. Thou win'st the day indeed, give me
          thy hand ;
I 'll challenge thee no more. My patient breast
Play'd thus the rebel, only for a jest.   125
Here 's the rank rider that breaks colts ; 't is he
Can tame the mad folks, and curst wives.
Bride.   Who ? Your man ?
Cand. My man ? My master, though his head
          be bare,
But he 's so courteous, he 'll put off his hair.
Lod. Nay, if your service be so hot a [130
man cannot keep his hair on, I 'll serve you no
longer.   [*Takes off his false hair.*]
Bride. Is this your schoolmaster ?
Lod. Yes, faith, wench, I taught him to take
thee down. I hope thou canst take him down [135
without teaching ;
You ha' got the conquest, and you both are
          friends.
Cand. Bear witness else.
Lod.   My prenticeship then ends.
Cand. For the good service you to me have
          done,
I give you all your years.
Lod.   I thank you, master. 140
I 'll kiss my mistress now, that she may say
My man was bound, and free all in one day.
                              Exeunt.

ACT III

[SCENE I.][1]

Enter INFELICE, *and* ORLANDO [*disguised as a*
Serving-man].

Inf. From whom say'st thou ?
Orl. From a poor gentlewoman, madam,
whom I serve.
Inf. And what 's your business ?
Orl. This madam : my poor mistress has a [5
waste piece of ground, which is her own by inheritance, and left to her by her mother.
There 's a lord now that goes about not to take
it clean from her, but to enclose it to himself,
and to join it to a piece of his lordship's.   10
Inf. What would she have me do in this ?
Orl. No more, madam, but what one woman
should do for another in such a case. My honourable lord your husband, would do any thing
in her behalf, but she had rather put herself [15
into your hands, because you, a woman, may
do more with the duke, your father.
Inf. Where lies this land ?
Orl. Within a stone's cast of this place. My
mistress, I think, would be content to let [20
him enjoy it after her decease, if that would

---

[1] A fencing contest. Cf. p. 414, note 5.   [2] Cudgels.

[3] An apartment in Hippolito's house

serve his turn, so my master would yield too;
but she cannot abide to hear that the lord
should meddle with it in her lifetime.

Inf. Is she then married? Why stirs not [25
her husband in it?

Orl. Her husband stirs in it underhand: but
because the other is a great rich man, my master
is loth to be seen in it too much.

Inf. Let her in writing draw the cause at
large,   30
And I will move the duke.

Orl. 'T is set down, madam, here in black
and white already. Work it so, madam, that
she may keep her own without disturbance,
grievance, molestation, or meddling of any [35
other; and she bestows this purse of gold on
your ladyship.

Inf. Old man, I 'll plead for her, but take no
fees.

Give lawyers them, I swim not in that flood;
I 'll touch no gold, till I have done her good.   40

Orl. I would all proctors' clerks were of your
mind, I should law more amongst them than I
do then. Here, madam, is the survey, not only
▼f the manor itself, but of the grange-house,
with every meadow pasture, plough-land, [45
cony-burrow, fish-pond, hedge, ditch, and bush,
that stands in it.   [*Gives a letter.*]

Inf. My husband's name, and hand and seal
at arms
To a love letter? Where hadst thou this writing?

Orl. From the foresaid party, madam, that [50
would keep the foresaid land out of the foresaid
lord's fingers.

Inf. My lord turn'd ranger now?

Orl. You 're a good huntress, lady; you ha'
found your game already. Your lord would [55
fain be a ranger, but my mistress requests you
to let him run a course in your own park. If
you 'll not do 't for love, then do 't for money!
She has no white money, but there 's gold; or
else she prays you to ring him by this token, [60
and so you shall be sure his nose will not be
rooting other men's pastures.
                    [*Gives purse and ring.*]

Inf. This very purse was woven with mine
own hands;
This diamond on that very night, when he
Untied my virgin girdle, gave I him;   65
And must a common harlot share in mine?
Old man, to quit thy pains, take thou the gold.

Orl. Not I, madam, old serving-men want no
money.

Inf. Cupid himself was sure his secretary;   70
These lines are even the arrows love let flies,
The very ink dropt out of Venus' eyes.

Orl. I do not think, madam, but he fetcht
off some poet or other for those lines, for they
are parlous hawks to fly at wenches.   75

Inf. Here 's honied poison! To me he ne'er
thus writ;
But lust can set a double edge on wit.

Orl. Nay, that 's true, madam, a wench will
whet any thing, if it be not too dull.

Inf. Oaths, promises, preferments, jewels,
gold,   80

What snares should break, if all these cannot
hold?
What creature is thy mistress?

Orl. One of those creatures that are contrary
to man; a woman.

Inf. What manner of woman?   85

Orl. A little tiny woman, lower than your
ladyship by head and shoulders, but as mad a
wench as ever unlaced a petticoat: these things
should I indeed have delivered to my lord, your
husband.   90

Inf. They are delivered better: why should
she
Send back these things?

Orl. 'Ware, 'ware, there 's knavery.

Inf. Strumpets, like cheating gamesters, will
not win
At first; these are but baits to draw him in.
How might I learn his hunting hours?   95

Orl. The Irish footman can tell you all his
hunting hours, the park he hunts in, the doe
he would strike; that Irish shackatory [1] beats
the bush for him, and knows all; he brought
that letter, and that ring; he is the carrier. 100

Inf. Knowest thou what other gifts have past
between them?

Orl. Little Saint Patrick knows all.

Inf. Him I 'll examine presently.

Orl. Not whilst I am here, sweet madam.   105

Inf. Be gone then, and what lies in me command.   *Exit* ORLANDO.

Enter BRYAN.

Inf. How much cost those satins,
And cloth of silver, which my husband sent
By you to a low gentlewoman yonder?   109

Bry. Faat satins? faat silvers, faat low gen-
tlefolks? Dow pratest dow knowest not what,
i' faat, la.

Inf. She there, to whom you carried letters,

Bry. By dis hand and bod dow saist true, if
I did so, oh how? I know not a letter a' de [115
book i' faat, la.

Inf. Did your lord never send you with a
ring, sir,
Set with a diamond?

Bry. Never, sa crees sa' me, never! He may
run at a towsand rings i' faat, and I never [120
hold his stirrup, till he leap into de saddle. By
St. Patrick, madam, I never touch my lord's
diamond, nor ever had to do, i' faat, la, with
any of his precious stones.   124

Enter HIPPOLITO.

Inf. Are you so close,[2] you bawd, you pan-
d'ring slave?   [*Strikes* BRYAN.]

Hip. How now? Why, Infelice; what 's
your quarrel?

Inf. Out of my sight, base varlet! get thee
gone.

Hip. Away, you rogue!

Bry. Slawne loot,[3] fare de well, fare de well.
Ah marragh frofat boddah breen![4]   *Exit.*

---

[1] Hound.   [2] Secret.
[3] Irish: *Slán leat,* fare thee well.
[4] Irish: *As a márach frómhadh bodach bréan* — On
the morrow of a feast, a clown is a beast. (Rhys.)

Hip. What, grown a fighter? Prithee, what 's
the matter?　　　　　　　　　　　　　131
Inf. If you 'll needs know, it was about the
clock.
How works the day, my lord, pray, by your
watch?
Hip. Lest you cuff me, I 'll tell you presently:[1]
I am near two.
Inf.　　　How, two? I 'm scarce at one. 135
Hip. One of us then goes false.
Inf.　　　　　　Then sure 't is you,
Mine goes by heaven's dial, the sun, and it goes
true.
Hip. I think, indeed, mine runs somewhat
too fast.
Inf. Set it to mine at one then.
Hip.　　　　　　One? 't is past :
'T is past one by the sun.
Inf.　　　　　Faith, then, belike, 140
Neither your clock nor mine does truly strike;
And since it is uncertain which goes true,
Better be false at one, than false at two.
Hip. Y' are very pleasant, madam.
If.　　　　　　Yet not merry.
Hip. Why, Infelice, what should make you
sad?　　　　　　　　　　　　　145
Inf. Nothing, my lord, but my false watch.
Pray, tell me, —
You see, my clock or yours is out of frame,
Must we upon the workmen lay the blame,
Or on ourselves that keep them?
Hip.　　　　　Faith on both.
He may by knavery spoil them, we by sloth. 150
But why talk you all riddle thus? I read
Strange comments in those margins of your looks.
Your cheeks of late are like bad printed books,
So dimly charact'red, I scarce can spell
One line of love in them. Sure all 's not well. 155
Inf. All is not well indeed, my dearest lord;
Lock up thy gates of hearing, that no sound
Of what I speak may enter.
Hip.　　　　　What means this?
Inf. Or if my own tongue must myself betray,
Count it a dream, or turn thine eyes away, 160
And think me not thy wife.　　*She kneels.*
Hip.　　　　　Why do you kneel?
Inf. Earth is sin's cushion : when the sick
soul feels
Herself growing poor, then she turns beggar,
cries,
And kneels for help. Hippolito, for husband
I dare not call thee, I have stolen that jewel 165
Of my chaste honour, which was only thine,
And given it to a slave.
Hip.　　　　　Ha?
Inf.　　　　　On thy pillow
Adultery and lust have slept; thy groom
Hath climb'd the unlawful tree, and pluckt the
sweets;
A villain hath usurp'd a husband's sheets. 170
Hip. S'death, who? — a cuckold! — who?
Inf.　　　　　This Irish footman.
Hip. Worse than damnation! a wild kerne,[2]
a frog.

A dog : whom I 'll scarce spurn. Long'd you for
shamrock?
Were it my father's father, heart, I 'll kill him,
Although I take him on his death-bed gasping
'Twixt Heaven and hell! A shag-hair'd cur!
Bold strumpet,　　　　　　　　175
Why hang'st thou on me? Think'st I 'll be a
bawd
To a whore, because she 's noble?
Inf.　　　　　I beg but this
Set not my shame out to the world's broad eye
Yet let thy vengeance, like my fault, soar high,
So it be in dark'ned clouds.
Hip.　　　　Dark'ned! my horns 181
Cannot be dark'ned, nor shall my revenge.
A harlot to my slave? The act is base,
Common, but foul, so shall not thy disgrace.
Could not I feed your appetite? O women 185
You were created angels, pure and fair;
But since the first fell, tempting devils you are
You should be men's bliss, but you prove their
rods :
Were there no women, men might live like
gods.
You ha' been too much down already; rise, 190
Get from my sight, and henceforth shun my
bed;
I 'll with no strumpet's breath be poisoned.
As for your Irish lubrican,[3] that spirit
Whom by prepost'rous charms thy lust hath
raised
In a wrong circle, him I 'll damn more black 195
Then any tyrant's soul.
Inf.　　　　Hippolito!
Hip. Tell me, didst thou bait hooks to draw
him to thee,
Or did he bewitch thee?
Inf.　　　　The slave did woo me.
Hip. Tu-whoos in that screech-owl's lan-
guage! Oh, who 'd trust
Your cork-heel'd sex? I think to sate your lust
You'd love a horse, a bear, a croaking toad, 201
So your hot itching veins might have their
bound :
Then the wild Irish dart was thrown? Come,
how?
The manner of this fight?
Inf. 'T was thus, he gave me this battery
first. — Oh, I　　　　　　　　205
Mistake — believe me, all this in beaten gold;
Yet I held out, but at length thus was charm'd.
　　　　　[*Gives letter, purse and ring.*]
What? change your diamond, wench? The act
is base,
Common, but foul, so shall not your disgrace.
Could not I feed your appetite? O men 210
You were created angels, pure and fair,
But since the first fell, worse than devils you
are.
You should our shields be, but you prove our
rods.
Were there no men, women might live like
gods.
Guilty, my lord?
Hip.　　　　Yes, guilty, my good lady. 215

---

[1] At once.
[2] An Irish foot-soldier : often used contemptuously.

[3] Leprechaun, a pigmy sprite in Irish folk-lore.

Inf. Nay, you may laugh, but henceforth shun my bed,
With no whore's leavings I 'll be poisoned.
                                        Exit.
Hip. O'er-reached so finely? 'T is the very diamond
And letter which I sent. This villany   219
Some spider closely weaves, whose poison'd bulk
I must let forth. Who 's there without?
Ser. (*within.*) My lord calls?
Hip. Send me the footman.
Ser. (*within.*) Call the footman to my lord. —
Bryan, Bryan!   224

Re-enter BRYAN.

Hip. It can be no man else, that Irish Judas,
Bred in a country where no venom prospers
But in the nation's blood, hath thus betray'd me.—
Slave, get you from your service.
Bry. Faat meanest thou by this now?
Hip. Question me not, nor tempt my fury, villain!   230
Couldst thou turn all the mountains in the land
To hills of gold, and give me, here thou stayest not.
Bry. I' faat, I care not.
Hip. Prate not, but get thee gone, I shall send else.   234
Bry. Ay, do predy, I had rather have thee make a scabbard of my guts, and let out all de Irish puddings in my poor belly, den to be a false knave to de, i' faat! I will never see dine own sweet face more. *A mawhid deer a gra,*[1] fare dee well, fare dee well; I will go steal [240 cows again in Ireland.   *Exit.*
Hip. He 's damn'd that raised this whirl-wind, which hath blown
Into her eyes this jealousy: yet I 'll on,
I 'll on, stood armed devils staring in my face.
To be pursued in flight, quickens the race,   245
Shall my blood-streams by a wife's lust be barr'd?
Fond[2] woman, no: iron grows by strokes more hard;
Lawless desires are seas scorning all bounds,
Or sulphur, which being ramm'd up, more confounds;
Struggling with madmen madness nothing tames;   250
Winds wrestling with great fires incense the flames.   *Exit.*

[SCENE II.][3]

Enter BELLAFRONT, *and* ORLANDO [*disguised as a* Serving-man], MATHEO [*following*].

Bell. How now, what ails your master?
Orl. Has taken a younger brother's purge, forsooth, and that works with him.
Bell. Where is his cloak and rapier?
Orl. He has given up his cloak, and his ra- [5 pier is bound to the peace. If you look a little higher, you may see that another hath ent'red

---

[1] Irish: *A maighisdir a grádh,* O master, O love.
[2] Foolish.   [3] A room in Matheo's house.

into hatband for him too. Six and four[4] have put him into this sweat.
Bell. Where 's all his money?   10
Orl. 'T is put over by exchange; his doublet was going to be translated, but for me. If any man would ha' lent but half a ducat on his beard, the hair of it had stuft a pair of breeches by this time. I had but one poor penny, and [15 that I was glad to niggle out,[5] and buy a holly-wand to grace him through the street. As hap was, his boots were on, and them I dustied, to make people think that he had been riding, and I had run by him. —   20
Bell. Oh me! — How does my sweet Matheo?
                        [MATHEO *comes forward.*]
Mat. Oh rogue, of what devilish stuff are these dice made of, — the parings of the devil's corns of his toes, that they run thus damnably?
Bell. I prithee, vex not.   25
Mat. If any handicraft's-man was ever suf-f'red to keep shop in hell, it will be a dice-maker; he 's able to undo more souls than the devil; I play'd with mine own dice, yet lost. Ha' you any money?   30
Bell. 'Las, I ha' none.
Mat. Must have money, must have some, must have a cloak, and rapier, and things. Will you go set your lime-twigs, and get me some birds, some money?   35
Bell. What lime-twigs should I set?
Mat. You will not then? Must have cash and pictures, do ye hear, frailty? Shall I walk in a Plymouth cloak,[6] that 's to say, like a rogue, in my hose and doublet, and a crabtree cudgel [40 in my hand, and you swim in your satins? Must have money, come! [*Taking off her gown.*]
Orl. Is 't bed-time, master, that you undo my mistress?
Bell. Undo me? Yes, yes, at these riflings I Have been too often.
Mat.   Help to flay, Pacheco. 45
Orl. Flaying call you it?
Mat. I 'll pawn you, by th' lord, to your very eyebrows.
Bell. With all my heart, since Heaven will have me poor;
As good be drown'd at sea, as drown'd at shore.
Orl. Why, hear you, sir? I 'faith, do not make away her gown.   51
Mat. Oh! it 's summer, it 's summer; your only fashion for a woman now is to be light, to be light.
Orl. Why, pray sir, employ some of that [55 money you have of mine.
Mat. Thine? I 'll starve first, I 'll beg first; when I touch a penny of that, let these fingers' ends rot.
Orl. [*Aside.*] So they may, for that 's past [60 touching. I saw my twenty pounds fly high.
Mat. Knowest thou never a damn'd broker about the city?
Orl. Damn'd broker? Yes, five hundred.
Mat. The gown stood me in[7] above twenty [65

---

[4] *I. e.* dicing.   [6] *I. e.* with a staff.
[5] Draw out unwillingly.   [7] Cost me.

ducats ; borrow ten of [1] it. Cannot live without
silver.

Orl. I 'll make what I can of it, sir, I 'll be
your broker, —
[*Aside*] But not your damn'd broker. Oh thou
    scurvy knave !
What makes a wife turn whore, but such a
    slave ? *Exit* [*with* BELLAFRONT'S *gown*].

Mat. How now, little chick, what ailest ?
Weeping for a handful of tailor's shreds ? Pox
on them, are there not silks enow at mercer's ?

Bell. I care not for gay feathers, I.   75

Mat. What dost care for then ? Why dost
grieve ?

Bell. Why do I grieve ? A thousand sorrows
    strike
At one poor heart, and yet it lives. Matheo,
Thou art a gamester ; prithee, throw at all, 80
Set all upon one cast. We kneel and pray,
And struggle for life, yet must be cast away.
Meet misery quickly then, split all, sell all,
And when thou 'st sold all, spend it ; but, I be-
    seech thee,
Build not thy mind on me to coin thee more ; 85
To get it wouldst thou have me play the whore ?

Mat. 'T was your profession before I married
you.

Bell. Umh ? it was indeed. If all men should
    be branded
For sins long since laid up, who could be saved ?
The quarter-day 's at hand, how will you do 91
To pay the rent, Matheo ?

Mat. Why, do as all of our occupation do
against [2] quarter-days : break up house, remove,
shift your lodgings : pox a' your quarters ! 95

Enter LODOVICO.

Lod. Where 's this gallant ?

Mat. Signor Lodovico ? how does my little
Mirror of Knighthood ? [3] This is kindly done, i'
faith : welcome, by my troth.

Lod. And how dost, frolic ? — Save you fair
    lady. — 100
Thou lookest smug and bravely, noble Mat.

Mat. Drink and feed, laugh and lie warm.

Lod. Is this thy wife ?

Mat. A poor gentlewoman, sir, whom I make
use of a'nights. 105

Lod. Pay custom to your lips, sweet lady.
    [*Kisses her.*]

Mat. Borrow some shells [4] of him. — Some
    wine, sweetheart.

Lod. I 'll send for 't then, i 'faith.

Mat. You send for 't ! — Some wine, I prithee.

Bell. I ha' no money. 110

Mat. 'Sblood, nor I. — What wine love you,
signor ?

Lod. Here ! [*offering money*] or I 'll not stay, I
protest ; trouble the gentlewoman too much ?
    Exit BELLAFRONT.
And what news flies abroad, Matheo ? 114

Mat. Troth, none. Oh, signor, we ha' been
merry in our days.

Lod. And no doubt shall again.

    [1] On.   [2] In preparation for.
    [3] An allusion to a well-known romance.
    [4] A cant term for money.

The divine powers never shoot darts at men
Mortal, to kill them.

Mat. You say true. 120

Lod. Why should we grieve at want ? Say
    the world made thee
Her minion, that thy head lay in her lap,
And that she danc'd thee on her wanton knee,
She could but give thee a whole world : that 's
    all, 124
And that all's nothing ; the world's greatest part
Cannot fill up one corner of thy heart.
Say the three corners were all fill'd, alas !
Of what art thou possest ? A thin blown glass,
Such as is by boys puft into the air !
Were twenty kingdoms thine, thou 'dst live in
    care : 130
Thou couldst not sleep the better, nor live
    longer,
Nor merrier be, nor healthfuller, nor stronger.
If, then, thou want'st, thus make that want thy
    pleasure,
No man wants all things, nor has all in measure.

Mat. I am the most wretched fellow : sure 135
some left-handed priest hath christ'ned me, I
am so unlucky ; I am never out of one puddle or
another ; still falling.

Re-enter BELLAFRONT [*with wine*] *and* ORL-
    ANDO.

Fill out wine to my little finger. — With my
heart, i' faith.   [*Drinks.*] 140

Lod. Thanks, good Matheo. To your own
sweet self.   [*Drinks.*]

Re-enter ORLANDO.

Orl. All the brokers' hearts, sir, are made of
flint. I can with all my knocking strike but six
sparks of fire out of them ; here 's six ducats, if
you 'll take them. 146

Mat. Give me them ! [*Taking money.*] An evil
conscience gnaw them all ! Moths and plagues
hang upon their lousy wardrobes !

Lod. Is this your man, Matheo ? 150

[*Mat.*] An old serving-man.

Orl. You may give me t' other half too, sir ;
that 's the beggar.

Lod. What hast there, — gold ? 154

Mat. A sort [5] of rascals are in my debt, God
knows what, and they feed me with bits, with
crumbs, a pox choke them.

Lod. A word, Matheo ; be not angry with me ;
Believe it that I know the touch of time, 159
And can part copper, though it be gilded o 'er,
From the true gold : the sails which thou dost
    spread,
Would show well if they were not borrowed.
The sound of thy low fortunes drew me hither,
I give my self unto thee ; prithee, use me,
I will bestow on you a suit of satin, 165
And all things else to fit a gentleman,
Because I love you.

Mat.   Thanks, good, noble knight !

Lod. Call on me when you please ; till then
    farewell.   *Exit.*

Mat. Hast angled ? Hast cut up this fresh
salmon ? 170

    [5] Band.

Bell. Wouldst have me be so base?

Mat. It's base to steal, it's base to be a whore: Thou'lt be more base, I'll make thee keep a door.[1]   *Exit.*

Orl. I hope he will not sneak away with all the money, will he?   175

Bell. Thou seest he does.

Orl. Nay then, it's well. I set my brains upon an upright last;[2] though my wits be old, yet they are like a wither'd pippin, wholesome. Look you, mistress, I told him I had but six [180 ducats of the knave broker, but I had eight, and kept these two for you.

Bell. Thou should'st have given him all.

Orl.   What, to fly high?

Bell. Like waves, my misery drives on misery.
                                                     Exit.

Orl. Sell his wife's clothes from her back? [185 Does any poulterer's wife pull chickens alive? He riots all abroad, wants all at home: he dices, whores, swaggers, swears, cheats, borrows, pawns. I'll give him hook and line, a little more for all this;   190 Yet sure i'th' end he'll delude all my hopes, And show me a French trick danc'd on the ropes.[3]   *Exit.* 185

[SCENE III.]

Enter at one door LODOVICO *and* CAROLO; *at another* BOTS, *and* Mistress HORSELEECH. CANDIDO *and his* Wife *appear in the Shop.*

Lod. Hist, hist, Lieutenant Bots! How dost, man?

Car. Whither are you ambling, Madam Horseleech?

Mis. H. About worldly profit, sir: how [5 do your worships?

Bots. We want tools, gentlemen, to furnish the trade: they wear out day and night, they wear out till no metal be left in their back. We hear of two or three new wenches are come [10 up with a carrier, and your old goshawk here is flying at them.

Lod. And, faith, what flesh have you at home?

Mis. H. Ordinary dishes; by my troth, [15 sweet men, there's few good i' th' city. I am as well furnisht as any, and, though I say it, as well custom'd.

Bots. We have meats of all sorts of dressing; we have stew'd meat for your Frenchman, [20 pretty light picking meat for your Italian, and that which is rotten roasted for Don Spaniardo.

Lod. A pox on 't.

Bots. We have poulterer's ware for your sweet bloods, as dove, chicken, duck, teal, [25 woodcock, and so forth: and butcher's meat for the citizen: yet muttons[4] fall very bad this year.

Lod. Stay, is not that my patient linen-draper yonder, and my fine young smug mistress, [30 his wife?

Car. Sirrah,[5] grannam, I'll give thee for thy

[1] *I. e.* turn bawd.   [2] *I. e.* My expectation was just.
[3] Will be hanged.   [4] Prostitutes.
[5] Formerly used to both sexes.

fee twenty crowns, if thou canst but procure me the wearing of yon velvet cap.

Mis. H. You'd wear another thing be- [35 sides the cap. You're a wag.

Bots. Twenty crowns? We'll share, and I'll be your pully to draw her on.

Lod. Do't presently; we'll ha' some sport.

Mis. H. Wheel you about, sweet men: [40 do you see? I'll cheapen wares of the man, whilst Bots is doing with his wife.

Lod. To 't: if we come into the shop to do you grace, we'll call you madam.

Bots. Pox a' your old face, give it the [45 badge of all scurvy faces, a mask.

[*Mistress* HORSELEECH *puts on a mask.*]

Cand. What is 't you lack, gentlewoman? Cambric or lawns, or fine hollands? Pray draw near; I can sell you a pennyworth.

Bots. Some cambric for my old lady.   50

Cand. Cambric? You shall, the purest thread in Milan.

Lod., Car. Save you, Signor Candido.

Lod. How does my noble master? How my fair mistress?   55

Cand. My worshipful good servant. — View it well, for 't is both fine and even.

                                    [*Shows cambric.*]

Car. Cry you mercy, madam; though mask'd, I thought it should be you by your man. — Pray, signor, show her the best, for she commonly deals for good ware.   61

Cand. Then this shall fit her. — This is for your ladyship.

Bots. [*to Bride.*] A word, I pray. There is a waiting gentlewoman of my lady's — her [65 name is Ruyna — says she's your kinswoman, and that you should be one of her aunts.

Bride. One of her aunts? Troth, sir, I know her not.   69

Bots. If it please you to bestow the poor labour of your legs at any time, I will be your convoy thither.

Bride. I am a snail, sir, seldom leave my house. If 't please her to visit me, she shall be welcome.   75

Bots. Do you hear? The naked truth is, my lady hath a young knight, her son, who loves you; you're made, if you lay hold upon 't; this jewel he sends you.   [*Offers jewel.*] 79

Bride. Sir, I return his love and jewel with scorn. Let go my hand, or I shall call my husband. You are an arrant knave.   *Exit.*

Lod. What will she do?

Bots. Do? They shall all do if Bots sets upon them once. She was as if she had profest [85 the trade, squeamish at first; at last I showed her this jewel, said a knight sent it her.

Lod. Is 't gold, and right stones?

Bots. Copper, copper; I go a fishing with these baits. She nibbled, but would not swallow the hook, because the conger-head, her [91 husband, was by; but she bids the gentleman name any afternoon, and she'll meet him at her garden house,[6] which I know.

[6] Gardens with summer-houses were very common in the suburbs of London at the time, and were often used as places of intrigue. (Dyce.)

Lod. Is this no lie now ?   95
Bots. Damme, if —
Lod. Oh, prithee, stay there.
Bots. The twenty crowns, sir.
Lod. Before he has his work done ? — But
on my knightly word he shall pay 't thee.   100

Enter ASTOLFO, BERALDO, FONTINELL, *and*
the Irish footman [BRYAN].

Ast. I thought thou hadst been gone into
thine own country.
Bry. No, faat, la, I cannot go dis four or
tree days.   104
Ber. Look thee, yonder 's the shop, and that 's
the man himself.
Fon. Thou shalt but cheapen, and do as we
told thee, to put a jest upon him, to abuse his
patience,   109
Bry. I' faat, I doubt my pate shall be
knocked : but, sa crees sa' me, for your shakes,
I will run to any linen-draper in hell. Come,
predee.
All. Save you, gallants.
Lod., Car. Oh, well met !   115
Cand. You 'll give no more, you say ? I can-
not take it.
Mis. H. Truly, I 'll give no more.
Cand. It must not fetch it.
What would you have, sweet gentlemen.   120
Ast. Nay, here 's the customer.
    Exeunt BOTS *and* Mistress HORSE-
    LEECH.

Lod. The garden-house, you say ? We 'll bolt ¹
out your roguery.
Cand. I will but lay these parcels by — my
men
Are all at custom house unloading wares.   125
If cambric you would deal in, there 's the best ;
All Milan cannot sample it.
Lod. Do you hear it ? one, two, three, —
'Sfoot, there came in four gallants ! Sure
your wife is slipt up, and the fourth man, I
hold my life, is grafting your warden tree.²   131
Cand. Ha, ha, ha ! you gentlemen are full of
jest,
If she be up, she 's gone some wares to show ;
I have above as good wares as below.
Lod. Have you so ? Nay, then —   135
Cand. Now, gentlemen, is 't cambrics ?
Bry. I predee now, let me have de best
waures.
Cand. What 's that he says, pray, gentlemen ?
Lod. Marry, he says we are like to have the
best wars.   141
Cand. The best wars ? All are bad, yet wars
do good,
And, like to surgeons, let sick kingdom's
blood.
Bry. Faat a devil pratest tow so ? a pox on
dee ! I preddee, let me see some hollen, to make
linen shirts, for fear my body be lousy.   146
Cand. Indeed, I understand no word he
speaks.
Car. Marry, he says that at the siege in
Holland

¹ Sift.   ² Pear-tree.

There was much bawdry us'd among the sol-
diers,
Though they were lousy.   15
Cand. It may be so, that 's likely. — True,
indeed,
In every garden, sir, does grow that weed.
Bry. Pox on de gardens, and de weeds,
and de fool's cap dere, and de clouts ! Hear ?
dost make a hobby-horse of me.   155
    [*Tearing the cambric.*]
All. Oh, fie ! he has torn the cambric.
Cand.   'T is no matter.
Ast. It frets me to the soul.
Cand.   So does 't not me.
My customers do oft for remnants call,
These are two remnants, now, no loss at all.
But let me tell you, were my servants here,   160
It would ha' cost more. — Thank you, gentle-
men,
I use you well, pray know my shop again.
    Exit.
All. Ha, ha, ha ! come, come, let 's go, let 's go.
    Exeunt.

[ACT IV]

[SCENE I.] ³

Enter MATHEO *brave,*⁴ *and* BELLAFRONT.

Mat. How am I suited, Front ? Am I not gallant, ha ?
Bell. Yes, sir, you are suited well.
Mat. Exceeding passing well, and to the
time.⁵   ⁴
Bell. The tailor has play'd his part with you.
Mat. And I have play'd a gentleman's part
with my tailor, for I owe him for the making
of it.
Bell. And why did you so, sir ?
Mat. To keep the fashion ; it 's your only [10
fashion now, of your best rank of gallants, to
make their tailors wait for their money ; neither were it wisdom indeed to pay them upon
the first edition⁶ of a new suit ; for commonly the suit is owing for, when the linings [15
are worn out, and there 's no reason, then, that
the tailor should be paid before the mercer.
Bell. Is this the suit the knight bestowed
upon you ?
Mat. This is the suit, and I need not shame
to wear it, for better men than I would be [20
glad to have suits bestowed on them. It 's a generous fellow, — but — pox on him — we whose
pericranions are the very limbecks and stilla-
tories of good wit and fly high, must drive
liquor out of stale gaping oysters. Shallow [25
knight, poor squire Tinacheo : I 'll make a wild
Cataian⁷ of forty such : hang him, he 's an ass,
he 's always sober.
Bell. This is your fault to wound your friends
still.   31
Mat. No, faith, Front, Lodovico is a noble

³ A room in Matheo's house.   ⁵ In the fashion.
⁴ Finely attired.   ⁶ Delivery.
⁷ " It would take forty such knights to make a thief."
Cataia is China ; the Chinese were supposed to be great
thieves.

Slavonian: it's more rare to see him in a woman's company, than for a Spaniard to go into England, and to challenge the English [35 fencers there. — [*Knocking within.*] One knocks, — see. — [*Exit* BELLAFRONT.] — La, fa, sol, la, fa, la, [*sings*] rustle in silks and satins! There's music in this, and a taffeta petticoat, it makes both fly high. *Catso.*   40

Re-enter BELLAFRONT; *after her* ORLANDO, *like himself, with four men after him.*

Bell. Matheo! 't is my father.
Mat. Ha! father? It's no matter, he finds no tatter'd prodigals here.
Orl. Is not the door good enough to hold your blue coats? Away, knaves, wear not your [45 clothes threadbare at knees for me; beg Heaven's blessing, not mine. [*Exeunt* Servants.] — Oh cry your worship mercy, sir; was somewhat bold to talk to this gentlewoman, your wife here.   50
Mat. A poor gentlewoman, sir.
Orl. Stand not, sir, bare to me; I ha' read oft
That serpents who creep low, belch ranker poison
Than winged dragons do that fly aloft.
Mat. If it offend you, sir, 't is for my pleasure.   55
Orl. Your pleasure be 't, sir. Umh, is this your palace?
Bell. Yes, and our kingdom, for 't is our content.
Orl. It's a very poor kingdom then; what, are all your subjects gone a sheep-shearing? Not a maid? not a man? not so much as a cat? You keep a good house belike, just like one [61 of your profession, every room with bare walls, and a half-headed bed to vault upon, as all your bawdy-houses are. Pray who are your upholsters? Oh, the spiders, I see, they bestow hangings upon you.   66
Mat. Bawdy-house? Zounds, sir —
Bell. Oh sweet Matheo, peace. Upon my knees
I do beseech you, sir, not to arraign me
For sins, which Heaven, I hope, long since hath pardoned!   70
Those flames, like lightning flashes, are so spent,
The heat no more remains, than where ships went,
Or where birds cut the air, the print remains.
Mat. Pox on him, kneel to a dog.
Bell. She that's a whore,   75
Lives gallant, fares well, is not, like me, poor.
I ha' now as small acquaintance with that sin,
As if I had never known 't, that never been.
Orl. No acquaintance with it? What maintains thee then? How dost live then? Has thy husband any lands, any rents coming in, any [81 stock going, any ploughs jogging, any ships sailing? Hast thou any wares to turn,[1] so much as to get a single penny by?
Yes thou hast ware to sell;   85
Knaves are thy chapmen, and thy shop is hell.
Mat. Do you hear, sir?

Orl. So, sir, I do hear, sir, more of you than you dream I do.
Mat. You fly a little too high, sir.   90
Orl. Why, sir, too high?
Mat. I ha' suff'red your tongue, like a barr'd cater-tray,[2] to run all this while, and ha' not stopt it.
Orl. Well, sir, you talk like a gamester.   95
Mat. If you come to bark at her because she's a poor rogue, look you, here's a fine path, sir, and there, there, the door.
Bell. Matheo!
Mat. Your blue coats stay for you, sir. I love a good honest roaring boy, and so —   101
Orl. That's the devil.
Mat. Sir, sir, I'll ha' no Joves in my house to thunder avaunt. She shall live and be maintained when you, like a keg of musty stur- [105 geon, shall stink. Where? In your coffin. How? Be a musty fellow, and lousy.
Orl. I know she shall be maintained, but how? She like a quean, thou like a knave; she like a whore, thou like a thief.   110
Mat. Thief? Zounds! Thief?
Bell. Good, dearest Mat! — Father!
Mat. Pox on you both! I'll not be braved. New satin scorns to be put down with bare bawdy velvet. Thief!   115
Orl. Ay, thief, th' art a murderer, a cheater, a whoremonger, a pot-hunter, a borrower, a beggar —
Bell. Dear father —
Mat. An old ass, a dog, a churl, a chuff, an usurer, a villain, a moth, a mangy mule, [121 with an old velvet foot-cloth on his back, sir.
Bell. Oh me!
Orl. Varlet, for this I'll hang thee.
Mat. Ha, ha, alas!
Orl. Thou keepest a man of mine here, [126 under my nose.
Mat. Under thy beard.
Orl. As arrant a smell-smock, for an old mutton-monger[3] as thyself.   130
Mat. No, as yourself.
Orl. As arrant a purse-taker as ever cried, Stand! yet a good fellow I confess, and valiant; but he'll bring thee to th' gallows. You both have robb'd of late two poor country pedlars.   136
Mat. How's this? How's this? Dost thou fly high? Rob pedlars? — Bear witness, Front — rob pedlars? My man and I a thief?
Bell. Oh, sir, no more.
Orl. Ay, knave, two pedlars. Hue and cry [141 is up, warrants are out, and I shall see thee climb a ladder.
Mat. And come down again as well as a bricklayer or a tiler. — [*Aside.*] How the vengeance knows he this? — If I be hanged, [146 I'll tell the people I married old Friscobaldo's daughter; I'll frisco you, and your old carcass.
Orl. Tell what thou canst; if I stay here longer, I shall be hang'd too, for being in thy company; therefore, as I found you, I leave [151 you —

---

[1] Turn over. sell.

[2] A kind of false dice.   [3] Whoremonger.

Mat. Kneel, and get money of him.

Orl. A knave and a quean, a thief and a strumpet, a couple of beggars, a brace of bag- 156
gages.

Mat. Hang upon him — Ay, ay, sir, fare you well; we are so — follow close — we are beggars — in satin — to him.

Bell. Is this your comfort, when so many years 160
You ha' left me frozen to death?

Orl. Freeze still, starve still!

Bell. Yes, so I shall: I must: I must and will.
If, as you say, I'm poor, relieve me then,
Let me not sell my body to base men.
You call me strumpet, Heaven knows I am none: 165
Your cruelty may drive me to be one:
Let not that sin be yours; let not the shame
Of common whore live longer than my name.
That cunning bawd, Necessity, night and day
Plots to undo me; drive that hag away, 170
Lest being at lowest ebb, as now I am,
I sink for ever.

Orl. Lowest ebb, what ebb?

Bell. So poor, that, though to tell it be my shame,
I am not worth a dish to hold my meat;
I am yet poorer, I want bread to eat. 175

Orl. It's not seen by your cheeks.

Mat. [*Aside.*] I think she has read an homily to tickle the old rogue.

Orl. Want bread! There's satin: bake that.

Mat. 'Sblood, make pasties of my clothes? 180

Orl. A fair new cloak, stew that; an excellent gilt rapier.

Mat. Will you eat that, sir?

Orl. I could feast ten good fellows with these hangers.[1]

Mat. The pox, you shall! 185

Orl. I shall not, till thou begg'st, think thou art poor;
And when thou begg'st I'll feed thee at my door,
As I feed dogs, with bones; till then beg, borrow,
Pawn, steal, and hang, turn bawd, when thou art whore, —
[*Aside.*] My heart-strings sure would crack,
were they strain'd more. *Exit.* 190

Mat. This is your father, your damn'd — Confusion light upon all the generation of you!
He can come bragging hither with four white herrings a 's tail in blue coats, without roes in their bellies; but I may starve ere he give me so much as a cob.[2] 196

Bell. What tell you me of this? alas!

Mat. Go, trot after your dad, do you capitulate; I'll pawn not for you; I'll not steal to be hanged for such an hypocritical, close, common harlot: away, you dog! — 201
Brave i' faith! Udsfoot, give me some meat.

Bell. Yes, sir. *Exit.*

Mat. Goodman slave, my man too, is gallop'd

---

to the devil a' the t' other side: Pacheco, I'll checo you. Is this your dad's day? Eng- [206
land, they say, is the only hell for horses, and only paradise for women: pray get you to that paradise, because you're called an honest whore; there they live none but honest whores with a pox. Marry, here in our city, all your [211
sex are but foot-cloth nags:[3] the master no sooner lights but the man leaps into the saddle.

Re-enter BELLAFRONT [*with meat and drink*].

Bell. Will you sit down, I pray, sir?

Mat. [*sitting down.*] I could tear, by th' Lord, his flesh, and eat his midriff in salt, as I eat [216
this: — must I choke? — My father Friscobaldo, I shall make a pitiful hog-louse of you, Orlando, if you fall once into my fingers — Here's the savourest meat! I ha' got a stomach with chafing.[4] What rogue should tell him of those [221
two pedlars? A plague choke him, and gnaw him to the bare bones! — Come fill.

Bell. Thou sweatest with very anger, good sweet. Vex not, 'las, 't is no fault of mine. 225

Mat. Where didst buy this mutton? I never felt better ribs.

Bell. A neighbour sent it me.

Re-enter ORLANDO [*disguised as a Serving-man*].

Mat. Hah, neighbour? Foh, my mouth stinks. You whore, do you beg victuals for me? Is this satin doublet to be bombasted[5] with broken [231
meat? *Takes up the stool.*

Orl. What will you do, sir?

Mat. Beat out the brains of a beggarly — 234

Orl. Beat out an ass's head of your own. —
Away, Mistress! [*Exit* BELLAFRONT.] Zounds, do but touch one hair of her, and I'll so quilt your cap with old iron, that your coxcomb shall ache the worse these seven years for 't. Does she look like a roasted rabbit, that you must have the head for the brains? 241

Mat. Ha, ha! go out of my doors, you rogue! Away, four marks; trudge.

Orl. Four marks? No, sir, my twenty pound that you ha' made fly high, and I am gone. 245

Mat. Must I be fed with chippings? You're best get a clapdish,[6] and say y' are proctor to some spittle-house.[7] — Where hast thou been, Pacheco? Come hither my little turkey-cock.

Orl. I cannot abide, sir, to see a woman wrong'd, not I. 251

Mat. Sirrah, here was my father-in-law to-day.

Orl. Pish, then y' are full of crowns.

Mat. Hang him! he would ha' thrust crowns upon me, to have fall'n in again, but I scorn cast clothes, or any man's gold. 256

Orl. [*Aside.*] — But mine. How did he brook that, sir?

Mat. Oh, swore like a dozen of drunken tinkers; at last growing foul in words, he and [260
four of his men drew upon me, sir.

---

[1] The straps attached to the girdle, from which a dagger or sword hung. They were often richly embroidered.

[2] Herring's head.

[3] Horses with long housings.

[4] An appetite with anger.   [5] Stuffed out.

[6] A dish carried by beggars, with a lid used to rattle to attract notice.

[7] Hospital.

Orl. In your house ? Would I had been by !

Mat. I made no more ado, but fell to my old lock,[1] and so thrashed my blue-coats and old crab-tree-face my father-in-law, and then walkt like a lion in my grate.[2] 266

Orl. O noble master !

Mat. Sirrah, he could tell me of the robbing the two pedlars, and that warrants are out for us both. 270

Orl. Good sir, I like not those crackers.[3]

Mat. Crackhalter,[4] wou't set thy foot to mine?

Orl. How, sir ? at drinking.

Mat. We 'll pull that old crow my father: rob thy master. I know the house, thou [275 the servants : the purchase[5] is rich, the plot to get it is easy ; the dog will not part from a bone.

Orl. Pluck't out of his throat, then. I 'll snarl for one, if this[6] can bite.

Mat. Say no more, say no more, old coal ; [280 meet me anon at the sign of the Shipwrack.

Orl. Yes, sir.

Mat. And dost hear, man ? — the Shipwrack.
Exit.

Orl. Th' art at the shipwrack now, and like a swimmer,
Bold, but unexpert, with those waves dost play, 285
Whose dalliance, whorelike, is to cast thee away.

Enter HIPPOLITO *and* BELLAFRONT.

And here 's another vessel, better fraught,
But as ill-mann'd ; her sinking will be wrought,
If rescue come not : like a man of war
I 'll therefore bravely out ; somewhat I 'll do, 291
And either save them both, or perish too.
Exit.

Hip. It is my fate to be bewitched by those eyes.

Bell. Fate? your folly.
Why should my face thus mad you ? 'Las, those colours 295
Are wound up long ago, which beauty spread :
The flowers that once grew here, are withered.
You turn'd my black soul white, made it look new,
And should I sin, it ne'er should be with you.

Hip. Your hand, I 'll offer you fair play.
When first 300
We met i' th' lists together, you remember
You were a common rebel ; with one parley
I won you to come in.

Bell. You did.

Hip. I 'll try
If now I can beat down this chastity
With the same ordnance. Will you yield this fort, 305
If the power of argument now, as then,
I get of you the conquest : as before
I turn'd you honest, now to turn you whore,
By force of strong persuasion ?

Bell. If you can,
I yield.

Hip. The alarum 's struck up ; I 'm your man.

Bell. A woman gives defiance.

Hip. Sit. [*They seat themselves.*]

Bell. Begin : 311
'T is a brave battle to encounter sin.

Hip. You men that are to fight in the same war
To which I 'm prest, and plead at the same bar,
To win a woman, if you 'd have me speed, 315
Send all your wishes !

Bell. No doubt you 're heard ; proceed.

Hip. To be a harlot, that you stand upon,
The very name 's a charm to make you one.
Harlotta[7] was a dame of so divine 319
And ravishing touch[8] that she was concubine
To an English king ; her sweet bewitching eye
Did the king's heart-strings in such love-knots tie
That even the coyest was proud when she could hear
Men say, " Behold, another Harlot there ! "
And after her all women that were fair 325
Were harlots call'd, as to this day some are :
Besides, her dalliance she so well does mix,
That she 's in Latin call'd the *Meretrix.*
Thus for the name ; for the profession, this :
Who lives in bondage, lives lac'd ; the chief bliss 330
This world below can yield, is liberty :
And who, than whores, with looser wings dare fly ?
As Juno's proud bird spreads the fairest tail,
So does a strumpet hoist the loftiest sail,
She 's no man's slave ; men are her slaves ; her eye 335
Moves not on wheels screw'd up with jealousy,
She, hors'd or coach'd, does merry journeys make,
Free as the sun in his gilt zodiac :
As bravely does she shine, as fast she 's driven,
But stays not long in any house of heaven ; 340
But shifts from sign to sign, her amorous prizes
More rich being when she 's down, than when she rises.
In brief, gentlemen haunt them, soldiers fight for them,
Few men but know them, few or none abhor them.
Thus for sport's sake speak I, as to a woman
Whom, as the worst ground, I would turn to common : 346
But you I would enclose for mine own bed.

Bell. So should a husband be dishonoured.

Hip. Dishonour'd ? Not a whit : to fall to one
Besides your husband is to fall to none, 350
For one no number is.

Bell. Faith, should you take
One in your bed, would you that reckoning make ?
'T is time you found retreat.

Hip. Say, have I won,
Is the day ours ?

---

[1] Trick. [3] Boasters. [5] Booty.
[2] Cage. [4] Gallows-bird. [6] His sword.

[7] The mistress of the father of William the Conqueror.
[8] Quality.

Bell.   The battle 's but half done,
None but yourself have yet sounded alarms, 355
Let us strike too, else you dishonour arms.
Hip. If you can win the day, the glory's yours.
Bell. To prove a woman should not be a
whore :
When she was made, she 'd one man, and no
more ;   359
Yet she was tied to laws then, for even than, [1]
'T is said, she was not made for men, but man.
Anon, t' increase earth's brood, the law was
varied,
Men should take many wives : and though they
married
According to that act, yet 't is not known
But that those wives were only tied to one. 365
New parliaments were since : for now one
woman
Is shar'd between three hundred, nay she 's
common,
Common ! as spotted leopards, whom for sport
Men hunt to get the flesh, but care not for 't.
So spread they nets of gold, and tune their
calls,   370
To enchant silly women to take falls ;
Swearing they 're angels, which that they may
win
They 'll hire the devil to come with false dice
in.
Oh Sirens' subtle tunes ! yourselves you flatter,
And our weak sex betray : so men love water ;
It serves to wash their hands, but being once
foul,   376
The water down is pour'd, cast out of doors ;
And even of such base use do men make
whores.
A harlot, like a hen, more sweetness reaps,
To pick men one by one up, than in heaps : 380
Yet all feeds but confounding.[2] Say you should
taste me,
I serve but for the time, and when the day
Of war is done, am cashier'd out of pay :
If like lame soldiers I could beg, that 's all,
And there 's lust's rendezvous, an hospital. 385
Who then would be a man's slave, a man's
woman ?
She 's half starv'd the first day that feeds in
common.
Hip. You should not feed so, but with me
alone.
Bell. If I drink poison by stealth, is 't not
all one ?
Is 't not rank poison still with you alone ? 390
Nay, say you spi'd a courtesan, whose soft side
To touch you 'd sell your birth-right, for one kiss
Be rack'd ; she 's won, you 're sated : what fol-
lows this ?
Oh, then you curse that bawd that toll'd[3] you
in,
The night ; you curse your lust, you loathe the
sin,   395
You loathe her very sight, and ere the day
Arise, you rise glad when y' are stol'n away.
Even then when you are drunk with all her
sweets,

There 's no true pleasure in a strumpet's sheets.
Women whom lust so prostitutes to sale, 400
Like dancers upon ropes, once seen, are stale.
Hip. If all the threads of harlot's lives are
spun,
So coarse as you would make them, tell me
why
You so long lov'd the trade ?
Bell.   If all the threads
Of harlot's lives be fine as you would make
them,   405
Why do not you persuade your wife turn
whore,
And all dames else to fall before that sin ?
Like an ill husband, though I knew the same
To be my undoing, followed I that game.
Oh, when the work of lust had earn'd my
bread,   410
To taste it how I trembled, lest each bit,
Ere it went down, should choke me chewing it !
My bed seem'd like a cabin hung in hell,
The bawd, hell's porter, and the lickerish[4]
wine
The pander fetch'd, was like an easy fine, 415
For which, methought, I leas'd away my soul ;
And oftentimes, even in my quaffing bowl,
Thus said I to myself, I am a whore,
And have drunk down thus much confusion
more.   419
Hip. It is a common rule, and 't is more true,
Two of one trade ne'er love : no more do you.
Why are you sharp 'gainst that you once pro-
fest ?
Bell. Why dote you on that, which you did
once detest ?
I cannot, seeing she 's woven of such bad stuff,
Set colours on a harlot base enough. 421
Nothing did make me, when I lov'd them best,
To loathe them more than this : when in the
street
A fair young modest damsel I did meet,
She seem'd to all a dove, when I pass'd by,
And I to all a raven : every eye 430
That followed her went with a bashful glance,
At me each bold and jeering countenance
Darted forth scorn ; to her as if she had been
Some tower unvanquished, would they vail,[5]
'Gainst me swoln rumour hoisted every sail ;
She, crown'd with reverend praises, pass'd by
them,   436
I, though with face mask'd, could not scape
the " Hem ! "
For, as if Heaven had set strange marks on
whores,
Because they should be pointing stocks to
man,
Drest up in civilest shape, a courtesan — 440
Let her walk saint-like, noteless, and unknown,
Yet she 's betray'd by some trick of her own.
Were harlots therefore wise, they 'd be sold
dear :
For men account them good but for one year,
And then like almanacs whose dates are
gone,   445
They are thrown by, and no more look'd upon.

Who 'll therefore backward fall, who will launch
forth
In seas so foul, for ventures no more worth ?
Lust's voyage hath, if not this course, this
cross,
Buy ne'er so cheap, your ware comes home
with loss.   450
What, shall I sound retreat ? The battle 's
done :
Let the world judge which of us two have won.
  Hip. I !
  Bell. You ? nay then as cowards do in fight,
What by blows cannot, shall be sav'd by
flight.   *Exit.*
  Hip. Fly to earth's fixed centre : to the caves
Of everlasting horror, I 'll pursue thee,   456
Though loaden with sins, even to hell's brazen
doors.
Thus wisest men turn fools, doting on whores.
                                          Exit.

[SCENE II.]¹

Enter the DUKE, LODOVICO, *and* ORLANDO
[*disguised as a* Serving-man] ; *after them* IN-
FELICE, CAROLO, ASTOLFO, BERALDO, *and*
FONTINELL.

  Orl. I beseech your grace, though your eye
be so piercing as under a poor blue coat to cull
out an honest father from an old serving-man,
yet, good my lord, discover not the plot to any,
but only this gentleman that is now to be an [5
actor in our ensuing comedy.
  Duke. Thou hast thy wish, Orlando, pass unknown,
Sforza shall only go along with thee,
To see that warrant serv'd upon thy son.
  Lod. To attach him upon felony, for two [10
pedlars : is 't not so ?
  Orl. Right, my noble knight : those pedlars
were two knaves of mine ; he fleec'd the men
before, and now he purposes to flay the master.
He will rob me ; his teeth water to be nib- [15
bling at my gold ; but this shall hang him by th'
gills, till I pull him on shore.
  Duke. Away : ply you the business.
  Orl. Thanks to your grace : but, my good
lord, for my daughter —   20
  Duke. You know what I have said.
  Orl. And remember what I have sworn. She 's
more honest, on my soul, than one of the Turks'
wenches, watcht by a hundred eunuchs.
  Lod. So she had need, for the Turks make [25
them whores.
  Orl. He 's a Turk that makes any woman a
whore ; he 's no true Christian, I 'm sure. I
commit your grace.
  Duke. Infelice.   30
  Inf. Here, sir.
  Lod. Signor Friscobaldo.
  Orl. Frisking again ? Pacheco.
  Lod. Uds so, Pacheco ! We 'll have some
sport with this warrant : 't is to apprehend [35
all suspected persons in the house. Besides,
there 's one Bots, a pander, and one Madam
Horseleech, a bawd, that have abus'd my friend ;

¹ An apartment in the Duke's Palace.

those two conies will we ferret into the purse-
net.²   40
  Orl. Let me alone for dabbing them o' th'
neck. Come, come.
  Lod. Do ye hear, gallants ? Meet me anon
at Matheo's.
  All. Enough.   45
        Exeunt LODOVICO *and* ORLANDO.
  Duke. Th' old fellow sings that note thou
didst before,
Only his tunes are, that she is no whore,
But that she sent his letters and his gifts,
Out of a noble triumph o'er his lust,
To show she trampled his assaults in dust.   50
  Inf. 'T is a good honest servant, that old man.
  Duke. I doubt no less.
  Inf.   And it may be my husband,
Because when once this woman was unmaskt,
He levell'd all her thoughts, and made them fit,
Now he 'd mar all again, to try his wit.   55
  Duke. It may be so too, for to turn a harlot
Honest, it must be by strong antidotes ;
'T is rare, as to see panthers change their spots.
And when she 's once a star fix'd and shines
bright,
Though 't were impiety then to dim her light, 60
Because we see such tapers seldom burn,
Yet 't is the pride and glory of some men,
To change her to a blazing star again,
And it may be, Hippolito does no more. —
It cannot be but you 're acquainted all   64
With that same madness of our son-in-law,
That dotes so on a courtesan.
  All.   Yes, my lord.
  Car. All the city thinks he 's a whoremonger.
  Ast. Yet I warrant he 'll swear no man marks
him.   70
  Ber. 'T is like so, for when a man goes a
wenching, is as if he had a strong stinking
breath, every one smells him out, yet he feels
it not, though it be ranker than the sweat of
sixteen bear warders.   75
  Duke. I doubt then you have all those stink-
ing breaths ;
You might be all smelt out.
  Car. Troth, my lord, I think we are all as
you ha' been in your youth when you went a-
maying ; we all love to hear the cuckoo sing [80
upon other men's trees.
  Duke. It 's well ; yet you confess. But, girl,
thy bed
Shall not be parted with a courtesan.
'T is strange,
No frown of mine, no frown of the poor lady, 85
My abus'd child, his wife, no care of fame,
Of honour, heaven, or hell, no not that name
Of common strumpet, can affright, or woo him
To abandon her ; the harlot does undo him ;   89
She has bewitcht him, robb'd him of his shape,
Turn'd him into a beast ; his reason 's lost ;
You see he looks wild, does he not ?
  Car.   I ha' noted
New moons in 's face, my lord, all full of change.
  Duke. He 's no more like unto Hippolito

² A net, the mouth of which was drawn together with
a string.

Than dead men are to living — never sleeps,   95
Or if he do, it 's dreams : and in those dreams
His arms work, and then cries, "Sweet" —
what 's her name.
What 's the drab's name ?
    Ast.   In troth, my lord, I know not,
I know no drabs, not I.
    Duke.   Oh, Bellafront! —   99
And, catching her fast, cries, "My Bellafront!"
    Car. A drench that 's able to kill a horse
cannot kill this disease of smock-smelling, my
lord, if it have once eaten deep.
    Duke. I 'll try all physic, and this medicine
first :   104
I have directed warrants strong and peremptory
To purge our city Milan, and to cure
The outward parts, the suburbs, for the at-
taching
Of all those women, who, like gold, want
weight :
Cities, like ships, should have no idle freight. 109
    Car. No, my lord, and light wenches are no
idle freight ; but what 's your grace's reach [1] in
this ?
    Duke. This, Carolo. If she whom my son
dotes on,
Be in that muster-book enroll'd, he 'll shame
Ever t' approach one of such noted name.   115
    Car. But say she be not?
    Duke.   Yet on harlots' heads
New laws shall fall so heavy, and such blows
Shall give to those that haunt them, that Hippolito
If not for fear of law, for love to her,
If he love truly, shall her bed forbear.   120
    Car. Attach all the light heels i' the city and
clap 'em up? Why, my lord, you dive into a
well unsearchable : all the whores within the
walls, and without the walls ? I would not be [124
he should meddle with them for ten such dukedoms ; the army that you speak on is able to fill
all the prisons within this city, and to leave not
a drinking-room in any tavern besides.
    Duke. Those only shall be caught that are of
note ;   130
Harlots in each street flow :
The fish being thus i' th' net, ourself will sit,
And with eye most severe dispose of it.
Come, girl.   [*Exeunt* DUKE *and* INFELICE.]
    Car. Arraign the poor whores !
    Ast. I 'll not miss that sessions.   135
    Font. Nor I.
    Ber. Nor I, though I hold up my hand there
myself.   *Exeunt.*

[SCENE III.] [2]

Enter MATHEO, LODOVICO, *and* ORLANDO [*disguised as a* Serving-man].

    Mat. Let who will come, my noble cheva-
lier ; I can but play the kind host, and bid 'em
welcome.
    Lod. We 'll trouble your house, Matheo, but
as Dutchmen do in taverns, drink, be merry, [5
and be gone.

    Orl. Indeed, if you be right Dutchmen ; if
you fall to drinking, you must be gone.
    Mat. The worst is, my wife is not at home ;
but we 'll fly high, my generous knight, for all
that. There 's no music when a woman is in [11
the concert.
    Orl. No ; for she 's like a pair of virginals,
Always with jacks at her tail.

Enter ASTOLFO, CAROLO, BERALDO, *and* FON-
TINELL.

    Lod. See, the covey is sprung.   15
    All. Save you, gallants.
    Mat. Happily encounter'd, sweet bloods.
    Lod. Gentlemen, you all know Signor Can-
dido, the linen-draper, he that 's more patient
than a brown baker upon the day when he heats
his oven, and has forty scolds about him.   21
    All. Yes, we know him all ; what of him ?
    Lod. Would it not be a good fit of mirth, to
make a piece of English cloth of him, and to
stretch him on the tenters,[3] till the threads of
his own natural humour crack, by making [26
him drink healths, tobacco, dance, sing bawdy
songs, or to run any bias[4] according as we think
good to cast him ?   29
    Car. 'T were a morris-dance worth the seeing.
    Ast. But the old fox is so crafty, we shall
hardly hunt him out of his den.
    Mat. To that train I ha' given fire already ;
and the hook to draw him hither, is to see certain pieces of lawn, which I told him I have [34
to sell, and indeed have such ; fetch them down,
Pacheco.
    Orl. Yes, sir, I 'm your water-spaniel, and will
fetch any thing — [*Aside.*] but I 'll fetch one
dish of meat anon shall turn your stomach, and
that 's a constable.   *Exit.*   41

Enter BOTS *ushering* Mistress HORSELEECH.

    All. How now ? how now ?
    Car. What galley-foist [5] is this ?
    Lod. Peace, two dishes of stewed prunes,[6] a
bawd and a pander. My worthy lieutenant Bots ;
why, now I see thou 'rt a man of thy word, [46
welcome. — Welcome Mistress Horseleech. —
Pray, gentlemen, salute this reverend matron.
    Mis. H. Thanks to all your worships.   48
    Lod. I bade a drawer send in wine, too : did
none come along with thee, grannam, but the
lieutenant ?
    Mis. H. None came along with me but Bots,
if it like your worship.
    Bots. Who the pox should come along with
you but Bots.   54

Enter two Vintners [*with wine*].

    All. Oh brave ! march fair.
    Lod. Are you come ? That 's well.
    Mat. Here 's ordnance able to sack a city.
    Lod. Come, repeat, read this inventory.   60
    1 Vint. Imprimis, a pottle [7] of Greek wine, a

---

[1] Aim.   [2] A room in Matheo's house.

[3] A frame used for stretching cloth.
[4] In any direction.   [5] A state barge.
[6] A common dish in the brothels of the time.
[7] Two quarts.

pottle of Peter-sameene,[1] a pottle of Char-
neco,[2] and a pottle of Leatica.[3]

Lod. You 're paid ?

2 Vint. Yes, Sir. *Exeunt* Vintners.

Mat. So shall some of us be anon, I fear. 66

Bots. Here 's a hot day towards : but
zounds, this is the life out of which a soldier
sucks sweetness ! When this artillery goes off
roundly, some must drop to the ground : cannon, demi-cannon, saker, and basilisk.[4] 71

Lod. Give fire, lieutenant.

Bots. So, so : must I venture first upon the
breach ? To you all, gallants ; Bots sets upon
you all. [*Drinks.*] 75

All. It 's hard, Bots, if we pepper not you, as
well as you pepper us.

Enter CANDIDO.

Lod. My noble linen-draper !—Some wine ! —
Welcome, old lad !

Mat. You 're welcome, signor. 80

Cand. These lawns, sir ?

Mat. Presently ; my man is gone for them.
We ha' rigged a fleet, you see here, to sail about
the world.

Cand. A dangerous voyage, sailing in such
ships. 86

Bots. There 's no casting over board yet.

Lod. Because you are an old lady, I will have
you be acquainted with this grave citizen. Pray
bestow your lips upon him, and bid him welcome. 91

Mis. H. Any citizen shall be most welcome
to me : — I have used to buy ware at your shop.

Cand. It may be so, good madam. 94

Mis. H. Your prentices know my dealings
well ; I trust your good wife be in good case.
If it please you, bear her a token from my
lips, by word of mouth. [*Kisses him.*]

Cand. I pray, no more ; forsooth, 't is very
well ;
Indeed I love no sweetmeats. —[*Aside.*] Sh'as
a breath 100
Stinks worse than fifty polecats. — Sir, a word,
Is she a lady ?

Lod. A woman of a good house, and an
ancient ; she 's a bawd.

Cand. A bawd ? Sir, I 'll steal hence, and see
your lawns 105
Some other time.

Mat. Steal out of such company ? Pacheco,
my man, is but gone for 'em. Lieutenant Bots,
drink to this worthy old fellow, and teach him
to fly high. 110

All. Swagger ; and make him do 't on his
knees.

Cand. How, Bots ? Now bless me, what do I
with Bots ?
No wine in sooth, no wine, good master Bots. [114

Bots. Gray-beard, goat's pizzle, 't is a health;
have this in your guts, or this, there [*touching
his sword*]. I will sing a bawdy song, sir, be-

cause your verjuice [5] face is melancholy, to
make liquor go down glib. Will you fall on your
marrowbones, and pledge this health ? 'T is to
my mistress, a whore. 121

Cand. Here 's ratsbane upon ratsbane, Master
Bots.
I pray, sir, pardon me : you are a soldier,
Press me not to this service, I am old,
And shoot not in such pot-guns.[6]

Bots. Cap, I 'll teach you. 12r

Cand. To drink healths, is to drink sickness.
— Gentlemen,
Pray rescue me.

Bots. Zounds, who dare ?

All. We shall ha' stabbing then ?

Cand. I ha' reckonings to cast up, good Master Bots. 130

Bots. This will make you cast 'em up better.

Lod. Why does your hand shake so ?

Cand. The palsy, signors, danceth in my blood.

Bots. Pipe with a pox, sir, then, or I 'll make
your blood dance — 135

Cand. Hold, hold, good Master Bolts, I drink.
[*Kneels.*]

All. To whom ?

Cand. To the old countess there. [*Drinks.*]

Mis. H. To me, old boy ? This is he that never
drunk wine ! Once again to 't. 140

Cand. With much ado the poison is got down,
Though I can scarce get up ; never before
Drank a whore's health, nor will never more.

Re-enter ORLANDO *with lawns.*

Mat. Hast been at gallows ?

Orl. Yes, sir, for I make account to suffer to-
day. 145

Mat. Look, signor ; here 's the commodity.

Cand. Your price ?

Mat. Thus.[7]

Cand. No ; too dear : thus. 150

Mat. No. O fie, you must fly higher. Yet
take 'em home, trifles shall not make us quarrel ; we 'll agree ; you shall have them, and a
pennyworth. I 'll fetch money at your shop. 155

Cand. Be it so, good signor, send me going.

Mat. Going ? A deep bowl of wine for Signor
Candido.

Orl. He would be going.

Cand. I 'll rather stay than go so : stop your
bowl.

Enter Constable *and* Billmen.

Lod. How now ? 160

Bots. Is 't Shrove-Tuesday, that these ghosts
walk ? [8]

Mat. What 's your business, sir ?

Const. From the duke : you are the man we
look for, signor. I have warrant here from [165
the duke, to apprehend you upon felony for robbing two pedlars. I charge you i' th' duke's
name, go quickly.

---

[1] A corruption of *Pedro Ximenes;* a sweet Spanish
wine.

[2] A Portuguese wine.

[3] *I. e.* Aleatico, a red Italian muscatel wine.

[4] Kinds of cannon.

[5] An acid liquor made from green fruit.

[6] A play upon " pop-guns."

[7] The price was here probably indicated by display-
ing the fingers. (Rhys.)

[8] On Shrove Tuesday the city authorities made a search
for brothel-keepers.

Mat. Is the wind turn'd ? Well, this is that
old wolf, my father-in-law.—Seek out your
mistress, sirrah.   171
Orl. Yes, Sir.—[*Aside.*] As shafts by piecing
are made strong,
So shall thy life be straight'ned by this wrong.
     Exit.
All. In troth, we are sorry.   174
Mat. Brave men must be crost ; pish, it 's
but Fortune's dice roving[1] against me. Come,
sir, pray use me like a gentleman ; let me not
be carried through the streets like a pageant.
Const. If these gentlemen please, you shall
go along with them.   180
All. Be 't so : come.
Const. What are you, sir ?
Bots. I, sir ? Sometimes a figure, sometimes
a cipher, as the State has occasion to cast up
her accounts. I 'm a soldier.   185
Const. Your name is Bots, is 't not ?
Bots. Bots is my name ; Bots is known to this
company.
Const. I know you are, sir : what 's she ?
Bots. A gentlewoman, my mother.   190
Const. Take 'em both along.
Bots. Me, sir ?
Billmen. [Ay,] sir !
Const. If he swagger, raise the street.   194
Bots. Gentlemen, gentlemen, whither will
you drag us ?
Lod. To the garden house. Bots, are we even
with you ?
Const. To Bridewell with 'em.
Bots. You will answer this.   200
Const. Better than a challenge. I have war-
rant for my work, sir.
Lod. We 'll go before.
Const. Pray do.—
     Exeunt [MATHEO *with* LODOVICO, As-
     TOLFO, CAROLO, BERALDO, *and*
     FONTINELL ; BOTS *and* Mistress
     HORSELEECH, *with* Billmen.]
Who, Signor Candido ? a citizen   205
Of your degree consorted thus, and revelling
In such a house ?
Cand.   Why, sir ? what house, I pray ?
Const. Lewd, and defam'd.
Cand.   Is 't so ? thanks, sir : I 'm gone.
Const. What have you there ?
Cand. Lawns which I bought, sir, of the
gentleman   210
That keeps the house.
Const.   And I have warrant here,
To search for such stol'n ware : these lawns
are stol'n,
Cand. Indeed !
Const. So he 's the thief, you the receiver :   213
I 'm sorry for this chance, I must commit you.
Cand. Me, sir, for what ?
Const.   These goods are found upon you,
And you must answer 't.
Cand.   Must I so ?
Const.   Most certain.
Cand. I 'll send for bail.
Const.   I dare not : yet because

[1] Thrown at random (?)

You are a citizen of worth, you shall not
Be made a pointing stock, but without guard,
Pass only with myself.
Cand.   To Bridewell too ?   220
Const. No remedy.
Cand.   Yes, patience. Being not mad.
They had me once to Bedlam, now I 'm drawn
To Bridewell, loving no whores.
Const.   You will buy lawn ! *Exeunt.*

[ACT V]

[SCENE I.][2]

Enter at one door HIPPOLITO ; *at another,* LOD-
OVICO, ASTOLFO, CAROLO, BERALDO, *and*
FONTINELL.

Lod. Yonder 's the Lord Hippolito ; by any
means leave him and me together. Now will I
turn him to a madman.
All. Save you my lord.
     Exeunt [*all except* HIPPOLITO *and*
     LODOVICO].
Lod. I ha' strange news to tell you.   5
Hip. What are they ?
Lod. Your mare 's i' th' pound.
Hip. How 's this ?
Lod. Your nightingale is in a limebush.
Hip. Ha ?   10
Lod. Your puritanical honest whore sits in a
blue gown.[3]
Hip. Blue gown !
Lod. She 'll chalk out your way to her now :
she beats chalk.[4]   15
Hip. Where ? who dares ? —
Lod. Do you know the brick-house of casti-
gation, by the river side that runs by Milan,—
the school where they pronounce no letter well
but O ?   20
Hip. I know it not.
Lod. Any man that has borne office of con-
stable or any woman that has fallen from a
horse-load to a cart-load,[5] or like an old hen
that has had none but rotten eggs in her nest, [25
can direct you to her : there you shall see your
punk amongst her back-friends.[6]
There you may have her at your will,
For there she beats chalk, or grinds in the mill,
Witn a whip deedle, deedle, deedle, deedle ;   30
Ah, little monkey !
Hip. What rogue durst serve that warrant,
knowing I loved her ?
Lod. Some worshipful rascal, I lay my life.
Hip. I 'll beat the lodgings down about their
ears   35
That are her keepers.
Lod. So you may bring an old house over her
head.
Hip. I 'll to her —
I 'll to her, stood armed fiends to guard the doors.
     Exit.

[2] A street.
[3] Strumpets had to do penance in a blue gown.
[4] Crushing chalk was one of the occupations assigned
to the prisoners.
[5] An allusion to the carting of prostitutes.
[6] Former friends.

Lod. Oh me ! what monsters are men made by
  whores !   40
If this false fire do kindle him, there 's one fag-
  got
More to the bonfire. Now to my Bridewell birds ;
What song will they sing ?   *Exit.*

[SCENE II.] [1]

Enter DUKE, INFELICE, CAROLO, ASTOLFO,
BERALDO, FONTINELL, *and three or four* Masters of Bridewell.

Duke. Your Bridewell ? that the name ? For
  beauty, strength,
Capacity and form of ancient building,
Besides the river's neighbourhood, few houses
Wherein we keep our court can better it.
  1 *Mast.* Hither from foreign courts have
    princes come,   5
And with our duke did acts of State commence.
Here that great cardinal had first audience,
The grave Campayne ; that duke dead, his son
That famous prince, gave free possession
Of this, his palace, to the citizens,   10
To be the poor man's ware-house ; and endow'd
  it
With lands to th' value of seven hundred mark,[2]
With all the bedding and the furniture, once
  proper,
As the lands then were, to an hospital
Belonging to a Duke of Savoy. Thus   15
Fortune can toss the world ; a prince's court
Is thus a prison now.
  Duke.   'T is Fortune's sport:
These changes common are : the wheel of fate
Turns kingdoms up, till they fall desolate.
But how are these seven hundred marks by th'
  year   20
Employ'd in this your work-house ?
  1 *Mast.*   War and peace
Feed both upon those lands : when the iron
  doors
Of war burst open, from this house are sent
Men furnisht in all martial complement.
The moon hath through her bow scarce drawn
  to th' head,   25
Like to twelve silver arrows, all the months,
Since sixteen hundred soldiers went aboard.
Here providence and charity play such parts,
The house is like a very school of arts ;
For when our soldiers, like ships driven from
  sea,   30
With ribs all broken, and with tatter'd sides,
Cast anchor here again, their ragged backs
How often do we cover ! that, like men,
They may be sent to their own homes again.   34
All here are but one swarm of bees, and strive
To bring with wearied thighs honey to the hive.
The sturdy beggar, and the lazy loon,[3]
Gets here hard hands, or lac'd [4] correction.
The vagabond grows staid and learns t' obey,

---

[1] A room in Bridewell.
[2] The allusions here really refer of course to the
London Bridewell. The cardinal, duke, and prince are
Campeius, Henry VIII, and Edward VI ; and the other
details are substantially historical.
[3] Rascal.   [4] By whipping.

The drone is beaten well, and sent away.   40
As other prisons are, some for the thief,
Some, by which undone credit gets relief
From bridled debtors ; others for the poor,
So this is for the bawd, the rogue, the whore.
  Car. An excellent team of horse !
  1 *Mast.*   Nor is it seen   45
That the whip draws blood here, to cool the
  spleen
Of any rugged bencher ; [5] nor does offence
Feel smart on spiteful or rash evidence ;
But pregnant testimony forth must stand,
Ere justice leave them in the beadle's hand.   50
As iron, on the anvil are they laid,
Not to take blows alone, but to be made
And fashion'd to some charitable use.
  Duke. Thus wholsom'st laws spring from the
    worst abuse.

Enter ORLANDO. [*disguised as a* Serving-man,]
before BELLAFRONT.

  Bell. Let mercy touch your heart-strings,
    gracious lord,   55
That it may sound like music in the ear
Of a man desperate, being i' th' hands of law.
  Duke. His name ?
  Bell.   Matheo.
  Duke.   For a robbery ?
Where is he ?
  Bell.   In this house.
          Exeunt BELLAFRONT *and one of
          the* Masters of Bridewell.
  Duke.   Fetch you him hither —
Is this the party ?   60
  Orl. This is the hen, my lord, that the cock
with the lordly comb, your son-in-law, would
crow over, and tread.
  Duke. Are your two servants ready ?
  Orl. My two pedlars are pack'd together, my
good lord.   65
  Duke. 'T is well ; this day in judgment shall
be spent :
Vice, like a wound lanc'd, mends by punishment.
  Inf. Let me be gone, my lord, or stand un-
seen ;
'T is rare when a judge strikes and that none
die,
And 't is unfit then women should be by.   70
  1 *Mast.* We 'll place you, lady, in some pri-
vate room.
  Inf. Pray do so.
          Exit [*with a* Master, *who returns alone*].
  Orl. Thus nice dames swear, it is unfit their
eyes
Should view men carv'd up for anatomies,[6]
Yet they 'll see all, so they may stand unseen ;
Many women sure will sin behind a screen.   76

Enter LODOVICO.

  Lod. Your son, the Lord Hippolito, is ent'red.
  Duke. Tell him we wish his presence. A word,
Sforza ;
On what wings flew he hither ?   79
  Lod. These : — I told him his lark whom he
loved, was a Bridewell-bird ; he 's mad that

---

[5] Tavern loafers.   [6] Subjects for dissection.

this cage should hold her, and is come to let her out.

Duke. 'T is excellent : away, go call him hither.   *Exit* LODOVICO. [85

Re-enter one of the Governors *of the House;* BELLAFRONT *after him with* MATHEO ; *after him the* Constable ; *enter at another door* LODOVICO *and* HIPPOLITO. ORLANDO *steps forth and brings in two [of his* Servants *disguised as]* Pedlars.

Duke. You are to us a stranger, worthy lord ; 'T is strange to see you here.

Hip.   It is most fit That where the sun goes, atomies [1] follow it.

Duke. Atomies neither shape nor honour bear : Be you yourself, a sunbeam to shine clear. — 90 Is this the gentleman? Stand forth and hear Your accusation.

Mat. I 'll hear none ; I fly high in that : rather than kites shall seize upon me, and [94 pick out mine eyes to my face, I 'll strike my talons through mine own heart first, and spit my blood in theirs. I am here for shriving those two fools of their sinful pack. When those jack-daws have caw'd over me, then must I cry [99 guilty, or not guilty. The law has work enough already and therefore I 'll put no work of mine into his hands ; the hangman shall ha 't first. I did pluck those ganders, did rob them.

Duke. 'T is well done to confess.   104

Mat. Confess and be hanged, and then I fly high, is 't not so? That for that ; a gallows is the worst rub [2] that a good bowler can meet with ; I stumbled against such a post, else this night I had play'd the part of a true son in [109 these days, undone my father-in-law ; with him would I ha' run at leap-frog, and come over his gold, though I had broke his neck for 't : but the poor salmon-trout is now in the net.

Hip. And now the law must teach you to fly high.   114

Mat. Right, my lord, and then may you fly low ; no more words : — a mouse, mum, you are stopp'd.

Bell. Be good to my poor husband, dear my lords.

Mat. Ass !   119 Why shouldst thou pray them to be good to me, When no man here is good to one another?

Duke. Did any hand work in this theft but yours?

Mat. O yes, my lord, yes : — the hangman has never one son at a birth, his children al-ways come by couples. Though I cannot give [125 the old dog, my father, a bone to gnaw, the daughter shall be sure of a choke-pear. — Yes, my lord, there was one more that fiddled my fine pedlars, and that was my wife.

Bell. Alas, I?   130

Orl. [*Aside.*] O everlasting, supernatural, su-perlative villain !

All. Your wife, Matheo?

Hip. Sure it cannot be.   134

Mat. Oh, sir, you love no quarters of mutton

---

[1] Atoms.   [2] Obstruction.

that hang up, you love none but whole mutton. She set the robbery, I perform'd it ; she spurr'd me on, I gallop'd away.

Orl. My lords, —

Bell. My lords, — fellow, give me speech, — if my poor life   146 May ransom thine, I yield it to the law. Thou hurt'st thy soul, yet wip'st off no offence, By casting blots upon my innocence. Let not these spare me, but tell truth ; no, see Who slips his neck out of the misery,   145 Though not out of the mischief. let thy servant That shar'd in this base act accuse me here, Why should my husband perish, he go clear?

Orl. [*Aside.*] A good child, hang thine own father !

Duke. Old fellow, was thy hand in too?   150

Orl. My hand was in the pie, my lord, I con-fess it. My mistress, I see, will bring me to the gallows, and so leave me ; but I 'll not leave her so : I had rather hang in a woman's com- [154 pany, than in a man's ; because if we should go to hell together, I should scarce be letten in, for all the devils are afraid to have any women come amongst them. As I am true thief, she neither consented to this felony, nor knew of it.   161

Duke. What fury prompts thee on to kill thy wife?

Mat. It is my humour, sir, 't is a foolish bag-pipe that I make myself merry with. Why should I eat hemp-seed at the hangman's thir-teen-pence halfpenny [3] ordinary, and have this whore laugh at me, as I swing, as I totter? 166

Duke. Is she a whore?

Mat. A six-penny mutton pasty, for any to cut up.

Orl. Ah, toad, toad, toad.   169

Mat. A barber's cittern [4] for every serving-man to play upon ; that lord, your son, knows it.

Hip. I, sir? Am I her bawd then?

Mat. No, sir, but she 's your whore then.

Orl. [*Aside.*] Yea, spider ; dost catch at great flies?

Hip. My whore?   175

Mat. I cannot talk, sir, and tell of your rems and your rees and your whirligigs and devices : but, my lord, I found 'em like sparrows in one nest, billing together, and bulling of me. I took 'em in bed, was ready to kill him, was up [180 to stab her —

Hip. Close thy rank jaws : — pardon me, I am vex'd. — Thou art a villain, a malicious devil ; Deep as the place where thou art lost, thou liest. Since I am thus far got into this storm,   185 I 'll through, and thou shalt see I 'll through untoucht, When thou shalt perish in it.

Re-enter INFELICE.

Inf.   'T is my cue To enter now. — Room ! let my prize [5] be play'd ;

---

[3] The amount of the hangman's fee.
[4] Musical instruments hung in the barbers' shops of the period.   [5] Bout. A term in fencing.

I ha' lurked in clouds, yet heard what all have
said ;
What jury more can prove sh'as wrong'd my
bed,   190
Than her own husband? She must be punished.
I challenge law, my lord ; letters and gold
And jewels from my lord that woman took.
   Hip. Against that black-mouth'd devil,
   against letters and gold,
And against a jealous wife, I do uphold   195
Thus far her reputation ; I could sooner
Shake th' Appenine and crumble rocks to dust
Than, though Jove's shower rain'd down, tempt
her to lust.
   Bell. What shall I say ?
   Orl. (*discovers himself.*) Say thou art not a [200
whore, and that 's more than fifteen women
amongst five hundred dare swear without lying,
this shalt thou say — no, let me say 't for thee ;
— thy husband 's a knave, this lord 's an honest
man ; thou art no punk, this lady 's a right [205
lady. Pacheeo is a thief as his master is, but old
Orlando is as true a man as thy father is. I ha'
seen you fly high, sir, and 1 ha' seen you fly low,
sir, and to keep you from the gallows, sir, a
blue coat have I worn, and a thief did I turn. [210
Mine own men are the pedlars, my twenty
pounds did fly high, sir, your wife's gown did
fly low, sir : whither fly you now, sir ? You ha'
scap'd the gallows, to the devil you fly next, sir.
Am I right, my liege ?   215
   Duke. Your father has the true physician
   play'd.
   Mat. And I am now his patient.
   Hip.   And be so still ;
'T is a good sign when our cheeks blush at ill.
   Const. The linen-draper, Signor Candido,
He whom the city terms the patient man,   220
Is likewise here for buying of those lawns
The pedlars lost.
   Inf.   Alas, good Candido !
   Duke. Fetch him ; and when these payments
   up are cast,   *Exit* Constable.
Weigh out your light gold, but let 's have them
last.

Enter CANDIDO *and* Constable, [*who presently
goes out.*]

   Duke. In Bridewell, Candido ?
   Cand.   Yes, my good lord.   225
   Duke. What make you here ?
   Cand.   My lord, what make you here ?
   Duke. I 'm here to save right, and to drive
   wrong hence.
   Cand. And I to bear wrong here with patience.
   Duke. You ha' bought stol'n goods.
   Cand.   So they do say, my lord,
Yet bought I them upon a gentleman's word,
And I imagine now, as I thought then,   231
That there be thieves, but no thieves, gentlemen.
   Hip. Your credit 's crack'd, being here.
   Cand.   No more than gold,
Being crack'd, which does his estimation hold.
I was in Bedlam once, but was I mad ?   235
They made me pledge whores' healths, but am
   I bad
Because I 'm with bad people ?

   Duke.   Well, stand by ;
If you take wrong, we 'll cure the injury.

Re-enter Constable, *after him* BOTS, *after them
two* Beadles, *one with hemp, the other with a
beetle.*[1]

   Duke. Stay, stay, what 's he ? A prisoner ?
   Const. Yes, my lord.   240
   Hip. He seems a soldier ?
   Bots. I am what I seem, sir, one of fortune's
bastards, a soldier and a gentleman, and am
brought in here with master constable's band of
billmen, because they face me down that I [245
live, like those that keep bowling alleys, by the
sins of the people, in being a squire of the body.
   Hip. Oh, an apple-squire.[2]
   Bots. Yes, sir, that degree of scurvy squires ;
and that I am maintained by the best part [250
that is commonly in a woman, by the worst
players of those parts ; but I am known to all
this company.
   Lod. My lord, 't is true, we all know him ;
't is lieutenant Bots.   255
   Duke. Bots, and where ha' you served, Bots ?
   Bots. In most of your hottest services in the
Low-countries : at the Groyne I was wounded
in this thigh, and halted upon 't, but 't is now
sound. In Cleveland I mist but little, having
the bridge of my nose broken down with [261
two great stones, as I was scaling a fort. I ha'
been tried, sir, too, in Gelderland, and scap'd
hardly there from being blown up at a breach :
I was fired, and lay i' th' surgeon's hands [265
for 't, till the fall of the leaf following.
   Hip. All this may be, and yet you no soldier.
   Bots. No soldier, sir ? I hope these are services that your proudest commanders do venture
upon, and never come off sometimes.   270
   Duke. Well, sir, because you say you are a
   soldier,
I 'll use you like a gentlemen. — Make room
there,
Plant him amongst you ; we shall have anon
Strange hawks fly here before us. If none light
On you, you shall with freedom take your flight ;
But if you prove a bird of baser wing,   276
We 'll use you like such birds, here you shall
sing.
   Bots. I wish to be tried at no other weapon.
   Duke. Why, is he furnisht with those imple-
ments ?
   1 *Master.* The pander is more dangerous to a
   State   280
Than is the common thief ; and though our laws
Lie heavier on the thief, yet that the pander
May know the hangman's ruff should fit him
too,
Therefore he 's set to beat hemp.
   Duke.   This does savour
Of justice ; basest slaves to basest labour. 285
Now pray, set open hell, and let us see
The she-devils that are here.
   Inf.   Methinks this place
Should make e'en Lais honest.
   1 *Mast.*   Some it turns good,

---

1 A heavy mallet.   2 A pander.

But as some men, whose hands are once in blood,
Do in a pride spill more, so, some going hence
Are, by being here, lost in more impudence.   291
Let it not to them, when they come, appear
That any one does as their judge sit here ;
But that as gentlemen you come to see,
And then perhaps their tongues will walk more
    free.   295
Duke. Let them be marshall'd in. — [*Exeunt*
    Masters, Constable, *and* Beadles.] — Be
    cover'd all,
Fellows, now to make the scene more comical.
Car. Will not you be smelt out, Bots ?
Bots. No, your bravest whores have the worst
    noses.

Re-enter two of the Masters ; *a* Constable *after
them, then* DOROTHEA TARGET, *brave* ;[1] *after
her two* Beadles, th' *one with a wheel, the other
with a blue gown.*

Lod. Are not you a bride, forsooth ?   300
Dor. Say ye ?
Car. He would know if these be not your
    bridemen.
Dor. Vuh ! yes, sir : and look ye, do you
see ? the bride-laces that I give at my wedding,
will serve to tie rosemary to both your coffins
when you come from hanging — Scab !   306
Orl. Fie, punk, fie, fie, fie !
Dor. Out, you stale, stinking head of garlic,
foh, at my heels.
Orl. My head 's cloven.   310
Hip. O, let the gentlewoman alone, she 's go-
ing to shrift.
Ast. Nay, to do penance.
Car. Ay, ay, go, punk, go to the cross and be
whipt.   315
Dor. Marry mew, marry muff,[2] marry, hang
you, goodman dog. Whipt ? do ye take me
for a base, spital-whore ? In troth, gentlemen,
you wear the clothes of gentlemen, but you
carry not the minds of gentlemen, to abuse [320
a gentlewoman of my fashion.
Lod. Fashion ? Pox a' your fashions ! Art
not a whore ?
Dor. Goodman slave.
Duke. O fie, abuse her not, let us two talk,
What mought I call your name, pray ?   326
Dor. I 'm not ashamed of my name, sir ; my
name is Mistress Doll Target, a Western gentle-
woman.   329
Lod. Her target against any pike in Milan.
Duke. Why is this wheel borne after her ?
1 Mast. She must spin.
Dor. A coarse thread it shall be, as all threads
are.
Ast. If you spin, then you 'll earn money here
too ?   334
Dor. I had rather get half-a-crown abroad,
than ten crowns here.
Orl. Abroad ? I think so.
Inf. Dost thou not weep now thou art here ?
Dor. Say ye ? weep ? Yes, forsooth, as you [340
did when you lost your maidenhead. Do you
aot hear how I weep ?   *Sings.*

[1] Finely attired.   [2] A term of contempt.

Lod. Farewell, Doll.
Dor. Farewell, dog.   *Exit.*
Duke. Past shame : past penitence ! Why is
that blue gown ?   346
1 Mast. Being stript out of her wanton loose
    attire,
That garment she puts on, base to the eye,
Only to clothe her in humility.
Duke. Are all the rest like this ?
1 Mast.   No, my good lord.
You see, this drab swells with a wanton rein. 350
The next that enters has a different strain.
Duke. Variety is good, let 's see the rest.
                              Exit 1 Master.
Bots. Your grace sees I 'm sound yet, and no
bullets hit me.
Duke. Come off so, and 't is well.
All. Here 's the second mess.   356

Re-enter the two Masters, *after them* Constable,
after him PENELOPE WHOREHOUND, *like a*
Citizen's Wife ; *after her two* Beadles, *one
with a blue gown, another with chalk and a
mallet.*

Pen. I ha' worn many a costly gown, but I
was never thus guarded[3] with blue coats, and
beadles, and constables, and —
Car. Alas, fair mistress, spoil not thus your
    eyes.   360
Pen. Oh, sweet sir, I feel the spoiling of other
places about me that are dearer than my eyes ;
if you be gentlemen, if you be men, or ever came
of a woman, pity my case ! Stand to me, stick
to me, good sir, you are an old man.   365
Orl. Hang not on me, I prithee ; old trees
bear no such fruit.
Pen. Will you bail me, gentlemen ?
Lod. Bail thee ? Art in for debt ?   369
Pen. No ; God is my judge, sir, I am in for no
debts ; I paid my tailor for this gown, the last
five shillings a-week that was behind, yesterday.
Duke. What is your name. I pray ?
Pen. Penelope Whorehound, I come of the
Whorehounds. How does lieutenant Bots ?   375
All. Aha, Bots ?
Bots. A very honest woman, as I 'm a soldier
— a pox Bots ye.
Pen. I was never in this pickle before ; and
yet if I go amongst citizens' wives, they [380
jeer at me ; if I go among the loose-bodied
gowns,[4] they cry a pox on me, because I go civilly attired, and swear their trade was a good
trade, till such as I am took it out of their [384
hands. Good lieutenant Bots, speak to these
captains to bail me.
1 Mast. Begging for bail still ? You are a
trim gossip. Go give her the blue gown, set
her to her chare. Work,[5] huswife, for your
bread, away.   390
Pen. Out, you dog ! — a pox on you all ! —
women are born to curse thee — but I shall live
to see twenty such flat-caps shaking dice for
a penny-worth of pippins. Out, you blue-eyed
rogue !   *Exit.* 395

[3] A play upon the word, which also signifies
"trimmed."
[4] Prostitutes.   [5] Chore, task work.

All. Ha, ha, ha.

Duke. Even now she wept, and pray'd ; now does she curse ?

1 *Mast.* Seeing me ; if still she had stay'd, this had been worse. 400

Hip. Was she ever here before ?

1 *Mast.*   Five times at least, And thus, if men come to her, have her eyes Wrung, and wept out her bail.

All.   Bots, you know her ?

Bots. Is there any gentleman here, that knows not a whore, and is he a hair the worse for that ? 406

Duke. Is she a city-dame ? She 's so attired.

1 *Mast.* No, my good lord, that 's only but the veil To her loose body. I have seen her here In gayer masking suits ; as several sauces 410 Give one dish several tastes, so change of habits In whores is a bewitching art : to-day She 's all in colours to besot gallants, then In modest black, to catch the citizen, And this from their examination 's drawn. 415 Now shall you see a monster both in shape And nature quite from these, that sheds no tear Nor yet is nice, 't is a plain ramping bear ; Many such whales are cast upon this shore. 419

All. Let 's see her.

1 *Mast.*   Then behold a swaggering whore.

Exeunt [Masters *and* Constable].

Orl. Keep your ground, Bots.

Bots. I do but traverse to spy advantage how to arm myself.

Re-enter the two Masters *first ; after them the Constable ; after them a* Beadle *beating a basin,*[1] *then* CATHERINA BOUNTINALL, *with* Mistress HORSELEECH ; *after them another* Beadle *with a blue head guarded*[2] *with yellow.*

Cat. Sirrah, when I cry, hold your hands, hold, you rogue-catcher, hold. — Bawd, are [425 the French chilblains in your heels, that you can come no faster ? Are not you, bawd, a whore's ancient,[3] and must not I follow my colours ?

Mis. H. O Mistress Catherine, you do me wrong to accuse me here as you do, before [430 the right worshipful. I am known for a motherly, honest woman, and no bawd.

Cat. Marry foh, honest ? Burnt[4] at fourteen, seven times whipt, six times carted, nine times duck'd, search'd by some hundred and [435 fifty constables, and yet you are honest ? Honest Mistress Horseleech, is this world a world to keep bawds and whores honest ? How many times hast thou given gentlemen a quart of wine in a gallon pot ? How many twelve-penny fees, nay two shillings fees, nay, when any [441 ambassadors ha' been here, how many half-crown fees hast thou taken ? How many carriers hast thou bribed for country wenches ? How often have I rinst your lungs in *aqua vitae*, and yet you are honest ? 446

Duke. And what were you the whilst ?

Cat. Marry hang you, master slave, who made you an examiner ?

Lod. Well said ! belike this devil spares no man. 451

Cat. What art thou, prithee ?   [*To* BOTS.]

Bots. Nay, what art thou, prithee ?

Cat. A whore, art thou a thief ? 454

Bots. A thief, no, I defy[5] the calling ; I am a soldier, have borne arms in the field, been in many a hot skirmish, yet come off sound.

Cat. Sound, with a pox to ye, ye abominable rogue ! You a soldier ? You in skirmishes ? [459 Where ? Amongst pottle pots in a bawdy-house ? Look, look here, you Madam Worm-eaten, do you not know him ?

Mis. H. Lieutenant Bots, where have ye been this many a day ?

Bots. Old bawd, do not discredit me, seem not to know me. 466

Mis. H. Not to know ye, Master Bots ? As long as I have breath, I cannot forget thy sweet face.

Duke. Why, do you know him ? He says he is a soldier. 471

Cat. He a soldier ? A pander, a dog that will lick up sixpence. Do ye hear, you master swines'-snout, how long is 't since you held the door for me, and cried, " To 't again, no [475 body comes ! " Ye rogue, you ?

All. Ha, ha, ha ! y' are smelt out again, Bots.

Bots. Pox ruin her nose for 't ! An I be not revenged for this — um, ye bitch !

Lod. D' ye hear ye, madam ? Why does your ladyship swagger thus ? You 're very brave, [481 methinks.

Cat. Not at your cost, master cod's-head ; Is any man here blear-eyed to see me brave ?

Ast. Yes, I am, 485 Because good clothes upon a whore's back Is like fair painting upon a rotten wall.

Cat. Marry muff, master whoremaster, you come upon me with sentences.

Ber. By this light, has small sense for 't. 490

Lod. O fie, fie, do not vex her ! And yet methinks a creature of more scurvy conditions should not know what a good petticoat were.

Cat. Marry, come out ; you 're so busy [494 about my petticoat, you 'll creep up to my placket, an ye could but attain the honour : but the outsides offend your rogue-ships, look o' the lining, 't is silk.

Duke. Is 't silk 't is lined with, then ? 499

Cat. Silk ? Ay, silk, master slave, you would be glad to wipe your nose with the skirt on 't. This 't is to come among a company of cod's-heads[6] that know not how to use a gentle-woman.

Duke. Tell her the duke is here. 505

1 *Mast.* Be modest, Kate, the duke is here.

Cat. If the devil were here, I care not. Set forward, ye rogues, and give attendance according to your places ! Let bawds and whores [509 be sad, for I 'll sing an the devil were a-dying.

Exit [*with* Mistress HORSELEECH *and* Beadles].

---

[1] At the carting of bawds and prostitutes they were preceded by a mob beating basins and performing other rough music. (Rhys.)

[2] Head-dress trimmed.   [3] Ensign.   [4] Branded.

[5] Disdain.   [6] Fools.

Duke. Why before her does the basin ring?
1 *Mast.* It is an emblem of their revelling.
The whips we use let forth their wanton blood,
Making them calm; and. more to calm their
    pride,
Instead of coaches they in carts do ride.   515
Will your grace see more of this bad ware?
Duke. No, shut up shop, we'll now break up
    the fair.
Yet ere we part — you, sir, that take upon ye
The name of soldier, that true name of worth,
Which, action, not vain boasting, best sets forth,
To let you know how far a soldier's name   521
Stands from your title, and to let you see
Soldiers must not be wrong'd where princes be;
This be your sentence : —
    All. Defend yourself, Bots.   525
    Duke. First, all the private sufferance that
Inflicts upon offenders, you, as the basest,
Shall undergo it double, after which
You shall be whipt, sir, round about the city,
Then banisht from the land.   530
    Bots. Beseech, your grace!
    Duke. Away with him, see it done. Panders
    and whores
Are city-plagues, which, being kept alive,
Nothing that looks like goodness ere can thrive.
Now good Orlando, what say you to your bad
    son-in-law?   535
    Orl. Marry this, my lord, he is my son-in-law,
and in law will I be his father: for if law can
pepper him, he shall be so parboil'd, that he
shall stink no more i' th' nose of the commonwealth.   540
    Bell. Be yet more kind and merciful, good
father.
    Orl. Dost thou beg for him, thou precious
man's meat, thou? Has he not beaten thee,

kickt thee, trod on thee, and dost thou fawn [544
on him like his spaniel? Has he not pawn'd thee
to thy petticoat, sold thee to thy smock, made
ye leap at a crust, yet wouldst have me save
him?
    Bell. Oh yes, good sir, women shall learn of me,
To love their husbands in greatest misery;   550
Then show him pity, or you wrack myself.
    [*Orl.*] Have ye eaten pigeons, that you're
so kindhearted to your mate? Nay, you're a
couple of wild bears, I'll have ye both baited
at one stake: but as for this knave, the gal- [555
lows is thy due, and the gallows thou shalt have.
I'll have justice of the duke, the law shall have
thy life. — What, dost thou hold him? Let go
his hand. If thou dost not forsake him, a [559
father's everlasting blessing fall upon both
your heads! Away, go, kiss out of my sight,
play thou the whore no more, nor thou the thief
again; my house shall be thine, my meat shall
be thine, and so shall my wine, but my money
shall be mine, and yet when I die, so thou dost
not fly high, take all;   566
Yet, good Matheo, mend.
Thus for joy weeps Orlando, and doth end.
    Duke. Then hear, Matheo : all your woes are
    stayed
By your good father-in-law: all your ills   570
Are clear purg'd from you by his working
    pills. —
Come, Signor Candido, these green young wits,
We see by circumstance, this plot have laid
Still to provoke thy patience, which they find
A wall of brass; no armour's like the mind. 575
Thou hast taught the city patience, now our
    court
Shall be thy sphere, where from thy good report,
Rumours this truth unto the world shall sing,
A patient man's a pattern for a king. *Exeunt.*

THE MALCONTENT

BY

JOHN MARSTON

BENIAMINO JONSONIO, POETAE ELEGANTISSIMO, GRAVISSIMO, AMICO SVO, CANDIDO ET CORDATO, IOHANNES MARSTON, MVSARVM ALVMNVS, ASPERAM HANC SVAM THALIAM D.D.

[Members of the Company of His Majesty's Servants appearing in the INDUCTION

W. SLY.	D. BURBADGE.	J. LOWIN.
SINKLO.	H. CONDELL.	A Tire-man.]

DRAMATIS PERSONAE

GIOVANNI ALTOFRONTO, disguised as MALEVOLE, sometime Duke of Genoa.
PIETRO JACOMO, Duke of Genoa.
MENDOZA, a minion to the Duchess of Pietro Jacomo.
CELSO, a friend to Altofronto.
BILIOSO, an old choleric marshal.
PREPASSO, a gentleman-usher.
FERNEZE, a young courtier, and enamoured on the Duchess.
FERRARDO, a minion to Duke Pietro Jacomo.

EQUATO, } two courtiers.
GUERRINO, }
PASSARELLO, fool to Biliosa.

AURELIA, Duchess to Duke Pietro Jacomo.
MARIA, Duchess to Duke Altofronto.
EMILIA, } two ladies attending on Aurelia.
BIANCA, }
MAQUERELLE, an old panderess.

[THE SCENE. — *Genoa.*]

TO THE READER

I AM an ill orator; and, in truth, use to indite more honestly than eloquently, for it is my custom to speak as I think, and write as I speak.

In plainness, therefore, understand that in some things I have willingly erred, as in supposing a Duke of Genoa, and in taking names different from that city's families: for which some may wittily accuse me: but my defence shall be as honest as many reproofs unto me have been most malicious; since, I heartily protest, it was my care to write so far from reasonable offence, that even strangers, in whose state I laid my scene, should not from thence draw any disgrace to any, dead or living. Yet, in despite of my endeavours, I understand some have been most unadvisedly over-cunning in misinterpreting me, and with subtlety as deep as hell have maliciously spread ill rumours, which, springing from themselves, might to themselves have heavily returned. Surely I desire to satisfy every firm spirit, who, in all his actions, proposeth to himself no more ends than God and virtue do, whose intentions are always simple: to such I protest that, with my free understanding, I have not glanced at disgrace of any, but of those whose unquiet studies labour innovation, contempt of holy policy, reverend, comely superiority, and establisht unity: for the rest of my supposed tartness, I fear not but unto every worthy mind it will be approved so general and honest as may modestly pass with the freedom of a satire. I would fain leave the paper; only one thing afflicts me, to think that scenes, invented merely to be spoken, should be enforcively published to be read, and that the least hurt I can receive is to do myself the wrong. But, since others otherwise would do me more, the least inconvenience is to be accepted. I have myself, therefore, set forth this comedy; but so, that my enforced absence must much rely upon the printer's discretion: but I shall entreat slight errors in orthography may be as slightly overpassed, and that the unhandsome shape which this trifle in reading presents, may be pardoned for the pleasure it once afforded you when it was presented with the soul of lively action.

Sine aliqua dementia nullus Phoebus. [1]

[1] Some copies of Q₁ read *Me mea sequentur fata.*

[THE INDUCTION[1]

TO

THE MALCONTENT, AND THE ADDITIONS[2] ACTED BY THE KING'S MAJESTY'S SERVANTS.

WRITTEN BY JOHN WEBSTER

Enter W. SLY, *a* Tire-man *following him with a stool.*

Tire-man. Sir, the gentlemen will be angry if you sit here.

Sly. Why, we may sit upon the stage at the private house. Thou dost not take me for a country gentleman, dost? Dost think I fear [5 hissing? I'll hold my life thou tookest me for one of the players.

Tire-man. No, sir.

Sly. By God's slid,[3] if you had, I would have given you but sixpence for your stool. Let [10 them that have stale suits sit in the galleries. Hiss at me! He that will be laught out of a tavern or an ordinary, shall seldom feed well, or be drunk in good company. — Where's Harry Condell, Dick Burbadge, and William Sly? [15 Let me speak with some of them.

Tire-man. An't please you to go in, sir, you may.

Sly. I tell you, no: I am one that hath seen this play often, and can give them intelli- [20 gence for their action. I have most of the jests here in my table-book.[4]

Enter SINKLO.

Sinklo. Save you coz!

Sly. O, cousin, come, you shall sit between my legs here.   25

Sinklo. No, indeed, cousin: the audience then will take me for a viol-de-gambo, and think that you play upon me.

Sly. Nay, rather that I work upon you, coz.

Sinklo. We stayed for you at supper last [30 night at my cousin Honeymoon's, the woollen-draper. After supper we drew cuts for a score of apricocks, the longest cut still to draw an apricock: by this light, 't was Mistress Frank Honeymoon's fortune still to have the long- [35 est cut: I did measure for the women. — What be these, coz?

Enter D. BURBADGE, H. CONDELL, *and* J. LOWIN.

Sly. The players. — God save you!

Burbadge. You are very welcome.

Sly. I pray you, know this gentleman, my [40 cousin; 't is Master Doomsday's son, the usurer.

Condell. I beseech you, sir, be cover'd.

Sly. No, in good faith, for mine ease. Look

you, my hat's the handle to this fan. God's [45 so, what a beast was I. I did not leave my feather at home! Well, but I'll take an order with you. *Puts his feather in his pocket.*

Burbadge. Why do you conceal your feather, sir?   50

Sly. Why, do you think I'll have jests broken upon me in the play, to be laught at? This play hath beaten all your gallants out of the feathers. Blackfriars hath almost spoiled Blackfriars for feathers.[5]   55

Sinklo. God's so, I thought 't was for some-what our gentlewomen at home counsell'd me to wear my feather to the play: yet I am loth to spoil it.

Sly. Why, coz?   60

Sinklo. Because I got it in the tilt-yard; there was a herald broke my pate for taking it up: but I have worn it up and down the Strand, and met him forty times since, and yet he dares not challenge it.   65

Sly. Do you hear, sir? this play is a bitter play.

Condell. Why, sir, 't is neither satire nor moral, but the mean passage of a history: yet there are a sort of discontented creatures that [70 bear a stingless envy to great ones, and these will wrest the doings of any man to their base, malicious applyment;[6] but should their interpretation come to the test, like your marmoset, they presently turn their teeth to their tail [75 and eat it.

Sly. I will not go so far with you; but I say, any man that hath wit may censure,[7] if he sit in the twelve-penny room;[8] and I say again, the play is bitter.   80

Burbadge. Sir, you are like a patron that, presenting a poor scholar to a benefice, enjoins him not to rail against anything that stands within compass of his patron's folly. Why should not we enjoy the ancient freedom of poesy? [85 Shall we protest to the ladies that their painting makes them angels? or to my young gallant that his expense in the brothel shall gain him reputation? No, sir, such vices as stand not accountable to law should be cured as [90 men heal tetters,[9] by casting ink upon them. Would you be satisfied in anything else, sir?

---

[5] The meaning is that in *The Malcontent*, which had been originally acted in Blackfriars Theatre, the practice of wearing feathers had been so ridiculed that the feather-makers of Blackfriars had suffered injury in their business. See V. iv. (Bullen.)

[6] Application.   [8] Box.
[7] Judge.   [9] Scabs.

---

[1] The induction appears first in Q$_2$.
[2] The Additions are enclosed in brackets throughout.
[3] Corruption of (eye-)lid.   [4] Note-book.

Sly. Ay, marry, would I: I would know how you came by this play?

Condell. Faith, sir, the book was lost; and [95 because 't was pity so good a play should be lost, we found it, and play it.

Sly. I wonder you would play it, another company having interest in it.

Condell. Why not Malevole in folio with [100 us, as Jeronimo in decimo-sexto with them? [1] They taught us a name for our play; we call it *One For Another.*

Sly. What are your additions?

Burbadge. Sooth, not greatly needful; only [105 as your salad to your great feast, to entertain a little more time, and to abridge the not-received custom of music in our theatre. I must leave you, sir.   *Exit.*

Sinklo. Doth he play the Malcontent?   110

Condell. Yes, sir.

Sinklo. I durst lay four of mine ears the play is not so well acted as it hath been.

Condell. O, no, sir, nothing *ad Parmenonis suem.*[2]   115

Lowin. Have you lost your ears, sir, that you are so prodigal of laying them?

Sinklo. Why did you ask that, friend?

Lowin. Marry, sir, because I have heard of a fellow would offer to lay a hundred-pound [120 wager, that was not worth five baubees:[3] and in this kind you might venture four of your elbows; yet God defend[4] your coat should have so many!

Sinklo. Nay, truly, I am no great censu-[125 rer;[5] and yet I might have been one of the college of critics once. My cousin here hath an excellent memory, indeed, sir.

Sly. Who? I? I'll tell you a strange thing of myself; and I can tell you, for one that [130 never studied the art of memory, 'tis very strange too.

Condell. What's that, sir?

Sly. Why, I'll lay a hundred pound, I'll walk but once down by the Goldsmith's [135 Row in Cheap, take notice of the signs, and tell you them with a breath instantly.

Lowin. 'T is very strange.

Sly. They begin the world did, with Adam and Eve. There's in all just five and fifty. [140 I do use to meditate much when I come to plays too. What do you think might come into a man's head now, seeing all this company?

[1] *I. e.* Why should not the King's company of grown up (folio) actors play *The Malcontent* (which was the property of the children's company playing at Blackfriars), since the children (16mo actors) have appropriated *The Spanish Tragedy*, in which the King's company had rights?

[2] "'T is reported that Parmeno, being very famous for imitating the grunting of a pig, some endeavoured to rival and outdo him. And when the hearers, being prejudiced, cried out, ' Very well, indeed, but nothing comparable to Parmeno's sow,' one took a pig under his arm and came upon the stage; and when, tho' they heard the very pig, they still continued, ' This is nothing comparable to Parmeno's sow,' he threw the pig among them to show them that they judged according to opinion and not truth." (Plutarch's *Symposium*, V. I., cited by " L. S." and Bullen.)

[3] Halfpennies.   [4] Forbid.   [5] Judge.

Condell. I know not, sir.

Sly. I have an excellent thought. If some [145 fifty of the Grecians that were cramm'd in the horse' belly had eaten garlic, do you not think the Trojans might have smelt out their knavery?

Condell. Very likely.

Sly. By God, I would [they] had, for I [150 love Hector horribly.

Sinklo. O, but, coz, coz!

" Great Alexander, when he came to the tomb of Achilles,

Spake with a big loud voice, O thou thrice blessed and happy!"[6]

Sly. Alexander was an ass to speak so well [155 of a filthy cullion.[7]

Lowin. Good sir, will you leave the stage? I'll help you to a private room.

Sly. Come, coz, let's take some tobacco. — Have you never a prologue?   160

Lowin. Not any, sir.

Sly. Let me see, I will make one extempore.
        *Come to them, and fencing of a con-
        gee*[8] *with arms and legs, be round
        with them.*

Gentlemen, I could wish for the women's sakes you had all soft cushions; and gentlewomen, I could wish that for the men's sakes you [165 had all more easy standings.

What would they wish more but the play now? and that they shall have instantly.
                                          [*Exeunt.*]]

ACT I[9]

SCENE I.[10]

The vilest out-of-tune music being heard, enter BILIOSO *and* PREPASSO.

Bil. Why, how now! Are ye mad, or drunk, or both, or what?

Pre. Are ye building Babylon there?

Bil. Here's a noise in court? You think you are in a tavern, do you not?   5

Pre. You think you are in a brothel-house, do you not? — This room is ill-scented.

Enter One with a perfume.

So, perfume, perfume: some upon me, I pray thee.

The duke is upon instant entrance; so, make place there!

SCENE II.[11]

Enter the DUKE PIETRO, FERRARDO, COUNT EQUATO, COUNT CELSO *before, and* GUERRINO.

Pietro. Where breathes that music?

Bil. The discord rather than the music is heard from the malcontent Malevole's chamber.

Fer. [*calling.*] Malevole!

Mal. (*out of his chamber.*) Yaugh, god-a-[5

[6] Petrarch's 153rd Sonnet, trans. by John Harvey.
[7] Rascal.   [8] Salute.
[9] In the margin of the Qq. here: *Vexat censura columbas.*
[10] Palace of the Duke of Genoa.   [11] The same.

man, what dost thou there? Duke's Gany-
mede, Juno's jealous of thy long stockings.
Shadow of a woman, what wouldst, weasel?
Thou lamb o' court, what dost thou bleat for?
Ah, you smooth chinn'd catamite![1]   10

Pietro. Come down, thou rugged[2] cur, and
snarl here; I give thy dogged sullenness free
liberty; trot about and bespurtle[3] whom thou
pleasest.

Mal. I'll come among you, you goat- [15
ish-blooded toderers,[4] as gum into taffeta, to
fret, to fret. I'll fall like a sponge into water,
to suck up, to suck up. Howl again;[5] I'll go
to church and come to you.   [*Exit above.*]

Pietro. This Malevole is one of the most [20
prodigious affections that ever converst with
nature: a man, or rather a monster, more discontent than Lucifer when he was thrust out of
the presence. His appetite is insatiable as the
grave; as far from any content as from [25
heaven. His highest delight is to procure
others vexation, and therein he thinks he truly
serves heaven; for 't is his position, whosoever
in this earth can be contented is a slave and
damned; therefore does he afflict all in [30
that to which they are most affected.[6] The
elements struggle within him; his own soul is
at variance [within herself];[7] his speech is hal-
ter-worthy at all hours. I like him, faith: he
gives good intelligence to my spirit, makes [35
me understand those weaknesses which others'
flattery palliates. Hark! they sing.

SCENE III.[8]

A Song.

Enter MALEVOLE *after the song.*

[*Pietro.*] See, he comes. Now shall you hear
the extremity of a malcontent: he is as free as
air; he blows over every man. — And, sir,
whence come you now?   4

Mal. From the public place of much dissimulation, [the church.][9]

Pietro. What didst there?

Mal. Talk with a usurer; take up at interest.   9

Pietro. I wonder what religion thou art
[of]?[9]

Mal. Of a soldier's religion.

Pietro. And what dost thou think makes
most infidels now?   14

Mal. Sects, sects. I have seen seeming Piety
change her robe so oft, that sure none but some
arch-devil can shape her a new petticoat.

Pietro. O, a religious policy.

Mal. But, damnation on a politic religion!
I am weary: would I were one of the duke's
hounds now!   21

Pietro. But what's the common news abroad,
Malevole? Thou dogg'st rumour still.

Mal. Common news? Why, common words
are, "God save ye," "Fare ye well;" common [25
actions, flattery and cozenage; common things,
women and cuckolds. — And how does my little
Ferrard? Ah, ye lecherous animal! — my little
ferret, he goes sucking up and down the palace into every hen's nest, like a weasel: — [30
and to what dost thou addict thy time to now
more than to those antique painted drabs that
are still affected of[10] young courtiers, Flattery,
Pride, and Venery?   34

Fer. I study languages. Who dost think to
be the best linguist of our age?

Mal. Phew! the devil: let him possess thee;
he'll teach thee to speak all languages most
readily and strangely; and great reason, marry,
he's travel'd greatly i' the world, and is everywhere.   4:

Fer. Save i' th' court.

Mal. Ay, save i' th' court. — (*To* BILIOSO.)
And how does my old muckhill, overspread
with fresh snow? Thou half a man, half a [45
goat, all a beast! how does thy young wife, old
huddle?

Bil. Out, you improvident rascal!

Mal. Do, kick thou hugely-horn'd old duke's
ox, good Master Make-pleas.   50

Pietro. How dost thou live nowadays, Malevole?

Mal. Why, like the knight, Sir Patrick Pen-
lolians, with killing o' spiders for my lady's
monkey.   55

Pietro. How dost spend the night? I hear
thou never sleep'st.

Mal. O, no; but dream the most fantastical!
O heaven! O fubbery, fubbery![11]

Pietro. Dream! What dream'st thou?   60

Mal. Why, methinks I see that signior pawn
his footcloth,[12] that metreza[13] her plate: this
madam takes physic that t' other monsieur may
minister to her: here is a pander jewel'd;
there a fellow in shift of satin this day, that [65
could not shift a shirt t' other night: here
a Paris supports that Helen; there's a Lady
Guinever bears up that Sir Lancelot. Dreams,
dreams, visions, fantasies, chimeras, imaginations, tricks, conceits! — (*To* PREPASSO.) Sir [70
Tristram, Trimtram, come aloft, Jack-an-apes,[14]
with a whim-wham: here's a knight of the
land of Catito shall play at trap[15] with any page
in Europe; do the sword-dance with any morris-
dancer in Christendom; ride at the ring till [75
the fin[16] of his eyes look as blue as the welkin;
and run the wildgoose-chase even with Pompey the Huge.

Pietro. You run!   79

Mal. To the devil. Now, signior Guerrino,
that thou from a most pitied prisoner shouldst
grow a most loath'd flatterer! — Alas, poor
Celso, thy star's opprest: thou art an honest
lord: 't is pity.

---

[1] Male prostitute.   [2] Q₂ *ragged.*   [3] Bespatter.
[4] Nares suggests "dealers in wool or mutton," *i. e.*
mutton-mongers, lascivious fellows.
[5] Bullen prints *Howls again* as a stage direction.
[6] Which they care most for.
[7] Q₁ omits.   [8] The same.   [9] Q₁ omits.

[10] Liked by.   [12] Housings of his horse.
[11] Deceit.   [13] Ital., mistress.
[14] The ape-leader's call to his monkey.
[15] A game played with a ball, a bat, and a wooden
trap.
[16] Lid.

Equato. Is 't pity?   85

Mal. Ay, marry is 't, philosophical Equato;
and 't is pity that thou, being so excellent a
scholar by art, should be so ridiculous a fool
by nature. — I have a thing to tell you, duke:
bid 'em avaunt, bid 'em avaunt.   90

Pietro. Leave us, leave us.

        Exeunt all saving PIETRO *and*
        MALEVOLE.

Now, sir, what is 't?

Mal. Duke, thou art a becco,[1] a cornuto.[2]

Pietro. How!

Mal. Thou art a cuckold.   95

Pietro. Speak, unshale[3] him quick.

Mal. With most tumbler-like nimbleness.

Pietro. Who? By whom? I burst with de-
sire.   99

Mal. Mendoza is the man makes thee a
horn'd beast; duke, 't is Mendoza cornutes
thee.

Pietro. What conformance?[4] Relate; short,
short.

Mal. As a lawyer's beard.   105
There is an old crone in the court, her name is
    Maquerelle,
She is my mistress, sooth to say, and she doth
    ever tell me.
Blirt[5] o' rhyme, blirt o' rhyme! Maquerelle is
a cunning bawd; I am an honest villain; thy
wife is a close drab;[6] and thou art a notorious
cuckold. Farewell, duke.   111

Pietro. Stay, stay.

Mal. Dull, dull duke, can lazy patience make
lame revenge? O God, for a woman to make a
man that which God never created, never
made?   116

Pietro. What did God never make?

Mal. A cuckold: to be made a thing that 's
hoodwinkt with kindness, whilst every rascal
fillips his brows; to have a coxcomb with [120
egregious horns pinn'd to a lord's back, every
page sporting himself with delightful laughter,
whilst he must be the last must know it. Pistols and poniards! pistols and poniards!

Pietro. Death and damnation!   125

Mal. Lightning and thunder!

Pietro. Vengeance and torture!

Mal. Catso![7]

Pietro. O, revenge!

Mal. [8Nay, to select among ten thousand
    fairs   130
A lady far inferior to the most,
In fair proportion both of limb and soul;
To take her from austerer check of parents,
To make her his by most devoutful rites,
Make her commandress of a better essence   135
Than is the gorgeous world, even of a man;
To hug her with as rais'd an appetite
As usurers do their delv'd-up treasury
(Thinking none tells[9] it but his private self);
To meet her spirit in a nimble kiss,   140
Distilling panting ardour to her heart;

True to her sheets, nay, diets strong his blood,
To give her height of hymeneal sweets, —

Pietro. O God!

Mal. Whilst she lisps, and gives him some
    court-*quelquechose*,   145
Made only to provoke, not satiate:
And yet, even then, the thaw of her delight
Flows from lewd heat of apprehension,
Only from strange imagination's rankness,
That forms the adulterer's presence in her
    soul,   150
And makes her think she clips the foul knave's
    loins.

Pietro. Affliction to my blood's root!

Mal. Nay, think, but think what may proceed of this; adultery is often the mother of
incest.   155

Pietro. Incest!

Mal. Yes, incest: mark: — Mendoza of his
wife begets perchance a daughter: Mendoza
dies, his son marries this daughter: say you?
nay, 't is frequent, not only probable, but no [160
question often acted, whilst ignorance, fearless
ignorance, clasps his own seed.

Pietro. Hideous imagination!

Mal. Adultery! Why, next to the sin of
simony, 't is the most horrid transgression under the cope of salvation.[10]   166

Pietro. Next to simony!

Mal. Ay, next to simony, in which our men
in next age shall not sin.

Pietro. Not sin! why?   170

Mal. Because (thanks to some churchmen)
our age will leave them nothing to sin with.
But adultery, O dulness! should show[11] exemplary punishment, that intemperate bloods may
freeze but to think it.] I would damn him [175
and all his generation: my own hands should
do it; ha, I would not trust heaven with my
vengeance anything.

Pietro. Anything, anything, Malevole: thou
shalt see instantly what temper my spirit [180
holds. Farewell; remember I forget thee not;
farewell.   *Exit* PIETRO.

    [12*Mal.* Farewell.
Lean thoughtfulness, a sallow meditation,
Suck thy veins dry! Distemperance rob thy
    sleep!   185
The heart's disquiet is revenge most deep:
He that gets blood, the life of flesh but spills,
But he that breaks heart's peace, the dear soul
    kills.
Well, this disguise doth yet afford me that
Which kings do seldom hear, or great men
    use, —   190
Free speech: and though my state 's usurpt,
Yet this affected strain gives me a tongue
As fetterless as is an emperor's.
I may speak foolishly, ay, knavishly,   194
Always carelessly, yet no one thinks it fashion
To poise[13] my breath; for he that laughs and
strikes

---

[1] Ital., cuckold.
[2] A horned one.
[3] Unshell.
[4] Corroboration.
[5] Outburst.
[6] Secret harlot.
[7] Exclamation of contempt.
[8] Q₁ omits these forty-five lines.
[9] Counts.

[10] Under heaven (?) In spite of which a man can
purchase salvation (?)
[11] Q₂ reads *shue, should.*
[12] Q₁ omits the rest of this scene.
[13] Weigh seriously.

Is lightly felt, or seldom struck again.
Duke, I'll torment thee now : my just revenge
From thee than crown a richer gem shall part:
Beneath God, naught's so dear as a calm
    heart.]   200

SCENE IV.[1]

Enter CELSO.

Celso. My honour'd lord, —
Mal. Peace, speak low, peace ! O Celso, con-
    stant lord,
(Thou to whose faith I only rest discovered,
Thou, one of full ten millions of men,
That lovest virtue only for itself ;   5
Thou in whose hands old Ops[2] may put her
    soul)
Behold forever-banisht Altofront,
This Genoa's last year's duke. O truly noble !
I wanted those old instruments of state,
Dissemblance and suspect : I could not time it,
    Celso ;   10
My throne stood like a point in midst of a
    circle,
To all of equal nearness ; bore with none ;
Rein'd all alike ; so slept in fearless virtue,
Suspectless, too suspectless ; till the crowd,
(Still likerous of[3] untried novelties)   15
Impatient with severer government,
Made strong with Florence, banisht Alto-
    front.
Celso. Strong with Florence ! ay, thence your
    mischief rose ;
For when the daughter of the Florentine
Was match'd once with this Pietro, now duke,
No stratagem of state untri'd was left,   21
Till you of all —
    Mal.   Of all was quite bereft :
Alas, Maria too, close prisoned,
My true faith'd duchess, i' the citadel !   24
    Celso. I'll still adhere: let's mutiny and die.
    Mal. O, no, climb not a falling tower, Celso ;
'T is well held desperation, no zeal,
Hopeless to strive with fate. Peace ! Tem-
    porize !
Hope, hope, that never forsak'st the wretched'st
    man,   29
Yet bidd'st me live, and lurk in this disguise !
What, play I well the free-breath'd discontent?
Why,[4] man, we are all philosophical mon-
    archs
Or natural fools. Celso, the court's a-fire ;
The duchess' sheets will smoke for't ere't be
    long :
Impure Mendoza, that sharp-nos'd lord, that
    made   35
The cursed match that linkt Genoa with Flo-
    rence,
Now broad-horns the duke, which he now
    knows.
Discord to malcontents is very manna :
When the ranks are burst, then scuffle, Alto-
    front.
    Celso. Ay, but durst, —   40

---

[1] The same.   [2] The goddess of plenty.
[3] Having an appetite for.
[4] Qq print the rest of this speech as prose, perhaps
rightly.

Mal. 'T is gone; 't is swallowed like a min-
    eral :
Some say 't will work ; pheut, I'll not shrink :
He's resolute who can no lower sink :

[[5] BILIOSO *entering,* MALEVOLE *shifteth his
speech.*

O the father of May-poles ! did you never see a
fellow whose strength consisted in his breath, [45
respect in his office, religion in his lord, and love
in himself, why, then, behold !
    Bil. Signior, —
    Mal. My right worshipful lord, your court
night-cap makes you have a passing high forehead.   51
    Bil. I can tell you strange news, but I am
sure you know them already: the duke speaks
much good of you.
    Mal. Go to, then: and shall you and I now
enter into a strict friendship ?   56
    Bil. Second one another ?
    Mal. Yes.
    Bil. Do one another good offices ?   59
    Mal. Just : what though I call'd thee old ox,
egregious wittol, broken-bellied coward, rotten
mummy ? yet, since I am in favour —
    Bil. Words of course, terms of disport. His
grace presents you by me a chain, as his grateful remembrance for — I am ignorant for [65
what ; marry, ye may impart: yet howsoever —
come — dear friend ; dost know my son ?
    Mal. Your son !
    Bil. He shall eat wood-cocks, dance jigs.
make possets, and play at shuttle-cock with [70
any young lord about the court: he has as sweet
a lady, too ; dost know her little bitch ?
    Mal. 'T is a dog, man.
    Bil. Believe me, a she-bitch. O, 't is a good
creature ! thou shalt be her servant. I'll [75
make thee acquainted with my young wife too :
what ! I keep her not at court for nothing. 'T is
grown to supper-time ; come to my table : that,
anything I have, stands open to thee.
    Mal. (*Aside to* CELSO.) How smooth to him
that is in state of grace,   80
How servile is the rugged'st courtier's face !
What profit, nay, what nature would keep down,
Are heav'd to them as minions to a crown.
Envious ambition never sates his thirst,
Till, sucking all, he swells and swells, and
    bursts.   85
    Bil. I shall now leave you with my always-
best wishes ; only let's hold betwixt us a
firm correspondence, a mutual friendly-recipro-
cal kind of a steady-unanimous-heartily-
leagued ——   90
    Mal. Did your signorship ne'er see a pigeon-
house that was smooth, round, and white without, and full of holes and stink within ? Ha' ye
not, old courtier ?   94
    Bil. O, yes, 't is the form, the fashion of
them all.
    Mal. Adieu, my true court-friend ; farewell,
my dear Castilio.[6]   *Exit* BILIOSO.]

---

[5] Q₁ omits ll. 44–98.
[6] An allusion to Castiglione, author of *The Courtier*

Celso. Yonder 's Mendoza.

Descries MENDOZA.

Mal.　　　　　　　　True, the privy-key. 99
Celso. I take my leave, sweet lord.
Mal.　　　　　　　'T is fit; away! *Exit* CELSO.

SCENE V.[1]

Enter MENDOZA *with three or four* Suitors.

Men. Leave your suits with me; I can and
will. Attend my secretary; leave me.
　　　　　　　　　　　　[*Exeunt* Suitors.]
Mal. Mendoza, hark ye, hark ye. You are a
treacherous villain: God b' wi' ye!
Men. Out, you base-born rascal! 　　　　5
Mal. We are all the sons of heaven, though
a tripe-wife were our mother: ah, you whore-
son, hot-rein'd he-marmoset! Aegisthus! didst
ever hear of one Aegisthus?
Men. Gisthus? 　　　　　　　　　　10
Mal. Ay, Aegisthus: he was a filthy incon-
tinent flesh-monger, such a one as thou art.
Men. Out, grumbling rogue!
Mal. Orestes, beware Orestes!
Men. Out, beggar! 　　　　　　　　15
Mal. I once shall rise!
Men. Thou rise!
Mal. At the resurrection.
No vulgar seed but once may rise and shall;
No king so huge but 'fore he die may fall. 　20
　　　　　　　　　　　　　　　Exit.
Men. Now, good Elysium! what a delicious
heaven is it for a man to be in a prince's fa-
vour! O sweet God! O pleasure! O fortune!
O all thou best of life! What should I think,
what say, what do to be a favourite, a minion? [25
to have a general timorous respect observe[2] a
man, a stateful silence in his presence, solitariness in his absence, a confused hum and busy
murmur of obsequious suitors training[3] him;
the cloth held up, and way proclaim'd be- [30
fore him; petitionary vassels licking the pavement with their slavish knees, whilst some
odd palace-lampreels[4] that engender with
snakes, and are full of eyes on both sides, with
a kind of insinuating humbleness, fix all [35
their delights upon his brow. O blessed state!
what a ravishing prospect doth the Olympus of
favour yield! Death, I cornute the duke!
Sweet women! most sweet ladies! nay, angels!
by heaven, he is more accursed than a devil [40
that hates you, or is hated by you; and happier
than a god that loves you, or is beloved by
you. You preservers of mankind, life-blood of
society, who would live, nay, who can live without you? O paradise! how majestical is your [45
austerer presence! how imperiously chaste is
your more modest face! but, O, how full of
ravishing attraction is your pretty, petulant,
languishing, lasciviously-composed countenance! these amorous smiles, those soul- [50
warming sparkling glances, ardent as those
flames that singed the world by heedless Phaeton! in body how delicate, in soul how witty, in

discourse how pregnant, in life how wary, in favours how judicious, in day how sociable, and [55
in night how — O pleasure unutterable! indeed, it is most certain, one man cannot deserve
only to enjoy a beauteous woman: but a
duchess! In despite of Phoebus, I 'll write a
sonnet instantly in praise of her. 　*Exit.* [60

SCENE VI.[5]

Enter FERNEZE *ushering* AURELIA, EMILIA *and*
MAQUERELLE *bearing up her train,* BIANCA
attending; then exeunt EMILIA *and* BIANCA.

Aurel. And is 't possible? Mendoza slight
me! Possible?
Fer. Possible!
What can be strange in him that 's drunk with
　　favour,
Grows insolent with grace? — Speak, Maquer-
　　elle, speak. 　　　　　　　　　5
Maq. To speak feelingly, more, more richly
in solid sense than worthless words, give me
those jewels of your ears to receive my enforced
duty. As for my part, 't is well known I can
put up anything (FERNEZE *privately feeds* MA- [10
QUERELLE'*s hands with jewels during this speech*);
can bear patiently with any man: but when I
heard he wronged your precious sweetness, I
was enforced to take deep offence. 'T is most
certain he loves Emilia with high appetite: [15
and, as she told me (as you know we women
impart our secrets one to another), when she re-
pulsed his suit, in that he was possessed with
your endeared grace, Mendoza most ingrate-
fully renounced all faith to you. 　　20
Fer. Nay, call'd you — Speak, Maquerelle,
　　speak.
Maq. By heaven, witch, dri'd biscuit; and
contested blushlessly he lov'd you but for a
spurt or so.
Fer. For maintenance. 　　　　　25
Maq. Advancement and regard.
Aurel. O villain! O impudent Mendoza!
Maq. Nay, he is the rustiest-jaw'd, the foul-
est mouth'd knave in railing against our sex:
he will rail again' women — 　　　　30
Aurel. How? how?
Maq. I am asham'd to speak 't, I.
Aurel. I love to hate him: speak.
Maq. Why, when Emilia scorn'd his base un-
steadiness, the black-throated rascal scolded,
and said — 　　　　　　　　　　35
Aurel. What?
Maq. Troth, 't is too shameless.
Aurel. What said he?
Maq. Why, that, at four, women were [40
fools; at fourteen, drabs; at forty, bawds; at
fourscore, witches; and [at] a hundred, cats.
Aurel. O unlimitable impudency!
Fer. But as for poor Ferneze's fixed heart,
Was never shadeless meadow drier parcht 　45
Under the scorching heat of heaven's dog,
Than is my heart with your enforcing eyes.
Maq. A hot simile.

---

[1] The same.
[2] Pay obsequious attention to.
[3] Following.
[4] Lampreys.

[5] The same.

Fer. Your smiles have been my heaven, your
    frowns my hell:
O, pity, then! grace should with beauty dwell. 50
    Maq. Reasonable perfect, by 'r lady.
Aurel. I will love thee, be it but in despite
Of that Mendoza: — witch! Ferneze,— witch! —
Ferneze, thou art the duchess' favourite:
Be faithful, private: but 't is dangerous.   55
    Fer. His love is lifeless that for love fears
        breath:
The worst that 's due to sin, O, would 't were
    death!
Aurel. Enjoy my favour. I will be sick in-
stantly and take physic: therefore in depth of
night visit —   60
    Maq. Visit her chamber, but conditionally
you shall not offend her bed: by this diamond!
    Fer. By this diamond.   *Gives it to* MAQ.
    Maq. Nor tarry longer than you please: by
this ruby!   65
    Fer. By this ruby.   *Gives again.*
    Maq. And that the door shall not creak.
    Fer. And that the door shall not creak.
    Maq. Nay, but swear.
    Fer. By this purse.   *Giving her his purse.*
    Maq. Go to, I 'll keep your oaths for you: [71
remember, visit.

Enter MENDOZA, *reading a sonnet.*

Aurel. Dried biscuit! — Look where the base
wretch comes.   74
    Men. "Beauty's life, heaven's model, love's
queen," —
    Maq. That 's his Emilia.
    Men. "Nature's triumph, best of earth," —
    Maq. Meaning Emilia.   79
    Men. "Thou only wonder that the world
hath seen," —
    Maq. That 's Emilia.
    Aurel. Must I, then, hear her prais'd? —
Mendoza!
    Men. Madam, your excellency is graciously [85
encount'red: I have been writing passionate
flashes in honour of —   *Exit* FERNEZE.
    Aurel. Out, villain, villain!
O judgment, where have been my eyes? what
Bewitch'd election made me dote on thee?   90
What sorcery made me love thee? But, be gone;
Bury thy head. O, that I could do more
Than loath thee! hence, worst of ill!
No reason else,[1] our reason is our will.
                        Exit with MAQUERELLE.
    Men. Women! nay, Furies; nay, worse; [95
for they torment only the bad, but women good
and bad. Damnation of mankind! Breath, hast
thou prais'd them for this? and is 't you, Ferneze, are wriggled into smock-grace? Sit sure.
O, that I could rail against these monsters [100
in nature, models of hell, curse of the earth,
women! that dare attempt anything, and what
they attempt they care not how they accomplish; without all premeditation or prevention;
rash in asking, desperate in working, impa- [105
tient in suffering, extreme in desiring, slaves
unto appetite, mistresses in dissembling, only

constant in unconstancy, only perfect in counterfeiting; their words are feigned, their eyes
forg'd, their sighs dissembled, their looks [110
counterfeit, their hair false, their given hopes
deceitful, their very breath artificial; their
blood is their only god; bad clothes and old age
are only the devils they tremble at. That I
could rail now!   115

SCENE VII.[2]

Enter PIETRO, *his sword drawn.*

Pietro. A mischief fill thy throat, thou foul-
jaw'd slave!
Say thy prayers.
    Men.   I ha' forgot 'em.
Pietro.   Thou shalt die.
    Men. So shalt thou. I am heart-mad.
Pietro.   I am horn-mad.
    Men. Extreme mad.
Pietro.   Monstrously mad.
    Men.   Why?
Pietro. Why! thou, thou hast dishonoured
    my bed.   5
    Men. I! Come, come, sit; here 's my bare
        heart to thee,
As steady as is the[3] centre to this[4] glorious
        world:
And yet, hark, thou art a cornuto, — but by
    me?
Pietro. Yes, slave, by thee.
    Men. Do not, do not with tart and spleenful
        breath   10
Lose him can lose thee. I offend my duke!
Bear record, O ye dumb and raw-air'd nights,
How vigilant my sleepless eyes have been
To watch the traitor! Record, thou spirit of
        truth,
With what debasement I ha' thrown myself 15
To under offices, only to learn
The truth, the party, time, the means, the
        place,
By whom, and when, and where thou wert dis-
    grac'd!
And am I paid with "slave"? Hath my intru-
        sion
To places private and prohibited,   20
Only to observe the closer passages,
Heaven knows with vows of revelation,
Made me suspected, made me deem'd a villain?
What rogue hath wrong'd us?
Pietro.   Mendoza, I may err.
    Men. Err! 't is too mild a name: but err and
        err,   25
Run giddy with suspect, 'fore through me thou
        know
That which most creatures, save thyself, do
        know:
Nay, since my service hath so loath'd reject,
'Fore I 'll reveal, shalt find them clipt[5] to-
        gether.   29
    Pietro. Mendoza, thou know'st I am a most
plain-breasted man.
    Men. The fitter to make a cuckold: would
your brows were most plain too!

1 Q₀ *asks.*   2 The same.   3 Qq. *this.*   4 Qq. *the*   5 Embraced

Pietro. Tell me : indeed, I heard thee rail —
Men. At women, true : why, what cold
   phlegm could choose,   35
Knowing a lord so honest, virtuous,
So boundless loving, bounteous, fair-shap'd,
   sweet,
To be contemn'd, abus'd, defam'd, made cuckold ?
Heart! I hate all women for 't: sweet sheets, [39
wax lights, antique bedposts, cambric smocks,
villanous curtains, arras pictures, oil'd hinges,
and all ye tongue-tied lascivious witnesses of
great creatures' wantonness, — what salvation
can you expect?
   Pietro. Wilt thou tell me?   45
   Men. Why, you may find it yourself ; observe,
observe.
   Pietro. I ha' not the patience. Wilt thou de-
serve me, tell, give it.
   Men. Take 't : why, Ferneze is the man, [50
Ferneze : I 'll prove 't ; this night you shall take
him in your sheets. Will 't serve ?
   Pietro. It will ; my bosom 's in some peace :
   till night —
   Men. What?
   Pietro. Farewell.
   Men.   God! how weak a lord are you !
Why, do you think there is no more but so?   55
   Pietro. Why!
   Men. Nay, then, will I presume to counsel
   you :
It should be thus. You with some guard upon
   the sudden
Break into the princess' chamber : I stay be-
   hind,
Without the door, through which he needs must
   pass: 60
Ferneze flies ; let him : to me he comes ; he 's
   kill'd
By me, observe, by me : you follow : I rail,
And seem to save the body. Duchess comes,
On whom (respecting her advanced birth,   64
And your fair nature), I know, nay, I do know,
No violence must be us'd ; she comes : I storm,
I praise, excuse Ferneze, and still maintain
The duchess' honour ; she for this loves me.
I honour you ; shall know her soul, you mine :
Then naught shall she contrive in vengeance   70
(As women are most thoughtful in revenge)
Of her Ferneze, but you shall sooner know 't
Than she can think 't. Thus shall his death
   come sure,
Your duchess brain-caught : so your life se-
   cure.
   Pietro. It is too well : my bosom and my
   heart   75
When nothing helps, cut off the rotten part.
                              Exit.
   Men. Who cannot feign friendship can ne'er
produce the effects of hatred. Honest fool duke !
subtle lascivious duchess ! silly novice Ferneze !
I do laugh at ye. My brain is in labour till it [80
produce mischief, and I feel sudden throes,
proofs sensible, the issue is at hand.
As bears shape young, so I 'll form my device,
Which grown proves horrid : vengeance makes
   men wise.   [*Exit.*]

[SCENE VIII.]¹

   [*Enter* MALEVOLE *and* PASSARELLO.

   Mal. Fool, most happily encount'red : canst
sing, fool ?
   Pass. Yes, I can sing, fool, if you 'll bear the
burden ; and I can play upon instruments, scurvily, as gentlemen do. O, that I had been [5
gelded ! I should then have been a fat fool for
a chamber, a squeaking fool for a tavern, and a
private fool for all the ladies.
   Mal. You are in good case since you came to
court, fool : what, guarded,² guarded !   10
   Pass. Yes, faith, even as footmen and bawds
wear velvet, not for an ornament of honour,
but for a badge of drudgery ; for, now the duke
is discontented, I am fain to fool him asleep
every night.   15
   Mal. What are his griefs ?
   Pass. He hath sore eyes.
   Mal. I never observed so much.
   Pass. Horrible sore eyes ; and so hath every
cuckold, for the roots of the horns spring in [20
the eyeballs, and that 's the reason the horn of
a cuckold is as tender as his eye, or as that
growing in the woman's forehead, twelve years
since, that could not endure to be toucht.³ The
duke hangs down his head like a columbine.   25
   Mal. Passarello, why do great men beg
fools?⁴
   Pass. As the Welshman stole rushes when
there was nothing else to filch ; only to keep
begging in fashion.   30
   Mal. Pooh, thou givest no good reason ; thou
speakest like a fool.
   Pass. Faith, I utter small fragments, as your
knight courts your city widow with jingling of
his gilt spurs,⁵ advancing his bush-coloured [35
beard, and taking tobacco : this is all the mirror of their knightly complements.⁶ Nay, I shall
talk when my tongue is a-going once ; 't is like
a citizen on horseback, evermore in a false
gallop.   40
   Mal. And how doth Maquerelle fare nowadays?
   Pass. Faith, I was wont to salute her as our
English women are at their first landing in
Flushing ;⁷ I would call her whore : but now [45
that antiquity leaves her as an old piece of
plastic to work by, I only ask her how her
rotten teeth fare every morning, and so leave
her. She was the first that ever invented perfum'd smocks for the gentlewomen, and [50
woollen shoes, for fear of creaking for the visitant. She wears an excellent lady, but that her
face peeleth like Muscovy glass.⁸

   ¹ The same. Q₁ omits this scene.
   ² With facings on his coat, such as fools wore.
   ³ An extant pamphlet records this monstrosity.
   ⁴ Seek to be made guardians to idiots, in order to enjoy their revenues.
   ⁵ Some copies read *something of his guilt: some advancing his high-colored.*
   ⁶ Accomplishments.
   ⁷ Flushing was in the hands of the English as security for a loan, and presumably the garrison was unpopular with the towns people.   ⁸ Talc.

Mal. And how doth thy old lord, that hath wit enough to be a flatterer, and conscience enough to be a knave ?   56

Pass. O, excellent : he keeps beside me fifteen jesters, to instruct him in the art of fooling, and utters their jests in private to the duke and duchess. He 'll lie like to your Switzer or [60 lawyer ; he 'll be of any side for most money.

Mal. I am in haste, be brief.

Pass. As your fiddler when he is paid. — He 'll thrive, I warrant you, while your young [64 courtier stands like Good Friday in Lent ; men long to see it, because more fatting days come after it ; else he 's the leanest and pitifullest actor in the whole pageant. Adieu, Malevole.

Mal. O world most vile, when thy loose vanities,   69
Taught by this fool, do make the fool seem wise !

Pass. You 'll know me again, Malevole.

Mal. O, ay, by that velvet.

Pass. Ay, as a pettifogger by his buckram bag. I am as common in the court as an host- [74 ess's lips in the country ; knights, and clowns, and knaves, and all share me ; the court cannot possibly be without me. Adieu, Malevole.
   [*Exeunt.*]]

ACT II

SCENE I.[1]

Enter MENDOZA, *with a sconce,[2] to observe* FER-
NEZE'S *entrance, who, whilst the act is playing,
enters unbraced, two* Pages *before him with
lights ; is met by* MAQUERELLE *and convey'd
in ; the* Pages *are sent away.*

Men. He 's caught, the woodcock's head is i' th' noose.
Now treads Ferneze in dangerous path of lust,
Swearing his sense is merely [3] deified :
The fool grasps clouds, and shall beget Cen-
taurs :
And now, in strength of panting faint delight, 5
The goat bids heaven envy him. — Good goose,
I can afford thee nothing
But the poor comfort of calamity, pity.
Lust 's like the plummets hanging on clock-
lines,
Will ne'er ha' done till all is quite undone ; 10
Such is the course salt sallow lust doth run ;
Which thou shalt try. I 'll be reveng'd. Duke,
thy suspect ;
Duchess, thy disgrace ; Ferneze, thy rivalship ;
Shall have swift vengeance. Nothing so holy,
No band of nature so strong,   15
No law of friendship so sacred,
But I 'll profane, burst, violate, 'fore I 'll
Endure disgrace, contempt, and poverty.
Shall I, whose very "Hum" struck all heads
bare,
Whose face made silence, creaking of whose
shoe   20
Forc'd the most private passages fly ope,

Scrape like a servile dog at some latch'd door ?
Learn how to make a leg, and cry "Beseech ye,
Pray ye, is such a lord within ? " be aw'd
At some odd usher's scoff'd formality ?   25
First sear my brains ! *Unde cadis non quo, re-
fert ;* [4]
My heart cries, "Perish all ! " How ! how ! what
fate
Can once avoid revenge, that 's desperate ?   28
I 'll to the duke ; if all should ope — If ! tush.
Fortune still dotes on those who cannot blush.
   [*Exit.*]

SCENE II.[5]

Enter MALEVOLE *at one door ;* BIANCA, EMILIA,
and MAQUERELLE *at the other door.*

Mal. Bless ye, cast [6] o' ladies ! — Ha, Dipsas !
how dost thou, old coal ?

Maq. Old coal !

Mal. Ay, old coal ; methinks thou liest like
a brand under these billets of green wood. He [5
that will inflame a young wench's heart, let
him lay close to her an old coal that hath first
been fir'd, a panderess, my half-burnt lint, who
though thou canst not flame thyself, yet art
able to set a thousand virgin's tapers afire. [10
— And how does Janivere thy husband, my little
periwinkle ? Is he troubled with the cough o'
the lungs still ? Does he hawk o' nights still ?
He will not bite.

Bian. No, by my troth, I took him with [15
his mouth empty of old teeth.

Mal. And he took thee with thy belly full of
young bones : marry, he took his maim by the
stroke of his enemy.   19

Bian. And I mine by the stroke of my friend.

Mal. The close stock ! [7] O mortal wench !
Lady, ha' ye no restoratives for your decayed Jasons ? Look ye, crab's guts bak'd, distill'd ox-pith, the pulverized hairs of a lion's
upper-lip, jelly of cock-sparrows, he-mon- [25
key's marrow, or powder of fox-stones ? — And
whither are all you ambling now ?

Bian. Why, to bed, to bed.

Mal. Do your husbands lie with ye ?

Bian. That were country fashion, i' faith.   30

Mal. Ha' ye no foregoers about you ? Come,
whither in good deed, la' now ?

Maq. In good indeed, la now, to eat the most
miraculously, admirably, astonishable compos'd
posset with three curds, without any drink. [35
Will ye help me with a he-fox ? — Here 's the
duke.   *Exeunt Ladies.*

[*Mal.* Fri'd frogs are very good, and French-
like too.] [8]

SCENE III.[9]

Enter DUKE PIETRO, COUNT CELSO, COUNT
EQUATO, BILIOSO, FERRARDO, *and* MEN-
DOZA.

Pietro. The night grows deep and foul : what
hour is 't ?

Celso. Upon the stroke of twelve.

---

1 Chamber in the Duke's Palace.
2 Lantern.   3 Absolutely.

4 "It is whence you fall, not whither, that matters."
5 Chamber in the Duke's Palace.   6 Pair.
7 Stuck, stoccado, a thrust.   8 Q1 omits.
9 The same.

Mal. Save ye, Duke!

Pietro. From thee: begone, I do not love [5
thee! Let me see thee no more; we are displeas'd.

Mal. Why, God b' wi' thee! Heaven hear
my curse, — may thy wife and thee live long
together!　　　　　　　　　　　　　　1c

Pietro. Begone, sirrah!

Mal. "When Arthur first in court began," —
Agamemnon — Menelaus — was ever any duke
a cornuto?

Pietro. Begone, hence!　　　　　　　　15

Mal. What religion wilt thou be of next?

Men. Out with him!

Mal. With most servile patience.— Time will
come
When wonder of thy error will strike dumb
Thy bezzled¹ senses.—　　　　　　　　20
Slaves! ay, favour: ay, marry, shall he rise:
Good God! how subtle hell doth flatter vice!
Mounts him aloft, and makes him seem to fly,
As fowl the tortoise mock'd, who to the sky
The ambitious shell-fish rais'd! The end of all
Is only, that from height he might dead fall. 26

[²*Bil.* Why, when? Out, ye rogue! begone,
ye rascal!

Mal. I shall now leave ye with all my best
wishes.　　　　　　　　　　　　　30

Bil. Out, ye cur!

Mal. Only let's hold together a firm correspondence.

Bil. Out!

Mal. A mutual-friendly-reciprocal-perpetual
kind of steady-unanimous-heartily-leagued — 36

Bil. Hence, ye gross-jaw'd, peasantly — out,
go!

Mal. Adieu, pigeon-house; thou burr, that
only stickest to nappy fortunes. The serpigo,³ [40
the strangury, an eternal uneffectual priapism
seize thee!

Bil. Out, rogue!

Mal. May'st thou be a notorious wittolly pander to thine own wife, and yet get no office, [45
but live to be the utmost misery of mankind, a
beggarly cuckold!]　　　　　　*Exit.*

Pietro. It shall be so.

Men. It must be so, for where great states
revenge,　　　　　　　　　　　50
'T is requisite the parts be closely dogg'd,
(Which piety and soft respect forbears).⁴
Lay one into his breast shall sleep with him,
Feed in the same dish, run in self-faction,
Who may discover any shape of danger;
For once disgrac'd, displayed in offence,　55
It makes man blushless, and man is (all confess)
More prone to vengeance than to gratefulness.
Favours are writ in dust; but stripes we feel
Depraved nature stamps in lasting steel.

Pietro. You shall be leagu'd with the duchess.

Equato. The plot is very good.　　　61

Men. You shall both kill, and seem the corse
to save.

¹ Drunken.　² Q₁ omits ll. 27–47.　³ An eruption.
⁴ Bullen's emend. Qq. read
　　'T is requisite, the parts with piety
　　And soft respect forbears, be closely dogd.
For *soft*, other copies read *loft*, *lost*.

Fer. A most fine brain-trick.

Celso. (*Aside.*) Of a most cunning knave.　64

Pietro. My lords, the heavy action we intend
Is death and shame, two of the ugliest shapes
That can confound a soul; think, think of it.
I strike, but yet, like him that 'gainst stone
walls
Directs, his shafts rebound in his own face;
My lady's shame is mine, O God, 't is mine! 70
Therefore I do conjure all secrecy:
Let it be as very little as may be,
Pray ye, as may be,
Make frightless entrance, salute her with soft
eyes,
Stain nought with blood; only Ferneze dies, 75
But not before her brows. O gentlemen,
God knows I love her! Nothing else, but this: —
I am not well: if grief, that sucks veins dry,
Rivels⁵ the skin, casts ashes in men's faces,
Be-dulls the eye, unstrengthens all the blood, 80
Chance to remove me to another world,
As sure I once must die, let him succeed:
I have no child; all that my youth begot
Hath been your loves, which shall inherit me:
Which as it ever shall, I do conjure it,　85
Mendoza may succeed: he's nobly born;
With me of much desert.

Celso. (*Aside.*) Much!

Pietro. Your silence answers, "Ay."
I thank you. Come on now. O, that I might
die　　　　　　　　　　　　　90
Before her shame's display'd! Would I were
forc'd
To burn my father's tomb, unheal⁶ his bones,
And dash them in the dirt, rather than this!
This both the living and the dead offends:　94
Sharp surgery where naught but death amends.
　　　　　　　　　　　　　Exeunt.

Scene IV.⁷

Enter Maquerelle, Emilia, *and* Bianca *with
a posset.*

Maq. Even here it is, three curds in three regions individually distinct, most methodically
according to art compos'd, without any drink.

Bian. Without any drink!

Maq. Upon my honour. Will ye sit and eat? 4

Emil. Good; the composure, the receipt,
how is 't?

Maq. 'T is a pretty pearl; by this pearl (how
does 't with me?⁸) thus it is: Seven and thirty
yolks of Barbary hens' eggs; eighteen spoon-[10
fuls and a half of the juice of cock-sparrow
bones; one ounce, three drams, four scruples,
and one quarter of the syrup of Ethiopian
dates; sweetened with three quarters of a pound
of pure candied Indian eringoes; strewed [15
over with the powder of pearl of America,
amber of Cataia, and lamb-stones of Muscovia.

Bian. Trust me, the ingredients are very
cordial, and, no question, good, and most powerful in restoration.　　　　　　20

Maq. I know not what you mean by restoration; but this it doth, — it purifieth the

⁵ Wrinkles.　　　　⁷ The same.
⁶ Uncover.　　　　⁸ How does it become me?

blood, smootheth the skin, enliveneth the eye, strengtheneth the veins, mundifieth [1] the teeth, comforteth the stomach, fortifieth the back, [25] and quickeneth the wit; that 's all.

Emil. By my troth, I have eaten but two spoonfuls, and methinks I could discourse most swiftly and wittily already.

Maq. Have you the art to seem honest? 30

Bian. Ay, thank advice and practice.

Maq. Why, then, eat me o' this posset, quicken your blood, and preserve your beauty. Do you know Doctor Plaster-face? by this curd, he is the most exquisite in forging of veins, [35] sprightening of eyes, dying of hair, sleeking of skins, blushing of cheeks, surphling[2] of breasts, blanching and bleaching of teeth, that ever made an old lady gracious by torchlight; by this curd, la. 40

Bian. Well, we are resolved, what God has given us we 'll cherish.

Maq. Cherish anything saving your husband; keep him not too high, lest he leap the pale: but, for your beauty, let it be your saint; [45] bequeath two hours to it every morning in your closet. I ha' been young, and yet, in my conscience, I am not above five and twenty: but, believe me, preserve and use your beauty; for youth and beauty once gone, we are like bee- [50] hives without honey, out-o'-fashion apparel that no man will wear: therefore use me your beauty.

Emil. Ay, but men say —

Maq. Men say! let men say what they [55] will: life o' woman! they are ignorant of our wants. The more in years, the more in perfection they grow; if they lose youth and beauty, they gain wisdom and discretion: but when our beauty fades, good-night with us. There [60] cannot be an uglier thing than to see an old woman: from which, O pruning, pinching, and painting, deliver all sweet beauties!

[Music within.]

Bian. Hark! music! 64

Maq. Peace, 't is i' the duchess' bed-chamber. Good rest, most prosperously-graced ladies.

Emil. Good night, sentinel.

Bian. Night, dear Maquerelle.

Exeunt all but MAQ.

Maq. May my posset's operation send you my wit and honesty; and me, your youth and [70] beauty; the pleasing'st rest! *Exit.*

SCENE V.[3]

A Song [within].

Whilst the song is singing, enter MENDOZA *with his sword drawn, standing ready to murder* FERNEZE *as he flies from the duchess' chamber. — Tumult within.* 40

All [within.] Strike, strike!

Aur. [within.] Save my Ferneze! O, save my Ferneze!

---

[1] Cleanseth.
[2] Treating with cosmetics.
[3] The same.

Enter FERNEZE *in his shirt, and is receiv'd upon* MENDOZA'S *sword.*

All [within.] Follow, pursue!

Aur. [within.] O, save Ferneze!

Men. Pierce, pierce! — Thou shallow fool, drop there!

He that attempts a princess' lawless love 5
Must have broad hands, close heart, with Argus' eyes,
And back of Hercules, or else he dies.

Thrusts his rapier in FER.

Enter AURELIA, PIETRO, FERRARDO, BILIOSO, CELSO, *and* EQUATO.

All. Follow, follow!

Men. Stand off, forbear, ye most uncivil lords!

Pietro. Strike!

Men. Do not; tempt not a man resolv'd: 10

MENDOZA *bestrides the wounded body of* FERNEZE, *and seems to save him.*

Would you, inhuman murderers, more than death?

Aur. O poor Ferneze!

Men. Alas, now all defence too late!

Aur. He 's dead.

Pietro. I am sorry for our shame. — Go to your bed! 15
Weep not too much, but leave some tears to shed
When I am dead.

Aur. What, weep for thee! my soul no tears shall find.

Pietro. Alas, alas, that women's souls are blind!

Men. Betray such beauty! 20
Murder such youth! Contemn civility!
He loves him not that rails not at him.

Pietro. Thou canst not move us: we have blood enough. —
And please you, lady, we have quite forgot
All your defects: if not, why, then — 25

Aur. Not.

Pietro. Not: the best of rest: good-night.

Exit PIETRO, *with other* Courtiers.

Aur. Despite go with thee!

Men. Madam, you ha' done me foul disgrace; you have wrong'd him much loves you too much: go to, your soul knows you have. 31

Aur. I think I have.

Men. Do you but think so?

Aur. Nay, sure, I have: my eyes have witnessed thy love: thou hast stood too firm for me. 35

Men. Why, tell me, fair-cheekt lady, who even in tears art powerfully beauteous, what unadvised passion struck ye into such a violent heat against me? Speak, what mis- [40] chief wrong'd us? What devil injur'd us? Speak.

Aur. The thing ne'er worthy of the name of man, Ferneze;
Ferneze swore thou lov'st Emilia;
Which to advance, with most reproachful breath 45
Thou both didst blemish and denounce my love.

Men. Ignoble villain! did I for this bestride

Thy wounded limbs? for this, rank opposite
Even to my sovereign? for this, O God, for this, 49
Sunk all my hopes, and with my hopes my life?
Ripp'd bare my throat unto the hangman's
    axe? —
Thou most dishonour'd trunk! — Emilia!
By life, I know her not — Emilia — !
Did you believe him?
    Aur.   Pardon me, I did.
    Men. Did you? And thereupon you graced
    him?   55
    Aur. I did.
    Men. Took him to favour, nay even clasp'd
With him?
    Aur.   Alas, I did!
    Men.   This night?
    Aur.   This night.
    Men. And in your lustful twines the duke
    took you?
    Aur. A most sad truth.
    Men. O God, O God! how we dull honest
    souls,   60
Heavy brain'd men, are swallowed in the bogs
Of a deceitful ground, whilst nimble bloods,
Light-jointed spirits, speed;[1] cut good men's
    throats,
And scape! Alas, I am too honest for this age,
Too full of phlegm and heavy steadiness;   65
Stood still whilst this slave cast a noose about
    me;
Nay, then to stand in honour of him and her,
Who had even slic'd my heart!
    Aur.   Come, I did err,
And am most sorry I did err.
    Men. Why, we are both but dead: the duke
    hates us;   70
And those whom princes do once groundly[2]
    hate,
Let them provide to die, as sure as fate.
Prevention is the heart of policy.
    Aur. Shall we murder him?
    Men. Instantly?   75
    Aur. Instantly; before he casts a plot,
Or further blaze my honour's much-known blot,
Let's murder him.
    Men. I would do much for you: will ye marry
    me?
    Aur. I'll make thee duke. We are of Med-
    icis;   80
Florence our friend; in court my faction
Not meanly strengthful; the duke then dead;
We well prepar'd for change; the multitude
Irresolutely reeling; we in force;
Our party seconded; the kingdom maz'd;   85
No doubt of[3] swift success all shall be grac'd.
    Men. You do confirm me, we are resolute.
To-morrow look for change: rest confident.
'T is now about the immodest waist of night:
The mother of moist dew with pallid light   90
Spreads gloomy shades about the numbed
    earth.
Sleep, sleep, whilst we contrive our mischief's
    birth.
This man I'll get inhum'd. Farewell: to bed;

Ay, kiss thy pillow, dream the duke is dead.
So, so, good night.   *Exit* AURELIA.
                How fortune dotes on impudence! 95
I am in private the adopted son
Of yon good prince:
I must be duke: why, if I must, I must.
Most silly lord, name me! O heaven! I see
God made honest fools to maintain crafty
    knaves.   100
The duchess is wholly mine too; must kill her
    husband
To quit her shame. Much! then marry her! Ay.
O, I grow proud in prosperous treachery!
As wrestlers clip, so I'll embrace you all,
Not to support, but to procure your fall.   105

            Enter MALEVOLE.

    Mal. God arrest thee!
    Men. At whose suit?
    Mal. At the devil's. Ah, you treacherous,
damnable monster, how dost? how dost, thou
treacherous rogue? Ah, ye rascal! I am ban- [110
ished the court, sirrah.
    Men. Prithee, let's be acquainted; I do love
thee, faith.
    Mal. At your service, by the Lord, la: shall's
go to supper? Let's be once drunk together, [115
and so unite a most virtuously-strength'ned
friendship: shall's Huguenot? shall's?
    Men. Wilt fall upon my chamber to-morrow
morn?
    Mal. As a raven to a dunghill. They say [120
there's one dead here: prickt for the pride of
the flesh.
    Men. Ferneze: there he is; prithee, bury him.
    Mal. O, most willingly: I mean to turn pure
Rochelle churchman, I.[4]   125
    Men. Thou churchman! Why, why?
    Mal. Because I'll live lazily, rail upon au-
thority, deny kings' supremacy in things indifferent, and be a pope in mine own parish.
    Men. Wherefore dost thou think churches
were made?   131
    Mal. To scour plough-shares: I ha' seen oxen
plough up altars; *et nunc seges ubi Sion fuit.*[5]
    Men. Strange!   134
    Mal. Nay, monstrous! I ha' seen a sumptu-
ous steeple turned to a stinking privy; more
beastly, the sacredest place made a dogs' kennel; nay, most inhuman, the stoned coffins of
long-dead Christians burst up, and made hogs'
troughs: *hic finis Priami.*[6] Shall I ha' some [140
sack and cheese at thy chamber? Good night,
good mischievous incarnate devil; good night,
Mendoza; ah, ye inhuman villain, good night!
night, fub.[7]   144
    Men. Good night: to-morrow morn?   *Exit.*
    Mal. Ay, I will come, friendly damnation, I
will come. I do descry cross-points; honesty
and courtship straddle as far asunder as a true
Frenchman's legs.
    Fer. O!   150
    Mal. Proclamations! more proclamations!
    Fer. O! a surgeon!

---

[1] Dodsley's emend. Q₁ *pent;* Q₂ *spent.*
[2] Thoroughly.   [3] *By.*
[4] *I. e.* a Huguenot.
[5] Ovid, *Her. Epist.* i. 53, with *Troja* for *Sion.*
[6] Virgil, *Aeneid,* ii. 554.   [7] *Cheat.*

Mal. Hark! lust cries for a surgeon. What
news from Limbo? How does the grand cuckold, Lucifer?   155
Fer. O, help, help! conceal and save me.

> FERNEZE *stirs, and* MALEVOLE *helps*
> *him up and conveys him away.*

Mal. Thy shame more than thy wounds do
    grieve me far:
Thy wounds but leave upon thy flesh some scar;
But fame ne'er heals, still rankles worse and
    worse;
Such is of uncontrolled lust the curse.   160
Think what it is in lawless sheets to lie;
But, O, Ferneze, what in lust to die!
Then thou that shame respect'st, O, fly con-
    verse
With women's eyes and lisping wantonness! 164
Stick candles 'gainst a virgin wall's white back,
If they not burn, yet at the least they'll black.
Come, I'll convey thee to a private port,
Where thou shalt live (O happy man!) from
    court.
The beauty of the day begins to rise,
From whose bright form night's heavy shadow
    flies.   170
Now 'gin close plots to work; the scene grows
    full,
And craves his eyes who hath a solid skull.
                                 Exeunt.

ACT III

Scene I.[1]

Enter PIETRO, MENDOZA, EQUATO, *and* BILI-
OSO.

Pietro. 'T is grown to youth of day: how
    shall we waste this light?
My heart's more heavy than a tyrant's crown.
Shall we go hunt? Prepare for field.
                        Exit EQUATO.
Men. Would ye could be merry!
Pietro. Would God I could! Mendoza, bid
    'em haste.   *Exit* MENDOZA. 5
I would fain shift place; O vain relief!
Sad souls may well change place, but not change
    grief:
As deer, being struck, fly thorough many soils,[2]
Yet still the shaft sticks fast, so ——
Bil. A good old simile, my honest lord.   10
Pietro. I am not much unlike to some sick
    man
That long desired hurtful drink; at last
Swills in and drinks his last, ending at once
Both life and thirst. O, would I ne'er had
    known
My own dishonour! Good God, that men should
    desire   15
To search out that, which, being found, kills all
Their joy of life! to taste the tree of knowledge,
And then be driven from out paradise! ——
Canst give me some comfort?
Bil. My lord, I have some books which [20
have been dedicated to my honour, and I ne'er
read 'em, and yet they had very fine names,

*Physic for Fortune, Lozenges of Sanctified Sin-
cerity;* very pretty works of curates, scriveners,
and schoolmasters. Marry, I remember one [25
Seneca, Lucius Annaeus Seneca ——
Pietro. Out upon him! he writ of temperance
and fortitude, yet lived like a voluptuous epi-
cure, and died like an effeminate coward. —
Haste thee to Florence: 30
Here, take our letters; see 'em seal'd; away!
Report in private to the honour'd duke
His daughter's forc'd disgrace; tell him at
    length
We know too much: due compliments[3] ad-
    vance:
There 's naught that 's safe and sweet but ig-
    norance.   *Exit.* 35

> [*Enter*[4] BIANCA.

Bil. Madam, I am going ambassador for
Florence; 't will be great charges to me.
Bian. No matter, my lord, you have the
lease of two manors come out next Christmas;
you may lay your tenants on the greater rack [40
for it: and when you come home again, I 'll
teach you how you shall get two hundred pounds
a-year by your teeth.
Bil. How, madam?
Bian. Cut off so much from house-keep- [45
ing: that which is saved by the teeth, you know,
is got by the teeth.
Bil. 'Fore God, and so I may; I am in wondrous credit, lady.
Bian. See the use of flattery: I did ever [50
counsel you to flatter greatness, and you have
profited well: any man that will do so shall be
sure to be like your Scotch barnacle,[5] now a
block, instantly a worm, and presently a great
goose: this it is to rot and putrefy in the bosom
of greatness.   55
Bil. Thou art ever my politician. O, how
happy is that old lord that hath a politician to
his young lady! I 'll have fifty gentlemen shall
attend upon me: marry, the most of them [60
shall be farmer's sons, because they shall bear
their own charges; and they shall go apparelled
thus, — in sea-water-green suits, ash-colour
cloaks, watchet stockings, and popinjay-green
feathers: will not the colours do excellent?   65
Bian. Out upon 't! they 'll look like citizens
riding to their friends at Whitsuntide; their
apparel just so many several parishes.
Bil. I 'll have it so; and Passarello, my fool,
shall go along with me; marry, he shall be in
velvet.   70
Bian. A fool in velvet!
Bil. Ay, 't is common for your fool to wear
satin; I 'll have mine in velvet.
Bian. What will you wear, then, my lord? 75
Bil. Velvet too; marry, it shall be embroidered, because I 'll differ from the fool somewhat.
I am horribly troubled with the gout: nothing
grieves me, but that my doctor hath forbidden
me wine, and you know your ambassador [80

---

[3] So Q2. Q1 *complaints.*   [4] Q1 omits ll. 36–176.
[5] A kind of wild geese were supposed to grow from
barnacles.

must drink. Didst thou ask thy doctor what was good for the gout?

Bian. Yes; he said, ease, wine, and women, were good for it.

Bil. Nay, thou hast such a wit! What was good to cure it, said he? 86

Bian. Why, the rack. All your empirics could never do the like cure upon the gout the rack did in England, or your Scotch boot.[1] The French harlequin will instruct you. 90

Bil. Surely, I do wonder how thou, having for the most part of thy lifetime been a country body, shouldst have so good a wit.

Bian. Who, I? why, I have been a courtier thrice two months. 95

Bil. So have I this twenty year, and yet there was a gentleman-usher called me coxcomb t' other day, and to my face too : was 't not a backbiting rascal? I would I were better travelled, that I might have been better acquainted with the fashions of several countrymen : [101 but my secretary, I think, he hath sufficiently instructed me.

Bian. How, my lord?

Bil. "Marry, my good lord," quoth he, [105 "your lordship shall ever find amongst a hundred Frenchmen forty hot-shots; amongst a hundred Spaniards, three-score braggarts; amongst a hundred Dutchmen, four-score drunkards; amongst an hundred Englishmen, four-score [110 and ten madmen; and amongst an hundred Welshmen "——

Bian. What, my lord?

Bil. "Four-score and nineteen gentlemen." [2]

Bian. But since you go about a sad embassy, I would have you go in black, my lord. 116

Bil. Why, dost think I cannot mourn, unless I wear my hat in cypress,[3] like an alderman's heir? That 's vile, very old, in faith. 119

Bian. I 'll learn of you shortly : O, we should have a fine gallant of you, should not I instruct you! How will you bear yourself when you come into the Duke of Florence' court?

Bil. Proud enough, and 't will do well enough. As I walk up and down the chamber, I 'll [125 spit frowns about me, have a strong perfume in my jerkin, let my beard grow to make me look terrible, salute no man beneath the fourth button; and 't will do excellent.

Bian. But there is a very beautiful lady [130 there; how will you entertain her?

Bil. I 'll tell you that, when the lady hath entertained me : but to satisfy thee, here comes the fool.

Enter PASSARELLO.

Fool, thou shalt stand for the fair lady. 135

Pass. Your fool will stand for your lady most willingly and most uprightly.

Bil. I 'll salute her in Latin.

Pass. O, your fool can understand no Latin.

Bil. Ay, but your lady can. 140

Pass. Why, then, if your lady take down

your fool, your fool will stand no longer for your lady.

Bil. A pestilent fool! 'fore God, I think the world be turned upside down too. 145

Pass. O, no, sir; for then your lady and all the ladies in the palace should go with their heels upward, and that were a strange sight, you know. 149

Bil. There be many will repine at my preferment.

Pass. O, ay, like the envy of an elder sister, that hath her younger made a lady before her.

Bil. The duke is wondrous discontented.

Pass. Ay, and more melancholic than a [155 usurer having all his money out at the death of a prince.

Bil. Didst thou see Madam Floria to-day?

Pass. Yes, I found her repairing her face to-day; the red upon the white showed as if [160 her cheeks should have been served in for two dishes of barberries in stewed broth, and the flesh to them a woodcock.

Bil. A bitter fool![4] Come, madam, this night thou shalt enjoy me freely, and tomorrow [165 for Florence.

Pass. What a natural fool is he that would be a pair of bodies[5] to a woman's petticoat, to be trussed and pointed to them! Well, I 'll dog my lord; and the word is proper: for when I [170 fawn upon him, he feeds me; when I snap him by the fingers, he spits in my mouth. If a dog 's death were not strangling, I had rather be one than a serving-man; for the corruption of coin is either the generation of a usurer or a lousy [175 beggar.   *Exeunt* BIANCA *and* PASSARELLO.]

SCENE II.[6]

Enter MALEVOLE *in some frieze gown, whilst* BILIOSO *reads his patent.*

Mal. I cannot sleep; my eyes' ill-neighbouring lids
Will hold no fellowship. O thou pale sober night,
Thou that in sluggish fumes all sense dost steep;
Thou that giv'st all the world full leave to play,
Unbend'st the feebled veins of sweaty labour!
The galley-slave, that all the toilsome day   5
Tugs at his oar against the stubborn wave,
Straining his rugged veins, snores fast;
The stooping scythe-man, that doth barb[7] the field,
Thou mak'st wink sure : in night all creatures sleep;   10
Only the malcontent, that 'gainst his fate
Repines and quarrels,—alas he 's goodman tell-clock!
His sallow jaw-bones sink with wasting moan;
Whilst others' beds are down, his pillow 's stone.

Bil. Malevole!   15

Mal. Elder of Israel, thou honest defect of

---

[1] A form of torture.
[2] Welshmen were notoriously proud of their pedigree.
[3] Crape.

[4] Qq. *fowl.* Perhaps a pun.   [6] The same.
[5] Pair of stays, bodice.   [7] Shave; here, mow.

wicked nature and obstinate ignorance, when
did thy wife let thee lie with her?

Bil. I am going ambassador to Florence.

Mal. Ambassador! Now, for thy country's [20
honour, prithee, do not put up mutton and porridge i' thy cloak-bag. Thy young lady wife
goes to Florence with thee too, does she not?

Bil. No, I leave her at the palace.   24

Mal. At the palace! Now, discretion shield,
man! For God's love, let's ha' no more cuck-
olds! Hymen begins to put off his saffron robe:[1]
keep thy wife i' the state of grace. Heart o'
truth, I would sooner leave my lady singled in
a bordello than in the Genoa palace: 30
Sin there appearing in her sluttish shape,
Would soon grow loathsome, even to blushes'
sense;
Surfeit would choke [2] intemperate appetite,
Make the soul scent the rotten breath of lust.
When in an Italian lascivious palace,   35
A lady guardianless,
Left to the push of all allurement,
The strongest incitements to immodesty,
To have her bound, incens'd with wanton
sweets,
Her veins fill'd high with heating delicates,   40
Soft rest, sweet music, amorous masquerers,
Lascivious banquets, sin itself gilt o'er,
Strong fantasy tricking up strange delights,
Presenting it dress'd pleasingly to sense,
Sense leading it unto the soul, confirm'd   45
With potent examples, impudent custom,
Entic'd by that great bawd, Opportunity;
Thus being prepar'd, clap to her easy ear
Youth in good clothes, well-shap'd, rich,
Fair-spoken, promising, noble, ardent, blood-
full,   50
Witty, flattering, — Ulysses absent,
O Ithaca, can chastest Penelope hold out?

Bil. Mass, I'll think on 't. Farewell.

Mal. Farewell. Take thy wife with thee.
Farewell.   *Exit* BILIOSO.
To Florence; um! it may prove good, it may!
And we may once unmask our brows.   56

Enter COUNT CELSO.

Celso. My honour'd lord —,

Mal. Celso, peace! how is 't? Speak low:
pale fears
Suspect that hedges, walls, and trees, have
ears:
Speak, how runs all?

Celso. I' faith, my lord, that beast with many
heads,   5
The staggering multitude, recoils apace:
Though thorough great men's envy, most men's
malice,
Their much-intemperate heat hath banish'd
you,
Yet now they find envy and malice ne'er
Produce faint reformation.   10
The duke, the too soft duke, lies as a block

[1] The usual costume of Hymen in masques.
[2] So Bullen. Qq. *cloake, cloke.*
[3] The same

For which two tugging factions seem to saw;
But still the iron through the ribs they draw.

Mal. I tell thee, Celso, I have ever found
Thy breast most far from shifting cowardice   15
And fearful baseness: therefore I'll tell thee,
Celso,
I find the wind begins to come about;
I'll shift my suit of fortune.
I know the Florentine, whose only force,[4]
By marrying his proud daughter to this
prince,   20
Both banish'd me and made this weak lord
duke,
Will now forsake them all; be sure he will.
I'll lie in ambush for conveniency,
Upon their severance to confirm myself.

Celso. Is Ferneze interr'd?   25

Mal. Of that at leisure: he lives.

Celso. But how stands Mendoza? How is 't
with him?

Mal. Faith, like a pair of snuffers, snibs filth
in other men, and retains it in himself.   30

Celso. He does fly from public notice, methinks, as a hare does from hounds; the feet
whereon he flies betray him.

Mal. I can track him, Celso.
O, my disguise fools him most powerfully!   35
For that I seem a desperate malcontent,
He fain would clasp with me: he's the true
slave
That will put on the most affected grace
For some vile second cause.

Enter MENDOZA.

Celso. He's here.

Mal. Give place.   *Exit* CELSO.
Illo, ho, ho, ho! art there, old truepenny?
Where hast thou spent thyself this morning?
I see flattery in thine eyes, and damnation in
thy soul. Ha, ye huge rascal!   45

Men. Thou art very merry.

Mal. As a scholar, *futuens gratis.* How does
the devil go with thee now?

Men. Malevole, thou art an arrant knave.

Mal. Who, I? I have been a sergeant, [50
man.

Men. Thou art very poor.

Mal. As Job, an alchymist, or a poet.

Men. The duke hates thee.

Mal. As Irishmen do bum-cracks.   55

Men. Thou hast lost his amity.

Mal. As pleasing as maids lose their virginity.

Men. Would thou wert of a lusty spirit!
Would thou wert noble!   60

Mal. Why, sure my blood gives me I am
noble, sure I am of noble kind; for I find myself possessed with all their qualities; — love
dogs, dice, and drabs, scorn wit in stuff-clothes;
have beat my shoemaker, knocked my seam- [65
stress, cuckold[ed] my 'pothecary, and undone
my tailor. Noble! why not? since the stoic[5]
said, *Neminem servum non ex regibus, neminem
regem non ex servis esse oriundum;* only busy
Fortune touses, and the provident Chances [70

[4] Whose force alone.   [5] Seneca. *Epist.* xliv

blend them together. I'll give you a simile:
did you e'er see a well with two buckets,
whilst one comes up full to be emptied, another
goes down empty to be filled? Such is the
state of all humanity. Why, look you, I may [75
be the son of some duke; for, believe me, intemperate lascivious bastardy makes nobility
doubtful: I have a lusty daring heart, Mendoza.　　　　　　　　　　　　　　　　　79
　Men. Let's grasp; I do like thee infinitely.
Wilt enact one thing for me?
　Mal. Shall I get by it? (MEN. *gives him his
purse.*) Command me; I am thy slave, beyond
death and hell.
　Men. Murder the duke.　　　　　　　85
　Mal. My heart's wish, my soul's desire, my
fantasy's dream, my blood's longing, the only
height of my hopes! How, O God, how! O,
how my united spirits throng together, to
strengthen my resolve!　　　　　　　90
　Men. The duke is now a-hunting.
　Mal. Excellent, admirable, as the devil would
have it! Lend me, lend me, rapier, pistol,
cross-bow: so, so, I'll do it.
　Men. Then we agree.　　　　　　　95
　Mal. As Lent and fishmongers. Come, a-cap-
a-pe, how? Inform.
　Men. Know that this weak-brain'd duke,
who only stands
On Florence' stilts, hath out of witless zeal
Made me his heir, and secretly confirm'd　100
The wreath to me after his life's full point.
　Mal. Upon what merit?
　Men.　　　　　Merit! by heaven, I horn him.
Only Ferneze's death gave me state's life.
Tut, we are politic, he must not live now.　104
　Mal. No reason, marry: but how must he
die now?
　Men. My utmost project is to murder the
duke, that I might have his state, because he
makes me his heir; to banish the duchess, that
I might be rid of a cunning Lacedaemon- [110
ian, because I know Florence will forsake her;
and then to marry Maria, the banished Duke
Altofront's wife, that her friends might
strengthen me and my faction: that is all,
la.　　　　　　　　　　　　　　　　　115
　Mal. Do you love Maria?
　Men. Faith, no great affection, but as wise men
do love great women, to ennoble their blood and
augment revenue. To accomplish this now, thus
now. The duke is in the forest, next the sea: [120
single him, kill him, hurl him i' the main, and
proclaim thou sawest wolves eat him.
　Mal. Um! Not so good. Methinks when he
is slain,
To get some hypocrite, some dangerous
wretch
That's muffled o('e)r with feigned holiness,　125
To swear he heard the duke on some steep cliff
Lament his wife's dishonour, and, in an agony
Of his heart's torture, hurl'd his groaning sides
Into the swollen sea, – this circumstance
Well made sounds probable: and hereupon　130
The duchess ——
　Men.　　　　May well be banish'd:

O unpeerable invention! rare!
Thou god of policy! it honeys me.
　Mal. Then fear not for the wife of Alto-
front;
I'll close to her.　　　　　　　　　135
　Men. Thou shalt, thou shalt. Our excellency
is pleas'd:
Why wert not thou an emperor? When we
Are duke, I'll make thee some great man,
sure.
　Mal. Nay. Make me some rich knave, and
I'll make myself
Some great man.
　Men.　　　　In thee be all my spirit:　140
Retain ten souls, unite thy virtual powers:
Resolve; ha, remember greatness! Heart,
farewell;
The fate of all my hopes in thee doth dwell.
　　　　　　　　　　　　　　　[*Exit.*]

　　　　　　　Re-enter CELSO.

　Mal. Celso, didst hear? — O heaven, didst
hear
Such devilish mischief? Suffer'st thou the
world　　　　　　　　　　　　　　145
Carouse damnation even with greedy swallow,
And still dost wink, still does thy vengeance
slumber?
If now thy brows are clear, when will they
thunder?　　　　　　　　　　　*Exeunt.*

　　　　　　　　SCENE IV.[1]

Enter PIETRO, FERRARDO, PREPASSO, *and*
　　　　　　Three Pages.

　Fer. The dogs are at a fault.
　　　　　　　　　　Cornets like horns.
　Pietro. Would God nothing but the dogs were
at it! Let the deer pursue safety,[2] the dogs follow the game, and do you follow the dogs: as
for me, 'tis unfit one beast should hunt an- [5
other; I ha' one chaseth me: an't please you, I
would be rid of ye a little.
　Fer. Would your grief would, as soon as we,
leave you to quietness!
　Pietro. I thank you.　　　　　　　10
　　　　　　Exeunt [FERRARDO *and* PREPASSO].
Boy, what dost thou dream of now?
　1 Page. Of a dry summer, my lord; for
here's a hot world towards: but, my lord, I
had a strange dream last night.
　Pietro. What strange dream?　　　　15
　1 Page. Why, methought I pleased you with
singing, and then I dreamt that you gave me
that short sword.
　Pietro. Prettily begged: hold thee, I'll prove
thy dream true; take 't.　　[*Giving sword.*] 20
　1 Page. My duty: but still I dreamt on, my
lord; and methought, an't shall please your
excellency, you would needs out of your royal
bounty give me that jewel in your hat.
　Pietro. O, thou didst but dream, boy; do [25
not believe it: dreams prove not always true;
they may hold in a short sword, but not in a
jewel. But now, sir, you dreamt you had

─────────────

　[1] A forest near the sea.　　[2] Qq. *safely.*

pleased me with singing; make that true, as I
ha' made the other.   30
  1 Page. Faith, my lord, I did but dream,
and dreams, you say, prove not always true;
they may hold in a good sword, but not in a
good song. The truth is, I ha' lost my voice.
  Pietro. Lost thy voice! How?   35
  1 Page. With dreaming, faith: but here's a
couple of sirenical rascals shall enchant ye.
What shall they sing, my good lord?
  Pietro. Sing of the nature of women: and
then the song shall be surely full of variety, [40
old crotchets, and most sweet closes; it shall be
humorous, grave, fantastic, amorous, melancholy, sprightly, one in all, and all in one.
  1 Page. All in one!
  Pietro. By'r lady, too many. Sing: my [45
speech grows culpable of unthrifty idleness: 1
sing.

Song [by 2 and 3 Pages].

SCENE V.2

[*To Pietro*] *Enter* MALEVOLE, *with cross-bow
and pistol.*

  Pietro, Ah, so, so, sing. I am heavy: walk
off; I shall talk in my sleep: walk off.
Exeunt Pages.
  Mal. Brief, brief: who? The Duke! Good
    heaven, that fools
Should stumble upon greatness! — Do not sleep,
    duke;   4
Give ye good-morrow. I 3 must be brief, duke;
I am fee'd to murder thee: — start not: — Men-
    doza,
Mendoza hir'd me; here's his gold, his pistol,
Cross-bow, [and] sword: 'tis all as firm as earth.
O fool, fool, choked with the common maze
Of easy idiots, credulity!   10
Make him thine heir! What, thy sworn mur-
    derer!
  Pietro. O, can it be?
  Mal. Can!
  Pietro. Discover'd he not Ferneze?
  Mal. Yes, but why? but why? For love to
    thee?   15
Much, much! To be reveng'd upon his rival,
Who had thrust his jaws awry;
Who being slain, suppos'd by thine own hands,
Defended by his sword, made thee most loath-
    some,
Him most gracious with thy loose princess: 20
Thou, closely 4 yielding egress and regress to her,
Madest him heir; whose hot unquiet lust
Straight tous'd thy sheets, and now would seize
    thy state.
Politician! Wise man! Death! to be
Led to the stake like a bull by the horns;   25
To make even kindness cut a gentle throat!
Life, why art thou numb'd? Thou foggy dul-
    ness, speak:
Lives not more faith in a home-thrusting
    tongue
Than in those fencing tip-tap courtiers?

---

1 Vanity, frivolity.   3 Q1 omits; Q2 *you.*
2 The same. continued.   4 Secretly

Enter CELSO, *with a hermit's gown and beard.*

  [*Pietro.*] 5 Lord Malevole, if this be true —
  Mal. If! Come, shade thee with this dis- [31
guise. If! Thou shalt handle it; he shall
thank thee for killing thyself. Come, follow my
directions, and thou shalt see strange sleights.
  Pietro. World, whither wilt thou?   31
  Mal. Why, to the devil. Come, the morn
    grows late:
A steady quickness is the soul of state.
Exeunt,

ACT IV

SCENE I.6

Enter MAQUERELLE, *knocking at the ladies'
door.*

  Maq. Medam, medam, are you stirring, medam? If you be stirring, medam, — if I thought
I should disturb ye —

[*Enter* Page.]

  Page. My lady is up, forsooth.
  Maq. A pretty boy, faith: how old art thou?
  Page. I think fourteen.   6
  Maq. Nay, an ye be in the teens — are ye a
gentleman born? Do you know me? My name
is Medam Maquerelle; I lie in the old Cunny-
court.   10

Enter BIANCA *and* EMILIA.

  [*Page.*] See, here the ladies.
  Bian. A fair day to ye, Maquerelle.
  Emil. Is the duchess up yet, sentinel?
  Maq. O ladies, the most abominable mischance! O dear ladies the most piteous dis- [15
aster! Ferneze was taken last night in the duchess' chamber. Alas, the duke catcht him and
kill'd him!
  Bian. Was he found in bed?
  Maq. O, no; but the villanous certainty is, [20
the door was not bolted, the tongue-tied hatch
held his peace: so the naked troth is, he was
found in his shirt, whilst I, like an arrant beast,
lay in the outward chamber, heard nothing;
and yet they came by me in the dark, and [25
yet I felt them not, like a senseless creature as
I was. O beauties, look to your busk-points; 7
if not chastely, yet charily: be sure the door
be bolted. — Is your lord gone to Florence?
  Bian. Yes, Maquerelle.   30
  Maq. I hope you'll find the discretion to purchase a fresh gown 'fore his return. — Now, by
my troth, beauties, I would ha' ye once wise.
He loves ye; pish! He is witty; bubble! Fair-
proportioned; mew! Nobly-born; wind! Let [35
this be still your fixed position: esteem me
every man according to his good gifts, and so
ye shall ever remain most worthy to be most
dear ladies.

---

5 Qq. *Cel.*   6 Palace of the Duke.
7 The tags of the laces fastening the "busk,' th
whale-bone in the front of the stays.

Emil. Is the duke returned from hunting
yet?   40
Maq. They say not yet.
Bian. 'T is now in midst of day.
Emil. How bears the duchess with this blemish now?
Maq. Faith, boldly; strongly defies defame,
as one that has a duke to her father. And [45
there 's a note to you : be sure of a stout friend
in a corner, that may always awe your husband. Mark the behaviour of the duchess now :
she dares defame ; cries, " Duke, do what thou
canst, I 'll quit mine honour : " nay, as one [50
confirmed in her own virtue against ten thousand mouths that mutter her disgrace, she 's
presently for dances.

Enter FERRARDO.

Bian. For dances !
Maq. Most true.   55
Emil. Most strange. See, here 's my servant,[1] young Ferrardo. How many servants
thinkest thou I have, Maquerelle ?[2]
Maq. The more, the merrier. 'T was well [59
said, use your servants as you do your smocks ;
have many, use one, and change often ; for that 's
most sweet and courtlike.
Fer. Save ye, fair ladies ! Is the duke return'd ?
Bian. Sweet sir, no voice of him as yet in
court.
Fer. 'T is very strange.   65
Bian. And how like you my servant, Maquerelle ?
Maq. I think he could hardly draw Ulysses'
bow ; but, by my fidelity, were his nose narrower, his eyes broader, his hands thinner, [69
his lips thicker, his legs bigger, his feet lesser,
his hair blacker, and his teeth whiter, he were
a tolerable sweet youth, i' faith. And he will
come to my chamber, I will read him the fortune of his beard.   *Cornets sound.* 74
Fer. Not yet return'd ! I fear — but the
duchess approacheth.

SCENE II.[3]

Enter MENDOZA *supporting the* Duchess *and*
GUERRINO: *the ladies that are on the stage
rise:* FERRARDO *ushers in the* Duchess, *and
then takes a lady to tread a measure.*[4]

Aur. We will dance : music ! — we will dance.
Guer. Les quanto,[5] lady, Pensez bien, Passa
regis, or Bianca's brawl ?
Aur. We have forgot the brawl.
Fer. So soon ? 'T is wonder.   5
Guer. Why, 't is but two singles on the left,
two on the right, three doubles forward, a traverse of six round : do this twice, three singles
side, galliard trick-of-twenty, coranto-pace ; a

---

[1] Lover.
[2] This speech should probably be given to Bianca.
[3] The same, continued.
[4] A slow dance.
[5] Dyce cites *Les Guanto* from Munday as the name of
a courtly dance.

figure of eight, three singles broken down, [10
come up, meet, two doubles, fall back, and then
honour.
Aur. O Daedalus, thy maze ! I have quite
forgot it.
Maq. Trust me, so have I, saving the falling-
back, and then honour.   16

Enter PREPASSO.

Aur. Music, music !
Prep. Who saw the duke ? the duke ?

Enter EQUATO.

Aur. Music !
Equato. The duke ? is the duke returned ? 20
Aur. Music !

Enter CELSO.

Celso. The duke is either quite invisible, or
else is not.
Aur. We are not pleased with your intrusion
upon our private retirement ; we are not [25
pleased : you have forgot yourselves.

Enter a Page.

Celso. Boy, thy master? Where 's the duke ?
Page. Alas, I left him burying the earth with
his spread joyless limbs : he told me he was
heavy, would sleep ; bade me walk off, [30
for that the strength of fantasy oft made him
talk in his dreams. I straight obeyed, nor ever
saw him since : but whereso'er he is, he 's sad.
Aur. Music, sound high, as is our heart !
Sound high !   35

SCENE III.[6]

[*To them*] *enter* MALEVOLE, *and* PIETRO *disguised like an hermit.*

Mal. The duke, — peace ! — the duke is dead.
Aur. Music !
Mal. Is 't music ?
Men. Give proof.
Fer. How ?   5
Celso. Where ?
Prep. When ?
Mal. Rest in peace, as the duke does : quietly
sit : for my own part, I beheld him but dead ;
that 's all. Marry, here 's one can give you a [10
more particular account of him.
Men. Speak, holy father, nor let any brow
Within this presence fright thee from the
truth :
Speak confidently and freely.
Aur.   We attend.
Pietro. Now had the mounting sun's all-rip-
ening wings   15
Swept the cold sweat of night from earth's dank
breast,
When I, whom men call Hermit of the Rock,
Forsook my cell, and clambered up a cliff,
Against whose base the heady Neptune dash'd
His high-curl'd brows ; there 't was I eas'd my
limbs :
When, lo ! my entrails melted with the moan

---

[6] The same, continued.

Some one, who far 'bove me was climb'd, did
    make —
I shall offend.
    Men. Not.
    Aur. On.   25
    Pietro. Methinks I hear him yet : — " O fe-
male faith !
Go sow the ingrateful sand, and love a woman !
And do I live to be the scoff of men ?
To be their wittol-cuckold, even to hug
My poison ? Thou knowest, O truth !   30
Sooner hard steel will melt with southern wind,
A seaman's whistle calm the ocean,
A town on fire be extinct with tears,
Than women, vow'd to bluish impudence,
With sweet behaviour and soft minioning   35
Will turn from that where appetite is fix'd.
O powerful blood ! how thou dost slave their
    soul !
I wash'd an Ethiop, who, for recompense,
Sullied my name : and must I, then, be forc'd   39
To walk, to live thus black ? Must ! must ! fie !
He that can bear with ' must,' he cannot die."
With that he sigh'd so passionately deep,
That the dull air even groan'd : at last he cries,
" Sink shame in seas, sink deep enough ! " so
    dies ;
For then I viewed his body fall, and souse   45
Into the foamy main. O, then I saw,
That which methinks I see, it was the duke ;
Whom straight the nicer-stomach'd sea belch'd
    up :
But then ——
    Mal. Then came I in ; but, 'las, all was too
    late !   50
For even straight he sunk.
    Pietro.   Such was the duke's sad fate.
    Celso. A better fortune to our Duke Mendoza !
    Omnes. Mendoza !   *Cornets flourish.*
    Men. A guard, a guard !

                    Enter a Guard.

                         We, full of hearty tears,
For our good father's loss,   55
(For so we well may call him
Who did beseech your loves for our succession),
Cannot so lightly over-jump his death
As leave his woes revengeless. — (*To* AURELIA.)
                    Woman of shame,
We banish thee for ever to the place   60
From whence this good man comes ; nor permit,
On death, unto thy body any ornament ;
But, base as was thy life, depart away.
    Aur. Ungrateful !
    Men. Away !   65
    Aur. Villain, hear me !

PREPASSO *and* GUERRINO *lead away* AURELIA.

    Men. Begone ! My lords,
Address to [1] public council ; 't is most fit :
The train of fortune is borne up by wit.
Away ! our presence shall be sudden ; haste.   70
        All depart saving MENDOZA, MAL-
        EVOLE, *and* PIETRO.
    Mal. Now, you egregious devil ! Ha, ye mur-

                                                    ----
[1] Prepare for.

dering politician ! How dost, duke ? How dost
look now ? Brave duke, i' faith.
    Men. How did you kill him ?
    Mal. Slatted his brains out, then soused him
in the briny sea.   75
    Men. Brained him, and drowned him too ?
    Mal. O 't was best, sure work ; for he that
strikes a great man, let him strike home, or
else 'ware, he 'll prove no man. Shoulder not [80
a huge fellow, unless you may be sure to lay
him in the kennel.
    Men. A most sound brain-pan ! I 'll make you
both emperors.
    Mal. Make us Christians, make us Christians.
    Men. I 'll hoist ye, ye shall mount.   85
    Mal. To the gallows, say ye ? Come : *prae-
mium incertum petit, certum scelus.*[2] How stands
the progress ?
    Men. Here, take my ring unto the citadel ; 90
                         [*Giving ring.*]
Have entrance to Maria, the grave duchess
Of banish'd Altofront. Tell her we love her ;
Omit no circumstance to grace our person : do 't.
    Mal. I 'll make an excellent pander : duke,
farewell ; 'dieu, adieu, duke.   95
    Men. Take Maquerelle with thee ; for 't is
    found
None cuts a diamond but a diamond.
                         Exit MALEVOLE.
                                         Hermit,
Thou art a man for me, my confessor ;
O thou selected spirit, born for my good,
Sure thou wouldst make   100
An excellent elder in a deform'd church.
Come, we must be inward,[3] thou and I all one.
    Pietro. I am glad I was ordained for ye.
    Men. Go to, then ; thou must know that Mal-
evole is a strange villain ; dangerous, very [105
dangerous : you see how broad 'a speaks ; a
gross-jawed rogue : I would have thee poison
him : he 's like a corn upon my great toe, I can-
not go for him ; he must be cored out, he must.
Wilt do 't, ha ?   110
    Pietro. Anything, anything.
    Men. Heart of my life ! thus, then. To the
    citadel ;
Thou shalt consort with this Malevole ;
There being at supper, poison him. It shall be laid
Upon Maria, who yields love or dies.   115
Scud quick.
    Pietro. Like lightning : good deeds crawl,
    but mischief flies.   *Exit.*

            Re-enter MALEVOLE.

    Mal. Your devilship's ring has no virtue :
the buff-captain, the sallow Westphalian gam-
mon-faced zaza cries, " Stand out ! " must have
a stiffer warrant, or no pass into the castle [121
of comfort.
    Men. Command our sudden letter. — Not en-
ter ! sha't ; what place is there in Genoa but
thou shalt ? Into my heart, into my very heart :
come, let 's love : we must love, we two, soul [126
and body.

                                                    ----
[2] Adapted from Seneca, *Phoen.* 632. " He seeks an
uncertain reward, but certain guilt."
[3] Intimate.

Mal. How didst like the hermit? A strange
hermit, sirrah.
Men. A dangerous fellow, very perilous. He
must die.   131
Mal. Ay, he must die.
Men. Thou 'st kill him. We are wise; we
must be wise.
Mal. And provident.   135
Men. Yea, provident: beware an hypocrite;
A churchman once corrupted, O, avoid!
A fellow that makes religion his stalking-horse.[1]
He breeds a plague. Thou shalt poison him.
Mal. O, 't is wondrous necessary: how?   140
Men. You both go jointly to the citadel;
There sup, there poison him: and Maria,
Because she is our opposite,[2] shall bear
The sad suspect; on which she dies or loves us.
Mal. I run.   *Exit.*
Men. We that are great, our sole self-good
still moves us.   146
They shall die both, for their deserts crave more
Than we can recompense: their presence still
Imbraids[3] our fortunes with beholdingness,
Which we abhor; like deed, not doer: then
conclude,   150
They live not to cry out "Ingratitude!"
One stick burns t' other, steel cuts steel alone:
'T is good trust few; but, O, 't is best trust
none!   *Exit.*

Scene IV.[4]

Enter Malevole *and* Pietro, *still disguised,*
at several doors.

Mal. How do you? How dost duke?
Pietro. O, let
The last day fall! drop, drop on our curs'd
heads!
Let heaven unclasp itself, vomit forth flames.
Mal. O, do not rave, do not turn player; [5
there 's more of them than can well live one by
another already. What, art an infidel still?
Pietro. I am amazed, struck in a swoon with
wonder: I am commanded to poison thee —
Mal. I am commanded to poison thee at [10
supper —
Pietro. At supper —
Mal. In the citadel —
Pietro. In the citadel.
Mal. Cross capers! tricks! Truth o' [15
heaven! he would discharge us as boys do
eldern guns, one pellet to strike out another.
Of what faith art now?
Pietro. All is damnation; wickedness extreme:
There is no faith in man.   20
Mal. In none but usurers and brokers; they
deceive no man: men take 'em for blood-suck-
ers, and so they are. Now, God deliver me from
my friends!
Pietro. Thy friends!   25
Mal. Yes, from my friends; for from mine
enemies I 'll deliver myself. O, cut-throat
friendship is the rankest villainy! Mark this

¹ Qq. note on margin: *Shoots under his belly.*
² Opponent.   ³ Upbraids.   ⁴ Court of the Palace.

Mendoza; mark him for a villain: but heaven
will send a plague upon him for a rogue.   30
Pietro. O world!
Mal. World! 't is the only region of death,
the greatest shop of the devil; the cruelest
prison of men, out of the which none pass without paying their dearest breath for a fee; [35
there 's nothing perfect in it but extreme, extreme calamity, such as comes yonder.

Scene V.[5]

Enter Aurelia, *two halberts before and two after,*
supported by Celso *and* Ferrardo; Aurelia *in base mourning attire.*

Aur. To banishment! led on to banishment!
Pietro. Lady, the blessedness of repentance
to you!
Aur. Why, why, I can desire nothing but
death,
Nor deserve anything but hell.   5
If heaven should give sufficiency of grace
To clear my soul, it would make heaven grace-
less:
My sins would make the stock of mercy poor;
O, they would tire heaven's goodness to re-
claim them!
Judgment is just, yet from that vast villain,   10
But, sure, he shall not miss sad punishment
'Fore he shall rule. — On to my cell of shame!
Pietro. My cell 't is, lady; where, instead of
masks,
Music, tilts, tourneys, and such court-like
shows,
The hollow murmur of the checkless winds   15
Shall groan again; whilst the unquiet sea
Shakes the whole rock with foamy battery.
There usherless the air comes in and out:
The rheumy vault will force your eyes to weep,
Whilst you behold true desolation.   20
A rocky barrenness shall pain your eyes,
Where all at once one reaches where he stands,
With brows the roof, both walls with both his
hands.
Aur. It is too good. — Bless'd spirit of my
lord,
O, in what orb so'er thy soul is thron'd,   25
Behold me worthily most miserable!
O, let the anguish of my contrite spirit
Entreat some reconciliation!
If not, O, joy, triumph in my just grief!
Death is the end of woes and tears' relief.   30
Pietro. Belike your lord not lov'd you, was
unkind.
Aur. O heaven!
As the soul loves[6] the body, so lov'd he:
'T was death to him to part my presence,
heaven
To see me pleas'd.   35
Yet I, like a wretch given o'er to hell,
Brake all the sacred rites of marriage,
To clip[7] a base ungentle faithless villain;
O God! a very pagan reprobate —
What should I say? ungrateful, throws me
out,   40

⁵ The same.   ⁶ Qq. *lov'd.*   ⁷ Embrace.

For whom I lost soul, body, fame, and honour.
But 't is most fit : why should a better fate
Attend on any who forsake chaste sheets ;
Fly the embrace of a devoted heart,
Join'd by a solemn vow 'fore God and man,   45
To taste the brackish [1] flood [2] of beastly lust
In an adulterous touch? O ravenous immodesty !
Insatiate impudence of appetite !
Look, here 's your end ; for mark, what sap in
      dust,
What good in sin,[3] even so much love in lust.   50
Joy to thy ghost, sweet lord ! pardon to me !
Celso. 'T is the duke's pleasure this night you
rest in court.
Aur. Soul, lurk in shades ; run, shame, from
      brightsome skies ;
In night the blind man misses not his eyes.   55
      Exit [with CELSO, FERRARDO, and
      halberts].
Mal. Do not weep, kind cuckold : take com-
fort, man ; thy betters have been beccos :[4]
Agamemnon, emperor of all the merry Greeks,
that tickled all the true Trojans, was a cornuto ;
Prince Arthur, that cut off twelve kings' [60
beards, was a cornuto ; Hercules, whose back
bore up heaven, and got forty wenches with
child in one night, —
Pietro. Nay, 't was fifty.
Mal. Faith, forty 's enow, o' conscience, — [65
yet was a cornuto. Patience ; mischief grows
proud : be wise.
Pietro. Thou pinchest too deep ; art too keen
upon me.
Mal. Tut, a pitiful surgeon makes a dan- [70
gerous sore ; I 'll tent [5] thee to the ground.
Thinkest I 'll sustain myself by flattering thee,
because thou art a prince ? I had rather follow
a drunkard, and live by licking up his vomit,
than by servile flattery.   75
Pietro. Yet great men ha' done 't.
Mal. Great slaves fear better than love, born
naturally for a coal-basket ; [6] though the common usher of princes' presence, Fortune, ha'
blindly given them better place. I am [80
vowed to be thy affliction.
Pietro. Prithee, be :
I love much misery, and be thou son to me.
Mal. Because you are an usurping duke. —

Enter BILIOSO.

Your lordship 's well returned from Florence.
Bil. Well return'd, I praise my horse.   85
Mal. What news from the Florentines ?
Bil. I will conceal the great duke's pleasure ;
only this was his charge : his pleasure is, that
his daughter die ; Duke Pietro be banished [90
for publishing [7] his blood's dishonour ; and that
Duke Altofront be re-accepted. This is all : but
I hear Duke Pietro is dead.
Mal. Ay, and Mendoza is duke : what will
you do ?   95
Bil. Is Mendoza strongest ?
Mal. Yet he is.

[1] Salt, licentious.   [2] Qq. *bloud.*
[3] Qq. *sinne in good.*   [4] Cuckolds.   [5] Probe.
[6] "Carrying coals," menial employment.
[7] Deighton's emend. Qq. *banishing.*

Bil. Then yet I 'll hold with him.
Mal. But if that Altofront should turn
straight again ?   100
Bil. Why, then, I would turn straight again.
'T is good run still with him that has most
      might :
I had rather stand with wrong, than fall with
      right.
Mal. What religion will you be of now ?
Bil. Of the Duke's religion, when I know
what it is.   105
Mal. O Hercules !
Bil. Hercules ! Hercules was the son of Jupi-
ter and Alcmena.
Mal. Your lordship is a very wit-all.   110
Bil. Wittal !
Mal. Aye, all-wit.
Bil. Amphitryo was a cuckold.
Mal. Your lordship swears ; your young lady
will get you a cloth for your old worship's [115
brows. (*Exit* BILIOSO.) Here 's a fellow to do
damn'd : this is his inviolable maxim, — flatter
the greatest and oppress the least : a whoreson
flesh-fly, that still knaws upon the lean galled
backs.   120
Pietro. Why dost, then, salute him ?
Mal. Faith, as bawds go to church, for fashion sake. Come, be not confounded ; thou 'rt
but in danger to lose a dukedom. Think this :
— this earth is the only grave and Golgotha [125
wherein all things that live must rot ; 't is but
the draught wherein the heavenly bodies discharge their corruption ; the very muck-hill on
which the sublunary orbs cast their excrements : man is the slime of this dung pit, [130
and princes are the governors of these men ; for,
for our souls, they are as free as emperors, all
of one piece ; there goes but a pair of shears betwixt [7] an emperor and the son of a bagpiper ;
only the dying, dressing, pressing, glossing, [135
makes the difference.
Now, what art thou like to lose ?
A gaoler's office to keep men in bonds,
Whilst toil and treason all life's good con-
      founds.
Pietro. I here renounce for ever regency : 140
O Altofront, I wrong thee to supplant thy right,
To trip thy heels up with a devilish sleight !
For which I now from throne am thrown :
      world-tricks abjure ;
For vengeance, though 't comes slow, yet it
      comes sure.
O, I am chang'd ! for here, 'fore the dread
      power,   145
In true contrition, I do dedicate
My breath to solitary holiness,
My lips to prayer, and my breast's care shall
      be,
Restoring Altofront to regency.
Mal. Thy vows are heard, and we accept thy
      faith.   *Undisguiseth himself.*

Re-enter FERNEZE *and* CELSO.

Banish amazement: come, we four must
      stand   151

[7] Are cut out of the same cloth.

Full shock of fortune: be not so wonder-
    stricken.
Pietro. Doth Ferneze live?
Fer. For your pardon.
Pietro. Pardon and love. Give leave to recol-
    lect   155
My thoughts dispers'd in wild astonishment.
My vows stand fix'd in heaven, and from hence
I crave all love and pardon.
Mal. Who doubts of providence,
That sees this change? A hearty faith to all!
He needs must rise who can no lower fall: 161
For still impetuous vicissitude
Touseth the world; then let no maze intrude
Upon your spirits: wonder not I rise;
For who can sink that close can temporize?   165
The time grows ripe for action: I'll detect
My privat'st plot, lest ignorance fear suspect.
Let's close to counsel, leave the rest to fate:
Mature discretion is the life of state.   *Exeunt.*

ACT V

[Scene Ia.[1]

Enter Bilioso *and* Passarello.

Bil. Fool, how dost thou like my calf in a
long stocking?
Pass. An excellent calf, my lord.
Bil. This calf hath been a reveller this twenty
year. When Monsieur Gundi lay here am- [5
bassador, I could have carried a lady up and
down at arm's end in a platter; and I can tell
you, there were those at that time who, to try
the strength of a man's back and his arm, would
be coistered.[2] I have measured calves with [10
most of the palace, and they come nothing near
me; besides, I think there be not many armours in the arsenal will fit me, especially for
the headpiece. I'll tell thee —
Pass. What, my lord?   15
Bil. I can eat stewed broth as it comes seeth-
ing off the fire; or a custard as it comes reeking
out of the oven; and I think there are not many
lords can do it. A good pomander,[3] a little decayed in the scent; but six grains of musk, [20
ground with rose-water, and tempered with
a little civet, shall fetch her again presently.
Pass. O, ay, as a bawd with aqua-vitae.
Bil. And, what, dost thou rail upon the ladies
as thou wert wont?   25
Pass. I were better roast a live cat, and might
do it with more safety. I am as secret to [the]
thieves as their painting. There's Maquerelle,
oldest bawd and a perpetual beggar — did you
never hear of her trick to be known in the [30
city?
Bil. Never.
Pass. Why, she gets all the picture-makers

to draw her picture; when they have done, she
most courtly finds fault with them one after [35
another, and never fetcheth them. They, in revenge of this, execute her in pictures as they do
in Germany, and hang her in their shops. By
this means is she better known to the stinkards[4]
than if she had been five times carted.   40
Bil. 'Fore God, an excellent policy.
Pass. Are there any revels to-night, my lord?
Bil. Yes.
Pass. Good my lord, give me leave to break
a fellow's pate that hath abused me.   45
Bil. Whose pate?
Pass. Young Ferrardo, my lord.
Bil. Take heed, he's very valiant; I have
known him eight quarrels in five days,
believe it.   50
Pass. O, is he so great a quarreller? Why,
then, he's an arrant coward.
Bil. How prove you that?
Pass. Why, thus. He that quarrels seeks to
fight; and he that seeks to fight seeks to [55
die; and he that seeks to die seeks never to
fight more; and he that will quarrel, and seeks
means never to answer a man more, I think he's
a coward.
Bil. Thou canst prove anything.   60
Pass. Anything but a rich knave; for I can
flatter no man.
Bil. Well, be not drunk, good fool: I shall
see you anon in the presence.   *Exeunt.*]

Scene I.[5]

Enter, from opposite sides, Malevole *and* Ma-
    QUERELLE, *singing.*

Mal. "The Dutchman for a drunkard," —
Maq. "The Dane for golden locks," —
Mal. "The Irishman for usquebaugh," —
Maq. "The Frenchman for the (   )."
Mal. O, thou art a blessed creature! Had [5
I a modest woman to conceal, I would put her
to thy custody; for no reasonable creature
would ever suspect her to be in thy company.
Ah, thou art a melodious Maquerelle, — thou
picture of a woman, and substance of a beast!

[6*Enter* Passarello *with wine.*

Maq. O fool, will ye be ready anon to go [11
with me to the revels? The hall will be so pestered[7] anon.
Pass. Ay, as the country is with attorneys.
Mal. What hast thou there, fool?   15
Pass. Wine; I have learned to drink since I
went with my lord ambassador: I'll drink to
the health of Madam Maquerelle,
Mal. Why, thou wast wont to rail upon her.
Pass. Ay; but since I borrowed money of [20
her, I'll drink to her health now; as gentlemen visit brokers, or as knights send venison
to the city, either to take up more money, or
to procure longer forbearance.
Mal. Give me the bowl. I drink a health [25
to Altofront, our deposed duke.   [*Drinks.*]

---

[1] A room in the Palace. Q₁ omits this scene.
[2] Meaning uncertain. "Coiled up into a small compass," Nares. "Inconvenienced," Halliwell. Deighton
would read *hoistered*, "an Essex word meaning 'supported,' 'held up,' an extension of 'hoisted,' as 'hoisted'
is an extension of 'hoised.'"
[3] A perfume ball.

[4] Stinking fellows: the mob.   [6] Q₁ omits ll. 11-43.
[5] Before the Citadel.   [7] Crowded.

Pass. I 'll take it [*drinks*] : — so. Now I 'll begin a health to Madam Maquerelle. [*Drinks.*]

Mal. Pooh ! I will not pledge her.

Pass. Why, I pledged your lord.   30

Mal. I care not.

Pass. Not pledge Madam Maquerelle ! Why, then, will I spew up your lord again with this fool's finger.

Mal. Hold ; I 'll take it.   [*Drinks.*]

Maq. Now thou hast drunk my health, [36 fool, I am friends with thee.

Pass. Art ? art ?

When Griffon [1] saw the reconciled quean
Offering about his neck her arms to cast,   40
He threw off sword and heart's malignant spleen,[2]
And lovely her below the loins embrac'd. —

Adieu, Madam Maquerelle.   *Exit.*]

Mal. And how dost thou think o' this transformation of state now ?   45

Maq. Verily, very well ; for we women always note, the falling of the one is the rising of the other ; some must be fat, some must be lean ; some must be fools, and some must be lords ; some must be knaves, and some must be officers ; some [50 must be beggars, some must be knights ; some must be cuckolds, and some must be citizens. As for example, I have two court-dogs, the most fawning curs, the one called Watch, the other Catch : now I, like Lady Fortune, sometimes love this dog, sometimes raise that [55 dog, sometimes favour Watch, most commonly fancy Catch. Now, that dog which I favour I feed ; and he 's so ravenous, that what I give he never chaws it, gulps it down whole, without any relish of what he has, but with a greedy [61 expectation of what he shall have. The other dog now —

Mal. No more dog, sweet Maquerelle, no more dog. And what hope hast thou of the [65 Duchess Maria ? Will she stoop to the duke's lure ? Will she come, thinkest ?

Maq. Let me see, where 's the sign now ? Ha' ye e'er a calendar ? Where 's the sign, trow you ?   70

Mal. Sign ! why is there any moment in that ?

Maq. O, believe me, a most secret power : look ye, a Chaldean or an Assyrian, I am sure 't was a most sweet Jew, told me, court any woman in the right sign, you shall not miss. But you must take her in the right vein [76 then ; as, when the sign is in Pisces, a fishmonger's wife is very sociable ; in Cancer, a precisian's wife is very flexible ; in Capricorn, a merchant's wife hardly holds out ; in Libra, a lawyer's wife is very tractable, especially if [81 her husband be at the term ; only in Scorpio 't is very dangerous meddling. Has the duke sent any jewel, any rich stones ?

Enter CAPTAIN.

Mal. Ay, I think those are the best signs to [85 take a lady in. By your favour, signior, I must discourse with the Lady Maria, Altofront's duchess ; I must enter for the duke.

Capt. She here shall give you interview. I [89 received the guardship of this citadel from the good Altofront, and for his use I 'll keep 't, till I am of no use.

Mal. Wilt thou ? O heavens, that a Christian should be found in a buff-jerkin ! Captain Conscience, I love thee, captain. (*Exit* Captain.) 95 We attend. And what hope hast thou of this duchess' easiness ?

Maq. 'T will go hard, she was a cold creature ever ; she hated monkeys, fools, jesters, [99 and gentlemen-ushers extremely ; she had the vile trick on 't, not only to be truly modestly honourable in her own conscience, but she would avoid the least wanton carriage that might incur suspect ; as, God bless me, she had almost brought bed-pressing out of fashion ; I [105 could scarce get a fine for the lease of a lady's favour once in a fortnight.

Mal. Now, in the name of immodesty, how many maidenheads has thou brought to the block ?   110

Maq. Let me see : heaven forgive us our misdeeds ! — Here 's the duchess.

Scene II.[3]

[To them] enter MARIA *with* Captain.

Mal. God bless thee, lady !

Maria. Out of thy company !

Mal. We have brought thee tender of a husband.

Maria. I hope I have one already.   5

Maq. Nay, by mine honour, madam, as good ha' ne'er a husband as a banished husband ; he 's in another world now. I 'll tell ye, lady, I have heard of a sect that maintained, when the husband was asleep the wife might law- [10 fully entertain another man, for then her husband was as dead ; much more when he is banished.

Maria. Unhonest creature !   14

Maq. Pish, honesty is but an art to seem so : Pray ye, what 's honesty, what 's constancy, But fables feign'd, odd old fools' chat, devis'd By jealous fools to wrong our liberty ?

Mal. Molly, he that loves thee is a duke, Mendoza ; he will maintain thee royally, love [20 thee ardently, defend thee powerfully, marry thee sumptuously, and keep thee in despite of Rosicleer [4] or Donzel del Phebo. There 's jewels : if thou wilt, so ; if not, so.

Maria. Captain, for God's love, save poor wretchedness   25 From tyranny of lustful insolence ! Enforce me in the deepest dungeon dwell, Rather than here ; here round about is hell.— O my dear'st Altofront ! where'er thou breathe, Let my soul sink into the shades beneath,   30 Before I stain thine honour ! 'T is [5] thou has 't, And long as I can die, I will live chaste.

Mal. 'Gainst him that can enforce how vain is strife !

---

1 A hero in *Orlando Furioso*. (Reed.)
2 Bullen's emend. Qq. *stream.*

3 The same.   4 Heroes in *The Mirrour of Knighthood.*
5 Q2 *this.*

Maria. She that can be enforc'd has ne'er a
knife:
She that through force her limbs with lust en-
rolls,   35
Wants Cleopatra's asps and Portia's coals.
God amend you !   *Exit with* Captain.
Mal. Now, the fear of the devil for ever go
with thee ! — Maquerelle, I tell thee, I have
found an honest woman : faith, I perceive, [40
when all is done, there is of women, as of all
other things, some good, most bad ; some saints,
some sinners : for as nowadays no courtier but
has his mistress, no captain but has his cock- [44
atrice, no cuckold but has his horns, and no fool
but has his feather ; even so, no woman but has
her weakness and feather too, no sex but has his
— I can hunt the letter no farther. — (*Aside.*) O
God, how loathsome this toying is to me ! That [49
a duke should be forced to fool it ! Well, *stulto-
rum plena sunt omnia:*[1] better play the fool lord
than be the fool lord. — Now, where's your
sleights, Madam Maquerelle ?
Maq. Why, are ye ignorant that 't is said a
squeamish affected niceness is natural to [55
women, and that the excuse of their yielding is
only, forsooth, the difficult obtaining ? You
must put her to 't : women are flax, and will
fire in a moment.
Mal. Why, was the flax put into thy mouth,
and yet thou —   60
Thou set fire, thou inflame her !
Maq. Marry, but I 'll tell ye now, you were
too hot.
Mal. The fitter to have inflamed the flax,
woman.   65
Maq. You were too boisterous, spleeny, for,
indeed —
Mal. Go, go, thou art a weak pandress ; now
I see,
Sooner earth's fire heaven itself shall waste,   69
Than all with heat can melt a mind that's chaste.
Go ; thou the duke's lime-twig ! I 'll make the
duke turn thee out of thine office : what, not get
one touch of hope, and had her at such advan-
tage !   74
Maq. Now, o' my conscience, now I think in
my discretion, we did not take her in the right
sign ; the blood was not in the true vein, sure.
                                                              Exit.

SCENE III.

[*Enter*[2] BILIOSO.

Bil. Make way there ! The duke returns from
the enthronement. — Malevole —
Mal. Out, rogue !
Bil. Malevole, —
Mal. "Hence, ye gross-jawed, peasantly [5
— out, go ! "[3]
Bil. Nay, sweet Malevole, since my return I
hear you are become the thing I always prophe-
sied would be, — an advanced virtue, a worth-
ily-employed faithfulness, a man o' grace, [10
dear friend. Come ; what ! *Si quoties peccant
homines*[4] — if as often as courtiers play the

knaves, honest men should be angry — why,
look ye, we must collogue[5] sometimes, forswear
sometimes.   15
Mal. Be damned sometimes.
Bil. Right : *nemo omnibus horis sapit ;* "no
man can be honest at all hours : " necessity
often depraves virtue.
Mal. I will commend thee to the duke.   20
Bil. Do : let us be friends, man.
Mal. And knaves, man.
Bil. Right : let us prosper and purchase : our
lordships shall live, and our knavery be for-
gotten.   25
Mal. He that by any ways gets riches, his
means never shames him.
Bil. True.
Mal. For impudency and faithlessness are the
main stays to greatness.   30
Bil. By the Lord, thou art a profound lad.
Mal. By the Lord, thou art a perfect knave :
out, ye ancient damnation !
Bil. Peace, peace ! and thou wilt not be a
friend to me as I am a knave, be not a knave to
me as I am thy friend, and disclose me. Peace !
cornets !]   37

Enter PREPASSO *and* FERRARDO, *two Pages
with lights,* CELSO *and* EQUATO, MENDOZA *in
duke's robes, and* GUERRINO.

Men. On, on ; leave us, leave us.
                Exeunt all saving MALEVOLE [*and*
                MENDOZA].
Stay, where is the hermit ?
Mal. With Duke Pietro, with Duke Pietro.   40
Men. Is he dead ? Is he poisoned ?
Mal. Dead, as the duke is.
Men. Good, excellent : he will not blab : se-
cureness lives in secrecy. Come hither, come
hither.   45
Mal. Thou hast a certain strong villainous
scent about thee my nature cannot endure.
Men. Scent, man ! What returns Maria, what
answer to our suit ?
Mal. Cold, frosty ; she is obstinate.   50
Men. Then she 's but dead ; 't is resolute, she
dies :
"Black deed only through black deed safely
flies."
Mal. Pooh ! *per scelera semper sceleribus tutum
est iter.*[6]
Men. What, art a scholar ? Art a politician ?
Sure, thou art an arrant knave.   55
Mal. Who, I ? I ha' been twice an under-sher-
iff, man.[7]
[Well, I will go rail upon some great man, that
I may purchase the bastinado, or else go marry
some rich Genoan lady, and instantly go travel.
Men. Travel, when thou art married ?   62

<hr>

[1] Cicero, *Ad Fam.* ix. 22. (Bullen.)
[2] Q₁ omits ll. 1-37.   [3] Cf. II. ii. 64.
[4] Ovid, *Tristia,* ii. 33. (Bullen.)

[5] Talk closely together, as if conspiring.
[6] Seneca, *Agam.* 115. (Bullen.)
[7] Q₂ inserts here :
    Mend. *Hast been with Maria?*
    Mal. *As your scrivener to your usurer, I have dealt
    about taking of this commodity, but she 's cold-frosty.*
    These lines seem to have been meant to take the place
of ll. 48-58, which were left in by mistake. Q₁ omits
ll. 59-72.

Mal. Ay, 't is your young lord 's fashion to do so, though he was so lazy, being a bachelor, that he would never travel so far as the uni- [65 versity: yet, when he married her, tales off, and, Catso, for England !

Men. And why for England ?

Mal. Because there is no brothel-houses there.

Men. Nor courtesans ? 70

Mal. Neither ; your whore went down with the stews, and your punk came up with your puritan.]

Men. Canst thou empoison? Canst thou empoison? 75

Mal. Excellently ; no Jew, 'pothecary, or politician better. Look ye, here 's a box : whom wouldst thou empoison? Here 's a box *(giving it)*, which, opened and the fume ta'en up in con- [80 duits thorough which the brain purges it-self, doth instantly for twelve hours' space bind up all show of life in a deep senseless sleep: here 's another *(giving it)*, which, being opened under the sleeper's nose, chokes all the pores of life, kills him suddenly. 85

Men. I 'll try experiments ; 't is good not to be deceived. — So, so ; catso !

Seems to poison MALEVOLE *[who falls]*.

Who would fear that may destroy ?
Death hath no teeth nor tongue ;
And he that 's great, to him are slaves, 90
Shame, murder, fame, and wrong. —

Celso !

Enter Celso.

Celso. My honour'd lord ?

Men. The good Malevole, that plain-tongu'd man,
Alas, is dead on sudden, wondrous strangely !
He held in our esteem good place. Celso, 96
See him buried, see him buried.

Celso. I shall observe ye.

Men. And, Celso, prithee, let it be thy care to-night
To have some pretty show, to solemnize 100
Our high instalment ; some music, masquery.
We 'll give fair entertain unto Maria,
The duchess to the banish'd Altofront :
Thou shalt conduct her from the citadel
Unto the palace. Think on some masquery. 105

Celso. Of what shape, sweet lord ?

Men. What[1] shape ! Why, any quick-done fiction ;
As some brave spirits of the Genoan dukes,
To come out of Elysium, forsooth,
Led in by Mercury, to gratulate 110
Our happy fortune ; some such anything,
Some far-fet trick good for ladies, some stale toy
Or other, no matter, so 't be of our devising.
Do thou prepare 't ; 't is but for fashion sake.
Fear not, it shall be grac'd, man, it shall take.

Celso. All service. 116

Men. All thanks ; our hand shall not be close[2] to thee ; farewell.

[1] *Qu. Why.* [2] Niggardly.

(Aside.) Now is my treachery secure, nor can we fall:
Mischief that prospers, men do virtue call.
I 'll trust no man: he that by tricks gets wreaths 120
Keeps them with steel; no man securely breathes
Out of deserved ranks ; the crowd will mutter, " fool ! "
Who cannot bear with spite, he cannot rule.
The chiefest secret for a man of state
Is, to live senseless of a strengthless hate. *Exit.*

Mal. (starts up and speaks.) Death of the [126 damned thief ! I 'll make one i' the masque ; thou shalt ha' some brave spirits of the antique dukes.

Celso. My lord, what strange delusion ? 130

Mal. Most happy, dear Celso, poisoned with an empty box : I 'll give thee all, anon. My lady comes to court; there is a whirl of fate comes tumbling on ; the castle's captain stands for me, the people pray for me, and the [135 great leader of the just stands for me : then courage, Celso ;
For no disastrous chance can ever move him
That leaveth[3] nothing but a God above him.

Exeunt.

[SCENE IV.][4]

Enter BILIOSO *and* PREPASSO, *two Pages before them ;* MAQUERELLE, BIANCA, *and* EMILIA.

Bil. Make room there, room for the ladies !
Why, gentlemen, will not ye suffer the ladies to be entered in the great chamber? Why, gallants ! and you, sir, to drop your torch where the beauties must sit too ? 5

Pre. And there 's a great fellow plays the knave ; why dost not strike him ?

Bil. Let him play the knave, o' God's name ; thinkest thou I have no more wit than to strike a great fellow ? — The music ! more lights ! [10 revelling-scaffolds ! do you hear ? Let there be oaths enow ready at the door, swear out the devil himself. Let 's leave the ladies, and go see if the lords be ready for them.

Exeunt BILIOSO, PREPASSO, *ana* Pages.

Maq. And, by my tooth, beauties, why do [15 you not put you into the fashion ? This is a stale cut ; you must come in fashion: look ye, you must be all felt, felt and feather, a felt upon your bare hair. Look ye, these tiring things[5] are justly out of request now : and, do ye [20 hear ? you must wear falling-bands,[6] you must come into the falling fashion: there is such a deal o' pinning these ruffs, when the fine clean fall is worth all : and again, if ye should chance to take a nap in the afternoon, your falling- [25 band requires no poting-stick[7] to recover his form: believe me, no fashion to the falling, I say.

[3] Deighton suggests *feareth.*
[4] The Presence-Chamber. [5] Head-dresses.
[6] A part of dress, now usually called a vandyke ; it fell flat upon the dress from the neck, and succeeded the stiff ruffs. (Nares.)
[7] Or poking-stick, for setting the plaits of ruffs.

Bian. And is not Signior St. Andrew a gallant
fellow now.   30
Maq. By my maidenhead, la, honour and he
agree as well together as a satin suit and woollen
stockings.
Emilia. But is not Marshal Make-room, my
servant in reversion, a proper gentleman?   35
Maq. Yes, in reversion, as he had his office;
as, in truth, he hath all things in reversion : he
has his mistress in reversion, his clothes in reversion, his wit in reversion; and, indeed, is a
suitor to me for my dog in reversion : but, [40
in good verity, la, he is as proper a gentleman in
reversion as — and, indeed, as fine a man as may
be, having a red beard and a pair of warpt legs.
Bian. But, i' faith, I am most monstrously
in love with Count Quidlibet-in-quodlibet : [45
is he not a pretty, dapper, unidle[1] gallant ?
Maq. He is even one of the most busy-fingered
lords ; he will put the beauties to the squeak
most hideously.

Re-enter BILIOSO.

Bil. Room ! make a lane there ! the duke [50
is entering : stand handsomely for beauty's sake,
take up the ladies there ! So, cornets, cornets !

SCENE V.

Re-enter PREPASSO, *joins to* BILIOSO ; *then enter*
    two Pages with lights, FERRARDO, MENDOZA ;
    at the other door, two Pages *with lights, and*
    the Captain *leading in* MARIA ; MENDOZA
    meets MARIA *and closeth with her ; the rest fall*
    back.

Men. Madam, with gentle ear receive my suit ;
A kingdom's safety should o'er-peise[2] slight rites ;
Marriage is merely nature's policy :
Then, since unless our royal beds be join'd,
Danger and civil tumults fright the state,   5
Be wise as you are fair, give way to fate.
Maria. What wouldst thou, thou affliction to
    our house ?
Thou ever-devil, 't was thou that banished'st
My truly noble lord !
Men. I !   10
Maria. Ay, by thy plots, by thy black strat-
    agems :
Twelve moons have suffer'd change since I be-
    held
The loved presence of my dearest lord.
O thou far worse than Death ! he parts but soul
From a weak body ; but thou soul from soul   15
Dissever'st, that which God's own hand did
    knit ;
Thou scant of honour, full of devilish wit !
Men. We 'll check your too-intemperate lav-
    ishness :
I can and will.
Maria. What canst ?   20
Men. Go to ; in banishment thy husband dies.
Maria. He ever is at home that 's ever wise.
Men. You 'st ne'er meet more : reason should
    love control.

---

[1] So Q$_2$. Some copies of Q$_1$ *windle.* Bullen suggests
wimble, nimble.
[2] Outweigh.

Maria. Not meet !   24
She that dear loves, her love 's still in her soul.
Men. You are but a woman, lady, you must
    yield.
Maria. O, save me, thou innated bashfulness
Thou only ornament of woman's modesty !
Men. Modesty ! death, I 'll torment thee.   29
Maria. Do, urge all torments, all afflictions try ;
I 'll die my lord's as long as I can die.
Men. Thou obstinate, thou shalt die.— Cap-
    tain, that lady's life
Is forfeited to justice : we have examin'd her,
And we do find she hath empoisoned   34
The reverend hermit ; therefore we command
Severest custody.— Nay, if you 'll do 's no good,
You 'st do 's no harm : a tyrant's peace is blood.
Maria. O, thou art merciful ; O gracious devil,
Rather by much let me condemned be   38
For seeming murder than be damn'd for thee !
I 'll mourn no more ; come, girt my brows with
    flowers :
Revel and dance, soul, now thy wish thou hast ;
Die like a bride, poor heart, thou shalt die
    chaste.

Enter AURELIA *in mourning habit.*

Aur. " Life is a frost of cold felicity,[3]
And death the thaw of all our vanity : "[4]   45
Was 't not an honest priest that wrote so ?
Men. Who let her in ?
Bil. Forbear !
Pre. Forbear !
Aur. Alas, calamity is everywhere :   50
Sad misery, despite your double doors,
Will enter even in court.
Bil. Peace !
Aur. I ha' done.
Bil.[5] One word,— take heed !   55
Aur. I ha' done.

Enter MERCURY *with loud music.*

Mer. Cyllenian Mercury, the god of ghosts,
From gloomy shades that spread the lower
    coasts,[6]
Calls four high-famed Genoan dukes to come,
And make this presence their Elysium,   60
To pass away this high triumphal night
With song and dances, court's more soft delight.
Aur. Are you god of ghosts ? I have a suit
pending in hell betwixt me and my conscience ;
I would fain have thee help me to an advocate.
Bil. Mercury shall be your lawyer, lady.   66
Aur. Nay, faith, Mercury has too good a face
to be a right lawyer.
Pre. Peace, forbear ! Mercury presents the
    masque.

Cornets : the song to the cornets, which playing
    the masque enters ; MALEVOLE, PIETRO, FER-
    NEZE, *and* CELSO, *in white robes, with duke's*
    crowns upon laurel wreaths, pistolets and short
    swords under their robes.

Men. Celso, Celso, court Maria for our love.—
Lady, be gracious, yet grace.   71

---

[2] Some copies of Q$_1$ give this line to Maria.
[4] From Thomas Bastard's *Chrestoleros,* 1598. (Bullen.)
[5] Qq. gives this line to Aurelia.   [6] Regions.

Maria. With me, sir ?

MALEVOLE *takes* MARIA *to dance.*

Mal.   Yes, more loved than my breath ;
With you I 'll dance.

Maria.   Why, then, you dance with death.
But, come, sir, I was ne'er more apt for mirth.
Death gives eternity a glorious breath :   75
O, to die honour'd, who would fear to die ?

Mal. They die in fear who live in villainy.

Men. Yes, believe him, lady, and be rul'd by
him.

Pietro. Madam, with me.

PIETRO *takes* AURELIA *to dance.*

Aur. Wouldst, then, be miserable ?   80

Pietro. I need not wish.

Aur. O, yet forbear my hand ! away ! fly !
fly !

O, seek not her that only seeks to die !

Pietro. Poor loved soul !

Aur. What, wouldst court misery ?   85

Pietro. Yes.

Aur. She 'll come too soon : — O my grieved
heart !

Pietro. Lady, ha' done, ha' done :
Come, let us dance : be once from sorrow free.

Aur. Art a sad man ?   90

Pietro. Yes, sweet.

Aur. Then we 'll agree.

FERNEZE *takes* MAQUERELLE *and*
CELSO, BIANCA : *then the cornets
sound the measure, one change and
rest.*

Fer. (*to* BIANCA.) Believe it, lady ; shall I
swear ? Let me enjoy you in private, and I 'll
marry you, by my soul.   95

Bian. I had rather you would swear by your
body : I think that would prove the more regarded oath with you.

Fer. I 'll swear by them both, to please you.

Bian. O, damn them not both to please [100
me, for God's sake !

Fer. Faith, sweet creature, let me enjoy you
to-night, and I 'll marry you to-morrow fortnight, by my troth, la.

Maq. On his troth, la ! believe him not ; [105
that kind of cony-catching [1] is as stale as Sir
Oliver Anchovy's perfumed jerkin : promise of
matrimony by a young gallant, to bring a virgin
lady into a fool's paradise ; make her a great
woman, and then cast her off ; — 't is as com- [110
mon [and] [2] natural to a courtier, as jealousy
to a citizen, gluttony to a puritan, wisdom to an
alderman, pride to a tailor, or an empty hand-
basket to one of these six-penny damnations :
of his troth, la ! believe him not ; traps to [115
catch pole-cats.

Mal. (*to* MARIA.) Keep your face constant,
let no sudden passion
Speak in your eyes.

Maria. O my Altofront !

Pietro. (*to* AURELIA.) A tyrant's jealousies
Are very nimble : you receive it all ?   121

Aur. My heart, though not my knees, doth
humbly fall
Low as the earth, to thee.

[Mal.] [3] Peace ! next change ; no words.

Maria. Speech to such, ay, O, what will affords !   125

*Cornets sound the measure over
again ; which danced, they unmask.*

Men. Malevole !

They environ MENDOZA, *bending
their pistols on him.*

Mal. No.

Men. Altofront ! Duke Pietro ! Ferneze ! ha !

All. Duke Altofront ! Duke Altofront !

Cornets, a flourish.— They seize upon
MENDOZA.

Men. Are we surpris'd ? What strange de-
lusions mock   130
Our senses ? Do I dream ? or have I dreamt
This two days' space ? Where am I ?

Mal. Where an arch-villain is.

Men. O, lend me breath till I am fit to die !
For peace with heaven, for your own souls' sake,
Vouchsafe me life !   135

Pietro. Ignoble villain ! whom neither heaven
nor hell,
Goodness of God or man, could once make
good !

Mal. Base, treacherous wretch ! what grace
canst thou expect,
That hast grown impudent in gracelessness ? [140]

Men. O, life !

Mal. Slave, take thy life.
Wert thou defenced, th(o)rough blood and
wounds,
The sternest horror of a civil fight,   144
Would I achieve thee ; but prostrate at my feet,
I scorn to hurt thee : 't is the heart of slaves
That deigns to triumph over peasants' graves ;
For such thou art, since birth doth ne'er enroll
A man 'mong monarchs, but a glorious soul.
[4 O, I have seen strange accidents of state !   150
The flatterer, like the ivy, clip the oak,
And waste it to the heart ; lust so confirm'd,
That the black act of sin itself not sham'd
To be term'd courtship.
O, they that are as great as be their sins,   155
Let them remember that th' inconstant people
Love many princes merely for their faces
And outward shows ; and they do covet more
To have a sight of these than of their virtues.
Yet thus much let the great ones still conceive,[5]
When they observe not heaven's impos'd con-
ditions,   160
They are no kings, but forfeit their commis-
sions.

Maq. O good my lord, I have lived in the court
this twenty year : they that have been old
courtiers, and come to live in the city, they [165
are spited at, and thrust to the walls like apricocks, good my lord.

Bil. My lord, I did know your lordship in
this disguise ; you heard me ever say, if Altofront did return, I would stand for him : [170
besides, 't was your lordship's pleasure to call
me wittol and cuckold : you must not think,
but that I knew you, I would have put it up so
patiently.]

[1] Deceiving.   [2] Qq. *as.*   [3] Qq. Pietro.   [4] Q₄ omits ll. 148-172.   [5] Qq. *conceale.*

Mal. You o'er-joy'd spirits, wipe your long-
wet eyes.   *To* PIETRO *and* AURELIA.
Hence with this man (*kicks out* MENDOZA): an
eagle takes not flies.   176
You to your vows (*to* PIETRO *and* AURELIA):
and thou into the suburbs.[1]
                To MAQUERELLE.
You to my worst friend I would hardly give;
Thou art a perfect old knave (*to* BILIOSO): all-
pleas'd live
You two unto my breast (*to* CELSO *and the*
Captain): thou to my heart. (*To* MARIA.)
The rest of idle actors idly part :   181
And as for me, I here assume my right,
To which I hope all 's pleas'd: to all, good-
night.
       Cornets, a flourish. Exeunt omnes.

AN IMPERFECT ODE, BEING BUT ONE STAFF

SPOKEN BY THE PROLOGUE.

To wrest each hurtless thought to private sense
Is the foul use of ill-bred impudence :
    Immodest censure now grows wild,
       All over-running.
    Let innocence be ne'er so chaste,   5
       Yet to the last
       She is defil'd
With too nice-brained cunning.

[1] The disreputable district.

           O you of fairer soul,
             Control   10
     With an Herculean arm
          This harm ;
And once teach all old freedom of a pen,
Which still must write of fools, whiles 't writes
of men !

EPILOGUS

YOUR modest silence, full of heedy stillness,
Makes me thus speak : a voluntary illness
Is merely[2] senseless ; but unwilling error,
Such as proceeds from too rash youthful fer-
vour,
May well be call'd a fault, but not a sin :   5
Rivers take names from founts where they be-
gin.
Then let not too severe an eye peruse
The slighter brakes[3] of our reformed Muse,
Who could herself herself of faults detect,
But that she knows 't is easy to correct,   10
Though some men's labour: troth, to err is fit,
As long as wisdom 's not profess'd, but wit.
Then till another's[4] happier Muse appears,
Till his Thalia feast your learned ears,
To whose desertful lamps pleased Fates impart
Art above nature, judgment above art,   16
Receive this piece, which hope nor fear yet
daunteth :
He that knows most knows most how much he
wanteth.

[2] Wholly.   [3] Flaws.   [4] Ben Jonson's.

A WOMAN KILLED WITH KINDNESS

BY

THOMAS HEYWOOD

[DRAMATIS PERSONAE

SIR FRANCIS ACTON, Brother to Mistress Frankford.
SIR CHARLES MOUNTFORD.
MASTER JOHN FRANKFORD.
MASTER MALBY, friend to Sir Francis.
MASTER WENDOLL, friend to Frankford.
MASTER CRANWELL.
MASTER SHAFTON, false friend to Sir Charles.
OLD MOUNTFORD, Uncle to Sir Charles.
MASTER SANDY.
MASTER RODER.
MASTER TIDY, Cousin to Sir Charles.

NICHOLAS, ROGER BRICKBAT,
JENKIN, JACK SLIME,
SPIGOT, Butler,
} Household Servants to Frankford.
Sheriff.
Keeper of Prison.
Sheriff's Officers, Serjeant, Huntsmen, Falconers, Coachmen, Carters, Servants, Musicians.

MISTRESS ANNE FRANKFORD.
SUSAN, Sister to Sir Charles Mountford.
CICELY, Maid to Mistress Frankford.
Women Servants in Master Frankford's household.]

PROLOGUE

I COME but like a harbinger, being sent
To tell you what these preparations mean.
Look for no glorious state ; our Muse is bent
Upon a barren subject, a bare scene.
We could afford this twig a timber-tree,   5
Whose strength might boldly on your favours build ;
Our russet, tissue ; drone, a honey-bee ;
Our barren plot, a large and spacious field ;
Our coarse fare, banquets ; our thin water, wine ;
Our brook, a sea ; our bat's eyes, eagle's sight ;   10
Our poet's dull and earthy Muse, divine ;
Our ravens, doves ; our crow's black feathers, white.
     But gentle thoughts, when they may give the foil,[1]
     Save them that yield, and spare where they may spoil.

[ACT I]

[SCENE I.][2]

Enter MASTER JOHN FRANKFORD, MISTRESS [FRANKFORD],[3] SIR FRANCIS ACTON, SIR CHARLES MOUNTFORD, MASTER MALBY, MASTER WENDOLL, AND MASTER CRANWELL.

Sir F. Some music, there ! None lead the bride a dance ?
Sir C. Yes, would she dance *The Shaking of*
But that 's the dance her husband means to lead her.
Wen. That 's not the dance that every man must dance,
According to the ballad.[4]

---

[1] Defeat.
[2] Room in Frankford's house.   [3] Q₂ *Acton.*
[4] *The Shaking of the Sheets, or The Dance of Death,* was a well-known ballad and dance tune.

Sir F.   Music, ho !   5
By your leave, sister, — by your husband's leave,
I should have said, — the hand that but this day
Was given you in the church I 'll borrow. — Sound !
This marriage music hoists me from the ground.
Frank. Ay, you may caper ; you are light and free !   10
Marriage hath yok'd my heels ; pray, then, pardon me.
Sir F. I 'll have you dance too, brother !
Sir C.   Master Frankford,
You are a happy man, sir, and much joy
Succeed your marriage mirth : you have a wife
So qualified, and with such ornaments   15
Both of the mind and body. First, her birth
Is noble, and her education such
As might become the daughter of a prince ;
Her own tongue speaks all tongues, and her own hand

Can teach all strings to speak in their best
    grace,   20
From the shrill'st treble to the hoarsest base.
To end her many praises in one word,
She 's Beauty and Perfection's eldest daughter,
Only found by yours, though many a heart hath
    sought her.
    Frank. But that I know your virtues and
        chaste thoughts,   25
I should be jealous of your praise, Sir Charles.
    Cran. He speaks no more than you approve.
    Mal. Nor flatters he that gives to her her due.
    Mrs. F. I would your praise could find a fitter
    theme
Than my imperfect beauties to speak on !   30
Such as they be, if they my husband please,
They suffice me now I am marrièd.
His sweet content is like a flattering glass,
To make my face seem fairer to mine eye ;
But the least wrinkle from his stormy brow   35
Will blast the roses in my cheeks that grow.
    Sir F. A perfect wife already, meek and
        patient !
How strangely the word husband fits your
    mouth,
Not married three hours since ! Sister, 't is
    good ;   39
You that begin betimes thus must needs prove
Pliant and duteous in your husband's love. —
Gramercies, brother ! Wrought her to 't al-
    ready, —
' Sweet husband,' and a curtsey, the first day ?
Mark this, mark this, you that are bachelors,
And never took the grace [1] of honest man ;   45
Mark this, against you marry, [2] this one phrase :
In a good time that man both wins and woos
That takes his wife down [3] in her wedding shoes.
    Frank. Your sister takes not after you, Sir
    Francis,
All his wild blood your father spent on you ;   50
He got her in his age, when he grew civil.
All his mad tricks were to his land entail'd,
And you are heir to all ; your sister, she
Hath to her dower her mother's modesty.
    Sir C. Lord, sir, in what a happy state live
    you !   55
This morning, which to many seems a burden,
Too heavy to bear, is unto you a pleasure.
This lady is no clog, as many are ;
She doth become you like a well-made suit,
In which the tailor hath us'd all his art ;   60
Not like a thick coat of unseason'd frieze,
Forc'd on your back in summer. She 's no chain
To tie your neck, and curb you to the yoke ;
But she 's a chain of gold to adorn your neck.
You both adorn each other, and your hands,   65
Methinks, are matches. There 's equality
In this fair combination ; you are both
Scholars, both young, both being descended
    nobly.
There 's music in this sympathy ; it carries
Consort and expectation of much joy,   70
Which God bestow on you from this first day
Until your dissolution, — that 's for aye !

---

[1] Gained the dignity.
[2] In preparation for marrying.
[3] Reduces her to submission.

    Sir F. We keep you here too long, good
    brother Frankford.
Into the hall ; away ! Go cheer your guests.
What ! Bride and bridegroom both withdrawn
    at once ?   75
If you be mist, the guests will doubt their wel-
    come,
And charge you with unkindness.
    Frank.   To prevent it,
I 'll leave you here, to see the dance within.
    Mrs. F. And so will I.
         Exeunt [MASTER AND MISTRESS
               FRANKFORD].
    Sir. F.   To part you it were sin. —
Now, gallants, while the town musicians   80
Finger their frets [4] within, and the mad lads
And country lasses, every mother's child,
With nosegays and bride-laces [5] in their hats,
Dance all their country measures, rounds, and
    jigs,
What shall we do ? Hark ! They 're all on the
    hoigh ; [6]   85
They toil like mill-horses, and turn as round,—
Marry, not on the toe ! Ay, and they caper,
[Not] [7] without cutting ; you shall see, to-
    morrow,
The hall-floor peckt and dinted like a mill-
    stone,
Made with their high shoes. Though their skill
    be small,   90
Yet they tread heavy where their hobnails fall.
    Sir C. Well, leave them to their sports ! —
Sir Francis Acton,
I 'll make a match with you ! Meet me to-
    morrow
At Chevy Chase ; I 'll fly my hawk with yours.
    Sir F. For what ? For what ?
    Sir C.   Why, for a hundred pound.   95
    Sir F. Pawn me some gold of that !
    Sir C.   Here are ten angels ; [8]
I 'll make them good a hundred pound to-mor-
    row
Upon my hawk's wing.
    Sir. F.   'T is a match ; 't is done.
Another hundred pound upon your dogs ; —
Dare ye, Sir Charles ?
    Sir C.   I dare ; were I sure to lose,
I durst do more than that ; here is my hand,   100
The first course for a hundred pound !
    Sir F.   A match.
    Wen. Ten angels on Sir Francis Acton's
    hawk ;
As much upon his dogs !
    Cran. I 'm for Sir Charles Mountford : I have
    seen   105
His hawk and dog both tried. What ! Clap ye
    hands, [9]
Or is 't no bargain ?
    Wen.   Yes, and stake them down.
Were they five hundred, they were all my own.
    Sir F. Be stirring early with the lark to-
    morrow ;

---

[4] The points where the strings of a musical instrument are stopped.
[5] Streamers.   [6] Boisterous.   [7] Q[1] *But.*
[8] Gold coins worth about $2.50.
[9] Shake hands on it.

I 'll rise into my saddle ere the sun   110
Rise from his bed.
    Sir C.   If there you miss me, say
I am no gentleman! I 'll hold my day.
    Sir F. It holds on all sides. — Come, to-night
let 's dance;
Early to-morrow let 's prepare to ride :   114
We 'd need be three hours up before the bride.
                      Exeunt.

[SCENE II.]¹

Enter NICHOLAS *and* JENKIN, JACK SLIME,
ROGER BRICKBAT, *with* Country Wenches,
and two or three Musicians.

    Jen. Come, Nick, take you Joan Miniver, to
trace withal; Jack Slime, traverse you with
Cicely Milkpail; I will take Jane Trubkin, and
Roger Brickbat shall have Isabel Motley. And
now that they are busy in the parlour, come, [5
strike up; we 'll have a crash² here in the
yard.
    Nich. My humour is not compendious: danc-
ing I possess not, though I can foot it; yet,
since I am fallen into the hands of Cicely [10
Milkpail, I consent.
    Slime. Truly, Nick, though we were never
brought up like serving courtiers, yet we have
been brought up with serving creatures, — ay,
and God's creatures, too; for we have been [15
brought up to serve sheep, oxen, horses, hogs,
and such like; and, though we be but country
fellows, it may be in the way of dancing we can
do the horse-trick as well as the serving-men.
    Brick. Ay, and the cross-point too.   20
    Jen. O Slime! O Brickbat! Do not you know
that comparisons are odious? Now we are odious ourselves, too; therefore there are no comparisons to be made betwixt us.
    Nich. I am sudden, and not superfluous;   25
I am quarrelsome, and not seditious;
I am peaceable, and not contentious;
I am brief, and not compendious.
    Slime. Foot it quickly! If the music overcome
not my melancholy, I shall quarrel; and if [30
they suddenly do not strike up, I shall presently
strike thee down.
    Jen. No quarrelling, for God's sake! Truly,
if you do, I shall set a knave between ye.
    Slime. I come to dance, not to quarrel. [35
Come, what shall it be? *Rogero*?³
    Jen. Rogero? No; we will dance *The Begin-
ning of the World.*
    Cicely. I love no dance so well as *John come
kiss me now.*   40
    Nich. I that have ere now deserv'd a cush-
ion, call for the *Cushion-dance.*
    Brick. For my part, I like nothing so well as
Tom Tyler.
    Jen. No; we 'll have *The Hunting of the* [45
Fox.
    Slime. The Hay, The Hay! There 's nothing
like *The Hay.*
    Nich. I have said, I do say, and I will say
again ——   50

¹ Yard of the same.   ² Frolic, bout.
³ The names of the dance-tunes here were all familiar.

    Jen. Every man agree to have it as Nick says!
    All. Content.
    Nich. It hath been, it now is, and it shall
be ——
    Cicely. What, Master Nicholas? What?   55
    Nich. Put on your Smock a' Monday.
    Jen. So the dance will come cleanly off! Come,
for God's sake, agree of something : if you like
not that, put it to the musicians; or let me
speak for all, and we 'll have *Sellenger's* [60
Round.
    All. That, that, that!
    Nich. No, I am resolv'd thus it shall be;
First take hands, then take ye to your heels.
    Jen. Why, would you have us run away?   65
    Nich. No; but I would have you shake your
heels. — Music, strike up!
       They dance; NICK *dancing, speak
         stately and scurvily, the rest after
         the country fashion.*
    Jen. Hey! Lively, my lasses! Here 's a turn
for thee!   *Exeunt.*

[SCENE III.]⁴

Wind horns. Enter SIR CHARLES MOUNTFORD,
SIR FRANCIS ACTON, MALBY, CRANWELL,
WENDOLL, Falconer, *and* Huntsmen.

    Sir C. So; well cast off! Aloft, aloft! Well
flown!
Oh, now she takes her at the souse,⁵ and strikes
her
Down to the earth, like a swift thunder-clap.
    Wen. She hath struck ten angels out of my
way.
    Sir F. A hundred pound from me.   5
    Sir C. What, falconer!
    Falc. At hand, sir!
    Sir C. Now she hath seiz'd the fowl and 'gins
to plume⁶ her,
Rebeck⁷ her not; rather stand still and check
her!
So, seize her gets,⁸ her jesses,⁹ and her bells!   10
Away!
    Sir F. My hawk kill'd, too.
    Sir C.   Ay, but 't was at the querre,¹⁰
Not at the mount like mine.
    Sir F.   Judgment, my masters!
    Cran. Yours mist her at the ferre.¹¹
    Wen. Ay, but our merlin first had plum'd
the fowl,   15
And twice renew'd¹² her from the river too.
Her bells, Sir Francis, had not both one weight,
Nor was one semi-tune above the other.
Methinks, these Milan bells do sound too full,
And spoil the mounting of your hawk.
    Sir C.   'T is lost.   20
    Sir F. I grant it not. Mine likewise seiz'd a
fowl
Within her talons, and you saw her paws

---

⁴ Chevy Chase.   ⁶ Pluck.
⁵ On the descent.   ⁷ Call back.
⁸ Verity explains as " booty," but apparently it is
the same as *jesses.*   ⁹ Leg-straps.
¹⁰ Quarry: " the swoop upon the bird." (N. E. D.)
¹¹ Not satisfactorily explained.
¹² Attacked afresh.

Full of the feathers ; both her petty singles [1]
And her long singles grip'd her more than
  other ;
The terrials [2] of her [3] legs were stain'd with
  blood,   25
Not of the fowl only ; she did discomfit
Some of her feathers ; but she brake away.
Come, come ; your hawk is but a rifler. [4]
  Sir C.   How !
  Sir F. Ay, and your dogs are trindle-tails [5]
  and curs.
  Sir C. You stir my blood.   30
You keep not one good hound in all your ken-
  nel,
Nor one good hawk upon your perch.
  Sir F.   How, knight !
  Sir F. So, knight. You will not swagger,
  sir ?
  Sir F. Why, say I did ?
  Sir C.   Why, sir,
I say you would gain as much by swagg'ring   35
As you have got by wagers on your dogs.
You will come short in all things.
  Sir F.   Not in this !
Now I 'll strike home.   [*Strikes* Sir Charles.]
  Sir C.   Thou shalt to thy long home,
Or I will want my will.
  Sir F. All they that love Sir Francis, follow
  me !   40
  Sir C. All that affect Sir Charles, draw on
  my part !
  Cran. On this side heaves my hand.
  Wen.   Here goes my heart.
    They divide themselves. Sir Charles
      Mountford, Cranwell, Fal-
      coner, *and* Huntsman, *fight*
      against Sir Francis Acton,
      Wendoll, *his* Falconer *and*
      Huntsman ; *and* Sir Charles
      hath the better, and beats them
      away, killing both of Sir Fran-
      cis's *men.* [*Exeunt all but* Sir
      Charles Mountford.]
  Sir C. My God, what have I done ! What
  have I done !
My rage hath plung'd into a sea of blood,
In which my soul lies drown'd. Poor inno-
  cents,   45
For whom we are to answer ! Well, 't is done,
And I remain the victor. A great conquest,
When I would give this right hand, nay, this
  head,
To breathe in them new life whom I have
  slain ! —
Forgive me, God ! 'T was in the heat of
  blood,   50
And anger quite removes me from myself.
It was not I, but rage, did this vile murder ;
Yet I, and not my rage, must answer it.
Sir Francis Acton, he is fled the field ;
With him all those that did partake his quarrel ;
And I am left alone with sorrow dumb,   55
And in my height of conquest overcome.

  [1] Toes.   [2] Unexplained.
  [3] The rest of the speech seems to refer to Mountford's
  hawk.
  [4] Bungler.   [5] Curly-tailed.

Enter Susan.

  Susan. O God ! My brother wounded 'mong
  the dead !
Unhappy jest, that in such earnest ends !
The rumour of this fear stretcht to my ears,   60
And I am come to know if you be wounded.
  Sir C. Oh, sister, sister ! Wounded at the
  heart.
  Susan. My God forbid !
  Sir. C. In doing that thing which he for-
  bad,
I am wounded, sister.
  Susan.   I hope, not at the heart.   65
  Sir C. Yes, at the heart.
  Susan.   O God ! A surgeon, there.
  Sir C. Call me a surgeon, sister, for my
  soul !
The sin of murder, it hath pierc'd my heart
And made a wide wound there ; but for these
  scratches,
They are nothing, nothing.
  Susan.   Charles, what have you done ?   70
Sir Francis hath great friends, and will pursue
  you
Unto the utmost danger [6] of the law.
  Sir C. My conscience is become mine enemy,
And will pursue me more than Acton can.
  Susan. Oh ! Fly, sweet brother !
  Sir C.   Shall I fly from thee ?   75
Why, Sue, art weary of my company ?
  Susan. Fly from your foe !
  Sir C.   You, sister, are my friend,
And flying you, I shall pursue my end.
  Susan. Your company is as my eyeball
  dear ;
Being far from you, no comfort can be near.   80
Yet fly to save your life ! What would I care
To spend my future age in black despair,
So you were safe ? And yet to live one week
Without my brother Charles, through every
  cheek
My streaming tears would downwards run so
  rank,   85
Till they could set on either side a bank,
And in the midst a channel ; so my face
For two salt-water brooks shall still find place.
  Sir C. Thou shalt not weep so much ; for I
  will stay,
In spite of danger's teeth. I 'll live with thee, 90
Or I 'll not live at all. I will not sell
My country and my father's patrimony,
Nor thy sweet sight, for a vain hope of life.

Enter Sheriff, *with* Officers.

  Sher. Sir Charles, I am made the unwilling
  instrument
Of your attach [8] and apprehension.   95
I 'm sorry that the blood of innocent men
Should be of you exacted. It was told me
That you were guarded with a troop of friends,
And therefore I come thus arm'd.
  Sir C.   Oh, Master Sheriff !
I came into the field with many friends,   100

  [6] Limit of liability.   [7] Abundantly.
            [8] Arrest.

But see, they all have left me ; only one
Clings to my sad misfortune, my dear sister.
I know you for an honest gentleman ;
I yield my weapons, and submit to you.
Convey me where you please !
Sher.   To prison, then, 105
To answer for the lives of these dead men.
Susan. O God ! O God !
Sir C.   Sweet sister, every strain
Of sorrow from your heart augments my pain ;
Your grief abounds,[1] and hits against my
breast.
Sher. Sir, will you go ?
Sir C.   Even where it likes you best. 110
                    [*Exeunt.*]

[ACT II]

[SCENE I.]

Enter MASTER FRANKFORD *in a study.*

Frank. How happy am I amongst other men,
That in my mean estate embrace content !
I am a gentleman, and by my birth
Companion with a king ; a king 's no more.
I am possess'd of many fair revenues,   5
Sufficient to maintain a gentleman ;
Touching my mind, I am studied in all arts ;
The riches of my thoughts and of my time
Have been a good proficient ;[2] but, the chief
Of all the sweet felicities on earth,   10
I have a fair, a chaste, and loving wife, —
Perfection all, all truth, all ornament.
If man on earth may truly happy be,
Of these at once possess, sure, I am he.

Enter NICHOLAS.

Nich. Sir, there 's a gentleman attends with-
out   15
To speak with you.
Frank.   On horseback ?
Nich.   Yes, on horseback.
Frank. Entreat him to alight, I will attend
him.
Know'st thou him, Nick ?
Nich. Know him ? Yes ; his name 's Wendoll.
It seems, he comes in haste : his horse is booted[3]
Up to the flank in mire, himself all spotted   20
And stain'd with plashing. Sure, he rid in
fear,
Or for a wager. Horse and man both sweat ;
I ne'er saw two in such a smoking heat.
Frank. Entreat him in : about it instantly !
                    [*Exit* NICHOLAS.]
This Wendoll I have noted, and his carriage   25
Hath pleas'd me much ; by observation
I have noted many good deserts in him.
He 's affable, and seen[4] in many things ;
Discourses well ; a good companion ;
And though of small means, yet a gentleman   30
Of a good house, though somewhat prest by
want.
I have preferr'd him to a second place
In my opinion and my best regard.

Enter WENDOLL, MISTRESS FRANKFORD, *and*
NICHOLAS.

Mrs. F. Oh, Master Frankford ! Master Wen-
doll here
Brings you the strangest news that e'er you
heard.   35
Frank. What news, sweet wife ? What news,
good Master Wendoll ?
Wen. You knew the match made 'twixt Sir
Francis Acton
And Sir Charles Mountford ?
Frank. True ; with their hounds and hawks.
Wen. The matches were both play'd.
Frank.   Ha ? And which won ?
Wen. Sir Francis, your wife's brother, had
the worst,   40
And lost the wager.
Frank.   Why, the worse his chance ;
Perhaps the fortune of some other day
Will change his luck.
Mrs. F.   Oh, but you hear not all.
Sir Francis lost, and yet was loth to yield.   44
At length the two knights grew to difference,
From words to blows, and so to banding sides ;[5]
Where valorous Sir Charles slew, in his spleen,
Two of your brother's men, — his falconer,
And his good huntsman, whom he lov'd so
well.
More men were wounded, no more slain out-
right.   50
Frank. Now, trust me, I am sorry for the
knight.
But is my brother safe ?
Wen.   All whole and sound,
His body not being blemish'd with one wound.
But poor Sir Charles is to the prison led,
To answer at th' assize for them that 's dead.
Frank. I thank your pains, sir. Had the news
been better,   56
Your will was to have brought it, Master Wen-
doll.
Sir Charles will find hard friends ; his case is
heinous
And will be most severely censur'd[6] on.
I 'm sorry for him. Sir, a word with you !   60
I know you, sir, to be a gentleman
In all things ; your possibilities[7] but mean :
Please you to use my table and my purse ;
They 're yours.
Wen.   O Lord, sir ! I shall ne'er deserve it.
Frank. O sir, disparage not your worth too
much :   65
You are full of quality[8] and fair desert.
Choose of my men which shall attend on you,
And he is yours. I will allow you, sir,
Your man, your gelding, and your table, all
At my own charge ; be my companion !   70
Wen. Master Frankford, I have oft been
bound to you
By many favours ; this exceeds them all,
That I shall never merit your least favour ;
But when your last remembrance I forget,
Heaven at my soul exact that weighty debt !   75

Frank. There needs no protestation; for I
know you
Virtuous, and therefore grateful. — Prithee,
Nan,
Use him with all thy loving'st courtesy !
Mrs. F. As far as modesty may well extend,
It is my duty to receive your friend.   80
Frank. To dinner ! Come, sir, from this pre-
sent day,
Welcome to me for ever ! Come, away !
            Exeunt [FRANKFORD, MISTRESS
            FRANKFORD, *and* WENDOLL].
Nich. I do not like this fellow by no means :
I never see him but my heart still yearns.[1]
Zounds ! I could fight with him, yet know not
why ;   85
The devil and he are all one in mine eye.

            Enter JENKIN.

Jen. O Nick ! What gentleman is that comes
to lie at our house ? My master allows him one
to wait on him, and I believe it will fall to thy
lot.   90
Nich. I love my master ; by these hilts, I do ;
But rather than I 'll ever come to serve him,
I 'll turn away my master.

            Enter CICELY.

Cic. Nich'las ! where are you, Nich'las ? You
must come in, Nich'las, and help the young
gentleman off with his boots.   96
Nich. If I pluck off his boots, I 'll eat the
spurs,
And they shall stick fast in my throat like burrs.
Cic. Then, Jenkin, come you !
Jen. Nay, 't is no boot[2] for me to deny it. [100
My master hath given me a coat here, but he
takes pains himself to brush it once or twice a
day with a holly wand.
Cic. Come, come, make haste, that you may
wash your hands again, and help to serve [105
in dinner !
Jen. You may see, my masters, though it be
afternoon with you, 't is yet but early days with
us, for we have not din'd yet. Stay but a little ;
I 'll but go in and help to bear up the first [110
course, and come to you again presently.
                                        Exeunt.

            [SCENE II.][3]

            Enter MALBY *and* CRANWELL.

Mal. This is the sessions-day ; pray can you
tell me
How young Sir Charles hath sped ? Is he ac-
quit,
Or must he try the laws' strict penalty ?
Cran. He 's clear'd of all, spite of his ene-
mies,
Whose earnest labour was to take his life.   5
But in this suit of pardon he hath spent
All the revenues that his father left him ;
And he is now turn'd a plain countryman,
Reform'd[4] in all things. See, sir, here he
comes.

            ---

1 Grieves.   3 The Gaol.
2 Use.   4 Changed.

            Enter SIR CHARLES *and his* Keeper.

Keep. Discharge your fees, and you are then
at freedom.   10
Sir C. Here, Master Keeper, take the poor
remainder
Of all the wealth I have ! My heavy foes
Have made my purse light ; but, alas ! to me
'T is wealth enough that you have set me free.
Mal. God give you joy of your delivery !   15
I am glad to see you abroad, Sir Charles.
Sir C. The poorest knight in England, Mas-
ter Malby.
My life has cost me all my patrimony
My father left his son. Well, God forgive them
That are the authors of my penury !   20

            Enter SHAFTON.

Shaft. Sir Charles ! A hand, a hand ! At lib-
erty ?
Now, by the faith I owe, I am glad to see it.
What want you ? Wherein may I pleasure you ?
Sir C. Oh me ! Oh, most unhappy gentle-
man !
I am not worthy to have friends stirr'd up,   25
Whose hands may help me in this plunge of
want.
I would I were in Heaven, to inherit there
Th' immortal birthright which my Saviour
keeps,
And by no unthrift can be bought and sold ;
For here on earth what pleasures should we
trust !   30
Shaft. To rid you from these contemplations,
Three hundred pounds you shall receive of
me ;
Nay, five for fail.[5] Come, sir, the sight of gold
Is the most sweet receipt for melancholy,
And will revive your spirits. You shall hold
law   35
With your proud adversaries. Tush ! let Frank
Acton
Wage, with his knighthood, like expense with
me,
And he will sink, he will. — Nay, good Sir
Charles,
Applaud your fortune and your fair escape
From all these perils.
Sir C.   Oh, sir ! they have undone me. 40
Two thousand and five hundred pound a year
My father at his death possest me of ;
All which the envious Acton made me spend ;
And, notwithstanding all this large expense,
I had much ado to gain my liberty ;   45
And I have only now a house of pleasure,
With some five hundred pounds reserv'd,
Both to maintain me and my loving sister.
Shaft. [*Aside.*] That must I have, it lies con-
venient for me.
If I can fasten but one finger on him,   50
With my full hand I 'll gripe him to the heart.
'T is not for love I proffer'd him this coin,
But for my gain and pleasure. — Come, Sir
Charles,
I know you have need of money ; take my offer.

            ---

5 To prevent failure.

Sir C. Sir, I accept it, and remain indebted
Even to the best of my unable [1] power.　　56
Come, gentlemen, and see it tend'red down ! [2]

[*Exeunt.*]

[SCENE III.] [3]

Enter WENDOLL, *melancholy.*

Wen. I am a villain, if I apprehend [4]
But such a thought ! Then, to attempt the deed,
Slave, thou art damn'd without redemption. —
I 'll drive away this passion with a song.　　4
A song ! Ha, ha ! A song ! As if, fond [5] man,
Thy eyes could swim in laughter, when thy soul
Lies drench'd and drowned in red tears of blood !
I 'll pray, and see if God within my heart
Plant better thoughts. Why, prayers are meditations,
And when I meditate (oh, God forgive me !)　　10
It is on her divine perfections.
I will forget her ; I will arm myself
Not t' entertain a thought of love to her ;
And, when I come by chance into her presence,
I 'll hale these balls until my eye-strings crack.　　15
From being pull'd and drawn to look that way.

Enter, over the Stage, FRANKFORD, *his* Wife,
and NICHOLAS [*and exit*].

O God, O God ! With what a violence
I 'm hurried to mine own destruction !
There goest thou, the most perfectest man
That ever England bred a gentleman,　　20
And shall I wrong his bed ? — Thou God of thunder !
Stay, in Thy thoughts of vengeance and of wrath,
Thy great, almighty, and all-judging hand
From speedy execution on a villain, —
A villain and a traitor to his friend.　　25

Enter JENKIN.

Jen. Did your worship call ?
Wen. He doth maintain me ; he allows me largely
Money to spend.
Jen. By my faith, so do not you me : I cannot
get a cross of you.　　30
Wen. My gelding, and my man.
Jen. That 's Sorrel and I.
Wen. This kindness grows of no alliance [6]
'twixt us.
Jen. Nor is my service of any great acquaintance.
Wen. I never bound him to me by desert.　　35
Of a mere stranger, a poor gentleman,
A man by whom in no kind he could gain,
He hath plac'd me in the height of all his thoughts,
Made me companion with the best and chiefest
In Yorkshire. He cannot eat without me,　　40
Nor laugh without me ; I am to his body

1 Feeble.
2 Paid over.
3 Frankford's house.
4 Conceive.
5 Foolish.
6 Relationship.

As necessary as his digestion,
And equally do make him whole or sick.
And shall I wrong this man ? Base man ! Ingrate !
Hast thou the power, straight with thy gory hands,　　45
To rip thy image from his bleeding heart,
To scratch thy name from out the holy book
Of his remembrance, and to wound his name
That holds thy name so dear ? Or rend his heart
To whom thy heart was knit and join'd together ? —　　50
And yet I must. Then Wendoll, be content !
Thus villains, when they would, cannot repent.
Jen. What a strange humour is my new master in ! Pray God he be not mad ; if he should
be so, I should never have any mind to serve [55
him in Bedlam. It may be he 's mad for missing of me.
Wen. What, Jenkin ! Where 's your mistress ?
Jen. Is your worship married ?　　60
Wen. Why dost thou ask ?
Jen. Because you are my master ; and if I
have a mistress, I would be glad, like a good
servant, to do my duty to her.
Wen. I mean Mistress Frankford.　　65
Jen. Marry, sir, her husband is riding out of
town, and she went very lovingly to bring him
on his way to horse. Do you see, sir ? Here she
comes, and here I go.
Wen. Vanish !　　[*Exit* JENKINS.] 70

Enter MISTRESS FRANKFORD.

Mrs. F. You are well met, sir ; now, in troth, my husband
Before he took horse, had a great desire
To speak with you ; we sought about the house,
Halloo'd into the fields, sent every way,
But could not meet you. Therefore, he enjoin'd me　　75
To do unto you his most kind commends, —
Nay, more : he wills you, as you prize his love,
Or hold in estimation his kind friendship,
To make bold in his absence, and command
Even as himself were present in the house ;　　80
For you must keep his table, use his servants,
And be a present Frankford in his absence.
Wen. I thank him for his love. —
[*Aside.*] Give me a name, you, whose infectious tongues
Are tipt with gall and poison : as you would
Think on a man that had your father slain,　　85
Murd'red your children, made your wives base strumpets,
So call me, call me so ; print in my face
The most stigmatic [7] title of a villain,
For hatching treason to so true a friend !　　90
Mrs. F. Sir, you are much beholding to my husband ;
You are a man most dear in his regard.
Wen. I am bound unto your husband, and you too.

7 Opprobrious.

[*Aside.*] I will not speak to wrong a gentle-
man
Of that good estimation, my kind friend.   95
I will not ; zounds ! I will not. I may choose,
And I will choose. Shall I be so misled,
Or shall I purchase [1] to my father's crest
The motto of a villain ? If I say
I will not do it, what thing can enforce me ?   100
What can compel me ? What sad destiny
Hath such command upon my yielding
thoughts ?
I will not ; — ha ! Some fury pricks me on ;
The swift fates drag me at their chariot
wheel,
And hurry me to mischief. Speak I must :   105
Injure myself, wrong her, deceive his trust !
Mrs. F. Are you not well, sir, that you seem
thus troubled ?
There is sedition in your countenance.
Wen. And in my heart, fair angel, chaste
and wise.   109
I love you ! Start not, speak not, answer not ;
I love you, — nay, let me speak the rest ;
Bid me to swear, and I will call to record
The host of Heaven.
Mrs. F.   The host of Heaven forbid
Wendoll should hatch such a disloyal thought ?
Wen. Such is my fate ; to this suit was I
born,   115
To wear rich pleasure's crown, or fortune's
scorn.
Mrs. F. My husband loves you.
Wen.   I know it.
Mrs. F.   He esteems you,
Even as his brain, his eye-ball, or his heart.
Wen. I have tried it.
Mrs. F. His purse is your exchequer, and his
table   120
Doth freely serve you.
Wen.   So I have found it.
Mrs. F. Oh ! With what face of brass, what
brow of steel,
Can you, unblushing, speak this to the face
Of the espous'd wife of so dear a friend ?   124
It is my husband that maintains your state. —
Will you dishonour him that in your power
Hath left his whole affairs ? I am his wife,
It is to me you speak.
Wen.   O speak no more ;
For more than this I know, and have recorded
Within the red-leav'd table of my heart.   130
Fair, and of all belov'd, I was not fearful
Bluntly to give my life into your hand,
And at one hazard all my earthly means.
Go, tell your husband ; he will turn me off,
And I am then undone. I care not, I ;   135
'Twas for your sake. Perchance, in rage he 'll
kill me ;
I care not, 't was for you, Say I incur
The general name of villain through the world,
Of traitor to my friend ; I care not, I.
Beggary, shame, death, scandal, and re-
proach, —   140
For you I 'll hazard all. Why, what care I ?
For you I 'll live, and in your love I 'll die.

---

[1] Acquire, add.

Mrs. F. You move me, sir, to passion and to
pity.
The love I bear my husband is as precious
As my soul's health.
Wen.   I love your husband too,   145
And for his love I will engage my life.
Mistake me not ; the augmentation
Of my sincere affection borne to you
Doth no whit lessen my regard to him.
I will be secret, lady, close as night ;   150
And not the light of one small glorious star
Shall shine here in my forehead, to bewray
That act of night.
Mrs. F.   What shall I say ?
My soul is wandering, hath lost her way.
Oh, Master Wendoll ! Oh !
Wen.   Sigh not, sweet saint ; 1x
For every sigh you breathe draws from my
heart
A drop of blood.
Mrs. F.   I ne'er offended yet:
My fault, I fear, will in my brow be writ.
Women that fall, not quite bereft of grace,
Have their offences noted in their face.   16x
I blush, and am asham'd. Oh, Master Wen-
doll,
Pray God I be not born to curse your tongue,
That hath enchanted me ! This maze I am
in
I fear will prove the labyrinth of sin.

Enter NICHOLAS [*behind*].

Wen. The path of pleasure and the gate to
bliss,   165
Which on your lips I knock at with a kiss !
Nich. I 'll kill the rogue.
Wen. Your husband is from home, your bed's
no blab.
Nay, look not down and blush !
                    [*Exeunt* WENDOLL *and* MISTRESS
                         FRANKFORD.]
Nich.   Zounds ! I 'll stab.
Ay, Nick, was it thy chance to come just in the
nick ?   170
I love my master, and I hate that slave ;
I love my mistress, but these tricks I like
not.
My master shall not pocket up this wrong ;
I 'll eat my fingers first. What say'st thou,
metal ?
Does not that rascal Wendoll go on legs   175
That thou must cut off ? Hath he not ham-
strings
That thou must hough ? Nay, metal, thou shalt
stand
To all I say. I 'll henceforth turn a spy,
And watch them in their close conveyances.[2]
I never look'd for better of that rascal,   180
Since he came miching [3] first into our house.
It is that Satan hath corrupted her ;
For she was fair and chaste. I 'll have an
eye
In all their gestures. Thus I think of them :
If they proceed as they have done before,   185
Wendoll 's a knave, my mistress is a ——
                                        Exit.

---

[2] Secret proceedings.   [3] Sneaking.

[ACT III]

[SCENE I.][1]

Enter SIR CHARLES MOUNTFORD *and* SUSAN.

Sir C. Sister, you see we are driven to hard
    shift,
To keep this poor house we have left unsold.
I 'm now enforc'd to follow husbandry,
And you to milk ; and do we not live well ?
Well, I thank God.
Susan.   Oh, brother ! here 's a change,   5
Since old Sir Charles died in our father's house.
Sir C. All things on earth thus change,
    some up, some down ;
Content 's a kingdom, and I wear that crown.

Enter SHAFTON, *with a* Sergeant.

Shaft. Good morrow, morrow, Sir Charles !
    What ! With your sister,   9
Plying your husbandry ? — Sergeant, stand off ! —
You have a pretty house here, and a garden,
And goodly ground about it. Since it lies
So near a lordship that I lately bought,
I would fain buy it of you. I will give you ——
Sir C. Oh, pardon me ; this house succes-
    sively   15
Hath long'd to me and my progenitors
Three hundred years. My great-great-grand-
    father,
He in whom first our gentle style began,
Dwelt here, and in this ground increast this
    mole-hill
Unto that mountain which my father left me.
Where he the first of all our house began,   21
I now the last will end, and keep this house, —
This virgin title, never yet deflower'd
By any unthrift of the Mountfords' line.
In brief, I will not sell it for more gold   25
Than you could hide or pave the ground withal.
Shaft. Ha, ha ! a proud mind and a beggar's
    purse !
Where 's my three hundred pounds, besides the
    use ?[2]
I have brought it to an execution   29
By course of law. What ! Is my money ready ?
Sir C. An execution, sir, and never tell me
You put my bond in suit ? You deal extremely.[3]
Shaft. Sell me the land, and I 'll acquit you
    straight.
Sir C. Alas, alas ! 'T is all trouble hath left
    me
To cherish me and my poor sister's life.   35
If this were sold, our names should then be
    quite
Raz'd from the bead-roll[4] of gentility.
You see what hard shift we have made to keep
    it
Allied still to our name. This palm you see,
Labour hath glow'd within ; her silver brow,   40
That never tasted a rough winter's blast
Without a mask or fan, doth with a grace
Defy cold winter, and his storms outface.

[1] Sir Charles Mountford's house.
[2] Interest.   [3] Extremely rigorously.
[4] List. Properly a list of names to be prayed for.

Susan. Sir, we feed sparing, and we labour
    hard,
We lie uneasy, to reserve to us   45
And our succession this small spot of ground.
Sir C. I have so bent my thoughts to hus-
    bandry,
That I protest I scarcely can remember
What a new fashion is ; how silk or satin
Feels in my hand. Why, pride is grown to us   50
A mere, mere stranger. I have quite forgot
The names of all that ever waited on me.
I cannot name ye any of my hounds,
Once from whose echoing mouths I heard all
    music
That e'er my heart desir'd. What should I
    say ?   55
To keep this place, I have chang'd myself
    away.
Shaft. Arrest him at my suit ! — Actions and
    actions
Shall keep thee in perpetual bondage fast ;
Nay, more, I 'll sue thee by a late appeal,
And call thy former life in question.   60
The keeper is my friend ; thou shalt have irons,
And usage such as I 'll deny to dogs. —
Away with him !
Sir C.   You are too timorous.[5]
But trouble is my master,
And I will serve him truly. — My kind sister,
Thy tears are of no use to mollify   65
The flinty man. Go to my father's brother,
My kinsmen, and allies ; entreat them for me,
To ransom me from this injurious man
That seeks my ruin.
Shaft.   Come, irons ! Come away ;   70
I 'll see thee lodg'd far from the sight of day.
                            Exeunt [except SUSAN].
Susan. My heart 's so hard'ned with the frost
    of grief,
Death cannot pierce it through. — Tyrant too
    fell !
So lead the fiends condemned souls to hell.

Enter SIR FRANCIS ACTON *and* MALBY.

Sir F. Again to prison ! Malby, hast thou
    seen   75
A poor slave better tortur'd ? Shall we hear
The music of his voice cry from the grate,[6]
Meat, for the Lord's sake? No, no ; yet I am
    not
Throughly reveng'd. They say, he hath a pretty
    wench
Unto his sister ; shall I, in mercy-sake   80
To him and to his kindred, bribe the fool
To shame herself by lewd, dishonest lust ?
I 'll proffer largely ; but, the deed being done,
I 'll smile to see her base confusion.
Mal. Methinks, Sir Francis, you are full re-
    veng'd   85
For greater wrongs than he can proffer you.
See where the poor sad gentlewoman stands !
Sir F. Ha, ha ! Now will I flout her poverty,
Deride her fortunes, scoff her base estate ;
My very soul the name of Mountford hates.   90
But stay, my heart ! Oh, what a look did fly

[5] Ed. conj. *tyrannous.*   [6] Of the debtor's prison.

To strike my soul through with thy piercing
eye!
I am enchanted; all my spirits are fled.
And with one glance my envious spleen struck
dead.
Susan. Acton! That seeks our blood!
Runs away.
Sir F. O chaste and fair! ⁹⁵
Mal. Sir Francis! Why, Sir Francis! Zounds,
in a trance?
Sir Francis! What cheer, man? Come, come,
how is 't?
Sir F. Was she not fair? Or else this judg-
ing eye
Cannot distinguish beauty.
Mal. She was fair. ⁹⁹
Sir F. She was an angel in a mortal's shape,
And ne'er descended from old Mountford's line.
But soft, soft, let me call my wits together!
A poor, poor wench, to my great adversary
Sister, whose very souls denounce stern war
One against other! How now, Frank, turn'd ¹⁰⁵
fool
Or madman, whether? But no! Master of
My perfect senses and directest wits.
Then why should I be in this violent humour
Of passion and of love? And with a person
So different every way, and so oppos'd ¹¹⁰
In all contractions ¹ and still-warring actions?
Fie, fie! How I dispute against my soul!
Come, come; I 'll gain her, or in her fair quest
Purchase my soul free and immortal rest.
[Exeunt.]

[SCENE II.] ²

Enter three or four Serving-men, *one with a voi-
der* ³ *and a wooden knife, to take away all;
another the salt and bread; another with the
table-cloth and napkins; another the carpet;* ⁴
JENKIN *with two lights after them.*

Jen. So; march in order, and retire in
battle array! My master and the guests have
supp'd already; all 's taken away. Here, now
spread for the serving-men in the hall! — Butler, it belongs to your office. ⁵
But. I know it, Jenkin. What d' ye call the
gentleman that supp'd there to-night?
Jen. Who? My master?
But. No, no; Master Wendoll, he 's a daily
guest. I mean the gentleman that came [¹⁰
but this afternoon.
Jen. His name 's Master Cranwell. God's
light! Hark, within there; my master calls to
lay more billets ⁵ upon the fire. Come, come!
Lord, how we that are in office here in the [¹⁵
house are troubled! One spread the carpet in
the parlour, and stand ready to snuff the lights;
the rest be ready to prepare their stomachs!
More lights in the hall, there! Come, Nicholas.
Exeunt [all but NICHOLAS].
Nich. I cannot eat; but had I Wendoll's
heart, ²⁰
I would eat that. The rogue grows impudent,
Oh! I have seen such vile, notorious tricks,

¹ Legal transactions.
² Frankford's house.
³ Tray for removing dishes.
⁴ Table-cover.
⁵ Small logs.

Ready to make my eyes dart from my head.
I 'll tell my master; by this air, I will;
Fall what may fall, I 'll tell him. Here he
comes. ²⁵

Enter MASTER FRANKFORD, *as it were brushing
the crumbs from his clothes with a napkin, as
newly risen from supper.*

Frank. Nicholas, what make you here? Why
are not you
At supper in the hall, among your fellows?
Nich. Master, I stay'd your rising from the
board,
To speak with you.
Frank. Be brief then, gentle Nicholas;
My wife and guests attend⁶ me in the parlour. ³⁰
Why dost thou pause? Now, Nicholas, you
want money,
And, uuthrift-like, would eat into your
wages
Ere you had earn'd it. Here, sir, 's half-a-crown;
Play the good husband,⁷ — and away to supper!
Nich. By this hand, an honourable gentle-
man! I will not see him wrong'd. ³⁵
Sir, I have serv'd you long; you entertain'd me
Seven years before your beard; you knew me,
sir,
Before you knew my mistress.
Frank. What of this, good Nicholas?
Nich. I never was a make-bate ⁸ or a knave; ⁴⁰
I have no fault but one — I 'm given to quarrel,
But not with women. I will tell you, master,
That which will make your heart leap from
your breast,
Your hair to startle from your head, your ears
to tingle.
Frank. What preparation 's this to dismal
news? ⁴⁵
Nich. 'Sblood! sir, I love you better than
your wife.
I 'll make it good.
Frank. You are a knave, and I have much
ado
With wonted patience to contain my rage,
And not to break thy pate. Thou art a knave.
I 'll turn you, with your base comparisons, ⁵⁰
Out of my doors.
Nich. Do, do.
There is not room for Wendoll and me too,
Both in one house. O master, master,
That Wendoll is a villain!
Frank. Ay, saucy? ⁵⁵
Nich. Strike, strike, do strike; yet hear me!
I am no fool;
I know a villain, when I see him act
Deeds of a villain. Master, master, the base
slave
Enjoys my mistress, and dishonours you.
Frank. Thou hast kill'd me with a weapon,
whose sharp point ⁶⁰
Hath prick'd quite through and through my
shiv'ring heart,
Drops of cold sweat sit dangling on my hairs,
Like morning's dew upon the golden flowers,

⁶ Await.
⁷ Economist.
⁸ Maker of quarrels.

And I am plung'd into strange agonies.
What did'st thou say? If any word that 65
　toucht
His credit, or her reputation,
It is as hard to enter my belief,
As Dives into heaven.
　　Nich.　　　　　　I can gain nothing:
They are two that never wrong'd me. I knew
　before
'T was but a thankless office, and perhaps 70
As much as is my service, or my life
Is worth. All this I know; but this, and
　more,
More by a thousand dangers, could not hire
　me
To smother such a heinous wrong from you.
I saw, and I have said. 75
　　Frank. 'T is probable. Though blunt, yet he
　　is honest.
Though I durst pawn my life, and on their
　faith
Hazard the dear salvation of my soul,
Yet in my trust I may be too secure.
May this be true? Oh, may it? Can it be? 80
Is it by any wonder possible?
Man, woman, what thing mortal can we trust,
When friends and bosom wives prove so un-
　just? —
What instance[1] hast thou of this strange re-
　port?
　　Nich. Eyes, [master,] eyes. 85
　　Frank. Thy eyes may be deceiv'd, I tell
　　thee;
For should an angel from the heavens drop
　down,
And preach this to me that thyself hast told,
He should have much ado to win belief;
In both their loves I am so confident. 90
　　Nich. Shall I discourse the same by circum-
　　stance?
　　Frank. No more! To supper, and command
　　your fellows
To attend us and the strangers! Not a word,
I charge thee, on thy life! Be secret then;
For I know nothing. 95
　　Nich. I am dumb; and, now that I have
　　eas'd my stomach,[2]
I will go fill my stomach.　　　　*[Exit.]*
　　Frank.　　　　Away! Begone! —
She is well born, descended nobly;
Virtuous her education; her repute
Is in the general voice of all the country 100
Honest and fair; her carriage, her demeanour,
In all her actions that concern the love
To me her husband, modest, chaste, and godly.
Is all this seeming gold plain copper?
But he, that Judas that hath borne my purse,
Hath sold me for a sin. O God! O God! 106
Shall I put up these wrongs? No! Shall I
　trust
The bare report of this suspicious groom,
Before the double-gilt, the well-hatch'd[3] ore
Of their two hearts? No, I will lose these
　thoughts; 110
Distraction I will banish from my brow,

And from my looks exile sad discontent.
Their wonted favours in my tongue shall
　flow;
Till I know all, I 'll nothing seem to know. —
Lights and a table there! Wife, Master
　Wendoll, 115
And gentle Master Cranwell!

Enter MISTRESS FRANKFORD, MASTER WEN-
　DOLL, MASTER CRANWELL, NICHOLAS, *and*
　JENKIN *with cards, carpets, stools, and other*
　necessaries.

　　Frank. O! Master Cranwell, you are a
　　stranger here,
And often balk[4] my house; faith, y' are a
　churl! —
Now we have supp'd, a table, and to cards!
　　Jen. A pair[5] of cards, Nicholas, and a carpet
　　to cover the table! Where 's Cicely, with her 121
　　counters and her box? Candles and candlesticks,
　　there! Fie! We have such a household of ser-
　　ving-creatures! Unless it be Nick and I, there 's
　　not one amongst them all that can say bo to a
　　goose. — Well said,[6] Nick! 126
　　　　　　They spread a carpet: set down
　　　　　　　　lights and cards.
　　Mrs. F. Come, Mr. Frankford, who shall take
　　my part?[7]
　　Frank. Marry, that will I, sweet wife. 129
　　Wen. No, by my faith, when you are to-
　　gether, I sit out. It must be Mistress Frank-
　　ford and I, or else it is no match.
　　Frank. I do not like that match.
　　Nich. [*Aside.*] You have no reason, marry,
　　knowing all. 135
　　Frank. 'T is no great matter, neither. —
Come, Master Cranwell, shall you and I take
them up?[8]
　　Cran. At your pleasure, sir. 139
　　Frank. I must look to you, Master Wendoll,
for you 'll be playing false. Nay, so will my
wife, too.
　　Nich. [*Aside.*] Ay, I will be sworn she will.
　　Mrs. F. Let them that are taken playing false,
forfeit the set! 145
　　Frank. Content; it shall go hard but I 'll take
　　you.
　　Cran. Gentlemen, what shall our game be?
　　Wen. Master Frankford, you play best at
noddy.[9]
　　Frank. You shall not find it so; indeed, you
shall not.
　　Mrs. F. I can play at nothing so well as
double-ruff.[10] 150
　　Frank. If Master Wendoll and my wife be
together, there 's no playing against them at
double-hand.
　　Nich. I can tell you, sir, the game that Mas-
ter Wendoll is best at. 155
　　Wen. What game is that, Nick?
　　Nich. Marry, sir, knave out of doors.
　　Wen. She and I will take you at lodam.
　　Mrs. F. Husband, shall we play at saint?

---

　　　1 Evidence.　　　2 Resentment.　　　3 Of noble origin.

　　4 Avoid.　　　　　　8 Be their opponents.
　　5 Pack.　　　　　　9 A game like cribbage.
　　6 Well done.　　　10 An earlier kind of whist.
　　7 Be my partner.

Frank. [*Aside.*] My saint's turn'd devil. —
No, we 'll none of saint :　　　　　　160
You are best at new-cut, wife, you 'll play at
that.
Wen. If you play at new-cut, I 'm soonest hit-
ter of any here, for a wager.
Frank. [*Aside.*] 'T is me they play on. —
Well, you may draw out ;　　　　　　164
For all your cunning, 't will be to your shame ;
I 'll teach you, at your new-cut, a new game.
Come, come !
Cran. If you cannot agree upon the game,
To post and pair !
Wen. We shall be soonest pairs ; and my good
host,　　　　　　170
When he comes late home, he must kiss the
post.[1]
Frank. Whoever wins, it shall be to thy
cost.
Cran. Faith, let it be vide-ruff, and let 's
make honours !
Frank. If you make honours, one thing let
me crave :
Honour the king and queen, except the
knave.　　　　　　175
Wen. Well, as you please for that. — Lift,[2]
who shall deal ?
Mrs. F. The least in sight. What are you,
Master Wendoll ?
Wen. I am a knave.
Nich. [*Aside.*]　　　　　I 'll swear it.
Mrs. F.　　　　　　　　　I a queen.
Frank. [*Aside.*] A quean, thou should'st say.
— Well, the cards are mine :
They are the grossest pair[3] that e'er I felt.　180
Mrs. F. Shuffle, I 'll cut : would I had never
dealt !
Frank. I have lost my dealing.
Wen.　　　　　　Sir, the fault 's in me ;
This queen I have more than mine own, you see.
Give me the stock ![3]
Frank.　　　　　My mind 's not on my game.
Many a deal I 've lost ; the more 's your shame.
You have serv'd me a bad trick, Master Wen-
doll.　　　　　　186
Wen. Sir, you must take your lot. To end
this strife,
I know I have dealt better with your wife.
Frank. Thou hast dealt falsely, then.
Mrs. F. What 's trumps ?　　　　　190
Wen. Hearts. Partner, I rub.
Frank. [*Aside.*] Thou robb'st me of my soul,
of her chaste love ;
In thy false dealing thou hast robb'd my
heart. —
Booty you play ; I like a loser stand,
Having no heart, or here or in my hand.　195
I will give o'er the set, I am not well.
Come, who will hold my cards ?
Mrs. F. Not well, sweet Master Frankford ?
Alas, what ails you ? 'T is some sudden qualm.
Wen. How long have you been so, Master
Frankford ?　　　　　200
Frank. Sir, I was lusty, and I had my
health,

But I grew ill when you began to deal. —
Take hence this table ! — Gentle Master Cran-
well,
Y' are welcome ; see your chamber at your
pleasure !
I am sorry that this megrim takes me so,　205
I cannot sit and bear you company. —
Jenkin, some lights, and show him to his
chamber ![4]
Mrs. F. A nightgown for my husband ;
quickly, there !
It is some rheum or cold.
Wen.　　　　　　Now, in good faith,
This illness you have got by sitting late　210
Without your gown.
Frank.　　　　I know it, Master Wendoll.
Go, go to bed, lest you complain like me ! —
Wife, prithee, wife, into my bed-chamber !
The night is raw and cold, and rheumatic.
Leave me my gown and light ; I 'll walk away
my fit.　　　　　　215
Wen. Sweet sir, good night !
Frank. Myself, good night ! [*Exit Wendoll.*]
Mrs. F.　　　　　Shall I attend you, husband ?
Frank. No, gentle wife, thou 'lt catch cold
in thy head.
Prithee, begone, sweet ; I 'll make haste to
bed.
Mrs. F. No sleep will fasten on mine eyes,
you know,　　　　　　220
Until you come.　　　　　　[*Exit.*]
Frank.　　　Sweet Nan, I prithee, go ! —
I have bethought me ; get me by degrees
The keys of all my doors, which I will mould
In wax, and take their fair impression,
To have by them new keys. This being com-
past,　　　　　　225
At a set hour a letter shall be brought me,
And when they think they may securely
play,
They nearest are to danger. — Nick, I must
rely
Upon thy trust and faithful secrecy.
Nich. Build on my faith !
Frank.　　　　　To bed, then, not to rest !
Care lodges in my brain, grief in my breast.　231
[*Exeunt.*]

[SCENE III.][5]

Enter SIR CHARLES'S *Sister*, OLD MOUNTFORD,
SANDY, RODER, *and* TIDY.

Old Mount. You say my nephew is in great
distress ;
Who brought it to him but his own lewd life ?
I cannot spare a cross. I must confess,
He was my brother's son ; why, niece, what
then ?
This is no world in which to pity men.　　5
Susan. I was not born a beggar, though his
extremes
Enforce this language from me. I protest
No fortune of mine own could lead my tongue
To this base key. I do beseech you, uncle,

---

[1] Be shut out.　　　[2] Cut.　　　[3] Pack.

[4] This line should probably be given to Mrs F. If
not, Cranwell exit here with Jenkin.
[5] Old Mountford's house.

For the name's sake, for Christianity, — 10
Nay, for God's sake, to pity his distress.
He is deni'd the freedom of the prison,
And in the hole is laid with men condemn'd ;
Plenty he hath of nothing but of irons,
And it remains in you to free him thence. 15
    Old Mount. Money I cannot spare ; men
        should take heed.
He lost my kindred when he fell to need. *Exit.*
    Susan. Gold is but earth ; thou earth enough
        shalt have,
When thou hast once took measure of thy grave.
You know me, Master Sandy, and my suit. 20
    Sandy. I knew you, lady, when the old man
        liv'd ;
I knew you ere your brother sold his land.
Then you were Mistress Sue, trick'd up in
        jewels ;
Then you sung well, play'd sweetly on the lute ;
But now I neither know you nor your suit. 25
                                        [*Exit.*]
    Susan. You, Master Roder, was my brother's
        tenant ;
Rent-free he plac'd you in that wealthy farm,
Of which you are possest.
    Roder.   True, he did ;
And have I not there dwelt still for his sake ?
I have some business now ; but, without doubt,
They that have hurl'd him in, will help him
        out.   *Exit.* 31
    Susan. Cold comfort still. What say you,
        cousin Tidy ?
    Tidy. I say this comes of roysting, ¹ swag-
        g'ring.
Call me not cousin ; each man for himself !
Some men are born to mirth, and some to sor-
        row :   35
I am no cousin unto them that borrow. *Exit.*
    Susan. O Charity, why art thou fled to
        heaven,
And left all things [up]on this earth uneven ?
Their scoffing answers I will ne'er return,
But to myself his grief in silence mourn. 40

Enter Sir Francis *and* Malby.

    Sir F. She is poor, I 'll therefore tempt her
        with this gold.
Go, Malby, in my name deliver it,
And I will stay thy answer.
    Mal. Fair mistress, as I understand your grief
Doth grow from want, so I have here in store
A means to furnish you, a bag of gold, 46
Which to your hands I freely tender you.
    Susan. I thank you, Heavens ! I thank you,
        gentle sir :
God make me able to requite this favour !
    Mal. This gold Sir Francis Acton sends by
        me,   50
And prays you——
    Susan. Acton? O God ! That name I 'm born
        to curse.
Hence, bawd ; hence, broker ! See, I spurn his
        gold.
My honour never shall for gain be sold.
    Sir F. Stay, lady, stay !

                ¹ Rioting.

    Susan.   From you I 'll posting hie, 55
Even as the doves from feather'd eagles fly.
                                        Exit.
    Sir F. She hates my name, my face ; how
        should I woo ?
I am disgrac'd in every thing I do.
The more she hates me, and disdains my love,
The more I am rapt in admiration 60
Of her divine and chaste perfections.
Woo her with gifts I cannot, for all gifts
Sent in my name she spurns ; with looks I can-
        not,
For she abhors my sight ; nor yet with letters,
For none she will receive. How then ? how then ?
Well, I will fasten such a kindness on her, 65
As shall o'ercome her hate and conquer it.
Sir Charles, her brother, lies in execution
For a great sum of money ; and, besides,
The appeal is sued still for my huntsmen's
        death,   70
Which only I have power to reverse.
In her I 'll bury all my hate of him. —
Go seek the Keeper, Malby, bring him to me !
To save his body, I his debts will pay ; 74
To save his life, I his appeal will stay. [*Exeunt.*]

[ACT IV]

[SCENE I.]²

Enter Sir Charles [Mountford], *in prison,
with irons, his feet bare, his garments all ragged
and torn.*

    Sir C. Of all on the earth's face most miser-
        able,
Breathe in this hellish dungeon thy laments !
Thus like a slave ragg'd, like a felon gyv'd,—
That hurls thee headlong to this base estate.
Oh, unkind uncle ! Oh, my friends ingrate ! 5
Unthankful kinsmen ! Mountford 's all too base,
To let thy name be fetter'd in disgrace.
A thousand deaths here in this grave I die ;
Fear, hunger, sorrow, cold, all threat my death,
And join together to deprive my breath ; 10
But that which most torments me, my dear
        sister
Hath left ³ to visit me, and from my friends
Hath brought no hopeful answer ; therefore, I
Divine they will not help my misery.
If it be so, shame, scandal, and contempt 15
Attend their covetous thoughts ; need make
        their graves !
Usurers they live, and may they die like slaves !

Enter Keeper.

    Keep. Knight, be of comfort, for I bring thee
        freedom
From all thy troubles.
    Sir C.   Then, I am doom'd to die :
Death is the end of all calamity. 20
    Keep. Live ! Your appeal is stay'd ; the exe-
        cution
Of all your debts discharg'd ; your creditors
Even to the utmost penny satisfied.

                ² York Castle.   ³ Ceased.

In sign whereof your shackles I knock off.
You are not left so much indebted to us   25
As for your fees; all is discharg'd; all paid.
Go freely to your house, or where you please;
After long miseries, embrace your ease.

Sir C. Thou grumblest out the sweetest
    music to me
That ever organ play'd. — Is this a dream?   30
Or do my waking senses apprehend
The pleasing taste of these applausive[1] news?
Slave that I was, to wrong such honest friends,
My loving kinsman, and my near allies!   34
Tongue, I will bite thee for the scandal breath'd
Against such faithful kinsmen; they are all
Compos'd of pity and compassion,
Of melting charity and of moving ruth.
That which I spoke before was in my rage;
They are my friends, the mirrors of this age; 40
Bounteous and free. The noble Mountford's
    race
Ne'er bred a covetous thought, or humour base.

Enter SUSAN.

Susan. I cannot longer stay from visiting
My woful brother. While I could, I kept
My hapless tidings from his hopeful ear.   45

Sir C. Sister, how much am I indebted to
    thee
And to thy travail!

Susan.   What, at liberty?

Sir C. Thou seest I am, thanks to thy indus-
    try.
Oh! Unto which of all my courteous friends
Am I thus bound? My uncle Mountford, he   50
Even of an infant lov'd me; was it he?
So did my cousin Tidy; was it he?
So Master Roder, Master Sandy, too.
Which of all these did this high kindness do?

Susan. Charles, can you mock me in your
    poverty,   55
Knowing your friends deride your misery?
Now, I protest I stand so much amaz'd,
To see your bonds free, and your irons knock'd
    off,
That I am rapt into a maze of wonder;
The rather for I know not by what means   60
This happiness hath chanc'd.

Sir C.   Why, by my uncle,
My cousins, and my friends; who else, I pray,
Would take upon them all my debts to pay?

Susan. Oh, brother! they are men [made] all
    of flint,
Pictures of marble, and as void of pity   65
As chased bears. I begg'd, I sued, I kneel'd,
Laid open all your griefs and miseries,
Which they derided; more than that, deni'd us
A part in their alliance; but, in pride,
Said that our kindred with our plenty died.   70

Sir C. Drudges too much,[2] — what did they?
    Oh, known evil!
Rich fly the poor, as good men shun the devil.
Whence should my freedom come? Of whom
    alive,
Saving of those, have I deserv'd so well?
Guess, sister, call to mind, remember me!   75

These have I rais'd, they follow the world's
    guise,
Whom rich [they][3] honour, they in woe despise.

Susan. My wits have lost themselves; let's
    ask the keeper!

Sir C. Gaoler!

Keep. At hand, sir.   80

Sir C. Of courtesy resolve me one demand!
What was he took the burden of my debts
From off my back, staid my appeal to death,
Discharg'd my fees, and brought me liberty?

Keep. A courteous knight, one call'd Sir
    Francis Acton.   85

Sir C. Ha! Acton! Oh me! More distress'd
    in this
Than all my troubles! Hale me back,
Double my irons, and my sparing meals
Put into halves, and lodge me in a dungeon
More deep, more dark, more cold, more com-
    fortless!   90
By Acton freed! Not all thy manacles
Could fetter so my heels, as this one word
Hath thrall'd my heart; and it must now lie
    bound
In more strict prison than thy stony gaol.
I am not free, I go but under bail.   95

Keep. My charge is done, sir, now I have my
    fees.
As we get little, we will nothing leese.[4]

Sir C. By Acton freed, my dangerous oppo-
    site!
Why, to what end? On what occasion? Ha!
Let me forget the name of enemy,   100
And with indifference balance[5] this high fa-
    vour!
Ha!

Susan. [*Aside.*] His love to me, upon my soul,
    'tis so!
That is the root from whence these strange
    things grow.

Sir C. Had this proceeded from my father, he
That by the law of Nature is most bound   106
In offices of love, it had deserv'd
My best employment to requite that grace.
Had it proceeded from my friends, or him,   109
From them this action had deserv'd my life,—
And from a stranger more, because from such
There is less execution[6] of good deeds.
But he, nor father, nor ally, nor friend,
More than a stranger, both remote in blood,
And in his heart oppos'd my enemy,   115
That this high bounty should proceed from
    him, —
Oh! there I lose myself. What should I say,
What think, what do, his bounty to repay?

Susan. You wonder, I am sure, whence this
    strange kindness
Proceeds in Acton; I will tell you, brother. 120
He dotes on me, and oft hath sent me gifts,
Letters, and tokens; I refus'd them all.

Sir C. I have enough, though poor: my heart
    is set,
In one rich gift to pay back all my debt.
                                    Exeunt.

---

[3] Ed. conj. Qq. *in.*   [4] Lose.   [5] Weigh impartially.
[6] Verity emends to *expectation.*

[1] Joyful.   [2] Too base in their conduct. (Ward.)

[SCENE II.[1]]

Enter FRANKFORD *and* NICHOLAS, *with keys
and a letter in his hand.*

Frank. This is the night that I must play my
　part,
To try two seeming angels.—Where 's my keys?
Nich. They are made according to your
　mould in wax.
I bade the smith be secret, gave him money,
And here they are. The letter, sir!　　5
Frank. True, take it, there it is ;
And when thou seest me in my pleasant'st vein,
Ready to sit to supper, bring it me !
Nich. I 'll do 't ; make no more question, but
　I 'll do it.　　　　　　　　　　　*Exit.*

Enter MISTRESS FRANKFORD, CRANWELL,
WENDOLL, *and* JENKIN.

Mrs. F. Sirrah, 't is six o'clock already
　struck ;　　10
Go bid them spread the cloth, and serve in
　supper !
Jen. It shall be done, forsooth, mistress.
Where 's Spigot, the butler, to give us out salt
and trenchers ?　　14
Wen. We that have been a hunting all the day,
Come with prepared stomachs.— Master Frank-
　ford,
We wish'd you at our sport.
Frank. My heart was with you, and my mind
　was on you. —
Fie, Master Cranwell ! You are still thus sad.—
A stool, a stool ! Where 's Jenkin, and where 's
　Nick ?　　20
'T is supper time at least an hour ago.
What 's the best news abroad ?
Wen. I know none good.
Frank. [*Aside.*] But I know too much bad.

Enter Butler *and* JENKIN, *with a table-cloth,
bread, trenchers, and salt ; [then exeunt.]*

Cran. Methinks, sir, you might have that
　interest[2]
In your wife's brother, to be more remiss[3]　　25
In his hard dealing against poor Sir Charles,
Who, as I hear, lies in York Castle, needy
And in great want.
Frank. Did not more weighty business of
　mine own
Hold me away, I would have labour'd peace　30
Betwixt them with all care ; indeed I would,
　sir.
Mrs. F. I 'll write unto my brother earnestly
In that behalf.
Wen. 　　　　　A charitable deed,
And will beget the good opinion
Of all your friends that love you, Mistress
　Frankford.　　35
Frank. That 's you, for one ; I know you
　love Sir Charles,
[*Aside.*] And my wife too, well.
Wen. 　　　　　　He deserves the love
Of all true gentlemen ; be yourselves judge !

---

[1] Frankford's house.　　[2] Influence with.
[3] Less severe.

Frank. But supper, ho !— Now, as thou
　lov'st me, Wendoll,　　39
Which I am sure thou dost, be merry, pleasant,
And frolic it to-night !— Sweet Mr. Cranwell,
Do you the like !— Wife, I protest, my heart
Was ne'er more bent on sweet alacrity.
Where be those lazy knaves to serve in supper ?

Enter NICHOLAS.

Nich. Here 's a letter, sir.
Frank. Whence comes it, and who brought it ?
Nich. A stripling that below attends your
　answer,　　46
And, as he tells me, it is sent from York.
Frank. Have him into the cellar, let him
　taste
A cup of our March beer ; go, make him
　drink !
Nich. I 'll make him drunk, if he be a Tro-
　jan.[4]　　50
Frank. [*after reading the letter.*] My boots
　and spurs ! Where 's Jenkin ? God forgive
　me,
How I neglect my business !— Wife, look here !
I have a matter to be tri'd to-morrow
By eight o'clock ; and my attorney writes me,
I must be there betimes with evidence,　　55
Or it will go against me. Where 's my boots ?

Enter JENKIN, *with boots and spurs.*

Mrs. F. I hope your business craves no such
　despatch,
That you must ride to-night ?
Wen. [*Aside.*] 　　　　　I hope it doth.
Frank. God's me ! No such despatch ?
Jenkin, my boots ! Where 's Nick ? Saddle my
　roan,　　60
And the grey dapple for himself !— Content ye,
It much concerns me. — Gentle Master Cran-
　well,
And Master Wendoll, in my absence use
The very ripest pleasure of my house !
Wen. Lord ! Master Frankford, will you ride
　to-night ?　　65
The ways are dangerous.
Frank. 　　　　　Therefore will I ride
Appointed[5] well ; and so shall Nick, my man.
Mrs. F. I 'll call you up by five o'clock to-
　morrow.
Frank. No, by my faith, wife, I 'll not trust
　to that :
'T is not such easy rising in a morning　　70
From one I love so dearly. No, by my faith,
I shall not leave so sweet a bedfellow,
But with much pain. You have made me a
　sluggard
Since I first knew you.
Mrs. F. 　　　　Then, if you needs will go
This dangerous evening, Master Wendoll,　　75
Let me entreat you bear him company.
Wen. With all my heart, sweet mistress.—
　My boots, there !
Frank. Fie, fie, that for my private busines
I should disease[6] a friend, and be a trouble
To the whole house !— Nick !

---

[4] Good fellow.　　[5] Armed.　　[6] Cause discomfort to.

Nich. Anon, sir!   80
Frank. Bring forth my gelding!—As you
love me, sir,
Use no more words: a hand, good Master Cran-
well!
Cran. Sir, God be your good speed!
Frank. Good night, sweet Nan; nay, nay, a
kiss, and part!
[*Aside.*] Dissembling lips, you suit not with my
heart.   85
            Exeunt [FRANKFORD *and* NICHOLAS].
Wen. [*Aside.*] How business, time, and hours,
all gracious prove,
And are the furtherers to my new-born love!
I am husband now in Master Frankford's place,
And must command the house.—My pleasure
is
We will not sup abroad so publicly,   90
But in your private chamber, Mistress Frank-
ford.
Mrs. F. Oh, sir! you are too public in your
love,
And Master Frankford's wife ——
Cran. Might I crave favour,
I would entreat you I might see my chamber.
I am on the sudden grown exceeding ill,   95
And would be spar'd from supper.
Wen. Light there, ho!—
See you want nothing, sir, for if you do,
You injure that good man, and wrong me too.
Cran. I will make bold; good night! [*Exit.*]
Wen. How all conspire
To make our bosom[1] sweet, and full entire! 100
Come, Nan, I pr'ythee, let us sup within!
Mrs. F. Oh! what a clog unto the soul is sin!
We pale offenders are still full of fear;
Every suspicious eye brings danger near;
When they, whose clear hearts from offence
are free,   105
Despise report, base scandals do outface,
And stand at mere defiance with disgrace.
Wen. Fie, fie! You talk too like a puritan.
Mrs. F. You have tempted me to mischief,
Master Wendoll:
I have done I know not what. Well, you plead
custom;   110
That which for want of wit I granted erst,
I now must yield through fear. Come, come,
let 's in;
Once over shoes, we are straight o'er head in sin.
Wen. My jocund soul is joyful beyond meas-
ure;   114
I 'll be profuse in Frankford's richest treasure.
                                    Exeunt.

[SCENE III.][2]

Enter CICELY, JENKIN, Butler, *and other* Serving-men.

Jen. My mistress and Master Wendoll, my
master, sup in her chamber to-night. Cicely,
you are preferr'd, from being the cook, to be
chambermaid. Of all the loves betwixt thee and
me, tell me what thou think'st of this?   5
Cic. Mum; there 's an old proverb,—when
the cat 's away, the mouse may play.

---

[1] Intimacy.   [2] Another part of the house.

Jen. Now you talk of a cat, Cicely, I smell a
rat.
Cic. Good words, Jenkin, lest you be call'd [10
to answer them!
Jen. Why, God make my mistress an honest
woman! Are not these good words? Pray God
my new master play not the knave with my old
master! Is there any hurt in this? God send [15
no villainy intended; and if they do sup together, pray God they do not lie together! God
make my mistress chaste, and make us all His
servants! What harm is there in all this? Nay,
more; here in my hand, thou shalt never have [20
my heart, unless thou say, Amen.
Cic. Amen; I pray God, I say.

Enter Serving-man.

Serving-man. My mistress sends that you
should make less noise. So, lock up the doors,
and see the household all got to bed! You, [25
Jenkin, for this night are made the porter, to
see the gates shut in.
Jen. Thus by little and little I creep into
office. Come, to kennel, my masters, to kennel;
't is eleven o'clock already.   30
Serving-man. When you have lock'd the gates
in, you must send up the keys to my mistress.
Cic. Quickly, for God's sake, Jenkin; for I
must carry them. I am neither pillow nor bol-
ster, but I know more than both.   35
Jen. To bed, good Spigot; to bed, good honest serving-creatures; and let us sleep as snug
as pigs in pease-straw!   *Exeunt.*

[SCENE IV.][3]

Enter FRANKFORD *and* NICHOLAS.

Frank. Soft, soft! We 've tied our geldings
to a tree,
Two flight-shot[4] off, lest by their thundering
hoofs
They blab our coming back. Hear'st thou no
noise?
Nich. Hear? I hear nothing but the owl and
you.
Frank. So; now my watch's hand points upon
twelve,   5
And it is dead midnight. Where are my keys?
Nich. Here, sir.
Frank. This is the key that opes my outward
gate;
This, the hall-door; this, the withdrawing-
chamber;   9
But this, that door that 's bawd unto my shame,
Fountain and spring of all my bleeding thoughts,
Where the most hallowed order and true knot
Of nuptial sanctity hath been profan'd.
It leads to my polluted bed-chamber,
Once my terrestrial heaven, now my earth's
hell,   15
The place where sins in all their ripeness
dwell.—
But I forget myself; now to my gate!
Nich. It must ope with far less noise than
Cripplegate, or your plot 's dash'd.

---

[3] Outside the house.   [4] Bow-shots.

Frank. So ; reach me my dark lantern to the
    rest !   20
Tread softly, softly !
Nich.   I will walk on eggs this pace.
Frank. A general silence hath surpris'd the
    house,
And this is the last door. Astonishment,
Fear, and amazement, beat upon my heart,
Even as a madman beats upon a drum.   25
Oh, keep my eyes, you Heavens, before I enter,
From any sight that may transfix my soul ;
Or, if there be so black a spectacle,
Oh, strike mine eyes stark blind ; or if not so,
Lend me such patience to digest my grief,   30
That I may keep this white and virgin hand
From any violent outrage, or red murder ! —
And with that prayer I enter.
                       [*Exeunt into the house.*]

[SCENE V.]¹

[*Enter* NICHOLAS.]

Nich. Here 's a circumstance ! ²
A man may be made cuckold in the time
That he 's about it. An the case were mine,
As 't is my master's, 'sblood ! (that he makes me
    swear !),   4
I would have plac'd his action,³ enter'd there ;
I would, I would !

[*Enter* FRANKFORD.]

Frank.   Oh ! oh !
Nich. Master ! 'Sblood ! Master, master !
Frank. Oh me unhappy ! I have found them
    lying
Close in each other's arms, and fast asleep.   9
But that I would not damn two precious souls,
Bought with my Saviour's blood, and send them,
    laden
With all their scarlet sins upon their backs,
Unto a fearful judgment, their two lives
Had met upon my rapier.
Nich. Master, what, have you left them sleep-
    ing still ?   15
Let me go wake 'em !
Frank.   Stay, let me pause awhile ! —
Oh, God ! Oh, God ! That it were possible
To undo things done ; to call back yesterday ;
That Time could turn up his swift sandy glass,
To untell⁴ the days, and to redeem these hours !
Or that the sun   21
Could, rising from the west, draw his coach
    backward ;
Take from th' account of time so many minutes,
Till he had all these seasons call'd again,
Those minutes, and those actions done in them,
Even from her first offence ; that I might take
    her   26
As spotless as an angel in my arms !
But, oh ! I talk of things impossible,
And cast beyond the moon. God give me
    patience ;
For I will in, and wake them.   *Exit.*

¹ The hall of the house. Note that in the Qq. these
scenes are continuous.
² Delay.   ³ Established his case. (Ward.)
⁴ Count backwards.

Nich.   Here 's patience perforce ! 30
He needs must trot afoot that tires his horse.
                                   [*Exit.*]

Enter WENDOLL, *running over the stage in a
    night-gown,*⁵ FRANKFORD *after him with his
    sword drawn ; a maid in her smock stays his
    hand, and clasps hold on him. He pauses for a
    while.*

Frank. I thank thee, maid ; thou, like the
    angel's hand,
Hast stay'd me from a bloody sacrifice. —
Go, villain ; and my wrongs sit on thy soul
As heavy as this grief doth upon mine !   35
When thou record'st my many courtesies,
And shalt compare them with thy treacherous
    heart,
Lay them together, weigh them equally, —
'T will be revenge enough. Go, to thy friend
A Judas ; pray, pray, lest I live to see   40
Thee, Judas-like, hang'd on an elder-tree !

Enter MISTRESS FRANKFORD *in her smock,
    night-gown, and night-attire.*

Mrs. F. Oh, by what word, what title, or
    what name,
Shall I entreat your pardon ? Pardon ! Oh !
I am as far from hoping such sweet grace,
As Lucifer from Heaven. To call you hus-
    band, —   45
(Oh me, most wretched !) I have lost that name ;
I am no more your wife.
Nich.   'Sblood, sir, she swoons.
Frank. Spare thou thy tears, for I will weep
    for thee ;
And keep thy count'nance, for I 'll blush for
    thee.
Now, I protest, I think 't is I am tainted,   50
For I am most asham'd ; and 't is more hard
For me to look upon thy guilty face
Than on the sun's clear brow. What ! Would'st
    thou speak ?
Mrs. F. I would I had no tongue, no ears, no
    eyes,
No apprehension, no capacity.   55
When do you spurn me like a dog ? When tread
    me
Under feet ? When drag me by the hair ?
Though I deserve a thousand, thousand fold,
More than you can inflict — yet, once my hus-
    band,
For womanhood, to which I am a shame,   60
Though once an ornament — even for His sake,
That hath redeem'd our souls, mark not my
    face,
Nor hack me with your sword ; but let me go
Perfect and undeformed to my tomb !
I am not worthy that I should prevail   65
In the least suit ; no, not to speak to you,
Nor look on you, nor to be in your presence ;
Yet, as an abject,⁶ this one suit I crave ; —
This granted, I am ready for my grave.
Frank. My God, with patience arm me ! —
    Rise, nay, rise,   70
And I 'll debate with thee. Was it for want

⁵ Dressing-gown.   ⁶ Outcast.

Thou play'dst the strumpet? Wast thou not
  suppli'd
With every pleasure, fashion, and new toy, —
Nay, even beyond my calling?[1]
  Mrs. F.　　　　　　　　　I was.
  Frank.　Was it, then, disability in me ;　　75
Or in thine eye seem'd he a properer man?
  Mrs. F.　Oh, no !
  Frank.　Did I not lodge thee in my bosom ?
Wear thee here in my heart ?
  Mrs. F.　　　　　　　　You did.
  Frank.　I did, indeed ; witness my tears, I
  did —
Go, bring my infants hither ! —

　　　　　　[*Two* Children *are brought in.*]
　　　　　　　　　　Oh, Nan ! Oh, Nan !
If neither fear of shame, regard of honour,　81
The blemish of my house, nor my dear love,
Could have withheld thee from so lewd a fact ;
Yet for these infants, these young, harmless
  souls,　　　　　　　　　　　　　　84
On whose white brows thy shame is character'd,
And grows in greatness as they wax in years, —
Look but on them, and melt away in tears ! —
Away with them ; lest, as her spotted body
Hath stain'd their names with stripe of bas-
  tardy,
So her adulterous breath may blast their spirits
With her infectious thoughts ! Away with
  them !　　　　　[*Exeunt* Children.]　91
  Mrs. F.　In this one life, I die ten thousand
  deaths.
  Frank.　Stand up, stand up ! I will do nothing
  rashly.
I will retire awhile into my study,
And thou shalt hear thy sentence presently.
　　　　　　　　　　　　　　Exit.
  Mrs. F.　'T is welcome, be it death. Oh me,
  base strumpet,　　　　　　　　　96
That, having such a husband, such sweet chil-
  dren,
Must enjoy neither ! Oh, to redeem mine hon-
  our,
I 'd have this hand cut off, these my breasts
  sear'd ;
Be rack'd, strappado'd, put to any torment: 100
Nay, to whip but this scandal out, I 'd hazard
The rich and dear redemption of my soul !
He cannot be so base as to forgive me,
Nor I so shameless to accept his pardon.
Oh, women, women, you that yet have kept 105
Your holy matrimonial vow unstain'd,
Make me your instance ; when you tread awry,
Your sins, like mine, will on your conscience
  lie.

Enter CICELY, SPIGOT, *all the* Serving-men, *and*
  JENKIN, *as newly come out of bed.*

  All.　Oh, mistress, mistress ! What have you
  done, mistress ?
  Nich.　'Sblood, what a caterwauling keep you
  here !　　　　　　　　　　　　110
  Jen.　O Lord, mistress, how comes this to
pass ?　My master is run away in his shirt, and

never so much as call'd me to bring his clothes
after him.
  Mrs. F.　See what guilt is ! Here stand I in
  this place,　　　　　　　　　　115
Asham'd to look my servants in the face.

Enter FRANKFORD *and* CRANWELL ; *whom seeing, she falls on her kneees.*

  Frank.　My words are regist'red in Heaven al-
  ready.
With patience hear me ! I 'll not martyr thee,
Nor mark thee for a strumpet ; but with usage
Of more humility torment thy soul,　　120
And kill thee even with kindness.
  Cran.　Master Frankford——
  Frank.　Good Master Cranwell ! — Woman,
  hear thy judgment !
Go make thee ready in thy best attire ;　124
Take with thee all thy gowns, all thy apparel ;
Leave nothing that did ever call thee mistress,
Or by whose sight, being left here in the house,
I may remember such a woman by.
Choose thee a bed and hangings for thy cham-
  ber ;
Take with thee every thing which hath thy
  mark,　　　　　　　　　　　130
And get thee to my manor seven mile off,
Where live ; — 't is thine ; I freely give it thee.
My tenants by[2] shall furnish thee with wains
To carry all thy stuff within two hours ;
No longer will I limit[3] thee my sight.　　135
Choose which of all my servants thou lik'st
  best,
And they are thine to attend thee.
  Mrs. F.　　　　　　　A mild sentence.
  Frank.　But, as thou hop'st for Heaven, as
  thou believ'st
Thy name's recorded in the book of life,
I charge thee never after this sad day　　140
To see me, or to meet me ; or to send,
By word or writing, gift or otherwise,
To move me, by thyself, or by thy friends ;
Nor challenge any part in my two children.
So farewell, Nan ; for we will henceforth be 145
As we had never seen, ne'er more shall see.
  Mrs. F.　How full my heart is, in mine eyes
  appears ;
What wants in words, I will supply in tears.
  Frank.　Come, take your coach, your stuff ;
  all must along.
Servants and all make ready ; all begone !　150
It was thy hand cut two hearts out of one.
　　　　　　　　　　　　　[*Exeunt.*]

[ACT V]

[SCENE I.][4]

Enter SIR CHARLES MOUNTFORD, *gentleman-
  like, and his* Sister, *gentlewoman-like.*

  Susan.　Brother, why have you trick'd[5] me
  like a bride,
Bought me this gay attire, these ornaments ?
Forget you our estate, our poverty ?

---

[1] Rank.
[2] Nearby.　　　　　　　　　[3] Permit.
[4] Before Sir Francis Acton's house.　[5] Dressed.

Sir C. Call me not brother, but imagine me
Some barbarous outlaw, or uncivil kern ; [1]   5
For if thou shutt'st thine eye, and only hear'st
The words that I shall utter, thou shalt judge me
Some staring ruffian, not thy brother Charles.
Oh, sister !
  Susan. Oh, brother ! what doth this strange
    language mean ?   10
Sir C. Dost love me, sister ? Wouldst thou
    see me live
A bankrupt beggar in the world's disgrace,
And die indebted to mine enemies ?
Wouldst thou behold me stand like a huge beam
In the world's eye, a bye-word and a scorn ?   15
It lies in thee of these to acquit me free,
And all my debt I may outstrip by thee.
  Susan. By me ? Why, I have nothing, nothing
    left ;
I owe even for the clothes upon my back ;
I am not worth ——
  Sir C.   O sister, say not so !   20
It lies in you my downcast state to raise ;
To make me stand on even points with the
    world.
Come, sister, you are rich ; indeed you are,
And in your power you have, without delay
Acton's five hundred pounds back to repay.   25
  Susan. Till now I had thought you lov'd me.
    By my honour
(Which I have kept as spotless as the moon),
I ne'er was mistress of that single doit [2]
Which I reserv'd not to supply your wants ;
And do you think that I would hoard from
    you ?   30
Now, by my hopes in Heaven, knew I the
    means
To buy you from the slavery of your debts
(Especially from Acton, whom I hate),
I would redeem it with my life or blood !   34
  Sir C. I challenge it, and, kindred set apart,
Thus, ruffian-like, I lay siege to thy heart.
What do I owe to Acton ?
  Susan. Why, some five hundred pounds ; to-
    wards which, I swear,
In all the world I have not one denier.[3]
  Sir C. It will not prove so. Sister, now re-
    solve [4] me :   40
What do you think (and speak your conscience)
Would Acton give, might he enjoy your bed ?
  Susan. He would not shrink to spend a thou-
    sand pound
To give the Mountfords' name so deep a wound.
  Sir C. A thousand pound ! I but five hundred
    owe :   45
Grant him your bed ; he 's paid with interest so.
  Susan. Oh, brother !
  Sir C.   Oh, sister ! only this one way,
With that rich jewel you my debts may pay.
In speaking this my cold heart shakes with
    shame ;
Nor do I woo you in a brother's name,   50
But in a stranger's. Shall I die in debt
To Acton, my grand foe, and you still wear
The precious jewel that he holds so dear ?

Susan. My honour I esteem as dear and pre-
    cious
As my redemption.
  Sir C.   I esteem you, sister,   55
As dear, for so dear prizing it.
  Susan.   Will Charles
Have me cut off my hands, and send them
    Acton ?
Rip up my breast, and with my bleeding heart
Present him as a token ?
  Sir C.   Neither, sister ;
But hear me in my strange assertion !   60
Thy honour and my soul are equal in my re-
    gard ;
Nor will thy brother Charles survive thy shame.
His kindness, like a burden, hath surcharg'd
    me,
And under his good deeds I stooping go,
Not with an upright soul. Had I remain'd   65
In prison still, there doubtless I had died.
Then, unto him that freed me from that
    prison,
Still do I owe this life. What mov'd my foe
To enfranchise me ? 'T was, sister, for your
    love ;
With full five hundred pounds he bought your
    love ; —   70
And shall he not enjoy it ? Shall the weight
Of all this heavy burden lean on me,
And will not you bear part ? You did partake
The joy of my release ; will you not stand
In joint-bond bound to satisfy the debt ?   75
Shall I be only charg'd ?
  Susan.   But that I know
These arguments come from an honour'd mind,
As in your most extremity of need
Scorning to stand in debt to one you hate, —
Nay, rather would engage your unsustain'd
    honour,   80
Than to be held ingrate, — I should condemn
    you.
I see your resolution, and assent ;
So Charles will have me, and I am content.
  Sir C. For this I trick'd [5] you up.
  Susan.   But here 's a knife,
To save mine honour, shall slice out my life.   85
  Sir C. I know thou pleasest me a thousand
    times
More in that resolution than thy grant. —
Observe her love ; to soothe it to my suit,
Her honour she will hazard, though not lose ;
To bring me out of debt, her rigorous hand   90
Will pierce her heart, — O wonder ! — that will
    choose,
Rather than stain her blood, her life to lose.
Come, you sad sister to a woful brother,
This is the gate. I 'll bear him such a present,
Such an acquittance for the knight to seal,   95
As will amaze his senses, and surprise
With admiration all his fantasies.

Enter SIR FRANCIS ACTON *and* MALBY.

Susan. Before his unchaste thoughts shall
    seize on me,
'T is here shall my imprison'd soul set free.

---

[1] A Celtic foot-soldier; often used in contempt.
[2] A small coin.   [3] Penny.   [4] Tell.

[5] Dressed finely.

Sir F. How! Mountford with his sister, hand
in hand! 100
What miracle 's afoot?
Mal. It is a sight
Begets in me much admiration.[1]
Sir C. Stand not amaz'd to see me thus at-
tended!
Acton, I owe thee money, and, being unable
To bring thee the full sum in ready coin, 105
Lo! for thy more assurance, here 's a pawn, —
My sister, my dear sister, whose chaste honour
I prize above a million. Here! Nay, take her;
She 's worth your money, man; do not forsake
her.
Sir F. I would he were in earnest! 110
Susan. Impute it not to my immodesty.
My brother, being rich in nothing else
But in his interest that he hath in me,
According to his poverty hath brought you 114
Me, all his store; whom, howsoe'er you prize,
As forfeit to your hand, he values highly,
And would not sell, but to acquit your debt,
For any emperor's ransom.
Sir F. Stern heart, relent,
Thy former cruelty at length repent!
Was ever known, in any former age, 120
Such honourable, wrested courtesy?
Lands, honours, life, and all the world forego,
Rather than stand engag'd to such a foe!
Sir C. Acton, she is too poor to be thy bride,
And I too much oppos'd to be thy brother. 125
There, take her to thee; if thou hast the heart
To seize her as a rape, or lustful prey;
To blur our house, that never yet was stain'd;
To murder her that never meant thee harm;
To kill me now, whom once thou sav'dst from
death: — 130
Do them at once; on her all these rely,
And perish with her spotless chastity.
Sir F. You overcome me in your love, Sir
Charles.
I cannot be so cruel to a lady
I love so dearly. Since you have not spar'd 135
To engage your reputation to the world,
Your sister's honour, which you prize so dear,
Nay, all the comforts which you hold on earth,
To grow out of my debt, being your foe, —
Your honour'd thoughts, lo! thus I recompense. 141
Your metamorphos'd foe receives your gift
In satisfaction of all former wrongs.
This jewel I will wear here in my heart;
And where before I thought her, for her wants,
Too base to be my bride, to end all strife, 145
I seal you my dear brother, her my wife.
Susan. You still exceed us. I will yield to
fate,
And learn to love, where I till now did hate.
Sir C. With that enchantment you have
charm'd my soul
And made me rich even in those very words! 150
I pay no debt, but am indebted more;
Rich in your love, I never can be poor.
Sir F. All 's mine is yours; we are alike in
state;
Let 's knit in love what was oppos'd in hate!

[1] Wonder.

Come, for our nuptials we will straight provide,
Blest only in our brother and fair bride. 156
[*Exeunt.*]

[SCENE II.] [2]

Enter CRANWELL, FRANKFORD, *and* NICHOLAS.

Cran. Why do you search each room about
your house,
Now that you have despatch'd your wife away?
Frank. Oh, sir! To see that nothing may be
left
That ever was my wife's. I lov'd her dearly;
And when I do but think of her unkindness, 5
My thoughts are all in hell; to avoid which tor-
ment,
I would not have a bodkin or a cuff,
A bracelet, necklace, or rabato wire,[3]
Nor anything that ever was call'd hers,
Left me, by which I might remember her.— 10
Seek round about.
Nich. 'Sblood! master, here 's her lute flung
in a corner.
Frank. Her lute! Oh, God! Upon this in-
strument
Her fingers have rung quick division,[4]
Sweeter than that which now divides our
hearts. 15
These frets have made me pleasant,[5] that have
now
Frets of my heart-strings made. Oh, Master
Cranwell,
Oft hath she made this melancholy wood
(Now mute and dumb for her disastrous chance)
Speak sweetly many a note, sound many a
strain 20
To her own ravishing voice; which being well
strung,
What pleasant strange airs have they jointly
sung!—
Post with it after her! — Now nothing 's left;
Of her and hers I am at once bereft.
Nich. I 'll ride and overtake her; do my
message, 25
And come back again. [*Exit.*]
Cran. Meantime, sir, if you please,
I 'll to Sir Francis Acton, and inform him
Of what hath past betwixt you and his sister.
Frank. Do as you please.— How ill am I be-
sted,
To be a widower ere my wife be dead! 30
[*Exeunt.*]

[SCENE III.] [6]

Enter MISTRESS FRANKFORD; *with* JENKIN,
her maid CICELY, *her Coachmen, and three*
Carters.

Mrs. F. Bid my coach stay! Why should I
ride in state,
Being hurl'd so low down by the hand of fate?
A seat like to my fortunes let me have,—
Earth for my chair, and for my bed a grave!
Jen. Comfort, good mistress; you have [5
watered your coach with tears already. You
have but two miles now to go to your manor.

[2] Frankford's house. [4] Variation.
[3] Wire used to support a ruff. [5] Merry.
[6] Road near Mistress Frankford's manor.

A man cannot say by my old master Frankford
as he may say by me, that he wants manors ;
for he hath three or four, of which this is one
that we are going to now.   11
Cic. Good mistress, be of good cheer ! Sorrow,
you see, hurts you, but helps you not ; we all
mourn to see you so sad.
Carter. Mistress, I spy one of my landlord's
men   15
Come riding post : 't is like he brings some news.
Mrs. F. Comes he from Master Frankford, he
is welcome ;
So is his news, because they come from him.

Enter NICHOLAS.

Nich. There !
Mrs. F. I know the lute. Oft have I sung to
thee ;   20
We both are out of tune, both out of time.
Nich. Would that had been the worst instrument that e'er you played on ! My master commends him to ye ; there 's all he can find was
ever yours ; he hath nothing left that ever you
could lay claim to but his own heart,— and [26
he could afford you that ! All that I have to
deliver you is this : he prays you to forget him ;
and so he bids you farewell.   29
Mrs. F. I thank him ; he is kind, and ever was.
All you that have true feeling of my grief,
That know my loss, and have relenting hearts,
Gird me about, and help me with your tears
To wash my spotted sins ! My lute shall groan ;
It cannot weep, but shall lament my moan.   35
                                            [*She plays.*]

Enter WENDOLL [*behind*].

Wen. Pursu'd with horror of a guilty soul,
And with the sharp scourge of repentance
lash'd,
I fly from mine own shadow. O my stars !
What have my parents in their lives deserv'd, 39
That you should lay this penance on their son ?
When I but think of Master Frankford's love,
And lay it to my treason, or compare
My murdering him for his relieving me,
It strikes a terror like a lightning's flash,
To scorch my blood up. Thus I, like the owl, 45
Asham'd of day, live in these shadowy woods,
Afraid of every leaf or murmuring blast,
Yet longing to receive some perfect knowledge
How he hath dealt with her. [*Seeing* MISTRESS
FRANKFORD.] O my sad fate !
Here, and so far from home, and thus attended !
Oh, God ! I have divorc'd the truest turtles 51
That ever liv'd together, and, being divided,
In several places make their several moan ;
She in the fields laments, and he at home ;
So poets write that Orpheus made the trees 55
And stones to dance to his melodious harp,
Meaning the rustic and the barbarous hinds,
That had no understanding part in them :
So she from these rude carters tears extracts,
Making their flinty hearts with grief to rise, 60
And draw down rivers from their rocky eyes.
Mrs. F. [*to* NICHOLAS.] If you return unto
my master, say
(Though not from me, for I am all unworthy

To blast his name so with a strumpet's tongue)
That you have seen me weep, wish myself
dead !   65
Nay, you may say, too (for my vow is past),[1]
Last night you saw me eat and drink my last.
This to your master you may say and swear ;
For it is writ in heaven, and decreed here.
Nich. I 'll say you wept ; I 'll swear you made
me sad.   70
Why, how now, eyes ? What now ? What 's
here to do ?
I 'm gone, or I shall straight turn baby too.
Wen. [*Aside.*] I cannot weep, my heart is all
on fire.
Curs'd be the fruits of my unchaste desire !
Mrs. F. Go, break this lute upon my coach's
wheel,   75
As the last music that I e'er shall make,—
Not as my husband's gift, but my farewell
To all earth's joy ; and so your master tell !
Nich. If I can for crying.
Wen. [*Aside.*]   Grief, have done,
Or, like a madman, I shall frantic run.   80
Mrs. F. You have beheld the wofull'st wretch
on earth,—
A woman made of tears ; would you had words
To express but what you see ! My inward grief
No tongue can utter ; yet unto your power
You may describe my sorrow, and disclose 85
To thy sad master my abundant woes.
Nich. I 'll do your commendations.[2]
Mrs. F.   Oh, no !
I dare not so presume ; nor to my children !
I am disclaim'd in both ; alas ! I am.
Oh, never teach them, when they come to
speak,   90
To name the name of mother : chide their
tongue,
if they by chance light on that hated word ;
Tell them 't is naught ; for when that word
they name,
Poor, pretty souls ! they harp on their own
shame.
Wen. [*Aside.*] To recompense their wrongs,
what canst thou do ?   95
Thou hast made her husbandless, and childless
too.
Mrs. F. I have no more to say.— Speak not
for me ;
Yet you may tell your master what you see.
Nich. I 'll do 't.   *Exit*
Wen. [*Aside.*] I 'll speak to her, and comfort
her in grief.   100
Oh, but her wound cannot be cur'd with words !
No matter, though ; I 'll do my best good will
To work a cure on her whom I did kill.
Mrs. F. So, now unto my coach, then to my
home,
So to my death-bed ; for from this sad hour, 105
I never will nor eat, nor drink, nor taste
Of any cates[3] that may preserve my life.
I never will nor smile, nor sleep, nor rest ;
But when my tears have wash'd my black soul
white,
Sweet Saviour, to thy hands I yield my sprite.

<hr>

[1] Sworn.   [2] Commands.   [3] Food.

Wen. [*coming forward.*] Oh, Mistress Frankford!
Mrs F. Oh, for God's sake, fly! 111
The devil doth come to tempt me, ere I die.
My coach!—This sin, that with an angel's
face
Conjur'd[1] mine honour, till he sought my
wrack,
In my repentant eye seems ugly, black. 115
      Exeunt all [*except* WENDOLL *and*
JENKIN]; *the* Carters *whistling.*
Jen. What, my young master, that fled
in his shirt! How come you by your clothes
again? You have made our house in a sweet
pickle, ha' ye not, think you? What, shall I
serve you still, or cleave to the old house? 120
Wen. Hence, slave! Away, with thy unsea-
son'd mirth!
Unless thou canst shed tears, and sigh, and
howl,
Curse thy sad fortunes, and exclaim on fate,
Thou art not for my turn.
Jen. Marry, an you will not, another will;
farewell, and be hang'd! Would you had [126
never come to have kept this coil[2] within our
doors! We shall ha' you run away like a sprite
again. [*Exit.*]
Wen. She 's gone to death; I live to want
and woe, 130
Her life, her sins, and all upon my head.
And I must now go wander, like a Cain,
In foreign countries and remoted climes,
Where the report of my ingratitude
Cannot be heard. I 'll over first to France, 135
And so to Germany and Italy;
Where, when I have recovered, and by travel
Gotten those perfect tongues,[3] and that these
rumours
May in their height abate, I will return:
And I divine (however now dejected), 140
My worth and parts being by some great man
prais'd,
At my return I may in court be rais'd. *Exit.*

[SCENE IV.][4]

Enter SIR FRANCIS ACTON, SIR CHARLES
MOUNTFORD, CRANWELL, [MALBY,] *and*
SUSAN.

Sir F. Brother, and now my wife, I think
these troubles,
Fall on my head by justice of the heavens,
For being so strict to you in your extremi-
ties;
But we are now aton'd. I would my sister
Could with like happiness o'ercome her griefs 5
As we have ours.
Susan. You tell us, Master Cranwell, won-
drous things
Touching the patience of that gentleman,
With what strange virtue he demeans[5] his
grief.

[1] Enchanted, seduced.
[2] Made this trouble.
[3] Acquired these languages perfectly.
[4] Before the Manor House.
[5] Conducts

Cran. I told you what I was a witness of; 10
It was my fortune to lodge there that night.
Sir F. Oh, that same villain, Wendoll!
'T was his tongue
That did corrupt her; she was of herself
Chaste and devoted well.[6] Is this the house?
Cran. Yes, sir; I take it, here your sister
lies.[7] 15
Sir F. My brother Frankford show'd too
mild a spirit
In the revenge of such a loathed crime.
Less than he did, no man of spirit could do.
I am so far from blaming his revenge,
That I commend it. Had it been my case, 20
Their souls at once had from their breasts been
freed;
Death to such deeds of shame is the due meed.

Enter JENKIN *and* CICELY.

Jen. Oh, my mistress, mistress! my poor mistress!
Cicely. Alas! that ever I was born; what [25
shall I do for my poor mistress?
Sir C. Why, what of her?
Jen. Oh, Lord, sir! she no sooner heard that
her brother and her friends had come to see
how she did, but she, for very shame of her [30
guilty conscience, fell into such a swoon, that
we had much ado to get life in her.
Susan. Alas, that she should bear so hard a
fate!
Pity it is repentance comes too late.
Sir F. Is she so weak in body? 35
Jen. Oh, sir! I can assure you there 's no hope
of life in her; for she will take no sust'nance: she
hath plainly starv'd herself, and now she 's as
lean as a lath. She ever looks for the good hour.
Many gentlemen and gentlewomen of the [40
country are come to comfort her.

[SCENE V.][8]

[SIR CHARLES MOUNTFORD, SIR FRANCIS AC-
TON, MALBY, CRANWELL, *and* SUSAN.]

Enter MISTRESS FRANKFORD *in her bed.*

Mal. How fare you, Mistress Frankford?
Mrs. F. Sick, sick, oh, sick! Give me some
air, I pray you!
Tell me, oh, tell me, where is Master Frank-
ford?
Will not he deign to see me ere I die?
Mal. Yes, Mistress Frankford; divers gentle-
men, 5
Your loving neighbours, with that just request
Have mov'd, and told him of your weak estate:[9]
Who, though with much ado to get belief,
Examining of the general circumstance,
Seeing your sorrow and your penitence, 10
And hearing therewithal the great desire
You have to see him, ere you left the world,
He gave to us his faith to follow us,
And sure he will be here immediately.

[6] Dutiful.   [7] Dwells.
[8] The Manor House. The scene was really unchanged.
[9] Condition.

Mrs. F. You have half reviv'd me with the
pleasing news,   15
Raise me a little higher in my bed.—
Blush I not, brother Acton? Blush I not, Sir
Charles?
Can you not read my fault writ in my cheek?
Is not my crime there? Tell me, gentlemen.
Sir C. Alas, good mistress, sickness hath not
left you   20
Blood in your face enough to make you blush.
Mrs. F. Then, sickness, like a friend, my
fault would hide. —
Is my husband come? My soul but tarries
His arrive; then I am fit for heaven.
Sir F. I came to chide you, but my words of
hate   25
Are turn'd to pity and compassionate grief.
I came to rate you, but my brawls, you see,
Melt into tears, and I must weep by thee. —
Here 's Master Frankford now.

Enter FRANKFORD.

Frank. Good morrow, brother; morrow,
gentlemen!   30
God, that hath laid this cross upon our heads,
Might (had He pleas'd) have made our cause of
meeting
On a more fair and more contented ground;
But He that made us made us to this woe.
Mrs. F. And is he come? Methinks, that
voice I know.   35
Frank. How do you, woman?
Mrs. F. Well, Master Frankford, well; but
shall be better,
I hope within this hour. Will you vouchsafe,
Out of your grace and your humanity,
To take a spotted strumpet by the hand?   40
Frank. This hand once held my heart in
faster bonds,
Than now 't is gripp'd by me. God pardon
them
That made us first break hold!
Mrs. F.   Amen, amen!
Out of my zeal to Heaven, whither I 'm now
bound,
I was so impudent to wish you here;   45
And once more beg your pardon. O, good
man,
And father to my children, pardon me.
Pardon, oh, pardon me: my fault so heinous
is,
That if you in this world forgive it not,
Heaven will not clear it in the world to come.   50
Faintness hath so usurp'd upon my knees,
That kneel I cannot; but on my heart's knees
My prostrate soul lies thrown down at your
feet,
To beg your gracious pardon. Pardon, oh, par-
don me!
Frank. As freely, from the low depth of my
soul,   55
As my Redeemer hath forgiven His death,
I pardon thee. I will shed tears for thee;
pray with thee;
And, in mere pity of thy weak estate,
I 'll wish to die with thee.
All.   So do we all.

Nich.   So will not I ·
I 'll sigh and sob, but, by my faith, not
die.   60
Sir F. Oh, Master Frankford, all the near
alliance
I lose by her, shall be suppli'd in thee.
You are my brother by the nearest way;
Her kindred hath fall'n off, but yours doth
stay.
Frank. Even as I hope for pardon, at that
day   65
When the Great Judge of heaven in scarlet
sits,
So be thou pardon'd! Though thy rash of-
fence
Divorc'd our bodies, thy repentant tears
Unite our souls.
Sir C.   Then comfort, Mistress Frankford!
You see your husband hath forgiven your
fall;   70
Then rouse your spirits, and cheer your fainting
soul!
Susan. How is it with you?
Sir F.   How d' ye feel yourself?
Mrs. F. Not of this world.
Frank. I see you are not. and I weep to see
it.
My wife, the mother to my pretty babes!   75
Both those lost names I do restore thee back,
And with this kiss I wed thee once again.
Though thou art wounded in thy honour'd
name,
And with that grief upon thy death-bed liest,
Honest in heart, upon my soul, thou diest.   80
Mrs. F. Pardon'd on earth, soul, thou in
heaven art free;
Once more thy wife, dies thus embracing
thee.[1]   [*Dies.*]
Frank. New-married, and new-widow'd. —
Oh! she 's dead,
And a cold grave must be her nuptial bed.
Sir C. Sir, be of good comfort, and your
heavy sorrow   85
Part equally amongst us; storms divided
Abate their force, and with less rage are
guided.
Cran. Do, Master Frankford; he that hath
least part,
Will find enough to drown one troubled heart.
Sir. F. Peace with thee, Nan! — Brothers
and gentlemen,   90
All we that can plead interest in her grief,
Bestow upon her body funeral tears!
Brother, had you with threats and usage bad
Punish'd her sin, the grief of her offence
Had not with such true sorrow touch'd her
heart.   95
Frank. I see it had not; therefore, on her
grave
Will I bestow this funeral epitaph,
Which on her marble tomb shall be engrav'd.
In golden letters shall these words be fill'd:[2]
Here lies she whom her husband's kindness kill'd.

---

[1] Verity suggests, *Once more* (*i. e.* Kiss me once
more); *thy wife dies*, etc.
[2] Cut and filled in with gold.

THE EPILOGUE

An honest crew, disposed to be merry,
  Came to a tavern by, and call'd for wine.
The drawer brought it, smiling like a cherry,
  And told them it was pleasant, neat[1] and
    fine.
'Taste it,' quoth one. He did so. 'Fie!'
    (quoth he)   5
'This wine was good ; now 't runs too near the
    lee.'

Another sipp'd, to give the wine his due,
  And said unto the rest, it drunk too flat ;

[1] Pure.

The third said, it was old ; the fourth, too new ;
  Nay, quoth the fifth, the sharpness likes me
    not.   10
Thus, gentlemen, you see how, in one hour,
The wine was new, old, flat, sharp, sweet, and
    sour.

Unto this wine we do allude[2] our play,
  Which some will judge too trivial, some too
    grave :
You as our guests we entertain this day,   15
  And bid you welcome to the best we have.
Excuse us, then ; good wine may be disgrac'd,
When every several mouth hath sundry taste.

[2] Compare.

THE KNIGHT OF THE BURNING PESTLE

BY

FRANCIS BEAUMONT AND JOHN FLETCHER

[DRAMATIS PERSONAE

PROLOGUE.	WILLIAM HAMMERTON.
A CITIZEN.	GEORGE GREENGOOSE.
HIS WIFE.	Host.
RALPH,[1] his Apprentice.	Tapster.
Boys.	Barber.
	Three Men, supposed captives.
VENTUREWELL, a Merchant.	Sergeant.
HUMPHREY.	Soldiers and Attendants.
MERRYTHOUGHT.	
JASPER, } His Sons.	LUCE, Daughter of Venturewell.
MICHAEL, }	MISTRESS MERRYTHOUGHT.
TIM, } Apprentices.	POMPIONA, Daughter of the King of Moldavia.
GEORGE, }	Woman, supposed a captive.

SCENE. — *London and the neighbouring Country, excepting Act IV, Scene II, where it is in Moldavia.*]

TO THE READERS OF THIS COMEDY[2]

GENTLEMEN;

The world is so nice[3] in these our times, that for apparel there is no fashion; for music (which is a rare art, though now slighted) no instrument; for diet, none but the French kickshaws that are delicate; and for plays, no invention but that which now runneth an invective way, touching some particular persons, or else it is contemned before it is thoroughly understood. This is all that I have to say: that the author had no intent to wrong any one in this comedy; but, as a merry passage, here and there interlaced it with delight, which he hopes will please all, and be hurtful to none.

PROLOGUE[4]

WHERE the bee can suck no honey, she leaves her sting behind; and where the bear cannot find origanum[5] to heal his grief, he blasteth all other leaves with his breath. We fear it is like to fare so with us; that, seeing you cannot draw from our labours sweet content, you leave behind you a sour mislike,[6] and with open reproach blame our good meaning, because you cannot reap the wonted mirth. Our intent was at this time to move inward delight, not outward lightness; and [5 to breed (if it might be) soft smiling, not loud laughing; knowing it, to the wise, to be a great pleasure to hear counsel mixed with wit, as to the foolish, to have sport mingled with rudeness. They were banished the theatre of Athens, and from Rome hissed, that brought parasites on the stage with apish actions, or fools with uncivil habits, or courtesans with immodest words. We have endeavoured to be as far from unseemly speeches, to make your ears glow, as we hope you [10 will be free from unkind reports, or mistaking the authors'[7] intention, (who never aimed at any one particular in this play,) to make our cheeks blush. And thus I leave it, and thee to thine own censure, to like or dislike. — VALE.

[INDUCTION]

[*Several* Gentlemen *sitting on Stools upon the Stage. The* Citizen, *his* Wife, *and* RALPH *sitting below among the Audience.*]

Enter PROLOGUE.

[*Prol.*]" From all that 's near the court, from all that 's great,

Within the compass of the city-walls,
We now have brought our scene —— "

Citizen [*leaps on the stage*].

Cit. Hold your peace, goodman boy!
Prol. What do you mean, sir? 5
Cit. That you have no good meaning: this

---

[1] The Q spellings *Rafe* and *Raph* indicate the pronunciation.
[2] From the Second Edition, 1635.   [3] Fastidious.
[4] *Idem.* " This Prologue is almost an exact Transcript of ' The Prologue at the Black fryers ' prefixed to Lyly's *Sapho and Phaon.*" (Murch.)
[5] Marjoram.   [6] Disapproval.   [7] Q₂ *authors.*

seven years there hath been plays at this house,[1]
I have observed it, you have still girds[2] at citi-
zens; and now you call your play "The London
Merchant." Down with your title,[3] boy! down
with your title!   11
Prol. Are you a member of the noble city?
Cit. I am.
Prol. And a freeman?
Cit. Yea, and a grocer.[4]   15
Prol. So, grocer, then, by your sweet favour,
we intend no abuse to the city.
Cit. No, sir! yes, sir. If you were not resolv'd
to play the Jacks,[5] what need you study for
new subjects, purposely to abuse your bet- [20]
ters? Why could not you be contented, as well
as others, with "The legend of Whittington,"[6]
or "The Life and Death of Sir Thomas Gresh-
am, with the building of the Royal Exchange,"[7] or "The story of Queen Eleanor, [25]
with the rearing of London Bridge upon wool-
sacks?"[8]
Prol. You seem to be an understanding man:
what would you have us do, sir?   29
Cit. Why present something notably in honour of the commons of the city.
Prol. Why, what do you say to "The Life
and Death of fat Drake, or the Repairing of
Fleet-privies?"   34
Cit. I do not like that; but I will have a citi-
zen, and he shall be of my own trade.
Prol. Oh, you should have told us your mind
a month since; our play is ready to begin now.
Cit. 'T is all one for that; I will have a
grocer, and he shall do admirable[9] things.   40
Prol. What will you have him do?
Cit. Marry, I will have him ——
Wife. (*below.*) Husband, husband!
Ralph. [*below.*] Peace, mistress.   44
Wife. [*below.*] Hold thy peace, Ralph; I know
what I do, I warrant 'ee. — Husband, hus-
band!
Cit. What sayst thou, cony?[10]
Wife. [*below.*] Let him kill a lion with a [49]
pestle, husband! Let him kill a lion with a
pestle!
Cit. So he shall. — I 'll have him kill a lion
with a pestle.
Wife. [*below.*] Husband! shall I come up,
husband?   55
Cit. Ay, cony. — Ralph, help your mistress
this way. — Pray, gentlemen, make her a little
room. — I pray you, sir, lend me your hand to
help up my wife: I thank you, sir. — So.
[*Wife comes on the stage.*]
Wife. By your leave, gentlemen all; I 'm [60]
something troublesome. I 'm a stranger here;
I was ne'er at one of these plays, as they

say, before; but I should have seen[11] "Jane
Shore"[12] once; and my husband hath promised
me, any time this twelvemonth, to carry me [65]
to "The Bold Beauchamps,"[13] but in truth he
did not. I pray you, bear with me.
Cit. Boy, let my wife and I have a couple
of stools and then begin; and let the grocer do
rare things.   [*Stools are brought.*] 70
Prol. But, sir, we have never a boy[14] to play
him: every one hath a part already.
Wife. Husband, husband, for God's sake,
let Ralph play him! Beshrew me, if I do not
think he will go beyond them all.   75
Cit. Well remem'bred, wife. — Come up,
Ralph. — I 'll tell you, gentlemen; let them but
lend him a suit of reparel[15] and necessaries,
and, by gad, if any of them all blow wind in the
tail on him,[16] I 'll be hang'd.   80

[RALPH *comes on the stage.*]

Wife. I pray you, youth, let him have a suit
of reparel! — I 'll be sworn, gentlemen, my
husband tells you true. He will act you sometimes at our house, that all the neighbours [84]
cry out on him; he will fetch you up a courag-
ing part so in the garret, that we are all as
fear'd, I warrant you, that we quake again:
we 'll fear our children with him; if they be
never so unruly, do but cry, "Ralph comes,
Ralph comes!" to them, and they 'll be as [90]
quiet as lambs. — Hold up thy head, Ralph;
show the gentlemen what thou canst do; speak
a huffing[17] part; I warrant you, the gentlemen
will accept of it.   95
Cit. Do, Ralph, do.
Ralph. "By Heaven, methinks, it were an
        easy leap
To pluck bright honour from the pale-fac'd
        moon;
Or dive into the bottom of the sea,
Where never fathom-line toucht any ground,
And pluck up drowned honour from the lake of
        hell."[18]   100
Cit. How say you, gentlemen, is it not as I
told you?
Wife. Nay, gentlemen, he hath play'd
before, my husband says, "Mucedorus,"[19] be-
fore the wardens of our company.   105
Cit. Ay, and he should have play'd Jeron-
imo[20] with a shoemaker for a wager.
Prol. He shall have a suit of apparel, if he
will go in.
Cit. In, Ralph, in, Ralph; and set out the
grocery in their kind, if thou lov'st me.   111
                                    [*Exit* RALPH.]
Wife. I warrant, our Ralph will look finely
when he 's drest.
Prol. But what will you have it call'd?

---

[1] Probably Whitefriars, a private theatre.
[2] Jeers.
[3] The placard announcing the name of the play.
[4] *I. e.* a member of the Grocers' Guild, one of the great livery companies.
[5] Behave trickily.
[6] A lost play, author unknown.
[7] Heywood's *If you know not me, you know nobody,* pt. II.
[8] Peele's *Edward I*   [9] Wonderful.   [10] Dear.

[11] Was to have seen.
[12] Perhaps *Edward IV*, ascribed to Heywood.
[13] A lost play.
[14] This play was first acted by the children of Her Majesty's Revels.
[15] Apparel.   [16] Disparage.   [17] Swaggering.
[18] With slight changes from *1 Henry IV*, I. iii. 201.
[19] An early play of unknown authorship.
[20] See *The Spanish Tragedy, ante.*

Cit. "The Grocer's Honour." 115
Prol. Methinks " The Knight of the Burning Pestle " were better.
Wife. I 'll be sworn, husband, that 's as good a name as can be.
Cit. Let it be so. — Begin, begin ; my wife and I will sit down. 121
Prol. I pray you, do.
Cit. What stately music have you ? You have shawms ? [1]
Prol. Shawms ? No.
Cit. No ! I 'm a thief if my mind did not [126 give me so. Ralph plays a stately part, and he must needs have shawms. I 'll be at the charge of them myself, rather than we 'll be without them. 130
Prol. So you are like to be.
Cit. Why, and so I will be : there 's two shillings ; — [*Gives money.*] — let 's have the waits of Southwark ; they are as rare fellows as any are in England ; and that will fetch them all o 'er the water with a vengeance, as if they [136 were mad.
Prol. You shall have them. Will you sit down then ?
Cit. Ay. — Come, wife. 140
Wife. Sit you merry all, gentlemen ; I 'm bold to sit amongst you for my ease.
            [*Citizen and Wife sit down.*]
Prol. " From all that 's near the court, from all that 's great,
Within the compass of the city-walls,
We now have brought our scene. Fly far from hence 145
All private taxes, [2] immodest phrases,
Whatever may but show like vicious !
For wicked mirth never true pleasure brings,
But honest minds are pleas'd with honest things." —
Thus much for that we do ; but for Ralph's part you must answer for yourself. 151
Cit. Take you no care for Ralph ; he 'll discharge himself, I warrant you.
            [*Exit* PROLOGUE.]
Wife. I' faith, gentlemen, I 'll give my word for Ralph. 155

ACT I

SCENE I.[3]

Enter Merchant [VENTUREWELL] *and* JASPER, *his Prentice.*

Vent. Sirrah, I 'll make you know you are my prentice,
And whom my charitable love redeem'd
Even from the fall of fortune ; gave thee heat
And growth, to be what now thou art, new-cast thee ;
Adding the trust of all I have, at home,
In foreign staples,[4] or upon the sea,
To thy direction ; tied the good opinions

---

[1] A pipe resembling a hautboy.
[2] Attacks on individuals.
[3] A room in the house of Venturewell.
[4] Markets.

Both of myself and friends to thy endeavours ;
So fair were thy beginnings. But with these,
As I remember, you had never charge 10
To love your master's daughter, and even then
When I had found a wealthy husband for her ;
I take it, sir, you had not : but, however,
I 'll break the neck of that commission,
And make you know you are but a merchant's factor. 1⌄
Jasp. Sir, I do liberally confess I am yours,
Bound both by love and duty to your service,
In which my labour hath been all my profit :
I have not lost in bargain, nor delighted
To wear your honest gains upon my back ; 20
Nor have I given a pension to my blood,[5]
Or lavishly in play consum'd your stock ;
These, and the miseries that do attend them,
I dare with innocence proclaim are strangers 2⌄
To all my temperate actions. For your daughter,
If there be any love to my deservings
Borne by her virtuous self, I cannot stop it ;
Nor am I able to refrain her wishes.
She 's private to herself, and best of knowledge[6]
Whom she will make so happy as to sigh for : 3⌄
Besides, I cannot think you mean to match her
Unto a fellow of so lame a presence,[7]
One that hath little left of nature in him.
Vent. 'T is very well, sir : I can tell your wisdom
How all this shall be cur'd.
Jasp.   Your care becomes you. 3⌄
Vent. And thus it must be, sir : I here discharge you
My house and service ; take your liberty ;
And when I want a son, I 'll send for you. *Exit.*
Jasp. These be the fair rewards of them that love !
Oh, you that live in freedom, never prove 4⌄
The travail of a mind led by desire !

Enter LUCE.

Luce. Why, how now, friend ? Struck with my father's thunder !
Jasp. Struck, and struck dead, unless the remedy
Be full of speed and virtue ; I am now,
What I expected long, no more your father's. 4⌄
Luce. But mine.
Jasp.   But yours, and only yours, I am ;
That 's all I have to keep me from the statute.[8]
You dare be constant still ?
Luce.   Oh, fear me not !
In this I dare be better than a woman :
Nor shall his anger nor his offers move me, 5⌄
Were they both equal to a prince's power.
Jasp. You know my rival !
Luce.   Yes, and love him dearly,
Even as I love an ague or foul weather.
I prithee, Jasper, fear him not.
Jasp.   Oh, no !
I do not mean to do him so much kindness. 5⌄
But to our own desires : you know the plot
We both agreed on ?

---

[5] Indulged my passions.
[6] Is her own confidant, and knows best.
[7] So feeble a personality.
[8] Against masterless men.

Luce.   Yes, and will perform
My part exactly.
    Jasp.   I desire no more.
Farewell, and keep my heart; 'tis yours.
    Luce.   I take it;
He must do miracles makes me forsake it.   60
                    Exeunt [*severally*].

Cit. Fie upon 'em, little infidels! what a
matter's here now! Well, I'll be hang'd for a
halfpenny, if there be not some abomination
knavery in this play. Well; let 'em look to 't;
Ralph must come, and if there be any tricks [65
a-brewing ——
    Wife. Let 'em brew and bake too, husband,
a' God's name; Ralph will find all out, I warrant you, an they were older than they are.—
[*Enter* Boy.] — I pray, my pretty youth, is [70
Ralph ready?
    Boy. He will be presently.
    Wife. Now, I pray you, make my commend-
ations unto him, and withal carry him this stick
of liquorice. Tell him his mistress sent it to [75
him; and bid him bite a piece; 't will open his
pipes the better, say.   [*Exit* Boy.]

[Scene II.][1]

Enter Merchant [VENTUREWELL] *and* Master
HUMPHREY.

Vent. Come, sir, she's yours; upon my faith,
    she's yours;
You have my hand: for other idle lets[2]
Between your hopes and her, thus with a wind
They are scattered and no more. My wanton
    prentice,
That like a bladder blew himself with love,   5
I have let out, and sent him to discover
New masters yet unknown.
    Hum.   I thank you, sir,
Indeed, I thank you, sir; and, ere I stir,
It shall be known, however you do deem,
I am of gentle blood and gentle seem.   10
    Vent. Oh, sir, I know it certain.
    Hum.   Sir, my friend,
Although, as writers say, all things have end,
And that we call a pudding hath his two,
Oh, let it not seem strange, I pray, to you,
If in this bloody simile I put   15
My love, more endless than frail things or gut!

Wife. Husband, I prithee, sweet lamb, tell
me one thing; but tell me truly. — Stay, youths,
I beseech you, till I question my husband.
    Cit. What is it, mouse?   20
    Wife. Sirrah, didst thou ever see a prettier
child? how it behaves itself, I warrant ye, and
speaks and looks, and perts up the head! — I
pray you, brother, with your favour, were you
never none of Master Moncaster's[3] scholars?   25
    Cit. Chicken, I prithee heartily, contain[4] thy-
self: the childer are pretty childer; but when
Ralph comes, lamb ——

[1] Another room in the same.   [2] Hindrances.
[3] Richard Mulcaster, headmaster of St. Paul's School,
1596-1608. He trained the pupils to act.
[4] Restrain.

Wife. Ay, when Ralph comes, cony! — Well,
my youth, you may proceed.   36

Vent. Well, sir, you know my love, and rest,
    I hope,
Assur'd of my consent; get but my daughter's,
And wed her when you please. You must be
    bold,
And clap in close unto her: come, I know
You have language good enough to win a
    wench.   35

Wife. A whoreson tyrant! h'as been an old
stringer[5] in 's days, I warrant him.

Hum. I take your gentle offer, and withal
Yield love again for love reciprocal.
    Vent. What, Luce! within there!

Enter LUCE.

Luce.   Call'd you, sir?
    Vent.   I did: 40
Give entertainment to this gentleman;
And see you be not froward. — To her, sir:
My presence will but be an eye-sore to you.
                        Exit.
    Hum. Fair Mistress Luce, how do you do?
    Are you well?
Give me your hand, and then I pray you tell   45
How doth your little sister and your brother;
And whether you love me or any other.
    Luce. Sir, these are quickly answered.
    Hum.   So they are,
Where women are not cruel. But how far
Is it now distant from the place we are in,   50
Unto that blessed place, your father's warren?
    Luce. What makes you think of that, sir?
    Hum.   Even that face;
For, stealing rabbits whilom in that place,
God Cupid, or the keeper, I know not whether,
Unto my cost and charges brought you thither,
And there began ——
    Luce.   Your game, sir.
    Hum.   Let no game,   56
Or any thing that tendeth to the same,
Be evermore remem'red, thou fair killer,
For whom I sat me down, and brake my
    tiller.[6]

Wife. There's a kind gentleman, I war- [60
rant you; when will you do as much for me,
George?

Luce. Beshrew me, sir, I am sorry for your
    losses,
But, as the proverb says, I cannot cry.
I would you had not seen me!
    Hum.   So would I,   65
Unless you had more maw[7] to do me good.
    Luce. Why, cannot this strange passion be
    withstood?
Send for a constable, and raise the town.
    Hum. Oh, no! my valiant love will batter
    down
Millions of constables, and put to flight   70

[5] Rake.   [6] Crossbow.   [7] Inclination.

Even that great watch of Midsummer-day at
　　　night.[1]
Luce. Beshrew me, sir, 't were good I yielded,
　　　then;
Weak women cannot hope, where valiant men
Have no resistance.
　　Hum.　　　　　　　Yield, then; I am full
Of pity, though I say it, and can pull　　75
Out of my pocket thus a pair of gloves.
Look, Lucy, look; the dog's tooth nor the
　　　dove's
Are not so white as these; and sweet they be,
And whipt[2] about with silk, as you may see.
If you desire the price, shoot from your eye　　80
A beam to this place, and you shall espy
F S, which is to say, my sweetest honey,
They cost me three and twopence, or no money.
Luce. Well, sir, I take them kindly, and I
　　　thank you:
What would you more?
　　Hum.　　　　　　　Nothing.
　　Luce.　　　　　Why, then, farewell.　　85
　　Hum. Nor so, nor so; for, lady, I must tell,
Before we part, for what we met together:
God grant me time and patience and fair
　　　weather!
Luce. Speak, and declare your mind in terms
　　　so brief.
Hum. I shall: then, first and foremost, for
　　　relief　　90
I call to you, if that you can afford it;
I care not at what price, for, on my word, it
Shall be repaid again, although it cost me
More then I'll speak of now; for love hath tost
　　　me
In furious blanket like a tennis-ball,　　95
And now I rise aloft, and now I fall.
Luce. Alas, good gentleman, alas the day!
Hum. I thank you heartily; and, as I say,
Thus do I still continue without rest,
I' th' morning like a man, at night a beast,　　100
Roaring and bellowing mine own disquiet,
That much I fear, forsaking of my diet
Will bring me presently to that quandary,
I shall bid all adieu.
Luce.　　　　　　Now, by St. Mary,
That were great pity!
Hum.　　　　　　So it were, beshrew me;　　105
Then, ease me, lusty Luce, and pity show me.
Luce. Why, sir, you know my will is nothing
　　　worth
Without my father's grant; get his consent,
And then you may with assurance try me.
Hum. The worshipful your sire will not deny
　　　me;　　110
For I have askt him, and he hath repli'd,
"Sweet Master Humphrey, Luce shall be thy
　　　bride."
Luce. Sweet Master Humphrey, then I am
　　　content.
Hum. And so am I, in truth.
Luce.　　　　　　Yet take me with you;[3]

There is another clause must be annext,　　115
And this it is: I swore, and will perform it,
No man shall ever joy me as his wife
But he that stole me hence. If you dare vent-
　　　ure,
I am yours (you need not fear; my father loves
　　　you);
If not, farewell for ever!
　　Hum.　　　　　Stay, nymph, stay:　　120
I have a double gelding, colour'd bay,
Sprung by his father from Barbarian kind;
Another for myself, though somewhat blind,
Yet true as trusty tree.
Luce.　　　　　I am satisfied;
And so I give my hand. Our course must
　　　lie　　125
Through Waltham-forest, where I have a
　　　friend
Will entertain us. So, farewell, Sir Humphrey,
And think upon your business.　　　　　*Exit.*
　　Hum.　　　　　　Though I die,
I am resolv'd to venture life and limb
For one so young, so fair, so kind, so trim.　　130
　　　　　　　　　　　　　　　　Exit.

Wife. By my faith and troth, George, and as
I am virtuous, it is e'en the kindest young man
that ever trod on shoe-leather. — Well, go thy
ways; if thou hast her not, 't is not thy fault,
'faith.　　135
Cit. I prithee, mouse, be patient; 'a shall
have her, or I'll make some of 'em smoke
for 't.
Wife. That's my good lamb, George. — Fie,
this stinking tobacco kills me![4] would there　　140
were none in England! — Now, I pray, gentlemen, what good does this stinking tobacco do
you? Nothing, I warrant you: make chimneys
o' your faces! Oh, husband, husband, now, now!
there's Ralph, there's Ralph.　　145

[SCENE III.]

Enter RALPH, *like a Grocer in's shop with two*
Prentices [TIM *and* GEORGE], *reading "Palmerin of England."*

Cit. Peace, fool! let Ralph alone. — Hark
you, Ralph; do not strain yourself too much at
the first. — Peace! — Begin, Ralph.

Ralph. [*reads.*] Then Palmerin and Trineus,
snatching their lances from their dwarfs, [5
and clasping their helmets, gallopt amain after
the giant; and Palmerin, having gotten a sight
of him, came posting amain, saying, "Stay,
traitorous thief! for thou mayst not so carry
away her, that is worth the greatest lord in [10
the world;" and, with these words, gave him a
blow on the shoulder, that he struck him besides[5] his elephant. And Trineus, coming to
the knight that had Agricola behind him, set
him soon besides his horse, with his neck [15
broken in the fall; so that the princess, getting
out of the throng, between joy and grief, said,
"All happy knight, the mirror of all such as

---

[1] The "annual military muster of the citizens, em-
bodying all the companies, for the purpose of forming a
regular guard for the city during the ensuing year."
(Dyce.)
[2] Embroidered.　　　　[3] Hear me out.

[4] Qq. *men.*　　　　[5] Off.

follow arms, now may I be well assured of the
love thou bearest me." [1] I wonder why the [20
kings do not raise an army of fourteen or fifteen hundred thousand men, as big as the army
that the Prince of Portigo brought against
Rosicleer, and destroy these giants; they do
much hurt to wand'ring damsels, that go in [25
quest of their knights.

Wife. Faith, husband, and Ralph says true;
for they say the King of Portugal cannot sit at
his meat, but the giants and the ettins[2] will
come and snatch it from him.   30
Cit. Hold thy tongue.—On, Ralph!

Ralph. And certainly those knights are much
to be commended, who, neglecting their possessions, wander with a squire and a dwarf through
the deserts to relieve poor ladies.   35

Wife. Ay, by my faith, are they, Ralph;
let 'em say what they will, they are indeed.
Our knights neglect their possessions well
enough, but they do not the rest.

Ralph. There are no such courteous and [40
fair well-spoken knights in this age: they will
call one "the son of a whore," that Palmerin
of England would have called "fair sir;" and
one that Rosicleer would have call'd "right
beauteous damsel," they will call "damn'd [45
bitch."

Wife. I'll be sworn will they, Ralph; they
have call'd me so an hundred times about a
scurvy pipe of tobacco.

Ralph. But what brave spirit could be [50
content to sit in his shop, with a flappet of
wood,[3] and a blue apron before him, selling mith-
ridatum[4] and dragon's-water[4] to visited houses,[5]
that might pursue feats of arms, and, through
his noble achievements, procure such a fam- [55
ous history to be written of his heroic prowess?

Cit. Well said, Ralph; some more of those
words, Ralph!
Wife. They go finely, by my troth.

Ralph. Why should not I, then, pursue [60
this course, both for the credit of myself and
our company? for amongst all the worthy books
of achievements, I do not call to mind that I yet
read of a grocer-errant. I will be the said knight.
—Have you heard of any that hath wand'red [65
unfurnished of his squire and dwarf? My elder
prentice Tim shall be my trusty squire, and
little George my dwarf. Hence, my blue apron!
Yet, in remembrance of my former trade, upon
my shield shall be portray'd a Burning Pestle, [70
and I will be call'd the Knight of the Burning
Pestle.

---

[1] The passage is condensed from *Palmerin d'Oliva*,
the romance to which *Palmerin of England* is a sequel.
[2] Giants.   [3] *I. e.* a counter.
[4] Specifics used against the plague.
[5] *I. e.* visited by the plague.

Wife. Nay, I dare swear thou wilt not forget thy old trade; thou wert ever meek.

Ralph. Tim!   75
Tim. Anon.
Ralph. My beloved squire, and George my
dwarf, I charge you that from henceforth you
never call me by any other name but "the right
courteous and valiant Knight of the Burning [80
Pestle;" and that you never call any female by
the name of a woman or wench, but "fair lady,"
if she have her desires, if not, "distressed damsel;" that you call all forests and heaths "deserts," and all horses "palfreys."   85

Wife. This is very fine, faith.— Do the gentlemen like Ralph, think you, husband?
Cit. Ay, I warrant thee; the players would
give all the shoes in their shop for him.

Ralph. My beloved squire Tim, stand out. [90
Admit this were a desert, and over it a knight-
errant pricking,[6] and I should bid you inquire
of his intents, what would you say?
Tim. Sir, my master sent me to know whither
you are riding?   95
Ralph. No, thus: "Fair sir, the right courteous and valiant Knight of the Burning Pestle
commanded me to inquire upon what adventure
you are bound, whether to relieve some distressed damsels, or otherwise."   100

Cit. Whoreson blockhead, cannot remember!
Wife. I' faith, and Ralph told him on 't before: all the gentlemen heard him.— Did he not,
gentlemen? Did not Ralph tell him on 't?

George. Right courteous and valiant [105
Knight of the Burning Pestle, here is a distressed damsel to have a halfpenny-worth of
pepper.

Wife. That's a good boy! See, the little boy
can hit it; by my troth, it's a fine child.   110

Ralph. Relieve her, with all courteous language. Now shut up shop; no more my prentices, but my trusty squire and dwarf. I must
bespeak my shield and arming[7] pestle.
                 [*Exeunt* TIM *and* GEORGE.]

Cit. Go thy ways, Ralph! As I'm a true[8] [115
man, thou art the best on 'em all.
Wife. Ralph, Ralph!
Ralph. What say you, mistress?
Wife. I prithee, come again quickly, sweet
Ralph.   120
Ralph. By and by.   *Exit.*

[SCENE IV.][9]

Enter JASPER *and his mother,* MISTRESS MERRY-
THOUGHT.

Mist. Mer. Give thee my blessing? No, I'll
ne'er give thee my blessing; I'll see thee

---

[6] Spurring.   [7] Heraldic.   [8] Honest.
[9] A room in Merrythought's house.

hang'd first; it shall ne'er be said I gave thee
my blessing. Th' art thy father's own son, of
the right blood of the Merrythoughts. I may [5
curse the time that e'er I knew thy father; he
hath spent all his own and mine too; and when
I tell him of it, he laughs, and dances, and
sings, and cries, "A merry heart lives long-a."
And thou art a wastethrift, and art run [10
away from thy master that lov'd thee well,
and art come to me; and I have laid up a
little for my younger son Michael, and thou
think'st to bezzle ¹ that, but thou shalt never
be able to do it. — Come hither, Michael!   15

Enter MICHAEL.

Come, Michael, down on thy knees; thou shalt
have my blessing.
Mich. [*kneels.*] I pray you, mother, pray to
God to bless me.
Mist. Mer. God bless thee! but Jasper shall [20
never have my blessing; he shall be hang'd
first; shall he not, Michael? How sayst thou?
Mich. Yes, forsooth, mother, and grace of
God.
Mist. Mer. That's a good boy!   25

Wife. I' faith, it's a fine spoken child.

Jasp. Mother, though you forget a parent's love
I must preserve the duty of a child.
I ran not from my master, nor return
To have your stock maintain my idleness.   30

Wife. Ungracious child, I warrant him;
hark, how he chops logic with his mother! —
Thou hadst best tell her she lies; do, tell her
she lies.
Cit. If he were my son, I would hang him [35
up by the heels, and flay him, and salt him,
whoreson haltersack.²

Jasp. My coming only is to beg your love,
Which I must ever, though I never gain it;
And, howsoever you esteem of me,   40
There is no drop of blood hid in these veins
But, I remember well, belongs to you
That brought me forth, and would be glad for you
To rip them all again, and let it out.
Mist. Mer. I' faith, I had sorrow enough [45
for thee, God knows; but I'll hamper thee
well enough. Get thee in, thou vagabond, get
thee in, and learn of thy brother Michael,
        [*Exeunt* JASPER *and* MICHAEL.]
Mer. (within.)

    Nose, nose, jolly red nose,
    And who gave thee this jolly red nose?   50

Mist. Mer. Hark, my husband! he's singing
and hoiting; and I'm fain to cark ³ and care,
and all little enough. — Husband! Charles!
Charles Merrythought!

Enter old MERRYTHOUGHT.

Mer. [*sings.*]

    Nutmegs and ginger, cinnamon and cloves;   55
    And they gave me this jolly red nose.

: Squander.   ² Gallows-bird.   ³ To be careful.

Mist. Mer. If you would consider your state,
you would have little list to sing, i-wis.⁴
Mer. It should never be considered, while it
were an estate, if I thought it would spoil [60
my singing.
Mist. Mer. But how wilt thou do, Charles?
Thou art an old man, and thou canst not work,
and thou hast not forty shillings left, and thou
eatest good meat, and drinkest good drink, [65
and laughest.
Mer. And will do.
Mist. Mer. But how wilt thou come by it,
Charles?
Mer. How! why, how have I done hitherto [70
this forty years? I never came into my dining
room, but, at eleven and six o'clock,⁵ I found
excellent meat and drink a' th' table; my
clothes were never worn out, but next morning
a tailor brought me a new suit: and with- [75
out question it will be so ever; use makes per-
fectness. If all should fail, it is but a little
straining myself extraordinary, and laugh myself to death.

Wife. It's a foolish old man this; is not [80
he, George?
Cit. Yes, cony.
Wife. Give me a penny i' th' purse while I
live, George.
Cit. Ay, by lady, cony, hold thee there.⁶   85

Mist. Mer. Well, Charles; you promis'd to
provide for Jasper, and I have laid up for Michael. I pray you, pay Jasper his portion: he's
come home, and he shall not consume Michael's
stock, he says his master turn'd him away, [90
but, I promise you truly, I think he ran away.

Wife. No, indeed, Mistress Merrythought;
though he be a notable gallows,⁷ yet I'll assure
you his master did turn him away, even in this
place; 't was, i' faith, within this half- [95
hour, about his daughter; my husband was
by.
Cit. Hang him, rogue! he serv'd him well
enough: love his master's daughter! By my
troth, cony, if there were a thousand boys, [100
thou wouldst spoil them all with taking their
parts; let his mother alone with him.
Wife. Ay, George; but yet truth is truth.

Mer. Where is Jasper? He's welcome, however. Call him in; he shall have his portion. [105
Is he merry?
Mist. Mer. Ah, foul chive ⁸ him, he is too
merry! — Jasper! Michael!

Re-enter JASPER *and* MICHAEL.

Mer. Welcome, Jasper! though thou run'st
away, welcome! God bless thee! 'T is thy [110
mother's mind thou shouldst receive thy portion; thou hast been abroad, and I hope hast
learn'd experience enough to govern it; thou
art of sufficient years. Hold thy hand — one,

⁴ Certainly.   ⁷ Gallows-bird.
⁵ Dinner and supper hours.   ⁸ Ill luck to him.
⁶ Stick to your opinion.

two, three, four five, six, seven, eight, nine, [115
there 's ten shillings for thee. [*Gives money.*]
Thrust thyself into the world with that, and
take some settled course. If fortune cross thee,
thou hast a retiring place ; come home to me ; I
have twenty shillings left. Be a good hus- [120
band ;[1] that is, wear ordinary clothes, eat the
best meat, and drink the best drink ; be merry,
and give to the poor, and, believe me, thou hast
no end of thy goods.

Jasp. Long may you live free from all
thought of ill,   125
And long have cause to be thus merry still !
But, father——

Mer. No more words, Jasper ; get thee gone.
Thou hast my blessing ; thy father's spirit upon
thee !
Farewell, Jasper !   [*Sings.*] 130

But yet, or ere you part (oh, cruel ?)
Kiss me, kiss me, sweeting, mine own dear
jewel !

So, now begone ; no words.   *Exit* JASPER.
Mist. Mer. So, Michael, now get thee gone
too.   135
Mich. Yes, forsooth, mother ; but I 'll have
my father's blessing first.
Mist. Mer. No, Michael ; 't is no matter for
his blessing ; thou hast my blessing ; begone.
I 'll fetch my money and jewels, and follow [140
thee ; I 'll stay no longer with him, I warrant
thee. [*Exit* MICHAEL.] — Truly, Charles, I 'll
be gone too.
Mer. What ! you will not ?
Mist. Mer. Yes, indeed will I.   145
Mer. [*sings.*]

Heigh-ho, farewell, Nan !
I 'll never trust wench more again, if I can.

Mist. Mer. You shall not think, when all
your own is gone, to spend that I have been
scraping up for Michael.   150
Mer. Farewell, good wife ; I expect it not :
all I have to do in this world, is to be merry ;
which I shall, if the ground be not taken from
me ; and if it be,   [*Sings.*]

When earth and seas from me are reft,   155
The skies aloft for me are left.

Exeunt [*severally*].

Wife. I 'll be sworn he 's a merry old gentleman for all that. (*Music.*) Hark, hark, husband, hark ! fiddles, fiddles ! now surely they go
finely. They say 't is present death for these [160
fiddlers, to tune their rebecks[2] before the great
Turk's grace ; it 's not, George ? (Boy *danceth.*) But, look, look ! here 's a youth dances !
— Now, good youth, do a turn a' th' toe. —
Sweetheart, i' faith, I 'll have Ralph [165
come and do some of his gambols. — He 'll ride
the wild mare[3] gentlemen, 't would do your
hearts good to see him. — I thank you, kind
youth ; pray, bid Ralph come.   169
Cit. Peace, cony ! — Sirrah, you scurvy boy,

bid the players send Ralph ; or, by God's —— 4
an they do not, I 'll tear some of their periwigs
beside their heads : this is all riff-raff.

[*Exit* BOY.]

ACT II

SCENE I.[5]

Enter Merchant [VENTUREWELL] *and* HUM-
PHREY.

Vent. And how, faith, how goes it now, son
Humphrey ?
Hum. Right worshipful, and my beloved
friend
And father dear, this matter 's at an end.
Vent. 'T is well ; it should be so. I 'm glad
the girl
Is found so tractable.
Hum.   Nay, she must whirl   6
From hence (and you must wink ; for so, I say,
The story tells,) to-morrow before day.

Wife. George, dost thou think in thy conscience now 't will be a match ? Tell me but
what thou think'st, sweet rogue. Thou seest [10
the poor gentleman, dear heart, how it labours
and throbs, I warrant you, to be at rest ! I 'll go
move the father for 't.
Cit. No, no ; I prithee, sit still, honeysuckle ;
thou 'lt spoil all. If he deny him, I 'll bring [15
half-a-dozen good fellows myself, and in the
shutting[6] of an evening, knock 't up, and
there 's an end.
Wife. I 'll buss thee for that, i' faith, boy.
Well, George, well, you have been a wag in [20
your days, I warrant you ; but God forgive you,
and I do with all my heart.

Vent. How was it, son ? You told me that
to-morrow
Before day-break, you must convey her hence.
Hum. I must, I must ; and thus it is agreed :
Your daughter rides upon a brown-bay steed, 25
I on a sorrel, which I bought of Brian,
The honest host of the Red roaring Lion,
In Waltham situate. Then, if you may,
Consent in seemly sort ; lest, by delay,   30
The Fatal Sisters come, and do the office,
And then you 'll sing another song.
Vent.   Alas,
Why should you be thus full of grief to me,
That do as willing as yourself agree
To any thing, so it be good and fair ?   35
Then, steal her when you will, if such a pleas-
ure
Content you both ; I 'll sleep and never see it,
To make your joys more full. But tell me why
You may not here perform your marriage ?

Wife. God's blessing a' thy soul, old man ! 40
I' faith, thou art loth to part true hearts. I see
'a has her, George ; and I 'm as glad on 't ! —
Well, go thy ways, Humphrey, for a fair-spoken

___

[1] Be frugal.   [2] A kind of a violin.
[3] The game of see-saw.

[4] Ed. 1778, *God's wounds.*   [6] Close.
[5] A room in the house of Venturewell.

man; I believe thou hast not thy fellow within the walls of London; an I should say the [45 suburbs too, I should not lie.— Why dost not rejoice with me, George?

Cit. If I could but see Ralph again, I were as merry as mine host, i' faith.

Hum. The cause you seem to ask. I thus de-
　　clare —　　　　　　　　　　　　　　　　50
Help me, O Muses nine! Your daughter sware
A foolish oath, and more it was the pity;
Yet no one but myself within this city
Shall dare to say so, but a bold defiance　54
Shall meet him, were he of the noble science; [1]
And yet she sware, and yet why did she swear?
Truly, I cannot tell, unless it were
For her own ease; for, sure, sometimes an oath,
Being sworn thereafter, is like cordial broth;
And this it was she swore, never to marry　　60
But such a one whose mighty arm could carry
(As meaning me, for I am such a one)
Her bodily away, through stick and stone,
Till both of us arrive, at her request,　　64
Some ten miles off, in the wild Waltham-forest.

Vent. If this be all, you shall not need to fear
Any denial in your love: proceed;
I 'll neither follow, nor repent the deed.

Hum. Good night, twenty good nights, and
　　twenty more,
And twenty more good nights,— that makes
　　three-score!　　　　　*Exeunt [severally].* 70

[SCENE II.] [2]

Enter MISTRESS MERRYTHOUGHT *and her son*
MICHAEL.

Mist. Mer. Come, Michael; art thou not weary, boy?
Mich. No, forsooth, mother, not I.
Mist. Mer. Where be we now, child?
Mich. Indeed, forsooth, mother, I cannot [5 tell, unless we be at Mile-End. Is not all the world Mile-End, mother?
Mist. Mer. No, Michael, not all the world, boy; but I can assure thee, Michael, Mile-End is a goodly matter: there has been a pitch- [10 field,[3] my child, between the naughty Spaniels[4] and the Englishmen; and the Spaniels ran away, Michael, and the Englishmen followed: my neighbor Coxstone was there, boy, and kill'd them all with a birding-piece.[5]　　15
Mich. Mother, forsooth —
Mist. Mer. What says my white boy? [6]
Mich. Shall not my father go with us too?
Mist. Mer. No, Michael, let thy father go snick-up; [7] he shall never come between a [20 pair of sheets with me again while he lives; let him stay at home, and sing for his supper, boy. Come, child, sit down, and I 'll show my boy fine knacks, indeed. [*They sit down: and she takes out a casket.*] Look here Michael; here 's

---

[1] A master of fencing.
[2] This seems to be an allusion to a sham-battle at Mile-End, the green at which was used as a training ground.
[4] Spaniards.　　　　　[6] A term of endearment.
[5] Fowling-piece.　　　[7] Go hang.

---

a ring, and here 's a brooch, and here 's a [26 bracelet, and here 's two rings more, and here 's money and gold by th' eye,[8] my boy.
Mich. Shall I have all this, mother?
Mist. Mer. Ay, Michael, thou shalt have [30 all, Michael.
Cit. How likest thou this, wench?
Wife. I cannot tell; I would have Ralph, George; I 'll see no more else, indeed, la; and I pray you, let the youths understand so [35 much by word of mouth; for, I tell you truly, I 'm afraid a' my boy. Come, come, George, let 's be merry and wise: the child 's a father-less child; and say they should put him into a strait pair of gaskins,[9] 't were worse than [40 knot-grass;[10] he would never grow after it.

Enter RALPH, *Squire* [TIM], *and* Dwarf
[GEORGE].

Cit. Here 's Ralph, here 's Ralph!
Wife. How do you do, Ralph? you are wel-come, Ralph, as I may say. It 's a good boy, hold up thy head, and be not afraid; we are thy friends, Ralph; the gentlemen will praise thee, Ralph, if thou play'st thy part with auda- [47 city. Begin, Ralph, a' God's name!

Ralph. My trusty squire, unlace my helm;
　　give me my hat.
Where are we, or what desert may this be?　50
George. Mirror of knighthood, this is, as I
take it, the perilous Waltham-down; in whose
bottom stands the enchanted valley.
Mist. Mer. Oh, Michael, we are betray'd, we
are betray'd! Here be giants! Fly, boy! fly,
boy, fly!　　　　　　　　　　　　　　55
　　　　　Exit with MICHAEL [*leaving the
　　　　　casket*].
Ralph. Lace on my helm again. What noise
　　is this?
A gentle lady, flying the embrace
Of some uncourteous knight! I will relieve her.
Go, squire, and say, the Knight that wears this
　　Pestle　　　　　　　　　　　　　　　60
In honour of all ladies, swears revenge
Upon that recreant coward that pursues her;
Go, comfort her, and that same gentle squire
That bears her company.
Tim.　　　　　　　I go, brave knight. [*Exit.*]
Ralph. My trusty dwarf and friend, reach me
　　my shield;　　　　　　　　　　　　65
And hold it while I swear. First, by my knight-
　　hood;
Then by the soul of Amadis de Gaul,
My famous ancestor; then by my sword
The beauteous Brionella [11] girt about me;
By this bright burning Pestle, of mine honour
The living trophy; and by all respect　　　71
Due to distressed damsels; here I vow
Never to end the quest of this fair lady
And that forsaken squire till by my valour
I gain their liberty!

---

[8] In abundance.　　　　　[9] Breeches.
[10] An infusion of knot-grass was supposed to retard growth.
[11] The mistress of Ptolme, the friend of Palmerin.

George.   Heaven bless the knight 75
That thus relieves poor errant gentlewomen!
                                    Exeunt.

Wife. Ay, marry, Ralph, this has some savour in 't; I would see the proudest of them all
offer to carry his books after him. But, George,
I will not have him go away so soon; I shall be
sick if he go away, that I shall. Call Ralph [81
again, George, call Ralph again; I prithee,
sweetheart, let him come fight before me, and
let 's ha' some drums and some trumpets, and
let him kill all that comes near him, an thou
lov 'st me, George!   86
Cit. Peace a little, bird : he shall kill them
all, an they were twenty more on 'em than there
are.

                Enter JASPER.

Jasp. Now, Fortune, if thou be'st not only
    ill,   90
Show me thy better face, and bring about
Thy desperate wheel, that I may climb at
    length,
And stand. This is our place of meeting,
If love have any constancy. Oh, age
Where only wealthy men are counted happy! 95
How shall I please thee, how deserve thy smiles,
When I am only rich in misery!
My father's blessing and this little coin
Is my inheritance; a strong revénue!
From earth thou art, and to the earth I give
    thee :   [*Throws away the money.*]
There grow and multiply, whilst fresher air 101
Breeds me a fresher fortune. — How! illusion?
                            Spies the casket.
What, hath the devil coin'd himself before me ?
'T is metal good, it rings well ; I am waking,
And taking too, I hope. Now, God's dear bless-
    ing   105
Upon his heart that left it here! 'T is mine ;
These pearls, I take it, were not left for swine.
                        Exit [*with the casket*].

Wife. I do not like that this unthrifty youth
should embezzle away the money; the poor
gentlewoman his mother will have a heavy
heart for it, God knows.   111
Cit. And reason good, sweetheart.
Wife. But let him go ; I 'll tell Ralph a tale
in 's ear shall fetch him again with a wanion,[1] I
warrant him, if he be above ground ; and besides, George, here are a number of suffi- [116
cient gentlemen can witness, and myself, and
yourself, and the musicians, if we be call'd in
question. But here comes Ralph, George ; thou
shalt hear him speak as he were an emperal.[2]

                [SCENE III.][3]

Enter RALPH *and* Dwarf [GEORGE].

Ralph. Comes not sir squire again ?
George.   Right courteous knight,

Your squire doth come, and with him comes the
    lady,

Enter MISTRESS MERRYTHOUGHT, MICHAEL,
            and Squire [TIM].

For and [4] the Squire of Damsels, as I take it.
Ralph. Madam, if any service or devoir   4
Of a poor errant knight may right your wrongs,
Command it ; I am prest [5] to give you succour ;
For to that holy end I bear my armour.
Mist. Mer. Alas, sir, I am a poor gentle-
woman, and I have lost my money in this forest!
Ralph. Desert, you would say, lady ; and not
    lost   10
Whilst I have sword and lance. Dry up your
    tears,
Which ill befits the beauty of that face,
And tell the story, if I may request it,
Of your disastrous fortune.
Mist. Mer. Out, alas! I left a thousand [15
pound, a thousand pound, e'en all the money I
had laid up for this youth, upon the sight of
your mastership, you lookt so grim, and, as I
may say it, saving your presence, more like a
giant than a mortal man.   20
Ralph. I am as you are, lady ; so are they ;
All mortal. But why weeps this gentle squire ?
Mist. Mer. Has he not cause to weep, do you
think, when he hath lost his inheritance ?
Ralph. Young hope of valour, weep not ; I am
    here   25
That will confound thy foe, and pay it dear
Upon his coward head, that dares deny
Distressed squires and ladies equity.
I have but one horse, on which shall ride
This fair lady behind me, and before,   30
This courteous squire : fortune will give us more
Upon our next adventure. Fairly speed
Beside us, squire and dwarf, to do us need !
                                    Exeunt.

Cit. Did not I tell you, Nell, what your man
would do ? By the faith of my body, wench, [35
for clean action and good delivery, they may all
cast their caps at him.[6]
Wife. And so they may, i' faith ; for I dare
speak it boldly, the twelve companies [7] of London cannot match him, timber for timber.[8]
Well, George, an he be not inveigled by some [41
of these paltry players, I ha' much marvel: but,
George, we ha' done our parts, if the boy have
any grace to be thankful.
Cit. Yes, I warrant thee, duckling.   45

                [SCENE IV.] [9]

        Enter HUMPHREY *and* LUCE.

Hum. Good Mistress Luce, however I in fault
    am
For your lame horse, you 're welcome unto Wal-
    tham ;
But which way now to go, or what to say,
I know not truly, till it be broad day.

---

    [1] With a vengence.
    [2] Imperial, *i. e.* emperor.
    [3] Another part of the forest.
    [4] And also.   [5] Ready.
    [6] Salute him as superior. (Moorman.)
    [7] *I. e.* Livery companies, guilds.
    [8] Man for man.   [9] Another part of the forest.

Luce. Oh, fear not, Master Humphrey ; I am
   guide   5
For this place good enough.
   Hum.   Then, up and ride ;
Or, if it please you, walk, for your repose ;
Or sit, or, if you will, go pluck a rose ;[1]
Either of which shall be indifferent
To your good friend and Humphrey, whose con-
   sent   10
Is so entangled ever to your will,
As the poor harmless horse is to the mill.
   Luce. Faith, an you say the word, we 'll e'en
   sit down,
And take a nap.
   Hum.   'T is better in the town,
Where we may map together ; for, believe me,
To sleep without a snatch would mickle grieve
   me.   16
   Luce. You 're merry, Master Humphrey.
   Hum.   So I am,
And have been ever merry from my dam.
   Luce. Your nurse had the less labour.
   Hum.   Faith, it may be,
Unless it were by chance I did beray[2] me.   20

Enter JASPER.

   Jasp. Luce ! dear friend Luce !
   Luce.   Here, Jasper.
   Jasp.   You are mine.
   Hum. If it be so, my friend, you use me fine.
What do you think I am ?
   Jasp.   An arrant noddy.
   Hum. A word of obloquy! Now, by God's body,
I 'll tell thy master ; for I know thee well.   25
   Jasp. Nay, an you be so forward for to tell,
Take that, and that ; and tell him, sir, I gave it :
And say, I paid you well.   [*Beats him.*]
   Hum.   Oh, sir, I have it,
And do confess the payment ! Pray, be quiet.
   Jasp. Go, get [you] to your night-cap and the
   diet,   30
To cure your beaten bones.
   Luce.   Alas, poor Humphrey ;
Get thee some wholesome broth, with sage and
   comfrey ;[3]
A little oil of roses and a feather
To 'noint thy back withal.
   Hum.   When I came hither,
Would I had gone to Paris with John Dory![4]
   Luce. Farewell, my pretty nump ; I am very
   sorry   36
I cannot bear thee company.
   Hum.   Farewell :
The devil's dam was ne'er so bang'd in hell.
                   Exeunt LUCE *and* JASPER.

   Wife. This young Jasper will prove me another thing, a' my conscience, an he may be
suffered. George, dost not see, George, how 'a
swaggers, and flies at the very heads a' folks, [42

---

   [1] Cf. *Changeling,* I. ii. 76 and note.
   [2] Befoul.   [3] A healing herb.
   [4] John Dory, according to the legend, engaged with
the King of France to bring the crew of an English
ship prisoners to Paris, but was himself captured whilst
making the attempt. The song and tune were for a long
time popular in England. (Strachey.)

as he were a dragon ? Well, if I do not do his
lesson[5] for wronging the poor gentleman, I am
no true woman. His friends that brought him
up might have been better occupied, i-wis, than
ha' taught him these fegaries :[6] he 's e'en in [47
the high way to the gallows, God bless him !
   Cit. You 're too bitter, cony ; the young man
may do well enough for all this.   50
   Wife. Come hither, Master Humphrey ; has
he hurt you ? Now, beshrew his fingers
for 't ! Here, sweetheart, here 's some green ginger for thee. Now, beshrew my heart, but 'a
has peppernel[7] in 's head, as big as a pullet's
egg ! Alas, sweet lamb, how thy temples [56
beat ! Take the peace on him,[8] sweetheart, take
the peace on him.
   Cit. No, no ; you talk like a foolish woman :
I 'll ha' Ralph fight with him, and swinge him
up well-favour'dly. — Sirrah boy, come hither.
(*Enter* Boy.) Let Ralph come in and fight [62
with Jasper.
   Wife. Ay, and beat him well ; he 's an unhappy[9] boy.   65
   Boy. Sir, you must pardon ; the plot of our
play lies contrary ; and 't will hazard the spoiling of our play.
   Cit. Plot me no plots ! I 'll ha' Ralph come
out ; I 'll make your house too hot for you else.
   Boy. Why, sir, he shall ; but if any thing fall
out of order, the gentlemen must pardon us.   72
   Cit. Go your ways, goodman boy ! [*Exit* Boy.]
I 'll hold[10] him a penny, he shall have his bellyful of fighting now. Ho, here comes Ralph ! No
more ![11]   76

[SCENE V.][12]

[HUMPHREY *manet.*] *Enter* RALPH, MISTRESS
   MERRYTHOUGHT, MICHAEL, Squire [TIM],
   and Dwarf [GEORGE].

   Ralph. What knight is that, squire ? Ask
   him if he keep
The passage, bound by love of lady fair,
Or else but prickant.[13]
   Hum.   Sir, I am no knight,
But a poor gentleman, that this same night
Had stolen from me, on yonder green,   5
My lovely wife, and suffered (to be seen
Yet extant on my shoulders) such a greeting,
That whilst I live I shall think of that meeting.

   Wife. Ay, Ralph, he beat him unmercifully,
Ralph ; an thou sparest him, Ralph, I would [10
thou wert hang'd.
   Cit. No more, wife, no more.

   Ralph. Where is the caitiff-wretch hath done
   this deed ?
Lady, your pardon, that I may proceed
Upon the quest of this injurious knight. —   15
And thou, fair squire, repute me not the worse,
In leaving the great venture of the purse
And the rich casket, till some better leisure.

---

   [5] Teach him.   [6] Vagaries.   [7] A lump.
   [8] Appease (?) (Moorman.) Perhaps, have him bound
to keep the peace.
   [9] Mischievous.   [10] Wager.   [11] Silence !
   [12] The same.   [13] Traveling, spurring along.

Enter JASPER *and* LUCE.

Hum. Here comes the broker hath purloin'd
my treasure.
Ralph. Go, squire, and tell him I am here,   20
An errant knight-at-arms, to crave delivery
Of that fair lady to her own knight's arms.
If he deny, bid him take choice of ground,
And so defy him.
Tim.   From the Knight that bears
The Golden Pestle, I defy thee, knight,   25
Unless thou make fair restitution
Of that bright lady.
Jasp.   Tell the knight that sent thee,
He is an ass; and I will keep the wench,
And knock his head-piece.
Ralph.   Knight, thou art but dead
If thou recall not thy uncourteous terms.   30

Wife. Break 's pate, Ralph; break 's pate,
Ralph, soundly!

Jasp. Come, knight; I am ready for you.
Now your Pestle (*Snatches away his pestle.*)
Shall try what temper, sir, your mortar 's of.
" With that he stood upright in his stirrups, [35
and gave the Knight of the calf-skin such a
knock [*Knocks* RALPH *down.*] that he forsook
his horse, and down he fell ; and then he leaped
upon him, and plucking off his helmet ——"
Hum. Nay, an my noble knight be down so
soon,   40
Though I can scarcely go, I needs must run.
          Exeunt HUMPHREY *and* RALPH.

Wife. Run, Ralph, run, Ralph ; run for thy
life, boy ;
Jasper comes, Jasper comes !

Jasp. Come Luce, we must have other arms
for you :
Humphrey, and Golden Pestle, both adieu !   45
          Exeunt.

Wife. Sure the devil (God bless us !) is in this
springald ! [1] Why, George, didst ever see such
a fire-drake ? [2] I am afraid my boy's miscarried :
if he be, though he were Master Merrythought's
son a thousand times, if there be any law in [50
England, I 'll make some of them smart for 't.
Cit. No, no ; I have found out the matter,
sweetheart ; Jasper is enchanted ; as sure as we
are here, he is enchanted : he could no more
have stood in Ralph's hands than I can in [55
my lord mayor's. I 'll have a ring to discover
all enchantments, and Ralph shall beat him yet.
Be no more vext, for it shall be so.

[SCENE VI.] [3]

Enter RALPH, MISTRESS MERRYTHOUGHT,
MICHAEL, Squire [TIM], *and* Dwarf [GEORGE].

Wife. Oh, husband, here's Ralph again ! —
Stay, Ralph, let me speak with thee. How
dost thou, Ralph ? Art thou not shrewdly [4]

[1] Youth.   [2] Fiery dragon.
[3] Before the Bell Inn, Waltham.   [4] Severely.

hurt ? — The foul great lungies [5] laid unmercifully on thee : there 's some sugar-candy for [5
thee. Proceed ; thou shalt have another bout
with him.
Cit. If Ralph had him at the fencing-school,
if he did not make a puppy of him, and drive
him up and down the school, he should ne'er [10
come in my shop more.

Mist. Mer. Truly Master Knight of the Burn-
ing Pestle, I am weary.
Mich. Indeed, la, mother, and I am very
hungry.   15
Ralph. Take comfort, gentle dame, and you
fair squire ;
For in this desert there must needs be plac'd
Many strong castles held by courteous knights ;
And till I bring you safe to one of those,
I swear by this my order ne'er to leave you.   20

Wife. Well said, Ralph ! — George, Ralph
was ever comfortable, [6] was he not ?
Cit. Yes, duck.
Wife. I shall ne'er forget him. When we had
lost our child, (you know it was stray'd al- [25
most, alone, to Puddle-Wharf, and the criers
were abroad for it, and there it had drown'd
itself but for a sculler,) Ralph was the most
comfortablest to me : " Peace, mistress," says
he, " let it go ; I 'll get you another as good." [30
Did he not, George, did he not say so ?
Cit. Yes, indeed did he, mouse.

George. I would we had a mess of pottage and
a pot of drink, squire, and were going to bed !
Tim. Why, we are at Waltham town's [35
end, and that 's the Bell Inn.
George. Take courage, valiant knight, dam-
sel, and squire !
I have discovered, not a stone cast off,
An ancient castle, held by the old knight
Of the most holy order of the Bell,   40
Who gives to all knights-errant entertain.
There plenty is of food, and all prepar'd
By the white hands of his own lady dear.
He hath three squires that welcome all his
guests ;
The first, hight Chamberlino, who will see   45
Our beds prepar'd, and bring us snowy sheets,
Where never footman stretch'd his butter'd
hams ; [7]
The second, hight Tapstero, who will see
Our pots full filled, and no froth therein ;
The third, a gentle squire, Ostlero hight,   50
Who will our palfreys slick with wisps of straw,
And in the manger put them oats enough,
And never grease their teeth with candle-
snuff. [8]

Wife. That same dwarf 's a pretty boy, but
the squire 's a groutnol. [9]   55

[5] Great dirty lout.   [6] Consoling.
[7] Running footmen had their legs greased to keep
them supple.
[8] A common trick of the ostlers of the time to prevent the horses from eating the hay. (Weber.)
[9] Blockhead.

Ralph. Knock at the gates, my squire, with
stately lance.   [TIM *knocks at the door.*]

Enter TAPSTER.

Tap. Who 's there ? — You 're welcome, gen-
tlemen : will you see a room ?
George. Right courteous and valiant Knight
of the Burning Pestle, this is the Squire [60
Tapstero.
Ralph. Fair Squire Tapstero, I a wandering
knight,
Hight of the Burning Pestle, in the quest
Of this fair lady's casket and wrought purse,
Losing myself in this vast wilderness,   65
Am to this castle well by fortune brought :
Where, hearing of the goodly entertain
Your knight of holy order of the Bell
Gives to all damsels and all errant knights,
I thought to knock, and now am bold to en-
ter.   70
Tap. An 't please you see a chamber, you are
very welcome.   *Exeunt.*

Wife. George, I would have something done,
and I cannot tell what it is.
Cit. What is it, Nell ?   75
Wife. Why, George, shall Ralph beat nobody
again ? Prithee, sweetheart, let him.
Cit. So he shall, Nell ; and if I join with him,
we 'll knock them all.

[SCENE VII.][1]

Enter HUMPHREY *and* Merchant [VENTURE-
WELL.]

Wife. Oh, George, here 's Master Humphrey
again now, that lost Mistress Luce, and Mistress Luce's father. Master Humphrey will do
somebody's errand, I 'll warrant him.

Hum. Father, it 's true in arms I ne'er shall
clasp her ;   5
For she is stoln away by your man Jasper.

Wife. I thought he would tell him.

Vent. Unhappy that I am, to lose my child !
Now I begin to think on Jasper's words,
Who oft hath urg'd [to] me thy foolishness.   10
Why didst thou let her go ? Thou lov'st her not,
That wouldst bring home thy life, and not
bring her.
Hum. Father, forgive me. Shall I tell you
true ?
Look on my shoulders, they are black and blue.
Whilst to and fro fair Luce and I were wind-
ing,   15
He came and basted me with a hedge-binding.[2]
Vent. Get men and horses straight : we will
be there
Within this hour. You know the place again ?
Hum. I know the place where he my loins
did swaddle ;

I 'll get six horses, and to each a saddle.   20
Vent. Mean time I will go talk with Jasper's
father.   *Exeunt [severally].*

Wife. George, what wilt thou lay with me
now, that Master Humphrey has not Mistress
Luce yet ? Speak, George, what wilt thou lay
with me ?   25
Cit. No, Nell ; I warrant thee Jasper is at
Puckeridge[3] with her by this.
Wife. Nay, George, you must consider Mistress Luce's feet are tender ; and besides 't is
dark ; and, I promise you truly, I do not see [30
how he should get out of Waltham-forest with
her yet.
Cit. Nay, cony, what wilt thou lay with me,
that Ralph has her not yet ?
Wife. I will not lay against Ralph, honey, [35
because I have not spoken with him. But look,
George, peace ! here comes the merry old
gentleman again.

[SCENE VIII.][4]

Enter old MERRRTHOUGHT.

Mer. [*sings.*]

When it was grown to dark midnight,
    And all were fast asleep,
In came Margaret's grimly ghost,
    And stood at William's feet.

I have money, and meat, and drink before- [5
hand, till to-morrow at noon ; why should I be
sad ? Methinks I have half-a-dozen jovial spirits
within me !   [*Sings.*]

I am three merry men, and three merry men !

To what end should any man be sad in this [10
world ? Give me a man who when he goes to
hanging cries,

Troul[5] the black bowl to me !

and a woman that will sing a catch in her travail ! I have seen a man come by my door [15
with a serious face, in a black cloak, without a
hatband, carrying his head as if he lookt for pins
in the street ; I have lookt out of my window
half a year after, and have spied that man's
head upon London-bridge.[6] ' T is vile : never [20
trust a tailor that does not sing at his work ; his
mind is of nothing but filching.

Wife. Mark this, George ; 't is worth noting :
Godfrey my tailor, you know, never sings, and
he had fourteen yards to make this gown : [25
and I 'll be sworn, Mistress Penistone the draper's wife had one made with twelve.

Mer. [*sings.*]

'T is mirth that fills the veins with blood,
    More than wine, or sleep, or food ;
Let each man keep his heart at ease,   30
    No man dies of that disease.

---

[1] A room in the house of Venturewell.
[2] Something used to bind together the bushes composing a hedge. (N. E. D.)
[3] Thirteen miles beyond Waltham.
[4] A room in Merrythought's house.   [5] Pass.
[6] Where the heads of traitors and heretics were ex
posed.

He that would his body keep
From diseases, must not weep ;
But whoever laughs and sings,
Never he his body brings   35
Into fevers, gouts, or rheums,
Or ling'ringly his lungs consumes,
Or meets with aches in the bone,
Or catarrhs or griping stone ;
But contented lives for aye ;   40
The more he laughs, the more he may.

Wife. Look, George ; how sayest thou by
this, George ? Is 't not a fine old man ? — Now,
God's blessing a' thy sweet lips ! — When wilt
thou be so merry, George ? Faith, thou art [45
the frowning'st little thing, when thou art
angry, in a country.

Enter Merchant [VENTUREWELL].

Cit. Peace, cony ; thou shalt see him taken
down too, I warrant thee. Here 's Luce's
father come now.   50

Mer. [*sings.*]

As you came from Walsingham,
From that holy land,
There met you not with my true love
By the way as you came ?

Vent. Oh, Master Merrythought, my daughter 's gone !   55
This mirth becomes you not ; my daughter 's
gone !
Mer. [*sings.*]

Why, an if she be, what care I ?
Or let her come, or go, or tarry.

Vent. Mock not my misery ; it is your son
(Whom I have made my own, when all forsook
him)   60
Has stoln my only joy, my child, away.
Mer. [*sings.*]

He set her on a milk-white steed,
And himself upon a grey ;
He never turn'd his face again,
But he bore her quite away.   65

Vent. Unworthy of the kindness I have
shown
To thee and thine ! too late I well perceive
Thou art consenting to my daughter's loss.
Mer. Your daughter ? what a stir 's here wi'
your daughter ? Let her go, think no more [70
on her, but sing loud. If both my sons were on
the gallows, I would sing,

Down, down, down they fall ;
Down, and arise they never shall.

Vent. Oh, might I behold her once again,   75
And she once more embrace her aged sire !
Mer. Fie, how scurvily this goes ! "And she
once more embrace her aged sire ? " You 'll
make a dog on her, will ye ? She cares much
for her aged sire, I warrant you.   [*Sings.*]

She cares not for her daddy, nor   81
She cares not for her mammy,
For she is, she is, she is, she is
My lord of Lowgave's lassy.

Vent. For this thy scorn I will pursue that
son   85
Of thine to death.
Mer.   Do ; and when you ha' kill'd him,
[*Sings.*]
Give him flowers enow, palmer, give him flowers enow ;
Give him red, and white, and blue, green, and yellow.

Vent. I 'll fetch my daughter ——
Mer. I 'll hear no more a' your daughter ; it
spoils my mirth.   91
Vent. I say, I 'll fetch my daughter.
Mer. [*sings.*]

Was never man for lady's sake,
Down, down,
Tormented as I, poor Sir Guy,   95
De derry down,
For Lucy's sake, that lady bright,
Down, down,
As ever men beheld with eye,
De derry down.   100

Vent. I 'll be reveng'd, by Heaven !
Exeunt [*severally*].

Music.

Wife. How dost thou like this, George ?
Cit. Why, this is well, cony ; but if Ralph
were hot once, thou shouldst see more.
Wife. The fiddlers go again, husband.   105
Cit. Ay, Nell ; but this is scurvy music. I
gave the whoreson gallows money, and I think
he has not got me the waits of Southwark. If
I hear 'em anon, I 'll twinge him by the
ears. — You musicians, play *Baloo* !   110
Wife. No, good George, let 's ha' *Lachrymae* !
Cit. Why, this is it, cony.
Wife. It 's all the better, George. Now,
sweet lamb, what story is that painted upon
the cloth ? The Confutation of St. Paul ?   115
Cit. No, lamb ; that 's Ralph and Lucrece.
Wife. Ralph and Lucrece ! Which Ralph ?
Our Ralph ?
Cit. No, mouse ; that was a Tartarian.[1]
Wife. A Tartarian ! Well, I would the [120
fiddlers had done, that we might see our Ralph
again !

ACT III

SCENE I.[2]

Enter JASPER and LUCE.

Jasp. Come, my dear dear ; though we have
lost our way,
We have not lost ourselves. Are you not weary
With this night's wand'ring, broken from your
rest,
And frighted with the terror that attends
The darkness of this wild unpeopled place ?   5
Luce. No, my best friend ; I cannot either
fear,
Or entertain a weary thought, whilst you
(The end of all my full desires) stand by me.
Let them that lose their hopes, and live to lan-
guish

---

[1] Thief.   [2] Waltham-forest.

Amongst the number of forsaken lovers, 10
Tell the long weary steps, and number time,
Start at a shadow, and shrink up their blood,
Whilst I (possest with all content and quiet)
Thus take my pretty love, and thus embrace
    him.
  Jasp. You have caught me, Luce, so fast,
    that, whilst I live, 15
[shall become your faithful prisoner,
And wear these chains for ever. Come, sit
    down,
And rest your body, too, too delicate
For these disturbances. — [*They sit down.*] So :
    will you sleep?
Come, do not be more able ¹ than you are ; 20
I know you are not skilful in these watches,
For women are no soldiers. Be not nice,²
But take it ; ³ sleep, I say.
  Luce.   I cannot sleep ;
Indeed, I cannot, friend.
  Jasp.   Why, then we 'll sing,
And try how that will work upon our senses. 25
  Luce. I 'll sing, or say, or any thing but
    sleep.
  Jasp. Come, little mermaid, rob me of my
    heart
With that enchanting voice.
  Luce.   You mock me, Jasper. [*They sing.*]

           SONG.

  Jasp. Tell me, dearest, what is love ?
  Luce. 'T is a lightning from above ; 30
      'T is an arrow, 't is a fire,
      'T is a boy they call Desire ;
        'T is a smile
        Doth beguile
  Jasp. The poor hearts of men that prove. 35

      Tell me more, are women true ?
  Luce. Some love change, and so do you.
  Jasp. Are they fair and never kind ?
  Luce. Yes, when men turn with the wind.
  Jasp.   Are they froward ? 40
  Luce.   Ever toward
      Those that love, to love anew.

  Jasp. Dissemble it no more ; I see the god 44
Of heavy sleep lay on his heavy mace
Upon your eyelids.
  Luce.   I am very heavy. [*Sleeps.*]
  Jasp. Sleep, sleep ; and quiet rest crown thy
    sweet thoughts !
Keep from her fair blood distempers, startings,
Horrors, and fearful shapes ! Let all her
    dreams
Be joys, and chaste delights, embraces,
    wishes,
And such new pleasures as the ravisht soul 50
Gives to the senses ! — So ; my charms have
    took. —
Keep her, you powers divine, whilst I contem-
    plate
Upon the wealth and beauty of her mind !
She is only fair and constant, only kind,
And only to thee, Jasper. Oh, my joys ! 55
Whither will you transport me ? Let not ful-
    ness

Of my poor buried hopes come up together
And overcharge my spirits ! I am weak.
Some say (however ill) the sea and women
Are govern'd by the moon ; both ebb and 60
    flow,
Both full of changes ; yet to them that know,
And truly judge, these but opinions are,
And heresies, to bring on pleasing war
Between our tempers, that without these were
Both void of after-love and present fear ; 65
Which are the best of Cupid. Oh, thou child
Bred from despair, I dare not entertain thee,
Having a love without the faults of women,
And greater in her perfect goods than men !
Which to make good, and please myself the 70
    stronger,
Though certainly I am certain of her love,
I 'll try her, that the world and memory
May sing to after-times her constancy.—
                [*Draws his sword.*]
Luce ! Luce ! awake !
  Luce.   Why do you fright me, friend,
With those distempered looks? What makes⁴ 75
    your sword
Drawn in your hand ? Who hath offended you ?
I prithee, Jasper, sleep ; thou art wild with
    watching.
  Jasp. Come, make your way to Heaven, and
    bid the world,
With all the villanies that stick upon it,
Farewell ; you 're for another life.
  Luce.   Oh, Jasper, 80
How have my tender years committed evil,
Especially against the man I love,
Thus to be cropt untimely ?
  Jasp.   Foolish girl,
Canst thou imagine I could love his daugh-
    ter 84
That flung me from my fortune into nothing ?
Discharged me his service, shut the doors
Upon my poverty, and scorn'd my prayers,
Sending me, like a boat without a mast,
To sink or swim ? Come ; by this hand you
    die ;
I must have life and blood, to satisfy 90
Your father's wrongs.

  Wife. Away, George, away ! raise the watch
at Ludgate, and bring a mittimus ⁵ from the
justice for this desperate villain ! — Now, I
charge you, gentlemen, see the king's peace [95
kept ! — Oh, my heart, what a varlet 's this
to offer manslaughter upon the harmless gentle-woman !
  Cit. I warrant thee, sweetheart, we 'll have
him hampered.

  Luce. Oh, Jasper, be not cruel ! 100
If thou wilt kill me, smile, and do it quickly,
And let not many deaths appear before me.
I am a woman, made of fear and love,
A weak, weak woman ; kill not with thy eyes,
They shoot me through and through. Strike, I 105
    am ready ;
And, dying, still I love thee.

---

¹ Capable of endurance.   ² Foolish.   ³ Give in.   ⁴ Does.   ⁵ Warrant for arrest.

Enter Merchant [VENTUREWELL], HUMPHREY,
and his men.

Vent. Whereabouts?
Jasp. No more of this ; now to myself again.
[Aside.]
Hum. There, there he stands, with sword,
like martial knight,
Drawn in his hand ; therefore beware the fight,
You that be wise ; for, were I good Sir Bevis,
I would not stay his coming, by your leaves. 111
Vent. Sirrah, restore my daughter !
Jasp. Sirrah, no.
Vent. Upon him, then !
[They attack JASPER, *and force
LUCE from him.]*

Wife. So ; down with him, down with him,
down with him !
Cut him i' th' leg, boys, cut him i' th' leg ! 116

Vent. Come your ways, minion : I 'll provide
a cage
For you, you 're grown so tame. — Horse her
away.
Hum. Truly, I 'm glad your forces have the
day. *Exeunt all except* JASPER.
Jasp. They are gone, and I am hurt ; my
love is lost, 120
Never to get again. Oh, me unhappy !
Bleed, bleed and die ! I cannot. Oh, my folly,
Thou hast betray'd me ! Hope, where art thou
fled ?
Tell me, if thou be'st any where remaining,
Shall I but see my love again ? Oh, no ! 125
She will not deign to look upon her butcher,
Nor is it fit she should ; yet I must venture.
Oh, Chance, or Fortune, or whate'er thou art,
That men adore for powerful, hear my cry,
And let me loving live, or losing die ! *Exit.*

Wife. Is 'a gone, George ? 131
Cit. Ay, cony.
Wife. Marry, and let him go, sweetheart. By
the faith a' my body, 'a has put me into such
a fright, that I tremble (as they say) as [135
't were an aspen-leaf. Look a' my little finger,
George, how it shakes. Now, i' truth, every
member of my body is the worse for 't.
Cit. Come, hug in mine arms, sweet
mouse ; he shall not fright thee any more. Alas,
mine own dear heart, how it quivers ! 141

[SCENE II.][1]

Enter MISTRESS MERRYTHOUGHT, RALPH, MI-
CHAEL, Squire [TIM], Dwarf [GEORGE], Host,
and Tapster.

Wife. Oh, Ralph ! how dost thou, Ralph ?
How hast thou slept to-night ? Has the knight
us'd thee well ?
Cit. Peace, Nell ; let Ralph alone.

Tap. Master, the reckoning is not paid. 5
Ralph. Right courteous knight, who, for the
order's sake

[1] A room in the Bell Inn, Waltham.

Which thou hast ta'en, hang'st out the holy
Bell,
As I this flaming Pestle bear about,
We render thanks to your puissant self,
Your beauteous lady, and your gentle squires, 10
For thus refreshing of our wearied limbs,
Stiff'ned with hard achievements in wild desert.
Tap. Sir, there is twelve shillings to pay.
Ralph. Thou merry Squire Tapstero, thanks
to thee
For comforting our souls with double jug : 15
And, if advent'rous fortune prick thee forth,
Thou jovial squire, to follow feats of arms,
Take heed thou tender every lady's cause,
Every true knight, and every damsel fair ;
But spill the blood of treacherous Saracens, 20
And false enchanters that with magic spells
Have done to death full many a noble knight.
Host. Thou valiant Knight of the Burning
Pestle, give ear to me ; there is twelve shillings
to pay, and, as I am a true knight, I will not [25
bate a penny.

Wife. George, I prithee, tell me, must Ralph
pay twelve shillings now ?
Cit. No, Nell, no ; nothing but the old knight
is merry with Ralph. 30
Wife. Oh, is 't nothing else ? Ralph will be
as merry as he.

Ralph. Sir Knight, this mirth of yours be-
comes you well ;
But, to requite this liberal courtesy,
If any of your squires will follow arms, 35
He shall receive from my heroic hand
A knighthood, by the virtue of this Pestle.
Host. Fair knight, I thank you for your
noble offer :
Therefore, gentle knight,
Twelve shillings you must pay, or I must cap [2]
you. 40

Wife. Look, George ! did not I tell thee as
much ? The knight of the Bell is in earnest.
Ralph shall not be beholding to him : give him
his money, George, and let him go snick up.[3]
Cit. Cap Ralph ? No. — Hold your hand, [45
Sir Knight of the Bell ; there 's your money
[Gives money.]: have you any thing to say to
Ralph now ? Cap Ralph !
Wife. I would you should know it, Ralph has
friends that will not suffer him to be capt [50
for ten times so much, and ten times to the end
of that. — Now take thy course, Ralph.

Mist. Mer. Come, Michael ; thou and I will
go home to thy father ; he hath enough left to
keep us a day or two, and we 'll set fellows [55
abroad to cry our purse and our casket : shall
we, Michael ?
Mich. Ay, I pray, mother ; in truth my feet
are full of chilblains with travelling.

Wife. Faith, and those chilblains are a [60
foul trouble. Mistress Merrythought, when

[2] Arrest.   [3] Go hang.

your youth comes home, let him rub all the soles of his feet, and his heels, and his ancles, with a mouse-skin; or, if none of your people can catch a mouse, when he goes to bed, let [65 him roll his feet in the warm embers, and, I warrant you, he shall be well; and you may make him put his fingers between his toes, and smell to them; it's very sovereign for his head, if he be costive. 70

Mist. Mer. Master Knight of the Burning Pestle, my son Michael and I bid you farewell: I thank your worship heartily for your kindness.
Ralph. Farewell, fair lady, and your tender squire. 75
If pricking through these deserts, I do hear
Of any traitorous knight, who through his guile
Hath light upon your casket and your purse,
I will dispoil him of them, and restore them.
Mist. Mer. I thank your worship. 80
Exit with Michael.
Ralph. Dwarf, bear my shield; squire, elevate my lance: —
And now farewell, you Knight of holy Bell.

Cit. Ay, ay, Ralph, all is paid.

Ralph. But yet, before I go, speak, worthy knight,
If aught you do of sad[1] adventures know, 85
Where errant knight may through his prowess win
Eternal fame, and free some gentle souls
From endless bonds of steel and ling'ring pain.
Host. Sirrah, go to Nick the barber, and bid him prepare himself, as I told you before, [90 quickly.
Tap. I am gone, sir. *Exit.*
Host. Sir Knight, this wilderness affordeth none
But the great venture, where full many a knight
Hath tri'd his prowess, and come off with shame; 95
And where I would not have you lose your life
Against no man, but furious fiend of hell.
Ralph. Speak on, Sir Knight; tell what he is and where:
For here I vow, upon my blazing badge,
Never to blaze a day in quietness, 100
But bread and water will I only eat,
And the green herb and rock shall be my couch,
Till I have quell'd[2] that man, or beast, or fiend,
That works such damage to all errant knights.
Host. Not far from hence, near to a craggy cliff, 105
At the north end of this distressed town,
There doth stand a lowly house,
Ruggedly builded, and in it a cave
In which an ugly giant now doth won,[3]
Ycleped Barbaroso: in his hand 110

He shakes a naked lance of purest steel,
With sleeves turn'd up; and him before he wears
A motley garment, to preserve his clothes
From blood of those knights which he massacres,
And ladies gent:[4] without his door doth hang
A copper basin on a prickant[5] spear; 116
At which no sooner gentle knights can knock,
But the shrill sound fierce Barbaroso hears,
And rushing forth, brings in the errant knight
And sets him down in an enchanted chair; 120
Then with an engine, which he hath prepar'd,
With forty teeth, he claws his courtly crown;
Next makes him wink, and underneath his chin
He plants a brazen piece of mighty bord.[6]
And knocks his bullets[7] round about his cheeks; 125
Whilst with his fingers, and an instrument
With which he snaps his hair off, he doth fill
The wretch's ears with a most hideous noise.
Thus every knight-adventurer he doth trim,
And now no creature dares encounter him. 130
Ralph. In God's name, I will fight him. Kind sir,
Go but before me to this dismal cave,
Where this huge giant Barbaroso dwells,
And, by that virtue that brave Rosicleer
That damned brood of ugly giants slew, 135
And Palmerin Frannarco overthrew,
I doubt not but to curb this traitor foul,
And to the devil send his guilty soul.
Host. Brave-sprighted knight, thus far I will perform
This your request: I'll bring you within sight
Of this most loathsome place, inhabited 141
By a more loathsome man; but dare not stay,
For his main force swoops all he sees away.
Ralph. Saint George, set on before! March squire and page! *Exeunt.*

Wife. George, dost think Ralph will confound the giant? [145
Cit. I hold my cap to a farthing he does. Why, Nell, I saw him wrastle with the great Dutchman, and hurl him.
Wife. Faith, and that Dutchman was a goodly man, if all things were answerable to his [151 bigness. And yet they say there was a Scotchman higher than he, and that they two and a knight met, and saw one another for nothing. But of all the sights that ever were in Lon- [155 don, since I was married, methinks the little child that was so fair grown about the members was the prettiest; that and the hermaphrodite.
Cit. Nay, by your leave, Nell, Ninivie[8] was better. 160
Wife. Ninivie! Oh, that was the story of Jone and the wall,[9] was it not, George?
Cit. Yes, lamb.

4 Elegant, courteous, noble.
5 Pointing upward. The reference is, of course, to the usual sign of the barber-surgeon.
6 Circumference. 7 Balls of soap.
8 *I. e.* The puppet-show of Nineveh.
9 Jonah and the whale.

1 Serious. 2 Killed. 3 Dwell.

[SCENE III.] [1]

Enter MISTRESS MERRYTHOUGHT.

Wife. Look, George, here comes Mistress Merrythought again! and I would have Ralph come and fight with the giant; I tell you true, I long to see 't.

Cit. Good Mistress Merrythought, begone, [5 I pray you, for my sake; I pray you, forbear a little; you shall have audience presently; I have a little business.

Wife. Mistress Merrythought, if it please you to refrain your passion a little, till Ralph [10 have despatcht the giant out of the way, we shall think ourselves much bound to you. I thank you, good Mistress Merrythought.

Exit MISTRESS MERRYTHOUGHT.

Enter a Boy.

Cit. Boy, come hither. Send away Ralph and this whoreson giant quickly.

Boy. In good faith, sir, we cannot; you 'll [15 utterly spoil our play, and make it to be hist; and it cost money; you will not suffer us to go on with our plot. — I pray, gentlemen, rule him.

Cit. Let him come now and despatch this, [20 and I 'll trouble you no more.

Boy. Will you give me your hand of that?

Wife. Give him thy hand, George, do; and I 'll kiss him. I warrant thee, the youth means plainly. 25

Boy. I 'll send him to you presently.[2]

Wife. [*kissing him.*] I thank you, little youth. (*Exit* Boy.) Faith, the child hath a sweet breath, George; but I think it be troubled with the worms; *carduus benedictus* and mare's milk [30 were the only thing in the world for 't.

[SCENE IV.] [3]

Enter RALPH, Host, TIM, *and* GEORGE.

Wife. Oh, Ralph 's here, George! — God send thee good luck, Ralph!

Host. Puissant knight, yonder his mansion is. Lo, where the spear and copper basin are! Behold that string, on which hangs many a tooth, 5 Drawn from the gentle jaw of wand'ring knights! I dare not stay to sound; he will appear.[4]

Exit.

Ralph. Oh, faint not, heart! Susan, my lady dear, The cobbler's maid in Milk-street, for whose sake 9 I take these arms, oh, let the thought of thee Carry thy knight through all adventurous deeds; And, in the honour of thy beauteous self, May I destroy this monster Barbaroso! — Knock, squire, upon the basin, till it break 14 With the shrill strokes, or till the giant speak.

[TIM *knocks upon the basin.*]

Enter Barber.

Wife. Oh, George, the giant, the giant! — Now, Ralph for thy life!

Bar. What fond [5] unknowing wight is this, that dares So rudely knock at Barbaroso's cell, Where no man comes but leaves his fleece behind? 20

Ralph. I, traitorous caitiff, who am sent by fate To punish all the sad enormities Thou hast committed against ladies gent And errant knights. Traitor to God and men, Prepare thyself! This is the dismal hour 25 Appointed for thee to give strict account Of all thy beastly treacherous villanies.

Bar. Fool-hardy knight, full soon thou shalt aby [6] This fond reproach: thy body will I bang; 29

Takes down his pole.

And, lo, upon that string thy teeth shall hang! Prepare thyself, for dead soon shalt thou be.

Ralph. Saint George for me! *They fight.*

Bar. Gargantua for me!

Wife. To him, Ralph, to him! hold up the giant; set out thy leg before, Ralph! 35

Cit. Falsify [7] a blow, Ralph, falsify a blow! The giant lies open on the left side.

Wife. Bear 't off, bear 't off still! there, boy! — Oh, Ralph 's almost down, Ralph 's almost down!

Ralph. Susan, inspire me! Now have up again. 40

Wife. Up, up, up, up, up! so, Ralph! down with him, down with him, Ralph!

Cit. Fetch him o'er the hip, boy!

[RALPH *knocks down the* Barber.]

Wife. There, boy! kill, kill, kill, kill, kill, Ralph!

Cit. No, Ralph; get all out of him first. 45

Ralph. Presumptuous man, see to what desperate end Thy treachery hath brought thee! The just gods, Who never prosper those that do despise them, For all the villanies which thou hast done To knights and ladies, now have paid thee home 50 By my stiff arm, a knight adventurous. But say, vile wretch, before I send thy soul To sad Avernus, whither it must go, What captives holdst thou in thy sable cave?

Bar. Go in, and free them all; thou hast the day. 55

Ralph. Go, squire and dwarf, search in this dreadful cave, And free the wretched prisoners from their bonds. *Exeunt* TIM *and* GEORGE.

[1] The street before Merrythought's house.
[2] At once.
[3] Before a barber's shop, Waltham.   [4] Knock.
[5] Foolish.   [6] Pay for.   [7] Feign.

Bar. I crave for mercy, as thou art a knight,
And scorn'st to spill the blood of those that
 beg.
Ralph. Thou show'd'st no mercy, nor shalt
 thou have any ;   60
Prepare thyself, for thou shalt surely die.

Re-enter Squire [TIM], *leading one winking, with
a Basin under his Chin.*

Tim. Behold, brave knight, here is one
 prisoner,
Whom this wild man hath used as you see.

Wife. This is the first wise word I heard the
squire speak.   65

Ralph. Speak what thou art, and how thou
 hast been us'd,
That I may give him condign punishment.
1 Kn. I am a knight that took my journey
 post
Northward from London ; and in courteous
 wise
This giant train'd me to his loathsome den, 70
Under pretence of killing of the itch ;
And all my body with a powder strew'd,
That smarts and stings ; and cut away my
 beard,
And my curl'd locks wherein were ribands ti'd ;
And with a water washt my tender eyes, 75
(Whilst up and down about me still he skipt,)
Whose virtue is, that, till my eyes be wipt
With a dry cloth, for this my foul disgrace,
I shall not dare to look a dog i' th' face.

Wife. Alas, poor knight ! — Relieve him, [80
Ralph ; relieve poor knights, whilst you live.

Ralph. My trusty squire, convey him to the
 town,
Where he may find relief.— Adieu, fair knight.
      Exit 1 Knight.

Re-enter Dwarf [GEORGE], *leading one, with a
patch o'er his nose.*

George. Puissant Knight, of the Burning Pes-
 tle hight,   84
See here another wretch, whom this foul beast
Hath scorcht [1] and scor'd in this inhuman wise.
Ralph. Speak me thy name, and eke thy
 place of birth,
And what hath been thy usage in this cave.
2 Kn. I am a knight, Sir Pockhole is my
 name,
And by my birth I am a Londoner, 90
Free by my copy,[2] but my ancestors
Were Frenchmen [3] all ; and riding hard this
 way
Upon a trotting horse, my bones did ache ;
And I, faint knight, to ease my weary limbs,
Light at this cave ; when straight this furious 95
 fiend,
With sharpest instruments of purest steel,

 [1] Old form of *scotched*, cut.
 [2] Certificate of citizenship.
 [3] The pox or syphilis was also known as the **French**
disease.

Did cut the gristle of my nose away,
And in the place this velvet plaster stands.
Relieve me, gentle knight, out of his hands ! 99

Wife. Good Ralph, relieve Sir Pockhole, and
send him away ; for in truth his breath stinks.

Ralph. Convey him straight after the other
 knight. —
Sir Pockhole, fare you well.
2 Kn.   Kind sir, good night. *Exit.*
Man. [*within.*] Deliver us ! *Cries within.*
Woman. [*within.*] Deliver us ! 105

Wife. Hark, George, what a woeful cry there
is ! I think some woman lies-in there.

Man. [*within.*] Deliver us !
Women. [*within.*] Deliver us !
Ralph. What ghastly noise is this ? Speak,
 Barbaroso,   110
Or, by this blazing steel, thy head goes off !
Bar. Prisoners of mine, whom I in diet keep.
Send lower down into the cave,
And in a tub that 's heated smoking hot,
There may they find them, and deliver them. 115
Ralph. Run, squire and dwarf ; deliver them
 with speed. *Exeunt* TIM *and* GEORGE.

Wife. But will not Ralph kill this giant ?
Surely I am afeard, if he let him go, he will do
as much hurt as ever he did.
Cit. Not so, mouse, neither, if he could convert him.   121
Wife. Ay, George, if he could convert him ;
but a giant is not so soon converted as one of us
ordinary people. There 's a pretty tale of a
witch, that had the devil's mark about her,
(God bless us !) that had a giant to her son, [126
that was call'd Lob-lie-by-the-fire ; didst never
hear it, George ?

Re-enter Squire [TIM], *leading a* Man, *with a
glass of lotion in his hand, and* Dwarf [GEORGE],
leading a Woman, *with diet-bread and drink
[in her hand].*

Cit. Peace, Nell, here comes the prisoners.

George. Here be these pined wretches, man-
 ful knight,   130
That for this six weeks have not seen a wight.
Ralph. Deliver what you are, and how you
 came
To this sad cave, and what your usage was ?
Man. I am an errant knight that followed
 arms
With spear and shield ; and in my tender years
I stricken was with Cupid's fiery shaft, 135
And fell in love with this my lady dear,
And stole her from her friends in Turnbull-
 street,[4]
And bore her np and down from town to town,
Where we did eat and drink, and music hear ;
Till at the length at this unhappy town 141
We did arrive, and coming to this cave,

 [4] The resort of prostitutes.

This beast us caught, and put us in a tub,
Where we this two months sweat,[1] and should
          have done
Another month, if you had not reliev'd us.   145
    Woman. This bread and water hath our diet
          been,
Together with a rib cut from a neck
Of burned mutton ; hard hath been our fare.
Release us from this ugly giant's snare !
    Man. This hath been all the food we have
          receiv'd ;   150
But only twice a-day, for novelty,
He gave a spoonful of this hearty broth
To each of us, through this same slender quill.
                              Pulls out a syringe.
    Ralph. From this infernal monster you shall
          go,
That useth knights and gentle ladies so ! —   155
Convey them hence.
                    Exeunt Man *and* Woman.

    Cit. Cony, I can tell thee, the gentlemen like
Ralph.
    Wife. Ay, George, I see it well enough. —
Gentlemen, I thank you all heartily for [160
gracing my man Ralph ; and I promise you,
you shall see him oft'ner.

    Bar. Mercy, great knight ! I do recant my
          ill,
And henceforth never gentle blood will spill.
    Ralph. I give thee mercy ; but yet shalt thou
          swear   165
Upon my Burning Pestle, to perform
Thy promise uttered.
    Bar. I swear and kiss.   [*Kisses the Pestle.*]
    Ralph.   Depart, then, and amend.—
                              [*Exit* Barber.]
Come, squire and dwarf ; the sun grows towards
          his set,
And we have many more adventures yet.   170
                              Exeunt.

    Cit. Now Ralph is in this humour, I know he
would ha' beaten all the boys in the house, if
they had been set on him.
    Wife. Ay, George, but it is well as it is. I
warrant you, the gentlemen do consider what
it is to overthrow a giant. But, look, [176
George ; here comes Mistress Merrythought,
and her son Michael.— Now you are welcome,
Mistress Merrythought ; now Ralph has done,
you may go on.

                    [SCENE V.] [2]

Enter MISTRESS MERRYTHOUGHT *and* MI-
                    CHAEL.

    Mist. Mer. Mick, my boy —
    Mich. Ay, forsooth, mother.
    Mist. Mer. Be merry, Mick ; we are at home
now ; where, I warrant you, you shall find the
house flung out of the windows. [*Music within.*] 5
Hark ! hey, dogs, hey ! this is the old world,[3]
i' faith, with my husband. If I get in among

    [1] A common method of treating syphilis.
    [2] The street before Merrythought's house.
    [3] His old habits.

'em, I 'll play 'em such a lesson, that they shall
have little list to come scraping hither again. —
Why, Master Merrythought ! husband ! Charles
Merrythought !   11
    Mer. [*appearing above, and singing.*]

        If you will sing, and dance, and laugh,
          And hollow, and laugh again,
        And then cry, " There, boys, there ! " why, then,
          One, two, three, and four,   15
        We shall be merry within this hour.

    Mist. Mer. Why, Charles, do you not know
your own natural wife ? I say, open the door,
and turn me out those mangy companions ; 't is
more than time that they were fellow and [20
fellow-like with you. You are a gentleman,
Charles, and an old man, and father of two
children ; and I myself, (though I say it) by my
mother's side niece to a worshipful gentleman
and a conductor ; [4] he has been three times [25
in his majesty's service at Chester, and is now
the fourth time, God bless him and his charge,
upon his journey.
    Mer. [*sings.*]

        Go from my window, love, go ;
          Go from my window, my dear !   30
        The wind and the rain
          Will drive you back again ;
          You cannot be lodged here.

Hark you, Mistress Merrythought, you that
walk upon adventures, and forsake your hus- [35
band, because he sings with never a penny
in his purse ; what, shall I think myself the
worse ? Faith, no, I 'll be merry. You come not
here ; here 's none but lads of mettle, lives of
a hundred years and upwards ; care never [40
drunk their bloods, nor want made 'em warble
" Heigh-ho, my heart is heavy."
    Mist. Mer. Why, Master Merrythought, what
am I, that you should laugh me to scorn thus
abruptly ? Am I not your fellow-feeler, as [45
we may say, in all our miseries ? your comforter
in health and sickness ? Have I not brought
you children ? Are they not like you, Charles ?
look upon thine own image, hard-hearted man !
and yet for all this ——   50
    Mer. [*sings.*]

        Begone, begone, my juggy, my puggy,
        Begone, my love, my dear !
        The weather is warm,
        'T will do thee no harm :
        Thou canst not be lodged here. —   55

Be merry, boys ! some light music, and more
wine !   [*Exit above.*]

    Wife. He 's not in earnest, I hope, George,
is he ?
    Cit. What if he be, sweetheart ?   60
    Wife. Marry, if he be, George, I 'll make
bold to tell him he 's an ingrant [5] old man to use
his bed-fellow so scurvily.
    Cit. What ! how does he use her, honey ?
    Wife. Marry, come up, sir saucebox ! I think
you'll take his part, will you not ? Lord, how [65
hot you are grown ! You are a fine man, an
you had a fine dog ; it becomes you sweetly !

    [4] Military leader.   [5] Ignorant (?) ingrate(?)

Cit. Nay, prithee, Nell, chide not; for, as I am an honest man and a true Christian grocer, [70 I do not like his doings.

Wife. I cry you mercy, then, George! you know we are all frail and full of infirmities. — D'ye hear, Master Merrythought? May I crave a word with you?   75

Mer. [*appearing above.*] Strike up lively, lads!

Wife. I had not thought, in truth, Master Merrythought, that a man of your age and discretion, as I may say, being a gentleman, [80 and therefore known by your gentle conditions,[1] could have used so little respect to the weakness of his wife; for your wife is your own flesh, the staff of your age, your yoke-fellow, with whose help you draw through the mire to this [85 transitory world; nay, she's your own rib: and again ——

Mer. [*sings.*]

> I come not hither for thee to teach,
> I have no pulpit for thee to preach,
> I would thou hadst kist me under the breech,   90
> As thou art a lady gay.

Wife. Marry, with a vengeance! I am heartily sorry for the poor gentlewoman: but if I were thy wife, i' faith, greybeard, i' faith —

Cit. I prithee, sweet honeysuckle, be con- [95 tent.

Wife. Give me such words, that am a gentlewoman born! Hang him, hoary rascal! Get me some drink, George; I am almost molten with fretting: now, beshrew his knave's heart [100 for it!   [*Exit* Citizen.]

Mer. Play me a light lavolta.[2] Come, be frolic. Fill the good fellows wine.

Mist. Mer. Why, Master Merrythought, are you disposed to make me wait here? You'll [105 open, I hope; I'll fetch them that shall open else.

Mer. Good woman, if you will sing, I'll give you something; if not ——   [*Sings.*]

> You are no love for me, Margaret,   110
> I am no love for you.—

Come aloft,[3] boys, aloft!   [*Exit above.*]

Mist. Mer. Now a churl's fart in your teeth, sir! — Come, Mick, we'll not trouble him; 'a shall not ding us i' th' teeth with his bread [115 and his broth, that he shall not. Come, boy; I'll provide for thee, I warrant thee. We'll go to Master Venturewell's, the merchant: I'll get his letter to mine host of the Bell in Waltham; there I'll place thee with the tapster: [120 will not that do well for thee, Mick? And let me alone for that old cuckoldly knave your father; I'll use him in his kind,[4] I warrant ye.   [*Exeunt.*]

[*Re-enter* Citizen *with Beer.*]

Wife. Come, George, where's the beer?

Cit. Here, love.   125

Wife. This old fornicating fellow will not out

---

1 Qualities.   2 A lively dance.   3 Be lively.
4 After his own nature.

---

of my mind yet. — Gentlemen, I'll begin to you all; and I desire more of your acquaintance with all my heart. [*Drinks.*] Fill the gentlemen some beer, George. *Music. Boy danceth.* [130 Look,[5] George, the little boy's come again: methinks he looks something like the Prince of Orange in his long stocking, if he had a little harness[6] about his neck. George, I will have him dance *Fading.—Fading* is a fine jig, [135 I'll assure you, gentlemen. — Begin, brother. — Now 'a capers, sweetheart! — Now a turn i' th' toe, and then tumble! cannot you tumble, youth?

Boy. No, indeed, forsooth.   140

Wife. Nor eat fire?

Boy. Neither.

Wife. Why, then, I thank you heartily; there's twopence to buy you points[7] withal.

ACT IV

Scene I.[8]

Enter Jasper *and* Boy.

Jasp. There, boy, deliver this; but do it well.
Hast thou provided me four lusty fellows,
                [*Gives a letter.*]
Able to carry me? and art thou perfect
In all thy business?

Boy.   Sir, you need not fear;
I have my lesson here, and cannot miss it: 5
The men are ready for you, and what else
Pertains to this employment.

Jasp.   There, my boy;
Take it, but buy no land.   [*Gives money.*]

Boy.   Faith, sir, 't were rare
To see so young a purchaser. I fly,
And on my wings carry your destiny.   10

Jasp. Go and be happy! [*Exit* Boy.] Now, my latest hope,
Forsake me not, but fling thy anchor out,
And let it hold! Stand fixt, thou rolling stone,
Till I enjoy my dearest! Hear me, all
You powers, that rule in men, celestial! *Exit.* 15

Wife. Go thy ways; thou art as crooked a sprig as ever grew in London. I warrant him, he'll come to some naughty end or other; for his looks say no less: besides, his father (you know, George) is none of the best; you heard [20 him take me up like a flirt-gill,[9] and sing bawdy songs upon me; but i' faith, if I live, George ——

Cit. Let me alone, sweetheart: I have a trick in my head shall lodge him in the Arches[10] for one year, and make him sing *peccavi* ere [25 I leave him; and yet he shall never know who hurt him neither.

Wife. Do, my good George, do!

---

5 Qq. begin Act IV here.   6 Armour.
7 Tagged laces used to attach the hose or breeches to the doublet.
8 A street.   9 A loose woman.
10 Apparently a prison attached to the Court of Arches.

Cit. What shall we have Ralph do now, [30 boy?

Boy. You shall have what you will, sir.

Cit. Why, so, sir; go and fetch me him then, and let the Sophy of Persia come and christen him a child.[1] 35

Boy. Believe me, sir, that will not do so well; 't is stale; it has been had before at the Red Bull.[2]

Wife. George, let Ralph travel over great hills, and let him be very weary, and come [40 to the King of Cracovia's house, covered with velvet; and there let the king's daughter stand in her window, all in beaten gold, combing her golden locks with a comb of ivory; and let her spy Ralph, and fall in love with him, and [45 come down to him, and carry him into her father's house; and then let Ralph talk with her.

Cit. Well said, Nell; it shall be so. — Boy, let 's ha 't done quickly.

Boy. Sir, if you will imagine all this to be [50 done already, you shall hear them talk together; but we cannot present a house covered with black velvet, and a lady in beaten gold.

Cit. Sir boy, let 's ha 't as you can, then.

Boy. Besides, it will show ill-favouredly [55 to have a grocer's prentice to court a king's daughter.

Cit. Will it so, sir? You are well read in histories![3] I pray you, what was Sir Dagonet? Was not he prentice to a grocer in London? [60 Read the play of "The Four Prentices of London,"[4] where they toss their pikes so. I pray you, fetch him in, sir, fetch him in.

Boy. It shall be done. — It is not our fault, gentlemen. *Exit.* 65

Wife. Now we shall see fine doings, I warrant 'ee, George.

[SCENE II.][5]

Enter the Lady [POMPIONA], RALPH, Squire, *and* Dwarf.

Wife. Oh, here they come, how prettily the King of Cracovia's daughter is drest!

Cit. Ay, Nell, it is the fashion of that country, I warrant 'ee.

Pomp. Welcome, Sir Knight, unto my father's court, 5
King of Moldavia : unto me Pompiona,
His daughter dear! But, sure, you do not like
Your entertainment, that will stay with us
No longer but a night.

Ralph. Damsel right fair,
I am on many sad[6] adventures bound, 10
That call me forth into the wilderness;
Besides, my horse's back is something gall'd,
Which will enforce me ride a sober pace.
But many thanks, fair lady, be to you
For using errant knight with courtesy! 15

Pomp. But say, brave knight, what is your name and birth?

Ralph. My name is Ralph; I am an Englishman,
As true as steel, a hearty Englishman,
And prentice to a grocer in the Strand
By deed indent,[7] of which I have one part : 20
But fortune calling me to follow arms,
On me this holy order I did take
Of Burning Pestle, which in all men's eyes
I bear, confounding ladies' enemies.

Pomp. Oft have I heard of your brave countrymen, 25
And fertile soil, and store of wholesome food;
My father oft will tell me of a drink
In England found, and nipitato[8] call'd,
Which driveth all the sorrow from your hearts.

Ralph. Lady, 't is true ; you need not lay your lips 30
To better nipitato than there is.

Pomp. And of a wild fowl he will often speak,
Which powd'red[9] -beef-and-mustard called is :
For there have been great wars 'twixt us and you;
But truly, Ralph, it was not 'long of me. 35
Tell me then, Ralph, could you contented be
To wear lady's favour in your shield?

Ralph. I am a knight of religious order,
And will not wear a favour of a lady 39
That trusts in Antichrist and false traditions.

Cit. Well said, Ralph! convert her, if thou canst.

Ralph. Besides, I have a lady of my own
In merry England, for whose virtuous sake
I took these arms ; and Susan is her name, 45
A cobbler's maid in Milk Street; whom I vow
Ne'er to forsake whilst life and Pestle last.

Pomp. Happy that cobbling dame, whoe'er she be,
That for her own, dear Ralph, hath gotten thee!
Unhappy I, that ne'er shall see the day 50
To see thee more, that bear'st my heart away!

Ralph. Lady, farewell; I needs must take my leave.

Pomp. Hard-hearted Ralph, that ladies dost deceive!

Cit. Hark thee, Ralph: there 's money for thee [*gives money*]; give something in the King of Cracovia's house; be not beholding to him. 56

Ralph. Lady, before I go, I must remember
Your father's officers, who truth to tell,
Have been about me very diligent.
Hold up thy snowy hand, thou princely maid!
There 's twelve-pence for your father's chamberlain; 61
And another shilling for his cook,

---

[1] An allusion to an incident in a play called *The Travailes of the Three English Brothers*, by Day, Rowley, and Wilkins.
[2] Another theatre. [3] Tales.
[4] By Heywood. But Dagonet is in Malory.
[5] A Hall in the King of Moldavia's Court. [6] Serious.
[7] Indenture.
[8] A mock learned form of nipitate, or strong ale.
[9] Salted.

For, by my troth, the goose was roasted well;
And twelve-pence for your father's horse-
keeper,
For nointing my horse' back, and for his but-
ter [1]   65
There is another shilling; to the maid
That washt my boot-hose [2] there 's an English
groat,
And two-pence to the boy that wipt my boots;
And last, fair lady, there is for yourself
Three-pence, to buy you pins at Bumbo Fair.
  Pomp. Full many thanks; and I will keep
    them safe   71
Till all the heads be off, for thy sake, Ralph.
  Ralph. Advance, my squire and dwarf! I
    cannot stay.
  Pomp. Thou kill'st my heart in passing thus
    away.   *Exeunt.*

Wife. I commend Ralph yet, that he will [75
not stoop to a Cracovian; there 's properer [3]
women in London than any are there, I-wis. But
here comes Master Humphrey and his love
again now, George.
  Cit. Ay, cony; peace.   80

Scene III.[4]

Enter Merchant [VENTUREWELL], HUMPHREY,
LUCE, *and* Boy.

  Vent. Go, get you up; [5] I will not be en-
treated;
And, gossip mine, I 'll keep you sure hereafter
From gadding out again with boys and un-
thrifts.
Come, they are women's tears; I know your
fashion, —
Go, sirrah, lock her in, and keep the key   5
Safe as you love your life.
                    Exeunt LUCE *and* Boy.
Now, my son Humphrey,
You may both rest assured of my love
In this, and reap your own desire.
  Hum. I see this love you speak of, through
your daughter,
Although the hole be little; and hereafter   10
Will yield the like in all I may or can,
Fitting a Christian and a gentleman.
  Vent. I do believe you, my good son, and
thank you;
For 't were an impudence to think you flat-
tered.
  Hum. It were, indeed: but shall I tell you
why?   15
I have been beaten twice about the lie.
  Vent. Well, son, no more of compliment. My
daughter
Is yours again: appoint the time and take
her.
We 'll have no stealing for it; I myself
And some few of our friends will see you mar-
ried.   20

  Hum. I would you would, i' faith! for, be it
known,
I ever was afraid to lie alone.
  Vent. Some three days hence, then.
  Hum.   Three days! let me see:
'T is somewhat of the most; [6] yet I agree,
Because I mean against [7] the appointed day   25
To visit all my friends in new array.

Enter Servant.

  Serv. Sir, there 's a gentlewoman without
would speak with your worship.
  Vent. What is she?
  Serv. Sir, I askt her not.   30
  Vent. Bid her come in.   [*Exit* Servant.]

Enter MISTRESS MERRYTHOUGHT *and* MI-
CHAEL.

  Mist. Mer. Peace be to your worship! I come
as a poor suitor to you, sir, in the behalf of this
child.
  Vent. Are you not wife to Merrythought?
  Mist. Mer. Yes, truly. Would I had ne'er [36
seen his eyes! Ha has undone me and himself
and his children; and there he lives at home,
and sings and hoits and revels among his
drunken companions! but, I warrant you, [40
where to get a penny to put bread in his mouth
he knows not: and therefore, if it like your
worship, I would entreat your letter to the
honest host of the Bell in Waltham, that I
may place my child under the protection of his
tapster, in some settled course of life.   46
  Vent. I 'm glad the heavens have heard my
prayers. Thy husband,
When I was ripe in sorrows, laught at me;
Thy son, like an unthankful wretch, I having
Redeem'd him from his fall, and made him
mine,   50
To show his love again, first stole my daugh-
ter,
Then wronged this gentleman, and, last of all,
Gave me that grief had almost brought me
down
Unto my grave, had not a stronger hand
Reliev'd my sorrows. Go, and weep as I did, 55
And be unpitied: for I here profess
An everlasting hate to all thy name.
  Mist. Mer. Will you so, sir? how say you by
that?—Come, Mick; let him keep his wind to
cool his porridge. We 'll go to thy nurse's, [60
Mick: she knits silk stockings, boy; and we 'll
knit too, boy, and be beholding to none of
them all.   *Exit with* MICHAEL.

Enter a Boy *with a letter.*

  Boy. Sir, I take it you are the master of this
house.   65
  Vent. How then, boy?
  Boy. Then to yourself, sir, comes this let-
ter.
  Vent. From whom, my pretty boy?
  Boy. From him that was your servant; but
no more
Shall that name ever be, for he is dead: 70

---

[1] Used as ointment.
[2] Stockings without feet, worn with boots.
[3] Handsomer.
[4] A room in the house of Venturewell.
[5] Upstairs.

[6] Pretty long.   [7] In anticipation of.

Grief of your purchas'd [1] anger broke his
      heart.
I saw him die, and from his hand receiv'd
This paper, with a charge to bring it hither:
Read it, and satisfy yourself in all.
    Vent. [*reads.*] Sir, that I have wronged your
love I must confess ; in which I have pur-   [76
chast to myself, besides mine own undoing,
the ill opinion of my friends. Let not your
anger, good sir, outlive me, but suffer me to
rest in peace with your forgiveness : let my   [80
body (if a dying man may so much prevail with
you) be brought to your daughter, that she may
truly know my hot flames are now buried, and
withal receive a testimony of the zeal I bore
her virtue. Farewell for ever, and be ever   [85
happy !   JASPER.
God's hand is great in this. I do forgive him ;
Yet I am glad he 's quiet, where I hope
He will not bite again. — Boy, bring the body,
And let him have his will, if that be all.   90
    Boy. 'T is here without, sir.
    Vent.   So, sir ; if you please,
You may conduct it in ; I do not fear it.
    Hum. I 'll be your usher, boy ; for, though I
      say it,
He ow'd me something once, and well did pay
  it.   *Exeunt.*

                  [SCENE IV.] [2]

                  Enter LUCE.

    Luce. If there be any punishment inflicted
Upon the miserable, more than yet I feel,
Let it together seize me, and at once
Press down my soul ! I cannot bear the pain
Of these delaying tortures. — Thou that art   5
The end of all, and the sweet rest of all,
Come, come, oh, Death ! bring me to thy peace,
And blot out all the memory I nourish
Both of my father and my cruel friend ! —   9
Oh, wretched maid, still living to be wretched,
To be a say to Fortune in her changes,
And grow to number times and woes together !
How happy had I been, if, being born,
My grave had been my cradle !

                  Enter Servant.

    Serv.   By your leave,
Young mistress ; here 's a boy hath brought a
      coffin :   15
What 'a would say, I know not ; but your
      father
Charg'd me to give you notice. Here they come.
                                       [*Exit.*]

    Enter two bearing a Coffin, JASPER *in it.*

    Luce. For me I hope 't is come, and 't is most
      welcome.
    Boy. Fair mistress, let me not add greater
      grief
To that great store you have already. Jasper   20
(That whilst he liv'd was yours, now dead
And here enclos'd) commanded me to bring
His body hither, and to crave a tear

_____
[1] Acquired.
[2] Another room in the house of Venturewell.

From those fair eyes, (though he deserv'd not
      pity,)
To deck his funeral ; for so he bid me   25
Tell her for whom he died.
    Luce.   He shall have many. —
Good friends, depart a little, whilst I take
My leave of this dead man, that once I lov'd.
                      Exeunt Coffin-carrier *and* Boy.
Hold yet a little, life ! and then I give thee
To thy first heavenly being. Oh, my friend !   30
Hast thou deceiv'd me thus, and got before me ?
I shall not long be after. But, believe me,
Thou wert too cruel, Jasper, 'gainst thyself,
In punishing the fault I could have pardon'd,
With so untimely death : thou didst not wrong
      me,   35
But ever wert most kind, most true, most lov-
      ing ;
And I the most unkind, most false, most cruel !
Didst thou but ask a tear ? I 'll give thee all,
Even all my eyes can pour down, all my sighs,
And all myself, before thou goest from me.   40
These are but sparing rites ; but if thy soul
Be yet about this place, and can behold
And see what I prepare to deck thee with,
It shall go up, borne on the wings of peace,
And satisfied. First will I sing thy dirge,   45
Then kiss thy pale lips, and then die myself,
And fill one coffin and one grave together.

                  SONG.

  Come, you whose loves are dead,
        And, whiles I sing,
        Weep, and wring   50
  Every hand, and every head
  Bind with cypress and sad yew ;
  Ribands black and candles blue
  For him that was of men most true !

  Come with heavy moaning,[3]   55
        And on his grave
        Let him have
  Sacrifice of sighs and groaning ;
  Let him have fair flowers enow,
  White and purple, green and yellow,   60
  For him that was of men most true !

Thou sable cloth, sad cover of my joys,
I lift thee up, and thus I meet with death.
        [*Removes the Cloth, and* JASPER
                  rises out of the Coffin.]
    Jasp. And thus you meet the living.
    Luce.   Save me, Heaven !
    Jasp. Nay, do not fly me, fair ; I am no
      spirit :   65
Look better on me ; do you know me yet ?
    Luce. Oh, thou dear shadow of my friend !
    Jasp.   Dear substance,
I swear I am no shadow ; feel my hand,
It is the same it was ; I am your Jasper,
Your Jasper that 's yet living, and yet loving.   70
Pardon my rash attempt, my foolish proof [4]
I put in practice of your constancy ;
For sooner should my sword have drunk my
      blood,
And set my soul at liberty, than drawn
The least drop from that body : for which bold-
      ness   75

_____
[3] So ed. 1750. Qq. *mourning.*   [4] Test.

Doom me to any thing ; if death, I take it,
And willingly.
　　Luce.　　　　This death I 'll give you for it;
　　　　　　　　　　　　　　[*Kisses him.*]
So, now I am satisfied you are no spirit,
But my own truest, truest, truest friend :
Why do you come thus to me ?
　　Jasp.　　　　First, to see you ;　80
Then to convey you hence.
　　Luce.　　　　It cannot be ;
For I am lockt up here, and watcht at all hours,
That 't is impossible for me to scape.
　　Jasp. Nothing more possible. Within this
　　　　coffin
Do you convey yourself. Let me alone,　85
I have the wits of twenty men about me ;
Only I crave the shelter of your closet
A little, and then fear me not.[1] Creep in,
That they may presently convey you hence :　89
Fear nothing, dearest love ; I 'll be your second;
　　　[*Luce lies down in the Coffin, and
　　　　Jasper covers her with the cloth.*]
Lie close :[2] so ; all goes well yet. — Boy !

　　　[*Re-enter Boy and Men.*]

　　Boy.　　　　　　　　　At hand, sir.
　　Jasp. Convey away the coffin, and be wary.
　　Boy. 'T is done already.
　　　　　　　　　[*Exeunt Men with the Coffin.*]
　　Jasp.　　　　Now must I go conjure.
　　　　　　　　　　Exit [*into a Closet*].

　　　Enter Merchant [VENTUREWELL].

　　Vent. Boy, boy !
　　Boy. Your servant, sir.　　　　95
　　Vent. Do me this kindness, boy ; (hold, here 's
　　　a crown ;)
Before thou bury the body of this fellow,
Carry it to his old merry father, and salute him
From me, and bid him sing ; he hath cause.[3]
　　Boy. I will, sir.　　　　　　100
　　Vent. And then bring me word what tune he
　　　is in,
And have another crown ; but do it truly.
I have fitted him a bargain now will vex him.
　　Boy. God bless your worship's health, sir !
　　Vent.　　Farewell, boy ! *Exeunt* [*severally*].

　　　　　　[SCENE V.][4]

　　　Enter MERRYTHOUGHT.

　　Wife. Ah, old Merrythought, art thou there
again ? Let 's hear some of thy songs.

　　Mer. [*sings.*]

　　　Who can sing a merrier note
　　　Than he that cannot change a groat ?

Not a denier[5] left, and yet my heart leaps. I [5
do wonder yet, as old as I am, that any man
will follow a trade, or serve, that may sing and
laugh, and walk the streets. My wife and both

1 Fear not for me.　　2 Hidden.
3 In Qq. this speech is in prose : probably correctly.
4 A street before Merrythought's house.
5 Penny.

my sons are I know not where ; I have nothing
left, nor know I how to come by meat to sup- [10
per; yet am I merry still, for I know I shall find
it upon the table at six o'clock ; therefore, hang
thought !　　　　　　　　[*Sings.*]

　　　I would not be a serving-man
　　　　To carry the cloak-bag[6] still,　　1r
　　　Nor would I be a falconer
　　　　The greedy hawks to fill ;
　　　But I would be in a good house,
　　　　And have a good master too ;
　　　But I would eat and drink of the best,　2c
　　　　And no work would I do.

This is it that keeps life and soul together,
— mirth ; this is the philosopher's stone that
they write so much on, that keeps a man ever
young.　　　　　　　　　　　25

　　　　　Enter a Boy.

　　Boy. Sir, they say they know all your money
is gone, and they will trust you for no more
drink.
　　Mer. Will they not ? let 'em choose ! The
best is, I have mirth at home, and need not [30
send abroad for that ; let them keep their drink
to themselves.　　　　　　　[*Sings.*]

　　　For Jillian of Berry, she dwells on a hill,
　　　And she hath good beer and ale to sell,
　　　And of good fellows she thinks no ill ;　35
　　　And thither will we go now, now, now,
　　　And thither will we go now.

　　　And when you have made a little stay,
　　　You need not ask what is to pay,
　　　But kiss your hostess, and go your way ;　40
　　　And thither will we go now, now, now,
　　　And thither will we go now.

　　　　Enter another Boy.

　　2 Boy. Sir, I can get no bread for supper.
　　Mer. Hang bread and supper ! Let 's preserve
our mirth, and we shall never feel hunger, [45
I 'll warrant you. Let 's have a catch ; boy, follow me, come sing this catch.

　　　Ho, ho, nobody at home !
　　　Meat, nor drink, nor money ha' we none.
　　　Fill the pot, Eedy,　　　　50
　　　Never more need I.

　　Mer. So, boys ; enough. Follow me : let 's
change our place, and we shall laugh afresh.
　　　　　　　　　　　　Exeunt.

　　Wife. Let him go, George ; 'a shall not have
any countenance from us, nor a good word from
any i' th' company, if I may strike stroke[7] in 't.
　　Cit. No more 'a sha'not, love. But, Nell, I [57
will have Ralph do a very notable matter now,
to the eternal honour and glory of all grocers.
—Sirrah ! you there, boy ! Can none of you
hear ?　　　　　　　　　　61

　　　　[*Enter Boy.*]

　　Boy. Sir, your pleasure ?
　　Cit. Let Ralph come out on May-day in the
morning, and speak upon a conduit, with all his

6 Portmanteau.　　7 Have a say

scarfs about him, and his feathers, and his rings, and his knacks. 66

Boy. Why, sir, you do not think of our plot; what will become of that, then?

Cit. Why, sir, I care not what become on 't: I 'll have him come out, or I 'll fetch him [70 out myself; I 'll have something done in honour of the city. Besides, he hath been long enough upon adventures. Bring him out quickly; or, if I come in amongst you ——

Boy. Well, sir, he shall come out, but if our play miscarry, sir, you are like to pay for 't. 76

Cit. Bring him away then!

Exit Boy.

Wife. This will be brave, i ' faith! George, shall not he dance the morris too, for the credit of the Strand? 80

Cit. No, sweetheart, it will be too much for the boy. Oh, there he is, Nell! he 's reasonable well in reparel: but he has not rings enough.

Enter RALPH [*dressed as a May-lord*].

Ralph. London, to thee I do present the merry month of May; 85
Let each true subject be content to hear me what I say:
For from the top of conduit-head, as plainly may appear,
I will both tell my name to you, and wherefore I came here.
My name is Ralph, by due descent though not ignoble I [1]
Yet far inferior to the flock [2] of gracious grocery; 90
And by the common counsel of my fellows in the Strand,
With gilded staff and crossed scarf, the May-lord here I stand.
Rejoice, oh, English hearts, rejoice! rejoice, oh, lovers dear!
Rejoice, oh, city, town, and country! rejoice, eke every shire!
For now the fragrant flowers do spring and sprout in seemly sort, 95
The little birds do sit and sing, the lambs do make fine sport;
And now the birchen-tree doth bud, that makes the schoolboy cry;
The morris rings, while hobby-horse doth foot it featously; [3]
The lords and ladies now abroad, for their disport and play,
Do kiss sometimes upon the grass, and sometimes in the hay; 100
Now butter with a leaf of sage is good to purge the blood;
Fly Venus and phlebotomy, [4] for they are neither good;
Now little fish on tender stone begin to cast their bellies, [5]
And sluggish snails, that erst were mew'd, [6] do creep out of their shellies;

[1] Cf. *Spanish Tragedy*, I. 1   [2] Dyce emends to *stock*.
[3] Neatly, expertly.   [4] Blood-letting.   [5] Spawn.
[6] Shut up, confined. Sympson emend. Qq. *mute*.

The rumbling rivers now do warm, for little boys to paddle; 165
The sturdy steed now goes to grass, and up they hang his saddle;
The heavy hart, the bellowing buck, the rascal, [7] and the pricket, [8]
Are now among the yeoman's peas, and leave the fearful thicket:
And be like them, oh, you, I say, of this same noble town,
And lift aloft your velvet heads, and slipping off your gown, 110
With bells on legs, and napkins clean unto your shoulders tied,
With scarfs and garters as you please, and " Hey for our town!" cried,
March out, and show your willing minds, by twenty and by twenty,
To Hogsdon [9] or to Newington, where ale and cakes are plenty;
And let it ne'er be said for shame, that we the youths of London 115
Lay thrumming of our caps [10] at home, and left our custom undone.
Up, then, I say, both young and old, both man and maid a-maying,
With drums, and guns that bounce aloud, and merry tabor playing!
Which to prolong, God save our king, and send his country peace,
And root out treason from the land! and so, my friends, I cease.   *Exit.* 120

ACT V

Scene I.[11]

Enter Merchant [VENTUREWELL].

Vent. I will have no great store of company at the wedding; a couple of neighbours and their wives; and we will have a capon in stewed broth, with marrow, and a good piece of beef stuck with rosemary. 5

Enter JASPER, *his face mealed.*

Jasp. Forbear thy pains, fond [12] man! it is too late.

Vent. Heaven bless me! Jasper!

Jasp.   Ay, I am his ghost,
Whom thou hast injur'd for his constant love,
Fond worldly wretch! who dost not understand
In death that true hearts cannot parted be. 10
First know, thy daughter is quite borne away
On wings of angels, through the liquid air,
To far out of thy reach, and never more
Shalt thou behold her face: but she and I
Will in another world enjoy our loves; 15
Where neither father's anger, poverty,
Nor any cross that troubles earthly men,
Shall make us sever our united hearts.
And never shalt thou sit or be alone

[7] A lean deer.
[8] A buck in his second year.   [9] Hoxton
[10] Setting thrums or tufts on a cap. (Murch.) Fingering. (Moorman.)
[11] A room in the house of Venturewell.   [12] Foolish

In any place, but I will visit thee   20
With ghastly looks, and put into thy mind
The great offences which thou didst to me.
When thou art at thy table with thy friends,
Merry in heart, and fill'd with swelling wine,
I 'll come in midst of all thy pride and mirth, 25
Invisible to all men but thyself,
And whisper such a sad tale in thine ear
Shall make thee let the cup fall from thy hand,
And stand as mute and pale as death itself.

Vent. Forgive me, Jasper! Oh, what might
          I do,   30
Tell me, to satisfy thy troubled ghost ?

Jasp. There is no means ; too late thou
          think'st of this.

Vent. But tell me what were best for me to
          do ?

Jasp. Repent thy deed, and satisfy my
          father,
And beat fond Humphrey out of thy doors.   35
                                        Exit.

Wife. Look, George ; his very ghost would
have folks beaten.

Enter HUMPHREY.

Hum. Father, my bride is gone, fair Mistress
          Luce :
My soul 's the fount of vengeance, mischief's
          sluice.

Vent. Hence, fool, out of my sight with thy
          fond passion !
Thou hast undone me.   [*Beats him.*]

Hum.   Hold, my father dear,
For Luce thy daughter's sake, that had no
          peer !

Vent. Thy father, fool ! There 's some blows
          more ; begone.—   [*Beats him.*]
Jasper, I hope thy ghost be well appeas'd
To see thy will perform'd. Now will I go   45
To satisfy thy father for thy wrongs.   *Exit.*

Hum. What shall I do ? I have been beaten
          twice,
And Mistress Luce is gone. Help me, device !
Since my true love is gone, I never more,
Whilst I do live, upon the sky will pore ;   50
But in the dark will wear out my shoe-soles
In passion[1] in Saint Faith's church under
Paul's.   *Exit.*

Wife. George, call Ralph hither ; if you love
me, call Ralph hither : I have the bravest thing
for him to do, George ; prithee, call him quickly.

Cit. Ralph ! why, Ralph, boy !   55

Enter RALPH.

Ralph. Here, sir.

Cit. Come hither, Ralph ; come to thy mistress, boy.

Wife. Ralph, I would have thee call all [60
the youths together in battle-ray, with drums,
and guns, and flags, and march to Mile-End in
pompous[2] fashion, and there exhort your soldiers to be merry and wise, and to keep their
beards from burning, Ralph ; and then skir- [65

[1] Sorrow, melancholy.   [2] Magnificent.

mish, and let your flags fly, and cry, "Kill,
kill, kill !" My husband shall lend you his jerkin, Ralph, and there 's a scarf ; for the rest,
the house shall furnish you, and we 'll pay for 't,
Do it bravely, Ralph ; and think before [70
whom you perform, and what person you represent.

Ralph. I warrant you, mistress ; if I do it
not for the honour of the city and the credit
of my master, let me never hope for free- [75
dom ![3]

Wife. 'T is well spoken, i' faith. Go thy
ways ; thou art a spark indeed.

Cit. Ralph, Ralph, double your files bravely,
Ralph !   80

Ralph. I warrant you, sir.   *Exit.*

Cit. Let him look narrowly to his service ; I
shall take him else. I was there myself a pike-
man once, in the hottest of the day, wench ;
had my feather shot sheer away, the fringe of
my pike burnt off with powder, my pate [86
broken with a scouring-stick,[4] and yet, I thank
God, I am here.   *Drum within.*

Wife. Hark, George, the drums !

Cit. Ran, tan, tan, tan ; ran, tan ! Oh, wench,
an thou hadst but seen little Ned of Aldgate, [91
Drum Ned, how he made it roar again, and
laid on like a tyrant, and then struck softly till
the ward[5] came up, and then thund'red again,
and together we go ! "Sa, sa, sa, bounce !" [95
quoth the guns ; "Courage, my hearts !"
quoth the captains ; "Saint George !" quoth
the pikemen ; and withal, here they lay, and
there they lay : and yet for all this I am here,
wench.   100

Wife. Be thankful for it, George ; for indeed
't is wonderful.

[SCENE II.][6]

Enter RALPH *and Company of* Soldiers (*among
whom are* WILLIAM HAMMERTON, *and*
GEORGE GREENGOOSE), *with drums and
colours.*

Ralph. March fair, my hearts ! Lieutenant,
beat the rear up.—Ancient,[7] let your colours
fly ; but have a great care of the butchers'
hooks at Whitechapel ; they have been the
death of many a fair ancient.—Open your [5
files, that I may take a view both of your persons and munition.—Sergeant, call a muster.

Serg. A stand !—William Hammerton, pew-
terer !

Ham. Here, captain !   10

Ralph. A corselet and a Spanish pike ; 't is
well : can you shake it with a terror ?

Ham. I hope so, captain.

Ralph. Charge upon me. [*He charges on*
RALPH.]—'T is with the weakest : put more [15
strength, William Hammerton, more strength.
As you were again !—Proceed, Sergeant.

Serg. George Greengoose, poulterer !

[3] *I. e.* full membership in his Company.
[4] Ramrod.
[5] Guard (Moorman) ; regiment (Murch).
[6] A street (and afterwards Mile-End).
[7] Ensign (the flag or its bearer).

Green. Here!

Ralph. Let me see your piece,[1] neighbour [20 Greengoose: when was she shot in?

Green. An't like you, master captain, I made a shot even now, partly to scour her, and partly for audacity.

Ralph. It should seem so certainly, for her [25 breath is yet inflamed; besides, there is a main[2] fault in the touch-hole, it runs and stinketh; and I tell you moreover, and believe it, ten such touch-holes would breed the pox in the army. Get you a feather, neighbour, get you [30 a feather, sweet oil, and paper, and your piece may do well enough yet. Where's your powder?

Green. Here.

Ralph. What, in a paper! As I am a soldier and a gentleman, it craves a martial court! [35 You ought to die for 't. Where's your horn? Answer me to that.

Green. An't like you, sir, I was oblivious.

Ralph. It likes me not you should be so; 't is a shame for you, and a scandal to all our [40 neighbours, being a man of worth and estimation, to leave your horn behind you: I am afraid 't will breed example. But let me tell you no more on 't. — Stand, till I view you all. What's become o' th' nose of your flask?   45

1 Sold. Indeed, la, captain, 'twas blown away with powder.

Ralph. Put on a new one at the city's charge. — Where's the stone[3] of this piece?

2 Sold. The drummer took it out to light [50 tobacco.

Ralph. 'T is a fault, my friend; put it in again. — You want a nose, — and you a stone. — Sergeant, take a note on 't, for I mean to stop it in the pay. — Remove, and march! [*They* [55 *march.*] Soft and fair, gentlemen, soft and fair! Double your files! As you were! Faces about! Now, you with the sodden[4] face, keep in there! Look to your match, sirrah, it will be in your fellow's flask anon. So; make a crescent now: [60 advance your pikes: stand and give ear! — Gentlemen, countrymen, friends, and my fellow-soldiers, I have brought you this day, from the shops of security and the counters of content, to measure out in these furious fields honour by [65 the ell, and prowess by the pound. Let it not, oh, let it not, I say, be told hereafter, the noble issue of this city fainted; but bear yourselves in this fair action like men, valiant men, and free men! Fear not the face of the enemy, [70 nor the noise of the guns, for, believe me, brethren, the rude rumbling of a brewer's car is far more terrible, of which you have a daily experience; neither let the stink of powder offend you, since a more valiant stink is nightly with you.   75

To a resolved mind his home is every-where:
I speak not this to take away
The hope of your return; for you shall see
(I do not doubt it) and that very shortly   80
Your loving wives again and your sweet children,
Whose care doth bear you company in baskets.

Remember, then, whose cause you have in hand,
And, like a sort[5] of true-born scavengers,
Scour me this famous realm of enemies.   85
I have no more to say but this: stand to your tacklings,[6] lads, and show to the world you can as well brandish a sword as shake an apron.
Saint George, and on, my hearts!

All. Saint George, Saint George!   *Exeunt.* 90

Wife. 'T was well done, Ralph! I 'll send thee a cold capon a-field and a bottle of March beer; and, it may be, come myself to see thee.

Cit. Nell, the boy has deceived me much; I [95 did not think it had been in him. He has performed such a matter, wench, that, if I live, next year I 'll have him captain of the galley-foist[7] or I 'll want my will.

[SCENE III.][8]

Enter MERRYTHOUGHT.

Mer. Yet, I thank God, I break not a wrinkle more than I had. Not a stoop,[9] boys? Care, live with cats; I defy thee! My heart is as sound as an oak; and though I want drink to wet my whistle, I can sing;   [*Sings.*] 5
    Come no more there, boys, come no more there;
    For we shall never whilst we live come any more there.

Enter Boy, [*and two* Men] *with a Coffin.*

Boy. God save you, sir!

Mer. It 's a brave boy. Canst thou sing?

Boy. Yes, sir, I can sing; but 't is not so [10 necessary at this time.

Mer. [*sings.*]
    Sing we, and chant it;
    Whilst love doth grant it.

Boy. Sir, sir, if you knew what I have brought you, you would have little list to [15 sing.

Mer. [*sings.*]
    Oh, the Mimon round,
    Full long, long I have thee sought,
    And now I have thee found,
    And what hast thou here brought?   20

Boy. A coffin, sir, and your dead son Jasper in it.   [*Exit with* Men.]

Mer. Dead!   [*Sings.*]
    Why, farewell he!
    Thou wast a bonny boy,   25
    And I did love thee.

Enter JASPER.

Jasp. Then, I pray you, sir, do so still.

Mer. Jasper's ghost!   [*Sings.*]
    Thou art welcome from Stygian lake so soon;
    Declare to me what wondrous things in Pluto's court
        are done.   30

Jasp. By my troth, sir, I ne'er came there: 't is too hot for me, sir.

Mer. A merry ghost, a very merry ghost!
    [*Sings.*]
    And where is your true love? Oh, where is yours?

---

[5] Band.   [6] Weapons.   [7] The Lord Mayor's barge.   [8] A room in Merrythought's house.   [9] Tankard.

Jasp. Marry, look you, sir!   35
                              Heaves up coffin.
Mer. Ah, ha! art thou good at that, i' faith?
                                        [*Sings.*]
          With hey, trixy, terlery-whiskin,
          The world it runs on wheels:
          When the young man's —— ,[1]
          Up goes the maiden's heels.   40

MRS. MERRYTHOUGHT *and* MICHAEL *within.*

Mist. Mer. [*within.*] What, Master Merrythought! will you not let's in? What do you
think shall become of us?
Mer. [*sings.*]
     What voice is that, that calleth at our door.
Mist. Mer. [*within.*] You know me well [45
enough; I am sure I have not been such a
stranger to you.
Mer. [*sings.*]
        And some they whistled, and some they sung,
                Hey, down, down!
          And some did loudly say,   50
        Ever as the Lord Barnet's horn blew,
                Away, Musgrave, away!

Mist. Mer. [*within.*] You will not have us
starve here, will you, Master Merrythought?
Jasp. Nay, good sir, be persuaded; she is   55
     my mother.
If her offences have been great against you,
Let your own love remember she is yours,
And so forgive her.
Luce.   Good Master Merrythought.
Let me entreat you; I will not be denied.
Mist. Mer. [*within.*] Why, Master Merry- [60
thought, will you be a vext thing still?
Mer. Woman, I take you to my love again;
but you shall sing before you enter; therefore
despatch your song and so come in.
Mist. Mer. [*within.*] Well, you must have [65
your will, when all's done. — Mick, what song
canst thou sing, boy?
Mich. [*within.*] I can sing none, forsooth, but
A Lady's Daughter, of Paris properly.
Mist. Mer. [*Song.*]
        It was a lady's daughter, &c.   70

[MERRYTHOUGHT *opens the Door*; *enter* MIS-
TRESS MERRYTHOUGHT *and* MICHAEL.]

Mer. Come, you're welcome home again.
                                       [*Sings.*]
          If such danger be in playing,
          And jest must to earnest turn,
          You shall go no more a-maying—

Vent. (*within.*) Are you within, sir? Master [75
Merrythought!
Jasp. It is my master's voice! Good sir, go
     hold him
In talk, whilst we convey ourselves into
Some inward room.   [*Exit with* LUCE.]
Mer.   What are you? Are you merry?
You must be very merry, if you enter.   80
Vent. [*within.*] I am, sir.
Mer. Sing, then.
Vent. [*within.*] Nay, good sir, open to me.
Mer. Sing, I say, or, by the merry heart, you
come not in!   85

                  ¹ So printed in Qq.

Vent. [*within.*] Well, sir, I 'll sing. [*Sings.*]
                Fortune, my foe, &c.

[MERRYTHOUGHT *opens the Door*: *Enter* VEN-
TUREWELL.]

Mer. You are welcome, sir, you are welcome:
you see your entertainment; pray you, be
merry.   90
Vent. Oh, Master Merrythought, I'm come
     to ask you
Forgiveness for the wrongs I offered you
And your most virtuous son! They're infinite;
Yet my contrition shall be more than they:
I do confess my hardness broke his heart,   95
For which just Heaven hath given me punish-
     ment
More than my age can carry. His wand'ring
     spirit,
Not yet at rest, pursues me every where,
Crying, "I 'll haunt thee for thy cruelty."
My daughter, she is gone, I know not how,   100
Taken invisible, and whether living
Or in [the] grave, 't is yet uncertain to me.
Oh, Master Merrythought, these are the
     weights
Will sink me to my grave! Forgive me, sir,
Mer. Why, sir, I do forgive you; and be
     merry.   105
And if the wag in 's lifetime play'd the knave,
Can you forgive him too?
Vent.   With all my heart, sir.
Mer. Speak it again, and heartily.
Vent.   I do, sir;
Now, by my soul, I do.

                Re-enter LUCE *and* JASPER.

Mer. [*sings.*]
        With that came out his paramour;   116
        She was as white as the lily flower:
                Hey, troul, troly, jolly!
        With that came out her own dear knight;
        He was as true as ever did fight, &c.

Sir, if you will forgive him, clap their hands [115
together; there's no more to be said i' th'
matter.
Vent. I do, I do.

Cit. I do not like this. Peace, boys! Hear
me, one of you! Every body's part is come to
an end but Ralph's, and he's left out.   121
Boy. 'T is 'long of yourself, sir; we have
nothing to do with his part.
Cit. Ralph, come away! — Make [an end] [2] on
him, as you have done of the rest, boys;
come.   126
Wife. Now, good husband, let him come out
and die.
Cit. He shall, Nell. — Ralph, come away
quickly, and die, boy!   130
Boy. 'T will be very unfit he should die, sir,
upon no occasion — and in a comedy too.
Cit. Take you no care of that, sir boy; is
not his part at an end, think you, when he's
dead? — Come away, Ralph!   135

              ² Qq. omit. Added in Ed. of 1778.

Enter RALPH, *with a forked Arrow through his Head.*

Ralph. When I was mortal, this my costive corps
Did lap up figs and raisins in the Strand ;
Where sitting, I espi'd a lovely dame,
Whose master wrought with lingel[1] and with awl,
And underground he vamped many a boot. 140
Straight did her love prick forth me, tender sprig,
To follow feats of arms in warlike wise
Through Waltham-desert ; where I did perform
Many achievements, and did lay on ground
Huge Barbaroso, that insulting giant, 145
And all his captives soon set at liberty.
Then honour prickt me from my native soil
Into Moldavia, where I gain'd the love
Of Pompiona, his beloved daughter ;
But yet prov'd constant to the black thumb'd maid 150
Susan, and scorned Pompiona's love ;
Yet liberal I was, and gave her pins,
And money for her father's officers.
I then returned home, and thrust myself
In action, and by all men chosen was 155
Lord of the May, where I did flourish it,
With scarfs and rings, and posy in my hand.
After this action I preferred was,
And chosen city-captain at Mile-End, 159
With hat and feather, and with leading-staff,[2]
And train'd my men, and brought them all off clear,
Save one man that beray'd him[3] with the noise.
But all these things I Ralph did undertake
Only for my beloved Susan's sake.
Then coming home, and sitting in my shop 165
With apron blue, Death came into my stall
To cheapen[4] *aqua vitae ;* but ere I
Could take the bottle down and fill a taste,
Death caught a pound of pepper in his hand,
And sprinkled all my face and body o'er, 170
And in an instant vanished away.

Cit. 'T is a pretty fiction, i' faith.

Ralph. Then took I up my bow and shaft in hand,
And walkt into Moorfields to cool myself ;
But there grim cruel Death met me again, 175
And shot this forked arrow through my head ;

[1] Shoemaker's thread.
[2] Baton.   [3] Befouled himself.
[4] Ask the price of, bargain for.

And now I faint ; therefore be warn'd by me,
My fellows every one, of forked heads !
Farewell, all you good boys in merry London !
Ne'er shall we more upon Shrove-Tuesday meet, 180
And pluck down houses of iniquity ;[5] —
My pain increaseth — I shall never more
Hold open, whilst another pumps both legs,
Nor daub a satin gown with rotten eggs ;
Set up a stake, oh, never more I shall ! 185
I die ! fly, fly, my soul, to Grocers' Hall !
Oh, oh, oh, &c.[6]

Wife. Well said, Ralph ! do your obeisance to the gentlemen, and go your ways : well said, Ralph ! 190

RALPH [*rises, makes obeisance and*] *exit.*

Mer. Methinks all we, thus kindly and unexpectedly reconciled, should not depart[7] without a song.

Vent. A good motion.

Mer. Strike up, then ! 195

SONG.

Better music ne'er was known
Than a choir of hearts in one.
Let each other, that hath been
Troubled with the gall or spleen,
Learn of us to keep his brow 200
Smooth and plain, as ours are now :
Sing, though before the hour of dying ;
He shall rise, and then be crying,
" Hey, ho, 't is nought but mirth
That keeps the body from the earth ! " 205

Exeunt.

EPILOGUS.

Cit. Come, Nell, shall we go ? The play 's done.

Wife. Nay, by my faith, George, I have more manners than so ; I 'll speak to these gentlemen first. — I thank you all, gentlemen, for [210 your patience and countenance to Ralph, a poor fatherless child ; and if I might see you at my house, it should go hard but I would have a pottle of wine and a pipe of tobacco for you : for, truly, I hope you do like the youth, but [215 I would be glad to know the truth ; I refer it to your own discretions, whether you will applaud him or no ; for I will wink, and whilst[8] you shall do what you will. I thank you with all my heart. God give you good night ! — Come, [220 George. [*Exeunt.*]

[5] As the London prentices did on Shrove Tuesday.
[6] Cf. the speech of Andrea's Ghost in *The Spanish Tragedy,* I. i., many lines of which are here parodied.
[7] Part.   [8] Meanwhile.

PHILASTER

OR

LOVE LIES A-BLEEDING

BY

FRANCIS BEAUMONT AND JOHN FLETCHER

[DRAMATIS PERSONAE

THE KING OF SICILY.
PHILASTER, Heir to the Crown.
PHARAMOND, Prince of Spain.
DION, a Lord.
CLEREMONT, } Noble Gentlemen,
THRASILINE, } his associates.
An Old Captain.
Five Citizens.
A Country Fellow.

Two Woodmen.
The King's Guard and Train.

ARETHUSA, Daughter of the King.
EUPHRASIA, Daughter of Dion, but disguised like a Page
    and called BELLARIO.
MEGRA, a lascivious Lady.
GALATEA, a wise, modest Lady attending the Princess.
Two other Ladies.

SCENE. — *Sicily.*][1]

ACT I

SCENE I.[2]

Enter DION, CLEREMONT, *and* THRASILINE.

Cler. Here 's nor lords nor ladies.

Dion. Credit me, gentlemen, I wonder at it. They receiv'd strict charge from the King to attend here; besides, it was boldly published that no officer should forbid any gentleman [5 that desired to attend and hear.

Cle. Can you guess the cause?

Dion. Sir, it is plain, about the Spanish Prince that 's come to marry our kingdom's heir and be our sovereign. 10

Thra. Many that will seem to know much say she looks not on him like a maid in love.

Dion. Faith, sir, the multitude, that seldom know any thing but their own opinions, speak that they would have; but the prince, be- [15 fore his own approach, receiv'd so many confident messages from the state, that I think she 's resolv'd to be rul'd.

Cle. Sir, it is thought, with her he shall enjoy both these kingdoms of Sicily and Calabria.

Dion. Sir, it is without controversy so [21 meant. But 't will be a troublesome labour for him to enjoy both these kingdoms with safety, the right heir to one of them living, and living so virtuously: especially, the people admir- [25 ing the bravery of his mind and lamenting his injuries.

Cle. Who? Philaster?

Dion. Yes; whose father, we all know, was by our late King of Calabria unrighteously [30 deposed from his fruitful Sicily. Myself drew

[1] This list is taken with slight changes from Q₈. Q₂ omits it.
[2] The presence chamber in the palace.

some blood in those wars, which I would give my hand to be washed from.

Cle. Sir, my ignorance in state-policy will not let me know why, Philaster being heir to one [35 of these kingdoms, the King should suffer him to walk abroad with such free liberty.

Dion. Sir, it seems your nature is more constant than to inquire after state-news. But the King, of late, made a hazard of both the [40 kingdoms, of Sicily and his own, with offering but to imprison Philaster; at which the city was in arms, not to be charm'd down by any state-order or proclamation, till they saw Philaster ride through the streets pleas'd and [45 without a guard: at which they threw their hats and their arms from them; some to make bonfires, some to drink, all for his deliverance: which wise men say is the cause the King labours to bring in the power of a foreign nation to awe his own with. 51

Enter GALATEA, *a Lady, and* MEGRA.

Thra. See, the ladies! What 's the first?

Dion. A wise and modest gentlewoman that attends the princess.

Cle. The second? 55

Dion. She is one that may stand still discreetly enough and ill-favour'dly dance her measure; simper when she is courted by her friend, and slight her husband.

Cle. The last? 60

Dion. Faith, I think she is one whom the state keeps for the agents of our confederate princes; she 'll cog[3] and lie with a whole army, before the league shall break. Her name is common through the kingdom, and the tro- [65

[3] Cheat.

phies of her dishonour advanced beyond Hercules' Pillars. She loves to try the several con-
stitutions of men's bodies ; and, indeed, has
destroyed the worth of her own body by making
experiment upon it for the good of the com- [70
monwealth.

Cle. She 's a profitable member.

Meg. Peace, if you love me ! You shall see these
gentlemen stand their ground and not court us.

Gal. What if they should ?   75

La. What if they should !

Meg. Nay, let her alone. — What if they
should ! Why, if they should, I say they were
never abroad. What foreigner would do so ? [79
It writes them directly untravell'd.

Gal. Why, what if they be ?

La. What if they be !

Meg. Good madam, let her go on. — What if
they be ! Why, if they be, I will justify, [84
they cannot maintain discourse with a judicious
lady, nor make a leg [1] nor say "Excuse me."

Gal. Ha, ha, ha !

Meg. Do you laugh, madam ?

Dion. Your desires upon you, ladies !

Meg. Then you must sit beside us.   90

Dion. I shall sit near you then, lady.

Meg. Near me, perhaps ; but there 's a lady
endures no stranger ; and to me you appear a
very strange fellow.   94

La. Methinks he 's not so strange ; he would
quickly be acquainted.

Thra. Peace, the King !

Enter KING, PHARAMOND, ARETHUSA, *and
Train.*

King. To give a stronger testimony of love
Than sickly promises (which commonly
In princes find both birth and burial   100
In one breath) we have drawn you, worthy
    sir,
To make your fair endearments to our daugh-
    ter,
And worthy services known to our subjects,
Now lov'd and wondered at ; next, our intent
To plant you deeply our immediate heir   105
Both to our blood and kingdoms. For this lady,
(The best part of your life, as you confirm me,
And I believe,) though her few years and sex
Yet teach her nothing but her fears and
    blushes,
Desires without desire, discourse and know-
    ledge   110
Only of what herself is to herself,
Make her feel moderate health ; and when she
    sleeps,
In making no ill day, knows no ill dreams.
Think not, dear sir, these undivided parts,
That must mould up a virgin, are put on   115
To show her so, as borrowed ornaments
To speak her perfect love to you, or add
An artificial shadow to her nature, —
No, sir ; I boldly dare proclaim her yet
No woman. But woo her still, and think her
    modesty   120
A sweeter mistress than the offer'd language

Of any dame, were she a queen, whose eye
Speaks common loves and comforts to her ser-
    vants.[2]
Last, noble son (for so I now must call you),
What I have done thus public, is not only   125
To add a comfort in particular
To you or me, but all ; and to confirm
The nobles and the gentry of these kingdoms
By oath to your succession, which shall be
Within this month at most.   130

Thra. This will be hardly done.

Cle. It must be ill done, if it be done.

Dion. When 't is at best, 't will be but half
    done, whilst
So brave a gentleman is wrong'd and flung off.

Thra. I fear.   135

Cle. Who does not ?

Dion. I fear not for myself, and yet I fear
    too.
Well, we shall see, we shall see. No more.

Pha. Kissing your white hand, mistress, I
    take leave
To thank your royal father ; and thus far   140
To be my own free trumpet. Understand,
Great King, and these your subjects, mine that
    must be,
(For so deserving you have spoke me, sir,
And so deserving I dare speak myself,)
To what a person, of what eminence,   145
Ripe expectation, of what faculties,
Manners and virtues, you would wed your king-
    doms ;
You in me have your wishes. Oh, this country !
By more than all the gods, I hold it happy ;   149
Happy in their dear memories that have been
Kings great and good ; happy in yours that is ;
And from you (as a chronicle to keep
Your noble name from eating age) do I
Opine myself most happy. Gentlemen,
Believe me in a word, a prince's word,   155
There shall be nothing to make up a kingdom
Mighty and flourishing, defenced, fear'd,
Equal to be commanded and obeyed,
But through the travails of my life I 'll find it,
And tie it to this country. By all the gods,   160
My reign shall be so easy to the subject,
That every man shall be his prince himself,
And his own law — yet I his prince and law.
And dearest lady, to your dearest self
(Dear in the choice of him whose name and lus-
    tre   165
Must make you more and mightier) let me say,
You are the blessed'st living ; for, sweet prin-
    cess,
You shall enjoy a man of men to be
Your servant ; you shall make him yours, for
    whom
Great queens must die.   170

Thra. Miraculous !

Cle. This speech calls him Spaniard, being
nothing but a large inventory of his own commendations.

Dion. I wonder what 's his price ; for cer-
    tainly   175
He 'll sell himself, he has so prais'd his shape.

Enter PHILASTER.

But here comes one more worthy those large
  speeches,
Than the large speaker of them.
Let me be swallowed quick, if I can find,
In all the anatomy of yon man's virtues,   180
One sinew sound enough to promise for him,
He shall be constable. By this sun,
He 'll ne'er make king unless it be of trifles,
In my poor judgment.
    Phi. [*kneeling.*] Right noble sir, as low as my
    obedience,   185
And with a heart as loyal as my knee,
I beg your favour.
    King.   Rise ; you have it, sir.
                [PHILASTER *rises.*]
    Dion. Mark but the King, how pale he looks !
He fears !
Oh, this same whorson conscience, how it jades
us !
    King. Speak your intents, sir.
    Phi.   Shall I speak 'em freely ?   190
Be still my royal sovereign.
    King.   As a subject,
We give you freedom.
    Dion.   Now it heats.
    Phi.   Then thus I turn
My language to you, prince ; you, foreign man !
Ne'er stare nor put on wonder, for you must
Endure me, and you shall. This earth you tread
  upon   195
(A dowry, as you hope, with this fair princess),
By my dead father (oh, I had a father,
Whose memory I bow to !) was not left
To your inheritance, and I up and living —
Having myself about me and my sword,   200
The souls of all my name and memories,
These arms and some few friends beside the
  gods —
To part so calmly with it, and sit still
And say, " I might have been." I tell thee,
  Pharamond,   204
When thou art king, look I be dead and rot-
  ten,
And my name ashes: [1] for, hear me, Pharamond !
This very ground thou goest on, this fat earth,
My father's friends made fertile with their
  faiths,
Before that day of shame shall gape and swal-
  low
Thee and thy nation, like a hungry grave,   210
Into her hidden bowels. Prince, it shall :
By the just gods, it shall !
    Pha.   He 's mad ; beyond cure, mad.
    Dion. Here is a fellow has some fire in 's
  veins :
The outlandish prince looks like a tooth-drawer.
    Phi. Sir Prince of popinjays, I 'll make it
  well   215
Appear to you I am not mad.
    King.   You displease us :
You are too bold.
    Phi.   No, sir, I am too tame,
Too much a turtle, a thing born without pas-
  sion,

    [1] Q₂ and Q₃ insert *as I.*

A faint shadow, that every drunken cloud
Sails over, and makes nothing.
    King.   I do not fancy this.   220
Call our physicians ; sure, he 's somewhat
  tainted.[2]
    Thra. I do not think 't will prove so.
    Dion. H'as given him a general purge al-
  ready,
For all the right he has ; and now he means
To let him blood. Be constant, gentlemen :   225
By heaven, I 'll run his hazard,
Although I run my name out of the kingdom !
    Cle. Peace, we are all one soul.
    Pha. What you have seen in me to stir offence
I cannot find, unless it be this lady,   230
Offer'd into mine arms with the succession ;
Which I must keep, (though it hath pleas'd
  your fury
To mutiny within you,) without disputing
Your genealogies, or taking knowledge
Whose branch you are. The King will leave it
  me,   235
And I dare make it mine. You have your an-
  swer.
    Phi. If thou wert sole inheritor to him
That made the world his,[3] and couldst see no
  sun
Shine upon any thing but thine ; were Phara-
  mond
As truly valiant as I feel him cold,   240
And ring'd amongst the choicest of his friends
(Such as would blush to talk such serious follies,
Or back such bellied [4] commendations),
And from this presence, spite of all these bugs,[5]
You should hear further from me.   245
    King. Sir, you wrong the prince ; I gave you
  not this freedom
To brave our best friends. You deserve our
  frown.
Go to ; be better temper'd.
    Phi. It must be, sir, when I am nobler us'd.
    Gal. Ladies,   250
This would have been a pattern of succession, [6]
Had he ne'er met this mischief. By my life,
He is the worthiest the true name of man
This day within my knowledge.
    Meg. I cannot tell what you may call your
  knowledge ;   255
But the other is the man set in mine eye.
Oh, 't is a prince of wax ! [7]
    Gal.   A dog it is,[8]
    King. Philaster, tell me
The injuries you aim at [9] in your riddles.   259
    Phi. If you had my eyes, sir, and sufferance,
My griefs upon you, and my broken fortunes,
My wants great, and now nought but hopes and
  fears,
My wrongs would make ill riddles to be laught at.
Dare you be still my king, and right me not ?
    King. Give me your wrongs in private.

    [2] Unbalanced in mind.
    [3] *I. e.* Alexander the Great.
    [4] Swollen. Q₁ and Q₂ *belied.*   [6] To succeeding kings.
    [5] Bugbears.   [7] A model prince
    [8] The phrase, *a dog of wax,* is used elsewhere in a
contemptuous sense, but has not been explained.
    [9] Refer to.

Phi.   Take them,   265
And ease me of a load would bow strong Atlas.
                            They whisper.
Cle. He dares not stand the shock.
Dion. I cannot blame him ; there 's danger
in 't. Every man in this age has not a soul of
crystal, for all men to read their actions [270
through : men's hearts and faces are so far asun-
der, that they hold no intelligence. Do but view
yon stranger well, and you shall see a fever
through all his bravery,[1] and feel him shake
like a true tenant.[2] If he give not back his [275
crown again upon the report of an elder-gun, I
have no augury.
King. Go to ;
Be more yourself, as you respect our favour ; 279
You 'll stir us else. Sir, I must have you know,
That y' are and shall be, at our pleasure, what
Fashion we will put upon you. Smooth your
        brow,
Or by the gods ——
Phi. I am dead, sir ; y' are my fate. It was
        not I
Said, I was wrong'd : I carry all about me   285
My weak stars lead me to, all my weak for-
        tunes.
Who dares in all this presence speak, (that is
But man of flesh, and may be mortal,) tell me
I do not most entirely love this prince,
And honour his full virtues !
King.   Sure, he 's possess'd. 290
Phi. Yes, with my father's spirit. It 's here,
        O King,
A dangerous spirit ! Now he tells me, King,
I was a king's heir, bids me be a king,
And whispers to me, these are all my subjects.
'T is strange he will not let me sleep, but dives
Into my fancy, and there gives me shapes   296
That waken me and do me service, cry me king.
But I 'll suppress him ; he 's a factious spirit,
And will undo me. — [*To* PHAR.] Noble sir,
        your hand ;
I am your servant.
King.   Away ! I do not like this : 360
I 'll make you tamer, or I 'll dispossess you
Both of your life and spirit. For this time
I pardon your wild speech, without so much
As your imprisonment.
            Exeunt KING, PHARAMOND, ARE-
                THUSA [*and* Train].
Dion. I thank you, sir ; you dare not for the
        people.   305
Gal. Ladies, what think you now of this
        brave fellow ?
Meg. A pretty talking fellow, hot at hand.
But eye yon stranger : is he not a fine complete
gentleman ? Oh, these strangers, I do affect[3]
them strangely ! They do the rarest home- [310
things, and please the fullest ! As I live, I could
love all the nation over and over for his sake.
Gal. Gods comfort your poor head-piece,
lady ! 'T is a weak one, and had need of a night-
cap.   *Exeunt* Ladies. 315

---

[1] Ostentation, swagger.
[2] Probably corrupt. Q1 *truant.* Mod. edd. conjecture
tyrant ; recreant ; in a true tertian.
[3] Love.

Dion. See, how his fancy labours ! Has he
        not
Spoke home and bravely ? What a dangerous
        train
Did he give fire to ! How he shook the King,
Made his soul melt within him, and his blood
Run into whey ! It stood upon his brow   320
Like a cold winter dew.
Phi.   Gentlemen,
You have no suit to me ? I am no minion.
You stand, methinks, like men that would be
        courtiers,
If I[4] could well be flatter'd at a price
Not to undo your children. You're all honest :
Go, get you home again, and make your coun-
        try   326
A virtuous court, to which your great ones
        may,
In their diseased age, retire and live recluse.
Cle. How do you, worthy sir ?
Phi.   Well, very well ;
And so well that, if the King please you, I find
I may live many years.
Dion.   The King must please, 331
Whilst we know what you are and who you are,
Your wrongs and virtues.[5] Shrink not, worthy
        sir,
But add your father to you ; in whose name
We 'll waken all the gods, and conjure up   335
The rods of vengeance, the abused people,
Who, like to raging torrents, shall swell high,
And so begirt the dens of these male-dragons,
That, through the strongest safety, they shall
        beg
For mercy at your sword's point.
Phi.   Friends, no more ; 340
Our ears may be corrupted ; t is an age
We dare not trust our wills to. Do you love
        me ?
Thra. Do we love Heaven and Honour ?
Phi. My Lord Dion, you had
A virtuous gentlewoman call'd you father ;   345
Is she yet alive ?
Dion.   Most honour'd sir, she is ;
And, for the penance but of an idle dream
Has undertook a tedious pilgrimage.

                Enter a Lady.

Phi. Is it to me, or any of these gentlemen,
        you come ?
Lady. To you, brave lord ; the princess would
        entreat   350
Your present company.
Phi. The princess send for me ! You are mis-
        taken.
Lady. If you be called Philaster, 't is to you.
Phi. Kiss her fair hand, and say I will attend
her.   [*Exit* Lady.]
Dion. Do you know what you do ?   355
Phi. Yes ; go to see a woman.
Cle. But do you weigh the danger you are
        in ?
Phi. Danger in a sweet face !
By Jupiter, I must not fear a woman !

---

[4] Mason conj. Qq. F. *you.* If you could flatter me
without ruining your families by antagonizing the king.
[5] Q1, Other edd. *injuries.*

Thra. But are you sure it was the princess
sent ? 360
It may be some foul train to catch your life.
Phi. I do not think it, gentlemen; she's noble.
Her eye may shoot me dead, or those true red
And white friends in her cheeks may steal my
soul out; 354
There's all the danger in 't. But, be what may,
Her single [1] name hath arm'd me. *Exit.*
Dion. Go on,
And be as truly happy as thou 'rt fearless!—
Come, gentlemen, let's make our friends ac-
quainted,
Lest the King prove false. *Exeunt.*

[SCENE II.] [2]

Enter ARETHUSA *and a* Lady.

Are. Comes he not ?
Lady. Madam ?
Are. Will Philaster come ?
Lady. Dear madam, you were wont to credit
me
At first.
Are. But didst thou tell me so ?
I am forgetful, and my woman's strength 5
Is so o'ercharg'd with dangers like to grow
About my marriage, that these under-things
Dare not abide in such a troubled sea.
How lookt he when he told thee he would come ?
Lady. Why, well. 10
Are. And not a little fearful ?
Lady. Fear, madam! Sure, he knows not
what it is.
Are. You all are of his faction; the whole
court
Is bold in praise of him; whilst I
May live neglected, and do noble things, 15
As fools in strife throw gold into the sea,
Drown'd in the doing. But, I know he fears.
Lady. Fear, madam! Methought, his looks
hid more
Of love than fear.
Are. Of love! To whom ? To you ?
Did you deliver those plain words I sent, 20
With such a winning gesture and quick look
That you have caught him ?
Lady. Madam, I mean to you.
Are. Of love to me! Alas, thy ignorance
Lets thee not see the crosses of our births!
Nature, that loves not to be questioned 25
Why she did this or that, but has her ends,
And knows she does well, never gave the world
Two things so opposite, so contrary
As he and I am : if a bowl of blood
Drawn from this arm of mine would poison 30
thee,
A draught of his would cure thee. Of love to me !
Lady. Madam, I think I hear him.
Are. Bring him in. [*Exit* Lady.]
You gods, that would not have your docms
withstood,
Whose holy wisdoms at this time it is
To make the passion of a feeble maid 35
The way unto your justice, I obey.

[*Re*]-*enter* [Lady *with*] PHILASTER.

Lady. Here is my Lord Philaster.
Are. Oh, 't is well.
Withdraw yourself. [*Exit* Lady.]
Phi. Madam, your messenger
Made me believe you wish'd to speak with me.
Are. 'T is true, Philaster; but the words are
such 40
I have to say, and do so ill beseem
The mouth of woman, that I wish them said,
And yet am loth to speak them. Have you
known
That I have aught detracted from your worth?
Have I in person wrong'd you, or have set 45
My baser instruments to throw disgrace
Upon your virtues ?
Phi. Never, madam, you.
Are. Why, then, should you, in such a public
place,
Injure a princess, and a scandal lay
Upon my fortunes, fam'd to be so great, 50
Calling a great part of my dowry in question ?
Phi. Madam, this truth which I shall speak
will be
Foolish : but, for your fair and virtuous self,
I could afford myself to have no right
To any thing you wish'd.
Are. Philaster, know, 55
I must enjoy these kingdoms.
Phi. Madam, both ?
Are. Both, or I die: by heaven, I die, Phil-
aster,
If I not calmly may enjoy them both.
Phi. I would do much to save that noble life;
Yet would be loth to save posterity 60
Find in our stories, that Philaster gave
His right unto a sceptre and a crown
To save a lad'y's longing.
Are. Nay, then, hear :
I must and will have them, and more——
Phi. What more ?
Are. Or lose that little life the gods prepared 65
To trouble this poor piece of earth withal.
Phi. Madam, what more ?
Are. Turn, then, away thy face
Phi. No.
Are. Do.
Phi. I can endure it. Turn away my face ! 70
I never yet saw enemy that lookt
So dreadfully, but that I thought myself
As great a basilisk [3] as he ; or spake
So horrible, but that I thought my tongue
Bore thunder underneath, as much as his ; 75
Nor beast that I could turn from. Shall I then
Begin to fear sweet sounds ? A lady's voice,
Whom I do love ? Say you would have my life ;
Why, I will give it you ; for 't is of me
A thing so loath'd, and unto you that ask 80
Of so poor use, that I shall make no price :
If you entreat, I will unmov'dly hear.
Are. Yet, for my sake, a little bend thy looks.
Phi. I do.
Are. Then know, I must have them and thee.
Phi. And me ?

---

[3] Mere. [2] Arethusa's apartment in the palace. [3] A fabulous serpent that killed with a glance.

Are. Thy love ; without which, all the land
Discovered yet will serve me for no use   86
But to be buried in.
Phi.   Is 't possible ?
Are. With it, it were too little to bestow
On thee. Now, though thy breath do strike me
    dead,
(Which, know, it may,) I have unript my
    breast.   90
Phi. Madam, you are too full of noble
    thoughts,
To lay a train for this contemned life,
Which you may have for asking. To suspect
Were base, where I deserve no ill. Love you !
By all my hopes, I do, above my life !   95
But how this passion should proceed from you
So violently, would amaze a man
That would be jealous.[1]
Are. Another soul into my body shot
Could not have fill'd me with more strength and
    spirit   100
Than this thy breath. But spend not hasty
    time
In seeking how I came thus : 't is the gods,
The gods, that make me so ; and, sure, our love
Will be the nobler and the better blest,
In that the secret justice of the gods   105
Is mingled with it. Let us leave, and kiss ;
Lest some unwelcome guest should fall betwixt
    us,
And we should part without it.
Phi.   'T will be ill
I should abide here long.
Are.   'T is true ; and worse
You should come often. How shall we devise
To hold intelligence, that our true loves,   111
On any new occasion, may agree
What path is best to tread ?
Phi.   I have a boy,
Sent by the gods, I hope, to this intent,   114
Not yet seen in the court. Hunting the buck,
I found him sitting by a fountain's side,
Of which he borrow'd some to quench his thirst,
And paid the nymph again as much in tears.
A garland lay him by, made by himself
Of many several flowers bred in the vale,   120
Stuck in that mystic order that the rareness
Delighted me : but ever when he turn'd
His tender eyes upon 'em, he would weep,
As if he meant to make 'em grow again.
Seeing such pretty helpless innocence   125
Dwell in his face, I ask'd him all his story.
He told me that his parents gentle died,
Leaving him to the mercy of the fields,
Which gave him roots ; and of the crystal
    springs,   129
Which did not stop their courses ; and the sun,
Which still, he thank'd him, yielded him his
    light.
Then took he up his garland, and did show
What every flower, as country-people hold,
Did signify, and how all, ordered thus,
Exprest his grief ; and, to my thoughts, did
    read   135
The prettiest lecture of his country-art

[1] Suspicious.

That could be wisht : so that methought I
    could
Have studied it. I gladly entertain'd
Him, who was glad to follow ; and have got
The trustiest, loving'st, and the gentlest boy 140
That ever master kept. Him will I send
To wait on you, and bear our hidden love.
Are. 'T is well ; no more.

Re-enter Lady.

Lady. Madam, the prince is come to do his
    service.
Are. What will you do, Philaster, with your-
    self ?   145
Phi. Why, that which all the gods have
    pointed out for me.
Are. Dear, hide thyself. —
Bring in the prince.   [*Exit* Lady.]
Phi.   Hide me from Pharamond !
When thunder speaks, which is the voice of
    God,
Though I do reverence, yet I hide me not ;   150
And shall a stranger-prince have leave to brag
Unto a foreign nation, that he made
Philaster hide himself ?
Are.   He cannot know it.
Phi. Though it should sleep for ever to the
    world,
It is a simple sin to hide myself,   155
Which will for ever on my conscience lie.
Are. Then, good Philaster, give him scope
    and way
In what he says ; for he is apt to speak
What you are loth to hear. For my sake, do.
Phi. I will.   160

[*Re*]-*enter* [Lady *with*] PHARAMOND.

Pha. My princely mistress, as true lovers
    ought,   [*Exit* Lady.]
I come to kiss these fair hands, and to show,
In outward ceremonies, the dear love
Writ in my heart.   164
Phi. If I shall have an answer no directlier,
I am gone.
Pha. To what would he have answer ?
Are. To his claim unto the kingdom.
Pha. Sirrah, I forbare you before the King —
Phi. Good sir, do so still ; I would not talk
    with you.   170
Pha. But now the time is fitter. Do but offer
To make mention of right to any kingdom,
Though it be scarce habitable ——
Phi.   Good sir, let me go.
Pha. And by the gods —
Phi.   Peace, Pharamond ! if thou ——
Are. Leave us, Philaster.
Phi.   I have done. [*Going.*]   175
Pha. You are gone ! by Heaven I 'll fetch
    you back.
Phi. You shall not need.   [*Returning.*]
Pha.   What now ?
Phi.   Know, Pharamond,
I loathe to brawl with such a blast as thou,
Who art nought but a valiant voice ; but if
Thou shalt provoke me further, men shall
    say,
Thou wert, and not lament it.

Pha.   Do you slight 181
My greatness so, and in the chamber of
The princess?
  Phi. It is a place to which I must confess
I owe a reverence ; but were 't the church, 185
Ay, at the altar, there 's no place so safe,
Where thou dar'st injure me, but I dare kill
    thee.
And for your greatness, know, sir, I can grasp
You and your greatness thus, thus into nothing.
Give not a word, not a word back ! Farewell.
                                    Exit.
  Pha. 'T is an odd fellow, madam ; we must
    stop   191
His mouth with some office when we are
    married.
  Are. You were best make him your controller.
  Pha. I think he would discharge it well. But,
    madam,
I hope our hearts are knit ; but yet so slow 195
The ceremonies of state are, that 't will be
    long
Before our hands be so. If then you please,
Being agreed in heart, let us not wait
For dreaming form, but take a little stolen
Delights, and so prevent[1] our joys to come. 200
  Are. If you dare speak such thoughts,
I must withdraw in honour.   *Exit.*
  Pha. The constitution of my body will never
hold out till the wedding ; I must seek else-
where.   *Exit.* [205

ACT II

SCENE I.[2]

Enter PHILASTER *and* BELLARIO.

  Phi. And thou shalt find her honourable,
    boy ;
Full of regard unto thy tender youth,
For thine own modesty ; and, for my sake,
Apter to give than thou wilt be to ask,
Ay, or deserve.
  Bel.   Sir, you did take me up   5
When I was nothing ; and only yet am some-
    thing
By being yours. You trusted me unknown ;
And that which you were apt to conster[3]
A simple innocence in me, perhaps
Might have been craft, the cunning of a boy 10
Hard'ned in lies and theft: yet ventur'd you
To part my miseries and me: for which,
I never can expect to serve a lady
That bears more honour in her breast than you.
  Phi. But, boy, it will prefer[4] thee. Thou
    art young,   15
And bear'st a childish overflowing love
To them that clap thy cheeks and speak thee
    fair yet ;
But when thy judgment comes to rule those
    passions,
Thou wilt remember best those careful friends
That plac'd thee in the noblest way of life. 20
She is a princess I prefer thee to.

[1] Anticipate.   [2] An apartment in the palace.
[3] Construe, interpret.   [4] Advance.

  Bel. In that small time that I have seen the
    world,
I never knew a man hasty to part
With a servant he thought trusty. I remember,
My father would prefer the boys he kept   26
To greater men than he ; but did it not
Till they were grown too saucy for himself.
  Phi. Why, gentle boy, I find no fault at all
In thy behaviour.
  Bel.   Sir, if I have made
A fault in ignorance, instruct my youth :   30
I shall be willing, if not apt, to learn ;
Age and experience will adorn my mind
With larger knowledge ; and if I have done
A wilful fault, think me not past all hope
For once. What master holds so strict a hand 35
Over his boy, that he will part with him
Without one warning ? Let me be corrected
To break my stubbornness, if it be so,
Rather than turn me off ; and I shall mend.   39
  Phi. Thy love doth plead so prettily to stay,
That, trust me, I could weep to part with thee.
Alas, I do not turn thee off ! Thou knowest
It is my business that doth call thee hence ;
And when thou art with her, thou dwell'st
    with me,
Think so, and 't is so; and when time is full, 45
That thou hast well discharg'd this heavy trust,
Laid on so weak a one, I will again
With joy receive thee ; as I live, I will !
Nay, weep not, gentle boy. 'T is more than
    time
Thou didst attend the princess.
  Bel.   I am gone.   50
But since I am to part with you, my lord,
And none knows whether I shall live to do
More service for you, take this little prayer :
Heaven bless your loves, your fights, all your
    designs !   54
May sick men, if they have your wish, be well ;
And Heaven hate those you curse, though I be
    one !   *Exit.*
  Phi. The love of boys unto their lords is
    strange ;
I have read wonders of it : yet this boy
For my sake (if a man may judge by looks
And speech) would out-do story. I may see 60
A day to pay him for his loyalty.   *Exit.*

[SCENE II.][5]

Enter PHARAMOND.

  Pha. Why should these ladies stay so long?
They must come this way. I know the queen
employs 'em not ; for the reverend mother[6]
sent me word, they would all be for the garden.
If they should all prove honest[7] now, I were [8
in a fair taking ; I was never so long without
sport in my life, and, in my conscience, 't is not
my fault. Oh, for our country ladies !

Enter GALATEA.

Here 's one bolted ; I 'll hound at her.— Madam !
  Gal. Your grace !

[5] A gallery in the palace.
[6] In charge of the maids of honor.   [7] Chaste.

Pha. Shall I not be a trouble?
Gal.   Not to me, sir. 11
Pha. Nay, nay, you are too quick. By this
sweet hand——
Gal. You'll be forsworn, sir; 't is but an old
glove.
If you will talk at distance, I am for you:
But, good prince, be not bawdy, nor do not
brag;   15
These two I bar;
And then, I think, I shall have sense enough
To answer all the weighty apophthegms
Your royal blood shall manage.
Pha. Dear lady, can you love?   20
Gal. Dear prince! how dear? I ne'er cost
you a coach yet, nor put you to the dear repentance of a banquet. Here's no scarlet, sir, to
blush the sin out it was given for. This wire
mine own hair covers; and this face has [25
been so far from being dear to any, that it ne'er
cost penny painting; and, for the rest of my
poor wardrobe, such as you see, it leaves no
hand[1] behind it, to make the jealous mercer's
wife curse our good doings.   30
Pha. You mistake me, lady.
Gal. Lord, I do so; would you or I could
help it!
[*Pha.* You're very dangerous bitter, like a
potion.
Gal. No, sir, I do not mean to purge you,
though
I mean to purge a little time on you.][2]   35
Pha. Do ladies of this country use to give
No more respect to men of my full being?
Gal. Full being! I understand you not, unless your grace means growing to fatness; and
then your only remedy (upon my knowledge, [40
prince) is, in a morning, a cup of neat white
wine brewed with carduus,[3] then fast till supper; about eight you may eat; use exercise,
and keep a sparrow-hawk; you can shoot in a
tiller:[4] but, of all, your grace must fly phle- [45
botomy,[5] fresh pork, conger,[6] and clarified
whey; they are all duller of the vital spirits.
Pha. Lady, you talk of nothing all this while.
Gal. 'T is very true, sir; I talk of you. 49
Pha. [*Aside.*] This is a crafty wench; I like
her wit well; 't will be rare to stir up a leaden
appetite. She's a Danaë, and must be courted
in a shower of gold. — Madam, look here; all
these, and more than ——   54
Gal. What have you there, my lord? Gold!
now, as I live, 't is fair gold! You would have
silver for it, to play with the pages. You could
not have taken me in a worse time; but, if
you have present use, my lord, I'll send my
man with silver and keep your gold for you. 60
Pha. Lady, lady!
Gal. She's coming, sir, behind, will take
white money.—
[*Aside.*] Yet for all this I'll match ye.
                            Exit behind the hangings.
Pha. If there be but two such more in this
kingdom, and near the court, we may even [65

---

[1] Note of indebtedness.   [2] Only in Q₁.
[3] A kind of thistle used as a medicine.
[3] Cross-bow.   [5] Blood letting.   [6] Conger-eel.

hang up our harps. Ten such camphire[7] con-
stitutions as this would call the golden age
again in question, and teach the old way for
every ill-fac'd husband to get his own children;
and what a mischief that would breed, let all
consider!   71

Enter MEGRA.

Here's another: if she be of the same last, the
devil shall pluck her on.— Many fair mornings,
lady!
Meg. As many mornings bring as many days,
Fair, sweet and hopeful to your grace!   76
Pha. [*Aside.*] She gives good words yet; sure
this wench is free. — [8]
If your more serious business do not call you,
Let me hold quarter with you; we will talk
An hour out quickly.
Meg.   What would your grace talk of? 80
Pha. Of some such pretty subject as yourself:
I'll go no further than your eye, or lip;
There's theme enough for one man for an age.
Meg. Sir, they stand right, and my lips are
yet even,
Smooth, young enough, ripe enough, and red
enough,   85
Or my glass wrongs me.
Pha. Oh, they are two twinn'd cherries dy'd
in blushes
Which those fair suns above with their bright
beams
Reflect upon and ripen. Sweetest beauty,
Bow down those branches, that the longing
taste   90
Of the faint looker-on may meet those blessings,
And taste and live.   *They kiss*
Meg. [*Aside.*]   Oh, delicate sweet prince!
She that hath snow enough about her heart
To take the wanton spring of ten such lines off,
May be a nun without probation. — Sir,   95
You have in such neat poetry gathered a kiss,
That if I had but five lines of that number,
Such pretty begging blanks,[9] I should com-
mend
Your forehead or your cheeks, and kiss you
too.
Pha. Do it in prose; you cannot miss it,
madam.   100
Meg. I shall, I shall.
Pha.   By my life, but you shall not;
I'll prompt you first. [*Kisses her.*] Can you do
it now?
Meg. Methinks 't is easy, now you ha' done 't
before me;
But yet I should stick at it.   [*Kisses him.*]
Pha.   Stick till to-morrow;
I'll ne'er part you, sweetest. But we lose time:
Can you love me?   105
Meg. Love you, my lord! How would you
have me love you?
Pha. I'll teach you in a short sentence,
'cause I will not load your memory; this is all:
love me, and lie with me.   110
Meg. Was it "lie with you" that you said?
'T is impossible.

---

[7] *I. e.* cold.   [8] Responsive.   [9] Blank verses.

Pha. Not to a willing mind, that will endeavour. If I do not teach you to do it as easily in one night as you 'll go to bed, I 'll lose my royal blood for 't.   116

Meg. Why, prince, you have a lady of your own
That yet wants teaching.

Pha. I 'll sooner teach a mare the old measures[1] than teach her anything belonging to [120 the function. She 's afraid to lie with herself if she have but any masculine imaginations about her. I know, when we are married, I must ravish her.

Meg. By mine honour, that 's a foul fault, indeed;   125
But time and your good help will wear it out, sir.

Pha. And for any other I see, excepting your dear self, dearest lady, I had rather be Sir Tim the schoolmaster, and leap a dairy-maid, madam.   130

Meg. Has your grace seen the court-star, Galatea?

Pha. Out upon her! She 's as cold of her favour as an apoplex; she sail'd by but now.

Meg. And how do you hold her wit, sir?   135

Pha. I hold her wit? The strength of all the guard cannot hold it, if they were tied to it; she would blow 'em out of the kingdom. They talk of Jupiter; he 's but a squib-cracker to her: look well about you, and you may find a tongue- [140 bolt. But speak, sweet lady, shall I be freely welcome.

Meg. Whither?

Pha. To your bed. If you mistrust my faith, you do me the unnoblest wrong.   145

Meg. I dare not, prince, I dare not.

Pha. Make your own conditions, my purse shall seal 'em, and what you dare imagine you can want, I 'll furnish you withal. Give two hours to your thoughts every morning about it. Come I know you are bashful;   151
Speak in my ear, will you be mine? Keep this,
And with it, me: soon I will visit you.

Meg. My lord, my chamber 's most unsafe; but when 't is night,   154
I 'll find some means to slip into your lodging;
Till when ——   [thee!

Pha. Till when, this and my heart go with
         Exeunt several ways.

Re-enter GALATEA *from behind the hangings.*

Gal. Oh, thou pernicious petticoat prince! are these your virtues? Well, if I do not lay a train to blow your sport up, I am no woman: and, Lady Towsabel, I 'll fit you for 't. *Exit.* 160

[SCENE III.][2]

Enter ARETHUSA *and a* Lady.

Are. Where 's the boy?
Lady. Within, madam.
Are. Gave you him gold to buy him clothes?

---

[1] Stately dances.
[2] Arethusa's apartment in the palace.

Lady. I did.
Are. And has he done 't?   5
Lady. Yes, madam.
Are. 'T is a pretty sad-talking boy, is it not? Asked you his name?
Lady. No, madam.   9

Enter GALATEA.

Are. Oh, you are welcome. What good news?
Gal. As good as any one can tell your grace, That says she has done that you would have wish'd.
Are. Hast thou discovered?
Gal. I have strain'd a point of modesty for you.
Are. I prithee, how?   15
Gal. In list'ning after bawdry. I see, let a lady live never so modestly, she shall be sure to find a lawful time to hearken after bawdry. Your prince, brave Pharamond, was so hot on 't!   20
Are. With whom?
Gal. Why, with the lady I suspected. I can tell the time and place.
Are. Oh, when, and where?
Gal. To-night, his lodging.   25
Are. Run thyself into the presence; mingle there again
With other ladies; leave the rest to me.
         [*Exit* GALATEA.]
If destiny (to whom we dare not say,
" Why didst thou this?") have not decreed it so,
In lasting leaves (whose smallest characters   30
Were never alter'd yet), this match shall break. —
Where 's the boy?
Lady. Here, madam.

Enter BELLARIO.

Are. Sir, you are sad to change your service; is 't not so?
Bel. Madam, I have not chang'd; I wait on you,   35
To do him service.
Are.   Thou disclaim'st in me.
Tell me thy name.
Bel. Bellario.
Are. Thou canst sing and play?
Bel. If grief will give me leave, madam, I can.   40
Are. Alas, what kind of grief can thy years know?
Hadst thou a curst master when thou went'st to school?
Thou art not capable of other grief;
Thy brows and cheeks are smooth as waters be
When no breath troubles them. Believe me, boy,   45
Care seeks out wrinkled brows and hollow eyes,
And builds himself caves, to abide in them
Come, sir, tell me truly, doth your lord love me?
Bel. Love, madam! I know not what it is.
Are. Canst thou know grief, and never yet knew'st love?   50
Thou art deceiv'd, boy. Does he speak of me
As if he wish'd me well?

Bel.   If it be love
To forget all respect of his own friends
With thinking of your face ; if it be love
To sit cross-arm'd and sigh away the day,   55
Mingled with starts, crying your name as loud
And hastily as men i' the streets do fire ;
If it be love to weep himself away
When he but hears of any lady dead
Or kill'd, because it might have been your
    chance ;   60
If, when he goes to rest (which will not be),
'Twixt every prayer he says, to name you once,
As others drop a bead, be to be in love,
Then, madam, I dare swear he loves you.
Are. Oh you 're a cunning boy, and taught
    to lie   65
For your lord's credit ! But thou know'st a lie
That bears this sound is welcomer to me
Than any truth that says he loves me not.
Lead the way, boy. — [*To* Lady.] Do you attend
    me too. —   69
'T is thy lord's business hastes me thus. Away !
                    Exeunt.

[SCENE IV.] [1]

Enter DION, CLEREMONT, THRASILINE, MEGRA,
    and GALATEA.

Dion. Come, ladies, shall we talk a round ?
    As men
Do walk a mile, women should talk an hour
After supper : 't is their exercise.
Gal. 'T is late.
Meg. 'T is all   5
My eyes will do to lead me to my bed.
Gal. I fear, they are so heavy, you 'll scarce
    find
The way to your own lodging with 'em to-night.

Enter PHARAMOND.

Thra. The prince !
Pha. Not a-bed, ladies ? You 're good sit-
    ters-up.   10
What will you of a pleasant dream, to last
Till morning ?
Meg. I should choose, my lord, a pleasing
    wake before it.

Enter ARETHUSA *and* BELLARIO.

Are. 'T is well, my lord ; you 're courting of
    these ladies. —
Is 't not late, gentlemen ?   15
Cle. Yes, madam.
Are. Wait you there.   *Exit.*
Meg. [*Aside.*] She 's jealous, as I live. — Look
    you, my lord,
The princess has a Hylas, an Adonis.
Pha. His form is angel-like.   20
Meg. Why, this is he that must, when you
    are wed,
Sit by your pillow, like young Apollo, with
His hand and voice binding your thoughts in
    sleep ,
The princess does provide him for you and for
    herself.

[1] Before Pharamond's lodging in the court of the
palace.

Pha. I find no music in these boys.
Meg.   NOR I :   25
They can do little, and that small they do,
They have not wit to hide.
Dion.   Serves he the princess ?
Thra. Yes.   [keeps him !
Dion.   'T is a sweet boy : how brave [2] she
Pha. Ladies all, good rest ; I mean to kill a
    buck
To-morrow morning ere you 've done your
    dreams.   30
Meg. All happiness attend your grace ! [*Exit*
    PHARAMOND.] Gentlemen, good rest. —
Come, shall we go to bed ?
Gal.   Yes. — All good night.
Dion. May your dreams be true to you ! —
                    Exeunt GALATEA *and* MEGRA.
What shall we do, gallants ? 't is late. The
    King
Is up still : see, he comes ; a guard along   35
With him.

Enter KING, ARETHUSA, *and* Guard.

King.   Look your intelligence be true.
Are. Upon my life, it is ; and I do hope
Your highness will not tie me to a man
That in the heat of wooing throws me off,
And takes another.
Dion.   What should this mean ? 40
King. If it be true,
That lady had been better have embrac'd
Cureless diseases. Get you to your rest :
You shall be righted.
                    Exeunt ARETHUSA *and* BELLARIO.
        — Gentlemen, draw near ;
We shall employ you. Is young Pharamond   45
Come to his lodging ?
Dion.   I saw him enter there.
King. Haste, some of you, and cunningly dis-
    cover
If Megra be in her lodging.   [*Exit* DION.]
Cle. Sir,
She parted hence but now, with other ladies. 50
King. If she be there, we shall not need to
    make
A vain discovery of our suspicion.
[*Aside.*] You gods, I see that who unrighteously
Holds wealth or state from others shall be curst
In that which meaner men are blest withal :   55
Ages to come shall know no male of him
Left to inherit, and his name shall be
Blotted from earth ; if he have any child,
It shall be crossly match'd ; the gods them-
    selves
Shall sow wild strife betwixt her lord and her.
Yet, if it be your wills, forgive the sin   61
I have committed ; let it not fall
Upon this understanding child of mine !
She has not broke your laws. But how can I
Look to be heard of gods that must be just,   65
Praying upon the ground I hold by wrong ?

Re-enter DION.

Dion. Sir, I have asked, and her women swear
she is within ; but they, I think, are bawds.

[2] Finely dressed.

I told 'em, I must speak with her; they laught,
and said, their lady lay speechless. I said, [70]
my business was important; they said, their
lady was about it. I grew hot, and cried, my
business was a matter that concern'd life and
death; they answered, so was sleeping, at which
their lady was. I urg'd again, she had scarce [75]
time to be so since last I saw her: they smil'd
again, and seem'd to instruct me that sleeping was nothing but lying down and winking.[1]
Answers more direct I could not get: in short,
sir, I think she is not there.   80
  King. 'T is then no time to dally. — You o'
the guard,
Wait at the back door of the prince's lodging,
And see that none pass thence, upon your lives.
                            [*Exeunt* Guards.]
Knock, gentlemen; knock loud; louder yet.
      [DION, CLER., &c. *knock at the door*
        of PHARAMOND'S *Lodging.*]
What, has their pleasure taken off their hear-
ing? —   85
I 'll break your meditations. — Knock again. —
Not yet? I do not think he sleeps, having this
Larum by him. — Once more. — Pharamond!
  prince! PHARAMOND [*appears*] *above.*
  Pha. What saucy groom knocks at this dead
of night?
Where be our waiters? By my vexed soul,   90
He meets his death that meets me, for his bold-
ness.
  King. Prince, prince, you wrong your
thoughts; we are your friends:
Come down.
  Pha.   The King!
  King.   The same, sir. Come down, sir:
We have cause of present counsel with you.
  Pha. If your grace please   95
To use me, I 'll attend you to your chamber.

       Enter PHARAMOND *below.*

  King. No, 't is too late, prince; I 'll make
bold with yours.
  Pha. I have some private reasons to myself
Makes me unmannerly, and say you cannot. —
              They press to come in.
Nay, press not forward, gentlemen; he must 100
Come through my life that comes here.
  King. Sir, be resolv'd[2] I must and will come.
  — Enter.
  Pha. I will not be dishonour'd.
He that enters, enters upon his death.
Sir, 't is a sign you make no stranger of me, 105
To bring these renegadoes to my chamber
At these unseasoned hours.
  King.   Why do you
Chafe yourself so? You are not wrong'd nor
shall be;
Only I 'll search your lodging, for some cause
To ourself known. — Enter, I say.
  Pha.   I say, no. 110

       Enter MEGRA *above.*

  Meg. Let 'em enter, prince, let 'em enter;
I am up and ready:[3] I know their business;

---

  [1] Closing the eyes.   [2] Convinced.   [3] Dressed.

'T is the poor breaking of a lady's honour
They hunt so hotly after; let 'em enjoy it. — 114
You have your business, gentlemen; I lay here.
Oh, my lord the King, this is not noble in you
To make public the weakness of a woman!
  King. Come down.
  Meg. I dare, my lord. Your hootings and your
  clamours,   119
Your private whispers and your broad fleerings,
Can no more vex my soul than this base car-
  riage.[4]
But I have vengeance yet in store for some
Shall, in the most contempt you can have of me,
Be joy and nourishment.
  King.   Will you come down?
  Meg. Yes, to laugh at your worst; but I shall
  wring you,   125
If my skill fail me not.   [*Exit above.*
  King. Sir, I must dearly chide you for this
  looseness;
You have wrong'd a worthy lady; but, no
  more. —
Conduct him to my lodging and to bed.
      [*Exeunt* PHARAMOND *and* Attendants.]
  Cle. Get him another wench, and you bring
him to bed indeed.   131
  Dion. 'T is strange a man cannot ride a stage
Or two, to breathe himself, without a warrant.
If his gear hold, that lodgings be search'd thus,
Pray God we may lie with our own wives in
  safety,   135
That they be not by some trick of state mis-
  taken!

    Enter [Attendants] *with* MEGRA [*below*].

  King. Now, lady of honour, where 's your
honour now?
No man can fit your palate but the prince.
Thou most ill-shrouded rottenness, thou piece
Made by a painter and a 'pothecary,   140
Thou troubled sea of lust, thou wilderness
Inhabited by wild thoughts, thou swoln cloud
Of infection, thou ripe mine of all diseases,
Thou all-sin, all-hell, and last, all-devils, tell me,
Had you none to pull on with your courtesies 145
But he that must be mine, and wrong my
  daughter?
By all the gods, all these, and all the pages,
And all the court, shall hoot thee through the
  court,
Fling rotten oranges, make ribald rhymes,
And sear thy name with candles upon walls! 150
Do you laugh, Lady Venus?
  Meg. Faith, sir, you must pardon me;
I cannot choose but laugh to see you merry.
If you do this, O King! nay, if you dare do it,
By all those gods you swore by, and as many 155
More of my own, I will have fellows, and such
Fellows in it, as shall make noble mirth!
The princess, your dear daughter, shall stand
  by me
On walls, and sung in ballads, any thing.   159
Urge me no more; I know her and her haunts,
Her lays, leaps, and outlays, and will discover
  all;
Nay, will dishonour her. I know the boy

---

             [4] Behavior.

She keeps ; a handsome boy, about eighteen ;
Know what she does with him, where, and
when.   164
Come, sir, you put me to a woman's madness,
The glory of a fury ; and if I do not
Do 't to the height ——
    King.   What boy is this she raves at ?
    Meg. Alas ! good-minded prince, you know
    not these things !
I am loth to reveal 'em. Keep this fault,
As you would keep your health from the hot
air   170
Of the corrupted people, or, by Heaven,
I will not fall alone. What I have known
Shall be as public as a print ; all tongues
Shall speak it as they do the language they
Are born in, as free and commonly ; I 'll set it,
Like a prodigious [1] star, for all to gaze at,   176
And so high and glowing, that other kingdoms
    far and foreign
Shall read it there, nay, travel with it, till they
    find
No tongue to make it more, nor no more peo-
    ple ;
And then behold the fall of your fair princess !
    King. Has she a boy ?   181
    Cle. So please your grace, I have seen a boy
On her, a fair boy.
    King.   Go, get you to your quarter :
For this time I will study to forget you.
    Meg. Do you study to forget me, and I 'll
study   185
To forget you.
        Exeunt KING, MEGRA, *and* Guard.
    Cle. Why, here 's a male spirit fit for Her-
cules. If ever there be Nine Worthies of women,
this wench shall ride astride and be their captain.   190
    Dion. Sure, she has a garrison of devils in her
tongue, she uttered such balls of wild-fire. She
has so nettled the King, that all the doctors in
the country will scarce cure him. That boy was
a strange-found-out antidote to cure her [195
infection ; that boy, that princess' boy ; that
brave, chaste, virtuous lady's boy ; and a fair
boy, a well-spoken boy ! All these considered,
can make nothing else — but there I leave you,
gentlemen.   200
    Thra. Nay, we 'll go wander with you.
                    Exeunt.

ACT III

SCENE I.[2]

Enter DION, CLEREMONT, *and* THRASILINE.

    Cle. Nay, doubtless, 't is true.
    Dion. Ay ; and 't is the gods
That rais'd this punishment, to scourge the
    King
With his own issue. Is it not a shame
For us that should write noble in the land,   5
For us that should be freemen, to behold
A man that is the bravery of his age,

Philaster, prest down from his royal right
By this regardless King ? and only look
And see the sceptre ready to be cast   10
Into the hands of that lascivious lady
That lives in lust with a smooth boy, now to be
    married
To yon strange prince, who, but that people
    please
To let him be a prince, is born a slave
In that which should be his most noble part,   15
His mind ?
    Thra. That man that would not stir with you
To aid Philaster, let the gods forget
That such a creature walks upon the earth !
    Cle. Philaster is too backward in 't himself.
The gentry do await it, and the people,   20
Against their nature, are all bent for him,
And like a field of standing corn, that 's moved
With a stiff gale, their heads bow all one way.
    Dion. The only cause that draws Philaster
    back
From this attempt is the fair princess' love,   25
Which he admires, and we can now confute.
    Thra. Perhaps he 'll not believe it.
    Dion. Why, gentlemen, 't is without question
    so.
    Cle. Ay, 't is past speech she lives dishon-
estly.
But how shall we, if he be curious,[3] work   30
Upon his faith ?
    Thra. We all are satisfied within ourselves.
    Dion. Since it is true, and tends to his own
    good,
I 'll make this new report to be my know-
    ledge ;
I 'll say I know it ; nay, I 'll swear I saw it.   35
    Cle. It will be best.
    Thra.   'T will move him.

              Enter PHILASTER.

    Dion.   Here he comes.
Good morrow to your honour : we have spent
Some time in seeking you.
    Phi.   My worthy friends,
You that can keep your memories to know
Your friend in miseries, and cannot frown   40
On men disgrac'd for virtue, a good day
Attend you all ! What service may I do
Worthy your acceptation ?
    Dion.   My good lord,
We come to urge that virtue, which we know
Lives in your breast, forth. Rise, and make a
    head ; [4]   45
The nobles and the people are all dull'd
With this usurping king ; and not a man,
That ever heard the word, or knew such a
    thing
As virtue, but will second your attempts.
    Phi. How honourable is this love in you   50
To me that have deserv'd none ! Know, my
    friends,
(You, that were born to shame your poor Phi-
    laster
With too much courtesy,) I could afford
To melt myself in thanks : but my designs

Are not yet ripe. Suffice it, that ere long   55
I shall employ your loves ; but yet the time
Is short of what I would.
  Dion. The time is fuller, sir, than you ex-
    pect ;
That which hereafter will not, perhaps, be
  reach'd
By violence, may now be caught. As for the
  King,   60
You know the people have long hated him ;
But now the princess, whom they lov'd ——
  Phi. Why, what of her ?
  Dion.   Is loath'd as much as he.
  Phi. By what strange means ?
  Dion.   She 's known a whore.
  Phi.   Thou liest.
  Dion. My lord ——   65
  Phi. Thou liest,
             Offers to draw and is held.
And thou shalt feel it ! I had thought thy
  mind
Had been of honour. Thus to rob a lady
Of her good name is an infectious sin
Not to be pardon'd. Be it false as hell,   70
'T will never be redeem'd, if it be sown
Amongst the people, fruitful to increase
All evil they shall hear. Let me alone
That I may cut off falsehood whilst it springs !
Set hills on hills betwixt me and the man   75
That utters this, and I will scale them all,
And from the utmost top fall on his neck,
Like thunder from a cloud.
  Dion.   This is most strange :
Sure, he does love her.
  Phi.   I do love fair truth.
She is my mistress, and who injures her   80
Draws vengeance from me. Sirs, let go my
  arms.
  Thra. Nay, good my lord, be patient.
  Cle. Sir, remember this is your honour'd
  friend,
That comes to do his service, and will show you
Why he utter'd this.
  Phi.   I ask your pardon, sir ;   85
My zeal to truth made me unmannerly :
Should I have heard dishonour spoke of you,
Behind your back, untruly, I had been
As much distemper'd and enrag'd as now.
  Dion. But this, my lord, is truth.
  Phi.   Oh, say not so !   90
Good sir, forbear to say so : 't is then truth,
That womankind is false : urge it no more ;
It is impossible. Why should you think
The princess light ?
  Dion.   Why, she was taken at it.   94
  Phi. 'T is false ! by Heaven, 't is false ! It
  cannot be !
Can it ? Speak, gentlemen ; for God's love,
  speak !
Is 't possible ? Can women all be damn'd ?
  Dion. Why, no, my lord.
  Phi.   Why, then, it cannot be.
  Dion. And she was taken with her boy.
  Phi.   What boy ?   99
  Dion. A page, a boy that serves her.
  Phi.   Oh, good gods !
A little boy ?

  Dion.   Ay ; know you him my lord ?
  Phi. [*Aside.*] Hell and sin know him ! — Sir,
  you are deceiv'd ;
I 'll reason it a little coldly with you.
If she were lustful, would she take a boy,
That knows not yet desire ? She would have
  one   105
Should meet her thoughts and know the sin he
  acts,
Which is the great delight of wickedness.
You are abus'd,[1] and so is she, and I.
  Dion. How you, my lord ?
  Phi.   Why, all the world 's abus'd   100
In an unjust report.
  Dion.   Oh, noble sir, your virtues
Cannot look into the subtle thoughts of wo-
  man !
In short, my lord, I took them ; I myself.
  Phi. Now, all the devils, thou didst ! Fly
  from my rage !
Would thou hadst ta'en devils engend'ring
  plagues,
When thou did'st take them ! Hide thee from
  mine eyes !   115
Would thou hadst taken thunder on thy breast,
When thou didst take them ; or been strucken
  dumb
For ever ; that this foul deed might have
  slept
In silence !
  Thra. Have you known him so ill-temper'd ?
  Cle. Never before.
  Phi.   The winds that are let loose   120
From the four several corners of the earth,
And spread themselves all over sea and land,
Kiss not a chaste one. What friend bears a
  sword
To run me thorough ?
  Dion.   Why, my lord, are you
So mov'd at this ?
  Phi.   When any fall from virtue,   125
I am distract ; I have an interest in 't.
  Dion. But, good my lord, recall yourself, and
  think
What 's best to be done.
  Phi.   I thank you ; I will do it.
Please you to leave me ; I 'll consider of it.
To-morrow I will find your lodging forth,   130
And give you answer.
  Dion.   All the gods direct you
The readiest way !
  Thra.   He was extreme impatient.
  Cle. It was his virtue and his noble mind.
    Exeunt DION, CLEREMONT, *and*
      THRASILINE.
  Phi. I had forgot to ask him where he took
  them ;
I 'll follow him. Oh that I had a sea   135
Within my breast, to quench the fire I feel !
More circumstances will but fan this fire :
It more afflicts me now, to know by whom
This deed is done, than simply that 't is done ;
And he that tells me this is honourable,   140
As far from lies as she is far from truth.
Oh, that, like beasts, we could not grieve our-
  selves

---

[1] Deceived.

With that we see not! Bulls and rams will
    fight
To keep their females standing in their sight;
But take 'em from them, and you take at
    once   145
Their spleens away; and they will fall again
Unto their pastures, growing fresh and fat,
And taste the waters of the springs as sweet
As 't was before, finding no start in sleep;   149
But miserable man ——

Enter BELLARIO.

           See, see, you gods,
He walks still; and the face you let him wear
When he was innocent is still the same,
Not blasted! Is this justice? Do you mean
To intrap mortality, that you allow
Treason so smooth a brow? I cannot now   155
Think he is guilty.
   Bel.   Health to you, my lord!
The princess doth commend her love, her life,
And this, unto you.   *Gives a letter.*
   Phi.   Oh, Bellario,
Now I perceive she loves me: she does show it
In loving thee, my boy, she has made thee
    brave.   160
   Bel. My lord, she has attir'd me past my wish,
Past my desert; more fit for her attendant,
Though far unfit for me who do attend.
   Phi. Thou art grown courtly, boy. — Oh, let
    all women,   164
That love black deeds, learn to dissemble here,
Here, by this paper! She does write to me
As if her heart were mines of adamant
To all the world besides; but, unto me,
A maiden-snow that melted with my looks. —
Tell me, my boy, how doth the princess use
    thee?   170
For I shall guess her love to me by that.
   Bel. Scarce like her servant, but as if I
    were,
Something allied to her, or had preserv'd
Her life three times by my fidelity;
As mothers fond do use their only sons,   175
As I 'd use one that 's left unto my trust,
For whom my life should pay if he met harm,
So she does use me.
   Phi.   Why, this is wondrous well:
But what kind language does she feed thee
    with?
   Bel. Why, she does tell me she will trust my
    youth   180
With all her loving secrets, and does call me
Her pretty servant; bids me weep no more
For leaving you; she 'll see my services
Regarded: and such words of that soft strain
That I am nearer weeping when she ends   185
Than ere she spake.
   Phi.   This is much better still.
   Bel. Are you not ill, my lord?
   Phi.   Ill? No, Bellario.
   Bel. Methinks your words
Fall not from off your tongue so evenly,
Nor is there in your looks that quietness   190
That I was wont to see.
   Phi.   Thou art deceiv'd, boy:
And she strokes thy head?

   Bel.   Yes.
   Phi. And she does clap thy cheeks?
   Bel.   She does, my lord.
   Phi. And she does kiss thee, boy? ha!
   Bel.   How, my lord?   194
   Phi. She kisses thee?
   Bel.   Never, my lord, by heaven.
   Phi. That 's strange, I know she does.
   Bel.   No, by my life.
   Phi. Why then she does not love me. Come,
    she does.
I bade her do it; I charg'd her, by all charms
Of love between us, by the hope of peace
We should enjoy, to yield thee all delights   200
Naked as to her bed; I took her oath
Thou shouldst enjoy her. Tell me, gentle boy,
Is she not parallelless? Is not her breath
Sweet as Arabian winds when fruits are ripe?
Are not her breasts two liquid ivory balls?   205
Is she not all a lasting mine of joy?
   Bel. Ay, now I see why my disturbed
    thoughts
Were so perplex'd. When first I went to her,
My heart held augury. You are abus'd;
Some villain hath abus'd you; I do see   210
Whereto you tend. Fall rocks upon his head
That put this to you! 'T is some subtle train
To bring that noble frame of yours to nought.
   Phi. Thou think'st I will be angry with
    thee. Come,   214
Thou shalt know all my drift. I hate her more
Than I love happiness, and plac'd thee there
To pry with narrow eyes into her deeds.
Hast thou discovered? Is she fallen to lust,
As I would wish her? Speak some comfort to
    me.
   Bel. My lord, you did mistake the boy you
    sent.   220
Had she the lust of sparrows or of goats,
Had she a sin that way, hid from the world,
Beyond the name of lust, I would not aid
Her base desires; but what I came to know
As servant to her, I would not reveal,   225
To make my life last ages.
   Phi.   Oh, my heart!
This is a salve worse than the main disease. —
Tell me thy thoughts; for I will know the
    least
That dwells within thee, or will rip thy heart
To know it. I will see thy thoughts as plain   230
As I do now thy face.
   Bel.   Why, so you do.
She is (for aught I know) by all the gods,
As chaste as ice! But were she foul as hell,
And I did know it thus, the breath of kings,
The points of swords, tortures, nor bulls of
    brass,   235
Should draw it from me.
   Phi.   Then it is no time
To dally with thee; I will take thy life,
For I do hate thee. I could curse thee now,
   Bel. If you do hate, you could not curse me
    worse;
The gods have not a punishment in store   240
Greater for me than is your hate.
   Phi.   Fie, fie,
So young and so dissembling! Tell me when

And where thou didst enjoy her, or let plagues
Fall on me, if I destroy thee not!
                        Draws his sword.
  Bel. By heaven, I never did; and when I
lie   245
To save my life, may I live long and loath'd!
Hew me asunder, and, whilst I can think,
I'll love those pieces you have cut away
Better than those that grow, and kiss those
limbs   249
Because you made 'em so.
  Phi.   Fear'st thou not death?
Can boys contemn that?
  Bel.   Oh, what boy is he
Can be content to live to be a man,
That sees the best of men thus passionate,
Thus without reason?
  Phi.   Oh, but thou dost not know
What 't is to die.
  Bel.   Yes, I do know, my lord: 255
'T is less than to be born; a lasting sleep;
A quiet resting from all jealousy,
A thing we all pursue. I know, besides,
It is but giving over a game   259
That must be lost.
  Phi.   But there are pains, false boy,
For perjur'd souls. Think but on those, and
then
Thy heart will melt, and thou wilt utter all.
  Bel. May they fall all upon me whilst I live,
If I be perjur'd, or have ever thought
Of that you charge me with! If I be false, 265
Send me to suffer in those punishments
You speak of; kill me!
  Phi.   Oh, what should I do?
Why, who can but believe him? He does
swear
So earnestly, that if it were not true,
The gods would not endure him. Rise, Bel-
lario: 270
Thy protestations are so deep, and thou
Dost look so truly when thou utter'st them,
That, though I know 'em false as were my
hopes,
I cannot urge thee further. But thou wert
To blame to injure me, for I must love 275
Thy honest looks, and take no revenge upon
Thy tender youth. A love from me to thee
Is firm, whate'er thou dost; it troubles me
That I have call'd the blood out of thy cheeks,
That did so well become thee. But, good boy,
Let me not see thee more: something is
done   281
That will distract me, that will make me mad,
If I behold thee. If thou tender'st me,
Let me not see thee.
  Bel.   I will fly as far
As there is morning, ere I give distaste 285
To that most honour'd mind. But through
these tears,
Shed at my hopeless parting, I can see
A world of treason practis'd upon you,
And her, and me. Farewell for evermore! 289
If you shall hear that sorrow struck me dead,
And after find me loyal, let there be
A tear shed from you in my memory,
And I shall rest in peace.   ***Exit.***

  Phi.   Blessing be with thee,
Whatever thou deserv'st! Oh, where shall I
Go bathe this body? Nature too unkind; 295
That made no medicine for a troubled mind!
                          Exit.

[Scene II.][1]

Enter ARETHUSA.

  Are. I marvel my boy comes not back again:
But that I know my love will question him
Over and over, — how I slept, wak'd, talk'd,
How I rememb'red him when his dear name
Was last spoke, and how when I sigh'd, wept,
sung,   5
And ten thousand such, — I should be angry at
his stay.

Enter KING.

  King. What, at your meditations! Who at-
tends you?
  Are. None but my single self. I need no
guard;
I do no wrong, nor fear none.
  King. Tell me, have you not a boy?
  Are.   Yes, sir. 10
  King. What kind of boy?
  Are.   A page, a waiting-boy.
  King. A handsome boy?
  Are.   I think he be not ugly:
Well qualified and dutiful I know him;
I took him not for beauty.
  King. He speaks and sings and plays?
  Are.   Yes, sir. 16
  King. About eighteen?
  Are.   I never ask'd his age.
  King. Is he full of service?
  Are. By your pardon, why do you ask?
  King. Put him away.
  Are.   Sir!
  King.   Put him away, I say.
H'as done you that good service shames me to
speak of.   20
  Are. Good sir, let me understand you.
  King.   If you fear me,
Show it in duty; put away that boy.
  Are. Let me have reason for it, sir, and then
Your will is my command.
  King. Do not you blush to ask it? Cast him
off,   26
Or I shall do the same to you. You're one
Shame with me, and so near unto myself,
That, by my life, I dare not tell myself
What you, myself, have done.
  Are. What have I done, my lord? 30
  King. 'T is a new language, that all love to
learn:
The common people speak it well already;
They need no grammar. Understand me well;
There be foul whispers stirring. Cast him off,
And suddenly. Do it! Farewell.   ***Exit.*** 34
  Are. Where may a maiden live securely free,
Keeping her honour fair? Not with the living.
They feed upon opinions, errors, dreams,
And make 'em truths; they draw a nourish-
ment

---

[1] Arethusa's apartment in the palace.

Out of defamings, grow upon disgraces,   40
And, when they see a virtue fortified
Strongly above the batt'ry of their tongues,
Oh, how they cast [1] to sink it! and, defeated,
(Soul-sick with poison) strike the monuments 44
Where noble names lie sleeping, till they sweat,
And the cold marble melt.

Enter PHILASTER.

Phi. Peace to your fairest thoughts, dearest
    mistress!
Are. Oh, my dearest servant,[2] I have a war
    within me!
Phi. He must be more than man that makes
    these crystals
Run into rivers. Sweetest fair, the cause?   50
And, as I am your slave, tied to your goodness,
Your creature, made again from what I was
And newly-spirited, I 'll right your honour.
Are. Oh, my best love, that boy?
Phi.   What boy?
Are. The pretty boy you gave me——
Phi.   What of him? 55
Are. Must be no more mine.
Phi.   Why?
Are.   They are jealous of him.
Phi. Jealous! Who?
Are.   The King.
Phi. [*Aside.*]   Oh, my misfortune!
Then 't is no idle jealousy. — Let him go.
Are. Oh, cruel!
Are you hard-hearted too? Who shall now tell
    you   60
How much I lov'd you? Who shall swear it to
    you,
And weep the tears I send? Who shall now
    bring you
Letters, rings, bracelets? Lose his health in
    service?
Wake tedious nights in stories of your praise?
Who shall now sing your crying elegies,   65
And strike a sad soul into senseless pictures,
And make them mourn? Who shall take up his
    lute,
And touch it till he crown a silent sleep
Upon my eye-lids, making me dream, and cry,
" Oh, my dear, dear Philaster! "
Phi. [*Aside.*]   Oh, my heart! 70
Would he had broken thee, that made me know
This lady was not loyal! — Mistress,
Forget the boy; I 'll get thee a far better.
Are. Oh, never, never such a boy again
As my Bellario!
Phi.   'T is but your fond affection. 75
Are. With thee, my boy, farewell for ever
All secrecy in servants! Farewell, faith,
And all desire to do well for itself!
Let all that shall succeed thee for thy wrongs
Sell and betray chaste love!   80
Phi. And all this passion for a boy?
Are. He was your boy, and you put him to me,
And the loss of such must have a mourning
    for.
Phi. Oh, thou forgetful woman!
Are.   How, my lord?

     [1] Plan.   [2] Lover.

Phi. False Arethusa!   85
Hast thou a medicine to restore my wits,
When I have lost 'em? If not, leave to talk,
And do thus.
Are.   Do what, sir? Would you sleep?
Phi. For ever, Arethusa. Oh, you gods
Give me a worthy patience! Have I stood,   90
Naked, alone, the shock of many fortunes?
Have I seen mischiefs numberless and mighty
Grow like a sea upon me? Have I taken
Danger as stern as death into my bosom,
And laught upon it, made it but a mirth,   95
And flung it by? Do I live now like him,
Under this tyrant King, that languishing
Hears his sad bell and sees his mourners? Do I
Bear all this bravely, and must sink at length
Under a woman's falsehood? Oh, that boy, 100
That cursed boy! None but a villain boy
To ease your lust?
Are.   Nay, then, I am betrayed:
I feel the plot cast for my overthrow.
Oh, I am wretched!
Phi. Now you may take that little right I
    have   105
To this poor kingdom. Give it to your joy;
For I have no joy in it. Some far place,
Where never womankind durst set her foot
For [3] bursting with her poisons, must I seek,
And live to curse you;   110
There dig a cave, and preach to birds and beasts
What woman is, and help to save them from
    you;
How heaven is in your eyes, but in your hearts
More hell than hell has; how your tongues, like
    scorpions,
Both heal and poison; [4] how your thoughts are
    woven   115
With thousand changes in one subtle web,
And worn so by you; how that foolish man,
That reads the story of a woman's face
And dies believing it, is lost for ever;
How all the good you have is but a shadow, 120
I ' the morning with you, and at night behind
    you,
Past and forgotten; how your vows are frosts,
Fast for a night, and with the next sun gone;
How you are, being taken all together,
A mere confusion, and so dead a chaos,   125
That love cannot distinguish. These sad texts,
Till my last hour, I am bound to utter of you.
So, farewell all my woe, all my delight! *Exit.*
Are. Be merciful, ye gods, and strike me
    dead!
What way have I deserv'd this? Make my
    breast   130
Transparent as pure crystall, that the world,
Jealous of me, may see the foulest thought
My heart holds. Where shall a woman turn her
    eyes,
To find out constancy?

Enter BELLARIO.

          Save me, how black
And guiltily, methinks, that boy looks now! 135

    [3] For fear of.
    [4] It was believed that scorpions, applied to the wound
they made, cured it.

Oh, thou dissembler, that, before thou spak'st,
Wert in thy cradle false, sent to make lies
And betray innocents ! Thy lord and thou
May glory in the ashes of a maid
Fool'd by her passion ; but the conquest is   140
Nothing so great as wicked. Fly away !
Let my command force thee to that which
  shame
Would do without it. If thou understood'st
The loathed office thou hast undergone,
Why, thou wouldst hide thee under heaps of
  hills,   145
Lest men should dig and find thee.
  Bel.   Oh, what god,
Angry with men, hath sent this strange dis-
  ease
Into the noblest minds ! Madam, this grief
You add unto me is no more than drops   149
To seas, for which they are not seen to swell.
My lord hath struck his anger through my
  heart,
And let out all the hope of future joys.
You need not bid me fly ; I came to part,
To take my latest leave. Farewell for ever !
I durst not run away in honesty   155
From such a lady, like a boy that stole
Or made some grievous fault. The power of
  gods
Assist you in your sufferings ! Hasty time
Reveal the truth to your abused lord
And mine, that he may know your worth ;
  whilst I   160
Go seek out some forgotten place to die ! *Exit.*
  Are. Peace guide thee ! Thou hast overthrown
  me once ;
Yet, if I had another Troy to lose,
Thou, or another villain with thy looks,   164
Might talk me out of it, and send me naked,
My hair dishevell'd, through the fiery streets.

Enter a Lady.

  Lady. Madam, the King would hunt, and
  calls for you
With earnestness.
  Are.   I am in tune to hunt !
Diana, if thou canst rage with a maid
As with a man,[1] let me discover thee   170
Bathing, and turn me to a fearful hind,
That I may die pursued by cruel hounds,
And have my story written in my wounds !
                                Exeunt.

ACT IV

SCENE I.[2]

Enter KING, PHARAMOND, ARETHUSA, GALA-
TEA, MEGRA, DION, CLEREMONT, THRASI-
LINE, *and* Attendants.

  King. What, are the hounds before and all
  the woodmen?
Our horses ready and our bows bent?
  Dion.   All, sir.
  King. [*to* PHARAMOND.] You are cloudy, sir.
  Come, we have forgotten

[1] Actaeon.   [2] Before the palace.

Your venial trepass ; let not that sit heavy
Upon your spirit; here's none dare utter it.   5
  Dion. He looks like an old surfeited stallion,
dull as a dormouse. See how he sinks ! The
wench has shot him between wind and water,
and, I hope, sprung a leak.
  Thra. He needs no teaching, he strikes [10
sure enough. His greatest fault is, he hunts too
much in the purlieus ; would he would leave off
poaching !
  Dion. And for his horn, h'as left it at the
lodge where he lay late. Oh, he's a precious [15
limehound ![3] Turn him loose upon the pursuit
of a lady, and if he lose her, hang him up i' the
slip. When my fox-bitch Beauty grows proud,
I'll borrow him.
  King, Is your boy turn'd away ?   20
  Are. You did command, sir, and I obey'd
you.
  King. 'T is well done. Hark ye further.
                      [*They talk apart.*]
  Cle. Is 't possible this fellow should repent ?
Methinks, that were not noble in him; and [25
yet he looks like a mortified member, as if he
had a sick man's salve[4] in 's mouth. If a worse
man had done this fault now, some physical[5]
justice or other would presently (without the
help of an almanack[6]) have opened the ob- [30
structions of his liver, and let him blood with a
dog-whip.
  Dion. See, see how modestly yon lady looks,
as if she came from churching with her neighbours ! Why, what a devil can a man see in [35
her face but that she's honest ![7]
  Thra. Faith, no great matter to speak of ; a
foolish twinkling with the eye, that spoils her
coat ;[8] but he must be a cunning herald that
finds it.   40
  Dion. See how they muster one another ! Oh,
there's a rank regiment where the devil carries
the colours and his dam drum-major ! Now the
world and the flesh come behind with the carriage.[9]   45
  Cle. Sure this lady has a good turn done her
against her will; before she was common talk,
now none dare say cantharides[10] can stir her.
Her face looks like a warrant, willing and commanding all tongues, as they will answer it, [50
to be tied up and bolted when this lady means
to let herself loose. As I live, she has got her a
goodly protection and a gracious ; and may use
her body discreetly for her health's sake, once
a week, excepting Lent and dog-days. Oh, [55
if they were to be got for money, what a great
sum would come out of the city for these
licences !
  King. To horse, to horse ! we lose the morning,
gentlemen.   *Exeunt.*   60

[3] A hunting dog. Lyme = *leash.*
[4] An allusion to a religious work, Thomas Bacon's *The Sicke Man's Salve,* 1561.
[5] Acting as a doctor.
[6] Almanacs gave the proper seasons for blood-letting.
[7] Chaste.
[8] Coat of arms. Mason explains that the reference is to the introduction of stars into a coat of arms, denot-ing a younger branch.
[9] Baggage.   [10] Spanish fly, used as a provocative.

[Scene II.] [1]

Enter two Woodmen.

1 *Wood.* What, have you lodged the deer?
2 *Wood.* Yes, they are ready for the bow.
1 *Wood.* Who shoots?
2 *Wood.* The princess.
1 *Wood.* No, she 'll hunt.
2 *Wood.* She 'll take a stand, I say.
1 *Wood.* Who else?
2 *Wood.* Why, the young stranger-prince.
1 *Wood.* He shall shoot in a stone-bow [2] for
me. I never lov'd his beyond-sea-ship since [10]
he forsook the say, [3] for paying ten shillings.
He was there at the fall of a deer, and would
needs (out of his mightiness) give ten groats
for the dowcets; marry, his steward would
have the velvet-head [4] into the bargain, to [15]
turf [5] his hat withal. I think he should love
venery; he is an old Sir Tristrem; for, if you be
rememb'red, he forsook the stag once to strike a
rascal [6] miching [7] in a meadow, and her he
kill'd in the eye. Who shoots else?   20
2 *Wood.* The Lady Galatea.
1 *Wood.* That 's a good wench, an she would
not chide us for tumbling of her women in the
brakes. She 's liberal, and by the Gods, they
say she 's honest, and whether that be a [25]
fault, I have nothing to do. There 's all?
2 *Wood.* No, one more; Megra.
1 *Wood.* That 's a firker, [8] i' faith, boy.
There 's a wench will ride her haunches as
hard after a kennel of hounds as a hunting [30]
saddle, and when she comes home, get 'em
clapt, and all is well again. I have known her
lose herself three times in one afternoon (if the
woods have been answerable), [9] and it has been
work enough for one man to find her, and [35]
he has sweat for it. She rides well and she pays
well. Hark! let 's go.   *Exeunt.*

Enter PHILASTER.

Phi. Oh, that I had been nourish'd in these
    woods
With milk of goats and acorns, and not known
The right of crowns nor the dissembling trains
Of women's looks; but digg'd myself a cave [41]
Where I, my fire, my cattle, and my bed,
Might have been shut together in one shed;
And then had taken me some mountain-girl,
Beaten with winds, chaste as the hard'ned
    rocks   45
Whereon she dwelt, that might have strewed
    my bed
With leaves and reeds, and with the skins of
    beasts,
Our neighbours, and have borne at her big
    breasts

---

[1] A forest.
[2] With a cross-bow for shooting stones.
[3] The assay or slitting of the deer, in order to test
the quality of the flesh, which involved a fee to the
keeper.
[4] The hart's horns, which are covered with velvet
pile when new.
[5] Re-cover.   [7] Creeping stealthily.   [9] Suitable.
[6] A lean doe.   [8] A fast one.

My large coarse issue! This had been a life
Free from vexation.

Enter BELLARIO.

Bel.   Oh, wicked men!   50
An innocent may walk safe among beasts;
Nothing assaults me here. See, my griev'd lord
Sits as his soul were searching out a way
To leave his body! — Pardon me, that must
Break thy last commandment; for I must
    speak.   55
You that are griev'd can pity; hear, my lord!
Phi. Is there a creature yet so miserable,
That I can pity?
Bel.   Oh, my noble lord,
View my strange fortune, and bestow on me,
According to your bounty (if my service   60
Can merit nothing), so much as may serve
To keep that little piece I hold of life
From cold and hunger!
Phi.   Is it thou? Be gone!
Go, sell those misbeseeming clothes thou wear'st,
And feed thyself with them.   65
Bel. Alas, my lord, I can get nothing for
    them!
The silly country-people think 't is treason
To touch such gay things.
Phi.   Now, by the gods, this is
Unkindly done, to vex me with thy sight.
Thou 'rt fallen again to thy dissembling trade;
How shouldst thou think to cozen me again? [71]
Remains there yet a plague untried for me?
Even so thou wept'st, and lookt'st, and spok'st
    when first
I took thee up.
Curse on the time! If thy commanding tears [75]
Can work on any other, use thy art;
I 'll not betray it. Which way wilt thou take,
That I may shun thee, for thine eyes are poison
To mine, and I am loth to grow in rage?
This way, or that way?   80
Bel. Any will serve; but I will choose to
    have
That path in chase that leads unto my grave.
        Exeunt severally.

Enter [on one side] DION, *and [on the other] the
    two* Woodmen.

Dion. This is the strangest sudden chance!
    — You, woodmen!
1 *Wood.* My lord Dion?
Dion. Saw you a lady come this way on a sable
    horse studded with stars of white?   85
2 *Wood.* Was she not young and tall?
Dion. Yes. Rode she to the wood or to the
    plain?
2 *Wood.* Faith, my lord, we saw none.
        Exeunt Woodmen.
Dion. Pox of your questions then!

Enter CLEREMONT.

        What, is she found?
Cle. Nor will be, I think.   90
Dion. Let him seek his daughter himself.
She cannot stray about a little necessary natural
business, but the whole court must be in arms.
When she has done, we shall have peace.

Cle. There's already a thousand father- [95
less tales amongst us. Some say, her horse ran
away with her; some, a wolf pursued her;
others, 't was a plot to kill her, and that arm'd
men were seen in the wood: but questionless
she rode away willingly. 100

Enter KING *and* THRASILINE.

King. Where is she?
Cle.   Sir, I cannot tell.
King.   How's that?
Answer me so again!
Cle.   Sir, shall I lie?
King. Yes, lie and damn, rather than tell me
that.
I say again, where is she? Mutter not! —
Sir, speak you; where is she?
Dion.   Sir, I do not know. 105
King. Speak that again so boldly, and, by
Heaven,
It is thy last! — You, fellows, answer me;
Where is she? Mark me, all; I am your
king:
I wish to see my daughter; show her me;
I do command you all, as you are subjects, 110
To show her me! What! am I not your king?
If ay, then am I not to be obeyed?
Dion. Yes, if you command things possible
and honest.
King. Things possible and honest! Hear me,
thou,—
Thou traitor, that dar'st confine thy King to
things 115
Possible and honest! Show her me,
Or, let me perish, if I cover not
All Sicily with blood!
Dion.   Faith, I cannot,
Unless you tell me where she is.
King. You have betray'd me; you have let
me lose 120
The jewel of my life. Go, bring her to me,
And set her here before me. 'T is the king
Will have it so; whose breath can still the
winds,
Uncloud the sun, charm down the swelling sea,
And stop the floods of heaven. Speak, can it
not? 125
Dion. No.   [this?
King.   No! cannot the breath of kings do
Dion. No; nor smell sweet itself, if once the
lungs
Be but corrupted.
King.   Is it so? Take heed!
Dion. Sir, take you heed how you dare the
powers
That must be just.
King.   Alas! what are we kings! 130
Why do you gods place us above the rest,
To be serv'd, flatter'd, and ador'd, till we
Believe we hold within our hands your thunder?
And when we come to try the power we have,
There's not a leaf shakes at our threat'nings.
I have sinn'd, 't is true, and here stand to be
punish'd; 135
Yet would not thus be punish'd. Let me choose
My way, and lay it on!
Dion. [*Aside.*] He articles with the gods.

Would somebody would draw bonds for the
performance of covenants betwixt them! 141

Enter PHARAMOND, GALATEA, *and* MEGRA.

King. What, is she found?
Pha.   No; we have ta'en her horse;
He gallopt empty by. There is some treason.
You, Galatea, rode with her into the wood;
Why left you her?
Gal.   She did command me. 145
King. Command! you should not.
Gal.   'T would ill become my fortunes and
my birth
To disobey the daughter of my king.
King. You're all cunning to obey us for our
hurt;
But I will have her.
Pha.   If I have her not, 150
By this hand, there shall be no more Sicily.
Dion. [*Aside.*] What, will he carry it to Spain
in's pocket?
Pha. I will not leave one man alive, but the
king,
A cook, and a tailor. 154
Dion. [*Aside.*] Yes; you may do well to spare
your lady-bedfellow; and her you may keep
for a spawner.
King. [*Aside.*] I see the injuries I have done
must be reveng'd.
Dion. Sir, this is not the way to find her out.
King. Run all, disperse yourselves. The man
that finds her, 160
Or (if she be kill'd) the traitor, I'll make him
great.
Dion. I know some would give five thousand
pounds to find her.
Pha. Come, let us seek.
King. Each man a several way; here I my-
self.
Dion. Come, gentlemen, we here. 165
Cle. Lady, you must go search too.
Meg. I had rather be search'd myself.
Exeunt [*severally*].

[SCENE III.]¹

Enter ARETHUSA.

Are. Where am I now? Feet, find me out a
way,
Without the counsel of my troubled head.
I'll follow you boldly about these woods,
O'er mountains, thorough brambles, pits, and
floods.
Heaven, I hope, will ease me: I am sick. 5
Sits down.

Enter BELLARIO.

Bel. [*Aside.*] Yonder's my lady. God knows
I want nothing,
Because I do not wish to live; yet I
Will try her charity. — Oh hear, you have
plenty!
From that flowing store drop some on dry
ground. — See,
The lively red is gone to guard her heart! 10

¹ Another part of the forest.

I fear she faints. — Madam, look up ! — She
  breathes not.—
Open once more those rosy twins, and send
Unto my lord your latest farewell ! — Oh, she
  stirs. —
How is it, Madam ? Speak comfort.
  Are.   'T is not gently done,
To put me in a miserable life,   15
And hold me there. I prithee, let me go ;
I shall do best without thee ; I am well.

Enter PHILASTER.

Phi. I am to blame to be so much in rage.
I 'll tell her coolly when and where I heard
This killing truth. I will be temperate   20
In speaking, and as just in hearing. ——
Oh, monstrous ! Tempt me not, you gods ! good
  gods,
Tempt not a frail man ! What 's he, that has
  a heart,
But he must ease it here !
  Bel. My lord, help, help ! The princess !   25
  Are. I am well : forbear.
  Phi. [*Aside.*] Let me love lightning, let me
  be embrac'd
And kist by scorpions, or adore the eyes
Of basilisks, rather than trust the tongues
Of hell-bred women ! Some good god look
  down,   30
And shrink these veins up ! Stick me here a
  stone,
Lasting to ages in the memory
Of this damn'd act ! — Hear me, you wicked
  ones !
You have put hills of fire into this breast,
Not to be quench'd with tears ; for which may
  guilt   35
Sit on your bosoms ! At your meals and beds
Despair await you ! What, before my face ?
Poison of asps between your lips ! Diseases
Be your best issues ! Nature make a curse,
And throw it on you !
  Are.   Dear Philaster, leave 40
To be enrag'd, and hear me.
  Phi.   I have done ;
Forgive my passion. Not the calmed sea,
When Aeolus locks up his windy brood,
Is less disturb'd than I. I 'll make you
  know 't.
Dear Arethusa, do but take this sword,   45
                    Offers his drawn sword.
And search how temperate a heart I have ;
Then you and this your boy may live and reign
In lust without control. — Wilt thou, Bellario ?
I prithee kill me ; thou art poor, and
  may'st   49
Nourish ambitious thoughts ; when I am dead,
Thy way were freer. Am I raging now ?
If I were mad, I should desire to live.
Sirs,[1] feel my pulse, whether you have known
A man in a more even tune to die.
  Bel. Alas, my lord, your pulse keeps mad-
  man's time !   55
So does your tongue.
  Phi.   You will not kill me, then ?

  Are. Kill you !
  Bel.   Not for the world.
  Phi.   I blame not thee,
Bellario ; thou hast done but that which gods
Would have transform'd themselves to do. Be
  gone,
Leave me without reply ; this is the last   60
Of all our meetings — (*Exit* BELLARIO.) Kill
  me with this sword ;
Be wise, or worse will follow : we are two
Earth cannot bear at once. Resolve to do,
Or suffer.   64
  Are. If my fortune be so good to let me fall
Upon thy hand, I shall have peace in death.
Yet tell me this, will there be no slanders,
No jealousy in the other world ; no ill there ?
  Phi. No.
  Are. Show me, then, the way.   70
  Phi. Then guide my feeble hand,
You that have power to do it, for I must
Perform a piece of justice ! — If your youth
Have any way offended Heaven, let prayers
Short and effectual reconcile you to it.   75
  Are. I am prepared.

Enter a Country Fellow.

  C. Fell. I 'll see the King, if he be in the
forest ; I have hunted him these two hours. If
I should come home and not see him, my sisters would laugh at me. I can see nothing [80
but people better hors'd than myself, that out-
ride me ; I can hear nothing but shouting.
These kings had need of good brains ; this
whooping is able to put a mean man out of
his wits. There 's a courtier with his sword [85
drawn ; by this hand, upon a woman, I think !
  Phi. Are you at peace ?
  Are.   With heaven and earth.
  Phi. May they divide thy soul and body !
                              Wounds her.
  C. Fell. Hold, dastard ! strike a woman !
Thou 'rt a craven. I warrant thee, thou [90
wouldst be loth to play half a dozen venies[2] at
wasters[3] with a good fellow for a broken head.
  Phi. Leave us, good friend,
  Are. What ill-bred man art thou, to intrude
thyself
Upon our private sports, our recreation ?   95
  C. Fell. God 'uds[4] me, I understand you not ;
but
I know the rogue has hurt you.
  Phi. Pursue thy own affairs : it will be ill
To multiply blood upon my head ; which thou
Wilt force me to.   100
  C. Fell. I know not your rhetoric ; but I can
lay it on, if you touch the woman.
  Phi. Slave, take what thou deservest !
                              They fight.
  Are.   Heavens guard my lord !
  C. Fell. Oh, do you breathe ?   104
  Phi. I hear the tread of people. I am hurt.
The gods take part against me : could this
  boor
Have held me thus else ? I must shift for life,
Though I do loathe it. I would find a course

---

[1] Formerly used to women as well as to men.

[2] Bouts.   [3] Cudgels.   [4] God judge.

To lose it rather by my will than force.
Exit.

C. Fell. I cannot follow the rogue. I pray
thee, wench, come and kiss me now. 111

Enter PHARAMOND, DION, CLEREMONT,
THRASILINE, *and* Woodmen.

Pha. What art thou?
C. Fell. Almost kill'd I am for a foolish
woman; a knave has hurt her. 114
Pha. The princess, gentlemen! — Where's
the wound, madam! Is it dangerous?
Are. He has not hurt me.
C. Fell. By God, she lies; h'as hurt her in
the breast;
Look else.
Pha. O sacred spring of innocent blood!
Dion. 'T is above wonder! Who should dare
this? 120
Are. I felt it not.
Pha. Speak, villain, who has hurt the prin-
cess?
C. Fell. Is it the princess?
Dion. Ay.
C. Fell. Then I have seen something yet. 125
Pha. But who has hurt her?
C. Fell. I told you, a rogue; I ne'er saw
him before, I.
Pha. Madam, who did it?
Are. Some dishonest wretch;
Alas, I know him not, and do forgive him!
C. Fell. He's hurt too; he cannot go far; [130
I made my father's old fox[1] fly about his ears.
Pha. How will you have me kill him?
Are. Not at all; 't is some distracted fellow.
Pha. By this hand, I 'll leave ne'er a piece
of him bigger than a nut, and bring him [135
all to you in my hat.
Are. Nay, good sir,
If you do take him, bring him quick[2] to me,
And I will study for a punishment
Great as his fault. 140
Pha. I will.
Are. But swear.
Cha. By all my love, I will. ——
Woodmen, conduct the princess to the King,
And bear that wounded fellow to dressing. ——
Come, gentlemen, we 'll follow the chase close.
Exeunt [*on one side*] PHARAMOND,
DION, CLEREMONT, *and* THRA-
SILINE; [*exit on the other*] ARE-
THUSA [*attended by*] 1 Woodman.
C. Fell. I pray you, friend, let me see [145
the King.
2 *Wood.* That you shall, and receive
thanks.
C. Fell. If I get clear with this, I 'll go see
no more gay sights. *Exeunt.* 150

[SCENE IV.][3]

Enter BELLARIO.

Bel. A heaviness near death sits on my brow,
And I must sleep. Bear me, thou gentle bank,

For ever, if thou wilt. You sweet ones all,
[*Lies down.*]
Let me unworthy press you; I could wish
I rather were a corse strew'd o'er with you 5
Than quick above you. Dulness[4] shuts mine
eyes,
And I am giddy: oh, that I could take
So sound a sleep that I might never wake!
[*Sleeps.*]

Enter PHILASTER.

Phi. I have done ill; my conscience calls me
false
To strike at her that would not strike at me. 10
When I did fight, methought I heard her
pray
The gods to guard me. She may be abus'd,
And I a loathed villain; if she be,
She will conceal who hurt her. He has wounds
And cannot follow; neither knows he me. 15
Who's this? Bellario sleeping! If thou be'st
Guilty, there is no justice that thy sleep
Should be so sound, and mine, whom thou hast
wrong'd,
So broken. (*Cry within.*) Hark! I am pursued.
You gods
I 'll take this offer'd means of my escape. 20
They have no mark to know me but my blood,
If she be true; if false, let mischief light
On all the world at once! Sword, print my
wounds
Upon this sleeping boy! I ha' none, I think,
Are mortal, nor would I lay greater on thee. 25
Wounds BELLARIO.
Bel. Oh, death, I hope, is come! Blest be
that hand!
It meant me well. Again, for pity's sake!
Phi. I have caught some. *Falls.*
The loss of blood hath stay'd my flight. Here,
here, 29
Is he that struck thee: take thy full revenge;
Use me, as I did mean thee, worse than death;
I 'll teach thee to revenge. This luckless hand
Wounded the princess; tell my followers[5]
Thou didst receive these hurts in staying me,
And I will second thee; get a reward. 35
Bel. Fly, fly, my lord, and save yourself!
Phi. How's this?
Wouldst thou I should be safe?
Bel. Else were it vain
For me to live. These little wounds I have
Ha' not bled much. Reach me that noble
hand;
I 'll help to cover you.
Phi. Art thou then true to me? 40
Bel. Or let me perish loath'd! Come, my
good lord,
Creep in amongst those bushes; who does
know
But that the gods may save your much-lov'd
breath?
Phi. Then I shall die for grief, if not for
this,
That I have wounded thee. What wilt thou
do? 45

---

[1] Broad sword.   [2] Alive.
[3] Another part of the forest.

[4] Sleepiness.   [5] Pursuers.

Bel. Shift for myself well. Peace! I hear 'em
come.   [PHILASTER *creeps into a bush.*]
[*Voices*] *within.* Follow, follow, follow! that
    way they went.
Bel. With my own wounds I'll bloody my
    own sword.
I need not counterfeit to fall; Heaven knows
That I can stand no longer.   *Falls.* 50

Enter PHARAMOND, DION, CLEREMONT, *and*
    THRASILINE.

Pha. To this place we have trackt him by
    his blood.
Cle. Yonder, my lord, creeps one away.
Dion. Stay, sir! what are you?
Bel. A wretched creature, wounded in these
    woods   54
By beasts. Relieve me, if your names be men,
Or I shall perish.
Dion.   This is he, my lord,
Upon my soul, that hurt her. 'T is the boy,
That wicked boy, that serv'd her.
Pha.   Oh, thou damn'd
In thy creation! What cause couldst thou shape
To hurt the princess?
Bel.   Then I am betrayed. 60
Dion. Betrayed! No, apprehended,
Bel.   I confess,
(Urge it no more) that, big with evil thoughts
I set upon her, and did make my aim,
Her death. For charity let fall at once
The punishment you mean, and do not load 65
This weary flesh with tortures.
Pha.   I will know
Who hir'd thee to this deed.
Bel.   Mine own revenge.
Pha. Revenge! for what?
Bel.   It pleas'd her to receive
Me as her page and, when my fortunes ebb'd,
That men strid o'er them careless, she did
    shower   70
Her welcome graces on me, and did swell
My fortunes till they overflow'd their banks,
Threat'ning the men that crost 'em; when, as
    swift
As storms arise at sea, she turn'd her eyes
To burning suns upon me, and did dry 75
The streams she had bestow'd, leaving me
    worse
And more contemn'd than other little brooks,
Because I had been great. In short, I knew
I could not live, and therefore did desire
To die reveng'd.
Pha.   If tortures can be found 80
Long as thy natural life, resolve to feel
The utmost rigour.
        PHILASTER *creeps out of the bush.*
Cle.   Help to lead him hence.
Phi. Turn back, you ravishers of innocence!
Know ye the price of that you bear away
So rudely?
Pha. Who's that?
Dion.   'T is the Lord Philaster. 85
Phi. 'T is not the treasure of all kings in one,
The wealth of Tagus, nor the rocks of pearl
That pave the court of Neptune, can weigh
    down

That virtue. It was I that hurt the princess.
Place me, some god, upon a pyramis [1] 90
Higher than hills of earth, and lend a voice
Loud as your thunder to me, that from hence
I may discourse to all the under-world
The worth that dwells in him!
Pha.   How's this?
Bel.   My lord, some man 95
Weary of life, that would be glad to die.
Phi. Leave these untimely courtesies, Bel-
    lario.
Bel. Alas, he's mad! Come, will you lead
    me on?
Phi. By all the oaths that men ought most
    to keep,
And gods to punish most when men do break,
He touch'd her not. —Take heed, Bellario, 100
How thou dost drown the virtues thou hast
    shown
With perjury. — By all that's good, 't was I!
You know she stood betwixt me and my right.
Pha. Thy own tongue be thy judge!
Cle.   It was Philaster.
Dion. Is 't not a brave boy? 105
Well, sirs, I fear me we were all deceived.
Phi. Have I no friend here?
Dion.   Yes.
Phi.   Then show it: some
Good body lend a hand to draw us nearer.
Would you have tears shed for you when you
    die?
Then lay me gently on his neck, that there 110
I may weep floods and breathe forth my spirit.
'T is not the wealth of Plutus, nor the gold
                [*Embraces Bel.*]
Lockt in the heart of earth, can buy away
This arm-full from me; this had been a ran-
    som   115
To have redeem'd the great Augustus Cæsar,
Had he been taken. You hard-hearted men,
More stony than these mountains, can you see
Such clear pure blood drop, and not cut your
    flesh
To stop his life, to bind whose bitter wounds,
Queens ought to tear their hair, and with their
    tears   120
Bathe 'em? — Forgive me, thou that art the
    wealth
Of poor Philaster!

Enter KING, ARETHUSA, *and* Guard.

King.   Is the villain ta'en?
Pha. Sir, here be two confess the deed; but
    sure
It was Philaster.
Phi.   Question it no more;
It was.
King. The fellow that did fight with him, 125
Will tell us that.
Are.   Aye me! I know he will.
King. Did not you know him?
Are.   Sir, if it was he,
He was disguis'd.
Phi.   I was so.— Oh, my stars,
That I should live still.   *Aside.*

---

[1] Pyramid.

King.   Thou ambitious fool,
Thou that hast laid a train for thy own life ! —
Now I do mean to do, I 'll leave to talk.   131
Bear them to prison.

Are. Sir, they did plot together to take hence
This harmless life ; should it pass unreveng'd,
I should to earth go weeping. Grant me, then,
By all the love a father bears his child,   136
Their custodies, and that I may appoint
Their tortures and their deaths.

Dion. Death ! Soft ; our law will not reach
that for this fault.

King. 'T is granted ; take 'em to you with a
guard. —   140
Come, princely Pharamond, this business past,
We may with security go on
To your intended match.

[*Exeunt all except* DION, CLERE-
MONT, *and* THRASILINE.]

Cle. I pray that this action lose not Philaster the hearts of the people.   145

Dion. Fear it not ; their over-wise heads will
think it but a trick.   *Exeunt.*

ACT V

SCENE I.[1]

Enter DION, CLEREMONT, *and* THRASILINE.

Thra. Has the King sent for him to death ?

Dion. Yes ; but the King must know 't is not
in his power to war with Heaven.

Cle. We linger time ; the King sent for Philaster and the headsman an hour ago.   5

Thra. Are all his wounds well ?

Dion. All ; they were but scratches ; but the
loss of blood made him faint.

Cle. We dally, gentlemen.

Thra. Away !   10

Dion. We 'll scuffle hard before we perish.
Exeunt.

[SCENE II.][2]

Enter PHILASTER, ARETHUSA, *and* BELLARIO.

Are. Nay, faith, Philaster, grieve not ; we are
well.

Bel. Nay, good my lord, forbear ; we 're
wondrous well.

Phi. Oh, Arethusa, oh, Bellario,
Leave to be kind !
I shall be shut from Heaven, as now from earth,
If you continue so. I am a man   6
False to a pair of the most trusty ones
That ever earth bore ; can it bear us all ?
Forgive, and leave me. But the King hath sent
To call me to my death : oh, shew it me,   10
And then forget me ! And for thee, my boy,
I shall deliver words will mollify
The hearts of beasts to spare thy innocence.

Bel. Alas, my lord, my life is not a thing
Worthy your noble thoughts ! 'T is not a life,   15
'T is but a piece of childhood thrown away.
Should I outlive you, I should then outlive
Virtue and honour ; and when that day comes,

If ever I shall close these eyes but once,
May I live spotted for my perjury,   20
And waste my limbs to nothing !

Are. And I (the woful'st maid that ever was,
Forc'd with my hands to bring my lord to
death)
Do by the honour of a virgin swear
To tell no hours beyond it !

Phi.   Make me not hated so.   25

Are. Come from this prison all joyful to our
deaths !

Phi. People will tear me, when they find you
true
To such a wretch as I ; I shall die loath'd.
Enjoy your kingdoms peacably, whilst I
For ever sleep forgotten with my faults.   30
Every just servant, every maid in love,
Will have a piece of me, if you be true.

Are. My dear lord, say not so.

Bel.   A piece of you !
He was not born of woman that can cut
It and look on.   35

Phi. Take me in tears betwixt you, for my
heart
Will break with shame and sorrow.

Are.   Why, 't is well.

Bel. Lament no more.

Phi.   Why, what would you have done
If you had wrong'd me basely, and had found
Your[3] life no price compar'd to mine ?[3] For
love, sirs,   40
Deal with me truly.

Bel.   'T was mistaken, sir.

Phi. Why, if it were ?

Bel.   Then, sir, we would have ask'd
You pardon.

Phi.   And have hope to enjoy it ?

Are. Enjoy it ! ay.

Phi.   Would you indeed ? Be plain.

Bel. We would, my lord.

Phi.   Forgive me, then.

Are.   So, so.   45

Bel. 'T is as it should be now.

Phi.   Lead to my death. *Exeunt.*

[SCENE III.][4]

Enter KING, DION, CLEREMONT, THRASILINE
[*and* Attendants].

King. Gentlemen, who saw the prince ?

Cle. So please you, sir, he 's gone to see the
city
And the new platform, with some gentlemen
Attending on him.

King.   Is the princess ready
To bring her prisoner out ?

Thra.   She waits your grace.   5

King. Tell her we stay.   *Exit* THRASILINE.

Dion. [*Aside.*] King, you may be deceiv'd yet.
The head you aim at cost more setting on
Than to be lost so lightly. If it must off, —
Like a wild overflow, that swoops before him
A golden stack, and with it shakes down
bridges,   10

---

[3] Mason conj. Qq. F. *my . . . yours.*

[1] Before the palace.   [2] A prison.   [4] A state-room in the palace.

Cracks the strong hearts of pines, whose cable-
   roots
Held out a thousand storms, a thousand thun-
   ders,
And, so made mightier, takes whole villages
Upon his back, and in that heat of pride   14
Charges strong towns, towers, castles, palaces,
And lays them desolate ; so shall thy head,
Thy noble head, bury the lives of thousands,
That must bleed with thee like a sacrifice,
In thy red ruins.

Enter ARETHUSA, PHILASTER, BELLARIO *in a
   robe and garland* [*and* THRASILINE].

  King. How now ? What masque is this?   20
  Bel. Right royal sir, I should
Sing you an epithalamion of these lovers,
But having lost my best airs with my fortunes,
And wanting a celestial harp to strike
This blessed union on, thus in glad story   25
I give you all. These two fair cedar-branches,
The noblest of the mountain where they grew,
Straightest and tallest, under whose still shades
The worthier beasts have made their lairs, and
   slept
Free from the fervour of the Sirian star   30
And the fell thunder-stroke, free from the
   clouds
When they were big with humour, and deliver'd
In thousand spouts their issues to the earth ;
Oh, there was none but silent quiet there !
Till never-pleased Fortune shot up shrubs,   35
Base under-brambles, to divorce these branches;
And for a while they did so, and did reign
Over the mountain, and choke up his beauty
With brakes, rude thorns and thistles, till the
   sun
Scorcht them even to the roots and dried them
   there.   40
And now a gentle gale hath blown again,
That made these branches meet and twine to-
   gether,
Never to be divided. The god that sings
His holy numbers over marriage-beds
Hath knit their noble hearts ; and here they
   stand   45
Your children, mighty King ; and I have done.
  King. How, how ?
  Are.   Sir, if you love it in plain truth,
(For now there is no masquing in 't,) this gen-
   tleman,
The prisoner that you gave me, is become
My keeper, and through all the bitter throes 50
Your jealousies and his ill fate have wrought
   him,
Thus nobly hath he struggled, and at length
Arrived here my dear husband.
  King.   Your dear husband ! —
Call in the Captain of the Citadel —
There you shall keep your wedding. I 'll pro-
   vide   55
A masque shall make your Hymen turn his saf-
   fron
Into a sullen coat, and sing sad requiems
To your departing souls.
Blood shall put out your torches ; and, instead
Of gaudy flowers about your wanton necks, 60

An axe shall hang, like a prodigious meteor,
Ready to crop your loves' sweets. Hear, you
   gods !
From this time do I shake all title off
Of father to this woman, this base woman ;
And what there is of vengeance in a lion   65
Chaft among dogs or robb'd of his dear young,
The same, enforc'd more terrible, more mighty,
Expect from me !
  Are. Sir, by that little life I have left to
   swear by,   69
There 's nothing that can stir me from myself.
What I have done, I have done without repent-
   ance,
For death can be no bugbear unto me,
So long as Pharamond is not my headsman.
  Dion. [*Aside.*] Sweet peace upon thy soul,
   thou worthy maid,
Whene'er thou diest ! For this time I 'll excuse
   thee,   75
Or be thy prologue.
  Phi.   Sir, let me speak next ;
And let my dying words be better with you
Than my dull living actions. If you aim
At the dear life of this sweet innocent,
You are a tyrant and a savage monster,   80
[That feeds upon the blood you gave a life to ;][1]
Your memory shall be as foul behind you,
As you are living ; all your better deeds
Shall be in water writ, but this in marble ; 84
No chronicle shall speak you, though your own,
But for the shame of men. No monument,
Though high and big as Pelion, shall be able
To cover this base murder : make it rich
With brass, with purest gold, and shining jas-
   per,
Like the Pyramides ; lay on epitaphs   90
Such as make great men gods ; my little mar-
   ble,
That only clothes my ashes, not my faults,
Shall far outshine it. And for after-issues,
Think not so madly of the heavenly wisdoms,
That they will give you more for your mad
   rage   95
To cut off, unless it be some snake, or something
Like yourself, that in his birth shall strangle
   you.
Remember my father, King ! There was a
   fault,
But I forgive it. Let that sin persuade you
To love this lady ; if you have a soul,   100
Think, save her, and be saved. For myself,
I have so long expected this glad hour,
So languisht under you, and daily withered,
That, Heaven knows, it is a joy to die ;
I find a recreation in 't.   105

Enter a Messenger.

  Mess. Where is the King ?
  King.   Here.
  Mess.   Get you to your strength,
And rescue the Prince Pharamond from dan-
   ger ;
He 's taken prisoner by the citizens,
Fearing[2] the Lord Philaster.

    1 Q₁. Other edd. omit.   *I. e.* fearing for

Dion. [Aside.]   Oh, brave followers!
Mutiny, my fine dear countrymen, mutiny!   110
Now, my brave valiant foremen, shew your
        weapons
In honour of your mistresses!

Enter a Second Messenger.

2 Mess. Arm, arm, arm, arm!
King. A thousand devils take 'em!
Dion. [Aside.] A thousand blessings on 'em!
2 Mess. Arm, O King! The city is in mu-
        tiny,   115
Led by an old gray ruffian, who comes on
In rescue of the Lord Philaster.
King. Away to the citadel! I 'll see them
        safe,
And then cope with these burghers. Let the
        guard   120
And all the gentlemen give strong attendance.
        Exeunt all except DION, CLERE-
            MONT, *and* THRASILINE.
Cle. The city up! This was above our wishes.
Dion. Ay, and the marriage too. By my life,
This noble lady has deceiv'd us all.
A plague upon myself, a thousand plagues,   125
For having such unworthy thoughts of her dear
        honour!
Oh, I could beat myself! Or do you beat me,
And I 'll beat you; for we had all one thought.
Cle. No no, 't will but lose time.   129
Dion. You say true. Are your swords sharp?
— Well, my dear countrymen What-ye-lacks,[1]
if you continue, and fall not back upon the first
broken skin, I 'll have you chronicled and
chronicled, and cut and chronicled, and all-to
be-prais'd and sung in sonnets, and bawled [135
in new brave ballads, that all tongues shall troll
you in *saecula saeculorum*, my kind can-carriers.
Thra. What, if a toy[2] take 'em i' th' heels
now, and they run all away, and cry, " the
devil take the hindmost "?   140
Dion. Then the same devil take the foremost
too, and souse him for his breakfast! If they
all prove cowards, my curses fly among them,
and be speeding! May they have murrains
reign to keep the gentlemen at home un-   [145
bound in easy frieze! May the moths branch[3]
their velvets, and their silks only be worn before sore eyes! May their false lights undo
'em, and discover presses,[4] holes, stains, and
oldness in their stuffs, and make them shop- [150
rid! May they keep whores and horses, and
break; and live mewed up with necks of beef
and turnips! May they have many children,
and none like the father! May they know no
language but that gibberish they prattle to [155
their parcels, unless it be the goatish Latin they
write in their bonds — and may they write that
false, and lose their debts!

Re-enter KING.

King. Now the vengeance of all the gods confound them! How they swarm together! [160
What a hum they raise! — Devils choke your

wild throats! — If a man had need to use their
valours, he must pay a brokage for it, and then
bring 'em on, and they will fight like sheep.
'T is Philaster, none but Philaster, must allay
this heat. They will not hear me speak, but [166
fling dirt at me and call me tyrant. Oh, run,
dear friend, and bring the Lord Philaster! Speak
him fair; call him prince; do him all the courtesy you can; commend me to him. Oh, my [170
wits, my wits!   *Exit* CLEREMONT.
Dion. [Aside.] Oh, my brave countrymen!
as I live, I will not buy a pin out of your walls
for this. Nay, you shall cozen me, and I 'll
thank you, and send you brawn and bacon, and
soil[5] you every long vacation a brace of fore- [175
men,[6] that at Michaelmas shall come up fat
and kicking.
King. What they will do with this poor
prince, the gods know, and I fear.   180
Dion. [Aside.] Why, sir, they 'll flay him,
and make church-buckets on 's skin, to quench
rebellion; then clap a rivet in 's sconce, and
hang him up for a sign.

Enter CLEREMONT *with* PHILASTER.

King. Oh, worthy sir, forgive me! Do not
        make   185
Your miseries and my faults meet together,
To bring a greater danger. Be yourself,
Still sound amongst diseases. I have wrong'd
        you;
And though I find it last, and beaten to it,
Let first your goodness know it. Calm the peo-
        ple,   190
And be what you were born to. Take your
        love,
And with her my repentance, all my wishes,
And all my prayers. By the gods, my heart
        speaks this;
And if the least fall from me not perform'd,
May I be struck with thunder!
Phi.   Mighty sir, 195
I will not do your greatness so much wrong,
As not to make your word truth. Free the
        princess
And the poor boy, and let me stand the shock
Of this mad sea-breach, which I 'll either
        turn,
Or perish with it.
King.   Let your own word free them. 200
Phi Then thus I take my leave, kissing your
        hand,
And hanging on your royal word. Be kingly,
And be not mov'd, sir. I shall bring you peace
Or never bring myself back.
King. All the gods go with thee.   *Exeunt.*

[SCENE IV.][7]

Enter an old Captain *and* Citizens *with* PHAR-
        AMOND.

Cap. Come, my brave myrmidons, let us fall
        on.
Let your caps swarm, my boys, and your nimble
        tongues

Forget your mother-gibberish of "what do you lack?"
And set your mouths ope, children, till your palates
Fall frighted half a fathom past the cure   5
Of bay-salt and gross pepper, and then cry
"Philaster, brave Philaster!" Let Philaster
Be deeper in request, my ding-dongs,[1]
My pairs of dear indentures,[2] kings of clubs,[2]
Than your cold water-camlets,[3] or your paintings   10
Spitted with copper.[4] Let not your hasty silks,
Or your branch'd cloth of bodkin,[5] or your tissues,
Dearly belov'd of spiced cake and custards,
Your Robin Hoods, Scarlets, and Johns, tie your affections
In darkness to your shops. No dainty duckers,[6]
Up with your three-pil'd spirits, your wrought valours;[7]   16
And let your uncut cholers[8] make the King feel
The measure of your mightiness. Philaster!
Cry, my rose-nobles,[9] cry!
All.   Philaster! Philaster!
Cap. How do you like this, my lord-prince?
These are mad boys, I tell you; these are things   21
That will not strike their top-sails to a foist,[10]
And let a man of war, an argosy,
Hull[11] and cry cockles.[12]
Pha. Why, you rude slave, do you know what you do?   25
Cap. My pretty prince of puppets, we do know;
And give your greatness warning that you talk
No more such bug's-words,[13] or that solder'd crown
Shall be scratch'd with a musket.[14] Dear prince Pippin,
Down with your noble blood, or, as I live,   30
I'll have you coddled.[15] — Let him loose, my spirits:
Make us a round ring with your bills, my Hectors,
And let us see what this trim man dares do.
Now, sir, have at you! here I lie;
And with this swashing blow (do you see, sweet prince?)   35
I could hulk[16] your grace, and hang you up cross-legg'd,
Like a hare at a poulter's, and do this with this wiper.[17]

[1] Darlings.
[2] Apprentices, who were bound by indentures, and whose usual weapons were clubs. Throughout these scenes, it is, of course, London citizens who are in view.
[3] A cloth, made of wool, sometimes mixed with silk, with a watered surface.
[4] Colored cloth interwoven with copper.
[5] Embroidered cloth, originally of gold and silk.
[6] Cringers (?), duck-hunters (?).
[7] A pun on velour.   [8] A pun on collars.
[9] Another pun. Rose-nobles were gold coins.
[10] A small vessel.   [12] Be basely occupied.
[11] Float idly.   [13] Swaggering words.
[14] A male sparrow-hawk, with a pun on the weapon.
[15] Stewed.   [16] Disembowel.
[17] Instrument for cleaning a gun.

Pha. You will not see me murder'd, wicked villains?
1 Cit. Yes, indeed, will we, sir; we have not seen one
For a great while.
Cap. He would have weapons, would he?   40
Give him a broadside, my brave boys, with your pikes;
Branch me his skin in flowers like a satin,
And between every flower a mortal cut. —
Your royalty shall ravel![18] — Jag him, gentlemen;
I'll have him cut to the kell,[19] then down the seams.   45
O for a whip to make him galloon-laces![20]
I'll have a coach-whip.
Pha.   Oh, spare me, gentlemen!
Cap. Hold, hold;
The man begins to fear and know himself.
He shall for this time only be seel'd up,[21]   50
With a feather through his nose, that he may only
See heaven, and think whither he is going.
Nay, my beyond-sea sir, we will proclaim you:
You would be king!
Thou tender heir apparent to a church-ale,[22]   55
Thou slight prince of single sarcenet,[23]
Thou royal ring-tail,[24] fit to fly at nothing
But poor men's poultry, and have every boy
Beat thee from that too with his bread and butter!
Pha. Gods keep me from these hell-hounds!
1 Cit. Shall's geld him, captain?   61
Cap. No, you shall spare his dowcets, my dear donsels:[25]
As you respect the ladies, let them flourish.
The curses of a longing woman kill
As speedy as a plague, boys.   65
1 Cit. I'll have a leg, that's certain.
2 Cit.   I'll have an arm.
3 Cit. I'll have his nose, and at mine own charge build
A college and clap 't upon the gate.[26]
4 Cit. I'll have his little gut to string a kit[27] with;
For certainly a royal gut will sound like silver.
Pha. Would they were in thy belly, and I past   71
My pain once!
5 Cit. Good captain, let me have his liver to feed ferrets.
Cap. Who will have parcels else? Speak.
Pha. Good gods, consider me! I shall be tortur'd.   75
1 Cit. Captain, I'll give you the trimming of your two-hand sword,
And let me have his skin to make false scabbards.

[18] Fray out.   [19] The caul about the hart's paunch.
[20] Ribbons, tape.
[21] Have his eyelids sewed together like a hawk's.
[22] *I. e.* a bastard, one born after the convivialities of a church feast.
[23] Thin silk.
[24] A sort of kite.   [25] Diminutive of *dons*.
[26] In allusion to Brazenose College, Oxford.
[27] Cittern.

2 *Cit.* He had no horns, sir, had he?

Cap. No, sir, he 's a pollard.[1]

What wouldst thou do with horns?

2 *Cit.* Oh, if he had had, 80
I would have made rare hafts and whistles of
'em;
But his shin-bones, if they be sound, shall serve
me.

Enter PHILASTER.

All. Long live Philaster, the brave Prince
Philaster!

Phi. I thank you, gentlemen. But why are
these
Rude weapons brought abroad, to teach your
hands 85
Uncivil trades?

Cap. My royal Rosicleer,[2]
We are thy myrmidons, thy guard, thy roar-
ers;[3]
And when thy noble body is in durance,
Thus do we clap our musty murrions[4] on,
And trace the streets in terror. Is it peace, 90
Thou Mars of men? Is the King sociable,
And bids thee live? Art thou above thy foe-
men,
And free as Phoebus? Speak. If not, this
stand[5]
Of royal blood shall be abroach, a-tilt,
And run even to the lees of honour. 95

Phi. Hold, and be satisfied. I am myself;
Free as my thoughts are; by the gods, I am!

Cap. Art thou the dainty darling of the
King?
Art thou the Hylas to our Hercules?
Do the lords bow, and the regarded scarlets[6]
Kiss their gumm'd golls,[7] and cry, "We are
your servants"? 101
Is the court navigable and the presence stuck
With flags of friendship? If not, we are thy
castle,
And this man sleeps.

Phi. I am what I desire to be, your friend;
I am what I was born to be, your prince. 106

Pha. Sir, there is some humanity in you;
You have a noble soul. Forget my name,
And know my misery; set me safe aboard
From these wild cannibals, and as I live, 110
I 'll quit this land for ever. There is nothing,—
Perpetual prisonment, cold, hunger, sickness
Of all sorts, of all dangers, and all together,
The worst company of the worst men, madness,
age,
To be as many creatures as a woman, 115
And do as all they do, nay, to despair,—
But I would rather make it a new nature,
And live with all these, than endure one hour
Amongst these wild dogs.

Phi. I do pity you. — Friends, discharge your
fears; 120

1 Hornless animal.

2 A hero in *The Mirrour of Knighthood*, a romance
from the Spanish. See *The Knight of the Burning
Pestle*.

3 Roistering blades.

4 Steel caps.

5 Cask (Pharamond).

6 Courtiers clad in scarlet.

7 Perfumed hands.

Deliver me the prince. I 'll warrant you
I shall be old enough to find my safety.

3 *Cit.* Good sir, take heed he does not hurt
you;
He is a fierce man, I can tell you, sir.

Cap. Prince, by your leave, I 'll have a sur-
cingle,[8] 125
And make[9] you like a hawk. [PHAR.] *strives.*

Phi. Away, away, there is no danger in him:
Alas, he had rather sleep to shake his fit off!
Look you, friends, how gently he leads! Upon
my word,
He 's tame enough, he needs no further watch-
ing. 130
Good my friends, go to your houses,
And by me have your pardons and my love;
And know there shall be nothing in my power
You may deserve, but you shall have your
wishes.
To give you more thanks, were to flatter you.
Continue still your love; and for an earnest, 136
Drink this. [*Gives money.*]

All. Long mayst thou live, brave prince,
brave prince, brave prince!

Exeunt PHIL. *and* PHAR.

Cap. Go thy ways, thou art the king of court-
esy!
Fall off again, my sweet youths. Come, 140
And every man trace to his house again,
And hang his pewter up; then to the tavern,
And bring your wives in muffs. We will have
music;
And the red grape shall make us dance and rise,
boys. *Exeunt.*

[SCENE V.][10]

Enter KING, ARETHUSA, GALATEA, MEGRA,
DION, CLEREMONT, THRASILINE, BELLARIO,
and Attendants.

King. Is it appeas'd?

Dion. Sir, all is quiet as this dead of night,
As peaceable as sleep. My lord Philaster
Brings on the prince himself.

King. Kind gentleman!
I will not break the least word I have given 5
In promise to him. I have heap'd a world
Of grief upon his head, which yet I hope
To wash away.

Enter PHILASTER *and* PHARAMOND.

Cle. My lord is come.

King. My son!
Blest be the time that I have leave to call
Such virtue mine! Now thou art in mine arms,
Methinks I have a salve unto my breast 11
For all the stings that dwell there. Streams of
grief
That I have wrong'd thee, and as much of joy
That I repent it, issue from mine eyes;
Let them appease thee. Take thy right; take
her; 15
She is thy right too; and forget to urge
My vexed soul with that I did before.

Phi. Sir. it is blotted from my memory,

8 Band.

9 Train.

10 An apartment in the palace.

Past and forgotten. — For you, prince of Spain,
Whom I have thus redeem'd, you have full
　　leave　　　　　　　　　　　　　　　　20
To make an honourable voyage home.
And if you would go furnish'd to your realm
With fair provision, I do see a lady,
Methinks, would gladly bear you company.
How like you this piece ?
　　Meg.　　　　　　　Sir, he likes it well, 25
For he hath tried it, and hath found it worth
His princely liking. We were ta'en abed ;
I know your meaning. I am not the first
That nature taught to seek a fellow forth ;
Can shame remain perpetually in me,　　30
And not in others ? Or have princes salves
To cure ill names, that meaner people want ?
　　Phi. What mean you ?
　　Meg.　　　　　You must get another ship,
To bear the princess and her boy together.
　　Dion. How now !　　　　　　　　　35
　　Meg. Others took me, and I took her and
　　him
At that all women may be ta'en sometime.
Ship us all four, my lord ; we can endure
Weather and wind alike.
　　King. Clear thou thyself, or know not me
　　for father.　　　　　　　　　　　　40
　　Are. This earth, how false it is ! What means
is left for me
To clear myself ? It lies in your belief.
My lords, believe me ; and let all things else
Struggle together to dishonour me.
　　Bel. Oh, stop your ears, great King, that I
　　may speak　　　　　　　　　　　　45
As freedom would ! Then I will call this lady
As base as are her actions. Hear me, sir ;
Believe your heated blood when it rebels
Against your reason, sooner than this lady.
　　Meg. By this good light, he bears it hand-
　　somely.　　　　　　　　　　　　　50
　　Phi. This lady ! I will sooner trust the wind
With feathers, or the troubled sea with pearl,
Than her with any thing. Believe her not.
Why, think you, if I did believe her words,
I would outlive 'em ? Honour cannot take　55
Revenge on you ; then what were to be known
But death ?
　　King.　　　Forget her, sir, since all is knit
Between us. But I must request of you
One favour, and will sadly[1] be denied.
　　Phi. Command, whate'er it be.
　　King.　　　　　　Swear to be true　60
To what you promise.
　　Phi.　　　　By the powers above,
Let it not be the death of her or him,
And it is granted !
　　King.　　　Bear away that boy
To torture ; I will have her clear'd or buried.
　　Phi. Oh, let me call my word back, worthy sir !
Ask something else : bury my life and right　66
In one poor grave ; but do not take away
My life and fame at once.
　　King. Away with him ! It stands irrevocable.
　　Phi. Turn all your eyes on me. Here stands
　　a man,　　　　　　　　　　　　　70

[1] Shall be sorry to be denied.

The falsest and the basest of this world.
Set swords against this breast, some honest man,
For I have liv'd till I am pitied !
My former deeds were hateful ; but this last
Is pitiful, for I unwillingly　　　　　　75
Have given the dear preserver of my life
Unto his torture. Is it in the power
Of flesh and blood to carry this, and live ?
　　　　　　　　Offers to stab himself.
　　Are. Dear sir, be patient yet ! Oh, stay that
　　hand !
　　King. Sirs, strip that boy.
　　Dion.　　　Come, sir ; your tender flesh　80
Will try your constancy.
　　Bel.　　　　Oh, kill me, gentlemen !
　　Dion. No.— Help, sirs.
　　Bel.　　　　　Will you torture me ?
　　King.　　　　　Haste there ;
Why stay you ?
　　Bel.　　　Then I shall not break my vow,
You know, just gods, though I discover all.
　　King. How 's that ? Will he confess ?
　　Dion.　　　Sir, so he says. 85
　　King. Speak then.
　　Bel.　　　Great King, if you command
This lord to talk with me alone, my tongue
Urg'd by my heart, shall utter all the thoughts
My youth hath known ; and stranger things
　　than these
You hear not often.
　　King.　　　Walk aside with him. 90
　　　　　　[DION *and* BELLARIO *walk apart.*]
　　Dion. Why speak'st thou not ?
　　Bel.　　Know you this face, my lord ?
　　Dion. No.
　　Bel.　　Have you not seen it, nor the like ?
　　Dion. Yes, I have seen the like, but readily
I know not where.
　　Bel.　　　I have been often told
In court of one Euphrasia, a lady,　　　95
And daughter to you ; betwixt whom and me
They that would flatter my bad face would swear
There was such strange resemblance, that we
　　two
Could not be known asunder, drest alike.
　　Dion. By Heaven, and so there is !
　　Bel.　　　For her fair sake, 100
Who now doth spend the spring-time of her life
In holy pilgrimage, move to the King,
That I may scape this torture.
　　Dion.　　　But thou speak'st
As like Euphrasia as thou dost look.
How came it to thy knowledge that she lives 105
In pilgrimage ?
　　Bel.　　I know it not, my lord ;
But I have heard it, and do scarce believe it.
　　Dion. Oh, my shame ! is it possible ? Draw
　　near,
That I may gaze upon thee. Art thou she,
Or else her murderer ?[2] Where wert thou
　　born ?　　　　　　　　　　　　110
　　Bel. In Syracusa.
　　Dion.　　　What 's thy name ?
　　Bel.　　　　　Euphrasia.

[2] In some barbarous countries, it was believed that
the murderer inherited the form and qualities of his
victim. (Mason.)

Dion. Oh, 'tis just, 'tis she !
Now I do know thee. Oh, that thou hadst died,
And I had never seen thee nor my shame !
How shall I own thee ? Shall this tongue of
    mine   115
E'er call thee daughter more ?
    Bel. Would I had died indeed ! I wish it too ;
And so I must have done by vow, ere publish'd
What I have told, but that there was no means
To hide it longer. Yet I joy in this,   120
The princess is all clear.
    King.   What, have you done ?
    Dion. All is discovered.
    Phi.   Why then hold you me ?
All is discovered ! Pray you, let me go.
                Offers to stab himself.
    King. Stay him.
    Are.   What is discovered ?
    Dion.   Why, my shame.
It is a woman ; let her speak the rest.   125
    Phi. How ? That again !
    Dion.   It is a woman.
    Phi. Blest be you powers that favour inno-
    cence !
    King. Lay hold upon that lady.
                [MEGRA *is seized.*]
    Phi. It is a woman, sir ! — Hark, gentlemen,
It is a woman ! — Arethusa, take   130
My soul into thy breast, that would be gone
With joy. It is a woman ! Thou art fair,
And virtuous still to ages, in despite
Of malice.
    King. Speak you, where lies his shame ?
    Bel.   I am his daughter. 135
    Phi. The gods are just.
    Dion. I dare accuse none ; but, before you
    two,
The virtue of our age, I bend my knee
For mercy.   [*Kneels.*]
    Phi. [*raising him.*] Take it freely ; for I know,
Though what thou didst were undiscreetly
    done,   140
'T was meant well.
    Are.   And for me,
I have a power to pardon sins, as oft
As any man has power to wrong me.
    Cle. Noble and worthy !
    Phi.   But, Bellario,
(For I must call thee still so,) tell me why 145
Thou didst conceal thy sex. It was a fault,
A fault, Bellario, though thy other deeds
Of truth outweigh'd it : all these jealousies
Had flown to nothing if thou hadst discovered
What now we know.
    Bel.   My father oft would speak 150
Your worth and virtue ; and, as I did grow
More and more apprehensive,[1] I did thirst
To see the man so prais'd. But yet all this
Was but a maiden-longing, to be lost
As soon as found ; till, sitting in my window, 155
Printing my thoughts in lawn, I saw a god,
I thought, (but it was you,) enter our gates.
My blood flew out and back again, as fast
As I had puft it forth and suckt it in   159
Like breath. Then was I call'd away in haste

    [1] Quick to understand.

To entertain you. Never was a man,
Heav'd from a sheep-cote to a sceptre, rais'd
So high in thoughts as I. You left a kiss
Upon these lips then, which I mean to keep
From you for ever. I did hear you talk, 165
Far above singing. After you were gone,
I grew acquainted with my heart, and search'd
What stirr'd it so : alas, I found it love !
Yet far from lust ; for, could I but have liv'd
In presence of you, I had had my end. 170
For this I did delude my noble father
With a feign'd pilgrimage, and drest myself
In habit of a boy ; and, for I knew
My birth no match for you, I was past hope
Of having you ; and, understanding well 175
That when I made discovery of my sex
I could not stay with you, I made a vow,
By all the most religious things a maid
Could call together, never to be known,
Whilst there was hope to hide me from men's
    eyes, 180
For other than I seem'd, that I might ever
Abide with you. Then sat I by the fount,
Where first you took me up.
    King.   Search out a match
Within our kingdom, where and when thou wilt,
And I will pay thy dowry ; and thyself 185
Wilt well deserve him.
    Bel.   Never, sir, will I
Marry ; it is a thing within my vow :
But, if I may have leave to serve the princess,
To see the virtues of her lord and her,
I shall have hope to live.
    Are.   I, Philaster, 190
Cannot be jealous, though you had a lady
Drest like a page to serve you ; nor will I
Suspect her living here.— Come, live with me ;
Live free as I do, She that loves my lord,
Curst be the wife that hates her ! 195
    Phi. I grieve such virtue should be laid in
    earth
Without an heir. — Hear me, my royal father :
Wrong not the freedom of our souls so much,
To think to take revenge of that base woman ;
Her malice cannot hurt us. Set her free 200
As she was born, saving from shame and sin.
    King. Set her at liberty.— But leave the
    court :
This is no place for such.— You, Pharamond,
Shall have free passage, and a conduct home
Worthy so great a prince. When you come
    there, 205
Remember 't was your faults that lost you her,
And not my purpos'd will.
    Pha.   I do confess,
Renowned sir.
    King. Last, join your hands in one. Enjoy,
    Philaster,
This kingdom, which is yours, and, after me, 210
Whatever I call mine. My blessing on you !
All happy hours be at your marriage-joys,
That you may grow yourselves over all lands,
And live to see your plenteous branches spring
Wherever there is sun ! Let princes learn 215
By this to rule the passions of their blood ;
For what Heaven wills can never be withstood.
                    Exeunt omnes.

THE MAID'S TRAGEDY

BY

FRANCIS BEAUMONT AND JOHN FLETCHER

[DRAMATIS PERSONAE.]

KING.
LYSIPPUS, brother to the King..
AMINTOR, [a noble Gentleman.]
MELANTIUS, } brothers to Evadne.
DIPHILUS, }
CALIANAX, an old humorous Lord, and father to Aspatia.
CLEON, } Gentlemen.
STRATO, }
DIAGORAS, a servant.

[Lords, Gentlemen, Servants, etc.]

EVADNE, wife to Amintor.
ASPATIA, troth-plight wife to Amintor.
ANTIPHILA, } waiting gentlewomen to Aspatia.
OLYMPIAS, }
DULA, a Lady, [attendant on Evadne.]
[Ladies.]

MASQUERS.

Night, Cynthia, Neptune, Aeolus, [Sea Gods, Winds.]

[SCENE. — *The City of Rhodes.*]

ACT I

SCENE I.[1]

Enter CLEON, STRATO, LYSIPPUS, *and* DIPHILUS.

Cle. The rest are making ready, sir.
Lys. So let them; there's time enough.
Diph. You are the brother to the King, my lord;
We'll take your word.
Lys. Strato, thou hast some skill in poetry; 5
What think'st thou of the masque? Will it be well?
Stra. As well as masques can be.
Lys. As masques can be!
Stra. Yes; they must commend their king, and speak in praise
Of the assembly, bless the bride and bridegroom
In person of some god; they're tied to rules 10
Of flattery.
Cle. See, good my lord, who is return'd!

Enter MELANTIUS.

Lys. Noble Melantius, the land by me
Welcomes thy virtues home to Rhodes;
Thou that with blood abroad buyest our peace!
The breath of kings is like the breath of gods; 15
My brother wisht thee here, and thou art here.
He will be too kind, and weary thee
With often welcomes; but the time doth give thee
A welcome above his or all the world's.
Mel. My lord, my thanks; but these scratcht limbs of mine 20
Have spoke my love and truth unto my friends,
More than my tongue e'er could. My mind's the same

---

¹ An apartment in the palace.

It ever was to you: where I find worth,
I love the keeper till he let it go,
And then I follow it.
Diph. Hail, worthy brother! 25
He that rejoices not at your return
In safety is mine enemy for ever.
Mel. I thank thee, Diphilus. But thou art faulty:
I sent for thee to exercise thine arms
With me at Patria; thou cam'st not, Diphilus;
'T was ill.
Diph. My noble brother, my excuse 31
Is my king's strict command, which you, my lord,
Can witness with me.
Lys. 'T is most true, Melantius;
He might not come till the solemnities
Of this great match were past.
Diph. Have you heard of it? 35
Mel. Yes, and have given cause to those that here
Envy my deeds abroad to call me gamesome:
I have no other business here at Rhodes.
Lys. We have a masque to-night, and you must tread
A soldier's measure. 40
Mel. These soft and silken wars are not for me:
The music must be shrill and all confus'd
That stirs my blood; and then I dance with arms.
But is Amintor wed?
Diph. This day.
Mel. All joys upon him! for he is my friend.
Wonder not that I call a man so young my friend: 45
His worth is great; valiant he is and temperate;
And one that never thinks his life his own,
If his friend need it. When he was a boy,
As oft as I return'd (as, without boast, 50

I brought home conquest), he would gaze upon
    me
And view me round, to find in what one limb
The virtue lay to do these things he heard ;
Then would he wish to see my sword, and feel
The quickness of the edge, and in his hand   55
Weigh it. He oft would make me smile at this.
His youth did promise much, and his ripe years
Will see it all perform'd.

      Enter ASPATIA, *passing by.*

                 Hail, maid and wife !
Thou fair Aspatia, may the holy knot
That thou hast tied to-day last till the hand   60
Of age undo 't ! May'st thou bring a race
Unto Amintor, that may fill the world
Successively with soldiers !

Asp.   My hard fortunes
Deserve not scorn, for I was never proud
When they were good.   *Exit.*

Mel.   How 's this ?
Lys.   You are mistaken, sir ;   65
She is not married.
Mel.   You said Amintor was.
Diph. 'T is true ; but ——
Mel.   Pardon me ; I did receive
Letters at Patria from my Amintor,
That he should marry her.
Diph.   And so it stood
In all opinion long ; but your arrival   70
Made me imagine you had heard the change.
Mel. Who hath he taken then ?
Lys.   A lady, sir,
That bears the light about [1] her, and strikes
    dead
With flashes of her eye ; the fair Evadne,
Your virtuous sister.
Mel.   Peace of heart betwixt them !   75
But this is strange.
Lys.   The King, my brother, did it
To honour you ; and these solemnities
Are at his charge.
Mel. 'T is royal, like himself. But I am sad
My speech bears so unfortunate a sound   80
To beautiful Aspatia. There is rage
Hid in her father's breast, Calianax,
Bent long against me ; and he should not think,
If I could call it back, that I would take
So base revenges, as to scorn the state   85
Of his neglected daughter. Holds he still
His greatness with the King ?
Lys.   Yes. But this lady
Walks discontented, with her watery eyes
Bent on the earth. The unfrequented woods
Are her delight ; where, when she sees a bank
Stuck full of flowers, she with a sigh will tell   91
Her servants what a pretty place it were
To bury lovers in ; and make her maids
Pluck 'em, and strow her over like a corse.
She carries with her an infectious grief,   95
That strikes all her beholders : she will sing
The mournful'st things that ever ear hath
    heard,
And sigh, and sing again ; and when the rest

Of our young ladies, in their wanton blood,
Tell mirthful tales in course,[2] that fill the room
With laughter, she will, with so sad a look,   100
Bring forth a story of the silent death
Of some forsaken virgin, which her grief
Will put in such a phrase that, ere she end,
She 'll send them weeping one by one away.   105
Mel. She has a brother under my command,[3]
Like her ; a face as womanish as hers ;
But with a spirit that hath much outgrown
The number of his years.

          Enter AMINTOR.

Cle.   My lord the bridegroom !
Mel. I might run fiercely, not more hastily,
Upon my foe. I love thee well, Amintor ;   110
My mouth is much too narrow for my heart ;
I joy to look upon those eyes of thine ;
Thou art my friend, but my disordered speech
Cuts off my love.
Amin.   Thou art Melantius ;   115
All love is spoke in that. A sacrifice,
To thank the gods Melantius is return'd
In safety ! Victory sits on his sword,
As she was wont. May she build there and
    dwell !
And may thy armour be, as it hath been,   120
Only thy valour and thine innocence !
What endless treasures would our enemies give,
That I might hold thee still thus !
Mel.   I am poor
In words ; but credit me, young man, thy
    mother   124
Could do no more but weep for joy to see thee
After long absence. All the wounds I have
Fetcht not so much away, nor all the cries
Of widowed mothers. But this is peace,
And that was war.
Amin.   Pardon, thou holy god
Of marriage-bed, and frown not, I am forc'd,
In answer of such noble tears as those,   131
To weep upon my wedding-day !
Mel. I fear thou art grown too fickle ; for I
    hear
A lady mourns for thee, men say, to death,
Forsaken of thee, on what terms [4] I know not.
Amin. She had my promise ; but the King
    forbad it,   136
And made me make this worthy change, thy
    sister,
Accompanied with graces [far] [5] above [6] her,
With whom I long to lose my lusty youth
And grow old in her arms.
Mel.   Be prosperous !   140

         Enter Messenger.

Mess. My lord, the masquers rage for you.
Lys. Cleon, Strato, Diphilus ! We are gone.
Amin. We 'll all attend you. —
       Exeunt LYSIPPUS, CLEON, STRATO,
         DIPHILUS [*and* Messenger].
              We shall trouble you
With our solemnities.
Mel.   Not so, Amintor ;

---

[1] So Q2. Q1 *above.* The choice of reading depends on
whether *her* refers to Aspatia or Evadne.
[2] In turn.
[3] Cf. V. iii. 42.
[4] Under what circumstances.
[5] Theo. emend. Qq. omit.
[6] So Q3. Q1 and Q2 *about.*

But if you laugh at my rude carriage   145
In peace, I 'll do as much for you in war,
When you come thither. Yet I have a mistress
To bring to your delights ; rough though I
am,
I have a mistress, and she has a heart   149
She says ; but, trust me, it is stone, no better ;
There is no place that I can challenge in 't.
But you stand still, and here my way lies.
                                        Exeunt [severally].

[SCENE II.]¹

Enter CALIANAX *with* DIAGORAS.

Cal. Diagoras, look to the doors better, for
shame ! You let in all the world, and anon the
King will rail at me. Why, very well said.² By
Jove, the King will have the show i' th' court !
   Diag. Why do you swear so, my lord ? You
know he 'll have it here.   6
   Cal. By this light, if he be wise, he will not.
   Diag. And if he will not be wise, you are for-
sworn.
   Cal. One may wear his heart out with swear-
ing, and get thanks on no side. I 'll be gone, [11
look to 't who will.
   Diag. My lord, I shall never keep them out.
Pray, stay ; your looks will terrify them.
   Cal. My looks terrify them, you coxcom- [15
bly ass, you ! I 'll be judged by all the company
whether thou hast not a worse face than I.
   Diag. I mean, because they know you and
your office.
   Cal. Office ! I would I could put it off ! I [20
am sure I sweat quite through my office. I
might have made room at my daughter's wedding ; — they ha' near kill'd her among them ;
and now I must do service for him that hath
forsaken her. Serve that will !   *Exit.*   25
   Diag. He 's so humorous ³ since his daughter
was forsaken ! (*Knock within.*) Hark, hark !
there, there ! so, so ! codes, codes !⁴ What now ?
   Mel. (within.) Open the door.
   Diag. Who 's there ?   30
   Mel. [*within.*] Melantius.
   Diag. I hope your lordship brings no troop
with you ; for, if you do, I must return them.
                                  [*Opens the door.*]

Enter MELANTIUS *and a* Lady.

Mel. None but this lady, sir.
   Diag. The ladies are all plac'd above, save [35
those that come in the King's troop ; the best of
Rhodes sit there, and there 's room.
   Mel. I thank you, sir. — When I have seen you
placed, madam, I must attend the King ; but,
the masque done, I 'll wait on you again.   40
   Diag. [*opening another door.*] Stand back
there ! — Room for my Lord Melantius ! (*Exeunt* MELANTIUS *and* Lady, *other door.*) — Pray,
bear back — this is no place for such youth and
their trulls ⁵ — let the doors shut again. — No !
— do your heads itch ? I 'll scratch them for [46

¹ A hall in the palace, with a gallery full of spectators.
² Done.   ⁴ A corruption of God's (?)
³ Moody.   ⁵ Wenches.

you. [*Shuts the door.*] — So, now thrust and hang.
[*Knocking within.*] — Again ! who is 't now ? — I
cannot blame my Lord Calianax for going
away ; would he were here ! He would run [50
raging among them, and break a dozen wiser
heads than his own in the twinkling of an eye.
— What 's the news now ?
   [*Voice*] *within.* I pray you, can you help me
to the speech of the master-cook ?   55
   Diag. If I open the door, I 'll cook some of
your calves-heads. Peace, rogues ! [*Knocking
within.*] — Again ! who is 't ?
   Mel. (within.) Melantius.

Re-enter CALIANAX.

Cal. Let him not in.   60
   Diag. O, my lord, I must. [*Opening the door.*]
— Make room there for my lord. Is your lady
plac'd ?

Re-enter MELANTIUS.

Mel. Yes, sir.
I thank you. — My Lord Calianax, well met. 65
Your causeless hate to me I hope is buried.
   Cal. Yes, I do service for your sister here,
That brings my own poor child to timeless
death.
She loves your friend Amintor ; such another
False-hearted lord as you.
   Mel.   You do me wrong, 70
A most unmanly one, and I am slow
In taking vengeance : but be well advis'd.
   Cal. It may be so. — Who plac'd the lady
there
So near the presence of the King ?
   Mel.   I did.
   Cal. My lord, she must not sit there.
   Mel.   Why ? 75
   Cal. The place is kept for women of more
worth.
   Mel. More worth than she ! It misbecomes
your age
And place to be thus womanish : forbear !
What you have spoke, I am content to think
The palsy shook your tongue to.
   Cal.   Why, 't is well, 80
If I stand here to place men's wenches.
   Mel.   I
Shall quite forget this place, thy age, my safety,
And, through all, cut that poor sickly week
Thou hast to live away from thee.
   Cal. Nay, I know you can fight for your
whore.   85
   Mel. Bate me the King, and, be he flesh and
blood,
He lies that says it ! Thy mother at fifteen
Was black and sinful to her.
   Diag.   Good my lord —
   Mel. Some god pluck threescore years from
that fond ⁶ man,   89
That I may kill him, and not stain mine honour !
It is the curse of soldiers, that in peace
They shall be brav'd by such ignoble men
As, if the land were troubled, would with tears
And knees beg succour from 'em. Would that
blood,

⁶ Foolish.

That sea of blood, that I have lost in fight, 95
Were running in thy veins, that it might make
    thee
Apt to say less, or able to maintain,
Should'st thou say more! This Rhodes, I see, is
    nought
But a place privileg'd to do men wrong.
Cal. Ay, you may say your pleasure.

Enter AMINTOR.

Amin.   What vile injury 100
Has stirr'd my worthy friend, who is as slow
To fight with words as he is quick of hand?
Mel. That heap of age, which I should rever-
    ence
If it were temperate, but testy years
Are most contemptible.
Amin.   Good sir, forbear. 105
Cal. There is just such another as yourself.
Amin. He will wrong you, or me, or any man,
And talk as if he had no life to lose,
Since this our match. The King is coming in;
I would not for more wealth than I enjoy 110
He should perceive you raging. He did hear
You were at difference now, which hast'ned him.
                    Hautboys play within.
Cal. Make room there!

Enter KING, EVADNE, ASPATIA, Lords, *and*
    Ladies.

King. Melantius, thon art welcome, and my
    love
Is with thee still; but this is not a place 115
To brabble[1] in. — Calianax, join hands.
Cal. He shall not have mine hand.
King.   This is no time
To force you to 't. I do love you both: —
Calianax, you look well to your office; —
And you, Melantius, are welcome home. 120
Begin the masque.
Mel. Sister, I joy to see you and your choice;
You lookt with my eyes when you took that man.
Be happy in him!   *Recorders*[2] [*play*].
Evad.   O, my dearest brother,
Your presence is more joyful than this day 125
Can be unto me.

THE MASQUE

NIGHT *rises in mists.*

Night. Our reign is come; for in the raging[3]
    sea
The sun is drown'd, and with him fell the Day.
Bright Cynthia, hear my voice! I am the
    Night,
For whom thou bear'st about thy borrowed
    light.
Appear! no longer thy pale visage shroud, 5
But strike thy silver horns quite through a
    cloud,
And send a beam upon my swarthy face,
By which I may discover all the place
And persons, and how many longing eyes
Are come to wait on our solemnities. 10

Enter CYNTHIA.

How dull and black am I! I could not find
This beauty[4] without thee, I am so blind:
Methinks they show like to those eastern
    streaks,
That warn us hence before the morning breaks.
Back, my pale servant! for these eyes know 15
To shoot far more and quicker rays than
    thou.
Cynth. Great queen, they be a troop for
    whom alone
One of my clearest moons I have put on;
A troop, that looks as if thyself and I
Had pluckt our reins in and our whips laid
    by, 20
To gaze upon these mortals, that appear
Brighter than we.
Night.   Then let us keep 'em here,
And never more our chariots drive away,
But hold our places and outshine the Day.
Cynth. Great queen of shadows, you are
    pleas'd to speak 25
Of more than may be done. We may not
    break
The gods' decrees; but, when our time is
    come,
Must drive away, and give the Day our room.
Yet, while our reign lasts, let us stretch our
    power
To give our servants one contented hour, 30
With such unwonted solemn grace and state,
As may forever after force them hate
Our brother's glorious beams, and wish the
    Night
Crown'd with a thousand stars and our cold
    light:
For almost all the world their service bend 35
To Phoebus, and in vain my light I lend,
Gaz'd on unto my setting from my rise
Almost of none but of unquiet eyes.
Night. Then shine at full, fair queen, and by
    thy power
Produce a birth, to crown this happy hour, 40
Of nymphs and shepherds; let their songs dis-
    cover,
Easy and sweet, who is a happy lover;
Or, if thou woo[5] 't, then call thine own Endy-
    mion
From the sweet flow'ry bed he lies upon,
On Latmus' top, thy pale beams drawn away, 45
And of his long night let him make a day.
Cynth. Thou dream'st, dark queen; that fair
    boy was not mine,
Nor went I down to kiss him. Ease and wine
Have bred these bold tales: poets, when they
    rage,
Turn gods to men, and make an hour an age. 50
But I will give a greater state and glory,
And raise to time a nobler memory
Of what these lovers are. — Rise, rise, I say,
Thou power of deeps, thy surges laid away,
Neptune, great king of waters, and by me 55
Be proud to be commanded!

NEPTUNE *rises.*

Nept.   Cynthia, see
Thy word hath fetcht me hither : let me know
Why I ascend.
Cynth.   Doth this majestic show
Give thee no knowledge yet ?
Nept.   Yes, now I see
Something intended, Cynthia, worthy thee.   60
Go on ; I 'll be a helper.
Cynth.   Hie thee, then,
And charge the Wind fly from his rocky den,
Let loose his subjects ; only Boreas,
Too foul for our intentions as he was,
Still keep him fast chain'd : we must have none
         here   65
But vernal blasts and gentle winds appear,
Such as blow flowers, and through the glad
         boughs sing
Many soft welcomes to the lusty spring ;
These are our music. Next, thy wat'ry race
Bring on in couples (we are pleas'd to grace   70
This noble night), each in their richest things
Your own deeps or the broken vessel brings.
Be prodigal, and I shall be as kind
And shine at full upon you.
Nept.   Oh, the Wind !
Commanding Aeolus !

Enter AEOLUS *out of a Rock.*

Aeol.   Great Neptune !
Nept.   He.   75
Aeol. What is thy will ?
Nept.   We do command thee free
Favonius and thy milder winds, to wait
Upon our Cynthia ; but tie Boreas strait,
He 's too rebellious.
Aeol.   I shall do it. [*Exit* AEOLUS.]
Nept.   Do.
Aeol. [*within.*] Great master of the flood and
         all below,   80
Thy full command has taken.——Oh, the
         Main !
Neptune !
Nept.   Here.

[*Re-enter* AEOLUS, *followed by* FAVONIUS *and
other Winds.*]

Aeol.   Boreas has broken his chain,
And, struggling with the rest, has got away.
Nept. Let him alone, I 'll take him up at
         sea ;
I will not long be thence. Go once again,   85
And call out of the bottoms of the main
Blue Proteus and the rest ; charge them put on
Their greatest pearls, and the most sparkling
         stone
The beaten[1] rock breeds ; tell this night is
         done
By me a solemn honour to the Moon :   90
Fly, like a full sail.
Aeol.   I am gone.   [*Exit.*]
Cynth.   Dark Night,
Strike a full silence, do a thorough right
To this great chorus, that our music may

---

[1] Crushed (?) or beaten by the waves (?).

Touch high as Heaven, and make the east
         break day
At midnight.   *Music.* 95
                [FIRST] SONG.

[*During which* PROTEUS *and other* Sea-deities
         enter.]

    Cynthia, to thy power and thee
            We obey.
    Joy to this great company !
            And no day
    Come to steal this night away,   100
       Till the rites of love are ended,
    And the lusty bridegroom say,
       Welcome, light, of all befriended !

    Pace out, you watery powers below ;
            Let your feet,   105
    Like the galleys when they row,
            Even beat.
    Let your unknown measures, set
       To the still winds, tell to all,
    That gods are come, immortal, great,   110
    To honour this great nuptial.
                          The Measure.

                SECOND SONG.

Hold back thy hours, dark Night, till we have done ;
    The Day will come too soon :
Young maids will curse thee, if thou steal'st away,
And leav'st their losses open to the day :   115
    Stay, stay, and hide
    The blushes of the bride.

Stay, gentle Night, and with thy darkness cover
    The kisses of her lover ;
Stay, and confound her tears and her shrill cryings,
Her weak denials, vows, and often-dyings ;   121
    Stay, and hide all :
    But help not, though she call.

Nept. Great queen of us and Heaven, hear
         what I bring
To make this hour a full one.[2]
Cynth.   Speak, sea's king.   125
Nept. The tunes my Amphitrite joys to
         have,
When she will dance upon the rising wave,
And court me as she sails. My Tritons, play
Music to lay a storm ! I 'll lead the way.
            A Measure, NEPTUNE *leads it.*

                [THIRD] SONG.

    To bed, to bed ! Come, Hymen, lead the bride, 130
    And lay her by her husband's side ;
       Bring in the virgins every one,
       That grieve to lie alone,
    That they may kiss while they may say a maid ;
    To-morrow 't will be other kist and said.   135
       Hesperus, be long a-shining,
       Whilst these lovers are a-twining.

Aeol. [*within.*] Ho, Neptune !
Nept.   Aeolus !

                [*Re-enter* AEOLUS.]

Aeol.   The sea goes high,
Boreas hath rais'd a storm : go and apply
Thy trident ; else, I prophesy, ere day   140

---

[2] Q₁ adds here *if not her measure*, plausibly explained by Fleay as a stage-direction, *Another measure.*

Many a tall ship will be cast away.
Descend with all the gods and all their power,
To strike a calm.
Cynth. [We thank you for this hour:
My favour to you all.]¹ To gratulate   145
So great a service, done at my desire,
Ye shall have many floods, fuller and higher
Than you have wisht for ; and no ebb shall dare
To let the Day see where your dwellings are.
Now back unto your governments in haste,   150
Lest your proud charge should swell above the
          waste,
And win upon the island.
    Nept.   We obey.
        NEPTUNE *descends and the Sea-*
          Gods. [*Exeunt* FAVONIUS *and*
          other Winds.]
Cynth. Hold up thy head, dead Night ; see'st
    thou not Day ?
The east begins to lighten. I must down,
And give my brother place.
    Night.   Oh, I could frown 155
To see the Day, the Day that flings his light
Upon my kingdom and contemns old Night !
Let him go on and flame ! I hope to see
Another wild-fire in his axle-tree,
And all fall drencht. But I forget ; — speak,
          queen :   160
The Day grows on ; I must no more be seen.
    Cynth. Heave up thy drowsy head and see
A greater light, a greater majesty,
Between our set² and us ! Whip up the team :
The Day breaks here, and yon same flashing
          stream³   165
Shot from the south. Say, which way wilt thou
          go ?
Night. I 'll vanish into mists.
Cynth.   I into Day.
        Exeunt NIGHT *and* CYNTHIA.

        Finis Masque.

King. Take lights there ! — Ladies, get the
    bride to bed. —
We will not see you laid ; good night, Amintor ;
We 'll ease you of that tedious ceremony.   170
Were it my case, I should think time run
    slow.
If thou be'st noble, youth, get me a boy,
That may defend my kingdoms from my foes.
Amin. All happiness to you !
King.   Good night, Melantius. *Exeunt.*

ACT II

[SCENE I.]⁴

Enter EVADNE, ASPATIA, DULA, *and other*
          Ladies.

Dula. Madam, shall we undress you for this
    fight ?
The wars are nak'd that you must make to-
    night.

¹ So Q₁. Q₂ *A thanks to every one, and.*
² Setting, the West. Qq. *Sect,* emended by Seward.
³ The effulgence of the court. (Thorndike.)
⁴ Ante-room to Evadne's bed-chamber.

Evad. You are very merry, Dula.
Dula.   I should be
Far merrier, madam, if it were with me
As it is with you.
Evad.   How 's that ?
Dula.   That I might go 5
To bed with him wi' th' credit that you do.
Evad. Why, how now, wench ?
Dula.   Come, ladies, will you help ?
Evad. I am soon undone.
Dula.   And as soon done :
Good store of clothes will trouble you at both.
Evad. Art thou drunk, Dula ?
Dula.   Why, here 's none but we. 10
Evad. Thou think 'st belike there is no mod-
    esty
When we 're alone.
Dula. Ay, by my troth, you hit my thoughts
    aright.
Evad. You prick me, lady.
1 Lady.   'T is against my will.
Dula. Anon you must endure more and lie
    still ;   15
You 're best to practise.
Evad.   Sure, this wench is mad.
Dula. No, faith, this is a trick that I have
    had
Since I was fourteen.
Evad.   'T is high time to leave it.
Dula. Nay, now I 'll keep it till the trick
    leave me.
A dozen wanton words put in your head   20
Will make you livelier in your husband's bed.
Evad. Nay, faith, then take it.⁵
Dula.   Take it, madam ! Where ?
We all, I hope, will take it that are here.
Evad. Nay, then I 'll give you o 'er.
Dula.   So will I make
The ablest man in Rhodes, or his heart ache. 25
Evad. Wilt take my place to-night ?
Dula.   I 'll hold your cards
Against any two I know.
Evad.   What wilt thou do ?
Dula. Madam, we 'll do 't, and make 'em
    leave play too.
Evad. Aspatia, take her part.
Dula.   I will refuse it :
She will pluck down a side ;⁶ she does not
    use it.   30
Evad. Why, do, I prithee.
Dula.   You will find the play
Quickly, because your head lies well that way.
Evad. I thank thee, Dula. Would thou
    couldst instil
Some of thy mirth into Aspatia !
Nothing but sad thoughts in her breast do
    dwell :   35
Methinks, a mean betwixt you would do well.
Dula. She is in love : hang me, if I were
    so,
But I could run⁷ my country. I love too
To do those things that people in love do.
Asp. It were a timeless⁸ smile should prove
    my cheek.   40

⁵ *I. e.* the trick. (Thorndike.)
⁶ Cause the loss of the game.
⁷ Drive at a fast pace.   ⁸ Untimely.

It were a fitter hour for me to laugh,
When at the altar the religious priest
Were pacifying the offended powers
With sacrifice, than now. This should have
been
My rite;[1] and all your hands have been em-
ploy'd   45
In giving me a spotless offering
To young Amintor's bed, as we are now
For you. Pardon, Evadne: would my worth
Were great as yours, or that the King, or he,
Or both, thought so! Perhaps he found me
worthless: 50
But till he did so, in these ears of mine,
These credulous ears, he pour'd the sweetest
words
That art or love could frame. If he were false,
Pardon it, Heaven! and, if I did want
Virtue, you safely may forgive that too;   55
For I have lost none that I had from you.
  Evad. Nay, leave this sad talk, madam.
  Asp.   Would I could!
Then I should leave the cause.
  Evad. See, if you have not spoil'd all Dula's
mirth!
  Asp. Thou think'st thy heart hard; but, if
thou be'st caught,   60
Remember me; thou shalt perceive a fire
Shot suddenly into thee.
  Dula.   That's not so good;
Let 'em shoot anything but fire, I fear 'em
not.
  Asp. Well, wench, thou may'st be taken.
  Evad. Ladies, good-night; I'll do the rest
myself.   65
  Dula. Nay, let your lord do some.
  Asp. [*singing.*]

> Lay a garland on my hearse
>   Of the dismal yew —

  Evad. That's one of your sad songs, madam.
  Asp. Believe me, 't is a very pretty one.   70
  Evad. How is it, madam?
  Asp. [*singing.*]

> Lay a garland on my hearse
>   Of the dismal yew;
> Maidens, willow-branches bear;
>   Say I died true.   75
> My love was false, but I was firm
>   From my hour of birth:
> Upon my buried body lie
>   Lightly, gentle earth!

  Evad. Fie on 't, madam! The words are so
strange, they   80
Are able to make one dream of hobgoblins. —
"I could never have the power" — sing that,
Dula.
  Dula. [*singing.*]

> I could never have the power
>   To love one above an hour,
> But my heart would prompt mine eye   85
>   On some other man to fly.
> Venus, fix mine eyes fast,
> Or, if not, give me all that I shall see at last!

  Evad. So, leave me now.
  Dula. Nay, we must see you laid.   90

  Asp. Madam, good night. May all the mar-
riage-joys
That longing maids imagine in their beds
Prove so unto you! May no discontent
Grow 'twixt your love and you! but, if there do,
Inquire of me, and I will guide your moan;   95
Teach you an artificial [2] way to grieve,
To keep your sorrow waking. Love your lord
No worse than I; but, if you love so well,
Alas, you may displease him! so did I.
This is the last time you shall look on me. — 100
Ladies, farewell. As soon as I am dead,
Come all and watch one night about **my**
hearse;
Bring each a mournful story and a tear,
To offer at it when I go to earth;
With flattering ivy clasp my coffin round;   105
Write on my brow my fortune; let my bier
Be borne by virgins, that shall sing by course [3]
The truth of maids and perjuries of men.
  Evad. Alas, I pity thee.
  All.   Madam, good night. *Exit* EVADNE.
  1 Lady. Come, we'll let in the bridegroom.
  Dula.   Where's my lord? 110
  1 Lady. Here, take this light.

Enter AMINTOR.

  Dula.   You'll find her in the dark.
  1 Lady. Your lady's scarce a-bed yet; you
must help her.
  Asp. Go, and be happy in your lady's love.
May all the wrongs that you have done to me
Be utterly forgotten in my death!   115
I'll trouble you no more; yet I will take
A parting kiss, and will not be denied.
                  [*Kisses* AMINTOR.]
You'll come, my lord, and see the virgins
weep
When I am laid in earth, though you yourself
Can know no pity. Thus I wind myself   120
Into this willow-garland, and am prouder
That I was once your love, though now re-
fus'd,
Than to have had another true to me.
So with my prayers I leave you, and must try
Some yet unpractis'd way to grieve and die. 125
                       Exit.
  Dula. Come, ladies, will you go?
  All.   Good night, my lord.
  Amin. Much happiness unto you all!
              Exeunt [DULA *and*] Ladies.
I did that lady wrong. Methinks, I feel
A grief shoot suddenly through all my veins;
Mine eyes rain: this is strange at such a
time.   130
It was the King first mov'd me to 't; but **he**
Has not my will in keeping. Why do I
Perplex myself thus? Something whispers **me**,
Go not to bed. My guilt is not so great
As mine own conscience, too sensible,   135
Would make me think; I only brake a prom-
ise,
And 't was the King that forc'd me. Timorous
flesh,
Why shak'st thou so? Away, my idle fears!

Re-enter EVADNE.

Yonder she is, the lustre of whose eye
Can blot away the sad remembrance   140
Of all these things. — Oh, my Evadne, spare
That tender body ; let it not take cold !
The vapours of the night will not fall here.
To bed, my love: Hymen will punish us
For being slack performers of his rites.   145
Cam'st thou to call me ?
   Evad.   No.
   Amin.   Come, come, my love,
And let us lose ourselves to one another.
Why art thou up so long ?
   Evad.   I am not well.
   Amin. To bed then ; let me wind thee in
   these arms
Till I have banisht sickness.
   Evad.   Good my lord,   150
I cannot sleep.
   Amin.   Evadne, we will watch ;
I mean no sleeping.
   Evad.   I 'll not go to bed.
   Amin. I prithee, do.
   Evad.   I will not for the world.
   Amin. Why, my dear love ?
   Evad.   Why ! I have sworn I will not.
   Amin. Sworn !
   Evad.   Ay.
   Amin.   How ? Sworn, Evadne !   155
   Evad. Yes, sworn, Amintor ; and will swear
   again,
If you will wish to hear me.
   Amin. To whom have you sworn this ?
   Evad. If I should name him, the matter were
not great.
   Amin. Come, this is but the coyness of a
   bride.   160
   Evad. The coyness of the bride !
   Amin.   How prettily
That frown becomes thee !
   Evad.   Do you like it so ?
   Amin. Thou canst not dress thy face in such
   a look
But I shall like it.
   Evad.   What look likes [1] you best ?
   Amin. Why do you ask ?   165
   Evad. That I may show you one less pleas-
ing to you.
   Amin. How 's that ?
   Evad. That I may show you one less pleas-
ing to you.
   Amin. I prithee, put thy jests in milder
looks ;
It shows as thou wert angry.
   Evad.   So perhaps   170
I am indeed.
   Amin.   Why, who has done thee wrong ?
Name me the man, and by thyself I swear,
Thy yet unconquered self, I will revenge thee !
   Evad. Now I shall try thy truth. If thou
dost love me,
Thou weigh'st not anything compar'd with
me :   175
Life, honour, joys eternal, all delights

This world can yield, or hopeful people feign,
Or in the life to come, are light as air
To a true lover when his lady frowns,
And bids him, " Do this.'' Wilt thou kill this
man ?   180
Swear, my Amintor, and I 'll kiss the sin
Off from thy lips.
   Amin.   I wo' not swear, sweet love,
Till I do know the cause.
   Evad.   I would thou wouldst.
Why, it is thou that wrong'st me ; I hate
thee ;
Thou should'st have kill'd thyself.   185
   Amin. If I should know that, I should
quickly kill
The man you hated.
   Evad.   Know it, then, and do 't.
   Amin. Oh, no ! what look soe'er thou shalt
put on
To try my faith, I shall not think thee false ;
I cannot find one blemish in thy face,   190
Where falsehood should abide. Leave, and to
bed.
If you have sworn to any of the virgins
That were your old companions, to preserve
Your maidenhead a night, it may be done
Without this means.
   Evad.   A maidenhead, Amintor, 195
At my years !
   Amin.   Sure she raves ; this cannot be
Her natural temper. — Shall I call thy maids ?
Either thy healthful sleep hath left thee long,
Or else some fever rages in thy blood.
   Evad. Neither, Amintor : think you I am
mad,   200
Because I speak the truth ?
   Amin.   [Is this the truth ?] [2]
Will you not lie with me to-night ?
   Evad.   To-night !
You talk as if [you thought] [2] I would hereafter.
   Amin. Hereafter ! yes, I do.
   Evad.   You are deceiv'd.
Put off amazement, and with patience mark 205
What I shall utter, for the oracle
Knows nothing truer. 'T is not for a night
Or two that I forbear thy bed, but ever.
   Amin. I dream. Awake, Amintor !
   Evad.   You hear right:
I sooner will find out the beds of snakes,   210
And with my youthful blood warm their cold
flesh,
Letting them curl themselves about my limbs,
Than sleep one night with thee. This is not
feign'd,
Nor sounds it like the coyness of a bride.
   Amin. Is flesh so earthly to endure all
this ?   215
Are these the joys of marriage ? Hymen, keep
This story, that will make succeeding youth
Neglect thy ceremonies, from all ears ;
Let it not rise up, for thy shame and mine
To after-ages : we will scorn thy laws,   220
If thou no better bless them. Touch the heart
Of her that thou hast sent me, or the world
Shall know ; there 's not an altar that will
smoke

---

[1] Pleases.   [2] Only in Q₁.

In praise of thee ; we will adopt us sons ;
Then virtue shall inherit, and not blood.   225
If we do lust, we 'll take the next we meet,
Serving ourselves as other creatures do ;
And never take note of the female more,
Nor of her issue. — I do rage in vain ;
She can but jest. — Oh, pardon me, my love !   230
So dear the thoughts are that I hold of thee,
That I must break forth. Satisfy my fear ;
It is a pain, beyond the hand of death,
To be in doubt. Confirm it with an oath,
If this be true.
        Evad.   Do you invent the form ;   235
Let there be in it all the binding words
Devils and conjurers can put together,
And I will take it. I have sworn before,
And here by all things holy do again,
Never to be acquainted with thy bed !   240
Is your doubt over now ?
    Amin. I know too much ; would I had
        doubted still !
Was ever such a marriage-night as this !
You powers above, if you did ever mean
Man should be us'd thus, you have thought a
        way   245
How he may bear himself, and save his honour :
Instruct me in it ; for to my dull eyes
There is no mean, no moderate course to run ;
I must live scorn'd, or be a murderer.
Is there a third ? Why is this night so calm ?   250
Why does not Heaven speak in thunder to us,
And drown her voice ?
    Evad.   This rage will do no good.
    Amin. Evadne, hear me. Thou hast ta'en an
        oath,
But such a rash one, that to keep it were
Worse than to swear it. Call it back to thee ;   255
Such vows as that never ascend to Heaven ;
A tear or two will wash it quite away.
Have mercy on my youth, my hopeful youth,
If thou be pitiful ! for, without boast,
This land was proud of me. What lady was
        there,   260
That men call'd fair and virtuous in this isle,
That would have shunn'd my love ? It is in
        thee
To make me hold this worth. Oh, we vain
        men,
That trust [out] [1] all our reputation
To rest upon the weak and yielding hand   265
Of feeble woman ! But thou art not stone ;
Thy flesh is soft, and in thine eyes doth dwell
The spirit of love ; thy heart cannot be hard.
Come, lead me from the bottom of despair
To all the joys thou hast ; I know thou wilt ;   270
And make me careful lest the sudden change
O'ercome my spirits.
    Evad.   When I call back this oath,
The pains of hell environ me !
    Amin. I sleep, and am too temperate. Come
        to bed !
Or by those hairs, which, if thou hadst a soul   275
Like to thy locks, were threads for kings to
        wear
About their arms ——

        [1] In Q₄ only.

    Evad.   Why, so perhaps they are.
    Amin. I 'll drag thee to my bed, and make
        thy tongue
Undo this wicked oath, or on thy flesh
I 'll print a thousand wounds to let out life !   280
    Evad. I fear thee not : do what thou dar'st
        to me !
Every ill-sounding word or threat'ning look
Thou shew'st to me will be reveng'd at full.
    Amin. It will not sure, Evadne ?
    Evad. Do not you hazard that.
    Amin.   Ha' ye your champions ?   285
    Evad. Alas, Amintor, think'st thou I for-
        bear
To sleep with thee, because I have put on
A maiden's strictness ? Look upon these
        cheeks,
And thou shalt find the hot and rising blood
Unapt for such a vow. No ; in this heart   290
There dwells as much desire and as much will
To put that wished [2] act in practice as ever yet
Was known to woman ; and they have been
        shown
Both. But it was the folly of thy youth
To think this beauty, to what land [3] soe'er   295
It shall be call'd, shall stoop to any second.
I do enjoy the best, and in that height
Have sworn to stand or die. You guess the
        man.
    Amin. No ; let me know the man that wrongs
        me so,
That I may cut his body into motes,   300
And scatter it before the northern wind.
    Evad. You dare not strike him.
    Amin.   Do not wrong me so.
Yes, if his body were a poisonous plant
That it were death to touch, I have a soul
Will throw me on him.
    Evad.   Why, 't is the King.
    Amin.   The King !   305
    Evad. What will you do now ?
    Amin.   'T is not the King !
    Evad. What did he make this match for,
        dull Amintor ?
    Amin. Oh, thou hast nam'd a word, that
        wipes away
All thoughts revengeful ! In that sacred name,
"The King," there lies a terror. What frail
        man   310
Dares lift his hand against it ? Let the gods
Speak to him when they please : till when, let us
Suffer and wait.
    Evad. Why should you fill yourself so full of
        heat,
And haste so to my bed ? I am no virgin.   315
    Amin. What devil put it in thy fancy, then,
To marry me ?
    Evad.   Alas, I must have one
To father children, and to bear the name
Of husband to me, that my sin may be
More honourable !
    Amin.   What strange thing am I !   320
    Evad. A miserable one ; one that myself
Am sorry for.
    Amin.   Why, show it then in this :

    [2] So Q₁. Q₄ *wisht.*   [3] Bullen conjectures *hana*

If thou hast pity, though thy love be none,
Kill me ; and all true lovers, that shall live
In after ages crost in their desires,   325
Shall bless thy memory, and call thee good,
Because such mercy in thy heart was found,
To rid [1] a ling'ring wretch.
  Evad.   I must have one
To fill thy room again, if thou wert dead ;
Else, by this night, I would ! I pity thee.   330
  Amin. These strange and sudden injuries
      have fall'n
So thick upon me, that I lose all sense
Of what they are. Methinks, I am not wrong'd ;
Nor is it aught, if from the censuring world
I can but hide it. Reputation,   335
Thou art a word, no more ! — But thou hast
      shown
An impudence so high, that to the world
I fear thou wilt betray or shame thyself.
  Evad. To cover shame, I took thee ; never
      fear
That I would blaze [2] myself.
  Amin.   Nor let the King 340
Know I conceive he wrongs me ; then mine
      honour
Will thrust me into action, though [3] my flesh
Could bear with patience. And it is some ease
To me in these extremes, that I know this
Before I touch't thee ; else, had all the sins 345
Of mankind stood betwixt me and the King,
I had gone through 'em to his heart and thine.
I have lost [4] one desire : 'tis not his crown
Shall buy me to thy bed, now I resolve [5]
He has dishonour'd thee. Give me thy hand : 350
Be careful of thy credit, and sin close ; [6]
'T is all I wish. Upon thy chamber-floor
I 'll rest to-night, that morning visitors
May think we did as married people use :   354
And prithee, smile upon me when they come,
And seem to toy, as if thou hadst been pleased
With what we did.
  Evad.   Fear not ; I will do this.
  Amin. Come, let us practise ; and, as wantonly
As ever loving [7] bride and bridegroom met,
Let 's laugh and enter here.
  Evad.   I am content.   360
  Amin. Down all the swellings of my troubled
      heart !
When we walk thus intwin'd, let all eyes see
If ever lovers better did agree.   *Exeunt.*

[SCENE II.] [8]

Enter ASPATIA, ANTIPHILA, *and* OLYMPIAS.

  Asp. Away, you are not sad ! force it no fur-
      ther.
Good gods, how well you look ! Such a full
      colour
Young bashful brides put on : sure, you are
      new married !
  Ant. Yes, madam, to your grief.
  Asp.   Alas, poor wenches !

  [1] Despatch.   [2] Proclaim.
  [3] So edd. 1778. Early Qq. and F *that.*
  [4] Q₁ *left.*   [5] Am convinced.
  [6] Secretly.   [7] Q₁ *longing.*
  [8] An apartment in the house of Calianax.

Go learn to love first ; learn to lose yourselves ; [9]
Learn to be flattered, and believe and bless
The double tongue that did it ; make a faith
Out of the miracles of ancient lovers,
Such as spake truth and died in 't ; and, like
      me,
Believe all faithful, and be miserable.   10
Did you ne'er love yet, wenches ? Speak,
      Olympias :
Thou hast an easy temper, fit for stamp.
  Olym. Never.
  Asp.   Nor you, Antiphila ?
  Ant.   Nor I.
  Asp. Then, my good girls, be more than
      women, wise ;
At least be more than I was ; and be sure   15
You credit any thing the light gives life to,
Before a man. Rather believe the sea
Weeps for the ruin'd merchant, when he roars ;
Rather, the wind courts but the pregnant sails,
When the strong cordage cracks ; rather, the
      sun   20
Comes but to kiss the fruit in wealthy autumn,
When all falls blasted. If you needs must love,
(Forc'd by ill fate,) take to your maiden-bosoms
Two dead-cold aspics, and of them make lovers.
They cannot flatter nor forswear ; one kiss   25
Makes a long peace for all. But man —
Oh, that beast man ! Come, let 's be sad, my
      girls :
That down-cast of thine eye, Olympias,
Shows a fine sorrow. — Mark, Antiphila ;
Just such another was the nymph Oenone,   30
When Paris brought home Helen. — Now, a
      tear ;
And then thou art a piece expressing fully
The Carthage queen, when from a cold sea-
      rock,
Full with her sorrow, she tied fast her eyes   34
To the fair Trojan ships ; and, having lost them,
Just as thine does, down stole a tear. — An-
      tiphila,
What would this wench do, if she were Aspatia ?
Here she would stand, till some more pitying
      god
Turn'd her to marble ! — 'Tis enough, my
      wench !
Show me the piece of needlework you wrought.
  Ant. Of Ariadne, madam ?
  Asp.   Yes, that piece.—   41
This should be Theseus ; h'as a cozening face.—
You meant him for a man ?
  Ant.   He was so, madam.
  Asp. Why, then, 't is well enough. — Never
      look back ;
You have a full wind and a false heart, The-
      seus. —   45
Does not the story say, his keel was split,
Or his masts spent, or some kind rock or other
Met with his vessel ?
  Ant.   Not as I remember.
  Asp. It should ha' been so. Could the gods
      know this,
And not, of all their number, raise a storm ? 50
But they are all as evil. This false smile
Was well exprest ; just such another caught
      me.—

You shall not go so.[1] —
Antiphila, in this place work a quicksand,
And over it a shallow smiling water,   55
And his ship ploughing it ; and then a Fear:
Do that Fear to the life,[2] wench.
   Ant.   'T will wrong the story.
   Asp. 'T will make the story, wrong'd by
    wanton poets,
Live long and be believ'd. But where 's the
    lady ?
   Ant. There, madam.   60
   Asp. Fie, you have mist it here, Antiphila ;
You are much mistaken, wench.
These colours are not dull and pale enough
To show a soul so full of misery
As this sad lady's was. Do it by me,   65
Do it again by me, the lost Aspatia ;
And you shall find all true but the wild island.
I stand upon the sea-breach now, and think[3]
Mine arms thus, and mine hair blown with the
    wind,
Wild as that desert ; and let all about me   70
Tell that I am forsaken. Do my face
(If thou had'st ever feeling of a sorrow)
Thus, thus, Antiphila : strive to make me look
Like Sorrow's monument ; and the trees about
    me,
Let them be dry and leafless ; let the rocks   75
Groan with continual surges ; and behind me,
Make all a desolation. See, see, wenches,
A miserable life[4] of this poor picture !
   Olym. Dear madam !
   Asp.   I have done. Sit down ; and let us
Upon that point fix all our eyes, that point
    there.   80
Make a dull silence, till you feel a sudden sad-
    ness
Give us new souls.

             Enter CALIANAX.

   Cal. The King may do this, and he may not
    do it :
My child is wrong'd, disgrac'd. — Well, how
    now, huswives ?   84
What, at your ease ! Is this a time to sit still ?
Up, you young lazy whores, up, or I 'll swinge
    you !
   Olym. Nay, good my lord—
   Cal. You 'll lie down shortly. Get you in,
    and work !
What, are you grown so resty you want heats ?
We shall have some of the court-boys do that
    office.   90
   Ant. My lord, we do no more than we are
    charg'd :
It is the lady's pleasure we be thus
In grief she is forsaken.
   Cal.   There 's a rogue too,
A young dissembling slave ! — Well, get you
    in.—
I 'll have a bout with that boy. 'T is high time
Now to be valiant : I confess my youth   96
Was never prone that way. What, made an
    ass !

---

[1] Addressed to Theseus.   [2] Q₁ *bravely.*
[3] Q₁ reads *Suppose I . . . now.*
[4] Living representation.

A court-stale ![5] Well, I will be valiant,
And beat some dozen of these whelps ; I will !
And there 's another of 'em, a trim cheating
    soldier ;   100
I 'll maul that rascal ; has out-brav'd me
    twice ;
But now, I thank the gods, I am valiant.—
Go, get you in.— I 'll take a course with all.
                     Exeunt.

ACT III

[SCENE I.][6]

    Enter CLEON, STRATO, *and* DIPHILUS.

   Cle. Your sister is not up yet.
   Diph. Oh, brides must take their morning's
rest ; the night is troublesome.
   Stra. But not tedious.
   Diph. What odds, he has not my sister's [5
maidenhead to-night ?
   Stra. None ; it 's odds against any bridegroom
living, he ne'er gets it while he lives.
   Diph. You 're merry with my sister ; you 'll
please to allow me the same freedom with [10
your mother.
   Stra. She 's at your service.
   Diph. Then she 's merry enough of herself ;
she needs no tickling. Knock at the door.
   Stra. We shall interrupt them.   15
   Diph. No matter ; they have the year before
them.   [STRATO *knocks at the door.*]
Good morrow, sister. Spare yourself to-day ;
The night will come again.

             Enter AMINTOR.

   Amin. Who 's there ? My brother ! I 'm no
readier[7] yet.   20
Your sister is but now up.
   Diph. You look as you had lost your eyes to-
night :
I think you ha' not slept.
   Amin.   I' faith I have not.
   Diph. You have done better, then.
   Amin. We ventur'd for a boy ; when he is
    twelve,   25
'A shall command against the foes of Rhodes.
Shall we be merry ?
   Stra. You cannot ; you want sleep.
   Amin.   'T is true.— (*Aside.*) But she,
As if she had drank Lethe, or had made
Even with Heaven, did fetch so still a sleep,   30
So sweet and sound ——
   Diph.   What 's that ?
   Amin.   Your sister frets
This morning ; and does turn her eyes upon me,
As people on their headsman. She does chafe,
And kiss, and chafe again, and clap my cheeks :
She 's in another world.   35
   Diph. Then I had lost : I was about to lay
You had not got her maidenhead to-night.
   Amin. [*Aside.*] Ha ! does he not mock me ?
    You 'd lost indeed ;
I do not use to bungle.

---

[5] Laughing-stock.
[6] Ante-room to Evadne's bed-chamber.
[7] No more dressed.

Cleo.   You do deserve her.
Amin. (*Aside.*) I laid my lips to hers, and
    that wild breath,   40
That was so rude and rough to me last night,
Was sweet as April. I 'll be guilty too,
If these be the effects.

Enter MELANTIUS.

Mel. Good day, Amintor; for to me the name
Of brother is too distant: we are friends,   45
And that is nearer.
Amin.   Dear Melantius!
Let me behold thee. Is it possible?
Mel. What sudden gaze is this?
Amin.   'T is wondrous strange!
Mel. Why does thine eye desire so strict a
    view
Of that it knows so well? There 's nothing
    here   50
That is not thine.
Amin.   I wonder much, Melantius,
To see those noble looks, that make me think
How virtuous thou art: and, on the sudden,
'T is strange to me thou shouldst have worth
    and honour;
Or not be base, and false, and treacherous,   55
And every ill. But ——
Mel.   Stay, stay, my friend;
I fear this sound will not become our loves.
No more; embrace me.[1]
Amin.   Oh, mistake me not!
I know thee to be full of all those deeds   59
That we frail men call good; but by the course
Of nature thou shouldst be as quickly chang'd
As are the winds; dissembling as the sea,
That now wears brows as smooth as virgins' be,
Tempting the merchant to invade his face,
And in an hour calls his billows up,   65
And shoots 'em at the sun, destroying all
'A carries on him.—(*Aside.*) Oh, how near am
    I
To utter my sick thoughts.
Mel. But why, my friend, should I be so by
    nature?
Amin. I have wed thy sister, who hath vir-
    tuous thoughts   70
Enough for one whole family; and it is strange
That you should feel no want.
Mel. Believe me, this is compliment too cun-
    ning for me.
Diph. What should I be then by the course
    of nature,   74
They having both robb'd me of so much virtue?
Stra. Oh, call the bride, my Lord Amintor,
That we may see her blush, and turn her eyes
    down.
It is the prettiest sport!
Amin. Evadne!
Evad. (*within.*) My lord?
Amin.   Come forth, my love;
Your brothers do attend to wish you joy.   80
Evad. [*within.*] I am not ready yet.
Amin.   Enough, enough.
Evad. [*within.*] They 'll mock me.
Amin.   Faith, thou shalt come in.

---

[1] The Qq. have no point after *more*; F₂ has a comma.

Enter EVADNE.

Mel. Good morrow, sister. He that under-
    stands
Whom you have wed, need not to wish you joy;
You have enough: take heed you be not proud.
Diph. Oh, sister, what have you done?   86
Evad. I done! why, what have I done?
Stra. My Lord Amintor swears you are no
    maid now.
Evad. Pish!
Stra. I' faith, he does.
Evad.   I knew I should be mockt.   90
Diph. With a truth.
Evad.   If 't were to do again,
In faith I would not marry.
Amin. (*Aside.*) Nor I, by Heaven!
Diph.   Sister, Dula swears
She heard you cry two rooms off.
Evad.   Fie, how you talk!
Diph. Let 's see you walk, Evadne. By my
    troth,   95
You 're spoil'd.[2]
Mel. Amintor.—
Amin. Ha!
Mel.   Thou art sad.
Amin.   Who, I? I thank you for that.
Shall Diphilus, thou, and I, sing a catch?
Mel. How!   100
Amin. Prithee, let 's.
Mel. Nay, that 's too much the other way.
Amin. I 'm so light! wed with my happiness!—
How dost thou, love? Kiss me.
Evad. I cannot love you, you tell tales of
    me.   105
Amin. Nothing but what becomes us.—
    Gentlemen,
Would you had all such wives, and all the
    world,
That I might be no wonder! You 're all sad:
What, do you envy me? I walk, methinks,
On water, and ne'er sink, I am so light.   110
Mel. 'T is well you are so.
Amin.   Well! how can I be other,
When she looks thus?—Is there no music
    there?
Let 's dance.
Mel.   Why this is strange, Amintor!
Amin. I do not know myself; yet I could
    wish
My joy were less.   115
Diph. I 'll marry too, if it will make one
    thus.
Evad. (*Aside.*) Amintor, hark.
Amin. What says my love?—I must obey.
Evad. You do it scurvily, 't will be perceiv'd.
Cleo. My lord, the King is here.   120

Enter KING *and* LYSIPPUS.

Amin. Where?
Stra. And his brother.
King. Good morrow, all!—
Amintor, joy on joy fall thick upon thee!—
And, madam, you are alter'd since I saw you;

---

[2] In Qq. and F this sentence is given to Evadne, her
name becoming a speech-tag.

I must salute you ; you are now another's.   126
How lik'd you your night's rest ?
Evad.   Ill, sir.
Amin.   Indeed,
She took but little.
Lys.   You 'll let her take more,
And thank her too, shortly.
King. Amintor, wert thou truly honest till   130
Thou wert married ?
Amin.   Yes, sir.
King.   Tell me, then, how shows
The sport unto thee ?
Amin.   Why, well.
King.   What did you do ?
Amin. No more, nor less, than other couples
use ;
You know what 't is ; it has but a coarse name.
King. But, prithee, I should think, by her
black eye,   135
And her red cheek, she should be quick and
stirring
In this same business ; ha ?
Amin.   I cannot tell ;
I ne'er tried other, sir ; but I perceive
She is as quick as you delivered.
King. Well, you 'll trust me then, Amintor,
to choose   140
A wife for you again ?
Amin.   No, never, sir.
King. Why, like you this so ill ?
Amin.   So well I like her.
For this I bow my knee in thanks to you,
And unto Heaven will pay my grateful tribute
Hourly ; and do hope we shall draw out   145
A long contented life together here,
And die both, full of grey hairs, in one day :
For which the thanks is yours. But if the
powers
That rule us please to call her first away,
Without pride spoke, this world holds not a
wife   150
Worthy to take her room.
King. I do not like this.—All forbear the
room,
But you, Amintor, and your lady.
        [*Exeunt all but the* KING, AMINTOR,
        and EVADNE.]
I have some speech with you, that may concern
Your after living well.   155
Amin. [*Aside.*] 'A will not tell me that he
lies with her !
If he do, something heavenly stay my heart,
For I shall be apt to thrust this arm of mine
To acts unlawful !
King.   You will suffer me
To talk with her, Amintor, and not have   160
A jealous pang ?
Amin.   Sir, I dare trust my wife
With whom she dares to talk, and not be jeal-
ous.   [*Retires.*]
King. How do you like Amintor ?
Evad.   As I did, sir.
King. How 's that ?
Evad. As one that, to fulfil your will and
pleasure,   165
I have given leave to call me wife and love.
King. I see there is no lasting faith in sin ;

They that break word with Heaven will **break**
again
With all the world, and so dost thou with me.
Evad. How, sir ?
King.   This subtle woman's ignorance   170
Will not excuse you : thou hast taken oaths,
So great that, methought, they did misbecome
A woman's mouth, that thou wouldst ne'er en-
joy
A man but me.
Evad.   I never did swear so ;
You do me wrong.
King.   Day and night have heard it.   175
Evad. I swore indeed that I would neveᵣ
love
A man of lower place ; but, if your fortune
Should throw you from this height, I bade you
trust
I would forsake you, and would bend to him
That won your throne. I love with my ambi-
tion,   180
Not with my eyes. But, if I ever yet
Toucht any other, leprosy light here
Upon my face ! which for your royalty
I would not stain !
King.   Why, thou dissemblest, and
It is in me to punish thee.
Evad.   Why, it is in me,   185
Then, not to love you, which will more **afflict**
Your body than your punishment can mine.
King. But thou hast let Amintor lie with
thee.
Evad. I ha' not.
King.   Impudence ! he says himself **so.**
Evad. 'A lies.
King.   'A does not.
Evad.   By this light, he does,   190
Strangely and basely ! and I 'll prove it so.
I did not only shun him for a night,
But told him I would never close with him.
King. Speak lower ; it is false.
Evad.   I am no man
To answer with a blow ; or, if I were,   195
You are the King. But urge me not ; 't is most
true.
King. Do not I know the uncontrolled
thoughts
That youth brings with him, when his blood is
high
With expectation and desire of that
He long hath waited for ? Is not his spirit,   200
Though he be temperate, of a valiant strain
As this our age hath known ? What could he
do,
If such a sudden speech had met his blood,
But ruin thee for ever, if he had not kill'd
thee ?
He could not bear it thus : he is as we,   205
Or any other wrong'd man.
Evad.   It is dissembling.
King. Take him ! farewell : henceforth I am
thy foe ;
And what disgraces I can blot thee with, look
for.
Evad. Stay, sir !—Amintor !—You **shall**
hear.—Amintor !
Amin. [*coming forward.*] What, my love.   ₂₁₀

Evad. Amintor, thou hast an ingenious [1]
   look,
And shouldst be virtuous: it amazeth me
That thou canst make such base malicious lies!
Amin. What, my dear wife?
Evad.   Dear wife! I do despise thee.
Why, nothing can be baser than to sow   215
Dissension amongst lovers.
Amin.   Lovers! Who?
Evad. The king and me —
Amin.   Oh, God!
Evad. Who should live long, and love with-
   out distaste,
Were it not for such pickthanks [2] as thyself.
Did you lie with me? Swear now, and be pun-
   isht   220
In hell for this!
Amin.   The faithless sin I made
To fair Aspatia is not yet reveng'd;
It follows me. — I will not lose a word
To this vile woman: but to you, my King,   224
The anguish of my soul thrusts out this truth:
You 're a tyrant! and not so much to wrong
An honest man thus, as to take a pride
In talking with him of it.
Evad.   Now, sir, see
How loud this fellow lied!
Amin. You that can know to wrong, should
   know how men   230
Must right themselves. What punishment is due
From me to him that shall abuse my bed?
Is it not death? Nor can that satisfy,
Unless I send your limbs [3] through all the land,
To show how nobly I have freed myself.   235
King. Draw not thy sword; thou know'st I
   cannot fear
A subject's hand; but thou shalt feel the
   weight
Of this, if thou dost rage.
Amin.   The weight of that!
If you have any worth, for Heaven's sake, think
I fear not swords; for, as you are mere man,   240
I dare as easily kill you for this deed,
As you dare think to do it. But there is
Divinity about you that strikes dead
My rising passions: as you are my King,
I fall before you, and present my sword   245
To cut mine own flesh, if it be your will.
Alas, I am nothing but a multitude
Of walking griefs! Yet, should I murder you,
I might before the world take the excuse
Of madness: for, compare my injuries,   250
And they will well appear too sad a weight
For reason to endure. But, fall I first
Amongst my sorrows, ere my treacherous hand
Touch holy things! But why (I know not what
I have to say), why did you choose out me   255
To make thus wretched? There were thousands,
   fools
Easy to work on, and of state enough,
Within the island.
Evad.   I would not have a fool;
It were no credit for me.
Amin.   Worse and worse!   259

Thou, that dar'st talk unto thy husband thus,
Profess thyself a whore, and, more than so,
Resolve to be so still! —— It is my fate
To bear and bow beneath a thousand griefs,
To keep that little credit with the world! —
But there were wise ones too; you might have
   ta'en   265
Another.
King. No: for I believ'd thee honest,
As thou wert valiant.
Amin.   All the happiness [4]
Bestow'd upon me turns into disgrace.
Gods, take your honesty again, for I   270
Am loaden with it! — Good my lord the King,
Be private in it.
King.   Thou mayst live, Amintor,
Free as thy king, if thou wilt wink at this,
And be a means that we may meet in secret.
Amin. A bawd! Hold, hold, my breast! A
   bitter curse   275
Seize me, if I forget not all respects
That are religious, on another word
Sounded like that; and through a sea of sins
Will wade to my revenge, though I should call
Pains here and after life upon my soul!   280
King. Well, I am resolute [5] you lay not with
   her;
And so I leave you.   *Exit.*
Evad.   You must needs be prating;
And see what follows!
Amin.   Prithee, vex me not.
Leave me; I am afraid some sudden start
Will pull a murder on me.
Evad.   I am gone;   285
I love my life well.   *Exit.*
Amin.   I hate mine as much.
This 't is to break a troth! I should be glad,
If all this tide of grief would make me mad.
                       Exit.

[SCENE II.] [6]

Enter MELANTIUS.

Mel. I 'll know the cause of all Amintor's
   griefs,
Or friendship shall be idle.

Enter CALIANAX.

Cal.   Oh, Melantius,
My daughter will die!
Mel.   Trust me, I am sorry:
Would thou hadst ta'en her room!
Cal.   Thou art a slave,
A cut-throat slave, a bloody treacherous slave! [5]
Mel. Take heed, old man; thou wilt be heard
   to rave,
And lose thine offices.
Cal.   I am valiant grown
At all these years, and thou art but a slave!
Mel. Leave!
Some company will come, and I respect   10
Thy years, not thee, so much, that I could wish
To laugh there alone.
Cal.   I 'll spoil your mirth:
I mean to fight with thee. There lie, my cloak.

---

[1] Ingenuous.   [2] Tale-tellers.
[3] So Sympson. Qq. and F *lives.*

[4] Fortunate qualities.   [6] A room in the palace
[5] Convinced.

This was my father's sword, and he durst fight.
Are you prepar'd?
Mel.   Why wilt thou dote thyself   15
Out of thy life? Hence, get thee to bed,
Have careful looking-to, and eat warm things,
And trouble not me: my head is full of thoughts
More weighty than thy life or death can be.
Cal. You have a name in war, where you
    stand safe   20
Amongst a multitude; but I will try
What you dare do unto a weak old man
In single fight. You will give ground, I fear.
Come, draw,
Mel. I will not draw, unless thou pull'st thy
    death   25
Upon thee with a stroke. There's no one blow,
That thou canst give hath strength enough to
    kill me.
Tempt me not so far, then: the power of earth
Shall not redeem thee.
Cal. [*Aside.*]   I must let him alone;
He's stout and able; and, to say the truth,   30
However I may set a face and talk,
I am not valiant. When I was a youth,
I kept my credit with a testy trick
I had 'mongst cowards, but durst never fight.
Mel. I will not promise to preserve your life,
If you do stay.
Cal. [*Aside.*] I would give half my land   36
That I durst fight with that proud man a little.
If I had men to hold him, I would beat him
Till he askt me mercy.
Mel.   Sir, will you be gone?
Cal. [*Aside.*] I dare not stay; but I will go
home, and beat   40
My servants all over for this.   *Exit.*
Mel. This old fellow haunts me.
But the distracted carriage of mine Amintor
Takes deeply on me.[1] I will find the cause: 44
I fear his conscience cries, he wrong'd Aspatia.

Enter AMINTOR.

Amin. [*Aside.*] Men's eyes are not so subtle
    to perceive
My inward misery: I bear my grief
Hid from the world. How art thou wretched
    then?
For aught I know, all husbands are like me;
And every one I talk with of his wife   50
Is but a well dissembler of his woes,
As I am. Would I knew it! for the rareness
Afflicts me now.
Mel. Amintor, we have not enjoy'd our [54
friendship of late, for we were wont to change
our souls in talk.
Amin. Melantius, I can tell thee a good jest
of Strato and a lady the last day.
Mel. How was't?
Amin. Why, such an odd one!   60
Mel. I have long'd to speak with you; not of
an idle jest, that's forc'd, but of matter you are
bound to utter to me.
Amin. What is that, my friend?
Mel. I have observ'd your words fall from
    your tongue   65

Wildly; and all your carriage
Like one that strove to shew his merry mood,
When he were ill dispos'd. You were not wont
To put such scorn into your speech, or wear
Upon your face ridiculous jollity.   70
Some sadness sits here, which your cunning
    would
Cover o'er with smiles, and 't will not be. What
    is it?
Amin. A sadness here! What cause
Can fate provide for me to make me so?   74
Am I not lov'd through all this isle? The King
Rains greatness on me. Have I not received
A lady to my bed, that in her eye
Keeps mounting fire, and on her tender cheeks
Inevitable[2] colour, in her heart
A prison for all virtue? Are not you,   80
Which is above all joys, my constant friend?
What sadness can I have? No; I am light,
And feel the courses of my blood more warm
And stirring than they were. Faith, marry too;
And you will feel so unexprest a joy   85
In chaste embraces, that you will indeed
Appear another.
Mel.   You may shape, Amintor,
Causes to cozen the whole world withal,
And you yourself too; but 't is not like a friend
To hide your soul from me. 'T is not your
    nature   90
To be thus idle. I have seen you stand
As you were blasted 'midst of all your mirth;
Call thrice aloud, and then start, feigning joy
So coldly! — World, what do I here? A friend
Is nothing. Heaven, I would ha' told that man
My secret sins! I 'll search an unknown land, 96
And there plant friendship; all is withered here.
Come with a compliment! I would have fought,
Or told my friend 'a lied, ere sooth'd[3] him so.—
Out of my bosom!   100
Amin. But there is nothing.
Mel.   Worse and worse! farewell:
From this time have acquaintance, but no friend.
Amin. Melantius, stay: you shall know what
    that is.
Mel. See how you play'd with friendship! Be
    advis'd
How you give cause unto yourself to say   105
You ha' lost a friend.
Amin.   Forgive what I ha' done;
For I am so o'ergone with injuries
Unheard of, that I lose consideration
Of what I ought to do. Oh, oh!
Mel.   Do not weep.
What is't? May I once but know the man   110
Hath turn'd my friend thus!
Amin.   I had spoke at first,
But that——
Mel.   But what?
Amin.   I held it most unfit
For you to know. Faith, do not know it yet.
Mel. Thou see'st my love, that will keep
    company   114
With thee in tears; hide nothing, then, from me;
For when I know the cause of thy distemper,
With mine old armour I 'll adorn myself,

---

[1] Affects me deeply.

[2] Irresistible.   [3] Cajoled.

My resolution, and cut through thy foes,
Unto thy quiet, till I place thy heart
As peaceable as spotless innocence.　120
What is it?
　Amin. Why, 't is this —— it is too big
To get out —— let my tears make way awhile.
　Mel. Punish me strangely, Heaven, if he escape
Of life or fame, that brought this youth to this!
　Amin. Your sister ——
　Mel. 　　　　Well said.
　Amin. You will wish 't unknown,　125
When you have heard it.
　Mel. 　　　　No.
　Amin. 　　　　Is much to blame,
And to the King has given her honour up,
And lives in whoredom with him.
　Mel. 　　　　How 's this?
Thou art run mad with injury indeed;
Thou couldst not utter this else. Speak again;
For I forgive it freely; tell thy griefs.　131
　Amin. She 's wanton: I am loth to say, a whore,
Though it be true.
　Mel. Speak yet again, before mine anger grow
Up beyond throwing down. What are thy griefs?　135
　Amin. By all our friendship, these.
　Mel. 　　　　What, am I tame?
After mine actions, shall the name of friend
Blot all our family, and strike the brand
Of whore upon my sister, unreveng'd?
My shaking flesh, be thou a witness for me,　140
With what unwillingness I go to scourge
This railer, whom my folly hath call'd friend?
I will not take thee basely: thy sword　143
　　　　　　　　[Draws his sword.]
Hangs near thy hand: draw it, that I may whip
Thy rashness to repentance; draw thy sword!
　Amin. Not on thee, did thine anger go as high
As the wild surges. Thou shouldst do me ease
Here and eternally, if thy noble hand
Would cut me from my sorrows.
　Mel. 　　　　This is base
And fearful.[1] They that use to utter lies　150
Provide not blows but words to qualify[2]
The men they wrong'd. Thou hast a guilty cause.
　Amin. Thou pleasest me: for so much more
like this
Will raise my anger up above my griefs,
(Which is a passion easier to be borne,)　155
And I shall then be happy.
　Mel. 　　　　Take, then, more
To raise thine anger: 't is mere cowardice
Makes thee not draw; and I will leave thee dead,
However. But if thou art so much prest
With guilt and fear as not to dare to fight,　160
I 'll make thy memory loath'd, and fix a scandal
Upon thy name forever.
　Amin. [drawing his sword.] Then I draw,
As justly as our magistrates their swords
To cut offenders off. I knew before
'T would grate your ears; but it was base in you

To urge a weighty secret from your friend,　166
And then rage at it. I shall be at ease,
If I be kill'd; and, if you fall by me,
I shall not long outlive you.
　Mel. 　　　　Stay awhile. —
The name of friend is more than family,　170
Or all the world besides: I was a fool.
Thou searching human nature, that didst wake
To do me wrong, thou art inquisitive,　173
And thrusts me upon questions that will take
My sleep away! Would I had died, ere known
This sad dishonour! — Pardon me, my friend!
　　　　　　　[Sheaths his sword.]
If thou wilt strike, here is a faithful heart;
Pierce it, for I will never heave my hand
To thine. Behold the power thou hast in me!
I do believe my sister is a whore,　180
A leprous one. Put up thy sword, young man.
　Amin. How should I bear it, then, she being
so?
I fear, my friend, that you will lose me shortly;
　　　　　　　[Sheaths his sword.]
And I shall do a foul act on myself,
Through these disgraces.
　Mel. 　　　　Better half the land　185
Were buried quick[3] together. No, Amintor;
Thou shalt have ease. Oh, this adulterous King,
That drew her to 't! Where got he the spirit
To wrong me so?
　Amin. 　　　　What is it, then, to me,
If it be wrong to you?
　Mel. 　　　　Why, not so much.　190
The credit of our house is thrown away.
But from his iron den I 'll waken Death,
And hurl him on this King. My honesty
Shall steel my sword; and on its horrid point
I 'll wear my cause, that shall amaze the eyes
Of this proud man, and be too glitt'ring　196
For him to look on.
　Amin. I have undone my fame.
　Mel. Dry up thy watery eyes,
And cast a manly look upon my face;　200
For nothing is so wild as I, thy friend,
Till I have freed thee. Still this swelling breast.
I go thus from thee, and will never cease
My vengeance till I find thy heart at peace.
　Amin. It must not be so. Stay. Mine eyes
would tell　205
How loth I am to this; but, love and tears,
Leave me awhile! for I have hazarded
All that this world calls happy. — Thou hast
wrought
A secret from me, under name of friend,
Which art could ne'er have found, nor torture
wrung　210
From out my bosom. Give it me again;
For I will find it, wheresoe'er it lies,
Hid in the mortal'st part. Invent a way
To give it back.
　Mel. 　　　　Why would you have it back?
I will to death pursue him with revenge,　215
　Amin. Therefore I call it back from thee; for
I know
Thy blood so high, that thou wilt stir in this,
And shame me to posterity. Take to thy weapon!
　　　　　　　[Draws his sword.]

---

[1] Cowardly.　　　[2] Satisfy, make mild.　　　[3] Alive.

Mel. Hear thy friend, that bears more years
than thou.
Amin. I will not hear: but draw, or I —
Mel. Amintor ! 220
Amin. Draw, then ; for I am full as resolute
As fame and honour can enforce me be:
I cannot linger. Draw !
Mel. I do. But is not
My share of credit equal with thine,
If I do stir ?
Amin. No ; for it will be call'd 225
Honour in thee to spill thy sister's blood,
If she her birth abuse ; and, on the King
A brave revenge : but on me, that have walkt
With patience in it, it will fix the name
Of fearful cuckold. Oh, that word ! Be quick.
Mel. Then, join with me.
Amin. I dare not do a sin, 231
Or else I would. Be speedy.
Mel. Then, dare not fight with me ; for that's
a sin. —
His grief distracts him. — Call thy thoughts
again, 234
And to thyself pronounce the name of friend,
And see what that will work. I will not fight.
Amin. You must.
Mel. [*sheathing his sword.*] I will be kill'd first.
Though my passions
Offered the like to you, 't is not this earth
Shall buy my reason to it. Think awhile, 240
For you are (I must weep when I speak that)
Almost besides yourself.
Amin. [*sheathing his sword.*] Oh, my soft
temper !
So many sweet words from thy sister's mouth,
I am afraid would make me take her to 245
Embrace, and pardon her. I am mad indeed,
And know not what I do. Yet, have a care
Of me in what thou dost.
Mel. Why, thinks my friend
I will forget his honour ? or, to save
The bravery of our house, will lose his fame, 250
And fear to touch the throne of majesty ?
Amin. A curse will follow that ; but rather
live
And suffer with me.
Mel. I will do what worth
Shall bid me, and no more.
Amin. Faith, I am sick,
And desperately I hope ; yet, leaning thus, 255
I feel a kind of ease.
Mel. Come, take again
Your mirth about you.
Amin. I shall never do 't.
Mel. I warrant you ; look up ; we 'll walk to-
gether ;
Put thine arm here ; all shall be well again.
Amin. Thy love (oh, wretched !) ay, thy love
Melantius ; 260
Why, I have nothing else.
Mel. Be merry, then. *Exeunt.*

Re-enter MELANTIUS.

Mel. This worthy young man may do violence
Upon himself ; but I have cherisht him
To my best power, and sent him smiling from
me.

To counterfeit again. Sword, hold thine edge ;
My heart will never fail me.

Enter DIPHILUS.

Diphilus ! 266
Thou com'st as sent.
Diph. Yonder has been such laughing.
Mel. Betwixt whom ?
Diph. Why, our sister and the King.
I thought their spleens would break ; they
laught us all
Out of the room. 270
Mel. They must weep, Diphilus.
Diph. Must they ?
Mel. They must.
Thou art my brother ; and, if I did believe
Thou hadst a base thought, I would rip it out,
Lie where it durst.
Diph. You should not ; I would first
Mangle myself and find it.
Mel. That was spoke 275
According to our strain.[1] Come, join thy hands
to mine,
And swear a firmness to what project I
Shall lay before thee.
Diph. You do wrong us both.
People hereafter shall not say there past
A bond, more than our loves, to tie our lives
And deaths together. 281
Mel. It is as nobly said as I would wish.
Anon I 'll tell you wonders : we are wrong'd.
Diph. But I will tell you now, we 'll right
ourselves.
Mel. Stay not : prepare the armour in my
house ; 285
And what friends you can draw unto our side,
Not knowing of the cause, make ready too.
Haste, Diphilus, the time requires it, haste ! —
Exit DIPHILUS.
I hope my cause is just ; I know my blood
Tells me it is ; and I will credit it. 290
To take revenge, and lose myself withal,
Were idle ; and to scape impossible,
Without I had the fort, which (misery !)
Remaining in the hands of my old enemy
Calianax — but I must have it. See 295

Re-enter CALIANAX.

Where he comes shaking by me ! — Good my
lord,
Forget your spleen to me. I never wrong'd you,
But would have peace with every man.
Cal. 'T is well ;
If I durst fight, your tongue would lie at quiet.
Mel. You 're touchy without all cause.
Cal. Do, mock me. 300
Mel. By mine honour, I speak truth.
Cal. Honour ! where is 't ?
Mel. See, what starts you make
Into your idle hatred, to my love
And freedom to you. I come with resolution
To obtain a suit of you.
Cal. A suit of me ! 305
'T is very like it should be granted, sir.
Mel. Nay, go not hence.

[1] Race, stock.

'T is this ; you have the keeping of the fort,
And I would wish you, by the love you ought
To bear unto me, to deliver it   310
Into my hands.
    Cal.   I am in hope thou art mad,
To talk to me thus.
    Mel.   But there is a reason
To move you to it : I would kill the King,
That wrong'd you and your daughter.
    Cal.   Out, traitor !
    Mel. Nay, but stay: I cannot scape, the deed   315
once done,
Without I have this fort.
    Cal.   And should I help thee ?
Now thy treacherous mind betrays itself.
    Mel. Come, delay me not ;
Give me a sudden answer, or already
Thy last is spoke ! Refuse not offered love   320
When it comes clad in secrets.
    Cal. [*Aside.*]   If I say
I will not, he will kill me ; I do see 't
Writ in his looks ; and should I say I will,
He 'll run and tell the King. — I do not shun
Your friendship, dear Melantius ; but this cause
Is weighty : give me but an hour to think.   326
    Mel. Take it. — [*Aside.*] I know this goes
unto the King ;
But I am arm'd.   *Exit.*
    Cal.   Methinks I feel myself
But twenty now again. This fighting fool
Wants policy : I shall revenge my girl,   330
And make her red again. I pray my legs
Will last that pace that I will carry them :
I shall want breath before I find the King.
                            Exit.

ACT IV

[SCENE I.][1]

Enter MELANTIUS, EVADNE, *and* Ladies.

    Mel. Save you !
    Evad.   Save you, sweet brother.
    Mel. In my blunt eye, methinks, you look,
Evadne —
    Evad. Come, you would make me blush.
    Mel.   I would, Evadne ;
I shall displease my ends else.
    Evad.   You shall, if you
Commend me ; I am bashful. Come, sir, how
do   5
I look ?
    Mel. I would not have your women hear me
Break into commendation of you ; 't is not
Seemly.
    Evad. Go wait me in the gallery.
                      Exeunt Ladies.
Now speak.
    Mel.   I 'll lock the door first.
    Evad.   Why ?
    Mel. I will not have your gilded things, that
dance   10
In visitation with their Milan skins,[2]
Choke up my business.

    Evad.   You are strangely dispos'd, sir.
    Mel. Good madam, not to make you merry.
    Evad. No ; if you praise me, it will make me
sad.
    Mel. Such a sad commendation I have for you.
    Evad. Brother,   16
The court hath made you witty, and learn to
riddle.
    Mel. I praise the court for 't: has it learn'd
you nothing ?
    Evad. Me !
    Mel.   Ay, Evadne ; thou art young and
handsome,
A lady of a sweet complexion,   20
And such a flowing carriage, that it cannot
Choose but inflame a kingdom.
    Evad.   Gentle brother !
    Mel. 'T is yet in thy repentance, foolish
woman,
To make me gentle.
    Evad.   How is this ?
    Mel.   'T is base ;   24
And I could blush, at these years, through all
My honour'd scars, to come to such a parley.
    Evad. I understand you not.
    Mel.   You dare not, fool !
They that commit thy faults fly the remem-
brance.
    Evad. My faults, sir ! I would have you know,
I care not   29
If they were written here, here in my forehead.
    Mel. Thy body is too little for the story ;
The lusts of which would fill another woman,
Though [3] she had twins within her.
    Evad.   This is saucy:
Look you intrude no more ! There 's your way.
    Mel. Thou art my way, and I will tread upon
thee,   35
Till I find truth out.
    Evad.   What truth is that you look for ?
    Mel. Thy long-lost honour. Would the gods
had set me
Rather to grapple with the plague, or stand
One of their loudest bolts ! Come, tell me
quickly,
Do it without enforcement, and take heed   40
You swell me not above my temper.
    Evad.   How, sir !
Where got you this report ?
    Mel.   Where there was people,
In every place.
    Evad.   They and the seconds of it
Are base people : believe them not, they lied.   44
    Mel. Do not play with mine anger ; do not,
wretch !   [*Seizes her.*]
I come to know that desperate fool that drew
thee
From thy fair life. Be wise, and lay him open.
    Evad. Unhand me, and learn manners ! Such
another
Forgetfulness forfeits your life.
    Mel. Quench me this mighty humour, and
then tell me   50
Whose whore you are ; for you are one, I know it.

---

[1] An apartment of Evadne.
[2] Gloves manufactured at Milan.

[3] Theobald read, *As though sh'ad.* Other edd. take
fill in sense of " cover with writing ; " Dyce as " inflame," which is perhaps best.

Let all mine honours perish but I 'll find him
Though he lie lock'd up in thy blood ! Be sud-
den ;
There is no facing it ; and be not flattered.
The burnt air, when the Dog[1] reigns, is not
    fouler   55
Than thy contagious name, till thy repentance
(If the gods grant thee any) purge thy sickness.
  Evad. Begone ! you are my brother ; that 's
    your safety.
  Mel. I 'll be a wolf first. 'T is, to be thy
    brother,
An infamy below the sin of coward.   60
I am as far from being part of thee
As thou art from thy virtue. Seek a kindred
'Mongst sensual beasts, and make a goat thy
    brother ;
A goat is cooler. Will you tell me yet ?
  Evad. If you stay here and rail thus, I shall
    tell you   65
I 'll ha' you whipt ! Get you to your command,
And there preach to your sentinels, and tell
    them
What a brave man you are : I shall laugh at you.
  Mel. You 're grown a glorious whore ! Where
    be your fighters ?   69
What mortal fool durst raise thee to this daring,
And I alive ! By my just sword, he 'd safer
Bestrid a billow when the angry North
Ploughs up the sea, or made Heaven's fire his
    foe !
Work me no higher. Will you discover yet ?
  Evad. The fellow 's mad. Sleep, and speak
    sense.   75
  Mel. Force my swol'n heart no further ; I
    would save thee.
Your great maintainers are not here, they dare
    not.
Would they were all, and armed ! I would speak
    loud ;
Here 's one should thunder to 'em ! Will you
    tell me ? —
Thou hast no hope to scape. He that dares
    most,   80
And damns away his soul to do thee service,
Will sooner snatch meat from a hungry lion
Than come to rescue thee. Thou hast death
    about thee ; —
Has undone thine honour, poison'd thy virtue,
And, of a lovely rose, left thee a canker.[2]   85
  Evad. Let me consider.
  Mel.   Do, whose child thou wert,
Whose honour thou hast murdered, whose grave
    opened,
And so pull'd on the gods that in their justice
They must restore him flesh again and life,   89
And raise his dry bones to revenge this scandal.
  Evad. The gods are not of my mind ; they
    had better
Let 'em lie sweet still in the earth ; they 'll stink
    here.
  Mel. Do you raise mirth out of my easiness ?
Forsake me, then, all weaknesses of nature,
                            [*Draws his sword.*]

---
[1] The dog-star, Sirius.
[2] Dog-rose ; also used of the canker worm, a disease
attacking plants. Cf. V. i. 76.

That make men women ! Speak, you whore,
    speak truth,   95
Or, by the dear soul of thy sleeping father,
This sword shall be thy lover ! Tell, or I 'll kill
    thee ;
And, when thou hast told all, thou wilt deserve
    it.
  Evad. You will not murder me ?
  Mel. No ; 't is a justice, and a noble one,   100
To put the light out of such base offenders.
  Evad. Help !
  Mel. By thy foul self, no human help shall
    help thee,
If thou criest ! When I have kill'd thee, as I
Have vow'd to do, if thou confess not, naked   105
As thou hast left thine honour will I leave thee,
That on thy branded flesh the world may read
Thy black shame and my justice. Wilt thou
    bend yet ?
  Evad. Yes.
  Mel. Up, and begin your story.   110
  Evad. Oh, I am miserable !
  Mel. 'T is true, thou art. Speak truth still.
  Evad. I have offended : noble sir, forgive me !
  Mel. With what secure slave ?
  Evad.   Do not ask me, sir ;
Mine own remembrance is a misery   115
Too mighty for me.
  Mel.   Do not fall back again ;
My sword 's unsheathed yet.
  Evad.   What shall I do ?
  Mel. Be true, and make your fault less.
  Evad.   I dare not tell.
  Mel. Tell, or I 'll be this day a-killing thee.
  Evad. Will you forgive me, then ?   120
  Mel. Stay ; I must ask mine honour first.
I have too much foolish nature in me : speak.
  Evad. Is there none else here ?
  Mel. None but a fearful[3] conscience ; that 's
    too many.
Who is 't ?
  Evad. Oh, hear me gently ! It was the King.
  Mel. No more. My worthy father 's and my
    services   126
Are liberally rewarded ! King, I thank thee !
For all my dangers and my wounds thou hast
    paid me
In my own metal : these are soldiers' thanks ! —
How long have you liv'd thus, Evadne ?
  Evad.   Too long.   130
  Mel. Too late you find it. Can you be sorry ?[4]
  Evad. Would I were half as blameless !
  Mel. Evadne, thou wilt to thy trade again.
  Evad. First to my grave.
  Mel. Would gods thou hadst been so blest !
Dost thou not hate this King now ? Prithee,
    hate him :   135
Couldst thou not curse him ? I command thee,
    curse him ;
Curse till the gods hear, and deliver him
To thy just wishes. Yet I fear, Evadne,
You had rather play your game out.
  Evad.   No ; I feel
Too many sad confusions here, to let in   140
Any loose flame hereafter.

---
[3] Cowardly.   [4] Q *very sorry.*

Mel. Dost thou not feel, 'mongst all those,
    one brave anger,
That breaks out nobly, and directs thine arm
To kill this base King?
Evad.   All the gods forbid it!
Mel. No, all the gods require it;   145
They are dishonoured in him.
Evad.   'T is too fearful.
Mel. You're valiant in his bed, and bold
    enough
To be a stale whore, and have your madam's
    name
Discourse for grooms and pages; and hereafter,
When his cool majesty hath laid you by,   150
To be at pension with some needy sir
For meat and coarser clothes; thus far you
    know
No fear. Come, you shall kill him.
Evad.   Good sir!
Mel. An 't were to kiss him dead, thou 'dst
    smother him:
Be wise, and kill him. Canst thou live, and
    know   155
What noble minds shall make thee, see thyself
Found out with every finger, made the shame
Of all successions, and in this great ruin
Thy brother and thy noble husband broken?
Thou shalt not live thus. Kneel, and swear to
    help me,   160
When I shall call thee to it; or, by all
Holy in Heaven and earth, thou shalt not live
To breathe a full hour longer; not a thought!
Come 't is a righteous oath. Give me thy hands,
And, both to Heaven held up, swear, by that
    wealth   165
This lustful thief stole from thee, when I say it,
To let his foul soul out.
Evad.   Here I swear it; [*Kneels.*]
And, all you spirits of abused ladies,
Help me in this performance!
Mel. [*raising her.*] Enough. This must be
    known to none   170
But you and I, Evadne; not to your lord,
Though he be wise and noble, and a fellow
Dares step as far into a worthy action
As the most daring, ay, as far as justice.
Ask me not why. Farewell.   *Exit.*   175
Evad. Would I could say so to my black dis-
    grace!
Oh, where have I been all this time? How
    friended,
That I should lose myself thus desperately,
And none for pity show me how I wand'red?
There is not in the compass of the light   180
A more unhappy creature: sure, I am mon-
    strous;
For I have done those follies, those mad mis-
    chiefs,
Would dare [1] a woman. Oh, my loaden soul,
Be not so cruel to me; choke not up
The way to my repentance!

      Enter AMINTOR.

               Oh, my lord!   185

Amin. How now?

Evad.   My much abused lord! [*Kneels.*]
Amin.   This cannot be!
Evad. I do not kneel to live; I dare not hope
    it;
The wrongs I did are greater. Look upon me,
Though I appear with all my faults.
Amin.   Stand up.
This is a new way to beget more sorrow;   190
Heaven knows I have too many. Do not mock
    me:
Though I am tame, and bred up with my
    wrongs,
Which are my foster-brothers, I may leap,
Like a hand-wolf, [2] into my natural wildness, 194
And do an outrage. Prithee, do not mock me.
Evad. My whole life is so leprous, it infects
All my repentance. I would buy your pardon,
Though at the highest set, [3] even with my life:
That slight contrition, that 's no sacrifice   199
For what I have committed.
Amin.   Sure, I dazzle;
There cannot be a faith in that foul woman,
That knows no god more mighty than her mis-
    chiefs.
Thou dost still worse, still number on thy
    faults,
To press my poor heart thus. Can I believe
There 's any seed of virtue in that woman   205
Left to shoot up, that dares go on in sin
Known, and so known as thine is? Oh, Evadne!
Would there were any safety in thy sex,
That I might put a thousand sorrows off,
And credit thy repentance! but I must not. 210
Thou hast brought me to that dull calamity,
To that strange misbelief of all the world
And all things that are in it, that I fear
I shall fall like a tree, and find my grave,
Only rememb'ring that I grieve.
Evad.   My lord,   215
Give me your griefs: you are an innocent,
A soul as white as Heaven; let not my sins
Perish your noble youth. I do not fall here
To shadow by dissembling with my tears,
(As all say women can,) or to make less   220
What my hot will hath done, which Heaven
    and you
Know to be tougher than the hand of time
Can cut from man's remembrance; no, I do not;
I do appear the same, the same Evadne,
Drest in the shames I liv'd in, the same mon-
    ster.   225
But these are names of honour to what I am;
I do present myself the foulest creature,
Most poisonous, dangerous, and despis'd of men,
Lerna [4] e'er bred or Nilus. I am hell,   129
Till you, my dear lord, shoot your light into me,
The beams of your forgiveness; I am soul-sick,
And wither with the fear of one condemn'd,
Till I have got your pardon.
Amin.   Rise, Evadne.
Those heavenly powers that put this good into
    thee
Grant a continuance of it! I forgive thee: 235
Make thyself worthy of it; and take heed,

[1] Frighten.

[2] A tame wolf.   [3] Stake.
[4] The marsh where the Hydra lived which Hercules
slew.

Take heed, Evadne, this be serious.
Mock not the powers above, that can and dare
Give thee a great example of their justice
To all ensuing ages,[1] if thou play'st   240
With thy repentance, the best sacrifice.
    Evad. I have done nothing good to win belief,
My life hath been so faithless. All the crea-
        tures,
Made for Heaven's honours, have their ends,
        and good ones
All but the cozening crocodiles, false women.
They reign here like those plagues, those killing
        sores,   245
Men pray against; and when they die, like
        tales
Ill told and unbeliev'd, they pass away,
And go to dust forgotten. But, my lord,
Those short days I shall number to my rest   250
(As many must not see me) shall, though too late,
Though in my evening, yet perceive a will,
Since I can do no good, because a woman,
Reach constantly at something that is near it :
I will redeem one minute of my age,   255
Or, like another Niobe, I 'll weep,
Till I am water.
    Amin.   I am now dissolved :
My frozen soul melts. May each sin thou hast,
Find a new mercy ! Rise ; I am at peace.
Hadst thou been thus, thus excellently good,   260
Before that devil-king tempted thy frailty,
Sure thou hadst made a star. Give me thy
        hand :
From this time I will know thee ; and, as far
As virtue gives me leave, be thy Amintor.
When we meet next, I will salute thee fairly,   265
And pray the gods to give thee happy days :
My charity shall go along with thee,
Though my embraces must be far from thee.
I should ha' kill'd thee, but this sweet repent-
        ance
Locks up my vengeance : for which thus I kiss
        thee —   270
The last kiss we must take : and would to
        Heaven
The holy priest that gave our hands together
Had given us equal virtues ! Go, Evadne ;
The gods thus part our bodies. Have a care
My honour falls no farther : I am well, then.
    Evad. All the dear joys here, and above
        hereafter,   275
Crown thy fair soul ! Thus I take leave, my
        lord ;
And never shall you see the foul Evadne.
Till she have tried all honoured means, that
        may
Set her in rest and wash her stains away.   280
                Exeunt [*severally*].

[SCENE II.] [2]

A Banquet spread. Enter KING *and* CALIANAX.
        Hautboys play within.

    King. I cannot tell how I should credit this
From you, that are his enemy.
    Cal.   I am sure

He said it to me ; and I 'll justify it
What way he dares oppose — but with my sword.
    King. But did he break, without all circum-
        stance,
To you, his foe, that he would have the fort,   5
To kill me, and then scape ?
    Cal.   If he deny it,
I 'll make him blush.
    King.   It sounds incredibly.
    Cal. Ay, so does every thing I say of late.
    King. Not so, Calianax.
    Cal.   Yes, I should sit   10
Mute, whilst a rogue with strong arms cuts your
        throat.
    King. Well, I will try him ; and, if this be
        true,
I 'll pawn my life I 'll find it ; if 't be false,
And that you clothe your hate in such a lie,
You shall hereafter dote in your own house,   15
Not in the court.
    Cal.   Why, if it be a lie.
Mine ears are false, for I 'll be sworn I heard it.
Old men are good for nothing ; you were best
Put me to death for hearing, and free him
For meaning it. You would ha' trusted me   20
Once, but the time is altered.
    King.   And will still,
Where I may do with justice to the world.
You have no witness.
    Cal.   Yes, myself.
    King.   No more,
I mean, there were that heard it.
    Cal.   How ? no more !
Would you have more ? Why, am not I
        enough   25
To hang a thousand rogues ?
    King.   But so you may
Hang honest men too, if you please.
    Cal.   I may !
'T is like I will do so : there are a hundred
Will swear it for a need too, if I say it——
    King. Such witnesses we need not.
    Cal.   And 't is hard   30
If my word cannot hang a boisterous knave.
    King. Enough. — Where 's Strato ?

                Enter STRATO.

    Strato.   Sir ?
    King. Why, where 's all the company ? Call
        Amintor in ;
Evadne. Where 's my brother, and Melantius ?
Bid him come too ; and Diphilus. Call all   35
That are without there.   *Exit* STRATO.
                If he should desire
The combat of you, 't is not in the power
Of all our laws to hinder it, unless
We mean to quit 'em.
    Cal.   Why, if you do think
'T is fit an old man and a councillor   40
To fight for what he says, then you may grant
        it.

Enter AMINTOR, EVADNE, MELANTIUS, DIPH-
    ILUS, LYSIPPUS, CLEON, STRATO, *and* DIA-
    GORAS.

    King. Come, sirs ! — Amintor, thou art yet a
        bridegroom,

And I will use thee so; thou shalt sit down.—
Evadne, sit;—and you, Amintor, too;
This banquet is for you, sir.—Who has
brought   45
A merry tale about him, to raise laughter
Amongst our wine? Why, Strato, where art
thou?
Thou wilt chop out with them unseasonably,
When I desire 'em not.
    Stra. 'T is my ill luck, sir, so to spend them,
then.   50
    King. Reach me a bowl of wine.— Melantius,
thou
Art sad.
    Mel. I should be, sir, the merriest here,
But I ha' ne'er a story of mine own
Worth telling at this time.
    King.   Give me the wine. — 55
Melantius, I am now considering
How easy 't were for any man we trust
To poison one of us in such a bowl.
    Mel. I think it were not hard, sir, for a
knave.
    Cal. [*Aside.*] Such as you are.   60
    King. I' faith, 't were easy. It becomes us
well
To get plain-dealing men about ourselves;
Such as you all are here.— Amintor, to thee;
And to thy fair Evadne.   [*Drinks.*]
    Mel. [*Aside.*]   Have you thought
Of this, Calianax?
    Cal.   Yes, marry, have I.   65
    Mel. And what's your resolution?
    Cal.   You shall have it, —
[*Aside.*] Soundly, I warrant you.
    King. Reach to Amintor, Strato.
    Amin.   Here, my love;
        [*Drinks and then hands the cup to*
            EVADNE.]
This wine will do thee wrong, for it will set
Blushes upon thy cheeks; and, till thou dost 70
A fault, 't were pity.
    King.   Yet I wonder much
[At] the strange desperation of these men,
That dare attempt such acts here in our state:
He could not scape that did it.
    Mel.   Were he known,
Unpossible.
    King. It would be known, Melantius.   75
    Mel. It ought to be. If he got then away,
He must wear all our lives upon his sword:
He need not fly the island; he must leave
No one alive.
    King. No; I should think no man
Could kill me, and scape clear, but that old
man.   80
    Cal. But I! Heaven bless me! I! should I,
my liege?
    King. I do not think thou wouldst; but yet
thou mightst,
For thou hast in thy hands the means to scape,
By keeping of the fort.— He has, Melantius,
And he has kept it well.
    Mel.   From cobwebs, sir,   85
'T is clean swept; I can find no other art
In keeping of it now. 'T was ne'er besieg'd
Since he commanded.

    Cal.   I shall be sure
Of your good word; but I have kept it safe
From such as you.
    Mel.   Keep your ill temper in: 90
I speak no malice; had my brother kept it,
I should ha' said as much.
    King.   You are not merry.
Brother, drink wine. Sit you all still: — (*Aside.*)
        Calianax,
I cannot trust this. I have thrown out words,
That would have fetcht warm blood upon the
cheeks   95
Of guilty men, and he is never mov'd;
He knows no such thing.
    Cal.   Impudence may scape,
When feeble virtue is accus'd.
    King.   'A must,
If he were guilty, feel an alteration
At this our whisper, whilst we point at him:
You see he does not.
    Cal.   Let him hang himself;   100
What care I what he does? This he did say.
    King. Melantius, you can easily conceive
What I have meant; for men that are in fault
Can subtly apprehend when others aim   105
At what they do amiss: but I forgive
Freely before this man, — Heaven do so too!
I will not touch thee, so much as with shame
Of telling it. Let it be so no more.
    Cal. Why, this is very fine!
    Mel.   I cannot tell   110
What 't is you mean; but I am apt enough
Rudely to thrust into an ignorant fault.
But let me know it. Happily [1] 't is nought
But misconstruction; and, where I am clear,
I will not take forgiveness of the gods,   115
Much less of you.
    King. Nay, if you stand so stiff,
I shall call back my mercy.
    Mel.   I want smoothness
To thank a man for pardoning of a crime
I never knew.
    King. Not to instruct your knowledge, but
to show you   120
My ears are every where; you meant to kill me,
And get the fort to scape.
    Mel.   Pardon me, sir;
My bluntness will be pardoned. You preserve
A race of idle people here about you,
Facers [2] and talkers, to defame the worth   125
Of those that do things worthy. The man that
uttered this
Had perisht without food, be 't who it will,
But for this arm, that fenc'd him from the foe;
And if I thought you gave a faith to this,
The plainness of my nature would speak more.
Give me a pardon (for you ought to do 't)   131
To kill him that spake this.
    Cal. [*Aside.*]   Ay, that will be
The end of all; then I am fairly paid
For all my care and service.
    Mel.   That old man,
Who calls me enemy, and of whom I   135
(Though I will never match my hate so low)

----

[1] Haply.
[2] Shameless fellows. So Q₁. Q₂ ff. *Eaters.*

Have no good thought, would yet, I think, ex-
    cuse me,
And swear he thought me wrong'd in this,
    Cal.   Who, I ?
Thou shameless fellow ! didst thou not speak
    to me
Of it thyself ?
    Mel.   Oh, then it came from him !   140
    Cal. From me ! who should it come from but
        from me ?
    Mel. Nay, I believe your malice is enough ;
But I have lost my anger. — Sir, I hope
You are well satisfied.
    King.   Lysippus, cheer
Amintor and his lady. — There 's no sound   145
Comes from you ;   I will come and do 't my-
    self.
    Amin. [*Aside.*] You have done already, sir,
    for me, I thank you.
    King. I do credit this from him,
How slight soe'er you make 't.
    Mel.   'T is strange you should.
    Cal. 'T is strange 'a should believe an old
        man's word   150
That never lied in 's life !
    Mel.   I talk not to thee. —
Shall the wild words of this distempered man,
Frantic with age and sorrow, make a breach
Betwixt your majesty and me ? 'T was wrong
To hearken to him ; but to credit him,   155
As much at least as I have power to bear.
But pardon me — whilst I speak only truth,
I may commend myself — I have bestow'd
My careless blood with you, and should be loth
To think an action that would make me lose   160
That and my thanks too. When I was a boy,
I thrust myself into my country's cause,
And did a deed that pluckt five years from
    time,
And styl'd me man then. And for you, my
    King,
Your subjects all have fed by virtue of   165
My arm. This sword of mine hath plough'd
    the ground,
And reapt the fruit in peace ;
And you yourself have liv'd at home in ease.
So terrible I grew, that without swords,
My name hath fetcht you conquest : and my
    heart   170
And limbs are still the same ; my will as great
To do you service. Let me not be paid
With such a strange distrust.
    King.   Melantius,
I held it great injustice to believe
Thine enemy, and did not ; if I did,   175
I do not ; let that satisfy. — What, struck
With sadness all ? More wine !
    Cal.   A few fine words
Have overthrown my truth. Ah, thou 'rt a
    villain !
    Mel. (*Aside.*) Why, thou wert better let me
    have the fort :
Dotard, I will disgrace thee thus for ever ;   180
There shall no credit lie upon thy words.
Think better, and deliver it.
    Cal.   My liege,
He 's at me now again to do it. — Speak ;

Deny it, if thou canst. — Examine him
Whilst he is hot ; for, if he cool again,   185
He will forswear it.
    King.   This is lunacy,
I hope, Melantius.
    Mel.   He hath lost himself
Much, since his daughter mist the happinsss
My sister gain'd ; and, though he call me foe,
I pity him.
    Cal.   Pity ! A pox upon you !   190
    Mel. Mark his disordered words : and at the
        masque
Diagoras knows he rag'd and rail'd at me,
And call'd a lady " whore," so innocent
She understood him not. But it becomes
Both you and me too to forgive distraction :   195
Pardon him, as I do.
    Cal.   I 'll not speak for thee,
For all thy cunning. — If you will be safe,
Chop off his head ; for there was never known
So impudent a rascal.
    King.   Some, that love him,
Get him to bed. Why, pity should not let   200
Age make itself contemptible ; we must be
All old. Have him away.
    Mel. [*Aside.*]   Calianax,
The king believes you ; come, you shall go
    home,
And rest ;   you ha' done well. You 'll give it
    up,
When I have us'd you thus a month, I hope.   205
    Cal. Now, now, 't is plain, sir ; he does
    move me still.
He says, he knows I 'll give him up the fort,
When he has us'd me thus a month. I am mad,
Am I not, still ?
    All.   Ha, ha, ha !
    Cal. I shall be mad indeed, if you do thus.
Why should you trust a sturdy fellow there   211
(That has no virtue in him, all 's in his sword)
Before me ? Do but take his weapons from
    him,
And he 's an ass ; and I am a very fool,
Both with 'em [1] and without 'em,[1] as you use
    me.   215
    All. Ha, ha, ha !
    King. 'T is well, Calianax : but if you use
This once again, I shall entreat some other
To see your offices be well discharg'd. —
Be merry, gentlemen. — It grows somewhat
    late. —   220
Amintor, thou wouldst be a-bed again.
    Amin. Yes, sir.
    King.   And you, Evadne. — Let me take
Thee in my arms, Melantius, and believe
Thou art, as thou deserv'st to be, my friend
Still and for ever. — Good Calianax,   225
Sleep soundly ; it will bring thee to thyself.
        Exeunt all except MELANTIUS *and*
            CALIANAX.
    Cal. Sleep soundly ! I sleep soundly now, I
        hope ;
I could not be thus else. — How dar'st thou
    stay
Alone with me, knowing how thou hast us'd
    me ?

----

[1] So Dyce. Old edd. *him.*

Mel. You cannot blast me with your tongue,
　　and that's　　　　　　　　　　　　　230
The strongest part you have about you.
　Cal.　　　　　　　　　　　　　　　I
Do look for some great punishment for this ;
For I begin to forget all my hate,
And take 't unkindly that mine enemy
Should use me so extraordinarily scurvily.　235
　Mel. I shall melt too, if you begin to take
Unkindnesses : I never meant you hurt.
　Cal. Thou 'lt anger me again. Thou wretched
　　rogue,
Meant me no hurt ! Disgrace me with the
　　King !
Lose all my offices ! This is no hurt,　　　240
Is it ? I prithee, what dost thou call hurt ?
　Mel. To poison men, because they love me
　　not ;
To call the credit of men's wives in question ;
To murder children betwixt me and land ;　244
This is all hurt.
　Cal.　　　　　All this thou think'st is sport ;
For mine is worse : but use thy will with me ;
For betwixt grief and anger I could cry.
　Mel. Be wise, then, and be safe ; thou may'st
　　revenge —
　Cal. Ay, o' the King : I would revenge of
　　thee.
　Mel. That you must plot yourself.
　Cal.　　　　　　　　I 'm a fine plotter.
　Mel. The short is, I will hold thee with the
　　King　　　　　　　　　　　　　　251
In this perplexity, till peevishness
And thy disgrace have laid thee in thy grave.
But if thou wilt deliver up the fort,
I 'll take thy trembling body in my arms,　255
And bear thee over dangers. Thou shalt hold
Thy wonted state.
　Cal.　　　　　If I should tell the King,
Canst thou deny 't again ?
　Mel.　　　　　　Try, and believe.
　Cal. Nay, then, thou canst bring any thing
　　about.
Melantius, thou shalt have the fort.
　Mel.　　　　　　　　　Why, well.
Here let our hate be buried ; and this hand　261
Shall right us both. Give me thy aged breast
To compass.
　Cal.　　Nay, I do not love thee yet ;
I cannot well endure to look on thee ;
And if I thought it were a courtesy,　　　265
Thou shouldst not have it. But I am disgrac'd ;
My offices are to be ta'en away ;
And, if I did but hold this fort a day,
I do believe the King would take it from me,
And give it thee, things are so strangely car-
　　ried.　　　　　　　　　　　　　270
Ne'er thank me for 't ; but yet the King shall
　　know
There was some such thing in 't I told him of,
And that I was an honest man.
　Mel.　　　　　　　　　He 'll buy
That knowledge very dearly.

　　　　Re-enter DIPHILUS.

　　　　　　　　　　Diphilus,
What news with thee ?

Diph.　　　　　This were a night indeed
To do it in : the King hath sent for her.　276
　Mel. She shall perform it then. — Go, Diph-
　　ilus,
And take from this good man, my worthy
　　friend,
The fort ; he 'll give it thee.
　Diph.　　　　　　Ha' you got that ?
　Cal. Art thou of the same breed ? Canst thou
　　deny　　　　　　　　　　　　　280
This to the King too ?
　Diph.　　　　　With a confidence
As great as his.
　Cal.　　　Faith, like enough.
　Mel. Away, and use him kindly.
　Cal.　　　　　　　Touch not me ;
I hate the whole strain.[1] If thou follow me
A great way off, I 'll give thee up the fort ;　285
And hang yourselves.
　Mel.　　　　Begone.
　Diph.　　　　　He 's finely wrought.
　　　　Exeunt CALIANAX *and* DIPHILUS.
　Mel. This is a night, spite of astronomers,[2]
To do the deed in. I will wash the stain
That rests upon our house off with his blood.

　　　　Re-enter AMINTOR.

　Amin. Melantius, now assist me : if thou
　　be'st　　　　　　　　　　　　　290
That which thou say'st, assist me. I have lost
All my distempers, and have found a rage
So pleasing ! Help me.
　Mel. [*Aside.*]　　Who can see him thus,
And not swear vengeance ? — What 's the mat-
　　ter, friend ?
　Amin. Out with thy sword ; and, hand in
　　hand with me,　　　　　　　　　295
Rush to the chamber of this hated King,
And sink him with the weight of all his sins
To hell for ever.
　Mel.　　　　'T were a rash attempt,
Not to be done with safety. Let your reason
Plot your revenge, and not your passion.　300
　Amin. If thou refusest me in these extremes,
Thou art no friend. He sent for her to me ;
By Heaven, to me, myself ! and, I must tell
　　you,
I love her as a stranger : there is worth
In that vile woman, worthy things, Melantius ;
And she repents. I 'll do 't myself alone,　305
Though I be slain. Farewell.
　Mel. [*Aside.*]　　He 'll overthrow
My whole design with madness.— Amintor,
Think what thou dost : I dare as much as
　　valour ;
But 't is the King, the King, the King, Amin-
　　tor,　　　　　　　　　　　　　310
With whom thou fightest ! (*Aside.*) — I know he
　　is honest.[3]
And this will work with him.
　Amin.　　　　　I cannot tell
What thou hast said ; but thou hast charm'
　　my sword
Out of my hand, and left me shaking here,
Defenceless.

　　　　[1] Family.　　[2] Astrologers.　　[3] Loyal.

Mel.   I will take it up for thee.   315
Amin. What a wild beast is uncollected [1]
man !
The thing that we call honour bears us all
Headlong unto sin, and yet itself is nothing.
Mel. Alas, how variable are thy thoughts !
Amin. Just like my fortunes. I was run to
that   320
I purpos'd to have chid thee for. Some plot,
I did distrust, thou hadst against the King,
By that old fellow's carriage. But take heed ;
There 's not the least limb growing to a King
But carries thunder in 't.
Mel.   I have none   325
Against him.
Amin. Why, come, then ; and still remember
We may not think revenge.
Mel.   I will remember. *Exeunt.*

ACT V

[SCENE I.] [2]

Enter EVADNE *and a* Gentleman [*of the Bed-chamber*].

Evad. Sir, is the King a-bed ?
Gent.   Madam, an hour ago.
Evad. Give me the key, then, and let none
be near ;
'T is the King's pleasure.
Gent. I understand you, madam ; would
't were mine !   5
Evad. You talk, you talk.
Gent. 'T is all I dare do, madam ; but the
King
Will wake, and then, methinks —
Evad. Saving your imagination, pray, good
night, sir.
Gent. A good night be it, then, and a long
one, madam.   10
I am gone.   *Exit.*
Evad.[3] The night grows horrible ; and all
about me
Like my black purpose. Oh, the conscience
King abed.
Of a lost virgin,[4] whither wilt thou pull me ?
To what things dismal as the depth of hell   15
Wilt thou provoke me ? Let no woman dare
From this hour be disloyal, if her heart be flesh,
If she have blood, and can fear. 'T is a daring
Above that desperate fool's that left his peace,
And went to sea to fight : 't is so many sins,   20
An age cannot repent 'em ; and so great,
The gods want mercy for. Yet I must through
'em :
I have begun a slaughter on my honour,
And I must end it there. — 'A sleeps. Good
Heavens !   24
Why give you peace to this untemperate beast,
That hath so long transgrest you ? I must kill
him,
And I will do it bravely : the mere joy

Tells me, I merit in it. Yet I must not
Thus tamely do it as he sleeps — that were
To rock him to another world : my vengeance   30
Shall take him waking, and then lay before
him
The number of his wrongs and punishments.
I 'll shape his sins like Furies, till I waken
His evil angel, his sick conscience,
And then I 'll strike him dead. — King, by your
leave ; —   *Ties his arms to the bed.*   35
I dare not trust your strength ; your grace and I
Must grapple upon even terms no more.
So, if he rail me not from my resolution,
I shall be strong enough. — My lord the King !
My lord ! — 'A sleeps, as if he meant to wake   40
No more. — My lord ! — Is he not dead al-
ready ? —
Sir ! My lord !
King. Who 's that ?
Evad.   Oh, you sleep soundly sir !
King.   My dear Evadne,
I have been dreaming of thee ; come to bed.
Evad. I am come at length, sir ; but how
welcome ?
King. What pretty new device is this,   45
Evadne ?
What, do you tie me to you ? By my love,
This is a quaint one. Come, my dear, and kiss
me ;
I 'll by thee Mars ; to bed, my queen of love.
Let us be caught together, that the gods   50
May see and envy our embraces.
Evad.   Stay, sir, stay ;
You are too hot, and I have brought you physic
To temper your high veins.
King. Prithee, to bed, then ; let me take it
warm ;
There thou shalt know the state of my body
better.   55
Evad. I know you have a surfeited foul body ;
And you must bleed.   [*Draws a knife.*]
King.   Bleed !
Evad. Ay, you shall bleed. Lie still ; and, if
the devil,
Your lust, will give you leave, repent. This
steel
Comes to redeem the honour that you stole,   60
King, my fair name ; which nothing but thy
death
Can answer to the world.
King.   How 's this, Evadne ?
Evad. I am not she ; nor bear I in this breast
So much cold spirit to be call'd a woman :
I am a tiger ; I am any thing   65
That knows not pity. Stir not ! If thou dost,
I 'll take thee unprepar'd, thy fears upon thee,
That make thy sins look double, and so send
thee
(By my revenge, I will !) to look those torments
Prepar'd for such black souls.   70
King. Thou dost not mean this ; 't is impos-
sible ;
Thou art too sweet and gentle.
Evad.   No, I am not :
I am as foul as thou art, and can number
As many such hells here. I was once fair,
Once I was lovely : not a blowing rose   75

---

[1] Without self-control.   [2] A room in the palace.
[3] Most mod. edd. begin a new scene here.
[4] Q. *virtue.*

More chastely sweet, till thou, thou, thou, foul
canker,ᴧ
(Stir not!) didst poison me. I was a world of
virtue,
Till your curst court and you (Hell bless you
for 't!)
With your temptations on temptations
Made me give up mine honour; for which,
King,   80
I am come to kill thee.
    King.   No!
    Evad.   I am.
    King.   Thou art not!
I prithee speak not these things. Thou art
gentle,
And wert not meant thus rugged.
    Evad.   Peace, and hear me.
Stir nothing but your tongue, and that for
mercy
To those above us; by whose lights I vow,   85
Those blessed fires [2] that shot to see our sin,
If thy hot soul had substance with thy blood,
I would kill that too; which, being past my
steel,
My tongue shall reach. Thou art a shameless
villain;
A thing out of the overcharge of nature   90
Sent, like a thick cloud, to disperse a plague
Upon weak catching [3] women; such a tyrant,
That for his lust would sell away his subjects,
Ay, all his Heaven hereafter!
    King.   Hear, Evadne,
Thou soul of sweetness, hear! I am thy King.
    Evad. Thou art my shame! Lie still; there's
none about you,   96
Within your cries; all promises of safety
Are but deluding dreams. Thus, thus, thou foul
man,
Thus I begin my vengeance!   *Stabs him.*
    King.   Hold, Evadne!
I do command thee hold.
    Evad.   I do not mean, sir, 100
To part so fairly with you; we must change
More of these love-tricks yet.
    King.   What bloody villain
Provokt thee to this murder?
    Evad.   Thou, thou monster!
    King. Oh!
    Evad. Thou kept'st me brave [4] at court, and
whor'd me, King;   105
Then married me to a young noble gentleman,
And whor'd me still.
    King.   Evadne, pity me!
    Evad. Hell take me, then! This for my lord
Amintor.
This for my noble brother! And this stroke
For the most wrong'd of women!   *Kills him.*
    King.   Oh! I die. 110
    Evad. Die all our faults together! I forgive
thee.   *Exit.*

Enter two [Gentlemen] of the bed-chamber.

1 *Gent.* Come, now she's gone, let's enter; the
King expects it, and will be angry.

[1] A corroding disease. Ct. IV. i. 85, note.
[2] Shooting stars.
[3] Easily infected.   [4] Finely dressed.

2 *Gent.* 'T is a fine wench; we'll have a snap
at her one of these nights, as she goes from [115
him.
1 *Gent.* Content. How quickly he had done
with her! I see kings can do no more that way
than other mortal people.
2 *Gent.* How fast he is! I cannot hear him
breathe.   120
1 *Gent.* Either the tapers give a feeble light,
Or he looks very pale.
2 *Gent.*   And so he does:
Pray Heaven he be well; let's look. — Alas!
He's stiff, wounded, and dead! Treason,
treason!
1 *Gent.* Run forth and call.   125
2 *Gent.* Treason, treason!   *Exit.*
1 *Gent.*   This will be laid on us!
Who can believe a woman could do this?

Enter CLEON *and* LYSIPPUS.

Cleon. How now! where's the traitor?
1 *Gent.* Fled, fled away; but there her woe-
ful act
Lies still.   130
    Cleon. Her act! a woman!
    Lys.   Where's the body?
1 *Gent.* There.
    Lys. Farewell, thou worthy man! There were
two bonds
That tied our loves, a brother and a king,
The least of which might fetch a flood of tears;
But such the misery of greatness is,   135
They have no time to mourn; then, pardon me!
Sirs, which way went she?

Enter STRATO.

    Stra.   Never follow her;
For she, alas! was but the instrument.
News is now brought in that Melantius   140
Has got the fort, and stands upon the wall,
And with a loud voice calls those few that
pass
At this dead time of night, delivering
The innocence of this act.
    Lys.   Gentlemen,
I am your King.
    Stra.   We do acknowledge it.   145
    Lys. I would I were not! Follow, all; for this
Must have a sudden stop.   *Exeunt.*

[SCENE II.] [5]

Enter MELANTIUS, DIPHILUS, *and* CALIANAX,
on the Walls.

    Mel. If the dull people can believe I am
arm'd,
(Be constant, Diphilus,) now we have time
Either to bring our banisht honours home,
Or create new ones in our ends.
    Diph.   I fear not;
My spirit lies not that way. — Courage, Calianax! ᴧ
    Cal. Would I had any! you should quickly
know it.
    Mel. Speak to the people; thou art elo-
quent.

[5] Before the Fort.

Cal. 'T is a fine eloquence to come to the gallows:
You were born to be my end; the devil take you!
Now must I hang for company. 'T is strange, 10
I should be old, and neither wise nor valiant.

Enter LYSIPPUS, DIAGORAS, CLEON, STRATO, *and* Guard.

Lys. See where he stands, as boldly confident
As if he had his full command about him.
Stra. He looks as if he had the better cause, sir;
Under your gracious pardon, let me speak it!   15
Though he be mighty-spirited, and forward
To all great things, to all things of that danger
Worse men shake at the telling of, yet certainly
I do believe him noble, and this action
Rather pull'd on than sought: his mind was ever   20
As worthy as his hand.
Lys.   'T is my fear, too.
Heaven forgive all! — Summon him, Lord Cleon.
Cleon. Ho, from the walls there!
Mel.   Worthy Cleon, welcome:
We could have wisht you here, lord; you are honest.
Cal. (*Aside.*) Well, thou art as flattering a knave, though   25
I dare not tell thee so ——
Lys.   Melantius!
Mel.   Sir?
Lys. I am sorry that we meet thus; our old love
Never requir'd such distance. Pray to Heaven,
You have not left yourself, and sought this safety
More out of fear than honour! You have lost   30
A noble master, which your faith, Melantius,
Some think might have preserv'd: yet you know best.
Cal. [*Aside.*] When time was, I was mad: some that dares fight,
I hope will pay this rascal.
Mel. Royal young man, those tears look lovely on thee: 35
Had they been shed for a deserving one,
They had been lasting monuments. Thy brother,
Whilst he was good, I call'd him King, and serv'd him
With that strong faith, that most unwearied valour,
Pull'd people from the farthest sun to seek him,   40
And buy his friendship. I was then his soldier.
But since his hot pride drew him to disgrace me,
And brand my noble actions with his lust,
(That never-cur'd dishonour of my sister,
Base stain of whore, and, which is worse, the joy   45
To make it still so,) like myself, thus I

Have flung him off with my allegiance;
And stand here, mine own justice, to revenge
What I have suffer'd in him, and this old man
Wrong'd almost to lunacy.
Cal.   Who, I?   50
You would draw me in. I have had no wrong;
I do disclaim ye all.
Mel.   The short is this.
'T is no ambition to lift up myself
Urgeth me thus; I do desire again
To be a subject, so I may be free: 55
If not, I know my strength, and will unbuild
This goodly town. Be speedy, and be wise,
In a reply.
Stra.   Be sudden, sir, to tie
All up again. What 's done is past recall,
And past you to revenge; and there are thousands   60
That wait for such a troubled hour as this.
Throw him the blank.
Lys.   Melantius, write in that
Thy choice: my seal is at it.
                       [*Throws a paper to* MELANTIUS.]
Mel. It was our honours drew us to this act,
Not gain; and we will only work our pardons.   65
Cal. Put my name in too.
Diph.   You disclaim'd us all
But now, Calianax.
Cal.   That 's all one;
I 'll not be hang'd hereafter by a trick:
I 'll have it in.
Mel.   You shall, you shall. —
Come to the back gate, and we 'll call you King,   70
And give you up the fort.
Lys.   Away, away. *Exeunt.*

[SCENE III.][1]

Enter ASPATIA, *in man's apparel,* [*and with artificial scars on her face.*]

Asp. This is my fatal hour. Heaven may forgive
My rash attempt, that causelessly hath laid
Griefs on me that will never let me rest,
And put a woman's heart into my breast.
It is more honour for you that I die;   5
For she that can endure the misery
That I have on me, and be patient too,
May live and laugh at all that you can do.

Enter Servant.

God save you, sir!
Ser.   And you, sir! What 's your business?
Asp. With you, sir, now; to do me the fair office   10
To help me to your lord.
Ser.   What, would you serve him?
Asp. I 'll do him any service; but, to haste,
For my affairs are earnest, I desire
To speak with him.
Ser. Sir, because you are in such haste, I would   15
Be loth delay you longer: you can not.

---

[1] Anteroom to Amintor's apartments.

Asp. It shall become you, though, to tell
your lord.

Ser. Sir, he will speak with nobody;
[But in particular, I have in charge,
About no weighty matters.]¹

Asp. This is most strange. 20
Art thou gold-proof? There's for thee; help
me to him. [*Gives money.*]

Ser. Pray be not angry, sir: I'll do my best.
[*Exit.*

Asp. How stubbornly this fellow answer'd
me!
There is a vile dishonest trick in man,
More than in women. All the men I meet 25
Appear thus to me, are harsh and rude,
And have a subtilty in every thing,
Which love could never know; but we fond
women
Harbour the easiest and the smoothest thoughts,
And think all shall go so. It is unjust 30
That men and women should be matcht to-
gether.

Enter AMINTOR *and his man.*

Amin. Where is he?

Ser. There, my lord.

Amin. What would you, sir?

Asp. Please it your lordship to command
your man
Out of the room, I shall deliver things
Worthy your hearing.

Amin. Leave us. [*Exit* Servant.]

Asp. (*Aside.*) Oh, that that shape 35
Should bury falsehood in it!

Amin. Now your will, sir.

Asp. When you know me, my lord, you needs
must guess
My business; and I am not hard to know;
For, till the chance of war markt this smooth
face
With these few blemishes, people would call
me 40
My sister's picture, and her mine. In short,
I am brother to the wrong'd Aspatia.

Amin. The wrong'd Aspatia! Would thou
wert so too
Unto the wrong'd Amintor! Let me kiss
That hand of thine, in honour that I bear 45
Unto the wrong'd Aspatia. Here I stand
That did it. Would he could not! Gentle youth,
Leave me; for there is something in thy looks
That calls my sins in a most hideous form
Into my mind; and I have grief enough 50
Without thy help.

Asp. I would I could with credit!
Since I was twelve years old, I had not seen
My sister till this hour I now arriv'd:
She sent for me to see her marriage, —
A woful one! but they that are above 55
Have ends in everything. She us'd few words,
But yet enough to make me understand
The baseness of the injuries you did her.
That little training I have had is war:
I may behave myself rudely in peace; 60
I would not, though. I shall not need to tell
you

¹ Only in Q₁.

I am but young, and would be loth to lose
Honour, that is not easily gain'd again.
Fairly I mean to deal: the age is strict
For single combats; and we shall be stopt, 65
If it be publisht. If you like your sword,
Use it; if mine appear a better to you,
Change; for the ground is this, and this the
time,
To end our difference. [*Draws.*]

Amin. Charitable youth,
If thou be'st such, think not I will maintain 70
So strange a wrong: and, for thy sister's sake,
Know, that I could not think that desperate
thing
I durst not do; yet, to enjoy this world,
I would not see her; for, beholding thee,
I am I know not what. If I have aught 75
That may content thee, take it, and begone,
For death is not so terrible as thou;
Thine eyes shoot guilt into me.

Asp. Thus, she swore,
Thou wouldst behave thyself, and give me
words
That would fetch tears into my eyes; and so 80
Thou dost indeed, But yet she bade me watch
Lest I were cozen'd; and be sure to fight
Ere I return'd.

Amin. That must not be with me.
For her I'll die directly; but against her
Will never hazard it.

Asp. You must be urg'd. 85
I do not deal uncivilly with those
That dare to fight; but such a one as you
Must be us'd thus. [*She strikes him.*

Amin. I prithee, youth, take heed.
Thy sister is a thing to me so much 90
Above mine honour, that I can endure
All this — Good gods! a blow I can endure;
But stay not, lest thou draw a timeless² death
Upon thyself.

Asp. Thou art some prating fellow;
One that hath studied out a trick to talk, 95
And move soft hearted people; to be kickt.
[*She kicks him.*

Thus to be kickt. — (*Aside.*) Why should he
be so slow
In giving me my death?

Amin. A man can bear
No more, and keep his flesh. Forgive me,
then!
I would endure yet, if I could. Now show 100
[*Draws.*
The spirit thou pretend'st, and understand
Thou hast no hour to live.
[*They fight;* [ASPATIA *is wounded.*]
What dost thou mean?
Thou canst not fight: the blows thou mak'st at
me
Are quite besides; and those I offer at thee,
Thou spread'st thine arms, and tak'st upon thy
breast, 105
Alas, defenceless!

Asp. I have got enough.
And my desire. There is no place so fit
For me to die as here. [*Falls.*

² Untimely.

Enter EVADNE, *her hands bloody, with a knife.*

Evad. Amintor, I am loaden with events,
That fly to make thee happy ; I have joys,   110
That in a moment can call back thy wrongs,
And settle thee in thy free state again.
It is Evadne still that follows thee,
But not her mischiefs.   114
    Amin. Thou canst not fool me to believe
        again ;
But thou hast looks and things so full of news,
That I am stay'd.
    Evad. Noble Amintor, put off thy amaze,
Let thine eyes loose, and speak. Am I not fair ?
Looks not Evadne beauteous with these rites
        now ?   120
Were those hours half so lovely in thine eyes
When our hands met before the holy man ?
I was too foul inside to look fair then :
Since I knew ill, I was not free till now.
    Amin. There is presage of some important
        thing   125
About thee, which, it seems, thy tongue hath
        lost.
Thy hands are bloody, and thou hast a knife.
    Evad. In this consists thy happiness and
        mine.
Joy to Amintor ! for the King is dead.
    Amin. Those have most power to hurt us,
        that we love ;   130
We lay our sleeping lives within their arms.
Why, thou hast rais'd up mischief to his height,
And found one to out-name[1] thy other faults ;
Thou hast no intermission of thy sins
But all thy life is a continued ill.   135
Black is thy colour now, disease thy nature.
Joy to Amintor ! Thou hast toucht a life,
The very name of which had power to calm
Up all my rage, and calm my wildest wrongs.
    Evad. 'T is done ; and, since I could not find
        a way   140
To meet thy love so clear as through his life,
I cannot now repent it.
    Amin. Couldst thou procure the gods to speak
        to me,
To bid me love this woman and forgive,   144
I think I should fall out with them. Behold,
Here lies a youth whose wounds bleed in my
        breast,
Sent by a violent fate to fetch his death
From my slow hand ! And, to augment my woe,
You now are present, stain'd with a king's
        blood
Violently shed. This keeps night here,   150
And throws an unknown wilderness[2] about me.
    Asp. Oh, oh, oh !
    Amin. No more ; pursue me not.
    Evad.   Forgive me, then,
And take me to thy bed : we may not part.
        [*Kneels.*]
    Amin. Forbear, be wise, and let my rage go
        this way.   155
    Evad. 'T is you that I would stay, not it.
    Amin.   Take heed ;
It will return with me.

────────
[1] Surpass.   [2] Wildness.

    Evad.   If it must be,
I shall not fear to meet it. Take me home.
    Amin. Thou monster of cruelty, forbear !
    Evad. For Heaven's sake look more calm !
        Thine eyes are sharper   160
Than thou canst make thy sword.
    Amin.   Away, away !
Thy knees are more to me than violence.
I am worse than sick to see knees follow me
For that I must not grant. For God's sake,
        stand.
    Evad. Receive me, then.
    Amin.   I dare not stay thy language.   165
In midst of all my anger and my grief,
Thou dost awake something that troubles me,
And says, I lov'd thee once. I dare not stay ;
There is no end of woman's reasoning.
        Leaves her.
    Evad. [*rising.*] Amintor, thou shalt love me
        now again.   170
Go ; I am calm. Farewell, and peace for ever !
Evadne, whom thou hat'st, will die for thee.
        Stabs herself.
    Amin. (*returning.*) I have a little human na-
        ture yet,
That 's left for thee, that bids me stay thy
        hand.
    Evad. Thy hand was welcome, but it came
        too late.   175
Oh, I am lost ! the heavy sleep makes haste.
        She dies.
    Asp. Oh, oh, oh !
    Amin. This earth of mine doth tremble, and
        I feel
A stark affrighted motion in my blood.
My soul grows weary of her house, and I   180
All over am a trouble to myself.
There is some hidden power in these dead
        things,
That calls my flesh unto 'em ; I am cold.
Be resolute and bear 'em company.
There 's something yet, which I am loth to
        leave :   185
There 's man enough in me to meet the fears
That death can bring ; and yet would it were
        done !
I can find nothing in the whole discourse
Of death, I durst not meet the boldest way ;
Yet still, betwixt the reason and the act,   190
The wrong I to Aspatia did stands up ;
I have not such another fault to answer.
Though she may justly arm herself with scorn
And hate of me, my soul will part less troubled,
When I have paid to her in tears my sorrow.   195
I will not leave this act unsatisfied,
If all that 's left in me can answer it.
    Asp. Was it a dream ? There stands Amin-
        tor still ;
Or I dream still.
    Amin. How dost thou ? speak ; receive my
        love and help.   200
Thy blood climbs up to his old place again ;
There 's hope of thy recovery.
    Asp. Did you not name Aspatia ?
    Amin.   I did.
    Asp. And talkt of tears and sorrow unto
        her ?

Amin. 'T is true ; and, till these happy signs in thee   205
Did stay my course, 't was thither I was going.
Asp. Thou art there already, and these wounds are hers.
Those threats I brought with me sought not re-
      venge,
But came to fetch this blessing from thy hand :
I am Aspatia yet.   210
Amin. Dare my soul ever look abroad again ?
Asp. I shall sure live, Amintor ; I am well ;
A kind of healthful joy wanders within me.
Amin. The world wants lives to excuse thy loss ;   214
Come, let me bear thee to some place of help.
Asp. Amintor, thou must stay ; I must rest here ;
My strength begins to disobey my will.
How dost thou, my best soul ? I would fain live
Now, if I could. Wouldst thou have lov'd me, then ?
Amin. Alas,   220
All that I am 's not worth a hair from thee !
Asp. Give me thy hand ; mine hands grope up and down,
And cannot find thee ; I am wondrous sick.
Have I thy hand, Amintor ?
Amin. Thou greatest blessing of the world, thou hast.   225
Asp. I do believe thee better than my sense.
Oh, I must go ! farewell !   *Dies.*
Amin. She swoons.[1] — Aspatia ! — Help ! for God's sake, water,
Such as may chain life ever to this frame ! —
Aspatia, speak ! — What, no help yet ? I fool !
I 'll chafe her temples. Yet there 's nothing stirs.   231
Some hidden power tell her, Amintor calls,
And let her answer me ! — Aspatia, speak ! —
I have heard, if there be any life, but bow
The body thus, and it will show itself.   235
Oh, she is gone ! I will not leave her yet.
Since out of justice we must challenge nothing,
I 'll call it mercy, if you 'll pity me,
You heavenly powers, and lend for some few years
The blessed soul to this fair seat again !   240
No comfort comes ; the gods deny me too.
I 'll bow the body once again. — Aspatia ! —
The soul is fled for ever ; and I wrong
Myself, so long to lose her company.   244
Must I talk now ? Here 's to be with thee, love !
      Kills himself.

Re-enter Servant.

Serv. This is a great grace to my lord, to have the new king come to him. I must tell him he is ent'ring. — Oh, God ! — Help, help !

Enter LYSIPPUS, MELANTIUS, CALIANAX, CLEON, DIPHILUS, *and* STRATO.

Lys. Where 's Amintor ?
Stra.   Oh, there, there !

Lys. How strange is this !
Cal.   What should we do here ?   250
Mel. These deaths are such acquainted things with me,
That yet my heart dissolves not. May I stand
Stiff here for ever ! — Eyes, call up your tears !
This is Amintor. Heart, he was my friend ;
Melt ! now it flows. — Amintor, give a word   255
To call me to thee.
Amin. Oh !
Mel. Melantius calls his friend Amintor. Oh,
Thy arms are kinder to me than thy tongue !
Speak, speak !   260
Amin. What ?
Mel. That little word was worth all the sounds
That ever I shall hear again.
Diph.   Oh, brother,
Here lies your sister slain ! You lose yourself
In sorrow there.
Mel.   Why, Diphilus, it is   265
A thing to laugh at, in respect of this.
Here was my sister, father, brother, son ;
All that I had. — Speak once again ; what youth
Lies slain there by thee ?
Amin.   'T is Aspatia.
My last is said. Let me give up my soul   270
Into thy bosom.   [*Dies.*]
Cal. What 's that ? What 's that ? Aspatia !
Mel.   I never did
Repent the greatness of my heart till now ;
It will not burst at need.   275
Cal. My daughter dead here too ! And you
have all fine new tricks to grieve ; but I ne'er
knew any but direct crying.
Mel. I am a prattler : but no more.
      [*Offers to stab himself.*]
Diph.   Hold, brother !
Lys. Stop him.
Diph. Fie, how unmanly was this offer in you !   280
Does this become our strain ?[2]
Cal. I know not what the matter is, but I am
grown very kind, and am friends with you
all now. You have given me that among you
will kill me quickly ; but I 'll go home, and live
as long as I can.   [*Exit.*]   286
Mel. His spirit is but poor that can be kept
From death for want of weapons.
Is not my hands a weapon sharp enough
To stop my breath ? or, if you tie down those,
I vow, Amintor, I will never eat,   291
Or drink, or sleep, or have to do with that
That may preserve life ! This I swear to keep.
Lys. Look to him, though, and bear those bodies in.
May this a fair example be to me   295
To rule with temper ; for on lustful kings
Unlookt-for sudden deaths from God are sent ;
But curst is he that is their instrument.
      [*Exeunt.*]

THE FAITHFUL SHEPHERDESS

BY

JOHN FLETCHER

[DRAMATIS PERSONAE

PERIGOT.	Satyr.
THENOT.	Shepherds.
DAPHNIS.	
ALEXIS.	
Sullen Shepherd.	CLORIN.
Old Shepherd.	AMORET.
Priest of Pan.	AMARILLIS.
God of the River.	CLOE
	Shepherdesses.

SCENE. — *Thessaly*.]

TO THE READER

IF you be not reasonably assur'd of your knowledge in this kind of poem, lay down the book, or read this, which I would wish had been the prologue. It is a pastoral tragi-comedy, which the people seeing when it was play'd, having ever had a singular gift in defining, concluded to be a play of country hired shepherds in gray cloaks, with curtail'd dogs in strings, sometimes laughing together, and sometimes killing one another ; and, missing Whitsun-ales, cream, wassail, and mor-ris-dances, began to be angry. In their error I would not have you fall, lest you incur their cen-sure.[1] Understand, therefore, a pastoral to be a representation of shepherds and shepherdesses with their actions and passions, which must be such as may agree with their natures, at least not exceeding former fictions and vulgar traditions ; they are not to be adorn'd with any art, but such improper ones as nature is said to bestow, as singing and poetry ; or such as experience may teach them, as the virtues of herbs and fountains, the ordinary course of the sun, moon, and stars, and such like. But you are ever to remember shepherds to be such as all the ancient poets, and modern, of understanding, have received them ; that is, the owners of flocks, and not hirelings. A tragi-comedy is not so called in respect of mirth and killing, but in respect it wants deaths, which is enough to make it no tragedy, yet brings some near it, which is enough to make it no comedy, which must be a representation of familiar people, with such kind of trouble as no life be question'd ;[2] so that a god is as lawful in this as in a tragedy, and mean people as in a comedy. Thus much I hope will serve to justify my poem, and make you understand it ; to teach you more for nothing, I do not know that I am in conscience bound.

JOHN FLETCHER.

ACT I

SCENE I.

Enter CLORIN, *a shepherdess, having buried her love in an arbour.*

Clorin. Hail, holy earth, whose cold arms do embrace
The truest man that ever fed his flocks
By the fat plains of fruitful Thessaly !
Thus I salute thy grave ; thus do I pay
My early vows and tribute of mine eyes 5
To thy still-loved ashes ; thus I free
Myself from all ensuing heats and fires
Of love ; all sports, delights, and [jolly][3] games,
That shepherds hold full dear, thus put I off.

[1] *I. e.* the judgment which must be passed on them.
[2] Called in question ; endangered.
[3] Q3. Q1 omits. Some copies of Q3 read *merry*.

Now no more shall these smooth brows be be-girt 10
With youthful coronals,[4] and lead the dance ;
No more the company of fresh fair maids
And wanton shepherds be to me delightful,
Nor the shrill pleasing sound of merry pipes
Under some shady dell, when the cool wind 15
Plays on the leaves : all be far away,
Since thou art far away, by whose dear side
How often have I sat crown'd with fresh flowers
For summer's queen, whilst every shepherd's boy
Puts on his lusty green, with gaudy hook, 20
And hanging scrip of finest cordevan.[5]
But thou art gone, and these are gone with thee,
And all are dead but thy dear memory ;

[4] Garlands.   [5] Leather (from *Cordova* in Spain)

That shall outlive thee, and shall ever spring,
Whilst there are pipes or jolly shepherds sing. 25
And here will I, in honour of thy love,
Dwell by thy grave, forgetting all those joys
That former times made precious to mine
  eyes;
Only rememb'ring what my youth did gain
In the dark, hidden virtuous use of herbs; 30
That will I practise, and as freely give
All my endeavours, as I gain'd them, free.
Of all green wounds I know the remedies
In men or cattle, be they stung with snakes,
Or charm'd with powerful words of wicked
  art,   35
Or be they love-sick, or through too much heat
Grown wild or lunatic, their eyes or ears
Thick'ned with misty film of dulling rheum;
These I can cure, such secret virtue lies
In herbs applied by a virgin's hand.   40
My meat shall be what these wild woods afford,
Berries and chestnuts, plantains, on whose
  cheeks
The sun sits smiling, and the lofty fruit
Pull'd from the fair head of the straight-grown
  pine;
On these I'll feed with free content, and
  rest,   45
When night shall blind the world, by thy side
  blest.

Enter a Satyr [*with a basket of fruit*].

Sat. Through yon same bending plain,
That flings his arms down to the main,
And through these thick woods, have I run,
Whose bottom never kist the sun   50
Since the lusty spring began;
All to please my master Pan,
Have I trotted without rest
To get him fruit; for at a feast
He entertains, this coming night,   55
His paramour, the Syrinx bright. —
But, behold, a fairer sight!
                           He stands amazed.
By that heavenly form of thine,
Brightest fair, thou art divine,
Sprung from great immortal race   60
Of the gods; for in thy face
Shines more awful majesty
Than dull weak mortality
Dare with misty eyes behold,
And live: therefore on this mould   65
Lowly do I bend my knee
In worship of thy deity.
Deign it, goddess, from my hand
To receive what'er this land
From her fertile womb doth send   70
Of her choice fruits; and but lend
Belief to that the Satyr tells:
Fairer by the famous wells
To this present day ne'er grew,
Never better nor more true.   75
Here be grapes, whose lusty blood
Is the learned poets' good,
Sweeter yet did never crown
The head of Bacchus; nuts more brown
Than the squirrel's teeth that crack them; 80
Deign, O fairest fair, to take them!

For these black-ey'd Dryope
Hath oftentimes commanded me
With my clasped knee to climb:
See how well the lusty time   85
Hath deckt their rising cheeks in red,
Such as on your lips is spread!
Here be berries for a queen,
Some be red, some be green;
These are of that luscious meat,   90
The great god Pan himself doth eat:
All these, and what the woods can yield,
The hanging mountain or the field,
I freely offer, and ere long
Will bring you more, more sweet and strong; 95
Till when, humbly leave I take,
Lest the great Pan do awake,
That sleeping lies in a deep glade,
Under a broad beech's shade.
I must go, I must run   100
Swifter than the fiery sun.   *Exit.*
  Clo. And all my fears go with thee!
What greatness, or what private hidden power,
Is there in me, to draw submission
From this rude man and beast? Sure I am
  mortal,   105
The daughter of a shepherd; he was mortal,
And she that bore me mortal: prick my hand,
And it will bleed; a fever shakes me, and
The self-same wind that makes the young
  lambs shrink
Makes me a-cold: my fear says I am mortal. 110
Yet I have heard (my mother told it me,
And now I do believe it), if I keep
My virgin-flower uncropt, pure, chaste, and fair,
No goblin, wood-god, fairy, elf, or fiend, 114
Satyr, or other power that haunts these groves,
Shall hurt my body, or by vain illusion
Draw me to wander after idle fires;
Or voices calling me in dead of night,
To make me follow, and so toll[1] me on,
Through mires and standing pools [to find my
  ruin:]   120
Else why should this rough thing, who never
  knew
Manners nor smooth humanity,[2] whose heats[3]
Are rougher than himself and more mis-shapen,
Thus mildly kneel to me? Sure there is a
  power   124
In that great name of virgin, that binds fast
All rude uncivil bloods, all appetites
That break their confines. Then, strong chas-
  tity,
Be thou my strongest guard, for here I'll
  dwell
In opposition against fate and hell!
                  [*Retires into her bower.*]

[SCENE II.][4]

Enter an Old Shepherd, *with four couples of*
Shepherds *and* Shepherdesses, [*among whom
are* PERIGOT *and* AMORET.]

  Old Shep. Now we have done this holy festival

---

[1] Entice.   [2] Culture.   [3] Passions.
[4] In the neighbourhood of a village.

In honour of our great god, and his rites
Perform'd, prepare yourselves for chaste
And uncorrupted fires ; that as the priest
With powerful hand shall sprinkle on your
 brows   5
His pure and holy water, ye may be
From all hot flames of lust and loose thoughts
 free.
Kneel, shepherds, kneel ; here comes the priest
 of Pan.

Enter Priest.

Priest. Shepherds, thus I purge away
 [*Sprinkling them with water.*]
Whatsoever this great day,   10
Or the past hours, gave not good,
To corrupt your maiden blood.
From the high rebellious heat
Of the grapes, and strength of meat,
From the wanton quick desires   15
They do kindle by their fires
I do wash you with this water ;
Be you pure and fair hereafter !
From your livers and your veins
Thus I take away the stains ;   20
All your thoughts be smooth and fair :
Be ye fresh and free as air !
Never more let lustful heat
Through your purged conduits [1] beat,
Or a plighted troth be broken,   25
Or a wanton verse be spoken
In a shepherdess's ear :
Go your ways, ye are all clear.
They rise and sing in praise of PAN.

THE SONG.

Sing his praises that doth keep
 Our flocks from harm,
Pan, the father of our sheep ;   30
 And arm in arm
Tread we softly in a round,
 Whilst the hollow neighbouring ground
Fills the music with her sound.   35

Pan, O great god Pan, to thee
 Thus do we sing !
Thou that keep'st us chaste and free
 As the young spring ;
Ever be thy honour spoke,   40
 From that place the Morn is broke
To that place Day doth unyoke !

Exeunt omnes but PERIGOT *and*
 AMORET.

Peri. Stay, gentle Amoret, thou fair-brow'd
 maid ;
Thy shepherd prays thee stay, that holds thee
 dear,
Equal with his soul's good.
Amo.   Speak ; I give   45
Thee freedom, shepherd ; and thy tongue be
 still
The same it ever was, as free from ill
As he whose conversation never knew
The court or city ; be thou ever true !
Peri. When I fall off from my affection,   50

[1] Veins.

Or mingle my clean thoughts with foul desires,
First, let our great god cease to keep my flocks,
That, being left alone without a guard,
The wolf, or winter's rage, summer's great heat
And want of water, rots, or what to us   55
Of ill is yet unknown, fall speedily,
And in their general ruin let me go !
Amo. I pray thee, gentle shepherd, wish not
 so :
I do believe thee ; 't is as hard for me
To think thee false, and harder, than for thee
To hold me foul.
Peri.   Oh, you are fairer far   61
Than the chaste blushing morn, or that fair star
That guides the wand'ring seaman through the
 deep ;
Straighter than the straightest pine upon the
 steep
Head of an aged mountain ; and more white   65
Than the new milk we strip before day-light
From the full-freighted bags of our fair flocks :
Your hair more beauteous than those hanging
 locks
Of young Apollo !
Amo.   Shepherd, be not lost ;
Y' are sail'd too far already from the coast   70
Of your discourse.
Peri.   Did you not tell me once
I should not love alone, I should not lose
Those many passions, vows, and holy oaths,
I 've sent to heaven ? Did you not give your
 hand,
Even that fair hand, in hostage ? Do not, then,   75
Give back again those sweets to other men,
You yourself vow'd were mine.
Amo. Shepherd, so far as maiden's modesty
May give assurance, I am once more thine,
Once more I give my hand. Be ever free   80
From that great foe to faith, foul jealousy !
Peri. I take it as my best good ; and desire,
For stronger confirmation of our love,
To meet this happy night in that fair grove,   84
Where all true shepherds have rewarded been
For their long service : say, sweet, shall it hold?
Amo. Dear friend, you must not blame me,
 if I make
A doubt of what the silent night may do,
Coupled with this day 's heat, to move your
 blood.
Maids must be fearful. Sure you have not been
Wash'd white enough, for yet I see a stain   91
Stick in your liver : [2] go and purge again.
Peri. Oh, do not wrong my honest simple
 truth !
Myself and my affections are as pure
As those chaste flames that burn before the
 shrine   95
Of the great Dian : only my intent
To draw you thither was to plight our troths,
With interchange of mutual chaste embraces,
And ceremonious tying of our souls.
For to that holy wood is consecrate   100
A virtuous well, about whose flowery banks
The nimble-footed fairies dance their rounds
By the pale moonshine, dipping oftentimes

[2] Seat of the passions.

Their stolen children, so to make them free
From dying flesh and dull mortality.   105
By this fair fount hath many a shepherd sworn,
And given away his freedom, many a troth
Been plight, which neither envy nor old time
Could ever break, with many a chaste kiss
          given,
In hope of coming happiness ; by this   110
Fresh fountain many a blushing maid
Hath crown'd the head of her long-loved shep-
          herd
With gaudy flowers, whilst he happy sung
Lays of his love and dear captivity.   114
There grows all herbs fit to cool looser flames
Our sensual parts provoke, chiding our bloods,
And quenching by their power those hidden
          sparks
That else would break out, and provoke our
          sense
To open fires ; so virtuous is that place.
Then, gentle shepherdess, believe, and grant.
In troth, it fits not with that face to scant   121
Your faithful shepherd of those chaste desires
He ever aim'd at, and ——
          Amo. Thou hast prevail'd : farewell. This
          coming night
Shall crown thy chaste hopes with long-wish'd
          delight.   125
          Peri. Our great god Pan reward thee for
          that good
Thou hast given thy poor shepherd ! Fairest
          bud
Of maiden virtues, when I leave to be
The true admirer of thy chastity,
Let me deserve the hot polluted name   130
Of a wild woodman, or affect some dame
Whose often prostitution hath begot
More foul diseases than ever yet the hot
Sun bred thorough his burnings, whilst the Dog
Pursues the raging Lion, throwing fog   135
And deadly vapour from his angry breath,
Filling the lower world with plague and death !
          Exit AMORET.

Enter AMARILLIS, *another* Shepherdess *that is
          in love with* PERIGOT.

          Amar. Shepherd, may I desire to be believ'd,
What I shall blushing tell ?
          Peri.   Fair maid, you may.
          Amar. Then, softly thus : I love thee, Peri-
          got ;   140
And would be gladder to be lov'd again
Than the cold earth is in his frozen arms
To clip [1] the wanton spring. Nay, do not start,
Nor wonder that I woo thee ; thou that art
The prime of our young grooms, even the top
Of all our lusty shepherds. What dull eye,   146
That never was acquainted with desire,
Hath seen thee wrastle, run, or cast the stone
With nimble strength and fair delivery,
And hath not sparkled fire, and speedily   150
Sent secret heat to all the neighbouring veins ?
Who ever heard thee sing, that brought again
That freedom back was lent unto thy voice ?
Then, do not blame me, shepherd, if I be

One to be numb'red in this company,   155
Since none that ever saw thee yet were free.
          Peri. Fair shepherdess, much pity I can lend
To your complaints ; but sure I shall not love.
All that is mine, myself and my best hopes,
Are given already. Do not love him, then,   160
That cannot love again ; on other men
Bestow those heats, more free, that may return
You fire for fire, and in one flame equal burn.
          Amar. Shall I rewarded be so slenderly
For my affection, most unkind of men ?   165
If I were old, or had agreed with art
To give another nature to my cheeks,
Or were I common mistress to the love
Of every swain, or could I with such ease
Call back my love as many a wanton doth,   170
Thou mightst refuse me, shepherd ; but to thee
I am only fixt and set ; let it not be
A sport, thou gentle shepherd, to abuse
The love of silly [2] maid.
          Peri.   Fair soul, ye use
These words to little end : for, know, I may   175
Better call back that time was yesterday,
Or stay the coming night, than bring my love
Home to myself again, or recreant prove.
I will no longer hold you with delays :
This present night I have appointed been   180
To meet that chaste fair that enjoys my soul,
In yonder grove, there to make up our loves.
Be not deceiv'd no longer, choose again :
These neighbouring plains have many a comely
          swain,
Fresher and freer [3] far than I e'er was ;   185
Bestow that love on them, and let me pass.
Farewell : be happy in a better choice !   *Exit.*
          Amar. Cruel, thou hast struck me deader
          with thy voice
Than if the angry heavens with their quick
          flames
Had shot me through. I must not leave to love,
I cannot ; no, I must enjoy thee, boy,   191
Though the great dangers 'twixt my hopes and
          that
Be infinite. There is a shepherd dwells
Down by the moor, whose life hath ever shown
More sullen discontent than Saturn's brow   195
When he sits frowning on the births of men ;
One that doth wear himself away in loneness,
And never joys, unless it be in breaking
The holy plighted troths of mutual souls ;
One that lusts after every several beauty,   200
But never yet was known to love or like,
Were the face fairer or more full of truth
Than Phoebe in her fulness, or the youth
Of smooth Lyaeus ; whose nigh-starved flocks
Are always scabby, and infect all sheep   205
They feed withal ; whose lambs are ever last,
And die before their weaning : and whose dog
Looks, like his master, lean and full of scurf,
Not caring for the pipe or whistle. This man
          may,
If he be well wrought, do a deed of wonder,   210
Forcing me passage to my long desires :
And here he comes, as fitly to my purpose
As my quick thoughts could wish for.

1 Embrace.   2 Weak.   3 More gracious.

Enter Sullen Shepherd.

Sull. Shep. Fresh beauty, let me not be
    thought uncivil,
Thus to be partner of your loneness : 't was 215
My love (that ever-working passion) drew
Me to this place, to seek some remedy
For my sick soul. Be not unkind and fair,
For such the mighty Cupid in his doom
Hath sworn to be aveng'd on ; then, give room
To my consuming fires, that so I may   221
Enjoy my long desires, and so allay
Those flames that else would burn my life
    away.
  Amar. Shepherd, were I but sure thy heart
    were sound
As thy words seem to be, means might be
    found   225
To cure thee of thy long pains ; for to me
That heavy youth-consuming misery
The love-sick soul endures never was pleasing.
I could be well content with the quick easing
Of thee and thy hot fires, might it procure 230
Thy faith and farther service to be sure.
  Sull. Shep. Name but that work, danger, or
    what can
Be compass'd by the wit or art of man ;
And, if I fail in my performance, may
I never more kneel to the rising day !   235
  Amar. Then, thus I try thee, shepherd. This
    same night
That now comes stealing on, a gentle pair
Have promis'd equal love, and do appoint
To make yon wood the place where hands and
    hearts
Are to be tied for ever. Break their meeting 240
And their strong faith, and I am ever thine.
  Sull. Shep. Tell me their names, and if I do
    not move
By my great power, the centre of their love
From his fixt being, let me never more
Warm me by those fair eyes I thus adore.   245
  Amar. Come ; as we go, I 'll tell thee what
    they are,
And give thee fit directions for thy work.
                       Exeunt.

[SCENE III.][1]

Enter CLOE.

Cloe. How have I wrong'd the times or men,
    that thus,
After this holy feast, I pass unknown
And unsaluted ? 'T was not wont to be
Thus frozen with the younger company
Of jolly shepherds ; 't was not then held good 5
For lusty grooms to mix their quicker blood
With that dull humour, most unfit to be
The friend of man, cold and dull chastity.
Sure I am held not fair, or am too old,
Or else not free enough, or from my fold   10
Drive not a flock sufficient great to gain
The greedy eyes of wealth-alluring swain.
Yet, if I may believe what others say,
My face has foil [2] enough ; nor can they lay
Justly too strict a coyness to my charge ;   15

My flocks are many, and the downs as large
They feed upon. Then, let it ever be
Their coldness, not my virgin-modesty
Makes me complain.

Enter THENOT.

  The.   Was ever man but I
Thus truly taken with uncertainty ;   20
Where shall that man be found that loves a
    mind
Made up in constancy, and dares not find
His love rewarded ? Here, let all men know,
A wretch that lives to love his mistress so.
  Cloe. Shepherd, I pray thee stay. Where hast
    thou been ?   25
Or whither go'st thou ? Here be woods as green
As any ; air [likewise] [3] as fresh and sweet
As where smooth Zephyrus plays on the fleet
Face of the curled streams ; with flowers as
    many
As the young spring gives, and as choice as
    any ;   30
Here be all new delights, cool streams and
    wells,
Arbours o'ergrown with woodbines, caves, and
    dells ;
Choose where thou wilt, whilst I sit by and sing,
Or gather rushes, to make many a ring
For thy long fingers ; tell thee tales of love, —
How the pale Phoebe, hunting in a grove,   36
First saw the boy Endymion, from whose eyes
She took eternal fire that never dies ;
How she convey'd him softly in a sleep,
His temples bound with poppy, to the steep 40
Head of old Latmus, where she stoops each
    night,
Gilding the mountain with her brother's light,
To kiss her sweetest.
  The.   Far from me are these
Hot flashes, bred from wanton heat and ease ;
I have forgot what love and loving meant ;   45
Rhymes, songs, and merry rounds, that oft are
    sent
To the soft ear of maid, are strange to me :
Only I live t' admire a chastity,
That neither pleasing age, smooth tongue, nor
    gold,
Could ever break upon, so sure [4] a mould   50
Is that her mind was cast in ; 't is to her
I only am reserv'd ; she is my form I stir
By, breathe and move ; 't is she, and only she,
Can make me happy, or give misery.
  Cloe. Good shepherd, may a stranger crave
    to know   55
To whom this dear observance [5] you do owe ?
  The. You may, and by her virtue learn to
    square
And level out your life ; for to be fair,
And nothing virtuous, only fits the eye
Of gaudy youth and swelling vanity.
Then, know, she 's call'd the Virgin of the
    Grove,
She that hath long since buri'd her chaste love
And now lives by his grave, for whose dear
    soul

---

[1] Another part of the wood.   [2] Beauty.

[3] Q$_1$–Q$_4$ omit.   [4] F$_2$ *pure.*   [5] Worship.

She hath vow'd herself into the holy roll
Of strict virginity : 't is her I so admire,   65
Not any looser blood or new desire.   [*Exit.*]
  Cloe. Farewell, poor swain ! thou art not for
    my bend ;[1]
I must have quicker souls, whose words may
    tend
To some free action. Give me him dare love
At first encounter, and as soon dare prove !   70

                    THE SONG.

[*Sings.*] Come, shepherds, come !
      Come away
      Without delay,
         Whilst the gentle time doth stay.
         Green woods are dumb,   75
         And will never tell to any
      Those dear kisses, and those many
      Sweet embraces that are given;
      Dainty pleasures, that would even
         Raise in coldest age a fire,   80
      And give virgin-blood desire.
         Then, if ever,
         Now or never,
      Come and have it :
         Think not I   85
         Dare deny,
      If you crave it.

                Enter DAPHNIS.

[*Aside.*] Here comes another. Better be my
    speed,
Thou god of blood ! But certain, if I read
Not false, this is that modest shepherd, he   90
That only dare salute, but ne'er could be
Brought to kiss any, hold discourse, or sing,
Whisper, or boldly ask that wished thing
We all are born for; one that makes loving
    faces,
And could be well content to covet graces,   95
Were they not got by boldness. In this thing
My hopes are frozen; and, but fate doth bring
Him hither, I would sooner choose
A man made out of snow, and freer use
An eunuch to my ends; but since he 's here,   100
Thus I attempt him. — Thou, of men most
    dear,
Welcome to her that only for thy sake
Hath been content to live ! Here, boldly take
My hand in pledge, this hand, that never yet
Was given away to any ; and but sit   105
Down on this rushy bank, whilst I go pull
Fresh blossoms from the boughs, or quickly cull
The choicest delicates from yonder mead,
To make thee chains or chaplets, or to spread
Under our fainting bodies, when delight   110
Shall lock up all our senses. How the sight
Of those smooth rising cheeks renew the story
Of young Adonis, when in pride and glory
He lay infolded 'twixt the beating arms
Of willing Venus ! Methinks stronger charms 115
Dwell in those speaking eyes, and on that brow
More sweetness than the painters can allow
To their best pieces. Not Narcissus, he
That wept himself away in memory
Of his own beauty, nor Silvanus' boy,[2]   120

Nor the twice-ravish'd maid, for whom old Troy
Fell by the hand of Pyrrhus, may to thee
Be otherwise compar'd, than some dead tree
To a young fruitful olive.
  Daph.   I can love,
But I am loth to say so, lest I prove   125
Too soon unhappy.
  Cloe.   Happy, thou wouldst say.
My dearest Daphnis, blush not ; if the day
To thee and thy soft heats be enemy,
Then take the coming night ; fair youth, 't is
    free
To all the world. Shepherd, I 'll meet thee
    then   130
When darkness hath shut up the eyes of men,
In yonder grove. Speak, shall our meeting hold ?
Indeed you are too bashful ; be more bold,
And tell me ay.
  Daph.   I am content to say so,
And would be glad to meet, might I but pray
    so   135
Much from your fairness, that you would be
    true.
  Cloe. Shepherd, thou hast thy wish.
  Daph.   Fresh maid, adieu.
Yet one word more : since you have drawn me
    on
To come this night, fear not to meet alone
That man that will not offer to be ill,   140
Though your bright self would ask it, for his
    fill
Of this world's goodness ; do not fear him, then,
But keep your 'pointed time. Let other men
Set up their bloods to sale, mine shall be ever
Fair as the soul it carries, and unchaste never.
                            Exit.
  Cloe. Yet am I poorer than I was before.   146
Is it not strange, among so many a score
Of lusty bloods, I should pick out these things
Whose veins, like a dull river far from springs,
Is still the same, slow, heavy, and unfit   150
For stream or motion, though the strong winds
    hit
With their continual power upon his sides ?
Oh, happy be your names that have been brides,
And tasted those rare sweets for which I pine !
And far more heavy be thy grief and tine,[3]   155
Thou lazy swain, that mayst relieve my needs,
Than his, upon whose liver always feeds
A hungry vulture !

                Enter ALEXIS.

  Alex.   Can such beauty be
Safe in his[4] own guard, and not draw the eye
Of him that passeth on, to greedy gaze   160
Or covetous desire, whilst in a maze
The better part contemplates, giving rein,
And wished freedom to the labouring vein ?
Fairest and whitest, may I crave to know
The cause of your retirement, why you go   165
Thus all alone ? Methinks the downs are
    sweeter,
And the young company of swains more meeter,
Than these forsaken and untrodden places.
Give not yourself to loneness, and those graces

---

[1] Aim, purpose.
[2] Cyparissus, metamorphosed into a cypress.

[3] Sorrow.   [4] Its.

Hide from the eyes of men, that were intended
To live amongst us swains.
    Cloe.   Thou art befriended, 171
Shepherd : in all my life I have not seen
A man in whom greater contents hath been,
Than thou thyself art. I could tell thee more,
Were there but any hope left to restore 175
My freedom lost. Oh, lend me all thy red,
Thou shame-fast Morning, when from Tithon's[1]
    bed
Thou risest ever-maiden !
    Alex.   If for me,
Thou sweetest of all sweets, these flashes be,
Speak, and be satisfi'd. Oh, guide her tongue,
My better angel ; force my name among 181
Her modest thoughts, that the first word may
    be ——
    Cloe. Alexis, when the sun shall kiss the sea,
Taking his rest by the white Thetis' side,
Meet me in the holy wood, where I 'll abide 185
Thy coming, shepherd.
    Alex.   If I stay behind,
An everlasting dulness, and the wind,
That as he passeth by shuts up the stream
Of Rhine or Volga, whilst the sun's hot beam 190
Beats back again, seize me, and let me turn
To coldness more than ice ! Oh, how I burn
And rise in youth and fire ! I dare not stay.
    Cloe. My name shall be your word.
    Alex.   Fly, fly, thou day ! *Exit.*
    Cloe. My grief is great, if both these boys
    should fail : 194
He that will use all winds must shift his sail.
                      Exit.

ACT II

SCENE I.[2]

Enter Old Shepherd *with a bell ringing, and the*
    Priest of Pan *following.*

    Priest. Shepherds all, and maidens fair,
Fold your flocks up, for the air
'Gins to thicken, and the sun
Already his great course hath run.
See the dew-drops how they kiss 5
Every little flower that is ;
Hanging on their velvet heads,
Like a rope of crystal beads ;
See the heavy clouds down[3] falling,
And bright Hesperus loud[3] calling 10
The dead Night from under ground ;
At whose rising mists unsound,[4]
Damps and vapours fly apace,
Hovering o'er the wanton face
Of these pastures, where they come, 15
Striking dead both bud and bloom.
Therefore, from such danger lock
Every one his loved flock ;
And let your dogs lie loose without,
Lest the wolf come as a scout 20
From the mountain, and, ere day,
Bear a lamb or kid away ;

Or the crafty thievish fox
Break upon your simple flocks.
To secure yourselves from these, 25
Be not too secure in ease.
Let one eye his watches keep,
Whilst the t'other eye doth sleep ;
So you shall good shepherds prove,
And for ever hold the love 30
Of our great god. Sweetest slumbers,
And soft silence, fall in numbers
On your eyelids ! So, farewell :
Thus I end my evening's knell.   *Exeunt.*

[SCENE II.][5]

Enter CLORIN, the Shepherdess, *sorting of herbs,*
    and telling the natures of them.

    Clo. Now let me know what my best art hath
    done,
Helpt by the great power of the virtuous moon
In her full light. Oh, you sons of earth,
You only brood, unto whose [happy][6] birth
Virtue was given, holding more of nature 5
Than man, her first-born and most perfec'
    creature,
Let me adore you ! you, that only can
Help or kill nature, drawing out that span
Of life and breath even to the end of time ;
You, that these hands did [crop][7] long before
    prime 10
Of day, give me your names, and, next, your
    hidden power.
This is the clote,[8] bearing a yellow flower ;
And this, black horehound ; both are very good
For sheep or shepherd bitten by a wood[9]
Dog's venom'd teeth : these rhamnus[10] branches
    are, 15
Which, stuck in entries, or about the bar
That holds the door, kill all enchantments,
    charms
(Were they Medea's verses), that do harms
To men or cattle : these for frenzy be
A speedy and a sovereign remedy, 20
The bitter wormwood, sage, and marigold ;
Such sympathy with man's good they do hold :
This tormentil,[11] whose virtue is to part
All deadly killing poison from the heart ;
And, here, narcissus root, for swellings best : 25
Yellow lysimachus,[12] to give sweet rest
To the faint shepherd, killing, where it comes,
All busy gnats, and every fly that hums :
For leprosy, darnel and celandine,
With calamint, whose virtues do refine 30
The blood of man, making it free and fair
As the first hour it breath'd, or the best air :
Here, other two ; but your rebellious use
Is not for me, whose goodness is abuse :
Therefore, foul standergrass,[13] from me and
    mine 35
I banish thee, with lustful turpentine ;
You that entice the veins and stir the heat
To civil mutiny, scaling the seat
Our reason moves in, and deluding it

---

[1] Tithonus'. F₂ reads *Titans*.   [2] A pasture.
[3] Dyce emend. Qq. 1-4 transpose *down* and *loud*, F₂
low falling . . . down calling.
[4] Unwholesome.

[5] The wood before Clorin's bower.
[6] Q₁ *high*   [9] Mad.   [12] Loosestrife.
[7] Q₁ *lop.*   [10] Buckthorn.   [13] *Orchis mascula.*
[8] Water-lily.   [11] Septfoil.

With dreams and wanton [fancies] [1] till the fit
Of burning lust be quencht, by appetite   41
Robbing the soul of blessedness and light :
And thou, light vervain, too, thou must go after,
Provoking easy souls to mirth and laughter ;
No more shall I dip thee in water now,   45
And sprinkle every post and every bough
With thy well-pleasing juice, to make the grooms
Swell with high mirth, and with joy all the rooms.

Enter THENOT.

The. This is the cabin where the best of all
Her sex that ever breath'd, or ever shall   50
Give heat or happiness to the shepherd's side,
Doth only to her worthy self abide.
Thou blessed star, I thank thee for thy light,
Thou by whose power the darkness of sad night
Is banisht from the earth, in whose dull place
Thy chaster beams play on the heavy face   56
Of all the world, make the blue sea smile,
To see how cunningly thou dost beguile
Thy brother of his brightness, giving day
Again from chaos ; whiter than that way   60
That leads to Jove's high court, and chaster far
Than chastity itself, you blessed star
That brightly shines ! thou, all the constancy
That in all women was or e'er shall be ;
From whose fair eye-balls flies that holy fire   65
That styled is the mother of desire,
Infusing into every gentle breast
A soul of greater price, and far more blest,
Than that quick power which gives a difference
'Twixt man and creatures of a lower sense !   70
Clo. Shepherd, how cam'st thou hither to this place ?
No way is trodden ; all the verdant grass
The spring shot up stands yet unbruised here
Of any foot ; only the dappled deer,
Far from the feared sound of crooked horn,   75
Dwells in this fastness.
The.   Chaster than the morn,
I have not wand'red, or by strong illusion
Into this virtuous place have made intrusion :
But hither am I come (believe me, fair),
To seek you out, of whose great good the air   80
Is full, and strongly labours, whilst the sound
Breaks against heaven, and drives into a stound [2]
Th' amazed shepherd, that such virtue can
Be resident in lesser than a man.
Clo. If any art I have, or hidden skill,   85
May cure thee of disease or fest'red ill
Whose grief or greenness to another's eye
May seem unpossible of remedy,
I dare yet undertake it.
The.   'T is no pain
I suffer through disease, no beating vein   90
Conveys infection dangerous to the heart,
No part imposthum'd, to be cur'd by art,
This body holds ; and yet a feller grief
Than ever skilful hand did give relief,

Dwells on my soul, and may be heal'd by you,
Fair, beauteous virgin.
Clo.   Then, shepherd, let me sue   95
To know thy grief : that man yet never knew
The way to health that durst not show his sore.
The. Then, fairest, know, I love you.
Clo.   Swain, no more !
Thou hast abus'd the strictness of this place,   100
And off'red sacrilegious foul disgrace
To the sweet rest of these interred bones ;
For fear of whose ascending, fly at once,
Thou and thy idle passions, that the sight
Of death and speedy vengeance may not fright
Thy very soul with horror.
The.   Let me not,   106
Thou all perfection, merit such a blot
For my true zealous faith.
Clo.   Dar'st thou abide
To see this holy earth at once divide,
And give her body up ? for sure it will,   110
If thou pursu'st with wanton flame to fill
This hallowed place : therefore repent and go,
Whilst I with prayers appease his ghost below,
That else would tell thee what it were to be
A rival in that virtuous love that he   115
Embraces yet.
The.   'T is not the white or red
Inhabits in your cheek that thus can wed
My mind to adoration ; nor your eye,
Though it be full and fair, your forehead high
And smooth as Pelops' shoulder ; not the smile
Lies watching in those dimples to beguile   121
The easy soul ; your hands and fingers long,
With veins enamell'd richly ; nor your tongue,
Though it spoke sweeter than Arion's harp ;
Your hair woven into many a curious warp,   125
Able in endless error to enfold
The [wand'ring] [3] soul ; not the true perfect mould
Of all your body, which as pure doth show
In maiden-whiteness as the Alpine snow :
All these, were but your constancy away,   130
Would please me less than a black stormy day
The wretched seaman toiling through the deep.
But, whilst this honour'd strictness you do keep,
Though all the plagues that e'er begotten were
In the great womb of air were settled here,   135
In opposition, I would, like the tree,
Shake off those drops of weakness, and be free
Even in the arm of danger.
Clo.   Wouldst thou have
Me raise again, fond man, from silent grave
Those sparks, that long ago were buried here   140
With my dead friend's cold ashes ?
The.   Dearest dear,
I dare not ask it, nor you must not grant :
Stand strongly to your vow, and do not faint.
Remember how he lov'd you, and be still
The same opinion speaks you : let not will,   145
And that great god of women, appetite,
Set up your blood again ; do not invite
Desire and fancy from their long exile,
To seat them once more in a pleasing smile :
Be, like a rock, made firmly up 'gainst all   150

The power of angry heaven, or the strong fall
Of Neptune's battery. If you yield, I die
To all affection; 't is that loyalty
You tie unto this grave I so admire:
And yet there 's something else I would desire,
If you would hear me, but withal deny.　　156
Oh, Pan, what an uncertain destiny
Hangs over all my hopes! I will retire;
For, if I longer stay, this double fire
Will lick my life up.
　　Clo.　　　　Do; and let time wear out　160
What art and nature cannot bring about.
　　The. Farewell, thou soul of virtue, and be
　　blest
For ever, whilst [that here] [1] I wretched rest
Thus to myself! Yet grant me leave to dwell
In kenning [2] of this arbour: yon same dell,　165
O'ertopt with mourning cypress and sad yew,
Shall be my cabin, where I 'll early rue,
Before the sun hath kist this dew away,
The hard uncertain chance which faith doth lay
Upon his head.
　　Clo.　　　　The gods give quick release　170
And happy cure unto thy hard disease!
　　　　　　　　　　　　　　　　　　Exeunt.

[SCENE III.] [3]

Enter Sullen Shepherd.

　　Sull. Shep. I do not love this wench that I
　　should meet;
For ne'er did my unconstant eye yet greet
That beauty, were it sweeter or more fair
Than the new blossoms when the morning-air
Blows gently on them, or the breaking light,　5
When many maiden-blushes to our sight
Shoot from his early face: were all these set
In some neat form before me, 't would not get
The least love from me; some desire it might,
And present burning. All to me in sight　10
Are equal; be they fair, or black, or brown,
Virgin, or careless wanton, I can crown
My appetite with any; swear as oft,
And weep, as any; melt my words as soft
Into a maiden's ears, and tell how long　15
My heart has been her servant, and how strong
My passions are; call her unkind and cruel;
Offer her all I have to gain the jewel
Maidens so highly [prize]; [4] then loathe, and fly:
This do I hold a blessed destiny.　20

Enter AMARILLIS.

　　Amar. Hail, shepherd! Pan bless both thy
　　flock and thee,
For being mindful of thy word to me!
　　Sull. Shep. Welcome, fair shepherdess! Thy
　　loving swain
Gives thee the self-same wishes back again;　24
Who till this present hour ne'er knew that eye
Could make me cross mine arms, or daily die
With fresh consumings. Boldly tell me, then,
How shall we part their faithful loves, and
　　when?
Shall I belie him to her? Shall I swear
His faith is false and he loves every where?　30

I 'll say he mockt her th' other day to you;
Which will by your confirming show as true,
For [she] [5] is of so pure an honesty,
To think, because [she] [5] will not, none will lie.
Or else to him I 'll slander Amoret,　35
And say, she but seems chaste; I 'll swear she
　　met
Me 'mongst the shady sycamores last night,
And loosely off'red up her flame and sprite
Into my bosom; made a wanton bed　39
Of leaves and many flowers, where she spread
Her willing body to be prest by me;
There have I carv'd her name on many a tree,
Together with mine own. To make this show
More full of seeming, — Hobinal, you know,
Son to the aged shepherd of the glen,　45
Him I have sorted out of many men,
To say he found us at our private sport,
And rous'd us 'fore our time by his resort.
This to confirm, I 've promis'd to the boy
Many a pretty knack and many a toy;　50
As gins to catch him birds, with bow and bolt
To shoot at conies, [6] squirrels, in the holt;
A pair of painted buskins, and a lamb
Soft as his own locks or the down of swan.
This I have done to win you; which doth give
Me double pleasure: discord makes me live.　55
　　Amar. Lov'd swain, I thank ye. These tricks
　　might prevail
With other rustic shepherds, but will fail
Even once to stir, much more to overthrow,　59
His fixed love from judgment, who doth know
Your nature, my end, and his chosen's merit;
Therefore some stronger way must force his
　　spirit,
Which I have found: give second, and my love
Is everlasting thine.
　　Sull. Shep.　　　　Try me, and prove.
　　Amar. These happy pair of lovers meet
　　straightway,　65
Soon as they fold their flocks up with the day,
In the thick grove bordering upon yon hill,
In whose hard side nature hath carv'd a well,
And, but that matchless spring which poets
　　know,
Was ne'er the like to this. By it doth grow,　70
About the sides, all herbs which witches use,
All simples good for medicine or abuse,
All sweets that crown the happy nuptial day,
With all their colours; there the month of May
Is ever dwelling, all is young and green;　75
There 's not a grass on which was ever seen
The falling autumn or cold winter's hand;
So full of heat and virtue is the land
About this fountain, which doth slowly break,
Below yon mountain's foot, into a creek　80
That waters all the valley, giving fish
Of many sorts to fill the shepherd's dish.
This holy well, my grandam that is dead,
Right wise in charms, hath often to me said,
Hath power to change the form of any creature,
Being thrice dipt o'er the head, into what
　　feature　85
Or shape 't would please the letter-down to
　　crave,

---

[1] Q₁-Q₄ omit.　　　　[3] Another part of the wood.
[2] View.　　　　　　　[4] Q₁-Q₄ *praise.*

[5] Qq. F *he.*　　　　[6] Q₂ ff. *nimble.*

Who must pronounce this charm too, which she
    gave   [*Showing a scroll.*]
Me on her death-bed ; told me what, and how,
I should apply unto the patients' brow   90
That would be chang'd, casting them thrice
    asleep,
Before I trusted them into this deep.
All this she show'd me, and did charge me
    prove
This secret of her art, if crost in love.
I 'll this attempt now, shepherd ; I have here 95
All her prescriptions, and I will not fear
To be myself dipt. Come, my temples bind
With these sad herbs, and when I sleep you
    find,
As you do speak your charm, thrice down me
    let,
And bid the water raise me Amoret ;   100
Which being done, leave me to my affair,
And ere the day shall quite itself outwear,
I will return unto my shepherd 's arm ;
Dip me again, and then repeat this charm,
And pluck me up myself, whom freely take,
And the hott'st fire of thine affection slake. 105
  Sull. Shep. And if I fit thee not, then fit not
    me.
I long the truth of this well's power to see.
                        Exeunt.

SCENE IV.[1]

Enter DAPHNIS.

  Daph. Here will I stay, for this the covert is
Where I appointed Cloe. Do not miss,
Thou bright-ey'd virgin ; come, oh come, my
    fair !
Be not abus'd with fear, nor let cold care
Of honour stay thee from thy shepherd's
    arm,   5
Who would as hard be won to offer harm
To thy chaste thoughts, as whiteness from the
    day,
Or yon great round to move another way.
My language shall be honest, full of truth,
My flame as smooth and spotless as my
    youth ;   10
I will not entertain that wand'ring thought,
Whose easy current may at length be brought
To a loose vastness.
  Alexis. (*within.*) Cloe !
  Daph.   'T is her voice,
And I must answer. — Cloe ! — Oh, the
    choice
Of dear embraces, chaste and holy strains 15
Our hands shall give ! I charge you, all my
    veins,
Through which the blood and spirit take their
    way,
Lock up your disobedient heats, and stay
Those mutinous desires that else would grow
To strong rebellion; do not wilder show   20
Than blushing modesty may entertain.
  Alexis. (*within.*) Cloe !   [*again,*
  Daph.   There sounds that blessed name
And I will meet it. Let me not mistake ;

Enter ALEXIS,

This is some shepherd. Sure, I am awake:
What may this riddle mean ? I will retire, 25
To give myself more knowledge.   [*Retires.*]
  Alexis.   Oh, my fire,
How thou consum'st me ! — Cloe, answer me !
Alexis, strong Alexis, high and free,
Calls upon Cloe. See, mine arms are full
Of entertainment, ready for to pull   30
That golden fruit which too, too long hath
    hung
Tempting the greedy eye. Thou stay'st too
    long ;
I am impatient of those mad delays:
I must not leave unsought those many ways
That lead into this centre, till I find   35
Quench for my burning lust. I come, unkind !
                        Exit.
  Daph. [*coming forward.*] Can my imagina-
    tion work me so much ill,
That I may credit this for truth, and still
Believe mine eyes ? Or shall I firmly hold
Her yet untainted, and these sights but bold 40
Illusion ? Sure, such fancies oft have been
Sent to abuse true love, and yet are seen
Daring to blind the virtuous thought with
    error ;
But be they far from me with their fond ter-
    ror !
I am resolv'd my Cloe yet is true.   45
                (CLOE *within.*)
Cloe ! Hark ! Cloe ! Sure, this voice is new,
Whose shrillness, like the sounding of a bell,
Tells me it is a woman. — Cloe, tell
Thy blessed name again.
  Cloe. (*within.*)   Here !
  Daph. Oh, what a grief is this, to be so
    near,   50
And not encounter !

Enter CLOE.

  Cloe.   Shepherd, we are met:
Draw close into the covert, lest the wet,
Which falls like lazy mist upon the ground,
Soak through your startups.[2]
  Daph.   Fairest, are you found ?
How have we wand'red, that the better part
Of this good night is perisht? Oh, my heart !
How have I long'd to meet you, how to kiss 57
Those lily hands, how to receive the bliss
That charming tongue gives to the happy
    ear
Of him that drinks your language ! But I fear
I am too much unmanner'd, far too rude, 61
And almost grown lascivious, to intrude
These hot behaviours ; where regard of fame,
Honour and modesty, a virtuous name,
And such discourse as one fair sister may 65
Without offence unto the brother say,
Should rather have been tend'red. But, be-
    lieve,
Here dwells a better temper: do not grieve,
Then, ever-kindest, that my first salute
Seasons so much of fancy ; I am mute   70

---

[1] Another part of the wood.

[2] High laced boots.

Henceforth to all discourses but shall be
Suiting to your sweet thoughts and modesty.
Indeed, I will not ask a kiss of you,
No, not to wring your fingers, nor to sue
To those blest pair of fixed stars for smiles ;   75
All a young lover's cunning, all his wiles,
And pretty wanton dyings shall to me
Be strangers ; only to your chastity
I am devoted ever.
    Cloe.   Honest swain,
First let me thank you, then return again   80
As much of my love. — [*Aside.*] No, thou art
        too cold,
Unhappy boy, not temp'red to my mould ;
Thy blood falls heavy downward. 'T is not
        fear
To offend in boldness wins ; they never wear
Deserved favours that deny to take   85
When they are offered freely. Do I wake,
To see a man of his youth, years, and feature,
And such a one as we call goodly creature,
Thus backward ? What a world of precious
        art
Were merely lost, to make him do his part !   90
But I will shake him off, that dares not hold :
Let men that hope to be belov'd be bold.
Daphnis, I do desire, since we are met
So happily, our lives and fortunes set
Upon one stake, to give assurance now,   95
By interchange of hands and holy vow,
Never to break again. Walk you that way,
Whilst I in zealous meditation stray
A little this way. When we both have ended
These rites and duties, by the woods be-
        friended   100
And secrecy of night, retire and find
An aged oak, whose hollowness may bind
Us both within his body ; thither go ;
It stands within yon bottom.
    Daph.   Be it so.   *Exit.*
    Cloe. And I will meet there never more with
        thee,   105
Thou idle shamefastness !
    Alexis. (*within.*)   Cloe !
    Cloe.   'T is he
That dare, I hope, be bolder.
    Alexis. (*within.*)   Cloe !
    Cloe.   Now,
Great Pan, for Syrinx' sake, bid speed our
        plough !   *Exit.*

ACT III

Scene I.[1]

Enter Sullen Shepherd, *with* Amarillis *in a
        sleep.*

Sull. Shep. From thy forehead thus I take
These herbs, and charge thee not awake
Till in yonder holy well
Thrice, with powerful magic spell
Fill'd with many a baleful word   5
Thou hast been dipt. Thus, with my cord
Of blasted hemp, by moonlight twin'd
I do thy sleepy body bind.

I turn thy head unto the east,
And thy feet unto the west,   10
Thy left arm to the south put forth,
And thy right unto the north.
I take thy body from the ground,
In this deep and deadly swound,
And into this holy spring   15
I let thee slide down by my string. —
            [*Lets her down into the well.*]
Take this maid, thou holy pit,
To thy bottom ; nearer yet ;
In thy water pure and sweet,
By thy leave I dip her feet ;   20
Thus I let her lower yet,
That her ankles may be wet ;
Yet down lower, let her knee
In thy waters washed be ;
There stop. — Fly away,   25
Every thing that loves the day !
Truth, that hath but one face,
Thus I charm thee from this place.
Snakes that cast your coats for new,
Chameleons that alter hue,   30
Hares that yearly sexes change,
Proteus alt'ring oft and strange,
Hecate with shapes three,
Let this maiden changed be,
With this holy water wet,   35
To the shape of Amoret !
Cynthia, work thou with my charm ! —
Thus I draw thee, free from harm,
            [*Draws her out of the well, in the
                shape of* Amoret.]
Up out of this blessed lake.
Rise both like her and awake !   *She awaketh.*   40
    Amar. Speak, shepherd, am I Amoret to
        sight ?
Or hast thou mist in any magic rite,
For want of which any defect in me
May make our practices discovered be ?
    Sull. Shep. By yonder moon, but that I here
        do stand,   45
Whose breath hath thus transform'd [2] thee, and
        whose hand
Let thee down dry, and pluckt thee up thus
        wet,
I should myself take thee for Amoret !
Thou art in clothes, in feature, voice and hue,
So like, that sense cannot distinguish you.   50
    Amar. Then, this deceit, which cannot crossed
        be,
At once shall lose her him, and gain thee me.
Hither she needs must come, by promise made ;
And, sure, his nature never was so bad,
To bid a virgin meet him in the wood,   55
When night and fear are up, but understood
'T was his part to come first. Being come, I 'll
        say,
My constant love made me come first and stay ;
Then will I lead him further to the grove :
But stay you here, and, if his own true love   60
Shall seek him here, set her in some wrong
        path,
Which say her lover lately trodden hath ;
I 'll not be far from hence. If need there be,

---

[1] Part of the wood with the holy well.

[2] Q₁ and Q₂ *reformed.*

Here is another charm, whose power will free
                    [Gives a scroll.]
The dazzled sense, read by the moonbeams
        clear,   65
And in my own true shape make me appear.

Enter PERIGOT.

Sull. Shep. Stand close ; here 's Perigot, whose
        constant heart
Longs to behold her in whose shape thou art.
                    [Retires with AMARILLIS.]
Peri. This is the place. — Fair Amoret ! —
        The hour
Is yet scarce come. Here every sylvan power   70
Delights to be, about yon sacred well,
Which they have blest with many a powerful
        spell ;
For never traveller in dead of night,
Nor stray'd beasts have fall'n in ; but when
        sight
Hath fail'd them, then their right way they
        have found   75
By help of them, so holy is the ground.
But I will farther seek, lest Amoret
Should be first come, and so stray long un-
        met. —
My Amoret, Amoret !   *Exit.*
    [*Amar. coming forward.* Perigot !][1]
Peri. [*within.*] My love !
    Amar.   I come, my love ! *Exit.*
Sull. Shep.   Now she hath got
Her own desires, and I shall gainer be   81
Of my long-lookt-for hopes, as well as she.
How bright the moon shines here, as if she
        strove
To show her glory in this little grove

Enter AMORET.

To some new-loved shepherd ! Yonder is   85
Another Amoret. Where differs this
From that ? But that she Perigot hath met,
I should have ta'en this for the counterfeit.
Herbs, woods, and springs, the power that in
        you lies,
If mortal men could know your properties ! 90
    Amo. Methinks it is not night ; I have no fear,
Walking this wood, of lion or of bear,
Whose names at other times have made me
        quake,
When any shepherdess in her tale spake
Of some of them, that underneath a wood   95
Have torn true lovers that together stood ;
Methinks there are no goblins, and men's talk,
That in these woods the nimble fairies walk,
Are fables : such a strong heart I have got
Because I come to meet with Perigot.—   100
My Perigot ! Who 's that ? my Perigot ?
    Sull. Shep. (*coming forward.*) Fair maid !
    Amo.   Aye me, thou art not Perigot ?
    Sull. Shep. But I can tell you news of Peri-
        got.
An hour together under yonder tree
He sat with wreathed arms, and call'd on thee
And said, " Why, Amoret, stay'st thou so
        long ? "   106

───────

[1] Early edd. *Ex. Amaryllis, Perigot.*

Then starting up, down yonder path he flung,
Lest thou hadst miss'd thy way. Were it day-
        light,
He could not yet have borne him out of sight.
    Amo. Thanks, gentle shepherd ; and beshrew
        my stay,   110
That made me fearful I had lost my way.
As fast as my weak legs (that cannot be
Weary with seeking him) will carry me,
I 'll follow ; and, for this thy care of me,[2]
Pray Pan thy love may ever follow thee ! *Exit.*
    Sull. Shep. How bright she was, how lovely
        did she show !   116
Was it not pity to deceive her so ?
She pluckt her garments up, and tript away,
And with a virgin-innocence did pray   119
For me that perjur'd her. Whilst she was here,
Methought the beams of light that did appear
Were shot from her ; methought the moon gave
        none
But what it had from her. She was alone
With me ; if then her presence did so move,
Why did I not assay to win her love ?   125
[Would she][3] not sure have yielded unto me ?
Women love only opportunity,
And not the man ; or if she had deni'd,
Alone, I might have forc'd her to have tri'd
Who had been stronger. Oh, vain fool, to let
Such blest occasion pass ! I 'll follow yet ; 131
My blood is up ; I cannot now forbear.

Enter ALEXIS *and* CLOE.

I come, sweet Amoret ! — Soft, who is here ?
A pair of lovers ? He shall yield her me : 134
Now lust is up, alike all women be. [*Retires.*]
    Alexis. Where shall we rest ? But for the
        love of me,
Cloe, I know, ere this would weary be.
    Cloe. Alexis, let us rest here, if the place
Be private, and out of the common trace
Of every shepherd ; for, I understood,   140
This night a number are about the wood :
Then, let us choose some place, where, out of
        sight,
We freely may enjoy our stol'n delight.
    Alexis. Then, boldly here, where we shall
        ne'er be found.
No shepherd's way lies here, 't is hallow'd
        ground ;   145
No maid seeks here her strayed cow or sheep ;
Fairies and fawns and satyrs do it keep.
Then, carelessly rest here, and clip and kiss,
And let no fear make us our pleasures miss. 149
    Cloe. Then, lie by me : the sooner we begin,
The longer ere the day descry our sin.
                    [*They lie down.*]
    Sull. Shep. [*coming forward.*] Forbear to
        touch my love ; or, by yon flame,
The greatest power that shepherds dare to
        name,
Here where thou sit'st, under this holy tree,
Her to dishonour, thou shalt buried be !   155
    Alexis. If Pan himself should come out of
        the lawns,
With all his troops of satyrs and of fawns,

───────

[2] F2 *I 'll seek him out ; and for thy* Courtesie.
[3] Ed. conj. Early edd. *She would.*

And bid me leave, I swear by her two eyes
(A greater oath than thine), I would not rise!
Sull. Shep. Then, from the cold earth never
 thou shalt move,   160
But leave at one stroke both thy life and love.
     [*Wounds him with his spear.*]
Cloe. Hold, gentle shepherd!
Sull. Shep.   Fairest shepherdess,
Come you with me; I do not love you less
Than that fond man, that would have kept you
 there
From me of more desert.
Alexis.   Oh, yet forbear 165
To take her from me! Give me leave to die
By her!

Enter Satyr; Sullen Shepherd *runs one way,*
  and CLOE *another.*

Sat. Now, whilst the moon doth rule the sky,
And the stars, whose feeble light
Gives a pale shadow to the night,
Are up, great Pan commanded me 170
To walk this grove about, whilst he,
In a corner of the wood,
Where never mortal foot hath stood,
Keeps dancing, music, and a feast,
To entertain a lovely guest; 175
Where he gives her many a rose,
Sweeter than the breath that blows
The leaves; grapes, berries of the best;
I never saw so great a feast.
But, to my charge. Here must I stay, 180
To see what mortals lose their way,
And by a false fire, seeming bright,
Train them in and leave them right,
Then must I watch if any be
Forcing of a chastity; 185
If I find it, then in haste
Give my wreathed horn a blast,
And the fairies all will run,
Wildly dancing by the moon.
And will pinch him to the bone, 190
Till his lustful thoughts be gone.
Alexis. Oh, death!
Sat. Back again about this ground;
Sure, I hear a mortal sound. —
I bind thee by this powerful spell, 195
By the waters of this well,
By the glimmering moonbeams bright,
Speak again, thou mortal wight!
Alexis. Oh!
Sat. Here the foolish mortal lies, 200
Sleeping on the ground. — Arise! —
The poor wight is almost dead;
On the ground his wounds have bled,
And his clothes foul'd with his blood:
To my goddess in the wood 205
Will I lead him, whose hands pure
Will help this mortal wight to cure.
    [*Exit carrying* ALEXIS.]

Re-enter CLOE.

Cloe. Since I beheld yon shaggy man, my
 breast
Doth pant; each bush, methinks, should hide a
 beast.
Yet my desire keeps still above my fear: 210

I would fain meet some shepherd, knew I
 where;
For from one cause of fear I am most free,
It is impossible to ravish me,
I am so willing. Here upon this ground
I left my love, all bloody with his wound; 215
Yet, till that fearful shape made me begone,
Though he were hurt, I furnisht was of one;
But now both lost. — Alexis, speak or move,
If thou hast any life; thou art yet my love! —
He 's dead, or else is with this little might 220
Crept from the bank for fear of that ill
 sprite. —
Then, where art thou that struck'st my love?
 Oh, stay!
Bring me thyself in change, and then I 'll say
Thou hast some justice. I will make thee trim
With flowers and garlands that were meant for
 him; 225
I 'll clip thee round with both mine arms, as fast
As I did mean he should have been embrac'd.
But thou art fled. — What hope is left for me?
I 'll run to Daphnis in the hollow tree,
Whom I did mean to mock; though hope be
 small 230
To make him bold, rather than none at all,
I 'll try him; his heart, and my behaviour too,
Perhaps may teach him what he ought to do.
       Exit.

Re-enter Sullen Shepherd.

Sull. Shep. This was the place. 'T was but
 my feeble sight,
Mixt with the horror of my deed, and night, 235
That shapt these fears, and made me run away,
And lose my beauteous hardly-gotten prey. —
Speak, gentle shepherdess! I am alone,
And tender love for love. — But she is gone
From me, that, having struck her lover dead,
For silly fear left her alone and fled. 240
And see, the wounded body is remov'd
By her of whom it was so well belov'd.

Enter PERIGOT, *and* AMARILLIS *in the shape of*
  AMORET.

But all these fancies must be quite forgot.
I must lie close; here comes young Perigot, 245
With subtle Amarillis in the shape
Of Amoret. Pray, love, he may not scape!
       [*Retires.*]
Amar. Beloved Perigot, show me some place,
Where I may rest my limbs weak with the chase
Of thee, an hour before thou cam'st at least. 250
Peri. Beshrew my tardy steps! Here shalt
 thou rest
Upon this holy bank: no deadly snake
Upon this turf herself in folds doth make;
Here is no poison for the toad to feed;
Here boldly spread thy hands; no venom'd
 weed 255
Dares blister them; no slimy snail dare creep
Over thy face when thou art fast asleep;
Here never durst the babbling cuckoo spit;[1]
No slough of falling star did ever hit

---

[1] The popular explanation of the foam secreted by
the cicada.

Upon this bank : let this thy cabin be ;   260
This other, set with violets, for me.
          [*They lie down.*]
  Amar. Thou dost not love me, Perigot.
  Peri.   Fair maid,
You only love to hear it often said ;
You do not doubt.
  Amar.   Believe me, but I do.
  Peri. What, shall we now begin again to
woo ?   265
'T is the best way to make your lover last,
To play with him when you have caught him fast.
  Amar. By Pan I swear, beloved [1] Perigot,
And by yon moon, I think thou lov'st me not.
  Peri. By Pan I swear,— and, if I falsely
swear,   270
Let him not guard my flocks ; let foxes tear
My earliest lambs, and wolves, whilst I do
sleep,
Fall on the rest ; a rot among my sheep, —
I love thee better than the careful ewe   274
The new-yean'd [2] lamb that is of her own hue :
I dote upon thee more than that young lamb
Doth on the bag that feeds him from his dam !
Were there a sort [3] of wolves got in my fold,
And one ran after thee, both young and old
Should be devour'd, and it should be my strife
To save thee, whom I love above my life.   281
  Amar. How should I trust thee, when I see
thee choose
Another bed, and dost my side refuse ?
  Peri. 'T was only that the chaste thoughts
might be shown
'Twixt thee and me, although we were alone.
  Amar. Come, Perigot will show his power,
that he   286
Can make his Amoret, though she weary be,
Rise nimbly from her couch, and come to his.
Here, take thy Amoret ; embrace and kiss.
          [*Lies down beside him.*]
  Peri. What means my love ?
  Amar.   To do as lovers should,   290
That are to be enjoy'd, not to be woo'd.
There 's ne'er a shepherdess in all the plain
Can kiss thee with more art ; there 's none can
feign
More wanton tricks.
  Peri.   Forbear, dear soul, to try
Whether my heart be pure ; I 'll rather die   295
Than nourish one thought to dishonour thee.
  Amar. Still think 'st thou such a thing as
chastity
Is amongst women ? Perigot, there 's none
That with her love is in a wood alone,
And would come home a maid : be not abus'd
With thy fond first belief ; let time be us'd.   301
          [*PERIGOT rises.*]
Why dost thou rise ?
  Peri.   My true heart thou hast slain !
  Amar. Faith, Perigot, I 'll pluck thee down
again.
  Peri. Let go, thou serpent, that into my
breast
Hast with thy cunning div'd ! — Art not in
jest ?   305

[1] Q₈ ff. F₂ *I loved.*   [2] New-born.   [3] Band.

  Amar. Sweet love, lie down.
  Peri.   Since this I live to see,
Some bitter north wind blast my flocks and
me !
  Amar. You swore you lov'd, yet will not do
my will.
  Peri. Oh, be as thou wert once, I 'll love thee
still !
  Amar. I am as still I was, and all my kind ;
Though other shows we have, poor men to
blind.   311
  Peri. Then, here I end all love ; and, lest my
vain
Belief should ever draw me in again,
Before thy face, that hast my youth misled,
I end my life ! my blood be on thy head !   315
          [*Offers to kill himself with his spear.*]
  Amar. [*rising.*] Oh, hold thy hands, thy Amo-
ret doth cry !
  Peri. Thou counsel'st well ; first, Amoret
shall die,
That is the cause of my eternal smart !
  Amar. Oh, hold !   [*Exit.*]
  Peri.   This steel shall pierce thy lustful
heart !
          [*Exit,*] *running after her. The* Sul-
          *len Shepherd steps out and un-
          charms her.*
  Sull. Shep. Up and down, every where,   320
I strew the herbs, to purge the air :
Let your odour drive hence
All mists that dazzle sense.
Herbs and springs, whose hidden might
Alters shapes, and mocks the sight,   325
Thus I charge ye to undo
All before I brought ye to !
Let her fly, let her scape ;
Give again her own shape !   [*Retires.*]

Re-enter AMARILLIS *in her own shape,* [*and*
          PERIGOT *following with his spear.*]

  Amar. Forbear, thou gentle swain ! thou dost
mistake ;   330
She whom thou follow'st fled into the brake,
And as I crost thy way, I met thy wrath ;
The only fear of which near slain me hath.
  Peri. Pardon, fair shepherdess : my rage and
night
Were both upon me, and beguil'd my sight :   335
But far be it from me to spill the blood
Of harmless maids that wander in the wood !
          Exit AMARILLIS.

Enter AMORET.

  Amo. Many a weary step, in yonder path,
Poor hopeless Amoret twice trodden hath,
To seek her Perigot ; yet cannot hear   340
His voice. — My Perigot ! She loves thee dear
That calls.
  Peri.   See yonder where she is ! How fair
She shows ! and yet her breath infects the air.
  Amo. My Perigot !
  Peri.   Here.
  Amo.   Happy !
  Peri.   Hapless ! first
It lights on thee : the next blow is the worst.   345
          [*Wounds her.*]

Amo. Stay, Perigot! My love, thou art un-
just.   [*Falls.*]
Peri. Death is the best reward that 's due to
lust.   *Exit.*
Sull. Shep. Now shall their love be crost : for,
being struck,
I 'll throw her in the fount, lest being took
By some night-traveller, whose honest care   350
May help to cure her. —
                                    [*Comes forward.*]
                        Shepherdess, prepare
Yourself to die !
Amo.   No mercy I do crave ;
Thou canst not give a worse blow than I have.
Tell him that gave me this, who lov'd him
too,
He struck my soul, and not my body through ;
Tell him, when I am dead, my soul shall be   355
At peace, if he but think he injur'd me.
Sull. Shep. In this fount be thy grave. Thou
wert not meant
Sure for a woman, thou art so innocent. —
                        He flings her into the well.
She cannot scape, for, underneath the ground, 360
In a long hollow the clear spring is bound,
Till on yon side, where the morn's sun doth
look,
The struggling water breaks out in a brook.
                                              Exit.

The God of the River *riseth with* Amoret *in his
arms.*

God of the R. What powerful charms my
streams do bring
Back again unto their spring,   365
With such force that I their god,
Three times striking with my rod,
Could not keep them in their ranks?
My fishes shoot into the banks;
There 's not one that stays and feeds,   370
All have hid them in the weeds.
Here 's a mortal almost dead,
Fall'n into my river-head,
Hallowed so with many a spell,
That till now none ever fell.   375
'T is a female young and clear,
Cast in by some ravisher :
See, upon her breast a wound,
On which there is no plaster bound.
Yet, she 's warm, her pulses beat,   380
'T is a sign of life and heat. —
If thou be'st a virgin pure,
I can give a present cure :
Take a drop into thy wound,
From my watery locks, more round   385
Than orient pearl, and far more pure
Than unchaste flesh may endure.—
See, she pants, and from her flesh
The warm blood gusheth out afresh.
She is an unpolluted maid ;   390
I must have this bleeding stay'd.
From my banks I pluck this flower
With holy hand, whose virtuous power
Is at once to heal and draw.
The blood returns. I never saw   395
A fairer mortal. Now doth break
Her deadly slumber. — Virgin, speak.

Amo. Who hath restor'd my sense, given
me new breath,
And brought me back out of the arms of
death ?
God of the R. I have heal'd thy wounds.
Amo.   Aye, me ! 400
God of the R. Fear not him that succour'd
thee.
I am this fountain's god : below,
My waters to a river grow,
And 'twixt two banks with osiers set,
That only prosper in the wet,   405
Through the meadows do they glide,
Wheeling still on every side,
Sometimes winding round about,
To find the evenest channel out.
And if thou wilt go with me,   410
Leaving mortal company,
In the cool streams shalt thou lie,
Free from harm as well as I :
I will give thee for thy food
No fish that useth in the mud ;   415
But trout and pike, that love to swim
Where the gravel from the brim
Through the pure streams may be seen ;
Orient pearl fit for a queen,
Will I give, thy love to win,   420
And a shell to keep them in ;
Not a fish in all my brook
That shall disobey thy look,
But, when thou wilt, come sliding by,
And from thy white hand take a fly :   425
And, to make thee understand
How I can my waves command,
They shall bubble, whilst I sing,
Sweeter than the silver string.   [*Sings.*]

                THE SONG

        Do not fear to put thy feet   430
        Naked in the river sweet ;
        Think not leech, or newt, or toad,
        Will bite thy foot when thou hast trod ;
        Nor let the water rising high,
        As thou wad'st in, make thee cry   435
        And sob ; but ever live with me,
        And not a wave shall trouble thee.

Amo. Immortal power, that rul'st this holy
flood,
I know myself unworthy to be woo'd
By thee, a god ; for ere this, but for thee, 440
I should have shown my weak mortality :
Besides, by holy oath betwixt us twain,
I am betroth'd unto a shepherd-swain,
Whose comely face, I know, the gods above
May make me leave to see, but not to love. 445
God of the R. May he prove to thee as true !
Fairest virgin, now adieu :
I must make my waters fly,
Lest they leave their channels dry,
And beasts that come unto the spring   450
Miss their morning's watering ;
Which I would not ; for of late
All the neighbour-people sate
On my banks, and from the fold
Two white lambs of three weeks old   455
Offered to my deity ;
For which this year they shall be free

From raging floods, that, as they pass,
Leave their gravel in the grass ;
Nor shall their meads be overflown   460
When their grass is newly mown.
    Amo. For thy kindness to me shown,
Never from thy banks be blown
Any tree, with windy force,
Cross thy streams, to stop my course ;   465
May no beast that comes to drink,
With his horns cast down thy brink ;
May none that for thy fish do look,
Cut thy banks to dam thy brook ;
Barefoot may no neighbour wade   470
In thy cool streams, wife nor maid,
When the spawns on stones do lie,
To wash their hemp, and spoil the fry !
    God of the R. Thanks, virgin. I must down
again.
Thy wound will put thee to no pain.   475
Wonder not so soon 't is gone ;
A holy hand was laid upon   [*Descends.*]
    Amo. And I, unhappy born to be,
Must follow him that flies from me.   *Exit.*

ACT IV

Scene I.[1]

Enter Perigot.

    Peri. She is untrue, unconstant, and unkind ;
She 's gone, she 's gone ! Blow high, thou north-
west wind,
And raise the sea to mountains ; let the trees
That dare oppose thy raging fury leese [2]
Their firm foundation ; creep into the earth,   5
And shake the world, as at the monstrous birth
Of some new prodigy ; whilst I constant stand,
Holding this trusty boar-spear in my hand,
And falling thus upon it.
            [*Offers to fall on his spear.*]

Enter Amarillis *running.*

    Amar. Stay thy dead-doing hand ! Thou art
too hot   10
Against thyself. Believe me, comely swain,
If that thou diest, not all the showers of rain
The heavy clouds send down can wash away
That foul unmanly guilt the world will lay
Upon thee. Yet thy love untainted stands :   15
Believe me, she is constant ; not the sands
Can be so hardly numb'red as she won.
I do not trifle, shepherd ; by the moon,
And all those lesser lights our eyes do view,
All that I told thee, Perigot, is true.   20
Then, be a free man ; put away despair
And will to die ; smooth gently up that fair
Dejected forehead ; be as when those eyes
Took the first heat.
    Peri.   Alas, he double dies
That would believe, but cannot ! 'T is not well
You keep me thus from dying, here to dwell   25
With many worse companions. But, oh, death !
I am not yet enamour'd of this breath
So much but I dare leave it ; 't is not pain

In forcing of a wound, nor after-gain   30
Of many days, can hold me from my will.
'T is not myself, but Amoret, bids kill.
    Amar. Stay but a little, little ; but one hour ;
And if I do not show thee, through the power
Of herbs and words I have, as dark as night,   35
Myself turn'd to thy Amoret, in sight,
Her very figure, and the robe she wears,
With tawny buskins, and the hook she bears
Of thine own carving, where your names are set,
Wrought underneath with many a curious fret,   40
The primrose-chaplet, tawdry-lace,[3] and ring, 41
Thou gav'st her for her singing, with each
            thing
Else that she wears about her, let me feel
The first fell stroke of that revenging steel !
    Peri. I am contented, if there be a hope,   45
To give it entertainment for the scope
Of one poor hour. Go ; you shall find me next
Under yon shady beech, even thus perplext,
And thus believing.
    Amar.   Bind, before I go,   1
Thy soul by Pan unto me, not to do
Harm or outrageous wrong upon thy life,
Till my return.
    Peri.   By Pan, and by the strife
He had with Phoebus for the mastery,
When golden Midas judg'd their minstrelsy,
I will not !   *Exeunt [severally].*   5

[Scene II.][4]

Enter Satyr *with* Alexis.

    Sat. Softly gliding as I go,
With this burthen full of woe,
Through still silence of the night
Guided by the glow-worm's light,
Hither am I come at last.   5
Many a thicket have I past ;
Not a twig that durst deny me,
Not a bush that durst descry me
To the little bird that sleeps
On the slender spray ; nor creeps   10
That hardy worm with pointed tail,
But if I be under sail,
Flying faster than the wind,
Leaving all the clouds behind,
But doth hide her tender head   15
In some hollow tree, or bed
Of seeded nettles ; not a hare
Can be started from his fare
By my footing ; nor a wish
Is more sudden ; nor a fish   20
Can be found with greater ease
Cut the vast unbounded seas,
Leaving neither print nor sound,
Than I, when nimbly on the ground
I measure many a league an hour.   25
But, behold, the happy power [5]
That must ease me of my charge,
And by holy hand enlarge
The soul of this sad man, that yet
Lies fast bound in deadly fit :   30
Heaven and great Pan succour it ! —

---

[1] Part of the wood.   [2] Lose.

[3] Lace bought at St. Audrey's Fair at Ely.
[4] The wood before Clorin's bower.
[5] Q₁-Q₄ *lower.*

Hail, thou beauty of the bower,
Whiter than the paramour
Of my master ! Let me crave
Thy virtuous help, to keep from grave   35
This poor mortal, that here lies,
Waiting when the Destinies
Will undo [1] his thread of life :
View the wound, by cruel knife
Trencht into him.   40
   Clo. [*coming from the bower.*] What art thou
    call'st me from my holy rites,
And with the feared name of death affrights
My tender ears ? Speak me thy name and will.
   Sat. I am the Satyr that did fill
Your lap with early fruit ; and will,   45
When I hap to gather more,
Bring you better and more store.[2]
Yet I come not empty now :
See, a blossom from the bough ;
But beshrew his heart that pull'd it,   50
And his perfect sight that cull'd it
From the other springing blooms !
For a sweeter youth the grooms
Cannot show me, nor the downs,
Nor the many neighbouring towns.   55
Low in yonder glade I found him ;
Softly in mine arms I bound him ;
Hither have I brought him sleeping
In a trance, his wounds fresh weeping,
In remembrance such youth may   60
Spring and perish in a day.
   Clo. Satyr, they wrong thee that do term thee
    rude ;
Though thou be'st outward-rough and tawny-
    hu'd,
Thy manners are as gentle and as fair
As his who brags himself born only heir   65
To all humanity. — Let me see thy wound :
This herb will stay the current, being bound
Fast to the orifice, and this restrain
Ulcers and swellings, and such inward pain
As the cold air hath forc'd into the sore ; 70
This to draw out such putrefying gore
As inward falls.
   Sat. Heaven grant it may do good !
   Clo. Fairly wipe away the blood.
Hold him gently, till I fling   75
Water of a virtuous [3] spring
On his temples ; turn him twice
To the moonbeams ; pinch him thrice ;
That the labouring soul may draw
From his great eclipse.
   Sat.   I saw   80
His eyelids moving.
   Clo.   Give him breath ;
All the danger of cold death
Now is vanisht ! With this plaster
And this unction do I master
All the fest'red ill that may   85
Give him grief another day.
   Sat. See, he gathers up his sprite,
And begins to hunt for light ;
Now 'a gaps and breathes again :
How the blood runs to the vein   90
That erst was empty !

   Alexis.   O my heart !
My dearest, dearest Cloe ! Oh, the smart
Runs through my side ! I feel some pointed
    thing
Pass through my bowels, sharper than the sting
Of scorpion. ——   95
Pan, preserve me ! — What are you ?
Do not hurt me : I am true
To my Cloe, though she fly,
And leave me to this destiny.
There she stands, and will not lend   100
Her smooth white hand to help her friend.
But I am much mistaken, for that face
Bears more austerity and modest grace,
More reproving and more awe,
Than these eyes yet ever saw   105
In my Cloe. Oh, my pain
Eagerly renews again !
Give me your help for his sake you love best.
   Clo. Shepherd, thou canst not possibly take
    rest,
Till thou hast laid aside all heats, desires, 110
Provoking thoughts that stir up lusty fires,
Commerce with wanton eyes, strong blood, and
    will
To execute ; these must be purg'd until
The vein grow whiter ; then repent, and pray
Great Pan to keep you from the like decay,   115
And I shall undertake your cure with ease ;
Till when, this virtuous plaster will displease [4]
Your tender sides. Give me your hand, and
    rise !
Help him a little, Satyr ; for his thighs
Yet are feeble.
   Alexis. [*rising.*] Sure, I have lost much blood.
   Sat. 'T is no matter ; 't was not good.   121
Mortal, you must leave your wooing :
Though there be a joy in doing,
Yet it brings much grief behind it ;
They best feel it, that do find it.   125
   Clo. Come, bring him in ; I will attend his
    sore. —
When you are well, take heed you lust no more.
              [ALEXIS *is led into the bower.*]
   Sat. Shepherd, see, what comes of kissing ;
By my head, 't were better missing.
Brightest, if there be remaining   130
Any service, without feigning
I will do it ; were I set
To catch the nimble wind, or get
Shadows gliding on the green,
Or to steal from the great queen   135
Of fairies all her beauty ;
I would do it, so much duty
Do I owe those precious eyes.
   Clo. I thank thee, honest Satyr. If the cries
Of any other, that be hurt or ill   140
Draw thee unto them, prithee, do thy will
To bring them hither.
   Sat. I will ; and when the weather
Serves to angle in the brook,
I will bring a silver hook,   145
With a line of finest silk,
And a rod as white as milk,
To deceive the little fish.

---

   [1] F₂ *cut off.*   [2] **Abundance.**   [3] **Potent.**   [4] **Discomfort.**

So I take my leave, and wish
On this bower may ever dwell   150
Spring and summer!
   Clo.   Friend, farewell. *Exeunt.*

[SCENE III.] [1]

Enter AMORET.

Amo. This place is ominous; for here I lost
My love and almost life, and since have crost
All these woods over; ne'er a nook or dell,
Where any little bird or beast doth dwell,
But I have sought it; ne'er a bending brow   5
Of any hill, or glade the wind sings through,
Nor a green bank nor shade where shepherds
   use
To sit and riddle, sweetly pipe, or choose
Their valentines, that I have mist, to find
My love in. Perigot! Oh, too unkind,   10
Why hast thou fled me? Whither art thou
   gone?
How have I wrong'd thee. Was my love alone
To thee worthy this scorn'd recompense? 'T is
   well;
I am content to feel it. But I tell
Thee, shepherd, and these lusty woods shall
   hear,   15
Forsaken Amoret is yet as clear
Of any stranger fire, as heaven is
From foul corruption, or the deep abyss
From light and happiness; and thou mayst
   know
All this for truth, and how that fatal blow   20
Thou gav'st me, never from desert of mine
Fell on my life, but from suspect of thine,
Or fury more than madness. Therefore here,
Since I have lost my life, my love, my dear,
Upon this cursed place, and on this green   25
That first divorc'd us, shortly shall be seen
A sight of so great pity, that each eye
Shall daily spend his spring in memory
Of my untimely fall.

Enter AMARILLIS.

Amar. [*Aside.*]   I am not blind,
Nor is it through the working of my mind   30
That this shows Amoret. Forsake me, all
That dwell upon the soul, but what men call
Wonder, or, more than wonder, miracle!
For, sure, so strange as this, the oracle
Never gave answer of; it passeth dreams,   35
Or madmen's fancy, when the many streams
Of new imaginations rise and fall.
'T is but an hour since these ears heard her call
For pity to young Perigot; whilst he
Directed by his fury, bloodily   40
Lanc'd up her breast, which bloodless fell and
   cold;
And, if belief may credit what was told,
After all this, the Melancholy Swain
Took her into his arms, being almost slain,
And to the bottom of the holy well   45
Flung her, for ever with the waves to dwell.
'T is she, the very same; 't is Amoret,
And living yet; the great powers will not let

      *Part of the wood with the holy well.

Their virtuous love be crost. — Maid, wipe
   away
Those heavy drops of sorrow, and allay   50
The storm that yet goes high, which, not de-
   prest,
Breaks heart and life and all before it rest.
Thy Perigot ——
   Amo.   Where, which is Perigot?
   Amar. Sits there below, lamenting much,
   God wot,
Thee and thy fortune. Go, and comfort him; 55
And thou shalt find him underneath a brim
Of sailing pines, that edge yon mountain in.
   Amo. I go, I run. Heaven grant me I may
   win
His soul again!   *Exit.*

Enter SULLEN SHEPHERD.

   Sull. Shep.   Stay, Amarillis, stay!
You are too fleet; 't is two hours yet to day. 60
I have perform'd my promise; let us sit
And warm our bloods together, till the fit
Come lively on us.
   Amar.   Friend, you are too keen;
The morning riseth, and we shall be seen;
Forbear a little.
   Sull. Shep.   I can stay no longer.   65
   Amar. Hold, shepherd, hold! Learn not to be
   a wronger
Of your word. Was not your promise laid,
To break their loves first?
   Sull. Shep.   I have done it, maid.
   Amar. No; they are yet unbroken, met
   again,
And are as hard to part yet as the stain   70
Is from the finest lawn.
   Sull. Shep.   I say they are
Now at this present parted, and so far
That they shall never meet.
   Amar.   Swain, 't is not so;
For do but to yon hanging mountain go,
And there believe your eyes.
   Sull. Shep.   You do but hold 75
Off with delays and trifles. — Farewell, cold
And frozen bashfulness, unfit for men! —
Thus I salute thee, virgin!
           [*Attempts to seize her.*]
   Amar.   And thus, then,
I bid you follow: catch me if you can!   *Exit.*
   Sull. Shep. And, if I stay behind, I am no
   man!   *Exit, running after her.* 80

[SCENE IV.] [2]

Enter PERIGOT.

Peri. Night, do not steal away; I woo thee
   yet
To hold a hard hand o'er the rusty bit
That guides thy lazy team. Go back again,
Boötes, thou that driv'st thy frozen wain
Round as a ring, and bring a second night,   5
To hide my sorrows from the coming light;
Let not the eyes of men stare on my face,
And read my falling; give me some black place,
Where never sunbeam shot his wholesome
   light,

      [2] *A dale in the wood.*

That I may sit and pour out my sad sprite   10
Like running water, never to be known
After the forced fall and sound is gone.

    Enter AMORET, *looking for* PERIGOT.

  Amo. This is the bottom.[1] — Speak, if thou
    be here,
My Perigot ! Thy Amoret, thy dear,
Calls on thy loved name.
  Peri.   What art thou dare 15
Tread these forbidden paths, where death and
    care
Dwell on the face of darkness ?
  Amo.   'T is thy friend,
Thy Amoret, come hither, to give end
To these consumings. Look up, gentle boy :
I have forgot those pains and dear annoy   20
I suffer'd for thy sake, and am content
To be thy love again. Why hast thou rent
Those curled locks, where I have often hung
Ribands and damask-roses, and have flung
Waters distill'd, to make thee fresh and gay, 25
Sweeter than nosegays on a bridal day ?
Why dost thou cross thine arms, and hang thy
    face
Down to thy bosom, letting fall apace
From those two little heavens, upon the ground,
Showers of more price, more orient, and more
    round,   30
Than those that hang upon the moon's pale
    brow ?
Cease these complainings, shepherd : I am now
The same I ever was, as kind and free,
And can forgive before you ask of me ;
Indeed, I can and will.
  Peri.   So spoke my fair ! 35
Oh, you great working powers of earth and air,
Water and forming fire, why have you lent
Your hidden virtues of so ill intent ?
Even such a face, so fair, so bright of hue,
Had Amoret ; such words, so smooth and new,
Came flowing from her tongue ; such was her
    eye,   41
And such the pointed sparkle that did fly
Forth like a bleeding shaft; all is the same,
The robe and buskins, painted hook, and frame
Of all her body. Oh me, Amoret !   45
  Amo. Shepherd, what means this riddle? Why
    hath set
So strong a difference ' twixt myself and me,
That I am grown another ? Look, and see
The ring thou gav'st me, and about my wrist
That curious bracelet thou thyself dist twist 50
From those fair tresses. Know'st thou Amoret?
Hath not some newer love forc'd thee forget
Thy ancient faith ?
  Peri.   Still nearer to my love !
These be the very words she oft did prove
Upon my temper ; so she still would take 55
Wonder into her face, and silent make
Signs with her head and hand, as who would
    say,
" Shepherd, remember this another day."
  Amo. Am I not Amoret ? Where was I lost ?
Can there be heaven, and time, and men, and
    most   60

      [1] Dell.

Of these unconstant ? Faith, where art thou
    fled ?
Are all the vows and protestations dead,
The hands held up, the wishes and the heart ?
Is there not one remaining, not a part
Of all these to be found ? Why, then, I see   65
Men never knew that virtue, constancy.
  Peri. Men ever were most blessed, till cross
    fate
Brought love and women forth, unfortunate
To all that ever tasted of their smiles ;
Whose actions are all double, full of wiles ; 70
Like to the subtle hare, that 'fore the hounds
Makes many turnings, leaps, and many rounds,
This way and that way, to deceive the scent
Of her pursuers.
  Amo.   'T is but to prevent
Their speedy coming on, that seek her fall ; 75
The hands of cruel men, more bestial,
And of a nature more refusing good
Than beasts themselves, or fishes of the flood.
  Peri. Thou art all these, and more than na-
    ture meant
When she created all ; frowns, joys, content ; 80
Extreme fire for an hour, and presently
Colder than sleepy poison, or the sea
Upon whose face sits a continual frost ;
Your actions ever driven to the most,
Then down again as low, that none can find 85
The rise or falling of a woman's mind.
  Amo. Can there be any age, or days, or time,
Or tongues of men, guilty so great a crime
As wronging simple maid ? Oh, Perigot,
Thou that wast yesterday without a blot ; 90
Thou that wast every good and every thing
That men call blessed ; thou that wast the
    spring
From whence our looser grooms drew all their
    best ;
Thou that wast always just and always blest
In faith and promise ; thou that hadst the name 95
Of virtuous given thee, and made good the
    same
Ev'n from thy cradle ; thou that wast that all
That men delighted in ! Oh, what a fall
Is this, to have been so, and now to be
The only best in wrong and infamy !   100
And I to live to know this ! and by me,
That lov'd thee dearer than mine eyes, or that
Which we esteem'd our honour, virgin state !
Dearer than swallows love the early morn,
Or dogs of chase the sound of merry horn ; 105
Dearer than thou canst love thy new love, if
    thou hast
Another, and far dearer than the last ;
Dearer than thou canst love thyself, though all
The self-love were within thee that did fall 109
With that coy swain that now is made a flower,
For whose dear sake Echo weeps many a
    shower !
And am I thus rewarded for my flame ?
Lov'd worthily to get a wanton's name ?
Come, thou forsaken willow, wind my head,
And noise it to the world, my love is dead ! 115
I am forsaken, I am cast away,
And left for every lazy groom to say
I was unconstant, light, and sooner lost

Than the quick clouds we see, or the chill frost
When the hot sun beats on it! Tell me yet,   120
Canst thou not love again thy Amoret?
 Peri. Thou art not worthy of that blessed
      name;
I must not know thee. Fling thy wanton flame
Upon some lighter blood that may be hot
With words and feigned passions; Perigot   125
Was ever yet unstain'd, and shall not now
Stoop to the meltings of a borrowed brow.
 Amo. Then hear me, Heaven, to whom I call
      for right,
And you, fair twinkling stars, that crown the
      night;   129
And hear me, woods, and silence of this place,
And ye, sad hours, that move a sullen pace;
Hear me, ye shadows, that delight to dwell
In horrid darkness, and ye powers of hell,
Whilst I breathe out my last! I am that maid,
That yet-untainted Amoret, that play'd   135
The careless prodigal, and gave away
My soul to this young man that now dares say
I am a stranger, not the same, more vild;[1]
And thus with much belief I was beguil'd.
I am that maid, that have delay'd, deni'd,   140
And almost scorn'd the loves of all that tri'd
To win me, but this swain; and yet confess
I have been woo'd by many with no less
Soul of affection; and have often had
Rings, belts, and cracknels,[2] sent me from the
      lad   145
That feeds his flocks down westward; lambs
      and doves
By young Alexis; Daphnis sent me gloves;
All which I gave to thee: nor these nor they
That sent them did I smile on, or e'er lay
Up to my after-memory. But why   150
Do I resolve to grieve, and not to die?
Happy had been the stroke thou gav'st, if home;
By this time had I found a quiet room,
Where every slave is free, and every breast,
That living bred new care, now lies at rest;   155
And thither will poor Amoret.
 Peri.   Thou must.
Was ever any man so loth to trust
His eyes as I? or was there ever yet
Any so like as this to Amoret?
For whose dear sake I promise, if there be   160
A living soul within thee, thus to free
Thy body from it?   *He hurts her again.*
 Amo. [*falling.*] So, this work hath end.
Farewell, and live; be constant to thy friend
That loves thee next.

        Enter Satyr; PERIGOT *runs off.*

 Sat. See, the day begins to break,   165
And the light shoots like a streak
Of subtle fire; the wind blows cold,
Whilst the morning doth unfold;
Now the birds begin to rouse,
And the squirrel from the boughs   170
Leaps, to get him nuts and fruit.
The early lark, that erst was mute,
Carols to the rising day
Many a note and many a lay:

    [1] Vile. F[2] *wild.*   [2] Biscuits.

Therefore here I end my watch,   175
Lest the wand'ring swain should catch
Harm, or lose himself.
 Amo.   Ah me!
 Sat. Speak again, whate'er thou be;
I am ready; speak, I say;
By the dawning of the day,   180
By the power of night and Pan,
I enforce thee speak again!
 Amo. Oh, I am most unhappy.
 Sat. Yet more blood!
Sure, these wanton swains are wood.[3]   185
Can there be a hand or heart
Dare commit so vild a part
As this murder? By the moon,
That hid herself when this was done,
Never was a sweeter face: 190
I will bear her to the place
Where my goddess keeps, and crave
Her to give her life or grave.
        Exit [*carrying* AMORET].

            [SCENE V.][4]

        Enter CLORIN.

 Clo. Here whilst one patient takes his rest
      secure,
I steal abroad to do another cure. —
Pardon, thou buried body of my love,
That from thy side I dare so soon remove;
I will not prove unconstant, nor will leave   5
Thee for an hour alone. When I deceive
My first-made vow, the wildest of the wood
Tear me, and o'er thy grave let out my blood!
I go by wit to cure a lover's pain,
Which no herb can; being done, I'll come
      again.   *Exit.*   10

        Enter THENOT.

 The. Poor shepherd, in this shade for ever lie,
And seeing thy fair Clorin's cabin, die!
        [*Lying down.*]
Oh, hapless love, which being answer'd, ends!
And, as a little infant cries and bends
His tender brows, when, rolling of his eye,   15
He hath espi'd something that glisters nigh,
Which he would have; yet, give it him, away
He throws it straight, and cries afresh to play
With something else, such my affection, set
On that which I should loathe, if I could get.   20

        Re-enter CLORIN.

 Clo. [*Aside.*] See, where he lies! Did ever
      man but he
Love any woman for her constancy
To her dead lover, which she needs must end
Before she can allow him for her friend,
And he himself must needs the cause destroy   25
For which he loves, before he can enjoy?
Poor shepherd, Heaven grant I at once may
      free
Thee from thy pain, and keep my loyalty! —
Shepherd, look up.
 The.   Thy brightness doth amaze;
So Phoebus may at noon bid mortals gaze;   30

    [3] Mad.   [4] The wood before Clorin's bower.

Thy glorious constancy appears so bright,
I dare not meet the beams with my weak sight.
  Clo. Why dost thou pine away thyself for me?
  The. Why dost thou keep such spotless constancy ?
  Clo. Thou holy shepherd, see what for thy sake   35
Clorin, thy Clorin, now dare undertake.
                      He starts up.
  The. Stay there, thou constant Clorin! If there be
Yet any part of woman left in thee,
To make thee light, think yet before thou speak.
  Clo. See, what a holy vow for thee I break ;
I, that already have my fame far spread   41
For being constant to my lover dead.
  The. Think yet, dear Clorin, of your love ; how true,
If you had died, he would have been to you.
  Clo. Yet, all I 'll lose for thee ——
  The.   Think but how blest 45
A constant woman is above the rest !
  Clo. And offer up myself, here on this ground,
To be dispos'd by thee.
  The.   Why dost thou wound.
His heart with malice against women more,
That hated all the sex but thee before ?   50
How much more pleasant had it been to me
To die than to behold this change in thee !
Yet, yet return ; let not the woman sway !
  Clo. Insult not on her now, nor use delay,
Who for thy sake hath ventur'd all her fame. 55
  The. Thou hast not ventur'd, but bought certain shame ;
Your sex's curse, foul falsehood, must and shall,
I see, once in your lives, light on you all.
I hate thee now. Yet turn !
  Clo.   Be just to me :
Shall I at once lose both my fame and thee ? 60
  The. Thou hadst no fame ; that which thou didst like good
Was but thy appetite that sway'd thy blood
For that time to the best : for as a blast
That through a house comes, usually doth cast
Things out of order, yet by chance may come,
And blow some one thing to his proper room, 66
So did thy appetite, and not thy zeal,
Sway thee by chance to do some one thing well.
Yet turn !
  Clo.   Thou dost but try me, if I would
Forsake thy dear embraces for my old 70
Love's, though he were alive : but do not fear.
  The. I do contemn thee now, and dare come near,
And gaze upon thee ; for methinks that grace,
Austerity, which sate upon that face,
Is gone, and thou like others. False maid, see,
This is the gain of foul inconstancy !   *Exit.* 76
  Clo. 'T is done : great Pan, I give thee thanks for it ! —
What art could not have heal'd is cur'd by wit.

Re-enter THENOT.

  The. Will ye be constant yet ? Will ye remove
Into the cabin to your buried love ? 80

  Clo. No, let me die, but by thy side remain.
  The. There 's none shall know that thou didst ever stain
Thy worthy strictness, but shall honour'd be,
And I will lie again under this tree,
And pine and die for thee with more delight 85
Than I have sorrow now to know thee light.
  Clo. Let me have thee, and I 'll be where thou wilt.
  The. Thou art of women's race, and full of guilt.
Farewell all hope of that sex ! Whilst I thought
There was one good, I fear'd to find one naught :
But since their minds I all alike espy,   91
Henceforth I 'll choose, as others, by mine eye.
                            Exit.
  Clo. Blest be ye powers that gave such quick redress,
And for my labours sent so good success !
I rather choose, though I a woman be, 95
He should speak ill of all than die for me.
                [Exit into the bower.]

ACT V

Scene I.[1]

Enter Priest [of Pan] *and* Old Shepherd.

  Priest. Shepherds, rise, and shake off sleep !
See, the blushing morn doth peep
Through the windows, whilst the sun
To the mountain-tops is run,
Gilding all the vales below   5
With his rising flames, which grow
Greater by his climbing still.
Up, ye lazy grooms, and fill
Bag and bottle for the field !
Clasp your cloaks fast, lest they yield 10
To the bitter north-east wind.
Call the maidens up, and find
Who lay longest, that she may
Go without a friend all day ;
Then reward your dogs, and pray 15
Pan to keep you from decay :
So unfold, and then away !
What, not a shepherd stirring ? Sure, the grooms
Have found their beds too easy, or the rooms
Fill'd with such new delight and heat, that they 20
Have both forgot their hungry sheep and day.
Knock, that they may remember what a shame
Sloth and neglect lays on a shepherd's name.
  Old Shep.   *[after knocking at several doors.]*
It is to little purpose ; not a swain
This night hath known his lodging here, or lain
Within these cotes ; the woods, or some near town 26
That is a neighbour to the bordering down,
Hath drawn them thither 'bout some lusty sport,
Or spiced wassail bowl, to which resort
All the young men and maids of many a cote, 30
Whilst the trim minstrel strikes his merry note.

                    [1] A village.

Priest. God pardon sin ! — Show me the way
   that leads
To any of their haunts.
  Old Shep.   This to the meads,
And that down to the woods.
  Priest.   Then, this for me.
Come, shepherd, let me crave your company. 35
                       Exeunt.

[SCENE II]¹

Enter CLORIN *in her cabin,* ALEXIS *with her.*

Clo. Now your thoughts are almost pure,
And your wound begins to cure ;
Strive to banish all that 's vain,
Lest it should break out again.
  Alexis. Eternal thanks to thee, thou holy
    maid !   5
I find my former wand'ring thoughts well staid
Through thy wise precepts : and my outward
  pain
By thy choice herbs is almost gone again.
Thy sex's vice and virtue are reveal'd
At once ; for what one hurt another heal'd. 10
  Clo. May thy grief more appease !
Relapses are the worst disease.
Take heed how you in thought offend ;
So mind and body both will mend.

Enter Satyr, *carrying* AMORET.

Amo. Be'st thou the wildest creature of the
  wood,   15
That bear'st me thus away, drown'd in my
  blood,
And dying, know I cannot injur'd be ;
I am a maid ; let that name fight for me.
  Sat. Fairest virgin, do not fear
Me, that doth thy body bear,   20
Not to hurt, but heal'd to be ;
Men are ruder far than we. —
See, fair goddess, in the wood
They have let out yet more blood.
Some savage man hath struck her breast, 25
So soft and white, that no wild beast
Durst ha' toucht, asleep or 'wake ;
So sweet, that adder, newt, or snake,
Would have lain, from arm to arm,
On her bosom to be warm   30
All a night, and, being hot,
Gone away, and stung her not.
Quickly clap herbs to her breast.
A man, sure, is a kind of beast.
  Clo. With spotless hand on spotless breast 35
I put these herbs, to give thee rest ;
Which till I heal thee, will abide,
If both be pure ; if not, off slide. —
See, it falls off from the wound !
Shepherdess, thou art not sound,   40
Full of lust.
  Sat.   Who would have thought it ?
So fair a face !
  Clo.   Why, that hath brought it.
  Amo. For aught I know or think, these words
  my last,
Yet, Pan so help me as my thoughts are chaste !
  Clo. And so may Pan bless this my cure, 45

As all my thoughts are just and pure !
Some uncleanness nigh doth lurk,
That will not let my medicines work. —
Satyr, search if thou canst find it.
  Sat. Here away methinks I wind² it: 50
Stronger yet. — Oh, here they be ;
Here, here, in a hollow tree,
Two fond mortals have I found.
  Clo. Bring them out ; they are unsound.

Enter CLOE *and* DAPHNIS.

  Sat. By the fingers thus I wring ye, 55
To my goddess thus I bring ye ;
Strife is vain, come gently in. —
I scented them ; they 're full of sin.
  Clo. Hold, Satyr ; take this glass,
Sprinkle over all the place,   60
Purge the air from lustful breath,
To save this shepherdess from death :
And stand you still whilst I do dress
Her wound, for fear the pain increase.
  Sat. From this glass I throw a drop 65
Of crystal water on the top
Of every grass, on flowers a pair :
Send a fume, and keep the air
Pure and wholesome, sweet and blest,
Till this virgin's wound be drest. —   70
  Clo. Satyr, help to bring her in.
  Sat. By Pan, I think she hath no sin,
    [*Carrying* AMORET *into the bower.*]
She is so light. — Lie on these leaves.
Sleep, that mortal sense deceives,
Crown thine eyes and ease thy pain ; 75
May'st thou soon be well again !
  Clo. Satyr, bring the shepherd near.
  Sat. Shepherd, come.
  Daph.   My thoughts are pure.
  Sat. The better trial to endure.   80
  Clo. In this flame his finger thrust,
Which will burn him if he lust ;
But if not, away will turn,
As loth unspotted flesh to burn. —
    [*Satyr applies* DAPHNIS'S *finger to*
    the taper.]
See, it gives back ;³ let him go,   85
Farewell, mortal : keep thee so.
             [*Exit* DAPHNIS.]
Stay, fair nymph ; fly not so fast ;
We must try if you be chaste. —
Here 's a hand that quakes for fear ;
Sure, she will not prove so clear.   90
  Clo. Hold her finger to the flame ;
That will yield her praise or shame.
  Sat. To her doom she dares not stand,
    [*Applies* CLOE'S *finger to the taper.*]
But plucks away her tender hand ;
And the taper darting sends   95
His hot beams at her fingers' ends. —
Oh, thou art foul within, and hast
A mind, if nothing else, unchaste !
  Alex. Is not that Cloe ? 'T is my love, 't is
  she !
Cloe, fair Cloe !
  Cloe.   My Alexis !

¹ The wood before Clorin's bower.

² Scent.   ³ Withdraws.

Alex. He. 100
Cloe. Let me embrace thee.
Clo. Take her hence,
Lest her sight disturb his sense.
Alex. Take not her ; take my life first !
Clo. See his wound again is burst !
Keep her near, here in the wood, 105
Till I ha' stopt these streams of blood.
　　　　　[*Satyr leads off* CLOE.]
Soon again he ease shall find,
If I can but still his mind.
This curtain thus I do display,
To keep the piercing air away. 110
　　　　[*Draws a curtain before the bower.*]

[SCENE III.]¹

Enter Old Shepherd *and* Priest of Pan.

Priest. Sure, they are lost for ever ; 'tis in
　　　vain
To find them out with trouble and much pain
That have a ripe desire and forward will
To fly the company of all but ill.
What shall be counsell'd now ? Shall we retire,
Or constant follow still that first desire 6
We had to find them ?
Old Shep. Stay a little while ;
For, if the morning's mist do not beguile
My sight with shadows, sure I see a swain :
One of this jolly troop 's come back again. 10

Enter THENOT.

Priest. Dost thou not blush, young shepherd,
　　　to be known
Thus without care leaving thy flocks alone,
And following what desire and present blood
Shapes out before thy burning sense for good ;
Having forgot what tongue hereafter may 15
Tell to the world thy falling off, and say
Thou art regardless both of good and shame,
Spurning at virtue and a virtuous name ?
And like a glorious desperate man, that buys
A poison of much price, by which he dies, 20
Dost there lay out for lust, whose only gain
Is foul disease, with present age and pain,
And then a grave ? These be the fruits that
　　　grow
In such hot veins, that only beat to know
Where they may take most ease, and grow am-
　　　bitious 25
Through their own wanton fire and pride de-
　　　licious.
The. Right holy sir, I have not known this
　　　night
What the smooth face of mirth was, or the
　　　sight
Of any looseness ; music, joy, and ease,
Have been to me as bitter drugs to please 30
A stomach lost with weakness, not a game
That I am skill'd at throughly : nor a dame,
Went her tongue smoother than the feet of time,
Her beauty ever-living like the rhyme
Our blessed Tityrus² did sing of yore ; 35
No, were she more enticing than the store
Of fruitful summer, when the loaden tree

Bids the faint traveller be bold and free ;
'T were but to me like thunder 'gainst the bay,
Whose lightning may enclose, but never stay 40
Upon his charmed branches ; such am I
Against the catching flames of woman's eye.
Priest. Then, wherefore hast thou wand'red ?
The. 'T was a vow
That drew me out last night, which I have now
Strictly perform'd, and homewards go to give 45
Fresh pasture to my sheep, that they may live.
Priest. 'T is good to hear you, shepherd, if
　　　the heart
In this well-sounding music bear his part.
Where have you left the rest ?
The. I have not seen,
Since yesternight we met upon this green 50
To fold our flocks up, any of that train ;
Yet have I walkt those woods round, and have
　　　lain
All this long night under an aged tree ;
Yet neither wand'ring shepherd did I see,
Or shepherdess ; or drew into mine ear 55
The sound of living thing, unless it were
The nightingale, among the thick-leav'd spring
That sits alone in sorrow, and doth sing
Whole nights away in mourning ; or the owl,
Or our great enemy,³ that still doth howl 60
Against the moon's cold beams.
Priest. Go, and beware
Of after-falling.
The. Father, 't is my care. *Exit.*

Enter DAPHNIS.

Old Shep. Here comes another straggler ;
　　　sure I see
A shame in this young shepherd. — Daphnis ?
Daph. He.
Priest. Where hast thou left the rest, that
　　　should have been 65
Long before this grazing upon the green
Their yet-imprison'd flocks ?
Daph. Thou holy man,
Give me a little breathing, till I can
Be able to unfold what I have seen ;
Such horror, that the like hath never been 70
Known to the ear of shepherd. Oh, my heart
Labours a double motion to impart
So heavy tidings ! You all know the bower
Where the chaste Clorin lives, by whose great
　　　power
Sick men and cattle have been often cur'd ; 75
There lovely Amoret, that was assur'd⁴
To lusty Perigot, bleeds out her life,
Forc'd by some iron hand and fatal knife ;
And, by her, young Alexis.

Enter AMARILLIS, *running from her* Sullen
Shepherd.

Amar. If there be
Ever a neighbour-brook or hollow tree, 80
Receive my body, close me up from lust
That follows at my heels ! Be ever just,
Thou god of shepherds, Pan, for her dear sake
That loves the rivers' brinks, and still doth
　　　shake

---

¹ A pasture. ² Chaucer.

³ The wolf. ⁴ Betrothed.

In cold remembrance of thy quick pursuit ;   85
Let me be made a reed, and, ever mute,
Nod to the waters' fall, whilst every blast
Sings through my slender leaves that I was
                                   chaste !
  Priest. This is a night of wonder. — Amarill,
Be comforted : the holy gods are still   90
Revengers of these wrongs.
  Amar.   Thou blessed man,
Honour'd upon these plains, and lov'd of Pan,
Hear me, and save from endless infamy
My yet-unblasted flower, virginity !
By all the garlands that have crown'd that
                                   head,   95
By thy chaste office, and the marriage-bed
That still is blessed by thee ; by all the rites
Due to our god, and by those virgin-lights
That burn before his altar ; let me not
Fall from my former state, to gain the blot   100
That never shall be purg'd ! I am not now
That wanton Amarillis : here I vow
To Heaven, and thee, grave father, if I may
Scape this unhappy night, to know the day
A virgin, never after to endure   105
The tongues or company of men unpure !
I hear him come ; save me !
  Priest.   Retire a while
Behind this bush, till we have known that vile
Abuser of young maidens.   [*They retire.*]

               Enter Sullen [Shepherd].

  Sull. Shep.   Stay thy pace,
Most lov'd Amarillis ; let the chase   110
Grow calm and milder : fly me not so fast :
I fear the pointed brambles have unlac'd
Thy golden buskins. Turn again, and see
Thy shepherd follow, that is strong and free,
Able to give thee all content and ease.   115
I am not bashful, virgin ; I can please
At first encounter, hug thee in mine arm,
And give thee many kisses, soft and warm
As those the sun prints on the smiling cheek
Of plums or mellow peaches ; I am sleek   120
And smooth as Neptune when stern Aeolus
Locks up his surly winds, and nimbly thus
Can show my active youth. Why dost thou fly?
Remember, Amarillis, it was I
That kill'd Alexis for thy sake, and set   125
An everlasting hate 'twixt Amoret
And her beloved Perigot ; 't was I
That drown'd her in the well, where she must
                                   lie
Till time shall leave to be. Then, turn again,129
Turn with thy open arms, and clip[1] the swain
That hath perform'd all this ; turn, turn, I say ;
I must not be deluded.
  Priest [*coming forward.*] Monster, stay !
Thou that art like a canker to the state
Thou liv'st and breath'st in, eating with debate
Through every honest bosom, forcing still   135
The veins of any that may serve thy will ;
Thou that hast offer'd with a sinful hand
To seize upon this virgin, that doth stand
Yet trembling here !
  Sull. Shep.   Good holiness, declare

[1] Embrace.

What had the danger been, if being bare   14[?]
I had embrac'd her ; tell me, by your art,
What coming wonders would that sight impart.
  Priest. Lust and a branded soul.
  Sull. Shep.   Yet, tell me more ;
Hath not our mother Nature, for her store
And great encrease, said it is good and just, 145
And will'd that every living creature must
Beget his like ?
  Priest.   You 're better read than I,
I must confess, in blood and lechery. —
Now to the bower, and bring this beast along,
Where he may suffer penance for his wrong. 150
                                   Exeunt.

               [SCENE IV.][2]

          Enter PERIGOT, *with his hand bloody.*

  Peri. Here will I wash it in the morning's
                                   dew,
Which she on every little grass doth strew
In silver drops against the sun's appear ;[3]
'T is holy water, and will make me clear.
My hand will not be cleans'd. — My wronged
                                   love,   5
If thy chaste spirit in the air yet move,
Look mildly down on him that yet doth stand
All full of guilt, thy blood upon his hand ;
And though I struck thee undeservedly,
Let my revenge on her that injur'd thee   10
Make less a fault which I intended not,
And let these dew-drops wash away my spot ! —
It will not cleanse. Oh, to what sacred flood
Shall I resort, to wash away this blood ?
Amidst these trees the holy Clorin dwells,   15
In a low cabin of cut boughs, and heals
All wounds : to her I will myself address,
And my rash faults repentantly confess ;
Perhaps she 'll find a means, by art or prayer,
To make my hand, with chaste blood stained,
                                   fair.   20
That done, not far hence, underneath some tree
I 'll have a little cabin built, since she
Whom I ador'd is dead ; there will I give
Myself to strictness, and, like Clorin, live.
                                   Exit.

               [SCENE V.][4]

The curtain is drawn, CLORIN *appears sitting in
the cabin,* AMORET *sitting on the one side of her,*
ALEXIS *and* CLOE *on the other ; the* Satyr
standing by.

  Clo. Shepherd, once more your blood is staid :
Take example by this maid,
Who is heal'd ere you be pure ;
So hard it is lewd lust to cure.
Take heed, then, how you turn your eye   5
On this[5] other lustfully. —
And, shepherdess, take heed lest you
Move his willing eye thereto :
Let no wring, nor pinch, nor smile,
Of yours his weaker sense beguile. —   10
Is your love yet true and chaste,
And for ever so to last ?
  Alexis. I have forgot all vain desires,

[2] Part of the wood.   [3] Appearance.
[4] The wood before Clorin's bower.
[5] Q_1-Q_4 *these ;* F_2 *each.*

All looser thoughts, ill-temp'red fires:
True love I find a pleasant fume,   15
Whose moderate heat can ne'er consume.
  Cloe. And I a new fire feel in me,
Whose chaste flame is not quencht to be.
  Clo. Join your hands with modest touch,
And for ever keep you such.   20

Enter PERIGOT.

  Peri. [*Aside.*] Yon is her cabin : thus far off
    I 'll stand,
And call her forth ; for my unhallowed hand
I dare not bring so near yon sacred place. —
Clorin, come forth, and do a timely grace
To a poor swain.
  Clo.   What art thou that dost call ? 25
Clorin is ready to do good to all :
Come near.
  Peri. I dare not.
  Clo.   Satyr, see
Who it is that calls on me.
  Sat. [*coming from the bower.*] There, at hand,
    some swain doth stand,
Stretching out a bloody hand.   30
  Peri. Come, Clorin, bring thy holy waters
    clear,
To wash my hand.
  Clo. [*coming out.*] What wonders have been
    here
To-night ! Stretch forth thy hand, young
    swain ;
Wash and rub it, whilst I rain
Holy water.
  Peri.   Still you pour,   35
But my hand will never scour.
  Clo. Satyr, bring him to the bower :
We will try the sovereign power
Of other waters.
  Sat.   Mortal, sure,
'T is the blood of maiden pure   40
That stains thee so.
          The Satyr *leadeth him to the bower,
          where he* spieth AMORET, *and
          kneeling down, she knoweth him.*
  Peri.   Whate'er thou be,
Be'st thou her sprite, or some divinity,
That in her shape thinks good to walk this grove,
Pardon poor Perigot !
  Amo.   I am thy love,
Thy Amoret, for evermore thy love :   45
Strike once more on my naked breast, I 'll
    prove
As constant still. Oh, couldst thou love me yet,
How soon could I my former griefs forget !
  Peri. So over-great with joy that you live,
    now
I am, that no desire of knowing how   50
Doth seize me. Hast thou still power to for-
    give ?
  Amo. Whilst thou hast power to love, or I to
    live :
More welcome now than hadst thou never
    gone
Astray from me !
  Peri.   And when thou lov'st alone, 54
And not I [thee,] death, or some ling'ring pain
That 's worse, light on me !

  Clo.   Now your stain
Perhaps will cleans'd be ; [1] once again.
See, the blood that erst did stay,
With the water drops away.
All the powers again are pleas'd,   60
And with this new knot are appeas'd.
Join your hands, and rise together :
Pan be blest that brought you hither !

Enter Priest *of Pan and* Old Shepherd.

Go back again, whate'er thou art ; unless
Smooth maiden-thoughts possess thee, do not
    press   65
This hallowed ground. — Go, Satyr, take his
    hand,
And give him present trial.
  Sat.   Mortal, stand,
Till by fire I have made known
Whether thou be such a one
That mayst freely tread this place.   70
Hold thy hand up. — Never was
          [*Applying the* Priest's *hand to the
          taper.*]
More untainted flesh than this.
Fairest, he is full of bliss.
  Clo. Then boldly speak, why dost thou seek
    this place ?
  Priest. First, honour'd virgin, to behold thy
    face,   75
Where all good dwells that is ; next, for to try
The truth of late report was given to me, —
Those shepherds that have met with foul mis-
    chance
Through much neglect and more ill govern-
    ance,
Whether the wounds they have may yet en-
    dure   80
The open air, or stay a longer cure ;
And lastly, what the doom may be shall light
Upon those guilty wretches, through whose
    spite
All this confusion fell ; for to this place,
Thou holy maiden, have I brought the race   85
Of these offenders, who have freely told
Both why and by what means they gave this
    bold
Attempt upon their lives.
  Clo.   Fume all the ground,
And sprinkle holy water, for unsound
And foul infection 'gins to fill the air :   90
It gathers yet more strongly ; take a pair
          [*The* Satyr *fumes the ground, etc.*]
Of censers fill'd with frankincense and myrrh,
Together with cold camphire : quickly stir
Thee, gentle Satyr, for the place begins
To sweat and labour with th' abhorred sins   95
Of those offenders : let them not come nigh,
For full of itching flame and leprosy
Their very souls are, that the ground goes
    back,
And shrinks to feel the sullen weight of
    black
And so unheard-of venom. — Hie thee fast,   100
Thou holy man, and banish from the chaste

---

[1] Moorman's conj. for Qq. *cleanse thee.* F₂ reads, *This
perhaps will cleanse again.*

These manlike monsters; let them never
more
Be known upon these downs, but, long before
The next sun's rising, put them from the sight
And memory of every honest wight : 105
Be quick in expedition, lest the sores
Of these weak patients break into new gores.[1]
Exit Priest.

Peri. My dear, dear Amoret, how happy are
Those blessed pairs, in whom a little jar
Hath bred an everlasting love, too strong 110
For time, or steel, or envy to do wrong !
How do you feel your hurts ? Alas, poor heart,
How much I was abus'd ! Give me the smart,
For it is justly mine.

Amo. I do believe.
It is enough, dear friend ; leave off to grieve, 115
And let us once more, in despite of ill,
Give hands and hearts again.

Peri. With better will
Than e'er I went to find in hottest day
Cool crystal of the fountain, to allay 119
My eager thirst. May this band never break !
Hear us, oh, Heaven !

Amo. Be constant.
Peri. Else Pan wreak
With double vengeance my disloyalty !
Let me not dare to know the company
Of men, or any more behold those eyes !
Amo. Thus, shepherd, with a kiss all envy
dies. 125

Re-enter Priest of Pan.

Priest. Bright maid, I have perform'd your
will. The swain
In whom such heat and black rebellions reign
Hath undergone your sentence and disgrace ;
Only the maid I have reserv'd, whose face
Shows much amendment ; many a tear doth
fall 130
In sorrow of her fault. Great fair, recall
Your heavy doom, in hope of better days,
Which I dare promise ; once again upraise
Her heavy spirit, that near drowned lies
In self-consuming care that never dies. 135

Clo. I am content to pardon ; call her in.—
The air grows cool again, and doth begin
To purge itself : how bright the day doth show
After this stormy cloud ! — Go, Satyr, go,
And with this taper boldly try her hand. 140
If she be pure and good, and firmly stand
To be so still, we have perform'd a work
Worthy the gods themselves.

Satyr brings AMARILLIS *in.*

Sat. Come forward, maiden ; do not lurk,
Nor hide your face with grief and shame ; 145
Now or never get a name
That may raise thee, and re-cure
All thy life that was impure.
Hold your hand unto the flame ;
If thou be'st a perfect dame, 150
Or hast truly vow'd to mend,
This pale fire will be thy friend. —
[*Applies her hand to the taper.*]
See, the taper hurts her not !

Go thy ways ; let never spot
Henceforth seize upon thy blood : 155
Thank the gods, and still be good.
Clo. Young shepherdess, now ye are brought
again
To virgin-state, be so, and so remain
To thy last day, unless the faithful love 159
Of some good shepherd force thee to remove ;
Then labour to be true to him, and live
As such a one that ever strives to give
A blessed memory to after-time ;
Be famous for your good, not for your crime.—
Now, holy man, I offer up again 165
These patients, full of health and free from
pain.
Keep them from after-ills ; be ever near
Unto their actions ; teach them how to clear
The tedious way they pass through from sus-
pect ;
Keep them from wronging others, or neglect 170
Of duty in themselves ; correct the blood
With thrifty bits [2] and labour ; let the flood,
Or the next neighbouring spring, give remedy
To greedy thirst and travail, not the tree 174
That hangs with wanton clusters ; let not wine,
Unless in sacrifice or rites divine,
Be ever known of shepherds ; have a care,
Thou man of holy life ! Now do not spare
Their faults through much remissness, nor for-
get 179
To cherish him whose many pains and sweat
Hath giv'n increase and added to the downs.
Sort all your shepherds from the lazy clowns
That feed their heifers in the budded brooms.
Teach the young maidens strictness, that the
grooms
May ever fear to tempt their blowing youth. 185
Banish all compliment, but single truth,
From every tongue and every shepherd's heart ;
Let them still use persuading, but no art.
Thus, holy priest, I wish to thee and these
All the best goods and comforts that may
please. 190
All. And all those blessings Heaven did ever
give,
We pray upon this bower may ever live.
Priest. Kneel, every shepherd, whilst with
powerful hand
I bless your after-labours, and the land
You feed your flocks upon. Great Pan defend
you 195
From misfortune, and amend you ;
Keep you from those dangers still
That are followed by your will ;
Give ye means to know at length,
All your riches, all your strength, 200
Cannot keep your foot from falling
To lewd lust, that still is calling
At your cottage, till his power
Bring again that golden hour
Of peace and rest to every soul ; 205
May his care of you control
All diseases, sores, or pain,
That in after-time may reign
Either in your flocks or you ;

---

[1] Bleedings.

[2] Well-earned morsels. (Moorman.)

Give ye all affections new,   210
New desires, and tempers new,
That ye may be ever true !
Now rise, and go ; and, as ye pass away,
Sing to the God of Sheep that happy lay
That honest Dorus taught ye,— Dorus, he   215
That was the soul and god of melody.

*They all sing [and strew the ground
with flowers].*

THE SONG.

All ye woods, and trees, and bowers,
All ye virtues and ye powers
That inhabit in the lakes,
In the pleasant springs or brakes,   220
  Move your feet
  To our sound,
  Whilst we greet
  All this ground
With his honour and his name   225
That defends our flocks from blame.

He is great, and he is just,
He is ever good, and must
Thus be honour'd. Daffadillies,
Roses, pinks, and loved lilies,   230
  Let us fling,
  Whilst we sing,
  Ever holy,
  Ever holy,
Ever honour'd, ever young !   235
Thus great Pan is ever sung !

Exeunt [all except Clorin *and* Satyr].

Sat. Thou divinest, fairest, brightest,
Thou most powerful maid and whitest,
Thou most virtuous and most blessed,
Eyes of stars, and golden-tressed   240

Like Apollo ; tell me, sweetest,
What new service now is meetest
For the Satyr ? Shall I stray
In the middle air, and stay
The sailing rack,[1] or nimbly take   245
Hold by the moon, and gently make
Suit to the pale queen of night
For a beam to give thee light ?
Shall I dive into the sea,
And bring thee coral, making way   250
Through the rising waves that fall
In snowy fleeces ? Dearest, shall
I catch thee wanton fawns, or flies
Whose woven wings the summer dyes
Of many colours ? get thee fruit,   255
Or steal from Heaven old Orpheus' lute ?
All these I 'll venture for, and more,
To do her service all these woods adore.
  Clo. No other service, Satyr, but thy watch
About these thicks,[2] lest harmless people
        catch   260
Mischief or sad mischance.
  Sat.   Holy virgin, I will dance
Round about these woods as quick
As the breaking light, and prick [3]
Down the lawns and down the vales   265
Faster than the windmill sails.
So I take my leave, and pray
All the comforts of the day,
Such as Phoebus' heat doth send
On the earth, may still befriend   270
Thee and this arbour !
  Clo.   And to thee
All thy master's love be free !   *Exeunt.*

---

[1] Cloud-drift.   [2] Q₄ F₂ *thickets.*   [3] Speed.

THE WILD-GOOSE CHASE

BY

JOHN FLETCHER

DRAMATIS PERSONAE

De Gard, a noble staid Gentleman, that, being newly lighted from his travels, assists his sister Oriana in her chase of Mirabel the Wild-Goose. Acted by Mr. Robert Benfield.

La Castre, the indulgent father to Mirabel. Acted by Mr. Richard Robinson.

Mirabel the Wild-Goose, a travelled Monsieur, and great defier of all ladies in the way of marriage, otherwise their much loose servant, at last caught by the despised Oriana. Incomparably acted by Mr. Joseph Taylor.

Pinac, his fellow-traveller, of a lively spirit, and servant to the no less sprightly Lillia Bianca. Admirably well acted by Mr. Thomas Pollard.

Belleur, Companion to both, of a stout blunt humour, in love with Rosalura. Most naturally acted by Mr. John Lowin.

Nantolet, father to Rosalura and Lillia Bianca. Acted by Mr. William Penn.

Lugier, the rough and confident tutor to the ladies, and chief engine to entrap the Wild-Goose. Acted by Mr. Hilliard Swanston.

A Young [Man disguised as a] Factor. By Mr. John Hony-man.

[Gentlemen,] Foot-Boy, Singing-Boy, Two [Men disguised as] Merchants, Priest, Servants.

Oriana, the fair betrothed of Mirabel, and witty follower of the chase. Acted by Mr. Steph. Hammerton.

Rosalura,⎱ the airy daughters of Nantolet.
Lillia Bianca,⎰ William Trigg, Sander Gough.

Petella, their servant. Mr. Shanck.

Mariana, an English Courtesan.

Four Women.

SCENE. — *Paris.*

ACT I

SCENE I.[1]

Enter Monsieur DE GARD *and a* Foot-boy.

De Gard. Sirrah, you know I have rid hard ;
stir my horse well,
And let him want no litter.
F. Boy. I am sure I have run hard ;
Would somebody would walk me, and see me
litter'd,
For I think my fellow-horse cannot in reason 5
Desire more rest, nor take up his chamber be-
fore me :
But we are the beasts now, and the beasts are
our masters.
De Gard. When you have done, step to the
ten-crown ordinary ——
F. Boy. With all my heart, sir ; for I have a
twenty-crown stomach.
De Gard. And there bespeak a dinner.
F. Boy. [going.]   Yes, sir, presently.[2] 10
De Gard. For whom, I beseech you, sir ?
F. Boy.   For myself, I take it, sir.
De Gard. In truth, you shall not take it ; 'tis
not meant for you.
There 's for your provender. *[Gives money.]* Be-
speak a dinner
For Monsieur Mirabel and his companions ;
They 'll be in town within this hour. When you
have done, sirrah,   15

⎱ A hall in the house of La Castre.   ⎰ At once.

Make ready all things at my lodging for me,
And wait me there.
F. Boy.   The ten-crown ordinary ?
De Gard. Yes, sir, if you have not forgot it.
F. Boy. I 'll forget my feet first :
'T is the best part of a footman's faith.   *Exit.*
De Gard.   These youths, 20
For all they have been in Italy to learn thrift,
And seem to wonder at men's lavish ways,
Yet they cannot rub off old friends, their French
itches ;
They must meet sometimes to disport their
bodies
With good wine and good women, and good
store too.   25
Let 'em be what they will, they are arm'd at
all points,
And then hang saving, let the sea grow high !
This ordinary can fit 'em of all sizes.

Enter LA CASTRE *and* ORIANA.

They must salute their country with old cus-
toms.
Ori. Brother !
De Gard.   My dearest sister !
Ori.   Welcome, welcome ! 30
Indeed, ye are welcome home, most welcome !
De Gard.   Thank ye.
You are grown a handsome woman, Oriana
(Blush at your faults) : I am wondrous glad to
see ye.
Monsieur La Castre, let not my affection
To my fair sister make me be held unmannerly

I am glad to see ye well, to see ye lusty,   36
Good health about ye, and in fair company;
Believe me, I am proud ——
  La Cast.   Fair sir, I thank ye.
Monsieur De Gard, you are welcome from your
    journey;
Good men have still good welcome. Give me
    your hand, sir.   40
Once more, you are welcome home. You look
    still younger.
  De Gard. Time has no leisure to look after
    us;
We wander every where; Age cannot find us.
  La Cast. And how does all?
  De Gard.   All well, sir, and all lusty.
  La Cast. I hope my son be so. I doubt not,
    sir,   45
But you have often seen him in your journeys,
And bring me some fair news.
  De Gard.   Your son is well, sir,
And grown a proper gentleman; he is well and
    lusty.
Within this eight hours I took leave of him,
And over-hied him, having some slight business
That forc'd me out o' th' way. I can assure
    you,   51
He will be here to-night.
  La Cast.   Ye make me glad, sir,
For, o' my faith, I almost long to see him.
Methinks, he has been away ——
  De Gard.   'T is but your tenderness.
What are three years? A love-sick wench will
    allow it.   55
His friends that went out with him are come
    back too,
Belleur and young Pinac. He bid me say little,
Because he means to be his own glad messenger.
  La Cast. I thank ye for this news, sir. He
    shall be welcome,
And his friends too; indeed, I thank you
    heartily.   60
And how (for I dare say you will not flatter
    him)
Has Italy wrought on him? Has he mew'd[1] yet
His wild fantastic toys? They say that climate
Is a great purger of those humorous fluxes.
How is he improved, I pray ye?
  De Gard.   No doubt, sir, well;   65
H'as borne himself a full and noble gentleman:
To speak him farther is beyond my charter.
  La Cast. I am glad to hear so much good.
    Come, I see
You long to enjoy your sister; yet I must en-
    treat ye,
Before I go, to sup with me to-night,   70
And must not be deni'd.
  De Gard.   I am your servant.
  La Cast. Where you shall meet fair, merry,
    and noble company;
My neighbour Nantolet and his two fair daugh-
    ters.
  De Gard. Your supper's season'd well, sir; I
    shall wait upon ye.
  La Cast. Till then I'll leave ye; and y' are
    once more welcome.   *Exit.* 75

          [1] Moulted.

  De Gard. I thank ye, noble sir! Now, Oriana,
How have ye done since I went? Have ye had
    your health well?
And your mind free?
  Ori.   You see, I am not bated;
Merry, and eat my meat.
  De Gard.   A good preservative.
And how have you been us'd? You know,
    Oriana,   80
Upon my going out, at your request,
I left your portion in La Castre's hands,
The main means you must stick to. For that
    reason,
And 'tis no little one, I ask ye, sister,
With what humanity he entertains ye,   85
And how ye find his courtesy?
  Ori.   Most ready.
I can assure you, sir, I am us'd most nobly.
  De Gard. I am glad to hear it; but, I prithee,
    tell me
And tell me true, what end had you, Oriana,
In trusting your money here? He is no kins-
    man,   90
Nor any tie upon him of a guardian;
Nor dare I think ye doubt my prodigality.
  Ori. No, certain, sir; none of all this pro-
    voked[2] me;
Another private reason.
  De Gard.   'T is not private,
Nor carried so; 't is common, my fair sister;
Your love to Mirabel: your blushes tell it.   96
'T is too much known, and spoken of too
    largely;
And with no little shame I wonder at it.
  Ori. Is it a shame to love?
  De Gard.   To love undiscreetly:
A virgin should be tender of her honour,   100
Close, and secure.
  Ori.   I am as close as can be,
And stand upon as strong and honest guards
    too;
Unless this warlike age need a portcullis:
Yet I confess, I love him.
  De Gard.   Hear the people.
  Ori. Now, I say, hang the people! He that
    dares   105
Believe what they say dares be mad, and give
His mother, nay, his own wife, up to rumour.
All grounds of truth they build on is a tavern,
And their best censure 's sack, sack in abund-
    ance;   109
For, as they drink, they think: they ne'er speak
    modestly,
Unless the wine be poor, or they want money.
Believe them! Believe *Amadis de Gaul,*
The Knight o' the Sun, or *Palmerin of England,*
For these, to them, are modest and true stories.
Pray, understand me; if their tongues be truth,
And if *in vino veritas* be an oracle,   116
What woman is, or has been ever, honest?
Give 'em but ten round cups, they'll swear
    Lucretia
Died not for want of power to resist Tarquin,
But want of pleasure, that he stay'd no longer;
And Portia, that was famous for her piety   121

          [2] Incited.

To her lov'd lord, they 'll face ye out, died o'
th' pox.
De Gard. Well, there is something, sister.
Ori. If there be, brother,
'T is none of their things; 't is not yet so mon-
strous :
My thing is marriage ; and, at his return,   125
I hope to put their squint eyes right again.
De Gard. Marriage ? 'T is true his father is
a rich man,
Rich both in land and money ; he his heir,
A young and handsome man, I must confess,
too ;
But of such qualities, and such wild flings,   130
Such admirable imperfections, sister,
(For all his travel and bought experience,)
I should be loth to own him for my brother.
Methinks, a rich mind in a state indifferent
Would prove the better fortune.
Ori. If he be wild,   135
The reclaiming him to good and honest, brother,
Will make much for my honour ; which, if I
prosper,
Shall be the study of my love, and life too.
De Gard. Ye say well ; would he thought as
well, and loved too !
He marry ! He 'll be hanged first. He knows
no more   140
What the conditions and the ties of love are,
The honest purposes and grounds of marriage,
Nor will know, nor be ever brought t' endeav-
our,
Than I do how to build a church. He was ever
A loose and strong defier of all order ;   145
His loves are wanderers, they knock at each
door,
And taste each dish, but are no residents.
Or say, he may be brought to think of marriage,
(As 't will be no small labour,) thy hopes are
strangers.   149
I know there is a labour'd match now follow'd,
Now at this time, for which he was sent for
home too.
Be not abus'd : [1] Nantolet has two fair daugh-
ters,
And he must take his choice.
Ori. Let him take freely.
For all this I despair not ; my mind tells me
That I, and only I, must make him perfect ;   155
And in that hope I rest.
De Gard. Since y' are so confident,
Prosper your hope ! I 'll be no adversary ;
Keep yourself fair and right, he shall not wrong
ye.
Ori. When I forget my virtue, no man know
me !   *Exeunt.*

SCENE II. [2]

Enter MIRABEL, PINAC, BELLEUR, *and* Servants.

Mir. Welcome to Paris, once more, gentlemen !
We have had a merry and a lusty ordinary,
And wine, and good meat, and a bouncing reckoning ;

And let it go for once ; 't is a good physic.
Only the wenches are not for my diet ;   5
They are too lean and thin, their embraces
brawn-fallen.[3]
Give me the plump Venetian, fat and lusty,
That meets me soft and supple ; smiles upon me,
As if a cup of full wine leap'd to kiss me,
These slight things I affect not.
Pin. They are ill-built ;   10
Pin-buttock'd,[4] like your dainty Barbaries,[5]
And weak i' the pasterns ; they 'll endure no
hardness.
Mir. There 's nothing good or handsome bred
amongst us ;
Till we are travell'd, and live abroad, we are
coxcombs.
Ye talk of France — a slight unseason'd coun-
try,   15
Abundance of gross food, which makes us
blockheads.
We are fair set out indeed, and so are fore-
horses : —
Men say, we are great courtiers, — men abuse
us ;
We are wise, and valiant too, — *non credo, sig-
nor* ;
Our women the best linguists, — they are par-
rots ;   20
O' this side the Alps they are nothing but mere
drolleries.[6]
Ha ! *Roma la Santa*, Italy for my money !
Their policies, their customs, their frugalities,
Their courtesies so open, yet so reserv'd too,
As, when you think y' are known best, ye are a
stranger.   25
Their very pick-teeth [7] speak more man than
we do.
And season of more salt.
Pin. 'T is a brave country,
Not pester'd with your stubborn precise puppies,
That turn all useful and allow'd contentments
To scabs and scruples — hang 'em, capon-wor-
shippers.   30
Bel. I like that freedom well, and like their
women too,
And would fain do as others do ; but I am so
bashful,
So naturally an ass ! Look ye, I can look upon
'em,
And very willingly I go to see 'em,   34
(There 's no man willinger), and I can kiss 'em,
And make a shift ——
Mir. But, if they chance to flout ye,
Or say, " Ye are too bold ! Fie, sir, remember !
I pray, sit farther off —— "
Bel. 'T is true — I am humbled,
I am gone ; I confess ingenuously, I am silenced ;
The spirit of amber [8] cannot force me answer.   40
Pin. Then would I sing and dance ——
Bel. You have wherewithal, sir.
Pin. And charge her up again.
Bel. I can be hang'd first :
Yet, where I fasten well, I am a tyrant.
Mir. Why, thou dar'st fight ?

---

1 Deceived.   2 A street before the same house.

3 Feeble.   5 Barbary horses.
4 With narrow buttocks.   6 Puppets.
7 Tooth-picks.   8 Supposed to be a provocative.

Bel.   Yes, certainly, I dare fight,
And fight with any man at any weapon.   45
Would th' other were no more! But, a pox
on 't!
When I am sometimes in my height of hope,
And reasonable valiant that way, my heart
harden'd,
Some scornful jest or other chops between me
And my desire. What would ye have me to do,
then, gentlemen?   50
Mir. Belleur, you must be bolder. Travel
three years,
And bring home such a baby to betray ye
As bashfulness! A great fellow, and a soldier!
Bel. You have the gift of impudence; be
thankful.
Every man has not the like talent. I will study,
And, if it may be reveal'd to me ——
Mir.   Learn of me,   55
And of Pinac. No doubt, you 'll find employ-
ment;
Ladies will look for courtship.
Pin.   'T is but fleshing,
But standing one good brunt or two. Hast thou
any mind to marriage?
We 'll provide thee some soft-natur'd wench,
that 's dumb too.   60
Mir. Or an old woman that cannot refuse
thee in charity.
Bel. A dumb woman, or an old woman, that
were eager,
And car'd not for discourse, I were excellent
at.
Mir. You must now put on boldness, there 's
no avoiding it,
And stand all hazards, fly at all games bravely;
They 'll say, you went out like an ox, and re-
turn'd like an ass, else.   66
Bel. I shall make danger,[1] sure.
Mir.   I am sent for home now;
I know it is to marry; but my father shall par-
don me:
Although it be a weighty[2] ceremony,   69
And may concern me hereafter in my gravity,
I will not lose the freedom of a traveller,
A new strong lusty bark cannot ride at one an-
chor,
Shall I make divers suits to show to the same
eyes?
'T is dull and homespun; — study several pleas-
ures,
And want employments for 'em? I 'll be hang'd
first.   75
Tie me to one smock? Make my travels fruit-
less?
I 'll none of that; for every fresh behaviour,
By your leave, father, I must have a fresh mis-
tress,
And a fresh favour[3] too.
Bel.   I like that passingly;
As many as you will, so they be willing,   80
Willing, and gentle, gentle.
Pin.   There 's no reason
A gentleman, and a traveller, should be clapt
up,

[1] Attempt it.   [2] Old edd. *witty*.   [3] Countenance.

(For 't is a kind of bilboes[4] to be married),
Before he manifest to the world his good parts;
Tug ever, like a rascal, at one oar?   85
Give me the Italian liberty!
Mir.   That I study,
And that I will enjoy. Come, go in, gentlemen;
There mark how I behave myself, and follow.
                                        Exeunt.

SCENE III.[4]

Enter LA CASTRE, NANTOLET, LUGIER, ROSA-
LURA, *and* LILLIA BIANCA.

La Cast. You and your beauteous daughters
are most welcome.
Beshrew my blood, they are fair ones! — Wel-
come beauties,
Welcome, sweet birds.   [*courtesies.*
Nant.   They are bound much to your
La Cast. I hope we shall be nearer ac-
quainted.
Nant. That 's my hope too: 5
For, certain, sir, I much desire your alliance.
You see 'em; they are no gypsies. For their
breeding,
It has not been so coarse but they are able
To rank themselves with women of fair fash-
ion;
Indeed, they have been trained well.
Lug.   Thank me.   10
Nant. Fit for the heirs of that state I shall
leave 'em:
To say more, is to sell 'em. They say your son,
Now he has travell'd, must be wondrous curious
And choice in what he takes; these are no
coarse ones.
Sir, here 's a merry wench — let him look to
himself —   15
All heart, i' faith — may chance to startle him;
For all his care, and travell'd caution,
May creep into his eye. If he love gravity,
Affect a solemn face, there 's one will fit him.
La Cast. So young and so demure?
Nant.   She is my daughter,   20
Else I would tell you, sir, she is a mistress
Both of those manners and that modesty
You would wonder at. She is no often-speaker,
But, when she does, she speaks well; nor no
reveller,
Yet she can dance, and has studied the court
elements,   25
And sings, as some say, handsomely; if a
woman,
With the decency of her sex, may be a scholar,
I can assure ye, sir, she understands too.
La Cast. These are fit garments, sir.
Lug.   Thank them that cut 'em.
Yes, they are handsome women; they have
handsome parts too,   30
Pretty becoming parts.
La Cast.   'Tis like they have, sir.
Lug. Yes, yes, and handsome education they
have had too,
Had it abundantly; they need not blush at it.
I taught it, I 'll avouch it.

[4] A bar of iron with fetters attached.
[5] Room in the house of La Castre.

La Cast. Ye say well, sir.
Lug. I know what I say, sir, and I say but
   right, sir. 35
I am no trumpet of their commendations
Before their father; else I should say farther.
La Cast. Pray ye, what's this gentleman?
Nant. One that lives with me, sir;
A man well bred and learn'd, but blunt and
   bitter;
Yet it offends no wise man; I take pleasure
   in't. 40
Many fair gifts he has, in some of which,
That lie most easy to their understandings,
H'as handsomely bred up my girls, I thank him.
   [*Lug.*] I have put it to 'em, that's my part,
   I have urg'd it.
It seems, they are of years now to take hold
   on't. 45
Nant. He's wondrous blunt.
La Cast. By my faith, I was afraid of him.
Does he not fall out with the gentlewomen
   sometimes?
Nant. No, no; he's that way moderate and
   discreet, sir.
Ros. If he did, we should be too hard for
   him.
Lug. Well said, sulphur! 50
Too hard for thy husband's head, if he wear
   not armour.

Enter MIRABEL, PINAC, BELLEUR, DE GARD,
   and ORIANA.

Nant. Many of these bickerings, sir.
La Cast. I am glad they are no oracles.
Sure as I live, he beats them, he's so puissant.
Ori. Well, if ye do forget ——
Mir. Prithee, hold thy peace. 55
I know thou art a pretty wench; I know thou
   lov'st me;
Preserve it till we have a fit time to discourse
   on't,
And a fit place. I'll ease thy heart, I warrant
   thee.
Thou seest I have much to do now.
Ori. I am answer'd, sir:
With me ye shall have nothing on these condi-
   tions. 60
De Gard. Your father and your friends.
La Cast. You are welcome home, sir;
Bless ye, ye are very welcome! Pray, know this
   gentleman,
And these fair ladies.
Nant. Monsieur Mirabel,
I am much affected with your fair return, sir;
You bring a general joy.
Mir. I bring you service, 65
And these bright beauties, sir.
Nant. Welcome home, gentlemen,
Welcome with all my heart!
Bel. & Pin. We thank ye, sir.
La Cast. Your friends will have their share
   too.
Bel. Sir, we hope
They'll look upon us, though we show like
   strangers.
Nant. Monsieur De Gard, I must salute you
   also, 70

And this fair gentlewoman; you are welcome
   from your travel too.
All welcome, all.
De Gard. We render ye our loves, sir.
The best wealth we bring home. — By your
   favours, beauties. —
   [*Aside to Ori.*] One of these two: you know my
   meaning.
Ori. Well, sir;
They are fair and handsome, I must needs con-
   fess it, 75
And, let it prove the worst, I shall live after it.
Whilst I have meat and drink, love cannot
   starve me;
For, if I die o' th' first fit, I am unhappy,
And worthy to be buried with my heels upward.
Mir. To marry, sir?
La Cast. You know I am an old man, 80
And every hour declining to my grave,
One foot already in; more sons I have not,
Nor more I dare not seek whilst you are
   worthy.
In you lies all my hope, and all my name,
The making good or wretched of my memory, 85
The safety of my state.
Mir. And you have provided,
Out of this tenderness, these handsome gentle-
   women,
Daughters to this rich man, to take my choice
   of?
La Cast. I have, dear son.
Mir. 'T is true, ye are old and feebled;
Would ye were young again, and in full
   vigour! 90
I love a bounteous father's life, a long one;
I am none of those that, when they shoot to
   ripeness,
Do what they can to break the boughs they
   grew on.
I wish ye many years and many riches,
And pleasures to enjoy 'em; but, for mar-
   riage, 95
I neither yet believe in't, nor affect[1] it;
Nor think it fit.
La Cast. You will render me your reasons?
Mir. Yes, sir, both short and pithy, and these
   they are: —
You would have me marry a maid?
La Cast. A maid! what else?
Mir. Yes, there be things called widows, dead
   men's wills, 100
I never lov'd to prove those; nor never long'd
   yet
To be buried alive in another man's cold monu-
   ment.
And there be maids appearing, and maids
   being;
The appearing are fantastic things, mere shad-
   ows;
And, if you mark 'em well, they want their
   heads, too; 105
Only the world, to cozen[2] misty eyes,
Has clapt 'em on new faces: the maids being
A man may venture on, if he be so mad to
   marry,

---

[1] Desire.   [2] Cheat

If he have neither fear before his eyes, nor
    fortune;
And let him take heed how he gather these
    too;   110
For, look ye, father, they are just like melons,
Musk-melons are the emblems of these maids;
Now they are ripe, now cut 'em, they taste
    pleasantly,
And are a dainty fruit, digested easily;
Neglect this present time, and come to-mor-
    row,   115
They are so ripe they are rotten gone, their
    sweetness
Run into humour, and their taste to surfeit.
La Cast. Why, these are now ripe, son.
    Mir.   I 'll try them presently,
And, if I like their taste ——
    La Cast.   'Pray ye, please yourself, sir.
    Mir. That liberty is my due, and I 'll main-
    tain it.——   120
Lady, what think you of a handsome man now?
    Ros. A wholesome too, sir?
    Mir.   That 's as you make your bargain.
A handsome, wholesome man, then, and a kind
    man,
To cheer your heart up, to rejoice ye, lady?
    Ros. Yes, sir, I love rejoicing.
    Mir.   To lie close to ye?   125
Close as a cockle? Keep the cold nights from
    ye?
    Ros. That will be look'd for too; our bodies
    ask it.
    Mir. And get two boys at every birth?
    Ros.   That 's nothing?
I have known a cobbler do it, a poor thin cob-
    bler,
A cobbler out of mouldy cheese perform it,   130
Cabbage, and coarse black bread. Methinks, a
    gentleman
Should take foul scorn to have an awl out-
    name [1] him.
Two at a birth! Why, every house-dove has it.
That man that feeds well, promises as well too,
I should expect indeed something of worth
    from.   135
You talk of two!
    Mir. [*Aside.*] She would have me get two
    dozen,
Like buttons, at a birth.
    Ros.   You love to brag, sir.
If you proclaim these offers at your marriage,
(Ye are a pretty-timber'd man, take heed,)
They may be taken hold of, and expected,   140
Yes, if not hoped for at a higher rate too.
    Mir. I will take heed, and thank ye for your
    counsel.
Father, what think ye?
    La Cast.   'T is a merry gentlewoman;
Will make, no doubt, a good wife.
    Mir.   Not for me.
I marry her, and, happily,[2] get nothing: 145
In what a state am I then, father? I shall
    suffer,
For any thing I hear to the contrary, *more ma-
    jorum;*

I were as sure to be a cuckold, father,
A gentleman of antler ——
    La Cast.   Away, away, fool!
    Mir. As I am sure to fail her expectation.   150
I had rather get the pox than get her babies.
    La Cast. Ye are much to blame. If this do
    not affect[3] ye,
Pray, try the other; she 's of a more demure
    way.
    Bel. [*Aside.*] That I had but the audacity to
    talk thus!
I love that plain-spoken gentlewoman admir-
    ably;   155
And, certain, I could go as near to please her,
If down-right only — she has a per'lous coun-
    tenance —
If I could meet one that would believe me,
And take my honest meaning without circum-
    stance ——
    Mir. You shall have your will, sir; I will try
    the other;   160
But 't will be to small use. — I hope, fair lady,
(For, methinks, in your eyes I see more mercy,)
You will enjoin your lover a less penance;
And though I 'll promise much, as men are lib-
    eral,
And vow an ample sacrifice of service,   165
Yet your discretion, and your tenderness,
And thriftiness in love, good huswife's careful-
    ness
To keep the stock entire ——
    Lil.   Good sir, speak louder,
That these may witness, too, you talk of no-
    thing.
I should be loth alone to bear the burden   170
Of so much indiscretion.
    Mir.   Hark ye, hark ye!
'Ods-bobs,[4] you are angry, lady.
    Lil.   Angry! no, sir;
I never own'd an anger to lose poorly.
    Mir. But you can love, for all this; and de-
    light too,
For all your set austerity to hear   175
Of a good husband, lady?
    Lil.   You say true, sir;
For, by my troth, I have heard of none these
    ten year,
They are so rare; and there are so many, sir,
So many longing women on their knees too,
That pray the dropping-down of these good
    husbands —   180
The dropping-down from Heaven; for they are
    not bred here —
That you may guess at all my hope, but hear-
    ing ——
    Mir. Why may not I be one?
    Lil.   You were near 'em once, sir,
When ye came o'er the Alps; those are near
    Heaven.
But since ye miss'd that happiness, there 's no
    hope of ye,   185
    Mir. Can ye love a man?
    Lil.   Yes, if the man be lovely,
That is, be honest, modest. I would have him
    valiant,

---

[1] Surpass.   [2] Haply.   [3] Please.   [4] God's body!

His anger slow, but certain for his honour;
Travell'd he should be, but through himself
exactly,
For 't is fairer to know manners well than coun-
tries.   190
He must be no vain talker, nor no lover
To hear himself talk ; they are brags of a wan-
derer,
Of one finds no retreat for fair behaviour.
Would ye learn more ?
    Mir.   Yes.
    Lil.   Learn to hold your peace, then :
Fond [1] girls are got with tongues, women with
tempers.   195
    Mir. Women, with I know what ; but let that
vanish.
Go thy way, good-wife Bias ! Sure, thy hus-
band
Must have a strong philosopher's stone, he will
ne'er please thee else. —
Here 's a starch'd piece of austerity ! — Do you
hear, father ?
Do you hear this moral lecture ?
    La Cast.   Yes, and like it.   200
    Mir. Why, there 's your judgment now ;
there 's an old bolt shot !
This thing must have the strangest observa-
tion, [2]
(Do you mark me, father ?) when she is married
once,
The strangest custom too of admiration
On all she does and speaks, 't will be past suf-
ferance.   205
I must not lie with her in common language,
Nor cry, " Have at thee, Kate ! " — I shall be
hiss'd then ;
Nor eat my meat without the sauce of sen-
tences,
Your powder'd beef and problems, a rare diet !
My first son, Monsieur Aristotle, I know it,   210
Great master of the metaphysics, or so ;
The second, Solon, and the best law-setter ;
And I must look [3] Egyptian god-fathers,
Which will be no small trouble ; my eldest
daughter,
Sappho, or such a fiddling kind of poetess.   215
And brought up, *invita Minerva*, at her needle !
My dogs must look their names too, and all
Spartan,
Lelaps, Melampus ; no more Fox and Bawdy-
face.
I married to a sullen set of sentences !
To one that weighs her words and her behav-
iours   220
In the gold-weights [4] of discretion ! I 'll be
hang'd first.
    La Cast. Prithee, reclaim thyself.
    Mir.   Pray ye, give me time, then.
If they can set me any thing to play at,
That seems fit for a gamester, have at the
fairest,
Till I see more, and try more !
    La Cast.   Take your time, then ; 225
I 'll bar ye no fair liberty. — Come, gentlemen ;

And ladies, come ; to all, once more, a welcome !
And, now let 's in to supper.
            [*Exeunt* LA CASTRE, NANTOLET,
                LUGIER, ROSALURA, *and* LIL-
                LIA BIANCA.]
    Mir. How dost like 'em ?
    Pin. They are fair enough, but of so strange
behaviours ——   230
    Mir. Too strange for me. I must have those
have mettle,
And mettle to my mind. Come, let 's be merry.
    Bel. Bless me from this woman ! I would
stand the cannon,
Before ten words of hers.
            [*Exeunt* MIRABEL, PINAC, *and*
                BELLEUR.]
    De Gard.   Do you find him now ?
Do you think he will be ever firm ?
    Ori.   I fear not. *Exeunt.* 225

ACT II

SCENE I. [5]

Enter MIRABEL, PINAC, *and* BELLEUR.

    Mir. Ne'er tell me of this happiness ; 't is
nothing ;
The state [6] they bring with being sought-to, [7]
scurvy :
I had rather make mine own play, and I will do.
My happiness is in mine own content,
And the despising of such glorious [8] trifles,   5
As I have done a thousand more. For my
humour,
Give me a good free fellow, that sticks to me,
A jovial fair companion ; there 's a beauty !
For women, I can have too many of them ;
Good women too, as the age reckons 'em,   10
More than I have employment for.
    Pin.   You are happy.
    Mir. My only fear is, that I must be forced,
Against my nature, to conceal myself :
Health and an able body are two jewels.
    Pin. If either of these two women were
offered to me now,   15
I would think otherwise, and do accordingly ;
Yes, and recant my heresies ; I would, [9] sir ;
And be more tender of opinion,
And put a little of my travell'd liberty
Out of the way, and look upon 'em seriously.   20
Methinks, this grave-carried wench ——
    Bel. Methinks, the other,
The home-spoken gentlewoman, that desires to
be fruitful,
That treats of the full manage of the matter,
(For there lies all my aim,) that wench, me-
thinks,   25
If I were but well set on, for she is affable,
If I were but hounded right, and one to teach
me —
She speaks to th' matter, and comes home to
th' point —

---

[1] Foolish.   [2] Obsequious attention.
[3] Seek.   [4] *I. e.* with great precision.

[5] A garden belonging to the house of La Castre.
[6] Estate.   [8] Vain-glorious.
[7] Courted.   [9] F2 *would fain.*

Now do I know I have such a body to please
her
As all the kingdom cannot fit her with, I am
sure on 't,   30
If I could but talk myself into her favour.
Mir. That 's easily done.
Bel. That 's easily said ; would 't were done !
You should see then how I would lay about me.
If I were virtuous, it would never grieve me,
Or any thing that might justify my modesty ; 35
But when my nature is prone to do a charity,
And my calf's tongue will not help me ——
Mir.   Will ye go to 'em ?
They cannot but take it courteously.
Pin.   I 'll do my part,
Though I am sure 't will be the hardest I e'er
play'd yet   39
A way I never tried too, which will stagger me ;
And, if it do not shame me, I am happy.
Mir. Win 'em, and wear 'em ; I give up my
interest.
Pin. What say you, Monsieur Belleur ?
Bel.   Would I could say,
Or sing, or any thing that were but handsome !
I would be with her presently !
Pin.   Yours is no venture ; 45
A merry ready wench.
Bel.   A vengeance squibber ; [1]
She 'll fleer me out of faith too.
Mir.   I 'll be near thee ;
Pluck up thy heart ; I 'll second thee at all
brunts.[2]
Be angry, if she abuse thee, and beat her a
little ;
Some women are won that way.
Bel.   Pray, be quiet, 50
And let me think : I am resolv'd to go on ;
But how I shall get off again ——
Mir.   I am persuaded
Thou wilt so please her, she will go near to
ravish thee.
Bel. I would 't were come to that once ! Let
me pray a little.
Mir. Now, for thine honour, Pinac, board me
this modesty ;   55
Warm but this frozen snow-ball, 't will be a
conquest
(Although I know thou art a fortunate wencher,
And hast done rarely in thy days) above all thy
ventures.
Bel. You will be ever near ?
Mir.   At all necessities ; 59
And take thee off, and set thee on again, boy,
And cherish thee, and stroke thee.
Bel.   Help me out too ;
For I know I shall stick i' th' mire. If you see
us close once,
Be gone, and leave me to my fortune, suddenly,
For I am then determin'd to do wonders.
Farewell, and fling an old shoe. How my heart
throbs !   65
Would I were drunk ! Farewell, Pinac ; Heaven
send us
A joyful and a merry meeting, man !
Pin.   Farewell,

And cheer thy heart up ; and remember, Bel-
leur,
They are but women.
Bel.   I had rather they were lions.
Mir. About it ; I 'll be with you instantly. ——
                    Exeunt [BELLEUR *and* PINAC].

                    Enter ORIANA.

Shall I ne'er be at rest ? No peace of con-
science ?   71
No quiet for these creatures ? Am I ordain'd
To be devour'd quick [3] by these she-cannibals ?
Here 's another they call handsome ; I care not
for her,
I ne'er look after her. When I am half-tippled,
It may be I should turn her, and peruse her ; 76
Or, in my want of women, I might call for her ;
But to be haunted when I have no fancy,
No maw to th' matter — [*Aside.*] Now, why do
you follow me ?   79
Ori. I hope, sir, 't is no blemish to my virtue ;
Nor need you, out of scruple, ask that question,
If you remember ye, before your travel,
The contract you tied to me. 'T is my love, sir,
That makes me seek ye, to confirm your mem-
ory ;
And, that being fair and good, I cannot suffer.
I come to give ye thanks too.
Mir.   For what, prithee ? 86
Ori. For that fair piece of honesty you show'd
sir,
That constant nobleness.
Mir.   How ? for I am short-headed.
Ori. I 'll tell you then ; for refusing that free
offer
Of Monsieur Nantolet's, those handsome
beauties,   90
Those two prime ladies, that might well have
press'd ye
If not to have broken, yet to have bow'd your
promise.
I know it was for my sake, for your faith-sake,
You slipt 'em off ; your honesty compell'd ye ;
And let me tell ye, sir, it show'd most hand-
somely.   95
Mir. And let me tell thee, there was no such
matter ;
Nothing intended that way, of that nature.
I have more to do with my honesty than to fool it,
Or venture it in such leak barks as women.
I put 'em off because I lov'd 'em not,   100
Because they are too queasy [4] for my temper,
And not for thy sake, nor the contract-sake,
Nor vows, nor oaths ; I have made a thousand
of 'em ;
They are things indifferent, whether kept or
broken ;
Mere venial slips, that grow not near the con-
science ;   105
Nothing concerns those tender parts ; they are
trifles ;
For, as I think, there was never man yet hop'd
for
Either constancy or secrecy from a woman,
Unless it were an ass ordain'd for sufferance ;

---

[1] Satirist.   [2] Against all attacks.

[3] Alive.   [4] Fastidious.

Nor to contract with such can be a tie-all.   110
So let them know again ; for 't is a justice
And a main point of civil policy,
Whate'er we say or swear, they being repro-
    bates,
Out of the state of faith, we are clear of all
    sides,
And 't is a curious blindness to believe us.   115
    Ori. You do not mean this, sure ?
    Mir.   Yes, sure, and certain ;
And hold it positively, as a principle,
As ye are strange things, and made of strange
    fires and fluxes,
So we are allow'd as strange ways to obtain ye,
But not to hold ; we are all created errant.   120
    Ori. You told me other tales.
    Mir.   I not deny it ;
I have tales of all sorts for all sorts of women,
And protestations likewise of all sizes,
As they have vanities to make us coxcombs.
If I obtain a good turn, so it is,   125
I am thankful for it ; if I be made an ass,
The 'mends are in mine own hands, or the sur-
    geon's,
And there 's an end on 't.
    Ori.   Do not you love me, then ?
    Mir. As I love others ; heartily I love thee ;
When I am high and lusty, I love thee cruelly.
After I have made a plenteous meal, and satis-
    fied   131
My senses with all delicates, come to me,
And thou shalt see how I love thee.
    Ori. Will not you marry me ?
    Mir. No, certain, no, for any thing I know yet.
I must not lose my liberty, dear lady,   136
And, like a wanton slave, cry for more shackles.
What should I marry for ? Do I want any
    thing ?
Am I an inch the farther from my pleasure ?
Why should I be at charge to keep a wife of
    mine own,   140
When other honest married men will ease me,
And thank me too, and be beholding to me ?
Thou think'st I am mad for a maidenhead ;
    thou art cozen'd :
Or, if I were addicted to that diet,
Can you tell me where I should have one ? Thou
    art eighteen now,   145
And, if thou hast thy maidenhead yet extant,
Sure, 't is as big as cods-head ; and those grave
    dishes
I never love to deal withal. Dost thou see this
    book here ?   [*Shows a book.*]
Look over all these ranks ; all these are women,
Maids, and pretenders to maidenheads ; these
    are my conquests ;   150
All these I swore to marry, as I swore to thee,
With the same reservation, and most right-
    eously :
Which I need not have done neither ; for, alas,
    they made no scruple,
And I enjoy'd 'em at my will, and left 'em.
Some of 'em are married since, and were as pure
    maids again,   155
Ay, o' my conscience, better than they were
    bred for ;
The rest, fine sober women.

    Ori.   Are ye not ashamed, sir ?
    Mir. No, by my troth, sir ;[1] there 's no shame
    belongs to it ;
I hold it as commendable to be wealthy in plea-
    sure,
As others do in rotten sheep and pasture.   160

                Enter DE GARD.

    Ori. Are all my hopes come to this ? Is there
    no faith,
No troth, nor modesty, in men ?   [*Weeps.*]
    De Gard.   How now, sister ?
Why weeping thus ? Did I not prophesy ?
Come, tell me why ——
    Ori.   I am not well ; pray ye pardon me.
                                        Exit.
    De Gard. Now, Monsieur Mirabel, what ails
    my sister ?   165
You have been playing the wag with her.
    Mir.   As I take it,
She is crying for a cod-piece. Is she gone ?
Lord, what an age is this ! I was calling for ye ;
For, as I live, I thought she would have ravish'd
    me.
    De Gard. Ye are merry, sir.   170
    Mir. Thou know'st this book, De Gard, this
    inventory ?
    De Gard. The debt-book of your mistresses ;
    I remember it.
    Mir. Why, this was it that anger'd her ; she
    was stark mad
She found not her name here ; and cried down-
    right
Because I would not pity her immediately,   175
And put her in my list.
    De Gard. Sure, she had more modesty.
    Mir. Their modesty is anger to be overdone ;
They 'll quarrel sooner for precedence here,
And take it in more dudgeon to be slighted,
Than they will in public meetings ; 't is their
    natures :   180
And, alas, I have so many to despatch yet,
And to provide myself for my affairs too,
That, in good faith ——
    De Gard.   Be not too glorious[2] foolish ;
Sum not your travels up with vanities ;
It ill becomes your expectation.[3]   185
Temper your speech, sir : whether your loose
    story
Be true or false, (for you are so free, I fear it,)
Name not my sister in 't ; I must not hear it.
Upon your danger, name her not ! I hold her
A gentlewoman of those happy parts and car-
    riage,   190
A good man's tongue may be right proud to
    speak her.
    Mir. Your sister, sir ! D' ye blench at that ?
    D' ye cavil ?
Do you hold her such a piece she may not be
    play'd withal ?
I have had an hundred handsomer and nobler
Have su'd to me, too, for such a courtesy ;   195
Your sister comes i' the rear. Since ye are so
    angry,

    [1] Formerly used to women as well as to men.
    [2] Boastful.
    [3] The expectation formed of you.

And hold your sister such a strong recusant,
I tell ye, I may do it; and, it may be, will too;
It may be, have too; there 's my free confession;
Work upon that now!
  De Gard. If I thought ye had, I would work,
And work such stubborn work should make
    your heart ache: 201
But I believe ye, as I ever knew ye,
A glorious talker, and a legend-maker
Of idle tales and trifles; a depraver   204
Of your own truth: their honours fly about[1] ye!
And so, I take my leave; but with this caution,
Your sword be surer than your tongue; you 'll
    smart else.
  Mir. I laugh at thee, so little I respect thee;
And I 'll talk louder, and despise thy sister; 209
Set up a chamber-maid that shall outshine her,
And carry her in my coach too, and that will
    kill her.
Go, get thy rents up, go!
  De Gard.   Ye are a fine gentleman! *Exit.*
  Mir. Now, have at my two youths! I 'll see
how they do;
How they behave themselves; and then I 'll
    study
What wench shall love me next, and when I 'll
    loose [2] her.   *Exit.* 215

SCENE II.[3]

Enter PINAC *and* Servant.

  Pin. Art thou her servant, sayest thou?
  Serv.   Her poor creature;
But servant to her horse, sir.
  Pin.   Canst thou show me
The way to her chamber, or where I may con-
    veniently
See her, or come to talk to her?
  Serv.   That I can, sir;
But the question is, whether I will or no.
  Pin.   Why, I 'll content thee. 5
  Serv. Why, I 'll content thee, then; now ye
    come to me.
  Pin. There 's for your diligence.
                        [Gives money.]
  Serv.   There 's her chamber, sir,
And this way she comes out; stand ye but
    here, sir,
You have her at your prospect or your pleasure,
  Pin. Is she not very angry?
  Serv.   You 'll find that quickly.
May be she 'll call ye saucy, scurvy fellow, 11
Or some such familiar name; may be she knows
    ye
And will fling a piss-pot at ye, or a pantofle,[4]
According as ye are in acquaintance. If she
    like ye,
May be she 'll look upon ye; may be no; 15
And two months hence call for ye.
  Pin.   This is fine.
She is monstrous proud, then?
  Serv.   She is a little haughty;
Of a small body, she has a mind well mounted.
Can you speak Greek?

---

[1] Sympson suggests *above.*   [2] Get rid of. F[2] *lose.*
[3] A hall in the house of Nantolet.   [4] Slipper

  Pin.   No, certain.
  Serv.   Get ye gone, then! —
And talk of stars, and firmaments, and fire-
    drakes?   20
Do you remember who was Adam's schoolmas-
    ter,
And who taught Eve to spin? She knows all
    these,
And will run ye over the beginning o' th' world
As familiar as a fiddler.
Can you sit seven hours together, and say no-
    thing?   25
Which she will do, and, when she speaks, speak
    oracles,
Speak things that no man understands, nor her-
    self neither.
  Pin. Thou mak'st me wonder.
  Serv.   Can ye smile?
  Pin.   Yes, willingly;
For naturally I bear a mirth about me.
  Serv. She 'll ne'er endure ye, then; she is
    never merry;   30
If she see one laugh, she 'll swound past *aqua
    vitae.*
Never come near her, sir; if ye chance to ven-
    ture,
And talk not like a doctor, you are damn'd too.
I have told ye enough for your crown, and so,
    good speed you!   *Exit.*
  Pin. I have a pretty task, if she be thus cu-
    rious,   35
As, sure, it seems she is! If I fall off now,
I shall be laugh'd at fearfully; if I go forward,
I can but be abus'd, and that I look for;
And yet I may hit right, but 't is unlikely.
Stay: in what mood and figure shall I attempt
    her?   40
A careless way? No, no, that will not waken
    her:
Besides, her gravity will give me line still,
And let me lose myself: yet this way often
Has hit, and handsomely. A wanton method?
Ay, if she give it leave to sink into her considera-
    tion: 45
But there 's the doubt: if it but stir her blood
    once,
And creep into the crannies of her fancy,
Set her a-gog; — but, if she chance to slight
    it,
And by the power of her modesty fling it back,
I shall appear the arrant'st rascal to her,
The most licentious knave, for I shall talk
    lewdly,
To bear myself austerely? Rate my words?
And fling a general gravity about me,
As if I meant to give laws? But this I canno
    do.
This is a way above my understanding;
Or, if I could, 't is odds she 'll think I moc
    her;
For serious and sad things are ever still susp
    cious.
Well, I 'll say something:
But learning I have none, and less good man
    ners,
Especially for ladies. Well I 'll set my be
    face.

Enter LILLIA BIANCA *and* PETELLA.

I hear some coming. This is the first woman
I ever fear'd yet, the first face that shakes me.
                                    [*Retires.*]
Lil. Give me my hat, Petella; take this veil off,
This sullen cloud; it darkens my delights.
Come, wench, be free, and let the music war-
ble: —   65
Play me some lusty measure.
        [*Music within, to which presently*
        LILLIA *dances.*]
Pin. [*Aside.*]   This is she, sure,
The very same I saw, the very woman,
The gravity I wonder'd at. Stay, stay;
Let me be sure. Ne'er trust me, but she dan-
ceth!
Summer is in her face now, and she skippeth!
I 'll go a little nearer.   71
Lil. Quicker time, fellows!

Enter MIRABEL [*and remains at the side of the
stage.*]

I cannot find my legs yet — Now, Petella!
Pin. [*Aside.*] I am amaz'd; I am founder'd
in my fancy!
Mir. [*Aside.*] Ha! say you so? Is this your
gravity?   75
This the austerity you put upon you?
I 'll see more o' this sport.
Lil.   A song now!
Call in for a merry and a light song;
And sing it with a liberal spirit.

Enter a Man.

Man. Yes, madam.   80
Lil. And be not amaz'd, sirrah, but take us
for your own company. —
        [*A song by the* Man *who then exit.*]
Let 's walk ourselves; come, wench. Would we
had a man or two!
Pin. [*Aside.*] Sure, she has spi'd me, and will
abuse me dreadfully.
She has put on this for the purpose: yet I will
try her. —   [*Advances.*]
Madam, I would be loth my rude intrusion, 85
Which I must crave a pardon for ——
Lil.   Oh, ye are welcome,
Ye are very welcome, sir! We want such a
one.
Strike up again! — I dare presume ye dance
well:
Quick, quick, sir, quick! the time steals on.
Pin.   I would talk with you.
Lil. Talk as you dance.   [*They dance.*]
Mir. [*Aside.*]   She 'll beat him off his legs
first.   90
This is the finest masque!
Lil.   Now, how do ye, sir?
Pin. You have given me a shrewd heat.
Lil.   I 'll give you a hundred.
Come, sing now, sing: for I know ye sing well;
see ye have a singing face.
Pin. [*Aside.*]   A fine modesty!
If I could, she 'd never give me breath. —
Madam, would   95
I might sit and recover!

Lil.   Sit here, and sing now;
Let 's do things quickly, sir, and handsomely.—
Sit close, wench, close. — Begin, begin.
Pin. I am lesson'd.   *A song [by* PINAC].
Lil. 'T is very pretty, i' faith. Give me some
wine now.   100
Pin. I would fain speak to you.
Lil.   You shall drink first, believe me.
Here 's to you a lusty health.   [*They drink.*]
Pin.   I thank you, lady. —
[*Aside.*] Would I were off again! I smell my
misery;
I was never put to this rack: I shall be drunk
too.
Mir. [*Aside.*] If thou be'st not a right one, I
have lost mine aim much: 105
I thank Heaven that I have scaped thee. To
her, Pinac!
For thou art as sure to have her, and to groan
for her. —
I 'll see how my other youth does; this speeds
trimly.
A fine grave gentlewoman, and worth much
honour!   *Exit.*
Lil. Now, how do ye like me, sir?
Pin.   I like ye rarely.   110
Lil. Ye see, sir, though sometimes we are
grave and silent,
And put on sadder dispositions,
Yet we are compounded of free parts, and some-
times too
Our lighter, airy, and our fiery mettles
Break out, and show themselves: and what
think you of that, sir?   115
Pin. Good lady, sit (for I am very weary),
And then I 'll tell ye.
Lil.   Fie! a young man idle!
Up, and walk; be still in action;
The motions of the body are fair beauties;
Besides, 't is cold. 'Ods me, sir, let 's walk faster!
What think ye now of the Lady Felicia?   121
And Bellafronte, the duke's fair daughter? ha!
Are they not handsome things? There is Du-
arta,
And brown Olivia ——
Pin.   I know none of 'em.
Lil. But brown must not be cast away, sir.
If young Lelia   126
Had kept herself till this day from a husband,
Why, what a beauty, sir! You know Ismena,
The fair gem of Saint-Germains?
Pin.   By my troth, I do not.
Lil. And, then, I know, you must hear of
Brisac,
How unlike a gentleman ——
Pin.   As I live, I have heard nothing. 130
Lil. Strike me another galliard![1]
Pin.   By this light, I cannot!
In troth, I have sprain'd my leg, madam.
Lil.   Now sit ye down, sir,
And tell me why ye came hither? Why ye
chose me out?
What is your business? Your errand? De-
spatch, despatch.
Maybe, you are some gentleman's man, and I
mistook ye,   135

[1] A lively dance.

That have brought me a letter, or a haunch of
  venison,
Sent me from some friend of mine.
Pin.   Do I look like a carrier?
You might allow me, what I am, a gentleman.
Lil. Cry ye mercy, sir! I saw ye yesterday;
You are new-come out of travel; I mistook
  ye.   140
And how do all our impudent friends in Italy?
Pin. Madam, I came with duty, and fair
  courtesy,
Service, and honour to ye.
Lil.   Ye came to jeer me.
Ye see I am merry, sir; I have chang'd my
  copy;
None of the sages now: and, pray ye, proclaim
  it.   145
Fling on me what aspersion you shall please,
  sir,
Of wantonness or wildness; I look for it;
And tell the world I am an hypocrite,
Mask in a forc'd and borrow'd shape; I expect
  it;
But not to have you believ'd: for, mark ye,
  sir,   150
I have won a nobler estimation,
A stronger tie, by my discretion,
Upon opinion (howe'r you think I forc'd it)
Than either tongue or art of yours can slubber;
And, when I please, I will be what I please,
  sir,   155
So I exceed not mean;[1] and none shall brand it,
Either with scorn or shame, but shall be
  slighted.
Pin. Lady, I come to love ye.
Lil.   Love yourself, sir;
And, when I want observers,[2] I 'll send for ye.
Heigh-ho! my fit 's almost off; for we do all by
  fits, sir.   160
If ye be weary, sit till I come again to ye.
                    Exit [*with* PETELLA].
Pin. This is a wench of a dainty spirit; but
Hang me, if I know yet either what to think
Or make of her. She had her will of me,
And baited me abundantly, I thank her;   165
And, I confess, I never was so blurted,[3]
Nor never so abus'd. I must bear mine own
  sins.
Ye talk of travels; here 's a curious country!
Yet I will find her out, or forswear my faculty.
                                            Exit.

SCENE III.[4]

Enter ROSALURA *and* ORIANA.

Ros. Ne'er vex yourself, nor grieve; ye are
  a fool, then.
Ori. I am sure I am made so: yet, before I
  suffer
Thus like a girl, and give him leave to triumph——
Ros. You say right; for, as long as he per-
  ceives ye

---

[1] Moderation.   [2] Admirers.
[3] Contemptuously treated.
[4] A garden belonging to the house of Nantolet, with
  a summer-house in the back-ground.

Sink under his proud scornings, he 'll laugh at
  ye.   5
For me, secure yourself; and, for my sister,
I partly know her mind too: howsoever,
To obey my father, we have made a tender
Of our poor beauties to the travell'd monsieur;
Yet two words to a bargain. He slights us   10
As skittish things, and we shun him as curious.[5]
May be, my free behaviour turns his stomach,
And makes him seem to doubt a loose opinion.[6]
I must be so sometimes, though all the world
  saw it.
Ori. Why should not ye? Are our minds only
  measur'd?   15
As long as here ye stand secure——
Ros.   Ye say true;
As long as mine own conscience makes no ques-
  tion,
What care I for report? That woman 's miser-
  able,
That 's good or bad for their tongues' sake.
Come, let 's retire,
And get my veil, wench. By my troth, your
  sorrow,   20
And the consideration of men's humorous mad-
  dings,
Have put me into a serious contemplation.

Enter MIRABEL *and* BELLEUR.

Ori. Come, faith, let 's sit and think.
Ros.   That 's all my business.
    [*They go into the summer-house, and
      sit down,* ROSALURA *having taken
      her veil from a table, and put it
      on.*][7]
Mir. Why stand'st thou peeping here? Thou
  great slug, forward!
Bel. She is there; peace!
Mir.   Why stand'st thou here, then,   15
Sneaking and peeking[8] as thou wouldst steal
  linen?
Hast thou not place and time?
Bel.   I had a rare speech
Studied, and almost ready; and your violence
Has beat it out of my brains.
Mir.   Hang your rare speeches!
Go me on like a man.
Bel.   Let me set my beard up.   30
How has Pinac performed?
Mir.   He has won already;
He stands not thrumming[9] of caps thus.
Bel.   Lord, what should I ail!
What a cold I have over my stomach! Would
  I had some hum![10]
Certain I have a great mind to be at her,
A mighty mind.
Mir.   On, fool!
Bel.   Good words, I beseech ye;   3
For I will not be abus'd by both.
Mir.   Adieu, then
(I will not trouble you; I see you are valiant);
And work your own way.
Bel.   Hist, hist! I will be rul'd
I will, i' faith; I will go presently.

---

[5] Fastidious.   [8] Peeping.
[6] Reputation.   [9] Idly fingering.
[7] This S. D. is from Dyce.   [10] Strong ale.

Will ye forsake me now, and leave me i' th'
  suds ?   40
You know I am false-hearted this way. I be-
  seech ye,
Good sweet Mirabel — I 'll cut your throat, if
  ye leave me,
Indeed I will — sweet-heart —
  Mir.   I will be ready,
Still at thine elbow. Take a man's heart to
  thee,
And speak thy mind ; the plainer still the
  better.   45
She is a woman of that free behaviour,
Indeed, that common courtesy, she cannot deny
  thee.
Go bravely on.
  Bel.   Madam — keep close about me,
Still at my back — Madam, sweet madam —
  Ros.   Ha !
What noise is that? What saucy sound to
  trouble me ?   50
  Mir. What said she ?
  Bel.   I am saucy.
       [ROSALURA and ORIANA *rise and
        come forward.*]
  Mir.   'T is the better.
  Bel. She comes; must I be saucy still ?
  Mir.   More saucy.
  Ros. Still troubled with these vanities ?
  Heaven bless us !
What are we born to ? — Would you speak with
  any of my people ?
Go in, sir ; I am busy.
  Bel.   This is not she, sure : 55
Is this two children at a birth ? I 'll be hang'd,
  then :
Mine was a merry gentlewoman, talk'd daintily,
Talked of those matters that befitted women ;
This is a parcel prayer-book.[1] I'm serv'd
  sweetly !
And now I am to look to ; I was prepar'd for
  th' other way.   60
  Ros. Do you know that man ?
  Ori.   Sure, I have seen him, lady.
  Ros. Methinks 't is pity such a lusty fellow
Should wander up and down, and want em-
  ployment.
  Bel. She takes me for a rogue ! — You may
  do well, madam,
To stay this wanderer, and set him a-work,
  forsooth ;   65
He can do something that may please your
  ladyship.
I have heard of women that desire good breed-
  ings,
Two at a birth, or so.
  Ros.   The fellow 's impudent.
  Ori. Sure, he is craz'd.
  Ros. I have heard of men too that have had
  good manners.   70
Sure, this is want of grace : indeed, 't is great
  pity
The young man has been bred so ill ; but this
  lewd age
Is full of such examples.

           [1] Partly a prayer-book.

  Bel.   I am founder'd,
And some shall rue the setting of me on.
  Mir. Ha ! so bookish, lady ? Is it possible ?
Turn'd holy at the heart too ? I 'll be hang'd
  then :   75
Why, this is such a feat, such an activity,
Such fast and loose ! A veil too for your kna-
  very ?
O Dio, Dio !
  Ros.   What do you take me for, sir ?
  Mir. An hypocrite, a wanton, a dissembler,
Howe'er ye seem ; and thus ye are to be hand-
  led ! —   81
Mark me, Belleur ; — and this you love, I know
  it.   [*Attempts to remove the veil.*]
  Ros. Stand off, bold sir !
  Mir.   You wear good clothes to this end,
Jewels ; love feasts and masques.
  Ros.   Ye are monstrous saucy.
  Mir. All this to draw on fools: and thus,
  thus, lady,   [*Attempts to remove the veil.*]
You are to be lull'd.
  Bel.   Let her alone, I 'll swinge ye else, 86
I will, i' faith ! for, though I cannot skill o'
  this matter
Myself, I will not see another do it before me,
And do it worse.
  Ros.   Away ! ye are a vain thing.
You have travell'd far, sir, to return again 90
A windy and poor bladder. You talk of women,
That are not worth the favour of a common
  one,
The grace of her grew in an hospital !
Against a thousand such blown fooleries
I am able to maintain good women's honours,
Their freedoms, and their fames, and I will do
  it. —   96
  Mir. She has almost struck me dumb too.
  Ros.   And declaim
Against your base malicious tongues, your
  noises,
For they are nothing else. You teach behav-
  iours !
Or touch us for our freedoms ! Teach your
  selves manners,   100
Truth and sobriety, and live so clearly
That our lives may shine in ye ; and then task[2]
  us.
It seems ye are hot ; the suburbs[3] will supply
  ye :
Good women scorn such gamesters.[4] So, I 'll
  leave ye.
I am sorry to see this: faith, sir, live fairly. 105
             Exit [*with* ORIANA].
  Mir. This woman, if she hold on, may be vir-
  tuous ;
'T is almost possible : we 'll have a new day.
  Bel. Ye brought me on, ye forc'd me to this
  foolery.
I am sham'd, I am scorn'd, I am flurted ;[5] yes,
  I am so :
Though I cannot talk to a woman like your
  worship,   110

    [2] Accuse, tax.
    [3] Where the houses of ill-repute were situated.
    [4] Dissolute fellows.   [5] Flouted.

And use my phrases and my learn'd figures,
Yet I can fight with any man.
Mir.   Fie!
Bel.   I can, sir;
And I will fight.
Mir.   With whom?
Bel.   With you; with any man;
For all men now will laugh at me.
Mir.   Prithee, be moderate.
Bel. And I 'll beat all men. Come.
Mir.   I love thee dearly. 115
Bel. I [will] beat all that love; love has un-
    done me.
Never tell me; I will not be a history.
Mir.   Thou art not.
Bel. 'Sfoot, I will not! Give me room,
And let me see the proudest of ye jeer me;
And I 'll begin with you first.
Mir.   Prithee, Belleur —120
If I do not satisfy thee —
Bel.   Well, look ye do.
But, now I think on 't better, 't is impossible;
I must beat somebody. I am maul'd myself.
And I ought in justice —
Mir.   No, no, no; you are cozen'd:
But walk, and let me talk to thee,
Bel.   Talk wisely, 125
And see that no man laugh, upon no occasion;
For I shall think then 't is at me.
Mir.   I warrant thee.
Bel. Nor no more talk of this.
Mir.   Dost think I am maddish?
Bel. I must needs fight yet; for I find it con-
    cerns me:
A pox on 't: I must fight.
Mir.   I' faith, thou shalt not. 130
                    Exeunt.

ACT III

Scene I.[1]

Enter De Gard *and* Lugier.

De Gard. I know ye are a scholar, and can
do wonders.
Lug. There 's no great scholarship belongs to
    this, sir;
What I am, I am. I pity your poor sister,
And heartily I hate these travellers,
These gim-cracks, made of mops[2] and motions.[3]
There 's nothing in their houses here but hum-
    mings;   6
A bee has more brains. I grieve and vex too
The insolent licentious carriage
Of this out-facing fellow Mirabel;
And I am mad to see him prick his plumes up.
De Gard. His wrongs you partly know.
Lug.   Do not you stir, sir; 11
Since he has begun with wit, let wit revenge it:
Keep your sword close; we 'll cut his throat a
    new way.
I am asham'd the gentlewoman should suffer
Such base lewd wrongs.
De Gard.   I will be rul'd: he shall live, 15
And left to your revenge.

Lug.   Ay, ay, I 'll fit him.
He makes a common scorn of handsome women;
Modesty and good manners are his May-games;
He takes up maidenheads with a new commis-
    sion, —
The church-warrant 's out of date. Follow my
    counsel,   20
For I am zealous in the cause.
De Gard.   I will, sir,
And will be still directed; for the truth is,
My sword will make my sister seem more mon-
    strous.
Besides, there is no honour won on reprobates.
Lug. You are i' th' right. The slight he has
    show'd my pupils   25
Sets me a-fire too. Go; I 'll prepare your sister.
And as I told ye —
De Gard.   Yes; all shall be fit, sir.
Lug. And seriously, and handsomely.
De Gard.   I warrant ye.
Lug. A little counsel more.   [*Whispers.*]
De Gard.   'T is well.
Lug.   Most stately:
See that observ'd; and then —
De Gard.   I have ye every way. 30
Lug. Away, then, and be ready.
De Gard.   With all speed, sir. *Exit.*

Enter Lillia Bianca, Rosalura, *and* Oriana.

Lug. We 'll learn to travel too, may be, be-
    yond him. —
Good day, fair beauties!
Lil.   You have beautified us,
We thank ye, sir; ye have set us off most
    gallantly
With your grave precepts.
Ros.   We expected husbands 35
Out of your documents[1] and taught behaviours,
Excellent husbands; thought men would run
    stark mad on us,
Men of all ages and all states; we expected
An inundation of desires and offers,
A torrent of trim suitors; all we did,   40
Or said, or purpos'd, to be spells about us,
Spells to provoke.
Lil.   Ye have provok'd us finely!
We follow'd your directions, we did rarely,
We were stately, coy, demure, careless, light,
    giddy,
And play'd at all points: this, you swore,
    would carry.   45
Ros. We made love, and contemn'd love;
    now seem'd holy,
With such a reverent put-on reservation
Which could not miss, according to your prin-
    ciples;
Now gave more hope again; now close,[2] now
    public,
Still up and down we beat it like a billow;   50
And ever those behaviours you read to us,
Subtle and new: but all this will not help us.
Lil. They help to hinder us of all acquaint-
    ance,
They have frighted off all friends. What am
    better

---

[1] A public walk. [2] Grimaces. [3] Gestures, antics.

[1] Instructions. [2] Private.

For all my learning, if I love a dunce,   55
A handsome dunce? To what use serves my
          reading?
You should have taught me what belongs to
          horses,
Dogs, dice, hawks, banquets, masques, free
          and fair meetings,
To have studied gowns and dressings.
   Lug.   Ye are not mad, sure!
Ros. We shall be, if we follow your encour-
          agements.   60
I 'll take mine own way now.
   Lil.   And I my fortune;
We may live maids else till the moon drop mill-
          stones.
I see, your modest women are taken for mon-
          sters;
A dowry of good breeding is worth nothing.
   Lug. Since ye take it so to th' heart, pray ye,
          give me leave yet,   65
And ye shall see how I 'll convert this heretic.
Mark how this Mirabel ——
   Lil.   Name him no more;
For, though I long for a husband, I hate him,
And would be married sooner to a monkey,
Or to a Jack of Straw, than such a juggler.   70
Ros. I am of that mind too. He is too nimble,
And plays at fast and loose too learnedly,
For a plain-meaning woman; that 's the truth
          on 't.
Here 's one too, that we love well, would be
          angry;   [*Pointing to* ORIANA.]
And reason why. — No, no, we will not trouble
          ye,   75
Nor him at this time: may he make you happy!
We 'll turn ourselves loose now to our fair for-
          tunes;
And the downright way ——
   Lil.   The winning way we 'll follow;
We 'll bait that men may bite fair, and not be
          frighted.
Yet we 'll not be carried so cheap neither; we 'll
          have some sport,   80
Some mad-morris or other for our money, tutor.
   Lug. 'T is like enough: prosper your own de-
          vices!
Ye are old enough to choose. But, for this
          gentlewoman,
So please her give me leave ——
   Ori.   I shall be glad, sir,
To find a friend whose pity may direct me.   85
   Lug. I 'll do my best, and faithfully deal for
          ye;
But then ye must be rul'd.
   Ori.   In all, I vow to ye.
Ros. Do, do: he has a lucky hand sometimes,
          I 'll assure ye,
And hunts the recovery of a lost lover deadly.
   Lug. You must away straight.
   Ori.   Yes.
   Lug.   And I 'll instruct ye: 90
Here ye can know no more.
   Ori.   By your leave, sweet ladies;
And all our fortunes arrive at our own wishes!
   Lil. Amen, amen!
   Lug.   I must borrow your man.
   Lil.   Pray, take him:

He is within. To do her good, take any thing.
Take us and all.
   Lug.   No doubt, ye may find takers; 95
And so, we 'll leave ye to your own disposes.
           Exeunt [LUGIER *and* ORIANA].
   Lil. Now, which way, wench?
   Ros.   We 'll go a brave way, fear not;
A safe and sure way too; and yet a by-way.
I must confess I have a great mind to be mar-
          ried.
   Lil. So have I too a grudging [1] of good-will
          that way,   100
And would as fain be despatch'd. But this
          Monsieur Quicksilver ——
   Ros. No, no; we 'll bar him, bye and main.[2]
          Let him trample;
There is no safety in his surquedry.[3]
An army-royal of women are too few for him;
He keeps a journal of his gentleness,   105
And will go near to print his fair despatches,
And call it his "Triumph over time and
          women."
Let him pass out of memory! What think you
Of his two companions?
   Lil.   Pinac, methinks, is reasonable;
A little modesty he has brought home with
          him,   110
And might be taught, in time, some handsome
          duty.
   Ros. They say, he is a wencher too.
   Lil.   I like him better;
A free light touch or two becomes a gentleman,
And sets him seemly off: so he exceed not,
But keep his compass [4] clear, he may be lookt
          at.   115
I would not marry a man that must be taught,
And conjur'd up with kisses; the best game
Is play'd still by the best gamesters.
   Ros.   Fie upon thee!
What talk hast thou!
   Lil.   Are not we alone, and merry?
Why should we be ashamed to speak what we
          think? Thy gentleman,   120
The tall fat fellow, he that came to see thee ——
   Ros. Is 't not a goodly man?
   Lil.   A wondrous goodly!
H'as weight enough, I warrant thee. Mercy
          upon me,
What a serpent wilt thou seem under such a
          St. George!
   Ros. Thou art a fool! Give me a man brings
          mettle,   125
Brings substance with him, needs no broths to
          lare [5] him.
These little fellows shew like fleas in boxes,
Hop up and down, and keep a stir to vex us.
Give me the puissant pike; take you the small
          shot.   130
   Lil. Of a great thing, I have not seen a duller;
Therefore, methinks, sweet sister ——
   Ros.   Peace, he 's modest;
A bashfulness; which is a point of grace,
          wench:

---

[1] Secret inclination.
[2] Entirely: a phrase from the game of hazard.
[3] Arrogance.   [4] Limits.   [5] Perhaps lard, fatten.

But, when these fellows come to moulding,
 sister,
To heat, and handling — As I live, I like him ;

    Enter MIRABEL.

And, methinks, I could form him.
 Lil.   Peace ; the fire-drake. 135
 Mir. Bless ye, sweet beauties, sweet incom-
  parable ladies,
Sweet wits, sweet humours ! Bless you, learned
 lady !
And you, most holy nun, bless your devotions !
 Lil. And bless your brains, sir, your most
  pregnant brains, sir !
They are in travail ; may they be delivered 140
Of a most hopeful wild-goose !
 Ros.   Bless your manhood !
They say ye are a gentleman of action,
A fair accomplish'd man, and a rare engineer.
You have a trick to blow up maidenheads,
A subtle trick, they say abroad.
 Mir.   I have, lady. 145
 Ros. And often glory in their ruins.
 Mir.   Yes, forsooth ;
I have a speedy trick, please you to try it ;
My engine will despatch you instantly.
 Ros. I would I were a woman, sir, fit for
  you !
As there be such, no doubt, may engine you
 too ; 150
May, with a counter-mine, blow up your valour :
But, in good faith, sir, we are both too honest ;
And, the plague is, we cannot be persuaded ;
For, look you, if we thought it were a glory
To be the last of all your lovely ladies —— 155
 Mir. Come, come, leave prating : this has
  spoil'd your market !
This pride and puft-up heart will make ye fast,
 ladies,
Fast when ye are hungry too.
 Ros.   The more our pain, sir.
 Lil. The more our health, I hope too.
 Mir.   Your behaviours
Have made men stand amaz'd ; those men that
 lov'd ye, 160
Men of fair states[1] and parts. Your strange
 conversions [2]
Into I know not what, nor how, nor wherefore ;
Your scorns of those that came to visit ye ;
Your studied whim-whams and your fine set
 faces —
What have these got ye ? Proud and harsh
 opinions. 165
A travell'd monsieur was the strangest creature,
The wildest monster to be wond'red at ;
His person made a public scoff, his knowledge
(As if he had been bred 'mongst bears or ban-
 dogs) [3]
Shunn'd and avoided ; his conversation snuff'd
 at ; [4] — 170
What harvest brings all this ?
 Ros.   I pray you, proceed, sir.
 Mir. Now ye shall see in what esteem a trav-
 eller,

[1] Estates.   [2] Ff. *conventions.*
[3] Dogs kept chained on account of their fierceness.
[4] Treated contemptuously.

An understanding gentleman, and a monsieur,
Is to be held ; and, to your griefs, confess it,
Both to your griefs and galls.
 Lil.   In what, I pray ye, sir ? 175
We would be glad to understand your excel-
 lence.
 Mir. Go on, sweet ladies ; it becomes ye
 rarely !
For me, I have blest me from ye ; scoff on seri-
 ously,
And note the man ye mock'd. You, Lady
 Learning, 179
Note the poor traveller that came to visit you,
That flat unfurnish'd fellow ; note him
 throughly ;
You may chance to see him anon.
 Lil.   'T is very likely.
 Mir. And see him courted by a travell'd lady,
Held dear and honour'd by a virtuous virgin ;
May be, a beauty not far short of yours neither ;
It may be, clearer.
 Lil.   Not unlikely.
 Mir.   Younger : 185
As killing eyes as yours, a wit as poignant ;
May be, a state, too, that may top [5] your fortune.
Inquire how she thinks of him, how she holds
 him ; 189
His good parts, in what precious price already ;
Being a stranger to him, how she courts him ;
A stranger to his nation too, how she dotes on
 him.
Inquire of this ; be sick to know : curse, lady,
And keep your chamber ; cry, and curse : a
 sweet one,
A thousand in yearly land, well bred, well
 friended, 195
Travell'd, and highly followed for her fashions.
 Lil. Bless his good fortune, sir !
 Mir.   This scurvy fellow,
I think they call his name Pinac, this serving-
 man
That brought ye venison, as I take it, madam,
Note but this scab : 't is strange that this coarse
 creature, 200
That has no more set-off but his jugglings,
His travell'd tricks ——
 Lil.   Good sir, I grieve not at him,
Nor envy not his fortune : yet I wonder.
He 's handsome ; yet I see no such perfection.
 Mir. Would I had his fortune ! For 't is a
 woman 205
Of that sweet-temper'd nature, and that judg-
 ment,
Besides her state, that care, clear understand-
 ing,
And such a wife to bless him ——
 Ros.   Pray you, whence is she ?
 Mir. Of England, and a most accomplish'd
 lady ; 208
So modest that men's eyes are frighted at her,
And such a noble carriage —

    Enter a Boy.

       How now, sirrah ?
 Boy. Sir, the great English lady ——
 Mir.   What of her, sir ?

[5] Surpass.

Boy. Has newly left her coach, and coming
this way,
Where you may see her plain : Monsieur Pinac
The only man that leads her.

Enter PINAC, MARIANA, *and* Attendants.

Mir.   He is much honoured ; 215
Would I had such a favour !   [*Exit* Boy.]
                       Now vex, ladies,
Envy, and vex, and rail !
Ros.   You are short of us, sir.
Mir. Bless your fair fortune, sir !
Pin.   I nobly thank ye.
Mir. Is she married, friend ?
Pin.   No, no.
Mir.   A goodly lady ;
A sweet and delicate aspect ! — Mark, mark,
and wonder ! —   220
Hast thou any hope of her ?
Pin.   A little.
Mir.   Follow close, then ;
Lose not that hope.
Pin.   To you, sir.
         [MARIANA *courtesies to* MIRABEL.]
Mir.   Gentle lady !
Ros. She is fair, indeed.
Lil.   I have seen a fairer ; yet
She is well.
Ros.   Her clothes sit handsome too.
Lil.   She dresses prettily.
Ros. And, by my faith, she is rich ; she looks
still sweeter.   225
A well-bred woman, I warrant her.
Lil.   Do you hear, sir ?
May I crave this gentlewoman's name ?
Pin.   Mariana, lady.
Lil. I will not say I owe ye a quarrel, mon-
sieur,
For making me your stale : [1] a noble gentleman
Would have had more courtesy, at least more
faith,   230
Than to turn off his mistress at first trial.
You know not what respect I might have
show'd ye ;
I find ye have worth.
Pin.   I cannot stay to answer ye ;
Ye see my charge. I am beholding to ye
For all your merry tricks ye put upon me, 235
Your bobs,[2] and base accounts. I came to love
ye,
To woo ye, and to serve ye ; I am much in-
debted to ye
For dancing me off my legs, and then for walk-
ing me ;
For telling me strange tales I never heard of,
More to abuse me ; for mistaking me,   240
When you both knew I was a gentleman,
And one deserv'd as rich a match as you are.
Lil. Be not so bitter, sir.
Pin.   You see this lady :
She is young enough and fair enough to please
me ;
A woman of a loving mind, a quiet,   245
And one that weighs the worth of him that
loves her :

I am content with this, and bless my fortune.
Your curious wits, and beauties ——
Lil.   Faith, see me once more
Pin. I dare not trouble ye.
Lil.   May I speak to your lady ?
Pin. I pray ye, content yourself. I know ye
are bitter,   250
And, in your bitterness, ye may abuse her ;
Which if she comes to know (for she under-
stands ye not),
It may breed such a quarrel to your kindred,
And such an indiscretion fling on you too
(For she is nobly friended) ——
Lil. [*Aside.*]   I could eat her. 255
Pin. Rest as ye are, a modest noble gentle-
woman,
And afford your honest neighbours some of
your prayers.
         Exeunt [PINAC, MARIANA, *and*
                       Attendants].
Mir. What think you now ?
Lil.   Faith, she 's a pretty whiting ; [3]
She has got a pretty catch too.
Mir.   You are angry,
Monstrous angry now, grievously angry ;   260
And the pretty heart does swell now.
Lil.   No, in troth, sir.
Mir. And it will cry anon, " A pox upon it ! "
And it will curse itself, and eat no meat, lady ;
And it will sigh.[4]
Lil.   Indeed, you are mistaken ;
It will be very merry.
Ros.   Why, sir, do you think 265
There are no more men living, nor no hand-
somer,
Than he or you ? By this light, there be ten
thousand,
Ten thousand thousand ! Comfort yourself,
dear monsieur ;
Faces, and bodies, wits, and all abiliments [5] —
There are so many we regard 'em not.   270

Enter BELLEUR *and two* Gentlemen.

Mir. That such a noble lady — I could burst
now ! —
So far above such trifles ——
Bel.   You did laugh at me ;
And I know why ye laughed.
1 Gent.   I pray ye, be satisfied
If we did laugh, we had some private reason,
And not at you.
2 Gent.   Alas, we know you not, sir ! 275
Bel. I 'll make you know me. Set your faces
soberly ;
Stand this way, and look sad ; I 'll be no May-
game ;
Sadder, demurer yet.
Ros.   What is the matter ?
What ails this gentleman ?
Bel. Go off now backward, that I may be-
hold ye ;   280
And not a simper, on your lives !
         [*Exeunt* Gentlemen, *walking back-
                       wards.*]
Lil. He 's mad, sure.

---

[1] Stalking-horse.   [2] Bitter jests.

[3] Fair one.   [4] Old edd. *fight.*   [5] Accomplishments.

Bel.   Do you observe me too?
Mir.   I may look on ye.
Bel. Why do you grin? I know your mind.
Mir.   You do not.
You are strangely humorous. Is there no mirth
    nor pleasure
But you must be the object?   285
Bel. Mark, and observe me. Wherever I am
    nam'd,
The very word shall raise a general sadness,
For the disgrace this scurvy woman did me,
This proud pert thing. Take heed ye laugh
    not at me,
Provoke me not; take heed.
Ros.   I would fain please ye; 290
Do any thing to keep ye quiet.
Bel.   Hear me.
Till I receive a satisfaction
Equal to the disgrace and scorn ye gave me,
Ye are a wretched woman; till thou woo'st me,
And I scorn thee as much, as seriously   295
Jeer and abuse thee; ask what gill [1] thou art,
Or any baser name; I will proclaim thee,
I will so sing thy virtue, so be-paint thee ——
Ros. Nay, good sir, be more modest.
Bel.   Do you laugh again? —
Because ye are a woman, ye are lawless,   300
And out of compass of an honest anger.
Ros. Good sir, have a better belief of me.
Lil.   Away, dear sister!
                    Exit [*with* ROSALURA].
Mir. Is not this better now, this seeming
    madness,
Than falling out with your friends?
Bel.   Have I not frighted her?
Mir. Into her right wits, I warrant thee.
    Follow this humour,   305
And thou shalt see how prosperously 't will
    guide thee.
Bel. I am glad I have found a way to woo
    yet; I was afraid once
I never should have made a civil suitor.
Well, I 'll about it still.   *Exit.*
Mir.   Do, do, and prosper.
What sport do I make with these fools! What
    pleasure   310
Feeds me, and fats my sides at their poor inno-
    cence!

        Enter LUGIER, [*disguised.*]

Wooing and wiving — hang it! Give me mirth,
Witty and dainty mirth! I shall grow in love,
    sure,
With mine own happy head.
                    Who 's this? — To me, sir? —
[*Aside.*] What youth is this?
Lug.   Yes, sir, I would speak with you, 315
If your name be Monsieur Mirabel.
Mir.   You have hit it:
Your business, I beseech you?
Lug.   This it is, sir;
There is a gentlewoman hath long time affected
    you,
And lov'd you dearly.
Mir.   Turn over, and end that story;

'T is long enough: I have no faith in women,
    sir.   320
Lug. It seems so, sir. I do not come to woo
    for her,
Or sing her praises, though she well deserve
    'em;
I come to tell ye, ye have been cruel to her,
Unkind and cruel, falser of faith, and careless,
Taking more pleasure in abusing her,   325
Wresting her honour to your wild disposes,
Than noble in requiting her affection:
Which, as you are a man, I must desire ye
(A gentleman of rank) not to persist in,
No more to load her fair name with your in-
    juries.   330
Mir. Why, I beseech you, sir?
Lug.   Good sir, I 'll tell ye.
And I 'll be short; I 'll tell ye because I love
    ye,
Because I would have you shun the shame may
    follow.
There is a nobleman, new come to town, sir,
A noble and a great man, that affects her, 335
(A countryman of mine, a brave Savoyan,
Nephew to th' duke) and so much honours her,
That 't will be dangerous to pursue your old
    way,
To touch at any thing concerns her honour,
Believe, most dangerous. Her name is Oriana,
And this great man will marry her. Take heed,
    sir;   341
For howsoe'er her brother, a staid gentleman,
Lets things pass upon better hopes, this lord, sir,
Is of that fiery and that poignant metal,
(Especially provok'd on by affection)   345
That 't will be hard — but you are wise.
Mir. A lord, sir?
Lug.   Yes, and a noble lord.
Mir.   Send her good fortune!
This will not stir her lord. A baroness!
Say ye so? Say ye so? By 'r lady, a brave title!
Top and top-gallant now! Save her great lady-
    ship!   350
I was a poor servant of hers, I must confess, sir,
And in those days I thought I might be jovy,[2]
And make a little bold to call in to her;
But, *basta*;[2] now I know my rules and dis-
    tance;
Yet, if she want an usher, such an implement,
One that is throughly pac'd, a clean-made
    gentleman,   355
Can hold a hanging up with approbation,
Plant his hat formally, and wait with patience,
I do beseech you, sir ——
Lug.   Sir, leave your scoffing,
And, as ye are a gentleman, deal fairly.   360
I have given ye a friend's counsel; so, I 'll leave
    ye.
Mir. But, hark ye, hark ye, sir; is 't possible
I may believe what you say?
Lug.   You may choose, sir.
Mir. No baits, no fish-hooks, sir? No gins?
    no nooses?
No pitfals to catch puppies?
Lug.   I tell ye certain: 365

---

[1] Wanton wench   [2] Jovial.   [3] Ital. "enough."

You may believe; if not, stand to the danger!
                                                    Exit.
Mir. A lord of Savoy, says he? The duke's
nephew?
A man so mighty? By lady, a fair marriage!
By my faith, a handsome fortune! I must leave
prating:
For, to confess the truth, I have abus'd her,   370
For which I should be sorry, but that will
seem scurvy.
I must confess she was, ever since I knew her,
As modest as she was fair; I am sure she lov'd
me;
Her means good, and her breeding excellent;
And for my sake she has refus'd fair matches.
I may play the fool finely. — Stay: who are
these?   376

Re-enter DE GARD *with* ORIANA, [*both of them
disguised, and in rich dresses;*] *and* Attendants.

[*Aside.*] 'T is she, I am sure; and that the lord,
it should seem.
He carries a fair port, is a handsome man too.
I do begin to feel I am a coxcomb.[1]
    Ori. Good my lord, choose a nobler; for I
know   380
I am so far below your rank and honour,
That what ye can say this way I must credit
But spoken to beget yourself sport. Alas, sir,
I am so far off from deserving you,
My beauty so unfit for your affection,   385
That I am grown the scorn of common railers,
Of such injurious things that, when they cannot
Reach at my person, lie with my reputation!
I am poor, besides.
    De Gard.   Ye are all wealth and goodness;
And none but such as are the scum of men,   390
The ulcers of an honest state, spite-weavers,
That live on poison only, like swoln spiders,
Dare once profane such excellence, such sweet-
ness.
    Mir. This man speaks loud indeed.
    De Gard.   Name but the men, lady;
Let me but know these poor and base depravers,
Lay but to my revenge their persons open,   396
And you shall see how suddenly, how fully,
For your most beauteous sake, how direfully,
I 'll handle their despites. Is this thing one?
Be what he will—
    Mir.   Sir?   400
    De Gard. Dare your malicious tongue, sir—
    Mir. I know you not, nor what ye mean.
    Ori.   Good my lord—
    De Gard. If he, or any he—
    Ori.   I beseech your honour—
This gentleman 's a stranger to my knowledge;
And, no doubt, sir, a worthy man.
    De Gard.   Your mercy! —   405
But, had he been a tainter of your honour,
A blaster of those beauties reign within ye—
But we shall find a fitter time. Dear lady,
As soon as I have freed ye from your guardian,
And done some honour'd offices unto ye,   410
I 'll take ye with those faults the world flings
    on ye,

    [1] Fool.

And dearer than the whole world I 'll esteem
ye! *Exit* [*with* ORIANA *and* Attendants].
    Mir. This is a thund'ring lord: I am glad I
scap'd him.
How lovingly the wench disclaim'd my villany!
I am vex'd now heartily that he shall have
her;   415
Not that I care to marry, or to lose her,
But that this bilbo-lord[2] shall reap that maidenhead
That was my due; that he shall rig and top
her:
I 'd give a thousand crowns now, he might miss
her.

Enter a Servant.

    Serv. Nay, if I bear your blows, and keep
your counsel,   420
You have good luck, sir: I teach ye to strike
lighter.
    Mir. Come hither, honest fellow: canst thou
tell me
Where this great lord lies, this Savoy lord?
Thou mett'st him;
He now went by thee, certain.
    Serv.   Yes, he did, sir;
I know him, and I know you are fool'd.
    Mir.   Come hither: 425
Here 's all this, give me truth.   [*Gives money.*]
    Serv.   Not for your money,
(And yet that may do much) but I have been
beaten,
And by the worshipful contrivers beaten, and
I 'll tell ye:
This is no lord, no Savoy lord.
    Mir.   Go forward.
    Serv. This is a trick, and put upon you
grossly   430
By one Lugier. The lord is Monsieur De Gard,
sir,
An honest gentleman, and a neighbour here;
Their ends you understand better than I, sure.
    Mir. Now I know him; know him now plain.
    Serv. I have discharg'd my colours,[3] so God
b'y ye, sir!   *Exit.*
    Mir. What a purblind puppy was I. Now I
remember him;   435
All the whole cast on 's face, though it were
umber'd,[4]
And mask'd with patches. What a dunder-
whelp,[5]
To let him domineer thus! How he strutted,
And what a load of lord he clapt upon him! 440
Would I had him here again! I would so
bounce him,
I would so thank his lordship for his lewd[6]
plot!
Do they think to carry it away, with a great
band made of bird-pots,[7]
And a pair of pin-buttock'd breeches? — Ha!
't is he again;
He comes, he comes, he comes! have at him! 447

    [2] Swaggering lord.
    [3] Several editors read *choler.*
    [4] Browned.
    [5] Stupid dog.
    [6] Vile.
    [7] Apparently some extravagance of dress.

Re-enter DE GARD, ORIANA, [*both disguised as before and* Attendants.]

[MIRABEL *sings.*]

My Savoy lord, why dost thou frown on me?
And will that favour never sweeter be?
Wilt thou, I say, for ever play the fool?
De Gard, be wise, and, Savoy, go to school!
My lord De Gard, I thank you for your antic; 450
My lady bright, that will be sometimes frantic;
You worthy train, that wait upon this pair,
Send you more wit, and them[1] a bouncing hair?[2]

And so I take my humble leave of your honours!
                                    Exit.
De Gard. We are discover'd; there's no
    remedy.   455
Lillia Bianca's man, upon my life,
In stubbornness, because Lugier corrected
    him —
A shameless slave! Plague on him for a rascal!
    Ori. I was in a perfect hope. The bane on't
        is now,
He will make mirth on mirth, to persecute us.
    De Gard. We must be patient; I am vex'd
        to the proof too.   461
I'll try once more; then, if I fail, here's one
    speaks.   [*Puts his hand on his sword.*]
    Ori. Let me be lost and scorn'd first!
De Gard.   Well, we'll consider.
Away, and let me shift; I shall be hooted else.
                                    Exeunt.

ACT IV

SCENE I.[3]

Enter LUGIER, LILLIA BIANCA, *and* Servant
    [*carrying a willow garland*].

Lug. Faint not, but do as I direct ye: trust
    me;
Believe me too; for what I have told ye, lady,
As true as you are Lillia, is authentic;
I know it, I have found it: 'tis a poor courage
Flies off for one repulse. These travellers   5
Shall find, before we have done, a home-spun
    wit,
A plain French understanding, may cope with
    'em.
They have had the better yet, thank your sweet
    squire here!
And let 'em brag. You would be reveng'd?
    Lil.   Yes, surely.
Lug. And married too?
Lil.   I think so.
Lug.   Then be counsell'd; 10
You know how to proceed. I have other irons
Heating as well as yours, and I will strike
Three blows with one stone home. Be rul'd, and
    happy;
And so, I leave ye. Now is the time.
Lil.   I am ready.
If he do come to dor[4] me.   [*Exit* LUGIER.]
Serv.   Will ye stand here,   15

[1] Ff. *they.*   [2] Bairn.
[3] A street before the lodging of Pinac.
[4] Mock. So Sympson. Ff. *d—*

And let the people think ye are God knows
    what, mistress?
Let boys and prentices presume upon ye?
    Lil.   Prithee, hold thy peace.
Serv. Stand at his door that hates ye?
Lil.   Prithee, leave prating.
Serv. Pray ye, go to the tavern: I'll give ye
    a pint of wine there.
If any of the mad-cap gentlemen should come
    by,   20
That take up women upon special warrant,
You were in a wise case now.

Enter MIRABEL, PINAC, MARIANA, Priest,
    and Attendants.

Lil.   Give me the garland;
And wait you here.
          [*Takes the garland from* Servant,
                    who retires.]
Mir.   She is here to seek thee, sirrah.
I told thee what would follow; she is mad for
    thee.
Show, and advance. — So early stirring,
    lady?   25
It shows a busy mind, a fancy troubled.
A willow garland too? Is't possible?
'Tis pity so much beauty should lie musty;
But 'tis not to be help'd now.
    Lil.   The more's my misery. —
Good fortune to ye, lady! you deserve it;   30
To me, too-late repentance! I have sought it.
I do not envy, though I grieve a little,
You are mistress of that happiness, those joys,
That might have been, had I been wise — but
    fortune —
    Pin. She understands ye not; pray ye, do
        not trouble her: 35
And do not cross me like a hare thus; 'tis as
    ominous.
Lil. I come not to upbraid your levity
(Though ye made show of love, and though I
    lik'd ye),
To claim an interest (we are yet both strangers;
But what we might have been, had you per-
    sever'd, sir!)   40
To be an eye-sore to your loving lady:
This garland shows I give myself forsaken
(Yet, she must pardon me, 'tis most unwill-
    ingly);
And all the power and interest I had in ye
(As, I persuade myself, somewhat ye lov'd
    me)   45
Thus patiently I render up, I offer
To her that must enjoy ye, and so bless ye;
Only, I heartily desire this courtesy,
And would not be deni'd, to wait upon ye
This day, to see ye tied, then no more trouble
    ye.   50
Pin. It needs not, lady.
Lil.   Good sir, grant me so much.
Pin. 'Tis private, and we make no invita-
    tion.
Lil. My presence, sir, shall not proclaim it
    public.
Pin. May be, 'tis not in town.
Lil.   I have a coach, sir,
And a most ready will to do you service.   55

Mir. [*Aside to* PINAC.] Strike now or never ;
make it sure : I tell thee,
She will hang herself, if she have thee not.
　Pin. Pray ye, sir,
Entertain my noble mistress : only a word or
two
With this importunate woman, and I 'll relieve
ye. — 　　　　　　　　　　　　　　　60
Now ye see what your flings are, and your fan-
cies,
Your states, and your wild stubbornness ; now
ye find
What 't is to gird [1] and kick at men's fair ser-
vices,
To raise your pride to such a pitch and glory
That goodness shows like gnats, scorn'd under
ye. 　　　　　　　　　　　　　　　65
'T is ugly, naught ; a self-will in a woman,
Chain'd to an overweening thought, is pestilent,
Murders fair fortune first, then fair opinion.[2]
There stands a pattern, a true patient pattern,
Humble and sweet.
　Lil. 　　　I can but grieve my ignorance. 70
Repentance, some say too, is the best sacrifice ;
For, sure, sir, if my chance had been so happy
(As I confess I was mine own destroyer)
As to have arriv'd at you, I will not prophesy,
But certain, as I think, I should have pleas'd
ye ; 　　　　　　　　　　　　　　　75
Have made ye as much wonder at my courtesy,
My love, and duty, as I have dishearten'd ye.
Some hours we have of youth, and some of
folly ;
And being free-born maids, we take a liberty,
And, to maintain that, sometimes we strain
highly. 　　　　　　　　　　　　　　80
　Pin. Now you talk reason.
　Lil. 　　　　But, being yok'd and govern'd,
Married, and those light vanities purg'd from
us,
How fair we grow, how gentle, and how tender!
We twine about those loves that shoot up with
us !
A sullen woman fear, that talks not to ye ; 　85
She has a sad and darken'd soul, loves dully.
A merry and a free wench, give her liberty,
Believe her, in the lightest form she appears to
ye,
Believe her excellent, though she despise ye ;
Let but these fits and flashes pass, she will
show to ye 　　　　　　　　　　　　　90
As jewels rubb'd from dust, or gold new burn-
ish'd :
Such had I been, had you believ'd.
　Pin. 　　　　　　　Is 't possible ?
　Lil. And to your happiness, I dare assure ye,
If true love be accounted so : your pleasure,
Your will, and your command, had tied my
motions : 　　　　　　　　　　　　95
But that hope 's gone. I know you are young
and giddy,
And, till you have a wife can govern with ye,
You sail upon this world's sea light and empty,
Your bark in danger daily. 'T is not the name
neither

　　　[1] Scoff.　　　　　　[2] Reputation.

Of wife can steer you, but the noble nature, 100
The diligence, the care, the love, the patience :
She makes the pilot, and preserves the hus-
band,
That knows and reckons every rib he is built
on.
But this I tell ye, to my shame.
　Pin. 　　　　　　　　I admire ye ;
And now am sorry that I aim beyond ye. 　105
　Mir. [*Aside.*] So, so, so : fair and softly ! She
is thine own, boy ;
She comes now without lure.
　Pin. 　　　　　　But that it must needs
Be reckon'd to me as a wantonness,
Or worse, a madness, to forsake a blessing,
A blessing of that hope ——
　Lil. 　　　　　　I dare not urge ye ; 110
And yet, dear sir ——
　Pin. 　　　　'T is most certain, I had rather,
If 't were in mine own choice — for you are my
country-woman,
A neighbour here, born by me ; she a stranger,
And who knows how her friends ——
　Lil. 　　　　　　　Do as you please, sir ;
If ye be fast, not all the world — I love ye. 115
It is most true, and clear I would persuade ye ;
And I shall love ye still.
　Pin. 　　　　　　Go, get before me —
So much ye have won upon me — do it pre-
sently.
Here 's a priest ready — I 'll have you.
　Lil. 　　　　　　　Not now, sir ; 119
No, you shall pardon me. Advance your lady ;
I dare not hinder your most high preferment :
'T is honour enough for me I have unmask'd
you.
　Pin. How 's that ?
　Lil. I have caught ye, sir. Alas, I am no
stateswoman,
Nor no great traveller, yet I have found ye ; 125
I have found your lady too, your beauteous
lady ;
I have found her birth and breeding too, her
discipline,
Who brought her over, and who kept your
lady,
And, when he laid her by, what virtuous nun-
nery
Receiv'd her in : I have found all these. Are ye
blank now ? 　　　　　　　　　　　　130
Methinks, such travell'd wisdoms should not
fool thus, —
Such excellent indiscretions !
　Mir. 　　　　　How could she know this ?
　Lil. 'T is true she 's English-born ; but most
part French now,
And so I hope you 'll find her to your comfort.
Alas, I am ignorant of what she cost ye ! 　135
The price of these hired clothes I do not know,
gentlemen !
Those jewels are the broker's, how ye stand
bound for 'em !
　Pin. Will you make this good ?
　Lil. 　　　　　Yes, yes ; and to her face, sir,
That she is an English whore, a kind of fling-
dust, 　　　　　　　　　　　　　　139
One of your London light-o'-loves, a right one ;

Came over in thin pumps and half a petticoat,
One faith, and one smock, with a broken hab-
　erdasher –
I know all this without a conjurer.
Her name is Jumping Joan, an ancient sin-
　weaver;
She was first a lady's chambermaid, there
　slipp'd, 145
And broke her leg above the knee; departed,
And set up shop herself; stood the fierce con-
　flicts
Of many a furious term;[1] there lost her col-
　ours,
And last shipp'd over hither.

Mir.　　　　　　　　We are betray'd!
Lil. Do you come to fright me with this mys-
　tery? 150
To stir me with a stink none can endure, sir?
I pray ye, proceed; the wedding will become ye:
Who gives the lady? You? An excellent
　father!
A careful man, and one that knows a beauty!
Send ye fair shipping, sir! and so, I'll leave
　ye. 155
Be wise and manly; then I may chance to love
　ye!
　　　　　　　　　　　Exit [with Servant].
Mir. As I live, I am asham'd this wench has
　reach'd me,
Monstrous asham'd; but there's no remedy.
This skew'd-ey'd carrion——
Pin.　　　　　This I suspected ever.—
Come, come, uncase; we have no more use of
　ye; 160
Your clothes must back again.
Mari.　　　　　Sir, you shall pardon me;
'T is not our English use to be degraded.
If you will visit me, and take your venture,
You shall have pleasure for your properties.
And so, sweetheart——　　　　　[*Exit.*] 165
Mir. Let her go, and the devil go with her!
We have never better luck with these prelu-
　diums.
Come, be not daunted; think she is but a
　woman,
And, let her have the devil's wit, we'll reach
　her!　　　　　　　　　　　*Exeunt.*

Scene II.[2]

Enter Rosalura *and* Lugier.

Ros. You have now redeem'd my good opin-
　ion, tutor,
And ye stand fair again.
Lug.　　　　　I can but labour,
And sweat in your affairs. I am sure Belleur
Will be here instantly, and use his anger,
His wonted harshness.
Ros.　　　　　I hope he will not beat me. 5
Lug. No, sure, he has more manners. Be you
　ready.
Ros. Yes, yes, I am; and am resolv'd to fit
　him,
With patience to outdo all he can offer.
But how does Oriana?

1 In term-time London was full of strangers from the
country. (Dyce.)
2 A public walk.

Lug.　　　　　　Worse and worse still;
There is a sad house for her; she is now, 10
Poor lady, utterly distracted.
Ros.　　　　　　Pity,
Infinite pity! 't is a handsome lady:
That Mirabel's a beast, worse than a monster,
If this affliction work not.

Enter Lillia Bianca.

Lil.　　　　　　Are you ready?
Belleur is coming on here, hard behind me: 15
I have no leisure to relate my fortune;
Only I wish you may come off as handsomely.
Upon the sign, you know what.
Ros.　　　　　Well, well; leave me.
　　　Exeunt [Lillia Bianca *and* Lugier].

Enter Belleur.

Bel. How now?
Ros.　　　　　Ye are welcome, sir.
Bel.　　　　　'T is well ye have manners.
That court'sy again, and hold your countenance
　staidly. 20
That look's too light; take heed: so; sit ye
　down now;
And, to confirm me that your gall is gone,
Your bitterness dispers'd (for so I'll have it),
Look on me stedfastly, and, whatsoe'er I say
　to ye,
Move not, nor alter in your face; ye are gone,
　then; 25
For, if you do express the least distaste,
Or show an angry wrinkle, (mark me, woman!
We are now alone,) I will so conjure thee,
The third part of my execution
Cannot be spoke.
Ros.　　　　　I am at your dispose, sir. 30
Bel. Now rise, and woo me a little; let me
　hear that faculty:
But touch me not; nor do not lie, I charge
　ye.
Begin now.
Ros.　　　　If so mean and poor a beauty
May ever hope the grace——
Bel.　　　　Ye cog,[3] ye flatter;
Like a lewd[4] thing, ye lie: "May hope that
　grace!" 35
Why, what grace canst thou hope for? Answer
　not;
For, if thou dost, and liest again, I'll swinge
　thee.
Do not I know thee for a pestilent woman?
A proud at both ends? Be not angry,
Nor stir not, o' your life.
Ros.　　　　I am counsell'd, sir. 40
Bel. Art thou not now (confess, for I'll have
　the truth out)
As much unworthy of a man of merit,
Or any of ye all, nay, of mere man,
Though he were crooked, cold, all wants upon
　him,
Nay, of any dishonest thing that bears that
　figure, 45
As devils are of mercy?
Ros.　　　　　We are unworthy.

3 Cajole.　　　　　　　4 Vile.

Bel. Stick to that truth, and it may chance
to save thee.
And is it not our bounty that we take ye?
That we are troubled, vex'd, or tortur'd with ye,
Our mere and special bounty?
Ros.　　　　　　　　　　Yes.
Bel.　　　　　　　　　　　　Our pity, 50
That for your wickedness we swinge ye soundly;
Your stubbornness and stout hearts, we bela-
　　bour ye?
Answer to that!
Ros.　　　　　I do confess your pity.
Bel. And dost not thou deserve in thine own
　　person,
Thou impudent, thou pert — Do not change
　　countenance.　　　　　　　　　　55
Ros. I dare not, sir.
Bel.　　　　　For, if you do ——
Ros.　　　　　　　　　I am settled.
Bel. Thou wagtail, peacock, puppy, look on
　　me:
I am a gentleman.
Ros.　　　　　It seems no less, sir,
Bel. And dar'st thou in thy surquedry [1] ——
Ros.　　　　　　　　I beseech you! —
It was my weakness, sir, I did not view ye, 60
I took not notice of your noble parts,
Nor call'd your person nor your fashion proper.[2]
Bel. This is some amends yet.
Ros.　　　　　　I shall mend, sir, daily,
And study to deserve.
Bel.　　　　　Come a little nearer:
Canst thou repent thy villany?
Ros.　　　　　　　Most seriously. 65
Bel. And be asham'd?
Ros.　　　　　I am asham'd.
Bel.　　　　　　　　　Cry.
Ros. It will be hard to do, sir.
Bel.　　　　　　Cry now instantly;
Cry monstrously, that all the town may hear
　　thee;
Cry seriously, as if thou hadst lost thy monkey;
And, as I like thy tears ——

Enter LILLIA BIANCA, *and four* Women, *laughing.*

Ros.　　　Now!　　　　　[*To those within.*]
Bel.　　　How! how! Do ye jeer me? 70
Have ye broke your bounds again, dame?
Ros.　　　　　Yes, and laugh at ye,
And laugh most heartily.
Bel.　　　What are these? whirlwinds?
Is hell broke loose, and all the Furies flutter'd?
Am I greased [3] once again?
Ros.　　　　　Yes, indeed are ye;
And once again ye shall be, if ye quarrel:　 75
Do you come to vent your fury on a virgin?
Is this your manhood, sir?
1 *Wom.*　　　　　Let him do his best;
Let's see the utmost of his indignation;
I long to see him angry.— Come, proceed, sir.—
　　　　　　　　　[*The women display knives.*]
Hang him, he dares not stir; a man of timber!
2 *Wom.* Come hither to fright maids with
　　thy bull-faces!　　　　　　　　　81

To threaten gentlewomen! Thou a man! A
　　Maypole,
A great dry pudding.
　　[3] *Wom.*　　Come, come, do your worst, sir;
Be angry, if thou dar'st.
Bel.　　　　　The Lord deliver me!
4 *Wom.* Do but look scurvily upon this
　　lady,　　　　　　　　　　　　　　85
Or give us one foul word! — We are all mis-
　　taken;
This is some mighty dairy-maid in man's
　　clothes.
Lil. I am of that mind too.
Bel. [*Aside.*]　　What will they do to me?
Lil. And hired to come and abuse us. — A
　　man has manners;
A gentleman, civility and breeding: —　　90
Some tinker's trull, with a beard glu'd on.
1 *Wom.*　　　　　Let's search him,
And, as we find him ——
Bel.　　　　　Let me but depart from ye,
Sweet Christian women!
Lil.　　Hear the thing speak, neighbours.
Bel. 'T is but a small request: if e'er I trou-
　　ble ye,
If e'er I talk again of beating women,　　95
Or beating any thing that can but turn to me;
Of ever thinking of a handsome lady
But virtuously and well; of ever speaking
But to her honour, — this I 'll promise ye,
I will take rhubarb, and purge choler [4] mainly,[5]
Abundantly I 'll purge.
Lil.　　　　I 'll send ye broths, sir. 101
Bel. I will be laugh'd at, and endure it pa-
　　tiently;
I will do any thing.
Ros.　　　　I 'll be your bail, then.
When ye come next to woo, pray ye come not
　　boisterously,
And furnish'd like a bear-ward.[6]
Bel.　　　　No, in truth, forsooth. 105
Ros. I scented ye long since.
Bel.　　　　I was to blame, sure:
I will appear a gentleman.
Ros.　　　　　'T is the best for ye,
For a true noble gentleman 's a brave thing.
Upon that hope, we quit ye. You fear seri-
　　ously?
Bel. Yes, truly do I; I confess I fear ye, 110
And honour ye, and any thing.
Ros.　　　　　Farewell, then.
Wom. And, when ye come to woo next,
　　bring more mercy.
　　　　　　Exeunt [*all except* BELLEUR].

Enter two Gentlemen.

Bel. A dairy-maid! A tinker's trull! Heaven
　　bless me!
Sure, if I had provok'd 'em, they had quarter'd
　　me.
I am a most ridiculous ass, now I perceive it;
A coward, and a knave too.
1 *Gent.*　　　'T is the mad gentleman; 116
Let's set our faces right.

---

[1] Arrogance.　　[2] Handsome.　　[3] Gulled.
[4] Bile, the supposed cause of anger.
[5] Thoroughly.　　[6] Bear-keeper.

Bel.   No, no ; laugh at me,
And laugh aloud.
  2 Gent.   We are better manner'd, sir.
  Bel. I do deserve it ; call me patch[1] and
  puppy,
And beat me, if you please.
  1 Gent.   No, indeed ; we know ye. 120
  Bel. 'Death, do as I would have ye!
  2 Gent.   Ye are an ass, then,
A coxcomb, and a calf !
  Bel.   I am a great calf.
Kick me a little now. Why, when ! [*They kick
  him.*] Sufficient.
Now laugh aloud, and scorn me. So good b' ye!
And ever, when ye meet me, laugh.
  Gentlemen.   We will, sir. 125
      Exeunt [*on one side, the two* Gentle-
      men ; *on the other,* BELLEUR].

Scene III.[2]

Enter NANTOLET, LA CASTRE, DE GARD, LU-
  GIER, *and* MIRABEL.

  Mir. Your patience, gentlemen ; why do ye
  bait me ?
  Nant. Is 't not a shame you are so stubborn-
  hearted,
So stony and so dull, to such a lady,
Of her perfections and her misery ?
  Lug. Does she not love ye ? Does not her dis-
  traction   5
For your sake only, her most pitied lunacy
Of all but you, show ye ? Does it not compel ye ?
  Mir. Soft and fair, gentlemen ; pray ye, pro-
  ceed temperately.
  Lug. If ye have any feeling, any sense in ye,
The least touch of a noble heart ——   10
  La Cast. Let him alone :
It is his glory that he can kill beauty. —
Ye bear my stamp, but not my tenderness ;
Your wild unsavoury courses let[3] that in ye !
For shame, be sorry, though ye cannot cure
  her ;   15
Show something of a man, of a fair nature.
  Mir. Ye make me mad !
  De Gard. Let me pronounce this to ye :
You take a strange felicity in slighting
And wronging women, which my poor sister
  feels now ;   20
Heaven's hand be gentle on her ! Mark me, sir ;
That very hour she dies (there 's small hope
  otherwise),
That minute, you and I must grapple for it ;
Either your life or mine.
  Mir.   Be not so hot, sir ;
I am not to be wrought on by these policies, 25
In truth, I am not ; nor do I fear the tricks,
Or the high-sounding threats, of a Savoyan.
I glory not in cruelty, (ye wrong me,)
Nor grow up water'd with the tears of women.
This let me tell ye, howsoe'er I show to ye, 30
Wild, as you please to call it, or self-will'd,
When I see cause, I can both do and suffer,
Freely and feelingly, as a true gentleman.

---

[1] Fool.   [3] Hinder. Ff. *set.*
[2] A hall in the house of La Castre.

Enter ROSALURA *and* LILLIA BIANCA.

  Ros. Oh, pity, pity ! thousand, thousand
  pities !
  Lil. Alas, poor soul, she will die ! She is
  grown senseless ;   35
She will not know nor speak now.
  Ros.   Die for love !
And love of such a youth ! I would die for a dog
  first :
He that kills me, I 'll give him leave to eat me ;
I 'll know men better, ere I sigh for any of 'em.
  Lil. You have done a worthy act, sir, a most
  famous ;   40
Ye have kill'd a maid the wrong way ; ye are
  a conqueror.
  Ros. A conqueror? A cobbler ! Hang him,
  sowter ![4] —
Go hide thyself, for shame ! Go lose thy memory!
Live not 'mongst men ; thou art a beast, a mon-
  ster,
A blatant beast !
  Lil.   If ye have yet any honesty, 45
Or ever heard of any, take my counsel :
Off with your garters, and seek out a bough, —
A handsome bough, for I would have ye hang
  like a gentleman ;
And write some doleful matter to the world,
A warning to hard-hearted men.
  Mir.   Out, kitlings ! 50
What caterwauling 's here ! What gibbing ![5]
Do you think my heart is soft'ned with a black
  santis ?[6]
Show me some reason.

Enter ORIANA *on a bed.*

  Ros.   Here then, here is a reason.
  Nant. Now, if ye be a man, let this sight
  shake ye !
  La Cast. Alas, poor gentlewoman ! — Do ye
  know me, lady ?   55
  Lug. How she looks up, and stares !
  Ori.   I know ye very well ;
You are my godfather : and that 's the mon-
  sieur.
  De Gard. And who am I ?
  Ori.   You are Amadis de Gaul, sir. —
Oh, oh, my heart ! — Were you never in love,
  sweet lady ?
And do you never dream of flowers and gar-
  dens ?   60
I dream of walking fires : take heed ; it comes
  now.
Who 's that ? Pray, stand away. I have seen
  that face, sure. —
How light my head is !
  Ros.   Take some rest.
  Ori.   I cannot ;
For I must be up to-morrow to go to church,
And I must dress me, put my new gown on, 65
And be as fine to meet my love ! Heigh-ho !
Will you not tell me where my love lies buried?
  Mir. He is not dead. —[*Aside.*] Beshrew my
  heart, she stirs me !

---

[4] Cobbler.   [5] Cat-like behavior.
[6] *I. e.* black-sanctus, a burlesque hymn accompanied
by discordant noises.

Ori. He is dead to me.

Mir. [*Aside.*]   Is 't possible my nature
Should be so damnable to let her suffer ? —   70
Give me your hand.

Ori.   How soft ye feel, how gentle !
I 'll tell you your fortune, friend.

Mir.   How she stares on me !

Ori. You have a flattering face, but 't is a
    fine one ;
I warrant you may have a hundred sweethearts.
Will ye pray for me ? I shall die to-morrow ;   75
And will ye ring the bells ?

Mir.   I am most unworthy,
I do confess, unhappy. Do you know me ?

Ori. I would I did !

Mir.   Oh, fair tears, how ye take[1] me !

Ori. Do you weep too ? You have not lost
    your lover ?
You mock me : I 'll go home and pray.

Mir.   Pray ye, pardon me ;   80
Or, if it please ye to consider justly,
Scorn me, for I deserve it ; scorn and shame
    me,
Sweet Oriana !

Lil.   Let her alone ; she trembles :
Her fits will grow more strong, if ye provoke
    her.

La Cast. Certain she knows ye not, yet loves
    to see ye.   85
How she smiles now !

Enter BELLEUR.

Bel. Where are ye ? Oh, why do not ye
    laugh ? Come, laugh at me :
Why a devil art thou sad, and such a subject,
Such a ridiculous subject, as I am,
Before thy face ?

Mir.   Prithee, put off this lightness ;   90
This is no time for mirth, nor place ; I have
    us'd too much on 't.
I have undone myself and a sweet lady
By being too indulgent to my foolery,
Which truly I repent. Look here.

Bel.   What ails she ?

Mir. Alas, she 's mad !

Bel.   Mad !

Mir. Yes, too sure ; for me too.   95

Bel. Dost thou wonder at that ? By this good
    light, they are all so ;
They are coz'ning-mad, they are brawling-mad,
    they are proud-mad ;
They are all, all mad. I came from a world of
    mad women,
Mad as March hares. Get 'em in chains, then
    deal with 'em.
There 's one that 's mad ; she seems well, but
    she is dog-mad.   100
Is she dead, dost think ?

Mir.   Dead ! Heaven forbid !

Bel.   Heaven further it !
For, till they be key-cold dead, there 's no trust-
    ing of 'em :
Whate'er they seem, or howsoe'er they carry
    it,
Till they be chap-fallen, and their tongues at
    peace,

[1] Cast a spell on me.

Nail'd in their coffins sure, I 'll ne'er believe
    'em.   105
Shall I talk with her ?

Mir.   No, dear friend, be quiet,
And be at peace a while.

Bel.   I 'll walk aside,
And come again anon. But take heed to her :
You say she is a woman ?

Mir.   Yes.

Bel.   Take great heed ;
For, if she do not cozen thee, then hang me : 110
Let her be mad, or what she will, she 'll cheat
    thee !   *Exit.*

Mir. Away, wild fool ! — How vild this shows
    in him now ! —
Now take my faith, (before ye all I speak it,)
And with it my repentant love.

La Cast.   This seems well.

Mir. Were but this lady clear again, whose
    sorrows   115
My very heart melts for, were she but perfect,
(For thus to marry her would be two miseries,)
Before the richest and the noblest beauty,
France or the world could show me, I would
    take her.
As she is now, my tears and prayers shall wed
    her.   120

De Gard. This makes some small amends.

Ros.   She beckons to ye ;
To us, too, to go off.

Nant.   Let 's draw aside all.
          [*Exeunt all except* ORIANA *and* MI-
                    RABEL.]

Ori. Oh, my best friend ! I would fain ——

Mir. [*Aside.*]   What, she speaks well,
And with another voice.

Ori.   But I am fearful,
And shame a little stops my tongue ——

Mir.   Speak boldly.   125

Ori. Tell ye, I am well. I am perfect well
    (pray ye, mock not) ;
And that I did this to provoke your nature ;
Out of my infinite and restless love,
To win your pity. Pardon me !

Mir.   Go forward :
Who set ye on ?

Ori.   None, as I live, no creature ;   130
Not any knew or ever dream'd what I meant.
Will ye be mine ?

Mir.   'Tis true, I pity ye ;
But, when I marry ye, ye must be wiser.
Nothing but tricks ? devices ?

Ori.   Will ye shame me ?

Mir. Yes, marry, will I. — Come near, come
    near ! a miracle !   135
The woman 's well ; she was only mad for mar-
    riage,
Stark mad to be ston'd to death : give her good
    counsel.
Will this world never mend ? — Are ye caught,
    damsel ?

Enter BELLEUR, NANTOLET, LA CASTRE, DE
GARD, LUGIER, ROSALURA, *and* LILLIA BI-
ANCA.

Bel. How goes it now ?

Mir.   Thou art a kind of prophet;

The woman's well again, and would have gull'd
　　me ;　　　　　　　　　　　　　　　　　　140
Well, excellent well, and not a taint upon her.
　Bel. Did not I tell ye ? Let 'em be what can be,
Saints, devils, any thing, they will abuse us :
Thou wert an ass to believe her so long, a cox-
　　comb :
Give 'em a minute, they 'll abuse whole mil-
　　lions.　　　　　　　　　　　　　　　　　145
　Mir. And am not I a rare physician, gentle-
　　men,
That can cure desperate mad minds ?
　De Gard.　　　　　　　Be not insolent.
　Mir. Well, go thy ways : from this hour I
　　disclaim thee,
Unless thou hast a trick above this ; then I 'll
　　love thee.
Ye owe me for your cure. — Pray, have a care
　　of her,　　　　　　　　　　　　　　　　150
For fear she fall into relapse. — Come, Belleur ;
We 'll set up bills to cure diseased virgins.
　Bel. Shall we be merry ?
　Mir.　　　　　Yes.
　Bel.　　　　　　　But I 'll no more projects :
If we could make 'em mad, it were some mas-
　　tery.
　　　　　　Exeunt [MIRABEL *and* BELLEUR].
　Lil. I am glad she is well again.
　Ros.　　　　　　So am I, certain. —　155
Be not ashamed.
　Ori.　　　　I shall never see a man more.
　De Gard. Come, ye are a fool : had ye but
　　told me this trick,
He should not have gloried thus.
　Lug.　　　　He shall not long, neither.
　La Cast. Be rul'd, and be at peace. Ye have
　　my consent,　　　　　　　　　　　　159
And what power I can work with.
　Nant.　　　　　Come, leave blushing ;
We are your friends : an honest way compell'd
　　ye :
Heaven will not see so true a love unrecom-
　　pens'd.
Come in, and slight him too.
　Lug.　　　　The next shall hit him. *Exeunt.*

ACT V

SCENE I. [1]

Enter DE GARD *and* LUGIER.

De Gard. 'T will be discover'd.
Lug.　　　　That 's the worst can happen :
If there be any way to reach, and work upon
　　him,
Upon his nature suddenly, and catch him—That
　　he loves,
Though he dissemble it, and would show con-
　　trary,
And will at length relent, I 'll lay my fortune ;
Nay, more, my life.
De Gard.　　　Is she won ?
Lug.　　　　　Yes, and ready, 6
And my designments set.

---

[1] A street, before the house of La Castre.

De Gard.　　　　They are now for travel ;
All for that game again ; they have forgot
　　wooing.
Lug. Let 'em ; we 'll travel with 'em.
De Gard.　　　　Where 's his father ?
Lug. Within ; he knows my mind too, and
　　allows [2] it,　　　　　　　　　　　　10
Pities your sister's fortune most sincerely,
And has appointed, for our more assistance,
Some of his secret friends.
De Gard.　　　　Speed the plough !
Lug.　　　　　　　Well said !
And be you serious too.
De Gard.　　　　I shall be diligent.
Lug. Let's break the ice for one, the rest will
　　drink too　　　　　　　　　　　　　15
(Believe me, sir) of the same cup. My young
　　gentlewomen
Wait but who sets the game a-foot. Though
　　they seem stubborn,
Reserv'd, and proud now, yet I know their
　　hearts,
Their pulses how they beat, and for what cause,
　　sir,
And how they long to venture their abilities 20
In a true quarrel. Husbands they must and will
　　have,
Or nunneries and thin collations
To cool their bloods. Let 's all about our busi-
　　ness,
And, if this fail, let nature work.
De Gard.　　　Ye have arm'd me. *Exeunt.*

SCENE II. [3]

Enter MIRABEL, NANTOLET, *and* LA CASTRE.

La Cast. Will ye be wilful, then ?
Mir.　　　　　Pray, sir, your pardon ;
For I must travel. Lie lazy here,
Bound to a wife ! Chain'd to her subleties,
Her humours, and her wills, which are mere
　　fetters !
To have her to-day pleas'd, to-morrow peevish,
The third day mad, the fourth rebellious !　6
You see before they are married, what moris-
　　coes, [4]
What masques and mummeries they put upon
　　us :
To be tied here, and suffer their lavoltas ! [5]
Nant. 'T is your own seeking.
Mir.　　　　Yes, to get my freedom. 10
Were they as I could wish 'em ——
La Cast.　　　Fools and meacocks, [6]
To endure what you think fit to put upon 'em.
Come, change your mind.
Mir. Not before I have chang'd air, father.
When I know women worthy of my company,
I will return again, and wait upon 'em ; 15
Till then, dear sir, I 'll amble all the world over,
And run all hazards, misery, and poverty,

Enter PINAC *and* BELLEUR.

So I escape the dangerous bay of matrimony.
Pin. Are ye resolv'd ?

---

[2] Approves.
[3] A public walk.
[4] Morris-dances.
[5] Lively dances.
[6] Dastards.

Mir.   Yes, certain ; I will out again.
Pin. We are for ye, sir ; we are your servants
     once more ;   20
Once more we 'll seek our fortune in strange
     countries ;
Ours is too scornful for us.
Bel.   Is there ne'er a land
That you have read or heard of (for I care not
     how far it be,
Nor under what pestiferous star it lies),   24
A happy kingdom, where there are no women,
Nor have been ever, nor no mention
Of any such lewd things with lewder qualities,
(For thither would I travel) where 't is felony
To confess he had a mother ; a mistress, trea-
     son ?
La Cast. Are you for travel too ?
Bel.   For any thing,   30
For living in the moon, and stopping hedges,[1]
Ere I stay here to be abus'd and baffl'd.[2]
Nant. Why did ye not break your minds to
     me ? They are my daughters ;
And, sure, I think I should have that command
     over 'em,
To see 'em well bestow'd. I know ye are gen-
     tlemen,   35
Men of fair parts and states ; I know your
     parents :
And, had ye told me of your fair affections —
Make but one trial more, and let me second ye.
Bel. No ; I 'll make hob-nails first, and mend
     old kettles.
Can ye lend me an armour of high proof, to
     appear in,   40
And two or three field-pieces to defend me ?
The king's guard are mere pigmies.
Nant.   They will not eat ye.
Bel. Yes, and you too, and twenty fatter
     monsieurs,
If their high stomachs hold. They came with
     chopping-knives,
To cut me into rands[3] and sirloins, and so pow-
     der me. —   45
Come, shall we go ?
Nant.   You cannot be so discourteous,
If ye intend to go, as not to visit 'em,
And take your leaves.
Mir.   That we dare do, and civilly,
And thank 'em too.
Pin.   Yes, sir, we know that honesty.[4]
Bel. I 'll come i' the rear, forty foot off, I 'll
     assure ye,   50
With a good gun in my hand. I 'll no more
     Amazons,
I mean, no more of their frights. I 'll make my
     three legs,[5]
Kiss my hand twice, and, if I smell no danger,
If the interview be clear, may be I 'll speak to
     her ;
I 'll wear a privy coat[6] too, and behind me,   55
To make those parts secure, a bandog.
La Cast. You are a merry gentleman.
Bel. A wary gentleman, I do assure you.
I have been warn'd ; and must be arm'd.

---

[1] Like the man-in-the-moon with his bundle of sticks.
[2] Disgraced.   [4] Good breeding.
[3] Slices.   [5] Bows.   [6] Secret coat of mail.

La Cast.   Well, son,
These are your hasty thoughts ; when I see you
     are bent to it,   60
Then I 'll believe, and join with ye : so, we 'll
     leave ye. —
[Aside.] There 's a trick will make ye stay.
Nant. *[Aside].*   I hope so.
         Exeunt [LA CASTRE *and* NANTOLET].
Mir. We have won immortal fame now, if
     we leave 'em.
Pin. You have ; but we have lost.
Mir.   Pinac, thou art cozen'd.
I know they love ye ; and to gain ye hand-
     somely,   65
Not to be thought to yield, they would give
     millions.
Their father's willingness, that must needs
     show ye.
Pin. If I thought so ——
Mir. Ye shall be hang'd, you recreant !
Would ye turn renegado now ?
Bel.   No ; let 's away, boys,   70
Out of the air and tumult of their villanies.
Though I were married to that grasshopper,
And had her fast by the legs, I should think
     she would cozen me.

Enter a Young [Man, *disguised as a*] Factor.

Y. Man. Monsieur Mirabel, I take it ?
Mir.   Y' are i' th' right, sir.
Y. Man. I am come to seek ye, sir. I have
     been at your father's,   75
And, understanding you were here ——
Mir.   Ye are welcome.
May I crave your name ?
Y. Man.   Fosse, sir, and your servant.
That you may know me better, I am factor
To your old merchant, Leverdure.
Mir.   How does he ?
Y. Man. Well, sir, I hope ; he is now at Or-
     leans,   80
About some business.
Mir.   You are once more welcome.
Your master 's a right honest man, and one
I am much beholding to, and must very shortly
Trouble his love again.
Y. Man.   You may be bold, sir.
Mir. Your business, if you please now ?
Y. Man.   This, it is sir.   85
I know ye well remember in your travel
A Genoa merchant ——
Mir.   I remember many.
Y. Man. But this man, sir, particularly ;
     your own benefit
Must needs imprint him in ye ; one Alberto,
A gentleman you sav'd from being murther'd   90
A little from Bologna :
I was then myself in Italy, and supplied ye ;
Though haply you have forgot me now.
Mir.   No, I remember ye,
And that Alberto too ; a noble gentleman :
More to remember were to thank myself, sir.   95
What of that gentleman ?
Y. Man. He is dead.
Mir.   I am sorry.
Y. Man. But on his death-bed, leaving to his
     sister

All that he had, beside some certain jewels,
Which, with a ceremony, he bequeath'd to
   you   100
In grateful memory, he commanded strictly
His sister, as she lov'd him and his peace,
To see those jewels safe and true deliver'd,
And, with them, his last love. She, as tender
To observe his will, not trusting friend nor
   servant   105
With such a weight, is come herself to Paris
And at my master's house.
  Mir.   You tell me a wonder.
Y. Man. I tell ye a truth, sir. She is young
   and handsome,
And well attended ; of much state and riches ;
So loving and obedient to her brother,   110
That, on my conscience, if he had given her also,
She would most willingly have made her tender.
  Mir. May not I see her ?
  Y. Man.   She desires it heartily.
  Mir. And presently ?
  Y. Man.   She is now about some business,
Passing accounts of some few debts here
   owing,   115
And buying jewels of a merchant.
  Mir. Is she wealthy ?
  Y. Man. I would ye had her, sir, at all ad-
   venture !
Her brother had a main state.[1]
  Mir.   And fair too ?
  Y. Man. The prime of all those parts of
   Italy,   120
For beauty and for courtesy.
  Mir.   I must needs see her.
  Y. Man. 'T is all her business, sir. Ye may
   now see her ;
But to-morrow will be fitter for your visitation,
For she is not yet prepared.
  Mir.   Only her sight, sir ;
And, when you shall think fit, for further
   visit.   125
  Y. Man. Sir, ye may see her, and I 'll wait
   your coming.
  Mir. And I 'll be with ye instantly ; I know
   the house ; —
Meantime, my love and thanks, sir.
  Y. Man.   Your poor servant. *Exit.*
  Pin. Thou hast the strangest luck ! What
   was that Alberto ?
  Mir. An honest noble merchant 't was my
   chance   130
To rescue from some rogues had almost slain
   him ;
And he in kindness to remember this !
  Bel. Now we shall have you
For all your protestations and your forwardness,
Find out strange fortunes in this lady's eyes, 135
And new enticements to put off your journey ;
And who shall have honour then ?
  Mir.   No, no, never fear it :
I must needs see her to receive my legacy.
  Bel. If it be tied up in her smock, Heaven
   help thee !
May not we see too?
  Mir.   Yes, afore we go: 140

[1] Large fortune.

I must be known myself, ere I be able
To make thee welcome. Wouldst thou see more
   women ?
I thought you had been out of love with all.
  Bel.   I may be
(I find that), with the least encouragement ;
Yet I desire to see whether all countries   145
Are naturally possess'd with the same spirits,
For, if they be, I 'll take a monastery,
And never travel : for I had rather be a friar,
And live mew'd [2] up, than be a fool, and flouted.
  Mir. Well, well, I 'll meet ye anon, then tell
   you more, boys ;   150
However, stand prepared, prest [3] for our jour-
   ney ;
For certain we shall go, I think, when I have
   seen her,
And view'd her well.
  Pin.   Go, go, and we 'll wait for ye ;
Your fortune directs ours.
  Bel.   You shall find us i' th' tavern,
Lamenting in sack and sugar for our losses. 155
If she be right Italian, and want servants,[4]
You may prefer the properest man. How I
   could
Worry a woman now !
  Pin.   Come, come, leave prating :
Ye may have enough to do, without this boast
   ing.

       Exeunt [on one side, PINAC *and*
       BELLEUR ; *on the other* MIRABEL].

SCENE III.[5]

Enter LUGIER, DE GARD, ROSALURA, *and*
      LILLIA BIANCA.

  Lug. This is the last adventure.
  De Gard.   And the happiest,
As we hope, too.
  Ros.   We should be glad to find it.
  Lil. Who shall conduct us thither ?
  Lug.   Your man is ready,
For I must not be seen ; no, nor this gentleman ;
That may beget suspicion ; all the rest   5
Are people of no doubt. I would have ye, ladies,
Keep your old liberties, and as we instruct ye.
Come, look not pale ; you shall not lose your
   wishes,
Nor beg 'em neither; but be yourselves and
   happy.
  Ros. I tell you true, I cannot hold off longer,
Nor give no more hard language.
  De Gard.   You shall not need. 1s
  Ros. I love the gentleman, and must now
   show it :
Shall I beat a proper man out of heart?
  Lug.   There 's none advises ye.
  Lil. Faith, I repent me too.
  Lug.   Repent and spoil all ;
Tell what ye know, ye had best !
  Lil.   I 'll tell what I think ; 15
For, if he ask me now if I can love him,
I 'll tell him, yes, I can. The man 's a kind man,
And out of his true honesty affects me.

[2] Shut.   [3] Ready.   [4] Lovers.
[5] A room in the house of Nantolet.

Although he play'd the fool, which I requited,
Must I still hold him at the staff's end?
  Lug.   You are two strange women. 20
  Ros. We may be, if we fool still.
  Lug.   Dare ye believe me?
Follow but this advice I have set you in now,
And if ye lose — Would ye yield now so basely?
Give up without your honours sav'd?
  De Gard.   Fie, ladies!
Preserve your freedom still.
  Lil.   Well, well, for this time. 25
  Lug. And carry that full state —
  Ros.   That's as the wind stands;
If it begin to chop about, and scant us,
Hang me, but I know what I'll do! Come,
       direct us;
I make no doubt we shall do handsomely.
  De Gard. Some part o' th' way we'll wait
     upon ye, ladies;   30
The rest your man supplies.
  Lug.   Do well, I'll honour ye. *Exeunt.*

SCENE IV.[1]

ORIANA [*disguised as an Italian lady,*] *and two*
[*persons disguised as*] Merchants, [*discovered
above.*] *Enter,* [*below, the* Young Man *disguised
as a*] Factor, *and* MIRABEL.

  Y. Man. Look ye, sir, there she is; you see
     how busy.
Methinks you are infinitely bound to her for her
     journey.
  Mir. How gloriously she shows! She is a tall
     woman.
  Y. Man. Of a fair size, sir. My master not
     being at home,
I have been so out of my wits to get her com-
     pany!   5
I mean, sir, of her own fair sex and fashion ——
  Mir. Afar off, she is most fair too.
  Y. Man.   Near, most excellent. —
At length, I have entreated two fair ladies
(And happily you know 'em), the young
     daughters
Of Monsieur Nantolet.
  Mir.   I know 'em well, sir. 10
What are those? Jewels?
  Y. Man.   All.
  Mir.   They make a rich show.
  Y. Man. There is a matter of ten thousand
     pounds, too,
Was owing here. You see those merchants with
     her;
They have brought it in now.
  Mir.   How handsomely her shape shows!
  Y. Man. Those are still neat; your Italians
     are most curious.   15
Now she looks this way.
  Mir.   She has a goodly presence;
How full of courtesy! — Well, sir, I'll leave ye;
And, if I may be bold to bring a friend or two,
Good noble gentlemen ——
  Y. Man.   No doubt, ye may, sir;
For you have most command.
  Mir.   I have seen a wonder! *Exit.* 20

---

[1] A room in a neighboring house, with a gallery.

  Ori. Is he gone?
  Y. Man.   Yes.
  Ori.   How?
  Y. Man.   Taken to the utmost:
A wonder dwells about him.
  Ori.   He did not guess at me?
  Y. Man. No, be secure; ye show another
     woman.
He is gone to fetch his friends.
  Ori.   Where are the gentlewomen?
  Y. Man. Here, here: now they are come,   26
Sit still, and let them see ye.

Enter [*below*] ROSALURA, LILLIA BIANCA, *and*
Servant.

  Ros. Pray you, where's my friend, sir?
  Y. Man. She is within, ladies; but here's
     another gentlewoman,
A stranger to this town: so please you visit her.
'T will be well taken.
  Lil.   Where is she?
  Y. Man.   There, above, ladies.
  Serv. Bless me, what thing is this? Two pin-
     nacles   31
Upon her pate! Is't not a glode[2] to catch wood-
     cocks?
  Ros. Peace, you rude knave!
  Serv.   What a bouncing bum she has too!
There's sail enough for a carrack.[3]
  Ros.   What is this lady?   35
For, as I live, she is a goodly woman.
  Y. Man. Guess, guess.
  Lil.   I have not seen a nobler presence.
  Serv. 'T is a lusty wench: now could I spend
     my forty-pence,
With all my heart, to have but one fling at her,
To give her but a [s]washing blow.
  Lil.   Ye rascal!
  Serv. Ay, that's all a man has for 's good will.
     'T will be long enough   40
Before ye cry, "Come, Anthony, and kiss me."
  Lil. I'll have ye whipt.
  Ros.   Has my friend seen this lady?
  Y. Man. Yes, yes, and is well known to her.
  Ros. I much admire her presence.
  Lil.   So do I too;
For, I protest, she is the handsomest,   45
The rarest, and the newest to mine eye,
That ever I saw yet.
  Ros.   I long to know her;
My friend shall do that kindness.
  Ori.   So she shall, ladies:
Come, pray ye, come up.
  Ros.   Oh me!
  Lil.   Hang me, if I knew her! —
Were I a man myself, I should now love ye;
Nay, I should dote.
  Ros.   I dare not trust mine eyes; 50
For, as I live, ye are the strangest alter'd!
I must come up to know the truth.
  Serv.   So must I, lady:
For I'm a kind of unbeliever too.
  Lil.   Get ye gone, sirrah;

---

[2] Glade. The space between the pinnacles is compared
to the opening in a wood, where nets were spread to
snare woodcocks.

[3] A large ship of burden.

And what ye have seen be secret in; you are
paid else !   55
No more of your long tongue.

Y. Man.   Will ye go in, ladies,
And talk with her? These venturers will come
straight.
Away with this fellow.

Lil.   There, sirrah ; go, disport you.

Serv. I would the trunk-hos'd woman would
go with me.

> *Exeunt,* [*on one side,* ROSALURA,
> LILLIA BIANCA, *and the* Young
> Man *disguised as a* Factor ; *on the
> other,* Servant.]

SCENE V.[1]

Enter MIRABEL, PINAC, *and* BELLEUR.

Pin. Is she so glorious handsome ?

Mir.   You would wonder ;
Our women look like gipsies, like gills[2] to her ;
Their clothes and fashions beggarly and bank-
rupt,
Base, old, and scurvy.

Bel.   How looks her face ?

Mir. Most heavenly ;   5
And the becoming motion of her body
So sets her off !

Bel.   Why then, we shall stay.

Mir.   Pardon me,
That's more than I know. If she be that
woman
She appears to be ——

Bel.   As 't is impossible.

Mir. I shall then tell ye more.

Pin.   Did ye speak to her ?   10

Mir. No, no, I only saw her ; she was busy.
Now I go for that end ; and mark her, gentlemen,
If she appear not to ye one of the sweetest,
The handsomest, the fairest in behaviour !
We shall meet the two wenches there too ; they
come to visit her,   15
To wonder, as we do.

Pin.   Then we shall meet 'em.

Bel. I had rather meet two bears.

Mir. There you may take your leaves, despatch that business,
And, as ye find their humours ——

Pin.   Is your love there too ?

Mir. No, certain ; she has no great heart to
set out again.   20
This is the house ; I'll usher ye.

Bel.   I'll bless me,
And take a good-heart, if I can.

Mir. Come, nobly.   *Exeunt* [*into the house*].

SCENE VI.[3]

Enter [*the* Young Man *disguised as a*] Factor,
ROSALURA, LILLIA BIANCA, *and* ORIANA
[*disguised as before*].

Y. Man. They are come in. Sit you two off,
as strangers. ——
There, lady. —— Where's the boy ?

---

[1] The street, before the same house
[2] Sluts.   [3] A room in the same house.

[*Enter* Boy.]

Be ready, sirrah,
And clear your pipes. — The music now ; they
enter.   *Music.*

Enter MIRABEL, PINAC, *and* BELLEUR.

Pin. What a state she keeps ! How far off
they sit from her !
How rich she is ! Ay, marry, this shows
bravely !   5

Bel. She is a lusty wench, and may allure a
good man ;
But, if she have a tongue, I'll not give twopence for her.
There sits my Fury ; how I shake to see her !

Y. Man. Madam, this is the gentleman.

Mir.   How sweet she kisses !
    [MIRABEL *salutes* ORIANA.]
She has a spring dwells on her lips, a para-
dise !   10
This is the legacy ?

Song [*by the* Boy, *while he presents a casket to*
MIRABEL].

> From the honour'd dead I bring
> Thus his love and last off'ring.
> Take it nobly, 't is your due,
> From a friendship ever true ;   15
> From a faith, &c.

Ori. Most noble sir,
This from my now-dead brother, as his love,
And grateful memory of your great benefit ;
From me my thanks, my wishes, and my ser-
vice.   20
Till I am more acquainted, I am silent ;
Only I dare say this, — you are truly noble.

Mir. What should I think ?

Pin.   Think you have a handsome fortune:
Would I had such another !

Ros.   Ye are all well met, gentlemen ;
We hear ye are for travel.

Pin.   You hear true, lady ;   25
And come to take our leaves.

Lil.   We'll along with ye :
We see you are grown so witty by your journey,
We cannot choose but step out too. This lady
We mean to wait upon as far as Italy.

Bel. I'll travel into Wales, amongst the
mountains,   30
In hope they cannot find me.

Ros.   If you go further,
So good and free society we hold ye,
We'll jog along too.

Pin.   Are you so valiant, lady ?

Lil. And we'll be merry, sir, and laugh.

Pin.   It may be
We'll go by sea.

Lil.   Why, 't is the only voyage !   35
I love a sea-voyage, and a blust'ring tempest ;
And let all split !

Pin.   This is a dainty damosel ! —
I think 't will tame ye. Can ye ride post ?

Lil. Oh, excellently ! I am never weary that
way :
A hundred mile a day is nothing with me.   40

Bel. I 'll travel under ground. Do you hear,
    sweet lady ?
I find it will be dangerous for a woman.
Ros. No danger, sir, I warrant ; I love to be
    under.
Bel. I see she will abuse me all the world
    over. —
But say we pass through Germany, and drink
    hard ?   45
Ros. We 'll learn to drink, and swagger
    too.
Bel.   She 'll beat me ! —
Lady, I 'll live at home.
Ros.   And I 'll live with thee ;
And we 'll keep house together.
Bel.   I 'll keep hounds first :
And those I hate right heartily.
Pin.   I go for Turkey ;
And so, it may be, up into Persia.   50
Lil. We cannot know too much ; I 'll travel
    with ye.
Pin. And you 'll abuse me ?
Lil.   Like enough.
Pin.   'T is dainty !
Bel. I will live in a bawdy-house.
Ros.   I dare come to you.
Bel. Say I am dispos'd to hang myself ?
Ros.   There I 'll leave you.
Bel. I am glad I know how to avoid you.
Mir.   May I speak yet ?
Y. Man. She beckons to ye.   56
Mir. Lady, I could wish I knew to recom-
    pense,
Even with the service of my life, those pains,
And those high favours you have thrown upon
    me :
Till I be more desertful in your eye,   60
And till my duty shall make known I honour
    ye,
Noblest of women, do me but this favour,
To accept this back again as a poor testimony.
           [*Offering the casket.*]
Ori. I must have you too with 'em ; else the
    will,
That says they must rest with ye, is infring'd,
    sir ;   65
Which, pardon me, I dare not do.
Mir.   Take me then,
And take me with the truest love.
Ori.   'T is certain
My brother lov'd ye dearly, and I ought
As dearly to preserve that love : but, sir,
Though I were willing, these are but your cere-
    monies.   70
Mir. As I have life, I speak my soul !
Ori.   I like ye :
But how you can like me, without having tes-
    timony,
A stranger to ye ——
Mir.   I 'll marry ye immediately ;
A fair state [1] I dare promise ye.
Bel.   Yet she 'll cozen thee.
Ori. Would some fair gentleman durst prom-
    ise for ye !   75
Mir. By all that 's good ——

     [1] **Estate.**

Enter LA CASTRE, NANTOLET, LUGIER, *and*
    DE GARD.

La Cast., Nant., &c. And we 'll make up the
    rest, lady.
Ori. Then Oriana takes ye ! Nay, she has
    caught ye ;
If ye start now, let all the world cry shame on ye !
I have out-travell'd ye.
Bel. Did not I say she would cheat thee ?   80
Mir. I thank ye : I am pleas'd ye have de-
    ceiv'd me,
And willingly I swallow it, and joy in 't ;
And yet, perhaps, I knew [2] ye. Whose plot was
    this ?
Lug. He is not asham'd that cast [3] it ; he
    that executed,
Follow'd your father's will.
Mir.   What a world 's this !   85
Nothing but craft and cozenage !
Ori.   Who begun, sir ?
Mir. Well ; I do take thee upon mere com-
    passion ;
And I do think I shall love thee. As a testimony,
I 'll burn my book, and turn a new leaf over.
But these fine clothes you shall wear still.
Ori.   I obey you, sir, in all.   90
Nant. And how, how, daughters ? What say
    you to these gentlemen ?
What say ye, gentlemen, to the girls ?
Pin.   By my troth — if she can love me —
Lil. How long ?
Pin.   Nay, if once ye love ——
Lil.   Then take me,
And take your chance.
Pin.   Most willingly : ye are mine, lady ;
And, if I use ye not that ye may love me —— 95
Lil. A match, i' faith.
Pin.   Why, now ye travel with me.
Ros. How that thing stands !
Bel.   It will, if ye urge it :
Bless your five wits !
Ros.   Nay, prithee, stay ; I 'll have thee.
Bel. You must ask me leave first.
Ros.   Wilt thou use me kindly,
And beat me but once a week ?
Bel.   If you deserve no more. 100
Ros. And wilt thou get me with child ?
Bel. Dost thou ask me seriously ?
Ros. Yes, indeed, do I.
Bel. Yes, I will get thee with child. Come
    presently,
An 't be but in revenge, I 'll do thee that cour-
    tesy.   105
Well, if thou wilt fear God and me, have at thee !
Ros. I 'll love ye, and I 'll honour ye.
Bel.   I am pleas'd, then.
Mir. This *Wild-Goose Chase* is done ; we
    have won o' both sides.
Brother, your love : and now to church of all
    hands ;
Let 's lose no time.
Pin.   Our travelling lay by.   110
Bel. No more for Italy ; for the Low Coun-
    tries, [I.]   *Exeunt.*

     [2] Ft. *know.*   [3] **Planned.**

THE DUCHESS OF MALFI

BY

JOHN WEBSTER

DRAMATIS PERSONAE

FERDINAND [Duke of Calabria].
CARDINAL [his brother].
ANTONIO [BOLOGNA, Steward of the Household to the Duchess].
DELIO [his friend].
DANIEL DE BOSOLA [Gentleman of the Horse to the Duchess].
[CASTRUCCIO, an old Lord.]
MARQUIS OF PESCARA
[COUNT] MALATESTI.

RODERIGO, }
SILVIO, } [Lords.]
GRISOLAN, }
DOCTOR.
The Several Madmen.

DUCHESS [OF MALFI].
CARIOLA [her woman].
[JULIA, Castruccio's wife, and] the Cardinal's mistress.
[Old Lady.]

Ladies, Three Young Children, Two Pilgrims, Executioners, Court Officers, and Attendants.

[SCENE. — *Amalfi, Rome, Loretto, Milan.* TIME. — *Early Sixteenth Century.*]

ACT I

SCENE I.[1]

[Enter] ANTONIO *and* DELIO.

Delio. You are welcome to your country, dear Antonio;
You have been long in France, and you return
A very formal Frenchman in your habit.
How do you like the French court?
Ant.   I admire it.
In seeking to reduce both state and people   5
To a fix'd order, their judicious king
Begins at home; quits first his royal palace
Of flatt'ring sycophants, of dissolute
And infamous persons, — which he sweetly terms
His master's master-piece, the work of heaven;
Considering duly that a prince's court   11
Is like a common fountain, whence should flow
Pure silver drops in general, but if 't chance
Some curs'd example poison 't near the head,
Death and diseases through the whole land spread.   15
And what is 't makes this blessed government
But a most provident council, who dare freely
Inform him the corruption of the times?
Though some o' th' court hold it presumption
To instruct princes what they ought to do,   20
It is a noble duty to inform them
What they ought to forsee.[2] — Here comes Bosola,
The only court-gall; yet I observe his railing
Is not for simple love of piety:
Indeed, he rails at those things which he wants;   25

[1] Amalfi. The presence-chamber in the palace of the Duchess.
[2] Prevent.

Would be as lecherous, covetous, or proud,
Bloody, or envious, as any man,
If he had means to be so. — Here 's the cardinal.

[Enter CARDINAL *and* BOSOLA.]

Bos. I do haunt you still.
Card. So.   30
Bos. I have done you better service than to be slighted thus. Miserable age, where only the reward of doing well is the doing of it!
Card. You enforce your merit too much.
Bos. I fell into the galleys in your serv-   [35
ice; where, for two years together, I wore two towels instead of a shirt, with a knot on the shoulder, after the fashion of a Roman mantle. Slighted thus! I will thrive some way. Black-birds fatten best in hard weather; why not   [40
I in these dog-days?
Card. Would you could become honest!
Bos. With all your divinity do but direct me the way to it. I have known many travel far for it, and yet return as arrant knaves as   [45
they went forth, because they carried themselves always along with them. [*Exit* CARDINAL.] Are you gone? Some fellows, they say, are possessed with the devil, but this great fellow were able to possess the greatest devil, and make him   [50
worse.
Ant. He hath denied thee some suit?
Bos. He and his brother are like plum-trees that grow crooked over standing-pools; they are rich and o'erladen with fruit, but none but   [55
crows, pies, and caterpillars feed on them. Could I be one of their flatt'ring panders, I would hang on their ears like a horseleech, till I were full, and then drop off. I pray, leave me. Who would rely upon these miserable depend-encies, in expectation to be advanc'd to-   [61

morrow ? What creature ever fed worse than hoping Tantalus ? Nor ever died any man more fearfully than he that hop'd for a pardon. There are rewards for hawks and dogs when [65 they have done us service ; but for a soldier that hazards his limbs in a battle, nothing but a kind of geometry is his last supportation.

Delio. Geometry ?

Bos. Ay, to hang in a fair pair of slings, take his latter swing in the world upon an hon- [71 ourable pair of crutches, from hospital to hospital. Fare ye well, sir : and yet do not you scorn us ; for places in the court are but like beds in the hospital, where this man's head lies at that man's foot, and so lower and lower. [*Exit.*] 76

Del. I knew this fellow seven years in the galleys
For a notorious murder ; and 't was thought
The cardinal suborn'd it : he was releas'd
By the French general, Gaston de Foix,   80
When he recover'd Naples.

Ant.   'T is great pity
He should be thus neglected : I have heard
He 's very valiant. This foul melancholy
Will poison all his goodness ; for, I 'll tell you,
If too immoderate sleep be truly said   85
To be an inward rust unto the soul,
It then doth follow want of action
Breeds all black malcontents ; and their close rearing,
Like moths in cloth, do hurt for want of wearing.

SCENE II. [1]

ANTONIO, DELIO. [*Enter*] SILVIO, CASTRUCCIO, JULIA, RODERIGO, *and* GRISOLAN.

Delio. The presence 'gins to fill : you prom-is'd me
To make me the partaker of the natures
Of some of your great courtiers.

Ant.   The lord cardinal's
And other strangers' that are now in court ?
I shall. — Here comes the great Calabrian duke.

[*Enter* FERDINAND *and* Attendants.]

Ferd. Who took the ring oft'nest ? [2]   6

Sil. Antonio Bologna, my lord.

Ferd. Our sister duchess' great master of her household ? Give him the jewel. — When shall we leave this sportive action, and fall to action indeed ?   11

Cast. Methinks, my lord, you should not de-sire to go to war in person.

Ferd. Now for some gravity. — Why, my lord ?   15

Cast. It is fitting a soldier arise to be a prince, but not necessary a prince descend to be a cap-tain.

Ferd. No ?

Cast. No, my lord ; he were far better do it by a deputy.   21

Ferd. Why should he not as well sleep or eat by a deputy ? This might take idle, offensive,

and base office from him, whereas the other de-prives him of honour.   25

Cast. Believe my experience, that realm is never long in quiet where the ruler is a soldier.

Ferd. Thou told'st me thy wife could not en-dure fighting.

Cast. True, my lord.   30

Ferd. And of a jest she broke of [3] a captain she met full of wounds : I have forgot it.

Cast. She told him, my lord, he was a pitiful fellow, to lie, like the children of Ismael, all in tents.[4]   35

Ferd. Why, there 's a wit were able to undo all the chirurgeons [5] o' the city ; for although gallants should quarrel, and had drawn their weapons, and were ready to go to it, yet her persuasions would make them put up.   40

Cast. That she would, my lord. — How do you like my Spanish gennet ? [6]

Rod. He is all fire.

Ferd. I am of Pliny's opinion, I think he was begot by the wind ; he runs as if he were bal-las'd [7] with quicksilver.   46

Sil. True, my lord, he reels from the tilt often.

Rod. Gris. Ha, ha, ha !

Ferd. Why do you laugh ? Methinks you that are courtiers should be my touch-wood, [51 take fire when I give fire ; that is, laugh when I laugh, were the subject never so witty.

Cast. True, my lord : I myself have heard a very good jest, and have scorn'd to seem to have so silly a wit as to understand it.   56

Ferd. But I can laugh at your fool, my lord.

Cast. He cannot speak, you know, but he makes faces ; my lady cannot abide him.

Ferd. No ?   60

Cast. Nor endure to be in merry company ; for she says too full laughing, and too much company, fills her too much of the wrinkle.

Ferd. I would, then, have a mathematical in-strument made for her face, that she might not laugh out of compass. — I shall shortly visit [66 you at Milan, Lord Silvio.

Sil. Your grace shall arrive most welcome.

Ferd. You are a good horseman, Antonio : you have excellent riders in France ; what do you think of good horsemanship ?   71

Ant. Nobly, my lord : as out of the Grecian horse issued many famous princes, so out of brave horsemanship arise the first sparks of growing resolution, that raise the mind to noble action.   76

Ferd. You have bespoke it worthily.

Sil. Your brother, the lord cardinal, and sis-ter duchess.

[*Enter* CARDINAL, *with* DUCHESS, *and* CARI-OLA.]

Card. Are the galleys come about ?

Gris.   They are, my lord.   80

Ferd. Here 's the Lord Silvio is come to take his leave.

---

1 The same.
2 The reference is to the knightly sport of riding at the ring.

3 At the expense of.
4 Rolls of lint used to dress wounds.
5 Surgeons.   6 A small horse.   7 Ballasted.

Delio. Now, sir, your promise: what's that
   cardinal?
I mean his temper. They say he's a brave fellow,
Will play his five thousand crowns at tennis,
   dance,
Court ladies, and one that hath fought single
   combats.   85
Ant. Some such flashes superficially hang
on him for form; but observe his inward character: he is a melancholy churchman. The
spring in his face is nothing but the engend'ring
of toads; where he is jealous of any man, he
lays worse plots for them than ever was im- [91
pos'd on Hercules, for he strews in his way
flatterers, panders, intelligencers, atheists, and
a thousand such political monsters. He should
have been Pope; but instead of coming to it by
the primitive decency of the church, he did [96
bestow bribes so largely and so impudently as
if he would have carried it away without heaven's knowledge. Some good he hath done——
Delio. You have given too much of him.
   What's his brother?   100
Ant. The duke there? A most perverse and
   turbulent nature.
What appears in him mirth is merely outside;
If he laught heartily, it is to laugh
All honesty out of fashion.
Delio.   Twins?
Ant.   In quality.
He speaks with others' tongues, and hears
   men's suits   105
With others' ears; will seem to sleep o' th'
   bench
Only to entrap offenders in their answers;
Dooms men to death by information;
Rewards by hearsay.
Delio.   Then the law to him
Is like a foul, black cobweb to a spider,—   110
He makes it his dwelling and a prison
To entangle those shall feed him.
Ant.   Most true:
He never pays debts unless they be shrewd
   turns,
And these he will confess that he doth owe.
Last, for his brother there, the cardinal,   115
They that do flatter him most say oracles
Hang at his lips; and verily I believe them,
For the devil speaks in them.
But for their sister, the right noble duchess,
You never fix'd your eye on three fair medals
Cast in one figure, of so different temper.   121
For her discourse, it is so full of rapture,
You only will begin then to be sorry
When she doth end her speech, and wish, in
   wonder,
She held it less vain-glory to talk much,   125
Than your penance to hear her. Whilst she
   speaks,
She throws upon a man so sweet a look
That it were able to raise one to a galliard [1]
That lay in a dead palsy, and to dote
On that sweet countenance; but in that look 130
There speaketh so divine a continence

As cuts off all lascivious and vain hope.
Her days are practis'd in such noble virtue,
That sure her nights, nay, more, her very
   sleeps,
Are more in heaven than other ladies' shrifts.
Let all sweet ladies break their flatt'ring
   glasses,   136
And dress themselves in her.
Delio.   Fie, Antonio,
You play the wire-drawer with her commenda-
   tions.
Ant. I'll case the picture up: only thus
   much;
All her particular worth grows to this sum,—
She stains [2] the time past, lights the time to
   come.   141
Cari. You must attend my lady in the gal-
   lery,
Some half an hour hence.
Ant. I shall. [*Exeunt* ANTONIO *and* DELIO.]
Ferd. Sister, I have a suit to you.
Duch.   To me, sir?
Ferd. A gentlemen here, Daniel de Bosola,
One that was in the galleys——
Duch.   Yes, I know him.   146
Ferd. A worthy fellow he's: pray, let me en-
   treat for
The provisorship of your horse.
Duch.   Your knowledge of him
Commends him and prefers him.
Ferd.   Call him hither. [*Exit* Attendants.]
We [are] now upon [3] parting. Good Lord Silvio,
Do us commend to all our noble friends   151
At the leaguer.
Sil.   Sir, I shall.
[*Duch.*]   You are for Milan?
Sil. I am.
Duch. Bring the caroches.[4] —We'll bring
   you down
To the haven,
        [*Exeunt* DUCHESS, SILVIO, CAS-
        TRUCCIO, RODERIGO, GRISOLAN,
        CARIOLA, JULIA, *and* Attendants.]
Card. Be sure you entertain that Bosola   154
For your intelligence.[5] I would not be seen in 't;
And therefore many times I have slighted him
When he did court our furtherance, as this
   morning.
Ferd. Antonio, the great master of her house-
   hold,
Had been far fitter.
Card.   You are deceiv'd in him. 159
His nature is too honest for such business.—
He comes: I'll leave you.   [*Exit.*]

           [*Re-enter* BOSOLA.]

Bos.   I was lur'd to you.
Ferd. My brother, here, the cardinal could
   never
Abide you.
Bos.   Never since he was in my debt.
Ferd. May be some oblique character in your
   face
Made him suspect you.

---

[1] A lively dance.

[2] Throws into the shade.
[3] At the point of.

[4] Coaches.
[5] Spy.

Bos.   Doth he study physiognomy? 165
There 's no more credit to be given to th' face
Than to a sick man's urine, which some call
The physician's whore, because she cozens [1]
    him.
He did suspect me wrongfully.
    Ferd.   For that
You must give great men leave to take their
    times.   170
Distrust doth cause us seldom be deceiv'd.
You see the oft shaking of the cedar-tree
Fastens it more at root.
    Bos.   Yet take heed ;
For to suspect a friend unworthily
Instructs him the next way to suspect you, 175
And prompts him him to deceive you.
    Ferd.   There 's gold.
    Bos.   So :
What follows ? — ⸢*Aside.*⸣ Never rain'd such
    showers as these
Without thunderbolts i' th' tail of them. —
    Whose throat must I cut ?
    Ferd. Your inclination to shed blood rides
    post
Before my occasion to use you. I give you that
To live i' th' court here, and observe the
    duchess ;   181
To note all the particulars of her behaviour,
What suitors do solicit her for marriage,
And whom she best affects.[2] She 's a young
    widow :
I would not have her marry again.
    Bos.   No, sir ?   185
    Ferd. Do not you ask the reason ; but be
    satisfied.
I say I would not.
    Bos.   It seems you would create me
One of your familiars.
    Ferd.   Familiar ! What 's that ?
    Bos. Why, a very quaint invisible devil in
    flesh, —
An intelligencer. [3]
    Ferd.   Such a kind of thriving thing 190
I would wish thee ; and ere long thou mayst
    arrive
At a higher place by 't.
    Bos.   Take your devils,
Which hell calls angels ! These curs'd gifts
    would make
You a corrupter, me an impudent traitor ;
And should I take these, they 'd take me [to]
    hell.   195
    Ferd. Sir, I 'll take nothing from you that I
    have given.
There is a place that I procur'd for you
This morning, the provisorship o' th' horse ;
Have you heard on 't ?
    Bos.   No.
    Ferd.   'T is yours : is 't not worth thanks ?
    Bos. I would have you curse yourself now,
    that your bounty   200
(Which makes men truly noble) e'er should
    make me
A villain. O, that to avoid ingratitude
For the good deed you have done me, I must
    do

[1] Cheats.   [2] Likes.   [3] Spy.

All the ill man can invent ! Thus the devil
Candies all sins o'er : and what heaven terms
    vile,   205
That names he complimental.
    Ferd.   Be yourself ;
Keep your old garb of melancholy ; 't will ex-
    press
You envy those that stand above your reach,
Yet strive not to come near 'em. This will
    gain
Access to private lodgings, where yourself 210
May, like a politic dormouse ——
    Bos.   As I have seen some
Feed in a lord's dish, half asleep, not seeming
To listen to any talk ; and yet these rogues
Have cut his throat in a dream. What 's my
    place ?
The provisorship o' th' horse ? Say, then, my
    corruption   215
Grew out of horse-dung : I am your creature.
    Ferd.   Away ! [*Exit.*]
    Bos. Let good men, for good deeds, covet
    good fame,
Since place and riches oft are bribes of shame.
Sometimes the devil doth preach.   *Exit.*

[SCENE III.][4]

[*Enter* FERDINAND, DUCHESS, CARDINAL, *and*
    CARIOLA.]

    Card. We are to part from you ; and your
    own discretion
Must now be your director.
    Ferd.   You are a widow :
You know already what man is ; and therefore
Let not youth, high promotion, eloquence ——
    Card. No,   5
Nor anything without the addition, honour,
Sway your high blood.
    Ferd.   Marry ! They are most luxurious [5]
Will wed twice.
    Card.   O, fie !
    Ferd.   Their livers are more spotted
Than Laban's sheep.[6]
    Duch.   Diamonds are of most value,
They say, that have past through most jewel-
    lers' hands.   10
    Ferd. Whores by that rule are precious.
    Duch.   Will you hear me ?
I 'll never marry.
    Card.   So most widows say ;
But commonly that motion [7] lasts no longer
Than the turning of an hour-glass : the funeral
    sermon
And it end both together.
    Ferd.   Now hear me :   15
You live in a rank pasture, here, i' th' court ;
There is a kind of honey-dew that 's deadly ;
'T will poison your fame ; look to 't. Be not
    cunning ;
For they whose faces do belie their hearts
Are witches ere they arrive at twenty years, 20
Ay, and give the devil suck.
    Duch. This is terrible good counsel.

[4] Amalfi. Gallery in the Duchess's palace.
[5] Lustful.   [6] *Genesis* XXX. 31-42.   [7] Impulse.

Ferd. Hypocrisy is woven of a fine small
    thread,
Subtler than Vulcan's engine : [1] yet, believe 't,
Your darkest actions, nay, your privat'st
    thoughts,   25
Will come to light.
    Card.   You may flatter yourself,
And take your own choice ; privately be mar-
    ried
Under the eaves of night——
    Ferd.   Think 't the best voyage
That e'er you made ; like the irregular crab,
Which, though 't goes backward, thinks that it
    goes right   30
Because it goes its own way : but observe,
Such weddings may more properly be said
To be executed than celebrated.
    Card.   The marriage night
Is the entrance into some prison.
    Ferd.   And those joys,
Those lustful pleasures, are like heavy sleeps 35
Which do fore-run man's mischief.
    Card.   Fare you well.
Wisdom begins at the end : remember it.
                                          [*Exit.*]
    Duch. I think this speech between you both
    was studied,
It came so roundly off.
    Ferd.   You are my sister ;
This was my father's poniard, do you see ?   40
I 'd be loth to see 't look rusty, 'cause 't was
    his.
I would have you give o'er these chargeable
    revels :
A visor and a mask are whispering-rooms
That were nev'r built for goodness,— fare ye
    well —
And women like that part which, like the
    lamprey,   45
Hath nev'r a bone in 't.
    Duch.   Fie, sir !
    Ferd.   Nay,
I mean the tongue ; variety of courtship.
What cannot a neat knave with a smooth tale
Make a woman believe ? Farewell, lusty widow.
                                          [*Exit.*]
    Duch. Shall this move me ? If all my royal
    kindred   50
Lay in my way unto this marriage,
I 'd make them my low footsteps. And even
    now,
Even in this hate, as men in some great battles,
By apprehending danger, have achiev'd
Almost impossible actions (I have heard soldiers
    say so),   55
So I through frights and threat'nings will assay
This dangerous venture. Let old wives report
I wink'd and chose a husband. — Cariola,
To thy known secrecy I have given up
More than my life,— my fame.
    Cari.   Both shall be safe ;   60
For I 'll conceal this secret from the world
As warily as those that trade in poison
Keep poison from their children.
    Duch.   Thy protestation

Is ingenious and hearty ; I believe it.
Is Antonio come ?
    Cari.   He attends you.
    Duch.   Good dear soul, 65
Leave me ; but place thyself behind the arras,
Where thou mayest overhear us. Wish me good
    speed ;
For I am going into a wilderness,
Where I shall find nor path nor friendly clue
To be my guide.
            [*Cariola goes behind the arras.*]

            [*Enter* Antonio.]

                    I sent for you : sit down ;   70
Take pen and ink, and write : are you ready ?
    Ant.   Yes.
    Duch. What did I say ?
    Ant. That I should write somewhat.
    Duch.   O, I remember.
After these triumphs and this large expense
It 's fit, like thrifty husbands,[2] we inquire   75
What 's laid up for to-morrow.
    Ant. So please your beauteous excellence.
    Duch.   Beauteous !
Indeed, I thank you. I look young for your
    sake ;
You have ta'en my cares upon you.
    Ant.   I 'll fetch your grace
The particulars of your revenue and expense. 80
    Duch. O, you are
An upright treasurer, but you mistook ;
For when I said I meant to make inquiry
What 's laid up for to-morrow, I did mean
What 's laid up yonder for me.
    Ant.   Where ?
    Duch.   In heaven. 85
I am making my will (as 't is fit princes should,
In perfect memory), and, I pray, sir, tell me,
Were not one better make it smiling, thus,
Than in deep groans and terrible ghastly looks,
As if the gifts we parted with procur'd[3]   90
That violent distraction ?
    Ant.   O, much better.
    Duch. If I had a husband now, this care were
    quit :
But I intend to make you overseer.
What good deed shall we first remember ? Say.
    Ant. Begin with that first good deed began
    i' th' world   95
After man's creation, the sacrament of mar-
    riage.
I 'd have you first provide for a good husband ;
Give him all.
    Duch. All !
    Ant.   Yes, your excellent self.
    Duch. In a winding-sheet ?
    Ant.   In a couple.
    Duch. Saint Winifred, that were a strange
    will !   100
    Ant. 'T were stranger[4] if there were no will
    in you
To marry again.
    Duch.   What do you think of marriage ?
    Ant. I take 't, as those that deny purgatory,

---

[1] The net in which he caught Venus and Mars.
[2] Housekeepers.   [4] Qq. read *strange*.
[3] Produced.

It locally contains or heaven or hell;
There's no third place in 't.
Duch.   How do you affect it? 105
Ant. My banishment, feeding my melancholy,
Would often reason thus: —
Duch.   Pray, let 's hear it.
Ant. Say a man never marry, nor have
   children,
What takes that from him? Only the bare
   name
Of being a father, or the weak delight   110
To see the little wanton ride a-cock-horse
Upon a painted stick, or hear him chatter
Like a taught starling.
Duch.   Fie, fie, what 's all this?
One of your eyes is blood-shot; use my ring
   to 't.
They say 't is very sovereign. 'T was my wed-
   ding-ring.   115
And I did vow never to part with it
But to my second husband.
Ant. You have parted with it now.
Duch. Yes, to help your eye-sight.
Ant. You have made me stark blind.
Duch.   How? 120
Ant. There is a saucy and ambitious devil
Is dancing in this circle.
Duch.   Remove him.
Ant.   How?
Duch. There needs small conjuration, when
   your finger
May do it : thus. Is it fit?
      [*She puts the ring upon his finger*]:
      he kneels.
Ant.   What said you?
Duch.   Sir,
This goodly roof of yours is too low built; 125
I cannot stand upright in 't nor discourse,
Without I raise it higher. Raise yourself;
Or, if you please, my hand to help you : so.
                        [*Raises him.*]
Ant. Ambition, madam, is a great man's
   madness,
That is not kept in chains and close-pent rooms,
But in fair lightsome lodgings, and is girt 131
With the wild noise of prattling visitants,
Which makes it lunatic beyond all cure.
Conceive not I am so stupid but I aim [1]
Whereto your favours tend : but he 's a fool 135
That, being a-cold, would thrust his hands i'
   th' fire
To warm them.
Duch.   So, now the ground 's broke,
You may discover what a wealthy mine
I make you lord of.
Ant.   O my unworthiness!
Duch. You were ill to sell yourself :   140
This dark'ning of your worth is not like that
Which tradesmen use i' th' city; their false
   lights
Are to rid bad wares off : and I must tell you,
If you will know where breathes a complete
   man
(I speak it without flattery), turn your eyes, 145
And progress through yourself.

          [1] Guess.

Ant. Were there nor heaven nor hell,
I should be honest: I have long serv'd virtue,
And nev'r ta'en wages of her.
Duch.   Now she pays it.
The misery of us that are born great!   150
We are forc'd to woo, because none dare woo us;
And as a tyrant doubles with his words
And fearfully equivocates, so we
Are forc'd to express our violent passions
In riddles and in dreams, and leave the path 155
Of simple virtue, which was never made
To seem the thing it is not. Go, go brag
You have left me heartless; mine is in your
   bosom:
I hope 't will multiply love there. You do
   tremble:
Make not your heart so dead a piece of flesh, 160
To fear more than to love me. Sir, be confi-
   dent:
What is 't distracts you? This is flesh and
   blood, sir ;
'T is not the figure cut in alabaster
Kneels at my husband's tomb. Awake, awake,
   man!
I do here put off all vain ceremony,   165
And only do appear to you a young widow
That claims you for her husband, and, like a
   widow,
I use but half a blush in 't.
Ant.   Truth speak for me ;
I will remain the constant sanctuary
Of your good name.
Duch.   I thank you, gentle love: 170
And 'cause you shall not come to me in debt,
Being now my steward, here upon your lips
I sign your *Quietus est.*[2] This you should have
   begg'd now.
I have seen children oft eat sweetmeats thus,
As fearful to devour them too soon.   175
Ant. But for your brothers?
Duch.   Do not think of them :
All discord without this circumference
Is only to be pitied, and not fear'd :
Yet, should they know it, time will easily
Scatter the tempest.
Ant.   These words should be mine, 180
And all the parts you have spoke, if some part
   of it
Would not have savour'd flattery.
Duch.   Kneel.
      [CARIOLA *comes from behind the
      arras.*]
Ant.   Ha !
Duch. Be not amaz'd: this woman 's of my
   counsel.
I have heard lawyers say, a contract in a cham-
   ber
Per verba [de] presenti[3] is absolute marriage. 185
                  [*She and* ANTONIO *kneel.*]
Bless, heaven, this sacred gordian,[4] which let
   violence
Never untwine.

   [2] The phrase used to indicate that accounts had been
examined and found correct.
   [3] Using words of present time: *i. e.* "I take," not
"I will take."
   [4] Knot.

Ant. And may our sweet affections, like the
    spheres,
Be still in motion !
  Duch.   Quick'ning, and make
The like soft music !   190
  Ant. That we may imitate the loving palms,
Best emblem of a peaceful marriage,
That nev'r bore fruit, divided !
  Duch. What can the church force more ?
  Ant. That fortune may not know an acci-
    dent,   195
Either of joy or sorrow, to divide
Our fixed wishes !
  Duch.   How can the church build faster ?[1]
We now are man and wife, and 't is the church
That must but echo this. — Maid, stand apart :
I now am blind.
  Ant.   What 's your conceit in this ? 200
  Duch. I would have you lead your fortune by
    the hand
Unto your marriage-bed :
(You speak in me this, for we now are one.)
We 'll only lie and talk together, and plot
T' appease my humorous[2] kindred ; and if you
    please,   205
Like the old tale in *Alexander and Lodowick*,
Lay a naked sword between us, keep us chaste.
O, let me shroud my blushes in your bosom,
Since 't is the treasury of all my secrets !
          [Exeunt DUCHESS *and* ANTONIO.]
  Cari. Whether the spirit of greatness or of
    woman   210
Reign most in her, I know not ; but it shows
A fearful madness. I owe her much of pity.
                       Exit.

ACT II

Scene I.[3]

[Enter] BOSOLA *and* CASTRUCCIO.

  Bos. You say you would fain be taken for an
    eminent courtier ?
  Cast. 'T is the very main[4] of my ambition.
  Bos. Let me see : you have a reasonable good
face for 't already, and your night-cap expresses
your ears sufficient largely. I would have you [5
learn to twirl the strings of your band with a
good grace, and in a set speech, at th' end of
every sentence, to hum three or four times, or
blow your nose till it smart again, to recover
your memory. When you come to be a presi- [10
dent in criminal causes, if you smile upon a
prisoner, hang him ; but if you frown upon him
and threaten him, let him be sure to scape the
gallows.
  Cast. I would be a very merry president. 15
  Bos. Do not sup o' nights ; 't will beget you
an admirable wit.
  Cast. Rather it would make me have a good
stomach to quarrel ; for they say, your roaring
boys eat meat seldom, and that makes them so [20
valiant. But how shall I know whether the
people take me for an eminent fellow ?

  [1] More firmly   [2] Of difficult disposition.
  [3] Amalfi. An apartment in the palace of the Duchess.
  [4] Chief part.

  Bos. I will teach a trick to know it : give out
you lie a-dying, and if you hear the common
people curse you, be sure you are taken for one
of the prime night-caps.[5]   25

            [Enter an Old Lady.]

You come from painting now.
  Old Lady. From what ?
  Bos. Why, from your scurvy face-physic. To
behold thee not painted inclines somewhat near
a miracle. These in thy face here were deep ruts
and foul sloughs the last progress.[6] There was [31
a lady in France that, having had the small-pox,
flayed the skin off her face to make it more level ;
and whereas before she looked like a nutmeg-gra-
ter, after she resembled an abortive hedge-hog. 35
  Old Lady. Do you call this painting ?
  Bos. No, no, but you call [it] careening[7] of an
old morphew'd[8] lady, to make her disembogue[9]
again : there 's rough-cast phrase to your plastic.[10]
  Old Lady. It seems you are well acquainted [40
with my closet.
  Bos. One would suspect it for a shop of witchcraft, to find in it the fat of serpents, spawn of
snakes, Jews' spittle, and their young children's
ordure ; and all these for the face. I would [45
sooner eat a dead pigeon taken from the soles
of the feet of one sick of the plague, than kiss
one of you fasting. Here are two of you, whose
sin of your youth is the very patrimony of the
physician ; makes him renew his foot-cloth [50
with the spring, and change his high-pric'd
courtesan with the fall of the leaf. I do wonder
you do not loathe yourselves. Observe my medi-
tation now.
What thing is in this outward form of man 55
To be belov'd ? We account it ominous,
If nature do produce a colt, or lamb,
A fawn, or goat, in any limb resembling
A man, and fly from 't as a prodigy.
Man stands amaz'd to see his deformity 60
In any other creature but himself.
But in our own flesh though we bear diseases
Which have their true names only ta'en from
    beasts, —
As the most ulcerous wolf[11] and swinish
    measle,[12] —
Though we are eaten up of lice and worms, 65
And though continually we bear about us
A rotten and dead body, we delight
To hide it in rich tissue : all our fear,
Nay, all our terror, is, lest our physician 60
Should put us in the ground to be made sweet. —
Your wife 's gone to Rome : you two couple, and
get you to the wells at Lucca to recover your
aches. I have other work on foot.

      [Exeunt CASTRUCCIO *and* Old Lady.]

I observe our duchess 74
Is sick a-days, she pukes, her stomach seethes,

  [5] Bullies (Hazlitt) ; lawyers (Vaughan).
  [6] Royal journey.
  [7] Turning a boat on its side for repairs.
  [8] Scabbed.   [9] Empty.
  [10] Face-modelling. (Sampson.) "There 's a plain
statement of your practices."
  [11] Lupus.   [12] A disease of swine.

The fins of her eye-lids look most teeming
blue,[1]
She wanes i' th' cheek, and waxes fat i' th'
flank,
And, contrary to our Italian fashion,
Wears a loose-bodied gown : there 's somewhat
in 't.
I have a trick may chance discover it,   80
A pretty one ; I have bought some apricocks,
The first our spring yields.

[*Enter* ANTONIO *and* DELIO, *talking together
apart.*]

Delio.   And so long since married ?
You amaze me.
Ant.   Let me seal your lips for ever :
For, did I think that anything but th' air
Could carry these words from you, I should
wish   85
You had no breath at all. — Now, sir, in your
contemplation ?
You are studying to become a great wise fel-
low.
Bos. O, sir, the opinion of wisdom is a foul
tetter[2] that runs all over a man's body : if sim-
plicity direct us to have no evil, it directs us [90
to a happy being ; for the subtlest folly proceeds
from the subtlest wisdom. Let me be simply
honest.
Ant. I do understand your inside.
Bos.   Do you so ?
Ant. Because you would not seem to appear
to th' world   95
Puff'd up with your preferment, you continue
This out-of-fashion melancholy : leave it, leave
it.
Bos. Give me leave to be honest in any
phrase, in any compliment whatsoever. Shall I
confess myself to you ? I look no higher than [100
I can reach : they are the gods that must ride
on winged horses. A lawyer's mule of a slow
pace will both suit my disposition and business ;
for, mark me, when a man's mind rides faster
than his horse can gallop, they quickly both [105
tire.
Ant. You would look up to heaven, but I
think
The devil, that rules i' th' air, stands in your
light.
Bos. O, sir, you are lord of the ascendant,[3]
chief man with the duchess : a duke was your [110
cousin-german remov'd. Say you were lineally
descended from King Pepin, or he himself, what
of this ? Search the heads of the greatest rivers
in the world, you shall find them but bubbles of
water. Some would think the souls of princes [115
were brought forth by some more weighty cause
than those of meaner persons : they are deceiv'd,
there 's the same hand to them ; the like
passions sway them ; the same reason that
makes a vicar go to law for a tithe-pig, and [120
undo his neighbours, makes them spoil a whole
province, and batter down goodly cities with
the cannon.

---

[1] Blue like those of a woman with child.
[2] Scurf.   [3] Person of highest influence.

[*Enter* DUCHESS *and* LADIES.]

Duch. Your arm, Antonio : do I not grow fat ?
I am exceeding short-winded. — Bosola,   125
I would have you, sir, provide for me a litter ;
Such a one as the Duchess of Florence rode in.
Bos. The duchess us'd one when she was
great with child.
Duch. I think she did. — Come hither, mend
my ruff :   129
Here, when ? thou art such a tedious lady ; and
Thy breath smells of lemon-pills : wouldst thou
hadst done !
Shall I swoon under thy fingers ? I am
So troubled with the mother ![4]
Bos. [*Aside.*]   I fear, too much.
Duch. I have heard you say that the French
courtiers
Wear their hats on 'fore the king.   135
Ant. I have seen it.
Duch.   In the presence ?
Ant.   Yes.
Duch. Why should not we bring up that
fashion ?
'T is ceremony more than duty that consists
In the removing of a piece of felt.
Be you the example to the rest o' th' court ;   140
Put on your hat first.
Ant.   You must pardon me :
I have seen, in colder countries than in France,
Nobles stand bare to th' prince ; and the distinc-
tion
Methought show'd reverently.
Bos. I have a present for your grace.
Duch.   For me, sir ?   145
Bos. Apricocks, madam.
Duch.   O, sir, where are they ?
I have heard of none to-year.[5]
Bos. [*Aside.*]   Good ; her colour rises.
Duch. Indeed, I thank you : they are won-
drous fair ones.
What an unskilful fellow is our gardener !
We shall have none this month.   150
Bos. Will not your grace pare them ?
Duch. No : they taste of musk, methinks ; in-
deed they do.
Bos. I know not : yet I wish your grace had
par'd 'em.
Duch. Why ?
Bos. I forgot to tell you, the knave gardener
Only to raise his profit by them the sooner,   155
Did ripen them in horse-dung.
Duch.   O, you jest. —
You shall judge : pray, taste one.
Ant.   Indeed, madam,
I do not love the fruit.
Duch.   Sir, you are loth
To rob us of our dainties. 'T is a delicate fruit ;
They say they are restorative.
Bos.   'T is a pretty art,   160
This grafting.
Duch. 'T is so ; a bett'ring of nature.
Bos. To make a pippin grow upon a crab,
A damson on a black-thorn. — [*Aside.*] How
greedily she eats them !

---

[4] Hysteria.   [5] This year.

A whirlwind strike off these bawd farthingales !
For, but for that and the loose-bodied gown, 166
I should have discover'd apparently [1]
The young springal [2] cutting a caper in her
belly.
　　Duch. I thank you, Bosola: they were right
　　　good ones,
If they do not make me sick.
　　Ant.　　　　　　How, now, madam ! 170
　　Duch. This green fruit and my stomach are
　　　not friends :
How they swell me !
　　Bos. [*Aside.*] Nay, you are too much swell'd
　　　already.
　　Duch. O, I am in an extreme cold sweat !
　　Bos.　　　　　I am very sorry. [*Exit.*]
　　Duch. Lights to my chamber ! — O good An-
　　　tonio, 175
I fear I am undone !
　　Delio.　　　　　Lights there, lights !
　　　　　　　Exeunt DUCHESS [*and Ladies*].
　　Ant. O my most trusty Delio, we are lost !
I fear she 's fall'n in labour ; and there 's left
No time for her remove
　　Delio.　　　　Have you prepar'd
Those ladies to attend her ; and procur'd 180
That politic safe conveyance for the midwife
Your duchess plotted ?
　　Ant.　　　　　I have.
　　Delio. Make use, then, of this forc'd occa-
　　　sion.
Give out that Bosola hath poison'd her
With these apricocks ; that will give some
　　colour 185
For her keeping close.
　　Ant.　　　　Fie, fie, the physicians
Will then flock to her.
　　Delio. For that you may pretend
She 'll use some prepar'd antidote of her own,
Lest the physicians should re-poison her. 190
　　Ant. I am lost in amazement : I know not
what to think on 't.　　　　　　*Exeunt.*

SCENE II.[3]

[*Enter*] BOSOLA *and* Old Lady.

　　Bos. So, so, there 's no question but her tech-
iness [4] and most vulturous eating of the apricocks are apparent signs of breeding. — Now ?
　　Old Lady. I am in haste, sir.
　　Bos. There was a young waiting-woman had
a monstrous desire to see the glass-house —— 6
　　Old Lady. Nay, pray, let me go.
　　Bos. And it was only to know what strange
instrument it was should swell up a glass to the
fashion of a woman's belly. 10
　　Old Lady. I will hear no more of the glass-
house. You are still [5] abusing women !
　　Bos. Who ? I ? No ; only, by the way now and
then, mention your frailties. The orange-tree
bears ripe and green fruit and blossoms all [15
together ; and some of you give entertainment
for pure love, but more for more precious reward. The lusty spring smells well ; but droop-

ing autumn tastes well. If we have the same
golden showers that rained in the time of [20
Jupiter the thunderer, you have the same
Danäes still, to hold up their laps to receive
them. Didst thou never study the mathematics ?
　　Old Lady. What 's that, sir ? 25
　　Bos. Why, to know the trick how to make a
many lines meet in one centre. Go, go, give
your foster-daughters good counsel : tell them,
that the devil takes delight to hang at a woman's girdle, like a false rusty watch, that [30
she cannot discern how the time passes.
　　　　　　　　[*Exit* Old Lady.]

[*Enter* ANTONIO, RODERIGO, *and* GRISOLAN.]

　　Ant. Shut up the court-gates.
　　Rod.　　　　Why, sir ? What 's the danger ?
　　Ant. Shut up the posterns presently, and
　　call
All the officers o' th' court.
　　Gris.　　　　　I shall instantly. [*Exit.*]
　　Ant. Who keeps the key o' th' park-gate ?
　　Rod.　　　　　　　Forobosco. 35
　　Ant. Let him bring 't presently.

[*Re-enter* GRISOLAN *with* Servants.]

　　1 Serv. O, gentleman o' th' court, the foulest
　　　treason !
　　Bos. [*Aside.*] If that these apricocks should
　　　be poison'd now,
Without my knowledge ?
　　1 Serv. There was taken even now a Switzer
　　　in the duchess' bed-chamber —— 40
　　2 Serv. A Switzer !
　　1 Serv. With a pistol in his great codpiece.
　　Bos. Ha, ha, ha !
　　1 Serv. The codpiece was the case for 't.
　　2 Serv. There was a cunning traitor. Who
would have search'd his codpiece ? 45
　　1 Serv. True ; if he had kept out of the ladies' chambers. And all the moulds of his buttons were leaden bullets.
　　2 Serv. O wicked cannibal ! A fire-lock in 't
codpiece ! 50
　　1 Serv. 'T was a French plot, upon my life.
　　2 Serv. To see what the devil can do !
　　Ant. [Are] all the officers here ?
　　Servants. We are.
　　Ant. Gentlemen, 55
We have lost much plate you know ; and but
　　this evening
Jewels, to the value of four thousand ducats
Are missing in the duchess' cabinet.
Are the gates shut ?
　　Serv.　　　　Yes.
　　Ant.　　　　　'T is the duchess' pleasure
Each officer be lock'd into his chamber 60
Till the sun-rising ; and to send the keys
Of all their chests and of their outward doors
Into her bed-chamber. She is very sick.
　　Rod. At her pleasure.
　　Ant. She entreats you take 't not ill the in-
　　　nocent 65
Shall be the more approv'd by it.
　　Bos. Gentlemen o' th' wood-yard, where 's
your Switzer now ?

---

[1] Clearly.
[2] Youngster.
[3] A hall in the same palace.
[4] Crossness.
[5] Always.

1 *Serv.* By this hand, 'twas credibly reported
by one o' th' black guard.[1] 70
[*Exeunt all except* ANTONIO *and* DELIO.]
Delio. How fares it with the duchess?
Ant. She's expos'd
Unto the worst of torture, pain and fear.
Deli. Speak to her all happy comfort.
Ant. How I do play the fool with mine own
danger!
You are this night, dear friend, to post to
Rome. 75
My life lies in your service.
Delio. Do not doubt me.
Ant. O, 'tis far from me: and yet fear pre-
sents me
Somewhat that looks like danger.
Delio. Believe it,
'Tis but the shadow of your fear, no more.
How superstitiously we mind our evils! 80
The throwing down salt, or crossing of a hare,
Bleeding at nose, the stumbling of a horse,
Or singing of a cricket, are of power
To daunt whole man in us. Sir, fare you well:
I wish you all the joys of a bless'd father; 85
And, for my faith, lay this unto your breast, —
Old friends, like old swords, still are trusted
best. [*Exit.*]

[*Enter* CARIOLA.]

Cari. Sir, you are the happy father of a son:
Your wife commends him to you.
Ant. Blessed comfort! —
For heaven's sake, tend her well: I'll presently[2]
Go set a figure for 's nativity.[3] *Exeunt.* 91

SCENE III.[4]

[*Enter* BOSOLA, *with a dark lantern.*]

Bos. Sure I did hear a woman shriek: list,
ha!
And the sound came, if I receiv'd it right,
From the duchess' lodgings. There's some
stratagem
In the confining all our courtiers
To their several wards: I must have part of it;
My intelligence will freeze else. List, again! 6
It may be 'twas the melancholy bird,
Best friend of silence and of solitariness,
The owl, that scream'd so. — Ha! Antonio!

[*Enter* ANTONIO *with a candle, his sword
drawn.*]

Ant. I heard some noise. — Who's there?
What art thou? Speak. 10
Bos. Antonio, put not your face nor body
To such a forc'd expression of fear;
I am Bosola, your friend.
Ant. Bosola! —
Aside.] This mole does undermine me. —
Heard you not
A noise even now?
Bos. From whence?
Ant. From the duchess' lodging. 15
Bos. Not I: did you?

[1] The meaner servants. [3] Cast his horoscope.
[2] At once.
[4] The court of the same palace.

Ant. I did, or else I dream'd.
Bos. Let's walk towards it.
Ant. No: it may be 't was
But the rising of the wind.
Bos. Very likely.
Methinks 'tis very cold, and yet you sweat:
You look wildly.
Ant. I have been setting a figure[5] 20
For the duchess' jewels.
Bos. Ah, and how falls your question?
Do you find it radical?[6]
Ant. What's that to you?
'Tis rather to be question'd what design,
When all men were commanded to their lodg-
ings,
Makes you a night-walker.
Bos. In sooth, I'll tell you: 25
Now all the court's asleep, I thought the devil
Had ast to do 'ere: I came to say my prayers;
And do offend you I do so,
You are a fine courtier.
Ant. [*Aside.*] This fellow will undo me, —
You gave the duchess apricocks to-day: 30
Pray heaven they were not poison'd!
Bos. Poison'd! a Spanish fig
For the imputation!
Ant. Traitors are ever confident
Till they are discover'd. There were jewels
stol'n too:
In my conceit, none are to be suspected 35
More than yourself.
Bos. You are a false steward.
Ant. Saucy slave, I'll pull thee up by the
roots.
Bos. May be the ruin will crush you to pieces.
Ant. You are an impudent snake indeed, sir:
Are you scarce warm, and do you show your
sting? 40
You libel[7] well, sir?
Bos. No, sir: copy it out,
And I will set my hand to 't.
Ant. [*Aside.*] My nose bleeds.
One that were superstitious would count
This ominous, when it merely comes by chance.
Two letters, that are wrought here for my
name,[8] 45
Are drown'd in blood!
Mere accident. — For you, sir, I'll take order
I' th' morn you shall be safe. — [*Aside.*] 'Tis
that must colour
Her lying-in. — Sir, this door you pass not:
I do not hold it fit that you come near 50
The duchess' lodgings, till you have quit your-
self. —
[*Aside.*] The great are like the base, nay, they
are the same,
When they seek shameful ways to avoid shame.
Exit.
Bos. Antonio hereabout did drop a paper: —
Some of your help, false friend.[9] — O, here it is.
What's here? a child's nativity calculated! 55
[*Reads.*]
' The duchess was deliver'd of a son, 'tween the

[5] Making an astrological calculation.
[6] Going to the root of the matter.
[7] Write. [8] *I. e.* on his handkerchief.
[9] Addressing the lantern.

hours twelve and one in the night, Anno Dom.
1504.' — that 's this year — '*decimo nono Dec-*
embris,' — that 's this night — '*taken accord-* [60]
ing to the meridian of Malfi,' — that 's our duchess: happy discovery! — '*The lord of the first*
house being combust in the ascendant signifies
short life. and Mars being in a human sign,
joined to the tail of the Dragon, in the eighth [65]
house, doth threaten a violent death. Caetera non
scrutantur.'
Why now 't is most apparent: this precise fellow
Is the duchess' bawd: — I have it to my wish!
This is a parcel of intelligency [2]   70
Our courtiers were cas'd up for: it needs must
follow
That I must be committed on pretence
Of poisoning her; which I 'll endure, and laugh
at.
If one could find the father now! but that
Time will discover. Old Castruccio   75
I' th' morning posts to Rome: by him I 'll send
A letter that shall make her brothers' galls
O'erflow their livers. This was a thrifty [3] way!
Though Lust do mask in ne'er so strange dis-
guise,
She 's oft found witty, but is never wise.   80
                      [*Exit.*]

SCENE IV. [4]

[*Enter*] CARDINAL *and* JULIA.

Card. Sit: thou art my best of wishes. Pri-
thee, tell me
What trick didst thou invent to come to Rome
Without thy husband?
    Julia.   Why, my lord, I told him
I came to visit an old anchorite [5]
Here for devotion.
    Card.   Thou art a witty false one, —   5
I mean, to him.
    Julia.   You have prevail'd with me
Beyond my strongest thoughts; I would not
now
Find you inconstant.
    Card.   Do not put thyself
To such a voluntary torture. which proceeds
Out of your own guilt.
    Julia.   How, my lord!
    Card.   You fear   10
My constancy, because you have approv'd [6]
Those giddy and wild turnings in yourself.
    Julia. Did you e'er find them?
    Card.   Sooth, generally for women,
A man might strive to make glass malleable,
Ere he should make them fixed.
    Julia.   So, my lord.   15
    Card. We had need go borrow that fantastic
glass
Invented by Galileo the Florentine
To view another spacious world i' th' moon,
And look to find a constant woman there.
    Julia. This is very well, my lord.
    Card.   Why do you weep?   20

Are tears your justification? The self-same
tears
Will fall into your husband's bosom, lady,
With a loud protestation that you love him
Above the world. Come, I 'll love you wisely,
That 's jealously; since I am very certain   25
You cannot make me cuckold.
    Julia.   I 'll go home
To my husband.
    Card.   You may thank me, lady,
I have taken you off your melancholy perch,
Bore you upon my fist, and show'd you game,
And let you fly at it. — I pray thee, kiss
me. —   30
When thou wast with thy husband, thou wast
watch'd
Like a tame elephant: — still you are to thank
me: —
Thou hadst only kisses from him and high
feeding;
But what delight was that? 'T was just like
one
That hath a little fing'ring on the lute,   35
Yet cannot tune it · — still you are to thank
me.
    Julia. You told me of a piteous wound i' th'
heart,
And a sick liver, when you woo'd me first,
And spake like one in physic. [7]
    Card.   Who 's that? —

[*Enter* Servant.]

Rest firm for my affection to thee,   40
Lightning moves slow to 't.
    Serv.   Madam, a gentleman
That 's comes post from Malfi, desires to see
you.
    Card. Let him enter: I 'll withdraw. *Exit.*
    Serv.   He says
Your husband, old Castruccio, is come to
Rome,
Most pitifully tir'd with riding post. [*Exit.*]   45

[*Enter* DELIO.]

    Julia. [*Aside.*] Signior Delio! 't is one of my
old suitors.
    Delio. I was bold to come and see you.
    Julia.   Sir, you are welcome.
    Delio. Do you lie here?
    Julia.   Sure, your own experience
Will satisfy you no: our Roman prelates
Do not keep lodging for ladies.
    Delio.   Very well: 50
I have brought you no commendations from
your husband,
For I know none by him.
    Julia.   I hear he 's come to Rome.
    Delio. I never knew man and beast, of a
horse and a knight,
So weary of each other. If he had had a good
back,
He would have undertook to have borne his
horse,   55
His breech was so pitifully sore.
    Julia.   Your laughter
Is my pity.

---

[1] *The rest not considered.*
[2] A piece of news.   [3] Cleverly contrived.
[4] Rome. An apartment in the palace of the Cardinal.
[5] Religious recluse   [6] Experienced.
[7] Sick.

Delio. Lady, I know not whether
You want money, but I have brought you
    some.
Julia. From my husband ?
Delio.   No, from mine own allowance. 60
Julia. I must hear the condition, ere I be
    bound to take it.
Delio. Look on 't, 't is gold ; hath it not a
    fine colour ?
Julia. I have a bird more beautiful.
Delio.   Try the sound on 't.
Julia. A lute-string far exceeds it.
It hath no smell, like cassia or civet ;   65
Nor is it physical,[1] though some fond doctors
Persuade us seethe 't in cullises.[2] I 'll tell you,
This is a creature bred by ——

[*Re-enter* Servant.]

Serv.   Your husband 's come,
Hath deliver'd a letter to the Duke of Ca-
    labria
That, to my thinking, hath put him out of his
    wits.   *Exit.* 70
Julia. Sir, you hear :
Pray, let me know your business and your suit
As briefly as can be.
Delio. With good speed : I would wish you,
At such time as you are non-resident   75
With your husband, my mistress.
Julia. Sir, I 'll go ask my husband if I shall,
And straight return your answer.
Delio.   Very fine !
Is this her wit, or honesty, that speaks thus ?
I heard one say the duke was highly mov'd   80
With a letter sent from Malfi. I do fear
Antonio is betray'd. How fearfully
Shows his ambition now ! Unfortunate for-
    tune !
They pass through whirl-pools, and deep woes
    do shun,
Who the event weigh ere the action 's done.   85

SCENE V.[3]

[*Enter*] CARDINAL *and* FERDINAND *with a letter.*

Ferd. I have this night digg'd up a man-
    drake.[4]
Card.   Say you ?
Ferd. And I am grown mad with 't.
Card.   What 's the prodigy ?
Ferd. Read there,— a sister damn'd : she 's
    loose i' th' hilts ; [5]
Grown a notorious strumpet.
Card.   Speak lower.
Ferd.   Lower !
Rogues do not whisper 't now, but seek to pub-
    lish 't   5
(As servants do the bounty of their lords)
Aloud ; and with a covetous searching eye,
To mark who note them. O, confusion seize
    her !

She hath had most cunning bawds to serve her
    turn,
And more secure conveyances for lust   10
Than towns of garrison for service.
Card.   Is 't possible ?
Can this be certain ?
Ferd.   Rhubarb, O, for rhubarb
To purge this choler ! Here 's the cursed day
To prompt my memory ; and here 't shall stick
Till of her bleeding heart I make a sponge   15
To wipe it out.
Card.   Why do you make yourself
So wild a tempest ?
Ferd.   Would I could be one,
That I might toss her palace 'bout her ears,
Root up her goodly forests, blast her meads,
And lay her general territory as waste   20
As she hath done her honours.
Card.   Shall our blood,
The royal blood of Arragon and Castile,
Be thus attainted ?
Ferd.   Apply desperate physic :
We must not now use balsamum, but fire,
The smarting cupping-glass, for that 's the
    mean   25
To purge infected blood, such blood as hers.
There is a kind of pity in mine eye,—
I 'll give it to my handkercher ; and now 't is
    here,
I 'll bequeath this to her bastard.
Card.   What to do ?
Ferd. Why, to make soft lint for his mother's
    wounds,   30
When I have hew'd her to pieces.
Card.   Curs'd creature !
Unequal nature, to place women's hearts
So far upon the left side ! [6]
Ferd.   Foolish men,
That e'er will trust their honour in a bark
Made of so slight weak bulrush as is woman,   35
Apt every minute to sink it !
Card. Thus ignorance, when it hath pur-
    chas'd honour,
It cannot wield it.
Ferd.   Methinks I see her laughing,—
Excellent hyena ! Talk to me somewhat quickly
Or my imagination will carry me   40
To see her in the shameful act of sin.
Card. With whom ?   [*bargeman.*
Ferd.   Happily with some strong-thigh'd
Or one o' th' wood-yard that can quoit the
    sledge [7]
Or toss the bar, or else some lovely squire
That carries coals up to her privy lodgings.   45
Card. You fly beyond your reason.
Ferd.   Go to, mistress !
'T is not your whore's milk that shall quench
    my wild-fire,
But your whore's blood.
Card. How idly shows this rage, which
    carries you,
As men convey'd by witches through the air,   50
On violent whirlwinds ! This intemperate noise
Fitly resembles deaf men's shrill discourse,

---

[1] Medicinal.   [2] Strong broth.
[3] Another apartment in the same palace.
[4] The mandrake was supposed to give forth shrieks
when uprooted, which drove the hearer mad.
[5] Unchaste.

[6] Supposed to be a sign of folly.
[7] Throw the hammer.

Who talk aloud, thinking all other men
To have their imperfection.
Ferd.   Have not you
My palsy?
Card.   Yes, [but] I can be angry   55
Without this rupture. There is not in nature
A thing that makes man so deform'd, so beastly,
As doth intemperate anger. Chide yourself.
You have divers men who never yet express'd
Their strong desire of rest but by unrest,   60
By vexing of themselves. Come, put yourself
In tune.
Ferd.   So I will only study to seem
The thing I am not. I could kill her now,
In you, or in myself; for I do think
It s some sin in us heaven doth revenge   65
By her.
Card. Are you stark mad?
Ferd.   I would have their bodies
Burnt in a coal-pit with the ventage stopp'd,
That their curs'd smoke might not ascend to
heaven;
Or dip the sheets they lie in in pitch or sulphur, 70
Wrap them in 't, and then light them like a
match;
Or else to-boil [1] their bastard to a cullis,
And give 't his lecherous father to renew
The sin of his back.
Card.   I 'll leave you.
Ferd.   Nay, I have done.
I am confident, had I been damn'd in hell,   75
And should have heard of this, it would have
put me
Into a cold sweat. In, in; I 'll go sleep.
Till I know who leaps my sister, I 'll not stir:
That known, I 'll find scorpions to string my
whips,
And fix her in a general eclipse.   *Exeunt.* 80

ACT III

SCENE I.[2]

[*Enter*] ANTONIO *and* DELIO.

Ant. Our noble friend, my most beloved Delio!
O, you have been a stranger long at court:
Came you along with the Lord Ferdinand?
Delio. I did, sir: and how fares your noble
duchess?
Ant. Right fortunately well: she 's an excel-
lent   5
Feeder of pedigrees; since you last saw her,
She hath had two children more, a son and
daughter.
Delio. Methinks 't was yesterday. Let me
but wink,
And not behold your face, which to mine eye
Is somewhat leaner, verily I should dream   10
It were within this half hour.
Ant. You have not been in law, friend Delio,
Nor in prison, nor a suitor at the court,
Nor begg'd the reversion of some great man's
place,

Nor troubled with an old wife, which doth
make   15
Your time so insensibly hasten.
Delio.   Pray, sir, tell me,
Hath not this news arriv'd yet to the ear
Of the lord cardinal?
Ant.   I fear it hath:
The Lord Ferdinand, that 's newly come to
court,
Doth bear himself right dangerously.
Delio.   Pray, why? 20
Ant. He is so quiet that he seems to sleep
The tempest out, as dormice do in winter.
Those houses that are haunted are most still
Till the devil be up.
Delio.   What say the common people?
Ant. The common rabble do directly say   25
She is a strumpet.
Delio.   And your graver heads
Which would be politic, what censure they?
Ant. They do observe I grow to infinite pur-
chase,[3]
The left hand way; and all suppose the duchess
Would amend it, if she could; for, say they,   30
Great princes, though they grudge their officers
Should have such large and unconfined means
To get wealth under them, will not complain,
Lest thereby they should make them odious
Unto the people. For other obligation   35
Of love or marriage between her and me
They never dream of.
Delio.   The Lord Ferdinand
Is going to bed.

[*Enter* DUCHESS, FERDINAND, *and* Attendants.]

Ferd.   I 'll instantly to bed,
For I am weary.— I am to bespeak
A husband for you.
Duch.   For me, sir! Pray, who is 't? 40
Ferd. The great Count Malatesti.
Duch.   Fie upon him!
A count! He 's a mere stick of sugar-candy;
You may look quite through him. When I
choose
A husband, I will marry for your honour.
Ferd. You shall do well in 't. — How is 't,
worthy Antonio?   45
Duch. But, sir, I am to have private confer-
ence with you
About a scandalous report is spread
Touching mine honour.
Ferd.   Let me be ever deaf to 't:
One of Pasquil's paper-bullets,[4] court-calumny,
A pestilent air, which princes' palaces   50
Are seldom purg'd of. Yet, say that it were true,
I pour it in your bosom, my fix'd love
Would strongly excuse, extenuate, nay, deny
Faults, were they apparent in you. Go, be safe
In your own innocency.
Duch. [*Aside.*]   O bless'd comfort!   55
This deadly air is purg'd.
            Exeunt [DUCHESS,   ANTONIO,
                  DELIO, *and* Attendants.]
Ferd.   Her guilt treads on
Hot-burning coulters.[5]

---

[4] Boil to shreds. (Dyce.) Qq. *to boil.*
[2] Amalfi. An apartment in the palace of the Duchess.

[3] Wealth.   [4] Lampoons.   [5] Ploughshares

[*Enter* Bosola.]

Now, Bosola,
How thrives our intelligence ? [1]
Bos.   Sir, uncertainly:
'T is rumour'd she hath had three bastards, but
By whom we may go read i' th' stars.
Ferd.   Why, some 60
Hold opinion all things are written there.
Bos. Yet, if we could find spectacles to read
them.
I do suspect there hath been some sorcery
Us'd on the duchess.
Ferd.   Sorcery ! to what purpose ?
Bos. To make her dote on some desertless
fellow   65
She shames to acknowledge.
Ferd.   Can your faith give way
To think there 's power in potions or in charms,
To make us love whether we will or no ?
Bos. Most certainly.
Ferd. Away ! these are mere gulleries,[2] hor-
rid things,   70
Invented by some cheating mountebanks
To abuse us. Do you think that herbs or charms
Can force the will ? Some trials have been
made
In this foolish practice, but the ingredients
Were lenitive [3] poisons, such as are of force   75
To make the patient mad ; and straight the witch
Swears by equivocation they are in love.
The witch-craft lies in her rank blood. This
night
I will force confession from her. You told me
You had got, within these two days, a false key 80
Into her bed-chamber.
Bos.   I have.
Ferd.   As I would wish.
Bos. What do you intend to do ?
Ferd.   Can you guess ?
Bos.   No.
Ferd.   Do not ask, then :
He that can compass me, and know my drifts,
May say he hath put a girdle 'bout the world,
And sounded all her quick-sands.
Bos.   I do not   85
Think so.
Ferd. What do you think, then, pray ?
Bos.   That you
Are your own chronicle too much, and grossly
Flatter yourself.
Ferd.   Give me thy hand ; I thank thee :
I never gave pension but to flatterers,
Till I entertained thee. Farewell.   90
That friend a great man's ruin strongly checks,
Who rails into his belief all his defects.
                                        Exeunt.

SCENE II.[4]

Enter Duchess, Antonio, *and* Cariola.

Duch. Bring me the casket hither, and the
glass.—
You get no lodging here to-night, my lord.
Ant. Indeed, I must persuade one.

Duch.   Very good :
I hope in time 't will grow into a custom,
That noblemen shall come with cap and knee •
To purchase a night's lodging of their wives.
Ant. I must lie here.
Duch.   Must ! You are a lord of mis-rule.
Ant. Indeed, my rule is only in the night.
Duch. To what use will you put me ?
Ant.   We 'll sleep together.
Duch. Alas, what pleasure can two lovers find
in sleep ?   10
Cari. My lord, I lie with her often, and I
know
She 'll much disquiet you.
Ant.   See, you are complain'd of.
Cari. For she 's the sprawling'st bedfellow.
Ant. I shall like her the better for that.
Cari. Sir, shall I ask you a question ?   15
Ant. I pray thee, Cariola.
Cari. Wherefore still when you lie with my
lady
Do you rise so early ?
Ant.   Labouring men
Count the clock oft'nest, Cariola,
Are glad when their task 's ended.
Duch. I 'll stop your mouth. [*Kisses him.*] 20
Ant. Nay, that 's but one ; Venus had two
soft doves
To draw her chariot ; I must have another.—
                    [*She kisses him again.*]
When wilt thou marry, Cariola ?
Cari.   Never, my lord.
Ant. O, fie upon this single life ! forgo it.
We read how Daphne, for her peevish [flight,] [5]
Became a fruitless bay-tree ; Syrinx turn'd   26
To the pale empty reed ; Anaxarete
Was frozen into marble : whereas those
Which married, or prov'd kind unto their
friends,
Were by a gracious influence trans-shap'd   30
Into the olive, pomegranate, mulberry,
Became flowers, precious stones, or eminent
stars.
Cari. This is a vain poetry : but I pray you,
tell me,
If there were propos'd me, wisdom, riches, and
beauty,
In three several young men, which should I
choose ?   35
Ant. 'T is a hard question. This was Paris'
case,
And he was blind in 't, and there was a great
cause ;
For how was 't possible he could judge right,
Having three amorous goddesses in view,
And they stark naked ? 'T was a motion   40
Were able to benight the apprehension
Of the severest counsellor of Europe.
Now I look on both your faces so well form'd,
It puts me in mind of a question I would ask.
Cari. What is 't ?
Ant. I do wonder why hard-favour'd ladies,
For the most part, keep worse-favour'd waiting-
women   45
To attend them, and cannot endure fair ones.

---

[1] Spying.   [2] Deceptions.   [3] Soothing.
[4] The bed-chamber of the Duchess in the same.

[5] Qq. read *slight.*

Duch. O, that's soon answer'd.
Did you ever in your life know an ill painter
Desire to have his dwelling next door to the
    shop   50
Of an excellent picture-maker? 'T would dis-
    grace
His face-making, and undo him. I prithee,
When were we so merry? My hair tangles.
    Ant. Pray thee, Cariola, let's steal forth the
    room,
And let her talk to herself: I have divers times
Serv'd her the like, when she hath chaf'd ex-
    tremely.   56
I love to see her angry. Softly, Cariola.
          Exeunt [ANTONIO *and* CARIOLA].
    Duch. Doth not the colour of my hair 'gin to
    change?
When I wax gray, I shall have all the court
Powder their hair with arras,[1] to be like me. 60
You have cause to love me; I ent'red you into
    my heart

          [*Enter* FERDINAND *unseen*.]

Before you would vouchsafe to call for the
    keys.
We shall one day have my brothers take you
    napping.
Methinks his presence, being now in court,
Should make you keep your own bed; but you'll
    say   65
Love mixt with fear is sweetest. I'll assure you,
You shall get no more children till my brothers
Consent to be your gossips. Have you lost your
    tongue?
'T is welcome: 69
For know, whether I am doom'd to live or die,
I can do both like a prince.
    Ferd.   Die, then, quickly.
                   Giving her a poniard.
Virtue, where art thou hid? What hideous
    thing
Is it that doth eclipse thee?
    Duch.   Pray, sir, hear me.
    Ferd. Or is it true thou art but a bare name,
And no essential thing?
    Duch.   Sir ——
    Ferd.   Do not speak. 75
    Duch. No, sir:
I will plant my soul in mine ears, to hear you.
    Ferd. O most imperfect light of human
    reason,
That mak'st [us] so unhappy to foresee
What we can least prevent! Pursue thy wishes,
And glory in them: there's in shame no com-
    fort   81
But to be past all bounds and sense of shame.
    Duch. I pray, sir, hear me: I am married.
    Ferd.   So!
    Duch. Happily, not to your liking: but for
    that,
Alas, your shears do come untimely now   85
To clip the bird's wings that's already flown!
Will you see my husband?
    Ferd.   Yes, if I could change
Eyes with a basilisk.

        [1] Powder of orris-root.

Duch.   Sure, you came hither
By his confederacy.
    Ferd.   The howling of a wolf   90
Is music to thee, screech-owl: prithee, peace.—
Whate'er thou art that hast enjoy'd my sister,
For I am sure thou hear'st me, for thine own
    sake
Let me not know thee. I came hither prepar'd
To work thy discovery; yet am now persuaded
It would beget such violent effects   95
As would damn us both. I would not for ten
    millions
I had beheld thee: therefore use all means
I never may have knowledge of thy name;
Enjoy thy lust still, and a wretched life,
On that condition. — And for thee, vild woman,
If thou do wish thy lecher may grow old   101
In thy embracements, I would have thee build
Such a room for him as our anchorites
To holier use inhabit. Let not the sun
Shine on him till he's dead; let dogs and mon-
    keys   105
Only converse with him, and such dumb things
To whom nature denies use to sound his name;
Do not keep a paraquito, lest she learn it;
If thou do love him, cut out thine own tongue,
Lest it bewray him.
    Duch.   Why might not I marry?   110
I have not gone about in this to create
Any new world or custom.
    Ferd.   Thou art undone;
And thou hast ta'en that massy sheet of lead
That hid thy husband's bones, and folded it
About my heart.
    Duch.   Mine bleeds for't.
    Ferd.   Thine! thy heart! 115
What should I name't, unless a hollow bullet
Fill'd with unquenchable wild-fire?
    Duch.   You are in this
Too strict; and were you not my princely
    brother,
I would say, too wilful: my reputation
Is safe.
    Ferd. Dost thou know what reputation is?
I'll tell thee, — to small purpose, since th' in-
    struction   121
Comes now too late.
Upon a time Reputation, Love, and Death,
Would travel o'er the world; and it was con-
    cluded
That they should part, and take three several
    ways.   125
Death told them, they should find him in great
    battles,
Or cities plagu'd with plagues; Love gives
    them counsel
To inquire for him 'mongst unambitious shep-
    herds,
Where dowries were not talk'd of and some-
    times
'Mongst quiet kindred that had nothing left 130
By their dead parents: 'Stay,' quoth Reputa-
    tion,
'Do not forsake me; for it is my nature,
If once I part from any man I meet,
I am never found again.' And so for you:
You have shook hands with Reputation,   135

And made him invisible. So, fare you well:
I will never see you more.
   Duch.   Why should only I,
Of all the other princes of the world,
Be cas'd up, like a holy relic ? I have youth
And a little beauty.
   Ferd.   So you have some virgins 140
That are witches. I will never see thee more.
                       Exit.

Re-enter ANTONIO *with a pistol,* [*and* CARIOLA.]

   Duch. You saw this apparition ?
   Ant.   Yes : we are
Betray'd. How came he hither ? I should turn
This to thee, for that.
   Cari.   Pray, sir, do ; and when
That you have cleft my heart, you shall read
     there   145
Mine innocence.
   Duch.   That gallery gave him entrance.
   Ant. I would this terrible thing would come
again,
That, standing on my guard, I might relate
My warrantable love. —
             (*She shows the poniard.*)
              Ha ! what means this ?
   Duch. He left this with me,
   Ant.   And it seems did wish 150
You would use it on yourself.
   Duch.   His action seem'd
To intend so much.
   Ant.   This hath a handle to 't,
As well as a point : turn it towards him, and
So fasten the keen edge in his rank gall.
                 [*Knocking within.*]
How now ! who knocks ? More earthquakes ?
   Duch.   I stand 155
As if a mine beneath my feet were ready
To be blown up.
   Cari.   'T is Bosola.
   Duch.   Away !
O misery ! methinks unjust actions
Should wear these masks and curtains, and not
we.
You must instantly part hence : I have fashion'd
   it already.   *Exit* ANTONIO. 160

[*Enter* BOSOLA.]

   Bos. The duke your brother is ta'en up in a
    whirlwind ;
Hath took horse, and 's rid post to Rome.
   Duch.   So late ?
   Bos. He told me, as he mounted into th'
    saddle,
You were undone.
   Duch.   Indeed, I am very near it.
   Bos. What 's the matter ?   165
   Duch. Antonio, the master of our household,
Hath dealt so falsely with me in 's accounts.
My brother stood engag'd with me for money
Ta'en up of certain Neapolitan Jews,
And Antonio lets the bonds be forfeit.   170
   Bos. Strange ! — [*Aside.*] This is cunning.
   Duch.   And hereupon
My brother's bills at Naples are protested
Against. — Call up our officers.
   Bos.   I shall. *Exit.*

[*Re-enter* ANTONIO.]

   Duch. The place that you must fly to is An-
    cona :
Hire a house there ; I 'll send after you   175
My treasure and my jewels. Our weak safety
Runs upon enginous wheels : [1] short syllables
Must stand for periods. I must now accuse you
Of such a feigned crime as Tasso calls
Magnanima menzogna, a noble lie,   180
'Cause it must shield our honours. — Hark ! they
are coming.

[*Re-enter* BOSOLA *and* Officers.]

   Ant. Will your grace hear me ?
   Duch. I have got well by you ; you have
    yielded me
A million of loss : I am like to inherit
The people's curses for your stewardship.   185
You had the trick in audit-time to be sick,
Till I had sign'd your quietus ; [2] and that cur'd
    you
Without help of a doctor. — Gentlemen,
I would have this man be an example to you
    all ;
So shall you hold my favour ; I pray, let him ;
For h'as done that, alas, you would not think
    of,   191
And, because I intend to be rid of him,
I mean not to publish. — Use your fortune else-
    where.
   Ant. I am strongly arm'd to brook my over-
    throw,
As commonly men bear with a hard year.   195
I will not blame the cause on 't ; but do think
The necessity of my malevolent star
Procures this, not her humour. O, the incon-
    stant
And rotten ground of service ! You may see,
'T is even like him, that in a winter night,   200
Takes a long slumber o'er a dying fire,
A-loth to part from 't ; yet parts thence as cold
As when he first sat down.
   Duch.   We do confiscate,
Towards the satisfying of your accounts,
All that you have.
   Ant.   I am all yours ; and 't is very fit 205
All mine should be so.
   Duch.   So, sir, you have your pass.
   Ant. You may see, gentlemen, what 't is to
    serve
A prince with body and soul.   *Exit.*
   Bos. Here 's an example for extortion : what
moisture is drawn out of the sea, when foul [210
weather comes, pours down, and runs into the
sea again.
   Duch. I would know what are your opinions
Of this Antonio.   214
   2 Off. He could not abide to see a pig's head
gaping : I thought your grace would find him a
Jew.
   3 Off. I would you had been his officer, for
your own sake.
   4 Off. You would have had more money. 220

[1] Wheels of craft.
[2] Certificate that the books were found correct.

1 *Off.* He stopp'd his ears with black wool, and to those came to him for money said he was thick of hearing.

2 *Off.* Some said he was an hermaphrodite, for he could not abide a woman.   225

4 *Off.* How scurvy proud he would look when the treasury was full ! Well, let him go.

1 *Off.* Yes, and the chippings of the buttery fly after him, to scour his gold chain.[1]   229
Duch. Leave us. —— *Exeunt* [Officers].
What do you think of these ?

Bos. That these are rogues that in 's prosperity,
But to have waited on his fortune, could have wish'd
His dirty stirrup riveted through their noses,
And follow'd after 's mule, like a bear in a ring ;   235
Would have prostituted their daughters to his lust ;
Made their first-born intelligencers ; [2] thought none happy
But such as were born under his blest planet,
And wore his livery : and do these lice drop off now ?
Well, never look to have the like again :   240
He hath left a sort [3] of flatt'ring rogues behind him ;
Their doom must follow. Princes pay flatterers
In their own money : flatterers dissemble their vices,
And they dissemble their lies ; that 's justice.
Alas, poor gentleman !   245
Duch. Poor ! he hath amply fill'd his coffers.
Bos. Sure, he was too honest. Pluto,[4] the god of riches,
When he 's sent by Jupiter to any man,
He goes limping, to signify that wealth
That comes on God's name comes slowly ; but when he 's sent   250
On the devil's errand, he rides post and comes in by scuttles.[5]
Let me show you what a most unvalu'd jewel
You have in a wanton humour thrown away,
To bless the man shall find him. He was an excellent
Courtier and most faithful ; a soldier that thought it   255
As beastly to know his own value too little
As devilish to acknowledge it too much.
Both his virtue and form deserv'd a far better fortune :
His discourse rather delighted to judge itself than show itself :
His breast was fill'd with all perfection,   260
And yet it seem'd a private whisp'ring-room,
It made so little noise of 't.
Duch. But he was basely descended.
Bos. Will you make yourself a mercenary herald,
Rather to examine men's pedigrees than virtues ?   265
You shall want [6] him :
For know an honest statesman to a prince

Is like a cedar planted by a spring ;
The spring bathes the tree's root, the grateful tree
Rewards it with his shadow : you have not done so.   270
I would sooner swim to the Bermoothes on
Two politicians' rotten bladders, tied
Together with an intelligencer's heart-string,
Than depend on so changeable a prince's favour.
Fare thee well, Antonio ! Since the malice of the world   275
Would needs down with thee, it cannot be said yet
That any ill happen'd unto thee, considering thy fall
Was accompanied with virtue.
Duch. O, you render me excellent music !
Bos.   Say you ?
Duch. This good one that you speak of is my husband.   280
Bos. Do I not dream ? Can this ambitious age
Have so much goodness in 't as to prefer
A man merely for worth, without these shadows
Of wealth and painted honours ? Possible ?
Duch. I have had three children by him.
Bos.   Fortunate lady ! 285
For you have made your private nuptial bed
The humble and fair seminary of peace,
No question but : many an unbenefic'd scholar
Shall pray for you for this deed, and rejoice
That some preferment in the world can yet   290
Arise from merit. The virgins of your land
That have no dowries shall hope your example
Will raise them to rich husbands. Should you want
Soldiers, 't would make the very Turks and Moors
Turn Christians, and serve you for this act.   295
Last, the neglected poets of your time,
In honour of this trophy of a man,
Rais'd by that curious engine, your white hand,
Shall thank you in your grave for 't, and make that
More reverend than all the cabinets   300
Of living princes,
His fame shall likewise flow from many a pen,
When heralds shall want coats to sell to men.
Duch. As I taste comfort in this friendly speech,
So would I find concealment.   305
Bos. O, the secret of my prince,
Which I will wear on th' inside of my heart !
Duch. You shall take charge of all my coin and jewels,
And follow him ; for he retires himself
To Ancona.
Bos.   So.
Duch.   Whither, within few days, 310
I mean to follow thee.
Bos.   Let me think :
I would wish your grace to feign a pilgrimage
To our Lady of Loretto, scarce seven leagues
From fair Ancona ; so may you depart
Your country with more honour, and your flight

---

[1] The badge of a steward.   [4] For *Plutus.*
[2] Spies.   [5] Quick steps.
[3] Lot.   [6] Miss.

Will seem a princely progress, retaining   316
Your usual train about you.
  Duch.   Sir, your direction
Shall lead me by the hand.
  Cari.   In my opinion,
She were better progress to the baths at Lucca,
Or go visit the Spa   320
In Germany ; for, if you will believe me,
I do not like this jesting with religion,
This feigned pilgrimage.
  Duch. Thou art a superstitious fool :
Prepare us instantly for our departure.   325
Past sorrows, let us moderately lament them,
For those to come, seek wisely to prevent them.
        [*Exeunt* DUCHESS *and* CARIOLA.]
  Bos. A politician is the devil's quilted anvil ;
He fashions all sins on him, and the blows
Are never heard : he may work in a lady's
    chamber,   330
As here for proof. What rests¹ but I reveal
All to my lord ? O, this base quality²
Of intelligencer ! Why, every quality i' th'
    world
Prefers but gain or commendation :
Now, for this act I am certain to be rais'd,   335
And men that paint weeds to the life are
    prais'd.   *Exit.*

SCENE III.³

[*Enter*] CARDINAL, FERDINAND, MALATESTI,
    PESCARA, DELIO, *and* SILVIO.

  Card. Must we turn soldier, then ?
  Mal.   The emperor,
Hearing your worth that way, ere you attain'd
This reverend garment, joins you in commission
With the right fortunate soldier the Marquis of
    Pescara,
And the famous Lannoy.
  Card.   He that had the honour   5
Of taking the French king prisoner ?
  Mal.   The same.
Here 's a plot drawn for a new fortification
At Naples.
  Ferd. This great Count Malatesti, I perceive,
Hath got employment ?
  Delio.   No employment, my lord ;
A marginal note in the muster-book that he
    is   10
A voluntary lord.
  Ferd.   He 's no soldier ?
  Delio. He has worn gun-powder in 's hollow
    tooth for the tooth-ache.
  Sil. He comes to the leaguer with a full in-
    tent
To eat fresh beef and garlic, means to stay
Till the scent be gone, and straight return to
    court.   15
  Delio. He hath read all the late service
As the City Chronicle relates it ;
And keeps two pewterers going, only to express
Battles in model.
  Sil.   Then he 'll fight by the book.
  Delio. By the almanac, I think,   20

To choose good days and shun the critical ;
That 's his mistress' scarf.
  Sil.   Yes, he protests
He would do much for that taffeta.
  Delio. I think he would run away from a
    battle,
To save it from taking prisoner.
  Sil.   He is horribly afraid   25
Gun-powder will spoil the perfume on 't.
  Delio. I saw a Dutchman break his pate
    once
For calling him a pot-gun ; he made his head
Have a bore in 't like a musket.
  Sil. I would he had made a touch-hole to 't.   30
He is indeed a guarded sumpter-cloth,⁴
Only for the remove of the court.

[*Enter* BOSOLA.]

  Pes. Bosola arriv'd ! What should be the
    business ?
Some falling-out among the cardinals.
These factions amongst great men, they are
    like   35
Foxes, when their heads are divided,
They carry fire in their tails, and all the country
About them goes to wrack for 't.
  Sil.   What 's that Bosola ?
  Delio. I knew him in Padua, — a fantastical
scholar, like such who study to know how many
knots was in Hercules' club, of what colour [41
Achilles' beard was, or whether Hector were
not troubled with the tooth-ache. He hath
studied himself half blear-ey'd to know the
true symmetry of Caesar's nose by a shoeing- [45
horn ; and this he did to gain the name of a
speculative man.
  Pes. Mark Prince Ferdinand :
A very salamander lives in 's eye,
To mock the eager violence of fire.   50
  Sil. That cardinal hath made more bad faces
with his oppression than ever Michael Angelo
made good ones. He lifts up 's nose, like a foul
porpoise before a storm.
  Pes. The Lord Ferdinand laughs.
  Delio.   Like a deadly cannon   55
That lightens ere it smokes.
  Pes. These are your true pangs of death,
The pangs of life, that struggle with great
    statesmen.
  Delio. In such a deformed silence witches
    whisper their charms.
  Card. Doth she make religion her riding-
    hood   60
To keep her from the sun and tempest ?
  Ferd. That, that damns her. Methinks her
    fault and beauty,
Blended together, show like leprosy,
The whiter the fouler. I make it a question
Whether her beggarly brats were ever chris-
    t'ned.   65
  Card. I will instantly solicit the state of An-
    cona
To have them banish'd.
  Ferd.   You are for Loretto :

---

¹ Remains.   ² Profession.
³ An apartment in the Cardinal's palace at Rome.

⁴ A decorated horse-cloth, used only when the court
is traveling.

I shall not be at your ceremony, fare you well —
Write to the Duke of Malfi, my young nephew,
She had by her first husband, and acquaint
him   70
With 's mother's honesty.
  Bos.   I will.
  Ferd.   Antonio !
A slave that only smell'd of ink and counters,
And nev'r in 's life look'd like a gentleman,
But in the audit-time. — Go, go presently,
Draw me out an hundred and fifty of our
horse,   75
And meet me at the foot-bridge.   *Exeunt.*

SCENE IV.

[*Enter*] Two Pilgrims *to the Shrine of our* Lady
of Loretto.

  1 Pil. I have not seen a goodlier shrine than
this ;
Yet I have visited many.
  2 Pil.   The Cardinal of Arragon
Is this day to resign his cardinal's hat ;
His sister duchess likewise is arriv'd
To pay her vow of pilgrimage. I expect   5
A noble ceremony.
  1 Pil.   No question. — They come.
   [*Here the ceremony of the Cardinal's
   instalment in the habit of a soldier perform'd in delivering up
   his cross, hat, robes and ring at
   the shrine, and investing him with
   sword, helmet, shield, and spurs.
   Then* ANTONIO, *the* DUCHESS *and
   their children, having presented
   themselves at the shrine, are, by a
   form of banishment in dumb-show
   expressed towards them by the*
   CARDINAL *and the state of Ancona, banished : during all which
   ceremony, this ditty is sung, to
   very solemn music, by divers
   church-men ; and then exeunt* [*all
   except the* Two Pilgrims].

Arms and honours deck thy story,[1]
To thy fame's eternal glory !
Adverse fortune ever fly thee ;
No disastrous fate come nigh thee !   10
I alone will sing thy praises,
Whom to honour virtue raises,
And thy study, that divine is,
Bent to martial discipline is,
Lay aside all those robes lie by thee ;   15
Crown thy arts with arms, they 'll beautify thee.

O worthy of worthiest name, adorn'd in this manner,
Lead bravely thy forces on under war's warlike banner !
O, mayst thou prove fortunate in all martial courses !
Guide thou still by skill in arts and forces !   20
Victory attend thee nigh, whilst fame sings loud thy
   powers;
Triumphant conquest crown thy head, and blessings
   pour down showers !

  1 Pil. Here 's a strange turn of state ! who
would have thought
So great a lady would have match'd herself

---

[1] The first quarto has in the margin : " The author
disclaims this ditty to be his."

Unto so mean a person ? Yet the cardinal   25
Bears himself much too cruel.
  2 Pil.   They are banish'd.
  1 Pil. But I would ask what power hath this
state
Of Ancona to determine of a free prince ?
  2 Pil. They are a free state, sir, and her
brother show'd
How that the Pope, fore-hearing of her looseness,   30
Hath seiz'd into th' protection of the church
The dukedom which she held as dowager.
  1 Pil. But by what justice ?
  2 Pil.   Sure, I think by none,
Only her brother's instigation.
  1 Pil. What was it with such violence he
took   35
Off from her finger ?
  2 Pil.   'T was her wedding-ring ;
Which he vow'd shortly he would sacrifice
To his revenge.
  1 Pil.   Alas, Antonio !
If that a man be thrust into a well,   39
No matter who sets hand to 't, his own weight
Will bring him sooner to th' bottom. Come,
let 's hence.
Fortune makes this conclusion general,
All things do help th' unhappy man to fall.
                        Exeunt.

SCENE V.[2]

[*Enter*] DUCHESS, ANTONIO, Children, CARI-
OLA, *and* Servants.

  Duch. Banish'd Ancona !
  Ant.   Yes, you see what power
Lightens in great men's breath.
  Duch.   Is all our train
Shrunk to this poor remainder ?
  Ant.   These poor men,
Which have got little in your service, vow
To take your fortune : but your wiser bunt-
tings,[3]   5
Now they are fledg'd, are gone.
  Duch.   They have done wisely.
This puts me in mind of death : physicians
thus,
With their hands full of money, use to give o'er
Their patients.
  Ant.   Right the fashion of the world :
From decay'd fortunes every flatterer shrinks ;
Men cease to build where the foundation sinks.
  Duch. I had a very strange dream to-night.
  Ant.   What was 't ?
  Duch. Methought I wore my coronet of
state,
And on a sudden all the diamonds
Were chang'd to pearls.
  Ant.   My interpretation   15
Is, you 'll weep shortly ; for to me the pearls
Do signify your tears.
  Duch.   The birds, that live i' th' field
On the wild benefit of nature, live
Happier than we : for they may choose their
mates,
And carol their sweet pleasures to the spring.   20

---

[2] Near Loretto.   [3] Small birds.

[*Enter* Bosola *with a letter.*]

Bos. You are happily o'erta'en.
Duch.   From my brother?
Bos. Yes, from the Lord Ferdinand your
    brother
All love and safety.
Duch.   Thou dost blanch mischief,
Would'st make it white. See, see, like to
    calm weather
At sea before a tempest, false hearts speak
    fair   25
To those they intend most mischief. [*Reads.*]
" Send Antonio to me ; I want his head in a
    business."
A politic equivocation !
He doth not want your counsel, but your head;
That is, he cannot sleep till you be dead.   30
And here 's another pitfall that 's strew'd o'er
With roses ; mark it, 't is a cunning one:
                                       [*Reads.*]
" I stand engaged for your husband for several
debts at Naples : let not that trouble him ; I
had rather have his heart than his money." —
And I believe so too.
Bos.   What do you believe ? 36
Duch. That he so much distrusts my hus-
    band's love,
He will by no means believe his heart is with him
Until he see it : the devil is not cunning enough
To circumvent us in riddles.   40
Bos. Will you reject that noble and free
    league
Of amity and love which I present you ?
Duch. Their league is like that of some poli-
    tic kings,
Only to make themselves of strength and
    power
To be our after-ruin : tell them so.   45
Bos. And what from you ?
Ant.   Thus tell him ; I will not come.
Bos. And what of this ?
Ant.   My brothers have dispers'd
Bloodhounds abroad ; which till I hear are
    muzzl'd,
No truce, though hatch'd with ne'er such poli-
    tic skill,
Is safe, that hangs upon our enemies' will.   50
I 'll not come at them.
Bos.   This proclaims your breeding.
Every small thing draws a base mind to fear
As the adamant draws iron. Fare you well, sir ;
You shall shortly hear from 's.   *Exit.*
Duch.   I suspect some ambush ;
Therefore by all my love I do conjure you   55
To take your eldest son, and fly towards Milan,
Let us not venture all this poor remainder
In one unlucky bottom.
Ant.   You counsel safely.
Best of my life, farewell. Since we must part,
Heaven hath a hand in 't ; but no otherwise 60
Than as some curious artist takes in sunder
A clock or watch, when it is out of frame,
To bring 't in better order.
Duch. I know not which is best,
To see you dead, or part with you. Farewell,
    boy :   65

Thou art happy that thou hast not understand-
    ing
To know thy misery ; for all our wit
And reading brings us to a truer sense
Of sorrow. — In the eternal church, sir,
I do hope we shall not part thus.
Ant.   O, be of comfort !   70
Make patience a noble fortitude,
And think not how unkindly we are us 'd :
Man, like to cassia, is prov'd best, being bruis'd.
Duch. Must I, like to a slave-born Russian,
Account it praise to suffer tyranny ?   75
And yet, O heaven, thy heavy hand is in 't !
I have seen my little boy oft scourge his top,
And compar'd myself to 't : naught made me
    e'er
Go right but heaven's scourge-stick.
Ant.   Do not weep :
Heaven fashion'd us of nothing ; and we strive
To bring ourselves to nothing. — Farewell,
    Cariola,   81
And thy sweet armful. — If I do never see thee
    more,
Be a good mother to your little ones,
And save them from the tiger : fare you well.
Duch. Let me look upon you once more, for
    that speech   85
Came from a dying father. Your kiss is colder
Than that I have seen an holy anchorite
Give to a dead man's skull.
Ant. My heart is turn'd to a heavy lump of
    lead,
With which I sound my danger : fare you well.
        Exeunt [Antonio *and his son*].
Duch. My laurel is all withered.   91
Cari. Look, madam, what a troop of armed
    men
Make toward us !

Re-enter Bosola [*visarded,*] *with a Guard.*

Duch.   O, they are very welcome:
When Fortune's wheel is over-charg'd with
    princes,
The weight makes it move swift : I would have
    my ruin   95
Be sudden. — I am your adventure, am I not ?
Bos. You are : you must see your husband no
    more.
Duch. What devil art thou that counterfeit'st
    heaven's thunder ?
Bos. Is that terrible ? I would have you tell
    me whether
Is that note worse that frights the silly birds 100
Out of the corn, or that which doth allure them
To the nets ? You have heark'ned to the last
    too much.
Duch. O misery ! like to a rusty o'ercharg'd
    cannon,
Shall I never fly in pieces ? Come, to what
    prison ?
Bos. To none.
Duch.   Whither, then ?
Bos.   To your palace.
Duch.   I have heard   105
That Charon's boat serves to convey all o'er
The dismal lake, but brings none back again.
Bos. **Your brothers mean you safety and pity.**

Duch.   Pity !
With such a pity men preserve alive
Pheasants and quails, when they are not fat
     enough   110
To be eaten.
     Bos.   These are your children ?
     Duch.   Yes.
     Bos.   Can they prattle ?
     Duch. No :
But I intend, since they were born accurs'd,
Curses shall be their first language.
     Bos.   Fie, madam !
Forget this base, low fellow ——
     Duch.   Were I a man, 115
I 'd beat that counterfeit face [1] into thy other.
     Bos. One of no birth.
     Duch.   Say that he was born mean,
Man is most happy when 's own actions
Be arguments and examples of his virtue.
     Bos. A barren, beggarly virtue.   120
     Duch. I prithee, who is greatest ? Can you
     tell ?
Sad tales befit my woe : I 'll tell you one.
A salmon, as she swam unto the sea,
Met with a dog-fish, who encounters her
With this rough language ; ' Why art thou so
     bold   125
To mix thyself with our high state of floods,
Being no eminent courtier, but one
That for the calmest and fresh time o' th'
     year
Dost live in shallow rivers, rank'st thyself
With silly smelts and shrimps ? And darest
     thou   130
Pass by our dog-ship without reverence ? '
' O,' quoth the salmon, ' sister, be at peace :
Thank Jupiter we both have pass'd the net !
Our value never can be truly known,
Till in the fisher's basket we be shown :   135
I' th' market then my price may be the higher,
Even when I am nearest to the cook and
     fire.'
So to great men the moral may be stretched ;
Men oft are valu'd high, when they 're most
     wretched. —
But come, whither you please. I am arm'd
     'gainst misery ;   140
Bent to all sways of the oppressor's will.
There 's no deep valley but near some great
     hill.   *Exeunt.*

ACT IV

Scene I.[2]

[Enter] Ferdinand *and* Bosola.

Ferd. How doth our sister duchess bear her-
     self
In her imprisonment ?
     Bos.   Nobly : I 'll describe her.
She 's sad as one long us'd to 't, and she seems
Rather to welcome the end of misery
Than shun it ; a behaviour so noble   5
As gives a majesty to adversity :

[1] His vizard.
[2] Amalfi. An apartment in the palace of the Duchess.

You may discern the shape of loveliness
More perfect in her tears than in her smiles :
She will muse four hours together ; and her
     silence,
Methinks, expresseth more than if she spake. 10
     Ferd. Her melancholy seems to be fortified
With a strange disdain.
     Bos.   'T is so ; and this restraint,
Like English mastives that grow fierce with ty-
     ing,
Makes her too passionately apprehend
Those pleasures she is kept from.
     Ferd.   Curse upon her ! 15
I will no longer study in the book
Of another's heart. Inform her what I told
     you.   *Exit.*

[*Enter* Duchess *and* Attendants.]

     Bos. All comfort to your grace !
     Duch.   I will have none.
Pray thee, why dost thou wrap thy poison'd
     pills
In gold and sugar ?   20
     Bos. Your elder brother, the Lord Ferdi-
     nand,
Is come to visit you, and sends you word,
'Cause once he rashly made a solemn vow
Never to see you more, he comes i' th' night ;
And prays you gently neither torch nor taper 25
Shine in your chamber. He will kiss your hand,
And reconcile himself ; but for his vow
He dares not see you.
     Duch.   At his pleasure. —
Take hence the lights. — He 's come.

     [*Exeunt* Attendants *with lights.*]

     [*Enter* Ferdinand.]

     Ferd.   Where are you ?
     Duch.   Here, sir.
     Ferd. This darkness suits you well.
     Duch.   I would ask you pardon. 30
     Ferd. You have it ;
For I account it the honorabl'st revenge,
Where I may kill, to pardon. — Where are your
     cubs ?
     Duch. Whom ?
     Ferd.   Call them your children ;
For though our national law distinguish bas-
     tards   35
From true legitimate issue, compassionate na-
     ture
Makes them all equal.
     Duch.   Do you visit me for this ?
You violate a sacrament o' th' church
Shall make you howl in hell for 't.
     Ferd.   It had been well 30
Could you have liv'd thus always ; for, indeed,
You were too much i' th' light : — but no more ;
I come to seal my peace with you. Here 's a
     hand   *Gives her a dead man's hand.*
To which you have vow'd much love ; the ring
     upon 't
You gave.
     Duch. I affectionately kiss it.
     Ferd. Pray, do, and bury the print of it in
     your heart.   45
I will leave this ring with you for a love-token ;

And the hand as sure as the ring ; and do not doubt
But you shall have the heart too.　When you need a friend,
Send it to him that ow'd it ; you shall see
Whether he can aid you.
　　Duch.　　　　　　　You are very cold : 50
I fear you are not well after your travel. —
Ha ! lights ! —— O, horrible !
　　Ferd.　　Let her have lights enough. *Exit.*
　　Duch. What witchcraft doth he practise, that he hath left
A dead man's hand here ?
　　　　　Here is discover'd, behind a traverse,[1]
　　　　　the artificial figures of ANTONIO
　　　　　and his children, appearing as if
　　　　　they were dead.
　　Bos. Look you, here 's the piece from which 't was ta'en.　　55
He doth present you this sad spectacle,
That, now you know directly they are dead,
Hereafter you may wisely cease to grieve
For that which cannot be recovered.
　　Duch. There is not between heaven and earth one wish　60
I stay for after this. It wastes me more
Than ware 't my picture, fashion'd out of wax,
Stuck with a magical needle, and then buried
In some foul dung hill ; and yon 's an excellent property
For a tyrant, which I would account mercy.
　　Bos.　　　　　　What 's that ? 65
　　Duch. If they would bind me to that lifeless trunk,
And let me freeze to death.
　　Bos.　　　　Come, you must live.
　　Duch. That 's the greatest torture souls feel in hell,
In hell, that they must live, and cannot die.
Portia,[2] I 'll new kindle thy coals again,　70
And revive the rare and almost dead example
Of a loving wife.
　　Bos.　　　O, fie ! despair ? Remember
You are a Christian.
　　Duch.　　　The church enjoins fasting :
I 'll starve myself to death.
　　Bos.　　　Leave this vain sorrow.
Things being at the worst begin to mend : the bee　75
When he hath shot his sting into your hand,
May then play with your eye-lid.
　　Duch.　　　Good comfortable fellow,
Persuade a wretch that 's broke upon the wheel
To have all his bones new set ; entreat him live
To be executed again. Who must despatch me ?
I account this world a tedious theatre,　81
For I do play a part in 't 'gainst my will.
　　Bos. Come, be of comfort ; I will save your life.
　　Duch. Indeed, I have not leisure to tend so small a business.
　　Bos. Now, by my life, I pity you.
　　Duch.　　　Thou art a fool, then,　85
To waste thy pity on a thing so wretched

As cannot pity itself. I am full of daggers.
Puff, let me blow these vipers from me.

　　　　　　[*Enter* Servant.]

What are you ?
　　Serv.　　One that wishes you long life.
　　Duch. I would thou wert hang'd for the horrible curse　90
Thou hast given me : I shall shortly grow one
Of the miracles of pity. I 'll go pray ; —
　　　　　　　　　　　　[*Exit Serv.*
No, I 'll go curse.
　　Bos.　　　　O, fie !
　　Duch.　　　　I could curse the stars —
　　Bos.　　　　　　　O, fearful !
　　Duch. And those three smiling seasons of the year
Into a Russian winter ; nay, the world　95
To its first chaos.
　　Bos.　　Look you, the stars shine still.
　　Duch. O, but you must
Remember, my curse hath a great way to go. —
Plagues, that make lanes through largest families,
Consume them ! —
　　Bos.　　　Fie, lady !
　　Duch.　　　Let them, like tyrants,　100
Never be remembered but for the ill they have done ;
Let all the zealous prayers of mortified
Churchmen forget them ! —
　　Bos.　　　　O, uncharitable !
　　Duch. Let heaven a little while cease crowning martyrs,
To punish them ! —　105
Go, howl them this, and say, I long to bleed :
It is some mercy when men kill with speed.
　　　　　　　　　　　　　　　　Exit.

　　　　　　[*Re-enter* FERDINAND.]

　　Ferd. Excellent, as I would wish ; she 's plagu'd in art.[3]
These presentations are but fram'd in wax
By the curious master in that quality,[4]　110
Vincentio Lauriola, and she takes them
For true substantial bodies.
　　Bos.　　　Why do you do this ?
　　Ferd. To bring her to despair.
　　Bos.　　　　Faith, end here,
And go no farther in your cruelty :
Send her a penitential garment to put on　115
Next to her delicate skin, and furnish her
With beads and prayer-books.
　　Ferd.　　Damn her ! that body of hers,
While that my blood ran pure in 't, was more worth
Than that which thou wouldst comfort, call'd a soul.　119
I will send her masques of common courtesans,
Have her meat serv'd up by bawds and ruffians,
And, 'cause she 'll needs be mad, I am resolv'd
To move forth the common hospital
All the mad-folk, and place them near her lodging ;

---

[1] Curtain.
[2] The wife of Brutus, who died by swallowing fire.
[3] By artificial means.　　[4] Profession.

There let them practise together, sing and
    dance,   125
And act their gambols to the full o' th' moon:
If she can sleep the better for it, let her.
Your work is almost ended.

Bos.   Must I see her again ?

Ferd. Yes.

Bos.   Never.

Ferd.   You must.

Bos.   Never in mine own shape;
That 's forfeited by my intelligence [1]   130
And this last cruel lie: when you send me next,
The business shall be comfort.

Ferd.   Very likely,
Thy pity is nothing of kin to thee. Antonio
Lurks about Milan: thou shalt shortly thither,
To feed a fire as great as my revenge,   135
Which nev'r will slack till it hath spent his
    fuel:
Intemperate agues make physicians cruel.

                       Exeunt.

        [SCENE II.] [2]

     Enter DUCHESS *and* CARIOLA.

Duch. What hideous noise was that ?

Cari.   'T is the wild consort [3]
Of madmen, lady, which your tyrant brother
Hath plac'd about your lodging. This tyranny,
I think, was never practis'd till this hour.

Duch. Indeed, I thank him. Nothing but
    noise and folly   5
Can keep me in my right wits; whereas reason
And silence make me stark mad. Sit down ;
Discourse to me some dismal tragedy.

Cari. O, 't will increase your melancholy !

Duch.   Thou art deceiv'd :
To hear of greater grief would lessen mine.   10
This is a prison ?

Cari.   Yes, but you shall live
To shake this durance off.

Duch.   Thou art a fool :
The robin-red-breast and the nightingale
Never live long in cages.

Cari.   Pray, dry your eyes.
What think you of, madam ?

Duch.   Of nothing ;   15
When I muse thus, I sleep.

Cari. Like a madman, with your eyes open ?

Duch. Dost thou think we shall know one
    another
In th' other world ?

Cari.   Yes, out of question.

Duch. O, that it were possible we might   20
But hold some two days' conference with the
    dead !
From them I should learn somewhat, I am sure,
I never shall know here. I 'll tell thee a mir-
    acle :
I am not mad yet, to my cause of sorrow :
Th' heaven o'er my head seems made of molten
    brass,   25
The earth of flaming sulphur, yet I am **not**
    mad.
I am acquainted with sad misery

   [1] Spying.
   [2] Another room in the lodging of the Duchess.
   [3] Band.

As the tann'd galley-slave is with his oar ;
Necessity makes me suffer constantly,
And custom makes it easy. Who do I look like
    now ?   31

Cari. Like to your picture in the gallery,
A deal of life in show, but none in practice ;
Or rather like some reverend monument
Whose ruins are even pitied.

Duch.   Very proper ;
And Fortune seems only to have her eye-sight
To behold my tragedy.— How now !
What noise is that ?

        [*Enter* Servant.]

Serv.   I am come to tell you
Your brother hath intended you some sport.
A great physician, when the Pope was sick
Of a deep melancholy, presented him   40
With several sorts [4] of madmen, which wild ob-
    ject
Being full of change and sport, forc'd him to
    laugh,
And so th' imposthume [5] broke : the self-same
    cure
The duke intends on you.

Duch.   Let them come in.

Serv. There 's a mad lawyer ; and a secular
    priest ;   45
A doctor that hath forfeited his wits
By jealousy ; an astrologian
That in his works said such a day o' th' month
Should be the day of doom, and, failing of 't,
Ran mad ; an English tailor craz'd i' th' brain
With the study of new fashions ; a gentleman-
    usher   51
Quite beside himself with care to keep in mind
The number of his lady's salutations,
Or 'How do you,' she employ'd him in each
    morning ;
A farmer, too, an excellent knave in grain,[6]   55
Mad 'cause he was hind'red transportation : [7]
And let one broker that 's mad loose to these,
You 'd think the devil were among them.

Duch. Sit, Cariola. — Let them loose when
    you please,
For I am chain'd to endure all your tyranny.   60

        [*Enter* Madman.]

Here by a Madman *this song is sung to a dismal*
             kind of music.

    O, let us howl some heavy note,
      Some deadly dogged howl,
    Sounding as from the threat'ning throat
      Of beasts and fatal fowl !
    As ravens, screech-owls, bulls, and bears,   65
      We 'll bell, and bawl our parts,
    Till irksome noise have cloy'd your ears
      And corrosiv'd your hearts.
    At last, when as our choir wants breath,
      Our bodies being blest,   70
    We 'll sing, like swans, to welcome death,
      And die in love and rest.

1 *Madman.* Doom's-day not come yet ! I 'll
draw it nearer by a perspective,[8] or make a [74

   [4] Bands.   [5] Boil.
   [6] Punning on the two senses of " dye " and " corn."
   [7] From exporting his grain.   [7] Optical glass.

glass that shall set all the world on fire upon
an instant. I cannot sleep; my pillow is stuft
with a litter of porcupines.

2 Madman. Hell is a mere glass-house, where
the devils are continually blowing up women's
souls on hollow irons, and the fire never goes [80
out.

3 Madman. I will lie with every woman in
my parish the tenth night. I will tithe them
over like hay-cocks.   84

4 Madman. Shall my 'pothecary out-go me,
because I am a cuckold ? I have found out his
roguery : he makes alum of his wife's urine, and
sells it to Puritans that have sore throats with
over-straining.

1 Madman. I have skill in heraldry.   90

2 Madman. Hast ?

1 Madman. You do give for your crest a woodcock's head with the brains pickt out on 't;
you are a very ancient gentleman.   94

3 Madman. Greek is turn'd Turk : we are
only to be sav'd by the Helvetian translation.[1]

1 Madman. Come on, sir, I will lay the law
to you.

2 Madman. O, rather lay a corrosive : the
law will eat to the bone.   100

3 Madman. He that drinks but to satisfy nature is damn'd.

4 Madman. If I had my glass here, I would
show a sight should make all the women here
call me mad doctor.   105

1 Madman. What 's he ? A rope-maker ?

2 Madman. No, no, no ; a snuffling knave
that while he shows the tombs, will have his
hand in a wench's placket.[2]   109

3 Madman. Woe to the caroche [3] that brought
home my wife from the masque at three o'clock
in the morning ! It had a large feather-bed in
it.

4 Madman. I have pared the devil's nails
forty times, roasted them in raven's eggs, [115
and cur'd agues with them.

3 Madman. Get me three hundred milch-bats,
to make possets [4] to procure sleep.

4 Madman. All the college may throw their
caps at me : I have made a soap-boiler cos- [120
tive ; it was my masterpiece.

Here the dance, consisting of Eight Madmen,
with music answerable thereunto; after which,
Bosola, *like an old man, enters.*

Duch. Is he mad too ?

Serv. Pray, question him. I 'll leave you.
          [*Exeunt* Servant *and* Madmen.]

Bos. I am come to make thy tomb.

Duch.   Ha ! my tomb !
Thou speak'st as if I lay upon my death-bed,
Gasping for breath. Dost thou perceive me
    sick ?   125

Bos. Yes, and the more dangerously, since
thy sickness is insensible.

Duch. Thou art not mad, sure : dost know
me ?

Bos.   Yes.

Duch. Who am I ?

Bos. Thou art a box of worm-seed, at best
but a salvatory [5] of green mummy.[6] What 's
this flesh ? A little crudded [7] milk, fantasti- [131
cal puff-paste. Our bodies are weaker than
those paper-prisons boys use to keep flies in ;
more contemptible, since ours is to preserve
earth-worms. Didst thou ever see a lark in [135
a cage ? Such is the soul in the body : this
world is like her little turf of grass, and the
heaven o'er our heads, like her looking-glass,
only gives us a miserable knowledge of the
small compass of our prison.   140

Duch. Am I not thy duchess ?

Bos. Thou art some great woman, sure, for
riot begins to sit on thy forehead (clad in gray
hairs) twenty years sooner than on a merry
milk-maid's. Thou sleep'st worse than if a [145
mouse should be forc'd to take up her lodging
in a cat's ear : a little infant that breeds its
teeth, should it lie with thee, would cry out,
as if thou wert the more unquiet bedfellow.

Duch. I am Duchess of Malfi still.   150

Bos. That makes thy sleep so broken :
Glories, like glow-worms, afar off shine bright,
But, look'd to near, have neither heat nor
    light.

Duch. Thou art very plain.

Bos. My trade is to flatter the dead, not [155
the living ; I am a tomb-maker.

Duch. And thou com'st to make my tomb ?

Bos. Yes.

Duch. Let me be a little merry : — of what
stuff wilt thou make it ?   160

Bos. Nay, resolve me first, of what fashion ?

Duch. Why, do we grow fantastical on our
deathbed ?
Do we affect fashion in the grave ?

Bos. Most ambitiously. Princes' images on
their tombs do not lie, as they were wont, [165
seeming to pray up to heaven ; but with their
hands under their cheeks, as if they died of
the tooth-ache. They are not carved with their
eyes fix'd upon the stars, but as their minds
were wholly bent upon the world, the self- [170
same way they seem to turn their faces.[8]

Duch. Let me know fully therefore the effect
Of this thy dismal preparation,
This talk fit for a charnel.

Bos.   Now I shall : —

[*Enter* Executioners, *with*] a coffin, cords, and a
          bell.

Here is a present from your princely brothers ;
And may it arrive welcome, for it brings   175
Last benefit, last sorrow.

Duch.   Let me see it :
I have so much obedience in my blood,
I wish it in their veins to do them good.

Bos. This is your last presence-chamber.   180

Cari. O my sweet lady !

Duch.   Peace ; it affrights not me.

Bos. I am the common bellman

---

[1] The Geneva Bible.   [2] Petticoat.   [3] Coach.
[4] A warm drink containing milk, wine, etc.
[5] Receptacle.
[6] A drug supposed to ooze from embalmed bodies
[7] Curdled.   [8] Printed as verse in Qq.

That usually is sent to condemn'd persons
The night before they suffer.
Duch.   Even now thou said'st
Thou wast a tomb-maker.
Bos.   'T was to bring you 185
By degrees to mortification. Listen.

> Hark, now everything is still,
> The screech-owl and the whistler shrill
> Call upon our dame aloud,
> And bid her quickly don her shroud!   190
> Much you had of land and rent;
> Your length in clay 's now competent:
> A long war disturb'd your mind;
> Here your perfect peace is sign'd.
> Of what is 't fools make such vain keeping? 195
> Sin their conception, their birth weeping,
> Their life a general mist of error,
> Their death a hideous storm of terror.
> Strew your hair with powders sweet,
> Don clean linen, bathe your feet,   200
> And (the foul fiend more to check)
> A crucifix let bless your neck.
> 'T is now full tide 'tween night and day;
> End your groan, and come away.

Cari. Hence, villains, tyrants, murderers!
Alas!   205
What will you do with my lady? — Call for help!
Duch. To whom? To our next neighbours?
They are mad-folks.
Bos. Remove that noise.
Duch.   Farewell, Cariola.
In my last will I have not much to give:
A many hungry guests have fed upon me;   210
Thine will be a poor reversion.
Cari.   I will die with her.
Duch. I pray thee, look thou giv'st my little
boy
Some syrup for his cold, and let the girl
Say her prayers ere she sleep.
          [*Cariola is forced out by the Ex-
          ecutioners.*]
                    Now what you please:
What death?
Bos. Strangling; here are your executioners.
Duch. I forgive them: 215
The apoplexy, catarrh, or cough o' th' lungs,
Would do as much as they do.
Bos. Doth not death fright you?
Duch.   Who would be afraid on 't,
Knowing to meet such excellent company   220
In th' other world?
Bos. Yet, methinks,
The manner of your death should much afflict
you:
This cord should terrify you.
Duch.   Not a whit:
What would it pleasure me to have my throat
cut   225
With diamonds? or to be smothered
With cassia? or to be shot to death with pearls?
I know death hath ten thousand several doors
For men to take their exits; and 't is found
They go on such strange geometrical hinges,   230
You may open them both ways: any way, for
heaven-sake,
So I were out of your whispering. Tell my
brothers
That I perceive death, now I am well awake,

Best gift is they can give or I can take.
I would fain put off my last woman's-fault, 235
I 'd not be tedious to you.
1 Execut.   We are ready.
Duch. Dispose my breath how please you;
but my body
Bestow upon my women, will you?
1 Execut.   Yes.
Duch. Pull, and pull strongly, for your able
strength
Must pull down heaven upon me: —   240
Yet stay; heaven-gates are not so highly arch'd
As princes' palaces; they that enter there
Must go upon their knees [*kneels*].— Come, vio-
lent death,
Serve for mandragora to make me sleep! —
Go tell my brothers, when I am laid out,   245
They then may feed in quiet. *They strangle her.*
Bos. Where 's the waiting-woman?
Fetch her: some other strangle the children.

[*Enter* Cariola.]

Look you, there sleeps your mistress.
Cari.   O, you are damn'd
Perpetually for this! My turn is next;   250
Is 't not so ordered?
Bos.   Yes, and I am glad
You are so well prepar'd for 't.
Cari.   You are deceiv'd, sir,
I am not prepar'd for 't, I will first come to my answer,[1] and know
How I have offended.
Bos.   Come, despatch her.— 255
You kept her counsel; now you shall keep ours.
Cari. I will not die, I must not; I am con-
tracted
To a young gentleman.
1 Execut.   Here 's your wedding-ring.
Cari. Let me but speak with the duke. I 'll
discover
Treason to his person.
Bos.   Delays: — throttle her. 260
1 Execut. She bites and scratches.
Cari.   If you kill me now,
I am damn'd; I have not been at confession
This two years.
Bos. [*To Executioners.*] When![2]
Cari.   I am quick with child.
Bos.   Why, then,
Your credit 's saved.
          [*Executioners strangle* Cariola.]
          Bear her into th' next room; 265
Let these lie still.
          [*Exeunt* Executioners *with body of*
          Cariola.]

[*Enter* Ferdinand.]

Ferd.   Is she dead?
Bos.   She is what
You 'd have her. But here begin your pity:
          Shows the Children *strangled.*
Alas, how have these offended?
Ferd.   The death
Of young wolves is never to be pitied.

---

[1] Trial.   [2] An exclamation of impatience.

Bos. Fix your eye here.
Ferd.   Constantly.
Bos.   Do you not weep? 270
Other sins only speak ; murder shrieks out.
The element of water moistens the earth,
But blood flies upwards and bedews the heavens.
Ferd. Cover her face ; mine eyes dazzle : she
          died young.
Bos. I think not so ; her infelicity   275
Seem'd to have years too many.
Ferd. She and I were twins ;
And should I die this instant, I had liv'd
Her time to a minute.
Bos.   It seems she was born first :
You have bloodily approv'd the ancient truth,
That kindred commonly do worse agree   281
Than remote strangers.
Ferd.   Let me see her face
Again. Why didst thou not pity her ? What
An excellent honest man mightst thou have
been,
If thou hadst borne her to some sanctuary !   285
Or, bold in a good cause, — oppos'd thyself,
With thy advanced sword above thy head,
Between her innocence and my revenge !
I bade thee, when I was distracted of my wits,
Go kill my dearest friend, and thou hast done 't.
For let me but examine well the cause :   291
What was the meanness of her match to me ?
Only I must confess I had a hope,
Had she continu'd widow, to have gain'd
An infinite mass of treasure by her death :   295
And that was the main cause, — her marriage,
That drew a stream of gall quite through my
          heart.
For thee, as we observe in tragedies
That a good actor many times is curs'd
For playing a villain's part, I hate thee for 't.
And, for my sake, say, thou hast done much
          ill well.   301
Bos. Let me quicken your memory, for I
          perceive
You are falling into ingratitude : I challenge
The reward due to my service.
Ferd.   I 'll tell thee
What I 'll give thee.
Bos.   Do.
Ferd.   I 'll give thee a pardon 305
For this murder.
Bos.   Ha !
Ferd.   Yes, and 'tis
The largest bounty I can study to do thee.
By what authority didst thou execute
This bloody sentence ?
Bos.   By yours.
Ferd. Mine ! Was I her judge ?   310
Did any ceremonial form of law
Doom her to not-being ? Did a complete jury
Deliver her conviction up i' th' court ?
Where shalt thou find this judgment register'd,
Unless in hell ? See, like a bloody fool,   315
Thou 'st forfeited thy life, and thou shalt die
          for 't.
Bos. The office of justice is perverted quite
When one thief hangs another. Who shall dare
To reveal this ?
Ferd. O, I 'll tell thee ;

The wolf shall find her grave, and scrape it up,
Not to devour the corpse, but to discover   321
The horrid murder.
Bos.   You, not I, shall quake for 't.
Ferd. Leave me.
Bos.   I will first receive my pension.
Ferd. You are a villain.
Bos.   When your ingratitude
Is judge, I am so.
Ferd.   O horror,   325
That not the fear of him which binds the devils
Can prescribe man obedience ! —
Never look upon me more.
Bos.   Why, fare thee well.
Your brother and yourself are worthy men !
You have a pair of hearts are hollow graves, 330
Rotten, and rotting others ; and your vengeance,
Like two chain'd-bullets, still goes arm in arm :
You may be brothers ; for treason, like the
          plague,
Doth take much in a blood. I stand like one
That long hath ta'en a sweet and golden
          dream :   335
I am angry with myself now, that I wake.
Ferd. Get thee into some unknown part o'
          the world,
That I may never see thee.
Bos.   Let me know
Wherefore I should be thus neglected. Sir,
I serv'd your tyranny, and rather strove   340
To satisfy yourself than all the world :
And though I loath'd the evil, yet I lov'd
You that did counsel it ; and rather sought
To appear a true servant than an honest man.
Ferd. I 'll go hunt the badger by owl-light : 345
'T is a deed of darkness.   *Exit.*
Bos. He 's much distracted. Off, my painted
          honour !
While with vain hopes our faculties we tire,
We seem to sweat in ice and freeze in fire.
What would I do, were this to do again ?   350
I would not change my peace of conscience
For all the wealth of Europe. — She stirs ; here 's
          life : —
Return, fair soul, from darkness, and lead
          mine
Out of this sensible hell ! — she 's warm, she
          breathes : —
Upon thy pale lips I will melt my heart,   355
To store them with fresh colour. — Who 's
          there ?
Some cordial drink ! — Alas ! I dare not call :
So pity would destroy pity. — Her eye opes,
And heaven in it seems to ope, that late was
          shut,
To take me up to mercy.   360
Duch. Antonio !
Bos.   Yes, madam, he is living ;
The dead bodies you saw were but feign'd
          statues.
He 's reconcil'd to your brothers ; the Pope
          hath wrought
The atonement.
Duch.   Mercy !   *Dies.*
Bos. O, she 's gone again ! there the cords of
          life broke.   365
O sacred innocence, that sweetly sleeps

On turtles' feathers, whilst a guilty conscience
Is a black register wherein is writ
All our good deeds and bad, a perspective
That shows us hell ! That we cannot be suffer'd
To do good when we have a mind to it !   371
This is manly sorrow ;
These tears, I am very certain, never grew
In my mother's milk. My estate is sunk
Below the degree of fear : where were   375
These penitent fountains while she was living ?
O, they were frozen up ! Here is a sight
As direful to my soul as is the sword
Unto a wretch hath slain his father.
Come, I 'll bear thee hence,   380
And execute thy last will ; that 's deliver
Thy body to the reverend dispose
Of some good women : that the cruel tyrant
Shall not deny me. Then I 'll post to Milan,
Where somewhat I will speedily enact   385
Worth my dejection.   *Exit* [*with the body*].

ACT V

Scene I.[1]

[*Enter*] Antonio *and* Delio.

Ant. What think you of my hope of reconcilement
To the Arragonian brethren ?
Delio.   I misdoubt it ;
For though they have sent their letters of safe-conduct
For your repair to Milan, they appear
But nets to entrap you. The Marquis of Pescara,   5
Under whom you hold certain land in cheat,[2]
Much 'gainst his noble nature hath been mov'd
To seize those lands ; and some of his dependants
Are at this instant making it their suit
To be invested in your revenues.   10
I cannot think they mean well to your life
That do deprive you of your means of life,
Your living.
Ant.   You are still an heretic [3]
To any safety I can shape myself.
Delio. Here comes the marquis : I will make myself   15
Petitioner for some part of your land,
To know whither it is flying.
Ant.   I pray, do. [*Withdraws.*]

[*Enter* Pescara.]

Delio. Sir, I have a suit to you.
Pes.   To me ?
Delio.   An easy one :
There is the Citadel of Saint Bennet,
With some demesnes, of late in the possession
Of Antonio Bologna, — please you bestow them on me.   21
Pes. You are my friend ; but this is such a suit,
Nor fit for me to give, nor you to take.
Delio. No, sir ?

Pes.   I will give you ample reason for 't
Soon in private : — here 's the cardinal's mistress.   25

[*Enter* Julia.]

Julia. My lord, I am grown your poor petitioner,
And should be an ill beggar, had I not
A great man's letter here, the cardinal's,
To court you in my favour.   [*Gives a letter.*]
Pes.   He entreats for you
The Citadel of Saint Bennet, that belong'd   30
To the banish'd Bologna.
Julia.   Yes.
Pes. I could not have thought of a friend I could rather
Pleasure with it : 't is yours.
Julia.   Sir, I thank you ;
And he shall know how doubly I am engag'd
Both in your gift, and speediness of giving,   35
Which makes your grant the greater.   *Exit.*
Ant.   How they fortify
Themselves with my ruin !
Delio.   Sir, I am
Little bound to you.
Pes.   Why ?
Delio. Because you deni'd this suit to me, and gave 't
To such a creature.
Pes.   Do you know what it was ?
It was Antonio's land ; not forfeited   41
By course of law, but ravish'd from his throat
By the cardinal's entreaty. It were not fit
I should bestow so main a piece of wrong
Upon my friend ; 't is a gratification   45
Only due to a strumpet, for it is injustice.
Shall I sprinkle the pure blood of innocents
To make those followers I call my friends
Look ruddier upon me ? I am glad
This land, ta'en from the owner by such wrong,
Returns again unto so foul an use   51
As salary for his lust. Learn, good Delio,
To ask noble things of me, and you shall find
I 'll be a noble giver.
Delio.   You instruct me well.
Ant. [*Aside.*] Why, here 's a man now would fright impudence   55
From sauciest beggars.
Pes.   Prince Ferdinand 's come to Milan,
Sick, as they give out, of an apoplexy ;
But some say 't is a frenzy : I am going
To visit him.   *Exit.*
Ant.   'T is a noble old fellow.
Delio. What course do you mean to take, Antonio ?   60
Ant. This night I mean to venture all my fortune,
Which is no more than a poor ling'ring life,
To the cardinal's worst of malice. I have got
Private access to his chamber ; and intend
To visit him about the mid of night,   65
As once his brother did our noble duchess.
It may be that the sudden apprehension
Of danger, — for I 'll go in mine own shape, —
When he shall see it fraight[4] with love and duty,

May draw the poison out of him, and work   70
A friendly reconcilement. If it fail,
Yet it shall rid me of this infamous calling ;
For better fall once than be ever falling.
Delio. I 'll second you in all danger ; and,
howe'er,
My life keeps rank with yours.   75
Ant. You are still my lov'd and best friend.
                                        Exeunt.

[SCENE II.]¹

[Enter] PESCARA *and* DOCTOR.

Pes. Now, doctor, may I visit your patient ?
Doc. If 't please your lordship ; but he 's in-
stantly
To take the air here in the gallery
By my direction.
Pes.   Pray thee, what 's his disease ?
Doc. A very pestilent disease, my lord,   5
They call lycanthropia.
Pes.   What 's that?
I need a dictionary to 't.
Doc.   I 'll tell you.
In those that are possess'd with 't there o'er-
flows
Such melancholy humour they imagine
Themselves to be transformed into wolves ;   10
Steal forth to church-yards in the dead of night,
And dig dead bodies up : as two nights since
One met the duke 'bout midnight in a lane
Behind Saint Mark's church, with the leg of a
man
Upon his shoulder ; and he howl'd fearfully ;   15
Said he was a wolf, only the difference
Was, a wolf's skin was hairy on the outside,
His on the inside ; bade them take their swords,
Rip up his flesh, and try. Straight I was sent for,
And, having minister'd to him, found his grace
Very well recovered.   21
Pes. I am glad on 't.
Doc.   Yet not without some fear
Of a relapse. If he grow to his fit again,
I 'll go a nearer way to work with him
Than ever Paracelsus dream'd of ; if   25
They 'll give me leave, I 'll buffet his madness
out of him.
Stand aside ; he comes.

[Enter FERDINAND, CARDINAL, MALATESTI,
and BOSOLA.]

Ferd. Leave me.
Mal. Why doth your lordship love this soli-
tariness ?
Ferd. Eagles commonly fly alone : they are [30
crows, daws, and starlings that flock together.
Look, what 's that follows me ?
Mal. Nothing, my lord.
Ferd. Yes.
Mal. 'T is your shadow.   35
Ferd. Stay it ; let it not haunt me.
Mal. Impossible, if you move, and the sun
shine.
Ferd. I will throttle it.
      [Throws himself down on his shadow.]

¹ A gallery in the residence of the Cardinal and Ferdinand.

Mal. O, my lord, you are angry with nothing.
Ferd. You are a fool : how is 't possible I [40
should catch my shadow, unless I fall upon 't ?
When I go to hell, I mean to carry a bribe ; for,
look you, good gifts evermore make way for the
worst persons.
Pes. Rise, good mv lord.   45
Ferd. I am studying the art of patience.
Pes. 'T is a noble virtue.
Ferd. To drive six snails before me from this
town to Moscow ; neither use goad nor whip to
them, but let them take their own time ; — [50
the patient'st man i' th' world match me for an
experiment : — an I 'll crawl after like a sheep-
biter.²
Card. Force him up.   *[They raise him.]*
Ferd. Use me well, you were best. What I [55
have done, I have done : I 'll confess nothing.
Doc. Now let me come to him. — Are you
mad, my lord ?
Are you out of your princely wits ?
Ferd.   What 's he ?
Pes.   Your doctor.
Ferd. Let me have his beard saw'd off, and
his eye-brows fil'd more civil.   60
Doc. I must do mad tricks with him, for that
's the only way on 't. — I have brought your
grace a salamander's skin to keep you from sun-
burning.
Ferd. I have cruel sore eyes.   65
Doc. The white of a cockatrix's³ egg is pre-
sent remedy.
Ferd. Let it be a new-laid one, you were best.
Hide me from him : physicians are like kings, —
They brook no contradiction.   70
Doc. Now he begins to fear me : now let me
alone with him.
Card. How now ! put off your gown !
Doc. Let me have some forty urinals filled
with rose-water : he and I 'll go pelt one [75
another with them. — Now he begins to fear me.
— Can you fetch a frisk,⁴ sir ? — Let him go,
let him go, upon my peril : I find by his eye he
stands in awe of me ; I 'll make him as tame as
a dormouse.   80
Ferd. Can you fetch your frisks, sir ! — I will
stamp him into a cullis,⁵ flay off his skin to
cover one of the anatomies⁶ this rogue hath
set i' th' cold yonder in Barber-Chirurgeon's-
hall. — Hence, hence ! you are all of you like [85
beasts for sacrifice. *[Throws the* DOCTOR *down
and beats him.]* There 's nothing left of you but
tongue and belly, flattery and lechery. *[Exit.]*
Pes. Doctor, he did not fear you thoroughly.
Doc. True ; I was somewhat too forward.   90
Bos. Mercy upon me, what a fatal judgment
Hath fall'n upon this Ferdinand !
Pes.   Knows your grace
What accident hath brought unto the prince
This strange distraction ?
Card. *[Aside.]* I must feign somewhat. —
Thus they say it grew.   95
You have heard it rumour'd, for these many
years

² A dog which worries sheep.
³ A fabulous serpent that killed by its glance.
⁴ Cut a caper.   ⁵ Broth.   ⁶ Skeletons.

None of our family dies but there is seen
The shape of an old woman, which is given
By tradition to us to have been murder'd   99
By her nephews for her riches. Such a figure
One night, as the prince sat up late at 's book,
Appear'd to him ; when crying out for help,
The gentleman of 's chamber found his grace
All on a cold sweat, alter'd much in face
And language : since which apparition,   105
He hath grown worse and worse, and I much
        fear
He cannot live.
    Bos.   Sir, I would speak with you.
    Pes. We 'll leave your grace,
Wishing to the sick prince, our noble lord,
All health of mind and body.
    Card.   You are most welcome.
        [*Exeunt* PESCARA, MALATESTI, *and*
                DOCTOR.]
Are you come ? so. — [*Aside.*] This fellow must
        not know   111
By any means I had intelligence
In our duchess' death ; for, though I counsell'd
        it,
The full of all th' engagement seem'd to grow
From Ferdinand. — Now, sir, how fares our
        sister ?   115
I do not think but sorrow makes her look
Like to an oft-dy'd garment : she shall now
Take comfort from me. Why do you look so
        wildly ?
O, the fortune of your master here, the prince,
Dejects you ; but be you of happy comfort :   120
If you 'll do one thing for me I 'll entreat,
Though you had a cold tomb-stone o'er his bones,
I 'd make you what you would be.
    Bos.   Any thing ;
Give it me in a breath, and let me fly to 't.
They that think long small expedition win,   125
For musing much o' th' end cannot begin.

[*Enter* JULIA.]

Julia. Sir, will you come in to supper ?
Card.   I am busy ; leave me.
Julia. [*Aside.*] What an excellent shape hath
        that fellow !   *Exit.*
Card. 'T is thus. Antonio lurks here in Milan :
Inquire him out, and kill him. While he lives,
Our sister cannot marry ; and I have thought
Of an excellent match for her. Do this, and
        style me   132
Thy advancement.
    Bos. But by what means shall I find him
        out ?
Card. There is a gentleman call'd Delio   135
Here in the camp, that hath been long approv'd
His loyal friend. Set eye upon that fellow ;
Follow him to mass ; may be Antonio,
Although he do account religion
But a school-name, for fashion of the world   140
May accompany him ; or else go inquire out
Delio's confessor, and see if you can bribe
Him to reveal it. There are a thousand ways
A man might find to trace him ; as to know
What fellows haunt the Jews for taking up   145
Great sums of money, for sure he 's in want ;
Or else to go to th' picture-makers, and learn

Who bought [1] her picture lately : some of these
Happily may take.
    Bos.   Well, I 'll not freeze i' th' business :
I would see that wretched thing, Antonio,   150
Above all sights i' th' world.
    Card.   Do, and be happy. *Exit.*
    Bos. This fellow doth breed basilisks in 's
        eyes,
He 's nothing else but murder ; yet he seems
Not to have notice of the duchess' death.
'T is his cunning : I must follow his example ;
There cannot be a surer way to trace   155
Than that of an old fox.

[*Re-enter* JULIA, *with a pistol.*]

Julia. So, sir, you are well met.
Bos.   How now !
Julia. Nay, the doors are fast enough :
Now, sir, I will make you confess your treach-
        ery,   160
Bos. Treachery !
Julia.   Yes, confess to me
Which of my women 't was you hir'd to put
Love-powder into my drink ?
Bos. Love powder !
Julia.   Yes, when I was at Malfi.
Why should I fall in love with such a face else ?
I have already suffer'd for thee so much pain,
The only remedy to do me good   167
Is to kill my longing.
Bos.   Sure, your pistol holds
Nothing but perfumes or kissing-comfits.[2]
Excellent lady !   170
You have a pretty way on 't to discover
Your longing. Come, come, I 'll disarm you,
And arm you thus : yet this is wondrous
        strange.
Julia. Compare thy form and my eyes to-
        gether,
You 'll find my love no such great miracle.   175
Now you 'll say
I am wanton : this nice modesty in ladies
Is but a troublesome familiar
That haunts them.
Bos. Know you me, I am a blunt soldier.
Julia.   The better :
Sure, there wants fire where there are no lively
        sparks   181
Of roughness.
Bos.   And I want compliment.
Julia.   Why, ignorance
In courtship cannot make you do amiss,
If you have a heart to do well.
Bos.   You are very fair.
Julia. Nay, if you lay beauty to my charge,
I must plead unguilty.
Bos.   Your bright eyes   186
Carry a quiver of darts in them, sharper
Than sun-beams.
Julia.   You will mar me with commenda-   [tion,
Put yourself to the charge of courting me,
Whereas now I woo you.   190
    Bos. [*Aside.*] I have it, I will work upon this
        creature, —

----

1 So Dyce. Qq. *brought.*
2 Perfumed sweetmeats for the breath.

Let us grow most amorously familiar:
If the great cardinal now should see me thus,
Would he not count me a villain?
   Julia. No; he might count me a wanton, 195
Not lay a scruple of offence on you;
For if I see and steal a diamond,
The fault is not i' th' stone, but in me the thief
That purloins it. I am sudden with you.
We that are great women of pleasure use to cut off 200
These uncertain wishes and unquiet longings,
And in an instant join the sweet delight
And the pretty excuse together. Had you been i' th' street,
Under my chamber-window, even there
I should have courted you. 205
   Bos. O, you are an excellent lady!
   Julia. Bid me do somewhat for you presently
To express I love you.
   Bos. I will; and if you love me,
Fail not to effect it.
The cardinal is grown wondrous melancholy;
Demand the cause, let him not put you off 211
With feign'd excuse; discover the main ground on 't.
   Julia. Why would you know this?
   Bos. I have depended on him,
And I hear that he is fall'n in some disgrace
With the emperor: if he be, like the mice 215
That forsake falling houses, I would shift
To other dependance.
   Julia. You shall not need
Follow the wars: I 'll be your maintenance.
   Bos. And I your loyal servant: but I cannot
Leave my calling.
   Julia. Not leave an ungrateful 220
General for the love of a sweet lady!
You are like some cannot sleep in feather-beds,
But must have blocks for their pillows.
   Bos. Will you do this?
   Julia. Cunningly.
   Bos. To-morrow I 'll expect th' intelligence.
   Julia. To-morrow! Get you into my cabinet; 226
You shall have it with you. Do not delay me,
No more than I do you: I am like one
That is condemn'd; I have my pardon promis'd,
But I would see it seal'd. Go, get you in: 230
You shall see me wind my tongue about his heart
Like a skein of silk.   [*Exit* Bosola.]

     [*Re-enter* Cardinal.]

   Card. Where are you?

     [*Enter* Servants.]

   Servants. Here.
   Card. Let none, upon your lives, have conference
With the Prince Ferdinand, unless I know it. —
[*Aside.*] In this distraction he may reveal 235
The murder.   [*Exeunt* Servants.]
     Yond 's my lingering consumption:
I am weary of her, and by any means
Would be quit of.

   Julia. How now, my lord! what ails you?
   Card. Nothing.
   Julia. O, you are much alter'd:
Come, I must be your secretary, and remove
This lead from off your bosom: what 's the matter? 241
   Card. I may not tell you.
   Julia. Are you so far in love with sorrow
You cannot part with part of it? Or think you
I cannot love your grace when you are sad 245
As well as merry? Or do you suspect
I, that have been a secret to your heart
These many winters, cannot be the same
Unto your tongue?
   Card. Satisfy thy longing, —
The only way to make thee keep my counsel
Is, not to tell thee.
   Julia. Tell your echo this, 251
Or flatterers, that like echoes still report
What they hear, though most imperfect, and not me;
For if that you be true unto yourself,
I 'll know.
   Card. Will you rack me?
   Julia. No, judgment shall
Draw it from you: it is an equal fault, 256
To tell one's secrets unto all or none.
   Card. The first argues folly.
   Julia. But the last tyranny.
   Card. Very well: why, imagine I have committed 260
Some secret deed which I desire the world
May never hear of.
   Julia. Therefore may not I know it?
You have conceal'd for me as great a sin
As adultery. Sir, never was occasion
For perfect trial of my constancy 265
Till now; sir, I beseech you ——
   Card. You 'll repent it.
   Julia. Never.
   Card. It hurries thee to ruin: I 'll not tell thee.
Be well advis'd, and think what danger 't is
To receive a prince's secrets. They that do, 270
Had need have their breasts hoop'd with adamant
To contain them. I pray thee, yet be satisfi'd;
Examine thine own frailty; 't is more easy
To tie knots than unloose them. 'T is a secret
That, like a ling'ring poison, may chance lie
Spread in thy veins, and kill thee seven year hence. 276
   Julia. Now you dally with me.
   Card. No more; thou shalt know it.
By my appointment, the great Duchess of Malfi
And two of her young children, four nights since,
Were strangled.
   Julia. O heaven! sir, what have you done!
   Card. How now? How settles this? Think you your bosom 281
Will be a grave dark and obscure enough
For such a secret?
   Julia. You have undone yourself, sir.
   Card. Why?
   Julia. It lies not in me to conceal it.

Card.   No ?
Come, I will swear you to 't upon this book.
Julia. Most religiously.
Card.   Kiss it. [*She kisses the book.*] 286
Now you shall never utter it ; thy curiosity
Hath undone thee ; thou 'rt poison'd with that
    book.
Because I knew thou couldst not keep my
    counsel,
I have bound thee to 't by death.   290

[*Re-enter* BOSOLA.]

Bos. For pity sake, hold !
Card.   Ha, Bosola !
Julia.   I forgive you
This equal piece of justice you have done ;
For I betray'd your counsel to that fellow.
He over-heard it ; that was the cause I said
It lay not in me to conceal it.   295
Bos. O foolish woman,
Couldst not thou have poison'd him ?
Julia.   'T is weakness
Too much to think what should have been
    done. I go,
I know not whither.   [*Dies.*]
Card.   Wherefore com'st thou hither ?
Bos. That I might find a great man like
    yourself,   300
Not out of his wits, as the Lord Ferdinand,
To remember my service.
Card. I 'll have thee hew'd in pieces.
Bos. Make not yourself such a promise of
    that life
Which is not yours to dispose of.
Card.   Who plac'd thee here ?
Bos. Her lust, as she intended.
Card.   Very well : 306
Now you know me for your fellow-murderer.
Bos. And wherefore should you lay fair
    marble colours
Upon your rotten purposes to me ?
Unless you imitate some that do plot great trea-
    sons,   310
And when they have done, go hide themselves
    i' th' graves
Of those were actors in 't ?
Card.   No more ; there is
A fortune attends thee.
Bos. Shall I go sue to Fortune any longer ?
'T is the fool's pilgrimage.   315
Card. I have honours in store for thee.
Bos. There are a many ways that conduct to
    seeming
Honour, and some of them very dirty ones.
Card. Throw to the devil
Thy melancholy. The fire burns well ;   320
What need we keep a stirring of 't, and make
A greater smother ? [1] Thou wilt kill Antonio ?
Bos. Yes.
Card.   Take up that body.
Bos.   I think I shall
Shortly grow the common bier for church-yards.
Card. I will allow thee some dozen of attend-
    ants   325
To aid thee in the murder.

Bos. O, by no means. Physicians that apply
horse-leeches to any rank swelling use to cut off
their tails, that the blood may run through them
the faster : let me have no train when I go [330
to shed blood, less it make me have a greater
when I ride to the gallows.
Card. Come to me after midnight, to help to
    remove
That body to her own lodging. I 'll give out
She died o' th' plague ; 't will breed the less in-
    quiry   335
After her death.
Bos. Where 's Castruccio her husband ?
Card. He 's rode to Naples, to take posses-
    sion
Of Antonio's citadel.
Bos. Believe me, you have done a very happy
    turn.   340
Card. Fail not to come. There is the master-
    key
Of our lodgings ; and by that you may conceive
What trust I plant in you.
Bos.   You shall find me ready.
                        Exit CARDINAL.
O poor Antonio, though nothing be so needful
To thy estate as pity, yet I find   345
Nothing so dangerous ! I must look to my foot-
    ing :
In such slippery ice-pavements men had need
To be frost-nail'd well, they may break their
    necks else ;
The precedent 's here afore me. How this man
Bears up in blood ! seems fearless ! Why, 't is
    well :   350
Security some men call the suburbs of hell,
Only a dead wall between. Well, good Antonio,
I 'll seek thee out ; and all my care shall be
To put thee into safety from the reach
Of these most cruel biters that have got 355
Some of thy blood already. It may be,
I 'll join with thee in a most just revenge.
The weakest arm is strong enough that strikes
With the sword of justice. Still methinks the
    duchess
Haunts me : there, there ! — 'T is nothing but
    my melancholy.   360
O Penitence, let me truly taste thy cup,
That throws men down only to raise them up !
                                    Exit.

SCENE III. [2]

[*Enter*] ANTONIO *and* DELIO. ECHO (*from the*
        DUCHESS'S *Grave*).

Delio. Yond 's the cardinal's window. This
    fortification
Grew from the ruins of an ancient abbey ;
And to yond side o' th' river lies a wall,
Piece of a cloister, which in my opinion
Gives the best echo that you ever heard,   5
So hollow and so dismal, and withal
So plain in the distinction of our words,
That many have suppos'd it is a spirit
That answers.
Ant.   I do love these ancient ruins.
We never tread upon them but we set   10

---

[1] Smoke.   [2] A fortification.

Our foot upon some reverend history ;
And, questionless, here in this open court,
Which now lies naked to the injuries
Of stormy weather, some men lie interr'd
Lov'd the church so well, and gave so largely
   to 't,   15
They thought it should have canopied their
   bones
Till dooms-day. But all things have their end ;
Churches and cities, which have diseases like
   to men,
Must have like death that we have.
   Echo.   *Like death that we have.*
   Delio. Now the echo hath caught you.   20
   Ant. It groan'd methought, and gave
A very deadly accent.
   Echo.   *Deadly accent.*
   Delio. I told you 't was a pretty one. You
   may make it
A huntsman, or a falconer, a musician,
Or a thing of sorrow.
   Echo.   *A thing of sorrow.*   25
   Ant. Ay, sure, that suits it best.
   Echo.   *That suits it best.*
   Delio. Come, let us walk further from 't.
I would not have you go to the cardinal's to-
   night :
Do not.   30
   Echo. Do not.
   Delio. Wisdom doth not more moderate
   wasting sorrow
Than time. Take time for 't ; be mindful of
   thy safety.
   Echo. Be mindful of thy safety.
   Ant. Necessity compels me.   35
Make scrutiny throughout the passages
Of your own life, you 'll find it impossible
To fly your fate.
   Echo.   *O, fly your fate !*
   Delio. Hark ! the dead stones seem to have
   pity on you,
And give you good counsel.   40
   Ant. Echo, I will not talk with thee,
For thou art a dead thing.
   Echo.   *Thou art a dead thing.*
   Ant. My duchess is asleep now,
And her little ones, I hope sweetly. O heaven,
Shall I never see her more ?
   Echo.   *Never see her more.*   45
   Ant. I mark'd not one repetition of the echo
But that ; and on the sudden a clear light
Presented me a face folded in sorrow.
   Delio. Your fancy merely.
   Ant.   Come, I 'll be out of this ague.
For to live thus is not indeed to live :   50
It is a mockery and abuse of life.
I will not henceforth save myself by halves ;
Lose all, or nothing.
   Delio.   Your own virtue save you !
I 'll fetch your eldest son, and second you.
It may be that the sight of his own blood   55
Spread in so sweet a figure may beget
The more compassion. However, fare you
   well.
Though in our miseries Fortune have a part,

Yet in our noble suff'rings she hath none.
Contempt of pain, that we may call our own.   60
                           Exeunt.

SCENE IV.[1]

[*Enter*] CARDINAL, PESCARA, MALATESTI,
   RODERIGO, *and* GRISOLAN.

   Card. You shall not watch to-night by the
   sick prince ;
His grace is very well recover'd.
   Mal. Good my lord, suffer us.
   Card.   O, by no means ;
The noise, and change of object in his eye,
Doth more distract him. I pray, all to bed ;   5
And though you hear him in his violent fit,
Do not rise, I entreat you.
   Pes. So, sir ; we shall not.
   Card.   Nay, I must have you promise
Upon your honours, for I was enjoin'd to 't
By himself ; and he seem'd to urge it sensibly.
   Pes. Let our honours bind this trifle.   11
   Card. Nor any of your followers.
   Mal. Neither.
   Card. It may be, to make trial of your pro-
   mise,
When he 's asleep, myself will rise and feign   15
Some of his mad tricks, and cry out for help,
And feign myself in danger.
   Mal. If your throat were cutting,
I 'd not come at you, now I have protested
   against it.
   Card. Why, I thank you.
   Gris.   'T was a foul storm to-night.   20
   Rod. The Lord Ferdinand's chamber shook
   like an osier.
   Mal. 'T was nothing but pure kindness in the
   devil
To rock his own child.
          Exeunt [*all except the* CARDINAL].
   Card. The reason why I would not suffer
   these
About my brother, is, because at midnight   25
I may with better privacy convey
Julia's body to her own lodging. O, my con-
   science !
I would pray now ; but the devil takes away
   my heart
For having any confidence in prayer.
About this hour I appointed Bosola   30
To fetch the body. When he hath serv'd my
   turn,
He dies.   *Exit.*

Enter [BOSOLA].

   Bos. Ha ! 't was the cardinal's voice ; I heard
him name Bosola and my death. Listen ; I hear
one's footing.   35

[*Enter* FERDINAND.]

   Ferd. Strangling is a very quiet death.
   Bos. [*Aside.*] Nay, then, I see I must stand
   upon my guard.
   Ferd. What say to that ? Whisper softly : do
you agree to 't ? So ; it must be done i' th'

---

1 Milan. An apartment in the residence of the Cardinal and Ferdinand.

dark ; the cardinal would not for a thousand [40
pounds the doctor should see it.   *Exit.*
  Bos. My death is plotted ; here 's the consequence of murder.
We value not desert nor Christian breath,
When we know black deeds must be cur'd with
  death.

    [*Enter* ANTONIO *and* Servant.]

  Serv. Here stay, sir, and be confident, I pray ;
I 'll fetch you a dark lantern.   *Exit.* 46
  Ant. Could I take him at his prayers,
There were hope of pardon.
  Bos. Fall right, my sword ! —   [*Stabs him.*]
I 'll not give thee so much leisure as to pray. 50
  Ant. O, I am gone ! Thou hast ended a long suit
In a minute.
  Bos.   What art thou ?
  Ant.   A most wretched thing,
That only have thy benefit in death,
To appear myself.

    [*Re-enter* Servant *with a lantern.*]

  Serv. Where are you, sir ?   55
  Ant. Very near my home. — Bosola !
  Serv. O, misfortune !
  Bos. Smother thy pity, thou art dead else. —
  Antonio !
The man I would have sav'd 'bove mine own life !
We are merely the stars' tennis-balls, struck and
  banded [1]   60
Which way please them. — O good Antonio,
I 'll whisper one thing in thy dying ear
Shall make thy heart break quickly ! Thy fair
  duchess
And two sweet children ——
  Ant.   Their very names
Kindle a little life in me.
  Bos.   Are murder'd.   65
  Ant. Some men have wish'd to die
At the hearing of sad tidings ; I am glad
That I shall do 't in sadness.[2] I would not now
Wish my wounds balm'd nor heal'd, for I have
  no use   69
To put my life to. In all our quest of greatness,
Like wanton boys whose pastime is their care,
We follow after bubbles blown in th' air.
Pleasure of life, what is 't ? Only the good hours
Of an ague ; merely a preparative to rest,
To endure vexation. I do not ask   75
The process of my death ; only commend me
To Delio.
  Bos. Break, heart !
  Ant. And let my son fly the courts of princes.
                        [*Dies.*]
  Bos. Thou seem'st to have lov'd Antonio.
  Serv. I brought him hither,   80
To have reconcil'd him to the cardinal.
  Bos. I do not ask thee that.
Take him up, if thou tender thine own life,
And bear him where the lady Julia
Was wont to lodge. — O, my fate moves swift !
I have this cardinal in the forge already ;   85
Now I 'll bring him to th' hammer. O direful
  misprision ![3]

   [1] Bandied.   [2] Reality.   [3] Mistake.

I will not imitate things glorious,
No more than base ; I 'll be mine own example.—
On, on, and look thou represent, for silence, 90
The thing thou bear'st.[4]   *Exeunt.*

SCENE V.[5]

    [*Enter*] CARDINAL, *with a book.*

  Card. I am puzzl'd in a question about hell :
He says, in hell there 's one material fire,
And yet it shall not burn all men alike.
Lay him by. How tedious is a guilty conscience !
When I look into the fish-ponds in my garden, 5
Methinks I see a thing arm'd with a rake,
That seems to strike at me.

    [*Enter* BOSOLA, *and* Servant *bearing* ANTONIO'S
                body.]

               Now, art thou come ?
Thou look'st ghastly ;
There sits in thy face some great determination
Mix'd with some fear.
  Bos.   Thus it lightens into action : 10
I am come to kill thee.
  Card.   Ha ! — Help ! our guard !
  Bos. Thou art deceiv'd ; they are out of thy
  howling.
  Card. Hold ; and I will faithfully divide
Revenues with thee.
  Bos.   Thy prayers and proffers
Are both unseasonable.
  Card.   Raise the watch !   15
We are betray'd !
  Bos.   I have confin'd your flight :
I 'll suffer your retreat to Julia 's chamber,
But no further.
  Card.   Help ! we are betray'd !

    [*Enter, above,* PESCARA, MALATESTI, RODERIGO,
         and GRISOLAN.]

  Mal. Listen.
  Card. My dukedom for rescue !   20
  Rod. Fie upon his counterfeiting !
  Mal. Why, 't is not the cardinal.
  Rod. Yes, yes, 't is he :
But, I 'll see him hang'd ere I 'll go down to him.
  Card. Here 's a plot upon me ; I am as-
  saulted ! I am lost,   25
Unless some rescue !
  Gris.   He doth this pretty well ;
But it will not serve to laugh me out of mine
  honour.
  Card. The sword 's at my throat !
  Rod.   You would not bawl so loud then.
  Mal. Come, come, let 's go to bed : he told us
this much aforehand.   30
  Pes. He wish'd you should not come at him ;
  but, believe 't,
The accent of the voice sounds not in jest.
I 'll down to him, howsoever, and with engines
Force ope the doors.   [*Exit above.*]
  Rod.   Let 's follow him aloof,
And note how the cardinal will laugh at him.
    [*Exeunt, above,* MALATESTI, ROD-
        ERIGO, *and* GRISOLAN.]

   [4] *I. e.* the dead body.   [5] Another apartment in the same.

Bos. There's for you first, ₃₆
'Cause you shall not unbarricade the door
To let in rescue. *Kills the* Servant.
    Card.   What cause hast thou to pursue
    my life?
    Bos.   Look there.
    Cara. Antonio!
    Bos.   Slain by my hand unwittingly.
Pray, and be sudden. When thou kill'd'st thy
    sister, ₄₀
Thou took'st from Justice her most equal bal-
    ance,
And left her naught but her sword.
    Card.   O, mercy!
    Bos. Now it seems thy greatness was only
    outward;
For thou fall'st faster of thyself than calamity
Can drive thee. I'll not waste longer time;
    there!   *[Stabs him.]*
    Card. Thou hast hurt me.
    Bos.   Again!
    Card.   Shall I die like a leveret, ₄₆
Without any resistance? — Help, help, help!
I am slain!

    [Enter FERDINAND.*]*

    Ferd. Th' alarum! Give me a fresh horse;
Rally the vaunt-guard, or the day is lost,
Yield, yield! I give you the honour of arms ₅₀
Shake my sword over you; will you yield?
    Card. Help me; I am your brother!
    Ferd.   The devil!
My brother fight upon the adverse party!
    He wounds the CARDINAL, *and, in
    the scuffle, gives* BOSOLA *his
    death-wound.*
There flies your ransom.
    Card. O justice! ₅₅
I suffer now for what hath former bin:
Sorrow is held the eldest child of sin.
    Ferd. Now you're brave fellows. Caesar's
fortune was harder than Pompey's; Caesar died
in the arms of prosperity, Pompey at the [₆₀
feet of disgrace. You both died in the field.
The pain's nothing; pain many times is taken
away with the apprehension of greater, as the
tooth-ache with the sight of a barber that comes
to pull it out. There's philosophy for you. ₆₅
    Bos. Now my revenge is perfect. — Sink,
thou main cause   *Kills* FERDINAND.
Of my undoing! — The last part of my life
Hath done me best service.
    Ferd. Give me some wet hay; I am broken-
    winded.
I do account this world but a dog-kennel: ₇₀
I will vault credit and affect high pleasures
Beyond death.
    Bos.   He seems to come to himself,
Now he's so near the bottom.
    Ferd. My sister, O my sister! there's the
    cause on 't.
Whether we fall by ambition, blood, or lust, ₇₅
Like diamonds, we are cut with our own dust.
    [Dies.]
    Card. Thou hast thy payment too.
    Bos. Yes, I hold my weary soul in my teeth;

'T is ready to part from me. I do glory ₇₀
That thou, which stood'st like a hugh pyramid
Begun upon a large and ample base,
Shalt end in a little point, a kind of nothing.

    [Enter, below, PESCARA, MALATESTI, RODERIGO,
    and GRISOLAN.*]*

    Pes. How now, my lord!
    Mal.   O sad disaster!
    Rod.   How comes this?
    Bos. Revenge for the Duchess of Malfi mur-
    dered
By th' Arragonian brethren; for Antonio ₈₅
Slain by this hand; for lustful Julia
Poison'd by this man; and lastly for myself,
That was an actor in the main of all
Much 'gainst mine own good nature, yet i' th'
    end
Neglected.
    Pes.   How now, my lord!
    Card.   Look to my brother:
He gave us these large wounds, as we were
    struggling ₉₁
Here i' th' rushes. And now, I pray, let me
Be laid by and never thought of.   *[Dies.]*
    Pes. How fatally, it seems, he did withstand
His own rescue!
    Mal.   Thou wretched thing of blood, ₉₅
How came Antonio by his death?
    Bos. In a mist; I know not how;
Such a mistake as I have often seen
In a play. O, I am gone! ₉₉
We are only like dead walls or vaulted graves,
That, ruin'd, yields no echo. Fare you well!
It may be pain, but no harm, to me to die
In so good a quarrel. O, this gloomy world!
In what a shadow, or deep pit of darkness,
Doth womanish and fearful mankind live! ₁₀₅
Let worthy minds ne'er stagger in distrust
To suffer death or shame for what is just:
Mine is another voyage.   *[Dies.]*
    Pes. The noble Delio, as I came to th' palace,
Told me of Antonio's being here, and show'd
    me ₁₁₀
A pretty gentleman, his son and heir.

    [Enter DELIO, *and* ANTONIO's Son.*]*

    Mal. O sir, you come too late!
    Delio.   I heard so, and
Was arm'd for 't, ere I came. Let us make no-
    ble use
Of this great ruin; and join all our force
To establish this young hopeful gentleman ₁₁₅
In 's mother's right. These wretched eminent
    things
Leave no more fame behind 'em, than should
    one
Fall in a frost, and leave his print in snow;
As soon as the sun shines, it ever melts,
Both form and matter. I have ever thought ₁₂₀
Nature doth nothing so great for great men
As when she's pleas'd to make them lords of
    truth:
Integrity of life is fame's best friend,
Which nobly, beyond death, shall crown the
    end.   *Exeunt.*

A TRICK TO CATCH THE OLD ONE

BY

THOMAS MIDDLETON

[DRAMATIS PERSONAE

THEODORUS WITGOOD.
PECUNIUS LUCRE, his uncle.
WALKADINE HOARD
ONESIPHORUS HOARD, his brother.
LIMBER,
KIX,
LAMPREY,
SPICHCOCK, } friends of Hoard.
HARRY DAMPIT,
GULF, } usurers.
SAM FREEDOM, son of Mistress Lucre.
MONEYLOVE.
Host.
SIR LAUNCELOT.

Creditors.
Gentlemen.
GEORGE.
ARTHUR.
Drawer.
Boy.
Scrivener.
Servants, &c.

Courtesan.
MISTRESS LUCRE.
JOYCE, niece to Hoard.
LADY FOXTONE.
AUDREY, servant to Dampit.

SCENE. — *A country town; then London.*]

[ACT I

SCENE I.]¹

Enter WITGOOD, *a gentleman, solus.*

Wit. All 's gone! still thou 'rt a gentleman,
that 's all; but a poor one, that 's nothing.
What milk brings thy meadows forth now?
Where are thy goodly uplands, and thy down-
lands? All sunk into that little pit, lechery. [5
Why should a gallant pay but two shillings for
his ordinary that nourishes him, and twenty
times two for his brothel that consumes him?
But where 's Longacre?² In my uncle's conscience, which is three years' voyage about: [10
he that sets out upon his conscience ne'er finds
the way home again; he is either swallowed in
the quicksands of law-quillets, or splits upon
the piles of a *praemunire;*³ yet these old fox-
brain'd and ox-brow'd uncles have still de- [15
fences for their avarice, and apologies for their
practices, and will thus greet our follies:

He that doth his youth expose
   To brothel, drink, and danger,
Let him that is his nearest kin   20
   Cheat him before a stranger:

and that 's his uncle; 't is a principle in usury.
I dare not visit the city: there I should be too
soon visited by that horrible plague, my debts;
and by that means I lose a virgin's love, her [25
portion, and her virtues. Well, how should a

¹ A street in a country town.
² Used of any one's estate.
³ Used vaguely of a legal scrape.

man live now that has no living? Hum, — why,
are there not a million of men in the world that
only sojourn upon their brain, and make their
wits their mercers; and am I but one amongst
that million, and cannot thrive upon 't? Any [31
trick, out of the compass of law, now would
come happily to me.

Enter Courtesan.

Cour. My love!

Wit. My loathing! has thou been the se- [35
cret consumption of my purse, and now com'st
to undo my last means, my wits? Wilt leave
no virtue in me, and yet thou ne'er the better?
Hence, courtesan, round-webb'd tarantula,
That dry'st the roses in the cheeks of youth! 40
Cour. I've been true unto your pleasure;
      and all your lands
Thrice rackt⁴ was never worth the jewel which
I prodigally gave you, my virginity.
Lands mortgag'd may return, and more es-
      teem'd,
But honesty⁵ once pawn'd, is ne'er redeem'd. 45
Wit. Forgive; I do thee wrong
To make thee sin, and then to chide thee for 't.
Cour. I know I am your loathing now; fare-
      well.
Wit. Stay, best invention, stay.
Cour. I that "have been the secret con- [50
sumption of your purse," shall I stay now "to
undo your last means, your wits? Hence, cour-
tesan," away!
Wit. I prithee, make me not mad at my own
weapon: stay (a thing few women can do, I [55

⁴ Excessively rented.   ⁵ Chastity.

know that, and therefore they had need wear
stays), be not contrary. Dost love me? Fate has
so cast[1] it that all my means I must derive
from thee.

Cour. From me? be happy then;   60
What lies within the power of my performance
Shall be commanded of thee.

Wit.   Spoke like
An honest drab, i' faith. It may prove some-
thing;
What trick is not an embryon at first,
Until a perfect shape come over it?   65

Cour. Come, I must help you: whereabouts
left you?

I 'll proceed:
Though you beget, 't is I must help to breed.
Speak, what is 't? I 'd fain conceive it.

Wit. So, so, so: thou shalt presently take [70
the name and form upon thee of a rich country
widow, four hundred a-year valiant,[2] in woods,
in bullocks, in barns, and in rye-stacks. We 'll
to London, and to my covetous uncle.

Cour. I begin to applaud thee; our states [75
being both desperate, they are soon resolute.
But how for horses?

Wit. Mass, that 's true; the jest will be of
some continuance. Let me see; horses now, a
bots[3] on 'em! Stay, I have acquaintance with [80
a mad host, never yet bawd to thee. I have
rins'd the whoreson's gums in mull-sack[4] many
a time and often. Put but a good tale into his
ear now, so it come off cleanly, and there 's
horse and man for us, I dare warrant thee.   85

Cour. Arm your wits then
Speedily; there shall want nothing in me,
Either in behaviour, discourse, or fashion,
That shall discredit your intended purpose.
I will so artfully disguise my wants,   90
And set so good a courage on my state,
That I will be believed.

Wit. Why, then, all 's furnisht. I shall go
nigh to catch that old fox, mine uncle. Though
he make but some amends for my un- [95
doing, yet there 's some comfort in 't, he cannot
otherwise choose (though it be but in hope to
cozen[5] me again) but supply any hasty want
that I bring to town with me. The device well
and cunningly carried, the name of a rich [100
widow, and four hundred a-year in good earth,
will so conjure up a kind of usurer's love in him
to me, that he will not only desire my presence,
—which at first shall scarce be granted him,
I 'll keep off a' purpose, — but I shall find [105
him so officious to deserve, so ready to supply!
I know the state of an old man's affection so
well: if his nephew be poor indeed, why, he let's
God alone with him; but if he be once rich, then
he 'll be the first man that helps him.   110

Cour. 'T is right the world;[6] for, in these
days, an old man's love to his kindred is like
his kindness to his wife, 't is always done before
he comes at it.   114

---

[1] Planned.   [2] Worth.
[3] A disease caused by a parasite. Used as an execration.
[4] A white wine warm and spiced.
[5] Cheat.   [6] Precisely the way of the world.

Wit. I owe thee for that jest. Begone:
here 's all my wealth; prepare thyself, away.
I 'll to mine host with all possible haste; and
with the best art, and most profitable form,
pour the sweet circumstance into his ear, [119
which shall have the gift to turn all the wax to
honey. [*Exit* Courtesan.] — How now? O, the
right worshipful signors of our country!

[*Enter* ONESIPHORUS HOARD, LIMBER, *and*
KIX.]

[*O. Hoa.*][7] Who 's that?
[*Lim.*] O, the common rioter; take no note of
him.   125
Wit. [*Aside.*] You will not see me now; the
comfort is,
Ere it be long you will scarce see yourselves.
[*Exit.*]

[*O. Hoa.*] I wonder how he breathes; h'as
consum'd all
Upon that courtesan.

[*Lim.*]   We have heard so much.
[*O. Hoa.*] You 've heard all truth. His uncle
and my brother   130
Have been these three years mortal adver-
saries:
Two old tough spirits, they seldom meet but
fight,
Or quarrel when 't is calmest:
I think their anger be the very fire   134
That keeps their age alive.

[*Lim.*]   What was the quarrel, sir?
[*O. Hoa.*] Faith, about a purchase, fetching
over a young heir. Master Hoard, my brother,
having wasted much time in beating the bargain, what did me old Lucre, but as his con- [139
science mov'd him, knowing the poor gentleman, stept in between 'em and cozened him
himself.

[*Lim.*] And was this all, sir?
[*O. Hoa.*] This was e'en it, sir; yet for [144
all this, I know no reason but the match might
go forward betwixt his wife's son and my niece;
what though there be a dissension between the
two old men, I see no reason it should put a difference between the two younger; 't is as [149
natural for old folks to fall out, as for young to
fall in. A scholar comes a-wooing to my niece;
well, he 's wise, but he 's poor: her son comes
a-wooing to my niece; well, he 's a fool, but
he 's rich.

[*Lim.*] Ay, marry, sir.   155
[*O. Hoa.*] Pray, now, is not a rich fool better
than a poor philosopher?

[*Lim.*] One would think so, i' faith.
[*O. Hoa.*] She now remains at London [159
with my brother, her second uncle, to learn
fashions, practise music; the voice between her
lips, and the viol between her legs, she 'll be
fit for a consort[8] very speedily: a thousand
good pound is her portion; if she marry, we 'll
ride up and be merry.   165

[*Kix.*] A match, if it be a match.   *Exeunt.*

---

[7] In the Qq. O. Hoard, Limber, and Kix appear in
the speech tags as 1, 2, and 3.
[8] A pun on the two meanings, "concert" and
"consort."

[SCENE II.][1]

Enter at one door, WITGOOD, *at the other,* Host.

Wit. Mine host!

Host. Young Master Witgood.

Wit. I have been laying[2] all the town for thee.

Host. Why, what's the news, bully Had- [5 land?

Wit. What geldings are in the house, of thine own? Answer me to that first.

Host. Why, man, why? 9

Wit. Mark me what I say: I'll tell thee such a tale in thine ear, that thou shalt trust me spite of thy teeth, furnish me with some money willy nilly, and ride up with me myself *contra voluntatem et professionem.*[3] 14

Host. How? Let me see this trick, and I'll say thou hast more art than a conjuror.

Wit. Dost thou joy in my advancement?

Host. Do I love sack and ginger?

Wit. Comes my prosperity desiredly to thee? 20

Host. Come forfeitures to a usurer, fees to an officer, punks to an host, and pigs to a parson desiredly? Why, then, la.

Wit. Will the report of a widow of four hundred a-year, boy, make thee leap, and sing, and dance, and come to thy place again? 26

Host. Wilt thou command me now? I am thy spirit; conjure me into any shape.

Wit. I ha' brought her from her friends, [29 turn'd back the horses by a slight; not so much as one among her six men, goodly large yeomanly fellows, will she trust with this her purpose: by this light, all unmann'd,[4] regardless of her state, neglectful of vain-glorious ceremony, all for my love. O, 'tis a fine little voluble tongue, mine host, that wins a widow! 36

Host. No, 'tis a tongue with a great T, my boy, that wins a widow.

Wit. Now, sir, the case stands thus: good mine host, if thou lovest my happiness, assist me. 41

Host. Command all my beasts i' th' house.

Wit. Nay, that's not all neither: prithee take truce with thy joy, and listen to me. [44 Thou know'st I have a wealthy uncle i' th' city, somewhat the wealthier by my follies. The report of this fortune, well and cunningly carried, might be a means to draw some goodness from the usuring rascal; for I have put her in hope [49 already of some estate that I have either in land or money. Now, if I be found true in neither, what may I expect but a sudden breach of our love, utter dissolution of the match, and confusion of my fortunes for ever? 54

Host. Wilt thou but trust the managing of thy business with me?

Wit. With thee? Why, will I desire to thrive in my purpose? Will I hug four hundred a-year, I that know the misery of nothing? Will that man wish a rich widow, that has ne'er a [60

[1] Another street in the same town.
[2] Searching.
[3] "Contrary to your will and profession."
[4] Without escort.

hole to put his head in? With thee, mine host? Why, believe it, sooner with thee than with a covey of counsellors.

Host. Thank you for your good report, i' faith, sir; and if I stand you not in stead, [65 why then let an host come off *hic et haec hostis,* a deadly enemy to dice, drink, and venery. Come, where's this widow?

Wit. Hard at Park-end.

Host. I'll be her serving-man for once. 70

Wit. Why, there we let off together, keep full time; my thoughts were striking then just the same number.

Host. I knew 't: shall we then see our merry days again? 75

Wit. Our merry nights — [*Aside.*] which ne'er shall be more seen. *Exeunt.*

[SCENE III.][5]

Enter at several doors, old LUCRE *and old* HOARD; [LAMPREY, SPICHCOCK, FREEDOM, *and* MONEYLOVE,] *gentlemen coming between them to pacify them.*

Lam. Nay, good Master Lucre, and you, Master Hoard, anger is the wind which you're both too much troubled withal.

Hoa. Shall my adversary thus daily affront me, ripping up the old wound of our malice, [5 which three summers could not close up? into which wound the very sight of him drops scalding lead instead of balsamum.

Luc. Why, Hoard, Hoard, Hoard, Hoard, Hoard! may I not pass in the state of quiet- [10 ness to mine own house? Answer me to that, before witness, and why? I'll refer the cause to honest, even-minded gentlemen, or require the mere indifferences[6] of the law to decide this matter. I got the purchase,[7] true: was 't [15 not any man's case? Yes. Will a wise man stand as a bawd, whilst another wipes his nose[8] of the bargain? No; I answer no in that case.

Lam. Nay, sweet Master Lucre.

Hoa. Was it the part of a friend — no, [20 rather of a Jew; — mark what I say — when I had beaten the bush to the last bird, or, as I may term it, the price to a pound, then, like a cunning usurer, to come in the evening of the bargain, and glean all my hopes in a minute? [25 to enter, as it were, at the back door of the purchase? for thou ne'er camest the right way by it.

Luc. Hast thou the conscience to tell me so without any impeachment to thyself? 30

Hoa. Thou that canst defeat thy own nephew, Lucre, lap his lands into bonds, and take the extremity of thy kindred's forfeitures, because he's a rioter, a wastethrift, a brothel-master, and so forth, — what may a stranger expect [35 from thee but *vulnera dilacerata,* as the poet says, dilacerate dealing?

Luc. Upbraidest thou me with nephew? Is all imputation laid upon me? What acquaintance have I with his follies? If he riot, 'tis [40

[5] A street in London.
[6] Impartiality.
[7] The booty.
[8] Cheats him.

he must want it; if he surfeit, 't is he must
feel it; if he drab it, 't is he must lie by 't:
what 's this to me?

Hoa. What 's all to thee? Nothing, nothing;
such is the gulf of thy desire and the wolf of [45
thy conscience: but be assured, old Pecunius
Lucre, if ever fortune so bless me that I may
be at leisure to vex thee, or any means so favour me that I may have opportunity to mad
thee,[1] I will pursue it with that flame of hate, [50
spirit of malice, unrepressed wrath, that I will
blast thy comforts.

Luc. Ha, ha, ha!

Lam. Nay, Master Hoard, you 're a wise
gentleman ——   55

Hoa. I will so cross thee ——

Luc. And I thee.

Hoa. So without mercy fret thee ——

Luc. So monstrously oppose thee ——

Hoa. Dost scoff at my just anger? O, that [60
I had as much power as usury has over thee!

Luc. Then thou wouldst have as much power
as the devil has over thee.

Hoa. Toad!

Luc. Aspic![2]   65

Hoa. Serpent!

Luc. Viper!

Spi. Nay, gentlemen, then we must divide
you perforce.

Lam. When the fire grows too unreason- [70
able hot, there 's no better way than to take off
the wood.

> *Exeunt* [LAMPREY *and* SPICHCOCK,
> *drawing off* LUCRE *and* HOARD
> *different ways*].

Free. A word, good signior.

Mon. How now, what 's the news?

Free. 'T is given me to understand that [75
you are a rival of mine in the love of Mistress
Joyce, Master Hoard's niece: say me ay, say
me no?

Mon. Yes, 't is so.

Free. Then look to yourself, you cannot [80
live long. I 'm practising every morning; a
month hence I 'll challenge you.

Mon. Give me your hand upon 't; there 's
my pledge I 'll meet you. *Strikes him, and exit.*

Free. O, O! what reason had you for that, [85
sir, to strike before the month? You knew
I was not ready for you, and that made you so
crank:[3] I am not such a coward to strike again,
I warrant you. My ear has the law of her side,
for it burns horribly. I will teach him to strike
a naked face, the longest day of his life. [91
'Slid, it shall cost me some money but I 'll bring
this box into the chancery.   *Exit.*

[SCENE IV.][4]

Enter WITGOOD *and* Host.

Host. Fear you nothing, sir; I have lodg'd
her in a house of credit, I warrant you.

Wit. Hast thou the writings?

Host. Firm, sir.

---

[1] *Or any . . . mad thee*, omitted in Q_2.
[2] Asp.   [3] Lively.   [4] Another street.

Wit. Prithee, stay, and behold two the [5
most prodigious rascals that ever slipt into the
shape of men; Dampit, sirrah, and young Gulf,
his fellow-caterpillar.

Host. Dampit? Sure I have heard of that
Dampit?   10

Wit. Heard of him! Why, man, he that has
lost both his ears may hear of him; a famous
infamous trampler[5] of time; his own phrase.
Note him well: that Dampit, sirrah, he in the
uneven beard and the serge cloak, is the [15
most notorious, usuring, blasphemous, atheistical, brothel-vomiting rascal, that we have in
these latter times now extant; whose first beginning was the stealing of a masty[6] dog from
a farmer's house.   20

Host. He lookt as if he would obey the commandment[s] well, when he began first with
stealing.

Wit. True: the next town he came at, he set
the dogs together by th' ears.   25

Host. A sign he should follow the law, by my
faith.

Wit. So it followed, indeed; and being destitute of all fortunes, stakt his masty against a
noble,[7] and by great fortune his dog had the [30
day. How he made it up ten shillings, I know
not, but his own boast is, that he came to town
with but ten shillings in his purse, and now is
credibly worth ten thousand pound.

Host. How the devil came he by it?   35

[Enter DAMPIT *and* GULF.]

Wit. How the devil came he not by it? If
you put in the devil once, riches come with a
vengeance. Has been a trampler of the law, sir;
and the devil has a care of his footmen. The
rogue has spied me now; he nibbled me finely [40
once, too : — a pox search you! — O, Master
Dampit! — the very loins of thee! — Cry you
mercy, Master Gulf; you walk so low, I promise you I saw you not, sir.

Gulf. He that walks low walks safe, the [45
poets tell us.

Wit. [*Aside.*] And nigher hell by a foot and
a half than the rest of his fellows. — But, my
old Harry!

Dam. My sweet Theodorus!   50

Wit. 'T was a merry world when thou camest
to town with ten shillings in thy purse.

Dam. And now worth ten thousand pound,
my boy. Report it; Harry Dampit, a trampler
of time, say, he would be up in a morning, [55
and be here with his serge gown, dasht up to the
hams in a cause; have his feet stink about
Westminster Hall, and come home again; see
the galleons, the galleasses,[8] the great armadas
of the law; then there be hoys[9] and petty [60
vessels, oars and scullers of the time; there be
picklocks of the time too: then would I be
here; I would trample up and down like a
mule: now to the judges, " May it please your
reverend honourable fatherhoods; " then to [65
my counsellor, " May it please your worshipful

---

[5] A lawyer.
[6] Mastiff.
[7] A gold coin worth 6s. 8d.
[8] Heavy built galleys.
[9] Passenger sloops.

patience ; " then to the examiner's office, " May
it please your mastership's gentleness ; " then
to one of the clerks, " May it please your worshipful lousiness," — for I find him scrubbing [70
in his codpiece ; then to the hall again, then to
the chamber again —

Wit. And when to the cellar again ?

Dam. E'en when thou wilt again : tramplers
of time, motions [1] of Fleet Street, and visions [75
of Holborn ; here I have fees of one, there I
have fees of another ; my clients come about
me, the fooliaminy [2] and coxcombry of the
country : I still trasht [3] and trotted for other
men's causes. Thus was poor Harry Dampit [80
made rich by others' laziness, who though they
would not follow their own suits, I made 'em
follow me with their purses.

Wit. Didst thou so, old Harry ?

Dam. Ay, and I sous'd 'em with bills of [85
charges, i 'faith ; twenty pound a-year have I
brought in for boat-hire, and I ne'er stept into
boat in my life.

Wit. Tramplers of time !

Dam. Ay, tramplers of time, rascals of [90
time, bull-beggars ! [4]

Wit. Ah, thou 'rt a mad old Harry ! — Kind
Master Gulf, I am bold to renew my acquaintance.

Gulf. I embrace it, sir.   *Exeunt.* 95

MUSIC

ACT II

[SCENE I.] [5]

Enter LUCRE.

Luc. My adversary evermore twits me with
my nephew, forsooth, my nephew : why may
not a virtuous uncle have a dissolute nephew ?
What though he be a brotheller, a wastethrift,
a common surfeiter, and, to conclude, a beg- [5
gar, must sin in him call up shame in me ?
Since we have no part in their follies, why
should we have part in their infamies ? For my
strict hand toward his mortgage, that I deny
not : I confess I had an uncle's pen'worth ; [10
let me see, half in half, true. I saw neither
hope of his reclaiming, nor comfort in his being ;
and was it not then better bestow'd upon his
uncle than upon one of his aunts ? — I need not
say bawd, for every one knows what " aunt "
stands for in the last translation.   16

[*Enter* Servant.]

Now, Sir ?

Ser. There 's a country serving-man, sir, attends to speak with your worship.

Luc. I 'm at best leisure now ; send him in [20
to me.   [*Exit* Servant.]

---

[1] Puppet-shows.
[2] One of Dampit's self-explanatory coinages.
[3] Apparently, rushed about. See Nares.
[4] Bogies, bugbears.
[5] A room in Lucre's house.

Enter Host *like a serving-man.*

Host. Bless your venerable worship.

Luc. Welcome, good fellow.

Host. [*Aside.*] He calls me thief [6] at first
sight, yet he little thinks I am an host.

Luc. What 's thy business with me ?   26

Host. Faith, sir, I am sent from my mistress,
to any sufficient gentleman indeed, to ask advice upon a doubtful point : 't is indifferent,
sir, to whom I come, for I know none, nor [30
did my mistress direct me to any particular
man, for she 's as mere a stranger here as myself ;
only I found your worship within, and 't is a
thing I ever lov'd, sir, to be despatcht as soon
as I can.   35

Luc. [*Aside.*] A good, blunt honesty ; I like
him well.— What is thy mistress ?

Host. Faith, a country gentlewoman, and a
widow, sir. Yesterday was the first flight of
us ; but now she intends to stay till a little [40
term business be ended.

Luc. Her name, I prithee ?

Host. It runs there in the writings, sir, among
her lands ; Widow Medler.

Luc. Medler ? Mass, have I [7] ne'er heard [45
of that widow ?

Host. Yes, I warrant you, have you, sir ; not
the rich widow in Staffordshire ?

Luc. Cuds [8] me, there 't is indeed ; thou hast
put me into memory. There 's a widow in- [50
deed ; ah, that I were a bachelor again !

Host. No doubt your worship might do much
then ; but she 's fairly promist to a bachelor already.

Luc. Ah, what is he, I prithee ?   55

Host. A country gentleman too ; one of whom
your worship knows not, I 'm sure ; h'as spent
some few follies in his youth, but marriage, by
my faith, begins to call him home. My mistress
loves him, sir, and love covers faults, you [60
know : one Master Witgood, if ever you have
heard of the gentleman.

Luc. Ha ! Witgood, sayst thou ?

Host. That 's his name indeed, sir ; my mistress is like to bring him to a goodly seat [65
yonder ; four hundred a-year, by my faith.

Luc. But, I pray, take me with you. [9]

Host. Ay, sir.

Luc. What countryman might this young
Witgood be ?   70

Host. A Leicestershire gentleman, sir.

Luc. [*Aside.*] My nephew, by th' mass, my
nephew ! I 'll fetch out more of this, i' faith :
a simple country fellow, I 'll work 't out of him.
— And is that gentleman, sayst thou, presently
to marry her ?   76

Host. Faith, he brought her up to town, sir ;
h'as the best card in all the bunch for 't, her
heart ; and I know my mistress will be married
ere she go down ; [10] nay, I 'll swear that, for [80
she 's none of those widows that will go down

---

[6] " Good fellow " was then slang for a thief.
[7] Q[2] *I have.*   [8] A corruption of " Gods."
[9] Let me understand you.
[10] To the country, with a pun.

first, and be married after ; she hates that, I can tell you, sir.

Luc. By my faith, sir, she is like to have a proper gentleman, and a comely ; I 'll give [85 her that gift.

Host. Why, does your worship know him, sir ?

Luc. I know him ? Does not all the world know him ? Can a man of such exquisite [90 qualities be hid under a bushel ?

Host. Then your worship may save me a labour, for I had charge given me to inquire after him.

Luc. Inquire of him ? If I might counsel [95 thee, thou shouldst ne'er trouble thyself further ; inquire of him no more, but of me ; I 'll fit thee. I grant he has been youthful ; but is he not now reclaim'd ? Mark you that, sir : has not your mistress, think you, been wanton [100 in her youth ? If men be wags, are there not women wagtails ?

Host. No doubt, sir.

Luc. Does not he return wisest that comes home whipt with his own follies ?   105

Host. Why, very true, sir.

Luc. The worst report you can hear of him, I can tell you, is that he has been a kind gentleman, a liberal, and a worthy ; who but lusty Witgood, thrice-noble Witgood !   110

Host. Since your worship has so much knowledge in him, can you resolve me, sir, what his living might be ? My duty binds me, sir, to have a care of my mistress' estate ; she has been ever a good mistress to me, though I [115 say it. Many wealthy suitors has she nonsuited for his sake ; yet, though her love be so fixt, a man cannot tell whether his non-performance may help to remove it, sir ; he makes us believe he has lands and living.   120

Luc. Who, young Master Witgood ? Why, believe it, he has as goodly a fine living out yonder,— what do you call the place ?

Host. Nay, I know not, i' faith.

Luc. Hum — see, like a beast, if I have [125 not forgot the name — pooh ! and out yonder again, goodly grown woods and fair meadows : pax[1] on 't, I can ne'er hit of that place neither. — He ? Why, he 's Witgood of Witgood Hall ; he an unknown thing !   130

Host. Is he so, sir ? To see how rumour will alter ! Trust me, sir, we heard once he had no lands, but all lay mortgag'd to an uncle he has in town here.

Luc. Push ! 'tis a tale, 'tis a tale.   135

Host. I can assure you, sir, 't was credibly reported to my mistress.

Luc. Why, do you think, i' faith, he was ever so simple to mortgage his lands to his uncle, or his uncle so unnatural to take the extremity of such a mortgage ?   141

Host. That was my saying still, sir.

Luc. Pooh, ne'er think it.

Host. Yet that report goes current.

Luc. Nay, then you urge me :   145
Cannot I tell that best that am his uncle ?

[1] A corruption of " pox."

Host. How, sir ? what have I done !

Luc. Why, how now ! In a swoon, man ?

Host. Is your worship his uncle, sir ?

Luc. Can that be any harm to you, sir ?   151

Host. I do beseech you, sir, do me the favour to conceal it. What a beast was I to utter so much ! Pray, sir, do me the kindness to keep it in ; I shall have my coat pull'd o'er my ears, an 't should be known ; for the truth is, an 't [155 please your worship, to prevent much rumour and many suitors, they intend to be married very suddenly and privately.

Luc. And dost thou think it stands with my judgment to do them injury ? Must I needs [160 say the knowledge of this marriage comes from thee ? Am I a fool at fifty-four ? Do I lack subtlety now, that have got all my wealth by it ? There 's a leash of angels[2] for thee : come, let me woo thee speak where lie[3] they ?   165

Host. So I might have no anger, sir ——

Luc. Passion of me, not a jot : prithee, come.

Host. I would not have it known, sir, it came by my means.

Luc. Why, am I a man of wisdom ?   170

Host. I dare trust your worship, sir ; but I 'm a stranger to your house ; and to avoid all intelligencers, I desire your worship's ear.

Luc. [*Aside.*] This fellow 's worth a matter of trust. — Come, sir. [*Host whispers to him.*] Why, now, thou 'rt an honest lad. — Ah, [175 sirrah, nephew !

Host. Please you, sir, now I have begun with your worship, when shall I attend for your advice upon that doubtful point ? I must come warily now.   181

Luc. Tut, fear thou nothing ;
To-morrow's evening shall resolve the doubt.

Host. The time shall cause my attendance.
                                        Exit.

Luc. Fare thee well. — There 's more true [185 honesty in such a country serving-man than in a hundred of our cloak companions :[4] I may well call 'em companions,[4] for since blue[5] coats have been turn'd into cloaks, we can scarce know the man from the master. — George !   190

[*Enter* GEORGE.]

Geo. Anon, sir.

Luc. List hither : [*whispers*] keep the place secret ; commend me to my nephew ; I know no cause, tell him, but he might seem his uncle.

Geo. I will, sir.   195

Luc. And, do you hear, sir ?
Take heed to use him with respect and duty.

Geo. [*Aside.*] Here 's a strange alteration ; one day he must be turn'd out like a beggar, and now he must be call'd in like a knight.   200
                                        Exit.

Luc. Ah, sirrah, that rich widow ! — four hundred a-year ! beside, I hear she lays claim to a title of a hundred more. This falls unhappily that he should bear a grudge to me now, being likely to prove so rich. What [205

[2] Couple of gold coins, each worth from 6s. 8d. to 10s.
[3] Lodge.   [4] Fellows, contemptuously.
[5] The common livery of serving-men.

is 't, trow, that he makes me a stranger for?
Hum,— I hope he has not so much wit to apprehend that I cozened him: he deceives me
then. Good Heaven, who would have thought
it would ever have come to this pass! yet [210
he 's a proper gentleman, i' faith, give him his
due,— marry, that 's his mortgage; but that I
ne'er mean to give him. I 'll make him rich
enough in words, if that be good: and if it come
to a piece of money, I will not greatly stick [215
for 't; there may be hope some of the widow's
lands, too, may one day fall upon me, if things
be carried wisely.

[Re-enter GEORGE.]

Now, sir, where is he?
Geo. He desires your worship to hold him [220
excus'd; he has such weighty business, it commands him wholly from all men.
Luc. Were those my nephew's words?
Geo. Yes, indeed, sir.
Luc. [*Aside.*] When men grow rich, they [225
grow proud too, I perceive that. He would not
have sent me such an answer once within this
twelvemonth: see what 't is when a man comes
to his lands! Return to him again, sir; tell him
his uncle desires his company for an hour; [230
I 'll trouble him but an hour, say; 't is for his
own good, tell him: and, do you hear, sir? put
"worship" upon him. Go to, do as I bid you;
he 's like to be a gentleman of worship very
shortly.   235
Geo. [*Aside.*] This is good sport, i' faith.
                                              Exit.
Luc. Troth, he uses his uncle discourteously
now. Can he tell what I may do for him? Goodness may come from me in a minute, that comes
not in seven year again. He knows my hu- [240
mour; I am not so usually good; 't is no small
thing that draws kindness from me, he may
know that an he will. The chief cause that invites me to do him most good is the sudden as-
tonishing of old Hoard, my adversary. How [245
pale his malice will look at my nephew's advancement! With what a dejected spirit he
will behold his fortunes, whom but last day he
proclaim'd a rioter, penurious makeshift, despised brothel-master! Ha, ha! 't will do me [250
more secret joy than my last purchase, more
precious comfort than all these widow's revenues.

[Re-]enter [GEORGE, showing in] WITGOOD.

Now, sir?
Geo. With much entreaty he 's at length [255
come, sir.   [*Exit.*]
Luc. O, nephew, let me salute you, sir!
Your 're welcome, nephew.
Wit. Uncle, I thank you.
Luc. You 've a fault, nephew; you 're a [260
stranger here. Well, Heaven give you joy!
Wit. Of what, sir?
Luc. Hah, we can hear!
You might have known your uncle 's house, i'
faith,
You and your widow: go to, you were to
blame -

If I may tell you so without offence.   266
Wit. How could you hear of that, sir?
Luc. O, pardon me!
'T was your will to have kept it from me, I per-
ceive now.
Wit. Not for any defect of love, I protest,
uncle.   271
Luc. Oh, 't was unkindness, nephew! fie, fie,
fie.
Wit. I am sorry you take it in that sense, sir.
Luc. Pooh, you cannot colour it, i' faith, [275
nephew.
Wit. Will you but hear what I can say in my
just excuse, sir.
Luc. Yes, faith, will I, and welcome.   279
Wit. You that know my danger i' th' city,
sir, so well, how great my debts are, and how
extreme my creditors, could not out of your
pure judgment, sir, have wisht us hither.
Luc. Mass, a firm reason indeed.
Wit. Else, my uncle 's house! why, 't had [285
been the only make-match.
Luc. Nay, and thy credit.
Wit. My credit? Nay, my countenance. Pish,
nay, I know, uncle, you would have wrought it
so by your wit, you would have made her believe
in time the whole house had been mine.   291
Luc. Ay, and most of the goods too.
Wit. La, you there! Well, let 'em all prate
what they will, there 's nothing like the bringing of a widow to one's uncle's house.   295
Luc. Nay, let nephews be rul'd as they list,
they shall find their uncle's house the most natural place when all 's done.
Wit. There they may be bold.
Luc. Life, they may do anything there, [300
man, and fear neither beadle nor summoner.
An uncle's house! a very Cole-Harbour.[1] Sir-
rah, I 'll touch thee near now: hast thou so
much interest in thy widow, that by a token
thou couldst presently send for her?   305
Wit. Troth, I think I can, uncle.
Luc. Go to, let me see that.
Wit. Pray, command one of your men hither,
uncle.
Luc. George!   310

[Re-enter GEORGE.]

Geo. Here, sir.
Luc. Attend my nephew. [WITGOOD *whispers
to* GEORGE, *who then goes out.*] — [*Aside.*] I love
a' life[2] to prattle with a rich widow; 't is pretty,
methinks, when our tongues go together: [315
and then to promise much and perform little.
I love that sport a' life, i' faith; yet I am in the
mood now to do my nephew some good, if he
take me handsomely. What, have you despatcht?   320
Wit. I ha' sent, sir.
Luc. Yet I must condemn you of unkindness,
nephew.
Wit. Heaven forbid, uncle!
Luc. Yes, faith, must I. Say your debts be [325
many, your creditors importunate, yet the kind-

---

[1] A corruption of "Cold Harbour," where debtors
and vagabonds found sanctuary.
[2] As my life,

ness of a thing is all, nephew: you might have sent me close[1] word on 't, without the least danger or prejudice to your fortunes.   329

Wit. Troth, I confess it, uncle; I was to blame there; but, indeed, my intent was to have clapt it up suddenly, and so have broke forth like a joy to my friends, and a wonder to the world. Beside, there 's a trifle of a forty pound matter toward the setting of me forth; [335 my friends should ne'er have known on 't; I meant to make shift for that myself.

Luc. How, nephew? let me not hear such a word again, I beseech you. Shall I be beholding to you?   340

Wit. To me? Alas, what do you mean, uncle?

Luc. I charge you, upon my love, you trouble nobody but myself.

Wit. You 've no reason for that, uncle.

Luc. Troth, I 'll ne'er be friends with you while you live, an you do.   346

Wit. Nay, an you say so, uncle, here 's my hand; I will not do 't.

Luc. Why, well said! there 's some hope in thee when thou wilt be rul'd. I 'll make it [350 up fifty, faith, because I see thee so reclaim'd. Peace; here comes my wife with Sam, her t' other husband's son.

[*Enter* MISTRESS LUCRE *and* FREEDOM.]

Wit. Good aunt.   354

Free. Cousin Witgood, I rejoice in my salute; you 're most welcome to this noble city, gov- ern'd with the sword in the scabbard.

Wit. [*Aside.*] And the wit in the pommel. — Good Master Sam Freedom, I return the salute.

Luc. By the mass, she 's coming, wife; let [360 me see now how thou wilt entertain her.

Mis. L. I hope I am not to learn, sir, to en- tertain a widow; 't is not so long since I was one myself.

[*Enter* Courtesan.]

Wit. Uncle ——   365

Luc. She 's come indeed.

Wit. My uncle was desirous to see you, wi- dow, and I presumed to invite you.

Cour. The presumption was nothing, Master Witgood. Is this your uncle, sir?   370

Luc. Marry am I, sweet widow; and his good uncle he shall find me; ay, by this smack that I give thee, thou 'rt welcome. — Wife, bid the widow welcome the same way again.   374

Free. [*Aside.*] I am a gentleman now too by my father's occupation, and I see no reason but I may kiss a widow by my father's copy: [2] truly, I think the charter is not against it; surely these are the words, " The son once a gentleman may revel it, though his father were a dau- [380 ber;" 't is about the fifteenth page: I 'll to her. [*Offers to kiss the* Courtesan, *who repulses him.*]

Luc. You 're not very busy now; a word with thee, sweet widow.   385

---

[1] Secret.

[2] Membership in a livery company, one of the great trade guilds of London.

Free. Coads-nigs![3] I was never so disgrac'd since the hour my mother whipt me.

Luc. Beside, I have no child of mine own to care for; she 's my second wife, old, past bear- ing; clap sure to him, widow; he 's like to be my heir, I can tell you.   391

Cour. Is he so, sir?

Luc. He knows it already, and the knave 's proud on 't; jolly rich widows have been offer'd him here i' th' city, great merchants' wives; and do you think he will once look upon [396 'em? Forsooth, he 'll none. You are beholding to him i' th' country, then, ere we could be: nay, I 'll hold a wager, widow, if he were once known to be in town, he would be presently [400 sought after; nay, and happy were they that could catch him first.

Cour. I think so.

Luc. O, there would be such running to and fro, widow! He should not pass the streets for 'em: he 'd be took up in one great house or [406 other presently: faugh! they know he has it, and must have it. You see this house here, wi- dow; this house and all comes to him; goodly rooms, ready furnisht, ceil'd with plaster [410 of Paris, and all hung about with cloth of arras. — Nephew.

Wit. Sir.

Luc. Show the widow your house; carry her into all the rooms, and bid her welcome. — [415 You shall see, widow. — [*Aside to* WITGOOD.] Nephew, strike all sure above an thou beest a good boy, — ah!

Wit. Alas, sir, I know not how she would take it!   420

Luc. The right way, I warrant t' ee. A pox, art an ass? Would I were in thy stead! get you up, I am asham'd of you. [*Exeunt* WIT- GOOD *and* Courtesan.] So: let 'em agree as they will now: many a match has been struck up in my house a' this fashion: let 'em try all man-[426 ner of ways, still there's nothing like an uncle's house to strike the stroke in. I 'll hold my wife in talk a little. — Now Jenny, your son there goes a-wooing to a poor gentlewoman but of [430 a thousand pound portion: see my nephew, a lad of less hope, strikes at four hundred a-year in good rubbish.

Mis. L. Well, we must do as we may, sir.

Luc. I 'll have his money ready told for him again[3] he come down. Let me see, too; — by [436 th' mass, I must present the widow with some jewel, a good piece a' plate, or such a device; 't will hearten her on well. I have a very fair standing cup; and a good high standing cup [440 will please a widow above all other pieces.

Exit.

Mis. L. Do you mock us with your nephew? — I have a plot in my head, son; — i' faith, hus- band, to cross you.

Free. Is it a tragedy plot, or a comedy plot, good mother?   446

Mis. L. 'T is a plot shall vex him. I charge you, of my blessing, son Sam, that you presently

---

[3] A corrupt oath: God's nigs.

[4] Against, by the time that.

withdraw the action of your love from Master
Hoard's niece.   450

Free. How, mother?

Mis. L. Nay, I have a plot in my head, i' faith.
Here, take this chain of gold, and this fair diamond: dog me the widow home to her lodging,
and at thy best opportunity, fasten 'em [455
both upon her. Nay, I have a reach:[1] I can
tell you thou art known what thou art, son,
among the right worshipful, all the twelve
companies.

Free. Truly, I thank 'em for it.   460

Mis. L. He? he's a scab to thee: and so certify her thou hast two hundred a-year of thyself, besides thy good parts — a proper person
and a lovely. If I were a widow, I could find
in my heart to have thee myself, son; ay, [465
from 'em all.

Free. Thank you for your good will, mother;
but, indeed, I had rather have a stranger: and
if I woo her not in that violent fashion, that [469
I will make her be glad to take these gifts ere
I leave her, let me never be called the heir of
your body.

Mis. L. Nay, I know there's enough in you,
son, if you once come to put it forth.   474

Free. I'll quickly make a bolt or a shaft
on 't.[2]   *Exeunt.*

[SCENE II.][3]

Enter HOARD *and* MONEYLOVE.

Mon. Faith, Master Hoard, I have bestowed
many months in the suit of your niece, such was
the dear love I ever bore to her virtues: but
since she hath so extremely denied me, I am to
lay out for my fortunes elsewhere.   5

Hoa. Heaven forbid but you should, sir! I
ever told you my niece stood otherwise affected.[4]

Mon. I must confess you did, sir; yet, in regard of my great loss of time, and the zeal with
which I sought your niece, shall I desire one [10
favour of your worship?

Hoa. In regard of those two, 't is hard but
you shall, sir.

Mon. I shall rest grateful: 't is not full three
hours, sir, since the happy rumour of a rich [15
country widow came to my hearing.

Hoa. How? a rich country widow?

Mon. Four hundred a-year landed.

Hoa. Yea?

Mon. Most firm, sir; and I have learnt her [20
lodging. Here my suit begins, sir; if I might
but entreat your worship to be a countenance
for me, and speak a good word (for your words
will pass), I nothing doubt but I might set fair
for the widow; nor shall your labour, sir, end [25
altogether in thanks; two hundred angels ——

Hoa. So, so: what suitors has she?

Mon. There lies the comfort, sir; the report
of her is yet but a whisper; and only solicited

[1] Scheme.

[2] A proverb: I'll make the venture. A bolt was an
arrow with a round knob at its head; a shaft, sharp and
barbed.

[3] A street.

[4] In love with some one else.

by young riotous Witgood, nephew to your mortal adversary.   31

Hoa. Ha! art certain he's her suitor?

Mon. Most certain, sir; and his uncle very industrious to beguile the widow, and make up
the match.   35

Hoa. So: very good.

Mon. Now, sir, you know this young Witgood
is a spendthrift, dissolute fellow.

Hoa. A very rascal.

Mon. A midnight surfeiter.   40

Hoa. The spume of a brothel-house.

Mon. True, sir; which being well told in your
worship's phrase, may both heave him out of
her mind, and drive a fair way for me to the
widow's affections.   45

Hoa. Attend me about five.

Mon. With my best care, sir.   *Exit.*

Hoa. Fool, thou hast left thy treasure with a
         thief,
To trust a widower with a suit in love!
Happy revenge, I hug thee! I have not only [50
the means laid before me, extremely to cross my
adversary, and confound the last hopes of his
nephew, but thereby to enrich my estate, aug-
ment my revenues, and build mine own fortunes
greater: ha, ha!   55
I'll mar your phrase, o'erturn your flatteries,
Undo your windings, policies, and plots,
Fall like a secret and despatchful plague
On your secured comforts. Why, I am able
To buy three of Lucre; thrice outbid him,   60
Let my out-monies be reckoned and all.

Enter three [of WITGOOD'S] *Cred.tors.*

1 [*Cred.*] I am glad of this news.

2 [*Cred.*] So are we, by my faith.

3 [*Cred.*] Young Witgood will be a gallant
again now.   65

Hoa. Peace.   [*Listening.*]

1 *Cred.* I promise you, Master Cockpit, she's
a mighty rich widow.

2 *Cred.* Why, have you ever heard of her?

1 *Cred.* Who? Widow Medler? She lies [70
open to much rumour.

3 *Cred.* Four hundred a-year, they say, in
very good land.

1 *Cred.* [Nay,] take 't of my word, if you believe that, you believe the least.   75

2 *Cred.* And to see how close he keeps it!

1 *Cred.* O, sir, there's policy in that, to prevent better suitors.

3 *Cred.* He owes me a hundred pound, and I
protest I ne'er lookt for a penny.   80

1 *Cred.* He little dreams of our coming; he'll
wonder to see his creditors upon him.

                              Exeunt [Creditors].

Hoa. Good, his creditors: I'll follow. This
makes for me:
All know the widow's wealth; and 't is well
         known
I can estate her fairly, ay, and will.   85
In this one chance shines a twice happy
         fate;
I both deject my foe and raise my state.
                                       Exit.

                  MUSIC.

ACT III

[SCENE I.][1]

[*Enter*] WITGOOD *with his* Creditors.

Wit. Why, alas, my creditors, could you find no other time to undo me but now ? Rather your malice appears in this than the justness of the debt.

1 Cred. Master Witgood, I have forborne [5 my money long.

Wit. I pray, speak low, sir: what do you mean ?

2 Cred. We hear you are to be married suddenly to a rich country widow.   10

Wit. What can be kept so close but you creditors hear on 't ! Well, 't is a lamentable state, that our chiefest afflictors should first hear of our fortunes. Why, this is no good course, i' faith, sirs : if ever you have hope to be satis- [15 fied, why do you seek to confound the means that should work it ? There 's neither piety, no, nor policy in that. Shine favourably now : why, I may rise and spread again, to your great comforts.   20

1 Cred. He says true, i' faith.

Wit. Remove me now, and I consume for ever.

2 Cred. Sweet gentleman !

Wit. How can it thrive which from the sun you sever ?

3 Cred. It cannot, indeed.   25

Wit. O, then, show patience ! I shall have enough

To satisfy you all.

Cred.   Ay, if we could

Be content, a shame take us !

Wit.   For, look you ;

I am but newly sure[2] yet to the widow,

And what a rend might this discredit make ! 30

Within these three days will I bind you lands

For your securities.

1 Cred. No, good Master Witgood :

Would 't were as much as we dare trust you with !

Wit. I know you have been kind ; however, now,

Either by wrong report or false incitement, 35

Your gentleness is injured : in such

A state as this a man cannot want foes.

If on the sudden he begin to rise,

No man that lives can count his enemies.

You had some intelligence, I warrant ye, 40

From an ill-willer.

2 Cred. Faith, we heard you brought up a rich widow, sir, and were suddenly to marry her.   44

Wit. Ay, why there it was ; I knew 't was so ; but since you are so well resolv'd,[3] of my faith toward you, let me be so much favour'd of you, I beseech you all ——

All. O, it shall not need, i' faith, sir ! —— 49

Wit. As to lie still awhile, and bury my debts in silence, till I be fully possest of the widow ; for the truth is — I may tell you as my friends ——

All. O, O, O ! ——   5½

Wit. I am to raise a little money in the city, toward the setting forth of myself, for my own credit and your comfort. Now, if my former debts should be divulg'd, all hope of my proceedings were quite extinguisht.   59

1 Cred. Do you hear, sir ? I may deserve your custom hereafter ; pray, let my money be accepted before a stranger's. Here 's forty pound I receiv'd as I came to you ; if that may stand you in any stead, make use on 't. [*Offers him money, which he at first declines.*] Nay, pray, sir ; 't is at your service.   66

Wit. You do so ravish me with kindness, that

I am constrain'd to play the maid, and take it.

1 Cred. Let none of them see it, I beseech you.   70

Wit. Faugh !

1 Cred. I hope I shall be first in your remembrance

After the marriage rites.

Wit.   Believe it firmly.

1 Cred. So. — What, do you walk, sirs ?   74

2 Cred. I go. — [*Aside to* WITGOOD.] — Take no care, sir, for money to furnish you ; within this hour I send you sufficient. Come, Master Cockpit, we both stay for you.

3 Cred. I ha' lost a ring, i' faith ; I 'll follow you presently [*exeunt 1 and 2 Creditors*] — but [80 you shall find it, sir. I know your youth and expenses have disfurnisht you of all jewels : there 's a ruby of twenty pound price, sir ; bestow it upon your widow. [*Offers him the ring, which he at first declines.*] — What, man ! 't [85 will call up her blood to you ; beside, if I might so much work with you, I would not have you beholding to those bloodsuckers for any money.

Wit. Not I, believe it.

3 Cred. They 're a brace of cut-throats.   90

Wit. I know 'em.

3 Cred. Send a note of all your wants to my shop, and I 'll supply you instantly.

Wit. Say you so ? Why, here 's my hand then, no man living shalt do 't but thyself.   95

3 Cred. Shall I carry it away from 'em both, then ?

Wit. I' faith, shalt thou.

3 Cred. Troth, then, I thank you, sir.   99

Wit. Welcome, good Master Cockpit. *Exit* [3 Creditor]. — Ha, ha, ha ! why, is not this better now than lying a-bed ? I perceive there 's nothing conjures up wit sooner than poverty, and nothing lays it down sooner than wealth and lechery : this has some savour yet. O that [105 I had the mortgage from mine uncle as sure in possession as these trifles ! I would forswear brothel at noonday, and muscadine[4] and eggs, at midnight.

Enter Courtesan.

Cour. Master Witgood, where are you ?   11c

Wit. Holla !

Cour. Rich news !

Wit. Would 't were all in plate !

----

[1] Witgood's lodgings.   [2] Betrothed.   [3] Satisfied.

[4] A sweet wine, taken with eggs as an aphrodisiac.

Cour. There's some in chains and jewels. I am so haunted with suitors, Master Witgood, I know not which to despatch first.   116

Wit. You have the better term,[1] by my faith.

Cour. Among the number
One Master Hoard, an ancient gentleman.

Wit. Upon my life, my uncle's adversary.   120

Cour. It may well hold so, for he rails on you,
Speaks shamefully of him.

Wit.   As I could wish it.

Cour. I first denied him, but so cunningly,
It rather promis'd him assured hopes,
Than any loss of labour.

Wit.   Excellent !   125

Cour. I expect him every hour with gentlemen,
With whom he labours to make good his words,
To approve you riotous, your state consum'd.
Your uncle ——

Wit. Wench, make up thy own fortunes [130
now ; do thyself a good turn once in thy days.
He's rich in money, movables, and lands ;
marry him : he's an old doting fool, and that's
worth all ; marry him. 'Twould be a great comfort to me to see thee do well, i' faith ; marry [135
him. 'T would ease my conscience well to see
thee well bestow'd ; I have a care of thee,
i' faith.

Cour. Thanks, sweet Master Witgood.

Wit. I reach at farther happiness : first, I [140
am sure it can be no harm to thee, and there
may happen goodness to me by it. Prosecute it
well ; let's send up for our wits, now we require
their best and most pregnant assistance.

Cour. Step in, I think I hear 'em. [*Exeunt.*]

Enter HOARD *and* Gentlemen *with the* Host *as
serving-man.*

Hoa. Art thou the widow's man ? By my [146
faith, sh'as a company of proper men then.

Host. I am the worst of six, sir ; good enough
for blue coats.

Hoa. Hark hither : I hear say thou art in
most credit with her.   151

Host. Not so, sir.

Hoa. Come, come, thou 'rt modest. There's a
brace of royals ;[2] prithee, help me to th' speech
of her.   [*Gives him money.*] 155

Host. I'll do what I may, sir, always saving
myself harmless.

Hoa. Go to, do 't, I say ; thou shalt hear better from me.

Host. [*Aside.*] Is not this a better place [160
than five mark[3] a-year standing wages ? Say a
man had but three such clients in a day, methinks he might make a poor living on't ; beside, I was never brought up with so little honesty to refuse any man's money ; never. [165
What gulls there are a' this side the world ! Now
know I the widow's mind ; none but my young
master comes in her clutches : ha, ha, ha !
                                          Exit.

---

[1] Playing on the two meanings of "suitors," at law and for love.
[2] Gold pieces 15s. in value.
[3] The mark was worth 13s. 4d.

Hoa. Now, my dear gentlemen, stand firmly
to me ;
You know his follies and my worth.

1 [*Gent.*]   We do, sir.   170

2 [*Gent.*] But, Master Hoard, are you sure he
is not i' th' house now ?

Hoa. Upon my honesty, I chose this time
A' purpose, fit : the spendthrift is abroad.
Assist me ; here she comes.

                    Enter Courtesan.

                    Now, my sweet widow.   175

Cour. You 're welcome, Master Hoard.

Hoa. Despatch, sweet gentlemen, despatch.—
I am come, widow, to prove those my words
Neither of envy sprung nor of false tongues,
But such as their[4] deserts and actions   180
Do merit and bring forth ; all which these
gentlemen,
Well known, and better reputed, will confess.

Cour. I cannot tell
How my affections may dispose of me ;
But surely if they find him so desertless,   185
They 'll have that reason to withdraw themselves :
And therefore, gentlemen, I do entreat you,
As you are fair in reputation
And in appearing form, so shine in truth.
I am a widow, and, alas, you know,   190
Soon overthrown ! 'T is a very small thing
That we withstand, our weakness is so great :
Be partial unto neither, but deliver,
Without affection, your opinion.

Hoa. And that will drive it home.   195

Cour. Nay, I beseech your silence, Master
Hoard ;
You are a party.

Hoa.   Widow, not a word.

1 *Gent.* The better first to work you to belief,
Know neither of us owe him flattery,
Nor t' other malice ; but unbribed censure,[5] 200
So help us our best fortunes !

Cour.   It suffices.

1 *Gent.* That Witgood is a riotous, undone
man,
Imperfect both in fame and in estate,
His debts wealthier than he, and executions
In wait for his due body, we 'll maintain   205
With our best credit and our dearest blood.

Cour. Nor land nor living, say you ? Pray,
take heed
You do not wrong the gentleman.

1 *Gent.*   What we speak
Our lives and means are ready to make good.

Cour. Alas, how soon are we poor souls beguil'd !   210

2 *Gent.* And for his uncle ——

Hoa.   Let that come to me.
His uncle, a severe extortioner ;
A tyrant at a forfeiture ; greedy of others'
Miseries ; one that would undo his brother,
Nay, swallow up his father, if he can,   215
Within the fathoms of his conscience.

1 *Gent.* Nay, believe it, widow,

---

[4] Lucre's and Witgood's.   [5] Judgment.

You had not only matcht yourself to wants,
But in an evil and unnatural stock.
　　Hoa. [*Aside to* Gent.] Follow hard, gentle-
　　　men, follow hard.　　　　　　　　　　220
　　Cour. Is my love so deceiv'd? Before you
all
I do renounce him; on my knees I vow
He ne'er shall marry me.
　　Wit. [*looking in.*] Heaven knows he never
　　　meant it!
　　Hoa. [*Aside to* Gent.] There take her at the
　　　bound.　　　　　　　　　　　　　　225
　　1 *Gent.* Then, with a new and pure affection,
Behold yon gentleman; grave, kind, and rich,
A match worthy yourself: esteeming him,
You do regard your state.
　　Hoa. [*Aside to* Gent.] I'll make her a joint-
　　　ure, say.　　　　　　　　　　　　　230
　　1 *Gent.* He can join land to land, and will
　　　possess you
Of what you can desire.
　　2 *Gent.*　　　　　　Come, widow, come.
　　Cour. The world is so deceitful!
　　1 *Gent.*　　　　　There, 't is deceitful,
Where flattery, want, and imperfection lies;
But none of these in him: push!
　　Cour.　　　　　　Pray, sir ——　　235
　　1 *Gent.* Come, you widows are ever most backward when you should do yourselves most good;
but were it to marry a chin not worth a hair
now, then you would be forward enough. Come,
clap hands, a match.　　　　　　　　　240
　　Hoa. With all my heart, widow. [Hoard
　　　and Courtesan *shake hands.*] — Thanks,
　　　gentlemen:
I will deserve your labour, and [*to* Courtesan]
thy love.
　　Cour. Alas, you love not widows but for
wealth!
I promise you I ha' nothing, sir.
　　Hoa.　　　　　　　Well said, widow,
Well said; thy love is all I seek, before　　245
These gentlemen.
　　Cour.　　　　Now I must hope the best.
　　Hoa. My joys are such they want to be ex-
prest.
　　Cour. But, Master Hoard, one thing I must
remember you of, before these gentlemen, your
friends: how shall I suddenly avoid the [250
loathed soliciting of that perjur'd Witgood,
and his tedious, dissembling uncle? who this
very day hath appointed a meeting for the same
purpose too; where, had not truth come forth,
I had been undone, utterly undone!　　255
　　Hoa. What think you of that, gentlemen?
　　1 *Gent.* 'T was well devised.
　　Hoa. Hark thee, widow: train[1] out young
Witgood single; hasten him thither with thee,
somewhat before the hour; where, at the [260
place appointed, these gentlemen and myself
will wait the opportunity, when, by some slight
removing him from thee, we'll suddenly enter
and surprise thee, carry thee away by boat to
Cole-Harbour, have a priest ready, and there [265
clap it up instantly. How likest it, widow?

　　Cour. In that it pleaseth you, it likes me well.
　　Hoa. I'll kiss thee for those words. Come,
　　　gentlemen,
Still must I live a suitor to your favours,
Still to your aid beholding.　　　　　　270
　　1 *Gent.* We're engag'd, sir;
'T is for our credits now to see 't well ended.
　　Hoa. 'T is for your honours, gentlemen; nay,
　　　look to 't.
Not only in joy, but I in wealth excel:
No more sweet widow, but, sweet wife, fare-
　　　well.　　　　　　　　　　　　　　275
　　Cour. Farewell, sir.
　　　　　　　Exeunt [Hoard *and* Gentlemen].

　　　　　　　Re-enter Witgood.

　　Wit. O for more scope! I could laugh
eternally! Give you joy, Mistress Hoard, I
promise your fortune was good, forsooth; you've
fell upon wealth enough, and there's young [280
gentlemen enow can help you to the rest. Now
it requires our wits: carry thyself but heedfully
now, and we are both ——

　　　　　　　[*Re-enter* Host.]

　　Host. Master Witgood, your uncle.　　284
　　Wit. Cuds me![2] remove thyself awhile; I'll
serve for him. [*Exeunt* Courtesan *and* Host.]

　　　　　　　Enter Lucre.

　　Luc. Nephew, good morning, nephew.
　　Wit. The same to you, kind uncle.
　　Luc. How fares the widow? Does the meeting hold?
　　Wit. O, no question of that, sir.　　　290
　　Luc. I'll strike the stroke, then, for thee;
no more days.[3]
　　Wit. The sooner the better, uncle. O, she's
mightily follow'd!
　　Luc. And yet so little rumour'd!　　　295
　　Wit. Mightily: here comes one old gentleman, and he'll make her a jointure of three
hundred a year, forsooth; another wealthy
suitor will estate his son in his lifetime, and
make him weigh down the widow; here a [300
merchant's son will possess her with no less
than three goodly lordships at once, which were
all pawns to his father.
　　Luc. Peace, nephew, let me hear no more of
'em; it mads me. Thou shalt prevent[4] 'em [305
all. No words to the widow of my coming
hither. Let me see — 't is now upon nine: before twelve, nephew, we will have the bargain
struck, we will, faith, boy.　　　　　　309
　　Wit. O, my precious uncle!　　　*Exeunt.*

　　　　　　　[Scene II.][5]

　　　Enter Hoard *and* Niece [Joyce].

　　Hoa. Niece, sweet niece, prithee, have a care
to my house; I leave all to thy discretion. Be
content to dream awhile; I'll have a husband
for thee shortly: put that care upon me, wench,

---

[2] Gods me. Perhaps a corruption of "God save me!"
[3] Postponements.　　　　　　　[4] Anticipate.
[5] A room in Hoard's house.

[1] Entice.

for in choosing wives and husbands I am only [5
fortunate; I have that gift given me.   *Exit.*

Joy. But 't is not likely you should choose
for me,
Since nephew to your chiefest enemy
Is he whom I affect: but, O, forgetful!
Why dost thou flatter thy affections so,   10
With name of him that for a widow's bed
Neglects thy purer love? Can it be so,
Or does report dissemble?

[*Enter* GEORGE.]

How, now, sir?

Geo. A letter, with which came a private
charge.

Joy. Therein I thank your care.

[*Exit* GEORGE.]
— I know this hand — 15
(*Reads.*) Dearer than sight, what the world re-
ports of me, yet believe not; rumour will alter
shortly: be thou constant; I am still the same
that I was in love, and I hope to be the same in
fortunes.   20
Theodorus Witgood.
I am resolv'd:[1] no more shall fear or doubt
Raise their pale powers to keep affection out.
Exit.

[SCENE III.][2]

Enter, with a Drawer, HOARD *and two* Gentlemen.

Dra. You're very welcome, gentlemen. —
Dick, show those gentlemen the Pomegranate[3]
there.

Hoa. Hist!

Dra. Up those stairs, gentlemen.   5

Hoa. Hist! drawer!

Dra. Anon, sir.

Hoa. Prithee, ask at the bar if a gentlewoman
came not in lately.

Dra. William, at the bar, did you see any [10
gentlewoman come in lately? Speak you ay,
speak you no?

Within. No, none came in yet, but Mistress
Florence.

Dra. He says none came in yet, sir, but one [15
Mistress Florence.

Hoa. What is that Florence? A widow?

Dra. Yes, a Dutch widow.

Hoa. How?   19

Dra. That's an English drab, sir: give your
worship good morrow.   [*Exit.*]

Hoa. A merry knave, i'faith! I shall remember a Dutch widow the longest day of my life.

1 *Gent.* Did not I use most art to win the
widow?   25

2 *Gent.* You shall pardon me for that, sir;
Master Hoard knows I took her at best 'vantage.

Hoa. What's that, sweet gentlemen, what's
that?   30

2 *Gent.* He will needs bear me down, that his
art only wrought with the widow most.

1 Convinced.   2 A tavern.
3 Rooms in taverns had such individual names.

Hoa. O, you did both well, gentlemen, you
did both well, I thank you.

1 *Gent.* I was the first that mov'd her.   35

Hoa. You were, i'faith.

2 *Gent.* But it was I that took her at the
bound.

Hoa. Ay, that was you: faith, gentlemen,
't is right.

3 *Gent.* I boasted least, but 't was I join'd
their hands.

Hoa. By th' mass, I think he did: you did
all well,   40
Gentlemen, you did all well; contend no more.

1 *Gent.* Come, yon room's fittest.

Hoa. True, 't is next the door.   *Exeunt.*

Enter WITGOOD, Courtesan, Host [*and* Drawer].

Dra. You're very welcome: please you to
walk up stairs; cloth's laid, sir.   45

Cour. Up stairs? Troth, I am very weary,
Master Witgood.

Wit. Rest yourself here awhile, widow; we'll
have a cup of muscadine in this little room.

Dra. A cup of muscadine? You shall have
the best, sir.   51

Wit. But, do you hear, sirrah?

Dra. Do you call? Anon, sir.

Wit. What is there provided for dinner?

Dra. I cannot readily tell you, sir: if you
please you may go into the kitchen and see [56
yourself, sir; many gentlemen of worship do
use to do it, I assure you, sir.   *Exit.*

Host. A pretty familiar, prigging rascal; he
has his part without book.   60

Wit. Against you are ready to drink to me,
widow, I'll be present to pledge you.

Cour. Nay, I commend your care, 't is done
well of you. [*Exit* WITGOOD.] — 'Las, what have
I forgot!   65

Host. What, mistress?

Cour. I slipt my wedding ring off when I
washt, and left it at my lodging. Prithee, run;
I shall be sad without it. [*Exit* Host.] — So,
he's gone. Boy!   70

[*Enter* Boy.]

Boy. Anon, forsooth.

Cour. Come hither, sirrah: learn secretly if
one Master Hoard, an ancient gentleman, be
about house.

Boy. I heard such a one nam'd.   75

Cour. Commend me to him.

Re-enter HOARD *and* Gentlemen.

Hoa. Ay, boy, do thy commendations.

Cour. O, you come well: away, to boat, begone.

Hoa. Thus wise men are reveng'd, give two
for one.   *Exeunt.*

Re-enter WITGOOD *and* Vintner.

Wit. I must request   80
You, sir, to show extraordinary care:
My uncle comes with gentlemen, his friends,
And 't is upon a making.[4]

4 Matching.

Vin.   Is it so?
I'll give a special charge, good Master Wit-
    good.
May I be bold to see her?
    Wit.   Who? the widow?   85
With all my heart, i' faith, I'll bring you to her.
    Vin. If she be a Staffordshire gentlewoman,
't is much if I know her not.
    Wit. How now? Boy! drawer!
    Vin. Hie!   90

[*Re-enter* Boy.]

Boy. Do you call, sir?
    Wit. Went the gentlewoman up that was
here?
    Boy. Up, sir? She went out, sir.
    Wit. Out, sir?   95
    Boy. Out, sir: one Master Hoard, with a
guard of gentlemen, carried her out at back
door, a pretty while since, sir.
    Wit. Hoard? Death and darkness! Hoard?

[*Re-enter* Host.]

Host. The devil of ring I can find.   100
    Wit. How now? What news? Where's the
widow?
    Host. My mistress? Is she not here, sir?
    Wit. More madness yet!
    Host. She sent me for a ring.   105
    Wit. A plot, a plot!—To boat! she's stole
away.
    Host. What?

Enter LUCRE *and* Gentlemen.

Wit. Follow! Inquire old Hoard, my uncle's
adversary.   [*Exit* Host.]
    Luc. Nephew, what's that?   110
    Wit. Thrice-miserable wretch!
    Luc. Why, what's the matter?
    Vin. The widow's borne away, sir.
    Luc. Ha? passion of me!—A heavy wel-
come, gentlemen.
    1 Gent. The widow gone?   115
    Luc. Who durst attempt it?
    Wit. Who but old Hoard, my uncle's adver-
sary?
    Luc. How?
    Wit. With his confederates.
    Luc. Hoard, my deadly enemy?— Gentle-
men, stand to me,   120
I will not bear it; 't is in hate of me;
That villain seeks my shame, nay, thirsts my
blood;
He owes me mortal malice.
I'll spend my wealth on this despiteful plot,
Ere he shall cross me and my nephew thus.   125
    Wit. So maliciously!

Re-enter Host.

Luc. How now, you treacherous rascal?
    Host. That's none of my name, sir.
    Wit. Poor soul, he knew not on 't!
    Luc. I'm sorry. I see then 't was a mere plot.
    Host. I trac'd 'em nearly ——
    Luc.   Well?
    Host.   And hear for certain   131
They have took Cole-Harbour.

Luc.   The devil's sanctuary!
They shall not rest; I'll pluck her from his
    arms —
Kind and dear gentlemen,
If ever I had seats within your breasts ——   135
    1 Gent. No more, good sir; it is a wrong to
us
To see you injur'd; in a cause so just
We'll spend our lives but we will right our
    friends.
    Luc. Honest and kind! come we've delay'd
too long;
Nephew, take comfort; a just cause is strong.
        Exeunt [*all but* WITGOOD].   140
    Wit. That's all my comfort, uncle. Ha, ha,
ha!
Now may events fall luckily and well;
He that ne'er strives, says wit, shall ne'er excel.
                                    [*Exit.*]

[SCENE IV.] [1]

Enter DAMPIT, *the usurer, drunk.*

Dam. When did I say my prayers? In anno
88, when the great armada was coming; and in
anno 99, when the great thunder and lightning
was, I pray'd heartily then, i' faith, to overthrow Poovies' new buildings; I kneeled by [5]
my great iron chest, I remember.

[*Enter* AUDREY.]

Aud. Master Dampit, one may hear you before they see you: you keep sweet hours, Master Dampit; we were all a-bed three hours ago.
    Dam. Audrey?   10
    Aud. O, you 're a fine gentleman!
    Dam. So I am i' faith, and a fine scholar. Do
you use to go to bed so early, Audrey?
    Aud. Call you this early, Master Dampit?
    Dam. Why, is 't not one of clock i' th' [15]
morning? Is not that early enough? Fetch me
a glass of fresh beer.
    Aud. Here, I have warm'd your nightcap for
you, Master Dampit.
    Dam. Draw it on then. I am very weak [20]
truly: I have not eaten so much as the bulk of
an egg these three days.
    Aud. You have drunk the more, Master
Dampit.
    Dam. What's that?   25
    Aud. You mought,[2] an you would, Master
Dampit.
    Dam. I answer you, I cannot. Hold your
prating; you prate too much, and understand
too little: are you answered? Give me a glass [30]
of beer.
    Aud. May I ask you how you do, Master
Dampit?
    Dam. How do I? I' faith, naught.
    Aud. I ne'er knew you do otherwise.   35
    Dam. I eat not one pen'north of bread these
two years. Give me a glass of fresh beer. I am
not sick, nor I am not well.
    Aud. Take this warm napkin about your
neck, sir, whilst I help to make you unready.[3]

---

[1] A room in Dampit's house.
[2] Might.   [3] Undress you.

Dam. How now, Audrey-prater, with your scurvy devices, what say you now?   42

Aud. What say I, Master Dampit? I say nothing, but that you are very weak.

Dam. Faith, thou hast more cony-catch- [45 ing[1] devices than all London.

Aud. Why, Master Dampit, I never deceiv'd you in all my life.

Dam. Why was that? Because I never did trust thee.   50

Aud. I care not what you say, Master Dampit.

Dam. Hold thy prating: I answer thee, thou art a beggar, a quean, and a bawd: are you answer'd?   55

Aud. Fie, Master Dampit! a gentleman, and have such words?

Dam. Why, thou base drudge of infortunity, thou kitchen-stuff-drab of beggary, roguery, and coxcombry, thou cavernesed quean of [60 foolery, knavery, and bawdreaminy, I 'll tell thee what, I will not give a louse for thy fortunes.

Aud. No, Master Dampit? and there 's a gentleman comes a-wooing to me, and he doubts[2] [65 nothing but that you will get me from him.

Dam. I? If I would either have thee or lie with thee for two thousand pound, would I might be damn'd! Why, thou base, impudent quean of foolery, flattery, and coxcombry, are [70 you answer'd?

Aud. Come, will you rise and go to bed, sir?

Dam. Rise, and go to bed too, Audrey? How does Mistress Proserpine?

Aud. Fooh!   75

Dam. She 's as fine a philosopher of a stinkard's wife, as any within the liberties. Faugh, faugh, Andrey!

Aud. How now, Master Dampit?

Dam. Fie upon 't, what a choice of stinks [80 here is! What hast thou done, Audrey? Fie upon't, here 's a choice of stinks indeed! Give me a glass of fresh beer, and then I will to bed.

Aud. It waits for you above, sir.   85

Dam. Foh! I think they burn horns in Barnard's Inn. If ever I smelt such an abominable stink, usury forsake me,   [*Exit.*]

Aud. They be the stinking nails of his trampling feet, and he talks of burning horns. *Exit.*

ACT IV

[SCENE I.]

Enter at Cole-Harbour HOARD, *the Widow,* [LAMPREY, SPICHCOCK,] *and Gentlemen, he married now.*

1 [*Gent.*] Join hearts, join hands,
In wedlock's bands,
Never to part
Till death cleave your heart.
[*To* HOARD.] You shall forsake all other women;   5

[*To* Courtesan.] You lords, knights, gentlemen, and yeomen.
What my tongue slips
Make up with your lips.

Hoa. Give you joy, Mistress Hoard; let the kiss come about.   [*Knocking.*]
Who knocks? Convey my little pig-eater[3] out.

Luc. [*within.*] Hoard!   11

Hoa. Upon my life, my adversary, gentlemen!

Luc. [*within.*] Hoard, open the door, or we will force it ope:
Give us the widow.

Hoa.   Gentlemen, keep 'em out.

Lam. He comes upon his death that enters here.   15

Luc. [*within.*] My friends, assist me!

Hoa.   He has assistants, gentlemen.

Lam. Tut, nor him nor them we in this action fear.

Luc. [*within.*] Shall I, in peace, speak one word with the widow?

Cour. Husband, and gentlemen, hear me but a word.

Hoa. Freely, sweet wife.

Cour.   Let him in peaceably;   20
You know we 're sure from any act of his.

Hoa. Most true.

[Cour.][4] You may stand by and smile at his old weakness:
Let me alone to answer him.

Hoa. Content;   26
'T will be good mirth, i' faith. How think you, gentlemen?

Lam. Good gullery!

Hoa. Upon calm conditions let him in.

Luc. [*within.*] All spite and malice!

Lam. Hear me, Master Lucre: 30
So you will vow a peaceful entrance
With those your friends, and only exercise
Calm conference with the widow, without fury,
The passage shall receive you.

Enter LUCRE, [Gentlemen, *and* Host.]

Luc.   I do vow it.

Lam. Then enter and talk freely: here she stands.   35

Luc. O, Master Hoard, your spite has watcht the hour!
You 're excellent at vengeance, Master Hoard.

Hoa. Ha, ha, ha!

Luc. I am the fool you laugh at:
You are wise, sir, and know the seasons well.—
Come hither, widow: why is it thus?   41
O, you have done me infinite disgrace,
And your own credit no small injury!
Suffer mine enemy so despitefully
To bear you from my nephew? O, I had   45
Rather half my substance had been forfeit
And begg'd by some starv'd rascal!

Cour. Why, what would you wish me do, sir?
I must not overthrow my state for love:
We have too many precedents for that;   50
From thousands of our wealthy undone widows
One may derive some wit. I do confess

---

[1] Cheating.   [2] Fears.

[3] A term of endearment.
[4] Qq. give this speech to Lucre.

I lov'd your nephew, nay, I did affect him
Against the mind and liking of my friends ;
Believ'd his promises ; lay here in hope   55
Of flatter'd living, and the boast of lands.
Coming to touch his wealth and state indeed,
It appears dross ; I find him not the man ;
Imperfect, mean, scarce furnisht of his needs :
In words, fair lordships ; in performance, hovels :
Can any woman love the thing that is not ?   61
   Luc. Broke you for this ?
   Cour. Was it not cause too much ?
Send to inquire his state : most part of it
Lay two years mortgag'd in his uncle's hands.
   Luc. Why, say it did, you might have known
      my mind :   66
I could have soon restor'd it.
   Cour. Ay, had I but seen any such thing per-
      form'd,
Why, 't would have tied my affection, and con-
      tain'd
Me in my first desires. Do you think, i' faith,   70
That I could twine such a dry oak as this,
Had promise in your nephew took effect ?
   Luc. Why, and there 's no time past ; and
      rather than
My adversary should thus thwart my hopes,
I would ——   75
   Cour. Tut, you 've been ever full of golden
      speech :
If words were lands, your nephew would be rich.
   Luc. Widow, believe 't, I vow by my best bliss,
Before these gentlemen, I will give in
The mortgage to my nephew instantly,   80
Before I sleep or eat.
   1 Gent. [*friend to* LUCRE.] We 'll pawn our
      credits,
Widow, what he speaks shall be perform'd
In fulness.
   Luc.   Nay, more ; I will estate him
In farther blessings ; he shall be my heir ;
I have no son ;   85
I 'll bind myself to that condition.
   Cour. When I shall hear this done, I shall
      soon yield
To reasonable terms.
   Luc.   In the mean season,
Will you protest, before these gentlemen,   89
To keep yourself as you 're now at this present ?
   Cour. I do protest, before these gentlemen,
I will be as clear then as I am now.
   Luc. I do believe you. Here 's your own hon-
      est servant,
I 'll take him along with me.
   Cour.   Ay, with all my heart.
   Luc. He shall see all perform'd, and bring
      you word.   95
   Cour. That 's all I wait for.
   Hoa. What, have you finisht, Master Lucre ?
      Ha, ha, ha !
   Luc. So laugh, Hoard, laugh at your poor
      enemy, do ;
The wind may turn, you may be laught at too ;
Yes, marry may you, sir. — Ha, ha, ha !   100
         Exeunt [LUCRE, Gentlemen, *and*
            Host].
   Hoa. Ha, ha, ha ! if every man that swells in
      malice

Could be reveng'd as happily as I,
He would choose hate, and forswear amity. —
What did he say, wife, prithee ?
   Cour. Faith, spoke to ease his mind.
   Hoa.   O, O, O ! 105
   Cour. You know now, little to any purpose.
   Hoa.   True, true, true !
   Cour. He would do mountains now.
   Hoa.   Ay, ay, ay, ay.
   Lam. You 've struck him dead, Master Hoard.
   Spi. And his nephew desperate.
   Hoa.   I know 't sirs, I.
Never did man so crush his enemy. *Exeunt.* 110

[SCENE II.][1]

Enter LUCRE, Gentlemen, [*and* Host,] *meeting*
      SAM FREEDOM.

   Luc. My son-in-law, Sam Freedom, where 's
      my nephew ?
   Free. O man in lamentation,[2] father.
   Luc. How !
   Free. He thumps his breast like a gallant
dicer that has lost his doublet, and stands [5
in 's shirt to do penance.
   Luc. Alas, poor gentleman !
   Free. I warrant you may hear him sigh in a
still evening to your house at Highgate.
   Luc. I prithee send him in.   10
   Free. Were it to do a greater matter, I will
not stick with you, sir, in regard you married
my mother.   [*Exit.*]
   Luc. Sweet gentlemen, cheer him up ; I will
but fetch the mortgage and return to you [15
instantly.   *Exit.*
   1 [Gent.] We 'll do our best, sir. — See where
      he comes,
E'en joyless and regardless of all form.

[*Enter* WITGOOD.]

   2 [Gent.] Why, how now, Master Witgood ?
Fie ! you a firm scholar, and an understand- [20
ing gentleman, and give your best parts to pas-
sion ?[3]
   1 Gent. Come, fie fie !
   Wit. O, gentlemen ——
   1 Gent. Sorrow of me, what a sigh was there,
      sir !   25
Nine such widows are not worth it.
   Wit. To be borne from me by that lecher,
      Hoard !
   1 Gent. That vengeance is your uncle's ; be-
      ing done
More in despite to him than wrong to you :
But we bring comfort now.
   Wit.   I beseech you, gentlemen —— [30
   2 Gent. Cheer thyself, man ; there 's hope of
      her, i' faith.
   Wit. Too gladsome to be true.

Re-enter LUCRE.

   Luc.   Nephew, what cheer ?
Alas, poor gentleman, how art thou chang'd !

   [1] A room in Lucre's house.
   [2] " O man in desperation " is the name of an old
tune mentioned by Nashe and Peele.
   [3] Grief.

Call thy fresh blood into thy cheeks again:
She comes.

Wit. Nothing afflicts me so much, 35
But that it is your adversary, uncle,
And merely plotted in despite of you.

Luc. Ay, that 's it mads me, spites me ! I 'll
spend my wealth ere he shall carry her so, because I know 't is only to spite me. Ay, this [40
is it. Here, nephew [*giving a paper*], before
these kind gentlemen, I deliver in your mortgage, my promise to the widow ; see, 't is done.
Be wise, you 're once more master of your own.
The widow shall perceive now you are not [45
altogether such a beggar as the world reputes
you ; you can make shift to bring her to three
hundred a-year, sir.

1 Gent. By'rlady, and that 's no toy, sir.

Luc. A word, nephew. 50

1 Gent. [*to Host.*] Now you may certify the
widow.

Luc. You must conceive it aright, nephew,
now ;
To do you good I am content to do this.

Wit. I know it, sir. 55

Luc. But your own conscience can tell I
had it
Dearly enough of you.

Wit. Ay, that 's most certain.

Luc. Much money laid out, beside many a
journey
To fetch the rent ; I hope you 'll think on 't,
nephew.

Wit. I were worse than a beast else, i' faith.

Luc. Although to blind the widow and the
world, 61
I out of policy do 't, yet there 's a conscience,
nephew.

Wit. Heaven forbid else !

Luc. When you are full possest,
'T is nothing to return it.

Wit. Alas, a thing quickly done, uncle ! 65

Luc. Well said ! you know I give it you but
in trust.

Wit. Pray, let me understand you rightly,
uncle :
You give it me but in trust ?

Luc. No.

Wit. That is, you trust me with it ? 70

Luc. True, true.

Wit. [*Aside.*] But if ever I trust you with it
again,
Would I might be truss'd up for my labour !

Luc. You can all witness, gentlemen ; and
you, sir yeoman ? 75

Host. My life for yours, sir, now, I know my
mistress's mind too well toward your nephew ;
let things be in preparation ; and I 'll train her
hither in most excellent fashion. *Exit.*

Luc. A good old boy ! — Wife ! Jenny ! 80

Enter Wife.

Mis. L. What 's the news, sir ?

Luc. The wedding-day 's at hand : prithee,
sweet wife, express thy housewifery. Thou 'rt
a fine cook, I know 't ; thy first husband married thee out of an alderman's kitchen ; go [85
to, he rais'd thee for raising of paste. What !

here 's none but friends ; most of our beginnings must be winkt at. — Gentlemen, I invite
you all to my nephew's wedding against Thursday morning. 90

1 Gent. With all our hearts, and we shall joy
to see
Your enemy so mockt.

Luc. He laught at me, gentlemen ; ha, ha,
ha ! *Exeunt* [*all but* WITGOOD].

Wit. He has no conscience, faith, would
laugh at them :
They laugh at one another ; 95
Who then can be so cruel ? Troth, not I ;
I rather pity now, than ought envy.
I do conceive such joy in mine own happiness,
I have no leisure yet to laugh at their follies.
Thou soul of my estate, I kiss thee ! 100
[*To the mortgage.*]
I miss life's comfort when I miss thee
O, never will we part again,
Until I leave the site of men !
We 'll ne'er trust conscience of our kin,
Since cozenage brings that title in. *Exit.* 105

[SCENE III.][1]

Enter three Creditors.

1 Cred. I 'll wait these seven hours but I 'll
see him caught.

2 Cred. Faith, so will I.

3 Cred. Hang him, prodigal ! He 's stript of
the widow. 5

1 Cred. A' my troth, she 's the wiser ; she
has made the happier choice : and I wonder of
what stuff those widows' hearts are made of,
that will marry unfledg'd boys before comely
thrum-chinn'd [2] gentlemen. 10

Enter Boy.

Boy. News, news, news !

1 Cred. What, boy ?

Boy. The rioter is caught.

1 Cred. So, so, so, so ! it warms me at the
heart ;
I love a' life to see dogs upon men. 15
O, here he comes.

Enter WITGOOD, *with* Sergeants.

Wit. My last joy was so great, it took away
the sense of all future afflictions. What a day is
here o'ercast ! How soon a black tempest rises !

1 Cred. O, we may speak with you now, [20
sir ! What 's become of your rich widow ? I
think you may cast your cap at the widow, may
you not, sir ?

2 Cred. He a rich widow ? Who, a prodigal,
a daily rioter, and a nightly vomiter ? He a [25
widow of account ? He a hole i' th' Counter.[3]

Wit. You do well, my masters, to tyrannise
over misery, to afflict the afflicted ; 't is a custom
you have here amongst you ; I would wish you
never leave it, and I hope you 'll do as I bid
you. 31

---

[1] A street.
[2] Rough-chinned. "Thrum" is the end of the warp
in weaving.
[3] A debtors' prison.

1 *Cred.* Come, come, sir, what say you extempore now to your bill of a hundred pound?
A sweet debt for froating[1] your doublets?
2 *Cred.* Here 's mine of forty.   35
3 *Cred.* Here 's mine of fifty.
Wit. Pray, sirs, — you 'll give me breath?
1 *Cred.* No, sir, we 'll keep you out of breath
still; then we shall be sure you will not run away
from us.   40
Wit. Will you but hear me speak?
2 *Cred.* You shall pardon us for that, sir; we
know you have too fair a tongue of your own;
you overcame us too lately, a shame take you!
We are like to lose all that for want of wit- [45
nesses; we dealt in policy then: always when
we strive to be most politic we prove most coxcombs: *non plus ultra* I perceive by us, we 're
not ordain'd to thrive by wisdom, and therefore
we must be content to be tradesmen.   50
Wit. Give me but reasonable time, and I protest I 'll make you ample satisfaction.
1 *Cred.* Do you talk of reasonable time to
us?
Wit. 'T is true, beasts know no reasonable
time.   55
2 *Cred.* We must have either money or carcass.
Wit. Alas, what good will my carcass do you?
3 *Cred.* O, 't is a secret delight we have [60
amongst us! We that are us'd to keep birds in
cages, have the heart to keep men in prison, I
warrant you.
Wit. [*Aside.*] I perceive I must crave a little
more aid from my wits: do but make shift for [65
me this once, and I 'll forswear ever to trouble
you in the like fashion hereafter; I 'll have
better employment for you, an I live. — You 'll
give me leave, my masters, to make trial of
my friends, and raise all means I can?   70
1 *Cred.* That 's our desires, sir.

Enter HOST.

Host. Master Witgood.
Wit. O, art thou come?
Host. May I speak one word with you in private, sir?   75
Wit. No, by my faith, canst thou; I am in
hell here, and the devils will not let me come
to thee.
1 *Cred.* Do you call us devils? You shall
find us puritans. — Bear him away; let [80
'em talk as they go: we 'll not stand to hear 'em.
— Ah, sir, am I a devil? I shall think the better of myself as long as I live: a devil, i'faith!
                                         Exeunt.

[SCENE IV.][2]

Enter HOARD.

Hoa. What a sweet blessing hast thou, Master Hoard, above a multitude! Wilt thou never
be thankful? How dost thou think to be blest
another time? Or dost thou count this the full
measure of thy happiness? By my troth, I [5
think thou dost: not only a wife large in posses-

sions, but spacious in content; she 's rich, she 's
young, she 's fair, she 's wise. When I wake, I
think of her lands — that revives me; when I
go to bed, I dream of her beauty — and that 's [10
enough for me: she 's worth four hundred a-year
in her very smock, if a man knew how to use it.
But the journey will be all, in troth, into the
country; to ride to her lands in state and order
following; my brother, and other worshipful [15
gentlemen, whose companies I ha' sent down
for already, to ride along with us in their goodly
decorum beards, their broad velvet cassocks,
and chains of gold twice or thrice double;
against which time I 'll entertain some ten [20
men of mine own into liveries, all of occupations
or qualities; I will not keep an idle man about
me: the sight of which will so vex my adversary
Lucre — for we 'll pass by his door a' purpose,
make a little stand for [the] nonce, and have [25
our horses curvet before the window — certainly
he will never endure it, but run up and hang
himself presently.

[*Enter* Servant.]

How now, sirrah, what news? Any that offer
their service to me yet?   30
Ser. Yes, sir, there are some i' th' hall that
wait for your worship's liking, and desire to be
entertain'd.
Hoa. Are they of occupation?
Ser. They are men fit for your worship, sir. 35
Hoa. Sayest so? Send 'em all in. [*Exit* Servant.] — To see ten men ride after me in watchet[3] liveries, with orange-tawny capes, — 't will
cut his comb, i' faith.

Enter All [Tailor, Barber, Perfumer, Falconer,
and Huntsman].

How now? Of what occupation are you, sir? 40
Tai. A tailor, an 't please your worship.
Hoa. A tailor? O, very good: you shall serve
to make all the liveries. — What are you, sir?
Bar. A barber, sir.
Hoa. A barber? very needful: you shall shave
all the house, and, if need require, stand for [46
a reaper i' th' summer time. — You, sir?
Per. A perfumer.
Hoa. I smelt you before. Perfumers, of all
men, had need carry themselves uprightly; [50
for if they were once knaves, they would be
smelt out quickly. — To you, sir?
Fal. A falconer, an 't please your worship.
Hoa. Sa ho, sa ho, sa ho![4] — And you, sir?
Hunt. A huntsman, sir.   55
Hoa. There, boy, there, boy, there, boy![5] I
am not so old but I have pleasant days to come.
I promise you, my masters, [I take such a good
liking to you, that I entertain you all;] I put
you already into my countenance, and you [60
shall be shortly in my livery; but especially you
two, my jolly falconer and my bonny huntsman;
we shall have most need of you at my wife's
manor-houses i' th' country; there 's goodly
parks and champion[6] grounds for you; we [65

---

[1] Rubbing with perfume.
[2] A room in Hoard's house.
[3] Light blue.
[4] A hawking cry.
[5] A hunting cry.
[6] Champaign.

shall have all our sports within ourselves; all
the gentlemen a' th' country shall be beholding
to us and our pastimes.

Fal. And we 'll make your worship admire,
sir.   70

Hoa. Sayest thou so? Do but make me
admire, and thou shall want for nothing. — My
tailor.

Tai. Anon, sir.

Hoa. Go presently in hand with the liveries. 75

Tai. I will, sir.

Hoa. My barber.

Bar. Here, sir.

Hoa. Make 'em all trim fellows, louse 'em
well, — especially my huntsman, — and cut [80
all their beards of the Polonian fashion. — My
perfumer.

Per. Under your nose, sir.

Hoa. Cast a better savour upon the knaves,
to take away the scent of my tailor's feet, and
my barber's lotium-water.   86

Per. It shall be carefully perform'd, sir.

Hoa. But you, my falconer and huntsman,
the welcom'st men alive, i' faith!

Hunt. And we 'll show you that, sir, shall [90
deserve your worship's favour.

Hoa. I prithee, show me that. — Go, you
knaves all, and wash your lungs i' th' buttery,
go. [*Exeunt* Tailor, Barber, &c.] — By th'
mass, and well remem'red! I 'll ask my wife [95
that question. — Wife, Mistress Jane Hoard!

Enter Courtesan, *alter'd in apparel.*

Cour. Sir, would you with me?

Hoa. I would but know, sweet wife, which
might stand best to thy liking, to have the wedding dinner kept here or i' th' country?   100

Cour. Hum : — faith, sir, 't would like me
better here ; here you were married, here let all
rites be ended.

Hoa. Could a marquesse [1] give a better answer? Hoard, bear thy head aloft, thou 'st a
wife will advance it.   106

Enter Host *with a letter.*

What haste comes here now? Yea, a letter?
Some dreg of my adversary's malice. Come
hither; what 's the news?   109

Host. A thing that concerns my mistress, sir.
                              Giving a letter to Courtesan.

Hoa. Why then it concerns me, knave.

Host. Ay, and you, knave, too (cry your worship mercy). You are both like to come into
trouble, I promise you, sir ; a pre-contract. [2]

Hoa. How? a pre-contract, sayest thou? 115

Host. I fear they have too much proof on 't,
sir: old Lucre, he runs mad up and down, and
will to law as fast as he can ; young Witgood
laid hold on by his creditors, he exclaims [119
upon you a' t' other side, says you have wrought
his undoing by the injurious detaining of his
contract.

Hoa. Body a' me!

---

[1] Marchioness.

[2] A pre-contract of marriage could not be set aside
without the mutual consent of the parties. (Bullen.)

Host. He will have utmost satisfaction ;
The law shall give him recompense, he says. 125

Cour. [*Aside.*] Alas, his creditors so merciless ! my state being yet uncertain, I deem it
not unconscionable to further him.

Host. True, sir.

Hoa. Wife, what says that letter? Let me
construe it.   131

Cour. Curst be my rash and unadvised words !
          [*Tears the letter and stamps on it.*]
I 'll set my foot upon my tongue,
And tread my inconsiderate grant to dust.

Hoa. Wife ——   135

Host. [*Aside.*] A pretty shift, i' faith ! I commend a woman when she can make away a letter from her husband handsomely, and this was
cleanly done, by my troth.

Cour. I did, sir ;   140
Some foolish words I must confess did pass,
Which now litigiously he fastens on me.

Hoa. Of what force? Let me examine 'em.

Cour. Too strong, I fear : would I were well
freed of him !   145

Hoa. Shall I compound?

Cour. No, sir, I 'd have it done some nobler
                                              way
Of your side ; I 'd have you come off with honour ;
Let baseness keep with them. Why, have you not
The means, sir? The occasion 's offer'd you. 150

Hoa. Where, how, dear wife?

Cour. He is now caught by his creditors ; the
slave 's needy; his debts petty ; he 'll rather
bind himself to all inconveniences than rot in
prison ; by this only means you may get a release
from him. 'T is not yet come to his uncle's [156
hearing ; send speedily for the creditors ; by
this time he 's desperate ; he 'll set his hand to
anything : take order for his debts, or discharge
'em quite: a pax on him, let 's be rid of a
rascal !   161

Hoa. Excellent !
Thou dost astonish me. — Go, run, make haste ;
Bring both the creditors and Witgood hither.

Host. [*Aside.*] This will be some revenge yet.
                                              [*Exit.*]

Hoa. In the mean space I 'll have a release
drawn. —   166
Within there !

                    [*Enter* Servant.]

[*Ser.*] Sir?

Hoa. Sirrah, come take directions ; go to my
scrivener.

Cour. [*Aside, while* HOARD *gives directions to
the* Servant.] I 'm yet like those whose
riches lie in dreams,   170
If I be wakt, they 're false ; such is my fate,
Who venture deeper than the desperate state.
Though I have sinn'd, yet could I become new,
For where I once vow, I am ever true.

Hoa. Away, despatch, on my displeasure,
quickly.   [*Exit* Servant.]   175
Happy occasion ! pray Heaven he be in the
right vein now to set his hand to 't, that nothing
alter him ; grant that all his follies may meet
in him at once, to besot him enough ! I pray for
him, i' faith, and here he comes.   180

[*Enter* WITGOOD *and* Creditors.]

Wit. What would you with me now, my uncle's spiteful adversary?

Hoa. Nay, I am friends.

Wit.   Ay, when your mischief's spent.

Hoa. I heard you were arrested.

Wit.   Well, what then?
You will pay none of my debts, I am sure.   185

Hoa. A wise man cannot tell ;
There may be those conditions 'greed upon
May move me to do much.

Wit.   Ay, when? —
'T is thou, perjured woman ! (O, no name
Is vile enough to match thy treachery !)   190
That art the cause of my confusion.

Cour. Out, you penurious slave !

Hoa.   Nay, wife, you are too froward ;
Let him alone ; give losers leave to talk.

Wit. Shall I remember thee of another promise
Far stronger than the first?

Cour.   I'd fain know that.   195

Wit. 'T would call shame to thy cheeks.

Cour.   Shame !

Wit.   Hark in your ear. — [*They converse
apart.*]
Will he come off, think'st thou, and pay my
debts roundly?

Cour. Doubt nothing ; there's a release a-
drawing and all, to which you must set your
hand.   201

Wit. Excellent !

Cour. But methinks, i' faith, you might have
made some shift to discharge this yourself, having in the mortgage, and never have burd'ned
my conscience with it.   206

Wit. A' my troth, I could not, for my creditors' cruelties extend to the present.

Cour. No more. —
Why, do your worst for that, I defy you.   210

Wit. You 're impudent : I 'll call up witnesses.

Cour. Call up thy wits, for thou hast been
devoted
To follies a long time.

Hoa.   Wife, you 're too bitter. —
Master Witgood, and you, my masters, you shall
hear a mild speech come from me now, and [215
this it is : 't has been my fortune, gentlemen, to
nave an extraordinary blessing poured upon me
a' late, and here she stands ; I have wedded
her, and bedded her, and yet she is little the
worse. Some foolish words she hath past to you
in the country, and some peevish[1] debts you [221
owe here in the city ; set the hare's head to the
goose-giblet,[2] release you her of her words, and
I 'll release you of your debts, sir.

Wit. Would you so ?   I thank you for that,
sir ; I cannot blame you, i' faith.   226

Hoa. Why, are not debts better than words,
sir ?

Wit. Are not words promises, and are not
promises debts, sir ?   230

Hoa. [*Aside.*] He plays at back-racket[3] with
me.

<hr>

[1] Trifling.   [2] A proverbial phrase.
[3] A return in tennis ; a *tu quoque.*

1 *Cred.* Come hither, Master Witgood, come
hither ; be rul'd by fools once.

2 *Cred.* We are citizens, and know what belongs to 't.   236

1 *Cred.* Take hold of his offer : pax on her,
let her go. If your debts were once discharg'd,
I would help you to a widow myself worth ten
of her.   240

3 *Cred.* Mass, partner, and now you remember me on 't, there 's Master Mulligrub's sister
newly fallen a widow.

1 *Cred.* Cuds me, as pat as can be !   There 's
a widow left for you ; ten thousand in money,
beside plate, jewels, *et cetera:* I warrant it a [246
match ; we can do all in all with her. Prithee,
despatch ; we 'll carry thee to her presently.

Wit. My uncle will ne'er endure me when he
shall hear I set my hand to a release.   250

2 *Cred.* Hark, I 'll tell thee a trick for that.
I have spent five hundred pound in suits in
my time, I should be wise. Thou 'rt now a
prisoner ; make a release ; take 't of my word,
whatsoever a man makes as long as he is in [255
durance, 't is nothing in law, not thus much.
                    [*Snaps his fingers.*]

Wit. Say you so, sir ?

3 *Cred.* I have paid for 't ; I know 't.

Wit. Proceed then ; I consent.

3 *Cred.* Why, well said.   260

Hoa. How now, my masters, what have you
done with him ?

1 *Cred.* With much ado, sir, we have got him
to consent.

Hoa. Ah — a — a ! and what come his debts
to now ?   266

1 *Cred.* Some eight score odd pounds, sir.

Hoa. Naw, naw, naw, naw, naw ! tell me the
second time ; give me a lighter sum. They are
but desperate debts, you know ; ne'er call'd [270
in but upon such an accident ; a poor, needy
knave, he would starve and rot in prison. Come,
come, you shall have ten shillings in the pound,
and the sum down roundly.

1 *Cred.* You must make it a mark, sir.   275

Hoa. Go to then, tell your money in the
meantime ; you shall find little less there. [*Giving them money.*] — Come, Master Witgood,
you are so unwilling to do yourself good now !

[*Enter* Scrivener.]

Welcome, honest scrivener. — Now you shall
hear the release read.   281

Scri. [*reads.*] Be it known to all men, by
these presents, that I, Theodorus Witgood,
gentleman, sole nephew to Pecunius Lucre,
having unjustly made title and claim to one [285
Jane Medler, late widow of Anthony Medler,
and now wife to Walkadine Hoard, in consideration of a competent sum of money to discharge my debts, do for ever hereafter disclaim
any title, right, estate, or interest in or to [290
the said widow, late in the occupation of the
said Anthony Medler, and now in the occupation of Walkadine Hoard ; as also neither to
lay claim by virtue of any former contract,
grant, promise, or demise, to any of her [295
manors, manor-houses, parks, groves, meadow-

grounds, arable lands, barns, stacks, stables, dove-holes, and coney-burrows; together with all her cattle, money, plate, jewels, borders, chains, bracelets, furnitures, hangings, [300 moveables or immoveables. In witness where-of, I the said Theodorus Witgood, have inter-changeably set to my hand and seal before these presents, the day and date above written.

Wit. What a precious fortune hast thou slipt here, like a beast as thou art!　　　　　306

Hoa. Come, unwilling heart, come.

Wit. Well, Master Hoard, give me the pen; I see 'T is vain to quarrel with our destiny.

[*Signs the paper.*]

Hoa. O, as vain a thing as can be! you [310 cannot commit a greater absurdity, sir. So, so; give me that hand now; before all these pres-ents, I am friends for ever with thee.

Wit. Troth, and it were pity of my heart now, if I should bear you any grudge, i' faith. [315

Hoa. Content: I 'll send for thy uncle against the wedding dinner; we will be friends once again.

Wit. I hope to bring it to pass myself, sir.

Hoa. How now? Is 't right, my masters? 320

1 Cred. 'T is something wanting, sir; yet it shall be sufficient.

Hoa. Why, well said; a good conscience makes a fine show now-a-days. Come, my mas-ters, you shall all taste of my wine ere you de-part.　　　　　326

All. We follow you, sir.

[*Exeunt* HOARD *and* Scrivener.]

Wit. [*Aside.*] I 'll try these fellows now. — A word, sir: what, will you carry me to that widow now?　　　　　330

1 Cred. Why, do you think we were in ear-nest, i' faith? Carry you to a rich widow? We should get much credit by that: a noted rioter! a contemptible prodigal! 'T was a trick we have amongst us to get in our money: fare you well, sir.　　　　　*Exeunt* [Creditors]. 336

Wit. Farewell, and be hang'd, you short pig-hair'd, ram-headed rascals! He that believes in you shall ne'er be sav'd, I warrant him. By this new league I shall have some access unto my love.　　　　　341

[JOYCE *appears above.*]

Joyce. Master Witgood!

Wit. My life!

Joyce. Meet me presently; that note directs you [*throws him a letter*]: I would not be sus- [345 pected. Our happiness attends us: farewell.

Wit. A word 's enough.　　　*Exeunt* [*severally*].

[SCENE V.][1]

DAMPIT *the usurer in his bed;* AUDREY *spin-ning by;* [Boy.]

[*Aud. singing.*]

Let the usurer cram him, in interest that excel,
There 's pits enow to damn him, before he comes to hell;

　　　　　[1] Dampit's bed-chamber.

In Holborn some, in Fleet Street some,
Where'er he come there 's some, there 's some.

Dam. *Trahe, trahito,* draw the curtain; give me a sip of sack more.　　　　　6

[*While he drinks,*] *enter* Gentlemen, [LAMPREY *and* SPICHCOCK.]

Lam. Look you; did not I tell you he lay like the devil in chains, when he was bound for a thousand year?

Spi. But I think the devil had no steel [10 bedstaffs; he goes beyond him for that.

Lam. Nay, do but mark the conceit of his drinking; one must wipe his mouth for him with a muckinder,[2] do you see, sir?

Spi. Is this the sick trampler? Why, he [15 is only bed-rid with drinking.

Lam. True, sir. He spies us.

Dam. What, Sir Tristram? You come and see a weak man here, a very weak man.

Lam. If you be weak in body, you should [20 be strong in prayer, sir.

Dam. O, I have prayed too much, poor man!

Lam. There 's a taste of his soul for you!

Spi. Faugh, loathsome!

Lam. I come to borrow a hundred pound [25 of you, sir.

Dam. Alas, you come at an ill time! I can-not spare it i' faith; I ha' but two thousand i' th' house.

Aud. Ha, ha, ha!　　　　　30

Dam. Out, you gernative[3] quean, the mulli-pood[3] of villany, the spinner of concupiscency!

Enter [SIR LAUNCELOT *and*] *other* Gentlemen.

Sir L. Yea, gentlemen, are you here before us? How is he now?

Lam. Faith, the same man still: the tav- [35 ern bitch has bit him i' the head.[4]

Sir L. We shall have the better sport with him: peace. — And how cheers Master Dampit now?

Dam. O, my bosom, Sir Launcelot, how cheer I! Thy presence is restorative.　　　　　41

Sir L. But I hear a great complaint of you, Master Dampit, among gallants.

Dam. I am glad of that, i' faith: prithee, what?　　　　　45

Sir L. They say you are wax'd proud a' late, and if a friend visit you in the afternoon, you 'll scarce know him.

Dam. Fie, fie; proud? I cannot remember any such thing: sure I was drunk then.　　　50

Sir L. Think you so, sir?

Dam. There 't was, i' faith; nothing but the pride of the sack; and so certify 'em. — Fetch sack, sirrah.

Boy. A vengeance sack you once!　　　　55

[*Exit, and returns presently with sack.*]

Aud. Why, Master Dampit, if you hold on as you begin, and lie a little longer, you need

　　　　　[2] Handkerchief.
　　　　　[3] As before, Dampit's words must be interpreted by the context.
　　　　　[4] *I. e.* he is drunk.

not take care how to dispose your wealth; you'll make the vintner your heir.　　59

Dam. Out, you babliaminy, you unfeathered, cremitoried quean, you cullisance of scabiosity!

Aud. Good words, Master Dampit, to speak before a maid and a virgin!

Dam. Hang thy virginity upon the pole of carnality!　　65

Aud. Sweet terms! My mistress shall know 'em.

Lam. Note but the misery of this usuring slave: here he lies, like a noisome dunghill, full of the poison of his drunken blasphemies; [70 and they to whom he bequeaths all, grudge him the very meat that feeds him, the very pillow that eases him. Here may a usurer behold his end. What profits it to be a slave in this world, and a devil i' th' next?　　75

Dam. Sir Launcelot, let me buss[1] thee, Sir Launcelot; thou art the only friend that I honour and respect.

Sir L. I thank you for that, Master Dampit.

Dam. Farewell, my bosom Sir Launcelot.　80

Sir L. Gentlemen, an you love me, let me step behind you, and one of you fall a-talking of me to him.

Lam. Content.— Master Dampit ——

Dam. So, sir.　　85

Lam. Here came Sir Launcelot to see you e'en now.

Dam. Hang him, rascal!

Lam. Who? Sir Launcelot?

Dam. Pythagorical rascal!　　90

Lam. Pythagorical?

Dam. Ay, he changes his cloak when he meets a sergeant.

Sir L. What a rogue's this!

Lam. I wonder you can rail at him, sir; [95 he comes in love to see you.

Dam. A louse for his love! his father was a comb-maker; I have no need of his crawling love. He comes to have longer day,[2] the superlative rascal!　　100

Sir L. 'Sfoot, I can no longer endure the rogue!— Master Dampit, I come to take my leave once again, sir.

Dam. Who? my dear and kind Sir Launcelot, the only gentleman of England? Let me hug thee; farewell, and a thousand.　106

Lam. Compos'd of wrongs and slavish flatteries!

Sir L. Nay, gentlemen, he shall show you more tricks yet; I'll give you another taste [110 of him.

Lam. Is't possible?

Sir L. His memory is upon departing.

Dam. Another cup of sack!　　114

Sir L. Mass, then 't will be quite gone! Before he drink that, tell him there's a country client come up, and here attends for his learned advice.

Lam. Enough.

Dam. One cup more, and then let the bell [120 toll: I hope I shall be weak enough by that time.

Lam. Master Dampit ——

Dam. Is the sack spouting?

Lam. 'T is coming forward, sir. Here's [125 a countryman, a client of yours, waits for your deep and profound advice, sir.

Dam. A coxcomb, where is he? Let him approach: set me up a peg higher.

Lam. [*to* Sir Laun.] You must draw near, sir.　　131

Dam. Now, good man fooliaminy, what say you to me now?

Sir L. Please your good worship, I am a poor man, sir ——　　135

Dam. What make you in my chamber then?

Sir L. I would entreat your worship's device[3] in a just and honest cause, sir.

Dam. I meddle with no such matters; I refer 'em to Master No-man's office.　140

Sir L. I had but one house left me in all the world, sir, which was my father's, my grandfather's, my great-grandfather's, and now a villain has unjustly wrung me out, and took possession on 't.　　145

Dam. Has he such feats? Thy best course is to bring thy *ejectione firmae*, and in seven year thou mayst shove him out by the law.

Sir L. Alas, an 't please your worship, I have small friends and less money!　　150

Dam. Hoyday! this gear will fadge well.[4] Hast no money? Why, then, my advice is, thou must set fire a' th' house, and so get him out.

Lam. That will break strife, indeed.　155

Sir L. I thank your worship for your hot counsel, sir.— Altering but my voice a little, you see he knew me not: you may observe by this, that a drunkard's memory holds longer in the voice than in the person. But, gentle- [160 men, shall I show you a sight? Behold the little dive-dapper[5] of damnation, Gulf the usurer, for his time worse than t'other.

Enter Hoard *with* Gulf.

Lam. What's he comes in with him?

Sir L. Why, Hoard, that married lately [165 the Widow Medler.

Lam. O, I cry you mercy, sir.

Hoa. Now, gentlemen visitants, how does Master Dampit?　　169

Sir L. Faith, here he lies, e'en drawing in, sir, good canary as fast as he can, sir; a very weak creature, truly, he is almost past memory.

Hoa. Fie, Master Dampit! you lie lazing a-bed here, and I come to invite you to my [175 wedding-dinner: up, up, up!

Dam. Who's this? Master Hoard? Who hast thou married, in the name of foolery?

Hoa. A rich widow.

Dam. A Dutch widow?[6]　　180

Hoa. A rich widow; one Widow Medler.

Dam. Medler? She keeps open house.

Hoa. She did, I can tell you, in her t'other husband's days; open house for all comers;

---

[1] Kiss.　　[2] Time to repay borrowed money.

[3] Used designedly for "advice."　　[4] Work well.

[5] The didapper or dabchick, a small water-bird.

[6] See III. iii. 17–19.

horse and man was welcome, and room enough
for 'em all.   185

Dam. There 's too much for thee, then ; thou
mayst let out some to thy neighbours.

Gulf. What, hung alive in chains ? O spectacle ! bed-staffs oi steel ? *O monstrum hor-* [190
rendum, informe, ingens, cui lumen ademptum ! [1]
O Dampit, Dampit, here 's a just judgment
shown upon usury, extortion, and trampling
villany !

Sir L. This is excellent, thief rails upon [195
the thief !

Gulf. Is this the end of cut-throat usury,
brothel, and blasphemy ? Now mayst thou see
what race a usurer runs.

Dam. Why, thou rogue of universality, [200
do not I know thee ? Thy sound is like the
cuckoo, the Welsh ambassador ; [2] thou cowardly slave, that offers to fight with a sick man
when his weapon 's down ! Rail upon me in my
naked [3] bed ? Why, thou great Lucifer's [205
little vicar ! I am not so weak but I know a
knave at first sight. Thou inconscionable rascal ! thou that goest upon Middlesex juries,
and wilt make haste to give up thy verdict
because thou wilt not lose thy dinner ! Are [210
you answered ?

Gulf. An 't were not for shame ——
              Draws his dagger.

Dam. Thou wouldst be hang'd then.

Lam. Nay, you must exercise patience, Master Gulf, always in a sick man's chamber.   215

Sir L. He 'll quarrel with none, I warrant
you, but those that are bed-rid.

Dam. Let him come, gentlemen, I am arm'd :
reach my close-stool hither.

Sir L. Here will be a sweet fray anon : [220
I 'll leave you, gentlemen.

Lam. Nay, we 'll go along with you.— Master Gulf ——

Gulf. Hang him, usuring rascal !

Sir L. Pish, set your strength to his, your [225
wit to his !

Aud. Pray, gentlemen, depart ; his hour 's
come upon him.— Sleep in my bosom, sleep.

Sir L. Nay, we have enough of him, i' faith ;
keep him for the house.   230
Now make your best :
For thrice his wealth I would not have his breast.

Gulf. A little thing would make me beat him
now he 's asleep.

Sir L. Mass, then 't will be a pitiful day [235
when he wakes : I would be loath to see that
day : come.

Gulf. You overrule me, gentlemen, i' faith.
              Exeunt.

ACT V

[SCENE I.] [4]

Enter LUCRE *and* WITGOOD.

Wit. Nay, uncle, let me prevail with you so
much ; I' faith, go, now he has invited you.

[1] Virg. *Aen.* iii. 658.

[2] So named, Nares conjectures, from the bird's migrat-
ing from the west.

[3] *I. e.* Naked in bed.   [4] A room in Lucre's house.

Luc. I shall have great joy there when he
has borne away the widow !

Wit. Why, la, I thought where I should [5
find you presently. Uncle, a' my troth, 't is
nothing so.

Luc. What 's nothing so, sir ? Is not he married to the widow ?

Wit. No, by my troth, is he not, uncle.   10

Luc. How ?

Wit. Will you have the truth on' t ? He is
married to a whore, i' faith.

Luc. I should laugh at that.

Wit. Uncle, let me perish in your favour [15
if you find it not so ; and that 't is I that have
married the honest woman.

Luc. Ha ! I 'd walk ten mile 'a foot to see
that, i' faith.

Wit. And see 't you shall, or I 'll ne'er see [20
you again.

Luc. A quean, i' faith ? Ha, ha, ha ! *Exeunt.*

[SCENE II.] [5]

Enter HOARD, *tasting wine,* Host *following in
a livery cloak.*

Hoa. Pup, pup, pup, pup, pup, I like not this
wine : is there never a better tierce in the
house ?

Host. Yes, sir, there are as good tierces in the
house as any are in England.   5

Hoa. Desire your mistress, you knave, to
taste 'em all over ; she has best skill.

Host. [*Aside.*] Has she so ? The better for
her, and the worse for you.   *Exit.*

Hoa. Arthur !   10

[*Enter* ARTHUR.]

Is the cupboard of plate set out ?

Arth. All 's in order, sir.   [*Exit.*]

Hoa. I am in love with my liveries every
time I think on 'em ; they make a gallant show,
by my troth. Niece !   15

[*Enter* JOYCE.]

Joyce. Do you call, sir ?

Hoa. Prithee, show a little diligence, and
overlook the knaves a little ; they 'll filch and
steal to-day, and send whole pasties home to
their wives ; an thou be'st a good niece, do [20
not see me purloin'd.

Joyce. Fear it not, sir — [*Aside.*] I have cause :
though the feast be prepared for you, yet it
serves fit for my wedding-dinner too.   [*Exit.*]

Enter two Gentlemen [LAMPREY *and* SPICH-
COCK].

Hoa. Master Lamprey and Master Spich- [25
cock, two the most welcome gentlemen alive !
Your fathers and mine were all free a' th' fishmongers. [6]

Lam. They were indeed, sir. You see bold
guests, sir ; soon entreated.   30

Hoa. And that 's best, sir.

[5] A room in Hoard's house.

[6] Members of the Fishmongers' Company.

[*Enter* Servant.]

How now, sirrah?

Ser. There's a coach come to th' door, sir.
                                    [*Exit.*]

Hoa. My Lady Foxtone, a' my life! — Mistress Jane Hoard! wife! — Mass, 't is her lady-[35 ship indeed!

[*Enter* Lady FOXTONE.]

Madam, you are welcome to an unfurnisht house, dearth of cheer, scarcity of attendance.

L. Fox. You are pleas'd to make the worst, sir.   40

Hoa. Wife!

[*Enter* Courtesan.]

L. Fox. Is this your wife?

Hoa. Yes, madam. — Salute my Lady Foxtone.

Cour. Please you, madam, awhile to taste [45 the air in the garden?

L. Fox. 'T will please us well.

                Exeunt [L. FOXTONE *and* Courtesan].

Hoa. Who would not wed? The most delicious life!

No joys are like the comforts of a wife.   49

Lam. So we bachelors think, that are not troubled with them.

[*Re-enter* Servant.]

Ser. Your worship's brother, with other ancient gentlemen, are newly alighted, sir. [*Exit.*]

Hoa. Master Onesiphorus Hoard? Why, now our company begins to come in.   55

[*Enter* ONESIPHORUS HOARD, LIMBER, *and* KIX.]

My dear and kind brother, welcome, i' faith.

O. Hoa. You see we are men at an hour, brother.

Hoa. Ay, I 'll say that for you, brother; you keep as good an hour to come to a feast as [60 any gentleman in the shire. — What, old Master Limber and Master Kix! Do we meet, i' faith, jolly gentlemen?

Lim. We hope you lack guests, sir?   64

Hoa. O, welcome, welcome! We lack still such guests as your worships.

O. Hoa. Ah, sirrah brother, have you catcht up Widow Medler?

Hoa. From 'em all, brother; and I may tell you I had mighty enemies, those that stuck [70 sore; old Lucre is a sore fox, I can tell you, brother.

O. Hoa. Where is she? I 'll go seek her out;

I long to have a smack at her lips.   74

Hoa. And most wishfully,[1] brother, see where she comes.

[*Re-enter* Courtesan *and* LADY FOXTONE.]

Give her a smack now we may hear it all the house over. (Courtesan *and* O. Hoard *turn back.*)

Cour. O Heaven, I am betray'd! I know that face.   80

¹ Just on your wish.

Hoa. Ha, ha, ha! why, how now? Are you both asham'd? — Come, gentlemen, we 'll look another way.

O. Hoa. Nay, brother, hark you: come, you 're dispos'd to be merry.   85

Hoa. Why do we meet else, man?

O. Hoa. That 's another matter: I was ne'er so 'fraid in my life but that you had been in earnest.

Hoa. How mean you, brother?   90

O. Hoa. You said she was your wife.

Hoa. Did I so? By my troth, and so she is.

O. Hoa. By your troth, brother?

Hoa. What reason have I to dissemble [94 with my friends, brother? If marriage can make her mine, she is mine. Why ——

O. Hoa. Troth, I am not well of a sudden. I must crave pardon, brother; I came to see you, but I cannot stay dinner, i' faith.

Hoa. I hope you will not serve me so, brother?   101

Lim. By your leave, Master Hoard ——

Hoa. What now? what now? Pray, gentlemen: — you were wont to show yourselves wise men.   105

Lim. But you have shown your folly too much here.

Hoa. How?

Kix. Fie, fie! a man of your repute and name!

You 'll feast your friends, but cloy 'em first with shame.

Hoa. This grows too deep; pray, let us reach the sense.   110

Lim. In your old age dote on a courtesan!

Hoa. Ha!

Kix. Marry a strumpet!

Hoa. Gentlemen!

O. Hoa. And Witgood's quean!   114

Hoa. O! nor lands nor living?

O Hoa. Living!

Hoa. [*to* Courtesan.] Speak.

Cour. Alas, you know, at first, sir,

I told you I had nothing!   120

Hoa. Out, out! I am cheated; infinitely cozened!

Lim. Nay, Master Hoard ——

Enter LUCRE, WITGOOD, [*and* JOYCE.]

Hoa. A Dutch widow! a Dutch widow! a Dutch widow!

Luc. Why, nephew, shall I trace thee still a liar?

Wilt make me mad? Is not yon thing the widow?   124

Wit. Why, la, you are so hard a' belief, uncle!

By my troth, she 's a whore.

Luc. Then thou 'rt a knave.

Wit. Negatur argumentum, uncle.   129

Luc. Probo tibi, nephew: he that knows a woman to be a quean must needs be a knave; thou sayst thou knowest her to be one; *ergo*, if she be a quean, thou 'rt a knave.

Wit. Negatur sequela majoris, uncle; he that knows a woman to be a quean must needs be a knave; I deny that.   135

Hoa. Lucre and Witgood, you're both villains; get you out of my house!

Luc. Why, didst not invite me to thy wedding-dinner?   140

Wit. And are not you and I sworn perpetual friends before witness, sir, and were both drunk upon 't?

Hoa. Daintily abus'd! You've put a junt[1] upon me!

Luc. Ha, ha, ha!   145

Hoa. A common strumpet!

Wit. Nay, now
You wrong her, sir; if I were she, I 'd have
The law on you for that; I durst depose for her   149
She ne'er had common use nor common thought.

Cour. Despise me, publish me, I am your wife;
What shame can I have now but you 'll have part?
If in disgrace you share, I sought not you;
You pursued, nay, forc'd me; had I friends would follow it,
Less than your action has been prov'd a rape.

O. Hoa. Brother!   156

Cour. Nor did I ever boast of lands unto you,
Money, or goods; I took a plainer course,
And told you true, I 'd nothing:
If error were committed, 't was by you;   160
Thank your own folly. Nor has my sin been
So odious, but worse has been forgiven;
Nor am I so deform'd, but I may challenge
The utmost power of any old man's love.   164
She that tastes not sin before, twenty to one
but she 'll taste it after: most of you old men
are content to marry young virgins, and
take that which follows; where, marrying one
of us, you both save a sinner and are quit from
a cuckold for ever: 170
And more, in brief, let this your best thoughts win,
She that knows sin, knows best how to hate sin.

Hoa. Curst be all malice! black are the fruits of spite,
And poison first their owners. O, my friends,
I must embrace shame, to be rid of shame!   175
Conceal'd disgrace prevents a public name.
Ah, Witgood! ah, Theodorus!

Wit. Alas, sir, I was prickt in conscience to
see her well bestowed, and where could I bestow
her better than upon your pitiful worship? [180
Excepting but myself, I dare swear she 's a
virgin; and now, by marrying your niece, I
have banisht myself for ever from her. She 's

---

mine aunt now, by my faith, and there 's no
meddling with mine aunt, you know: a sin
against my nuncle.   186

Cour. Lo, gentlemen, before you all
                                        [*Kneels.*]
In true reclaimed form I fall.
Henceforth for ever I defy[2]
The glances of a sinful eye,   190
Waving of fans (which some suppose
Tricks of fancy[3]), treading of toes,
Wringing of fingers, biting the lip,
The wanton gait, th' alluring trip;
All secret friends and private meetings,   195
Close-borne letters and bawds' greetings;
Feigning excuse to women's labours
When we are sent for to th' next neighbour's;
Taking false physic, and ne'er start
To be let blood though sign[4] be at heart;   200
Removing chambers, shifting beds,
To welcome friends in husbands' steads,
Them to enjoy, and you to marry,
They first serv'd, while you must tarry,
They to spend, and you to gather,   205
They to get, and you to father,
These, and thousand, thousand more,
New reclaim'd, I now abhor.

Luc. [*to* WITGOOD.] Ah, here 's a lesson, rioter, for you!

Wit. I must confess my follies; I 'll down too: [*Kneels.*] 210
And here for ever I disclaim
The cause of youth's undoing, game,
Chiefly dice, those true outlanders,
That shake out beggars, thieves, and panders;
Soul-wasting surfeits, sinful riots,   215
Queans' evils, doctors' diets,
'Pothecaries' drugs, surgeons' glisters;
Stabbing of arms[5] for a common mistress;
Riband favours, ribald speeches;
Dear perfum'd jackets, penniless breeches;   220
Dutch flapdragons,[6] healths in urine;
Drabs that keep a man too sure in:
I do defy you all.
Lend me each honest hand, for here I rise
A reclaim'd man, loathing the general vice.   225

Hoa. So, so, all friends! the wedding-dinner cools:
Who seem most crafty prove ofttimes most fools.   [*Exeunt.*]

---

[2] Renounce.   [3] Love.

[4] "According to the directions for bleeding in old almanacs, blood was to be taken from particular parts under particular planets." (Dyce.)

[5] "To stab their arms with daggers, and drink off the blood mixed with wine, to the health of their mistresses, was formerly a frequent practice among gallants." (Dyce.) Cf. *Lear*, II. i. 36.

[6] "Dutchmen had the reputation of being very expert in swallowing flapdragons." (Bullen.)

---

[1] A trick. Some mod. edd. emend to *punk*.

THE CHANGELING

BY

THOMAS MIDDLETON AND WILLIAM ROWLEY

DRAMATIS PERSONAE

VERMANDERO, [governor of the castle of Alicant,] father
  to Beatrice.
TOMASO DE PIRACQUO, a noble lord.
ALONZO DE PIRACQUO, his brother, suitor to Beatrice.
ALSEMERO, a nobleman, afterwards married to Beatrice.
JASPERINO, his friend.
ALIBIUS, a jealous doctor.
LOLLIO, his man.
PEDRO, friend to Antonio.

ANTONIO, the changeling.
FRANCISCUS, the counterfeit madman.
DE FLORES, servant to Vermandero.
Madmen.
Servants.

BEATRICE [-JOANNA], daughter to Vermandero.
DIAPHANTA, her waiting-woman.
ISABELLA, wife of Alibius.

SCENE. — *Alicant.*

ACT I

[SCENE I.] [1]

Enter ALSEMERO.

Als. 'T was in the temple where I first be-
  held her,
And now again the same : what omen yet
Follows of that ? None but imaginary.
Why should my hopes or fate be timorous ?
The place is holy, so is my intent :   5
I love her beauties to the holy purpose ;
And that, methinks, admits comparison
With man's first creation, the place blessed,[2]
And is his right home back, if he achieve it.
The church hath first begun our interview,   10
And that 's the place must join us into one ;
So there 's beginning and perfection too.

Enter JASPERINO.

Jas. O sir, are you here ? Come, the wind 's
  fair with you ;
You 're like to have a swift and pleasant pas-
  sage.
Als. Sure, you 're deceived, friend, 't is con-
  trary,   15
In my best judgment.
Jas.   What, for Malta ?
If you could buy a gale amongst the witches,[3]
They could not serve you such a lucky penny-
  worth
As comes a' God's name.
Als.   Even now I observ'd
The temple's vane to turn full in my face ;   20
I know it is against me.
Jas.   Against you ?
Then you know not where you are.
Als.   Not well, indeed.
Jas. Are you not well, sir ?
Als.   Yes, Jasperino,

Unless there be some hidden malady
Within me, that I understand not.
Jas.   And that 25
I begin to doubt, sir. I never knew
Your inclinations to travels at a pause
With any cause to hinder it, till now.
Ashore you were wont to call your servants up,
And help to trap your horses for the speed ;   30
At sea I 've seen you weigh the anchor with'em,
Hoist sails for fear to lose the foremost breath,
Be in continual prayers for fair winds ;
And have you chang'd your orisons ?
Als.   No, friend ;
I keep the same church, same devotion.   35
Jas. Lover I 'm sure you 're none ; the stoic
  was
Found in you long ago ; your mother nor
Best friends, who have set snares of beauty, ay,
And choice ones too, could never trap you that
  way.
What might be the cause ?
Als.   Lord, how violent 40
Thou art ! I was but meditating of
Somewhat I heard within the temple.
Jas.   Is this
Violence ? 'T is but idleness compar'd
With your haste yesterday.
Als.   I 'm all this while
A-going, man.

Enter Servants.

Jas.   Backwards, I think, sir. Look, 45
Your servants.
1 Ser. The seamen call ; shall we board your
  trunks ?
Als. No, not to-day.
Jas. 'T is the critical day, it seems, and the
  sign in Aquarius.   51
2 Ser. We must not to sea to-day ; this smoke
  will bring forth fire.
Als. Keep all on shore ; I do not know the
  end,

---

[1] A street.   [2] Q. *blest.*   [3] Cf. *Macbeth*, I. iii.

Which needs I must do, of an affair in hand 55
Ere I can go to sea.
1 Ser.   Well, your pleasure.
2 Ser. Let him e'en take his leisure too; we
are safer on land.   *Exeunt* Servants.

Enter BEATRICE, DIAPHANTA, *and* Servants
[ALSEMERO *accosts* BEATRICE *and then kisses
her*].

Jas. [*Aside.*] How now? The laws of the
Medes are chang'd sure; salute a woman! He
kisses too; wonderful! Where learnt he [61
this? and does it perfectly too. In my conscience, he ne'er rehearst it before. Nay, go on;
this will be stranger and better news at Valen-
cia than if he had ransom'd half Greece from
the Turk.   66
Beat. You are a scholar, sir?
Als.   A weak one, lady.
Beat. Which of the sciences is this love you
speak of?
Als. From your tongue I take it to be music.
Beat. You 're skilful in it, can sing at first
sight.   70
Als. And I have show'd you all my skill at
once;
I want more words to express me further,
And must be forc'd to repetition;
I love you dearly.
Beat.   Be better advis'd, sir:
Our eyes are sentinels unto our judgments, 75
And should give certain judgment what they
see;
But they are rash sometimes, and tell us won-
ders
Of common things, which when our judgments
find,
They can then check the eyes, and call them
blind.
Als. But I am further, lady; yesterday 80
Was mine eyes' employment, and hither now
They brought my judgment, where are both
agreed.
Both houses then consenting, 't is agreed;
Only there wants the confirmation
By the hand royal; that 's your part, lady. 85
Beat. Oh, there 's one above me, sir.—[*Aside.*]
For five days past
To be recall'd! Sure mine eyes were mistaken;
This was the man was meant me. That he
should come
So near his time, and miss it!
Jas. We might have come by the carriers [90
from Valencia, I see, and sav'd all our sea-
provision; we are at farthest sure. Methinks I
should do something too;
I meant to be a venturer in this voyage.
Yonder 's another vessel, I 'll board her; 95
If she be lawful prize, down goes her topsail.
                        [*Accosts* DIAPHANTA.]

Enter DE FLORES.

De F. Lady, your father——
Beat.   Is in health, I hope.
De F. Your eye shall instantly instruct you,
lady;
He 's coming hitherward.

Beat.   What needed then
Your duteous preface? I had rather 100
He had come unexpected; you must stall [1
A good presence with unnecessary blabbing;
And how welcome for your part you are.
I 'm sure you know.
De F. [*Aside.*]   Will 't never mend, this
scorn,
One side nor other? Must I be enjoin'd 105
To follow still whilst she flies from me? Well,
Fates, do your worst, I 'll please myself with
sight
Of her at all opportunities,
If but to spite her anger. I know she had
Rather see me dead than living; and yet 120
She knows no cause for 't but a peevish will.
Als. You seem'd displeas'd, lady, on the sud-
den.
Beat. Your pardon, sir, 't is my infirmity;
Nor can I other reason render you
Than his or hers, of [2 some particular thing 115
They must abandon as a deadly poison,
Which to a thousand other tastes were whole-
some;
Such to mine eyes is that same fellow there,
The same that report speaks of the basilisk.[3]
Als. This is a frequent frailty in our nature;
There 's scarce a man amongst a thousand
found 121
But hath his imperfection: one distastes
The scent of roses, which to infinites
Most pleasing is and odoriferous;
One oil, the enemy of poison; 125
Another wine, the cheerer of the heart
And lively refresher of the countenance.
Indeed this fault, if so it be, is general;
There 's scarce a thing but is both lov'd and
loath'd: 129
Myself, I must confess, have the same frailty.
Beat. And what may be your poison, sir?
I 'm bold with you.
Als. What [4 might be your desire, perhaps;
a cherry.
Beat. I am no enemy to any creature
My memory has, but yon gentleman.
Als. He does ill to tempt your sight, if he
knew it. 135
Beat. He cannot be ignorant of that, sir,
I have not spar'd to tell him so; and I want
To help myself, since he 's a gentleman
In good respect with my father, and follows
him.
Als. He 's out of his place then now. 140
                        [*They talk apart.*]
Jas. I am a mad wag, wench.
Dia. So methinks; but for your comfort, I
can tell you, we have a doctor in the city that
undertakes the cure of such.
Jas. Tush, I know what physic is best for the
state of mine own body. 145
Dia. 'T is scarce a well-govern'd state, I be-
lieve.
Jas. I could show thee such a thing with an
ingredient that we two would compound to- [150

---

[1] Forestall. Mod. edd. *stale.*   [2] Q. *or.*
[3] A fabulous animal said to kill with a glance.
[4] Q. *And what.*

gether, and if it did not tame the maddest blood
i' th' town for two hours after, I 'll ne'er profess physic again.

Dia. A little poppy, sir, were good to cause
you sleep.   155

Jas. Poppy? I 'll give thee a pop i' th' lips
for that first, and begin there. Poppy is one
simple indeed, and cuckoo (what-you-call 't)
another. I 'll discover no more now; another
time I 'll show thee all.   [*Exit.*] 160

Enter VERMANDERO *and Servants.*

Beat. My father, sir.
Ver.   O Joanna, I came to meet thee.
Your devotion 's ended?
Beat.   For this time, sir. —
[*Aside.*] I shall change my saint, I fear me; I
                                                    find
A giddy turning in me. — Sir, this while   165
I am beholding to this gentleman,
Who left his own way to keep me company,
And in discourse I find him much desirous
To see your castle. He hath deserv'd it, sir,
If ye please to grant it.
Ver.   With all my heart, sir.
Yet there 's an article between; I must know
Your country; we use not to give survey   171
Of our chief strengths to strangers; our citadels
Are plac'd conspicuous to outward view,
On promonts' [1] tops, but within our secrets.
Als. A Valencian, sir.
Ver.   A Valencian?   175
That 's native, sir. Of what name, I beseech
                                                    you?
Als. Alsemero, sir.
Ver.   Alsemero? Not the son
Of John de Alsemero?
Als.   The same, sir.
Ver. My best love bids you welcome.
Beat.   He was wont   180
To call me so, and then he speaks a most
Unfeign'd truth.
Ver.   O sir, I knew your father;
We two were in acquaintance long ago,
Before our chins were worth iulan [2] down,
And so continued till the stamp of time   185
Had coin'd us into silver. Well, he 's gone;
A good soldier went with him.
Als. You went together in that, sir.
Ver. No, by Saint Jacques, I came behind
                                                    him;
Yet I 've done somewhat too: an unhappy day
Swallowed him at last at Gibraltar,   190
In fight with those rebellious Hollanders.
Was it not so?
Als.   Whose death I had reveng'd,
Or followed him in fate, had not the late
                                                    league
Prevented me.
Ver.   Ay, ay, 't was time to breathe. —
O Joanna, I should ha' told thee news;   195
I saw Piracquo lately.
Beat. [*Aside.*]   That 's ill news.

---

[1] Promontories'.

[2] A coinage from the Greek, meaning the first growth
of the beard.

Ver. He 's hot preparing for this day of tri-
                                                    umph:
Thou must be a bride within this sevennight.
Als. [*Aside.*] Ha!
Beat. Nay, good sir, be not so violent; with
                                        speed   200
I cannot render satisfaction
Unto the dear companion of my soul,
Virginity, whom I thus long have liv'd with,
And part with it so rude and suddenly.
Can such friends divide, never to meet again,
Without a solemn farewell?
Ver.   Tush, tush! there 's a toy.[3] 206
Als. [*Aside.*] I must now part, and never
                                        meet again
With any joy on earth. — Sir, your pardon;
My affairs call on me.
Ver.   How, sir? By no means:
Not chang'd so soon, I hope? You must see my
                                        castle,   210
And her best entertainment, e'er we part;
I shall think myself unkindly us'd else.
Come, come, let 's on; I had good hope your
                                        stay
Had been a while with us in Alicant;
I might have bid you to my daughter's wed-
                                        ding.   215
Als. [*Aside.*] He means to feast me, and poi-
                                        sons me beforehand. —
I should be dearly glad to be there, sir,
Did my occasions suit as I could wish.
Beat. I shall be sorry if you be not there
When it is done, sir; but not so suddenly.   220
Ver. I tell you, sir, the gentleman 's complete,
A courtier and a gallant, enricht
With many fair and noble ornaments;
I would not change him for a son-in-law
For any he in Spain, the proudest he,   225
And we have great ones, that you know.
Als.   He 's much
Bound to you, sir.
Ver.   He shall be bound to me
As fast as this tie can hold him; I 'll want
My will else.
Beat. [*Aside.*]   I shall want mine, if you do
                                        it.
Ver. But come, by the way I 'll tell you more
of him.   230
Als. [*Aside.*] How shall I dare to venture in
                                        his castle,
When he discharges murderers [4] at the gate?
But I must on, for back I cannot go.
Beat. [*Aside.*] Not this serpent gone yet?
                                        [*Drops a glove.*]
Ver.   Look, girl, thy glove 's fallen.
Stay, stay; De Flores, help a little.   235
            [*Exeunt* VERMANDERO, ALSE-
                MERO, *and Servants.*]
De F. Here, lady. [*Offers her the glove.*]
Beat. Mischief on your officious forwardness;
Who bade you stoop? They touch my hand no
                                        more:
There! For t' other's sake I part with this;
                [*Takes off and throws down the
                    other glove.*]

---

[3] Trifling fancy.   [4] Cannon.

Take 'em, and draw thine own skin off with
'em!   240
    Exit [*with* DIAPHANTA *and* Servants].
De F. Here's a favour come with a mischief
now! I know
She had rather wear my pelt[1] tann'd in a pair
Of dancing pumps, than I should thrust my fin-
    gers
Into her sockets here. I know she hates me,
Yet cannot choose but love her. No matter, 245
If but to vex her, I will haunt her still ;
Though I get nothing else, I 'll have my will.
                        Exit.

[SCENE II.][2]

Enter ALIBIUS *and* LOLLIO.

Alib. Lollio, I must trust thee with a secret,
But thou must keep it.
Lol. I was ever close to a secret, sir.
Alib. The diligence that I have found in
    thee,
The care and industry already past,   5
Assures me of thy good continuance.
Lollio, I have a wife.
Lol. Fie, sir, 't is too late to keep her secret ;
she 's known to be married all the town and
country over.   10
Alib. Thou goest too fast, my Lollio. That
    knowledge
I allow no man can be barr'd it ;
But there is a knowledge which is nearer,
Deeper, and sweeter, Lollio.
Lol. Well, sir, let us handle that between
you and I.   15
Alib. 'T is that I go about, man. Lollio,
My wife is young.
Lol. So much the worse to be kept secret, sir.
Alib. Why, now thou meet'st the substance
of the point ;
I am old, Lollio.   20
Lol. No, sir, 't is I am old Lollio.
Alib. Yet why may not this concord and
sympathize ?
Old trees and young plants often grow together,
Well enough agreeing.   24
Lol. Ay, sir, but the old trees raise them-
selves higher and broader than the young
plants.
Alib. Shrewd application ! There 's the fear,
    man ;
I would wear my ring on my own finger ;
Whilst it is borrowed, it is none of mine,   30
But his that useth it.
Lol. You must keep it on still then, if it but
lie by, one or other will be thrusting into 't.
Alib. Thou conceiv'st me, Lollio ; here thy
    watchful eye
Must have employment · I cannot always be 35
At home.
Lol. I dare swear you cannot.
Alib. I must look out.
Lol. I know 't, you must look out ; 't is every
man's case.
Alib. Here, I do say, must thy employ-
ment be ;   40

To watch her treadings, and in my absence
Supply my place.
Lol. I 'll do my best, sir ; yet surely I cannot
see who you should have cause to be jealous
of.   45
Alib. Thy reason for that, Lollio ? It is
A comfortable question.
Lol. We have but two sorts of people in the
house, and both under the whip, that 's fools[3]
and madmen ; the one has not wit enough to [50
be knaves, and the other not knavery enough
to be fools.
Alib. Ay, those are all my patients, Lollio ;
I do profess the cure of either sort ;
My trade, my living 't is ; I thrive by it ;   55
But here 's the care that mixes with my thrift :
The daily visitants, that come to see
My brain-sick patients, I would not have
To see my wife. Gallants I do observe
Of quick enticing eyes, rich in habits,   60
Of stature and proportion very comely :
These are most shrewd temptations, Lollio.
Lol. They may be easily answered, sir ; if
they come to see the fools and madmen, you
and I may serve the turn, and let my mis- [65
tress alone ; she 's of neither sort.
Alib. 'T is a good ward ;[4] indeed, come they
    to see
Our madmen or our fools, let 'em see no more
Than what they come for ; by that consequent
They must not see her ; I 'm sure she 's no
    fool.   70
Lol. And I 'm sure she 's no madman.
Alib. Hold that buckler fast ; Lollio, my
    trust
Is on thee, and I account it firm and strong.
What hour is 't, Lollio ?
Lol.   Towards belly-hour, sir.
Alib. Dinner-time ? Thou mean'st twelve
o'clock ?   75
Lol. Yes, sir, for every part has his hour : we
wake at six and look about us, that 's eye hour ;
at seven we should pray, that 's knee-hour : at
eight walk, that 's leg-hour ; at nine gather
flowers and pluck a rose,[5] that 's nose-hour ; [80
at ten we drink, that 's mouth-hour ; at eleven
lay about us for victuals, that 's hand-hour ; at
twelve go to dinner, that 's belly-hour.
Alib. Profoundly, Lollio ! It will be long
Ere all thy scholars learn this lesson, and   85
I did look to have a new one ent'red ; — stay,
I think my expectation is come home.

Enter PEDRO, *and* ANTONIO [*disguised*] *like
an idiot.*

Ped. Save you, sir ; my business speaks it-
    self :
This sight takes off the labour of my tongue.
Alib. Ay, ay, sir, it is plain enough, you
mean   90
Him for my patient.
Ped. And if your pains prove but commodi-
ous, to give but some little strength to his sick
and weak part of nature in him, these are

---

  ³ **Skin.**   ² A room in the house of Alibius.
                      ³ Idiots.   ⁴ Guard (in fencing). (Dyce.)
                      ⁵ "Pluck a rose " = *alvum exonerare.* (Bullen.)

[gives him money] but patterns to show you [95 of the whole pieces that will follow to you, beside the charge of diet, washing, and other necessaries, fully defrayed.

Alib. Believe it, sir, there shall no care be wanting.

Lol. Sir, an officer in this place may de- [100 serve something. The trouble will pass through my hands.

Ped. 'T is fit something should come to your hands then, sir. *[Gives him money.]*

Lol. Yes, sir, 't is I must keep him sweet, [105 and read to him: what is his name?

Ped. His name is Antonio; marry, we use but half to him, only Tony.

Lol. Tony, Tony, 't is enough, and a very good name for a fool. — What 's your name, [110 Tony?

Ant. He, he, he! well, I thank you, cousin; he, he, he!

Lol. Good boy! hold up your head. — He can laugh; I perceive by that he is no beast. 115

Ped. Well, sir,
If you can raise him but to any height,
Any degree of wit; might he attain,
As I might say, to creep on but all four
Towards the chair of wit, or walk on crutches,
'T would add an honour to your worthy pains, 121
And a great family might pray for you,
To which he should be heir, had he discretion
To claim and guide his own. Assure you, sir,
He is a gentleman. 125

Lol. Nay, there 's nobody doubted that; at first sight I knew him for a gentleman, he looks no other yet.

Ped. Let him have good attendance and sweet lodging.

Lol. As good as my mistress lies in, sir; [130 and as you allow us time and means, we can raise him to the higher degree of discretion.

Ped. Nay, there shall no cost want, sir.

Lol. He will hardly be stretcht up to the wit of a magnifico. 135

Ped. O no, that 's not to be expected; far shorter will be enough.

Lol. I 'll warrant you I 'll make him fit to bear office in five weeks; I 'll undertake to wind him up to the wit of constable. 140

Ped. If it be lower than that, it might serve turn.

Lol. No, fie; to level him with a headborough,[1] beadle, or watchman, were but little better than he is. Constable I 'll able[2] him; [145 if he do come to be a justice afterwards, let him thank the keeper: or I 'll go further with you; say I do bring him up to my own pitch, say I make him as wise as myself.

Ped. Why, there I would have it. 150

Lol. Well, go to; either I 'll be as arrant a fool as he, or he shall be as wise as I, and then I think 't will serve his turn.

Ped. Nay, I do like thy wit passing well.

Lol. Yes, you may; yet if I had not been [155

---

a fool, I had had more wit than I have too. Remember what state[3] you found me in.

Ped. I will, and so leave you. Your best cares, I beseech you. *Exit* PEDRO.

Alib. Take you none with you, leave 'em [160 all with us.

Ant. O, my cousin 's gone! cousin, cousin, O!

Lol. Peace, peace, Tony; you must not cry, child, you must be whipt if you do; your cousin is here still; I am your cousin, Tony. 165

Ant. He, he! then I 'll not cry, if thou be'st my cousin; he, he, he!

Lol. I were best try his wit a little, that I may know what form to place him in.

Alib. Ay, do, Lollio, do. 170

Lol. I must ask him easy questions at first. — Tony, how many true[4] fingers has a tailor on his right hand?

Ant. As many as on his left, cousin.

Lol. Good: and how many on both? 175

Ant. Two less than a deuce,[5] cousin.

Lol. Very well answered. I come to you again, cousin Tony; how many fools goes to a wise man?

Ant. Forty in a day sometimes, cousin. 180

Lol. Forty in a day? How prove you that?

Ant. All that fall out amongst themselves, and go to a lawyer to be made friends.

Lol. A parlous fool! he must sit in the fourth form at least. I perceive that. — I come [185 again, Tony; how many knaves make an honest man?

Ant. I know not that, cousin.

Lol. No, the question is too hard for you. I 'll tell you, cousin; there 's three knaves [190 may make an honest man, — a sergeant, a jailor, and a beadle; the sergeant catches him, the jailor holds him, and the beadle lashes him; and if he be not honest then, the hangman must cure him. 195

Ant. Ha, ha, ha! that 's fine sport, cousin.

Alib. This was too deep a question for the fool, Lollio.

Lol. Yes, this might have serv'd yourself, though I say 't. — Once more and you shall go play, Tony. 200

Ant. Ay, play at push-pin, cousin; ha, he!

Lol. So thou shalt: say how many fools are here ——

Ant. Two, cousin; thou and I. 205

Lol. Nay, you 're too forward there, Tony. Mark my question; how many fools and knaves are here; a fool before a knave, a fool behind a knave, between every two fools a knave; how many fools, how many knaves? 210

Ant. I never learnt so far, cousin.

Alib. Thou puttest too hard questions to him, Lollio.

Lol. I 'll make him understand it easily. — Cousin, stand there. 215

Ant. Ay, cousin.

Lol. Master, stand you next the fool.

Alib. Well, Lollio.

Lol. Here 's my place. Mark now, Tony, there 's a fool before a knave. 220

---

[1] Constable.
[2] Answer for. warrant; or, make him able for.

[3] Business. [4] Honest. [5] Two.

Ant. That 's I, cousin.

Lol. Here 's a fool behind a knave, that 's I; and between us two fools there is a knave, that 's my master, 't is but we three, that 's all.

Ant. We three, we three, cousin.   225

Madmen within.

1 *Mad.* [*within.*] Put 's head i' th' pillory, the bread 's too little.

2 *Mad.* [*within.*] Fly, fly, and he catches the swallow.

3 *Mad.* [*within.*] Give her more onion, or the devil put the rope about her crag.[1]   231

Lol. You may hear what time of day it is, the chimes of Bedlam goes.

Alib. Peace, peace, or the wire[2] comes !

3 *Mad.* [*within.*] Cat whore, cat whore ! her permasant, her permasant ![3]   236

Alib. Peace, I say ! — Their hour 's come, they must be fed, Lollio.

Lol. There 's no hope of recovery of that Welsh madman; was undone by a mouse that spoil'd him a permasant; lost his wits for 't.   241

Alib. Go to your charge, Lollio; I 'll to mine.

Lol. Go you to your madmen's ward, let me alone with your fools.   245

Alib. And remember my last charge, Lollio.   *Exit.*

Lol. Of which your patients do you think I am?   Come, Tony, you must amongst your school-fellows now; there 's pretty scholars [250 amongst 'em, I can tell you; there 's some of 'em at *stultus, stulta, stultum.*

Ant. I would see the madmen, cousin, if they would not bite me.

Lol. No, they shall not bite thee, Tony.   255

Ant. They bite when they are at dinner, do they not, coz ?

Lol. They bite at dinner, indeed, Tony. Well, I hope to get credit by thee; I like thee the best of all the scholars that ever I [260 brought up, and thou shalt prove a wise man, o I 'll prove a fool myself.   *Exeunt.*

ACT II

[SCENE I.][4]

Enter BEATRICE *and* JASPERINO *severally.*

Beat. O sir, I 'm ready now for that fair service
Which makes the name of friend sit glorious on you !
Good angels and this conduct be your guide !
    [*Giving a paper.*]
Fitness of time and place is there set down, sir.

Jas. The joy I shall return rewards my service.   *Exit.* 5

Beat. How wise is Alsemero in his friend !
It is a sign he makes his choice with judgment;
Then I appear in nothing more approv'd
Than making choice of him; for 't is a principle,

[1] Neck.
[2] Whip.
[3] Parmesan cheese.
[4] An apartment in the Castle.

He that can choose   10
That bosom well who of his thoughts par- takes,
Proves most discreet in every choice he makes.
Methinks I love now with the eyes of judg- ment,
And see the way to merit, clearly see it.
A true deserver like a diamond sparkles;   15
In darkness you may see him, that 's in ab- sence,
Which is the greatest darkness falls on love;
Yet is he best discern'd then
With intellectual eyesight. What 's Piracquo,
My father spends his breath for? And his blessing   20
Is only mine as I regard his name,
Else it goes from me, and turns head against me,
Transform'd into a curse. Some speedy way
Must be remem'bred. He 's so forward too,
So urgent that way, scarce allows me breath   25
To speak to my new comforts.

Enter DE FLORES.

De F. [*Aside.*]   Yonder 's she;
Whatever ails me, now a-late especially,
I can as well be hang'd as refrain seeing her;
Some twenty times a day, nay, not so little,
Do I force errands, frame ways and excuses,   30
To come into her sight; and I 've small reason for 't,
And less encouragement, for she baits me still
Every time worse than other; does profess herself
The cruellest enemy to my face in town;
At no hand can abide the sight of me,   35
As if danger or ill-luck hung in my looks.
I must confess my face is bad enough,
But I know far worse has better fortune,
And not endur'd alone, but doted on;
And yet such pick-hair'd faces, chins like witches',   40
Here and there five hairs whispering in a cor- ner,
As if they grew in fear one of another,
Wrinkles like troughs, where swine-deformity swills
The tears of perjury, that lie there like wash
Fallen from the sliny and dishonest eye, —   45
Yet such a one plucks sweets without restraint,
And has the grace of beauty to his sweet.
Though my hard fate has thrust me out to servitude,
I tumbled into th' world a gentleman.
She turns her blessed eye upon me now,   50
And I 'll endure all storms before I part with 't.

Beat. [*Aside.*] Again ?
This ominous ill-fac'd fellow more disturbs me
Than all my other passions.

De F. [*Aside.*] Now 't begins again;   55
I 'll stand this storm of hail, though the stones pelt me.

Beat. Thy business ? What 's thy business ?

De F. [*Aside.*]   Soft and fair !
I cannot part so soon now.

Beat. [*Aside.*]   The villain 's fixt.—
Thou standing toad-pool ——

De F. [*Aside.*] The shower falls amain now.
Beat. Who sent thee? What 's thy errand?
Leave my sight!   60
De F. My lord your father, charg'd me to
deliver
A message to you.
Beat.   What, another since?
Do 't, and be hang'd then; let me be rid of thee.
De F. True service merits mercy.
Beat.   What 's thy message?
De F. Let beauty settle but in patience,   65
You shall hear all.
Beat.   A dallying, trifling torment!
De F. Signor Alonzo de Piracquo, lady,
Sole brother to Tomaso de Piracquo ——
Beat. Slave, when wilt make an end?
De F.   Too soon I shall.
Beat. What all this while of him?
De F.   The said Alonzo,   70
With the foresaid Tomaso ——
Beat.   Yet again?
De F. Is new alighted.
Beat.   Vengeance strike the news!
Thou thing most loath'd, what cause was there
in this
To bring thee to my sight?
De F.   My lord your father
Charg'd me to seek you out.
Beat.   Is there no other   75
To send his errand by?
De F.   It seems 't is my luck
To be i' th' way still.
Beat.   Get thee from me!
De F. So: —
[*Aside.*] Why, am not I an ass to devise ways
Thus to be rail'd at? I must see her still!   80
I shall have a mad qualm within this hour
again,
I know 't; and, like a common Garden [1]-bull,
I do but take breath to be lugg'd [2] again.
What this may bode I know not; I 'll despair
the less,   84
Because there 's daily precedents of bad faces
Belov'd beyond all reason. These foul chops
May come into favour one day 'mongst [their] [3]
fellows.
Wrangling has prov'd the mistress of good
pastime;
As children cry themselves asleep, I ha' seen   90
Women have chid themselves a-bed to men.
                                        Exit.
Beat. I never see this fellow but I think
Of some harm towards me; danger 's in my
mind still;
I scarce leave trembling of an hour after.
The next good mood I find my father in,
I 'll get him quite discarded. O, I was   95
Lost in this small disturbance, and forgot
Affliction's fiercer torrent that now comes
To bear down all my comforts!

Enter VERMANDERO, ALONZO, *and* TOMASO.

Ver.   You 're both welcome,
But an especial one belongs to you, sir.   99

[1] Paris Garden, on the Bankside, where bull-baiting
was carried on.
[2] Dragged by the ear.   [3] Q. *his*

To whose most noble name our love presents
Th' addition [4] of a son, our son Alonzo.
Alon. The treasury of honour cannot bring
forth
A title I should more rejoice in, sir.
Ver. You have improv'd it well.— Daughter,
prepare;
The day will steal upon thee suddenly.   105
Beat. [*Aside.*] Howe'er, I will be sure to
keep the night,
If it should come so near me.
        [BEATRICE *and* VERMANDERO *talk
                apart.*]
Tom.   Alonzo.
Alon.   Brother?
Tom. In troth I see small welcome in her eye.
Alon. Fie, you are too severe a censurer [5]
Of love in all points, there 's no bringing on
you.   110
If lovers should mark everything a fault,
Affection would be like an ill-set book,
Whose faults might prove as big as half the
volume.
Beat. That 's all I do entreat.
Ver.   It is but reasonable;   114
I 'll see what my son says to 't.— Son Alonzo,
Here is a motion made but to reprieve
A maidenhead three days longer; the request
Is not far out of reason, for indeed
The former time is pinching.
Alon.   Though my joys
Be set back so much time as I could wish   120
They had been forward, yet since she desires
it,
The time is set as pleasing as before,
I find no gladness wanting.
Ver.   May I ever
Meet it in that point still! You 're nobly wel-
come, sirs.   *Exit with* BEATRICE.
Tom. So; did you mark the dulness of her
parting now?   125
Alon. What dulness? Thou art so excep-
tious still!
Tom. Why, let it go then; I am but a fool
To mark your harms so heedfully.
Alon.   Where 's the oversight?
Tom. Come, your faith 's cozened in her,
strongly cozened.
Unsettle your affection with all speed   130
Wisdom can bring it to; your peace is ruin'd
else.
Think what a torment 't is to marry one
Whose heart is leapt into another's bosom:
If ever pleasure she receive from thee,
It comes not in thy name, or of thy gift;   135
She lies but with another in thine arms,
He the half-father unto all thy children
In the conception; if he get 'em not,
She helps to get 'em for him; [6] and how dan-
gerous   139
And shameful her restraint may go in time to,
It is not to be thought on without sufferings.
Alon. You speak as if she lov'd some other
then.

[4] Title.   [5] Judge.
[6] After *him*, Q. inserts *in his passions.*

Tom. Do you apprehend so slowly?
Alon.   Nay, an that
Be your fear only, I am safe enough.
Preserve your friendship and your counsel,
        brother,   145
For times of more distress ; I should depart
An enemy, a dangerous, deadly one,
To any but thyself, that should but think
She knew the meaning of inconstancy,
Much less the use and practice : yet we 're
        friends.   150
Pray, let no more be urg'd ; I can endure
Much, till I meet an injury to her,
Then I am not myself. Farewell, sweet brother ;
How much we 're bound to Heaven to depart
        lovingly.   *Exit.*
Tom. Why, here is love's tame madness ;   155
        thus a man
Quickly steals into his vexation.   *Exit.*

[SCENE II.]¹

Enter DIAPHANTA *and* ALSEMERO.

Dia. The place is my charge ; you have kept
        your hour,
And the reward of a just meeting bless you !
I hear my lady coming. Complete gentleman,
I dare not be too busy with my praises,
They 're dangerous things to deal with.   *Exit.*
Als.   This goes well ;   5
These women are the ladies' cabinets,
Things of most precious trust are lockt into 'em.

Enter BEATRICE.

Beat. I have within mine eye all my desires.
Requests that holy prayers ascend Heaven for,
And brings 'em down to furnish our defects,   10
Come not more sweet to our necessities
Than thou unto my wishes.
Als.   We 're so like
In our expressions, lady, that unless I borrow
The same words, I shall never find their equals.
Beat. How happy were this meeting, this em-
        brace,   15
If it were free from envy ! This poor kiss
It has an enemy, a hateful one,
That wishes poison to 't. How well were I now,
If there were none such name known as Piracquo,
Nor no such tie as the command of parents !   20
I should be but too much bless'd.
Als.   One good service
Would strike off both your fears, and I 'll go
        near 't too,
Since you are so distrest. Remove the cause,
The command ceases ; so there 's two fears blown
        out
With one and the same blast.
Beat.   Pray, let me find² you, sir :   25
What might that service be, so strangely happy ?
Als. The honourablest piece about man, val-
        our :
I 'll send a challenge to Piracquo instantly.
Beat. How ? Call you that extinguishing of
        fear,
When 't is the only way to keep it flaming ?   30

¹ Another apartment in the Castle.   ² Understand.

Are not you ventured in the action,
That 's all my joys and comforts ? Pray, no
        more, sir.
Say you prevail'd, you 're danger's and not
        mine then ;
The law would claim you from me, or obscurity
Be made the grave to bury you alive.   35
I 'm glad these thoughts come forth ; O, keep
        not one
Of this condition, sir ! Here was a course
Found to bring sorrow on her way to death ;
The tears would ne'er ha' dried, till dust had
        chok'd 'em.
Blood-guiltiness becomes a fouler visage ; —   40
[*Aside.*] And now I think on one ; I was to
        blame,
I ha' marr'd so good a market with my scorn ;
'T had been done questionless : the ugliest
        creature
Creation fram'd for some use : yet to see   44
I could not mark so much where it should be !
Als. Lady ——
Beat. [*Aside.*] Why, men of art make much
        of poison,
Keep one to expel another. Where was my art ?
Als. Lady, you hear not me.
Beat.   I do especially, sir.
The present times are not so sure of our side
As those hereafter may be ; we must use 'em
        then   50
As thrifty folks their wealth, sparingly now,
Till the time opens.
Als.   You teach wisdom, lady.
Beat. Within there ! Diaphanta !

Re-enter DIAPHANTA.

Dia.   Do you call, madam ?
Beat. Perfect your service, and conduct this
        gentleman
The private way you brought him.
Dia.   I shall, madam.   55
Als. My love 's as firm as love e'er built upon.
                          Exit with DIAPHANTA.

Enter DE FLORES.

De F. [*Aside.*] I 've watcht this meeting, and
        do wonder much
What shall become of t' other ; I 'm sure both
Cannot be serv'd unless she transgress ; haply
Then I 'll put in for one ; for if a woman   60
Fly from one point, from him she makes a hus-
        band,
She spreads and mounts then like arithmetic ;
One, ten, a hundred, a thousand, ten thousand,
Proves in time sutler to an army royal.
Now do I look to be most richly rail'd at,   65
Yet I must see her.
Beat. [*Aside.*] Why, put case I loath'd him
As much as youth and beauty hates a sepul-
        chre,
Must I needs show it ? Cannot I keep that
        secret,
And serve my turn upon him ? See, he 's here.—
De Flores.
De F. [*Aside.*] Ha, I shall run mad with joy !
She call'd me fairly by my name De Flores,   71
And neither rogue nor rascal.

Beat.   What ha' you done
To your face a' late ? You 've met with some
   good physician ;
You 've prun'd [1] yourself, methinks : you were
   not wont
To look so amorously.[2]
De F.   Not I ; —   75
[*Aside.*] 'T is the same physnomy, to a hair and
   pimple,
Which she called scurvy scarce an hour ago :
How is this ?
Beat.   Come hither ; nearer, man.
De F. [*Aside.*] I 'm up to the chin in Heaven !
Beat.   Turn, let me see ;
Faugh, 't is but the heat of the liver, I per-
   ceive 't ;
I thought it had been worse.
De F. [*Aside.*]   Her fingers toucht me ! 81
She smells all amber.[3]
Beat. I 'll make a water for you shall cleanse
   this
Within a fortnight.
De F.   With your own hands, lady ? 84
Beat. Yes, mine own, sir ; in a work of cure
I 'll trust no other.
De F. [*Aside.*]   'T is half an act of pleasure
To hear her talk thus to me.
Beat.   When we 're us'd
To a hard face, it is not so unpleasing ;
It mends still in opinion, hourly mends ;
I see it by experience.
De F. [*Aside.*]   I was blest   90
To light upon this minute ; I 'll make use on 't.
Beat. Hardness becomes the visage of a man
   well ;
It argues service, resolution, manhood,
If cause were of employment.
De F.   'T would be soon seen
If e'er your ladyship had cause to use it ;   95
I would but wish the honour of a service
So happy as that mounts to.
Beat.   We shall try you. —
O my De Flores !
De F. [*Aside.*]   How 's that ? She calls me
   hers
Already ! *My* De Flores ! — You were about
To sigh out somewhat, madam ?
Beat.   No, was I ? 100
I forgot, — O ! —
De F. There 't is again, the very fellow on 't.
Beat. You are too quick, sir.
De F. There 's no excuse for 't now ; I heard
   it twice, madam ;
That sigh would fain have utterance : take pity
   on 't,
And lend it a free word. 'Las, how it labours
For liberty ! I hear the murmur yet   105
Beat at your bosom.
Beat.   Would creation ——
De F. Ay, well said, that is it.
Beat.   Had form'd me man !
De F. Nay, that 's not it.
Beat.   O, 't is the soul of freedom !
I should not then be forc'd to marry one   110

---

[1] Preen, set the feathers in order. Used of hawks.
[2] Like an object of love.   [3] Ambergris.

I hate beyond all depths ; I should have power
Then to oppose my loathings, nay, remove 'em
For ever from my sight.
De F. [*Aside.*]   O blest occasion ! ——
Without change to your sex you have your
   wishes ;
Claim so much man in me.
Beat.   In thee, De Flores ? 115
There is small cause for that.
De F.   Put it not from me,
It is a service that I kneel for to you. [*Kneels.*]
Beat. You are too violent to mean faithfully.
There 's horror in my service, blood, and
   danger ;
Can those be things to sue for ?
De F.   If you knew   120
How sweet it were to me to be employed
In any act of yours, you would say then
I fail'd, and us'd not reverence enough
When I receive[d] the charge on 't.
Beat. [*Aside.*]   This is much,
Methinks ; belike his wants are greedy ; and 125
To such gold tastes like angel's food. Rise.
De F. I 'll have the work first.
Beat. [*Aside.*]   Possible his need
Is strong upon him. — There 's to encourage
   thee ;   [*Gives money.*]
As thou art forward, and thy service dangerous,
Thy reward shall be precious.
De F.   That I 've thought on ; 130
I have assur'd myself of that beforehand,
And know it will be precious ; the thought rav-
   ishes !
Beat. Then take him to thy fury !
De F.   I thirst for him.
Beat. Alonzo de Piracquo.
De F. [*rising.*]   His end 's upon him ;
He shall be seen no more.
Beat.   How lovely now   135
Dost thou appear to me ! Never was man
Dearlier rewarded.
De F.   I do think of that.
Beat. Be wondrous careful in the execution.
De F. Why, are not both our lives upon the
   cast ?
Beat. Then I throw all my fears upon thy
   service.   140
De F. They ne'er shall rise to hurt you.
Beat.   When the deed 's done,
I 'll furnish thee with all things for thy flight ;
Thou may'st live bravely in another country.
De F. Ay, ay ;
We 'll talk of that hereafter.
Beat. [*Aside.*]   I shall rid myself 145
Of two inveterate loathings at one time,
Piracquo, and his dog-face.   *Exit.*
De F.   O my blood !
Methinks I feel her in mine arms already ;
Her wanton fingers combing out this beard,
And, being pleased, praising this bad face.   150
Hunger and pleasure, they 'll commend some-
   times
Slovenly dishes, and feed heartily on 'em,
Nay, which is stranger, refuse daintier for 'em :
Some women are odd feeders. — I am too loud.
Here comes the man goes supperless to bed, 155
Yet shall not rise to-morrow to his dinner.

Enter ALONZO.

Alon. De Flores.
De F. My kind, honourable lord ?
Alon. I'm glad I ha' met with thee.
De F. Sir ?
Alon. Thou canst show me
The full strength of the castle ?
De F. That I can, sir.
Alon. I much desire it.
De F. And if the ways and straits 160
Of some of the passages be not too tedious for
you,
I 'll assure you, worth your time and sight, my
lord.
Alon. Pooh, that shall be no hindrance.
De F. I 'm your servant, then.
'T is now near dinner-time ; 'gainst [1] your lord-
ship's rising
I 'll have the keys about me.
Alon. Thanks, kind De Flores. 165
De F. [*Aside.*] He 's safely thrust upon me
beyond hopes. *Exeunt* [*severally*].

ACT III

[SCENE I.] [2]

Enter ALONZO *and* DE FLORES. (*In the act-
time* [3] DE FLORES *hides a naked rapier*) [*behind a door.*]

De Flores. Yes, here are all the keys ; I was
afraid, my lord,
I 'd wanted for the postern, this is it.
I 've all, I 've all, my lord : this for the sconce.[4]
Alon. 'T is a most spacious and impregnable
fort.
De F. You 'll tell me more, my lord. This
descent 5
Is somewhat narrow, we shall never pass
Well with our weapons, they 'll but trouble us.
Alon. Thou sayest true.
De F. Pray, let me help your lordship.
Alon. 'T is done : thanks, kind De Flores.
De F. Here are hooks, my lord,
To hang such things on purpose. 10
[*Hanging up his own sword and
that of* ALONZO.]
Alon. Lead, I 'll follow thee. *Exeunt.*[5]

[SCENE II.] [6]

[*Enter* ALONZO *and* DE FLORES.]

De F. All this is nothing ; you shall see anon
A place you little dream on.
Alon. I am glad
I have this leisure ; all your master's house
Imagine I ha' taken a gondola.
De F. All but myself, sir, — [*aside*] which
makes up my safety. 5

[1] In anticipation of.
[2] A narrow passage in the Castle.
[3] *I. e.* Between the acts.
[4] Fortification.
[5] Q. Exeunt at one door and enter at the other.
[5] A vault.

My lord, I 'll place you at a casement here
Will show you the full strength of all the castle.
Look, spend your eye awhile upon that object.
Alon. Here 's rich variety, De Flores.
De F. Yes, sir.
Alon. Goodly munition.
De F. Ay, there 's ordnance, sir, 10
No bastard metal, will ring you a peal like
bells
At great men's funerals. Keep your eye
straight, my lord ;
Take special notice of that sconce [4] before you,
There you may dwell awhile.
[*Takes the rapier which he had hid
behind the door.*]
Alon. I am upon 't.
De F. And so am I. [*Stabs him.*]
Alon. De Flores ! O De Flores ! 15
Whose malice hast thou put on ?
De F. Do you question
A work of secrecy ? I must silence you.
[*Stabs him.*]
Alon. O, O, O !
De F. I must silence you. [*Stabs him.*]
So here 's an undertaking well accomplish'd.
This vault serves to good use now : ha, what 's
that 20
Threw sparkles in my eye ? O, 't is a diamond
He wears upon his finger ; 't was well found ;
This will approve the work.[7] What, so fast on ?
Not part in death ? I 'll take a speedy course
then.
Finger and all shall off. [*Cuts off the finger.*]
So, now I 'll clear 25
The passages from all suspect or fear.
Exit with body.

[SCENE III.] [8]

Enter ISABELLA *and* LOLLIO.

Isa. Why, sirrah, whence have you commis-
sion
To fetter the doors against me ?
If you keep me in a cage, pray, whistle to me,
Let me be doing something.
Lol. You shall be doing, if it please you ; 5
I 'll whistle to you, if you 'll pipe after.
Isa. Is it your master's pleasure, or your
own,
To keep me in this pinfold ?
Lol. 'T is for my master's pleasure, lest being
taken in another man's corn, you might be [10
pounded in another place.
Isa. 'T is very well, and he 'll prove very wise.
Lol. He says you have company enough in
the house, if you please to be sociable, of all
sorts of people. 15
Isa. Of all sorts ? Why, here 's none but fools
and madmen.
Lol. Very well : and where will you find any
other, if you should go abroad ? There 's my
master and I to boot too. 20
Isa. Of either sort one, a madman and a
fool.

[7] Prove it has been done.
[8] An apartment in the house of Alibius.

Lol. I would ev'n participate of both then if
I were as you ; I know you 're half mad already,
be half foolish too.   25

Isa. You 're a brave saucy rascal ! Come on,
sir,
Afford me then the pleasure of your bedlam.
You were commending once to-day to me
Your last-come lunatic ; what a proper [1]
Body there was without brains to guide it,   30
And what a pitiful delight appear'd
In that defect, as if your wisdom had found
A mirth in madness ; pray, sir, let me partake,
If there be such a pleasure.

Lol. If I do not show you the handsomest, [35
discreetest madman, one that I may call the
understanding madman, then say I am a fool.

Isa. Well, a match, I will say so.

Lol. When you have had a taste of the madman, you shall, if you please, see Fool's Col- [40
lege, o' th' [other] side. I seldom lock there ;
't is but shooting a bolt or two, and you are
amongst 'em. *Exit. Enter presently.* — Come
on, sir ; let me see how handsomely you 'll behave yourself now.   45

Enter FRANCISCUS.

Fran. How sweetly she looks ! O, but there 's
a wrinkle in her brow as deep as philosophy.
Anacreon, drink to my mistress' health, I 'll
pledge it. Stay, stay, there 's a spider in the
cup ! No, 't is but a grape-stone ; swallow it. [50
fear nothing, poet ; so, so, lift higher.

Isa. Alack, alack, it is too full of pity
To be laught at ! How fell he mad ? Canst thou
tell ?

Lol. For love, mistress. He was a pretty
poet, too, and that set him forwards first ; [55
the muses then forsook him ; he ran mad for a
chambermaid, yet she was but a dwarf neither.

Fran. Hail, bright Titania !
Why stand'st thou idle on these flow'ry banks ?
Oberon is dancing with his Dryades ;   60
I 'll gather daisies, primrose, violets,
And bind them in a verse of poesy.

Lol. [*holding up a whip.*] Not too near ! You
see your danger.

Fran. O, hold thy hand, great Diomede !   65
Thou feed'st thy horses well, they shall obey
thee :
Get up, Bucephalus kneels.   [*Kneels.*]

Lol. You see how I awe my flock ; a shepherd
has not his dog at more obedience.

Isa. His conscience is unquiet ; sure that
was   70
The cause of this : a proper gentleman !

Fran. Come hither, Aesculapius ; hide the
poison.

Lol. Well, 't is hid.   [*Hides the whip.*]

Fran. Didst thou ne'er hear of one Tiresias,
A famous poet ?

Lol.   Yes, that kept tame wild geese. 75

Fran. That 's he ; I am the man.

Lol. No ?

Fran. Yes ; but make no words on 't. I was
a man
Seven years ago.

[1] *Handsome.*

Lol.   A stripling, I think, you might.

Fran. Now I 'm a woman, all feminine.   80

Lol. I would I might see that !

Fran. Juno struck me blind.

Lol. I 'll ne'er believe that ; for a woman,
they say, has an eye more than a man.

Fran. I say she struck me blind.   85

Lol. And Luna made you mad : you have two
trades to beg with.

Fran. Luna is now big-bellied, and there 's
room
For both of us to ride with Hecate ;
I 'll drag thee up into her silver sphere,   90
And there we 'll kick the dog — and beat the
bush —
That barks against the witches of the night ;
The swift lycanthropi [2] that walks the round,
We 'll tear their wolvish skins, and save the
sheep.   [*Attempts to seize* LOLLIO.]

Lol. Is 't come to this ? Nay, then, my [95
poison comes forth again. [*Showing the whip.*]
Mad slave, indeed, abuse your keeper !

Isa. I prithee, hence with him, now he grows
dangerous.

Fran. [*sings.*]

Sweet love, pity me,
Give me leave to lie with thee.   100

Lol. No, I 'll see you wiser first. To your own
kennel !

Fran. No noise, she sleeps ; draw all the cur-
tains round,
Let no soft sound molest the pretty soul
But love, and love creeps in at a mouse-hole.

Lol. I would you would get into your hole !
(*Exit* FRANCISCUS.) — Now, mistress, I will [105
bring you another sort ; you shall be fool'd an-
other while. [*Exit, and brings in* ANTONIO.] —
Tony, come hither, Tony : look who 's yonder,
Tony.   110

Ant. Cousin, is it not my aunt ? [3]

Lol. Yes, 't is one of 'em, Tony.

Ant. He, he ! how do you, uncle ?

Lol. Fear him not, mistress, 't is a gentle
nigget ; [4] you may play with him, as safely with
him as with his bauble.   116

Isa. How long hast thou been a fool ?

Ant. Ever since I came hither, cousin.

Isa. Cousin ? I 'm none of thy cousins, fool.

Lol. O, mistress, fools have always so much
wit as to claim their kindred.   121

Madman. [*within.*] Bounce, bounce ! he falls,
he falls !

Isa. Hark you, your scholars in the upper
room
Are out of order.   125

Lol. Must I come amongst you there ? —
Keep you the fool, mistress ; I 'll go up and
play left-handed Orlando amongst the mad-
men.   *Exit.*

Isa. Well, sir.   130

Ant. 'T is opportuneful now, sweet lady ! nay,
Cast no amazing eye upon this change.

Isa. Ha !

[2] Persons suffering from *lycanthropia*, or wolf-mad-
ness. Cf. *Duchess of Malfi*, V. ii. 10.
[3] Cant term for bawd.   [4] Nidget, *i. e.* idiot.

Ant. This shape of folly shrouds your dearest
  love,
The truest servant to your powerful beauties,
Whose magic had this force thus to transform
  me.   136
Isa. You 're a fine fool indeed !
Ant.   O, 't is not strange !
Love has an intellect that runs through all
The scrutinous [1] sciences ; and, like a cunning
  poet,
Catches a quantity of every knowledge,   140
Yet brings all home into one mystery,
Into one secret that he proceeds in.
Isa. You 're a parlous fool.
Ant. No danger in me ; I bring nought but
  love
And his soft-wounding shafts to strike you
  with.   145
Try but one arrow ; if it hurt you, I
Will stand you twenty back in recompense.
                                    [*Kisses her.*]
Isa. A forward fool too !
Ant.   This was love's teaching :
A thousand ways I fashion'd out my way,
And this I found the safest and the nearest, 150
To tread the galaxia to my star.
Isa. Profound withal ! certain you dream'd
  of this,
Love never taught it waking.
Ant.   Take no acquaintance
Of these outward follies, there 's within
A gentleman that loves you.
Isa.   When I see him, 155
I 'll speak with him ; so, in the meantime, keep
Your habit, it becomes you well enough.
As you 're a gentleman, I 'll not discover you ;
That 's all the favour that you must expect. 159
When you are weary, you may leave the school,
For all this while you have but play'd the fool.

Re-enter LOLLIO.

Ant. And must again. — He, he ! I thank
  you, cousin ;
I 'll be your valentine to-morrow morning.
Lol. How do you like the fool, mistress ?
Isa. Passing well, sir.   165
Lol. Is he not witty, pretty well, for a fool ?
Isa. If he holds on as he begins, he 's like
To come to something.
Lol. Ay, thank a good tutor. You may put
him to 't ; he begins to answer pretty hard [170
questions. — Tony, how many is five times six ?
Ant. Five times six is six times five.
Lol. What arithmetician could have answer'd
better ? How many is one hundred and seven ?
Ant. One hundred and seven is seven hundred
and one, cousin.   176
Lol. This is no wit to speak on ! — Will you
be rid of the fool now ?
Isa. By no means ; let him stay a little.
Madman. [*within.*] Catch there, catch the last
couple in hell ! [2]   181

Lol. Again ! must I come amongst you ?
Would my master were come home ! I am not
able to govern both these wards together.
                                         Exit.
Ant. Why should a minute of love 's hour be
  lost ?   185
Isa. Fie, out again ! I had rather you kept
Your other posture ; you become not your
  tongue
When you speak from [3] your clothes.
Ant.   How can he freeze   189
Lives near so sweet a warmth ? Shall I alone
Walk through the orchard of th' Hesperides,
And, cowardly, not dare to pull an apple ?

Enter LOLLIO *above*.

This with the red cheeks I must venture for.
                          [*Attempts to kiss her.*]
Isa. Take heed, there 's giants keep 'em.
Lol. [*Aside.*] How now, fool, are you good at
that ? Have you read Lipsius ? [4] He 's past [196
Ars Amandi ; I believe I must put harder ques-
tions to him, I perceive that.
Isa. You 're bold without fear too.
Ant.   What should I fear,
Having all joys about me ? Do you smile,
And love shall play the wanton on your lip, 201
Meet and retire, retire and meet again ;
Look you but cheerfully, and in your eyes
I shall behold mine own deformity,
And dress myself up fairer. I know this shape
Becomes me not, but in those bright mir-
  rors   206
I shall array me handsomely.
          [*Cries of madmen are heard within,*]
            some as birds others as beasts.
Lol.   Cuckoo, cuckoo ! *Exit* [*above*].
Ant. What are these ?
Isa.   Of fear enough to part us ;
Yet are they but our schools of lunatics,
That act their fantasies in any shapes,   210
Suiting their present thoughts : if sad, they
  cry ;
If mirth be their conceit, they laugh again :
Sometimes they imitate the beasts and birds,
Singing or howling. braying, barking ; all
As their wild fancies prompt 'em.

Enter LOLLIO.

Ant.   These are no fears. 215
Isa. But here 's a large one, my man.
Ant. Ha, he ! that 's fine sport, indeed,
cousin.
Lol. I would my master were come home !
'T is too much for one shepherd to govern two
of these flocks ; nor can I believe that one [221
churchman can instruct two benefices at once ;
there will be some incurable mad of the one
side, and very fools on the other. — Come,
Tony.   225
Ant. Prithee, cousin, let me stay here still.
Lol. No, you must to your book now ; you
have play'd sufficiently.

----

[1] Scrutinizing.
   An allusion to the game of barley-break, the ground
for which was divided into three compartments, of
which the middle one was termed "hell." (Ellis).

[3] Out of keeping with.
[4] " Is it necessary to notice that the name of this
great scholar is introduced merely for the sake of its
first syllable ? " (Dyce.)

Isa. Your fool has grown wondrous witty.
Lol. Well, I 'll say nothing : but I do not think
but he will put you down one of these days.   231
                    Exit with ANTONIO.
Isa. Here the restrained current might make
      breach,
Spite of the watchful bankers. Would a woman
      stray,
She need not gad abroad to seek her sin,
It would be brought home one ways or
      [an]other :   235
The needle's point will to the fixed north ;
Such drawing arctics womens' beauties are.

                  Re-enter LOLLIO.

Lol. How dost thou, sweet rogue ?
Isa. How now ?
Lol. Come, there are degrees ; one fool may
be better than another.   241
Isa. What 's the matter ?
Lol. Nay, if thou giv'st thy mind to fool's
flesh, have at thee !
Isa. You bold slave, you !   245
Lol. I could follow now as t' other fool
did :
" What should I fear,
Having all joys about me ? Do you but smile,
And love shall play the wanton on your lip,   250
Meet and retire, retire and meet again ;
Look you but cheerfully, and in your eyes
I shall behold my own deformity,
And dress myself up fairer. I know this
      shape
Becomes me not — "   255
And so as it follows : but is not this the most
foolish way ? Come, sweet rogue ; kiss me, my
little Lacedaemonian ; let me feel how thy
pulses beat. Thou hast a thing about thee
would do a man pleasure, I 'll lay my hand
on 't.   261
Isa. Sirrah, no more ! I see you have discov-
ered
This love's knight errant, who hath made ad-
venture
For purchase of [1] my love : be silent, mute,
Mute as a statue, or his injunction   265
For me enjoying, shall be to cut thy throat ;
I 'll do it, though for no other purpose ; and
Be sure he 'll not refuse it.
Lol.   My share, that 's all ;
I 'll have my fool's part with you.
Isa.   No more ! Your master.

                  Enter ALIBIUS.

Alib. Sweet, how dost thou ?
Isa.   Your bounden servant, sir.   270
Alib. Fie, fie, sweetheart, no more of that.
Isa. You were best lock me up.
Alib. In my arms and bosom, my sweet Isa-
      bella,
I 'll lock thee up most nearly. — Lollio,
We have employment, we have task in hand.
At noble Vermandero's, our castle's captain,   275
There is a nuptial to be solemnis'd —
Beatrice-Joanna, his fair daughter, bride, —

For which the gentleman hath bespoke our
      pains,
A mixture of our madmen and our fools,   280
To finish, as it were, and make the fag [2]
Of all the revels, the third night from the
      first ;
Only an unexpected passage over,
To make a frightful pleasure, that is all,
But not the all I aim at. Could we so act it,
To teach it in a wild distracted measure,   285
Though out of form and figure, breaking time's
      head,
It were no matter, 't would be heal'd again
In one age or other, if not in this :
This, this, Lollio, there 's a good reward begun,
And will beget a bounty, be it known.   291
Lol. This is easy, sir, I 'll warrant you : you
have about you fools and madmen that can
dance very well ; and 't is no wonder, your best
dancers are not the wisest men ; the reason is,
with often jumping they jolt their brains [296
down into their feet, that their wits lie more in
their heels than in their heads.
Alib. Honest Lollio, thou giv'st me a good
      reason,
And a comfort in it.
Isa.   You 've a fine trade on 't.
Madmen and fools are a staple commodity.   300
Alib. O wife, we must eat, wear clothes, and
live.
Just at the lawyer's haven we arrive,
By madmen and by fools we both do thrive.
                            Exeunt.

                  [SCENE IV.] [3]

Enter VERMANDERO, BEATRICE, ALSEMERO,
      and JASPERINO.

Ver. Valencia speaks so nobly of you, sir,
I wish I had a daughter now for you.
Als. The fellow of this creature were a part-
ner
For a king's love.
Ver.   I had her fellow once, sir,
But Heaven has married her to joys eternal ;   5
'T were sin to wish her in this vale again.
Come, sir, your friend and you shall see the
      pleasures
Which my health chiefly joys in.
Als.   I hear
The beauty of this seat largely [commended]. [4]
Ver. It falls much short of that.
                  Exit with ALSEMERO *and* JASPER
                                              INO.
Beat.   So, here 's one step   10
Into my father's favour ; time will fix him ;
I 've got him now the liberty of the house.
So wisdom, by degrees, works out her freedom ;
And if that eye be dark'ned that offends me, —
I wait but that eclipse, — this gentleman   15
Shall soon shine glorious in my father 's liking,
Through the refulgent virtue of my love.

                  Enter DE FLORES.

De F. [*Aside.*] My thoughts are at a ban-
      quet ; for the deed,

---

[1] To gain.

[2] End.   [3] An apartment in the Castle.   [4] Q. omits.

I feel no weight in 't; 't is but light and cheap
For the sweet recompense that I set down for 't.
Beat. De Flores?
De F.   Lady?
Beat.   Thy looks promise cheerfully. ²¹
De F. All things are answerable, time, circumstance,
Your wishes, and my service.
Beat.   Is it done, then?
De F. Piracquo is no more.
Beat. My joys start at mine eyes; our sweet'st delights   ²⁵
Are evermore born weeping.
De F.   I 've a token for you.
Beat. For me?
De F. But it was sent somewhat unwillingly;
I could not get the ring without the finger.
                [*Producing the finger and ring.*]
Beat. Bless me, what hast thou done?
De F.   Why, is that more ³⁰
Than killing the whole man? I cut his heart-strings;
A greedy hand thrust in a dish at court,
In a mistake hath had as much as this.
Beat. 'T is the first token my father made me send him.
De F. And I [have] made him send it back again   ³⁵
For his last token. I was loth to leave it,
And I 'm sure dead men have no use of jewels;
He was as loth to part with 't, for it stuck
As if the flesh and it were both one substance.
Beat. At the stag's fall, the keeper has his fees;   ⁴⁰
'T is soon appli'd, all dead men's fees are yours, sir.
I pray, bury the finger, but the stone
You may make use on shortly; the true value,
Take 't of my truth, is near three hundred ducats.
De F. 'T will hardly buy a capcase ¹ for one 's conscience though,   ⁴⁵
To keep it from the worm, as fine as 't is.
Well, being my fees, I 'll take it;
Great men have taught me that, or else my merit
Would scorn the way on 't.
Beat.   It might justly, sir.
Why, thou mistak 'st, De Flores; 't is not given
In state ² of recompense.
De F.   No, I hope so, lady; ⁵¹
You should soon witness my contempt to 't then.
Beat. Prithee, — thou look'st as if thou wert offended.
De F. That were strange, lady; 't is not possible
My service should draw such a cause from you.   ⁵⁵
Offended! Could you think so? That were much
For one of my performance, and so warm
Yet in my service.
Beat. 'T were misery in me to give you cause, sir.

I know so much, it were so; misery ⁶⁰
In her most sharp condition.
Beat.   'T is resolv 'd then;
Look you, sir, here 's three thousand golden florins;
I have not meanly thought upon thy merit.
De F. What! salary? Now you move me.
Beat.   How, De Flores?
De F. Do you place me in the rank of verminous fellows,   ⁶⁵
To destroy things for wages? Offer gold
For the life-blood of man? Is anything
Valued too precious for my recompense?
Beat. I understand thee not.
De F.   I could ha' hir 'd
A journeyman in murder at this rate,   ⁷⁰
And mine own conscience might have [slept at ease],³
And have had the work brought home.
Beat. [*Aside.*]   I 'm in a labyrinth;
What will content him? I 'd fain be rid of him.
I 'll double the sum, sir.
De F.   You take a course
To double my vexation, that 's the good you do.
Beat. [*Aside.*] Bless me, I 'm now in worse plight than I was;   ⁷⁵
I know not what will please him. — For my fear's sake,
I prithee, make away with all speed possible;
And if thou be'st so modest not to name
The sum that will content thee, paper blushes not,   ⁸⁰
Send thy demand in writing, it shall follow thee;
But, prithee, take thy flight.
De F.   You must fly too, then.
Beat. I?
De F. I 'll not stir a foot else.
Beat.   What 's your meaning?
De F. Why, are not you as guilty? In, I 'm sure,
As deep as I; and we should stick together. ⁸⁵
Come, your fears counsel you but ill; my absence
Would draw suspect upon you instantly;
There were no rescue for you.
Beat. [*Aside.*]   He speaks home!
De F. Nor is it fit we two, engag'd so jointly,
Should part and live asunder.
Beat.   How now, sir? ⁹⁰
This shows not well.
De F.   What makes your lip so strange?
This must not be 'twixt ⁴ us.
Beat.   The man talks wildly!
De F. Come, kiss me with a zeal now.
Beat. [*Aside.*] Heaven, I doubt him!
De F. I will not stand so long to beg 'em shortly.   ⁹⁵
Beat. Take heed, De Flores, of forgetfulness,
'T will soon betray us.
De F.   Take you heed first;
Faith, you 're grown much forgetful, you 're to blame in 't.
Beat. [*Aside.*] He 's bold, and I am blam 'd for 't.
De F.   I have eas 'd you

¹ Band-box.   ² Place.   ³ Q. omits. Add. Ed. 1816.   ⁴ Q. betwixt.

Of your trouble, think on it; I am [1] in pain,   100
And must be eas'd of [2] you; 't is a charity,
Justice invites your blood to understand me.
   Beat. I dare not.
   De F.   Quickly!
   Beat.   O, I never shall!
Speak it yet further off, that I may lose
What has been spoken, and no sound remain on 't;
I would not hear so much offence again   106
For such another deed.
   De F.   Soft, lady, soft!
The last is not yet paid for. O, this act
Has put me into spirit; I was as greedy on 't
As the parcht earth of moisture, when the
   clouds weep.   110
Did you not mark, I wrought myself into 't,
Nay, su'd and kneel'd for 't? Why was all
   that pains took?
You see I 've thrown contempt upon your gold;
Not that I want it [not], [3] for I do piteously,   114
In order I 'll come unto 't, and make use on 't,
But 't was not held so precious to begin with,
For I place wealth after the heels of pleasure;
And were not I resolv'd in my belief
That thy virginity were perfect in thee,
I should but take my recompense with grudg-
   ing,   120
As if I had but half my hopes I agreed for.
   Beat. Why, 't is impossible thou canst be so
   wicked,
Or shelter such a cunning cruelty,
To make his death the murderer of my honour!
Thy language is so bold and vicious,   125
I cannot see which way I can forgive it
With any modesty.
   De F.   Pish! you forget yourself;
A woman dipt in blood, and talk of modesty!
   Beat. O misery of sin! would I 'd been bound
Perpetually unto my living hate   130
In that Piracquo, than to hear these words!
Think but upon the distance that creation
Set 'twixt thy blood and mine, and keep thee
   there.
   De F. Look but into your conscience, read
   me there;
'T is a true book, you 'll find me there your
   equal.   135
Pish! fly not to your birth, but settle you
In what the act has made you; you 're no more
   now.
You must forget your parentage to me;
You 're the deed 's creature; by that name
You lost your first condition, and I challenge
   you,   140
As peace and innocency has turn'd you out,
And made you one with me.
   Beat.   With thee, foul villain!
   De F. Yes, my fair murd'ress. Do you urge
   me,
Though thou writ'st maid, thou whore in thy
   affection?
'T was chang'd from thy first love, and that 's
   a kind   145
Of whoredom in thy heart; and he 's chang'd
   now

[1] Q. *on 't, I 'me.*   [2] By.   [3] Q. omits.

To bring thy second on, thy Alsemero,
Whom, by all sweets that ever darkness tasted,
If I enjoy thee not, thou ne'er enjoy'st!
I 'll blast the hopes and joys of marriage,   150
I 'll confess all; my life I rate at nothing.
   Beat. De Flores!   [then;
   De F.   I shall rest from all love's [4] plagues
I live in pain now; that shooting eye
Will burn my heart to cinders.
   Beat.   O sir, hear me!
   De F. She that in life and love refuses me,   155
In death and shame my partner she shall be.
   Beat. [*kneeling.*] Stay, hear me once for all ;
   I make thee master
Of all the wealth I have in gold and jewels;
Let me go poor unto my bed with honour,
And I am rich in all things!
   De F.   Let this silence thee :
The wealth of all Valencia shall not buy   161
My pleasure from me;
Can you weep Fate from its determin'd purpose?
So soon may you weep me.
   Bea.   Vengeance begins;
Murder, I see, is followed by more sins.   165
Was my creation in the womb so curst,
It must engender with a viper first?
   De F. [*raising her.*] Come, rise and shroud
   your blushes in my bosom;
Silence is one of pleasure's best receipts: 168
Thy peace is wrought for ever in this yielding.
'Las! how the turtle pants! Thou 'lt love anon
What thou so fear 'st and faint'st to venture on.
                                        Exeunt.

ACT IV

[DUMB SHOW.]

Enter Gentlemen, VERMANDERO *meeting them
   with action of wonderment at the flight of* PIR-
   ACQUO. *Enter* ALSEMERO *with* JASPERINO
   and gallants: VERMANDERO *points to him,
   the gentlemen seeming to applaud the choice.*
   ALSEMERO, JASPERINO, *and* Gentlemen;
   BEATRICE *the bride following in great state,
   accompanied with* DIAPHANTA, ISABELLA,
   and other gentlewomen; DE FLORES *after all,
   smiling at the accident:* ALONZO'S *ghost appears to* DE FLORES *in the midst of his smile,
   startles him, showing him the hand whose finger
   he had cut off. They pass over in great solemnity.* [5]

[SCENE I.] [6]

Enter BEATRICE.

   Beat. This fellow has undone me endlessly;
Never was bride so fearfully distrest.
The more I think upon th' ensuing night,
And whom I am to cope with in embraces,
One [who 's] [7] ennobled both in blood and mind,
So clear in understanding, — that 's my plague
   now —   8

[4] Q. *lovers.* Dyce would omit, and read *love-shooting*
in next line.
[5] Stately ceremony.
[6] Alsemero's apartment in the Castle.
[7] Q. *both.*

Before whose judgment will my fault appear
Like malefactors' crimes before tribunals.
There is no hiding on 't, the more I dive
Into my own distress. How a wise man   10
Stands for [1] a great calamity! There's no ven-
    turing
Into his bed, what course soe'er I light upon,
Without my shame, which may grow up to
    danger.
He cannot but in justice strangle me
As I lie by him ; as a cheater use me ;   15
'T is a precious craft to play with a false die
Before a cunning gamester. Here's his closet ;
The key left in 't, and he abroad i' th' park !
Sure 't was forgot ; I'll be so bold as look in 't.
                              [Opens closet.]
Bless me ! a right physician's closet 't is,   20
Set round with vials ; every one her mark too.
Sure he does practise physic for his own use,
Which may be safely call'd your great man's
    wisdom.
What manuscript lies here ? "The Book of
    Experiment,
Call'd Secrets in Nature." So 'tis : 't is so.   25
[Reads.] "How to know whether a woman
    be with child or no."
I hope I am not yet ; if he should try though !
Let me see [reads] "folio forty-five," here 't is,
The leaf tuckt down upon 't, the place suspi-
    cious.   29
[Reads.] "If you would know whether a woman
be with child or not, give her two spoonfuls of
the white water in glass C—"
Where's that glass C ? O yonder, I see 't now—
[Reads.] "and if she be with child, she sleeps
full twelve hours after ; if not, not : "   35
None of that water comes into my belly ;
I'll know you from a hundred ; I could break
    you now,
Or turn you into milk, and so beguile
The master of the mystery ; but I'll look to
    you.
Ha ! that which is next is ten times worse :   40
[Reads.] "How to know whether a woman be
a maid or not : "
If that should be appli'd, what would become
of me ?
Belike he has a strong faith of my purity,
That never yet made proof ; but this he calls   45
[Reads.] "A merry slight,[2] but true experi-
ment ; the author Antonius Mizaldus. Give the
party you suspect the quantity of a spoonful of
the water in the glass M, which, upon her that
is a maid, makes three several effects ; 't will [50
make her incontinently [3] gape, then fall into a
sudden sneezing, last into a violent laughing ;
else, dull, heavy, and lumpish."
Where had I been ?
I fear it, yet 't is seven hours to bed-time.   55

Enter DIAPHANTA.

Dia. Cuds,[4] madam, are you here?
Beat.   Seeing that wench now,
A trick comes in my mind ; 't is a nice piece

Gold cannot purchase. [*Aside.*] --I come hither,
    wench,
To look my lord.
Dia.   Would I had such a cause
To look him too ! — Why, he's i' th' park,
    madam.   60
Beat. There let him be.
Dia.   Ay, madam, let him compass
Whole parks and forests, as great rangers do,
At roosting-time a little lodge can hold 'em.
Earth-conquering Alexander, that thought the
    world
Too narrow for him, in th' end had but his pit-
    hole.   65
Beat. I fear thou art not modest, Diaphanta.
Dia. Your thoughts are so unwilling to be
    known, madam.
'T is ever the bride's fashion, towards bed-time,
To set light by her joys, as if she ow'd 'em
    not.
Beat. Her joys ? Her fears thou wouldst
    say.
Dia.   Fear of what ?   70
Beat. Art thou a maid, and talk'st so to a
    maid ?
You leave a blushing business behind ;
Beshrew your heart for 't !
Dia.   Do you mean good sooth, madam ?
Beat. Well, if I'd thought upon the fear at
    first,
Man should have been unknown.
Dia.   Is 't possible ?   75
Beat. I'd give a thousand ducats to that
    woman
Would try what my fear were, and tell me true
To-morrow, when she gets from 't ; as she
    likes,
I might perhaps be drawn to 't.
Dia.   Are you in earnest ?
Beat. Do you get the woman, then challenge
    me,   80
And see if I'll fly from 't ; but I must tell you
This by the way, she must be a true maid.
Else there's no trial, my fears are not her's
    else.
Dia. Nay, she that I would put into your
    hands, madam,
Shall be a maid.
Beat. You know I should be sham'd else,   85
Because she lies for me.
Dia.   'T is a strange humour ! [5]
But are you serious still ? Would you resign
Your first night's pleasure, and give money
    too ?
Beat. As willingly as live. — [*Aside.*] Alas,
    the gold
Is but a by-bet to wedge in the honour !   90
Dia. I do not know how the world goes
    abroad
For faith or honesty ; there's both requir'd in
    this.
Madam, what say you to me, and stray no
    further ?
I've a good mind, in troth, to earn your money.
Beat. You are too quick, I fear, to be a
    maid.   95

---

[1] Is open to.   [2] Trick.
    Immediately   [4] Gods.
                [5] Whim.

Dia. How? Not a maid? Nay, then you
     urge me, madam;
Your honourable self is not a truer,
With all your fears upon you ——
  Beat. [*Aside.*]   Bad enough then.
Dia. Than I with all my lightsome joys
     about me.
Beat. I 'm glad to hear 't. Then you dare
  put your honesty [1]   100
Upon an easy trial.
  Dia.   Easy? Anything.
Beat. I 'll come to you straight.
               [*Goes to the closet.*]
Dia.   She will not search me, will she,
Like the forewoman of a female jury? [2]
  Beat. Glass M : ay, this is it. [*Brings vial.*]
  Look, Diaphanta,
You take no worse than I do.   [*Drinks.*]
  Dia.   And in so doing, 105
I will not question what it is, but take it.
                   [*Drinks.*]
Beat. [*Aside.*] Now if th' experiment be true,
  't will praise itself,
And give me noble ease: begins already ;
            [DIAPHANTA *gapes.*]
There 's the first symptom; and what haste it
  makes
To fall into the second, there by this time ! 110
            [DIAPHANTA *sneezes.*]
Most admirable secret ! on the contrary,
It stirs not me a whit, which most concerns it.
  Dia. Ha, ha, ha !
  Beat. [*Aside.*] Just in all things, and in or-
  der
As if 't were circumscrib'd ; one accident [3]   115
Gives way unto another.
  Dia. Ha, ha, ha !
  Beat. How now, wench ?
  Dia.   Ha, ha, ha ! I 'm so, so light
At heart — ha, ha, ha ! — so pleasurable !
But one swig more, sweet madam.
  Beat.   Ay, to-morrow, 120
We shall have time to sit by 't.
  Dia.   Now I 'm sad again.
  Beat. [*Aside.*] It lays itself so gently too ! —
  Come, wench.
Most honest Diaphanta I dare call thee now.
  Dia. Pray, tell me, madam, what trick call
  you this ?
Beat. I 'll tell thee all hereafter ; we must
  study   125
The carriage of this business.
  Dia.   I shall carry 't well,
Because I love the burthen.
  Beat.   About midnight
You must not fail to steal forth gently,
That I may use the place.
  Dia.   O, fear not, madam,
I shall be cool by that time. The bride's place,
And with a thousand ducats ! I 'm for a justice
  now,   131
I bring a portion with me ; I scorn small fools.
                   Exeunt.

---

[1] Chastity.
[2] I suspect that there is an allusion here to the examination by matrons of the notorious Countess of
Essex. (Bullen.)
[3] Property, symptom.

[SCENE II.] [4]

Enter VERMANDERO *and* Servant.

Ver. I tell thee, knave, mine honour is in
  question,
A thing till now free from suspicion,
Nor ever was there cause. Who of my gentle-
  men
Are absent? Tell me, and truly, how many,
  and who ?
  Ser. Antonio, sir, and Franciscus.   5
  Ver. When did they leave the castle ?
  Ser. Some ten days since, sir ; the one intend-
  ing to
Briamata, th' other for Valencia.
  Ver. The time accuses 'em ; a charge of mur-
  der
Is brought within my castle-gate, Piracquo's
  murder ;   10
I dare not answer faithfully their absence.
A strict command of apprehension
Shall pursue 'em suddenly, and either wipe
The stain off clear, or openly discover it.
Provide me winged warrants for the purpose. 15
                   Exit Servant.
See, I am set on again.

Enter TOMASO.

Tom. I claim a brother of you.
  Ver.   You 're too hot ;
Seek him not here.
  Tom.   Yes, 'mongst your dearest bloods,
If my peace find no fairer satisfaction.
This is the place must yield account for him,
For here I left him ; and the hasty tie   21
Of this snatcht marriage gives strong testi-
  mony
Of his most certain ruin.
  Ver.   Certain falsehood !
This is the place indeed ; his breach of faith
Has too much marr'd both my abused love, 25
The honourable love I reserv'd for him,
And mockt my daughter's joy ; the prepar'd
  morning
Blusht at his infidelity ; he left
Contempt and scorn to throw upon those friends
Whose belief hurt 'em. O, 't was most ignoble
To take his flight so unexpectedly,   31
And throw such public wrongs on those that
  lov'd him !
  Tom. Then this is all your answer ?
  Ver.   'T is too fair
For one of his alliance ; and I warn you
That this place no more see you.   *Exit.*

Enter DE FLORES.

Tom. The best is,   35
There is more ground to meet a man's revenge
  on. —
Honest De Flores ?
  De F.   That 's my name indeed.
Saw you the bride? Good sweet sir, which way
  took she ?
  Tom. I 've blest mine eyes from seeing such
  a false one.   40

---

[4] Another apartment in the Castle.

De F. [*Aside.*] I'd fain get off, this man's
not for my company;
I smell his brother's blood when I come near
him.

Tom. Come hither, kind and true one; I remember
My brother lov'd thee well.

Dr F.   O, purely, dear sir! —
[*Aside.*] Methinks I'm now again a-killing on
him,   45
He brings it so fresh to me.

Tom.   Thou canst guess, sirrah —
[An][1] honest friend an instinct of jealousy —
At some foul guilty person.

De F.   Alas! sir,
I am so charitable, I think none
Worse than myself! You did not see the bride
then?   50

Tom. I prithee, name her not: is she not
wicked?

De F. No, no; a pretty, easy, round-packt
sinner,
As your most ladies are, else you might think
I flatter'd her; but, sir, at no hand wicked,
Till they 're so old their chins and noses[2] meet,
And they salute witches. I'm call'd, I think,
sir. —   55
[*Aside.*] His company ev'n overlays my con-
science.   *Exit.*

Tom. That De Flores has a wondrous honest
heart!
He 'll bring it out in time, I'm assur'd on 't.
O, here 's the glorious master of the day's joy!
'T[3] will not be long till he and I do reckon. — 61

Enter ALSEMERO.

Sir.

Als. You 're most welcome.

Tom.   You may call that word back;
I do not think I am, nor wish to be.

Als. 'T is strange you found the way to this
house, then.

Tom. Would I 'd ne'er known the cause! I'm
none of those, sir,   65
That come to give you joy, and swill your wine;
'T is a more precious liquor that must lay
The fiery thirst I bring.

Als.   Your words and you
Appear to me great strangers.

Tom.   Time and our swords
May made us more acquainted. This the busi-
ness: 70
I should have had a brother in your place;
How treachery and malice have dispos'd of
him,
I 'm bound to inquire of him which holds his
right,
Which never could come fairly.

Als.   You must look
To answer for that word, sir.

Tom.   Fear you not,   75
I 'll have it ready drawn at our next meeting.

Keep your day solemn;[4] farewell, I disturb it
not;
I 'll bear the smart with patience for a time.
                                           Exit.

Als. 'T is somewhat ominous this; a quarrel
ent'red
Upon this day; my innocence relieves me,   80
I should be wondrous sad else. — Jasperino,
I 've news to tell thee, strange news.

Enter JASPERINO.

Jasp.   I ha' some too,
I think as strange as yours. Would I might
keep
Mine, so my faith and friendship might be kept
in 't!
Faith, sir, dispense a little with my zeal,   85
And let it cool in this.

Als.   This puts me on,
And blames thee for thy slowness.

Jas.   All may prove nothing,
Only a friendly fear that leapt from me, sir.

Als. No question, 't may prove nothing; let 's
partake it though.

Jas. 'T was Diaphanta's chance — for to that
wench   90
I pretend[5] honest love, and she deserves it —
To leave me in a back part of the house,
A place we chose for private conference.
She was no sooner gone, but instantly
I heard your bride's voice in the next room to
me;   95
And lending more attention, found De Flores
Louder than she.

Als.   De Flores! Thou art out now.

Jas. You 'll tell me more anon.

Als.   Still I 'll prevent[6] thee,
The very sight of him is poison to her.

Jas. That made me stagger too; but Diaphanta   100
At her return confirm'd it.

Als.   Diaphanta!

Jas. Then fell we both to listen, and words
past
Like those that challenge interest in a woman.

Als. Peace: quench thy zeal, 't is dangerous
to thy bosom.

Jas. Then truth is full of peril.

Als.   Such truths are.
O, were she the sole glory of the earth,   106
Had eyes that could shoot fire into king's
breasts,
And toucht,[7] she sleeps not here! Yet I have
time,
Though night be near, to be resolv'd hereof;
And, prithee, do not weigh me by my passions.

Jas. I never weigh'd friend so.

Als.   Done charitably!   111
That key will lead thee to a pretty secret,
                                   [*Giving key.*]
By a Chaldean taught me, and I have
My study upon some. Bring from my closet
A glass inscrib'd there with the letter M,   115
And question not my purpose.

Jas.   It shall be done, sir.   *Exit.*
Als. How can this hang together? Not an
    hour since
Her woman came pleading her lady's fears,
Deliver'd her for the most timorous virgin
That ever shrunk at man's name, and so
    modest,   120
She charg'd her weep out her request to me,
That she might come obscurely to my bosom.

            Enter BEATRICE.

Beat. [*Aside.*] All things go well; my wo-
    man's preparing yonder
For her sweet voyage, which grieves me to lose;
Necessity compels it; I lose all, else.   125
Als. [*Aside.*] Pish! modesty's shrine is set in
    yonder forehead:
I cannot be too sure though. — My Joanna!
Beat. Sir, I was bold to weep a message to
    you;
Pardon my modest fears.
Als.   The dove's not meeker;
[*Aside.*] She's abus'd, questionless.

      Re-enter JASPERINO [*with vial*].

               O, are you come, sir?
Beat. [*Aside.*] The glass, upon my life! I see
    the letter.   131
Jas. Sir, this is M.   [*Giving vial.*]
Als.   'T is it.
Beat. [*Aside.*]   I am suspected.
Als. How fitly our bride comes to partake with
    us!
Beat. What is 't, my lord?
Als.   No hurt.
Beat.   Sir, pardon me,
I seldom taste of any composition.   135
Als. But this, upon my warrant, you shall
    venture on.
Beat. I fear 't will make me ill.
Als.   Heaven forbid that.
Beat. [*Aside.*] I'm put now to my cunning:
    th' effects I know,
If I can now but feign 'em handsomely.
                       [*Drinks.*]
Als. It has that secret virtue, it ne'er mist,
    sir,   140
Upon a virgin.
Jas.   Treble-qualitied?
     [BEATRICE *gapes and sneezes.*]
Als. By all that 's virtuous it takes there!
    proceeds!
Jas. This is the strangest trick to know a
    maid by.
Beat. Ha, ha, ha!
You have given me joy of heart to drink, my
    lord.   145
Als. No, thou hast given me such joy of heart,
That never can be blasted.
Beat.   What's the matter, sir?
Als. [*Aside.*] See now 't is settled in a melan-
    choly;
Keeps both the time and method. — My Joanna,
Chaste as the breath of Heaven, or morning's
    womb,   150
That brings the day forth! thus my love en-
    closes thee.   *Exeunt.*

              [SCENE III.] [1]

      Enter ISABELLA *and* LOLLIO.

Isa. O Heaven! is this the [waning] [2] moon?
Does love turn fool, run mad, and all at once?
Sirrah, here 's a madman, akin to the fool too,
A lunatic lover.
Lol. No, no, not he I brought the letter
    from?   5
Isa. Compare his inside with his out, and
    tell me.
Lol. The out 's mad, I 'm sure of that; I had
a taste on 't. [*Reads letter.*] "To the bright
Andromeda, chief chambermaid to the Knight
of the Sun, at the sign of Scorpio, in the [10
middle region, sent by the bellows-mender of
Aeolus. Pay the post." This is stark madness!
Isa. Now mark the inside. [*Takes the letter
and reads.*] "Sweet lady, having now cast off
this counterfeit cover of a madman, I appear [15
to your best judgment a true and faithful
lover of your beauty."
Lol. He is mad still.
Isa. [*reads.*] "If any fault you find, chide
those perfections in you which have made [20
me imperfect; 't is the same sun that causeth
to grow and enforceth to wither——"
Lol. O rogue!
Isa. [*reads.*] "Shapes and transhapes, destroys and builds again. I come in winter to [25
you, dismantled of my proper ornaments; by
the sweet splendour of your cheerful smiles, I
spring and live a lover."
Lol. Mad rascal still!
Isa. [*reads.*] "Tread him not under foot, [30
that shall appear an honour to your bounties.
I remain — mad till I speak with you, from
whom I expect my cure, yours all, or one be-
side himself, FRANCISCUS."
Lol. You are like to have a fine time on 't. [35
My master and I may give over our professions;
I do not think but you can cure fools and mad-
men faster than we, with little pains too.
Isa. Very likely.
Lol. One thing I must tell you, mistress: [40
you perceive that I am privy to your skill; if I
find you minister once, and set up the trade, I
put in for my thirds; I shall be mad or fool else.
Isa. The first place is thine, believe it, Lollio,
If I do fall.
Lol.   I fall upon you.
Isa.   So.   45
Lol. Well, I stand to my venture.
Isa. But thy counsel now; how shall I deal
with 'em?
Lol. [Why,] do you mean to deal with 'em?
Isa. Nay, the fair understanding, [3] how to
    use 'em.   50
Lol. Abuse [4] 'em! That 's the way to mad
the fool, and make a fool of the madman, and
then you use 'em kindly.
Isa. 'T is easy, I 'll practise; do thou ob-
serve it.
The key of thy wardrobe.   55

[1] A room in the house of Alibius.
[2] So Bullen. Q. *Waiting.*
[3] Take the words in their modest sense.   [4] Deceive.

Lol. There [*gives key*] ; fit yourself for 'em,
and I 'll fit 'em both for you.

Isa. Take thou no further notice than the
outside. *Exit.*

Lol. Not an inch ; I 'll put you to the inside.

Enter ALIBIUS.

Alib. Lollio, art there ? Will all be perfect,
think'st thou ? 60

To-morrow night, as if to close up the
Solemnity, Vermandero expects us.

Lol. I mistrust the madmen most ; the fools
will do well enough ; I have taken pains with
them. 65

Alib. Tush ! they cannot miss ; the more
absurdity,

The more commends it, so [1] no rough behaviours

Affright the ladies ; they 're nice [2] things, thou
know'st.

Lol. You need not fear, sir ; so long as we
are there with our commanding pizzles, they 'll
be as tame as the ladies themselves. 71

Alib. I 'll see them once more rehearse before they go.

Lol. I was about it, sir : look you to the madmen's morris, and let me alone with the other.
There is one or two that I mistrust their [76
fooling ; I 'll instruct them, and then they shall
rehearse the whole measure.

Alib. Do so ; I 'll see the music prepar'd :
but, Lollio,

By the way, how does my wife brook her restraint ? 80

Does she not grudge at it ?

Lol. So, so ; she takes some pleasure in the
house, she would abroad else. You must allow
her a little more length, she 's kept too short.

Alib. She shall along to Vermandero's with
us, 85

That will serve her for a month's liberty.

Lol. What 's that on your face, sir ?

Alib. Where, Lollio ? I see nothing.

Lol. Cry you mercy,[3] sir, 't is your nose ; it
show'd like the trunk of a young elephant.[4] 90

Alib. Away, rascal ! I 'll prepare the music,
Lollio. *Exit.*

Lol. Do, sir, and I 'll dance the whilst. —
Tony, where art thou, Tony ?

Enter ANTONIO.

Ant. Here, cousin ; where art thou ?

Lol. Come, Tony, the footmanship I taught
you. 95

Ant. I had rather ride, cousin.

Lol. Ay, a whip take you ! but I 'll keep you
out ; vault in : look you, Tony ; fa, la, la, la,
la. [*Dances.*]

Ant. Fa, la, la, la, la. [*Sings and dances.*] 100

Lol. There, an honour.

Ant. Is this an honour, coz ?

Lol. Yes, an it please your worship.

Ant. Does honour bend in the hams, coz ?

Lol. Marry does it, as low as worship, [105

---

squireship, nay, yeomanry itself sometimes,
from whence it first stiffened : there rise, a caper.

Ant. Caper after an honour, coz ?

Lol. Very proper, for honour is but a caper,
rises as fast and high, has a knee or two, and [110
falls to th' ground again. You can remember
your figure, Tony ?

Ant. Yes, cousin ; when I see thy figure, I
can remember mine.

Re-enter ISABELLA, [*dressed as a madwoman.*]

Isa. Hey, how he [5] treads the air ! Shough,
shough, t' other way ! he burns his wings else. [116
Here 's wax enough below, Icarus, more than
will be cancelled these eighteen moons. He 's
down, he 's down ! what a terrible fall he had !
Stand up, thou son of Cretan Daedalus, 120
And let us tread the lower labyrinth ;
I 'll bring thee to the clue.

Ant. Prithee, coz, let me alone.

Isa. Art thou not drown'd ?
About thy head I saw a heap of clouds
Wrapt like a Turkish turban ; on thy back 125
A crookt chameleon-colour'd rainbow hung
Like a tiara down unto thy hams.
Let me suck out those billows in thy belly ;
Hark, how they roar and rumble in the straits ! [6]
Bless thee from the pirates ! 130

Ant. Pox upon you, let me alone !

Isa. Why shouldst thou mount so high as
Mercury,
Unless thou hadst reversion of his place ?
Stay in the moon with me, Endymion,
And we will rule these wild rebellious waves,
That would have drown'd my love.

Ant. I 'll kick thee, if 136
Again thou touch me, thou wild unshapen
antic ;
I am no fool, you bedlam !

Isa. But you are, as sure as I am, mad.
Have I put on this habit of a frantic, 140
With love as full of fury, to beguile
The nimble eye of watchful jealousy,
And am I thus rewarded ?

Ant. Ha ! dearest beauty !

Isa. No, I have no beauty now, 144
Nor never had but what was in my garments.
You a quick-sighted lover ! Come not near me :
Keep your caparisons, you 're aptly clad ;
I came a feigner, to return stark mad. *Exit.*

Ant. Stay, or I shall change condition,
And become as you are. 150

Re-enter LOLLIO.

Lol. Why, Tony, whither now ? Why,
fool ——

Ant. Whose fool, usher of idiots ? You coxcomb !

I have fool'd too much.

Lol. You were best be mad another while then.

Ant. So I am, stark mad ; I have cause 155
enough ;

And I could throw the full effects on thee,
And beat thee like a fury.

Lol. Do not, do not ; I shall not forbear the

---

gentleman under the fool, if you do. Alas! I saw through your fox-skin before now! Come, I can give you comfort; my mistress loves [161 you; and there is as arrant a madman i' th' house as you are a fool, your rival, whom she loves not. If after the masque we can rid her of him, you earn her love, she says, and the fool shall ride her.   166

Ant. May I believe thee?

Lol. Yes, or you may choose whether you will or no.

Ant. She's eas'd of him; I've a good quarrel on 't.

Lol. Well, keep your old station yet, and be quiet.   170

Ant. Tell her I will deserve her love.
                      [*Exit.*]

Lol. And you are like to have your desert.

Enter FRANCISCUS.

Fran. [*sings.*] "Down, down, down, a-down a-down," — and then with a horse-trick
To kick Latona's forehead, and break her bow-string.

Lol. This is t' other counterfeit; I 'll put [175 him out of his humour. [*Aside. Takes out a letter and reads.*] "Sweet lady, having now cast this counterfeit cover of a madman, I appear to your best judgment a true and faithful lover of your beauty." This is pretty well for a madman.   180

Fran. Ha! what's that?

Lol. [*reads.*] "Chide those perfections in you which have made me imperfect."

Fran. I am discover'd to the fool.

Lol. I hope to discover the fool in you ere [185 I have done with you. [*Reads.*] "Yours all, or one beside himself, FRANCISCUS." This madman will mend sure.

Fran. What do you read, sirrah?

Lol. Your destiny, sir; you 'll be hang'd for this trick, and another that I know.   191

Fran. Art thou of counsel with thy mistress?

Lol. Next her apron-strings.

Fran. Give me thy hand.

Lol. Stay, let me put yours in my pocket first. [*Putting letter into his pocket.*] Your hand is [196 true,[1] is it not? It will not pick? I partly fear it, because I think it does lie.

Fran. Not in a syllable.

Lol. So if you love my mistress so well as you have handled the matter here, you are like [201 to be cur'd of your madness.

Fran. And none but she can cure it.

Lol. Well, I 'll give you over then, and she shall cast your water next.   205

Fran. Take for thy pains past.
                 [*Gives him money.*]

Lol. I shall deserve more, sir, I hope. My mistress loves you, but must have some proof of your love to her.

Fran. There I meet my wishes.   210

Lol. That will not serve, you must meet her enemy and yours.

Fran. He's dead already.

Lol. Will you tell me that, and I parted but now with him?   215

Fran. Show me the man.

Lol. Ay, that's a right course now; see him before you kill him, in any case; and yet it needs not go so far neither. 'T is but a fool that haunts the house and my mistress in the [220 shape of an idiot; bang but his fool's coat well-favouredly, and 't is well.

Fran. Soundly, soundly!

Lol. Only reserve him till the masque be past; and if you find him not now in the dance [225 yourself, I 'll show you. In, in! my master!
                      [*Dancing.*]

Fran. He handles him like a feather. Hey!
                        [*Exit.*]

Enter ALIBIUS.

Alib. Well said: in a readiness, Lollio?

Lol. Yes, sir.   229

Alib. Away then, and guide them in, Lollio:
Entreat your mistress to see this sight.
Hark, is there not one incurable fool
That might be begg'd?[2] I 've friends.

Lol.   I have him for you,
One that shall deserve it too.

Alib. Good boy, Lollio!
            The madmen and fools dance.
'T is perfect: well, fit but once these strains,   236
We shall have coin and credit for our pains.
                      Exeunt.

ACT V

[SCENE I.][3]

Enter BEATRICE: a clock strikes one.

Beat. One struck, and yet she lies by 't!
O my fears!
This strumpet serves her own ends, 't is apparent now,
Devours the pleasure with a greedy appetite,
And never minds my honour or my peace,   5
Makes havoc of my right. But she pays dearly for 't;
No trusting of her life with such a secret
That cannot rule her blood to keep her promise;
Beside, I 've some suspicion of her faith to me,
Because I was suspected of my lord,   10
And it must come from her. [*Strikes two.*] Hark! by my horrors,
Another clock strikes two!

Enter DE FLORES.

De F.   Pist! where are you?

Beat. De Flores?

De F.   Ay. Is she not come from him yet?

Beat. As I 'm a living soul, not!

De F.   Sure the devil
Hath sow'd his itch within her. Who would trust   15
A waiting-woman?

Beat.   I must trust somebody.

De F. Push! they 're termagants;
Especially when they fall upon their masters

---

[1] Honest.

[2] Whose custody, with the revenues of his estate, might be begged from the king.

[3] A gallery in the Castle.

And have their ladies' first fruits ; they 're mad
  whelps,
You cannot stave 'em off from game royal:
  then   20
You are so rash [1] and hardy, ask no counsel ;
And I could have helpt you to a 'pothecary's
  daughter
Would have fall'n off before eleven, and
  thank[t] you too.
    Beat. O me, not yet ! this whore forgets
  herself.
    De F. The rascal fares so well : look, you 're
  undone ;   25
The day-star, by this hand ! see Phosphorus [2]
  plain yonder.
    Beat. Advise me now to fall upon some ruin ;
There is no counsel safe else.
    De F.   Peace ! I ha 't now,
For we must force a rising, there's no remedy.
    Beat. How ? take heed of that.   30
    De F. Tush ! be you quiet, or else give over
  all.
    Beat. Prithee, I ha' done then.
    De F.   This is my reach : [3] I 'll set
Some part a-fire of Diaphanta's chamber.
    Beat. How ? Fire, sir ? That may endanger
  the whole house.
    De F. You talk of danger when your fame 's
  on fire ?   35
    Beat. That 's true ; do what thou wilt now.
    De F.   Push ! I aim
At a most rich success strikes all dead sure.
The chimney being a-fire, and some light par-
  cels
Of the least danger in her chamber only,
If Diaphanta should be met by chance then 40
Far from her lodging, which is now suspicious,
It would be thought her fears and affrights then
Drove her to seek for succour ; if not seen
Or met at all, as that 's the likeliest,
For her own shame she 'll hasten towards her
  lodging ;   45
I will be ready with a piece [4] high-charg'd,
As 't were to cleanse the chimney, there 't is
  proper now
But she shall be the mark.
    Beat.   I 'm forc'd to love thee now,
'Cause thou provid'st so carefully for my hon-
  our.
    De F. 'Slid, it concerns the safety of us
  both,   50
Our pleasure and continuance.
    Beat.   One word now,
Prithee ; how for the servants ?
    De F.   I 'll despatch them,
Some one way, some another in the hurry,
For buckets, hooks, ladders ; fear not you,
The deed shall find its time ; and I 've thought
  since   55
Upon a safe conveyance for the body too:
How this fire purifies wit ! Watch you your
  minute.
    Beat. Fear keeps my soul upon 't, I cannot
  stray from 't.

¹ Q. *harsh.*   ³ Scheme.
² Q. *Bosphorus.*   ⁴ Fire-arm.

Enter ALONZO'S Ghost.

    De F. Ha ! what art thou that tak'st away
  the light
Betwixt that star and me ? I dread thee
  not. —   60
'T was but a mist of conscience ; all 's clear
  again.   *Exit.*
    Beat. Who 's that, De Flores ? Bless me, it
  slides by !   [*Exit* Ghost.]
Some ill thing haunts the house ; 't has left behind it
A shivering sweat upon me ; I 'm afraid now.
This night hath been so tedious ! O this strumpet !   65
Had she a thousand lives, he should not leave
  her
Till he had destroy'd the last. List ! O my ter-
  rors !   *Struck three o'clock.*
Three struck by St. Sebastian's !
    Within. Fire, fire, fire !
    Beat. Already ? How rare is that man's
  speed !   70
How heartily he serves me ! his face loathes
  one ;
But look upon his care, who would not love
  him ?
The east is not more beauteous than his service.
    Within. Fire, fire, fire !

Re-enter DE FLORES : Servants *pass over : bell
  rings.*

    De F. Away, despatch ! hooks, buckets, lad-
  ders ! that 's well said.[5]   75
The fire-bell rings ; the chimney works, my
  charge ;
The piece is ready.   *Exit.*
    Beat.   Here's a man worth loving !

Enter DIAPHANTA.

O you're a jewel !
    Dia.   Pardon frailty, madam ;
In truth, I was so well, I ev'n forgot myself.
    Beat. You 've made trim work !
    Dia.   What ?
    Beat.   Hie quickly to your chamber ; 80
Your reward follows you.
    Dia.   I never made
So sweet a bargain.   *Exit.*

Enter ALSEMERO.

    Als.   O my dear Joanna,
Alas ! art thou risen too ? I was coming,
My absolute treasure !
    Beat.   When I mist you,
I could not choose but follow.
    Als.   Thou 'rt all sweetness : 85
The fire is not so dangerous.
    Beat.   Think you so, sir ?
    Als. I prithee, tremble not ; believe me, 't is
  not.

Enter VERMANDERO *and* JASPERINO.

    Ver. O bless my house and me !
    Als.   My lord your father.

⁵ Well done.

Re-enter DE FLORES *with a gun.*

Ver. Knave, whither goes that piece?
De F.   To scour the chimney.   *Exit.*
Ver. O, well said, well said !   90
That fellow 's good on all occasions.
Beat. A wondrous necessary man, my lord.
Ver. He hath a ready wit; he 's worth 'em
all, sir ;
Dog at a house of fire ; I ha' seen him singed ere
now. —   *The piece goes off.*
Ha, there he goes !
Beat.   'T is done !
Als.   Come, sweet, to bed now ;   95
Alas ! thou wilt get cold.
Beat.   Alas ! the fear keeps that out !
My heart will find no quiet till I hear
How Diaphanta, my poor woman, fares ;
It is her chamber, sir, her lodging chamber.
Ver. How should the fire come there ?   100
Beat. As good a soul as ever lady countenanc'd,
But in her chamber negligent and heavy :
She scapt a mine twice.
Ver.   Twice ?
Beat.   Strangely twice, sir.
Ver. Those sleepy sluts are dangerous in a
house,
An they be ne'er so good.

Re-enter DE FLORES.

De F.   O poor virginity,   105
Thou hast paid dearly for 't !
Ver.   Bless us, what 's that ?
De F. A thing you all knew once, Dia-
phanta 's burnt.
Beat. My woman ! O my woman !
De F.   Now the flames
Are greedy of her ; burnt, burnt, burnt to
death, sir !
Beat. O my presaging soul !
Als.   Not a tear more !   110
I charge you by the last embrace I gave you
In bed, before this rais'd us.
Beat.   Now you tie me ;
Were it my sister, now she gets no more.

Enter Servant.

Ver. How now ?
Ser. All danger 's past ; you may now take   115
your rests, my lords ; the fire is throughly
quencht.
Ah, poor gentlewoman, how soon was she
stifled !
Beat. De Flores, what is left of her inter,
And we as mourners all will follow her.
I will entreat that honour to my servant   120
Ev'n of my lord himself.
Als.   Command it, sweetness.
Beat. Which of you spied the fire first ?
De F.   'T was I, madam.
Beat. And took such pains in 't too ? A
double goodness !
'T were well he were rewarded.
Ver.   He shall be. —
De Flores, call upon me.
Als.   And upon me, sir.   125
          Exeunt [all except DE FLORES*].*

De F. Rewarded ? Precious ! here 's a trick
beyond me.
I see in all bouts, both of sport and wit,
Always a woman strives for the last hit.
                         Exit.

[SCENE II.]¹

Enter TOMASO.

Tom. I cannot taste the benefits of life
With the same relish I was wont to do.
Man I grow weary of, and hold his fellowship
A treacherous bloody friendship ; and because
I 'm ignorant in whom my wrath should settle,
I must think all men villains, and the next
I meet, whoe'er he be, the murderer
Of my most worthy brother. Ha ! what 's he ?
          DE FLORES *passes over the stage.*
O, the fellow that some call honest De Flores ;
But methinks honesty was hard bested   10
To come there for a lodging ; as if a queen
Should make her palace of a pest-house.
I find a contrariety in nature
Betwixt that face and me ; the least occasion
Would give me game upon him ; yet he 's so foul   15
One would scarce touch [him] with a sword he
lov'd
And made account of ; so most deadly veno-
mous,
He would go near to poison any weapon
That should draw blood on him ; one must re-
solve
Never to use that sword again in fight   20
In way of honest manhood that strikes him ;
Some river must devour it ; 't were not fit
That any man should find it. What, again ?

Re-enter DE FLORES.

He walks a' purpose by, sure, to choke me up,
T' infect my blood.
De F.   My worthy noble lord !   25
Tom. Dost offer to come near and breathe
upon me ?   [*Strikes him.*]
De F. A blow !   [*Draws.*]
Tom.   Yea, are you so prepar'd ?
I 'll rather like a soldier die by th' sword,
Than like a politician by thy poison. [*Draws.*]
De F. Hold, my lord, as you are honourable !
Tom. All slaves that kill by poison are still
cowards.   31
De F. [*Aside.*] I cannot strike ; I see his
brother's wounds
Fresh bleeding in his eye, as in a crystal. —
I will not question this, I know you 're noble ;
I take my injury with thanks given, sir,   35
Like a wise lawyer, and as a favour
Will wear it for the worthy hand that gave it. —
[*Aside.*] Why this from him that yesterday ap-
pear'd
So strangely loving to me ?
O, but instinct is of a subtler strain !   40
Guilt must not walk so near his lodge again ;
He came near me now.   *Exit.*
Tom. All league with mankind I renounce
for ever,
Till I find this murderer ; not so much

¹ Another apartment in the Castle.

As common courtesy but I 'll lock up ;   45
For in the state of ignorance I live in,
A brother may salute his brother's murderer,
And wish good speed to th' villain in a greeting.

Enter VERMANDERO, ALIBIUS, *and* ISABELLA.

Ver. Noble Piracquo !
  Tom.   Pray, keep on your way, sir ;
I 've nothing to say to you.
  Ver.   Comforts bless you, sir ; 50
  Tom. I 've forsworn compliment, in troth I
have, sir ;
As you are merely man, I have not left
A good wish for you, nor for any here.
  Ver. Unless you be so far in love with grief,
You will not part from 't upon any terms,   55
We bring that news will make a welcome for us.
  Tom. What news can that be ?
  Ver.   Throw no scornful smile
Upon the zeal I bring you, 't is worth more, sir.
Two of the chiefest men I kept about me   59
I hide not from the law of your just vengeance.
  Tom. Ha !
  Ver. To give your peace more ample satisfac-
tion,
Thank these discoverers.
  Tom.   If you bring that calm,
Name but the manner I shall ask forgiveness in
For that contemptuous smile [I threw] [1] upon you;
I 'll perfect it with reverence that belongs   66
Unto a sacred altar.   [*Kneels.*]
  Ver. [*raising him.*] Good sir, rise ;
Why, now you overdo as much a' this hand
As you fell short a' t' other. —Speak, Alibius.
  Alib. 'T was my wife's fortune, as she is most
lucky   70
At a discovery, to find out lately,
Within our hospital of fools and madmen,
Two counterfeits slipt into these disguises,
Their names Franciscus and Antonio.
  Ver. Both mine, sir, and I ask no favour for
'em.   75
  Alib. Now that which draws suspicion to their
habits,
The time of their disguisings agrees justly
With the day of the murder.
  Tom.   O blest revelation !
  Ver. Nay, more, nay, more, sir — I 'll not
spare mine own   79
In way of justice — they both feign'd a journey
To Briamata, and so wrought out [2] their leaves ;
My love was so abus'd [3] in 't.
  Tom.   Time 's too precious
To run in waste now ; you have brought a peace
The riches of five kingdoms could not purchase.
Be my most happy conduct ; I thirst for 'em : 85
Like subtle lightning will I wind about 'em,
And melt their marrow in 'em.   *Exeunt.*

[SCENE III.] [4]

Enter ALSEMERO *and* JASPERINO.

Jas. Your confidence, I 'm sure, is now of
proof ;

[1] Q. omits.   [2] Obtained.   [3] Deceived.
[4] Alsemero's apartment in the Castle.

The prospect from the garden has show'd
Enough for deep suspicion.
  Als.   The black mask
That so continually was worn upon 't
Condemns the face for ugly ere 't be seen,   5
Her despite to him, and so seeming bottomless.
  Jas. Touch it home then ; 't is not a shallow
probe
Can search this ulcer soundly ; I fear you 'll
find it
Full of corruption. 'T is fit I leave you,
She meets you opportunely from that walk ;   10
She took the back door at his parting with her.
                             Exit.
  Als. Did my fate wait for this unhappy
stroke
At my first sight of woman ? She is here.

Enter BEATRICE.

  Beat. Alsemero !
  Als.   How do you ?
  Beat.   How do I ?
Alas, sir ! how do you ? You look not well.   15
  Als. You read me well enough ; I am not well.
  Beat. Not well, sir ? Is 't in my power to bet-
ter you ?
  Als. Yes.
  Beat. Nay, then you 're cur'd again.
  Als. Pray, resolve [5] me one question, lady. 20
  Beat. If I can.
  Als. None can so sure : are you honest ?
  Beat. Ha, ha, ha ! that 's a broad question,
my lord.
  Als. But that 's not a modest answer, my
lady.
Do you laugh ? My doubts are strong upon me.
  Beat. 'T is innocence that smiles, and no
rough brow   26
Can take away the dimple in her cheek.
Say I should strain a tear to fill the vault,
Which would you give the better faith to ?
  Als. 'T were but hypocrisy of a sadder colour,
But the same stuff ; neither your smiles nor
tears   31
Shall move or flatter me from my belief :
You are a whore !
  Beat.   What a horrid sound it hath !
It blasts a beauty to deformity ;
Upon what face soever that breath falls,   35
It strikes it ugly. O, you have ruin'd
What you can ne'er repair again ?
  Als.   I 'll all
Demolish, and seek out truth within you,
If there be any left ; let your sweet tongue
Prevent your heart's rifling ; there I 'll ransack
And tear out my suspicion.
  Beat.   You may, sir ;   41
It is an easy passage ; yet, if you please,
Show me the ground whereon you lost your
love ;
My spotless virtue may but tread on that
Before I perish.
  Als.   Unanswerable ;   45
A ground you cannot stand on ; you fall down
Beneath all grace and goodness when you set

[5] Answer.

Your ticklish heel on 't. There was a visor
Over that cunning face, and that became you;
Now Impudence in triumph rides upon 't.   50
How comes this tender reconcilement else
'Twixt you and your despite, your rancorous
     loathing,
De Flores? he that your eye was sore at sight of,
He 's now become your arm's supporter, your
Lip 's saint !
     Beat.   Is there the cause ?
     Als.   Worse, your lust's devil,   55
Your adultery !
     Beat.   Would any but yourself say that,
'T would turn him to a villain !
     Als.   It was witnest
By the counsel of your bosom, Diaphanta.
     Beat. Is your witness dead then ?
     Als.   'T is to be fear'd
It was the wages of her knowledge; poor soul,
She liv'd not long after the discovery.   61
     Beat. Then hear a story of not much less horror
Than this your false suspicion is beguil'd with ;
To your bed's scandal I stand up innocence,
Which even the guilt of one black other deed   65
Will stand for proof of ; your love has made me
A cruel murd'ress.
     Als.   Ha !
     Beat.   A bloody one ;
I have kist poison for it, strokt a serpent :
That thing of hate, worthy in my esteem
Of no better employment, and him most worthy
To be so employ'd, I caus'd to murder   71
That innocent Piracquo, having no
Better means than that worst to assure
Yourself to me.
     Als.   O, the place itself e'er since
Has crying been for vengeance ! The temple,   75
Where blood and beauty first unlawfully
Fir'd their devotion and quench't the right one ;
'T was in my fears at first, 't will have it now :
O, thou art all deform'd !
     Beat.   Forget not, sir,   79
It for your sake was done. Shall greater dangers
Make the less welcome ?
     Als.   O, thou should'st have gone
A thousand leagues about to have avoided
This dangerous bridge of blood ! Here we are lost.
     Beat. Remember, I am true unto your bed.
     Als. The bed itself 's a charnel, the sheets
     shrouds   85
For murdered carcasses. It must ask pause
What I must do in this ; meantime you shall
Be my prisoner only: enter my closet ;
           Exit BEATRICE [*into closet*].
I 'll be your keeper yet. O, in what part
Of this sad story shall I first begin ? Ha !   90
This same fellow has put me in. — De Flores !

          Enter DE FLORES.

     De F. Noble Alsemero !
     Als.   I can tell you
News, sir ; my wife has her commended to you.
     De F. That 's news indeed, my lord ; I think
     she would
Commend me to the gallows if she could,   95
She ever lov'd me so well ; I thank her.

     Als. What 's this blood upon your band, De
     Flores ?
     De F. Blood ! no, sure 't was washt since.
     Als.   Since when, man ?
     De F. Since t' other day I got a knock
In a sword-and-dagger school ; I think 't is out.
     Als. Yes, 't is almost out, but 't is perceiv'd
     though.   101
I had forgot my message ; this it is,
What price goes murder ?
     De F.   How, sir ?
     Als.   I ask you, sir ;
My wife 's behindhand with you, she tells me,
For a brave bloody blow you gave for her sake
Upon Piracquo.
     De F. Upon ? 'T was quite through him sure :
Has she confest it ?
     Als.   As sure as death to both of you ;   107
And much more than that.
     De F.   It could not be much more ;
'T was but one thing, and that — she is a whore.
     Als. It could not choose but follow. O cunning devils !   110
How should blind men know you from fair-fac'd
     saints ?
     Beat. [*within.*] He lies ! the villain does belie
     me !
     De F. Let me go to her, sir.
     Als.   Nay, you shall to her. —
Peace, crying crocodile, your sounds are heard;
Take your prey to you ;— get you into her, sir :
           Exit DE FLORES [*into closet*].
I 'll be your pander now ; rehearse again   116
Your scene of lust, that you may be perfect
When you shall come to act it to the black audience,
Where howls and gnashings shall be music to you.
Clip [1] your adulteress freely, 't is the pilot   126
Will guide you to the *mare mortuum*,
Where you shall sink to fathoms bottomless.

    Enter VERMANDERO, TOMASO, ALIBIUS, ISABELLA, FRANCISCUS, *and* ANTONIO.

     Ver. O Alsemero ! I 've a wonder for you.
     Als. No, sir, 't is I, I have a wonder for you.
     Ver. I have suspicion near as proof itself   125
For Piracquo's murder.
     Als.   Sir, I have proof.
Beyond suspicion of Piracquo's murder.
     Ver. Beseech you, hear me ; these who have
been disguis'd
E'er since the deed was done.
     Als.   I have two other
That were more close disguis'd than your two
could be   130
E'er since the deed was done.
     Ver. You 'll hear me — these mine own servants —
     Als. Hear me — those nearer than your servants
That shall acquit them, and prove them guiltless.
     Fran. That may be done with easy truth,
sir.   135
     Tom. How is my cause bandied through your
delays !
             [1] Embrace.

'T is urgent in [my] blood and calls for haste.
Give me a brother [or] alive or dead ;
Alive, a wife with him ; if dead, for both
A recompense for murder and adultery.   140
    Beat. (*within.*) O, O, O!
    Als.   Hark ! 't is coming to you.
    De F. (*within.*) Nay, I 'll along for company.
    Beat. (*within.*)   O, O!
    Ver. What horrid sounds are these ?
    Als.   Come forth, you twins
Of mischief !

Re-enter DE FLORES, *bringing in* BEATRICE
    [*wounded*].

    De F.   Here we are ; if you have any more
To say to us, speak quickly, I shall not   145
Give you the hearing else ; I am so stout yet,
And so, I think, that broken rib of mankind.
    Ver. A host of enemies ent'red my citadel
Could not amaze like this : Joanna ! Beatrice !
    Joanna !
    Beat. O, come not near me, sir, I shall defile   150
you !
I that was of your blood was taken from you,
For your better health ; look no more upon 't,
But cast it to the ground regardlessly,
Let the common sewer take it from distinction.
Beneath the stars, upon yon meteor   155
        [*Pointing to* DE FLORES.]
Ever hung my fate 'mongst things corruptible ;
I ne'er could pluck it from him ; my loathing
Was prophet to the rest, but ne'er believ'd.
Mine honour fell with him, and now my life. —
Alsemero, I 'm a stranger to your bed ;   160
Your bed was coz'ned on the nuptial night, —
For which your false bride died.
    Als.   Diaphanta ?
    De F. Yes, and the while I coupled with
        your mate
At barley-break ; now we are left in hell.[1]
    Ver. We are all there, it circumscribes us   165
        here.
    De F. I lov'd this woman in spite of her
        heart :
Her love I earn'd out of Piracquo's murder.
    Tom. Ha ! my brother's murderer ?
    De F.   Yes, and her honour's prize
Was my reward ; I thank life for nothing
But that pleasure ; it was so sweet to me,   170
That I have drunk up all, left none behind
For any man to pledge me.
    Ver.   Horrid villain !
Keep life in him for future tortures.
    De F.   No !
I can prevent you ; here 's my pen-knife still ;
It is but one thread more [*stabbing himself*], and   175
    now 't is cut. —
Make haste, Joanna, by that token to thee,
Canst not forget, so lately put in mind ;
I would not go to leave thee far behind.
            Dies.
    Beat. Forgive me, Alsemero, all forgive !
'T is time to die when 't is a shame to live.   180
            Dies.
    Ver. O, my name 's ent'red now in that
        record
    [1] See III. iii. 181. note.

Where till this fatal hour 't was never read.
    Als. Let it be blotted out ; let your heart
        lose it,
And it can never look you in the face,
Nor tell a tale behind the back of life   185
To your dishonour. Justice hath so right
The guilty hit, that innocence is quit
By proclamation, and may joy again. —
Sir, you are sensible of what truth hath done ;
'T is the best comfort that your grief can find.
    Tom. Sir, I am satisfied ; my injuries   191
Lie dead before me ; I can exact no more,
Unless my soul were loose, and could o'ertake
Those black fugitives that are fled from
        hence,
To take[2] a second vengeance ; but there are
        wraths   195
Deeper than mine, 't is to be fear'd, about
        'em.
    Als. What an opacous body had that moon
That last chang'd on us ! Here is beauty
        chang'd
To ugly whoredom ; here servant-obedience
To a master-sin, imperious murder ;   200
I, a suppos'd husband, chang'd embraces
With wantonness, — but that was paid be-
        fore. —
Your change is come too, from an ignorant
        wrath
To knowing friendship. — Are there any more
        on 's ?   204
    Ant. Yes, sir, I was chang'd too from a little
ass as I was to a great fool as I am ; and
had like to ha' been chang'd to the gallows, but
that you know my innocence[3] always excuses
me.
    Fran. I was chang'd from a little wit to be
stark mad,   210
Almost for the same purpose.
    Isa.   Your change is still behind,
But deserve best your transformation :
You are a jealous coxcomb, keep schools of
        folly,
And teach your scholars how to break your own
        head.
    Alib. I see all apparent, wife, and will
        change now   215
Into a better husband, and ne'er keep
Scholars that shall be wiser than myself.
    Als. Sir, you have yet a son's duty living,
Please you, accept it ; let that your sorrow,
As it goes from your eye, go from your heart,
Man and his sorrow at the grave must part.   221

EPILOGUE

    Als. All we can do to comfort one another,
To stay a brother's sorrow for a brother,
To dry a child from the kind father's eyes,
Is to no purpose, it rather multiplies :   225
Your only smiles have power to cause re-
        live
The dead again, or in their rooms to give
Brother a new brother, father a child ;
If these appear, all griefs are reconcil'd.
            Exeunt omnes.

    [2] Receive.   [3] Idiocy

A NEW WAY TO PAY OLD DEBTS

BY

PHILIP MASSINGER

DRAMATIS PERSONAE

[LORD] LOVELL, an English Lord.
SIR GILES OVERREACH, a cruel extortioner.
[FRANK] WELLBORN, a Prodigal.
[TOM] ALLWORTH, a young Gentleman, Page to Lord Lovell.
GREEDY, a hungry Justice of Peace.
MARRALL, a Term-Driver ; a creature of Sir Giles Overreach.
ORDER [Steward],
AMBLE [Usher],
FURNACE [Cook],
WATCHALL [Porter], } Servants to the Lady Allworth.

WILLDO, a Parson.
TAPWELL, an Alehouse Keeper.
Three Creditors, Servants, &c.

The LADY ALLWORTH, a rich Widow.
MARGARET, Overreach his daughter.
FROTH, Tapwell's Wife.
Chambermaid.
Waiting Woman.

[SCENE. — *The Country near Nottingham.*]

ACT I

SCENE I.[1]

[*Enter*] WELLBORN [*in tattered apparel*], TAP-
WELL, *and* FROTH.

Well. No bouse?[2] nor no tobacco?
Tap.   Not a suck, sir ;
Nor the remainder of a single can
Left by a drunken porter, all night pall'd[3] too.
Froth. Not the dropping of the tap for your
      morning's draught, sir.
'T is verity, I assure you.
Well.   Verity, you brach![4] [5]
The devil turn'd precisian![5] Rogue, what am
      I ?
Tap. Troth, durst I trust you with a looking-
      glass,
To let you see your trim shape, you would quit
      me
And take the name yourself.
Well.   How, dog !
Tap.   Even so, sir.
And I must tell you, if you but advance   10
Your Plymouth cloak[6] you shall be soon in-
      structed
There dwells, and within call, if it please your
      worship,
A potent monarch call'd the constable,
That does command a citadel call'd the stocks ;
Whose guards are certain files of rusty billmen
Such as with great dexterity will hale   16
Your tatter'd, lousy ——
Well.   Rascal ! slave !
Froth.   No rage, sir.
Tap. At his own peril. Do not put yourself
In too much heat, there being no water near

To quench your thirst ; and sure, for other
      liquor,   20
As mighty ale, or beer, they are things, I take
      it,
You must no more remember ; not in a dream,
      sir.
Well. Why, thou unthankful villain, dar'st
      thou talk thus !
Is not thy house, and all thou hast, my gift ?
Tap. I find it not in chalk ; and Timothy Tap-
      well   26
Does keep no other register.
Well.   Am not I he
Whose riots fed and cloth'd thee ? Wert thou
      not
Born on my father's land, and proud to be
A drudge in his house ?
Tap.   What I was, sir, it skills[7] not ; 29
What you are, is apparent. Now, for a farewell,
Since you talk of father, in my hope it will
      torment you,
I 'll briefly tell your story. Your dead father,
My quondam master, was a man of worship,
Old Sir John Wellborn, justice of peace and
      quorum,[8]
And stood fair to be *custos rotulorum* ;[9]   35
Bore the whole sway of the shire, kept a great
      house,
Reliev'd the poor, and so forth ; but he dying,
And the twelve hundred a year coming to you,
Late Master Francis, but now forlorn Well-
      born ——
Well. Slave, stop ! or I shall lose myself.
Froth.   Very hardly ;[4] 40
You cannot out of your way.
Tap.   But to my story :

[1] Before Tapwell's house.   [2] Booze, drink.
[3] Staled.   [4] Hound.   [5] Puritan.   [6] Cudgel.
[7] Matters.
[8] A select number of the more learned justices, whose presence was necessary to constitute the bench.
[9] Keeper of the county records.

You were then a lord of acres, the prime gal-
　　lant,
And I your under-butler. Note the change now:
You had a merry time of 't ; hawks and hounds ;
With choice of running horses ; mistresses　　45
Of all sorts and all sizes, yet so hot,
As their embraces made your lordship melt ;
Which your uncle, Sir Giles Overreach, observ-
　　ing,
(Resolving not to lose a drop of 'em,)
On foolish mortgages, statutes, and bonds,　　50
For a while suppli'd your looseness, and then
　　left you.
　　Well. Some curate hath penn'd this invective,
　　　mongrel,
And you have studied it.
　　Tap.　　　　　　I have not done yet.
Your land gone, and your credit not worth a
　　token,
You grew a common borrower ; no man scap'd
Your paper-pellets,[1] from the gentleman　　55
To the beggars on highways, that sold you
　　switches
In your gallantry.
　　Well.　　　　I shall switch your brains out.
　　Tap. Where poor Tim Tapwell, with a little
　　　stock,
Some forty pounds or so, bought a small cot-
　　tage ;　　60
Humbled myself to marriage with my Froth
　　here,
Gave entertainment ——
　　Well.　　　　Yes, to whores and canters,[2]
Clubbers by night.
　　Tap.　　True, but they brought in profit,
And had a gift to pay for what they call'd for,
And stuck not like your mastership. The poor
　　income　　65
I glean'd from them hath made me in my
　　parish
Thought worthy to be scavenger, and in time
May rise to be overseer of the poor ;
Which if I do, on your petition, Wellborn,
May allow you thirteen-pence a quarter,　　70
And you shall thank my worship.
　　Well.　　　　　Thus, you dog-bolt,
And thus ——　　　　　*Beats and kicks him.*
　　Tap. [*to his wife.*] Cry out for help !
　　Well.　　　　　Stir, and thou diest :
Your potent prince, the constable, shall not save
　　you.
Hear me, ungrateful hell-hound ! Did not I
Make purses for you ? Then you lick'd my
　　boots,　　75
And thought your holiday cloak too coarse to
　　clean 'em.
'T was I that, when I heard thee swear if ever
Thou couldst arrive at forty pounds thou
　　wouldst
Live like an emperor, 't was I that gave it
In ready gold. Deny this, wretch !
　　Tap.　　　　　I must, sir ;　80
For, from the tavern to the taphouse, all,
On forfeiture of their licenses, stand bound

Ne'er to remember who their best guests were,
If they grew poor like you.
　　Well.　　　　They are well rewarded
That beggar themselves to make such cuckolds
　　rich.　　85
Thou viper, thankless viper ! impudent bawd !
But since you have grown forgetful, I will help
Your memory, and tread you into mortar,
Nor leave one bone unbroken.
　　　　　　　　　　[*Beats him again.*]
　　Tap.　　　　　　Oh !
　　Froth.　　　　　　Ask mercy.

Enter ALLWORTH.

　　Well. 'T will not be granted.
　　All.　　　　Hold — for my sake, hold.　　90
Deny me, Frank ? They are not worth your
　　anger.
　　Well. For once thou hast redeem'd them from
　　　this sceptre ;[3]
But let 'em vanish, creeping on their knees,
And, if they grumble, I revoke my pardon.
　　Froth. This comes of your prating, husband ;
　　　you presum'd　　95
On your ambling wit, and must use your glib
　　tongue,
Though you are beaten lame for 't.
　　Tap.　　　　　Patience, Froth ;
There's law to cure our bruises.
　　　　　　They go off on their hands and knees.
　　Well.　　　　Sent to your mother ?
　　All. My lady, Frank, my patroness, my all !
She's such a mourner for my father's death,
And, in her love to him, so favours me,　　101
That I cannot pay too much observance to her.
There are few such stepdames.
　　Well.　　　　　'T is a noble widow,
And keeps her reputation pure, and clear
From the least taint of infamy ; her life,　　105
With the splendour of her actions, leaves no
　　tongue
To envy or detraction. Prithee tell me,
Has she no suitors ?
　　All.　　Even the best of the shire, Frank,
My lord excepted ; such as sue and send,
And send and sue again, but to no purpose ;　110
Their frequent visits have not gain'd her pres-
　　ence.
Yet she's so far from sullenness and pride,
That I dare undertake you shall meet from her
A liberal entertainment. I can give you
A catalogue of her suitors' names.
　　Well.　　　　Forbear it,　115
While I give you good counsel : I am bound to
　　it,
Thy father was my friend, and that affection
I bore to him, in right descends to thee ;
Thou art a handsome and a hopeful youth,　119
Nor will I have the least affront stick on thee,
If I with any danger can prevent it.
　　All. I thank your noble care ; but, pray you,
　　in what
Do I run the hazard ?
　　Well.　　　　Art thou not in love ?
Put it not off with wonder.

---

[1] Acknowledgments of indebtedness.
[2] Whining beggars.

[3] *I. e.* his cudgel.

All.   In love, at my years !
Well. You think you walk in clouds, but are
    transparent.   125
I have heard all, and the choice that you have
    made,
And, with my finger, can point out the north
    star
By which the loadstone of your folly 's guided ;
And, to confirm this true, what think you of
Fair Margaret, the only child and heir   130
Of Cormorant Overreach ? Does it blush and
    start,
To hear her only nam'd ? Blush at your want
Of wit and reason.
All.   You are too bitter, sir.
Well. Wounds of this nature are not to be
    cur'd
With balms, but corrosives. I must be plain : 135
Art thou scarce manumis'd [1] from the porter's
    lodge [2]
And yet sworn servant to the pantofle,[3]
And dar'st thou dream of marriage ? I fear
'T will be concluded for impossible
That there is now, or e'er shall be hereafter, 140
A handsome page or player's boy of fourteen
But either loves a wench, or drabs love him ;
Court-waiters not exempted.
All.   This is madness.
Howe'er you have discover'd my intents,
You know my aims are lawful ; and if ever   145
The queen of flowers, the glory of the spring,
The sweetest comfort to our smell, the rose,
Sprang from an envious briar, I may infer
There 's such disparity in their conditions   149
Between the goodness of my soul, the daughter,
And the base churl of her father.
Well.   Grant this true,
As I believe it, canst thou ever hope
To enjoy a quiet bed with her whose father
Ruin'd thy state ?
All.   And yours too.
Well.   I confess it ; 154
True ; I must tell you as a friend, and freely,
That, where impossibilities are apparent,
'T is indiscretion to nourish hopes.
Canst thou imagine (let not self-love blind thee)
That Sir Giles Overreach, that, to make her
    great   159
In swelling titles, without touch of conscience
Will cut his neighbour's throat, and I hope his
    own too,
Will e'er consent to make her thine ? Give o'er,
And think of some course suitable to thy rank,
And prosper in it.
All.   You have well advis'd me. 164
But in the meantime you that are so studious
Of my affairs wholly neglect your own.
Remember yourself, and in what plight you are.
Well. No matter, no matter.
All.   Yes, 't is much material.
You know my fortune and my means ; yet
    something
I can spare from myself to help your wants.
Well.   How 's this ? 170

---

[1] Freed.
[2] Where servants used to be punished.
[3] Slipper.

All. Nay, be not angry ; there 's eight pieces
To put you in better fashion.
Well.   Money from thee !
From a boy. A stipendiary ! One that lives
At the devotion of a stepmother
And the uncertain favour of a lord !   175
I 'll eat my arms first. Howsoe'er blind For-
    tune
Hath spent the utmost of her malice on me ——
Though I am vomited out of an alehouse,
And thus accoutred — know not where to eat,
Or drink, or sleep, but underneath this can-
    opy — [4]   180
Although I thank thee, I despise thy offer ;
And as I in my madness broke my state
Without th' assistance of another's brain,
In my right wits I 'll piece it ; at the worst, 184
Die thus and be forgotten.
All.   A strange humour ! *Exeunt.*

SCENE II.[5]

[*Enter*] ORDER, AMBLE, FURNACE, *and*
    WATCHALL.

Ord. Set all things right, or, as my name is
    Order,
And by this staff of office that commands you,
This chain and double ruff, symbols of power,
Whoever misses in his function,
For one whole week makes forfeiture of his
    breakfast   5
And privilege in the wine-cellar.
Amb.   You are merry,
Good master steward.
Furn.   Let him ; I 'll be angry.
Amb. Why, fellow Furnace, 't is not twelve
    o'clock yet,
Nor dinner taking up ; then, 't is allow'd,
Cooks, by their places, may be choleric.   10
Furn. You think you have spoke wisely,
    goodman Amble,
My lady's go-before !
Ord.   Nay, nay, no wrangling.
Furn. Twit me with the authority of the
    kitchen !
At all hours, and all places, I 'll be angry ;
And thus provok'd, when I am at my prayers 15
I will be angry.
Amb.   There was no hurt meant.
Furn. I am friends with thee ; and yet I will
    be angry.
Ord.   With whom ?
Furn.   No matter whom : yet, now I
    think on it,
I am angry with my lady.
Watch.   Heaven forbid, man !
Ord. What cause has she given thee ?
Furn.   Cause enough, master steward. 20
I was entertain'd by her to please her palate,
And, till she forswore eating, I perform'd it.
Now, since our master, noble Allworth, died,
Though I crack my brains to find out tempting
    sauces,
And raise fortifications in the pastry   25

---

[4] *I. e.* the sky.
[5] A room in Lady Allworth's house.

Such as might serve for models in the Low
Countries,
Which, if they had been practised at Breda,
Spinola might have thrown his cap at it, and
ne'er took it[1] —
 Amb. But you had wanted matter there to
work on.
 Furn. Matter! with six eggs, and a strike[2]
of rye meal,   ₃₀
I had kept the town till doomsday, perhaps
longer.
 Ord. But what's this to your pet against my
lady?
 Furn. What's this? Marry this: when I am
three parts roasted
And the fourth part parboil'd to prepare her
viands,
She keeps her chamber, dines with a panada[3] ₃₅
Or water-gruel, my sweat never thought on.
 Ord. But your art is seen in the dining-room.
 Furn.   By whom?
By such as pretend love to her, but come
To feed upon her. Yet, of all the harpies
That do devour her, I am out of charity ₄₀
With none so much as the thin-gutted squire
That's stolen into commission.
 Ord.   Justice Greedy?
 Furn. The same, the same; meat's cast away
upon him,
It never thrives; he holds this paradox,
Who eats not well, can ne'er do justice well. ₄₅
His stomach's as insatiate as the grave,
Or strumpet's ravenous appetites. *Knocking.*
 Watch.   One knocks.

    Enter ALLWORTH.

 Ord. Our late young master!
 Amb.   Welcome, sir.
 Furn.   Your hand;
If you have a stomach, a cold bake-meat's
ready.
 Ord. His father's picture in little.
 Furn.   We are all your servants. ₅₀
 Amb. In you he lives.
 All.   At once, my thanks to all;
This is yet some comfort. Is my lady stirring?

Enter LADY ALLWORTH, *Waiting Woman, and*
Chambermaid.

 Ord. Her presence answers for us.
 L. All.   Sort those silks well.
I'll take the air alone.
   Exeunt W. Woman *and* Chambermaid.
 Furn.   You air and air;
But will you never taste but spoon-meat more?
To what use serve I?
 L. All.   Prithee, be not angry; ₅₅
I shall ere long: i' the mean time, there is gold
To buy thee aprons, and a summer suit.
 Furn. I am appeas'd, and Furnace now
grows cool.[4]

---

[1] The siege of Breda by Spinola in 1624–25 was one of
the great events of the time.
[2] Two bushels.
[3] Bread soaked in hot water and milk.
[4] Q. reads *Cooke.*

 L. All. And, as I gave directions, if this
morning   ₆₀
I am visited by any, entertain 'em
As heretofore; but say, in my excuse,
I am indispos'd.
 Ord.   I shall, madam.
 L. All.   Do, and leave them.
Nay, stay you, Allworth.
  Exeunt ORDER, AMBLE, FURNACE,
    and WATCHALL.
 All.   I shall gladly grow here,
To wait on your commands.
 L. All.   So soon turn'd courtier! ₆₅
 All. Style not that courtship, madam, which
is duty
Purchas'd on your part.
 L. All.   Well, you shall o'ercome
I'll not contend in words. How is it with
Your noble master?
 All.   Ever like himself,
No scruple lessen'd in the full weight of hon-
our.   ₇₀
He did command me, pardon my presumption,
As his unworthy deputy, to kiss
Your ladyship's fair hands.
 L. All.   I am honour'd in
His favour to me. Does he hold his purpose
For the Low Countries?
 All.   Constantly, good madam; ₇₅
But he will in person first present his service.
 L. All. And how approve you of his course?
You are yet
Like virgin parchment, capable of any
Inscription, vicious or honourable.
I will not force your will, but leave you free ₈₀
To your own election.
 All.   Any form you please
I will put on; but, might I make my choice,
With humble emulation I would follow
The path my lord marks to me.
 L. All.   'Tis well answer'd,
And I commend your spirit. You had a father,
Blest be his memory! that some few hours ₈₅
Before the will of Heaven took him from me,
Who did commend you, by the dearest ties
Of perfect love between us, to my charge;
And, therefore, what I speak you are bound to
hear   ₉₀
With such respect as if he liv'd in me.
He was my husband, and howe'er you are not
Son of my womb, you may be of my love,
Provided you deserve it.
 All.   I have found you,
Most honour'd madam, the best mother to me;
And, with my utmost strengths of care and ser-
vice,   ₉₅
Will labour that you never may repent
Your bounties shower'd upon me.
 L. All.   I much hope it.
These were your father's words: "If e'er my
son
Follow the war, tell him it is a school ₁₀₀
Where all the principles tending to honour
Are taught, if truly followed: but for such
As repair thither as a place in which
They do presume they may with license practise
Their lusts and riots, they shall never merit ₁₀₅

The noble name of soldiers. To dare boldly
In a fair cause, and for their country's safety
To run upon the cannon's mouth undaunted;
To obey their leaders, and shun mutinies;
To bear with patience the winter's cold 110
And summer's scorching heat, and not to faint,
When plenty of provision fails, with hunger;
Are the essential parts make up a soldier,
Not swearing, dice, or drinking."
    All.   There 's no syllable
You speak, but is to me an oracle, 115
Which but to doubt were impious.
    L. All.   To conclude:
Beware ill company, for often men
Are like to those with whom they do converse;
And, from one man I warn[1] you, and that 's
    Wellborn:
Not 'cause he 's poor, that rather claims your
    pity; 120
But that he 's in his manners so debauch'd,
And hath to vicious courses sold himself.
'T is true, your father lov'd him, while he was
Worthy the loving; but if he had liv'd
To have seen him as he is, he had cast him off,
As you must do.
    All.   I shall obey in all things. 125
    L. All. Follow me to my chamber, you shall
    have gold
To furnish you like my son, and still supplied,
As I hear from you.
    All.   I am still your creature. *Exeunt.*

SCENE III.[2]

[*Enter*] OVERREACH, GREEDY, ORDER, AMBLE,
    FURNACE, WATCHALL, *and* MARRALL.

    Greedy. Not to be seen!
    Over.   Still cloistered up! Her reason,
I hope, assures her, though she make herself
Close prisoner ever for her husband's loss,
'T will not recover him.
    Ord.   Sir, it is her will,
Which we, that are her servants, ought to
    serve it, 5
And not dispute. Howe'er, you are nobly wel-
    come;
And, if you please to stay, that you may think
    so,
There came, not six days since, from Hull, a
    pipe
Of rich Canary, which shall spend itself
For my lady's honour.
    Greedy.   Is it of the right race? 10
    Ord. Yes, Master Greedy.
    Amb.   How his mouth runs o'er!
    Furn. I 'll make it run, and run. Save your
    good worship!
    Greedy. Honest Master Cook, thy hand;
    again, how I love thee!
Are the good dishes still in being? Speak, boy.
    Furn. If you have a mind to feed, there is a
    chine[3] 15
Of beef, well seasoned.
    Greedy.   Good!

    Furn.   A pheasant, larded.
    Greedy. That I might now give thanks for 't!
    Furn.   Other kickshaws.
Besides, there came last night, from the forest
    of Sherwood,
The fattest stag I ever cook'd.
    Greedy.   A stag, man!
    Furn. A stag, sir; part of it prepar'd for
    dinner, 20
And bak'd in puff-paste.
    Greedy.   Puff-paste too! Sir Giles,
A ponderous chine of beef! a pheasant larded!
And red deer too, Sir Giles, and bak'd in puff-
    paste!
All business set aside, let us give thanks here.
    Furn. How the lean skeleton 's rapt!
    Over.   You know we cannot. 25
    Mar. Your worships are to sit on a commis-
    sion,
And if you fail to come, you lose the cause.
    Greedy. Cause me no causes. I 'll prove 't,
    for such dinner
We may put off a commission: you shall find it
Henrici decimo quarto.
    Over.   Fie, Master Greedy! 30
Will you lose me a thousand pounds for a din-
    ner?
No more, for shame! We must forget the belly
When we think of profit.
    Greedy.   Well, you shall o'er-rule me;
I could ev'n cry now.—Do you hear, Master
    Cook,
Send but a corner of that immortal pasty, 35
And I, in thankfulness, will, by your boy,
Send you — a brace of three-pences.
    Furn.   Will you be so prodigal?

Enter WELLBORN.

    Over. Remember me to your lady. Who
    have we here?
    Well. You know me.
    Over.   I did once, but now I will not;
Thou art no blood of mine. Avaunt, thou beg-
    gar! 40
If ever thou presume to own me more,
I 'll have thee cag'd and whipp'd.
    Greedy.   I 'll grant the warrant.
Think of Pie-corner, Furnace!
        Exeunt OVERREACH, GREEDY, *and*
        MARRALL.
    Watch.   Will you out, sir?
I wonder how you durst creep in.
    Ord.   This is rudeness,
And saucy impudence.
    Amb.   Cannot you stay 45
To be serv'd, among your fellows, from the
    basket,[4]
But you must needs press into the hall?
    Furn.   Prithee, vanish
Into some outhouse, though it be the pigstye;
My scullion shall come to thee.

Enter ALLWORTH.

    Well.   This is rare.
Oh, here 's Tom Allworth. Tom!

---

1 Q. *warn'd.*   2 A hall in the same.
3 Part of the back: ribs or sirloin.
4 The basket of broken meats given in alms.

All. We must be strangers; 50
Nor would I have you seen here for a million,
Exit.
Well. Better and better. He contemns me
too !

Enter Waiting Woman *and* Chambermaid.

Woman. Foh, what a smell 's here ! What
thing 's this ?
Cham. A creature
Made out of the privy ; let us hence, for love's
sake.
Or I shall swoon.
Woman. I begin to feel faint already. 55
Exeunt W. Woman *and* Chamber-
maid.
Watch. Will you know your way ;
Amb. Or shall we teach it you,
By the head and shoulders ?
Well. No ; I will not stir ;
Do you mark, I will not : let me see the wretch
That dares attempt to force me. Why, you
slaves,
Created only to make legs,[1] and cringe ; 60
To carry in a dish, and shift a trencher ;
That have not souls only to hope a blessing
Beyond black-jacks [2] or flagons ; you, that
were born
Only to consume meat and drink, and batten [3]
Upon reversions ! — who advances ? Who 65
Shews me the way ?
Ord. My lady !

Enter LADY ALLWORTH, Waiting Woman, *and*
Chambermaid.

Cham. Here 's the monster.
Woman. Sweet madam, keep your glove to
your nose.
Cham. Or let me
Fetch some perfumes may be predominant ;
You wrong yourself else.
Well. Madam, my designs
Bear me to you.
L. All. To me !
Well. And though I have met with 70
But ragged entertainment from your grooms
here,
I hope from you to receive that noble usage
As may become the true friend of your hus-
band,
And then I shall forget these.
L. All. I am amaz'd
To see and hear this rudeness. Dar'st thou
think, 75
Though sworn, that it can ever find belief,
That I, who to the best men of this country
Deni'd my presence since my husband's death,
Can fall so low as to change words with
thee ?
Thou son of infamy, forbear my house, 80
And know and keep the distance that 's be-
tween us ;
Or, though it be against my gentler temper,
I shall take order you no more shall be
An eyesore to me.

Well. Scorn me not, good lady ;
But, as in form you are angelical, 85
Imitate the heavenly natures, and vouchsafe
At the least awhile to hear me. You will grant
The blood that runs in this arm is as noble
As that which fills your veins ; those costly
jewels,
And those rich clothes you wear, your men's
observance 90
And women's flattery, are in you no virtues,
Nor these rags, with my poverty, in me vices.
You have a fair fame, and, I know, deserve it ;
Yet, lady, I must say, in nothing more
Than in the pious sorrow you have shewn 95
For your late noble husband.
Ord. How she starts !
Furn. And hardly can keep finger from the
eye,
To hear him nam'd.
L. All. Have you aught else to say ?
Well. That husband, madam, was once in
his fortune 99
Almost as low as I ; want, debts, and quarrels
Lay heavy on him : let it not be thought
A boast in me, though I say I reliev'd him.
'T was I that gave him fashion ; mine the
sword
That did on all occasions second his ;
I brought him on and off with honour, lady ; 105
And when in all men's judgments he was
sunk,
And, in his own hopes, not to be buoy'd [4] up,
I stepp'd unto him, took him by the hand,
And set him upright.
Furn. Are not we base rogues,
That could forget this ?
Well. I confess, you made him 110
Master of your estate ; nor could your friends,
Though he brought no wealth with him, blame
you for 't ;
For he had a shape, and to that shape a mind
Made up of all parts either great or noble ;
So winning a behaviour, not to be 115
Resisted, madam.
L. All. 'T is most true, he had.
Well. For his sake, then, in that I was his
friend,
Do not contemn me.
L. All. For what 's past excuse me,
I will redeem it. Order, give the gentleman
A hundred pounds.
Well. No, madam, on no terms : 120
I will nor beg nor borrow sixpence of you,
But be suppli'd elsewhere, or want thus ever.
Only one suit I make, which you deny not
To strangers ; and 't is this. *Whispers to her.*
L. All. Fie ! nothing else ?
Well. Nothing, unless you please to charge
your servants 125
To throw away a little respect upon me.
L. All. What you demand is yours.
Well. I thank you, lady.
Now what can be wrought out of such a suit
Is yet in supposition : I have said all ;
When you please, you may retire.—
[Exit LADY ALL.*]*

---

[1] Bow.   [2] Leather beer cans.   [3] Feed.

[4] Q. *bung'd*

Nay, all's forgotten; [*To the* Servants.]
And, for a lucky omen to my project,   131
Shake hands, and end all quarrels in the cellar.
Ord. Agreed, agreed.
Furn.   Still merry Master Wellborn.
Exeunt.

ACT II

SCENE I.[1]

Enter OVERREACH *and* MARRALL.

Over. He's gone, I warrant thee; this com-
          mission crush'd him.
Mar. Your worships have the way on't, and
          ne'er miss
To squeeze these unthrifts into air; and yet,
The chapfallen[2] justice did his part, returning
For your advantage the certificate,   5
Against his conscience, and his knowledge too,
With your good favour, to the utter ruin
Of the poor farmer.
Over.   'T was for these good ends
I made him a justice; he that bribes his belly,
Is certain to command his soul.
Mar.   I wonder,   10
Still with your license, why your worship hav-
          ing
The power to put his thin-gut in commission,
You are not in't yourself?
Over.   Thou art a fool;
In being out of office I am out of danger;
Where, if I were a justice, besides the trouble,
I might, or out of wilfulness or error,   16
Run myself finely into a *premunire*,[3]
And so become a prey to the informer.
No, I'll have none of't; 'tis enough I keep
Greedy at my devotion; so he serve   20
My purposes, let him hang or damn, I care not;
Friendship is but a word.
Mar.   You are all wisdom.
Over. I would be worldly wise; for the other
          wisdom,
That does prescribe us a well govern'd life,
And to do right to others as ourselves,   25
I value not an atom.
Mar.   What course take you,
With your good patience, to hedge in the manor
Of your neighbour, Master Frugal? as 'tis said
He will nor sell, nor borrow, nor exchange;
And his land, lying in the midst of your many
          lordships,   30
Is a foul blemish.
Over.   I have thought on't, Marrall,
And it shall take. I must have all men sellers,
And I the only purchaser.
Mar.   'Tis most fit, sir.
Over. I'll therefore buy some cottage near
          his manor,
Which done, I'll make my men break ope his
          fences,   35
Ride o'er his standing corn, and in the night
Set fire on his barns, or break his cattle's legs.

[1] A room in Overreach's house.   [2] Hollow-cheeked.
[3] A writ issued for the offence of acknowledging foreign authority within the realm, or some offence with
the same penalties.

These trespasses draw on suits and suits ex-
          penses,
Which I can spare, but will soon beggar him.
When I have harried him thus two or three
          year,   40
Though he sue *in forma pauperis*, in spite
Of all his thrift and care, he'll grow behindhand.
Mar. The best I ever heard! I could adore
          you.
Over. Then, with the favour of my man of
          law,
I will pretend some title. Want will force him
To put it to arbitrement; then, if he sell   46
For half the value, he shall have ready money,
And I possess his land.
Mar.   'Tis above wonder!
Wellborn was apt to sell, and needed not
Those fine arts, sir, to hook him in.
Over.   Well thought on.   50
This varlet, Marrall, lives too long, to upbraid
          me
With my close cheat upon him. Will nor cold
Nor hunger kill him?
Mar.   I know not what to think on't.
I have us'd all means; and the last night I
          caus'd   54
His host, the tapster, to turn him out of doors;
And have been since with all your friends and
          tenants,
And, on the forfeit of your favour, charg'd
          them,
Though a crust of mouldy bread would keep
          him from starving,
Yet they should not relieve him. This is done,
          sir.
Over. That was something, Marrall; but thou
          must go further,   60
And suddenly, Marrall.
Mar.   Where, and when you please, sir.
Over. I would have thee seek him out, and, if
          thou canst,
Persuade him that 'tis better steal than beg;
Then, if I prove he has but robb'd a henroost,
Not all the world shall save him from the gal-
          lows.   65
Do any thing to work him to despair;
And 'tis thy masterpiece.
Mar.   I will do my best, sir.
Over. I am now on my main work with the
          Lord Lovell,
The gallant-minded, popular Lord Lovell,
The minion of the people's love. I hear   70
He's come into the country, and my aims are
To insinuate myself into his knowledge,
And then invite him to my house.
Mar.   I have you;
This points at my young mistress.
Over.   She must part with
That humble title, and write honourable,
Right honourable, Marrall, my right honourable
          daughter,   76
If all I have, or e'er shall get, will do it.
I'll have her well attended; there are ladies
Of errant knights decay'd and brought so
          low,
That for cast clothes and meat will gladly serve
          her.   80

And 't is my glory, though I come from the city,
To have their issue whom I have undone,
To kneel to mine as bondslaves.
 Mar.   'T is fit state, sir.
 Over. And therefore, I 'll not have a cham-
bermaid
That ties her shoes, or any meaner office, 85
But such whose fathers were right worshipful.
'T is a rich man's pride ! there having ever been
More than a feud, a strange antipathy,
Between us and true gentry.

Enter WELLBORN.

 Mar.   See, who 's here, sir.
 Over. Hence, monster ! prodigy !
 Well.   Sir, your wife's nephew ; 90
She and my father tumbled in one belly.
 Over. Avoid my sight ! thy breath 's infec-
tious, rogue !
I shun thee as a leprosy, or the plague.
Come hither, Marrall — [*aside*] this is the time
  to work him.   *Exit.*
 Mar. I warrant you, sir,
 Well. By this light I think he 's mad. 95
 Mar. Mad ! had you ta'en compassion on
  yourself,
You long since had been mad.
 Well.   You have ta'en a course,
Between you and my venerable uncle,
To make me so.
 Mar.   The more pale-spirited you.
That would not be instructed. I swear
deeply ——   100
 Well. By what ?
 Mar.   By my religion.
 Well.   Thy religion !
The devil's creed : — but what would you have
done ?
 Mar. Had there been but one tree in all the
  shire,
Nor any hope to compass a penny halter,
Before, like you, I had outliv'd my fortunes, 105
A withe had serv'd my turn to hang myself.
I am zealous in your cause ; pray you hang
  yourself,
And presently,[1] as you love your credit.
 Well.   I thank you.
 Mar. Will you stay till you die in a ditch, or
  lice devour you ? ——   110
Or, if you dare not do the feat yourself,
But that you 'll put the state to charge and
  trouble,
Is there no purse to be cut, house to be broken,
Or market-woman with eggs, that you may
  murder,
And so dispatch the business ?
 Well.   Here 's variety,
I must confess ; but I 'll accept of none 115
Of all your gentle offers, I assure you.
 Mar. Why, have you hope ever to eat again,
Or drink ? or be the master of three farthings ?
If you like not hanging, drown yourself ! Take
  some course
For your reputation.
 Well.   'T will not do, dear tempter, 120

[1] At once.

With all the rhetoric the fiend hath taught you.
I am as far as thou art from despair ;
Nay, I have confidence, which is more than
  hope,
To live, and suddenly, better than ever.
 Mar. Ha ! ha ! these castles you build in the
  air   125
Will not persuade me to give or lend
A token to you.
 Well.   I 'll be more kind to thee :
Come, thou shalt dine with me.
 Mar.   With you !
 Well.   Nay more, dine gratis.
 Mar. Under what hedge, I pray you ? or at
  whose cost ?
Are they padders[2] or abram-men[3] that are your
  consorts ?   130
 Well. Thou art incredulous ; but thou shalt
  dine
Not alone at her house, but with a gallant lady ;
With me, and with a lady.
 Mar.   Lady ! what lady ?
With the Lady of the Lake, or Queen of Fair-
  ies ?
For I know it must be an enchanted dinner. 135
 Well. With the Lady Allworth, knave.
 Mar.   Nay, now there 's hope
Thy brain is crack'd.
 Well. Mark there, with what respect
I am entertain'd.
 Mar. With choice, no doubt, of dog-whips.
Why, dost thou ever hope to pass her porter ?
 Well. 'T is not far off, go with me ; trust
  thine own eyes.   140
 Mar. Troth, in my hope, or my assurance
  rather,
To see thee curvet[4] and mount like a dog in a
  blanket,
If ever thou presume to pass her threshold,
I will endure thy company.
 Well.   Come along then. *Exeunt.*

SCENE II.[5]

[*Enter*] ALLWORTH, Waiting Woman, Chambermaid, ORDER, AMBLE, FURNACE, *and*
 WATCHALL.

 Woman. Could you not command your lei-
  sure one hour longer ?
 Cham. Or half an hour ?
 All. I have told you what my haste is :
Besides, being now another's, not mine own,
Howe'er I much desire to enjoy you longer,
My duty suffers, if, to please myself, 5
I should neglect my lord.
 Woman. Pray you do me the favour
To put these few quince-cakes into your pocket ;
They are of mine own preserving.
 Cham. And this marmalade ;
'T is comfortable for your stomach.
 Woman.   And, at parting,
Excuse me if I beg a farewell from you. 10

[2] Footpads.
[3] Beggars pretending lunacy.
[4] Bound. The reference is to the game of tossing in a blanket.
[5] A room in Lady Allworth's house.

Cham. You are still before me. I move the
    same suit, sir.
        [ALLWORTH] *kisses them severally.*
Furn. How greedy these chamberers are of a
    beardless chin !
I think the tits [1] will ravish him.
All.   My service
T₀ both.
Woman. Ours waits on you.
Cham.   And shall do ever.
Ord. You are my lady's charge, be therefore
    careful   15
That you sustain your parts.
Woman.   We can bear, I warrant you.
    Exeunt W. Woman *and* Chambermaid.
Furn. Here, drink it off ; the ingredients are
    cordial,
And this the true elixir ; it hath boil'd
Since midnight for you. 'T is the quintessence
Of five cocks of the game, ten dozen of spar-
    rows,   20
Knuckles of veal, potato-roots and marrow,
Coral and ambergris. Were you two years
    older,
And I had a wife, or gamesome mistress,
I durst trust you with neither. You need not
    bait
After this, I warrant you, though your jour-
    ney's long ;   25
You may ride on the strength of this till to-
    morrow morning.
All. Your courtesies overwhelm me : I much
    grieve
To part from such true friends ; and yet find
    comfort,
My attendance on my honourable lord,
Whose resolution holds to visit my lady,   30
Will speedily bring me back.
                Knocking at the gate.
Mar. (*within.*) Dar'st thou venture fur-
    ther ?
Well. (*within.*) Yes, yes, and knock again.
Ord.   'T is he ; disperse !
Amb. Perform it bravely.
Furn.   I know my cue, ne'er doubt me.
           Exeunt [*all but* ALLWORTH].

[*Enter* WATCHALL, *ceremoniously introducing*
    WELLBORN *and* MARRALL.]

Watch. Beast that I was, to make you stay !
    Most welcome ;   34
You were long since expected.
Well.   Say so much
To my friend, I pray you.
Watch.   For your sake, I will, sir.
Mar. For his sake !
Well.   Mum ; this is nothing.
Mar.   More than ever
I would have believ'd, though I had found it in
    my primer.
All. When I have given your reasons for my
    late harshness,
You 'll pardon and excuse me; for, believe
    me,   40
Though now I part abruptly, in my service
I will deserve it.
         [1] *Wenches.*

Mar.   Service ! with a vengeance !
Well. I am satisfied : farewell, Tom.
All.   All joy stay with you ! *Exit.*
           Re-enter AMBLE.

Amb. You are happily encounter'd ; I yet
    never
Presented one so welcome as I know   45
You will be to my lady.
Mar.   This is some vision,
Or, sure, these men are mad, to worship a
    dunghill ;
It cannot be a truth.
Well.   Be still a pagan,
An unbelieving infidel ; be so, miscreant,
And meditate on "blankets, and on dog-
    whips ! "   50

        Re-enter FURNACE.

Furn. I am glad you are come ; until I know
    your pleasure
I knew not how to serve up my lady's dinner.
Mar. His pleasure ! is it possible ?
Well.   What 's thy will ?
Furn. Marry, sir, I have some grouse, and
    turkey chicken,
Some rails [2] and quails, and my lady will'd me
    ask you,   55
What kind of sauces best affect your palate,
That I may use my utmost skill to please it.
Mar. [*Aside.*] The devil 's enter'd this cook.
    Sauce for his palate !
That, on my knowledge, for almost this twelve-
    month,
Durst wish but cheese-parings and brown bread
    on Sundays.   60
Well. That way I like 'em best.
Furn.   It shall be done, sir. *Exit.*
Well. What think you of " the hedge we
    shall dine under ? "
Shall we feed gratis ?
Mar.   I know not what to think;
Pray you make me not mad.

        Re-enter ORDER.

Ord.   This place becomes you not ; 64
Pray you walk, sir, to the dining room.
Well.   I am well here,
Till her ladyship quits her chamber.
Mar.   Well here, say you ?
'T is a rare change ! But yesterday you thought
Yourself well in a barn, wrapp'd up in peas-
    straw.

Re-enter Waiting Woman *and* Chambermaid.

Woman. O ! sir, you are wish'd for.
Cham.   My lady dreamt, sir, of you,
Woman. And the first command she gave,
    after she rose,   70
Was (her devotions done) to give her notice
When you approach'd here.
Cham.   Which is done, on my virtue.
Mar. I shall be converted ; I begin to grow
Into a new belief, which saints nor angels   74
Could have won me to have faith in.
Woman.   Sir, my lady !
        [2] *Marsh birds.*

Enter LADY ALLWORTH.

L. All. I come to meet you, and languish'd
till I saw you.
This first kiss is for form ; I allow a second
To such a friend.   [*Kisses* WELLBORN.]
  Mar. To such a friend ! Heaven bless me !
  Well. I am wholly yours ; yet, madam, if you
please
To grace this gentleman with a salute ——   80
  Mar. Salute me at his bidding !
  Well.   I shall receive it
As a most high favour.
  L. All.   Sir, you may command me.
          [*Advances to kiss* MARRALL, *who
          retires.*]
  Well. Run backward from a lady ! and such
a lady !
  Mar. To kiss her foot is, to poor me, a favour
I am unworthy of.   *Offers to kiss her foot.*
  L. All.   Nay, pray you rise ;   85
And since you are so humble, I 'll exalt you.
You shall dine with me to-day, at mine own table.
  Mar. Your ladyship's table ! I am not good
enough
To sit at your steward's board.
  L. All.   You are too modest ;
I will not be deni'd.

Re-enter FURNACE.

  Furn.   Will you still be babbling   90
Till your meat freeze on the table ? The old
trick still ;
My art ne'er thought on !
  L. All.   Your arm, Master Wellborn : ——
Nay, keep us company.   [*To* MARRALL.]
  Mar.   I was ne'er so grac'd.
          Exeunt WELLBORN, LADY ALL-
          WORTH, AMBLE, MARRALL, W.
          Woman, [*and* Chambermaid.]
  Ord. So ! we have play'd our parts, and are
come off well ;
But if I know the mystery, why my lady   95
Consented to it, or why Master Wellborn
Desir'd it, may I perish !
  Furn.   Would I had
The roasting of his heart that cheated him,
And forces the poor gentleman to these shifts !
By fire ! for cooks are Persians, and swear by
it,   100
Of all the griping and extorting tyrants
I ever heard or read of, I ne'er met
A match to Sir Giles Overreach.
  Watch.   What will you take
To tell him so, fellow Furnace ?
  Furn.   Just as much
As my throat is worth, for that would be the
price on 't.   105
To have a usurer that starves himself,
And wears a cloak of one and twenty years
On a suit of fourteen groats, bought of the
hangman,
To grow rich, and then purchase, is too com-
mon ;
But this Sir Giles feeds high, keeps many ser-
vants,   110
Who must at his command do any outrage ;

Rich in his habit, vast in his expenses ;
Yet he to admiration [1] still increases
In wealth and lordships.
  Ord.   He frights men out of their estates,
And breaks through all law-nets, made to curb
ill men,   115
As they were cobwebs. No man dares reprove
him.
Such a spirit to dare and power to do were
never
Lodg'd so unluckily.

Re-enter AMBLE [*laughing*].

  Amb.   Ha ! ha ! I shall burst.
  Ord. Contain thyself, man.
  Furn.   Or make us partakers
Of your sudden mirth.
  Amb.   Ha ! ha ! my lady has got   120
Such a guest at her table ! — this term-driver,
Marrall,
This snip of an attorney ——
  Furn.   What of him, man ?
  Amb. The knave thinks still he 's at the cook's
shop in Ram Alley,[2]
Where the clerks divide, and the elder is to
choose ;
And feeds so slovenly !
  Furn.   Is this all ?
  Amb.   My lady   125
Drank to him for fashion sake, or to please
Master Wellborn ;
As I live, he rises, and takes up a dish
In which there were some remnants of a boil'd
capon,
And pledges her in white broth !
  Furn.   Nay, 't is like
The rest of his tribe.
  Amb.   And when I brought him wine,   130
He leaves his stool, and, after a leg or two,
Most humbly thanks my worship.
  Ord.   Risen already !
  Amb. I shall be chid.

Re-enter LADY ALLWORTH, WELLBORN, *and*
MARRALL.

  Furn.   My lady frowns.
  L. All.   You wait well ! [*To* AMBLE.]
Let me have no more of this : I observ'd your
jeering.
Sirrah, I 'll have you know, whom I think
worthy   135
To sit at my table, be he ne'er so mean,
When I am present, is not your companion.
  Ord. Nay, she 'll preserve what 's due to her.
  Furn.   This refreshing
Follows your flux of laughter.
  L. All. [*to* WELLBORN.]   You are master
Of your own will. I know so much of manners,
As not to inquire your purposes ; in a word,   141
To me you are ever welcome, as to a house
That is your own.
  Wel. [*Aside to* MARRALL.] Mark that.
  Mar.   With reverence, sir,
An it like your worship.

----

[1] Marvellously.
[2] Off Fleet Street, famous for its restaurants.

Well. Trouble yourself no further,
Dear madam; my heart 's full of zeal and ser-
    vice, 145
However in my language I am sparing.
Come, Master Marrall.
    Mar. I attend your worship.
        Exeunt WELLBORN *and* MARRALL.
L. All. I see in your looks you are sorry,
    and you know me
An easy mistress. Be merry; I have forgot all.
Order and Furnace, come with me; I must
    give you 150
Further directions.
    Ord. What you please,
    Furn. We are ready. *Exeunt.*

SCENE III.[1]

[*Enter*] WELLBORN, *and* MARRALL [*bare-
headed*].

Well. I think I am in a good way.
    Mar. Good! Sir, the best way,
The certain best way.
    Well. There are casualties
That men are subject to.
    Mar. You are above 'em;
And as you are already worshipful,
I hope ere long you will increase in worship, 5
And be right worshipful.
    Well. Prithee do not flout me:
What I shall be, I shall be. Is 't for your ease,
You keep your hat off?
    Mar. Ease! an it like your worship!
I hope Jack Marrall shall not live so long,
To prove himself such an unmannerly beast, 10
Though it hail hazel-nuts, as to be cover'd
When your worship 's present.
    Well. (*Aside.*) Is not this a true rogue,
That, out of mere hope of a future coz'nage,[2]
Can turn thus suddenly? 'T is rank already.
    Mar. I know your worship 's wise, and needs
no counsel, 15
Yet if, in my desire to do you service,
I humbly offer my advice, (but still
Under correction,) I hope I shall not
Incur your high displeasure.
    Well. No; speak freely.
    Mar. Then, in my judgment, sir, my simple
judgment, 20
(Still with your worship's favour,) I could wish
    you
A better habit, for this cannot be
But much distasteful to the noble lady
(I say no more) that loves you; for, this morn-
    ing,
To me, and I am but a swine to her, 25
Before th' assurance of her wealth perfum'd
    you,
You savour'd not of amber.[3]
    Well. I do now then!
    Mar. This your batoon hath got a touch of
it.—— *Kisses the end of his cudgel.*
Yet, if you please, for change, I have twenty
    pounds here,

---

[1] The country near Lady Allworth's house.
[2] Cheating.
[3] Ambergris, a fashionable perfume.

Which, out of my true love, I 'll presently 30
Lay down at your worship's feet; 't will serve
    to buy you
A riding suit.
    Well. But where 's the horse?
    Mar. My gelding
Is at your service; nay, you shall ride me,
Before your worship shall be put to the trouble
To walk afoot. Alas, when you are lord 35
Of this lady's manor, as I know you will be,
You may with the lease of glebe land, called
    Knave's-acre,
A place I would manure,[4] requite your vassal.
    Well. I thank thy love, but must make no
    use of it;
What 's twenty pounds?
    Mar. 'T is all that I can make, sir. 40
    Well. Dost thou think, though I want
    clothes, I could not have 'em,
For one word to my lady?
    Mar. As I know not that!
    Well. Come, I will tell thee a secret, and so
    leave thee.
I will not give her the advantage, though she
    be
A gallant-minded lady, after we are married, 45
(There being no woman but is sometimes fro-
    ward,)
To hit me in the teeth, and say, she was forc'd
To buy my wedding-clothes, and took me on
With a plain riding-suit, and an ambling nag.
No, I 'll be furnish'd something like myself, 50
And so farewell: for thy suit touching Knave's-
    acre,
When it is mine, 't is thine.
    Mar. I thank your worship. *Exit* WELL.
How was I cozen'd[5] in the calculation
Of this man's fortune! My master cozen'd too,
Whose pupil I am in the art of undoing men; 55
For that is our profession! Well, well, Master
    Wellborn,
You are of a sweet nature, and fit again to be
    cheated:
Which, if the Fates please, when you are pos-
    sess'd
Of the land and lady, you, sans question, shall
    be.
I 'll presently think of the means.
        Walks by, musing.

Enter OVERREACH, [*speaking to a Servant
    within.*]

Over. Sirrah, take my horse. 60
I 'll walk to get me an appetite; 't is but a mile,
And exercise will keep me from being pursy.[6]
Ha! Marrall! Is he conjuring? Perhaps
The knave has wrought the prodigal to do
Some outrage on himself, and now he feels 65
Compunction in his conscience for 't: no matter,
So it be done. Marrall!
    Mar. Sir.
    Over. How succeed we
In our plot on Wellborn?
    Mar. Never better, sir.
    Over. Has he hang'd or drown'd himself?

---

[4] Cultivate. [5] Cheated. [6] Fat and short winded.

Mar.   No, sir, he lives;
Lives once more to be made a prey to you,   70
A greater prey than ever.
Over.   Art thou in thy wits?
If thou art, reveal this miracle, and briefly.
Mar. A lady, sir, is fall'n in love with him.
Over. With him? What lady?
Mar.   The rich Lady Allworth.
Over. Thou dolt! how dar'st thou speak this?
Mar. I speak truth;   75
And I do so but once a year, unless
It be to you, sir. We din'd with her ladyship,
I thank his worship.
Over.   His worship!
Mar.   As I live, sir,
I din'd with him, at the great lady's table,
Simple as I stand here; and saw when she
    kiss'd him,   80
And would, at his request, have kiss'd me too:
But I was not so audacious as some youths are,
That dare do anything, be it ne'er so absurd,
And sad after performance.
Over.   Why, thou rascal!
To tell me these impossibilities.   85
Dine at her table! and kiss him! or thee!——
Impudent varlet, have not I myself,
To whom great countesses' doors have oft flew
    open,
Ten times attempted, since her husband's
    death,
In vain, to see her, though I came—a suitor?
And yet your good solicitorship, and rogue
    Wellborn,   91
Were brought into her presence, feasted with
    her!——
But that I know thee a dog that cannot blush,
This most incredible lie would call up one
On thy buttermilk cheeks.
Mar. Shall I not trust my eyes, sir,   95
Or taste? I feel her good cheer in my belly.
Over. You shall feel me, if you give not over,
    sirrah:
Recover your brains again, and be no more
    gull'd
With a beggar's plot, assisted by the aids
Of serving-men and chambermaids, for beyond
    these   100
Thou never saw'st a woman, or I'll quit you
From my employments.
Mar.   Will you credit this yet?
On my confidence of their marriage, I offer'd
    Wellborn——
(*Aside.*) I would give a crown now I durst say
    "his worship"——
My nag and twenty pounds.
Over. Did you so, idiot! (*Strikes him down.*)
Was this the way to work him to despair,   106
Or rather to cross me?
Mar.   Will your worship kill me?
Over. No, no; but drive the lying spirit out
    of you.
Mar. He's gone.
Over.   I have done then: now, forgetting
Your late imaginary feast and lady,   110
Know, my Lord Lovell dines with me to-mor-
    row.
Be careful nought be wanting to receive him;

And bid my daughter's women trim her up,
Though they paint her, so she catch the lord,
    I'll thank them.
There's a piece for my late blows.
Mar. (*Aside.*)   I must yet suffer: 115
But there may be a time——
Over.   Do you grumble?
Mar.   No, sir. [*Exeunt.*]

ACT III

SCENE I.[1]

[*Enter* LORD] LOVELL, ALLWORTH, *and Ser-*
    vants.

Lov. Walk the horses down the hill: some-
            thing in private
I must impart to Allworth.   *Exeunt* Servants.
All.   O, my lord,
What a sacrifice of reverence, duty, watching,
Although I could put off the use of sleep,
And ever wait on your commands to serve
    'em;   5
What dangers, though in ne'er so horrid shapes,
Nay death itself, though I should run to meet
    it,
Can I, and with a thankful willingness, suffer!
But still the retribution will fall short
Of your bounties shower'd upon me.
Lov.   Loving youth,   10
Till what I purpose be put into act,
Do not o'erprize it; since you have trusted me
With your soul's nearest, nay, her dearest
    secret,
Rest confident 't is in a cabinet lock'd
Treachery shall never open. I have found you   15
(For so much to your face I must profess,
Howe'er you guard your modesty with a blush
    for 't)
More zealous in your love and service to me
Than I have been in my rewards.
All.   Still great ones,
Above my merit.
Lov.   Such your gratitude calls 'em;   20
Nor am I of that harsh and rugged temper
As some great men are tax'd[2] with, who imagine
They part from the respect due to their hon-
    ours
If they use not all such as follow 'em,   24
Without distinction of their births, like slaves.
I am not so condition'd; I can make
A fitting difference between my footboy
And a gentleman by want compell'd to serve
    me.
All. 'T is thankfully acknowledg'd: you
    have been
More like a father to me than a master.   30
Pray you, pardon the comparison.
Lov.   I allow it:
And, to give you assurance I am pleas'd in 't,
My carriage and demeanour to your mistress,
Fair Margaret, shall truly witness for me
I can command my passions.
All.   'T is a conquest   35

---

[1] The country near Overreach's house.   [2] Charged.

Few lords can boast of when they are tempted
— Oh!
    Lov. Why do you sigh? Can you be doubt-
ful of me?
By that fair name I in the wars have pur-
    chas'd,
And all my actions, hitherto untainted,
I will not be more true to mine own honour   40
Than to my Allworth!
    All.   As you are the brave Lord Lovell,
Your bare word only given is an assurance
Of more validity and weight to me
Than all the oaths, bound up with impreca-
    tions,
Which, when they would deceive, most court-
    iers practise;   45
Yet being a man, (for, sure, to style you more
Would relish of gross flattery,) I am forc'd,
Against my confidence of your worth and vir-
    tues,
To doubt, nay, more, to fear.
    Lov.   So young, and jealous!
    All. Were you to encounter with a single foe,
The victory were certain; but to stand   51
The charge of two such potent enemies,
At once assaulting you, as wealth and beauty,
And those too seconded with power, is odds
Too great for Hercules.
    Lov.   Speak your doubts and fears,   55
Since you will nourish 'em, in plainer lan-
    guage,
That I may understand them.
    All.   What 's your will,
Though I lend arms against myself, (provided
They may advantage you,) must be obeyed.
My much-lov'd lord, were Margaret only fair,   60
The cannon of her more than earthly form,
Though mounted high, commanding all be-
    neath it,
And ramm'd with bullets of her sparkling
    eyes,
Of all the bulwarks that defend your senses
Could batter none, but that which guards your
    sight.   65
But when the well-tun'd accents of her tongue
Make music to you, and with numerous [1] sounds
Assault your hearing, (such as if Ulysses
Now liv'd again, howe'er he stood the Syrens,
Could not resist,) the combat must grow doubt-
    ful   70
Between your reason and rebellious passions.
Add this too; when you feel her touch, and
    breath
Like a soft western wind when it glides o'er
Arabia, creating gums and spices;
And, in the van, the nectar of her lips,   75
Which you must taste, bring the battalia on,
Well arm'd, and strongly lin'd [2] with her dis-
    course,
And knowing manners, to give entertain-
    ment; —
Hippolytus himself would leave Diana,
To follow such a Venus.
    Lov.   Love hath made you   80
Poetical, Allworth.

    All.   Grant all these beat off,
Which if it be in man to do, you 'll do it,
Mammon, in Sir Giles Overreach, steps in
With heaps of ill-got gold, and so much land,
To make her more remarkable, as would tire   85
A falcon's wings in one day to fly over.
O my good lord! these powerful aids, which
    would
Make a mis-shapen negro beautiful,
(Yet are but ornaments to give her lustre,
That in herself is all perfection,) must   90
Prevail for her. I here release your trust;
'T is happiness enough for me to serve you
And sometimes, with chaste eyes, to look upon
    her.
    Lov. Why, shall I swear?
    All.   O, by no means, my lord;
And wrong not so your judgment to the world
As from your fond indulgence to a boy,   95
Your page, your servant, to refuse a blessing
Divers great men are rivals for.
    Lov.   Suspend
Your judgment till the trial. How far is it
To Overreach's house?
    All. At the most, some half hour's riding;   100
You 'll soon be there.
    Lov.   And you the sooner freed
From your jealous fears.
    All.   O that I durst but hope it! *Exeunt.*

SCENE II.[3]

[Enter] OVERREACH, GREEDY, *and* MARRALL.

    Over. Spare for no cost; let my dressers
    crack with the weight
Of curious viands.
    Greedy.   " Store indeed 's no sore," sir.
    Over. That proverb fits your stomach, Mas-
    ter Greedy.
And let no plate be seen but what 's pure gold,
Or such whose workmanship exceeds the
    matter   5
That it is made of; let my choicest linen
Perfume the room, and, when we wash, the
    water,
With precious powders mix'd, so please my
    lord
That he may with envy wish to bathe so ever.
    Mar. 'T will be very chargeable.
    Over.   Avaunt, you drudge!   10
Now all my labour'd ends are at the stake,
Is 't a time to think of thrift? Call in my
    daughter.   [*Exit* MARRALL.]
And, Master Justice, since you love choice
    dishes,
And plenty of 'em ——
    Greedy.   As I do, indeed, sir,
Almost as much as to give thanks for 'em.   15
    Over. I do confer that providence,[4] with my
    power
Of absolute command to have abundance,
To your best care.
    Greedy.   I 'll punctually discharge it,
And give the best directions. Now am I,

---

    [1] Rhythmical.   [2] Reinforced. Q. *lin'd.*

    [3] A room in Overreach's house.
    [4] Responsibility for providing.

In mine own conceit, a monarch ; at the least,
Arch-president of the boil'd, the roast, the
　　　bak'd ;　　　　　　　　　　　　　　　　21
For which I will eat often, and give thanks
When my belly 's brac'd up like a drum, and
　　　that 's pure justice.　　　　　　　　*Exit.*
　　Over. It must be so. Should the foolish girl
　　　prove modest,
She may spoil all ; she had it not from me,　25
But from her mother ; I was ever forward,
As she must be, and therefore I 'll prepare her.

　　　[*Enter*] MARGARET.

Alone — and let your women wait without.
　　Marg. Your pleasure, sir ?
　　Over.　　　　　Ha ! this is a neat dressing !
These orient pearls and diamonds well plac'd
　　too !　　　　　　　　　　　　　　　　30
The gown affects me not, it should have been
Embroider'd o'er and o'er with flowers of gold ;
But these rich jewels and quaint fashion help
　　it.
And how below ? since oft the wanton eye
The face observ'd, descends unto the foot,　35
Which being well proportion'd, as yours is,
Invites as much as perfect white and red,
Though without art. How like you your new
　　　woman,
The Lady Downfall'n ?
　　Marg.　　　　Well, for a companion ;
Not as a servant.
　　Over.　　　Is she humble, Meg,　40
And careful too, her ladyship forgotten ?
　　Marg. I pity her fortune.
　　Over.　　　　　Pity her ! trample on her.
I took her up in an old tamin [1] gown,
(Even starv'd for want of twopenny chops,) to
　　serve thee ;
And if I understand she but repines　　45
To do thee any duty, though ne'er so servile,
I 'll pack her to her knight, where I have
　　lodg'd him,
Into the Counter [2] and there let 'em howl to-
　　gether.
　　Marg. You know your own ways ; but for me,
　　　I blush
When I command her, that was once attended
With persons not inferior to myself　　　51
In birth.
　　Over. In birth ! why, art thou not my
　　　daughter,
The blest child of my industry and wealth ?
Why, foolish girl, was 't not to make thee great
That I have run, and still pursue, those ways　55
That hale down curses on me, which I mind not ?
Part with these humble thoughts, and apt [3] thy-
　　self
To the noble state I labour to advance thee ;
Or, by my hopes to see thee honourable,
I will adopt a stranger to my heir,　　　60
And throw thee from my care. Do not provoke
　　me.
　　Marg. I will not, sir ; mould me which way
　　　you please.

¹ A coarse cloth.　　　　　　　　　³ Fit.
² One of the London prisons.

　　　　　Re-enter GREEDY.

　　Over. How ! Interrupted !
　　Greedy.　　　'T is matter of importance.
The cook, sir, is self-will'd, and will not learn
From my experience. There 's a fawn brought
　　in, sir,　　　　　　　　　　　　　　　65
And, for my life, I cannot make him roast it
With a Norfolk dumpling in the belly of it ;
And, sir, we wise men know, without the dump-
　　ling
'T is not worth three-pence.
　　Over.　　　Would it were whole in thy belly,
To stuff it out ! Cook it any way ; prithee, leave
　　me.　　　　　　　　　　　　　　　　70
　　Greedy. Without order for the dumpling ?
　　Over.　　　　　Let it be dumpl'd
Which way thou wilt ; or tell him, I will scald him
In his own caldron.
　　Greedy.　　　I had lost my stomach
Had I lost my mistress dumpling ; I 'll give
thanks for 't.　　　　　　　　　　[*Exit.*]
　　Over. But to our business, Meg ; you have
　　heard who dines here ?　　　　　　　　75
　　Marg. I have, sir.
　　Over.　　　　'T is an honourable man ;
A lord, Meg, and commands a regiment
Of soldiers, and, what 's rare, is one himself,
A bold and understanding one ; and to be
A lord and a good leader, in one volume,　80
Is granted unto few but such as rise up
The kingdom's glory.

　　　　　Re-enter GREEDY.

　　Greedy.　　　　I 'll resign my office,
If I be not better obey'd.
　　Over.　　　'Slight, art thou frantic ?
　　Greedy. Frantic ! 'T would make me frantic
　　and stark mad,
Were I not a justice of peace and quorum too,
Which this rebellious cook cares not a straw
　　for.　　　　　　　　　　　　　　　85
There are a dozen of woodcocks ——
　　Over.　　　　　Make thyself
Thirteen, the baker's dozen.
　　Greedy.　　　　I am contented,
So they may be dress'd to my mind ; he has
　　found out
A new device for sauce, and will not dish 'em
With toasts and butter. My father was a
　　tailor,　　　　　　　　　　　　　　91
And my name, though a justice, Greedy Wood-
　　cock ;
And, ere I 'll see my lineage so abus'd,
I 'll give up my commission.
　　Over. [*loudly.*]　Cook ! — Rogue, obey him !
I have given the word, pray you now remove
　　yourself　　　　　　　　　　　　　95
To a collar of brawn,[4] and trouble me no further.
　　Greedy. I will, and meditate what to eat at
　　dinner.　　　　　　　　　　　　*Exit.*
　　Over. And as I said, Meg, when this gull [5]
　　disturb'd us,
This honourable lord, this colonel,
I would have thy husband.

⁴ Neck of a boar.　　　　　　　　　Fool.

Marg.   There's too much disparity 100
Between his quality and mine, to hope it.
　Over. I more than hope 't, and doubt not to
effect it.
Be thou no enemy to thyself, my wealth
Shall weight his titles down, and make you
　　equals.
Now for the means to assure him thine, ob-
　　serve me :   105
Remember he's a courtier and a soldier,
And not to be trifled with ; and, therefore,
　　when
He comes to woo you, see you do not coy it :
This mincing modesty has spoil'd many a match
By a first refusal, in vain after hop'd for.   110
　Marg. You'll have me, sir, preserve the dis-
　　tance that
Confines a virgin ?
　Over.   Virgin me no virgins !
I must have you lose that name, or you lose me.
I will have you private — start not — I say,
　　private ;
If thou art my true daughter, not a bastard, 115
Thou wilt venture alone with one man, though
　　he came
Like Jupiter to Semele, and come off, too ;
and therefore, when he kisses you, kiss close.
　Marg. I have heard this is the strumpet's
　　fashion, sir,
Which I must never learn.
　Over.   Learn any thing, 120
And from any creature that may make thee
　　great ;
From the devil himself.
　Marg. [*Aside.*]   This is but devilish doc-
　　trine !
　Over. Or, if his blood grow hot, suppose he
　　offer
Beyond this, do not you stay till it cool,
But meet his ardour ; if a couch be near,   125
Sit down on 't, and invite him.
　Marg.   In your house,
Your own house, sir ! For Heaven's sake, what
　　are you then ?
Or what shall I be, sir ?
　Over.   Stand not on form ;
Words are no substances.
　Marg.   Though you could dispense
With your own honour, cast aside religion,   130
The hopes of Heaven, or fear of hell, excuse me,
In worldly policy this is not the way
To make me his wife ; his whore, I grant it
　　may do.
My maiden honour so soon yielded up,
Nay, prostituted, cannot but assure him   135
I, that am light to him, will not hold weight
Whene'er [1] tempted by others ; so, in judg-
　　ment,
When to his lust I have given up my honour,
He must and will forsake me.
　Over.   How ! forsake thee !
Do I wear a sword for fashion ? or is this arm
Shrunk up or wither'd ? Does there live a
　　man   141
Of that large list I have encounter'd with

Can truly say I e'er gave inch of ground
Not purchas'd with his blood that did oppose
　　me ?
Forsake thee when the thing is done ! He dares
　　not.   145
Give me but proof he has enjoy'd thy person,
Though all his captains, echoes to his will,
Stood arm'd by his side to justify the wrong,
And he himself in the head of his bold troop,
Spite of his lordship, and his colonelship,   150
Or the judge's favour, I will make him render
A bloody and a strict account, and force him,
By marrying thee, to cure thy wounded hon-
　　our !
I have said it.

　　　　　Re-enter MARRALL.

　Mar.   Sir, the man of honour's come,
Newly alighted.
　Over.   In, without reply.   155
And do as I command, or thou art lost.
　　　　　　　　　Exit MARGARET.
Is the loud music I gave order for
Ready to receive him ?
　Mar.   'T is, sir.
　Over.   Let 'em sound
A princely welcome. [*Exit* MARRALL.] Rough-
　　ness awhile leave me ;
For fawning now, a stranger to my nature,   160
Must make way for me.

Loud music. Enter LORD LOVELL, GREEDY,
　　ALLWORTH, *and* MARRALL.

　Lov.   Sir, you meet your trouble.
　Over. What you are pleas'd to style so is an
　　honour
Above my worth and fortunes.
　All. [*Aside.*]   Strange, so humble.
　Over. A justice of peace, my lord.
　　　　　　　Presents GREEDY *to him.*
　Lov.   Your hand, good sir.
　Greedy. [*Aside.*] This is a lord, and some
　　think this a favour ;   165
But I had rather have my hand in my dump-
　　ling.
　Over. Room for my lord.
　Lov.   I miss, sir, your fair daughter
To crown my welcome.
　Over.   May it please my lord
To taste a glass of Greek wine first, and sud-
　　denly
She shall attend my lord.
　Lov.   You'll be obey'd, sir. 170
　　　　　　　Exeunt all but OVERREACH.
　Over. 'T is to my wish : as soon as come, ask
　　for her !
Why, Meg ! Meg Overreach.—

　　　　　[*Re-enter* MARGARET.]

　　　　　　　　How ! tears in your eyes !
Hah ! dry 'em quickly, or I'll dig 'em out.
Is this a time to whimper ? Meet that great-
　　ness
That flies into thy bosom, think what 't is   175
For me to say, " My honourable daughter ; "
And thou, when I stand bare, to say, " Put
　　on ; "

Or, " Father, you forget yourself." No more:
But be instructed, or expect —— He comes.

Re-enter LORD LOVELL, GREEDY, ALLWORTH,
and MARRALL.

A black-brow'd girl, my lord,
  Lov.   As I live, a rare one. *They salute.* 180
  All. [*Aside.*] He 's took already : I am lost.
  Over. [*Aside.*]   That kiss
Came twanging off, I like it.— Quit the room.
      [*Exeunt all but* OVERREACH, LOV-
      ELL, *and* MARGARET.]
A little bashful, my good lord, but you,
I hope, will teach her her boldness.
  Lov.   I am happy
In such a scholar : but ——
  Over.   I am past learning, 185
And therefore leave you to yourselves.— Re-
  member ! *Aside to* MARGARET *and exit.*
  Lov. You see, fair lady, your father is so-
licitous
To have you change the barren name of virgin
Into a hopeful wife.
  Marg.   His haste, my lord,
Holds no power o'er my will.
  Lov.   But o'er your duty. 190
  Marg. Which forc'd too much, may break.
  Lov.   Bend rather, sweetest :
Think of your years.
  Marg.   Too few to match with yours :
And choicest fruits too soon pluck'd, rot and
  wither.
  Lov. Do you think I am old ?
  Marg.   I am sure I am too young.
  Lov. I can advance you.
  Marg.   To a hill of sorrow, 195
Where every hour I may expect to fall,
But never hope firm footing. You are noble,
I of a low descent, however rich ;
And tissues match'd with scarlet [1] suit but ill.
O, my good lord, I could say more, but that 200
I dare not trust these walls.
  Lov.   Pray you, trust my ear then.

Re-enter OVERREACH [*behind*], *listening.*

  Over. Close at it ! whispering ! this is excellent !
And, by their postures, a consent on both parts.

Re-enter GREEDY *behind.*

  Greedy. Sir Giles, Sir Giles !
  Over.   The great fiend stop that clapper !
  Greedy. It must ring out, sir, when my belly
  rings noon. 205
The bak'd-meats are run out, the roasts turn'd
  powder.
  Over. I shall powder you.
  Greedy.   Beat me to dust, I care not ;
In such a cause as this, I 'll die a martyr.
  Over. Marry, and shall, you barathrum [2] of
  the shambles !   *Strikes him.*
  Greedy. How ! strike a justice of peace ! 'T is
  petty treason, 210
Edwardi quinto : but that you are my friend,

[1] Silks matched with woolen.
[2] Gulf : here, insatiable glutton.

I would commit you without bail or main-
  prize.[1]
  Over. Leave your bawling, sir, or I shall
  commit you
Where you shall not dine to-day. Disturb my
  lord,
When he is in discourse !
  Greedy.   Is 't a time to talk 215
When we should be munching !
  Lov.   Hah ! I heard some noise.
  Over. Mum, villain ; vanish ! Shall we break
  a bargain
Almost made up ?   *Thrusts* GREEDY *off.*
  Lov.   Lady, I understand you.
And rest most happy in your choice, believe
  it ;
I 'll be a careful pilot to direct 220
Your yet uncertain bark to a port of safety.
  Marg. So shall your honour save two lives,
  and bind us
Your slaves for ever.
  Lov.   I am in the act rewarded.
Since it is good ; howe'er, you must put on
An amorous carriage towards me to delude 225
Your subtle father.
  Marg.   I am prone to that.
  Lov. Now break we off our conference. —
  Sir Giles !
Where is Sir Giles ?
      [OVERREACH *comes forward.*]

Re-enter ALLWORTH, MARRALL, *and* GREEDY.

  Over.   My noble lord ; and how
Does your lordship find her ?
  Lov.   Apt, Sir Giles, and coming ;
And I like her the better.
  Over.   So do I too. 230
  Love. Yet should we take forts at the first
  assault,
'T were poor in the defendant; I must confirm
  her
With a love-letter or two, which I must have
Deliver'd by my page, and you give way to 't.
  Over. With all my soul : — a towardly gen-
  tleman ! 235
Your hand, good Master Allworth: know my
  house
Is ever open to you.
  All. (*Aside.*)   'T was shut till now.
  Over. Well done, well done, my honourable
  daughter !
Thou 'rt so already. Know this gentle youth,
And cherish him, my honourable daughter. 240
  Marg. I shall, with my best care.
      Noise within, as of a coach.
  Over.   A coach !
  Greedy.   More stops
Before we go to dinner ! O my guts !

Enter LADY ALLWORTH *and* WELLBORN.

  L. All.   If I find welcome,
You share in it ; if not, I 'll back again,
Now I know your ends ; for I come arm'd for
  all
Can be objected.

[3] A writ commanding the sheriff to take bail.

Lov.   How! the Lady Allworth! 245
Over. And thus attended!
    LOVELL *salutes* LADY ALLWORTH,
    LADY ALLWORTH *salutes* MAR-
    GARET.
Mar.   No, " I am a dolt!
The spirit of lies had ent'red me! "
Over.   Peace, Patch; [1]
'T is more than wonder! an astonishment
That does possess me wholly!
Lov.   Noble lady,
This is a favour, to prevent [2] my visit,   250
The service of my life can never equal.
L. All. My lord, I laid wait for you, and
  much hop'd
You would have made my poor house your first
  inn:
And therefore doubting that you might forget
  me,
Or too long dwell here, having such ample
  cause,   255
In this unequall'd beauty, for your stay,
And fearing to trust any but myself
With the relation of my service to you,
I borrow'd so much from my long restraint
And took the air in person to invite you.   260
Lov. Your bounties are so great, they rob me,
  madam,
Of words to give you thanks.
L. All.   Good Sir Giles Overreach.
       Salutes him.
—How dost thou, Marrall? Lik'd you my meat
  so ill,
You 'll dine no more with me?
Greedy.   I will, when you please, 264
An it like [3] your ladyship.
L. All. When you please, Master Greedy;
If meat can do it, you shall be satisfied.
And now, my lord, pray take into your know-
  ledge
This gentleman; howe'er his outside 's coarse,
      Presents WELLBORN.
His inward linings are as fine and fair   269
As any man's; wonder not I speak at large:
And howsoe'er his humour carries him
To be thus accoutred, or what taint soever,
For his wild life, hath stuck upon his fame,
He may ere long, with boldness, rank himself
With some that have contemn'd him. Sir Giles
  Overreach,   275
If I am welcome, bid him so.
Over.   My nephew!
He has been too long a stranger. Faith you
  have,
Pray let it be mended.
    LOVELL *confers aside with* WELLBORN.
Mar.   Why, sir, what do you mean?
This is " rogue Wellborn, monster, prodigy,
That should hang or drown himself; " no man
  of worship,   280
Much less your nephew.
Over.   Well, sirrah, we shall reckon
For this hereafter.
Mar.   I 'll not lose my jeer,
Though I be beaten dead for 't.

[1] Fool.   [2] Anticipate.   [3] If it please.

Well.   Let my silence plead
In my excuse, my lord, till better leisure
Offer itself to hear a full relation   285
Of my poor fortunes.
Lov.   I would hear, and help 'em.
Over. Your dinner waits you.
Lov.   Pray you lead, we follow.
L. All. Nay, you are my guest; come, dear
  Master Wellborn.
      Exeunt all but GREEDY.
Greedy. " Dear Master Wellborn! " so she
  said: Heaven! Heaven!
If my belly would give me leave, I could rumi-
  nate   290
All day on this. I have granted twenty war-
  rants
To have him committed, from all prisons in the
  shire,
To Nottingham gaol; and now " Dear Master
  Wellborn! "
And, " My good nephew! " — but I play the
  fool   294
To stand here prating, and forget my dinner.

     Re-enter MARRALL.

Are they set, Marrall?
Mar.   Long since; pray you a word, sir.
Greedy. No wording now.
Mar.   In troth, I must. My master,
Knowing you are his good friend, makes bold
  with you,
And does entreat you, more guests being come
  in
Than he expected, especially his nephew,   300
The table being full too, you would excuse
  him,
And sup with him on the cold meat.
Greedy.   How! No dinner,
After all my care?
Mar.   'T is but a penance for
A meal; besides, you broke your fast.
Greedy.   That was
But a bit to stay my stomach. A man in com-
  mission   305
Give place to a tatterdemalion!
Mar.   No bug [4] words, sir;
Should his worship hear you ——
Greedy.   Lose my dumpling too,
And butter'd toasts, and woodcocks!
Mar.   Come, have patience.
If you will dispense a little with your wor-
  ship,
And sit with the waiting women, you 'll have
  dumpling,   310
Woodcock, and butter'd toasts too.
Greedy.   This revives me:
I will gorge there sufficiently.
Mar.   This is the way, sir. *Exeunt.*

      SCENE III.[5]

   [*Enter*] OVERREACH, *as from dinner.*

Over. She 's caught! O women! — she neglects my lord,

[4] Terrifying.
[5] Another room in Overreach's house.

And all her compliments appli'd to Wellborn!
The garments of her widowhood laid by,
She now appears as glorious as the spring,
Her eyes fix'd on him, in the wine she drinks, 5
He being her pledge, she sends him burning
    kisses,
And sits on thorns, till she be private with him.
She leaves my meat to feed upon his looks,
And if in our discourse he be but nam'd,
From her a deep sigh follows. And why grieve
    I   10
At this? It makes for me; if she prove his,
All that is hers is mine, as I will work him.

Enter MARRALL.

Mar. Sir, the whole board is troubled at
    your rising.
Over. No matter, I'll excuse it. Prithee,
    Marrall,
Watch an occasion to invite my nephew   15
To speak with me in private.
Mar.   Who? " The rogue
The lady scorn'd to look on"?
Over.   You are a wag.

Enter LADY ALLWORTH *and* WELLBORN.

Mar. See, sir, she's come, and cannot be with-
    out him.
L. All. With your favour, sir, after a plente-
    ous dinner,
I shall make bold to walk a turn or two,   20
In your rare garden.
Over.   There's an arbour too,
If your ladyship please to use it.
L. All.   Come, Master Wellborn.
        Exeunt LADY ALLWORTH *and*
            WELLBORN.
Over. Grosser and grosser! Now I believe
    the poet
Feign'd not, but was historical, when he wrote
Pasiphae was enamour'd of a bull: 25
This lady's lust's more monstrous. — My good
    lord,

Enter LORD LOVELL, MARGARET, *and the rest.*

Excuse my manners.
Lov.   There needs none, Sir Giles,
I may ere long say father, when it pleases
My dearest mistress to give warrant to it.
Over. She shall seal to it, my lord, and make
    me happy.   30

Re-enter WELLBORN *and* LADY ALLWORTH.

Marg. My lady is return'd.
L. All.   Provide my coach,
I'll instantly away. My thanks, Sir Giles,
For my entertainment.
Over.   'T is your nobleness
To think it such.
L. All.   I must do you a further wrong
In taking away your honourable guest.   35
Lov. I wait on you, madam; farewell, good
    Sir Giles.
L. All. Good Mistress Margaret! Nay, come,
    Master Wellborn,
I must not leave you behind; in sooth, I must
    not.

Over. Rob me not, madam, of all joys at
    once;
Let my nephew stay behind. He shall have my
    coach,   40
And, after some small conference between us,
Soon overtake your ladyship.
L. All.   Stay not long, sir.
Lov. This parting kiss: [*kisses* MARGARET]
    you shall every day hear from me,
By my faithful page.
All.   'T is a service I am proud of.
        Exeunt LORD LOVELL, LADY ALL-
            WORTH, ALLWORTH, *and* MAR-
            RALL.
Over. Daughter, to your chamber. —
                        Exit MARGARET.
        — You may wonder, nephew, 45
After so long an enmity between us,
I should desire your friendship.
Well.   So I do, sir;
'T is strange to me.
Over.   But I'll make it no wonder;
And what is more, unfold my nature to you.
We worldly men, when we see friends and kins-
    men   50
Past hopes sunk in their fortunes, lend no
    hand
To lift 'em up, but rather set our feet
Upon their heads, to press 'em to the bottom;
As, I must yield,[1] with you I practis'd it:
But, now I see you in a way to rise,   55
I can and will assist you. This rich lady
(And I am glad of 't) is enamour'd of you;
'T is too apparent, nephew.
Well.   No such thing:
Compassion rather, sir.
Over.   Well, in a word,   59
Because your stay is short, I'll have you seen
No more in this base shape; nor shall she say
She married you like a beggar, or in debt.
Well. (*Aside.*) He'll run into the noose, and
    save my labour.
Over. You have a trunk of rich clothes, not
    far hence,
In pawn; I will redeem 'em; and that no clam-
    our   65
May taint your credit for your petty debts,
You shall have a thousand pounds to cut 'em
    off,
And go a free man to the wealthy lady.
Well. This done, sir, out of love, and no ends
    else ——
Over. As it is, nephew.
Well.   Binds me still your servant. 70
Over. No compliments; you are staid for. Ere
    you have supp'd
You shall hear from me. My coach, knaves,
    for my nephew.
To-morrow I will visit you.
Well.   Here's an uncle
In a man's extremes! How much they do be-
    lie you,
That say you are hard-hearted!
Over.   My deeds, nephew, 75
Shall speak my love; what men report I weigh
    not.   *Exeunt.*

        1 Admit.

ACT IV

SCENE I.[1]

[*Enter* LORD] LOVELL *and* ALLWORTH.

Lov. 'T is well; give me my cloak; I now dis-
charge you
From further service. Mind your own affairs;
I hope they will prove successful.
All.   What is blest
With your good wish, my lord, cannot but pros-
per.
Let aftertimes report, and to your honour,   5
How much I stand engag'd, for I want language
To speak my debt; yet if a tear or two
Of joy, for your much goodness, can supply
My tongue's defects, I could ——
Lov.   Nay, do not melt:
This ceremonial thanks to me 's superfluous.   10
Over. (*within.*) Is my lord stirring?
Lov. 'T is he! oh, here 's your letter. Let him
in.

Enter OVERREACH, GREEDY, *and* MARRALL.

Over. A good day to my lord!
Lov.   You are an early riser,
Sir Giles.
Over. And reason, to attend your lordship.   15
Lov. And you, too, Master Greedy, up so
soon!
Greedy. In troth, my lord, after the sun is up,
I cannot sleep, for I have a foolish stomach
That croaks for breakfast. With your lordship's
favour,
I have a serious question to demand   20
Of my worthy friend Sir Giles.
Lov.   Pray you use your pleasure.
Greedy. How far, Sir Giles, and pray you
answer me
Upon your credit, hold you it to be
From your manor-house, to this of my Lady's
Allworth's?
Over. Why, some four mile.
Greedy. How! four mile, good Sir Giles ——
Upon your reputation, think better;   26
For if you do abate but one half-quarter
Of five, you do yourself the greatest wrong
That can be in the world; for four miles riding
Could not have rais'd so huge an appetite   30
As I feel gnawing on me.
Mar.   Whether you ride,
Or go afoot, you are that way still provided,
An it please your worship.
Over.   How now, sirrah? Prating
Before my lord! No difference? Go to my
nephew,
See all his debts discharg'd, and help his wor-
ship   35
To fit on his rich suit.
Mar. [*Aside.*]   I may fit you too.
Toss'd like a dog still!   *Exit.*
Lov.   I have writ this morning
A few lines to my mistress, your fair daughter.
Over. 'T will fire her, for she 's wholly yours
already. ——

Sweet Master Allworth, take my ring; 't will
carry you   40
To her presence, I dare warrant you; and there
plead
For my good lord, if you shall find occasion.
That done, pray ride to Nottingham, get a li-
cence,
Still by this token. I 'll have it dispatch'd,
And suddenly, my lord, that I may say,   45
My honourable, nay, right honourable daughter.
Greedy. Take my advice, young gentleman,
get your breakfast;
'T is unwholesome to ride fasting. I 'll eat with
you,
And eat to purpose.
Over.   Some Fury 's in that gut;
Hungry again! Did you not devour, this morn-
ing,   50
A shield of brawn, and a barrel of Colchester
oysters?
Greedy. Why, that was, sir, only to scour my
stomach,
A kind of a preparative. Come, gentleman,
I will not have you feed like the hangman of
Flushing,
Alone, while I am here.
Lov.   Haste your return.   55
All. I will not fail, my lord.
Greedy.   Nor I, to line
My Christmas coffer.
                Exeunt GREEDY *and* ALLWORTH.
Over.   To my wish: we are private.
I come not to make offer with my daughter
A certain portion, — that were poor and trivial:
In one word, I pronounce all that is mine,   60
In lands or leases, ready coin or goods,
With her, my lord, comes to you; nor shall you
have
One motive to induce you to believe
I live too long, since every year I 'll add
Something unto the heap, which shall be yours
too.   65
Lov. You are a right kind father.
Over.   You shall have reason
To think me such. How do you like this seat?
It is well wooded, and well water'd, the acres
Fertile and rich; would it not serve for change,
To entertain your friends in a summer progress?
What thinks my noble lord?
Lov.   'T is a wholesome air,   71
And well-built pile; and she that 's mistress of
it,
Worthy the large revénue.
Over.   She the mistress!
It may be so for a time: but let my lord
Say only that he likes it, and would have it, 75
I say, ere long 't is his.
Lov.   Impossible.
Over. You do conclude too fast, not knowing
me,
Nor the engines [2] that I work by. 'T is not
alone
The Lady Allworth's lands, for those once
Wellborn's   79
(As by her dotage on him I know they will be,)

Shall soon be mine ; but point out any man's
In all the shire, and say they lie convenient
And useful for your lordship, and once more
I say aloud, they are yours.
    Lov.   I dare not own
What 's by unjust and cruel means extorted ; 85
My fame and credit are more dear to me,
Than so to expose 'em to be censur'd by
The public voice.
    Over.   You run, my lord, no hazard.
Your reputation shall stand as fair,
In all good men's opinions, as now ;   90
Nor can my actions, though condemn'd for ill,
Cast any foul aspersion upon yours.
For, though I do contemn report myself
As a mere sound, I still will be so tender   94
Of what concerns you, in all points of honour,
That the immaculate whiteness of your fame,
Nor your unquestioned integrity,
Shall e'er be sullied with one taint or spot
That may take from your innocence and can-
    dour.[1]
All my ambition is to have my daughter 100
Right honourable, which my lord can make her :
And might I live to dance upon my knee
A young Lord Lovell, borne by her unto you,
I write *nil ultra* [2] to my proudest hopes.
As for possessions and annual rents,   105
Equivalent to maintain you in the port
Your noble birth and present state requires,
I do remove that burthen from your shoulders,
And take it on mine own : for, though I ruin
The country to supply your riotous waste, 110
The scourge of prodigals, want, shall never find
    you.
    Lov. Are you not frighted with the impreca-
    tions
And curses of whole families, made wretched
By your sinister practices ?
    Over.   Yes, as rocks are,
When foamy billows split themselves against
Their flinty ribs ; or as the moon is mov'd 116
When wolves, with hunger pin'd, howl at her
    brightness.
I am of a solid temper, and, like these,
Steer on a constant course. With mine own
    sword,   119
If call'd into the field, I can make that right,
Which fearful enemies murmur'd at as wrong.
Now, for these other piddling complaints
Breath'd out in bitterness ; as when they call
    me
Extortioner, tyrant, cormorant, or intruder 124
On my poor neighbour's right, or grand incloser
Of what was common, to my private use ;
Nay, when my ears are pierc'd with widows'
    cries,
And undone orphans wash with tears my thresh-
    old,
I only think what 't is to have my daughter 129
Right honourable ; and 't is a powerful charm
Makes me insensible of remorse, or pity,
Or the least sting of conscience.
    Lov.   I admire [3]
The toughness of your nature.

    Over.   'T is for you,
My lord, and for my daughter, I am marble ;
Nay more, if you will have my character 135
In little, I enjoy more true delight
In my arrival to my wealth these dark
And crooked ways, than you shall e'er take
    pleasure
In spending what my industry hath compass'd.
My haste commands me hence ; in one word,
    therefore,   140
Is it a match ?
    Lov.   I hope, that is past doubt now.
    Over. Then rest secure ; not the hate of all
    mankind here,
Nor fear of what can fall on me hereafter,
Shall make me study aught but your advance-
    ment
One story higher : an earl ! if gold can do it. 145
Dispute not my religion, nor my faith ;
Though I am borne thus headlong by my will,
You may make choice of what belief you
    please,
To me they are equal ; so, my lord, good mor-
    row.   *Exit.*
    Lov. He 's gone — I wonder how the earth can
    bear   150
Such a portent ! I, that have liv'd a soldier,
And stood the enemy's violent charge un-
    daunted,
To hear this blasphemous beast am bath'd all
    over
In a cold sweat : yet, like a mountain, he
(Confirm'd in atheistical assertions) 155
Is no more shaken than Olympus [4] is
When angry Boreas loads his double head
With sudden drifts of snow.

Enter LADY ALLWORTH, *Waiting Woman, and*
    AMBLE.

    L. All.   Save you, my lord !
Disturb I not your privacy ?
    Lov.   No, good madam ;
For your own sake I am glad you came no
    sooner,   160
Since this bold bad man, Sir Giles Overreach,
Made such a plain discovery of himself,
And read this morning such a devilish matins,
That I should think it a sin next to his
But to repeat it.
    L. All.   I ne'er press'd, my lord, 165
On others' privacies ; yet, against my will,
Walking, for health' sake, in the gallery
Adjoining to your lodgings, I was made
(So vehement and loud he was) partaker
Of his tempting offers.
    Lov.   Please you to command 170
Your servants hence, and I shall gladly hear
Your wiser counsel.
    L. All.   'T is, my lord, a woman's,
But true and hearty ; — wait in the next room,
But be within call ; yet not so near to force me
To whisper my intents.
    Amb.   We are taught better 175
By you, good madam.
    W. Wom.   And well know our distance.

---

[1] Stainlessness.   [2] Nothing beyond.   [3] Wonder at.

[4] Apparently a slip for " Parnassus."

L. All. Do so, and talk not; 't will become
    your breeding,
              Exeunt AMBLE *and* W. Woman.
Now, my good lord; if I may use my freedom,
As to an honour'd friend ——
    Lov.   You lessen else
Your favour to me.
    L. All.   I dare then say thus: 180
As you are noble (howe'er common men
Make sordid wealth the object and sole end
Of their industrious aims) 't will not agree
With those of eminent blood, who are engag'd
More to prefer [1] their honours than to increase
The state left to 'em by their ancestors,   186
To study large additions to their fortunes,
And quite neglect their births: — though I
    must grant,
Riches, well got, to be a useful servant,
But a bad master.
    Lov.   Madam, 't is confessed;   190
But what infer you from it?
    L. All.   This, my lord;
That as all wrongs, though thrust into one scale,
Slide of themselves off when right fills the other
And cannot bide the trial; so all wealth,
I mean if ill-acquir'd, cemented to honour   195
By virtuous ways achiev'd, and bravely pur-
    chas'd,
Is but as rubbish pour'd into a river,
(Howe'er intended to make good the bank,)
Rendering the water, that was pure before,
Polluted and unwholesome. I allow   200
The heir of Sir Giles Overreach, Margaret,
A maid well qualified and the richest match
Our north part can make boast of; yet she can-
    not,
With all that she brings with her, fill their
    mouths,
That never will forget who was her father;   205
Or that my husband Allworth's lands, and Well-
    born's,
(How wrung from both needs now no repeti-
    tion,)
Were real motives that more work'd your lord-
    ship
To join your families, than her form and vir-
    tues:
You may conceive the rest.
    Lov.   I do, sweet madam,   210
And long since have consider'd it. I know,
The sum of all that makes a just man happy
Consists in the well choosing of his wife:
And there, well to discharge it, does require
Equality of years, of birth, of fortune;   215
For beauty being poor, and not cried up
By birth or wealth, can truly mix with neither.
And wealth, where there 's such difference in
    years,
And fair descent, must make the yoke un-
    easy: —
But I come nearer.
    L. All.   Pray you do, my lord.   220
    Lov. Were Overreach's states thrice centu-
    pl'd, his daughter
Millions of degrees much fairer than she is,

Howe'er I might urge precedents to excuse me,
I would not so adulterate my blood
By marrying Margaret, and so leave my issue
Made up of several pieces, one part scarlet,   225
And the other London blue. In my own tomb
I will inter my name first.
    L. All. (*Aside.*) I am glad to hear this. ——
Why then, my lord, pretend you marriage to
    her?
Dissimulation but ties false knots   230
On that straight line by which you, hitherto,
Have measur'd all your actions.
    Lov.   I make answer,
And aptly, with a question. Wherefore have
    you,
That, since your husband's death, have liv'd a
    strict
And chaste nun's life, on the sudden given your
    self   235
To visits and entertainments? Think you,
    madam,
'T is not grown public conference? [2] Or the fa-
    vours
Which you too prodigally have thrown on Well-
    born,
Being too reserv'd before, incur not censure?
    L. All. I am innocent here; and, on my life,
    I swear   240
My ends are good.
    Lov.   On my soul, so are mine
To Margaret; but leave both to the event:
And since this friendly privacy does serve
But as an offer'd means unto ourselves,
To search each other farther, you having shewn
Your care of me, I my respect to you,   245
Deny me not, but still in chaste words, madam,
An afternoon's discourse.
    L. All.   So I shall hear you. [*Exeunt.*]

SCENE II.[3]

[Enter] TAPWELL *and* FROTH.

    Tap. Undone, undone! this was your coun-
    sel, Froth.
    Froth. Mine! I defy thee. Did not Master
    Marrall
(He has marr'd all, I am sure) strictly command
    us,
On pain of Sir Giles Overreach' displeasure,
To turn the gentleman out of doors?
    Tap.   'T is true;   5
But now he 's his uncle's darling, and has got
Master Justice Greedy, since he fill'd his belly,
At his commandment, to do anything.
Woe, woe to us!
    Froth.   He may prove merciful.   9
    Tap. Troth, we do not deserve it at his hands.
Though he knew all the passages of our house,
As the receiving of stolen goods, and bawdry,
When he was rogue Wellborn no man would be-
    lieve him,
And then his information could not hurt us;
But now he is right worshipful again,   15
Who dares but doubt his testimony? Methinks,
I see thee, Froth, already in a cart,

---

[1] Promote.

[2] Gossip.   [3] Before Tapwell's house.

For a close[1] bawd, thine eyes ev'n pelted out
With dirt and rotten eggs ; and my hand hissing
If I scape the halter, with the letter R[2]   20
Printed upon it.
   Froth.   Would that were the worst !
That were but nine days' wonder : as for credit,
We have none to lose, but we shall lose the
    money
He owes us, and his custom ; there 's the hell
   on 't.
   Tap. He has summon'd all his creditors by
    the drum,   25
And they swarm about him like so many sol-
    diers
On the pay day : and has found out such A NEW
    WAY
To PAY HIS OLD DEBTS, as 't is very likely
He shall be chronicled for it !
   Froth.   He deserves it
More than ten pageants. But are you sure his
    worship   30
Comes this way, to my lady's ?
   A cry within : Brave Master Wellborn !
   Tap.   Yes : — I hear him.
   Froth. Be ready with your petition and pre-
    sent it
To his good grace.

Enter WELLBORN *in a rich habit,* [MARRALL,]
  GREEDY, ORDER, FURNACE, *and* Creditors ;
  TAPWELL *kneeling, delivers his bill of debt.*

   Well.   How 's this ? Petition'd to ?
But note what miracles the payment of
A little trash, and a rich suit of clothes,   35
Can work upon these rascals ! I shall be,
I think, Prince Wellborn.
   Mar.   When your worship 's married,
You may be — I know what I hope to see you.
   Well. Then look thou for advancement.
   Mar.   To be known
Your worship's bailiff, is the mark I shoot at.
   Well. And thou shalt hit it.
   Mar.   Pray you, sir, despatch   41
These needy followers, and for my admittance,[3]
Provided you 'll defend me from Sir Giles,
Whose service I am weary of, I 'll say something
You shall give thanks for.
   Well.   Fear not Sir Giles.[4]   45
   Greedy. Who, Tapwell ? I remember thy wife
    brought me
Last new-year's tide, a couple of fat turkeys.
   Tap. And shall do every Christmas, let your
    worship
But stand my friend now.
   Greedy.   How ! with Master Wellborn ?
I can do anything with him on such terms. —
See you this honest couple ; they are good
    souls   51
As ever drew out faucet ; have they not
A pair of honest faces ?
   Well.   I o'erheard you,
And the bribe he promis'd. You are cozen'd in
    them ;
For, by all the scum that grew rich by my riots,

<hr>

[1] Secret.   [2] For "Rogue."   [3] Appointment.
[4] Q. gives s. d., *This interim, Tapwell and Froth flattering and bribing Justice Greedy.*

This, for a most unthankful knave, and this,   55
For a base bawd and whore, have worst de-
    serv'd me,
And therefore speak not for 'em. By your place
You are rather to do me justice. Lend me your
    ear ;
— Forget his turkeys, and call in his license, 60
And, at the next fair, I 'll give you a yoke of
    oxen
Worth all his poultry.
   Greedy.   I am chang'd on the sudden
In my opinion ! Come near ; nearer, rascal.
And, now I view him better, did you e'er see
One look so like an archknave ? His very coun-
    tenance,   65
Should an understanding judge but look upon
    him,
Would hang him, though he were innocent.
   Tap. Froth.   Worshipful sir.
   Greedy. No, though the great Turk came, in-
    stead of turkeys,
To beg my favour, I am inexorable.
Thou hast an ill name : besides thy musty ale, 70
That hath destroy'd many of the king's liege
    people,
Thou never hadst in thy house, to stay men's
    stomachs,
A piece of Suffolk cheese or gammon of bacon,
Or any esculent, as the learned call it,
For their emolument, but sheer drink only,   75
For which gross fault I here do damn thy license,
Forbidding thee ever to tap or draw ;
For, instantly, I will, in mine own person,
Command the constable to pull down thy sign,
And do it before I eat.
   Froth.   No mercy ?
   Greedy.   Vanish !   80
If I shew any, may my promis'd oxen gore me !
   Tap. Unthankful knaves are ever so re-
    warded.
     Exeunt GREEDY, TAPWELL, *and* FROTH.
   Well. Speak, what are you ?
   1 Cred.   A decay'd vintner, sir,
That might have thriv'd, but that your worship
    broke me
With trusting you with muscadine[5] and eggs,
And five pound suppers, with your after drink-
    ings,   85
When you lodg'd upon the Bankside.
   Well.   I remember.
   1 Cred. I have not been hasty, nor e'er laid
    to arrest you ;
And therefore, sir ——
   Well.   Thou art an honest fellow,
I 'll set thee up again ; see his bill paid. —   90
What are you ?
   2 Cred. A tailor once, but now mere botcher.[6]
I gave you credit for a suit of clothes,
Which was all my stock, but you failing in pay-
    ment,
I was remov'd from the shopboard, and confin'd
    Under a stall.
   Well. See him paid ; — and botch no more.   95
   2 Cred. I ask no interest, sir.
   Well.   Such tailors need not ;

<hr>

[5] Wine from muscadel grapes.   [6] Repairer

If their bills are paid in one and twenty year,
They are seldom losers. — O, I know thy face,
　　　　　　　　　　　　　　[*To* Creditor.]
Thou wert my surgeon. You must tell no tales ;
Those days are done. I will pay you in private.
　Ord. A royal gentleman !
　Furn.　　　　　Royal as an emperor !　101
He 'll prove a brave master ; my good lady knew
To choose a man.
　Well.　　　　See all men else discharg'd ;
And since old debts are clear'd by a new way,
A little bounty will not misbecome me ;　105
There 's something, honest cook, for thy good
　　　breakfasts ;
And this, for your respect : [*to* ORDER] take 't,
　't is good gold,
And I able to spare it.
　Ord.　　　　　You are too munificent.
　Furn. He was ever so.
　Well.　　　　Pray you, on before.
　3 *Cred.*　　　　　Heaven bless you !
　Mar. At four o'clock ; the rest know where
　　to meet me.　110
　　　Exeunt ORDER, FURNACE, *and* Creditors.
　Well. Now, Master Marrall, what 's the
　　weighty secret
You promis'd to impart ?
　Mar.　　　　　Sir, time nor place
Allow me to relate each circumstance ;
This only, in a word : I know Sir Giles
Will come upon you for security　115
For his thousand pounds, which you must not
　consent to.
As he grows in heat, as I am sure he will,
Be you but rough, and say he 's in your debt
Ten times the sum, upon sale of your land ;
I had a hand in 't (I speak it to my shame)　120
When you were defeated [1] of it.
　Well.　　　　That 's forgiven.
　Mar. I shall deserve 't. Then urge him to
　　produce
The deed in which you pass'd it over to him,
Which I know he 'll have about him, to deliver
To the Lord Lovell, with many other writings,　125
And present monies ; I 'll instruct you further,
As I wait on your worship. If I play not my
　prize
To your full content, and your uncle's much
　vexation,
Hang up Jack Marrall.
　Well.　　　　I rely upon thee. *Exeunt.*

SCENE III.[2]

Enter ALLWORTH *and* MARGARET.

　All. Whether to yield the first praise to my
　　lord's
Unequall'd temperance or your constant sweet-
　　ness
That I yet live, my weak hands fasten'd on
Hope's anchor, spite of all storms of despair,
I yet rest doubtful.
　Marg.　　　　Give it to Lord Lovell :　5
For what in him was bounty, in me 's duty.
I make but payment of a debt to which

My vows, in that high office regist'red,
Are faithful witnesses.
　All.　　　　'T is true, my dearest :
Yet, when I call to mind how many fair ones　10
Make wilful shipwrecks of their faiths, and
　　oaths
To God and man, to fill the arms of greatness,
And you rise up [no] [3] less than a glorious star,
To the amazement of the world, — hold out
Against the stern authority of a father,　15
And spurn at honour when it comes to court
　you ;
I am so tender of your good, that faintly,
With your wrong, I can wish myself that right
You yet are pleas'd to do me.
　Marg.　　　　Yet, and ever.
To me what 's title, when content is want-
　ing ?　20
Or wealth, rak'd up together with much care.
And to be kept with more, when the heart
　pines
In being dispossess'd of what it longs for
Beyond the Indian mines ? or the smooth brow
Of a pleas'd sire, that slaves me to his will,　25
And, so his ravenous humour may be feasted
By my obedience, and he see me great,
Leaves to my soul nor faculties nor power
To make her own election ?
　All.　　　　But the dangers
That follow the repulse ——
　Marg.　　　　To me they are nothing ;　30
Let Allworth love, I cannot be unhappy.
Suppose the worst, that, in his rage, he kill me,
A tear or two, by you dropt on my hearse
In sorrow for my fate, will call back life
So far as but to say, that I die yours ;　35
I then shall rest in peace : or should he prove
So cruel, as one death would not suffice
His thirst of vengeance, but with ling'ring tor-
　ments
In mind and body I must waste to air,
In poverty join'd with banishment ; so you
　share　40
In my afflictions, which I dare not wish you,
So high I prize you, I could undergo 'em
With such a patience as should look down
With scorn on his worst malice.
　All.　　　　Heaven avert
Such trials of your true affection to me !　45
Nor will it unto you, that are all mercy,
Shew so much rigour : but since we must run
Such desperate hazards, let us do our best
To steer between them.
　Marg.　　　　Your lord 's ours, and sure :
And, though but a young actor, second me　50
In doing to the life what he has plotted.

Enter OVERREACH [*behind*].

The end may yet prove happy. Now, my All-
　worth —　　　　　　[*Seeing her father.*]
　All. To your letter, and put on a seeming
　　anger.
　Marg. I 'll pay my lord all debts due to his
　　title ;
And when with terms, not taking from his
　honour,　55

---

[1] Robbed.　　　　[2] A room in Overreach's house.
[3] Inserted by Dodsley.

He does solicit me, I shall gladly hear him.
But in this peremptory, nay, commanding way,
To appoint a meeting, and without my know-
    ledge,
A priest to tie the knot can ne'er be undone
Till death unloose it, is a confidence   60
In his lordship will deceive him.
    All.   I hope better,
Good lady.
    Marg.   Hope, sir, what you please : for me
I must take a safe and secure course ; I have
A father, and without his full consent,
Though all lords of the land kneel'd for my
    favor,   65
I can grant nothing.
    Over. I like this obedience : [*Comes forward.*]
But whatso'er my lord writes, must and shall
    be
Accepted and embrac'd. Sweet Master All-
    worth,
You shew yourself a true and faithful servant
To your good lord ; he has a jewel of you.   70
How ! frowning, Meg ? Are these looks to re-
    ceive
A messenger from my lord ? What 's this ?
    Give me it.
    Marg. A piece of arrogant paper, like th'
    inscriptions.
    Over. (*reads.*) " Fair mistress, from your
    servant learn all joys
That we can hope for, if deferr'd, prove toys ;[1]
Therefore this instant, and in private, meet   76
A husband, that will gladly at your feet
Lay down his honours, tend'ring them to you
With all content, the church being paid her
    due."
— Is this the arrogant piece of paper ? Fool ![80]
Will you still be one ? In the name of madness
    what
Could his good honour write more to content
    you ?
Is there aught else to be wish'd, after these
    two,
That are already offer'd ; marriage first,
And lawful pleasure after : what would you
    more ?   85
    Marg. Why, sir, I would be married like
    your daughter ;
Not hurried away i' th' night I know not
    whither,
Without all ceremony ; no friends invited
To honour the solemnity.
    All.   An 't please your honour,
For so before to-morrow I must style you,   90
My lord desires this privacy, in respect
His honourable kinsmen are afar off,
And his desires to have it done brook not
So long delay as to expect[2] their coming ;
And yet he stands resolv'd, with all due   95
    pomp,
As running at the ring, plays, masques, and
    tilting,
To have his marriage at court celebrated,
When he has brought your honour up to Lon-
    don.

    Over. He tells you true ; 'tis the fashion, on
    my knowledge :
Yet the good lord, to please your peevish-
    ness,   100
Must put it off, forsooth ! and lose a night,
In which perhaps he might get two boys on
    thee.
Tempt me no further, if you do, this goad
                    [*Points to his sword.*]
Shall prick you to him.
    Marg.   I could be contented,
Were you but by, to do a father's part,   105
And give me in the church.
    Over.   So my lord have you,
What do I care who gives you ? Since my lord
Does purpose to be private, I 'll not cross him.
I know not, Master Allworth, how my lord
May be provided, and therefore there 's a
    purse   110
Of gold, 't will serve this night 's expense ; to-
    morrow
I 'll furnish him with any sums. In the mean
    time,
Use my ring to my chaplain ; he is benefic'd
At my manor of Gotham, and call'd Parson
    Willdo.
'T is no matter for a licence, I 'll bear him out
    in 't ;   115
    Marg. With your favour, sir, what warrant
    is your ring ?
He may suppose I got that twenty ways,
Without your knowledge ; and then to be re-
    fus'd
Were such a stain upon me ! — If you pleas'd,
    sir,
Your presence would do better.
    Over.   Still perverse ! 120
I say again, I will not cross my lord ;
Yet I 'll prevent[3] you too. — Paper and ink,
    there !
    All. I can furnish you.
    Over.   I thank you, I can write then.
                    Writes on his book.
    All. You may, if you please, put out the
    name of my lord,
In respect he comes disguis'd, and only write, 125
" Marry her to this gentleman."
    Over.   Well advis'd.
'T is done ; away ; — (MARGARET *kneels.*) My
    blessing, girl ? Thou hast it.
Nay, no reply, be gone. — Good Master All-
    worth,
This shall be the best night's work you ever
    made.
    All. I hope so, sir.   130
        Exeunt ALLWORTH *and* MAR-
            GARET.
    Over. Farewell ! — Now all 's cocksure :
Methinks I hear already knights and ladies
Say, Sir Giles Overreach, how is it with
Your honourable daughter ? Has her honour
Slept well to-night ? or, will her honour
    please   135
To accept this monkey, dog, or paraquit[4]
(This is state in ladies), or my eldest son

---

[1] Trifles.   [2] Wait for.   [3] Anticipate your objections.   [4] Parrot.

To be her page, and wait upon her trencher?
My ends, my ends are compass'd! — then for
        Wellborn
And the lands: were he once married to the
        widow,   140
I have him here. — I can scarce contain myself,
I am so full of joy, nay, joy all over.   *Exit.*

ACT V

Scene I.[1]

[*Enter* Lord] Lovell, Lady Allworth, *and*
        Amble.

L. All. By this you know how strong the
        motives were
That did, my lord, induce me to dispense
A little with my gravity to advance,
In personating some few favours to him,
The plots and projects of the down-trod Well-
        born.   5
Nor shall I e'er repent, although I suffer
In some few men's opinions for 't, the action:
For he that ventur'd all for my dear husband
Might justly claim an obligation from me
To pay him such a courtesy; which had I   10
Coyly or over-curiously [2] denied,
It might have argu'd me of little love
To the deceas'd.

Lov.   What you intended, madam,
For the poor gentleman hath found good suc-
        cess;
For, as I understand, his debts are paid,   15
And he once more furnish'd for fair employ-
        ment:
But all the arts that I have us'd to raise
The fortunes of your joy and mine, young All-
        worth,
Stand yet in supposition, though I hope well;
For the young lovers are in wit more pregnant
Than their years can promise; and for their
        desires,   21
On my knowledge, they are equal.

L. All.   As my wishes
Are with yours, my lord; yet give me leave to
        fear
The building, though well grounded: to deceive
Sir Giles, that's both a lion and a fox   25
In his proceedings, were a work beyond
The strongest undertakers; not the trial
Of two weak innocents.

Lov.   Despair not, madam:
Hard things are compass'd oft by easy means;
And judgment, being a gift deriv'd from
        Heaven,   30
Though sometimes lodg'd i' th' hearts of
        worldly men,
That ne'er consider from whom they receive it,
Forsakes such as abuse the giver of it.
Which is the reason that the politic
And cunning statesman, that believes he fath-
        oms   35
The counsels of all kingdoms on the earth,
Is by simplicity oft over-reach'd.

L. All. May he be so! Yet, in his name to
        express it,
Is a good omen.

Lov.   May it to myself
Prove so, good lady, in my suit to you!   40
What think you of the motion?

L. All.   Troth, my lord,
My own unworthiness may answer for me;
For had you, when that I was in my prime,
My virgin flower uncropp'd, presented me
With this great favour; looking on my lowness
Not in a glass of self-love, but of truth,   45
I could not but have thought it as a blessing
Far, far beyond my merit.

Lov.   You are too modest,
And undervalue that which is above
My title, or whatever I call mine.   50
I grant, were I a Spaniard, to marry
A widow might disparage me; but being
A true-born Englishman, I cannot find
How it can taint my honour: nay, what's more,
That which you think a blemish is to me   55
The fairest lustre. You already, madam,
Have given sure proofs how dearly you can cher-
        ish
A husband that deserves you; which confirms
        me
That, if I am not wanting in my care
To do you service, you 'll be still the same   60
That you were to your Allworth: in a word,
Our years, our states, our births are not un-
        equal,
You being descended nobly, and alli'd so;
If then you may be won to make me happy,
But join your lips to mine, and that shall be   65
A solemn contract.

L. All.   I were blind to my own good
Should I refuse it; [*kisses him*] yet, my lord,
        receive me
As such a one, the study of whose whole life
Shall know no other object but to please you.

Lov. If I return not, with all tenderness,   70
Equal respect to you, may I die wretched!

L. All. There needs no protestation, my lord,
To her that cannot doubt, —

Enter Wellborn [*handsomely apparelled.*]

        You are welcome, sir.
Now you look like yourself.

Well.   And will continue
Such in my free acknowledgment that I am   75
Your creature, madam, and will never hold
My life mine own, when you please to command
        it.

Lov. It is a thankfulness that well becomes
        you.
You could not make choice of a better shape
To dress your mind in.

L. All.   For me, I am happy   80
That my endeavours prosper'd. Saw you of late
Sir Giles, your uncle?

Well.   I heard of him, madam,
By his minister, Marrall; he 's grown into
        strange passions
About his daughter. This last night he look'd
        for
Your lordship at his house, but missing you.   85

And she not yet appearing, his wise head
Is much perplex'd and troubl'd.
 Lov.   It may be,
Sweetheart, my project took.
 L. All.   I strongly hope.
 Over. [*within.*] Ha! find her, booby, thou
  huge lump of nothing,
I 'll bore thine eyes out else.
 Well.   May it please your lordship, 90
For some ends of mine own, but to withdraw
A little out of sight, though not of hearing,
You may, perhaps, have sport.
 Lov. You shall direct me. *Steps aside.*

Enter OVERREACH, *with distracted looks, driving in* MARRALL *before him* [*with a box*].[1]

 Over. I shall *sol fa* you, rogue!
 Mar.   Sir, for what cause
Do you use me thus?
 Over. Cause, slave! Why, I am angry, 95
And thou a subject only fit for beating,
And so to cool my choler. Look to the writing;
Let but the seal be broke upon the box
That hast slept in my cabinet these three
 years,
I 'll rack thy soul for 't.
 Mar. (*Aside.*) I may yet cry quittance, 100
Though now I suffer, and dare not resist.
 Over. Lady, by your leave, did you see my
  daughter lady?
And the lord her husband? Are they in your
 house?
If they are, discover, that I may bid 'em joy;
And, as an entrance to her place of honour, 105
See your ladyship be on her left hand, and make
 courtesies
When she nods on you; which you must receive
As a special favour.
 L. All.   When I know, Sir Giles,
Her state requires such ceremony, I shall pay
 it;
But in the meantime, as I am myself, 110
I give you to understand, I neither know
Nor care where her honour is.
 Over.   When you once see her
Supported, and led by the lord her husband,
You 'll be taught better. —— Nephew.
 Well.   Sir.
 Over.   No more?
 Well. 'T is all I owe you.
 Over. Have your redeem'd rags 115
Made you thus insolent?
 Well. (*in scorn.*) Insolent to you!
Why, what are you, sir, unless in your years,
At the best, more than myself?
 Over. [*Aside.*] His fortune swells him.
'T is rank[2] he 's married.
 L. All.   This is excellent!
 Over. Sir, in calm language, though I seldom
  use it, 120
I am familiar with the cause that makes you
Bear up thus bravely; there 's a certain buzz
Of a stol'n marriage, do you hear? of a stol'n
 marriage,

In which, 't is said, there 's somebody hath been
 cozen'd;
I name no parties.
 Well. Well, sir, and what follows? 125
 Over. Marry, this; since you are peremptory.
  Remember,
Upon mere hope of your great match, I lent you
A thousand pounds: put me in good security,
And suddenly, by mortgage or by statute, 129
Of some of your new possessions, or I 'll have you
Dragg'd in your lavender robes[3] to the goal.
 You know me,
And therefore do not trifle.
 Well.   Can you be
So cruel to your nephew, now he 's in
The way to rise? Was this the courtesy
You did me " in pure love, and no ends else? "
 Over. End me no ends! Engage the whole
  estate, 136
And force your spouse to sign it, you shall have
Three or four thousand more, to roar and swag-
 ger
And revel in bawdy taverns.
 Well.   And beg after;
Mean you not so?
 Over. My thoughts are mine, and free. 140
Shall I have security?
 Well.   No, indeed, you shall not,
Nor bond, nor bill, nor bare acknowledgment;
Your great looks fright not me.
 Over.   But my deeds shall.
Outbrav'd!   *Both draw.*
 L. All. Help, murder! murder!

     Enter Servants.

 Well.   Let him come on,
With all his wrongs and injuries about him, 145
Arm'd with his cut-throat practices to guard
 him;
The right that I bring with me will defend me,
And punish his extortion.
 Over.   That I had thee
But single in the field!
 L. All.   You may; but make not
My house your quarrelling scene.
 Over. Were 't in a church, 150
By Heaven and Hell, I 'll do 't!
 Mar.   Now put him to
The shewing of the deed.
     [*Aside to* WELLBORN.]
 Well.   This rage is vain, sir;
For fighting, fear not, you shall have your
 hands full,
Upon the least incitement; and whereas
You charge me with a debt of a thousand
 pounds, 155
If there be law, (howe'er you have no con-
 science,)
Either restore my land or I 'll recover
A debt, that 's truly due to me from you,
In value ten times more than what you chal-
 lenge.
 Over. I in thy debt! O impudence! did I not
  purchase 160

---

 [1] In Q. this entrance occurs after " took," above.
 [2] Obvious.

 [3] Clothes in pawn were said to be " laid up in laven
der."

The land left by thy father, that rich land,
That had continued in Wellborn's name
Twenty descents; which, like a riotous fool,
Thou didst make sale of it? Is not here in-
　　clos'd
The deed that does confirm it mine?
　Mar.　　　　　　　Now, now! 165
　Well. I do acknowledge none; I ne'er pass'd
　　o'er
Any such land. I grant for a year or two
You had it in trust; which if you do dis-
　　charge,
Surrend'ring the possession, you shall ease
Yourself and me of chargeable suits in law, 170
Which, if you prove not honest, as I doubt it,
Must of necessity follow.
　L. All.　　　　　In my judgment,
He does advise you well.
　Over.　　　　Good! good! Conspire
With your new husband, lady; second him
In his dishonest practices; but when 175
This manor is extended[1] to my use,
You'll speak in humbler key, and sue for fa-
　　vour.
　L. All. Never: do not hope it.
　Well.　　　　Let despair first seize me.
　Over. Yet, to shut up thy mouth, and make
　　thee give
Thyself the lie, the loud lie, I draw out 180
The precious evidence; if thou canst forswear
Thy hand and seal, and make a forfeit of
　　　　*Opens the box [and displays the
　　　　　bond].*
Thy ears to the pillory, see! here's that will
　　make
My interest clear — ha!
　L. All.　　　　A fair skin of parchment.
　Well. Indented, I confess, and labels too; 185
But neither wax nor words. How! thunder-
　　struck?
Not a syllable to insult with? My wise uncle,
Is this your precious evidence? Is this that
　　makes
Your interest clear?
　Over.　　　I am o'erwhelm'd with wonder!
What prodigy is this? What subtle devil 190
Hath raz'd out the inscription, the wax
Turn'd into dust? The rest of my deeds whole
As when they were deliver'd, and this only
Made nothing! Do you deal with witches, ras-
　　cal?
There is a statute[2] for you, which will bring 195
Your neck in an hempen circle; yes, there is;
And now 't is better thought for, cheater,
　　know
This juggling shall not save you.
　Well.　　　　To save thee
Would beggar the stock of mercy.
　Over.　　　　Marrall!
　Mar.　　　　　　　　Sir.
　Over. (*flattering him.*) Though the witnesses
　　are dead, your testimony 200
Help with an oath or two: and for thy master,
Thy liberal master, my good honest servant,
I know thou wilt swear anything, to dash

This cunning sleight: besides, I know thou art
A public notary, and such stand in law 205
For a dozen witnesses: the deed being drawn too
By thee, my careful Marrall, and deliver'd
When thou wert present, will make good my
　　title.
Wilt thou not swear this?
　Mar.　　　　　I! No, I assure you: 209
I have a conscience not sear'd up like yours;
I know no deeds.
　Over.　　　Wilt thou betray me?
　Mar.　　　　　　　Keep him
From using of his hands, I'll use my tongue,
To his no little torment.
　Over.　　　Mine own varlet
Rebel against me!
　Mar.　　　Yes, and uncase[3] you too.
"The idiot, the patch, the slave, the booby, 215
The property fit only to be beaten
For your morning exercise," your "football," or
"Th' unprofitable lump of flesh," your
　　"drudge,"
Can now anatomise you, and lay open 219
All your black plots, and level with the earth
Your hill of pride, and, with these gabions[4]
　　guarded
Unload my great artillery, and shake,
Nay pulverize, the walls you think defend you.
　L. All. How he foams at the mouth with
　　rage!
　Well.　　To him again.
　Over. O that I had thee in my gripe, I would
　　tear thee 225
Joint after joint!
　Mar.　　　I know you are a tearer,
But I'll have first your fangs par'd off, and
　　then
Come nearer to you; when I have discover'd,[5]
And made it good before the judge, what
　　ways
And devilish practices you us'd to cozen 230
With an army of whole families, who yet live,
And, but enroll'd for soldiers, were able
To take in[6] Dunkirk.
　Well.　　　All will come out.
　L. All.　　　　　The better.
　Over. But that I will live, rogue, to torture
　　thee, 234
And make thee wish, and kneel in vain, to die,
These swords that keep thee from me should
　　fix here,
Although they made my body but one wound,
But I would reach thee.
　Lov. (*Aside.*)　　Heaven's hand is in this;
One bandog[7] worry the other!
　Over.　　　　I play the fool,
And make my anger but ridiculous; 240
There will be a time and place, there will be,
　　cowards,
When you shall feel what I dare do.
　Well.　　　　I think so:
You dare do any ill, yet want true valour
To be honest, and repent.

[3] Flay.
[4] Wicker baskets filled with earth, used to protect
soldiers when digging trenches.
[5] Revealed.　[6] Capture.　[7] Fierce watchdog.

[1] Seized.　　[2] The law against witchcraft.

Over.   They are words I know not,
Nor e'er will learn. Patience, the beggar's
          virtue,   245

Enter GREEDY *and* PARSON WILLDO.

Shall find no harbour here : — after these
          storms
At length a calm appears. Welcome, most wel-
          come !
There 's comfort in thy looks. Is the deed done?
Is my daughter married? Say but so, my
          chaplain,
And I am tame.
          Willdo.   Married! Yes I assure you. 250
Over. Then vanish all sad thoughts! There 's
          more gold for thee.
My doubts and fears are in the titles drown'd
Of my honourable, my right honourable
          daughter.
Greedy. Here will [1] be feasting! At least for
          a month
I am provided : empty guts, croak no more. 255
You shall be stuff'd like bagpipes, not with wind,
But bearing [2] dishes.
Over.   Instantly be here?
                    (*Whispering to* WILLDO.)
To my wish! to my wish! Now you that plot
          against me,
And hop'd to trip my heels up, that contemn'd me,
Think on 't and tremble. — (*Loud music*) —
          They come! I hear the music.   260
A lane there for my lord!
Well.   This sudden heat
May yet be cool'd, sir.
Over.   Make way there for my lord!

Enter ALLWORTH *and* MARGARET.

Marg. Sir, first your pardon, then your bless-
          ing, with
Your full allowance of the choice I have made.
As ever you could make use of your reason, 265
                    Kneeling.
Grow not in passion; since you may as well
Call back the day that 's past, as untie the knot
Which is too strongly fasten'd. Not to dwell
Too long on words, this is my husband.
Over.   How!   269
All. So I assure you; all the rites of marriage,
With every circumstance, are past. Alas! sir,
Although I am no lord, but a lord's page,
Your daughter and my lov'd wife mourns not
          for it ;
And, for right honourable son-in-law, you may
          say,
Your dutiful daughter.
Over.   Devil! are they married? 275
Willdo. Do a father's part, and say, "Heaven
          give 'em joy !"
Over. Confusion and ruin! Speak, and speak
          quickly,
Or thou art dead.
Willdo.   They are married.
Over.   Thou hadst better
Have made a contract with the king of fiends,
Than these : — my brain turns!

          [1] Q. *will I.*   [2] Solid.

Willdo.   Why this rage to me? 280
Is not this your letter, sir, and these the words?
" Marry her to this gentleman."
Over.   It cannot —
Nor will I e'er believe it; 'sdeath! I will not;
That I, that in all passages I touch'd
At worldly profit have not left a print   285
Where I have trod for the most curious search
To trace my footsteps, should be gull'd by
          children,
Baffl'd and fool'd, and all my hopes and labours
Defeated and made void.
Well.   As it appears,
You are so, my grave uncle.
Over.   Village nurses 290
Revenge their wrongs with curses ; I 'll not
          waste
A syllable, but thus I take the life
Which, wretched, I gave to thee.
                    Offers to kill MARGARET.
Lov. [*coming forward.*] Hold, for your own
          sake !
Though charity to your daughter hath quite
          left you,   295
Will you do an act, though in your hopes lost here,
Can leave no hope for peace or rest hereafter?
Consider; at the best you are but a man,
And cannot so create your aims but that
They may be cross'd.
Over.   Lord! thus I spit at thee, 300
And at thy counsel; and again desire thee,
And as thou art a soldier, if thy valour
Dares shew itself where multitude and example
Lead not the way, let's quit the house, and
          change
Six words in private.
Lov.   I am ready.
L. All.   Stay, sir, 305
Contest with one distracted !
Well.   You 'll grow like him,
Should you answer his vain challenge.
Over.   Are you pale?
Borrow his help, though Hercules call it odds,
I 'll stand against both as I am, hemm'd in
          thus.
Since, like a Libyan lion in the toil,   310
My fury cannot reach the coward hunters,
And only spends itself, I 'll quit the place.
Alone I can do nothing; but I have servants
And friends to second me; and if I make not
This house a heap of ashes (by my wrongs, 315
What I have spoke I will make good !) or leave
One throat uncut, — if it be possible,
Hell, add to my afflictions!   *Exit.*
Mar.   Is 't not brave sport?
Greedy. Brave sport! I am sure it has ta'en
          away my stomach ;
I do not like the sauce.
All.   Nay, weep not, dearest, 320
Though it express your pity ; what 's decreed
Above, we cannot alter.
L. All.   His threats move me
No scruple, madam.
Mar.   Was it not a rare trick,
An it please your worship, to make the deed
          nothing?
I can do twenty neater, if you please   325

To purchase and grow rich ; for I will be
Such a solicitor and steward for you,
As never worshipful had.
    Well.   I do believe thee ;
But first discover the quaint[1] means you us'd
To raze out the conveyance ?
    Mar.   They are mysteries 330
Not to be spoke in public : certain minerals
Incorporated in the ink and wax —
Besides, he gave me nothing, but still fed me
With hopes and blows ; but that was the in-
    ducement   334
To this conundrum. If it please your worship
To call to memory, this mad beast once caus'd me
To urge you or to drown or hang yourself ;
I 'll do the like to him, if you command me.
    Well. You are a rascal ! He that dares be
    false   339
To a master, though unjust, will ne'er be true
To any other. Look not for reward
Or favour from me ; I will shun thy sight
As I would do a basilisk's. Thank my pity
If thou keep thy ears ; howe'er, I will take order
Your practice shall be silenc'd.
    Greedy.   I 'll commit him, 345
If you 'll have me, sir.
    Well.   That were to little purpose ;
His conscience be his prison. Not a word,
But instantly be gone.
    Ord.   Take this kick with you.
    Amb. And this.
    Furn.   If that I had my cleaver here,
I would divide your knave's head,
    Mar.   This is the haven 350
False servants still arrive at.   *Exit.*

        Re-enter OVERREACH.

    L. All.   Come again !
    Lov. Fear not, I am your guard.
    Well.   His looks are ghastly.
    Willdo. Some little time I have spent, under
your favours,
In physical studies, and if my judgment err not,
He 's mad beyond recovery : but observe him,
And look to yourselves.
    Over.   Why, is not the whole world
Included in myself ? To what use then 357
Are friends and servants ? Say there were a
    squadron
Of pikes, lin'd through with shot, when I am
    mounted
Upon my injuries, shall I fear to charge 'em ?
No : I 'll through the battalia, and, that routed,
    Flourishing his sword sheathed.[2]
I 'll fall to execution — Ha ! I am feeble : 362
Some undone widow sits upon mine arm,
And takes away the use of 't ; and my sword,
Glu'd to my scabbard with wrong'd orphans'
    tears,   365
Will not be drawn. Ha ! what are these ? Sure,
    hangmen
That come to bind my hands, and then to drag me
Before the judgment-seat : now they are new
    shapes,
And do appear like Furies, with steel whips 369

To scourge my ulcerous soul. Shall I then fall
Ingloriously, and yield ? No ; spite of Fate,
I will be forc'd to hell like to myself.
Though you were legions of accursed spirits,
Thus would I fly among you.
          [*Rushes forward and flings himself
             on the ground.*]
    Well.   There 's no help ;
Disarm him first, then bind him.
    Greedy.   Take a *mittimus.*[3] 37?
And carry him to Bedlam.
    Lov.   How he foams !
    Well. And bites the earth !
    Willdo.   Carry him to some dark room
There try what art can do for his recovery.
    Marg. O my dear father !
            They force OVERREACH *off.*
    All.   You must be patient, mistress.
    Lov. Here is a precedent to teach wicked
    men   380
That when they leave religion, and turn athe-
    ists,
Their own abilities leave 'em. Pray you take
    comfort,
I will endeavour you shall be his guardians
In his distractions : and for your land, Master
    Wellborn,
Be it good or ill in law, I 'll be an umpire 385
Between you, and this, th' undoubted heir
Of Sir Giles Overreach. For me, here 's the
    anchor
That I must fix on.
    All.   What you shall determine,
My lord, I will allow of.
    Well.   'T is the language 389
That I speak too ; but there is something else
Beside the repossession of my land,
And payment of my debts, that I must prac-
    tise.
I had a reputation, but 't was lost
In my loose course, and until I redeem it
Some noble way, I am but half made up. 395
It is a time of action ; if your lordship
Will please to confer a company upon me
In your command, I doubt not in my service
To my king and country but I shall do some-
    thing
That may make me right again.
    Lov.   Your suit is granted 400
And you lov'd for the motion.
    Well. [*coming forward.*] Nothing wants then
But your allowance —

THE EPILOGUE

BUT your allowance. and in that our all
Is comprehended ; it being known, nor we,
Nor he that wrote the comedy, can be free 405
Without your manumission ; which if you
Grant willingly, as a fair favour due
To the poet's and our labours, (as you may,
For we despair not, gentlemen, of the play,)
We jointly shall profess your grace hath might
To teach us action, and him how to write. 411
                    [*Exeunt.*]

---

[1] Crafty.   [2] Q. *unsheathed.*   [3] A writ of committal.

THE BROKEN HEART

BY

JOHN FORD

THE SPEAKERS' NAMES FITTED TO THEIR QUALITIES

AMYCLAS, *Common to the Kings of Laconia.*
ITHOCLES, *Honour of loveliness*, a Favourite.
ORGILUS, *Angry*, son to Crotolon.
BASSANES, *Vexation*, a jealous Nobleman.
ARMOSTES, *an Appeaser*, a Councillor of State.
CROTOLON, *Noise*, another Councillor.
PROPHILUS, *Dear*, Friend to Ithocles.
NEARCHUS, *Young Prince*, Prince of Argos.
TECNICUS, *Artist*, a Philosopher.
HEMOPHIL, *Glutton*, } two Courtiers.
GRONEAS, *Tavern-haunter*, }
AMELUS, *Trusty*, Friend to Nearchus.
PHULAS, *Watchful*, Servant to Bassanes.
Lords, Courtiers, Officers, Attendants, etc.

CALANTHA, *Flower of beauty*, the King's Daughter.
PENTHEA, *Complaint*, Sister to Ithocles [and Wife to Bassanes].
EUPHRANEA, *Joy*, a Maid of honour [Daughter to Crotolon].
CHRISTALLA, *Christal*, } Maids of honour.
PHILEMA, *A Kiss*, }
GRAUSIS,[1] *Old Beldam*, Overseer of Penthea.

PERSONS INCLUDED.

THRASUS, *Fierceness*, Father of Ithocles.
APLOTES, *Simplicity*, Orgilus so disguised.

SCENE — *Sparta.*

PROLOGUE

OUR scene is Sparta. He whose best of art
Hath drawn this piece calls it THE BROKEN HEART.
The title lends no expectation here
Of apish laughter, or of some lame jeer
At place or persons ; no pretended clause
Of jests fit for a brothel courts applause
From vulgar admiration : such low songs,
Tun'd to unchaste ears, suit not modest tongues.
The Virgin Sisters then deserv'd fresh bays
When Innocence and Sweetness crown'd their lays ;
Then vices gasp'd for breath, whose whole commerce
Was whipp'd to exile by unblushing verse.
This law we keep in our presentment now,
Not to take freedom more than we allow ;
What may be here thought fiction,[2] when time's youth
Wanted some riper years, was known a truth :
In which, if words have cloth'd the subject right,
You may partake a pity with delight.

ACT I

SCENE I.[3]

Enter CROTOLON *and* ORGILUS.

Crot. Dally not further ; I will know the reason
That speeds thee to this journey.
Org.　　　　　　Reason ! good sir,
I can yield many.
Crot.　　　　Give me one, a good one ;
Such I expect, and ere we part must have.

Athens ! Pray, why to Athens ? You intend not
To kick against the world, turn cynic, stoic,
Or read the logic lecture, or become
An Areopagite,[4] and judge in cases
Touching the commonwealth ; for, as I take it,
The budding of your chin cannot prognosticate
So grave an honour.
Org.　　　　All this I acknowledge. 11
Crot. You do ! Then, son, if books and love of knowledge
Inflame you to this travel, here in Sparta
You may as freely study.

---

[1] Q. *Gransis*, throughout.
[3] A room in Crotolon's house.
[2] Q. *a fiction.*
[4] A member of the Areopagus, the highest judicial court in Athens.

Org.   'T is not that, sir.
Crot. Not that, sir! As a father, I command
thee   15
To acquaint me with the truth.
Org.   Thus I obey ye.
After so many quarrels as dissension,
Fury, and rage had broacht in blood, and some-
times
With death to such confederates as sided
With now-dead Thrasus and yourself, my lord;
Our present king, Amyclas, reconcil'd   21
Your eager swords and seal'd a gentle peace:
Friends you profest yourselves; which to con-
firm,
A resolution for a lasting league
Betwixt your families was entertain'd,   25
By joining in a Hymenean bond
Me and the fair Penthea, only daughter
To Thrasus.
Crot.   What of this?
Org.   Much, much, dear sir.
A freedom of converse, an interchange
Of holy and chaste love, so fixt our souls   30
In a firm growth of union, that no time
Can eat into the pledge: we had enjoy'd
The sweets our vows expected, had not cruelty
Prevented all those triumphs we prepar'd for,
By Thrasus his untimely death.
Crot.   Most certain. 35
Org. From this time sprouted up that poison-
ous stalk
Of aconite, whose ripened fruit hath ravisht
All health, all comfort of a happy life;
For Ithocles, her brother, proud of youth,
And prouder in his power, nourisht closely   40
The memory of former discontents,
To glory in revenge. By cunning partly,
Partly by threats, 'a woos at once and forces
His virtuous sister to admit a marriage
With Bassanes, a nobleman, in honour   45
And riches, I confess, beyond my fortunes.
Crot. All this is no sound reason to impor-
tune
My leave for thy departure.
Org.   Now it follows.
Beauteous Penthea, wedded to this torture
By an insulting brother, being secretly   50
Compell'd to yield her virgin freedom up
To him who never can usurp her heart,
Before contracted mine, is now so yok'd
To a most barbarous thraldrom, misery,
Affliction, that he savours not humanity,   55
Whose sorrow melts not into more than pity
In hearing but her name.
Crot.   As how, pray?
Org.   Bassanes,
The man that calls her wife, considers truly
What heaven of perfections he is lord of
By thinking fair Penthea his: this thought   59
Begets a kind of monster-love, which love
Is nurse unto a fear so strong and servile
As brands all dotage with a jealousy:
All eyes who gaze upon that shrine of beauty
He doth resolve [1] do homage to the miracle;   65
Some one, he is assur'd, may now or then,

If opportunity but sort, [2] prevail.
So much, out of a self-unworthiness,
His fears transport him; not that he finds
cause
In her obedience, but his own distrust.   70
Crot. You spin out your discourse.
Org.   My griefs are violent:
For knowing how the maid was heretofore
Courted by me, his jealousies grow wild
That I should steal again into her favours,
And undermine her virtues; which the gods   75
Know I nor dare nor dream of. Hence, from
hence
I undertake a voluntary exile;
First, by my absence to take off the cares
Of jealous Bassanes; but chiefly, sir,
To free Penthea from a hell on earth;   80
Lastly, to lose the memory of something
Her presence makes to live in me afresh.
Crot. Enough, my Orgilus, enough. To Ath
ens,
I give a full consent. — Alas, good lady! —
We shall hear from thee often?
Org.   Often.
Crot.   See,   85
Thy sister comes to give a farewell.

Enter EUPHRANEA.

Euph.   Brother!
Org. Euphranea, thus upon thy cheeks I
print
A brother's kiss; more careful of thine honour,
Thy health, and thy well-doing, than my life.
Before we part, in presence of our father,   90
I must prefer a suit t' ye.
Euph.   You may style it,
My brother, a command.
Org.   That you will promise
To pass never to any man, however
Worthy, your faith, till, with our father's
leave,
I give a free consent.
Crot.   An easy motion!   95
I 'll promise for her, Orgilus.
Org.   Your pardon;
Euphranea's oath must yield me satisfaction.
Euph. By Vesta's sacred fires I swear.
Crot.   And I,
By Great Apollo's beams, join in the vow,
Not without thy allowance to bestow her   100
On any living.
Org.   Dear Euphranea,
Mistake me not: far, far 't is from my thought,
As far from any wish of mine, to hinder
Preferment to an honourable bed
Or fitting fortune; thou art young and hand-
some;   105
And 't were injustice, — more, a tyranny, —
Not to advance thy merit. Trust me, sister,
It shall be my first care to see thee match'd
As may become thy choice and our contents. 109
I have your oath.
Euph.   You have. But mean you, brother,
To leave us, as you say?
Crot.   Ay, ay, Euphranea;

He has just grounds direct him. I will prove
A father and a brother to thee.
 Euph.   **Heaven**
Does look into the secrets of all hearts:
Gods, you have mercy with ye, else —
 Crot.   Doubt nothing ; 115
Thy brother will return in safety to us.
 Org. Souls sunk in sorrows never are without
  'em ;
They change fresh airs, but bear their griefs
 about 'em.   *Exeunt omnes.*

SCENE II.[1]

Flourish. Enter AMYCLAS the King, ARMOS-
TES, PROPHILUS, [Courtiers,] *and* Attendants.

 Amy. The Spartan gods are gracious ; our
  humility
Shall bend before their altars, and perfume
Their temples with abundant sacrifice.
See, lords, Amyclas, your old king, is ent'ring
Into his youth again ! I shall shake off 5
This silver badge of age, and change this snow
For hairs as gay as are Apollo's locks ;
Our heart leaps in new vigour.
 Arm.   May old time
Run back to double your long life, great sir !
 Amy. It will, it must, Armostes : thy bold
  nephew, 10
Death-braving Ithocles, brings to our gates
Triumphs and peace upon his conquering
  sword.
Laconia is a monarchy at length ;
Hath in this latter war trod under foot
Messene's pride ; Messene bows her neck 15
To Lacedaemon's royalty. O, 't was
A glorious victory, and doth deserve
More than a chronicle — a temple, lords,
A temple to the name of Ithocles.—
Where didst thou leave him, Prophilus ?
 Pro.   At Pephon, 20
Most gracious sovereign ; twenty of the noblest
Of the Messenians there attend your pleasure,
For such conditions as you shall propose
In settling peace, and liberty of life.
 Amy. When comes your friend, the general ?
 Pro.   He promis'd 25
To follow with all speed convenient.

Enter CALANTHA, EUPHRANEA ; CHRISTALLA
and PHILEMA [*with a garland ;*] *and* CROTO-
LON.

 Amy. Our daughter ! — Dear Calantha, the
  happy news,
The conquest of Messene, hath already
Enrich'd thy knowledge.
 Cal.   With the circumstance
And manner of the fight, related faithfully 30
By Prophilus himself.— But, pray, sir, tell me
How doth the youthful general demean
His actions in these fortunes ?
 Pro.   Excellent princess,
Your own fair eyes may soon report a truth
Unto your judgment, with what moderation, 35

[1] A room in the palace.

Calmness of nature, measure, bounds, and limits
Of thankfulness and joy, 'a doth digest
Such amplitude of his success as would
In others, moulded of a spirit less clear,
Advance 'em to comparison with heaven : 40
But Ithocles —
 Cal.   Your friend —
 Pro.   He is so, madam,
In which the period of my fate consists :
He, in this firmament of honour, stands
Like a star fixt, not mov'd with any thunder
Of popular applause or sudden lightning 45
Of self-opinion ; he hath serv'd his country,
And thinks 't was but his duty.
 Crot.   You describe
A miracle of man.
 Amy.   Such, Crotolon,
On forfeit of a king's word, thou wilt find
  him.—   *Flourish.* 49
Hark, warning of his coming ! All attend him.

Enter ITHOCLES, HEMOPHIL, *and* GRONEAS ;
the rest of the Lords *ushering him in.*

Return into these arms, thy home, thy sanctu-
  ary,
Delight of Sparta, treasure of my bosom,
Mine own, own Ithocles !
 Ith.   Your humblest subject.
 Arm. Proud of the blood I claim an interest
  in,
As brother to thy mother, I embrace thee, 55
Right noble nephew.
 Ith.   Sir, your love 's too partial.
 Crot. Our country speaks by me, who by thy
  valour,
Wisdom, and service, shares in this great ac-
  tion ;
Returning thee, in part of thy due merits,
A general welcome.
 Ith.   You exceed in bounty. 60
 Cal. Christalla, Philema, the chaplet. [*Takes
the chaplet from them.*] — Ithocles,
Upon the wings of Fame the singular
And chosen fortune of an high attempt
Is borne so past the view of common sight,
That I myself with mine own hands have
  wrought, 65
To crown thy temples, this provincial garland : [2]
Accept, wear, and enjoy it as our gift
Deserv'd, not purchas'd.
 Ith.   Y' are a royal maid.
 Amy. She is in all our daughter.
 Ith.   Let me blush,
Acknowledging how poorly I have serv'd, 70
What nothings I have done, compar'd with th'
  honours
Heap'd on the issue of a willing mind ;
In that lay mine ability, that only :
For who is he so sluggish from his birth,
So little worthy of a name or country, 75
That owes not out of gratitude for life
A debt of service, in what kind soever
Safety or counsel of the commonwealth
Requires, for payment ?

[2] The laurel wreath . . . conferred on those who
added a province to the empire. (Gifford.)

Cal.   'A speaks truth.
Ith.   Whom heaven
Is pleas'd to style victorious, there to such   80
Applause runs madding, like the drunken
          priests
In Bacchus' sacrifices, without reason,
Voicing the leader-on a demi-god ;
Whenas, indeed, each common soldier's blood
Drops down as current coin in that hard pur-
          chase   85
As his whose much more delicate condition
Hath suckt the milk of ease : judgment com-
          mands,
But resolution executes. I use not,
Before this royal presence, these fit slights [1]
As in contempt of such as can direct ;   90
My speech hath other end ; not to attribute
All praise to one man's fortune, which is
          strengthen'd
By many hands. For instance, here is Prophilus,
A gentleman — I cannot flatter truth —
Of much desert ; and, though in other rank, 95
Both Hemophil and Groneas were not missing
To wish their country's peace ; for, in a word,
All there did strive their best, and 't was our
          duty.
Amy. Courtiers turn soldiers ! — We vouch-
          safe our hand.
          [HEMOPHIL *and* GRONEAS *kiss his*
          hand.]
Observe your great example.
Hem.   With all diligence. 100
Gron. Obsequiously and hourly.
Amy.   Some repose
After these toils is [2] needful. We must think
          on
Conditions for the conquered ; they expect [3]
          'em.
On ! — Come, my Ithocles.
Euph.   Sir, with your favour,
I need not a supporter.
Pro.   Fate instructs me. 105
          Exeunt. HEMOPHIL *stays* CHRIS-
          TALLA ; GRONEAS, PHILEMA.
Chris. With me ?
Phil.   Indeed, I dare not stay.
Hem.   Sweet lady.
Soldiers are blunt,— your lip.
Chris.   Fie, this is rudeness :
You went not hence such creatures.
Gro.   Spirit of valour
Is of a mounting nature.
Phil.   It appears so.—
Pray, in earnest, how many men apiece   110
Have you two been the death of ?
Gro.   'Faith, not many ;
We were compos'd of mercy.
Hem.   For our daring,
You heard the general's approbation
Before the king.
Chris. You " wish'd your country's peace ; "
That show'd your charity : where are your
          spoils,   115
Such as the soldier fights for ?

Phil.   They are coming.
Chris. By the next carrier, are they not ?
Gro.   Sweet Philema,
When I was in the thickest of mine enemies,
Slashing off one man's head, another's nose,
Another's arms and legs,—
Phil.   And all together. 120
Gro. Then would I with a sigh remember
          thee,
And cry " Dear Philema, 't is for thy sake
I do these deeds of wonder ! " — Dost not love
          me
With all thy heart now ?
Phil.   Now as heretofore.
I have not put my love to use ; the principal 125
Will hardly yield an interest.
Gro.   By Mars,
I 'll marry thee !
Phil.   By Vulcan, you 're forsworn,
Except my mind do alter strangely.
Gro.   One word.
Chris. You lie beyond all modesty : — for-
          bear me.   129
Hem. I 'll make thee mistress of a city ; 't is
Mine own by conquest.
Chris.   By petition ; sue for 't
In forma pauperis.— City ! kennel. — Gallants,
Off with your feathers, put on aprons, gallants ;
Learn to reel, thrum,[4] or trim a lady's dog, 134
And be good quiet souls of peace, hobgoblins !
Hem. Christalla !
Chris.   Practise to drill hogs, in hope
To share in the acorns.— Soldiers ! corncutters,
But not so valiant ; they ofttimes draw blood,
Which you durst never do. When you have
          practis'd
More wit or more civility, we 'll rank ye   140
I' th' list of men : till then, brave things-at-
          arms,
Dare not to speak to us, — most potent Gro-
          neas ! —
Phil. And Hemophil the hardy ! — at your
          services.
          Exeunt CHRISTALLA *and* PHILEMA.
Gro. They scorn us as they did before we
          went.
Hem. Hang 'em ! let us scorn them, and be
          reveng'd.   145
Gro. Shall we ?
Hem. We will : and when we slight them thus,
Instead of following them, they 'll follow us ;
It is a woman's nature,
Gro.   'T is a scurvy one. *Exeunt.*

SCENE III.[5]

Enter TECNICUS, *a philosopher, and* ORGILUS
disguised like a Scholar *of his.*

Tec. Tempt not the stars ; young man, thou
          canst not play
With the severity of fate : this change
Of habit and disguise in outward view
Hides not the secrets of thy soul within thee
From their quick-piercing eyes, which dive at
          all times   5

----

[1] Appropriately belittling terms.
[2] Q. *are.*   [3] **Await.**

[4] **Weave.**   [5] The gardens of the palace. A grove.

Down to thy thoughts: in thy aspect I note
A consequence of danger.
   Org.   Give me leave,
Grave Tecnicus, without foredooming destiny,
Under thy roof to ease my silent griefs,
By applying to my hidden wounds the balm 10
Of thy oraculous lectures. If my fortune
Run such a crooked by-way as to wrest
My steps to ruin, yet thy learned precepts
Shall call me back and set my footings straight.
I will not court the world.
   Tec.   Ah, Orgilus, 15
Neglects in young men of delights and life
Run often to extremities; they care not
For harms to others who contemn their own.
   Org. But I, most learned artist, am not so
     much
At odds with nature that I grudge the thrift 20
Of any true deserver; nor doth malice
Of present hopes so check them with despair
As that I yield to thought of more affliction
Than what is incident to frailty: wherefore
Impute not this retired course of living 25
Some little time to any other cause
Than what I justly render, — the information
Of an unsettled mind; as the effect
Must clearly witness.
   Tec.   Spirit of truth inspire thee!
On these conditions I conceal thy change, 30
And willingly admit thee for an auditor. —
I'll to my study.
   Org.   I to contemplations
In these delightful walks. — *Exit* TECNICUS.
                Thus metamorphos'd
I may without suspicion hearken after
Penthea's usage and Euphranea's faith. 35
Love, thou art full of mystery! The deities
Themselves are not secure [1] in searching out
The secrets of those flames, which, hidden,
    waste
A breast made tributary to the laws
Of beauty: physic yet hath never found 40
A remedy to cure a lover's wound. —
Ha! who are those that cross yon private walk
Into the shadowing grove in amorous foldings?

PROPHILUS *passeth over, supporting* [2] EUPHRA-
    NEA, *and whispering.*

My sister! O, my sister! 't is Euphranea
With Prophilus: supported too! I would 45
It were an apparition! Prophilus
Is Ithocles his friend: it strangely puzzles me.
Again! help me, my book; this scholar's habit
Must stand my privilege: my mind is busy,
Mine eyes and ears are open.
                Walks by, reading.

Re-enter PROPHILUS *and* EUPHRANEA.

   Pro.   Do not waste 50
The span of this stol'n time, lent by the gods
For precious use, in niceness.[3] Bright Eu-
    phranea,
Should I repeat old vows, or study new,
For purchase of belief to my desires, —

  [1] Certain.
  [2] With his arm round her waist. (Dyce.)
  [3] Coyness; over-particular scruples.

   Org. [*Aside.*] Desires!
   Pro.   My service, my integrity, — 55
   Org. [*Aside.*] That's better.
   Pro.   I should but repeat a lesson
Oft conn'd without a prompter but thine eyes.
My love is honourable.
   Org. [*Aside*]   So was mine
To my Penthea, chastely honourable.
   Pro. Nor wants there more addition to my
    wish 60
Of happiness than having thee a wife;
Already sure of Ithocles, a friend
Firm and unalterable.
   Org. [*Aside.*]   But a brother
More cruel than the grave.
   Euph.   What can you look for,
In answer to your noble protestations, 65
From an unskilful maid, but language suited
To a divided mind?
   Org. [*Aside.*]   Hold out, Euphranea!
   Euph. Know, Prophilus, I never undervalu'd,
From the first time you mentioned worthy love,
Your merit, means, or person: it had been 70
A fault of judgment in me, and a dulness
In my affections, not to weigh and thank
My better stars that offered me the grace
Of so much blissfulness. For, to speak truth,
The law of my desires kept equal pace 75
With yours; nor have I left that resolution:
But only, in a word, whatever choice
Lives nearest in my heart must first procure
Consent both from my father and my brother,
Ere he can own me his.
   Org. [*Aside.*]   She is forsworn else. 80
   Pro. Leave me that task.
   Euph.   My brother, ere he parted
To Athens, had my oath.
   Org. [*Aside.*]   Yes, yes, 'a had, sure.
   Pro. I doubt not, with the means the court
    supplies,
But to prevail at pleasure.
   Org. [*Aside.*]   Very likely!
   Pro. Meantime, best, dearest, I may build
    my hopes 85
On the foundation of thy constant suff'rance
In any opposition.
   Euph.   Death shall sooner
Divorce life and the joys I have in living
Than my chaste vows from truth.
   Pro.   On thy fair hand
I seal the like. 90
   Org. [*Aside.*] There is no faith in woman.
Passion, O, be contain'd! My very heart-strings
Are on the tenters.[4]
   Euph.   Sir, we are overheard.
Cupid protect us! 'T was a stirring, sir,
Of some one near.
   Pro.   Your fears are needless, lady; 95
None have access into these private pleasures
Except some near in court, or bosom-student
From Tecnicus his oratory, granted
By special favour lately from the king
Unto the grave philosopher.
   Euph.   Methinks 100
I hear one talking to himself, — I see him.

  [4] Hooks for stretching cloth; on the rack.

Pro. 'T is a poor scholar, as I told you, lady.

Org. [*Aside.*] I am discovered. — [*Half aloud to himself, as if studying.*] Say it; is it possible,
With a smooth tongue, a leering countenance,
Flattery, or force of reason — I come t' ye, sir — 105
To turn or to appease the raging sea?
Answer to that. — Your art! what art to catch
And hold fast in a net the sun's small atoms?
No, no; they 'll out, they 'll out: ye may as easily
Outrun a cloud driven by a northern blast 110
As fiddle-faddle so! Peace, or speak sense,

Euph. Call you this thing a scholar? 'Las, he 's lunatic.

Pro. Observe him, sweet; 't is but his recreation.

Org. But will you hear a little? You 're so tetchy,
You keep no rule in argument. Philosophy 115
Works not upon impossibilities,
But natural conclusions. — Mew! — absurd!
The metaphysics are but speculations
Of the celestial bodies, or such accidents
As not mixt perfectly, in the air engend'red 120
Appear to us unnatural; that 's all.
Prove it; yet, with a reverence to your gravity,
I 'll balk illiterate sauciness, submitting
My sole opinion to the touch of writers.

Pro. Now let us fall in with him.
           [*They come forward.*]

Org.   Ha, ha, ha! 125
These apish boys, when they but taste the grammates [1]
And principles of theory, imagine
They can oppose their teachers. Confidence
Leads many into errors.

Pro.   By your leave, sir.

Euph. Are you a scholar, friend?

Org.   I am, gay creature, 130
With pardon of your deities, a mushroom
On whom the dew of heaven drops now and then;
The sun shines on me too, I thank his beams!
Sometime I feel their warmth; and eat and sleep.

Pro. Does Tecnicus read to thee?

Org.   Yes, forsooth, 135
He is my master surely; yonder door
Opens upon his study.

Pro.   Happy creatures!
Such people toil not, sweet, in heats of state,
Nor sink in thaws of greatness; their affections
Keep order with the limits of their modesty; 140
Their love is love of virtue. — What 's thy name?

Org. Aplotes, sumptuous master, a poor wretch.

Euph. Dost thou want anything?

Org. Books, Venus, books.

Pro. Lady, a new conceit comes in my thought,
And most available for both our comforts. 145

Euph. My lord, —

Pro.   Whiles I endeavour to deserve
Your father's blessing to our loves, this scholar
May daily at some certain hours attend [2]
What notice I can write of my success, 149
Here in this grove, and give it to your hands;
The like from you to me: so can we never,
Barr'd of our mutual speech, want sure intelligence,
And thus our hearts may talk when our tongues cannot.

Euph. Occasion is most favourable; use it.

Pro. Aplotes, wilt thou wait us twice a day,
At nine i' the morning and at four at night, 156
Here in this bower, to convey such letters
As each shall send to other? Do it willingly,
Safely, and secretly, and I will furnish
Thy study, or what else thou canst desire. 160

Org. Jove, make me thankful, thankful, I beseech thee,
Propitious Jove! I will prove sure and trusty:
You will not fail me books?

Pro.   Nor aught besides
Thy heart can wish. This lady's name 's Euphranea,
Mine Prophilus.

Org.   I have a pretty memory; 165
It must prove my best friend. I will not miss
One minute of the hours appointed.

Pro.   Write
The books thou wouldst have bought thee in a note,
Or take thyself some money.

Org.   No, no money;
Money to scholars is a spirit invisible, 170
We dare not finger it: or books, or nothing.

Pro. Books of what sort thou wilt: do not forget
Our names.

Org.   I warrant ye, I warrant ye.

Pro. Smile, Hymen, on the growth of our desires;
We 'll feed thy torches with eternal fires! 175
       Exeunt PROPHILUS *and* EUPHRANEA.

Org. Put out thy torches, Hymen, or their light
Shall meet a darkness of eternal night!
Inspire me, Mercury, with swift deceits.
Ingenious Fate has leapt into mine arms,
Beyond the compass of my brain. [3] Mortality 180
Creeps on the dung of earth, and cannot reach
The riddles which are purpos'd by the gods.
Great arts best write themselves in their own stories;
They die too basely who outlive their glories.
                  Exit.

ACT II

SCENE I. [4]

Enter BASSANES *and* PHULAS.

Bass. I 'll have that window next the street damm'd up;

---

[1] Rudiments.
[2] Wait for.
[3] Beyond what I could have planned.
[4] A room in Bassanes' house.

It gives too full a prospect to temptation,
And courts a gazer's glances. There 's a lust
Committed by the eye, that sweats and trav-
ails,
Plots, wakes, contrives, till the deformed bear-
whelp,   5
Adultery, be lick'd into the act,
The very act. That light shall be damm'd up ;
D' ye hear, sir ?
Phu.   I do hear, my lord ; a mason
Shall be provided suddenly.[1]
Bass.   Some rogue,
Some rogue of your confederacy, — factor[2]   10
For slaves and strumpets ! — to convey close
packets
From this spruce springal[3] and t' other young-
ster,
That gaudy earwig, or my lord your patron,
Whose pensioner you are. — I 'll tear thy throat
out,
Son of a cat, ill-looking hound's-head, rip-up   15
Thy ulcerous maw, if I but scent a paper,
A scroll, but half as big as what can cover
A wart upon thy nose, a spot, a pimple,
Directed to my lady ; it may prove
A mystical preparative to lewdness.   20
Phu. Care shall be had : I will turn every
thread
About me to an eye. — [*Aside.*] Here 's a sweet
life !
Bass. The city housewives, cunning in the
traffic
Of chamber merchandise, set all at price
By wholesale ; yet they wipe their mouths and
simper,   25
Cull,[4] kiss, and cry " sweetheart," and stroke
the head
Which they have branch'd ;[5] and all is well
again !
Dull clods of dirt, who dare not feel the rubs
Stuck on the[ir] foreheads.
Phu.   'T is a villanous world ;
One cannot hold his own in 't.
Bass.   Dames at court, 30
Who flaunt in riots, run another bias ;[6]
Their pleasure heaves the patient ass that suf-
fers
Up on the stilts of office, titles, incomes ;
Promotion justifies the shame, and sues for 't.
Poor honour, thou art stabb'd, and bleed'st to
death   35
By such unlawful hire ! The country mistress
Is yet more wary, and in blushes hides
Whatever trespass draws her troth to guilt.
But all are false : on this truth I am bold,
No woman but can fall, and doth, or would. —
Now for the newest news about the city ;   41
What blab the voices, sirrah ?
Phu.   O, my lord,
The rarest, quaintest, strangest, tickling news
That ever —
Bass.   Hey-day ! up and ride me, rascal !
What is 't ?

[1] At once.   [2] Agent.   [3] Youth.   [4] Embrace.
[5] Cuckolded : the inevitable jest on the cuckold's
horns.
[6] Direction.

Phu.   Forsooth, they say the king has
mew'd[7]   45
All his gray beard, instead of which is budded
Another of a pure carnation colour,
Speckled with green and russet.
Bass.   Ignorant block !
Phu. Yes, truly ; and 't is talkt about the
streets
That, since Lord Ithocles came home, the lions
Never left roaring, at which noise the bears 51
Have danc'd their very hearts out.
Bass.   Dance out thine too.
Phu. Besides, Lord Orgilus is fled to Athens
Upon a fiery dragon, and 't is thought
'A never can return.
Bass.   Grant it, Apollo !   55
Phu. Moreover, please your lordship, 't is re-
ported
For certain, that whoever is found jealous
Without apparent proof that 's wife is wanton
Shall be divorce'd : but this is but she-news ;
I had it from a midwife. I have more yet.   60
Bass. Antic, no more ! Idiots and stupid fools
Grate my calamities. Why to be fair
Should yield presumption of a faulty soul --
Look to the doors.
Phu. [*Aside.*] The horn of plenty crest him !
Exit.
Bass. Swarms of confusion huddle in my
thoughts   65
In rare distemper. — Beauty ! O, it is
An unmatcht blessing or a horrid curse.

Enter PENTHEA *and* GRAUSIS, *an old* Lady.

She comes, she comes ! so shoots the morning
forth,
Spangled with pearls of transparent dew. —
The way to poverty is to be rich,   70
As I in her am wealthy ; but for her,
In all contents a bankrupt. —
Lov'd Penthea !
How fares my heart's best joy ?
Grau.   In sooth, not well,
She is so over-sad.
Bass.   Leave chattering, magpie. —
Thy brother is return'd, sweet, safe, and hon-
our'd   75
With a triumphant victory ; thou shalt visit
him :
We will to court, where, if it be thy pleasure,
Thou shalt appear in such a ravishing lustre
Of jewels above value, that the dames
Who brave it there, in rage to be outshin'd,   80
Shall hide them in their closets, and unseen
Fret in their tears ; whiles every wond'ring eye
Shall crave none other brightness but thy pres-
ence.
Choose thine own recreations ; be a queen
Of what delights thou fanciest best, what com-
pany,   85
What place, what times ; do anything, do all
things
Youth can command, so thou wilt chase these
clouds
From the pure firmament of thy fair looks.

[7] Moulted.

Grau. Now 't is well said, my lord. — What,
 lady ! laugh,
Be merry ; time is precious.
 Bass. [*Aside.*]   Furies whip thee ! 90
 Pen. Alas, my lord, this language to your
 hand-maid
Sounds as would music to the deaf ; I need
No braveries nor cost of art to draw
The whiteness of my name into offence :
Let such, if any such there are, who covet 95
A curiosity of admiration,
By laying-out their plenty to full view,
Appear in gaudy outsides ; my attires
Shall suit the inward fashion of my mind ;
From which, if your opinion, nobly plac'd, 100
Change not the livery your words bestow,
My fortunes with my hopes are at the highest.
 Bass. This house, methinks, stands some-
 what too much inward,
It is too melancholy ; we 'll remove 104
Nearer the court : or what thinks my Penthea
Of the delightful island we command ?
Rule me as thou canst wish.
 Pen.   I am no mistress.
Whither you please, I must attend ; all ways
Are alike pleasant to me.
 Grau.   Island ; prison !
A prison is as gaysome : we 'll no islands ; 110
Marry, out upon 'em ! Whom shall we see
 there ?
Sea-gulls, and porpoises, and water-rats,
And crabs, and mews, and dog-fish ; goodly
 gear
For a young lady's dealing, — or an old one's !
On no terms islands ; I 'll be stew'd first.
 Bass. [*Aside to* GRAUSIS.] Grausis, 115
You are a juggling bawd. — This sadness,
 sweetest,
Becomes not youthful blood. — [*Aside to* GRAU-
 SIS.] I 'll have you pounded. —
For my sake put on a more cheerful mirth ;
Thou 'lt mar thy cheeks, and make me old in
 griefs. —
[*Aside to* GRAUSIS.] Damnable bitch-fox !
 Grau.   I am thick of hearing, 120
Still, when the wind blows southerly. — What
 think ye,
If your fresh lady breed young bones, my
 lord ?
Would not a chopping boy d' ye good at heart ?
But, as you said —
 Bass. [*Aside to* GRAUSIS.] I 'll spit thee on a
 stake,
Or chop thee into collops !
 Grau.   Pray, speak louder. 125
Sure, sure the wind blows south still.
 Pen.   Thou prat'st madly.
 Bass. 'T is very hot ; I sweat extremely.

    Re-enter PHULAS.

           Now ?
 Phu. A herd of lords, sir.
 Bass.   Ha !
 Phu.   A flock of ladies.
 Bass. Where ?
 Phu.   Shoals of horses.
 Bass.   Peasant, how ?

Phu.   Caroches [1]
In drifts ; th' one enter, th' other stand with-
 out, sir :   130
And now I vanish.   *Exit.*

Enter PROPHILUS, HEMOPHIL, GRONEAS,
  CHRISTALLA, *and* PHILEMA.

 Pro.   Noble Bassanes !
 Bass. Most welcome, Prophilus ; ladies, gen-
 tlemen,
To all my heart is open ; you all honour me, —
[*Aside.*] A tympany [2] swells in my head al-
 ready, —
Honour me bountifully. — [*Aside.*] How they
 flutter,   135
Wagtails and jays together !
 Pro.   From your brother
By virtue of your love to him, I require
Your instant presence, fairest.
 Pen.   He is well, sir ?
 Pro. The gods preserve him ever ! Yet, dear
 beauty,
I find some alteration in him lately, 140
Since his return to Sparta. — My good lord,
I pray, use no delay.
 Bass. We had not needed
An invitation, if his sister's health
Had not fallen into question. — Haste, Penthea,
Slack not a minute. — Lead the way, good
 Prophilus ;   145
I 'll follow step by step.
 Pro.   Your arm, fair madam.
   Exeunt all but BASSANES *and* GRAUSIS.
 Bass. One word with your old bawdship : th'
 hadst been better
Rail'd at the sins [3] thou worshipp'st than have
 thwarted
My will : I 'll use thee cursedly.
 Grau.   You dote,
You are beside yourself. A politician 150
In jealousy ? No, y' are too gross, too vulgar.
Pish, teach not me my trade ; I know my cue.
My crossing you sinks me into her trust,
By which I shall know all ; my trade 's a sure
 one.
 Bass. Forgive me, Grausis, 't was considera-
 tion   155
I relish'd not ; [4] but have a care now.
 Grau.   Fear not,
I am no new-come-to 't.
 Bass.   Thy life 's upon it,
And so is mine. My agonies are infinite.
          Exeunt.

     SCENE II.[5]

   Enter ITHOCLES, *alone.*

 Ith. Ambition ! 't is of vipers' breed : it
 gnaws
A passage through the womb that gave it mo-
 tion.
Ambition, like a seeled [6] dove, mounts upward,
Higher and higher still, to perch on clouds,
But tumbles headlong down with heavier ruin.

---

[1] Coaches.   [3] Gifford emend. *saints.*
[2] Swelling.   [4] I did not see the point of.
[5] The palace. Ithocles' apartment.
[6] Blinded by sewing up the eye-lids.

So squibs and crackers fly into the air,   6
Then, only breaking with a noise, they vanish
In stench and smoke. Morality, appli'd
To timely practice, keeps the soul in tune,
At whose sweet music all our actions dance: 10
But this is form of books and school-tradition ;
It physics not the sickness of a mind
Broken with griefs : strong fevers are not eas'd
With counsel, but with best receipts and means ;
Means, speedy means and certain ; that 's the
    cure.   15

Enter ARMOSTES *and* CROTOLON.

Arm. You stick, Lord Crotolon, upon a point
Too nice and too unnecessary ; Prophilus
Is every way desertful. I am confident
Your wisdom is too ripe to need instruction
From your son's tutelage.
Crot.   Yet not so ripe,   20
My Lord Armostes, that it dares to dote
Upon the painted meat[1] of smooth persuasion,
Which tempts me to a breach of faith.
Ith.   Not yet
Resolv'd, my lord ? Why, if your son's consent
Be so available, we 'll write to Athens   25
For his repair to Sparta. The king's hand
Will join with our desires ; he has been mov'd
    to 't.
Arm. Yes, and the king himself impórtun'd
    Crotolon
For a dispatch.
Crot.   Kings may command ; their wills
Are laws not to be questioned.
Ith.   By this marriage 30
You knit an union so devout, so hearty,
Between your loves to me and mine to yours,
As if mine own blood had an interest in it ;
For Prophilus is mine, and I am his.
Crot. My lord, my lord ! —
Ith. What, good sir ? Speak your thought.   35
Crot. Had this sincerity been real once,
My Orgilus had not been now unwiv'd,
Nor your lost sister buried in a bride-bed.
Your uncle here, Armostes, knows this truth ;
For had your father Thrasus liv'd, — but peace
Dwell in his grave ! I have done.
Arm.   Y' are bold and bitter. 41
Ith. [*Aside.*] 'A presses home the injury ; it
    smarts. —
No reprehensions, uncle ; I deserve 'em.
Yet, gentle sir, consider what the heat
Of an unsteady youth, a giddy brain,   45
Green indiscretion, flattery of greatness,
Rawness of judgment, wilfulness in folly,
Thoughts vagrant as the wind and as uncertain,
Might lead a boy in years to : — 't was a fault,
A capital fault ; for then I could not dive   50
Into the secrets of commanding love ;
Since when, experience, by the extremes[2] (in
    others),
Hath forc'd me collect.[3] And, trust me, Croto-
    lon,
I will redeem those wrongs with any service
Your satisfaction can require for current.   55

[1] Gifford suggests *bait*.
[2] Q. *extremities*.
[3] Infer, understand.

Arm. The[4] acknowledgment is satisfaction :
What would you more ?
Crot.   I 'm conquer'd : if Euphranea
Herself admit the motion, let it be so ;
I doubt not my son's liking.
Ith.   Use my fortunes,
Life, power, sword, and heart, — all are your
    own.   60
Arm. The princess, with your sister.

Enter CALANTHA, PENTHEA, EUPHRANEA,
    CHRISTALLA, PHILEMA, GRAUSIS, BASSANES,
    and PROPHILUS.

Cal.   I present ye
A stranger here in court, my lord ; for did not
Desire of seeing you draw her abroad,
We had not been made happy in her company.
Ith. You are a gracious princess. — Sister,
    wedlock   65
Holds too severe a passion in your nature,
Which can engross all duty to your husband,
Without attendance on so dear a mistress. —
[*To* BASSANES.] 'T is not my brother's pleasure,
    I presume,
T' immure her in a chamber.
Bass.   'T is her will ; 70
She governs her own hours. Noble Ithocles,
We thank the gods for your success and wel-
    fare :
Our lady has of late been indispos'd,
Else we had waited on you with the first.
Ith. How does Penthea now ?
Pen.   You best know, brother, 75
From whom my health and comforts are de-
    riv'd.
Bass. [*Aside.*] I like the answer well ; 'tis
    sad and modest.
There can be tricks yet, tricks. — Have an eye,
    Grausis !
Cal. Now, Crotolon, the suit we join'd in
    must not
Fall by too long demur.
Crot.   'T is granted, princess, 80
For my part.
Arm.   With condition, that his son
Favour the contract.
Cal.   Such delay is easy. —
The joys of marriage make thee, Prophilus,
A proud deserver of Euphranea's love,
And her of thy desert !
Pro.   Most sweetly gracious ! 85
Bass. The joys of marriage are the heaven on
    earth,
Life's paradise, great princess, the soul's quiet,
Sinews of concord, earthly immortality,
Eternity of pleasures ; — no restoratives
Like to a constant woman ! — [*Aside.*] But
    where is she ?   90
'T would puzzle all the gods but to create
Such a new monster. — I can speak by proof,
For I rest in Elysium ; 'tis my happiness.
Crot. Euphranea, how are you resolv'd, speak
    freely,
In your affections to this gentleman ?   95
Euph. Nor more nor less than as his love as-
    sures me ;
                                      [4] Q. *Thy*.

Which — if your liking with my brother's war-
rants —
I cannot but approve in all points worthy.
   Crot. So, so ! — [*To* PROPHILUS.] I know your
answer.
   Ith.   'T had been pity
To sunder hearts so equally consented.   100

Enter HEMOPHIL.

   Hem. The king, Lord Ithocles, commands
your presence ; —
And, fairest princess, yours.
   Cal.   We will attend him.

Enter GRONEAS.

   Gro. Where are the lords ? All must unto the
king
Without delay: the Prince of Argos —
   Cal.   Well, sir?
   Gro. Is coming to the court, sweet lady.
   Cal.   How ! 105
The Prince of Argos ?
   Gro.   'T was my fortune, madam,
T' enjoy the honour of these happy tidings.
   Ith. Penthea ! —
   Pen.   Brother ?
   Ith.   Let me an hour hence
Meet you alone within the palace-grove ;   109
I have some secret with you. — Prithee, friend,
Conduct her thither, and have special care
The walks be clear'd of any to disturb us.
   Pro. I shall.
   Bass. [*Aside.*] How 's that?
   Ith.   Alone, pray be alone. —
I am your creature, princess. — On, my lords !
                 Exeunt all but BASSANES.
   Bass. Alone ! alone ! What means that word
" alone "?   115
Why might not I be there ? — hum ! — he 's
her brother.
Brothers and sisters are but flesh and blood,
And this same whoreson court-ease is tempta-
tion
To a rebellion in the veins ; — besides,   119
His fine friend Prophilus must be her guar-
dian :
Why may not he dispatch a business nimbly
Before the other come ? — or — pand'ring, pan-
d'ring
For one another, — be 't to sister, mother,
Wife, cousin, anything, — 'mongst youths of
mettle
Is in request ; it is so — stubborn fate !   125
But if I be a cuckold, and can know it,
I will be fell, and fell.

Re-enter GRONEAS.

   Gro.   My lord, y 'are call'd for.
   Bass. Most heartily I thank ye. Where 's my
wife, pray ?
   Gro. Retir'd amongst the ladies.
   Bass.   Still I thank ye.
There 's an old waiter with her ; saw you her
too ?   130
   Gro. She sits i' th' presence-lobby fast asleep,
sir.
   Bass. Asleep ! asleep, sir !

   Gro.   Is your lordship troubled ?
You will not to the king ?
   Bass.   Your humblest vassal.
   Gro. Your servant, my good lord.
   Bass.   I wait your footsteps.
                         Exeunt.

SCENE III.[1]

Enter PROPHILUS *and* PENTHEA.

   Pro. In this walk, lady, will your brother find
you :
And, with your favour, give me leave a little
To work a preparation. In his fashion
I have observ'd of late some kind of slackness
To such alacrity as nature [once]   5
And custom took delight in ; sadness grows
Upon his recreations, which he hoards
In such a willing silence, that to question
The grounds will argue little skill in friendship,
And less good manners.
   Pen.   Sir, I 'm not inquisitive   10
Of secrecies without an invitation.
   Pro. With pardon, lady, not a syllable
Of mine implies so rude a sense ; the drift —

Enter ORGILUS, [*disguised as before.*]

[*To* ORG.] Do thy best
To make this lady merry for an hour. *Exit.* 15
   Org. Your will shall be a law, sir.
   Pen.   Prithee, leave me ;
I have some private thoughts I would account
with ;
Use thou thine own.
   Org.   Speak on, fair nymph ; our souls
Can dance as well to music of the spheres
As any 's who have feasted with the gods.   20
   Pen. Your school-terms are too troublesome.
   Org.   What Heaven
Refines mortality from dross of earth
But such as uncompounded beauty hallows
With glorified perfection ?
   Pen.   Set thy wits
In a less wild proportion.
   Org.   Time can never   25
On the white table of unguilty faith
Write counterfeit dishonour ; turn those eyes,
The arrows of pure love, upon that fire,
Which once rose to a flame, perfum'd with
vows
As sweetly scented as the incense smoking   30
On Vesta's altars, ...[2]
. . . the holiest odours, virgin's tears,
. . . . . sprinkled, like dews, to feed 'em
And to increase their fervour.
   Pen.   Be not frantic.
   Org. All pleasures are but mere imagination,
Feeding the hungry appetite with steam   35
And sight of banquet, whilst the body pines,
Not relishing the real taste of food :
Such is the leanness of a heart divided
From intercourse of troth-contracted loves ;   40

---

[1] The gardens of the palace. A grove.
[2] Gifford's emend. Q. reads
     as the incense smoking
The holiest altars, virgin tears (like
On Vesta's odours) sprinkled dews to feed 'em,
And to increase.

No horror should deface that precious figure
Seal'd with the lively stamp of equal souls.
  Pen. Away ! some Fury hath bewitch'd thy
  tongue.
The breath of ignorance, that flies from thence,
Ripens a knowledge in me of afflictions   45
Above all suff'rance. — Thing of talk, begone !
Begone, without reply !
  Org.   Be just, Penthea,
In thy commands ; when thou send'st forth a
  doom
Of banishment, know first on whom it lights.
Thus I take off the shroud, in which my cares 50
Are folded up from view of common eyes.
              [*Throws off his* Scholar's *dress.*]
What is thy sentence next ?
  Pen.   Rash man ! thou layest
A blemish on mine honour, with the hazard
Of thy too-desperate life : yet I profess,
By all the laws of ceremonious wedlock,   55
I have not given admittance to one thought
Of female change since cruelty enforc'd
Divorce betwixt my body and my heart.
Why would you fall from goodness thus ?
  Org.   O, rather
Examine me, how I could live to say   60
I have been much, much wrong'd. 'T is for thy
  sake
I put on this imposture : dear Penthea,
If thy soft bosom be not turn'd to marble,
Thou 'lt pity our calamities ; my interest
Confirms me thou art mine still.
  Pen.   Lend your hand ;   65
With both of mine I clasp it thus, thus kiss it,
Thus kneel before ye.
  Org.   You instruct my duty.
  Pen. We may stand up. — Have you aught
    else to urge
Of new demand ? As for the old, forget it ;
'T is buried in an everlasting silence,   70
And shall be, shall be ever. What more would
  ye ?
  Org. I would possess my wife ; the equity
Of very reason bids me.
  Pen.   Is that all ?
  Org. Why, 't is the all of me, myself.
  Pen.   Remove
Your steps some distance from me : — at this
  space   75
A few words I dare change ; but first put on
Your borrowed shape.
  Org.   You are obey'd ; 't is done.
              [*He resumes his disguise.*]
  Pen. How, Orgilus, by promise I was thine
The heavens do witness : they can witness too
A rape done on my truth : how I do love thee   80
Yet, Orgilus, and yet, must best appear
In tendering thy freedom ; for I find
The constant preservation of thy merit,
By thy not daring to attempt my fame
With injury of any loose conceit,   85
Which might give deeper wounds to discon-
  tents.
Continue this fair race : [1] then, though I cannot
Add to thy comfort, yet I shall more often

Remember from what fortune I am fallen,   89
And pity mine own ruin. — Live, live happy,—
Happy in thy next choice, that thou mayst peo-
  ple
This barren age with virtues in thy issue !
And O, when thou art married, think on me
With mercy, not contempt ! I hope thy wife,
Hearing my story, will not scorn my fall. —   6
Now let us part.
  Org.   Part ! yet advise thee better :
Penthea is the wife to Orgilus,
And ever shall be.
  Pen.   Never shall nor will.
  Org. How !
  Pen. Hear me ; in a word I 'll tell thee why.
The virgin-dowry which my birth bestow'd   10b
Is ravish'd by another ; my true love
Abhors to think that Orgilus deserv'd
No better favours than a second bed.
  Org. I must not take this reason.
  Pen.   To confirm it
Should I outlive my bondage, let me meet   10a.
Another worse than this and less desir'd,
If, of all men alive, thou shouldst but touch
My lip or hand again !
  Org.   Penthea, now
I tell ye, you grow wanton in my sufferance :
Come, sweet, th' art mine.
  Pen.   Uncivil sir, forbear ! 110
Or I can turn affection into vengeance ;
Your reputation, if you value any,
Lies bleeding at my feet. Unworthy man,
If ever henceforth thou appear in language,
Message, or letter, to betray my frailty,   115
I 'll call thy former protestations lust,
And curse my stars for forfeit of my judgment.
Go thou, fit only for disguise, and walks,[2]
To hide thy shame : this once I spare thy life.
I laugh at mine own confidence ; my sorrows
By thee are made inferior to my fortunes.   121
If ever thou didst harbour worthy love,
Dare not to answer. My good genius guide me,
That I may never see thee more ! — Go from
  me !
  Org. I 'll tear my veil of politic French off,
And stand up like a man resolv'd to do :   126
Action, not words, shall show me. — O Penthea !
                                           Exit.
  Pen. 'A sighed my name, sure, as he parted
  from me :
I fear I was too rough. Alas, poor gentleman
'A look'd not like the ruins of his youth,   130
But like the ruins of those ruins. Honour,
How much we fight with weakness to preserve
  thee !   [*Walks aside.*]

Enter BASSANES *and* GRAUSIS.

  Bass. Fie on thee ! damn thee, rotten mag-
    got, damn thee !
Sleep ? sleep at court ? and now ? Aches,[3] con-
    vulsions,
Imposthumes, rheums, gouts, palsies, clog thy
  bones   135
A dozen years more yet !

---

[1] Course.

[2] Apparently corrupt.
[3] The word was pronounced *aitches.*

Grau.   Now y' are in humours.
Bass. She 's by herself, there 's hope of that;
  she 's sad too ;
She 's in strong contemplation ; yes, and fixt :
The signs are wholesome.
Grau.   Very wholesome, truly.
Bass. Hold your chops,[1] nightmare ! — Lady,
  come ; your brother   140
Is carried to his closet ; you must thither.
Pen. Not well, my lord ?
Bass.   A sudden fit ; 't will off !
Some surfeit or disorder. — How dost, dearest ?
Pen. Your news is none o' the best.

Re-enter PROPHILUS.

Pro.   The chief of men,
The excellentest Ithocles, desires   145
Your presence, madam.
Bass.   We are hasting to him.
Pen. In vain we labour in this course of life
To piece our journey out at length, or crave
Respite of breath : our home is in the grave.
Bass. Perfect philosophy !
[*Pen.*]   Then let us care   150
To live so, that our reckonings may fall even
When we 're to make account.
Pro.   He cannot fear
Who builds on noble grounds : sickness or pain
Is the deserver's exercise ;[2] and such
Your virtuous brother to the world is known.
Speak comfort to him, lady ; be all gentle :   155
Stars fall but in the grossness of our sight ;
A good man dying, th' earth doth lose a light.
                              Exeunt omnes.

ACT III

SCENE I.[3]

Enter TECNICUS, *and* ORGILUS *in his own
shape.*

Tec. Be well advis'd ; let not a resolution
Of giddy rashness choke the breath of reason.
Org. It shall not, most sage master.
Tec.   I am jealous ;[4]
For if the borrowed shape so late put on
Inferr'd a consequence, we must conclude   5
Some violent design of sudden nature
Hath shook that shadow off, to fly upon
A new-hatch'd execution. Orgilus,
Take heed thou hast not, under our integrity,
Shrouded unlawful plots ; our mortal eyes   10
Pierce not the secrets of your heart, the gods
Are only privy to them.
Org.   Learned Tecnicus,
Such doubts are causeless ; and, to clear the
  truth
From misconceit, the present state commands
  me.
The Prince of Argos comes himself in person   15
In quest of great Calantha for his bride,
Our kingdom's heir ; besides, mine only sister,
Euphranea, is dispos'd to Prophilus ;
Lastly, the king is sending letters for me

To Athens, for my quick repair to court :   20
Please to accept these reasons.
Tec.   Just ones, Orgilus,
Not to be contradicted : yet beware
Of an unsure foundation ; no fair colours
Can fortify a building faintly jointed.
I have observ'd a growth in thy aspéct   25
Of dangerous extent, sudden, and — look to 't —
I might add, certain —
Org.   My aspéct ! Could art
Run through mine inmost thoughts, it should
  not sift
An inclination there more than what suited
With justice of mine honour.
Tec.   I believe it.   30
But know then, Orgilus, what honour is.
Honour consists not in a bare opinion
By doing any act that feeds content,
Brave in appearance, 'cause we think it brave ;
Such honour comes by accident, not nature,   35
Proceeding from the vices of our passion,
Which makes our reason drunk : but real hon-
  our
Is the reward of virtue, and acquir'd
By justice, or by valour which for basis
Hath justice to uphold it. He then fails   40
In honour, who for lucre [or] revenge
Commits thefts, murders, treasons, and adul-
  teries,
With suchlike, by intrenching on just laws,
Whose sovereignty is best preserv'd by justice.
Thus, as you see how honour must be grounded
On knowledge, not opinion,— for opinion   46
Relies on probability and accident,
But knowledge on necessity and truth,—
I leave thee to the fit consideration
Of what becomes the grace of real honour,   50
Wishing success to all thy virtuous meanings.
Org. The gods increase thy wisdom, reverend
  oracle,
And in thy precepts make me ever thrifty ![5]
Tec. I thank thy wish.   *Exit.*
                    Much mystery of fate
Lies hid in that man's fortunes ; curiosity   55
May lead his actions into rare attempts : —
But let the gods be moderators still ;
No human power can prevent their will.

Enter ARMOSTES [*with a casket*].

From whence come ye ?
Arm.   From King Amyclas, — pardon
My interruption of your studies.— Here,   60
In this seal'd box, he sends a treasure [to you,]
Dear to him as his crown. 'A prays your grav-
  ity
You would examine, ponder, sift, and bolt
The pith and circumstance of every tittle
The scroll within contains.
Tec.   What is 't, Armostes ? 65
Arm. It is the health of Sparta, the king's
  life,
Sinews and safety of the commonwealth ;
The sum of what the oracle deliver'd
When last he visited the prophetic temple
At Delphos : what his reasons are, for which. 70

---

[1] Jaws.
[2] Discipline.
[3] The study of Tecnicus.
[4] Suspicious.
[5] Make me ever avail myself of thy precepts.

After so long a silence, he requires
Your counsel now, grave man, his majesty
Will soon himself acquaint you with.
    Tec. [*Takes the casket.*]   Apollo
Inspire my intellect ! — The Prince of Argos
Is entertain'd ?
    Arm.   He is ; and has demanded   75
Our princess for his wife ; which I conceive
One special cause the king importunes you
For resolution of the oracle.
    Tec. My duty to the king, good peace to
        Sparta,
And fair day to Armostes !
    Arm.   Like to Tecnicus ! *Exeunt.* 80

                    [SCENE II.]¹

Soft music, during which time enter PROPHILUS,
BASSANES, PENTHEA, GRAUSIS, *passing over
the stage.* BASSANES *and* GRAUSIS *enter again
softly, stealing to several stands, and listen.*

                    A SONG.

        Can you paint a thought ? or number
        Every fancy in a slumber ?
        Can you count soft minutes roving
        From a dial's point by moving ?
        Can you grasp a sigh ? or, lastly,   5
        Rob a virgin's honour chastely ?
        No, O, no ! yet you may
        Sooner do both that and this,
        This and that, and never miss,
        Than by any praise display   10
        Beauty's beauty ; such a glory,
        As beyond all fate, all story,
            All arms, all arts,
            All loves, all hearts,
        Greater than those or they,   15
        Do, shall, and must obey.

    Bass. All silent, calm, secure.— Grausis, no
        creaking ?
No noise ? Dost hear nothing ?
    Grau.   Not a mouse,
Or whisper of the wind.
    Bass.   The floor is matted ;
The bedposts sure are steel or marble. — Sol-
        diers   20
Should not affect, methinks, strains so effem-
        inate :
Sounds of such delicacy are but fawnings
Upon the sloth of luxury, they heighten
Cinders of covert lust up to a flame.
    Grau. What do you mean, my lord ? — speak
        low ; that gabbling   25
Of yours will but undo us.
    Bass.   Chamber-combats
Are felt, not heard.
    Pro. [*within.*]   'A wakes.
    Bass.   What's that ?
    Ith. [*within.*]   Who's there ?
Sister ? — All quit the room else.
    Bass.   'T is consented !

                Re-enter PROPHILUS.

    Pro. Lord Bassanes, your brother would be
        private,

¹ The palace. Ithocles' apartment.

We must forbear ; his sleep hath newly left
        him.   30
Please ye withdraw.
    Bass.   By any means ; 't is fit.
    Pro. Pray, gentlewoman, walk too.
    Grau.   Yes, I will, sir. *Exeunt omnes.*

ITHOCLES *discovered in a chair, and* PENTHEA
        [*beside him*].

    Ith. Sit nearer, sister to me ; nearer yet.
We had one father, in one womb took life,   34
Were brought up twins together, yet have liv'd
At distance, like two strangers. I could wish
That the first pillow whereon I was cradled
Had prov'd to me a grave.
    Pen.   You had been happy :
Then had you never known that sin of life
Which blots all following glories with a ven-
        geance,   40
For forfeiting the last will of the dead,
From whom you had your being.
    Ith.   Sad Penthea,
Thou canst not be too cruel ; my rash spleen
Hath with a violent hand pluck'd from thy
        bosom
A love-blest ² heart, to grind it into dust ;   45
For which mine 's now a-breaking.
    Pen.   Not yet, Heaven,
I do beseech thee ! First let some wild fires
Scorch, not consume it ! may the heat be cher-
        isht
With desires infinite, but hopes impossible !
    Ith. Wrong'd soul, thy prayers are heard.
    Pen.   Here, lo, I breathe,   50
A miserable creature, led to ruin
By an unnatural brother !
    Ith.   I consume
In languishing affections for that trespass ;
Yet cannot die.
    Pen.   The handmaid to the wages   54
Of country toil drinks the untroubled streams
With leaping kids and with the bleating lambs,
And so allays her thirst secure ; whiles I
Quench my hot sighs with fleetings ³ of my
        tears.
    Ith. The labourer doth eat his coarsest
        bread,
Earn'd with his sweat, and lies him down to
        sleep ;   60
While ⁴ every bit I touch turns in digestion
To gall as bitter as Penthea's curse.
Put me to any penance for my tyranny,
And I will call thee merciful.
    Pen.   Pray kill me,
Rid me from living with a jealous husband ;   65
Then we will join in friendship, be again
Brother and sister.— Kill me, pray ; nay, will
        ye ?
    Ith. How does thy lord esteem thee ?
    Pen.   Such an one
As only you have made me ; a faith-breaker,
A spotted whore : — forgive me, I am one   70
In act, not in desires, the gods must witness.
    Ith. Thou dost belie thy friend.
    Pen.   I do not, Ithocles ;

² Q. *lover-blest.*   ³ Streams.   ⁴ Q. *Which.*

For she that's wife to Orgilus, and lives
In known adultery with Bassanes,
Is at the best a whore. Wilt kill me now?   75
The ashes of our parents will assume
Some dreadful figure, and appear to charge
Thy bloody guilt, that hast betray'd their name
To infamy in this reproachful match.
   Ith. After my victories abroad, at home   80
I meet despair; ingratitude of nature
Hath made my actions monstrous. Thou shalt
     stand
A deity, my sister, and be worshipp'd
For thy resolved martyrdom; wrong'd maids
And married wives shall to thy hallowed
     shrine   85
Offer their orisons, and sacrifice
Pure turtles, crown'd with myrtle; if thy pity
Unto a yielding brother's pressure lend
One finger but to ease it.
   Pen.   O, no more!
   Ith. Death waits to waft me to the Stygian
     banks,   90
And free me from this chaos of my bondage;
And till thou wilt forgive, I must endure.
   Pen. Who is the saint you serve?
   Ith.   Friendship, or [nearness] [1]
Of birth to any but my sister, durst not
Have mov'd that question; ['t is] [2] a secret,
     sister,   95
I dare not murmur to myself.
   Pen.   Let me,
By your new protestations I conjure ye,
Partake her name.
   Ith. Her name? — 'tis — 'tis — I dare not.
   Pen. All your respects are forg'd. [3]
   Ith.   They are not. — Peace!
Calantha is — the princess — the king's daugh-
     ter —   100
Sole heir of Sparta.— Me, most miserable
Do I now love thee? For my injuries
Revenge thyself with bravery, and gossip
My treasons to the king's ears, do: — Calantha
Knows it not yet, nor Prophilus, my nearest.   105
   Pen. Suppose you were contracted to her,
     would it not
Split even your very soul to see her father
Snatch her out of your arms against her will,
And force her on the Prince of Argos?
   Ith.   Trouble not
The fountains of mine eyes with thine own
     story;   110
I sweat in blood for 't.
   Pen.   We are reconcil'd.
Alas, sir, being children, but two branches
Of one stock, 'tis not fit we should divide:
Have comfort, you may find it.
   Ith.   Yes, in thee;
Only in thee, Penthea mine.
   Pen.   If sorrows   115
Have not too much dull'd my infected brain,
I 'll cheer invention for an active strain. [4]
   Ith. Mad man! why have I wrong'd a maid
     so excellent!

Enter BASSANES *with a poniard;* PROPHILUS,
    GRONEAS, HEMOPHIL, *and* GRAUSIS.

   Bass. I can forbear no longer; more, I will
    not.
Keep off your hands, or fall upon my point.—
Patience is tir'd; for, like a slow-pac'd ass,   121
Ye ride my easy nature, and proclaim
My sloth to vengeance a reproach and property. [5]
   Ith. The meaning of this rudeness?
   Pro.   He 's distracted.
   Pen. O, my griev'd lord!—
   Grau.   Sweet lady, come not near him;   125
He holds his perilous weapon in his hand
To prick 'a cares not whom nor where,— see,
     see, see!
   Bass. My birth is noble: though the popu-
    lar blast
Of vanity, as giddy as thy youth,
Hath rear'd thy name up to bestride a cloud,   130
Or progress in the chariot of the sun,
I am no clod of trade, to lackey pride,
Nor, like your slave of expectation, [6] wait
The bawdy hinges of your doors, or whistle
For mystical conveyance to your bed-sports.   135
   Gro. Fine humours! they become him.
   Hem.   How 'a stares,
Struts, puffs, and sweats! Most admirable [7]
    lunacy!
   Ith. But that I may conceive the spirit of
    wine
Has took possession of your soberer custom,
I 'd say you were unmannerly.
   Pen.   Dear brother!—   140
   Bass. Unmannerly! — mew, kitling! —
    smooth Formality
Is usher to the rankness of the blood,
But Impudence bears up the train. Indeed, sir,
Your fiery mettle, or your springal [8] blaze
Of huge renown, is no sufficient royalty   145
To print upon my forehead the scorn, " cuck-
    old."
   Ith. His jealousy has robb'd him of his wits;
'A talks 'a knows not what.
   Bass.   Yes, and 'a knows
To whom 'a talks; to one that franks [9] his lust
In swine-security of bestial incest.   150
   Ith. Ha, devil!
   Bass. I will haloo 't; [10] though I blush more
To name the filthiness than thou to act it.
   Ith. Monster!   [*Draws his sword.*]
   Pro.   Sir, by our friendship —
   Pen.   By our bloods —
Will you quite both undo us, brother?
   Grau.   Out on him!
These are his megrims, firks, [11] and melancho-
    lies.   155
   Hem. Well said, old touch-hole.
   Gro.   Kick him out of doors.
   Pen. With favour, let me speak.— My lord,
    what slackness
In my obedience hath deserv'd this rage?
Except humility and silent duty

---

1 Q. omits.   2 *'Tis*, Dyce emend. Q. *as.*
3 *I. e.* You do not care for me as you say.
4 I will attempt to devise something.

5 Personal characteristics.   7 Wonderful.
6 Attendant slave.   8 Youthful.
9 Feeds; fattens, as one fattens swine.
10 Proclaim.   11 Freaks.

Have drawn on your unquiet, my simplicity 160
Ne'er studied your vexation.
Bass. Light of beauty,
Deal not ungently with a desperate wound !
No breach of reason dares make war with
  her
Whose looks are sovereignty, whose breath is
  balm.
O, that I could preserve thee in fruition 165
As in devotion !
Pen. Sir, may every evil
Lock'd in Pandora's box shower, in your pre-
  sence,
On my unhappy head, if, since you made me
A partner in your bed, I have been faulty
In one unseemly thought against your honour !
Ith. Purge not his griefs, Penthea.
Bass. Yes, say on, 171
Excellent creature ! — [*To* ITHOCLES.] Good,
  be not a hindrance
To peace and praise of virtue. — O, my senses
Are charm'd with sounds celestial ! — On, dear,
  on :
I never gave you one ill word ; say, did I ? 175
Indeed I did not.
Pen. Nor, by Juno's forehead,
Was I e'er guilty of a wanton error.
Bass. A goddess ! let me kneel.
Grau. Alas, kind animal !
Ith. No ; but for penance.
Bass. Noble sir, what is it ?
With gladness I embrace it ; yet, pray let not
My rashness teach you to be too unmerciful. 181
Ith. When you shall show good proof that
  manly wisdom,
Not oversway'd by passion or opinion,
Knows how to lead [your] judgment, then
  this lady,
Your wife, my sister, shall return in safety 185
Home, to be guided by you ; but, till first
I can out of clear evidence approve it,
She shall be my care.
Bass. Rip my bosom up,
I 'll stand the execution with a constancy ;
This torture is unsufferable.
Ith. Well, sir, 190
I dare not trust her to your fury.
Bass. But
Penthea says not so.
Pen. She needs no tongue
To plead excuse who never purpos'd wrong.
Hem. Virgin of reverence and antiquity,
Stay you behind.
Gro. [*to* GRAUSIS.] The court wants not
  your diligence. 195
Exeunt all but BASS. *and* GRAU.
Grau. What will you do, my lord ? My lady's
  gone ;
I am deni'd to follow.
Bass. I may see her,
Or speak to her once more ?
Grau. And feel her too, man ;
Be of good cheer, she 's your own flesh and
  bone.
Bass. Diseases desperate must find cures
  alike. 200
She swore she has been true.

Grau. True, on my modesty.
Bass. Let him want truth who credits not
  her vows !
Much wrong I did her, but her brother infinite ;
Rumour will voice me the contempt of man-
  hood, 204
Should I run on thus. Some way I must try
To outdo art, and [jealousy decry.] [1] *Exeunt.*

[SCENE III.] [2]

Flourish. Enter AMYCLAS, NEARCHUS, *leading*
CALANTHA, ARMOSTES, CROTOLON, EU-
PHRANEA, CHRISTALLA, PHILEMA, *and* AM-
ELUS.

Amy. Cousin of Argos, what the heavens
  have pleas'd,
In their unchanging counsels to conclude
For both our kingdoms' weal, we must submit
  to :
Nor can we be unthankful to their bounties,
Who, when we were even creeping to our
  grave, 5
Sent us a daughter, in whose birth our hope
Continues of succession. As you are
In title next, being grandchild to our aunt,
So we in heart desire you may sit nearest
Calantha's love ; since we have ever vow'd 10
Not to enforce affection by our will,
But by her own choice to confirm it gladly.
Near. You speak the nature of a right just
  father.
I come not hither roughly to demand
My cousin's thraldom, but to free mine own. 15
Report of great Calantha's beauty, virtue,
Sweetness, and singular perfections, courted
All ears to credit what I find was publish'd
By constant truth ; from which, if any service
Of my desert can purchase fair construction, 20
This lady must command it.
Cal. Princely sir,
So well you know how to profess observance, [3]
That you instruct your hearers to become
Practitioners in duty ; of which number
I 'll study to be chief.
Near. Chief, glorious virgin, 25
In my devotions, as in all men's wonder.
Amy. Excellent cousin, we deny no liberty ;
Use thine own opportunities. — Armostes,
We must consult with the philosophers ;
The business is of weight.
Arm. Sir, at your pleasure. 30
Amy. You told me, Crotolon, your son 's re-
  turn'd
From Athens : wherefore comes he not to court,
As we commanded ?
Crot. He shall soon attend
Your royal will, great sir.
Amy. The marriage
Between young Prophilus and Euphranea 35
Tastes of too much delay.
Crot. My lord, —
Amy. Some pleasures
At celebration of it would give life

---

[1] Q. *cry a Iealousie.*
[2] A room in the palace.
[3] Worship, courtship.

To th' entertainment of the prince our kins-
man;
Our court wears gravity more than we relish.
  Arm. Yet the heavens smile on all your high
    attempts,   40
Without a cloud.
  Crot.   So may the gods protect us.
  Cal. A prince a subject?
  Near.   Yes, to beauty's sceptre;
As all hearts kneel, so mine.
  Cal.   You are too courtly.

Enter ITHOCLES, ORGILUS, *and* PROPHILUS.

  Ith. Your safe return to Sparta is most wel-
    come:
I joy to meet you here, and, as occasion   45
Shall grant us privacy, will yield you reasons
Why I should covet to deserve the title
Of your respected friend; for, without compli-
    ment,
Believe it, Orgilus, 't is my ambition.
  Org. Your lordship may command me, your
    poor servant.   50
  Ith. [*Aside.*] So amorously close! — so soon!
    — my heart!
  Pro. What sudden change is next?
  Ith.   Life to the king!
To whom I here present this noble gentleman,
New come from Athens: royal sir, vouchsafe
Your gracious hand in favour of his merit.   55
    [*The King gives* ORGILUS *his hand
    to kiss.*]
  Crot. [*Aside.*] My son preferr'd by Ithocles!
  Amy.   Our bounties
Shall open to thee, Orgilus; for instance, —
Hark in thine ear, — if, out of those inventions
Which flow in Athens, thou hast there en-
    grost [1]
Some rarity of wit, to grace the nuptials   60
Of thy fair sister, and renown our court
In th' eyes of this young prince, we shall be
    debtor
To thy conceit: think on 't.
  Org.   Your highness honours me.
  Near. My tongue and heart are twins.
  Cal.   A noble birth,
Becoming such a father. — Worthy Orgilus,   65
You are a guest most wish'd for.
  Org.   May my duty
Still rise in your opinion, sacred princess!
  Ith. Euphranea's brother, sir; a gentleman
Well worthy of your knowledge.
  Near.   We embrace him,
Proud of so dear acquaintance.
  Amy.   All prepare   70
For revels and disport; the joys of Hymen,
Like Phoebus in his lustre, put to flight
All mists of dulness, crown the hours with
    gladness:
No sounds but music, no discourse but mirth!
  Cal. Thine arm, I prithee, Ithocles. — Nay,
    good   75
My lord, keep on your way; I am provided.
  Near. I dare not disobey.
  Ith.   Most heavenly lady!   *Exeunt.*

    [1] Acquired.

[SCENE IV.] [2]

Enter CROTOLON *and* ORGILUS.

  Crot. The king hath spoke his mind.
  Org.   His will he hath;
But were it lawful to hold plea against
The power of greatness, not the reason, haply
Such undershrubs as subjects sometimes might
Borrow of nature justice, to inform   5
That license sovereignty holds without check
Over a meek obedience.
  Crot.   How resolve you
Touching your sister's marriage? Prophilus
Is a deserving and a hopeful youth.
  Org. I envy not his merit, but applaud it;   10
Could wish him thrift [3] in all his best desires,
And with a willingness inleague our blood
With his, for purchase of full growth in friend-
    ship.
He never touch'd on any wrong that malic'd
The honour of our house nor stirr'd our peace:
Yet, with your favour, let me not forget   15
Under whose wing he gathers warmth and com-
    fort,
Whose creature he is bound, made, and must
    live so.
  Crot. Son, son, I find in thee a harsh condi-
    tion; [4]
No courtesy can win it; 't is too rancorous.   20
  Org. Good sir, be not severe in your construc-
    tion;
I am no stranger to such easy calms
As sit in tender bosoms: lordly Ithocles
Hath grac'd my entertainment in abundance,
Too humbly hath descended from that height   25
Of arrogance and spleen which wrought the
    rape
On griev'd Penthea's purity; his scorn
Of my untoward fortunes is reclaim'd
Unto a courtship, almost to a fawning: —
I 'll kiss his foot, since you will have it so.   30
  Crot. Since I will have it so! Friend, I will
    have it so,
Without our ruin by your politic plots,
Or wolf of hatred snarling in your breast.
You have a spirit, sir, have ye? A familiar
That posts i' th' air for your intelligence?   35
Some such hobgoblin hurried you from Athens,
For yet you come unsent for.
  Org.   If unwelcome,
I might have found a grave there.
  Crot.   Sure, your business
Was soon dispatch'd, or your mind alter'd
    quickly.
  Org. 'T was care, sir, of my health cut short
    my journey;   40
For there a general infection
Threatens a desolation.
  Crot.   And I fear
Thou hast brought back a worse infection with
    thee, —
Infection of thy mind; which, as thou say'st,
Threatens the desolation of our family.   45
  Org. Forbid it, our dear genius! I will rather

    [2] A room in the house of Crotolon.
    [3] Prosperity.   [4] Disposition.

ℬe made a sacrifice on Thrasus' monument,
Or kneel to Ithocles, his son, in dust,
Than woo a father's curse. My sister's mar-
    riage
With Prophilus is from my heart confirm'd ; 50
May I live hated, may I die despis'd,
If I omit to further it in all
That can concern me !
    Crot.   I have been too rough.
My duty to my king made me so earnest ;
Excuse it, Orgilus.
    Org.   Dear sir ! —
    Crot.   Here comes 55
Euphranea with Prophilus and Ithocles.

Enter PROPHILUS, EUPHRANEA, ITHOCLES,
    GRONEAS, *and* HEMOPHIL.

    Org. Most honoured ! — ever famous !
    Ith.   Your true friend ;
On earth not any truer. — With smooth eyes
Look on this worthy couple ; your consent
Can only make them one.
    Org.   They have it. — Sister, 60
Thou pawn'dst to me an oath, of which engage-
    ment
I never will release thee, if thou aim'st
At any other choice than this.
    Euph.   Dear brother,
At him, or none.
    Crot.   To which my blessing 's added.
    Org. Which, till a greater ceremony per-
    fect, —   65
Euphranea, lend thy hand, — here, take her,
    Prophilus ;
Live long a happy man and wife ; and further,
That these in presence may conclude an omen,
Thus for a bridal song I close my wishes :

[*Sings.*]   Comforts lasting, loves increasing,   70
        Like soft hours never ceasing :
        Plenty's pleasure, peace complying,
        Without jars, or tongues envying ;
        Hearts by holy union wedded,
        More than theirs by custom bedded ;   75
        Fruitful issues ; life so graced,
        Not by age to be defaced,
        Budding, as the year ensu'th,
        Every spring another youth :
        All what thought can add beside   80
        Crown this bridegroom and this bride !

    Pro. You have seal'd joy close to my soul. —
    Euphranea,
Now I may call thee mine.
    Ith.   I but exchange
One good friend for another.
    Org.   If these gallants
Will please to grace a poor invention   85
By joining with me in some slight device,
I 'll venture on a strain my younger days
Have studied for delight.
    Hem.   With thankful willingness
I offer my attendance.
    Gro.   No endeavour
Of mine shall fail to show itself.
    Ith.   We will   90
All join to wait on thy directions, Orgilus.
    Org. O, my good lord, your favours flow to-
    wards

A too unworthy worm ; — but as you please ;
I am what you will shape me.
    Ith.   A fast friend.
    Crot. I thank thee, son, for this acknowledg-
    ment ;   95
It is a sight of gladness.
    Org.   But my duty. *Exeunt.*

[SCENE V.][1]

Enter CALANTHA, PENTHEA, CHRISTALLA, *and*
    PHILEMA.

    Cal. Whoe'er would speak with us, deny his
    entrance ;
Be careful of our charge.
    Chris.   We shall, madam.
    Cal. Except the king himself, give none ad-
    mittance ;
Not any.
    Phil.   Madam, it shall be our care.
          Exeunt [CHRISTALLA *and* PHIL-
          EMA].
    Cal. Being alone, Penthea, you have granted
The opportunity you sought, and might   6
At all times have commanded.
    Pen.   'T is a benefit
Which I shall owe your goodness even in death
    for.
My glass of life, sweet princess, hath few minutes
Remaining to run down ; the sands are spent ;
For by an inward messenger I feel   11
The summons of departure short and certain.
    Cal. You feel too much your melancholy.
    Pen.   Glories
Of human greatness are but pleasing dreams
And shadows soon decaying : on the stage   15
Of my mortality my youth hath acted
Some scenes of vanity, drawn out at length
By varied pleasures, sweet'ned in the mixture,
But tragical in issue : beauty, pomp,
With every sensuality our giddiness   20
Doth frame an idol, are unconstant friends,
When any troubled passion makes assault
On the unguarded castle of the mind.
    Cal. Contemn not your condition for the proof
Of bare opinion only : to what end   25
Reach all these moral texts ?
    Pen.   To place before ye
A perfect mirror, wherein you may see
How weary I am of a ling'ring life,
Who count the best a misery.
    Cal.   Indeed
You have no little cause ; yet none so great   30
As to distrust a remedy.
    Pen.   That remedy
Must be a winding-sheet, a fold of lead,
And some untrod-on corner in the earth. —
Not to detain your expectation, princess,
I have an humble suit.
    Cal.   Speak ; I enjoy [2] it.   35
    Pen. Vouchsafe, then, to be my executrix,
And take that trouble on ye to dispose
Such legacies as I bequeath, impartially :
I have not much to give, the pains are easy ;

---

1 Calantha's apartment in the palace.
2 So Q. Dyce suggests *enjoin*.

Heaven will reward your piety, and thank it 40
When I am dead; for sure I must not live;
I hope I cannot.

Cal.   Now, beshrew thy sadness,
Thou turn'st me too much woman.   [*Weeps.*]

Pen. [*Aside.*]   Her fair eyes
Melt into passion. — Then I have assurance
Encouraging my boldness. In this paper   45
My will was character'd; which you, with par-
     don,
Shall now know from mine own mouth.

Cal.   Talk on, prithee;
It is a pretty earnest.

Pen.   I have left me
But three poor jewels to bequeath. The first is
My youth; for though I am much old in griefs,
In years I am a child.

Cal.   To whom that [jewel]? 51

Pen. To virgin-wives, such as abuse not wed-
     lock
By freedom of desires, but covet chiefly
The pledges of chaste beds for ties of love,   54
Rather than ranging of their blood; and next
To married maids, such as prefer the number
Of honourable issue in their virtues
Before the flattery of delights by marriage:
May those be ever young!

Cal.   A second jewel
You mean to part with?

Pen.   'T is my fame, I trust 60
By scandal yet untouch'd: this I bequeath
To Memory, and Time's old daughter, Truth.
If ever my unhappy name find mention
When I am fall'n to dust, may it deserve
Beseeming charity without dishonour!   65

Cal. How handsomely thou play'st with
     harmless sport
Of mere imagination! Speak the last.
I strangely like thy will.

Pen.   This jewel, madam,
Is dearly precious to me; you must use
The best of your discretion to employ   70
This gift as I intend it.

Cal.   Do not doubt me.

Pen. 'T is long agone since first I lost my
     heart:
Long I have liv'd without it, else for certain
I should have given that too; but instead
Of it, to great Calantha, Sparta's heir,   75
By service bound and by affection vow'd,
I do bequeath, in holiest rites of love,
Mine only brother, Ithocles.

Cal.   What saidst thou?

Pen. Impute not, heaven-blest lady, to am-
     bition
A faith as humbly perfect as the prayers   80
Of a devoted suppliant can endow it.
Look on him, princess, with an eye of pity;
How like the ghost of what he late appear'd
'A moves before you.

Cal.   Shall I answer here,
Or lend my ear too grossly?

Pen.   First his heart   85
Shall fall in cinders, scorch'd by your disdain,
Ere he will dare, poor man, to ope an eye
On these divine looks, but with low-bent
     thoughts

Accusing such presumption · as for words,
'A dares not utter any but of service: 90
Yet this lost creature loves ye. — Be a princess
In sweetness as in blood; give him his doom,
Or raise him up to comfort.

Cal.   What new change
Appears in my behaviour, that thou dar'st
Tempt my displeasure?

Pen.   I must leave the world 95
To revel in Elysium, and 't is just
To wish my brother some advantage here;
Yet, by my best hopes, Ithocles is ignorant
Of this pursuit. But if you please to kill him,
Lend him one angry look or one harsh word, 100
And you shall soon conclude how strong a
     power
Your absolute authority holds over
His life and end.

Cal.   You have forgot, Penthea,
How still I have a father.

Pen.   But remember
I am a sister, though to me this brother   105
Hath been, you know, unkind, O, most unkind!

Cal. Christalla, Philema, where are ye? —
Lady,
Your check lies in my silence.

Re-enter CHRISTALLA *and* PHILEMA.

Chris. and Phil.   Madam, here.

Cal. I think ye sleep, ye drones: wait on
     Penthea
Unto her lodging. — [*Aside.*] Ithocles? Wrong'd
     lady!   110

Pen. My reckonings are made even; death or
     fate
Can now nor strike too soon, nor force too late.
                                        Exeunt.

ACT IV

SCENE I.[1]

Enter ITHOCLES *and* ARMOSTES.

Ith. Forbear your inquisition: curiosity
Is of too subtle and too searching nature,
In fears of love too quick, too slow of credit. —
I am not what you doubt me.

Arm.   Nephew, be, then,
As I would wish; — all is not right. — Good
     heaven
Confirm your resolutions for dependence
On worthy ends, which may advance your quiet?

Ith. I did the noble Orgilus much injury,
But griev'd Penthea more: I now repent it, —
Now, uncle, now; this "now" is now too late.
So provident is folly in sad issue,   11
That after-wit, like bankrupts' debts, stands
     tallied,
Without all possibilities of payment.
Sure, he 's an honest, very honest gentleman;
A man of single [2] meaning.

Arm.   I believe it: 15
Yet, nephew, 't is the tongue informs our ears;
Our eyes can never pierce into the thoughts,

---

[1] The palace. Ithocles' apartment.
[2] Sincere.

For they are lodg'd too inward: — but I question
No truth in Orgilus. — The princess, sir.

Ith. The princess! ha!

Arm.   With her the Prince of Argos. 20

Enter NEARCHUS, *leading* CALANTHA; AMELUS, CHRISTALLA, PHILEMA.

Near. Great fair one, grace my hopes with
   any instance
Of livery,[1] from the allowance of your favour;
This little spark —

   [*Attempts to take a ring from her finger.*]

Cal.   A toy!

Near.   Love feasts on toys,
For Cupid is a child; — vouchsafe this bounty:
It cannot be deni'd.

Cal.   You shall not value,   25
Sweet cousin, at a price, what I count cheap;
So cheap, that let him take it who dares stoop
   for 't,
And give it at next meeting to a mistress:
She 'll thank him for 't, perhaps.

                    Casts the ring to ITHOCLES.

Ame.   The ring, sir, is
The princess's; I could have took it up.   30

Ith. Learn manners, prithee. — To the blessed
   owner,
Upon my knees —

                    Kneels and offers it to CALANTHA.

Near.   Y' are saucy.

Cal.   This is pretty!
I am, belike, "a mistress" — wondrous pretty!
Let the man keep his fortune, since he found
   it;
He 's worthy on 't. — On, cousin!

Ith. [*to* AMELUS.]   Follow, spaniel; 35
I 'll force ye to a fawning else.

Ame.   You dare not.

                    Exeunt. Manent ITH. *and* ARM.

Arm. My lord, you were too forward.

Ith.   Look ye, uncle,
Some such there are whose liberal contents
Swarm without care in every sort of plenty;
Who after full repasts can lay them down   40
To sleep; and they sleep, uncle: in which silence
Their very dreams present 'em choice of pleasures,
Pleasures — observe me, uncle — of rare object;
Here heaps of gold, there increments of honours,
Now change of garments, then the votes of
   people;   45
Anon varieties of beauties, courting,
In flatteries of the night, exchange of dalliance:
Yet these are still but dreams. Give me felicity
Of which my senses waking are partakers,
A real, visible, material happiness;   50
And then, too, when I stagger in expectance
Of the least comfort that can cherish life. ——
I saw it, sir, I saw it; for it came
From her own hand.

Arm.   The princess threw it t' ye.

Ith. True; and she said — well I remember
   what —   55
Her cousin prince would beg it.

Arm.   Yes, and parted
In anger at your taking on 't.

Ith.   Panthea,
O, thou hast pleaded with a powerful language!
I want a fee to gratify thy merit;
But I will do —

Arm.   What is 't you say?

Ith.   In anger!   60
In anger let him part; for could his breath,
Like whirlwinds, toss such servile slaves as lick
The dust his footsteps print into a vapour,
It durst not stir a hair of mine, it should not;
I 'd rend it up by th' roots first. To be anything   65
Calantha smiles on, is to be a blessing
More sacred than a petty prince of Argos
Can wish to equal, or in worth or title.

Arm. Contain yourself, my lord: Ixion, aiming
To embrace Juno, bosom'd but a cloud,   70
And begat Centaurs; 't is an useful moral.
Ambition hatch'd in clouds of mere opinion
Proves but in birth a prodigy.

Ith.   I thank ye;
Yet, with your licence, I should seem uncharitable
To gentler fate, if, relishing the dainties   75
Of a soul's settled peace, I were so feeble
Not to digest it.

Arm.   He deserves small trust
Who is not privy-counsellor to himself.

Re-enter NEARCHUS *and* AMELUS, *with* ORGILUS.

Near. Brave me!

Org.   Your excellence mistakes his temper;
For Ithocles in fashion of his mind   80
Is beautiful, soft, gentle, the clear mirror
Of absolute perfection.

Ame.   Was 't your modesty
Term'd any of the prince's servants "spaniel"?
Your nurse, sure, taught you other language.

Ith.   Language!

Near. A gallant man-at-arms is here, a
   doctor   85
In feats of chivalry, blunt and rough-spoken,
Vouchsafing not the fustian of civility,
Which [less][1] rash spirits style good manners!

Ith.   Manners!

Org. No more, illustrious sir; 't is matchless
   Ithocles.

Near. You might have understood who I am.

Ith.   Yes.   90
I did; else — but the presence calm'd th' affront —
Y' are cousin to the princess.

Near.   To the king, too;
A certain instrument that lent supportance
To you colossic greatness — to that king too,
You might have added.

Ith.   There is more divinity
In beauty than in majesty.   95

Arm. O fie, fie!
Near. This odd youth's pride turns heretic
 in loyalty.
Sirrah! low mushrooms never rival cedars.
                    Exeunt NEARCHUS *and* AMELUS.
Ith. Come back! — What pitiful dull thing
 am I
So to be tamely scolded at! come back! — 100
Let him come back, and echo once again
That scornful sound of mushroom! painted
 colts —
Like heralds' coats gilt o'er with crowns and
 sceptres —
May bait a muzzled lion.
Arm.   Cousin, cousin,
Thy tongue is not thy friend.
Org.   In point of honour 105
Discretion knows no bounds. Amelus told me
'T was all about a little ring.
Ith.   A ring
The princess threw away, and I took up.
Admit she threw 't to me, what arm of brass
Can snatch it hence? No; could he grind the
 hoop 110
To powder, 'a might sooner reach my heart
Than steal and wear one dust on 't. — Orgilus,
I am extremely wrong'd.
Org.   A lady's favour
Is not to be so slighted.
Ith.   Slighted!
Arm.   Quiet
These vain unruly passions, which will render
 ye 115
Into a madness.
Org.   Griefs will have their vent.

Enter TECNICUS [*with a scroll*].

Arm. Welcome; thou com'st in season, rev-
 erend man,
To pour the balsam of a suppling [1] patience
Into the festering wound of ill-spent fury.
Org. [*Aside.*] What makes he here?
Tec.   The hurts are yet but [2] mortal, 120
Which shortly will prove deadly. To the king,
Armostes, see in safety thou deliver
This seal'd-up counsel; bid him with a con-
 stancy
Peruse the secrets of the gods. — O Sparta,
O Lacedaemon! double-nam'd, but one 125
In fate: when kingdoms reel, — mark well my
 saw. —
Their heads must needs be giddy. Tell the
 king
That henceforth he no more must inquire after
My aged head; Apollo wills it so:
I am for Delphos.
Arm.   Not without some conference 130
With our great master?
Tec.   Never more to see him:
A greater prince commands me. — Ithocles,
*When youth is ripe, and age from time doth
 part,
The lifeless trunk shall wed the broken heart.*
Ith. What 's this, if understood?
Tec.   List, Orgilus; 135

Remember what I told thee long before,
These tears shall be my witness.
Arm.   'Las, good man!
*Tec. Let craft with courtesy a while confer,
 Revenge proves its own executioner.*
Org. Dark sentences are for Apollo's priests;
I am not Oedipus.
Tec.   My hour is come; 141
Cheer up the king; farewell to all.— O Sparta,
O Lacedaemon!   *Exit.*
Arm.   If prophetic fire
Have warm'd this old man's bosom, we might
 construe
His words to fatal sense.
Ith.   Leave to the powers 145
Above us the effects of their decrees;
My burthen lies within me: servile fears
Prevent no great effects. — Divine Calantha!
Arm. The gods be still propitious!
                    Exeunt ITHOCLES *and* ARMOSTES.
Org.   Something oddly
The book-man prated, yet 'a talk'd it weeping;
Let craft with courtesy a while confer, 151
Revenge proves its own executioner.
Con it again; — for what? It shall not puzzle
 me;
'T is dotage of a withered brain. — Penthea
Forbade me not her presence; I may see her,
And gaze my fill. Why see her, then, I may, 156
When, if I faint to speak — I must be silent.
                    Exit.

[SCENE II.] [3]

Enter BASSANES, GRAUSIS, *and* PHULAS.

Bass. Pray, use your recreations, all the ser-
 vice
I will expect is quietness amongst ye;
Take liberty at home, abroad, at all times,
And in your charities appease the gods,
Whom I, with my distractions, have offended. 5
Grau. Fair blessings on thy heart!
Phu. [*Aside.*]   Here 's a rare change!
My lord, to cure the itch, is surely gelded;
The cuckold in conceit hath cast his horns.
Bass. Betake ye to your several occasions;
And wherein I have heretofore been faulty, 10
Let your constructions mildly pass it over.
Henceforth I 'll study reformation, — more
I have not for employment.
Grau.   O, sweet man!
Thou art the very "Honeycomb of Honesty." [4]
Phu. The "Garland of Good-will." — Old
 lady, hold up 15
Thy reverend snout, and trot behind me softly,
As it becomes a moil [3] of ancient carriage.
                    Exeunt GRAUSIS *and* PHULAS.
Bass. Beasts, only capable of sense, enjoy
The benefit of food and ease with thankful-
 ness;
Such silly creatures, with a grudging, kick not
Against the portion nature hath bestow'd: 21
But men, endow'd with reason and the use

---

[1] Q. *supplying.*   [2] Gifford suggests *not.*

[3] A room in Bassanes' house.
[4] The *Honeycomb of Honesty*, like the *Garland of
Goodwill*, was probably one of the popular miscellanies
of the day. (Gifford.) See Additional Notes.
[5] Mule.

Of reason, to distinguish from the chaff
Of abject scarcity the quintessence,
Soul, and elixir of the earth's abundance,   25
The treasures of the sea, the air, nay, heaven,
Repining at these glories of creation
Are verier beasts than beasts; and of those
  beasts
The worst am I: I, who was made a monarch
Of what a heart could wish for,— a chaste
  wife,—   30
Endeavour'd what in me lay to pull down
That temple built for adoration only,
And level 't in the dust of causeless scandal.
But, to redeem a sacrilege so impious,
Humility shall pour, before the deities   35
I have incenst, a largess of more patience
Than their displeased altars can require:
No tempests of commotion shall disquiet
The calms of my composure.

Enter ORGILUS.

Org.   I have found thee,
Thou patron of more horrors than the bulk   40
Of manhood, hoop'd about with ribs of iron,
Can cram within thy breast: Penthea, Bas-
  sanes,
Curst by thy jealousies,— more, by thy dot-
  age,—
Is left a prey to words.
Bass.   Exercise
Your trials for addition to my penánce;   45
I am resolv'd.
Org.   Play not with misery
Past cure: some angry minister of fate hath
Depos'd the empress of her soul, her reason,
From its most proper throne; but, what 's the
  miracle
More new, I, I have seen it, and yet live!   50
Bass. You may delude my senses, not my
  judgment;
'T is anchor'd into a firm resolution;
Dalliance of mirth or wit can ne'er unfix it:
Practise[1] yet further.
Org.   May thy death of love to her
Damn all thy comforts to a lasting fast   55
From every joy of life! Thou barren rock,
By thee we have been split in ken[2] of harbour.

Enter ITHOCLES, PENTHEA *her hair about her
  ears,* [ARMOSTES,] PHILEMA, *and* CHRIS-
  TALLA.

Ith. Sister, look up; your Ithocles, your
  brother,
Speaks t' ye; why do you weep? Dear, turn
  not from me.—
Here is a killing sight; lo, Bassanes,   60
A lamentable object!
Org.   Man, dost see 't?
Sports are more gamesome; am I yet in merri-
  ment?
Why dost not laugh?
Bass.   Divine and best of ladies,
Please to forget my outrage; mercy ever
Cannot but lodge under a roof so excellent.   65
I have cast off that cruelty of frenzy

Which once appear'd imposture,[3] and then
  juggled
To cheat my sleeps of rest.
Org.   Was I in earnest?
Pen. Sure, if we were all Sirens, we should
  sing pitifully.
And 't were a comely music, when in parts   70
One sung another's knell. The turtle sighs
When he hath lost his mate; and yet some say
He must be dead first. 'T is a fine deceit
To pass away in a dream; indeed, I 've slept
With mine eyes open a great while. No false-
  hood   75
Equals a broken faith; there 's not a hair
Sticks on my head but, like a leaden plum-
  met,
It sinks me to the grave. I must creep thither;
The journey is not long.
Ith.   But, thou, Penthea,
Hast many years, I hope, to number yet,   80
Ere thou canst travel that way.
Bass.   Let the sun first
Be wrapp'd up in an everlasting darkness,
Before the light of nature, chiefly form'd
For the whole world's delight, feel an eclipse
So universal!
Org.   Wisdom, look ye, begins   85
To rave!— Art thou mad too, antiquity?
Pen. Since I was first a wife, I might have
  been
Mother to many pretty prattling babes;
They would have smil'd when I smil'd, and for
  certain
I should have cri'd when they cri'd:— truly,
  brother,   90
My father would have pick'd me out a hus-
  band,
And then my little ones had been no bastards;
But 't is too late for me to marry now,
I am past child-bearing; 't is not my fault.
Bass. Fall on me, if there be a burning
  Aetna,   95
And bury me in flames! Sweats hot as sulphur
Boil through my pores! Affliction hath in store
No torture like to this.
Org.   Behold a patience!
Lay by thy whining gray dissimulation,
Do something worth a chronicle; show justice
Upon the author of this mischief; dig out   101
The jealousies that hatch'd this thraldom first
With thine own poniard. Every antic rapture
Can roar as thine does.
Ith.   Orgilus, forbear.
Bass. Disturb him not; it is a talking motion[4]
Provided for my torment. What a fool am I   106
To bandy[5] passion! Ere I 'll speak a word,
I will look on and burst.
Pen.   I lov'd you once. [*To* ORGILUS.]
Org. Thou didst, wrong'd creature: in de-
  spite of malice,
For it I love thee ever.
Pen.   Spare your hand;   110
Believe me, I 'll not hurt it.
Org.   My[6] heart too.

---

[1] Test me.   [2] Sight.

[3] Q. *appear'd, Impostors.*   [4] Puppet.   [5] Q. *baudy*
[6] Q. *Paine my,* and omits [*Pen.*] in next line.

[*Pen.*] Complain not though I wring it hard.
    I 'll kiss it ;
O, 't is a fine soft palm ! — hark, in thine ear ;
Like whom do I look, prithee ? — Nay, no
    whispering.
Goodness ! we had been happy ; too much hap-
    piness   115
Will make folk proud, they say — but that is
    he —   *Points at* ITHOCLES.
And yet he paid for 't home ; alas, his heart
Is crept into the cabinet of the princess ;
We shall have points [1] and bride-laces. Re-
    member,
When we last gather'd roses in the garden, 120
I found my wits ; but truly you lost yours.
That 's he, and still 't is he.
             [*Again pointing at* ITHOCLES.]
  Ith.   Poor soul, how idly
Her fancies guide her tongue !
  Bass. [*Aside.*]   Keep in, vexation,
And break not into clamour.
  Org. [*Aside.*]   She has tutor'd me :
Some powerful inspiration checks my lazi-
    ness.—   125
Now let me kiss your hand, griev'd beauty.
  Pen.   Kiss it.—
Alack, alack, his lips be wondrous cold.
Dear soul, h'as lost his colour : have ye seen
A straying heart ? All crannies ! every drop
Of blood is turned to an amethyst,   130
Which married bachelors hang in their ears.
  Org. Peace usher her into Elysium ! —
If this be madness, madness is an oracle. *Exit.*
  Ith. Christalla, Philema, when slept my sister,
Her ravings are so wild ?
  Chris.   Sir, not these ten days. 135
  Phil. We watch by her continually ; besides,
We can not any way pray her to eat.
  Bass. O, misery of miseries !
  Pen.   Take comfort ;
You may live well, and die a good old man.
By yea and nay, an oath not to be broken,   140
If you had join'd our hands once in the
    temple, —
'T was since my father died, for had he liv'd
He would have done 't, — I must have call'd
    you father.—
O, my wrack'd honour ! ruin'd by those tyrants,
A cruel brother and a desperate dotage !   145
There is no peace left for a ravish'd wife
Widow'd by lawless marriage ; to all memory
Penthea's, poor Penthea's name is strumpeted :
But since her blood was season'd by the forfeit
Of noble shame with mixtures of pollution, 150
Her blood — 't is just — be henceforth never
    height'ned
With taste of sustenance ! Starve ; let that ful-
    ness
Whose plurisy [2] hath fever'd faith and mod-
    esty —
Forgive me ; O, I faint !
      [*Falls into the arms of her* Attendants.]
  Arm.   Be not so wilful,
Sweet niece, to work thine own destruction.
  Ith.   Nature 155

Will call her daughter monster ! — What ! not
    eat ?
Refuse the only ordinary means
Which are ordain'd for life ? Be not, my sister,
A murderess to thyself.— Hear'st thou this,
    Bassanes ?
  Bass. Foh ! I am busy ; for I have not
    thoughts   160
Enow to think : all shall be well anon.
'T is tumbling in my head ; there is a mastery
In art to fatten and keep smooth the outside ;
Yes, and to comfort up the vital spirits   164
Without the help of food, fumes or perfumes,
Perfumes or fumes. Let her alone ; I 'll search
    out
The trick on 't.
  Pen.   Lead me gently ; heavens reward ye.
Griefs are sure friends ; they leave without
    control
Nor cure nor comforts for a leprous soul.
         Exeunt the maids *supporting* PEN-
         THEA.
  Bass. I grant ye ; and will put in practice in-
    stantly   170
What you shall still admire : 't is wonderful,
'T is super-singular, not to be match'd ;
Yet, when I 've done 't, I 've done 't : — ye shall
    all thank me.   *Exit.*
  Arm. The sight is full of terror.
  Ith.   On my soul
Lies such an infinite clog of massy dulness, 175
As that I have not sense enough to feel it. —
See, uncle, th' angry [3] thing returns again ;
Shall 's welcome him with thunder ? We are
    haunted,
And must use exorcism to conjure down
This spirit of malevolence.
  Arm.   Mildly, nephew. 180

    Enter NEARCHUS *and* AMELUS.

  Near. I come not, sir, to chide your late dis-
    order,
Admitting that th' inurement to a roughness
In soldiers of your years and fortunes, chiefly,
So lately prosperous, hath not yet shook off
The custom of the war in hours of leisure ; 185
Nor shall you need excuse, since y' are to ren-
    der
Account to that fair excellence, the princess,
Who in her private gallery expects it
From your own mouth alone : I am a messenger
But to her pleasure.
  Ith.   Excellent Nearchus,   190
Be prince still of my services, and conquer
Without the combat of dispute ; I honour ye.
  Near. The king is on a sudden indispos'd,
Physicians are call'd for ; 't were fit, Armostes,
You should be near him.
  Arm.   Sir, I kiss your hands. 195
         Exeunt ITHOCLES *and* ARMOSTES.
  Near. Amelus, I perceive Calantha's bosom
Is warm'd with other fires than such as can
Take strength from any fuel of the love
I might address to her. Young Ithocles,
Or ever I mistake, is lord ascendant   200

---

[1] Tagged laces.   [2] Excess.   [3] Q. *augury.*

Ot her devotions; one, to speak him truly,
In every disposition nobly fashioned.

Ame. But can your highness brook to be so
rivall'd,
Considering the inequality of the persons? 204

Near. I can, Amelus; for affections injur'd
By tyranny or rigour of compulsion,
Like tempest-threat'ned trees unfirmly rooted,
Ne'er spring to timely growth: observe, for in-
stance,
Life-spent Penthea and unhappy Orgilus.

Ame. How does your grace determine?

Near.   To be jealous 210
In public of what privately I'll further;
And though they shall not know, yet they shall
find it.   *Exeunt.*

[SCENE III.]¹

Enter HEMOPHIL *and* GRONEAS *leading* AMY-
CLAS, *and placing him in a chair; followed by*
ARMOSTES [*with a box*], CROTOLON, *and*
PROPHILUS.

Amy. Our daughter is not near?

Arm.   She is retir'd, sir,
Into her gallery.

Amy.   Where's the prince our cousin?

Pro. New walk'd into the grove, my lord.

Amy.   All leave us
Except Armostes, and you, Crotolon;
We would be private.

Pro.   Health unto your majesty! 5
Exeunt PROPHILUS, HEMOPHIL,
and GRONEAS.

Amy. What! Tecnicus is gone?

Arm. He is to Delphos;
And to your royal hands presents this box.

Amy. Unseal it, good Armostes; therein lie
The secrets of the oracle; out with it:
[ARMOSTES *takes out the scroll.*]
Apollo live our patron! Read, Armostes. 10

Arm. [*reads.*] *The plot in which the vine
takes root
Begins to dry from head to foot;
The stock soon withering, want of sap
Doth cause to quail the budding grape;
But from the neighbouring elm a dew 15
Shall drop, and feed the plot anew.*

Amy. That is the oracle: what exposition
Makes the philosopher?

Arm.   This brief one only.
[*Reads.*] *The plot is Sparta, the dri'd vine the
king;
The quailing grape his daughter; but the thing* 20
*Of most importance, not to be reveal'd,
Is a near prince, the elm: the rest conceal'd.*
TECNICUS.

Amy. Enough; although the opening of this
riddle
Be but itself a riddle, yet we construe
How near our labouring age draws to a rest. 25
But must Calantha quail too? that young
grape
Untimely budded! I could mourn for her;
Her tenderness hath yet deserv'd no rigour
So to be crost by fate.

---

¹ An apartment in the palace.

Arm.   You misapply, sir,—
With favour let me speak it,—what Apollo 30
Hath clouded in hid sense. I here conjecture
Her marriage with some neighb'ring prince, the
dew
Of which befriending elm shall ever strengthen
Your subjects with a sovereignty of power.

Crot. Besides, most gracious lord, the pith of
oracles 35
Is to be then digested when th' events
Expound their truth, not brought as soon to
light
As utter'd. Truth is child of Time; and herein
I find no scruple, rather cause of comfort,
With unity of kingdoms.

Amy.   May it prove so, 40
For weal of this dear nation!—Where is
Ithocles?—
Armostes, Crotolon, when this wither'd vine
Of my frail carcass, on the funeral pile
Is fir'd into its ashes, let that young man
Be hedg'd about still with your cares and
loves. 45
Much owe I to his worth, much to his service.—
Let such as wait come in now.

Arm.   All attend here!

Enter CALANTHA, ITHOCLES, PROPHILUS,
ORGILUS, EUPHRANEA, HEMOPHIL, *and*
GRONEAS.

Cal. Dear sir! king! father!

Ith.   O my royal master!

Amy. Cleave not my heart, sweet twins of
my life's solace,
With your forejudging fears; there is no
physic 50
So cunningly restorative to cherish
The fall of age, or call back youth and vigour,
As your consents in duty. I will shake off
This languishing disease of time, to quicken
Fresh pleasures in these drooping hours of
sadness. 55
Is fair Euphranea married yet to Prophilus?

Crot. This morning, gracious lord.

Org.   This very morning;
Which, with your highness' leave, you may ob-
serve too.
Our sister looks, methinks, mirthful and
sprightly,
As if her chaster fancy could already 60
Expound the riddle of her gain in losing
A trifle maids know only that they know not.
Pish! prithee, blush not; 'tis but honest
change
Of fashion in the garment, loose for strait,
And so the modest maid is made a wife. 65
Shrewd business—is't not, sister?

Euph.   You are pleasant.

Amy. We thank thee, Orgilus; this mirth be-
comes thee.
But wherefore sits the court in such a silence?
A wedding without revels is not seemly.

Cal. Your late indisposition, sir, forbade
it. 70

Amy. Be it thy charge, Calantha, to set forward
The bridal sports, to which I will be present;

If not, at least consenting. — Mine own Ithocles,
I have done little for thee yet.
Ith.   Y' have built me
To the full height I stand in.
Cal. [*Aside.*]   Now or never ! —   75
May I propose a suit ?
Amy.   Demand, and have it.
Cal. Pray, sir, give me this young man, and
            no further
Account him yours than he deserves in all
            things
To be thought worth mine : I will esteem him
According to his merit
Amy.   Still thou 'rt my daughter,   80
Still grow'st upon my heart. — [*To* ITHOCLES.]
            Give me thine hand ; —
Calantha, take thine own : in noble actions
Thou 'lt find him firm and absolute.— I would not
Have parted with thee, Ithocles, to any
But to a mistress who is all what I am.   85
Ith. A change, great king, most wisht for,
            'cause the same.
Cal. [*Aside to* ITHOCLES.] Th' art mine. Have
            I now kept my word ?
Ith. [*Aside to* CALANTHA.] Divinely.
Org. Rich fortunes guard, [the] [1] favour of a
            princess
Rock thee, brave man, in ever-crowned plenty !
Y' are minion of the time ; be thankful for
            it. —   90
[*Aside.*] Ho ! here 's a swing in destiny — ap-
            parent !
The youth is up on tiptoe, yet may stumble.
Amy. On to your recreations. — Now convey
            me
Unto my bed-chamber : none on his forehead
Wear a distempered look.
All.   The gods preserve ye ! 95
Cal. [*Aside to* ITHOCLES.] Sweet, be not from
            my sight.
Ith. [*Aside to* CALANTHA.] My whole felicity !
            Exeunt carrying out the king. ORGI-
            LUS *stays* ITHOCLES.
Org. Shall I be bold, my lord ?
Ith.   Thou canst not, Orgilus.
Call me thine own ; for Prophilus must hence-
            forth
Be all thy sister's : friendship, though it cease
            not   100
In marriage, yet is oft at less command
Than when a single freedom can dispose it.
Org. Most right, my most good lord, my most
            great lord,
My gracious princely lord, I might add, royal.
Ith. Royal ! A subject royal ?
Org.   Why not, pray, sir ? 105
The sovereignty of kingdoms in their nonage
Stoop'd to desert, not birth ; there 's as much
            merit
In clearness of affection as in puddle
Of generation : you have conquer'd love
Even in the loveliest ; if I greatly err not,   110
The son of Venus hath bequeath'd his quiver
To Ithocles his manage, [2] by whose arrows
Calantha's breast is open'd.

Ith.   Can 't be possible ?
Org. I was myself a piece of suitor once,
And forward in preferment too ; so forward 115
That, speaking truth, I may without offence,
            sir,
Presume to whisper that my hopes, and — hark
            ye —
My certainty of marriage stood assured
With as firm footing — by your leave — as   85
            any's
Now at this very instant— but —
Ith.   'T is granted : 120
And for a league of privacy between us,
Read o'er my bosom and partake a secret ;
The princess is contracted mine.
Org.   Still, why not ?
I now applaud her wisdom : when your king-
            dom
Stands seated in your will, secure and settled, 125
I dare pronounce you will be a just monarch ;
Greece must admire and tremble.
Ith.   Then the sweetness
Of so imparadis'd a comfort, Orgilus !
It is to banquet with the gods.
Org.   The glory
Of numerous children, potency of nobles,   130
Bent knees, hearts pav'd to tread on !
Ith.   With a friendship
So dear, so fast as thine.
Org.   I am unfitting
For office ; but for service —
Ith.   We 'll distinguish
Our fortunes merely in the title ; partners
In all respects else but the bed.
Org.   The bed ! 135
Forfend it Jove's own jealousy ! — till lastly
We slip down in the common earth together,
And there our beds are equal ; save some mon-
            ument
To show this was the king, and this the sub-
            ject. —   *Soft sad music.*
List, what sad sounds are these, — extremely
            sad ones ?   140
Ith. Sure, from Penthea's lodgings.
Org.   Hark ! a voice too.

A SONG [*within*].

O, no more, no more, too late
    Sighs are spent ; the burning tapers
Of a life as chaste as fate,
    Pure as are unwritten papers,
Are burnt out : no heat, no light   145
Now remains ; 't is ever night.

Love is dead ; let lovers' eyes,
Lock'd in endless dreams,
    Th' extremes of all extremes,   150
Ope no more, for now Love dies,
    Now Love dies, — implying
Love's martyrs must be ever, ever dying.

Ith. O, my misgiving heart !
Org.   A horrid stillness
Succeeds this deathful air ; let 's know the rea-
            son :   155
Tread softly ; there is mystery in mourning.
            Exeunt.

---

[1] Q. *to.*   [2] To the control of Ithocles.

SCENE [IV].[1]

Enter CHRISTALLA *and* PHILEMA, *bringing in*
PENTHEA *in a chair, veiled: two other* Servants
*placing two chairs, one on the one side, and the
other with an engine* [2] *on the other. The Maids
sit down at her feet, mourning. The Servants
go out: meet them* ITHOCLES *and* ORGILUS.

1 *Ser.* [*Aside to* ORGILUS.] 'T is done; that on
her right hand.
Org.   Good: begone.
                                [*Exeunt* Servants.]
Ith. Soft peace enrich this room!
Org.   How fares the lady?
Phil. Dead!
Chris.   Dead!
Phil.   Starv'd!
Chris.   Starv'd!
Ith.   Me miserable!
Org.   Tell us
How parted she from life.
Phil.   She call'd for music,
And begg'd some gentle voice to tune a fare-
        well   5
To life and griefs: Christalla touch'd the
        lute;
I wept the funeral song.
Chris.   Which scarce was ended
But her last breath seal'd up these hollow
        sounds,
"O, cruel Ithocles and injur'd Orgilus!"
So down she drew her veil, so died.
Ith.   So died! 10
Org. Up! you are messengers of death; go
        from us;
Here's woe enough to court without a prompter:
Away: and — hark ye — till you see us next,
No syllable that she is dead. — Away,
Keep a smooth brow.
        Exeunt CHRISTALLA *and* PHILEMA.
                  My lord, —
Ith.   Mine only sister! 15
Another is not left me.
Org.   Take that chair;
I 'll seat me here in this: between us sits
The object of our sorrows; some few tears
We 'll part among us: I perhaps can mix
One lamentable story to prepare 'em. —   20
There, there; sit there, my lord.
Ith.   Yes, as you please.
        ITHOCLES *sits down, and is catcht
                in the engine.*
What means this treachery?
Org.   Caught! you are caught,
Young master; 't is thy throne of coronation,
Thou fool of greatness! See, I take this veil off;
Survey a beauty wither'd by the flames   25
Of an insulting Phaëton, her brother.
Ith. Thou mean'st to kill me basely?
Org.   I foreknew
The last act of her life, and train'd thee hither
To sacrifice a tyrant to a turtle.
You dreamt of kingdoms, did ye? How to
        bosom   30

The delicacies of a youngling princess;
How with this nod to grace that subtle courtier,
How with that frown to make this noble trem-
        ble,
And so forth; whiles Penthea's groans and tor-
        tures,
Her agonies, her miseries, afflictions,   35
Ne'er toucht upon your thought: as for my in-
        juries,
Alas, they were beneath your royal pity;
But yet they liv'd, thou proud man, to con-
        found thee.
Behold thy fate; this steel! [*Draws a dagger.*]
Ith.   Strike home! A courage
As keen as thy revenge shall give it welcome:
But prithee faint not; if the wound close up, 41
Tent[3] it with double force, and search it deeply.
Thou look'st that I should whine and beg com-
        passion,
As loth to leave the vainness of my glories.
A statelier resolution arms my confidence,   45
To cozen thee of honour; neither could I
With equal trial of unequal fortune
By hazard of a duel; 't were a bravery
Too mighty for a slave intending murder.
On to the execution, and inherit   50
A conflict with thy horrors.
Org.   By Apollo,
Thou talk'st a goodly language! for requital
I will report thee to thy mistress richly.
And take this peace along: some few short
        minutes
Determin'd, my resolves shall quickly follow 55
Thy wrathful ghost; then, if we tug for mas-
        tery,
Penthea's sacred eyes shall lend new courage.
Give me thy hand: be healthful in thy part-
        ing
From lost mortality! thus, thus I free it.
                                Kills him.

Ith. Yet, yet, I scorn to shrink.
Org.   Keep up thy spirit: 60
I will be gentle even in blood; to linger
Pain, which I strive to cure, were to be cruel.
                                [*Stabs him again.*]
Ith. Nimble in vengeance, I forgive thee.
        Follow
Safety, with best success: O, may it prosper! —
Penthea, by thy side thy brother bleeds;   65
The earnest of his wrongs to thy forc'd faith.
Thoughts of ambition, or delicious banquet
With beauty, youth, and love, together perish
In my last breath, which on the sacred altar
Of a long-look'd-for peace — now — moves — to
        heaven.   *Dies.* 70
Org. Farewell, fair spring of manhood!
        Henceforth welcome
Best expectation of a noble suff'rance.
I 'll lock the bodies safe, till what must fol-
        low
Shall be approv'd. — Sweet twins, shine stars
        for ever! —
In vain they build their hopes whose life is
        shame: 75
No monument lasts but a happy name.   *Exit.*

----

[1] Penthea's apartment in the palace.
[2] A piece of mechanism.

[3] Probe.

ACT V

Scene I.[1]

Enter Bassanes, *alone.*

Bass. Athens — to Athens I have sent, the
    nursery
Of Greece for learning and the fount of know-
    ledge ;
For here in Sparta there's not left amongst us
One wise man to direct ; we're all turn'd mad-
    caps.
'T is said Apollo is the god of herbs,   5
Then certainly he knows the virtue of 'em :
To Delphos I have sent too. If there can be
A help for nature, we are sure yet.

Enter Orgilus.

Org.   Honour
Attend thy counsels ever !
Bass.   I beseech thee
With all my heart, let me go from thee quietly ;
I will not aught to do with thee, of all men.   11
The doubles[2] of a hare, — or, in a morning,
Salutes from a splay-footed witch, — to drop
Three drops of blood at th' nose just and no
    more, —
Croaking of ravens, or the screech of owls,   15
Are not so boding mischief as thy crossing
My private meditations. Shun me, prithee ,
And if I cannot love thee heartily,
I'll love thee as well as I can.
Org.   Noble Bassanes,
Mistake me not.
Bass. Phew ! then we shall be troubled.   20
Thou wert ordain'd my plague — heaven make
    me thankful,
And give me patience too, heaven, I beseech
    thee.
Org. Accept a league of amity ; for hence-
    forth,
I vow, by my best genius, in a syllable,
Never to speak vexation. I will study   25
Service and friendship, with a zealous sorrow
For my past incivility towards ye.
Bass. Hey-day, good words, good words ! I
    must believe 'em,
And be a coxcomb for my labour.
Org.   Use not
So hard a language ; your misdoubt is cause-
    less.   30
For instance, if you promise to put on
A constancy of patience, such a patience
As chronicle or history ne'er mentioned,
As follows not example, but shall stand
A wonder and a theme for imitation,   35
The first, the index[3] pointing to a second,
I will acquaint ye with an unmatch'd secret,
Whose knowledge to your griefs shall set a pe-
    riod.
Bass. Thou canst not, Orgilus ; 't is in the
    power
Of the gods only : yet, for satisfaction,   40
Because I note an earnest in thine utterance,

Unforc'd and naturally free, be resolute[4]
The virgin-bays shall not withstand the light-
    ning
With a more careless danger than my constancy
The full of thy relation. Could it move   45
Distraction in a senseless marble statue,
It should find me a rock : I do expect now
Some truth of unheard moment.
Org.   To your patience
You must add privacy, as strong in silence
As mysteries lock'd-up in Jove's own bosom.   50
Bass. A skull hid in the earth a treble age
Shall sooner prate.
Org.   Lastly, to such direction
As the severity of a glorious action
Deserves to lead your wisdom and your judg-
    ment,
You ought to yield obedience.
Bass.   With assurance   55
Of will and thankfulness.
Org.   With manly courage
Please, then, to follow me.
Bass.   Where'er, I fear not.
                         Exeunt omnes.

Scene II.[5]

Loud music. Enter Groneas *and* Hemophil,
leading Euphranea ; Christalla *and* Philema, *leading* Prophilus ; Nearchus *supporting* Calantha ; Crotolon *and* Amelus.
Cease loud music, all make a stand.

Cal. We miss our servant Ithocles and Orgilus ;
On whom attend they ?
Crot.   My son, gracious princess,
Whisper'd some new device, to which these revels
Should be but usher : wherein I conceive
Lord Ithocles and himself are actors.   5
Cal. A fair excuse for absence : as for Bass-
    anes,
Delights to him are troublesome : Armostes
Is with the king ?
Crot.   He is.
Cal.   On to the dance ! —
Dear cousin, hand you the bride ; the bride-
    groom must be
Intrusted to my courtship, Be not jealous,   10
Euphranea ; I shall scarcely prove a tempt-
    ress. —
Fall to our dance.

Music.

Nearchus *dances with* Euphranea, Prophilus *with* Calantha, Christalla *with* Hemophil, Philema *with* Groneas.

They dance the first change ; during which Armostes *enters.*

Arm. (*in* Calantha's *ear.*) The king your
    father's dead.
Cal. To the other change.
Arm.   Is't possible ?   *They dance again.*

Enter Bassanes.

Bass. [*whispers* Calantha.]   O, madam !
Penthea, poor Penthea's starved.

---

[1] A room in Bassanes' house.
[2] Q. *doublers.*   [3] The index-hand.
[4] Satisfied.   [5] A state-room in the palace.

Cal.   Beshrew thee !—
Lead to the next.
Bass.   Amazement dulls my senses. 15
                                        They dance again.

                Enter ORGILUS.

Org. [*whispers* CALANTHA.] Brave Ithocles is
    murder'd, murder'd cruelly.
Cal. How dull this music sounds ! Strike up
    more sprightly ;
Our footings are not active like our heart,
Which treads the nimbler measure.
Org.   I am thunderstruck.
                    The last change. Cease music.
Cal. So ! let us breathe awhile.— Hath not
    this motion,   20
Rais'd fresher colour on your cheeks ?
Near.   Sweet princess,
A perfect purity of blood enamels
The beauty of your white.
Cal.   We all look cheerfully ;
And, cousin, 't is, methinks, a rare presumption
In any who prefer our lawful pleasures   25
Before their own sour censure, t' interrupt
The custom of this ceremony bluntly.
Near. None dares, lady.
Cal. Yes, yes ; some hollow voice deliver'd
to me
How that the king was dead.
Arm.   The king is dead : 30
That fatal news was mine ; for in mine arms
He breath'd his last, and with his crown be-
    queath'd ye
Your mother's wedding ring ; which here I ten-
    der.
Crot. Most strange !
Cal. Peace crown his ashes ! We are queen,
    then.   35
Near. Long live Calantha ! Sparta's sovereign
    queen !
All. Long live the queen !
Cal.   What whispered Bassanes ?
Bass. That my Penthea, miserable soul,
Was starv'd to death.
Cal.   She 's happy ; she hath finish'd
A long and painful progress.— A third mur-
    mur
Pierc'd mine unwilling ears.
Org.   That Ithocles   41
Was murder'd ;— rather butcher'd, had not
    bravery
Of an undaunted spirit, conquering terror,
Proclaim'd his last act triumph over ruin.
Arm. How ! murder'd !
Cal.   By whose hand ?
Org.   By mine ; this weapon 45
Was instrument to my revenge : the reasons
Are just, and known ; quit him of these, and
    then
Never liv'd gentleman of greater merit,
Hope or abiliment [1] to steer a kingdom.
Crot. Fie, Orgilus !
Euph.   Fie, brother !
Cal.   You have done it ? 50
Bass. How it was done let him report, the
    forfeit

[1] Capacity.

Of whose allegiance to our laws doth covet
Rigour of justice ; but that done it is,
Mine eyes have been an evidence of credit
Too sure to be convinc'd.[2] Armostes, rent not
Thine arteries with hearing the bare circum-
    stances   55
Of these calamities ; thou 'st lost a nephew,
A niece, and I a wife : continue man still ;
Make me the pattern of digesting evils,
Who can outlive my mighty ones, not shrink-
    ing   60
At such a pressure as would sink a soul
Into what 's most of death, the worst of hor-
    rors.
But I have seal'd a covenant with sadness,
And enter'd into bonds without condition,
To stand these tempests calmly ; mark me,
    nobles,   65
I do not shed a tear, not for Penthea !
Excellent misery !
Cal.   We begin our reign
With a first act of justice : thy confession,
Unhappy Orgilus, dooms thee a sentence ;
But yet thy father's or thy sister's presence 70
Shall be excus'd.— Give, Crotolon, a blessing
To thy lost son ;— Euphranea, take a fare-
    weil ;—
And both be gone.
Crot. [*to* ORGILUS.] Confirm thee, noble sor-
    row,
In worthy resolution !
Euph.   Could my tears speak,
My griefs were slight.
Org.   All goodness dwell amongst ye ! 75
Enjoy my sister, Prophilus : my vengeance
Aim'd never at thy prejudice.
Cal.   Now withdraw.
            Exeunt CROTOLON, PROPHILUS,
                and EUPHRANEA.
Bloody relater of thy stains in blood,
For that thou hast reported him, whose for-
    tunes
And life by thee are both at once snatch'd
    from him,   80
With honourable mention, make thy choice
Of what death likes thee best ; there 's all our
    bounty.—
But to excuse delays, let me, dear cousin,
Intreat you and these lords see execution
Instant before ye part.
Near.   Your will commands us. 85
Org. One suit, just queen, my last : vouch-
    safe my clemency,
That by no common hand I be divided
From this my humble frailty.
Cal.   To their wisdoms
Who are to be spectators of thine end
I make the reference. Those that are dead   90
Are dead ; had they not now died, of necessity
They must have paid the debt they ow'd to
    nature
One time or other.— Use dispatch, my lords ;
We 'll suddenly prepare our coronation.
            Exeunt CALANTHA, PHILEMA, *and*
                CHRISTALLA.

[2] Confuted.

Arm. 'T is strange these tragedies should
    never touch on   95
Her female pity.
    Bass.   She has a masculine spirit;
And wherefore should I pule, and, like a girl,
Put finger in the eye? Let 's be all toughness,
Without distinction betwixt sex and sex.
    Near. Now, Orgilus, thy choice?
    Org.   To bleed to death. 100
    Arm. The executioner?
    Org.   Myself, no surgeon;
I am well skill'd in letting blood. Bind fast
This arm, that so the pipes may from their con-
    duits
Convey a full stream; here 's a skilful instru-
    ment.   *[Shows his dagger.]*
Only I am a beggar to some charity   105
To speed me in this execution
By lending th' other prick to th' tother arm,
When this is bubbling life out.
    Bass.   I am for ye;
It most concerns my art, my care, my credit. —
Quick, fillet both his arms.
    Org.   Gramercy, friendship! 110
Such courtesies are real which flow cheerfully
Without an expectation of requital.
Reach me a staff in this hand.
               [They give him a staff.]
               —If a proneness
Or custom in my nature from my cradle
Had been inclin'd to fierce and eager blood-
    shed,   115
A coward guilt, hid in a coward quaking,
Would have betray'd fame to ignoble flight
And vagabond pursuit of dreadful safety:
But look upon my steadiness, and scorn not
The sickness of my fortune, which, since Bass-
    anes   120
Was husband to Penthea, had lain bed-rid.
We trifle time in words: — thus I show cunning
In opening of a vein too full, too lively.
            [Pierces the vein with his dagger.]
    Arm. Desperate courage!
    [Near.][1]   Honourable infamy!
    Hem. I tremble at the sight.
    Gro.   Would I were loose! 125
    Bass. It sparkles like a lusty wine new
    broacht;
The vessel must be sound from which it is-
    sues. —
Grasp hard this other stick — I 'll be as nim-
    ble —
But prithee, look not pale — have at ye! stretch
    out
Thine arm with vigour and [with][2] unshook vir-
    tue.   *[Opens the vein.]*
Good! O, I envy not a rival, fitted   131
To conquer in extremities. This pastime
Appears majestical; some high-tun'd poem
Hereafter shall deliver to posterity
The writer's glory and his subject's triumph.135
How is 't, man? Droop not yet.
    Org.   I feel no palsies.
On a pair-royal do I wait in death;
My sovereign, as his liegeman; on my mistress,

As a devoted servant; and on Ithocles,
As if no brave, yet no unworthy enemy.   140
Nor did I use an engine to entrap
His life, out of a slavish fear to combat
Youth, strength, or cunning;[3] but for that I
    durst not
Engage the goodness of a cause on fortune,
By which his name might have outfac'd my
    vengeance.   145
O, Tecnicus, inspir'd with Phoebus' fire!
I call to mind thy augury, 't was perfect;
Revenge proves its own executioner.
When feeble man is bending to his mother,
The dust 'a was first fram'd on, thus he totters.
    Bass. Life's fountain is dri'd up.
    Org.   So falls the standard 151
Of my prerogative in being a creature!
A mist hangs o'er mine eyes, the sun's bright
    splendour
Is clouded in an everlasting shadow;
Welcome, thou ice, that sitt'st about my heart
No heat can ever thaw thee.   *Dies.*
    Near.   Speech hath left him. 156
    Bass. 'A has shook hands with time; his
    funeral urn
Shall be my charge: remove the bloodless body.
The coronation must require attendance;
That past, my few days can be but one mourn-
    ing.   *Exeunt.* 160

Scene III.[4]

*An altar covered with white; two lights of virgin
wax, during which music of recorders; enter
four bearing* Ithocles *on a hearse, or in a chair,
in a rich robe, with a crown on his head; place
him on one side of the altar. After him enter*
Calantha *in a white robe and crown'd;* Euphranea, Philema, *and* Christalla, *in
white;* Nearchus, Armostes, Crotolon,
Prophilus, Amelus, Bassanes, Hemophil, *and* Groneas.

Calantha *goes and kneels before the altar, the
rest stand off, the women kneeling behind, the
recorders cease during her devotions. Soft
music.* Calantha *and the rest rise, doing obeisance to the altar.*

    Cal. Our orisons are heard; the gods are
    merciful. —
Now tell me, you whose loyalties pay tribute
To us your lawful sovereign, how unskilful
Your duties or obedience is to render
Subjection to the sceptre of a virgin,   5
Who have been ever fortunate in princes
Of masculine and stirring composition.
A woman has enough to govern wisely
Her own demeanours, passions, and divisions.
A nation warlike and inur'd to practice   10
Of policy and labour cannot brook
A feminate authority: we therefore
Command your counsel, how you may advise
    us
In choosing of a husband whose abilities
Can better guide this kingdom.
    Near.   Royal lady, 15
Your law is in your will.

---

[1] Q. *Org.*   [2] Dyce's suggestion. Q. omits.

[3] Skill.   [4] A temple.

Arm.   We have seen tokens
Of constancy too lately to mistrust it.

Crot. Yet, if your highness settle on a choice
By your own judgment both allow'd and lik'd of,
Sparta may grow in power, and proceed   20
To an increasing height.

Cal.   Hold you the same mind?

Bass. Alas, great mistress, reason is so clouded
With the thick darkness of my infinite woes,
That I forecast nor dangers, hopes, or safety.
Give me some corner of the world to wear out   25
The remnant of the minutes I must number,
Where I may hear no sounds but sad complaints
Of virgins who have lost contracting partners;
Of husbands howling that their wives were ravisht
By some untimely fate; of friends divided   30
By churlish opposition; or of fathers
Weeping upon their children's slaughtered carcases;
Or daughters groaning o'er their fathers' hearses;
And I can dwell there, and with these keep consort
As musical as theirs. What can you look for   35
From an old, foolish, peevish, doting man
But craziness of age?

Cal. Cousin of Argos, —

Near.   Madam?

Cal.   Were I presently
To choose you for my lord, I 'll open freely
What articles I would propose to treat on   40
Before our marriage.

Near.   Name them, virtuous lady.

Cal. I would presume you would retain the royalty
Of Sparta in her own bounds; then in Argos
Armostes might be viceroy; in Messene
Might Crotolon bear sway; and Bassanes —   45

Bass. I, queen! alas, what I?

Cal.   Be Sparta's marshal.
The multitudes of high employments could not
But set a peace to private griefs. These gentlemen,
Groneas and Hemophil, with worthy pensions,
Should wait upon your person in your chamber. —   50
I would bestow Christalla on Amelus.
She 'll prove a constant wife; and Philema
Should into Vesta's Temple.

Bass.   This is a testament!
It sounds not like conditions on a marriage.

Near. All this should be perform'd.

Cal.   Lastly, for Prophilus,   55
He should be, cousin, solemnly invested
In all those honours, titles, and preferments
Which his dear friend and my neglected husband
Too short a time enjoy'd.

Pro.   I am unworthy
To live in your remembrance.

Euph.   Excellent lady!   60

Near. Madam, what means that word, "neglected husband"?

Cal. Forgive me: — now I turn to thee, thou shadow
Of my contracted lord! Bear witness all,
I put my mother's wedding-ring upon
His finger; 't was my father's last bequest.   65
    [*Places a ring on the finger of* ITHOCLES.]
Thus I new-marry him whose wife I am;
Death shall not separate us. O, my lords,
I but deceiv'd your eyes with antic gesture,
When one news straight came huddling on another
Of death! and death! and death! still I danced forward;   70
But it struck home, and here, and in an instant.
Be such mere women, who with shrieks and outcries
Can vow a present end to all their sorrows,
Yet live to [court][1] new pleasures, and outlive them.
They are the silent griefs which cut the heart-strings;   75
Let me die smiling.

Near.   'T is a truth too ominous.

Cal. One kiss on these cold lips, my last!
    [*Kisses* ITHOCLES.] — Crack, crack! —
Argos now 's Sparta's king. — Command the voices
Which wait at th' altar now to sing the song
I fitted for my end.

Near.   Sirs, the song!   80

A SONG.

All. Glories, pleasures, pomps, delights, and ease,
      Can but please
    Outward senses when the mind
    Is [or][2] untroubled or by peace refin'd.

1 [*Voice.*] Crowns may flourish and decay,   85
      Beauties shine, but fade away.

2 [*Voice.*] Youth may revel, yet it must
      Lie down in a bed of dust.

3 [*Voice.*] Earthly honours flow and waste,
      Time alone doth change and last.   90

All. Sorrows mingled with contents prepare
      Rest for care;
    Love only reigns in death; though art
    Can find no comfort for a broken heart.

            [CALANTHA *dies.*]

Arm. Look to the queen!

Bass.   Her heart is broke, indeed.   95
O, royal maid, would thou hadst mist this part!
Yet 't was a brave one. I must weep to see
Her smile in death.

Arm.   Wise Tecnicus! thus said he;
When youth is ripe, and age from time doth part,
The Lifeless Trunk shall wed the Broken Heart
Is here fulfill'd.

Near.   I am your king.

All.   Long live   101
Nearchus, King of Sparta!

Near.   Her last will
Shall never be digrest from: wait in order

---

    1 Q. *vow.*   2 Q. *not.*

Upon these faithful lovers, as becomes us. —
The counsels of the gods are never known　　105
Till men can call th' effects of them their own.
　　　　　　　　　　　　　　　　[*Exeunt.*]

THE EPILOGUE

WHERE noble judgments and clear eyes are
　　fix'd
To grace endeavour, there sits truth, not mix'd
With ignorance ; those censures may command
Belief which talk not till they understand.

Let some say, " This was flat ; " some, " Here
　　the scene　　　　　　　　　　　　　　5
Fell from its height ; " another, that the mean
Was " ill observ'd " in such a growing passion
As it transcended either state or fashion :
Some few may cry, " 'T was pretty well," or
　　so,
" But—" and there shrug in silence ; yet we
　　know　　　　　　　　　　　　　　　10
Our writer's aim was in the whole addrest
Well to deserve of *all*, but please the *best ;*
Which granted, by th' allowance of this strain
The BROKEN HEART may be piec'd up again.

THE LADY OF PLEASURE

BY

JAMES SHIRLEY

[DRAMATIS PERSONAE]

LORD ——.
SIR THOMAS BORNWELL.
SIR WILLIAM SCENTLOVE, ⎫
MASTER ALEXANDER KICKSHAW, ⎬ [Gallants.]
MASTER JOHN LITTLEWORTH, ⎭
MASTER HAIRCUT, [a Barber.]
MASTER FREDERICK, [nephew to Lady Bornwell.]
Steward to the Lady Aretina.
Steward to the Lady Celestina.

Secretary [to Lord ——].
Servants, etc.

ARETINA, Sir Thomas Bornwell's **Lady.**
CELESTINA, a young widow.
ISABELLA, ⎱ [Friends of Celestina.]
MARIANA, ⎰
MADAM DECOY, [a Procuress.]
[Gentlewoman.]

SCENE. — *The Strand.*

ACT I

[SCENE I.] [1]

Enter Lady BORNWELL,[2] *and her* Steward.

Stew. Be patient, madam ; you may have
　your pleasure.
Lady B.[2] 'T is that I came to town for. I
　would not
Endure again the country conversation,
To be the lady of six shires ! The men,
So near the primitive making, they retain　5
A sense of nothing but the earth ; their brains,
And barren heads standing as much in want
Of ploughing as their ground. To hear a fellow
Make himself merry and his horse, with whist-
　ling
Sellinger's Round ![3] To observe with what sol-
　emnity　　　　　　　　　　　　　　10
They keep their wakes, and throw for pewter
　candle-sticks !
How they become the morris, with whose bells
They ring all in to Whitsun-ales ; and sweat,
Through twenty scarfs and napkins, till the
　hobby-horse [4]
Tire, and the Maid Marian,[4] dissolv'd to a jelly,
Be kept for spoon meat !　　　　　　　16
Stew.　　These, with your pardon, are no argu-
　ment
To make the country life appear so hateful ;
At least to your particular, who enjoy'd
A blessing in that calm, would you be pleas'd　20
To think so, and the pleasure of a kingdom ;
While your own will commanded what should
　move
Delights, your husband's love and power join'd

To give your life more harmony. You liv'd
　there
Secure, and innocent, belov'd of all ;　　　25
Prais'd for your hospitality, and pray'd for :
You might be envi'd, but malice knew
Not where you dwelt. I would not prophesy,
But leave to your own apprehension,
What may succeed your change.
Lady B.　　You do imagine, 30
No doubt, you have talk'd wisely, and confuted
London past all defence. Your master should
Do well to send you back into the country,
With title of superintendent-bailiff.
Stew. How, madam !
Lady B.　　Even so, sir.
Stew.　　I am a gentleman,　35
Though now your servant.
Lady B.　　A country gentleman,
By your affection to converse with stubble.
His tenants will advance your wit, and plump
　it so
With beef and bag-pudding !
Stew.　　You may say your pleasure,
It becomes not me dispute.
Lady B.　　Complain to　40
The lord of the soil, your master.
Stew.　　You 're a woman
Of an ungovern'd passion, and I pity you.

Enter Sir THOMAS BORNWELL.

Born. How now ? What 's the matter ?
Stew.　　Nothing, sir. [*Exit.*]
Born. Angry, sweetheart ?
Lady B.　　I am angry with myself,
To be so miserably restrain'd in things,　　45
Wherein it doth concern your love and honour
To see me satisfied.
Born.　　In what, Aretina,
Dost thou accuse me ? Have I not obey'd
All thy desires ? Against mine own opinion
Quitted the country, and remov'd the hope　50

---

[1] A room in Sir Thomas Bornwell's house.
[2] In the Q, Lady Bornwell is called *Aretina* throughout in stage directions and speech-tags.
[3] A common country-dance tune. Cf. p. 487.
[4] Characters in the morris-dance

Of our return, by sale of that fair lordship
We liv'd in? Chang'd a calm and retir'd life
For this wild town, compos'd of noise and
charge?[1]
   Lady B. What charge, more than is neces-
sary for
A lady of my birth and education?   55
   Born. I am not ignorant how much nobility
Flows in your blood; your kinsmen great and
powerful
I' th' state; but with this, lose not you mem-
ory
Of being my wife. I shall be studious,
Madam, to give the dignity of your birth   60
All the best ornaments which become my for-
tune;
But would not flatter it, to ruin both,
And be the fable of the town, to teach
Other men loss of wit by mine, employ'd
To serve your vast expenses.
   Lady B.   Am I then   65
Brought in the balance? So, sir!
   Born.   Though you weigh
Me in a partial[2] scale, my heart is honest,
And must take liberty to think you have
Obey'd no modest counsel, to affect,[3]   69
Nay, study ways of pride and costly ceremony:
Your change of gaudy furniture, and pictures
Of this Italian master, and that Dutchman's;
Your mighty looking-glasses, like artillery,
Brought home on engines; the superfluous
plate,
Antique and novel; vanities of tires;[4]   75
Fourscore-pound suppers for my lord, your kins-
man,
Banquets for t' other lady aunt, and cousins,
And perfumes that exceed all: train of ser-
vants,
To stifle us at home, and show abroad
More motley than the French or the Venetian,   80
About your coach, whose rude postillion
Must pester[5] every narrow lane, till passengers
And tradesmen curse your choking up their
stalls;
And common cries pursue your ladyship,
For hind'ring o' their market.
   Lady B.   Have you done, sir?   85
   Born. I could accuse the gaiety of your ward-
robe,
And prodigal embroideries, under which
Rich satins, plushes, cloth of silver, dare
Not show their own complexions; your jewels,
Able to burn out the spectators' eyes,   90
And show like bonfires on you by the tapers.
Something might here be spar'd, with safety of
Your birth and honour, since the truest wealth
Shines from the soul, and draws up just ad-
mirers.—
I could urge something more.
   Lady B.   Pray do, I like   95
Your homily of thrift.
   Born.   I could wish, madam,
You would not game so much.
   Lady B.   A gamester too!

   Born. But are not come to that acquaintance
yet,
Should teach you skill enough to raise your
profit.
You look not through the subtilty of cards,   100
And mysteries of dice; nor can you save
Charge with the box, buy petticoats and pearls,
And keep your family by the precious income;
Nor do I wish you should: my poorest servant
Shall not upbraid my tables, nor his hire,   105
Purchas'd beneath my honour. You make play
Not a pastime but a tyranny, and vex
Yourself and my estate by it.
   Lady B.   Good! proceed.
   Born. Another game you have, which con-
sumes more
Your fame than purse; your revels in the
night,   110
Your meetings called the "Ball," to which re-
pair,
As to the Court of Pleasure, all your gallants
And ladies, thither bound by a subpoena
Of Venus, and small Cupid's high displeasure;
'Tis but the Family of Love[6] translated   115
Into more costly sin! There was a play on 't,[7]
And had the poet not been brib'd to a modest
Expression of your antic gambols in 't,
Some darks had been discovered, and the deeds
too.
In time he may repent, and make some blush,
To see the second part danc'd on the stage.   120
My thoughts acquit you for dishonouring me
By any foul act; but the virtuous know
'Tis not enough to clear ourselves, but the
Suspicions of our shame.
   Lady B.   Have you concluded   125
Your lecture?
   Born.   I ha' done; and howsoever
My language may appear to you, it carries
No other than my fair and just intent
To your delights, without curb to their mod-
est[8]
And noble freedom.
   Lady B.   I 'll not be so tedious   130
In my reply; but, without art or elegance,
Assure you, I keep still my first opinion:
And though you veil your avaricious meaning
With handsome names of modesty and thrift,
I find you would intrench and wound the lib-
erty   135
I was born with. Were my desires unprivileg'd
By example, while my judgment thought 'em
fit,
You ought not to oppose; but when the prac-
tice
And track of every honourable lady
Authorise me, I take it great injustice   140
To have my pleasures circumscrib'd, and taught
me.
A narrow-minded husband is a thief
To his own fame, and his preferment too;
He shuts his parts and fortunes from the
world,

   [6] A religious sect often accused of licentiousness.
   [7] "The Ball," a comedy by Shirley and Chapman,
1632.
   [8] Moderate.

   [1] Expense.   [3] Desire.
   [2] Unjust.   [4] Headdresses.   [5] Obstruct.

While, from the popular vote and knowledge,
　men　　　　　　　　　　　　　　　　　　145
Rise to employment in the state.
　Born.　　　　　　　　　　　　　　　　I have
No great ambition to buy preferment at
So dear a rate.
　Lady B.　　　Nor I to sell my honour,
By living poor and sparingly. I was not
Bred in that ebb of fortune, and my fate　150
Shall not compel me to it.
　Born.　　　　　　　　　　　　I know not,
Madam ; but you pursue these ways —
　Lady B.　　　　　　　　　What ways ?
　Born. In the strict sense of honesty, I dare
Make oath they are innocent.
　Lady B.　　　　　　　Do not divert,
By busy troubling of your brain, those thoughts
That should preserve 'em.
　Born.　　　　　　　　How was that ?
　Lady B.　　　　　　　'T is English.　156
　Born. But carries some unkind sense.

Enter MADAM DECOY.

　Dec. Good morrow, my sweet madam.
　Lady B.　　　　　　Decoy ! welcome ;
This visit is a favour.
　Dec.　　　　　　　Alas, sweet madam,
I cannot stay : I came but to present　　160
My service to your ladyship ; I could not
Pass by your door, but I must take the bold-
　ness
To tender my respects.
　Lady B.　　　　　　You oblige me, madam ;
But I must not dispense so with your absence.
　Dec. Alas, the coach, madam, stays for me
　at the door.　　　　　　　　　　　　165
　Lady B. Thou sha't command mine ; prithee,
　sweet Decoy —
　Dec. I would wait on you, madam, but I
　have many
Visits to make this morning ; I beseech —
　Lady B. So you will promise to dine with
　me.
　Dec.　　　　　　　　I shall
Present a guest.
　Lady B.　　Why, then good morrow, madam.
　Dec. A happy day shine on your ladyship !　171
　　　　　　　　　　　　　　　　　Exit.

Re-enter Steward.

　Lady B. What 's your news, sir ?
　Stew.　　　　　Madam, two gentlemen.
　Lady B. What gentlemen ? Have they no
　names ?
　Stew.　　　　They are
The gentleman with his own head of hair,
Whom you commended for his horsemanship　175
In Hyde Park, and becoming so the saddle,
The t' other day.
　Lady B.　　　What circumstance is this
To know him by ?
　Stew.　　　His name 's at my tongue's end : —
He lik'd the fashion of your pearl chain,
　madam ;
And borrowed it for his jeweller to take　180
A copy by it.
　Born. [*Aside.*] What cheating gallant 's this ?

　Stew. That never walks without a lady's
　busk,[1]
And plays with fans — Master Alexander Kick-
　shaw, —
I thought I should remember him.
　Lady B.　　　　　　What 's the other ?
　Stew. What an unlucky memory I have !　185
The gallant that still danceth in the street,
And wears a gross of ribbon in his hat ;
That carries oringado [2] in his pocket,
And sugar-plums, to sweeten his discourse ;
That studies compliment, defies all wit　190
In black, and censures plays that are not
　bawdy —
Master John Littleworth.
　Lady B.　　　　They are welcome ; but
Pray entertain them a small time, lest I
Be unprovided.
　Born.　　　Did they ask for me ?
　Stew. No, sir.
　Born. It matters not, they must be welcome.
　Lady B. Fie ! how 's this hair disordered ?
Here 's a curl　　　　　　　　　　　　195
Straddles most impiously. I must to my closet.
　　　　　　　　　　　　　　　　　Exit.
　Born. Wait on 'em ; my lady will return
again.　　　　　　　　　[*Exit* Steward.]
I have to such a height fulfill'd [3] her humour,
All application 's [4] dangerous : these gallants　200
Must be receiv'd, or she will fall into
A tempest, and the house be shook with names
Of all her kindred. 'T is a servitude
I may in time shake off.

Enter ALEXANDER [KICKSHAW] *and* LITTLE-
　WORTH.

　Kick. and Little.　　　Save you, Sir Thomas !
　Born. Save you, gentlemen !
　Kick.　　　　　　　I kiss your hand.　205
　Born. What [5] day is it abroad ?
　Little.　The morning rises from your lady's
　eye :
If she look clear, we take the happy omen
Of a fair day.
　Born.　　　She 'll instantly appear,
To the discredit of your compliment ;　　210
But you express your wit thus.
　Kick.　　　　　　　And you modesty,
Not to affect [6] the praises of your own.
　Born. Leaving this subject, what game 's
now on foot ?
What exercise carries the general vote
O' the town ? Nothing moves without your
　knowledge.　　　　　　　　　　　　215
　Kick. The cocking now has all the noise ; I 'll
　have
A hundred pieces of one battle. — Oh,
These birds of Mars !
　Little.　　　Venus is Mars his bird too.
　Kick. Why, and the pretty doves are Venus's,
To show that kisses draw the chariot.　　220
　Little. I am for that skirmish.
　Born.　　　　　When shall we have

---

[1] Corset.
[2] Candied orange-peel.
[3] Indulged.
[4] Appeal, demand (?).
[5] What sort of.
[6] Like.

More booths and bagpipes upon Banstead
      downs?
No mighty race is expected? — But my lady
Returns!

Re-enter LADY BORNWELL.

Lady B.   Fair morning to you, gentlemen!
You went not late to bed by your early visit. 225
You do me honour.
    Kick.   It becomes our service.
Lady B. What news abroad? You hold pre-
      cious intelligence.
Little. All tongues are so much busy with
      your praise,
They have not time to frame other discourse.
Will 't please you, madam, taste a sugar-plum?
Born. What does the goldsmith think the
      pearl is worth   231
You borrowed of my lady?
    Kick.   'T is a rich one.
Born. She has many other toys, whose fash-
      ion you
Will like extremely: you have no intention
To buy any of her jewels?
    Kick.   Understand me — 235
Born. You had rather sell, perhaps. But,
      leaving this,
I hope you 'll dine with us.
    Kick.   I came a' purpose.
Lady B. And where were you last night?
    Kick.   I, madam? Where
I slept not; it had been sin, where so much
Delight and beauty was to keep me waking. 240
There is a lady, madam, will be worth
Your free society; my conversation
Ne'er knew so elegant and brave a soul,
With most incomparable flesh and blood;
So spirited! so courtly! speaks the lan-
      guages,   245
Sings, dances, plays o' th' lute to admiration!
Is fair, and paints not; games too, keeps a table,
And talks most witty satire; has a wit
Of a clean Mercury —
    Little.   Is she married?
    Kick.   No.
Lady B. A virgin?
    Kick.   Neither.
    Little.   What! a widow! Something
Of this wide commendation might have   251
Excus'd. This such a prodigy!
    Kick.   Repent,
Before I name her: she did never see
Yet full sixteen, an age, in the opinion
Of wise men, not contemptible. She has   255
Mourn'd out her year, too, for the honest
      knight
That had compassion of her youth, and died
So timely. Such a widow is not common;
And now she shines more fresh and tempting
Than any natural virgin.
    Lady B.   What 's her name? 260
    Kick. She was christened Celestina; by her
      husband,
The Lady Bellamour: this ring was hers.
Born. You borrowed it to copy out the posy.
Kick. Are they not pretty rubies? 't was a
      grace

She was pleas'd to show me, that I might have
      one   265
Made of the self-same fashion; for I love
All pretty forms.
    Lady B.   And is she glorious?
Kick. She is full of jewels, madam; but I
      am
Most taken with the bravery of her mind,
Although her garments have all grace and or-
      nament.   270
Lady B. You have been high in praises.
    Kick.   I come short;
No flattery can reach her.
    Born. [Aside.]   Now my lady
Is troubled, as she fear'd to be eclips'd:
This news will cost me somewhat.
    Lady B.   You deserve
Her favour, for this noble character.   275
    Kick. And I possess it, by my stars benevo-
      lence.
Lady B. You must bring us acquainted.
    Born.   I pray do, sir;
I long to see her too. — Madam, I have
Thought upon 't, and corrected my opinion.
Pursue what ways of pleasure your desires   280
Incline you to, not only with my state,
But with my person; I will follow you.
I see the folly of my thrift, and will
Repent in sack and prodigality,
To your own heart's content.
    Lady B.   But do not mock. 285
Born. Take me to your embraces, gentlemen,
And tutor me.
    Little.   And will you kiss the ladies?
Born. And sing and dance. I long to see this
      beauty;
I would fain lose a hundred pounds at dice now.
Thou sha't have another gown and petticoat 290
To-morrow. Will you sell my running-horses?
We have no Greek wine in the house, I think;
Pray send one of our footmen to the merchant,
And throw the hogshead of March-beer into 294
The kennel,[1] to make room for sack and claret.
What think you to be drunk yet before dinner?
We will have constant music, and maintain
Them and their fiddles in fantastic liveries:
I 'll tune my voice to catches. I must have
My dining-room enlarg'd, to invite ambassa-
      dors.   300
We 'll feast the parish in the fields, and teach
The military men new discipline,
Who shall charge all their great artillery
With oranges and lemons, boy, to play
All dinner upon our capons.
    Kick.   He 's exalted! 305
Born. I will do anything to please my lady,
Let that suffice; and kiss o' th' same condition.
I am converted; do not you dispute,
But patiently allow the miracle.
    Lady B. I am glad to hear you, sir, in so
      good tune.   310

Enter Servant.

Serv. Madam, the painter.
Lady B.   I am to sit this morning.

---

[1] Gutter.

Born. Do, while I give new directions to my
    steward.
Kick. With your favour, we 'll wait on you:
    sitting 's but
A melancholy exercise without
Some company to discourse.
    Lady B.   It does conclude 315
A lady's morning work. We rise, make fine,
Sit for our picture, and 't is time to dine.
  Little. Praying 's forgot.
  Kick.   'T is out of fashion.
                            Exeunt.

[SCENE II.] [1]

Enter CELESTINA *and her* Steward.

  Cel. Fie! what an air this room has!
  Stew.   'T is perfum'd.
  Cel. With some cheap stuff. Is it your wis-
    dom's thrift
To infect my nostrils thus? Or is 't to favour
The gout in your worship's hand, you are
    afraid
To exercise your pen in your account book? 5
Or do you doubt my credit to discharge
Your bills?
  Stew.   Madam, I hope you have not found
My duty, with the guilt of sloth or jealousy,
Unapt to your command.
  Cel.   You can extenuate
Your faults with language, sir; but I expect 10
To be obey'd. What hangings have we here!
  Stew. They are arras, madam.
  Cel.   Impudence! I know 't.
I will have fresher, and more rich; not
    wrought
With faces that may scandalize a Christian, 14
With Jewish stories stuft with corn and camels.
You had best wrap all my chambers in wild
    Irish,
And make a nursery of monsters here,
To fright the ladies come to visit me.
  Stew. Madam, I hope —
  Cel.   I say I will have other,
Good Master Steward, of a finer loom; 20
Some silk and silver, if your worship please
To let me be at so much cost. I 'll have
Stories to fit the seasons of the year,
And change as often as I please.
  Stew.   You shall, madam.
  Cel. I am bound to your consent, forsooth!
    And is 25
My coach brought home?
  Stew.   This morning I expect it.
  Cel. The inside, as I gave direction,
Of crimson plush?
  Stew.   Of crimson camel plush.
  Cel. Ten thousand moths consume 't! Shall
    I ride through
The streets in penance, wrapt up round in hair
    cloth? 30
Sell 't to an alderman, 't will serve his wife
To go a feasting to their country-house;
Or fetch a merchant's nurse-child, and come
    home
Laden with fruit and cheese-cakes. I despise
    it!

              [1] A room in Celestina's house.

  Stew. The nails adorn it, madam, set in
    method, 35
And pretty forms.
  Cel.   But single gilt, I warrant.
  Stew. No, madam.
  Cel.   Another solecism! Oh fie!
This fellow will bring me to a consumption
With fretting at his ignorance. Some lady
Had rather never pray than go to church in't.[40]
The nails not double gilt! To market wo 't? [2]
'T will hackney out to Mile-end, or convey
Your city tumblers [3] to be drunk with cream
And prunes at Islington.[4]
  Stew.   Good madam, hear me.
  Cel. I 'll rather be beholding to my aunt, 45
The countess, for her mourning coach, than be
Disparag'd so. Shall any juggling tradesman
Be at charge to shoe his running-horse with
    gold,
And shall my coach nails be but single gilt!
How dare these knaves abuse me so?
  Stew.   Vouchsafe 50
To hear me speak.
  Cel.   Is my sedan yet finish'd,
And liveries for my men-mules,[5] according
As I gave charge?
  Stew.   Yes, madam, it is finish'd,
But without tilting-plumes at the four corners;
The scarlet 's pure, but not embroidered. 55
  Cel. What mischief were it to your con-
    science
Were my coach lin'd with tissue, and my har-
    ness
Cover'd with needle-work? if my sedan
Had all the story of the prodigal
Embroidered with pearl?
  Stew.   Alas, good madam, 60
I know 't is your own cost; I am but your
    steward,
And would discharge my duty the best way.
You have been pleas'd to hear me; 't is not for
My profit that I manage your estate
And save expense, but for your honour, madam.
  Cel. How, sir! my honour?
  Stew.   Though you hear it not, 65
Men's tongues are liberal in your character,
Since you began to live thus high. I know
Your fame is precious to you.
  Cel.   I were best
Make you my governor. Audacious varlet! 70
How dare you interpose your doting connsel?
Mind your affairs with more obedience,
Or I shall ease you of an office, sir.
Must I be limited to please your honour,
Or, for the vulgar breath, confine my pleasures?
I will pursue 'em in what shapes I fancy, 76
Here, and abroad; my entertainments shall
Be oft'ner, and more rich. Who shall control
    me?
I live i' th' Strand, whither few ladies come
To live, and purchase more than fame. I will
Be hospitable then, and spare no cost 81
That may engage all generous report
To trumpet forth my bounty and my bravery,[5]

    [2] Will it? Gifford reads *with* 't.   [3] Courtesans.
    [4] A suburban resort for cakes and cream.
    [5] Chair-men.   [6] Splendor.

Till the court envy, and remove. I 'll have
My house the academy of wits, who shall   85
Exalt their genius with rich sack and sturgeon,
Write panegyrics of my feasts, and praise
The method of my witty superfluities.
The horses shall be taught, with frequent wait-
  ing
Upon my gates, to stop in their career   90
Toward Charing-cross, spite of the coachman's
  fury ;
And not a tilter but shall strike [1] his plume,
When he sails by my window : my balcony
Shall be the courtier's idol, and more gaz'd at
Than all the pageantry at Temple Bar,   95
By country clients.
  Stew.   Sure my lady 's mad.
  Cel. Take that for your ill manners.
                                    [*Strikes him.*]
  Stew.   Thank you, madam.—
I would there were less quicksilver in your fin-
  gers.   *Exit.*
  Cel. There 's more than simple honesty in a
  servant
Requir'd to his full duty ; none should dare   100
But with a look, much less a saucy language,
Check at their mistress' pleasure. I 'm resolv'd
To pay for some delight, my estate will bear it;
I 'll rein it shorter when I please.

              Re-enter Steward.

  Stew.   A gentleman
Desires to speak with your ladyship.
  Cel.   His name ?   105
  Stew. He says you know him not ; he seems
  to be
Of quality.
  Cel.   Admit him.   [*Exit* Steward.]

              Enter HAIRCUT.

                    Sir, with me ?
  Hair. Madam, I know not how you may re-
  ceive
This boldness from me ; but my fair intents
Known, will incline you to be charitable.   110
  Cel. No doubt, sir.
  Hair.   He must live obscurely, madam,
That hath not heard what virtues you possess ;
And I, a poor admirer of your fame,
Am come to kiss your hand.
  Cel.   That all your business ?
  Hair. Though it were worth much travel, I
  have more   115
In my ambition.
  Cel.   Speak it freely, sir.
  Hair. You are a widow.
  Cel.   So !
  Hair.   And I a bachelor.
  Cel. You come a wooing, sir, and would per-
  haps
Show me a way to reconcile the two ?
  Hair. And bless my stars for such a happi-
  ness.   120
  Cel. I like you, sir, the better, that you do
  not
Wander about, but shoot home to the mean-
  ing ;

                  [1] Lower.

It is a confidence will make a man
Know sooner what to trust to : but I never
Saw you before, and I believe you come not   125
With hope to find me desperate upon marriage.
If maids, out of their ignorance of what
Men are, refuse these offers, widows may,
Out of their knowledge, be allow'd some coy·
  ness :
And yet I know not how much happiness   136
A peremptory answer may deprive me of ; —
You may be some young lord, and though I see
  not
Your footmen and your groom, they may not
  be
Far off, in conference with your horse. Please
  you
To instruct me with your title, against which
I would not willingly offend.
  Hair.   I am   135
A gentleman ; my name is Haircut, madam.
  Cel. Sweet Master Haircut, are you a court-
  ier ?
  Hair. Yes.
  Cel.   I did think so, by your confidence.
Not to detain you, sir, with circumstance,   140
I was not so unhappy in my husband,
But that 't is possible I may be a wife
Again ; but I must tell you, he that wins
My affection, shall deserve me.
  Hair.   I will hope,
If you can love, I shall not present, madam,   145
An object to displease you in my person :
And when time, and your patience, shall pos-
  sess you
With further knowledge of me, and the truth
Of my devotion, you will not repent
The offer of my service.
  Cel.   You say well.   150
How long do you imagine you can love, sir ?
Is it a quotidian, or will it hold
But every other day ?
  Hair.   You are pleasant,[2] madam.
  Cel. Does it take you with a burning at the
  first,
Or with a cold fit ? for you gentlemen   155
Have both your summer and your winter ser-
  vice.
  Hair. I am ignorant what you mean ; but I
  shall never
Be cold in my affection to such beauty.
  Cel. And 't will be somewhat long ere I be
  warm in' t.
  Hair. If you vouchsafe me so much honour,
  madam,   160
That I may wait on you sometimes, I sha' not
Despair to see a change.
  Cel.   But now I know
Your mind, you shall not need to tell it when
You come again ; I shall remember it.
  Hair. You make me fortunate.

              Re-enter Steward.

  Stew.   Madam, your kinswomen,   165
The lady Novice, and her sister, are
New lighted from their coach.

                  [2] Jocular.

Cel.   I did expect 'em,
They partly are my pupils. I 'll attend 'em.
                              [*Exit* Steward.]
  Hair. Madam, I have been too great a tres-
      passer
Upon your patience ; I will take my leave.   170
You have affairs, and I have some employment
Calls me to court ; I shall present again
A servant to you.   *Exit.*
  Cel.   Sir, you may present,
But not give fire, I hope. — Now to the ladies.
This recreation 's past, the next must be   175
To read to them some court philosophy.   *Exit.*

ACT II

Scene I.[1]

Enter Sir Thomas Bornwell.

  Born. 'T is a strange humour I have under-
      taken,
To dance, and play, and spend as fast as she
      does ;
But I am resolv'd : it may do good upon her,
And fright her into thrift. Nay, I 'll endeavour
To make her jealous too ; if this do not   5
Allay her gamboling, she 's past a woman,
And only a miracle must tame her.

Enter Steward.

  Stew. 'T is master Frederick, my lady's
      nephew.
  Born.   What of him ?
  Stew. Is come from the university.
  Born.   By whose directions ?
  Stew. It seems, my lady's.
  Born.   Let me speak with him   10
Before he see his aunt. [*Exit* Stew.] — I do not
like it.—

Enter [Steward, *with*] Master Frederick, [*in
    his college dress.*]

Master Frederick, welcome ! I expected not
So soon your presence ; what 's the hasty cause ?
  Fred. These letters, from my tutor, will ac-
      quaint you.   [*Gives* Bornwell *letters.*]
  Stew. Welcome home, sweet Master Fred-
      erick !
  Fred.   Where 's my aunt ?   15
  Stew. She 's busy about her painting, in her
      closet ;
The outlandish man of art is copying out
Her countenance.
  Fred.   She is sitting for her picture ?
  Stew. Yes, sir ; and when 't is drawn she will
      be hang'd
Next the French cardinal, in the dining-room.
But when she hears you 're come, she will dis-
      miss   21
The Belgic gentleman, to entertain
Your worship.
  Fred.   Change of air has made you witty.
  Born. Your tutor gives you a handsome
      character.

<hr>

[1] A room in Sir Thomas Bornwell's house.

Frederick, and is sorry your aunt's pleasure   25
Commands you from your studies ; but I hope
You have no quarrel to the liberal arts.
Learning is an addition[2] beyond
Nobility of birth. Honour of blood,
Without the ornament of knowledge, is   30
A glorious[3] ignorance.
  Fred. I never knew more sweet and happy
      hours
Than I employ'd upon my books. I heard
A part of my philosophy, and was so
Delighted with the harmony of nature,   35
I could have wasted my whole life upon 't.
  Born. [*Aside.*] 'T is pity a rash indulgence
      should corrupt
So fair a genius ! She 's here ; I 'll observe.

Enter Lady Bornwell, Kickshaw, *and*
    Littleworth.

  Fred. My most lov'd aunt !
  Lady B.   Support me, I shall faint.
  Lttle. What ails your ladyship ?
  Lady B.   Is that Frederick,   40
In black ?
  Kick. Yes, madam ; but the doublet's satin.
  Lady B. The boy 's undone !
  Fred.   Madam, you appear troubled.
  Lady B. Have I not cause ? Was not I
      trusted with
Thy education, boy, and have they sent thee
Home like a very scholar !
  Kick.   'T was ill done,   45
Howe'er they us'd him in the university,
To send him to his friends thus.
  Fred.   Why, sir ? Black,
(For 't is the colour that offends your eye-sight,)
Is not, within my reading, any blemish ;
Sables are no disgrace in heraldry.   50
  Kick. 'T is coming from the college thus,
      that makes it
Dishonourable. While you wore it for
Your father, it was commendable ; or were
Your aunt dead, you might mourn, and justify.
  Lady B. What luck[4] I did not send him
      into France !   55
They would have given him generous education,
Taught him another garb, to wear his lock,[5]
And shape, as gaudy as the summer ; how
To dance, and wag his feather *à-la-mode*,
To compliment, and cringe ; to talk not mod-
      estly,   60
Like, " ay forsooth," and " no forsooth ; " to
      blush,
And look so like a chaplain ! — There he might
Have learn'd a brazen confidence, and observ'd
So well the custom of the country, that
He might, by this time, have invented fashions   65
For us, and been a benefit to the kingdom ;
Preserv'd our tailors in their wits, and sav'd
The charge of sending into foreign courts
For pride and antic fashions.— Observe
In what a posture he does hold his hat now !   70
  Fred. Madam, with your pardon, you have
      practis'd

<hr>

[2] Title, ornament.
[3] Vain-glorious.
[4] *I. e.* Bad luck.
[5] Hair.

Another dialect than was taught me when
I was commended to your care and breeding.
I understand not this; Latin or Greek
Are more familiar to my apprehension: 75
Logic was not so hard in my first lectures
As your strange language.

Lady B.   Some strong waters; oh!

Little. Comfits will be as comfortable to
your stomach, madam. [*Offers his box.*]

Lady B. I fear he 's spoil'd for ever! He did
name
Logic, and may, for aught I know, be gone   80
So far to understand it. I did always
Suspect they would corrupt him in the col-
lege.—
Will your Greek saws and sentences discharge
The mercer? Or is Latin a fit language
To court a mistress in?—Master Alexander,   85
If you have any charity, let me
Commend him to your breeding.— I suspect
I must employ my doctor first, to purge
The university that lies in 's head;
It alters his complexion.

Kick.   If you dare   90
Trust me to serve him—

Lady B.   Master Littleworth,
Be you join'd in commission.

Little.   I will teach him
Postures and rudiments.

Lady B.   I have no patience
To see him in this shape; it turns my stomach.
When he has cast his academic skin   95
He shall be yours. I am bound in conscience
To see him bred; his own state shall maintain
The charge, while he 's my ward. — Come
hither, sir.

Fred. What does my aunt mean to do with
me?

Stew. To make you a fine gentleman, and
translate you   100
Out of your learned language, sir, into
The present Goth and Vandal, which is French.

Born. [*Aside.*] Into what mischief will this
humour ebb?
She will undo the boy; I see him ruin'd.
My patience is not manly; but I must   105
Use stratagem to reduce her: open ways
Give me no hope.

Stew.   You shall be obey'd, madam.
Exeunt [*all but* FREDERICK *and*
Steward].

Fred. Master Steward, are you sure we do
not dream?
Was 't not my aunt you talkt to?

Stew.   One that loves you
Dear as her life. These clothes do not become
you,   110
You must have better, sir—

Fred.   These are not old.

Stew. More suitable to the town and time;
we keep
No Lent here, nor is 't my lady's pleasure you
Should fast from anything you have a mind to;
Unless it be your learning, which she would
have you   115
Forget with all convenient speed that may be,
For the credit of your noble family.

The case is alter'd since we liv'd i' th' country;
We do not now invite the poor o' th' parish
To dinner, keep a table for the tenants;   120
Our kitchen does not smell of beef; the cellar
Defies the price of malt and hops; the footmen
And coach-drivers may be drunk like gentle-
men,
With wine; nor will three fiddlers upon holi-
days,
With aid of bag-pipes, that call'd in the coun-
try   125
To dance, and plough the hall up with their
hob-nails,
Now make my lady merry. We do feed
Like princes, and feast nothing else but princes;
And are these robes fit to to be seen amongst
'em?

Fred. My lady keeps a court then! Is Sir
Thomas   130
Affected [1] with this state and cost?

Stew.   He was not,
But is converted: and I hope you wo' not
Persist in heresy, but take a course
Of riot, to content your friends; you shall
Want nothing, if you can be proud, and spend
it   135
For my lady's honour. Here are a hundred
Pieces, will serve you till you have new clothes;
I will present you with a nag of mine,
Poor tender of my service, please you accept;
My lady's smile more than rewards me for it.   140
I must provide fit servants to attend you,
Monsieurs, for horse and foot.

Fred.   I shall submit,
If this be my aunt's pleasure, and be rul'd;
My eyes are open'd with this purse already,
And sack will help to inspire me. I must spend
it?   145

Stew. What else, sir?

Fred.   I 'll begin with you: to encourage
You to have still a special care of me,
There is five pieces,—not for your nag.

Stew. No, sir; I hope it is not.

Fred.   Buy a beaver
For thy own block; [2] I shall be rul'd. Who
does   150
Command the wine cellar?

Stew.   Who commands but you, sir?

Fred. I 'll try to drink a health or two, my
aunt's,
Or anybody's; and if that foundation
Stagger me not too much, I will commence
In all the arts of London.

Stew.   If you find, sir,   155
The operation of the wine exalt
Your blood to the desire of any female
Delight, I know your aunt wo' not deny
Any of her chambermaids to practise on;
She loves you but too well.

Fred.   I know not how   160
I may be for that exercise. — Farewell, Aris-
totle,
Prithee commend me to the library
At Westminster; my bones I bequeath thither,

---

[1] Pleased.
[2] Usually, a mould for shaping a hat; here, head.

And to the learned worms that mean to visit
        'em.
I will compose myself ; I begin to think   165
I have lost time indeed. — Come to the wine
        cellar.   *Exeunt.*

[SCENE II.][1]

Enter CELESTINA, MARIANA, *and* ISABELLA.

Mar. But shall we not, madam, expose our-
        selves
To censure for this freedom ?
Cel.   Let them answer
That dare mistake us. Shall we be so much
Cowards, to be frighted from our pleasure,
Because men have malicious tongues, and show
What miserable souls they have ? No, cousin, 6
We hold our life and fortunes upon no
Man's charity ; if they dare show so little
Discretion to traduce our fames, we will
Be guilty of so much wit to laugh at 'em.   10
Isab. 'T is a becoming fortitude.
Cel.   My stars
Are yet kind to me ; for, in a happy minute
Be 't spoke, I 'm not in love, and men shall
        never
Make my heart lean with sighing, nor with
        tears
Draw on my eyes the infamy of spectacles.   15
'T is the chief principle to keep your heart
Under your own obedience ; jest, but love not.
I say my prayers, yet can wear good clothes,
And only satisfy my tailor for 'em
I will not lose my privilege.   20
Mar. And yet they say your entertainments
        are,
Give me your pardon, madam, to proclaim
Yourself a widow, and to get a husband.
Cel. As if a lady of my years, some beauty,
Left by her husband rich, that had mourn'd for
        him   25
A twelvemonth too, could live so obscure i' th'
        town,
That gallants would not know her, and invite
Themselves, without her chargeable[2] proclama-
        tions !
Then we are worse than citizens : no widow
Left wealthy can be thoroughly warm in mourn-
        ing,   30
But some one noble blood, or lusty kindred,
Claps in, with his gilt coach, and Flandrian[3]
        trotters,
And hurries her away to be a countess.
Courtiers have spies, and great ones with large
        titles,
Cold in their own estates, would warm them-
        selves   35
At a rich city bonfire.
Isab.   Most true, madam.
Cel. No matter for corruption of the blood :
Some undone courtier made her husband rich,
And this new lord receives it back again.
Admit it were my policy, and that   40
My entertainments pointed to acquaint me
With many suitors, that I might be safe

        [1] A room in Celestina's house.
        [2] Expensive.   [3] Flemish.

And make the best election, could you blame
        me ?
Mar. Madam, 't is wisdom.
Cel.   But I should be
In my thoughts miserable, to be fond[4]   45
Of leaving the sweet freedom I possess,
And court myself into new marriage fetters.
I now observe men's several wits and windings,[5]
And can laugh at their follies.
Mar.   You have given
A most ingenious satisfaction.   50
Cel. One thing I 'll tell you more, and this I
        give you
Worthy your imitation, from my practice :
You see me merry, full of song and dancing,
Pleasant in language, apt to all delights
That crown a public meeting ; but you cannot
Accuse me of being prodigal of my favours   56
To any of my guests. I do not summon,
By any wink, a gentleman to follow me
To my withdrawing chamber ; I hear all
Their pleas in court, nor can they boast abroad,
And do me justice, after a salute,[6]   61
They have much conversation with my lip.
I hold the kissing of my hand a courtesy,
And he that loves me, must, upon the strength
Of that, expect till I renew his favour.   65
Some ladies are so expensive in their graces
To those that honour 'em, and so prodigal,
That in a little time they have nothing but
The naked sin left to reward their servants ;
Whereas, a thrift in our rewards will keep   70
Men long in their devotion, and preserve
Ourselves in stock, to encourage those that
        honour us.
Isab. This is an art worthy a lady's practice.
Cel. It takes not from the freedom of our
        mirth,
But seems to advance it, when we can possess
Our pleasures with security of our honour ; 76
And, that preserv'd, I welcome all the joys
My fancy can let in. In this I have given
The copy of my mind, nor do I blush
You understand it.
Isab.   You have honour'd us.   80

Enter CELESTINA'S Gentlewoman.

Gentlew. Madam, Sir William Scentlove's
        come to wait on you.
Cel. There 's one would be a client. — Make
        excuse
For a few minutes.   [*Exit* Gentlewoman.]
Mar.   One that comes a wooing ?
Cel. Such a thing he would seem, but in his
        guiltiness
Of little land, his expectation is not   85
So valiant as it might be. He wears rich clothes,
And feeds with noblemen ; to some, I hear,
No better than a wanton emissary,
Or scout for Venus' wild fowl ; which made
        tame,
He thinks no shame to stand court sentinel,   90
In hope of the reversion.
Mar.   I have heard

        [4] Foolishly eager.   [6] Ordinary kiss of salutation.
        [5] Devices, schemings.

That some of them are often my lord's tasters,
The first fruits they condition for, and will
Exact as fees, for the promotion.
    Cel. Let them agree ; there 's no account shall
lie   95
For me among their traffic.

        Re-enter Gentlewoman.

    Gentlew.   Master Haircut, madam,
Is new come in, to tender you his service.
    Cel. Let him discourse a little with Sir Wil-
liam.   *Exit* Gentlewoman.
    Mar. What is this gentleman, Master Hair-
cut, madam ?
I note him very gallant, and much courted   100
By gentlemen of quality.
    Cel.   I know not,
More than a trim gay man ; he has some great
office,
Sure, by his confident behaviour.
He would be entertain'd under the title
Of servant [1] to me, and I must confess,   105
He is the sweetest of all men that visit me.
    Isab. How mean you, madam ?
    Cel.   He is full of powder ;
He will save much in perfume for my chamber,
Were he but constant here. — Give 'em access.

Enter Sir William Scentlove *and* Haircut.

    Scent. Madam, the humblest of your servants is
Exalted to a happiness, if you smile   111
Upon your visit.
    Hair.   I must beg your charity
Upon my rudeness, madam ; I shall give
That day up lost to any happiness,
When I forget to tender you my service.   115
    Cel. You practise courtship, gentlemen.
    Scent.   But cannot
Find where with more desert to exercise it.
What lady 's this, I pray ?
    Cel.   A kinswoman
Of mine, Sir William.
    Scent.   I am more her servant.
    Cel. You came from court, now, I presume ?
    Hair.   'T is, madam,   120
The sphere I move in, and my destiny
Was kind to place me there, where I enjoy
All blessings that a mortal can possess,
That lives not in your presence ; and I should
Fix my ambition, when you would vouchsafe   125
Me so much honour, to accept from me
An humble entertainment there.
    Cel.   But by
What name shall I be known ? In what degree
Shall I be of kindred to you ?
    Hair.   How mean you, madam ?
    Cel. Perhaps you 'll call me sister, I shall
take it   130
A special preferment ; or it may be
I may pass under title of your mistress,
If I seem rich, and fair enough, to engage
Your confidence to own me.
    Hair.   I would hope —
    Cel. But 't is not come to that yet : you will,
sir,   135
Excuse my mirth.

        [1] Lover.

    Hair.   Sweet madam !
    Cel.   Shall I take
Boldness to ask what place you hold in court ?
'T is an uncivil curiosity ;
But you 'll have mercy to a woman's question.
    Hair. My present condition, madam, carries
Honour and profit, though not to be nam'd   141
With that employment I expect i' th' state,
Which shall discharge the first maturity
Upon your knowledge ; until then, I beg
You allow a modest silence.
    Cel.   I am charm'd, sir ;   145
And if you scape ambassador, you cannot
Reach a preferment wherein I 'm against you.
But where is Sir William Scentlove ?
    Hair.   Give him leave
To follow his nose, madam, while he hunts
In view, — he 'll soon be at a fault.[2]
    Cel.   You know him ?   150
    Hair. Know Scentlove ? Not a page but can
decipher him ;
The waiting-women know him to a scruple ;
He 's called the blister-maker of the town.
    Cel. What 's that ?
    Hair.   The laundry ladies can resolve you,
And you may guess : an arrant epicure,   155
As this day lives, born to a pretty wit,
A knight, too ; but no gentleman. I must
Be plain to you ; — your ladyship may have
Use of this knowledge, but conceal the author.
    Scent. I kiss your fairest hand.
    Mar.   You make a difference ;   160
Pray reconcile them to an equal whiteness.
    Scent. You wound my meaning, lady.
    Cel.   Nay, Sir William
Has the art of compliment.
    Scent.   Madam, you honour me
'Bove my desert of language.
    Cel.   Will you please
To enrich me with your knowledge of that
gentleman ?   165
    Scent. Do you not know him, madam ?
    Cel.   What is he ?
    Scent. A camphire ball ; you shall know more
hereafter ;
He shall tell you himself, and save my charac-
ter ;
Till then, — you see he 's proud.
    Cel.   One thing, gentlemen,
I observe in your behaviour, which is rare   170
In two that court one mistress : you preserve
A noble friendship ; there 's no gum within
Your hearts ; you cannot fret,[3] or show an envy
Of one another's hope ; some would not govern
Their passions with that temper !
    Scent.   The whole world   175
Shall nor divorce our friendship. — Master Hair-
cut !
Would I had lives to serve him ! He is lost
To goodness does not honour him.
    Hair.   My knight !
    Cel. [*Aside.*] This is right playing at court
shuttlecock.   179

    [2] Lose the scent.
    [3] Cf. 1 *Henry IV*, II. ii. 2, "I have hid Falstaff's
horse, and he frets like gumm'd velvet." (Gifford.)

Re-enter Gentlewoman.

Gentlew. Madam, there is a gentleman desires
To speak wi' ye, one Sir Thomas Bornwell.
   Cel.   Bornwell?
   Gentlew. He says he is a stranger to your
     ladyship.
   Scent. I know him.
   Hair.   Your neighbour, madam.
   Scent.   Husband to
The lady that so revels in the Strand.
   Hair. He has good parts, they say, but can-
     not help   185
His lady's bias.
   Cel.   They have both much fame
I' th' town, for several merits. Pray admit him.
                          [*Exit* Gentlewoman.]
   Hair. [*Aside.*] What comes he for?

Enter Sir THOMAS BORNWELL.

   Born. Your pardon, noble lady, that I have
Presum'd a stranger to your knowledge, —
                    [*Salutes* CELESTINA.]
   Cel.   Sir, 190
Your worth was here before you, and your person
Cannot be here ungrateful.
   Born.   'T is the bounty
Of your sweet disposition, madam. — Make me
Your servant, lady, by her fair example,
To favour me. [*Offers to salute* ISABELLA, *who
     turns from him. Aside.*] — I never knew
     one turn   195
Her cheek to a gentleman that came to kiss her,
But she 'd a stinking breath. — Your servant,
   gentlemen.
Will Scentlove, how is 't?
   Cel.   I am sorry, coz,
To accuse you ; we in nothing more betray
Ourselves to censure of ridiculous pride, 200
Than answering a fair salute too rudely.
Oh, it shows ill upon a gentlewoman
Not to return the modest lip, if she
Would have the world believe her breath is not
Offensive.
   Born.   Madam, I have business 205
With you.
   Scent.   His looks are pleasant.
   Cel.   With me, sir?
   Born. I hear you have an exc'llent wit,
   madam ;
I see you are fair.
   Cel.   The first is but report ;
And do not trust your eye-sight for the last,
'Cause I presume y' are mortal, and may err.
   Hair. He is very gamesome.
   Born.   Y' have an exc'llent voice, 211
(They say you catcht it from a dying swan,)
[With] which, join'd to the harmony of your
   lute,
You ravish all mankind.
   Cel.   Ravish mankind?
   Born. With their consent.
   Cel.   It were the stranger rape ; 215
But there 's the less indictment lies against it :
And there is hope your little honesties [1]

          [1] Chastities.

Cannot be much the worse, for men do rather
Believe they had a maidenhead, than put
Themselves to th' rack of memory how long 220
'T is since they left the burden of their inno-
   cence.
   Born. Why, you are bitter, madam!
   Cel.   So is physic ;
I do not know your constitution.
   Born. You shall, if 't please you, madam.
   Cel.   Y' are too hasty,
I must examine what certificate 225
You have first, to prefer you.
   Born.   Fine ! certificate ?
   Cel. Under your lady's hand and seal.
   Born.   Go to ;
I see you are a wag.
   Cel.   But take heed how
You trust to 't.
   Born.   I can love you in my wedlock,
As well as that young gallant o' th' first
   hair,
Or the knight-bachelor ; and can return 231
As amorous delight to thy soft bosom.
   Cel. Your person and your language are both
   strangers.
   Born. But may be more familiar; I have
   those
That dare make affidavit for my body. 234
   Cel. D' ye mean your surgeon ?
   Born.   My surgeon, madam ?
I know not how you value my abilities,
But I dare undertake as much, to express
My service to your ladyship, and with
As fierce ambition fly to your commands, 240
As the most valiant of these lay siege to you.
   Cel. You dare not, sir.
   Born.   How, madam ?
   Cel.   I will justify 't.
You dare not marry me; and I imagine
Some here, should I consent, would fetch a
   priest
Out of the fire.
   Born.   I have a wife indeed. 245
   Cel. And there 's a statute not repeal'd, I
   take it.
   Born. Y' are in the right ; I must confess y'
   have hit
And bled me in a master vein.
   Cel.   You think
I took you on the advantage ; use your best
Skill at defence, I 'll come up to your valour, 250
And show another work you dare not do :
You dare not, sir, be virtuous.
   Born.   I dare,
By this fair hand I dare ; and ask a pardon,
If my rude words offend your innocence,
Which, in a form so beautiful, would shine 255
To force a blush in them suspected it,
And from the rest draw wonder.
   Hair.   I like not
Their secret parley ; shall I interrupt them ?
   Isab. By no means, sir.
   Scent.   Sir Thomas was not wont
To show so much a courtier.
   Mar.   He cannot 260
Be prejudicial to you; suspect not
Your own deserts so much ; he 's married.

Born. I have other business, madam. You
    keep music:
I came to try how you can dance.
    Cel. You did ? — [*Aside.*] I 'll try his hu-
    mour out of breath.   265
Although I boast no cunning, sir, in revels,
If you desire to show your art that way,
I can wait on you.
    Born.   You much honour me;
Nay. all must join to make a harmony.
                            They dance.
    Born. I have nothing now, madam, but to be-
    seech,   270
After a pardon for my boldness, you
Would give occasion to pay my gratitude.
I have a house will be much honoured,
If you vouchsafe your presence; and a wife
Desires to present herself your servant.   275
I came with the ambition to invite you,
Deny me not; your person you shall trust
On fair security.
    Cel.   Sir, although I use not
This freedom with a stranger, you shall have
No cause to hold me obstinate.
    Born.   You grace me.   280
Sir William Scentlove —
    Hair.   I must take my leave.
You will excuse me, madam; court attend-
    ances —
    Cel. By any means.
    Born.   Ladies, you will vouchsafe
Your company ?
    Isab.   We wait upon you, sir. *Exeunt.*

ACT III

[SCENE I.][1]

Table and looking-glass. Enter LORD —— *unready.*[2] HAIRCUT *preparing his periwig.*

    Lord. What hour is 't ?
    Hair.   'Bout three o'clock, my lord.
    Lord. 'T is time to rise.
    Hair.   Your lordship went but late
To bed last night.
    Lord.   'T was early in the morning.
    Sec. [*within.*] Expect[3] awhile, my lord is
busy.

    Enter Secretary.

    Lord. What 's the matter ?
    Sec.   Here is a lady   5
Desires access to you upon some affairs,
She says, may specially concern your lordship.
    Lord. A lady ? What 's her name ?
    Sec.   Madam Decoy.
    Lord. Decoy ? Prithee admit her.
                    [*Exit* Secretary.]

    Enter DECOY.

            Have you business, madam,
With me ?
    Dec.   And such, I hope, as will not be   10
Offensive to your lordship.

    Lord.   I pray speak it.
    Dec. I would desire your lordship's ear more
private.
    Lord. Wait i' th' next chamber till I call. —
Now, madam.   *Exit* [HAIRCUT].
    Dec. Although I am a stranger to your lord-
ship,
I would not lose a fair occasion offer'd   15
To show how much I honour, and would serve
you.
    Lord. Please you to give me the particular,
That I may know the extent of my engage-
ment.[4]
I am ignorant by what desert you should
Be encourag'd to have care of me.
    Dec.   My lord, 20
I will take boldness to be plain; beside
Your other excellent parts, you have much
fame
For your sweet inclination to our sex.
    Lord. How d' ye mean, madam ?
    Dec.   I' that way your lordship
Hath honourably practis'd upon some   25
Not to be nam'd. Your noble constancy
To a mistress hath deserv'd our general vote;
And I, a part of womankind, have thought
How to express my duty.
    Lord.   In what, madam ?
    Dec. Be not so strange, my lord. I knew the
beauty   30
And pleasures of your eyes; that handsome
creature
With whose fair life all your delight took
leave,
And to whose memory you have paid too much
Sad tribute.
    Lord.   What 's all this ?
    Dec.   This : if your lordship
Accept my service, in pure zeal to cure   35
Your melancholy, I could point where you
might
Repair your loss.
    Lord.   Your ladyship, I conceive,
Doth traffic in flesh merchandize.
    Dec.   To men
Of honour, like yourself. I am well known   39
To some in court, and come not with ambition
Now to supplant your officer.
    Lord.   What is
The lady of pleasure you prefer ?
    Dec.   A lady
Of birth and fortune, one upon whose virtue
I may presume, the lady Aretina.
    Lord. Wife to Sir Thomas Bornwell ?
    Dec.   The same, sir. 45
    Lord. Have you prepar'd her ?
    Dec. Not for your lordship, till I have found
your pulse.
I am acquainted with her disposition,
She has a very appliable[5] nature.
    Lord. And, madam, when expect you to be
whipt   50
For doing these fine favours ?
    Dec.   How, my lord ?
Your lordship does but jest, I hope ; you make

---

[1] Lord ——'s house.   [2] Undressed.   [3] Wait.

[4] Obligation.   [5] Accessible.

A difference between a lady that
Does honourable offices, and one   54
They call a bawd. Your lordship was not wont
To have such coarse opinion of our practice.
    Lord. The Lady Aretina is my kinswoman.
    Dec. What if she be, my lord? The nearer
        blood,
The dearer sympathy.
    Lord.   I 'll have thee carted.[1]
    Dec. Your lordship will not so much stain
        your honour   60
And education, to use a woman
Of my quality —
    Lord.   'T is possible you may
Be sent off with an honourable convoy
Of halberdiers.
    Dec.   Oh, my good lord !   64
    Lord. Your ladyship shall be no protection,
If you but stay three minutes.
    Dec.   I am gone. —
When next you find rebellion in your blood,
May all within ten mile o' th' court turn hon-
        est ![2]   *Exit.*
    Lord. I do not find that proneness, since the
        fair
Bella Maria died ; my blood is cold,   70
Nor is there beauty enough surviving
To heighten me to wantonness. — Who waits ?

            Re-enter HAIRCUT [*and* Secretary].

And what said my lady ?
    Hair. The silent language of her face, my
        lord,
Was not so pleasant, as it show'd upon   75
Her entrance.
    Lord.   Would any man that meets
This lady take her for a bawd ?
    Hair.   She does
The trade an honour, credit to the profession.
We may in time see baldness, quarter noses,   79
And rotten legs to take the wall of footcloths.
    Lord. I ha' thought better ; call the lady
        back. --
I wo' not lose this opportunity. —
Bid her not fear. [*Exit* Secretary.] — The fa-
        vour is not common,
And I 'll reward it. I do wonder much
Will Scentlove was not here to-day.   85
    Hair. I heard him say this morning he would
        wait
Upon your lordship. — She is return'd, sir.

            Re-enter Secretary *and* DECOY.

    Sec. Madam, be confident, my lord 's not
        angry.
    Lord. You return welcome, madam ; you are
        better
Read in your art, I hope, than to be frighted 90
With any shape of anger, when you bring
Such news to gentlemen. Madam, you shall
Soon understand how I accept the office.
    Dec. You are the first lord, since I studied
        carriage,
That show'd such infidelity and fury   95

    [1] The punishment of bawds was to be whipt and
carted.
    [2] Chaste.

Upon so kind a message. Every gentleman
Will show some breeding ; but if one right
        honourable
Should not have noble blood —
    Lord.   You shall return
My compliment, in a letter, to my lady   99
Aretina. Favour me with a little patience. —
Show her that chamber.
    Dec.   I 'll attend your lordship.
            Exeunt [DECOY *and* HAIRCUT. —
                Secretary *seats himself at a table*].
    Lord. Write, — " Madam, where your honour
is in danger, my love must not be silent."

    Enter [Sir WILLIAM] SCENTLOVE *and* KICK-
                SHAW.

Scentlove and Kickshaw !
    Kick.   Your lordship's busy.   104
    Lord. Writing a letter ; — nay, it sh' not bar
Any discourse.
            [*Walks alternately to the* Secretary
                and to SCENTLOVE *and* KICK-
                SHAW.]
    Sec. " Silent."
    Lord. " Though I be no physician, I may
prevent a fever in your blood." —
And where have you spent the morning's con-
        versation ?   110
    Scent. Where you would have given the best
        barbary
In your stable to have met on honourable
        terms.
    Lord. What new beauty ? You acquaint
        yourselves
With none but wonders.
    Scent.   'T is too low, — a miracle.
    Lord. It will require a strong faith.   115
    Sec. " Your blood."
    Lord. " If you be innocent, preserve your
fame, lest this Decoy-madam betray it, to your
repentance" —
By what name is she known ?
    Scent.   Ask Alexander ;   120
He knows her.
    Kick.   Whom ?
    Scent.   The lady Celestina.
    Lord. He has a vast knowledge of ladies.
'Las, poor Alexander !
When dost thou mean thy body shall lie fal-
        low ?
    Kick. When there is mercy in a petticoat :
I must turn pilgrim for some breath.
    Lord.   I think
'T were cooler travel, if you examine it,   125
Upon the hoof through Spain.
    Scent.   Through Ethiopia.
    Lord. Nay, less laborious to serve a prentice-
        ship
In Peru, and dig gold out of the mine,
Though all the year were dog-days.   130
    Sec. " To repentance."
    Lord. " In brief, this lady, could you fall
from virtue, within my knowledge, will not
blush to be a bawd."
    Scent. But hang 't, 't is honourable journey-
        work ;   135
Thou art famous by it, and thy name 's up.

Kick. So, sir!
Let me ask you a question, my dear knight:
Which is less servile, to bring up the pheasant,
And wait, or sit at table uncontroll'd,　　140
And carve to my own appetite?
　　Scent.　　　　　　　　No more;
Thou 'rt witty, as I am.
　　Sec.　　　　　　" A bawd."
　　Scent.　　　　　　　　How 's that?
Kick. Oh, you are famous by 't, and your
name 's up, sir.
Lord. " Be wise, and reward my caution
with timely care of yourself, so I shall not [145
repent to be known your loving kinsman and
servant " —
Gentlemen, the lady Celestina,
Is she so rare a thing?
　　Kick.　　　　　　If you 'll have my
Opinion, my lord, I never saw　　150
So sweet, so fair, so rich a piece of nature.
Lord. I 'll show thee a fairer presently, to
shame
Thy eyes and judgment; look o' that. [*Gives
him a miniature.*]—So; I 'll subscribe.
[*Signs his name to the letter.*]
Seal it; I 'll excuse your pen for the direction.
Kick. Bella Maria's picture! she was handsome.　　155
Scent. But not to be compar'd —
Lord. Your patience, gentlemen; I 'll return
instantly.　　　　　　　　*Exit.*
Kick. Whither is my lord gone?
Sec. To a lady i' th' next chamber.
Scent.　　　　　　What is she?
Sec. You shall pardon me, I am his secretary.　　160
Scent. I was wont to be of his counsel. A new
officer,
And I not know 't? I am resolv'd to batter
All other with the praise of Celestina:
I must retain him.

　　　　　Re-enter LORD.

Lord.　　　　　　Has not that object
Convinc'd your erring judgments?
Kick.　　　　　What! this picture? 165
Lord. Were but your thoughts as capable as
mine
Of her idea, you would wish no thought
That were not active in her praise, above
All worth and memory of her sex.
　　Scent.　　　　　　　She was fair,
I must confess; but had your lordship look'd 170
With eyes more narrow, and some less affection,
Upon her face, —
　　Kick.　　　　I do not love the copies
Of any dead, they make me dream of goblins;
Give me a living mistress, with but half
The beauty of Celestina. Come, my lord,　175
'T is pity that a lord of so much flesh
Should waste upon a ghost, when they are living
Can give you a more honourable consumption.
　　Scent. Why, do you mean, my lord, to live
an infidel?

Do, and see what will come on 't; observe [1]
still,　　180
And dote upon your vigils; build a chamber
Within a rock, a tomb among the worms,
Not far off, where you may, in proof apocryphal,
Court 'em not to devour the pretty pile
Of flesh your mistress carried to the grave.　185
There are no women in the world; all eyes,
And tongues, and lips, are buried in her coffin!
Lord. Why, do you think yourselves competent judges
Of beauty, gentlemen?
　　Both.　　　　What should hinder us? 189
Kick. I have seen and tried as many as another,
With a mortal back.
　　Lord.　　　　　Your eyes are brib'd,
And your hearts chain'd to some desires; you cannot
Enjoy the freedom of a sense.
　　Kick.　　　　　　Your lordship
Has a clear eyesight, and can judge and penetrate.
Lord. I can, and give a perfect censure of 195
Each line and point; distinguish beauty from
A thousand forms, which your corrupted optics
Would pass for natural.
　　Scent.　　　　　I desire no other
Judge should determine us, and if your lordship
Dare venture but your eyes upon this lady,　200
I 'll stand their justice, and be confident
You shall give Celestina victory
And triumph o'er all beauties past and living.
Kick. I dare, my lord, venture a suit of
clothes,
You 'll be o'ercome.
Lord.　　You do not know my fortitude. 205
Scent. Nor frailty; you dare not trust yourself to see her.
Lord. Think you so, gentlemen? I dare see
this creature
To make you know your errors, and the difference
Of her whose memory is my saint. Not trust
My senses! I dare see, and speak with her.　210
Which holds the best acquaintance to prepare
My visit to her?
　　Scent.　　　　I will do 't, my lord.
Kick. She is a lady free in entertainments.
Lord. I would give this advantage to your
cause,
Bid her appear in all the ornaments　215
Did ever wait on beauty, all the riches
Pride can put on, and teach her face more
charm
Than ever poet drest up Venus in;
Bid her be all the Graces, and the Queen
Of Love in one, I 'll see her, Scentlove. and 220
Bring off my heart, arm'd but [with a] single
thought
Of one that 's dead, without a wound; and
when

　　　　　[1] Pay observance. worship.

I have made your folly prisoner, I 'll laugh at
you.

Scent. She shall expect you ; trust to me for
knowledge.

Lord. I 'm for the present somewhere else
engag'd ;   225

Let me hear from you.   [*Exit.*]

Scent.   So ! I am glad he 's yet
So near conversion.

Kick.   I am for Aretina.

Scent. No mention of my lord.

Kick.   Prepare his lady,
'T is time he were reduc'd [1] to the old sport ; 229
One lord like him more would undo the court.

Exeunt.

[SCENE II.] [2]

Enter LADY BORNWELL, *with a letter, and* DE-
COY.

Dec. He is the ornament of your blood,
madam ;
I am much bound to his lordship.

Lady B.   He gives you
A noble character.

Dec.   'T is his goodness, madam.

Lady B. [*Aside.*] I wanted such an engine.
My lord has
Done me a courtesy, to disclose her nature ;   5
I now know one to trust, and will employ her.—
Touching my lord, for reasons which I shall
Offer to your ladyship hereafter, I
Desire you would be silent ; but, to show   9
How much I dare be confident in your secrecy,
I pour my bosom forth. I love a gentleman,
One whom there wo' not need much conjuration
To meet.— Your ear.   [*Whispers her.*]

Dec.   I apprehend you, and I shall
Be happy to be serviceable. I am sorry
Your ladyship did not know me before now : 15
I have done offices : and not a few
Of the nobility but have done feats
Within my house, which is convenient
For situation, and artful chambers,
And pretty pictures to provoke the fancy.   20

Enter LITTLEWORTH.

Little. Madam, all pleasures languish in your
absence.

Lady B. Your pardon a few minutes, sir. —
You must
Contrive it thus.   [*Walks aside with* DECOY.]

Little.   I attend, and shall account it
Honour to wait on your return.

Lady B.   He may not
Have the least knowledge of my name or per-
son.   25

Dec. I have practis'd that already for some
great ones,
And dare again, to satisfy you, madam ;
I have a thousand ways to do sweet offices.

Little. If this Lady Aretina should be honest,
I ha' lost time. She 's free as air ; I must   30
Have closer conference, and if I have art,
Make her affect me in revenge.

[1] Brought back.
[2] A room in Sir Thomas Bornwell's house.

Dec.   This evening ?
Leave me to manage things.

Lady B.   You will oblige me.

Dec. You shall commend my art, and thank
me after.   *Exit.*

Lady B. I hope the revels are maintain'd
within ?   35

Little. By Sir Thomas and his mistress.

Lady B.   How ? His mistress ?

Little. The lady Celestina ; I ne'er saw
Eyes shoot more amorous interchange.

Lady B.   Is 't so ?

Little. He wears her favour with mere [3]
pride —

Lady B.   Her favour ?

Little. A feather that he ravish'd from her
fan ;   40
And is so full of courtship, which she smiles on.

Lady B. 'T is well.

Little.   And praises her beyond all poetry.

Lady B. I 'm glad he has so much wit.

Little. [*Aside.*]   Not jealous !

Lady B. [*Aside.*] This secures me. What
would make other ladies pale
With jealousy, gives but license to my wand-
'rings.   45
Let him now tax [4] me, if he dare ; and yet
Her beauty 's worth my envy, and I wish
Revenge upon it, not because he loves,
But that it shines above my own.

Enter KICKSHAW.

Kick.   Dear madam !

Lady B. I have it. — You two gentlemen
profess   50
Much service to me ; if I have a way
To employ your wit and secrecy ? —

Both.   You 'll honour us.

Lady B. You gave a high and worthy character
Of Celestina.

Kick.   I remember, madam.

Lady B. Do either of you love her ?

Kick.   Not I, madam. 55

Little. I would not, if I might.

Lady B.   She 's now my guest
And, by a trick, invited by my husband,
To disgrace me.— You, gentlemen, are held
Wits of the town, the consuls that do govern
The senate here, whose jeers are all authentic.
The taverns and the ordinaries are   61
Made academies, where you come, and all
Your sins and surfeits made the time's ex-
ample.
Your very nods can quell a theatre,
No speech or poem good without your seal ; 65
You can protect scurrility, and publish ;
By your authority believ'd, no rapture
Ought to have honest meaning.

Kick.   Leave our characters.

Little. And name the employment.

Lady B.   You must exercise
The strength of both your wits upon this lady,
And talk her into humbleness or anger,   71
Both which are equal, to my thought. If you

[3] Absolute, unmixed.   [4] Accuse.

Dare undertake this slight thing for my sake,
My favour shall reward it; but be faithful,
And seem to let all spring from your own free-
dom.   75
 Kick. This all! We can defame her; if you
please,
My friend shall call her whore, or any thing,
And never be endanger'd to a duel.
 Lady B. How's that?
 Kick. He can endure a cudgelling, and no
man   80
Will fight after so fair a satisfaction:
But leave us to our art, and do not limit us.
 Lady B. They are here; begin not till I
whisper you.

Enter SIR THOMAS BORNWELL, CELESTINA,
MARIANA, *and* ISABELLA.

 Lady B. *Je vous prie, madame, d'excuser
l'importunité de mes affaires, qui m'ont fait of-* [85
*fenser, par mon absence, une dame de laquelle
j'ai reçu tant d'obligations.*
 Cel. *Pardonnez moi, madame; vous me faites
trop d'honneur.*   89
 Lady B. *C'est bien de la douceur de votre nat-
urel, que vous tenez cette langage; mais j'espère
que mon mari n'a pas manqué de vous entretenir
en mon absence.*
 Cel. *En vérité, monsieur nous a fort obligé.* 94
 Lady B. *Il eût trop failli, s'il n'eut taché de
tout son pouvoir à vous rendre toutes sortes de
services.*
 Cel. *C'est de sa bonté qu'il nous a tant favorisé.*
 Lady B. *De la vôtre plutôt, madame, que vous
fait donner d'interprétation si bénigne à ses ef-
forts.*   101
 Cel. *Je vois bien que la victoire sera toujours
à madame, et de langage et de la courtesie.*
 Lady B. *Vraiment, madame, que jamais per-
sonne a plus désiré l'honneur de votre compagnie
que moi.*   106
 Cel. *Laissons-en, je vous supplie, des compli-
mens, et permettez à votre servante de vous baiser
les mains.*
 Lady B. *Vous m'obligez trop.*   110
 Born. I have no more patience; let's be
merry again
In our own language: madam, our mirth cools.
Our nephew!

Enter FREDERICK [*intoxicated, and* Steward].

 Lady B. Passion of my brain!   114
 Fred. Save you, gentlemen! save you, ladies!
 Lady B. I am undone.
 Fred. I must salute; no matter at which
end I begin.   [*Salutes* CELESTINA.]
 Lady B. There's a compliment!
 Cel. Is this your nephew, madam?   120
 Lady B. *Je vous prie, madame, d'excuser les
habits et le rude comportement de mon cousin. Il
est tout fraîchement venu de l'université, où on
l'a tout gâté.*
 Cel. *Excusez moi, madame, il est bien accom-
pli.*   126
 Fred. This language should be French by
the motions of your heads, and the mirth of
your faces.

 Lady B. I am dishonour'd.   130
 Fred. 'Tis one of the finest tongues for ladies
to show their teeth in: if you'll Latin it, I am
for you, or Greek it; my tailor has not put me
into French yet. *Mille basia, basia mille.*
 Cel. *Je ne vous entends pas, monsieur;* 135
I understand you not, sir.
 Fred. Why, so!
You and I then shall be in charity;
For though we should be abusive, we ha' the
benefit
Not to understand one another. Where's my
aunt?   140
I did hear music somewhere; and my brains,
Tun'd with a bottle of your capering claret,
Made haste to show their dancing.
 Little.   Please you, madam,
   [*Offering his box of sweetmeats to*
      CELESTINA.]
They are very uncomfortable.[1]
 Stew.   Alas, madam,
How would you have me help it? I did use 145
All means I could, after he heard the music,
To make him drunk, in hope so to contain
him;
But the wine made him lighter, and his head
Flew hither, ere I mist his heels.
 Kick. Nay, he spoke Latin to the lady. 150
 Lady B. O most unpardonable! Get him off
Quickly, and discreetly too; or, if I live——
 Stew. It is not in my power; he swears I am
An absurd sober fellow; and if you keep
A servant in his house to cross his humour, 155
When the rich sword and belt comes home,
he'll kill him.
 Lady B. What shall I do? Try your skill.
Master Littleworth.
 Little. He has ne'er a sword.—Sweet master
Frederick—
 Born. 'Tis pity, madam, such a scion should
Be lost;—but you are clouded.
 Cel.   Not I, sir, 160
I never found myself more clear at heart.
 Born. I could play with a feather; your fan,
lady.—
Gentlemen, Aretina, ta, ra, ra, ra! Come,
madam.
 Fred. Why, my good tutor in election,
You might have been a scholar.
 Little.   But I thank 165
My friends, they brought me up a little better.
Give me the town wits, that deliver jests
Clean from the bow, that whistle in the air,
And cleave the pin at twelvescore! Ladies do
But laugh at a gentleman that has any learn-
ing;   170
'T is sin enough to have your clothes suspected.
Leave us, and I will find a time to instruct you.
Come, here are sugar plums; 't is a good Fred-
erick.
 Fred. Why, is not this my aunt's house in
the Strand?   175
The noble rendezvous? Who laughs at me? 175
Go, I will root here if I list, and talk
Of rhetoric, logic, Latin, Greek, or any thing,

---

[1] Comforting.

And understand 'em too; who says the con-
    trary?
Yet, in a fair way, I contemn all learning,
And will be as ignorant as he, or he,   180
Or any taffeta, satin, scarlet, plush,
Tissue, or cloth o' bodkin [1] gentleman,
Whose manners are most gloriously infected.—
Did you laugh at me, lady?
    Cel.   Not I, sir;
But if I did show mirth upon your question, 185
I hope you would not beat me, little gentleman?
    Fred. How! "little gentleman?" You dare
    not say
These words to my new clothes, and fighting
    sword.
    Lady B. Nephew Frederick!
    Fred.   "Little gentleman!"
'T is an affront both to my blood and person. 190
I am a gentleman of as tall a birth
As any boast [2] nobility; though my clothes
Smell o' the lamp, my coat is honourable,
Right honourable, full of or and argent.—
A "little gentleman!"
    Born. Coz, you must be patient;   195
My lady meant you no dishonour, and
You must remember she 's a woman.
    Fred. Is she a woman? That 's another mat-
    ter.—
Do you hear? My uncle tells me what you are.
    Cel. So, sir.   200
    Fred. You call'd me "little gentleman."
    Cel. I did, sir.
    Fred. A little pink [3] has made a lusty ship
Strike her top-sail; the crow may beard the ele-
    phant,
A whelp may tame the tiger, spite of all   205
False decks and murderers; [4] and a "little
    gentleman"
Be hard enough to grapple with your ladyship,
Top and top-gallant.— Will you go drink, uncle,
T' other enchanted bottle? You and I
Will tipple, and talk philosophy.
    Born.   Come, nephew.— 210
You will excuse a minute's absence, madam.—
Wait you on us.
    Stew.   My duty, sir.
        Exeunt Sir Thomas Bornwell,
            Frederick, *and* Steward.
    Lady B.   Now, gentlemen.
    Kick. Madam, I had rather you excuse my
    language
For speaking truth, than virtue suffer in
My further silence; and it is my wonder   215
That you, whose noble carriage hath deserv'd
All honour and opinion, should now
Be guilty of ill manners.
    Cel.   What was that
You told me, sir?
    Little.   Do you not blush, madam,
To ask that question?
    Cel.   You amaze rather   220
My cheek to paleness. What mean you by this?
I am not troubled with the hiccup, gentlemen,
You should bestow this fright upon me.

[1] Made of silk and gold thread.
[2] Q. reads *least*.   [3] A small vessel.
[4] Cannon charged with grape-shot.

    Little.   Then
Pride and ill memory go together.
    Cel.   How, sir?
    Kick. The gentleman on whom you exercis'd
Your thin wit, was a nephew to the lady   225
Whose guest you are; and though her modesty
Look calm on the abuse of one so near
Her blood, the affront was impious.
    Little.   I am asham'd on 't.
You an ingenious lady, and well manner'd! 230
I 'll teach a bear as much civility.
    Cel. You may be master of the college, sir,
For aught I know.
    Little.   What college?
    [*Cel.*] [5]   Of the bears.
Have you a plot upon me? Do you possess
Your wits, or know me, gentlemen?

        Re-enter Sir Thomas Bornwell [*behind*].

    Born.   How 's this? 235
    Kick. Know you? Yes; we do know you to
    an atom.
    Little. Madam, we know what stuff your soul
    is made on.
    Cel. But do not bark so like a mastiff, pray.—
Sure they are mad.— Let your brains stand
    awhile,
And settle, gentlemen; you know not me;   240
What am I?
    Little. Th' art a puppet, a thing made
Of clothes and painting, and not half so hand-
    some
As that which play'd Susanna in the fair.
    Cel. I heard you visited those canvas trage-
    dies,   244
One of their constant audience, and so taken
With Susan, that you wish'd yourself a rival
With the two wicked elders.
    Kick.   You think this
Is wit now. Come, you are —
    Cel.   What, I beseech you?
Your character will be full of salt and satire,
No doubt. What am I?
    Kick.   Why, you are a woman — 250
    Cel. And that 's at least a bow wide of your
    knowledge.
    Kick. Would be thought handsome, and
    might pass i' th' country
Upon a market day; but so miserably
Forfeit to pride and fashions, that if Heaven
Were a new gown, you'd not stay in 't a fort-
    night.   255
    Cel. It must be miserably out of fashion then,
Have I no sin but pride?
    Kick.   Hast any virtue,
Or but a good face, to excuse that want?
    Cel. You prais'd it yesterday.
    Kick.   That made you proud.
    Cel. More pride!
    Kick.   You need not: — to close up the
    praise,   260
I have seen a better countenance in a sybil.
    Cel. When you wore spectacles of sack,[6] mis-
    took

[5] Q. continues *of the bears* to Littleworth.
[6] *I. e.* Were drunk.

The painted cloth,[1] and kist it for your mistress.

Kick. Let me ask you a question: how much
Have you consum'd in expectation   265
That I would love you?

Cel.   Why, I think as much
As you have paid away in honest debts
This seven year. 'Tis a pretty impudence,
But cannot make me angry.

Little.   Is there any
Man that will cast away his limbs upon her ? 270

Kick. You do not sing so well as I imagin'd,
Nor dance ; you reel in your coranto,[2] and pinch
Your petticoat too hard : y' have no good ear
To th' music, and incline too much one shoulder,
As you were dancing on the rope, and falling.   275
You speak abominable French, and make
A curtsey like a dairy-maid. — [*Aside.*] Not mad !

Little. Do we not sting her handsomely ?

Born.   A conspiracy !

Kick. Your state is not so much as 't is reported,
When you confer notes, all your husband's debts,   280
And your own reconcil'd ; but that 's not it
Will so much spoil your marriage.

Cel.   As what, sir ?
Let me know all my faults.

Kick.   Some men do whisper
You are not over honest.[3]

Cel.   All this shall not
Move me to more than laughter, and some pity,   285
Because you have the shapes of gentlemen ;
And though you have been insolent upon me,
I will engage no friend to kick or cudgel you,
To spoil your living and your limbs together :
I leave that to diseases that offend you   290
And spare my curse, poor silken vermin ! and
Hereafter shall distinguish men from monkeys.

Born. [*coming forward.*] Brave soul ! — You
brace of horse-leeches ! ~ - I have heard
Their barbarous language, madam ; y' are too merciful :
They shall be silent to your tongue ; pray punish 'em.   295

Cel. They are things not worth my character,[4] nor mention
Of any clean breath ; so lost in honesty,
They cannot satisfy for wrongs enough,
Though they should steal out of the world at Tyburn.[5]

Little. We are hang'd already.   300

Cel. Yet I will talk a little to the pilchards. — [6]
You two, that have not 'twixt you both the hundred
Part of a soul, coarse woollen-witted fellows,
Without a nap, with bodies made for burdens !
You, that are only stuffings for apparel,   305

As you were made but engines[7] for your tailors
To frame their clothes upon, and get them custom,
Until men see you move ; yet, then you dare not,
Out of your guilt [8] of being the ignobler beast,
But give a horse the wall, whom you excel   310
Only in dancing of the brawls,[9] because
The horse was not taught the French way.
Your two faces,
One fat, like Christmas, t' other lean, like Candlemas,
And prologue to a Lent, both bound together,
Would figure Janus, and do many cures   315
On agues, and the green disease,[10] by frighting ;
But neither can, with all the characters
And conjuring circles, charm a woman, though
She 'd fourscore years upon her, and but one
Tooth in her head, to love, or think well of you :   320
And I were miserable to be at cost
To court such a complexion as your malice
Did impudently insinuate. But I waste time,
And stain my breath in talking to such tadpoles.
Go home, and wash your tongues in barley-water,   325
Drink [11] clean tobacco, be not hot i' th' mouth,
And you may scape the beadle ; so I leave you
To shame, and your own garters ! —Sir, I must
Entreat you, for my honour, do not penance them,
They are not worth your anger. How shall I   330
Acquit your lady's silence ?

Born.   Madam, I
Am sorry to suspect, and dare revenge.

Cel. No cause of mine,

Born. It must become me to attend you home.

Cel. You are noble.— Farewell, mushrooms.
          [*Exit with* SIR THOMAS BORNWELL.]

Lady B.   Is she gone ? 325

Little. I think we pepper'd her.

Kick.   I 'm glad 't is over ;
But I repent no service for you, madam.—

Enter Servant, *with a letter* [*and a jewel, which
he delivers to* KICKSHAW].

To me ? From whence ? — A jewel ! a good preface.
Be happy the conclusion. *He smiles upon 't.*

Lady B.   Some love letter.

Little. He has a hundred mistresses: you may   340
Be charitable, madam, I ha' none ;
He surfeits, and I fall away i' th' kidneys.

Kick. I 'll meet.—   [*Exit Servant.*]
[*Aside.*] 'T is some great lady, questionless,
that has
Taken notice, and would satisfy her appetite.

Lady B. Now, Master Alexander, you look
bright o' the sudden ;   345
Another spirit 's in your eye.

---

[1] A cheap substitute for tapestry.
[2] A quick, lively dance.   [4] Characterizing.
[3] Chaste.   [5] The place of execution.
[6] A contemptuous term, sometimes associated with
pilchard, a small fish like a herring.

[7] Devices.
[8] Guilty consciousness.   [10] Jaundice (?)
[9] A dance like a cotillion.   [11] Smoke.

Kick.   Not mine, madam ;
Only a summons to meet a friend.
Lady B. What friend ?
Little.   By this jewel, I know her not.
Lady B. 'T is a she-friend. I 'll follow, gen-
tlemen ;   350
We may have a game at cent[1] before you go.
Kick. I shall attend you, madam.
Little.   'T is our duty.
    [*Exeunt* KICKSHAW *and* LITTLEWORTH.]
Lady B. I blush while I converse with my
own thoughts.
Some strange fate governs me, but I must on ;
The ways are cast already, and we thrive   355
When our sin fears no eye nor perspective.
                                      Exit.

ACT IV

[SCENE I.][2]

Enter two men leading KICKSHAW *blinded, and
go off suddenly.*

Kick. I am not hurt ; my patience to obey 'em,
Not without fear to ha' my throat cut else,
Did me a courtesy. Whither ha' they brought
me ?   [*Pulls off a bandage.*]
'T is devilish dark ; the bottom of a well
At midnight, with but two stars on the top,   5
Were broad day to this darkness. I but think
How like a whirlwind these rogues caught me up,
And smothered my eyesight. Let me see,
These may be spirits, and, for aught I know,
Have brought me hither over twenty steeples. 10
Pray Heaven they were not bailiffs ! that 's more
worth
My fear, and this a prison. All my debts
Reek in my nostril, and my bones begin
To ache with fear to be made dice ; and yet
This is too calm and quiet for a prison. —   15
What if the riddle prove I am robb'd ? And
yet
I did not feel 'em search me. How now ! music !
                           [*Music within.*]

Enter DECOY, *like an old Woman, with a light.*

And a light ! What beldam 's this ? I cannot
pray. —
What art ?
Dec.   A friend. Fear not, young man, I am
No spirit.
Kick.   Off !
Dec.   Despise me not for age,   20
Or this coarse outside, which I wear not out
Of poverty. Thy eyes be witness, 't is
No cave, or beggar's cell, th' art brought to ;
let
That gold speak here 's no want, which thou
mayst spend,
And find a spring to tire even prodigality,   25
If thou be'st wise.   [*Gives him a purse.*]
Kick.   The devil was a coiner
From the beginning ; yet the gold looks current.
Dec. Th' art still in wonder : know, I am
mistress of

---
[1] A game at cards.   [2] A room in Decoy's house.

This house, and of a fortune that shall serve
And feed thee with delights ; 't was I sent for
thee ;   30
The jewel and the letter came from me.
It was my art thus to contrive our meeting,
Because I would not trust thee with my fame,
Until I found thee worth a woman's honour.
Kick [*Aside.*] Honour and fame ! the devil
means to have   35
A care on 's credit. Though she sent for me,
I hope she has another customer
To do the trick withal ; I would not turn
Familiar to a witch.
Dec.   What say 'st ? Canst thou
Dwell in my arms to-night ? Shall we change
kisses,   40
And entertain the silent hours with pleasure,
Such as old Time shall be delighted with,
And blame the too swift motion of his wings,
While we embrace ?
Kick. [*Aside.*] Embrace ! She has had no teeth
This twenty years, and the next violent cough 45
Brings up her tongue ; it cannot possibly
Be sound at root. I do not think but one
Strong sneeze upon her, and well meant, would
make
Her quarters fall away ; one kick would blow 49
Her up like gunpowder, and loose all her limbs.
She is so cold, an incubus would not heat her ;
Her phlegm would quench a furnace, and her
breath
Would damp a musket bullet.
Dec.   Have you, sir,
Consider'd ?
Kick.   What ?
Dec.   My proposition.   54
Canst love ?
Kick. I could have done ; whom do you mean ?
I know you are pleas'd but to make sport.
Dec.   Thou art not
So dull of soul as thou appear'st.
Kick. [*Aside.*]   This is
But some device ; my grannam has some trick
in 't. —
Yes, I can love.
Dec.   But canst thou affect me ?
Kick. Although to reverence so grave a ma-
tron   60
Were an ambitious word in me, yet since
You give me boldness, I do love you.
Dec.   Then
Thou art my own.
Kick. [*Aside.*]   Has she no cloven foot ?
Dec. And I am thine, and all that I com-
mand
Thy servants ; from this minute thou art happy,
And fate in thee will crown all my desires.   66
I griev'd a proper man should be compell'd
To bring his body to the common market.
My wealth shall make thee glorious ; and, the
more
To encourage thee, howe'er this form may
fright   70
Thy youthful eyes, yet thou wo't find, by light
Of thy own sense, for other light is banish'd
My chamber, when our arms tie lovers' knots,
And kisses seal the welcome of our lips.

I shall not there affright thee, nor seem old, 75
With rivell'd [1] veins; my skin is smooth and
    soft
As ermines, with a spirit to meet thine,
Active, and equal to the Queen of Love's
When she did court Adonis.
    Kick. [Aside.]   This doth more
Confirm she is a devil, and I am   80
Within his own dominions. I must on,
Or else be torn a' pieces. I have heard
These succubae must not be crost.
    Dec.   We trifle
Too precious time away; I 'll show you a pros-
    pect
Of the next chamber, and then out the candle. 85
    Kick. Have you no sack i' th' house? I
        would go arm'd
Upon this breach.
    Dec.   It sh' not need.
    Kick.   One word,
Mother; have not you been a cat in your days?
    Dec. I am glad you are so merry, sir. You
        observe
That bed?   [Opens a door.]
    Kick. A very brave one.
    Dec.   When you are 90
Disrob'd, you can come thither in the dark.
You sha' not stay for me? Come, as you wish
For happiness.   Exit.
    Kick.   I am preferr'd, if I
Be modest and obey: she cannot have   94
The heart to do me harm, an she were Hecate
Herself. I will have a strong faith, and think
I march upon a mistress, the less evil.
If I scape fire now, I defy the devil.   Exit.

[SCENE II.] [2]

Enter FREDERICK [gaily dressed,] LITTLE-
    WORTH, and Steward.

    Fred. And how d' ye like me now?
    Stew.   Most excellent.
    Fred. Your opinion, Master Littleworth.
    Little.   Your French tailor
Has made you a perfect gentleman; I may
Converse now with you, and preserve my credit.
D' ye find no alteration in your body   5
With these new clothes?
    Fred.   My body alter'd? No.
    Little. You are not yet in fashion then. That
        must
Have a new motion, garb, and posture too,
Or all your pride is cast away; it is not
The cut of your apparel makes a gallant,   10
But the geometrical wearing of your clothes.
    Stew. Master Littleworth tells you right; you
        wear your hat
Too like a citizen.
    Little.   'T is like a midwife;
Place it with best advantage of your hair.   14
Is half your feather moulted? This does make
No show; it should spread over, like a canopy;
Your hot-rein'd monsieur wears it for a shade
And cooler to his back. Your doublet must

[1] Wrinkled, shrivelled.
[2] A room in Sir Thomas Bornwell's house.

Be more unbutton'd hereabouts; you 'll not
Be a sloven else, a foul shirt is no blemish;   20
You must be confident, and outface clean linen.
Your doublet and your breeches must be al-
    low'd
No private meeting here; your cloak 's too long,
It reaches to your buttock, and doth smell
Too much of Spanish gravity; the fashion   21
Is to wear nothing but a cape; a coat
May be allow'd a covering for one elbow,
And some, to avoid the trouble, choose to walk
In querpo,[3] thus.
    Stew. [Aside.]   Your coat and cloak's a
        brushing
In Long-Lane, Lombard.[4]
    Fred.   But what if it rain? 30
    Little. Your belt about your shoulder is suffi-
        cient
To keep off any storm; beside, a reed
But wav'd discreetly, has so many pores,
It sucks up all the rain that falls about one. 34
With this defence, when other men have been
Wet to the skin through all their cloaks, I
    have
Defied a tempest, and walk'd by the taverns
Dry as a bone.
    Stew. [Aside.] Because he had no money
To call for wine.
    Fred.   Why, do you walk enchanted?
Have you such pretty charms in town? But
    stay;   40
Who must I have to attend me?
    Little.   Is not that
Yet thought upon?
    Stew.   I have laid out [5] for servants.
    Little. They are everywhere.
    Stew.   I cannot yet be furnish'd
With such as I would put into his hands.
    Fred. Of what condition must they be, and
        how   45
Many in number, sir?
    Little.   Beside your fencing,
Your singing, dancing, riding, and French
    master,
Two may serve domestic, to be constant wait-
    ers
Upon a gentleman; a fool, a pimp.
    Stew. For these two officers I have enquir'd,
And I am promis'd a convenient whiskin.[6]   51
I could save charges, and employ the pie-wench,
That carries her intelligence in whitepots; [7]
Or 't is but taking order [8] with the woman
That [trolls] [9] the ballads, she could fit him
    with   55
A concubine to any tune; but I
Have a design to place a fellow with him
That has read all Sir Pandarus' works; a Tro-
    jan [10]
That lies conceal'd, and is acquainted with
Both city and suburban fripperies,[11]   60

[3] Span. Cuerpo, stripped of the upper garment.
[4] Lombard Street: pawn-shops were common in Long
Lane.
[5] Been on the look-out.   [8] Make arrangements.
[6] Go-between.   [9] Q. reads holds.
[7] A kind of milk-pudding.   [10] Bravo.
[11] Gay women, prostitutes.

Can fetch 'em with a spell at midnight to him,
And warrant which are for his turn ; can, for
A need, supply the surgeon too.

Fred. I like thy providence ;[1] such a one deserves
A livery twice a year.   65

Stew. It sha' not need ; a cast suit of your worship's
Will serve ; he 'll find a cloak to cover it,
Out of his share with those he brings to bed to you.

Fred. But must I call this fellow pimp ?

Little,   It is
Not necessary ; [Tom,] or Jack, or Harry,   70
Or what he 's known abroad by, will sound better,
That men may think he is a Christian.

Fred. But hear you, Master Littleworth: is there not
A method, and degrees of title in
Men of this art ?

Little.   According to the honour   75
Of men that do employ 'em. An emperor
May give this office to a duke ; a king
May have his viceroy to negociate for him ;
A duke may use a lord ; the lord a knight,
A knight may trust a gentleman ; and when   80
They are abroad, and merry, gentlemen
May pimp to one another.

Fred.   Good, good fellowship !
But for the fool now, that should wait on me,
And break me jests ?

Little.   A fool is necessary.

Stew. By any[2] means.

Fred.   But which of these two servants 85
Must now take place ?[3]

Little.   That question, Master Frederick,
The school of heraldry should conclude upon:
But if my judgment may be heard, the fool
Is your first man ; and it is known a point
Of state to have a fool.

Stew.   But, sir, the other   90
Is held the finer servant ; his employments
Are full of trust, his person clean and nimble,
And none so soon can leap into preferment,
Where fools are poor.

Little.   Not all ; there 's story for 't ;
Princes have been no wiser than they should be.   95
Would any nobleman, that were no fool,
Spend all in hope of the philosopher's stone,
To buy new lordships in another country ?
Would knights build colleges, or gentlemen
Of good estates challenge the field, and fight,100
Because a whore wo' not be honest ? Come,
Fools are a family over all the world ;
We do affect one naturally ; indeed
The fool is leiger[4] with us.

Stew.   Then the pimp
Is extraordinary.

Fred.   Do not you fall out   105
About their places. — Here 's my noble aunt !

Enter LADY BORNWELL.

Little. How do you like your nephew, madam, now ?

---

[1] Foresight. [2] All. [3] Precedence. [4] Resident.

Lady B. Well ! — Turn about, Frederick. — Very well !

Fred. Am I not now a proper gentleman ?
The virtue of rich clothes ! Now could I take
The wall of Julius Caesar, or affront   111
Great Pompey's upper lip, and defy the senate.
Nay, I can be as proud as your own heart, madam,
You may take that for your comfort ; I put on
That virtue with my clothes, and I doubt not
But in a little time I shall be impudent   116
As any page, or player's boy. I am
Beholding to this gentleman's good discipline ;
But I shall do him credit in my practice.
Your servant has some pretty notions, too,   120
In moral mischief.

Lady B.   Your desert in this
Exceeds all other service, and shall bind me
Both to acknowledge and reward.

Little.   Sweet madam,
Think me but worth your favour ; I would creep
Upon my knees to honour you, and for every   125
Minute you lend to my reward, I 'll pay
A year of serviceable tribute.

Lady B.   You
Can compliment.

Little. (*Aside.*) Thus still she puts me off ;
Unless I speak the downright word, she 'll never
Understand me. A man would think that creeping   130
Upon one's knees were English to a lady.

Enter KICKSHAW.

Kick. How is 't, Jack. — Pleasures attend you, madam !
How does my plant of honour ?

Lady B.   Who is this ?

Kick. 'T is Alexander.

Lady B.   Rich and glorious !

Little. 'T is Alexander the Great.

Kick.   And my Bucephalus 135
Waits at the door.

Lady B.   Your case is alter'd, sir.

Kick. I cannot help these things, the Fates will have it ;
'T is not my land does this.

Little,   But thou hast a plough
That brings it in.

Lady B.   Now he looks brave and lovely.

Fred. Welcome, my gallant Macedonian.   140

Kick. Madam, you gave your nephew for my pupil,
I read[5] but in a tavern ; if you 'll honour us,
The Bear at the Bridge foot shall entertain you.
A drawer[6] is my Ganymede, he shall skink[7]
Brisk nectar to us ; we will only have   145
A dozen partridge in a dish ; as many pheasants,
Quails, cocks, and godwits shall come marching up
Like the train'd-band ;[8] a fort of sturgeon
Shall give most bold defiance to an army,
And triumph o'er the table. —

---

[5] Lecture. [6] Waiter. [7] Pour out. [8] City militia.

Lady B.   Sir, it will 150
But dull the appetite to hear more, and mine
Must be excus'd. Another time I may be
Your guest.
     Kick. 'T is grown in fashion now with ladies;
When you please, I 'll attend you. Little-
     worth. —
Come, Frederick.
     Fred.   We 'll have music; I love noise. 155
We will outroar the Thames, and shake the
     bridge, boy.   *Exit [with* KICKSHAW].
     Little. Madam, I kiss your hand; would you
     think
Of your poor servant: flesh and blood is frail,
And troublesome to carry, without help.
     Lady B. A coach will easily convey it, or 160
You may take water at Strand Bridge.
     Little.   But I
Have taken fire.
     Lady B.   The Thames will cool [it, sir].
     Little. But never quench my heart; your
     charity
Can only do that.
     Lady B.   I will keep it cold
Of purpose.
     Little.   Now you bless me, and I dare 165
Be drunk in expectation.   [*Exit.*]
     Lady B.   I am confident
He knows me not, and I were worse than mad
To be my own betrayer. — Here 's my husband.

          Enter Sir THOMAS BORNWELL.

     Born. Why, how now, Aretina? What!
     alone?
The mystery of this solitude? My house 170
Turn desert o' the sudden! All the gamesters
Blown up! Why is the music put to silence?
Or have their instruments caught a cold, since
     we
Gave 'em the last heat? I must know thy
     ground
Of melancholy.
     Lady B.   You are merry, as 175
You came from kissing Celestina.
     Born.   I
Feel her yet warm upon my lip; she is
Most excellent company: I did not think
There was that sweetness in her sex. I must
Acknowledge, 't was thy cure to disenchant
     me 180
From a dull husband to an active lover.
With such a lady I could spend more years
Than since my birth my glass hath run soft
     minutes,
And yet be young; her presence hath a spell
To keep off age; she has an eye would strike 185
Fire through an adamant.
     Lady B.   I have heard as much
Bestow'd upon a dull-fac'd chambermaid,
Whom love and wit would thus commend. True
     beauty
Is mock'd when we compare thus, itself being
Above what can be fetch'd[1] to make it lovely;
Or,[2] could our thoughts reach something to de-
     clare 191

The glories of a face, or body's elegance
(That touches but our sense), when beauty
     spreads
Over the soul, and calls up understanding
To look [what][3] thence is offer'd, and ad-
     mire!   194
In both I must acknowledge Celestina
Most excellently fair, fair above all
The beauties I ha' seen, and one most worthy
Man's love and wonder.
     Born.   Do you speak, Aretina,
This with a pure sense to commend? Or is 't 200
The mockery of my praise?
     Lady B.   Although it shame
Myself, I must be just, and give her all
The excellency of women; and were I
A man —
     Born.   What then?
     Lady B.   I know not with what loss
I should attempt her love. She is a piece 205
So angelically moving, I should think
Frailty excus'd to dote upon her form,
And almost virtue to be wicked with her.
                                        Exit.
     Born. What should this mean? This is no
     jealousy,
Or she believes I counterfeit. I feel 210
Something within me, like a heat, to give
Her cause, would Celestina but consent.
What a frail thing is man! It is not worth
Our glory to be chaste, while we deny
Mirth and converse with women. He is good 215
That dares the tempter, yet corrects his blood.
                                        Exit.

               [SCENE III.][4]

[*Enter*] CELESTINA, MARIANA, *and* ISABELLA.

     Cel. I have told you all my knowledge: since
     he is pleas'd
To invite himself, he shall be entertain'd,
And you shall be my witnesses.
     Mar.   Who comes with him?
     Cel. Sir William Scentlove, that prepar'd me
     for
The honourable encounter. I expect   5
His lordship every minute.

          Enter Sir WILLIAM SCENTLOVE.

     Scent.   My lord is come.
     Cel. He has honour'd me.

          Enter Lord — *and* HAIRCUT.

     Scent. My Lord, your periwig is awry.
     Lord. You, sir —
          While HAIRCUT *is busy about his*
          hair, SIR WILLIAM SCENTLOVE
          goes to CELESTINA.
     Scent.   You may guess at the gentleman
that 's with him.
It is his barber, madam, d' ye observe?
An your ladyship wants a shaver.
     Hair.   She is here, sir. 10
I am betray'd. — Scentlove, your plot. I may
Have opportunity to be reveng'd.   *Exit.*
     Scent. She in the midst.

----

[1] Brought in comparison.   [2] Perhaps, *Oh.*

[3] Q. reads *when.*   [4] A room in Celestina's house.

Lord. She's fair, I must confess;
But does she keep this distance out of state?
Cel. Though I am poor in language to ex- 15
　　press
How much your lordship honours me, my heart
Is rich and proud in such a guest. I shall
Be out of love with every air abroad,
And for his grace done my unworthy house,
Be a fond prisoner, become anchorite, 20
And spend my hours in prayer, to reward
The blessing and the bounty of this presence.
Lord. Though you could turn each place you
　　move in to
A temple, rather than a wall should hide
So rich a beauty from the world, it were 25
Less want to lose our piety and your prayer.
A throne were fitter to present you to
Our wonder, whence your eyes, more worth than
　　all
They look on, should chain every heart a pri-
　　soner.
Scent. 'T was pretty well come off.
Lord. By your example 30
I shall know how to compliment; in this,
You more confirm my welcome.
Cel. I shall love
My lips the better, if their silent language
Persuade your lordship but to think so truly.
Lord. You make me smile, madam.
Cel. I hope you came not 35
With fear that any sadness here should shake
One blossom from your eye. I should be mis-
　　erable
To present any object should displease you.
Lord. You do not, madam.
Cel. As I should account
It no less sorrow, if your lordship should 40
Lay too severe a censure on my freedom.
I wo' not court a prince against his justice,
Nor bribe him with a smile to think me honest.
Pardon, my lord, this boldness, and the mirth
That may flow from me. I believe my father 45
Thought of no winding-sheet when he begot me.
Lord. She has a merry soul. — It will become
Me ask your pardon, madam, for my rude
Approach, so much a stranger to your know-
　　ledge.
Cel. Not, my lord, so much stranger to my
　　knowledge; 50
Though I have but seen your person afar off,
I am acquainted with your character,
Which I have heard so often, I can speak it.
Lord. You shall do me an honour.
Cel. If your lordship will
Be patient.
Lord. And glad to hear my faults. 55
Cel. That as your conscience can agree upon
　　'em;
However, if your lordship give me privilege,
I'll tell you what's the opinion of the world.
Lord. You cannot please me better.
Cel. Y' are a lord
Born with as much nobility as would, 60
Divided, serve to make ten noblemen,
Without a herald; but with so much spirit
And height of soul, as well might furnish
　　twenty.

You are learn'd, a thing not compatible now
With native honour; and are master of 65
A language that doth chain all ears,[1] and charm
All hearts, where you persuade; a wit so flow-
　　ing,
And prudence to correct it, that all men
Believe they only meet in you, which, with 69
A spacious memory, make up the full wonders:
To these you have [joined][2] valour and upon
A noble cause, know how to use a sword
To honour's best advantage, though you wear[3]
You are as bountiful as the showers that fall
Into the spring's green bosom; as you were 75
Created lord of Fortune, not her steward;
So constant to the cause in which you make
Yourself an advocate, you dare all dangers;
And men had rather you should be their friend,
Than justice or the bench bound up together. 80
Lord. But did you hear all this?
Cel. And more, my lord.
Lord. Pray let me have it, madam.
Cel. To all these virtues there is added
　　one, —
(Your lordship will remember, when I name it,
I speak but what I gather from the voice 85
Of others) — it is grown to a full fame
That you have lov'd a woman.
Lord. But one, madam?
Cel. Yes, many; give me leave to smile, my
　　lord,
I shall not need to interpret in what sense;
But you have show'd yourself right honour-
　　able, 90
And, for your love to ladies, have deserv'd,
If their vote might prevail, a marble statue.
I make no comment on the people's text, —
My lord, I should be sorry to offend.
Lord. You cannot, madam; these are things
　　we owe 95
To nature for.
Cel. And honest men will pay.
Their debts.
Lord. If they be able, or compound.
Cel. She had a hard heart would be unmer-
　　ciful,
And not give day to men so promising;
But you ow'd women nothing.
Lord. Yes, I am 100
Still in their debt, and I must owe them love,
It was part of my character.
Cel. With your lordship's
Pardon, I only said you had a fame
For loving women; but of late, men say
You have, against the imperial laws of love, 105
Restrain'd the active flowings of your blood,
And with a mistress buried all that is
Hop'd for in love's succession, as all beauty
Had died with her, and left the world be-
　　nighted!
In this you more dishonour all our sex. 110
Than you did grace a part; when everywhere
Love tempts your eye to admire a glorious
　　harvest,
And everywhere as full blown ears submit

---

[1] Q. *yeares.*　　　[2] Q. *knowne.*　　　[3] Q. *were.*

Their golden heads, the laden trees bow down
Their willing fruit, and court your amorous
    tasting.   115
    Lord. I see men would dissect me to a fibre ;
But do you believe this ?
    Cel.   It is my wonder,
I must confess, a man of nobler earth
Than goes to vulgar composition,
(Born and bred high, so unconfin'd, so rich   120
In fortunes, and so read in all that sum
Up human knowledge, to feed gloriously,
And live at court, the only sphere wherein
True beauty moves, nature's most wealthy
    garden,
Where every blossom is more worth than all 125
The Hesperian fruit by jealous dragon watch'd,
Where all delights do circle appetite,
And pleasures multiply by being tasted,)
Should be so lost with thought of one turn'd
    ashes.
There 's nothing left, my lord, that can excuse
    you,   130
Unless you plead, what I am asham'd to prompt
Your wisdom to ?
    Lord.   What 's that ?
    Cel.   That you have play'd
The surgeon with yourself.
    Lord.   And am made eunuch ?
    Cel. It were much pity.
    Lord.   Trouble not yourself,
I could convince your fears with demonstra-
    tion   135
That I am man enough, but knew not where,
Until this meeting, beauty dwelt. The court
You talk'd of must be where the Queen of Love
    is,
Which moves but with your person ; in your eye
Her glory shines, and only at that flame   140
Her wanton boy doth light his quick'ning torch.
    Cel. Nay, now you compliment ; I would it
    did,
My lord, for your own sake.
    Lord.   You would be kind,
And love me then ?
    Cel.   My lord, I should be loving,
Where I found worth to invite it, and should
    cherish   145
A constant man.
    Lord.   Then you should me, madam.
    Cel. But is the ice about your heart fallen off ?
Can you return to do what love commands ? —
Cupid, thou shalt have instant sacrifice,
And I dare be the priest.
    Lord.   Your hand, your lip ; 150
                           [Kisses her.]
Now I am proof 'gainst all temptation.
    Cel. Your meaning, my good lord ?
    Lord.   I, that have strength
Against thy voice and beauty, after this
May dare the charms of womankind. — Thou
    art,
Bella Maria, unprofaned yet ;   155
This magic has no power upon my blood. —
Farewell, madam ! if you durst be the example
Of chaste as well as fair, thou wert a brave one.
    Cel. I hope your lordship means not this for
    earnest :

Be pleas'd to grace a banquet.
    Lord.   Pardon, madam. — 160
Will Scentlove, follow ; I must laugh at you.
    Cel. My lord, I must beseech you stay, for
    honour,
For her whose memory you love best.
    Lord.   Your pleasure.
    Cel. And by that virtue you have now profest,
I charge you to believe me too ; I can   165
Now glory that you have been worth my trial,
Which, I beseech you, pardon. Had not you
So valiantly behaved in this conflict,
You had been my triumph, without hope of
    more
Than my just scorn upon your wanton flame ;
Nor will I think these noble thoughts grew
    first   171
From melancholy, for some female loss,
As the fantastic world believes, but from
Truth, and your love of innocence, which shine
So bright in the two royal luminaries [1]   175
At court, you cannot lose your way to chastity.
Proceed, and speak of me as honour guides you.
                       Exit LORD.
I am almost tir'd. — Come, ladies, we 'll beguile
Dull time, and take the air another while.
                        Exeunt.

ACT V

[SCENE I.] [2]

Enter Lady BORNWELL, *and a* Servant *[with a
purse].*

    Lady B. But hath Sir Thomas lost five hun-
    dred pounds
Already ?
    Serv.   And five hundred more he borrow'd.
The dice are notable devourers, madam ;
They make no more of pieces than of pebbles,
But thrust their heaps together, to engender. 5
" Two hundred more the caster ! " [3] cries this
    gentleman.
" I am wi' ye. — I ha' that to nothing, sir.
    The caster
Again." 'T is covered, and the table too,
With sums that frighted me. Here one sneaks
    out,
And with a martyr's patience smiles upon   10
His money's executioner, the dice ;
Commands a pipe of good tobacco, and
I' th' smoke on 't vanishes. Another makes
The bones vault o'er his head, swears that ill-
    throwing
Has put his shoulder out of joint, calls for   15
A bone-setter. That looks to th' box, to bid
His master send him some more hundred
    pounds,
Which lost, he takes tobacco, and is quiet.
Here a strong arm throws in and in, with which
He brusheth all the table, pays the rooks [4]   20
That went their smelts [5] a piece upon his hand,

---

  [1] Charles I and Henrietta Maria.
  [2] A room in Sir Thomas Bornwell's house.
  [3] Thrower of the dice.
  [4] Gulls, simpletons.
  [5] Staked their coins (?).

Yet swears he has not drawn a stake this seven
 year.
But I was bid make haste ; my master may
Lose this five hundred pounds ere I come thither.
            Exit.
  Lady B. If we both waste so fast, we shall
  soon find   25
Our state is not immortal. Something in
His other ways appear not well ready.

Enter Sir THOMAS BORNWELL, [*and* Servants,
  one with a purse.]

  Born. Ye tortoises, why make ye no more
  haste ?
Go pay to th' master of the house that money,
And tell the noble gamesters I have another 30
Superfluous thousand pound ; at night I 'll visit
 'em.
D' ye hear ?
  Serv. Yes, an please you.
  Born.   Do 't ye drudges.
          [*Exeunt* Servants.]
Ta, ra, ra ! — Aretina !
  Lady B. You have a pleasant humour, sir.
  Born. What ! should a gentleman be sad ?
  Lady B.   You have lost —
  Born. A transitory sum ; as good that way 35
As another.
  Lady B. Do you not vex within for 't ?
  Born. I had rather lose a thousand more, than
  one
Sad thought come near my heart for 't. Vex for
 trash !
Although it go from other men like drops
Of their life blood, we lose with the alacrity 40
We drink a cup of sack, or kiss a mistress.
No money is considerable with a gamester ;
They have souls more spacious than kings. Did
 two
Gamesters divide the empire of the world,
They 'd make one throw for 't all, and he that
 lost   45
Be no more melancholy than to have play'd for
A morning's draught. Vex a rich soul for dirt,
The quiet of whose every thought is worth
A province !
  Lady B. But when dice have consum'd all,
Your patience will not pawn for as much more.
  Born. Hang pawning ! Sell outright, and the
 fear 's over.   51
  Lady B. Say you so ? I 'll have another
 coach to-morrow
If there be rich above ground.
  Born.   I forgot
To bid the fellow ask my jeweller
Whether the chain of diamonds be made up ; 55
I will present it to my Lady Bellamour,
Fair Celestina.
  Lady B. This gown I have worn
Six days already ; it looks dull, I 'll give it
My waiting-woman, and have one of cloth
Of gold embroidered ; shoes and pantables[1] 60
Will show well of the same.
  Born.   I have invited
A covey of ladies, and as many gentlemen

       [1] Slippers.

To-morrow, to the Italian ordinary ;
I shall have rarities and regalias [2]
To pay for, madam ; music, wanton songs,
And tunes of silken petticoats to dance to.
  Lady B. And to-morrow have I invited half
 the court
To dine here. What misfortune 't is your com-
 pany
And ours should be divided ! After dinner
I entertain 'em with a play.
  Born.   By that time 70
Your play inclines to the epilogue, shall we
Quit our Italian host ; and whirl in coaches
To the Dutch magazine of sauce, the Steelyard,
Where deal,[3] and backrag,[4] and what strange
 wine else
They dare but give a name to in the reckoning,
Shall flow into our room, and drown Westphal-
 ias,[5]   75
Tongues, and anchovies, like some little town
Endangered by a sluice, through whose fierce
 ebb
We wade, and wash ourselves into a boat,
And bid our coachmen drive their leather ten-
 ements   80
By land, while we sail home, with a fresh tide,
To some new rendezvous.
  Lady B.   If you have not
'Pointed the place, pray bring your ladies
 hither ;
I mean to have a ball to-morrow night, 84
And a rich banquet for 'em, where we 'll dance
Till morning rise, and blush to interrupt us.
  Born. Have you no ladies i' th' next room,
 to advance [6]
A present mirth ? What a dull house you govern !
Farewell ! a wife 's no company. — Aretina,
I 've summ'd up my estate, and find we may
 have   90
A month good yet.
  Lady B. What mean you ?
  Born.   And I 'd rather
Be lord one month of pleasures, to the height
And rapture of our senses, than be years
Consuming what we have in foolish temperance,
Live in the dark, and no fame wait upon us ! 95
I will live so, posterity shall stand
At gaze when I am mentioned.
  Lady B.   A month good !
And what shall be done then ?
  Born.   I 'll over sea,
And trail a pike. With watching, marching,
 lying
In trenches, with enduring cold and hunger, 100
And taking here and there a musket-shot,
I can earn every week four shillings, madam ;
And if the bullets favour me to snatch
Any superfluous limb, when I return,
With good friends, I despair not to be enroll'd
Poor knight of Windsor.[7] For your course,
 madam,   105

 [2] Choice viands.
 [3] " Some unidentified kind of wine." (N. E. D.)
 [4] Baccarach, a famous Rhine wine.
 [5] Hams.   [6] Rouse.
 [7] One of a small order of military knights with pensions and apartments in Windsor Castle.

No doubt you may do well; your friends are
  great;
Or if your poverty and their pride cannot
Agree, you need not trouble much invention
To find a trade to live by; there are custom-
  ers.   110
Farewell, be frolic, madam! If I live,
I will feast all my senses, and not fall
Less than a Phaeton from my throne of pleas-
  ure,
Though my estate flame like the world about
  me.   *Exit.*
  Lady B. 'T is very pretty! —

                Enter DECOY.

                      Madam Decoy!
  Dec.   What! melancholy, 115
After so sweet a night's work? Have not I
Show'd myself mistress of my art?
  Lady B.   A lady.
  Dec. That title makes the credit of the act
A story higher. Y' have not seen him yet?
I wonder what he 'll say.
  Lady B.   He 's here.

      Enter KICKSHAW *and* FREDERICK.

  Kick.   Bear up, 120
My little myrmidon; does not Jack Little-
  worth
Follow?
  Fred. Follow? He fell into the Thames
At landing.
  Kick.   The devil shall dive for him,
Ere I endanger my silk stockings for him.
Let the watermen alone, they have drags and
  engines.[1]   125
When he has drunk his julep, I shall laugh
To see him come in pickled the next tide.
  Fred. He'll never sink, he has such a cork
  brain.
  Kick. Let him be hang'd or drown'd, all 's
  one to me;
Yet he deserves to die by water, cannot   130
Bear his wine credibly.
  Fred.   Is not this my aunt?
  Kick. And another handsome lady; I must
  know her.   [*Goes up to* DECOY.]
  Fred. My blood is rampant too, I must court
  somebody;
As good my aunt as any other body.
  Lady B. Where have you been, cousin?
  Fred.   At the Bridge, 135
At the Bear's foot, where our first health be-
  gan
To the fair Aretina, whose sweet company
Was wished by all. We could not get a lay,
A tumbler, a device, a *bona roba,*[2]
For any money; drawers were grown dull: 140
We wanted our true firks,[3] and our vagaries.—
When were you in drink, aunt?
  Lady B.   How?
  Fred.   Do not ladies

Play the good fellows too? There 's no true
  mirth
Without 'em. I have now such tickling fancies!
That doctor of the chair of wit has read   145
A precious lecture, how I should behave
Myself to ladies; as now, for example.
                  [*Goes up to* LADY BORNWELL.]
  Lady B. Would you practise upon me?
  Fred.   I first salute you,
You have a soft hand, madam; are you so
All over?
  Lady B. Nephew!
  Fred.   Nay, you should but smile. 150
And then again I kiss you; and thus draw
Off your white glove, and start, to see your hand
More excellently white. I grace my own
Lip with this touch, and turning gently thus,
Prepare you for my skill in palmistry,   155
Which, out of curiosity, no lady
But easily applies[4] to. The first line
I look with most ambition to find out,
Is Venus' girdle, a fair semicircle,
Enclosing both the mount of Sol and Saturn; 160
If that appear, she 's for my turn; a lady
Whom nature has prepar'd for the career;
And, Cupid at my elbow, I put forward:
You have this very line, aunt.
  Lady B.   The boy 's frantic!
  Fred. You have a couch or pallet; I can shut
The chamber door. Enrich a stranger, when   166
Your nephew 's coming into play!
  Lady B.   No more.
  Fred. Are you so coy to your own flesh and
  blood?
  Kick. Here, take your playfellow; I talk of
  sport,
And she would have me marry her.   170
  Fred. Here 's Littleworth.

          Enter LITTLEWORTH, *wet.*

Why, how now, tutor?
  Little.   I have been fishing.
  Fred. And what ha' you caught?
  Little.   My belly full of water.
  Kick. Ha, ha! Where 's thy rapier?
  Little.   My rapier is drown'd,
And I am little better. I was up by th' heels, 175
And out came a tun of water, beside wine.
  Kick. 'T has made thee sober.
  Little.   Would you have me drunk
With water?
  Lady B. I hope your fire is quench'd by this
  time.
  Fred. It is not now, as when your worship
  "walk'd
By all the taverns, Jack, dry as a bone."   180
  Kick. You had store of fish under water,
  Jack.
  Little. It has made a poor John of me.
  Fred. I do not think but if we cast an angle
Into his belly, we might find some pilchards.[5]
  Little. And boil'd, by this time. — Dear
  madam, a bed.   185
  Kick. Carry but the water-spaniel to a grass-
  plot,

---

[1] Contrivances.

[2] All four terms are euphemisms for courtesan.

[3] A vague piece of contemporary slang, the meaning
of which has usually to be derived from the context.

[4] Yields.   [5] A small fish, like a herring.

Where he may roll himself ; let him but shake
His ears twice in the sun, and you may grind him
Into a posset.
    Fred.   Come, thou shalt to my bed,
Poor pickerel.
    Dec.   Alas, sweet gentleman !   190
    Little. I have ill luck an I should smell by
this time ;
I am but new ta'en, I am sure. — Sweet gentle-
woman !
    Dec. Your servant.
    Little.   Pray do not pluck off my skin ;
It is so wet, unless you have good eyes,
You 'll hardly know it from a shirt.
    Dec.   Fear nothing. 195
        Exeunt [*all but* KICKSHAW *and*
          Lady BORNWELL.]
    Lady B. [*Aside.*] He has sack enough, and I
may find his humour.
    Kick. And how is 't with your ladyship ? You
look
Without a sunshine in your face.
    Lady B.   You are glorious
In mind and habit.
    Kicks.   Ends of gold and silver !
    Lady B. Your other clothes were not so rich.
    Who was   200
Your tailor, sir ?
    Kick.   They were made for me long since ;
They have known but two bright days upon my
back.
I had a humour, madam, to lay things by ;
They will serve two days more : I think I ha'
gold enough
To go to th' mercer. I 'll now allow myself   205
A suit a week, as this, with necessary
Dependances, beaver, silk stockings, garters,
And roses, in their due conformity ;
Boots are forbid a clean leg, but to ride in.
My linen every morning comes in new,   210
The old goes to great bellies.
    Lady B.   You are charitable.
    Kick. I may dine wi' ye sometime, or at the
court,
To meet good company, not for the table.
My clerk o' th' kitchen 's here, a witty epicure,
A spirit, that, to please me with what 's rare,
Can fly a hundred mile a day to market,   216
And make me lord of fish and fowl. I shall
Forget there is a butcher ; and to make
My footman nimble, he shall feed on nothing
But wings of wild fowl.
    Lady B.   These ways are costly. 220
    Kick. Therefore I 'll have it so ; I ha' sprung
a mine.
    Lady B. You make me wonder, sir, to see
this change
Of fortune : your revenue was not late
So plentiful.
    Kick.   Hang dirty land, and lordships !
I wo' not change one lodging I ha' got,   225
For the Chamber of London.
    Lady B.   Strange, of such a sudden,
To rise to this estate !
At dice could lift you up so, for 't is since
Last night : yesterday, you were no such mon-
arch.

    Kick. There be more games than dice.
    Lady B.   It cannot be 230
A mistress, though your person is worth love ;
None possibly are rich enough to feed
As you have cast the method of your riots.
A princess, after all her jewels, must
Be forc'd to sell her provinces.
    Kick.   Now you talk 235
Of jewels, what do you think of this ?
    Lady B.   A rich one.
    Kick. You 'll honour me to wear 't ; this
other toy
I had from you ; this chain I borrowed of you,
A friend had it in keeping. [*Gives her the jewel
and chain.*] — If your ladyship
Want any sum, you know your friend, and
Alexander.   240
    Lady B. Dare you trust my security ?
    Kick.   There 's gold,
I shall have more to-morrow.
    Lady B.   You astonish me ;
Who can supply these ?
    Kick.   A dear friend I have.
She promis'd we should meet again i' th' morn-
ing.
    Lady B. Not that I wish to know   245
More of your happiness than I have already
Heart to congratulate,— be pleas'd to lay
My wonder.
    Kick.   'T is a secret —
    Lady B.   Which I 'll die
Ere I 'll betray.
    Kick.   You have always wish'd me well ;
But you shall swear not to reveal the party. 250
    Lady B. I 'll lose the benefit of my tongue.
    Kick.   Nor be
Afraid at what I say. What think you first
Of an old witch, a strange ill-favour'd hag,
That, for my company last night, has wrought
This cure upon my fortune ? I do sweat   255
To think upon her name.
    Lady B.   How, sir ! a witch ?
    Kick. I would not fright your ladyship too
much
At first, but witches are akin to spirits.
The truth is — Nay, if you look pale already,
I ha' done.
    Lady B. Sir, I beseech you.
    Kick.   If you have 260
But courage then to know the truth, I 'll tell
you
In one word ; my chief friend is — the devil !
    Lady B. What devil ? how I tremble !
    Kick.   Have a heart ;
'T was a she-devil too, a most insatiate,
Abominable devil, with a tail   265
Thus long.
    Lady B. Goodness defend me ! Did you see
her ?
    Kick. No, 't was i' th' dark ; but she appear'd
first to me
I' th' likeness of a beldam, and was brought,
I know not how, nor whither, by two goblins,
More hooded than a hawk.
    Lady B.   But would you venture 270
Upon a devil !
    Kick.   Ay, for means.

Lady B. [*Aside.*]   How black
An impudence is this ! — But are you sure
It was the devil you enjoy'd ?
Kick.   Say nothing ;
I did the best to please her ; but as sure
As you live, 't was a hell-cat.
  Lady B.   D' ye not quake ? 275
  Kick. I found myself in the very room [1] i' th'
    morning,
Where two of her familiars had left me.

Enter Servant.

Serv. My lord is come to visit you.
  Kick.   No words,
As you respect my safety. I ha' told tales
Out of the devil's school ; if it be known,   280
I lose a friend. 'T is now about the time
I promis'd her to meet again ; at my
Return I 'll tell you wonders. Not a word. *Exit.*
  Lady B. 'T is a false glass ; sure I am more
    deform'd : [*Looks in her pocket mirror.*]
What have I done ? — My soul is miserable. 285

Enter LORD ——.

Lord. I sent you a letter, madam.
  Lady B.   You exprest
Your noble care of me, my lord.

Re-enter Sir THOMAS BORNWELL *with* CELES-
    TINA.

Born.   Your lordship
Does me an honour.
  Lord.   Madam, I am glad
To see you here ; I meant to have kist your
    hand,
Ere my return to court.
  Cel.   Sir Thomas has   290
Prevail'd to bring me, to his trouble, hither.
  Lord. You do him grace.
  Born.   Why, what 's the matter, madam ?
Your eyes are tuning *Lachrimae.*[2]
  Lady B.   As you
Do hope for Heaven, withdraw, and give me
    but
The patience of ten minutes.
  Born.   Wonderful ! 295
I will not hear you above that proportion.
She talks of Heaven : — Come, where must we
    to counsel ?
  Lady B. You shall conclude me when you
    please.   [*Exit.*]
  Born. I follow.
  Lord. [*Aside.*] What alteration is this ? I,
    that so late
Stood the temptation of her eye and voice,   300
Boasted a heart 'bove all licentious flame,
At second view turn renegade, and think
I was too superstitious, and full
Of phlegm, not to reward her amorous courtship
With manly freedom.
  Cel.   I obey you, sir.   305
  Born. I 'll wait upon your lordship presently.
                              [*Exit.*]

---

[1] Gifford conj. Q. *myself the very same.*

[2] A punning allusion to Dowland's *Lacrimae or Seven
Tears,* etc., a popular musical work of the time for
stringed instruments.

Lord. She could not want a cunning to seem
    honest
When I neglected her. I am resolv'd.—
You still look pleasant, madam.
  Cel.   I have cause, 309
My lord, the rather for your presence, which
Hath power to charm all trouble in my thoughts.
  Lord. I must translate that compliment, and
All that is cheerful in myself to these
All-quick'ning smiles ; and rather than such
    bright
Eyes should repent their influence upon me, 315
I would release the aspects, and quit the bounty
Of all the other stars. Did you not think me
A strange and melancholy gentleman,
To use you so unkindly ?
  Cel.   Me, my lord ?
  Lord. I hope you made no loud complaint ; I
    would not   320
Be tried by a jury of ladies.
  Cel.   For what, my lord ?
  Lord. I did not meet that noble entertain-
    ment
You were late pleas'd to show me.
  Cel.   I observ'd
No such defect in your lordship, but a brave
And noble fortitude.
  Lord.   A noble folly ;   325
I bring repentance for 't. I know you have,
Madam, a gentle faith, and wo' not ruin
What you have built to honour you.
  Cel.   What 's that ?
  Lord. If you can love, I 'll tell your ladyship.
  Cel. I have a stubborn soul else.
  Lord   You are all 330
Compos'd of harmony.
  Cel.   What love d' ye mean ?
  Lord. That which doth perfect both. Ma-
    dam, you have heard
I can be constant, and if you consent
To grace it so, there is a spacious dwelling
Prepar'd within my heart for such a mistress, 335
  Cel. Your mistress, my good lord ?
  Lord.   Why, my good lady,
Your sex doth hold it no dishonour
To become mistress to a noble servant
In the now court Platonic way. Consider
Who 't is that pleads to you ; my birth and
    present   340
Value can be no stain to your embrace ;
But these are shadows when my love appears,
Which shall, in his first miracle, return
Me in my bloom of youth, and thee a virgin ;
When I, within some new Elysium,   345
Of purpose made and meant for us, shall be
In every thing Adonis, but in his
Contempt of love ; and court thee from a
    Daphne
Hid in the cold rind of a bashful tree,
With such warm language and delight, till
    thou   350
Leap from that bay [2] into the Queen of Love,
And pay my conquest with composing garlands
Of thy own myrtle for me.

---

[2] Daphne was transformed into a bay-tree.

Cel.   What's all this?
Lord. Consent to be my mistress, Celestina,
And we will have it spring-time all the year ; 355
Upon whose invitations, when we walk,
The winds shall play soft descant to our feet,
And breathe rich odours to re-pure the air :
Green bowers on every side shall tempt our stay,
And violets stoop to have us tread upon 'em. 360
The red rose shall grow pale, being near thy
      cheek,
And the white blush, o'ercome with such a fore-
      head.
Here laid, and measuring with ourselves some
      bank,
A thousand birds shall from the woods repair,
And place themselves so cunningly behind 365
The leaves of every tree, that while they pay
Us tribute of their songs, thou sha't imagine
The very trees bear music, and sweet voices
Do grow in every arbour.   Here can we
Embrace and kiss, tell tales, and kiss again, 370
And none but Heaven our rival.
Cel.   When we are
Weary of these, what if we shift our paradise,
And through a grove of tall and even pine,
Descend into a valley, that shall shame
All the delights of Tempe ; upon whose 375
Green plush the Graces shall be call'd to dance
To please us, and maintain their fairy revels,
To the harmonious murmurs of a stream
That gently falls upon a rock of pearl. 379
Here doth the nymph, forsaken Echo, dwell,
To whom we 'll tell the story of our love,
Till at our surfeit and her want of joy,
We break her heart with envy. Not far off,
A grove shall call us to a wanton river,
To see a dying swan give up the ghost, 385
The fishes shooting up their tears in bubbles,
That they must lose the genius of their
      waves —
And such love linsey woolsey, to no purpose.
Lord. You chide me handsomely ; pray tell
      me how
You like this language.
Cel.   Good my lord, forbear. 390
Lord. You need not fly out of this circle,
      madam ;
These widows are so full of circumstance ! —
I 'll undertake, in this time I ha' courted
Your ladyship for the toy, to ha' broken ten,
Nay, twenty colts, virgins I mean, and taught
      'em 395
The amble, or what pace I most affected.
Cel. You 're not, my lord, again, the lord I
      thought you ;
And I must tell you now, you do forget
Yourself and me.
Lord.   You 'll not be angry, madam ?
Cel. Nor rude, (though gay men have a pri-
      vilege,) 400
It shall appear : — there is a man, my lord,
Within my acquaintance, rich in worldly for-
      tunes,
But cannot boast any descent of blood,
Would buy a coat of arms.
Lord.   He may, and legs
Booted and spurr'd, to ride into the country. 405

Cel. But these will want antiquity, my
      lord,
The seal of honour. What 's a coat cut out
But yesterday, to make a man a gentleman ?
Your family, as old as the first virtue
That merited an escutcheon, doth owe [1]   410
A glorious coat of arms ; if you will sell now
All that your name doth challenge in that en-
      sign,
I 'll help you to a chapman that shall pay,
And pour down wealth enough for 't.
Lord.   Sell my arms !
I cannot, madam.
Cel.   Give but your consent,   415
You know not how the state may be inclin'd
To dispensation ; we may prevail
Upon the Herald's office afterward.
Lord. I 'll sooner give these arms to th'
      hangman's axe,
My head, my heart, to twenty executions, 420
Than sell one atom from my name.
Cel.   Change that,
And answer him would buy my honour from
      me ;
Honour, that is not worn upon a flag
Or pennon, that, without the owner's dangers,
An enemy may ravish, and bear from me ; 425
But that which grows and withers with my
      soul,
Beside the body's stain : think, think, my
      lord,
To what you would unworthily betray me,
If you would not, for price of gold, or pleasure,
(If that be more your idol,) lose the glory 430
And painted honour of your house. — I ha'
      done.
Lord. Enough to rectify a satyr's blood.
Obscure my blushes here.

Enter Sir WILLIAM SCENTLOVE *and* HAIRCUT.

Hair.   Or this, or fight with me ;
It shall be no exception that I wait
Upon my lord ; I am a gentleman, 435
You may be less and be a knight : the office
I do my lord is honest, sir. How many
Such you have been guilty of, Heaven knows.
Scent. 'T is no fear of your sword, but that I
      would not 439
Break the good laws establish'd against duels.
Hair. Off with your periwig, and stand bare.
      [Sir WILLIAM SCENTLOVE *takes
      off his periwig.*]
Lord.   From this
Minute I 'll be a servant to thy goodness ;
A mistress in the wanton sense is common,
I 'll honour you with chaste thoughts, and call
      you so.
Cel. I 'll study to be worth your fair opinion.
Lord. Scentlove, your head was us'd to a
      covering, 445
Beside a hat ; when went the hair away ?
Scent. I laid a wager, my lord, with Hair-
      cut,
Who thinks I shall catch cold, that I 'll stand
      bare
This half hour.
            [1] Own.

Hair.   Pardon my ambition,   450
Madam, I told you truth; I am a gentleman,
And cannot fear that name is drown'd in my
Relation to my lord.
Cel.   I dare not think so.
Hair. From henceforth call my service duty,
          madam.
That pig's head, that betray'd me to your
          mirth,   455
Is doing penance for 't.
Scent.   Why may not I,
My lord, begin a fashion of no hair?
Cel. Do you sweat, Sir William?
Scent.   Not with store of nightcaps.

Re-enter Sir Thomas *and* Lady Bornwell.

Lady B. Heaven has dissolv'd the clouds
          that hung upon
My eyes, and if you can with mercy meet   460
A penitent, I throw my own will off,
And now in all things obey yours. My nephew
Send back again to th' college, and myself
To what place you 'll confine me.
Born.   Dearer now
Than ever to my bosom, thou sha't please   465
Me best to live at thy own choice. I did
But fright thee with a noise of my expenses;
The sums are safe, and we have wealth enough,
If yet we use it nobly. My lord — madam,
Pray honour us to-night.
Lady B.   I beg your presence,   470
And pardon.
Born.   I know not how my Aretina
May be dispos'd to-morrow for the country.
Cel. You must not go before you have done
Me honour to accept an entertainment
Where I have power; on those terms I 'm your
          guest.   475
Born. You grace us, madam.
Lady B. [*Aside.*]   Already
I feel a cure upon my soul, and promise
My after life to virtue. Pardon, Heaven,
My shame, yet hid from the world's eye.

Re-enter Decoy.

Dec.   Sweet madam!
Lady B. Not for the world be seen here!
          We are lost.   480
I 'll visit you at home. — [*Aside.*] But not to
          practise
What she expects: my counsel may recover
          her.   [*Exit* Decoy.]

Re-enter Kickshaw.

Kick. Where 's madam? — Pray lend me a
          little money,
My spirit has deceiv'd me; Proserpine
Has broke her word.
Lady B.   Do you expect to find   485
The devil true to yon?
Kick.   Not too loud.
Lady B.   I 'll voice it
Louder, to all the world, your horrid sin,
Unless you promise me religiously,
To purge your foul blood by repentance, sir.
Kick. Then I 'm undone.
Lady B.   Not while I have power   490
To encourage you to virtue. I 'll endeavour
To find you out some nobler way at court,
To thrive in.
Kick.   Do 't and I 'll forsake the devil,
And bring my flesh to obedience. You shall
          steer me. —
My lord, your servant.
Lord.   You are brave again.   495
Kick. Madam, your pardon.
Born.   Your offence requires
Humility.
Kick.   Low as my heart. — Sir Thomas,
I 'll sup with you, a part of satisfaction.
Born. Our pleasures cool. Music! and when
          our ladies
Are tir'd with active motion, to give   500
Them rest, in some new rapture to advance
Full mirth, our souls shall leap into a dance.
          Exeunt.

THE CARDINAL

JAMES SHIRLEY

PERSONS

ᴋɪɴɢ ᴏғ Nᴀᴠᴀʀʀᴇ.
Tʜᴇ Cᴀʀᴅɪɴᴀʟ.
Cᴏʟᴜᴍʙᴏ, the Cardinal's Nephew.
[Cᴏᴜɴᴛ] ᴅ' Aʟᴠᴀʀᴇᴢ.
Hᴇʀɴᴀɴᴅᴏ, a Colonel.
Aʟᴘʜᴏɴsᴏ, [a Captain.]
Lords.
[Aɴᴛᴏɴɪᴏ,] Secretary to the Duchess.
Colonels.
Aɴᴛᴏɴᴇʟʟɪ, the Cardinal's Servant.

[Gentleman-Usher.]
Surgeon.
[Jᴀǫᴜᴇs, Pᴇᴅʀᴏ, and other Servants.]
Guard.
Attendants, etc.

Dᴜᴄʜᴇss Rᴏsᴀᴜʀᴀ.
Vᴀʟᴇʀɪᴀ, } Ladies.
Cᴇʟɪɴᴅᴀ, }
Pʟᴀᴄᴇɴᴛɪᴀ, a Lady that waits upon the Duchess.

Sᴄᴇɴᴇ.— *Navarre.*

THE PROLOGUE

Tʜᴇ Cᴀʀᴅɪɴᴀʟ ! 'Cause we express no scene,
We do believe most of you, gentlemen,
Are at this hour in France, and busy there,
Though you vouchsafe to lend your bodies here ;
But keep your fancy active, till you know,　　　　5
By th' progress of our play, 't is nothing so.
A poet's art is to lead on your thought
Through subtle paths and workings of a plot ;
And where your expectation does not thrive,
If things fall better, yet you may forgive.　　　　1
I will say nothing positive ; you may
Think what you please ; we call it but a Play :
Whether the comic Muse, or ladies' love,
Romance, or direful tragedy it prove,
The bill determines not ; and would you be　　　15
Persuaded, I would have 't a Comedy,
For all the purple in the name and state
Of him that owns it ; but 't is left to fate.
Yet I will tell you, ere you see it play'd,
What the author, and he blusht too, when he said,　　20
Comparing with his own, (for 't had been pride,
He thought, to build his wit a pyramid
Upon another's wounded fame,) this play
Might rival with his best, and dar'd to say —
Troth, I am out ⁚ he said no more. You, then,　　25
When 't 's done, may say your pleasures, gentlemen.

ACT I

[Scene I.]¹

Enter two Lords *at one door ; secretary [Aɴ-
ᴛᴏɴɪᴏ]² at the other.*

1 *Lord.* Who is that ?
2 *Lord.* The duchess' secretary.

¹ An apartment in the palace.
² In stage directions and speech-tags throughout, Antonio is called *Secretary.*

1 *Lord.* Signior !
Ant. Your lordship's servant.
1 *Lord.* How does her grace, since she left off
　　her mourning　　　　5
For the young Duke Mendoza, whose timeless
　　death
At sea left her a virgin and a widow ?
2 *Lord.* She 's now inclining to a second
　　bride.³ ——

³ Bridegroom, as often.

When is the day of mighty marriage
To our great Cardinal's nephew, Don Columbo?
  Ant. When they agree; they will not steal to
    church,   11
I guess the ceremonies will be loud and pub-
    lic.
Your lordships will excuse me.   *Exit.*
  1 *Lord.* When they agree! Alas! poor lady,
    she
Dotes not upon Columbo, when she thinks   15
Of the young Count d'Alvarez, divorc'd from
    her
By the king's power.
  2 *Lord.*   And counsel of the Cardinal,
To advance his nephew to the duchess' bed;
It is not well.
  1 *Lord.*   Take heed; the Cardinal holds
Intelligence with every bird i' th' air.   20
  2 *Lord.* Death on his purple pride! He gov-
    erns all;
And yet Columbo is a gallant gentleman.
  1 *Lord.* The darling of the war, whom victory
Hath often courted; a man of daring,
And most exalted spirit. Pride in him   25
Dwells like an ornament, where so much hon-
    our
Secures his praise.
  2 *Lord.*   This is no argument
He should usurp, and wear Alvarez' title
To the fair duchess; men of coarser blood,
Would not so tamely give this treasure up.   30
  1 *Lord.* Although Columbo's name is great
    in war,
Whose glorious art and practice is above
The greatness of Alvarez, yet he cannot
Want soul, in whom alone survives the virtue
Of many noble ancestors, being the last   35
Of his great family.
  2 *Lord.*   'T is not safe, you 'll say,
To wrastle with the king.
  1 *Lord.* More danger if the Cardinal be dis-
    pleas'd,
Who sits at helm of state. Count d'Alvarez
Is wiser to obey the stream, than by   40
Insisting on his privilege to her love,
Put both their fates upon a storm.
  2 *Lord.*   If wisdom,
Not inborn fear, make him compose,[1] I like it.
How does the duchess bear herself?
  1 *Lord.* She moves by the rapture [2] of another
    wheel,   45
That must be obey'd; like some sad passenger,
That looks upon the coast his wishes fly to,
But is transported by an adverse wind,
Sometimes a churlish pilot.
  2 *Lord.* She has a sweet and noble nature.
  1 *Lord.*   That   50
Commends Alvarez; Hymen cannot tie
A knot of two more equal hearts and blood.

             Enter ALPHONSO.

  2 *Lord.* Alphonso!
  Alph.   My good lord.
  1 *Lord.*   What great affair
Hath brought you from the confines?

---

  [1] Agree.   [2] Force, momentum.

  Alph.   Such as will
Be worth your counsels, when the king hath
    read   55
My letters from the governor: the Arragonians,
Violating their confederate oath and league,
Are now in arms: they have not yet marcht to-
    wards us;
But 't is not safe to expect,[3] if we may timely
Prevent invasion.
  2 *Lord.*   Dare they be so insolent?   60
  1 *Lord.* This storm I did foresee.
  2 *Lord.*   What have they, but
The sweetness of the king, to make a crime?
  1 *Lord.* But how appears the Cardinal at this
    news?
  Alph. Not pale, although
He knows they have no cause to think him in-
    nocent,   65
As by whose counsel they were once surpris'd.
  1 *Lord.* There is more
Than all our present art can fathom in
This story, and I fear I may conclude
This flame has breath at home to cherish it.   70
There 's treason in some hearts, whose faces are
Smooth to the state.
  Alph.   My lord, I take my leave.
  2 *Lord.* Your friends, good captain. *Exeunt.*

             [SCENE II.] [4]

  Enter DUCHESS, VALERIA, *and* CELINDA.

  Val. Sweet madam, be less thoughtful; this
    obedience [5]
To passion will destroy the noblest frame
Of beauty that this kingdom ever boasted.
  Cel. This sadness might become your other
    habit,
And ceremonies black, for him that died.   5
The times of sorrow are expir'd; and all
The joys that wait upon the court, your birth,
And a new Hymen, that is coming towards you,
Invite a change.
  Duch.   Ladies, I thank you both;
I pray excuse a little melancholy   10
That is behind; my year of mourning hath not
So clear'd my account with sorrow, but there
    may
Some dark thoughts stay, with sad reflections,
Upon my heart, for him I lost. Even this
New dress and smiling garment, meant to
    show   15
A peace concluded 'twixt my grief and me,
Is but a sad remembrance. But I resolve
To entertain more pleasing thoughts; and if
You wish me heartily to smile, you must
Not mention grief, not in advice to leave it.   20
Such counsels open but afresh the wounds
Ye would close up, and keep alive the cause,
Whose bleeding you would cure. Let 's talk of
    something
That may delight. You two are read in all
The histories of our court: tell me, Valeria,   25
Who has thy vote for the most handsome
    man? —

---

  [3] Wait.   [5] Yielding.
  [4] A room in the Duchess 's house.

[*Aside.*] Thus I must counterfeit a peace, when all
Within me is at mutiny.
   Val.   I have examin'd
All that are candidates for the praise of ladies,
But find — may I speak boldly to your grace?
And will you not return it in your mirth,   31
To make me blush?
   Duch.   No, no; speak freely.
   Val. I wo' not rack your patience, madam; but
Were I a princess, I should think the Count d'Alvarez
Had sweetness to deserve me from the world. 35
   Duch. [*Aside.*] Alvarez! she 's a spy upon my heart.
   Val. He 's young and active, and compos'd most sweetly.
   Duch. I have seen a face more tempting.
   Val.   It had then
Too much of woman in 't: his eyes speak movingly,
Which may excuse his voice, and lead away 40
All female pride his captive; his hair, black,
Which, naturally falling into curls —
   Duch. Prithee, no more; thou art in love with him. —
The man in your esteem, Celinda, now?
   Cel. Alvarez is, I must confess, a gentleman 45
Of handsome composition; but with
His mind, the greater excellence, I think
Another may delight a lady more,
If man be well considered, that's Columbo,
Now, madam, voted to be yours.
   Dutch. [*Aside.*]   My torment! 50
   Val. [*Aside.*] She affects him not.
   Cel. He has a person, and a bravery beyond
All men, that I observe.
   Val.   He is a soldier,
A rough-hewn man, and may show well at distance.
His talk will fright a lady; War, and grim- 55
Fac'd Honour are his mistresses; he raves
To hear a lute; Love meant him not his priest. —
Again your pardon, madam. We may talk,
But you have art to choose, and crown affection. [*CELINDA and VALERIA walk aside.*]
   Duch. What is it to be born above these ladies, 60
And want their freedom! They are not constrain'd,
Nor slav'd by their own greatness, or the king's,
But let their free hearts look abroad, and choose
By their own eyes to love. I must repair
My poor afflicted bosom, and assume 65
The privilege I was born with, which now prompts me
To tell the king, he hath no power nor art
To steer a lover's soul. —

       Enter Secretary [ANTONIO].

            What says Count d'Alvarez?
   Ant. Madam, he 'll attend you.

   Duch. Wait you, as I directed. When he comes, 70
Acquaint me privately.
   Ant.   Madam, I have news;
'T is now arriv'd the court; we shall have wars.
   Duch. [*Aside.*] I find an army here of killing thoughts.
   Ant. The king has chosen Don Columbo general,
Who is immediately to take his leave. 75
   Duch. [*Aside.*] What flood is let into my heart! — How far
Is he to go?
   Ant.   To Arragon.
   Duch.   That 's well
At first; he should not want a pilgrimage
To the unknown world, if my thoughts might convey him.
   Ant. 'T is not impossible he may go thither. 80
   Duch. How?
   Ant. To the unknown world; he goes to fight,
That 's in his way: such stories are in nature.
   Duch. Conceal this news.
   Ant.   He wo' not be long absent;
The affair will make him swift
To kiss your grace's hand.   [*Exit.*]
   Duch.   He cannot fly 85
With too much wing to take his leave. — I must
Be admitted to your conference; you have
Enlarg'd my spirits; they shall droop no more.
   Cel. We are happy, if we may advance one thought
To your grace's pleasure. 90
   Val. Your eye before was in eclipse; these smiles
Become you, madam.
   Duch. [*Aside.*] I have not skill to contain myself.

       Enter PLACENTIA.

   Pla. The Cardinal's nephew, madam, Don Columbo.
   Duch. Already! Attend him.
                Exit PLACENTIA.
   Val.   Shall we take our leave? 95
   Duch. He shall not know, [Celinda,] [1] how you prais'd him.
   [*Cel.*] [2] If he did, madam, I should have the confidence
To tell him my free thoughts.

       Enter COLUMBO.

   Duch. My lord, while I 'm in study to requite
The favour you ha' done me, you increase 100
My debt to such a sum, still by a new honouring
Your servant, I despair of my own freedom.
   Colum. Madam, he kisseth your white hand, that must
Not surfeit in this happiness — and, ladies,
I take your smiles for my encouragement! 105
I have not long to practise these court tactics.
                [*Kisses them.*]
   Cel. He has been taught to kiss.

---

[1] Q. *Valeria*, but cf. vv. 45-57, above.   [2] Q. *Val.*

Duch.   There 's something, sir,
Upon your brow I did not read before.
Colum. Does the character please you, madam?
Duch.   More,
Because it speaks you cheerful.
Colum.   'T is for such 110
Access of honour, as must make Columbo
Worth all your love ; the king is pleas'd to
    think
Me fit to lead his army.
Duch.   How ! an army ?
Colum. We must not use the priest, till I
    bring home
Another triumph that now stays for me,   115
To reap it in the purple field of glory.
Duch. But do you mean to leave me, and ex-
    pose
Yourself to the devouring war ? No enemy
Should divide us ; the king is not so cruel.
Colum. The king is honourable ; and this
    grace   120
More answers my ambition, than his gift
Of thee, and all thy beauty, which I can
Love, as becomes thy soldier, and fight
To come again, a conqueror of thee.
                           She weeps.
Then I must chide this fondness.[1]   125

Re-enter Secretary [ANTONIO].

Ant. Madam, the king, and my lord Cardinal.
                           [*Exit.*]

Enter KING, CARDINAL, *and* Lords.

King. Madam, I come to call a servant from
    you,
And strengthen his excuse ; the public cause
Will plead for your consent ; at his return
Your marriage shall receive triumphant cere-
    monies ;   130
Till then you must dispense.
Car.   She appears sad
To part with him. — I like it fairly, nephew.
    [*Cel.*][2] Is not the general a gallant man ?
What lady would deny him a small courtesy ?
    [*Val.*] Thou hast converted me, and I begin 135
To wish it were no sin.
    [*Cel.*] Leave that to narrow consciences.
    [*Val.*] You are pleasant.
    [*Cel.*] But he would please one better. Do
        such men
Lie with their pages?
    [*Val.*]   Wouldst thou make a shift ?
    [*Cel.*] He is going to a bloody business ;   140
'T is pity he should die without some heir.
That lady were hard-hearted now, that would
Not help posterity, for the mere good
O' th' king and commonwealth.
    [*Val.*] Thou art wild ; we may be observ'd.
Duch. Your will must guide me ; happiness
    and conquest   146
Be ever waiting on his sword !
Colum.   Farewell.
        Exeunt KING, COLUMBO, CARDI-
            NAL *and* Lords.

[1] Foolishness.
[2] Q. transposes *Cel.* and *Val.* throughout this conversation.

Duch. Pray give leave to examine a few
    thoughts ;
Expect[3] me in the garden.
Ladies. We attend. *Exeunt* Ladies. 150
Duch. This is above all expectation happy.
Forgive me, Virtue, that I have dissembled,
And witness with me, I have not a thought
To tempt or to betray him, but secure
The promise I first made, to love and honour. 155

Re-enter Secretary [ANTONIO].

Ant. The Count d'Alvarez, madam.
Duch.   Admit him,
And let none interrupt us. [*Exit* ANTONIO.] —
                           How shall I
Behave my looks ? The guilt of my neglect,
Which had no seal from hence, will call up blood
To write upon my cheeks the shame and story 160
In some red letter.

Enter ALVAREZ.

Alv.   Madam, I present
One that was glad to obey your grace, and come
To know what your commands are.
Duch.   Where I once
Did promise love, a love that had the power
And office of a priest to chain my heart   165
To yours, it were injustice to command.
Alv. But I can look upon you, madam, as
Becomes a servant ; with as much humility,
In tenderness of your honour and great fortune,
Give up, when you call back your bounty, all
    that   170
Was mine, as I had pride to think them favours.
Duch. Hath love taught thee no more assur-
    ance in
Our mutual vows, thou canst suspect it possible
I should revoke a promise, made to heaven
And thee, so soon ? This must arise from some
Distrust of thy own faith.
Alv.   Your grace's pardon ; 176
To speak with freedom, I am not so old
In cunning to betray, nor young in time,
Not to see when and where I am at loss,
And how to bear my fortune, and my wounds, 180
Which, if I look for health, must still bleed in-
    ward,
A hard and desperate condition.
I am not ignorant your birth and greatness
Have plac'd you to grow up with the king's grace
And jealousy, which to remove, his power   185
Hath chosen a fit object for your beauty
To shine upon, Columbo, his great favourite.
I am a man on whom but late the king
Has pleas'd to cast a beam, which was not meant
To make me proud, but wisely to direct,   190
And light me to my safety. Oh, dear madam !
I will not call more witness of my love
(If you will let me still give it that name)
Than this, that I dare make myself a loser,
And to your will give all my blessings up.   195
Preserve your greatness, and forget a trifle,
That shall, at best, when you have drawn me up,
But hang about you like a cloud, and dim
The glories you are born to.

[3] Await.

Duch.   Misery
Of birth and state ! That I could shift into 200
A meaner blood, or find some art to purge
That part which makes my veins unequal ! Yet
Those nice distinctions have no place in us ;
There 's but a shadow difference, a title :
Thy stock partakes as much of noble sap   205
As that which feeds the root of kings ; and he
That writes a lord hath all the essence of
Nobility.
Alv.   'T is not a name that makes
Our separation ; the king's displeasure
Hangs a portent to fright us, and the matter 210
That feeds this exhalation is the Cardinal's
Plot to advance his nephew ; then Columbo,
A man made up for some prodigious act,
Is fit to be considered : in all three
There is no character you fix upon   215
But has a form of ruin to us both.
Duch. Then you do look on these with fear ?
Alv.   With eyes
That should think tears a duty, to lament
Your least unkind fate ; but my youth dares
     boldly
Meet all the tyranny o' th' stars, whose black
Malevolence but shoots my single tragedy.   221
You are above the value of many worlds
Peopled with such as I am.
Duch.   What if Columbo,
Engag'd to war, in his hot thirst of honour,
Find out the way to death ?
Alv.   'T is possible.   225
Duch. Or say, (no matter by what art or
     motive,)
He give his title up, and leave me to
My own election?
Alv.   If I then be happy
To have a name within your thought, there can 229
Be nothing left to crown me with new blessing.
But I dream thus of heaven, and wake to find
My amorous soul a mockery. When the priest
Shall tie you to another, and the joys
Of marriage leave no thought at leisure to
Look back upon Alvarez, that must wither   235
For loss of you ; yet then I cannot lose
So much of what I was once in your favour,
But, in a sigh, pray still you may live happy.
                                    Exit.
Duch. My heart is in a mist ; some good star
     smile
Upon my resolution, and direct   240
Two lovers in their chaste embrace to meet !
Columbo's bed contains my winding sheet.
                                    Exit.

ACT II

[SCENE I.][1]

General COLUMBO, HERNANDO, *two* Colonels,
ALPHONSO, *two* Captains, *and other* Officers,
as at a Council of War.

Colum. I see no face in all this council that
Hath one pale fear upon 't, though we arriv'd not

[1] Before the walls of the frontier city.— Columbo's
tent.

So timely to secure the town, which gives
Our enemy such triumph.
1 *Col.*   'T was betray'd.
Alph. The wealth of that one city   5
Will make the enemy glorious.[2]
1 *Col.*   They dare
Not plunder it.
Alph.   They give fair quarter yet :
They only seal up men's estates, and keep
Possession for the city's use : they take up
No wares without security ; and he,   10
Whose single credit will not pass, puts in
Two lean comrades, upon whose bonds 't is not
Religion to deny 'em.
Colum.   To repair this
With honour, gentlemen ?
Her.   My opinion is
To expect awhile.
Colum.   Your reason ?
Her.   Till their own   15
Surfeit betray 'em ; for their soldier[s,]
Bred up with coarse and common bread, will
     show
Such appetites on the rich cates they find,
They 'll spare our swords a victory, when their
     own
Riot and luxury destroys 'em.
Col.   That   20
Will show our patience too like a fear.
With favour of his excellence, I think
The spoil of cities takes not off the courage,
But doubles it on soldiers ; besides,
While we have tameness to expect, the noise 25
Of their success and plenty will increase
Their army.
Her.   'T is considerable ; we do not
Exceed in foot or horse, our muster not
'Bove sixteen thousand both ; and the infantry
Raw, and not disciplin'd to act.
Alph.   Their hearts, 30
But with a brave thought of their country's
     honour,
Will teach 'em how to fight, had they not seen
A sword. But we decline[3] our own too much ;
The men are forward in their arms, and take
The use[4] with avarice of fame.
                     They rise, and talk privately.
Colum.   — Colonel,   35
I do suspect you are a coward.
Her.   Sir !
Colum. Or else a traitor ; take your choice.
     No more.
I call'd you to a council, sir, of war ;
Yet keep your place.
Her.   I have worn other names.
Colum. Deserve 'em. Such   40
Another were enough to unsoul an army.
Ignobly talk of patience, till they drink
And reel to death ! We came to fight, and force
     'em
To mend their pace : thou hast no honour in
     thee,
Not enough noble blood to make a blush   45
For thy tame eloquence.

[2] Boastful.   [3] Depreciate.
[4] Learn to use their arms.

Her.   My lord, I know
My duty to a general : yet there are
Some that have known me here. Sir, I desire
To quit my regiment.
Colum.   You shall have license. —
Ink and paper !   50

[*Enter* Attendant *with ink and paper, and exit.*]

1 *Col.* The general 's displeas'd.
2 *Col.*   How is 't, Hernando ?
Her. The general has found out employment
    for me ;
He is writing letters back.
Alph. and Capt.   To his mistress ?
Her. Pray do not trouble me ; yet, prithee,
    speak,
And flatter not thy friend· Dost think I dare 55
Not draw my sword, and use it, when a cause,
With honour, calls to action ?
Alph. and Col. With the most valiant man
    alive.
Her. You 'll do me some displeasure in your
    loves :
Pray to your places.   60
Colum. So ; bear those letters to the king ;
They speak my resolution, before
Another sun decline, to charge the enemy.
Her. [*Aside.*] A pretty court way
Of dismissing an officer. — I obey ; success 65
Attend your counsels !   *Exit.*
Colum. If here be any dare not look on dan-
    ger,
And meet it like a man, with scorn of death,
I beg his absence ; and a coward's fear
Consume him to a ghost !
1 *Col.*   None such [are] here. 70
Colum. Or, if in all your regiments you find
One man that does not ask to bleed with hon-
    our,
Give him a double pay to leave the army ;
There 's service to be done will call the spirits
And aid of men.
1 *Col.*   You give us all new flame. 75
Colum. I am confirm'd, and you must lose no
    time ;
The soldier that was took last night, to me
Discover'd their whole strength, and that we
    have
A party in the town. The river, that
Opens the city to the west, ['s] unguarded ; — 80
We must this night use art and resolution
We cannot fall ingloriously.
1 *Capt.*   That voice
Is every man's.

Enter Soldier *and* Secretary [ANTONIO] *with a
    letter.*

Colum. What now ?
Sold. Letters.   85
Colum. Whence ?
Sold. From the duchess.
Colum. They are welcome.—[*Takes the letter.*]
Meet at my tent again this evening ;
Yet stay, some wine.— The duchess' health ! 90
                              [*Drinks.*]
See it go round.   [*Opens the letter.*]
Ant. It wo' not please his excellence.

1 *Col.* The duchess' health !   [*Drinks.*]
2 *Capt.* To me ! more wine.
Ant. The clouds are gathering, and his eyes
    shoot fire ;   95
Observe what thunder follows.
2 *Capt.* The general has but ill news. I sus-
    pect
The duchess sick, or else the king.
1 *Capt.*   May be
The Cardinal.
2 *Capt.*   His soul has long been look'd for. 100
Colum. She dares not be so insolent. It is
The duchess' hand. How am I shrunk in
    fame
To be thus play'd withal ! She writes, and coun-
    sels,
Under my hand, to send her back a free
Resign of all my interest to her person,
Promise, or love ; that there 's no other way,
With safety of my honour, to revisit her. 105
The woman is possess't with some bold devil,
And wants an exorcism ; or, I am grown
A cheap, dull, phlegmatic fool, a post that 's
    carv'd
I' th' common street, and holding out my fore-
    head   110
To every scurril wit to pin disgrace
And libels on 't.— Did you bring this to me,
    sir ?
My thanks shall warm your heart.
                              Draws a pistol.
Ant.   Hold, hold ! my lord !
I know not what provokes this tempest, but
Her grace ne'er show'd more freedom from a
    storm   115
When I receiv'd this paper. If you have
A will to do an execution,
Your looks, without that engine, sir, may
    serve.—
I did not like the employment.
Colum.   Ha ! had she
No symptom, in her eye or face, of anger, 120
When she gave this in charge ?
Ant.   Serene, as I
Have seen the morning rise upon the spring ;
No trouble in her breath, but such a wind
As came to kiss, and fan the smiling flowers.
Colum. No poetry.
Ant.   By all the truth in prose, 125
By honesty, and your own honour, sir,
I never saw her look more calm and gentle.
Colum. I am too passionate ; you must for-
    give me.
I have found it out ; the duchess loves me
    dearly ;
She exprest a trouble in her when I took 130
My leave, and chid me with a sullen eye :
'T is a device to hasten my return ;
Love has a thousand arts. I 'll answer it
Beyond her expectation, and put
Her soul to a noble test. — Your patience, gen-
    tlemen ;   135
The king's health will deserve a sacrifice
Of wine.   [*Retires to the table and writes.*]
Ant. [*Aside.*] I am glad to see this change,
    and thank my wit
For my redemption.

1 *Col.*   Sir, the soldier's curse
On him loves not our master !
2 *Col.*   And they curse 140
Loud enough to be heard.
2 *Capt.* Their curse has the nature of gun-
powder.
Ant. They do not pray with half the noise.
1 *Col.* Our general is not well mixt ;
He has too great a portion of fire.   145
2 *Col.* His mistress cool him, (her complexion
Carries some phlegm,) when they two meet in
bed !
2 *Capt.* A third may follow.
1 *Capt.* 'T is much pity   149
The young duke liv'd not to take the virgin off.
1 *Col.* 'T was the king's act, to match two
rabbit-suckers.[1]
2 *Col.* A common trick of state ;
The little great man marries, travels then
Till both grow up, and dies when he should do
The feat ; these things are still unlucky   155
On the male side.
Colum. This to the duchess' fair hand.
                        [*Gives* ANTONIO *a letter.*]
Ant.   She will think
Time hath no wing, till I return.   [*Exit.*]
Colum.   Gentlemen,
Now each man to his quarter, and encourage
The soldier. I shall take a pride to know 160
Your diligence, when I visit all your
Several commands.
All.   We shall expect.
2 *Col.*   And move
By your directions.
Colum.   Y' are all noble.   *Exeunt.*

[SCENE II.][2]

Enter CARDINAL, DUCHESS, *and* PLACENTIA.

Car. I shall perform a visit daily, madam,
In th' absence of my nephew, and be happy
If you accept my care.
Duch.   You have honour'd me ;
And if your entertainment have not been
Worthy your grace's person, 't is because   5
Nothing can reach it in my power ; but where
There is no want of zeal, other defect
Is only a fault to exercise your mercy.
Car. You are bounteous in all. I take my
leave,
My fair niece, shortly, when Columbo has 10
Purchas'd more honours to prefer his name
And value to your noble thoughts ; meantime,
Be confident you have a friend, whose office
And favour with the king shall be effectual
To serve your grace.
Duch. Your own good deeds reward you, 15
Till mine rise equal to deserve their benefit. —
                              Exit CARDINAL.
Leave me awhile. —   *Exit* PLACENTIA.
Do not I walk upon the teeth of serpents,
And, as I had a charm against their poison,
Play with their stings ? The Cardinal is subtle,
Whom 't is not wisdom to incense, till I   21

Hear to what destiny Columbo leaves me.
May be the greatness of his soul will scorn
To own what comes with murmur ; — if he can
Interpret me so happily. — Art come ?   25

Enter Secretary [ANTONIO] *with a letter.*

Ant. His excellence salutes your grace.
Duch.   Thou hast
A melancholy brow. How did he take my letter ?
Ant. As he would take a blow ; with so much
sense
Of anger, his whole soul boil'd in his face ;
And such prodigious flame in both his eyes, 30
As they 'd been th' only seat of fire, and at
Each look a salamander leaping forth,
Not able to endure the furnace.
Duch.   Ha ! thou dost
Describe him with some horror.
Ant.   Soon as he
Had read again, and understood your mean-
ing,   35
His rage had shot me with a pistol, had not
I us'd some soft and penitential language,
To charm the bullet.
Duch.   Wait at some more distance. —
My soul doth bathe itself in a cold dew ;
Imagine I am opening of a tomb ;   40
                      [*Opens the letter.*]
Thus I throw off the marble, to discover
What antic posture death presents in this
Pale monument to fright me.— Ha !   *Reads.*
My heart, that call'd my blood and spirits to
Defend it from the invasion of my fears,   45
Must keep a guard about it still, lest this
Strange and too mighty joy crush it to no-
                    thing.—
Antonio.
Ant. Madam.
Duch.   Bid my steward give thee
Two thousand ducats. Art sure I am awake ?
Ant. I shall be able to resolve you, madam, 50
When he has paid the money.
Duch. Columbo now is noble.   *Exit.*
Ant.   This is better
Than I expected, — if my lady be
Not mad, and live to justify her bounty. *Exit.*

[SCENE III.][1]

Enter KING, ALVAREZ, HERNANDO, *and*
Lords.

King. The war is left to him ; but we must
have
You reconcil'd, if that be all your difference.
His rage flows like a torrent, when he meets
With opposition ; leave to wrastle with him,
And his hot blood retreats into a calm,   5
And then he chides his passion. You shall back
With letters from us.
Her.   Your commands are not
To be disputed.
King.   Alvarez.   [*Takes him aside.*]
1 *Lord.*   Lose not
Yourself by cool submission ; he will find
His error, and the want of such a soldier. 10

---

[1] Young rabbits, youngsters.
[2] A room in the Duchess's house.
[3] An apartment in the palace.

2 *Lord.* Have you seen the Cardinal?
Her.   Not yet.
1 *Lord.* He wants no plot —
Her.   The king I must obey;
But let the purple gownman place his engines
I' th' dark, that wound [1] me.
   2 *Lord.*   Be assur'd
Of what we can to friend you; and the king   15
Cannot forget your service.
Her.   I am sorry
For that poor gentleman.
Alv.   I must confess, sir,
The duchess has been pleas'd to think me
    worthy
Her favours, and in that degree of honour
That has oblig'd my life to make the best   20
Return of service, which is not, with bold
Affiance in her love, to interpose
Against her happiness, and your election.
I love so much her honour, I have quitted   24
All my desires; yet would not shrink to bleed
Out my warm stock of life, so the last drop
Might benefit her wishes.
King.   I shall find
A compensation for this act, Alvarez;
It hath much pleased us.

Enter DUCHESS *with a letter;* Gentleman-Usher.

Duch.   Sir, you are the king,
And in that sacred title it were sin   30
To doubt a justice: all that does concern
My essence in this world, and a great part
Of the other's bliss, lives in your breath.
King. What intends the duchess?
Duch. That will instruct you, sir. [*Gives the
  letter.*] — Columbo has,   35
Upon some better choice, or discontent,
Set my poor soul at freedom.
King.   'T is his character. *Reads.*
"Madam, I easily discharge all my pretensions
to your love and person; I leave you to your own
choice; and in what you have obliged yourself to
me, resume a power to cancel, if you please. [41
Columbo."
This is strange!
Duch.   Now do an act to make
Your chronicle belov'd and read for ever.
King. Express yourself.
Duch.   Since by divine infusion,— 45
For 't is no art could force the general to
This change, second this justice, and bestow
The heart you would have given from me, by
Your strict commands to love Columbo, where
'T was meant by Heaven; and let your breath
   return   50
Whom you divorc'd, Alvarez, mine.
Lords.   This is
But justice, sir.
King.   It was decreed above;
And since Columbo has releas'd his interest,
Which we had wrought him, not without some
   force
Upon your will, I give you your own wishes: 55
Receive your own Alvarez. When you please
To celebrate your nuptial, I invite
Myself your guest.

    [1] Q. *wounds.*

Duch.   Eternal blessings crown you!
All. And every joy your marriage!
        Exit KING, *who meets the* CARDI-
        NAL; *they converse.*
Alv. I know not whether I shall wonder
   most,   60
Or joy to meet this happiness.
Duch.   Now the king
Hath planted us, methinks we grow already,
And twist our loving souls, above the wrath
Of thunder to divide us.
Alv.   Ha! the Cardinal
Has met the king! I do not like this confer-
  ence;   65
He looks with anger this way. I expect
A tempest.
Duch.   Take no notice of his presence;
Leave me to meet, and answer it. If the king
Be firm in 's royal word, I fear no lightning.
Expect me in the garden.
Alv.   I obey;   70
But fear a shipwrack on the coast.   *Exit.*
Car.   Madam.
Duch. My lord.
Car. The king speaks of a letter that has
   brought
A riddle in 't.
Duch.   'T is easy to interpret.   74
Car. From my nephew? May I deserve the
  favour?   [DUCHESS *gives him the letter.*]
Duch. [*Aside.*] He looks as though his eyes
   would fire the paper.
They are a pair of burning glasses, and
His envious blood doth give 'em flame.
Car. [*Aside.*] What lethargy could thus un-
   spirit him?
I am all wonder. — Do not believe, madam,   80
But that Columbo's love is yet more sacred
To honour and yourself, than thus to forfeit
What I have heard him call the glorious wreath
To all his merits, given him by the king,
From whom he took you with more pride than
   ever   85
He came from victory: his kisses hang
Yet panting on your lips; and he but now
Exchang'd religious farewell to return,
But with more triumph, to be yours.
Duch.   My lord,
You do believe your nephew's hand was not   90
Surpris'd or strain'd to this?
Car. Strange arts and windings in the world!
   most dark
And subtle progresses! Who brought this let-
   ter?
Duch. I enquir'd not his name; I thought it
   not
Considerable [2] to take such narrow knowledge.
Car. Desert and honour urg'd it here, nor
   can   90
I blame you to be angry; yet his person
Oblig'd you should have given a nobler pause,
Before you made your faith and change so vio-
   lent,
From his known worth, into the arms of one,
However fashioned to your amorous wish,   100

    [2] *Important.*

Not equal to his cheapest fame, with all
The gloss of love and merit.
    Duch.   This comparison,
My good lord Cardinal, I cannot think
Flows from an even justice ; it betrays   105
You partial where your blood runs.
    Car.   I fear, madam,
Your own takes too much license, and will soon
Fall to the censure of unruly tongues.
Because Alvarez has a softer cheek,
Can, like a woman, trim his wanton hair,   110
Spend half a day with looking in the glass
To find a posture to present himself,
And bring more effeminacy than man,
Or honour, to your bed, must he supplant him ?
Take heed, the common murmur, when it
    catches   115
The scent of a lost fame —
    Duch.   My fame, lord Cardinal ?
It stands upon an innocence as clear
As the devotions you pay to Heaven.
I shall not urge, my lord, your soft indulgence
At my next shrift.
    Car.   You are a fine court lady ! 120
    Duch. And you should be a reverend church-
    man.
    Car.   One
That, if you have not thrown off modesty,
Would counsel you to leave Alvarez.
    Duch.   'Cause
You dare do worse than marriage, must not I
Be admitted what the church and law allows
    me ?   125
    Car. Insolent ! Then you dare marry him ?
    Duch.   Dare !
Let your contracted flame and malice, with
Columbo's rage, higher than that, meet us
When we approach the holy place, clasp'd
    hand
In hand we 'll break through all your force, and
    fix   130
Our sacred vows together there.
    Car.   I knew
When, with as chaste a brow, you promis'd
    fair
To another. You are no dissembling lady !
    Duch. Would all your actions had no falser
    lights
About 'em !   135
    Car. Ha !
    Duch. The people would not talk, and curse
    so loud.
    Car, I 'll have you chid into a blush for this.
    Duch. Begin at home, great man, there 's
    cause enough :
You turn the wrong end of the perspective [1] 140
Upon your crimes, to drive them to a far
And lesser sight ; but let your eyes look right,
What giants would your pride and surfeit seem !
How gross your avarice, eating up whole fami-
    lies !
How vast are your corruptions and abuse   145
Of the king's ear ! at which you hang a pen-
    dant,
Not to adorn, but ulcerate, while the honest

Nobility, like pictures in the arras,
Serve only for court ornament. If they speak,
'T is when you set their tongues, which you
    wind up   150
Like clocks, to strike at the just hour you
    please.
Leave, leave, my lord, these usurpations,
And be what you were meant, a man to cure,
Not let in, agues to religion :
Look on the church's wounds.
    Car.   You dare presume, 155
In your rude spleen to me, to abuse the
    church ?
    Duch. Alas, you give false aim, my lord ; 't is
    your
Ambition and scarlet sins, that rob
Her altar of the glory, and leave wounds
Upon her brow ; which fetches grief and pale-
    ness   160
Into her cheeks, making her troubled bosom
Pant with her groans, and shroud her holy
    blushes
Within your reverend purples.
    Car.   Will you now take breath ?
    Duch. In hope, my lord, you will behold your-
    self
In a true glass, and see those injust acts   165
That so deform you, and by timely cure
Prevent a shame, before the short-haired men ⌐
Do crowd and call for justice ; I take leave.
                             Exit.
    Car. This woman has a spirit, that may rise
To tame the devil's : there 's no dealing with
Her angry tongue ; 't is action and revenge 171
Must calm her fury. Were Columbo here,
I could resolve ; but letters shall be sent
To th' army, which may wake him into sense
Of his rash folly, or direct his spirit   175
Some way to snatch his honour from this
    flame.
All great men know the soul of life is fame.
                             Exit.

ACT III

[SCENE I.] [3]

Enter VALERIA *and* CELINDA.

    Val. I did not think, Celinda, when I prais'd
Alvarez to the duchess, that things thus
Would come about. What does your ladyship
Think of Columbo now ? It staggers all
The court, he should forsake his mistress ; I 5
Am lost with wonder yet.
    Cel.   'T is very strange,
Without a spell ; but there 's a fate in love ; —
I like him ne'er the worse.

Enter two Lords.

    1 *Lord.* Nothing but marriages and triumph
    now !
    Val. What new access of joy makes you, my
    lord,   10
So pleasant ?

---

[1] Here, a telescope.

[2] Apparently, an allusion to the Puritans.
[3] An apartment in the palace.

1 Lord. There 's a packet come to court
Makes the king merry; we are all concern'd in 't.
Columbo hath given the enemy a great
And glorious defeat, and is already
Preparing to march home.   15
Cel. He thriv'd the better for my prayers.
2 Lord.   You have been
His great admirer, madam.
1 Lord.   The king longs
To see him.
Val.   This news exalts the Cardinal.

Enter Cardinal.

1 Lord. He 's here !
He appears with discontent; the marriage   20
With Count d'Alvarez hath a bitter taste,
And not worn off his palate: but let us leave
   him.
Cel. and Val. We 'll to the duchess. *Exeunt.*
Car. He has not won so much upon the Ar-
   ragon
As he has lost at home; and his neglect   25
Of what my studies had contriv'd to add
More lustre to our family by the access
Of the great duchess' fortune, cools his triumph,
And makes me wild.

Enter HERNANDO.

Her.   My good lord Cardinal !
Car. You made complaint to th' king about
   your general ?   30
Her. Not a complaint, my lord; I did but
   satisfy
Some questions o' the king's,
Car.   You see he thrives
Without your personal valour or advice,
Most grave and learned in the wars.
Her.   My lord,
I envy not his fortune.
Car.   'T is above   35
Your malice, and your noise not worth his
   anger;
'T is barking 'gainst the moon.
Her.   More temper would
Become that habit.
Car. The military thing would show some
   spleen.
I 'll blow an army of such wasps about   40
The world. — Go look your sting you left i' th'
   camp, sir.

Enter King *and* Lords.

Her. The king ! — This may be one day
   counted for.   *Exit.*
King. All things conspire, my lord, to make
   you fortunate.
Your nephew's glory —
Car.   'T was your cause and justice
Made him victorious; had he been so valiant   45
At home, he had had another conquest to
Invite, and bid her welcome to new wars.
King. You must be reconcil'd to providence,
My lord.
I heard you had a controversy with   50
The duchess; I will have you friends.
Car. I am not angry.
King.   For my sake, then,

You shall be pleas'd, and with me grace the
   marriage.
A churchman must show charity, and shine
With first example : she 's a woman.   55
Car. You shall prescribe in all things, sir.
   You cannot
Accuse my love, if I still wish my nephew
Had been so happy, to be constant to
Your own, and my election; yet my brain
Cannot reach how this comes about; I know   60
My nephew lov'd her with a near affection.

Re-enter HERNANDO.

King. He 'll give you fair account at his re-
   turn. —
Colonel, your letters may be spar'd; the gen-
   eral
Has finish'd, and is coming home.   *Exit.*
Her. I am glad on 't, sir. — My good lord
   Cardinal,   65
'T is not impossible but some man provok'd
May have a precious mind to cut your throat.
Car. You shall command me, noble Colonel;
I know you wo' not fail to be at the wedding.
Her. 'T is not Columbo that is married, sir.
Car. Go teach the postures of the pike and
   musket;   71
Then drill your myrmidons into a ditch,
Where starve, and stink in pickle. — You shall
   find
Me reasonable; you see the king expects me.
                                   [*Exit.*]
Her. So does the devil. —   75
Some desperate hand may help you on your
   journey.   *Exit.*

[SCENE II.] [1]

Enter Secretary [ANTONIO] *and* Servants, [*with
   masques, dresses, etc.*]

Ant. Here, this; ay, this will fit your part:
you shall wear the slashes, because you are a
soldier. Here 's for the blue mute. [2]
1 Serv. This doublet will never fit me; pox
on 't ! Are these breeches good enough for a [5
prince too? Pedro plays but a lord, and he has
two laces more in a seam.
Ant. You must consider Pedro is a foolish
lord; he may wear what lace he please.
2 Serv. Does my beard fit my clothes well, [10
gentlemen ?
Ant. Pox o' your beard !
3 Serv. That will fright away the hair.
1 Serv. This fellow plays but a mute, and he
is so troublesome, and talks.   15
3 Serv. Master Secretary might have let
Jaques play the soldier; he has a black patch
already.
2 Serv. By your favour, Master Secretary, I
was ask'd who writ this play for us ?   20
Ant. For us ? Why, art thou any more than
a blue mute ?
2 Serv. And, by my troth, I said, I thought
it was all your own.

[1] A room in the Duchess's house.
[2] *I. e.* For the mute who was to take the servant's
part, blue being the general colour of a servant's livery.

Ant. Away, you coxcomb ! ²⁵

4 *Serv.* Dost think he has no more wit than
to write a comedy ? My lady's chaplain made
the play, though he is content, for the honour
and trouble of the business, to be seen in 't.

5 *Serv.* Did anybody see my head, gentle- [³⁰
men ? 'T was here but now.—I shall have
never a head to play my part in.

Ant. Is thy head gone ? 'T was well thy part
was not in 't. Look, look about ; has not
Jaques it ? ³⁵

4 *Serv.* I his head ? 'T wo' not come on upon
my shoulders.

Ant. Make haste, gentlemen ; I 'll see whether
the king has supp'd. Look every man to his
wardrobe and his part.   *Exit.* ⁴⁰

2 *Serv.* Is he gone ? In my mind, a masque
had been fitter for a marriage.

4 *Serv.* Why, mute ? There was no time for 't,
and the scenes are troublesome.

2 *Serv.* Half a score deal tack'd together [⁴⁵
in the clouds, what 's that ? A throne, to come
down and dance ; all the properties have been
paid forty times over, and are in the court
stock : — but the secretary must have a play, to
show his wit. ⁵⁰

4 *Serv.* Did not I tell thee 't was the chaplain's ? Hold your tongue, mute.

1 *Serv.* Under the rose, and would this cloth
of silver doublet might never come off again,
if there be any more plot than you see in the [⁵⁵
back of my hand.

2 *Serv.* You talk of a plot ! I 'll not give this
for the best poet's plot in the world, an if it be
not well carried.

4 *Serv.* Well said, mute. ⁶⁰

3 *Serv.* Ha, ha ! Pedro, since he put on his
doublet, has repeated but three lines, and he
has broke five buttons.

2 *Serv.* I know not ; but by this false beard,
and here 's hair enough to hang a reasonable [⁶⁵
honest man, I do not remember, to say, a strong
line indeed in the whole comedy, but when the
chambermaid kisses the captain.

3 *Serv.* Excellent, mute !

5 *Serv.* They have almost supp'd, and I [⁷⁰
cannot find my head yet.

4 *Serv.* Play in thine own.

5 *Serv.* Thank you for that ! so I may have
it made a property. If I have not a head found
me, let Master Secretary play my part him- [⁷⁵
self without it.

Re-enter Secretary [ANTONIO].

Ant. Are you all ready, my masters ? The
king is coming through the gallery. Are the
women drest ?

1 *Serv.* Rogero wants a head. ⁸⁰

Ant. Here, with a pox to you ! take mine.
You a player ! you a puppy-dog. Is the music
ready ?

Enter Gentleman-Usher.

Gent. Gentlemen, it is my lady's pleasure that
you expect till she call for you. There are [⁸⁵
a company of cavaliers in gallant equipage,
newly alighted. have offer'd to present their

Revels in honour of this Hymen ; and 't is her
grace's command, that you be silent till their
entertainment be over. ⁹⁰

1 *Serv.* Gentlemen ?

2 *Serv.* Affronted ?

5 *Serv.* Master Secretary, there 's your head
again ; a man 's a man. Have I broken my
sleep to study fifteen lines for an ambassa- [⁹⁵
dor, and after that a constable, and is it come
to this ?

Ant. Patience, gentlemen, be not so hot ; 't is
but deferr'd, and the play may do well enough
cold. ¹⁰⁰

4 *Serv.* If it be not presented, the chaplain
will have the greatest loss ; he loses his wits.
                              (*Hautbois.*)

Ant. This music speaks the king upon entrance. Retire, retire, and grumble not.
                    Exeunt [*all but* ANTONIO].

Enter KING, CARDINAL, ALVAREZ, DUCHESS,
CELINDA, VALERIA, PLACENTIA, Lords, *and*
HERNANDO. *They being set, enter* COLUMBO
*and five more, in rich habits, vizarded ; be-
tween every two a* Torch-bearer. *They dance,
and afterwards beckon to* ALVAREZ, *as if desirous to speak with him.*

Alv. With me ! (*They embrace and whisper.*) ¹⁰⁵

King. Do you know the masquers, madam ?

Duch. Not I, sir.

Car. There 's one, — but that my nephew is
    abroad,
And has more soul than thus to jig upon
Their hymeneal night, I should suspect ¹¹⁰
'T were he. (The Masquers *lead in* ALVAREZ.)

Duch. Where 's my Lord Alvarez ?
                              (*Recorders.*¹)

King. Call in the bridegroom.

Re-enter COLUMBO. *Four* Masquers *bring in* AL-
VAREZ *dead, in one of their habits, and having
laid him down, exeunt.*

Duch. What mystery is this ?

Car. We want the bridegroom still. ¹¹⁵

King. Where is Alvarez ?

        COLUMBO *points to the body ; they
        unvizard it, and find* ALVAREZ
        bleeding.

Duch. Oh, 't is my lord ! He 's murder'd !

King. Who durst commit this horrid act ?

Colum.   I, sir. [*Throws off his disguise.*]

King. Columbo ? Ha !

Colum. Yes ; Columbo, that dares stay ¹²⁰
To justify that act.

Her.   Most barbarous !

Duch. Oh, my dearest lord !

King. Our guard seize on them all :
This sight doth shake all that is man within me.
Poor Alvarez, is this thy wedding day ? ¹²⁵

Enter Guard.

Duch. If you do think there is a Heaven, or
    pains
To punish such black crimes i' th' other world,
Let me have swift, and such exemplar justice,

¹ Flageolets.

As shall become this great assassinate ;   129
You will take off our faith else : and, if here
Such innocence must bleed, and you look on,
Poor men, that call you gods on earth, will
    doubt
To obey your laws, nay, practise to be devils,
As fearing, if such monstrous sins go on,
The saints will not be safe in Heaven.
   King.   You shall,   135
You shall have justice.
   Car. [*Aside.*]   Now to come off were brave.

Enter Servant.

   Serv. The masquers, sir, are fled ; their horse,
    prepar'd
At gate, expected to receive 'em, where
They quickly mounted : coming so like friends,
None could suspect their haste, which is se-
    cur'd   140
By advantage of the night.
   Colum. I answer for 'em all ; 't is stake
    enough
For many lives : but if that poniard
Had voice, it would convince they were but all
Spectators of my act. And now, if you   145
Will give your judgments leave, though at the
    first
Face of this object your cool bloods were
    frighted,
I can excuse this deed, and call it justice ;
An act your honours and your office, sir,
Is bound to build a law upon, for others   150
To imitate. I have but took his life,
And punish'd her with mercy, who had both
Conspir'd to kill the soul of all my fame.
Read there ; and read an injury as deep
In my dishonour, as the devil knew   155
A woman had capacity or malice
To execute : read there, how you were cozen'd,
    sir.
        [*Gives the* DUCHESS'S *letter to the*
        KING.]
Your power affronted, and my faith ; her
    smiles,
A juggling witchcraft to betray, and make
My love her horse to stalk withal, and catch   160
Her curled minion.
   Car.   Is it possible
The duchess could dissemble so, and forfeit
Her modesty with you, and to us all ?
Yet I must pity her. My nephew has
Been too severe ; though this affront would
    call   165
A dying man from prayers, and turn him tiger ;
There being nothing dearer than our fame,
Which, if a common man, whose blood has no
Ingredient of honour, labour to
Preserve, a soldier (by his nearest tie   170
To glory) is, above all others, bound
To vindicate : — and yet it might have been
Less bloody.
   Her.   Charitable devil !
   King. [*Reads.*] " I pray, my lord, release un-
der your hand, what you dare challenge in [175
my love or person, as a just forfeit to myself ;
this act will speak you honourable to my
thoughts ; and when you have conquered thus

yourself, you may proceed to many victories,
and after, with safety of your fame, visit [180
again   The lost Rosaura.''
To this your answer was a free resign ?
   Colum. Flatter'd with great opinion of her
    faith,
And my desert of her (with thought that she,
Who seem'd to weep and chide my easy will   185
To part with her, could not be guilty of
A treason, or apostasy so soon,
But rather meant this a device to make
Me expedite the affairs of war), I sent
That paper, which her wickedness, not justice,
Applied (what I meant trial,) her divorce.   191
I lov'd her so, I dare call heaven to witness,
I knew not whether I lov'd most ; while she,
With him, whose crimson penitence I pro-
    vok'd,[1]
Conspir'd my everlasting infamy :   195
Examine but the circumstance.
   Car.   'T is clear ;
This match was made at home, before she
    sent
That cunning writ, in hope to take him off,
As knowing his impatient soul would scorn
To own a blessing came on crutches to him.   200
It was not well to raise his expectation,
(Had you, sir, no affront ?) to ruin him
With so much scandal and contempt.
   King.   We have
Too plentiful a circumstance to accuse
You, madam, as the cause of your own sor-
    rows ;   205
But not without an accessory more
Than young Alvarez.
   Car.   Any other instrument ?
   King. Yes ; I am guilty, with herself, and
    Don
Columbo, though our acts look'd several ways,
That thought a lover might so soon be ran-
    som'd ;[2]   210
And did exceed the office of a king,
To exercise dominion over hearts,
That owe to the prerogative of Heaven
Their choice or separation : you must, there-
    fore,
When you do kneel for justice and revenge,   215
Madam, consider me a lateral agent
In poor Alvarez' tragedy.
   1 *Lord.* It was your love to Don Columbo,
    sir.
   Her. So, so ! the king is charm'd. Do you
    observe
How, to acquit Columbo, he would draw   220
Himself into the plot. Heaven, is this justice ?
   Car. Your judgment is divine in this.
   King.   And yet
Columbo cannot be secure, and we
Just in his pardon, that durst make so great
And insolent a breach of law and duty.   225
   2 *Lord.* Ha ! will he turn again ?
   King.   And should we leave
This guilt of blood to Heaven, which cries, and
    strikes
With loud appeals the palace of eternity ;

---

[1] Brought about.   [2] Bought off, transferred.

Yet here is more to charge Columbo than
Alvarez' blood, and bids me punish it,   230
Or be no king.
    Her.   'T is come about, my lords.
    King. And if I should forgive
His timeless [1] death, I cannot the offence,
That with such boldness struck at me. Has my
Indulgence to your merits, which are great,   235
Made me so cheap, your rage could meet no
        time
Nor place for your revenge, but where my eyes
Must be affrighted, and affronted with
The bloody execution? This contempt
Of majesty transcends my power to pardon,   240
And you shall feel my anger, sir.
    Her.   Thou shalt
Have one short prayer more for that.
    Colum.   Have I,
I' th' progress of my life,
No actions to plead me up deserving
Against this ceremony? [2]
    Car.   Contain yourself.   245
    Colum. I must be dumb then. Where is hon-
        our,
And gratitude of kings, when they forget
Whose hand secur'd their greatness? Take my
        head off;
Examine then which of your silken lords,
As I have done, will throw himself on dangers;   251
Like to a floating island move in blood;
And where your great defence calls him to
        stand
A bulwark, upon his bold breast to take
In death, that you may live:— but soldiers are
Your valiant fools, whom, when your own se-
        curities   255
Are bleeding, you can cherish; but when once
Your state and nerves are knit, not thinking
        when
To use their surgery again, you cast
Them off, and let them hang in dusty armor-
        ies,
Or make it death to ask for pay.
    King.   No more;   260
We thought to have put your victory and merits
In balance with Alvarez' death, which, while
Our mercy was to judge, had been your safety;
But the affront to us, made greater by
This boldness to upbraid our royal bounty,   265
Shall tame, or make you nothing.
    Lord.   Excellent!
    Her. The Cardinal is not pleas'd.
    Car.   Humble yourself
To th' king.
    Colum.   And beg my life? Let cowards
        do 't
That dare not die; I 'll rather have no head   269
Than owe it to his charity.
    King.   To th' castle with him!—
        [COLUMBO *is led off by the* Guard.]
Madam, I leave you to your grief, and what
The king can recompense to your tears, or hon-
        our   272
Of your dead lord, expect.
    Duch.   This shows like justice. *Exeunt.*

---

[1] Untimely.   [2] Formal justice.

ACT IV

[SCENE I.] [3]

Enter two Lords *and* HERNANDO.

1 Lord. This is the age of wonders.
2 Lord.   Wondrous mischiefs!
Her. Among those guards, which some call
        tutelar angels,
Whose office is to govern provinces,
Is there not one will undertake Navarre?
Hath Heaven forsook us quite?
1 Lord.   Columbo at large! [5]
2 Lord. And grac'd now more than ever.
1 Lord.   He was not pardon'd;
That word was prejudicial to his fame.
Her. But, as the murder done had been a
        dream
Vanish'd to memory, he 's courted as
Preserver of his country. With what chains   10
Of magic does this Cardinal hold the king?
2 Lord. What will you say, my lord, if they
        enchant
The duchess now, and by some impudent art,
Advance a marriage to Columbo yet?
Her. Say!   15
I 'll say no woman can be sav'd; nor is 't
Fit, indeed, any should pretend to Heaven,
After one such impiety in their sex:
And yet my faith has been so stagger'd, since
The king restor'd Columbo, I 'll be now   20
Of no religion.
1 Lord.   'T is not possible
She can forgive the murder; I observ'd
Her tears.
Her.   Why, so did I, my lord;
And if they be not honest, 't is to be
Half damn'd, to look upon a woman weeping. 25
When do you think the Cardinal said his pray-
        ers?
2 Lord. I know not.
Her.   Heaven forgive my want of charity!
But, if I were to kill him, he should have
No time to pray; his life could be no sacrifice,
Unless his soul went too.
1 Lord.   That were too much. 30
Her. When you mean to dispatch him, you
        may give
Time for confession: they have injur'd me
After another rate.
2 Lord. You are too passionate, cousin.

Enter COLUMBO, Colonels, ALPHONSO, *and*
        Courtiers. *They pass over the stage.*

Her. How the gay men do flutter, to con-
        gratulate   35
His gaol delivery! There 's one honest man:
What pity 't is a gallant fellow should
Depend on knaves for his preferment!
1 Lord. Except this cruelty upon Alvarez,
Columbo has no mighty stain upon him;   40
But for his uncle—
Her.   If I had a son
Of twelve years old that would not fight with
        him,

---

[3] An apartment in the palace.

And stake his soul against his cardinal's cap,
I would disinherit him. Time has took a lease
But for three lives, I hope ; a fourth may see 45
Honesty walk without a crutch.
    2 Lord.   This is
But air and wildness.
    Her.   I will see the duchess.
[1 *Lord.*] You may do well to comfort her ;
    we must
Attend the king.
    Her.   Your pleasures.   *Exit.*

    Enter KING *and* CARDINAL.

    1 Lord. A man of a brave soul.
    2 Lord.   The less his safety. — 50
The king and Cardinal in consult !
    King. Commend us to the duchess, and em-
    ploy
What language you think fit and powerful
To reconcile her to some peace. — My lords.
    Car. Sir, I possess all for your sacred uses. 55
                   Exeunt severally.

    [SCENE II.] [1]

Enter Secretary [ANTONIO] *and* CELINDA.

    Ant. Madam, you are the welcom'st lady
    living.
    Cel. To whom, Master Secretary ?
    Ant.   If you have mercy
To pardon so much boldness, I durst say,
To me — I am a gentleman.
    Cel.   And handsome.
    Ant. But my lady has   5
Much wanted you.
    Cel.   Why, Master Secretary ?
    Ant. You are the prettiest, —
    Cel. So !
    Ant. The wittiest, —
    Cel. So !   10
    Ant. The merriest lady i' th' court.
    Cel. And I was wish'd, to make the duchess
    pleasant ? [2]
    Ant. She never had so deep a cause of sor-
    row ;
Her chamber 's but a coffin of a larger
Volume, wherein she walks so like a ghost, 15
'T would make you pale to see her.
    Cel.   Tell her grace
I attend here.
    Ant.   I shall most willingly. —
A spirited lady ! would I had her in my closet !
She is excellent company among the lords.
Sure she has an admirable treble. — Madam. 20
                      Exit.
    Cel. I do suspect this fellow would be nib-
    bling,
Like some, whose narrow fortunes will not rise
To wear things when the invention 's rare and
    new :
But treading on the heel of pride, they hunt 24
The fashion when 't is crippled, like fell tyrants.
I hope I am not old yet ; I had the honour
To be saluted by our Cardinal's nephew
This morning : there 's a man !

    Re-enter Secretary [ANTONIO].

    Ant.   I have prevail'd.
Sweet madam, use what eloquence you can
Upon her ; and if ever I be useful   30
To your ladyship's service, your least breath
    commands me.   [*Exit.*]

    Enter Duchess.

    Duch. Madam, I come to ask you but one
    question :
If you were in my state, my state of grief,
I mean, an exile from all happiness
Of this world, and almost of Heaven, (for my 36
Affliction is finding out despair,)
What would you think of Don Columbo ?
    Cel.   Madam ?
    Duch. Whose bloody hand wrought all this
    misery.
Would you not weep, as I do, and wish rather
An everlasting spring of tears to drown   40
Your sight, than let your eyes be curst to see
The murderer again, and glorious ?
So careless of his sin, that he is made
Fit for new parricide, even while his soul   44
Is purpled o'er, and reeks with innocent blood?
But do not, do not answer me ; I know
You have so great a spirit, (which I want,
The horror of his fact [3] surprising all
My faculties), you would not let him live :
But I, poor I, must suffer more. There 's not 50
One little star in Heaven will look on me,
Unless to choose me out the mark, on whom
It may shoot down some angry influence.

    Enter PLACENTIA.

    Pla. Madam, here 's Don Columbo says he
    must
Speak with your grace.
    Duch.   But he must not, I charge you. 55
                [*Exit* PLACENTIA.]
None else wait ? — Is this well done,
To triumph in his tyranny ? Speak, madam,
Speak but your conscience.

    Enter COLUMBO *and* Secretary [ANTONIO].

    Ant.   Sir, you must not see her.
    Colum. Not see her ? Were she cabled up
    above
The search of bullet or of fire, were she   60
Within her grave, and that the toughest mine
That ever nature teem'd and groan'd withal,
I would force some way to see her. — Do not
    fear
I come to court you, madam ; y' are not worth
The humblest of my kinder thoughts. I come 65
To show the man you have provok'd, and lost,
And tell you what remains of my revenge. —
Live, but never presume again to marry ;
I 'll kill the next at th' altar, and quench all
The smiling tapers with his blood : if after, 70
You dare provoke the priest and Heaven so
    much
To take another, in thy bed I 'll cut him from
Thy warm embrace, and throw his heart to ra-
    vens.

        [1] A room in the Duchess's house.   [2] Merry.   [3] Deed.

Cel. This will appear an unexampled cruelty.
Colum. Your pardon, madam; rage, and my
 revenge,   75
Not perfect, took away my eyes. You are
A noble lady, this not worth your eye-beam;
One of so slight a making, and so thin,
An autumn leaf is of too great a value
To play, which shall be soonest lost i' th' air. 80
Be pleas'd to own me by some name in your
Assurance, I despise to be receiv'd
There; let her witness that I call you mistress;
Honour me to make these pearls your carka-
  net.   [*Gives her a necklace.*]
 Cel. My lord, you are too humble in your
  thoughts.   85
 Colum. [*Aside.*] There's no vexation too great
  to punish her.   *Exit.*
 Ant. Now, madam.
 Cel. Away, you saucy fellow!—Madam, I
Must be excus'd, if I do think more honourably
Than you have cause, of this great lord.
 Duch.   Why, is not 90
All womankind concern'd to hate what's im-
 pious?
 Cel. For my part—
 Duch.   Antonio, is this a woman?
 Ant. I know not whether she be man or wo-
  man;
I should be nimble to find out the experiment.
She look'd with less state when Columbo came.
 Duch. Let me entreat your absence. [*Aside.*]
  I am cozen'd in her.—   96
I took you for a modest, honest lady.
 Cel. Madam, I scorn any accuser; and
Deducting the great title of a duchess,
I shall not need one grain of your dear honour
To me make full weight: if your grace be jeal-
 ous,   101
I can remove.   *Exit.*
 Ant.   She is gone.
 Duch.   Prithee remove
My fears of her return. [*Exit* ANT.]—She is
 not worth
Considering; my anger's mounted higher.
He need not put in caution for my next 105
Marriage.—Alvarez, I must come to thee,
Thy virgin wife, and widow; but not till
I ha' paid those tragic duties to thy hearse
Become my piety and love. But how?
Who shall instruct a way?

    Enter PLACENTIA.

 Pla.   Madam, Don 110
Hernando much desires to speak with you.
 Duch. Will not thy own discretion think I am
Unfit for visit?
 Pla.   Please your grace, he brings
Something, he says, imports your ear, and love
Of the dead lord, Alvarez.
 Duch. Then admit him. [*Exit* PLACENTIA.] 115

  Enter [PLACENTIA *with*] HERNANDO.

 Her. I would speak, madam, to yourself.
 Duch. Your absence. [*Exit* PLACENTIA.]
 Her. I know not how your grace will censure so
Much boldness, when you know the affairs I
 come for.

 Duch. My servant has prepar'd me to receive it
If it concern my dead lord.
 Her.   Can you name 120
So much of your Alvarez in a breath,
Without one word of your revenge? O, madam,
I come to chide you, and repent my great
Opinion of your virtue, that can walk,
And spend so many hours in naked solitude; 125
As if you thought that no arrears were due
To his death, when you had paid his funeral
 charges,
Made your eyes red, and wept a handkerchief.
I come to tell you that I saw him bleed;
I, that can challenge nothing in his name 130
And honour, saw his murder'd body warm,
And panting with the labour of his spirits,
Till my amaz'd soul shrunk and hid itself:
While barbarous Columbo grinning stood,
And mock'd the weeping wounds. It is too
 much,   135
That you should keep your heart alive so long
After this spectacle, and not revenge it.
 Duch. You do not know the business of my
 heart,
That censure me so rashly; yet I thank you;
And, if you be Alvarez' friend, dare tell 140
Your confidence, that I despise my life,
But know not how to use it in a service
To speak me his revenger: this will need
No other proof, than that to you, who may
Be sent with cunning to betray me, I 145
Have made this bold confession. I so much
Desire to sacrifice to that hovering ghost
Columbo's life, that I am not ambitious
To keep my own two minutes after it.
 Her. If you will call me coward, which is
 equal   150
To think I am a traitor, I forgive it
For this brave resolution, which time
And all the destinies must aid. I beg
That I may kiss your hand for this; and may
The soul of angry honour guide it—
 Duch.   Whither? 155
 Her. To Don Columbo's heart.
 Duch. It is too weak, I fear, alone.
 Her. Alone? Are you in earnest? Why, will
 it not
Be a dishonour to your justice, madam,
Another arm should interpose? But that 160
It were a saucy act to mingle with you,
I durst, nay, I am bound in the revenge
Of him that's dead, (since the whole world has
 interest
In every good man's loss,) to offer it.
Dare you command me, madam?
 Duch.   Not command; 165
But I should more than honour such a truth
In man, that durst, against so mighty odds,
Appear Alvarez' friend, and mine. The Car-
 dinal—
 Her. Is for the second course; Columbo must
Be first cut up; his ghost must lead the
 dance: 170
Let him die first.
 Duch.   But how?
 Her. How! with a sword; and, if I under-
 take it,

I wo' not lose so much of my own honour,
To kill him basely.

Duch.   How shall I reward
This infinite service ? 'T is not modesty   175
While now my husband groans beneath his
    tomb,
And calls me to his marble bed, to promise,
What this great act might well deserve, my-
    self,
If you survive the victor ; but if thus
Alvarez' ashes be appeas'd, it must   180
Deserve an honourable memory ;
And though Columbo (as he had all power,
And grasp'd the fates) has vow'd to kill the
    man
That shall succeed Alvarez —

Her.   Tyranny !
Duch. Yet, if ever   185
I entertain a thought of love hereafter,
Hernando from the world shall challenge it ;
Till when, my prayers and fortune shall wait
    on you.

Her. This is too mighty recompense.
Duch.   'T is all just.
Her. If I outlive Columbo, I must not   190
Expect security at home.

Duch.   Thou canst
Not fly where all my fortunes, and my love
Shall not attend to guard thee.

Her.   If I die —
Duch. Thy memory   194
Shall have a shrine, the next within my heart,
To my Alvarez.

Her.   Once again your hand.
Your cause is so religious, you need not
Strengthen it with your prayers ; trust it to me.

Re-enter PLACENTIA, *and the* CARDINAL.

Pla. Madam, the Cardinal.
Duch.   Will you appear ?
Her. An he had all the horror of the devil   200
In 's face, I would not baulk him.

He stares upon the CARDINAL *in his exit.*
Car. [*Aside.*] What makes Hernando here ?
    I do not like
They should consult ; I 'll take no note. — The
    king
Fairly salutes your grace ; by whose command
I am to tell you, though his will and actions   205
Illimited, stoop not to satisfy
The vulgar inquisition, he is
Yet willing to retain a just opinion
With those that are plac'd near him ; and al-
    though
You look with nature's eye upon yourself,   210
Which needs no perspective to reach, nor art
Of any optic to make greater, what
Your narrow sense applies[1] an injury,
(Ourselves still nearest to ourselves,) but there 's
Another eye that looks abroad, and walks   215
In search of reason, and the weight of things,
With which, if you look on him, you will find
His pardon to Columbo cannot be
So much against his justice, as your erring
Faith would persuade your anger.

Duch.   Good my lord,   220
Your phrase has too much landscape, and I
    cannot
Distinguish at this distance you present[2]
The figure perfect ; but indeed my eyes
May pray your lordship find excuse, for tears
Have almost made them blind.

Car.   Fair peace restore 'em !   225
To bring the object nearer, the king says,
He could not be severe to Don Columbo
Without injustice to his other merits,
Which call more loud for their reward and
    honour,
Than you for your revenge ; the kingdom
    made   230
Happy by those ; you only, by the last,
Unfortunate : — nor was it rational,
I speak the king's own language, he should die
For taking one man's breath, without whose
    valour
None now had been alive without dishonour.   235

Duch. In my poor understanding, 't is the
    crown
Of virtue to proceed in its own track,
Not deviate from honour. If you acquit
A man of murder, 'cause he has done brave
Things in the war, you will bring down his val-
    our   240
To a crime, nay, to a bawd, if it secure
A rape, and but teach those that deserve well
To sin with greater license. But dispute
Is now too late, my lord ; 't is done ; and you,
By the good king, in tender of my sorrows,   245
Sent to persuade me 't is unreasonable
That justice should repair me.

Car.   You mistake ;
For if Columbo's death could make Alvarez
Live, the king had given him up to law,
Your bleeding sacrifice ; but when his life   250
Was but another treasure thrown away,
To obey a clamorous statute, it was wisdom
To himself, and common safety, to take off
This killing edge of law, and keep Columbo
To recompense the crime by noble acts,   255
And sorrow, that in time might draw your pity.

Duch. This is a greater tyranny than that
Columbo exercis'd ; he kill'd my lord ;
And you have not the charity to let
Me think it worth a punishment.

Car.   To that,   260
In my own name, I answer : I condemn,
And urge the bloody guilt against my nephew ;
'T was violent and cruel, a black deed ;
A deed, whose memory doth make me shudder ;
An act, that did betray a tyrannous nature,   265
Which he took up[3] in war, the school of ven-
    geance ;
And though the king's compassion spare him
    here,
Unless his heart
Weep itself out in penitent tears, —

Duch.   This sounds
As you were now a good man.
Car.   Does your grace   270
Think I have conscience to allow the murder ?

---

[1] Regards.   [2] Whether you present.   [3] Acquired.

Although, when it was done, I did obey
The stream of nature, as he was my kinsman,
To plead he might not pay his forfeit life,
Could I do less for one so near my blood?   275
Consider, madam, and be charitable;
Let not this wild injustice make me lose
The character I bear, and reverend habit.
To make you full acquainted with my innocence,
I challenge here my soul, and Heaven to wit-
    ness,   230
If I had any thought, or knowledge with
My nephew's plot, or person, when he came,
Under the smooth pretence of friend, to vio-
    late
Your hospitable laws, and do that act,
Whose frequent mention draws this tear, a
    whirlwind   285
Snatch me to endless flames!
    Duch.   I must believe,
And ask your grace's pardon. I confess
I have not lov'd you since Alvarez' death,
Though we were reconcil'd.
    Car.   I do not blame
Your jealousy, nor any zeal you had   290
To prosecute revenge against me, madam,
As I then stood suspected, nor can yet
Implore your mercy to Columbo. All
I have to say is, to retain my first
Opinion and credit with your grace;   295
Which you may think I urge not out of fear,
Or ends upon you, (since, I thank the king,
I stand firm on the base of royal favour,)
But for your own sake, and to show I have
Compassion of your sufferings.
    Duch.   You have clear'd   300
A doubt, my lord; and by this fair remon-
    strance,
Given my sorrow so much truce, to think
That we may meet again, and yet be friends.—
But be not angry, if I still remember
By whom Alvarez died, and weep, and wake 305
Another justice with my prayers.
    Car.   All thoughts
That may advance a better peace dwell with
    you!   *Exit.*
    Duch. How would this cozening statesman
    bribe my faith
With flatteries, to think him innocent!
No; if his nephew die, this Cardinal must
    not   310
Be long-liv'd. All the prayers of a wrong'd
    widow
Make firm Hernando's sword! and my own
    hand
Shall have some glory in the next revenge.
I will pretend my brain with grief distracted,
It may gain easy credit; and beside   315
The taking off examination
For great Columbo's death, it makes what act
I do in that believ'd[1] want of my reason,
Appear no crime, but my defence.— Look
    down,
Soul of my lord, from thy eternal shade,   320
And unto all thy blest companions boast
Thy duchess busy to revenge thy ghost!   *Exit.*

---

[1] Supposed.

[SCENE III.][2]

Enter [on one side] COLUMBO *and* ALPHONSO:
    [*on the other,*] HERNANDO *and a Colonel.*

    Colum. Hernando, now I love thee, and do
        half
Repent the affront my passion threw upon thee.
    Her. You will not be too prodigal o' your
        penitence.
    Colum. This makes good thy nobility of
        birth;   4
Thou may'st be worth my anger and my sword,
If thou dost execute as daringly
As thou provok'st a quarrel. I did think
Thy soul a starveling, or asleep.
    Her.   You 'll find it
Active enough to keep your spirit waking;
Which, to exasperate, for yet I think   10
It is not high enough to meet my rage—
Do you smile?
    Colum. This noise is worth it.— Gentlemen,
I 'm sorry this great soldier has engag'd
Your travail; all his business is to talk.
    Her. A little of your lordship's patience, 15
You shall have other sport, and swords that
    will
Be as nimble 'bout your heart as you can
    wish.
'Tis pity more than our two single lives
Should be at stake.
    Colum.   Make that no scruple, sir.
    Her. To him then that survives, if fate al-
        low   1'
That difference, I speak, that he may tell
The world, I came not hither on slight anger,
But to revenge my honour, stain'd and trampled
    on
By this proud man; when general, he com-
    manded
My absence from the field.
    Colum.   I do remember,   20
And I 'll give your soul now a discharge.
    Her.   I come
To meet it, if your courage be so fortunate.
But there is more than my own injury
You must account for, sir, if my sword pros-
    per;   20
Whose point and every edge is made more keen
With young Alvarez' blood, in which I had
A noble interest. Does not that sin benumb
Thy arteries, and turn the guilty flowings
To trembling jelly in thy veins? Canst hear
Me name that murder, and thy spirits not   25
Struck into air, as thou wert shot by some
Engine from Heaven?
    Colum. You are the duchess' champion!
Thou hast given me a quarrel now. I grieve
It is determin'd all must fight, and I
Shall lose much honour in his fall.
    Her.   That duchess,   40
(Whom but to mention with thy breath is sacri-
    lege,
An orphan of thy making, and condemn'd
By thee to eternal solitude, I come
To vindicate; and while I am killing thee.

---

[2] A retired spot without the city.

By virtue of her prayers sent up for justice, 45
At the same time, in Heaven I am pardon'd
for 't.
Colum. I cannot hear the bravo.
Her. Two words more,
And take your chance. Before you all I must
Pronounce that noble lady without knowledge
Or thought of what I undertake for her. 50
Poor soul! she 's now at her devotions,
Busy with Heaven, and wearing out the earth
With her stiff knees, and bribing her good an-
gel
With treasures of her eyes, to tell her lord
How much she longs to see him. My attempt 55
Needs no commission from her: were I
A stranger in Navarre, the inborn right
Of every gentleman to Alvarez' loss
Is reason to engage their swords and lives
Against the common enemy of virtue. 60
Colum. Now have you finish'd? I have an in-
strument
Shall cure this noise, and fly up to thy tongue,
To murder all thy words.
Her. One little knot
Of phlegm, that clogs my stomach, and i ha'
done : —
You have an uncle, call'd a Cardinal, 65
Would he were lurking now about thy heart,
That the same wounds might reach you both,
and send
Your reeling souls together! Now have at
you.
Alph. We must not, sir, be idle.
[*They fight* ; COLUMBO'S *second*
[ALPHONSO], *slain.*
Her. What think you now of praying?
Colum. Time enough. 70
He kills HERNANDO'S *second.*
Commend me to my friend; the scales are
even.
I would be merciful, and give you time
Now to consider of the other world ;
You 'll find your soul benighted presently.
Her. I 'll find my way i' the dark.
They fight, and close ; COLUMBO
gets both the swords, and HER-
NANDO *takes up the second's*
weapon.
Colum. A stumble 's dangerous. 75
Now ask thy life.—Ha!
Her. I despise to wear it,
A gift from any but the first bestower.
Colum. I scorn a base advantage. —
COLUMBO *throws away one of the*
swords: they fight ; HERNANDO
wounds COLUMBO. —
Ha!
Her. I am now
Out of your debt.
Colum. Thou 'st don 't, and I forgive thee.
Sive me thy hand ; when shall we meet again ?
Her. Never, I hope. 81
Colum. I feel life ebb apace : yet I 'll look
upwards,
And show my face to Heaven. [*Dies.*]
Her. The matter 's done ;
I must not stay to bury him. *Exit.*

ACT V

[SCENE I.]¹

Enter two Lords.

1 *Lord.* Columbo's death doth much afflict
the king.
2 *Lord.* I thought the Cardinal would have
lost his wits
At first, for 's nephew ; it drowns all the talk
Of the others that were slain.
1 *Lord.* We are friends.
I do suspect Hernando had some interest, 5
And knew how their wounds came.
2 *Lord.* His flight confirms it,
For whom the Cardinal has spread his nets.
1 *Lord.* He is not so weak to trust himself at
home
To his enemy's gripe.
2 *Lord.* All strikes not me so much
As that the duchess, most oppressed lady, 10
Should be distracted, and before Columbo
Was slain.
1 *Lord.* But that the Cardinal should be
made
Her guardian, is to me above that wonder.
2 *Lord.* So it pleas'd the king ; and she, with
that small stock
Of reason left her, is so kind and smooth 15
Upon him.
1 *Lord.* She 's turn'd a child again: a madness,
That would ha' made her brain and blood boil
high,
In which distemper she might ha' wrought
something —
2 *Lord.* Had been to purpose.
1 *Lord.* The Cardinal is cunning ; and how-
e'er 20
His brow does smile, he does suspect Hernando
Took fire from her, and waits a time to punish
it.
2 *Lord.* But what a subject of disgrace and
mirth
Hath poor Celinda made herself by pride,
In her belief Columbo was her servant ! 25
Her head hath stoop'd much since he died, and
she
Almost ridiculous at court.

Enter CARDINAL, ANTONELLI, *and* Servant.

1 *Lord.* The Cardinal
Is come into the garden, now —
Car. Walk off. — [*Exeunt* Lords.]
It troubles me the duchess by her loss
Of brain, is now beneath my great revenge. 30
She is not capable to feel my anger,
Which, like to unregarded thunder spent
In woods, and lightning aim'd at senseless
trees,
Must idly fall, and hurt her not, not to
That sense her guilt deserves : a fatal stroke, 35
Without the knowledge for what crime, to
fright her
When she takes leave, and make her tug with
death,

¹ A garden.

Until her soul sweat, is a pigeon's torment,
And she is sent a babe to the other world.
Columbo's death will not be satisfied,　　40
And I but wound her with a two-edg'd feather.
I must do more : I have all opportunity,
(She by the king now made my charge,) but she's
So much a turtle, I shall lose by killing her,
Perhaps do her a pleasure and preferment;　45
That must not be.

Enter CELINDA *with a parchment.*

Anton. [*stopping her.*] — Is not this she, that
　　would be thought to have been
Columbo's mistress? — Madam, his grace is
　　private,
And would not be disturb'd ; you may displease
　　him.
　Cel. What will your worship wager that he
　　shall　　50
Be pleas'd again before we part?
Anton. I'll lay this diamond, madam, 'gainst
　　a kiss,
And trust yourself to keep the stakes.
　Cel.　　　　　　'T is done. [*Comes forward.*]
Anton. I have long had an appetite to this
　　lady ;
But the lords keep her up so high — this toy　55
May bring her on.
　Car. This interruption tastes not of good
　　manners.
　Cel. But where necessity, my lord, compels,
The boldness may meet pardon, and when you
Have found my purpose, I may less appear　60
Unmannerly.
　Car.　　　To the business.
　Cel.　　　　　　　It did please
Your nephew, sir, before his death, to credit me
With so much honourable favour, I
Am come to tender to his near'st of blood,
Yourself, what does remain a debt to him.　65
Not to delay your grace with circumstance,
That deed, if you accept, makes you my heir
Of no contemptible estate. — [*Aside.*] This way
　　　　　　　　　　　　　　He reads.
Is only left to tie up scurrile tongues
And saucy men, that since Columbo's death　70
Venture to libel on my pride and folly ;
His greatness and this gift, which I enjoy
Still for my life, (beyond which term a king-
　　dom's
Nothing,) will curb the giddy spleens of men
That live on impudent rhyme, and railing at　75
Each wandering fame they catch.
　Car.　　　　　　Madam, this bounty
Will bind my gratitude, and care to serve you.
　Cel. I am your grace's servant.
　Car.　　　　　　Antonelli! — *Whisper.*
And when this noble lady visits me,
Let her not wait.　　80
　Cel. What think you, my officious sir? His
　　grace
Is pleas'd, you may conjecture : I may keep
Your gem ; the kiss was never yours.
　Anton.　　　　　　Sweet madam —
　Cel. Talk if you dare ; you know I must not
　　wait ;
And so, farewell for this time.　　[*Exit.*]　85

Car. 'T is in my brain already, and it forms
Apace — good, excellent revenge, and pleasant!
She's now within my talons : 't is too cheap
A satisfaction for Columbo's death,
Only to kill her by soft charm or force.　　90
I'll rifle first her darling chastity ;
'T will be after time enough to poison her,
And she to th' world be thought her own de-
　　stroyer.
As I will frame the circumstance, this night
All may be finished: for the colonel,　　95
Her agent in my nephew's death, (whom I
Disturb'd at counsel with her,) I may reach him
Hereafter, and be master of his fate.
We starve our conscience when we thrive in
　　state.　　　　　　　　　　*Exeunt.*

[SCENE II.][1]

Enter Secretary [ANTONIO] *and* PLACENTIA.

　Ant. Placentia, we two are only left
Of all my lady's servants ; let us be true
To her, and one another ; and be sure,
When we are at prayers, to curse the Cardinal.
　Pla. I pity my sweet lady.　　5
　Ant. I pity her too, but am a little angry ;
She might have found another time to lose
Her wits.
　Pla. That I were a man !
　Ant. What would'st thou do, Placentia?　10
　Pla. I would revenge my lady.
　Ant. 'T is better, being a woman ; thou
　　may'st do
Things that may prosper better, and the fruit
Be thy own another day.
　Pla.　　　　Your wit still loves
To play the wanton.
　Ant.　　　　'T is a sad time, Placentia ;　15
Some pleasure would do well: the truth is, I
Am weary of my life, and I would have
One fit of mirth before I leave the world.
　Pla. Do not you blush to talk thus wildly ?
　Ant. 'T is good manners　　20
To be a little mad after my lady ;
But I ha' done. Who is with her now ?
　Pla. Madam Valeria.
　Ant. Not Celinda? There's a lady for my
　　humour !
A pretty book of flesh and blood, and well　25
Bound up, in a fair letter too. Would I
Had her with all the errata !
　Pla.　　　　She has not
An honourable fame.
　Ant.　　　　Her fame ! that's nothing ;
A little stain ; her wealth will fetch again
The colour, and bring honour into her cheeks　30
As fresh ; —
If she were mine, and I had her exchequer,
I know the way to make her honest ;
Honest to th' touch, the test, and the last
　　trial.
　Pla. How, prithee ?　　35
　Ant. Why,
First I would marry her, that's a verb material ;
Then I would print her with an *index
Expurgatorius*; a table drawn

---

[1] A room in the Duchess's house.

Of her court heresies ; and when she's read, 40
Cum privilegio, who dares call her whore ?
  Pla. I 'll leave you, if you talk thus.
  Ant.   I ha' done ;
Placentia, thou may'st be better company
After another progress ; and now tell me,
Didst ever hear of such a patient madness 45
As my lady is possest with ? She has rav'd
But twice : — an she would fright the Cardinal,
Or at a supper if she did but poison him,
It were a frenzy I could bear withal.
She calls him her dear governor. —

  Enter HERNANDO *disguised, having a letter.*

  Pla.   Who is this ? 50
  Her. Her secretary ! — Sir,
Here is a letter, if it may have so
Much happiness to kiss her grace's hand.
  Ant.   From whom ?
  Her. That 's not in your commission, sir,
To ask, or mine to satisfy ; she will want 55
No understanding when she reads.
  Ant.   Alas !
Under your favour, sir, you are mistaken ;
Her grace did never more want understanding.
  Her. How ?
  Ant. Have you not heard ? Her skull is
    broken, sir, 60
And many pieces taken out ; she 's mad.
  Her. The sad fame of her distraction
Has too much truth, it seems.
  Pla.   If please you, sir,
To expect awhile, I will present the letter.
  Her. Pray do. —   *Exit* PLACENTIA. 65
How long has she been thus distemper'd, sir ?
  Ant. Before the Cardinal came to govern
here,
Who, for that reason, by the king was made
Her guardian. We are now at his devotion.
  Her. A lamb given up to a tiger ! May dis-
    eases 70
Soon eat him through his heart !
  Ant.   Your pardon, sir.
I love that voice ; I know it too a little.
Are not you — be not angry, noble sir,
I can with ease be ignorant again,
And think you are another man ; but if 75
You be that valiant gentleman they call —
  Her. Whom ? what ?
  Ant. That kill'd — I would not name him, if
I thought
You were not pleas'd to be that very gentleman.
  Her. Am I betray'd ?
  Ant.   The devil sha' not 80
Betray you here : kill me, and I will take
My death you are the noble colonel.
We are all bound to you for the general's
death,
Valiant Hernando ! When my lady knows
You are here, I hope 't will fetch her wits
again. 85
But do not talk too loud ; we are not all
Honest [1] i' th' house ; some are the Cardinal's
creatures.
  Her. Thou wert faithful to thy lady. I am
glad
        [1] Loyal (to the Duchess).

'T is night. But tell me how the churchman
uses
The duchess. 90

  Enter ANTONELLI.

  Ant. He carries angels in his tongue and face,
but I
Suspect his heart : this is one of his spawns.—
Signor Antonelli.
  Anton. Honest Antonio !
  Ant. And how, and how — a friend of mine
— where is 9L
The Cardinal's grace ?
  Her. [*Aside.*] That will be never answered.
  Anton. He means to sup here with the duch-
ess.
  Ant. Will he ?
  Anton. We 'll have the charming bottles at
my chamber. 100
Bring that gentleman ; we 'll be mighty merry.
  Her. [*Aside.*] I may disturb your jollity.
  Anton. Farewell, sweet —   [*Exit.*]
  Ant. Dear Antonelli ! — A round pox con-
found you !
This is court rhetoric at the back-stairs. 105

  Enter PLACENTIA.

  Pla. Do you know this gentleman ?
  Ant. Not I.
  Pla. My lady presently dismist Valeria,
And bade me bring him to her bed-chamber.
  Ant. The gentleman has an honest face.
  Pla.   Her words 110
Fell from her with some evenness and joy.—
Her grace desires your presence.
  Her.   I 'll attend her.
                  Exit [*with* PLACENTIA].
  Ant. I would this soldier had the Cardinal
Upon a promontory, with what a spring
The churchman would leap down ! It were a
spectacle 115
Most rare, to see him topple from the preci-
pice,
And souse in the salt water with a noise
To stun the fishes ; and if he fell into
A net, what wonder would the simple sea-gulls
Have, to draw up the o'ergrown lobster,[2] 120
So ready boil'd ! He shall have my good wishes.
This colonel's coming may be lucky ; I
Will be sure none shall interrupt 'em.

  Enter CELINDA.

  Cel.   Is
Her grace at opportunity ?
  Ant.   No, sweet madam ;
She is asleep, her gentlewoman says. 126
  Cel. My business is but visit. I 'll expect.[3]
  Ant. That must not be, although I like your
company.
  Cel. You are grown rich, Master Secretary.
  Ant. I, madam ? Alas !
  Cel. I hear you are upon another purchase. 130
  Ant. I upon a purchase !
  Cel. If you want any sum —

  [2] Referring, of course, to the color of the Cardinal's
robes.   [3] Wait.

Ant. If I could purchase your sweet favour, madam.

Cel. You shall command me, and my fortune, sir.

Ant. [*Aside.*] How 's this?   135

Cel. I have observ'd you, sir, a staid
And prudent gentleman — and I shall want —

Ant. Not me?

Cel. A father for some infant: he has credit
I' th' world. — [*Aside.*] I am not the first cast   140
lady
Has married a secretary.

Ant. Shall I wait upon you?

Cel. Whither?

Ant. Any whither.

Cel. I may chance lead you then —   145

Ant. I shall be honour'd to obey. My blood
Is up, and in this humour I 'm for anything.

Cel. Well, sir, I 'll try your manhood.

Ant.   'T is my happiness;
You cannot please me better.

Cel. [*Aside.*]   This was struck
I' th' opportunity.

Ant.   I am made for ever.   150
                    [*Exit, following her.*]

[SCENE III.]¹

Enter HERNANDO *and* DUCHESS.

Her. Dear madam, do not weep.

Duch. Y' are very welcome;
I ha' done; I wo' not shed a tear more
Till I meet Alvarez, then I 'll weep for joy.
He was a fine young gentleman, and sung
sweetly;   5
An you had heard him but the night before
We were married, you would ha' sworn he had
been
A swan, and sung his own sad epitaph.
But we 'll talk o' the Cardinal.

Her.   Would his death
Might ransom your fair sense! he should not
live   10
To triumph in the loss. Beshrew my manhood,
But I begin to melt.

Duch.   I pray, sir, tell me, —
For I can understand, although they say
I have lost my wits; but they are safe enough,
And I shall have 'em when the Cardinal dies; —   15
Who had a letter from his nephew, too,
Since he was slain?

Her.   From whence?

Duch. I know not where he is. But in some
bower
Within a garden he is making chaplets,
And means to send me one; but I 'll not take it;
I have flowers enough, I thank him, while I live.

Her. But do you love your governor?   22

Duch. Yes, but I 'll never marry him; I am
promis'd
Already.

Her. To whom, madam?

Duch.   Do not you
Blush when you ask me that? Must not you be   25
My husband? I know why, but that 's a secret.

Indeed, if you believe me, I do love
No man alive so well as you: the Cardinal
Shall never know 't; he 'll kill us both; and yet
He says he loves me dearly, and has promis'd   30
To make me well again; but I 'm afraid,
One time or other, he will give me poison.

Her. Prevent him, madam, and take nothing
from him.

Duch. Why, do you think 't will hurt me?

Her.   It will kill you.

Duch. I shall but die, and meet my dear-
lov'd lord,   35
Whom, when I have kist, I 'll come again and
work
A bracelet of my hair for you to carry him,
When you are going to Heaven; the posy
shall
Be my own name, in little tears, that I
Will weep next winter, which congeal'd i' th'
frost,   40
Will show like seed-pearl. You'll deliver it?
I know he 'll love, and wear it for my sake.

Her. She is quite lost.

Duch.   I pray give me, sir, your pardon:
I know I talk not wisely; but if you had
The burthen of my sorrow, you would miss   45
Sometimes your better reason. Now I 'm well;
What will you do when the Cardinal comes?
He must not see you for the world.

Her.   He sha' not;
I 'll take my leave before he come.

Duch.   Nay, stay;
I shall have no friend left me when you go.   50
He will but sup; he sha' not stay to lie with me.
I have the picture of my lord abed;
Three are too much this weather.

Enter PLACENTIA.

Pla.   Madam, the Cardinal.

Her. He shall sup with the devil.

Duch.   I dare not stay;
The red cock² will be angry. I 'll come again.   55
                Exeunt [DUCHESS *and* PLACENTIA.]

Her. This sorrow is no fable. Now I find
My curiosity is sadly satisfied. —
Ha! if the duchess in her straggled wits
Let fall words to betray me to the Cardinal,
The panther will not leap more fierce to meet   60
His prey, when a long want of food hath parch'd
His starved maw, than he to print his rage,
And tear my heart-strings. Everything is fatal;
And yet she talk'd sometimes with chain of
sense,
And said she lov'd me. Ha! they come not yet.
I have a sword about me, and I left   66
My own security to visit death.
Yet I may pause a little, and consider
Which way does lead me to 't most honourably.
Does not the chamber that I walk in tremble?
What will become of her, and me, and all   71
The world in one small hour? I do not think
Ever to see the day again; the wings
Of night spread o'er me like a sable hearse-cloth;
The stars are all close mourners too; but I   75
Must not alone to the cold silent grave,

---

¹ Another room in the same.

² The Cardinal.

I must not. — If thou canst, Alvarez, open
That ebon curtain, and behold the man,
When the world's justice fails, shall right thy
    ashes,
And feed their thirst with blood! Thy duchess is
Almost a ghost already, and doth wear   81
Her body like an useless upper garment,
The trim and fashion of it lost. — Ha!

Re-enter PLACENTIA.

Pla. You need not doubt me, sir. — My lady
    prays
You would not think it long ; she in my ear   85
Commanded me to tell you, that when last
She drank, she had happy wishes to your health.
Her. And did the Cardinal pledge it ?
Pla.   He was not
Invited to 't, nor must he know you are here.
Her. What do they talk of, prithee ?   90
Pla. His grace is very pleasant
                   A lute is heard.
And kind to her ; but her returns [1] are after
The sad condition of her sense, sometimes
Unjointed.
Her.   They have music.
Pla.   A lute only,   94
His grace prepar'd ; they say, the best of Italy,
That waits upon my lord.
Her.   He thinks the duchess
Is stung with a tarantula.
Pla.   Your pardon ;
My duty is expected.   *Exit.*
Her.   Gentle lady ! —
A voice too!

SONG *within.*

Strep. Come, my Daphne, come away,   100
    We do waste the crystal day ;
    'T is Strephon calls. *Dap.* What says my love ?
Strep. Come, follow to the myrtle grove,
    Where Venus shall prepare
    New chaplets for thy hair.   105
Dap. Were I shut up within a tree,
    I 'd rend my bark to follow thee.
Strep. My shepherdess, make haste,
    The minutes slide too fast.
Dap. In those cooler shades will I,   110
    Blind as Cupid, kiss thine eye.
Strep. In thy bosom then I'll stay ;
    In such warm snow who would not lose his
        way ?
Chor. We 'll laugh, and leave the world behind,
    And gods themselves that see,   115
    Shall envy thee and me,
        But never find
    Such joys, when they embrace a deity.

Her. If at this distance I distinguish, 't is not
Church music ; and the air 's wanton, and no
    anthem   120
Sung to 't, but some strange ode of love and
    kisses.
What should this mean ? — Ha ? he is coming
    hither.   *[Draws his sword.]*
I am betray'd ; he marches in her hand.
I 'll trust a little more ; mute as the arras,
My sword and I here.   125
        *He [conceals himself behind the
        arras, and] observes.*

Enter CARDINAL, DUCHESS, ANTONELLI, *and*
    Attendants.

Car. Wait you in the first chamber, and let
    none
Presume to interrupt us.—
       Exeunt [ANTONELLI *and* Attendants.]
                    She is pleasant ;
Now for some art, to poison all her innocence.
Duch. I do not like the Cardinal's humour; he
Little suspects what guest is in my chamber. 130
Car. Now, madam, you are safe.
                   [Embraces her.]
Duch.   How means your lordship ?
Car. Safe in my arms, sweet duchess.
Duch.   Do not hurt me.
Car. Not for the treasures of the world ! You
    are
My pretty charge. Had I as many lives
As I have careful thoughts to do you service, 135
I should think all a happy forfeit, to
Delight your grace one minute ; 't is a Heaven
To see you smile.
Duch.   What kindness call you this ?
Car. It cannot want a name while you pre-
    serve
So plentiful a sweetness ; it is love.   140
Duch. Of me ? How shall I know 't, my lord?
Car. By this, and this, swift messengers to
    whisper
Our hearts to one another.   *Kisses her.*
Duch. Pray, do you come a wooing ?
Car.   Yes, sweet madam ;
You cannot be so cruel to deny me.   145
Duch. What, my lord?
Car.   Another kiss.
Duch.   Can you
Dispense with this, my lord ? — *(Aside.)* Alas ; I
    fear
Hernando is asleep, or vanish'd from me.
Car. *[Aside.]* I have mock'd my blood into a
    flame ; and what
My angry soul had form'd for my revenge,   150
Is now the object of my amorous sense.
I have took a strong enchantment from her lips,
And fear I shall forgive Columbo's death,
If she consent to my embrace.— Come, madam.
Duch. Whither, my lord ?
Car.   But to your bed or couch, 155
Where, if you will be kind, and but allow
Yourself a knowledge, love, whose shape and
    raptures
Wise poets have but glorified in dreams,
Shall make your chamber his eternal palace ;
And with such active and essential streams   160
Of new delights glide o'er your bosom, you
Shall wonder to what unknown world you are
By some blest change translated. Why d' ye
    pause,
And look so wild ? Will you deny your gov-
    ernor ?
Duch. How came you by that cloven foot ?
Car.   Your fancy
Would turn a traitor to your happiness.   165
I am your friend ; you must be kind.
Duch.   Unhand me,
Or I 'll cry out a rape.

Car.   You wo' not, sure?

Duch. I have been cozen'd with Hernando's
   shadow ;

Here 's none but Heaven to hear me.— Help ! a
   rape !   170

Car. Are you so good at understanding ?
   Then,

I must use other argument.

          He forces her. [HERNANDO *rushes*
          from the arras.]

Her. Go to, Cardinal.

          Strikes him ; exit DUCHESS.

Car. Hernando ? Murder ! treason ! help !

Her. An army sha' not rescue thee. Your
   blood   175

Is much inflam'd ; I have brought a lancet wi'
   me

Shall open your hot veins, and cool your fever.—

To vex thy parting soul, it was the same

Engine that pierc'd [1] Columbo's heart.

Car.   Help ! murder ! [*Stabs him.*]

     Enter ANTONELLI *and* Servants.

Anton. Some ring the bell, 't will raise the
   court ;   180

My lord is murder'd ! 'T is Hernando.

              The bell rings.

Her. I 'll make you all some sport.— [*Stabs
   himself.*] — So ; now we are even.

Where is the duchess ? I would take my leave

Of her, and then bequeath my curse among you.

                    He falls.

Enter KING, DUCHESS, VALERIA, Lords, *and*
     Guard.

King. How come these bloody objects ?   185

Her. With a trick my sword found out. I
   hope he 's paid.

1 *Lord.* [*Aside.*] I hope so too.— A surgeon

For my lord Cardinal !

King. Hernando ?

Duch. Justice ! oh, justice, sir, against a ravisher !   190

Her. Sir, I ha' done you service.

King.   A bloody service.

Her. 'T is pure scarlet.

          Enter Surgeon.

Car. [*Aside.*] After such care to perfect my
   revenge,

Thus bandied out o' th' world by a woman's
   plot !

Her. I have preserv'd the duchess from a
   rape.   195

Good night to me and all the world for ever.

                    Dies.

King. So impious !

Duch. 'T is most true ; Alvarez' blood

Is now reveng'd ; I find my brain return,

And every straggling sense repairing home.   200

Car. I have deserv'd you should turn from
   me, sir,

My life hath been prodigiously wicked ;

My blood is now the kingdom's balm. Oh, sir,

I have abus'd your ear, your trust, your people,

And my own sacred office ; my conscience   205

Feels now the sting. Oh, show your charity,

And with your pardon, like a cool soft gale,

Fan my poor sweating soul, that wanders
   through

Unhabitable climes, and parched deserts.

But I am lost, if the great world forgive me,   21'

Unless I find your mercy for a crime

You know not, madam, yet, against your life,

I must confess, more than my black intents

Upon your honour ; you 're already poison'd.

King. By whom ?   215

Car.   By me,

In the revenge I ow'd Columbo's loss ;

With your last meat was mixt a poison, that

By subtle, and by sure degrees, must let

In death.

King.   Look to the duchess, our physicians !

Car. Stay ;   221

I will deserve her mercy, though I cannot

Call back the deed. In proof of my repentance,

If the last breath of a now dying man

May gain your charity and belief, receive   225

This ivory box ; in it an antidote,

'Bove that they boast the great magistral medicine :

That powder, mixt with wine, by a most rare

And quick access to the heart, will fortify it

Against the rage of the most nimble poison.   230

I am not worthy to present her with it.

Oh, take it, and preserve her innocent life.

1 *Lord.* Strange, he should have a good thing
   in such readiness.

Car. 'T is that, which in my jealousy and
   state,

Trusting to false predictions of my birth,   235

That I should die by poison, I preserv'd

For my own safety ; wonder not, I made

That my companion was to be my refuge.

   Enter Servant *with a bowl of wine.*

1 *Lord.* Here 's some touch of grace.

Car. In greater proof of my pure thoughts, I
   take   240

This first, and with my dying breath confirm

My penitence ; it may benefit her life,

But not my wounds. [*He drinks.*] Oh, hasten
   to preserve her ;

And though I merit not her pardon, let not

Her fair soul be divorc'd.   24

     [*The* DUCHESS *takes the bowl and drinks.*]

King. This is some charity ; may it prosper,
   madam !

Val. How does your grace ?

Duch. And must I owe my life to him, whose
   death

Was my ambition ? Take this free acknowledgment ;

I had intent, this night, with my own hand   250

To be Alvarez' justicer.

King.   You were mad,

And thought past apprehension of revenge.

Duch. That shape I did usurp, great sir, to
   give

My heart more freedom and defence ; but when

Hernando came to visit me, I thought   25~

I might defer my execution ;

Which his own rage suppli'd without my guilt,
And when his lust grew high, met with his
    blood.
  1 *Lord.* The Cardinal smiles.
  Car.   Now my revenge has met
With you, nimble duchess ! I have took   260
A shape [1] to give my act more freedom too,
And now I am sure she 's poison'd with that dose
I gave her last.
  King.   Thou'rt not so horrid ?
  Duch. Ha ! some cordial.
  Car.   Alas, no preservative
Hath wings to overtake it ; were her heart   265
Lock'd in a quarry, it would search and kill
Before the aids can reach it. I am sure
You sha' not now laugh at me.
  King. How come you by that poison ?
  Car.   I prepar'd it,
Resolving, when I had enjoy'd her, which   270
The colonel prevented, by some art
To make her take it, and by death conclude
My last revenge. You have the fatal story.
  King. This is so great a wickedness, it will
Exceed belief.
  Car.   I knew I could not live.   275
  Surg. Your wounds, sir, were not desperate.
  Car. Not mortal ? Ha ! were they not mor-
    tal ?
  Surg. If I have skill in surgery.
  Car. Then I have caught myself in my own
    engine.
  2 *Lord.* It was your fate, you said, to die by
    poison.   280
  Car. That was my own prediction, to abuse
Your faith ; no human art can now resist it :
I feel it knocking at the seat of life ;
It must come in ; I have wrackt all my own
To try your charities : now it would be rare,   285
If you but waft me with a little prayer ;
My wings that flag may catch the wind ; but
    't is
In vain, the mist is risen, and there 's none
To steer my wand'ring bark.   *Dies.*
  1 *Lord.*   He 's dead.
  King.   With him
Die all deceived trust.
  2 *Lord.*   This was a strange   290
    Impiety.
  King. When men
Of gifts and sacred function once decline
From virtue, their ill deeds transcend example.
  Duch. The minute 's come that I must take
    my leave, too.

            [1] Disguise.

Your hand, great sir ; and though you be a
    king,   295
We may exchange forgiveness. Heaven forgive,
And all the world ! I come, I come, Alvarez.
                         Dies.
  King. Dispose their bodies for becoming fu-
    neral.
How much are kings abus'd by those they take
To royal grace, whom, when they cherish most
By nice indulgence, they do often arm   301
Against themselves ! from whence this maxim
    springs :
None have more need of perspectives [2] than
    kings.   *Exeunt.*

EPILOGUE

Within. Master Pollard ! Where 's Master
    Pollard, for the epilogue ?
          He is thrust upon the stage, and falls.
  Epi. [*rising.*] I am coming to you, gentle-
    men ; the poet
Has help'd me thus far on my way, but I 'll
Be even with him : the play is a tragedy,
The first that ever he compos'd for us,   5
Wherein he thinks he has done prettily,

          Enter Servant.

And I am sensible. — I prithee look,
Is nothing out of joint ? Has he broke nothing ?
  Serv. No, sir, I hope.
  Epi. Yes, he has broke his epilogue all to
    pieces.   10
Canst thou put it together again ?
  Serv. Not I, sir.
  Epi. Not I ; prithee be gone. [*Exit* Serv.] —
    Hum ! — Master poet,
I have a teeming mind to be reveng'd. —
You may assist, and not be seen in 't now,   15
If you please, gentlemen, for I do know
He listens to the issue of his cause ;
But blister not your hands in his applause ;
Your private smile, your nod, or hem ! to tell
My fellows that you like the business well ;   20
And when, without a clap, you go away,
I 'll drink a small-beer health to his second day ;
And break his heart, or make him swear and
    rage
He 'll write no more for the unhappy stage.
But that 's too much ; so we should lose ; faith,
    shew it,   25
And if you like his play, 't 's as well he knew
    it.

         [2] Telescopes ; used also of other optical instruments.

SEJANUS, HIS FALL

Sejanus was first performed in 1603, but, as Jonson admits, failed to please the audience. It was published in 1605, and again in the folio of 1616. On this latter the present text is based. It is not necessary to discuss the sources of this impressive tragedy, since Jonson has supplied us in his ample foot-notes with documentary evidence for nearly every fact in the play. These notes have been reproduced in the present edition, through the first scene, which is probably as far as the modern reader will care to study them. The delineation of Tiberius is one of the most successful attempts in our literature to recreate a highly complex historical character.

VOLPONE, OR THE FOX

Volpone was performed in 1605 or 1606 at the Globe theatre and at both Oxford and Cambridge, and in 1607 was printed in quarto. It was included in the folio of 1616, on which the present text is based. The main plot is founded on an episode in the *Satiricon* of Petronius Arbiter ; but the parts of Celia and of Sir Politic and Lady Would-be are of Jonson's own invention. The song, "Drink to me only with thine eyes," is practically a translation from Philostratus, and "Come, my Celia " is imitated from Catullus. The comedy is a terrible satire on some of the most sordid aspects of human nature, and the superb skill with which it is constructed barely suffices to counteract the depressing effect of the types of character it displays.

THE ALCHEMIST

The Alchemist, which may, perhaps, be regarded as Jonson's supreme masterpiece in comedy, was performed in 1610, and published in quarto in 1612. The present text is based on that of the folio of 1616. It has been frequently stated that for the plot of this play Jonson was indebted to Plautus, but the borrowing is very slight. In the *Mostellaria* there is a scene which might have suggested the opening dialogue of *The Alchemist*, and another which bears a slight resemblance to Face's attempt to hoodwink his master in V. i. In the *Poenulus*, a man speaks Punic, and is misunderstood somewhat as Surly's Spanish is misunderstood in IV. iii. But the plot as a whole is Jonson's own, and the alchemical and astrological matter is drawn from a wide acquaintance with current treatises on these subjects. Attempts have been made to identify Subtle and Face with the famous Dee and Kelley, but identification is much too strong a word. Hathaway has pointed out a more striking correspondence with the activities of Simon Forman, a notorious quack of Jonson's day. *The Alchemist* has been credited with a considerable effectiveness in clearing London of the type of impostors which it ridicules and exposes so trenchantly and amusingly.

THE SHOEMAKERS' HOLIDAY

This, the first of Dekker's comedies, was acted in 1599, and printed in the following year. On the text of this quarto, as reprinted by Warnke and Proescholdt, the present text is based. The story of the partly historical Simon Eyre was found by Dekker in one of the tales in Thomas Deloney's *Gentle Craft*, 1597; but the main interest of the play lies in its picture of London tradespeople in the author's own day, and for this Dekker needed no literary source.

THE HONEST WHORE

From a passage in Henslowe's *Diary* it appears that Middleton had some share in the first part of *The Honest Whore*, but it is not supposed that he wrote any considerable portion of it. The second part is wholly Dekker's, and is generally regarded as superior to the first. The first edition of part i. appeared in 1604, of part ii. in 1630. Pearson's reprint, on which the present text is based, follows the 1605 quarto of part i. and the 1630 of part ii. A copy of the 1635 quarto of the double play has been used to check Pearson's text. No source of the plot has been discovered. The play is a highly characteristic product of the time, both in its picture of the vices of the city, and in its sound and straightforward, if somewhat coarse, handling of the moral issues involved. The character of Friscobaldo, in part ii., afforded Hazlitt the theme for what he himself justly regarded as one of his finest pieces of critical interpretation.

THE MALCONTENT

The Malcontent was first issued in 1604; and in the same year a second quarto appeared with the title-page, "The Malcontent. Augmented by Marston. With the Additions played by the Kings Maiesties servants. Written by Ihon Webster. 1604. At London Printed by V. S. for William Aspley, and are to be sold at his shop in Paules Church-yard." The title-page of the first edition gives John Marston as author; the date and publisher are the same. The second edition, on which the present text is directly based, contains, as new matter, the Induction and a number of additions, marked in the present text by brackets and specified in the foot-notes. Its title-page has proved highly misleading; the facts seem to be that Webster supplied the Induction when the play was revived by the King's men; and that the other additions are restorations of passages from Marston's original play which had been cut for acting purposes. Stoll, who has made this clear, places the composition of the play in 1600, and has given the tragi-comedy a new importance, in addition to its intrinsic vigor and effectiveness, by arguing forcibly for it as an influence on the characters of Shakespeare's Jaques and Hamlet. The source of the plot has so far not been discovered.

A WOMAN KILLED WITH KINDNESS

This tragedy, one of the earliest and most pathetic examples of domestic drama, was first published in 1607; and the present text is based on Pearson's reprint of this quarto. The play was acted in 1603, as appears from an entry in Henslowe's *Diary*. The title, like those of several other plays by Heywood, was a proverbial phrase. Creizenach (IV. 264) states that Heywood borrowed the two plots of this drama from Margaret of Navarre and from Bandello. The thirty-second tale in the *Heptameron* does indeed tell of a husband who refrained from killing a wife taken in adultery, but the resemblance is far from close.

THE KNIGHT OF THE BURNING PESTLE

The Knight of the Burning Pestle was printed in quarto in 1613, and on Murch's reproduction of this edition the present text is based. A second and a third quarto were issued in 1635, and the play was included in the second folio edition of Beaumont and Fletcher in 1679. The date of composition is uncertain, but recent opinion tends to place it about 1610. It cannot be said that there is as yet a general agreement as to the respective shares of the two authors in this comedy, but according to the most careful examination of the question so far made, that of Dr. Murch, most of the play should be ascribed to Beaumont, Fletcher having probably written only the three love scenes, I. i. 1-60; III. i.; and IV. iv. 18-93. In spite of the similarity between the satirical purpose of this play and of *Don Quixote*, it has not been shown that the authors had any knowledge of the work of Cervantes, or that they could read Spanish. (The first English translation of *Don Quixote* appeared in 1612.) In the mock-heroic part of the play, the object of the satire was the type of play founded upon medieval romance and popular at that time among the tradespeople of London; and of this type, Heywood's *Four Prentices of London* seems to have been especially in view. Koeppel has pointed out the resemblance between the coffin scene in Act IV. and an episode in Marston's *Antonio and Mellida* (1602). The love-plot is too commonplace to have a definitely assignable source, and the scenes between Merrythought and his wife, like those of the Induction, are, one may be sure, due to direct observation of contemporary life and manners.

PHILASTER

The first quarto of *Philaster*, issued in 1620, seems to have been unauthorized, and to have been made up in part from a report taken down at a performance. At the beginning and end it is quite different from the other quartos. The second quarto, 1622, as reprinted by Thorndike, is the basis for the present text, with occasional readings from the later quartos and the folio of 1679. The play was probably written about 1608-10. The respective shares of the two authors are difficult to assign. Oliphant and Thorndike give to Fletcher I. i. 99-369; II. ii.; II. iv. 69-203; passages in III. ii.; V. iii.; and V. iv.; the rest to Beaumont; the prose scenes with less assurance. Macaulay gives little beyond V. iii., iv. to Fletcher. This distribution is made mainly on the grounds of the characteristics of the metre; it does not exclude the probability of intimate collaboration in plot and characterization. The story of the play seems to have been original, though several of the motives are common enough. There is marked indebtedness to *Hamlet*, and much resemblance to *Cymbeline*, though Thorndike has argued plausibly for the view that in the latter case Shakespeare was the borrower.

THE MAID'S TRAGEDY

As in the case of *Philaster*, the first quarto of the *The Maid's Tragedy* (1619) is corrupt and unauthorized. The second quarto (1622), with Thorndike's collations of the first and third (1630), is the basis for the present text. The date of composition is probably about 1609-11. There is more agreement here than in the case of *Philaster* as to the respective shares of the joint authors. Most critics give Fletcher II. ii; IV. i; V. i. 1-111; V. ii; the rest to Beaumont, with the exception of I. ii, which is uncertain. Macaulay gives II. ii. also to Beaumont. The source of the plot has not been found, though minor resemblances have been noted, such as that of the duel between Aspatia and Amintor, to the fight between Parthenia and Amphialus in Sidney's *Arcadia*, book iii, and that of the quarrel between Melantius and Amintor to that between Brutus and Cassius in *Julius Caesar*.

THE FAITHFUL SHEPHERDESS

The first quarto of *The Faithful Shepherdess* is undated, but it was certainly issued before May, 1610, and the play had been unsuccessfully produced not long before, perhaps in 1608 or 1609. The present text is based on the first edition, and is dependent on the collations in the Glover and Waller edition of Beaumont and Fletcher. Fletcher's chief model in this pastoral seems to have been Guarini's *Pastor Fido*, and some few details are borrowed from Spenser; but the plot itself seems to be original. The play, as Fletcher confesses in his address *To the Reader*, was unsuccessful on the stage, but the beauty of its lyric and descriptive poetry has given it, in spite of its weak dramatic quality, a distinguished place in literature. It is notable also as having in part suggested Milton's *Comus*.

THE WILD-GOOSE CHASE

The Wild-Goose Chase, we are told by the publisher of the first folio edition of Beaumont and Fletcher, was lost when that volume was compiled; it reappeared later, and was issued separately, in folio, in 1652. A second edition appeared in the folio of 1679. The present text is based on the reprint of Waller, following, however, the edition of 1652 in preference to that of 1679. The comedy is known to have been acted as early as 1621. No source for the plot seems as yet to have been found. Farquhar based on it his comedy of *The Inconstant*, a fact which points to the obvious relationship between the Fletcherian comedy, of which this is a typical example, and the drama of the Restoration.

THE DUCHESS OF MALFI

The first edition of *The Duchess of Malfi* appeared in quarto in 1623, and was followed by others in 1640, 1678, and 1708. The present text follows chiefly the Harvard copy of the first quarto, with occasional readings supplied by Sampson's collation of the other editions. The date of first performance cannot be later than 1614, since the actor who created the part of Antonio died in that year. The main plot is taken from Painter's *Palace of Pleasure*, vol. II, Nov. 23(1567). Painter translated his story from Belle-Forest's paraphrase (1565) of the twenty-sixth novella of Bandello (1554). The story appears in many places, and had been dramatized by Lope de Vega. Crawford (*Notes and Queries*, Sept. 17-Nov. 12, 1904) has shown many incidental and even literal borrowings from Sidney's *Arcadia*. Among the elements in the play not found in Painter are the underplot of Julia and the Cardinal, the scenes of torture, and the most of the fifth act. Some of these are derived from the tradition of the tragedy of revenge, especially as represented by Shakespeare, Marston, and Tourneur; but, in spite of frequent echoes, this impressive tragedy, almost the last of its kind, derives its vitality mainly from the powerful and sombre imagination of Webster.

A TRICK TO CATCH THE OLD ONE

This comedy was licensed October 7, 1607, and published in quarto in 1608. A second edition appeared in 1616. The present text is based directly on the copy of the first quarto in the Boston Public Library, with the aid of the readings from the second quarto given by Bullen. The plot is supposed to have given Massinger a suggestion for *A New Way to Pay Old Debts*, but where Middleton found it, if he did not originate it, is not known. This play is an excellent example of Middleton's comedies of intrigue and manners, full of bustle and fun, more careful of theatrical effect than of moral or aesthetic consistency.

THE CHANGELING

The Changeling was performed as early as 1623, but did not appear in print till 1653. On a copy of this quarto in the Harvard Library the present text is based. The source of the tragic plot is the fourth history in book i. of John Reynolds's *Triumph of God's Revenge against Murder* (1621), but the prose narrative is not followed closely. The under-plot, which gives its title to the play, may be original. Miss Wiggin assigns to Rowley the whole under-plot, and the opening and closing scenes of the main plot. Symons finds the greatness of the play as a whole due to the collaboration of the two authors, and beyond the powers of either alone (Cf. Camb. Hist. of Eng. Lit., vi. 76-7).

A NEW WAY TO PAY OLD DEBTS

This play, Massinger's masterpiece in comedy, appeared in quarto in 1633, and on the Harvard Library copy of this edition the present text is based. The play was acted before 1626, and Fleay places it as early as 1622. Few plays of this whole period have held the English stage so continuously or so long as this. The central idea of the plot seems to have been taken from Middleton's *A Trick to Catch the Old One;* but there is almost as great a difference in the dramatic method between the two plays as there is in moral tone. Massinger's didacticism here finds eloquent expression, without destroying theatrical effectiveness. Prototypes of Sir Giles Overreach and Greedy have been found in the notorious monopolist, Sir Giles Mompesson and his tool, Michael.

THE BROKEN HEART

The only early edition of *The Broken Heart* was published in 1633, and the present text is based on a copy of this quarto in the Boston Public Library. There is no evidence as to the date of composition except the hitherto unnoted fact that *The Garland of Good Will*, mentioned in IV. ii. 15, was published in 1631. The prologue seems to imply that the plot of the play is founded on fact, and Sherman has argued plausibly that the reference is to the story of Penelope Devereux, Sidney's "Stella," whose second husband Ford had eulogised in his first publication, *Fame's Memorial* (1606). It is certain that Ford was interested in both Sidney and Stella, and there are many correspondences between their situation and that of Orgilus and Penthea. The catastrophe is, of course, entirely changed; but in the spiritual situation there is much to recall the sonnets of Astrophel to Stella. There are traces of the influence of the *Arcadia* also in the play, such as the laying of the plot in Sparta; and in the delineation of the jealousy of Bassanes Ford draws upon Burton's *Anatomy of Melancholy*.

THE LADY OF PLEASURE

The Lady of Pleasure was published in quarto in 1637, and the present text is based on a copy of this edition in the Harvard Library. The play, a good example of Shirley's comedy of manners, was produced in 1635. No source has been discovered for the plot. Like Fletcher's *Wild-Goose Chase*, this type of Shirley's comedies is important in measuring the approach made toward the Restoration comedy before the Puritan Revolution.

THE CARDINAL

This tragedy, regarded by Shirley as his greatest play, and in fact no unworthy piece to close a volume representing the drama of that age, appeared in a volume of *Six New Plays* in 1653, the date on the title-page of *The Cardinal* being 1652. On a copy of this octavo in the Harvard Library the present text is based. The play was acted in 1641, and thus belongs to the last few months before the theatres were closed by the Long Parliament. It is probable that Webster's *Duchess of Malfi* afforded more than a suggestion for the plot, but otherwise no source has been found. The play was popular both on its first appearance and when it was revived after the Restoration.

BIBLIOGRAPHIES

GENERAL WORKS ON THE ELIZABETHAN DRAMA

REGISTER OF THE STATIONERS' COMPANY, 1554-1640. Transcript by E. Arber. 5 vols. 1875–94.
HENSLOWE'S DIARY. Ed. W. W. Greg. 2 vols. 1904.
COLLIER (J. P.), History of English Dramatic Poetry. New ed. 3 vols. 1879.
FLEAY (F. G.), Biographical Chronicle of the English Drama, 1559-1642. 2 vols. 1891.
FLEAY (F. G.), A Chronicle History of the London Stage, 1890.
WARD (A. W.), History of English Dramatic Literature to the Death of Queen Anne. 2d ed. 3 vols. 1899.
GREG (W. W.), A List of English Plays written before 1643 and printed before 1700. Bibliographical Society. 1900.
CREIZENACH (W.), Geschichte des neueren Dramas. Vols. I-IV. Halle, 1893-1909.
THORNDIKE (A. H.), Tragedy. Boston, 1908.
SCHELLING (F. E.), Elizabethan Drama. Boston, 1908.
HAZLITT (W.), Lectures on the Dramatic Poets of the Age of Elizabeth, in Works, ed. Waller and Glover, vol. VI., 1903.
LAMB (C.), Specimens of English Dramatic Poets. Ed. Gollancz (I.), 2 vols. 1908.
COLERIDGE (S. T.), Literary Remains, vol. II., 1836.
SYMONDS (J. A.), Shakespere's Predecessors in the English Drama. 1881.
LOWELL (J. R.), The Old English Dramatists, 1892.
SWINBURNE (A. C.), The Age of Shakespeare, 1908.
The Cambridge History of English Literature, vols. V and VI. Cambridge, 1910.
The Dictionary of National Biography (for lives of the dramatists).

JOHN LYLY

ORIGINAL EDITIONS

Campaspe, 1584. Sapho and Phao, 1584. Endymion, 1591. Gallathea, 1592. Midas, 1592. Mother Bombie, 1594. The Woman in the Moon, 1597. Love's Metamorphosis, 1601.

COLLECTED EDITIONS

Blount (E.), Six Court Comedies, 1632. — Fairholt (F. W.), 2 vols., 1858. — Bond (R. W.), 3 vols., Oxford, 1902.

ENDYMION

Ed. Baker (G. P.), New York, 1894.

CRITICISM, etc.[1]

Child (C. G.), John Lyly and Euphuism, in Münchener Beiträge, VII, Erlangen and Leipzig, 1894. — Halpin (N. J.), Oberon's Vision in M. N. Dream, illustrated by comparison with Lyly's Endymion, [Old] Shakespeare Soc. Pub. 1843. — Long (P. W.), The Purport of Lyly's Endymion, Pub. Mod. Lang. Ass. Amer., XXIV., 1909. — Feuillerat (A.), John Lyly, Cambridge, 1910. — Brooke (C. F. T.), The Allegory in Lyly's Endymion, Mod. Lang. Notes, Jan. 1911.

GEORGE PEELE

ORIGINAL EDITIONS

Arraignment of Paris, 1584. Edward I, 1593. Battle of Alcazar, 1594. Old Wives Tale, 1595. David and Bethsabe, 1599.

COLLECTED EDITIONS

Dyce (A.), 3 vols. 1828-39; 1861, 1879. — Bullen (A. H.), 2 vols. 1888.

OLD WIVES TALE

Ed. Gummere (F. B.), in Gayley's Representative English Comedies, 1903. — Greg (W. W.), in Malone Society Reprints, 1907.

[1] Critical and biographical articles contained in the General Works listed above, or in collected editions, or in editions of separate plays, are not repeated in this paragraph.

CRITICISM, etc.

Lämmerhirt (R.), George Peele, Untersuchungen über sein Leben und seine Werke. Rostock, 1882. — Bayley (A. R.), Peele as a Dramatic Artist. The Oxford Point of View, 15 Feb. 1903. — Odell (G. C.), Peele as a Dramatist. The Bibliographer, vol. II., 1903.

ROBERT GREENE

ORIGINAL EDITIONS

Orlando Furioso, 1594; 1599. Friar Bacon and Friar Bungay, 1594; 1599; 1630; 1655. James the Fourth, 1598. Alphonsus of Aragon, 1599. A Looking Glass for London and England (with Lodge), 1594.

COLLECTED EDITIONS

Dyce (A.), 2 vols. 1831; 1861, 1879. — Grosart (A. B.), 15 vols. 1881-6. — Collins (J. C.), 2 vols. Oxford, 1905. — Dickinson (T. A.), six plays in Mermaid Series, 1909.

FRIAR BACON AND FRIAR BUNGAY

Ed. Manly (J. M.), in Specimens of Pre-Shakespearean Drama, Boston, 1897-8. — Ward (A. W.), in Old English Drama, Oxford, 1878; New ed. 1901. — Gayley (C. M.), in Representative English Comedies, 1903.

CRITICISM, etc.

Conrad (H.), Robert Greene als Dramatiker, in Shak. Jahrbuch, XXIX., 1894. — Ehrke (K.), Robert Greene's Dramen, 1904. — Woodberry (G.), Greene's Place in Comedy, in Gayley's Representative English Comedies, 1903. — Ritter (O.), De Rob. Greeni Fabula, Fr. Bacon et Fr. Bungay, Thorn, 1886.

CHRISTOPHER MARLOWE

ORIGINAL EDITIONS

Tamburlaine the Great (parts i and ii), 1590; 1592; part i, 1605; part ii, 1606. Dr. Faustus, 1604; 1609; 1616; 1619; 1620; 1624; 1631; 1663. The Jew of Malta, 1633. Edward II, 1594; 1598; 1612; 1622. The Massacre at Paris, n. d. Dido, Queen of Carthage (with Nashe), 1594.

COLLECTED EDITIONS

Robinson (G.), 3 vols. 1826. — Dyce (A.), 3 vols., 1850, 1858; 1 vol., 1865, 1876. — Cunningham (F.), 1871. — Bullen (A. H.), 3 vols., 1884-5. — Breymann (H.), and Wagner (A.), 1885-9. — Ellis (H.), five plays in Mermaid Series, 1887. — Brooke (C. F. T.), 1 vol., Oxford, 1910.

TAMBURLAINE

Ed. Vollmöller (K.), Heilbronn, 1885.

DR. FAUSTUS

Ed. Wagner (W.), 1877. — Ward (A. W.), in Old English Drama, Oxford, new ed. 1891. — Gollancz, (I.), in Temple Dramatists, 1897.

THE JEW OF MALTA

Ed. Thayer (W. R.), in Best Elizabethan Plays, Boston, 1890.

EDWARD II

Ed. Wagner (W.), Hamburg, 1871. — Fleay (F. G.), 1873, 1877. — Tancock (O. W.), Oxford, 1879, 1899. — Verity (A. W.), in Temple Dramatists, 1896. — McLaughlin (E. T.), New York, 1894.

CRITICISM, etc.

Ingram (J. H.), Christopher Marlowe and his Associates, 1904, q. v. for further bibliography. — Tzschaschel (C.), Marlowe's Edward II und seine Quelle, Halle, 1902.

THOMAS KYD

ORIGINAL EDITIONS

Cornelia, 1594, 1595. The Spanish Tragedy, 1592 (?), 2d ed. n. d., 1594, 1599; with additions, 1602, 1610, 1615, 1618, 1623, 1633. The First Part of Jeronimo, 1605. Soliman and Perseda, 1599.

COLLECTED EDITIONS

Boas (F. S.), Oxford, 1901.

THE SPANISH TRAGEDY

Ed. Manly (J. M.), in Specimens, vol. II., 1897-8. — Schick (J.), in Temple Dramatists, 1898. — Markscheffel (K.), in Litterarhist. Forsch., Berlin, 1901.

CRITICISM, etc.

Sarrazin (G.), Thomas Kyd und sein Kreis, Berlin, 1892. (Cf. Schick in Herrig's Archiv, xc.; Koeppel in Englische Studien, XVIII. 125.) — Bang (W.), Engl. Stud. XXVIII. 229. — Brereton (J. LeG.), Notes on the text of Kyd, Engl. Stud., XXXVII. — Crawford (C.), Concordance to the Works of T. Kyd, in Bang's Materialien, Louvain, 1909.

GEORGE CHAPMAN

ORIGINAL EDITIONS

The Blind Beggar of Alexandria, 1598. A Humorous Day's Mirth, 1599. All Fools, 1605. Monsieur D'Olive, 1606. The Gentleman Usher, 1606. Bussy D'Ambois, 1607, 1608, 1641, 1646, 1657. The Conspiracy and Tragedy of Charles, Duke of Byron, 1608. May-Day, 1611. The Widow's Tears, 1612. The Revenge of Bussy D'Ambois, 1613. Pompey and Cæsar, 1631, 1653. Alphonsus of Germany (?), 1654. Revenge for Honour, 1654. Chabot, Admiral of France (with Shirley), 1639.

COLLECTED EDITIONS

Pearson (J.), 1873. — Shepherd (R. H.), 3 vols., 1874; 1889. Phelps (W. L.), five plays in Mermaid Series, 1895.

BUSSY D'AMBOIS

Ed. Boas (F. S.), in Belles Lettres Series, Boston, 1906.

CRITICISM, etc.

Coleridge (S. T.), Literary Remains, I. 259, 1836. — Koeppel (E.), Quellenstudien zu Dramen George Chapman's, etc., in Quellen und Forschungen, LXXXII., Strassburg, 1897. — Parrott (T. M.), Notes on the Text of Chapman's Plays, Anglia, XXX., 1907. — Stoll (E. E.), On the Dates of Some of Chapman's Plays, Mod. Lang. Notes, XX., 1905.

BEN JONSON

ORIGINAL EDITIONS

Every Man Out of his Humour, 1600. Every Man in his Humour, 1601 (S. R. 1600). Cynthia's Revels, 1601. The Poetaster, 1602 (S. R. 1601). Sejanus, 1605 (S. R. 1604). Volpone, 1607. The Case is Altered, 1606. Catiline, 1611. The Alchemist, 1612 (S. R. 1610). Epicoene, or The Silent Woman, 1609 (?), 1612 (?), (Acted 1609; S. R. 1610), Fol. 1616. The New Inn, 1631 (Acted 1629). Bartholomew Fair, 1631 (Acted 1614). The Devil is an Ass, 1631 (Acted 1616). The Staple of News, 1631 (Acted 1625). The Magnetic Lady, 1640 (S. R. 1632). A Tale of a Tub, 1640 (S. R. 1633). The Sad Shepherd, 1640. Mortimer, his Fall, 1640.

COLLECTED EDITIONS

First Folio, 1616. — Second Folio, 1640. — Whalley (P.), 7 vols., 1756. — Gifford (W.), 9 vols., 1816. — Cunningham (F.), rep. of Gifford, 1871, 1875. — Morley (H.), Plays and Poems of Ben Jonson, 1885. — Herford (C. H.), and Nicholson (B.), 3 vols. in Mermaid Series, 1893-4. — Bang (W.), Reprints from Folios and Quartos in his Materialien; in process. — Eight of the plays have appeared in Yale Studies in English, 1903-8. A new edition by Herford (C. H.) and Simpson (P.) is announced, Oxford.

EVERY MAN IN HIS HUMOUR

Rep. from Q. of 1601 by Grabau (C.), Shakespeare Jahrbuch, XXXVIII., 1903; and by Bang (W.) and Greg (W. W.), in Bang's Materialien, XI, 1905. — Wheatley (H. B.), 1877. — Dixon (W. M.), in Temple Dramatists, 1905.

VOLPONE

Ed. Wilkins (H. B.), New York, 1905, in Yale Studies in English.

THE ALCHEMIST

Ed. Thayer (W. R.), Boston, 1890, in Best Elizabethan Plays. — Hathaway (C. H.), New York, 1903, in Yale Studies in English. — Hart (H. C.), 1903, in The King's Library. — Schelling (F. E.), Boston, 1903, in Belles Lettres Series.

CRITICISM, etc.

Castelain (M.), Ben Jonson: l'Homme et l'Œuvre, Paris, 1907. — Koeppel (E.), Quellenstudien zu den Dramen Ben Jonson's, etc., in Münchener Beiträge, XI., Erlangen and Leipzig, 1895. — Swinburne (A. C.), A Study of Ben Jonson, 1889. — Symonds (J. A.), Ben Jonson, 1886. — Woodbridge (E.), Studies in Jonson's Comedy, Boston, 1898.

THOMAS DEKKER

ORIGINAL EDITIONS

The Shoemakers' Holiday, 1600, 1610, 1618, 1631, 1657. Old Fortunatus, 1600. Satiro-mastix, 1602. The Honest Whore, part i, 1604, 1605, 1615, 1616, 1635. The Whore of Babylon, 1607. If it be not Good, the Devil is in it, 1612. The Honest Whore, part ii, 1630. Match me in London, 1631. A Wonder of a Kingdom, 1636. Patient Grisel (with Chettle and Haughton), 1603. Westward Ho ! (with Webster), 1607. Northward Ho ! (with Webster), 1607. Sir Thomas Wyatt (with Webster), 1607. The Witch of Edmonton (with W. Rowley and Ford), 1658. The Roaring Girl (with Middleton), 1611. The Virgin Martyr (with Massinger), 1622.

COLLECTED EDITIONS

Pearson (J.), 4 vols., 1873. — Rhys (E.), five plays in Mermaid Series, 1895.

THE SHOEMAKERS' HOLIDAY

Ed. Fritsche (H.), Thorn, 1862. — Warnke (K.) and Proescholdt (L.), Halle, 1886.

CRITICISM, etc.

Swinburne (A. C.), Thomas Dekker, The Nineteenth Century, Jan. 1887. — Stoll (E. E.), The Influence of Jonson on Dekker, Mod. Lang. Notes, XXI.

JOHN MARSTON

ORIGINAL EDITIONS

Antonio and Mellida, 1602. Antonio's Revenge, 1602. The Dutch Courtesan, 1605. Parasitaster, or The Fawn, 1606. The Wonder of Women, or Sophonisba, 1606. What you Will, 1607. The Insatiate Countess, 1613. The Malcontent (with Webster), 1604. Eastward Hoe ! (with Chapman and Jonson), 1605.

COLLECTED EDITIONS

Plays. 1633. — Halliwell [-Phillipps] (J. O.), 3 vols., 1856. — Bullen (A. H.), 3 vols., 1887.

CRITICISM, etc.

Koeppel (E.), Quellenstudien zu den Dramen Ben Jonson's, John Marston's, etc. Münchener Beiträge, XI., Erlangen and Leipzig, 1895. — Swinburne (A. C.) in Nineteenth Century, XXIV, 1888. — Wurzbach (W. von), in Shak. Jahrbuch, XXXIII, 1897. — Stoll (E. E.), John Webster, chap. ii, sect. ii, Boston, 1905. — Stoll (E. E.), Shakspere, Marston and the Malcontent Type, in Modern Philology, III., 1906.— Aronstein (P.), Marston als Dramatiker, Eng. Studien, XX.

THOMAS HEYWOOD

ORIGINAL EDITIONS

Edward the Fourth, parts i and ii, 1600. If You Know Not Me, You Know Nobody, part i, 1605; part ii, 1606. A Woman Killed with Kindness, 1607, 1617. The Rape of Lucrece, 1608. The Four Prentices of London, 1615; rev. 1632. The Fair Maid of the West, part i, 1631; part ii, 1631. The Golden Age, 1610. The Silver Age, 1613. The Brazen Age, 1613. The Iron Age, part i, 1632; part ii, 1632. The English Traveller, 1633. A Maidenhead Well Lost, 1634. A Challenge for Beauty, 1636. The Royal King and the Loyal Subject, 1637. The Wise Woman of Hogsdon, 1638. Love's Mistress, 1636. The Late Lancashire Witches (with Brome), 1634. Fortune by Land and Sea (with W. Rowley), 1655.

COLLECTED EDITIONS

Pearson's Reprint, 6 vols., 1874. — Verity (A. W.), five plays in Mermaid Series, 1888.

A WOMAN KILLED WITH KINDNESS

Ed. Collier (J. P.), in Shak. Soc. Pub., 1850. — Ward (A. W.), in Temple Dramatists, 1897. — Cox (F. J.), 1907.

BEAUMONT AND FLETCHER

ORIGINAL EDITIONS OF SINGLE PLAYS BY BOTH AUTHORS

The Woman Hater (probably by Beaumont alone), 1607, 1648, 1649. The Knight of the Burning Pestle, 1613, 1635. Cupid's Revenge, 1615, 1630, 1635. The Scornful Lady, 1616, 1625, 1630, 1635, 1639, 1651, 1677, 1691, 1695. A King and No King, 1619, 1625, 1631, 1639, 1655, 1661, 1676, 1693. The Maid's Tragedy, 1619, 1622, 1630,

1638, 1641, 1650, 1661, 1686. Philaster, 1620, 1622, 1630, 1634, 1639, 1651, 1652 (2 edd.), 1660(?), 1687. Thierry and Theodoret, 1621, 1648, 1649.

ORIGINAL EDITIONS OF SINGLE PLAYS BY FLETCHER ALONE

The Faithful Shepherdess, n. d. (prob. 1609), 1629, 1634, 1656, 1665. Henry VIII (with Shakespeare), in Shakespeare Folio of 1623. The Two Noble Kinsmen (with Shakespeare), 1634. The Elder Brother, 1637, 1651, 1661, 1678. Wit Without Money, 1639, 1661. Monsieur Thomas, 1639. The Bloody Brother, 1639, 1640. Rule a Wife and Have a Wife, 1696, 1697. The Night-Walker, 1640, 1661. The Wild-Goose Chase, 1652. The Humorous Lieutenant, 1830 (from a MS. dated 1625).

FIRST FOLIO EDITION OF BEAUMONT AND FLETCHER'S PLAYS (1647)

The Mad Lover. The Spanish Curate. The Little French Lawyer. The Custom of the Country. The Noble Gentleman. The Captain.* The Beggar's Bush. The Coxcomb.* The False One. The Chances. The Loyal Subject. The Laws of Candy. The Lover's Progress. The Island Princess. The Humorous Lieutenant. The Nice Valour, or The Passionate Madman. The Maid in the Mill. The Prophetess. Bonduca. The Sea Voyage. The Double Marriage. The Pilgrim. The Knight of Malta. The Woman's Prize, or The Tamer Tamed. Love's Cure, or The Martial Maid.* The Honest Man's Fortune. The Queen of Corinth. Women Pleased. A Wife for a Month. Wit at Several Weapons.* Valentinian. The Fair Maid of the Inn. Love's Pilgrimage. The Masque at the Marriage of the Prince and Princess Palatine of the Rhine. Four Plays in One.*
(Plays followed by an asterisk are believed to be in part by Beaumont: the rest by Fletcher.)

COLLECTED EDITIONS

First Folio, 1647. Fifty Comedies and Tragedies (Second Folio), 1679. — Works of B. and F. (pub. Tonson), 7 vols., 1711. — Theobald, Seward, and Sympson, 10 vols., 1750. — Colman (G.), 10 vols., 1778. — Colman (G.), (with Jonson's Works), 4 vols., 1811; (without Jonson) 3 vols., 1811. — Weber (H.), 14 vols. Edin. 1812. — Darley (G.), 2 vols., 1839 (text of Weber). — Dyce (A.), 11 vols., 1843-6; 2 vols., Boston, 1852. — Strachey (J. St. L.), in Mermaid Series, ten plays in 2 vols., 1887. — Bullen (A. H.), General editor of Variorum edition by various editors, 12 vols., 1904, (in process). — Glover (A.) and Waller (A. R.), in Cambridge English Classics, 10 vols., 1905. (In process, Text of folio of 1679 with collations of other edd.)

THE KNIGHT OF THE BURNING PESTLE

Ed. Morley (H.) in Burlesque Plays and Poems, Universal Library, 1885. — Moorman (F. W.), in Temple Dramatists, 1898. — Murch (H. S.), in Yale Studies in English, New York, 1908. — Alden (R. M.), in Belles Lettres Series, Boston, 1910.

PHILASTER

Ed. Thayer (W. R.), in Best Elizabethan Plays, Boston, 1890. — Boas (F. S.), in Temple Dramatists, 1898. — Thorndike (A. H.), in Belles Lettres Series, Boston, 1906.

THE MAID'S TRAGEDY

Ed. Thorndike (A. H.), in Belles Lettres Series, Boston, 1906. — Cox (F. J.), 1908.

THE FAITHFUL SHEPHERDESS

Ed. Moorman (F. W.), in Temple Dramatists, 1897. — Fletcher (J. B.), in Belles Lettres Series, announced.

CRITICISM, etc.

Koeppel (E.), Quellenstudien zu den Dramen . . . Beaumont's and Fletcher's, in Münchener Beiträge, XI. 1895. — Leonhardt (B.), Ueber B. and F.'s Knight of the Burning Pestle, Annaberg, 1885. Cf. also Anglia, VIII. 424; XIX. 34; XIX. 509; XXIII. 14; in Engl. Studien, XII. 307; 1885-1903. — Macaulay (G. C.), Francis Beaumont, a critical study, 1883. — Hatcher (O. L.), John Fletcher, a study in dramatic method, Chicago, 1905. — Swinburne (A. C.), Beaumont and Fletcher, in Studies in Prose and Poetry, 1894. — Thorndike (A. H.), Influence of B. and F. on Shakespeare, Worcester, Mass., 1901. — Greg (W. W.), Pastoral Poetry and Pastoral Drama, London, 1906.

JOHN WEBSTER

ORIGINAL EDITIONS

The White Devil, 1612. The Duchess of Malfi, 1623, 1640, 1678. The Devil's Law-case, 1623. Appius and Virginia, 1654. A Cure for a Cuckold (with W. Rowley), 1661. The Thracian Wonder (with W. Rowley), 1661. Induction to The Malcontent, 1604.

COLLECTED EDITIONS

Dyce (A.), 4 vols., 1830, 1857. — Hazlitt (W.), 4 vols., 1857.—Symonds (J. A.), two plays in **Mermaid Series**, 1888.

THE DUCHESS OF MALFI

Ed. Thayer (W. R.), in Best Elizabethan Plays, Boston, 1890. — Vaughan (C. E.), in Temple Dramatists, 1896. — Sampson (M. W.), in Belles Lettres Series, Boston, 1904.

CRITICISM, etc.

Gosse (E.), in Seventeenth Century Studies, 1883. — Stoll (E. E.), John Webster, the Periods of his work, Boston, 1905. — Pierce (F. E.), The Collaboration of Webster and Dekker, in Yale Studies in English, New York, 1909. — Kiesow (K.), Die Verschiedenen Bearbeitungen der Novelle von der Herzogin v. Amalfi, Anglia, XVII. 198.

THOMAS MIDDLETON

ORIGINAL EDITIONS

Blurt, Master-Constable, 1602. The Phœnix, 1607, 1630. Michaelmas Term, 1607. A Trick to Catch the Old One, 1608, 1616. The Family of Love, 1608. A Mad World, my Masters, 1608. Your Five Gallants, n. d. (lic. 1608). A Game at Chess, 1625. A Chaste Maid in Cheapside, 1630. Women Beware Women, 1657. More Dissemblers Besides Women, 1657. No Wit, No Help like a Woman's, 1657. The Mayor of Quinborough, 1661. Anything for a Quiet Life, 1662. The Witch, 1778. A Fair Quarrel (with W. Rowley), 1617. The Changeling (with W. Rowley), 1653. The Spanish Gipsy (with W. Rowley), 1653. The Old Law (with Massinger and W. Rowley), 1656. The Roaring Girl (with Dekker), 1611. The Widow (with Jonson and Fletcher), 1652.

COLLECTED EDITIONS

Dyce (A.), 5 vols., 1840.—Bullen (A. H.), 8 vols., 1885-6.— Swinburne (A. C.), and Ellis (H.), ten plays, in Mermaid Series, 1890.

CRITICISM, etc.

Wiggin (P. G.), An Enquiry into the authorship of the Middleton-Rowley Plays, in Radcliffe College Monographs, Boston, 1897. — Christ (K.), Quellenstudien zu den Dramen Thomas Middleton's, 1905.

WILLIAM ROWLEY

ORIGINAL EDITIONS

A Search for Money, 1609. A New Wonder, a Woman Never Vext, 1632. A Match at Midnight, 1633. All's Lost by Lust, 1633. A Shoemaker a Gentleman, 1638. The Changeling (with Middleton), 1653. And many other collaborated plays.

CRITICISM, etc.

Stork (C. W.), Rowley's Place in the Drama, in his ed. of All's Lost by Lust, etc., Philadelphia, 1910. — Wiggin (P. G.), An Enquiry into the authorship of the Middleton-Rowley Plays, Boston, 1897.

PHILIP MASSINGER

ORIGINAL EDITIONS

The Virgin Martyr (with Dekker), 1622. The Duke of Milan, 1623. The Bondman, 1624. The Roman Actor, 1629. The Renegado, 1630. The Picture, 1630. The Maid of Honour, 1632. The Emperor of the East, 1632. The Fatal Dowry (with N. Field), 1632. A New Way to Pay Old Debts, 1633. The Great Duke of Florence, 1636. The Unnatural Combat, 1639. The Guardian, 1655. A Very Woman, 1655. The Bashful Lover, 1655. The City Madam, 1658. The Parliament of Love (lic. 1624), 1805. Believe as you List (S. R. 1653), 1849.

COLLECTED EDITIONS

Coxeter (T.), 4 vols., 1759, 1761. — Mason (T. M.), 4 vols., 1779. — Gifford (W.), 4 vols., 1805, 1813, 1845, 1850; ed. Cunningham (F.), 1870. — Coleridge (H.), with Ford, 1 vol., 1840. — Symons (A.), in Mermaid Series, ten plays in two vols., 1887-89.

A NEW WAY TO PAY OLD DEBTS

Ed. Stronach (G.), in Temple Dramatists, 1904.

CRITICISM, etc.

Stephen (Sir L.), in Cornhill Magazine, Oct., 1877 (also in Hours in a Library, III, 1879). — Swinburne (A. C.), in Fortnightly Review, July. 1889. — Tréverret (A. de), Étude sur Massinger, Revue de l'enseignement des langues vivantes, Dec. 1886, Jan. 1887. — Wurzbach (W. von), in Shakespeare Jahrbuch, XXXV. 214, XXXVI. 128. — Koeppel (E.), Quellenstudien, in Quellen und Forschungen, LXXXII, Strassburg, 1897. — Gardiner (S. R.), The Political Element in Massinger, Contemporary Review, XXVIII., 1876 (also New Shak. Soc. Trans., 1876). — Phelan (J.), Anglia, II., 1879.

JOHN FORD

ORIGINAL EDITIONS

The Lover's Melancholy, 1629. The Broken Heart, 1633. Love's Sacrifice, 1633. 'T is Pity She's a Whore, 1633. Perkin Warbeck, 1634. The Fancies, Chaste and Noble, 1638. The Lady's Trial, 1639. The Witch of Edmonton (with Dekker and W. Rowley), 1658.

COLLECTED EDITIONS

Weber (H.), 2 vols., 1811. — Gifford (W.), 2 vols., 1827; w. additions by Dyce (A.), 3 vols., 1869, 1895. — Coleridge (H.), (with Massinger's Works), 1840. — Ellis (H.), five plays in Mermaid Series, 1888. —Bang (W.), Louvain, 1908 (in process).

THE BROKEN HEART

Ed. Scollard (C.), New York, 1905. — Smeaton (O.), in Temple Dramatists, 1906.

CRITICISM, etc.

Koeppel (E.), Quellenstudien zu den Dramen . . . John Ford's, in Quellen und Forschungen, LXXXII, Strassburg, 1897. — Swinburne (A. C.), in Essays and Studies, 1888. — Wolff (M.), John Ford, ein Nachahmer Shakespeare's, Heidelberg, 1880. — Sherman (S. P.), Stella and The Broken Heart, in Publ. Mod. Lang. Ass. Amer. XXIV., 274, 1909; see also his Introduction to Bang's Ford, and his MS. dissertation in the archives of Harvard University Library. — Pierce (F. E.), The Sequence of Ford's Plays, The Nation, N. Y., Jan. 5, 1911.

JAMES SHIRLEY

ORIGINAL EDITIONS

The Wedding, 1629. The Grateful Servant, 1630. The School of Compliment, 1631, as Love Tricks, 1637, 1667. Changes, or Love in a Maze, 1632. The Witty Fair One, 1633. The Bird in a Cage, 1633. The Traitor, 1635. Hyde Park, 1637. The Gamester, 1637. The Young Admiral, 1637. The Example, 1637. The Lady of Pleasure, 1637. The Duke's Mistress, 1638. The Royal Master, 1638. The Maid's Revenge, 1639. Love's Cruelty, 1640. The Opportunity, 1640. The Coronation (lic. 1635), 1640. The Constant Maid, 1640, as Love Will Find Out a Way, 1667. St Patrick for Ireland, 1640. The Humorous Courtier, 1640. The Arcadia, 1640. Six New Plays, viz., The Brothers, The Doubtful Heir, The Imposture, The Cardinal, The Sisters, The Court Secret, 1652-3. The Politician, 1655. The Gentleman of Venice, 1655. Honoria and Mammon, 1659. The Contention of Ajax and Ulysses, 1659. The Ball (with Chapman), 1639. Chabot, Admiral of France (with Chapman), 1639.

COLLECTED EDITIONS

Gifford (W.) and Dyce (A.), 6 vols., 1833. — Gosse (E.), six plays, in Mermaid Series, 1888.

CRITICISM, etc.

Swinburne (A. C.), in Fortnightly Review, April, 1890. — Stiefel (A. L.), Die Nachahmung spanischer Komödien in England, in Romanische Forschungen, v. 193, 1890. — Nissen (P.), James Shirley, Hamburg, 1901. — Gärtner (O.), Shirley, sein Leben und Werken, Halle, 1904.

BIOGRAPHICAL SKETCHES

JOHN LYLY

John Lyly was born in Kent about 1554. His father was Peter Lyly, Registrar of Canterbury, and his grandfather the well-known grammarian, William Lyly, the friend of Colet and More. He entered Magdalen College, Oxford, in 1569, whence he graduated B. A. in 1573, and M. A. in 1575. Here he was more distinguished for wit than for scholarship. Going up to London, and living at first under the protection of Burleigh, he produced in 1578 his *Euphues : the Anatomy of Wit*, which was followed in 1580 by *Euphues and his England*, both of which gained a great and immediate popularity. He was now attached to the Earl of Oxford. *Campaspe*, his first play, was performed in 1581, and most of his dramatic work was done in that decade. *The Woman in the Moon*, however, may have been produced as late as 1594-5. In 1583, Lyly married Beatrice Browne, a well-connected lady, who bore him eight children. From 1588 he seems to have held an honorary position as Esquire of the Body to the Queen, and he lived for years in the vain hope of succeeding to the office of Master of the Revels. Between 1589 and 1601 he sat in four parliaments, and in his *Pappe with an Hatchet* (1589) he took part with the Bishops in the Marprelate controversy. In spite of the distinction which Lyly won by his literary work, he failed to obtain from the Queen the substantial preferment which he craved, and he died in 1606, a disappointed place-seeker. Lyly's reputation has depended largely on the extraordinary vogue of his *Euphues*, and the immense influence of the style of that work on the prose of the time; but he holds also a highly important position in the development of polite comedy in England.

GEORGE PEELE

The date of Peele's birth is unknown, but is conjecturally placed about 1558. In 1565 he was a free scholar at Christ's Hospital, of which his father was clerk, and in 1571 he went to Oxford. He was a student first at Broadgates Hall (now Pembroke College), and later at Christ Church, whence he graduated B. A. in 1577, and M. A. in 1579. From the University, where he had already achieved some reputation as a poet, he went to London, and apparently plunged at once into the irregularities that wrecked his career, for in the same year the governors of Christ's Hospital forced his father to turn him out of the precincts of the hospital. His wife, whom he had married by 1583, brought him some property, which he soon dissipated; and he became a member of that group of authors who wrote plays, pageants, and all sorts of occasional productions, in the uncertain hope of earning a living. The famous *Jests*, fathered on Peele, are probably quite unauthentic; but there is an unfortunate appropriateness in many of them to his known mode of life. He seems to have been an actor as well as a playwright. Meres mentions him in *Palladis Tamia* (1598) as dead.

Peele's claims to distinction rest upon his treatment of metre, and on his humor. He did much to refine and supple the diction of the drama, and before Marlowe placed his stamp upon blank verse, Peele was writing it with great sweetness and a charming musical quality. In the present play, the realistic element in the dialogue is more notable than the decorative, and this realism is employed in the service of a new type of humor. "He was the first," says Gummere, "to blend romantic drama with a realism which turns romance back upon itself, and produces the comedy of subconscious humor."

ROBERT GREENE

Greene was much given to the mingling of autobiography with his fiction, and this has resulted in a much larger body of possibly true biographical details than we possess concerning most of his contemporaries. He was born in Norwich of a respectable family, probably about 1560; entered St. John's College, Cambridge, in 1575; graduated B. A. in 1578; travelled in Spain and Italy, and, by his own account, lived up to the proverbial reputation of the Italianate Englishman; returned to Cambridge and took his M. A. in 1581; and during the rest of his short life busied himself in the production of the very considerable mass of romances, tracts, songs, and plays which to-day give him his place in literature. About 1585 he married a Lincolnshire woman, who bore him a son, and whom he deserted after spending her portion. The annals of literature hardly bear the record of a more sordid career than that of this university-bred man of letters; and his death was only too fitting a close to it. He died in 1592 in the house of a poor shoemaker, to whom he gave a bond for ten pounds, leaving the following letter to his deserted wife: "Doll, I charge thee by the love of our youth and by my soul's rest that thou wilt see this man paid, for if he and his wife had not succoured me I had died in the streets.

Robert Greene." Following his own wish, the shoemaker's wife crowned his head with a garland of bay.

In spite of the self-confessed wickedness of his ways, Greene was not a hardened criminal, and no themes are more frequent in his tracts than moral exhortation and repentance. It is further notable that his work is freer from grossness than that of most of his contemporary playwrights, and he is distinguished for the freshness and purity of his female creations. He seems also, to judge from his plays, to have retained a love for the country, where he often chose to lay his scenes; and he ranks high among the lyrists of the time. The vivacity and variety of his humor are well exemplified in the play here printed.

CHRISTOPHER MARLOWE

Christopher Marlowe was the eldest son of a substantial burgess of Canterbury, and he was born in that city on February 6, 1564. He entered the King's School in January, 1579, and two years later became a scholar of Corpus Christi College, Cambridge, whence he graduated B. A. in 1584, and M. A. in 1587. As *Tamburlaine* was acted in that year, it appears that Marlowe's academic and his literary life overlapped. Little is certainly known of his later life, apart from the production of his plays and poems. He belonged to a circle of which Sir Walter Raleigh was the centre, and which contained men like the Earl of Oxford, and Harriot, the mathematician. These men seem to have engaged in scientific and theological speculation, and were suspected of atheism by the narrower spirits of the time. This connection was probably the basis for certain extreme charges made against Marlowe after his death; but there is little evidence worthy of consideration. Even the documents connected with Kyd, in which that author seeks to save his own reputation for orthodoxy at Marlowe's expense, are under suspicion in point of genuineness. Marlowe died by the hand of a certain Francis Archer, at Deptford, in 1593, but the circumstances are obscure. The later reports, such as that according to which he was stabbed by a serving man in a brawl over a mistress, are inconsistent with one another, and are little worthy of credit. The prevailing impression of the dissoluteness of Marlowe's life is not based on substantial evidence such as we have, for example, in the case of Greene.

No such uncertainty as surrounds his character and career attaches to the quality of his work. Born in the same year as Shakespeare, he left behind him at twenty-nine work which far surpasses anything his great contemporary had written by that time. In the vastness and intensity of his imagination, the splendid dignity of his verse, and the dazzling brilliance of his poetry at its best, Marlowe exhibited the greatest genius that had so far appeared in the English drama.

THOMAS KYD

The date of Kyd's birth may with practical certainty be placed in 1558. His father was a London scrivener, and the son was educated at Merchant Taylors' School, which he entered in 1565. Mulcaster was then headmaster, and Edmund Spenser was among his schoolfellows. He does not seem to have attended a university. A habit of anonymity has thrown a cloud over the extent of Kyd's literary activity, and the list of his plays and translations has been compiled with difficulty and much less than complete certainty. His fame depends upon *The Spanish Tragedy*, and upon the importance of his contribution to the Senecan tragedy of revenge in this play and probably in the lost pre-Shakespearean *Hamlet*, which is now usually ascribed to him.

The later years of his life seem to have been unfortunate, and he was arrested on charges of sedition and atheism in 1593. From the latter he sought, if the letter to Puckering (Boas, p. cviii.) is genuine, to clear himself by ascribing the ownership of the incriminating documents to the dead Marlowe, and he endeavored to minimise the closeness of his intimacy with his great contemporary. These charges, it appears, lost him his patron, and perhaps in some degree his theatrical popularity. He died in 1594.

Kyd seems to have been a man of gloomy temperament, and the vividness and intensity with which he presents in his work the darker sides of human nature and experience are probably in some degree the outcome of his own disposition. In spite of tendencies to melodrama that, to the modern taste, border on the ludicrous, Kyd rises at times to the utterance of genuine passion, and even his sensationalism is frequently impressive. But his historical importance in the development of the type of tragedy of which *Hamlet* is the climax must be granted to be greater than his intrinsic value.

GEORGE CHAPMAN

George Chapman was born in Hitchin, Hertfordshire, in 1557 or 1559, and was educated at Oxford, and perhaps also at Cambridge. His earliest extant work is *The Shadow of Night* (1594), which was followed in 1595 by *Ovid's Banquet of Sense*, *The Amorous Zodiac*, and other poems, works curiously obscure and contorted in style, though containing distinguished passages. In 1598, he finished Mar lowe's incomplete *Hero and Leander*, and when Meres published his *Palladis Tamia* in that year, Chapman was already well-known as a playwright. His reputation, however, is most firmly based on his translations from Homer, issued in detachments in 1598, 1609, 1611, and 1614, and complete in folio in 1616. In this work he was encouraged by Prince Henry, to whom he was "sewer in ordinary." He was imprisoned in 1605 along with Jonson and Marston on account of the passages against the Scots in *Eastward Ho!* and in 1608 he again had difficulties with the authorities on account of a scene in *Charles, Duke of Byron*. He continued his work in translation and in the drama till his death in 1634.

Though one can hardly feel that Chapman's natural gifts were those of a dramatist, the evidences of intellectual power, and the almost Shakespearean splendor of the poetry in occasional passages throughout his work, entitle him to an honorable place among the writers of the time.

BEN JONSON

Ben Jonson came of an Annandale family, and was born at Westminster in 1573. He followed his stepfather's trade of bricklaying for a short time, and later served as a soldier in Flanders. He probably began play-writing about 1595, and two years later we find him in the Admiral's Company of actors. In 1598 he is mentioned by Meres as a writer of tragedy, and in the same year he killed a fellow-actor in a duel. In prison he became a Roman Catholic, but returned to the Church of England twelve years later. He scored a success with *Every Man in his Humour* in 1598, Shakespeare acting a part in the play. After several years of work on satirical drama, Jonson turned to tragedy; and on the accession of James I, he began his long series of masques and court entertainments. In 1605 he was again in prison, this time for his share in *Eastward Ho!* From this date till about 1617 Jonson was at the height of his fame, and was the leading literary figure in London. He visited France in 1613 as tutor to Raleigh's son; and in 1616 issued a folio edition of his works. In 1618, he visited Scotland, and held his famous conversations with Drummond of Hawthornden; and, on his return, Oxford made him an M. A. After the death of James I, Jonson was less fortunate in court favor, suffered from ill health, and was unsuccessful at the theatre. In 1628, however, he succeeded Middleton as chronologer to the city of London, and the King sent him £100 in his sickness, later raising his salary. But fortune turned against him again; he lost his city office, made further attempts to regain theatrical favor, and died August 6, 1637. Besides plays, he left an interesting prose work, *Timber, or Discoveries*, and a considerable amount of non-dramatic verse. A second folio edition of his *Works* appeared in 1640.

Jonson's artistic ideals were classical rather than romantic, and he stands, in significant respects, in opposition to some of the main literary currents of his time. The plays in the present volume include an example of the "comedy of humours" introduced by him, a typical example of his tragedy, and two of his satirical masterpieces. In these alone one can find abundant evidence that, despite a lack of charm and geniality, one is dealing with the work of a deep student of human nature, a vigorous and independent thinker, and a master of eloquent and virile expression.

THOMAS DEKKER

Dekker's career is an extreme instance of the hazardous life led by the professional author in the time of Shakespeare. Born in London about 1570, Dekker first appears certainly as a dramatist about 1597, when we find him working on plays in collaboration with other dramatists in the pay of Henslowe. He wrote, in partnership or alone, many dramas; and when the market for these was dull, he turned to the writing of entertainments, occasional verses, and prose pamphlets on a great variety of subjects. No writer of the time gives us a more vivid picture of Elizabethan London. But all his activity seems to have failed to supply a decent livelihood, for he was often in prison for debt, at one time for a period of three years; and most of the biographical details about him which have come down to us are connected with borrowing money, or getting into jail or out of it. He disappears from view in the thirties of the seventeenth century.

In spite of the impression of gloom left by such a record, Dekker's plays abound in high spirits, and their general tendency in plot and characterization is sane and wholesome. Evidences of hasty and careless workmanship are easily found, yet he was far from an uninspired hack, and passages of a noble and delicate poetry are frequent throughout his work.

JOHN MARSTON

John Marston came of an old Shropshire family, and was born, probably at Coventry, about 1575. His father, who bore the same name, was lecturer of the Middle Temple, and there is evidence that the son was trained for the law. He entered Brasenose College, Oxford, in 1592, and, according to Bullen, graduated B. A. in 1594. His first work in poetry was his *Metamorphosis of Pigmalion's Image and Certain Satires*, 1598; and later in the same year appeared his *Scourge of Villany*. In the following year both books were burned on account of their licentiousness by the order of the Archbishop of Canterbury, though Marston had professed a reformatory purpose in both. In 1599 he turned to play-writing; but the turgid style of his *Antonio and Mellida* and *Antonio's Revenge* brought down on him the ridicule of Jonson in *The Poetaster*. *The Malcontent* was written during a period of reconciliation with Jonson, and in 1605 Marston collaborated with him and Chapman in *Eastward Ho*, a comedy containing a passage reflecting on the Scots, which landed all three dramatists in prison.

Marston gave up play-writing in 1607, and later became a clergyman. From 1616 to 1631 he held the living of Christ Church, Hampshire, and in 1634 died in London, and was buried in the Temple Church.

The extreme tendency to fustian which Jonson had attacked in Marston's early work no longer appears to any great extent in *The Malcontent*, and the play exhibits favorably Marston's capacity for the creation of well marked character and effective stage situations. An attempt has recently been made to show that he exerted a considerable influence on Shakespeare, especially in *Hamlet*.

THOMAS HEYWOOD

The early records of this, the most prolific of the dramatic writers of the time, are extremely scanty. The date of his birth is conjecturally placed about 1575, and he refers to himself as a native of Lincolnshire, and at one time resident at Cambridge. He begins to figure in Henslowe's accounts in 1596, and he appears as a member of the Lord Admiral's Company in 1598. He began writing plays with *The Four Prentices of London*, and in the *Address to the Reader* prefixed to his *English Traveller* (1633) he claims to have written or had a "main finger" in two hundred and twenty plays. Outside of the drama, he tried his hand at almost all sorts of literature, and the quality of his work is extremely uneven. He was still alive in 1648, but probably died soon thereafter.

Heywood's characteristic power of eliciting powerful emotions by a sympathetic treatment of everyday conditions and events, is well illustrated by the play here printed. While much is perfunctory in his work, one constantly finds evidences of a genuine and pious spirit moved by a keen appreciation of the pathos of human life.

FRANCIS BEAUMONT

Francis Beaumont was born 1584, the son of Sir Francis Beaumont of Grace-Dieu, Leicestershire, a judge of the common pleas. He was educated at Broadgates Hall (now Pembroke College), Oxford, which he entered in 1597. On the death of his father in 1598, he left the university without a degree, and in 1600 became a member of the Inner Temple. The law, however, if he ever really studied it, was soon abandoned for poetry; and Beaumont became an intimate of Jonson and his circle at the Mermaid. His collaboration with Fletcher began early, and seems to have been brought about by personal preference, not, like most collaboration at that time, by the exigencies of the theatrical manager. Aubrey has preserved the tradition of their domestic intimacy and similarity of tastes. Their joint-production seems to have begun about 1605, and there is no evidence that Beaumont wrote any plays after 1612. About 1613 he married, and three years later died and was buried in Westminster Abbey. He had achieved a high contemporary reputation for his non-dramatic poetry, but he survives as a dramatist.

JOHN FLETCHER

John Fletcher came of a family which has given many distinguished names to English literature. His father was Richard Fletcher, Bishop of London. Giles Fletcher the elder was his uncle, and Giles and Phineas Fletcher his cousins. The dramatist was born at Rye, Sussex, in 1579, and entered Benet College (now Corpus Christi), Cambridge, in 1591; but of the details of his life from this time till his appearance as a dramatist little is known. He collaborated with Beaumont from about 1605 till 1612; and, after Beaumont's withdrawal, with Shakespeare, Jonson, Massinger, and others. He died of the plague in 1625.

The men who laid the foundations of the Elizabethan drama were generally of somewhat obscure origin; and though some of them had been educated at the universities, they were all poor. Beaumont and Fletcher were the first recruits to the profession of play-writing who came of distinguished families and habitually moved in wealthy circles; and this social environment was early suggested as an explanation of their power of representing naturally the conversation of high-born ladies and gentlemen. The general style of their plays has been thus admirably characterized by Thorndike: "Their plots, largely invented, are ingenious and complicated. They deal with royal or noble persons, with heroic actions, and are placed in foreign localities. The conquests, usurpations, and passions that ruin kingdoms are their themes, there are no battles or pageants, and the action is usually confined to the rooms of the palace or its immediate neighborhood. Usually contrasting a story of gross sensual passion with one of idyllic love, they introduce a great variety of incidents, and aim at constant but varied excitement. . . . The plays depend for interest not on their observation or revelation of human nature, or the development of character, but on the variety of situations, the clever construction that holds the interest through one suspense to another up to the unravelling at the very end, and on the naturalness, felicity, and vigor of the poetry."

JOHN WEBSTER

The dates 1580–1625 are usually given as conjectures for Webster's birth and death, exact information being entirely lacking. His father was a member of the Merchant Taylors' Company, of which the son was likewise a freeman; but this does not imply that he was actually a tailor. In 1602, we find him collaborating with seven others in the production of four plays for Henslowe, and the rest of his biography consists in the discussion of the dates of his works.

Webster's tragedies come towards the close of the great series of tragedies of blood and revenge in which *The Spanish Tragedy* and *Hamlet* are landmarks, but before decadence can fairly be said to have set in. Webster, indeed, loads his scene with horrors almost past the point which modern taste can bear; but the intensity of his dramatic situations, and his superb power of flashing in a single line a light into the recesses of the human heart at the crises of supreme emotion, redeem him from mere sensationalism, and place his best plays in the first rank of dramatic writing.

THOMAS MIDDLETON

The date of Middleton's birth is unknown, but is conjecturally placed about 1570. He came of good family, and his writings indicate that he received a good education. We know, however, nothing about his early training before his entering Gray's Inn, probably in 1593. His plays abound in allusions to law and pictures of lawyers.

The earliest evidence of his writing for the stage is in the date of *The Old Law*, which was probably composed by Middleton about 1599, and later revised by Massinger and W. Rowley. He was much employed in the writing of pageants and masques, especially by the city, and in 1621 he obtained the post of city chronologer. In 1624 he gave expression to the popular hatred of Spain in his allegorical play, *A Game at Chess*, which scored a great success, but which was ultimately suppressed at the instigation of the Spanish ambassador, and led to a warrant for Middleton's arrest. He died in 1627.

In his comedies Middleton shows himself a keen observer of contemporary life and manners, and few writers of the time have left a more vivacious picture of the London of James I. "His later plays," says Herford, "show more concentrated as well as more versatile power. His habitual occupation with depraved types becomes an artistic method; he creates characters which fascinate without making the smallest appeal to sympathy, tragedy which harrows without rousing either pity or terror, and language which disdains charm, but penetrates by remorseless veracity and by touches of strange and sudden power."

WILLIAM ROWLEY

William Rowley was born about 1585. He was an actor as well as a dramatist, and is sometimes confused with two other actors, Ralph and Samuel Rowley. In his earlier years he wrote some non-dramatic verse, mostly of a conventional kind. His most important work was done in collaboration with Middleton, with whom he worked from 1614, but he had many other literary partners. His verse is apt to be rough and irregular, his humor broad and rollicking rather than fine, his serious scenes tending to extravagance and bombast. But his constant employment to coöperate with greater men, or revise their work, points to a general serviceableness and a capacity for theatrical effectiveness. His death is conjecturally placed about 1642.

PHILIP MASSINGER

Philip Massinger was born at Salisbury, in November, 1583. His father was in the service of the Earls of Pembroke, and it has been conjectured that the future dramatist was named after the Countess's brother, Sir Philip Sidney. He entered St. Alban Hall, Oxford, in 1602, and left four years later without a degree, having, according to Wood, "applied his mind more to poetry and romances than to logic and philosophy." On coming to London he seems to have turned at once to writing for the stage; and, after Beaumont retired from play-writing, Massinger became Fletcher's chief partner and warm friend. All Massinger's relations with his fellow-authors of which we have record seem to have been pleasant; and the impression of his personality which one derives from his work is that of a dignified, hard-working, and conscientious man. He seems to have been much interested in public affairs, and he at times came into collision with the authorities on account of the introduction into his plays of more or less veiled allusions to political personages and events. He died in 1640, and was buried in St. Saviour's, Southwark, in the same grave, it is said by Cokayne, as his friend Fletcher.

Massinger's great merit lies in his masterly conduct of plot. His characters are usually of a some what conventional type, his pictures of passion tend to sheer extravagance, and his ethical quality has in it something mechanical. His verse is often eloquent, but the dialogue is often preposterously remote from life. Yet so skillful was he in the manipulation of the action that he usually holds the attention without difficulty; and in the present play this power is combined with a singularly forceful presentation of the main character and a fairly obvious didacticism that together kept the drama on the stage almost down to modern times.

JOHN FORD

John Ford was born at Ilsington in Devonshire in April, 1586, of good family. A man of his name entered Exeter College, Oxford, in 1601; but if this was our Ford, his stay was short, for he became a member of the Middle Temple in November, 1602. Of the rest of his career we know almost nothing, except the names of people to whom he dedicated his plays and verses. He disappears after the publication of his last play in 1639. He seems to have been a man of a somewhat melancholy temperament, independent in his attitude towards the public taste, and capable of espousing unpopular causes.

Ford's dramas show a tendency to deal with illicit and even incestuous love in a peculiar mood, the dramatist frequently creating strong sympathy for the tempted and the sinner, and leaving the question of guilt open. This, along with his fondness for the theatrical and the sensational, has led to his being frequently chosen as an example of the decadence of the drama. The charge is not to be denied; but in spite of these defects, he shows a power of insight into suffering and perplexity, and writes at times poetry of such beauty and tenderness, that he remains a figure of much intrinsic interest as well as historical importance.

JAMES SHIRLEY

James Shirley, often called " the last of the Elizabethans," was born in London in September, 1596, and was educated at Merchant Taylors' School and St. John's College, Oxford. Later he went to Catherine Hall, Cambridge, whence he graduated. About 1619 he took orders, and obtained a living at St. Albans, Hertfordshire; but resigned to enter the church of Rome, and became master of the St. Albans grammar school in 1623. His first play was licensed in 1625, and from this time till the closing of the theatres he devoted himself to the writing of plays and masques, gaining both popular success and the patronage of the court. With the outbreak of the Civil War, Shirley followed his patron, the Earl of Newcastle, to the field; but after Marston Moor he returned to London, published some of his earlier writings, and resumed teaching. Some of his plays were revived at the Restoration, but he wrote no more. He and his second wife were driven from their home by the fire of London in 1666, and both died from shock on the same day.

Shirley wrote many non-dramatic poems, graceful enough but conventional; few of them are read to-day. Out of nearly forty dramas, seven are tragedies, the rest chiefly romantic comedies and comedies of manners. He was a careful student of the work of his predecessors, and he reproduced many of their dramatic effects with skill. He had a distinct comic gift, and his power in tragedy may be judged by *The Cardinal*. With Shirley, more than with any of his fellow-playwrights, one feels the disadvantage of coming so late in the development of this phase of the drama that originality of conception seems almost impossible. That he is still able to amuse and to thrill with the old instruments is proof of his capacity as a literary workman; and he should not be denied the possession of passages where he displays touches of imagination all his own.

INDEX OF CHARACTERS

INDEX OF SONGS

INDEX OF AUTHORS

INDEX OF PLAYS